INTERSTATE
HIGHWAY
GUIDE

2015

THE MOST ACCURATE INTERSTATE HIGHWAY SERVICE GUIDE EVER PRINTED™

the Next EXIT® will save time, money and frustration.

This tool will help you find services along the USA Interstate Highways like nothing you have ever used.

D1444773

GA... ...RANTS • RV CAMPING • ... MORE

**PO Box 888
Garden City, UT 84028**

www.theNextExit.com

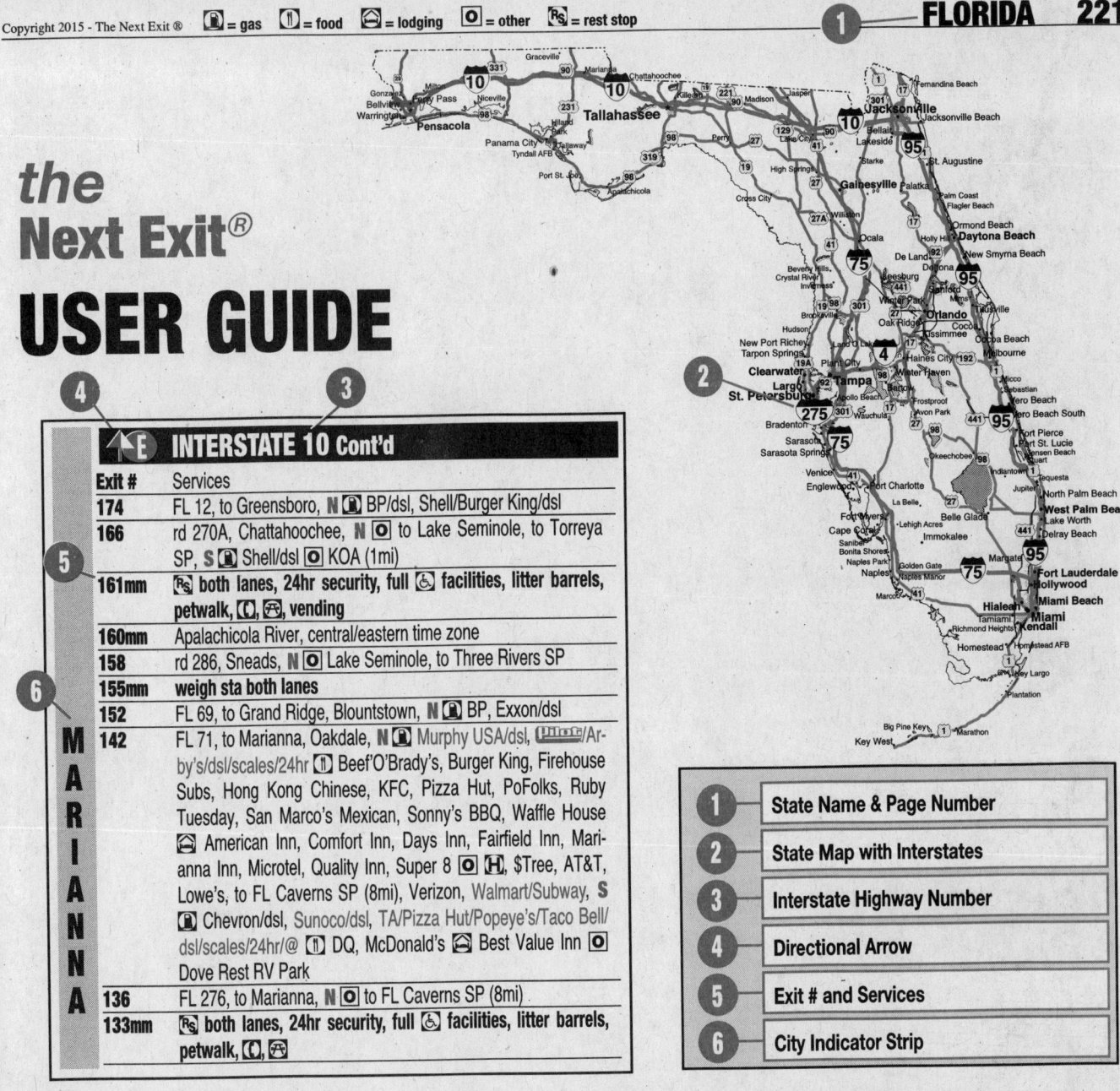

the Next Exit®

USER GUIDE

⬆E	**INTERSTATE 10 Cont'd**
Exit #	**Services**
174	FL 12, to Greensboro, **N** 🅖 BP/dsl, Shell/Burger King/dsl
166	rd 270A, Chattahoochee, **N** 🄾 to Lake Seminole, to Torreya SP, **S** 🅖 Shell/dsl 🄾 KOA (1mi)
161mm	🆁🆂 both lanes, 24hr security, full ♿ facilities, litter barrels, petwalk, 🅲, 🕮, vending
160mm	Apalachicola River, central/eastern time zone
158	rd 286, Sneads, **N** 🄾 Lake Seminole, to Three Rivers SP
155mm	weigh sta both lanes
152	FL 69, to Grand Ridge, Blountstown, **N** 🅖 BP, Exxon/dsl
142	FL 71, to Marianna, Oakdale, **N** 🅖 Murphy USA/dsl, 🅸🅷🅾🅿/Arby's/dsl/scales/24hr 🍴 Beef'O'Brady's, Burger King, Firehouse Subs, Hong Kong Chinese, KFC, Pizza Hut, PoFolks, Ruby Tuesday, San Marco's Mexican, Sonny's BBQ, Waffle House 🏠 American Inn, Comfort Inn, Days Inn, Fairfield Inn, Marianna Inn, Microtel, Quality Inn, Super 8 🄾 🄷, $Tree, AT&T, Lowe's, to FL Caverns SP (8mi), Verizon, Walmart/Subway, **S** 🅖 Chevron/dsl, Sunoco/dsl, TA/Pizza Hut/Popeye's/Taco Bell/dsl/scales/24hr/@ 🍴 DQ, McDonald's 🏠 Best Value Inn 🄾 Dove Rest RV Park
136	FL 276, to Marianna, **N** 🄾 to FL Caverns SP (8mi)
133mm	🆁🆂 both lanes, 24hr security, full ♿ facilities, litter barrels, petwalk, 🅲, 🕮

Left margin vertical text: **MARIANNA**

1	**State Name & Page Number**
2	**State Map with Interstates**
3	**Interstate Highway Number**
4	**Directional Arrow**
5	**Exit # and Services**
6	**City Indicator Strip**

Right margin vertical text: **the Next EXIT® USER GUIDE**

Exit

Most states number exits by the nearest mile marker(mm). A few states use consecutive numbers, in which case mile markers are given in ( ). Mile markers are the little green vertical signs beside the interstate at one mile intervals which indicate distance from the southern or western border of a state. Odd numbered interstates run north/south, even numbered run east/west.

Services

Services are listed alphabetically by category 🅖=gas 🍴=food 🏠=lodging 🆁🆂=rest stop 🄾=other services including camping.

"🄷" indicates an exit from which a hospital may be accessed, but it may not be close to the exit.

Services located away from the exit may be referred to by "access to," or "to" and a distance may be given.

A directional notation is also given, such as **N, S, E** or **W**

Directional Arrows

Follow exits DOWN the page if traveling from North to South or East to West, UP the page if traveling South to North or West to East.

TABLE OF CONTENTS

Abbreviations & Symbols used in the Next EXIT ®

AFB	Air Force Base	pk	park
B&B	Bed&Breakfast	pkwy	parkway
Bfd	Battlefield	rest.	restaurant
Ctr	Center	nb	northbound
Coll	College	sb	southbound
Cyn	canyon	eb	eastbound
dsl	diesel	wb	westbound
$	Dollar	SP	state park
Mem	Memorial	SF	state forest
Mkt	Market	Sprs	springs
Mtn	Mountain	st	street, state
mm	mile marker	sta	station
N	north side of exit	TPK	Turnpike
S	south side of exit	USPO	Post Office
E	east side of exit	vet	veterinarian
W	west side of exit	whse	warehouse
NM	National Monument	@	truckstop (full service)
NHS	Nat Hist Site	red print	RV accessible
NWR	Nat Wildlife Reserve	🚻	Handicapped accessible
NF	National Forest	📞	Telephone
H	Hospital	⛽	Gas
✈	Airport	🍴	Food
🏕	Picnic Tables	🏠	Lodging
NP	National Park	O	Other
NRA	Nat Rec Area	Rs	Rest Stop / Rest Area

For Trans Canada Highway (TCH) information and more, please visit us on the web at **www.thenextexit.com**

TABLE OF CONTENTS

HAVE PEACHES - WILL TRAVEL

Mark Watson – Winter 2015

Consider the peach, that delicious, succulent, fruit of the South whose ripening defines the boundaries of summer. Sure, California creates them too, and I did discover a few the size of grapefruits in eastern Pennsylvania recently. Utah yields them from mountain benches, but somehow peaches produced a long way from home, you know, *home*, are simply not as good. It could be the soil, the climate or all in my head, but mostly it is the manner by which these peaches are procured. They are sold in groceries and supermarkets everywhere, but to buy them there seems dishonest. Purchasing them at fruit stands and farmers markets, while legitimate, still falls short of the real thing.

Who doesn't like peaches? My brother is the only person on Earth I know, and that has something to do with peach fuzz rubbing across his teeth. What? My father the farmer proclaimed that more peaches are grown in one county in South Carolina than in all of Georgia, the "Peach State." He tried starting his own little orchard, but insects and varmints liked the fruit as much as he did and were ultimately his undoing. Not to be beaten, he began a new custom that we now observe every season: get into the truck and drive up Highway 151 into the sand hills past orchards laden with this year's harvest, turn right on US 1, cross the railroad track then right again into the last driveway before the overpass. Park in front of the shed's open doors through which can be seen at least two pallets stacked with packing boxes, one for grade A, the other for seconds. At the height of the run a man stands on the platform directing traffic in the warehouse. He answers questions, sells you crates of fruit and may allow you to walk back to get a view of the sorting machines. Heading out with several cases of seconds and an occasional grade A feels as good as money in the bank. Select a few specimens off the top to enjoy on the way home, and in just moments you wonder how it could get any better.

The only problem with buying peaches in bulk is time; it becomes the enemy the moment they come off the tree. It makes little sense to overbuy unless they are going to supply a crowd, be preserved or you are serious about consuming many peaches. Sadly, the winding down of the season signals that summer and all things fuzzy, juicy and tasty are nearing an end, causing us aficionados to use poor judgment on exactly how many to get on that final trip.

So several Septembers ago, we said goodbye to our kinfolk, drove up 151 and took two rights for our last load before wandering west. We were standing there beholding all those peaches when I heard a voice say "we'll take three cases of seconds." I protested, but then the same voice

HAVE PEACHES - WILL TRAVEL

reassured "it's only 2000 miles, just two weeks, they'll last," so I happily peeled off the bills, handed them to the man and opened the trunk. Next thing I knew, we were barreling back toward the big road, biting into the latest batch, flush with a feeling of plenty. That September was warm.

We left them in the car the first night and by next afternoon, the box we had moved into the back seat began to emit the faint aroma of ripening fruit. This was not a problem since Debby had wisely brought along dishes, a knife and spoons. She began handing me bowls of peeled, sliced peaches, drenched in evaporated milk, after breakfast, lunch and supper. How delightful, I thought, to have all these superb peaches at hand and a servant to fix them up for me. That night she suggested we take them into the hotel and place them near the air conditioner. "All three cases?" I asked. "They are ripening quickly," she said. Considering this development, inside they went along with all our baggage.

The next several days were much like the first few, only now the peaches required attention near the top of our daily list. We started on them right after breakfast, continued for our mid-morning snack and soon they became lunch. After nearly a week, every afternoon she asked what I wanted to eat and I named all the things we did not have, then said, "oh well, let's just have some PEACHES!" And so we did. Since it is a sin to waste anything so wonderfully appointed as peaches from home, we ate them morning, afternoon and most times in between, always selecting the ripest, sometimes mere moments ahead of the fruit flies. We hauled them in and out of lodging to the curious gaze of many, celebrating milestones as three boxes became two, then one and finally, a light one. And so it went.

That autumn we climbed Colorado bottom to top. Somewhere near its center we rolled into motel parking and unpacked, reckoning this would be near the last time. Overlooking a stream, gazing out at the Rocky Mountains as they colored up for fall, Debby peeled and I ate the last of the peaches. It was a melancholy moment, but we immediately saw the positives. Even the most ardent peach lovers can lose the edge down toward the end of that third box.

As with many traditions, this one has survived so that when our children from distant states visit peach country, they stock up like their parents and grandparents before them. Our family from Arizona recently headed back with a goodly quantity, expecting to dispatch them before their trip ended. If enough were leftover at journey's end for a cobbler in the desert, that would be fine too. All went as planned until it didn't. First, the cases claimed more than their fair share of space in the vehicle. Then the five children rebelled at eating so much fruit and at last the box unexpectedly opened, rolling peaches all around the minivan. Frustrated, but not wanting to waste perfectly good peaches, the dad began giving them away at rest areas, offering ripe fruit free--shipping and handling included--to fellow travelers.

At first I was disappointed when I heard the tale. You don't simply discard such a great treasure all for a little inconvenience, do you? Peaches? Food of the gods? After some thought, I concluded that while it may not have been the perfect solution, it did meet all standards and violated no protocol. They were enjoyed by somebody, and that was the thing. And that's when I heard the voice say, "Now, why didn't we think of that?"

🅴 INTERSTATE 10

Exit #	Services
66.5mm	Alabama/Florida state line
66mm	**Welcome Ctr, full 🚻 facilities, litter barrels, petwalk, 🅿, 🛏, vending**
53	rd 64, Wilcox Rd, N 📓 BP/Oasis/Chester's/Stuckey's/Subway/dsl/scales/24hr/@ ⊙ Riverside RV Park, Styx River Resort, S 📓 Chevron/dsl, Outpost/dsl ⊙ Azalea Acres RV Park, fireworks, Hilltop RV Park (1.5 mi), Wilderness RV Park
44	AL 59, Loxley, N 📓 ♥Loves/Arby's/dsl/scales/24hr 🛏 Bay Inn, S 📓 Chevron/dsl, Exxon/dsl, RaceWay/dsl 🍴 Burger King, Hardee's, McDonald's, Waffle House 🛏 Loxley Motel (3mi), WindChase Inn ⊙ to Gulf SP
38	AL 181, Malbis, N 🍴 CA Dreaming, Chick-fil-A, Cracker Barrel, Hibachi Grill, Logan's Roadhouse, McDonald's, Moe's SW Grill, Olive Garden, Panera Bread, Poor Mexican, Ruby Tuesday, Starbucks, Stix Asian, Taco Bell, Wendy's, Wintzell's Oyster House 🛏 Best Western, Country Inn&Suites, Holiday Inn Express, La Quinta ⊙ $Tree, Advance Parts, Barnes&Noble, Belk, Best Buy, Dillard's, Goodyear/auto, Michael's, Old Navy, Petsmart, Publix, Ross, Tuesday Morning, Verizon, Walgreens, World Mkt, S 📓 Chevron/dsl, Shell/LA Subs, Texaco/dsl 🍴 Burger King, Don Carlos, Firehouse Subs, Mellow Mushroom, Zaxby's 🛏 Malbis Motel (1mi), ValuePlace ⊙ AT&T, Honda, Hyundai, Lowe's, Nissan, Sam's Club/gas, Toyota/Scion, URGENT CARE, Walmart
35	US 90, US 98, N 📓 BP, Shell 🍴 Beef O'Brady's, China Fun 🛏 Courtyard, Fairfield Inn ⊙ Bass Pro Shops, Books-A-Million, JC Penney, Kohl's, Rite Aid, USPO, S 📓 Exxon/dsl, Shell 🍴 5 Guys Burgers, Arby's, Bangkok Thai, Baumhower's, Burger King, Domino's, Dragon City Buffet, El Rancho Mexican, Firehouse Subs, Grand Buffet, Hooters, IHOP, Longhorn Steaks, Los Tacos, Marble Slab, McAlister's Deli, McDonald's, O'Charley's, Papa John's, Pizza Hut, S China Rest., Smoothie King, Starbucks, Subway, Taco Bell, Top of the Bay, Waffle House, Wendy's, Zaxby's 🛏 Comfort Suites, Eastern Shore Motel, Hampton Inn, Hilton Garden, Homewood Suites, Microtel ⊙ 🏥, AT&T, Dick's, GNC, Hancock Fabrics, Hobby Lobby, Home Depot, Office Depot, Radio Shack, SteinMart, TJ Maxx, to Blakeley SP
30	US 90/98, Battleship Pkwy, same as 27
27	US 90/98, Battleship Pkwy, Gov't St, S 🍴 Capt's Table Seafood, Felix's Fish Camp, R&R Seafood, Tacky Jack's Rest, Word's Rest 🛏 Battleship Inn ⊙ Lap's Grocery, to USS Alabama
26b	Water St, Mobile, downtown, N 🛏 Adventure Inn, Hampton Inn, Holiday Inn, Quality Inn, Renaissance, to Visitors Ctr
26a	Canal St (from eb), same as 26b
25b	Virginia St, Mobile, N 📓 Shell/dsl
25a	Texas St (from wb, no return)
24	Broad St, to Duval St, Mobile, N 📓 Chevron
23	Michigan Ave, N 📓 Shell/dsl ⊙ $General

M O B I L E

22b a	AL 163, Dauphin Island Pkwy, N 📓 Citgo ⊙ Family$, S 📓 Exxon/Subway, Shell/dsl 🍴 Checker's, Chester's, Hart's Chicken, Kim's Palace, Waffle House ⊙ $General
20	I-65 N, to Montgomery
17	AL 193, Tillmans Corner, to Dauphin Island, N 📓 Chevron 🍴 Boiling Pot, Crazy Hibachi, Firehouse Subs, Five Guys, Golden Corral, IHOP, Ruby Tuesday, Zaxby's ⊙ 🏥, AT&T, auto repair, Lowe's, Office Depot, Radio Shack, URGENT CARE, Verizon, Walmart/Subway
15b a	US 90, Tillmans Corner, to Mobile, N 📓 Chevron, RaceWay/dsl, Valero 🍴 Arby's, Aztecas Mexican, Burger King, Checkers, Domino's, Godfather's, Hooters, KFC, King's Buffet, Little Caesar's, McDonald's, Papa John's, Popeye's, Russell's BBQ, Shrimp Basket, Subway, Taco Bell, Waffle House 🛏 Baymont Inn, Best Inn, Best Value Inn, Comfort Suites, Days Inn, EconoLodge, Hampton Inn, Holiday Inn, InTown Suites, La Quinta, Motel 6, Quality Inn, Rodeway Inn, Super 8, Wingate Inn ⊙ $General, $Tree, AutoZone, BigLots, CarQuest, Family$, Firestone/auto, Mike's Transmissions, O'Reilly Parts, PepBoys, Rite Aid, vet, Walgreens, Winn-Dixie, S 📓 Chevron/Circle K, Exxon, RaceWay/dsl, Shell/dsl 🍴 Hardee's, Waffle House ⊙ Advance Parts, auto repair, B&R Campers, Johnnys RV Ctr, Peterbilt, tires, transmissions, USPO, vet

AL

T H E O D O R E

⬆️E INTERSTATE 10 Cont'd

Exit #	Services
13	to Theodore, N 🅖 Clark/dsl, 🅖Wendy's/dsl/scales/24hr, Shell/Subway, Texaco/McDonald's 🍴 Burger King, Church's, Waffle House 🅞 Advance Parts, auto repair, Family$, Greyhound Prk, Rite Aid, Rouse's Mkt, transmissions, S 🅖 Chevron/dsl 🅞 Bellingraf Gardens, I-10 Kamping, Paynes RV Park (4mi)
10	rd 39, Bayou La Batre, Dawes, N 🍴 Waffle House 🅞 Kenworth
4	AL 188 E, to Grand Bay, N 🅖 Energize/Blimpie, Shell/Subway, TA/Country Pride/dsl/scales/24hr/@ 🍴 Arby's, McDonald's, Sam's Super Burger, Waffle House 🅞 Bumper Parts, S 🅖 Chevron 🍴 Hardee's 🅞 Trav-L-Kamp
1mm	Welcome Ctr eb, full ♿ facilities, info, litter barrels, petwalk, 🅒, 🚻, RV dump
0mm	Alabama/Mississippi state line

⬆️E INTERSTATE 20

Exit #	Services
215mm	Alabama/Georgia state line, Central/Eastern time zone
213mm	Welcome Ctr wb, 24hr security, full ♿ facilities, info, litter barrels, petwalk, 🅒, 🚻, RV dump, vending
210	AL 49, Abernathy, N fireworks, S fireworks
209mm	Tallapoosa River, weigh sta wb
208mm	no services
205	AL 46, to Heflin, N 🅖 BP/dsl 🍴 205 Cafe 🅞 Cane Creek RV Park (2mi), Exit 205 Tire Ctr, Smith Farms, S 🅖 Shell/dsl/24hr 🅞 Truck Repair
199	AL 9, Heflin, N 🍴 Hardee's, McDonald's, Vallarta Grill ⛺ Best Value Inn 🅞 Chevrolet, Ford, S 🅖 Chevron/dsl, SuperMart/dsl
198mm	Talladega Nat Forest eastern boundary
191	US 431, to US 78
188	to US 78, to Anniston, N 🅖 Exxon/Subway, Samco/dsl, Shell/dsl 🍴 Cracker Barrel, Fuji Japanese, IHOP, KFC, LoneStar Steaks, Los Mexicanos, Mellow Mushroom, Waffle House, Wendy's, Zaxby's ⛺ Comfort Suites, Country Inn&Suites, Courtyard, Fairfield Inn, Hampton Inn, Hilton Garden, Holiday Inn Express, Home 2 Suites, Quality Inn, Sleep Inn 🅞 Dandy RV Ctr, Harley-Davidson, Honda, KOA, Lowe's, Nissan, O'Reilly Parts, Toyota/Scion, S 🅖 Chevron/dsl 🍴 Arby's, Ezell's Fish Camp, Firehouse Subs, Golden Corral, Golden Rule BBQ, Longhorn Steaks, Mexico Lindo Grill, Olive Garden, Panera Bread 🅞 AAA, AT&T, Best Buy, Dick's, GNC, Hobby Lobby, Home Depot, Kohl's, Old Navy, Petsmart, Publix, Ross, Sams Club/gas, Target, TJ Maxx, Verizon
185	AL 21, to Ft McClellan, to Anniston, N 🅖 Chevron/dsl, GrubMart/dsl, Texaco 🍴 Applebee's, Arby's, Bojangles, Burger King, Capt D's, China Luck, CiCi's Pizza, Hardee's, HoneyBaked Ham, Jack's Rest., Logan's Roadhouse, Los Mexicanos, McAlister's Deli, McDonald's, O'Charley's, Pizza Hut, Red Lobster, Red Pepper Grill, Shoney's, Sonic, Starbucks, Super Buffet, Taco Bell, Waffle House, Western Sizzlin ⛺ Best Value Inn, Liberty Inn, Red Carpet Inn 🅞 $General, Advance Parts, Aldi Foods, BooksAMillion, CVS Drug, Dillard's, Firestone/auto, Ford, JC Penney, Martin's Foods, Rite Aid, Sears/auto, Verizon, S 🅖 Chevron/dsl, Delta Express, Kangaroo/dsl/scales, Murphy USA/dsl, RaceWay, Valero/Subway/dsl 🍴 Chick-fil-A, Jefferson's Rest, Outback Steaks, Waffle House, Wendy's ⛺ Comfort Inn, EconoLodge, Key West Inn, Motel 6, Super 8 🅞 H, $Tree, tires/repair, Walmart

A N N I S T O N

P E L L   C I T Y

L E E D S

Exit #	Services
179	AL 202, to US 78, to Munford, Coldwater, N 🅖 Chevron/Subway/dsl 🍴 China King, Jack's Rest 🅞 $General, Anniston Army Depot, Rite Aid, Winn Dixie, S 🅖 Texaco/dsl
173	AL 5, Eastaboga, S 🅖 MapCo/cafe 🍴 Stuckey's 🅞 to Speedway/Hall of Fame
168	AL 77, to Talladega, N 🅖 Citgo/dsl, Marathon/KFC/Taco Bell, QV/Domino's 🍴 Jack's Rest, Waffle House, S 🅖 AOC/Burger King, Chevron/Subway/dsl, Race City TC/diner/dsl/scales 🍴 McDonald's, MT Grill, Rana's Mexican ⛺ Comfort Inn, Days Inn, Lincoln Inn 🅞 Hall of Fame, to Speedway
165	Embry Cross Roads, N 🅖 Hi-Tech/dsl, 🅖/Subway/dsl/scales/24hr 🅞 Paradise Island RV Park, S 🅖 165 TP/Huddle House/dsl, I-20TrkStp/rest./dsl/scales/24hr 🍴 Doghouse Grill ⛺ McCaig Motel
164mm	Coosa River
162	US 78, Riverside, N 🅞 Safe Harbor RV Park, S 🅖 Texaco/dsl ⛺ Best Value Inn/rest
158	US 231, Pell City, N 🅖 Marathon/dsl, Murphy USA/dsl 🍴 Arby's, Chick-fil-A, Cracker Barrel, El Cazador, Golden Rule BBQ, Jade E Chinese, Krystal, Wendy's, Zaxby's ⛺ Comfort Suites, Hampton Inn, Holiday Inn Express 🅞 $Tree, City Tire, Home Depot, Radio Shack, URGENT CARE, Walgreens, Walmart/Subway, S 🅖 Chevron, Shell/dsl, Texaco/dsl, Valero 🍴 Akita Japanese, Burger King, Hardee's, Jack's Rest., KFC, McDonald's, Pell City Steaks, Pizza Hut, Subway, Taco Bell, Waffle House ⛺ Quality Inn 🅞 H, $General, AutoZone, CVS Drug, Ford, Fred's, Verizon
156	US 78 E, to Pell City, S 🅖 Chevron/dsl, Shell/dsl
153	US 78, Chula Vista
152	Cook Springs
147	Brompton, N 🅖 Citgo, Valero TC/dsl/scales/24hr, S 🅖 Loves/McDonalds/Subway/dsl/scales/24hr, Valero/dsl/deli
144	US 411, Leeds, N 🅖 Marathon/dsl, RaceWay/dsl, Shell/Subway 🍴 Arby's, Bojangles, Burger King, Cracker Barrel, Krystal, Logan's Roadhouse, Milo's Burgers, Pizza Hut, Ruby Tuesday, Waffle House, Wendy's, Zaxby's ⛺ Best Western, Comfort Inn, Super 8 🅞 $Tree, Food Giant, Verizon, S 🅖 Chevron, RaceWay/dsl 🍴 Capt D's, Chick-fil-A, El Cazador Mexican, Guadalajara Jalisco Mexican, Hardee's, KFC, Little Caesars, McDonald's, Supreme East Buffet, Taco Bell, Waffle House ⛺ Days Inn 🅞 $General, Advance Parts, AT&T, AutoZone, Lowe's, O'Reilly Parts, Radio Shack, Walgreens, Walmart/Subway
140	US 78, Leeds, N 🅞 Distinctive Outlets/famous brands, S 🅖 Chevron, Marathon 🍴 Subway ⛺ Best Value Inn, Hampton Inn 🅞 Bass Pro Shop
139mm	Cahaba River
136	I-459 S, to Montgomery, Tuscaloosa
135	US 78, Old Leeds Rd, N 🅖 Shell/dsl 🅞 B'ham Race Course
133	US 78, to Kilgore Memorial Dr, (wb return at 132), N 🅖 Chevron, Exxon/dsl 🍴 Golden Rule BBQ, Hamburger Heaven, Jack's, Krystal, Waffle House ⛺ Best Value Inn, Siesta Motel 🅞 same as 132, S 🅖 BP 🍴 McDonald's, Zaxby's ⛺ Hampton Inn, Holiday Inn Express, Quality Inn, Rime Inn/Suites 🅞 Sam's Club/dsl, Tire Engineers
132b a	US 78, Crestwood Blvd, N 🅖 Chevron, Exxon/dsl 🍴 Golden Rule BBQ, Hamburger Heaven, Jack's, Krystal, Subway, Villa Fiesta Mexican, Waffle House ⛺ Best Value Inn, Siesta Motel 🅞 $General, Aamco, O'Reilly Parts, same as 133, S 🅖 Chevron, Exxon, Marathon, Murphy Express/dsl, Shell, Texaco/dsl 🍴 Arby's, Bojangles, Burger King, Capt D's,

🆎 INTERSTATE 20 Cont'd

Exit #	Services
132b a	Continued
	Chick-fil-A, Domino's, El Cazador Mexican, Hacienda Mexican, Honeybaked Ham, IHOP, KFC, Logan's Roadhouse, Los Arcos Mexican, McDonald's, Milo's Burgers, New China Buffet, Olive Garden, Pizza Hut, Starbucks, Taco Bell, Wendy's, Zaxby's 🛏 Comfort Inn, Delux Inn, Garden Suites 🄾 🎗, $Tree, Advance Parts, Aldi Foods, Burlington Coats, Firestone/auto, Food Smart, Home Depot, Office Depot, Radio Shack, Ross, TJ Maxx, Tuesday Morning, URGENT CARE, Verizon, Walgreens, Walmart
130b	US 11, 1st Ave, N 🗋 Chevron, Marathon, Petro 🄾 AutoZone, Family$, Piggly Wiggly, S 🗋 Exxon/dsl 🍴 McDonald's, Pacific Seafood 🛏 Relax Inn, Sky Inn
130a	I-59 N, to Gadsden
I-59 S and I-20 W run together from B'ham to Meridian, MS	
129	Airport Blvd, N 🛏 Clarion 🄾 🎗, S 🗋 BP, Shell/dsl, Shell/dsl 🍴 Hardee's, Kabob House 🛏 Best Inn, Holiday Inn
128	AL 79, Tallapoosa St, N 🗋 Exxon/Wings/dsl, Kangaroo/Subway/dsl/scales
126b	31st St, N 🗋 Shell/dsl, Texaco/dsl 🍴 McDonald's 🄾 Family$
126a	US 31, US 280, 26th St, Carraway Blvd, N 🍴 Church's, KFC, Rally's
125b	22nd St, N 🍴 Subway 🛏 Sheraton, Westin
125a	17th St, to downtown
124b a	I-65, S to Montgomery, N to Nashville
123	US 78, Arkadelphia Rd, N 🗋, Chevron, Jet-Pep, 🚚/Wendy's/dsl/scales/24hr(0.5mi), Shell/dsl 🍴 Popeye's 🛏 Days Inn, S 🄾 🎗, to Legion Field
121	Bush Blvd (from wb, no return), Ensley, N 🗋 Exxon, Marathon
120	AL 269, 20th St, Ensley Ave, N 🗋 Jet-Pep 🍴 KFC 🄾 Honda, S 🗋 BP 🄾 🎗, Toyota/Scion
119b	Ave I (from wb)
119a	Lloyd Noland Pkwy, N 🗋 Chevron/dsl, Sunoco/dsl 🍴 Burger King, Fairfield Seafood, McDonald's, Subway, S 🗋 Mobil, Texaco 🄾 🎗
118	AL 56, Valley Rd, Fairfield, S 🗋 Shell 🍴 Papa John's 🛏 Best Inn 🄾 Advance Parts, Home Depot, URGENT CARE
115	Allison-Bonnett Memorial Dr, N 🗋 Marathon/dsl, RaceWay/dsl, Shell/dsl 🍴 Church's, Jack's, Los Reyes, Subway, Zaxby's 🄾 Advance Parts, O'Reilly Parts, USPO
113	18th Ave, to Hueytown, S 🗋 Chevron/dsl, Marathon 🍴 McDonald's
112	18th St, 19th St, Bessemer, N 🗋 RaceWay/dsl, Shell 🍴 Jack's Rest. 🄾 tire/repair, S 🗋 Chevron, Sunoco/dsl 🍴 KFC, Muffaletta's Italian, Rally's, Subway, Sykes BBQ 🄾 Advance Parts, FMS Drug, Lowe's, NAPA, O'Reilly Parts, Walgreens
110	AL Adventure Pkwy, N 🄾 🎗, Splash Adventure Funpark
108	US 11, AL 5 N, Academy Dr, N 🗋 Marathon 🍴 Applebee's, Carnation Buffet, Catfish Cabin, Cracker Barrel, Waffle House 🛏 Best Western, Comfort Inn, Country Inn&Suites, Fairfield Inn, Holiday Inn Express, Quality Inn, ValuePlace 🄾 Chevrolet, Chrysler/Dodge/Jeep, Nissan, S 🗋 BP, Texaco/Church's/dsl 🍴 Burger King, Domino's, Jade Garden, Little Caesars, McDonald's, Milo's Burgers, Ruby Tuesday, Sonic, Wendy's, Zaxby's 🛏 Economy Inn, Hampton Inn, Knights Inn, Motel 6 🄾 🎗, $Tree, BigLots, Ford, PepBoys, Radio Shack, to civic ctr, Verizon, Walmart/Subway

106	I-459 N, to Montgomery
104	Rock Mt Lake, S 🗋 ✈FLYING J/Subway/dsl/LP/24hr
100	to Abernant, N 🗋 🅻🅾🆅🅴🆂/McDonald's/Subway/dsl/scales/24hr, S 🗋 BP, Exxon, Petro/Valero/Iron Skillet/Popeyes/dsl/scales/24hr/@ 🄾 $General, Tannehill Ironworks Camping, Tannehill SP (3mi)
97	US 11 S, AL 5 S, to W Blocton, S 🗋 Chevron/KFC/dsl, Exxon/Subway/dsl, Texaco/dsl 🍴 Jack's Rest., La Tortilla Grill 🄾 Cahaba River NWR
89	Mercedes Dr, N 🛏 Greystone Inn, S 🄾 Mercedes Auto Plant
86	Vance, to Brookwood, N 🗋 BP/Huddle House/Subway/dsl, Shell/dsl/rest./24hr
85mm	🅡🆂 both lanes, full 🎗 facilities, litter barrels, petwalk, 🄰, 🄰, RV dump, vending
79	US 11, University Blvd, Coaling, S 🗋 Chevron/dsl, Texaco/dsl
77	Cottondale, N 🗋 Chevron/McDonald's, TA/BP/Taco Bell/dsl/scales/24hr/@, Wilco/Wendy's/dsl/scales/24hr 🍴 Arby's, Pizza Hut, Ruby Tuesday 🛏 Hampton Inn, Microtel 🄾 Blue Beacon, SpeedCo, USPO, S 🄾 Chevrolet
76	US 11, E Tuscaloosa, Cottondale, N 🗋 BP, Chevron, Shell/dsl 🍴 Burger King, Cracker Barrel, Waffle House 🛏 Centerstone Inn, Howard Johnson, ValuePlace, Western Motel, Wingate Inn 🄾 Sunset 2 RV Park, transmissions, S 🗋 🚚/Subway/dsl/scales/24hr, Texaco/dsl 🛏 Rodeway Inn
73	US 82, McFarland Blvd, Tuscaloosa, N 🗋 BP, Chevron/dsl, Marathon, RaceWay 🍴 5 Guys Burgers, Applebee's, Arby's, Buffalo Wild Wings, Burger King, Capt D's, Chick-fil-A, Chipotle, Full Moon BBQ, Jason's Deli, Krystal, Longhorn Steaks, Moe's SW Grill, O'Charley's, Olive Garden, Panera Bread, Popeyes, Red Lobster, Shrimp Basket, Starbucks, TCBY, Waffle House 🛏 Best Value Inn, Best Western, Comfort Suites, Guest Lodge, Holiday Inn Express, Masters Inn 🄾 🎗, $General, Aamco, Advance Parts, AT&T, Barnes&Noble, Belk, Best Buy, CVS Drug, Firestone/auto, Gander Mtn, Goodyear/auto, Home Depot, JC Penney, Michael's, OK Tire, Old Navy, PepBoys, Rite Aid, Ross, Sears/auto, SteinMart, Target, Verizon, vet, S 🗋 Jet-Pep/dsl, Marathon 🍴 Buffet City, Checkers, Cheddar's, Chili's, Hardee's, KFC, Logan's Roadhouse, McDonald's, Papa John's, Pizza Hut, Sonic, Subway, Taco Bell, Taco Casa, Trey Yuen Cinese 🛏 Ambassador Inn, Candlewood Suites, Country Inn&Suites, Days Inn, EconoLodge, La Quinta, Motel 6, Quality Inn, Ramada Inn, Super 8 🄾 $General, $Tree, Chrysler/Dodge/Jeep, NAPA, Office Depot, Rite Aid, Sam's Club/gas, TJ Maxx, U-Haul, Walmart/Subway
71b	I-359, Al 69 N, to Tuscaloosa, N 🄾 🎗, to Stillman Coll, U of AL

Side labels: BIRMINGHAM · BESSEMER · TUSCALOOSA

INTERSTATE 20 Cont'd

Exit #	Services
71a	AL 69 S, to Moundville, S 🚰 Chevron, Citgo/dsl, Mapco/Quiznos/dsl, Shell/dsl 🍴 Arby's, Chick-fil-A, Costa BBQ, Hooters, IHOP, LoneStar Steaks, OutBack Steaks, Pizza Hut, Ryan's, Southern Dining Room, Waffle House, Wendy's, Zaxby's 🛏 Baymont Inn, Courtyard, Fairfield Inn, Hilton Garden ⊙ Advance Parts, Goodyear/auto, Kia/Mazda/VW, K-Mart, Lowe's, O'Reilly Parts, PepBoys, to Mound SM, URGENT CARE
68	Northport-Tuscaloosa Western Bypass
64mm	Black Warrior River
62	Fosters, N 🚰 Chevron/Subway/dsl ⊙ Foodland, USPO, vet
52	US 11, US 43, Knoxville, N 🚰 Marathon/dsl
45	AL 37, Union, S 🚰 Chevron/Subway/dsl, Texaco/dsl 🍴 South Fork Rest 🛏 Best Inn, Comfort Inn ⊙ Greene Co Greyhound Park
40	AL 14, Eutaw, N ⊙ to Tom Bevill Lock/Dam, S 🚰 BP ⊙ 🏥
39mm	℞ˢ wb, full 🚻 facilities, litter barrels, petwalk, 🕿, 🏧, RV dump, vending
38mm	℞ˢ eb, full 🚻 facilities, litter barrels, petwalk, 🕿, 🏧, RV dump, vending
32	Boligee, N 🚰 Marathon/rest./dsl/24hr, S 🚰 Chevron/Subway/dsl
27mm	Tenn-Tom Waterway, Tombigbee River
23	rd 20, Epes, to Gainesville
17	AL 28, Livingston, S 🚰 Chevron/Subway/dsl, Shell/dsl, Texaco/L&B/dsl/24hr 🍴 Burger King, Diamond Jim's/Mrs Donna's, McDonald's, Pizza Hut 🛏 Comfort Inn, Western Inn ⊙ repair/24hr
8	AL 17, York, S 🚰 BP/New Orleans Grill/dsl/scales/@ 🛏 Best Inn ⊙ 🏥
1	to US 80 E, Cuba, S 🚰 Chevron/dsl, Citgo/rest./dsl
.5mm	Welcome Ctr eb, full 🚻 facilities, litter barrels, petwalk, 🕿, 🏧, RV dump, vending
	I-20 E and I-59 N run together from Meridian, MS to B'ham
0mm	Alabama/Mississippi state line

INTERSTATE 22 (FUTURE)

Exit #	Services
93	rd 77, (I-22 future begins/ends)
91	rd 105, to Brookside
89	rd 65, to Adamsville, Graysville
87	rd 112, to Graysville
85	US 78, Birmingham
81	rd 45, W Jefferson
78	rd 81, Dora, Sumiton, N 🚰 TJ's/dsl
72	rd 61, Cordova
70	rd 22, Cordova, Parish
65	Bevill Ind Pkwy, Jasper, N 🚰 RaceWay/dsl 🛏 Hampton Inn (3mi) ⊙ 🏥, to Walker Co Lake, S 🚰 Loves/McDonald's/Subway/dsl/scales/24hr ⊙ Buick/Cadillac/Chevrolet/GMC
63	AlL 269, Jasper, Parish, N 🚰 Chevron/deli/dsl
61	AL 69, Jasper, Tuscaloosa, N 🚰 RJ's
57	AL 118 E, Jasper, S 🚰 Chevron, Exxon 🍴 Panter's Place Rest
52	AL 118, Carbon Hill, S 🛏 Shadowbrook Inn
46	rd 11, Carbon Hill, Nauvoo, S 🚰 Shell
39	AL 13, Natural Bridge, Eldridge
34	AL 233, Glen Allen, Natural Bridge
30	AL 129, Brilliant, Winfield, S 🚰 Shell/deli/dsl, Texaco/deli/dsl 🛏 EconoLodge, Hampton Inn

26	AL 44, Brilliant, Guin, S 🛏 Holiday Inn Express ⊙ 🍴
22	rd 45
16	US 43, US 278, Hamilton, Guin, S 🚰 Shell/deli/dsl
14	Hamilton, N 🚰 Texaco/dsl 🍴 Huddle House 🛏 Days Inn (1mi), EconoLodge (1mi), Keywest Inn
11	AL 17, Hamilton, Sulligent, N 🚰 Citgo/dsl ⊙ 🍴
7	Hamilton, Weston, N ⊙ 🍴
3	rd 33
0mm	Alabama/Mississippi State Line

INTERSTATE 59

Exit #	Services
241.5mm	Alabama/Georgia state line, Central/Eastern time zone
241mm	Welcome Ctr sb, full 🚻 facilities, litter barrels, petwalk, 🕿, 🏧, RV dump, vending
239	to US 11, Sulphur Springs Rd, E ⊙ camping
231	AL 40, AL 117, Hammondville, Valley Head, E ⊙ camping (5mi), DeSoto SP, W 🚰 Victory Fuel
224	49th St, to Ft Payne
222	US 11, to Ft Payne, 1 mi E 🚰 Delta 🍴 Arby's, Hardee's, Jack's Rest., KFC, Krystal, New Asian Buffet, Pizza Hut, SteviB's Pizza, Subway 🛏 Country Hearth Inn ⊙ Chevrolet, Foodland/dsl, W 🚰 JetPep/dsl 🍴 Waffle King
218	AL 35, Ft Payne, E 🍴 Capt D's, Don Chico Mexican, DQ, Jack's, Jefferson's Burgers, McDonald's, New China, Papa John's, Quiznos, Taco Bell, Wendy's, Western Sizzlin, Zaxby's ⊙ $General, Advance Parts, AutoZone, BigLots, Buick/GMC, Chrysler/Dodge/Jeep, O'Reilly Parts, W 🚰 Kangaroo/dsl, MapCo, Murphy USA/dsl, Victory Fuel 🍴 Burger King, Chow King, Cracker Barrel, Hardee's, Ruby Tuesday, Ryan's, Santa Fe Steaks, Subway, Waffle House 🛏 Days Inn, EconoLodge, Hampton Inn, Holiday Inn Express ⊙ 🍴, $Tree, AT&T, Ford/Lincoln, GNC, K-Mart, Lowe's, Radio Shack, Verizon, Walgreens, Walmart, Will's Creek RV Park
205	AL 68, Collinsville, E 🚰 Delta 🍴 Jack's Rest. 🛏 Traveler's Inn ⊙ to Little River Canyon, Weiss Lake, W 🚰 BP/dsl, MapCo
188	AL 211, to US 11, Gadsden, E 🚰 Jet-Pep ⊙ Noccalula Falls Camping, W 🚰 Clean Fuels/dsl/E85
183	US 431, US 278, Gadsden, E 🚰 Jet-Pep/dsl, Shell, Texaco/dsl 🍴 Magic Burger, Waffle House 🛏 Days Inn, Rodeway Inn, Travelodge ⊙ st police, W 🚰 Chevron, Exxon, Jet-Pep 🍴 Krystal, McDonald's, Pizza Hut, Subway, Taco Bell
182	I-759, to Gadsden
181	AL 77, Rainbow City, to Gadsden, E 🚰 Petro/rest./dsl/scales/24hr/@ 🍴 Ezell's Fishcamp 🛏 Days Inn, W 🚰 Citgo, Kangaroo/dsl, Murphy Express/dsl, Pure/dsl 🍴 Arby's, Bubba Rito's SW Grill, Cracker Barrel, Domino's, Hardee's, Los Arcos, Lucky Wok, Old Mexico Grille, Ray's BBQ, Ruby Tuesday, Subway, Waffle House, Wendy's 🛏 Best Western, Comfort Suites, Fairfield Inn, Hampton Inn, Holiday Inn Express ⊙ $General, $Tree, O'Reilly Parts, Radio Shack, Walmart/Papa John's
174	to Steele, E 🚰 Loves/Subway/Chester's/dsl/scales/24hr, W 🚰 JetPep/dsl, Shell/rest/dsl
168mm	℞ˢ sb, full 🚻 facilities, litter barrels, petwalk, 🕿, 🏧, RV dump, vending
166	US 231, Whitney, to Ashville, E 🚰 BP, W 🚰 Texaco/dsl 🍴 Huddle House, Jack's Rest., Subway
165mm	℞ˢ nb, full 🚻 facilities, litter barrels, petwalk, 🕿, 🏧, RV dump, vending
156	AL 23, to US 11, Springville, to St Clair Springs, W 🚰 Citgo/dsl 🍴 Azteca's Mexican, China Stix, Hardee's, Pizza Hut,

(Vertical side text: FT PAYNE · GADSDEN)

⬆N INTERSTATE 59 Cont'd

Exit #	Services
156	Continued Waffle House 🅾 $Tree, AT&T, Walmart/Subway
154	AL 174, Springville, to Odenville, **W** 🅶 Chevron, MapCo, Shell/dsl, Valero/Subway 🍴 Choppin Block Rest., Huck's Ribshack, Jack's Rest., McDonald's, Sal's Rest., Smokin Grill BBQ 🅾 vet
148	to US 11, Argo, **E** 🅶 BP
143	Mt Olive Church Rd, Deerfoot Pkwy, **E** 🅶 Chevron/dsl/CNG, Shell/dsl (1mi) 🅾 Publix (1mi)
141	to Trussville, Pinson, **E** 🅶 Bama Gas, Shell/Subway/dsl, Texaco/dsl 🍴 Applebee's, Cracker Barrel, LoneStar Steaks, McDonald's, Papa John's, Pizza Hut, Taco Bell, Waffle House, Wendy's 🛏 Comfort Inn, Holiday Inn Express, Quality Inn 🅾 Harley-Davidson, **W** 🅶 BP, Chevron, Shell/dsl 🍴 Arby's, Buffalo Wild Wings, Burger King, Chick-fil-A, Costa's Italian, DQ, East Buffet, Frontera Grill, Jack's, Konomi Japanese, Krystal, Little Caesars, Milo's Burgers, Moe's SW Grill, Momma Goldberg's Deli, Palace Asian, Paul's Hotdogs, Ruby Tuesday, Seafood&Chicken Box, Whataburger, Zaxby's 🅾 $Tree, Ace Hardware, Advance Parts, Aldi Foods, AT&T, BigLots, CVS Drug, GNC, K-Mart, Kohl's, Marshalls, Office Depot, Petsmart, Sam's Club/gas, vet, Walgreens, Walmart/Subway
137	I-459 S, to Montgomery, Tuscaloosa
134	to AL 75, Roebuck Pkwy, **W** 🅶 Chevron, Marathon/Kangaroo, Murphy USA/dsl, Shell/dsl 🍴 Arby's, Burger King, Chick-fil-A, Krystal, McDonald's, Milo's Burgers, Pizza Hut, Ruby Tuesday, Taco Bell, Waffle House 🛏 Best Inn 🅾 🏥, $Tree, Aldi Foods, AT&T, CVS Drug, GNC, Honda, NTB, O'Reilly Parts, Rite Aid, V Tires, Walgreens, Walmart
133	4th St, to US 11 (from nb), **W** 🍴 Papa John's 🅾 $General, same as 134, Suzuki, USPO
132	US 11 N, 1st Ave, **E** same as 131, **W** 🅶 Chevron, Shell 🍴 Krispy Kreme 🅾 city park
131	Oporto-Madrid Blvd (from nb), **E** 🅶 Chevron, Marathon/Subway 🍴 Church's, Little Caesars, Rally's 🅾 CVS Drug, Family$, O'Reilly Parts, same as 132, U-Haul
130	I-20, **E** to Atlanta, **W** to Tuscaloosa

I-59 S and I-20 W run together from B'ham to Mississippi. See Alabama I-20, exits 129-1.

⬆N INTERSTATE 65

Exit #	Services
366mm	Alabama/Tennessee state line
365	AL 53, to Ardmore, **E** 🅶 Pure 🛏 Budget Inn
364mm	**W** Welcome Ctr sb, full ♿ facilities, info, litter barrels, petwalk, 🚻, 🛗, RV dump, vending
361	Elkmont, **W** 🅶 BP/dsl, HQ/rest./dsl 🍴 Momma D's Rest. 🅾 antiques, repair
354	US 31 S, to Athens, **W** 🅶 Chevron/dsl, Texaco/dsl 🍴 Capt D's, China Dragon, Domino's, Jack's Rest., Little Caesars, McDonald's, Pizza Hut, Rooster's Cafe, Subway 🛏 Mark Motel 🅾 🏥, $General, Advance Parts, city park, CVS Drug, HomeTown Mkt, K-Mart, Northgate RV Park, Rite Aid, Walgreens
351	US 72, to Athens, Huntsville, **E** 🅶 Exxon, RaceWay/dsl, Shell/Subway, Texaco/dsl 🍴 Burger King, Casa Blanca Mexican, Clark's Rest., Cracker Barrel, Jack's, Las Tejanas Mexican, Lawler's BBQ, McDonald's/RV Parking, New China Buffet, Pepper's Deli, Waffle House, Wendy's 🛏 Country Hearth Inn, Hampton Inn, Quality Inn, Travel Inn 🅾 $General, AT&T, Publix, Russell Stover, Verizon, vet, **W** 🅶 BP, Chevron/dsl,

Exit #	Services
351	Continued Citgo/dsl, Murphy USA 🍴 Applebee's, Arby's, Bojangles, Burger King, Catfish Cabin, Chick-fil-A, DQ, Firehouse Subs, Hardee's, IHOP, KFC, Krystal, Logan's Roadhouse, Papa John's, Papa Murphy's, Pizza Hut, Ruby Tuesday, Shoney's, Sonic, Starbucks, Steak-Out, Subway, Taco Bell, Zaxby's 🛏 Best Western, Days Inn, Fairfield Inn, Holiday Inn Express, Sleep Inn, Super 8 🅾 🏥, $General, $Tree, Advance Parts, Big 10 Tire, Big Lots, Chevrolet, Chrysler/Dodge/Jeep, Ford, Goodyear/auto, Lowe's, O'Reilly Parts, Pepboys, Radio Shack, SaveALot Foods, Staples, to Joe Wheeler SP, Tuesday Morning, Verizon, Walmart
347	Brownsferry Rd, Huntsville, Swan Creek RV Park
340b	I-565, to Huntsville, **E** to Alabama Space & Rocket Ctr
340a	AL 20, to Decatur, **W** 🅶 Chevron/dsl, RaceWay 🛏 Courtyard, Hampton Inn, Holiday Inn
337mm	Tennessee River
334	AL 67, Priceville, to Decatur, **E** 🅶 BP/dsl, RaceWay/dsl 🍴 JW's Steaks 🛏 Days Inn, Super 8 🅾 $General, Family$, Foodland, **W** 🅶 Chevron/dsl, ▨▨▨/Subway/Wendy's/dsl/scales/24hr 🍴 Burger King, DQ, Hardee's, Krystal, McDonald's/playplace, Pizza Hut, Smokehouse BBQ, Taste of China, Waffle House 🛏 Comfort Inn 🅾 🏥, Hood RV Ctr
328	AL 36, Hartselle, **E** 🍴 Cracker Barrel, **W** 🅶 Cowboys/dsl, Jet-Pep/dsl, Shell/dsl, Ztrac 🍴 Huddle House 🛏 Best Value Inn 🅾 vet
325	Thompson Rd, to Hartselle
322	AL 55, to US 31, to Falkville, Eva, **E** 🅶 BP/Chester's/dsl, **W** 🅶 Chevron, ▨Loves▨/McDonald's/Subway/dsl/scales/24hr 🍴 Momma's Grill 🅾 $General
318	US 31, to Lacon, **E** 🅶 BP/Stuckey's 🛏 Lacon Motel
310	AL 157, Cullman, West Point, **E** 🅶 Chevron, Conoco/Subway/dsl, Marathon/dsl, Shell/dsl, Texaco/Wendy's/dsl 🍴 Arby's, Backyard Burger, Burger King, Cracker Barrel, Denny's, KFC, Logan's Roadhouse, McDonald's, New China, Ruby Tuesday, Taco Bell, Waffle House 🛏 Best Western, Comfort Suites, Hampton Inn, Holiday Inn Express, Quality Inn, Sleep Inn 🅾 🏥, Buick/GMC, Ford/Lincoln, Piggly Wiggly, **W** 🅶 BP/dsl, Exxon/dsl 🛏 Best Value Inn
308	US 278, Cullman, **E** 🛏 Days Inn 🅾 Smith Farms, **W** 🅶 Chevron 🅾 Chrysler/Dodge/Jeep, flea mkt
304	AL 69 N, Good Hope, to Cullman, **E** 🅶 Exxon/dsl, Jet-Pep/dsl, Shell/rest/dsl/scales, Wilco/Hess/Wendy's/Dunkin Donuts/dsl/scales/24hts 🍴 Hardee's, Jack's Rest., Waffle House 🛏 EconoLodge 🅾 🏥, dsl/rv repair, Good Hope Camping, Kountry Mile RV Ctr, **W** 🅶 Jet-Pep, to Smith Lake Camping 🅾 $General
301mm	**E** 🆁🆂 both lanes, full ♿ facilities, litter barrels, petwalk, 🚻, 🛗, RV dump, vending

D E C A T U R   **C U L L M A N**   **A T H E N S**

AL

⬆N INTERSTATE 65 Cont'd

Exit #	Services
299	AL 69 S, to Jasper, **E** 🅶 Sunoco/dsl 🅾 Millican RV Ctr, repair/tires, **W** 🅶 HQ, Petro/Conoco/Iron Skillet/dsl/scales/24hr, Shell/McDonald's/dsl, Texaco/dsl 🍴 Jack's Rest., Subway 🅾 $General, Parts City
291mm	Warrior River
291	AL 91, to Arkadelphia, **E** 🅶 Jet-Pep/dsl 🅾 Country View RV Park (1mi), **W** 🅶 Shell/rest./dsl/24hr/@ 🍴 Southern Sunrise Cafe
289	to Blount Springs, **W** 🅶 BP/DQ/Stuckey's 🅾 to Rickwood Caverns SP
287	US 31 N, to Blount Springs, **E** 🅶 Citgo, Jet-Pep/dsl
284	US 31 S, AL 160 E, Hayden, **E** 🅶 Shamrock/dsl, Valero 🅾 URGENT CARE, **W** 🅾 tires
282	AL 140, Warrior, **E** 🅶 Chevron/Subway/dsl, Exxon/McDonald's, FuelZ/Dunkin Donuts/Little Caesars/dsl 🍴 Hardee's, Pizza Hut, Taco Bell, **W** 🅶 BP
281	US 31, to Warrior, **E** 🅾 Chevrolet
280	to US 31, to Warrior, **E** 🅶 Chevron/dsl 🅾 Chevrolet, vet
279mm	Warrior River
275	to US 31, Morris
272	Mt Olive Rd, **E** 🅶 Shell/dsl 🅾 LDS Temple, **W** 🅶 BP/dsl, Chevron/dsl 🍴 Jack's Rest. 🅾 $General
271	Fieldstown Rd, **E** 🅶 BP/Circle K, Chevron/dsl, Exxon, Murphy USA/dsl, RaceWay/dsl 🍴 Arby's, Buffalo Wild Wings, Capt D, Chick-fil-A, DQ, Guthrie's Diner, Habanero's Mexican, Jim'n Nick's BBQ, KFC, Little Caesars, McDonald's, Milo's Burgers, Panera Bread, Pasquales Pizza, Pizza Hut, Ryan's, Sonic, Subway, Taco Bell, Waffle House, Wendy's, Zaxby's 🛏 Microtel 🅾 $General, $Tree, Advance Parts, AT&T, AutoZone, CVS, Hobby Lobby, Kia, NAPA, PepBoys, Publix, Radio Shack, URGENT CARE, Verizon, Walgreens, Walmart/McDonald's, **W** 🅶 Shell/dsl 🍴 Cracker Barrel 🛏 Best Western
267	Walkers Chapel Rd, to Fultondale, **E** 🅶 Chevron/dsl, Jet-Pep, Murphy Express/dsl, Shell/Subway/dsl 🍴 5 Guys Burgers, Applebee's, Arby's, Bojangles, Burger King, Casa Fiesta, Chick-fil-A, Chili's, Domino's, Firehouse Subs, Fullmoon BBQ, Hardee's, Jack's Rest., Jalisco Mexican, Logan's Roadhouse, McDonald's, O'Charley's, Outback Steaks, Stix Asian, Waffle House, Whataburger, Zaxby's 🛏 Comfort Suites, Fairfield Inn, Hampton Inn, Holiday Inn Express, La Quinta 🅾 $General, AAA, Aldi Foods, AT&T, Best Buy, Books-A-Million, CVS Drug, GNC, JC Penney, Lowe's, O'Reilly Parts, Rite Aid, Ross, Target, URGENT CARE, USPO, Verizon, Volvo/Mack Trucks, Winn-Dixie, **W** 🅶 Chevron/dsl 🍴 Porky's Pride BBQ
266	US 31, Fultondale, **E** 🅶 Chevron/dsl 🛏 Days Inn, Super 8
265	I-22 W, to Memphis
264	41st Ave, **W** 🅶 ⚜FLYING J/Denny's/dsl/LP/scales/24hr
263	33rd Ave, **E** 🅶 Chevron/dsl 🛏 Apex Motel, **W** 🅶 Exxon
262 b a	16th St, Finley Ave, **E** 🅶 Chevron, Marathon/dsl, Sunoco/dsl 🅾 Kenworth, **W** 🅶 Chevron, Fuel City/dsl, Mobil/dsl/scales 🍴 Capt D's, McDonald's, Popeye's
261 b a	I-20/59, E to Gadsden, W to Tuscaloosa
260 b a	6th Ave N, **E** 🅶 Citgo, Shell, Texaco 🍴 Mrs Winner's 🛏 Tourway Inn 🅾 Chevrolet, Chrysler/Dodge/Jeep, Hyundai, Nissan, Subaru, **W** 🅶 Chevron/dsl 🅾 Tire Pros, to Legion Field
259 b a	University Blvd, 4th Ave, 5th Ave, **E** 🅶 Chevron/dsl 🍴 Capt D's, McDonald's, Ted's Cafeteria 🅾 H, **W** 🅶 Chevron/dsl 🅾 Goodyear
258	Green Springs Ave, **E** 🅶 Chevron, Shell, Sunoco/dsl 🍴 Exotic Wings

B I R M I N G H A M

256 b a	Oxmoor Rd, **E** 🅶 Exxon, Marathon, Mobil/dsl, Shell 🍴 Acapulco Grill, Alfredo's Pizza, Burger King, Domino's, Firehouse Subs, Hunan Rest., KFC, McDonald's, Papa Murphy's, Paw Paw Patch, Popeyes, Purple Onion, San Miguel Mexican, Taco Bell, The Baskits, Zaxby's 🛏 Howard Johnson 🅾 $Tree, Aldi Foods, AutoZone, BigLots, Firestone/auto, Food World, Fred's, K-Mart, Midas, Office Depot, Omega Tire Pros, PepBoys, Publix, Tire Engineers, Tuesday Morning, URGENT CARE, Walgreens, Walmart Mkt, **W** 🅶 Chevron, Texaco/dsl 🍴 Hamburger Heaven, Hardee's, Jim'n Nick's BBQ, Waffle House 🛏 Best Inn, Best Value Inn, Comfort Inn, EconoLodge, Motel 6, Quality Inn, Super 8 🅾 Batteries+, Valley Tire, vet
255	Lakeshore Dr, **E** 🅶 BP/Circle K 🅾 H, to Samford U, URGENT CARE, **W** 🅶 Chevron, Shell 🍴 Arby's, Chick-fil-A, Chili's, Costas BBQ, Hooters, IHOP, La Catrina Mexican, Landry's Seafood, McAlister's Deli, McDonald's, Milo's Burger, Moe's SW Grill, Mr Wang's, O'Charley's, Okinawa Grill, Outback Steaks, Starbucks, Subway, Taco Bell, Taco Casa, Wendy's 🛏 Best Western, Candlewood Suites, Country Inn&Suites, Drury Inn, Extended Stay, Hampton Inn, Hilton Garden, Holiday Inn, La Quinta, Residence Inn, TownePlace Suites 🅾 $Tree, AT&T, Goodyear/auto, Hobby Lobby, Lowe's, Radio Shack, Sam's Club/gas, Verizon, Walmart/Subway
254	Alford Ave, Shades Crest Rd, **E** 🅶 Chevron 🅾 vet, **W** 🅶 BP/dsl, Shell/dsl
252	US 31, Montgomery Hwy, **E** 🅶 Chevron, Shell, Sunoco, Texaco/dsl 🍴 Arby's, Backyard Burger, Bruster's, Capt D's, ChuckECheese's, Hardee's, Ichiban Japanese, Milo's Burger, Waffle House 🛏 Baymont Inn, Days Inn 🅾 H, Aamco, GMC, NAPA, PepBoys, Verizon, vet, Volvo, VW, **W** 🅶 Exxon/dsl, Shell/dsl, Sunoco/dsl 🍴 Burger King, Chick-fil-A, FishMkt Rest., Full Moon BBQ, Golden Rule BBQ, Habanero's Mexican, Krispy Kreme, Krystal, Mandarin House, McDonald's, Outback Steaks, Papa John's, Papa Murphy's, Purple Onion, Salvatore's Pizza, Starbucks, Subway, Waffle House 🛏 EconoLodge 🅾 $Tree, Acura, Advance Parts, AutoZone, Cadillac, Chevrolet, Chrysler/Dodge/Jeep, Firestone, Goodyear/auto, Honda, Hyundai, Mr Transmission, Nissan, Publix, Rite Aid, Staples, TJ Maxx, vet
250	I-459, to US 280
247	rd 17, Valleydale Rd, **E** 🅶 BP/Circle K 🍴 Hardee's, Jeffersons Wings 🅾 Goodyear/auto, Lowe's, **W** 🅶 Marathon, RaceWay/dsl, Shell/dsl 🍴 Arby's, Backyard Burger, IHOP, Milo's Burgers, Papa John's, RagTime Café, Subway, Waffle House, Zapatas Mexican 🛏 Homewood Suites, InTown Suites, La Quinta 🅾 Publix, Rite Aid, vet, Walgreens
246	AL 119, Cahaba Valley Rd, **E** 🅾 to Oak Mtn SP, **W** 🅶 Chevron, Kangaroo/Subway/dsl/scales, Murphy USA/dsl, RaceWay/dsl, Shell/dsl 🍴 2 Pesos Mexican, Applebee's, Arby's, Burger King, Capt D's, Chick-fil-A, Cracker Barrel, DQ, Dunkin Donuts, Golden Corral, Hooters, Johnny Ray's BBQ, KFC, Krystal, Margarita Grill, McAlister's Deli, McDonald's, Pizza Hut, Purple Onion, Ruby Tuesday, Sonic, Taco Bell, TX Roadhouse, Waffle House, Wendy's, Whataburger 🛏 Best Western, Comfort Suites, Fairfield Inn, Hampton Inn, Holiday Inn Express, Quality Inn, Ramada, Sleep Inn, Travelodge, ValuePlace 🅾 H, $Tree, Advance Parts, AutoZone, Firestone/auto, Harley-Davidson, Kia, Mazda, NAPA, O'Reilly Parts, Verizon, Walmart
242	rd 52, Pelham, **E** 🅶 Chevron/dsl, Exxon/dsl, Shell/dsl 🍴 Johnny Ray's BBQ, Subway 🅾 CVS Drug, Publix, **W** 🛏 Shelby Motel (2mi) 🅾 H, Good Sam Camping (1mi)

FULTONDALE (vertical side label)

HOOVER (vertical side label)

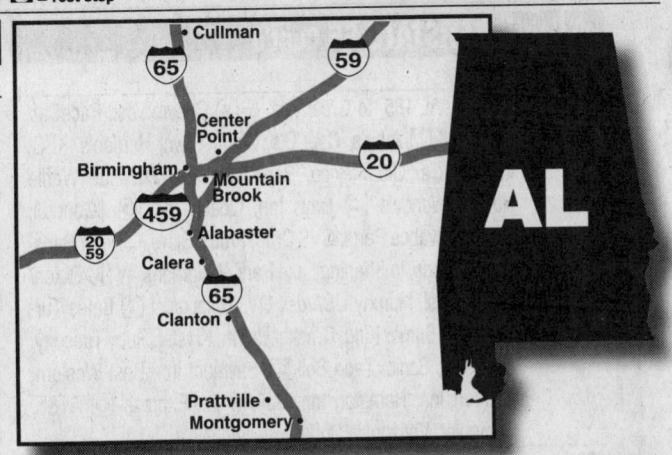

INTERSTATE 65 Cont'd

Exit #	Services
238	US 31, Alabaster, Saginaw, **E** 🅖 Murphy USA/dsl 🍴 Arby's, Buffalo Wild Wings, Chick-fil-A, DQ, Firehouse Subs, Full Moon BBQ, Habanero's Mexican, HoneyBaked Ham, Jim'n Nick's BBQ, Longhorn Steaks, McDonald's, Mizu Japanese, Moe's SW Grill, Momma Goldberg Deli, O'Charley's, Olive Garden, Panda House, Panera Bread, Ruby Tuesday, Starbucks, Steak'n Shake, Taco Bell 🛏 Candlewood Suites 🅞 $Tree, AT&T, Belk, Best Buy, Books-A-Million, Dick's, GNC, JC Penney, Lowe's, NTB, Old Navy, Petsmart, Radio Shack, Ross, Target, TJ Maxx, URGENT CARE, Walmart/Subway, **W** 🅖 Chevron/dsl, Shell/dsl 🍴 Waffle House, Whataburger 🛏 Shelby Motel 🅞 🅷
234	Shelby County 🆁🆂, **E** 🅖 BP/Subway/dsl, **W** 🅖 Chevron/dsl, Shell/dsl 🅞 Buick/GMC, Camping World RV Ctr
231	US 31, Saginaw, **E** 🅖 GasBoy, Murphy USA/dsl, Shell/dsl 🍴 Bojangles, Capt D's, Cracker Barrel, Ezell's Catfish Cabin, McDonald's, Milo's Burgers, Pizza Hut, Subway, Taco Bell, Waffle House, Zaxby's, Zopapan Mexican 🛏 Hampton Inn, Quality Inn 🅞 $Tree, AT&T, Burton RV Ctr, Publix, Radio Shack, Rolling Hills RV Park, URGENT CARE, Verizon, Walmart/Subway
228	AL 25, to Calera, **E** 🅖 Marathon/dsl, Shell/dsl 🛏 Calera Inn, **W** 🅖 Chevron/dsl 🍴 Little Caesar's, Subway 🅞 $General, Family$, to Brierfield Iron Works SP (15mi)
227mm	Buxahatchie Creek
219	Union Grove, Thorsby, **E** 🅖 Chevron/dsl, Exxon/Subway/dsl 🅞 Peach Queen Camping, **W** 🅖 Shell/dsl 🍴 Jack's Rest., Smokey Hollow Rest.
213mm	🆁🆂 both lanes, full 🛏 facilities, litter barrels, petwalk, 🅒, 🅰, RV dump, vending
212	AL 145, Clanton, **E** 🅖 Chevron/dsl 🅞 Nissan, Toyota/Scion, **W** 🅖 Headco/dsl, Texaco/Subway 🅞 🅷 Buick/Chevrolet/GMC, Chrysler/Dodge/Jeep, One Big Peach
208	Clanton, **E** 🅖 ♥Love's/Arby's/dsl/scales/24hr 🅞 Higgins Ferry RV Park (8mi), **W** 🅖 Exxon/dsl 🍴 Shoney's 🛏 Clanton Inn 🅞 Dandy RV Park/Ctr, Heaton Pecans, KOA
205	US 31, AL 22, to Clanton, **E** 🅖 Jet-Pep/dsl/E85, Shell/dsl, Texaco/dsl 🍴 McDonald's, Waffle House, Whataburger 🛏 Best Western, Days Inn, Holiday Inn Express, Scottish Inn 🅞 Peach Park, to Confed Mem Park (9mi), **0-2 mi W** 🅖 Chevron/dsl, Murphy USA/dsl, Shell/dsl 🍴 Boomerang's Grill, Burger King, Capt D's, Jack's Rest., KFC, New China Buffet, Papa John's, Pizza Hut, San Marcos Mexican, Subway, Taco Bell, Wendy's, Zaxby's 🛏 Key West Inn 🅞 $General, $Tree, auto repair, Durbin Farms Mkt, Verizon, Walmart
200	to Verbena, **E** 🅖 Texaco/dsl, **W** 🅖 Sunoco
195	Worlds Largest Confederate Flag
186	US 31, Pine Level, **E** 🅞 Confederate Mem Park (13mi), **W** 🅖 Chevron/dsl, Exxon/dsl, Texaco/Subway/dsl 🍴 Shann's Kitchen 🅞 🅷
181	AL 14, to Prattville, **E** 🅖 Chevron/dsl, Entec/dsl 🍴 Jack's, **W** 🅖 BP, Marathon/Kangaroo, QV, Shell/DQ/dsl 🍴 Cracker Barrel, Los Toros, McDonald's, Ruby Tuesday, Subway, Waffle House, Wendy's 🛏 EconoLodge, Hometowne Suites, La Quinta, Quality Inn, Super 8 🅞 🅷
179	US 82 W, Millbrook, **E** 🅖 Chevron/dsl 🛏 Country Inn&Suites, Key West Inn, Sleep Inn 🅞 K&K RV Ctr/Park, **0-2 mi W** 🅖 Liberty/dsl, Murphy Express/dsl, RaceWay/dsl, Shell/dsl 🍴 Applebee's, Arby's, Beef'O'Brady's, Bruster's, Burger King, Capt. D's, Chappy's Deli, Chick-fil-A, Chipotle, CiCi's Pizza,

MILLBROOK

MONTGOMERY

CLANTON

Exit #	Services
179	Continued City Buffet, El Patron, Five Guys, Hardee's, IHOP, Jim'n Nick's BBQ, KFC, Krystal, Las Casitas Mexican, Logan's Roadhouse, Longhorn Steaks, McAlister's Deli, McDonald's, Mellow Mushroom, Mexico Tipico, Moe's SW Grill, O'Charley's, Olive Garden, Outback Steaks, Panda Express, Popeyes, Ryan's, Shoney's, Sonic, Starbucks, Steak'n Shake, Subway, Waffle House, Zaxby's 🛏 Courtyard, Days Inn, Hampton Inn, Holiday Inn Express, Howard Johnson, Rodeway Inn 🅞 $General, $Tree, AT&T, AutoZone, Bass Pro Shops, Belk, Best Buy, BigLots, Books-A-Million, Chevrolet, CVS Drug, Firestone/auto, Ford, GNC, Hobby Lobby, Home Depot, JC Penney, K-Mart, Kohl's, Lowe's, Michael's, Office Depot, O'Reilly Parts, PepBoys, Petsmart, Publix, Ross, Target, TJ Maxx, URGENT CARE, Verizon, vet, Walmart
176	AL 143 N (from nb, no return), Millbrook, Coosada
173	AL 152, North Blvd, to US 231
172mm	Alabama River
172	Clay St, Herron St, **E** 🛏 Embassy Suites, Hampton Inn, Renaissance Hotel, **W** 🅖 Chevron/dsl
171	I-85 N, Day St
170	Fairview Ave, **E** 🅖 Citgo/Subway, Sunoco/dsl 🍴 Church's, McDonald's, Wing Master 🅞 Advance Parts, AutoZone, CVS Drug, Family$, O'Reilly Parts, Piggly Wiggly, Rite Aid, **W** 🅖 Exxon/dsl 🅞 Calhoun Foods, Family$
169	Edgemont Ave (from sb), **E** 🅖 Liberty
168	US 80 E, US 82, South Blvd, **E** 🅖 Entec/dsl, Kangaroo/dsl, TA/Marathon/Country Pride/dsl/24hr/@ 🍴 Arby's, Burger King, Capt D's, KFC, McDonald's, Pizza Hut, Popeye's, Taco Bell, Waffle House 🛏 Best Inn, Economy Inn 🅞 🅷, The Woods RV Park, **W** 🅖 Chevron/dsl, RaceWay/dsl, Shell/Subway/dsl 🍴 DQ, Hardee's, Wendy's 🛏 Candlelight Inn, Comfort Inn, KeyWest Inn
167	US 80 W, to Selma
164	US 31, Hyundai Blvd, Hope Hull, **E** 🅖 Liberty, Saveway/dsl/scales/24hr, Shell/dsl 🍴 El Amigo Mexican 🅞 auto repair, Montgomery Camping, **W** 🅖 BP, Chevron, Liberty/Subway 🍴 Burger King, McDonald's, Waffle House 🛏 Best Western, Comfort Suites, Fairfield Inn, Hampton Inn, Holiday Inn, Motel 6 🅞 auto repair
158	to US 31, Tyson, **E** 🅖 BP/DQ/Stuckey's 🅞 Montgomery South RV Park, **W** 🅖 🅳FLYING J/Denny's/dsl/scales/24hr
151	AL 97, to Letohatchee, **E** 🅖 Marathon/dsl, **W** 🅖 BP, PaceCar/dsl
142	AL 185, to Ft Deposit, **E** 🅖 Petro+/dsl 🍴 Priester's Pecans, Subway 🅞 auto parts, **W** 🅖 Chevron
133mm	🆁🆂 both lanes, full 🛏 facilities, litter barrels, petwalk, 🅒, 🅰, RV dump, vending

🅖 = gas 🍴 = food 🛏 = lodging 🄾 = other 🆁🆂 = rest stop

AL

G R E E N V I L L E   E V E R G R E E N   A T M O R E

Exit #	Services
▲🅽 **INTERSTATE 65 Cont'd**	
130	AL10 E, AL 185, to Greenville, **E** 🅖 Chevron/dsl, PaceCar/dsl, Shell 🍴 Arby's, Capt D's, China Town, Hardee's, KFC, McDonald's, Old Mexico, Papa John's, Pizza Hut, Waffle House, Wendy's 🛏 Days Inn, Quality Inn 🄾 $General, $Tree, Advance Parts, CVS Drug, Fred's Store, O'Reilly Parts, Super Foods, to Sherling Lake Park, Walgreens, **W** 🅖 Exxon/Subway/dsl, Murphy USA/dsl, QV, Texaco/dsl 🍴 Bates Turkey Cafe, Burger King, Cracker Barrel, Krystal, Ruby Tuesday, Shoney's, Sonic, Taco Bell 🛏 Baymont Inn, Best Western, Comfort Inn, Hampton Inn, Holiday Inn Express 🄾 AT&T, Chevrolet, Verizon, Walmart/Subway
128	AL 10, to Greenville, **E** 🅖 Shell/Smokehouse 🄾 🍴, **W** 🅖 Marathon
114	AL 106, to Georgiana, **E** 🄾 Hank Williams Museum, **W** 🅖 Chevron, Marathon 🄾 auto repair
107	rd 7, to Garland
101	to Owassa, **E** 🅖 Marathon/dsl, **W** 🅖 Exxon/dsl 🄾 dsl repair, Owassa RV Park
96	AL 83, to Evergreen, **E** 🅖 Chevron, Shell 🍴 Burger King, Hardee's, Jalisco Mexican, KFC/Taco Bell, McDonald's, Shrimp Basket 🛏 Sleep Inn 🄾🍴, vet, **W** 🅖 Spirit/Subway/dsl 🍴 Black Angus Rest., Bubba's BBQ, Waffle House 🛏 Best Value Inn, EconoLodge, Quality Inn, 🍴 Pizza Hut
93	US 84, to Evergreen, **E** 🅖 Liberty/dsl, **W** 🅖 BP/dsl, Love's/Arby's/dsl/scales/24hr
89mm	🆁🆂 sb, full 🚻 facilities, litter barrels, petwalk, 🅲, 🅵, RV dump, vending
85mm	🆁🆂 nb, full 🚻 facilities, litter barrels, petwalk, 🅲, 🅵, RV dump, vending
83	AL 6, to Lenox, **E** 🅖 Marathon/dsl 🄾 RV Park (4mi)
77	AL 41, to Range, to Range, **W** 🅖 Shell/dsl
69	AL 113, to Flomaton, **E** 🅖 Chevron/dsl, Jet-Pep/Subway/dsl, Shell/dsl/scales/24hr 🄾 dsl repair, Magnolia Branch Camping
57	AL 21, to Atmore, **E** 🅖 Chevron/dsl, Shell/dsl 🍴 Hardee's, Heritage Steaks, McDonald's, Waffle House 🛏 Hampton Inn, Holiday Inn Express, Muskogee Inn 🄾 Wind Creek Indian Gaming, **W** 🅖 BP/dsl 🄾 to Kelley SP
54	Escambia Cty Rd 1, **E** 🅖 BP/Subway/dsl 🄾 to Creek Indian Res, **W** 🅖 Shell/diner/dsl 🄾 $General
45	to Perdido, **W** 🅖 Chevron/dsl
37	AL 287, Gulf Shores Pkwy, to Bay Minette, **E** 🅖 BP/dsl 🄾🍴
34	to AL 59, to Bay Minette, Stockton
31	AL 225, to Stockton, **E** 🄾 Confederate Mem Bfd, to Blakeley SP, **W** 🅖 Shell/Subway/dsl 🄾 Landing RV Park (2mi)
29mm	Tensaw River
28mm	Middle River
25mm	Mobile River
22	Creola, **E** River Delta RV Park (1mi)
19	US 43, to Satsuma, **E** 🅖 Chevron/dsl/24hr, Pilot/Arby's/dsl/scales/24hr 🍴 McDonald's, Waffle House 🛏 La Quinta, **W** 🅖 Chevron/dsl, Shell 🄾 I-65 RV Park (1.5mi)
15	AL 41, **E** 🅖 Chevron, Shell/Pizza Inn/DQ/dsl 🍴 China Chef, Church's, Godfather's Pizza, Pizza Hut 🄾 Family$, O'Reilly Parts, Rite Aid, Rouse's Mkt, Walgreens, **W** 🅖 Circle K, Shell/Subway/dsl 🄾 $General
13	AL 158, AL 213, to Saraland, **E** 🅖 Murphy USA/dsl, Shell/dsl 🍴 Goldberg's Deli, Krystal, Marble Slab, Rotolo's Pizza,

M O B I L E

Exit #	Services
13	Continued
	Ruby Tuesday, Waffle House, Wintzell's Oyster House 🛏 Best Western, Comfort Suites, Country Inn Suites, Days Inn, EconoLodge, Microtel, Quality Inn 🄾 $Tree, AT&T, Radio Shack, URGENT CARE, Walmart/McDonald's, **W** 🍴 Exxon/Subway 🛏 Hampton Inn, Holiday Inn Express 🄾 to Chickasabogue Campground
10	W Lee St, **E** 🅖 Kangaroo, Shell/Subway 🍴 Huddle House 🛏 Best Inn
9	I-165 S, to I-10 E, to Mobile
8b a	US 45, to Prichard, **E** 🅖 Chevron/Circle K/dsl, Shell/dsl, Texaco/dsl 🍴 Church's 🛏 Star Motel 🄾 $General, Family$, tires/repair, **W** 🍴 1st Stop, BP, Energize/dsl, Pride Trkstp/dsl/scales, RaceWay/dsl, Texaco/dsl 🍴 Burger King, Domino's, Golden Egg Café, McDonald's 🄾 $General, Advance Parts, CVS Drug, Family$, O'Reilly Parts
5b	US 98, Moffett Rd, **E** 🅖 Exxon/dsl, Texaco/dsl 🍴 BJ's BBQ, Burger King, Church's, McDonald's, Sub King 🄾 AutoZone, Family$, PepBoys, **W** 🍴 Hardee's 🛏 Super 8 🄾 auto repair
5a	Spring Hill Ave, **E** 🍴 Burger King, Dreamland BBQ, McDonald's 🄾🍴, Mr Transmission, PepBoys, **W** 🅖 Chevron/dsl, Shell/dsl 🍴 Hibachi Express, Starbucks, Subway, Waffle House, Zaxby's 🛏 Extended Stay America, Wingate Inn
4	Dauphin St, **E** 🅖 BP/Circle K/dsl, Shell/dsl 🍴 Checkers, Chick-fil-A, Cracker Barrel, Krystal, McDonald's, Taco Bell, Taco Bell, Waffle House, Wendy's 🛏 Comfort Suites, Jamison Inn, Red Roof Inn, Rodeway Inn 🄾 $General, Buick/GMC, FoodChamps, Lowe's, Mercedes, same as 3 & 5a, Walmart/McDonald's, **W** 🄾🍴
3	Airport Blvd, **E** 🅖 Shell 🍴 Burger King, Cane's, Logan's Roadhouse, Macaroni Grill, McDonald's, Morrison's Cafeteria, Santa Fe Grill, Starbucks, Waffle House, Wendy's 🛏 Marriott 🄾🍴, $Tree, Acura, Belk, Best Buy, BigLots, Cadillac, Dillard's, Firestone/auto, Ford, Goodyear/auto, Harley-Davidson, Honda, Infiniti, Land Rover, mall, Marshalls, Michaels, Nissan, Old Navy, Sam's Club/gas, Sears/auto, Staples, Target, Verizon, **W** 🍴 BudgetZone/dsl, Shell/dsl 🍴 Arby's, Bamboo Japanese, Baumhowers, Boiling Pot, Burger King, Carrabba's, Cheddar's, China Doll, Chipotle, ChuckECheese, Denny's, Dunkin Donuts, Firehouse Subs, Goldberg's Deli, Honeybaked Ham, Hooters, IHOP, Jason's Deli, Lenny's Subs, Los Rancheros Mexican, Marble Slab, Melting Pot, Moe's SW Grill, Newk's Cafe, O'Charley's, Olive Garden, Osaka Japanese, Outback Steaks, Panda Express, Panera Bread, Popeye's, Red Lobster, Ruby Tuesday, Starbucks, Subway, Taco Bell, Waffle House 🛏 Ashberry Suites, Baymont Inn, Best Value Inn, Comfort Inn, Courtyard, Drury Inn, EconoLodge, Fairfield Inn, Family Inn, Hampton Inn, Hilton Garden, Holiday Inn, Homewood Suites, InTowne Suites, La Quinta, Motel 6, Quality Inn, Residence Inn, ValuePlace 🄾 $General, $Tree, AT&T, BooksAMillion, Fresh Mkt Foods, Hancock Fabrics, Home Depot, Jo-Ann Fabrics, Office Depot, PepBoys, Petsmart, Radio Shack, Ross, SteinMart, TJ Maxx, to USAL, U-Haul, vet, Walgreens
1b a	US 90, Government Blvd, **E** 🅖 Raceway/dsl, Snell/dsl 🍴 McAlister's Deli, Steak'n Shake 🄾 Audi/Porsche/VW, BMW, Chevrolet, Dodge, Family$, Kia, Lexus, Lincoln/Volvo, Mazda, Subaru, Toyota/Scion, **W** 🅖 Shell/dsl 🍴 Waffle House
0mm	I-10, E to Pensacola, W to New Orleans
I-65 begins/ends on I-10, exit 20.	

↑N   INTERSTATE 85

Exit #	Services
80mm	Alabama/Georgia state line, Chattahoochee River
79	US 29, to Lanett, **E** 🅖 Murphy USA, Shell/Circle K 🍴 Arby's, Burger King, Capt D's, Chuck's BBQ, KFC, Krystal, Little Caesars, McDonald's, Pizza Hut, Popeyes, San Marcos Mexican, Subway, Taco Bell, Waffle House, Wendy's, Wing Stop 🅞🅗 $General, $Tree, Advance Parts, repair, to West Point Lake, Verizon, Walmart, **W** 🅖 JetPep, QV, RaceWay/dsl 🍴 Domino's, Jin Japanese Steaks, Sonic 🛏 Days Inn, EconoLodge 🅞 AutoZone, CVS Drug, Kroger, O'Reilly Parts, vet
78.5mm	Welcome Ctr sb, full 🅖 facilities, litter barrels, petwalk, 🄲, 🄰, vending
77	AL 208, to Huguley, **E** 🅖 Jet Pep/Church's/dsl, Shell/Circle K/dsl 🍴 Waffle House 🛏 Holiday Inn Express 🅞 Chevrolet, Chrysler/Dodge/Ford/Lincoln, **W** 🛏 Hampton Inn 🅞 fireworks
76mm	Eastern/Central time zone
70	AL 388, to Cusseta, **E** 🅖 BigCat/dsl, Trvl Plaza/Shell/Subway/dsl/scales/24hr/@, **W** 🅞 fireworks
66	Andrews Rd, to US 29
64	US 29, to Opelika, **E** 🅖 Sunoco/dsl, **W** 🅖 Tiger/dsl
62	US 280/431, to Opelika, **E** 🅖 Big Cat/dsl, Chevron/dsl, Eagle/dsl, Shell/Circle K/Church's/dsl 🍴 Burger King, Durango Mexican, McDonald's, Subway, Wasabi Japanese, Wok'n Roll Rest. 🛏 Best Value Inn, Budget Inn, Days Inn, EconoLodge, Motel 6, Quality Inn 🅞 Lakeside RV Park (4.5mi), **W** 🅖 GrubMart, JetPep 🍴 Capt. D's, Cracker Barrel, Sizzlin Steaks, Waffle House 🛏 Comfort Inn, Travelodge 🅞 Buick/Chevrolet/GMC, Chrysler/Dodge/Jeep, Ford, H&W Tire, Harley-Davidson, USA Stores/famous brands
60	AL 51, AL 169, to Opelika, **E** 🅖 RaceWay/dsl 🍴 Hardee's 🅞 $General, **W** 🅞🅗, auto repair
58	US 280 W, to Opelika, **E** 🛏 Hampton Inn, Holiday Inn Express 🅞 golf, museum, **W** 🅖 Shell/Subway/dsl 🍴 Arby's, Brick Oven Pizza, Buffalo Wild Wings, Chick-fil-A, El Patron Mexican, Huddle House, Jersey Mike's, Jim Bob's, Logan's Roadhouse, Longhorn Steaks, Marble Slab, McDonald's, Moe's SW Grill, New Tokyo, Newk's Eatery, O'Charley's, Olive Garden, Sonic, Starbucks, Steak'n Shake, Waffle House, Zaxby's 🛏 Fairfield Inn, Microtel, Motel 6 🅞🅗, Best Buy, Books-A-Million, Dick's, Hobby Lobby, Home Depot, Kohl's, Kroger/dsl, Lowe's, Office Depot, Old Navy, PetCo, Ross, Target, TJ Maxx, URGENT CARE, World Mkt
57	Bent Creek Rd, **W** 🅖 Mapco, QV 🍴 Bob's Victory Grille, Shakey's Pizza, Venditori's Italian, Waffle House, Wendy's 🛏 Hilton Garden, Sleep Inn 🅞 Sam's Club/gas
51	US 29, to Auburn, **E** 🅖 Chevron/dsl, Grub Mart 🛏 Hampton Inn 🅞 Cadillac/Chevrolet, Leisure Time RV Park/Camping, Nissan, to Chewacla SP, Toyota/Scion, vet, **W** 🅖 Chevron/Subway/dsl, Murphy USA 🍴 Arby's, Burger King, Dunkin Donuts, El Dorado Mexican, Firehouse Subs, Jack's, Jim'n Nick's BBQ, KJ's Fish Camp, Krystal, Little Caesars, McDonald's, Ozzio's Italian, Philly Connection, Pizza Hut, Ruby Tuesday, Shrimp Basket, Sonic, Taco Bell, Waffle House, Wendy's, Zaxby's 🛏 Clarion, EconoLodge, Holiday Inn Express, Microtel, Pannie George's Kitchen, Quality Inn, Sleep Inn 🅞 $General, Advance Parts, Ford/Lincoln, Kia, tires/repair, to Auburn U, URGENT CARE, Walmart, Winn-Dixie
50	Cox Rd
44mm	🆁🆂 both lanes, 24hr security, full 🅖 facilities, litter barrels, petwalk, 🄲, 🄰, RV dump, vending
42	US 80, AL 186 E, Wire Rd, **E** 🅞 dsl repair/tires, to Tuskegee NF, **W** 🅖 Torch 85/rest./dsl/24hr
38	AL 81, to Tuskegee, **E** to Tuskegee NHS, Tuskegee University
32	AL 49 N, to Tuskegee, **E** 🅖 Sunoco/dsl
26	AL 229 N, to Tallassee, **E** 🅖 Shell/Guthrie's/dsl, **W** 🅞🅗
22	US 80, to Shorter, **E** 🅖 BP/dsl, Marathon/dsl, Petro/Valero/rest./dsl/scales/24hr 🛏 Days Inn 🅞 Wind Drift RV Park
16	Waugh, to Cecil, **E** 🅖 BP/Subway/dsl 🅞 auto repair
11	US 80, AL 110, to Mitylene, to Mt Meigs, **E** 🅖 Exxon/Subway/dsl, Liberty/dsl, Murphy USA/dsl 🍴 Anthony's Rest., Bruster's, Burger King, Cracker Barrel, Jose's Grill, McDonald's, Taco Bell, Top China, Waffle House 🛏 Candlewood Suites, Comfort Inn, Country Inn&Suites, Fairfield Inn, Holiday Inn Express, Sleep Inn 🅞 auto repair, Home Depot, Walmart/Subway, **W** 🅖 Chevron/dsl 🛏 Microtel
9	AL 271, to AL 110, to Auburn U/Montgomery, **E** 🍴 5 Guys Burgers, Arby's, BoneFish Grill, Chick-fil-A, Chili's, Chipotle Mexican, Del Taco, Firebirds Grill, Genghis Grill, Ixtapa Mexican, La Jolla Rest., Moe's SW Grill, Panera Bread, Red Robin, Ruby Tuesday, Sonic, Starbucks, Taziki's Cafe, TX Roadhouse, Wendy's, Zoe's Kitchen 🛏 Hampton Inn, Staybridge Suites 🅞 AT&T, Books-A-Million, Costco/gas, Dick's, Dillard's, EarthFare Foods, Firestone/auto, Jo-Ann Fabrics, Kohl's, Michael's, Old Navy, Petsmart, Radio Shack, Ross, Target, URGENT CARE, Verizon, vet, World Mkt, **W** 🅞🅗
6	US 80, US 231, AL 21, East Blvd, 0-2 mi **E** 🅖 Chevron, Exxon/dsl, RaceWay/dsl, Shell 🍴 Arby's, Baumhowers Rest., Burger King, Carrabba's, Chick-fil-A, Gangnam Grill, Golden Corral, Hardee's, Jason's Deli, KFC, Longhorn Steaks, Los Cabos, Los Vaqueros Mexican, McDonald's, Ming's Garden, Olive Garden, Piccadilly Cafe, Popeyes, Rock Bottom Cafe, Schlotzsky's, Starbucks, Subway, Sushiyama, Taco Bell, Waffle House, Wendy's, Zaxby's 🛏 Arlington Lodge, Best Inn, Comfort Inn, Country Inn&Suites, Courtyard, Extended Stay America, Home-Towne Suites, La Quinta, Quality Inn, Quality Roof Inn, Residence Inn, Sleep Inn, Springhill Suites, ValuePlace, Wingate Inn 🅞 $General, $Tree, Acura, Best Buy, Books-A-Million, Family$, Ford/Lincoln, Fresh Mkt Foods, Home Depot, Honda, Hyundai, Lowe's, Office Depot, Pepboys, PetCo, Radio Shack, Subaru, TJ Maxx, Tuesday Morning, UHaul, USPO, Walmart/McDonald's, Winn-Dixie, **W** 🅖 Chevron, Liberty, Mapco/dsl, Shell 🍴 Arby's, Capt D's, Hardee's, Hibachi Buffet, IHOP, Jan's Rest., Krispy Kreme, Krystal, McDonald's, Outback Steaks, Red Lobster, Saigon Bistro, Taco Bell, Waffle House 🛏 Alabama Hotel, Baymont Inn, Comfort Suites, Drury Inn, Express Inn, Motel 6, Ramada Inn 🅞 $General, Audi/VW, BMW, Buick/Cadillac/GMC, Chevrolet, Chrysler/Dodge/Jeep, Firestone/auto, Fred's Store,

LANETT · OPELIKA · AUBURN

MONTGOMERY

AL
AZ

⬆N INTERSTATE 85 Cont'd

Exit #	Services
6	Continued
	Infiniti, JC Penney, Kia, Lexus, mall, Mercedes, Nissan, Sam's Club/gas, Sears/auto, to Gunter AFB, Toyota/Scion, Volvo
4	Perry Hill Rd, **E** 🍴 Chappy's Deli, Marco's Pizza 🄾 Fresh Mkt, **W** 🅟 Cannon/dsl, Chevron 🍴 Hardee's, Subway 🛏 Hilton Garden, Homewood Suites 🄾 $General, Express Oil Change, Rite Aid, vet
3	Ann St, **E** 🅟 Big Cat/dsl, Chevron 🍴 Arby's, Capt D's, Country's BBQ, Domino's, KFC, Krystal, McDonald's, Taco Bell, Waffle House, Wendy's, Zaxby's 🛏 Days Inn 🄾 Pepboys, **W** 🅟 Entec, Murphy USA/dsl, PaceCar, Ztec 🍴 Burger King, Chick-fil-A, CiCi's Pizza, Hardee's, Popeye's 🛏 Stay Lodge 🄾 $Tree, AT&T, Office Depot, O'Reilly Parts, Radio Shack, Ross, Verizon, Walmart/Subway
2	Forest Ave, **E** 🄾 CVS Drug, **W** 🄾 🄷
1	Court St, Union St, downtown, **E** 🅟 BP/dsl, Exxon/dsl, **W** 🄾 to Ala St U
0mm	**I-85 begins/ends on I-65, exit 171 in Montgomery**

⬆N INTERSTATE 459 (BIRMINGHAM)

Exit #	Services
33b a	I-59, N to Gadsden, S to Birmingham
32	US 11, Trussville, **N** 🅟 BP/24hr, **S** 🅟 BP, Chevron/dsl/24hr, RaceWay/dsl/24hr, Shell/dsl 🍴 Arby's, Chili's, China Palace, Coldstone, Firehouse Subs, Habanero's Rest., Hooters, Jack's Rest., Jim'n Nick's BBQ, KFC, Lee Garden, Logan's Roadhouse, McDonald's, Red Robin, Starbucks, Subway, Waffle House, Wendy's 🛏 Courtyard, Hampton Inn, Hilton Garden 🄾 AT&T, Belk, Best Buy, Big 10 Tires, Books-A-Million, Buick/GMC, Harley-Davidson, Home Depot, JC Penney, Lowe's, Mazda, Michael's, Old Navy, Staples, Target, TJ Maxx, Verizon
31	Derby Parkway, **N** 🄾 B'ham Race Course
29	I-20, E to Atlanta, W to Birmingham
27	Grants Mill Rd, **N** 🛏 Hampton Inn 🄾 Fiat, **S** 🅟 Chevron/dsl 🄾 Audi/Porsche, BMW/Lexus, Chrysler/Dodge/Jeep, Land Rover, Mini
23	Liberty Parkway, **S** 🍴 Billy's Grill, DQ, Tazaki's Greek 🛏 Hilton Garden
19	US 280, Mt Brook, Childersburg, **N** 🅟 Chevron 🍴 CA Pizza Kitchen, Cheesecake Factory, Flemings Rest., Macaroni Grill, Panera Bread, PF Chang's, Village Tavern 🄾 Barnes&Noble, **0-3 mi S** 🅟 BP/Circle K, Chevron, Exxon, RaceWay.dsl, Shell 🍴 Arby's, Baha Burger, Burger King, Carrabba's, Chick-fil-A, Chili's, Chipotle Mexican, Cracker Barrel, DQ, Edgar's Rest., Fox&Hound Grille, Full Moon BBQ, Hamburger Heaven, Hooters, IHOP, Jade Palace, Jason's Deli, Joe's Crabshack, Kobe Japanese, Lloyd's Rest., Logan's Roadhouse, Longhorn Steaks, Max's Deli, McAlister's Deli, McDonald's, Milo's Burgers, Ming's Chinese, Outback Steaks, Pablo's, Papa John's, Petruccelli's Italian, Pizza Hut, Ralph&Kacoos, Schlotzsky's, Shogun Japanese, Subway, Superior Grill, Suria 280, Taco Bell, Taziki's Greek, TCBY, Tilted Kilt, Wendy's, Zaxby's 🛏 Best Western, Candlewood Suites, Courtyard, Drury Inn, Fairfield Inn, Hampton Inn, Hilton, Holiday Inn Express, Homestead Suites, Homewood Suites, Hyatt Place, La Quinta, Marriott, Residence Inn, SpringHill Suites, Wingate Inn 🄾 AT&T, Best Buy, BigLots, Books-A-Million, CVS Drug, Dick's, Firestone/auto, Fresh Mkt Foods, Goodyear/auto, Hancock Fabrics, Home Depot, Kohl's, Lowe's, Michael's, NTB, PetCo,

B I R M I N G H A M

Exit #	Services
19	Continued
	Petsmart, Ross, Staples, SteinMart, Target, TJMaxx, Verizon, vet, Walgreens, Walmart
17	Acton Rd, **N** 🅟 Shell/dsl/24hr 🍴 Krystal, McDonald's, **S** 🛏 Comfort Inn
15b a	I-65, N to Birmingham, S to Montgomery
13	US 31, Hoover, Pelham, **N** 🅟 Exxon/dsl, Shell/dsl, Sunoco/dsl 🍴 Burger King, Chick-fil-A, Fish Mkt Rest., Full Moon BBQ, Golden Rule BBQ, Habanero's, Krispy Kreme, Krystal, McDonald's, Outback Steaks, Papa John's, Purple Onion, Salvatori's Pizza, Starbucks, Subway 🛏 Econolodge 🄾 $Tree, Acura, AutoZone, Cadillac, Chevrolet, Firestone/auto, Goodyear/auto, Honda, Hyundai, Mr Transmission, Nissan, Publix, Rite Aid, Staples, TJ Maxx, vet, **S** 🅟 Jet-Pep, Shell/dsl/24hr 🍴 Arby's, Bonefish Grill, CA Pizza Kitchen, Carino's, Chipotle Mexican, Guthrie's, J Alexander's Rest., Jason's Deli, Jim'n Nicks BBQ, McDonald's, Michael's Steaks, Moe's SW Grill, Olive Garden, Panera Bread, Pizza Hut, Quiznos, Ruby Tuesday, Shula's Steaks, Starbucks, Subway, Taco Bell, Ted's MT Grill, Top China, Wendy's 🛏 Courtyard, Days Inn, Embassy Suites, Hampton Inn, Hyatt Place, Microtel, Residence Inn, Wynfrey Hotel 🄾 Barnes&Noble, Belk, Best Buy, Big 10 Tire, Bruno's Foods, Costco/gas, CVS Drug, Dick's, Hancock Fabrics, Home Depot, Infiniti, JC Penney, Jo-Ann Fabrics, Macy's, mall, Marshall's, Mercedes, Michael's, NTB, Office Depot, Petsmart, Ross, Sam's Club/gas, Sears/auto, Smart Car, Tuesday Morning, Verizon, Walmart (1mi)
10	AL 150, Waverly, **N** 🅟 Chevron (1mi), Shell (1mi) 🍴 Frontera Mexican Grill 🄾 $Tree, Kohl's, PetCo, Target, **S** 🅟 BP/dsl/24hr, Exxon 🛏 Hampton Inn, Hyatt Place 🄾 Ford, Publix/deli, Toyota, URGENT CARE, Walgreens
6	AL 52, to Bessemer, **N** 🅟 BP/dsl, **S** 🅟 BP, Jet-Pep, Texaco/Taco Bell 🍴 Arby's, China Wok, Domino's, Hickory Grill, McDonald's, Pizza Hut, Quiznos, Subway, Waffle House, Wendy's 🛏 Sleep Inn 🄾 $General, CVS Drug, RV Camping, TrueValue, Winn-Dixie
1	AL 18, Bessemer, **N** 🅟 Exxon, Shell/dsl 🍴 Burger King, Chick-fil-A, East Palace, Full Moon BBQ, Habanero's Mexican, Logan's Roadhouse, McAlister's Deli, Taco Bell 🄾 AT&T, GNC, JC Penney, Publix, Ross, Target, Verizon, **S** 🅟 BP/dsl 🍴 Bojangles, China King, McDonald's, Momma's Rest., San Antonio Grill, Subway, Zaxby's 🄾 Advance Parts, CVS Drug, Piggly Wiggly, to Tannehill SP
0mm	**I-459 begins/ends on I-20/59, exit 106**

H O O V E R

B E S S E M E R

ARIZONA

⬆E INTERSTATE 8

Exit #	Services
178b a	I-10, **I-8 begins/ends on I-10, exit 199**, E to Tucson, W to Phoenix
174	Trekell Rd, to Casa Grande, **2-4 mi N** 🄾 🄷, food, gas, lodging
172	Thornton Rd, to Casa Grande, **5-8 mi N** 🅟 gas 🍴 food 🛏 Francisco Grande Resort, Holiday Inn
171mm	Santa Cruz River
169	Bianco Rd
167	Montgomery Rd
163mm	Santa Rosa Wash
161	Stanfield Rd
151mm	**litter barrels, picnic area wb,** 🄿

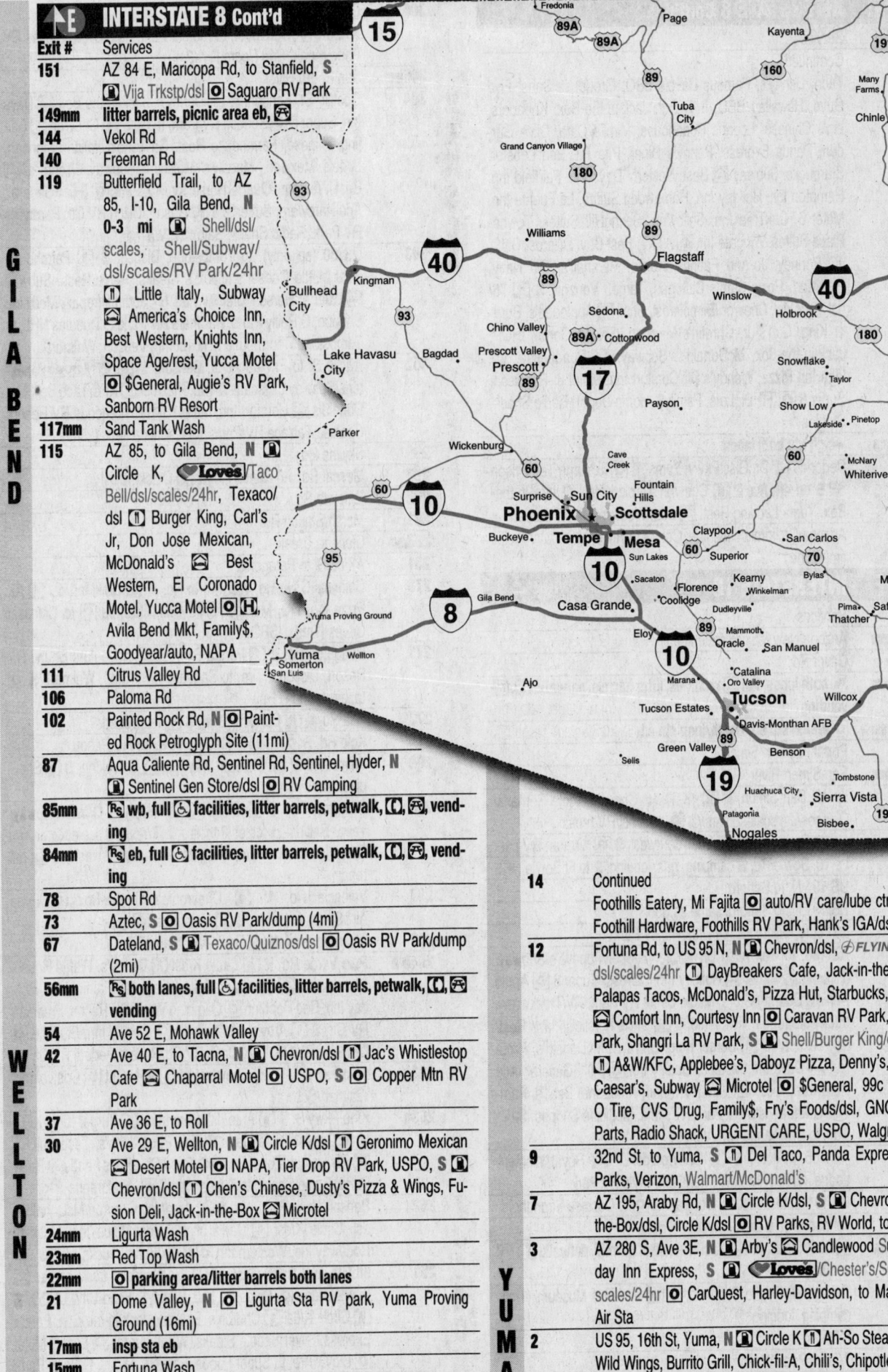

⬆E   INTERSTATE 8 Cont'd   🛡15

Exit #	Services
151	AZ 84 E, Maricopa Rd, to Stanfield, **S** 🅖 Vija Trkstp/dsl 🅞 Saguaro RV Park
149mm	litter barrels, picnic area eb, 🆁🆂
144	Vekol Rd
140	Freeman Rd
119	Butterfield Trail, to AZ 85, I-10, Gila Bend, **N** 0-3 mi 🅖 Shell/dsl/scales, Shell/Subway/dsl/scales/RV Park/24hr 🅕 Little Italy, Subway 🛏 America's Choice Inn, Best Western, Knights Inn, Space Age/rest, Yucca Motel 🅞 $General, Augie's RV Park, Sanborn RV Resort
117mm	Sand Tank Wash
115	AZ 85, to Gila Bend, **N** 🅖 Circle K, ♥Loves/Taco Bell/dsl/scales/24hr, Texaco/dsl 🅕 Burger King, Carl's Jr, Don Jose Mexican, McDonald's 🛏 Best Western, El Coronado Motel, Yucca Motel 🅞🅗, Avila Bend Mkt, Family$, Goodyear/auto, NAPA
111	Citrus Valley Rd
106	Paloma Rd
102	Painted Rock Rd, **N** 🅞 Painted Rock Petroglyph Site (11mi)
87	Aqua Caliente Rd, Sentinel Rd, Sentinel, Hyder, **N** 🅖 Sentinel Gen Store/dsl 🅞 RV Camping
85mm	🆁🆂 wb, full ♿ facilities, litter barrels, petwalk, 🅞🆁🆂, vending
84mm	🆁🆂 eb, full ♿ facilities, litter barrels, petwalk, 🅞🆁🆂, vending
78	Spot Rd
73	Aztec, **S** 🅞 Oasis RV Park/dump (4mi)
67	Dateland, **S** 🅖 Texaco/Quiznos/dsl 🅞 Oasis RV Park/dump (2mi)
56mm	🆁🆂 both lanes, full ♿ facilities, litter barrels, petwalk, 🅞🆁🆂 vending
54	Ave 52 E, Mohawk Valley
42	Ave 40 E, to Tacna, **N** 🅖 Chevron/dsl 🅕 Jac's Whistlestop Cafe 🛏 Chaparral Motel 🅞 USPO, **S** 🅞 Copper Mtn RV Park
37	Ave 36 E, to Roll
30	Ave 29 E, Wellton, **N** 🅖 Circle K/dsl 🅕 Geronimo Mexican 🛏 Desert Motel 🅞 NAPA, Tier Drop RV Park, USPO, **S** 🅖 Chevron/dsl 🅕 Chen's Chinese, Dusty's Pizza & Wings, Fusion Deli, Jack-in-the-Box 🛏 Microtel
24mm	Ligurta Wash
23mm	Red Top Wash
22mm	🅞 parking area/litter barrels both lanes
21	Dome Valley, **N** 🅞 Ligurta Sta RV park, Yuma Proving Ground (16mi)
17mm	insp sta eb
15mm	Fortuna Wash
14	Foothills Blvd, **N** 🅞 Sundance RV Park, **S** 🅕 Domino's,

14	Continued Foothills Eatery, Mi Fajita 🅞 auto/RV care/lube ctr, Family$, Foothill Hardware, Foothills RV Park, Hank's IGA/dsl
12	Fortuna Rd, to US 95 N, **N** 🅖 Chevron/dsl, ⟁FLYING J/Giant/dsl/scales/24hr 🅕 DayBreakers Cafe, Jack-in-the-Box, Las Palapas Tacos, McDonald's, Pizza Hut, Starbucks, Taco Bell 🛏 Comfort Inn, Courtesy Inn 🅞 Caravan RV Park, Oasis RV Park, Shangri La RV Park, **S** 🅖 Shell/Burger King/dsl, SP/dsl 🅕 A&W/KFC, Applebee's, Daboyz Pizza, Denny's, DQ, Little Caesar's, Subway 🛏 Microtel 🅞 $General, 99c Store, Big O Tire, CVS Drug, Family$, Fry's Foods/dsl, GNC, O'Reilly Parts, Radio Shack, URGENT CARE, USPO, Walgreens
9	32nd St, to Yuma, **S** 🅕 Del Taco, Panda Express 🅞 RV Parks, Verizon, Walmart/McDonald's
7	AZ 195, Araby Rd, **N** 🅖 Circle K/dsl, **S** 🅖 Chevron/Jack-in-the-Box/dsl, Circle K/dsl 🅞 RV Parks, RV World, to AZWU
3	AZ 280 S, Ave 3E, **N** 🅕 Arby's 🛏 Candlewood Suites, Holiday Inn Express, **S** 🅖 ♥Loves/Chester's/Subway/dsl/scales/24hr 🅞 CarQuest, Harley-Davidson, to Marine Corp Air Sta
2	US 95, 16th St, Yuma, **N** 🅖 Circle K 🅕 Ah-So Steaks, Buffalo Wild Wings, Burrito Grill, Chick-fil-A, Chili's, Chipotle Mexican, ChuckeCheese, Coldstone Creamery, Cracker Barrel, Del

AZ / **YUMA**

▲E INTERSTATE 8 Cont'd

Exit #	Services
2	Continued
	Taco, Denny's, Famous Dave's BBQ, Firehouse Subs, Five Guys, Hawaiian BBQ, In-N-Out, Jack-in-the-Box, Kneaders, Lin's Chinese, Logans Roadhouse, Mimi's Cafe, Olive Garden, Panda Express, Penny's Diner, Pita Pit, Red Lobster, Starbucks, Subway 🛏 Best Western, Days Inn, Fairfield Inn, Hampton Inn, Holiday Inn, Homewood Suites, La Fuente Inn, Motel 6, OakTree Inn, Shilo Inn, SpringHill Suites, Towne-Place Suites, Wingate Inn 🅞 AT&T, Best Buy, Dillards, GNC, JC Penney, Jo-Ann Fabrics, Kohl's, Marshall's, Old Navy, PetsMart, Ross, Sam's Club/gas, Target, Verizon, S 🅟 76/dsl, Arco/dsl, Chevron/Blimpie/dsl, Shell 🍴 Applebee's, Burger King, Carl's Jr, Chretin's Mexican, Golden Corral, IHOP, Jack-in-the-Box, McDonald's, Subway, TX Roadhouse, Village Inn Pizza, Wendy's 🛏 Comfort Inn, Motel 6, Radisson, Super 8 🅞 Ħ, BigLots, Family$, Home Depot, Radio Shack, Staples
1.5mm	weigh sta both lanes
1	Redondo Ctr Dr, Giss Pkwy, Yuma, N 🅞 to Yuma Terr Prison SP S on 4th Ave E 🅟 Chevron, Circle K/dsl 🍴 Jack-in-the-Box, Yuma Landing Rest. 🛏 Best Western, Hilton Garden
0mm	Arizona/California state line, Colorado River, Mountain/Pacific time zone

▲E INTERSTATE 10

Exit #	Services
391mm	Arizona/New Mexico state line
390	Cavot Rd
389mm	🅡ˢ both lanes, full ♿ facilities, litter barrels, petwalk, 🚻, vending
383mm	🅞 weigh sta eb, weigh/insp sta wb
382	Portal Rd, San Simon
381mm	San Simon River
378	Lp 10, San Simon, N 🅟 4K Trkstp/Chevron/Noble Romans/Quiznos/dsl/scales/24hrs/@ 🅞 auto/dsl/RV repair
366	Lp 10, Bowie Rd, N 🅟 Shell/Jerky/dsl, S 🅞 Alaskan RV park
362	Lp 10, Bowie Rd, N camping, gas, lodging, S to Ft Bowie NHS
355	US 191 N, to Safford
352	US 191 N, to Safford, same as 355
344	Lp 10, to Willcox, N 🅞 Lifestyle RV Park
340	AZ 186, to Rex Allen Dr, N 🅟 TA/Shell/Popeye's/Subway/dsl/scales/24hr/@ 🛏 Holiday Inn Express, Super 8 🅞 Apple Annie's Country Store, Magic Circle RV Park, RV/Truckwash, truck/auto repair, visitor info, S 🅟 Circle K, Doc's/Plaza Rest/dsl, Texaco/dsl 🍴 Burger King, Carl's Jr, Pizza Hut 🛏 Days Inn, Motel 6, Quality Inn 🅞 Ħ, $General, Ace Hardware, Alco, auto/tire/RV repair, AutoZone, Beall's, Family$, Grande Vista RV Park, KT's Mkt, Medicine Shoppe, Safeway, to Chiricahua NM, Verizon
336	AZ 186, Willcox, S 🅟 Chevron/dsl/LP 🛏 Royal Western Lodge 🅞 Ft Willcox RV Park, Life Style RV Park
331	US 191 S, to Sunsites, Douglas, S 🅞 to Cochise Stronghold
322	Johnson Rd, S 🅟 Shell/DQ/dsl/gifts
320mm	🅡ˢ both lanes, full ♿ facilities, litter barrels, petwalk, 🚻, vending
318	Triangle T Rd, to Dragoon, S 🅞 Amerind Museum (1mi), camping, lodging
312	Sibyl Rd
309mm	Adams Peak Wash
306	AZ 80, Pomerene Rd, Benson, 1-2 mi S 🅟 Circle K, Shell 🍴

WILCOX

BENSON / **TUCSON**

Exit #	Services
306	Continued
	86 Cafe 🅞 CarQuest, El Rio RV Park, Pato Blanco Lakes RV Park, repair, San Pedro RV (2mi)
305mm	San Pedro River
304	Ocotillo St, Benson, N 🍴 Denny's, Jack-in-the-Box 🛏 Days Inn, Super 8 🅞 Benson RV Park, KOA, S 🅟 Chevron 🍴 Beijing Chinese, Farmhouse Rest, Galleano's Italian-American, Lupe's Mexican, Magaly's Mexican, Subway, Wendy's 🛏 Best Western, QuarterHorse Inn/RV Park 🅞 Ħ, $General, Ace Hardware, Butterfield RV Resort, Dillon RV Ctr, Pardner's RV Park, Radio Shack, Safeway, Walmart
303	US 80 (eb only), to Tombstone, Bisbee, S 🍴 Farmhouse Rest., Little Caesar's, Pablo's Steaks, Reb's Rest., Subway 🛏 Quarter Horse Motel/RV Park 🅞 auto/dsl/repair, Medicine Shoppe, O'Reilly Parts, Pardners RV Park, to Douglas NHL, to Tombstone Courthouse SHP (26mi), Verizon, Walmart
302	AZ 90 S, to Ft Huachuca, Benson, S 🅟 ❤Loves/Chester's/Subway/dsl/scales/24hr, Shell/dsl 🍴 KFC/Taco Bell, McDonald's 🛏 Comfort Inn, Motel 6 🅞 AZ Legends RV Resort, Cochise Terrace RV Park, Ft Huachuca NHS (25mi)
299	Skyline Rd
297	Mescal Rd, J-6 Ranch Rd, N 🅟 QuickPic/dsl
292	Empirita Rd
291	Marsh Station Rd
288mm	Cienega Creek
281	AZ 83 S, to Patagonia
279	Colossal Cave Rd, Wentworth Rd, N 🅟 QuikMart/dsl 🍴 AZ Pizza Co, DQ, Montgomery's Grill, Quiznos 🅞 to Colossal Caves (7mi), USPO
275	Houghton Rd, N 🍴 Panda Express 🅞 Adventure Bound RV Resort, Discount Tire, to Saguaro NP (10mi), Walmart, S 🅞 to fairgrounds (1mi)
273	Rita Rd, N 🅟 Conoco (2mi), S 🅞 fairgrounds
270	Kolb Rd, S 🅞 Bay RV Resort, Voyager RV Resort
269	Wilmot Rd, N 🅟 Chevron/A&W/dsl 🛏 Travel Inn, S 🅟 Shell/pizza/subs/dsl
268	Craycroft Rd, N 🅟 Circle K, Mr T/dsl/LP, ⬛⬛/Subway/Taco Bell/dsl/lp/scales/24hr@, TTT/rest/dsl/scales/24hr 🅞 Crazy Horse RV Park, Frieghtliner, truck/RV wash, S 🅞 dsl repair
267	Valencia Rd, N 🅟 Chevron/Jack-in-the-Box 🅞 Pima Air&Space Museum, S 🅟 Valero/dsl 🅞 🖂
265	Alvernon Way, N 🅞 Davis-Monthan AFB
264b a	Palo Verde Rd, N 🅟 Circle K/dsl 🍴 Denny's, Waffle House, Wendy's/dsl 🛏 Crossland Suites, Days Inn, Fairfield Inn, Holiday Inn, Red Roof Inn 🅞 Camping World RV Resort, Freedom RV Ctr, S 🍴 Arby's, McDonald's 🛏 Quality Inn, Studio 6 🅞 La Mesa RV Ctr, Lazy Days RV Ctr/Resort, Pedata RV Ctr
263b	Kino Pkwy N, N 🅟 Chevron/dsl 🍴 In-N-Out 🅞 Costco/gas, Walmart/Subway
263a	Kino Pkwy S, S 🅟 Arco/dsl, Shamrock 🍴 Burger King, KFC, Little Caesar's, Mandarin Buffet, Papa John's, Taco Bell 🅞 Ħ $Tree, AutoZone, Family$, Food City, Fry's Foods, O'Reilly Parts, Radio Shack, to Tucson Intn'l 🖂, Walgreens
262	Benson Hwy, Park Ave, S 🅟 Arco/dsl, Chevron/McDonald's/dsl, Circle K/dsl 🍴 Carl's Jr. 🛏 Best Value Inn, Motel 6, Rodeway Inn, Western Inn 🅞 Mack/Volvo Trucks, USPO
261	6th/4th Ave, N 🅟 GasCo 🍴 Little Caesars, Los Portales 🛏 EconoLodge 🅞 Discount Tire, Family$, Food City, USPO, S 🅟 Circle K/dsl 🍴 Church's, El Indio, Jack-in-the-Box, Panda Express, Silver Saddle Steaks, Whataburger 🛏 Lazy 8 Motel 🅞 Big O Tire, El Super Foods, Family$, Midas, O'Reilly Parts
260	I-19 S, to Nogales

INTERSTATE 10 Cont'd

Exit #	Services
259	22nd St, Starr Pass Blvd, N □ Circle K/dsl, S Ⅱ Kettle, Waffle House □ Clarion, Regal Inn, Silverbell Inn, Super 8, Travel Inn
258	Congress St, Broadway St, N □ Circle K Ⅱ Hotel Tuscan, S Ⅱ Carl's Jr □ Days Inn, Howard Johnson, Motel 6, River Park Inn, Travelodge
257a	St Mary's Rd, N □ Ⓗ, S □ Shell/dsl Ⅱ Burger King, Church's, Denny's, Eegee's Cafe, Furr's Cafeteria, Jack-in-the-Box, Little Caesar's, Whataburger □ Country Inn&Suites, Ramada Ltd. □ Family$, Food City, Pima Comm Coll
257	Speedway Blvd, N □ Best Western, EconoLodge □ Ⓗ, U of AZ, Victory Motorcycles, S □ Arco/dsl □ museum, Old Town Tucson
256	Grant Rd, N □ Circle K Ⅱ auto/dsl repair, Burger King, Jack-in-the-Box, Sonic □ Walgreens, S □ Circle K, QT/dsl, Shell/dsl Ⅱ Arby's, Del Taco, Eegee's Cafe, IHOP, Waffle House □ Comfort Inn, Grant Inn, Hampton Inn, Holiday Inn Express, Super 8 □ Ace Hardware, Safeway, Walgreens
255	AZ 77 N, to Miracle Mile
254	Prince Rd, N □ Circle K, Valero/dsl □ $General, O'Reilly Parts, Walgreens, S □ golf, Kenworth, Prince of Tucson RV Park
252	El Camino del Cerro, Ruthrauff Rd, N □ Arco □ Ruthrauff RV Ctr, S □ Chevron/Jack-in-the-Box/dsl
251	Sunset Rd
250	Orange Grove Rd, N □ Arco/dsl, Circle K/dsl Ⅱ Burger King, Culver's, Domino's, Firehouse Subs, Golden Corral, Little Caesar's, Subway, Tulioberto's, Wendy's □ Big O Tire, Costco/gas, diesel repair, Home Depot, Petsmart, South Forty RV Park, Sprouts Mkt, Staples, URGENT CARE, vet
248	Ina Rd, N □ Chevron/dsl, Circle K/dsl, Shell/dsl Ⅱ Bisbee Breakfast Club, Carl's Jr, ChickeNuevo, Chuy's Mesquite, DQ, Eegee's Cafe, Five Guys, Hooters, Jack-in-the-Box, Jade Garden, Losbetos Cafe, Lupita's Cafe, McDonald's, Miss Saigon, Molinitas Mexican, Papa John's, Peter Piper's Pizza, Pollo Loco, Starbucks, Subway, Taco Bell, Waffle House □ InTown Suites, Motel 6 □ $Tree, 99c Store, auto repair, AutoZone, BigLots, CarQuest, CVS Drug, Discount Tire, Firestone/auto, Fry's Foods/dsl, Goodyear/auto, Hancock Fabrics, Lowe's, Michael's, Midas, O'Reilly Parts, PepBoys, Radio Shack, Target, U-Haul, Walgreens, Walmart Mkt, S □ Circle K Ⅱ Denny's, Starbucks □ Best Western, Red Roof Inn, Travelodge □ Ace Hardware, Freedom RV Ctr, Harley-Davidson
246	Cortaro Rd, N □ Circle K/Arby's/dsl, QT/dsl Ⅱ IHOP, Wendy's, S □ Shell/dsl Ⅱ Boston's Rest, Burger King, Chili's, Chopstix, Cracker Barrel, Eegee's Rest., In-N-Out, KFC/Taco Bell, Little Caesars, McDonald's, Nana's Mexican, Native New Yorker, New Town Asian, Panda Express, Starbucks, Subway, TX Roadhouse □ Comfort Inn, Days Inn, Holiday Inn Express, La Quinta, Super 8 □ access to RV camping, Ace Hardware, AT&T, Batteries+, GNC, Kohl's, O'Reilly Parts, USPO, Verizon, Walmart/McDonald's
244	Twin Peaks Rd
242	Avra Valley Rd, S □ □ □, RV camping, Saguaro NP (13mi)
240	Tangerine Rd, to Rillito, N □ A-A RV Park, S □ USPO
236	Marana, S □ Chevron/dsl/LP, Circle K/dsl Ⅱ R&R Pizza □ auto repair, Family$, Sun RV Park
232	Pinal Air Park Rd, S □ Pinal Air Park (3mi)
228mm	to frontage rd, wb pulloff

TUCSON (vertical margin label)

CASA GRANDE (vertical margin label)

Exit #	Services
226	Red Rock, S □ USPO
219	Picacho Peak Rd, N □ Shell/DQ, Shell/Subway/dsl, S □ Ostrich Ranch, Pichaco Peak RV Park, to Picacho Peak SP
212	Picacho (from wb), S □ KOA
211b	AZ 87 N, AZ 84 W, to Coolidge, S □ KOA
211a	Picacho (from eb), S □ KOA, state prison
208	Sunshine Blvd, to Eloy, N □ Ⓟⓘⓛⓞⓣ/Subway/DQ/dsl/scales/24hr □ dsl repair, S □ FLYING J/Denny's/dsl/scales/24hr □ Blue Beacon
203	Toltec Rd, to Eloy, N □ Circle K/dsl, Shell/McDonald's/playplace/24hr Ⅱ Carl's Jr, El Caballito Mexican □ Best Value Inn, Super 8 □ Desert Valley RV Park, dsl/tire repair, S □ TA/A&W/Taco Bell/dsl/RV dump/24hr/@ Ⅱ Pizza Hut □ golf, truckwash
200	Sunland Gin Rd, Arizona City, N □ Petro/Iron Skillet/dsl/scales/24hr/@, Pride/Subway/dsl/24hr Ⅱ Burger King, Eva's Mexican □ Days Inn, Travelodge □ Blue Beacon, Eagle Truckwash, Las Colinas RV Park, S □ Loves/Arby's/Baskin-Robbins/dsl/24hr Ⅱ Golden 9 Rest □ Motel 6 □ Speedco Lube
199	I-8 W, to Yuma, San Diego
198	AZ 84, to Eloy, Casa Grande, N □ Robson Ranch Rest./golf (3mi), S □ Casa Grande Outlets/famous brands
194	AZ 287, Florence Blvd, to Casa Grande, N Ⅱ Cactus Moon Grill, Chick-fil-A, Culver's, In-N-Out, Krispy Kreme, Mimi's Cafe, Olive Garden, Rubio's, Subway □ Dillard's, GNC, JC Penney, Kohl's, Marshall's, Michael's, Petsmart, Radio Shack, Ross, Sam's Club/dsl, Staples, Sunscape RV Park (7mi), Target, Verizon, Walgreens, World Mkt, 0-2 mi S □ 76/DQ, Arco/dsl, Chevron/Little Caesars/dsl, Circle K/gas Ⅱ Arby's, Burger King, Carl's Jr, Chili's, China Buffet, Chipotle Mexican, Church's, Coldstone, Cracker Barrel, Del Taco, Denny's, Eegee's, Filiberto's Mexican, Golden Corral, IHOP, Jack-in-the-Box, JB's, Jimmy John's, LJ Silver/Taco Bell, Macayo's Mexican, McDonald's, Panda Express, Papa John's, Papa Murphy's, Peter Piper Pizza, Sonic, Starbucks, Subway, T&M Italian, Wendy's □ Best Western, Comfort Inn, Holiday Inn Express, Legacy Suites, Mainstay Suites, Super 8 □ Ⓗ, $Tree, 99¢ Store, AT&T, AutoZone, Big Lots, Big O Tire, CVS Drug, Discount Tire, Encore Camping (2mi), Family$, Fiesta Grande RV Resort, Food City, Fry's Food/drug/dsl, Goodyear/auto, Home Depot, Jo-Ann Fabrics, K-Mart, Lowe's, U-Haul, URGENT CARE, Verizon, vet, Walgreens, Walmart/McDonalds
190	McCartney Rd, N □ to Central AZ Coll, S Ⅱ Barro's Pizza (3mi)
185	AZ 387, to Casa Grande, Casa Grande Ruins NM, S Ⅱ Eva's Mexican (6mi) □ Fransisco Grande (6mi), Holiday Inn (6mi) □ Fry's Food/gas (6mi), hwy patrol, to Casa Grande Ruins

AZ

⬆E INTERSTATE 10 Cont'd

C H A N D L E R

Exit #	Services
185	Continued NM, Val Vista RV camping (3mi)
183mm	🆁🆂 wb, full ♿ facilities, litter barrels, petwalk, 🚻, 🛒, vending
181mm	🆁🆂 eb, full ♿ facilities, litter barrels, petwalk, 🚻, 🛒, vending
175	AZ 587 N, Casa Blanca Rd, Chandler, Gilbert, S 🅿 Shell/dsl
173mm	Gila River
167	Riggs Rd, to Sun Lake, N 🅿 Shell/dsl 🅾 Akimel Smoke Shop
164	AZ 347 S, Queen Creek Rd, to Maricopa, N 🅾 gas, to Chandler 🔄
162b a	Wild Horse Pass Rd, Sundust Rd, N 🅿 ⓛⓞⓥⓔⓢ/Arby's/dsl/scales/24hr 🍴 McDonald's, S 🅿 Chevron/dsl 🛏 Sheraton Resort, Wildhorse Pass Hotel/Casino 🅾 Firebird Sports Park, Gila River Casino, Phoenix Outlets/famous brands
161	AZ 202 E, Pecos Rd
160	Chandler Blvd, to Chandler, N 🅿 Chevron/dsl, Circle K, Circle K/dsl 🍴 Can't Stop Smokin' BBQ, Denny's, Filiberto's Mexican, Marie's Rest., McDonald's, Rudy's BBQ, Sandella's Flatbread Cafe, Starbucks, Subway, US Egg Cafe, Wendy's, Whataburger 🛏 Comfort Inn, Fairfield Inn, Hampton Inn, Hawthorn Suites, Homewood Suites, Motel 6, Quality Inn, Radisson, Super 8 🅾 $Tree, Aamco, ADS Auto Repair, CVS, Firestone/auto, Harley-Davidson, to Compadre Stadium, U-Haul, vet, Walmart Mkt, Williams AFB, auto repair, S 🅿 7-11, Chevron/dsl, Circle K/dsl, Shell/dsl 🍴 Bell Italian Pizza, Brazilian Bull Steaks, Carl's Jr, Cracker Barrel, Del Taco, Dunkin Donuts, Hong Kong Buffet, Jersey Mike's, Qdoba, Spinato's Pizzaria, Starbucks, Tukee's Grille, Waffle House, Wendy's 🛏 Extended Stay America, Holiday Inn Express, InTown Suites, La Quinta 🅾 🏥, AT&T, AutoZone, Discount Tire, Kohl's, URGENT CARE
159	Ray Rd, N 🅿 Circle K, Shell 🍴 Buca Italian, Carrabba's, Charleston's Rest., Chipotle Mexican, Fleming's Steaks, Frederico's Mexican, Genghis Grill, Habit Burger, In-N-Out, Jasons Deli, Jimmy John's, Longhorn Steaks, McDonald's, Nabers Rest., Outback Steaks, Paradise Cafe, Pei Wei Asian, Red Lobster, Roy's Hawaiian, Rumbi Grill, Sandbar Mexican, Starbucks, Subway, Tejas, Zoe's Kitchen 🛏 Courtyard 🅾 AJ's Fine Foods, Audi, BMW, Chevrolet, Ford, Home Depot, Lexus, Lowe's Whse, Mercedes, PetsMart, Sam's Club/gas, Verizon, S 🅿 Circle K/dsl 🍴 Barro's Pizza, Boston Mkt, Chick-Fil-A, Five Guys, Honeybaked Ham, IHOP/24hr, Jack-in-the-Box, Kneaders Cafe, Mellow Mushroom, Mimi's Café, Native Grill, Neo Tokyo, On-the-Border, Peter Piper Pizza, Pizza Hut, Rubio's, Subway, Uncle Bear's Grill, Vincent's Pizza, Wendy's 🛏 Extended Stay America, Extended Stay America 🅾 AT&T, auto repair, Barnes&Noble, Best Buy, Fresh&Easy Mkt, Hobby Lobby, JC Penney, Jo-Ann Fabrics, Marshall's, Michael's, PetCo, Ross, Sprouts Mkt, Target, Verizon
158	Warner Rd, N 🅿 Circle K/dsl, QT 🍴 Carl's Jr, Dunkin Donuts, Forefathers Cheesesteaks, Port of Subs, Topical Smoothie 🛏 Drury Inn 🅾 Dick's, IKEA, S 🅿 Circle K/dsl, Minute Mart/dsl 🍴 AZ Sandwich Co., Burger King, ChuckeCheese, DQ, Hillside Spot Cafe, Macayo's Mexican, McDonald's, Nello's Pizza, Panda Garden, Ruffino's Italian, Taco Bell, Zipp's Grill 🅾 Ace Hardware, Basha's Foods, Big O Tire, Goodyear/auto, vet
157	Elliot Rd, N 🅿 Chevron/dsl, QT/dsl, Shell/Circle K/dsl 🍴 Applebee's, Arby's, Burger King, Crackers Cafe, Crazy Buffet, Fuddrucker's, Jimmy John's, Kabab Palace, Kobe Japanese,

P H O E N I X

157	Continued McDonald's, Olive Garden, Oregano's Pizza Bistro, Panda Express, Red Robin Rest., Sonic, Starbucks, Subway, Taco Bell, Wendy's, YC Mongolian Grill 🛏 Days Inn&Suites 🅾 $Tree, Acura, Buick, Cadillac/GMC, Chrysler/Dodge/Jeep, Costco/gas, Discount Tire, Fiat, Honda, Hyundai, Kia, Mazda, Mini, NAPA, Nissan, PetsMart, Ross, Savers, Staples, Toyota/Scion, URGENT CARE, Volvo, Walmart, S 🅿 Circle K/Dsl, Shell/Circle K/dsl 🍴 Biscuits, Cactus Jack's, Niros Gyros, Original Burrito, Pacific Gardens Asian, Starbucks, Sub Factory, Subway 🛏 Clarion, Sheraton 🅾 auto repair, O'Reilly Parts, Safeway, vet, Walgreens
155	Baseline Rd, Guadalupe, N 🅿 Circle K/dsl, Shell/Circle K/Popeye's/dsl 🍴 Carl's Jr, ClaimJumper, Ell Pollo Loco, Joe's Crabshack, KFC, McDonald's, Poliberto's Tacos, Rainforest Cafe, Subway, Taco Bell, Waffle House, Wendy's 🛏 Best Western, Candlewood Studios, Holiday Inn Express, InnSuites, Ramada, Residence Inn, SpringHill Suites, TownePlace Suites 🅾 AutoZone, AZ Mills/Famous Brands, CVS Drug, Food City, Home Depot, Marshall's, Parts Authority, Ross, Walgreens, S 🅿 7-11, Arco/dsl, QT 🍴 Aunt Chilada's Mexican, China Town, Denny's, Little Caesar's, Sonic, Subway 🅾 Fry's Electronics, Fry's Foods, URGENT CARE
154	US 60 E, AZ 360, Superstition Frwy, to Mesa, N 🅾 to Camping World (off Mesa Dr)
153b	Broadway Rd E, N 🍴 Denny's 🛏 Comfort Suites, Extended Stay America, La Quinta, Quality Inn, Red Roof Inn, Sheraton 🅾 to Diablo Stadium, S 🅿 Chevron/dsl, Shell/Circle K/Del Taco/24hr 🍴 Goodcents Deli, Panda Express, Papa John's, Pizza Hut, Port of Subs, Taco Bell, Whataburger 🛏 Country Inn & Suites, Homewood Suites 🅾 Staples
153a	AZ 143 N, N 🍴 Denny's 🛏 Courtyard, Fairfield Inn, Hilton, Holiday Inn, La Quinta, Sleep Inn 🅾 to Diablo Stadium, S same as 153b
152	40th St, N 🅿 Shell/dsl 🅾 U Phoenix, S 🅿 Shell/Circle K 🍴 Burger King, Quiznos
151mm	Salt River
151b a	28th St, 32nd St, University Ave, N 🍴 Waffle House 🛏 Drury Inn, Extended Stay America, Hilton Garden, Holiday Inn Express 🅾 AZSU, U Phoenix, S 🅿 Circle K/dsl, QT/dsl 🍴 McDonald's
150b	24th St E (from wb), N 🛏 Motel 6 🅾 Air Nat Guard, S 🛏 Best Western/rest.
150a	I-17 N, to Flagstaff
149	Buckeye Rd, N 🅾 Sky Harbor 🔄
148	Washington St, Jefferson St, N 🅿 Chevron/dsl, Shell, Tiemco/dsl 🍴 Carl's Jr, McDonald's 🛏 Motel 6, Sterling Hotel 🅾 to Sky Harbor 🔄, S 🅿 Circle K 🅾 🏥
147b a	AZ 51 N, AZ 202 E, to Squaw Peak Pkwy
146	16th St (from sb), N 🅿 Shell/Circle K 🍴 Filiberto's Mexican, S 🅿 Circle K, Shamrock/dsl 🍴 Church's, Jack-in-the-Box, Little Caesar's, Salsita's Mexican 🅾 🏥, O'Reilly Parts, Ranch Mkt
145	7th St, N 🍴 Chicos Tacos, McDonald's, Sonic, Starbucks, Subway, Taco Bell, Whataburger 🅾 Safeway Foods, Walgreens, S 🅿 Circle K, Shell, Sinclair/dsl 🍴 Jimmy John's 🛏 Holiday Inn Express, Hyatt, Sheraton, Springhill Suites 🅾 🏥, to Chase Field
144	7th Ave, N 🅿 Circle K 🍴 Chipotle, Five Guys, Habit Burger, Jersey Mike's, NY Pizza, Peiwei Asian, Potbelly, Starbucks, Zoe's Kitchen, S 🅿 Circle K 🅾 central bus dist
143c	US 60, 19th Ave (from wb), downtown
143b a	I-17, N to Flagstaff, S to Phoenix

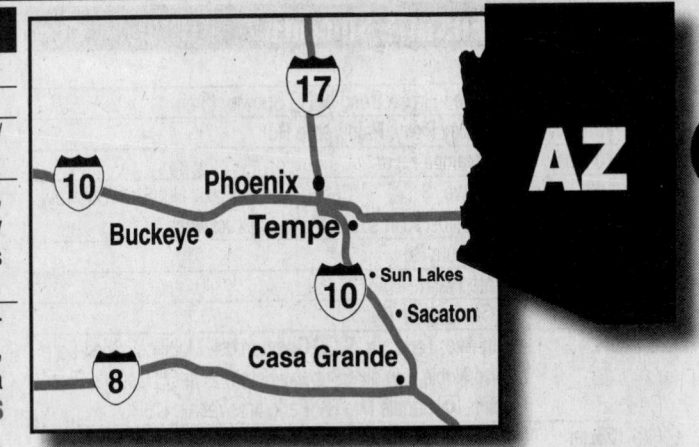

INTERSTATE 10 Cont'd

Exit #	Services
142	27th Ave (from eb, no return), N 🛏 Comfort Inn
141	35th Ave, N 🍴 Jack-in-the-Box, Rita's Mexican, S 📟 Shell/Circle K
140	43rd Ave, N 📟 7-11, Circle K/dsl, Shell 🍴 Filberto's Mexican, KFC, Little Caesar's, Pizza Hut, Salsita's Mexican, Subway 🛏 ValuePlace Hotel 🅾 AutoZone, Family$, Food City, Fry's Mercado/gas, Radio Shack, Walgreens
139	51st Ave, N 📟 Chevron/dsl, Circle K 🍴 Burger King, Domino's, El Pollo Loco, McDonald's, Sonic 🛏 Best Value Inn, Budget Inn, Crossland Suites, Holiday Inn, InTown Suites, La Quinta, Motel 6, Red Roof Inn, Travelodge 🅾 Food City, S 📟 QT/dsl/scales, Shell/dsl 🍴 Carl's Jr, Filberto's Mexican, IHOP, Port of Subs, Taco Bell 🛏 Comfort Inn, Days Inn, Super 8, Travelers Inn
138	59th Ave, N 📟 Circle K, Valero 🍴 Los Armandos Mexican, Papa John's, Subway 🅾 7-11, AutoZone, Family$, O'Reilly Parts, URGENT CARE, Walgreens, S 📟 Liberty/Chester's/dsl/24hr 🍴 Waffle House 🅾 Blue Beacon/scales
137	67th Ave, N 📟 Circle K/dsl, QT, Shell/dsl 🍴 Church's, S 📟 *FLYING J*/Denny's/dsl/LP/24hr
136	75th Ave, N 📟 Chevron/dsl, Circle K 🍴 A&W/LJ Silver, CiCi's Pizza, Coco's, Denny's, Hooters, IHOP, Lin's Buffet, Longhorn Steaks, McDonald's, Olive Garden, Pizza Hut/Taco Bell, Red Lobster, Starbucks, Subway, TX Roadhouse, Wendy's, Whataburger 🅾 $Tree, AT&T, Big Lots, Big O Tire, Dillards, Home Depot, La Mesa RV Ctr, Lowe's, Radio Shack, Ross, Sears, Target, Walmart, S 📟 Arco
135	83rd Ave, N 📟 Circle K, QT 🍴 Burger King, Jack-in-the-Box, Waffle House 🛏 Best Western, Premier Inn, Victory Inn 🅾 K-Mart, Sam's Club/gas
134	91st Ave, Tolleson, N 📟 Circle K/dsl
133b	Lp 101 N
133a	99th Ave, N 📟 Chevron/dsl 🍴 Cafe Rio, Cane's, Carrabba's, Chick-fil-A, China City, Chipotle Mexican, ClaimJumper, HoneyBaked Ham, Ichiban Rest., Island's Burgers, Jimmy John's, McDonald's, Native Grill, Panda Express, Paradise Cafe, Peter Piper Pizza, Pita Kitchen, Red Robin, Rumbi Grill, Smashburger, Starbucks, Subway, Taco Bell, Village Inn 🛏 Courtyard 🅾 Best Buy, Costco/gas, Discount Tire, GNC, Hobby Lobby, Marshall's, Old Navy, PetCo, Ross, URGENT CARE, Verizon, S 🍴 🏨/Subway/Wendy's/dsl/scales/24hr 🅾 CarMax, Chevrolet
132	107th Ave, N 🅾 Walgreens, S 🅾 Camping World RV Ctr, Chrysler/Jeep, Dodge/Ram, Fiat, Honda, Hyundai, Kia, Mazda, Nissan, Toyota/Scion, VW
131	Avondale Blvd, to Cashion, N 📟 Circle K/dsl, S 🍴 Culver's, Jack-in-the-Box, Panda Express, Ruby Tuesday 🛏 Hilton Garden, Homewood Suites 🅾 CVS Drug, to Phoenix Intnl Raceway
129	Dysart Rd, to Avondale, N 📟 Chevron/dsl, Shell/Circle K/dsl 🍴 Buffalo Wild Wings, Chick-fil-A, ChuckECheese, Fiesta Mexican, In-N-Out, Jack-in-the-Box/24hr, Manuel's Mexican, Mimi's Cafe, Nakomo Japanese, NYPD Pizza, Ono Hawaiian BBQ, Panda Express, Peiwei Asian, Starbucks, Subway, Taco Bell, Tomo Japanese 🛏 Holiday Inn Express 🅾 $Tree, AT&T, AutoZone, Discount Tire, Fry's Foods, JC Penney, JoAnn Fabrics, Kohl's, Lowe's, PetsMart, Sprouts Mkt, Tuesday Morning, Verizon, vet, Walmart, S 📟 QT 🍴 AZ Frybread, Black Bear Diner, Del Taco, Golden Corral, IHOP, KFC, McDonald's, Peter Piper Pizza, Subway, Waffle House,

Exit #	Services
129	**Continued** Whataburger 🛏 Quality Inn, Super 8 🅾 Brakemasters, Food City, Home Depot, Pepboys, S&S Tire/repair, Sam's Club/gas, Walgreens
128	Litchfield Rd, N 📟 Circle K/dsl 🍴 Applebee's, Black Angus Steaks, Caballero, Carl's Jr, Chili's, Chipotle Mexican, Cracker Barrel, Denny's, Five Guys, Freddy's Steakburger, Gus' NY Pizza, Hayashi Japanese, Jimmy John's, Macaroni Grill, Macavo's Mexican, McDonald's, Raul&Theresa's Mexican, Starbucks, Subway, Wendy's, Wildflower Bread Co. 🛏 Hampton Inn, Holiday Inn Express, Residence Inn 🅾 🏨 Barnes&Noble, Best Buy, Michael's, Ross, Target, to Luke AFB, URGENT CARE, Wigwam Resort/rest (3mi), S 📟 Circle K/dsl 🍴 Arby's, Burger King, Eggs&More, Little Caesar's, Ramiro's Mexican, Rudy's BBQ, Schlotsky's 🛏 Best Western, TownePlace Suites 🅾 AutoZone, BigLots, Buick/GMC, Ford, O'Reilly Parts
127	Bullard Ave, N 🍴 PF Chang's, Red Robin
126	PebbleCreek Pkwy, to Estrella Park, N 🍴 Ah-So Steaks, Aribba Mexican, Barro's Pizza, Native Grill, Olive Garden, Paradise Cafe, Red Lobster, Rubio's, Taco Bell, TX Roadhouse 🅾 $Tree, Cal Ranch, Firestone/auto, Old Navy, PetCo, Staples, TJ Maxx, Walgreens, S 📟 QT/dsl 🍴 Augie's Grill, Austin's Rest., Burger Joint, Filiberto's Mexican, McDonald's, Panda Express, Pizza Hut, Senor Taco, Starbucks, Subway, Yan's Chinese 🛏 Comfort Suites 🅾 Ace Hardware, Fletcher Tire, Radio Shack, Safeway Foods/dsl, Verizon, vet, Walgreens, Walmart
125mm	Roosevelt Canal
125	Sarival Ave, Cotton Lane (from wb)
124	AZ 303
123	Citrus Rd, to Cotton Ln, S 🅾 Phoenix RV Park
122	Perryville Rd
121	Jackrabbit Trail, N 📟 Chevron/dsl, S 📟 Circle K/dsl 🅾 CarQuest
120	Verrado Way
117	Watson Rd, S 📟 Circle K/dsl 🍴 Carl's Jr, Chipotle Mexican, Cracker Barrel, Denny's, Dunkin Donuts, El Pollo Loco, Federico's Mexican, Jack-in-the-Box, KFC, Little Caesar's, McDonald's, Native NY Grill, Palermo's Pizza, Panda Express, Papa John's, Peter Piper Pizza, Subway, Taco Bell, Wendy's 🅾 $Tree, AT&T, AutoZone, Discount Tire, Fletcher's Tire, Fry's Foods/dsl, Lowe's, PetsMart, URGENT CARE, Verizon, vet, Walgreens, Walmart/McDonald's
114	Miller Rd, to Buckeye, S 📟 Chevron Travel Ctr/Sams Deli/grill/dsl/E85/LP/24hr, *Loves*/Chester's/Subway/dsl/scales/24hr, QT/dsl 🍴 Burger King 🛏 Days Inn 🅾 Leaf Verde RV Park

AZ

Q U A R T Z S I T E

⬆E INTERSTATE 10 Cont'd

Exit #	Services
112	AZ 85, to I-8, Gila Bend, **S** 🍴 Subway (3mi)
109	Sun Valley Pkwy, Palo Verde Rd
104mm	Hassayampa River
103	339th Ave, **S** 🅖 TA/Country Pride/Pizza Hut/Shell/Subway/Taco Bell/dsl/scales/LP/24hr/@ 🅞 truckwash
98	Wintersburg Rd
97mm	Coyote Wash
95.5mm	Old Camp Wash
94	411th Ave, Tonopah, **S** 🅖 Chevron/dsl, Mobil/dsl, Shell/Cafe Charro/Noble Roman's/Subway/dsl/LP/24hr 🍴 Oscar's Place Cantina 🅞 Saddle Mtn RV Park, tires/repair, USPO
86mm	🅡ₛ both lanes, full 🅿 facilities, litter barrels, petwalk, 🛇, 🚮 vending
81	Salome Rd, Harquahala Valley Rd
69	Ave 75E
53	Hovatter Rd
52mm	🅡ₛ both lanes, full 🅿 facilities, litter barrels, petwalk, 🛇, 🚮 vending
45	Vicksburg Rd, **N** 🅖 Zip TC/Chevron/Subway/dsl/scales/LP/24hr, **S** 🅖 Pride/dsl/rest./scales/24hr 🅞 Jobski's dsl Repair/towing, Kofa NWR, RV Park, tires
31	US 60 E, to Wickenburg, **12 mi N** 🅞 camping, food
26	Gold Nugget Rd
19	Quartzsite, to US 95, Yuma, **N** 🅖 Arco/dsl, Chevron/dsl, Shell/dsl 🍴 Taco Mio 🅞 Beall's, Family$, Roadrunner Foods, RV camping
18mm	Tyson Wash
17	US 95, AZ 95, Quartzsite, **N** 🅖 Mobil/Burger King/LP/dsl, (📶)/DQ/Subway/dsl/scales/24hr 🍴 Carl's Jr, McDonald's, Quartzsite Yacht Grill, Times 3 Rest. 🏠 Stagecoach Motel/rest. 🅞 $General, RV camping, tires/repair, **S** 🅖 ♥Love's/Chester's/Subway/dsl/24hr 🏠 Super 8 🅞 Desert Gardens RV Park, Lifestyles RV Ctr
11	Dome Rock Rd
5	Tom Wells Rd, **N** 🅖 Texaco/SunMart/Quizno's/dsl/scales
4.5mm	🅡ₛ both lanes, full 🅿 facilities, litter barrels, petwalk, 🛇, 🚮 vending
3.5mm	AZ Port of Entry, **weigh sta**
1	Ehrenberg, to Parker, **N** 🅖 Texaco 🅞 River Lagoon RV Resort, **S** 🅖 ⛟FLYING J/Wendy's/dsl/LP/scales/lube/repair/tires/24hr 🏠 Best Western
0mm	Arizona/California state line, Colorado River, Mountain/Pacific time zone

⬆N INTERSTATE 15

Exit #	Services
29.5mm	Arizona/Utah state line
27	Black Rock Rd
21mm	turnout sb
18	Cedar Pocket, **S** 🅞 **parking area**, Virgin River Canyon RA/camping
16mm	**truck parking both lanes**
15mm	**truck parking nb**
14mm	**truck parking nb**
10mm	**truck parking nb**
9	Desert Springs
8.5mm	Virgin River
8	Littlefield, Beaver Dam, **E** 🅞 RV park, **1 mi W** 🅞 camping, food, gas/dsl, lodging
0mm	Arizona/Nevada state line, Pacific/Mountain time zone

F L A G S T A F F

S E D O N A

⬆N INTERSTATE 17

Exit #	Services
341	McConnell Dr, **I-17 begins/ends**, **N** 🅖 Chevron/dsl, Circle K, Conoco/dsl, Giant/dsl, Mobil/dsl, Shell, Texaco/Wendy's/dsl 🍴 5 Guys Burgers, Arby's, August Moon Chinese, Baskin-Robbins, Buffalo Wild Wings, Burger King, Buster's Rest., Cafe Rio, Carl's Jr, Chick-fil-A, Chili's, China Garden, Chipotle Mexican, Coco's, Coldstone, Del Taco, Denny's, Domino's, DQ, Freddy's Steakburgers, IHOP, Jack-in-the-Box, Jimmy John's, KFC, Little Caesars, Mandarin Buffet, McDonald's, Native New Yorker, Ni Marco's Pizza, Olive Garden, Panda Express, Papa John's, Papa Murphy's, Peter Piper Pizza, Picazzo's Pizza, Pizza Hut, Quiznos, Red Lobster, Sizzler, Starbucks, Subway, Taco Bell 🏠 Best Inn, Budget Inn, Canyon Inn, Comfort Inn, Courtyard, Days Inn, Drury Inn, EconoLodge, EconoLodge, Embassy Suites, Fairfield Inn, Hampton Inn, Knights Inn, La Quinta, Motel 6, Quality Inn, Ramada Ltd, Rodeway Inn, SpringHill Suites, Super 8 🅞 🄷, $Tree, AT&T, Barnes&Noble, Basha's Foods, Discount Tire, Hastings Books, Jo-Ann Crafts, Kohl's, Michael's, O'Reilly Parts, Petsmart, Ross, Safeway, Sprouts Mkt, Staples, Target, Verizon, Walgreens, Walmart
340b a	I-40, E to Gallup, W to Kingman
339	Lake Mary Rd (from nb), Mormon Lake, **E** 🅖 Circle K/dsl 🏠 AZ Mtn Inn 🅞 access to same as 341
337	AZ 89A S, to Sedona, Ft Tuthill RA, **W** 🅞 camping
333	Kachina Blvd, Mountainaire Rd, **E** 🍴 Mountainaire Rest. (1mi) 🏠 Abineau B&B, **W** 🅖 Shell/Subway/dsl 🅞 county park
331	Kelly Canyon Rd
328	Newman Park Rd
326	Willard Springs Rd
322mm	Munds Canyon
322	Pinewood Rd, to Munds Park, **E** 🅖 Shell/dsl, Woody's/dsl 🍴 Lone Pine Rest. 🅞 golf, Motel in the Pines, **W** 🅖 Chevron/dsl 🅞 Munds RV Park
320	Schnebly Hill Rd
317	Fox Ranch Rd
316mm	Woods Canyon
315	Rocky Park Rd
313mm	scenic view sb, litter barrels
306	Stoneman Lake Rd
300mm	**runaway truck ramp sb**
298	AZ 179, to Sedona, Oak Creek Canyon, **7-15 mi W** 🍴 Burger King, Cowboy Club Rest., Joey's Bistro 🏠 Belrock Inn, Diamond Resort, Hilton, La Quinta, Radisson/cafe, Wildflower Inn 🅞 Rancho Sedona RV Park
297mm	🅡ₛ both lanes, full 🅿 facilities, litter barrels, petwalk, 🛇, 🚮 vending
293mm	Dry Beaver Creek
293	Cornville Rd, McGuireville Rd, to Rimrock, **E** 🅖 McGuireville 🍴 Nikki's Grill, **W** 🅖 76/dsl, Conoco/Beaver Hollow/dsl 🍴 El Patio Grill
289	Middle Verde Rd, Camp Verde, **E** 🅖 Chevron/dsl 🍴 Sonic, The Gathering Rest. 🏠 Cliff Castle Hotel/casino/rest. 🅞 to Montezuma Castle NM, **W** 🅞 Distant Drums RV Park
288mm	Verde River
287	AZ 260, to AZ 89A, Cottonwood, Payson, **E** 🅖 Shell/Subway/dsl/RV dump/LP/24hr 🍴 Burger King, Carl's Jr, Denny's, DQ, Gabriela's Mexican, Los Betos Mexican, McDonald's, Starbucks, Taco Bell 🏠 Comfort Inn, Days Inn, Super 8 🅞 Territorial RV Park (1mi), Trails End RV Park, Zane Grane RV Park (9mi), **W** 🅖 Chevron/Wendy's/dsl/24hr 🅞 RV camping, to Jerome SP

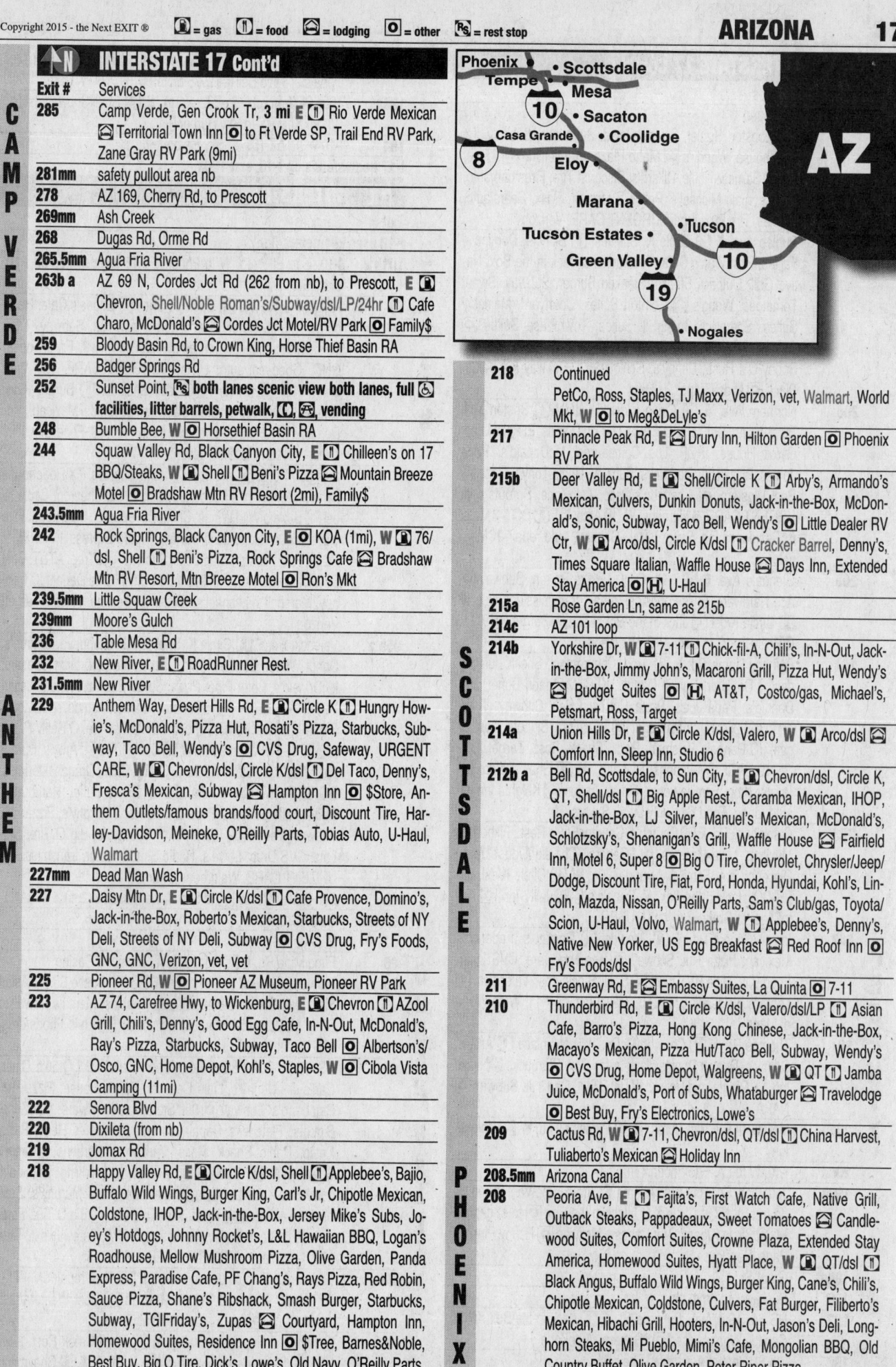

INTERSTATE 17 Cont'd

CAMP VERDE

Exit #	Services
285	Camp Verde, Gen Crook Tr, **3 mi** E 🍴 Rio Verde Mexican 🛏 Territorial Town Inn ⊙ to Ft Verde SP, Trail End RV Park, Zane Gray RV Park (9mi)
281mm	safety pullout area nb
278	AZ 169, Cherry Rd, to Prescott
269mm	Ash Creek
268	Dugas Rd, Orme Rd
265.5mm	Agua Fria River
263b a	AZ 69 N, Cordes Jct Rd (262 from nb), to Prescott, E 🖐 Chevron, Shell/Noble Roman's/Subway/dsl/LP/24hr 🍴 Cafe Charo, McDonald's 🛏 Cordes Jct Motel/RV Park ⊙ Family$
259	Bloody Basin Rd, to Crown King, Horse Thief Basin RA
256	Badger Springs Rd
252	Sunset Point, 🆁🆂 **both lanes scenic view both lanes, full ♿ facilities, litter barrels, petwalk, 🆗, 🖐, vending**
248	Bumble Bee, W ⊙ Horsethief Basin RA
244	Squaw Valley Rd, Black Canyon City, E 🍴 Chilleen's on 17 BBQ/Steaks, W 🖐 Shell 🍴 Beni's Pizza 🛏 Mountain Breeze Motel ⊙ Bradshaw Mtn RV Resort (2mi), Family$
243.5mm	Agua Fria River
242	Rock Springs, Black Canyon City, E ⊙ KOA (1mi), W 🖐 76/dsl, Shell 🍴 Beni's Pizza, Rock Springs Cafe 🛏 Bradshaw Mtn RV Resort, Mtn Breeze Motel ⊙ Ron's Mkt
239.5mm	Little Squaw Creek
239mm	Moore's Gulch
236	Table Mesa Rd
232	New River, E 🍴 RoadRunner Rest.
231.5mm	New River

ANTHEM

Exit #	Services
229	Anthem Way, Desert Hills Rd, E 🖐 Circle K 🍴 Hungry Howie's, McDonald's, Pizza Hut, Rosati's Pizza, Starbucks, Subway, Taco Bell, Wendy's ⊙ CVS Drug, Safeway, URGENT CARE, W 🖐 Chevron/dsl, Circle K/dsl 🍴 Del Taco, Denny's, Fresca's Mexican, Subway 🛏 Hampton Inn ⊙ $Store, Anthem Outlets/famous brands/food court, Discount Tire, Harley-Davidson, Meineke, O'Reilly Parts, Tobias Auto, U-Haul, Walmart
227mm	Dead Man Wash
227	Daisy Mtn Dr, E 🖐 Circle K/dsl 🍴 Cafe Provence, Domino's, Jack-in-the-Box, Roberto's Mexican, Starbucks, Streets of NY Deli, Streets of NY Deli, Subway ⊙ CVS Drug, Fry's Foods, GNC, GNC, Verizon, vet, vet
225	Pioneer Rd, W ⊙ Pioneer AZ Museum, Pioneer RV Park
223	AZ 74, Carefree Hwy, to Wickenburg, E 🖐 Chevron 🍴 AZool Grill, Chili's, Denny's, Good Egg Cafe, In-N-Out, McDonald's, Ray's Pizza, Starbucks, Subway, Taco Bell ⊙ Albertson's/Osco, GNC, Home Depot, Kohl's, Staples, W ⊙ Cibola Vista Camping (11mi)
222	Senora Blvd
220	Dixileta (from nb)
219	Jomax Rd
218	Happy Valley Rd, E 🖐 Circle K/dsl, Shell 🍴 Applebee's, Bajio, Buffalo Wild Wings, Burger King, Carl's Jr, Chipotle Mexican, Coldstone, IHOP, Jack-in-the-Box, Jersey Mike's Subs, Joey's Hotdogs, Johnny Rocket's, L&L Hawaiian BBQ, Logan's Roadhouse, Mellow Mushroom Pizza, Olive Garden, Panda Express, Paradise Cafe, PF Chang's, Rays Pizza, Red Robin, Sauce Pizza, Shane's Ribshack, Smash Burger, Starbucks, Subway, TGIFriday's, Zupas 🛏 Courtyard, Hampton Inn, Homewood Suites, Residence Inn ⊙ $Tree, Barnes&Noble, Best Buy, Big O Tire, Dick's, Lowe's, Old Navy, O'Reilly Parts,

SCOTTSDALE

Exit #	Services
218	Continued PetCo, Ross, Staples, TJ Maxx, Verizon, vet, Walmart, World Mkt, W ⊙ to Meg&DeLyle's
217	Pinnacle Peak Rd, E 🛏 Drury Inn, Hilton Garden ⊙ Phoenix RV Park
215b	Deer Valley Rd, E 🖐 Shell/Circle K 🍴 Arby's, Armando's Mexican, Culvers, Dunkin Donuts, Jack-in-the-Box, McDonald's, Sonic, Subway, Taco Bell, Wendy's ⊙ Little Dealer RV Ctr, W 🖐 Arco/dsl, Circle K/dsl 🍴 Cracker Barrel, Denny's, Times Square Italian, Waffle House 🛏 Days Inn, Extended Stay America ⊙ Ⓗ, U-Haul
215a	Rose Garden Ln, same as 215b
214c	AZ 101 loop
214b	Yorkshire Dr, W 🖐 7-11 🍴 Chick-fil-A, Chili's, In-N-Out, Jack-in-the-Box, Jimmy John's, Macaroni Grill, Pizza Hut, Wendy's 🛏 Budget Suites ⊙ Ⓗ, AT&T, Costco/gas, Michael's, Petsmart, Ross, Target
214a	Union Hills Dr, E 🖐 Circle K/dsl, Valero, W 🖐 Arco/dsl 🛏 Comfort Inn, Sleep Inn, Studio 6
212b a	Bell Rd, Scottsdale, to Sun City, E 🖐 Chevron/dsl, Circle K, QT, Shell/dsl 🍴 Big Apple Rest., Caramba Mexican, IHOP, Jack-in-the-Box, LJ Silver, Manuel's Mexican, McDonald's, Schlotzsky's, Shenanigan's Grill, Waffle House 🛏 Fairfield Inn, Motel 6, Super 8 ⊙ Big O Tire, Chevrolet, Chrysler/Jeep/Dodge, Discount Tire, Fiat, Ford, Honda, Hyundai, Kohl's, Lincoln, Mazda, Nissan, O'Reilly Parts, Sam's Club/gas, Toyota/Scion, U-Haul, Volvo, Walmart, W 🍴 Applebee's, Denny's, Native New Yorker, US Egg Breakfast 🛏 Red Roof Inn ⊙ Fry's Foods/dsl
211	Greenway Rd, E 🛏 Embassy Suites, La Quinta ⊙ 7-11
210	Thunderbird Rd, E 🖐 Circle K/dsl, Valero/dsl/LP 🍴 Asian Cafe, Barro's Pizza, Hong Kong Chinese, Jack-in-the-Box, Macayo's Mexican, Pizza Hut/Taco Bell, Subway, Wendy's ⊙ CVS Drug, Home Depot, Walgreens, W 🖐 QT 🍴 Jamba Juice, McDonald's, Port of Subs, Whataburger 🛏 Travelodge ⊙ Best Buy, Fry's Electronics, Lowe's
209	Cactus Rd, W 🖐 7-11, Chevron/dsl, QT/dsl 🍴 China Harvest, Tuliaberto's Mexican 🛏 Holiday Inn

PHOENIX

Exit #	Services
208.5mm	Arizona Canal
208	Peoria Ave, E 🍴 Fajita's, First Watch Cafe, Native Grill, Outback Steaks, Pappadeaux, Sweet Tomatoes 🛏 Candlewood Suites, Comfort Suites, Crowne Plaza, Extended Stay America, Homewood Suites, Hyatt Place, W 🖐 QT/dsl 🍴 Black Angus, Buffalo Wild Wings, Burger King, Cane's, Chili's, Chipotle Mexican, Coldstone, Culvers, Fat Burger, Filiberto's Mexican, Hibachi Grill, Hooters, In-N-Out, Jason's Deli, Longhorn Steaks, Mi Pueblo, Mimi's Cafe, Mongolian BBQ, Old Country Buffet, Olive Garden, Peter Piper Pizza,

AZ

⬆N	INTERSTATE 17 Cont'd
Exit #	Services
208	Continued
	Red Lobster, Sizzler, Souper Salad, Starbucks, Subway, TX Roadhouse, Wendy's 🛏 Metro Plaza, Premier Inn 🅞 $Tree, AT&T, Barnes&Noble, Dillard's, Discount Tire, Firestone/auto, Macy's, mall, Michael's, PetCo, Petsmart, Ross, Sears/auto, Staples, Tire Pros/repair, URGENT CARE, Verizon
207	Dunlap Ave, E 🅖 Circle K, Shell/dsl 🍴 Blimpie, Domino's, Fajitas, First Watch Cafe, Fuddrucker's, Jack-in-the-Box, Native Grill, Outback Steaks, Steaken Burger, Subway, Sweet Tomatoes, Wong's 🛏 Comfort Suites, Courtyard, Mainstay Suites, Sheraton, SpringHill Suites, TownPlace Suites 🅞 Aamco, CVS Drug, URGENT CARE, W 🅖 Chevron/dsl 🍴 Bobby-Q's Rest., Denny's, Schlotzsky's, Subway 🛏 ValuePlace 🅞 Midas, repair, U-Haul
206	Northern Ave, E 🅖 Circle K/dsl, Shell/dsl 🍴 Boston Mkt, Burger King, Del Taco, Denny's, Dunkin Donuts, El Pollo Loco, Gyros House, IHOP, Los Compadres, McDonald's, Papa John's, Pizza Hut, Starbucks, Subway, Uncle Tony's Pizza 🛏 Best Western 🅞 Albertson's/Osco, AutoZone, Sprouts Mkt, URGENT CARE, Walgreens, W 🅖 Arco, QT 🍴 DQ 🛏 Motel 6, Residence Inn, Super 8 🅞 $General, auto repair, K-Mart, vet
205	Glendale Ave, E 🅖 7-11, QT 🍴 Pizza Patron, Subway 🅞 Ace Hardware, Fry's Foods/dsl, repair, transmissions, vet, W 🅖 Circle K/dsl 🍴 Jack-in-the-Box, Lenny's Burger 🅞 7-11, O'Reilly Parts, to Luke AFB, Walgreens
204	Bethany Home Rd, E 🅖 Arco, Chevron/dsl, Shell/Church's/dsl 🍴 Carl's Jr, Dunkin Donuts, KFC, Mandarin Buffet, McDonald's, Papa Joe's, Pizza Hut/Taco Bell, Subway, Tulioberto's Mexican, Whataburger 🅞 H, $Tree, BigLots, Costco/gas, JC Penney, Petsmart, Radio Shack, Ross, Target, URGENT CARE, Walgreens, Walmart, W 🅖 Shell, Valero 🍴 Burger King, Familia Lorito, Great Dragon 🛏 Knights Inn 🅞 auto repair, Food City, Jiffy Lube, Savers
203	Camelback Rd, E 🍴 Church's, Country Boy's Rest., Filiberto's Mexican, Little Caesars 🅞 $General, Chrysler/Dodge/Jeep, Discount Tire, Family$, Hyundai, Kia, W 🅖 Circle K/dsl, QT 🍴 DQ, Jack-in-the-Box, McDonald's 🛏 Quality Inn 🅞 AutoZone, to Grand Canyon U, USPO
202	Indian School Rd, E 🅖 Arco/dsl 🍴 Domino's, Federico's Mexican, Pizza Hut, Subway 🅞 Ace Hardware, CVS Drug, Food City, Little RV Ctr, W 🅖 Shell, Sinclair/dsl, Valero/dsl 🍴 Lenny's Burgers 🛏 Motel 6, Travel Inn 🅞 7-11, Wide World of Maps
201	Thomas Rd, E 🅖 Chevron/McDonald's/playplace 🍴 Arby's, Denny's, Dunkin Donuts, Jack-in-the-Box, Starbucks 🛏 Days Inn, La Quinta 🅞 Circle K, W 🅖 QT 🍴 Carl's Jr, Subway 🅞 NAPA
200b	McDowell Rd, Van Buren, E 🅞 Purcell's Tire, W 🛏 Knights Inn
200a	I-10, W to LA, E to Phoenix
199b	Jefferson St (from sb), Adams St (from nb), Van Buren St (from nb), E 🅖 Circle K 🍴 Jack-in-the-Box 🅞 to st capitol, W 🅖 Circle K/gas 🍴 La Canasta Mexican 🅞 Penny Pincher Parts, PepBoys
199a	Grant St
198	Buckeye Rd (from nb)
197	US 60, 19th Ave, Durango St, E 🍴 Jack-in-the-Box, to St Capitol, Whataburger 🅞 $General, AutoZone
196	7th St, Central Ave, W 🅖 Shell/dsl

PHOENIX

195b	7th St, Central Ave, E 🅖 Circle K/dsl 🍴 Jack-in-the-Box, McDonald's, Taco Bell 🛏 EZ 8 Motel 🅞 H, NAPA Care
195a	16th St (from sb, no EZ return), E 🅖 Shell/Subway/dsl 🍴 Burger King 🅞 to Sky Harbor ✈
194	I-10 W, to AZ 151, to Sky Harbor ✈

I-17 begins/ends on I-10, exit 150a

⬆N	INTERSTATE 19
Exit #	Services
I-19 uses kilometers (km)	
101b a	I-10, E to El Paso, W to Phoenix, **I-19 begins/ends on I-10, exit 260.**
99	AZ 86, Ajo Way, E 🅖 Circle K, Shell 🍴 Eegee's Cafe, Hamburger Stand, Peter Piper Pizza, Pizza Hut, Subway, Taco Bell, Wienerschnitzel 🅞 auto repair, Family$, Fry's Foods, GNC, Goodyear/auto, U-Haul, URGENT CARE, vet, Walgreens, W 🅖 Circle K, QT/dsl, Shell/dsl 🍴 Burger King, Church's, Domino's, Little Caesars, Losbetos Mexican, McDonald's 🅞 H, $General, city park, Family$, Food City, Jiffy Lube, museum, to Old Tucson
98	Irvington Rd, E 🅖 Arco/dsl 🍴 Jimmy John's, TX Roadhouse 🅞 AutoZone, Fry's Foods/drug/dsl, W 🅖 Chevron, Circle K/dsl 🍴 Buffalo Wild Wings, China Olive Buffet, Coldstone, Five Guys, McDonald's, Olive Garden, Panda Express, Peter Piper Pizza, Red Lobster, Starbucks, Subway 🅞 $Tree, AT&T, Best Buy, Discount Tire, Family$, Food City, Home Depot, JC Penney, Marshall's, Michael's, Old Navy, Petsmart, Ross, Target, Verizon
95b a	Valencia Rd, E 🅖 Circle K, Shell 🍴 Chickenuevo, Church's, Donut Wheel, Eegee's Cafe, Jack-in-the-Box, Little Caesars, McDonald's, Peter Piper Pizza, Sonic, Subway, Whataburger, Yokohama Asian 🅞 $General, $Tree, Aamco, AutoZone, Brake Masters, Family$, Food City, Jiffy Lube, O'Reilly Parts, to ✈, USPO, Walgreens, W 🅖 Circle K/dsl 🍴 Arby's, Burger King, Carl's Jr, Casa Valencia, Chili's, China Dragon, Denny's, DQ, El Taco Tote, Golden Corral, Grand Buffet, Hamburger Stand, Little Caesars, Papa John's, Papa Murphy's, Pizza Hut, Subway, Taco Bell, Wendy's 🅞 99c Store, Big O Tire, BigLots, CVS Drug, Lowe's, Radio Shack, repair, transmissions, URGENT CARE, Walgreens, Walmart
92	San Xavier Rd, W 🅞 to San Xavier Mission (2mi)
91.5km	Santa Cruz River
87	Papago Rd
80	Pima Mine Rd, E 🍴 Agave Rest., Diamond Casino
75	Helmut Peak Rd, to Sahuarita, E 🅖 Shell/dsl/e-85 🍴 Asian Sky Rest., Dunkin Donuts/Baskin Robbins, Mama's Hawaiian BBQ, McDonald's, Starbucks, Subway 🅞 Fry's Foods/drug, USPO, vet
69	US 89 N, Duval Mine Rd., Green Valley, E 🍴 50's Diner, Carl's Jr., Denny's, Little Caesars, Panda House, Pizza Hut, Rigoberto's, Subway 🅞 99c Store, Ace Hardware, AutoZone, BigLots, Fletcher's Repair, Jo-Ann Fabrics, O'Reilly Parts, Petco, Radio Shack, Ross, Verizon, Walgreens, Walmart/Subway, W 🅖 Circle K 🍴 Arby's, Burger King, Domino's, Jerry Bob's Rest., Manuel's Mexican, Papa Murphy's, Starbucks, Taco Bell 🛏 Holiday Inn Express 🅞 Big O Tire, Ford/Hyundai, Green Valley RV Resort, NAPA, Safeway/dsl, Titan Missile Museum, URGENT CARE, USPO, vet
65	Esperanza Blvd, to Green Valley, E 🅖 Shell/repair/dsl, W 🍴 AZ Family Rest., La Placita Mexican 🛏 Best Western/rest, Comfort Inn 🅞 Ace Hardware, Walgreens
63	Continental Rd, Green Valley, E 🍴 Quail Creek Rest. (7mi) 🅞 golf, San Ignacio Golf Club/rest., USPO, W 🅖 Chevron/

TUCSON

GREEN VALLEY

INTERSTATE 19 Cont'd

Exit #	Services
63	Continued
	HotStuff Pizza 🍴 KFC, McDonald's, Starbucks 🔲 CVS Drug, Merle's Parts, repair/tires, Safeway, to Madera Cyn RA, TrueValue, Verizon, Walgreens
56	Canoa Rd, W 🛏 San Ignacio Inn, Wyndham Resort
54km	🆁🆂 both lanes, full 🛢 facilities, litter barrels, petwalk, 🅲, 🗑 vending
48	Arivaca Rd, Amado, 2-3 mi E 🛏 Amado Inn 🔲 DeAnza RV Resort (2mi), Mtn View RV Park, W 🍴 Cow Palace Rest. 🔲 Amado Mkt/gas, JJ's Auto Repair
42	Agua Linda Rd, to Amado, E 🔲 Mtn View RV Park
40	Chavez Siding Rd, Tubac, E 🔲 Tubac Golf Resort
34	Tubac, E 🅖 El Mercado 🍴 Elvira's Cafe, Tubac Deli, Tubac Hamburgers, Tubac Jack's Rest., Tubac Pizza 🔲 to Tubac Presidio SP, Tubac Golf Resort, Tubac Mkt, USPO
29	Carmen, Tumacacori, E 🔲 to Tumacacori Nat Hist Park, food, gas, lodging
25	Palo Parado Rd
22	Pec Canyon Rd
17	Rio Rico Dr, Calabasas Rd, W 🅖 Chevron/dsl/LP 🍴 Hua Mei Chinese, Nickles Diner, Wood Oven Pizza 🛏 Esplendor Resort 🔲 IGA Foods, JC Auto Repair/Lube, USPO, vet
12	AZ 289, to Ruby Rd, E 🅖 🚂 /Wendy's/dsl/scales/24hr, W 🔲 to Pena Blanca Lake RA
8	AZ 82 (exits left from sb, no return), Nogales, E 🅖 Circle K 🔲 Mi Casa RV Park
4	AZ 189 S, Mariposa Rd, Nogales, E 🅖 FasTrip/dsl 🍴 Bella Mia Rest., China Buffet, Chuyitos Hotdogs, City Salads, DQ, Dragon Buffet, Exquisito Mexican, Gorilla Pizza, Jack-in-the-Box, KFC, Little Caesars, McDonald's, Panda Express, Panda Express, Pizza Pollis, Subway, Toscanos 🛏 Mariposa Hotel, Motel 6 🔲 $General, $Tree, Ace Hardware, AutoZone, Buick/GMC, Chevrolet, Ford, GNC, Home Depot, JC Penney, K-Mart, Petsmart, Radio Shack, Ross, Safeway, Walgreens, Walmart/McDonald's (N Grand Ave), W 🅖 Circle K/dsl 🍴 Carl's Jr, IHOP 🛏 Best Western, Candlewood Suites, Holiday Inn Express 🔲 Mexico Insurance
1b	Western Ave, Nogales
1a	International St
0km	**I-19 begins/ends in Nogales**, Arizona/Mexico Border, 1/2 mi N 🅖 Circle K, Jr's Fuel Depot/dsl, Shell 🍴 Church's, Denny's, Jack-in-the-Box, McDonald's, Peter Piper Pizza, Pizza Hut, Subway 🔲 AutoZone, CarQuest, Family$, Food City, museum, NAPA, O'Reilly Parts, PepBoys

INTERSTATE 40

Exit #	Services
359.5mm	Arizona/New Mexico state line
359	Grants Rd, to Lupton, N **Welcome Ctr**/🆁🆂 both lanes, full 🛢 facilities, litter barrels, petwalk, 🅲, 🗑 🅖 Speedy's/dsl/rest./24hr 🔲 Tee Pee Trading Post/rest., YellowHorse Indian Gifts
357	AZ 12 N, Lupton, to Window Rock, N 🔲 USPO
354	Hawthorne Rd
351	Allentown Rd, N 🔲 Chee's Indian Store, Indian City Gifts
348	St Anselm Rd, Houck, N 🔲 Ft Courage Food/gifts
347.5mm	Black Creek
346	Pine Springs Rd
345mm	Box Canyon
344mm	Querino Wash

343	Querino Rd
341	Ortega Rd, Cedar Point, N 🅖 Armco/gas/gifts
340.5mm	insp/weigh sta both lanes
339	US 191 S, to St Johns, S 🅖 Conoco/dsl 🔲 Family$, RV Park, USPO
333	US 191 N, Chambers, N 🅖 Rte 66 Gas/dsl 🔲 to Hubbell Trading Post NHS, USPO, S 🅖 Mobil/dsl 🛏 Chieftain Inn/rest.
330	McCarrell Rd
325	Navajo, S 🅖 Shell/Subway/Navajo Trading Post/dsl/24hr
323mm	Crazy Creek
320	Pinta Rd
316mm	Dead River
311	Painted Desert, N 🅖 Chevron 🔲 Painted Desert, Petrified Forest NP
303	Adamana Rd, N 🔲 Stewarts/gifts, S 🔲 Painted Desert Indian Ctr
302.5mm	Big Lithodendron Wash
301mm	Little Lithodendron Wash
300	Goodwater
299mm	Twin Wash
294	Sun Valley Rd, N 🛏 Root 66 RV camping, S 🔲 Knife City
292	AZ 77 N, to Keams Canyon, N 🅖 Conoco/Burger King/dsl/24hr 🔲 dsl repair
289	Lp 40, Holbrook, N 🅖 Chevron/dsl, Hatch's/dsl 🍴 Denny's, Jerry's Rest., Mesa Rest. 🛏 Best Inn, Best Western, Comfort Inn, Days Inn, EconoLodge, Motel 6, Ramada Ltd, Sahara Inn, Travelodge 🔲 Goodyear
286	Navajo Blvd, Holbrook, N 🅖 Chevron/dsl, Circle K, Maverik/dsl 🍴 Aliberto's Mexican, Burger King, Hilltop Cafe, KFC, McDonald's, Pizza Hut, Taco Bell 🛏 66 Motel, Holiday Inn Express, Super 8 🔲 $General, Alco, KOA, OK RV Park, O'Reilly Parts, S 🅖 Chevron/dsl, Fuel Express/dsl, Jack's/repair/LP, MiniMart/gas, Speedy Dsl 🍴 DQ, Rte 66 Cafe 🛏 Best Value, El Rancho Motel/rest., Knights Inn 🔲 🅷 Dodge/Ford/Lincoln, museum, rockshops, Scotty & Son Repair, SW Transmissions
285	US 180 E, AZ 77 S, Holbrook 1 mi S 🅖 Giant/dsl 🍴 Butterfield Steaks, Wayside Mexican 🛏 Best Western, Economy Inn, Globetrotter Hotel, Wigwam Motel 🔲 Best Hardware, Family$, repair, 🆁🆂/🗑 litter barrels, Safeway, to Petrified Forest NP
284mm	Leroux Wash
283	Perkins Valley Rd, Golf Course Rd, S 🅖 Fuel Express/dsl/rest./scales/24hr/@
280	Hunt Rd, Geronimo Rd, N 🔲 Geronimo Trading Post
277	Lp 40, Joseph City, N 🅖 Loves/Chester's/Subway/scales/dsl/24h, S 🔲 RV camping, to Cholla Lake CP
274	Lp 40, Joseph City, N food, gas, lodging, RV camping

AZ

WINSLOW

🔼E INTERSTATE 40 Cont'd

Exit #	Services
269	Jackrabbit Rd, S 🅞 Jackrabbit Trading Post
264	Hibbard Rd
257	AZ 87 N, to Second Mesa, N 🅞 camping, to Homolovi Ruins SP, S 🅞 trading post
256.5mm	Little Colorado River
255	Lp 40, Winslow, N 🅖 Winslow Fuel/dsl 🅛 Best Western 🅞 Mi Pueblo Mexican, Take-A-Rest RV Park, S 🅖 ⊕FLYING J /Denny's/dsl/LP/scales/RV Dump/24hr 🅕 Sonic 🅞 Chrysler/ Dodge/Jeep, Nissan, 🆁🆂
253	N Park Dr, Winslow, N 🅖 Chevron, Maverik/dsl 🅕 Arby's, Capt Tony's Pizza, Denny's, Pizza Hut 🅞 $General, Ford, O'Reilly Parts, tires/lube, Walmart/truck parking, S 🅕 Alfon- so's Mexican, KFC, LJ Silver/Taco Bell, McDonald's, Subway 🅛 Motel 6, Oak Tree Inn, Quality Inn 🅞🅗 Family$, NAPA
252	AZ 87 S, Winslow, S 🅖 Shell/dsl 🅕 Entre Chinese 🅛 Best Value, Rest Inn, Super 8, The Lodge
245	AZ 99, Leupp Corner
239	Meteor City Rd, Red Gap Ranch Rd, S 🅞 Meteor City Trading Post, to Meteor Crater
235mm	🆁🆂 both lanes, full 🅰 facilities, info, litter barrels, petwalk, 🅒, 🅰, vending
233	Meteor Crater Rd, S 🅖 Mobil/Meteor Crater RV Park/dump 🅞 to Meteor Crater NL
230	Two Guns
229.5mm	Canyon Diablo
225	Buffalo Range Rd
219	Twin Arrows
218.5mm	Padre Canyon
211	Winona, N 🅖 Shell/dsl/repair
207	Cosnino Rd
204	to Walnut Canyon NM
201	US 89, Flagstaff, to Page, N 🅖 Chevron, Express Stop/dsl, Shell, Texaco 🅕 Arby's, Burger King, Del Taco, Jack-in-the- Box, LJ Silver/Taco Bell, McDonald's, Pizza Hut, Quiznos, Roma Pizza, Ruby Tuesday, Sizzler, Smokehouse BBQ, Vil- lage Inn, Wendy's 🅛 Best Western, Days Inn, Hampton Inn, Howard Johnson, Luxury Inn, Super 8 🅞🅗, auto repair, Best Buy, CVS Drug, Dillard's, Discount Tire, Family$, Flagstaff RV Ctr/LP, Goodyear/auto, Home Depot, JC Penney, KOA, mall, Marshall's, Old Navy, O'Reilly Parts, PetCo, PitStop Lube, Safeway/dsl, Sears/auto, Toyota, World Mkt, S 🅖 Mobil/dsl 🅛 Residence Inn

FLAGSTAFF

198	Butler Ave, Flagstaff, N 🅖 Chevron, Conoco/dsl, Shell 🅕 Burger King, Country Host Rest., Cracker Barrel, Denny's, Hogs Rest., McDonald's, Outback Steaks, Sonic, Taco Bell 🅛 EconoLodge, Holiday Inn Express, Howard Johnson, Motel 6, Quality Inn, Ramada, Rodeway Inn, Super 8, Travelodge 🅞 Ace Hardware, NAPA, Sam's Club/gas, U-Haul, vet, Walmart, S 🅖 Mobil, Sinclair/Little America/dsl/motel/@ 🅕 Black Bart's Steaks/RV Park
197.5mm	Rio de Flag
195b	US 89A N, McConnell Dr, Flagstaff, N 🅖 Chevron/dsl, Circle K, Conoco/dsl, Giant/dsl, Mobil/dsl, Shell, Texaco/Wendy's/dsl 🅕 5 Guys Burgers, Arby's, August Moon Chinese, Baskin- Robbins, Buffalo Wild Wings, Burger King, Buster's Rest., Carl's Jr, Chili's, China Garden, Chipotle Mexican, Coco's, Coldstone, Del Taco, Denny's, Domino's, DQ, Freddy's Steak- burgers, IHOP, Jack-in-the-Box, KFC, Little Caesars, Manda- rin Buffet, McDonald's, Native New Yorker, Ni Marco's Pizza, Olive Garden, Panda Express, Papa John's, Papa Murphy's,

195b	Continued Peter Piper Pizza, Picazzo's Pizza, Pizza Hut, Quiznos, Red Lobster, Sizzler, Starbucks, Subway, Taco Bell 🅛 Best Inn, Budget Inn, Canyon Inn, Comfort Inn, Country Inn, Courtyard, Days Inn, Drury Inn, EconoLodge, Embassy Suites, Executive Inn, Fairfield Inn, Hampton Inn, Knights Inn, La Quinta, Motel 6, Quality Inn, Ramada Ltd, Rodeway Inn, SpringHill Suites, Super 8 🅞🅗, $Tree, AT&T, auto/RV repair, Barnes&Noble, Basha's Foods, Discount Tire, Hastings Books, Jo-Ann Crafts, Kohl's, Michael's, O'Reilly Parts, Petsmart, Ross, Safeway, Staples, Target, Verizon, Walgreens, Walmart
195a	I-17 S, AZ 89A S, to Phoenix
192	Flagstaff Ranch Rd
191	Lp 40, to Grand Canyon, Flagstaff, 5 mi N 🅖 Chevron, Maver- ik, Whistle Stop/dsl 🅕 Galaxy Diner 🅛 Best Value, Budget Host, Comfort Inn, Days Inn, EconoLodge, Radisson, Super 8, Travel Inn, Travelodge 🅞 CarQuest, Chevrolet/Cadillac, Home Depot, Kia, Kit Carson RV Park, O'Reilly Parts, vet, Woody Mtn Camping
190	A-1 Mountain Rd
189.5mm	Arizona Divide, elevation 7335
185	Transwestern Rd, Bellemont, N 🅕🅖🅛/McDonald's/Sub- way/dsl/scales/24hr/@ 🅛 Motel 6, S 🅞 Camping World, Harley-Davidson/Roadside Grill
178	Parks Rd, N 🅖 Texaco/dsl
171	Pittman Valley Rd, Deer Farm Rd, S 🅛 Mountain Ranch Re- sort
167	Garland Prairie Rd, Circle Pines Rd, N 🅞 KOA
165	AZ 64, to Williams, Grand Canyon, N 🅖 76 (8mi), Shell/dsl (4mi) 🅞 KOA (4mi), to Grand Canyon, S 🅛 Super 8 (1mi)

WILLIAMS

163	Williams, N 🅖 Chevron/dsl, ⬭Loves/Arby's/dsl/ scales/24hr 🅛 Quality Inn 🅞 Canyon Gateway RV Park, S 🅖 Circle K, Mobil/dsl, Mustang/dsl, Shell/dsl 🅕 Jack-in-the- Box, KFC/Taco Bell, McDonald's, Old Town Rest., Pancho's Mexican, Pine Country Rest., Pizza Hut, Red Garter Rest., Rod's Steaks, Rte 66 Diner, Twisters Soda Fountain 🅛 Can- yon Motel/RV Park, EconoLodge, El Rancho Motel, Grand Canyon Railway Hotel, Howard Johnson, Knights Inn, Moun- tainside Motel, Ramada Inn, Rodeway Inn, Rodeway Inn, The Lodge Motel, Travelodge 🅞 $General, same as 161, USPO
161	Lp 40, Golf Course Dr, Williams, N 🅞 RV camping, 0-3 mi S 🅖 Circle K, Conoco/dsl/LP, Shell 🅕 Buffalo Pointe Inn, DQ, Jessica's Rest., Maria's Tacos 🅛 AZ Motel, Best Value, Best Western, Budget Host, Canyon Country Inn, Comfort Inn, Days Inn, Grand Canyon Hotel, Highlander Motel, Motel 6, Westerner Motel 🅞🅗, Family$, Safeway, to Grand Canyon Railway
157	Devil Dog Rd
155.5mm	litter barrels, safety pullout wb
151	Welch Rd
149	Monte Carlo Rd, N 🅞 dsl repair
148	County Line Rd
146	AZ 89, to Prescott, Ash Fork, N 🅖 Mobil/dsl, Shell/dsl 🅕 Lulu Belle's BBQ, Ranch House Cafe 🅛 Ash Fork Inn 🅞 Family$
144	Ash Fork, N 🅛 Ash Fork Inn 🅞 Grand Canyon RV Park, mu- seum/info, USPO, S 🅖 Chevron/Piccadilly's/dsl, Texaco/dsl/ RV Park 🅞 auto/RV repair
139	Crookton Rd, to Rte 66
123	Lp 40, to Rte 66, to Grand Canyon Caverns, Seligman, N 🅖 Chevron/A&W, Shell/dsl 🅕 Copper Cart Cafe, Lilo's Rest., Pizza Joint, Snow Cap Burgers 🅛 Canyon Lodge, Deluxe Inn, Stagecoach 66 Motel, Supai Motel 🅞 KOA (1mi), repair, USPO, S 🅖 Chevron/Subway/dsl, 🅞 (same as 121)

AZ

AR

⬆E INTERSTATE 40 Cont'd

Exit #	Services
121	Lp 40, to Rte 66, Seligman, N 🅰 76/dsl, Chevron/A&W 🍴 Copper Cart Cafe, Lilo's Rest., Roadkill Cafe 🏠 Canyon Lodge, Route 66 Motel/pizza, Supai Motel 🅾 KOA (1mi), repair (same as 123), to Grand Canyon Caverns, USPO
109	Anvil Rock Rd
108mm	Markham Wash
103	Jolly Rd
96	Cross Mountain Rd
91	Fort Rock Rd
87	Willows Ranch Rd
86mm	Willow Creek
79	Silver Springs Rd
75.5mm	Big Sandy Wash
73.5mm	Peacock Wash
71	US 93 S, to Wickenburg, Phoenix
66	Blake Ranch Rd, N 🅰 Petro/Iron Skillet/dsl/scales/24hr/@ 🅾 Blake Ranch RV Park, SpeedCo Lube
60mm	Frees Wash
59	DW Ranch Rd, N 🅰❤Loves/Chester's/Subway/dsl/scales/24hr 🅾 Hualapai Mtn Park (9mi), truckwash
57mm	Rattlesnake Wash
53	AZ 66, Andy Devine Ave, to Kingman, N 🅰 ⊕FLYING J/Denny's/dsl/LP/scales/24hr, Chevron/dsl, Maverik/dsl, Terrible's/dsl, Texaco/dsl 🍴 Arby's, Burger King, Denny's, Jack-in-the-Box, McDonald's, Pizza Hut, Taco Bell 🏠 Days Inn, EconoLodge, Knights Inn, Motel 6, Super 8, Travelodge 🅾 $General, Basha's Foods, Blue Beacon, dsl/tire repair, Freightliner, Goodyear, Harley-Davidson, K-Mart, KOA (1mi), S 🅰 Mobil/dsl, Shell/dsl/repair 🍴 ABC Chinese, JB's, Oyster's Mexican, Sonic 🏠 Best Western, Comfort Inn, Days Inn, High Desert Inn, Holiday Inn Express, Magnuson, Rodeway Inn, Rte 66 Motel, SpringHill Suites 🅾 Chrysler/Dodge/Jeep, Kia, NAPA, Sunrise RV Park, Uptown Drug
51	Stockton Hill Rd, Kingman, N 🅰 Arco/dsl, Chevron, Circle K/dsl 🍴 Carl's Jr, Chili's, Chipotle Mexican, Cracker Barrel, Del Taco, Domino's, Five Guys, Golden Corral, IHOP, In-N-Out, KFC, McDonald's, Panda Express, Papa John's, Papa Murphy, Plaza Bonita, Scotty's Rest., Sonic, Starbucks, Subway, Taco Bell 🏠 Hampton Inn 🅾🅷, $General, $Tree, AutoZone, AZ RV Depot/repair, BigLots, BrakeMasters, Buick/Chevrolet,

51	Continued CVS Drug, Discount Tire, Ford/Lincoln, Home Depot, Honda, Hyundai, Oil Can Henry's, O'Reilly Parts, PetCo, Petsmart, Ross, Safeway/gas, Smith's Foods/dsl, Staples, Superior Tire, TrueValue, Verizon, vet, Walgreens, Walmart, S 🅰 Circle K 🍴 Kingman Co Steaks, Little Caesars, Paco's Mexican, Pizza Hut 🅾 99¢ Store, CarQuest, Family$, Hastings Books, JC Penney, Radio Shack, Safeway/dsl, Sears
48	US 93 N, Beale St, Kingman, N 🅰 76/dsl, Chevron/dsl, Mobil/dsl, Shell/dsl, TA/Country Pride/Popeye's/dsl/scales/24hr/@, Texaco/dsl, USA/Subway/dsl, Woody's 🍴 Wendy's 🏠 Budget Inn, Economy Inn, Tristate Inn 🅾 4A Tire/auto/RV repair, S 🅰 Chevron/Quiznos/dsl 🍴 Calico's Rest., Carl's Jr 🏠 AZ Inn, Motel 6 🅾 city park, Ft Beale RV Park, Mohave Museum
46.5mm	Holy Moses Wash
44	AZ 66, Oatman Hwy, McConnico, to Rte 66, S 🅰 Crazy Fred's/café/dsl 🅾 Canyon West RV Camping (3mi), truckwash
40.5mm	Griffith Wash
37	Griffith Rd
35mm	Black Rock Wash
32mm	Walnut Creek
28	Old Trails Rd
26	Proving Ground Rd, S 🅾 AZ Proving Grounds
25	Alamo Rd, to Yucca, N 🅾 USPO
23mm	℞ˢ both lanes, full ♿ facilities, litter barrels, petwalk, 🕭, 🔀 vending
21mm	Flat Top Wash
20	Santa Fe Ranch Rd
18.5mm	Illavar Wash
15mm	Buck Mtn Wash
13.5mm	Franconia Wash
13	Franconia Rd
9	AZ 95 S, to Lake Havasu City, Parker, London Br, S 🅰 Chevron/dsl, ❤Loves/Carl's Jr/Subway/dsl/scales/24hr, 🍴/Wendy's/dsl/scales/24hr 🅾 Havasu RV Park, Prospectors RV Resort
4mm	weigh sta both lanes
2	Needle Mtn Rd
1	Topock Rd, to Bullhead City, Oatman, N 🅾 camping, food, gas, to Havasu NWR
0mm	Arizona/California state line, Colorado River, Mountain/Pacific time zone

ARKANSAS

⬆E INTERSTATE 30

Exit #	Services
I-30 begins/ends on I-40, exit 153b	
143b a	I-40, E to Memphis, W to Ft Smith
142	15th St, S 🅰 Super Stop/dsl
141mm	Arkansas River
141b	US 70, Broadway St, downtown, N 🅰 Exxon, US Fuel/dsl 🍴 Burger King 🅾 U-Haul, Verizon Arena, S 🅰 Citgo, Valero/dsl 🍴 KFC/LJ Silver, McDonald's, Popeye's, Taco Bell, Wendy's
141a	AR 10, Cantrell Rd, Markham St (from wb), W 🅾 to downtown
140	9th St, 6th St, downtown, N 🅰 Exxon/dsl, Phillips 66, Shell 🍴 Pizza Hut 🏠 Holiday Inn 🅾 USPO, S 🅰 SuperStop 🏠 Comfort Inn
139b	I-630, downtown

139a	AR 365, Roosevelt Rd, N 🅰 Exxon 🍴 Sim's BBQ 🅾 AutoZone, S 🅰 Shell 🅾 Family$, Kroger, NAPA
138b	I-530 S, US 167 S, US 65 S, to Pine Bluff
138a	I-440 E, to Memphis, 🅾🔀
135	W 65th St, N 🅰 Exxon/dsl, MapCo, Shell/dsl 🏠 Days Inn, S 🏠 Rodeway Inn
134	Scott Hamilton Dr, S 🅰 Exxon/dsl 🏠 Best Value Inn, Motel 6
133	Geyer Springs Rd, N 🅰 Exxon, Hess 🍴 Church's, Sonic, Subway, S 🅰 Exxon, Phillips 66, Shell 🍴 Arby's, Burger King, El Chico, KFC, Little Caesars, McDonald's, Panda Chinese, Rallys, Shark's Rest., Taco Bell, Waffle House, Wendy's 🏠 Baymont Inn, Best Western, Comfort Inn, Quality Inn, Rest Inn 🅾 Advance Parts, Family$, Goodyear/auto, Kroger/gas, Radio Shack, Walgreens
132	US 70b, University Ave, N 🅰 RaceWay/dsl, SuperStop, Valero 🏠 Best Value Inn 🅾 Chevrolet, S 🍴 Luigi's Pizza

S E L I G M A N

K I N G M A N

Y U C C A

AR

MABELVALE

▲E INTERSTATE 30 Cont'd	
Exit #	**Services**
131	McDaniel Dr, N 🅞 U-Haul, S 🛏 Knights Inn, Super 7 Inn 🅞 Firestone
130	AR 338, Baseline Rd, Mabelvale, N 🛏 Best Inn 🅞 Harley-Davidson, Suzuki, S 🅖 Shell/Popeye's 🅕 #1 Buffet, Applebee's, China Buffet, Dixie Cafe, McDonald's, Pizza Hut, Sonic, Taco Bueno, Wendy's 🅞 $Tree, AT&T, Chevrolet, Crain RV Ctr, Home Depot, Walmart/Subway
129	I-430 N
128	Otter Creek Rd, Mabelvale West, N 🅖 Loves/Hardee's/Subway/dsl/scales/24hr, S 🅖 Exxon/dsl 🛏 La Quinta 🅞 🅷, Goodyear
126	AR 111, County Line Rd, Alexander, N 🅖 Phillips 66/dsl, Shell/dsl, S 🅖 Citgo/Subway 🅞 Cherokee RV Park/dump (4mi)
123	AR 183, Reynolds Rd, to Bryant, Bauxite, N 🅖 Murphy USA/dsl, Shell, SuperStop 🅕 Arby's, Backyard Burgers, Burger King, Catfish Barn, Cracker Barrel, D-Light Chinese, Domino's, Firehouse Subs, IHOP, KFC, Papa Murphy's, Pizza Hut, Quiznos, Ruby Tuesday, Subway, TaMolly's, Waffle House 🛏 Best Value Inn, Comfort Inn, Hampton Inn, Holiday Inn Express, Hometown Hotel, La Quinta, Vista Inn 🅞 $Tree, AT&T, AutoZone, Radio Shack, Walgreens, Walmart/Subway, S 🅖 Conoco/dsl, Exxon/dsl 🅕 Chick-fil-A, Little Caesars, Logan's Roadhouse, McDonald's, Mi Ranchito, Sonic, Taco Bell, Wendy's, Zaxby's 🛏 Super 8 🅞 $General, Lowe's, O'Reilly Parts, USPO
121	Alcoa Rd, N 🅖 Citgo, ▨▨/Subway/dsl/scales/24hr/@ 🅕 McDonald's, Taco Bueno 🅞 Chrysler/Dodge/Jeep, Fiat, Firestone, S 🅕 Chili's, McAlister's Deli, Moe's SW Grill, Sakura Japanese, Sonic, Starbucks, Subway 🅞 AT&T, Best Buy, Buick/GMC, GNC, Kohl's, Old Navy, PetCo, Target
118	Congo Rd, N 🅕 Applebee's, Brown's Rest, CiCi's, Dixie Café, Patrone Mexican, Santa Fe Grill 🅞 Chevrolet/Hummer, Home Depot, Williams Tire, S 🅖 Exxon 🅕 Burger King 🛏 Days Inn, Ramada Inn 🅞 Ford, I-30 Travel Park, RV City, USPO

BENTON

117	US 64, AR 5, AR 35, N 🅖 Shell 🅕 Denny's, IHOP, Papa John's, Pizza Hut, Waffle House 🛏 Best Inn, Best Western, EconoLodge, S 🅖 Exxon, Fina, Murphy USA, Shell, Valero 🅕 Arby's, Backyard Burger, Buffet City, Burger King, Capt D's, Chicken Express, Colton's Steaks, IHOP, KFC, La Hacienda Mexican, McDonald's, Pasta Jack's Italian, Rib Crib, Sonic, Subway, Taco Bell, Wendy's, Western Sizzlin 🛏 Days Inn 🅞 🅷, $General, $Tree, Advance Parts, AT&T, AutoZone, BigLots, Fred's, GNC, Hastings Books, Kroger, Office Depot, O'Reilly Parts, Radio Shack, Tuesday Morning, Verizon, Walgreens, Walmart
116	Sevier St, N 🅖 Citgo/dsl, Shell/dsl 🅕 Hunan Place Chinese 🛏 Troutt Motel, S 🅖 Phillips 66 🛏 Capri Inn
114	US 67 S, Benton, S 🅖 Valero/McDonald's/dsl 🅕 Sonic
113mm	insp sta both lanes

MALVERN

111	US 70 W, Hot Springs, N 🅞 Cloud 9 RV Park, to Hot Springs NP
106	Old Military Rd, N 🅖 Fina/JJ's Rest./dsl/scales/@, S 🅞 JB'S RV Park
99	US 270 E, Malvern, N 🅞 🅷
98b a	US 270, Malvern, Hot Springs, N 🛏 Super 8, S 🅖 Murphy USA/dsl, Phillips 66/dsl, Shell/dsl, Valero/Baskin-Robbins 🅕 Burger King, Chile Peppers, Cotija Mexican, El Parian, Great Wall Buffet, McDonald's, Pizza Hut, Sonic, Subway, Taco Bell, Waffle House, Wendy's, Western Sizzlin 🛏 Best

ARKADELPHIA

98b a	Continued Value Inn, Comfort Inn, Holiday Inn Express, Super 8 🅞 🅷, $General, $Tree, AutoZone, Buick/GMC, Chevrolet, city park, Ford,O'Reilly Parts, Radio Shack, USPO, Verizon, Walmart/Subway
97	AR 84, AR 171, N 🅞 Lake Catherine SP, RV camping
93mm	🆁🆂 both lanes (exit left), full ♿ facilities, litter barrels, petwalk, 🚻, 🐾, vending
91	AR 84, Social Hill
83	AR 283, Friendship, S 🅖 Shell/dsl
78	AR 7, Caddo Valley, N 🅖 Conoco/dsl/scales/24hr, Shell/dsl, Valero/dsl 🅕 Cracker Barrel 🛏 Holiday Inn Express 🅞 Arkadelphia RV Park, to Hot Springs NP, S 🅖 Exxon/Subway/dsl, Phillips 66, Shell/dsl 🅕 McDonald's, Taco Bell, TaMolly's Mexican, Waffle House, Wendy's 🛏 Best Value Inn, Best Western, Comfort Inn, Days Inn, Hampton Inn, Motel 6, Quality Inn, Super 8 🅞 De Gray SP
73	AR 8, AR 26, AR 51, Arkadelphia, N 🅖 Citgo/dsl, Shell/Stuckey's 🅕 Chicken Express, Domino's, Great Wall Buffet, McDonald's, Western Sizzlin 🅞 $Tree, AT&T, Radio Shack, to Crater of Diamond SP, Verizon, Walmart/Subway, S 🅖 Exxon/dsl, Shell 🅕 Andy's Rest., Burger King, Little Italy, Mazzio's Pizza, Subway, Taco Tico 🅞 🅷, $General, Ace Hardware, AT&T, AutoZone, Brookshire Foods, Fred's, O'Reilly Parts, tires/repair, vet, Walgreens
69	AR 26 E, Gum Springs
63	AR 53, Gurdon, N 🅖 South Fork Trkstp/Citgo/rest./dsl 🛏 Best Value Inn, S 🅖 Shell/rest/dsl 🅞 to White Oak Lake SP
56mm	🆁🆂 both lanes, full ♿ facilities, litter barrels, petwalk, 🐾 vending
54	AR 51, Gurdon, Okolona
46	AR 19, Prescott, N 🅖 Valero/Horizon/cafe/dsl/24hr 🅞 Crater of Diamonds SP (31mi), White Oaks SP, S 🅖 Loves/Hardee's/dsl/scales/24hr 🅕 Los Agave's Mexican
44	AR 24, Prescott, N 🅖 TA/Country Fare/Subway/Taco Bell/dsl/scales/24hr/@, S 🅖 Norman's 44 Trkstp/rest/dsl/scales/@ 🛏 Best Value Inn 🅞 🅷, to S Ark U, truckwash
36	AR 299, to Emmett
31	AR 29, Hope, N 🅖 Shell/dsl 🅕 Uncle Henry's BBQ 🛏 Relax Inn, Village Inn/RV park 🅞 st police, S 🅖 Exxon/dsl, Valero/dsl 🅕 KFC 🛏 Best Value Inn 🅞 🅷

HOPE

30	AR 4, Hope, N 🅖 Murphy USA, Valero/dsl 🅕 Dos Loco Gringos 🛏 Best Western, Hampton Inn, Holiday Inn Express, Super 8 🅞 Millwood SP, Verizon, Walmart/Subway, S 🅖 Exxon/Baskin-Robbins/Wendy's, Shell 🅕 Amigo Juan Mexican, Burger King, Little Caesars, McDonald's, Panda Chinese, Pizza Hut, Sonic, Subway, Taco Bell, Waffle House 🛏 Days Inn 🅞 🅷, $Tree, AT&T, AutoZone, Buick/Chevrolet/GMC, Bumper Parts, Ford, Fred's, Old Washington Hist SP, O'Reilly Parts, Super 1 Foods/gas, Walgreens
26mm	weigh sta both lanes
18	rd 355, Fulton, N 🅖 Red River Trkstp/dsl
17mm	Red River
12	US 67 (from eb), Fulton
7mm	Welcome Ctr eb, full ♿ facilities, info, litter barrels, petwalk, 🚻, 🐾, vending
7	AR 108, Mandeville, N 🅖 ⊕FLYING J/Denny's/dsl/LP/24hr 🛏 Sunrise RV Park 🅞 truckwash
3	AR 549
2	US 67, AR 245, Texarkana, N 🅖 RoadRunner/dsl, Shell/Circle K/dsl, S 🅕 T-Town Diner 🅞 Nick's RV Ctr
1	US 71, Jefferson Ave, Texarkana, N 🛏 Holiday Inn Express 🅞 KOA, S 🛏 Country Host Inn
0mm	Arkansas/Texas state line

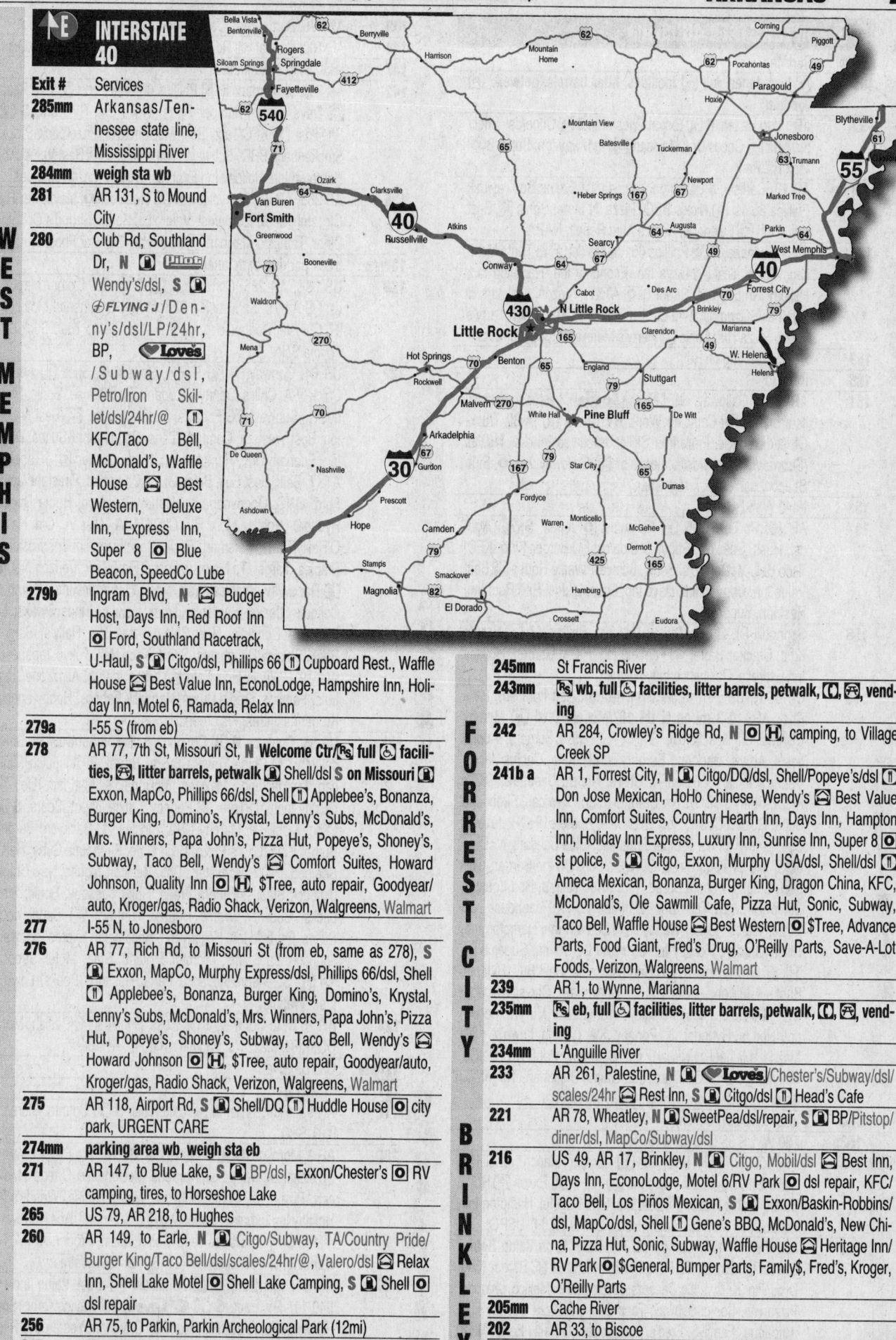

WEST MEMPHIS

Exit #	Services
285mm	Arkansas/Tennessee state line, Mississippi River
284mm	weigh sta wb
281	AR 131, S to Mound City
280	Club Rd, Southland Dr, **N** 🛢️ Pilot/Wendy's/dsl, **S** 🛢️ FLYING J/Denny's/dsl/LP/24hr, BP, ♥Loves/Subway/dsl, Petro/Iron Skillet/dsl/24hr/@ 🍴 KFC/Taco Bell, McDonald's, Waffle House 🏠 Best Western, Deluxe Inn, Express Inn, Super 8 🅾️ Blue Beacon, SpeedCo Lube
279b	Ingram Blvd, **N** 🏠 Budget Host, Days Inn, Red Roof Inn 🅾️ Ford, Southland Racetrack, U-Haul, **S** 🛢️ Citgo/dsl, Phillips 66 🍴 Cupboard Rest., Waffle House 🏠 Best Value Inn, EconoLodge, Hampshire Inn, Holiday Inn, Motel 6, Ramada, Relax Inn
279a	I-55 S (from eb)
278	AR 77, 7th St, Missouri St, **N** Welcome Ctr/🆁🆂 full ♿ facilities, 🚮, litter barrels, petwalk 🛢️ Shell/dsl **S on Missouri** 🛢️ Exxon, MapCo, Phillips 66/dsl, Shell 🍴 Applebee's, Bonanza, Burger King, Domino's, Krystal, Lenny's Subs, McDonald's, Mrs. Winners, Papa John's, Pizza Hut, Popeye's, Shoney's, Subway, Taco Bell, Wendy's 🏠 Comfort Suites, Howard Johnson, Quality Inn 🅾️ Ⓗ, $Tree, auto repair, Goodyear/auto, Kroger/gas, Radio Shack, Verizon, Walgreens, Walmart
277	I-55 N, to Jonesboro
276	AR 77, Rich Rd, to Missouri St (from eb, same as 278), **S** 🛢️ Exxon, MapCo, Murphy Express/dsl, Phillips 66/dsl, Shell 🍴 Applebee's, Bonanza, Burger King, Domino's, Krystal, Lenny's Subs, McDonald's, Mrs. Winners, Papa John's, Pizza Hut, Popeye's, Shoney's, Subway, Taco Bell, Wendy's 🏠 Howard Johnson 🅾️ Ⓗ, $Tree, auto repair, Goodyear/auto, Kroger/gas, Radio Shack, Verizon, Walgreens, Walmart
275	AR 118, Airport Rd, **S** 🛢️ Shell/DQ 🍴 Huddle House 🅾️ city park, URGENT CARE
274mm	parking area wb, weigh sta eb
271	AR 147, to Blue Lake, **S** 🛢️ BP/dsl, Exxon/Chester's 🅾️ RV camping, tires, to Horseshoe Lake
265	US 79, AR 218, to Hughes
260	AR 149, to Earle, **N** 🛢️ Citgo/Subway, TA/Country Pride/Burger King/Taco Bell/dsl/scales/24hr/@, Valero/dsl 🏠 Relax Inn, Shell Lake Motel 🅾️ Shell Lake Camping, **S** 🛢️ Shell 🅾️ dsl repair
256	AR 75, to Parkin, Parkin Archeological Park (12mi)
247	AR 38 E, to Widener

FORREST CITY BRINKLEY

245mm	St Francis River
243mm	🆁🆂 wb, full ♿ facilities, litter barrels, petwalk, 🚻, 🚮, vending
242	AR 284, Crowley's Ridge Rd, **N** 🅾️ Ⓗ, camping, to Village Creek SP
241b a	AR 1, Forrest City, **N** 🛢️ Citgo/DQ/dsl, Shell/Popeye's/dsl 🍴 Don Jose Mexican, HoHo Chinese, Wendy's 🏠 Best Value Inn, Comfort Suites, Country Hearth Inn, Days Inn, Hampton Inn, Holiday Inn Express, Luxury Inn, Sunrise Inn, Super 8 🅾️ st police, **S** 🛢️ Citgo, Exxon, Murphy USA/dsl, Shell/dsl 🍴 Ameca Mexican, Bonanza, Burger King, Dragon China, KFC, McDonald's, Ole Sawmill Cafe, Pizza Hut, Sonic, Subway, Taco Bell, Waffle House 🏠 Best Western 🅾️ $Tree, Advance Parts, Food Giant, Fred's Drug, O'Reilly Parts, Save-A-Lot Foods, Verizon, Walgreens, Walmart
239	AR 1, to Wynne, Marianna
235mm	🆁🆂 eb, full ♿ facilities, litter barrels, petwalk, 🚻, 🚮, vending
234mm	L'Anguille River
233	AR 261, Palestine, **N** 🛢️ ♥Loves/Chester's/Subway/dsl/scales/24hr 🏠 Rest Inn, **S** 🛢️ Citgo/dsl 🍴 Head's Cafe
221	AR 78, Wheatley, **N** 🛢️ SweetPea/dsl/repair, **S** 🛢️ BP/Pitstop/diner/dsl, MapCo/Subway/dsl
216	US 49, AR 17, Brinkley, **N** 🛢️ Citgo, Mobil/dsl 🏠 Best Inn, Days Inn, EconoLodge, Motel 6/RV Park 🅾️ dsl repair, KFC/Taco Bell, Los Piños Mexican, **S** 🛢️ Exxon/Baskin-Robbins/dsl, MapCo/dsl, Shell 🍴 Gene's BBQ, McDonald's, New China, Pizza Hut, Sonic, Subway, Waffle House 🏠 Heritage Inn/RV Park 🅾️ $General, Bumper Parts, Family$, Fred's, Kroger, O'Reilly Parts
205mm	Cache River
202	AR 33, to Biscoe
200mm	White River

AR

🔼E INTERSTATE 40 Cont'd

Exit #	Services
199mm	🆁🆂 both lanes, full 🏛 facilities, litter barrels, petwalk, 🎍 vending
193	AR 11, to Hazen, N 🅖 Exxon/Chester's, S 🅖 Citgo/dsl, Shell/dsl/24hr 🍴 Cocos Dos Mexican 🛏 Rodeway Inn, Super 8 🄾 T-rix RV Park
183	AR 13, Carlisle, S 🅖 Citgo, Conoco/dsl, Exxon/Subway/dsl, Phillips 66/dsl 🍴 Nick's BBQ, Pizza 'N More, Sonic 🛏 Best Value Inn 🄾 $General, Keith's Auto Repair, NAPA
175	AR 31, Lonoke, N 🅖 Phillips 66, Valero/dsl 🍴 El Torito Mexican, McDonald's 🛏 Days Inn, Economy Inn, Hampton Inn, Holiday Inn Express, Super 8 🄾 AT&T, Verizon, Walmart, S 🅖 Shell/Subway 🍴 I-40 Catfish Rest., KFC/Taco Bell, Larry's Pizza, Pizza Hut, Sonic 🛏 Perry's Motel 🄾 Goodyear/auto
169	AR 15, Remington Rd
165	Kerr Rd
161	AR 391, Galloway, N 🅖 Loves/Chester's/subs/dsl/scales/24hr 🄾 Camping World RV Ctr, S 🅖 IA-80 Truck-O/Mat/dsl/scales, Petro/Iron Skillet/dsl/scales/24hr/@, Pilot/Subway/Chester's/dsl/scales/24hr 🛏 Galloway Inn 🄾 Blue Beacon, dsl repair, Freightliner
159	I-440 W, S 🅿
157	AR 161, to US 70, N 🅖 Exxon/dsl 🄾 repair, S 🅖 Citgo/dsl, Hess, Shell/dsl, Super S Stop/dsl 🍴 Burger King, KFC/Taco Bell, McDonald's, Sonic, Subway, Waffle House 🛏 Best Value Inn, Comfort Inn, Days Inn, EconoLodge, Red Roof Inn, Rest Inn, Super 8
156	Springhill Dr, N 🅖 Murphy USA/dsl, Phillips 66 🍴 Burger King, Cracker Barrel 🛏 Fairfield Inn, Hilton Garden, Holiday Inn Express, Residence Inn, Walmart
155	US 67 N, US 167, to Jacksonville (exits left from eb), Little Rock AFB, 0-3 mi on N US 167/McCain Blvd 🅖 Murphy USA/dsl, Phillips 66/dsl, Shell 🍴 5 Guys Burgers, Applebee's, Arby's, Backyard Burger, Burger King, Cactus Jacks, Carino's Italian, Chick-fil-A, Chili's, ChuckECheese's, CiCi's Pizza, Corky's BBQ, Dixie Cafe, El Porton Mexican, Firehouse Subs, Golden Corral, Hog Wild Cafe, Hooters, IHOP, Jason's Deli, Jimmy John's, Kanpai Japanese, Little Caesars, McDonald's, Old Chicago Pizza, Olive Garden, On-the-Border, Outback Steaks, Panera Bread, Pizza Hut, Rally's, Red Lobster, Sonic, Subway, Taco Bell, TGIFriday's, TX Roadhouse, US Pizza, Waffle House, Wendy's 🛏 Comfort Inn, Hampton Inn, Hilton Garden, Holiday Inn Express, La Quinta, Super 8 🄾 🏥, $Tree, Aamco, AT&T, Barnes&Noble, Best Buy, BigLots, Books-A-Million, Buick/GMC, Chevrolet, Chrysler/Dodge/Jeep, Dillard's, Firestone/auto, Ford, Gander Mtn, Home Depot, Honda, Hyundai, JC Penney, Kia, Lincoln, Lowe's, mall, Mazda, Michael's, Nissan, Office Depot, PepBoys, PetCo, Petsmart, Sam's Club/gas, Sears/auto, Steinmart, Target, TJ Maxx, Toyota/Scion, Verizon, vet, VW, Walmart
154	to Lakewood (from eb)
153b	I-30 W, US 65 S, to Little Rock
153a	AR 107 N, JFK Blvd, N 🅖 Exxon, Mapco, Shell 🍴 Schlotzsky's 🛏 Best Value Inn 🄾 vet, S 🅖 Exxon 🍴 Royal Buffet, Waffle House 🛏 Best Western, Bugetel, Hampton Inn, Holiday Inn, Motel 6, Simply Home Suites 🄾 🏥, USPO
152	AR 365, AR 176, Camp Pike Rd, Levy, N on Camp Robinson Rd 🅖 Exxon, EZ Mart, Phillips 66, Shell 🍴 Burger King, Dixie Pig, KFC, Little Caesars, McDonald's, Mexico Chiquito, Pizza Hut, Sonic, Subway, Taco Bell, US Pizza, Wendy's 🄾 AutoZone, Family$, Fred's, Kroger/gas, O'Reilly Parts, S 🅖 Shell 🍴 Chicken King 🄾 🏥, Family$, Kroger, Radio Shack

150	AR 176, Burns Park, Camp Robinson, S 🄾 camping, info
148	AR 100, Crystal Hill Rd, N 🅖 Shell, S 🅖 Citgo/dsl 🄾 KOA
147	I-430 S, to Texarkana
142	AR 365, to Morgan, N 🅖 Phillips 66, Valero/dsl 🍴 I-40 Rest. 🛏 Days Inn 🄾 Bumper Parts, Trails End RV Park, S 🅖 Shell/dsl 🍴 KFC/Taco Bell, McDonald's, Razorback Pizza, Smokeshack BBQ, Subway, Waffle House 🛏 Best Value Inn, Hampton Inn, Holiday Inn Express, Quality Inn 🄾 antiques
135	AR 365, AR 89, Mayflower, N 🅖 Hess/dsl 🄾 Mayflower RV Ctr (1mi), S 🅖 Exxon/dsl, Valero 🍴 Sonic, Stroud's Country Diner, Tampico Mexican 🄾 $General, Big Star Food/Drug
134mm	truck parking both lanes
129	US 65B, AR 286, Conway, S 🅖 Citgo/dsl, Exxon, MapCo/dsl 🍴 Arby's, Subway 🛏 Budget Inn, Continental Motel 🄾 🏥 Chrysler/Dodge/Jeep, Honda, st police, to Toad Suck SP, Toyota/Scion
127	US 64, Conway, N 🅖 Exxon, Satterfield, Shell 🍴 Arby's, Chick-fil-A, Chili's, Denny's, Logan's Roadhouse, Sonic, Starbucks, Subway, TGIFriday's, Waffle House 🛏 Best Value Inn, Best Western, Comfort Suites, Country Inn&Suites, Days Inn, Economy Inn, Hampton Inn, Hilton Garden 🄾 $General, AT&T, Belk, Best Buy, Buick/GMC, Chevrolet, Firestone/auto, Ford, GNC, Goodyear/auto, Harley-Davidson, Home Depot, Hyundai, Kohl's, Moix RV Ctr, NAPA, Nissan, Old Navy, O'Reilly Parts, Petsmart, Radio Shack, repair/transmissions, Staples, Target, TJ Maxx, to Lester Flatt Park, Verizon, vet, S 🅖 RaceWay, Shell/dsl, Valero/dsl 🍴 Burger King, Church's, Colton's Steaks, Hardee's, Jimmy John's, Kings Steaks, LJ Silver, McDonald's, New China, Pizza Inn, Rally's, Saigon Rest., Shipley Doughnuts, Sonic, Taco Bell, Tokyo Japanese, Wendy's, Whole Hog Cafe 🛏 Kings Inn 🄾 AutoZone, Big-Lots, Family$, Fred's Drugs, Hancock Fabrics, Hobby Lobby, Kroger/gas, tires, Walgreens
125	US 65, Conway, N 🅖 Conoco/dsl, Exxon/Subway/dsl, Shell/dsl/24hr 🍴 China Town, Cracker Barrel, El Acapulco Mexican, La Hacienda Mexican, McDonald's, MktPlace Deli 🛏 Quality Inn 🄾 $Tree, JC Penney, Office Depot, Sears, S 🅖 Citgo, Mobil/dsl, Murphy USA, Sinclair 🍴 Backyard Burger, Burger King, CiCi's Pizza, Dixie Cafe, Firehouse Subs, Hart's Seafood, IHOP, McAlister's Deli, Mexico Chiquito, New China, Outback Steaks, Panera Bread, Ruby Tuesday, Sonic, Starbucks, Subway, Waffle House, Wendy's 🛏 Candlewood Suites, Fairfield Inn, Holiday Inn, Holiday Inn Express, Howard Johnson, La Quinta, Microtel, Motel 6, Stacy Motel, Super 8 🄾 🏥, $General, Advance Parts, Hastings Books, Lowe's, tires, Walmart
124	AR 25 N, to Conway, S 🅖 Hess, Shell/dsl 🍴 Catfish&More, DQ, KFC, Mazzio's, Popeye's 🄾 🏥, U-Haul
120mm	Cadron River
117	to Menifee
112	AR 92, Plumerville, N 🅖 Exxon/dsl, S 🅖 Country Store/dsl 🄾 USPO
108	AR 9, Morrilton, S 🅖 Murphy USA, Shell/Pizza Pro/dsl, Valero 🍴 Bonanza, Chop Stix, Hardees, McDonald's, Ortega's Mexican, Pizza Hut, Sonic, Subway, Waffle House, Wendy's 🛏 Holiday Inn Express, Super 8 🄾 🏥, $General, Ace Hardware, AT&T, Chrysler/Dodge/Jeep, Ford/Lincoln, Kroger, NAPA, RV camping, to Petit Jean SP (21mi), Verizon, Walmart
107	AR 95, Morrilton, N 🅖 Shell/dsl 🛏 Best Value Inn 🄾 I-40/107 RV Park, S 🅖 Loves/Subway/dsl/24hr, Shell 🍴 Mom&Pop's Waffles, Morrilton Drive Inn, Yesterdays Rest. 🛏 Days Inn 🄾 Bumper Parts

*(left margin, top to bottom)*
L O N O K E   **L I T T L E   R O C K**

*(right margin, top to bottom)*
C O N W A Y   **M O R R I L T O N**

⬆️E INTERSTATE 40 Cont'd

Exit #	Services
101	Blackwell, **N** 🅖 Blackwell TrkStp/Citgo/Domino's/diner/dsl/scales/24hr 🅞 Utility Trailer Sales
94	AR 105, Atkins, **N** 🅖 Exxon/Subway/dsl, Shell/McDonald's/dsl 🍴 Berky's Diner, El Parian Mexican, Sonic 🅞 $General, repair, **S** 🅞 Sexton Foods
88	Pottsville, **S** 🍴 Pottsville Country Cafe 🅞 truck repair/wash
84	US 64, AR 331, Russellville, **N** 🅖 ✈FLYING J/Denny's/dsl/scales/LP/24hr, Shell/dsl 🅞 Ivys Cove RV Retreat, trucklube, **S** 🅖 Phillips 66, 🅻🅾🆅🅴🆂/Subway/Wendy's/dsl/scales 🍴 CiCi's Pizza, Hardee's, Hunan Chinese, McDonald's, Sonic, Waffle House 🛏 Comfort Inn, Quality Inn 🅞 🅷, $Tree, AutoZone, Belk, Buick/Chevrolet/GMC, Chrysler/Dodge/Jeep, Hastings Books, Hobby Lobby, Hyundai, JC Penney, K-Mart, Lowe's, Nissan, Petsmart, Staples, TJ Maxx, Toyota, USPO
83	AK 326, Weir Rd, **S** 🅖 Murphy USA/dsl, Phillips 66 🍴 DQ, McAlisters Deli, Popeye's, Ryan's, Starbucks, Subway, Taco Bueno 🛏 Comfort Inn 🅞 $General, AT&T, AutoZone, Ford, Mazda, NAPA, O'Reilly Parts, Verizon, Walmart
81	AR 7, Russellville, **N** 🅖 SuperStop/dsl 🍴 7-40 Rest., CJ's Burgers 🛏 Motel 6 🅞 Outdoor RV Ctr/Park, **S** 🅖 Exxon/dsl, Phillips 66/dsl/24hr, Shell 🍴 Arby's, Burger King, Colton's Steaks, Cracker Barrel, Dixie Café, IHOP, La Huerta Mexican, New China, Ruby Tuesday, Subway, Waffle House 🛏 Best Value, Best Western, Days Inn, Economy Inn, Fairfield Inn, Hampton Inn, Hawthorn Park Inn, La Quinta, Super 8 🅞 RV camping, to Lake Dardanelle SP
80mm	Dardanelle Reservoir
78	US 64, Russellville, **S** 🍴 Fat Daddy's BBQ 🅞 🅷, Darrell's Mkt, Mission RV Park, to Lake Dardanelle SP
74	AR 333, London
72mm	🆁🆂 wb, full ♿ facilities, litter barrels, petwalk, 🚻, 🛒, vending
70mm	litter barrels, overlook wb lane
68mm	🆁🆂 eb, full ♿ facilities, litter barrels, petwalk, 🚻, 🛒, vending
67	AR 315, Knoxville, **S** 🅖 Citgo, Knoxville Mkt 🅞 USPO
64	US 64, Clarksville, Lamar, **S** 🅖 Valero/Pizza Pro/dsl 🅞 Dad's Dream RV Park
58	AR 21, AR 103, Clarksville, **N** 🅖 Shell/dsl, Valero 🍴 Emerald Dragon Chinese, KFC, Larry's Pizza, McDonald's, Pasta Grill, Pizza Hut, Sonic, Subway, Taco Bell, Waffle House 🛏 Best Western, Executive Inn, Quality Inn, Super 8 🅞 🅷, $General, Buick/Chevrolet, **S** 🅖 Murphy USA/dsl 🍴 Arby's, China Fun, Wendy's 🅞 $Tree, Chrysler/Dodge/Jeep, Ford, Walmart/Subway
57	AR 109, Clarksville, **N** 🅖 Fuel Stop/dsl 🍴 Subway 🅞 Family$, Harvest Foods/drug, **S** 🅖 Shell/Chester's/dsl 🅞 repair, TrueValue
55	US 64, AR 109, Clarksville, **N** 🍴 Crosswoods Rest., Hardee's 🛏 Days Inn, Hampton Inn, Holiday Inn Express, **S** 🅖 Exxon/dsl 🍴 Jackson Family Steaks 🅞 Radio Shack, st police
47	AR 164, Coal Hill
41	AR 186, Altus, **S** 🍴 Swiss Family Rest., Wiederkehr Rest. 🅞 Pine Ridge RV Park, winery
37	AR 219, Ozark, **S** 🅖 ❤Loves/Subway/dsl/scales/24hr, Shell/McDonald's/dsl 🍴 KFC/Taco Bell 🛏 Days Inn 🅞 🅷
36mm	🆁🆂 both lanes, full ♿ facilities, litter barrels, petwalk, 🚻, 🛒 vending
35	AR 23, Ozark, **3 mi S** 🅖 Valero/Subway/dsl 🍴 Hardee's, Hillbilly Hideout Rest., Subway 🛏 Oxford Inn, Ozark Inn 🅞 🅷, Aux Arc Park (5mi), to Mt Magnus SP (20 mi)

Exit #	Services
24	AR 215, Mulberry, **S** Vine Prairie Park
20	Dyer, **N** 🅖 Conoco/dsl 🅞 Freightliner/Western Star, **S** 🅖 Phillips 66/dsl, Shell/dsl 🛏 Mill Creek Inn
13	US 71 N, to Fayetteville, **N** 🅖 Phillips 66/dsl, Shell 🍴 Burger King, Catfish Hole, China Fun, Cracker Barrel, KFC, La Fiesta Mexican, Mazzio's, Pizza Parlor, Subway, Taco Bell 🛏 Comfort Inn, Meadors Inn 🅞 $General, Crabtree RV Ctr/Park, KOA (2mi), Lake Ft Smith SP, O'Reilly Parts, to U of AR, **S** 🅖 Murphy USA/dsl, Shamrock, Valero/dsl 🍴 Braum's, El Trio, Geno's Pizza, McDonald's, Sonic 🛏 Days Inn 🅞 Alma Drug, AT&T, C&H Tires, CV's Foods, Harp's Foods, Walgreens, Walmart
12	I-540 N, to Fayetteville, **N** 🅞 to Lake Ft Smith SP
9mm	weigh sta both lanes
7	I-540 S, US 71 S, to Ft Smith, Van Buren, **S** 🅞 🅷
5	AR 59, Van Buren, **N** 🅖 Citgo/dsl, Murphy USA/dsl, Phillips 66 🍴 Arby's, Burger King, Chili's, China Buffet, Domino's, Firehouse Subs, Frank's Italian, Golden Wok, La Fiesta Mexican, McDonald's, Popeye's, Zaxby's 🛏 Best Western, Hampton Inn 🅞 $Tree, Advance Parts, AT&T, Cooley's Tire, Lowe's, NAPA, Radio Shack, USPO, Verizon, Walmart, **S** 🅖 Shell/dsl/24hr 🍴 Big Jake's Steaks, Braum's, Geno's Pizza, Home Run Pizza, KFC/Taco Bell, La Fresas Mexican, Rick's Rib House, Sonic, Subway, Waffle House, Wendy's 🛏 Holiday Inn Express, Motel 6, Sleep Inn, Super 8 🅞 $General, CV's Foods, Grizzle Tire, Outdoor RV Ctr, truckwash, Walgreens
3	Lee Creek Rd, **N** 🅖 Shell 🅞 Park Ridge Camping
2.5mm	Welcome Ctr eb, full ♿ facilities, info, litter barrels, petwalk, 🚻, 🛒, vending
1	to Ft Smith (from wb), Dora
0mm	Arkansas/Oklahoma state line

⬆️N INTERSTATE 49

Exit #	Services
93	US 71B, Bentonville, **I-49 begins/ends on US 71 N.**
88	AR 72, Bentonville, Pea Ridge, **E** 🅖 Conoco 🍴 River Grille 🛏 Courtyard, Simmon's Suites, **W** 🅖 Kum&Go/dsl 🍴 Smokin' Joe's Ribs 🅞 Walmart Visitors Ctr
86	US 62, AR 102, Bentonville, Rogers, **E** 🛏 TownePlace Suites 🅞 Pea Ridge NMP, Sam's Club/gas, Walmart Mkt, **W** 🅖 Phillips 66/McDonald's/dsl, Shell/dsl 🍴 Arby's, Sonic, Subway, Taco Bell 🛏 ValuePlace
85	US 71B, AR 12, Bentonville, Rogers, **E** 🅖 Conoco/dsl 🍴 Abuelo's, Applebee's, Arby's, Atlanta Bread, Bob Evans, Carino's Italian, Chick-fil-A, Chili's, Colton's Steaks, Copeland's Rest., Dixie Café, Famous Dave's, Freddy's Burgers, IHOP, Logan's Roadhouse, McDonald's, Napoli's Pizza, On-the-Border, Outback Steaks, Quiznos, Red Robin, Sonic,

Russellville / Clarksville / Van Buren

AR

◤N	**INTERSTATE 49 Cont'd**

Exit #	Services
85	Continued
	Starbucks 🛏 Candlewood Suites, Country Inn&Suites, Fairfield Inn, Hampton Inn, Homewood Suites, Hyatt Place, Mainstay Suites, Residence Inn 🅾 AT&T, Barnes&Noble, Beaver Lake SP, Belk, Firestone/auto, Kohl's, Lowe's, Marshalls, Office Depot, Old Navy, PetCo, Prairie Creek SP, Ross, Staples, Verizon, **W** 🅿 Kum&Go, Murphy Express/dsl, Phillips 66/dsl 🍴 Braum's, Buffalo Wild Wings, Denny's, Firehouse Subs, HoneyBaked Ham, Joe's Italian, Jonny Brusco's Pizza, Krispy Kreme, Lenny's Subs, Lin's Garden, Mama Fu's Asian, McAlister's Deli, Panera Bread, Shogun Japanese, Starbucks, Subway, Taco Bueno, Village Inn, Waffle House, Whole Hog Cafe, Zaxby's 🛏 Best Western, Comfort Suites, Days Inn, DoubleTree Hotel, EconoLodge, Hilton Garden, Holiday Inn Express, La Quinta, Microtel, Motel 6, SpringHill Suites, Suburban Lodge, Super 8 🅾 🄷, Buick/GMC, Chevrolet, Christian Bros Auto, Honda, Hyundai, Kia, Mazda, Nissan, Toyota/Scion, URGENT CARE
83	AR 94 E, Pinnacle Hills Pkwy, **E** 🅿 Phillips 66 🍴 5 Guys Burgers, After 5 Grill, Bariola's Pizza, ChuckECheese's, Dickey's BBQ, Firehouse Subs, Genghis Grill, Jimmy John's, Mojitos Mexican, Olive Garden, Panda Express, Qdoba, Red Lobster, Slim Chickens, Starbucks, Steak'n Shake, Taco Bell 🅾 🄷, Home Depot, Horse Shoe Bend Park, Walgreens, **W** 🍴 Bonefish Grill, Carrabba's, Coldstone, Crabby's Seafood Grill, Grub's Grille, Mellow Mushroom, Ruth's Chris Steaks, Subway, The Egg&I, Tropical Smoothie 🛏 ALoft, Embassy Suites, Holiday Inn, Staybridge Suites
82	Promenade Blvd, **E** 🍴 Fish City Grill, Food Pavilion, Houlihan's, PF Changs 🅾 🄷, AT&T, Best Buy, Cabela's, Dillard's, Fresh Mkt, GNC, Gordman's, Hancock Fabrics, JC Penney, Old Navy, Target, TJMaxx, Walmart Mkt/dsl
81	Pleasant Grove Rd, **E** 🅿 Murphy USA/dsl 🍴 Backyard Burger, Chick-fil-A, Golden Corral, Mad Pizza, McDonald's, Starbucks, Subway, Taco Bueno 🅾 Firestone/auto, Walgreens, Walmart, **W** 🅿 Casey's/dsl
78	AR 264, Lowell, Cave Sprgs, Rogers, **E** 🅿 Kum&Go, Shell 🍴 Arby's, Dickey's BBQ, Domino's, DQ, KFC, LJ Silver, Mazzio's Pizza, McDonald's, Sonic, Subway, Taco Bell 🅾 $General, AT&T, Camping World RV Ctr, Super 8, **W** 🅿 Kum&Go/dsl
76	Wagon Wheel Rd, **E** 🅿 Shell/Subway/dsl 🅾 to Hickory Creek Park
73	Elm Springs Rd, **E** 🅿 Kum&Go/dsl, Shell/dsl, VP/dsl 🍴 Eureka Pizza, Patrick's Burgers 🛏 ValuePlace 🅾 Chevrolet, Family$
72mm	**weigh sta nb**
72	US 412, Springdale, Siloam Springs, **E** 🅿 Conoco, Phillips 66/Subway 🍴 Applebee's, Bleu Monkey Grill, Braum's, Denny's, Golden Dragon Buffet, Guadalajara Grill, Joe's Italian, Little Caesars, McDonald's, Mkt Place Rest., Sonic, Taco Bell, Waffle House, Wendy's, Western Sizzlin 🛏 DoubleTree Hotel, Extended Stay America, Fairfield Inn, Hampton Inn, Holiday Inn, La Quinta, Residence Inn, Royal Inn, Sleep Inn, Super 8 🅾 $General, AT&T, Big O Tire, Harp's Mkt, Kenworth/Volvo Trucks, Lowe's, Office Depot, O'Reilly Parts, Radio Shack, Verizon, Walgreens, Walmart Mkt, **W** 🅿 Murphy Express/dsl, 🚛Burger King/dsl/scales/24hr 🍴 Arby's, Buffalo Wild Wings, Cracker Barrel, Jose's Mexican, McDonald's, Quiznos, Rib Crib, Subway, Taco Bueno 🅾 BigLots, Buick/GMC, Harp's Mkt/dsl, Hobby Lobby, vet

Exit #	Services
71mm	**weigh sta sb**
69	Johnson Mill Blvd, Johnson, **1-2 mi E** 🍴 Chick-fil-A, Eureka Pizza, Fire Mtn Grill, Hooters, Inn at the Mill Rest, James Rest, Shogun Japanese 🛏 Inn at the Mill, TownePlace Suites
67	US 71B, Fayetteville, **E** 🅾 🄷
66	AR 112, Garland Ave, **E** 🅿 Phillips 66/dsl 🛏 Motel 6, **W** 🅾 Acura, Chevrolet, Fiat, Honda, Sam's Club/gas, Toyota/Scion
65	Porter Rd
64	AR 16 W, AR 112 E, Wedington Dr, **E** 🍴 Eureka Pizza (2mi), **W** 🅿 Murphy Express/dsl, Phillips 66/McDonald's/dsl 🍴 Boar's Nest BBQ, El Matador Mexican, Gusano's Pizza, IHOP, Pizza Hut, Sonic, Subway, Taco Bell 🛏 Comfort Inn, Hilton Garden, Holiday Inn Express, Homewood Suites 🅾 Harp's Food/gas, vet, Walmart Mkt
62	US 62, AR 180, Farmington, **E** 🅿 Phillips 66, Shell 🍴 Arby's, Braum's, Burger King, Burger Shack, Charlie's Chicken, Chick-fil-A, Hardee's, KFC, McDonald's, Mexico Viejo, Panda Express, Popeye's, Sonic, Starbucks, Subway, Taco Bell, Taco Bueno, Waffle House, Wendy's, Zaxby's 🛏 Best Western, Candlewood Suites, EconoLodge 🅾 AT&T, Bumper Parts, **W** 🅿 Murphy USA/dsl 🍴 Braum's, Denny's, Firehouse Subs, Gino's Pizza, King Pizza, Lucy's Diner, Papa Murphy's, Pavilion Buffet, Ruby Tuesday 🛏 Guesthouse Inn, Hampton Inn, Quality Inn, Regency 7 Motel, Super 8, Travelodge, ValuePlace 🅾 $Tree, Aldi Foods, AutoZone, Lowe's, Radio Shack, Verizon, Walgreens, Walmart
61	US 71, to Boston Mtn Scenic Lp, sb only
60	AR 112, AR 265, Razorback Rd, **E** 🛏 Staybridge Suites 🅾 Southgate RV Park, to U of AR
58	Greenland, **W** 🅿 Phillips 66/McDonalds/dsl/scales/24hr 🍴 Sonic
53	AR 170, West Fork, **E** 🅿 Harp's/dsl 🅾 Harp's Mkt, Winn Creek RV Resort (4mi), **W** 🅾 to Devils Den SP
45	AR 74, Winslow, **W** 🅾 to Devils Den SP
41mm	Bobby Hopper Tunnel
34	AR 282, to US 71, Chester, **W** 🅾 USPO
29	AR 282, to US 71, Mountainburg, **1 mi E** 🅾 $General, to Lake Ft Smith SP
24	AR 282, to US 71, Rudy, **E** 🅿 Shell/dsl 🍴 Red Hog BBQ 🅾 Boston Mtns Scenic Lp, KOA
21	Collum Ln
20	(from sb) to US 71, **E** 🅿 Shell 🍴 KFC, Taco Bell 🛏 Comfort Inn, Days Inn

I-49 N begins/ends on I-40, exit 12.

◤N	**INTERSTATE 55**

Exit #	Services
72mm	Arkansas/Missouri state line
72	State Line Rd, **weigh sta sb**
71	AR 150, Yarbro
68mm	**Welcome Ctr sb, full 🛁 facilities, litter barrels, petwalk, 🄲,** 🖼
67	AR 18, Blytheville, **E** 🅿 Murphy Express/dsl 🍴 Burger King, Subway, Waffle Inn, Zaxby's 🛏 Best Value Inn, Days Inn/RV park 🅾 $Tree, Lowe's, Verizon, Walmart/Subway, **W** 🅿 Citgo/dsl, QuikStop/dsl, Shell 🍴 7 Mayors Rest, Cotton Patch Buffet, El Acapulco Mexican, GreatWall Chinese, Grecian Steaks, Hardee's, McDonald's, Olympia Steaks, Perkins, Pizza Inn, Sonic, Subway, Taco Bell, Wendy's 🛏 Comfort Inn, Fairview Suites, Hampton Inn, Holiday Inn, Quality Inn, Super 8 🅾 🄷, AT&T, AutoZone, CarQuest, Family$, Ford/Lincoln, Fred's, JC Penney, Nissan, Toyota

🅖 = gas   🍴 = food   🛏 = lodging   🅞 = other   🆁🆂 = rest stop

◤N INTERSTATE 55 Cont'd

Exit #	Services
63	US 61, to Blytheville, **E** 🅞 Shearins RV Park (2mi), **W** 🅖 Dodge's Store/dsl, Exxon/Baskin-Robbins/Chester's/Pizza Hut/dsl, Shell/McDonald's/dsl 🛏 Best Western, Relax Inn 🅞 🄷, truckwash
57	AR 148, Burdette, **E** 🅞 NE AR Coll
53	AR 158, Victoria, Luxora
48	AR 140, to Osceola, **E** 🅖 Mobil/dsl, Shell/Baskin-Robbins/Chester's/ds 🍴 McDonald's, Pizza Inn, Sonic, Subway 🛏 Days Inn, Deerfield Inn, EconoLodge, Fairview Inn 🅞 🄷, Cotton Inn Rest., Huddle House
45mm	litter barrels, truck parking nb
44	AR 181, Keiser
41	AR 14, Marie, **E** 🅞 to Hampson SP/museum
36	AR 181, to Wilson, Bassett
35mm	litter barrels, truck parking sb
34	AR 118, Joiner
23b a	US 63, AR 77, to Marked Tree, Jonesboro, ASU, **E** 🅖 Citgo/chicken/pizza
21	AR 42, Turrell, **W** 🅖 Exxon/rest./dsl/scales/24hr
17	AR 50, to Jericho
14	rd 4, to Jericho, **E** 🅖 Citgo/dsl/scales/24hr, **W** 🅖 Citgo/Stuckey's 🅞 Chevrolet, KOA
10	US 64 W, Marion, **E** 🅖 Citgo/Baskin-Robbins/Subway/scales, Shell/McDonald's 🍴 Ameca Mexican, KFC/Taco Bell, Sonic, Tops BBQ 🛏 Comfort Inn, Hallmarc Inn 🅞 $General, Family$, Marion Tire/repair, Mkt Place Foods, USPO, **W** 🅖 JP Mkt, Shell 🍴 Burger King, Colton's Steaks, Mi Pueblo, Wendy's, Zaxby's 🛏 Best Western, Journey Inn 🅞 AutoZone, Neats Repair, to Parkin SP (23mi)
9mm	truck parking nb, weigh sta sb
8	I-40 W, to Little Rock
I-55 and I-40 run together 3 mi. See I-40, exits 278-279b	
5	(279 .b from I-40) Ingram Blvd, **E** 🍴 Margaritas Mexican 🛏 Days Inn, Homegate Inn, Knights Inn, Red Roof Inn 🅞 Ford, Southland Racetrack, U-Haul, **W** 🅖 Citgo/dsl, Shell/dsl 🍴 Cupboard Rest., Waffle House 🛏 Best Value Inn, EconoLodge, Hampshire Inn, Holiday Inn, Motel 6, Ramada, Relax Inn
4	King Dr, Southland Dr, **E** 🅖 ⚡FLYING J/Denny's/dsl/LP/scales/RV dump, 💗Loves/Subway/dsl/scales/@, Petro/Iron Skillet/rest./dsl/24hr/@, TA/Subway/Wendy's/dsl/scales/24hr 🍴 KFC/Taco Bell, McDonald's 🛏 Best Western, Deluxe Inn, Express Inn, Super 8 🅞 Blue Beacon, SpeedCo Lube, **W** 🍴 Poncho's Mexican 🛏 Sunset Inn
3b a	US 70, Broadway Blvd, AR 131, Mound City Rd (exits left from nb), **W** 🛏 Budget Inn
2mm	weigh sta nb
1	Bridgeport Rd
0mm	Arkansas/Tennessee state line, Mississippi River

◤N INTERSTATE 430 (LITTLE ROCK)

Exit #	Services
13b a	I-430 begins/ends on I-40, exit 147.
12	AR 100, Maumelle, **W** 🅖 Citgo 🅞 NAPA, O'Reilly Parts, vet
10mm	Arkansas River
9	AR 10, Cantrell Rd., **W** 🅞 Maumelle Park, Pinnacle Mtn SP
8	Rodney Parham Rd, **E** 🅖 Conoco, Shell 🍴 Arby's, Baskin-Robbins, El Chico, Firehouse Subs, KFC, McAlister's Grill, McDonald's, Mt Fuji Japanese, New China Buffet, Sonic, Starbucks, Subway, Taco Bell, Terri Lynn's BBQ, US Pizza

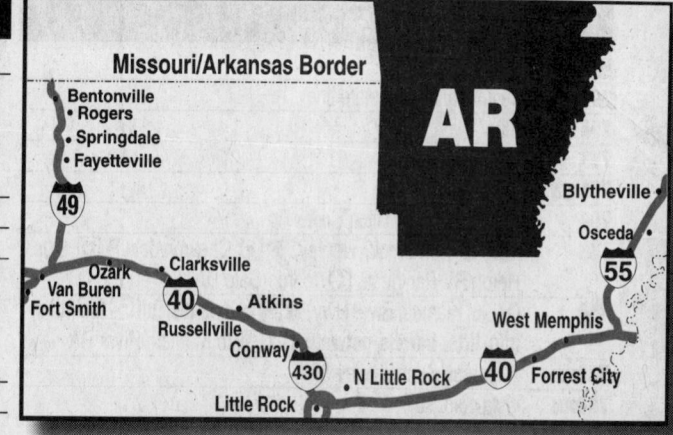

Missouri/Arkansas Border

AR

Bentonville • Rogers • Springdale • Fayetteville • 49 • Ozark • Clarksville • Van Buren Fort Smith • 40 • Atkins • Russellville • Conway • 430 • N Little Rock • Little Rock • 40 • West Memphis • Forrest City • Blytheville • Osceda • 55

L I T T L E R O C K	

8	Continued
	🛏 La Quinta 🅞 $Days, $General, Advance Parts, AutoZone, Drug Emporium, Kroger, Walgreens, **W** 🅖 Exxon 🍴 Burger King, Chili's, Chizi's Pizza, ChuckeCheese, Dixie Cafe, Dominos, Franke's Café, Heavenly Ham, LoneStar Steaks, Olive Garden, Shorty Small's Ribs, Wendy's 🛏 Best Western 🅞 Firestone/auto, GNC, K-Mart, Radio Shack, USA Drug, vet, Whole Foods Mkt
6	I-630, Kanis Rd, Markham St, to downtown, **E** 🍴 McDonald's 🛏 Candlewood Suites, Comfort Inn, Motel 6, SpringHill Suites, **W** 🅖 Exxon 🍴 Cozymel's Grill, Denny's, Famous Dave's BBQ, IHOP, Jason's Deli, Kobe Japanese, Lenny's Subs, Macaroni Grill, McAlister's Deli, Mimi's Cafe, On-the-Border, PF Chang's, Shotgun Dan's Pizza, Starbucks, Taco Bell, Waffle House, Wendy's 🛏 Courtyard, Crowne Plaza, Embassy Suites, Extended Stay America, Jameson Inn, La Quinta, Ramada Ltd 🅞 AT&T, Barnes&Noble, Best Buy, PetsMart, Walmart
5	Kanis Rd, Shackleford Rd, **E** 🍴 Cracker Barrel, Panda Garden, Samurai Steaks, TX Roadhouse 🛏 Candlewood Suites, Comfort Inn, Motel 6, SpringHill Suites, Towneplace Suites 🅞 Gordman's, JC Penney, **W** 🅖 Shell 🍴 Krispy Kreme 🛏 Hampton Inn, Holiday Inn Select, La Quinta, Residence Inn, Studio+, Wingate Inn 🅞 🄷, Lexus
4	AR 300, Col Glenn Rd, **E** 🍴 Subway, Wendy's 🛏 Holiday Inn Express, ValuePlace Hotel 🅞 Toyota/Scion, **W** 🅖 Valero/Burger King/dsl 🅞 Honda, Hyundai, Jaguar, Land Rover, Mazda, Mercedes, Nissan
1	AR 5, Stagecoach Rd, **E** 🍴 Our Place Grill, **W** 🅖 Phillips 66, Valero 🍴 Grandpa's Catfish, Jordan's BBQ, Subway 🅞 Tires
0mm	I-430 begins/ends on I-30, exit 129.

◤N INTERSTATE 440 (LITTLE ROCK)

Exit #	Services
11	I-440 begins/ends on I-40, exit 159.
10	US 70, **W** 🅞 Peterbilt
8	Faulkner Lake Rd, **W** 🅖 Pioneer/dsl
7	US 165, to England, **S** 🅞 Agricultural Museum, Toltec Mounds SP, Willow Beach SP
6mm	Arkansas River
5	Fourche Dam Pike, LR Riverport, **N** 🅖 Exxon, Shell/Subway 🍴 McDonald's 🛏 Travelodge 🅞 Kenworth, **S** 🅖 Phillips 66/dsl, Valero/dsl
4	Lindsey Rd
3	Bankhead Dr, **N** 🛏 Comfort Inn 🅞 LR ✈, **S** 🅖 Valero 🅞 🍴 Boston's Rest., Waffle House 🛏 Days Inn, Holiday Inn, Holiday Inn Express
1	AR 365, Springer Blvd, **S** 🅞 Little Rock Ntl Cemetery
0mm	I-440 begins/ends on I-30, exit 138.

CA

⬆N INTERSTATE 5

Exit #	Services
797mm	California/Oregon state line
796	Hilt
793	Bailey Hill Rd
791mm	**inspection sta sb**
790	Hornbrook Hwy, Ditch Creek Rd
789	A28, to Hornbrook, Henley, E 🅖 Chevron/dsl/LP 🅞 Blue Heron RV Park/rest., 🚻, to Iron Gate RA
786	CA 96, Klamath River Hwy, W 🆁🆂 **both lanes, full ♿ facilities, info, litter barrels, petwalk, 🚻, 🐾, to Klamath River RA**
782mm	Anderson Summit, elev 3067
780mm	vista point sb
779mm	Shasta River
776	Yreka, Montague, E 🅛 Holiday Inn Express 🅞 Yreka RV Park, W 🅖 Mobil/dsl 🅕 Casa Ramos Mexican, J&D Diner, Puerto Vallarta 🅛 Mtn View Inn, Super 8 🅞 Grocery Outlet
775	Miner St, Central Yreka, W 🅖 76/dsl, Chevron/dsl 🅕 China Dragon, Grandma's House, Purple Plum Rest., RoundTable Pizza, Subway 🅛 Best Western, Budget Inn, EconoLodge, Klamath Motel, Relax Inn, Rodeway Inn, Yreka Motel 🅞 🏥, Ace Hardware, Baxter Parts, CarQuest, Clayton Tire, Honda, museum, Rite Aid, USPO
773	CA 3, to Ft Jones, Etna, E 🅞 Les Schwab, tires, Trailer Haven RV Park, W 🅖 Shell/dsl, Valero/dsl 🅕 BlackBear Diner, Burger King, Carl's Jr, KFC, McDonald's, Pizza Factory, Siskiyou Roadhouse Grill, Starbucks, Subway, Taco Bell 🅛 Baymont Inn, Comfort Inn, Motel 6 🅞 🏥, $Tree, AAA, AT&T, CHP, Ford/Lincoln, JC Penney, NAPA, O'Reilly Parts, Radio Shack, Raley's Foods, Walmart
770	Shamrock Rd, Easy St, W 🅖 Beacon/LP, Fuel 24/7/dsl 🅞 RV camping
766	A12, to Gazelle, Grenada, E 🅖 76/dsl, W 🅖 Texaco/dsl 🅞 RV camping
759	Louie Rd
753	Weed Airport Rd, 🆁🆂 **both lanes, full ♿ facilities, litter barrels, petwalk, 🚻, 🐾**
751	Stewart Springs Rd, Edgewood, E 🅞 Lake Shasta RA/RV camp (2mi), W 🅞 RV camp (7mi)
748	to US 97, to Klamath Falls, Weed, E 🅖 Chevron, Shell/dsl, Spirit/dsl 🅕 Ellie's Cafe, Pizza Factory, Subway 🅛 Hi-Lo Motel/rest., Motel 6, Summit Inn, Townhouse Motel 🅞 auto repair, golf, NAPA, Ray's Foods, RV camping
747	Central Weed, E 🅞 auto repair, same as 748, W Coll of Siskiyou
745	S Weed Blvd, E 🅖 Chevron/dsl, 🅕/Subway/dsl/scales/24hr, Shell/dsl 🅕 Burger King, Dos Amigos Mexican, McDonald's/RV parking, Silva's Rest., Taco Bell 🅛 Comfort Inn, Quality Inn, Sis-Q Inn 🅞 Friendly RV Park
743	Summit Dr, Truck Village Dr
742mm	Black Butte Summit, elev 3912
741	Abrams Lake Rd, E 🅞 Schwab Tire, W 🅛 Abrams Lake RV Park
740	Mt Shasta City (from sb), E 🅖 Pacific Pride/dsl/LP, Shell/dsl/CFN 🅛 Cold Creek Inn 🅞 Tire Factory, vet
738	Central Mt Shasta, E 🅖 Chevron/dsl, Shell/dsl/LP, Spirit/dsl 🅕 BlackBear Diner, Burger King, KFC/Taco Bell, RoundTable Pizza, Subway 🅛 Best Western/Treehouse Rest., Mt Shasta Inn, Travel Inn 🅞 🏥, Best Hardware, NAPA, O'Reilly Parts, Radio Shack, Ray's Foods, Rite Aid, USPO, visitors info, W 🅛 Lake Siskiyou RV Park, Mt Shasta Resort/rest., Sisson Museum

Left margin vertical labels: **YREKA**, **WEED**, **MT SHASTA**

Exit #	Services
737	Mt Shasta City (from nb), E 🅕 Casa Ramos, LaiLai Chinese, Lily's Rest., Piemont Italian, Wayside Grill 🅛 Alpine Lodge, Choice Inn, Evergreen Lodge, Swiss Holiday Lodge 🅞 McCloud RV Park, same as 738
736	CA 89, to McCloud, to Reno, E 🅛 Swiss Holiday Lodge
735mm	weigh sta sb
734	Mott Rd, to Dunsmuir
732	Dunsmuir Ave, Siskiyou Ave, E 🅕 Penny's Diner 🅛 Oak Tree Inn, W 🅖 Chevron/dsl 🅛 Acorn Inn, Cedar Lodge
730	Central Dunsmuir, E 🅕 Burger Barn, Cornerstone Cafe, Dumsmuir Brewery Rest., Hot Dog Depot, Pizza Factory 🅛 Dunsmuir Inn, Hotel Dunsmuir/Rest 🅞 True Value, USPO, Value King Foods, W 🅖 Chevron/dsl/LP 🅕 Hitching Post, Micki's Burgers 🅛 Cave Springs Motel 🅞 city park
729	Dunsmuir (from nb), E 🅖 Manfredi's/deli/dsl 🅛 auto repair, Dunsmuir Lodge 🅞 to hist dist
728	Crag View Dr, Dunsmuir, Railroad Park Rd, W 🅞 Railroad Park Motel/RV Park
727	(from nb) Crag View Dr, RV Camping
726	Soda Creek Rd, to Pacific Crest Trail
724	Castella, W 🅖 Chevron/dsl 🅞 Castle Crags SP, RV camping, USPO
723mm	vista point nb
723	Sweetbrier Ave
721	Conant Rd
720	Flume Creek Rd
718	Sims Rd, W 🅞 RV camping
714	Gibson Rd
712	Pollard Flat, E 🅖 Pollard Flat/dsl/LP 🅕 Pollard Flat Diner
710	Slate Creek Rd, La Moine
707	Delta Rd, Dog Creek Rd, to Vollmers
705mm	🆁🆂 **sb, full ♿ facilities, litter barrels, 🚻, 🐾**
704	Riverview Dr, E 🅕 Klondike Diner 🅛 Lakehead Lodge/RV Camping
702	Antlers Rd, Lakeshore Dr, to Lakehead, E 🅖 Shell/Subway/dsl 🅛 Antlers RV Park, Lakehead Camping, Neu Lodge Motel 🅞 auto repair, USPO, W 🅖 Jack's/dsl 🅕 Allyson's Rest., Bass Hole Rest. 🅛 Lakeshore Mkt, Shasta Lake Motel/RV 🅞 Villa RV Park
698	Salt Creek Rd, Gilman Rd, W 🅛 Salt Creek Resort/RV Park 🅞 Trail In RV Park
695	Shasta Caverns Rd, to O'Brien
694mm	🆁🆂 **nb, full ♿ facilities, litter barrels, petwalk, 🚻, 🐾**
693	(from sb) Packers Bay Rd
692	Turntable Bay Rd
690	Bridge Bay Rd, W 🅕 Tail of a Whale Rest. 🅛 Bridge Bay Motel
689	Fawndale Rd, Wonderland Blvd, E 🅛 Fawndale Lodge, Fawndale Oaks RV Park, W 🅛 Wonderland RV Park
687	Wonderland Blvd, Mountain Gate, E 🅖 Chevron/dsl/LP 🅕 La Fogata 🅞 Mountain Gate RV Park, Ranger Sta, W 🅖 Shell/dsl/LP
685	CA 151, Shasta Dam Blvd, Project City, Central Valley, W 🅖 76/Circle K/dsl, Chevron/Burger King/dsl/LP, Valero/dsl 🅕 McDonald's, Pizza Factory, Taco Shop 🅛 Shasta Dam Motel 🅞 NAPA, Rite Aid, Sentry Foods, USPO, vet
684	Pine Grove Ave, E 🅞 Cousin Gary's RV Ctr, W 🅖 76/dsl/LP
682	Oasis Rd, E 🅞 CA RV Ctr, Peterbilt, W 🅖 Arco, Shell/Subway/dsl 🅞 CHP, Redding RV Ctr, U-Haul
681b	(from sb, no re-entry) CA 273, Market St, Johnson Rd, to Central Redding, W 🅞 🏥
681a	Twin View Blvd, E 🅖 Chevron/dsl 🅛 Motel 6, Ramada Ltd 🅞

Right margin vertical label: **DUNSMUIR**

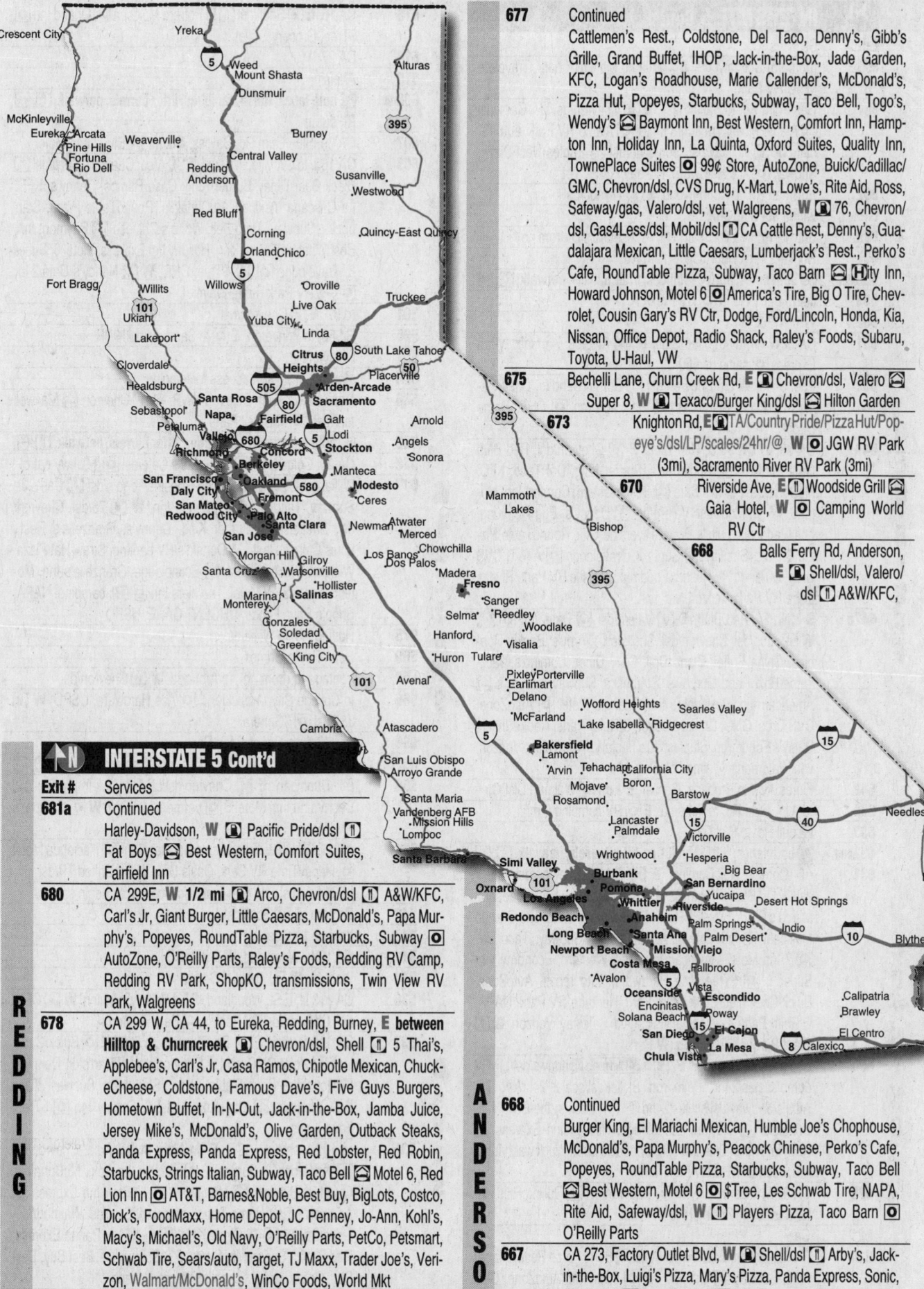

CA

677 Continued
Cattlemen's Rest., Coldstone, Del Taco, Denny's, Gibb's Grille, Grand Buffet, IHOP, Jack-in-the-Box, Jade Garden, KFC, Logan's Roadhouse, Marie Callender's, McDonald's, Pizza Hut, Popeyes, Starbucks, Subway, Taco Bell, Togo's, Wendy's 🛏 Baymont Inn, Best Western, Comfort Inn, Hampton Inn, Holiday Inn, La Quinta, Oxford Suites, Quality Inn, TownePlace Suites 🅞 99¢ Store, AutoZone, Buick/Cadillac/GMC, Chevron/dsl, CVS Drug, K-Mart, Lowe's, Rite Aid, Ross, Safeway/gas, Valero/dsl, vet, Walgreens, **W** 🅖 76, Chevron/dsl, Gas4Less/dsl, Mobil/dsl 🍴 CA Cattle Rest, Denny's, Guadalajara Mexican, Little Caesars, Lumberjack's Rest., Perko's Cafe, RoundTable Pizza, Subway, Taco Barn 🛏 🅗ity Inn, Howard Johnson, Motel 6 🅞 America's Tire, Big O Tire, Chevrolet, Cousin Gary's RV Ctr, Dodge, Ford/Lincoln, Honda, Kia, Nissan, Office Depot, Radio Shack, Raley's Foods, Subaru, Toyota, U-Haul, VW

675 Bechelli Lane, Churn Creek Rd, **E** 🅖 Chevron/dsl, Valero 🛏 Super 8, **W** 🅖 Texaco/Burger King/dsl 🛏 Hilton Garden

673 Knighton Rd, **E** 🅖 TA/Country Pride/Pizza Hut/Popeye's/dsl/LP/scales/24hr/@, **W** 🅞 JGW RV Park (3mi), Sacramento River RV Park (3mi)

670 Riverside Ave, **E** 🍴 Woodside Grill 🛏 Gaia Hotel, **W** 🅞 Camping World RV Ctr

668 Balls Ferry Rd, Anderson, **E** 🅖 Shell/dsl, Valero/dsl 🍴 A&W/KFC,

668 Continued
Burger King, El Mariachi Mexican, Humble Joe's Chophouse, McDonald's, Papa Murphy's, Peacock Chinese, Perko's Cafe, Popeyes, RoundTable Pizza, Starbucks, Subway, Taco Bell 🛏 Best Western, Motel 6 🅞 $Tree, Les Schwab Tire, NAPA, Rite Aid, Safeway/dsl, **W** 🍴 Players Pizza, Taco Barn 🅞 O'Reilly Parts

667 CA 273, Factory Outlet Blvd, **W** 🅖 Shell/dsl 🍴 Arby's, Jack-in-the-Box, Luigi's Pizza, Mary's Pizza, Panda Express, Sonic, Starbucks 🛏 Baymont Inn 🅞 AT&T, Shasta Outlets/famous brands, Tire Factory, Verizon, Walmart/Subway

---

↑N **INTERSTATE 5 Cont'd**

Exit #	Services
681a	Continued

Harley-Davidson, **W** 🅖 Pacific Pride/dsl 🍴 Fat Boys 🛏 Best Western, Comfort Suites, Fairfield Inn

680 CA 299E, **W** 1/2 mi 🅖 Arco, Chevron/dsl 🍴 A&W/KFC, Carl's Jr, Giant Burger, Little Caesars, McDonald's, Papa Murphy's, Popeyes, RoundTable Pizza, Starbucks, Subway 🅞 AutoZone, O'Reilly Parts, Raley's Foods, Redding RV Camp, Redding RV Park, ShopKO, transmissions, Twin View RV Park, Walgreens

678 CA 299 W, CA 44, to Eureka, Redding, Burney, **E** between Hilltop & Churncreek 🅖 Chevron/dsl, Shell 🍴 5 Thai's, Applebee's, Carl's Jr, Casa Ramos, Chipotle Mexican, ChuckeCheese, Coldstone, Famous Dave's, Five Guys Burgers, Hometown Buffet, In-N-Out, Jack-in-the-Box, Jamba Juice, Jersey Mike's, McDonald's, Olive Garden, Outback Steaks, Panda Express, Panda Express, Red Lobster, Red Robin, Starbucks, Strings Italian, Subway, Taco Bell 🛏 Motel 6, Red Lion Inn 🅞 AT&T, Barnes&Noble, Best Buy, BigLots, Costco, Dick's, FoodMaxx, Home Depot, JC Penney, Jo-Ann, Kohl's, Macy's, Michael's, Old Navy, O'Reilly Parts, PetCo, Petsmart, Schwab Tire, Sears/auto, Target, TJ Maxx, Trader Joe's, Verizon, Walmart/McDonald's, WinCo Foods, World Mkt

677 Cypress Ave, Hilltop Dr, Redding, **E** 🅖 76/dsl, Chevron/dsl, Valero/dsl 🍴 Black Bear Diner, Burger King, Carl's Jr,

REDDING

ANDERSON

CA

INTERSTATE 5 Cont'd

Exit #	Services
665	(from sb) Cottonwood, **E** 🄷 Alamo Motel/RV park, Travelers Motel/RV Park
664	Gas Point Rd, to Balls Ferry, **E** 🄶 Chevron/dsl/LP, Gas+/dsl 🄷 Alamo Motel, Travelers Motel 🄾 Alamo RV Park, auto repair, **W** 🄶 Holiday/dsl, Sunshine/dsl 🄵 Eagles Nest Pizza, Subway 🄾 Ace Hardware, Holiday Foods, vet
662	Bowman Rd, to Cottonwood, **E** 🄶 Texaco/dsl
660mm	**weigh sta both lanes**
659	Snively Rd, Auction Yard Rd, (Sunset Hills Dr from nb)
657	Hooker Creek Rd, Auction Yard Rd
656mm	🅁🅂 **both lanes, full** ♿ **facilities, litter barrels, petwalk, 🅲, 🅯**
653	Jellys Ferry Rd, **E** 🄾 RV Park/LP
652	Wilcox Golf Rd
651	CA 36W (from sb), Red Bluff, **W** 🄶 Arco/dsl 🄷 Holiday Inn Express 🄾 same as 650
650	Adobe Rd, **W** 🄶 Chevron/dsl 🄵 Burrito Bandito, Casa Ramos Mexican, Starbucks 🄷 Hampton Inn 🄾 CHP, Home Depot
649	CA 36, to CA 99 S, Red Bluff, **E** 🄶 Chevron/dsl, Red Bluff Gas, Shell/dsl 🄵 Applebee's, Burger King, Del Taco, KFC, McDonald's, Perko's Cafe 🄷 Best Western, Comfort Inn, Motel 6, **W** 🄶 Mobil/dsl, Valero/dsl 🄵 Denny's, Egg Roll King, Los Mariachis, Luigi's Pizza, Riverside Grill, RoundTable Pizza, Shari's, Subway 🄷 Super 8, Travelodge 🄾 AT&T, CVS Drug, Durango RV Resort, Foodmaxx, O'Nite RV Park, River's Edge RV Park, Verizon, vet
647a b	S Main St, Red Bluff, **E** 🄶 Valero/dsl 🄷 Days Inn 🄾 🄷, **W** 🄶 Arco/dsl, Chevron/dsl, Shell/dsl 🄵 Arby's, Baskin-Robbins, China Buffet, China Doll, Cozy Diner, Domino's, Jack-in-the-Box, Papa Murphy's, Starbucks, Subway, Wendy's 🄷 American Inn, Best Value Inn, Triangle Motel 🄾 AutoZone, CVS Drug, GNC, Grocery Outlet, O'Reilly Parts, Radio Shack, Raley's Food/drug, Staples, Tire Factory, True Value, Verizon, vet, Walgreens, Walmart/McDonald's
642	Flores Ave, to Proberta, Gerber, **E 1 mi** 🄾 Walmart Dist Ctr
636	rd A11, Gyle Rd, to Tehama, **E** 🄾 RV camping (7mi)
633	Finnell Rd, to Richfield
632mm	🅁🅂 **both lanes, full** ♿ **facilities, litter barrels, petwalk, 🅲, 🅯**
631	A9, Corning Rd, Corning, **E** 🄶 76/dsl, Chevron/dsl, Shell/dsl/LP 🄵 Burger King, Casa Ramos Mexican, Little Caesars, Marco's Pizza, Olive Pit Rest., Papa Murphy's, Rancho Grande Mexican, RoundTable Pizza, Starbucks, Subway, Taco Bell 🄷 7 Inn Motel, American Inn, Best Western, Economy Inn, Super 8 🄾 $Tree, Ace Hardware, auto repair, AutoZone, Buick/Chevrolet, Clark Drug, Ford, Heritage RV Park, NAPA, O'Reilly Parts, Radio Shack, Rite Aid, Safeway, Verizon, **W** 🄵 Giant Burger 🄷 Corning RV Park
630	South Ave, Corning, **E** 🄶 ▰Loves/Denny's/dsl/LP/RV dump/scales/24hr, Petro/Iron Skillet/dsl/scales/24hr/@, TA/Arby's/Subway/dsl/scales/24hr/@ 🄵 Jack-in-the-Box, McDonald's 🄷 CA Inn, Econolodge, Holiday Inn Express 🄾 Ace Hardware, Blue Beacon, SpeedCo Lube, truck wash/lube, Woodson Br SRA/RV Park (6mi)
628	CA 99W, Liberal Ave, **W** 🄶 Chevron/dsl 🄷 Rolling Hills Hotel/Casino 🄾 Rolling Hills RV Park
621	CA 7
619	CA 32, Orland, **E** 🄶 76/dsl, Arco 🄵 Berry Patch Rest., Burger King, Subway 🄷 Orlanda Inn 🄾 $General, AutoZone, CVS Drug, Walgreens, **W** 🄶 Shell/dsl 🄵 I-5 Cafe, Taco Bell 🄾 Old Orchard RV Park, Parkway RV Park

618	CA 16, **E** 🄶 Shell/dsl 🄵 El Potrero Mexican 🄷 Orland Inn 🄾 $Tree, Grocery Outlet
614	CA 27
610	Artois
608mm	🅁🅂 **both lanes, full** ♿ **facilities, litter barrels, petwalk, 🅲, 🅯 RV dump**
607	CA 39, Blue Gum Rd, Bayliss, **E 2 mi** 🄷 Blue Gum Motel
603	CA 162, to Oroville, Willows, **E** 🄶 Arco, Chevron, Shell/dsl 🄵 Black Bear Diner, Burger King, Casa Ramos, Denny's, KFC, La Cascada Mexican, McDonald's, RoundTable Pizza, Starbucks, Subway, Taco Bell, Wong's Chinese 🄷 Baymont Inn, Best Western/RV parking, Holiday Inn Express, Motel 6, Super 8, Travelodge 🄾 🄷, $Tree, CHP, **W** 🄵 Nancy's Café/24hr 🄾 🄵, RV Park (8mi), Walmart
601	rd 57, **E** 🄶 Chevron/dsl
595	Rd 68, to Princeton, **E** 🄾 to Sacramento NWR
591	Delevan Rd
588	Maxwell (from sb), access to camping
586	Maxwell Rd, **E** 🄾 Delavan NWR, **W** 🄶 Chevron 🄷 Maxwell Inn/rest. 🄾 Maxwell Parts
583	🅁🅂 **both lanes, full** ♿ **facilities, litter barrels, petwalk, 🅲, 🅯**
578	CA 20, Colusa, **W** 🄶 Shell/Orv's Cafe/dsl 🄾 🄷, hwy patrol
577	Williams, **E** 🄶 Shell/Baskin-Robbins/Togo's/dsl 🄵 Carl's Jr, Subway, Taco Bell 🄷 Ramada Inn, **W** 🄶 76/dsl, Chevron/dsl, Shell/dsl 🄵 Burger King, Denny's, Granzella's Rest., Louis Cairo's Rest., McDonald's/RV parking, Straw Hat Pizza, Williams Chinese Rest. 🄷 Econolodge, Granzella's Inn, Motel 6, StageStop Motel, Travelers Inn 🄾 🄷, camping, NAPA, Shop'n Save Foods, URGENT CARE, USPO
575	Husted Rd, to Williams
569	Hahn Rd, to Grimes
567	frontage rd (from nb), to Arbuckle, **W** 🄶 Chevron/dsl
566	to College City, Arbuckle, **E** 🄾 Ace Hardware, USPO, **W** 🄶 J&J/dsl 🄾 $General
559	Yolo/Colusa County Line Rd
557mm	🅁🅂 **both lanes, full** ♿ **facilities, litter barrels, petwalk, 🅲, 🅯**
556	E4, Dunnigan, **E** 🄶 Chevron/dsl/LP 🄵 Jack-in-the-Box 🄷 Best Value Inn, Motel 6 🄾 Farmers Mkt Deli, **W** 🄾 Camper's RV Park/golf (1mi)
554	rd 8, **E** ▰/Wendy's/dsl/scales/24hr 🄷 Hacienda Motel 🄾 HappyTime RV Park, Oasis Grill, **W** 🄶 United TP/dsl
553	I-505 (from sb), to San Francisco, callboxes begin sb
548	Zamora, **E** 🄶 Shell/dsl
542	Yolo, **E 1 mi** gas
541	CA 16W, Woodland, **W 3 mi** 🄾 🄷
540	West St, **W** 🄶 Arco 🄵 Denny's
538	CA 113 N, E St, Woodland, **E** 🄷 Valley Oaks Inn, **W** 🄶 CFN/dsl, Chevron/dsl 🄵 Perry's 🄷 Best Western
537	CA 113 S, Main St, to Davis (same as 536), **E** 🄾 Buick/Cadillac/Chevrolet/GMC, **W** 🄶 Chevron/dsl 🄵 Carl's Jr, Denny's, McDonald's, RoundTable Pizza, Starbucks, Subway, Taco Bell, Wendy's 🄷 Days Inn, Motel 6, Quality Inn 🄾 $Tree, Food4Less
536	rd 102 (same as 537), **E on Main St** 🄶 Arco, Chevron/dsl 🄵 Applebee's, Burger King, Jack-in-the-Box, McDonald's, Quiznos, Subway 🄷 Hampton Inn, Holiday Inn Express 🄾 America's Tire, Home Depot, museum, Staples, Walmart/McDonald's, **W** 🄶 76/Circle K/dsl 🄵 In-N-Out, Panda Express, Red Robin, Spoon Me, Starbucks, Subway 🄾 Best Buy, Best Buy, Costco/gas, Michael's, Target, Verizon
531	rd 22, W Sacramento
530mm	Sacramento River

RED BLUFF

CORNING

WILLIAMS

DAVIS

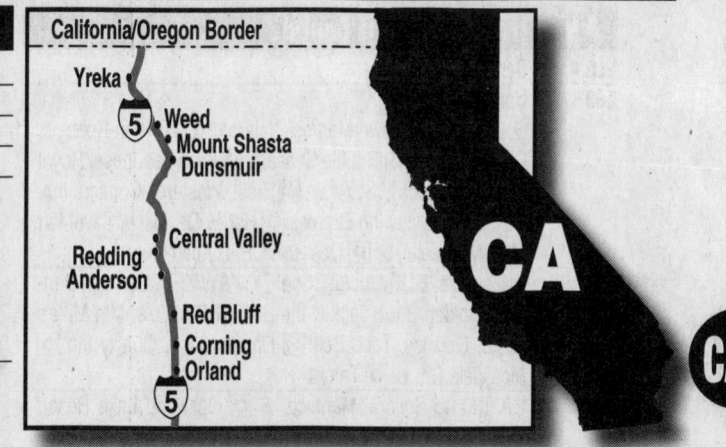

INTERSTATE 5 Cont'd

Exit #	Services
529mm	🅿️ sb, full 🛏 facilities, litter barrels, petwalk, 🚻, 🐾
528	Airport Rd, E 🅶 Arco 🅾️ 🖨
525b	CA 99, to CA 70, to Marysville, Yuba City
525a	Del Paso Rd, E 🅶 Chevron 🍴 A&W/KFC, Chicken'n Waffles, Denny's, IHOP, In-N-Out, Jack-in-the-box, Malabar Rest., Panda Express, Panera Bread, Papa Murphy's, Sizzler, Sizzler, Taco Bell 🛏 Hampton Inn, Holiday Inn Express, Homewood Suites 🅾️ Rite Aid, Safeway Foods/dsl, W 🍴 Subway 🛏 Sheraton 🅾️ Walgreens
524	Arena Blvd, E 🍴 Papa John's, Subway 🅾️ Power Balance Arena, W 🍴 RoundTable Pizza, Starbucks 🅾️ Bel-Air Food/Drug/dsl
522	I-80, E to Reno, W to San Francisco
521b a	Garden Hwy, West El Camino, W 🅶 Shell/dsl 🍴 Carl's Jr, Jack-in-the-Box, Jamba Juice, Starbucks, Subway, Togo's/Baskin-Robbins 🛏 Courtyard, Hilton Garden, Residence Inn, SpringHill Suites
520	Richards Blvd, E 🅶 Chevron/dsl 🍴 Grill Master's Steaks, McDonald's, Sekou's BBQ 🛏 Governor's Inn, Hawthorn Suites, Ramada Ltd, Super 8, W 🅶 Arco, Shell 🍴 Coyote Jct Mexican 🛏 Best Value Inn, Best Western, Comfort Suites, Days Inn, La Quinta, Motel 6 🅾️ waterfront park
519b	J St, Old Sacramento, E 🍴 Denny's 🛏 Holiday Inn, Vagabond Inn, W 🛏 Embassy Suites 🅾️ Railroad Museum
519a	Q St, downtown, Sacramento, W 🛏 Embassy Suites, to st capitol
518	US 50, CA 99, Broadway, E services downtown
516	Sutterville Rd, E 🅶 76/dsl, Land Park/dsl 🍴 La Bou Cafe, Macau Cafe 🅾️ Sunflower Mkt, Wm Land Park, zoo
515	Fruitridge Rd, Seamas Rd
514	43rd Ave, Riverside Blvd (from sb), E 🅶 76/repair
513	Florin Rd, E 🅶 Arco, Chevron 🍴 Rosalinda's Mexican, RoundTable Pizza, Sizzling Wok 🅾️ $Tree, Bel Air Foods, CVS Drug, O'Reilly Parts, URGENT CARE, W 🍴 Burger King, Coldstone, JimBoy's Tacos, L&L Hawaiian BBQ, Panda Garden, Shari's, Starbucks, Subway, Wings Stop 🅾️ AAA, Marshall's, Nugget Mkt, Radio Shack, Rite Aid
512	CA 160, Pocket Rd, Meadowview Rd, to Freeport, E 🅶 Shell/dsl, Valero/dsl 🍴 IHOP, KFC/LJ Silver, McDonald's, Starbucks, Wendy's 🅾️ AT&T, Home Depot, Staples, vet, Walgreens
508	Laguna Blvd, E 🅶 76/Circle K/dsl/LP, Chevron/McDonald's/dsl, Shell 🍴 A&W/KFC, Starbucks, Subway, Wendy's 🛏 Extended Stay America, Hampton Inn 🅾️ Jiffy Lube, Laguna Tire, U-Haul
506	Elk Grove Blvd, E 🅶 Arco/dsl, Chevron/dsl, Shell 🍴 Carl's Jr, Nick-N-Willy's Pizza, Pete's Grill, Vallarta Mexican, Wasabi Grill 🛏 Holiday Inn Express
504	Hood Franklin Rd
498	Twin Cities Rd, to Walnut Grove
493	Walnut Grove Rd, Thornton, E 🅶 CFN/dsl, Chevron/Subway/dsl
490	Peltier Rd
487	Turner Rd
485	CA 12, Lodi, E 🅶 ✈FLYING J/Denny's/dsl/scales/24hr, 76/Rocky's Rest./dsl/scales/24hr, Arco/Subway/dsl/24hr, Chevron/dsl, Shell/dsl 🍴 Burger King, Carl's Jr, McDonald's, Taco Bell 🛏 Best Western, Microtel 🅾️ Blue Beacon, Flag City RV Resort, Profleet Trucklube, W 🅾️ KOA (5mi)
481	Eight Mile Rd, W 🅶 Chevron/Jack-in-the-Box/dsl 🍴 Baskin-

(left margin, vertical) **SACRAMENTO**

481	Continued Robbins, Del Taco, Hawaiian BBQ, Jalapeno's, Jamba Juice, McDonald's, MooMoo's Burgers, Panda Express, Panera Bread, RoundTable Pizza, Sonic, Starbucks, Strings Italian, Subway, Wendy's 🅾️ AAA, AT&T, Jo-Ann Fabrics, KOA, Kohl's, Lowe's, Office Depot, Petsmart, Ross, Target, Verizon, Walmart
478	Hammer Lane, Stockton, E 🅶 76/dsl, Arco 🍴 Adalberto's Mexican, Carl's Jr, KFC, Little Caesars, McDonald's, Subway 🅾️ AutoZone, Radio Shack, Rally's Foods, Walgreens, W 🅶 Chevron/dsl, QuikStop 🍴 Jack-in-the-Box, Lupe's Mexican, Taco Bell
477	Benjamin Holt Dr, Stockton, E 🅶 Arco, Chevron/dsl, Qwik-Stop 🍴 Pizza Guys 🛏 Motel 6 🅾️ Quikstop, W 🅶 7-11 🍴 Casa Flores, Eddie's Pizza, Fon Wong Chinese, Lumber Jack's Rest., McDonald's, Subway/TCBY 🅾️ Ace Hardware, Marina Foods, vet
476	March Lane, Stockton, E 🅶 7-11 🍴 Applebee's, Carl's Jr, Denny's, El Torito, Jack-in-the-Box, Marie Callender's, McDonald's, Olive Garden, Red Lobster, StrawHat Pizza, Taco Bell, Toot Sweets Bakery, Wendy's 🛏 Comfort Inn, Hilton 🅾️ CVS Drug, Marshall's, SMart Foods, W 🅶 76/dsl 🍴 Carrow's Rest., In-N-Out, Italian Cuisine, Jamba Juice, Krispy Kreme, Old Spaghetti Factory, RoundTable Pizza, Starbucks, Subway, Wong's Chinese 🛏 Courtyard, Extended Stay America, La Quinta, Quality Inn, Residence Inn 🅾️ Home Depot
475	Alpine Ave, Country Club Blvd, same as 474 b
474b	Country Club Blvd (from nb), E 🅶 76/dsl, W 🅶 7-11, Shell/Subway/dsl 🅾️ BigLots, Safeway/gas
474a	Monte Diablo Ave
473	Pershing Ave (from nb), W 🅶 Arco 🛏 Red Roof Inn
472	CA 4 E, to CA 99, Fresno Ave, downtown
471	CA 4 W, Charter Way, E 🅶 Chevron/dsl, Shell, United 🍴 Burger King, Denny's, Little Ceasars, McDonald's, Quiznos 🛏 Days Inn 🅾️ O'Reilly Parts, W 🅶 76/dsl/scales/24hr, Valero/Subway 🍴 Jack-in-the-Box, Taco Bell 🛏 Motel 6 🅾️ Les Schwab Tire, truck repair
470	8th St, Stockton, W 🅶 CA Stop/dsl, Shell/Subway/dsl 🛏 I-5 Inn
469	Downing Ave, W 🍴 China Express, Lou's Chinese, Mtn Mike's Pizza, Subway 🅾️ AutoZone, Food4Less/gas
468	French Camp, E 🅶 76/Togo's/dsl 🅾️ Pan Pacific RV Ctr, W 🅾️ 🏥
467b	Mathews Rd, E 🅶 J&L Mkt/dsl 🅾️ tires/repair, W 🅾️ 🏥
467a	El Dorado St (from nb)
465	Roth Rd, Sharpe Depot, E 🅶 FL/dsl 🅾️ Freightliner, Kenworth, truck/rv repair
463	Lathrop Rd, E 🅶 Chevron/dsl/LP, Joe's Trkstp/Texaco/To

(middle margin, vertical) **STOCKTON**

⬆↕ N INTERSTATE 5 Cont'd

Exit #	Services
463	Continued
	go's/dsl/scales, TowerMart/dsl, Valero/dsl 🍴 Baskin-Robbins, China Wok, CK Grill, Little Ceasars, Mi Kasa Japanese, Royal Pizza, Starbucks, Subway 🏨 Best Western, Comfort Inn, Days Inn, Holiday Inn Express ⊙ Harley-Davidson, SaveMart Mkt, Walgreens, **W** ⊙ Dos Reis CP, RV camping
462	Louise Ave, **E** ⛽ Arco/dsl, Shell 🍴 A&W/KFC, Carl's Jr, Denny's, Golden Bowl, Jack-in-the-Box, McDonald's, Mtn Mike's Pizza, Quiznos, Taco Bell 🏨 Hampton Inn, Quality Inn ⊙ Mossdale CP, **W** ⊙ Target
461	CA 120, to Sonora, Manteca, **E** ⊙ Oakwood Lake Resort Camping, to Yosemite
460	Mossdale Rd, **E** ⛽ Arco/dsl, **W** 🍴 fruit stand/cafe
458b	I-205, to Oakland (from sb, no return)
458a	11th St, to Tracy, Defense Depot, **W 2 mi** ⛽ gas/dsl/food
457	Kasson Rd, to Tracy, **W** ⛽ Valley Pacific/dsl
452	CA 33 S, Vernalis
449b a	CA 132, to Modesto, **E** ⊙ The Orchard Campground
446	I-580 (from nb, exits left, no return)
445mm	**Westley** ℞ **both lanes, full** ♿ **facilities, litter barrels, petwalk, ⟨🄲⟩, 🚮, RV dump**
441	Ingram Creek, Howard Rd, Westley, **E** ⛽ 76/dsl, Chevron/dsl, Joe's Trvl Plaza/dsl/scales/24hr, Triangle TruckStp/dsl 🍴 Antojito's Mexican, Carl's Jr, McDonald's, Subway 🏨 Best Value Inn, Days Inn, EconoLodge, Holiday Inn Express, **W** ⛽ Shell/dsl 🍴 fruits, Ingram Creek Rest. ⊙ truck repair
434	Sperry Ave, Del Puerto, Patterson, **E** ⛽ 76/Subway/dsl, Chevron 🍴 A&W/KFC, Carl's Jr, Denny's, El Rosal Mexican, Golden Lion Chinese, Jack-in-the-Box, Lamp Post Pizza, Starbucks, Strings Italian 🏨 Best Western ⊙ Kit Fox RV Park
430mm	vista point nb
428	Fink Rd, Crow's Landing
423	Stuhr Rd, Newman, **E 5 mi** ⊙ Ⓗ, food, lodging, RV camping
422mm	vista point sb
418	CA 140E, Gustine
409	**weigh sta both lanes**
407	CA 33, Santa Nella, **E** ⛽ Arco/Subway, Loves/Del Taco/dsl/scales/24hr, TA/Buckhorn Rest./Popeye's/dsl/scales/24hr/@ 🍴 Andersen's Rest, Carl's Jr, Wendy's 🏨 Best Western/Andersen's, Holiday Inn Express, **W** ⛽ Chevron, Rotten Robbie/dsl/scales, Shell/Circle K/Jack-in-the-Box/dsl, Valero/dsl 🍴 Denny's, In-N-Out, McDonald's, Quiznos, Starbucks, Taco Bell 🏨 Hotel de Oro, Motel 6 ⊙ Santa Nella RV Park
403b a	CA 152, Los Banos, **E 6 mi** ⊙ Ⓗ, **W** ⛽ (1mi), Petro/dsl/24hr ⊙ KOA, San Luis RV Park
391	CA 165N, Mercy Springs Rd, **E** ⊙ Ⓗ, **W** ⛽ Shell
388	vista point (from nb)
386mm	℞ **both lanes, full** ♿ **facilities, litter barrels, petwalk, ⟨🄲⟩, 🚮**
385	Nees Ave, to Firebaugh, **W** ⛽ Chevron/CFN/Subway/dsl/scales
379	Shields Ave, to Mendota
372	Russell Ave
368	Panoche Rd, **W** ⛽ 76/dsl, Chevron/McDonald's, Mobil/Taco Bell/dsl, Shell/dsl 🍴 Apricot Tree Rest., Fosters Freeze, Subway 🏨 Best Western ⊙ country store
365	Manning Ave, to San Joaquin
357	Kamm Ave
349	CA 33 N, Derrick Ave
337	CA 33 S, CA 145 N, to Coalinga

334	CA 198, to Lemoore, Huron, **E** ⛽ Shell/Subway/dsl/24hr 🏨 Harris Ranch Inn/rest., **W** ⛽ 76, Chevron, Valero/dsl 🍴 Burger King, Carl's Jr, Denny's, McDonald's, Oriental Express Chinese, Taco Bell 🏨 Best Western, Motel 6, Travelodge ⊙ Ⓗ
325	Jayne Ave, to Coalinga, **W** ⛽ Arco, Shell/Baja Fresh/dsl 🏨 Sommerville RV Park/LP ⊙ Ⓗ
320mm	℞ **both lanes, full** ♿ **facilities, litter barrels, petwalk, ⟨🄲⟩, 🚮**
319	CA 269, Lassen Ave, to Avenal, **W** ⛽ Hillcrest TP/76/dsl/scales/24hr
309	CA 41, Kettleman City, **E** ⛽ 76/Subway/TCBY, CFN/dsl, Chevron/McDonald's, Mobil/Starbucks/dsl/24hr, Shell/dsl, Valero/dsl 🍴 Carl's Jr, Denny's, In-N-Out, Jack-in-the-Box, Pizza Hut/Taco Bell 🏨 Best Western, Super 8 ⊙ Travelers RV Park
305	Utica Ave
288	Twisselman Rd
278	CA 46, Lost Hills, **E** ⛽ Buford Star Mart/dsl/LP ⊙ to Kern NWR, **W** ⛽ 76/Quiznos, Chevron/dsl, Loves/Arby's/dsl/scales/24hr, Mobil/McDonald's/dsl/LP, Wendy's/dsl/scales/24hr, Shell/Pizza Hut/Subway/Taco Bell/dsl, Valero/dsl 🍴 Carl's Jr, Denny's, Jack-in-the-Box, McDonald's 🏨 Days Inn, Motel 6 ⊙ K&S Truck Wash, Lost Hills RV Park
268	Lerdo Hwy, to Shafter
262	7th Standard Rd, Rowlee Rd, to Buttonwillow
259mm	**Buttonwillow** ℞ **both lanes, full** ♿ **facilities, litter barrels, petwalk, ⟨🄲⟩, 🚮**
257	CA 58, to Bakersfield, Buttonwillow, **E** ⛽ 76/Circle K/Quiznos/dsl, Arco/dsl, Bruce's/dsl/wash, Chevron/dsl, Shell/dsl, TA/Pizza Hut/Taco Bell/dsl/scales/24hr/@ 🍴 Carl's Jr, Denny's, McDonald's, Starbucks, Subway, Tita's Mexican, Willow Ranch BBQ 🏨 EconoLodge, Knights Inn, Motel 6 ⊙ Castro's Tire/Truckwash, **W** ⛽ Valero/dsl
253	Stockdale Hwy, **E** ⛽ Chevron/dsl, Shell/dsl/24hr 🍴 IHOP, Jack-in-the-Box 🏨 Best Western, Vagabond Inn, **W** ⊙ Tule Elk St Reserve
246	CA 43, to Taft, Maricopa, ⊙ to Buena Vista RA
244	CA 119, to Pumpkin Center, **E** ⛽ Mobil/dsl, **W** ⛽ Chevron, dsl/LP
239	CA 223, Bear Mtn Blvd, to Arvin, **W** ⊙ RV camping, to Buena Vista RA, ⊙ Bear Mtn. RV Resort
234	Old River Rd
228	Copus Rd, Murray Farms Mkt
225	CA 166, to Mettler, **E 2-3 mi** food, gas/dsl
221	I-5 and CA 99 (from nb, exits left, no return)
219b a	Laval Rd, Wheeler Ridge, **E** ⛽ TA/Chevron/Popeye's/Subway/scales/@ 🍴 Burger King, Pizza Hut, Taco Bell 🏨 Microtel ⊙ Blue Beacon, **W** ⛽ Chevron/dsl, Mobil/dsl, Petro/Iron Skillet/Subway/dsl/scales/24hr/@ 🍴 Baskin-Robbins, Chipotle Mexican, Del Taco, In-N-Out, McDonald's, Panda Express, Starbucks, Subway, Wendy's, Yogurtland 🏨 Best Western
218	**truck weigh sta sb**
215	Grapevine, **E** ⛽ Valero/dsl 🍴 Denny's, Jack-in-the-Box, **W** ⛽ Shell/dsl 🍴 Don Perico Grill 🏨 Ramada Ltd.
210	Ft Tejon Rd, **W** ⊙ to Ft Tejon Hist SP, towing/repair
209mm	**brake check area nb**
207	Lebec Rd, **W** ⊙ antiques, CHP, towing, USPO
206mm	℞ **both lanes, full** ♿ **facilities, petwalk, ⟨🄲⟩, 🚮 litter barrels, vending**
205	Frazier Mtn Park Rd, **W** ⛽ FLYING J/Denny's/dsl/LP/24hr/@, 76, Chevron/Subway/dsl/24hr, Shell/Quiznos/dsl/LP 🍴 Jack-in-the-Box, Los Pinos Mexican 🏨 Holiday Inn Express, Motel 6 ⊙ auto repair/towing, NAPA, to Mt Pinos RA

Side markers (vertical, left column): **CA** | **WESTLEY** | **SANTA NELLA**

Side markers (vertical, right column): BUTTONWILLOW | **FT TEJON**

INTERSTATE 5 Cont'd

Exit #	Services
204	elev 4144, Tejon Pass, **truck brake insp sb**
202	Gorman Rd, to Hungry Valley, **E** 🅶 76/dsl, Chevron/dsl/LP 🍴 Carl's Jr, El Grullense, Ranch House Rest. 🛏 EconoLodge, **W** 🅶 Shell 🍴 McDonald's 🅾 auto repair
199	CA 138 E, Lancaster Rd, to Palmdale
198b a	Quail Lake Rd, CA 138 E (from nb)
195	Smokey Bear Rd, Pyramid Lake, **W** 🅾 Pyramid Lake RV Park
191	Vista del Lago Rd, **W** 🅾 visitors ctr
186mm	**brake inspection area sb**, motorist callboxes begin sb
183	Templin Hwy, **W** 🅾 Ranger Sta, RV camping
176b a	Lake Hughes Rd, Parker Rd, Castaic, **E** 🅶 7-11, Castaic Trk-stp/dsl/24hr, 🚛/Wendy's/dsl/scales/24hr/@, Shell/dsl 🍴 Baskin-Robbins, Burger King, Carl's Jr, Denny's, Domino's, El Pollo Loco, Fosters Freeze, Jersey Mikes, McDonald's, Mike's Diner, Mike's Diner, Panda Express, Pizza Factory, Popeye's, Starbucks, Subway, Telly's Drive-in, Vinny's Pizza, Wok's Chinese 🛏 Castaic Inn, Days Inn, Rodeway Inn 🅾 $Tree, Benny's Tire/repair, Castaic Lake RV Park, O'Reilly Parts, Ralph's Food, Rite Aid, to Castaic Lake, vet, **W** 🅶 76/repair, Mobil 🍴 Jack-in-the-Box, Taco Bell 🅾 auto repair, Walgreens
173	Hasley Canyon Rd, **W** 🍴 Amici Pizza, Las Delicias, Pizza Hut, Subway 🅾 Ralph's Foods
172	CA 126 W, to Ventura, **E** 🛏 Courtyard, Embassy Suites
171mm	**weigh sta nb**
171	Rye Canyon Rd (from sb), **W** 🅶 Chevron, Shell 🍴 Del Taco, Jack-in-the-Box, Jimmy Deans, Starbucks, Subway, Tommy's Burgers 🅾 6 Flags
170	CA 126 E, Magic Mtn Pkwy, Saugus, **E** 🍴 Denny's, Geisha Japanese, Sam's Grille, Starbucks 🛏 Best Western/rest., Holiday Inn Express, **W** 🅶 Chevron/dsl 🍴 El Torito, Game Day Cafe, Marie Callender's, Red Lobster, Wendy's 🛏 Hilton Garden 🅾 Six Flags of CA
169	Valencia Blvd, **W** 🍴 Fat Burger, Nick'n Willy's Pizza, Panda Express, Robeks, Starbucks, Subway 🅾 Albertson's/Sav-On, Verizon
168	McBean Pkwy, **E** 🅾 H, **W** 🍴 Baskin-Robbins, Cabo Cabana, Chili's, ChuckeCheese, ClaimJumper, Jamba Juice, Jersey Mikes Subs, Macaroni Grill, Mamma Mia Italian, Pick up Stix, Starbucks, Subway, Urbane Cafe 🅾 Michael's, Old Navy, Verizon, Vons Foods, WorldMkt
167	Lyons Ave, Pico Canyon Rd, **E** 🅶 76/Circle K/dsl, Chevron/dsl, Shell/dsl 🍴 Burger King, Wendy's, **W** 🅶 Arco, Shell/dsl 🍴 Carl's Jr, Chuy's, Coco's, Del Taco, Denny's, El Pollo Loco, Fortune Express Chinese, Golden Spoon, IHOP, In-N-Out, Jack-in-the-Box, Kinza Asian, McDonald's, Outback Steaks, Spumoni Italian, Taco Bell, Wood Ranch BBQ, Yamato Japanese 🛏 Comfort Suites, Extended Stay America, Fairfield Inn, Hampton Inn, La Quinta, Residence Inn 🅾 AT&T, Camping World RV Ctr, GNC, Jiffy Lube, Marshall's, Petsmart, Ralph's Foods, Ross, Staples, SteinMart, Tire World, Walmart/McDonald's
166	Calgrove Blvd
162	CA 14 N, to Palmdale
161b	Balboa Blvd (from sb)
160a	I-210, to San Fernando, Pasadena
159	Roxford St, Sylmar, **E** 🅶 Chevron/dsl, Mobil/dsl 🍴 Denny's/24hr, McDonald's 🛏 Good Nite Inn, Motel 6
158	I-405 S (from sb, no return)
157b a	SF Mission Blvd, Brand Blvd, **E** 🅶 76, Arco, Chevron,

Vertical labels: CASTAIC / SANTA CLARITA

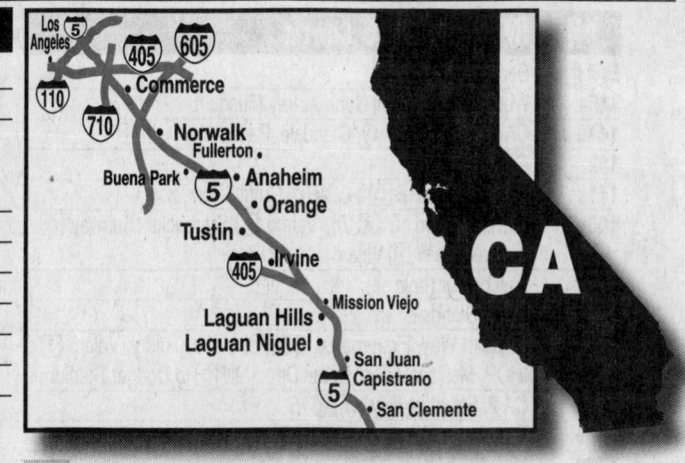

Exit #	Services
157b a	Continued Mobil/dsl, Shell 🍴 Carl's Jr, In-N-Out, Little Caesars, New Asia, Pollo Gordo, Popeye's, Subway, Taco Bell, Winchell's 🅾 H, Honda, Rite Aid
156b	CA 118
156a	Paxton St, Brand Ave (from nb), **E** 🅶 Shell/dsl 🅾 7-11
155b	Van Nuys Blvd (no EZ nb return), **E** 🅶 Eagle 🍴 Jack-in-the-Box, KFC/LJ Silver, McDonald's, Pizza Hut, Popeye's 🅾 Discount Parts, USPO, **W** 🍴 Domino's 🅾 auto repair
155a	Terra Bella St (from nb), **E** 🅶 Arco
154	Osborne St, to Arleta, **E** 🅶 Arco, Chevron/dsl 🍴 El Pollo Loco, Knight's Pizza, Papa's Tacos 🅾 AutoZone, BigLots, Food4Less, Superior Grocers, Target, **W** 🅶 76, Mobil/Burger King 🅾 7-11
153b	CA 170 (from sb), to Hollywood
152a	Sheldon St, **E** 🍴 Big Jim's Rest. 🅾 H, auto repair, Big O Parts
152	Lankershim Blvd, Tuxford, **E** 🅶 Superfine/dsl/scales
151	Penrose St
150b	Sunland Blvd, Sun Valley, **E** 🅶 76/dsl, Mobil 🍴 Acapulco Rest., Carl's Jr, El Pollo Loco, Old Time Burgers, Quiznos, Subway, Town Café, Yoshinoya 🛏 Economy Inn 🅾 7-11, Ralph's Foods, **W** 🅶 76, Shell 🍴 Big Boy, McDonald's
150a	GlenOaks Blvd (from nb), **E** 🅶 Superior/dsl 🛏 Willows Motel
149	Hollywood Way, **W** 🅶 Shell/dsl 🅾 ⛽, U-Haul
148	Buena Vista St, **E** 🅶 Hampton Inn, **W** 🅶 76/dsl 🍴 Jack-in-the-Box 🛏 Quality Inn, Ramada Inn
147	Scott Rd, to Burbank, **E** 🅶 Sevan/dsl, **W** 🍴 Hometown Buffet, Krispy Kreme, Outback Steaks, Panda Express, Starbucks, Wendy's 🛏 Courtyard, Extended Stay America 🅾 Best Buy, Lowe's, Marshall's, Michael's, Staples, Target, Verizon
146b	Burbank Blvd, **E** 🅶 76/repair 🍴 Baskin-Robbins, CA Pizza Kitchen, Carl's Jr, Chevy's Mexican, ChuckECheese's, Corner Cafe, Harry's Rest., Hooters, IHOP, In-N-Out, McDonald's, Pizza Hut, Popeye's, Quiznos, Robek's Juice, Shakey's Pizza, Starbucks, Subway, Taco Bell, Tommy's Burgers, Yoshinoya 🛏 Holiday Inn 🅾 Barnes&Noble, CVS Drug, Henry's Mkt, K-Mart, Loehmanns, Macy's, Office Depot, Old Navy, Ralph's Foods, Ross, Sears, **W** 🍴 McDonald's, Subway 🅾 Costco/gas, Discount Tire
146a	Olive Ave, Verdugo, **E** 🍴 BJ's Rest., Black Angus 🛏 Holiday Inn 🅾 Radio Shack, USPO, **W** 🅾 H, 7-11, Chevrolet, Metro RV Ctr
145b	Alameda Ave, **E** 🅶 Chevron 🍴 Baskin-Robbins/Togo's, Del Taco, Habit Burgers, Starbucks 🅾 CarMax, CVS Drug, Home Depot, Ralph's Foods, Trader Joes, Walgreens, **W** 🅶 Arco, Shell 🛏 Burbank Inn 🅾 U-Haul

Vertical labels: ARLETA / SUN VALLEY

CA

LOS ANGELES AREA

⬆N INTERSTATE 5 Cont'd

Exit #	Services
145a	Western Ave, **W** 🅞 Gene Autrey Museum
144b a	CA 134, Ventura Fwy, Glendale, Pasadena
142	Colorado St
141a	Los Feliz Blvd, **E** 🅞 🅗, **W** 🅞 Griffith Park, zoo
140b	Glendale Blvd, **E** 🅖 76, Valero 🍴 Starbucks, Subway 🅞 auto repair, **W** 🅖 Valero
140a	Fletcher Dr (from sb)
139b a	CA 2, Glendale Fwy
138	Stadium Way, Figueroa St, **E** 🅖 Chevron, Thrifty, Valero 🍴 IHOP, McDonald's 🅞 Home Depot, **W** 🅞 to Dodger Stadium
137b a	CA 2, Glendale Fwy, **W** 🅖 76
136b	Broadway St (from sb), **W** 🅖 76
136a	Main St, **E** 🅖 76, Chevron/24hr 🍴 Chinatown Express, Jack-in-the-Box, McDonald's, Mr Pizza 🅞 🅗, Parts+
135c	I-10 W (from nb), Mission Rd (from sb), **E** 🅖 76/dsl, Chevron 🍴 Jack-in-the-Box, McDonald's 🅞 🅗
135b	Cesar Chavez Ave, **W** 🅞 🅗
135a	4th St, Soto St, **E** 🅖 76/dsl, Shell/Subway/dsl, **W** 🅖 Arco/dsl 🅞 city park
134b	Ca 60 E (from sb), Soto St (from nb)
134a	CA 60 W, Santa Monica Fwy
133	Euclid Ave (from sb), Grand Vista (from nb), **E** 🅖 Arco, USA/dsl, **W** 🅖 Mobil, Shell 🅞 🅗
132	Calzona St, Indiana St, **E** 🅖 Arco/dsl
131b	Indiana St (from nb), **E** 🅖 Arco/dsl, Valero/dsl
131a	Olympic Blvd, **E** 🍴 McDonald's, **W** 🍴 Jack-in-the-Box, King Taco 🅞 🅗
130c b	I-710 (exits left from nb), to Long Beach, Eastern Ave, **E** 🍴 McDonald's
130a	Triggs St (from sb), **E** 🅞 outlet mall, **W** 🍴 Denny's/24hr 🛏 Destiny Inn
129	Atlantic Blvd N, Eastern Ave (from sb), **E** 🍴 Carl's Jr, Fresca's Mexican, Panda Express, Ruby's Diner, Starbucks, Subway 🛏 Doubletree 🅞 Hyundai, outlets/famous brands, **W** 🍴 Denny's, Steven's Steaks
128b	Washington Blvd, Commerce, **E** 🅖 Chevron/dsl/repair/24hr 🍴 McDonald's 🛏 Crowne Plaza Hotel/casino, Doubletree 🅞 Costco, outlets/famous brands, **W** 🅖 Arco 🍴 Del Taco, Subway
128a	Garfield Blvd, **E** 🛏 Commerce/Hotel/casino 🅞 Home Depot, Office Depot, **W** 🅖 76
126b	Slauson Ave, Montebello, **E** 🅖 Shell, Valero/dsl 🍴 Ozzie's Diner, Quiznos, Starbucks 🛏 Quality Inn, Super 8, **W** 🅖 Arco 🍴 Denny's 🛏 Budget Inn, Ramada Inn
126a	Paramount Blvd, Downey, **E** 🅖 Shell/Jack-in-the-Box/dsl
125	CA 19 S, Lakewood Blvd, Rosemead Blvd, **E** 🅖 Mobil, Thrifty 🍴 Arthurs Cafe, Foster's Freeze, Sam's Burgers, Starbucks, Taco Bell 🛏 EconoLodge, **W** 🍴 China Wok, Chris&Pitt's BBQ, McDonald's, Subway 🅞 Ralph's Foods
124	I-605
123	Florence Ave, to Downey, **E** 🅖 Mobil, **W** 🅞 Honda, repair
122	Imperial Hwy, Pioneer Blvd, **E** 🅖 Chevron 🍴 Applebee's, Habit Burgers, IHOP, Jack-in-the-Box, McDonald's, Subway, Wendy's, Wood Grill Buffet 🅞 Firestone/auto, Rite Aid, Target, **W** 🅖 7-11, Chevron 🍴 Alberts Mexican, Denny's, HongKong Express, Panda King, Pizza Hut, Rally's, Shakey's Pizza, Sizzler, Wienerschnitzel 🛏 Comfort Inn, Keystone Motel, Rodeway Inn 🅞 Toyota/Scion, Walmart
121	San Antonio Dr, to Norwalk Blvd, **E** 🅖🍴 IHOP, Jack-in-the-Box, McDonald's, Outback Steaks, Starbucks, Wood Grill Buffet 🛏 Doubletree Inn 🅞 Rite Aid, Target, **W** 🅖 76 🅞 auto repair

NORWALK

Exit #	Services
120b	Firestone Blvd (exits left from nb)
120a	Rosecrans Ave, **E** 🅖 Valero/dsl 🍴 Jim's Burgers, KFC, Little Caesars, Starbucks, Taco Joe 🅞 🅗, BigSaver Foods, **W** 🅖 Arco/24hr 🍴 El Pollo Loco, Fosters Freeze 🛏 Guesthouse Inn 🅞 Camping World RV Ctr, El Monte RV Ctr, Tune-Up Masters
119	Carmenita Rd, Buena Park, **E** 🅖 Arco 🍴 Burger King 🅞 Ford Trucks, Lowe's, **W** 🍴 Galaxy Burgers 🛏 Budget Inn, Dynasty Suites
118	Valley View Blvd, **E** 🍴 Carl's Jr, Elephant Bar Rest, In-N-Out, Northwoods Rest, Red Robin, Subway 🛏 Extended Stay America, Holiday Inn Select, Residence Inn 🅞 Staples, **W** 🅖 Chevron 🍴 Burger King, El Pollo Loco 🅞 Thompson's RV Ctr, to Camping World
117	Artesia Blvd, Knott Ave, **E** 🅖 76/24hr, Chevron 🛏 Extended Stay America 🅞 CarMax, **W** 🅞 Chrysler, Knotts Berry Farm, to Camping World RV Ctr
116	CA 39, Beach Blvd, **E** 🅖 Chevron 🅞 🅗, Acura, BMW, Buick/GMC, CarMax, Honda, Hyundai, Mercedes, Nissan, Toyota/Scion, VW, **W** 🅖 Chevron 🍴 Arby's, Black Angus, Denny's, Fuddruckers, KFC, Pizza Hut, Subway, Wendy's 🛏 Holiday Inn, Red Roof Inn 🅞 Stater Bros, Target, to Knotts Berry Farm
115	Manchester (from nb), same as 116
114b	CA 91 E, Riverside Fwy, **W** to 🔁
114a	Magnolia Ave, Orangethorpe Ave, **E** 🅖 Mobil/dsl 🍴 Burger King, Burger Town, Taco Bell 🅞 Harley-Davidson
113c	CA 91 W (from nb)
113b a	Brookhurst St, LaPalma, **E** 🅖 Chevron/dsl 🍴 Subway, **W** 🅖 Arco, Texaco/dsl 🍴 Carl's Jr., Quiznos, Starbucks 🅞 Home Depot, Staples
112	Euclid St, **E** 🅖 Arco 🍴 IHOP, Marie Callender's, McDonald's, Starbucks, Taco Bell, Wendy's 🅞 7-11, AAA, PetCo, Ross, TJ Maxx, Walmart, **W** 🅖 76, Mobil 🍴 Burger King, Charley's Subs, Denny's, KFC/LJ Silver, Subway 🅞 Radio Shack, Target, Verizon
111	Lincoln Ave, to Anaheim, **E** 🍴 El Triunfo Mexican, La Casa Garcia Mexican, Ruby's Diner, Starbucks, Subway 🅞 vet, **W** 🅞 Discount Auto Repair
110b	Ball Rd (from sb), **E** 🅖 7-11, Chevron/dsl, Shell 🍴 Burger King, El Pollo Loco, McDonald's, Shakey's Pizza, Starbucks, Subway, Taco Bell 🛏 Best Inn, Best Value Inn, Days Inn, Hotel Menage 🅞 Anaheim RV, Traveler's World RV Park, **W** 🅖 Arco/24hr, Shell/dsl 🛏 Best Western, Budget Inn, Holiday Inn, Rodeway Inn, Sheraton, Travelodge 🅞 Camping World RV Ctr, Disneyland, USPO
110a	Harbor Blvd, **E** 🅖 Chevron, Shell 🍴 Carrow's, Shakey's Pizza, Taco Bell 🛏 Days Inn, EconoLodge, Frontier Harbor Hotel, Hotel Menage, Ramada Ltd 🅞 Anaheim Harbor RV Park, **W** 0-2 mi 🍴 Acapulco Mexican, Captain Kidd's, Coldstone, Del Sol, Dennys, IHOP, McDonald's, Millie's Rest., Mimi's Cafe, Mortons Steaks, Overland Sage BBQ, Quiznos, Tony Roma's 🛏 Anaheim Resort, Best Inn, Best Western, Camelot Inn, Candy Cane Inn, Carousel Inn, Castle Inn Suites, Clarion, Courtyard, Desert Inn, Fairfield Inn, Hampton Inn, Hilton Garden, Howard Johnson, ParkVue Inn, Portofino Inn, Ramada Inn, Red Lion, Saga Inn, Sheraton, Travelodge, Tropicana Inn 🅞 same as 109, to Disneyland
109	Katella Ave, Disney Way, **E** 🅖 Arco 🍴 Baskin-Robbins, Carl's Jr, Catch Seafood, Denny's, El Torito, McDonald's, Mr Stox Dining, Panda Express, Subway, Togo's 🛏 Angel Inn, TownePlace Suites 🅞 Angels Stadium, **W** 🅖 Chevron 🍴 Bubba Gump Shrimp, CA Pizza Kitchen, Cheesecake

ANAHEIM

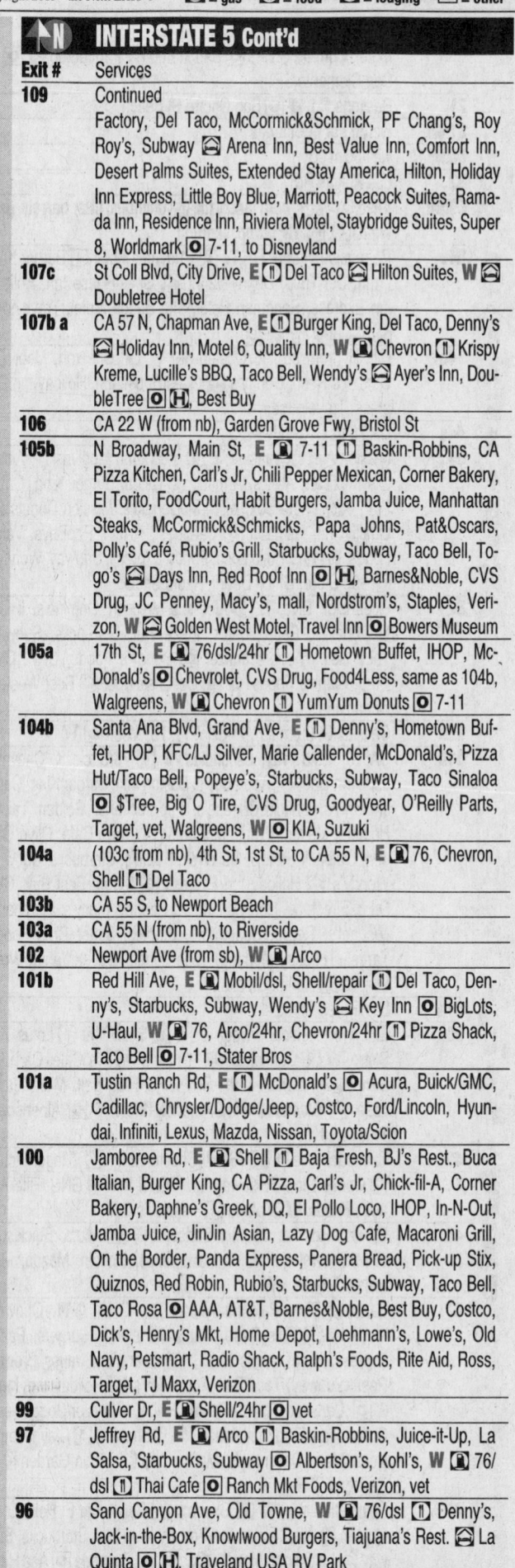

INTERSTATE 5 Cont'd

Exit #	Services
109	Continued
	Factory, Del Taco, McCormick&Schmick, PF Chang's, Roy Roy's, Subway 🏨 Arena Inn, Best Value Inn, Comfort Inn, Desert Palms Suites, Extended Stay America, Hilton, Holiday Inn Express, Little Boy Blue, Marriott, Peacock Suites, Ramada Inn, Residence Inn, Riviera Motel, Staybridge Suites, Super 8, Worldmark 🅾 7-11, to Disneyland
107c	St Coll Blvd, City Drive, E 🍴 Del Taco 🏨 Hilton Suites, W 🏨 Doubletree Hotel
107b a	CA 57 N, Chapman Ave, E 🍴 Burger King, Del Taco, Denny's 🏨 Holiday Inn, Motel 6, Quality Inn, W 🅰 Chevron 🍴 Krispy Kreme, Lucille's BBQ, Taco Bell, Wendy's 🏨 Ayer's Inn, DoubleTree 🅾 Ⓗ, Best Buy
106	CA 22 W (from nb), Garden Grove Fwy, Bristol St
105b	N Broadway, Main St, E 🅰 7-11 🍴 Baskin-Robbins, CA Pizza Kitchen, Carl's Jr, Chili Pepper Mexican, Corner Bakery, El Torito, FoodCourt, Habit Burgers, Jamba Juice, Manhattan Steaks, McCormick&Schmicks, Papa Johns, Pat&Oscars, Polly's Café, Rubio's Grill, Starbucks, Subway, Taco Bell, To-go's 🏨 Days Inn, Red Roof Inn 🅾 Ⓗ, Barnes&Noble, CVS Drug, JC Penney, Macy's, mall, Nordstrom's, Staples, Verizon, W 🏨 Golden West Motel, Travel Inn 🅾 Bowers Museum
105a	17th St, E 🅰 76/dsl/24hr 🍴 Hometown Buffet, IHOP, McDonald's 🅾 Chevrolet, CVS Drug, Food4Less, same as 104b, Walgreens, W 🅰 Chevron 🍴 YumYum Donuts 🅾 7-11
104b	Santa Ana Blvd, Grand Ave, E 🍴 Denny's, Hometown Buffet, IHOP, KFC/LJ Silver, Marie Callender, McDonald's, Pizza Hut/Taco Bell, Popeye's, Starbucks, Subway, Taco Sinaloa 🅾 $Tree, Big O Tire, CVS Drug, Goodyear, O'Reilly Parts, Target, vet, Walgreens, W 🅾 KIA, Suzuki
104a	(103c from nb), 4th St, 1st St, to CA 55 N, E 🅰 76, Chevron, Shell 🍴 Del Taco
103b	CA 55 S, to Newport Beach
103a	CA 55 N (from nb), to Riverside
102	Newport Ave (from sb), W 🅰 Arco
101b	Red Hill Ave, E 🅰 Mobil/dsl, Shell/repair 🍴 Del Taco, Denny's, Starbucks, Subway, Wendy's 🏨 Key Inn 🅾 BigLots, U-Haul, W 🅰 76, Arco/24hr, Chevron/24hr 🍴 Pizza Shack, Taco Bell 🅾 7-11, Stater Bros
101a	Tustin Ranch Rd, E 🍴 McDonald's 🅾 Acura, Buick/GMC, Cadillac, Chrysler/Dodge/Jeep, Costco, Ford/Lincoln, Hyundai, Infiniti, Lexus, Mazda, Nissan, Toyota/Scion
100	Jamboree Rd, E 🅰 Shell 🍴 Baja Fresh, BJ's Rest., Buca Italian, Burger King, CA Pizza, Carl's Jr, Chick-fil-A, Corner Bakery, Daphne's Greek, DQ, El Pollo Loco, IHOP, In-N-Out, Jamba Juice, JinJin Asian, Lazy Dog Cafe, Macaroni Grill, On the Border, Panda Express, Panera Bread, Pick-up Stix, Quiznos, Red Robin, Rubio's, Starbucks, Subway, Taco Bell, Taco Rosa 🅾 AAA, AT&T, Barnes&Noble, Best Buy, Costco, Dick's, Henry's Mkt, Home Depot, Loehmann's, Lowe's, Old Navy, Petsmart, Radio Shack, Ralph's Foods, Rite Aid, Ross, Target, TJ Maxx, Verizon
99	Culver Dr, E 🅰 Shell/24hr 🅾 vet
97	Jeffrey Rd, E 🅰 Arco 🍴 Baskin-Robbins, Juice-it-Up, La Salsa, Starbucks, Subway 🅾 Albertson's, Kohl's, W 🅰 76/dsl 🍴 Thai Cafe 🅾 Ranch Mkt Foods, Verizon, vet
96	Sand Canyon Ave, Old Towne, W 🅰 76/dsl 🍴 Denny's, Jack-in-the-Box, Knowlwood Burgers, Tiajuana's Rest. 🏨 La Quinta 🅾 Ⓗ, Traveland USA RV Park
95	CA 133 (toll), Laguna Fwy, N to Riverside, S Laguna Beach
94b	Alton Pkwy, E 🅰 Shell/Subway/dsl 🍴 Cabo Grill, Carl's Jr, Homestead Suites, Quiznos, Starbucks, W 🍴 CA Pizza, Cheesecake Factory, Chipotle Mexican, Dave&Buster's, Johnny Rockets, Panda Express, PF Chang's, Wahoo's Fish Tacos, Wood Ranch, Yardhouse Rest. 🏨 Doubletree Inn 🅾 Barnes&Noble, Macy's, Nordstrom, Old Navy, Target
94a	I-405 N (from nb)
92b	Bake Pkwy, same as 92a
92a	Lake Forest Dr, Laguna Hills, E 🅰 Chevron/24hr, Shell/dsl 🍴 Buffalo Wild Wings, Del Taco, Jack-in-the-Box, McDonald's, Panera Bread, Pizza Hut, RoundTable Pizza, Subway, Taco Bell, The Hat 🏨 Best Value Inn, Holiday Inn, Irvine Suites Hotel, Quality Inn 🅾 America's Tire, Buick/GMC, Chrysler/Dodge/Jeep, Ford/Lincoln, Honda, Hyundai, Mazda, Nissan, Subaru, Volvo, VW, W 🅰 Chevron/24hr, Shell 🍴 Carl's Jr, Coco's, Del Taco, McDonald's, Quiznos, Subway 🏨 Comfort Inn, Courtyard 🅾 AZ Leather, Best Buy, BMW/Mini
91	El Toro Rd, E 🅰 Chevron/dsl, USA 🍴 Arby's, Asia Buffet, Baskin-Robbins, Cafe Rio, Chipotle Mexican, Chronic Tacos, Denny's, El Pollo Loco, Flamebroiler, Fuddrucker's, Hooters, Jack-in-the-Box, Lucille's BBQ, McDonald's, Mr Wok, Panda Express, PeiWei Asian, Quiznos, Scarantino's Rest., Sizzler, Starbucks, Subway, Tommy's Burgers, Wendy's 🅾 99¢ Store, CVS Drug, Firestone/auto, Home Depot, PetCo, Petsmart, Ralph's Foods, Ross, Staples, W 🅰 76/Circle K, Chevron/dsl/24hr, Shell/24hr 🍴 BJ's Rest., Carrow's, El Torito, In-N-Out, King's Fishhouse, LoneStar Steaks, Nami Seafood, Starbucks, Woody's Diner 🏨 Laguna Hills Lodge 🅾 Ⓗ CVS Drug, Firestone/auto, JC Penney, Just Tires, Macy's, mall, Marshall's, Sears/auto, Trader Joe's, USPO, Walgreens
90	Alicia Pkwy, Mission Viejo, E 🍴 Del Taco, Denny's, Subway 🅾 $Tree, Albertson's, America's Tire, CVS Drug, O'Reilly Parts, Target, W 🅰 76/dsl, Chevron 🍴 Carl's Jr, It's a Grind, Togo's, Wendy's 🅾 AAA, BigLots, Mazda, vet
89	La Paz Rd, Mission Viejo, E 🅰 Arco/24hr, Shell 🍴 Chronic Tacos, Pizza Hut, Starbucks, Taco Bell, TK Burgers 🅾 Albertson's/Sav-On, vet, W 🅰 76 🍴 Claim Jumper Rest., DQ, Flamingos Mexican, Hot Off the Grill, Jack-in-the-Box, Krispy Kreme, La Salsa, McDonald's, Outback Steaks, Spasso's Italian, Starbucks, Subway, Villa Roma, Wienerschnitzel, Yamato Japanese 🏨 Hills Hotel 🅾 7-11, Best Buy, Goodyear/auto, Jo-Ann Fabrics, PetCo, to Laguna Niguel Pk, URGENT CARE
87	Oso Pkwy, Pacific Park Dr, E 🅰 76/dsl/repair, Chevron/repair 🍴 Carl's Jr, Starbucks, Subway 🏨 Fairfield Inn 🅾 golf
86	Crown Valley Pkwy, E 🅰 76, Arco, Chevron 🍴 Buffalo Wild Wings, Chili's, Coco's, Islands Grill 🅾 Ⓗ, Macy's, mall, vet, W 🅰 Chevron/dsl 🅾 Aamco, Costco/gas

📷 = gas 🍴 = food 🛏 = lodging ▣ = other Ⓡ = rest stop   Copyright 2015 - the Next EXIT ®

Exit #	Services
↖N	**INTERSTATE 5 Cont'd**
85b	Avery Pkwy, **E** 📷 Shell/dsl 🍴 Alberto's Mexican, Carrow's, Del Taco, Jack-in-the-Box, Mongolian BBQ, Papa John's, Starbucks, Subway ▣ Acura, America's Tire/auto, Audi/Infiniti, Jaguar/Land Rover, Lexus, Parts+, World Mkt, **W** 📷 Chevron, Shell/dsl/24hr 🍴 A's Burgers, Carl's Jr, In-N-Out 🛏 Best Value Laguna Inn ▣ Aamco, Cadillac/GMC, Costco/gas, Firestone/auto, Hyundai, Mercedes
85a	CA 73 N (toll)
83	Junipero Serra Rd, to San Juan Capistrano, **W** 📷 Shell, Spirit/service/dsl
82	CA 74, Ortego Hwy, **E** 📷 76, Chevron/dsl, Shell 🍴 Bad to the Bone BBQ, Ballpark Pizza, Bravo Burgers, Denny's, Subway 🛏 Best Western ▣ vet, **W** 📷 Chevron/24hr 🍴 Arby's, Carl's Jr, Del Taco, Jack-in-the-Box, KFC, Marie Callender's, McDonald's, Oeeshi Japanese, Pedro's Tacos, Quiznos, RoundTable Pizza, Ruby's Cafe, Starbucks, Taco Bell 🛏 Cedar Creek Inn, Mission Inn ▣ Capistrano Trading Post, GNC, Marshall's, Ralph's Foods, Ross, San Juan Capistrano Mission, TrueValue
81	Camino Capistrano, **E** ▣ VW, **W on Capistrano** 📷 Chevron 🍴 El Adobe Rest., El Pollo Loco, Eng's Chinese, KFC, Papa John's, Pizza Hut, Ricardo's Mexican, Starbucks ▣ Aamco, BigLots, CHP, Costco, Ford, Goodyear/auto, Honda, KIA, Nissan, PetCo, Petsmart, Radio Shack, Rite Aid, Ross, San Juan Capistrano SP (1mi), Staples, Toyota/Scion, URGENT CARE, Vons Foods
79	CA 1, Pacific Coast Hwy, Capistrano Bch, Capistrano, **W 1 mi** 📷 76/dsl, Arco/24hr 🍴 A's Burgers, Carl's Jr, Del Taco, Denny's, Jack-in-the-Box, JuiceSpot, McDonald's, Rib Joint, Subway 🛏 DoubleTree, Harbor Inn, Holiday Inn Express ▣ Ralph's Foods, Rite Aid, USPO, vet
78	Camino de Estrella, San Clemente, **E** 📷 76/dsl 🍴 Carl's Jr, China Well, Coldstone, Crispins, Flame Broiler, Jamba Juice, Melting Pot, Papa Murphy's, RoundTable Pizza, Rubio's, Starbucks, Subway, Wahoo's Fish Taco ▣ H, AT&T, CVS Drug, Ralph's Foods, Stater Bros Foods, Trader Joe's, vet, **W** 📷 Arco/dsl 🍴 Las Golondrinas ▣ BigLots, O'Reilly Parts, Sears Essentials
77	Ave Vista Hermosa
76	Ave Pico, **E** 📷 Mobil 🍴 Buono Pizza, Carrow's, Golden Spoon, Juice it Up, McDonald's, Panda Express ▣ Albertson's/Sav-On, GNC, **W** 📷 Chevron, Shell/dsl 🍴 Bad to the Bone BBQ, BurgerStop, Del Taco, Denny's/24hr, Pick-up-Stix, Pizza Hut, Stuft Pizza, Subway 🛏 Holiday Inn Express ▣ 99¢ Store, Staples, tires/repair, Tuesday Morning, USPO, vet
75	Ave Palizada, Ave Presidio, **W** 📷 Valero 🍴 Baskin-Robbins, Coffee Bean, Mr. Pete's Burgers, Sonny's Pizza, Starbucks, Subway, Taka-O Japanese 🛏 Holiday Inn ▣ 7-11, TrueValue
74	El Camino Real, **E** 📷 Chevron/dsl/24hr 🍴 El Mariachi Rest., Pipes Cafe 🛏 Budget Lodge, San Clemente Inn, Tradewinds Motel ▣ same as 75, vet, **W** 📷 76/dsl, Exxon 🍴 FatBurger, KFC, Pizza Hut/Taco Bell, Subway, Taste Of China, Tommy's Rest./24hr ▣ 7-11, O'Reilly Parts, Radio Shack, Ralph's Foods
73	Ave Calafia, Ave Magdalena, **E** 📷 76/dsl, Shell 🍴 Jack-in-the-Box, Molly Bloom's Cafe, Pedro's Tacos, Sugar Shack Cafe 🛏 Budget Inn, Calafia Beach Motel, C-Vu Inn, Hampton Inn, LaVista Inn, San Clemente Motel, Travelodge ▣ 7-11, repair, San-O Tire, **W** to San Clemente SP
72	Cristianitos Ave, **E** 🍴 Café Del Sol, Carl's Jr. 🛏 Carmelo

72	Continued Motel, Comfort Suites ▣ San Mateo RV Park/dump, **W** ▣ to San Clemente SP
71	Basilone Rd, **W** ▣ San Onofre St Beach
67mm	**weigh sta both lanes**
66mm	viewpoint sb
62	Las Pulgas Rd
59mm	**Aliso Creek** Ⓡ **both lanes, full ♿ facilities, litter barrels, pet-walk, ℂ, 🚰, RV dump, vending**
54c	Oceanside Harbor Dr, **W** 📷 Chevron, Mobil 🍴 Burger King (1mi), Del Taco, Denny's/24hr 🛏 GuestHouse Inn, Holiday Inn Express, Sandman Hotel, The Bridge Motel, Travelodge ▣ to Camp Pendleton
54b	Hill St (from sb), to Oceanside, **W** 📷 Chevron, Mobil 🍴 Carrow's Rest., Denny's 🛏 GuestHouse Inn, Holiday Inn Express, Travelodge
54a	CA 76 E, Coast Hwy
53	Mission Ave, Oceanside, **E** 📷 Arco/24hr, Mobil/dsl 🍴 Alberto's Mexican, Arby's, Armando's Tacos, Burger King, China Star, Jack-in-the-Box, KFC, McDonald's, Mission Donuts 🛏 Quality Inn, Ramada ▣ CarQuest, NAPA, PepBoys, Valu+ Foods, **W** 🍴 El Pollo Loco, Panda Express, Subway, Wendy's ▣ 99¢ Store, Office Depot, Radio Shack
52	Oceanside Blvd, **E** 🍴 Alberto's Mexican, Domino's, IHOP, McDonald's, Papa John's, Pizza Hut, Starbucks, Subway, Taco Bell, Wienerschnitzel ▣ Boney's Foods, CHP, CVS Drug, Ralph's Foods, **W** 📷 Oceanside/dsl 🛏 Best Western Oceanside
51c	Cassidy St (from sb), **W** 📷 7-11, 76, Mobil ▣ H
51b	CA 78, Vista Way, Escondido, **E** 📷 76/Circle K, Chevron/dsl/24hr, Shell 🍴 Applebee's, Boston Mkt, Burger King, Carl's Jr, Chili's, ChuckECheese's, Fuddrucker's, Golden Taipei, Hooters, Macaroni Grill, McDonald's, Mimi's Café, Olive Garden, Outback Steaks, QuikWok, Rubio's, Starbucks, Subway, Wendy's 🛏 Holiday Inn Express ▣ $Tree, Best Buy, CVS Drug, Firestone, Henry's Mkt, JC Penney, Macy's, Marshall's, Michael's, PetCo, Sears/auto, Staples, Stater Bros Foods, Target, Tuesday Morning, Vons Foods, Walmart/auto, World Mkt, **W** 🍴 Hunter Steaks
51a	Las Flores Dr
50	Elm Ave, Carlsbad Village Dr, **E** 📷 Shell/24hr 🍴 Lotus Thai Bistro, **W** 📷 Carlsbad/dsl/LP, Valero 🍴 Al's Cafe, Carl's Jr, Denny's/24hr, Jack-in-the-Box, KFC/Taco Bell, Mikko Japanese 🛏 Extended Stay America, Motel 6 ▣ Albertson's, TrueValue
49	Tamarack Ave, **E** 📷 76/dsl, Chevron/24hr 🍴 Village Kitchen 🛏 Comfort Inn, Rodeway Inn, Travel Inn ▣ GNC, Rite Aid, Vons Foods, **W** 📷 Arco 🍴 Hensley's Grill
48	Cannon Rd, Car Country Carlsbad, **E** ▣ Acura, Buick, Cadillac/Chevrolet, Ford, Honda, Lexus, Lincoln, Mazda, Mercedes, Toyota, VW
47	Carlsbad Blvd, Palomar Airport Rd, **E** 📷 7-11, Chevron, Mobil/dsl 🍴 BJ's Rest., Carl's Jr, Islands Burgers, Panda Express, Pat&Oscar's Rest., PF Chang's, Strauss Brewery Rest., Subway, Taco Bell, TGIFriday's 🛏 Holiday Inn, Motel 6 ▣ Carlsbad Ranch/Flower Fields, Chrysler/Dodge/Jeep, Costco/gas, Ford, outlet mall, **W** 📷 Shell/dsl 🍴 ClaimJumper Rest., Marie Callender's, McDonald's 🛏 Hilton Garden ▣ S Carlsbad St Bch
45	Poinsettia Lane, **W** 📷 Chevron 🍴 Benihana, El Pollo Loco, Golden Spoon, Jack-in-the-Box, Pick-Up Stix, Starbucks, Subway 🛏 La Quinta, Motel 6, Quality Inn, Ramada ▣ Ace Hardware, Porsche/Volvo, Ralph's Foods, Rite Aid

Sidebar labels: CA / CAPISTRANO / SAN CLEMENTE / OCEANSIDE / CARLSBAD

INTERSTATE 5 Cont'd

Exit #	Services
44	La Costa Ave, **E** vista point, **W** 🅟 Chevron/dsl
43	Leucadia Blvd, **E** 🏠 Howard Johnson, **W** 🅟 Shell/service
41b	Encinitas Blvd, **E** 🅟 Chevron/dsl, O'Brien Sta., Valero 🍴 Coco's Cafe, Del Taco, Gusto Trattoria, HoneyBaked Ham, Oggi's Pizza 🅞 CVS Drug, NAPA, to Quail Botanical Gardens, vet, **W** 🅟 Shell 🍴 Denny's, Little Caesar's, Subway, Wendy's 🏠 Best Western/rest., Days Inn 🅞 PetCo
41a	Santa Fe Dr, to Encinitas, **E** 🅟 Shell 🍴 Carl's Jr, El Nopalito, Papa Toni's Pizza 🅞 7-11, **W** 🍴 Today's Pizza 🅞 🅷, Rite Aid, vet, Vons Foods
40	Birmingham Dr, **E** 🅟 Chevron, Valero 🍴 Mandarin City 🏠 Holiday Inn Express, **W** 🅟 Arco/24hr
39mm	viewpoint sb
39	Manchester Ave, **E** 🅟 76 🅞 to MiraCosta College
37	Lomas Santa Fe Dr, Solana Bch, **E** 🍴 Baskin-Robbins, Pizza Nova, Samurai Rest., Starbucks 🅞 Ross, Vons Foods, We-R-Fabrics, **W** 🅟 Mobil 🍴 Carl's Jr, Golden Spoon, Jamba Juice, Panda Express, Panera Bread, RoundTable Pizza, Starbucks, Togo's 🅞 CVS Drug, Discount Tire, GNC, Henry's Foods, Marshall's, Staples
36	Via de La Valle, Del Mar, **E** 🅟 Chevron, Mobil 🍴 Chevy's Mexican, Coffee Bean, McDonald's, Milton's Deli, Pappachino's Italian, Paradise Grille, Pasta Pronto, Pick-Up Stix, Taste of Thai 🅞 Albertson's/SavOn, PetCo, Radio Shack, **W** 🅟 Arco/24hr, Shell/dsl 🍴 Denny's, FishMkt Rest., Red Tracton's Rest. 🏠 Hilton 🅞 racetrack
34	Del Mar Heights Rd, **E** 🅟 Shell/dsl, **W** 🅟 7-11 🍴 Elijah's Rest., Jack-in-the-Box, Mexican Grill 🅞 CVS Drug, vet, Vons Foods
33	Carmel Mtn Rd, **E** 🅟 Arco, Shell/repair 🍴 Taco Bell, Tio Leo's Mexican 🏠 DoubleTree Hotel, Hampton Inn, Marriott
32	CA 56 E, Carmel Valley Rd
31	I-805 (from sb)
30	Sorrento Valley Rd
29	Genesee Ave, **E** 🅞 🅷
28b	La Jolla Village Dr, **E** 🍴 Italian Bistro 🏠 Embassy Suites, Hyatt, Marriott 🅞 🅷, to LDS Temple, **W** 🅟 Mobil/dsl 🍴 BJ's Grill, CA Pizza Kitchen, Chipotle Mexican, Dominos, El Torito, Elijah's Deli, Flame Broiler, Islands Burgers, Mrs Gooch's, Pick-Up Stix, RockBottom Café, Rubio's, TGIFriday's 🏠 Sheraton 🅞 🅷, AT&T, Best Buy, CVS Drug, Marshall's, PetsMart, Radio Shack, Ralph's Foods, Ross, Staples, Trader Joe's, Whole Foods Mkt
28a	Nobel Dr (from nb), **E** 🏠 Hyatt 🅞 LDS Temple, **W** same as 28b
27	Gilman Dr, La Jolla Colony Dr
26b	CA 52 E
26a	La Jolla Rd (from nb)
23b	CA 274, Balboa Ave, **E 1 mi** 🅟 Shell 🍴 Del Taco 🅞 Albertson's, **W** 🅟 7-11, 76/repair, Mobil 🍴 In-N-Out, McDonald's, Rubio's, Wienerschnitzel 🏠 Days Inn, Holiday Inn Express, Mission Bay Inn, San Diego Motel 🅞 🅷, Discount Tire, Express Tire, Ford, Mission Bay Pk, Nissan, Toyota/Scion
23a	Grand Ave, Garnet Ave, same as 23b
22	Clairemont Dr, Mission Bay Dr, **E** 🅟 Arco, Shell 🏠 Best Western 🅞 Chevrolet/VW, **W** to Sea World Dr
21	Sea World Dr, Tecolote Dr, **E** 🅟 Shell 🏠 Seaside Inn 🅞 Aamco, CarQuest, Circle K, PetCo, **W** 🏠 Hilton 🅞 Old Town SP, Seaworld

20	I-8, W to Nimitz Blvd, E to El Centro, CA 209 S (from sb), to Rosecrans St
19	Old Town Ave, **E** 🅟 Arco/24hr, Shell 🏠 Courtyard, La Quinta
18b	Washington St, **E** 🏠 Comfort Inn
18a	Pacific Hwy Viaduct, Kettner St
17b	India St, Front St, Sassafras St, **E** 🅟 Mobil, Rte 66 Gas, **W** 🅞 🅂, civic ctr
17a	Hawthorn St, Front St, **W** 🅟 Exxon/dsl 🏠 Holiday Inn, Motel 6, Radisson 🅞 🅷
16b	6th Ave, downtown
16a	CA 163 N, 10th St, **E** 🅞 AeroSpace Museum, **W** 🅟 Shell 🍴 Del Taco, Jack-in-the-Box, McDonald's 🏠 Days Inn, Downtown Lodge, El Cortez Motel, Holiday Inn, Marriott 🅞 🅷
15c b	CA 94 E (from nb), Pershing Dr, B St, civic ctr
15a	CA 94 E, J St, Imperial Ave (from sb),
14b	Cesar Chavez Pkwy
14a	CA 75, to Coronado, **W toll rd to Coronado**
13b	National Ave SD, 28th St, **E** 🍴 Little Caesar's, Starbucks, Subway 🅞 AutoZone, **W** 🅟 Shell 🍴 Burger King, Del Taco, El Pollo Loco
13a	CA 15 N, to Riverside
12	Main St, National City
11b	8th St, National City, **E** 🅟 Arco, Shell/24hr 🍴 Jack-in-the-Box 🏠 Holiday Inn, Howard Johnson, Ramada Inn, Super 8, Value Inn, **W** 🅟 Chevron/dsl
11a	Harbor Dr, Civic Center Dr
10	Bay Marina, 24th St, Mile of Cars Way, **E 1/2 mi** 🍴 Denny's, In-N-Out
9	CA 54 E
8b	E St, Chula Vista, **E** 🏠 Motel 6, **W** 🍴 Anthony's Fish Grotto 🏠 GoodNite Inn
8a	H St
7b	J St (from sb)
7a	L St, **E** 🅟 7-11, 76, Shell/dsl 🍴 Mandarin Chinese 🏠 Best Western 🅞 AutoZone, NAPA, Office Depot, Parts+
6	Palomar St, **E** 🅟 Arco 🍴 China King, Del Taco, DQ, HomeTown Buffet, KFC, Little Caesar's, McDonald's, Subway 🏠 Palomar Inn 🅞 7-11, Costco/gas, **E on Broadway** 🍴 Food-4Less, Jack-in-the-Box, KFC, Michael's, Office Depot, Panda Express, Quizno's, Ross, Target, Walmart, Yoshinoya
5b	Main St, to Imperial Beach, **E** 🅟 Arco 🏠 AZ Chinese
5a	CA 75 (from sb), Palm Ave, to Imperial Beach, **E** 🅟 Arco 🍴 Armando's Mexican, Papa John's, Wahshing Chinese 🅞 7-11, Discount Tire, Soto's Transmissions, **W** 🅟 7-11, Arco, Shell/repair/24hr, Thrifty 🍴 Boll Weevil Diner, Burger King, Carl's Jr, Carrow's, Coldstone Creamery, El Chile Mexican, Los Pancho's Tacos, McDonald's, Rally's, Red Hawk Steaks, Roberto's Mexican, Subway, Taco Bell, Wienerschnitzel 🏠

🅖 = gas 🍴 = food 🛏 = lodging 🅞 = other 🆁🆂 = rest stop   Copyright 2015 - the Next EXIT ®

CA

SAN YSIDRO

🔼N INTERSTATE 5 Cont'd

Exit #	Services
5a	Continued
	Super 8, Travelodge 🅞 99¢ Store, AutoZone, CVS Drug, Home Depot, Jiffy Lube, Von's Foods
4	Coronado Ave (from sb), **E** 🅖 Chevron/service, Shell/service 🍴 Denny's, Taco Bell 🛏 EZ 8 Motel 🅞 7-11, **W** 🅖 Shell/dsl 🛏 Days Inn 🅞 to Border Field SP
3	CA 905, Tocayo Ave, **W** 🅖 7-11
2	Dairy Mart Rd, **E** 🅖 Arco/24hr, Circle K 🍴 Burger King, Carl's Jr, Coco's, KFC, McDonald's, Roberto's Mexican 🛏 Americana Inn, Best Value, Super 8, Valli-Hi Motel 🅞 CarQuest, Pacifica RV Resort, Radio Shack
1b	Via de San Ysidro, **W** 🅖 Chevron, Mobil/dsl 🍴 Denny's 🛏 Knights/RV park, Motel 6, Travelodge
1a	I-805 N (from nb), Camino de la Plaza (from sb), **E** 🍴 Burger King, El Pollo Loco, Jack-in-the-Box, KFC, McDonald's, Subway 🛏 Holiday Motel 🅞 AutoZone, **W** 🍴 Achiato Mexican, IHOP, Iron Wok, McDonald's, Starbucks, Sunrise Buffet 🅞 $Tree, Baja Duty-Free, border parking, factory outlet, K-Mart, Marshall's, Old Navy, Ross, TJ Maxx
0	US/Mexico Border, California state line, customs, **I-5 begins/ends.**

🔼E INTERSTATE 8

YUMA

Exit #	Services
172.5mm	California/Arizona state line, Colorado River, Pacific/Mountain time zone
172	4th Ave, Yuma, **N** 🅞 Paradise Casino, **S** 🅖 Chevron, Circle K/dsl 🍴 Jack-in-the-Box, Yuma Landing Rest. 🛏 Best Western, Hilton Garden 🅞 to Yuma SP
170	Winterhaven Dr, **S** Rivers Edge RV Park
166	CA 186, Algodones Rd, Andrade, **S** Cocopah RV Resort/golf, Quechan Hotel/Casino, to Mexico
165mm	**CA Insp/weigh sta**
164	Sidewinder Rd, **N** 🅞 st patrol, **S** 🅖 Shell/LP/dsl 🅞 Pilot Knob RV Park
159	CA 34, Ogilby Rd, to Blythe
156	Grays Well Rd, **N** Imperial Dunes RA
155mm	🆁🆂 **both lanes (exits left), full facilities, litter barrels, petwalk,** 🚻
151	Gordons Well
146	Brock Research Ctr Rd
143	CA 98, to Calexico, Midway Well
131	CA 115, VanDerLinden Rd, to Holtville, **N 5 mi** 🅞 food, gas, lodging, RV camping
128	Bonds Corner Rd
125	CA 7 S, Orchard Rd, Holtville, **N 4 mi** 🅞 food, gas/dsl
120	Bowker Rd
118b a	CA 111, to Calexico, **N** 🅞 Country Life RV Park
116	Dogwood Rd, **S** 🅖 Arco/dsl 🍴 Burger King, Carino's, Chili's, ChuckeCheese, Denny's, Famous Dave's BBQ, Fortune Garden, Jack-in-the-Box, Olive Garden, Sombrero Mexican, Starbucks, Subway 🛏 Fairfield Inn, TownePlace Suites 🅞 $Tree, 99c, Americas Tire, Best Buy, Dillard's, JC Penney, Kohl's, Macy's, mall, Marshall's, Michael's, PetCo, Ross, Sears/auto, Staples
115	CA 86, 4th St, El Centro, **N** 🅖 7-11/dsl, Arco/dsl, Chevron/dsl, FillCo/dsl, Shell/dsl 🍴 Carl's Jr, Exotic Thai, Jack-in-the-Box, Las Palmitas Tacos, Lucky Chinese, McDonald's 🛏 Holiday Inn Express, Motel 6 🅞 Family$, O'Reilly Parts, U-Haul, **S** 🅖

EL CENTRO

Exit #	Services
115	Continued
	7-11/Subway, Mobil/dsl/scales 🍴 IHOP, In-N-Out, Johnny's Burritos, Panda Express, Taco Bell 🛏 Best Western, Comfort Inn, Rodeway Inn 🅞 AutoZone, Buick/Chevrolet/GMC/Cadillac, Desert Trails RV Park, Home Depot, Honda, Hyundai, Lucky Foods
114	Imperial Ave, El Centro, **N** 🅖 7-11/dsl, Arco, Chevron/dsl, Chevron/dsl, USA/dsl 🍴 Applebee's, Broken Yolk Cafe, Burger King, Carl's Jr, Carrow's, Church's, Coldstone, Del Taco, Denny's, Domino's, El Pollo Loco, Farmer Boys, Golden Corral, Jack-in-the-Box, Jack-in-the-Box, KFC, La Resaca, Little Caesars, McDonald's, Mexicali Grill, Papa John's, Pizza Hut, Rally's, Sizzler, Sonic, Starbucks, Subway, Taco Bell, Tastee-Freez Burgers, Wendy's 🛏 Clarion, Crown Motel, Super 8, SuperStar Inn, Vacation Inn/RV Park, Value Inn 🅞 🏥, $General Mkt, $Tree, 99¢ Store, Chrysler/Dodge/Jeep, Costco/gas, Discount Tire, Food4Less, Ford, Goodyear/auto, Jo-Ann, K-Mart, Lowe's, Nissan, O'Reilly Parts, PepBoys, Radio Shack, Rite Aid, st patrol, Target, Toyota/Scion, Verizon, Von's Foods, Walgreens, Walmart
111	Forrester Rd, to Westmorland
108mm	Sunbeam 🆁🆂 **both lanes, full** 🛏 **facilities, litter barrels, petwalk,** 🚻, 🐾, **RV dump,**
107	Drew Rd, Seeley, **N** 🅞 Sunbeam RV Park, to Sunbeam Lake, **S** 🅞 Rio Bend RV Park
101	Dunaway Rd, Imperial Valley, **N** st prison, elev 0 ft
89	Imperial Hwy, CA 98, Ocotillo, **N** 🅞 Red Feathers Mkt/Cafe, RV camping, USPO, **S** 🅖 Chevron/dsl 🅞 Desert Museum
87	CA 98 (from eb), to Calexico
81mm	**eb, runaway truck ramp**
80	Mountain Springs Rd
77	In-ko-pah Park Rd, **N** 🚻, towing
75mm	**brake insp area eb,** 🚻
73	Jacumba, **S** 🅖 Chevron/dsl, Shell/Subway/dsl/24hr 🅞 RV camping
65	CA 94, Boulevard, to Campo, **S** 🅖 MtnTop/dsl 🛏 Back Country Inn 🅞 auto repair, to McCain Valley RA (7mi), USPO
63mm	elev 4140 ft, Tecate Divide
62mm	Crestwood Summit, elev 4190 ft
61	Crestwood Rd, Live Oak Springs, **S** 🅖 Golden Acorn Trkstp/casino/dsl 🛏 Live Oak Sprs Country Inn 🅞 info
54	Kitchen Creek Rd, Cameron Station, **S** food, RV camping
51	rd 1, Buckman Spgs Rd, to Lake Morena, 🆁🆂 **both lanes, full** 🛏 **facilities, litter barrels, petwalk,** 🚻🐾, **RV dump S** food, gas/dsl/LP, lodging, Lake Morena CP (7mi), Potrero CP (19mi), RV camping
48	**insp sta, wb**
47	rd 1, Sunrise Hwy, Laguna Summit, elev 4055 ft, **N** to Laguna Mtn RA
45	Pine Valley, Julian, **N** 🍴 Calvin's Rest., Frosty Burger, Major's Diner 🛏 Pine Valley Inn 🅞 city park, Mtn Mkt, Pine Valley/gas, to Cuyamaca Rancho SP, USPO, vet
44mm	Pine Valley Creek
42mm	elev 4000 ft
40	CA 79, Japatul Rd, Descanso, **N** 🍴 Descanso Rest. 🅞 to Cuyamaca Rancho SP
37mm	elev 3000 ft, vista point eb
36	E Willows, **N** Alpine Sprs RV Park, casino, Viejas Indian Res
33	W Willows Rd, to Alpine, **N** Alpine Sprs RV Park, casino, same as 36, Viejas Outlets/famous brands, **S** ranger sta
31mm	elev 2000 ft

⬆Ⓔ INTERSTATE 8 Cont'd

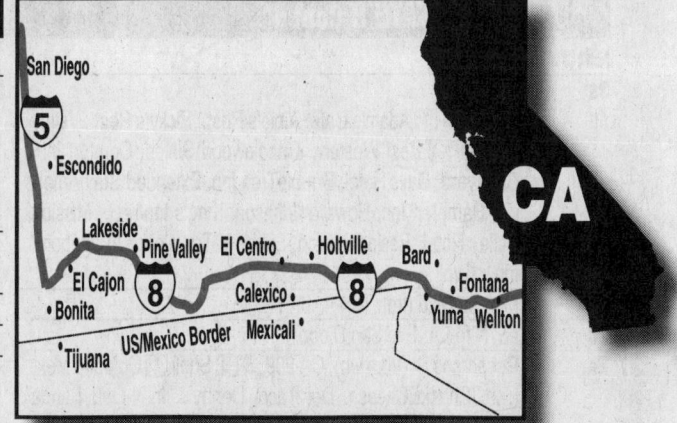

Exit #	Services
30	Tavern Rd, to Alpine, N ⛽ Chevron/dsl, Shell/dsl, S ⛽ 76/Circle K 🍴 American Grill, Carl's Jr, Greek Village Grill, La Carreta, Little Caesars, Mananas Mexican, Mediterraneo Grill, Panda Machi Chinese, Subway 🛏 Ayre's Lodge Ⓞ Ace Hardware, city park, CVS Drug, Farmers Mkt, Rite Aid
27	Dunbar Lane, Harbison Canyon, N Ⓞ Flinn Sprgs CP, RV camping
25mm	elev 1000 ft
24mm	⛽
23	Lake Jennings Pk Rd, Lakeside, N ⛽ Arco/Jack-in-the-Box/dsl/24hr, to Lake Jennings CP Ⓞ RV camping, S ⛽ 7-11 🍴 Burger King, Karla's Mexican, Marechiaro's Pizza
22	Los Coches Rd, Lakeside, N ⛽ 7-11, Eagle/dsl/LP, East County Gas 🍴 Albert's Mexican, Giant Pizza, Laposta Mexican Ⓞ RV camping/dump, S ⛽ Shell/dsl 🍴 Denny's, Giant NY Pizza, McDonald's, Panda Express, Subway, Taco Bell Ⓞ Radio Shack, Vons Foods, Walmart
20b	Greenfield Dr, to Crest, N ⛽ Chevron/dsl, Sky Fuel/dsl 🍴 Jack-in-the-Box, Marieta's Mexican, McDonald's, Panchos Tacos, Subway Ⓞ 7-11, 99¢ Store, Albertson's, auto repair, AutoZone, Ford, RV camping, st patrol, URGENT CARE, vet, S ⛽ Mobil/dsl/LP
20a	E Main St (from wb, no EZ return), N 🛏 Budget Inn Ⓞ Ford, repair, Vacationer RV Park, S ⛽ Arco Ⓞ Cadillac
19	2nd St, CA 54, El Cajon, N ⛽ 76/dsl, Arco, Chevron/dsl 🍴 Marechio's Italian, Pancake House Ⓞ CVS Drug, Meineke, USPO, Vons Foods, Walgreens, S ⛽ Gas Depot, Golden State/dsl, Shell 🍴 Arby's, Baskin-Robbins, Burger King, Carl's Jr, Estrada's Mexican, IHOP, Jack-in-the-Box, KFC, Little Caesar's, McDonald's, Popeye's, Subway, Taco Bell, Taco Shop, Wings n Things 🛏 Best Value Inn Ⓞ $Tree, 7-11, CarQuest, Firestone/auto, Jiffy Lube, PepBoys, PetCo, Radio Shack, Sprouts Mkt, Walgreens, Walmart Mkt
18	Mollison Ave, El Cajon, N ⛽ Chevron 🍴 Denny's 🛏 Best Western, Days Inn, S ⛽ Arco, QuickTrip/dsl 🍴 Los Garcia's 🛏 EconoLodge
17c	Magnolia Ave, CA 67 (from wb), to Santee, N ⛽ Arco 🍴 Del Taco, El Pollo Loco, Jack-in-the-Box, Jersey Mike's, Panda Express, Starbucks Ⓞ AT&T, Food4Less, Target, S ⛽ Shell/service 🍴 New East Buffet, Panda Express, Perry's Cafe, Rubio's 🛏 Motel 6, Super 8 Ⓞ Nudo's Drug, Ross
17b	CA 67 (from eb), same as 17 a&c
17a	Johnson Ave (from eb), N 🍴 Applebee's, Boston Mkt, Burger King, Carl's Jr, Coco's, Five Guys, Hacienda Mexican, Jamba Juice, KFC, Little Caesar's, LJ Silver, McDonald's, New Century Buffet, On the Border, O's American Kitchen, Rubio's, Ruby's Diner, Subway Ⓞ $Tree, Best Buy, CVS Drug, Dick's, Goodyear/auto, Home Depot, Honda, JC Penney, Lexus, Macy's, mall, Marshall's, Mazda, Office Depot, PetsMart, Sears/auto, Subaru, Toyota/Scion, Walmart, S Ⓞ Aamco, KIA, vet
16	Main St, N ⛽ Arco 🍴 Denny's, Sombrero Mexican 🛏 Relax Inn Ⓞ 7-11, S ⛽ Chevron/dsl, Super Star Ⓞ brakes/transmissions, Nissan
15	El Cajon Blvd (from eb), N 🛏 Quality Inn, S ⛽ 76/dsl 🍴 Wrangler BBQ Ⓞ BMW
14c	Severin Dr, Fuerte Dr (from wb), N ⛽ USA/dsl 🍴 Anthony's Fish Grotto, Charcoal House Rest., La Casa Blanca 🛏 Holiday Inn Express, S 🍴 Brigantine Seafood Rest.
14b a	CA 125, to CA 94

13b	Jackson Dr, Grossmont Blvd, N ⛽ Chevron 🍴 Arby's, BJ's Rest., Casa de Pico, Chili's, ChuckeCheese, ClaimJumper, Fuddrucker's, Olive Garden, Panera Bread, Red Lobster, Shakey's Pizza, Starbucks Ⓞ 🏥, $Tree, Best Buy, CVS Drug, Macy's, mall, O'Reilly Parts, Staples, Target, USPO, Verizon, vet, Walmart, World Mkt, S ⛽ 76 🍴 Honeybaked Ham, Jack-in-the-Box Ⓞ Discount Tire, Ford, Hyundai, Ross, Walmart Mkt
13a	Spring St (from eb), El Cajon Blvd (from wb), S 🍴 El Pollo Loco, Starbucks, Subway 🛏 Hitching Post Ⓞ 99¢ Store, AutoZone
12	Fletcher Pkwy, to La Mesa, N ⛽ Shell/dsl 🍴 Carl's Jr, Chipotle Mexican, McDonald's, Pick Up Stix 🛏 Heritage Inn Ⓞ 7-11, Costco, S 🍴 El Torito, Starbucks, Subway 🛏 Motel 6 Ⓞ 99¢ Store, Chevrolet, San Diego RV Resort
11	70th St, Lake Murray Blvd, N ⛽ Shell/dsl 🍴 Subway, S ⛽ Shell/7-11/dsl 🍴 Aiken's Deli, Denny's, Marie Callender's Ⓞ 🏥, auto repair, URGENT CARE
10	College Ave, N ⛽ Chevron/dsl Ⓞ Windmill Farms Mkt, S Ⓞ 🏥, to SDSU
9	Waring Rd, N 🛏 Days Inn, Rodeway Inn
8	Fairmount Ave (7 from eb), to Mission Gorge Rd, N ⛽ 7-11, Mobil, Sky/dsl, USA/dsl 🍴 Arby's, Black Angus, Carl's Jr, Chili's, Coco's, El Pollo Loco, Filippi's Pizza, Jack-in-the-Box, Jamba Juice, Jersey Mike's, McDonald's, Roberto's Tacos, Rubio's, Sombrero Mexican, Starbucks, Subway, Szechuan Chinese, Togo's, Wendy's 🛏 Motel 6 Ⓞ 🏥, AutoZone, CVS Drug, Discount Tire, Home Depot, Honda, Radio Shack, Rite Aid, Toyota/Scion, Tuesday Morning, Vons Foods
7b a	I-15 N, CA 15 S, to 40th St
6b	I-805, N to LA, S to Chula Vista
6a	Texas St, Qualcomm Way, N 🍴 Dave&Buster's, same as 5
5	Mission Ctr Rd, N ⛽ Chevron 🍴 Broken Yolk Cafe, Chipotle Mexican, Corner Cafe, El Pollo Loco, Fuddrucker's, Gordon Biersch Rest., Habit Burger, Hooters, In-N-Out, King's Fishouse, Lazy Dog Rest., Mimi's Cafe, On The Border, Outback Steaks, Panda Express, Peiwei Asian, Pick-Up Stix, Robek Juice, Rubio's, Sammy's Woodfired Pizza, Starbucks, Subway, Taco Bell, Tilted Kilt 🛏 Marriott, Sheraton Ⓞ AT&T, Best Buy, Chevrolet, Lincoln, Macy's, mall, Marshall's, Michael's, Nordstrom Rack, Old Navy, Staples, Target, Trader Joe's, S ⛽ Arco 🍴 Benihana, Denny's, Fuji Japanese, Mission Valley Cafe, Wendy's 🛏 Comfort Suites, Hilton, La Quinta, Sheraton Ⓞ Buick/GMC/Cadillac, Chrysler/Dodge/Jeep, Mazda
4c b	CA 163, Cabrillo Frwy, S Ⓞ to downtown, zoo
4a	Hotel Circle Dr (from eb), CA 163 (from wb)
3a	Hotel Circle, Taylor St, N 🍴 Hunter Steaks 🛏 Comfort Suites, Crowne Plaza, Handlery Hotel, Motel 6, Town&Country Motel

EL CAJON

SAN DIEGO AREA

CA **POINT LOMA** **BLYTHE**

⬆E INTERSTATE 8 Cont'd

Exit #	Services
3a	Continued
	🅞 golf, **S** 🍴 Adam's Cafe, Albie's Rest., Ricky's Rest., Valley Kitchen 🛏 Best Western, Candlewood Suites, Comfort Inn, Courtyard, Days Hotel, DoubleTree Inn, Extended Stay America, Hampton Inn, Howard Johnson, King's Inn/rest., Mission Valley Hotel, Residence Inn, Super 8, Travelodge, Vagabond Inn 🅞 vet
2c	Morena Blvd (from wb)
2b	I-5, N to LA, S to San Diego
2a	Rosecrans St (from wb), CA 209, **S** 🅖 Shell 🍴 Chipotle Mexican, ChuckECheese, Del Taco, Denny's, In-N-Out, Panda Express, Starbucks, Subway 🛏 Goodnite Inn, Hampton Inn 🅞 Staples
1	W Mission Bay Blvd, Sports Arena Blvd (from wb), **N** 🅞 to SeaWorld, **S** 🍴 Arby's, Buffalo Wild Wings, Chick-fil-A, Chili's, Jack-in-the-Box, McDonald's, Phil's BBQ, Red Lobster, Wendy's 🛏 Ramada Ltd, Wyndham Garden 🅞 Dick's, Home Depot, Ralph's, Target, U-Haul, Von's
0mm	**I-8 begins/ends on Sunset Cliffs Blvd, W** 1/4 mi 🅖 76, Shell/repair 🍴 Jack-in-the-Box, Kaiserhof Cafe, **N** 🅞 Mission Bay Park

⬆E INTERSTATE 10

Exit #	Services
245mm	California/Arizona state line, Colorado River, Pacific/Mountain time zone
244mm	**inspection sta wb**
243	Riviera Dr, **S** 🅞 Riviera RV Park
241	US 95, Intake Blvd, to Needles, Blythe, **N** 🅖 Mobil/dsl, Shell/dsl 🍴 Lalo's Mexican, Steaks'n Cakes Rest. 🛏 Days Inn, Relax Inn, Rodeway Inn 🅞 auto/RV repair/24hr, Burton's RV Park, **S** 🛏 Hampton Inn 🅞 McIntyre Park
240	7th St, **N** 🅖 76/dsl, EZ Mart 🍴 China Garden 🛏 Blue Line Motel, Budget Inn, Knights Inn, Solar City Inn 🅞 $General, Albertson's, AutoZone, Ford, repair, Rite Aid, **S** 🅞 Buick/Chevrolet, Chrysler/Dodge/Jeep
239	Lovekin Blvd, Blythe, **N** 🅖 Mobil/dsl, Shell/Quiznos 🍴 Carl's Jr, Del Taco, Domino's, Jack-in-the-Box, McDonald's, Pizza Hut, Popeye's, Rebel BBQ, Rosita's Mexican, Sizzler, Starbucks, Wang's Chinese 🛏 Best Value Inn, Best Western, Budget Host, Clarion, Regency Inn, Willow Inn 🅞🅷, $Tree, Ace Hardware, Goodyear/auto, K-Mart/Little Caesars, O'Reilly Parts, Radio Shack, Verizon, **S** 🅖 76/dsl, Chevron/dsl, USA/Chester's/dsl, Valero/Circle K 🍴 Burger King, Denny's, Red Cactus Grill, Subway, Taco Bell 🛏 Comfort Suites, Motel 6, Quality Inn, Super 8 🅞 city park
236	CA 78, Neighbours Blvd, to Ripley, **N** 🅖 Valero/dsl, **S** to Cibola NWR
232	Mesa Dr, **N** 🅖 76/dsl/rest./scales/24hr/@, Valero/dsl 🅞 🚬
231	**weigh sta wb**
222mm	Wileys Well Rd, **N** 🆁ₛ **both lanes, full** ♿ **facilities, litter barrels, petwalk,** 🚬🏕, **S** to st prison
217	Ford Dry Lake Rd
201	Corn Springs Rd
192	CA 177, Rice Rd, to Lake Tamarisk, **N** 🅞 camping, USPO
189	Eagle Mtn Rd
182	Red Cloud Rd
177	Hayfield Rd
173	Chiriaco Summit, **N** 🅖 Chevron/Foster's Freeze/dsl/24hr 🍴 Chiriaco Rest 🅞 Patton Museum, truck/tire repair

INDIO **PALM SPRINGS**

168	to Twentynine Palms, to Mecca, Joshua Tree NM
162	frontage rd
159mm	**Cactus City** 🆁ₛ **both lanes, full** ♿ **facilities, litter barrels, petwalk,** 🏕
147mm	0 ft elevation
146	Dillon Rd, to CA 86, to CA 111 S, Coachella, **N** 🅖 Chevron, Loves/Carl's Jr/dsl/24hr 🍴 Del Taco, **S** 🅖 Chevron/Jack-in-the-Box, TA/Shell/Country Pride/Taco Bell/dsl/24hr/@ 🅞 Spotlight Casino, truckwash
145	(from eb), CA 86 S
144	CA 111 N, CA 86 S, Indio, **N** 🛏 Holiday Inn Express, Quality Inn 🅞 Classic RV Park, Fantasy Sprgs Casino/Hotel/Cafe
143	Jackson St, Indio, **N** 🅖 Arco/dsl 🍴 IHOP, KFC, La Casita Mexican, McDonald's, Panda Express, Starbucks, Subway, Taco Bell 🅞 $Tree, AT&T, AutoZone, BigLots, CVS Drug, GNC, Home Depot, Marshall's, PetCo, Ramona Tire/auto, Ross, Target, Verizon, Walgreens, WinCo Foods, **S** 🅞 7-11
142	Monroe St, Central Indio, **N** 🅞 RV camping, Walmart, **S** 🅖 76, Circle K, Shell/dsl/LP 🍴 Mexicali Cafe, Subway, Taco Jalisco 🛏 Best Value Inn 🅞 $General
139	Jefferson St, Indio Blvd, **N** 🅞 hwy patrol, Shadow Hills RV Resort
137	Washington St, Country Club Dr, to Indian Wells, **N** 🅖 Arco, Chevron/dsl 🍴 Burger King, Coco's, Del Taco, Legends and Icons Grill, Mario's Italian, Papa John's, Popeye's, Starbucks, Winchell's 🛏 Comfort Suites, Motel 6 🅞 1000 Trails RV Park, Buick/GMC, Ford, Honda, McMahon's RV Ctr, Rite Aid, Stater Bros, Toyota/Scion, TrueValue, VW, Walgreens, **S** 🅖 76/Circle K, Mobil/Circle K 🍴 Carl's Jr, China Wok, Domino's, Goody's Cafe, La Casita Mexican, Lili's Chinese, Pizza Hut, Pronto Mexican, Quiznos, Subway, TJ's Mexican, ToGo's/Baskin-Robbins, Wendy's 🅞 Firestone/auto, Goodyear/auto
134	Cook St, to Indian Wells, **S** 🅖 Arco, Mobil/Circle K/dsl 🍴 Applebees, Carl's Jr, Coldstone, Firehouse Grill, Goody's Cafe, Jack-in-the-Box, Pueblo Viejo Grill, Starbucks, Subway 🛏 Courtyard, Hampton Inn, Hilton/Homewood Suites, Residence Inn 🅞 vet
131	Monterey Ave, Thousand Palms, **N** 🅖 Arco 🍴 Jack-in-the-Box, **S** 🍴 Clark's Cafe/Food Mkt, Del Taco, El Pollo Loco, Hibachi City, IHOP, Maracas Cantina, McDonald's, Panda Express, Red Robin, Santana's Mexican, Starbucks, Subway, Wendy's 🅞 $Tree, 99¢ Store, America's Tire, Costco/gas, Goodyear/auto, Home Depot, Kohls, Lowe's, PetsMart, Sam's Club/gas, Walmart
130	Ramon Rd, Bob Hope Dr, **N** 🅖 FLYING J/dsl/LP/rest./24hr, Chevron/dsl, Shell/dsl, Valero/dsl 🍴 Carl's Jr, Del Taco, Denny's, Domino's, Goody's Cafe, In-N-Out, McDonald's, San Miguel Mexican 🛏 Red Roof Inn 🅞 truckwash, **S** 🅞🅷, Agua Caliente Casino/rest.
126	Date Palm Dr, Rancho Mirage, **S** 🅖 Arco/dsl, Mobil, Valero 🅞 Walgreens
123	Palm Dr, to Desert Hot Sprgs, **N** 🅖 Arco/dsl, Chevron/Jack-in-the-Box/dsl 🅞 Caliente Springs Camping, **S** 🅞 to Gene Autry Trail (3mi)
120	Indian Ave, to N Palm Sprgs, **N** 🅖 76/Circle K, Arco/dsl, Shell/dsl 🛏 Motel 6 🅞 Harley-Davidson, **S** 🅖 Chevron, Wendy's/dsl/scales/24hr 🍴 Del Taco, Jack-in-the-Box 🅞🅷
117	CA 62, to Yucca Valley, Twentynine Palms, to Joshua Tree NM
114	Whitewater, many windmills
113mm	🆁ₛ **both lanes, full** ♿ **facilities, litter barrels,** 🚬, 🏕
112	CA 111 (from eb), to Palm Springs

⬆️E INTERSTATE 10 Cont'd

Exit #	Services
110	Haugeen-Lehmann
106	Main St, to Cabazon, N 🅖 Shell/dsl 🅕 Burger King, S 🅖 Valero/Circle K/dsl
104	Cabazon, same as 103
103	Fields Rd, N 🅖 Chevron, Morongo/dsl 🅕 In-N-Out, McDonald's, Ruby's Diner 🅞 Hadley Fruit Orchards, Morongo Reservation/casino, Premium Outlets/famous brands
102.5mm	Banning weigh sta both lanes
102	Ramsey St (from wb)
101	Hargrave St, Banning, N 🅖 76/Church's, Arco/dsl 🅛 Country Inn, Stagecoach Motel 🅞 tires
100	CA 243, 8th St, Banning, N 🅖 Chevron/dsl 🅕 IHOP, Jack-in-the-Box, Subway 🅞 Rite Aid
99	22nd St, to Ramsey St, N 🅖 Arco/dsl, Shell/dsl 🅕 Carl's Jr, Carrow's, Chelos Tacos, Del Taco, Fishermans Grill, KFC, Little Caesar's, McDonald's, Pizza Hut, Russo's Italian, Sizzler, Starbucks, Wall Chinese 🅛 Days Inn, Super 8, Travelodge 🅞 $General, Banning RV Ctr, Family$, Goodyear/auto
98	Sunset Ave, Banning, N 🅖 Chevron/dsl 🅕 Domino's, Gramma's Kitchen, Gus Jr #7 Burger 🅛 Holiday Inn Express 🅞 $Tree, AutoZone, BigLots, Buick/Chevrolet/GMC, Ray's RV Ctr, repair, Rio Ranch Mkt, vet
96	Highland Springs Ave, N 🅖 Arco, Chevron/dsl, Shell/dsl 🅕 Applebee's, Burger King, Denny's, FarmHouse Rest., Guy's Italian, Jack-in-the-Box, Little Caesar's, Orchid Thai, Papa John's, Subway, Wendy's 🅛 Hampton Inn 🅞 H, Best Hardware, Food4Less, O'Reilly Parts, Stater Bros Foods, Walgreens, S 🅖 Mobil 🅕 Carl's Jr, Chili's, Dickey's BBQ, El Pollo Loco, FarmerBoys, Good China, La Casita, McDonald's, Palermo's Pizza, Quiznos, Starbucks, Taco Bell, Wienerschnitzel 🅞 $Tree, Albertson's, Best Buy, GNC, Home Depot, hwy patrol, Kohls, PetCo, Ramona Tire/auto, Rite Aid, Ross, Verizon, Walmart/Subway
95	Pennsylvania Ave (from wb), Beaumont, N 🅕 Country Jct Rest., Jasmine Thai, Marla's Rest. 🅛 Rodeway Inn 🅞 AutoZone, Meineke, Miller RV Ctr
94	CA 79, Beaumont, N 🅖 76/dsl, USA 🅕 Baker's DriveThru, BMG Mexican, Casa Palacios, McDonald's, Popeye's, YumYum Donuts 🅛 Best Value Inn, Best Western 🅞 Family$, NAPA, O'Reilly Parts, S 🅖 Arco/dsl, Shell/Circle K/dsl 🅕 Del Taco, Denny's, Jack-in-the-Box, Subway 🅞 RV camping, vet
93	CA 60 W, to Riverside
92	San Timoteo Canyon Rd, Oak Valley Pkwy, N 🅖 Chevron/dsl 🅕 Sand Trap Grill, Subway 🅛 Holiday Inn Express 🅞 golf, Rite Aid, S 🅞 golf
91mm	🆁🆂 wb, full 🍴 facilities, litter barrels, petwalk, 🚻, 🐾
90	Cherry Valley Blvd, N 🅞 truck/tire repair
89	Singleton Rd (from wb), to Calimesa
88	Calimesa Blvd, N 🅖 Arco/dsl, Chevron/dsl, Shell/dsl 🅕 Best Wok, Burger King, Carl's Jr, Denny's, Isabella's Italian, McDonald's, NY Pizzaria, Subway, Taco Bell, Tang's Chinese 🅛 Calimesa Inn 🅞 Fresh&Easy Foods, Stater Bros Foods, Walgreens, S 🅕 Big Boy, Jack-in-the-Box
87	County Line Rd, to Yucaipa, N 🅖 FasTrip/dsl, Shell/dsl 🅕 Baker's DriveThru, Del Taco 🅛 Best Value 🅞 $General, auto repair/tires, SavALot Foods, USPO, vet
86mm	Wildwood 🆁🆂 eb, full 🍴 facilities, litter barrels, petwalk, 🚻, 🐾
85	Live Oak Canyon Rd, Oak Glen
83	Yucaipa Blvd, N 🅖 Arco/dsl, Chevron/dsl, Mobil 🅕 Baker's DriveThru, Starbucks, S 🅕 Subway

82	Wabash Ave (from wb)
81	Redlands Blvd, Ford St, S 🅖 76
80	Cypress Ave, University St, N 🅞 H, to U of Redlands
79b a	CA 38, 6th St, Orange St, Redlands, N 🅖 Chevron, USA 🅕 Redlands Rest. 🅛 Budget Inn, Stardust Motel 🅞 Stater Bros Foods, S 🅖 76, Shell 🅕 Chipotle Mexican, Corner Cafe, Domino's, Eureka Burger, Las Cuentes Mexican, Phoenicia Greek, Rubio's, Starbucks, Subway 🅞 Firestone/auto, Office Depot, O'Reilly Parts, Trader Joe's, Verizon, Von's Foods
77c	(77b from wb) Tennessee St, N 🅖 7-11 🅕 Jack-in-the-Box, Shakey's Pizza 🅞 Home Depot, Toyota/Scion, S 🅖 Shell 🅕 Arby's, Bakers DriveThru, Burger King, Carl's Jr, Coco's, El Burrito, El Pollo Loco, LJ Silver, Papa John's, Subway, Taco Bell 🅛 Ayers Hotel, Comfort Suites, Dynasty Suites, Motel 6 🅞 American Tire Depot, Ford, USPO, vet
77b	(77c from wb) CA 210, to Highlands
77a	Alabama St, N 🅖 76/Circle K/dsl 🅕 Buffet Star, Cafe Rio, Chick-fil-A, Chili's, Coldstone Creamery, Denny's, Famous Dave's BBQ, Five Guys, Hawaiian BBQ, Jamba Juice, Jersey Mike's, Macaroni Grill, Magic Wok, Noodle 21 Asian, Red Robin, Starbucks, Subway, Tom's Charburgers 🅛 Best Value Inn, Motel 7 West, Super 8 🅞 AT&T, Barnes&Noble, GNC, JC Penney, Jo-Ann Superstore, Kohl's, Marshall's, Michael's, PetCo, Target, U-Haul, Verizon, World Mkt, S 🅖 Chevron, Shell 🅕 Del Taco, IHOP, McDonald's, Nick's Burgers, Old Spaghetti Factory, Pizza Hut, Zabella's Mexican 🅛 Country Inn&Suites, GoodNite Inn 🅞 $Tree, 7-11, 99¢ Store, BigLots, Chevrolet, CVS Drug, Discount Tire, Goodyear/auto, K-Mart, Lowe's, Midas, Nissan, PepBoys, Ross, Tuesday Morning
76	California St, N 🅕 Mill Creek Rest. 🅞 funpark, museum, S 🅖 Arco, Shell/LP/dsl 🅕 Applebee's, Bravo Burger, Jack-in-the-Box, Jose's Mexican, Little Caesar's, Panda Express, Red Chili Szechuan, Subway, Wendy's, Wienerschnitzel 🅞 AT&T, AutoZone, Food4Less, Just Tires, Mission RV Park, Radio Shack, Walmart
75	Mountain View Ave, Loma Linda, N 🅖 Valero/dsl, S 🅕 Domino's, FarmerBoys Burgers, Lupe's Mexican, Subway
74	Tippecanoe Ave, Anderson St, N 🅕 BJ's Rest., Chipotle Mexican, El Pollo Loco, Hawaiian BBQ, In-N-Out, Jack-in-the-Box, Jamba Juice, Panera Bread, Pick-Up Stix, Pollo Campero, Starbucks, Subway, Tasty Goody 🅛 Fairfield Inn, Hampton Inn, Homewood Suites, Residence Inn 🅞 Costco/gas, Sam's Club/gas, Staples, S 🅖 76/dsl 🅕 Baker's DriveThru, Del Taco, HomeTown Buffet, KFC, Napoli Italian, Wienerschnitzel 🅞 auto repair, Honda, Hyundai, to Loma Linda U
73b a	Waterman Ave, N 🅖 76, Shell/dsl 🅕 Baja Fresh, Black Angus, Buffalo Wild Wings, Chili's, ChuckeCheese, ClaimJumper, Coco's, El Torito, Five Guys, IHOP, King Buffet, Lotus

⨁ INTERSTATE 10 Cont'd

S A N   B E R N A R D I N O

Exit #	Services
73b a	Continued Garden Chinese, Mimi's Café, Olive Garden, Outback Steaks, Panda Express, Red Lobster, Sizzler, Souplantation, Subway, TGIFriday's, Togo's 🏠 Best Western, Days Inn, Hilton Garden, La Quinta, Quality Inn, San Bernardino Hotel, Super 8 ⊙ 7-11, Best Buy, Home Depot, Office Depot, PetsMart, S ⛽ Arco 🍴 Burger King, Carl's Jr, Gus Jr Burger #8, McDonald's, Popeye's, Starbucks, Taco Bell 🏠 Motel 6 ⊙ Camping World RV Ctr, El Monte RV Ctr, repair
72	I-215, CA 91
71	Mt Vernon Ave, Sperry Ave, N ⛽ 7-11, Trkstp/dsl/LP 🍴 Alberto's Mexican 🏠 Colony Inn, Colton Motel, Comfort Inn ⊙ repair
70b	9th St, N ⛽ Mobil 🍴 Denny's, Domino's, McDonald's, P&G Burgers, Starbucks, Subway 🏠 Hampton Inn ⊙ NAPA, Stater Bros Foods, USPO
70a	Rancho Ave, N 🍴 Del Taco, Jack-in-the-Box, KFC/Taco Bell, Wienerschnitzel
69	Pepper Dr, N ⛽ Valero 🍴 Baker's DriveThru
68	Riverside Ave, to Rialto, N ⛽ Chevron/dsl, I-10 Trkstp/dsl/scales, USA 🍴 Burger King, Burger King, Coco's, El Pollo Loco, HomeTown Buffet, Jack-in-the-Box, McDonald's, Panda Express, Starbucks, Subway, Taco Joe's 🏠 American Inn, Days Inn, ValleyView Inn ⊙ dsl repair, Midas, Pepboys, Walmart, S ⛽ Shell/Circle K/dsl
66	Cedar Ave, to Bloomington, N ⛽ Arco, Valero/dsl 🍴 Baker's DriveThru, Burger King, DQ, FarmerBoys Burgers, Subway, Taco Bell, S ⊙ 7-11
64	Sierra Ave, to Fontana, N ⛽ Arco, Mobil, Shell, Valero/dsl 🍴 Arby's, Billy J's Rest., China Cook, China Panda, ChuckeCheese, Del Taco, Denny's, El Gallo Giro, Hawaiian BBQ, IHOP, In-N-Out, Jack-in-the-Box, KFC, Little Caesars, Little Caesar's, McDonald's, Pancho Villa's, Papa John's, Pizza Hut/Taco Bell, Popeye's, Sizzler, Sub Shop, Subway, Wendy's, Wienerschnitzel, Yoshinoya 🏠 Best Value Inn, EconoLodge, Motel 6, Valley Motel ⊙ Ⓗ, $Tree, AutoZone, BigLots, Cardenas Foods, CVS Drug, Food4Less, GNC, Just Tires, K-Mart, PepBoys, Radio Shack, Rite Aid, Stater Bros Foods, Verizon, S ⛽ Chevron/dsl 🍴 Alvaro's Mexican, Brandon's Diner, China Buffet, Circle K, Del Taco, Los Jalapeños, Shakey's Pizza, Shrimp House, Subway, Tasty Goody 🏠 Hilton Garden ⊙ AutoZone, Ross, Target, TJ Maxx
63	Citrus Ave, N ⛽ 76, Gasco 🍴 Baker's DriveThru, Subway ⊙ Ford, S ⛽ 7-11/dsl, Arco/dsl
61	Cherry Ave, N ⛽ Arco, Chevron, Fontana Trkstp/dsl/24hr, Valero/dsl 🍴 Carl's Jr, Del Taco, Jack-in-the-Box ⊙ Mack/Volvo, truck sales, S ⛽ 3 Sisters Trkstp/dsl/@, 76/Circle K, North American Trkstp/dsl 🍴 Farmer Boy's Rest., La Chaquita ⊙ Peterbilt
59	Etiwanda Ave, Valley Blvd
58b a	I-15, N to Barstow, S to San Diego
57	Milliken Ave, N ⛽ 76/dsl, Arco/24hr, Chevron, Mobil/Albertos Mexican/dsl, Shell 🍴 Applebee's, Arby's, Baja Fresh, BJ's Rest., Boston's, Burger King, Carl's Jr, Chevy's Mexican, Chipotle, Coco's, Coldstone, Dave&Buster's, Del Taco, El Pollo Loco, Famous Dave's BBQ, Fat Burger, Fuddruckers, Hooters, IHOP, In-n-Out, Jack-in-the-Box, Jamba Juice, KFC, Krispy Kreme, McDonald's, Mkt Broiler, New City Buffet, NY Grill, Olive Garden, Outback Steaks, Rain Forest Cafe, Red Lobster, Rubio's, Sonic, Starbucks, Subway, Tokyo Tokyo,

O N T A R I O

Exit #	Services
57	Continued Wendy's, Wienerschnitzel, Wing Place 🏠 Ayre's Suites, Country Inn&Suites, Courtyard, Hampton Inn, Hilton Garden, Holiday Inn Express, Homewood Suites, Hyatt, TownePlace Suites ⊙ America's Tire, Best Buy, Big O Tire, Carmax, Costco/gas, JC Penney, Jo-Ann Fabrics, Kohl's, Marshalls, Ontario Mills Mall, Petsmart, Sam's Club/gas, Staples, Target, Verizon, S ⛽ TA/Shell/Pizza Hut/Subway/Taco Bell/dsl/rest./24hr/@ 🏠 Rodeway Inn
56	Haven Ave, Rancho Cucamonga, N ⛽ Mobil 🍴 Benihana, Black Angus, Pizza Factory 🏠 Aloft Hotel, Best Western, Extended Stay America, Hilton, La Quinta, Ontario Grand Suites, S 🍴 Panda Chinese, TGIFriday's 🏠 Fairfield Inn
55b a	Holt Blvd, to Archibald Ave, N ⛽ Arco, Mobil/dsl 🍴 Baker's Drive-thru, Burgertown USA, Hawaiian BBQ, Subway, Weinerschnitzel
54	Vineyard Ave, N ⛽ 76/Circle K 🍴 Carl's Jr, Del Taco, El Pollo Loco, Great China, Pizza Hut/Taco Bell, Popeye's, Quiznos, Rocky's Pizza ⊙ AutoZone, Ralph's Foods, Rite Aid, Stater Bros Foods, S ⛽ 76, Mobil, Valero 🍴 Basil Rest., Cowboy Burgers, Denny's, Garden Square Rest., In-N-Out, Jack-in-the-Box, Marie Callenders, Quiznos, Rosa's Italian, Spires Rest., Wendy's, Yoshinoya Japanese 🏠 Ayers Suites, Best Western, Comfort Suites, Countryside Suites, DoubleTree Inn, Holiday Inn, Motel 6, Ontario Airport Inn, Quality Inn, Ramada Inn, Red Roof Inn, Residence Inn, Sheraton ⊙ Buick/Cadillac/Chevrolet/GMC, to ✈, USPO
53	San Bernardino Ave, 4th St, to Ontario, N ⛽ 7-11, 76, Arco, Shell 🍴 Burger King, Carl's Jr, Jack-in-the-Box 🏠 EconoLodge, Motel 6 ⊙ K-Mart, Radio Shack, S ⛽ 76, Arco/24hr, Valero 🍴 Denny's, Little Caesars, Subway, YumYum Donuts 🏠 Days Inn, Rodeway Inn ⊙ city park, Jax Mkt
51	CA 83, Euclid Ave, to Ontario, Upland, N ⊙Ⓗ
50	Mountain Ave, to Mt Baldy, N ⛽ Chevron, Mobil/dsl, Shell/dsl 🍴 Carrow's, Denny's, El Torito, Fresh&Easy, HoneyBaked Ham, Mi Taco, Mimi's Café, Rubio's, Subway, Trader Joe's, Wendy's 🏠 Super 8 ⊙ $Tree, AT&T, CVS Drug, Home Depot, Kohl's, Michaels, Radio Shack, Staples, S ⛽ 76/dsl 🍴 Baskin-Robbins, Carl's Jr, Chopstix, Coldstone, Jo-Anne's Cafe, Pizza Hut, Quiznos, Roundtable Pizza, Starbucks, Wingnuts ⊙ Albertsons, Rite Aid, USPO, vet

M O N T C L A I R

Exit #	Services
49	Central Ave, to Montclair, N 🍴 Carl's Jr., Chipotle Mexican, Del Taco, El Pollo Loco, Hometown Buffet, John's Incredible Pizza, McDonald's, Panda Garden Buffet, Pizza Hut, Quiznos, Starbucks, Subway, Taco Bell ⊙ 99¢ Store, America's Tire, AT&T, AutoZone, Barnes&Noble, Best Buy, Firestone/auto, Giant RV Ctr, Goodyear/auto, Harley-Davidson, JC Penney, Just Tires, Macy's, mall, PepBoys, PetCo, Ross, same as 48, Sears/auto, Target, Tuesday Morning, vet, S ⛽ Chevron, Thrifty 🍴 Alberto's Mexican, Fulin Chinese, Jack-in-the-Box, LJ Silver, Subway, Wienerschnitzel ⊙ 7-11, Acura/Honda/Infiniti, Costco/gas, Nissan, Stater Bro's
48	Monte Vista, N ⛽ Shell 🍴 Acapulco Mexican, Applebee's, Black Angus, Chilis, Elephant Bar Rest., Macaroni Grill, Olive Garden, Red Lobster ⊙ Ⓗ, Macy's, mall, Nordstrom's, same as 49
47	Indian Hill Blvd, to Claremont, N ⛽ Mobil 🍴 BC Cafe, Garden Square 🏠 Claremont Lodge, Howard Johnson, S ⛽ 76/dsl, Chevron/McDonald's 🍴 Burger King, Carl's Jr, Denny's, In-N-Out, Norm's Rest., RoundTable Pizza, Starbucks, World Famous Grill ⊙ 7-11, Toyota/Scion

INTERSTATE 10 Cont'd

Exit #	Services
46	Towne Ave, N 7-11, 76/dsl Jack-in-the-Box
45b	Garey Ave, to Pomona, N Arco H, vet, S Chevron, Shell/dsl Del Taco
45	White Ave, Garey Ave, to Pomona
44	(43 from eb) Dudley St, Fairplex Dr, N Arco/dsl Denny's LemonTree Motel, Sheraton, S Chevron/24hr Jack-in-the-Box, McDonald's, Starbucks 7-11
42b	CA 71 S (from eb), to Corona
42a	I-210 W, CA 57 S
41	Kellogg Dr, S to Cal Poly Inst
40	Via Verde
38b	Holt Ave, to Covina, N Hamiltons Steaks Radisson
38a	Grand Ave, N Arco/dsl, United Baily's Rest, Denny's Best Western
37b	Barranca St, Grand Ave, N 76, Shell/dsl BJ's Rest., Carinos, Carl's Jr, Chili's, Chipotle Mexican, Dockside Grill, El Torito, Habit Burgers, Hooters, Islands Burgers, Marie Callender, Mariposa Mexican, Starbucks Best Western, Clarion, Fairfield Inn, Hampton Inn Albertsons, CVS Drug, Dick's, IKEA, Marshalls, Office Depot, Old Navy, Petsmart, Target, Verizon, S In-N-Out, McDonald's 5 Star Inn, Days Inn, same as 37a
37a	Citrus Ave, to Covina, N Chevron Buffalo Wild Wings, Burger King, Del Taco, IHOP, Jack-in-the-Box, Millie's Rest., Starbucks, Subway, TGIFriday's, Yum Yum Donuts Acura, Albertsons, Baja Ranch Foods, Buick/GMC, CVS Drug, KIA, Marshall's, Nissan, VW, S 76/autocare Classic Burger H, Cadillac, same as 37b
36	CA 39, Azusa Ave, to Covina, N 76/dsl, Arco/24hr Dennys, Green Field Brazillian, McDonald's, Norm's Rest., Papa John's, Quiznos, Subway BigLots, Chrysler/Dodge/Jeep, CVS Drug, Food4Less, Stater Bros, S Mobil, Shell/dsl Carrow's Audi, Chevrolet, Ford, Honda, Hummer, Mercedes, Toyota
35	Vincent Ave, Glendora Ave, N 76/dsl/autocare, S 76 Applebee's, Baja Fresh, CA Pizza Kitchen, Elephant Bar Rest., Fresh&Easy, Grand Buffet, Jamba Juice, Panera Bread, Pizza Hut, Red Robin, Starbucks, Subway, Weinerschnitzel Best Buy, Big O Tire, Firestone, JC Penney, Macy's, mall, Sears/auto, USPO, Verizon
34	Pacific Ave, N 76, S Mobil, Valero H, Discount Tire, K-Mart, mall, same as 35, Sears Outlet
33	Puente Ave, N Chevron Denny's, Farmer Boy's, Guadalajara Grill, McDonald's, Panda Express, Sizzler, Starbucks Courtyard, Motel 6 AT&T, Home Depot, Verizon, Walmart, S Valero/dsl Jack-in-the-Box Regency Inn Harley-Davidson, U-Haul
32b	Francisquito Ave, to La Puente, N V&G hwy patrol, S 76 Carl's Jr, In-N-Out, Wienerschnitzel Grand Park Inn
32a	Baldwin Pk Blvd, N Chevron/McDonald's Burger King, Fronteiras, IHOP, Jack-in-the-Box, Papa Johns, Pizza Hut/Taco Bell, Starbucks, Subway, Wok'n Go, Yum Yum Donuts H, CVS Drug, Food4Less, Target, transmissions, S In-N-Out
31c	(31b from wb) Frazier St, N 7-11
31b a	(31a from wb) I-605 N/S, to Long Beach
30	Garvey Ave, S Rte 66
29b	Valley Blvd, Peck Rd, N Chevron Baskin-Robbins, Carl's Jr., Denny's, Hometown Buffet, Jamba Juice, KFC,

COVINA (vertical left margin)

29b	Continued Papa Johns, Shakey's Pizza, Subway, Taco Bell, Yoshinoya Motel 6 Honda, Hyundai, Lexus, Nissan, Radio Shack, Sears Essentials, Staples, Toyota/Scion, Walgreens, S McDonald's, Pepe's Seafood, Tommy's Burgers
29a	S Peck Rd (from eb)
28	Santa Anita Ave, to El Monte, S 76/dsl 7-11, vet
27	Baldwin Avenue, Temple City Blvd, S Arco/24hr Denny's, same as 26b a
26b	CA 19, Rosemead Blvd, Pasadena, N Coldstone, Denny's, IHOP, Jamba Juice, Mayumba Cuban, Subway Knights Inn $Tree, GNC, Goodyear/auto, Office Depot, Radio Shack, Target, S Del Taco, Jack-in-the-Box, Quiznos, Starbucks
26a	Walnut Grove Ave
25b	San Gabriel Blvd, N Shell Carl's Jr, Pizza Hut/Taco Bell, Popeye's, Wienerschnitzel Budget Inn, S 7-11
25a	Del Mar Ave, to San Gabriel, N 76 auto repair, S Arco, Chevron/dsl Rodeway Inn
24	New Ave, to Monterey Park, N KFC, to Mission San Gabriel
23b	Garfield Ave, to Alhambra, S Arco Grand Inn H
23a	Atlantic Blvd, Monterey Park, N 76, Mobil Pizza Hut, Popeye's, Starbucks H, S Best Western auto repair, Ralph's Foods
22	Fremont Ave, N H, tuneup, S Papa Johns 7-11
21	I-710, Long Beach Fwy, Eastern Ave (from wb)
20b a	Eastern Ave, City Terrace Dr, S Chevron/service, Mobil Burger King, McDonald's
19c	Soto St (from wb), N Chevron/dsl Burger King H, city park, S 76, Mobil
19b	I-5 (from wb), US 101 S, N to Burbank, S to San Diego
19a	State St, N H
17	I-5 N
16b	I-5 S (from eb)
16a	Santa Fe Ave, San Mateo St, S 76/dsl industrial area, Penske Trucks
15b	Alameda St, N 76/dsl Jack-in-the-Box, to downtown, S industrial area
15a	Central Ave, N Shell/repair
14b	San Pedro Blvd, S industrial
14a	LA St, N conv ctr, S El Pollo Loco, McDonald's 99¢ Store, O'Reilly Parts, Radio Shack, Rite Aid, URGENT CARE
13	I-110, Harbor Fwy
12	Hoover St, Vermont Ave, N Mobil Burger King, McDonald's, Subway AutoZone, Honda, PepBoys, Rite Aid, S 76, Arco, Chevron Jack-in-the-Box, Papa Johns, Yoshinoya Ralph's Foods
11	Normandie Ave, Western Ave

EL MONTE (vertical margin)

LOS ANGELES AREA (vertical margin)

Ⓖ = gas　Ⓕ = food　Ⓛ = lodging　Ⓞ = other　℞ = rest stop　Copyright 2015 - the Next EXIT ®

➤E　INTERSTATE 10 Cont'd

Exit #	Services
10	Arlington Ave, N Ⓖ 76, Chevron
9	Crenshaw Blvd, S Ⓖ 76, Chevron, Mobil, Thrifty Ⓕ El Pollo Loco, McDonald's, Pizza Hut/Taco Bell, Subway, Yoshinoya Ⓞ U-Haul
8	La Brea Ave, N Ⓖ Valero/dsl Ⓞ USPO, S Ⓖ Chevron Ⓞ AutoZone
7b	Washington Blvd, Fairfax Ave, S Ⓖ Mobil, same as 8
7a	La Cienega Blvd, Venice Ave (from wb), N Ⓖ Chevron/24h, Mobil Ⓕ Carl's Jr., Del Taco Ⓞ Firestone/auto, S Ⓕ Subway Ⓞ Aamco
6	Robertson Blvd, Culver City, N Ⓖ Chevron, Valero Ⓕ Domino's, Taco Bell Ⓞ EZ Lube, Goodyear, S Ⓕ Del Taco Ⓞ Albertsons, CVS Drug, Ross
5	National Blvd, N Ⓖ 76, United Oil Ⓕ Starbucks, Subway, Taco+ Ⓞ Rite Aid, Von's Foods, S Ⓖ Arco
4	Overland Ave, S Ⓖ Mobil/dsl
3b a	I-405, N to Sacramento, S to Long Beach
2c b	Bundy Dr, N Ⓖ Chevron, Shell/dsl Ⓕ Taco Bell Ⓞ Cadillac/GMC, Staples
2a	Centinela Ave, to Santa Monica, N Ⓕ Taco Bell, S Ⓕ McDonald's, Trader Joe's Ⓛ Santa Monica Hotel
1c	20th St (from wb), Cloverfield Blvd, 26th St (from wb), N Ⓖ 76/dsl, Arco, Shell/repair Ⓞ Ⓗ
1b	Lincoln Blvd, CA 1 S, N Ⓖ Mobil Ⓕ Arbys, Denny's, Jack-in-the-Box, McDonald's, Norm's Rest., Starbucks Ⓛ Holiday Inn Ⓞ BrakeMasters, Jo-Ann Fabrics, Sears, Toyota, Tuesday Morning, USPO, Vons Foods, S Ⓖ 76, Chevron/dsl, Mobil, Shell, World Gas Ⓕ Dominos, Hawaiian BBQ, Jack-in-the-Box, Subway, Taco Bell, Tommy's Burgers Ⓛ Doubletree Suites Ⓞ 7-11, EZ Lube, Firestone/auto, U-Haul
1a	4th, 5th, (from wb), N Ⓞ mall, Sears
0	Santa Monica Blvd, to beaches, I-10 begins/ends on CA 1.

➤N　INTERSTATE 15

Exit #	Services
298	California/Nevada state line, facilities located at state line, Nevada side
291	Yates Well Rd
286	Nipton Rd, E Mojave Nat Preserve, to Searchlight
281	Bailey Rd
276mm	brake check area for trucks, nb
272	Cima Rd, E Ⓖ Shell/cafe/dsl/towing
270mm	**Valley Wells ℞ both lanes, full Ⓐ facilities, litter barrels, petwalk, Ⓒ, ⛽**
265	Halloran Summit Rd
259	Halloran Springs Rd
248	to Baker (from sb), same as 246
246	CA 127, Kel-Baker Rd, Baker, to Death Valley, W Ⓖ 76/dsl, Arco, Chevron/Taco Bell, Shell/Jack-in-the-Box/dsl, Valero/A&W/Pizza Hut/Subway/TCBY, Valero/DQ/Quiznos/dsl Ⓕ Arby's, Big Boy Rest., Burger King, Carl's Jr, Del Taco, Dennys, IHOP, Mad Greek Café Ⓛ BunBoy Hotel, Will's Fargo Motel Ⓞ Alien Fresh Jerky, Baker Mkt Foods, Country Store, repair, USPO, World's Tallest Thermometer
245	to Baker (from nb), same as 246
239	Zzyzx Rd
233	Rasor Rd, E Ⓖ Shell/Rasor Sta/dsl/towing/24hr
230	Basin Rd
221	Afton Rd, to Dunn, W Ⓞ Mini Mkt

Exit #	Services
217mm	℞ both lanes, full Ⓐ facilities, litter barrels, petwalk, Ⓒ, ⛽
213	Field Rd
206	Harvard Rd, to Newberry Springs
198	Minneola Rd, W gas/dsl
197mm	**agricultural insp sta sb**
196	Yermo Rd, Yermo
194	Calico Rd
191	Ghost Town Rd, E Ⓖ Arco/24hr, Mohsen Oil Trkstp/dsl/24hr Ⓕ Jack-in-the-Box, Peggy Sue's 50s Diner, Penny's Diner Ⓛ OakTree Inn, W Ⓖ 76, Shell/dsl/24hr Ⓞ Calico GhostTown (3mi), KOA
189	Ft Irwin Rd
186	CA 58 W, to Bakersfield, W Ⓕ Idle Spur Steaks
184a	I-40 E (from nb), I-40 begins/ends
184	E Main, Barstow, Montera Rd (from eb), to I-40, E Ⓖ 76/dsl Ⓕ Grill It, Hollywood Subs, McDonald's, Mega Tom's Burgers, Panda Express, Popeye's, Starbucks, Straw Hat Pizza Ⓛ Arco, Best Western, Travelodge Ⓞ Walmart/McDonald's/auto, W Ⓖ Chevron, Circle K, Shell/dsl, Thrifty/dsl, Valero Ⓕ Burger King, Carl's Jr, China Town Buffet, Coco's, Del Taco, Denny's, FireHouse Italian, IHOP, Jack-in-the-Box, Jenny's Grill, Little Caesars, LJ Silver, Sizzler, Taco Bell, Wienerschnitzel Ⓛ Astrobudget Motel, Best Motel, Budget Inn, CA Inn, Days Inn, Desert Inn, EconoLodge, Economy Inn, Motel 6, Quality Inn/rest, Ramada Inn, Rodeway Inn, Super 8 Ⓞ $Tree, 99Cent Store, AutoZone, Family$, O'Reilly Parts, Radio Shack, U-Haul/LP, vet, Von's Foods
183	CA 247, Barstow Rd, E Ⓖ Circle K, Valero/dsl Ⓕ Jimenez Mexican, Pizza Hut, Subway Ⓞ $General, Rite Aid, W Ⓖ Chevron Ⓞ Ⓗ, Food4Less, Mojave River Valley Museum, st patrol
181	L St, W Main, Barstow, W Ⓖ Chevron, Thrifty Ⓕ Foster's Freeze Ⓛ Best Value Inn, Holiday Inn Express Ⓞ Home Depot, NAPA, tires/towing
179	CA 58, to Bakersfield
178	Lenwood, to Barstow, E Ⓖ ⊕FLYING J/Denny's/dsl/24hr, 76/dsl, Arco/dsl, Chevron, Shell/dsl, Valero Ⓕ Arby's, Big Boy, Burger King, Carl's Jr, Chili's, Chipotle Mexican, Del Taco, El Pollo Loco, In-N-Out, Jack-in-the-Box, Panda Express, Starbucks, Subway, Tommy's Burgers Ⓛ Comfort Suites, Country Inn&Suites, Hampton Inn, Holiday Inn Express Ⓞ Blue Beacon, Old Navy, Tanger Outlet/famous brands/food ct, W Ⓖ ♥Love's/Chester's/Godfather's/dsl/scales/24hr/@, ⊞/Subway/dsl/scales/24hr, TA/Shell/Country Fare/Subway/dsl/scales/24hr/@ Ⓕ McDonald's Ⓛ Days Inn Ⓞ repair, truckwash, Zippy Lube
175	Outlet Ctr Dr, Sidewinder Rd
169	Hodge Rd
165	Wild Wash Rd
161	Dale Evans Pkwy, to Apple Valley
157	Stoddard Wells Rd, to Bell Mtn
154	Stoddard Wells Rd, to Bell Mtn, E Ⓞ Shady Oasis Camping/LP, W Ⓖ 76/dsl, Mobil Ⓕ Frankie's Diner Ⓛ Motel 6, Queens Motel
153.5mm	Mojave River
153b	E St
153a	CA 18 E, D St, to Apple Valley, E Ⓖ Arco Ⓞ Ⓗ, repair, W Ⓖ Arco/Subway/dsl
151b	Mojave Dr, Victorville, E Ⓖ Gasmart/dsl Ⓛ Budget Inn, W Ⓖ Valero/dsl Ⓛ Economy Inn, Sunset Inn
151a	La Paz Dr, Roy Rogers Dr, E Ⓖ Chevron, Shell/dsl Ⓕ Bravo Burgers, Burger King, Carl's Jr, El Pollo Loco, Home

*Side tabs: SANTA MONICA · BAKER ; BARSTOW · LENWOOD ; CA*

⬆N   INTERSTATE 15 Cont'd

Exit #   Services

V I C T O R V I L L E

151a   Continued
Town Buffet, IHOP, Jack-in-the-Box, McDonald's, Wendy's 🅞 $General, $Tree, 99¢ Store, AutoZone, BigLots, Costco/ gas, Food4Less, Harley-Davidson, Pepboys, Radio Shack, Rite Aid, same as 144, Toyota/Scion, **W** 🅖 Arco 🅕 Carl's Jr, Domino's, Farmer Boys, Golden ChopStix, Hawaiian BBQ, In-N-Out, Panda Express, Papa John's, Starbucks, Subway, Taco Grande 🅞 Americas Tire, Buick/GMC, Chrysler/Dodge/ Jeep, Home Depot, Honda, Kia, Nissan, Stater Bros, Verizon, Walgreens, WinCo Foods

150   CA 18 W, Palmdale Rd, Victorville, **E** 🅕 Baker's Drive-Thru, Burger King, Denny's, KFC, Richie's Diner 🅛 Greentree Inn, Red Roof Inn, **W** 🅖 Arco, Circle K 🅕 Coco's, Del Taco, House of Joy, La Casita Mexican, McDonald's, Pizza Hut, Raul's Mexican, Starbucks, Subway, Taco Bell, Tom's Rest. 🅛 Ambassador Inn, Budget Inn, Days Inn 🅞 🄷, Aamco, AutoZone, CVS Drug, Ford, Hyundai, Kamper's Korner RV, Mazda, Target, Town&Country Tire, vet

147   Bear Valley Rd, to Lucerne Valley, **E 0-2 mi** 🅖 76/Circle K/dsl, Arco, Chevron, Mobil 🅕 Arby's, Baker's Drive-Thru, Blimpie, Burger King, Carl's Jr, Del Taco, Dragon Express, John's Pizza, KFC, Los Alazanes Mexican, Los Toritos, Marie Callender's, McDonald's, Panda Express, Red Robin, Star-bucks, Steer'n Stein, Subs'n Salads, Tacos Mexico, Wiener-schnitzel 🅛 Comfort Suites, Day&Night Inn, EconoLodge, Extended Studio Hotel, Hilton Garden, La Quinta, Super 8, Travelodge 🅞 Affordable RV Ctr, America's Tire, AutoZone, Firestone/auto, Food4Less, Home Depot, Michael's, O'Reilly Parts, Range RV, Rite Aid, Scandia Funpark, Tire Depot, Tire Guys, Vallarta Foods, vet, Walmart/McDonald's/auto, **W** 🅖 76/Circle K, Arco, Chevron/dsl, Valero/dsl 🅕 Applebee's, Ar-chibald's Drive-Thru, Baja Fresh, Baskin-Robbins, Carino's, Chili's, Chipotle Mexican, ChuckeCheese, Del Taco, El Pollo Loco, El Tio Pepe Mexican, Farmer Boy's Rest., Freddy's Custard, Giuseppe's, Jack-in-the-Box, Little Caesar's, Mc-Donald's, Mimi's Cafe, Olive Garden, Outback Steaks, Pan-cho Villa's, Red Lobster, RoadHouse Grill, Sonic, Starbucks, Subway, Tokyo Steaks, Wendy's 🅛 Hawthorn Suites 🅞 99¢ Store, AAA, Albertson's, AT&T, Barnes&Noble, Best Buy, CVS Drug, Goodyear/auto, Hobby Lobby, JC Penney, Kohl's, Lowe's, Macy's, mall, Petsmart, Rite Aid, Stater Bros., Veri-zon, Walgreens, Walmart

H E S P E R I A

143   Main St, to Hesperia, Phelan, **E** 🅖 Chevron/dsl, Shell/Pop-eye's/dsl, Valero/Alberto's 🅕 Arby's, Burger King, Del Taco, Denny's, IHOP, In-N-Out, Jack-in-the-Box, Quiznos, Star-bucks 🅛 Courtyard, SpringHill Suites, **W** 🅖 76/dsl, Arco/dsl 🅕 Baker's Drive-thru, Farmer Boys, Golden Corral, Subway 🅛 Holiday Inn Express, Motel 6 🅞 Desert Willow RV Park, GNC, Jo-Ann Fabrics, Marshall's, Radio Shack, Ross, Super-Target, URGENT CARE, Verizon

141   US 395, Joshua St, Adelanto, **W** 🅖 Arco/dsl, 🄻🄻🄻🄻/Wen-dy's/dsl/scales/24hr 🅕 Outpost Café 🅞 repair, RV supply ctr, truck/RV wash, Zippy Lube

138   Oak Hill Rd, **E** 🅖 Chevron/dsl 🅕 Summit Inn Café, **W** 🅞 Oak Hills RV Village/LP

137mm   brake check sb, Cajon Summit, elevation 4260

131   CA 138, to Palmdale, Silverwood Lake, **E** 🅖 Chevron 🅕 Mc-Donald's 🅞 Silverwood SRA, **W** 🅖 76/Circle K/Del Taco/LP, Shell/Subway/dsl/LP 🅛 Best Western

130mm   elevation 3000, **weigh sta both lanes**

---

129   Cleghorn Rd
124   Kenwood Ave
123   I-215 S, to San Bernardino, **E** 🅖 Arco, to Glen Helen Park
122   Glen Helen Parkway
119   Sierra Ave, **W** 🅖 Arco/dsl, Chevron/dsl, Shell/Del Taco/dsl, Valero/dsl 🅕 Jack-in-the-Box, McDonalds 🅞 to Lytle Creek RA

116   Summit Ave, **E** 🅖 7-11, Chevron 🅕 Chili's, Coldstone, Del Taco, El Ranchero, Hawaiian BBQ, Jack-in-the-Box, Juice It Up, Little Beijing, Little Caesars, Panera Bread, Quiznos, Roundtable Pizza, Starbucks, Subway, Taco Bell, Wendy's 🅞 CVS Drug, GNC, Kohl's, Marshall's, Michael's, Petsmart, Ross, Staples, Stater Bros, Target, Verizon

115b a   CA 210, Highland Ave, **E** to Lake Arrowhead

113   Base Line Rd, **E** 🅖 USA 🅕 Denny's, Jack-in-the-Box, Lo-gans Roadhouse, Pizza Hut, Rosa Maria's, Starbucks 🅛 Comfort Inn

C U C A M O N G A

112   CA 66, Foothill Blvd, **E** 🅖 Chevron 🅕 Asia Buffet, Claim-Jumper, Golden Spoon, In-N-Out, Panda Express, Subway, Taco Bell, Tutti Frutti Yogurt, Wienerschnitzel 🅞 $City, Food-4Less, Jiffy Lube, Radio Shack, Walmart, **W 1-2 mi** 🅖 76/ dsl, Chevron/dsl 🅕 Baker's, Buffalo Wild Wings, Carino's, Cheesecake Factory, Chick-fil-A, Chipotle Mexican, Del Taco, Denny's, El Pollo Loco, El Torito, Flemings Steaks, Islama-dora Fish Co, Jack-in-the-Box, Joe's Crab Shack, Johnny Rockets, Kings Fishouse, Lucille's BBQ, Old Spagetti Factory, Paisano's Rest., PF Chang's, Popeyes, Red Robin, Richie's Diner, Shakey's Pizza, Starbucks, TGIFriday's, The Hat Grill, Wendy's 🅛 Sheraton 4 Points 🅞 AT&T, AutoZone, Bass Pro Shops, Best Buy, Discount Tire, Fresh&Easy Mkt, Home De-pot, JC Penney, Macy's, Office Depot, Sears Grand

110   4th St, **E** 🅖 Arco/dsl 🅕 Baker's, Subway, **W** 🅖 76/dsl, Arco, Chevron/Alberto's Mexican/dsl, Shell/dsl 🅕 Applebee's, Ar-by's, Baja Fresh, Baskin-Robbins, BJ's Rest., Boston's, Burger King, Carl's Jr, Chevy's Mexican, Chick-fil-A, Chipotle, Chop Sticks, Chu Chinese, Coco's, Coldstone, Daphne's Greek, Del Taco, Denny's, El Pollo Loco, Famous Dave's BBQ, Fat Burger, Fuddruckers, Hooters, IHOP, In-N-Out, Jack-in-the-Box, Jamba Juice, Juice It Up, KFC, Krispy Kreme, Lazy Dog Cafe, McDonald's, Mkt Broiler, New City Buffet, NY Grill, Olive Garden, Oporto Chicken Burgers, Outback Steaks, Panera Bread, Quiznos, Rain Forest Cafe, Red Brick Pizza, Red Lob-ster, Rubio's, Sonic, Starbucks, Subway, Tokyo Tokyo, To-kyo Wako, Wendy's, Wienerschnitzel, Wing Place 🅛 Ayre's Suites, Country Inn&Suites, Courtyard, Hampton Inn, Hilton Garden, Holiday Inn Express, Homewood Suites, Hyatt Place, TownePlace Suites 🅞 $Tree, America's Tire, Costco/gas, JC Penney, Jo-Ann Fabrics, Kohl's, Marshall's, Ontario Mills Mall, Petsmart, Sam's Club/gas, Staples, Target, Tire Pros, Verizon

CA

ONTARIO · NORCO · EL CERRITO

⬆N INTERSTATE 15 Cont'd

Exit #	Services
109b a	I-10, E to San Bernardino, W to LA
108	Jurupa St, E ⛽ Chevron/dsl 🍴 Burger King, Del Taco, El Gran Burrito, Starbucks, Subway ⊙ Affordable RV, BMW, Chrysler/Dodge/Jeep, Family RV Ctr, Fiat, Honda, Hyundai, Lexus, Mazda, Mini, Nissan, Subaru, Toyota/Scion, Volvo, VW, W ⛽ Arco 🍴 Carl's Jr ⊙ Ford, Kia, Scandia funpark
106	CA 60, E to Riverside, W to LA
105	Cantu-Galleano Ranch Rd
103	Limonite Ave, E 🍴 5 Guys Burgers, Alberto's Mexican, Carl's Jr, Del Taco, Denny's, Hawaiian BBQ, Jamba Juice, Subway ⊙ Lowe's, Michael's, PetCo, Ross, W ⛽ Chevron 🍴 Applebee's, Carino's, Coldstone, El Gran Burrito, Farmer Boys, Golden Chop Sticks, Golden Spoon, Johnny Rockets, L&L BBQ, Little Caesars, McDonald's, On-the-Border, Panda Express, Pick Up Stix, Quiznos, Red Brick Pizza, Starbucks, Subway, Taco Bell, Tasty Chinese, Tutti Frutti Yogurt, Wendy's ⊙ AT&T, Best Buy, GNC, Home Depot, Kohl's, Nestle Tollhouse, Petsmart, Radio Shack, Ralph's Foods/gas, Staples, Target, TJ Maxx, URGENT CARE, Verizon, Vons Foods/gas, Walgreens
100	6th St, Norco Dr, Old Town Norco, E ⛽ 76/dsl, Chevron 🍴 Jack-in-the-Box, McDonald's, Starbucks ⊙ Rite Aid, W ⛽ Arco, Valero/dsl 🍴 Big Boy, Norco's Burgers, Senior Tacos, Wienerschnitzel, Zaky's Kabob 🏠 Knights Inn ⊙ Brake Masters, Jiffy Lube, USPO, vet
98	2nd St, W ⛽ Mobil, Shell/dsl, Thrifty 🍴 Baja Fish Tacos, Burger Basket, Burger King, Carl's Jr, Del Taco, Domino's, In-N-Out, Magic Wok, Pizza Hut, Polly's Cafe, Sizzler, Subway ⊙ $Tree, 7-11, Ace Hardware, America's Tire, Mazda, Norco Tires, Stater Bros
97	Yuma Dr, Hidden Valley Pkwy, E ⛽ 7-11 🍴 Baja Fresh, Chick-fil-A, Fat Burger, Hot Dog Shoppe, Shogun Japanese, Starbucks, Subway ⊙ Kohl's, Stater Bros, Walgreens, W ⛽ 76/dsl, Chevron, Shell/dsl 🍴 5 Guys Burgers, Alberto's Mexican, Burger City Grill, Carl's Jr, Chipotle, Denny's, Domino's, DQ, Hawaiian BBQ, Hickory Joe's BBQ, Jack-in-the-Box, Jamba Juice, Jersey Mikes, KFC, Magic Wok, McDonald's, Miguel's Jr, Papa John's, Pizza Hut/Taco Bell, Rodrigo's Mexican, Rubio's, Starbucks 🏠 Hampton Inn, Howard Johnson Express ⊙ Albertson's/Sav-On, America's Tire, AT&T, AutoZone, BigLots, GNC, K-Mart, O'Reilly Parts, Radio Shack, Staples, Target, Verizon, Walgreens
96b a	CA 91, to Riverside, beaches
95	Magnolia Ave, E ⛽ Chevron/Jack-in-the-Box/dsl 🍴 Islands Burgers, Lonestar Steaks, Shamrock's Grill 🏠 Residence Inn ⊙ AAA, Lowe's, Office Depot, W ⛽ Mobil/Circle K, Shell 🍴 Baskin-Robbins, Burger King, Coco's, Golden China, Jersey's Pizza, Little Caesars, McDonald's, Sizzler, Subway 🏠 Holiday Inn Express ⊙ $Tree, AT&T, CVS Drug, El Tapatio Mkt, O'Reilly Parts, Rite Aid, Stater Bros Foods
93	Ontario Ave, to El Cerrito, E ⛽ Shell/dsl 🍴 Sombrero Mexican, Starbucks ⊙ Mtn View Tire, vet, W ⛽ 76/Circle K, Arco, Chevron 🍴 Chopstix, Denny's, Eatza Pizza, El Pollo Loco, Hawaiian BBQ, In-N-Out, Jack-in-the-Box, Juice It Up, KFC, Magic Wok, McDonald's, Miguel's Jr, Papa John's, Porky's Pizza, Quiznos, Rubio's, SpringHill Suites, Subway, Taco Bell, Tommy's Burgers, Wienerschnitzel ⊙ Albertson's/Sav-On, America's Tire, AutoZone, CVS Drug, Fresh&Easy Mkt, Home Depot, Long's Drug, Radio Shack, Sam's Club/gas, USPO, vet, Walmart

LAKE ELSINORE

Exit #	Services
92	El Cerrito Rd
91	Cajalco Rd, E 🍴 5 Guys Burgers, BJ's Grill, Bubba Jack's Roadhouse, Buffalo Wild Wings, Chick-fil-A, Chili's, Jamba Juice, King's Fish House, Macaroni Grill, Panera Bread, Starbucks, Wendy's ⊙ AT&T, Barnes&Noble, Best Buy, Kohl's, Marshall's, Michael's, Old Navy, PetCo, Ross, See's Candies, Staples, Target, World Mkt, W ⛽ Mobil/dsl 🍴 Jack-in-the-Box, Juice It Up, NY Pizza, Subway ⊙ Stater Bros, vet
90	Weirick Rd, Dos Lagos Dr, E ⛽ Arco/dsl 🍴 Citrus City Grille, Miguel's, Tap's Rest., TGIFriday's, Wood Ranch BBQ ⊙ 7 Oaks Gen Store, Trader Joe's
88	Temescal Cyn Rd, Glen Ivy, E ⛽ Shell, W ⛽ Arco/dsl 🍴 Carl's Jr, Tom's Farms/BBQ
85	Indian Truck Trail, W 🍴 Pizza Hut, Starbucks, Subway ⊙ CVS Drug, Von's Foods/dsl
81	Lake St
78	Nichols Rd, W ⛽ Arco/dsl ⊙ Outlets/famous brands
77	CA 74, Central Ave, Lake Elsinore, E ⛽ Arco, Chevron, Mobil/Circle K/dsl 🍴 Archibald's, Burger King, Chili's, Del Taco, Douglas Burgers, Hawaiian BBQ, Juice It Up, Panda Express, Submarina, Taco Del Mar, Tom's ChiliBurgers, Wendy's ⊙ $Tree, AT&T, Costco/gas, Lowe's, Petsmart, Staples, Valvoline, W 🍴 El Pollo Loco, Farmer Boys, Golden Chop Stix, IHOP, McDonald's, Papa John's, Starbucks, Subway, Wienerschnitzel ⊙ 99¢ Store, Home Depot, PetCo, Target, Verizon, Walgreens
75	Main St, Lake Elsinore, W ⛽ Main St Gas/dsl 🍴 Gina's Rest. ⊙ Circle K, tires/repair
73	Railroad Cyn Rd, to Lake Elsinore, E ⛽ 76/7-11, Shell/Circle K/dsl 🍴 Alberto's Mexican, Denny's, El Pollo Loco, In-N-Out, KFC, Peony Chinese, Starbucks 🏠 Holiday Inn Express ⊙ Albertson's, GNC, Jiffy Lube, O'Reilly Parts, URGENT CARE, Verizon, vet, Von's Foods, Walmart/McDonald's, W ⛽ Arco, Chevron, Mobil/Circle K/dsl 🍴 Annie's Cafe, Cafe China, Carl's Jr, Coco's, Del Taco, Don Jose's Mexican, King Kabob, Kokoro Japanese, Los Gallos Mexican, McDonald's, My Buddies Pizza, Pizza Hut, Sizzler, Subway, Taco Bell, Vincenzo's 🏠 Best Western Lake Elsinore, Quality Inn, Travel Inn ⊙ 7-11, AutoZone, BigLots, Buick/GMC, Chevrolet, CVS Drug, Express Tire/auto, Firestone/auto, Ford, NAPA, Radio Shack, Rite Aid, Stater Bro's, vet, Walgreens
71	Bundy Cyn Rd, W ⛽ Arco 🍴 Jack-in-the-Box
69	Baxter Rd, E 🍴 Pizza Factory
68	Clinton Keith Rd, E ⛽ Chevron/dsl, USA 🍴 Denny's, Golden Spoon, Los Jilbetos Tacos, Los Reyes Grill, McDonald's, Panda Express, Starbucks, Subway ⊙ 🏥, Ace Hardware, Albertsons/sav-on, W ⛽ 7-11, Arco/dsl 🍴 Arriba Grill, Checkerboard Deli, D'Canter's Grill, Del Taco, Jack-in-the-Box, KFC/LJ Silver, Stadium Pizza, Starbucks, Submarina, Tresino's Italian, Yellow Basket Burgers ⊙ Baron's Mkt, Rite Aid, Stater Bro's
65	California Oaks Rd, Kalmia St, E ⛽ 76/Circle K/dsl, Chevron, Shell/7-11/dsl 🍴 Big Cheese Pizza, Burger King, Carl's Jr, Chili's, Chiptole Mexican, DQ, Jade Chinese, Jamba Juice, Jersey's, Jimenez Mexican, KFC, Little Caesars, Papa John's, Starbucks, Subway, Wings'N Things 🏠 Comfort Inn ⊙ $Tree, Albertson's/Sav-On, AutoZone, Express Tire, O'Reilly Parts, Radio Shack, Ralphs, Rite Aid, Target, Tuesday Morning, vet, Walgreens, W ⛽ Arco/dsl, Chevron 🍴 Applebee's, Carrow's, Chick-fil-A, Farmer Boys, Jack-in-the-Box, Juice It Up, Pick Up Stix, Sizzlin Steer, Subway, Taco Bell ⊙ America's Tire, fun ctr, Giant RV Ctr, Kohl's, Lowe's, Office Depot, PetCo, Verizon

M U R R I E T A	**🔼N INTERSTATE 15 Cont'd**

Exit #   Services

64 Murrieta Hot Springs Rd, to I-215, E🅿 7-11, Shell/dsl 🍴 Buffalo Wild Wings, Carl's Jr, El Pollo Loco, Hungry Bull, Richie's Diner, Rubio's, Sizzler, Starbucks, Wendy's ⊙ Ralph's Foods, Rite Aid, Ross, Sam's Club/gas, Walgreens, W🅿 7-11, Shell/Popeye's/dsl 🍴 Arby's, Chuy's, Coldstone, Denny's, IHOP, Jersey Mike's Subs, McDonald's, Panda Express, Starbucks, Subway, Tom's Burgers, Wienerschnitzel ⊙ 99¢ Store, AAA, American Tire Depot, AT&T, Best Buy, BigLots, Home Depot, Petsmart, Staples, Walmart/McDonald's

63 I-215 N (from nb), to Riverside

62 French Valley Pkwy (from sb, no return), W🍴 Los Cabos ⊙ BMW, O'Reilly Parts, VW

61 CA 79 N, Winchester Rd, E🅿 76/dsl, Chevron 🍴 5 Guys Burgers, Baja Fresh, Baskin-Robbins/Togo's, BF Greek Rest., BJ's Rest., Burger King, CA Pizza Kitchen, Chick-fil-A, Chipotle Mexican, Coldstone, Corner Cafe, Del Taco, Dickey's BBQ, El Torito, Famous Dave's, Fatburger, Freebirds Burrito, Harry's Grill, Hometown Buffet, Islands Burgers, Jamba Juice, Lazy Dog Cafe, Lucille's BBQ, Macaroni Grill, McDonald's, Mimi's Cafe, Ming's, Olive Garden, Outback Steaks, Panda Express, Panera Bread, PF Chang's, Red Ginger Chinese, Red Lobster, Red Robin, Shakey's Pizza, Shogun Chinese, Souplantation, Starbucks, Subway, Taco Bell, TGIFriday's, Tilted Kilt, Wahoo's, Yellow Basket Hamburgers ⊙ $Tree, 99¢ Store, America's Tire, AT&T, AutoZone, Barnes&Noble, Costco/gas, CVS Drug, Express Tire, Express Tire, Food-4Less, GNC, Hobby Lobby, Hyundai, JC Penney, Jo-Ann Fabrics, K-Mart, Lowe's, Macy's, Nissan, Office Depot, Old Navy, PepBoys, PetCo, Radio Shack, Ramona Tire, Roots Mkt, Sears/auto, See's Candies, TJ Maxx, Trader Joe's, Verizon, WinCo Foods, World Mkt, W🅿 Arco, Chevron/dsl 🍴 Arby's, Banzai Japanese, Chin's Gourmet Chinese, Del Taco, El Pollo Loco, Farmer Boys, In-N-Out, Jack-in-the-Box, Patsy's Country Kitchen, Serrano's Grill, Starbucks, Subway, Super China, Tacos El Gallo, Vail Ranch Steakhouse, Wendy's 🏨 Best Western, Extended Stay America, Fairfield Inn, Holiday Inn Express, La Quinta, Quality Inn ⊙ NAPA, Richardson's RV Ctr, st patrol, tires/repair, vet

T E M E C U L A	**59** Rancho California Rd, E🅿 Arco, Mobil/Circle K/dsl, Shell/dsl 🍴 Black Angus, Chili's, ClaimJumper, Del Taco, Golden Spoon, Jilberto's Mexican, Little Caesars, Marie Callender's, Pat&Oscar's Rest., Peony Chinese, Pizza Hut, RoundTable Pizza, Rubio's, Starbucks, Subway, Times Square NY Pizza 🏨 Embassy Suites ⊙ BigLots, CVS Drug, Ford, Mazda, Michael's, Subaru, Target, URGENT CARE, Verizon, vet, Von's Foods, W🅿 76/Circle K/dsl, Chevron 🍴 Alberto's Mexican, Denny's, McDonald's, Mr Kabob Grill, Penfold's Cafe, Rosa's Café, Starbucks, Vince's Spaghetti 🏨 Hampton Inn, Motel 6, Rancho California Inn, Rodeway Inn, SpringHill Suites ⊙ to Old Town Temecula, USPO
	58 CA 79 S, to Indio, Temecula, E🅿 Mobil/Circle K/dsl, Valero/Circle K/dsl 🍴 Carl's Jr, Del Taco, Domino's, Domino's, Francesca's Italian, Golden Bowl Asian, In-N-Out, Los Jilberto's, Starbucks, Utopizza, Wing-n-Things ⊙ 7-11, Ace Hardware, America's Tire, CVS Drug, Valvoline, W🅿 Arco, Shell/dsl 🍴 Baskin-Robbins, Eldorado Mexican, Garage Rest., Hungry Howie's, Leinzo Charro Mexican, Wienerschnitzel 🏨 Ramada Inn ⊙ Express Tire, Harley-Davidson

55mm check sta nb

54 Rainbow Valley Blvd, E 2 mi ⊙ food, gas, W⊙ CA Insp Sta

---

51 Mission Rd, to Fallbrook, W⊙ 🇭

46 CA 76, to Oceanside, Pala, E⊙ RV camp, W🅿 Mobil/Circle K 🍴 McGrath's Grill 🏨 Quality Inn ⊙ Pala Meas Mkt

44mm San Luis Rey River

43 Old Hwy 395

41 Gopher Canyon Rd, Old Castle Rd, E 1 mi 🏨 Welk Resort ⊙ gas, RV camping

37 Deer Springs Rd, Mountain Meadow Rd, W🅿 Arco

34 Centre City Pkwy (from sb)

33 El Norte Pkwy, E🅿 Arco, Shell/dsl 🍴 Arby's, DQ, IHOP, Papa John's, Starbucks 🏨 Best Western ⊙ CVS Drug, Express Tire/auto repair, Radio Shack, RV Resort, vet, Von's Foods, W🅿 76/7-11/dsl, Circle K 🍴 Jack-in-the-Box, Killer Pizza, Rita's Custard, Subway, Wendy's ⊙ vet, Von's Foods

32 CA 78, to Oceanside

E S C O N D I D O	**31** Valley Pkwy, E🅿 Arco 🍴 Chili's, ChuckeCheese, Cocina del Charro, Firehouse Subs, McDonald's, Olive Garden, Panda Express, Rock'N Jenny's Subs, Thai Kitchen ⊙ 🇭, Barnes&Noble, Meineke, Michael's, PetCo, URGENT CARE, W🅿 Express 🍴 5 Guys Burgers, Applebee's, Burger King, Carl's Jr, Chipotle Mexican, Coco's, Del Taco, El Pollo Loco, In-N-Out, Jamba Juice, Mike's BBQ, Panera Bread, Pick Up Stix, Port of Subs, Primo's Mexican, Soup Plantation, Starbucks, Subway, Wendy's 🏨 Comfort Inn, Holiday Inn Express ⊙ 7-11, Albertson's, AT&T, BigLots, CVS Drug, Dick's, GNC, Home Depot, Lexus, Ross, Staples, Target, TJ Maxx, Verizon, World Mkt

30 9th Ave, Auto Parkway, E⊙ Infiniti, Mercedes, W same as 31

29 Felicita Rd

28 Centre City Pkwy (from nb, no return), E🍴 Center City Café 🏨 Escondido Lodge ⊙ vet

27 Via Rancho Pkwy, to Escondido, E🅿 Chevron/dsl, Shell 🍴 BJ's Rest., Cheesecake Factory, Macaroni Grill, On-the-Border, Panera Bread, Red Robin ⊙ JC Penney, Macy's, Nordstrom, San Diego Animal Park, Sears/auto, Target, W🅿 Shell/Quiznos/dsl 🍴 McDonald's, Starbucks, Subway ⊙ Verizon

26 W Bernardo Dr, to Highland Valley Rd, Palmerado Rd

24 Rancho Bernardo Rd, to Lake Poway, E🅿 Arco, Mobil/Circle K 🍴 Chef Chin, Cojita's Taco, Pizza Hut, Soup Plantation, Starbucks, Stirfresh, Sub Marina, Subway 🏨 Hilton Garden ⊙ AT&T, Barons Mkt, GNC, Von's Foods, W🅿 76/Circle K, Chevron/7-11 🍴 Elephant Bar Rest., Starbucks 🏨 Holiday Inn Express, Radisson

23 Bernardo Ctr Dr, E🅿 Chevron 🍴 Burger King, Carl's Jr, Coco's, Denny's, Hibachi Buffet, Jack-in-the-Box, Little Caesars, McDonald's, Quiznos, Robeks Juice, RoundTable Pizza, Rubio's ⊙ 7-11, CVS Drug, Express Tire/auto, Firestone/auto, Radio Shack, vet

[map of Riverside / Moreno Valley / Lake Elsinore / Murrieta / Temecula area with CA]

N INTERSTATE 15 Cont'd

Exit #	Services
22	Camino del Norte
21	Carmel Mtn Rd, **E** 🅖 Chevron, Shell/dsl 🍴 Athens Greek, Baskin-Robbins, Boston Mkt, Broken Yolk Cafe, CA Pizza Kitchen, Carl's Jr, Chick-fil-A, China Fun, Chipotle Mexican, ClaimJumper, DQ Orange Julius, El Pollo Loco, Habit Burgers, In-N-Out, Islands Burgers, Jamba Juice, Little Tokyo, Marie Callender's, McDonald's, Olive Garden, O's American Kitchen, Panda Express, Panera Bread, Rubio's, Sombrero Mexican, Subway, Taco Bell, TGIFriday's, Wendy's, Which Wich? 🛏 Residence Inn 🅞 AT&T, Barnes&Noble, Best Buy, Costco/gas, GNC, Home Depot, Marshall's, Michael's, PetCo, Radio Shack, Ralph's Foods, Rite Aid, Ross, Sears Outlet, See's Candies, Sprouts Mkt, Staples, TJ Maxx, Trader Joe's, USPO, Valvoline, Verizon, **W** 🅖 Chevron 🍴 Jack-in-the-Box, Starbucks 🅞 7-11, Albertson's, Big O Tire, Office Depot
19	CA 56 W, Ted Williams Pkwy
18	Rancho Penasquitos Blvd, Poway Rd, **E** 🅖 Arco 🍴 Alvero's Mexican, Papa John's 🅞 AAA, **W** 🅖 76/dsl, Mobil/dsl 🍴 IHOP, McDonald's, Mi Ranchito Mexican, MXN Cafe, NY Pizza, Starbucks, Subway 🛏 La Quinta 🅞 7-11
17	Mercy Rd, Scripps Poway Pkwy, **E** 🅖 USA/dsl 🍴 Chili's, Wendy's, Yanni's Grill 🛏 Residence Inn, SpringHill Suites, **W** 🅖 Chevron 🍴 KFC, Que Pasa Mexican, Starbucks
16	Mira Mesa Blvd, to Lake Miramar, **E** 🍴 Bruski Burgers, ChuckeCheese, Denny's, Filippi's Pizza, Filippi's Pizza, Gyu-Kaku Japanese, Lucio's Mexican, Nok Thai, Pizza Hut, Shozen BBQ 🛏 Comfort Suites, Holiday Inn Express 🅞 Trader Joe's, USPO, **W** 🅖 Arco, Shell 🍴 Applebee's, Arby's, Buca Italian, Coldstone, El Patron, In-N-Out, Islands Burgers, Jack-in-the-Box, Jamba Juice, Jersey Mike's Subs, McDonald's, Mimi's Café, MXN Mexican, On the Border, Panera Bread, Pick Up Stix, Popeye's, Rubio's, Starbucks, Subway, Wings n Things 🅞 Albertson's/Sav-On, AutoZone, Barnes&Noble, Best Buy, BigLots, CVS Drug, Discount Tire, GNC, Home Depot, Old Navy, Ralph's Foods, Rite Aid, Ross, USPO, Verizon
15	Carroll Canyon Rd, to Miramar College, **E** 🍴 Carl's Jr, Subway
14	Pomerado Rd, Miramar Rd, **W** 🅖 Chevron/dsl, Mobil, Shell/dsl, USA/dsl 🍴 Carl's Jr, Chin's Rest., IHOP, Rice King, Subway 🛏 Best Western, Holiday Inn, Quality Inn 🅞 Audi/Porsche, aviation museum, Land Rover, vet
13	Miramar Way, US Naval Air Station
12	CA 163 S (from sb), to San Diego
11	to CA 52
10	Clairemont Mesa Blvd, **W** 🍴 Boll Weevil Rest., Carl's Jr, China Express, Giovanni's, Giovanni's Pizza, Jack-in-the-Box, Jersey Mike's, La Salsa, McDonald's, Panda Express, Primo's Mexican, Robeks, Rubio's, Spice House Cafe, Starbucks, Subway, Sunny Donuts, Taco Bell, Taco Bell, Togo's, Wendy's 🅞 7-11, vet
9	CA 274, Balboa Ave
8	Aero Dr, **W** 🅖 Arco, Chevron/dsl 🍴 Baskin-Robbins/Togo's, Jack-in-the-Box, McDonald's, Papa John's, Pick Up Stix, Rubio's, Sizzler, SmashBurger, Starbucks, Submarina, Subway, Taco Bell 🛏 Holiday Inn 🅞 $Tree, AT&T, Express Tire/auto, Fry's Electronics, Petsmart, Radio Shack, Verizon, Von's Foods, Walmart/McDonald's
7b	Friars Rd W, **W** 🍴 Coldstone, Dragon Chinese, IHOP, Islands Burgers, Luna Grill, McDonald's, Oggi's Pizza, Playa Grill, Starbucks, Subway 🅞 Costco/gas, Lowe's, San Diego Stadium

S A N D I E G O

Exit #	Services
7a	Friars Rd E
6b	I-8, E to El Centro, W to beaches
6a	Adams Ave, downtown
5b	El Cajon Blvd, **E** 🅖 Pearson/dsl/E85/NG 🍴 Subway 🅞 Carquest, Ford, **W** 🅖 Chevron/dsl, United Oil 🍴 Church's 🅞 PepBoys
5a	University Ave, **E** 🅖 Chevron/dsl 🍴 Burger King, Jack-in-the-Box
3	I-805, N to I-5, S to San Ysidro
2b	(2c from nb) CA 94 W, downtown
2a	Market St, downtown
1c	National Ave, Ocean View Blvd
1b	(from sb) I-5 S, to Chula Vista
1a	(from sb) I-5 N. **I-15 begins/ends on I-5**

E INTERSTATE 40

Exit #	Services
155	California/Arizona state line, Colorado River, Pacific/Mountain time zone
153	Park Moabi Rd, to Rte 66, **N** boating, camping
149mm	insp both lanes
148	5 Mile Rd, to Topock, Rte 66 (from eb)
144	US 95 S, E Broadway, Needles, **N** 🅖 Chevron/dsl, Mobil, Shell/dsl/LP 🍴 Domino's 🅞 Basha's Foods, Harris Repair/towing, Rite Aid, **S** 🛏 Best Value Inn 🅞 $Tree, Stout Tires/repair
142	J St, Needles, **N** 🅖 76, Valero/dsl 🍴 Jack-in-the-Box, McDonald's 🛏 Travelers Inn 🅞 Big O Tire, NAPA, **S** 🍴 Denny's 🛏 Days Inn, Motel 6 🅞 🅗
141	W Broadway, River Rd, Needles, **N** 🍴 River City Pizza 🛏 Best Motel, Desert Mirage Inn, River Valley Motel, **S** 🅖 Chevron/dsl, Mobil/dsl, Shell/DQ/dsl 🍴 Carl's Jr, China Garden, River Cafe, Taco Bell, Wagon Wheel Rest. 🛏 Best Western, Budget Inn, Needles Inn, Relax Inn, Rio Del Sol Inn 🅞 auto/RV/tire/repair
139	River Rd Cutoff (from eb), **N** 🅞 Desert View RV Park, KOA, Hist Rte 66, rec area
133	US 95 N, to Searchlight, to Rte 66
120	Water Rd
115	Mountain Springs Rd, elev 2770, High Springs Summit
107	Goffs Rd, Essex, **N** gas/dsl/food, Hist Rte 66
106mm	🆁🆂 both lanes, full 🚾 facilities, litter barrels, petwalk, 🅲, 🛗
100	Essex Rd, Essex, **N** Mitchell Caverns, to Providence Mtn SP
78	Kelbaker Rd, to Amboy, E Mojave Nat Preserve, Kelso, **S** 🅞 RV camping (14mi), Hist Rte 66
50	Ludlow, **N** 🅖 76/DQ, **S** 🅖 Chevron/dsl 🍴 Ludlow Cafe 🛏 Ludlow Motel
33	Hector Rd, to Hist Rte 66
28mm	🆁🆂 both lanes, full 🚾 facilities, litter barrels, petwalk, 🅲, 🛗
23	Ft Cady Rd, to Newberry Spgs, **S** 🅞 Newberry Mtn RV Park, Twins Lake RV Park (8mi)
18	Newberry Springs, **S** 🅖 Chevron/Subway/dsl/LP
12	Barstow-Daggett 🛬, **N** 🅞 🛬
7	Daggett, **N** 🅞 RV camping (2mi), to Calico Ghost Town
5	Nebo St (from eb), to Hist Rte 66
2	USMC Logistics Base, **N** 🛏 Pennywise Inn
1	E Main St, Montara Rd, Barstow, **N** 1 mi 🅖 76/dsl, Chevron, Circle K, Shell/dsl, Thrifty/dsl, Valero 🍴 Burger King, Carl's Jr, China Town Buffet, Coco's, Del Taco, Denny's, FireHouse Italian, Grill It, Hollywood Subs, IHOP, Jack-in-the-Box, Jenny's Grill, Little Caesars, LJ Silver, McDonald's, Panda Express, Popeye's, Sizzler, Starbucks, Taco Bell, Tom's Burgers,

⬆E INTERSTATE 40 Cont'd

**B
A
R
S
T
O
W**

Exit #	Services
1	Continued
	Wienerschnitzel 🛏 Astrobudget Motel, Best Motel, Best Western, Budget Inn, CA Inn, Days Inn, Desert Inn, EconoLodge, Economy Inn, Motel 6, Quality Inn/rest, Ramada Inn, Rodeway Inn, Super 8, Travelodge ⊙ $Tree, 99Cent Store, AutoZone, Family$, O'Reilly Parts, Radio Shack, U-Haul/LP, vet, Von's Foods, S ⛽ Arco ⊙ Walmart/McDonald's/auto
0mm	**I-40 begins/ends on I-15 in Barstow**

⬆E INTERSTATE 80

**T
R
U
C
K
E
E**

Exit #	Services
208	California/Nevada state line
201	Farad
199	Floristan
194	Hirschdale Rd, N Stampede Dam, to Boca Dam, S RV Park
191	(from wb), **inspection sta, weigh sta**
190	Overland Trail
188	CA 89 N, CA 267, to N Shore Lake Tahoe, N ⊙ Coachland RV Park, USFS, S same as 186
186	Central Truckee (no eb return), S ⛽ 76/dsl, Beacon 🍴 Burger Me, Casa Baeza Mexican, El Toro Bravo Mexican, Jax Truckee Diner, Marg's Taco Bistro, Wagon Train Café 🛏 Hilltop Lodge, Truckee Hotel
185	CA 89 S, to N Lake Tahoe, N 🍴 DQ, El Sancho, Jiffy's Pizza, Panda Express, Port of Subs, RoundTable Pizza, Starbucks, Zano's Pizza ⊙ H, 7-11, Ace Hardware, hwy patrol, NAPA, New Moon Natural Foods, Rite Aid, Safeway Foods, URGENT CARE, Verizon, S ⛽ Shell/dsl 🍴 Bill's Rotisseire, McDonald's, Subway, Village Pizzaria ⊙ auto repair, CVS Drug, O'Reilly Parts, RV camping, SaveMart Foods, to Squaw Valley
184	Donner Pass Rd, Truckee, N ⛽ Shell/dsl 🍴 La Bamba Mexican, Smokey's Kitchen, Taco Station 🛏 Sunset Inn ⊙ vet, S ⛽ 76, Chevron/dsl 🍴 Taco Bell 🛏 Truckee Donner Lodge ⊙ chain service, RV camp/dump, to Donner SP
181mm	vista point both lanes
180	Donner Lake (from wb), S 🛏 Donner Lake Village Resort
177mm	Donner Summit, elev 7239, Rs both lanes, full ♿ facilities, litter barrels, petwalk, ⟨C⟩, ⛽, view area
176	Castle Park, Boreal Ridge Rd, S 🛏 Boreal Inn/rest. ⊙ Pacific Crest Trailhead, skiing
174	Soda Springs, Norden, S ⛽ Sugar Bowl/dsl 🍴 Summit Rest. 🛏 Donner Summit Lodge ⊙ chain services
171	Kingvale, S ⛽ Shell
168	Rainbow Rd, to Big Bend, S 🛏 Rainbow Lodge/rest. ⊙ RV camping
166	Big Bend (from eb), no facilities
165	Cisco Grove, N ⊙ RV camp/dump, skiing, snowmobiling, S ⛽ Chevron/dsl ⊙ chain services
164	Eagle Lakes Rd
161	CA 20 W, to Nevada City, Grass Valley
160	Yuba Gap, S ⊙ boating, camping, ⟨C⟩, ⛽, skiing, snowpark
158a	Emigrant Gap (from eb), S 🛏 Sierra Woods Lodge/café ⊙ USPO
158	Laing Rd, S 🛏 Sierra Woods Lodge/café ⊙ USPO
157mm	**brake check area, wb**
156mm	**brake check area**
156	Nyack Rd, Emigrant Gap, S ⛽ Shell/Burger King/dsl 🍴 Nyack Café ⊙ USPO
155	Blue Canyon

Exit #	Services
150	Drum Forebay
148b	Baxter, N ⊙ chainup services, food, ⟨C⟩, RV camping
148a	Crystal Springs
146	Alta
145	Dutch Flat, N 🍴 Monte Vista Rest., S ⛽ 76/dsl ⊙ chainup services, Dutch Flat RV Resort, hwy patrol
144	Gold Run (from wb), N chainup, food, gas/dsl, ⟨C⟩
143mm	Rs both lanes, full ♿ facilities, litter barrels, petwalk, ⟨C⟩, ⛽
143	Magra Rd, Gold Run, N chainup services
140	Magra Rd, Rollins Lake Rd, Secret Town Rd
139	Rollins Lake Road (from wb), RV camping
135	CA 174, to Grass Valley, Colfax, N ⛽ 76/dsl, Beacon/dsl 🍴 Colfax Max Burgers, McDonald's, Pizza Factory, Starbucks, Taco Bell, TJ's Roadhouse 🛏 Colfax Motel ⊙ NAPA, Sierra Mkt Foods, S ⛽ Chevron/dsl, Valero/dsl 🍴 Shang Garden Chinese, Subway
133	Canyon Way, to Colfax, S 🍴 Dine'n Dash Cafe ⊙ Chevrolet, Plaza Tire
131	Cross Rd, to Weimar, no facilites
130	W Paoli Lane, to Weimar, S ⛽ Weimar Store/dsl
129	Heather Glen, elev 2000 ft
128	Applegate, N ⛽ Valero/dsl/LP ⊙ chainup services
125	Clipper Gap, Meadow Vista
124	Dry Creek Rd, ⊙ no services
123	Bell Rd
122	Foresthill Rd, Ravine Rd, Auburn, N ⊙ RV camping/dump, S 🍴 Burger King, La Bonte's Rest., Sizzler, Starbucks, Subway 🛏 Best Western, Quality Inn ⊙ same as 121
121	(from eb) Lincolnway, Auburn, N ⛽ Flyers/dsl, Mobil, Valero/dsl 🍴 Denny's, JimBoy's Tacos, Starbucks, Taco Bell, Wienerschnitzel 🛏 Comfort Inn, Foothills Motel, Motel 6, Super 8, S ⛽ Arco, Beacon/dsl, Chevron/dsl, Gas&Shop, Shell/dsl 🍴 Black Bear Diner, Burger King, Burrito Shop, Carl's Jr, Hawaiian BBQ, Jack-in-the-Box, Joe Caribe Bistro, KFC, La Bonte's Rest., McDonald's, Pete's Grill, Sierra Grill, Sizzler, Starbucks, Subway 🛏 Best Western, Quality Inn ⊙ Ikeda's Mkt, Raley's Foods, Verizon
120	Russell Ave (from wb), same as 121, to Lincolnway from eb
119c	Elm Ave, Auburn, N ⛽ 76/dsl, Shell/dsl 🍴 Foster's, Starbucks 🛏 Holiday Inn ⊙ CVS Drug, Grocery Outlet, Rite Aid, SaveMart Foods, Staples, Verizon
119b	CA 49, to Grass Valley, Auburn, N ⛽ 76/dsl, Shell/dsl 🍴 In-N-Out 🛏 Holiday Inn ⊙ RV Connection, Staples
119a	Maple St, Nevada St, Old Town Auburn, S ⛽ Valero 🍴 Cafe Delicias, Mary Belle's, Tio Pepe Mexican ⊙ USPO
118	Ophir Rd (from wb)
116	CA 193, to Lincoln
115	Indian Hill Rd, Newcastle, N ⊙ transmissions, USPO, S ⛽ Flyers/dsl, Valero/dsl 🍴 Denny's ⊙ CHP

**C
O
L
F
A
X**

**A
U
B
U
R
N**

 = gas = food = lodging = other = rest stop   Copyright 2015 - the Next EXIT ®

INTERSTATE 80 Cont'd

CA

ROCKLIN

Exit #	Services
112	Penryn, N 76/dsl, Valero/dsl Ground Cow Rest., Subway
110	Horseshoe Bar Rd, to Loomis, N Burger King, RoundTable Pizza, Starbucks, Taco Bell Raley's Food
109	Sierra College Blvd, N 7-11/dsl, Arco/dsl, Chevron/McDonald's/dsl Blast Pizza, Carl's Jr, Chipotle, Noodles&Co, Panera Bread, Subway Camping World RV Ctr, Rocklin RV Ctr, Ross, Steinmart, Target, Tesla, Verizon, S Starbucks Petsmart, Walmart
108	Rocklin Rd, N Valero/dsl A&W/KFC, Adalberto's Mexican, Arby's, Baskin-Robbins, Denny's, Golden Dragon, Jack-in-the-Box, Jamba Juice, Milo's, Mongolian BBQ, Papa Murphy's, RoundTable Pizza, Starbucks, Subway, Taco Bell Days Inn, Heritage Inn, Howard Johnson CVS Drug, GNC, Land Rover, Mercedes, Porsche, Radio Shack, Safeway Foods, S Arco Little Caesar's Rocklin Park Hotel vet
106	CA 65, to Lincoln, Marysville, N **1 mi on Stanford Ranch Rd** 76, Arco, Shell Black Bear Diner, Carl's Jr, Cheesecake Factory, Chipotle, IHOP, Jack-in-the-Box, KFC, Olive Garden, On-the-Border, PF Changs, TGIFriday Holiday Inn Express AutoZone, Barnes&Noble, Best Buy, Costco, Goodyear/auto, JC Penney, Macy's, Marshall's, Michael's, Nordstrom's, Old Navy, Ross, Sears/auto, Sprouts Mkt, Staples
105b	Taylor Rd, to Rocklin (from eb), N Cattlemen's Rest., S 76/Burger King/dsl, Chevron Islands Burgers, Subway, Tahoe Joe's Courtyard, Fairfield Inn, Hilton Garden, Holiday Inn Express, Larkspur Suites, Residence Inn H, funpark
105a	Atlantic St, Eureka Rd, S 76/7-11/dsl, Shell/Circle K Brookfield's Rest., Chicago Fire Rest., In-N-Out, Taco Bell, Wendy's H, Acura, America'sTire, Buick/GMC, Carmax, Chevrolet, Chrysler/Dodge/Jeep, Fiat, Ford, Home Depot, Honda, Hyundai, Infiniti, Kia, Lexus, Mazda, Nissan, Petsmart, Subaru, Target, Toyota/Scion, VW

CITRUS HEIGHTS

103b a	Douglas Blvd, N 76/dsl, Arco/dsl, Chevron/7-11, Shell/dsl Burger King, Carolina's Mexican, Claim Jumper, McDonald's, Mongolian BBQ, Popeyes, Starbucks, Subway Best Western, Extended Stay America, Heritage Inn $Tree, Ace Hardware, Autozone, Big O Tire, BigLots, BrakeMasters, Goodyear, Grocery Outlet, Midas, O'Reilly Parts, Rite Aid, Trader Joe's, S Carl's Jr, Carrow's, Chevy's, Del Taco, Denny's, Jack-in-the-Box, Lorenzo's Mexican, Outback Steaks, Panera Bread, Rubio's, Sizzler, Subway Best Western, Hampton Inn H, Fry's Electronics, Hobby Lobby, Office Depot, Ross, Target
102	Riverside Ave, Auburn Blvd, to Roseville, N Arco/dsl, Valero/dsl Starbucks auto repair, Meineke, S Chevron/7-11, Shell, Towne Mart Back 40 TX BBQ, Baskin-Robbins, CA Burgers, Jack-in-the-Box, Subway, The Station Bistro $General, auto repair, AutoZone, BMW Motorcycles, Camping World RV Ctr, K-Mart, NAPA, Schwab Tire
100mm	**weigh sta both lanes**
100	Antelope Rd, to Citrus Heights, N 76 Carl's Jr, Extreme Hummus, Giant Pizza, McDonald's, Papa Murphy's, Popeye's, RoundTable Pizza, Subway, Taco Bell, Wendy's $Tree, 7-11, O'Reilly Parts, Raley's Foods, vet
98	Greenback Lane, Elkhorn Blvd, Orangedale, Citrus Heights, N Baskin Robbins, Carl's Jr, Little Caesar's, McDonald's, Pizza Hut, Subway, Taco Bell $General, CVS Drug, Radio Shack, Safeway Foods

SACRAMENTO

96	Madison Ave, N Chevron/dsl, Valero/dsl Brookfield's Rest., Denny's, El Malecon Mexican, Jack-in-the-Box, Mongolian BBQ, Starbucks Motel 6, Super 8 funpark, to McClellan AFB, S Arco, Shell/dsl Boston Mkt, Burger King, Chipotle Mexican, El Pollo Loco, IHOP, In-N-Out, Jack-in-the-Box, McDonald's, Panda Express, Starbucks, Strings Italian, Subway, Wienerschnitzel Crowne Plaza, La Quinta 7-11, Acura, AT&T, Chevrolet, Firestone/auto, Ford, Office Depot, PepBoys, Schwab Tire, Target, Verizon, Walgreens
95	CA 99 S
94b	Auburn Blvd
94a	Watt Ave, N 76/dsl, Arco Carl's Jr, Golden Corral, Jack-in-the-Box, KFC, McDonald's, Panda Express, Starbucks, Subway, Taco Bell Courtyard Inn, Mega Inn $Tree, Firestone/auto, McClellan AFB, Walmart, S 76/dsl, Arco, Chevron, Shell China Taste, Denny's, Jimboy's Tacos, Kim Long Noodle House, Quiznos, Starbucks, Wendy's Economy Inn AutoZone, Grocery Outlet
93	Longview Dr
92	Winters St
91	Raley Blvd, Marysville Blvd, to Rio Linda, N Arco, Chevron/dsl, S $General, Hooten Tires, Mkt Basket Foods, USPO
90	Norwood Ave, N Arco/Jack-in-the-Box, Valero Little Caesar's, McDonald's, RoundTable Pizza, Starbucks, Subway Rite Aid, Viva Foods, Walgreens, S $General
89	Northgate Blvd, Sacramento, N Cilantro's Mexican, L&L Hawaiian BBQ, Subway, Wendy's Fry's Electronics, S Arco, Shell, Valero/Circle K 524 Mexican, Carl's Jr, Classic Burgers, El Pollo Loco, IHOP, KFC, LampPost Pizza, LJ Silver, McDonald's/playplace, Subway, Taco Bell Extended Stay America, Quality Inn $Tree, Foodsco Foods, O'Reilly Parts, PepBoys, Schwab Tire
88	Truxel Rd, N Chevron/McDonald's, Shell/dsl Applebee's, BJ's Rest, Buffalo Wild Wings, Chili's, Chipotle Mexican, Del Taco, Firehouse Subs, Hooters, In-N-Out, Logan's Roadhouse, Mimi's Cafe, On the Border, Panda Express, Panera Bread, Rubio's, Sandwich Spot, Starbucks, Subway, Tokyo Steakhouse Staybridge Suites AT&T, Barnes&Noble, Best Buy, GNC, Home Depot, Michael's, Old Navy, Petsmart, Power Balance Pavilion, Radio Shack, Ross, See's Candies, Staples, Target, Verizon, Walmart, World Mkt
86	I-5, N to Redding, S to Sacramento, to CA 99 N
85	W El Camino, N 49er Trkstp/Silver Skillet/dsl/scales/24hr/@, Chevron/Subway/dsl/24hr Burger King Fairfield Inn, Super 8
83	Reed Ave, N 76/dsl Hawaiian BBQ, Jack-in-the-Box, Los Amigo's, Panda Express, Quizno's, Starbucks, Subway Extended Stay America, Hampton Inn dsl repair, S Arco/24hr, Shell/McDonald's/dsl In-N-Out, Taco Bell Home Depot, Walmart Super Ctr
82	US 50 E, W Sacramento
81	Enterprise Blvd, W Capitol Ave, W Sacramento, N Chevron/dsl/24hr, Valero/dsl Eppie's Rest/24hr Granada Inn, S 7-11 Denny's, JR's BBQ, Starbucks, Subway KOA
78	Rd 32A, E Chiles Rd, S Fruit Stand
75	Mace Blvd, N Arco, S Chevron/24hr, Valero/dsl Burger King, Cindy's Rest., McDonald's, Mtn Mike's Pizza, Subway, Taco Bell/24hr Howard Johnson, Motel 6 Chevrolet, Chrysler/Dodge/Jeep, Ford, Honda, Nissan, Nugget Mkt Foods, Schwab Tire, to Mace Ranch, Toyota/Scion, Tuesday Morning
73	Olive Dr (from wb, no EZ return)

INTERSTATE 80 Cont'd

Exit #	Services
72b a	Richards Blvd, Davis, N 🅿 Shell/24hr 🍴 Caffe Italia, In-N-Out, Redrum Burger 🏠 University Park Inn ⊡ NAPA, S 🅿 Chevron 🍴 Applebee's, Del Taco, IHOP, KFC, Wendy's 🏠 Comfort Suites, Hotel Davis ⊡ Jiffy Lube, O'Reilly Parts
71	to UC Davis
70	CA 113 N, to Woodland, N ⊡ Ⓗ
69	Kidwell Rd
67	Pedrick Rd, N 🅿 76/LP, Chevron/dsl ⊡ produce
66b	Milk Farm Rd (from wb)
66a	CA 113 S, Currey Rd, to Dixon, S 🅿 Arco, CFN/dsl, Shell/dsl, Valero/Popeye's/dsl 🍴 Cattlemen's Rest., Jack-in-the-Box, Papa Murphy's, Subway, Taco Del Mar, Wendy's 🏠 Comfort Suites ⊡ Walmart
64	Pitt School Rd, to Dixon, S 🅿 Chevron/24hr, Valero/24hr 🍴 Arby's, Asian Garden, Burger King, Chevy's Mexican, Denny's, IHOP, Little Ceasar's, Maria's Mexican, Mary's Pizza, McDonald's, Pizza Guys, Quizno's, Solano Bakery, Starbucks, Subway, Taco Bell 🏠 Best Western, Microtel ⊡ Ford, O'Reilly Parts, Safeway/dsl
63	Dixon Ave, Midway Rd, N 🅿 Truck Stp/dsl, S 🅿 Chevron/LP/lube, USA/24hr 🍴 Carl's Jr, Mr Taco 🏠 Super 8 ⊡ Dixon Fruit Mkt, RV Dump
60	Midway Rd, Lewis Rd, Elmyra, N ⊡ Produce Mkt, RV camping
59	Meridian Rd, Weber Rd
57	Leisure Town Rd, N ⊡ Ⓗ, Camping World, S 🅿 76/McDonald's, Arco, Chevron, KwikStop/dsl 🍴 Black Oak Rest., Island Grill, Jack-in-the-Box, King's Buffet, Omlette Bistro, Popeye's, Quizno's 🏠 Best Value, Extended Stay America, Fairfield Inn, Holiday Inn Express, Motel 6, Quality Inn, Residence Inn ⊡ Buick/GMC, Chevrolet, Chrysler/Dodge/Jeep, Harley-Davidson, Home Depot, Honda, Kohl's, Nissan, Toyota, VW
56	I-505 N, to Winters
55	Nut Tree Pkwy, Monte Vista Dr, Allison Dr, N 🅿 7-11, 76/Circle K, Valero 🍴 Amici Pizza, Arby's, Burger King, Denny's, Elephant Bar Rest., Hisui Japanese, IHOP, Jamba Juice, McDonald's, Murillo's Mexican, Nations Burger, Panera Bread, Pelayo's Mexican, Rubio's, Subway, Taco Bell, Wendy's 🏠 Best Value Inn, Best Western, Super 8 ⊡ Ⓗ, America's Tire, Best Buy, Big O Tire, Firestone/auto, Lowe's Whse, Nugget Foods, Old Navy, Petsmart, See's Candies, transmissions, U-Haul, S 🅿 Arco/24hr, Chevron/24hr 🍴 Applebee's, Baja Fresh, BJ's Grill, Black Oak Rest., Carl's Jr, Chevy's Mexican, Chili's, Coldstone Creamery, Fresh Choice Rest., In-N-Out, Jack-in-the-Box, Jamba Juice, KFC, Mel's Diner, Olive Garden, Omlette Bistro, Popeye's, Quizno's, Starbucks, String's Italian, Tahoe Joe's Steaks, TGIFriday, Togo's 🏠 Comfort Suites, Courtyard, Fairfield Inn, Holiday Inn Express, Motel 6, Residence Inn ⊡ GMC, GNC, Jo-Ann Fabrics, Marshall's, Michael's, PetCo, Radio Shack, Ross, Safeway, Sam's Club, Staples, Target, Vacaville Stores/famous brands, Walmart/auto
54b	Mason St, Peabody Rd, N 🅿 Chevron, Valero 🍴 A&W/LJ Silver 🏠 Hampton Inn ⊡ NAPA, Schwab Tire, S 🅿 USA 🍴 Domino's, Starbucks, Subway ⊡ 7-11, Costco/gas
54a	Davis St, N 🅿 Chevron/McDonald's 🍴 Outback Steaks 🏠 Hampton Inn, S 🅿 QuikStop ⊡ repair, WinCo Foods
53	Merchant St, Alamo Dr, N 🅿 Chevron, Shell/dsl, Valero 🍴 Bakers Square, Baldo's Mexican, Baskin-Robbins, Lyon's/24hr, RoundTable Pizza, Subway, Tin Tin Buffet 🏠

53	Continued Alamo Inn ⊡ BigLots, vet, S 🅿 76/dsl 🍴 Jack-in-the-Box, KFC, McDonald's, Pizza Hut, Starbucks ⊡ Radio Shack
52	Cherry Glen Rd (from wb)
51b	Pena Adobe Rd, S 🏠 Ranch Hotel
51a	Lagoon Valley Rd, Cherry Glen
48	N Texas St, Fairfield, S 🅿 Arco/24hr, Chevron, Shell 🍴 El Pollo Loco, Jim Boy's Tacos, Panda Express, RoundTable Pizza, Starbucks, Subway, Texas Roadhouse ⊡ CVS Drugs, Raley's Foods
47	Waterman Blvd, N 🍴 Dynasty Chinese, Loard's Icecream, RoundTable Pizza, Starbucks, Strings Italian ⊡ Chevrolet/Cadillac, Safeway, to Austin's Place, S ⊡ museum, to Travis AFB
45	Travis Blvd, Fairfield, N 🅿 Arco/24hr, Chevron/24hr 🍴 Baskin-Robbins, Burger King, Denny's, In-N-Out, McDonald's, Peking Rest., Subway, Taco Bell 🏠 Courtyard, Motel 6 ⊡ CHP, Ford, Harley-Davidson, Hyundai, Nissan, PetCo, Raley's Foods, S 🍴 BizWiz Tasty Burgers, Carino's Italian, Chevy's Mexican, Chipotle Mexican, Coldstone Creamery, FreshChoice Rest., Marie Callender's, Mimi's Café, Panda Express, Quizno's, Red Lobster, Redbrick Pizza, Starbucks 🏠 Hilton Garden ⊡ Ⓗ, Barnes&Noble, Best Buy, Cost+, JC Penney, Macy's, mall, Michael's, Ross, Sears/auto, Trader Joe's, World Mkt
44	W Texas St, same as 45, Fairfield, N 🅿 Shell/dsl, Valero/dsl 🍴 ChuckeCheese, Gordito's Mexican, Starbucks 🏠 Extended Stay America ⊡ Staples, S 🅿 Valero 🍴 Baldo's Mexican, McDonald's, Paleyo's Mexican, Scenario's Pizza ⊡ Acura/Honda, Chrysler/Jeep/Dodge, FoodMaxx, Home Depot, Hyundai, Infiniti, Mitsubishi, Nissan, Target, Toyota, Volvo, Walgreens
43	CA 12 E, Abernathy Rd, Suisun City, S ⊡ Budweiser Plant, Walmart
42mm	☕, weigh sta both lanes
41	Suisan Valley Rd, N 🏠 Homewood Suites, Staybridge Suites, S 🅿 76/dsl/24hr, Arco/24hr, Chevron, Shell/dsl, Valero 🍴 Arby's, Bravo's Pizza, Burger King, Carl's Jr, Denny's, Green Bamboo, Jack-in-the-Box, McDonald's, Starbucks, Subway, Taco Bell, Wendy's 🏠 Best Western, Comfort Inn, Days Inn, Fairfield Inn, Holiday Inn Express ⊡ Ray's RV Ctr, Scandia FunCtr
40	I-680 (from wb)
39b	Green Valley Rd, I-680 (from eb), N 🍴 Hawaiian BBQ, Peloyas Mexican, RoundTable Pizza, Starbucks, Sticky Rice Bistro, Subway 🏠 Homewood Suites, Staybridge Suites ⊡ Costco/gas, CVS Drug, Safeway, TJ Maxx, S 🅿 Arco
39a	Red Top Rd, N 🅿 76/Circle K/24hr 🍴 Jack-in-the-Box

Left margin labels: **DAVIS**, **VACAVILLE**, **FAIRFIELD**

INTERSTATE 80 Cont'd

Exit #	Services
36	American Canyon Rd
34mm	🆁🆂 wb, full ♿ facilities, info, litter barrels, petwalk, 🔧, 🚮, vista parking
33b a	CA 37, to San Rafael, Columbus Pkwy, N 🅿️ Chevron/dsl 🍴 Baskin-Robbins, Carl's Jr. 🏨 Best Western, Courtyard 🅾️ funpark, S same as 32
32	Redwood St, to Vallejo, N 🅿️ 76 🍴 Denny's, Panda Garden 🏨 Best Inn, Motel 6 🅾️ 🏥, S 🅿️ Arco, BonFair, Shell 🍴 Applebee's, Black Angus, Chevy's Mexican, Coldstone Creamery, IHOP, Jamba Juice, Lyon's Rest., McDonald's, Mtn. Mike's Pizza, Olive Garden, Panda Express, Red Lobster, Rubio's, Starbucks, Subway, Taco Bell, Wendy's 🏨 Comfort Inn, Ramada Inn 🅾️ AutoZone, Best Buy, Cadillac/Chevrolet, Costco/gas, Hancock Fabrics, Home Depot, Honda, Hyundai, CVS Drug, Marshall's, Mazda, Michael's, Old Navy, PepBoys, PetCo, Radio Shack, Ross, Safeway, Toyota
31b	Tennessee St, to Vallejo, S 🅿️ Valero/dsl 🍴 Jack-in-the-Box, Pacifica Pizza, Pizza Guys 🏨 Great Western Inn, Quality Inn 🅾️ Grocery Outlet
31a	Solano Ave, Springs Rd, N 🍴 Burger King, Church's, El Rey Mexican, Taco Bell 🏨 Deluxe Inn, Relax Inn 🅾️ Rite Aid, U-Haul, S 🅿️ Chemco, Chevron, Grand Gas, QuikStop 🍴 Domino's, DQ, Pizza Hut, Starbucks, Subway, Wok 🏨 Islander Motel 🅾️ Island Pacific Foods, O'Reilly Parts
30c	Georgia St, Central Vallejo, N 🅿️ Safeway/gas, S 🅿️ Shell/Starbucks/dsl 🍴 McDonald's 🏨 California Motel
30b	Benicia Rd (from wb), S 🅿️ Shell/dsl 🍴 McDonald's, Starbucks
30a	I-780, to Martinez
29b	Magazine St, Vallejo, N 🅿️ BPG 🍴 Starbucks, Subway 🏨 7 Motel, Budget Inn, El Rancho 🅾️ Tradewinds RV Park, S 🍴 McDonald's 🏨 Travel Inn 🅾️ 7-11
29a	CA 29, Maritime Academy Dr, Vallejo, N 🅿️ 5 Star Gas, Chevron/dsl/24hr 🍴 Subway 🏨 Motel 6, Vallejo Inn
28mm	pay toll from eb, toll plaza
27	Pomona Rd, Crockett, N 🍴 Dead Fish Seafood, vista point
26	Cummings Skyway, to CA 4 (from wb), to Martinez
24	Willow Ave, to Rodeo, N 🍴 Straw Hat Pizza, Subway 🅾️ Safeway/24hr, USPO, S 🅿️ 76/Circle K/dsl 🍴 Burger King, Mazatlan, Starbucks, Willow Garden Chinese
23	CA 4, to Stockton, Hercules, N 🅿️ Shell 🍴 Extreme Pizza, Jack-in-the-Box, Starbucks 🅾️ Radio Shack, S 🍴 McDonald's, RoundTable Pizza, Subway, Taco Bell 🅾️ BigLots, Home Depot, Lucky Foods, Rite Aid, USPO
22	Pinole Valley Rd, S 🅿️ Arco/24hr, Chevron/dsl 🍴 Jack-in-the-Box, Jamba Juice, NY Pizza, Red Onion Rest., Subway 🅾️ 7-11, Trader Joe's, Walgreens
21	Appian Way, N 🅿️ Pinole Express 🍴 China Delite, McDonald's, Pizza Hut 🅾️ O'Reilly Parts, CVS Drug, Safeway, S 🅿️ Valero/dsl 🍴 Burger King, Carl's Jr, Coldstone Creamery, Hawaiian BBQ, HomeTown Buffet, HotDog Sta, In-N-Out, KFC, Krispy Kreme, Panda Express, Papa Murphy's, RoundTable Pizza, Sizzler, Starbucks, Subway, Taco Bell, Wendy's, Wing Stop 🏨 Days Inn, Motel 6 🅾️ $Tree, AutoZone, Best Buy, K-Mart, Lucky Foods, Radio Shack
20	Richmond Pkwy, to I-580 W, N 🅿️ Chevron 🍴 Ground Round Rest., IHOP, McDonald's, Me&Ed's Pizza, Subway 🅾️ 99¢ Store, Barnes&Noble, Chrysler/Dodge/Jeep, Ford, Petsmart, Ross, S 🅿️ Chevron, Shell/dsl 🍴 Applebee's, Chuck Steak, In-N-Out, Krispy Kreme, Outback Steaks, Panda Express,

Exit #	Services
20	Continued RoundTable Pizza 🅾️ FoodMaxx, O'Reilly Parts, Michael's, Old Navy, Staples, Target
19b	Hilltop Dr, to Richmond, N 🅿️ Chevron 🍴 Chevy's Mexican, Olive Garden, Red Lobster, Tokyo Rest. 🏨 Courtyard, Extended Stay America 🅾️ Firestone, JC Penney, Jo-Ann Fabrics, Macy's, mall, Nissan, Sears/auto, Walmart, S 🅿️ Hilltop Fuel/dsl
19a	El Portal Dr, to San Pablo, S 🅿️ SMP 🍴 KFC, McDonalds, Mtn. Mike's Pizza, Subway 🅾️ Raley's Foods, Walgreens
18	San Pablo Dam Rd, N 🅿️ Chevron 🍴 Burger King, Denny's, El Pollo Loco, Empire Buffet, Jack-in-the-Box, Jamba Juice, Nations Burgers, Popeye's, RoundTable Pizza, Starbucks, Subway, Taco Bell 🏨 Holiday Inn Express 🅾️ 🏥, $Tree, AutoZone, FoodMaxx, Lucky Foods, Walgreens, S 🅾️ CamperLand RV Ctr
17	Macdonald Ave (from eb), McBryde Ave (from wb), Richmond, N 🅿️ Arco/24hr 🍴 Burger King, Church's, S 🅿️ Chevron/24hr 🍴 Wendy's 🅾️ auto repair, Safeway
16	San Pablo Ave, to Richmond, San Pablo, S 🅿️ Chevron 🍴 KFC, LJ Silver, Subway, Wendy's 🅾️ Safeway
15	Cutting Blvd, Potrero St, to I-580 Br (from wb), to El Cerrito, N 🅿️ Arco 🍴 Panda Express 🅾️ Target, S 🅿️ Chevron 🍴 Carrow's Rest., Church's, Denny's, IHOP, Jack-in-the-Box, Little Caesar's, McDonald's, Starbucks 🅾️ $Tree, Home Depot, Honda, Staples, Walgreens
14b	Carlson Blvd, El Cerrito, N 🅿️ 76 🏨 40 Flags Motel, S 🏨 Best Value Inn
14a	Central Ave, El Cerrito, S 🅿️ 76, Valero 🍴 Burger King, KFC, Nations Burgers
13	to I-580 (from eb), Albany
12	Gilman St, to Berkeley, N 🅾️ Golden Gate Fields Racetrack, S 🅾️ Target
11	University Ave, to Berkeley, S 🅿️ 76, University Gas 🏨 La Quinta 🅾️ to UC Berkeley
10	CA 13, to Ashby Ave
9	Powell St, Emeryville, N 🅿️ Shell 🍴 Chevy's Mexican 🏨 Hilton Garden, S 🅿️ 76 🍴 Burger King, CA Pizza Kitchen, Denny's, Elephant Bar/Grill, Jamba Juice, PF Chang's, Starbucks, Togo's 🏨 Courtyard, Sheraton, Woodfin Suites 🅾️ Barnes&Noble, Old Navy, Ross, Trader Joe's
8c b	Oakland, to I-880, I-580
8a	W Grand Ave, Maritime St
7mm	**toll plaza wb**
5mm	SF Bay
4a	Treasure Island (exits left)
2c b	Fremont St, Harrison St, Embarcadero (from wb)
2a	4th st (from eb), S 🅿️ Shell
1	9th St, Civic Ctr, downtown SF
1b a	**I-80 begins/ends on US 101 in SF**

INTERSTATE 110 (Los Angeles)

Exit #	Services
21	I-110 begins/ends on I-10.
20c	Adams Blvd, E 🍴 Chevron 🅾️ Audi, Chrysler/Dodge/Jeep, LA Convention Ctr., Mercedes, Nissan, Office Depot, VW
20b	37th St, Exposition Blvd, W 🅿️ Chevron/McDonald's 🏨 Radisson 🅾️ Chevrolet
20a	MLK Blvd, Expo Park, W 🅿️ Chevron 🍴 McDonald's, Subway
19b	Vernon Ave, E 🅿️ Mobil 🍴 Tacos El Gavilan, W 🅿️ 76/24hr, Shell 🍴 Burger King, Jack-in-the-Box 🅾️ Rite Aid, Ross
18b	Slauson Ave, E 🅿️ Mobil, W 🅿️ 76

* VALLEJO, CA, RICHMOND, BERKELEY*

⬆E INTERSTATE 110 (Los Angeles) Cont'd

Exit #	Services
18a	Gage Blvd, E 🅶 Arco 🍴 Church's, Hercules Burgers
17	Florence Ave, E 🅶 Shell 🍴 Jack-in-the-Box, W 🅶 Chevron, Valero 🍴 Burger King, Little Caesars, McDonald's, Pizza Hut, Subway
16	Manchester Ave, E 🅶 Arco 🍴 El Pollo Loco, Little Caesars, McDonald's, Subway, Winchell's 🅾 AutoZone, W 🅶 76/Circle K 🍴 Church's, Jack-in-the-Box, Popeye's, Tam's Burgers
15	Century Blvd, E 🅶 Arco, Shell/Subway/dsl 🍴 Burger King, McDonald's, W 🅶 76/dsl
14b	Imperial Hwy, W 🅶 Chevron/dsl 🍴 Jack-in-the-Box, McDonald's
14a	I-105
13	El Segundo Blvd, E 🍴 Dominos, Taco Bell, W 🅶 Mobil, Shell 🛏 Executive Inn
12	Rosecrans Ave, E 🅶 Arco/24hr, Valero, W 🅶 Chevron/McDonald's, Valero 🍴 Jack-in-the-Box, KFC/LJ Silver, Pizza Hut, Popeye's, Subway, Yoshinoya 🅾 7-11, AutoZone, casino
11	Redondo Beach Blvd, E 🍴 McDonald's, W 🅶 Mobil 🅾 H, casino
10b a	CA 91, 190th St, W 🅶 Arco 🍴 Carl's Jr, Jack-in-the-Box, Krispy Kreme, McDonald's, Pizza Hut/Taco Bell, Subway 🅾 Food4Less, Ranch Mkt, Sam's Club
9	I-405, San Diego Fwy
8	Torrance Blvd, Del Amo, E 🍴 Burger King, Chile Verde, Hawaiian BBQ, Starbucks 🅾 K-mart, W 🅶 Mobil, Shell/Subway/dsl
7b	Carson St, E 🍴 KFC 🛏 Cali Inn 🅾 vet, W 🅶 76, Shell 🍴 FatBurger, Hong Kong Deli, In-N-Out, Jack-in-the-Box, Louis Burgers, McDonalds, Pizza Hut, Polly's Pies, Starbucks, Subway, Wienerschnitzel 🅾 H, Autozone, Carson Drug, Costsaver Mkt, O'Reilly Parts, Rite Aid
5	Sepulveda Blvd, E 🍴 McDonald's 🅾 Albertson's, Home Depot, Staples, Target, W 🅶 Arco/24hr, Chevron, Mobil 🍴 Burger King, Carl's Jr, McDonald's, Pizza Hut/Taco Bell, Popeye's, Starbucks, Subway 🛏 Motel 6 🅾 $Tree, 99¢ Store, AT&T, Food4Less, Rite Aid, Ross
4	CA 1, Pacific Coast Hwy, E 🅶 76, Arco 🍴 Jack-in-the-Box, Pizza Hut, Wienerschnitzel, W 🅶 Circle K, United/dsl 🍴 Del Taco, Denny's, El Pollo Loco, Subway 🛏 Best Western 🅾 H Discount Parts, PepBoys, Rite Aid, transmissions
3b	Anaheim St, W 🅶 Mobil/dsl, Thrifty 🅾 Conoco/Phillips Refinery, radiators
3a	C St
1b	Channel St, W 🅶 Arco, Chevron 🍴 Subway 🅾 7-11, Home Depot, Target
1a	CA 47, Gaffey Ave
0mm	I-110 begins/ends

⬆E INTERSTATE 205 (Tracy)

Exit #	Services
12	I-205 begins wb, ends eb, accesses I-5 nb
9	MacArthur Dr, Tracy, S 🅶 Chevron/Jack-in-the-Box/Subway/dsl 🅾 Prime Outlet Ctr/famous brands
8	Tracy Blvd, Tracy, N 🅶 76/Mean Gene's Burger/dsl, Chevron, Shell/dsl 🍴 Denny's 🛏 Holiday Inn Express, Motel 6, S 🅶 Arco 🍴 Arby's, Burger King, In-N-Out, McDonald's, McHenry's Rest., Milano Pizza, Nations Burgers, Pizza Guys, Starbucks, Straw Hat Pizza, Subway, Wendy's, Wok King 🛏 Best Western, Microtel, Quality Inn 🅾 H, CHP, CVS Drug, Mi Pueblo Mkt, O'Reilly Parts

Exit #	Services
6	Grant Line Rd, Antioch, N 🅶 Chevron/dsl 🍴 Applebee's, Burger King, Cavey's Grille, Chevy's Mexican, Famous Dave's BBQ, Golden Corral, Hometown Buffet, IHOP, Jamba Juice, Olive Garden, Panda Express, RoundTable Pizza, Rubio's, Sonic, Starbucks, Strings Italian, Subway, Taco Bell, TX Roadhouse, Wienerschnitzel 🛏 Extended Stay America, Fairfield Inn, Hampton Inn, Squeeze Inn 🅾 America's Tire, AT&T, Barnes&Noble, Best Buy, Chevrolet, Chrysler/Dodge/Jeep, Costco/gas, Ford, Home Depot, Honda, Hyundai, JC Penney, Les Schwab Tire, Macy's, mall, Marshall's, Michael's, Nissan, PetCo, Petsmart, Ross, Sears/auto, See's Candies, Staples, Target, Toyota/Scion, Verizon, Walmart/McDonald's/auto, WinCo Foods, World Mkt, S 🅾 7-11, 76/dsl, Arco, Shell/dsl 🍴 A&W/KFC, Black Bear Diner, Carl's Jr, Chili's, Hawaiian BBQ, Mtn Mike's Pizza, Popeye's, Taco Del Mar 🅾 Rite Aid
4	11th St (from eb), to Tracy, Defense Depot
2	Mtn House Pkwy, to I-580 E
0mm	I-205 begins eb/ends wb, accesses I-580 wb.

⬆E INTERSTATE 210 (Pasadena)

Exit #	Services
74	I-215 N to Barstow S to San Bernardino
73	State St, University Pkwy, N 🅶 Thrifty, Valero
71	Riverside Ave, N 🍴 Carl's Jr, Del Taco, Starbucks, Subway 🅾 Fresh&Easy, Ralph's Foods, Rite Aid, Walgreens, S 🅶 Arco 🍴 Jack-in-the-Box 🅾 7-11
70	Ayala Dr, S 🅾 Target
68	Alder Ave
67	Sierra Ave, N 🍴 Applebee's, Carl's Jr, Dickie's BBQ, El Pollo Loco, Hawaiian BBQ, Jamba Juice, Mimi's Cafe, Panda Express, Pizza Hut, Subway, Teo's Mexican 🅾 $Tree, Costco/gas, Lowe's Whse, S 🅾 Chevrolet, Nissan
66	Citrus Ave, N 🍴 El Gran Burrito, FarmerBoys Rest., Marble Slab Creamery, Pick Up Stix, Quizno's, Red Brick Pizza, Wienerschnitzel 🅾 Home Depot, Ralph's Foods, Walgreens
64	Cherry Ave
63	I-15 N to Barstow, S to San Diego
62	Day Creek Blvd, S 🅶 Arco/dsl, Shell 🍴 Chinese Food, Jack-in-the-Box, Marble Slab Creamery, Pizza Factory, Starbucks, Wendy's 🅾 Ralph's Foods
60	Milliken Ave, S 🅶 Mobil 🍴 Taco Bell 🅾 Albertsons, CVS Drug, O'Reilly Parts
59	Haven Ave, N 🅾 7-11, 76, Mobil 🍴 Del Taco, Domino's, Jack-in-the-Box, McDonald's, Subway, Teo's Mexican 🅾 Trader Joe's, Vons Foods, Walgreens
58	Archibald Ave, S 🍴 Barboni's Pizza, Blimpie, Carl's Jr 🅾 Stater Bros, vet

LA AREA (vertical side label)

TRACY (vertical side label)

CA

⬆E INTERSTATE 210 (Pasadena) Cont'd

Exit #	Services
57	Carnelion St, **S** 🅟 76 🍴 Baskin-Robbins, Del Taco, El Ranchero Mexican, Papa John's, Starbucks 🄾 Radio Shack, Rite Aid, Vons Foods, Walgreens
56	Campus Ave, **S** 🍴 Carl's Jr, Chick-fil-A, Golden Spoon Yogurt, Hawaiian BBQ, IHOP, Jamba Juice, Magic Wok, Qdoba Mexican, Quizno's, Starbucks, Subway 🄾 Albertsons, Goodyear, Home Depot, Kohl's, Office Depot, Petsmart, Target
54	Mtn Ave, Mount Balde
52	Baseline Rd
50	Towne Ave
48	Fruit St, Via Verde, **S** 🅟 Shell 🍴 El Pollo Loco, Magic Wok, McDonald's, Myiabi, Panda Express, Pizza Hut, Quizno's, Round Table Pizza, Rubio's, Subway 🄾 Kohl's, Marshall's, Office Depot, Pet Depot, U of LaVerne, vet, Vons Foods
47	Foothill Blvd, LaVerne, **N** 🅟 Mobil/Taco Bell 🍴 Denny's, **S** 🅟 Chevron/dsl, Shell 🍴 IHOP, Starbucks, Togo's 🄾 GNC, Radio Shack
46	San Dimas Ave, San Dimas, **N** San Dimas Canyon CP
45	CA 57 S
44	Lone Hill Ave, Santa Ana, **S** 🅟 Chevron 🍴 Baja Fresh, Chili's, Coco's, In-N-Out, Subway, Wendy's 🄾 Barnes&Noble, Best Buy, Chevrolet, Chrysler/Dodge/Jeep, Ford, Home Depot, Hyundai, Kohl's, Old Navy, Petsmart, Sam's Club/gas, Staples, Toyota, Walmart/auto
43	Sunflower Ave
42	Grand Ave, to Glendora, **N** 🅟 76, Valero/dsl 🍴 Denny's 🄾 🄷
41	Citrus Ave, to Covina
40	CA 39, Azusa Ave, **N** 🅟 Arco/24hr, Chevron, Mobil, Shell/Del Taco 🍴 Jack-in-the-Box 🛏 Rodeway Inn, Super 8, **S** 🅟 Chevron, Valero 🍴 Baskin-Robbins, In-N-Out, Marquez Mexican 🛏 Best Value 🄾 7-11, Rite Aid
39	Vernon Ave (from wb), same as 38
38	Irwindale, **N** 🅟 Arco 🍴 Carl's Jr, Denny's, FarmerBoys Rest., McDonald's, Shanghai Buffet, Taco Bell 🄾 Costco/gas, NAPA
36b	Mt Olive Dr
36a	I-605 S
35b a	Mountain Ave, **N** 🅟 Arco, Chevron 🍴 Denny's, Old Spaghetti Factory, Tommy's Hamburgers, Wienerschnitzel 🛏 Oak Park Motel 🄾 Best Buy, BMW/Mini, Buick/Chevrolet, CarMax, Ford, Honda, Infiniti, Nissan, Staples, Subaru, Target, Walgreens, **S** 🍴 IHOP, Panda Express, Roasty Toasty Chicken, Senor Fish, Subway 🄾 Home Depot, Ross, Walmart
34	Myrtle Ave, **S** 🅟 76, Chevron 🍴 Jack-in-the-Box
33	Huntington Dr, Monrovia, **N** 🅟 Shell/dsl 🍴 Acapulco Rest., Applebee's, Black Angus, Burger King, Chili's, ChuckeCheese, Domino's, LeRoy's Rest., McDonald's, Mimi's Cafe, Panda Express, Popeye's, Quizno's, RoundTable Pizza, Rubio's, Starbucks 🛏 Courtyard 🄾 GNC, King Ranch Foods, Marshall's, Office Depot, Pepboy's, Radio Shack, Rite Aid, Trader Joe's, **S** 🅟 Chevron 🍴 Baja Fresh, BJ's Grill, Capistrano's, ClaimJumper, Daphne's Rest., Derby Rest., Fusion Grill, Golden Dragon, Macaroni Grill, Olive Garden, Outback Steaks, Red Lobster, Sesame Grill, Soup Plantation, Starbucks, Subway, Taisho Rest., Togo's, Tokyo Wako 🛏 Double Tree, Embassy Suites, Extended Stay America, Hampton Inn, Hilton Garden, Homestead Suites, OakTree Inn, Residence Inn, SpringHill Suites
32	Santa Anita Ave, Arcadia, **N** 🅟 76, Arco 🍴 KFC, McDonald's, Pizza Hut, Subway 🄾 Ralph's Foods, Rite Aid, **S** 🅟 Chevron/dsl 🍴 In-N-Out 🄾 carwash

S A N D I M A S

M O N R O V I A

Exit #	Services
31	Baldwin Ave, to Sierra Madre
30b a	Rosemead Blvd, **N** 🅟 76/dsl, Arco 🍴 Boston Mkt, Chuck-eCheese, Jamba Juice, Starbucks 🄾 CVS Drug, EZ Lube, Marshall's, Ralph's Foods, Rite Aid, Sears/auto, Whole Foods Mkt, **S** 🅟 76 🍴 Coco's, Jack-in-the-Box 🛏 Days Inn 🄾 Big O Tires
29b a	San Gabriel Blvd, Madre St, **N** 🅟 76 🍴 Chipotle Mexican, El Torito, Starbucks, Togo's 🄾 Best Buy, Old Navy, Petsmart, Ross, **S** 🅟 76 🍴 Jack–in-the-Box 🛏 Best Western, Holiday Inn Express, Quality Inn 🄾 Buick/Chevrolet/GMC, Cadillac, Hyundai, Jiffy Lube, Land Rover Staples, Target, Toyota
28	Altadena Dr, Sierra Madre, **S** 🅟 Chevron, Mobil 🄾 Just Tires
27b	Allen
27a	Hill Ave
26	Lake Ave, **N** 🅟 Mobil 🄾 Jo-Ann Fabrics
25b	CA 134, to Ventura
25a	Del Mar Blvd, CA Blvd, CO Blvd (exits left from eb)
24	Mountain St
23	Lincoln Ave, **S** 🛏 Lincoln Motel 🄾 auto repair
22b	Arroyo Blvd, **N** 🍴 Jack-in-the-Box, **S** to Rose Bowl
22a	Berkshire Ave, Oak Grove Dr
21	Gould Ave, **S** 🅟 Arco 🍴 Dominos, McDonald's, RoundTable Pizza, Trader Joes 🄾 Firestone, Just Tires, Ralph's Foods
20	CA 2, Angeles Crest Hwy
19	CA 2, Glendale Fwy, **S** 🄾 🄷
18	Ocean View Blvd, to Montrose
17b a	Pennsylvania Ave, La Crescenta, **N** 🅟 76, Shell, Valero 🍴 Baja Fresh, Burger King, Domino's, Starbucks, Subway, Togo's, Wienerschnitzel 🄾 GNC, Nissan, Office Depot, Ralph's Foods, Rite Aid, Toyota, USPO, Vons Foods, Walgreens, **S** 🄾 7-11, Gardenia Mks/deli
16	Lowell Ave
14	La Tuna Cyn Rd
11	Sunland Blvd, Tujunga, **N** 🅟 76, Mobil, Shell 🍴 Coco's, Jack-in-the-Box, KFC, Sizzler, Yum Yum Donuts 🄾 7-11, city park, Ralph's Foods, Rite Aid
9	Wheatland Ave
8	Osborne St, Lakeview Terrace, **N** 🍴 Ranch Side Cafe 🄾 7-11
6b	CA 118
6a	Paxton St
5	Maclay St, to San Fernando, **S** 🅟 76/dsl, Chevron 🍴 El Pollo Loco, KFC, McDonald's, Quizno's, Subway, Taco Bell 🄾 Home Depot, Office Depot, Radio Shack, Sam's Club
4	Hubbard St, **N** 🅟 Chevron 🍴 Denny's, Yum Yum Donuts 🄾 AutoZone, Radio Shack, Rite Aid, Valley Foods, **S** 🅟 Mobil/dsl, Shell 🍴 El Caporal Mexican, Jack-in-the-Box, Shakey's Pizza, Subway 🄾 Vons Foods
3	Polk St, **S** 🅟 Arco, Chevron/24hr 🍴 KFC 🄾 🄷, 7-11
2	Roxford St, **N** 🅟 Arco/dsl 🍴 Topia Pizza/Subs 🄾 🄷, Jiffy Lube, **S** 🛏 Country Side Inn
1c	Yarnell St
1b a	I-210 begins/ends on I-5, exit 160.

P A S A D E N A

⬆N INTERSTATE 215 (Riverside)

Exit #	Services
55	I-215 begins/ends on I-15.
54	Devore, **E** 🅟 Arco/dsl, Shell, **W** 🍴 Tony's Diner
50	Palm Ave, Kendall Dr, **E** 🅟 7-11, Arco 🍴 Albertacos, Burger King, Mi Cocina Mexican, Starbucks, Subway, **W** 🍴 Denny's
48	University Pkwy, **E** 🅟 76/Circle K, Chevron/dsl 🍴 Alberto's, Baskin Robbins/Togo's, Carl's Jr, Del Taco, Domino's, IHOP,

INTERSTATE 215 (Riverside) Cont'd

Exit #	Services
48	Continued

S A N   B E R N A R D I N O

48 KFC, Little Ceasars, McDonald's, Papa John's, Starbucks, Subway, Wienerschnitzel 🅞 AT&T, Jiffy Lube, Radio Shack, Ralph's Foods, Staples, **W** 🅖 Arco, Mobil/dsl/LP 🍴 Don Martin Grill, Jack-in-the-Box, Taco Bell 🏨 Days Inn, Motel 6 🅞 Verizon, Walmart/Subway

46c a CA 210, Redlands, to Pasadena, **E** 🅞 golf, **W** 🅞 golf

46b Highland Ave

45a CA 210 E, Highlands

45 Baseline Rd, **E** 🅖 76, Arco

44a CA 66 W, 5th St, **E** 🍴 In-N-Out 🏨 Best Value Inn, Country Inn, Golden Star Inn, Leisure Inn, Rodeway Inn

43 2nd St, Civic Ctr, **E** 🅖 Chevron/dsl 🍴 Del Taco, Honeybaked Ham, In-N-Out, McDonald's, Starbucks, Subway, Taco Bell 🏨 Best Value Inn 🅞 $Tree, Food4Less, Ford, Marshall's, Ross

42b Mill St, **E** 🍴 Carl's Jr, Jack-in-the-Box 🅞 AutoZone, **W** 🅖 Shell 🍴 Yum-yum Donuts

42a Inland Ctr Dr, **E** 🅖 Chevron/dsl 🍴 Carl's Jr, Jack-in-the-Box, Wienerschnitzel 🅞 AutoZone, Macy's, mall, O'Reilly Parts, Sears/auto, **W** 🅖 Arco/dsl

41 Orange Show Rd, **E** 🅖 76/dsl, World 🍴 Burger Mania, ChuckECheese, Jose's Mexican, Subway, Sundowners Rest., Viva Villa Grill 🏨 Knights Inn, Orange Show Inn 🅞 7-11, 99¢ Store, BigLots, Chrysler/Dodge/Jeep, Firestone/auto, Kelly Tire, Radio Shack, Target, **W** 🅞 AT&T, Kia, Mitsubishi, Nissan, Subaru, Toyota/Scion, VW

40b a I-10, E to Palm Springs, W to LA

39 Washington St, Mt Vernon Ave, **E** 🅖 5 Point/repair, 76/Circle K, Arco 🍴 Baker's Drive-Thru, China Town, DQ, George's Burgers, Siquio's Mexican, Starbucks, Taco Joe's 🏨 Colton Inn 🅞 BigLots, Goodyear/auto, Jiffy Lube, **W** 🍴 Buffet Star, Carl's Jr, Church's, Del Taco, Denny's, Graziano's Pizza, Jack-in-the-Box, McDonald's, Starbucks, Subway, Taco Patron 🏨 Red Tile Inn 🅞 99¢ Store, GNC, multiple RV dealers, Radio Shack, Ross, Walmart/auto

38 Barton Rd, **E** 🅖 Arco, Shell/Circle K/dsl 🍴 Miguel's Mexican, Quiznos 🅞 AutoZone, Stater Bros., **W** 🍴 Demetri's Burgers 🅞 vet

37 La Cadena Dr, (Iowa Ave from sb), **E** 🅖 Shell/dsl 🍴 Jack-in-the-Box, YumYum Rest. 🏨 Holiday Inn Express

36 Center St, to Highgrove, **E** 🅖 Chevron/Subway/dsl, **W** 🅖 Valero/dsl

35 Columbia Ave, **E** 🅖 Arco/dsl, **W** 🅞 Circle K

34b a CA 91, CA 60, Main St, Riverside, to beach cities

R I V E R S I D E

33 Blaine St, 3rd St, **E** 🅖 76, Shell, Valero 🍴 Baker's Drive-Thru, Jack-in-the-Box, Starbucks 🅞 K-Mart, Stater Bros., Valvoline

32 University Ave, Riverside, **W** 🅖 Mobil/dsl, Shell, Thrifty 🍴 Canton Chinese, Carl's Jr, Coco's, Denny's, Domino's, Fatburger, Gus Jr, IHOP, Jack-in-the-Box, Jersey Mike's, Little Ceasars, Mandarin Chinese, Papa John's, Pizza Hut, Rubio's, Santana's Mexican, Shakey's Pizza, Starbucks, Subway, Taco Bell, Wienerschnitzel 🏨 Comfort Inn, Courtyard, Motel 6 🅞 $Tree, AT&T, Food4Less, O'Reilly Parts, Radio Shack, Rite Aid, USPO, Walgreens

31 MLK Blvd, El Cerrito

30b Central Ave, Watkins Dr

30a Fair Isle Dr, Box Springs, **E** 🅞 Marjon RV Ctr, **W** 🅖 76/Circle K/Subway/dsl 🍴 Jack-in-the-Box 🅞 Ford, Nissan

29 CA 60 E, to Indio, **E** 🅖 Arco, Shell/dsl 🍴 Applebee's, Buffalo Wild Wings, Baker's Drive-Thru, BJ's Rest., Burger Boss, Carl's Jr, Chick-fil-A, Chili's, Chipotle Mexican, El Pollo Loco, Five Guys, Golden Chop Stix, Hawaiian BBQ, Home Town Buffet, Hooters, Jamba Juice, Jason's Deli, Jersey Mike's, John's Pizza, McDonald's, Miguel's Mexican, Mimi's Cafe, Olive Garden, Outback Steaks, Panda Express, Panera Bread, Portillo's Hot Dogs, Round Table Pizza, Rubio's, Starbucks, Subway, Waba Grill, Wendy's, Wienerschnitzel 🏨 Ayres Hotel, Hampton Inn 🅞 $Tree, 99¢ Store, Best Buy, Costco/gas, JC Penney, Jo-Ann Fabrics, Lowe's, Macy's, mall, Marshall's, Michael's, Old Navy, PetCo, Petsmart, Ross, Sears/auto, Staples, Target, TJ Maxx, Verizon, Walmart, WinCo Foods, World Mkt

28 Eucalyptus Ave, Eastridge Ave, **E** 🍴 Bravo Burgers, Hooters 🅞 Sam's Club/gas, Target, Walmart, 🅞 same as 29

27b (27c from sb) Alessandro Blvd, **E** 🅖 Arco/dsl 🅞 auto repair, Big O Tire, **W** 🅖 Chevron 🍴 Farmer Boys

27a Cactus Ave to March ARB, **E** 🅖 76/Circle K/dsl, Chevron/dsl 🍴 Carl's Jr, Gus Jr

25 Van Buren Blvd, **E** 🅞 March Field Museum, **W** 🅞 Riverside Nat Cem

23 Harley Knox Blvd

22 Ramona Expswy, **E** 🅖 Arco, Chevron/dsl, Mobil/Circle K, Shell/Subway/dsl 🍴 Farmer Boys, Harry's Cafe, McDonald's, Papa John's, Starbucks, Subway, Valentino's Pizza, **W** 🅖 76/Circle K/dsl/LP, Arco/dsl/scales/24hr 🍴 Jack-in-the-Box

19 Nuevo Rd, **E** 🅖 Arco, Chevron/dsl, Mobil/Circle K 🍴 Baskin-Robbins, Burger King, Carl's Jr, China Palace, Del Taco, El Pollo Loco, IHOP, Jenny's Rest., McDonald's, Pizza Hut, Sizzler, Starbucks, Subway 🅞 AutoZone, Food4Less, GNC, Radio Shack, Rite Aid, Stater Bros Foods, Walmart

P E R R I S

17 CA 74 W, 4th St, to Perris, Lake Elsinore, **E** 🅖 Shell, **W** 🅖 Chevron 🍴 Del Taco, Denny's, Jack-in-the-Box, Jimenez Mexican, Little Caesar's, Popeye's 🏨 Holiday Inn Express 🅞 AutoZone, Chrysler/Dodge/Jeep/Kia

15 CA 74 E, Hemet, **E** 🍴 Jack-in-the-Box 🏨 Sun Leisure Motel

14 Ethanac Rd, **E** 🍴 KFC/Taco Bell 🅞 Richardson's RV, **W** 🅖 76/dsl, Circle K/dsl 🍴 Carl's Jr, Del Taco, Ono Hawaiian BBQ, Starbucks, Subway 🅞 Home Depot, Just Tires, Verizon, WinCo Foods

12 McCall Blvd, Sun City, **E** 🅖 Valero/dsl 🍴 Wendy's 🏨 Best Value Inn, Motel 6 🅞 🅗, **W** 🅖 Chevron/dsl, United Oil 🍴 Coco's, Domino's, McDonald's, Papa Murphy's, Santana's Mexican, Subway 🅞 $Tree, Rite Aid, Stater Bros, Von's Foods, Walgreens

10 Newport Rd, Quail Valley, **E** 🅖 Shell/Del Taco/dsl 🍴 Cathay Chinese, Jack-in-the-Box, Papa John's, Subway, Taco Bell

🅖 = gas   🅕 = food   🅛 = lodging   🅞 = other   🆁🆂 = rest stop

CA

MURRIETA

SAN FRANCISCO

⬆️N INTERSTATE 215 (Riverside) Cont'd

Exit #	Services
10	Continued
	🅞 $Tree, AutoZone, GNC, Ralph's Foods, Ross, vet, **W** 🅖 Circle K/dsl 🅕 Applebee's, Baskin-Robbins, BJ's Rest., Chipotle Mexican, In-N-Out, Miguel's Mexican, NY Pizza, Panda Express, Panera Bread, Red Robin, Starbucks, Subway, TX Roadhouse, Yellow Basket Cafe 🅞 AT&T, Best Buy, CVS Drug, Kohl's, Lowe's, Michael's, Old Navy, PetCo, Radio Shack, Staples, SuperTarget, TJ Maxx, URGENT CARE, Verizon, vet
7	Scott Rd, **E** 🅖 7-11, Arco/dsl 🅕 Carl's Jr, Del Taco, Jack-in-the-Box, Submarina, Subway, Wood Rock Fire Pizza 🅞 Albertson's/SavOn, Verizon, vet, Walgreens, **W** 🅕 Marco's Pizza
4	Clinton Keith Rd, **W** 🅖 Arco/dsl 🅕 Del Taco, Jersey Mike's, Juice It Up, Starbucks, Subway 🅞 Mtn View Tire, Target, URGENT CARE, Verizon, Walgreens
2	Los Alamos, **E** 🅖 Shell 🅕 Board'z Grill, Cojito's Mexican, In-N-Out, Miguel's Jr Mexican, Peony Chinese, Starbucks, Taco Bell 🅞 USPO, **W** 🅖 Mobil/Circle K/dsl 🅕 ChuckeCheese, Jack-in-the-Box, McDonald's, Pizza Hut, Starbucks, Subway, TJ's Pizza 🅞 CVS Drug, Stater Bros., vet
1	Murrieta Hot Springs, **E** 🅖 7-11, Shell/dsl 🅕 Alberto's Mexican, Buffalo Wild Wings, Carl's Jr, El Pollo Loco, Habit Burger, Hungry Bull, Richie's Diner, Rubio's, Sizzler, Starbucks, Submarina, Wendy's 🅞 $Tree, Dick's, Ralph's Foods, Rite Aid, Ross, Sam's Club/gas, Verizon, vet, Walgreens, **W** 🅕 Richie's Diner, Starbucks
0mm	**I-215 begins/ends on I-15.**

⬆️E INTERSTATE 280 (Bay Area)

Exit #	Services
58	4th St, **I-280 begins/ends, N** 🅞 Whole Foods Mkt, **S** 🅖 Shell
57	7th St, to I-80, downtown
56	Mariposa St, downtown
55	Army St, Port of SF
54	US 101 S, Alemany Blvd, Mission St, **E** 🅖 Shell
52	San Jose Ave, Bosworth St (from nb, no return)
51	Geneva Ave
50	CA 1, 19th Ave, **W** 🅖 Chevron 🅞 SFSU, to Bay Bridge
49	Daly City, Daly City, **E** 🅖 76/dsl/LP 🅞 Toyota, Walgreens, **W** 🅖 Arco 🅕 Carl's Jr, Domino's, IHOP, In-N-Out, Krispy Kreme, McDonald's, Val's Rest. 🅛 Hampton Inn
47b	CA 1, Mission St (from nb), Pacifica, **E** 🅕 Hawaiian BBQ, RoundTable Pizza, Sizzler 🅞🅗, Chrysler/Jeep/Dodge, Drug Barn, Fresh Choice Foods, Home Depot, Infiniti, Isuzu, Jo-Ann Fabrics, Lexus, mall, Mitsubishi, Nordstrom's, PetCo, Target
47a	Serramonte Blvd, Daly City (from sb), **E** 🅖 Silver Gas 🅞 Cadillac, Chevrolet, Ford, Home Depot, Honda, Nissan, Target, **W** 🅖 76, Olympian 🅕 Boston Mkt, Elephant Bar Rest., McDonald's, Sizzler, Starbucks 🅞 CVS Drugs, Macy's, Office Depot, PetsMart, Ross, Target
46	Hickey Blvd, Colma, **E** 🅖 Chevron/dsl/24hr, Shell, **W** 🅖 Shell/dsl/24hr 🅕 Boston Mkt, Celia's Rest., Koi Palace, Moonstar, Outback Steaks, Sizzler 🅞 7-11, Ross
45	Avalon Dr (from sb), Westborough, **W** 🅖 Arco/24hr, Valero/dsl 🅕 Denny's, McDonald's, Subway 🅞 Pak'n Save Foods, Skyline Coll, Walgreens/24hr
44	(from nb)
43b	I-380 E, to US 101, to SF ⬆️

Exit #	Services
43a	San Bruno Ave, Sneath Ave, **E** 🅕 Au's Kitchen, Baskin-Robbins, Carl's Jr, Jamba Juice, Quizno's, Starbucks, Taco Bell 🅞 GNC, CVS Drugs, Mollie Stones Mkt, Radio Shack, **W** 🅖 76, Chevron 🅕 Baker's Square 🅞 7-11
42	Crystal Springs (from sb), county park
41	CA 35 N, Skyline Blvd (from wb, no EZ return), to Pacifica, **W 1 mi** 🅖 Chevron
40	Millbrae Ave, Millbrae, **E** 🅖 Chevron
39	Trousdale Dr, to Burlingame, **E** 🅞 🅗
36mm	**Crystal Springs** 🆁🆂 wb, full 🅗 **facilities, litter barrels, petwalk, 🅒, picnic table**
36	Black Mtn Rd, Hayne Rd, **W** 🅞 vista point, golf
35	CA 35, CA 92W (from eb), to Half Moon Bay
34	Bunker Hill Dr
33	CA 92, to Half Moon Bay, San Mateo
32mm	vista point both lanes
29	Edgewood Rd, Canada Rd, to San Carlos, **E** 🅞 🅗
27	Farm Hill Blvd, **E** 🅞 Cañada Coll, 🅒
25	CA 84, Woodside Rd, Redwood City, **W 1 mi** 🅖 Chevron/dsl 🅕 Buck's Rest., John Bentley's Rest. 🅞 Robert's Mkt, USPO
24	Sand Hill Rd, Menlo Park, **E 1 mi** 🅖 Shell 🅕 Starbucks 🅞 CVS Drug, Safeway
22	Alpine Rd, Portola Valley, **E** 🅞 🅗, **W** 🅖 Shell/autocare 🅕 Red Lotus Cafe, RoundTable Pizza 🅞 Curves
20	Page Mill Rd, to Palo Alto, **E** 🅞 🅗, to Stanford U
16	El Monte Rd, Moody Rd
15	Magdalena Ave
13	Foothill Expswy, Grant Rd, **E** 🅖 Chevron/24hr 🅕 Starbucks, Woodpecker Grill 🅞 Rite Aid, Trader Joe's, **W** 🅞 to Rancho San Antonio CP
12b a	CA 85, N to Mtn View, S to Gilroy
11	Saratoga, Cupertino, Sunnyvale, **E** 🅖 Chevron 🅕 Carl's Jr, Quizno's 🅛 Cupertino Inn 🅞 Goodyear, Michael's, repair, Rite Aid, TJ Maxx, **W** 🅖 76, Chevron, Dianza Gas, USA 🅕 BJ's Rest., Outback Steaks 🅛 Cypress Hotel 🅞 Apple Computer HQ, PetsMart
10	Wolfe Rd, **E** 🅖 Arco/24hr 🅕 Starbucks, Teppan Steaks 🅛 Courtyard, Hilton Garden 🅞 Ranch Mkt, **W** 🅖 76 🅕 Alexander Steaks, Benihana, Vallco Dynasty Chinese 🅞 FreshChoice Foods, JC Penney, Jiffy Lube, Sears/auto, Vallco Fashion Park
9	Lawrence Expswy, Stevens Creek Blvd (from eb), **N** 🅕 El Pollo Loco, McDonalds, Mtn Mikes Pizza, Panda Express, Quizno's, Starbucks 🅞 Land Rover, Marshalls, Nissan, Safeway, **S** 🅖 76, Rotten Robbie 🅕 IHOP, Subway 🅛 7-11, Woodcrest Hotel
7	Saratoga Ave, **N** 🅖 Arco/24hr, Chevron/24hr 🅕 Black Angus, Burger King, Garden City Rest., Happi House, Lion Rest., McDonald's, Taco Bell 🅞 7-11, Cadillac, Chevrolet, Ford, Goodyear, Jiffy Lube, PepBoys, **S** 🅖 76, Shell, Valero 🅕 Applebee's, Tony Roma's 🅛 MoorPark Hotel
5c	Winchester Blvd, Campbell Ave (from eb)
5b	CA 17 S, to Santa Cruz, I-880 N, to San Jose
5a	Leigh Ave, Bascom Ave
4	Meridian St (from eb), **N** 🅖 76 🅞 Big O Tire, FoodMaxx, **S** 🅖 Chevron 🅕 KFC, Subway, Wienerschnitzel 🅞 7-11
3b	Bird Ave, Race St
3a	CA 87, **N** 🅛 Hilton, Holiday Inn, Hotel Sainte Claire, Marriott
2	7th St, to CA 82, **N** conv ctr
1	10th St, 11th St, **N** 🅞 7-11, to San Jose St U
0mm	**I-280 begins/ends on US 101.**

SAN JOSE

INTERSTATE 405 (Los Angeles)

Exit #	Services
73	I-5, N to Sacramento, I-5, S to LA
72	Rinaldi St, Sepulveda, **E** 🅖 76, Chevron/dsl 🍴 Arby's, McDonald's, Presidente Mexican, Subway 🅞 🄷, Nissan, Toyota, **W** 🅖 Shell 🏠 Best Value Inn
71	CA 118 W, Simi Valley
70	Devonshire St, Granada Hills, **E** 🅖 76, Arco, GasMart/dsl 🍴 Holiday Burger, Millie's Rest., Papa John's, Quiznos, Safari Room Rest, Subway 🅞 Bare's RV Ctr, Radio Shack, Ralph's Foods, Rite Aid, Verizon, Vons Foods
69	Nordhoff St, **E** 🅖 Mobil/dsl 🍴 7 Mares, China Wok, Coldstone, Del Taco, KFC, Panda Express, Pollo Campero, Starbucks 🏠 Hillcrest Inn 🅞 7-11, Marshalls, Vallarta Foods, Walgreens, **W** 🅖 76/dsl, Arco 🍴 Jack-in-the-Box, Pizza Hut
68	Roscoe Blvd, to Panorama City, **E** 🅖 76/dsl, Shell 🍴 Burger King, Country Folks Rest., Denny's, Galpin Rest., Jack-in-the-Box, Little Caesars, McDonald's, Panda Express, Taco Bell, Yoshinoya 🏠 Holiday Inn Express 🅞 7-11, AutoZone, Ford, Jaguar/Volvo, Lincoln, U-Haul, **W** 🅖 Chevron/dsl, Shell/dsl 🍴 Tommy's Burgers 🏠 Motel 6
66	Sherman Blvd, Reseda, **E** 🅖 Chevron, Mobil/LP 🍴 Golden Chicken, KFC, McDonald's, Starbucks 🏠 Motel 6 🅞 BigLots, CVS Drug, Jon's Foods, **W** 🅖 76/dsl/24hr 🍴 Taco Bell 🅞 🄷 USPO
65	Victory Blvd, Van Nuys, **E** 🍴 Carl's Jr, El Pollo Loco, Jack-in-the-Box, Subway, Wendy's 🅞 Costco/gas, CVS Drug, El Monte RV Ctr, Office Depot, PepBoys, Staples, **W** 🅖 Arco/24hr 🅞 🄷
64	Burbank Blvd, **E** 🅖 Chevron, Shell 🍴 Denny's 🏠 Best Western, Hampton Inn 🅞 Target
63b	US 101, Ventura Fwy
63a	Ventura Blvd (from nb), **E** 🅖 Mobil 🍴 Cheesecake Factory, El Pollo Loco 🅞 mall, Whole Foods Mkt, **W** 🅖 76 🍴 Ameci Pizza, CA Chicken Cafe, Corner Bakery Cafe, IHOP, McDonald's 🏠 Courtyard, Valley Inn
63a	Valley Vista Blvd (from sb)
61	Mulholland Dr, Skirvall Dr
59	Sepulveda Blvd, Getty Ctr Dr, **W** 🅞 to Getty Ctr
57	Sunset Blvd, Morega Dr, **E** 🅖 76/dsl, Chevron/24hr 🅞 to UCLA, **W** 🏠 Luxe Hotel
56	Waterford St, Montana Ave (from nb)
55c b	Wilshire Blvd, **E** downtown, **W** 🅞 🄷
55a	CA 2, Santa Monica Blvd, **E** 🅖 Chevron, Mobil, Shell, Thrifty 🍴 Coffee Bean, Jack-in-the-Box, Jamba Juice, Quiznos, Starbucks, Winchell's, Yoshinoya, Zankau Chicken 🅞 7-11, Firestone/auto, LDS Temple, Staples, vet, **W** 🅖 76/24hr, Chevron/dsl 🍴 Subway 🏠 Holiday Inn Express
54	Olympic Blvd, Peco Blvd, **E** 🅖 Mobil 🍴 Islands Burgers, Jack-in-the-Box, La Salsa, Norm's Rest., Stabucks 🅞 Barnes&Noble, Nordstroms, **W** 🍴 Big Tomy's Rest. 🅞 Best Buy, Marshall's, USPO
53	I-10, Santa Monica Fwy
52	Venice Blvd, **E** 🅖 Chevron/service, Shell/dsl 🍴 Carl's Jr, Subway 🏠 Ramada 🅞 7-11, services on Sepulveda, **W** 🅖 SP/dsl 🍴 FatBurger
51	Culver Blvd, Washington Blvd, **E** 🍴 Dear John's Café, Taco Bell 🅞 vet, **W** 🅖 76/repair
50b	CA 90, Slauson Ave, to Marina del Rey, **E** 🅖 Arco/24hr 🍴 Del Taco, El Pollo Loco, HoneyBaked Ham, Shakey's Pizza, Winchell's 🅞 $Tree, BigLots, Firestone/auto, Goodyear/auto, Just Tires, Office Depot, Old Navy, Staples, transmissions, **W** 🅖 76 🍴 Denny's 🅞 Albertson's

50a	Jefferson Blvd (from sb), **E** 🍴 Coco's, Jack-in-the-Box 🅞 PetsMart, Rite Aid, Target, **W** to LA 🄷
49	Howard Hughes Pkwy, to Centinela Ave, **E** 🅖 Chevron/dsl, Mobil/dsl 🍴 BJ's Brewhouse, Quiznos, Sizzler 🏠 Courtyard, Sheraton 🅞 Best Buy, CVS Drug, Ford, Honda, JC Penney, Macy's, mall, Marshall's, Target, **W** 🅖 Chevron 🍴 Dinah's Rest., Habuki Japanese, Islands Burgers, Marie Callender's, Rubio's, Starbucks, Subway, Wild Thai 🏠 Extended Stay America, Radisson 🅞 Howard Hughes Ctr, Nordstrom
48	La Tijera Blvd, **E** 🅖 Mobil/sl 🍴 Burger King, ChuckeCheese, El Pollo Loco, Jamba Juice, KFC, McDonald's, Starbucks, Subway, Taco Bell, TGIFriday's 🏠 Best Western 🅞 99¢ Store, CVS Drug, Ralph's Foods, Ross, Vons Foods, **W** 🅖 76/Circle K, Chevron/dsl/24hr 🍴 Buggy Whip Rest., Wendy's 🅞 USPO
47	CA 42, Manchester Ave, Inglewood, **E** 🅖 76/Circle K/dsl/24hr 🍴 Carl's Jr, Subway 🏠 Best Western, Economy Inn 🅞 7-11, repair, **W** 🅖 76, Arco, Circle K, Shell, Valero 🍴 Arby's, Burger King, Denny's, El Pollo Loco, Jack-in-the-Box, Louis Burgers 🏠 Days Inn 🅞 CarMax, Chrysler/Dodge/Jeep, Home Depot, Hyundai
46	Century Blvd, **E** 🅖 Chevron/dsl 🍴 Casa Gamino Mexican, El Pollo Loco, Flower Drum Chinese, Hawaiian BBQ, Little Caesars, Panda Express, Rally's 🏠 Best Value Inn, Best Western, Comfort Inn, Motel 6, Tivoli Hotel 🅞 7-11, LAX Transmissions, **W** 🅖 76/Circle K, Arco/24hr, Chevron/dsl, Shell 🍴 Carl's Jr, Denny's, McDonald's, Pizza Hut/Taco Bell 🏠 Hampton Inn, Hilton, Holiday Inn, La Quinta, Marriott, Travelodge, Westin Hotel 🅞 to LAX
45	I-105, Imperial Hwy, **E** 🅖 76/dsl, Shell, Valero 🍴 El Pollo Loco, El Tarasco Mexican, Jack-in-the-Box, KFC/Taco Bell, McDonald's 🏠 Best Value Inn, Candlewood Suites, Holiday Inn Express 🅞 J&S Transmissions, repair, **W** 🍴 Wild Goose Rest./Theater (1mi)
44	El Segundo Blvd, to El Segundo, **E** 🅖 Chevron/24hr, Thrifty, Valero 🍴 Burger King, Christy's Donuts, Cougars Burgers, Jack-in-the-Box, Jase Burgers, Subway 🏠 El Segundo Inn 🅞 transmissions, **W** 🍴 Denny's 🏠 Ramada Inn
43b a	Rosecrans Ave, to Manhattan Beach, **E** 🅖 76, Shell 🍴 Denny's, El Pollo Loco, Pizza Hut, Starbucks, Subway 🅞 Best Buy, CVS Drug, Food4Less, Ford/Lincoln, Home Depot, Marshall's, Michael's, Office Depot, Ross, **W** 🅖 Thrifty 🍴 Cafe Rio, Carl's Jr, Chipotle Mexican, Flemings Rest., Hawaiian BBQ, Houston's, Luigi's Rest., Macaroni Grill, McDonald's, Qdoba Mexican, Robeks Juice, Sansai Japanese, Starbucks, Subway 🏠 Ayres Hotel, Hyatt, SpringHill Suites, TownePlace Suites 🅞 AT&T, Barnes&Noble, Costco/gas, CVS Drug, Fresh&Easy, Nissan, Office Depot, Old Navy, Staples, Trader Joe's, VW

L O S   A N G E L E S   A R E A

H A W T H O R N E

CA

T O R R A N C E

C A R S O N

Exit #	Services
⬆⬇N INTERSTATE 405 (Los Angeles) Cont'd	
42b	Inglewood Ave, **E** 🅖 Shell 🍴 Baskin-Robbins, Del Taco, Denny's, Domino's, In-N-Out, Quiznos 🅾 CVS Drug, Marshall's, PetCo, Vons Foods, **W** 🅖 76, Shell/dsl/24hr 🍴 La Salsa Mexican, Subway 🅾 99¢ Store, repair
42a	CA 107, Hawthorne Blvd, **E** 🅖 Chevron 🍴 Carl's Jr, Jack-in-the-Box, Little Caesars, McDonald's, Panda Express, Papa John's, Wendy's, Wienerschnitzel 🛏 Baymont Inn, Best Western, Days Inn 🅾 99¢ Store, CVS Drug, O'Reilly Parts, PepBoys, Radio Shack, Value+ Foods, vet, **W** 🅖 Arco/24hr, Chevron/dsl, Thrifty 🍴 Boston Mkt, Marie Callendar's, Quiznos, Sizzler, Starbucks, Subway, Taco Bell, Yoshinoya 🅾 AutoZone, Macy's, Nordstom
40b	Redondo Beach Blvd (no EZ sb return), Hermosa Beach, **E** 🅖 76, Arco/24hr 🍴 ChuckeCheese, Jack-in-the-Box 🅾 golf, **W** 🍴 RoundTable Pizza, Starbucks 🅾 AutoZone, CVS Drug, URGENT CARE
40a	CA 91 E, Artesia Blvd, to Torrance, **W** 🅖 Chevron 🅾 Carl's Jr, Starbucks, YumYum Donuts
39	Crenshaw Blvd, to Torrance, **E** 🅖 Arco/24hr, Shell 🍴 Burger King, El Pollo Loco, McDonald's 🅾 Ralph's Foods, USPO, **W** 🅖 Mobil/dsl, Shell/Subway/dsl 🅾 Jiffy Lube
38b	Western Ave, to Torrance, **E** 🅖 76/dsl, Arco, Chevron 🍴 Del Taco, Denny's, Hong Kong Express, Local Place, Papa John's, Quiznos, Starbucks, Wendy's, Yorgo's Burgers 🛏 Dynasty Inn 🅾 Albertson's/Sav-On, GNC, Toyota/Scion, **W** 🅖 Mobil 🍴 Mill's Rest. 🛏 Courtyard 🅾 Lexus
38a	Normandie Ave, to Gardena, **E** 🛏 Comfort Inn, **W** 🅖 Shell/dsl 🍴 Big Island BBQ, Carl's Jr, Chile Verde Mexican, Hong Kong Cafe, Pizza Hut/Taco Bell, Quiznos, Starbucks, Subway, Wienerschnitzel 🛏 Extended Stay America 🅾 $Tree, Walmart
37b	Vermont Ave (from sb), **W** 🛏 Holiday Inn 🅾 hwy patrol
37a	I-110, Harbor Fwy
36mm	**weigh sta both lanes**
36	Main St (from nb)
35	Avalon Blvd, to Carson, **E** 🅖 Chevron, Mobil 🍴 5 Guys Burgers, Carson Buffet, Chili's, ChuckeCheese, Denny's, FoodCourt, Jack-in-the-Box, Jamba Juice, McDonald's, Panda Express, Panera Bread, Pizza Hut, Quiznos, Sensai Grill, Shakey's Pizza, Sizzler, Starbucks, Tokyo Grill, Tony Roma, WingStop 🛏 Clarion 🅾 America's Tire, AT&T, Bestway Foods, Firestone/auto, Goodyear/auto, Ikea, JC Penney, Just Tires, mall, PepBoys, Radio Shack, Sears/auto, Target, USPO, Verizon, **W** 🅖 Arco/24hr, Mobil 🍴 Carl's Jr, McDonald's 🅾 Kia, O'Reilly Parts, Ralph's Foods
34	Carson St, to Carson, **E** 🛏 EconoLodge, **W** 🅖 76/dsl/24hr, Mobil 🍴 Carl's Jr, Jack-in-the-Box, Subway 🛏 DoubleTree Inn
33b	Wilmington Ave, **E** 🅖 Mobil/dsl 🍴 Carson Burgers, **W** 🅖 Chevron/Jack-in-the-Box/dsl, Shell/Subway/dsl 🍴 Del Taco, Spires Rest. 🅾 Chevrolet/Hyundai, Honda, Nissan, Toyota/Scion
33a	Alameda St
32d	Santa Fe Ave (from nb), **E** 🅖 Arco/24hr, **W** 🅖 Chevron/24hr, United/dsl 🍴 Fantastic Burgers
32c b	I-710, Long Beach Fwy
32a	Pacific Ave (from sb)
30b	Long Beach Blvd, **E** 🅖 Arco/dsl 🍴 Subway 🅾 7-11, **W** 🅖 Exxon 🅾 H

Exit #	Services
30a	Atlantic Blvd, **E** 🅖 Chevron/dsl 🍴 Arby's, Carl's Jr, Denny's/24hr, El Torito, Jack-in-the-Box, Polly's Cafe 🅾 CVS Drug, NAPACare, Staples, Target, vet, Walgreens, **W** 🅾 H, $Tree, Home Depot, PetCo, Ross
29c	Orange Ave (from sb), **W** 🅾 Dodge/GMC/Nissan
29b a	Cherry Ave, to Signal Hill, **E** 🅖 Mobil/dsl 🍴 Fantastic Burgers 🅾 auto repair, Ford, Lincoln, Mazda, **W** 🅖 76 🅾 America's Tire, Best Buy, BMW/Mini, Buick, Dodge, Firestone, Honda, Mercedes, Nissan
27	CA 19, Lakewood Blvd, **E** 🛏 Marriott 🅾 ⊙, **W** 🅖 Chevron, Shell/24hr 🍴 Spires Rest. 🛏 Extended Stay America, Holiday Inn, Residence Inn 🅾 H, Ford, Goodyear/auto
26b	Bellflower Blvd, **E** 🅖 76 🍴 Burger King, Carl's Jr, Denny's, Jamba Juice, KFC, Papa John's, Subway, Togo's 🅾 Ford, K-Mart, Lowe's, **W** 🅖 Chevron, Mobil/dsl, Shell 🍴 Baja Fresh, Hof's Hut, IHOP, McDonald's, Pick-Up Stix, Quiznos, Wendy's 🅾 H, BigLots, CVS Drug, Goodyear/auto, Rite Aid/24hr, Sears, See's Candies, Target, USPO
26a	Woodruff Ave (from nb)
25	Palo Verde Ave, **W** 🅖 76 🍴 Dave's Burgers, Del Taco, Domino's, Pizza Hut/Taco Bell, Starbucks, Subway
24b	Studebaker Rd (from sb)
24a	I-605 N
23	CA 22 W, 7th St, to Long Beach
22	Seal Beach Blvd, Los Alamitos Blvd, **E** 🅖 76/dsl, Chevron/repair/24hr, Mobil/dsl 🍴 Baja Fresh, CA Pizza Kitchen Daphne's Greek, Hot Off the Grill, Islands Burgers, Jamba Juice, KFC, Kobe Japanese, Macaroni Grill, Marie Callenders, Pei-wei Asian, Pick-Up Stix, Quiznos, Rubio's, Spaghettini Grill, Starbucks, Z Pizza 🛏 Ayres Hotel 🅾 AT&T, CVS Drug, GNC, Kohl's, Marshall's, Ralph's Foods, Sprouts Mkt, Target, **W** 1 mi 🅖 76/dsl, Chevron 🍴 Carl's Jr, Del Taco, Domino's 🛏 Hampton Inn
21	CA 22 E, Garden Grove Fwy, Valley View St, **E** 🅾 Ford
19	Westminster Ave, to Springdale St, **E** 🅖 76/Circle K, Arco/24hr, Chevron/dsl, Thrifty 🍴 Café Westminster, Carl's Jr, In-N-Out, KFC, McDonald's 🛏 Knights Inn, Motel 6, Travelodge 🅾 7-11, America's Tire, AutoZone, BigLots, Home Depot, O'Reilly Parts, Radio Shack, Rite Aid, Ross, **W** 🅖 Chevron/dsl/24hr 🍴 Ranchito Mkt, Starbucks, Subway 🛏 Best Western, Courtyard Inn
18	Bolsa Ave, Golden West St, **W** 🅖 76, Mobil/dsl 🍴 Coco's, El Torito, IHOP, Jack-in-the-Box, Outback Steaks, Rodrigo's Mexican, Starbucks, Wendy's 🅾 $Tree, CVS Drug, JC Penney, Jo-Ann Fabrics, Jons Foods, Macy's, mall, Sears/auto, Target
16	CA 39, Beach Blvd, to Huntington Bch, **E** 🅖 Chevron, Shell 🍴 Jack-in-the-Box, Subway 🛏 Super 8 🅾 H, PepBoys, Toyota, U-Haul, **W** 🅖 Mobil/service 🍴 Arby's, BJ's Rest., Buca Italian, Burger King, CA Pizza Kitchen, Chipotle Mexican, Islands Burgers, Jack-in-the-Box, Macaroni Grill, Marie Callender's, McDonald's, Panera Bread, Popeye's, Quiznos, Starbucks, Subway 🛏 Comfort Suites 🅾 AT&T, Barnes&Noble, Big O Tire, Chrysler/Dodge/Jeep, Firestone/auto, Kohl's, Office Depot, See's Candies, Staples, Target, Verizon, Whole Foods Mkt
15b a	Magnolia St, Warner Ave, **E** 🍴 Del Taco, Sizzler 🅾 Fresh&Easy, **W** 🅖 Chevron, Mobil 🍴 Carrow's, Magnolia Café, Starbucks, Tommy's Burgers 🛏 Days Inn 🅾 7-11, CVS Drug, Grocery Outlet, Tuesday Morning, Winchell's
14	Brookhurst St, Fountain Valley, **E** 🅖 Arco/24hr, Chevron, Mobil, Shell 🍴 Alerto's Mexican, Carl's Jr, Coco's, Del Taco,

INTERSTATE 405 (Los Angeles) Cont'd

Exit #	Services
14	Continued
	KFC, Taco Bell 🏠 Courtyard, Residence Inn 🅞 America's Tire, Sam's Club/gas, Thompson's RV Ctr, W 🅖 76/dsl, Arco, Shell/dsl 🍴 Applebee's, Black Angus, Chop Stix, ClaimJumper, Coco's, Coldstone, Corner Bakery Cafe, Islands Burgers, Mandarin, Mimi's Cafe, Quiznos, Rubio's, Starbucks, Subway, Togo's, Wendy's 🅞 H, Albertson's, Office Depot, Ralph's Foods, Rite Aid, TJ Maxx, vet
12	Euclid Ave, E 🍴 Cancun Fresh, Carl's Jr, Coffee Bean, FlameBroiler, Panda Express, Pita Fresh Grill, Quiznos, Souplantation, Starbucks, Subway, Taco Bell, Z Pizza 🅞 H, $Tree, Big Lots, Costco/gas, PetsMart, Staples, Tire Whse
11b	Harbor Blvd, to Costa Mesa, E 🍴 Hooters 🏠 La Quinta, W 🅖 7-11, Arco, Chevron, Mobil, Shell/dsl 🍴 Burger King, Denny's, Domino's, El Pollo Loco, IHOP, Jack-in-the-Box, KFC, LJ Silver, McDonald's, Subway 🏠 Costa Mesa Inn, Motel 6, Super 8, Vagabond Inn 🅞 Acura/Dodge, Albertson's, Big O Tire, Buick, Cadillac, Chevrolet, Ford/Lincoln, Honda, Infiniti, JustTires, Mazda, Radio Shack, Rite Aid, Target, Vons Foods, Winchell's
11a	Fairview Rd, E 🅞 Barnes&Noble, Best Buy, Marshall's, Nordstrom's, Old Navy, W 🅖 76, Chevron, Shell 🍴 Del Taco, Jack-in-the-Box, Round Table Pizza, Taco Bell 🅞 CVS Drug, O'Reilly Parts, Stater Bros
10	CA 73, to CA 55 S (from sb), Corona del Mar, Newport Beach
9b	Bristol St, E 🅖 Chevron/dsl 🍴 Antonello's Italian, Baja Fresh, Baskin-Robbins, Boudin SF Cafe, Capital Grill, Carrow's, Chick-fil-A, China Olive, Chipotle Mexican, ClaimJumper, Corner Bakery, Darya Persian, In-N-Out, Jack-in-the-Box, Jade Palace, Maggiano's Rest., McDonald's, Morton's Steaks, Pat&Oscar's, Pizza Hut, Quiznos, Red Robin, Sabores Mexican, Scott Seafood, South Coast Rest, Starbucks, Subway, Z Pizza, Ztejas Rest 🏠 Marriott Suites, Westin Hotel 🅞 BigLots, Bloomingdale's, CVS Drug, Firestone/auto, GNC, Macy's, mall, Michael's, Office Depot, PetCo, Radio Shack, Rite Aid, Ross, Sears/auto, Staples, Target, TJ Maxx, Trader Joe's, Vons Foods, World Mkt, W 🅖 76/Circle K/dsl, Chevron/dsl 🍴 Del Taco/24hr, El Pollo Loco, McDonald's, Orchid Rest., Subway, Wahoo's Fish Taco 🏠 Hanford Hotel, Hilton 🅞 7-11, PepBoys, vet
9a	CA 55, Costa Mesa Fwy, to Newport Bch, Riverside
8	MacArthur Blvd, E 🅖 Chevron, Mobil/Subway 🍴 Carl's Jr, El Torito, McCormick&Schmick's, McDonald's, Quiznos, Starbucks 🏠 Crowne Plaza, Embassy Suites 🅞 Pepperdine U, W 🅖 Chevron 🍴 El Torito, Gulliver's Ribs, IHOP 🏠 Atrium Hotel, Hilton, to ✈
7	Jamboree Rd, Irvine, E 🅖 Shell 🍴 Andrei's Rest., Burger King, Soup Plantation 🏠 Courtyard, Hyatt, Residence Inn, W 🍴 CA Pizza Kitchen, Daily Grill, FatBurger, Flamebroiler, Houston's, Melting Pot, Ruth's Chris Steaks, Starbucks, Subway, Taleo Mexico, Wahoo's Fish Taco 🏠 Marriott 🅞 Office Depot
5	Culver Dr, W 🅖 Alfie's Gas, Chevron/dsl 🍴 Carl's Jr, Subway 🅞 Ace Hardware, Rite Aid, Wholesome Foods Mkt
4	Jeffrey Rd, University Dr, E 🅖 Chevron, Circle K/gas 🍴 Baja Fresh, Coffee Bean, Daphney's Greek, El Cholo Cantina, El Pollo Loco, Golden Spoon, Juice It Up, McDonald's, NY Pizza, Peiwei Asian, Pick-Up Stix, Pomodoro Italian, Starbucks, Togo's, Z Pizza 🅞 H, Ace Hardware, CVS Drug, Gelson's Mkt, Office Depot, Ralph's Foods, Walgreens, W 🅖 Mobil/dsl 🍴 IHOP, Korean BBQ, Subway 🅞 Ralph's Foods, vet

COSTA MESA / IRVINE (side tab)

3	Sand Canyon Ave, E 🅞 H, W 🅖 Arco/dsl 🏠 Crystal Jade Asian, Lucca Cafe, Mitsui Grill, Red Brick Pizza, Sharkey's Mexican, Starbucks, Subway, Thai Bamboo 🅞 Albertson's, CVS Drug, Starbucks
2	CA 133, to Laguna Beach, E 🏠 DoubleTree Inn
1c	Irvine Center Dr, E 🍴 Cheesecake Factory, Chipotle Mexican, Dave&Buster's, Oasis Cafes, Panda Express, PF Chang's, Wahoo's Fish Tacos 🅞 Barnes&Noble, Macy's, Nordstrom, Target, W 🅖 7-11 🍴 Burger King, La Salsa, NY Deli 🅞 Big O Tire
1b	Bake Pkwy, W 🅞 Carmax, Toyota
1a	Lake Forest
0mm	I-405 begins/ends on I-5, exit 132.

INTERSTATE 505 (Winters)

Exit #	Services
33	I-5. I-505 begins/ends on I-5.
31	CA 12A
28	CA 14, Zamora
24	CA 19
21	CA 16, to Esparto, Woodland, W 🅖 Guy's Food/fuel 🍴 La Plazita
17	CA 27
15	CA 29A
11	CA 128 W, Russell Blvd, W 🅖 Chevron/24hr, Interstate/dsl 🍴 RoundTable Pizza, Subway 🅞 Lorenzo's Mkt, vet
10	Putah Creek Rd, no crossover...same as 11
6	Allendale Rd
3	Midway Rd, E 🅞 RV camping
1c	Vaca Valley Pkwy
1b	I-80 E. I-505 begins/ends on I-80.

INTERSTATE 580 (Bay Area)

Exit #	Services
79	I-580 begins/ends, accesses I-5 sb.
76b a	CA 132, Chrisman Rd, to Modesto, E 🅖 76/dsl 🅞 RV camping (5mi)
72	Corral Hollow Rd
67	Patterson Pass Rd, W 🅖 76/dsl/24hr
65	I-205 (from eb), to Tracy
63	Grant Line Rd, to Byron
59	N Flynn Rd, S Brake Check Area, many wind-turbines, Altamont Pass, elev 1009
57	N Greenville Rd, Laughlin Rd, Altamont Pass Rd, to Livermore Lab, S 🅖 Chevron/Subway/dsl 🏠 Best Western, La Quinta 🅞 Harley-Davidson
56mm	weigh sta both lanes

INTERSTATE 580 (Bay Area) Cont'd

Exit #	Services
55	Vasco Rd, to Brentwood, N 🅖 76, Arco, Chevron, QuikStop/dsl, Shell/dsl/deli 🅵 A&W/KFC, McDonald's, S 🅖 Citgo/7-11, Valero/dsl 🅵 Blimpie, Jack-in-the-Box, Taco Bell 🅛 Quality Inn
54	CA 84, 1st St, Springtown Blvd, Livermore, N 🅖 Chevron 🅛 DoubleTree, Holiday Inn, Motel 6, Springtown Inn 🅞 7-11, S 🅖 76/24hr, Shell, Valero/Circle K 🅵 Applebee's, Arby's, Burger King, Chevy's Mexican, Chili's, Crazy Buffet, IHOP, Italian Express, McDonald's, Panda Express, Starbucks, Subway, Taco Bell, Togo's 🅞 America's Tire, CVS Drug, Lowe's Whse, Office Depot, Radio Shack, Ross, Safeway/gas, Target
52	N Livermore Ave, S 🅖 Chevron/Jack-in-the-Box, Citgo/7-11 🅵 Baja Fresh, Coldstone, In-N-Out, Popeye's, Quizno's, String's Italian 🅛 Hawthorn Suites 🅞 Home Depot, Honda, Schwab Tire, Walmart/auto
51	Portola Ave, Livermore (no EZ eb return)
50	Airway Blvd, Collier Canyon Rd, Livermore, N 🅖 Shell/dsl 🅵 Baskin-Robbins, Wendy's 🅛 Courtyard, Hampton Inn, Hilton Garden, Holiday Inn Express, Residence Inn 🅞 Costco/gas, S 🅵 Cattlemen's Rest., Chicago Pizza, Starbucks 🅛 Extended Stay America 🅞 7-11, Chrysler/Jeep, Ford/Lincoln, Mazda
48	El Charro Rd, O'Fallon Rd
47	Santa Rita Rd, Tassajara Rd, N 🅞 Buick/GMC Safeway Foods, S 🅖 Shell 🅵 Bakers Square, Korea Garden, McDonald's, Quizno's, Subway, Taco Bell, TGI Friday, Thai Quisine 🅞 Acura, BMW, Cadillac, GMC, Hummer, Infiniti, Lexus, Long's Drug, MiniCooper, Mitsubishi, Rose Pavilion Trader Joe's, Volvo
46	Hacienda Dr, Pleasanton, N 🅖 Shell 🅵 Applebee's, Black Angus, Fuddruckers, Macaroni Grill, Mimi's Cafe, On-the-Border, Papa John's, Woks Up 🅛 AmeriSuites 🅞 Barnes&Noble, Best Buy, Ford, Old Navy, TJ Maxx, S 🅵 Red Robin 🅞 🅷, Kohl's, Staples, Walmart/auto
45	Hopyard Rd, Pleasanton, N 🅖 76/Circle K, Minimart, Shell/dsl 🅛 Hilton, Holiday Inn Express 🅞 America's Tire, Dodge, El Monte RV Ctr, Goodyear, Honda, Nissan, Office Depot, Pak'n Sav, RV Ctr, Toyota, U-Haul, S 🅖 Chevron, Shell/dsl 🅵 Arby's, Burger King, Chef India, Chevy's Mexican, Chili's, Denny's, El Balazo, In-N-Out, Nations Burgers, Pleasant Asian, Starbucks, Taco Bell 🅛 Candlewood Suites, Courtyard, Hilton, Larkspur Landing, Marriott, Motel 6, Sheraton, Super 8 🅞 Home Depot, Mercedes
44b	I-680, N to San Ramon, S to San Jose
44a	Foothills Rd, San Ramon Rd, N 🅖 CA Fuel, Chevron, Shell, Valero 🅵 Burger King, Casa Orozco, China Wall, Chipotle Mexican, ChuckeCheese, Country Waffles, Elephant Bar, Frankie's Johnny's & Luigi's Too, Hooters, Korean BBQ, Outback Steaks, Panera Bread, Popeye's, RoundTable Pizza, Starbucks 🅛 Radisson 🅞 $Tree, Big Lots, O'Reilly Parts, Long's Drug, Marshall's, Michael's, PetCo, PetsMart, Ranch Mkt Foods, Ross, Target, S 🅵 Cheesecake Factory, PF Chang's 🅛 Marriott, Residence Inn, Sheraton 🅞 JC Penney, Macy's, mall, Nordstrom's, Sears
39	Eden Canyon Rd, Palomares Rd, S 🅞 rodeo park
37	Center St, Crow Canyon Rd, S 🅖 76/dsl, Arco/24hr, Chevron/dsl/, Quikstop 🅵 McDonald's, Starbucks, Subway, same as 35
35	Redwood Rd (from eb), Castro Valley, N 🅖 76/dsl, Chevron, Shell/dsl 🅵 Baker's Square, Chipotle Mexican, KFC, McDonald's, Quizno's, RoundTable Pizza, Sizzler, Taco Bell,
35	Continued Wendy's 🅞 Comfort Suites, Goodyear, Holiday Inn Express, CVS Drug, Lucky Foods, NAPA, Radio Shack, Rite Aid, Safeway, Walgreens
34	I-238 W, to I-880, CA 238, W off I-238 🅵 Jack-in-the-Box, McDonald's 🅞 99¢ Store, Chrysler/Jeep
33	164th Ave, Miramar Ave, E 🅖 Chevron/dsl, Valero 🅛 Fairmont Inn
32	150th Ave, Fairmont, E 🅞 🅷, W 🅖 76/dsl, Shell 🅵 Arby's, Burger King, Carrows, Chili's, Denny's, McDonald's, Round-Table Pizza, Starbucks, Tito's Cafe 🅞 Goodyear, Kohl's, Long's Drug, Macy's, Pepboys, Staples, Target
31	Grand Ave (from sb), Dutton Ave, W 🅖 Coast 🅞 Rite Aid
30	106th Ave, Foothill Blvd, MacArthur Blvd, W 🅖 Arco 🅵 Church's
29	98th Ave, Golf Links Rd, E 🅖 Shell 🅞 Oakland Zoo, W 🅖 76, Valero
27b	Keller Ave, Mtn Blvd, E 🅞 repair
27a	Edwards Ave (from sb, no EZ return), E 🅞 US Naval 🅷
26b	Seminary Rd, E 🅞 Observatory/Planetarium, W 🅖 Arco/24hr
26a	CA 13, Warren Frwy, to Berkeley (from eb)
25b a	High St, to MacArthur Blvd, E 🅖 76 🅵 Razzo's Pizza, Subway 🅞 Lucky Foods, O'Reilly Parts, USPO, W 🅖 76 🅞 Walgreens
24	35th Ave (no EZ sb return), E 🅖 76 🅵 Taco Bell, W 🅖 76, Chevron, QuikStop
23	Coolidge Ave, Fruitvale, E 🅖 Shell/24hr 🅵 China Gourmet, McDonald's, Subway 🅞 Farmer Joe's, CVS Drug, Radio Shack
22	Park Blvd, E 🅖 Shell, W 🅖 Arco, Quikstop 🅞 🅷
21b	Grand Ave, Lake Shore, E 🅖 76/24hr, Chevron/dsl 🅵 KFC, Subway 🅞 Long's Drug, Trader Joe's, USPO, Walgreens, W 🅖 Chevron/dsl/24hr
21a	Harrison St, Oakland Ave, E 🅖 Quikstop, W 🅞 Honda
19d c	CA 24 E, I-980 W, to Oakland
19b	West St, San Pablo Ave, E 🅛 Extended Stay America 🅞 Best Buy, Home Depot, Jo-Ann Fabrics, Michael's, Office Depot
19a	I-80 W
18c	Market St, to San Pablo Ave, downtown
18b	Powell St, Emeryville, E 🅖 76 🅵 Burger King, CA Pizza Kitchen, Denny's, Elephant Bar/Grill, Jamba Juice, PF Chang's, Starbucks, Togo's 🅛 Courtyard, Sheraton, Woodfin Suites 🅞 Barnes&Noble, Old Navy, Ross, Trader Joe's, W 🅖 Shell 🅵 Chevy's Mexican 🅛 Hilton Garden
18a	CA 13, Ashby Ave, Bay St, same as 18b
17	University Ave, Berkeley, E 🅖 76, University Gas 🅛 La Quinta 🅞 to UC Berkeley
16	Gilman St, E 🅞 Golden Gate Fields Race Track, W 🅞 Target
13	Albany St, Buchanan St (from eb)
12	Central Ave (from eb), El Cerrito, E 🅖 Shell, Valero 🅞 Costco/gas
11	Bayview Ave, Carlson Blvd, E 🅖 76
10b	Regatta Blvd, E 🅖 Golden Gate/dsl
10a	S 23rd St, Marina Bay Pkwy, E 🅖 Stop and Save/dsl 🅵 Subway, W 🅵 Cafe Tiatro, El Molchaete, Quizno's, Wing Stop 🅞 CVS Drugs
9	Harbour Way, Cutting Blvd, E 🅖 Arco, W 🅵 Burger King
8	Canal Blvd, Garrard Blvd, W 🅖 Chevron/dsl 🅛 Days Inn
7b	Castro St, to I-80 E, Point Richmond, downtown industrial
7a	Western Drive (from wb), Point Molate
5mm	Richmond-San Rafael Toll Bridge

LIVERMORE PLEASANTON CASTRO VALLEY

CA

OAKLAND AREA

⬆E INTERSTATE 580 (Bay Area) Cont'd

Exit #	Services
2a	Francis Drake Blvd, to US 101 S, E 🛏 Extended Stay Deluxe ⭕ BMW, Home Depot
1b	Francisco Blvd, San Rafael, E ⛽ Beacon, Circle K, Francisco 🍴 Burger King, La Croissant 🛏 Motel 6, Travelodge ⭕ Mazda, tires, U-Haul, W 🍴 Subway, Wendy's ⭕ Office Depot, to San Quentin, USPO
1a	US 101 N to San Rafael, **I-580 begins/ends on US 101.**

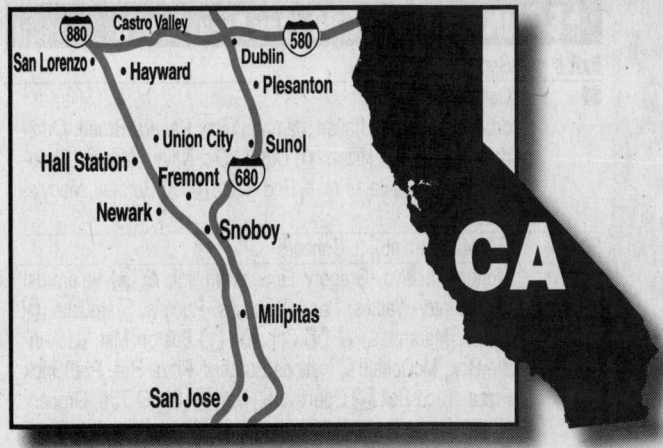

⬆E INTERSTATE 605 (Los Angeles)

Exit #	Services
27c	Huntington Dr. **I-605 begins/ends.** ⛽ Mobil 🍴 Subway ⭕ CVS Drug, Fresh&Easy Foods
27	I-210
26	Arrow Hwy, Live Oak, E ⭕ Santa Fe Dam, W ⭕ Irwindale Speedway
24	Lower Azusa Rd, LA St
23	Ramona Blvd, E ⛽ Mobil 🍴 Del Taco/24hr
22	I-10, E to San Bernardino, W to LA
21	Valley Blvd, to Industry, E ⛽ 76, Chevron/Chester's/Subway/dsl 🍴 7 Mares Rest., El Charro, Las Milpas Mexican, Winchell's Donuts 🛏 Valley Inn
19	CA 60, Pamona Fwy
18	Peck Rd, E ⛽ Shell, W ⭕ Ford Trucks
17	RoseHills Rd, W ⭕ Sports Arena
16	Beverly Blvd
15	Whittier Blvd, E ⛽ 76/dsl, Arco 🍴 Carl's Jr, Taco Bell, YumYum Donuts 🛏 GoodNite Inn ⭕ 7-11, W ⛽ Chevron, Shell 🍴 DQ, Pizza Hut, Shakey's Pizza, Starbucks, Subway, Taco's Mexico, Tommy's Burgers 🛏 Howard Johnson ⭕ AutoZone, Rite Aid
14	Washington Blvd, to Pico Rivera, E ⭕ Firestone/auto
13	Slauson Ave, E ⛽ Arco, Mobil 🍴 Denny's 🛏 Motel 6, W ⭕ Ⓗ
12mm	I-5
12	Telegraph Rd, to Santa Fe Springs, E ⛽ 76, Chevron 🍴 Del Taco, Jack-in-the-Box, KFC, Subway, Taco Bell, Yoshinoya ⭕ URGENT CARE, W ⛽ Arco/dsl
11	Florence Ave, to Downey, E ⛽ Mobil ⭕ Cadillac, Chevrolet, Honda
10	Firestone Blvd, E ⛽ 76 🍴 ChuckeCheese, KFC, McDonald's, Norm's Burgers, Sam's Burgers, Subway 🛏 Best Western ⭕ 99¢ Store, Audi/BMW/Porsche, Costco, Food4Less, Staples, Verizon, Walgreens, W ⛽ Chevron/repair 🍴 Starbucks ⭕ Chrysler/Dodge/Jeep, Office Depot, Target
9	Rosecrans Ave, to Norwalk, E ⛽ Chevron, Mobil 🍴 Del Taco, Little Caesars, McDonald's, Subway ⭕ Ⓗ, Food Basket Foods, Fresh&Easy, vet, Walgreens, W 🍴 Carrow's Rest 🛏 Motel 6
8	I-105, Imperial Hwy, E ⛽ 76 🍴 Domino's, KFC, LJ Silver, McDonald's, Pizza Hut/Taco Bell ⭕ CVS Drug, Food4Less, W ⛽ Arco
7	Alondra Blvd, E ⛽ 7-11, Chevron 🍴 A&W, Alondra's Mexican, Frantone's Rest., KFC, Red Chili ⭕ CVS Drug, Home Depot, Staples, W ⛽ Shell/Subway/24hr 🍴 Del Taco
6	CA 91
5	South St, E 🍴 5 Guys, BJ's Rest., CA Pizza Kitchen, Carl's Jr, Chick-fil-A, Coco's, Coldstone, Hometown Buffet, Jamba Juice, Lazy Dog Cafe, Luecille's BBQ, Panda Express, Panera Bread, Quiznos, Red Robin, Starbucks ⭕ AT&T, Firestone, Macy's, mall, Nordstrom's, Sears/auto, Target, Verizon, W ⛽

Exit #	Services
5	Continued Shell/service, Valero ⭕ Acura, Buick/GMC, Chevrolet, Chrysler/Dodge/Jeep, Ford, Honda, Hyundai, Infiniti, KIA, Lexus, Mazda, Nissan, Smartcar, Suzuki, Toyota/Scion, VW
4	Del Amo Blvd, to Cerritos, E 🍴 Del Taco, Omega Burgers, Starbucks ⭕ Ralph's Foods, W ⛽ Mobil
3	Carson St, E ⛽ 76, Price Saver/dsl 🍴 Alberto's Mexican, Jack-in-the-Box, KFC, Little Caesar's, McDonald's, Pizza Hut, Popeye's, Subway, Taco Bell, Wienerschnitzel 🛏 Lakewood Inn ⭕ 7-11, CVS Drug, Food4Less, O'Reilly Parts, Price Right Foods, W ⛽ Chevron/Subway/dsl 🍴 Carl's Jr, Chick-fil-A, Del Taco, Denny's, El Pollo Loco, El Torito, FoodCourt, In-N-Out, Island's Burgers, Jack-in-the-Box, Leucille's BBQ, Panda Express, Roadhouse Grill, Starbucks, SuperMex, TGIFriday's, Yashi Japanese ⭕ America's Tire, Barnes&Noble, Lowe's, Michael's, Old Navy, Petsmart, Radio Shack, Ross, Sam's Club, Staples, Walmart/auto
1	Katella Ave, Willow St, E ⛽ Shell 🍴 Madera's Steaks, McDonald's, Polly's Cafe, Starbucks ⭕ Ⓗ, Rite Aid, W Eldorado Regional Park
0mm	**I-605 begins/ends on I-405.**

⬆E INTERSTATE 680 (Bay Area)

Exit #	Services
71b a	I-80 E, to Sacramento, W to Oakland, **I-680 begins/ends on I-80.**
70	Green Valley Rd (from eb), Cordelia, N ⛽ Arco am/pm ⭕ Costco/gas, CVS Drug, Safeway
69	Gold Hill Rd, W ⛽ TowerMart/dsl
65	Marshview Rd
63	Parish Rd
61	Lake Herman Rd, E ⛽ Arco/Jack-in-the-Box/dsl, W ⛽ Gas City/dsl, Shell/Carl's Jr/dsl/24hr ⭕ vista point
60	Bayshore Rd, industrial park
58	I-780, to Benicia, toll plaza
56	Marina Vista, to Martinez
55mm	Martinez-Benicia Toll Br
54	Pacheco Blvd, Arthur Rd, Concord, W ⛽ 76, Shell/dsl
53	CA 4 E to Pittsburg, W to Richmond, Pittsburg
52	CA 4 E, Concord, Pacheco, E 🍴 Hometown Buffet, Marie Calender's, Starbucks, Taco Bell 🛏 Crowne Plaza, Holiday Inn ⭕ Chevrolet, Ford, Hyundai, Infiniti/VW, Sam's Club, Toyota, Trader Joe's, USPO, W ⛽ 76, Grand Gas, Shell/24hr 🍴 Denny's, McDonald's, Wendy's ⭕ AutoZone, Barnes&Noble, Firestone, K-Mart, O'Reilly Parts, Pepboys, Safeway Foods, Schwab Tire, Target, Toyota
51	Willow Pass Rd, Taylor Blvd, E 🍴 Benihana Rest., Buffet City, Claim Jumper, Denny's, El Torito, Elephant Bar Rest., Fud

CA

INTERSTATE 680 (Bay Area) Cont'd

Exit #	Services
51	Continued
	druckers, Grissini Italian, Jamba Juice, Panera Bread, Quizno's, Sizzler 🏨 Hilton ⭕ Cost+, Old Navy, Willows Shopping Ctr, W 🍴 Baja Fresh, Red Robin ⭕ JC Penney, Macy's, Sears/auto
50	CA 242 (from nb), to Concord
49b	Monument Blvd, Gregory Lane (from sb), E ⛽ Valero/dsl 🍴 Country Waffles, Panda Express, Rubio's, Starbucks ⭕ Kohl's, Marshall's, W ⛽ Chevron 🍴 Boston Mkt, Jack-in-the-Box, McDonald's, Nations Burgers, Pizza Hut, Red Brick Pizza, Taco Bell 🏨 Courtyard, Hyatt ⭕ Big O Tire, Grocery Outlet, Lucky Foods, Michael's, Radio Shack, Rite Aid, Ross, Safeway Foods, Staples, Tuesday Morning
49a	Contra Costa Blvd (from nb)
48	Treat Blvd, Geary Rd, E ⛽ Chevron 🍴 Back 40 BBQ, Heavenly Cafe, Subway 🏨 Embassy Suites, Extended Stay America ⭕ 7-11, Best Buy, Office Depot, W ⛽ Chevron, Shell 🍴 Black Angus, Primavera Pasta, Quizno's, Starbucks, Wendy's, Yan's China Bistro ⭕ Walgreens
47	N Main St, to Walnut Creek, E ⛽ Chevron 🍴 Fuddrucker's, Jack-in-the-Box, Taco Bell 🏨 Marriott, Motel 6, Walnut Cr Motel ⭕ Cadillac, Chevrolet, Chrysler/Dodge/Jeep, Harley-Davidson, Honda, Jaguar, Land Rover, Mercedes, Nissan, Target, W ⛽ 76/7-11/dsl/24hr ⭕ Domino's ⭕ NAPA, Porsche
46b	Ygnacio Valley Rd
46a	SR-24 W
45b	Olympic Blvd, Oakland
45a	S Main St, Walnut Creek, E ⭕ Ⓗ
44	Rudgear (from nb)
43	Livorna Rd
42b a	Stone Valley Rd, Alamo, W ⛽ Chevron, Shell/dsl 🍴 Papa Murphy's, Starbucks, Subway, Taco Bell, Xenia's ⭕ 7-11, CVS Drugs, Rite Aid, Safeway, vet
41	El Pintado Rd, Danville
40	El Cerro Blvd
39	Diablo Rd, Danville, E ⛽ 76/24hr 🍴 Chinese Cuisine, Taco Bell ⭕ Mt Diablo SP (12mi), Walgreens, W ⛽ Diablo
38	Sycamore Valley Rd, E ⛽ Shell 🍴 Denny's 🏨 Best Western, W ⛽ 76/dsl, Valero/dsl
36	Crow Canyon Rd, San Ramon, E ⛽ Shell 🍴 Burger King, Carl's Jr, Cheesesteak, Chili's, El Ballazo, Jamba Juice, Max's Diner, O'Zachary's Rest., Starbucks, Subway 🏨 Extended Stay America ⭕ Ⓗ, Big O Tire, Costco, Lucky Foods, Marshall's, Office Depot, PetCo, Rite Aid, Sea's Candies, USPO, W ⛽ 76, Chevron/repair/24hr, Shell/autocare, Valero 🍴 Chipotle Mexican, Giuseppe's Italian, In-N-Out, McDonald's, Nation's Burger's, Quizno's, Subway, Taco Bell, Togo's 🏨 Hotel Sierra ⭕ 7-11, Home Depot, Jo-Ann Fabrics, CVS Drug, repair/tires, Safeway, Staples, vet
34	Bollinger Canyon Rd, E ⛽ Valero 🍴 Baja Fresh, El Ballazo, Izzy's Steaks, Subway 🏨 Marriott, Residence Inn ⭕ Long's Drug, Target, Whole Foods, W ⛽ Chevron 🍴 Applebee's, Chevy's Mexican, Marie Callender's 🏨 Courtyard, Homestead Village
31	Alcosta Blvd, to Dublin, E ⛽ 76/7-11, W ⛽ Chevron, Shell/dsl 🍴 DQ, McDonalds, Mtn Mike's Pizza, Papa John's, Rulu's Cafe, Subway, Taco Bell ⭕ Lucky Foods, Walgreens
30	I-580, W to Oakland, E to Tracy
29	Stoneridge, Dublin, E 🏨 Hilton, W 🍴 Cheesecake Factory, PF Chang's, Taco Bell ⭕ JC Penney, Macy's, mall, Nordstrom's, Sears

SAN RAMON

FREMONT / SAN JOSE

26	Bernal Ave, Pleasanton, E ⛽ Shell/Jack-in-the-Box 🍴 Lindo's Mexican
25	Sunol Blvd, Pleasanton
21b a	CA 84, Calvaras Rd, Sunol, W to Dumbarton Bridge
20	Andrade Rd, Sheridan Rd (from sb), E ⛽ Sunol Super Stp/dsl
19mm	weigh sta nb
19	Sheridan Rd (from nb)
18	Vargas Rd
16	CA 238, Mission Blvd, to Hayward, E ⛽ Shell 🍴 McDonald's, W ⭕ Ⓗ
15	Washington Blvd, Irvington Dist, E ⛽ QuikStop
14	Durham Rd, to Auto Mall Pkwy, W ⛽ 76/Circle K/Subway/24hr, Shell/Jack-in-the-Box ⭕ Fry's Electronics, Home Depot, Walmart
12	CA 262, Mission Blvd, to I-880, Warm Springs Dist, W ⛽ 76, Valero 🍴 Burger King, Carl's Jr, Denny's, KFC, RoundTable Pizza, Starbucks, Subway, Taco Bell 🏨 Extended Stay America ⭕ 7-11, GNC, CVS Drug, Radio Shack, Ross, Safeway, Walgreens
10	Scott Creek Rd
9	Jacklin Rd, E ⭕ Bonfare Mkt, W ⛽ Shell
8	CA 237, Calaveras Blvd, Milpitas, E ⛽ 76, Shell/repair 🍴 Domino's, Flames CoffeeShop, RoadTable Pizza, Sizzler, Subway 🏨 Exectuive Inn ⭕ 7-11, Oceans SuperMkt, W ⛽ Shell 🍴 El Torito, Giorgio's Italian, It's a Grind, Lyon's Rest., McDonald's, Red Lobster 🏨 Embassy Suites, Extended Stay America ⭕ CVS Drug, Lucky Foods, Safeway, Staples
6	Landess Ave, Montague Expswy, E ⛽ 76, Arco, Chevron 🍴 Burger King, Jack-in-the-Box, McDonald's, Taco Bell, Togo's, Wienerschnitzel ⭕ Firestone, Lucky Foods, Radio Shack, Rite Aid, Target, Walgreens
5	Capitol Ave, Hostetter Ave, E ⛽ Shell 🍴 Carl's Jr, Popeye's ⭕ SaveMart Foods, W ⛽ Valero ⭕ Jiffy Lube
4	Berryessa Rd, E ⛽ Arco/24hr, USA, Valero/repair 🍴 Denny's, Lee's Sandwiches, McDonald's, Taco Bell ⭕ AutoZone, CVS Drug, Safeway
2b	McKee Rd, E ⛽ 76, Chevron, Shell 🍴 Burger King, HomeTown Buffet, Pizza Hut, Quizno's, Starbucks, Togo's, Wienerschnitzel ⭕ $Tree, PaknSave Foods, Ross, Target, Walgreens, W ⛽ World Gas 🍴 Baskin-Robbins, Foster's Freeze, Lee's Sandwiches, McDonald's, RoundTable Pizza, Wendy's, Yum Yum Doughnut ⭕ Ⓗ, Kohl's
2a	Alum Rock Ave, E ⛽ Shell/dsl/24hr 🍴 Jack-in-the-Box, Taco Bell, W ⛽ 76/24hr, Chevron 🍴 Carl's Jr
1d	Capitol Expswy
1c	King Rd, Jackson Ave (from nb), E ⛽ L&D Gas, Shell 🍴 El Gallo Giro, Jamba Juice, Kings Burger, Panda Express, Starbucks, Super Buffet, Taco Bell ⭕ Target, Walgreens
1b	US 101, to LA, SF
1a	(exits left from sb) I-680 begins/ends on I-280.

INTERSTATE 710 (Los Angeles)

Exit #	Services
23	I-710 begins/ends on Valley Blvd, E ⛽ Arco
22b a	I-10
20c	Chavez Ave
20b	CA 60, Pamona Fwy, E 🍴 King Taco, Monterrey Hill Rest., W ⛽ Shell
20a	3rd St
19	Whittier Blvd, Olympic Blvd, W ⛽ Shell 🍴 McDonald's
17b	Washington Blvd, Commerce, W ⛽ Commerce Trkstp/dsl/rest.

⬆E INTERSTATE 710 (Los Angeles) Cont'd

Exit #	Services
17a	Bandini Blvd, Atlantic Blvd, industrial
15	Florence Ave, E 🍴 Alfredo's Mexican, Applebee's, Coldstone, El Pescador Mexican, El Pollo Loco, IHOP, KFC, McDonald's, Panda Express, Quiznos, Red Brick Pizza, Starbucks, Subway, Taco Bell, Yoshinoya 🏠 Comfort Inn 🅾 $Tree, casino, Food4Less, Marshall's, Rite Aid, Ross, W 🅾 truck repair
13	CA 42, Firestone Blvd, E 🅰 Arco 🍴 Burger King, Denny's, McDonald's, Panda Express, Subway 🏠 Guesthouse Inn 🅾 El Super Foods, Ford, GNC, Radio Shack, Sam's Club, Target
12b a	Imperial Hwy, E 🅰 Shell/dsl 🍴 Abierto's Mexican, Carl's Jr., El Pollo Loco, Subway, W 🅰 76, Chevron/dsl, Shell 🍴 KFC, McDonald's, Panda Express, Pizza Patron, Starbucks, Subway, Taco Bell, Wienerschnitzel, Winchell's 🅾 AutoZone, Manny's Repair, Radio Shack, Valu+ Foods, Walgreens
11b a	I-105
10	Rosecrans Ave
9b a	Alondra Ave, E 🅰 Chevron/dsl 🍴 Jack-in-the-Box 🅾 Home Depot
8b a	CA 91
7b a	Long Beach Blvd, E 🅰 Chevron, Mobil, United/dsl, Valero 🍴 El Ranchito Mexican, McDonald's, Sizzler 🅾 CVS Drug, W 🅰 Arco/24hr 🍴 Jack-in-the-Box, Mocasalitos, Subway 🏠 Luxury Inn
6	Del Amo Blvd
4	I-405, San Diego Freeway
3b a	Willow St, E 🅰 Arco, Chevron 🍴 Baskin-Robbins, Chee Chinese, Dominos, Pizza Hut 🅾 Radio Shack, Walgreens, W 🅰 76, Arco 🍴 KFC, Little Caesars, Popeye's 🅾 AutoZone, Big Saver Foods
2	CA 1, Pacific Coast Hwy, E 🅰 76/dsll, Arco/mart, Chevron, Mobil 🍴 Hong Kong Express, KFC, McDonald's 🏠 Beacon Inn, Don Chente Tacos, King Taco, La Mirage Inn, Travel Eagle Inn 🅾 auto repair, Ranch Mkt, W 🅰 76/service, PCH Trkstp/dsl, Shell/Carl's Jr/dsl 🍴 Alberto's Mexican, Golden Star Rest., Jack-in-the-Box, McDonald's, Taco Bell, Tom's Burgers, Winchell's 🏠 Hiland Motel, SeaBreeze Motel 🅾 truckwash, TrueValue
1d	Anaheim St, W 🅰 Speedy Fuel 🅾 dsl repair/scales
1c	Ahjoreline Dr, Piers B, C, D, E, Pico Ave
1b	Pico Ave, Piers F-J, Queen Mary
1a	Harbor Scenic Dr, Piers S, T, Terminal Island, E 🏠 Hilton
0mm	I-710 begins/ends in Long Beach

⬆E INTERSTATE 780 (Vallejo)

Exit #	Services
7	I-780 begins/ends on I-680.
6	E 5th St, Benicia, N 🅰 Fast&Easy, S 🅰 Citgo/7-11, Valero/dsl 🍴 China Garden 🅾 Big O Tire, repair, vet
5	E 2nd St, Central Benicia, N 🅰 Valero 🏠 Best Western, S 🍴 McDonald's, Pappa's Rest.
4	Southampton Rd, Benicia, N 🍴 Asian Bistro, Burger King, Coldstone Creamery, Country Waffles, Jamba Juice, Rickshaw Express, RoundTable Pizza, Starbucks, Subway 🅾 Ace Hardware, Radio Shack, Raley's Foods, vet
3b	Military West
3a	Columbus Pkwy, N 🅰 Shell 🍴 Burger King, Napoli Pizza, Subway 🅾 Jiffy Lube, CVS Drugs, S to Benicia RA
1d	Glen Cove Pkwy, N 🅾 Hwy Patrol, S 🍴 Baskin-Robbins, Subway, Taco Bell 🅾 Safeway
1c	Cedar St
1b a	I-780 begins/ends on I-80.

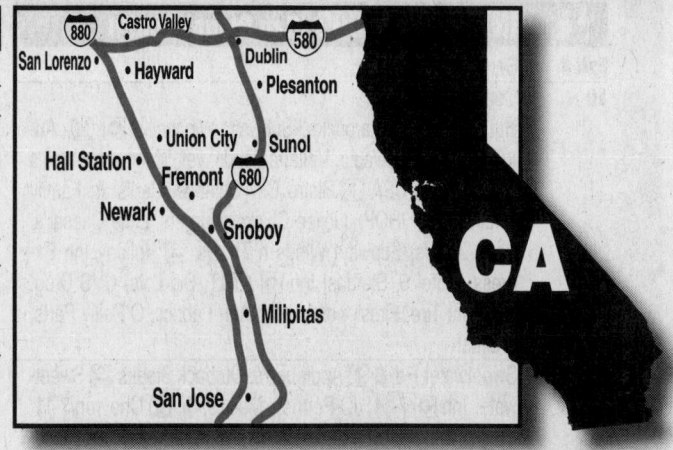

⬆N INTERSTATE 805 (San Diego)

Exit #	Services
28mm	I-5 (from nb). I-805 begins/ends on I-5.
27.5	CA 56 E (from nb)
27	Sorrento Valley Rd, Mira Mesa Blvd
26	Vista Sorrento Pkwy, E 🅰 Mobil/dsl 🍴 Chili's, Flame Broiler, Jamba Juice, McDonald's, Quizno's, Rubio's, Starbucks, Subway 🏠 Country Inn, Courtyard, Extended Stay America, Holiday Inn Express, Hyatt House 🅾 Staples
25b a	La Jolla Village Dr, Miramar Rd, E 1 mi 🅰 76/dsl 🅾 Discount Tire, Firestone, W 🍴 Corner Cafe, Cozymel's Cantina, Donovan's Grill, Harry's Grill, PF Chang's, Seasons Fresh Grill 🏠 Embassy Suites, Marriott 🅾 H, Macy's, mall, Nordstom's, Sears
24	Governor Dr
23	CA 52
22	Clairemont Mesa Blvd, E 🅰 7-11/dsl, Chevron/dsl, Mega/Subway/dsl, Shell 🍴 Arby's, Burger King, Carl's Jr, Chipotle Mexican, Coco's, Godfather Rest., Jersey Mike's, McDonald's, Rubio's Grill, Souplantation, Starbucks, Subway, Tommy's Burgers 🅾 Food4Less, Ford/Kia, Nissan, Ranch Mkt, Verizon, Walmart, W 🅰 Gas 🍴 Buga Korean BBQ, Subway 🏠 Best Western, CA Suites, Motel 6
21	CA 274, Balboa Ave, E 🅰 7-11, 76, Arco/dsl, Chevron/dsl 🍴 Applebee's, Islands Burger, Jack-in-the-Box 🅾 CarMax, Chevrolet, Chrysler/Dodge/Jeep, Jaguar, VW
20a	Mesa College Dr, Kearney Villa Rd, W 🅾 H
20	CA 163 N, to Escondido
18	Murray Ridge Rd, to Phyllis Place
17b	I-8, E to El Centro, W to beaches
16	El Cajon Blvd, E 🅰 Arco, Ultra 🅾 Pancho Villa Mkt, W 🅰 76 🍴 Carl's Jr, Jack-in-the-Box, Rudford's Rest., Subway, Wendy's 🅾 O'Reilly Parts
15	University Ave, E 🅰 Chevron 🍴 Subway 🅾 Radio Shack, W 🅰 76/dsl, USA/dsl 🍴 Starbucks 🅾 CVS Drug, Fresh&Easy Mkt, Walgreens
14	CA 15 N, 40th St, to I-15
13b	Home Ave, MLK Ave
13a	CA 94
12b	Market St
12a	Imperial Ave, E 🅰 Homeland Gas/dsl, United, W 🍴 Asia Wok, Cojita's Taco, Domino's, KFC/LJ Silver, Sizzler, Subway 🅾 99¢ Store, Home Depot
11b	47th St
11a	43rd St, W 🍴 Giant Pizza, Jack-in-the-Box, Subway 🅾 AutoZone, CVS Drug, Northgate Mkt
10	Plaza Blvd, National City, E 🍴 Chow King, McDonald's, Pizza

⬆N INTERSTATE 805 (San Diego) Cont'd

Exit #	Services
10	Continued
	Hut, Popeye's, Starbucks, Subway, Winchell's 🅞 🅷, AutoZone, Firestone/auto, Vallarta Foods, vet, Walgreens, Well's Drug, **W** 🅶 USA 🅕 Bistro City Chinese, Carl's Jr, Family House Rest., IHOP, Jubilee Chicken/burgers, Little Caesar's, Papa John's, Subway, Wings n Things 🅛 Holiday Inn Express; Motel 6, Stardust Inn 🅞 AT&T, Big Lots, CVS Drug, Discount Tire, Firestone/auto, Jo-Ann Fabrics, O'Reilly Parts, Walmart
9	Sweetwater Rd, **E** 🅕 Applebee's, Outback Steaks 🅛 Sweetwater Inn 🅞 7-11, JC Penney, Macy's, **W** 🅶 Chevron/7-11/dsl 🅕 Ben's Rest., Carl's Jr, Denny's, Hanaoka Japanese, Mike's NY Pizza, Pizza Hut, Pizza Hut, Starbucks, Subway, Taco Bell 🅞 CVS Drug, Food4Less, Goodyear/auto, Staples
8	CA 54
7c	E St, Bonita Rd, **E on Bonita Plaza Rd** 🅕 Applebee's, El Torito, Outback Steaks, Red Robin, Starbucks, Subway 🅞 JC Penney, Macy's, mall, Target, **W** 🅶 Chevron/dsl, Circle K, Shell/dsl 🅕 Burger King, Denny's, La Tequila Mexican 🅛 Comfort Inn, La Quinta
7b a	H St, **E** 🅶 Shell 🅕 China China, Coldstone, Daphne's CA Greek, D'Lish Pizza, Honeybaked, Jack-in-the-Box, Robeks Juice, Subway, Taco Bell 🅞 CVS Drug, Marshall's, Radio Shack, Vons Foods, **W** 🅕 Caffe Tazza
6	L St, Telegraph Canyon Rd, **E** 🅶 Arco/dsl 🅕 Little Caesar's, Mandarin Canyon, McDonald's, Starbucks, Subway 🅞 🅷, Olympic Training Ctr, Rite Aid, vet, Von's Foods, **W** 🅶 76/Circle K/dsl, USA 🅕 Canada Steakburger 🅞 7-11
4	Orange Ave, **E** 🅛 Olympic Training Ctr
3	Main St, Otay Valley Rd, **E** 🅶 Shell/dsl 🅕 Panda Express, Souplantation 🅞 Ford/Kia, Honda, Kohl's, Nissan, PetsMart, Staples, Toyota/Scion, **W** 🅶 Circle K/dsl 🅛 Best Western
2	Palm Ave, **E** 🅶 Arco, Chevron 🅕 Carl's Jr, Hometown Buffet, Starbucks, Subway, Taco Bell 🅞 AT&T, Home Depot, Meineke, Radio Shack, Tire Pros, USPO, Von's Foods, Walmart/McDonald's, **W** 🅶 Chevron 🅕 Golden House Chinese, KFC, Little Caesar's, McDonald's
1b	CA 905, **E** Brown Field ⊙, Otay Mesa Border Crossing
1a	San Ysidro Blvd, **E** 🅶 Shell/dsl, Valero 🅕 Church's 🅞 99¢ Store, CVS Drug, Factory2U, O'Reilly Parts, **W** 🅶 76, Chevron, Mobil/dsl, Shell 🅕 Denny's, McDonald's 🅛 Motel 6
	I-805 begins/ends on I-5.

⬆N INTERSTATE 880 (Bay Area)

Exit #	Services
46b a	I-80 W (exits left) . I-80 E/580 W.
44	7th St, Grand Ave, downtown
42b a	Broadway St, **E** 🅕 KFC 🅛 Marriott, **W** 🅛 Jack London Inn 🅞 to Jack London Square
41a	Oak St, Lakeside Dr, downtown
40	5th Ave, Embarcadero, **E** 🅕 Burger King, **W** 🅕 Quizno's, Starbucks 🅛 Executive Inn, Homewood Suites, Motel 6
39b a	29th Ave, 23rd Ave, to Fruitvale, **E** 🅶 Shell 🅕 Boston Mkt, Burger King, DonutStar, Popeye's, Starbucks 🅞 AutoZone, Lucky Foods, Office Depot, Radio Shack, **W** 🅞 7-11
38	High St, to Alameda, **E** 🅛 Bay Breeze Inn, Coliseum Motel 🅞 El Monte RV Ctr, **W** 🅶 Shell/dsl 🅕 McDonald's 🅞 Home Depot
37	66th Ave, Zhone Way, **E** coliseum
36	Hegenberger Rd, **E** 🅶 Arco/24hr, Shell/dsl 🅕 Burger King,

Exit #	Services
36	Continued
	Chubby Freeze, Denny's, Jack-in-the-Box/24hr, McDonald's, Taco Bell 🅛 Day's Hotel, Fairfield Inn, La Quinta, Motel 6, Quality Inn 🅞 Freightliner, GMC/Volvo, Pak'n Save Foods, **W** 🅶 76/Circle K/dsl, Shell 🅕 Carrows Rest., Francesco's Rest., Hegen Burger, In-N-Out, Jamba Juice, Panda Express, Quizno's, Red Barn Pizza, Starbucks, Subway, Wing Stop 🅛 Best Western, Courtyard, Econolodge, Hilton, Holiday Inn, Holiday Inn Express, Marriott, Park Plaza Motel 🅞 /auto, Harley-Davidson, Infiniti, Lexus, to Oakland ⊙, Walmart
35	98th Ave, **W** 🅞 ⊙
34	Davis St, **W** 🅶 Shell/Burger King 🅕 Hawaiian BBQ, Jamba Juice, Starbucks, Togo's 🅞 /McDonald's, Costco/gas, Home Depot, Office Depot, See's Candy, Walmart
33b a	Marina Blvd, **E** 🅶 Valero 🅕 Jack-in-the-Box, La Salsa Mexican, Panda Express, Starbucks, Taco Bell 🅞 Buick/GMC, Chevrolet, Ford, Honda, Hyundai, Kia, Marshall's, Nissan, Nordstrom's, Radio Shack, Volvo, **W** 🅶 Flyers/dsl 🅕 A&W/KFC, DairyBelle, Denny's
32	Washington Ave (from nb), Lewelling Blvd (from sb), **W** 🅶 76, Arco, TechCo 🅕 Hometown Buffet, Jack-in-the-Box, McDonald's, Papa Murphy's, Subway 🅛 Nimitz Motel 🅞 99¢ Store, Big Lots, Big O Tire, Food Maxx, GNC, Home Depot, CVS Drugs, Radio Shack, Safeway/24hr, same as 30, Walgreens/24hr
31	I-238 (from sb), to I-580, Castro Valley
30	Hesperian Blvd, **E** 🅶 76 🅕 In-N-Out, KFC, Quizno's, Starbucks 🅞 O'Reilly Parts, Walmart, Wheelworks Repair, **W** 🅶 76, Arco, Chevron 🅕 Black Angus, Hometown Buffet 🅛 Hilton Garden, Nimitz Inn 🅞 99¢ Store, BigLots, Food Maxx, CVS Drugs, Lucky Foods, Radio Shack, same as 32, USPO, vet
29	A St, San Lorenzo, **E** 🅶 76/Circle K 🅕 McDonald's 🅛 Best Western 🅞 Costco, tires/repair, **W** 🅶 76/Circle K, KB/dsl, Valero 🅕 Burger King, Carrow's, Chef Ming, Hawaiian BBQ, Jamba Juice, Pizza Hut, Starbucks, Subway 🅛 Days Inn, Heritage Inn, La Quinta, MainStay Suites, Phoenix Lodge 🅞 $Tree, Home Depot, Mi Pueblo Foods, Target
28	Winton Ave, **W** 🅶 Chevron, Valero/dsl 🅕 Applebee's, Coldstone, Elephant Grill, Hawaiian BBQ, Hometown Buffet, Marie Callendar's, Mimi's Cafe, Olive Garden, Panda Express, Panera Bread, Sizzler, Subway 🅞 Firestone/auto, Goodyear/auto, JC Penney, Macy's, mall, O'Reilly Parts, Ross, Sears/auto
27	CA 92, Jackson St, **E** 🅶 76, Beacon, Valero/24hr 🅕 Asian Wok, Baskin-Robbins, Hawaiian BBQ, Mnt Mike's Pizza, Nations Burgers, Papa Murphy's, Popeye's, Starbucks, Subway, Taco Bell 🅞 7-11, Grocery Outlet, CVS Drug, Lucky Foods, Radio Shack, Safeway, Walgreens, **W** San Mateo Br
26	Tennyson Rd, **E** 🅶 76, All American/dsl 🅕 Jack-in-the-Box, KFC, RoundTable Pizza 🅞 O'Reilly Parts, Walgreens, **W** 🅶 76 🅞 🅷
25	Industrial Pkwy (from sb), **E** 🅶 Industrial/dsl 🅕 Lite Wok, Quizno's, Starbucks, **W** 🅛 Pheonix Lodge
24	Whipple Rd, Dyer St, **E** 🅶 76, Chevron/dsl/24hr 🅕 Country Waffles, Del Taco, Denny's, McDonald's, Panda Express, Taco Bell, Wing Stop 🅛 Best Value Inn, Motel 6 🅞 FoodMaxx, Home Depot, PepBoys, Target, **W** 🅶 Shell 🅕 Applebee's, Baskin-Robbins, Burger King, Chili's, FreshChoice, Fuddrucker's, IHOP, In-N-Out, Jamba Juice, Jollibee, Krispy Kreme, La Salsa Mexican, Pasta Pormadora, Starbucks, Texas Roadhouse, TGIFriday, Togo's, Tony Roma's 🅛 Extended

⬆N INTERSTATE 880 (Bay Area) Cont'd

Exit #	Services
24	Continued
	Stay America, Holiday Inn Express 🅞 Best Buy, Lowe's Whse, Lucky Foods, Michael's, PetCo, Radio Shack, Walmart/auto
23	Alvarado-Niles Rd, **E** 🅖 Shell 🛏 Crowne Plaza 🅞 7-11, **W** 🅖 Shell 🅞 Walmart/auto, (same as 24)
22	Alvarado Blvd, Fremont Blvd, **E** 🍴 Phoenix Garden Chinese, Subway 🛏 Motel 6 🅞 Lucky Foods
21	CA 84 W, Decoto Rd to Dumbarton Br, **E** 🅖 7-11 🍴 McDonald's 🅞 Walgreens
19	CA 84 E, Thornton Ave, Newark, **E** 🅞 U-Haul, **W** 🅖 Chevron/dsl/24hr, Shell 🍴 Carl's Jr, KFC, Mtn Mike's Pizza, Taco Bell 🅞 7-11, BigLots, Home Depot
17	Mowry Ave, Fremont, **E** 🅖 76/Circle K, Chevron/dsl, Quik-Stop, Valero 🍴 Applebee's, Burger King, Chinese Buffet, Denny's, HoneyBaked Ham, KFC, Olive Garden, Starbucks, Subway, T&D Sandwiches 🛏 Best Western, Extended Stay Deluxe, Residence Inn 🅞 🏥, Lucky Foods, **W** 🅖 76 🍴 Arby's, BJ's Rest., Bombay Garden, El Burro Mexican, Jack-in-the-Box, McDonald's, Red Robin, Subway, Taco Bell, TK Noodles 🛏 Chase Suites, Comfort Inn, EZ 8 Motel, Homewood Suites, Motel 6, Towneplace Suites 🅞 Firestone, Goodyear/auto, JC Penney, Jiffy Lube, Lion Mkt., Macy's, mall, Mazda, Sears/auto, Target, TJ Maxx
16	Stevenson Blvd, **E** 🅖 Arco/dsl, Shell 🍴 Jack-in-the-Box, Outback Steaks, **W** 🅖 Chevron 🍴 Chevy's Mexican, Chuck-eCheese, Palm Gardens Rest., Starbucks, Togo's 🛏 Hilton 🅞 FoodMaxx, Ford, Harley-Davidson, Nissan, Tuesday Morning, Walmart
15	Auto Mall Pkwy, **E** 🅖 Arco, Chevron 🍴 Subway, **W** 🅖 Shell/dsl 🍴 Applebee's, Asian Pearl, Carino's, Chipotle Mexican, ClaimJumper, Coldstone Creamery, Dickey's BBQ, Hawaiian BBQ, In-N-Out, Jamba Juice, Panda Express, Panera Bread, PF Chang's, Quizno's, Rubio's, Starbucks, Subway, Tandoori Grill, Wendy's, Wing Stop 🅞 BMW, Chrysler/Dodge/Jeep, Costco/gas, Honda, Jaguar, Jo-Ann Fabrics, Kia, Kohl's, Land Rover, Lexus, Lowes Whse, Mercedes, Office Depot, Old Navy, Porsche, Radio Shack, Staples, Toyota, Volvo
14mm	**weigh sta both lanes**
13a	Gateway Blvd (from nb), **E** 🛏 Holiday Inn Express
13	Fremont Blvd, Irving Dist, **W** 🅖 Valero/Subway 🍴 McDonald's, SmartBrew 🛏 GoodNite Inn, Homestead Suites, La Quinta, Marriott

Exit	Services
12	Mission Blvd, **E** 🅖 76, Valero 🍴 Carl's Jr, Denny's, Jack-in-the-Box, KFC, Togo's 🛏 Holiday Inn Express, Quality Inn 🅞 7-11, CVS Drugs, Safeway, Walgreens, to I-680, **W** 🛏 Courtyard, Hampton Inn, Hyatt Place
10	Dixon Landing Rd, **E** 🍴 McDonald's 🛏 Residence Inn 🅞 7-11
8b	CA 237, Alviso Rd, Calaveras Rd, to McCarthy Rd, Milpitas, **E** 🅖 76, CA Fuel 🍴 Burger King, Carl's Jr, Chili Palace, Denny's, Lee's Sandwiches, Marie Callender's 🛏 Best Western, Days Inn, Travelodge 🅞 7-11, BigLots, **W** on McCarthy Rd 🅖 O'Reilly Parts, SaveMart Foods, vet, Walgreens, 🍴 Applebee's, Black Angus, Happi House, HomeTown Buffet, In-N-Out, Jamba Juice, Macaroni Grill, McDonald's, On the Border, Pasta Pomodoro, RedBrick Pizza, Starbucks, Subway, Taco Bell 🛏 Crowne Plaza, Hampton Inn, Hilton Garden, Homestead Suites, Larkspur Landing Hotel, Staybridge Suites 🅞 Best Buy, Chevron, GNC, Michael's, Petsmart, RanchMkt Foods, Ross, Walmart/McDonald's/auto
8a	Great Mall Parkway, Tasman Dr, **E** 🅞 Toyota
7	Montague Expswy, **E** 🅖 Shell/dsl, Valero 🍴 Jack-in-the-Box 🛏 Sleep Inn 🅞 U-Haul, **W** 🅖 Chevron/dsl 🍴 Dave&Buster's 🛏 Beverly Heritage Hotel, Sheraton
5	Brokaw Rd, **E** 🅞 Lowe's Whse, **W** 🅞 CHP, Ford Trucks, Fry's Electronics
4d	Gish Rd (nb only), **W** 🅞 auto/dsl repair/transmissions
4c b	US 101, N to San Francisco, S to LA
4a	1st St, **E** 🅖 76, Shell/repair 🍴 Subway, **W** 🅖 76 🍴 Cathay Chinese, Denny's/24hr, Empire Buffet, Genji Japanese 🛏 Clarion, Comfort Suites, Days Inn, Executive Inn, EZ 8 Motel, Holiday Inn Express, Homestead Suites, Radisson, Red Roof Inn, Vagabond Inn, Wyndham Garden 🅞 7-11
3	Coleman St, **E** 🅖 Valero/dsl 🍴 Quizno's, **W** 🅞 🍽
2	CA 82, The Alameda, **W** 🅖 Shell/repair 🍴 Starbucks, Subway, Taco Bell 🛏 Best Western, Santa Clara Inn, St. Francis Hotel, Sterling Motel, Valley Inn 🅞 Safeway, Santa Clara U
1d	Bascom Ave, to Santa Clara, **W** 🅖 Rotten Robbie/dsl, Valero 🍴 Burger King
1c	Stevens Creek Blvd, San Carlos St, **E** 🅖 Valero/dsl, Valley/dsl 🛏 Valley Park Hotel 🅞 🏥, **W** 🅖 76 🍴 Arby's, Cheese-Cake Factory, Jack-in-the-Box, RoundTable Pizza 🅞 7-11, Audi/VW, Best Buy, Ford, Goodyear/auto, Lexus, CVS Drugs, Macy's, mall, Nordstrom's, Old Navy, Safeway, Subaru
1b	**I-280. I-880 begins/ends on I-280**
1a	Ca 17 to Santa Cruz.

Sidebar labels: SAN JOSE, FREMONT, CA / CO

COLORADO

⬆N INTERSTATE 25

Exit #	Services
299	Colorado/Wyoming state line
296	point of interest both lanes
293	to Carr, Norfolk
288	Buckeye Rd
281	Owl Canyon Rd, **E** 🅞 KOA Campground, truck repair
278	CO 1 S, to Wellington, **W** 🅖 Kum&Go/dsl, Loaf'N Jug/dsl, Shell/dsl 🍴 Burger King, McDonald's, Subway, Taco John's 🛏 Days Inn 🅞 Bella Mkt, Family$, USPO, vet
271	Mountain Vista Dr, **W** 🅞 Budweiser Brewery
269b a	CO 14, to US 87, Ft Collins, **E** 🍴 CF&G Cookhouse, McDon-

Exit	Services
269b a	Continued
	ald's 🛏 Guesthouse Inn, **W** 🅖 Conoco, Shell/dsl, Valero 🍴 Denny's, DQ, Hacienda Real, Papa John's, Qdoba Mexican, Waffle House 🛏 9 Motel, Comfort Inn, Days Inn, La Quinta, Motel 6, Plaza Inn, Sleep Inn, Super 8 🅞 Home Depot, Radio Shack, RV Service, to CO St U, truck repair, U-Haul, vet, Walmart
268	Prospect Rd, to Ft Collins, **W** 🅞 🏥, Welcome Ctr/🆁🆂 both lanes, full 🚻 facilities, litter barrels, 🧺, petwalk
267mm	**weigh sta both lanes**
266mm	**W** 🅞 st patrol
265	CO 68 W, Timnath, **E** 🅖 Murphy USA/dsl 🅞 Walmart/Subway, **W** 2-3 mi 🅖 Shell/dsl 🍴 5 Guys Burgers, Austin's

N **INTERSTATE 25 Cont'd**

Exit #	Services
265	Continued
	Grill, Carrabba's, Chipotle, Coldstone, Firehouse Subs, Golden Corral, Huhot Chinese, IHOP, Macaroni Grill, McAlister's Deli, Old Chicago, Outback Steaks, Panera Bread, Papa John's, Qdoba, Quiznos, SmashBurger, Starbucks, Subway, Texas Roadhouse, Village Inn Rest. 🏨 Cambria Suites, Courtyard, Hampton Inn, Hiltson Garden, Marriott, Residence Inn 🅞 AT&T, Lowe's, Office Depot, Safeway/gas, Sam's Club, Target, Verizon, Walgreens, World Mkt
262	CO 392 E, to Windsor, E 🅖 7-11/dsl, Conoco/dsl, Shell/Subway/dsl 🍴 Arby's, Pueblo Viejo, Taco John's 🏨 AmericInn, Super 8, W 🅞 Powder River RV Ctr
259	Crossroads Blvd, E 🅖 Shell/dsl 🍴 Boot Grill, Carl's Jr, Nordy's, Palomino Mexican, Perkins, Qdoba Mexican, Subway 🏨 Candlewood Suites, Embassy Suites, Holiday Inn Express, ValuePlace Inn, W 🍴 Hooters 🅞 BMW, Buick/GMC, Chevrolet, Harley-Davidson, Hyundai, Mercedes, Mini, Subaru, to 🏨
257b a	US 34, to Loveland, E 🅖 7-11/dsl, Shell/dsl 🍴 Biaggi Italian, BoneFish Grill, Cafe Athens, Culver's, On-the-Border, PF Chang's, Red Robin, Rock Bottom Rest., Starbucks 🅞 AT&T, Barnes&Noble, Best Buy, Dick's, GNC, Macy's, See's Candies, Verizon, W 🅖 Conoco/dsl 🍴 Arby's (2mi), Buffalo Wild Wings, Carino's Italian, Chick-fil-A, Chili's, Chipotle Mexican, Cracker Barrel, IHOP, Jimmy Johns, KFC/Taco Bell, LoneStar Steaks, McDonald's, Mimi's Cafe, Noodles&Co, Old Chicago, Panera Bread, Qdoba, Starbucks, Subway, Wendy's 🏨 Best Western, Fairfield Inn, Hampton Inn, Residence Inn, Super 8 (2mi) 🅞 🏨, JoAnn Fabrics, Loveland Outlets/famous brands, Loveland RV Resort, Marshall's, museum, Old Navy, Petsmart, Ross, Sportsman's Whse, Staples, Target, to Rocky Mtn NP
255	CO 402 W, to Loveland
254	to CO 60 W, to Campion, E 🅖 Johnson's Corner/Sinclair/café/dsl/scales/motel/24hr 🏨 Budget Host 🅞 RV retreat/service
252	CO 60 E, to Johnstown, Milliken, W 🅖 Loaf'n Jug/Subway/dsl
250	CO 56 W, to Berthoud, W 🏨 Berthoud B&B 🅞 to Carter Lake
245	to Mead
243	CO 66, to Longmont, Platteville, E 🅖 Conoco/dsl, Kum&Go/dsl, Shell/7-11 🍴 Rancheros, Red Rooster Rest. 🅞 Big John's RV Ctr, Camping World/K&C RV Ctr, tires, W 🅞 to Estes Park, to Rocky Mtn NP
241mm	St Vrain River
240	CO 119, to Longmont, E 🅖 Shell/7-11/dsl 🍴 Burger King, Carl's Jr, Del Taco, Good Times Grill, Pizza Hut, Popeye's, Qdoba, Quiznos, Starbucks, Wendy's 🏨 Best Western, Comfort Suites, Value Place Inn 🅞 Century RV Ctr, Home Depot, Kia, Lexus, Toyota/Scion, Transwest RV Ctr, W 🅖 7-11/Subway/dsl, Conoco/dsl/scales/24hr, Shell/Circle K/dsl 🍴 Arby's, McDonald's, Pizza Hut/Taco Bell, Waffle House 🏨 1st Inn, Best Value Inn, Days Inn, Quality Inn, Super 8 🅞 museum, to Barbour Ponds SP, truckwash, Valley Camper RV Ctr
235	CO 52, Dacono, E 🅖 Kum&Go/dsl 🅞 Ford, Infiniti, W 🅖 Conoco/dsl/LP 🍴 McDonald's, Pepper Jacks Grille, Starbucks, Subway 🅞 Harley-Davidson, to Eldora Ski Area
232	to Erie, Dacono
229	CO 7, to Lafayette, Brighton, E 🍴 Buffalo Wild Wings, Chick-fil-A, Chili's, Famous Dave's BBQ, Goodtimes Burgers, Gunther Toody's, La Fogata, Starbucks, Subway, Village Inn 🅞

229	Continued
	AT&T, Costco/gas, Dick's, Home Depot, Petsmart, Sears Grand
228	E-470 (tollway), to Limon
226	144th Ave, E 🅞 Cabela's, W 🍴 HuHot Mongolian, Marco's Pizza, Mimi's Cafe, Mooyah Burgers, Red Robin, Starbucks 🅞 🏨, $Tree, AT&T, GNC, JC Penney, Macy's, Old Navy, REI, Ross, Staples, Target, Verizon
225	136th Ave, W 🅖 Valero/dsl 🍴 Big Burrito, Carl's Jr, KFC/LJ Silver's, Starbucks, Subway 🅞 Advance Parts, Lowe's, Walmart/McDonald's
223	CO 128, 120th Ave, to Broomfield, E 🅖 Conoco, Valero/dsl 🍴 Applebee's, Burger King, Café Rio, Chick-fil-A, Chipotle Mexican, Coldstone, Damon's, Fazoli's, Jimmy John's, Jim'N Nick's BBQ, Krispy Kreme, LoneStar Steaks, McDonald's, Olive Garden, Outback Steaks, Panda Express, Panera Bread, Pizza Hut, Smash Burger, Sonic, Starbucks, Subway, TGIFriday's 🏨 DoubleTree, EconoLodge, Hampton Inn, Holiday Inn Express, Ramada Inn 🅞 $Tree, Albertson's, Barnes&Noble, Big O Tire, Brakes+, CarQuest, Discount Tire, Meineke, Michael's, O'Reilly Parts, PetCo, Sprouts Mkt, Target, Tires+, vet, Walgreens, W 🅖 Conoco/dsl, Shell/Circle K/Popeye's/dsl, Valero/dsl 🍴 CB Potts Rest., Chili's, Cracker Barrel, DQ, Hooters, Laguna's Mexican, Perkins, Qdoba, Starbucks, Subway, Village Inn Rest., Wendy's 🏨 Comfort Suites, Cottonwood Suites, Extended Stay America, Fairfield Inn, La Quinta, Super 8
221	104th Ave, to Northglenn, E 🅖 Conoco, Shell 🍴 Buffalo Wild Wings, Burger King, CiCi's Pizza, Denny's, DQ, Firehouse Subs, Old Chicago, Qdoba, Subway, Texas Roadhouse 🅞 🏨, Gander Mtn, GNC, Home Depot, King's Soopers, Tires+, Walgreens, W 🅖 7-11, Shell/Circle K/dsl 🍴 Applebee's, Atlanta Bread, Blackeyed Pea, Cinzzetti's Italian, GoodTimes Burger, Gunther Toody's, McDonald's, Seoul BBQ, Starbucks, Taco Bell, The Armadillo 🅞 Best Buy, Fiat, Firestone/auto, Ford, Goodyear/auto, Hyundai, Jo-Ann Fabrics, Lowe's, Marshalls, Office Depot, Petsmart, Radio Shack, Ross, Sheplar's
220	Thornton Pkwy, E 🍴 Golden Corral, Rico Pollo 🅞 🏨, AT&T, Hobby Lobby, Sam's Club/gas, Thornton Civic Ctr, Walmart/McDonald's, W 🅖 Shell, Valero/dsl, Western/dsl 🍴 Subway
219	84th Ave, to Federal Way, E 🅖 Shell/dsl, Valero/dsl 🍴 Arby's, McDonald's, Quiznos, Sonic, Starbucks, Subway, Taco Bell, Taco Star, Waffle House 🅞 O'Reilly Parts, W 🅖 Econogas, Valero/dsl 🍴 Burger King, DQ, El Fogon, McDonald's, Popeye's, Santiago's Mexican, Village Inn Rest. 🏨 Motel 6 🅞 🏨, AutoZone, CarQuest, Discount Tire, Meineke, Save-A-Lot, vet
217	US 36 W (exits left from nb), to Boulder, W 🅖 Ammco 🍴 Subway 🅞 Chevrolet, Toyota/Scion
216b a	I-76 E, to I-270 E
215	58th Ave, E 🍴 Burger King, McDonald's, Steak Escape, Subway, Wendy's 🏨 Comfort Inn 🅞 URGENT CARE, W 🅖 Conoco/dsl, Shamrock/dsl 🏨 Super 8 🅞 O'Reilly Parts
214c	48th Ave, E 🅞 🏨, coliseum, W 🍴 Village Inn Rest. 🏨 Quality Inn, Ramada
214b a	I-70, E to Limon, W to Grand Junction
213	Park Ave, W 38th Ave, 23rd St, downtown, E 🅖 Conoco 🍴 Domino's, McDonald's, Starbucks 🏨 La Quinta, W 🏨 Town&Country Motel
212c	20th St, downtown, Denver
212b a	Speer Blvd, E 🅞 museum, downtown, W 🅖 Conoco/dsl, Shell/dsl 🍴 Starbucks, Subway 🏨 Hampton Inn, Ramada, Residence Inn, Super 8 🅞 AutoZone, Walgreens

CO

LOVELAND

BROOMFIELD

THORNTON

	INTERSTATE 25 Cont'd
Exit #	**Services**
211	23rd Ave, E [other] funpark
210c	CO 33 (from nb)
210b	US 40 W, Colfax Ave, W [food] Denny's, KFC [lodging] Ramada Inn/rest., Red Lion Inn [other] Mile High Stadium
210a	US 40 E, Colfax Ave, E [other] civic center, U-Haul, downtown
209c	8th Ave
209b	6th Ave W, US 6, W [gas] Shell/dsl
209a	6th Ave E, downtown, Denver
208	CO 26, Alameda Ave (from sb), E [gas] Shamrock/dsl [food] Burger King, Denny's [other] Home Depot, same as 207b, W [gas] Conoco/dsl
207b	US 85 S, Santa Fe Dr, same as 208
207a	Broadway, Lincoln St, E [food] Griff's Burgers [other] USPO
206b	Washington St, Emerson St, E [other] Whole Foods Mkt, W [other][H]
206a	Downing St (from nb)
205b a	University Blvd, W [gas] to U of Denver
204	CO 2, Colorado Blvd, E [gas] Conoco/dsl, Loaf'n Jug, Shamrock, Shell/Circle K [food] Arby's, Black Eyed Pea, Chili's, Domino's, GoodTimes Grill, Hacienda Colorado, IHOP, Jimmy John's, McDonald's, Noodles&Co, Old Chicago Pizza, Pizza Hut, Qdoba, Smashburger, Starbucks, Subway, Taco Bell, Tokyo Joe's, Village Inn Rest., Wahoo's, Whole Foods Mkt [lodging] Belcaro Motel, Courtyard, Fairfield Inn, Hampton Inn [other] Barnes&Noble, Best Buy, Chevrolet, Home Depot, Mercedes/BMW, Petco, Ross, Safeway Foods, Staples, vet, VW, Walgreens, W [gas] Conoco [food] A&W/KFC, Dave&Buster's, McDonald's, Pei Wei, Perkins, Which Wich [lodging] La Quinta [other] Natural Grocers, Office Depot, USPO
203	Evans Ave, E [lodging] Rockies Inn, W [lodging] Cameron Motel [other] Ford
202	Yale Ave, W [food] BeauJo's CO Pizza, Chipotle Mexican [other] GNC, King's Sooper, Michaels, Petsmart

201	US 285, CO 30, Hampden Ave, to Englewood, Aurora, E [gas] Conoco/Circle K/LP, Shamrock, Shell [food] Chick-fil-A, Chipotle Mexican, Coldstone, Domino's, Firehouse Subs, Jimmy John's, McDonald's, Noodles&Co, NY Deli, Panera Bread, Qdoba, Smashburger, Starbucks, Subway, Wahoos Fish Taco, Zanitas Mexican [lodging] Embassy Suites [other] Discount Tire, King's Sooper/dsl, Omaha Steaks, Petco, Target, URGENT CARE, Verizon, vet, Walgreens, Whole Food Mkt, W [gas] Conoco/7-11 [food] Burger King, Starbucks [other] Safeway
200	I-225 N, to I-70
199	CO 88, Belleview Ave, to Littleton, E [food] Baker St Grill, Chipotle Mexican, Cool River Cafe, Fiocchi's Pizzeria, Fornaio Rest., Garcia's Mexican, Great Northern Rest., Noodles&Co, Pancake House, Panera Bread, Qdoba, Starbucks, Wendy's, Which Wich [lodging] Hampton Inn, Hilton Garden, Hyatt Place, Marriott, W [gas] Conoco, Shamrock [food] McDonald's, Pappadeaux Café, Pizza Hut/Taco Bell [lodging] Extended Stay Am, Extended Stay America [other] Lexus
198	Orchard Rd, E [food] Del Frisco's Steaks [other] Shepler's, W [gas] Shell/Circle K/dsl [food] Subway [lodging] DoubleTree [other] vet
197	Arapahoe Blvd, E [gas] Conoco/dsl, Shell/Circle K/dsl [food] A&W/KFC, Bros BBQ, Burger King, Chick-fil-A, Del Taco, Dickie's BBQ, Domino's, El Parral, El Tapatio Mexican, Gunther Toody's Rest., Hoong's Palace, McDonald's, Outback Steaks, Pat's Cheesesteak, Pizza Hut, Qdoba, Schlotsky's, Smashburger, Sonic, Starbucks, Subway, Volcano Chinese, Wendy's [lodging] Best Western, Courtyard, Extended Stay America, Hawthorn Suites, Hyatt House, LaQuinta, Motel 6, Sleep Inn [other] Chrysler/Jeep, Discount Tire, Ford, Home Depot, Honda, Hyundai, Kia, Lowe's Whse, Mazda, Nissan, Subaru, Target, Toyota/Scion, USPO, Walmart, W [gas] Phillips 66/dsl, Shell/dsl, Valero/dsl [food] Arby's, Boston Mkt, CB & Potts, Chipotle

D E N V E R   A R E A *(left margin)*

D E N V E R   A R E A *(right margin)*

⬆N INTERSTATE 25 Cont'd

Exit #	Services
197	**Continued**
	Mexican, DQ, Elephant Bar Rest., Five Guys, Garbanzo Grill, Goodtimes, Jamba Juice, Jimmy John's, Macaroni Grill, Mc-Donald's, Papa Murphy's, Qdoba, Red Robin, Starbucks, Subway, Taco Bell, Twin Peaks Grill 🛏 Residence Inn, Wingate Inn 🅞 Advance Parts, AT&T, Big O Tire, Brakes+, Firestone/auto, GNC, Goodyear/auto, Office Depot, Safeway, Sprouts Mkt, URGENT CARE, vet
196	Dry Creek Rd, **E** 🍴 IHOP, Landry's Seafood, Maggiano's Italian, Purple Ginger Asian 🛏 Comfort Suites, Days Inn, Extended Stay America, Holiday Inn Express, La Quinta, Quality Inn, Sheraton, Staybridge Suites, **W** 🅖 7-11/dsl 🍴 Bono's BBQ 🛏 Drury Inn
195	County Line Rd, **E** 🍴 Fleming's 🛏 Courtyard, Homewood Suites, Residence Inn, **W** 🅖 Conoco 🍴 Buffalo Wild Wings, Burger King, CA Pizza Kitchen, Chick-fil-A, Chipotle Mexican, Earl's Kitchen, Firehouse Subs, Genghis Grill, J Alexander's, Jason's Deli, Panda Express, PF Changs, Red Lobster, Red Robin, Rock Bottom Brewery/Cafe, Smashburger, Starbucks, TGIFriday's, Thai Basil, Tokyo Joe's 🛏 Hyatt Place 🅞 AT&T, Barnes&Noble, Best Buy, Costco/gas, Dick's, Dillard's, Home Depot, JC Penney, Jo-Ann Fabrics, Macy's, Marshall's, Michaels, Nordstrom, Old Navy, PetsMart, REI, Ross, Verizon
194	CO 470 W, CO 470 E **(tollway)**
193	Lincoln Ave, to Parker, **E** 🅖 7-11/dsl, Conoco, Valero/dsl 🍴 Carl's Jr, Hacienda Colorado, Starbucks, Subway 🛏 Candlewood Suites, Hilton Garden, **W** 🅖 Conoco/dsl 🍴 Chili's, Chipotle Mexican, Firehouse Subs, Five Guys, Garbanzo Grill, Heidi's, KFC, McDonald's, Noodles&Co, Papa John's, Papa Murphy's, Pizza Hut/Taco Bell, Qdoba, Starbucks, Subway 🛏 Hampton Inn, Marriott 🅞 Ⓗ, Discount Tire, GNC, Safeway, Sprouts Mkt, Target
192	Ridgegate Pkwy, **W** 🅞 Ⓗ, Cabela's
191	no services
190	Surrey Ridge
188	Castle Pines Pkwy, **W** 🅖 Conoco/dsl, Shell/Circle K/Taco Bell/dsl 🍴 La Dolce Vita, Las Fajitas Mexican, Papa John's, Papa Murphy's, Starbucks, Subway, Wendy's 🅞 Big O Tires, Discount Tire, King's Sooper/dsl, Safeway, URGENT CARE, vet, Wlagreens
187	Happy Canyon Rd, **W services 2 mi**
184	Founders Pkwy, Meadows Pkwy, to Castle Rock, **E** 🅖 Conoco/dsl, Shell/Circle K/dsl 🍴 A&W/KFC, Applebee's, Baskin-Robbins, Chick-fil-A, Chipotle Mexican, Coldstone, Five Guys, Goodtimes Grill, Jimmy John's, Little Caesars, Noodles&Co, Outback Steaks, Panera Bread, Parry's Pizza, Qdoba, Red Robin, Sonic, Starbucks, Subway, Taco Bell, Wendy's 🅞 $Tree, Advance Parts, AT&T, Brakes+, Discount Tire, Firestone/auto, GNC, Goodyear/auto, Grease Monkey, Home Depot, Just Brakes, King's Sooper, Kohl's, Michael's, Natural Grocers, Office Depot, O'Reilly Parts, Petsmart, Radio Shack, Sprouts Mkt, Target, Verizon, vet, Walgreens, Walmart, **W** 🅖 Loaf'n Jug/dsl 🍴 Arby's, Blackeyed Pea, Chili's, Food Court, Freddy's Steakburger, IHOP, McDonald's, Rockyard Grill 🛏 Best Western, Comfort Suites, Days Inn, Hampton Inn, Holiday Inn Express 🅞 Castle Rock Outlet/famous brands, Lowe's, Midas, st patrol
182	CO 86, Castle Rock, Franktown, **E** 🅖 7-11/dsl, Conoco/dsl, Phillips 66/dsl 🍴 Augustine Grill, B&B Cafe, Castle Cafe, El Meson Mexican 🛏 Castle Pines Motel 🅞 vet, **W** 🅖 Shell/

182	**Continued**
	Circle K/dsl, Valero/dsl 🍴 Burger King, Domino's, Guadalajara Mexican, Jack-in-the-Box, McDonald's, Old West BBQ, Santiago's Mexican, Village Inn, Waffle House, Wendy's 🛏 Castle Inn, LaQuinta, Super 8 🅞 NAPA
181	CO 86, Wilcox St, Plum Creek Pkwy, Castle Rock, **E** 🍴 Conoco, Valero/dsl, Western/dsl 🍴 Blimpie, DQ, El Meson Mexican, Papa John's, Papa Murphy's, Pizza Hut, Quiznos, Starbucks, Stumpy's Pizzaria, Subway, Taco Bell 🛏 Castle Rock Motel 🅞 AutoZone, Big O Tire, Buick/Chevrolet/GMC, Chrysler/Dodge/Jeep, Ford, Midas, Safeway/dsl, Tuesday Morning, URGENT CARE, USPO, Walgreens⁕
174	Tomah Rd, **W** 🅞 Yogi Bear's Campground
173	Larkspur (from sb, no return), **W 3 mi** 🅖 Conoco/Larkspur Cafe/dsl/🅒
172	Upper Lake Gulch Rd, Larkspur, **W 2 mi** 🅖 Conoco/dsl/🅒 🍴 Larkspur Pizza Cafe, Spur Grill 🅞 USPO
167	Greenland
163	County Line Rd
162.5mm	Monument Hill, elev 7352
162mm	**weigh sta both lanes**
161	CO 105, Woodmoor Dr, **E** 🅖 Conoco 🍴 3 Margaritas Mexican, Papa John's 🛏 Sundance Mtn Lodge/rest 🅞 CO Hts RV Park (2mi), **W** 🅖 7-11, Conoco/Circle K/dsl 🍴 Arby's, Domino's, La Casa Fiesta New Mexican, McDonald's, Rosie's Diner, Starbucks, Subway, Taco Bell, Village Inn 🅞 Big O Tire, Natural Grocers, Safeway/dsl, USPO, Walgreens
158	Baptist Rd, **E** 🅖 Shell/Circle K/Popeye's/dsl/24hr 🍴 Borriello Bros. Pizza, Carlos Miguel's, Chili's, Coldstone, Freddy's Steakburgers, McDonald's, Papa Murphy's, Subway, TX Roadhouse 🛏 Fairfield Inn 🅞 AutoZone, Christian Bros. Auto, Discount Tire, GNC, Home Depot, King's Sooper, Kohl's, O'Reilly Parts, Petsmart, Staples, URGENT CARE, Verizon, Walgreens, Walmart/Subway, Jiffy Lube, **W** 🅖 Shamrock/dsl/scales, **N** 🍴 Mexican Grill
156b	N Entrance to USAF Academy, **E** 🍴 Bourbon Bros Kitchen, C B & Potts Rest., Jimmy John's 🅞 Bass Pro Shops, **W** 🅞 visitors center
156a	Gleneagle Dr, **E** 🅞 mining museum
153	InterQuest Pkwy, **E** 🅖 Kum&Go/dsl 🍴 Cheddar's, CO Mtn Brewery/rest. 🛏 Hampton Inn, Residence Inn
152	scenic overlook on sb
151	Briargate Pkwy, **E** 🅖 7-11 🍴 Biaggi's, CA Pizza Kitchen, Garbanzo Grill, Marco's Pizza, Panera Bread, PF Changs, Qdoba, Salsa Brava Mexican, Starbucks, Ted's MT Grill 🛏 Hilton Garden, Homewood Suites 🅞 AT&T, to Black Forest
150b a	CO 83, Academy Blvd, **E** 🅖 Shamrock/dsl, Shell/Circle K/dsl 🍴 5 Guys Burgers, A&W, Amanda's Fonda, Applebee's, Baskin-Robbins, Buffalo Wild Wings, Burger King, Chick-fil-A, Chipotle Mexican, Coldstone, Cracker Barrel, Crave Burgers, Culver's, Del Taco, Denny's, Drifters Hamburgers, Egg&I Café, Elephant Bar Rest., Extreme Pizza, Famous Dave's, Firehouse Subs, HuHot Mongolian, IHOP, Jason's Deli, Jimmy John's, KFC, McDonald's, Mimi's Café, Noodles&Co, Olive Garden, Olive Garden, On-the-Border, Panera Bread, Pei Wei, Qdoba, Red Robin, Salt Grass Steaks, Schlotzsky's, Sonic, Starbucks, Steak'n Shake, Subway, Tokyo Joe's Grill, Wendy's 🛏 Academy Hotel, Comfort Suites, Days Inn, Drury Inn, EconoLodge, Howard Johnson, Super 8 🅞 $Tree, Advance Parts, AT&T, Barnes&Noble, Best Buy, Chevrolet, Dick's, Dillard's, Firestone/auto, Ford, Hobby Lobby, Home Depot, Hyundai, JC Penney, Kia, King's Sooper, Macy's,

Ⓓ Ⓔ Ⓝ Ⓥ Ⓔ Ⓡ Ⓐ Ⓡ Ⓔ Ⓐ

CO

Ⓒ Ⓐ Ⓢ Ⓣ Ⓛ Ⓔ Ⓡ Ⓞ Ⓒ Ⓚ

Ⓛ Ⓐ Ⓡ Ⓚ Ⓢ Ⓟ Ⓤ Ⓡ

↑N	**INTERSTATE 25 Cont'd**
Exit #	**Services**
150b a	Continued

Marshall's, Michael's, Midas, Natural Grocers, Old Navy, O'Reilly Parts, PepBoys, Petsmart, REI, Ross, Sam's Club/gas, Sears/auto, to Peterson AFB, URGENT CARE, Verizon, VW, Walmart/Subway, Whole Foods Mkt, **W** S Entrance to USAF Academy

149 Woodmen Rd, **E** 🍴 Carl's Jr, Carraba's 🄾 Nissan, **W** 🅖 Shell/Circle K/dsl 🍴 Hooters, Old Chicago Pizza, Outback Steaks, TGIFriday's, Zio's Italian 🛏 Comfort Inn, Embassy Suites, Fairfield Inn, Hampton Inn, Holiday Inn Express, Microtel, Staybridge Suites

148 Corporate Ctr Dr, Nevada Ave, **E** 🍴 BJ's Rest, Bonefish Grill, Chipotle Mexican, Hacienda Colorado, Noodles&Co, Panera Bread, Pita Pit, Smashburger, Tokyo Joe's Grill, Which Wich 🛏 The Lodges 🄾 Costco/gas, Harley-Davidson, Kohl's, Lowe's, Petco, SteinMart, **W** 🅖 Shell/Circle K 🛏 Crestwood Suites, Extended Stay America, Hyatt House, Marriott 🄾 to Rodeo Hall of Fame

146 Garden of the Gods Rd, **E** 🅖 Conoco/7-11, Shell/Circle K/dsl 🍴 Carl's Jr, Caspian Cafe, Drifter's Burgers, McDonald's 🛏 Best Value Inn, La Quinta 🄾 Aamco, **W** 🅖 7-11, Conoco/Circle K, Shamrock/dsl, Shell/dsl 🍴 Applebee's, Arby's, Arceo's Mexican, Blackeyed Pea, Chick-fil-A, Freddy's Steakburgers, Jimmy John's, Mollica's Italian, Sonic, Souper Salad, Subway, Taco Bell, Village Inn, Wendy's 🛏 Days Inn, Hyatt Place, Quality Inn, Super 8 🄾 $Tree, AutoZone, Discount Tire, to Garden of Gods, vet

145 CO 38 E, Fillmore St, **E** 🅖 7-11, Shamrock/dsl, Western/dsl 🍴 Arby's, Burger King, Carl's Jr, DQ, Lucky Dragon, McDonald's, Subway, Taco Bell 🛏 Budget Host 🄾 🅷, Advance Parts, Walgreens, **W** 🍴 Waffle House 🛏 Motel 6, Super 8

144 Fontanero St

143 Uintah St, **E** 🅖 7-11 🄾 Uintah Fine Arts Ctr

142 Bijou St, Bus Dist, **E** 🛏 Hilton 🄾 Firestone/auto, visitor info, **W** 🍴 Denny's 🛏 Clarion, Quality Inn 🄾 7-11

141 US 24 W, Cimarron St, to Manitou Springs, **W** 🅖 Conoco/dsl, Shell/7-11/dsl 🍴 Arby's, Capt D's, La Casita Mexican, McDonald's, Popeye's, Sonic, TX Roadhouse 🄾 Acura, Audi, AutoZone, Brakes+, Buick/GMC, Cadillac, Chevrolet, Chrysler/Dodge/Jeep, Discount Tire, Ford, Grease Monkey, Hobby Lobby, Hyundai, Infiniti, Kia, Land Rover/Jaguar, Lexus, Lincoln, Mazda, Meineke, Mercedes, NAPA, Office Depot, Porsche, Radio Shack, Subaru, to Pikes Peak, Toyota/Scion, Volvo, VW, Walmart/McDonald's

140b US 85 S, Tejon St, **E** 🄾 Peerless Tires, **W** 🅖 Conoco/dsl 🄾 access to same as 141

140a Nevada Ave, **E** 🅖 Kum & Go/dsl 🛏 Chateau Motel, Howard Johnson 🄾 repair, **W** 🅖 7-11, Shamrock 🍴 Arceo's Mexican, Burger King, China Kitchen, Chipotle Mexican, IHOP, KFC, McDonald's, Noodles&Co, On the Border, Panda Express, Panera Bread, Rancho Alegre Mexican, Red Robin, Schlotzsky's, Starbucks, Subway, Taco Bell, Taco Express, Wendy's 🛏 Rodeway Inn, Sunsprings Motel, Travel Star Inn 🄾 $Tree, access to auto dealers at 141, Big O Tire, Family$, Michael's, Midas, Natural Grocers, Office Depot, O'Reilly Parts, Petsmart, Ross, Safeway Foods, Sears, Tuesday Morning, Walgreens

139 US 24 E, to Lyman, Peterson AFB

138 CO 29, Circle Dr, **E** 🅖 Conoco, Shell/Circle K/dsl 🍴 McDonald's 🛏 Days Inn, Hotel Elegante, Super 8 🄾 🖳, Kohl's,

138 Continued

URGENT CARE, zoo, **W** 🅖 7-11 🍴 Arby's, Buffalo Wild Wings, Burger King, Carl's Jr, Carrabba's, Chili's, ChuckeCheese, Culver's, Denny's, Fazoli's, Flatiron Grill, Macaroni Grill, Outback Steaks, Smoothie King, Subway, Village Inn 🛏 Best Western, Comfort Inn, Courtyard, DoubleTree Hotel, Fairfield Inn, Hampton Inn, La Quinta, Residence Inn 🄾 AT&T, GNC, PetCo, Radio Shack, Target

135 CO 83, Academy Blvd, **E** to 🖳, to Cheyenne Mtn SP, **W** Ft Carson

132 CO 16, Wide Field Security, **E** 🅖 ♥Loves♥/Subway/dsl 🄾 Camping World RV Ctr, KOA

128 to US 85 N, Fountain, Security, **E** 🅖 7-11, Loaf'n Jug/Subway/dsl 🄾 Family$, USPO, **W** 🅖 Tomahawk/Shell/rest/dsl/24hr/@ 🛏 Fountain Inn, Super 8 🄾 Freightliner

125 Ray Nixon Rd

123 no services

122 to Pikes Peak Meadows, **W** 🄾 Pikes Peak Intn'l Raceway

119 Rancho Colorado Blvd, Midway

116 county line rd

115mm 🆁🆂 nb, full 🚻 facilities, litter barrels, petwalk, 🐾

114 Young Hollow

112mm 🆁🆂 sb, full 🚻 facilities, litter barrels, petwalk, 🐾

110 Pinon

108 Purcell Blvd, Bragdon, **E** 🄾 racetrack, **W** 🄾 KOA

106 Porter Draw

104 Eden, **W** 🅖 ♥Loves♥/Chester's/Subway/dsl/scales/24hr 🄾 Peterbilt

102 Eagleridge Blvd, **E** 🅖 Loaf'n Jug/dsl 🍴 Burger King, Subway, TX Roadhouse 🛏 Holiday Inn Express 🄾 Big O Tire, Home Depot, Sam's Club/gas, **W** 🅖 Shell/dsl 🍴 Buffalo Wild Wings, Cactus Flower Mexican, Chili's, Cracker Barrel, IHOP, Starbucks, Taco Star, Village Inn, Wonderful Bistro 🛏 Best Western, Comfort Inn, EconoLodge, Hampton Inn, La Quinta, Ramada, Wingate Inn 🄾 Best Buy, frontage rds access 101, Harley-Davidson, Kohl's, Old Navy, PetCo

101 US 50 W, Pueblo, **E** 🍴 Capt D's, Coldstone, Country Buffet, Denny's, Margaritas Mexican, Ruby Tuesday, Souper Salad 🛏 Sleep Inn 🄾 Barnes&Noble, CO Tire, Dillard's, JC Penney, Jo-Ann, mall, Petsmart, Ross, Sears/auto, Target, TJ Maxx, U-Haul, Verizon, Walmart/Subway, **W** 🅖 7-11, Loaf'n Jug/dsl, Shell/dsl, Valero/dsl 🍴 Applebee's, Arby's, Arriba Mexican, Blackeyed Pea, Carl's Jr, China Rest., Chipotle Mexican, Country Kitchen, DJ's Steaks, Domino's, DQ, Fazoli's, Golden Corral, Jack-in-the-Box, Little Caesars, Manhattan's Pizza, McAlister's Deli, McDonald's, Noodles&Co, Olive Garden, Papa John's, Papa Murphy's, Pass Key Rest., Pizza Hut, Popeye's, Red Lobster, Starbucks, Subway, SW Grill,

⬆⬇N INTERSTATE 25 Cont'd

Exit #	Services
101	Continued
	Taco Bell, Wendy's 🛏 Clarion, Days Inn, Motel 6, Quality Inn, Rodeway Inn, Super 8 🅞 Aamco, Advance Parts, Albertson's, AT&T, AutoZone, Brakes+, Chevrolet, Chrysler/Dodge/Jeep, Discount Tire, EmergiCare, Ford/Lincoln, frontage rds access 102, Hyundai, Kia/Mazda, K-Mart, Lowe's, Midas, NAPA, Nissan, O'Reilly Parts, Staples, Subaru, Toyota, vet, Walgreens
100b	29th St, Pueblo, E 🍴 Country Buffet, Mongolian Grill 🅞 $Tree, Car Dr, Hobby Lobby, King's Sooper Foods, Natural Grocers, Peerless Tires, Tuesday Morning, W 🅖 Conoco 🍴 Sonic 🛏 USA Motel 🅞 Grease Monkey, Safeway
100a	US 50 E, to La Junta, E 🅖 Loaf'n Jug/dsl, Shell 🍴 Little Caesars, McDonald's, Pizza Hut, Wendy's 🅞 Advance Parts, AutoZone, Belmont Tire/repair, Family$, Save-A-Lot Foods, Walgreens
99b a	Santa Fe Ave, 13th St, downtown, W 🍴 Subway, Taco Bell, Wendy's 🛏 Bramble Tree Inn, Travelers Motel 🅞 🛏, Buick/Cadillac/GMC, CarQuest, Honda
98b	CO 96, 1st St, Union Ave Hist Dist, Pueblo, W 🅖 Loaf'n Jug/dsl 🍴 Carl's Jr 🛏 Courtyard
98a	US 50E bus, to La Junta, W 🍴 Sonic
97b	Abriendo Ave
97a	Central Ave, W 🅖 Alta/dsl 🍴 McDonald's 🅞 $General
96	Indiana Ave, W 🅞 🛏
95	Illinois Ave (from sb) W 🅞 to dogtrack
94	CO 45 N, Pueblo Blvd, W 🅖 Loaf'n Jug/dsl, Western/dsl 🍴 Subway, Taco Bell 🛏 Hampton Inn, Microtel 🅞 fairgrounds/racetrack, Forts RV Park, to Lake Pueblo SP
91	Stem Beach
88	Burnt Mill Rd
87	Verde Rd
83	no services
77	Hatchet Ranch Rd, Cedarwood
74	CO 165 W, Colo City, E 🅖 Shamrock/deli/dsl/24hr, 🍴 Obie's BBQ 🅞 KOA, W 🆁🆂 both lanes, full 🚻 facilities, litter barrels, petwalk, 🅒, 🐾, vending 🅖 Sinclair/Subway/dsl 🍴 Los Cuervo's 🛏 Days Inn/rest.
71	Graneros Rd
67	to Apache
64	Lascar Rd
60	Huerfano
59	Butte Rd
56	Redrock Rd
55	Airport Rd
52	CO 69 W, to Alamosa, Walsenburg, W 🅖 Conoco/A&W/dsl, Loaf'n Jug/dsl (2mi), Western/dsl 🍴 Carl's Jr (2mi), George's Rest., KFC/Taco Bell, Subway (2mi) 🛏 Best Western, Budget Host 🅞 Country Host RV Park, Dakota RV Park/camping, Family$ (2mi), San Luis Valley, to Great Sand Dunes NM
50	CO 10 E, to La Junta, W 🅞 🛏, tourist info
49	Lp 25, to US 160 W, Walsenburg, W 1 mi 🅖 Loaf'n Jug/dsl 🍴 Carl's Jr., Subway 🅞 Lathrop SP, to Cuchara Ski Valley
42	Rouse Rd, to Pryor
41	Rugby Rd
34	Aguilar
30	Aguilar Rd
27	Ludlow, W 🅞 Ludlow Memorial
23	Hoehne Rd
18	El Moro Rd, W 🆁🆂 both lanes, full 🚻 facilities, litter barrels, petwalk, 🐾

Exit #	Services
15	US 350 E, Goddard Ave, E 🍴 Burger King, Pizza Hut 🛏 Super 8 🅞 🛏, AutoZone, Big R Ranch Store, Family$, W 🅖 Shell/dsl 🛏 Frontier Motel/café
14	Commercial St, downtown, Trinidad, same as 13b
13b	Main St, Trinidad, E CO Welcome Ctr 🅖 Shell/dsl 🍴 KFC/Taco Bell, KFC/Taco Bell, McDonald's, McDonald's, Sonic, Sonic 🛏 Days Inn 🅞 CarQuest, CarQuest, Safeway Foods/dsl, Safeway Foods/dsl, Trinidad Motor Inn, Trinidad Motor Inn, W 🅖 Conoco/dsl 🍴 DQ, Great Wall Chinese, Wonderful House Chinese 🅞 Monument Lake, RV camping, to Trinidad Lake
13a	Santa Fe Trail, Trinidad, E 🅞 RV camping
11	Starkville, E 🅖 Shell/Wendy's/dsl/24hr 🍴 Tequila's Mexican 🛏 Budget Host/RVPark, Holiday Inn, Rodeway Inn 🅞 Summit RV Park, to Santa Fe Trail, **weigh/check sta**, W 🛏 La Quinta, Quality Inn/rest 🅞 Big O Tire, Grease Monkey, O'Reilly Parts, Toyota, Walmart
8	Springcreek
6	Gallinas
2	Wootten
1mm	scenic area pulloff nb
0mm	Colorado/New Mexico state line, Raton Pass, elev 7834, **weigh sta sb**

⬆E INTERSTATE 70

Exit #	Services
450mm	Colorado/Kansas state line
438	US 24, Rose Ave, Burlington, N 🅖 Conoco/dsl 🛏 Hi-Lo Motel, Sloan's Motel 🅞 🛏, $General, Buick/Cadillac/Chevrolet/GMC, CarQuest, Family$, Ford/Lincoln, NAPA, Safeway Foods, S 🅖 Shell/Reynaldo's Mexican/dsl/24hr 🅞 Bonny SRA, RV Camping, truck repair
437.5mm	**Welcome Ctr wb, full 🚻 facilities, historical site, info, litter barrels, petwalk, 🅒, 🐾**
437	US 385, Burlington, N 🅖 Conoco/dsl, Western/dsl 🍴 Arby's, Burger King, Denny's, McDonald's, Pizza Hut, Route Steaks, Subway 🛏 Best Value Inn, Burlington Inn, Chaparral Motel, Comfort Inn, Western Motel 🅞 🛏, Alco, to Bonny St RA, S 🛏 Best Western/rest
429	Bethune
419	CO 57, Stratton, N 🅖 Cenex/dsl, Conoco/dsl 🍴 Dairy Treat 🛏 Claremont Inn/café, I-70 Inn 🅞 Marshall Ash Village Camping, Trails End Camping
412	Vona, N 1/2 mi 🅞 gas, 🅒
405	CO 59, Seibert, N 🅞 Shady Grove Camping/RV dump, S 🅖 Conoco/dsl 🅞 tire repair
395	Flagler, N 🅖 Loaf'N Jug/dsl 🍴 I-70 Diner, Subway 🛏 Little England Motel 🅞 Flagler SWA, G&B RV camping, NAPA, S 🅖 Cenex/dsl 🅞 golf
383	Arriba, N 🅖 DJ/café/dsl, motel, S 🆁🆂 **both lanes full 🚻 facilities, litter barrels, petwalk, 🐾, point of interest, RV camping**
376	Bovina
371	Genoa, N food, gas, 🅒, point of interest, S 🅞 🛏
363	US 24, US 40, US 287, to CO 71, to Hugo, Limon, S 13 mi 🅞 🛏
361	CO 71, Limon, N 🅞 Ace Hardware, Chrysler/Dodge/Jeep, S 🅖 Conoco/dsl, Shell/Wendy's/dsl 🍴 Golden China, Pizza Hut 🛏 1st Inn Gold, Knights Inn 🅞 Alco, KOA, RV camping, st patrol, vet
360.5mm	**weigh/check sta both lanes**
359	to US 24, to CO 71, Limon, N 🅖 ⭐FLYING J/IHOP/dsl/scales/LP/24hr 🅞 dsl repair, RV camping, S 🅖 Phillips 66,

(side tab: CO)

(side tab right: TRINIDAD)

(side tab right: BURLINGTON)

(side tab right: LIMON)

(side tab left: WALSENBURG)

INTERSTATE 70 Cont'd

Exit #	Services
359	Continued
	Qwest/dsl, TA/Shell/Subway/Country Pride/dsl/scales/24hr/@ 🍴 Arby's, Denny's, McDonald's, Oscar's Grill 🛏 Comfort Inn, EconoLodge, Holiday Inn Express, Quality Inn, Super 8, TS Inn 🅞 camping
354	no services
352	CO 86 W, to Kiowa
348	to Cedar Point
340	Agate, S 1/4 mi gas/dsl, 🅒
336	to Lowland
332mm	🆁🆂 wb, full 🦽 facilities, info, litter barrels, petwalk, 🅒, 🛅, vending
328	to Deer Trail, N 🅖 Phillips/dsl, S 🅖 Shell/dsl 🅞 USPO
325mm	East Bijou Creek
323.5mm	Middle Bijou Creek
322	to Peoria
316	US 36 E, Byers, N 🅖 Sinclair 🛏 Budget Host 🅞 Thriftway Foods/Drug, S 🅖 Tri Valley 🍴 Country Burger Rest. 🅞 USPO
310	Strasburg, N 🅖 Conoco/dsl, Ray's 🍴 Patio Cafe, Subway 🛏 Strasburg Inn 🅞 Country Gardens RV Camping (3mi), dsl/auto repair, KOA, NAPA, USPO, Western Hardware
306mm	Kiowa, Bennett, N 🆁🆂 both lanes, full 🦽 facilities, litter barrels, petwalk, 🅒, 🛅
305	Kiowa (from eb)
304	CO 79 N, Bennett, N 🅖 Conoco/Hotstuff Pizza/dsl, ♥Love's/McDonald's/dsl/scales/24hr 🍴 Chesters, China Kitchen, High Plains Diner, Starbucks, Subway 🅞 Family$, King Soopers Foods/dsl, USPO, S 🅞 Ace Hardware
299	CO 36, Manila Rd, S 🅖 Shamrock/dsl
295	Lp 70, Watkins, N 🅖 Shell/Tomahawk/rest/dsl/24hr/@ 🍴 Biscuit's Cafe, Lulu's Cafe 🛏 Country Manor Motel 🅞 USPO
292	CO 36, Airpark Rd
289	**E-470 Tollway**, 120th Ave, CO Springs
288	US 287, US 40, Lp 70, Colfax Ave (exits left from wb)
286	CO 32, Tower Rd, N 🅖 Murphy Express/dsl 🍴 Chili's, Chipotle Mexican, Del Taco, McAlister's Deli, Starbucks, Wendy's 🅞 $Tree, Best Buy, Brakes+, Discount Tire, GNC, Home Depot, Les Schwab Tire, Office Depot, O'Reilly Parts, PetCo, Verizon, Walmart/Subway
285	Airport Blvd, N 🅞 Denver Int ✈, S 🅖 ⚡FLYING J/Denny's/dsl/scales/24hr, Shell/McDonald's/dsl 🛏 Comfort Inn, Crystal Inn 🅞 Harley-Davidson
284	I-225 N (from eb)
283	Chambers Rd, N 🅖 Conoco, Shell/Circle K/Popeye's 🍴 A&W/KFC, Anthony's Pizza, Applebees, Chicago Grill, Jimmy John's, LJ Silver/Taco Bell, Outback Steaks, Pizza Hut, Qdoba, Sonic, Subway, Ted's MT Grill, Urban Sombrero, Wendy's 🛏 A Loft, Cambria Suites, Country Inn&Suites, Crowne Plaza, Hampton Inn, Hilton Garden, Homewood Suites, Hyatt Place, Marriott, Residence Inn, Sleep Inn 🅞 Tires+, U-haul, S 🅖 Shamrock 🍴 Burger King 🛏 Crossland Suites 🅞 America East RV Ctr
282	I-225 S, to Colorado Springs
281	Peoria St, N 🅖 7-11, Conoco, Shell/dsl 🍴 Burger King, Del Taco, Domino's, El Patron Mexican, GoodTimes Burgers, McDonald's, Peoria Grill, Subway 🛏 Drury Inn, La Quinta, Timbers Motel 🅞 Big O Tire, Family$, S 🅖 Conoco/dsl, Shamrock/dsl 🍴 Bennett's BBQ, Chester's Grill, Church's, Denny's, Ho Mei Chinese, Pizza Hut/Taco Bell, Real Deminas Mexican,

CO

🆁🆂

281	Continued
	Subway, Waffle House, Wendy's 🛏 Motel 6, Quality Inn, Star Hotel, Stay Inn 🅞 auto/RV repair, Goodyear/auto, Tires For Less, vet
280	Havana St, N 🛏 Embassy Suites
279	I-270 W, US 36 W (from wb), to Ft Collins, Boulder
278	CO 35, Quebec St, N 🅖 Sapp Bros/Sinclair/Subway/dsl/@, TA/dsl/rest./24hr/@ 🍴 Coldstone, Del Taco, Jim'n Nick's BBQ, Marco's Pizza, Olive Garden, Qdoba, Red Lobster, Starbucks, TGIFriday's, Wahoo's 🛏 Best Inn, Comfort Inn, Studio Suites 🅞 AT&T, Bass Pro Shops, JC Penney, Macys, mall, Old Navy, Super Target, Verizon, S 🍴 Arby's, Buffalo Wild Wings, Country Buffet, Famous Dave's BBQ, IHOP, Jimmy John's, McDonald's, Panda Express, Panera Bread, Papa John's, Red Robin, Sonic, Subway 🛏 Courtyard, DoubleTree Hotel, Holiday Inn, Red Lion Inn, Renaissance Inn, Super 8 🅞 AT&T, GNC, Home Depot, Office Depot, Radio Shack, Ross, Sam's Club/gas, Tires+, Walgreens, Walmart/Subway
277	to Dahlia St, Holly St, Monaco St, frontage rd
276b	US 6 E, US 85 N, CO 2, Colorado Blvd, S 🅖 Conoco/Subway/dsl 🍴 Carl's Jr, Domino's, KT'S BBQ, Starbucks
276a	Vasquez Ave, N 🅖 ⛽/Wendy's/dsl/scales/24hr 🛏 Colonial Motel, Western Inn 🅞 Blue Beacon, Ford/Mack Trucks, S 🅖 7-11 🍴 Burger King
275c	York St (from eb), N 🛏 Colonial Motel
275b	CO 265, Brighton Blvd, Coliseum, N 🅖 7-11
275a	Washington St, N 🍴 Pizza Hut, S 🅖 Conoco 🍴 McDonald's, Quiznos, Subway
274b a	I-25, N to Cheyenne, S to Colorado Springs
273	Pecos St, N 🅖 7-11 🍴 Quiznos 🅞 CO Ranch Mkt, Family$, transmissions, True Value
272	US 287, Federal Blvd, N 🅖 Conoco/dsl, Sinclair 🍴 Burger King, Goodtimes Burgers, Little Caesar's, McCoy's Rest., McDonald's, Pizza Hut, Rico Pollo, Subway, Taco Bell, Village Inn, Wendy's, Winchell's 🛏 Motel 6 🅞 $Tree, Advance Parts, tires, S 🅖 Conoco/Circle K 🍴 El Padrino Mexican, Popeye's, Starbucks 🛏 Howard Johnson
271b	Lowell Blvd, Tennyson St (from wb)
271a	CO 95, S 🅞 funpark
270	Sheridan Blvd, N 🅖 Shell/dsl, S 🍴 El Paraiso Mexican 🅞 Family$, Firestone/auto, fun park, Radio Shack, repair
269b	I-76 E (from eb), to Ft Morgan, Ft Collins
269a	CO 121, Wadsworth Blvd, N 🅖 7-11, Conoco, Shell 🍴 Alamos Verdes Mexican, Anthony's Pizza, Applebee's, Bennet's BBQ, Burger King, Chipotle Mexican, Coldstone, El Tapatio, Fazoli's, Gunther Toody's Diner, IHOP, Kukoro Japanese, LoneStar Steaks, McDonald's/playplace, Red Robin, Ruby Tuesday, Smiling Moose Deli, Starbucks, Subway, Taco Bell,

[P] = gas   [¶] = food   [⌂] = lodging   [O] = other   [Rs] = rest stop   Copyright 2015 - the Next EXIT ®

W H E A T   R I D G E | L A K E W O O D

CO

↖E INTERSTATE 70 Cont'd

Exit #	Services
269a	Continued TX Roadhouse [O] $Tree, Advance Parts, Brakes+, city park, Costco/gas, Discount Tire, Goodyear/auto, Home Depot, Lowe's, mall, Office Depot, Petsmart, Radio Shack, Sam's Club, Tires+, URGENT CARE
267	CO 391, Kipling St, Wheat Ridge, N [P] Conoco, Shell/Carl's Jr/Circle K/dsl [¶] Burger King, Einstein Bros, Furr's Dining, Jack-in-the-Box, Lil Nick's Pizza, Margarita's Mexican, Panda Express, Qdoba, Quiznos, Starbucks, Subway [⌂] American Inn, Motel 6 [O] 7-11, Cadillac/Chevrolet, Chrysler/Jeep, GNC, NAPA, repair, Target, Verizon, vet, S [P] Conoco/Circle K, Phillips 66, Shell [¶] Pizza Hut/Taco Bell, Smokin' Joe's Grill, Village Inn, Winchell's [⌂] Affordable Inn, Best Value Inn, Comfort Inn, Holiday Inn Express, Ramada [O] Ketelesen RV Ctr
266	CO 72, W 44th Ave, Ward Rd, Wheat Ridge, N [P] Conoco/dsl [O] transmissions, S [¶] Shamrock/dsl, TA/rest./scales/dsl/24hr/@ [⌂] Howard Johnson [O] RV America
265	CO 58 W (from wb), to Golden, Central City
264	Youngfield St, W 32nd Ave, N [P] Conoco/Circle K [¶] Denny's, GoodTimes Burgers [⌂] La Quinta, S [¶] Abrusci's Italian, Chili's, DQ, McDonald's, Old Chicago Pizza, Pizza Hut/Taco Bell, Qdoba, SmashBurger, Starbucks, Subway [O] Camping World RV Ctr, King's Sooper/24hr, Petsmart, Tuesday Morning, Walgreens, Walmart
263	Denver West Blvd, N [⌂] Marriott/rest., S [¶] Coldstone, Jamba Juice, Keg Steaks, Macaroni Grill, McGrath's Fishouse, Mimi's Cafe, Qdoba [O] Barnes&Noble, Best Buy, Office Depot, Old Navy, same as 262, Whole Foods Mkt
262	US 40 E, W Colfax, Lakewood, N [P] Sinclair/dsl [¶] Jack-in-the-Box, Little Ricky's Cafe, Subway [⌂] Hampton Inn [O] Buick/GMC, Camping World RV Ctr, Chrysler/Jeep, Dodge, Home Depot, Honda, Hyundai, Kohl's, NAPA, PetCo, Staples, Subaru, transmissions, U-Haul, vet, S [P] Shell/Circle K/dsl/LP [¶] Chipotle Mexican, Hops Brewery, Jamba Juice, Mimi's Cafe, On-the-Border, Outback Steaks, Pei Wei Asian, Quiznos, Wendy's [⌂] Courtyard, Days Inn/rest., Holiday Inn, Mtn View Inn, Residence Inn [O] Chevrolet, Lexus, mall, Old Navy, same as 263, Target, Toyota
261	US 6 E (from eb), W 6th Ave, to Denver
260	CO 470, to Colo Springs
259	CO 26, Golden, N [P] Conoco [⌂] Hampton Inn (2mi) [O] Heritage Sq Funpark, S [O] Music Hall, to Red Rocks SP
257mm	runaway truck ramp eb
256	Lookout Mtn, N [O] to Buffalo Bill's Grave
254	Genesee, Lookout Mtn, N [O] to Buffalo Bill's Grave, S [P] Conoco/Genesee Store, LP [¶] Chart House Rest., Christie's Rest., Genesee Towne Cafe, Guido's Pizza [O] vet
253	Chief Hosa, S [O] RV Camping, [¶]
252	(251 from eb), CO 74, Evergreen Pkwy, S [P] Conoco [¶] Burger King, El Rancho Rest., McDonald's, Qdoba, Smiling Moose Deli, Subway [⌂] Quality Suites [O] Big O Tire, Echo Mtn Ski Area, Home Depot, King's Sooper, Walmart
248	(247 from eb), Beaver Brook, Floyd Hill, S [O] antiques
244	US 6, to CO 119, to Golden, Central City, Eldora Ski Area
243	Hidden Valley
242mm	tunnel
241b a	rd 314, Idaho Springs West, N [P] Conoco/McDonald's/dsl, Shell/dsl, Sinclair, Western/dsl/e85 [¶] Carl's Jr, Cherry Blossom Chinese, Marion's Rest., Quiznos, Smokin' Yards BBQ,

I D A H O   S P G S | S I L V E R T H O R N E | F R I S C O

Exit #	Services
241b a	Continued Starbucks, Subway, Wildfire Rest. [⌂] 6&40 Motel, Argo Inn, Columbine Inn, H&H Motel, Idaho Springs Hotel, JC Motel, Marion's Rest. [O] CarQuest, Safeway Foods/Drug, USPO
240	CO 103, Mt Evans, N [P] Kum&Go/dsl, Shell, Sinclair/dsl [¶] 2 Bros Deli, Azteca Mexican, Beaujo's Pizza, Buffalo Rest., Jiggie's Cafe, Main St Rest., Mangia Italian, Picci Pizza, same as 241, Tommy Knocker Grill, West Winds Cafe, S to Mt Evans
239	Idaho Springs, S [O] camping
238	Fall River Rd, to St Mary's Glacier
235	Dumont (from wb)
234	Downeyville, Dumont, N [P] Conoco/Subway/dsl [¶] Burger King, Starbucks [O] ski rentals, weigh sta both lanes
233	Lawson (from eb)
232	US 40 W, to Empire, N [O] Rocky Mtn NP, to Berthoud Pass, Winterpark/Sol Vista ski areas
228	Georgetown, S [P] Conoco/Subway/dsl, Shell/dsl, Valero [¶] Mountain Buzz Cafe [⌂] Chateau Chamonix, Super 8 [O] visitors ctr
226.5mm	scenic overlook eb
226	Georgetown, Silver Plume Hist Dist, N [O] Buckley Bros Mkt, repair
221	Bakerville
220mm	Arapahoe NF eastern boundary
219	parking area (eb only)
218	no services
216	US 6 W, Loveland Valley, Loveland Basin, ski areas
214mm	Eisenhower/Johnson Tunnel, elev 11013
213mm	parking area eb
205	US 6 E, CO 9 N, Dillon, Silverthorne, N [P] 7-11, Conoco/dsl, Shell/7-11/dsl [¶] Asian Oven, China Gourmet, Chipotle Mexican, Dominos, Mint Cafe, Mtn Lyon Café, Murphy's Cafe, Quiznos, Village Inn, Wendy's [⌂] 1st Interstate Inn, Days Inn, La Quinta, Luxury Suites, Quality Inn, Silver Inn [O] Buick/Cadillac/Chevrolet/GMC, CarQuest, Chrysler/Dodge/Jeep, Ford, Old Navy, Outlets/famous brands, Subaru, Target, TrueValue, S [P] Shamrock, Shell/dsl [¶] Arby's, Bamboo Garden, Blue Moon Deli, Burger King, Dam Brewery/Rest., DQ, Fiesta Mexican, Jimmy John's, McDonald's, Nick'n Willy's Pizza, Noodles&Co, Pizza Hut, Qdoba, Red Mtn Grill, Ruby Tuesday, SmashBurger, Smiling Moose Cafe, Starbucks, Subway, Sunshine Cafe [⌂] Comfort Suites, Dillon Inn, Super 8 [O] City Mkt Foods/gas, Natural Grocery, Outlets/famous brands, Tuesday Morning, Verizon, vet, Walgreens
203.5mm	scenic overlook both lanes
203	CO 9 S, to Breckenridge, Frisco, S [P] 7-11, Conoco/Wendy's/dsl, Shell, Valero/dsl [¶] A&W, Carlos Miguel's Mexican, Hacienda Real Mexican, KFC, Q4U BBQ, Starbucks, Subway, Szechuan Chinese, Taco Bell [⌂] Alpine Inn, Best Western, Holiday Inn, Ramada Ltd, Summit Inn [O] Big O Tire, NAPA, Radio Shack, RV Resort (6mi), Safeway Foods, to Breckenridge Ski Area, vet, Walmart/McDonald's
201	Main St, Frisco, S [P] Loaf N' Jug [¶] Alpine Deli, Backcountry Brew Pub, Boatyard Pizzaria, Butterhorn Cafe, Cowboy Pizza, Log Cabin Cafe, Lost Cajun Rest., Rainbow Ct Rest. [⌂] Blue Spruce Inn, Frisco Lodge, Hotel Frisco, Snowshoe Motel [O] Bighorn Reservations, museum/visitor info, RV camping, to Breckenridge Ski Area, USPO
198	Officers Gulch, emergency callbox
196mm	scenic area (wb only)
195	CO 91 S, to Leadville, S 1 mi [P] Conoco/dsl [¶] Quiznos [⌂] Copper Lodging [O] to Copper Mtn Ski Resort

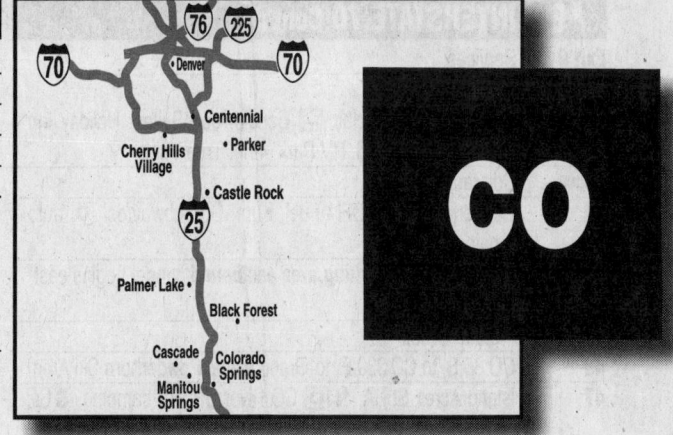

↑E	
Exit #	**Services**
190	**S** ⓡ⒮ **both lanes, full** ♿ **facilities, litter barrels,** 🗑, 🏞
189mm	elev 10662 ft, **parking area both lanes**, Vail Pass Summit
180	Vail East Entrance, 🗑, **S services 3-4 mi**
176	Vail, ⊡ Ⓗ, ski info/lodging
173	Vail Ski Area, **N** 🅖 Phillips 66, Shell/dsl 🍴 Bearfish Grill, Gohanya Chinese, McDonald's, Qdoba, Subway, Taco Bell, Wendy's 🛏 Holiday Inn, Roost Lodge ⊡ 7-11, Ace Hardware, City Mkt Foods/deli, Safeway Food/Drug, USPO, **S** 🅖 Conoco/dsl/LP 🛏 Black Bear Inn, Marriott/Streamside Hotel
171	US 6 W, US 24 E, to Minturn, Leadville, **N** ⊡ Ski Cooper ski area, **S 2 mi** 🅖 Shell 🍴 Magusto's Italian, Minturn Steaks 🛏 Minturn Inn ⊡ RV Camping, USPO
169	Eaglevale, (from wb), no return
168	William J. Post Blvd, **S** 🍴 Zaccazai Cafe ⊡ Home Depot, Walmart/McDonald's
167	Avon, **N** 🅖 Conoco/7-11/dsl, Shell 🍴 Pizza Hut ⊡ Goodyear, vet, **S** 🍴 Burger King, Denny's, Domino's, Fiesta Jalisco Mexican, Panda City, Pazzo's Pizza, Starbucks, Subway 🛏 Avon Ctr Lodge, Christie Lodge, Comfort Inn, Sheraton, Westin ⊡ City Mkt/drugs, GNC, Office Depot, ski info, to Beaver Creek/Arrowhead Ski, URGENT CARE, USPO
163	Edwards, **S** ⓡ⒮ **both lanes, full** ♿ **facilities, litter barrel,** 🏞, **RV dump** 🅖 Conoco/dsl, Shell/Wendy's/dsl 🍴 Cafe Milano, Cosmos BBQ, Dish Cafe, Gashouse Rest., Gore Range Brewery, Marble Slab Creamery, Marko's Pizza, Old Forge Pizza, Smiling Moose, Subway, Zino's Italian 🛏 Riverwalk Inn ⊡ to Arrowhead Ski Area, USPO, Villiage Mkt
162mm	scenic area eb
159mm	Eagle River
157	CO 131 N, Wolcott, **N** to Steamboat Ski Area
147	Eagle, **N** 🅖 Kum&Go/pizza/dsl 🍴 Burger King, Starbucks 🛏 AmericInn, Comfort Inn, Holiday Inn Express ⊡ City Mkt Foods, **S** ⓡ⒮ **both lanes, full** ♿ **facilities, info** 🅖 Conoco/dsl, Sinclair/Subway/dsl 🍴 Eagle Diner, El Pariente, Gourmet China, Grand Ave Grill, Moe's Original BBQ, Pazzo's Pizzaria, Taco Bell, Wendy's 🛏 Eagle Lodge&Suites, Silverleaf Suites ⊡ Costco/gas (3mi), USPO
140	Gypsum, **S** 🅖 Kum&Go, Shell 🍴 Columbine Mkt Deli, Ritten House Rest., Salsa's Mexican ⊡ 🔧, auto/truck repair, USPO, River Dance Resort camping
134mm	Colorado River
133	Dotsero, **N** ⊡ River Dance RV Camping (3mi)
129	Bair Ranch, **S** ⓡ⒮ **both lanes, full** ♿ **facilities, litter barrels, petwalk,** 🏞
128.5mm	**parking area eb**
127mm	tunnel wb
125mm	tunnel
125	to Hanging Lake (no return eb)
123	Shoshone (no return eb)
122.5mm	exit to river (no return eb)
121	to Hanging Lake, Grizzly Creek, **S** ⓡ⒮ **both lanes, full** ♿ **facilities, litter barrels,** 🏞
119	**No Name,** ⓡ⒮ **both lanes, full** ♿ **facilities, rafting, RV camping**
118mm	tunnel
116	CO 82 E, to Aspen, Glenwood Springs, **N** 🅖 Conoco/dsl, Shell/dsl 🍴 Chomp's Rest., Fiesta Guadalajara, KFC, Qdoba, Subway, Tequilas Rest., Village Inn 🛏 Best Western, Glenwood Springs Inn, Hampton Inn, Holiday Inn Express, Hotel Colorado, Ramada Inn, Silver Spruce Motel, Starlight Motel

INTERSTATE 70 Cont'd *(header for left column)*

GLENWOOD SPRINGS / RIFLE		
116	Continued ⊡ funpark, Hot Springs Bath, Land Rover, NAPA, Toyota, **S 0-2 mi** 🅖 Conoco, Phillips 66/dsl, Shamrock/dsl, Shell, Sinclair 🍴 19th St Diner, Arby's, Bears Loft Rest., China Town, Domino's, Little Ceasar's, McDonald's, Pizza Hut, Rib City Grill, Starbucks, Subway, Taco Bell, Taipei Japanese, Wendy's 🛏 Caravan Inn, Cedar Lodge, Frontier Lodge, Hotel Denver ⊡ Ⓗ, 7-11, Alpine Tire, AutoZone, B.Thornal DDS, City Mkt Foods, city park, NAPA, Office Depot, Rite Aid, Safeway Foods, to Ski Sunlight, USPO, Walmart
115mm	ⓡ⒮ **eb, full** ♿ **facilities, litter barrels,** 🏞
114	W Glenwood Springs, **N** 🅖 7-11, Phillips 66/dsl, Shell 🍴 Burger King, Jilbirtito's Mexican, Porker's BBQ, Rte 6 Grill House, Vicco's Charcoal Burger 🛏 Affordable Inn, Best Value Inn, Ponderosa Motel, Red Mtn Inn, Rodeway Inn ⊡ AT&T, Big O Tire, Checker Parts, Ford, JC Penney, K-Mart, mall, Radio Shack, Staples, Subaru, Verizon, **S** 🅖 Conoco/DQ/dsl 🍴 Chili's, Moe's SW Grill, Russo's Pizza, Starbucks 🛏 Courtyard, Glenwood Suites, Quality Inn, Residence Inn ⊡ Audi/VW, Harley-Davidson, Lowe's, PetCo, Target, URGENT CARE
111	South Canyon
109	Canyon Creek
108mm	**parking area both lanes**
105	New Castle, **N** 🅖 Conoco/dsl, Kum&Go/dsl 🍴 McDonald's, New Castle Diner, Subway 🛏 Rodeway Inn ⊡ City Mkt Foods/deli, Elk Creek Campground (4mi), **S** ⊡ Best Hardware
97	Silt, **N** 🅖 Conoco/dsl/24hr, Kum&Go, Phillips 66/dsl 🛏 Red River Inn ⊡ auto repair, to Harvey Gap SP, **S** 🍴 Red Brick BBQ 🛏 Holiday Inn Express, Ruby River Cabins ⊡ Heron's Nest RV Park
94	Garfield County Airport Rd
90	CO 13 N, Rifle, **N** ⓡ⒮ **both lanes, full** ♿ **facilities, litter barrels, NF Info,** 🏞, **RV dump,** 🅖 Conoco, Kum&Go, Phillips 66/dsl, Shell 🍴 KFC 🛏 Winchester Motel (1mi) ⊡ Rifle Gap SP, USPO, **S** 🅖 Kum&Go, Phillips 66/Subway/dsl, Shell 🍴 Burger King, Domino's, Little Caesar's, McDonald's/playplace, Rib City Grill, Sonic, Starbucks, Taco Bell 🛏 Comfort Inn, Hampton Inn, La Quinta, Red River Inn/rest., Rusty Cannon Motel ⊡ Ⓗ, Checker Parts, Radio Shack, Walmart/Subway
87	to CO 13, West Rifle
81	Rulison
75	Parachute, **N** ⓡ⒮ **both lanes, full** ♿ **facilities, info, litter barrels, petwalk,** 🗑, 🏞 🅖 Shell/dsl/24hr, Sinclair/dsl 🍴 El Tapatio Mexican, Hong's Garden Chinese, Outlaws Rest., Subway 🛏 Comfort Inn, Parachute Inn ⊡ NAPA, Radio Shack, USPO, Verizon, vet, **S** 🅖 Phillips 66/Domino's/dsl,

CO

�baE INTERSTATE 70 Cont'd

Exit #	Services
75	Continued
	Shell/Wendy's, Sinclair 🛏 Candlewood Suites, Holiday Inn Express 🅞 Family$, RV Park (4mi), True Value
63mm	Colorado River
62	De Beque, **N** 🍴 CFN Fuel, Kum&Go/Subway/dsl 🅞 auto repair, food, 🅒
50mm	Colorado River, **parking area eastbound**, tunnel begins eastbound
49mm	Plateau Creek
49	CO 65 S, to CO 330 E, to Grand Mesa, Powderhorn Ski Area
47	Island Acres St RA, **N** 🅞 CO River SP, RV camping, **S** 🅖 Conoco/rest./dsl
46	Cameo
44	Lp 70 W, to Palisade, **S 3 mi** 🅞 food, gas, lodging
43.5mm	Colorado River
42	US 6, Palisade, **S 1 mi** 🛏 Wine Country Inn 🅞 Fruitstand/store, gas, wineries
37	to US 6, to US 50 S, Clifton, Grand Jct, **S 0-1 mi** 🅖 Conoco/dsl, Maverik/dsl, Shamrock/dsl, Sinclair 🍴 Burger King, Cactus Canyon, Chin Chin Oriental, Dos Hombres, Jimmy Johns, KFC, Little Caesar's, McDonald's/playplace, Papa Johns, Papa Murphy's, Pizza Hut, Qdoba, Sonic, Starbucks, Subway, Taco Bell, Wendy's 🛏 Best Western 🅞 Ace Hardware, AutoZone, City Mkt Food/gas, Family$, Murdoch's Store, O'Reilly Parts, repair, USPO, Walgreens, Walmart (2mi)
31	Horizon Dr, Grand Jct, **N** 🅖 Shell/dsl 🍴 Enzo's Pizza, Las Palmas Mexican, Pepper's Rest., Village Inn, Wendy's 🛏 Best Value Inn, Clarion, Comfort Inn, Courtyard, Grand Vista Hotel, Holiday Inn, La Quinta, Motel 6, Ramada Inn, Residence Inn 🅞 🖭, Harley-Davidson, USPO, Zarlingo's Repair, **S** 🅖 Conoco/Subway/dsl, Shell/dsl 🍴 Applebee's, Burger King/playland, Denny's, Good Pastures Rest., Herford Steaks, Nick'n Willy's Pizza, Pizza Hut, Sang Garden, Starbucks, Taco Bell 🛏 Affordable Inn, Best Western, Country Inn, Doubletree Hotel, Mesa Inn, Quality Inn, Super 8 🅞 🖭, CO NM, golf, Safeway Food/drug/gas, to Mesa St Coll, **visitors ctr**
28	Redlands Pkwy, 24 Rd, **N** 🅞 Kenworth, **S 0-2 mi** 🛏 Candlewood Suites, city park, same as 26
26	US 6, US 50, Grand Jct, **N** 🅞 Hyundai, Jct W RV Park, **S 0-4 mi** 🅖 Conoco/A&W/dsl 🍴 Boston's Grill, Burger King, Cafe Rio, Carino's Italian, Carl's Jr, Chick-fil-A, Chili's, Chipotle Mexican, Coldstone, Famous Dave's BBQ, Genghis Grill, Golden Corral, Grand Buffet, IHOP, Jimmy John's, McDonald's/playplace, Olive Garden, Outback Steaks, Papa Murphys, Qdoba, Red Lobster, Red Robin, Schlotzky's, Sonic, Starbucks, Subway, Taco Bell, Wendy's 🛏 Holiday Inn Express, West Gate Inn 🅞 $Tree, AutoZone, Barnes&Noble, Best Buy, Big O Tire, Buick/Chevrolet, Cabela's, Chrysler/Dodge/Jeep, City Mkt, Ford, Freightliner, Hobby Lobby, Home Depot, Honda, JC Penney, Kohl's, Lowe's, mall, Michael's, Mobile City RV Park, Nissan, Office Depot, Old Navy, PetCo, Petsmart, Rite Aid, Ross, Sam's Club/gas, Scott RV Ctr, Sears/auto, Subaru, Suzuki, Target, Toyota, Verizon, Walmart/McDonald's
19	US 6, CO 340, Fruita, **N** 🅖 Conoco/dsl 🍴 Burger King, Munchie's Burgers/Pizza 🛏 Balanced Rock Motel 🅞 🖭, City Mkt Foods/deli/24hr, USPO, Walgreens, **S Welcome Ctr, full 🖭 facilities, litter barrels, petwalk, 🅒, 🏞, RV dump** 🅖 Conoco/Subway/dsl/24hr, Shell/Wendy's/dsl/24hr 🍴 Dragon Treasure Chinese, El Tapatio Mexican, McDonald's/playplace, Rib City Grill, Taco Bell 🛏 Comfort Inn, La Quinta, Super 8

Exit #	Services
19	Continued
	🅞 dinosaur museum, Monument RV Park, Peterbilt/Volvo, to CO, NM, Verizon, vet
17mm	Colorado River
15	CO 139 N, to Loma, Rangely, **N** gas/dsl, 🅒, to Highline Lake SP
14.5mm	🅒, **weigh/check sta both lanes**
11	Mack, **N 2-3 mi** 🅞 food, gas/dsl
2	Rabbit Valley, to Dinosaur Quarry Trail
0mm	Colorado/Utah state line

�baE INTERSTATE 76

Exit #	Services
185mm	**I-76 begins/ends on NE I-80, Exit 102.**
184mm	Colorado/Nebraska state line
180	US 385, Julesburg, **N Welcome Ctr/🆁🆂 both lanes, full 🖭 facilities, info, RV dump** 🅖 Shell 🍴 Subway 🛏 Budget Host 🅞 🖭 **S** 🅖 Conoco/dsl
172	Ovid
165	CO 59, to Haxtun, Sedgewick, **N** 🍴 Lucy's Cafe
155	Red Lion Rd
149	CO 55, to Fleming, Crook, **S** 🅖 Sinclair/dsl/café
141	Proctor
134	Iliff
125	US 6, Sterling, **N 0-3 mi** 🆁🆂 **both lanes** 🖭 **facilities, 🏞, litter barrels, petwalk, vending, RV dump** 🅖 Cenex/dsl, Sinclair 🍴 Arby's, Bamboo Garden, Burger King, Domino's, DQ, KFC/LJ Silver, McDonald's, Old Town Bistro, Papa Murphy's, Pizza Hut, Sonic, Subway, Taco Bell, Taco John's, Village Inn, Wendy's 🛏 1st Interstate Inn, Best Western 🅞 🖭, $General, $Tree, AutoZone, Buick/Chevrolet, Chrysler/Dodge/Jeep, Ford/Lincoln, Goodyear/auto, Home Depot, museum, N Sterling SP, NAPA, O'Reilly Parts, Radio Shack, st patrol, Sun Mart Foods, USPO, Verizon, Walgreens, Walmart, **S** 🅖 Reata/Quiznos/dsl 🍴 Country Kitchen 🛏 Comfort Inn, Ramada Inn, Super 8, Travelodge 🅞 RV Camping
115	CO 63, Atwood, **N** 🅖 Sinclair/dsl 🅞 🖭, **S** 🍴 Steakhouse
102	Merino
95	Hillrose
92	to US 6 E, to US 34, CO 71 S
90b a	CO 71 N, to US 34, Brush, **N** 🅖 Tomahawk Trkstp/Shell/rest./dsl/24hr 🍴 China Buffet, Pizza Hut, Wendy's 🛏 Econolodge, **S** 🅖 Conoco/dsl 🍴 McDonald's 🛏 Microtel
89	Hospital Rd, **S** 🅞 🖭, golf
86	Dodd Bridge Rd
82	Barlow Rd, **N** 🅖 Conoco/dsl 🍴 Maverick's Grill 🛏 Comfort Inn, Rodeway Inn, **S** 🅖 Reata/Quiznos/dsl/scales, USA/dsl 🍴 Burger King 🅞 $Tree, Walmart/Subway
80	CO 52, Ft Morgan, **N** 🅞 City Park, Golf, RV Camping, **S** 🅖 Conoco/dsl, Maverik/dsl, Sinclair/dsl, Western/dsl 🍴 Arby's, DQ, McDonald's, Sonic, Subway, Taco John's, Wonderful House Chinese 🛏 Central Motel, Hampton Inn, Sands Inn, Super 8 🅞 🖭, AutoZone, Toyota, Verizon, Walgreens
79	CO 144, to Weldona, (no wb return)
75	US 34 E, to Ft Morgan, **S** 🅖 Shell/pizza/dsl 🍴 Embers Rest. 🛏 Clarion 🅞 st patrol
74.5mm	**weigh sta both lanes**
73	Long Bridge Rd
66b	US 34 W (from wb), to Greeley
66a	CO 39, CO 52, to Goodrich, **N** 🅖 Phillips 66/dsl 🅞 RV Camping, to Jackson Lake SP, **S** 🆁🆂 **both lanes, full 🖭 facilities, 🏞, litter barrels, petwalk, vending** 🅖 Sinclair/cafe/dsl/e-85

Sidebar labels: **GRAND JCT** | **STERLING** | **FT MORGAN** | **CO**

INTERSTATE 76 Cont'd

Exit #	Services
64	Wiggins
60	to CO 144 E, to Orchard
57	rd 91
49	Painter Rd (from wb)
48	to Roggen, N 🅿 Conoco/dsl, S 🅾 USPO
39	Keensburg, S 🅿 Shell/dsl 🍴 Rooster's Rest. 🛏 Keene Motel
34	Kersey Rd
31	CO 52, Hudson, N 🅿 Loves/Subway/Carl's Jr/scales/24hr/dsl, S 🅿 Conoco/dsl, Shell/dsl 🍴 El Faro Mexican, Pepper Pod Rest. 🅾 RV camping, USPO
25	CO 7, Lochbuie, N 🅿 Shell/dsl
22	Bromley, N 🅿 Valero/dsl 🍴 KFC/LJ Silver, Wendy's 🛏 Hampton Inn (4mi) 🅾 Ⓗ, Lowe's, S 🅾 Barr Lake SP
21	144th Ave, Eagle Blvd, N 🍴 Buffalo Wild Wings, Chick-fil-A, Chili's, Heidi's Deli, McDonald's, Quiznos, Subway, Taco Bell 🛏 Candlewood Suites, Holiday Inn Express 🅾 Ⓗ, $Tree, Dick's, GNC, Home Depot, JC Penney, Kohl's, Michael's, Office Depot, Petsmart, Ross, Target, Verizon
20	136th Ave, N 🅾 Barr Lake RV Park, same as 21
18	E-470 tollway, to Limon (from wb)
16	CO 2, Sable Blvd, Commerce City, N 🅿 Shell/diner/dsl/24hr/@, to Denver 🔁
12	US 85 N, to Brighton (exits left from eb), Greeley
11	96th Ave, N 🅾 dsl repair, S 🅾 Buick/GMC
10	88th Ave, N 🅿 Shell/dsl 🛏 La Quinta, Super 8, S 🅾 flea mkt
9	US 6 W, US 85 S (no EZ wb return), Commerce City, S 🅾 Freightliner, st patrol, transmissions
8	CO 224, 74th Ave (no EZ eb return), N 1 mi 🅾 NAPA
6b a	I-270 E, to Limon, to 🔁, to I-25 N
5	I-25, N to Ft Collins, S to Colo Springs
4	Pecos St
3	US 287, Federal Blvd, N 🅿 Shamrock/dsl, S 🅾 Advance Parts, Family$, vet
1b	CO 95, Sheridan Blvd
1a	CO 121, Wadsworth Blvd, N 🅿 7-11/gas, Conoco, Phillips 66 🍴 Alamos Verdes Mexican, Applebee's, Bennet's BBQ, Burger King, Chipotle Mexican, Coldstone Creamery, Fazoli's, Gunther Toody's Diner, IHOP, Koro Japanese, LoneStar Steaks, McDonald's/playplace, Red Robin, Ruby Tuesday, Starbucks, Subway, Taco Bell 🅾 $Tree, Advance Parts, Brakes+, Costco/gas, Discount Tire, Goodyear/auto, Home Depot, Lowe's Whse, mall, Office Depot, Petsmart, Radio Shack, Sam's Club, Tires+
0mm	I-76 begins/ends on I-70, exit 269b.

INTERSTATE 225 (Denver)

Exit #	Services
12b a	I-70, W to Denver, E to Limon
10	US 40, US 287, Colfax Ave, E 🅿 7-11, Conoco/dsl, Phillips 66, Shell, Sinclair 🍴 Arby's, Burger King, Del Taco, DQ, KFC, McDonald's, Pizza Hut/Taco Bell, Popeye's, Starbucks, Subway, Village Inn, Wendy's 🅾 Aamco, Advance Parts, Chevrolet, Family$, King's Sooper/gas, K-Mart, NAPA, RV camping, Walgreens, W 🅿 Conoco/dsl 🍴 Anthony's, Caribou Coffee, Chipotle Mexican, Noodles&Co, Spicy Pickle 🅾 Ⓗ, U-Haul
9	Co 30, 6th Ave, E 🅿 Conoco/dsl 🍴 Denny's 🛏 Super 8, ValuePlace Inn 🅾 Hobby Lobby, W 🅿 Phillips 66/dsl 🅾 Ⓗ
8	Alameda Ave, E 🅿 Conoco, Shamrock 🍴 Atlanta Bread, Baja Fresh, Benny's Cafe, BJ's Rest., Chili's, FatBurger, Jamba Juice, L&L BBQ, Macaroni Grill, Mimi's Cafe, Panda Express, Starbucks, TGIFriday, Wingstop 🅾 Barnes&Noble, Dillards, Gordman's, JC Penney, Macys, Old Navy, Petsmart, Ross, Sears/auto, Super Target, W 🅿 Conoco/dsl, Shell/Circle K 🅾 $Tree
7	Mississippi Ave, Alameda Ave, E 🍴 Arby's, Bono's BBQ, Burger King, Chubby's Mexican, ChuckeCheese, CiCi's, Fazoli's, Guadalajara Mexican, Schlotsky's, Sonic, Subway, Village Inn 🛏 Best Western, Holiday Inn Express, La Quinta 🅾 Best Buy, Burlington Coats, Home Depot, JoAnn Fabrics, Sam's Club/gas, Tires +, Walmart, W 🍴 IHOP, McDonald's, Senor Ric's, Waffle House 🅾 7-11, AutoZone, Office Depot, Pepboys, PetCo
5	Iliff Ave, E 🅿 7-11 🍴 Applebee's, Boston Mkt, Carrabba's, Fuddrucker's, Hibachi Japanese, Joe's Crabshack, Outback Steaks, Rosie's Diner, Ruby Tuesday, Sweet Tomatoes, TX Roadhouse 🛏 Comfort Inn, Crestwood Suites, Extended Stay Deluxe, Fairfield Inn, Homestead Suites, Motel 6, W 🅿 Phillips 66 🍴 Dragon's Boat, Subway 🛏 DoubleTree
4	CO 83, Parker Rd, E 🛏 Red Lion 🅾 Cherry Creek SP, W 🅿 Phillips 66/dsl 🍴 Bent Noodle, Big Burrito, DQ, Little Caesars, Popeyes, Starbucks, Subway, Table Steaks, Taco Bell, Wendy's 🅾 $Tree, 7-11, Firestone/auto, King Sooper/dsl
2b	no services
2	DTC Blvd, Tamarac St, W 🅿 Conoco 🍴 La Fogata Mexican, Quizno's, Sonic 🅾 7-11, Goodyear, vet
1b a	I-25. I-225 begins/ends on I-25, exit 200.

INTERSTATE 270 (Denver)

Exit #	Services
4	I-70
3	N 🅿 TA/Burger King/Country Pride/Popeye's/Pizza Hut/dsl/24hr/@, S 🅿 Sapp Bros/Sinclair/Subway/dsl/@
2b a	US 85, CO 2, Vasquez Ave, N 🍴 Arby's, Carls Jr, Chipotle Mexican, GoodTimes Grill, KFC/LJ Silver, McDonald's, Taco John's, Wendy's 🅾 TDS, Walgreens, Walmart
1c	I-25 S, to Denver
1b	York St
1a	I-76 E, to Ft Morgan

CO

CT

▲E INTERSTATE 84

Exit #	Services
98mm	**Connecticut/Massachusetts state line**
74 (97)	CT 171, Holland, S 🍴 Traveler's Book Rest. 🄾 RV camping
95mm	**weigh sta wb**
73 (95)	CT 190, Stafford Springs, N 🄾 camping (seasonal), motor speedway, st police
72 (93)	CT 89, Westford, N 🄾 camping (seasonal), Red Carpet Inn
71 (88)	CT 320, Ruby Rd, S 🅟 TA/Shell/Burger King/Country Pride/dsl/scales/24hr/@ 🍴 Dunkin Donuts 🛏 Rodeway Inn
70 (86)	CT 32, Willington, N 🄾 🅷, S 🅟 Mobil/dsl, Sunoco/dsl 🄾 RV Camping
85mm	**🆁 both lanes, campers, full ♿ facilities, info, litter barrels, petwalk, 🄲, 🆔, vending**
69 (83)	CT 74, to US 44, Willington, S food, gas, 🄲, RV camping, st police
68 (81)	CT 195, Tolland, N 🅟 Gulf/dsl, Mobil 🍴 Dunkin Donuts, Papa T's Rest., Subway 🄾 NAPA, RV camping, S 🅟 Citgo 🄾 Big Y Foods, Radio Shack
67 (77)	CT 31, Rockville, N 🅟 Mobil, Shell 🍴 Beni's Grill, Burger King, China Taste, Dunkin Donuts, McDonald's, Subway 🄾 🅷, RV Camping, S 🄾 Nathan Hale Mon
66 (76)	Tunnel Rd, Vernon
65 (75)	CT 30, Vernon Ctr, N 🅟 Mobil/dsl, Shell 🍴 Brick Oven Pizza, Burger King, Joy Luck, KFC, Lotus Rest., Oki Asian, Rein's Deli, Vernon Diner 🛏 Howard Johnson, Quality Inn 🄾 CarQuest, Firestone/auto, K-Mart, Meineke, Stop&Shop/gas
64 (74)	Vernon Ctr, N 🅟 Mobil/24hr, Sunoco 🍴 99 Rest., Angellino's Italian, Anthony's Pizza, Denny's, Dunkin Donuts, Friendly's, McDonald's, Rita's Custard, Taco Bell, Wood'n Tap 🛏 Holiday Inn Express 🄾 $Tree, AutoZone, CVS Drug, GNC, Goodyear/auto, PriceChopper, Staples, TJ Maxx, vet, S 🛏 Motel 6
63 (72)	CT 30, CT 83, Manchester, S Windsor, N 🍴 Applebee's, Azteca Mexican, Chipotle Mexican, Dunkin Donuts, HomeTown Buffet, Longhorn Steaks, McDonald's, Outback Steaks, Panera Bread, Red Robin, Starbucks, TGIFriday's 🛏 Courtyard, Residence Inn 🄾 AT&T, Barnes&Noble, Best Buy, Dick's, JC Penney, Macy's, Marshall's, PetCo, same as 62, Sears/auto, Walgreens, Walmart, S 🅟 Shell/dsl, Sunoco/dsl, Xtra 🍴 Misaki Buffet, Shea's Grill 🛏 Baymont Inn, Best Value Inn, Extended Stay America, Motel 6 🄾 🅷, Big Y Mkt, Hyundai, Kohl's, Nissan, Subaru, Toyota/Scion, U-Haul
62 (71)	Buckland St, N 🅟 Mobil/Dunkin Donuts/dsl 🍴 Bonefish Grill, Boston Mkt, Boston's, Chili's, Friendly's, Hooters, Johnny Rocket's, KFC, Moe's SW Grill, Olive Garden, Starbucks, Taco Bell, Ted's MT Grill, Tullycross Tavern 🛏 Fairfield Inn, Hampton Inn 🄾 $Tree, BigLots, Home Depot, Jo-Ann Fabrics, Lowe's, mall, Michael's, PetsMart, same as 63, Sam's Club, Target, S 🅟 Xtra/dsl 🍴 Buffalo Wild Wings, Carrabba's, ChuckeCheese, Dunkin Donuts, Golden Dragon, McDonald's, Sonic, Subway, TX Roadhouse, Wendy's 🄾 BJ's Whse/gas, Firestone/auto, GNC, Honda, USPO
61 (70)	I-291 W, to Windsor
60 (69)	US 6, US 44, Burnside Ave (from eb)
59 (68)	I-384 E, Manchester
58 (67)	Roberts St, Burnside Ave, N 🍴 Margarita's Grill 🛏 Comfort Inn, Ramada, S 🅟 Mobil, Sunoco 🍴 Dunkin Donuts 🄾 Cabelas
57 (66)	CT 15 S, to I-91 S, Charter Oak Br
56 (65)	Governor St, E Hartford, S 🄾 ⬇
55 (64)	CT 2 E, New London, downtown
54 (63)	Old State House, N 🄾 Chevrolet, Ford, Lexus, Lincoln

53 (62)	CT Blvd (from eb), S 🛏 Holiday Inn
52 (61)	W Main St (from eb), downtown
51 (60)	I-91 N, to Springfield
50 (59.8)	to I-91 S (from wb), N 🛏 Ramada, S 🛏 Hilton, Residence Inn
48 (59.5)	Asylum St, downtown, N 🛏 Ramada, S 🛏 Holiday Inn Express 🄾 🅷
47 (59)	Sigourney St, downtown, N 🄾 Hartford Seminary, Mark Twain House
46 (58)	Sisson St, downtown (from wb, exits left), S 🄾 UConn Law School
45 (57)	Flatbush Ave (from wb, exits left)
44 (56.5)	Prospect Ave, N 🅟 Mobil, Shell/dsl 🍴 Burger King, D'angelo's, Hibachi Grill, McDonald's, Prospect Pizza, Wendy's 🄾 ShopRite Foods
43 (56)	Park Rd, W Hartford, N 🄾 to St Joseph Coll
42 (55)	Trout Brk Dr (exits left from wb), to Elmwood
41 (54)	S Main St, Elmwood, S 🄾 American School for the Deaf
40 (53)	CT 71, New Britain Ave, S 🅟 Shell, Sunoco 🍴 Brio Grille, Burger King, CA Pizza, Chili's, China Pan, Chipotle Mexican, Dunkin Donuts, McDonald's, Olive Garden, Panera Bread, PF Chang's, Red Robin, Starbucks, Subway, Wendy's 🛏 Courtyard 🄾 Barnes&Noble, Best Buy, JC Penney, Macy's, mall, Michael's, Nordstrom, Office Depot, Old Navy, PetCo, Radio Shack, Sears/auto, Target, TJ Maxx, Trader Joe's, Verizon
39a (52)	CT 9 S, to New Britain, Newington, S 🄾 🅷
39 (51.5)	CT 4, (exits left from eb), Farmington, N 🄾 🅷
38 (51)	US 6 W (from wb), Bristol, N 🅟 same as 37
37 (50)	Fienemann Rd, to US 6 W, N 🅟 Shell 🍴 Dunkin Donuts, Stonewell Rest., Subway 🛏 Hampton Inn, Marriott, S 🛏 Extended Stay America
36 (49)	Slater Rd (exits left from eb), S 🄾 🅷
35 (48)	CT 72, to CT 9 (exits left from both lanes), New Britain, S 🄾 🅷
34 (47)	CT 372, Crooked St, N 🅟 Gulf/dsl, Sunoco 🍴 Applebee's, Friendly's, McDonald's, Starbucks 🛏 Fairfield Inn 🄾 Big Y Mkt, Dick's, Ford/Lincoln, Kohl's, Lowe's, Marshall's, Old Navy, Petsmart, VW
33 (46)	CT 72 W, to Bristol (exits left from eb)
32 (45)	Ct 10, Queen St, Southington, N 🅟 Cumberland Farms, Exxon, Shell/dsl 🍴 Bertucci's, Buffalo Wild Wings, Burger King, Chili's, D'angelos, Denny's, Dunkin Donuts, JD's Rest., KFC, Liberty Pizza, Luenhop, McDonald's, Moe's SW Grill, Outback Steaks, Puerto Vallarta, Ruby Tuesday, Starbucks, Subway, Taco Bell 🛏 Motel 6 🄾 🅷, $Tree, 7-11, CVS Drug, GNC, Home Depot, PetCo, Radio Shack, ShopRite Foods, Staples, TJ Maxx, TownFair Tire, S 🅟 Hess, Mobil, Sunoco 🍴 Aziagos Italian, Dunkin Donuts, El Sombrero, Friendly's, Nordelli's Cafe, Pizza Hut, Rita's Custard, Subway, TD Homer's Grill, Wendy's, Wood'n Tap Grill 🛏 Days Inn, Holiday Inn Express, Knights Inn 🄾 Advance Parts, AT&T, Firestone, Midas, Monro, PriceChopper Foods, Rite Aid, Walmart
31 (44)	CT 229, West St, N 🅟 Mobil, Sunoco/dsl 🄾 Lowe's, Target, S 🅟 Citgo, Valero 🍴 Dunkin Donuts, Giovanni's Pizza, Subway 🛏 Residence Inn
30 (43)	Marion Ave, W Main, Southington, N 🄾 ski area, S 🅟 Mobil/dsl 🄾 🅷
29 (42)	CT 10, from wb, exits left, Milldale (exits left from wb)
41.5mm	**🆁 eb, full ♿ facilities, info, litter barrels, petwalk, 🄲, 🆔**
28 (41)	CT 322, Marion, S 🅟 Fleet/dsl, Mobil, TA/Country Pride/Pizza Hut/Popeye's/Taco Bell/dsl/scales/24hr/@ 🍴 Blimpie, Burger King, DQ, Dunkin Donuts, Manor Inn Rest., Subway, Young Young Chinese 🛏 Comfort Suites, EconoLodge 🄾 Home Depot, repair

(left margin vertical text) **VERNON — VERNON CTR — WINDSOR — HARTFORD**

(right margin vertical text) **SOUTHINGTON**

INTERSTATE 84 Cont'd

Exit #	Services
27 (40)	I-691 E, to Meriden
26 (38)	CT 70, to Cheshire, **N** 🍴 Blackie's Cafe
25a (37)	Austin Rd, **N** ⛽ Winzz/dsl 🍴 Asian Garden, Subway 🅾 Costco/gas, funpark, Kohl's
25 (36)	Harper's Ferry Rd, Reed Dr, Scott Rd, E Main St, **N** ⛽ Gulf/dsl, Mobil/dsl 🍴 Dunkin Donuts, Subway 🅾 NAPA, **S** ⛽ Gulf 🍴 Burger King, Dunkin Donuts, Friendly's, Golden Wok, McDonald's, Nino's Rest., Subway 🛏 Quality Inn 🅾 Aldi Foods, BJ's Whse/gas, Cadillac/Chevrolet, CVS Drug, Super Stop&Shop/gas
23 (33.5)	CT 69, Hamilton Ave, **N** 🍴 Bertucci's, Buffalo Wild Wings, Chili's, HomeTown Buffet, IHOP, McDonald's, Olive Garden, TGIFriday's 🅾 🏥, Barnes&Noble, JC Penney, Macy's, mall, Michael's, Save-a-Lot Foods, Sears/auto, **S** ⛽ Shell 🍴 Dunkin Donuts
22 (33)	Baldwin St, Waterbury, **N** ⛽ Gulf 🛏 Courtyard 🅾 🏥, same as 23, USPO
21 (33)	Meadow St, Banks St, **N** ⛽ 7-11, Citgo, **S** ⛽ Exxon/dsl 🅾 Home Depot, PetsMart
20mm	end wb, motorist callboxes begin eb
20 (32)	CT 8 N (exits left from eb), to Torrington
19 (32)	CT 8 S (exits left from wb), to Bridgeport
18 (32)	W Main, Highland Ave, **N** 🍴 Dunkin Donuts, Lena's Deli, Subway 🛏 Hampton Inn 🅾 🏥, CVS Drug
17 (30)	CT 63, CT 64, to Watertown, Naugatuck, **N** 🍴 Maggie McFly's Rest., **S** ⛽ Mobil/dsl 🍴 Leo's Rest., Maples Rest., Subway
16 (25)	CT 188, to Middlebury, **N** ⛽ Mobil 🍴 Patty's Pantry Deli 🛏 Crowne Plaza
15 (22)	US 6 E, CT 67, Southbury, **N** ⛽ Citgo/deli, Mobil, Shell/repair 🍴 Dunkin Donuts, Friendly's (1mi), McDonald's, Subway 🛏 Heritage Hotel 🅾 K-Mart, Stop&Shop, TJ Maxx, **S** 🅾 to Kettletown SP
14 (20)	CT 172, to S Britain, **N** ⛽ Mobil 🍴 Dunkin Donuts, Maggie McFly's, **S** 🅾 st police
13 (19)	River Rd (from eb), to Southbury
11 (16)	CT 34, to New Haven
10 (15)	US 6 W, Newtown, **N** 🍴 Fig's Rest., Foundry Kitchen, Subway, **S** ⛽ Citgo, Mobil/dsl 🍴 Blue Colony Diner, Pizza Palace, Starbucks 🅾 🏥
9 (11)	CT 25, to Hawleyville, **S** 🍴 McGuire's Alehouse
8 (8)	Newtown Rd, **N** ⛽ Global, Mobil/dsl 🍴 Outback Steaks 🛏 La Quinta 🅾 Best Buy, Harley-Davidson, Lowe's, Volvo, **S** ⛽ Shell, Sunoco 🍴 Bangkok Thai, Bertucci's Italian, Boston Mkt, Burger King, Chili's, Denny's, Dunkin Donuts, Friendly's, Ichiro Steaks, Little Caesars, McDonald's, Subway, Taco Bell

Exit #	Services
8 (8)	Continued 🛏 Best Western, Days Inn, Hampton Inn, Holiday Inn/rest. 🅾 Aldi Foods, Buick, Chrysler/Jeep, Goodyear/auto, Marshall's, Radio Shack, Staples, Stop&Shop, Target, Town Fair Tire, Verizon, Walmart
7 (7)	US 7N/202E, to Brookfield, (exits left from eb), New Milford, **N** **1 exit on Federal Rd** ⛽ Mobil, Shell, Sunoco 🍴 5 Guys Burgers, Applebee's, Arby's, KFC, McDonald's, Panera Bread, Pizza Hut, Starbucks, Subway, Wendy's 🅾 Bj's Whse/gas, CVS Drug, Firestone, Ford, GNC, Harley-Davidson, Home Depot, Jo-Ann Fabrics, Kohl's, Michael's, ShopRite Foods, Stew Leonards, Subaru, TJ Maxx, Town Fair Tire, Toyota/Scion, Walgreens
6 (6)	CT 37 (from wb), New Fairfield, **N** ⛽ Gulf 🍴 Burger King, Castello's Italian, Dunkin Donuts, Elmer's Diner, Grand Century Buffet, KFC, McDonald's, Moon Star Chinese 🅾 $Tree, A&P Foods, Radio Shack, Rite Aid, **S** ⛽ Citgo, Valero 🍴 KFC
5 (5)	CT 37, CT 39, CT 53, Danbury, **N** ⛽ Gulf/dsl, Shell 🛏 Best Value Inn, **S** ⛽ Mobil 🍴 Dunkin Donuts, Taco Bell 🅾 🏥, to Putnam SP
4 (4)	US 6 W/202 W, Lake Ave, **N** ⛽ Exxon, Gulf/dsl, Shell/dsl 🍴 Dunkin Donuts, McDonald's 🛏 Ethan Allen Hotel, Maron Hotel, Super 8 🅾 CVS Drug, Stop&Shop Foods, **S** 🍴 Chuck's Steaks 🛏 Residence Inn, to mall
3 (3)	US 7 S (exits left from wb), to Norwalk, **S** ⛽ Mobil 🍴 Brio Grille, Buffalo Wild Wings, Cheesecake Factory, Chucke-Cheese, Coldstone, Olive Garden, Panera Bread, Red Lobster 🅾 Barnes&Noble, Dick's, JC Penney, LL Bean, Macy's, mall, Petco, Sears/auto
2b a (1)	US 6, US 202, Mill Plain Rd, **N** ⛽ Mobil/dsl 🍴 Desert Moon Café, Rosy Tomorrows, Starbucks, Tuscanero's Pizza 🛏 Hilton Garden, Holiday Inn Express 🅾 Rite Aid, Staples, Trader Joe's, **S** **Welcome Ctr/weigh sta, full** ♿ **facilities, info,** 🚻, **litter barrels, petwalk,** 🛏 SpringHill Suites 🅾 to Old Ridgebury
1 (0)	Saw Mill Rd, **N** 🛏 Hilton Garden, Holiday Inn Express, Maron Hotel
0mm	Connecticut/New York state line

SOUTHBURY

🧭N	**INTERSTATE 91**
Exit #	Services
58mm	Connecticut/Massachusetts state line
49 (57)	US 5, to Longmeadow, MA, **E** 🅖 Pride/dsl, Valero 🍽 Backyard Grille, McDonald's 🛏 Holiday Inn 🅞 Meineke, repair, **W** 🅖 Sunoco/dsl 🍽 Baco's Pizza, Cloverleaf Café, DQ, Dunkin Donuts, Pizza Palace 🅞 $General, Chrysler/Dodge
48 (56)	CT 220, Elm St, **E** 🅖 Mobil/dsl 🍽 Arby's, Burger King, Denny's, Dunkin Donuts, Figaro, Friendly's, Jason's Seafood, McDonald's, Outback Steaks, Oyama Japanese, Panera Bread, Ruby Tuesday, TGIFriday's, Wendy's 🅞 $Tree, AutoZone, Best Buy, Costco/gas, Dick's, Firestone/auto, Home Depot, Honda, Hyundai, Jo-Ann Fabrics, Kohl's, Macy's, Nissan, Radio Shack, same as 47, Sears/auto, Target, TownFair Tire, Toyota, USPO, VW
47 (55)	CT 190, to Hazardville, **E** 🍽 99 Rest., Acapulcos Mexican, Cheng's Garden, Chipotle, D'angelo, Domino's, Dunkin Donuts, Longhorn Steaks, McDonald's, Moe's SW Grill, Olive Garden, Pizza Hut, Plaza Azteca Mexican, Red Robin, Starbucks, Subway, Taco Bell 🛏 Hampton Inn, Motel 6, Red Roof Inn 🅞 🅗, Advance Parts, Aldi Foods, AT&T, Barnes&Noble, Big Y Foods, CVS Drug, Ford, Goodyear, Marshall's, Michael's, NAPA, Old Navy, PetCo, Petsmart, Rite Aid, same as 48, ShopRite, Staples, Stop&Shop/gas, URGENT CARE, Verizon, Walgreens
46 (53)	US 5, King St, to Enfield, **E** 🅖 Mobil 🍽 Astro's Rest., **W** 🍽 Hacienda Del Sol 🛏 Enfield Inn
45 (51)	CT 140, Warehouse Point, **E** 🅖 Shell 🍽 Burger King, Chen's Chinese, Cracker Barrel, Dunkin Donuts, Friendly's, Jake's Burgers, Sofia's Rest., Subway 🛏 Comfort Inn 🅞 to Trolley Museum, **W** 🅖 Sunoco/dsl 🛏 Clarion 🅞 Advance Parts
44 (50)	US 5 S, to E Windsor, **E** 🅖 Sunoco/dsl 🍽 Dunkin Donuts, KFC, Sky Diner, Taco Bell, Wendy's 🛏 Baymont Inn 🅞 Walmart
49mm	Connecticut River
42 (48)	CT 159, Windsor Locks, **E** Longview RV Ctr, **W** same as 41
41 (47)	Center St (exits with 39), **W** 🍽 Ad's Pizzaria 🛏 HillPoint Hotel
40 (46.5)	CT 20, **W** 🅞 🔁, Old New-Gate Prison
39 (46)	Kennedy Rd (exits with 41), Community Rd, **E** 🅞 vet, **W** 🅖 Shell/dsl 🍽 Charkoon, Chili's 🅞 $Tree, GNC, PetCo, Radio Shack, Stop&Shop Foods, Target
38 (45)	CT 75, to Poquonock, Windsor Area, **E** 🅖 Mobil/dsl 🍽 Buffalo Wild Wings, Buffalo Wild Wings, China Sea, Dunkin Donuts, Izote SW Grill, Pizzarama, Subway 🅞 AT&T, PriceChopper Foods, to Ellsworth Homestead, **W** 🍽 River City Grill 🛏 Courtyard, Hilton Garden, Hyatt House Suites, Marriott
37 (44)	CT 305, Bloomfield Ave, Windsor Ctr, **E** 🅖 Mobil/dsl 🍽 McDonald's, **W** 🅖 Sunoco 🛏 Residence Inn
36 (43)	CT 178, Park Ave, to W Hartford
35b (41)	CT 218, to Bloomfield, to S Windsor, **E** food, gas/dsl
35a	I-291 E, to Manchester
34 (40)	CT 159, Windsor Ave, **E** 🅖 Shell/dsl, **W** 🅖 Citgo/dsl 🛏 Flamingo Inn, RanchHouse Rest. 🅞 🅗
33 (39)	Jennings Rd, Weston St, **E** 🅞 Cadillac, Fiat, Jaguar, VW, **W** 🅖 Mobil, Sunoco/dsl 🍽 Burger King, Dunkin Donuts, McDonald's, Subway 🛏 Super 8, Travel Inn 🅞 CarMax, Honda, Hyundai, Infiniti, Mazda, Mercedes, Midas, Nissan, Subaru, Toyota/Scion
32b (38)	Trumbull St (exits left from nb), **W** 🛏 Crowne Plaza, Hilton 🅞 🅗, Goodyear, to downtown

32a	(exit 30 from sb), I-84 W
29b (37)	I-84 E, Hartford
29a (36.5)	US 5 N, CT 15 N (exits left from nb), **W** 🅞 🅗, capitol, civic ctr, downtown
28 (36)	US 5, CT 15 S (from nb), **W** 🅖 Citgo 🍽 Burger King, Dunkin Donuts, Wendy's
27 (35)	Brainerd Rd, Airport Rd, **E** 🅖 Mobil/Dunkin Donuts/Subway/dsl, Shell/Dunkin Donuts/dsl 🍽 McDonald's, USS Chowder 🛏 Days Inn, Hartford Suites 🅞 Ford Trucks, to Regional Mkt
26 (33.5)	Marsh St, **E** 🅞 CT MVD, Silas Deane House, Webb House
25 (33)	CT 3, Glastonbury, Wethersfield
24 (32)	CT 99, Rocky Hill, Wethersfield, **E** 🅖 Phillips 66/dsl, Sunoco 🍽 Algarve Grill, Chuck's Steaks, Dakota Steaks, Dunkin Donuts, McDonald's, On-the-Border, Rita's Custard, Rockyhill Pizza, Saybrook Seafood, Subway 🛏 Hampton Inn, Howard Johnson, Super 8 🅞 Aldi Foods, Kohl's, Meineke, Monro, **W** 🅖 Mobil, Shell/dsl, Valero/dsl 🍽 Buffalo Wild Wings, Burger King, D'Angelo, Denny's, Dunkin Donuts, Friendly's, Ginza Cuisine, HomeTown Buffet, KFC, Ming Dynasty, Panera Bread, Pizza Hut, Red Lobster, Sake Japanese, Sophia's Pizzaria, Starbucks, Subway, Tamarind Rest., Tilted Kilt, Townline Diner, Wendy's, Wood-n-Tap Grill 🛏 Comfort Inn, Motel 6 🅞 $Tree, AT&T, CVS Drug, Goodyear/auto, Marshalls, Office Depot, Radio Shack, Stop&Shop, TJMaxx, TownFair Tire, TrueValue, Verizon, Walgreens, Walmart/Subway
23 (29)	to CT 3, West St, Rocky Hill, Vet Home, **E** 🛏 Sheraton 🅞 to Dinosaur SP, **W** 🅖 Mobil, Valero/dsl 🍽 Dunkin Donuts, Michelangeo's Pizza, Papa John's, Subway 🛏 Residence Inn 🅞 IGA Foods
22 (27)	CT 9, to New Britain, Middletown
21 (26)	CT 372, to Berlin, Cromwell, **E** 🅖 Sunoco/dsl/repair 🛏 Crowne Plaza, Quality Inn 🅞 Krauszer's Foods, Lowe's, **W** 🅖 Citgo/Subway/dsl, Mobil/dsl 🍽 Baci Grill, Burger King, Chili's, Cromwell Diner, Dunkin Donuts, McDonald's, Nordelli's, Oyama Japanese 🛏 Courtyard, Super 8 🅞 $Plus, Firestone/auto, Price Rite Foods, Verizon, vet, Walmart
20 (23)	Country Club Rd, Middle St
22mm	🅡ₛ /weigh sta nb, full 🛏 **facilities, info, litter barrels, petwalk, 🅒, 🔁, RV dump, vending**
19 (21)	Baldwin Ave (from sb)
18 (20.5)	I-691 W, to Marion, access to same as 16 & 17, ski area
17 (20)	CT 15 N (from sb), to I-691, CT 66 E, Meriden
16 (19)	CT 15, E Main St, **E** 🅖 Gulf/dsl, Mobil/dsl, Valero 🍽 American Steaks, Gianni's Rest., Huxley's Cafe, Kings Garden Chinese, Olympos Diner, Subway 🛏 Hampton Inn, Hawthorn Inn, The Meridan Inn 🅞 URGENT CARE, Volvo, **W** 🅖 Getty/dsl, Gulf/repair, Shell/dsl 🍽 Boston Mkt, Boston Mkt, Burger King, Dominos, Dunkin Donuts, KFC, Les' Dairy Bar, Little Caesar's, McDonald's, Nordelli's, Subway, Taco Bell, Wayback Burgers, Wendy's 🛏 Comfort Inn 🅞 🅗, CarQuest, CVS Drug, Hancock's Drug, Verizon, Walgreens
15mm	🅡ₛ sb, full 🛏 **facilities, info, litter barrels, petwalk, 🅒, 🔁**
15 (16)	CT 68, to Durham, **E** 🅞 golf, **W** 🛏 Courtyard, Fairfield Inn, Homewood Suites
14 (12)	CT 150 (no EZ return), Woodhouse Ave, Wallingford
13 (10)	US 5 (exits left from nb), Wallingford, **W** 2 mi on US 5 🅞 to Wharton Brook SP, services
12 (9)	US 5, Washington Ave, **E** 🅖 Shell, Sunoco, Valero 🍽 Boston Mkt, Burger King, D'angelo's, DQ, Dunkin Donuts, Hibachi Buffet, McDonald's, Popeyes, Starbucks, Subway, Wendy's 🅞 CVS Drug, Stop&Shop Food, Town Fair Tire, URGENT CARE, USPO, Walgreens, **W** 🅖 Citgo, Gulf/dsl, Mobil

Vertical left margin: CT

*Vertical text (left column):* ROCKY HILL · WINDSOR AREA

*Vertical text (right column):* WALLINGFORD

⬆N INTERSTATE 91 Cont'd

Exit #	Services
12 (9)	Continued
	🍴 Arby's, Athena II Diner, Dunkin Donuts, Outback Steaks 🏨 Best Western/Harry's Grill Ⓞ Advance Parts, BigY Foods/drug, vet
11 (7)	CT 22 (from nb), North Haven, same as 12
10 (6)	CT 40, to Cheshire, Hamden
9 (5)	Montowese Ave, **W** 🅶 Berkshire/dsl, Sunoco 🍴 Buffalo Wild Wings, Dunkin Donuts, Dynasty Chinese, Friendly's, Longhorn Steaks, McDonald's, Olive Garden, Panera Bread, Red Lobster, Ruby Tuesday, Subway, Wendy's Ⓞ $Tree, AT&T, Barnes&Noble, Best Buy, BigLots, BJ's Whse/gas, GNC, Home Depot, Michael's, Nissan/Jeep, PetCo, Petsmart, Radio Shack, Target, TJMaxx, URGENT CARE, Verizon
8 (4)	CT 17, CT 80, Middletown Ave, **E** 🅶 7-11, Citgo, Global/dsl, Mercury/dsl, Shell, Sunoco 🍴 Burger King, Country House Rest., Dunkin Donuts, Exit 8 Diner, KFC, McDonald's, Taco Bell 🏨 Days Inn Ⓞ Advance Parts, Aldi Foods, AutoZone, Lowe's, vet, Walgreens, Walmart/Subway
7 (3)	Ferry St (from sb), Fair Haven, **W** 🅶 Hess/dsl Ⓞ NAPA
6 (2.5)	Willow St (exits left from nb), Blatchley Ave, **E** Ⓞ repair
5 (2)	US 5 (from nb), State St, Fair Haven
4 (1.5)	State St (from sb), downtown
3 (1)	Trumbull St, downtown, **W** Ⓞ Peabody Museum
2 (.5)	Hamilton St, downtown, New Haven
1 (.3)	CT 34W (from sb), New Haven, **W** Ⓞ 🏥, downtown
0mm	I-91 begins/ends on I-95, exit 48.

⬆N INTERSTATE 95

Exit #	Services
94mm	Connecticut/Rhode Island state line
93 (111)	CT 216, Clarks Falls, **E** 🅶 Shell/dsl/repair 🍴 Dunkin Donuts, Subway, to Burlingame SP, **W** 🅶 Mobil/Dunkin Donuts/dsl, 🚛/Shell/Stuckey's/Roy Rogers/Sbarro's/dsl/scales/24hr 🍴 McDonald's 🏨 Budget Inn, Stardust Motel
92 (107)	CT 2, CT 49 (no EZ nb return), Pawcatuck, **E** 🅶 Shell 🍴 Dunkin Donuts 🏨 La Quinta Ⓞ 🏥, Stop&Shop, **W** 🏨 Cedar Park Suites Ⓞ FoxWoods (8mi), KOA
91 (103)	CT 234, N Main St, to Stonington, **E** Ⓞ 🏥
90 (101)	CT 27, Mystic, **E** 🅶 Mobil/Domino's/Dunkin Donuts/dsl 🍴 5 Guys Burgers, Boathouse Rest., Equinox Diner, Friendly's, Go Fish, McDonald's, Starbucks, Steak Loft, Ten Clams 🏨 EconoLodge, Hilton, Holiday Inn Express, Howard Johnson, Hyatt Place Ⓞ aquarium, Mystic Outlet Shops, Verizon, **W** 🅶 Shell/Subway/dsl 🍴 Dunkin Donuts, Jakes Burgers, Pizza Grille, Thai 1 🏨 Comfort Inn, Days Inn, Hampton Inn, Ramada Inn, Residence Inn Ⓞ Chevrolet, Chrysler/Dodge/Jeep, Ford, RV camping, TrueValue, VW
89mm	scenic overlook
89 (99)	CT 215, Allyn St, **W** Ⓞ camping (seasonal)
88 (98)	CT 117, to Noank, **E** Ⓞ 🚻, **W** 🍴 Octagon Steaks, Starbucks 🏨 Marriott
87 (97)	Sharp Hwy (exits left from sb), Groton, **E** 🏨 Hampton Inn Ⓞ 🚻, to Griswold SP
86 (96)	rd 184 (exits left from nb), Groton, **E** 🍴 99 Rest., Applebees 🏨 Hampton Inn, Knights Inn Ⓞ Walgreens, **W** 🅶 Cory's/dsl, Hess, Mobil, Shell/dsl 🍴 Chinese Kitchen, Dunkin Donuts, Flanagan's Diner, Groton Rest., KFC, NY Pizza, Russell's Ribs, Subway, Taco Bell 🏨 Best Western, Groton Inn, Super 8 Ⓞ $Tree, Advance Parts, GNC, Honda, Kia, Kohl's, Midas, Stop&Shop, to US Sub Base, Verizon
85 (95)	US 1 N, Groton, downtown, **E** Ⓞ NAPA

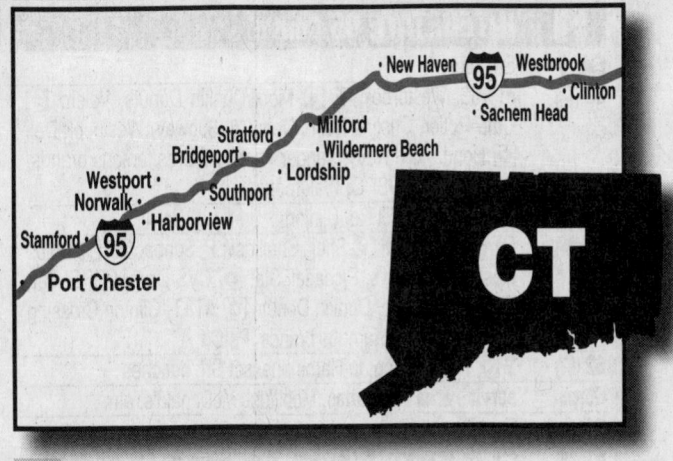

84 (94)	CT 32 (from sb), New London, downtown
83 (92)	CT 32, New London, **E** to Long Island Ferry
82a (90.5)	frontage rd, New London, **E** 🅶 Mobil 🍴 Panda Buffet, Pizza Hut Ⓞ AutoZone, NSA Foods, Radio Shack, same as 82, Staples, TownFair Tire, Verizon, **W** 🍴 Chili's, ChuckeCheese, Outback Steaks 🏨 Clarion, SpringHill Suites Ⓞ Marshall's, Petsmart, same as 82, ShopRite Foods
82 (90)	CT 85, to I-395 N, New London, **W** 🅶 Mobil/Dunkin Donuts 🍴 Coldstone, FoodCourt, Longhorn Steaks, Olive Garden, Panera Bread, Ruby Tuesday, Subway, Wendy's Ⓞ Best Buy, Dick's, Home Depot, JC Penney, Macy's, mall, Michael's, PetCo, Sears/auto, Target, Verizon
90mm	**weigh sta both directions**
81 (89.5)	Cross Road, **W** 🏨 Rodeway Inn Ⓞ BJ's Whse/gas, Lowe's, Walmart/McDonald's
80 (89.3)	Oil Mill Rd (from sb), **W** 🏨 Rodeway Inn
76 (89)	I-395 N (from nb, exits left), to Norwich
75 (88)	US 1, to Waterford
74 (87)	rd 161, to Flanders, Niantic, **E** 🅶 Citgo/dsl, Cory's/repair, Mobil 🍴 Burger King, Country Gourmet, Dunkin Donuts, Illiano's Grill, Quiznos, Shoreline Rest., Starbucks 🏨 Best Value Inn, Hilltop Inn, Motel 6, Sleep Inn Ⓞ Ford, Stop&Shop, Tires+, **W** 🅶 Shell 🍴 5 Guys Burgers, Flanders Pizza, Flanders Seafood, Kings Garden Chinese, McDonald's, Nanami Japanese, Shack Rest., Smokey O'Grady's BBQ, Yummy Yummy Pizza Ⓞ CVS Drug, IGA Foods, Rite Aid, RV camping, TrueValue, vet
73 (86)	Society Rd
72 (84)	to Rocky Neck SP, **E 2 mi** food, lodging, RV camping, to Rocky Neck SP
71 (83)	4 Mile Rd, River Rd, to Rocky Neck SP, **E 1 mi** camping (seasonal), beaches
70 (80)	US 1, CT 156, Old Lyme, **W** 🅶 Shell/dsl 🍴 Morning Glory Cafe, Subway 🏨 Old Lyme Inn/dining Ⓞ Big Y Foods, Griswold Museum, Rite Aid, USPO, vet
69 (77)	US 1, CT 9 N, to Hartford, **W** 🍴 Bangkok Sushi 🏨 Comfort Inn Ⓞ antiques, vet
68 (76.5)	US 1 S, Old Saybrook, **E** 🅶 Irving/dsl, Mobil 🍴 Cloud 9 Deli, Pat's Country Kitchen, **W** Ⓞ Buick/GMC, Chevrolet/Nissan, Chrysler/Dodge/Jeep, Kia, Mazda, NAPA, VW
67 (76)	CT 154, Elm St (no EZ sb return), Old Saybrook, **E** 🍴 Pasta Vita Itaian, same as 68
66 (75)	to US 1, Spencer Plain Rd, **E** 🅶 Citgo/dsl 🍴 Blue Crab Steaks, Brick Oven Pizza, Cuckoo's Nest Mexican, DQ, Dunkin Donuts, Fogo Grill, Luigi's Italian, Mike's Deli, Pizza Palace, Sal's Pizza, Samurai Japanese, Siagon City, Tiberio's Italian 🏨 Days Inn, EconoLodge, Saybrook Motel, Super 8 Ⓞ Benny's Mkt, transmissions, vet
74mm	Ⓡ𝐬 sb, full ♿ **facilities,** st police

⬆N	**INTERSTATE 95 Cont'd**

Exit # Services

65 (73) rd 153, Westbrook, **E** 🅿 Mobil/Dunkin Donuts, Valero 🍴 Cafe Rotier, Cristy's Rest., Denny's, Subway, Westbook Deli 🅾 Honda, Old Navy, Tanger Factory Stores/famous brands, Toyota/Scion, USPO, Walgreens

64 (70) rd 145, Horse Hill Rd, Clinton

63 (68) CT 81, Clinton, **E** 🅿 Shell, Shell/dsl/LP, Sunoco/dsl 🍴 Chips Rest., McDonald's, Piccadeli Sta. 🅾 CVS Drug, USPO, vet, **W** 🍴 Coldstone, Dunkin Donuts 🅾 AT&T, Clinton Crossing Premium Outlets/famous brands, PetCo

62 (67) **E** 🅾 RV camping, to Hammonasset SP, beaches

66mm **service area both lanes,** Mobil/dsl, McDonald's, atm

61mm East River

61 (64) CT 79, Madison, **E** 🅿 Gulf, Shell, Sunoco 🍴 Cafe Allegre, Starbucks, Subway, Village Pizza 🅾 CVS Drug, Stop&Shop, USPO

60 (63.5) Mungertown Rd (from sb, no return), **E** 🅾 food, lodging

59 (60) rd 146, Goose Lane, Guilford, **E** 🅿 Citgo, Mobil/24hr, Shell/DQ/dsl 🍴 Avest Pizza, Dunkin Donuts, First Garden Chinese, McDonald's, Nick&Tony's Pizza, Shoreline Diner, Splash American Grill, The Whole Enchilada, Wendy's 🏨 Comfort Inn, Tower Motel 🅾 NAPA, transmissions, **W** 🅾 st police, URGENT CARE

58 (59) CT 77, Guilford, **E on US 1** 🍴 BP, Hess, Mobil, Sunoco/dsl 🅾 CVS Drug, to Henry Whitfield Museum, Walgreens, **W** 🅾 st police

57 (58) US 1, Guilford, **E** 🅾 Extra/Dunkin Donuts/dsl, **W** 🅾 Land Rover

56 (55) rd 146, to Stony Creek, **E** 🏨 Rodeway Inn, **W** 🅿 Mobil, Shell/dsl, TA/Popeye's/Starbucks/Subway/dsl/scales/24hr/@ 🍴 Dunkin Donuts, Friendly's, USS Chowderpot 🏨 Baymont Inn, Best Value Inn 🅾 Freightliner, Stop&Shop Foods, Verizon

55 (54) US 1, **E** 🅿 Branford/repair, Cumberland, Global 🍴 Hornet's Nest Deli, Lynn's Rest, Marco Pizzaria, Rita's Custard, Sapori d'Italia, TNT Seafood Grill 🏨 Holiday Inn Express, Motel 6 🅾 Ford, vet, Walgreens, **W** 🅿 Gulf, Mobil/Dunkin Donuts/dsl 🍴 Brother's Deli, Chuck's Margarita Grill, Gourmet Wok, Parthenon Diner, Su Casa Mexican 🏨 Days Inn

54 (53) Cedar St, Branford, **E** 🅿 Citgo/repair, Mobil 🍴 Dragon East Chinese, Dunkin Donuts, La Luna Ristorante 🅾 AAA, Hyundai, Staples, Subaru, **W** 🅾 Krauszer's Foods

52mm **service area both lanes,** 🅿 Mobil/dsl/24hr 🍴 McDonald's, pizza 🅾 atm

52 (50) rd 100, North High St, **E** 🅾 to Trolley Museum, **W** 🅾 st police

51 (49.5) US 1, Easthaven, **E** 🅿 Hess/dsl, Sunoco, Valero/dsl 🍴 Boston Mkt, Chili's 🏨 Quality Inn 🅾 Chevrolet, Lexus, TJ Maxx, Verizon, **W** 🍴 Dunkin Donuts, Wendy's 🅾 AutoZone, CarMax, Home Depot, USPO

50 (49) Woodward Ave (from nb), **E** 🅾 Ft Nathan Hale, US Naval/Marine Reserve

49 (48.5) Stiles St (from nb)

48 (48) I-91 N, to Hartford

47 (47.5) CT 34, New Haven, **W** 🅿 Mobil/Dunkin Donuts/dsl 🍴 Brazi's Italian, Greek Olive Diner 🏨 La Quinta 🅾 Ikea, Long Wharf Theater, same as 46

46 (47) Long Wharf Dr, Sargent Dr, **E** 🍴 Lenny & Joe's Rest., **W** 🅿 Mobil/Dunkin Donuts/dsl 🍴 Brazi's Italian, Greek Olive Diner 🏨 La Quinta 🅾 Ikea, Long Warf Theater

45 (46.5) CT 10 (from sb), Blvd, **W** 🍴 Dunkin Donuts, McDonald's 🅾 same as 44

44 (46) CT 10 (from nb), Kimberly Ave, **E** 🏨 Super 8, **W** 🍴 DQ, Dunkin Donuts, McDonald's, Popeyes 🅾 same as 45

43 (45) CT 122, 1st Ave (no EZ return), West Haven, **W** 🅿 1st Fuel/dsl, Xtra 🅾 🍴 NAPA, to U of New Haven, vet

42 (44) CT 162, Saw Mill Rd, **E** 🍴 Pizza Hut 🏨 EconoLodge, **W** 🅿 Shell 🍴 American Steaks, Denny's, Dunkin Donuts, Starbucks, Subway, TX Roadhouse, Uncle Willie's BBQ 🏨 Best Western, Hampton Inn 🅾 Aldi Foods, Firestone/auto, Walmart/Subway

41 (42) Marsh Hill Rd, to Orange

41mm **service area both lanes,** 🅿 Mobil/dsl 🍴 Dunkin Donuts, McDonald's, Subway

40 (40) Old Gate Lane, Woodmont Rd, **E** 🅿 Citgo/dsl, 🚚/Wendy's/dsl/scales/24hr, Shell, Sunoco 🍴 Cracker Barrel, Duchess Rest., Dunkin Donuts, Gipper's Rest., Popeyes, Titlted Kilt 🏨 Hilton Garden, Holiday Inn Express, Mayflower Motel, Milford Inn 🅾 Blue Beacon, Lowe's, Midas

39 (39) US 1, to Milford, **E** 🅿 Cumberland Farms/dsl 🍴 Athenian Diner, Chicago Grill, Dunkin Donuts, Friendly's, Hooters, Mama Teresa's 🏨 Howard Johnson, Super 8 🅾 $Tree, CVS Drug, Firestone/auto, Mazda/Volvo, ShopRite Foods, URGENT CARE, vet, Walgreens, **W on US 1** 🅿 Mobil 🍴 Boston Mkt, Boston Mkt, Buffalo Wild Wings, Burger King, Chili's, Chipotle Mexican, DiBella Subs, Domino's, Dunkin Donuts, Hometown Buffet, HoneyBaked Ham, McDonald's, Panera Bread, Sonic, Starbucks, Subway, Taco Bell, Villano's Rest. 🅾 Acura, Advance Parts, AT&T, Barnes&Noble, BigLots, Chrysler/Dodge/Jeep, Costco/gas, Dick's, JC Penney, Jo-Ann Fabrics, Macy's, mall, Marshall's, Michael's, Old Navy, PetCo, Rite Aid, Sears/auto, Shop&Shop/gas, Staples, Target, TownFair Tire, Walmart/Subway, Whole Foods Mkt

38 (38) CT 15, Merritt Pkwy, Cross Pkwy

37 (37.5) High St (no ez nb return), **E** 🅿 Gulf, Sunoco, USA 🍴 Subway 🅾 7-11, Toyota/Scion, vet

36 Plains Rd, **E** 🍴 Dunkin Donuts, Gusto Italian 🏨 Hampton Inn 🅾 Aldi Foods

35 (37) Bic Dr, School House Rd, **E** 🅿 Citgo 🍴 Wendy's 🏨 Fairfield Inn 🅾 AutoZone, Buick/GMC, Chevrolet, CVS Drug, Dennis' Parts, Ford/Lincoln, Honda, Kia, Land Rover, Nissan, Stop&Shop Foods/gas, Subaru, Walgreens, **W** 🏨 Red Roof Inn, Residence Inn, SpringHill Suites

34 (34) US 1, Milford, **E on US 1** 🍴 Dunkin Donuts, McDonald's, Pizza Hut, Subway, Taco Bell 🏨 Devon Motel 🅾 $Tree, Hyundai, K-Mart, Radio Shack, Walgreens

33 (33.5) US 1 (from nb, no EZ return), CT 110, Ferry Blvd, **E** 🅿 Shell/dsl, Sunoco/dsl 🍴 Danny's Drive-In, Lumi Rest., Riverview Bistro, Subway 🅾 $Tree, BJ's Whse, PetCo, Staples, **W** 🍴 99 Rest., McDonalds, Villa Pizza 🅾 Home Depot, Marshall's, ShopRite Foods, Stop&Shop/dsl, USPO, Walmart/Subway

32 (33) W Broad St, Stratford, **E** 🅿 Petra/Subway/dsl, **W** 🅿 Gulf/dsl 🍴 Dunkin Donuts

31 (32) South Ave, Honeyspot Rd, **E** 🅿 Gulf/Dunkin Donuts 🏨 HoneySpot Motel, Quality Inn, **W** 🅿 Citgo/dsl 🅾 NAPA, TownFair Tire

30 (31.5) Lordship Blvd, Surf Ave, **E** 🅿 Gulf/dsl, Shell/dsl 🍴 Dunkin Donuts 🏨 Stratford Hotel 🅾 URGENT CARE, **W** 🅿 Massey/dsl

29 (31) rd 130, Stratford Ave, Seaview Ave, **W** 🅾 🍴

28 (30) CT 113, E Main St, Pembrook St

27a (29) CT 25, CT 8, to Waterbury

27 (29.5) Lafayette Blvd, downtown, **W** 🍴 Dunkin Donuts 🅾 🍴, Barnum Museum

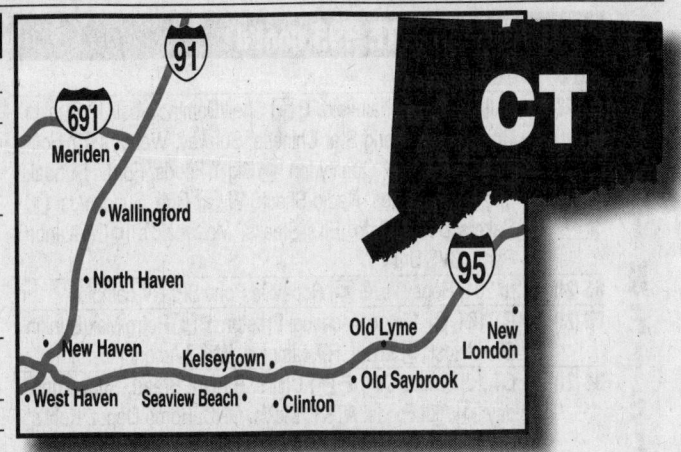

⬆N INTERSTATE 95 Cont'd

Exit #	Services
26 (28)	Wordin Ave
25 (27)	CT 130 (from sb, no EZ return), State St, Commerce Dr, Fairfield Ave, **E** 🅞 Audi, Infiniti, Mercedes, Porsche, USPO, **W** 🍴 McDonald's
24 (26.5)	Black Rock Tpk, **E** 🍴 Blackrock Oyster Bar, Fairfield Pizza, Rio Bravo, Sweet Basil 🛏 Best Western 🅞 BJ's Whse/Subway, Lexus, Porsche, Staples, USPO, Verizon, **W** 🅖 Gulf 🅞 Firestone/auto, Nissan
23 (26)	US 1, Kings Hwy, **E** 🅖 Sunoco/dsl 🍴 Chipotle, Five Guys 🅞 CVS Drug, Home Depot, Petco, Whole Foods Mkt
22 (24)	Round Hill Rd, N Benson Rd
23.5mm	**service area both lanes,** 🅖 Mobil/dsl 🍴 FoodCourt (sb), McDonald's
21 (23)	Mill Plain Rd, **E** 🅖 Citgo/dsl, Mobil/dsl 🍴 Avellino's Italian, DQ, Geronimo SW Grill, Kiraku Japanese, Rawley's Drive-In, Starbucks, Subway, Wilson's BBQ 🅞 Hemlock Hardware, Rite Aid
20 (22)	Bronson Rd (from sb)
19 (21)	US 1, Center St, **W** 🅖 BP, Shell/dsl 🍴 Athena Diner, Baskin-Robbins/Dunkin Donuts, Panera Bread, Subway 🛏 Westport Inn 🅞 Balducci's Mkt, Honda, Stop&Shop, TownFair Tire, Walgreens
18 (20)	to Westport, **E** 🅞 beaches, Sherwood Island SP, st police, **W** **1 mi on US 1** 🅖 Gulf, Mobil 🍴 Angelina's Trattoria, Arby's, Bertucci's Italian, Fresh Mkt, McDonald's, Sakura Japanese, Sherwood Diner, Starbucks, Subway 🅞 Barnes&Noble, Radio Shack, Toyota/Scion, URGENT CARE, Walgreens
17 (18)	CT 33, rd 136, Westport
16 (17)	E Norwalk, **E** 🅖 Citgo, Gulf, Mobil/dsl, Shell/dsl 🍴 Baskin-Robbins/Dunkin Donuts, Eastside Café, Penny's Diner, Subway 🅞 Rite Aid
15 (16)	US 7, to Danbury, Norwalk, **E** 🅖 Shell 🅞 Walgreens, **W** 🅖 Exxon, Sunoco
14 (15)	US 1, CT Ave, S Norwalk, **E** 🅞 st police, **W** 🅖 Shell/Dunkin Donuts 🍴 Burger King, Dunkin Donuts, Post Road Diner, Silver Star Diner, Subway, Wendy's 🅞 H, Barnes&Noble, Best Buy, CVS Drug, Kohl's, Old Navy, Petsmart, Radio Shack, same as 13, ShopRite Foods, Stop&Shop, TJ Maxx, TownFair Tire
13 (13)	US 1 (no EZ return), Post Rd, Norwalk, **W** 🅖 Mobil, Shell, Sunoco 🍴 American Steaks, Bertucci's, Chipotle Mexican, Darien Diner, Friendly's, KFC, McDonald's, Palmwich 🛏 DoubleTree Hotel 🅞 AT&T, Costco, Home Depot, Mini, same as 14, Staples, vet, Walmart
12.5mm	**service area nb, E** 🅖 Mobil/dsl 🍴 Dunkin Donuts, McDonald's, Subway
12 (12)	rd 136, Tokeneke Rd (from nb, no return), **W** 🍴 deli
11 (11)	US 1, Darien, **E** 🅖 Exxon 🛏 Chuck's Steaks 🅞 Chevrolet, Nissan, repair, vet, **W** 🅖 Gulf 🍴 Panera Bread 🅞 BMW, Whole Foods Mkt
10 (10)	Noroton, **W** 🅖 Shell, Standard 🅞 vet
9.5mm	**service area sb, W** 🅖 Mobil/dsl 🍴 McDonald's, Subway
9 (9)	US 1, rd 106, Glenbrook, **E** 🛏 Best Value Inn, **W** 🅖 Gulf 🍴 Dunkin Donuts, McDonald's, Subway 🅞 Advance Parts, Meineke
8 (8)	Atlantic Ave, Elm St, **E** 🅞 U-Haul, **W** 🅖 Sunoco 🛏 Marriott 🅞 H
7 (7)	CT 137, Atlantic Ave, **W** 🍴 PF Chang's 🛏 Hampton Inn, Marriott 🅞 Barnes&Noble, same as 8, USPO
6 (6)	Harvard Ave, West Ave, **E** 🅖 Gulf 🍴 City Limits Diner,

Vertical label: **NORWALK**

Exit #	Services
6 (6)	Continued Starbucks 🛏 La Quinta 🅞 Advance Parts, Petsmart, Subaru, USPO, **W** 🅖 Shell 🛏 Super 8 🅞 H
5 (5)	US 1, Riverside, Old Greenwich, **W** 🅖 BP, Mobil, Shell 🍴 Boston Mkt, Corner Deli, Hunan Cafe, McDonald's, Starbucks, Taco Bell, Valbello Ristorante 🛏 Hyatt Regency 🅞 A&P Mkt, CVS Drug, GNC, Staples, USPO, Walgreens
4 (4)	Indian Field Rd, Cos Cob, **W** 🅞 Bush-Holley House Museum
3 (3)	Arch St, Greenwich, **E** 🅞 Bruce Museum, **W** 🅖 Shell 🅞 H, Lexus
2mm	**weigh sta nb**
2 (1)	Delavan Ave, Byram
0mm	Connecticut/New York state line

Vertical label: **GREENWICH**

⬆N INTERSTATE 395

Exit #	Services
55.5mm	Connecticut/Massachusetts state line
100 (54)	E Thompson, to Wilsonville
99 (50)	rd 200, N Grosvenor Dale, **E** 🅞 W Thompson Lake Camping (seasonal)
98 (49)	to CT 12 (from nb, exits left), Grosvenor Dale, same as 99
97 (47)	US 44, to E Putnam, **E** 🍴 Dunkin Donuts, Empire Buffet, McDonald's/playplace, Subway, Wendy's 🅞 $Tree, Advance Parts, BigLots, CVS Drug, Giant Pizza, GNC, Radio Shack, Sears Essentials, Stop&Shop/gas, **W** 🅖 Shell/dsl/repair, Sunoco 🅞 Walmart/Subway
96 (46)	to CT 12, Putnam, **W** 🍴 Casa Mariachi 🛏 King's Inn 🅞 H
95 (45)	Kennedy Dr, to Putnam, **E** 🅞 Ford, **W** 🅞 H
94 (43)	Ballouville, **W** 🍴 Gold Eagle Rest. 🛏 Comfort Inn 🅞 truck parts
93 (41)	CT 101, to Dayville, **E** 🅖 Shell/dsl 🍴 Burger King, China Garden, Domino's, Dunkin Donuts, Nuccio's Pizza, Subway, Yamoto Japanese, Zip's Diner 🅞 $Tree, Aldi Foods, Walgreens, Wibberley Tire/repair, **W** 🅖 Mobil/dsl, Xtra/dsl 🍴 99 Rest., Dunkin Donuts, McDonald's, Mozzarella's Grill 🅞 AT&T, city park, GNC, Lowe's, Michael's, PetCo, Staples, Stop&Shop, Target, TJ Maxx, Verizon
92 (39)	to S Killingly, **W** 🍴 Dunkin Donuts, Giant Pizza 🅞 Bonneville Drug, st police
91 (38)	US 6 W, to Danielson, to Quinebaug Valley Coll
90 (36)	to US 6 E (from nb), to Providence
35mm	🆁🆂 **both lanes, full** ♿ **facilities,** 🅖 Mobil/dsl
89 (32)	CT 14, to Sterling, Central Village, **E** 🅖 Best Way, Gulf/repair 🍴 Johnny's Rest., Pizza Pizzaz 🅞 Rite Aid, RV camping, USPO, **W** 🅖 7-11/dsl, Shell/Dunkin Donuts/dsl 🍴 Music Lady Cafe, Subway 🛏 Knights Inn 🅞 transmissions
88 (30)	CT 14A to Plainfield, **E** 🅞 RV camping (seasonal), **W** 🅖 Mobil

Vertical label: **PUTNAM**

CT
DE

P L A I N F I E L D   N O R W I C H T O W N   M E R I D E N

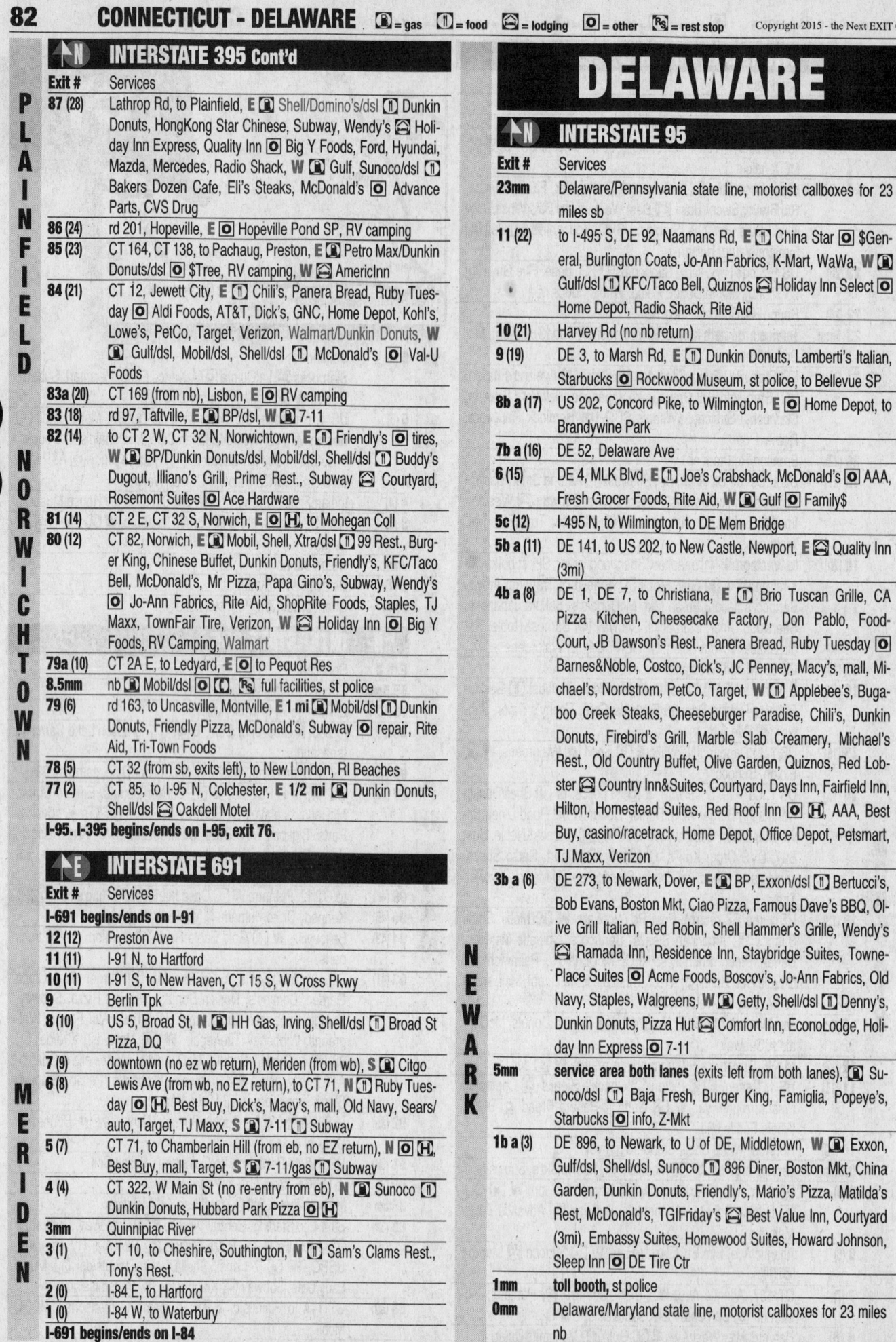

⬆N   INTERSTATE 395 Cont'd

Exit #	Services
87 (28)	Lathrop Rd, to Plainfield, E 🅖 Shell/Domino's/dsl 🍴 Dunkin Donuts, HongKong Star Chinese, Subway, Wendy's 🛏 Holiday Inn Express, Quality Inn 🅾 Big Y Foods, Ford, Hyundai, Mazda, Mercedes, Radio Shack, W 🅖 Gulf, Sunoco/dsl 🍴 Bakers Dozen Cafe, Eli's Steaks, McDonald's 🅾 Advance Parts, CVS Drug
86 (24)	rd 201, Hopeville, E 🅾 Hopeville Pond SP, RV camping
85 (23)	CT 164, CT 138, to Pachaug, Preston, E 🍴 Petro Max/Dunkin Donuts/dsl 🅾 $Tree, RV camping, W 🛏 AmericInn
84 (21)	CT 12, Jewett City, E 🍴 Chili's, Panera Bread, Ruby Tuesday 🅾 Aldi Foods, AT&T, Dick's, GNC, Home Depot, Kohl's, Lowe's, PetCo, Target, Verizon, Walmart/Dunkin Donuts, W 🅖 Gulf/dsl, Mobil/dsl, Shell/dsl 🍴 McDonald's 🅾 Val-U Foods
83a (20)	CT 169 (from nb), Lisbon, E 🅾 RV camping
83 (18)	rd 97, Taftville, E 🅖 BP/dsl, W 🅖 7-11
82 (14)	to CT 2 W, CT 32 N, Norwichtown, E 🍴 Friendly's 🅾 tires, W 🅖 BP/Dunkin Donuts/dsl, Mobil/dsl, Shell/dsl 🍴 Buddy's Dugout, Illiano's Grill, Prime Rest., Subway 🛏 Courtyard, Rosemont Suites 🅾 Ace Hardware
81 (14)	CT 2 E, CT 32 S, Norwich, E 🅾 🏥, to Mohegan Coll
80 (12)	CT 82, Norwich, E 🅖 Mobil, Shell, Xtra/dsl 🍴 99 Rest., Burger King, Chinese Buffet, Dunkin Donuts, Friendly's, KFC/Taco Bell, McDonald's, Mr Pizza, Papa Gino's, Subway, Wendy's 🅾 Jo-Ann Fabrics, Rite Aid, ShopRite Foods, Staples, TJ Maxx, TownFair Tire, Verizon, W 🛏 Holiday Inn 🅾 Big Y Foods, RV Camping, Walmart
79a (10)	CT 2A E, to Ledyard, E 🅾 to Pequot Res
8.5mm	nb 🅖 Mobil/dsl 🅾 🍴, 🆁🆂 full facilities, st police
79 (6)	rd 163, to Uncasville, Montville, E 1 mi 🅖 Mobil/dsl 🍴 Dunkin Donuts, Friendly Pizza, McDonald's, Subway 🅾 repair, Rite Aid, Tri-Town Foods
78 (5)	CT 32 (from sb, exits left), to New London, RI Beaches
77 (2)	CT 85, to I-95 N, Colchester, E 1/2 mi 🅖 Dunkin Donuts, Shell/dsl 🛏 Oakdell Motel
	I-95. I-395 begins/ends on I-95, exit 76.

⬆E   INTERSTATE 691

Exit #	Services
	I-691 begins/ends on I-91
12 (12)	Preston Ave
11 (11)	I-91 N, to Hartford
10 (11)	I-91 S, to New Haven, CT 15 S, W Cross Pkwy
9	Berlin Tpk
8 (10)	US 5, Broad St, N 🅖 HH Gas, Irving, Shell/dsl 🍴 Broad St Pizza, DQ
7 (9)	downtown (no ez wb return), Meriden (from wb), S 🅖 Citgo
6 (8)	Lewis Ave (from wb, no EZ return), to CT 71, N 🍴 Ruby Tuesday 🅾 🏥, Best Buy, Dick's, Macy's, mall, Old Navy, Sears/auto, Target, TJ Maxx, S 🅖 7-11 🍴 Subway
5 (7)	CT 71, to Chamberlain Hill (from eb, no EZ return), N 🅾 🏥, Best Buy, mall, Target, S 🅖 7-11/gas 🍴 Subway
4 (4)	CT 322, W Main St (no re-entry from eb), N 🅖 Sunoco 🍴 Dunkin Donuts, Hubbard Park Pizza 🅾 🏥
3mm	Quinnipiac River
3 (1)	CT 10, to Cheshire, Southington, N 🍴 Sam's Clams Rest., Tony's Rest.
2 (0)	I-84 E, to Hartford
1 (0)	I-84 W, to Waterbury
	I-691 begins/ends on I-84

DELAWARE

N E W A R K

⬆N   INTERSTATE 95

Exit #	Services
23mm	Delaware/Pennsylvania state line, motorist callboxes for 23 miles sb
11 (22)	to I-495 S, DE 92, Naamans Rd, E 🍴 China Star 🅾 $General, Burlington Coats, Jo-Ann Fabrics, K-Mart, WaWa, W 🅖 Gulf/dsl 🍴 KFC/Taco Bell, Quiznos 🛏 Holiday Inn Select 🅾 Home Depot, Radio Shack, Rite Aid
10 (21)	Harvey Rd (no nb return)
9 (19)	DE 3, to Marsh Rd, E 🍴 Dunkin Donuts, Lamberti's Italian, Starbucks 🅾 Rockwood Museum, st police, to Bellevue SP
8b a (17)	US 202, Concord Pike, to Wilmington, E 🅾 Home Depot, to Brandywine Park
7b a (16)	DE 52, Delaware Ave
6 (15)	DE 4, MLK Blvd, E 🍴 Joe's Crabshack, McDonald's 🅾 AAA, Fresh Grocer Foods, Rite Aid, W 🅖 Gulf 🅾 Family$
5c (12)	I-495 N, to Wilmington, to DE Mem Bridge
5b a (11)	DE 141, to US 202, to New Castle, Newport, E 🛏 Quality Inn (3mi)
4b a (8)	DE 1, DE 7, to Christiana, E 🍴 Brio Tuscan Grille, CA Pizza Kitchen, Cheesecake Factory, Don Pablo, FoodCourt, JB Dawson's Rest., Panera Bread, Ruby Tuesday 🅾 Barnes&Noble, Costco, Dick's, JC Penney, Macy's, mall, Michael's, Nordstrom, PetCo, Target, W 🍴 Applebee's, Bugaboo Creek Steaks, Cheeseburger Paradise, Chili's, Dunkin Donuts, Firebird's Grill, Marble Slab Creamery, Michael's Rest., Old Country Buffet, Olive Garden, Quiznos, Red Lobster 🛏 Country Inn&Suites, Courtyard, Days Inn, Fairfield Inn, Hilton, Homestead Suites, Red Roof Inn 🅾 🏥, AAA, Best Buy, casino/racetrack, Home Depot, Office Depot, Petsmart, TJ Maxx, Verizon
3b a (6)	DE 273, to Newark, Dover, E 🅖 BP, Exxon/dsl 🍴 Bertucci's, Bob Evans, Boston Mkt, Ciao Pizza, Famous Dave's BBQ, Olive Grill Italian, Red Robin, Shell Hammer's Grille, Wendy's 🛏 Ramada Inn, Residence Inn, Staybridge Suites, TownePlace Suites 🅾 Acme Foods, Boscov's, Jo-Ann Fabrics, Old Navy, Staples, Walgreens, W 🅖 Getty, Shell/dsl 🍴 Denny's, Dunkin Donuts, Pizza Hut 🛏 Comfort Inn, EconoLodge, Holiday Inn Express 🅾 7-11
5mm	service area both lanes (exits left from both lanes), 🅖 Sunoco/dsl 🍴 Baja Fresh, Burger King, Famiglia, Popeye's, Starbucks 🅾 info, Z-Mkt
1b a (3)	DE 896, to Newark, to U of DE, Middletown, W 🅖 Exxon, Gulf/dsl, Shell/dsl, Sunoco 🍴 896 Diner, Boston Mkt, China Garden, Dunkin Donuts, Friendly's, Mario's Pizza, Matilda's Rest., McDonald's, TGIFriday's 🛏 Best Value Inn, Courtyard (3mi), Embassy Suites, Homewood Suites, Howard Johnson, Sleep Inn 🅾 DE Tire Ctr
1mm	toll booth, st police
0mm	Delaware/Maryland state line, motorist callboxes for 23 miles nb

🔼N INTERSTATE 295 (Wilmington)

Exit #	Services
15mm	Delaware/New Jersey state line, Delaware River, Delaware Memorial Bridge
14.5mm	**toll plaza**
14	DE 9, New Castle Ave, to Wilmington, **E** 🅿 BP, Citgo 🍴 Giovanni's Cafe 🅾 Advance Parts, Family$, Firestone/auto, Harley-Davidson/rest., Rite Aid, SuperFresh Foods, **W** 🅿 Shell, Super/dsl 🍴 Dunkin Donuts, McDonald's 🛏 Budget Inn, Motel 6, SuperLodge
13	US 13, US 40, to New Castle, **E** 🅿 BP, Hess, Shell/dsl, Sunoco/dsl, WaWa 🍴 Applebee's, Arby's, Arner's Rest, Burger King, DogHouse, Dove Diner, Dunkin Donuts, Hadfield's Seafood, Hooters, IHOP, KFC, Lonestar Steaks, McDonald's, Pizza Hut, Popeye's, Season's Pizza, Subway, Taco Bell, TGIFriday's, Wendy's 🛏 EconoLodge, Quality Inn, Super 8 🅾 $Tree, 7-11, Acura, AutoZone, BJ's Whse/gas, Chevrolet, Chrysler/Jeep/Dodge, Cottman Transmissions, Fiat, Ford, Home Depot, Hyundai, Lincoln, Mazda, Nissan, PathMark Foods, PepBoys, Radio Shack, repair, Ross, Save-a-Lot, Staples, Toyota/Scion, Walgreens, Walmart, **W** 🅿 WaWa/dsl 🍴 Dunkin Donuts 🛏 Clarion 🅾 Ford Trucks, Freightliner, Lowe's
12	I-495, US 202, N to Wilmington
	I-295 begins/ends on I-95

🔼N INTERSTATE 495

Exit #	Services
11mm	I-95 N. **I-495 begins/ends on I-95.**
5 (10)	US 13, Phila Pike, Claymont, **W** 🅿 BP, Exxon/dsl, Sunoco/dsl 🍴 Arby's, Boston Mkt, Dunkin Donuts, McDonald's 🛏 Milan Motel 🅾 Family$, Food Lion, USPO
4 (5)	US 13, rd 3, Edgemoor Rd, to Fox Point Park
3 (4)	12th St
2 (3)	rd 9A, Terminal Ave, Port of Wilmington
1 (1)	US 13, **E** 🅿 WaWa/dsl 🍴 Dunkin Donuts 🛏 Clarion 🅾 Ford Trucks, Lowe's
0mm	I-95 S. **I-495 begins/ends on I-95.**

FLORIDA

🔼E INTERSTATE 4

Exit #	Services
132	I-95, S to Miami, N to Jacksonville, FL 400. **I-4 begins/ends on I-95, exit 260b**
129	to US 92 (from eb, exits left)
126mm	🆁🆂 eb, litter barrels, 🚻, no security
118	FL 44, to DeLand, N 🅿 BP/dsl 🛏 Howard Johnson 🅾 🅷
116	Orange Camp Rd, Lake Helen
114	FL 472, to DeLand, Orange City, N 🅾 Clark Campground (1mi), to Blue Sprgs SP
111b a	Deltona, N 🅿 Hess/dsl, RaceTrac/dsl, Shell/Circle K 🍴 Baskin-Robbins/Dunkin Donuts, Bob Evans, Chick-fil-A, Chili's, Denny's, Jimmy John's, KFC, Papa John's, Perkins, Pizza Hut, Quiznos, Ruby Tuesday, Sonic, Sonny's BBQ, Steak'n Shake, Subway, Taco Bell, Tijuana Flats, Zaxby's 🛏 Holiday Inn Express 🅾 🅷, $General, Firestone/auto, Home Depot, Lowe's, Office Depot, Publix/deli, Save-A-Lot Foods, Tire Kingdom, Tires+, URGENT CARE, Verizon, Walgreens,

SANFORD (vertical)

Exit #	Services
111b a	Continued Walmart, **S** 🅿 Chevron/repair 🍴 Wendy's 🅾 Family$, Publix, Walgreens
108	Dirksen Dr, DeBary, Deltona, N 🅿 Chevron 🍴 Burger King, IHOP 🛏 Hampton Inn, **S** 🅿 Kangaroo 🍴 McDonald's, Subway, Waffle House 🛏 Best Western 🅾 Publix (2mi)
104	US 17, US 92, Sanford, N 🍴 Captains Cove Rest. 🅾 La Mesa RV Ctr, **S** 🅿 Citgo/Subway
101c	rd 46, to Mt Dora, Sanford, N 🅿 7-11 🍴 Tijuana Flats 🅾 Ace Hardware, Ford, **S** 🅿 7-11, Chevron/dsl, Mobil, Murphy USA/dsl, RaceTrac 🍴 Baskin-Robbins/Dunkin Donuts, Big Boy, Burger King, Cracker Barrel, Denny's, Don Pablo, Firehouse Subs, Hooters, Joe's Crabshack, LJ Silver/Taco Bell, Logan's Roadhouse, McDonald's, Olive Garden, Outback Steaks, Panda Express, Panera Bread, Red Brick Pizza, Red Lobster, Rte 46 Smokehouse, Smokey Bones BBQ, Steak'n Shake, Subway, Wendy's 🛏 Comfort Inn, Days Inn, SpringHill Suites, Super 8 🅾 🅷, $Tree, Aldi Foods, Beall's, Belk, Best Buy, Big 10 Tire, BJ's Whse/gas, Books-A-Million, CVS Drug, Dillard's,

FL

HEATHROW

ALTAMONTE SPGS

ORLANDO

⬆ E   INTERSTATE 4 Cont'd

Exit #	Services
101c	Continued
	GNC, Goodyear/auto, Harley-Davidson, JC Penney, Jo-Ann Fabrics, Macy's, mall, Marshall's, Michael's, Old Navy, PetCo, Ross, Sears/auto, Target, Tire Kingdom, Tuffy Auto, URGENT CARE, Verizon, Walmart, World Mkt
101a b	rd 46a, FL 417 (toll), FL 46, Sanford, Heathrow, N 🅕 Applebee's, Carlos'n Charley's, Crisper's, FishBones, Moe's SW Grill, Papa Joe's Pizza, Rikka Asian Bistro, Ruth's Chris Steaks, Shula's 347 Grill, Subway, Vamonos ⌂ Hampton Inn, Marriott, Residence Inn, Westin 🅞 Publix, URGENT CARE, Walgreens, S 🅞 7-11, Acura, CarMax, CVS Drug, Honda, Kohl's, Sam's Club/gas, Toyota/Scion
98	Lake Mary Blvd, Heathrow, N 🅖 Shell 🅕 Luigino's Italian, Panera Bread, Peach Valley Cafe, Stonewood Grill, Subway ⌂ Courtyard, Hyatt Place 🅞 CVS Drug, Verizon, Walgreens, Winn-Dixie, S 🅖 7-11, BP/24hr, Chevron/24hr, Citgo, Mobil/dsl 🅕 Arby's, Baskin-Robbins/Dunkin Donuts, Bob Evans, Boston Mkt, Burger King, Checkers, Chick-fil-A, Chili's, Chipotle Mexican, Chop Stix, Domino's, Firehouse Subs, Frank&Naomi's, KFC, Krystal, Longhorn Steaks, Macaroni Grill, McDonald's, Panera Bread, Papa Joe's Pizza, Papa John's, Pizza Hut/Taco Bell, Quiznos, Starbucks, Steak'n Shake, Subway, Taste of China, Uno, Wendy's, WingZone ⌂ Candlewood Suites, Extended Stay America, Hilton Garden, Homestead Suites, Homewood Suites, La Quinta 🅞 Advance Parts, Albertsons, AT&T, Family$, Gander Mtn, Goodyear, Home Depot, K-Mart, mall, Office Depot, Petsmart, Publix, Radio Shack, Staples, Target, Tires+, TJ Maxx, USPO, vet, Walgreens
95mm	Ⓡs both lanes, 24hr security, full ♿ facilities, litter barrels, petwalk, 🅒, 🅡s, vending
94	FL 434, to Winter Springs, Longwood, N 🅖 7-11, Hess/dsl, Mobil/dsl 🅕 Burger King, East Buffet, Imperial Dynasty, Kobe Japanese, Melting Pot Rest., Miami Subs, Panera Bread, Papa Joe's Pizza, Starbucks, Tijuana Flats, Wendy's ⌂ Comfort Inn 🅞 CVS Drug, Publix, S 🅕 Bonefish Grill, Boston Mkt, Carmela's Rest., Crisper's, Pickle's NY ⌂ Candlewood Suites 🅞 Ⓗ
92	FL 436, Altamonte Springs, N 🅖 7-11, Shell/Circle K/dsl 🅕 Bojangles, Boston Mkt, Checkers, Chick-fil-A, Chipotle Mexican, ChuckeCheese, Cracker Barrel, Kobe Japanese, Little Caesars, Longhorn Steaks, McDonald's, Olive Garden, Perkins, Pollo Tropical, Popeye's, Red Lobster, Sweet Tomatoes, Taco Bell, TGIFriday's, Waffle House, WingHouse ⌂ Days Inn, Hampton Inn, Hotel Altamonte, Quality Suites, Remington Inn, Residence Inn, SpringHill Suites 🅞 Best Buy, CVS Drug, Family$, Firestone/auto, Goodyear/auto, Tire Kingdom, U-Haul, URGENT CARE, Walgreens, S 🅖 BP, Citgo, Hess/dsl, Mobil/dsl 🅕 5 Guys Burgers, Bahama Breeze, Burger King, Chili's, Denny's, Dunkin Donuts, Elephant Bar, Jason's Deli, Mimi's Cafe, Moe's SW Grill, Orlando Alehouse, Panda Express, Pizza Hut, Starbucks, Steak'n Shake, Subway, Wendy's ⌂ Embassy Suites, Hilton, Homestead Suites 🅞 Ⓗ Advance Parts, Albertsons, Barnes&Noble, CVS Drug, Dillard's, JC Penney, Marshall's, Michael's, Office Depot, PetCo, Publix, Ross, Sears/auto, TJMaxx, vet
90b a	FL 414, Maitland Blvd, N 🅖 7-11 🅕 Applebee's, Chick-fil-A, Oak Grill, Wendy's ⌂ Extended Stay America, Extended Stay Deluxe, Homewood Suites, Sheraton, S 🅞 Maitland Art Ctr

88	FL 423, Lee Rd, N 🅖 7-11 🅕 Arby's, Burger King, Del Frisco, IHOP, Little Caesars, LJ Silver/Taco Bell, McDonald's, Nick&Gina's Italian, Popeye's, Quiznos ⌂ Countryside Inn, InTown Suites, La Quinta, Motel 6 🅞 Aamco, Family$, Firestone/auto, Home Depot, Land Rover, Mini, Ross, Save-A-Lot Foods, Tires+, VW, S 🅖 Chevron/dsl, Sunoco 🅕 Denny's 🅞 BMW
87	FL 426, Fairbanks Ave (no eb re-entry), N 🅖 Hess/Blimpie/Dunkin Donuts/Godfather's/dsl, S 1 mi 🅕 Burger King, Chick-fil-A, Chipotle Mexican, Pizza Hut/Taco Bell, Popeye's, Steak'n Shake, Subway, Wendy's 🅞 Walgreens
86	Par St (from eb, no re-entry), S 🅖 Shell/Circle K
85	Princeton St, S 🅖 7-11, Chevron 🅞 Ⓗ
84	FL 50, Colonial Dr, Ivanhoe Blvd, N ⌂ Crowne Plaza
83b	US 17, US 92, FL 50, Amelia St (from eb), N ⌂ Crowne Plaza
83a	FL 526 (from eb), Robinson St, N ⌂ Sheraton
83	South St (from wb), downtown
82c	Anderson St E, Church St Sta Hist Dist, downtown
82b	Gore Ave (from wb), S 🅞 Ⓗ, downtown
82a	FL 408 (toll), to FL 526
81b c	Kaley Ave, S 🅖 Mobil 🅞 Ⓗ
81a	Michigan St (from wb), N 🅖 Citgo/dsl
80b a	US 17, US 441 S, US 92 W, S 🅖 Chevron, Citgo, RaceTrac, Shell, Sunoco 🅕 Checkers, Gyros, McDonald's, Subway ⌂ Days Inn 🅞 Aldi Foods, AutoZone, Goodyear/auto, Save-A-Lot Foods, Walgreens
79	FL 423, 33rd St, John Young Pkwy, N ⌂ Ramada Inn 🅞 Harley-Davidson, S 🅖 RaceTrac/dsl 🅕 IHOP ⌂ Days Inn
78	Conroy Rd, N 🅖 7-11, S 🅕 BJ's Rest., Bloomingdale's, Elephant Bar Rest., Green's Grill, Krispy Kreme, McDonald's, Mimi's Cafe, Moe's SW Grill, Olive Garden, Panda Express, Pollo Tropical, Subway, TGIFriday's, Village Tavern, Waffle Shop, Wendy's, Zaxby's 🅞 $Tree, AT&T, Best Buy, BJ's Whse, Dick's, Home Depot, Infiniti/Smart, Macy's, mall, Marshall's, Mercedes, Old Navy, PetCo, Super Target
77	FL 527, FL TPK (toll)
75b a	FL 435, International Dr (exits left from both lanes), N 🅖 Mobil 🅕 Cracker Barrel, Denny's, TGIFriday's ⌂ Days Inn, DoubleTree Motel, Fairfield Inn, Holiday Inn, Hyatt Place 🅞 to Universal Studios, S 🅖 7-11, Chevron 🅕 Bamboo Rest., Black Angus Steaks, Denny's, Great Western Steaks, IHOP, Ponderosa, Red Lobster, Sizzler, Sweet Tomatoes ⌂ Best Western, Clarion, Court of Flags Hotel, EconoLodge, Hampton Inn, Hilton Garden, Holiday Inn Express, Homewood Suites, Howard Johnson, International Gateway Inn, Lakefront Inn, Las Palmas Hotel, Motel 6, multiple hotels & resorts, Rodeway Inn, Sheraton, Super 8 🅞 Bass Pro Shops, Belz Outlet/famous Brands, Books A Million, Office Depot, Walgreens
74b	Universal Studios (from wb)
74a	FL 482, Sand Lake Rd, N 🅖 7-11, Chevron 🅕 Alexander's Rest., Chick-fil-A, McDonald's, multiple restaurants, Timpano Italian, Wendy's ⌂ Comfort Suites 🅞 K-Mart, Publix, Walgreens, Walmart, Whole Food Mkt, S 🅖 7-11, BP, Chevron, Mobil, Shell/Circle K/dsl 🅕 Asian Buffet, Bahama Breeze, Buffalo Wild Wings, Burger King, Cattleman's Steaks, Charley's Steaks, Checkers, Chili's, China Jade, CiCi's Pizza, Crabhouse, Denny's, Fish Bones Rest., Friendly's, Golden Corral, Houlihan's, IHOP, Italianni's, Kobe Japanese, Lobster Feast, McDonald's, Miller's Alehouse, Ming Court, Olive Garden, Perkins, Pizza Hut, Ponderosa, Popeye's, Sizzler, TGIFriday's, Tony Roma's, Uno, Vito's Chophouse, Wendy's, Wild Bean Cafe ⌂ Best Western, Castle Hotel, Comfort Inn,

🄴 INTERSTATE 4 Cont'd

Exit #	Services

ORLANDO

74a Continued
Courtyard, Crowne Plaza, EconoLodge, Embassy Suites, Fairfield Inn, Hampton Inn, Holiday Inn, Homewood Suites, Howard Johnson, Hyatt Place, La Quinta, Marriott, Masters Inn, Microtel, Peabody Hotel, Quality Inn, Radisson Inn, Ramada Inn, Red Roof Inn, Residence Inn, Rodeway Inn, Rosen Suites, Staybridge Suites, Wyndham Garden 🅞 🅗, Harley-Davidson, Ripley's Believe-it-or-not!, RV Park, Stouffer Resort, Walgreens

72 FL 528 E **(toll, no eb re-entry)**, to Cape Canaveral, **N** 🅞 USPO, **S** 🅞 to 🛩

71 Central FL Pkwy (from eb no re-entry), **S** 🅖 Chevron 🅕 Wendy's 🅛 Hilton Garden, Renaissance Resort, Residence Inn, to SeaWorld

68 FL 535, Lake Buena Vista, **N** 🅖 7-11, Mobil/dsl, Shell/Circle K/dsl 🅕 AleHouse, Amici Italian, Black Angus Steaks, Buffalo Wild Wings, Burger King, Chevy's Mexican, Chili's, China Buffet, CiCi's Pizza, Denny's, Dragon Super Buffet, El Patron, Flipper's Pizzaria, Fuddrucker's, Giordano's, Havana's Cuisine, Hooters, IHOP, Joe's Crabshack, Johnnie's Rest., Kobe Japanese, Macaroni Grill, McDonald's, Olive Garden, Perkins, Pizza Hut, Qdoba, Quiznos, Red Lobster, Shoney's, Sizzler, Steak'n Shake, Subway, Sweet Tomatoes, Taco Bell, TGIFriday's, The Crabhouse, Uno 🅛 Comfort Inn, Country Inn&Suites, Courtyard, DoubleTree, Embassy Suites, Extended Stay Deluxe, Hampton Inn, Hawthorn Suites, Hilton, Hilton Gargen, Holiday Inn, Holiday Inn Express, Homewood Suites, Hyatt Hotel, Orlando Vista Hotel, Quality Inn, Radisson, Residence Inn, Sheraton, StayBridge Suites 🅞 Gooding's Foods/drug, USPO, Walgreens, **S** 🅖 7-11, Chevron, Shell/dsl 🅕 Applebee's, Bahama Breeze, Carrabba's, Chick-fil-A, CiCi's Pizza, Dunkin Donuts, Golden Corral, Landry's Seafood, LoneStar Steaks, Panera Bread, Santa Fe Steaks, Starbucks, Wendy's 🅛 Blue Heron Resort, Buena Vista Suites, Courtyard, Fairfield Inn, Holiday Inn Resort, Marriott Village, Residence Inn, Sheraton, SpringHill Suites 🅞 CVS Drug, Orlando Premium Outlets, Verizon, Walgreens

67 FI 536, to Epcot, **N** 🅞 DisneyWorld, **S 1 mi** 🅖 7-11 🅕 Asian Harbor 🅛 Buena Vista, Marriott 🅞 CVS Drug, multiple resorts, to 🛩

65 Osceola Pkwy, to FL 417 **(toll)**, **N** 🅞 Animal Kingdom, Epcot, to DisneyWorld, Wide World of Sports

64b a US 192, FL 536, to FL 417 **(toll)**, to Kissimmee, **N** 🅖 7-11, MGM, to DisneyWorld, **S 0-3 mi** 🅖 7-11, Mobil/dsl, RaceTrac/dsl 🅕 Applebee's, Arby's, Bob Evans, Boston Lobster Feast, Burger King, Charley's Steakhouse, Checkers, Chick-fil-A, Chili's, Chinese Buffet, CiCi's Pizza, Cracker Barrel, Denny's, Domino's, Dunkin Donuts, Golden Corral, IHOP, Joe's Crabshack, Kabuki Oriental, KFC, Kobe Japanese, Krispy

ORLANDO

64b a Continued
Kreme, Logan's Roadhouse, Longhorn Steaks, Macaroni Grill, McDonald's, Ocean 11 Rest., Olive Garden, Pacino's Italian, Panda Express, Papa John's, Perkins, Pizza Hut, Ponderosa, Quiznos, Red Lobster, Rio Mexican Grill, Ruby Tuesday, Sizzlin Grill, Smokey Bones BBQ, Starbucks, Subway, Taco Bell, TGIFriday's, Uno, Waffle House, Wendy's 🅛 Best Inn, Celebration Suites, Comfort Suites, Days Inn, Holiday Inn, Howard Johnson, Knight Inn, Masters Inn, Mona Lisa Hotel, Motel 6, Orlando Palms, Parkway Resort, Quality Suites, Radisson, Ramada, Red Roof Inn, Rodeway Inn, Seralago Hotel, Sun Inn, Super 8, Travelodge 🅞 🅗, $General, AT&T, Camping World RV Ctr, CVS Drug, factory outlet/famous brands, Harley-Davidson, Jo-Ann Fabrics, Marshall's, Publix, Target, USPO, Walgreens

62 FL 417 **(toll, from eb)**, World Dr, **N** 🅞 to DisneyWorld, **S** 🅞 Celebration, to 🛩

60 FI 429 N **(toll)**, Apopka

58 FL 532, to Kissimmee, **N** 🅖 7-11, BP 🅕 Chili's, China One, McDonald's, Pizzaria, Subway 🅛 Championship Gate Resort 🅞 Publix, Walgreens, **S** 🅕 Dunkin Donuts (1mi) 🅛 Reunion Resort (2mi)

= gas   = food   = lodging   = other   = rest stop   Copyright 2015 - the Next EXIT ®

INTERSTATE 4 Cont'd

Exit #	Services
55	US 27, to Haines City, N 7-11, Sunoco/dsl Burger King, Cracker Barrel, Denny's, McDonald's, Waffle House, Wendy's Comfort Inn, Hampton Inn, Holiday Inn Express, Super 8 FL Camp Inn (5mi), Ford, S 7-11, BP/dsl, Marathon, RaceWay/dsl, Shell/dsl/service Bob Evans, CiCi's Pizza, Grand China, Perkins, Sake Steaks, Subway Days Inn, Microtel, Quality Inn, Southgate Inn , \$Tree, Belk, Best Buy, Books-A-Million, Deer Creek RV Resort, Dick's, GNC, JC Penney, KOA, Michael's, Petsmart, Ross, Staples, Target, Theme World RV Park, to Cypress Gardens, tourist info, Verizon
48	rd 557, to Winter Haven, Lake Alfred, S BP/dsl
46mm	both lanes, 24hr security, full facilities, litter barrels, petwalk, , , vending
44	FL 559, to Auburndale, S BP/dsl/scales/24hr, Loves/Arby's/dsl/scales/24hr
41	FL 570 W toll, Auburndale, Lakeland
38	FL 33, to Lakeland, Polk City
33	rd 582, to FL 33, Lakeland, N 7-11, BP, Exxon/24hr 5 Guys Burger, Applebee's, Cracker Barrel, McDonald's, Starbucks, Wendy's Country Inn&Suites, Crestwood Suites, Days Inn, Hampton Inn, Jameson Inn, La Quinta, Quality Inn, Ramada, Sleep Inn BMW, CVS Drug, GNC, Publix, S BP/dsl Waffle House ValuePlace , Harley-Davidson, Lakeland RV Resort, Nissan
32	US 98, Lakeland, N 7-11, BP, Mobil, Murphy USA/dsl Asian Buffet, Checkers, Chili's, ChuckeCheese, CiCi's Pizza, Domino's, DQ, Dunkin Donuts, Golden Corral, Hooters, IHOP, KFC, Ling's Buffet, LJ Silver, McDonald's, Moe's SW Grill, Olive Garden, Outback Steaks, Panera Bread, Papa John's, Place Garden, Red Lobster, Smokey Bones BBQ, Sonny's BBQ, Starbucks, Steak'n Shake, Subway, Taco Bell, TGIFriday's, Wendy's, Zaxby's Comfort Inn, La Quinta, Royalty Inn \$General, (2mi), Advance Parts, Aldi Foods, AT&T, AutoZone, Barnes&Noble, Beall's, Belk, Best Buy, CVS Drug, Dillard's, Firestone/auto, Goodyear/auto, JC Penney, JoAnn Fabrics, Lowe's, Macy's, PepBoys, PetCo, Publix, Sam's Club/gas, Sears/auto, Staples, Sweetbay Foods, Target, Tire Kingdom, Tires+, Verizon, vet, Walgreens, Walmart, S 7-11, Coastal, RaceTrac/dsl, Sunoco/dsl Bob Evans, Burger King, Denny's, LJ Silver, McDonald's, Popeye's, Waffle House Howard Johnson, Motel 6 , AutoZone, Beall's, Chrysler/Dodge, Family\$, Home Depot, NAPA, U-Haul
31	FL 539, to Kathleen, Lakeland, N Shell/Circle K Romeo's Pizza, Suwbay, Wendy's Publix/dsl, Walgreens, S hist dist
28	FL 546, to US 92, Memorial Blvd, Lakeland (from eb re-entry), S Shell/Circle K/dsl, Sunoco Hardee's
27	FL 570 E toll, Lakeland
25	County Line Rd, S Citgo/dsl, Shell/Circle K/Subway McDonald's, Wendy's Fairfield Inn FL Air Museum
22	FL 553, Park Rd, Plant City, N Chevrolet, S Shell/Circle K/Subway Arby's, Burger King, Denny's, Popeye's Comfort Inn, Holiday Inn Express
21	FL 39, Alexander St, to Zephyrhills, Plant City, S on FL 39 BP/dsl, Shell/dsl Days Inn, Red Rose Inn/rest.
19	FL 566, to Thonotosassa, N BP, S RaceTrac/dsl Applebee's, BuddyFreddy's Rest., Carrabba's, Lin's Chinese, Little Caesars, McDonald's, Mi Casa, OutBack Steaks, Pizza Hut/Taco Bell, Sonny's BBQ, Starbucks, Subway, Waffle

MANGO / TAMPA / JACKSONVILLE (vertical side labels)

Exit #	Services
19	Continued House , \$General, AT&T, Publix, Walgreens
17	Branch Forbes Rd, N Marathon, Sunoco Dinosaur World, S BP, Shell/Circle K/Subway/dsl Advance Parts, AutoZone
14	McIntosh Rd, N BP/dsl Longview RV Ctr, Windward RV Park (2mi), S 7-11/dsl, RaceWay/dsl Burger King, McDonald's/playplace Bates RV Ctr, East Tampa RV Park
12mm	both lanes, weigh sta
10	rd 579, Mango, Thonotosassa, N FLYING J/Denny's/dsl/LP/scales/24hr, Sunoco, TA/Arby's/Popeye's/dsl/scales/24hr/@ Bob Evans, Cracker Barrel Country Inn&Suites, Hampton Inn Camping World RV Ctr, Ford/Lincoln, Hillsboro River SP, Lazy Day's RV Ctr, Rally RV Park, S Shell/Circle K/dsl Hardee's, Subway, Wendy's Masters Inn
9	I-75, N to Ocala, S to Naples
7	US 92W, to US 301, Hillsborough Ave, N Chevron/dsl, Mobil Waffle House Hard Rock Hotel/casino, Knights Inn, S BP, Citgo, Hess/Dunkin Donuts/Quiznos 5 Guys Burgers, WingHouse Comfort Suites, Holiday Inn Express, La Quinta, Red Roof Inn FL Expo Fair
6	Orient Rd (from eb)
5	FL 574, MLK Blvd, N McDonald's truck/rv wash, S BP, Mobil, Sunoco/Subway Wendy's Fairfield Inn Kenworth
3	US 41, 50th St, Columbus Dr (exits left from eb), N Chevron/dsl, Shell/Subway/dsl Best Value Inn, Days Inn, Quality Inn to Busch Gardens, S Sunoco/dsl Checkers, Church's, KFC, McDonald's, Salem's Subs, Subway, Taco Bell Howard Johnson Advance Parts, Family\$, Save-A-Lot, Sweetbay Foods, URGENT CARE
1	FL 585, 22nd, 21st St, Port of Tampa, S Sunoco Burger King, McDonald's museum
0mm	I-4 begins/ends on I-275, exit 45b.

INTERSTATE 10

Exit #	Services
363mm	I-10 begins/ends on I-95, exit 351b.
362	Stockton St, to Riverside, S BP, Gate
361	US 17 S (from wb), S BP, Gate
360	FL 129, McDuff Ave, S BP Popeye's
359	Luna St, to Lenox Ave (from wb)
358	FL 111, Cassat Ave, N Hess/Godfather's/Quiznos/dsl, Shell/Subway/dsl Burger King, McDonald's, Popeye's, Wendy's AutoZone, Mr Transmission, S BP, RaceWay/dsl Baskin-Robbins/Dunkin Donuts, Domino's, Gorgi's BBQ, Pizza Hut, Taco Bell, Wendy's Advance Parts, Discount Tire, Lowe's, Walgreens
357	FL 103, Lane Ave, N Hess/dsl Andy's Sandwiches Knights Inn, Stars Rest Inn, S BP, Shell/dsl Applebee's, Cross Creek Steaks, Hardee's, KFC, Lee's Dragon, McDonald's, Piccadilly's Diamond Inn, Executive Inn, Sleep Inn Carquest, CVS Drug, Firestone/auto, Home Depot, Office Depot, PepBoys
356	I-295, N to Savannah, S to St Augustine
355	Marietta, N Exxon, S Hess/Dunkin Donuts/Godfather's/Quiznos/dsl, Shell/dsl Domino's
351	FL 115, Chaffee Rd, to Cecil Fields, N Kangaroo/dsl Rivers RV Ctr, S Chevron, KwikChek, Shell/Subway/dsl Cracker Barrel, King Wok, McDonald's, Mr Chubby's Wings, Perard's Italian, Wendy's Best Western, Fairfield Inn, Hampton Inn, Holiday Inn Express Family\$, Winn-Dixie

FL (side tab)

🔼E	**INTERSTATE 10 Cont'd**
Exit #	**Services**
350	FL 23, Cecil Commerce Ctr Pkwy
343	US 301, to Starke, Baldwin, **S** 🅖 Chevron, ▦/Subway/dsl/scales/24hr, TA/Shell/Arby's/dsl/scales/24hr/@ 🍴 Burger King, McDonald's, Waffle House 🛏 Best Western 🅞 NAPA
336	FL 228, to Maxville, Macclenny, **N** 🅖 Murphy USA/dsl 🍴 Starbucks 🅞 H, fireworks, Walmart/Subway
335	FL 121, to Lake Butler, Macclenny, **N** 🅖 BP/dsl, Kangaroo 🍴 China Dragon, Crystal River Seafood, Domino's, Hardee's, KFC, McDonald's, Pier 6, Pizza Hut, Subway, Taco Bell, Waffle House, Wendy's, Woody's BBQ, Zaxby's 🛏 American Inn 🅞 H, $General, $Tree, Advance Parts, AutoZone, repair, Save-A-Lot Foods, USPO, Verizon, Walgreens, Winn-Dixie, **S** 🅖 Exxon/dsl, RaceWay/dsl 🍴 Burger King, China Buffet, San Jose Mexican 🛏 EconoLodge, Travelodge
333	rd 125, Glen Saint Mary, **N** 🅖 Citgo/dsl/24hr
327	rd 229, to Raiford, Sanderson, **N** 1 mi 🅖 gas
324	US 90, to Olustee, Sanderson, **S** 🅖 Citgo/dsl, Osceola NF, to Olustee Bfd
318mm	🅡🅢 both lanes, 24hr security, full ♿ facilities, litter barrels, petwalk, 🅒, 🐾, vending
303	US 441, Lake City, **N** 🅖 Chevron/dsl 🅞 Lake City Camping (1mi), Oaks'n Pines RV Park, **S** 🅖 Shell/dsl, Sunoco/dsl 🍴 Huddle House 🛏 Days Inn 🅞 H
301	US 41, to Lake City, **N** 🅖 Busy Bee/dsl 🅞 to Stephen Foster Ctr, **S** 🅞 H
296b a	I-75, N to Valdosta, S to Tampa
294mm	🅡🅢 both lanes, 24hr security, full ♿ facilities, litter barrels, petwalk, 🅒, 🐾, vending
292	rd 137, to Wellborn
283	US 129, to Live Oak, **N** 🅖 Penn/dsl, to Boys Ranch, **S** 🅖 BP, Chevron/dsl, Exxon/dsl, Murphy USA/dsl, Shell/dsl 🍴 China Buffet, Huddle House, Krystal, McDonald's, Subway, Taco Bell, Waffle House, Wendy's, Zaxby's 🛏 Best Western, EconoLodge, Holiday Inn Express 🅞 H, $Tree, Lowe's, Verizon, Walmart
275	US 90, Live Oak, **N** 🅞 to Suwannee River SP, **S** 🅞 H
271mm	truck insp sta both lanes
269mm	Suwannee River
265mm	🅡🅢 both lanes, 24hr security, full ♿ facilities, litter barrels, petwalk, 🅒, 🐾, vending
264mm	weigh sta both lanes
262	rd 255, Lee, **N** 🅞 to Suwannee River SP, **S** 🅖 Jimmy's/Chevron/Red Onion Grill/dsl/scales/24hr/@, Loves, Arby's/dsl/scales/24hr
258	FL 53, **N** 🅖 Chevron/McDonald's/dsl, Mobil/DQ/Subway/Wendy's/dsl/scales/24hr 🍴 Denny's, Waffle House 🛏 Best Western, Days Inn, Super 8 🅞 H, **S** 🛏 Deerwood Inn 🅞 Jellystone Camping, Madison Camping
251	FL 14, to Madison, **N** 🅖 Mobil/Arby's/24hr 🅞 H
241	US 221, Greenville, **N** 🅖 Mobil/DQ
234mm	🅡🅢 both lanes, 24hr security, full ♿ facilities, litter barrels, petwalk, 🅒, 🐾
233	rd 257, Aucilla, **N** 🅖 Shell/dsl
225	US 19, to Monticello, **N** 🅞 Camper's World Camping, **S** 🅖 BP, Chevron/McDonald's/dsl, Mobil/Arby's/dsl, Sunoco/dsl 🍴 Huddle House 🛏 Days Inn, Super 8 🅞 A Stones Throw RV Park, dogtrack, KOA
217	FL 59, Lloyd, **S** 🅖 BP/rest/dsl/scales/24hr, Shell/Subway/dsl 🛏 EconoLodge 🅞 truckwash
209b a	US 90, Tallahassee, **N** 🛏 Staybrige Suites, **S** 🅖 Circle K/

209b a	Continued dsl, Shell/Subway/dsl 🍴 Eastern Chinese, Waffle House 🛏 Best Western, Country Inn&Suites 🅞 auto museum, Publix, Tallahassee RV Park
203	FL 61, US 319, Tallahassee, **N** 🅖 BP/dsl, Shell/Circle K, USA 🍴 5 Guys Burgers, Applebee's, Baskin-Robbins/Dunkin Donuts, Bonefish Grill, Firehouse Subs, Genghis Grill, Jimmy John's, McDonald's, Moe's SW Grill, Panda Buffet, Panera Bread, Popeye's, Sonny's BBQ, Starbucks, Subway, Taco Bell, Waffle House, Wendy's 🅞 $Tree, (3mi), AT&T, Books-A-Million, CVS Drug, Discount Tire, Fresh Mkt Foods, GNC, Hobby Lobby, Publix, Radio Shack, SteinMart, SuperLube, TJ Maxx, Walgreens, Walmart, **S** 🅖 BP, Citgo 🍴 Calico Jack's Oyster Bar, Carrabba's, Chick-fil-A, Los Amigos, McDonald's, Osaka Japanese, Outback Steaks, Steak'n Shake, Subway, Ted's MT Grill, TGIFriday's, Village Inn, Zaxby's 🛏 Cabot Lodge, Courtyard, Hampton Inn, Hilton Garden, Residence Inn, Sheraton, Studio+ 🅞 H, Advance Parts, Goodyear/auto, Home Depot, Infiniti, Office Depot, Petsmart, U-Haul, URGENT CARE, vet
199	US 27, Tallahassee, **N** 🅖 Chevron/dsl, Kangaroo/dsl, McKen-zie/dsl 🍴 Burger King, Domino's, McDonald's, Papa John's, Pizza Hut, Subway, Taco Bell, Waffle House 🛏 Baymont Inn, Country Inn&Suites, Days Inn, Fairfield Inn, Holiday Inn, Microtel, Quality Inn 🅞 $General, Ace Hardware, Advance Parts, Big Oak RV Park (2mi), CVS Drug, Family$, USPO, vet, Walgreens, Walmart, Winn-Dixie, **S** 🅖 Chevron/dsl, Shell/Circle K, USA/dsl 🍴 Arby's, Boston Mkt, Chick-fil-A, China Buffet, ChuckECheese, Cracker Barrel, Crystal River Sea-food, Denny's, DQ, El Jalisco, Firehouse Subs, Golden Cor-ral, Hooters, IHOP, Julie's Rest, Kacey's Rest, KFC, Krispy Kreme, Little Caesars, Longhorn Steaks, McDonald's, Melt-ing Pot, Ole Times Buffet, On-the-Border, Papa John's, Red Lobster, Shoney's, Sonic, Sonny's BBQ, Starbucks, Subway, TCBY, Wendy's, Whataburger, Zaxby's 🛏 Best Value Inn, EconoLodge, Guesthouse Inn, Howard Johnson, La Quinta, Red Roof Inn, Rodeway Inn, Super 8 🅞 $Tree, Advance Parts, AT&T, AutoZone, Barnes&Noble, Belk, city park, CVS Drug, PepBoys, Publix, Staples, Sun Tire, Tuffy Auto, U-Haul, Verizon, vet, Walgreens
196	FL 263, Tallahassee, **S** 🅖 Chevron/dsl, Inland/dsl, Shell/dsl, Stop'n Save Gas 🍴 Applebee's, Checker's, Dunkin Donuts, Firehouse Subs, KFC, McDonald's, Sonic, Steak'n Shake, Subway, Taco Bell, Waffle House, Wendy's, Zaxby's 🛏 Sleep Inn 🅞 Advance Parts, 🚗, Chrysler/Dodge/Jeep, Harley-Da-vidson, Home Depot, Lowe's, Mazda, Toyota, VW, Walgreens, Walmart

LAKE CITY LIVE OAK (vertical side label)

TALLAHASSEE (vertical side label)

◆E INTERSTATE 10 Cont'd

Exit #	Services

QUINCY

194mm 🆁🆂 both lanes, 24hr security, full ♿ facilities, litter barrels, petwalk, 🚻, 🖼, vending

192 US 90, to Tallahassee, Quincy, N 📱 ⊘FLYING J/Denny's/dsl/LP/scales/24hr, BP 🏠 Comfort Inn, Howard Johnson 🅾 Camping World RV Ctr (2mi), S 📱 🔲/Subway/dsl/scales/24hr 🍴 Waffle House 🏠 Best Western

181 FL 267, Quincy, N 1 mi 📱 Murphy USA/dsl 🍴 Domino's, Mayflower Chinese 🅾 🏥, Walmart, S 📱 BP/dsl, Pure 🏠 Hampton Inn, Holiday Inn Express, Parkway Inn, to Lake Talquin SF

174 FL 12, to Greensboro, N 📱 BP/dsl, Shell/Burger King/dsl

166 rd 270A, Chattahoochee, N 🅾 to Lake Seminole, to Torreya SP, S 📱 Shell/dsl 🅾 KOA (1mi)

161mm 🆁🆂 both lanes, 24hr security, full ♿ facilities, litter barrels, petwalk, 🚻, 🖼, vending

160mm Apalachicola River, central/eastern time zone

158 rd 286, Sneads, N 🅾 Lake Seminole, to Three Rivers SP

155mm weigh sta both lanes

152 FL 69, to Grand Ridge, Blountstown, N 📱 BP, Exxon/dsl

142 FL 71, to Marianna, Oakdale, N 📱 Murphy USA/dsl, 🔲/Arby's/dsl/scales/24hr 🍴 Beef'O'Brady's, Burger King, Firehouse Subs, Hong Kong Chinese, KFC, Pizza Hut, PoFolks, Ruby Tuesday, San Marco's Mexican, Sonny's BBQ, Waffle House 🏠 American Inn, Comfort Inn, Days Inn, Fairfield Inn, Marianna Inn, Microtel, Quality Inn, Super 8 🅾 🏥, $Tree, AT&T, Lowe's, to FL Caverns SP (8mi), Verizon, Walmart/Subway, S 📱 Chevron/dsl, Sunoco/dsl, TA/Pizza Hut/Popeye's/Taco Bell/dsl/scales/24hr/@ 🍴 DQ, McDonald's 🏠 Best Value Inn 🅾 Dove Rest RV Park

136 FL 276, to Marianna, N 🅾 to FL Caverns SP (8mi)

133mm 🆁🆂 both lanes, 24hr security, full ♿ facilities, litter barrels, petwalk, 🚻, 🖼

130 US 231, Cottondale, N 📱 BP/dsl, Chevron 🍴 Hardee's, Subway, S 📱 Loves/Chester's/McDonald's/dsl/scales/24hr/@, RaceWay/dsl

CHIPLEY

120 FL 77, to Panama City, Chipley, N 📱 BP/dsl, Exxon/Burger King/Stuckey's, Murphy USA/dsl, Shell/dsl 🍴 Arby's, Cancun Mexican, Hardee's, Hungry Howie's, JinJin Chinese, KFC, McDonald's, Pizza Hut, Sonic, Subway, Waffle House, Wendy's 🏠 Comfort Inn, Days Inn/rest., Executive Inn, Quality Inn, Super 8 🅾 🏥, $General, $Tree, Advance Parts, NAPA, O'Reilly Parts, Save-A-Lot Foods, Verizon, Walmart, S 🅾 Falling Water SP

112 FL 79, Bonifay, N 📱 Chevron, Citgo/Tom Thumb/dsl, Exxon/dsl 🍴 Burger King, Hardee's, Hungry Howie, McDonald's, Pizza Hut, Simbo's Rest, Subway, Waffle House 🏠 Bonifay Inn, Economy Lodge, Holiday Inn Express, Tivoli Inn 🅾 🏥, FL Springs RV Camping, Fred's, repair, S Panama City Beach

104 rd 279, Caryville

96 FL 81, Ponce de Leon, N 🅾 $General, to Ponce de Leon SRA, Vortex Spring Camping (5mi), S 🆁🆂 both lanes, 24hr security, full ♿ facilities, 🚻, 🖼, litter barrels, petwalk 📱 87 Depot/Subway/dsl, BP/dsl, Exxon/dsl 🏠 Ponce de Leon Motel

85 US 331, De Funiak Springs, N 📱 Chevron/dsl, Murphy USA/dsl 🍴 Arby's, Beef O'Brady's, Burger King, Hungry Howie's, McLain's Steaks, Pizza Hut, Sonic, Subway, Waffle House 🏠 Best Value Inn, Regency Inn, Sundown Inn, Super 8 🅾 🏥, $General, $Tree, AT&T, Lowe's, Verizon, Walgreens, Walmart, winery, Winn-Dixie, S 📱 87 Depot/dsl, BP,

85 Continued
Emerald Express/dsl 🍴 KFC, McDonald's, Whataburger 🏠 Best Western 🅾 🏥, camping (3mi)

70 FL 285, to Ft Walton Bch, Eglin AFB, N 📱 RaceWay/dsl, S 🏠 Rodeway Inn 🅾 Dixie RV Ctr, repair

60mm 🆁🆂 both lanes, 24hr security, full ♿ facilities, litter barrels, petwalk, 🚻, 🖼, vending

CRESTVIEW

56 FL 85, Crestview, Eglin AFB, N 📱 BP/dsl, Mobil/Chester's/dsl 🍴 Applebee's, Beef O'Brady's, Burger King, Capt D's, Chill Frozen Yogurt, China 1, Dunkin Donuts, Golden Asian, Hungry Howie's, Hunon Chinese, Lenny's Subs, McDonald's, Mia's Italian, Ryan's, Sonic, Starbucks, Steve&Joe's Diner, Taco Bell 🏠 Country Inn&Suites, EconoLodge 🅾 🏥, $General, Advance Parts, AT&T, AutoZone, BigLots, GNC, Lowe's, Publix, Radio Shack, Staples, URGENT CARE, Verizon, Walgreens, Walmart, S 📱 Citgo/Tom Thumb/dsl, Exxon/dsl 🍴 Arby's, Coach-n-Four Steaks, Cracker Barrel, Hardee's, Hooters, LaRumba Mexican, Waffle House, Wendy's, Whataburger 🏠 Baymont Inn, Best Value Inn, Comfort Inn, Hampton Inn, Holiday Inn Express, Jameson Inn, Rodeway Inn, Super 8 🅾 Buick/GMC, Chevrolet, Ford, museum, RV camping

45 rd 189, to US 90, Holt, N 📱 Chevron (1mi) 🅾 Eagle's Landing RV Park, to Blackwater River SP, S 🅾 River's Edge RV Park (1mi)

31mm 🆁🆂 both lanes, 24hr security, full ♿ facilities, litter barrels, petwalk, 🚻, 🖼

31 FL 87, to Ft Walton Beach, Milton, N 📱 Exxon/dsl 🍴 Waffle House 🏠 Holiday Inn Express 🅾 Blackwater River SP, KOA, S 📱 BP, Shell/dsl 🏠 Comfort Inn, Red Carpet Inn

28 rd 89, Milton, N 🅾 🏥

27mm Blackwater River

26 rd 191, Bagdad, Milton, N 📱 Shell/Circle K/dsl 🅾 🏥, $General, S 📱 Chevron/DQ/Stuckey's 🅾 Pelican Palms RV Park

22 N FL 281, Avalon Blvd, N 📱 RaceWay/dsl, Tom Thumb 🍴 Capt Pete's Oyster House, McDonald's, S 📱 Shell/Circle K/Subway/dsl 🍴 Waffle House 🏠 Red Roof Inn 🅾 Avalon Landing RV Park (3mi)

18mm Escambia Bay

17 US 90, Pensacola, N 📱 BP/dsl, S 📱 Exxon/DQ 🏠 Quality Inn/rest.

14mm truck inspection sta

PENSACOLA

13 FL 291, to US 90, Pensacola, N 📱 BP, Exxon, Shell/dsl 🍴 Arby's, Capt D's, Denny's, DQ, La Hacienda Mexican, McDonald's, Santino's Cafe, Subway, Taco Bell, Waffle House 🏠 Comfort Inn, Holiday Inn, La Quinta, Motel 6, Villager Lodge 🅾 $Tree, CVS Drug, Food World, Ross, U-Haul, Walgreens, S 🍴 ChuckECheese, Fazoli's, HoneyBaked Ham, Los Rancheros Mexican, Shrimp Basket Rest, Waffle House, Wendy's, Whataburger 🏠 Baymont Inn, Best Value Inn, Courtyard, Extended Stay America, Fairfield Inn, Hampton Inn, Mainstay Suites, Red Roof Inn, Super 6 Inn, TownePlace Suites 🅾 🏥, $General, Belk, Books-A-Million, Firestone/auto, Hobby Lobby, JC Penney, Jo-Ann Fabrics, PepBoys, Petsmart, Radio Shack, Sears/auto, TJ Maxx, U-Haul

12 I-110, to Pensacola, Hist Dist, Islands Nat Seashore

10b a US 29, Pensacola, N 📱 Kangaroo/dsl/scales, Murphy USA/dsl 🍴 Church's, Hardee's, Ryan's, Sonic, Vallarta Mexican, Waffle House 🅾 $Tree, Advance Parts, AT&T, AutoZone, Carpenter's RV Ctr, GNC, Office Depot, O'Reilly Parts, Radio Shack, Tires+, Walmart, S 0-2 mi 📱 RaceWay/dsl, Shell/Circle K, Tom Thumb 🍴 Burger King, Capt D's, Founaris Bro's Greek, IHOP, McDonald's, Pizza Hut, Ruby Tuesday,

FL

INTERSTATE 10 Cont'd

PENSACOLA

Exit #	Services
10b a	Continued Smokey's BBQ, Waffle House, Wendy's, Whataburger 🛏 Best Value Inn, Days Inn, Executive Inn, Howard Johnson, Key West Inn, Luxury Suites, Motel 6, Pensacola Inn, Quality Inn, Ramada Inn, Travelodge 🅞 Buick/Cadillac/GMC, Chevrolet, Dodge/Jeep, Ford, funpark, Harley-Davidson, Honda, Hyundai, Kia, Lincoln, Mazda, NAPA, Nissan, Subaru, Suzuki, Toyota/Scion
7b a	FI 297, Pine Forest Rd, N 🅖 Chevron 🍴 Beef'O'Brady's, Starbucks, Wendy's 🛏 Best Western, Comfort Inn, Garden Inn, Value Place 🅞 Publix, Tall Oaks Camping, transmissions, S 🅖 BP, Raceway/dsl, Tom Thumb 🍴 Burger King, Cracker Barrel, Figaro's Pizza, Hardee's, McDonald's, Ruby Tuesday, Sonny's BBQ, Subway, Waffle House, Wayne's Diner 🛏 Country Inn&Suites, Holiday Inn Express, Microtel, Quality Inn, Red Roof Inn 🅞 Big Lagoon SRA (12mi), Food World/24hr, museum
5	US 90 A, N 🅖 Kangaroo/Subway/dsl, Shell/Circle K 🍴 Beef'O Brady's, Hershey's Ice Cream, Starbucks, Wendy's 🅞 AT&T, Publix/gas, Walgreens, S 🅞 Leisure Lakes Camping
4mm	Welcome Ctr eb, 24hr security, full ♿ facilities, info, litter barrels, petwalk, 🅒, 🐾, vending, wi-fi
3mm	weigh sta both lanes
1mm	inspection sta eb
0mm	Florida/Alabama state line, Perdido River

INTERSTATE 75

Exit #	Services
471mm	Florida/Georgia state line. Motorist callboxes begin sb.
469mm	Welcome Ctr sb, full ♿ facilities, info, litter barrels, petwalk, 🅒, 🐾, vending
467	FL 143, Jennings, E 🅞 Budget Lodge, W 🅖 Exxon/dsl 🛏 Jennings House Inn, N Florida Inn 🅞 fireworks, Jennings Camping
460	FL 6, Jasper, E 🅖 BP/Burger King, Indian River Fruit/gas, Penn Oil/Huddle House/dsl 🛏 7 Oaks Inn, W 🅖 Shell/dsl, Sunoco/dsl 🍴 Sheffield's Country Kitchen 🛏 Scottish Inn 🅞 Suwanee River SP
451	US 129, Jasper, Live Oak, E 🅖 Loves/Arby's/dsl/scales/24hr, Mobil/DQ/Subway/dsl, W 🅖 BP/Lester's Grill/dsl 🅞 Suwanee Music Park (4mi), to FL Boys Ranch
448mm	weigh sta both lanes
446mm	insp sta both lanes
443mm	Historic Suwanee River
439	to FL 136, White Springs, Live Oak, E 🅖 Gate/dsl/e-85, Shell/dsl 🍴 McDonald's 🅞 Lee's Camping (3mi), Suwanee RV Camping (4mi), to S Foster Ctr, W 🛏 Best Value Inn
435	I-10, E to Jacksonville, W to Tallahassee
427	US 90, to Live Oak, Lake City, E 🅖 BP/dsl, Chevron/dsl, Exxon, Gas'n Go, Murphy USA/dsl, Shell/dsl 🍴 Applebee's, Arby's, Burger King, Cedar River Seafood, Cracker Barrel, Domino's, El Potro, Elliano's Coffee, Firehouse Subs, Gondolier Italian, Hardee's, IHOP, Ken's BBQ, Krystal, McDonald's, Moe's SW Grill, Ole Times Buffet, Papa John's, Pizza Hut, Player's Club, Red Lobster, Ruby Tuesday, Sonny's BBQ, Starbucks, Steak'n Shake, Subway, Taco Bell, TX Roadhouse, Waffle House, Wasabi, Wendy's, Zaxby's 🛏 Best Inn, Budget Inn, Cypress Inn, Days Inn, Driftwood Inn, Holiday Inn, Jameson Inn, Piney Woods Motel, Ramada Ltd, Rodeway Inn, Scottish Inn 🅞 🅗, Advance Parts, AT&T, AutoZone, Belk,

LAKE CITY

Exit #	Services
427	Continued BigLots, CVS Drug, Ford/Lincoln, Home Depot, Inn&Out RV Park, JC Penney, Kia, Lowe's, mall, Petsmart, Publix, Radio Shack, Tire Kingdom, TireMart, TJ Maxx, Toyota/Scion, Verizon, Walgreens, Walmart, W 🅖 BP, Chevron/dsl, Shell, Sunoco 🍴 Bob Evans, China One, Waffle House 🛏 Best Value Inn, Best Western, Cabot Lodge, Comfort Suites, Country Inn&Suites, EconoLodge, Fairfield Inn, Gateway Inn, Hampton Inn, Red Roof Inn, Travelodge 🅞 $General, Cadillac/Chevrolet, Camping World RV Ctr, Carquest, Chrysler/Dodge/Jeep, Family$, Harvey's Foods, Nissan, vet
423	FL 47, to Ft White, Lake City, E 🅖 Shell/dsl 🅞 Mack/Volvo Trucks, W 🅖 BP/dsl, Exxon/dsl, Stop-N-Go/USPO 🍴 Little Caesars, Subway 🛏 Motel 8, Super 8 🅞 $General, Casey Jones RV Park, Freightliner
414	US 41, US 441, to Lake City, High Springs, E 🅖 Chevron/dsl, Exxon, Pitstop 🛏 Traveler's Inn, Travelodge, W 🅖 BP/dsl, Shell/Wendy's/dsl 🍴 Subway 🅞 antiques, tires/repair, to O'Leno SP (5 mi)
413mm	🆁🆂 both lanes, 24hr security, full ♿ facilities, litter barrels, petwalk, 🅒, 🐾, vending
409mm	Santa Fe River
404	rd 236, to High Springs, E 🅖 Chevron/fruits/gifts, Citgo/dsl, Sunoco, W 🅞 High Springs Camping
399	US 441, to High Sprs, Alachua, E 🅖 BP, Kangaroo 🍴 Domino's, McDonald's, Moe's SW Grill, Pizza Hut, Sonny's BBQ, Subway, Taco Bell, Waffle House 🛏 EconoLodge, Quality Inn 🅞 $General, Advance Parts, AT&T, CVS Drug, Family$, Hitchcock's Foods, Lowe's, Traveler's Campground (1mi), vet, Walgreens, W 🅖 Chevron, Kangaroo/Wendy's, Mobil/Pizza-Vito/dsl 🍴 KFC, Mason's Grill 🛏 Best Value Inn, Royal Inn
390	FL 222, to Gainesville, E 🅖 Chevron/dsl, Kangaroo/Subway/dsl, Marathon/McDonald's/dsl 🍴 Burger King, La Fiesta Mexican, Pomodoro Cafe, Sonny's BBQ, Wendy's 🅞 Publix, Walgreens, W 🅖 BP/DQ/Dunkin Donuts/dsl 🛏 Best Western 🅞 Harley-Davidson, vet
387	FL 26, to Newberry, Gainesville, E 🅖 BP, Chevron/dsl, Shell/dsl, Sunoco 🍴 BJ's Rest., Bono's BBQ, Boston Mkt, Burger King, Dunkin Donuts, FoodCourt, HoneyBaked Ham, Jason's Deli, LJ Silver, Macaroni Grill, McAlister's Deli, McDonald's, Mr Tequila's Grill, Perkins, Red Lobster, Ruby Tuesday, Starbucks, Subway, Wendy's 🛏 La Quinta 🅞 🅗, Belk, Books-A-Million, Dillard's, JC Penney, Macy's, mall, Office Depot, PetCo, Sears/auto, SteinMart, to UF, Verizon, W 🅖 BP, Chevron/dsl, Exxon/dsl, Marathon/dsl 🍴 Asian Cafe, El Norteno's Mexican, Hardee's, Krystal, Moe's SW Grill, Napolatanos Rest., Pizza Hut, Taco Bell, Waffle House 🛏 Baymont Inn, Days Inn, EconoLodge, Gainesville Hotel 🅞 $Tree,

GAINESVILLE

INTERSTATE 75 Cont'd

Exit # | Services

387 | Continued
Advance Parts, Goodyear/auto, Home Depot, Jo-Ann Fabrics, K-Mart, PepBoys, Publix, tires/repair, TJ Maxx, vet, Walgreens

384 | FL 24, to Archer, Gainesville, **E** ⓖ Chevron/dsl, Exxon/dsl, Shell ⓕ 5 Guys Burgers, Arby's, Asian Wok, Backyard Burger, BoneFish Grill, Burger King, Checkers, Chick-fil-A, Chili's, Chipotle Mexican, Chuy's Mexican, CiCi's Pizza, Cody's Roadhouse, Coldstone, DQ, Dunkin Donuts, Firehouse Subs, Gainesville Alehouse, Genghis Grill, KFC, McAlister's Deli, McDonald's, Moe's SW Grill, Olive Garden, Outback Steaks, Panera Bread, Papa John's, Pizza Hut, Sonny's BBQ, Starbucks, Steak'n Shake, Subway, Taco Bell, TGIFriday's, Tijuana Flats, TX Roadhouse, Waffle House, Wendy's, Willy's Mexican Grill, Wing House, Zaxby's ⌂ Cabot Lodge, Comfort Inn, Courtyard, Extended Stay America, Hampton Inn, Hilton Garden, Homewood Suites, Motel 6, Red Roof Inn, Residence Inn, Sleep Inn, SpringHill Suites, Super 8 ⓞ $Tree, Barnes&Noble, Best Buy, CarQuest, CVS Drug, Discount Tire, Firestone/auto, GNC, Kohl's, Lowe's, Michael's, Old Navy, Petsmart, Publix, Radio Shack, Ross, Target, Tuffy Auto, Verizon, Walgreens, Walmart, **W** ⓖ Marathon/dsl ⓕ Cracker Barrel ⌂ Country Inn&Suites, Holiday Inn Express ⓞ Sunshine RV Park, to Bear Museum

382 | FL 121, to Williston, Gainesville, **E** ⓖ Marathon/dsl, Mobil/dsl ⓕ 1st Wok, Little Caesars, McDonald's, Subway ⓞ Publix, USPO, **W** ⓖ BP/dsl, Chevron/dsl, Kangaroo/dsl ⓕ 43rd St Deli ⌂ Quality Inn, Rodeway Inn, ValuePlace ⓞ Fred Bear Museum

381mm | Ⓡⓢ both lanes, 24hr security, full ⓕ facilities, litter barrels, petwalk, ⓒ, ⓕ, vending

374 | rd 234, Micanopy, **E** ⓖ BP, Chevron/dsl ⓞ antiques, to Paynes Prairie SP, **W** ⓕ Micanopy Inn ⓞ repair

368 | rd 318, Orange Lake, **E** ⓖ Chevron, Jim's/BBQ, Petro/BP/Iron Skillet/dsl/scales/24hr/@ ⓕ Wendy's ⓞ Grand Lake RV Park (3mi), **W** ⓞ Ocala N RV Camping

358 | FL 326, **E** ⓖ Marathon/McDonald's/dsl, ⓛ/Arby's/dsl/scales/24hr, ⓛ/Wendy's/dsl/scales/24hr, Sunoco/FL Citrus Ctr/dsl ⓞ auto/truck repair, Freightliner, **W** ⓖ Chevron/dsl, Loves/Chester's/Subway/dsl/scales/24hr ⓕ DQ

354 | US 27, to Silver Springs, Ocala, **E** ⓖ BP/dsl, RaceTrac/dsl ⓕ Burger King, Rascal's BBQ ⌂ Golden Palms Inn, **W** ⓖ BP/dsl, Chevron/dsl, Shell/dsl ⓕ Blanca's Cafe, China Taste, McDonald's, Roma Rest, Subway, Swampy's Grill ⌂ Budget Host, Comfort Suites, Days Inn, Howard Johnson, Ramada ⓞ $General, AT&T, Family$, GNC, Nelson's Trailers, Oaktree Village Camping, Publix, Walgreens, Winn-Dixie

352 | FL 40, to Silver Springs, Ocala, **E** ⓖ Chevron, Mobil/dsl, RaceTrac/dsl, Sunoco/dsl ⓕ Dunkin Donuts, McDonald's, Pizza Hut/Taco Bell, Subway, Wendy's, Zaxby's ⌂ Amadeus Inn, Days Inn/café, Economy Inn, Motor Inn/RV ⓞ Family$, to Silver River SP (8mi), **W** ⓖ Shell/dsl, Texaco/dsl ⓕ Denny's, Golden Coast Buffet, Waffle House ⌂ Red Roof Inn, Super 8, Travelodge ⓞ Gander Mtn, Holiday Trav-L Park

350 | FL 200, to Hernando, Ocala, **E** 0-2 mi ⓖ BP/dsl, Citgo/dsl, Texaco/dsl ⓕ 5 Guys Burgers, Applebee's, Arby's, Bob Evans, Boston Mkt, Burger King, Carrabba's, Checkers, Chick-fil-A, ChuckECheese, City Buffet, Cody's Roadhouse, Coldstone, Crispers, Domino's, El Toreo Mexican, Firehouse Subs, Golden Corral, Guadalajara Mexican, Hardee's, House of Japan, Krystal, Lee's Chicken, Logan's Roadhouse,

350 | Continued
McDonald's, Moe's SW Grill, Ocean Buffet, Olive Garden, Outback Steaks, Panera Bread, Papa John's, Red Lobster, Ruby Tuesday, Shane's Rib Shack, Smoothie King, Sonic, Sonny's BBQ, Starbucks, Stevie B's Pizza, Subway, Taco Bell, Wendy's, Zaxby's ⌂ Country Inn&Suites, Hilton, La Quinta ⓞ Ⓗ, $Tree, Acura, Advance Parts, Aldi Foods, Belk, Best Buy, Books-A-Million, Chevrolet, CVS Drug, Discount Tire, Goodyear/auto, Hobby Lobby, Home Depot, Honda, Hyundai, JC Penney, Jo-Ann Fabrics, Kia, Lowe's, Macy's, Mazda, Michael's, Nissan, Office Depot, O'Reilly Parts, PepBoys, Petsmart, Publix, Ross, Sears/auto, Staples, SteinMart, Target, Tire Kingdom, TJ Maxx, Toyota, Tuffy Auto, URGENT CARE, Verizon, Walgreens, Walmart, **W** ⓖ BP/dsl, Chevron ⓕ Bonefish Grill, Burger King, Cracker Barrel, Dunkin Donuts, KFC, McAlister's Deli, McDonald's, Mimi's Cafe, Panera Bread, Starbucks, Steak'n Shake, Tijuana Flats, Waffle House, Yamato Japanese ⌂ Best Western, Courtyard, Fairfield Inn, Hampton Inn, Holiday Inn, Homewood Suites, Residence Inn ⓞ Ⓗ, AT&T, Barnes&Noble, BMW, Buick/GMC, Cadillac, Camper Village RV Park, Dick's, Dillard's, Kohl's, Ocala RV Park, Old Navy, PetCo, Porsche, Sam's Club/gas, Tires+, Verizon, vet, VW, Walgreens

346mm | Ⓡⓢ both lanes, 24hr security, full ⓕ facilities, litter barrels, petwalk, ⓒ, ⓕ, vending

341 | rd 484, to Belleview, **E** ⓖ Chevron/fruit, Citgo/Baskin-Robbins/Dunkin Donuts, Exxon/dsl, Shell/dsl ⓕ Cracker Barrel, KFC/Taco Bell, Sonny's BBQ, Zaxby's ⌂ Microtel, Sleep Inn ⓞ drag racing museum, FL Citrus Ctr, **W** ⓖ ⓛ/DQ/Wendy's/dsl/scales/24hr ⓕ McDonald's, Subway, Waffle House ⌂ Hampton Inn ⓞ Ocala Sun RV Resort, outlets

338mm | weigh sta both lanes

329 | FL 44, to Inverness, Wildwood, **E** ⓖ Marathon/dsl, Sunoco/DQ, Wilco/Hess/Steak'n Shake/dsl/scales/24hr ⓕ Burger King, McDonald's, Waffle House, Wendy's ⓞ FL Citrus Ctr, Wild Wood RV Park, **W** ⓖ Citgo/dsl/repair/24hr, ⓛ/dsl/scales/24hr, TA/BP/Pizza Hut/Popeye's/Subway/dsl/scales/24hr/@ ⓕ IHOP, KFC ⌂ Best Value Inn, Days Inn, Super 8, Villager Lodge ⓞ truck repair, truckwash

328 | FL TPK (from sb), to Orlando

321 | rd 470, to Sumterville, Lake Panasoffkee, **E** ⓖ Spirit/deli/dsl/scales/24hr ⓞ Coleman Correctional, **W** ⓖ Chevron/7-11/dsl, Mobil/Hardee's/Subway/dsl

314 | FL 48, to Bushnell, **E** ⓖ Citgo, Murphy USA/dsl, Shell/Circle K/Subway, Texaco ⓕ Hong Kong Chinese, KFC/Taco Bell, McDonald's, Wendy's ⌂ Rodeway Inn ⓞ $Tree, AutoZone, BlueBerry Hill RV Camp, Red Oaks Camp (1mi), to Dade Bfd HS, Verizon, vet, Walmart, **W** ⓖ Shell/dsl, Sunoco/dsl ⓕ Beef'O'Brady's, Sonny's BBQ, Waffle House ⌂ Microtel ⓞ Flagship RV Ctr

309 | rd 476, to Webster, **E** ⓞ Breezy Oaks RV Park (1mi), Sumter Oaks RV Park (1mi)

307mm | Ⓡⓢ both lanes, 24hr security, coffee, full ⓕ facilities, litter barrels, petwalk, ⓒ, ⓕ, vending

301 | US 98, FL 50, to Dade City, **E** ⓖ RaceTrac/dsl ⓕ Beef'O'Brady's, Cracker Barrel, Denny's, McDonald's, Quinzos, Subway, Waffle House, Wendy's ⌂ Days Inn, Holiday Inn Express ⓞ $General, Advance Parts, Tall Pines RV Park, Winn-Dixie, **W** ⓖ Chevron/dsl ⓕ Burger King ⌂ Hampton Inn, Microtel, Quality Inn ⓞ Ⓗ

293 | rd 41, to Dade City, **E** ⓖ Citgo (2mi) ⓞ to Sertoma Youth Ranch, **W** ⓞ Travelers Rest Resort RV Park

Side labels: GAINESVILLE, OCALA, INVERNESS, DADE CITY, FL

INTERSTATE 75 Cont'd

Exit #	Services
285	FL 52, to Dade City, New Port Richey, **E** 🅖 ⭐FLYING J/ Denny's/dsl/LP/scales/24hr 🅞 🅗, Blue Beacon, **W** 🅖 Citgo/ dsl/scales/24hr 🅕 Waffle House
279	FL 54, to Land O' Lakes, Zephyrhills, **E** 🅖 Hess/Dunkin Donuts/Godfather's/Quiznos/dsl 🅕 Applebee's, Burger King, Gonna China, Papa's John's, Pizza Hut/Taco Bell, Sonny's BBQ, Subway, Waffle House, Wendy's, Winner's Grill 🅞 Ace Hardware, Beall's, Fiat, Ford, Happy Days RV Camping (9mi), Kia, Leasure Days RV Park (7mi), Nissan, Publix, Ralph's RV Camping (7mi), to Hillsborough River SP (18mi), Toyota/Scion, vet, Walgreens, **W** 🅖 7-11, Marathon, Mobil/Dunkin Donuts, Shell/Circle K/dsl 🅕 Beef'O'Brady's, Buffalo's, Cracker Barrel, DQ, Hungry Howie's, Marco's Pizza, McDonald's, Outback Steaks, Remington's Steaks, Shanghai Chinese 🅛 Best Western, Comfort Inn, Holiday Inn Express, Sleep Inn 🅞 $Tree, Advance Parts, AT&T, Best Buy, CVS Drug, Dick's, Encore RV Camping, GNC, Goodyear/auto, Honda, Hyundai, Mazda, Michael's, Petsmart, Quail Run RV Camping, Ross, Tire Kingdom, TJ Maxx, Tuffy Auto, URGENT CARE, Verizon
277mm	🆁🆂 both lanes, 24hr security, full ♿ facilities, litter barrels, petwalk, 🅒, 🗑, vending
275	FL 56, Land O Lakes, Tarpon Springs, **E** 🅖 BP/Dunkin Donuts/dsl 🅕 TX Roadhouse 🅛 Hampton Inn 🅞 Mini, Publix (2mi), **W** 🅖 Shell/dsl 🅞 Walgreens
274	I-275 (from sb), to Tampa, St Petersburg
270	rd 581, Bruce B Downs Blvd, **E** 🅖 7-11, Hess/dsl, Mobil, Shell/Circle K/Taco Bell/dsl 🅕 Baskin-Robbins/Dunkin Donuts, Boston Mkt, Chick-fil-A, Chili's, Coldstone, DQ, Firehouse Subs, Jimmy John's, KFC, Kobe Japanese, Liang's Asian Bistro, Macaroni Grill, McDonald's, Moe's SW Grill, Panera Bread, Papa John's, Pizza Hut, Ruby Tuesday, Selmon's Cafe, Starbucks, Steak'n Shake, Subway, TGIFriday's, Tijuana Flats, Wendy's 🅛 Holiday Inn Express, Wingate Inn 🅞 Best Buy, CVS Drug, GNC, Home Depot, Kauffman Tire, Michael's, Publix, Radio Shack, Tires+, URGENT CARE, Verizon, Walgreens, Walmart, **W** 🅖 7-11 🅕 McDonald's, Olive Garden, Panda Buffet, Red Lobster, Stonewood Grill 🅛 SpringHill Suites 🅞 $Tree, BJ's Whse/gas, CVS Drug, Jo-Ann Fabrics, Lowe's, Petsmart, Ross, Staples, USPO
266	rd 582A, Fletcher Ave, **W** 🅖 Shell/Circle K/dsl 🅕 Baskin-Robbins/Dunkin Donuts, Bob Evans, Lenny's Subs, Starbucks, Wendy's 🅛 Courtyard, Extended Stay America, Fairfield Inn, Hampton Inn, Hilton Garden, Holiday Inn Express, Residence Inn, Sleep Inn 🅞 🅗
265	FL 582, Fowler Ave, Temple Terrace, **E** 🅞 flea mkt, Happy Traveler RV Park, **W** 🅖 BP, Sunoco, Value/dsl 🅕 IHOP, Marco's Pizza 🅛 Ramada Inn 🅞 to Busch Gardens, to USF
261	I-4, W to Tampa, E to Orlando
260b a	FL 574, to Mango, Tampa, **E** 🅖 Chevron, Citgo/dsl, Shell/Circle K/Subway 🅕 Baskin-Robbins/Dunkin Donuts, China Wok, Quiznos, Waffle House 🅞 SweetBay Foods, Walgreens, **W** 🅖 BP, Mobil 🅛 Residence Inn, Sheraton, Staybridge Suites
257	FL 60, Brandon, **E** 🅖 Chevron, Citgo/dsl, Mobil, Mobil/dsl, Shell/Circle K, Sunoco 🅕 5 Guys Burgers, Anthony's Pizza, Arby's, Boston Mkt, Brandon Ale House, Buca Italian, Buffalo Wild Wings, Burger King, Checkers, Cheddars, Cheescake Factory, Chick-fil-A, Chili's, ChuckECheese, Crispers, Denny's, DQ, Dunkin Donuts, Firehouse Subs, Grill Smith Grill, Jesse's Steaks, Jimmy John's, Kabuki Japanese, KFC, Kobe Japanese, Krispy Kreme, Little Caesars, LJ Silver, Longhorn

TAMPA

257	Continued Steaks, Macaroni Grill, McDonald's, McDonald's, Moe's SW Grill, Olive Garden, Outback Steaks, Panda Express, Panera Bread, Papa John's, Popeye's, Qdoba, Quiznos, Red Lobster, Salad Works, Smokey Bones BBQ, Smoothie King, Starbucks, Steak'n Shake, Steak'n Shake, Subway, Tia's TexMex, Tops China Buffet, Tres Amigos Mexican, Waffle House, Wendy's, Wing House 🅛 Holiday Inn Express, HomeStead Suites, La Quinta 🅞 🅗, $General, $Tree, Aamco, Advance Parts, AT&T, AutoZone, Barnes&Noble, Best Buy, Books-A-Million, Cadillac, Costco/gas, CVS Drug, Dick's, Dillard's, Family$, Fiat, Firestone/auto, JC Penney, Jo-Ann Fabrics, Kia, K-Mart, Kohl's, Kohl's, Lowe's, Macy's, mall, Marshall's, Michael's, Office Depot, PepBoys, PetCo, Petsmart, Petsmart, Publix, Publix, Radio Shack, Ross, Sam's Club/gas, Sears/auto, Staples, Target, Tires+, TJ Maxx, Tuffy Auto, U-Haul, URGENT CARE, Walgreens, Walmart, **W** 🅖 Citgo/dsl, Marathon, Shell 🅕 Beef O'Brady's, Bob Evans, Burger King, Hooters, McDonald's, Sonny's BBQ, Subway, Sweet Tomatoes, Wendy's 🅛 Best Western, Comfort Suites, Country Inn&Suites, Courtyard, Embassy Suites, Fairfield Inn, Homewood Suites, La Quinta, Motel 6, Red Roof Inn, SpringHill Suites 🅞 Buick/GMC, Chevrolet, Chrysler/Dodge/Jeep, Ford, Harley-Davidson, Home Depot, Honda, Hyundai, Mazda, Nissan, Office Depot, Toyota/Scion, VW
256	FL 618 W (toll), to Tampa
254	US 301, Riverview, **E** 🅖 RaceTrac/dsl 🅕 Panda Express, Steak'n Shake 🅞 CVS Drug, Firestone, Home Depot, Target, **W** 🅖 7-11/dsl 🅕 China 1, Crazy Cafe, McDonald's 🅛 Hilton Garden 🅞 Publix
250	Gibsonton Dr, Riverview, **E** 🅖 RaceWay/dsl 🅕 Beef'O'Brady's, Burger King, DQ, Hungry Howie's, Little Caesars, Lucky Buffet, McDonald's, Pizza Hut, Ruby Tuesday, Subway, Taco Bell, Wendy's 🅞 $Tree, Alafia River RV Resort, Beall's, CVS Drug, Family$, Hidden River RV Resort (4mi), Lowe's, Save-a-Lot, USPO, Walgreens, Winn-Dixie, **W** 🅖 Murphy USA/dsl 🅞 Walmart/McDonald's
246	rd 672, Big Bend Rd, Apollo Bch, **E** 🅖 7-11, Hess/Dunkin Donuts/Godfather's Pizza/Quiznos/dsl 🅕 5 Guys Burgers, Applebee's, Beef'O'Brady's, Buffalo Wild Wings, Burger King, China Taste, East Coast Pizza, Little Caesars, McDonald's, Panera Bread, Pita, Poppi's Pizza, Qdoba, Sakura Japanese, Sonic, Starbucks, Subway, Village Inn, Wendy's 🅞 $Tree, Ace Hardware, Advance Parts, AT&T, AutoZone, Beall's, Firestone/auto, GNC, Goodyear/auto, Publix, Sam's Club/gas, Sweetbay Foods, Tire Choice, Tuffy Auto, URGENT CARE, Verizon, vet, Walgreens, **W** 🅖 Shell/Dunkin Donuts/dsl

BRANDON

FL

🅐 = gas 🍴 = food 🏠 = lodging 🅞 = other 🆁🆂 = rest stop   Copyright 2015 - the Next EXIT ®

🅽 INTERSTATE 75 Cont'd

Exit #	Services
240b a	FL 674, Sun City Ctr, Ruskin, **E** 🅐 Shell 🍴 Beef'O'Brady's, Bob Evans, Burger King, Denny's, Hungry Howie's, Pizza Hut, Seafood Dive, Sonny's BBQ, Subway, Taco Bell, Wendy's 🏠 Comfort Inn 🅞 �H, Beall's, GNC, Home Depot, Radio Shack, SunLake RV Resort (1mi), to Little Manatee River SP, **W** 🅐 Circle K/dsl, Hess/dsl, RaceTrac/dsl 🍴 China Wok, KFC, McDonald's 🏠 Ruskin Inn 🅞 auto repair, BigLots, NAPA
237mm	🆁🆂 both lanes, 24hr security, full ♿ facilities, litter barrels, petwalk, Ⓒ, 🚮, vending
229	rd 683, Moccasin Wallow Rd, to Parrish, **E** 🅞 Little Manatee Sprs SRA (10mi), **W** 🅞 Circle K, Fiesta Grove RV Park (3mi), Frog Creek RV Park (3mi), Terra Ceia RV Village (2mi), Winterset RV Park (3mi)
228	I-275 N, to St Petersburg
224	US 301, to Bradenton, Ellenton, **E** 🅐 Mobil, RaceWay/dsl, Shell/Circle K/dsl 🍴 Applebee's, Checkers, GioPizza, Hungry Howie's, Kings Wok, McDonald's, Peach's Rest., Ruby Tuesday, Subway, Wendy's, Woody's River Grill 🏠 Hampton Inn, Sleep Inn 🅞 $General, $Tree, Ace Hardware, Beall's, Ellenton Outlets/famous brands, GNC, Just Brakes, K-Mart, Publix, USPO, Walgreens, **W** 🅐 🚉/dsl 🍴 Anna Maria's, Crabtrap Seafood, Waffle House 🏠 GuestHouse Inn, Ramada Ltd
220b a	FL 64, to Zolfo Springs, Bradenton, **E** 🅞 Lake Manatee SRA, **W** 🅐 BP/dsl, Citgo/dsl, RaceTrac/dsl, Shell/Circle K/dsl 🍴 Burger King, Cracker Barrel, D. Americo's Pizza, Dunkin Donuts, KFC/LJ Silver, McDonald's, Sonny's BBQ, Subway, Waffle House, Wendy's 🏠 Best Western, Comfort Inn, Days Inn, EconoLodge, Motel 6 🅞 �H, Dream RV Ctr, Encore RV Resort (1mi), Harley-Davidson, Toyota/Scion, Walmart
217b a	FL 70, to Arcadia, **E** 🅐 Hess/Godfather's/Quiznos/dsl 🍴 Burger King, Crispers 🏠 Wingate Inn 🅞 Goodyear/auto, Sweetbay Foods, Walmart/Subway, **W** 🅐 7-11/dsl, BP/Dunkin Donuts/dsl, Shell/Circle K 🍴 Applebee's, Arby's, Bangkok Tokyo, Bob Evans, Bogey's Rest., Chick-fil-A, Dawson's Rest., DQ, Hungry Howie's, LJ Silver/Taco Bell, McDonald's, Papa John's, Peppermill Eatery, Rice Bowl, Starbucks, Subway 🏠 Country Inn&Suites 🅞 $Tree, Beall's, CVS Drug, Lowe's, Pleasant Lake RV Resort, Publix, Tire Kingdom, Tires+, Tuffy Auto, Verizon, vet
213	University Parkway, to Sarasota, **E** 🅐 Mobil/dsl 🍴 Chili's, Monty's Pizza, Ms JC Garden, Pizza Hut, Quiznos 🏠 Fairfield Inn, Holiday Inn 🅞 �H, GNC, Publix, URGENT CARE, Walgreens, **W** 🍴 5 Guys Burgers, Bellacino's, BoneFish Grill, Buffalo Wild Wings, Carrabba's, Chipotle Mexican, Jason's Deli, Jersey Mike's Subs, Jimmy John's, John Dough Cafe, Moe's SW Grill, Pei Wei, Red Elephant Grill, Ruby Tuesday, Selmon's Rest., Starbucks, Stonewood Grill, Sweet Tomatoes, Tijuana Flats, Wendy's 🏠 Comfort Suites, Hampton Inn 🅞 $Tree, Beall's, Best Buy, BJ's Whse/gas, CVS Drug, Fresh Mkt Foods, Home Depot, Jo-Ann Fabrics, Kohl's, Marshall's, Michael's, Old Navy, PetCo, Ross, SteinMart, Target, to Ringling Museum, Verizon
210	FL 780, Fruitville Rd, Sarasota, **E** 🅞 Sun-N-Fun RV Park (1mi), **W** 🅐 BP/dsl/LP, Mobil/7-11/dsl, RaceTrac/dsl, Sav-On/dsl, Shell 🍴 Applebee's, Bob Evans, Burger King, Cafe Italia, Checkers, Chick-fil-A, Don Pablo's, Dunkin Donuts, Firehouse Subs, KFC, Longhorn Steaks, McDonald's, Peking Tokyo, Perkins, Starbucks, Subway, Super Buffet, Taco Bell, Trader Vic's Grill 🏠 AmericInn, Homewood Suites (2mi) 🅞 $Tree, Advance Parts, AT&T, CVS Drug, GNC, Lowe's, Office Depot,

Exit #	Services
210	Continued Publix, Radio Shack, Sam's Club, Target, Tire Kingdom, Tuffy Auto, Verizon, Winn-Dixie
207	FL 758, Sarasota, **W** 🅐 BP/Subway/dsl, Marathon/Dunkin Donuts/Subway 🍴 Arby's, Cafe Amalfi, Chili's, Fortune Buffet, MadFish Grill, McDonald's, Panera Bread, Pizza Hut, Sarasota Alehouse, Starbucks, Steak'n Shake, Taco Bell 🏠 Hampton Inn 🅞 �H, Beall's, Home Depot, Publix, Radio Shack, to Selby Botanical Gardens (8mi), Verizon, vet, Walgreens, Walmart
205	FL 72, to Arcadia, Sarasota, **E** 🅞 Myakka River SP (9mi), **W** 🅐 BP/dsl, Mobil/7-11/dsl, Shell/Circle K 🍴 Applebee's, Burger King, Chick-fil-A, Dunkin Donuts, Gecko's Grill, Just Pizza, KFC, McDonald's, Quiznos, Starbucks, Subway, Waffle House, Wendy's, Wings&Weenies 🏠 Comfort Inn, Days Inn, Holiday Inn Express 🅞 Acura, AT&T, Beall's, BMW, CVS Drug, Jaguar, Land Rover, Lexus, Lotus, Mercedes/Smart, Publix, Tire Kingdom, Turtle Beach Camping (8mi), UPSO, vet, Walgreens, Windward Isle RV Park
200	FL 681 S (from sb), to Venice, Osprey, Gulf Bchs
195	Laurel Rd, Nokomis, **E** 🅐 BP/USPO/dsl 🍴 Subway 🅞 CVS Drug, **W** 🅞 Encore RV Park (2mi), Scherer SP (6mi)
193	Jaracanda Blvd, Venice, **W** 🅐 Hess/Godfather's/Quiznos/dsl, RaceTrac/dsl 🍴 BrewBurgers, Cracker Barrel, McDonald's, Ping's Chinese 🏠 Best Western, Fairfield Inn, Holiday Inn Express 🅞 �H, CVS Drug, Publix, Verizon
191	rd 777, Venice Rd, to Englewood, **W** 🅞 Encore RV Park (3mi), KOA (6mi), to Myakka SF (9mi)
182	rd 771, Sumter Blvd, to North Port
179	rd 779, Toledo Blade Blvd, North Port, **W 1-2 mi** 🅐 Mobil/Subway/dsl, Shell/Burger King 🅞 �H, Publix
170	rd 769, to Arcadia, Port Charlotte, **E** 🅐 7-11/dsl, Murphy USA/dsl, RaceTrac/dsl 🍴 Applebee's 🏠 Hampton Inn, Holiday Inn Express 🅞 Lettuce Lake Camping (7mi), Riverside Camping (5mi), Walmart, **W** 🅐 Hess/dsl, Mobil/Circle K/DQ/dsl, Shell/Circle K/Dunkin Donuts 🍴 Burger King, Cracker Barrel, Domino's, DQ, McDonald's, Peach Garden, Quiznos, Starbucks, Subway, Taco Bell, Top China, Waffle House, Wendy's 🏠 Country Inn&Suites, La Quinta, Sleep Inn 🅞 �H, $General, $Tree, Ace Hardware, Advance Parts, Beall's, CVS Drug, Publix, USPO, vet, Walgreens, Winn-Dixie
167	rd 776, Port Charlotte
164	US 17, Punta Gorda, Arcadia, **E** 🅐 Chevron/7-11/dsl, RaceWay/dsl, Shell/Circle K/dsl 🍴 King House Chinese, RV camping, Subway, vet 🅞 $General, Winn-Dixie, **W** 🍴 Fisherman's Village Rest. (2mi) 🅞 �H
161	rd 768, Punta Gorda, **E** 🆁🆂 both lanes, 24hr security security, full ♿ facilities, Ⓒ, vending, 🚮, litter barrels, petwalk, **W** 🅐 BP/DQ/Subway, Murphy USA/dsl, 🚉/Arby's/dsl/scales/24hr, Sunoco/dsl 🍴 Burger King, McDonald's, Pizza Hut, Waffle House, Wendy's 🏠 Best Value Inn, Knights Inn 🅞 Encore RV Park (2mi), Walmart
160mm	weigh sta both lanes
158	rd 762, Tropical Gulf Acres, Tuckers Grade, **E** 🅞 Babcock-Wells Wildlife Mgt Area
143	FL 78, to Cape Coral, N Ft Myers, **E** 🅐 Marathon/dsl 🅞 Seminole Camping (1mi), Up the River Camping, **W** 🏠 Encore RV Camping
141	FL 80, Palm Bch Blvd, Ft Myers, **E** 🅐 Marathon, Sunoco/dsl 🍴 Cracker Barrel, Waffle House 🏠 Comfort Inn, ValuePlace, **W** 🅐 7-11, Hess/Dunkin Donuts/dsl, Mobil 🍴 Domino's, Hardee's, KFC, Papa John's, Popeye's, Sonny's BBQ,

Vertical side labels (left): **B R A D E N T O N**, **S A R A S O T A**

Vertical side labels (right): **V E N I C E**, **P U N T A G O R D A**

FL

◆N   INTERSTATE 75 Cont'd

Exit #	Services
141	Continued Subway, Taco Bell ⊙ $General, BigLots, CVS Drug, North Trail RV Ctr, Radio Shack, Save-A-Lot, USPO, vet
139	Luckett Rd, Ft Myers, **E** ⊙ Camping World RV Service/supplies, Cypress Woods RV Resort, **W** 🅿 ⛽/Subway/dsl/scales/24hr/@
138	FL 82, to Lehigh Acres, Ft Myers, **E** 🅿 7-11/dsl 🛏 Hyatt Place, **W** 🅿 Mobil/dsl, Sunoco/dsl ⊙ Peterbilt
136	FL 884, Colonial Blvd, Ft Myers, **E** 🍽 5 Guys Burgers, Bajio, Buffalo Wild Wings, Starbucks, Subway 🛏 Candlewood Suites, Holiday Inn Express ⊙ Best Buy, Books-A-Million, GNC, Home Depot, PetCo, Ross, Staples, Target, **W** 🅿 7-11, BP, Marathon/dsl, Murphy USA/dsl, Shell/Circle K/dsl 🍽 Applebee's, Bob Evans, Burger King, Chick-fil-A, Chili's, Golden Corral, LJ Silver/Taco Bell, McDonald's, Panda Express, Steak'n Shake, Subway, TX Roadhouse 🛏 ValuePlace ⊙ 🄷, $Tree, AT&T, Beall's, BJ's Whse/gas, Hobby Lobby, Kohl's, Lowe's, Petsmart, Publix, Tire Choice/auto, Verizon, Walmart/McDonald's
131	rd 876, Daniels Pkwy, to Cape Coral, **E** 🆁🆂 **both lanes, 24hr security, full ♿ facilities, 🚻, vending, 🏞, litter barrels, petwalk,** 🅿 BP/Dunkin Donuts/Subway/dsl, RaceTrac/dsl 🍽 Cracker Barrel, Fat Katz 🛏 Comfort Inn, Floridian Airport Inn, Grand Stay ⊙ 🍴, CVS Drug, Porsche **W** 🅿 7-11, Hess/Dunkin Donuts/dsl, RaceWay/dsl, Shell/Circle K/dsl 🍽 Arby's, Beef'O'Brady's, Burger King, Denny's, DQ, Mac Daddy's, McDonald's, New China, Papa John's, Rib City, Sports Page Grill, Subway, Taco Bell, Waffle House, Wendy's 🛏 Baymont Inn, Best Western, Hampton Inn, La Quinta, Quality Inn, SpringHill Suites, Travelodge ⊙ 🄷, CVS Drug, Dream RV Ctr, Publix, Tire Choice/auto, Tuffy Auto, Walgreens
128	Alico Rd, San Carlos Park, **E** 🅿 7-11 🍽 Aurelio's Pizza, Bar Louie, Carrabba's, Chick-fil-A, Connor's Steaks, Elevation Burger, Famous Dave's BBQ, Longhorn Steaks, McDonald's, Miller's Alehouse, Moe's SW Grill, Olive Garden, Outback Steaks, Pincher's Crabshack, Pita Pit, Red Robin 🛏 Courtyard, Hilton Garden, Holiday Inn, Homewood Suites, Residence Inn ⊙ $Tree, AT&T, Bass Pro Shop/Islamorada Fish Co, Belk, Best Buy, Costco/gas, Dick's, GNC, JC Penney, Jo-Ann Fabrics, Marshall's, PetCo, Ross, Staples, Target, Verizon, **W** 🅿 7-11/dsl, Hess/Dunkin Donuts/dsl
123	rd 850, Corkscrew Rd, Estero, **E** 🅿 BP/Dunkin Donuts/dsl, Chevron/7-11/dsl 🍽 Beef'O'Brady's, China Gourmet, Marsala's Italian, McDonald's, Naples Flat Bread, Perkins, Subway ⊙ CVS Drug, Johnson Tire/auto, Miramar Outlet/famous brands, Publix, **W** 🅿 7-11, Hess/Dunkin Donuts/dsl, Shell/Blimpie/dsl 🍽 Applebee's, Arby's, Rib City, Ruby Tuesday, Subway 🛏 Embassy Suites, Hampton Inn ⊙ Chevrolet, Koreshan SHS (2mi), Lowe's, Tire Choice/auto, Woodsmoke RV Park (4mi)
116	Bonita Bch Rd, Bonita Springs, **E** 🅿 Mobil, Valero/7-11/dsl 🍽 Subway ⊙ Advance Parts, AT&T, Publix, Tire Choice/auto, **W** 🅿 Chevron/dsl, Hess/Dunkin Donuts/dsl, Shell/McDonald's 🍽 Waffle House 🛏 Best Western ⊙ CVS Drug, Home Depot, Imperial Bonita RV Park, Tire Kingdom, to Lovers Key SP (11mi), Walgreens
111	rd 846, Immokalee Rd, Naples Park, **E** 🅿 7-11, Mobil/dsl 🍽 Bob Evans, Burger King, Chili's, L'Appetite Pizza, Panera Bread 🛏 Hampton Inn ⊙ Staples, Target, World Mkt, **W** 🅿 Shell/Circle K/dsl 🍽 Bella's Pizza, Subway ⊙ 🄷, Publix, to Delnor-Wiggins SP, Verizon, Walmart/McDonald's

107	rd 896, Pinebridge Rd, Naples, **E** 🅿 BP/McDonald's/dsl 🍽 China Garden, Giovanni Ristorante, Starbucks, Subway ⊙ 🄷, Publix, vet, Walgreens, **W** 🅿 Chevron/dsl, RaceTrac/dsl, Shell/Circle K/dsl 🍽 5 Guys Burgers, Burger King, Hooters, IHOP, Perkins, Senor Tequilas, Sophia's Rest., Starbucks, Waffle House 🛏 Best Western, Hawthorn Suites, Spinnaker Inn ⊙ Harley-Davidson, Johnson Tire/auto, Nissan, Tire Choice/auto, vet
105	rd 886, to Golden Gate Pkwy, Golden Gate, **E** 🍽 Subway ⊙ CVS Drug, **W** 🅿 to 🍴, zoo
101	rd 951, to FL 84, to Naples, **E** 🅿 BP/Subway/pizza 🛏 Fairfield Inn, SpringHill Suites ⊙ 🄷, **W** 🅿 BP/dsl, Circle K, Mobil/dsl, Shell/dsl 🍽 BBQ Place, Cracker Barrel, McDonald's, Subway, Taco Bell, Waffle House 🛏 Comfort Inn, Days Inn, La Quinta, Super 8 ⊙ $Tree, AT&T, Club Naples RV Ctr, Endless Summer RV Park (3mi), KOA
100mm	**toll plaza eb**
80	FL 29, to Everglade City, Immokalee, **W** ⊙ Big Cypress NR, Everglades NP, Smallwoods Store
71mm	Big Cypress Nat Preserve, hiking, no security
63mm	**W** 🆁🆂 **both lanes, 24hr security, full ♿ facilities, litter barrels, petwalk, 🚻, 🏞, vending**
49	rd 833, Snake Rd, Big Cypress Indian Reservation, **E** 🅿 Miccosukee Service Plaza/deli/dsl ⊙ museum, swamp safari
41mm	**litter barrels, 🏞, rec area eb**
38mm	**litter barrels, 🏞, rec area wb**
35mm	**W** 🆁🆂 **/rec area both lanes, 24hr security, full ♿ facilities, litter barrels, petwalk, 🚻, 🏞, vending**
32mm	**litter barrels, 🏞, rec area both lanes**
25mm	motorist callboxes begin/end, **toll plaza wb**
23	US 27, FL 25, Miami, South Bay
22	FL 84 W, NW 196th, Glades Pkwy, **W** ⊙ Publix, same as 21
21	FL 84 W (from nb), Indian Trace, **W** 🅿 BP/dsl 🍽 Las Rikuras, Papa John's, Spain's Cuisine ⊙ $Days
19	I-595 E, FL 869 (**toll**), Sawgrass Expswy
15	Royal Palm Blvd, Weston, Bonaventure, **W** 🅿 Chevron, Mobil 🍽 Carolina Ale House, El Mariachi, Flanigan's Rest, Il Toscano Rest., La Granja, Lucille's Cafe, Offerdahl's Grill, Pollo Tropical, Sir Pizza, Wendy's 🛏 Comfort Suites, Courtyard, Residence Inn ⊙ 🄷, Meineke, Tires+, USPO
13b a	Griffin Rd, **E** 🅿 Shell/dsl 🍽 Burger King, Donato's Rest., DQ, Outback Steaks, Subway, Waffle House ⊙ Goodyear/auto, Publix, vet, **W** 🅿 7-11/dsl, Tom Thumb/dsl 🍽 Anthony's Pizza, Bone Fish Grill, Chick-fil-A, Chili's, Coldstone, Domino's, Dunkin Donuts, HoneyBaked Ham, Jimmy John's, McDonald's, Panera Bread, Pei Wei, Pizza Heaven, Starbucks, Weston Diner ⊙ AT&T, Fiat, Home Depot, Honda, Hyundai, Nissan/Volvo, Office Depot, Publix, Radio Shack, Toyota/

Side labels: FT MYERS · CAPE CORAL · ESTERO · NAPLES · FL

⬆N INTERSTATE 75 Cont'd

Exit #	Services
13b a	Continued Scion, vet, Walgreens
11b a	Sheridan St, **E** 🔲 Chevron 🔲 Cracker Barrel, Wendy's 🔲 Hampton Inn, Holiday Inn Express 🔲 Audi, BMW, **H** (3mi), Piccolo Park, **W** 🔲 Shell/dsl 🔲 Applebee's, Bistro 555, China One, Coldstone, Little Caesars, McDonald's, Original Pancake House, Romeus Cuban, Subway, TGIFriday's 🔲 Firestone/auto, GNC, Lowe's, Publix, URGENT CARE, Verizon, vet, Walgreens
9b a	FL 820, Pine Blvd, Hollywood Blvd, **E** 🔲 BP, Shell 🔲 Boston Mkt, Brimstone Woodfire Grill, Brio Italian, Cheesecake Factory, Chick-fil-A, Chili's, Fuddrucker's, HoneyBaked Ham, Jason's Deli, La Granja, Latin-American Grill, Lime Mexican Grill, Macaroni Grill, McDonald's, RA Grill, Sal's Italian, Starbucks, Stir Crazy, Subway, The Pub, Tijuana Flats, Village Tavern, Wendys 🔲 **H**, Barnes&Noble, BJ's Whse/gas, Dick's, Dodge, Mercedes, Old Navy, Petsmart, Publix, Radio Shack, USPO, Verizon, Walgreens, Walmart, **W** 🔲 BP/dsl, Citgo/dsl, Shell 🔲 Burger King, Chick-fil-A, Chipotle Mexican, Elevation Burger, KFC/Taco Bell, La Granja, Las Vegas Cuban, Marco's Pizza, McDonald's, Panda Express, Sal's Italian, SmashBurger, Starbucks, Sweet Tomatoes, Wendy's 🔲 Acura, Advance Parts, AT&T, AutoZone, Costco/gas, CVS Drug, GNC, Lexus, Publix, Sedano's Foods, Subaru, Tires+, Walgreens, Whole Foods Mkt
7b a	Miramar Pkwy, **E** 🔲 Chevron 🔲 Baskin-Robbins/Dunkin Donuts, Cancun Grill, La Carreta, McDonald's, Pollo Tropical, Quiznos, Sal's Italian, Starbucks, Subway, Tijuana Flats, Wendy's 🔲 Courtyard, Hilton Garden, Residence Inn, Wingate Inn 🔲 $Tree, Publix, USPO, Walgreens, **W** 🔲 Shell 🔲 Benihana, Chick-fil-A, Chili's, Coldstone, McDonald's, Orient Chef, Panera Bread, Starbucks, Subway, Yummy Asian 🔲 **H**, AT&T, city park, CVS Drug, Home Depot, Marshall's, Office Depot, Ross, SuperTarget, Winn-Dixie
5	to FL 821 (from sb), FL TPK (**toll**)
4	FL 860, NW 186th, Miami Gardens Dr, **E** 🔲 BP, Chevron 🔲 Carrabba's, Chicken Kitchen, Dunkin Donuts, McDonald's, Starbucks, Subway 🔲 AT&T, CVS Drug, GNC, Publix/deli, Sedanos Foods, vet
2	NW 138th, Graham Dairy Rd, **W** 🔲 Mobil, Shell/dsl 🔲 China Casa, China Wok, IHOP, Latin Cuban Cafe, Little Caesars, McDonald's, Starbucks, Subway, Wendy's 🔲 **H**, GNC, Publix, vet, Walgreens
1b a	I-75 begins/ends on FL 826, Palmetto Expswy, multiple services on FL 826.

⬆N INTERSTATE 95

Exit #	Services
382mm	Florida/Georgia state line, motorist callboxes begin/end., St Marys River
381mm	inspection sta both lanes
380	US 17, to Yulee, Kingsland, **E** 🔲 Osprey RV Park, **W** 🔲 Shell 🔲 American Inn
378mm	Welcome Ctr sb, 24hr security, full 🔲 facilities, litter barrels, petwalk, 🔲, 🔲, vending
376mm	weigh sta both lanes
373	FL 200, FL A1A, to Yulee, Callahan, Fernandina Bch, **E** 🔲 Flash/Krystal, Sunoco 🔲 Burger King, DQ, KFC/Pizza Hut, McDonald's, Wendy's 🔲 Comfort Inn, Holiday Inn Express, Nassau Holiday Motel (3mi) 🔲 RV Camping (3mi), to Ft Clinch SP (16mi), **W** 🔲 BP/Subway/dsl, Exxon/dsl

J A C K S O N V I L L E

366	Pecan Park Rd, **W** 🔲 Flea&Farmer's Mkt, Pecan Park RV Camping
363b a	Duval Rd, **E** 🔲 Mobil/7-11 🔲 5 Guys Burgers, Arby's, Boston's, Buffalo Wild Wings, Buffalo's Philly, Chick-fil-A, Chili's, Coldstone, Cracker Barrel, Green Papaya, Hardee's, Jimmy John's, Logan's Roadhouse, McDonald's, Olive Garden, Panda Express, Panera Bread, Pollo Tropical, Red Lobster, Salsaritas, Starbucks, Sticky Fingers, Subway, Taco Bell, Wasabi 🔲 A Loft 🔲 $Tree, AT&T, AutoZone, Best Buy, Dick's, Discount Tire, Gander Mtn, GNC, Goodyear/auto, Lowe's, Marshall's, Michael's, Old Navy, Petsmart, Ross, URGENT CARE, Verizon, Walgreens, Walmart/Subway, **W** 🔲 BP/dsl, Chevron, Exxon/dsl, Sunoco/Subway 🔲 Denny's, Longhorn Steaks, Millhouse Steaks, Ruby Tuesday, Waffle House, Zaxby's 🔲 Airport Inn, Best Western, Comfort Suites, Country Hearth Inn, Courtyard, Crowne Plaza, Fairfield Inn, Hampton Inn, Hilton Garden, Hyatt Place, Jacksonville Plaza Hotel, Jaxport Inn, Microtel, Quality Inn, Red Roof Inn, Residence Inn, SpringHill Suites, Travelodge, Wingate Inn 🔲 🔲, Gore's RV Ctr
362b a	I-295 S, FL 9A, to Blount Island, Jacksonville
360	FL 104, Dunn Ave, Busch Dr, **E** 🔲 Gate/dsl 🔲 Hardee's, Waffle House 🔲 Executive Inn 🔲 Sam's Club/gas, USPO, **W** 🔲 BP/dsl, Chevron, Hess, RaceTrac/dsl, Shell/dsl 🔲 Arby's, Burger King, Capt D's, Checker's, China Buffet, Country Cabin Rest., Firehouse Subs, KFC, Krystal, Little Caesars, McDonald's, New China, Pizza Hut, Popeye's, Sonny's BBQ, Starbucks, Subway, Taco Bell, Wendy's 🔲 EconoLodge, La Quinta, Motel 6 🔲 $Tree, Aamco, Advance Parts, BigLots, CVS Drug, Family$, Marshall's, Office Depot, PepBoys, Publix, Radio Shack, Tires+, Walgreens
358b a	FL 105, Broward Rd, Heckscher Dr, **E** 🔲 zoo, **W** 🔲 BP/dsl 🔲 USA Inn
357mm	Trout River
357	FL 111, Edgewood Ave, **W** 🔲 BP/dsl, Texaco/dsl
356b a	Fl 115, FL 117, Lem Turner Rd, Norwood Ave, **E** 🔲 Hardee's, **W** 🔲 BP/dsl, Hess/Dunkin Donuts, RaceWay/dsl, Shell 🔲 Burger King, Checker's, Golden EggRoll, Ho-Ho Chinese, Krystal, Popeye's, Subway, Taco Bell 🔲 Advance Parts, Save-A-Lot, Tires+, Walgreens
355	Golfair Blvd, **E** 🔲 Shell 🔲 McDonald's 🔲 Publix, **W** 🔲 Chevron/dsl, RaceWay/dsl
354b a	US 1, 20th St, to Jacksonville, to AmTrak, MLK Pkwy
353d	FL 114, to 8th St, **E** 🔲 McDonald's 🔲 **H**, Walgreens
353c	US 23 N, Kings Rd, downtown
353b	US 90A, Union St, 🔲 Sports Complex, downtown
353a	Church St, Myrtle Ave, Forsythe St, downtown
352d	I-10 W, Stockton St (from sb), Lake City
352c	Monroe St (from nb), downtown
352b a	Myrtle Ave (from nb), downtown
351mm	St Johns River
351d	Stockton St, 🔲 **H**, downtown
351c	Margaret St, downtown
351b	I-10 W, to Tallahassee
351a	Park St, College St, **H**, to downtown
350b	FL 13, San Marco Blvd, **E** 🔲 **H**
350a	Prudential Dr, Main St, Riverside Ave (from nb), to downtown, **E** 🔲 BP 🔲 Extended Stay America, Hampton Inn, Wyndham, **W** 🔲 Panera Bread 🔲 Hilton Garden
349	US 90 E (from sb), to beaches, **W** 🔲 Super 8, downtown
348	US 1 S (from sb), Philips Hwy, **W** 🔲 Scottish Inn, Super 8 🔲 Volvo

FL

M I A M I

Exit #	Services

INTERSTATE 95 Cont'd

347 US 1A, FL 126, Emerson St, E 🅿 Chevron/dsl, Shell 🍴 Hot Wok 🅾 Advance Parts, Family$, O'Reilly Parts, W 🅿 BP/dsl, Gate/dsl, Hess/dsl 🍴 McDonald's, Taco Bell 🛏 Emerson Inn 🅾 Chevrolet, Goodyear/auto

346b a FL 109, University Blvd, E 🅿 Exxon/dsl, Hess/dsl, Shell 🍴 Capt D's, Checkers, DQ, El Potro Mexican, Firehouse Subs, Happy Garden Chinese, Huddle House, Korean BBQ, Krystal, Pizza Hut, Popeye's, Ying's Chinese 🅾 Ⓗ, Ace Hardware, CarQuest, CVS Drug, Family$, Firestone/auto, NAPA, Sun Tire, Tire Kingdom, Tires+, Winn-Dixie, W 🅿 BP/dsl, Chevron, RaceTrac 🍴 Arby's, Baskin-Robbins/Dunkin Donuts, Burger King, Famous Amos, KFC, McDonald's, Papa John's, Sonny's BBQ, Taco Bell, Wendy's, Whataburger, Woody's BBQ 🛏 Days Inn, Ramada Inn, Super 8 🅾 auto repair, Family$, U-Haul

345 FL 109, University Blvd (from nb), E 🅿 Chevron, Gate/dsl/24hr, Hess/Blimpie/Godfather's Pizza/dsl 🍴 Bono's BBQ, Schnitzel House 🅾 Ⓗ

344 FL 202, Butler Blvd, E 🅿 Gate/dsl 🍴 Dave&Buster's 🛏 Best Western, Candlewood Suites, EconoLodge, Holiday Inn Express, Homestead Suites, Howard Johnson, Marriott, Radisson 🅾 Ⓗ, USPO, W 🅿 BP/dsl, Shell 🍴 Applebee's, Baskin-Robbins/Dunkin Donuts, Chick-fil-A, Cracker Barrel, Hardee's, McDonald's, Quiznos, Sonic, Starbucks, Waffle House, Wendy's, Whataburger/24hr, Zaxby's 🛏 Courtyard, Extended Stay Deluxe, Fairfield Inn, Jameson Inn, La Quinta, Microtel, Red Roof Inn, Wingate Inn

341 FL 152, Baymeadows Rd, E 🅿 BP/dsl, Gate/dsl, Shell/dsl 🍴 Arby's, Chili's, CiCi's Pizza, Hardee's, Krystal, Omaha Steaks, Panda Express, Quiznos, Subway 🛏 Bay Meadows Inn, Comfort Suites, Embassy Suites, Holiday Inn, HomeStead Suites 🅾 Advance Parts, Tires+, Walgreens, Winn-Dixie, W 🅿 Kangaroo, Shell 🍴 Al's Pizza, Bamboo Creek, Chicago Pizzaria, Denny's, Gator's Seafood, IHOP, KFC, Larry's Subs, Little Caesars, McDonald's, Pagoda Chinese, Red Lobster, Taco Bell, Wendy's, Woody's BBQ 🛏 Best Inn, Homewood Suites, La Quinta, Motel 6, Quality Inn, Residence Inn, Sheraton, Studio 6, Sun Suites 🅾 $Tree, BJ's Whse/gas, CVS Drug, Discount Tire, Goodyear/auto, Harley-Davidson, Lowe's, Office Depot

340 FL 115, Southside Blvd (from nb), E on FL 115 🅿 Kangaroo/dsl 🍴 5 Guys Burgers, Longhorn Steaks 🅾 AT&T, Home Depot, Michael's, Petsmart, same as 339, Target

339 US 1, Philips Hwy, E 🅿 Kangaroo/dsl, RaceTrac 🍴 Arby's, Bono's BBQ, Buca Italian, Burger King, Chick-fil-A, Coldstone, McDonald's, Mikado, Moe's SW Grill, Olive Garden, Ruby Tuesday, Starbucks, Taco Bell 🅾 $Tree, Belk, Best Buy, Chevrolet, Dillard's, Ford, JC Penney, mall, Mazda, Nissan, Sears/auto, Tire Kingdom, Toyota, Walmart, W 🅿 BP/dsl 🍴 Benito's Italian, Steak&Shake, Subway

337 I-295 N, to rd 9a, Orange Park, Jax Beaches

335 Old St Augustine Rd, E 🍴 Applebee's, Starbucks 🛏 Courtyard 🅾 Ⓗ, W 🅿 Gate/dsl, Shell 🍴 5 Guys Burgers, Bamboo Wok, Bono's BBQ, Chili's, Daruma Steaks, McDonald's, Panera Bread, Subway, Tijuana Flats, Zaxby's 🛏 Hampton Inn 🅾 AT&T, GNC, Goodyear/auto, Kohl's, Publix, Verizon, vet, Walgreens

331mm 🆁🆂 both lanes, 24hr security, full 🛏 facilities, litter barrels, petwalk, 🅿, 🛏, vending

---

329 rd 210, Green Cove Springs, Ponte Vedra Beach, E 🅿 Pilot /McDonald's/dsl/scales/24hr, Sunoco/fruit, TA/Shell/Subway/ dsl/scales/24hr/@ 🍴 Waffle House, W 🅿 BP/Subway/dsl/ USPO, Marathon/Kangaroo/dsl, Shell 🍴 Burger King, China Wok, Domino's, Dunkin Donuts, Firehouse Subs, Jenk's Pizza, Starbucks, Tropical Smoothie, Yummy Asian 🅾 AT&T, CVS Drug, fireworks, vet, Winn-Dixie

323 International Golf Pkwy, E 🅿 BP/dsl/USPO, Shell/Subway/dsl 🛏 Comfort Suites, W 🍴 Cino's Pizza, King Wok, Village Grill/ Subs 🛏 Renaissance Resort 🅾 vet, World Golf Village

318 FL 16, Green Cove Sprgs, St Augustine, E 🅿 BP/DQ/dsl, Gate/dsl/fruit, Kangaroo/dsl, Shell 🍴 Burger King, Dunkin Donuts, Krystal, McDonald's, NY Diner, Subway 🛏 Best Value Inn, Comfort Inn, Courtyard, Fairfield Inn, Holiday Inn Express, La Quinta, Quality Inn 🅾 Cadillac, Camping World RV Ctr, Ford/Lincoln, Gander Mtn, Gore's RV Ctr, St Augustine Outlets/Famous Brands, W 🅿 Exxon, RaceTrac/dsl 🍴 A-1 Chinese, Cracker Barrel, Denny's, Giovanni's Italian, IHOP, KFC, LemonGrass Asian, Ruby Tuesday, Sonny's BBQ, Taco Bell, Wendy's 🛏 Best Western, Days Inn, Hampton Inn, Ramada Ltd, Super 8, Wingate Inn 🅾 funpark, RV camping, St Augustine Outlets, Verizon

311 FL 207, St Augustine, E 🅿 Chevron, Hess/Subway/dsl, RaceTrac/dsl 🅾 Ⓗ, flea mkt/fireworks, Indian Forest RV Park (2mi), Indian River Fruit, KOA (7mi), St Johns RV Park, to Anastasia SP, W 🅿 Mobil/dsl/repair 🛏 Quality Inn

305 FL 206, to Hastings, Crescent Beach, E 🅿 FLYING J/Denny's/Subway/dsl/LP/scales/24hr 🅾 to Ft Matanzas NM, truck repair, W 🅾 truck repair

302mm 🆁🆂 both lanes, 24hr security, full 🛏 facilities, litter barrels, petwalk, 🅿, 🛏, vending

298 US 1, to St Augustine, E 🅿 BP/dsl, Indian River Fruit, Sunoco 🅾 to Faver-Dykes SP, W 🅿 Mobil/DQ/dsl, Sunrise/dsl

289 to FL A1A (toll br), to Palm Coast, E 🅿 Kangaroo/dsl, Mobil/7-11, RaceTrac/dsl, Shell 🍴 China Express, Colletti's Italian, Cracker Barrel, Denny's, Dunkin Donuts, Grand China, KFC, McDonald's, Salsa's Mexican, Starbucks, Wendy's 🛏 Best Western, Fairfield Inn, Microtel, Sleep Inn 🅾 Beall's, CVS Drug, Publix, Staples, vet, Walgreens, W 🅿 Chevron, Citgo, Kangaroo/dsl, Shell 🍴 Baskin-Robbins/Dunkin Donuts, Bob Evans, Brusters, China King, China One, Golden Corral, HoneyBaked Ham, Houligan's, Joe's NY Pizza, Nathan's Cafe, Outback Steaks, Perkins, Ruby Tuesday, Sakura Japanese, Sonny's BBQ, Steak'n Shake, Subway, Taco Bell, Wendy's 🛏 Days Inn 🅾 $General, Advance Parts, AutoZone, Beall's, Belk, CVS Drug, Ford, Home Depot, Kohl's, Lowe's, Publix, Radio Shack, Tire Kingdom, Tuffy Auto, USPO, Verizon, Walgreens, Walmart, Winn-Dixie

(Side labels: JACKSONVILLE, ST AUGUSTINE, PALM COAST)

🛢 = gas ⑪ = food 🛏 = lodging ⊙ = other Ⓡ🇸 = rest stop Copyright 2015 - the Next EXIT ®

Copyright 2015 - the Next EXIT ®

⬆N INTERSTATE 95 Cont'd

Exit #	Services
286mm	weigh sta both lanes, 🚻
284	FL 100, to Bunnell, Flagler Beach, E 🛢 Mobil/dsl, Valero/dsl ⑪ Burger King, Domino's, McDonald's, Oriental Garden, Subway, Woody's BBQ 🛏 Hampton Inn, Holiday Inn Express ⊙ Ace Hardware, Russell Stover's, vet, Winn-Dixie, W 🛢 BP 🛏 Hilton Garden ⊙ 🄷, Chevrolet, Chrysler/Dodge/Jeep, Dunkin Donuts, Panera Bread, Red Lobster
278	Old Dixie Hwy, E 🛢 7-11 ⑪ King Chinese, Plantation Grill ⊙ Bulow RV Park (3mi), Publix, to Tomoka SP, W 🛢 BP/dsl ⑪ Joe's Pizza 🛏 Country Hearth Inn ⊙ Holiday Travel Park, vet
273	US 1, E 🛢 Chevron, RaceTrac/dsl ⑪ McDonald's, Waffle House 🛏 Econo Inn, La Quinta ⊙ fruit/fireworks, Giant Rec RV Ctr, W 🛢 Exxon/Burger King, ♥Loves/Arby's/dsl/scales/24hr ⑪ Daytona Pig Stand BBQ, DQ, Houligan's 🛏 Days Inn, Daytona Hotel, Motel 6, Scottish Inn, Super 8 ⊙ Encore RV Park, Harley-Davidson
268	FL 40, Ormond Beach, E 🛢 Chevron/dsl, Hess/dsl ⑪ Applebee's, Boston Mkt, Chick-fil-A, Chili's, Crispers, Denny's, Dustin's BBQ, Houligan's, Mama Mia's Pizza, Papa John's, Starbucks, Steak'n Shake, Subway, Taco Bell, Takeya Steaks, The Dish, Wendy's, Wok&Roll 🛏 Sleep Inn ⊙ 🄷 $General, $Tree, AT&T, Beall's, Discount Tire, GNC, Lowe's, Publix, Ross, Tire Kingdom, to Tomoka SP, USPO, vet, Walmart, Whole Foods Mkt, W 🛢 7-11, BP/Dunkin Donuts, Mobil/dsl, RaceTrac/dsl, Texaco ⑪ Cracker Barrel, Little Italy, McDonald's, Salsa's Mexican 🛏 Hampton Inn, Jameson Inn ⊙ Walgreens
265	LPGA Blvd, Holly Hill, Daytona Beach, E 🛢 7-11, Shell/Circle K/Dunkin Donuts/dsl ⑪ Vince Carter Rest, Wendy's ⊙ CVS Drug, W 🛏 Holiday Inn ⊙ BMW, Chrysler/Dodge/Jeep, Fiat, Ford, Lincoln, Mazda, Nissan, VW
261b a	US 92, to DeLand, Daytona Bch, E 🛢 7-11, Citgo/dsl, Hess/Quiznos/Dunkin Donuts/dsl, RaceTrac, RaceWay/dsl, Sunoco ⑪ 5 Guys Burgers, Applebee's, Asian Grill, BJ's Rest., Bob Evans, Buffalo Wild Wings, Burger King, Carrabba's, Checkers, Chick-fil-A, Chili's, Chipotle Mexican, Cracker Barrel, Daytona Ale House, Denny's, Dickey's BBQ, Firehouse Subs, Gators, Hooters, Jersey Mike's Subs, Jimmy John's, KFC, Krystal, Longhorn Steaks, McDonald's, Olive Garden, Outback Steaks, Panera Bread, Piccadilly, Quiznos, Red Lobster, Ruby Tuesday, Subway, Taco Bell, Tijuana Flats, Waffle House, Wendy's, Winghouse 🛏 Comfort Suites, Hampton Inn, Hilton Garden, Holiday Inn Express, Homewood Suites, La Quinta, Quality Inn, Ramada Inn, Residence Inn ⊙ 🄷, $Tree, AT&T, Barnes&Noble, Beall's, Best Buy, BigLots, Books-A-Million, Dick's, Dillard's, Firestone/auto, Hobby Lobby, Home Depot, JC Penney, Jo-Ann Fabrics, K-Mart, Macy's, mall, Marshall's, Michael's, Old Navy, PepBoys, PetCo, Petsmart, Sears/auto, Staples, SteinMart, Target, TJMaxx, to Daytona Racetrack, Tuesday Morning, Verizon, World Mkt, W 🛢 BP/dsl ⑪ IHOP, McDonald's 🛏 Days Inn, Super 8 ⊙ flea mkt, KOA
260b a	I-4, to Orlando, FL 400 E, to S Daytona, E 🛢 Chevron/dsl, Citgo/7-11
256	FL 421, to Port Orange, E 🛢 BP, Shell/Circle K ⑪ Applebee's, Bob Evans, Boston Mkt, Burger King, Chick-fil-A, Chili's, Daily Grind Burgers, Denny's, Dustin's BBQ, Golden Corral, KFC, Marble Slab Creamery, McDonald's, Monterrey Grill, Panera Bread, Papa John's, Quiznos, Smoothie King, Sonny's BBQ, Stonewood Grill, TGIFriday's, Tijuana Flats
256	Continued 🛏 Country Inn&Suites, La Quinta ⊙ BigLots, CVS Drug, Daytona Beach RV Park, Home Depot, Lowe's, Save-a-Lot, Super Target, Tuffy Auto, vet, Walgreens, Walmart, W 🛢 7-11, BP, Citgo ⑪ 5 Guys Burgers, China Chef, Coldstone, Gatti's Pizza, Malibu Beach Grill, McDonald's, Olive Garden, Red Brick Pizza, Red Robin, Subway, Takara Steaks, TX Roadhouse, Wendy's ⊙ $Tree, AT&T, Belk, GNC, Kohl's, Marshall's, Michael's, PetCo, Publix, Walgreens, Whole Foods Mkt
249b a	FL 44, to De Land, New Smyrna Beach, E 🛢 Shell/dsl/fruit ⊙ New Smyrna RV Camp (3mi), W 🛢 Chevron/dsl ⑪ McDonald's ⊙ Walmart/Subway
244	FL 442, to Edgewater, E 🛢 BP/dsl ⊙ truck repair
231	rd 5A, Scottsmoor, E 🛢 BP/Stuckey's/dsl ⊙ Crystal Lake RV Park
227mm	Ⓡ🇸 sb, 24hr security, full ♿ facilities, litter barrels, petwalk, 🚻, 🅰, vending
225mm	Ⓡ🇸 nb, 24hr security, full ♿ facilities, litter barrels, petwalk, 🚻, 🅰, vending
223	FL 46, Mims, E 🛢 Chevron (2mi), RaceWay/dsl ⑪ McDonald's, W 🛢 BP, Shell ⊙ KOA/LP, Seasons RV Park
220	FL 406, Titusville, E 🛢 BP/dsl, Shell/Hungry Howie's/dsl ⑪ 1st Wok, Beef'O'Brady's, Kelsey's Pizza, McDonald's, Subway, Valentino's Rest, Wendy's 🛏 Super 8 ⊙ 🄷, $General, Advance Parts, AT&T, GNC, Publix, Tires+, to Canaveral Nat Seashore, Walgreens
215	FL 50, to Orlando, Titusville, E 🛢 BP/KFC/dsl, Circle K, Mobil/Subway/dsl, Murphy USA/dsl, Shell/DQ/dsl ⑪ Buddy Freddy's, Burger King, Denny's, Durango Steaks, McDonald's, Panda Express, Quiznos, Sonny's BBQ, Taco Bell, Waffle House, Wendy's 🛏 Best Western, Ramada Inn ⊙ Aldi Foods, Ford, GNC, Home Depot, Lowe's, Marshall's, PetCo, Radio Shack, Staples, Target, Tire Kingdom, to Kennedy Space Ctr, Walmart, W ⑪ Cracker Barrel, IHOP 🛏 Days Inn, Fairfield Inn, Hampton Inn, Holiday Inn, Quality Inn ⊙ Christmas RV Park (8mi), Great Outdoors RV/golf Resort
212	FL 407, to FL 528 **toll** (no re-entry sb)
208	Port St John
205	FL 528 (**toll 528**), to Cape Canaveral & Cape Port AFS, City Point
202	FL 524, Cocoa, E 🛢 Shell/dsl ⊙ Museum of History&Science, W 🛢 BP/dsl 🛏 Days Inn
201	FL 520, to Cocoa Bch, Cocoa, E 🛢 BP/dsl, Chevron, ▨▨▨/Subway/dsl/scales/24hr ⑪ IHOP, Waffle House 🛏 Best Western, Motel 6 ⊙ 🄷, fireworks, Sams Club/gas, W 🛢 Chevron/dsl, Shell/Burger King, Sunoco/dsl ⑪ McDonald's 🛏 Holiday Inn Express ⊙ Camping World RV Ctr
195	FL 519, Fiske Blvd, E 🛢 7-11, Mobil/dsl ⑪ Dominico Italian, Ruby Tuesday 🛏 Swiss Inn ⊙ 🄷, Discount Tire, Lowe's, Space Coast RV Park
191	rd 509, to Satellite Beach, Viera, E 🛢 7-11, BP, Hess/dsl, Sunoco/dsl ⑪ Bob Evans, Carrabba's, Chick-fil-A, Denny's, Domino's, DQ, Firehouse Subs, McDonald's, Papa John's, Perkins, Sonny's BBQ, Tropical Smoothie, Uno Grill, Wendy's 🛏 Hampton Inn, Holiday Inn ⊙ AT&T, CVS Drug, Publix, Radio Shack, Tires+, to Patrick AFB, Tuffy Auto, URGENT CARE, Walgreens, zoo, W 🛢 Chevron/dsl, Murphy USA ⑪ 5 Guys Burgers, Asian Too, Asian Wok, Burger King, Chili's, Coldstone, Cracker Barrel, Longhorn Steaks, Melting Pot, Mimi's Cafe, Moe's SW Grill, Panera Bread, Pita Pit, Pizza Gallery, Starbucks, Steak'n Shake, Subway 🛏 La Quinta

ORMOND BEACH DAYTONA

TITUSVILLE

FL

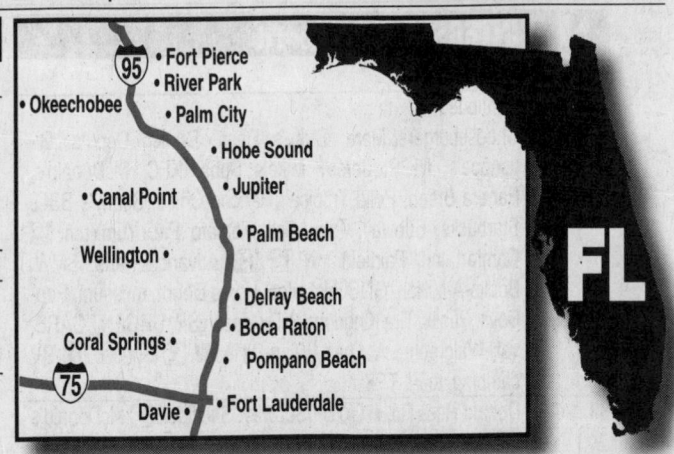

INTERSTATE 95 Cont'd

Exit #	Services
191	**Continued**
	🅾 H, $Tree, AT&T, Belk, Books-A-Million, GNC, Hobby Lobby, Kohl's, Lexus, Michael's, Office Depot, Old Navy, PetCo, Ross, SuperTarget, Tire Kingdom, Verizon, Walmart/McDonald's, World Mkt
188	FL 404, Patrick AFB, Satellite Beach
183	FL 518, Melbourne, Indian Harbour Beach, E 🍴 7-11, BP, Chevron/Baskin-Robbins/Dunkin Donuts/dsl, RaceTrac/dsl 🅾 H, art museum, AT&T, W 🅾 Flea Mkt
180	US 192, to Melbourne, E 🍴 7-11, BP/dsl, Circle K, Mobil/dsl, RaceTrac/dsl, Sunoco/dsl 🍴 ChuckECheese, Denny's, IHOP, Waffle House 🏠 Best Value Inn, Budget Inn, Days Inn, EconoLodge, Fairfield Inn, Hampton Inn, Holiday Inn Express 🅾 H, Ace Hardware, fireworks, Lowe's, Sam's Club/gas, vet, Volvo
176	rd 516, to Palm Bay, E 🍴 7-11, BP/dsl, Citgo, Murphy USA/dsl 🍴 Baskin Robbins/Dunkin Donuts, Bob Evans, Chick-fil-A, Cracker Barrel, Denny's, Golden Corral, Starbucks 🏠 Jameson Inn 🅾 Aldi Foods, BJ's Whse/gas, GNC, Harley-Davidson, Office Depot, vet, Walgreens, Walmart, W 🍴 7-11, Mobil/dsl, Shell 🍴 5 Guys Burgers, Buffalo Wild Wings, Burger King, Long Doggers, Longhorn Steaks, McDonald's, Michelli's Pizzeria, Moe's SW Grill, Panera Bread, Subway, Wendy's 🅾 $Tree, AT&T, CVS Drug, Discount Tire, Kohl's, Marshall's, Michael's, PetCo, Publix, Ross, Target, Walgreens
173	FL 514, to Palm Bay, E 🍴 RaceTrac/dsl, Shell, Sunoco/dsl 🏠 Holiday Inn Express 🅾 H, Firestone/auto, Ford, truck/RV repair, W 🍴 Hess/Quiznos, Mobil/dsl, Sunoco 🍴 Arby's, Burger King, IHOP, Japanese Buffet, McDonald's/playplace, Panda Express, Sonny's BBQ, Subway, Taco Bell, TX Roadhouse, Waffle House, Wendy's 🏠 Comfort Suites, Motel 6 🅾 $General, Advance Parts, Beall's, BigLots, CVS Drug, Home Depot, Lowe's, Publix, Tire Kingdom, URGENT CARE, USPO, Verizon, Walgreens, Walmart
168mm	🛉 both lanes, 24hr security, full ♿ facilities, litter barrels, petwalk, 🌳, 🚮, vending
156	rd 512, to Sebastian, Fellsmere, E 🍴 BP/DQ/Stuckey's/dsl, Chevron/McDonald's, RaceWay/dsl 🅾 H, Encore RV Park, Sebastian Inlet SRA, Vero Bch RV Park (8mi), W 🅾 Marsh Landing Camping, St Sebastian SP
147	FL 60, Osceola Blvd, E 🍴 7-11, BP/Dunkin Donuts/dsl, Citgo/dsl, Mobil/dsl, Sunoco, TA/BP/Popeye's/Subway/dsl/scales/24hr/@, Texaco/dsl, Valero/dsl 🍴 IHOP, Wendy's 🏠 Best Value Inn, Comfort Suites, Howard Johnson, Knights Inn, Vero Beach Resort 🅾 H, Hyundai, USPO, vet, W 🍴 Shell/dsl 🍴 Cracker Barrel, McDonald's, Steak'n Shake 🏠 Country Inn&Suites, Hampton Inn, Holiday Inn Express 🅾 Vero Beach Outlets/famous brands
138	FL 614, Indrio Rd, E 3 mi 🅾 Oceanographic Institute
133mm	🛉 both lanes, 24hr security, full ♿ facilities, litter barrels, petwalk, 🌳, 🚮, vending
131b a	FL 68, Orange Ave, E 🅾 H, to Ft Pierce SP, W 🍴 FLYING J/Denny's/Subway/dsl/LP/scales/24hr, Loves /Hardee's/dsl/scales/24hr 🅾 Blue Beacon
129	FL 70, to Okeechobee, E 🍴 Citgo, Hess/dsl, Murphy USA, RaceTrac/dsl, Shell/Circle K, Sunoco/dsl 🍴 Applebee's, Cowboys BBQ, Golden Corral, Sonic, Waffle House 🅾 H, $General, $Tree, Advance Parts, Firestone/auto, Home Depot, Radio Shack, truck tires, URGENT CARE, Walgreens, Walmart, W 🍴 BP/scales/dsl, Chevron, Loves /Arby's/

129	**Continued**
	dsl/24hr/@, Mobil/Dunkin Donuts/Subway, 🍴/McDonald's/dsl/scales/24hr 🍴 Burger King, Cracker Barrel, KFC, La Granja, LJ Silver, McDonald's, Red Lobster, Steak'n Shake, Waffle House, Wendy's 🏠 Best Value Inn, Best Western, Comfort Suites, Fairfield Inn, Hampton Inn, Holiday Inn Express, La Quinta, Motel 6, Quality Inn, Rodeway Inn, Sleep Inn, Treasure Coast Inn 🅾 Indian River Fruit, to FL TPK, Treasure Coast RV Park, UF R&E Ctr
126	rd 712, Midway Rd, E 🍴 BP/Subway/dsl
121	St Lucie West Blvd, E 🍴 7-11, BP/Dunkin Donuts, Mobil/7-11, Murphy USA/dsl, Shell/Subway/dsl 🍴 Arby's, Bob Evans, Burger King, Carrabba's, Chili's, Chipotle Mexican, Duffy's Grill, Frank&Al's Pizza, Friendly's, Hokkaido, Hurricane Grill, IHOP, Jimmy John's, KFC, Little Caesars, McDonald's, Moe's SW Grill, Outback Steaks, PA BBQ, Panda Express, Panera Bread, Ruby Tuesday, Starbucks, Stevi B's Pizza, Taco Bell, TGIFriday's, Wendy's 🏠 Hampton Inn, Holiday Inn Express, Residence Inn, SpringHill Suites 🅾 H, $Tree, AT&T, Beall's, CVS Drug, Outdoor Resorts Camping (2mi), PetCo, Publix/deli, Ross, Staples, SteinMart, Tire Kingdom, Tires+, URGENT CARE, USPO, Verizon, Walgreens, Walmart, W 🍴 Mobil/dsl 🏠 Hilton Garden, MainStay Suites, Sheraton Resort 🅾 PGA Village
120	Crosstown Pkwy
118	Gatlin Blvd, to Port St Lucie, E 🍴 BP/dsl/LP, Chevron/Dunkin Donuts/Subway/dsl, Shell, Sunoco/e-85 🍴 McDonald's, Taco Bell 🅾 AutoZone, Home Depot, Sam's Club/gas, Tires+, vet, Walgreens, Walmart, W 🍴 Longhorn Steaks, McDonald's, Olive Garden, Subway, Tropical Smoothie 🏠 Homewood Suites 🅾 H, GNC, Michael's, Old Navy, Petsmart, Publix, Radio Shack, Target, TJ Maxx
114	Becker Rd
112mm	weigh sta sb
110	FL 714, to Martin Hwy, Palm City, E 🅾 H
106mm	🛉 both lanes, 24hr security, full ♿ facilities, litter barrels, petwalk, 🌳, 🚮, vending
102	Rd 713, High Meadow Ave, Palm City
101	FL 76, to Stuart, Indiantown, E 🍴 Chevron/dsl, Sunoco/dsl 🍴 Baskin-Robbins/Dunkin Donuts, Cracker Barrel, McDonald's 🏠 Courtyard, Holiday Inn Express 🅾 H, city park, Publix, Walgreens, W 🍴 Marathon/DQ/dsl, Valero/dsl 🅾 RV camping
96	rd 708, to Hobe Sound, E 🅾 Dickinson SP (11mi), RV camping
92mm	weigh sta nb
87b a	FL 706, to Okeechobee, Jupiter, E 🍴 Citgo, Mobil/dsl, Shell/dsl, Sunoco 🍴 5 Guys Burgers, Applebee's,

MELBOURNE PALM BAY (vertical sidebar label, left)

OKEECHOBEE (vertical sidebar label, right)

FL (map label)

⬆N INTERSTATE 95 Cont'd

Exit #	Services
87b a	Continued Cheeseburgers&More, Duffy's Rest., Dunkin Donuts, Giuseppe's, IHOP, Jersey Mike's Subs, KFC, McDonald's, Panera Bread, Pollo Tropical, Rancho Chico, Sonny's BBQ, Starbucks, Subway, Taco Bell, Tomato Pie, YumYum ⌂ Comfort Inn, Fairfield Inn ◎ 🍴, Advance Parts, BMW, Books-A-Million, GNC, hist sites, Home Depot, museum, PepBoys, Publix, Tire Kingdom, to Dickinson SP, URGENT CARE, vet, Walgreens, Walmart, Winn-Dixie, **W** ◉ Sunoco ◎ RV camping, to FL TPK
83	Donald Ross Rd, **E** ◉ BP/Subway, Shell/deli 🍴 McDonald's ⌂ Hampton Inn, Holiday Inn Express, Homewood Suites ◎ 🍴, AT&T, CVS Drug, stadium, Walgreens
79c	FL 809 S (from sb), Military Tr, **W** same services as 79b, to FL TPK
79a b	FL 786, PGA Blvd, **E** ◉ Shell 🍴 Chili's, TGIFriday's, Yardhouse Rest ⌂ Hilton Garden, Marriott ◎ 🍴, Best Buy, Michael's, PetCo, Publix, Whole Foods Mkt, **W** ◉ Shell/dsl 🍴 3 Forks Rest, Cantina Laredo, China Kitchen, Chipotle Mexican, J Alexanders, Outback Steaks ⌂ DoubleTree Hotel, Embassy Suites ◎ CVS Drug, Publix
77	Northlake Blvd, to W Palm Bch, **E** ◉ BP, Hess/Dunkin Donuts, Shell/dsl 🍴 Aladdin Grill, Applebee's, Arby's, Burger King, Checkers, Chick-fil-A, Giovanni's Rest, Jimmy John's, KFC, La Granja, Little Caesars, McDonald's, Miami Subs, Panera Bread, Pollo Tropical, Starbucks, Taco Bell ◎ 🍴, $Tree, AT&T, Buick/Chevrolet/GMC, Chrysler/Dodge/Jeep, Costco, CVS Drug, Family$, Ford, Gander Mtn, Home Depot, Hyundai, K-Mart, Lowe's, PepBoys, Ross, Staples, Target, Verizon, vet, VW, Walgreens, **W** ◉ Chevron/dsl, Shell, Sunoco/dsl, Valero 🍴 Duffy's Grill, Dunkin Donuts, Original Pancakes, Papa John's, Pizza Hut, Wendy's ⌂ Inn of America ◎ Advance Parts, CVS Drug, Publix, Radio Shack, Verizon, vet, Winn-Dixie
76	FL 708, Blue Heron Blvd, **E** ◉ BP/dsl, Shell/dsl 🍴 Wendy's ⌂ Travelodge ◎ Honda, Kia, Nissan, Walgreens, **W** ◉ BP, Chevron/dsl, Cumberland Farms, RaceTrac/dsl, Texaco/dsl 🍴 Burger King, Denny's, McDonald's ⌂ Super 8
74	FL 702, 45th St, **E** ◉ Burger King, IHOP ⌂ Days Inn ◎ 🍴, Cadillac, URGENT CARE, Walgreens, **W** ◉ RaceTrac 🍴 Cracker Barrel, McDonald's, Pollo Tropical, Subway, Taco Bell, Wendy's ⌂ Courtyard, Extended Stay Deluxe, Holiday Inn Express, Homewood Suites, Red Roof Inn, Residence Inn, SpringHill Suites ◎ Family$, FoodTown, Goodyear/auto, Harley-Davidson, Sams Club/gas, Walmart
71	Lake Blvd, Palm Beach, **E** ◉ BP, Mobil/7-11/dsl 🍴 McDonald's, Wendy's ⌂ Best Western ◎ 🍴, Best Buy, Firestone/auto, Home Depot, JC Penney, Target, Tire Kingdom, **W** ◉ Texaco/dsl, Valero 🍴 Carrabba's, Chick-fil-A, Chipotle Mexican, Hooters, Manzo Italian, Palm Tree Cafe, Sweet Tomatoes ⌂ Comfort Inn, La Quinta ◎ URGENT CARE, vet, Walgreens
70b a	FL 704, Okeechobee Blvd, **E** 🍴 McCormick&Schmick, Ruth's Chris Steaks ⌂ Marriott ◎ museum, **W** ◉ BP/dsl, Chevron/dsl, Hess, Mobil/dsl, Shell, Texaco/dsl, Valero/dsl 🍴 Arby's, Burger King, Checkers, Denny's, Firehouse Grill, IHOP, McDonald's, Pizza Hut, Pollo Tropical, Starbucks, Subway, Taco Bell ◎ $Tree, AT&T, Audi/Porsche, BMW/Mini, Chevrolet, Firestone/auto, GNC, Hyundai, Mercedes, Michael's, Office Depot, Old Navy, Petsmart, Staples, Verizon, VW
69b	**W** ◎ to 🏖
69a	Belvedere Rd, **W** ◉ BP, Shell 🍴 Burger King, IHOP, Wendy's ⌂ Best Western, Courtyard, Crowne Plaza, DoubleTree, Hampton Inn, Hilton Garden, Holiday Inn/rest., Studio 6
68	US 98, Southern Blvd, **E** ◉ Texaco ◎ CVS Drug, Publix, Radio Shack, **W** ⌂ Hilton
66	Forest Hill Blvd, **W** ◉ Chevron/dsl, Sunoco 🍴 Bellante's Pizza ◎ Advance Parts
64	10th Ave N, **W** ◉ BP, Citgo 🍴 China Empire, Dunkin Donuts, Flanigans Grill, Wendy's ◎ CarQuest, CVS Drug, Family$, Ford, President Foods, Ross, Tires+, vet, Walgreens, Walmart/Subway
63	6th Ave S, **W** ◎ 🍴
61	FL 812, Lantana Rd, **E** ◉ Shell 🍴 Domino's, Dunkin Donuts, Golden Wok, KFC, Little Caesars, McDonald's, Pearl's Rest, Riggin's Crabhouse, Subway ⌂ Motel 6 ◎ $General, 7-11, Ace Hardware, CVS Drug, Publix, **W** ◎ 🍴, Costco/gas
60	Hypoluxo Rd, **E** ◉ BP, Mobil/dsl, Shell/dsl 🍴 IHOP, Popeye's, Subway, Taco Bell, Wendy's ⌂ Best Value Inn, Comfort Inn, Super 8 ◎ Family$, Sam's Club, Tire Kingdom, Tire Pros, Tires+, Winn-Dixie, **W** ◉ Valero/dsl 🍴 Anchor Inn Rest ◎ Advance Parts
59	Gateway Blvd, **W** ◉ Mobil/7-11/dsl 🍴 Bonefish Grill, Boynton Alehouse, Carrabba's, Chili's, Firehouse Subs, Friendly's, Golden Phoenix Chinese, Greek Cafe, McDonald's, Starbucks, Subway, Tropical Smoothie ⌂ Hampton Inn ◎ AT&T, CarMax, CVS Drug, Kohl's, Publix, Ross, Tuesday Morning, vet
57	FL 804, Boynton Bch Blvd, **E** ◉ Marathon/dsl 🍴 KFC ⌂ Boynton Beach Inn ◎ 🍴, USPO, **W** 0-2 mi ◉ BP, Mobil, Shell 🍴 Applebee's, Burger King, Checkers, Chick-Fil-A, Dunkin Donuts, Golden Corral, KFC, La Granja, Little Caesars, Sonic, Starbucks, Steak'n Shake, Subway, TGIFriday's, Wendy's ◎ 7-11, Barnes&Noble, BJ's Whse/gas, CVS Drug, Dick's, Dillard's, GNC, JC Penney, Macy's, Office Depot, Old Navy, PetCo, Petsmart, Publix, Radio Shack, Sears, SteinMart, TJ Maxx, USPO, vet, Walmart
56	Woolbright Rd, **E** ◉ Shell, Valero 🍴 Boynton Diner, McDonald's, Subway ◎ 🍴, 7-11, Jo-Ann Fabrics, Publix, vet, Walgreens, Winn-Dixie, **W** ◉ RaceTrac/dsl 🍴 Burger King, Cracker Barrel, Dunkin Donuts ◎ Advance Parts, Bravo Foods, Home Depot, Lowe's, Staples, Walgreens
52b a	FL 806, Atlantic Ave, **W** ◉ Chevron/dsl, Shell/dsl 🍴 Dunkin Donuts, Sandwich Man, Silver Wok ◎ 🍴, Tires+, transmissions, Verizon, vet, Walgreens
51	rd 782, Linton Blvd, **E** ◉ Shell 🍴 Applebee's, Arby's, Chipotle Mexican, DQ, Duffy's Grill, IHOP, KFC, McDonald's, Outback Steaks, Pollo Tropical, Steak'n Shake, Subway, Taco Bell, Wendy's ◎ AT&T, Chevrolet, Ford, Home Depot, Marshall's, Mercedes, Michael's, Petsmart, Publix, Ross, Staples, Target, Tire Kingdom, Verizon, **W** ◉ Shell 🍴 Little Caesars ◎ 🍴, Family$, Monterrey's Mkt, URGENT CARE
50	Congress Ave, **W** ◉ Mobil ⌂ Hilton Garden, Residence Inn
48b a	FL 794, Yamato Rd, **E** ◉ Mobil 🍴 Panera Bread ◎ CVS Drug, vet, **W** ◉ Chevron/dsl, Mobil 🍴 Blue Fin, Dunkin Donuts, Jersey Mike's Subs, Jimmy John's, McDonald's, Miller's Alehouse, Quiznos, Sal's Italian, Starbucks, Subway, Wendy's ⌂ DoubleTree, Embassy Suites, Guest Suites, Hampton Inn, SpringHill Suites, TownePlace Suites
45	FL 808, Glades Rd, **E** ◉ Chevron/dsl 🍴 J Alexander's Rest, Jamba Juice, PF Changs ⌂ Fairfield Inn ◎ Barnes&Noble, CVS Drug, museum, Whole Foods Mkt, **W** ◉ BP

FL

W PALM BEACH

PALM BEACH

INTERSTATE 95 Cont'd

Exit #	Services

45 Continued
🍴 Brewzzi Cafe, Brio Italian Grill, CA Pizza Kitchen, Capital Grille, Cheesecake Factory, Chili's, Chipotle Mexican, Coldstone, Hooters, Houston Rest., Macaroni Grill, Maggiano's Italian, Moe's SW Grill, Morton Steaks, Pinon Grill, Quiznos, Rosso Italian, Season's Rest, Starbucks, Stephane's, Stir Crazy, Subway, Wendy's 🛏 Courtyard, Holiday Inn, Marriott, Wyndham Garden 🄾 Macy's, Nordstrom, Publix, Sears/auto

44 Palmetto Park Rd, **E** 🅖 Valero/dsl 🍴 Denny's, Dunkin Donuts, Red's BBQ, Subway, Taco Bell, Tomasso's Pizza 🄾 AT&T, K-Mart, museums, Publix, **W** 🍴 McDonald's (2mi)

42b a FL 810, Hillsboro Blvd, **E** 🅖 BP, Shell/dsl 🍴 Hook Fish&Chicken, McDonald's, Popeye's, Wendy's 🛏 Hampton Inn, Hilton, La Quinta 🄾 Advance Parts, **W** 🅖 Chevron/dsl, Mobil/dsl 🍴 Boston Mkt, Checkers, Dunkin Donuts, Subway 🛏 Holiday Park Hotel, La Quinta 🄾 CVS Drug, Home Depot, Walgreens

41 FL 869 **(toll)**, SW 10th, to I-75, **E** 🅖 Mobil/7-11 🍴 Cracker Barrel, Pizza Express 🛏 Extended Stay America, **W** 🛏 Best Western, Comfort Suites

39 FL 834, Sample Rd, **E** 🅖 BP, Chevron/dsl, Hess/dsl, Shell/dsl 🍴 Taco Bell 🄾 Ⓗ, $General, Save-A-Lot, U-Haul, **W** 🅖 Chevron, Citgo/dsl, Mobil/dsl, Solo/dsl, Sunoco/dsl 🍴 Burger King, Checkers, IHOP, La Granja, McDonald's, Miami Subs, Subway 🄾 7-11, CarMax, Costco/gas, CVS Drug, Family$, Seabra Foods, vet

38b a Copans Rd, **E** 🅖 BP/7-11 🍴 McDonald's, Subway 🄾 Land Rover, Mercedes, PepBoys, Porche/Audi, Walmart, **W** 🅖 Chevron, Valero/dsl 🄾 Home Depot, NAPA

36b a FL 814, Atlantic Blvd, to Pompano Beach, **E** 🅖 RaceTrac/dsl 🍴 KFC/Pizza Hut/Taco Bell, Miami Subs, **W 1 mi** 🅖 BP, Chevron, Mobil/dsl, Murphy USA/dsl 🍴 Baskin-Robbins/Dunkin Donuts, Burger King, Golden Corral, KFC/LJ Silver, McDonald's, Pollo Tropical, Subway, Wendy's 🄾 $Tree, Chevrolet/Mazda, CVS Drug, Power Line Rd has many services, Radio Shack, to FL TPK, USPO, Walgreens, Walmart

33b a Cypress Creek Rd, **E** 🅖 7-11, BP, Hess 🍴 Duffy's Diner 🛏 Extended Stay America, Hampton Inn, Westin Hotel, **W** 🅖 Hess, Shell/repair 🍴 5 Guys Burgers, Arby's, Burger King, Carlucci's Italian, Champp's Grill, Chili's, Hooters, Longhorn Steaks, McDonald's, Moonlite Diner, Subway, Sweet Tomatoes, Wendy's 🛏 Courtyard, La Quinta, Marriott, Sheraton Suites 🄾 AT&T, GNC, Jaguar, Office Depot, Tires+, URGENT CARE

32 FL 870, Commercial Blvd, Lauderdale by the Sea, Lauderhill, **E** 🍴 Subway, **W** 🅖 BP, Circle K, Mobil/dsl, Shell, Sunoco/dsl 🍴 Dunkin Donuts, KFC, McDonald's, Miami Subs, Subway, Waffle House 🛏 Holiday Inn Express, Red Roof Inn, Universal Palms Motel 🄾 Advance Parts, auto repair, BJ's Whse/gas, Tire Kingdom

31b a FL 816, Oakland Park Blvd, **E** 🅖 7-11, Chevron, Mobil/dsl, Petro America/dsl 🍴 24 Diner, BBQ Jacks, Burger King, Checkers, Denny's, Domino's, Dunkin Donuts, Little Caesars, McDonald's, Miami Subs, Primanti Bros, Subway, Taco Bell, Wendy's 🄾 Advance Parts, K-Mart, Lowe's, Publix, Radio Shack, Walgreens, **W** 🅖 BP/dsl, RaceTrac/dsl, Shell, Texaco, Valero 🍴 Baskin-Robbins/Dunkin Donuts, Burger King, Checkers, IHOP, KFC, McDonald's, Pizza Hut, Subway 🛏 Days Inn 🄾 $General, Home Depot, Toyota/Scion, USPO, vet, Walgreens

29b a FL 838, Sunrise Blvd, **E** 🅖 BP, Shell, Sunoco/dsl/e-85, Valero/dsl 🍴 Burger King, Krystal, Miami Subs, Popeye's 🄾 Advance Parts, auto repair/tires, AutoZone, Family$, to Birch SP, Winn-Dixie, **W** 🅖 BP, Exxon/dsl, Marathon, Shell, Valero 🍴 China Bowl, Church's, KFC, McDonald's, Snapper's Fish&Chicken, Subway 🄾 Ⓗ, Family$

27 FL 842, Broward Blvd, Ft Lauderdale, **E** 🄾 Ⓗ

26 I-595 (from sb), FL 736 (from nb), Davie Blvd, **W** 🄾 to Ⓡ

25 FL 84, **E** 🅖 7-11, Marathon/dsl, RaceTrac/dsl, Sunoco/dsl, Texaco, Valero 🍴 Dunkin Donuts, Li'l Red's BBQ, McDonald's, Ruby Chinese, Subway, Wendy's 🛏 Best Western, Candlewood Suites, Holiday Inn Express, Motel 6, Sky Motel 🄾 $Tree, BigLots, Firestone/auto, Radio Shack, U-Haul, Winn-Dixie, **W** 🛏 Ramada Inn, Red Carpet Inn, Rodeway Inn

24 I-595 (from nb), to I-75, **E** 🄾 to Ⓡ

23 FL 818, Griffin Rd, **E** 🛏 Hilton, Sheraton, **W** 🅖 Mobil 🍴 Subway 🛏 Courtyard, Fairfield Inn, Homewood Suites 🄾 Bass Pro Shops, N Trail RV Ctr, Publix

22 FL 848, Stirling Rd, Cooper City, **E** 🅖 Mobil 🍴 AleHouse Grill, Burger King, Chipotle Mexican, Dave&Buster's, McDonald's, Moonlite Diner, Quiznos, Red Lobster, Sal's Italian, Sweet Tomatoes, Taco Bell, TGIFriday's, Wendy's, Yum Berry Yogurt 🛏 Comfort Inn, Hampton Inn, Hilton Garden, Hyatt House, Hyatt Place, La Quinta, SpringHill Suites 🄾 Advance Parts, BJ's Whse, GNC, Home Depot, K-Mart, Marshall's, Michael's, Old Navy, Petsmart, Radio Shack, Ross, to Lloyd SP, Verizon, **W** 🍴 Las Vegas Cuban, Mr M's Sandwiches, Subway 🛏 Best Western 🄾 CVS Drug, PepBoys, Tire Kingdom, vet, Walgreens, Winn-Dixie

21 FL 822, Sheridan St, **E** 🅖 BP, Chevron/dsl, Cumberland Farms/gas, same as 22, **W** 🅖 Shell 🍴 Denny's 🛏 Days Inn, Holiday Inn

20 FL 820, Hollywood Blvd, **E** 🅖 Shell 🍴 IHOP, Miami Subs 🛏 Hollywood Gateway Inn 🄾 Goodyear/auto, Office Depot, U-Haul, vet, **W** 🅖 BP, Chevron/dsl 🍴 Boston Mkt, China Hollywood, Coldstone, Firehouse Subs, Mama Fu's Asian, McDonald's, Offerdahl's Grill, Quiznos, Starbucks, Subway, Taco Bell, Waffle Works, Wendy's 🄾 Ⓗ, Publix, Radio Shack, Target, Verizon, Walgreens

19 FL 824, Pembroke Rd, **E** 🅖 Shell, **W** 🅖 Giant

18 FL 858, Hallandale Bch Blvd, **E** 🅖 7-11, Exxon, Shell 🍴 Baskin-Robbins/Dunkin Donuts, Burger King, Denny's, IHOP, KFC, La Granja, Little Caesars, McDonald's, Miami Subs, Pollo Tropical, Subway, Wendy's, Won Ton Garden 🛏 Best Western 🄾 Ⓗ, Family$, Goodyear/auto, Tire Kingdom, vet, Walgreens, Winn-Dixie, **W** 🅖 BP/dsl, RaceTrac/dsl 🄾 Advance Parts

16 Ives Dairy Rd, **E** 🄾 Ⓗ, mall, **W** 🅖 BP/7-11 🍴 Subway

(vertical margin text, left) **POMPANO BEACH   FT LAUDERDALE**

*(vertical margin text, center)* HOLLYWOOD

🅖 = gas 🍴 = food 🛏 = lodging 🅞 = other 🆁🆂 = rest stop   Copyright 2015 - the Next EXIT ®

⬆N INTERSTATE 95 Cont'd

Exit #	Services
14	FL 860, Miami Gardens Dr, N Miami Beach, **E** 🅞 🏥, Oleta River SRA **W** 🅖 BP, Valero/dsl
12c	US 441, FL 826, FL TPK, FL 9, **E** 🅖 7-11, BP, Chevron, Hess/dsl, Valero 🍴 Baskin-Robbins/Dunkin Donuts, Burger King, McDonald's, Wendy's 🛏 Holidays Hotel 🅞 🏥, PepBoys
12b	US 441 (from nb), same as 12c
12a	FL 868 (from nb), FL TPK N
11	NW 151st (from nb), **W** 🅖 Sunoco/dsl 🍴 McDonald's 🅞 Advance Parts, services on US 441 N, Winn-Dixie
10b	FL 916, NW 135th, Opa-Locka Blvd, **W** 🅖 Chevron, CR/dsl, Liberty 🍴 Checkers, Subway
10a	NW 125th, N Miami, Bal Harbour, **W** 🅖 Shell 🍴 Burger King, Wendy's
9	NW 119th (from nb), **W** 🅖 BP/McDonald's 🍴 KFC, Pollo Tropical, Popeye's 🅞 Advance Parts, AutoZone, CVS Drug, Family$, Walgreens, Winn-Dixie
8b	FL 932, NW 103rd, **E** 🅖 Shell, Texaco 🅞 7-11, **W** 🅖 BP, Sunoco 🍴 $General, Baskin-Robbins/Dunkin Donuts, Bravo Foods
8a	NW 95th, **E** 🅖 BP, **W** 🅖 CR/dsl, Mobil/dsl 🍴 McDonald's 🅞 🏥, Advance Parts, Walgreens
7	FL 934, NW 81st, NW 79th, **E** 🅖 BP/dsl, Chevron/dsl **W** 🅖 Sunoco 🍴 Checkers
6b	NW 69th (from sb)
6a	FL 944, NW 62nd, NW 54th, **W** 🍴 China Town, McDonald's, Subway, Wing Stop 🅞 Family$, Presidente Mkt, Walgreens
4b a	I-195 E, FL 112 W (**toll**), Miami Beach, **E** downtown, **W** 🅞✈
3b	NW 8th St (from sb)
3a	FL 836 W (**toll**) (exits left from nb), **W** 🅞 🏥, to ✈
2d	I-395 E (exits left from sb), to Miami Beach
2c	NW 8th, NW 14th (from sb), Miami Ave, **E** 🅞 Port of Miami
2b	NW 2nd (from nb), downtown Miami
2a	US 1 (exits left from sb), Biscayne Blvd, downtown Miami
1b	US 41, SW 7th, SW 8th, Brickell Ave, **E** 🅖 Chevron, Citgo 🍴 Burger King, Graziano's, McDonald's, Munchies, Subway, Wendy's 🛏 Extended Stay America, Hampton Inn 🅞 CVS Drug, GNC, Publix, **W** 🅖 Shell 🍴 Papa John's, Pepper's Mexican Grill
1a	SW 25th (from sb), downtown, to Rickenbacker Causeway, **E** 🅞 museum, to Baggs SRA
0mm	I-95 begins/ends on US 1. **S** 1 mi 🅖 BP 🍴 Quiznos

⬆N INTERSTATE 275 (Tampa)

Exit #	Services
59mm	**I-275 begins/ends on I-75, exit 274.**
53	Bearss Ave, **E** 🅖 Citgo/dsl 🅞 Carmax, **W** 🅖 Chevron/dsl, Marathon/Dunkin Donuts, RaceTrac/dsl, Shell 🍴 Burger King, IHOP, McDonald's, Subway 🛏 Vista Inn 🅞 Aldi Foods, BigLots, CVS Drug, GNC, Ross
52	Fletcher Ave, **E** 🅖 BP, Citgo/dsl, Hess, RaceTrac/dsl, Shell/dsl, Sunoco 🍴 Arby's, Bruno's Pizza, Church's, DQ, Hoho Chinese, Krystal, Little Caesars, McDonald's, Popeye's 🛏 Days Inn 🅞 🏥, Aldi Foods, AutoZone, Family$, to USF, Toyota/Scion, **W** 🅖 BP, Citgo, Mobil 🍴 Dunkin Donuts 🛏 Super 8 🅞 Advance Parts, Cadillac, Family$, Jaguar, Save-A-Lot, Sweetbay Foods
51	FL 582, Fowler Ave, **E** 🅖 BP, Citgo/dsl, GK, Mobil/dsl, Shell/Circle K 🍴 5 Guys Burgers, A&W/LJ Silver, Baskin-Robbins/Dunkin Donuts, Burger King, Checkers, Chili's, China Buffet, Chipotle Mexican, Denny's, Firehouse Subs, Jason's Deli,

51	Continued
	Jimmy John's, KFC, Longhorn Steaks, McAliter's Deli, McDonald's, Panera Bread, Pizza Hut, Quiznos, Sonic, Steak'n Shake, Subway, Taco Bell, TGIFriday's, Tia's TexMex, Waffle House, Wendy's 🛏 Clarion, Embassy Suites, Howard Johnson, Hyatt Place, La Quinta, Wingate Inn 🅞 $General, $Tree, 7-11, Advance Parts, AT&T, CarQuest, CVS Drug, Family$, Firestone/auto, Macy's, O'Reilly Parts, Sears/auto, Sweetbay Foods, Verizon, Walgreens, **W** 🛏 Economy Inn, Motel 6, Rodeway Inn 🅞 Audi, BMW
50	FL 580, Busch Blvd, **E** 🅖 BP, Chevron, Citgo 🍴 Arby's, McDonald's, Olive Garden, Popeye's, Red Lobster, Sonny's BBQ, Subway, Taco Bell 🛏 Days Inn, Holiday Inn Express, La Quinta, Red Roof Inn 🅞 $General, AutoZone, Busch Gardens, Family$, Walgreens, **W** 🅖 Chevron/dsl 🍴 Burger King, Pizza Hut 🅞 $Tree, Advance Parts, CVS Drug, Firestone/auto, Home Depot, Meineke, Radio Shack, Walmart Mkt
49	Bird Ave (from nb), **W** 🅖 Shell 🍴 Checkers, KFC, McDonald's, Wendy's 🅞 $General, K-Mart, Save-A-Lot
48	Sligh Ave, **E** 🅖 BP, Sunoco 🅞 USPO, **W** 🅞 zoo
47b a	US 92, to US 41 S, Hillsborough Ave, **E** 🅖 Circle K, Marathon, Mobil/dsl 🍴 Burger King, Checkers, McDonald's, Popeye's, Subway, Wendy's 🅞 Advance Parts, Ross, vet, Walgreens, **W** 🅖 BP, Shell/Circle K 🍴 Papa John's, Starbucks 🛏 Dutch Motel
46b	FL 574, MLK Blvd, **E** 🅖 BP 🅞 Advance Parts, Sweetbay Foods, Walgreens, **W** 🅖 Chevron/dsl 🍴 McDonald's 🅞 🏥
46a	Floribraska Ave (from sb, no return)
45b	I-4 E, to Orlando, I-75
45a	Jefferson St, downtown E
44	Ashley Dr, Tampa St, downtown W
42	Howard Ave, Armenia Ave, **W** 🅖 Texaco/dsl 🍴 Popeye's
41c	Himes Ave (from sb), **W** 🅞 RJ Stadium
41b a	US 92, Dale Mabry Blvd, **E** 🅖 BP, Marathon, Mobil/dsl, Shell/Circle K 🍴 Brickhouse Grill, Burger King, Carrabba's, Chick-Fil-A, Don Pan Cuban, Donatello Italian, Grill Smith, IHOP, J.Alexanders Rest, Jersey Mike's Subs, Little Caesars, Pei Wei, Pizza Hut, Red Elephant Cafe, Ruby Tuesday, Shells Rest., Starbucks, Subway, Village Inn 🛏 Best Western, Courtyard, Quality Inn, Tahitian Inn/cafe 🅞 AT&T, Barnes&Noble, CVS Drug, Hancock Fabrics, Office Depot, Tire Kingdom, to MacDill AFB, Verizon, **W** 🅖 Marathon/Dunkin Donuts 🍴 Burger King, Chili's, China 1, Crazy Buffet, Denny's, Jimmy John's, Joe's Pizza, Longhorn Steaks, Macaroni Grill, McDonald's, Moe's SW Grill, Sonic, Sonny's BBQ, Subway, Sweet Tomatoes, Wendy's 🛏 Hilton, Howard Johnson, Residence Inn, Stadium Inn 🅞 Best Buy, Chrysler/Dodge/Jeep, Family$, Home Depot, K-Mart, Petsmart, Staples, SweetBay Foods, Target, to RJ Stadium, Walmart, Whole Foods Mkt
40b	Lois Ave, **W** 🅖 Marathon/dsl 🍴 Charley's Rest. 🛏 DoubleTree Hotel, Sheraton
40a	FL 587, Westshore Blvd, **E** 🅖 BP, Chevron/dsl, Citgo/Subway 🍴 Burger King, Chipotle Mexican, Gogo's Greek, Maggiano's Rest., McDonald's, Panera Bread, PF Chang's, Season's Grill, Starbucks, Taco Bell, Waffle House 🛏 Crowne Plaza, Embassy Suites 🅞 Goodyear, JC Penney, Macy's, Old Navy, PetCo, Sears/auto, Walgreens, **W** 🅖 Shell/Subway 🍴 Blue Water Grill, Hurricane Grill 🛏 Hampton Inn, Marriott, Ramada Inn, SpringHill Suites, Wyndham
39b a	FL 60 W, **W** 🍴 Outback Steaks 🅞 to ✈
32	Fl 687 S, 4th St N, to US 92 (no sb re-entry)
31b a	9th St N, MLK St N (exits left from sb), 🅞 ✈, info

⬆N **INTERSTATE 275 (Tampa) Cont'd**

Exit #	Services
30	FL 686, Roosevelt Blvd, **W 0-2 mi** 🍴 Bascom's Chophouse, Bob Evans, Burger King, Chil-fil-A, Cracker Barrel, Kingfish Grill, McDonald's, Panchero's Mexican, Subway, Taco Bell 🛏 Courtyard, EconoLodge, Executive Inn, Extended Stay America, Fairfield Inn, Hampton Inn, Holiday Inn, La Quinta, Marriott, Quality Inn, Sleep Inn, SpringHill Suites ⊙ CVS Drug, Publix
28	FL 694 W, Gandy Blvd, Indian Shores, **W 0-2 mi** 🔲 Citgo, Hess/dsl, WaWa/dsl 🍴 Applebee's, BJ's Brewhouse, Bob Evans, Chili's, Cracker Barrel, Dunkin Donuts, Firehouse Subs, Godfather's, McDonald's, Pollo Tropical, Sonny's BBQ, Taco Bell, Wendy's 🛏 La Quinta ⊙ Bentley, Cadillac, Home Depot, Marshall's, Michael's, Office Depot, PetCo, Publix, Rolls Royce, Target, U-Haul
26b a	54th Ave N, **E** 🔲 Cracker Barrel 🛏 Comfort Inn, Holiday Inn Express, **W** 🔲 RaceTrac/dsl 🍴 Waffle House 🛏 Knights Inn, La Quinta ⊙ 🏥, Harley-Davidson, NAPA
25	38th Ave N, to beaches, **E** 🍴 Chick-fil-A, Hooters, McDonald's, **W** 🔲 Citgo/dsl 🍴 Burger King, Hardee's
24	22nd Ave N, **E** 🔲 Rally ⊙ Sunken Gardens, **W** 🔲 Citgo/dsl, RaceTrac/dsl 🍴 Taco Son ⊙ Home Depot, Lowe's, Tommy's Auto Service
23b	FL 595, 5th Ave N, **E** ⊙ 🏥
23a	I-375, **E** ⊙ The Pier, Waterfront, downtown
22	I-175 E, Tropicana Field, **W** ⊙ 🏥
21	28th St S, downtown
20	31st Ave (from nb), downtown
19	22nd Ave S, Gulfport, **W** 🔲 Chevron, Citgo, Shell 🍴 Church's, KFC ⊙ Bravo Foods, Family$
18	26th Ave S (from nb)
17	FL 682 W, 54th Ave S, Pinellas Bayway, **W services on US 19 (34th St)** 🔲 7-11, Sunoco/dsl 🍴 Beef'O'Brady's, Bob Evans, Burger King, China Wok, Denny's, Domino's, Dunkin Donuts, IHOP, McDonald's, Papa John's, Portofino Italian, Subway, Taco Bell, Wendy's 🛏 Bayway Inn, Crystal Inn ⊙ $Tree, AT&T, Beall's, CVS Drug, GNC, Publix, Radio Shack, St Pete Beach, to Ft DeSoto Pk, Walmart/McDonald's
16mm	**toll plaza sb**
16	Pinellas Point Dr, Skyway Lane, to Maximo Park, **E** 🛏 Holiday Inn Resort, **W** ⊙ marina
13mm	N Skyway Fishing Pier, **W** ℞ both lanes, full ♿ **facilities, litter barrels, petwalk, 🚮, 🐾, vending**
10mm	Tampa Bay
7mm	S Skyway Fishing Pier, **E** ℞ both lanes, full ♿ **facilities, litter barrels, petwalk, 🚮, 🐾, vending**
6mm	**toll plaza nb**
5	US 19, Palmetto, Bradenton
2	US 41, **(last nb exit before toll)**, Palmetto, Bradenton, **E** ⊙ Circle K, Fiesta Grove RV Resort, Frog Creek Campground, Terra Ceia Village Campground, Winterset RV Resort, **W** 🔲 BP/DQ/Subway/dsl
0mm	**I-275 begins/ends on I-75, exit 228.**

⬆N **INTERSTATE 295 (Jacksonville)**

Exit #	Services
61b a	**I-295 begins/ends on I-95, exit 337**
60	US 1, Philips Hwy, **E** 🔲 RaceTrac/dsl ⊙ Buick/GMC, Honda, VW, **W** 🔲 BP ⊙ Chevrolet, Ford, Mazda, Nissan
58	FL 9b
56	FL 152, Baymeadows Rd, **E** 🛏 Holiday Inn ⊙ Chrysler/ Dodge/Jeep, **W** 🔲 Shell 🍴 Bubba Burger, Carrabba's,

56	Continued
	Hampton Inn, Hurricane Grill, Outback Steaks, Sticky Fingers, Tequila's Mexican, Tony D's Pizza, Wendy's ⊙ Publix, SteinMart, URGENT CARE, Verizon, vet, Walgreens
54	Gate Pkwy, **W** 🍴 Joey's Pizzeria, Melting Pot
53	FL 202, Butler Blvd, **W 1 mi on Gate Pkwy** 🔲 Shell 🍴 Bahama Breeze, BJ's Rest, Bono's BBQ, Brio Grille, Capital Grill, Cheesecake Factory, Chipotle Mexican, Maggiano's Italian, Mimi's Cafe, Panda Express, Panera Bread, Pei Wei, PF Chang's, Pollo Tropical, Seasons Rest, Wasabi, Wendy's, Zaxby's 🛏 Sheraton ⊙ Barnes&Noble, Best Buy, Costco, CVS Drug, Dick's, Dillard's, Target
52	U of NF Dr, Town Center Pkwy, same as 53
51	US 90, Beach Blvd, **E** 🔲 Citgo 🍴 Burger King, Dunkin Donuts, Gene's Seafood, Jimmy John's, **W** 🔲 Shell 🍴 Arby's, KFC, McDonald's, Pizza Hut, Sonic, Taco Bell 🛏 InTown Suites ⊙ $Tree, Advance Parts, Walgreens, Winn-Dixie
49	St John's Bluff Rd (from nb), **E** 🔲 BP, Shell 🍴 Papa John's 🛏 Holiday Inn Express, InTown Suites ⊙ Nissan
48	FL 10, to Atlantic Blvd
47	Monument Rd, **E** 🔲 Marathon/Kangaroo/dsl 🍴 Mudville Grille ⊙ vet, **W** 🔲 Gate/dsl 🍴 Ruby Tuesday 🛏 Courtyard, Hampton Inn ⊙ Walmart
46	FL 116 E, Wonderwood Connector, Merrill Rd, **E** 🛏 Candlewood Suites
44mm	St John's River
41	FL 105, Heckscher Dr, Zoo Pkwy, **E** 🔲 Gate/dsl, **W** 🔲 Chevron/Kangaroo/dsl 🍴 Wendy's 🛏 Holiday Inn Express ⊙ zoo
40	Alta Dr, **E** 🍴 3 Lions Grill, Viva Mexican
37	Pulaski Rd, **E** 🔲 Kangaroo/dsl
36	US 17, Main St, **E** 🔲 Kangaroo/dsl 🍴 DQ, McDonald's ⊙ Winn-Dixie, **W** 🍴 Subway
35b a	I-95, S to Jacksonville, N to Savannah.
33	Duval Rd, **W** 🍴
32	FL 115, Lem Turner Rd, **E** 🍴 China Wok, Larry's Subs, McDonald's (1mi), Subway, Wendy's ⊙ Home Depot, Radio Shack, Walmart, **W** ⊙ Flamingo Lake RV Resort, Lakeside Cabins/RV Park
30	FL 104, Dunn Ave, **E** 🔲 Gate/dsl, Shell (1mi) 🍴 McDonald's (1mi), Wendy's (4mi), **W** ⊙ Big Tree RV Park
28b a	US 1, US 23, to Callahan, Jacksonville, **E** 🔲 Kangaroo, **W** 🔲 auto repair, BP/DQ/dsl, Chevron/Subway/dsl, RaceTrac/dsl
25	Pritchard Rd, **W** 🔲 Kangaroo/Subway/deli/dsl/24hr
22	Commonwealth Ave, **E** 🔲 BP/dsl 🍴 Burger King, Hardee's, Waffle House 🛏 Holiday Inn ⊙ dogtrack, **W** 🍴 Wendy's 🛏 Comfort Suites, Country Inn&Suites
21b a	I-10, W to Tallahassee, E to Jacksonville

🄖 = gas 🍴 = food 🛏 = lodging 🄾 = other 🆁🆂 = rest stop   Copyright 2015 - the Next EXIT ®

⬆N INTERSTATE 295 (Jacksonville) Cont'd

Exit #	Services
19	FL 228, Normandy Blvd, **E** 🄖 BP/dsl/24hr, Murphy USA/dsl 🍴 Arby's, Burger King, El Potro, Firehouse Subs, Golden Corral, Hot Wok, McDonald's, Panda Express, Papa John's, Sonic, Wendy's 🄾 $Tree, CVS Drug, Radio Shack, st patrol, Walgreens, Walmart, **W** 🄖 BP, Hess/dsl, RaceTrac/dsl, Shell 🍴 Famous Amos, Golden China, Hardee's, KFC, McDonald's, Pizza Hut, Popeye's, Whataburger 🄾 Advance Parts, CVS Drug, Family$, K-Mart, Publix, Walgreens, Winn-Dixie
17	FL 208, Wilson Blvd, **E** 🄖 BP/Subway/dsl, Hess/Dunkin Donuts/dsl 🍴 China Wok, Hardee's, McDonald's (1mi) 🄾 $General, Advance Parts, FL RV Ctr, **W** 🄖 Kangaroo
16	FL 134, 103rd St, Cecil Field, **E** 🄖 BP, Gate/dsl, Hess, Shell/dsl 🍴 Applebee's, Arby's, Capt D's, Firehouse Subs, Krystal, Papa John's, Popeye's, Red Apple Asian, Sonic, Wendy's, Ying's Chinese 🛏 🍴ity Inn 🄾 $General, Advance Parts, CVS Drug, Goodyear/auto, NAPA, Radio Shack, Save-A-Lot Foods, Tires+, U-Haul, Walmart/McDonald's, **W** 🄖 BP, Chevron, Exxon/dsl, Kangaroo, Shell 🍴 Burger King, DQ, Dunkin Donuts, IHOP, KFC, Little Caesars, McDonald's, Pizza Hut, Rosy's Mexican, Subway, Taco Bell 🄾 Aamco, AutoZone, Family$, Goodyear/auto, O'Reilly Parts, Publix, SavRite Foods, Sun Tires, vet, Walgreens
12	FL 21, Blanding Blvd, **E** 🄖 BP, Hess/Blimpie/Dunkin Donuts/Godfather's/dsl, RaceWay/dsl, Texaco 🍴 Burger King, Larry's Subs, McDonald's, Pizza Hut, Subway, Sunrise Cafe 🄾 $General, Acura, Audi, Best Buy, Buick/GMC, Cadillac, Chrysler/Dodge/Jeep, CVS Drug, Ford, Honda, Hyundai, Lexus, Lincoln, Mazda, Mercedes, Nissan, Office Depot, Petsmart, Subaru, U-Haul, USPO, VW, Walgreens, **W** 🄖 5 Guys Burgers, Arby's, BP, Buffalo's, Burger King, Carrabba's, Chick-fil-A, Chili's, China Buffet, Chipotle Mexican, ChuckeCheese, Denny's, El Potro, food: Applebee's, HoneyBaked Ham, Hooters, Kangaroo/dsl, KFC, Kyodai Steaks, Longhorn Steaks, Olive Garden, Orange Park Ale House, Outback Steaks, Panda Express, Panera Bread, Papa John's, Red Lobster, Ruby Tuesday, Shell, Smokey Bones, Sonic, Starbucks, Steak'n Shake, Sweet Tomatoes, Taco Bell, Ted's MT Grill, TGIFriday's, Thai Garden 🛏 Country Inn&Suites, Hampton Inn, La Quinta,

Exit #	Services
12	Continued Motel 6, Red Roof Inn, Suburban Lodge, Super 8 🄾 🍴 $Tree, Advance Parts, AT&T, Belk, Books-A-Million, Dick's, Dillard's, Discount Tire, Goodyear/auto, Home Depot, JC Penney, Jo-Ann Fabrics, mall, Michael's, Old Navy, O'Reilly Parts, PepBoys, Publix, Sam's Club/gas, Sears/auto, Target, Tire Kingdom, Tires+, TJMaxx, Toyota, Verizon, Walgreens
10	US 17, FL 15, Roosevelt Blvd, Orange Park, **E** 🛏 Best Western, **W** 🄖 BP, Chevron/dsl/24hr, Hess, RaceTrac/dsl 🍴 Aron's Pizza, Cracker Barrel, Krystal, McDonald's, Ramirez Rest., Subway, Waffle House, Wendy's 🛏 Comfort Inn, Days Inn, Fairfield Inn, Hilton Garden, Holiday Inn, Rodeway Inn 🄾 🍴, $General, CVS Drug, General RV Ctr, Harley-Davidson, Save-A-Lot Foods, Sun Tire, vet, Winn-Dixie
7mm	St Johns River, Buckman Br
5b a	FL 13, San Jose Blvd, **E** 🄖 Chevron/DQ/dsl, Hess 🍴 5 Guys Burgers, Arby's, Bob Evans, Bono's BBQ, Carrabba's, Domino's, Famous Amos, Firehouse Subs, HoneyBaked Ham, Krystal, McDonald's, Outback Steaks, Popeye's, Red Elephant Pizza, Smoothie King, Starbucks, Steak'n Shake, Subway, Tijuana Flats, Village Inn, Wendy's 🛏 La Quinta, Ramada Inn 🄾 Aamco, Advance Parts, auto repair, BigLots, CVS Drug, Firestone/auto, K-Mart, Office Depot, PepBoys, Publix, Sun Tire, Target, Tire Kingdom, Tires+, URGENT CARE, Verizon, vet, Walgreens, Whole Foods Mkt, **W** 🄖 BP, Citgo, Shell (1mi) 🍴 Al's Pizza, Brooklyn Pizza, Bruster's, Chili's, Chipotle Mexican, Golden China, Golden Corral, Hardee's, Krispy Kreme, Lee's Chicken, Mama Fu's, Mandarin Ale House, McDonald's, Moe's SW Grill, Osaka Grill, Panera Bread, Papa John's, Papa Murphy's, Pizza Hut, Subway, Taco Bell 🄾 $Tree, Ace Hardware, Advance Parts, AT&T, AutoZone, Barnes&Noble, Books-A-Million, Goodyear/auto, Marshall's, Michael's, NAPA, PetCo, Publix, Radio Shack, Staples, SteinMart, Tire Kingdom, TJMaxx, U-Haul, Walmart, Winn-Dixie, World Mkt
3	Old St Augustine Rd, **E** 🄖 BP, Shell 🍴 Burger King, Little Caesars, Little China, McDonald's, Taco Bell, Wendy's 🛏 Holiday Inn Express 🄾 $General, $Tree, CVS Drug, Family$, GNC, Hobby Lobby, Publix/deli, Winn-Dixie, **W** 🄖 Gate/dsl, Kangaroo/dsl 🍴 Firehouse Subs, KFC, Rosy's Mexican, Subway, Vino's Pizza 🄾 Lowe's, vet, Walgreens

GEORGIA

⬆E INTERSTATE 16

Exit #	Services
167b a	W Broad, Montgomery St, Savannah, **N** 0-1 mi 🄖 Chevron, Enmark, Parker's 🛏 Best Western, Courtyard, DoubleTree, Hampton Inn, Hilton Garden, Quality Inn, Residence Inn, Sheraton, **S** 🍴 Burger King, Popeye's, Wendy's. **I-16 begins/ends in Savannah.**
166	US 17, Gwinnet St, Savannah, Savannah Visitors Ctr
165	GA 204, 37th St (from eb), to Ft Pulaski NM, Savannah College
164b a	I-516, US 80, US 17, GA 21
162	Chatham Pkwy, **S** 🄖 Shell/dsl 🍴 Kan Pai Japanese, Larry's Subs, Nicky's Pizza, Sunrise Rest. 🄾 Kia, Lexus, Subaru, Toyota/Scion
160	GA 307, Dean Forest Rd, **N** 🄖 🚚/Subway/dsl/scales, Shell/dsl 🍴 Ronnie's Rest., Waffle House

Exit #	Services
157b a	I-95, S to Jacksonville, N to Florence
155	Pooler Pkwy, **N** 🄖 Murphy USA/dsl 🍴 Jalapeno's Mexican, Papa John's, Subway 🄾 Lowe's, **S** 🄖 BP/dsl, to 🏥
152	GA 17, to Bloomingdale
148	Old River Rd, to US 80
144mm	**weigh sta both lanes**
143	US 280, to US 80, **S** 🄖 El Cheapo/dsl, Zip'N Go/Subway/dsl
137	GA 119, to Pembroke, Ft Stewart
132	Ash Branch Church Rd
127	GA 67, to Pembroke, Ft Stewart, **N** 🄖 BP/dsl, Shell/dsl 🍴 Bay South Rest. 🄾 antiques
116	US 25/301, to Statesboro, **N** 🄖 Chevron/rest/dsl/scales/24hr 🍴 Magnolia Springs SP (45 mi), to GA S U, **S** 🄖 Sunoco/dsl 🛏 Scottish Inn
111	Pulaski-Excelsior Rd, **S** 🄖 Citgo/Grady's Grill/dsl 🄾 tires/repair
104	GA 22, GA 121, Metter, **N** 🄖 BP/dsl/scales/24hr, Chevron/

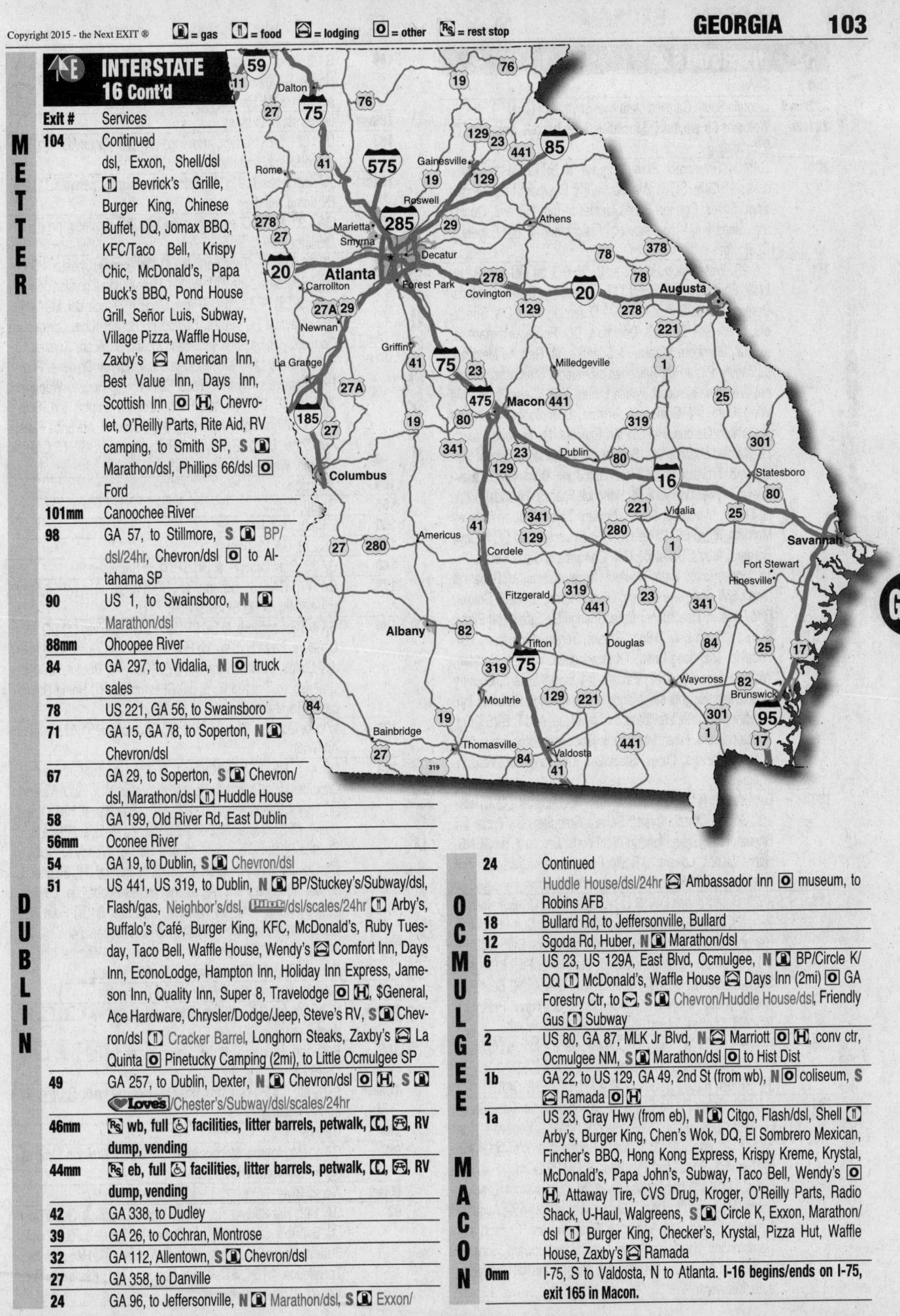

M E T T E R

INTERSTATE 16 Cont'd

Exit #	Services
104	Continued dsl, Exxon, Shell/dsl 🍴 Bevrick's Grille, Burger King, Chinese Buffet, DQ, Jomax BBQ, KFC/Taco Bell, Krispy Chic, McDonald's, Papa Buck's BBQ, Pond House Grill, Señor Luis, Subway, Village Pizza, Waffle House, Zaxby's 🏠 American Inn, Best Value Inn, Days Inn, Scottish Inn Ⓞ 🅷, Chevrolet, O'Reilly Parts, Rite Aid, RV camping, to Smith SP, S ⛽ Marathon/dsl, Phillips 66/dsl Ⓞ Ford
101mm	Canoochee River
98	GA 57, to Stillmore, S ⛽ BP/dsl/24hr, Chevron/dsl Ⓞ to Altahama SP
90	US 1, to Swainsboro, N ⛽ Marathon/dsl
88mm	Ohoopee River
84	GA 297, to Vidalia, N Ⓞ truck sales
78	US 221, GA 56, to Swainsboro
71	GA 15, GA 78, to Soperton, N ⛽ Chevron/dsl
67	GA 29, to Soperton, S ⛽ Chevron/dsl, Marathon/dsl 🍴 Huddle House
58	GA 199, Old River Rd, East Dublin
56mm	Oconee River
54	GA 19, to Dublin, S ⛽ Chevron/dsl
51	US 441, US 319, to Dublin, N ⛽ BP/Stuckey's/Subway/dsl, Flash/gas, Neighbor's/dsl, [truckstop]/dsl/scales/24hr 🍴 Arby's, Buffalo's Café, Burger King, KFC, McDonald's, Ruby Tuesday, Taco Bell, Waffle House, Wendy's 🏠 Comfort Inn, Days Inn, EconoLodge, Hampton Inn, Holiday Inn Express, Jameson Inn, Quality Inn, Super 8, Travelodge Ⓞ 🅷, $General, Ace Hardware, Chrysler/Dodge/Jeep, Steve's RV, S ⛽ Chevron/dsl 🍴 Cracker Barrel, Longhorn Steaks, Zaxby's 🏠 La Quinta Ⓞ Pinetucky Camping (2mi), to Little Ocmulgee SP
49	GA 257, to Dublin, Dexter, N ⛽ Chevron/dsl Ⓞ 🅷, S ⛽ Loves/Chester's/Subway/dsl/scales/24hr
46mm	℞ wb, full 🛉 facilities, litter barrels, petwalk, 🚻, RV dump, vending
44mm	℞ eb, full 🛉 facilities, litter barrels, petwalk, 🚻, RV dump, vending
42	GA 338, to Dudley
39	GA 26, to Cochran, Montrose
32	GA 112, Allentown, S ⛽ Chevron/dsl
27	GA 358, to Danville
24	GA 96, to Jeffersonville, N ⛽ Marathon/dsl, S ⛽ Exxon/

D U B L I N

Exit #	Services
24	Continued Huddle House/dsl/24hr 🏠 Ambassador Inn Ⓞ museum, to Robins AFB
18	Bullard Rd, to Jeffersonville, Bullard
12	Sgoda Rd, Huber, N ⛽ Marathon/dsl
6	US 23, US 129A, East Blvd, Ocmulgee, N ⛽ BP/Circle K/DQ 🍴 McDonald's, Waffle House 🏠 Days Inn (2mi) Ⓞ GA Forestry Ctr, to ✈, S ⛽ Chevron/Huddle House/dsl, Friendly Gus 🍴 Subway
2	US 80, GA 87, MLK Jr Blvd, N ⛽ Marriott Ⓞ 🅷, conv ctr, Ocmulgee NM, S ⛽ Marathon/dsl Ⓞ to Hist Dist
1b	GA 22, to US 129, GA 49, 2nd St (from wb), N Ⓞ coliseum, S 🏠 Ramada Ⓞ 🅷
1a	US 23, Gray Hwy (from eb), N ⛽ Citgo, Flash/dsl, Shell 🍴 Arby's, Burger King, Chen's Wok, DQ, El Sombrero Mexican, Fincher's BBQ, Hong Kong Express, Krispy Kreme, Krystal, McDonald's, Papa John's, Subway, Taco Bell, Wendy's Ⓞ 🅷, Attaway Tire, CVS Drug, Kroger, O'Reilly Parts, Radio Shack, U-Haul, Walgreens, S ⛽ Circle K, Exxon, Marathon/dsl 🍴 Burger King, Checker's, Krystal, Pizza Hut, Waffle House, Zaxby's 🏠 Ramada
0mm	I-75, S to Valdosta, N to Atlanta. **I-16 begins/ends on I-75, exit 165 in Macon.**

O C M U L G E E   M A C O N

GA

INTERSTATE 20

Exit #	Services
202mm	Georgia/South Carolina state line, Savannah River
201mm	Welcome Ctr wb, full ♿ facilities, litter barrels, petwalk, 🅲, 🚻, vending
200	GA 104, Riverwatch Pkwy, Augusta, N 🅶 ▦/Wendy's/dsl/scales/24hr 🍴 Waffle House 🛏 Baymont Inn, Candlewood Suites, Comfort Suites, Jameson Inn, Microtel, Quality Inn, Sleep Inn, ValuePlace 🅾 Freightliner, S 🅾 Cabela's, Costco/gas
199	GA 28, Washington Rd, Augusta, N 0-3 mi 🅶 BP, RaceWay, Shell/Circle K, Sprint 🍴 Applebee's, Baskin-Robbins/Dunkin Donuts, Burger King, CA Dreaming, Capt D's, Checkers, Chick-fil-A, Denny's, Domino's, DQ, Fujiyama Japanese, Krystal, Longhorn Steaks, McDonald's, Mi Rancho Mexican, Piccadilly, Pizza Hut, Rhinehart's Seafood, Starbucks, Steakout, Veracruz Mexican, Waffle House, Wife Saver Rest, Wild Wing Cafe 🛏 Clarion, Courtyard, Econolodge, Hampton Inn, Hilton Garden, Holiday Inn Express, Homewood Suites, La Quinta, Masters Inn, Scottish Inn, Sheraton, Sunset Inn, Super 8, Travelodge 🅾 $Tree, AutoZone, Buick/GMC, Chevrolet, Chrysler/Dodge/Jeep, Hancock Fabrics, Hyundai, Infiniti, Lexus, Mercedes, NAPA, Nissan, Toyota/Scion, Tuesday Morning, S 🅶 BP, Circle K/dsl, Shell/Circle K/dsl 🍴 5 Guys Burgers, Arby's, BoneFish Grill, Carrabba's, Crazy Turk's Pizza, HoneyBaked Ham, Hooters, Krispy Kreme, McDonald's, Moe's SW Grill, New Peking, Olive Garden, Outback Steaks, Red Lobster, Roadrunner Cafe, Shangri La, Straw Hat Pizza, Subway, Taco Bell, T-Bonz Steaks, Teresa's Mexican, TGIFriday's, Thai Jong Rest., TX Roadhouse, Vallarta Mexican, Waffle House, Wendy's, Zaxby's 🛏 Best Western, Country Inn&Suites, Knights Inn, Magnolia Inn, Motel 6, Parkway Inn, Staybridge Suites, Westbank Inn 🅾 $Tree, AT&T, CVS Drug, Firestone/auto, Fresh Mkt Foods, Goodyear/auto, Kroger/dsl, Midas, PepBoys, Publix, SteinMart, Tire Kingdom, Verizon, Walgreens
196b	GA 232 W, N 🅶 Enmark, Murphy Express/dsl 🍴 Checkers, Golden Corral, Krystal, Salsa's Grill, Stevi B's Pizza 🛏 Baymont Inn, Travel Inn 🅾 Aldi Foods, Discount Tire, GNC, Home Depot, Lowe's, O'Reilly Parts, Sam's Club/gas, Tire Kingdom, URGENT CARE, Walgreens, Walmart
196a	I-520, Bobby Jones Fwy, S 🍴 Atlanta Bread Co, Buffalo Wild Wings, Carolina Alehouse, Chick-fil-A, Chili's, Dunkin Donuts, Genghis Grill, Logan's Roadhouse, Macaroni Grill, McDonald's, O'Charley's, Panera Bread, Starbucks, Sticky Fingers, Subway, Waffle House 🛏 DoubleTree Hotel 🅾 �H, Best Buy, Hobby Lobby, Michael's, Office Depot, Old Navy, Petsmart, Rite Aid, Staples, Target, Tires+, to 🚇, Verizon, vet
195	Wheeler Rd, N 🅶 Sprint 🅾 CarMax, Gander Mtn, S 🅶 Shell/Circle K/Blimpie 🍴 Guiseppe's Pizza, Sonic 🛏 Days Inn 🅾 �H, BP/dsl, Harley-Davidson, Rite Aid, URGENT CARE
194	GA 383, Belair Rd, to Evans, N 🅶 Shell/Circle K/dsl, Sprint 🍴 Bojangles, Burger King, Hungry Howie's, Popeye's, Sun Kwong Chinese, Taco Bell, Waffle House, Wendy's 🛏 GA Inn 🅾 Family$, Food Lion, Fun Park, S 🅶 BP/DQ/dsl, Fuel Express, ▦/Subway/dsl/scales/24hr 🍴 Cookout, Cracker Barrel, McDonald"s, Steak'n Shake, Waffle House 🛏 Augusta Inn, Best Suites, Best Value Inn, Best Western, Comfort Inn, Hampton Inn, Hawthorn Suites, Holiday Inn, Howard Johnson, Quality Inn, Red Roof Inn, Super 8, Wingate Inn 🅾 Goodyear/auto, Kenworth
190	GA 388, to Grovetown, N 🅶 TPS/dsl/scales/24hr 🍴 Waffle House, S 🅶 Murphy Express/dsl 🍴 Applebee's, Arby's, Jersey Mike's, Mi Rancho 🅾 Verizon, Walmart
189mm	weigh sta both lanes
183	US 221, to Harlem, Appling, S 🅶 Exxon/dsl 🅾 to Laurel&Hardy Museum
182mm	🆁🆂 both lanes, full ♿ facilities, litter barrels, petwalk, 🅲, 🚻 RV dump, vending
175	GA 150, N 🅶 Chevron/rest/dsl/24hr 🛏 Express Inn 🅾 to Mistletoe SP
172	US 78, GA 17, Thomson, N 🅶 Loves/Chester's/Subway/dsl/scales/24hr 🍴 Waffle House 🅾 Chrysler/Dodge/Jeep, S 🅶 BP/DQ/dsl, BP/dsl, Circle K/Blimpie/dsl, M&A/dsl, RaceWay/dsl 🍴 Arby's, Bojangles, Burger King, Checkers, Domino's, Habaneros Mexican, Kiosco Mexican, Krystal, LJ Silver, Lucky Chinese, McDonald's, MingWah Chinese, Pizza Hut, Popeye's, Ryan's, Taco Bell, Waffle House, Wendy's, Zaxby's 🛏 Comfort Inn, EconoLodge, Hampton Inn, Scottish Inn, White Columns Inn 🅾 �H, $General, Advance Parts, AutoZone, Bi-Lo, Family$, O'Reilly Parts, URGENT CARE, Verizon, Walgreens
169	Thomson
165	GA 80, Camak
160	E Cadley Rd, Norwood
154	US 278, GA 12, Barnett
148	GA 22, Crawfordville, N 🅶 BP 🅾 to Stephens SP
138	GA 77, GA 15, Siloam, N 🅶 Flying J/Denny's/dsl/LP/scales/24hr, S 🅶 BP/dsl 🅾 �H
130	GA 44, Greensboro, N 🅶 BP/dsl, Valero/Subway 🍴 DQ, McDonald's, Pizza Hut, Waffle House, Wendy's, Zaxby's 🛏 Holiday Lodge, Jameson Inn 🅾 �H, $General, Buick/Chevrolet, Greensboro Tire/repair, S 🅶 Chevron/dsl 🅾 Home Depot/gas, 🅾 weigh sta
121	to Lake Oconee, Buckhead, S 🅶 Chevron/dsl 🅾 Museum of Art (3mi)
114	US 441, US 129, to Madison, N 🅶 Chevron/Subway/dsl, Citgo/dsl, ▦/Huddle House/dsl/scales/24hr, RaceWay/dsl 🍴 Arby's, Burger King, Chick-fil-A, Cracker Barrel, Hong Kong Buffet, KFC, Krystal, McDonald's, Pachos Mexican, Pizza Hut, Steak'n Shake, Taco Bell, Waffle House, Wendy's, Zaxby's 🛏 Comfort Inn, Hampton Inn, Quality Inn 🅾 �H, $General, $Tree, Advance Parts, AutoZone, Ingles Foods/gas, Lowe's, O'Reilly Parts, Rite Aid, Verizon, Walmart, S 🅶 Flash/dsl, Shell, TA/BP/Country Pride/Popeye's/dsl/scales/24hr/ @ 🍴 Waffle House 🛏 Deerfield Inn, Super 8, Wingate Inn 🅾 Country Boys RV Park (1mi), truckwash/service
113	GA 83, Madison, N 🅶 BP/dsl 🅾 �H, st patrol
108mm	N 🆁🆂 wb, full ♿ facilities, litter barrels, petwalk, 🅲, 🚻, RV dump, vending
105	Rutledge, Newborn, N 🅶 Valero/pizza/dsl 🅾 Hard Labor Creek SP
103mm	S 🆁🆂 eb, full ♿ facilities, litter barrels, petwalk, 🅲, 🚻, RV dump, vending
101	US 278
98	GA 11, to Monroe, Monticello, N 🛏 Blue Willow Inn (4mi), S 🅶 BP/Blimpie/dsl, Marathon
95mm	Alcovy River
93	GA 142, Hazelbrand Rd, N 🅾 Home Depot, S 🅶 QT/dsl 🍴 Bullrito's Cafe, IHOP, McDonald's, Shane's Rib Shack, Subway, Taco Bell, Waffle House, Wendy's 🛏 Hampton Inn, Travelodge 🅾 �H, $Tree, Aldi Foods, AT&T, Kauffman Tire, Verizon, Walmart/Subway

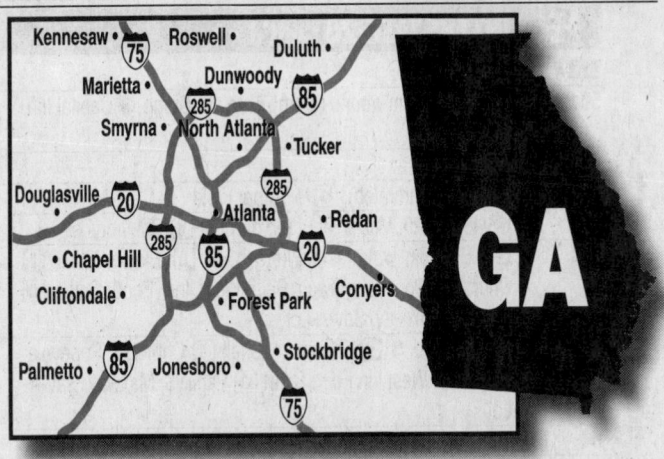

↑E	**INTERSTATE 20 Cont'd**
Exit #	Services
92	Alcovy Rd, N 🔃 Chevron/dsl, Shell/dsl 🍴 Waffle House 🏠 Baymont Inn, Best Value Inn, Covington Lodge, Days Inn, Super 8, S ⊙ H
90	US 278, GA 81, Covington, S 🔃 Citgo/dsl, QT, RaceWay/dsl 🍴 Applebee's, Arby's, Bojangles, Burrito Loco, Capt D's, Checkers, Chick-fil-A, Church's, Covington Diner, DQ, Dunkin Donuts/Baskin-Robbins, Firehouse Subs, Hardee's, Just Dogs/Burgers, KFC, Krystal, Little Caesars, LJ Silver, Longhorn Steaks, Mama Maria's, McDonald's, Moe's SW Grill, Pacho's Mexican, Papa John's, Pizza Hut, Stalvey's Rest., Stevi B's Pizza, Subway, Taco Bell, Waffle House, Wendy's, Zaxby's 🏠 Holiday Inn Express ⊙ $General, Ace Hardware, Advance Parts, AutoZone, BigLots, Chevrolet, CVS, Family$, Food Depot, GNC, Ingles Foods, K-Mart, Kroger/dsl, O'Reilly Parts, Radio Shack, Rite Aid, vet, Walgreens
88	Almon Rd, to Porterdale, N 🔃 Chevron/dsl, S 🔃 BP, Liberty 🍴 McDonald's, Subway (2mi) ⊙ Riverside Estates RV Camp, transmissions/repair
84	GA 162, Salem Rd, to Pace, N 🔃 BJ's Whse/gas, Marathon/dsl ⊙ Chrysler/Dodge/Jeep, S 🔃 Citgo, QT, RaceWay/dsl, Shell/dsl 🍴 Baskin-Robbins, Burger King, Dunkin Donuts, Hardee's, KFC, Los Bravos Mexican, McDonald's, Quiznos, Subway, Taco Bell, Waffle House, Wendy's ⊙ Advance Parts, Family$, Food Depot, Ingles/gas, Olympic Auto, O'Reilly Parts, PepBoys, Rite Aid
82	GA 138, GA 20, Conyers, N 🔃 BP/dsl, QT 🍴 Applebee's, Bruster's, Chili's, ChuckECheese, Coldstone, Cracker Barrel, Don Tello's, Golden Corral, IHOP, O'Charley's, Outback Steaks, Red Lobster, Sonic, Subway 🏠 Country Inn&Suites, Days Inn, Hampton Inn, Holiday Inn Express, Jameson Inn, La Quinta, Super 8 ⊙ AT&T, Belk, Chevrolet/Buick/GMC, Courtyard, Ford, Harley-Davidson, Home Depot, Jo-Ann, Kohl's, Michael's, Office Depot, Old Navy, Petsmart, Staples, Tires+, TJ Maxx, U-Haul, Walmart, S 🔃 Chevron, Shell/dsl 🍴 Blimpie, Burger King, Capt D's, Checkers, Chick-fil-A, CiCi's Pizza, Dunkin Donuts/Baskin-Robbins, Firehouse Subs, Folk's Rest., Frontera Mexican, Grand Buffet, HoneyBaked Ham, Hooters, Jim'n Nick's BBQ, KFC, Krystal, Little Caesar's, Mandarin Garden, McDonald's, Mellow Mushroom, Milano Cafe, Moe's SW Grill, Panda Express, Panera Bread, Piccadilly Cafe, Popeye's, Ruby Tuesday, Silver Dragon, Sonny's BBQ, Starbucks, Subway, Taco Bell, Waffle House 🏠 Microtel ⊙ $General, $Tree, Aldi Foods, BigLots, Discount Tire, Firestone/auto, GNC, Goodyear/auto, Hobby Lobby, Honda, Hyundai, Kauffman Tire, Kroger/gas, NTB, PepBoys, Publix, Radio Shack, Ross, Target, USPO, Verizon, Walgreens
80	West Ave, Conyers, N 🔃 Shell/dsl, Valero/dsl 🍴 Domino's, DQ, Subway, Waffle House 🏠 Best Value Inn, Motel 6 ⊙ Conyers Drug, Family$, Meineke, Piggly Wiggly, S 🔃 QT/dsl, Texaco/dsl 🍴 Fish House, Longhorn Steaks, McDonald's 🏠 Comfort Inn ⊙ Nissan, vet
79mm	parking area eb
78	Sigman Rd, N 🔃 Shell/dsl, Texaco 🍴 Waffle House
75	US 278, GA 124, Turner Hill Rd, N 🔃 BP/dsl, Citgo/dsl, S 🍴 Applebee's, Arizona's, Bruster's, Buffalo Wild Wings, Chicken&Waffles, Chick-fil-A, Chili's, Don Tello's Mexican, Firehouse Subs, Grand China, IHOP, Kampai's Steaks, McDonald's, Olive Garden, Panera Bread, Smokey Bones BBQ, Steak n'Shake, Steak'n Shake, Subway, Taco Bell, TGIFriday, Zaxby's 🏠 Comfort Inn, Comfort Suites, Fairfield Inn, Hilton

75	**Continued** Garden, Holiday Inn Express, Hyatt Place ⊙ $Tree, AT&T, Best Buy, Big Lots, Dillard's, JC Penney, Kia, Kohl's, Macy's, mall, Marshalls, PetCo, Rite Aid, Ross, Sam's Club/gas, Sears/auto, Staples, Target, Tires+, Toyota/Scion, Verizon, Walmart
74	Evans Mill Rd, GA 124, Lithonia, N 🔃 BP/Circle K, Chevron, Shell 🍴 Capt D's, McDonald's, Pizza Hut, SoulFood Rest., Subway, Wendy's ⊙ Advance Parts, CVS Drug, O'Reilly Parts, S 🔃 Citgo/dsl 🍴 Da-Bomb Wings/Seafood, DQ, Dudley's Rest., Krystal, Waffle House 🏠 Microtel ⊙ $General
71	Hillandale Dr, Farrington Rd, Panola Rd, N 🔃 QT/dsl, Shell/dsl 🍴 Burger King, Checkers, KFC, McDonald's, Rib Tips, Waffle House, Wings&Philly 🏠 Budgetel, Quality Inn, Super 8 ⊙ Family$, S 🔃 BP/dsl, Citgo, Murphy USA/dsl, Shell/dsl 🍴 Dunkin Donuts, IHOP, Marco's Pizza, New China, Popeye's, Ruby Tuesday, Subway, Taco Bell/LJ Silver, Town Wings, Wendy's 🏠 Red Roof Inn ⊙ Lowe's, Publix, Radio Shack, Tires+, Verizon, Walgreens, Walmart/McDonald's
68	Wesley Chapel Rd, Snapfinger Rd, N 🍴 Capt D's, Checkers, Chick-fil-A, China Cafeteria, Church's, Dunkin Donuts, KFC, Little Caesar's, New China, Subway, Taco Bell, Waffle House 🏠 Economy Inn ⊙ $General, DJ's Repair, Home Depot, Kroger, NTB, S 🔃 Chevron/dsl, Mobil, QT, Shell/dsl 🍴 Dragon Chinese, JJ's Fish& Chicken, McDonald's, Popeye's 🏠 Super Inn ⊙ Family$, USPO
67b a	I-285, S to Macon, N to Greenville
66	Columbia Dr (from eb, no return), N 🔃 Chevron
65	GA 155, Candler Rd, to Decatur, N 🔃 Chevron, Citgo, Marathon/dsl 🍴 Pizza Hut, Popeye's, Red Lobster, Wendy's 🏠 Best Value Inn ⊙ CVS Drug, U-Haul, S 🔃 BP, Chevron, Shell/dsl, Texaco 🍴 Baskin-Robbins/Dunkin Donuts, Burger King, Checkers, Church's, DQ, KFC, McDonald's, Subway, Taco Bell, Waffle King 🏠 Country Hearth Inn ⊙ BigLots, Firestone/auto, Macy's
63	Gresham Rd, N 🔃 Chevron, Citgo/dsl 🍴 American Deli ⊙ Walmart/Subway, S 🔃 Citgo, Marathon, Shell, Texaco/dsl 🍴 Church's
62	Flat Shoals Rd (from eb, no return)
61b	GA 260, Glenwood Ave, N 🔃 Chevron, Texaco/dsl
61a	Maynard Terrace (from eb, no return)
60b a	US 23, Moreland Ave, N 🔃 Exxon, Valero 🏠 Atlanta Motel ⊙ Advance Parts, S 🔃 Citgo/dsl, Shell 🍴 Checkers, Krystal, LJ Silver, McDonald's, Wendy's
59b	Memorial Dr, Glenwood Ave (from eb)
59a	Cyclorama, N 🔃 Chevron/Blimpie/dsl ⊙ MLK Site, S 🔃 BP/Subway ⊙ Confederate Ave Complex, CVS
58b	Hill St (from wb, no return), N 🔃 Shell 🍴 Mrs. Winners

Map labels: Kennesaw, Roswell, Duluth, Marietta, Dunwoody, 75, 85, Smyrna, North Atlanta, Tucker, Douglasville, 285, 20, Atlanta, Redan, Chapel Hill, 285, 85, Conyers, 20, Cliftondale, Forest Park, Palmetto, 85, Jonesboro, Stockbridge, 75, **GA**

INTERSTATE 20 Cont'd

Exit #	Services
58a	Capitol St (from wb, no return), N to GA Dome, S Capital Inn, downtown
57	I-75/85
56b	Windsor St (from eb), Ⓞ to Turner Field
56a	US 19, US 29, McDaniel St (eb only), N 🅖 Chevron/dsl
55b	Lee St (from wb), Ft McPherson, S 🅖 Exxon, Shell 🍴 Church's, Popeye's, Taco Bell, West Inn Food Court Ⓞ $Family, Maxway, Sav-A-Lot
55a	Lowery Blvd, S 🅖 Exxon/dsl, Shell 🍴 Church's, Popeye's, Taco Bell, West Inn Food Court Ⓞ Family$, Maxway, Sav-A-Lot
54	Langhorn St (from wb), to Cascade Rd
53	MLK Dr, to GA 139, N 🅖 Chevron, Shell/dsl, S 🅖 Texaco/dsl Ⓞ auto repair
52b a	GA 280, Holmes Dr, High Tower Rd, S 🅖 Chevron, Exxon/dsl 🍴 Hong Kong Chinese, McDonald's, Wendy's Ⓞ AutoZone, CVS Drug, Family$
51b a	I-285, S to Montgomery, N to Chattanooga
49	GA 70, Fulton Ind Blvd, N 🅖 Citgo/dsl, Shamrock/dsl 🍴 Wendy's 🏠 Days Inn, Majestick Lodge Ⓞ 🅡ˢ, S 🅖 BP/dsl, Chevron/dsl, Texaco/dsl, Valero 🍴 Grand Buffet, McDonald's, Waffle House 🏠 Fairview Inn, Red Roof Inn Ⓞ U-Haul
48mm	Chattahoochee River
47	Six Flags Pkwy (from wb), N 🅖 BP 🏠 EconoLodge, S 🏠 Knights Inn, Sleep Inn, Wingate Inn Ⓞ Six Flags Funpark
46b a	Riverside Parkway, N 🅖 Citgo/Church's, Marathon, QT 🍴 Hong Kong Buffet, Waffle House 🏠 Super 8 Ⓞ Family$, S 🅖 Citgo 🍴 Wendy's 🏠 Knights Inn, Sleep Inn, Wingate Inn Ⓞ Six Flags Funpark
44	GA 6, Thornton Rd, to Lithia Springs, N 🅖 BP, QT, RaceTrac/dsl, Shell/dsl, Valero 🍴 Applebee's, BBQ House, Bojangles, Burger King, Chick-fil-A, Church's, Domino's, Firehouse Subs, Golden Dragon Chinese, Hardee's, IHOP, KFC, Krystal, McDonald's, Olive Tree Rest., Popeye's, Ruby Tuesday, Shoney's, Sonic, Subway, Taco Bell, Waffle House, Wendy's, Zaxby's 🏠 Budget Inn, Holiday Inn Express, InTowne Suites, Knight's Inn, Quality Inn Ⓞ H, $General, AT&T, Atlanta West Camping (2mi), Autozone, Carmax, Chevrolet, Ford, Harley Davidson, Home Depot, Honda, Hyundai, Kroger/gas, Midas, Nissan, Office Depot, Tires+, Verizon, vet, VW, Walgreens, S 🅖 Shell 🍴 Bei Jin China, Cracker Barrel, Fiesta Mexican 🏠 Candlewood Suites, Country Inn&Suites, Courtyard, Fairfield Inn, Hampton Inn, Hilton Garden, Motel 6, SpringHill Suites Ⓞ Chrysler/Dodge/Jeep, Kia, to Sweetwater Creek SP, Toyota/Scion, Walmart
42mm	weigh sta eb
41	Lee Rd, to Lithia Springs, N 🅖 Marathon/dsl
37	GA 92, to Douglasville, N 🅖 RaceTrac/dsl, Shell/dsl 🍴 Blimpie, Checker's, Chick-fil-A, Church's, DQ, Kenny's Rest., Krystal, Longhorn Steaks, Martin's Rest., McDonald's, Pizza Hut, Popeye's, Subway, Taco Bell, Waffle House, Wendy's 🏠 Best Value Inn, Comfort Inn, Days Inn, EconoLodge, Quality Inn, Ramada Ltd, Royal Inn Ⓞ H, AutoZone, CVS Drug, Family$, Family$, Kroger/dsl, NAPA, O'Reilly Parts, Tires+, vet, Walgreens, S 🅖 Chevron/dsl, QT, Texaco/dsl 🍴 Domino's, Waffle House Ⓞ $General, Aamco, Advance Parts, Ingles Foods
36	Chapel Hill Rd, N Ⓞ H, S 🅖 BP, QT, Shell/dsl 🍴 $3 Cafe, 5 Guys Burgers, Arby's, Carrabba's, China Garden, Coldstone, Daruma, Joe's Crabshack, Johnny's Subs, Logan's

36	Continued Roadhouse, McDonald's, O'Charley's, Olive Garden, Outback Steaks, Panda Express, Provino's Italian, Shane's Rib Shack, Starbucks, Subway, TX Roadhouse, Waffle House 🏠 Hampton Inn Ⓞ $Tree, Aldi Foods, Belk, BigLots, Dillard's, Discount Tire, Firestone/auto, Hobby Lobby, JC Penney, Kohl's, Macy's, Marshall's, Michael's, Old Navy, Petsmart, Rite Aid, Ross, Sears/auto, Target, Verizon
34	GA 5, to Douglasville, N 🅖 RaceTrac/dsl, Texaco/dsl 🍴 Atlantic Grill, Cracker Barrel, Stevie B's Pizza, Waffle House, Williamson Bros BBQ, Zaxby's 🏠 Holiday Inn Express, La Quinta, Sleep Inn Ⓞ $Tree, Kauffman Tires, Sam's Club, URGENT CARE, Walmart, S 🅖 Chevron/dsl, Circle K, Shell/dsl 🍴 Applebee's, Bruster's, Buffalo Wild Wings, Burger King, Chick-fil-A, ChuckECheese, DQ, Dunkin Donuts, El Tio Mexican, Fiesta Mexican, Folk's Rest., Golden Corral, HoneyBaked Ham, IHOP, KFC, King Buffet, Krystal, La Salsa, LJ Silver, McDonald's, Moe's SW Grill, Monterrey Mexican, Papa John's, Pizza Buffet, Pizza Hut, Popeyes, Quiznos, Red Lobster, Seabreeze Seafood, S'more BBQ, Sonic, Steak'n Shake, Subway, Taco Bell, Taco Mac, Waffle House, Wasabi Japanese, Wendy's 🏠 InTown Suites Ⓞ Advance Parts, AT&T, Batteries+, Best Buy, Goodyear/auto, Home Depot, JoAnn Crafts, Kroger/dsl, Lowe's, Meineke, NTB, Office Depot, O'Reilly Parts, PepBoys, Publix, Tuesday Morning, U-Haul, vet, Walgreens
30	Post Rd, S 🅖 Shell/dsl
26	Liberty Rd, Villa Rica, N 🅖 Shell/dsl, Swifty/dsl 🍴 China Wok, Johnny's Pizza, McDonald's, Mex-Grill, Olive Tree Rest., Subway, Sumo Japanese, Waffle House Ⓞ H, $General, Publix, vet, Walgreens, S 🅖 Chevron, Wilco/Hess/Godfather's Pizza/Subway/dsl/scales/24hr 🏠 American Inn
24	GA 101, GA 61, Villa Rica, N 🅖 BP/dsl, RaceTrac/dsl, Shell/dsl 🍴 Arby's, Chick-fil-A, Hardee's, KFC/Taco Bell, Krystal, Lin's Garden Chinese, McDonald's, Pizza Hut, Romero's Italian, Sonic, Stix Grill, Subway, Waffle House, Wendy's 🏠 Comfort Inn, Days Inn, EconoLodge, Super 8 Ⓞ H, Advance Parts, AT&T, AutoZone, CVS Drug, Ingles Foods, Rite Aid, Walgreens, S 🅖 QT, Shell/dsl 🍴 Bojangles, Burger King, Capt D's, Domino's, El Ranchito Mexican, O'Charley's, Papa John's, Waffle House, Zaxby's Ⓞ $Tree, Chevrolet, GNC, Home Depot, Radio Shack, to W GA Coll, URGENT CARE, Verizon, Walmart/Subway
21mm	Little Tallapoosa River
19	GA 113, Temple, N 🅖 ⊕FLYING J/dsl/scales/24hr, 🍴 Subway/Wendy's/dsl/scales/24hr/ @ 🍴 El Tapatio's, Fortune Star Chinese, Hardee's, McDonald's, Temple Pizza, Waffle House Ⓞ Ingles Foods/gas, Truck-o-Mat/scales
15mm	weigh sta wb
11	US 27, Bremen, Bowdon, N 🅖 Chevron/dsl, Murphy USA/dsl, Texaco/dsl, Valero/Domino's/dsl 🍴 Arby's, Capt D's, Checker's, Chopsticks Chinese, Cracker Barrel, Juanito's, KFC/Taco Bell, McDonald's, Papa John's, Subway, Waffle House, Wendy's, Zaxby's 🏠 Bridgeview Inn, Hampton Inn, Holiday Inn Express, Microtel, Quality Inn Ⓞ H, $General, (1mi), Advance Parts, Ford, Ingles Foods/gas, URGENT CARE, Verizon, Walmart/McDonald's, S 🅖 BP/dsl, Kangaroo/dsl 🍴 John Tanner SP
9	Waco Rd, N 🅖 ♥Love's/Chesters/Subway/dsl/scales/24hr Ⓞ Jellystone RV Park (2mi)
5	GA 100, Tallapoosa, N 🅖 Citgo/dsl/24hr, Victory/dsl 🍴 Waffle House Ⓞ Big Oak RV park, S 🅖 Newborn TrkStp/rest/

Side labels: ATLANTA AREA · GA · DOUGLASVILLE · VILLA RICA · BREMEN

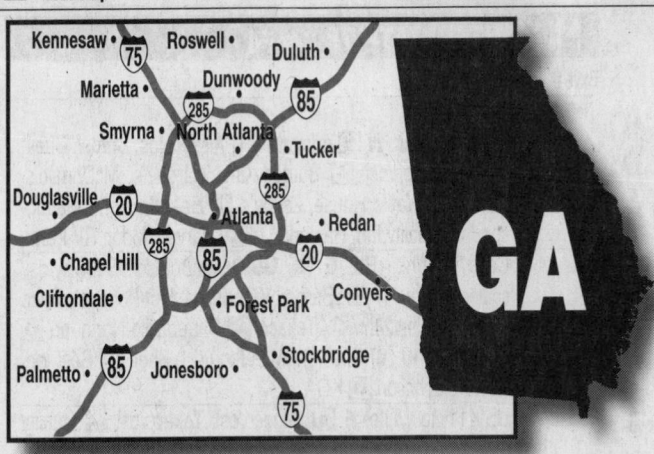

⬆E	**INTERSTATE 20 Cont'd**

Exit #	Services
5	**Continued**
	dsl/24hr/ @, 🚛/KFC/Taco Bell/dsl/scales/24hr, Robinson/Subway 🍴 DQ, GA Diner 🏠 Super 8 🅞 to John Tanner SP, truck repair/wash
1mm	**Welcome Ctr eb, full ♿ facilities, litter barrels, petwalk, 🚻, 🏧, vending**
0mm	Georgia/Alabama state line, Eastern/Central time zone

⬆N	**INTERSTATE 59**

Exit #	Services
	I-59 begins/ends on I-24, exit 167. For I-24, turn to Tennessee Interstate 24.
20mm	I-24, W to Nashville, E to Chattanooga
17	Slygo Rd, to New England, W 🅖 Midnite/dsl 🅞 KOA (2mi)
11	GA 136, Trenton, E 🅖 Chevron/dsl, Exxon/dsl, Marathon/Kangaroo 🍴 Asian Garden, Guthrie's, Hardee's, McDonald's, Pizza Hut, Subway 🏠 Days Inn 🅞 Advance Parts, CVS Drug, Family$, Ingles, O'Reilly Parts, to Cloudland Canyon SP, W 🅖 BP, Citgo/dsl, Marathon/Kangaroo/dsl 🍴 Huddle House, Krystal, Little Caesars, Taco Bell, Wendy's 🅞 $General, BiLo, Food Outlet
4	Rising Fawn, E 🅖 Citgo, W 🅖 BP/dsl, 🚛/Subway/dsl/scales/24hr 🅞 camping
0mm	Georgia/Alabama state line, eastern/central time zone

⬆N	**INTERSTATE 75**

Exit #	Services
355mm	Georgia/Tennessee state line
354mm	Chickamauga Creek
353	GA 146, Rossville, E 🅖 BP 🏠 Cloud Springs Lodge, W 🅖 BP/Subway/dsl, MegaStar/dsl 🅞 Costco/gas
352mm	**Welcome Ctr sb, full ♿ facilities, info, litter barrels, petwalk, 🚻, 🏧, vending**
350	GA 2, Bfd Pkwy, to Ft Oglethorpe, E 🅖 Chevron/dsl, Kangaroo/dsl 🏠 Hampton Inn, Hometown Inn, W 🅖 RaceTrac/dsl, Shell 🍴 BBQ Corral, Subway 🅞 🏥, KOA, to Chickamauga NP
348	GA 151, Ringgold, E 🅖 BP/dsl, FM 🍴 Cracker Barrel, Hardee's, KFC, Los Reyes Mexican, McDonald's, Pizza Hut, Subway, Taco Bell, Waffle House 🏠 Holiday Inn Express, Super 8 🅞 Advance Parts, AutoZone, Chevrolet, CVS Drug, Dunlap's RV Ctr, Ingles, Walgreens, W 🍴 Domino's, Guthries, New China, Wendy's 🅞 Ace Hardware, Family$, Food Lion, Peterbilt, truck repair
345	US 41, US 76, Ringgold, E 🅖 BP, W 🅖 Chevron, Cochran's/Midnite/rest/dsl/scales/24hr/ @, Kangaroo/Subway/dsl/scales/24hr 🍴 Waffle House
343mm	**weigh sta both lanes**
341	GA 201, to Varnell, Tunnel Hill, W 🅖 Chevron, Shell 🅞 carpet outlets
336	US 41, US 76, Dalton, Rocky Face, E 🅖 Murphy USA/dsl, RaceTrac/dsl, Shell 🍴 Checkers, Waffle House 🏠 EconoLodge 🅞 🏥, Ford/Lincoln, Home Depot, Kohl's, PetCo, Walmart, W 🅖 BP/dsl, Exxon 🍴 Los Pablos, Oyster Grill, Tijuana Mexican, Wendy's 🏠 Baymont Inn, carpet outlets, Guest Inn, Motel 6, Staylodge, Super 8
333	GA 52, Dalton, E 🅖 BP/dsl, Exxon/dsl, RaceTrac/dsl 🍴 Amici's Italian, Applebee's, Bruster's, Burger King, Capt D's, Chick-fil-A, CiCi's Pizza, Cracker Barrel, DQ, Five Guys Burgers, Fuji Japanese, IHOP, Jersey Mike's Subs,

DALTON *(vertical left margin)*

Exit #	Services
333	**Continued**
	Kani Japanese, KFC, LJ Silver, Longhorn Steaks, Los Pablos, Los Pablos Mexican, McDonald's, O'Charley's, Outback Steaks, Panda Express, Panera Bread, Pizza Hut, Schlotzsky's, Shoney's, Sonic, Starbucks, Steak'n Shake, Taco Bell, Waffle House, Wendy's 🏠 Best Inn, Days Inn, Hampton Inn, Travelodge 🅞 $Tree, AT&T, BigLots, Chevrolet, Chrysler/Jeep, Harley-Davidson, K-Mart, Kroger/dsl, TJ Maxx, Tuesday Morning, Walgreens, W 🍴 Chili's, Red Lobster, Zaxby's 🏠 Comfort Inn, Country Inn Suites, Courtyard, Holiday Inn, Holiday Inn Express, Jameson Inn, La Quinta, Quality Inn, Ramada 🅞 NW GA Trade/Conv Ctr
328	GA 3, to US 41, E 🅖 BP/Kangaroo/dsl, 🚛/Arby's/dsl/scales/24hr 🍴 Waffle House, Wendy's 🏠 Best Value Inn, Super Motel, W 🅞 carpet outlets
326	Carbondale Rd, E 🅖 🚛/McDonald's/Subway/dsl/scales, Smart/dsl, W 🅖 BP, Exxon
320	GA 136, to Lafayette, Resaca, E 🅖 FLYING J/Denny's/dsl/LP/24hr 🍴 truck repair/parts, truckwash
319mm	🆁🆂 sb, full ♿ facilities, litter barrels, Oostanaula River, petwalk, 🚻, 🏧, vending
318	US 41, Resaca, E 🅖 Hess/Wilco/DQ/Wendy's/scales/dsl/24hr 🍴 Hardee's 🏠 Relax Inn, W 🅖 Pure, Shell/dsl 🍴 Chuckwagon Rest. 🏠 Best Inn, Executive Inn
317	GA 225, to Chatsworth, E New Echota HS, Vann House HS, W 🅖 BP (1mi) 🏠 Express Inn
315	GA 156, Redbud Rd, to Calhoun, E 🅖 Citgo/dsl, Kangaroo 🍴 Waffle House 🅞 Food Lion, KOA (2mi), W 🅖 BP/dsl, Liberty/Subway/dsl, Shell 🍴 Arby's, Shoney's 🏠 Ramada Ltd 🅞 🏥 Rite Aid
312	GA 53, to Calhoun, E 🅖 Shell/dsl 🍴 Cracker Barrel, Longhorn Steaks 🏠 Country Inn&Suites, Days Inn, La Quinta 🅞 Calhoun Outlets/famous brands, W 🅖 BP/Arby's, Chevron/dsl, Marathon/Kangaroo, Murphy USA 🍴 Big John's Rest., Bojangles, Burger King, Capt D's, Checker's, Chick-fil-A, China Palace, Domino's, DQ, Eastern Cafe, El Nopal Mexican, Gondolier Pizza, Huddle House, IHOP, KFC, Krystal, Little Caesars, LJ Silver, Los Reyes Mexican, McDonald's, Papa's Pizza, Pizza Hut, Ruby Tuesday, Ryan's, Starbucks, Subway, Taco Bell, Tokyo Steaks, Wendy's, Zaxby's 🏠 Guest Inn, Hampton Inn, Holiday Inn Express, Jameson Inn, Motel 6, Scottish Inn 🅞 $General, Advance Parts, AutoZone, GNC, Goodyear/auto, Home Depot, Ingles, Kroger/gas, Office Depot, vet, Walmart
308mm	🆁🆂 nb, full ♿ facilities, litter barrels, petwalk, 🚻, 🏧, vending
306	GA 140, Adairsville, E 🅖 Cowboy's/dsl, QT/dsl/scales/24hrs, Shell 🍴 Cracker Barrel, Wendy's 🏠 Hampton Inn

RESACA CALHOUN *(vertical center margin)*

INTERSTATE 75 Cont'd

Exit #	Services

A D A I R S V I L L E

306 Continued

🅾 truck repair, **W** 🅖 Adairsville TP/dsl/scales, BP/dsl, Chevron/dsl, Exxon/dsl 🍴 Burger King, Hardee's, McDonald's, Taco Bell, Waffle House, Zaxby's 🛏 Best Western, Magnuson Inn, Quality Inn, Ramada Ltd 🅾 Harvest Moon RV Park

296 Cassville-White Rd, **E** 🅖 ▨▨▨/McDonald's/Subway/dsl/scales, Pure, TA/BP/Burger King/Pizza Hut/Popeye's/Taco Bell/dsl/scales/24hr/ @, Texaco 🛏 Cartersville North Inn 🅾 truckwash, **W** 🅖 Chevron, Marathon/dsl, Shell 🛏 Best Inn, Howard Johnson 🅾 KOA

293 US 411, to White, **E** 🅖 Sunoco/dsl, Texaco/dsl 🛏 Quality Inn, **W** 🅖 Chevron/dsl, Horizon, Marathon 🍴 AJ's Cafe, Waffle House 🛏 Holiday Inn 🅾 Harley-Davidson, mineral museum, RV camping, st patrol

290 GA 20, to Rome, **E** 🅖 Chevron/Subway/dsl, Exxon/dsl, Kangaroo/dsl 🍴 Arby's, Fruit Jar Cafe, McDonald's, Wendy's 🛏 Best Western, Country Inn Suites, EconoLodge, Motel 6, Ramada Ltd, Red Roof Inn, Super 8, **W** 🅖 BP, Murphy USA (1.5mi), Shell 🍴 Cracker Barrel, Michael's BBQ, Pruitt's BBQ, Shoney's, Waffle House 🛏 Days Inn, Hampton Inn 🅾 🏥, (1.5mi), RV camping (7mi), Walmart

288 GA 113, Cartersville, **W** 0-2 mi 🅖 BP/dsl, Exxon/Subway/dsl 🍴 Applebee's, Burger King, Chick-Fil-A, Chili's, Gondolier Pizza, IHOP, KFC, Krystal, Las Palmas Mexican, Longhorn Steaks, McDonald's, Moe's SW Grill, Mrs Winner's, Pizza Hut, Publix, Red Lobster, Starbucks, Taco Bell, Waffle House, Wing Moon 🛏 Fairfield Inn, Hampton Inn, Hilton Garden, Knights Inn, Quality Inn 🅾 Belk, Chrysler/Dodge/Jeep, K-Mart, Kohl's, Kroger, Rite Aid, Staples, Target, to Etowah Indian Mounds (6mi)

286mm Etowah River

285 Emerson, **E** 🅖 Sunoco 🛏 Red Top Mtn Lodge 🅾 to Allatoona Dam, to Red Top Mtn SP

283 Allatoona Rd, Emerson, **W** 🅖 ❤Loves/McDonald's/Subway/dsl/scales/24hr, Sunoco (1mi), 🍴 Allatoona Landing Resort (2mi), camping

280mm Allatoona Lake

A C W O R T H

278 Glade Rd, to Acworth, **E** 🅖 BP/dsl, Shell 🛏 Best Value 🅾 McKinney Camping (3mi), to Glade Marina, **W** 🅖 Chevron 🍴 Bojangles, Hong Kong Chinese, KFC, Krystal, Papa John's, Pizza Hut, Subway, Taco Bell, Waffle House 🛏 Best Inn 🅾 AutoZone, BigLots, Ingles/cafe, Rite Aid

277 GA 92, Acworth, **E** 🅖 BP, RaceTrac 🍴 Hardee's, Shoney's, Waffle House 🛏 Comfort Suites, La Quinta, Ramada Ltd, **W** 🅖 Chevron/dsl, Shell/DQ/dsl 🍴 Bamboo Garden, China Chef, Domino's, McDonald's, Ricardo's Mexican, Sonic, Subway, Taco 2 Go, Waffle House, Wendy's, Zaxby's 🛏 Best Western, Day's Inn, Econolodge, Motel 6, Super 8 🅾 Advance Parts, CVS Drug, Goodyear/auto, Publix, Walgreens

273 Wade Green Rd, **E** 🅖 BP, Pure, RaceTrac 🍴 Arby's, Burger King, Dunkin Donuts, Las Palmas Mexican, McDonald's, Mrs Winners, Papa John's, Pizza Hut/Taco Bell, Subway, Waffle House 🛏 Magnuson Motel, Sleep Inn 🅾 BigLots, GNC, Goodyear/auto, Publix, Rite Aid, **W** 🅖 Shell, Texaco/dsl 🍴 BBQ Street, Coldstone, Johnny's Pizza/Subs, Quiznos, Starbucks, Wendy's, Wing Zone 🅾 Home Depot, Kroger/gas, Walgreens

271 Chastain Rd, to I-575 N, **E** 🅖 Chevron 🍴 Brewsters, CA Dreaming, Chick-Fil-A, Chilito's Mexican, Cracker Barrel, Dunkin Donuts, Firehouse Subs, Five Guys Burgers,

271 Continued

Kayson's Grill, Little Zio, Los Reyes, McAlister's Deli, O'Charley's, Panda Express, Panera Bread, Sidelines Grille, Starbucks, Taco Mac, ToGo's/Baskin Robbins, Zaxby's, Zucca Pizza 🛏 Best Western, Comfort Inn, Embassy Suites, Extended Stay America, Fairfield Inn, La Quinta, Residence Inn, Suburban Lodge, Super 8 🅾 Goodyear/auto, Outlets Ltd Mall, **W** 🅖 Citgo, Shell/dsl, Swifty Save Gas/Blimpie 🍴 Arby's, Mrs Winners, Waffle House/24hr, Wendy's 🛏 Country Inn Suites, SpringHill Suites, Sun Suites 🅾 museum

269 to US 41, to Marietta, **E** 🅖 Chevron/24hr, Shell, Texaco/dsl 🍴 Applebee's, Burger King, Fuddrucker's, Highlands Grill, Honey Baked Ham, Longhorn Steaks, McDonald's, New China, Olive Garden, Pizza Hut, Provino's, Red Lobster, Shogun Japanese, Smokey Bones, Smoothie King, Starbucks, Subway, Twisted Taco, Waffle House 🛏 Comfort Inn, Econolodge, Holiday Inn Express, La Quinta, Red Roof Inn, Super 8 🅾 Barnes&Noble, Big 10 Tire, Firestone/auto, Home Depot, JC Penney, Macy's, mall, Marshall's, Publix, Sears/auto, TJ Maxx, **W** 🅖 BP, Exxon 🍴 Bahama Breeze, Bailey's Grill, Bugaboo, Carrabbas, Chick-fil-A, Chili's, ChuckeCheese, Coldstone, Copelands Grill, Creek Steaks, Golden Corral, Joe's Crabshack, Macaroni Grill, On-the-Border, Outback Steaks, Rafferty's, Starbucks, Steak'n Shake, Sweet Tomato, TGIFriday, Willy's Mexican 🛏 Day's Inn, Hampton Inn, Hilton Garden, Quality Inn, Wingate Inn 🅾 Best Buy, Buick/GMC, CarMax, Chevrolet, Costco/gas, Ford/Lincoln, Goodyear/auto, Jo-Anne Fabrics, Kia/Toyota, mall, Mitsubishi, Nissan, NTB, Office Depot, Old Navy, PetsMart, Target, to Kennesaw Mtn NP

268 I-575 N, GA 5 N, to Canton

267b a GA 5 N, to US 41, Marietta

M A R I E T T A

265 GA120, N Marietta Pkwy, **W** 🅖 Chevron, Shell/dsl 🍴 Arbys, Bojangles, Chick-fil-A, KFC 🛏 Days Inn, Suburban Lodge, Sun Inn, Travelers Motel

263 GA 120, to Roswell, **E** 🅖 Chevron/dsl/24hr, QT, Texaco/24hr, **W** 🅖 Exxon/dsl, RaceTrac 🍴 Applebee's, Capt D's, China Kitchen, DQ, Hardee's, Haveli Rest., Piccadilly's, Subway 🛏 Best Western, Crowne Plaza, Fairfield Inn, Hampton Inn, Marietta Motel, Ramada Ltd, Regency Inn, Super 8, Wyndham Garden 🅾 Atl-Marietta RV Resort, U-Haul

261 GA 280, Delk Rd, to Dobbins AFB, **E** 🅖 Exxon, RaceTrac, Shell/McDonald's 🍴 CC Cafeteria, China Wok, Hardee's, KFC/Taco Bell, Murphy's Deli, Ruby Tuesday, Spaghetti Whse 🛏 Budget Inn, Courtyard, Drury Inn, Motel 6, Scottish Inn, Sleep Inn, Super 8, Travelers Inn 🅾 Publix, **W** 🅖 BP, Chevron 🍴 Cracker Barrel, D&B Rest., Waffle House 🛏 Best Inn, Comfort Inn, Days Inn, Fairfield Inn, Holiday Inn, La Quinta, Quality Inn, Wingate Inn

S M Y R N A

260 Windy Hill Rd, to Smyrna, **E** 🅖 BP/dsl 🍴 Boston Mkt, Famous Dave's, Fuddrucker's, Houston's Rest., Jersey Mike's Subs, Mellow Mushroom, NY Pizza, Pappadeaux Seafood, Pappasito's Cantina, Philly Cafe, Rose&Crown, Sal Grosso Brazilian, Schlotzsky's, Starbucks, Subway, TGIFriday 🛏 Country Hearth Inn, EconoLodge, Extended Stay Deluxe, Hilton Garden, Hyatt, Marriott, Studio Lodge 🅾 CVS Drug, USPO, **W** 🅖 Chevron, Citgo, Shell 🍴 Arby's, Chick-fil-A, Fatburger, Halftime Grill, McDonald's, Panda Express, Popeye's, Starbucks, Waffle House, Wendy's 🛏 Best Western, Country Inn&Suites, Courtyard, Days Inn, DoubleTree, Hilton, Masters Inn, Red Roof Inn 🅾 🏥, Target

259b a I-285, W to Birmingham, E to Greenville, Montgomery

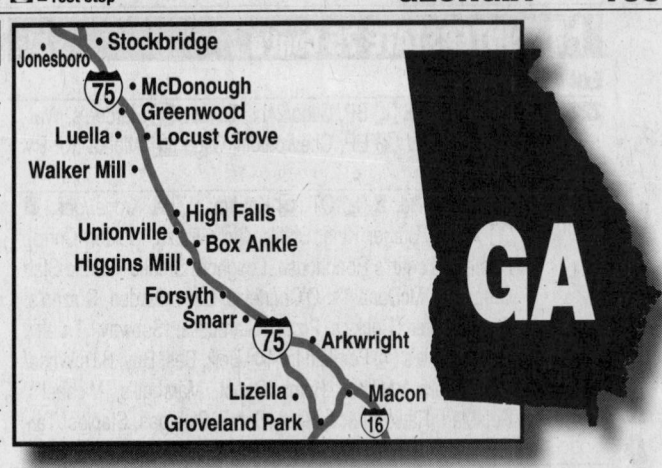

⬆N	**INTERSTATE 75 Cont'd**

Exit # | **Services**

258 Cumberland Pkwy, **W** 🍴 Chipotle Mexican, Copelands Rest, Hooters, Moe's SW Grill, Ray's On The River, Shane's Rib-shack, Subway

257mm Chattahoochee River

256 to US 41, Northside Pkwy

255 US 41, W Paces Ferry Rd, **E** 🅖 Chevron, Shell/dsl 🍴 Blue Ridge Grill, Caribou Coffee, Chick-fil-A, Houston's Rest., McDonald's/playplace, OK Café, Pero's Pizza, Starbucks, Steak'n Shake, Taco Bell, Willy's Rest. 🅞🅗 Ace Hardware, Publix, **W** 🅖 Exxon

254 Moores Mill Rd

252b Howell Mill Rd, **E** 🅖 Shell 🍴 Chick-fil-A, Domino's, McDonald's, Willy's Grill 🅞 Goodyear, Publix, Rite Aid, USPO, **W** 🅖 Shell 🍴 Arby's, Arthur's Italian, Chin Chin Chinese, Einstein Bro's, Kayson's, KFC/Pizza Hut, Mexican, Piccadilly, Rest., Sensational Subs, Starbucks, Subway, Taco Bell, US BBQ, Waffle House, Wendy's 🏠 Budget Inn, Holiday Inn 🅞 Ace Hardware, Firestrone/auto, GNC, Just Brakes, Kroger, Office Depot, Petsmart, Ross, TJ Maxx, Walmart

252a US 41, Northside Dr, **E** 🅞🅗, **W** 🅖 Shell 🍴 Krystal, Little Zio's, McDonald's, Waffle House 🏠 Days Inn

251 I-85 N, to Greenville

250 Techwood Dr (from sb), 10th St, 14th St, **E** 🏠 Travelodge

249d 10th St, Spring St (from nb), **E** 🅖 BP, Chevron/24hr 🍴 Checker's, Domino's, Pizza Hut, The Varsity 🏠 Fairfield Inn, Regency Suites, Renaissance Hotel, Residence Inn, **W** 🍴 McDonald's 🏠 Comfort Inn, Courtyard 🅞🅗, to GA Tech

249c Williams St (from sb), 🅞 to GA Dome, downtown

249b Pine St, Peachtree St (from nb), downtown, **W** 🏠 Hilton, Marriott

249a Courtland St (from sb), downtown, **W** 🏠 Hilton, Marriott 🅞 GA St U

248d Piedmont Ave, Butler St (from sb), downtown, **W** 🏠 Courtyard, Fairfield Inn, Radisson 🅞🅗, Ford, MLK NHS

248c GA 10 E, Intn'l Blvd, downtown, **W** 🏠 Hilton, Holiday Inn, Marriott Marquis, Radisson

248b Edgewood Ave (from nb), **W** 🅞🅗, downtown, hotels

248a MLK Dr (from sb), **W** st capitol, to Underground Atlanta

247 I-20, E to Augusta, W to Birmingham

246 Georgia Ave, Fulton St, **E** 🏠 Comfort Inn, Country Inn&Suites, Holiday Inn 🅞 stadium, **W** 🅖 BP 🍴 KFC 🅞 GSU, to Coliseum

245 Ormond St, Abernathy Blvd, **E** 🏠 Comfort Inn, Country Inn&Suites 🅞 stadium, **W** 🅞 st capitol

244 University Ave, **E** 🅖 Chevron, Exxon 🅞 NAPA, **W** 🍴 Mrs Winner's

243 GA 166, Lakewood Fwy, to East Point

242 I-85 S, 🅞 to ⛽

241 Cleveland Ave, **E** 🅖 BP, Chevron/Subway/dsl 🍴 Checkers, Church's, McDonald's 🅞 Advance Parts, **W** 🅖 Citgo/dsl, ExpressZone, Marathon 🍴 Ameican Deli, Burger King, Krystal, Papa John's 🏠 American Inn 🅞 $Tree, AutoZone, Big Lots, CVS Drug, Family$, Kroger, Walgreens

239 US 19, US 41, **E** 🅖 Chevron/dsl 🍴 Waffle House 🅞 USPO, **W** 🅖 Texaco 🍴 Chick-fil-A, IHOP, McDonald's, Wendy's 🏠 Best Western 🅞 to ⛽

238b a I-285 around Atlanta

237a GA 85 S (from sb)

237 GA 331, Forest Parkway, **E** 🅖 BP, Chevron/dsl, Shell/McDonald's, SunPetro/dsl 🍴 Burger King, Mr Taco, Subway,

---

237 Continued
Waffle House 🏠 Econolodge 🅞 Farmer's Mkt, **W** 🅖 BP, Exxon/Subway/dsl 🍴 Quizno's 🏠 Atlanta Inn, Ramada Ltd 🅞 Lee Tires/repair

235 US 19, US 41, GA 3, Jonesboro, **E** 🅖 Chevron/dsl, Exxon/Subway/dsl, Phillips 66, Valero 🍴 Waffle House 🏠 Travelodge, **W** 🅖 BP, Shell, Texaco/dsl 🍴 Applebee's, Burger King, Checker's, ChuckeCheese, Dunkin Donuts, Folk's Rest., Hooters, Krystal, Popeye's, Red Lobster, Tokyo Buffet, Waffle House, Zaxby's 🏠 Best Value, Econolodge, Holiday Inn, Motel 6 🅞🅗, Office Depot, O'Reilly Parts

233 GA 54, Morrow, **E** 🅖 BP, Citgo, Marathon 🍴 Cracker Barrel, IHOP, Krystal/24hr, Mrs Winner's, Papa Buffet, Taco Bell, Waffle House, Wendy's 🏠 Best Western, Days Inn, Drury Inn, Red Roof Inn 🅞 Walmart, **W** 🅖 Circle K, Exxon/24hr 🍴 China Café, KFC, Lenny's Subs, McDonald's, Quizno's, Subway, Waffle House 🏠 Hampton Inn, Quality Inn 🅞 Acura, Best Buy, Costco/gas, Harley-Davidson, Macy's, Nissan, TJ Maxx, Toyota, Tuesday Morning

231 Mt Zion Blvd, **E** 🅖 QT 🅞 Chrysler/Dodge/Jeep, Ford/Lincoln, Honda, **W** 🅖 Chevron, Exxon/dsl, Texaco/dsl 🍴 Arby's, Boston's Rest., Brewster's, Burger King, Burger Shack, Chick-fil-A, Chili's, Joe's Crabshack, Longhorn Steaks, McDonald's, Mo-Joe's, Panda Express, Papa John's, Pizza Hut, Steak'n Shake, Subway, Truett's Rest., Waffle House, Wendy's, Wok Asian 🏠 Country Inn&Suites, Extended Stay America, Sleep Inn, Sun Suites 🅞 Barnes & Noble, Best Buy, Home Depot, Michael's, NTB, Old Navy, PetsMart, Publix, Ross, Target

228 GA 54, GA 138, Jonesboro, **E** 🅖 Exxon, Raceway/24hr 🍴 Applebee's, Arby's, Broadway Diner, Burger King, Chick-fil-A, ChinChin Chinese, CiCi's, DQ, Frontera Mexican, Golden Corral, Honeybaked Ham, IHOP, KFC, Krystal, McDonald's, O'Charlie's, Piccadilly's, Subway, Taco Mac, Tokyo Seafood, Waffle House, Wendy's 🏠 Best Western, Comfort Inn, Day's Inn, Hampton Inn, Holiday Inn, Holiday Inn, Howard Johnson, La Quinta, Motel 6, Red Roof Inn 🅞🅗, GNC, Goodyear, K-Mart, Kroger/dsl, Lowes Whse, Office Depot, Tires+, **W** 🅖 BP/24hr, Marathon, Sunoco/Wendy's 🍴 Dragon Garden Chinese, Ranchero's Mexican 🅞 CarMax, CVS Drug, Kohl's

227 I-675 N, to I-285 E (from nb)

224 Hudson Bridge Rd, **E** 🅖 Shell, Texaco/dsl 🍴 Chick-fil-A, China Wok, DQ, KFC, La Hacienda, Outback Steaks, Pizza Hut, Starbucks, Subway, Waffle House, Wendy's 🏠 Baymont Inn 🅞🅗, Publix, Rite Aid, Walgreens, **W** 🅖 Murphy USA/dsl, QT 🍴 Arby's, China Cafe, Firehouse Subs, McDonald's, Mellow Mushroom, Subway, Taco Bell, Zaxby's 🏠 Super 8 🅞 $Tree, Discount Tire, Walmart/24hr

*(left margin, top to bottom: ATLANTA)*

(center margin: MORROW, JONESBORO)

(right tab: GA)

GA

M C D O N O U G H

F O R S Y T H

M A C O N

Exit #	Services
⬆N	**INTERSTATE 75 Cont'd**
222	Jodeco Rd, **E** 🅖 BP, Citgo/24hr, Texaco 🍽 Hardee's, Waffle House, **W** 🅖 BP, Chevron/dsl, Citgo 🅞 Atlanta So. RV Camping
221	Jonesboro Rd, **E** 🅖 QT 🅞 Kauffman Tire, Kroger/gas, **W** 🍽 Arby's, Burger King, Chili's, Cici's Pizza, Golden Corral, Hooter's, Logan's Roadhouse, Longhorn Steaks, Marble Slab Creamery, McDonald's, O'Charley's, Olive Garden, Quizno's, Red Lobster, Rocky's Pizza, Starbucks, Subway, Truett's Grill, Wendy's 🛏 Fairfield Inn 🅞 Belk, Best Buy, BJ's Whse/gas, Books-A-Million, Home Depot, Marshall's, Michael's, PetsMart, Radio Shack, Ross, Sam's Club/gas, Staples, Target
218	GA 20, GA 81, McDonough, **E** 🅖 BP, Murphy USA, QT, Texaco 🍽 3 Dollar Cafe, Applebee's, Arby's, Blimpie, Burger King, China Star, Cracker Barrel, DQ, IHOP, KFC, McDonald's, Moe's SW Grill, Mrs Winner's, OB's BBQ, Pizza Hut, Quizno's, Ruby Tuesday, Taco Bell, Tokyo Japanese, Waffle House, Wendy's, Zaxby's 🛏 Best Inn, Best Western, Economy Inn, Hampton Inn, Motel 6 🅞 $General, Aamco, Goodyear, Lowe's Whse, Office Depot, Rite Aid, Walmart, **W** 🅖 Citgo/dsl, RaceTrac, Shell/24hr 🍽 Chick-fil-A, El Agade Mexican, Firehouse Subs, Fuddruckers, Starbucks, Subway, Waffle House 🛏 Comfort Inn, Econolodge, Hilton Garden, Holiday Inn Express, Super 8 🅞 JC Penney, Kohl's, Toyota
216	GA 155, McDonough, Blacksville, **E** 🅖 Shell, Sunoco/Backyard Burger, Texaco/dsl 🍽 Blimpie 🛏 Best Value, Budget Inn, Day's Inn, Roadway Inn 🅞 Buick, Chevrolet, GMC, Lincoln, **W** 🅖 BP/dsl, Chevron, Citgo, Citgo/dsl/24hr, Mystik/dsl, QT 🍽 Da Vinci's Pizza, Krystal, Kuma Japanese, Legends Grill, Subway, Waffle House 🛏 Country Inn&Suites, Quality Inn
212	to US 23, Locust Grove, **E** 🅖 BP/McDonald's/dsl, Chevron/Burger King, Citgo/dsl, JP, Marathon/Subway, Shell/dsl 🍽 Capt D's, Country Steaks, Denny's, Gabino's Mexican, Huddle House, KFC/Pizza Hut/Taco Bell, Shane's Ribshack, Sunrise China, Waffle House, Wendy's, Zaxby's 🛏 Economy Inn, Executive Inn, La Quinta, Ramada Ltd, Red Roof Inn 🅞 Ingles/gas, NapaCare, Tanger Outlet/famous brands, **W** 🅖 Citgo/DQ/dsl, Exxon/dsl 🛏 Comfort Suites, Scottish Inn, Sundown Lodge, Super 8 🅞 Bumper Parts
205	GA 16, to Griffin, Jackson, **E** 🅖 BP, **W** 🅖 BP, Chevron/dsl 🅞 auto repair, Forest Glen RV Park
201	GA 36, to Jackson, Barnesville, **E** 🅖 Loves/McDonald's/dsl/grill/scales/24hr, TA/Subway/Taco Bell/dsl/scales/24hr/ @, Wilco/Hess/DQ/Stuckey's/Wendy's/dsl/scales/24hr/ @ 🅞 Blue Beacon, **W** 🅖 FLYING J/Denny's/dsl/LP/24hr, BP/dsl 🅞 Sagon RV Ctr, Speedco Lube, truckwash
198	Highfalls Rd, **E** 🅖 Exxon (1mi) 🍽 High Falls BBQ, Ken's Cafe 🛏 High Falls Lodge 🅞 High Falls SP, HighFalls RV Park (1mi)
193	Johnstonville Rd, **E** 🅖 BP
190mm	**weigh sta both lanes**
188	GA 42, **E** 🅖 Shell/24hr 🛏 Best Western, Budget Inn 🅞 RV camping, to Indian Spings SP
187	GA 83, Forsyth, **E** 🛏 Econolodge, New Forsyth Inn, Regency Inn, **W** 🅖 BP/Circle K, Citgo/dsl, Marathon, Shell 🍽 Burger King, Capt D's, China Inn, DQ, Hardee's, McDonald's, Pizza Hut, Subway, Taco Bell, Waffle House, Wendy's 🛏 Day's Inn, Tradewinds Motel 🅞 Advance Parts, Freshway Foods, O'Reilly Parts, Walmart

Exit #	Services
186	Tift College Dr, Juliette Rd, Forsyth, **E** 🅞 Jarrell Plantation HS (18mi), KOA, **W** 🅖 BP/dsl, Chevron, Marathon 🍽 Waffle House 🛏 Holiday Inn Express, Holiday Inn/rest., Super 8 🅞 🏥, CVS Drug, Ingles/Deli
185	GA 18, **E** 🅞 L&D RV Park (2mi), **W** 🅖 BP/Circle K/24hr, Shell/dsl 🍽 Shoney's 🛏 Comfort Inn 🅞 Ford, repair, st patrol
181	Rumble Rd, to Smarr, **E** 🅖 BP/dsl/24hr, Shell/dsl/24hr
179mm	🆁🆂 sb, full 🚻 facilities, litter barrels, petwalk, (🄲), 🅰, vending
177	I-475 S around Macon (from sb)
175	Pate Rd, Bolingbroke (from nb, no re-entry)
172	Bass Rd, **E** 🍽 McDonald's, Pig in a Pit BBQ, Quizno's, Zaxby's 🅞 Bass Pro Shop, **W** 🅖 Citgo/dsl/24hr 🍽 Homewood Suites, Magarita's Mexican, Mellow Mushroom 🅞 Publix, to Museum of Arts&Sciences
171	US 23, to GA 87, Riverside Dr, **E** 🅖 BP, Marathon/dsl 🍽 Bonefish Grill, Chili's, Jock&Jill's Grill, Mandarin Express, Sticky Fingers 🅞 Acura, Barnes & Noble, Belk, Dillards, KIA, Mercedes, Subaru, Volvo, **W** 🍽 Cracker Barrel 🅞 Lexus, same as 169 W, Toyota/Scion
169	to US 23, Arkwright Dr, **E** 🅖 Shell/Circle K/24hr 🍽 Carrabba's, Logan's Roadhouse, Outback Steaks, Waffle House, Wager's Grill 🛏 Candlewood Suites, Comfort Inn, Country Inn & Suites, Courtyard, Fairfield Inn, Hampton Inn, Holiday Inn, La Quinta, Red Roof Inn, Residence Inn, Sleep Inn, Super 8 🅞 Buick/Cadillac/GMC, **W** 🅖 BP/dsl, Chevron/24hr, Marathon/dsl 🍽 5 Guys Burgers, Arby's, Burger King, Cheddar's, Cheng's Kitchen, Chick-fil-A, Corky Bells, Cracker Barrel, Dunkin Donuts, El Azteca Mexican, Guiseppi's Italian, Hooters, KFC, Krystal, Longhorn Steaks, Mandarin Chinese, McDonald's, Panera Bread, Papa John's, Papoulis' Gyros, Pizza Hut, Shoki Japanese, Starbucks, Steak'n Shake, Steve B's Pizza, Subway, Taco Bell, Waffle House 🛏 Baymont Inn, Best Inn, Extended Stay Deluxe, Quality Inn, Travelodge, Wingate Inn 🅞 🏥, $Tree, Ace Hardware, Chrysler/Jeep/Dodge, Hyundai, K-Mart, Kroger, Mazda, Publix, Radio Shack, same as 167
167	GA 247, Pierce Ave, **E** 🛏 Days Inn, **W** 🅖 BP/Circle K/dsl, Chevron, Conoco, Exxon, LoBucks Gas, Marathon/Subway/dsl, Shell 🍽 Applebee's, Loco's Grill, Pier 97 Seafood, Pizza Hut, Red Lobster, San Marcos Mexican, Shogun Japanese, SteakOut Rest., Waffle House 🛏 Best Western/rest., Comfort Inn, Holiday Inn Express, Howard Johnson, Motel 6 🅞 Exper-Tire, Rite Aid
165	I-16 E, to Savannah
164	US 41, GA 19, Forsyth Ave, Macon, **E** 🍽 Sid's Rest. 🅞 hist dist, **W** 🅖 Citgo/dsl 🅞 🏥, museum
163	GA 74 W, Mercer U Dr, **E** 🛏 Hilton Garden 🅞 to Mercer U, **W** 🅖 Citgo, Marathon/dsl
162	US 80, GA 22, Eisenhower Pkwy, **W** 🅖 BP, Chevron, Lolo Gas 🍽 Burger King, Capt D's, Checker's, IHOP, Krispy Kreme, Krystal, LJ Silver, McDonald's, Mrs Winners, Subway, Taco Bell, Wendy's 🛏 InTown Suites 🅞 $Tree, Fred's, Meineke, Office Depot, O'Reilly Parts, PepBoys, Piggly Wiggly, Save-A-Lot Foods, Walgreens
160	US 41, GA 247, Pio Nono Ave, **E** 🅖 Flash/dsl, RaceWay/Dunkin Donuts/dsl 🍽 Waffle House, **W** 🅖 BP, Enmark/dsl 🍽 Arby's, DQ, KFC, McDonald's, Subway, Waffle House 🅞 $General, Advance Parts, Family$, O'Reilly Parts, Piggly Wiggly, Raffield Tire, Roses, same as 162
156	I-475 N around Macon (from nb)

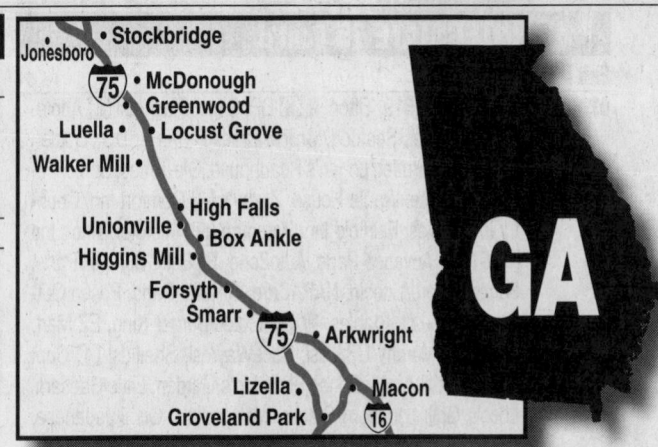

INTERSTATE 75 Cont'd

Exit #	Services
155	Hartley Br Rd, **E** 🅖 BP/KFC/dsl/24hr 🍴 Subway, Waffle House, Wendy's 🄾 Kroger/dsl, Verizon, **W** 🅖 Citgo/dsl, Exxon/dsl, Flash/DQ/dsl 🍴 McDonald's, Zaxby's 🏠 Best Value Inn 🄾 Advance Parts, CVS Drug
153	Sardis Church Rd
149	GA 49, Byron, **E** 🅖 Chevron/dsl, Marathon/dsl, Shell/dsl 🍴 Burger King, Denny's, GA Bob's BBQ, Krystal, McDonald's, Pizza Hut, Subway, Waffle House, Wendy's, Zaxby's 🏠 Best Western, Comfort Suites, Holiday Inn Express, Super 8 🄾 antiques, Campers Inn RV Ctr, Mid-State RV Ctr, Peach Stores/famous brands, **W** 🅖 Citgo/dsl/24hr, Flash/dsl, Marathon/dsl, RaceWay/dsl, Texaco/dsl 🍴 DQ, Huddle House, Waffle House 🏠 Budget Inn, Days Inn, EconoLodge, Quality Inn 🄾 Ace Hardware, Bumper Parts, Camping World RV Ctr, Chevrolet, Ford, O'Reilly Parts, USPO, Verizon
146	GA 247, to Centerville, **E** 🅖 Exxon, Flash/dsl, Shell 🍴 Subway, Waffle House 🏠 EconoLodge, Knights Inn 🄾 🏥, museum, to Robins AFB, **W** 🅖 ▭/Arby's/dsl/24hr
144	Russel Pkwy, **E** 🄾 aviation museum, Robins AFB
142	GA 96, Housers Mill Rd, **E** 🅖 Chevron/dsl 🄾 Ponderosa RV Park
138	Thompson Rd, **E** 🅖 Valero/dsl 🄾 🏥, **W** 🄾 🆂
136	US 341, Perry, **E** 🅖 Flash/dsl, Shell/dsl 🍴 Burger King, Capt D's, Chick-fil-A, China House, KFC, Krystal, Longhorn Steaks, McDonald's, Pizza Hut, Red Lobster, Sonny's BBQ, Steamers Seafood, Subway, Taco Bell, Waffle House, Wendy's, Zaxby's 🏠 Best Inn, Great Inn, Hampton Inn, Howard Johnson, Jameson Inn, Super 8 🄾 🏥, $Tree, Ace Hardware, Advance Parts, AT&T, Boland's RV Park, GNC, Kroger/dsl, NAPA, Radio Shack, Verizon, Walmart, **W** 🅖 Chevron/dsl, Marathon/dsl 🍴 Applebee's, Green Derby Rest., Grill Master BBQ 🏠 Ashburn Inn, EconoLodge, Knights Inn, Passport Inn, Quality Inn, Ramada Inn, Roadway Inn
135	US 41, GA 127, Perry, **E** 🅖 Flash/dsl, Marathon, Shell, Texaco 🍴 Cracker Barrel, DQ, Subway, Waffle House 🏠 Best Western, Comfort Inn, Red Carpet Inn, Relax Inn, Travelodge 🄾 Chrysler/Dodge/Jeep, GA Nat Fair, Kia, **W** 🄾 Fair Harbor RV Park, st patrol
134	South Perry Pkwy, **W** 🅖 Marathon 🏠 Microtel 🄾 Buick/Chevrolet/GMC, Priester's Pecans
127	GA 26, Henderson, **E** 🄾 Twin Oaks Camping, **W** 🅖 Chevron
122	GA 230, Unadilla, **E** 🅖 Chevron/dsl 🄾 Chevrolet/Ford, **W** 🏠 Red Carpet Inn
121	US 41, Unadilla, **E** 🅖 Borum/repair, Danfair, Flash/DQ/Stuckey's/dsl, Shell 🍴 Country Boys BBQ, Subway 🏠 Economy Inn, Scottish Inn 🄾 $General, Carquest, Family$, Firestone, Piggly Wiggly, Southern Trails RV Resort, **W** 🅖 Citgo/rest./dsl/scales/24hr
118mm	🆁🆂 sb, full ♿ facilities, litter barrels, petwalk, 🅲, 🆎, RV dump, vending
117	to US 41, Pinehurst
112	GA 27, Vienna
109	GA 215, Vienna, **E** 🅖 ▭/McDonalds/dsl/scales/24hrs, **W** 🅖 Citgo/dsl, Shell/Subway/dsl/e-85, Sunoco 🍴 Huddle House, Popeye's 🏠 Executive Inn 🄾 🏥, antiques, Cotton Museum
108mm	🆁🆂 nb, full ♿ facilities, litter barrels, petwalk, 🅲, 🆎, RV dump, vending
104	Farmers Mkt Rd, Cordele
102	GA 257, Cordele, **E** 🅖 Sunoco/dsl, **W** 🍴 Pecan House 🄾 🏥
101	US 280, GA 90, Cordele, **E** 🅖 Chevron, ▭/Arby's/dsl/scales/24hr, Shell 🍴 Denny's, Golden Corral, Waffle House 🏠 Days Inn, Fairfield Inn, Holiday Inn Express, Ramada Inn 🄾 Ford/Lincoln, st patrol, **W** 🅖 Flash, Gas'n Go, Pacecar Express, Sunoco 🍴 Burger King, Capt D's, Cracker Barrel, Cutter's Steaks, Domino's, DQ, Hardee's, KFC, Krystal, Little Caesars, Los Compadres, McDonald's, New China, Pizza Hut, Sonic, Subway, Taco Bell, TJ's Rest, Wendy's, Zaxby's 🏠 Ashburn Inn, Athens 8 Motel, Best Western, Comfort Inn, Hampton Inn, Quality Inn, Travelodge 🄾 $General, $Tree, Ace Hardware, Advance Parts, AutoZone, Belk, Harvey's Foods, Home Depot, J Carter HS, NAPA, O'Reilly Parts, Radio Shack, Save-A-Lot, to Veterans Mem SP, Verizon, Walgreens, Walmart
99	GA 300, GA/FL Pkwy, **E** 🅖 Citgo/DQ/dsl, **W** 🍴 Waffle House 🏠 Country Inn&Suites 🄾 to Chehaw SP
97	to GA 33, Wenona, **E** 🄾 Cordele RV Park, dsl repair, **W** 🄾 KOA, truckwash
92	Arabi, **E** 🅖 Shell/Plantation House, **W** 🅖 Citgo/dsl 🄾 Southern Gates RV Park
85mm	🆁🆂 nb, full ♿ facilities, litter barrels, petwalk, 🅲, 🆎, vending
84	GA 159, Ashburn, **W** 🅖 Chevron/DQ/Subway/dsl/24hr 🏠 Ashburn Inn/RV Park
82	GA 107, GA 112, Ashburn, **W** 🅖 BP, Shell, Sunoco/dsl 🍴 KFC, McDonald's, Pizza Hut, Shoney's, Waffle House, Zaxby's 🏠 Best Value Inn, Best Western, Days Inn, Super 8 🄾 $General, Auto Value Parts, Buick/Chevrolet/GMC, Fred's, O'Reilly Parts, Piggly Wiggly, Rite Aid, to Chehaw SP
80	Bussey Rd, Sycamore, **W** 🄾 Allen's Tires
78	GA 32, Sycamore, **E** to Jefferson Davis Mem Pk (14mi)
76mm	🆁🆂 sb, full ♿ facilities, litter barrels, petwalk, 🅲, 🆎, vending
75	Inaha Rd
71	Willis Still Rd, Sunsweet, **W** 🅖 BP/dsl
69	Chula-Brookfield Rd, **E** 🅖 Sunoco/dsl 🏠 Chula Carpet Inn
66	Brighton Rd
64	US 41, Tifton, **E** 🅖 BP/dsl 🄾 🏥, $General, Harvey's Foods, **W** 🅖 Shell
63b	8th St, Tifton, **E** 🅖 Flash/dsl/e-85 🍴 Los Compadres 🄾 Publix, **W** 🍴 Pit Stop BBQ 🄾 GA Museum of Agriculture
63a	2nd St, Tifton, **E** 🅖 BP, Marathon 🍴 Asahi Xpress, Checker's, El Cazador Mexican, Krystal, McDonald's, Pizza Hut, Ranchero's Grill, Red Lobster, Stevi B's Pizza, Subway, Taco Bell, Waffle House 🏠 EconoLodge, Super 8 🄾 $General, $Tree, Belk, Buick/Cadillac/GMC, JC Penney, K-Mart, **W** 🅖 Bob's/dsl 🍴 Coyoacan Mexican 🏠 Quality Inn, Travelodge

Side markers (top to bottom): **N** · **PERRY** · **CORDELE** · **WENONA** · **ASHBURN** · **TIFTON** · **GA**

🛢️ = gas   🍴 = food   🏨 = lodging   🅾️ = other   🅿️ₛ = rest stop   Copyright 2015 - the Next EXIT ®

⬆️N INTERSTATE 75 Cont'd

Exit #	Services
62	US 82, to US 319, Tifton, **E** 🛢️ BP, Citgo, Flash/dsl 🍴 Applebee's, Charles Seafood, Chili's, Cracker Barrel, DQ, Golden Corral, King Buffet, Logan's Roadhouse, Ole Times, Sonic, Tokyo Japanese, Waffle House, Zaxby's 🏨 Comfort Inn, Country Inn&Suites, Fairfield Inn, Hampton Inn, Microtel, Tifton Inn 🅾️ $Tree, Advance Parts, AutoZone, BigLots, Bumper Parts, Family$, Ford/Lincoln, NAPACare, O'Reilly Parts, Pecan Outlet, Save-A-Lot, Staples, **W** 🛢️ Exxon/Burger King, EZ Mart, Flash/dsl, Murphy USA/dsl, RaceWay/dsl, Shell/dsl 🍴 Capt D's, Chick-fil-A, HogBones BBQ, Lin's Garden, Little Caesars, Loco's Grill, Longhorn Steaks, McDonald's, Oishi Japanese, Ruby Tuesday, Shoney's, Starbucks, Subway, Waffle House, Wendy's 🏨 Days Inn, Hilton Garden, Rodeway Inn 🅾️ $General, Chevrolet, Chrysler/Dodge/Jeep, Honda, Lowe's, Radio Shack, Toyota, URGENT CARE, Verizon, Walmart/Subway
61	Omega Rd, **E** 🅾️ Nissan, **W** 🍴 Shell/Stuckey's/Country Diner/pizza/dsl/24hr 🏨 Motel 6 🅾️ Harley-Davidson, Pines RV Park
60	Central Ave, Tifton, **E** 🛢️ Chevron 🍴 Dragon 1 Chinese, **W** 🛢️ 🚚Steak'n Shake/Subway/dsl/scales/24hr 🅾️ Blue Beacon, KOA
59	Southwell Blvd, to US 41, Tifton, **E** 🛢️ ❤️Loves/Hardee's/dsl/24hr
55	to Eldorado, Omega, **E** 🛢️ Shell/Magnolia Plantation/dsl
49	Kinard Br Rd, Lenox, **E** 🛢️ Dixie/dsl 🏨 Knights Inn, **W** 🛢️ BP/dsl/24hr 🅾️ repair
47mm	🅿️ₛ both lanes, full ♿ facilities, litter barrels, petwalk, 🔌, 🏪 vending
45	Barneyville Rd, **E** 🏨 Economy Inn
41	Rountree Br Rd, **E** 🛢️ Citgo, **W** 🅾️ to Reed Bingham SP
39	GA 37, Adel, Moultrie, **E** 🛢️ Citgo/dsl, Dixie Gas, Quick Gas, Shell/McDonald's/dsl 🍴 DQ, Hardee's, Subway, Waffle House 🏨 Scottish Inn, Super 8 🅾️ 🏥, $General, Ace Hardware, Advance Parts, Family$, Harvey's Foods, O'Reilly Parts, Piggly Wiggly, Rite Aid, **W** 🛢️ BP, Citgo/dsl/scales 🍴 Burger King, Capt D's, China Buffet, IHOP, Taco Bell, Wendy's, Western Sizzlin 🏨 Days Inn, Hampton Inn 🅾️ to Reed Bingham SP
37	Adel
32	Old Coffee Rd, Cecil, **E** 🛢️ Citgo 🏨 Stagecoach Inn, **W** 🛢️ Chevron 🅾️ Cecil Bay RV Park
29	US 41 N, GA 122, Hahira, Sheriff's Boys Ranch, **E** 🍴 Subway 🅾️ NAPA, **W** 🛢️ Big Foot TC/cafe/dsl/24hr, Citgo/dsl 🏨 Hahira Inn
23mm	weigh sta both lanes
22	US 41 S, to Valdosta, **E** 🛢️ BP, Shell/Subway/dsl 🍴 Waffle House 🏨 Best Western 🅾️ 🏥, Buick/Chevrolet/GMC, golf, Mazda, **W** 🛢️ Citgo/Stuckey's 🍴 Burger King, DQ 🏨 Days Inn, Howard Johnson
18	GA 133, Valdosta, **E** 🛢️ Citgo/dsl, Exxon, Flash, Mobil 🍴 Applebee's, Arby's, Atl. Bread Co, Brusters, Buffalo Wild Wings, Burger King, Chick-fil-A, Chili's, Chow Town, CiCi's Pizza, Cracker Barrel, Crystal River Seafood, Denny's, El Potro Mexican, El Toreo, Fazoli's, Green Iguana Cafe, Honeybaked Ham, Hooters, KFC, Krystal, Little Caesars, Longhorn Steaks, Marble Slab, McAlister's Deli, McDonald's, Olive Garden, Outback Steaks, Quiznos, Red Lobster, Ruby Tuesday, Sonny's BBQ, Starbucks, Steak'n Shake, Subway, Taco Bell, TX Roadhouse, Waffle House, Wendy's, Zaxby's 🏨 Comfort Suites, Country Inn&Suites, Courtyard, Drury Inn,

18	Continued
	Hilton Garden, Holiday Inn Express, InTown Suites, Jameson Inn, Jolly Inn, La Quinta, Quality Inn 🅾️ $Tree, AT&T, Belk, Best Buy, Books-A-Million, Family$, Harvey's Foods, Hobby Lobby, Home Depot, JC Penney, Kohl's, Lowe's, mall, Michael's, Office Depot, Old Navy, Petsmart, Publix, repair, Ross, Sears/auto, Target, TJ Maxx, Tuesday Morning, Verizon, Walgreens, **W** 🛢️ BP/dsl, RaceWay/dsl, Shell 🏨 Days Inn, EconoLodge, Sleep Inn, Super 8 🅾️ RiverPark Camping, Toyota/Scion
16	US 84, US 221, GA 94, Valdosta, **E** 🛢️ Big Foot/dsl, BP/dsl, Citgo/DQ/dsl, Danfair Express, Murphy Express/dsl, Pure/dsl, Shell/dsl 🍴 Aligatou Japanese, Bojangles, Bubba Jax Crab Shack, Burger King, Cheddar's, IHOP, McDonald's, Pizza Hut, Sonic, Waffle House, Wendy's 🏨 Days Inn, Fairfield Inn, Hampton Inn, Holiday Inn, Motel 6, New Valdosta Inn, Quality Inn, Stay Inn, Super 8, Wingate Inn 🅾️ NAPA, repair, Sam's Club/gas, to Okefenokee SP, Walmart/Subway, **W** 🛢️ Horizon/Backyard Burger/pizza, Shell/dsl/24hr 🍴 Austin's Steaks 🏨 Clarion, Knights Inn
13	Old Clyattville Rd, Valdosta, **W** 🅾️ Wild Adventures Park
11	GA 31, Valdosta, **E** 🛢️ 🚚/Subway/dsl/24hr/ @, Wilco/Hess/Dunkin Donuts/Stuckey's/dsl/scales/24hr 🍴 Waffle House 🏨 Travelers Inn 🅾️ truckwash, **W** 🛢️ BP 🍴 Big Ed's BBQ 🅾️ $General
5	GA 376, to Lake Park, **E** 🛢️ Citgo, Flash Foods/Stuckey's/dsl, RaceWay/dsl, Shell 🍴 Chick-fil-A, Domino's, Farmhouse Rest., Krystal, Lin's Garden Chinese, Rodeo Mexican, Sonny's BBQ, Subway, Waffle House, Zaxby's 🏨 Guesthouse Inn, Quality Inn 🅾️ $Tree, antiques, Eagles Roost Camping, Family$, Fred's, Horizon RV Ctr, USPO, Winn-Dixie, **W** 🛢️ Citgo/dsl, Exxon/dsl, Shell/dsl 🍴 Cracker Barrel, McDonald's, Pizza Hut, Taco Bell, Wendy's 🏨 Ashburn Inn, Days Inn, Hampton Inn, Super 8 🅾️ KOA
3mm	Welcome Ctr nb, full ♿ facilities, litter barrels, petwalk, 🔌, 🏪, vending
2	Lake Park, Bellville, **E** 🛢️ Mobil/DQ, Shell/dsl, TA/BP/Arby's/dsl/scales/24hr/ @ 🅾️ SpeedCo, **W** 🛢️ 🟡FLYING J/Denny's/Subway/dsl/LP/scales/24hr 🏨 Motel 6 🅾️ lube/tires/wash
0mm	Georgia/Florida state line

⬆️N INTERSTATE 85

Exit #	Services
179mm	Georgia/South Carolina state line, Lake Hartwell, Tugaloo River
177	GA 77 S, to Hartwell, **E** 🛢️ BP/gifts/dsl 🍴 Dad's Grill 🅾️ to Hart SP, Tugaloo SP
176mm	Welcome Ctr sb, full ♿ facilities, info, litter barrels, petwalk, 🔌, 🏪, vending
173	GA 17, to Lavonia, **E** 🛢️ RaceTrac/dsl 🍴 Blimpie, La Cabana Mexican, McDonald's, Subway, Taco Bell, Waffle House 🏨 EconoLodge, Sleep Inn 🅾️ $General, Lavonia Foods, Rite Aid, **W** 🛢️ Chevron/dsl, Exxon/dsl 🍴 Burger King, Hardee's, Pizza Hut, Shoney's, Wendy's, Zaxby's 🏨 Holiday Inn Express, Super 8 🅾️ Chrysler/Dodge/Jeep, Ford, to Tugaloo SP
171mm	weigh sta nb
169mm	weigh sta sb
166	GA 106, to Carnesville, Toccoa, **E** 🛢️ Wilco/Hess/DQ/Wendy's/dsl/scales/24hr, **W** 🛢️ Echo Trkstp/Chevron/Echo Rest./dsl/scales/24hr 🅾️ truck repair

Side markers: GA, ADEL, VALDOSTA, VALDOSTA, LAVONIA

🅝	**INTERSTATE 85 Cont'd**
Exit #	**Services**
164	GA 320, to Carnesville, 🅖 Chevron/dsl
160	GA 51, to Homer, E 🅖 Shell/Subway/dsl/24hr 🅞 to Russell SP, Ty Cobb Museum, Victoria Bryant SP, W 🅖 ⊘FLYING J/dsl/24hr, Carnsville TrvlPlaza/dsl/scales/24hr 🅞 Blue Beacon
154	GA 63, Martin Br Rd
149	US 441, GA 15, to Commerce, Homer, E 🅖 Murphy USA, QT/dsl, TA/Buckhorn Rest/dsl/scales/24hr/ @ 🍴 Capt D's, Denny's, El Azteca, Grand Buffet, Krispy Kreme, Longhorn Steaks, Outback Steaks, Pizza Hut/Taco Bell, Sonny's BBQ, Zaxby's 🛏 Best Value Inn, Dandelion Inn, Hampton Inn, Scottish Inn 🅞 🅗, $General, $Tree, Funopolis, GNC, O'Reilly Parts, Radio Shack, Walmart, W 🅖 BP/Krystal/dsl, Citgo, RaceTrac/dsl 🍴 5 Guys Burgers, Applebee's, Arby's, Burger King, Checker's, Chick-fil-A, Cracker Barrel, DQ, La Fiesta, La Hacienda, McDonald's, Pizza Hut, Ruby Tuesday, Ryan's, Sonic, Starbucks, Subway, Wendy's 🛏 Best Inn, Best Western, Comfort Suites, Fairfield Inn, Holiday Inn Express, Howard Johnson, Jameson Inn, Motel 6, Quality Inn, Super 8 🅞 Home Depot, Pritchett Tires, Tanger Outlet/famous brands
147	GA 98, to Commerce, E 🅖 Flying J/Dunkin Donuts/dsl/24hr, FuelMart/dsl, Valero 🅞 🅗, W 🅞 Gulf
140	GA 82, Dry Pond Rd, E 🅞 Freightliner, W 🅞 RV & Truck Repair
137	US 129, GA 11 to Jefferson, E 🅖 RaceTrac/dsl 🍴 Arby's, El Jinete Mexican, KFC/Taco Bell, McDonald's, Waffle House, Zaxby's 🛏 Comfort Inn 🅞 museum, W 🅖 QT/dsl/scales/24hr 🍴 Burger King, Waffle House, Wendy's 🅞 flea mkt
129	GA 53, to Braselton, E 🅖 Chevron/dsl, Shell/Golden Pantry/dsl 🍴 La Hacienda Mexican, Waffle House 🛏 Best Western 🅞 USPO, W 🅖 🚃/McDonald's/dsl/scales/24hr 🍴 Cracker Barrel, Domino's, El Centinela, Stonewall's, Subway, Tea Garden Chinese, Wendy's, Zaxby's
126	GA 211, to Chestnut Mtn, E 🅖 Shell/dsl 🍴 Subway, Waffle House 🛏 Country Inn&Suites, W 🅖 BP/dsl 🍴 Blimpie, Chateau Elan Winery/rest., China Garden, Papa John's 🛏 Holiday Inn Express 🅞 Publix, vet
120	to GA 124, Hamilton Mill Rd, E 🅖 BP, QT/dsl 🍴 5 Guys Burgers, Arby's, Buffalo's Café, Burger King, Caprese Rest., Dos Copas Mexican, McDonald's, Moe's SW Grill, Shane's Rib Shack, Starbucks, Subway, Wendy's, Zaxby's 🅞 AT&T, auto repair, Home Depot, Kohl's, Publix/Deli, RV World of GA (1mi), vet, W 🅖 Chevron, Murphy USA/dsl, Shell/dsl 🍴 Barbarito's, Chick-fil-A, Chili's, El Molcajate, Hardee's, Italy's Pizza, Little Caesars 🅞 CVS Drug, O'Reilly Parts, Tires+, Walmart
115	GA 20, to Buford Dam, E 🅖 QT, W 🅖 QT/dsl 🍴 5 Guy's Burgers, Arby's, Bonefish Grill, Bruster's, Buck Head Pizza, Buffalo's Cafe, Burger King, Chick-fil-A, Chili's, Chipotle, ChuckeCheese, Einstein's Bagels, Firehouse Subs, Genghis Grill, Kani House, Krispy Kreme, Liu's Buffet, Longhorn Steaks, Macaroni Grill, McDonald's, Mimi's Cafe, Moe's SW Grill, O'Charley's, Olive Garden, On-the-Border, Panda Express, PF Chang's, Provino's Italian, Red Lobster, Shogun Japanese, Sonny's BBQ, Starbucks, Steak n' Shake, Subway, Taco Mac, Ted's MT Grill, TGIFriday's, Waffle House, Wendy's 🛏 Country Inn&Suites, Courtyard, Hampton Inn, SpringHill Suites, Wingate Inn 🅞 $Tree, AT&T, Belk, Best Buy, Costco/gas, Dick's, Dillard's, Discount Tire, Fiat, Firestone, Honda, Hyundai, JC Penney, Lowe's, Macy's, Mall of GA,

115	Continued Mazda, Michael's, Nissan, Nordstrom's, PetCo, Petsmart, Radio Shack, Ross, Sam's Club/gas, Staples, Target, TJ Maxx, to Lake Lanier Islands, Toyota/Scion, Verizon, VW, Walmart
113	I-985 N (from nb), to Gainesville
111	GA 317, to Suwanee, E 🅖 BP, Sims/dsl 🍴 Applebee's, Arby's, Checker's, Chick-fil-A, Cracker Barrel, Dunkin Donuts, Oriental Garden, Outback Steaks, Philly Connection, Pizza Hut/Taco Bell, Subway, Waffle House, Wendy's 🛏 Comfort Inn, Comfort Suites, Courtyard, Fairfield Inn, Mayqueen Hotel, Motel 6, Sun Suites 🅞 CVS Drug, GNC, W 🅖 Chevron/dsl, Murphy USA/dsl, RaceTrac/dsl, Shell 🍴 Atlanta Bread, CiCi's Pizza, HoneyBaked Ham, IHOP, KFC, McDonald's, Moe's SW Grill, Sonic, Subway, Taco Mac 🛏 Budgetel, Super 8 🅞 $Tree, AT&T, Lowe's, Office Depot, Tires&More, Walmart
109	Old Peachtree Rd, E 🅖 QT/dsl/24hr 🍴 McDonald's, Mi Casa Mexican 🛏 Hampton Inn 🅞 $World, Bass Pro Shops, Publix, W 🍴 5 Guys Burgers, Califonia Dreaming, Chick-fil-A, China Delight, Firehouse Subs, Jim&Nicks BBQ, Magnolia Bakery Cafe, Starbucks, Subway, Waffle House 🛏 Hilton Garden, Holiday Inn 🅞 Home Depot
108	Sugarloaf Pkwy (from nb), E 🛏 Hampton Inn, W 🍴 Carrabba's, Chick-fil-A 🛏 Hilton Garden, Holiday Inn 🅞 Gwinnett Civic Ctr
107	GA 120, to GA 316 E, Athens, E 🅖 Shell 🍴 Burger King, Carino's, Jillian's, Zaxby's 🅞 Bass Pro Shops, Books-a-Million, Burlington Coats, Discount Tire, Food Ct, Mercedes, Nieman-Marcus, Rite Aid, Ross, Saks 5th Ave, Sears, Suburban Tire, W 🅖 BP, Chevron 🍴 China Gate, McDonald's, Roadhouse Grill, Subway, Waffle House 🛏 La Quinta, Suburban Lodge
106	Boggs Rd (from sb, no return), Duluth, W 🅖 QT/dsl/24hr
104	Pleasant Hill Rd, E 🅖 Chevron/24hr, QT, Shell, Sim's/dsl 🍴 Arby's, Bahama Breeze, Burger King, Chick-fil-A, East Pearl, Fung Mi Chinese, GA Diner, Golden House, Grand Buffet, Ida's Pizza Kitchen, Joe's Crabshack, Krispy Kreme, Lobster House, McDonald's, Moe's SW Grill, Popeye's, Quiznos, Starbucks, Stevie B's Pizza, Subway, TGIFriday's, Waffle House, Wendy's 🛏 Candlewood Suites, Comfort Suites, Hampton Inn Suites, Holiday Inn Express, Marriott, Residence Inn 🅞 $General, $Tree, Advance Parts, Best Buy, Family$, Home Depot, Publix, URGENT CARE, Walgreens, W 🅖 BP/dsl, Chevron, Sim's/dsl 🍴 Applebee's, Arby's, Bruster's, Burger King, Checker's, Chili's, Chipotle Mexican, Hooters, IHOP, Jimmy John's, KFC, McDonald's, Olive Garden, On the Border, Panda Express, Red Lobster, Ryan's, Starbucks, Steak'n Shake, Subway, Sweet Tomatoes, Taco Bell, Wendy's 🛏 Courtyard, Days Inn, Extended Stay America, Holiday Inn, Hyatt Place, Quality Inn, Wingate Inn 🅞 AT&T, Audi,

COMMERCE · **JEFFERSON** · **SUWANEE DULUTH** · **ATLANTA AREA**

GA

🚪 = gas   🍴 = food   🛏 = lodging   ⊙ = other   ℞ = rest stop   Copyright 2015 - the Next EXIT ®

INTERSTATE 85 Cont'd

Exit #	Services
104	**Continiued** Barnes&Noble, Batteries+, Belk, BMW, Buick/GMC, Firestone/auto, Fry's Electronics, Goodyear/auto, Honda, JC Penney, Jo-Ann Fabrics, KIA, Macy's, mall, Marshall's, Nissan, Old Navy, PetCo, Rite Aid, Sears/auto, Staples, TJ Maxx, Toyota/Scion, Tuesday Morning, Verizon
103	Steve Reynolds Blvd (from nb, no return), **W** 🚪 QT, Shell 🍴 Dave&Buster's, Waffle House 🛏 InTown Suites ⊙ Costco/gas, Kohl's, Petsmart, same as 104, Sam's Club, Target
102	GA 378, Beaver Ruin Rd, **E** 🚪 QT, Shell/dsl, **W** 🚪 Citgo
101	Lilburn Rd, **E** 🚪 QT/dsl, Shell/dsl/24hr 🍴 Blimpie, Bruster's, Burger King, Hong Kong Buffet, KFC, Krystal, Manhattan Pizza, McDonald's/playplace, Quiznos, Starbucks, Taco Bell, Waffle House 🛏 Guesthouse Inn, InTown Suites ⊙ Jones RV Park, **W** 🚪 Chevron, Marathon, QT 🍴 Arby's, El Indo Mexican, El Taco Veloz, Grand Buffet, Papa John's, Pizza Plaza, Subway, Waffle House, Wendy's 🛏 Knights Inn, Red Roof Inn ⊙ CarMax, Lowe's
99	GA 140, Jimmy Carter Blvd, **E** 🚪 Phillips 66/dsl, Shell 🍴 Checker's, Chick-fil-A, Cracker Barrel, Denny's, Dunkin Donuts, El Nortino Mexican, KFC, McDonald's, Papa John's, Pizza Hut/Taco Bell, Pollo Campero, Wendy's 🛏 Best Inn, Courtyard, Horizon Inn, La Quinta, Motel 6, Ramada, Rite4Us Suites ⊙ Advance Parts, Aldi Foods, Family$, U-Haul, Walgreens, **W** 🚪 Chevron/24hr, Citgo/dsl, QT/dsl 🍴 5 Guys Burgers, Barnacle's Grill, Hong Kong Buffet, Pappadeaux Steak/seafood, Quiznos, Sonic, Waffle House, Wendy's 🛏 Country Inn&Suites, Days Inn, Drury Inn, Microtel ⊙ AutoZone, CarQuest, NTB, O'Reilly Parts, PepBoys
96	Pleasantdale Rd, Northcrest Rd, **E** 🍴 Burger King 🛏 Peachtree Inn, **W** 🚪 Exxon/dsl, QT/dsl 🍴 Subway, Waffle House 🛏 Atlanta Lodge
95	I-285
94	Chamblee-Tucker Rd, **E** 🚪 Chevron/dsl, Shell, **W** 🚪 QT/dsl, Shell 🍴 DQ, Waffle House 🛏 Motel 6, Super 8 ⊙ to Mercer U
93	Shallowford Rd, to Doraville, **E** 🚪 Shell 🍴 Blimpie, Hop Shing Chinese ⊙ Publix, U-Haul, **W** 🚪 Shell/dsl 🛏 Quality Inn
91	US 23, GA 155, Clairmont Rd, **E** 🚪 Chevron, Shell 🍴 IHOP, Mo's Pizza, Popeye's ⊙ IGA Foods, repair, **W** 🚪 BP 🍴 McDonald's, Mykonos Greek, Waffle House 🛏 Marriott, Wingate Inn ⊙ NTB, Sam's Club/dsl
89	GA 42, N Druid Hills, **E** 🚪 Chevron/Subway/dsl, QT/dsl/24hr, Shell 🍴 Arby's, Boston Mkt, Burger King, Chick-fil-A, Einstein Bro's, El Torero, Fortune Cookie, Jersey Mike's, Lettuce Souperise You, McDonald's, Moe's SW Grill, Piccadilly's, Starbucks, Taco Bell, Tin Roof Cantina 🛏 Courtyard ⊙ $Tree, Firestone/auto, GNC, Target, Walgreens, **W** 🚪 Chevron/dsl, Exxon, Shell 🍴 Atlanta Diner, HoneyBaked Ham, Krystal, Waffle House 🛏 DoubleTree, Hampton Inn, Red Roof Inn ⊙ CVS Drug, Just Brakes, vet
88	Lenox Rd, GA 400 N, Cheshire Br Rd (from sb), **E** 🚪 Shell 🛏 La Quinta
87	GA 400 N (from nb)
86	GA 13 S, Peachtree St, **E** 🚪 BP 🍴 Denny's, Wendy's 🛏 Intown Inn, La Quinta ⊙ Brake-O
85	I-75 N, to Marietta, Chattanooga
84	Techwood Dr, 14th St, **E** 🚪 BP, Shell 🍴 CheeseSteaks, La Bamba Mexican, Thai Cuisine, VVV Ristorante Italiano

Exit #	Services
84	**Continued** 🛏 Best Western, Hampton Inn, Marriott, Sheraton, Travelodge ⊙ Woodruff Arts Ctr, **W** 🍴 Blimpie 🛏 Courtyard, Knights Inn ⊙ CVS Drug, Dillard's, Office Depot, to Georgia Tech
77	I-75 S
76	Cleveland Ave, **E** 🚪 Citgo/dsl 🍴 Burger King, Papa John's ⊙ 🏥, $Tree, AutoZone, BigLots, CVS Drug, Family$, Kroger, Walgreens, **W** 🚪 Shell/dsl, Texaco/dsl 🍴 Chick-fil-A, Church's ⊙ CVS, O'Reilly Parts
75	Sylvan Rd, **E** 🚪 Shell/dsl
74	Loop Rd, ⊙ Aviation Commercial Center
73b a	Virginia Ave, **E** 🚪 Citgo/dsl 🍴 Jimmy John's, Jonny's Pizza, Landmark Diner, Malone's Grill, McDonald's, Pizza Hut, Ruby Tuesday, Schlotsky's, Spondivit's Rest., Waffle House, Wendy's, Willy's Mexican 🛏 Courtyard, Drury Inn, Hilton, Motel 6, Renaissance Hotel, Residence Inn, **W** 🚪 Chevron/Subway, Shell 🍴 Arby's, BBQ Kitchen, Blimpie, Giovanna's Italian, Happy Buddha Chinese, KFC, La Fiesta Mexican, Waffle House 🛏 Country Inn&Suites, Crowne Plaza, DoubleTree, EconoLodge, Fairfield Inn, Hampton Inn, Hilton Garden, Holiday Inn, Homewood Suites, Hyatt Place, Palms Hotel, Staybridge Inn, Wellesley Inn
72	Camp Creek Pkwy
71	Riverdale Rd, Atlanta ✈, **E** 🍴 Ruby Tuesday 🛏 Courtyard, Fairfield Inn, Hampton Inn, Holiday Inn, Hyatt Place, La Quinta, Microtel, Sheraton/grill, Sleep Inn, Super 8, **W** 🛏 Days Inn, Embassy Suites, Hilton Garden, Holiday Inn Express, Marriott, Westin Hotel
70	I-85 (from sb)
69	GA 14, GA 279, **E** 🚪 Chevron/dsl, Citgo, Exxon/dsl, Valero 🍴 Blimpie, Bojangles, Burger King, Checker's, China Cafe, Church's, Cozumel, KFC, Krystal, McDonald's, Piccadilly Cafeteria, Subway, Taco Bell, Waffle House, Wendy's 🛏 Comfort Inn, Days Inn, Quality Inn, Super 8, Travelodge, Windsor Atl Hotel ⊙ AutoZone, Family$, U-Haul, URGENT CARE, **W** 🚪 Chevron/dsl, Texaco 🍴 Waffle House 🛏 EconoLodge
68	I-285 Atlanta Perimeter (from nb)
66	Flat Shoals Rd, **W** 🚪 BP, Chevron/dsl, Shell/Blimpie 🍴 King's Rest., Waffle House 🛏 Motel 6
64	GA 138, to Union City, **E** 🚪 BP/dsl, RaceTrac/dsl 🍴 Waffle House 🛏 EconoLodge, Western Inn ⊙ BMW/Mini, Chevrolet, Chrysler/Dodge/Jeep, CVS Drug, Ford/Lincoln, Honda, Infiniti, Kia/Nissan, Lexus, Toyota/Scion, VW, **W** 🚪 Chevron/dsl, QT, Shell/dsl 🍴 Arby's, Burger King, Capt D's, China Garden, China King, Corner Cafe, Dunkin Donuts, IHOP, KFC, Krystal, McDonald's, Papa John's, Pizza Hut, Sonic, Southern Grill, Subway, Taco Bell, Wendy's, Zaxby's 🛏 Best Western, Comfort Inn, Country Hearth Inn, Garden Inn, La Quinta, Magnuson Hotel, Microtel ⊙ $Tree, Advance Parts, AT&T, BigLots, Firestone/auto, Kroger/dsl, NTB, O'Reilly Parts, PepBoys, Radio Shack, vet, Walgreens, Walmart/Subway
61	GA 74, to Fairburn, **E** 🚪 BP/Huddle House/dsl/scales/24hr, Los Mariachis, QT/dsl, RaceWay/dsl, Shell 🍴 Chick-fil-A, Cracker Barrel, Dunkin Donuts, Hardee's, McDonald's, Taco Bell, Waffle House, Wendy's, Zaxby's 🛏 Country Inn&Suites, Hampton Inn, Holiday Inn Express, Sleep Inn, Wingate Inn ⊙ Tire Depot, vet, **W** 🚪 Chevron/dsl, Citgo/dsl 🛏 Efficiency Motel
56	Collinsworth Rd, **W** 🚪 Marathon/dsl, Shell 🍴 Frank's Rest. ⊙ South Oaks Camping

A T L A N T A   A R E A (left margin)

GA (left margin)

A T L A N T A   A R E A (right margin)

F A I R B U R N (right margin)

⬆N   INTERSTATE 85 Cont'd

Exit #	Services
51	GA 154, to Sharpsburg, **E** 🅖 Phillips 66/dsl, Texaco/Blimpie/dsl 🅕 Hardee's, **W** 🅖 Chevron/dsl, Shell/Subway/dsl 🅕 Waffle House
47	GA 34, to Newnan, **E** 🅖 BP, Chevron/dsl, Marathon/Subway/dsl, QT, Shell/dsl 🅕 Applebee's, Arby's, Asian Chef, Capt D's, Chin Chin, Dunkin Donuts, Fried Tomato Buffet, Hooters, La Hacienda, Longhorn Steaks, Marco's Pizza, Moe's SW Grill, Panda Express, Red Lobster, Ruby Tuesday, Sprayberry's BBQ, Steak'n Shake, Stevi B's Pizza, TX Roadhouse, Waffle House, Wendy's 🏠 Country Inn&Suites, Hampton Inn, Quality Inn, Springhill Suites 🅞 GNC, Goodyear/auto, Hobby Lobby, Home Depot, Jo-Ann, Kauffman Tire, Kohl's, Lowe's, Petsmart, Ross, Walmart/McDonald's, **W** 🅕 RaceTrac/dsl 🅕 5 Guys Burgers, Burger King, Checkers, Chick-fil-A, Coldstone, Cracker Barrel, Firehouse Subs, Goldberg's Deli, Golden Corral, HoneyBaked Ham, IHOP, Jimmy John's, KFC, Krystal, La Parrilla Mexican, Newk's Cafe, O'Charley's, Olive Garden, Panera Bread, Red Robin, Rockback Pizza, Shane's BBQ, Shoney's, Starbucks, Taco Bell, Taco Mac, Thai Heaven, Tokyo Japanese, Yogli Mogli, Zaxby's 🏠 Best Western, Comfort Inn, La Quinta, Motel 6, Newnan Inn 🅞 🅷 $General, $Tree, AT&T, Barnes&Noble, Belk, Best Buy, BigLots, BJ's Whse/gas, Buick/Cadillac/GMC, Chevrolet, Dick's, Dillards, Ford/Lincoln, Hyundai, JC Penney, Michael's, Office Depot, Old Navy, Publix, Radio Shack, Target, Tires+, TJ Maxx, Toyota/Scion, Verizon, vet, Walgreens
41	US 27/29, Newnan, **E** 🅖 🅕/Subway/Wendy's/dsl/scales/24hr 🅞 Little White House NHS, Roosevelt SP, **W** 🅖 BP/dsl, Chevron/dsl 🅕 Huddle House, McDonald's, Waffle House 🏠 Best Value Inn, Economy Inn, Home Lodge, Super 8 🅞 $General, repair
35	US 29, to Grantville, **W** 🅖 BP/dsl, Phillips 66/dsl
28	GA 54, GA 100, to Hogansville, **E** 🅖 Valero/dsl, **W** 🅖 Chevron/dsl, Loves/Arby's/dsl/scales/24hr, Shell/dsl 🅕 Intnat'l Cafe, McDonald's, Nachos Mexican, Roger's BBQ, Subway, Waffle House, Wendy's 🏠 Garden Inn, Woodstream Inn 🅞 Ingles
23mm	Beech Creek
22mm	weigh sta both lanes
21	I-185 S, to Columbus
18	GA 109, to Mountville, **E** 🅖 Marathon/Domino's 🏠 Red Roof Inn, Wingate Inn 🅞 Little White House HS, to FDR SP, **W** 🅖 BP/dsl, Circle K/dsl, RaceTrac/dsl, Shell/dsl, Texaco/dsl 🅕 Applebee's, Banzai Japanese, Burger King, Chick-fil-A, Cracker Barrel, IHOP, Juanito's Mexican, Longhorn Steaks, Los Nopales, McDonald's, Mi Casa Mexican, Moe's SW Grill, Starbucks, Subway, Waffle House, Wendy's, Zaxby's 🏠 Baymont Inn, Comfort Inn, Holiday Inn Express, La Quinta, Lafayette Garden Inn, Quality Inn, Super 8 🅞 AT&T, Belk, Chrysler/Dodge/Jeep, Ford/Lincoln, Home Depot, Honda, Hyundai, JC Penney, mall, RV Park (3mi), TJ Maxx, Verizon
14	US 27, to La Grange, **W** 🅖 Pure, Shell, Summit/dsl 🏠 Hampton Inn
13	GA 219, to La Grange, **E** 🅕 Waffle House 🏠 Days Inn, **W** 🅖 🅕/Subway/dsl/scales/24hr, Shell/dsl 🅕 Arbys, McDonald's 🅞 🅷
10mm	Long Cane Creek
6	Kia Blvd, **W** Kia Plant
2	GA 18, to West Point, **E** 🅖 Shell/dsl, Summit/dsl 🏠 Best Value, **W** 🅕 Subway (1.5) 🅞 camping, to West Point Lake

| 0.5mm | Welcome Ctr nb, full 🚻 facilities, litter barrels, petwalk, 📞, 🍴, vending |
| 0mm | Georgia/Alabama state line, Chattahoochee River |

⬆N   INTERSTATE 95

Exit #	Services
113mm	Georgia/South Carolina state line, Savannah River
111mm	**Welcome Ctr/weigh sta sb, full 🚻 facilities, info, litter barrels, petwalk, 📞, 🍴, vending**
109	GA 21, to Savannah, Pt Wentworth, Rincon, **E** 🅖 Enmark/dsl, 🅕/McDonald's/Subway/dsl/scales/24hr 🅕 Waffle House 🏠 Country Inn&Suites, Hampton Inn, Mulberry Grove Inn, Wingate Inn 🅞 Peterbilt, **W** 🅖 Flash/dsl, Murphy Express/dsl, Shell/Circle K/Blimpie/dsl 🅕 El Ranchito, Happy Wok, Island Grill, Monte's Pizza, Silverado Kitchen, Wendy's, Zaxby's 🏠 Comfort Suites, Days Inn, Holiday Inn Express, Quality Inn, Ramada Ltd, Savannah Inn, Sleep Inn, Super 8 🅞 CVS Drug, Family$, FoodLion, Whispering Pines RV Park (3mi)
107mm	Augustine Creek
106	Jimmy DeLoach Pkwy
104	Savannah 🛫, **E** 🅖 BP, Shell/Wendy's/dsl 🅕 Sam Sneed's Grill, Waffle House 🏠 Cambria Suites, Candlewood Suites, Comfort Suites, Country Inn&Suites, Fairfield Inn, Hampton Inn, Hawthorn Suites, Hilton Garden, Holiday Inn Express, Sheraton, SpringHill Suites, Staybridge Suites, TownePlace Suites, Wingate Inn 🅞 to 🛫, **W** 🅖 Murphy USA/dsl, Parkers/dsl, Shell/Subway 🅕 Arby's, Cheddar's, Chick-fil-A, DQ, Fatz Cafe, Hilliard's Rest., Lemongrass Grill, Lenny's Subs, Longhorn Steaks, Mellow Mushroom, Ruby Tuesday, Shane's Rib Shack, Smokin' Hot BBQ, Sonic, Zaxby's 🏠 Embassy Suites, Red Roof Inn 🅞 Goodyear, Home Depot, Publix, Sam's Club/gas, Savannah Tire, URGENT CARE, Verizon, Walmart/McDonald's
102	US 80, to Garden City, **E** 🅖 BP/Baldinos Subs, Enmark/dsl, Flash/dsl 🅕 Cracker Barrel, Dickey's BBQ, Dizzy Dean's, Guerrero, Hirenos Steaks, Huddle House, KFC, Krystal, Larry's Subs, Masato Japanese, McDonald's, Peking Chinese, Pizza Hut/Taco Bell, Waffle House 🏠 Bradbury Suites, Jameson Inn, Microtel, Motel 6, Travelodge 🅞 Camping World RV Ctr, Family$, Food Lion, museum, to Ft Pulaski NM, **W** 🅖 BP, Gate/Subway/dsl, Shell, Texaco 🅕 Burger King, Domino's, Don's BBQ, El Potro Mexican, Hardee's, Italian Pizza, New China, Pizza Hut, Wendy's, Western Sizzlin 🏠 EconoLodge, Holiday Inn, La Quinta, Magnolia Inn, Savannah Conf Hotel, Sleep Inn 🅞 auto repair, NAPA
99b a	I-16, W to Macon, E to Savannah
94	GA 204, to Savannah, Pembroke, **E** 🅖 BP/dsl, Exxon, Murphy USA/dsl (2mi), Shell/dsl 🅕 Applebee's, Cracker Barrel,

INTERSTATE 95 Cont'd

SAVANNAH

Exit #	Services
94	Continued
	Denny's, Hardee's, Houlihan's, IHOP, McDonald's, Perkins, Ruby Tuesday, Sonic, Tony Popa's 🛏 Baymont Inn, Best Inn, Best Western, Clarion, Comfort Suites, Days Inn, EconoLodge, Fairfield Inn, Hampton Inn, Holiday Inn Express, Howard Johnson, La Quinta, Quality Inn, Red Roof Inn, San's Boutique Hotel, Scottish Inn, Sleep Inn, SpringHill Suites, Wingate Inn 🅞 🖸, Factory Stores/Famous Brands, GNC, Walmart (2mi), W 🅖 Chevron/dsl, Shell 🍴 Hooters, JT's Grill, Shellhouse Rest, Subway, Waffle House 🛏 Heritage Inn, Knights Inn, Microtel, Travel Inn 🅞 Harley-Davidson, Savannah Oaks RV Park (2mi)
91mm	Ogeechee River
90	GA 144, Old Clyde Rd, to Ft Stewart, Richmond Hill SP, E 🅖 Exxon/dsl, Parkers 🍴 DQ, Jalapeno's, Pizza Hut, Starbucks, Subway, Zaxby's 🅞 AT&T, Kroger/deli/dsl, URGENT CARE, Verizon, W 🅖 Loves/McDonald's/dsl/scales/24hr, Shell/dsl 🅞 Gore's RV Ctr
87	US 17, to Coastal Hwy, Richmond Hill, E 🅖 BP, Chevron/dsl, RaceWay/dsl 🍴 China 1, Denny's, Domino's, Fuji Japanese, Papa Murphy's, Smokin' Pig BBQ, Southern Image Rest., Steamer's Rest., Subway, Waffle House 🛏 Days Inn, Motel 6, Royal Inn, Scottish Inn, Travelodge 🅞 Food Lion, URGENT CARE, W 🅖 El Cheapo, Exxon/McDonald's/dsl, Shell/dsl, TA/BP/Pizza Hut/Popeye's/dsl/scales/24hr/ @ 🍴 Arby's, KFC/Taco Bell, Waffle House, Wendy's 🛏 Best Western, Comfort Suites, EconoLodge, Hampton Inn, Quality Inn, Savannah South Inn 🅞 KOA
85mm	Elbow Swamp
80mm	Jerico River
76	US 84, GA 38, to Midway, Sunbury, E hist sites, W 🅖 El Cheapo/dsl/scales, Parker's/dsl 🍴 Holton's Seafood, Huddle House 🅞 🖸
67	US 17, Coastal Hwy, to S Newport, E 🅖 Chevron/Subway/dsl, Citgo/dsl, El Cheapo, Shell/McDonald's 🍴 Jones BBQ 🅞 Harris Neck NWR, S Newport Camping (2mi), W 🅖 Texaco
58	GA 99, GA 57, Townsend Rd, Eulonia, E 🅖 BP/dsl, Citgo 🅞 $General, USPO, W 🅖 Chevron/dsl, El Cheapo, Shell/Stuckey's/dsl 🛏 7 Townsend Inn, Magnuson Inn 🅞 Lake Harmony RV Park, McIntosh Lake RV Park
55mm	🍴, weigh sta both lanes

DARIEN

49	GA 251, to Darien, E 🅖 Chevron, Mobil/dsl 🍴 DQ, McDonald's, Waffle House 🅞 Cathead RV Park, Ford, Inland Harbor RV Park, W 🅖 BP, El Cheapo/Larry's Subs/dsl/scales, Shell/Stuckey's/dsl 🍴 Burger King, KFC/Taco Bell, Ruby Tuesday, Wendy's 🛏 Comfort Inn, Days Inn, Hampton Inn, Quality Inn, Super 8 🅞 Darien Outlets/famous brands
47mm	Darien River
46.5mm	Butler River
46mm	Champney River
45mm	Altamaha River
42	GA 99, E to Hofwyl Plantation HS
41mm	🆁🆂 sb, full 🅰 facilities, info, litter barrels, petwalk, 🍴, 🚻, vending
38	US 17, GA 25, N Golden Isles Pkwy, Brunswick, E 🅖 RaceTrac/dsl 🛏 Comfort Suites, Country Inn&Suites, Embassy Suites (2mi), Fairfield Inn, Hawthorn Inn, Holiday Inn, Microtel 🅞 🖸, Nissan, W 🅖 BP, Chevron/dsl, Flash, Shell/dsl 🍴 China Town, Denny's, Huddle House, Logan's Roadhouse, Subway, Toucan's, Waffle House 🛏 Best Western,

BRUNSWICK

Exit #	Services
38	Continued
	Courtyard, EconoLodge, Guest Cottage Motel, Hampton Inn, Quality Inn, Sleep Inn 🅞 $General, Family$, Harley-Davidson, Harvey's Foods, Toyota/Scion
36b a	US 25, US 341, to Jesup, Brunswick, E 🅖 Chevron/Subway/dsl, Exxon/dsl, RaceWay/dsl 🍴 Cracker Barrel, IHOP, KFC, Krystal, McDonald's, Pizza Hut, Starbucks, Taco Bell, Wendy's 🛏 Brunswick Park Motel, Days Inn, Howard Johnson, La Quinta, Red Roof Inn 🅞 Jack's Tires, transmissions, W 🅖 Mr Pete's/dsl, Parker's/dsl, Sunoco/dsl 🍴 Capt Joe's Seafood, China Lee, Huddle House, Larry's Subs, Sonny's BBQ, Waffle House 🛏 Clarion, Comfort Inn, Magnuson Inn, Ramada Inn, Rodeway Inn, Super 8 🅞 $General, Advance Parts, CVS Drug, Family$, Fred's, Winn-Dixie
33mm	Turtle River
30mm	S Brunswick River
29	US 17, US 82, GA 520, S GA Pkwy, Brunswick, E 🅖 Citgo/Church's/dsl, Exxon, Loves/Steak'n Shake/Subway/dsl/scales/24hr 🍴 Huddle House, Krystal, McDonald's, Zaxby's 🛏 Comfort Suites 🅞 Blue Beacon, SpeedCo, W 🅖 Citgo, Flying J/Denny's/dsl/LP/scales/24hr, Goasis/BP/Burger King/Starbucks/Subway/dsl/24hr, Shell/dsl 🍴 Domino's, Larry's Subs, Waffle House, Zachry's Rest 🛏 EconoLodge, Microtel, Super 8 🅞 $General, Family$, Golden Isles Camping, Harvey's Foods, TA Truck Service
27.5mm	Little Satilla River
26	Dover Bluff Rd, E 🅖 Mobil/Stuckey's/dsl
22	Horse Stamp Church Rd
21mm	White Oak Creek
19mm	Canoe Swamp
15mm	Satilla River
14	GA 25, to Woodbine, W 🍴 Chevron/Sunshine/rest/dsl/scales/24hr 🛏 Stardust Motel (3mi)
7	Harrietts Bluff Rd, E 🅖 Exxon/dsl, Shell/Subway/e-85, W 🅖 BP/dsl 🅞 Walkabout Camping/RV Park
6.5mm	Crooked River
6	Laurel Island Pkwy, E 🅖 Green Cedar/Shell/dsl

ST MARYS

3	GA 40, Kingsland, to St Marys, E 🅖 BP/dsl, Chevron, El Cheapo, Exxon/Krystal, Mobil, Murphy USA/dsl, Shell/Subway 🍴 Applebee's, Burger King, Chick-fil-A, China Wok, DQ, Dunkin Donuts, Hong Kong Buffet, KFC, Little Caesars, Longhorn Steaks, McDonald's, Papa John's, Ruby Tuesday, Sonny's BBQ, Taco Bell, Waffle House, Wendy's, Zaxby's 🛏 Best Value Inn, Best Western, Comfort Inn, Country Inn&Suites, Days Inn, Fairfield Inn, Hawthorn Suites, Magnolia Inn, Microtel, Red Roof Inn, Rodeway Inn, Sleep Inn 🅞 🖸, $Tree, Buick/Chevrolet, Chrysler/Dodge/Jeep, CVS Drug, Ford, GNC, K-Mart, Lowe's, NAPA, Publix, Radio Shack, Suzuki, Tire Kingdom, to Crooked River SP, to Submarine Base, URGENT CARE, Verizon, Walgreens, Walmart, Winn-Dixie, W 🅖 Flash/dsl, Petro/Popeye's/dsl/scales/24hr/ @, RaceWay/dsl, Shell/dsl 🍴 Cracker Barrel, Domino's, IHOP, Millhouse Steaks, Subway, Waffle House 🛏 Clean Stay USA, Country Hearth Inn, EconoLodge, Hampton Inn, Jameson Inn, La Quinta, Springfield Suites 🅞 Ace Hardware, Fred's, Kiki RV Park, Welcome Ctr/info
1	St Marys Rd, to Cumberland Is Nat Seashoe, E Welcome Ctr nb, full 🅰 facilities, 🍴, vending, 🚻, litter barrels, petwalk, 🅖 Shell/dsl W 🅖 BP/dsl, Chevron/dsl, Wilco/Hess/Dunkin Donuts/Wendy's/dsl/scales/24hr 🍴 Jack's BBQ 🅞 GS RV Park, KOA
0mm	Georgia/Florida state line, St Marys River

⬆N   INTERSTATE 185 (Columbus)

Exit #	Services
48	**I-85. I-185 begins/ends on I-85.**
46	Big Springs Rd, **E** 🅖 Shell/dsl, **W** 🅞 tires
42	US 27, Pine Mountain, **E** 🅖 Shell/dsl, Summit/dsl 🍴 Waffle House 🅞 Little White House HS, Pine Mtn Camping, to Callaway Gardens
34	GA 18, to West Point, **E** 🅞 to Callaway Gardens
30	Hopewell Church Rd, Whitesville, **W** 🅖 Shell/dsl
25	GA 116, to Hamilton, **W** 🅞 RV camping
19	GA 315, Mulberry Grove, **W** 🅖 Chevron/dsl
14	Smith Rd
12	Williams Rd, **W** 🅖 Shell, Summit/dsl 🏠 Country Inn&Suites, Microtel 🅞 **Welcome Ctr/rest rooms**
10	US 80, GA 22, to Phenix City, **W** 🅞 Springer Opera House
8	Airport Thruway, **E** 🍴 Bojangles, Great Wall 🅞 $Tree, GNC, Home Depot, Walmart/Subway, **W** 🅖 Circle K/dsl, Shell/Circle K 🍴 Applebee's, Baskin Robbins, Ben's Chophouse, Blue Iguana Grill, Burger King, Cafe Le Rue, Capt D's, Country Road Buffet, Fuddruckers, Hardee's, Houlihan's, IHOP, McDonald's, Mikata Japanese, Outback Steaks, Pickle Barrel Cafe, Stevi B's Pizza, Subway, Taco Bell 🏠 Comfort Suites, DoubleTree, Extended Stay America, Hampton Inn, Sleep Inn 🅞 AAA, BigLots, Hancock Fabrics, K-Mart, Office Depot
7	45th St, Manchester Expswy, **E** 🍴 Applebee's, Burger King, Carino's Italian, Krystal, Ruby Tuesday 🏠 Courtyard, La Quinta, Super 8 🅞 Best Buy, Cadillac/Chevrolet, Dillard's, JC Penney, Macy's, mall, **W** 🅖 BP/dsl, Chevron/dsl, Circle K/dsl, Marathon 🍴 Arby's, China Express, Dunkin Donuts, Goldberg's Deli, Golden Corral, Jimmy John's, KFC, Little Caesar's, Logan's Roadhouse, Lucky China, McDonald's, Pizza Hut, Ryan's, Shogun Japanese, Sonic, Starbucks, SteakOut, Subway, Waffle House 🏠 Fairfield Inn, Holiday Inn, TownePlace Suites 🅞 Ⓗ, $General, Advance Parts, Big T Tire/repair, Civil War Naval Museum, Midas, Mr Transmission
6	GA 22, Macon Rd, **E** 🅖 Chevron/dsl, Circle K/dsl 🍴 Bruster's, Burger King, DQ, Little Caesars, Taco Bell, Waffle House 🏠 Best Western, Comfort Inn, Days Inn 🅞 $General, Rite Aid, U-Haul, vet, Walgreens, **W** 🅖 Chevron/dsl, Shell/dsl 🍴 American Deli, Capt D's, ChuckeCheese, Cici's, Country's BBQ, Denny's, DunkinDonuts/Baskin Robbins, Firehouse Subs, Jimmy John's, Longhorn Steaks, McDonald's, Subway, Zaxby's 🏠 Efficiency Lodge, La Quinta 🅞 AT&T, CVS Drug, Fred's, GNC, Goodyear/auto, K-Mart, Publix, Radio Shack, TJ Maxx, Tuesday Morning, Verizon
4	Buena Vista Rd, **E** 🅖 BP, Circle K, Solo 🍴 Burger King, Capt D's, Checkers, Church's, Krystal, McDonald's, Papa John's, Pizza Hut, Subway, Taco Bell, Waffle House, Zaxby's 🅞 $Tree, AutoZone, Family$, Firestone/auto, Goodyear/auto, O'Reilly Parts, Rainbow Foods, repair, USPO, vet, Walgreens, Walmart, Winn-Dixie, **W** 🅖 Marathon
3	St Marys Rd, **E** 🍴 Domino's 🏠 Microtel 🅞 Family$, **W** 🅖 FuelTech/dsl, Shell/dsl 🍴 Hardee's, Shark Seafood/Chicken 🅞 $General, Ace Hardware, Piggly Wiggly
1 b a	US 27, US 280, Victory Dr, **W 0-3 mi** 🅖 Chevron/dsl, Circle K, Liberty, RaceWay/dsl 🍴 Burger King, Capt D's, Checkers, Krystal, McDonald's, Papa John's, Sonic, Subway, Taco Bell, Waffle House, Wendy's 🏠 Candlewood Suites, Columbus Inn, EconoLodge, Holiday Inn Express, Motel 6, Suburban Lodge 🅞 $General, Advance Parts, AutoZone, CVS Drug, Family$, O'Reilly Parts, Piggly Wiggly, Verizon
0mm	**I-185 begins/ends on Victory Dr**

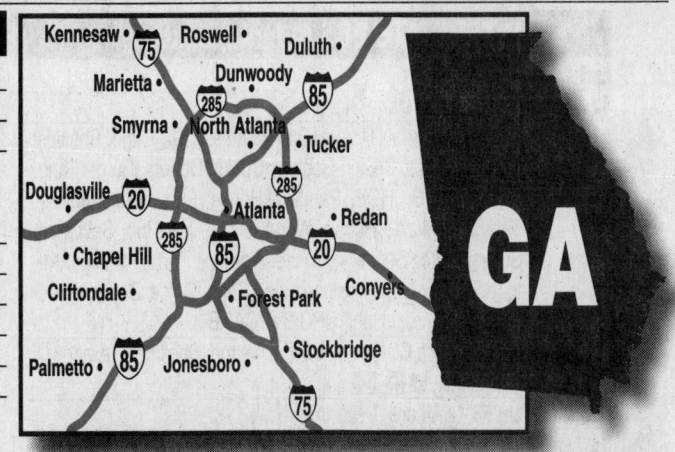

INTERSTATE 285 (Atlanta)

Exit #	Services
62	GA 279, S Fulton Hwy, Old Nat Hwy, **N** 🅖 Chevron, Texaco 🍴 City Cafe 🏠 Econolodge, **S** 🅖 Chevron, Exxon, Shell 🍴 Blimpie, Burger King, Checker's, China Cafeteria, Church's, El Nopal Mexican, KFC/Pizza Hut, Krystal, Longhorn Steaks, McDonald's, Mrs Winner's, Popeye's, Subway, Taco Bell, Waffle House, Wendy's 🏠 Clarion, Comfort Inn, Day's Inn, Howard Johnson, Motel 6, Quality Inn 🅞 AutoZone, Cottman Transmissions, Curves, Family$, NAPA, U-Haul
61	I-85, N to Atlanta, S to Montgomery, **E** 🍴 Ruby Tuesday 🏠 Comfort Suites, Courtyard, GA Conv Ctr, Hampton Inn, Microtel, Sheraton/grill, Sleep Inn, Sumner Suites, Super 8, Wingate Inn, **W** 🏠 Comfort Inn, Day's Inn, Embassy Suites, Marriott, Quality Inn, Ramada, Super 8, Travelodge, Westin Hotel
60	GA 139, Riverdale Rd, **N** 🏠 Fairfield Inn (2mi), Microtel (2mi), Wingate Inn (2mi), **S** 🅖 QT/dsl, Shell/dsl, Valero/dsl 🍴 Checkers, Church's, McDonald's, Papa John's, Waffle House 🏠 Best Western, Day's Inn, Quality Hotel 🅞 $General, Advance Parts, Family$
59	Clark Howell Hwy, **N** 🅞 air cargo
58	I-75, N to Atlanta, S to Macon (from eb), to US 19, US 41, to Hapeville, **S** 🅖 BP/dsl, Citgo/dsl, Exxon/dsl 🍴 American Deli, Jimmy John's, Rijuana Joe's, Subway, Waffle House, Wendy's 🏠 Home Lodge Motel
55	GA 54, Jonesboro Rd, **N** 🏠 Super 8, **S** 🅖 BP/dsl, Citgo/dsl, Shell/dsl, Texaco/dsl 🍴 DaiLai Vietnamese, McDonald's 🅞 Family$, Home Depot, repair
53	US 23, Moreland Ave, to Ft Gillem, **N** 🅖 BP/dsl, Citgo/dsl, **S** 🅖 Chevron/dsl, Citgo 🍴 Wendy's 🏠 EconoLodge 🅞 USPO
52	I-675, S to Macon
51	Bouldercrest Rd, **N** 🅖 BP, 🍴 Wendy's/dsl/24hr 🍴 Checkers, Domino's, Hardee's, KFC, WK Wings 🅞 Family$, Wayfield Foods, **S** 🅖 Exxon/dsl, Shell/Blimpie/dsl, Texaco/dsl
48	GA 155, Flat Shoals Rd, Candler Rd, **N** 🅖 BP, Chevron, Citgo/dsl, Shell/dsl, Texaco/dsl 🍴 Burger King, Checkers, Church's, DQ, Dunkin Donuts/BR, KFC, McDonald's, Taco Bell, Waffle King, WK Wings 🏠 Gulf American Inn 🅞 BigLots, Macy's, **S** 🅖 Citgo, QT, Texaco/dsl 🍴 Burger King, China One, Sonic, Subway 🅞 Family$
46 b a	I-20, E to Augusta, W to Atlanta
44	GA 260, Glenwood Rd, **E** 🅖 Sunoco/dsl 🏠 EconoLodge, **W** 🅖 Exxon/dsl, Texaco/dsl, Valero
43	US 278, Covington Hwy, **E** 🅖 Chevron/Subway, Citgo/dsl 🍴 Waffle House 🅞 U-Haul, **W** 🅖 BP, QT, RaceTrac/dsl, Shell/dsl, Texaco/dsl 🍴 HoneyBaked Ham, Mrs Winner's, Wendy's 🏠 Best Inn 🅞 Advance Parts, Family$

COLUMBUS (vertical text, left margin)

ATLANTA AREA

GA (right margin tab)

⛽ = gas   🍴 = food   🏠 = lodging   Ⓞ = other   Ⓡˢ = rest stop   Copyright 2015 - the Next EXIT ®

ATLANTA AREA **GA**

INTERSTATE 285 (Atlanta) Cont'd

Exit #	Services
42	(from nb), Ⓞ Marta Station
41	GA 10, Memorial Dr, Avondale Estates, **E** ⛽ Citgo, Shell/dsl 🍴 Applebee's, Baskin-Robbins/Dunkin Donuts, Burger King, Church's, DQ, IHOP, Pancake House, Pizza Hut, Subway, Taco Bell, Waffle House, Wendy's 🏠 Aloha Inn, Savannah Suites, United Suites Ⓞ $Tree, Advance Parts, Atl Tires, AutoZone, Family$, Firestone/auto, GNC, Office Depot, Ross, transmissions, U-Haul, URGENT CARE
40	Church St, to Clarkston, **E** ⛽ Chevron, Shell/dsl, Texaco Ⓞ auto repair, **W** Ⓞ 🏥
39b a	US 78, to Athens, Decatur
38	US 29, Lawrenceville Hwy, **E** ⛽ Phillips 66, QT/dsl, RaceTrac/dsl 🍴 Waffle House 🏠 Knights Inn, Super 8 Ⓞ 🏥 **W** ⛽ Citgo/dsl 🍴 Bruster's 🏠 Masters Inn, Motel 6 Ⓞ AutoZone, CVS Drug
37	GA 236, to LaVista, Tucker, **E** ⛽ Chevron/dsl, Texaco 🍴 Checkers, Folks Rest., IHOP, O'Charley's, Piccadilly's, Waffle House 🏠 Comfort Suites, Days Inn Ⓞ Firestone, Target, **W** ⛽ BP/repair, Chevron, Citgo/dsl, Shell/dsl 🍴 Arby's, Blackeyed Pea, Blue Ribbon Grill, Capt D's, Chick-fil-A, Chipotle, City Cafe, Coco Cabana Cuban, Dunkin Donuts, Eduardo's Mexican, HoneyBaked Ham, Jason's Deli, Kacey's Rest., Lucky Key Chinese, Madios Pizza, McDonald's, Mellow Mushroom, Panda Express, Red Lobster, Smoothie King, Starbucks, Wendy's 🏠 Courtyard, DoubleTree, Holiday Inn, Quality Inn Ⓞ $Tree, AT&T, Best Buy, Goodyear/auto, JC Penney, Kohl's, Kroger, Macy's, mall, Michael's, Office Depot, Petsmart, Publix, Sears/auto, TJ Maxx, Verizon
34	Chamblee-Tucker Rd, **E** ⛽ Chevron, Texaco 🍴 $3 Cafe, Galaxy Diner, Hunan Chinese, Jersey Mike's Subs, KFC/Taco Bell, Moe's SW Grill, S&S Cafeteria, Wendy's 🏠 Motel 6 Ⓞ Advance Parts, Goodyear, Kroger, Rite Aid, Verizon, **W** ⛽ Citgo, Shell 🍴 Little Cuba, McDonald's, Subway Ⓞ BigLots, vet
33b a	I-85, N to Greenville, S to Atlanta
32	US 23, Buford Hwy, to Doraville, **E** ⛽ BP/dsl 🍴 Burger King/playland, Checkers, Chick-fil-A, McDonald's, Waffle House, White Windmill Café, Zaxby's Ⓞ Advance Parts, auto repair, Firestone/auto, Marshalls, PepBoys, **W** ⛽ Citgo, QT/dsl 🍴 McDonald's, Monterrey Mexican, Pestones Cuban, Subway, Tostones Cuban, Waffle House 🏠 Comfort Inn Ⓞ $Tree, Meineke, transmissions
31b a	GA 141, Peachtree Ind, to Chamblee, **W** ⛽ Citgo/dsl, QT 🍴 Arby's, Baskin-Robbins/Dunkin Donuts, Chick-fil-A, IHOP, McDonald's, Pizza Hut, Subway, Wendy's Ⓞ Acura, Advance Parts, Audi/VW, Brands Mart, Buick/GMC, Chevrolet, CVS Drug, Fiat, Firestone/auto, Ford, Honda, Hyundai, Kia, Lexus, Mazda, Mini, Office Depot, Porsche Toyota, Walgreens
30	Chamblee-Dunwoody Rd, N Shallowford Rd, to N Peachtree Rd, **N** ⛽ BP, Shell, Texaco/dsl 🍴 Bagel&Co. Deli, Burger King, Guthrie's, Marco's Pizza, McDonald's, Starbucks, Subway, Waffle House Ⓞ Kroger, Tuesday Morning, **S** ⛽ Exxon/Blimpie/dsl, Mobil, Phillips 66/dsl, Shell, Valero/dsl 🍴 Bombay Grill, La Botana Mexican, Mad Italian Rest., Papa John's, Taco Bell, Wendy's, Wild Ginger Thai 🏠 Holiday Inn Select, Residence Inn Ⓞ vet
29	Ashford-Dunwoody Rd, **N** ⛽ BP, Exxon/Subway 🍴 Brio Tuscan, Broken Egg, CA Pizza Kitchen, Capital Grille, Cheesecake Factory, Chili's, Firebird's Rest., Goldfish, J. Alexander's, Jason's Deli, Maddio's Pizza, Maggiano's Little Italy,

Exit #	Services
29	Continued McCormick&Schmick's, McDonald's, McKendrick Steaks, Olive Garden, PF Chang's, Popeye's, Schlotzsky's, Seasons 32 Grill, Starbucks 🏠 Crowne Plaza Ⓞ Barnes&Noble, Best Buy, Dillard's, Goodyear/auto, Hobby Lobby, Macy's, mall, Marshalls, Nordstrom, Old Navy, USPO, Walmart, **S** Ⓞ Hilton Garden
28	Peachtree-Dunwoody Rd (no EZ return wb), **N** 🍴 5 Guys Burgers, Arby's, Chequer's Grill, Chipotle, Chuy's Mexican, Fleming's Steaks, Fuddrucker's, Genghis Grill, Mimi's Café, Panera Bread, Shane's Rib Shack, Taco Mac, Uncle Julio's Mexican 🏠 Comfort Suites, Courtyard, Extended Stay America, Extended Stay Deluxe, Fairfield Inn, Hampton Inn, Hilton Suites, Holiday Inn Express, Homestead Suites, La Quinta, Marriott, Microtel, Residence Inn, Sheraton, Westin Ⓞ Costco/gas, Firestone/auto, Home Depot, mall, Petsmart, Publix, Rite Aid, Ross, Target, TJ Maxx, Verizon, **S** Ⓞ 🏥
27	US 19 N, GA 400, **N 2 mi** Ⓞ LDS Temple
26	Glenridge Dr (from eb), Johnson Ferry Rd
25	US 19 S, Roswell Rd, Sandy Springs, **N** ⛽ BP, Shell/dsl 🍴 5 Guys Burgers, Applebee's, Bobbys Burgers, Boston Mkt, Burger King, Chick-fil-A, Chipotle Mexican, Domino's, Dunkin Donuts, Egg Harbor Café, El Azteca Mexican, Firehouse Subs, Hudson Grille, IHOP, Jason's Deli, Jimmy John's, Longhorn Steaks, Mandarin House, McDonald's, Mellow Mushroom, Moe's SW Grill, Pizza Hut, Ray's NY Pizza, Roasters, Ruth's Chris Steaks, SeaBass Kitchen, Smash Burger, Starbucks, Steak'n Shake, Subway, Taco Bell, Waffle House, Wendy's 🏠 Comfort Inn Ⓞ 🏥, $Tree, Aldi Foods, AT&T, CVS Drug, DeKalb Tire, Hancock Fabrics, Lowe's, Marshalls, Mr Transmission, NAPA AutoCare, Office Depot, PepBoys, PetCo, Publix, Radio Shack, Target, Toyota, Trader Joe's, Tuesday Morning, URGENT CARE, Verizon, Walgreens, Whole Foods Mkt, **S** ⛽ Chevron/dsl, Citgo, Shell 🍴 Barberitos, El Taco Veloz, Kobe Steaks, Seasons Rest., Starbucks, Subway, Taco Mac Ⓞ Publix, Staples, Target, URGENT CARE
24	Riverside Dr
22	New Northside Dr, to Powers Ferry Rd, **N** ⛽ Shell/Subway/dsl, **S** ⛽ BP, Chevron/dsl 🍴 Blimpie, McDonald's, Peter Cheng's Chinese, Ray's Rest., Waffle House 🏠 Candlewood Suites, Hawthorn Suites, Homestead Suites, Wyndham Ⓞ CVS Drug, Publix, vet
21	(from wb), **N** ⛽ Shell 🍴 Harry's Pizza, Homestead Village Ⓞ BMW/Mini
20	I-75, N to Chattanooga, S to Atlanta (from wb), to US 41 N
19	US 41, Cobb Pkwy, to Dobbins AFB, **N** ⛽ BP, Chevron/24hr, Citgo, Shell 🍴 Arby's, BBQ, Bruster's, Carrabba's, Chuck-eCheese, Denny's, Dunkin Donuts, Hardee's, IHOP, Jade Palace, Joe's Crabshack, KFC, McDonald's, Olive Garden, Papa John's, Pizza Hut, Red Lobster, Steak'n Shake, Subway, Sunny's BBQ, The Border Mexican, Waffle House, Wendy's, Wingate Inn 🏠 Hilton, Holiday Inn Express Ⓞ Best Buy, Buick/Subaru, Cadillac, Chevrolet, Honda, Hyundai, Lexus, Marshall's, Michael's, Office Depot, PetsMart, Ross, Target, Walgreen, **S** ⛽ Chevron/24hr 🍴 Buffalo's Café, Cheese Factory, Chick-fil-A, Chipotle Mexican, El Toro Mexican, Hooters, Jason's Deli, Johnny Rocket's, Longhorn Steaks, Maggiano's Italian, Malone's Grill, Olde Mill Steaks, PF Chang, Pizza Hut, Ruby Tuesday, Schlotsky's 🏠 Courtyard, Homewood Suites, Renaissance Motel, Sheraton Suites, Stouffer Waverly Hotel, Sumner Suites Ⓞ A&P, Barnes&Noble, Costco/gas, JC Penney, Macy's, mall, Sears/auto, USPO

INTERSTATE 285 (Atlanta) Cont'd	

Exit # **Services**

18 Paces Ferry Rd, to Vinings, **N** 🍴 Panera Bread 🛏 Fairfield Inn, La Quinta, **S** 🅖 QT/24hr 🍴 Chick-fil-A, Subway, Willy's Grill 🛏 Extended Stay Deluxe, Hampton Inn, Wyndham 🅞 Goodyear/auto, Home Depot, Publix

16 S Atlanta Rd, to Smyrna, **N** 🍴 Five Guys Burgers, Waffle House, Zio's Italian 🛏 Holiday Inn Express 🅞 🅷, **S** 🅖 ⛽/Wendy's/dsl/scales/24hr, Shell/dsl, Texaco 🅞 Kroger

15 GA 280, S Cobb Dr, **E** 🛏 Microtel 🅞 U-Haul, **W** 🅖 BP/dsl, RaceTrac, Shell 🍴 Arby's/Mrs Winners, Checker's, Chick-fil-A, China Buffet, IHOP, Krystal/24hr, McDonald's, Subway, Taco Bell, Wendy's, Zaxby's 🛏 AmeriHost, Comfort Inn, Country Inn Suites, Knight's Inn, Sun Suites 🅞 🅷

14mm Chattahoochee River

13 Bolton Rd (from nb)

12 US 78, US 278, Bankhead Hwy, **E** 🅖 Citgo/dsl, Petro/Iron Skillet/dsl/rest./scales/24hr/ @, Shell/dsl/24hr 🍴 Mrs Winner's 🅞 Blue Beacon, **W** 🅖 BP, Marathon

10b a I-20, W to Birmingham, E to Atlanta (exits left from nb), **W** 🅞 to Six Flags

9 GA 139, MLK Dr, to Adamsville, **E** 🅖 Phillips 66, Shell 🍴 Mrs Winner's 🅞 Family$, Wayfield Foods, **W** 🅖 Chevron, Shell 🍴 Checker's, Church's, Golden House Chinese, KFC/Taco Bell, McDonald's

7 Cascade Rd, **E** 🅖 Marathon 🍴 Papa John's 🅞 Kroger, **W** 🅖 BP, Phillips 66 🍴 Applebee's, China Express, KFC, McDonald's, Moe's SW Grill, Mrs Winner's, Pizza Hut, Quizno's, Starbucks, Subway, Up the Creek, Wendy's 🅞 🅷, GNC, Home Depot, Publix, Radio Shack, Tires+

5b a GA 166, Lakewood Fwy, **E** 🅖 Chevron, Shell 🍴 Blimpie, Burger King, Capt D's, Checker's, IHOP, KFC, Taco Bell, Wendy's 🅞 Firestone, Goodyear, Kroger, Macy's, mall, **W** 🅖 BP, Citgo/dsl, RaceWay, Shell/dsl/24hr 🍴 Church's, KFC, Mrs Winner's, Wendy's 🛏 Deluxe Inn 🅞 AutoZone, CVS Drug, Family$, Vet

2 Camp Creek Pkwy, to 🛬, **E** 🅖 BP, Exxon, Texaco 🍴 Checker's, McDonald's, Mrs Winner's 🛏 Comfort Suites, **W** 🍴 American Deli, Brewster's, Carino's, Chick-fil-A, Jason's Deli, LongHorn Steaks, Panda Express, Red Lobster, Ruby Tuesday, Wendys 🅞 Barnes&Noble, BJ's Whse/gas, Lowes Whse, Marshall's, Old Navy, PetsMart, Publix, Ross, Staples, Target, Walgreens

1 Washington Rd, **E** 🅖 Texaco/dsl, **W** 🅖 Chevron 🛏 Regency Inn

◤N **INTERSTATE 475 (Macon)**	

Exit # **Services**

16mm I-475 begins/ends on I-75, exit 177.

15 US 41, Bolingbroke, **E 1 mi** 🅖 Exxon/dsl/LP, Marathon/dsl

9 Zebulon Rd, **E** 🅖 Citgo, Murphy USA/dsl, Shell/Circle K/24hr 🍴 Buffalo's Café, Chen's Wok, Chick-fil-A, JL's BBQ, Krystal, Margarita's Mexican, McAlister's Deli, McDonald's, NU Way Wieners, Papa John's, Pizza Hut, Sonic, Subway, Taco Bell, Taki Japanese, Waffle House, Wendy's 🛏 Baymont Inn, Comfort Suites, Fairfield Inn, Sleep Inn 🅞 🅷, GNC, Goodyear/auto, Kohl's, Kroger/gas, Krystal, Lowe's, USPO, Walgreens, Walmart, **W** 🅖 Marathon 🍴 Polly's Café, Zaxby's 🅞 Advance Parts, CVS Drug

8mm 🆁🆂 nb, full ♿ facilities, litter barrels, petwalk, 🚻, 🏞, vending

5 GA 74, Macon, **E** 🅖 RaceWay 🍴 Waffle House 🅞 Harley-Davidson, to Mercer U, **W** 🅖 Flash/Subway/dsl, Texaco/Church's/dsl 🍴 Capt D's, Wok&Roll Chinese 🛏 Howard Johnson 🅞 $General, Food Lion, Tires+, to Lake Tobesofkee, vet

3 US 80, Macon, **E 0-2 mi** 🅖 Marathon/dsl, Murphy USA/dsl, RaceWay, Spectrum/Circle K/Subway, Sunoco/dsl 🍴 Applebee's, Burger King, Chick-fil-A, China Buffet, Cracker Barrel, DQ, Golden Corral, JL's BBQ, KFC, Krystal, McDonald's, Ryan's, S&S Cafeteria, Sonny's BBQ, Taco Bell, Waffle House, Zaxby's 🛏 Best Western, Country Hearth Inn, Days Inn, Discovery Inn, Economy Inn, Hampton Inn, Holiday Inn Express, La Quinta, Motel 6, Quality Inn, Ramada Inn, Red Roof Inn, Rodeway Inn, Super 8, Travelodge, ValuePlace, Villager Inn 🅞 Best Buy, BigLots, Books-A-Million, CVS Drug, Dick's, Dillard's, Firestone/auto, Home Depot, Honda, JC Penney, Kroger, Lowe's, Macy's, mall, Marshall's, Michael's, Nissan, Old Navy, Petsmart, Ross, Sam's Club/gas, Sears/auto, Staples, Target, VW, Walmart/24hr, **W** 🅖 Marathon/dsl, Shell/Circle K 🍴 Burger King 🛏 EconoLodge, Knights Inn, Scottish Inn

1 Hartley Bridge Rd, same as I-75 exit 156

0mm I-475 begins/ends on I-75, exit 156.

◤N **INTERSTATE 575**	

Exit # **Services**

30mm I-575 begins/ends on GA 5/515.

27 GA 5, Howell Br, to Ball Ground

24 Airport Dr

20 GA 5, to Canton, **E** 🅖 BP 🍴 Casey's rest., Chick-fil-A, Hooters, Ryan's, Stevi B's Pizza, Waffle Wouse, Wendy's 🛏 Comfort Inn, Homestead Inn 🅞 Chevrolet, Toyota, Walmart/24hr, **W** 🅖 Citgo, RaceTrac 🍴 Applebee's, Arby's, Cracker Barrel, Longhorn Steaks, McDonald's, O'Charley's, Outback Steaks, Panda Express, Red Lobster, Starbucks, Subway, Waffle House, Zaxby's 🛏 Holiday Inn Express 🅞 Belk, Home Depot, Michaels, Publix, Radio Shack, Ross

19 GA 20 E, Canton

17 GA 140, to Roswell (from sb), Canton

16 GA 20, GA 140, **E** 🅖 Pure, **W** 🅖 Citgo, Shell 🍴 BBQ, Burger King, KFC, LJ Silver, Mandarin House, Papa John's, Taco Bell, Waffle House 🅞 $General, K-Mart

14 Holly Springs, **E** 🅖 Citgo/dsl 🍴 Domino's, Pizza Hut 🛏 Pinecrest Motel, **W** 🅖 BP, Chevron, RaceTrac, Shell 🍴 Subway, Viva Mexico, Wendy's, Zaxby's 🅞 Kroger, Publix, Walgreens

11 Sixes Rd, **E** 🅖 Chevron, QT, **W** 🅖 Citgo

⬆⬇N INTERSTATE 575 Cont'd

Exit #	Services
8	Towne Lake Pkwy, to Woodstock, **E** 🅟 Citgo, Shell 🍴 McDonald's, Waffle House, Waffle King/24hr 🄾 Ford, Hyundai, **W** 🅟 Phillips 66
7	GA 92, Woodstock, **E** 🅟 Chevron, QT, Shell 🍴 Arby's, Bubba Q's Rest., Burger King, Capt D's, Checker's, Chick-fil-A, DQ, Firehouse Subs, Folk's Kitchen, KFC, McDonald's, Moe's SW Grill, Mrs Winner's, O'Charley's, Resturante Mexico, Ruby Tuesday, Subway, Taco Bell, Waffle House, Wendy's 🛏 Comfort Suites, Hampton Inn, Suburban Lodge 🄾 Big 10 Tire, Camping World, CVS Drug, Firestone/auto, Goodyear/auto, Ingles, Just Brakes, **W** 🅟 BP 🍴 Caribou Coffee, IHOP, Mi Casa Mexican, Schlotzky's, Steak'n Shake, Taco Mac 🄾 Atlanta Bread, Big Lots, BJ's Whse/gas, Discout Tire, Home Depot, Honda, Kohl's, Lowe's Whse, Office Depot, Old Navy, Target
4	Bells Ferry Rd, **W** 🅟 QT/24hr, Shell/dsl 🍴 Arby's, Burger King, Ralph's Grill, Subway, Waffle House
3	Chastain Rd, to I-75 N, **W** 🅟 Chevron, Citgo, Shell 🍴 Arby's, Cracker Barrel, Los Reyes, Mrs. Winner's, O'Charley's, Panda Express, Sidelines Grill, Subway, ToGo's/Baskin Robbins, Waffle House, Wendy's 🛏 Best Western, Comfort Inn, Country Inn&Suites, Fairfield Inn, Residence Inn, Springhill Suites, Suburban Inn 🄾 to Kennesaw St Coll
1	Barrett Pkwy, to I-75 N, US 41, **E** 🅟 Chevron, Murphy USA/dsl, QT 🍴 Barnacle's Cafe, Buffalo Wild Wings, Burger King, Fuddruckers, KFC, Moe's SW Grill, Quizno's, Starbucks, Texas Roadhouse, Waffle House, Wendy's, Zaxby's 🄾 $Tree, Atlanta Bread, Barnes&Noble, CVS Drug, Firestone, Publix, Ross, SteinMart, Walmart/dsl, **W** 🅟 Shell, Texaco 🍴 Applebee's, Fuddrucker's, McDonald's, Olive Garden, Provino's Italian, Red Lobster, Smokey Bones, Starbucks, Waffle House 🛏 Comfort Inn, Crestwood Suites, Day's Inn, Holiday Inn Express, La Quinta, Ramada Ltd, Red Roof Inn 🄾 Big 10 Tire, Firestone/auto, Home Depot, mall, Marshall's, Michael's, TJ Maxx
0mm	I-575 begins/ends on I-75, exit 268.

⬆⬇N INTERSTATE 675

Exit #	Services
10mm	I-285 W, to Atlanta ✈, E to Augusta. **I-675 begins/ends on I-285, exit 52.**
7	Anvil Block Rd, Ft Gillem, **E** 🅟 BP 🍴 Subway, **W** 🅟 Exxon
5	Forest Pkwy, **E** 🅟 Texaco/dsl, **W** 🅟 QT/dsl/scales 🍴 McDonald's, Waffle House
2	US 23, GA 42, **E** 🅟 BP, Texaco 🍴 Horizon/Backyard Burger, Mo-Joe's Café, **W** 🅟 Chevron/dsl, Citgo 🍴 Teapot Chinese, Waffle House 🄾 Family$, Food Depot, Goodyear/auto, USPO
1	GA 138, to I-75 N, Stockbridge, **E** 🅟 BP, Chevron/24hr, Citgo/dsl, Exxon, Murphy USA/dsl, QT, Shell 🍴 Arby's, Burger King, Capt D's, Checker's, Church's Chicken, DQ, Dunkin Donuts, Golden Corral, Hong Kong Buffet, KFC, McDonald's, Papa John's, Pizza Hut, Popeye's, Taco Bell, Waffle House, Wendy's, Zaxby's 🛏 Best Value, Country Hearth Inn, Motel 6, Quality Inn, Sleep Inn, Stockbridge Inn, Suburban Lodge 🄾 $General, $Tree, Ace Hardware, Advance Parts, Aldi Foods, Big10 Tire, BigLots, CVS Drug, Goodyear/auto, NAPA, Radio Shack, USPO, Walmart, **W** 🅟 Exxon, Raceway/24hr 🍴 Applebee's, Arby's, Broadway Diner, Burger King, Chick-fil-A, ChinChin Chinese, CiCi's, DQ, Folk's Rest., Frontera Mexican, Golden Corral, Honeybaked Ham, IHOP, KFC, Krystal,

1	Continued
	LJ Silver, McDonald's, Philly Connection, Piccadilly's, Shoney's, Subway, Taco Bell, Taco Mac, Tokyo Seafood, Waffle House, Wendy's 🛏 Best Western, Comfort Inn, Day's Inn, Hampton Inn, Holiday Inn, La Quinta, Motel 6, Red Roof Inn 🄾 H, GNC, Goodyear, K-Mart, Kroger, Lowes Whse, Office Depot, Tires+
	I-675 begins/ends on I-75, exit 227.

⬆⬇N INTERSTATE 985 (Gainesville)

Exit #	Services
	I-985 begins/ends on US 23, 25mm.
24	to US 129 N, GA 369 W, Gainesville, **N** 🄾 H, GA Mtn Ctr, **S** 🅟 BP/Subway/dsl, Chevron/dsl, Citgo 🍴 Double B Burger, Rabbit Trail Cafe
22	GA 11, Gainesville, **N** 🅟 BP/dsl, Citgo, QT/24hr 🍴 Burger King, McDonald's 🛏 Best Western/rest., **S** 🅟 Chevron, Shell/dsl 🍴 Waffle House 🛏 Motel 6
20	GA 60, GA 53, Gainesville, **N** 🍴 El Manarca, McDonald's, Mrs Winners 🛏 Best Value Inn, Hampton Inn, gas, Citgo/dsl, **S** 🅟 Kangaroo 🍴 Subway, Waffle House
16	GA 53, Oakwood, **N** 🅟 BP, Citgo 🍴 Arby's, Baskin-Robbins/Dunkin Donuts, Burger King, DQ, El Sombrero Mexican, Hardee's, KFC, McDonald's, Pizza Hut, Subway, Taco Bell, Waffle House, Zaxby's 🛏 Admiral Benbow Inn, Country Inn Suites, Jameson Inn 🄾 Chrysler/Jeep, CVS Drug, Food Lion, RV Ctr, Sam's Club, **S** 🅟 Citgo/dsl, QT/dsl 🍴 Checker's, Krystal, Mrs Winners, Sonny's BBQ, Waffle House, Wendy's 🛏 Comfort Inn 🄾 AutoZone, Goodyear/auto, Publix, Walgreens
12	Spout Springs Rd, Flowery Branch, **N** 🅟 Exxon/dsl, **S** 🅟 BP/Subway, Chevron/dsl 🍴 Burger&Shake, China Garden, CrossRoads Grill, Domino's, El Sombrero Mexican, TCBY, Thai Dish 🄾 Publix
8	GA 347, Friendship Rd, Lake Lanier, **N** 🅟 BP, Chevron, Shell, Texaco 🍴 3rd Coast, Backyard Burger, Blimpie, Burger King, China Garden, Huddle House, McDonald's, Sonia's Mexican, Subway, Vinny's NY Grill, Waffle House, Wendy's, Zaxby's 🄾 Advance parts, Publix, **S** Camper City RV Ctr, Harley Davidson
4	US 23 S, GA 20, Buford, **N** 🅟 QT, Shell 🍴 Arby's, Burger King, Capt D's, Checker's, Golden Buddah, Golden Corral, Huddle House, IHOP, KFC, McDonald's, Saigon Bangkok, Taco Bell, Wendy's, Zaxby's 🛏 Days Inn, Holiday Inn Express 🄾 Ace Hardware, Buick/GMC, Dodge/Jeep, Home Depot, KIA, Tuesday Morning, **S** 🅟 BP, Chevron, Citgo, Texaco 🍴 Ryan's, Sonny's BBQ, Waffle House 🄾 $Tree, Expert Tire, Honda, Lowes Whse, Walmart
0mm	I-985 begins/ends on I-85.

IDAHO

⬆⬇N INTERSTATE 15

Exit #	Services
196mm	Idaho/Montana state line, Monida Pass, continental divide, elev 6870
190	Humphrey
184	Stoddard Creek Area, **E** 🄾 Historical Site, RV camping, **W** 🄾 Stoddard Creek Camping
180	Spencer, **E** 🍴 Opal Country Café/gas 🄾 High Country Opal Store
172	no services

DUBOIS

🧭 N   INTERSTATE 15 Cont'd

Exit #	Services
167	ID 22, Dubois, **E** 📶 **both lanes, full ♿ facilities, litter barrels, petwalk,** 📕 Phillips 66/dsl 🍴 Dubois Cafe 🅾 city park, 🅲, 🏤USPO, **W** 🅾 Nez Pearce Tr, to Craters NM
150	Hamer, **E** 🅾 food, 🅲, Ron's Tire, USPO, **W** 🅾 Camus NWR
143	ID 33, ID 28, to Mud Lake, Rexburg, **W** 🅾 Sacajawea Hist Bywy, **weigh sta both lanes**
142mm	hist site, roadside parking
135	ID 48, Roberts, **E** 📕 Exxon/cafe/dsl/LP 🅾 city park
128	Osgood Area, **E** 📕 Osgood/dsl 🅾 camping (6mi)
119	US 20 E, to Rexburg, Idaho Falls, **E on Lindsay** 📕 Sinclair/dsl 🍴 Denny's, Jaker's Steaks, Outback Steaks, Sandpiper Rest. 🏠 Best Western, Guesthouse Inn, Hampton Inn, Hilton Garden, Hotel on the Falls, LeRitz Hotel, Safari Inn, Shilo Inn/rest., South Fork Inn, Super 8 🅾 LDS Temple, same as 118, Snake River RV Park/ camping, **W** 📕 Chevron/dsl

IDAHO FALLS

118	US 20, Broadway St, Idaho Falls, **E** 📕 Phillips 66/dsl 🍴 Applebee's, Arctic Circle, Buffalo Wild Wings, Carl's Jr, Cedric's Rest., Chili's, Domino's, Famous Dave's BBQ, Jimmy John's, MacKenzie River Grill, Olive Garden, Panda Express, Shari's Rest., Smitty's Pancakes, Starbucks, Wendy's 🏠 Candlewood Suites, Fairfield Inn, Hampton Inn, Hilton Garden, Residence Inn 🅾 🅷, Candy Jct, Ford, Harley-Davidson, LDS Temple, same as 119, tires, URGENT CARE, Verizon, Walmart/Subway **W** 📕 Exxon/dsl, Phillips 66/dsl, Sinclair/McDonald's 🍴 5 Buck Pizza, Arby's, Burger King, Fiesta Ole, Hong Kong Rest., Jack-in-the-Box, Los Adalaberto's Mexican, O'Brady's, Papa Murphy's, Pizza Hut, Subway 🏠 Comfort Inn, Motel 6, Motel West 🅾 Albertsons, AutoZone, O'Reilly Parts, Walgreens
116	US 26, Sunnyside Rd, Ammon, Jackson, **E** 🅾 🅷, Chevrolet, Honda, Sunnyside Acres RV Park, Toyota/Scion, VW, zoo, **W** 📕 Exxon/diesel 🍴 DoubleDown Grill 🏠 Sleep Inn
113	US 26, to Idaho Falls, Jackson, **E** 📕 Blu/dsl/LNG, Chevron/ Burger King/dsl, ❤Loves/McDonald's/dsl/scales/24hr, Sinclair/Dad's/dsl/24hr/@ 🍴 Subway 🅾 🅷 Jack's Tires, Peterbilt, Sunnyside RV Park, Targhee RV Park
108	Shelley, Firth Area, **E 1 mi** 🅾 RV Park/dump
101mm	📶 **both lanes, full ♿ facilities, geological site, litter barrels, petwalk,** 🅲, **picnic tables**
98	Rose-Firth Area
94.5mm	Snake River

93	US 26, ID 39, Blackfoot, **E** 📕 Chevron/dsl, Maverik/dsl, Stinker/dsl 🍴 Arby's, Burger King, Domino's, Golden China, Homestead Rest., Hong Kong Garden, Italiano's, Little Caesars, McDonald's, Papa Murphy's, Pizza Hut, Roberto's Mexican, Subway, Taco Bell, Taco Time, Wendy's, Wingers 🏠 Best Western, Super 8 🅾 AutoZone, Bealls, Chrysler/ Dodge/Ford/Jeep, city park, GNC, Kesler's Foods, O'Reilly Parts, Radio Shack, Ridley's Mkt, Schwab Tire, Tire Factory, URGENT CARE, Verizon, Walgreens, Walmart/Subway **W** 📕 Sinclair/A&W/dsl 🅾 Riverside Boot/saddleshop (4mi)
90.5mm	Blackfoot River
89	US 91, S Blackfoot, **W** 📕 Sinclair/Sage Cafe/dsl
80	Ft Hall, **W** 📕 Phillips 66/rest./dsl/casino 🏠 Shoshone Bannock Hotel/casino
72	I-86 W, to Twin Falls
71	Pocatello Creek Rd, Pocatello, **E** 📕 Chevron/Burger King/dsl, Phillips 66/dsl, Shell/ dsl 🍴 Applebee's, Jack-in-the-Box, Perkins, Sandpiper Rest., Subway 🏠 AmeriTel, Best Western, Clarion, Comfort Inn, Red Lion Inn, Super 8 🅾 KOA (1mi), **W 0-2 mi** 📕 Exxon, Maverik/dsl 🍴 Arby's, Bamboo

POCATELLO

71	Continued Garden, Butter Burr's Rest., Café Rio, Carl's Jr, Changs Garden Chinese, Coldstone, El Caparal, Golden Corral, Jamba Juice, KFC, Mandarin House, McDonald's, Papa Murphy's, Pizza Hut, Ridley's Mkt, Schlotzsky's, Senor Iguana's Mexican, SF Pizza, Sizzler, Sonic, Subway, Taco Bell, Taco Time, Thai Kitchen, Wendy's, Winger's 🅾 $Tree, AutoZone, Big-Lots, Buick/GMC, Chevrolet, Fred Meyer/dsl, Harley-Davidson, Honda, O'Reilly Parts, Radio Shack, Subaru, Toyota, Tuesday Morning, Walgreens, WinCo Foods
69	Clark St, Pocatello, **E** 📕 Chevron/cafe/dsl, Maverik/dsl, Sinclair/Arctic Circle/dsl 🍴 Ruby Tuesday 🏠 Hampton Inn, Holiday Inn Express, TownePlace Suites 🅾 🅷, **W** 🅾 museum, to ID St U
67	US 30/91, 5th St, Pocatello, **E** 📕 Exxon/dsl, **W 1-2 mi** 📕 Chevron/dsl, Shell/dsl 🍴 Elmer's Dining, Goody's Deli, Jimmy John's, McDonald's, Pizza Hut, Subway, Taco Bell 🏠 Rodeway Inn, Thunderbird Motel 🅾 🅷, city park, info, museum, Old Fort Hall, RV dump
63	Portneuf Area, **W** 🅾 RV camp/dump, to Mink Creek RA

🅖 = gas 🍴 = food 🛌 = lodging 🅞 = other 🆁🆂 = rest stop   Copyright 2015 - the Next EXIT ®

⬆N INTERSTATE 15 Cont'd

Exit #	Services
59mm	**weigh sta both lanes**
58	Inkom (from sb), **W** 1/2 mi 🅖 Sinclair/café/dsl 🅞 Bisharat's Mkt, Pebble Creek Ski Area, repair, USPO
57	Inkom (from nb), same as 58
47	US 30, to Lava Hot Springs, McCammon, **E** 🅖 *FLYING J* /dsl/scales/LP/RV dump/24hr, Chevron/A&W/Taco Time/dsl 🍴 Subway 🅞 Lava Hot Springs RA, McCammon RV Park, to KOA
44	Lp 15, Jenson Rd, McCammon, **E** access to food
40	Arimo, **E** 🅞 USPO
36	US 91, Virginia
31	ID 40, to Downey, Preston, **E** 🅖 Shell/Flags West/café/dsl/ motel/24hr/@ 🅞 Downata Hot Springs RV camping (6mi)
25mm	🆁🆂 sb, full ♿ **facilities, litter barrels, petwalk, 🚻, picnic tables**
24.5mm	elev 5574, Malad Summit
22	to Devil Creek Reservoir, **E** RV camping
17	ID 36, to Weston, to Preston
13	ID 38, Malad City, **W** 🅖 Chevron/Burger King, Phillips 66/café/ dsl, Texaco/dsl 🍴 Me&Lou's Rest., Pines Rest., Sperow's BBQ, Subway 🛌 Village Inn Motel 🅞 🅷 3R's Tire, Family$, pioneer museum, repair, RV dump
7mm	**Welcome Ctr nb, full** ♿ **facilities, info, litter barrels, petwalk, 🚻, 🆁🆂 vending**
3	to Samaria, Woodruff
0mm	Idaho/Utah state line

⬆E INTERSTATE 84

Exit #	Services
275mm	Idaho/Utah state line
270mm	🆁🆂 **both lanes, full** ♿ **facilities, geological site, litter barrels, petwalk, 🚻, picnic tables**
263	Juniper Rd
257mm	Sweetzer Summit, elev 5530, Sweetzer Summit
254	Sweetzer Rd
245	Sublett Rd, to Malta, **N** 🅖 Sinclair/dsl/café 🅞 camping
237	Idahome Rd
234mm	Raft River
229mm	🆁🆂/weigh sta both lanes, full ♿ **facilities, litter barrels, petwalk, 🚻, picnic tables**
228	ID 81, Yale Rd, to Declo
222	I-86, US 30, E to Pocatello
216	ID 77, ID 25, to Declo, **N** 🅖 Phillips 66/FoodCourt/dsl 🅞 🅷 to Walcott SP, Village of Trees RV Park, **S** 🅖 Shell/Pit Stop Grill/dsl
215mm	Snake River
211	ID 24, Heyburn, Burley, **N** 🅖 Sinclair/A&W/café/dsl 🍴 Wayside Cafe 🛌 Tops Motel 🅞 🅷 Country RV Village/park, **S** 🅖 ♥Loves/Carl's Jr./dsl/scales/24hr 🅞 Riverside RV Park, truck repair
208	ID 27, Burley, **N** 🅖 Phillips 66/dsl 🍴 Conner's Cafe 🛌 Super 8, **S** 🅖 Chevron/Subway/dsl/24hr, Maverik/dsl, Shell/dsl, Sinclair/dsl, Sinclair/dsl 🍴 Aguila's Mexican, Arby's, Burger King, El Caporal, Guadalajara Mexican, Jack-in-the-Box, JB's, KFC, Little Caesars, McDonald's, Morey's Steaks, Perkins, Wendy's 🛌 Best Western, Fairfield Inn 🅞 🅷 $Tree, Buick/GMC, Cal Ranch Store, CarQuest, Commercial Tire, JC Penney, NAPA, O'Reilly Parts, Radio Shack, to Snake River RA, Verizon, Walmart
201	ID 25, Kasota Rd, to Paul, 🅞 Kasota RV Park

Exit #	Services
194	ID 25, to Hazelton
188	Valley Rd, to Eden
182	ID 50, to Kimberly, Twin Falls, **N** 🅖 Sinclair/dsl 🅞 Gary's RV Ctr/park/dump, **S** 🅖 Shell/Blimpie/Taco Time/dsl/ scales/24hr/@ 🍴 Garden of Eden Cafe 🛌 Amber Inn 🅞 🅷, auto/truck/rv repair, to Shoshone Falls scenic attraction
173	US 93, Twin Falls, **N** 🅖 *FLYING J*/dsl/LP/24hr/@ 🍴 Subway 🛌 Comfort Inn, Days Inn 🅞 Blue Beacon, Freightliner, KOA (1mi), to Sun Valley, **S 5 mi** 🅖 Chevron/dsl, Exxon/dsl/ LP, Phillips 66, Shell, Sinclair 🍴 5 Guys Burgers, Applebee's, Arby's, Arctic Circle, Baskin-Robbins, Buffalo Wild Wings, Burger King, Cafe Rio, Carino's, Chili's, Coldstone, DQ, Golden Corral, Idaho Joe's, IHOP, Jack-in-the-Box, Jakers Grill, Jamba Juice, KFC, La Fiesta, Mandarin Chinese, McDonald's, Outback Steaks, Panda Express, Papa John's, Perkins, Pizza Hut, Quiznos, River Rock Grill, Shari's, Sizzler, Sonic, Subway, Taco Bell, Tomato's Grill, Wendy's, Wok In Grill 🛌 AmericInn, Best Western, Comfort Inn, Hampton Inn, Hilton Garden, Holiday Inn Express, La Quinta, Motel 6, Red Lion, Shilo Inn, Super 8, Weston Inn 🅞 🅷, $Tree, AutoZone, Barnes&Noble, Best Buy, Buick/GMC, Chevrolet, Chrysler/Dodge/Jeep, Coll of S ID, Commercial Tire, Costco/gas, Curves, Ford/Lincoln, Fred Meyer/dsl, Hancock Fabrics, Hastings Books, Home Depot, Honda, Hyundai, JC Penney, Jo-Ann Fabrics, LDS Temple, Les Schwab Tire, Lowe's, Macy's, Mazda/VW, Michael's, Nissan, Old Navy, O'Reilly Parts, Petsmart, Sears/ auto, ShopKO, Target, Tire Factory, TJ Maxx, Tuesday Morning, Verizon, Walgreens, Walmart/Subway, WinCo Foods
171mm	🆁🆂/weigh sta eb; full ♿ **facilities, litter barrels, petwalk, 🚻, 🆁🆂 vending**
168	ID 79, to Jerome, **N** 🅖 Chevron/dsl, Shell/Wendy's/dsl, Sinclair/dsl, USA 🍴 Burger King, DQ, Little Caesars, McDonald's 🛌 Best Western, Crest Motel, Holiday Motel 🅞 🅷, $Tree, AutoZone, Brockman RV Ctr, Les Schwab Tire, Walmart/Subway **S** 🍴 Subway 🅞 Chevrolet, ID RV Ctr/marine
165	ID 25, Jerome, **N** 🅖 Sinclair/dsl 🛌 Holiday Motel (1mi) 🅞 🅷 RV camping/dump
157	ID 46, Wendell, **N 1 mi** 🍴 Subway 🅞 🅷, CarQuest, Family$, Intermountain RV Park, **S** 🅖 Phillips 66/dsl 🍴 Farmhouse Rest.
155	ID 46, to Wendell, **N** 🅞 Intermountain RV Camp/ctr
147	to Tuttle, **S** 🅞 High Adventure RV Park/cafe, to Malad Gorge SP
146mm	Malad River
141	US 26, to US 30, Gooding, **N** 🅞 🅷, **S** 🅖 Phillips 66/café/dsl, Sinclair/dsl 🛌 Amber Inn, Hagerman Inn (9mi) 🅞 Hagerman RV Village (8mi)
137	Lp 84, to US 30, to Pioneer Road, Bliss, **S 2 mi** 🅖 Sinclair/ Stinker/Oxbow Rest/dsl/24hr 🅞 camping
133mm	🆁🆂 both lanes, full ♿ **facilities, info, litter barrels, petwalk, 🚻, picnic tables**
129	King Hill
128mm	Snake River
125	Paradise Valley
122mm	Snake River
121	Glenns Ferry, **S 1 mi** 🅖 Shell/dsl, Sinclair/dsl 🛌 Hansen Motel/cafe, Redford Motel 🅞 Carmela Winery/rest., fudge factory, NAPA, tires, to 3 Island SP, Trails Break RV camp/dump, Western Family Mkt
120	Glenns Ferry (from eb), same as 121
114	ID 78 (from wb), to Hammett, **S 1 mi** access to gas/dsl, to Bruneau Dunes SP

T W I N   F A L L S

B U R L E Y

ID

🚏 E	**INTERSTATE 84 Cont'd**
Exit #	**Services**

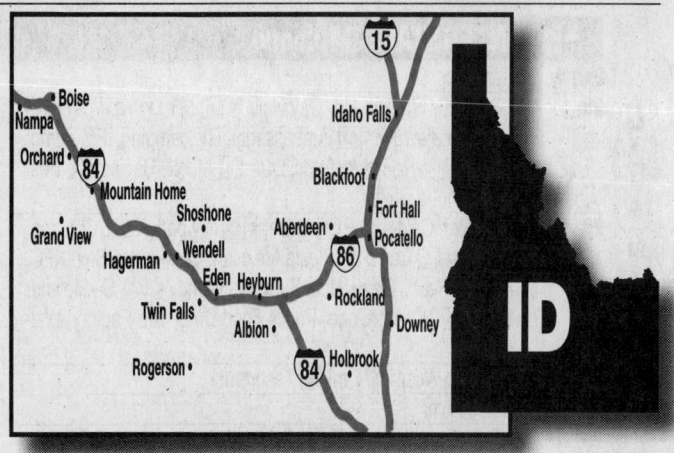

MOUNTAIN HOME

112	to ID 78, Hammett, **S 1 mi** food, gas/dsl, to Bruneau Dunes SP
99	ID 51, ID 67, to Mountain Home, **S 2 mi** 🛏 camping, Maple Cove Motel
95	US 20, Mountain Home, **N** 🅖 Chevron/KFC/dsl, ▨▨▨/Arby's/dsl/scales/24hr 🍴 AJ's Rest., Jack-in-the-Box, Subway, Wingers 🛏 Best Western, Hampton Inn, Mtn Home Inn, **S** 🅖 USA 🍴 Golden Crown Chinese, Jade Palace, McDonald's, Smoky Mtn Pizza, Wendy's 🛏 Hilander Motel (1mi), Towne Ctr Motel (1mi) 🅞 🅷, $Tree, AT&T, Chrysler/Dodge/Jeep, Family$, Ford/Lincoln, to Mtn Home RV Park, Verizon, visitors ctr, Walmart/Subway
90	to ID 51, ID 67, W Mountain Home, **S** 🅖 Chevron/Burger King/dsl 🍴 McDonald's (4mi) 🛏 Maple Cove Motel (4mi), to Hilander Motel (4mi), Towne Ctr Motel (4mi) 🅞 KOA
74	Simco Rd
71	Orchard, Mayfield, **S** 🅖 Sinclair/rest/StageStop Motel/dsl/24hr 🅞 🅒, truckwash
66mm	**weigh sta both lanes**
64	Blacks Creek, Kuna, historical site
62mm	🆁🆂 **both lanes, full** 🛁 **facilities, litter barrels, OR Trail info, petwalk,** 🅒, 🖾 **vending**
59b a	S Eisenman Rd, Memory Rd
57	ID 21, Gowen Rd, to Idaho City, **N** 🅖 Sinclair 🍴 Jack-in-the-Box, McDonald's, Quiznos, Subway, Sunrise Cafe, Taco Del Mar 🛏 Best Western/NW Lodge 🅞 Albertsons/Sav-On, Peterbilt, to Micron, **S** 🅖 Chevron 🍴 Burger King, FoodCourt 🅞 Boise Stores/famous brands, ID Ice World

BOISE

54	US 20/26, Broadway Ave, Boise, **N** 🅖 ⊕FLYING J/dsl/LP/24hr, Chevron/dsl, Shell/dsl 🍴 A&W/KFC, Arby's, Chili's, Fiesta Mexican, IHOP, Jack-in-the-Box, Mongolian Noodles, Nick'n Willy's Pizza, Port Of Subs, Sonic, Starbucks, Subway, Wendy's 🛏 Courtyard (3mi) 🅞 🅷, Big O Tire, Dowdie's Automotive, Fred Meyer, Goodyear/auto, Home Depot, Hyundai, Jo-Ann Fabrics, O'Reilly Parts, PetCo, Radio Shack, Ross, ShopKO, to Boise St U, vet, Walgreens, **S** 🅖 TA/Buckhorn Rest/Taco Bell/Subway/dsl/24hr/@ 🛏 Shilo Inn 🅞 Bretz RV Ctr, Kenworth, Mtn View RV Park
53	Vista Ave, Boise, **N** 🅖 Shell/dsl, Texaco/dsl 🍴 Applebee's, Pizza Hut 🛏 Boise Hotel, Comfort Suites, Extended Stay America, Fairfield Inn, Hampton Inn, Holiday Inn Express, Holiday Inn/rest., Super 8 🅞 museums, st capitol, st police, zoo, **S** 🅖 Chevron/McDonald's 🍴 Denny's, Kopper Kitchen 🛏 Best Western, Comfort Inn, InnAmerica, Motel 6, Sleep Inn 🅞 🖾
52	Orchard St, Boise, **N** 🅖 Shell/dsl 🅞 Fiat, GMC, Kia, Mazda/Nissan
50b a	Cole Rd, Overland Rd, **N** 🅖 Chevron/dsl, Shell, Sinclair 🍴 Cancun Mexican, Eddie's Rest., McDonald's, Outback Steaks, Pizza Hut, Subway, Taco Bell, Taco Time 🅞 Ace Hardware, LDS Temple, transmissions, **S** 🅖 Common Cents/dsl, Phillips 66/dsl 🍴 A&W/KFC, Black Bear Diner, Burger King, Carino's, Carl's Jr, Chapala Mexican, Chuck-a-Rama, Cracker Barrel, Fuddruckers, Goodwood BBQ, Jamba Juice, Legend's Grill, Lucky Palace Chinese, McGrath's FishHouse, On the Border, Panda Express, Panda Express, Papa John's, Perky's Pizza, Pollo Ray, Port Of Subs, Primo's, Sonic, Starbucks, Tucano's Brazilian Grill 🛏 Budget Host, Hampton Inn, Hilton Garden, Homewood Suites, Oxford Suites 🅞 AT&T, Commercial Tire, Costco/gas, Dillon RV Ctr, Les Schwab Tire, Lowe's, Verizon, vet, Walmart/McDonald's

49	I-184 (exits left from eb), to W Boise, **N** 🅞 🅷,,

EAGLE

46	ID 55, Eagle, **N** 🅖 Chevron/McDonald's/dsl 🍴 Blimpie, Buffalo Wild Wings, Del Taco, Ketchn Burritos, Ling&Louis, Los Beto's, Smash Burger, Starbucks, Subway 🛏 Comfort Suites, Hampton Inn, Meridian Inn 🅞 🅷, **S** 🅖 Chevron/dsl 🍴 Beef'O'Brady's, Chicago Connection, Dickey's BBQ, Don Diego Mexican, Jack-in-the-Box, Jimmy John's, Joy Garden, Moxie Java, Pita Pit, Port Of Subs, Qdoba, Quiznos, Rudy's Grill, Sakana Japanese, Taco Bell, TCBY 🛏 Candlewood Suites, Courtyard, TownePlace Suites 🅞 AAA, Harley-Davidson
44	ID 69, Meridian, **N** 🅖 Chevron/dsl, Sinclair 🍴 A&W/KFC, Blimpie, China Wok, DQ, McDonald's, Panda Express, Pizza Hut, Quiznos, Shari's, Starbucks, Subway, Taco Bell, Taco Time, Wendy's 🛏 Best Western, Motel 6 🅞 AT&T, Home Depot, Les Schwab Tire, Sierra Trading Post, URGENT CARE, Verizon, WinCo Foods, **S** 🅖 Shell/dsl 🍴 JB's, Papa John's 🛏 Mr Sandman Motel 🅞 Camping World RV Ctr, Ford, Lowe's, O'Reilly Parts, Walgreens, waterpark
42	Ten Mile Rd

NAMPA

38	Garrity Blvd, Nampa, **N** 🅖 Chevron/dsl 🍴 Jack-in-the-Box, Port of Subs 🛏 Hampton Inn 🅞 Buick/GMC, Cadillac/Chevrolet, Chrysler/Dodge/Jeep, Ford, Hyundai, Kia, Nissan, Subaru, Swiss Village Cheese, Toyota/Scion, Verizon, Walmart/gas **S** 🅖 Phillips 66/McDonald's/dsl, Shell/dsl 🍴 A&W/KFC, Panda Express, Pizza Hut, Subway 🛏 Holiday Inn Express 🅞 🅷, Garrity RV Park, JC Penney, Macy's, War Hawk Museum
36	Franklin Blvd, Nampa, **N** 🅖 Maverik 🍴 Jack-in-the-Box, Noodles Rest. 🛏 Shilo Inn/rest., **S** 🅖 Chevron/dsl, Shell/Subway/dsl/RV dump/scales/4hr 🛏 Sleep Inn 🅞 🅷, Bish's RV Ctr, Freightliner, Honda, Mason Cr RV Park
35	ID 55, Nampa, **S** 🅖 Shell/dsl 🍴 Denny's 🛏 Rodeway Inn, Shilo Inn, Super 8
33b a	ID 55 S, Midland Blvd, Marcine, **N** 🍴 McDonald's, Olive Garden, Port of Subs, Qdoba Mexican, Sonic, Subway, TGI-Friday's, Tulley's Coffee, Winger's 🛏 Fairfield Inn 🅞 AT&T, Best Buy, Costco/gas, Gordmans, Kohl's, Michael's, Old Navy, PetCo, Target, World Mkt, **S** 🅖 Shell/dsl 🍴 Applebee's, Arby's, Baskin-Robbins, Blimpie, Buffalo Wild Wings, Carl's Jr, Coldstone, DQ, Golden Corral, IHOP, Jack-in-the-Box, Jade Garden, Jalapeno's Grill, Mongolian BBQ, Outback Steaks, Papa Murphy's, Quiznos, Red Robin, Shari's Rest, Skipper's, Smokey Mtn Grill, Subway, TX Roadhouse, Wendy's 🅞 $Tree, Big O Tire, BigLots, Hastings Books, Home Depot, Jo-Ann Fabrics, K-Mart, Lowe's, NAPA, Radio Shack, Ross, Savers, ShopKO, Staples, Tire Factory, U-Haul, Verizon, Walgreens, WinCo Foods

ID

INTERSTATE 84 Cont'd

Exit #	Services
29	US 20/26, Franklin Rd, Caldwell, N ⛽ 🛑FLYING J/Denny's/dsl/LP/scales/24hr ⊙ Ambassador RV camping, RV dump, S ⛽ Sage/Sinclair/cafe/dsl/24hr 🍴 Magic Recipe 🏨 Best Western, La Quinta
28	10th Ave, Caldwell, N ⛽ Maverik ⊙ city park, S ⛽ Chevron, Shell/dsl 🍴 Carl's Jr, Fiesta Mexican, Jack-in-the-Box, KFC, Mr V's Rest., Pizza Hut, Subway, Wendy's 🏨 Sundowner Motel ⊙ Ⓗ, AutoZone, Paul's Food/Drug, Tire Factory, Walgreens
27	ID 19, to Wilder, S 1 mi ⛽ Tesoro/dsl
26.5mm	Boise River
26	US 20/26, to Notus, N ⊙ Caldwell Campground, S ⛽ Sinclair/dsl
25	ID 44, Middleton, N ⛽ Shell/dsl 🍴 44 Burgers/shakes, S Insp sta eb
17	Sand Hollow, N 🍴 Sand Hollow Café ⊙ Country Corners RV Park
13	Black Canyon Jct, S ⛽🍴⊙, Sinclair/rest./motel/dsl/scales/24hr
9	US 30, to New Plymouth
3	US 95, Fruitland, N ⛽ Chevron/A&W/dsl ⊙ Neat Retreat RV Park, to Hell's Cyn RA
1mm	Welcome Ctr eb, full ♿ facilities, info, litter barrels, petwalk, Ⓒ, picnic tables
0mm	Idaho/Oregon state line, Snake River

INTERSTATE 86

Exit #	Services
63b a	I-15, N to Butte, S to SLC. I-86 begins/ends on I-15, exit 72.
61	US 91, Yellowstone Ave, Pocatello, N ⛽ Exxon, Maverik/dsl, Shell/dsl 🍴 5 Mile Café, Arby's, Arctic Circle, Burger King, Chapala Mexican, Lei's BBQ, Papa Murphy's, Pizza Hut, Subway, Wendy's 🏨 Motel 6, Ramada Inn ⊙ $Tree, Crossroads RV Ctr, Family$, O'Reilly Parts, Smith's Foods/dsl, Tire Discounters, vet, S ⛽ Exxon/dsl, Phillips 66/dsl 🍴 5 Guys Burgers, Buffalo Wild Wings, Chili's, Costa Vida, Denny's, Great Wall, IHOP, Jimmy John's, MacKenzie River Grill, McDonald's, Panda Express, Pizza Pie Café, Red Lobster, Starbucks, Taco John's, TX Roadhouse ⊙ AT&T, Cal Ranch Store, Costco/gas, Dick's, Ford/Lincoln, Herbergers, Home Depot, JC Penney, Jo-Ann Fabrics, K-Mart/Little Caesars, Lowe's, PetCo, Radio Shack, Ross, Schwab Tire, ShopKo, Staples, TJ Maxx, Verizon, Walgreens, Walmart
58.5mm	Portneuf River
58	US 30, W Pocatello, N ⊙ Batise Springs RV Park/dump (1mi-seasonal)
56	N ⊙ Pocatello Reg ✈, S ⛽ Sinclair/dsl/24hr
52	Arbon Valley, S ⛽ Phillips 66/Bannock Peak/dsl ⊙ casino
51mm	Bannock Creek
49	Rainbow Rd
44	Seagull Bay
40	ID 39, American Falls, N ⛽ Phillips 66/dsl (1mi), Sinclair/dsl (1mi), Texaco 🍴 Pizza Hut, Subway, Tres Hermanos Mexican 🏨 American Motel ⊙ Ⓗ, Alco, auto repair, Family$ (1mi), Jiffy Lube, NAPA, Schwab Tire, to Am Falls RA, Willow Bay RV Park/dump, S 🏨 Hillview Motel
36	ID 37, to Rockland, American Falls, N 2 mi ⛽ Shell/dsl 🏨 Falls Motel ⊙ Ⓗ, S 2 mi ⊙ Indian Springs RV Resort
33	Neeley Area
31mm	Ⓡⓢ wb, full ♿ facilities, hist site, litter barrel, petwalk, Ⓒ, 🏪, vending

28	N ⊙ Register Rock Hist Site, RV camping/dump, to Massacre Rock SP
21	Coldwater Area
19mm	Ⓡⓢ eb, full ♿ facilities, hist site, litter barrel, petwalk, Ⓒ, 🏪 vending
15	Raft River Area
1	I-84 E, to Ogden. I-86 begins/ends on I-84, exit 222.

INTERSTATE 90

Exit #	Services
74mm	Idaho/Montana state line, Lookout Pass elev 4680, Pacific/Central time zone
73mm	scenic area/hist site wb
72mm	scenic area/hist site eb
71mm	runaway truck ramp wb
70mm	runaway truck ramp wb
69	Lp 90, Mullan, N ⛽ Sinclair/dsl 🏨 Lookout Motel (1mi) ⊙ Mullan Trail grocery/RV Park, museum, USPO
68	Lp 90 (from eb), Mullan, same as 69
67	Morning District, Morning District
66	Gold Creek (from eb)
65	Compressor District
64	Golconda District
62	ID 4, Wallace, S ⛽ Conoco 🍴 Pizza Factory, Smokehouse Rest. 🏨 Brooks Hotel, Stardust Motel ⊙ Depot RV Park, Harvest Foods, museum, TrueValue
61	Lp 90, Wallace, S ⛽ Conoco/dsl 🍴 Pizza Factory, Red Light Garage, Smokehouse Rest., Wallace Sta Rest./gifts 🏨 Brooks Hotel/rest., Molly B-Damm Inn, Wallace Inn ⊙ auto repair, info ctr, same as 62
60	Lp 90, Silverton, S 🏨 Molly B-Damm Inn ⊙ RV camping
57	Lp 90, Osburn, S ⛽ 76/dsl ⊙ Blue Anchor RV Park, Stein's Foods, USPO
54	Big Creek, N ⊙ hist site
51	Lp 90, Division St, Kellogg, N ⛽ Conoco/dsl 🏨 Trail Motel ⊙ Ⓗ, Buick/Cadillac/Chevrolet/GMC, Chrysler/Dodge/Jeep, Schwab Tire, Stein's Foods, Sunnyside Drug, vet, S 🍴 In Cahoots Cafe, Moose Creek Grill ⊙ USPO
50	Hill St (from eb), Kellogg, N 🍴 Humdinger Drive-In 🏨 Trail Motel ⊙ Ace Hardware, NAPA, Stein's Foods, Sunnyside Drug, tires, S ⛽ Conoco/dsl 🍴 Greek Deli ⊙ museum, Silver Mtn Ski/summer resort/rec area, Yoke's Foods
49	Bunker Ave, N ⛽ Conoco/dsl 🍴 McDonald's, Sam's Drive-In, Subway 🏨 Silverhorn Motel/rest. ⊙ Ⓗ, S 🍴 Noah's Canteen, Silver Mtn Rest. 🏨 GuestHouse Inn, Morning Star Lodge ⊙ city park, museum, RV dump, Silver Mtn RA
48	Smelterville, S ⊙ O'Reilly Parts, Tire Factory, USPO, Walmart
45	Pinehurst, S ⛽ Chevron/dsl/repair, Conoco/dsl ⊙ By-the-way Camping, Harvest Foods, TrueValue, USPO
43	Kingston, N ⛽ Conoco/dsl ⊙ RV camping, S ⛽ Exxon/dsl/rv dump, USPO
40	Cataldo, N 🍴 Mission Inn Rest., USPO, S ⊙ RV Park
39.5mm	Coeur d' Alene River
39	Cataldo Mission, S ⊙ Nat Hist Landmark, Old Mission SP
34	ID 3, to St Maries, Rose Lake, S ⛽ Conoco/dsl, Rose Lake/dsl 🍴 Rose Lake Cafe ⊙ White Pines Scenic Rte
33	chain removal eb
32mm	chainup area/weigh sta wb
31.5mm	4th of July Creek, eastern boundary, Idaho Panhandle NF
28	4th of July Pass RA, elev 3069, Mullan Tree HS, ski area, snowmobile area, turnout both lanes
24mm	chainup eb, removal wb

Vertical side labels: CALDWELL, POCATELLO, WALLACE, KELLOGG, ID

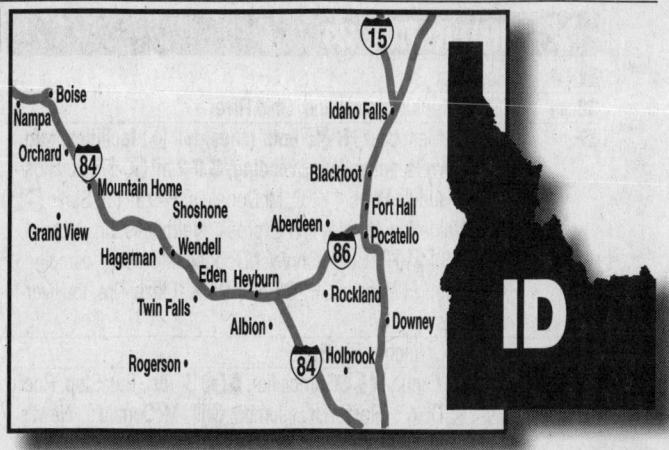

INTERSTATE 90 Cont'd

Exit #	Services
22	ID 97, to St Maries, L Coeur d' Alene Scenic ByWay, Wolf Lodge District, Harrison, **N 1 mi** 🅞 Wolf Lodge Camping, **S** 🅞 Lake Coeur d'Alene RV Park, Squaw Bay Resort (7mi)
20.5mm	Lake Coeur d' Alene
17	Mullan Trail Rd
15	Lp 90, Sherman Ave, Coeur d' Alene, **N** 🅞 forest info, Lake Coeur D' Alene RA/HS, **S** 🅖 Exxon/dsl, Tesoro/dsl/LP, Texaco 🍴 Jeffrey's Rest., Jimmy's Cafe, Michael D's Eatery, O'Shay's Rest., Roger's Burgers, Subway, Zip's Rest. 🏠 Bates Motel, BudgetSaver Motel, Cedar Motel/RV park, El Rancho Motel, Flaming Motel, Holiday Motel, Japan House Suites, La Quinta, State Motel 🅞 auto repair, Peterson's Foods, tourist info
14	15th St, Coeur d' Alene, **S** 🅖 TAJ Mart 🅞 Jordon's Grocery
13	4th St, Coeur d' Alene, **N** 🅖 A&D/dsl 🍴 Atilano's Mexican, Baskin Robbins, Carl's Jr, Davis Donuts, Denny's, DQ, Fiesta Mexican, IHOP, Jimmy John's, Little Caesars, Original Mongolian BBQ, Panda Express, Satay Bistro, Starbucks, Subway, Taco Time, Uva Trattoria, Wendy's 🏠 Comfort Inn 🅞 AutoZone, BigLots, CarQuest, Costco/gas, Hastings Books, NAPA, Radio Shack, same as 12, Schwab Tire, **S** 🅖 Exxon/dsl 🍴 Thai Bamboo
12	US 95, to Sandpoint, Moscow, **N** 🅖 Exxon/dsl, Holiday/dsl, Mobil/dsl 🍴 Applebee's, Arby's, Buffalo Wild Wings, Burger King, Cafe Rio, Chili's, Del Taco, Dragon House Chinese, Elmer's, Golden Corral, JB's Rest., Jimmy John's, MacKenzie River Pizza, McDonald's, Olive Garden, Panda Express, Papa Murphy's, Pizza Hut, Qdoba, Red Lobster, Skipper's, Taco Bell, Tomato St., TX Roadhouse 🏠 Best Western, Guesthouse Inn, Motel 6, Quality Inn, Shilo Suites, Super 8 🅞 $Tree, Albertson's, AT&T, Best Buy, Buick/GMC, Cadillac, Cour d' Alene RV, Discount Tire, Ford/Lincoln, Fred Meyer/dsl, Grocery Outlet, Home Depot, JC Penney, Jo-Ann Fabrics, Kia, K-Mart, Kohl's, Michael's, Natural Grocers, O'Reilly Parts, PetCo, Ross, RVs NW, Safeway/dsl, Sears/auto, Subaru, Super 1 Foods, Target, TireRama, TJ Maxx, Toyota/Scion, Tuesday Morning, U-Haul, URGENT CARE, Verizon, Walgreens, Walmart/Subway **S** 🅖 Conoco/dsl, Tesoro 🍴 Asian Twist, Jack-in-the-Box, Jamba Juice, Papa Murphy's, Qdoba Mexican, Quiznos, Schlotzsky's, Shari's, Starbucks 🏠 La Quinta 🅞 🅷, Albertson's, AT&T, GNC, Rite Aid, same as 13, Shop-KO/drugs, Staples
11	Northwest Blvd, **N** 🅖 Conoco/dsl 🍴 Jack-in-the-Box, Subway 🅞 Lowe's, WinCo Foods, **S** 🅖 Exxon/dsl, Texaco 🍴 Azteca Mexican, Bullman's Woodfired Pizza, Coldstone, McDonald's, Outback Steaks, Porky G's BBQ, Red Robin, SF Sourdough, Starbucks, Ugly Fish Rest. 🏠 Days Inn, Hampton Inn, Holiday Inn Express, Springhill Suites 🅞 🅷, Honda, Riverwalk RV Park, Verizon
8.5mm	**Welcome Ctr/weigh sta eb, full ♿ facilities, info, litter barrels, petwalk, 🅒, 🏠 🆁🆂 both lanes**
7	ID 41, to Rathdrum, Spirit Lake, **N** 🅖 76/dsl 🍴 Burger King, Del Taco, La Cocina Mexican, NY Pizza, Papa Murphy's, Pita Pit, Pizza Factory, Quiznos, Sonic, Starbucks, Subway, Wendy's 🅞 $Tree, AT&T, auto repair, Chevrolet, Chrysler/Dodge/Jeep, Couer d'Alene RV Park, Hyundai, Mazda, Nissan, Radio Shack, VW, Walmart/Subway **S** 🅖 Chevron/dsl, Coleman/dsl

Exit #	Services
7	Continued 🍴 A&W/KFC, Capone's Grill, DQ 🏠 Comfort Inn 🅞 Robins RV Ctr, truck repair, Verizon, vet
6	Seltice Way, **N** 🅖 7-11 🍴 La Cabana Mexican, Paul Bunyan Burgers, Pizza Hut 🅞 NAPA, Super 1 Foods, Walgreens, **S** 🅖 Conoco/dsl/LP 🍴 Denny's, Fuki Japanese, Lide St Cafe, Little Caesars, McDonald's, Moons Mongolian, Old European Cafe, Rancho Viejo Mexican, Taco Bell 🅞 Ace Hardware, O'Reilly Parts, TireRama, Trading Co Foods, USPO, vet
5	Lp 90, Spokane St, Treaty Rock HS, **N** 🅖 76/dsl, Exxon/dsl 🍴 Corner Cafe, Domino's, Hunter's Rest., Rob's Seafood/burgers, Subway, WhiteHouse Grill 🅞 AutoZone, Blue Dog RV Ctr, Meineke, Perfection Tire/repair, Schwab Tire, **S** 🅖 Handy Mart/Pacific Pride/dsl 🏠 Red Lion Inn 🅞 visitors ctr
2	Pleasant View Rd, **N** 🅖 ⓕ FLYING J/Conoco/Subway/dsl/LP/scales/24hr, Exxon/dsl, ◀Loves▶/Carl's Jr/dsl/scales/24hr 🍴 McDonald's, Toro Viejo Mexican 🏠 Silver Stone Inn 🅞 RV/truckwash, Suntree RV Park, **S** 🅖 Exxon/dsl 🍴 Zip's Drive-in 🏠 Riverbend Inn, Sleep Inn 🅞 dogtrack
1	Beck Rd, **N** 🅞 Cabela's, Walmart/Subway, **S** 🅞 greyhound track
0mm	Idaho/Washington state line

INTERSTATE 184 (Boise)

Exit #	Services
6mm	**I-184 begins/ends on 13th St, downtown,** 🅖 Shell 🍴 5 Guys Burgers, Chandler's Steaks, PF Chang's 🏠 Hampton Inn, Safari Inn, The Grove 🅞 Office Depot, USPO
5	River St (from eb), **W** 🅖 Chevron 🍴 McDonald's 🅞 Ford
4.5mm	Boise River
3	Fairview Ave, to US 20/26 E, **W** 🍴 Joe's Crabshack, McDonald's, Tepanyaki Japanese 🏠 Boise Inn, Budget Inn, Riverside Hotel, Shiloh Inn 🅞 Commercial Tire
2	Curtis Rd, to Garden City, **E** 🅖 Shell 🏠 Rodeway Inn 🅞 🅷
1b a	Cole Rd, Franklin Rd, **E** 🅖 Chevron/Subway 🏠 Harrison Hotel 🅞 Acura/Honda, Dodge, Jaguar, Land Rover, Volvo, **W** 🅖 Sinclair 🍴 Cafe Ole, Cafe Rio, Carl's Jr, Cheesecake Factory, Chili's, Hooters, Jack-in-the-Box, Jalapeno's, Keva Juice, Old Chicago Pizza, Olive Garden, Quiznos, Red Lobster, Red Robin, Shari's, Sizzler, Smash Burger, Starbucks, TGIFriday's, Wendy's 🏠 Ameritel, Candlewood Suites, Residence Inn 🅞 AT&T, Audi/VW, Best Buy, Cabela's, Dillard's, JC Penney, Kohl's, Macy's, mall, Michael's, Office Depot, Old Navy, PetCo, Petsmart, Ross, Sears/auto, Target, TJ Maxx, Verizon, vet
0mm	**I-184 begins/ends on I-84, exit 49.**

= gas = food = lodging = other = rest stop Copyright 2015 - the Next EXIT ®

INTERSTATE 24

Exit #	Services
38mm	Illinois/Kentucky state line, Ohio River
37	US 45, Metropolis, N both lanes, full facilities, info, litter barrels, petwalk, vending, S 0-2 mi BP/Quiznos/dsl Huddle House, KFC, McDonald's, Pizza Hut, Sonic Best Value Inn, Holiday Inn Express, Metropolis Inn, Motel 6, Super 8 , Buick/Chrysler/Dodge/GMC/Jeep, camping, Chevrolet, Ft Massac SP, O'Reilly Parts, Plaza Tire, to Riverboat Casino
27	to New Columbia, Big Bay
16	IL 146, Vienna, N Gambit Inn, S BP/dsl, FastStop, Roc/dsl Dolly's Rest., DQ, Jumbo Grill, McDonald's, Newt's Pizza, Subway Limited Inn
14	US 45, Vienna, S camping
7	to Goreville, Tunnel Hill, N Fast Stop/dsl winery, S camping, to Ferne Clyffe SP
1	I-57, N to Chicago, S to Memphis. I-24 begins/ends on I-57, exit 44.

INTERSTATE 39

Exit #	Services
	I-39 and I-90 run together into Wisconsin. See Illinois Interstate 90, exits 15mm through 1.
122b a	US 20 E, Harrison Ave, to Belvidere, W Mobil, Road Ranger/Subway/dsl Arby's, Bergner's, Burger King, DQ, Granite City Rest., Lung Fung, Rosati's Pizza, Sonic, Taco Bell, TGIFriday's Barnes&Noble, BMW, Buick/Chevrolet/GMC, Collier RV Ctr, Goodyear/auto, Harley-Davidson, JC Penney, Macy's, mall, Menards, Schnuck's Foods/gas, Sears/auto, Tires+, vet, VW, Walgreens, last nb exit before toll rd
119	US 20 W, Alpine Rd, to Rockford
116.5mm	Kishwaukee River
115	Baxter Rd, E Shell/Subway/dsl/scales/24hr/@
111	IL 72, to Monroe Center, E BP/Sunrise Family Rest./dsl/24hr, Marathon (1mi)
104	IL 64, to Oregon, Sycamore, W Grubsteakers Rest/truck parking (2mi)
99	IL 38, to De Kalb, Rochelle, W 0-2 mi Murphy USA/dsl, Petro/Iron Skillet/dsl/scales/RV Dump/@, Phillips 66/dsl, Road Ranger/Subway/dsl/scales/24hr, Shell/dsl Arby's, Butterfly Rest., Culver's, DQ, Jimmy John's, Little Ceasar's, McDonald's, New China, Pizza Hut, Subway, Taco Bell, Wendy's Comfort Inn, Holiday Inn Express, Red Roof Inn, Super 8 , $General, Blue Beacon, GNC, O'Reilly Parts, Sullivan's Foods, Verizon, Walgreens, Walmart
97b a	I-88 tollway, to Moline, Rock Island, Chicago
93	Steward
87	US 30, to Sterling, Rock Falls, E to Shabbona Lake SP, W Yogi Bear Camping (16mi)
84.5mm	both lanes, full facilities, litter barrels, petwalk, phones, playground, vending
82	Paw Paw, E 3 mi Casey's (3mi), W many wind turbines
72	US 34, to Mendota, Earlville, W BP/Cindy's/dsl/scales/24hr, Road Ranger/dsl/scales/24hr KFC/Taco Bell, McDonald's Comfort Inn, Super 8/truck parking ,
67.5mm	Little Vermilion River
66	US 52, Troy Grove, E KOA (1mi)
62.5mm	Tomahawk Creek
59b a	I-80, E to Chicago, W to Des Moines
57	US 6, to Peru, La Salle, W 1-2 mi Casey's Daniel's Motel city park

56mm	Abraham Lincoln Mem Bridge, Illinois River
54	Oglesby, E BP/dsl, Casey's, Phillips 66/dsl, Shell Burger King, Delaney's Rest., KFC/Taco Bell, McDonald's, Root Beer Stand, Subway Best Western, Days Inn Starved Rock SP, W Loves/Hardee's/dsl/scales/24hr
52	IL 251, to La Salle, Peru
51	IL 71, to Hennepin, Oglesby
48	Tonica, E Casey's city park
41	IL 18, to Streator, Henry
35	IL 17, to Wenona, Lacon, E BP/dsl, Casey's (2mi), Fast&Fresh/Burger King/dsl/RV dump Subway, Sunrise Rest. Super 8/truck parking NAPA Autocare
27	to Minonk, E Casey's (2mi), /Road Ranger/Subway/Woody's Rest./dsl/24hr Motel 6 NAPA
22	IL 116, to Peoria, Benson
14	US 24, to El Paso, Peoria, E Freedom/dsl, Shell/Subway/dsl/24hr Casey's/dsl, DQ, Hardee's, McDonald's, Woody's Family Rest. Days Inn Buick/Chevrolet/GMC, city park, Ford, IGA Foods, USPO, W Monical's Pizza Super 8 $General, Hickory Hill Camping (4mi), PROMPT CARE
9mm	Mackinaw River
8	IL 251, Lake Bloomington Rd, E Lake Bloomington, W Evergreen Lake, RV camping, to Comlara Park
5	Hudson, E 1 mi Casey's/dsl
2	US 51 bus, Bloomington, Normal
0mm	I-39 begins/ends on I-55, exit 164. Services located N on I-55, exit 165 E BP/Circle K/24hr, Mobil/Arby's/dsl, Qik-n-EZ, Shell/Burger King/24hr A&W/KFC, Denny's, McDonald's, Moe's SW Grill, Pizza Hut, Smoothie King, Steak'n Shake, Subway, Uncle Tom's Pancakes, Wendy's Best Western, Motel 6, Super 8 , $General, $Tree, Discount Tire, Schnucks Foods, to Ill St U, Walgreens, W dsl repair

INTERSTATE 55

Exit #	Services
295mm	I-55 begins/ends on US 41, Lakeshore Dr, in Chicago.
293a	to Cermak Rd (from nb)
292	I-90/94, W to Chicago, E to Indiana
290	Damen Ave, Ashland Ave (no EZ nb return), E Marathon, Shell Target
289	to California Ave (no EZ nb return), E Citgo, Speedway/dsl
288	Kedzie Ave, (from sb no ez return), E Citgo
287	Pulaski Rd, E Mobil/dsl, Shell Burger King, Domino's, Quiznos, Subway Advance Parts, Aldi Foods, Dodge, Family$, Honda, Pete's Mkt, Staples, Target, Walgreens
286	IL 50, Cicero Ave, E Citgo/dsl, Marathon, Mobil Burger King, Dunkin Donuts, JJ Fish, McDonald's, Pepe's Mexican, Popeye's, Starbucks, Subway Family$, O'Reilly Parts, to , Walgreens
285	Central Ave, E BP/dsl, Citgo, Marathon/Dunkin Donuts Burger King, Donald's HotDogs
283	IL 43, Harlem Ave, E Shell Baskin-Robbins/Dunkin Donuts, Burger King, Domino's, El Pollo Loco, Little Caesars, Portillo HotDogs, Subway AT&T, AutoZone, Fannie May Candies, Walgreens
282b a	IL 171, 1st Ave, W Brookfield Zoo, Mayfield Park
279b	US 12, US 20, US 45, La Grange Rd, W 0-2 mi BP, Mobil, Shell Al's Beef, Applebee's, Arby's, Baskin-Robbins/Dunkin Donuts, Boston Mkt, Brown's Chicken, Burger King, Cafe Salsa, Jimmy John's, Ledo's Pizza, LoneStar Steaks, McDonald's, Nancy's Pizza, NoNno's Pizza, Old Country Buffet, Panda Express, Pizza Hut, Popeye's, Subway, Taco Bell,

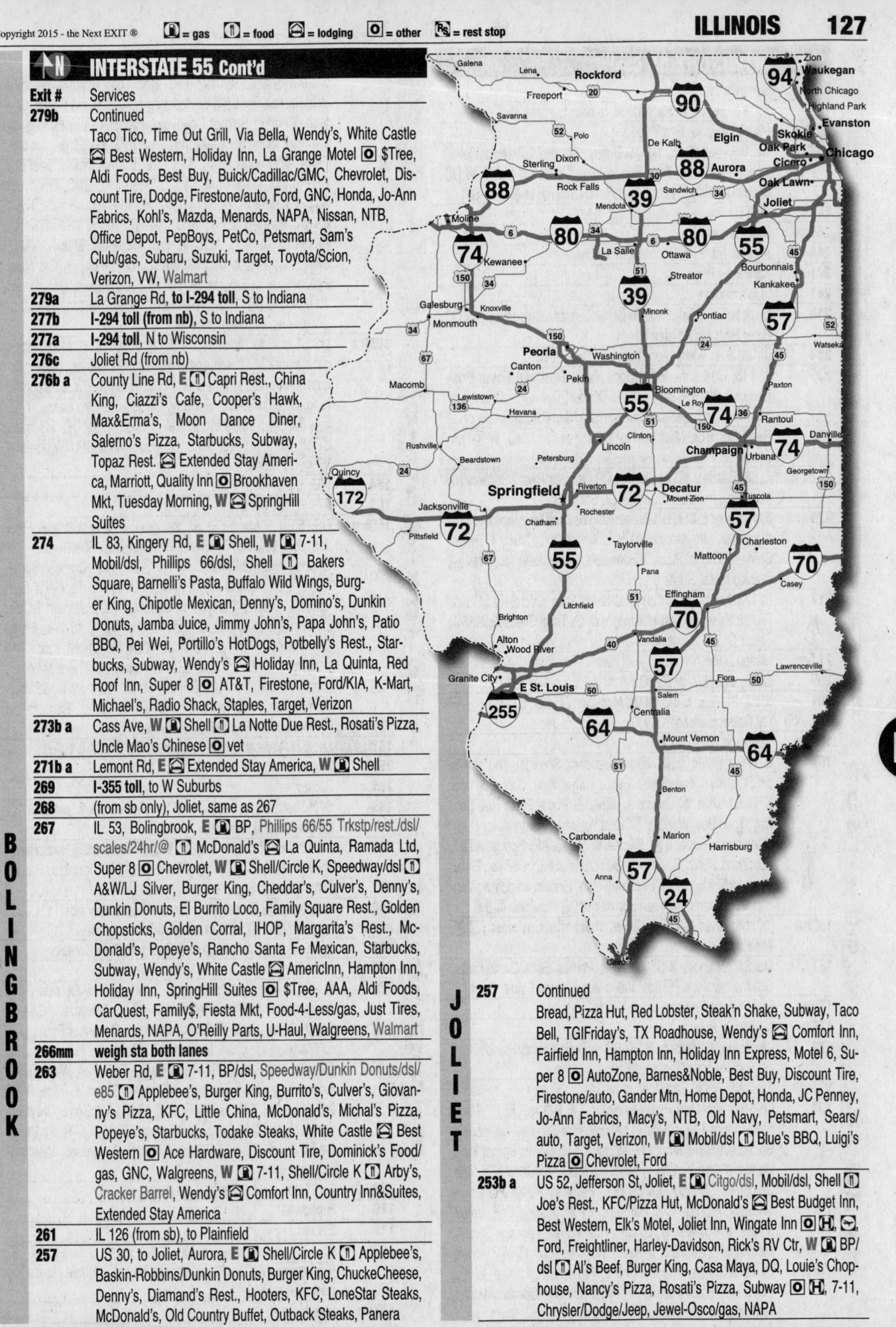

INTERSTATE 55 Cont'd

Exit #	Services
279b	Continued Taco Tico, Time Out Grill, Via Bella, Wendy's, White Castle 🏨 Best Western, Holiday Inn, La Grange Motel ⊙ $Tree, Aldi Foods, Best Buy, Buick/Cadillac/GMC, Chevrolet, Discount Tire, Dodge, Firestone/auto, Ford, GNC, Honda, Jo-Ann Fabrics, Kohl's, Mazda, Menards, NAPA, Nissan, NTB, Office Depot, PepBoys, PetCo, Petsmart, Sam's Club/gas, Subaru, Suzuki, Target, Toyota/Scion, Verizon, VW, Walmart
279a	La Grange Rd, to I-294 toll, S to Indiana
277b	I-294 toll (from nb), S to Indiana
277a	I-294 toll, N to Wisconsin
276c	Joliet Rd (from nb)
276b a	County Line Rd, E 🍴 Capri Rest., China King, Ciazzi's Cafe, Cooper's Hawk, Max&Erma's, Moon Dance Diner, Salerno's Pizza, Starbucks, Subway, Topaz Rest. 🏨 Extended Stay America, Marriott, Quality Inn ⊙ Brookhaven Mkt, Tuesday Morning, W 🏨 SpringHill Suites
274	IL 83, Kingery Rd, E 🅿 Shell, W 🅿 7-11, Mobil/dsl, Phillips 66/dsl, Shell 🍴 Bakers Square, Barnelli's Pasta, Buffalo Wild Wings, Burger King, Chipotle Mexican, Denny's, Domino's, Dunkin Donuts, Jamba Juice, Jimmy John's, Papa John's, Patio BBQ, Pei Wei, Portillo's HotDogs, Potbelly's Rest., Starbucks, Subway, Wendy's 🏨 Holiday Inn, La Quinta, Red Roof Inn, Super 8 ⊙ AT&T, Firestone, Ford/KIA, K-Mart, Michael's, Radio Shack, Staples, Target, Verizon
273b a	Cass Ave, W 🅿 Shell 🍴 La Notte Due Rest., Rosati's Pizza, Uncle Mao's Chinese ⊙ vet
271b a	Lemont Rd, E 🏨 Extended Stay America, W 🅿 Shell
269	I-355 toll, to W Suburbs
268	(from sb only), Joliet, same as 267
267	IL 53, Bolingbrook, E 🅿 BP, Phillips 66/55 Trkstp/rest./dsl/scales/24hr/@ 🍴 McDonald's 🏨 La Quinta, Ramada Ltd, Super 8 ⊙ Chevrolet, W 🅿 Shell/Circle K, Speedway/dsl 🍴 A&W/LJ Silver, Burger King, Cheddar's, Culver's, Denny's, Dunkin Donuts, El Burrito Loco, Family Square Rest., Golden Chopsticks, Golden Corral, IHOP, Margarita's Rest., McDonald's, Popeye's, Rancho Santa Fe Mexican, Starbucks, Subway, Wendy's, White Castle 🏨 AmericInn, Hampton Inn, Holiday Inn, SpringHill Suites ⊙ $Tree, AAA, Aldi Foods, CarQuest, Family$, Fiesta Mkt, Food-4-Less/gas, Just Tires, Menards, NAPA, O'Reilly Parts, U-Haul, Walgreens, Walmart
266mm	weigh sta both lanes
263	Weber Rd, E 🅿 7-11, BP/dsl, Speedway/Dunkin Donuts/dsl/e85 🍴 Applebee's, Burger King, Burrito's, Culver's, Giovanny's Pizza, KFC, Little China, McDonald's, Michal's Pizza, Popeye's, Starbucks, Todake Steaks, White Castle 🏨 Best Western ⊙ Ace Hardware, Discount Tire, Dominick's Food/gas, GNC, Walgreens, W 🅿 7-11, Shell/Circle K 🍴 Arby's, Cracker Barrel, Wendy's 🏨 Comfort Inn, Country Inn&Suites, Extended Stay America
261	IL 126 (from sb), to Plainfield
257	US 30, to Joliet, Aurora, E 🅿 Shell/Circle K 🍴 Applebee's, Baskin-Robbins/Dunkin Donuts, Burger King, ChuckeCheese, Denny's, Diamand's Rest., Hooters, KFC, LoneStar Steaks, McDonald's, Old Country Buffet, Outback Steaks, Panera

Exit #	Services
257	Continued Bread, Pizza Hut, Red Lobster, Steak'n Shake, Subway, Taco Bell, TGIFriday's, TX Roadhouse, Wendy's 🏨 Comfort Inn, Fairfield Inn, Hampton Inn, Holiday Inn Express, Motel 6, Super 8 ⊙ AutoZone, Barnes&Noble, Best Buy, Discount Tire, Firestone/auto, Gander Mtn, Home Depot, Honda, JC Penney, Jo-Ann Fabrics, Macy's, NTB, Old Navy, Petsmart, Sears/auto, Target, Verizon, W 🅿 Mobil/dsl 🍴 Blue's BBQ, Luigi's Pizza ⊙ Chevrolet, Ford
253b a	US 52, Jefferson St, Joliet, E 🅿 Citgo/dsl, Mobil/dsl, Shell 🍴 Joe's Rest., KFC/Pizza Hut, McDonald's 🏨 Best Budget Inn, Best Western, Elk's Motel, Joliet Inn, Wingate Inn ⊙ H, ⊡, Ford, Freightliner, Harley-Davidson, Rick's RV Ctr, W 🅿 BP/dsl 🍴 Al's Beef, Burger King, Casa Maya, DQ, Louie's Chophouse, Nancy's Pizza, Rosati's Pizza, Subway ⊙ H, 7-11, Chrysler/Dodge/Jeep, Jewel-Osco/gas, NAPA

BOLINGBROOK

JOLIET

IL

Exit #	Services
	INTERSTATE 55 Cont'd
251	IL 59 (from nb), to Shorewood, access to same as 253 W
250b a	I-80, W to Iowa, E to Toledo
248	US 6, Joliet, E 🅰 ⛽/Dunkin Donuts/Subway/dsl/24hr, Speedway/dsl 🍴 Taco Burrito King 🏠 Manor Motel, W 🅰 BP/McDonald's 🍴 Lone Star Rest. (2mi) 🅾 to Ill/Mich SP
247	Bluff Rd
245mm	Des Plaines River
244	Arsenal Rd, E 🅾 Exxon/Mobil Refinery
241mm	Kankakee River
241	to Wilmington
240	Lorenzo Rd, E 🅰 BP/dsl W 🅰 Mobil/pizza/dsl/scales/24hr 🍴 River Rest. 🏠 Knights Inn
238	IL 129 S, to Wilmington (from nb), Braidwood
236	IL 113, Coal City, E 🍴 Good Table Rest. 🅾 Fossil Rock Camping, W 🅰 Casey's, Shell/DQ/dsl 🍴 KFC/Taco Bell, Los 3 Burritos, WhistleStop Cafe 🅾 EZ Living RV Ctr
233	Reed Rd, E 🅰 Marathon/dsl 🍴 Jones-sez BBQ, W 🅾 antiques
227	IL 53, Gardner, E 🅰 Casey's 🍴 Gardner Rest., Subway 🅾 $General, truck/tire repair, W 🅾 Shell/dsl
220	IL 47, Dwight, E 🅰 BP/Burger King/dsl, ⛽Loves/Hardee's/dsl/scales/24hr, Marathon/Circle K/dsl/24hr 🍴 Arby's, Dwight Chinese, Dwight Pizza, McDonald's, Pete's Rest., Subway 🏠 Classic Motel, Super 8
217	IL 17, Dwight, E 🅰 Casey's, Shell/Circle K/dsl/24hr 🍴 DQ, Rte 66 Rest. 🅾 Best Hardware, Doc's Drug, Family$, NAPA, ShopKO
213mm	Mazon River
209	Odell, E 🅰 BP 🅾 USPO
201	IL 23, Pontiac, E 0-3 mi 🅰 Marathon 🍴 DQ, La Mex 🅾 4H RV Camp (seasonal) RV Ctr, W 🅾 truck repair
198mm	Vermilion River
197	IL 116, Pontiac, E 🅰 BP/dsl, Freedom, Shell/dsl, Thornton's/dsl 🍴 Arby's, Baby Bull's Rest., Burger King, Cafe Fontana, KFC, LJ Silver, McDonald's, Monical's Pizza, Pizza Hut, Subway, Taco Bell, Wendy's 🏠 Best Western, Fiesta Motel (1mi), Quality Inn, Super 8 🅾 $General, $Tree, Aldi Foods, AT&T, AutoZone, Big R Store, Buick/Chevrolet, Cadillac/GMC, Chrysler/Dodge/Jeep, Firestone/auto, Lincoln, st police, Verizon, Walgreens, Walmart/Subway W 🅰 Mobil/dsl 🅾 H
193mm	📱 both lanes, full 🦽 facilities, litter barrels, petwalk, 📱, 🎮 vending
187	US 24, Chenoa, E 🅰 Casey's, Phillips 66/McDonald's/dsl, Shell/Subway/dsl 🍴 Best Value Inn, Chenoa Family Rest.
179mm	Des Plaines River
178mm	Mackinaw River
178	Lexington, Lexington, E 🅰 BP/McDonalds/dsl, Freedom/dsl 🍴 Subway 🅾 $General, W 🅾 Chevrolet
171	Towanda, E 🅰 FastStop/dsl
167	Lp 55 S Veterans Pkwy, to Normal, E 0-3 mi 🅰 BP/Circle K, Marathon/Circle K/dsl 🍴 Alexander's Steaks, Applebee's, Bandana's BBQ, Biaggi's Ristorante, Bob Evans, Burger King, Carlos O'Kelly's, Chili's, Chipotle Mexican, ChuckeCheese, Coldstone, Destihl Rest., DQ, Fazoli's, Fiesta Ranchera Mexican, FlatTop Grill, Hardee's, IHOP, Jason's Deli, Jimmy John's, Krispy Kreme, Logan's Roadhouse, Lonestar Steaks, McDonald's, Monical's Pizza, Noodles&Co, Olive Garden, Outback Steaks, Panda Express, Panera Bread, Papa John's, Pizza Hut, Pizza Ranch, Popeyes, Potbelly, Qdoba Mexican, Red Lobster, Schlotzsky's, Smashburger, Sonic, Starbucks,

Exit #	Services
167	Continued Steak'n Shake, Subway, Taco Bell, Tony Roma's, Wendy's, Wild Berries Rest. 🏠 Baymont Inn, Candlewood Suites, Chateau, Comfort Suites, Courtyard, Hampton Inn, Holiday Inn Express, Motel 6, Quality Inn, Super8 🅾 H, $Tree, Advance Parts, Aldi Foods, AT&T, AutoZone, Barnes&Noble, Best Buy, Cub Foods, CVS Drug, Dick's, Fresh Mkt, GNC, Goodyear/auto, Gordman's, Hobby Lobby, Home Depot, Honda, Hyundai, JC Penney, Jewel-Osco, Jo-Ann Fabrics, K-Mart, Kohl's, Kroger/dsl, Lowe's, Macy's, mall, Meijer/dsl, Meineke, Menards, Michael's, Midas, Mitsubishi, Office Depot, Old Navy, PetCo, Sam's Club/gas, Schnuck's Foods, Sears/auto, Target, TJ Maxx, to 📱, Tuesday Morning, Tuffy, Verizon, Von Maur, Walgreens, Walmart/Subway
165b a	US 51 bus, to Bloomington, E 🅰 BP/Circle K, Mobil/Arby's/dsl, Qik-n-EZ, Shell/Burger King/dsl 🍴 Denny's, Dunkin Donuts, McDonald's, Moe's SW Grill, Rosati's Pizza, Smoothie King, Steak'n Shake, Subway, Uncle Tom's Pancakes, Wendy's 🏠 Best Value Inn, Motel 6, Super 8 🅾 H, $General, $Tree, Discount Tire, Schuncks Foods, to Ill St U, Walgreens, W 🅾 dsl repair
164	I-39, US 51, N to Peru
163	I-74 W, to Peoria
160b a	US 150, IL 9, Market St, Bloomington, E 🅰 BP/Circle K, Freedom/dsl, ⛽/Wendy's/dsl/scales/24hr, Shell/repair, TA/Country Pride/dsl/scales/24hr/@ 🍴 Arby's, Cracker Barrel, Culver's, JJ Fish&Chicken, KFC, McDonald's, Popeye's, Subway, Taco Bell 🏠 Days Inn, EconoLodge, Hawthorn Suites, La Quinta, Quality Suites, Red Roof Inn 🅾 H, Advance Parts, Blue Beacon, Family$, Peterbilt, W 🅰 Marathon/Circle K/dsl, Murphy USA/dsl 🍴 Bob Evans, Fiesta Ranchera Mexican, Steak'n Shake/24hr 🏠 Comfort Suites, Country Inn&Suites, Fairfield Inn, Hampton Inn, Holiday Inn Express, Ramada Ltd 🅾 Aldi Foods, Farm&Fleet, Walmart
157b	Lp 55 N, Veterans Pkwy, Bloomington, E 🅾 H, to 📱
157a	I-74 E, to Indianapolis, US 51 to Decatur
154	Shirley
149	W 📱 both lanes, full 🦽 facilities, litter barrels, petwalk, 📱 🎮 playground, vending
145	US 136, E 🅾 Quality RV Ctr, W 🅰 Dixie/⛽/Road Ranger/Subway/dsl/scales/24hr, Shell-dsl 🍴 McDonald's, Rte 66 Drive Thru 🏠 Super 8
140	Atlanta, E 🅾 RV camping (3mi), W 🅰 Casey's/dsl 🍴 Country-Aire Rest. 🏠 Atlanta Inn 🅾 $General, NAPA
133	Lp 55, Lincoln, E 2 mi 🅾 H, Camp-A-While Camping
127	I-155 N, to Peoria
126	IL 10, IL 121 S, Lincoln, E 0-2 mi 🅰 BP/Arby's/dsl/24hr, Thornton's/⛽/dsl/scales/24hr 🍴 Bonanza Steaks, Burger King, Cracker Barrel, Culver's, Daphne's Rest., DQ, El Mazatlan Mexican, Hardee's, McDonald's, Pizza Hut, Rio Grande Grill, Steak'n Shake, Subway, Taco Bell, Wendy's 🏠 EconoLodge, Hampton Inn, Holiday Inn Express, Super 8 🅾 H, $General, $Tree, Aldi Foods, AT&T, AutoZone, Chrysler/Dodge/Jeep, CVS Drug, Ford/Lincoln, Kroger, O'Reilly Parts, Radio Shack, Russell Stover, Verizon, Walgreens, Walmart/Subway
123	Lp 55, to Lincoln, E 🅾 H
119	Broadwell
115	Elkhart
109	IL 123, Williamsville, E 🅰 Casey's 🍴 Subway, W 🅰 ⛽Loves/McDonalds/dsl/scales/24hr 🍴 Huddle House 🅾 New Salem SHS
107mm	weigh sta sb

BLOOMINGTON

LINCOLN

PONTIAC

NORMAL

IL

INTERSTATE 55 Cont'd

Exit #	Services
105	Lp 55, to Sherman, **W** 🆁 Casey's 🍴 Cancun Mexican, Fairlane Diner, Fire&Ale Grill, Ricco's Pizza, Sam's Too Pizza, Subway 🅾 County Mkt Foods, hist sites, Military Museum, repair, Riverside Park Campground, to Prairie Capitol Conv Ctr, Verizon, Walgreens
103mm	🅿🆂 sb, full 🚻 facilities, litter barrels, petwalk, 🅲, 🖼 vending
102mm	Sangamon River
102mm	🅿🆂 nb, full 🚻 facilities, litter barrels, petwalk, 🅲, 🖼 vending
100b	IL 54, Sangamon Ave, Springfield, **W** 🆁 BP/Circle K, Marathon/Circle K, Murphy USA/dsl, Shell/dsl 🍴 Arby's, Buffalo Wild Wings, Burger King, Culver's, DQ, Hickory River BBQ, Jimmy John's, McDonald's, Parkway Cafe, Penn Sta Subs, Royal Buffet, Sonic, Steak'n Shake, Taco Bell, Thai Basil, Wendy's, Wings Etc, Xochimilco Mexican, Yummy House 🏨 Northfield Suites, Ramada 🅾 🏨, Aldi Foods, AT&T, GNC, Harley-Davidson, Lowe's, Menards, to Vet Mem, Verizon, Walmart/Subway
100a	Il 54, E to Clinton, **E** 🆁 Road Ranger/🛻/Subway/dsl/scales/24hr 🅾 Kenworth/Ryder/Volvo, truckwash
98b	I-72, IL 97, Springfield, **W** 🆁 BP/Circle K, Casey's, Shell/dsl 🍴 Chesapeake Seafood House, Freddy's Steakburger, Hardee's, Mario's Pizza, McDonald's, Starbucks, Subway 🏨 Best Western, Lincoln's Lodge 🅾 🏨, city park, Ford Trucks, K-Mart/Little Caesar's, to Capitol Complex, Walgreens
98a	I-72 E, US 36 E, to Decatur
96b a	IL 29 N, S Grand Ave, Springfield, **W** 🆁 Marathon/dsl, Road Ranger/dsl 🍴 Burger King, Godfather's, Popeye's 🏨 Red Roof Inn, Super 8 🅾 $General, Advance Parts, AutoZone, Buick/GMC, Hyundai, JC Penney, museum, O'Reilly Parts, Shop'n Save
94	Stevenson Dr, Springfield, **E** KOA (7mi), **W** 🆁 BP/Circle K/Dsl, Mobil/Subway/dsl, Shell/dsl 🍴 Applebee's, Arby's, Bob Evans, Cancun Rest., Cheddar's, Denny's, Gallina Pizza, Hardee's, Hooters, IHOP, La Fiesta Mexican, LJ Silver, Luca Pizza, McDonald's, Outback Steaks, Panera Bread, Papa John's, Red Lobster, Smokey Bones BBQ, Steak'n Shake, Taste of Thai 🏨 Candlewood Suites, Comfort Suites, Country Inn Suites, Crowne Plaza, Drury Inn, Hampton Inn, Hilton Garden, Holiday Inn Express, Microtel, Residence Inn 🅾 $General, auto repair, BigLots, CVS Drug, GNC, Walgreens, zoo (4mi)
92b a	I-72 W, US 36 W, 6th St, Springfield, **W** 🆁 Road Ranger/dsl, Thornton's 🍴 Arby's, Burger King, Chadito's Tacos, Cozy Drive In, Golden Corral, Jimmy John's, KFC, McDonald's, New China, Pizza Hut, Sgt. Pepper's Cafe, Starbucks, Subway, Taco Bell 🏨 Comfort Inn, La Quinta, Route 66, Springfield Lodge 🅾 🏨, Aldi, AutoZone, CarX, County Mkt Foods, Lincoln, Mazda, Walgreens, Walmart/McDonald's
90	Toronto Rd, **E** 🆁 Qik-n-EZ/Wendy's/dsl, Shell/Circle K 🍴 Antonio's Pizza, China Express, Cracker Barrel, Head West Subs, Hen House, McDonald's, Subway, Taco Bell 🏨 Baymont Inn, Day's Inn, Motel 6, **W** 🆁 🛻/Road Ranger/dsl/24hr
89mm	Lake Springfield
88	E Lake Dr, Chatham, **E** 🅾 KOA, to Lincoln Mem Garden/Nature Ctr, **W** 🅾 JJ RV Park/camping (2mi)
83	Glenarm, **W** 🅾 JJ RV Park/camping (4mi)

Exit #	Services
82	IL 104, to Pawnee, **E** 🅾 to Sangchris Lake SP, **W** 🆁 Mobil/Auburn Trvl Ctr/Subway/scales/dsl/rest/24hr 🍴 Myra's Rest 🅾 antiques/crafts
80	Hist 66, Divernon, **W** 🅾 antiques
72	Farmersville, **W** 🆁 Phillips 66/Subway/dsl/24hr, Shell/24hr
65mm	🅿🆂 both lanes, full 🚻 facilities, litter barrels, petwalk, 🅲, 🖼 playground, vending
63	IL 48, IL 127, to Raymond
60	IL 108, to Carlinville, **E** 🅾 Kamper Kampanion RV Park, **W** 🆁 Shell/dsl/LP/café 🏨 Magnuson Grand Hotel/cafe 🅾 antiques, to Blackburn Coll
56mm	weigh sta nb
52	IL 16, Hist 66, Litchfield, **E** 🆁 BP, Casey's, Conoco/Jack-in-the-Box/dsl, Faststop/deli/dsl/scales, Murphy USA/dsl, Shell 🍴 A&W/LJ Silver, Arby's, Ariston Café, Burger King, China Town, Denny's, DQ, El Rancherito Mexican, Jubelt's Rest., KFC, Maverick Steaks, McDonald's, Pizza Hut, Ruby Tuesday, Subway, Taco Bell, Wendy's 🏨 Best Value Inn, Hampton Inn, Holiday Inn Express, Quality Inn, Super 8 🅾 🏨, $General, $Tree, Aldi Foods, AT&T, Buick/Cadillac/Chevrolet/GMC, Ford, Goodyear/auto, IGA Foods, NAPA, O'Reilly Parts, Radio Shack, Rte 66 Museum, Verizon, vet, Walgreens, Walmart/Subway **W** 🅾 st police
44	IL 138, to Benld, Mt Olive, **E** 🍴 Crossroads Diner, Sunset Rest. 🅾 Mother Jones Mon
41	to Staunton, **E** 🅾 Country Classic Cars, **W** 🆁 Casey's 🍴 DQ, Las Cabanas Mexican 🏨 Super 8 🅾 🏨, $General
37	Livingston, New Douglas, **W** 🆁 Shell/dsl 🍴 Gasperoni's Café 🏨 Country Inn/cafe 🅾 IGA Foods, NAPA AutoCare, USPO
33	IL 4, to Staunton, Worden
30	IL 140, Hamel, **E** 🆁 Loves/McDonald's/Subway/dsl/scales/24hr 🏨 Innkeeper Motel, **W** 🆁 Shell 🍴 Weezy's Grill
28mm	🅿🆂 both lanes, full 🚻 facilities, litter barrels, petwalk, 🅲, 🖼 vending
23	IL 143, Edwardsville, **E** 🆁 Phillips 66/dsl, **W** 🅾 Red Barn Camping (apr-oct)
20b	I-270 W, to Kansas City
20a	I-70 E, to Indianapolis
I-55 S and I-70 W run together 18 mi	
18	IL 162, to Troy, **E** 🆁 Casey's/dsl, Phillips 66/Circle K/dsl, 🛻/Arby's/dsl/scales/24hr, TA/BP/Country Pride/dsl/scales/24hr/@, ZX 🍴 Alfonzo's Pizza, Burger King, China King, Domino's, DQ, Dunkin Donuts, El Potro Mexican, Jack-in-the-Box, Little Caesar's, McDonald's/playplace, Pizza Hut, Subway, Troy Rest. 🅾 🏨, $General, Ace Hardware, Speedco, SuperValu Foods, truckwash, USPO, vet, Walgreens, **W** 🆁 Mobil 🍴 Cracker Barrel, Joe's Pizza, Taco Bell 🏨 Holiday Inn Express, Motel 6, Red Roof Inn, Super 8 🅾 Freightliner, Verizon

(left margin, vertical) S P R I N G F I E L D

(right margin, vertical) L I T C H F I E L D

(right edge tab) IL

⬆N INTERSTATE 55 Cont'd

Exit #	Services
17	US 40 E, to Troy, to St Jacob
15b a	IL 159, Maryville, Collinsville, E 0-2 mi 🅟 Phillips 66/Circle K/ dsl, Shell, Zx Gas 🍴 Asia Garden, Carisillo's Mexican, KFC, McDonald's, Sonic, Subway ⊙ $General, Advance Parts, Aldi Foods, AutoZone, CVS Drug, Ford/Lincoln, O'Reilly Parts, vet, Walgreens, W 🏠 Rodeway Inn
14mm	weigh sta sb
11	IL 157, Collinsville, E 🅟 Casey's 🍴 A&W/LJ Silver, Denny's, Golden Corral, Little Caesar's, McDonald's, Penn Sta Subs, Qdoba Mexican, St Louis Bread Co, Starbucks, Waffle House, Wendy's 🏠 Best Value Inn ⊙ AT&T, Dobbs Tire, GNC, Home Depot, Midas, Radio Shack, Verizon, Walgreens, Walmart/Subway W 🅟 Motomart/dsl/24hr 🍴 Applebee's, Arby's, Bandana's BBQ, Bob Evans, Burger King, Culver's, DQ, Pizza Hut, Ponderosa, Porter's Steaks, Ruby Tuesday, Steak'n Shake, White Castle/24hr, Zapata's Mexican 🏠 Comfort Inn, Days Inn, DoubleTree Inn, Drury Inn, Extended Stay Suites, Fairfield Inn, Hampton Inn, Super 8 ⊙ Buick/GMC, st police
10	I-255, S to Memphis, N to I-270
9	Black Lane (from nb, no return), E Fairmount RaceTrack
6	IL 111, Great River Rd, Fairmont City, E 🅟 Phillips 66 🏠 Relax Inn, Royal Budget Inn ⊙ auto repair, W ⊙ Horseshoe SP
5mm	motorist callboxes begin at 1/2 mi intervals nb
4b a	IL 203, Granite City, E 🅟 BP/dsl 🏠 Western Inn, W 🅟 🅿ILOT/Subway/Taco Bell/dsl/scales/24hr/@ ⊙ Gateway Int Raceway
3	Exchange Ave
2b	3rd St
2a	M L King Bridge, to downtown E St Louis
2	I-64 E, IL 3 N, St Clair Ave
1	IL 3, to Sauget (from sb)
I-55 N and I-70 E run together 18 mi	
0mm	Illinois/Missouri state line, Mississippi River

⬆N INTERSTATE 57

Exit #	Services
358mm	I-94 E to Indiana. I-57 begins/ends on I-94, exit 63 in Chicago.
357	IL 1, Halsted St, E 🅟 BP, Mobil ⊙ auto repair, W 🅟 Citgo/ dsl, Shell/Dunkin Donuts 🍴 McDonald's, Shark's, Subway ⊙ Walgreens
355	111th St, Monterey Ave, W 🅟 BP, Citgo
354	119th St, W 🅟 Citgo/Dunkin Donuts 🍴 Chili's, Harold's Chicken, Panda Express, Subway ⊙ $Tree, Jewel-Osco, Marshall's, PetCo, Staples, Target
353	127th St, Burr Oak Ave, E 🅟 Citgo, Marathon, Shell 🍴 Burger King, Dillinger's Drive-In, McDonald's, Wendy's 🏠 Motel 6, Plaza Inn, Red Roof Inn ⊙ H, Ace Hardware, Advance Parts, Aldi Foods, Family$, Walgreens, W 🅟 BP, Citgo/dsl ⊙ JJ Fish&Chicken
352mm	Calumet Sag Channel
350	IL 83, 147th St, Sibley Blvd, E 🅟 Marathon/dsl 🍴 Checker's, Dunkin Donuts, Harold's Chicken, McDonald's, Subway ⊙ Aldi Foods, Family$, O'Reilly Parts, W ⊙ USPO
348	US 6, 159th St, E 🅟 Citgo/dsl, Clark, Marathon/dsl 🍴 Baskin-Robbins/Dunkin Donuts, Burger King, Harold's Chicken, McDonald's, Popeye's, Subway, Taco Bell, White Castle 🏠 Comfort Inn ⊙ $Tree, auto repair, AutoZone, BigLots, Family$, U-Haul, Walgreens, W 🅟 Citgo/dsl, Mobil/dsl

346	167th St, Cicero Ave, to IL 50, E 🅟 BP, Citgo/dsl 🍴 Applebee's, Baskin-Robbins/Dunkin Donuts, Bee's Steaks, Harold's Chicken, McDonald's, Panda Express, Shark's Fish&Chicken, Sonic, Subway, Thom's BBQ, Wendy's 🏠 Best Western Oak Forest ⊙ Radio Shack, Verizon, Walmart/Subway W 🅟 Shell ⊙ 7-11
345b a	I-80, W to Iowa, E to Indiana, to I-294 N toll to Wisconsin
342	Vollmer Rd, E 🅟 Shell/Circle K/dsl ⊙ H,
340b a	US 30, Lincoln Hwy, Matteson, E 🅟 BP, Citgo/dsl 🍴 A&W/ LJ Silver, Afusion Asian, Applebee's, Bocce's Grill, Burger King, ChuckeCheese, Cracker Barrel, Culver's, Dusties Buffet, Fuddrucker's, Hibachi Grill, IHOP, Jimmy John's, KFC, Knock-Outs Rest., McDonald's, Michael's Rest., Mr Benny's Rest., Olive Garden, Panda Express, Panera Bread, Pepe's, Perros Bros Gyros, Pizza Hut, Quiznos, Red Lobster, Shark's, Starbucks, Subway, Taco Bell, Wendy's, White Castle 🏠 Best Value Inn, Country Inn&Suites, Hampton Inn, La Quinta, Matteson Hotel ⊙ $Tree, Aldi Foods, AT&T, Best Buy, Chrysler/Dodge/Jeep, Discount Tire, Dominick's Foods, Firestone/ auto, Home Depot, JC Penney, Marshall's, Menards, NTB, Old Navy, PepBoys, Petsmart, Radio Shack, Sam's Club/gas, Sears/auto, Target, USPO, Verizon, Walgreens, Walmart W ⊙ Buick/Cadillac/GMC, Ford/Lincoln, Honda, Hyundai, Kia, Nissan, Toyota/Scion, Walgreens
339	Sauk Trail, to Richton Park, E 🅟 BP, Citgo/dsl 🍴 Domino's, McDonald's, Uncle John's BBQ/Ribs ⊙ Walgreens
335	Monee, E 🅟 BP/Dunkin Donuts/Subway/dsl, Petro/Iron Skillet/ dsl/e-85/scales/24hr/@, 🅿ILOT/McDonald's/dsl/scales/24hr 🍴 Burger King, Lucky Burrito, Quiznos, Schoops Rest. 🏠 Best Western, Country Host Motel, Red Roof Inn, Super 8 ⊙ Blue Beacon
332mm	Prairie View 🆁🆂 both lanes, full ♿ facilities, info, litter barrels, petwalk, ⊙, 🆖 vending
330mm	weigh sta both lanes
327	to Peotone, E 🅟 Casey's, Shell/Circle K 🍴 Bierstube German, McDonald's/RV parking
322	Manteno, E 🅟 Phillips 66/Subway, Shell/McDonald's 🍴 Jimmy John's, KFC/Pizza Hut/Taco Bell, Monical's Pizza, Wendy's 🏠 Country Inn&Suites, Howard Johnson ⊙ Curves, Harley-Davidson, W 🅟 BP/dsl
315	IL 50, Bradley, E 🅟 F&F, Shell/Circle K/Burger King 🍴 Buffalo Wild Wings, Cracker Barrel, LoneStar Steaks, McDonald's, Red Lobster, Ruby Tuesday, TGIFriday's, Tucci's Rest., White Castle 🏠 Best Inn, Fairfield Inn, Hampton Inn, Holiday Inn Express ⊙ Barnes&Noble, Best Buy, Chrysler/Dodge/Jeep, Dick's, JC Penney, Kohl's, mall, Marshall's, Michael's, PetCo, Petsmart, Sears/auto, Staples, Target, Verizon, Walmart/Subway W 🅟 Phillips 66/dsl, Shell/Circle K/dsl, Speedway/dsl 🍴 Applebee's, Arby's, Bakers Square, Coyote Canyon, Denny's, El Campesino Mexican, IHOP, LJ Silver, Mancino's Pizza, McDonald's, Oberweis Ice Cream, Old Country Buffet, Panda Express, Pizza Hut/Taco Bell, Starbucks, Steak'n Shake, Subway, VIP's Rest., Wendy's 🏠 Motel 6, Quality Inn, Super 8 ⊙ $Tree, Aldi Foods, AutoZone, Brown RV Ctr, Buick/GMC, Chevrolet, Hobby Lobby, Honda, Hyundai, Jo-Ann Fabrics, Kia, K-Mart, Lowe's, Menards, Nissan, to Kankakee River SP, Verizon, vet
312	IL 17, Kankakee, E ⊙ Twin River's Camping, W 🅟 BP/dsl, Marathon/dsl, Shell/Circle K 🍴 Capt Hook's Fish&Chicken, McDonald's/RV parking, PoorBoy Rest. ⊙ H, Advance Parts, auto repair, Family$, Walgreens
310.5mm	Kankakee River

COLLINSVILLE, CHICAGO ; MATTESON, BRADLEY ; IL

K A N K A K E E

INTERSTATE 57 Cont'd

Exit #	Services
308	US 45, US 52, to Kankakee, E ♥Loves/Arby's/dsl/scales/24hr ○ KOA (3mi), W Gas Depot, Speedway/Dunkin Donuts/Subway/dsl El Mexicano, KFC/Taco Bell Fairview Motel, Hilton Garden ○ $Tree, Aldi Foods, Walmart/Subway
302	Chebanse, W ○ truck repair
297	Clifton, W Phillips 66/DQ/dsl CharGrilled Cheeseburgers
293	IL 116, Ashkum, E Shell/Subway/dsl, W Loft Rest. ○ st police, tires
283	US 24, IL 54, Gilman, E Apollo/Marathon/dsl/scales/24hr, K&H Trkstp/BP/dsl/scales/24hr/@, Shell/dsl Burger King, DQ, McDonald's, Monical's Pizza, Red Door Rest. Motel 6, Super 8, W Shell/Subway/dsl
280	IL 54, Onarga, E Casey's, Phillips 66 ○ USPO, W ○ Lake Arrowhead RV camping
272	to Roberts, Buckley
268.5mm	both lanes, full facilities, litter barrels, petwalk, , vending
261	IL 9, Paxton, E 0-1 mi Casey's, Phillips 66/dsl Hardee's, Monical's Pizza, Pizza Hut, Subway ○ Buick/Cadillac/Chevrolet/GMC, Family$, IGA Foods, TrueValue, USPO, W BP, Marathon Country Garden Rest. Paxton Inn
250	US 136, Rantoul, E 0-1 mi BP/Circle K, Casey's/dsl Arby's, Baskin-Robbins/Dunkin Donuts, Burger King, Hardee's, KFC/Taco Bell, LJ Silver, McDonald's, Monical's Pizza, Papa John's, Red Wheel Rest., Subway Best Western, Days Inn, Super 8 ○ $General, camping, Chrysler/Dodge/Jeep, Ford, NAPA, to Chanute AFB, vet, Walgreens, Walmart/Subway
240	Market St, E Road Ranger//McDonald's/dsl/scales ○ D&W Lake Camping/RV Park, Kenworth/Volvo, truck/tire repair
238	Olympian Dr, to Champaign, W Mobil/dsl DQ Microtel ○ RV/dsl repair
237b a	I-74, W to Peoria, E to Urbana
235b	I-72 W, to Decatur
235a	University Ave, to Champaign, E ○ , U of Ill
232	Curtis Rd
229	to Savoy, Monticello, E Marathon/dsl
221.5mm	both lanes, full facilities, litter barrels, petwalk, phones, vending
220	US 45, Pesotum, E ○ st police
212	US 36, Tuscola, E FuelMart/dsl W Phillips 66/Circle K, /Road Ranger/dsl/scales/24hr Amish Land Country Buffet, Big Red Barn Rest., Burger King, Denny's, DQ, McDonald's, Monical's Pizza, Pantry Cafe, Pizza Hut, Subway, Tuscany Steaks Baymont Inn, Holiday Inn Express, Super 8 ○ Ford, IGA Foods, Radio Shack, ShopKO, Tanger Outlets/Famous Brands, Verizon
203	IL 133, Arcola, E Best Western, W Phillips 66/Subway/dsl, Sunrise/dsl DQ, Hen House, La Cazuela's, Mexican, Monical's Pizza Arcola Inn, Comfort Inn, Knights Inn ○ $General, city park, NAPA, Rockome Gardens (5mi), vet
192	CtyRd 1000 N, Rd 18
190b a	IL 16, to Mattoon, E BP/dsl ○ , Fox Ridge SP, to E IL U, W Huck's, Murphy USA/dsl, Phillips 66/Subway/dsl A&W/LJ Silver, Alamo Steaks, Arby's, Buffalo Wild Wings, Cody's Roadhouse, Cracker Barrel, Domino's, Don Sol Mexican, DQ, Fast Freddy's, Jumbo Buffet, KFC, Lee's Chicken, McDonald's/playplace, McHugh's, Papa Murphy's, Pizza Hut,

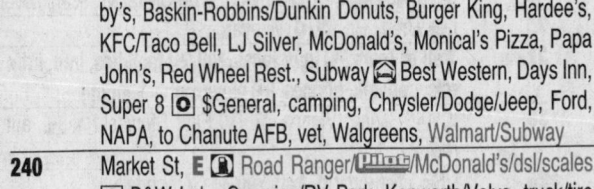

M A T T O O N

Exit #	Services
190b a	Continued Quiznos, Stadium Grill, Steak'n Shake, Super Jumbo Buffet, Taco Bell, Wendy's Baymont Inn, Comfort Suites, Days Inn, Hampton Inn, Holiday Inn Express, Super 8 ○ $General, $Tree, Aldi Foods, BigLots, CVS Drug, Home Depot, JC Penney, Petsmart, Sears, Staples, Verizon, Walgreens, Walmart/Subway
184	US 45, IL 121, to Mattoon, E Phillips 66/Subway/dsl, W McDonald's Budget Inn, Quality Inn ○ to Lake Shelbyville
177	US 45, Neoga, E FuelMart/Subway/dsl/e-85 ○ NAPA, W Casey's (1mi) ○ $General
166.5mm	both lanes, full facilities, litter barrels, petwalk, phones, vending
163	I-70 E, to Indianapolis

I-57 S and I-70 W run together 6 mi

Exit #	Services
162	US 45, Effingham, E Motomart ○ Harley-Davidson, W /McDonald's/dsl/scales/24hr Foxx's Den Smokehouse, Subway ○ Camp Lakewood (2mi), truck repair
160	IL 33, IL 32, Effingham, E Domino's, Jimmy John's, LoneStar Steaks, Papa John's, Pizza Hut Comfort Inn, Fairfield Inn, Hampton Inn ○ , $General, Aldi Foods, AutoZone, Family$, K-Mart, Midas, Save-a-Lot, Verizon, vet, W FLYING J/Denny's/dsl/LP/scales/24hr, BP/Quiznos/dsl, Marathon, Murphy USA/dsl, TA/Country Pride/Popeye's/dsl/@ Arby's, Bangkok Thai, Buffalo Wild Wings, Burger King, Cracker Barrel, Denny's, El Rancherito Mexican, KFC, LJ Silver, McDonald's, Ruby Tuesday, Ryan's, Starbucks, Steak'n Shake, Subway, Taco Bell, TGIFriday's, Wendy's Country Inn&Suites, Days Inn, Hilton Garden, Holiday Inn Express, Motel 6, Rodeway Inn, Super 8 ○ $Tree, AT&T, Blue Beacon, Camp Lakewood RV Park, Ford/Lincoln, Kohl's, Menards, Peterbilt, SpeedCo, Verizon, Walmart/Subway
159	US 40, Effingham, E BP/dsl/24hr, Marathon/dsl, Phillips 66/dsl China Buffet, Culver's, Hardee's, Little Caesars, Niemerg's Rest., Subway Abe Lincoln Motel, Best Value Inn, Comfort Suites, EconoLodge ○ O'Reilly Parts, tires/repair, Walgreens, W Petro/Iron Skillet/dsl/24hr/@ Best Western ○ Blue Beacon, Truck-O-Mat/IA-80/scales/wash

I-57 N and I-70 E run together 6 mi

Exit #	Services
157	I-70 W, to St Louis
151	Watson, E 5 mi ○ Percival Springs RV Park
150mm	Little Wabash River
145	Edgewood, E Phillips 66
135	IL 185, Farina, E BP/Subway/dsl ○ $General, Ford
127	to Kinmundy, Patoka
116	US 50, Salem, E Huck's/dsl, Shell/Circle K/dsl, Swifty Burger King, Domino's, Hardee's, La Cocina Mexican, LJ Silver, McDonald's, Pizza Hut, Pizza Man, Subway, Taco Bell,

E F F I N G H A M

S A L E M   MT VERNON   B E N T O N

M A R I O N

⬆N INTERSTATE 57 Cont'd

Exit #	Services
116	Continued
	Village Garden, Wendy's 🅞 🄷, AutoZone, Chrysler/Dodge/ Jeep, CVS Drug, GMC, NAPA, O'Reilly Parts, Save-A-Lot, to Forbes SP, USPO, **W** 🅖 Murphy USA/dsl, Phillips 66/dsl 🍴 Applebee's, Arby's, Denny's, KFC 🏠 Comfort Inn, Guest-house Inn, Salem Inn, Super 8 🅞 $Tree, AT&T, Buick/Chevrolet, Carlisle Lake (23mi), Ford, Salem Tires, Walmart
114mm	☕ **both lanes, full** ♿ **facilities, litter barrels, petwalk, phones,** 🎪 **playground, vending**
109	IL 161, to Centralia, **W** 🅖 Biggie's General Store/cafe/dsl
103	Dix, **E** 🍴 Austin's Rest 🏠 Red Carpet Inn
96	I-64 W, to St Louis
95	IL 15, Mt Vernon, **E** 🅖 Hucks, Phillips 66/Circle K/dsl 🍴 Agave Mexican, Asian Buffet, Bandana's BBQ, El Rancherito Mexican, Fazoli's, Hardee's, Hardee's, KFC, Little Caesar's, LJ Silver, McDonald's, Moe's SW Grill, Panda Express, Papa John's, Pizza Hut, Steak'n Shake, Subway, Taco Bell, Waffle Co, Wendy's 🏠 Best Inn, Best Value Inn, Comfort Suites, Drury Inn, Motel 6, Super 8 🅞 🄷, Aldi Foods, AutoZone, Big Lots, Chevrolet/Cadillac, Chrysler/Dodge/Jeep, CVS Drug, Ford/Lincoln, Harley-Davidson, Hobby Lobby, JC Penney, K-Mart, Kroger/dsl, Midas, O'Reilly Parts, Prompt Care, Radio Shack, Ross, Verizon, Walgreens, **W** 🅖 🚛FLYING J/Hucks/Country Cookin/dsl/scales/24hr, 🚛/Denny's/dsl/scales/24hr, Shell/Circle K/dsl, TA/Country Pride/Popeye's/dsl/24hr/@ 🍴 Applebee's, Arby's, Bob Evans, Buffalo Wild Wings, Burger King, Chili's, Cracker Barrel, Jimmy John's, Kriger's Grill, LoneStar Steaks, McDonald's, Ryan's, Sonic, Subway 🏠 Days Inn, Fairfield Inn, Hampton Inn, Holiday Inn, Quality Inn 🅞 $Tree, Archway RV Park, Buick/GMC, Freight-liner, Kohl's, Lowe's, NAPA, Staples, Toyota, truckwash, Verizon, Walmart
94	Veteran's Memorial Dr, 🅞🄷
92	I-64 E, to Louisville
83	Ina, **E** 🅖 ❤Loves/McDonald's/dsl/scales, Marathon/deli/dsl/scales/24hr 🅞 Sherwood Camping (2mi), **W** 🅞 to Rend Lake Coll
79mm	☕ **sb, full** ♿ **facilities, info, litter barrels, petwalk, phones,** 🎪 **playground, vending**
77	IL 154, to Whittington, **E** 🅖 Shell 🅞 Whittington Woods RV Park, **W** 🍴 Gibby's Grill 🏠 Seasons at Rend Lake Lodge/rest. 🅞 golf, to Rend Lake, Wayne Fitzgerrell SP
74mm	☕ **nb, full** ♿ **facilities, litter barrels, petwalk,** 🎪 **playground, vending**
71	IL 14, Benton, **E** 🅖 Jumpin' Jimmy's/dsl 🍴 Arby's, Hardee's, KFC/Taco Bell, Pizza Hut 🏠 Days Inn/rest., Gray Plaza Motel, Super 8 🅞 🄷, AutoZone, CVS Drug, KOA (1.5mi), O'Reilly Parts, Plaza Tire, **W** 🅖 BP/dsl, Murphy USA/dsl, Phillips 66/dsl/24hr 🍴 Applebee's, Burger King, McDonald's, Subway 🅞 Radio Shack, to Rend Lake, Verizon, Walmart
65	IL 149, W Frankfort, **E** 🅖 BP/dsl, Gas-4-Less, Marathon/dsl, Shell/dsl 🍴 China Star, Dixie Cream Deli, Hardee's, La Fiesta Mexican, LJ Silver, Mike's Drive-In, Miranda's Rest., Sonic, Subway 🏠 Gray Plaza Motel 🅞 🄷, CarQuest, MadPricer Foods, repair, **W** 🅖 Casey's 🍴 EEE BBQ, McDonald's, Pizza Hut 🏠 Best Value Inn 🅞 $General, $Tree, Buick/Chevrolet/GMC, K-Mart, Kroger, VF Factory Stores
59	to Herrin, Johnston City, **E** 🅖 ROC/dsl/e85, ZX/dsl 🍴 DQ, McDonald's, Subway 🅞 $General, camping (2mi), NAPA, Sandy Drug, **W** 🅞🄷, camping (4mi)

54b a	IL 13, Marion, **E** 🅖 Phillips 66/dsl 🍴 Arby's, Fazoli's, Hardee's, KFC, La Fiesta Mexican, LJ Silver, Papa John's, Pizza Hut, Quiznos, Subway, Tequila's Mexican, Wendy's, Western Sizzlin 🏠 Days Inn, EconoLodge 🅞 $General, Advance Parts, Aldi Foods, AutoZone, Cadillac/Chevrolet, Ford/Hyundai/Lincoln, Kroger/gas, Menards, Plaza Tire, Radio Shack, Sav-A-Lot Foods, USPO, Walgreens, **W** 🅖 Huck's/dsl, 🚛/Subway/dsl/scales/24h 🍴 17th St Grill, Applebee's, Asian Bistro, Backyard Burger, Bob Evans, Burger King, Hong Kong BBQ, Logan's Roadhouse, Mackie's Pizza, McAlister's Deli, McDonald's, O'Charley's, Panera Bread, Red Lobster, Ryan's, Sonic, Steak'n Shake, Taco Bell, Wok'n Roll Buffet 🏠 Best Inn, Comfort Inn, Country Inn&Suites, Drury Inn, Fairfield Inn, Hampton Inn, Holiday Inn Express, Motel 6, Super 8 🅞 🄷, Buick/Chevrolet/GMC, Chrysler/Dodge/Jeep, Dillard's, Harley-Davidson, Home Depot, Honda, mall, Menards, Mercedes, Nissan, Sam's Club/gas, Sears/auto, Subaru, Target, Toyota/Scion, Verizon, Walmart/Subway
53	Main St, Marion, **E** 🍴 DQ 🏠 Motel Marion 🅞 🄷, Marion Camping/RV Park, NAPA, **W** 🅖 Motomart 🍴 Cracker Barrel, HideOut Steaks 🏠 Comfort Suites, Holiday Inn Express, Quality Inn
47mm	**weigh sta both lanes**
45	IL 148, **E** 1 mi 🅖 King Tut's Food/dsl 🏠 Lake Tree Inn 🅞 camping, dsl repair
44	I-24 E to Nashville
40	Goreville Rd, **E** 🅞 camping, Ferne Clyffe SP, scenic overlook
36	Lick Creek Rd, **W** 🅞 vineyards
32mm	**Trail of Tears** ☕ **both lanes, full** ♿ **facilities, info, litter barrels, petwalk, phones,** 🎪 **playground, vending**
30	IL 146, Anna, Vienna, **W** 🅖 Fast Stop/dsl 🅞 🄷, auto/RV repair
25	US 51 N (from nb, exits left), to Carbondale
24	Dongola Rd, **E** 🅞 $General, **W** 🅖 BP/dsl
18	Ullin Rd, **W** 🅖 Fast Stop/dsl 🍴 EEE BBQ 🏠 Best Value Inn 🅞 Chevrolet, st police
8	Mounds Rd, to Mound City, **E** 🅞 K&K AutoTruck/dsl/repair
1	IL 3, to US 51, Cairo, **E** 🏠 Belvedere Motel (2mi), Days Inn 🅞 $General, camping, Mound City Nat Cem (4mi), **W** 🅞 camping
0mm	Illinois/Missouri state line, Mississippi River

⬆E INTERSTATE 64

Exit #	Services
131.5mm	Illinois/Indiana state line, Wabash River
131mm	**Skeeter Mtn Welcome Ctr wb, full** ♿ **facilities, litter barrels, petwalk,** ♿🎪, **vending**
130	IL 1, to Grayville, **N** 🅖 Casey's (2mi), 🚛/Road Ranger/dsl/scales/24hr, Shell/dsl/24hr 🍴 Season's Grill, Subway 🏠 Super 8, Windsor Oaks Inn/rest. 🅞 Beall Woods SP (10mi)
124mm	Little Wabash River
117	Burnt Prairie, **S** 🅖 CountryMark/DSL 🍴 ChuckWagon Charlie's Café 🅞 antiques
110	US 45, Mill Shoals
100	IL 242, to Wayne City, **N** 🅖 Citgo/dsl
94	Veterans Memorial Drive, **N** 🅞🄷
89	to Belle Rive, Bluford
86mm	☕ **wb, full** ♿ **facilities, litter barrels, petwalk,** ♿🎪, **vending**
82.5mm	☕ **eb, full** ♿ **facilities, litter barrels, petwalk,** ♿🎪, **vending**
80	IL 37, to Mt Vernon, **N** 2 mi 🅖 Hucks/dsl/24hr, Phillips 66/

IL

🛢️ = gas 🍴 = food 🏨 = lodging Ⓞ = other 🅁🅂 = rest stop

🔼🄴 INTERSTATE 64 Cont'd

Exit #	Services
80	Continued
	Circle K/Burger King/dsl Ⓞ $General
78	I-57, S to Memphis, N to Chicago
I-64 and I-57 run together 5 mi. See I-57, exits 95-94	
73	I-57, N to Chicago, S to Memphis
69	Woodlawn
61	US 51, to Centralia, Richview
50	IL 127, to Nashville, N Ⓞ to Carlyle Lake, S 🛢️ Citgo/rest/E-85/dsl, Little Nashville/Conoco/rest/dsl/scales/24hr, Shell/dsl 🍴 McDonald's 🏨 Best Western Ⓞ Ⓗ
41	IL 177, Okawville, S 🛢️ 🍴/Road Ranger/dsl/24hr 🍴 Burger King, DQ, Subway 🏨 Original Springs Motel, Super 8 Ⓞ $General, truck repair, USPO
37mm	Kaskaskia River
34	to Albers, N 3 mi 🛢️ Casey's
27	IL 161, New Baden, N 🛢️ Casey's/dsl, Shell/dsl 🍴 China King, Four Corners Pizza, Good Ol Days Rest., McDonald's, Subway Ⓞ $General, Chevrolet S 🛢️ Loves/Hardee's/dsl/scales/24hr
23	IL 4, to Mascoutah, N 🛢️ Mobil/dsl, Phillips 66/Huddle House/.dsl/RV dump 🏨 Best Western, S Ⓞ 🛢️
19b a	US 50, IL 158, N 🛢️ Motomart/dsl 🍴 Amore Italian, Subway 🏨 Super 8 Ⓞ Ⓗ, S Ⓞ to Scott AFB
18mm	**weigh sta eb**
16	to O'Fallon, Shiloh, N 🍴 Bella Milano, Sonic, The Egg & I 🏨 Hilton Garden Ⓞ CVS Drug, Harley-Davidson, URGENT CARE, S 🛢️ Motomart/dsl 🍴 54th St. Grille, Applebee's, Arby's, Aroy Thai, Buffalo Wild Wings, China King, Coldstone, Cracker Barrel, Golden Corral, Jersey Mike's, Jimmy John's, La Casa Mexicana, Little Caesar's, McAlister's Deli, McDonald's, Qdoba, Ravanelli's Rest., St. Louis Bread Co., Starbucks, Subway, TX Roadhouse, White Castle 🏨 Drury Inn, Holiday Inn Express Ⓞ AT&T, Dierbergs Foods, Dobb's Tire, Menard's, Michael's, Radio Shack, Target, vet, World Mkt
14	O'Fallon, N 🛢️ Motomart, Phillips 66/Circle K, Shell/dsl 🍴 IHOP, Japanese Garden, Steak'n Shake, Subway 🏨 Country Inn&Suites, Extended Stay America, La Quinta, Sleep Inn, Suburban Inn Ⓞ Cadillac, Chevrolet, Ford, O'Reilly Parts, S 🍴 Chevy's Mexican, Culver's, Hardee's, Jack-in-the-Box, KFC, La Parrilla Mexican, McDonald's, O'Charley's, Panda Express, Papa Murphy's, Sake Grill, Schiappa's Pizza, Syberg's Rest., Taco Bell 🏨 Candlewood Suites, Days Inn, Quality Inn Ⓞ Aldi Foods, BMW, Home Depot, Honda, Hyundai, Kia, Mazda, Nissan, Petsmart, Sam's Club/gas, Toyota, VW, Walmart
12	IL 159, to Collinsville, N 🛢️ Shell/Circle K 🍴 Agostino's, Applebee's, Bob Evans, Houlihan's, Joe's Crabshack, Lotawata Creek Grill, Olive Garden, Red Lobster, Shogun Japanese 🏨 Best Value Inn, Comfort Suites, Drury Inn, Fairfield Inn, Hampton Inn, Holiday Inn, Sheraton, Super 8 Ⓞ Fiat, Gordman's, S 🛢️ BP/dsl, Motomart/dsl 🍴 5 Guys Burgers, Arby's, Boston Mkt, Burger King, Capt D's, Cheddar's, Chick-fil-A, Chili's, Chipotle Mexican, ChuckECheese, Domino's, Dunkin Donuts, Fazoli's, Firehouse Subs, Honeybaked Ham, Hooters, Imo's Pizza, Jimmy John's, Krispy Kreme, Little Caesar's, LJ Silver, Logan's Roadhouse, Longhorn Steaks, McAlister's Deli, McDonald's, Popeye's, Red Robin, Ruby Tuesday, Smokey Bones BBQ, St. Louis Bread, Steak'n Shake, Subway, Taco Bell, Wasabi, Wendy's, White Castle Ⓞ $General, $Tree, Aamco, Advance Parts, AT&T, Barnes&Noble, Best Buy, BigLots, Burlington Coats, CarX, Dillard's, Dobb's Tire,

O'FALLON
COLLINSVILLE

12	Continued
	Firestone/auto, Hobby Lobby, JC Penney, Jo-Ann Fabrics, Kohl's, Lowe's, Macy's, Marshall's, Meineke, Midas, NTB, Old Navy, O'Reilly Parts, PetCo, Ross, Russell Stover, Schnuck's Foods, Sears/auto, TJ Maxx, Tuesday Morning, Verizon, vet, Walgreens
9	IL 157, to Caseyville, N 🛢️ Huck's/dsl, Phillips 66/Subway 🍴 Hardee's 🏨 Western Inn, S 🛢️ BP 🍴 Cracker Barrel, Domino's, DQ, McDonald's, Pizza Hut/Taco Bell 🏨 Best Inn, Motel 6, Quality Inn, Rodeway Inn
7	I-255, S to Memphis, N to Chicago
6	IL 111, Kingshighway, N 🛢️ BP, Mobil/ 🍴 Ray's Rest. 🏨 Econo Inn
5	25th St
4	15th St, Baugh
3	I-55 N, I-70 E, IL 3 N, to St Clair Ave, to stockyards
2b a	3rd St, S 🛢️
1	IL 3 S, 13th St, E St Louis, N Ⓞ Casino Queen
0mm	Illinois/Missouri state line, Mississippi River

🔼🄴 INTERSTATE 70

Exit #	Services
156mm	Illinois/Indiana state line
154	US 40 W
151mm	**weigh sta wb**
149mm	🅁🅂 wb, full 🏨 facilities, info, litter barrels, petwalk, 🅲🅲 vending
147	IL 1, Marshall, S 🛢️ Casey's (1mi), Jiffy/dsl/24hr, Marathon/Arby's/dsl 🍴 Burger King, Los Tres Caminos, McDonald's, Pizza Hut, Sam's Steaks, Subway, Wendy's 🏨 Lincoln Suites, Relax Inn, Super 8 Ⓞ antiques, camping, Ford, Lincoln Trail SP, Walmart
136	to Martinsville, S 🛢️ Fast Stop/dsl/24hr
134.5mm	N Fork Embarras River
129	IL 49, Casey, N Ⓞ KOA (seasonal), RV service, S 🛢️ BP/Subway/dsl, Casey's, Fast Stop/DQ, Marathon/Circle K/dsl 🍴 Hardee's, McDonald's, Pizza Hut 🏨 Comfort Inn Ⓞ IGA Foods
119	IL 130, Greenup, S 🛢️ Casey's, Marathon/dsl 🍴 Backyard BBQ, Dandy Kitchen, DQ, Subway 🏨 Budget Host, Greenup Motel Ⓞ $General, camping, hist sites
105	Montrose, N Ⓞ Spring Creek Camping (1mi), S 🛢️ BP/dsl, Marathon/dsl/24hr 🏨 Fairview Inn, Red Carpet Inn
98	I-57, N to Chicago
I-70 and I-57 run together 6 mi. See I-57, exits 159-162.	
92	I-57, S to Mt Vernon
91mm	Little Wabash River

⬆E INTERSTATE 70 Cont'd

Exit #	Services
87mm	🆁🆂 both lanes, full ♿ facilities, info, litter barrels, petwalk, 🅲, 🗑, playground, RV dump, vending
82	IL 128, Altamont, **N** 🅡 Casey's, Jumpin Jimmy's/Subway/dsl/24hr, Marathon/dsl 🍽 Dairy Bar, McDonald's 🏠 Altamont Motel 🅞 city park, **S** 🏠 Super 8
76	US 40, St Elmo, **N** 🅡 Casey's 🏠 Waldorf Motel 🅞 Timberline Camping (2mi)
71mm	weigh sta eb
68	US 40, Brownstown, **N** 🅞 Okaw Valley Kamping, **S** 🅞 truck repair
63.5mm	Kaskaskia River
63	US 51, Vandalia, **N** 🍽 Chuck Wagon Cafe, LJ Silver 🏠 Days Inn, **S** 🅡 BP/Burger King/24hr, Casey's, Phillips 66 🍽 Arby's, China Buffet, DQ, McDonald's, Pizza Hut, Rancho Nuevo Mexican, Sonic, Subway, Wendy's 🏠 Jay's Inn, Travelodge 🅞 🅷, Aldi Foods, city park, County Mkt Foods, hist site
61	US 40, Vandalia, **N** 🅡 Fast Stop/Denny's/dsl/scales/24hr **S** 🅡 Murphy USA/dsl 🍽 KFC/Taco Bell, Ponderosa 🏠 Holiday Inn Express, Ramada Ltd 🅞 AutoZone, Verizon, Walmart
52	US 40, Mulberry Grove, **N** 🅡 Jumpin Jimmy's/dsl 🅞 Timber Trail Camp-In (2mi), tires, **S** 🅞 Cedar Brook Camping (1mi)
45	IL 127, Greenville, **N** 🅡 Jumpin Jimmy's/Domino's/dsl, ❤Loves/Subway/dsl/scales/24hr, Shell/dsl/24hr 🍽 Cunetto's Rest., Huddle House, KFC/Taco Bell, Lu-Bob's Rest., McDonald's 🏠 2 Acre Motel, EconoLodge, M Hotel, Super 8 🅞 🅷, Ford, **S** 🍽 La Hacienda Mexican 🏠 Sleep Inn 🅞 American Farm Heritage Museum, RV Service, to Carlyle Lake
41	US 40 E, to Greenville
36	US 40 E, Pocahontas, **S** 🅡 Marathon/dsl/24hr, Phillips 66/dsl/24hr 🍽 Funderburks Grill 🏠 Lighthouse Lodge, Powhatan Motel/rest., Tahoe Motel 🅞 truck/tire repair
30	US 40, IL 143, to Highland, **S** 🅡 Shell/dsl/wi-fi/24hr 🍽 Blue Springs Café 🅞 🅷, Tomahawk RV Park (7mi)
26.5mm	Silver Lake 🆁🆂 both lanes, full ♿ facilities, litter barrels, petwalk, 🅲, 🗑 vending
24	IL 143, Marine, **S 4 mi** 🍽 Ponderosa 🏠 Holiday Inn Express 🅞 🅷,
21	IL 4, Troy
19mm	motorist callboxes begin wb every 1/2 mile
15b a	I-55, N to Chicago, S to St Louis, I-270 W to Kansas City
	I-70 and I-55 run together 18 mi. See I-55, exits 3-18.
0mm	Illinois/Missouri state line, Mississippi River

⬆E INTERSTATE 72

Exit #	Services
183mm	**1 mi E on University** 🅡 Thornton's/dsl 🍽 Arby's, Burger King, La Bamba Mexican, McDonald's, Monical's Pizza, Original Pancakes, Pizza Hut, Sonic, Taco Bell, Taffie's Rest., TX Roadhouse, Village Inn Pizza 🅞 Advance Parts, Aldi Foods, AutoZone, County Mkt Foods, CVS Drug, Schnuck's Foods/gas, Walgreens
182b a	I-57, N to Chicago, S to Memphis, to I-74
176	IL 47, to Mahomet
172	IL 10, Lodge, Seymour
169	White Heath Rd
166	IL 105 W, Market St, **N** 🅞 🅷, Ford, **S** 🅡 Mobil/Subway/dsl 🍽 Red Wheel Rest. 🏠 Best Western, Foster Inn 🅞 city park, railway museum
165mm	Sangamon River

Exit #	Services
164	Bridge St, **S 1 mi** 🅡 Mobil/dsl 🍽 China Star, DQ, Hardee's, McDonald's, Monical's Pizza, Pizza Hut, Subway 🅞 🅷, $General, Buick/Chevrolet, Chrysler/Dodge/Jeep, USPO
156	IL 48, to Weldon, Cisco, **S** 🅞 Friends Creek Camping (may-oct) (3mi)
153mm	🆁🆂 both lanes, full ♿ facilities, litter barrels, petwalk, 🅲, 🗑 vending
152mm	Friends Creek
150	Argenta
144	IL 48, Oreana, **S** 🅡 🚛/McDonald's/Subway/dsl/scales/24hr 🏠 Sleep Inn 🅞 🅷, Chrysler/Dodge, Honda, Hyundai, Tressley RV Ctr
141b a	US 51, Decatur, **N** 🅡 Shell/Circle K 🍽 Applebee's, Buffalo Wild Wings, Cheddar's, Cracker Barrel, HomeTown Buffet, McDonald's, Mi Jalapeno, O'Charley's, Pizza Hut, Red Lobster, Steak'n Shake, Subway, Taco Bell, TX Roadhouse 🏠 Baymont Inn, Country Inn&Suites, Fairfield Inn, Hampton Inn, Homewood Suites, Quality Inn, Ramada Ltd, Welcome Hotel 🅞 $Tree, AT&T, Bergner's, Best Buy, Bon-Ton, Buick/Cadillac/GMC, Harley-Davidson, JC Penney, Kohl's, Lowe's, mall, Menards, Petsmart, Sears/auto, Staples, Verizon, Von Maur, **S** 🍽 Arby's, Burger King, El Rodeo Mexican, Fuji Japanese, Monical's Pizza, Olive Garden, Panera Bread, Papa Murphy's, Starbucks 🅞 🅷, Jo-Ann Fabrics, Radio Shack, Sam's Club, Target, Verizon, Walgreens, Walmart/Subway
138	IL 121, Decatur, **S** 🅞 🅷,
133b a	US 36 E, US 51, Decatur, **S** 🅡 Phillips 66/Subway/dsl 🏠 Best Value Inn, Decatur Hotel/rest.
128	Niantic
122	to Mt Auburn, Illiopolis, **N** 🅡 FastStop/dsl
114	Buffalo, Mechanicsburg, **S** 🅡 Gas Depot/dsl (2mi) 🅞 USPO
108	Riverton, Dawson
107mm	Sangamon River
104	Camp Butler, **N 2 mi** 🍽 Arby's, McDonald's, Starbucks 🏠 Best Rest Inn, Best Western, Lincoln Inn, Park View Motel 🅞 golf
103b a	I-55, N to Chicago, S to St Louis, Il 97, to Springfield
	I-72 and I-55 run together 6 mi. See I-55, exits 92-98
96	MacArthur Blvd, **N** 🍽 Quaker Steak 🅞 Scheels
93	IL 4, Springfield, **N** 🅡 Hucks, Thorntons/dsl 🍽 Applebee's, Arby's, Bakers Square, Burger King, Cara BBQ, Chili's, Chipotle Mexican, Denny's, Ginger Asian, Hickory River, LoneStar Steaks, Longhorn Steaks, Los Rancheros Mexican, McDonald's, Noodles&Co, Olive Garden, Panda Express, Panera Bread, Sonic, Starbucks, Subway, Taco Bell, TGIFriday's, TX Roadhouse, Wendy's 🏠 Courtyard, Fairfield Inn, Quality Inn, Sleep Inn 🅞 AT&T, Barnes&Noble, Best Buy, County Mkt Foods, Dick's, Discount Tire, Gordman's, Jo-Ann Fabrics, K-Mart, Kohl's, Lowe's, Menards, Michael's, Office Depot, Old Navy, PetCo, Petsmart, Sam's Club/gas, Sears/auto, St Fair Camping, Staples, Target, TJ Maxx, Verizon, vet, Walgreens, Walmart **S** 🅡 Meijer/dsl/E85 🍽 Bob Evans, Monical's Pizza, O'Charley's, Steak'n Shake 🏠 Hampton Inn, Staybridge Suites 🅞 Cadillac, Chevrolet, Chrysler/Jeep, Fiat, Ford, Gander Mtn, Honda
91	Wabash Ave, to Springfield, **N** 🅡 Quik'n EZ 🍽 Bella Milano, Buffalo Wild Wings, Culver's, Firehouse Subs, IHOP, Mimosa Thai 🅞 Kia, Nissan, Toyota, **S** 🅞 Colmans RV Ctr
82	New Berlin, **S** 🅡 Phillips 66/Subway/dsl 🅞 $General
76	IL 123, to Ashland, Alexander
68	to IL 104, to Jacksonville, **N 2 mi** 🅡 BP 🅞 🅷,

(Vertical tab labels: **VANDALIA**, **DECATUR**, **SPRINGFIELD**)

🏳E	**INTERSTATE 72 Cont'd**
Exit #	**Services**
64	US 67, to Jacksonville, **N 2 mi** 🅖 BP/Circle K/dsl, Casey's, Clark/Quiznos/dsl/e-85, FastStop 🍴 DQ, KFC, McDonald's 🛏 Comfort Inn, Holiday Inn Express 🄾 H, H, $General, CVS Drug, Family$, Hopper RV Ctr, Walgreens
60	to US 67 N, to Jacksonville, **N 6 mi on IL 104** 🄾 H, food, gas, lodging
52	to IL 106, Winchester, **N** 🄾 golf, **S 2 mi** food, gas, lodging
46	IL 100, to Bluffs
42mm	Illinois River
35	US 54, IL 107, to Pittsfield, Griggsville, **N 4 mi** food, gas, lodging, **S** 🄾 H, Jellystone Camping (6mi), st police
31	to Pittsfield, New Salem, **S 5 mi** 🄾 H, Jellystone Camping, food, gas, lodging
20	IL 106, Barry, **S** 🅖 FastStop/dsl/24hr, Shell/dsl 🍴 Rodger's St Cafe (1mi), Wendy's 🄾 antiques, winery
10	IL 96, to Payson, Hull
4a	I-172, N to Quincy
1	IL 106, to Hull
0mm	Illinois/Missouri state line, Mississippi River.
	Exits 157 & 156 are in Missouri.
157	to Hannibal, MO 179, **S** 🅖 Ayerco, BP, Phillips 66, Shell/dsl 🍴 Mark Twain Dinette, Subway 🛏 Best Value Inn, Best Way Inn, Hotel Mark Twain 🄾 auto repair, visitor info
156	US 61, New London, Palmyra. **I-72 begins/ends in Hannibal, MO on US 61 N** 🅖 BP, Conoco/dsl, Murphy USA/dsl 🍴 Burger King, Country Kitchen, Domino's, Golden Corral, Hardee's, LJ Silver, Maya Mexican, McDonald's, Mi Mexico, Pizza Hut, Royal Garden, Sonic, Subway, Taco Bell 🄾 $General, $Tree, Aldi Foods, BigLots, Ford, JC Penney, Kroger, Lowe's, Radio Shack, Walmart, **S 0-2 mi** 🅖 Ayerco, Shell/dsl 🍴 Cassano's Subs, DQ, Gran Rio Mexican, Hardee's, Joe's Diner, KFC, Logue's Rest, Papa John's, Wendy's 🛏 Days Inn, EconoLodge, Hannibal Inn, Holiday Inn Express, Mark Twain Motel, Motel 6, Super 8 🄾 $General, AutoZone, Buick/Chevrolet, Chrysler/Dodge/Jeep, County Mkt Foods, Family$, Injun Joe's RV Camp, O'Reilly Parts, Walgreens

🏳E	**INTERSTATE 74**
Exit #	**Services**
221mm	Illinois/Indiana state line, Central/Eastern Time Zone
220	Lynch Rd, Danville, **N** 🅖 BP/dsl, Marathon/dsl (1mi) 🍴 Big Boy 🛏 Best Western, Comfort Inn, Danville Inn, Fairfield Inn, Hampton Inn, Holiday Inn Express, Sleep Inn, Super 8
216	Bowman Ave, Danville, **N** 🅖 Mobil/dsl, Phillips 66/dsl 🍴 Godfather's, KFC 🄾 city park
215b a	US 150, IL 1, Gilbert St, Danville, **N** 🅖 BP, Casey's/dsl, Circle K/dsl 🍴 Arby's, El Toro, La Potosina, LJ Silver, McDonald's, Pizza Hut, Steak'n Shake, Subway, Taco Bell 🛏 Best Western, Days Inn 🄾 H, Aldi Foods, BigLots, Ford/Lincoln, **S** 🅖 Casey's/dsl, Marathon/Circle K/dsl 🍴 Burger King, Green Jade Chinese, Mike's Grill, Monical's Pizza, Rich's Rest. 🄾 $General, AutoZone, Big R, Buick/Chevrolet/GMC, Family$, Forest Glen Preserve Camping (11mi), Toyota/Scion
214	G St, Tilton
210	US 150, MLK Dr, **N 2 mi** 🅖 Marathon 🍴 Little Nugget Steaks 🄾 H, to Kickapoo SP, **S** 🍴 PossumTrot Rest.
208mm	Welcome Ctr wb, full ♿ facilities, info, litter barrels, pet-walk, phones, 🅿 vending
206	Oakwood, **S** 🅖 Casey's (1mi), Oakwood TP/Shell/rest/dsl/scales/24hr, Phillips 66/Subway/dsl/scales 🍴 McDonald's 🄾 $General

200	IL 49 N, to Rankin
197	IL 49 S, Ogden, **S** 🅖 Phillips 66/Godfather's/dsl 🍴 Rich's Rest. 🄾 city park
192	St Joseph, **S** 🍴 DQ, Monical's Pizza 🄾 antiques
185	IL 130, University Ave
184	US 45, Cunningham Ave, Urbana, **N** 🅖 F&F 🄾 Hyundai, Kia, Mazda, Toyota/Scion, VW, **S** 🅖 Marathon/Circle K/Subway/dsl, Shell 🍴 Arby's, Cracker Barrel, Domino's, El Toro, Hickory River BBQ, McDonald's, MT Mike's Steaks, Steak'n Shake 🛏 Eastland Suites, Motel 6 🄾 $General, auto repair, vet
183	Lincoln Ave, Urbana, **S** 🅖 Circle K/dsl, Marathon/Circle K/dsl, Mobil/dsl 🍴 Urbana Garden Rest. 🛏 Comfort Suites, Holiday Inn Express, Holiday Inn/rest., Ramada Inn, Sleep Inn, Super 8 🄾 H, Harley-Davidson, to U of IL
182	Neil St, Champaign, **N** 🍴 Alexander's Steaks, Bob Evans, Chevy's Mexican, Food Court, McAlister's Deli, McDonald's, Old Chicago, Olive Garden, Panera Bread, Taco Bell, Zia's Italian 🛏 Baymont Inn, La Quinta, Quality Inn, Red Roof Inn, Super 8 🄾 Barnes&Noble, Bergner's, Cadillac/Chevrolet, Chrysler/Dodge/Jeep, Gordman's, Hobby Lobby, JC Penney, Kohl's, Macy's, mall, Mercedes/Volvo, Office Depot, Old Navy, same as 181, Sears/auto, TJ Maxx, **S** 🅖 Mobil 🄾 Jo-Ann Fabrics
181	Prospect Ave, Champaign, **N** 🅖 Meijer/dsl, Murphy USA/dsl 🍴 Applebee's, Best Wok, Buffalo Wild Wings, Burger King, Chili's, China Town, Culver's, Fazoli's, Hometown Buffet, LoneStar Steaks, Longhorn Steaks, O'Charley's, Oishi Asain, Outback Steaks, Panda Express, Penn Sta Subs, Red Lobster, Ruby Tuesday, Ryan's, Starbucks, Steak'n Shake, Subway, Wendy's 🛏 Candlewood Suites, Country Inn&Suites, Courtyard, Drury Inn, Extended Stay America, Fairfield Inn, ValuePlace Hotel, Wingate Inn 🄾 $Tree, Advance Parts, AT&T, Best Buy, Dick's, Lowe's, Menards, Michael's, Petsmart, Radio Shack, same as 182, Sam's Club/gas, Staples, Target, Tires+, Walmart/Subway **S** 🅖 Freedom/dsl, Marathon/Circle K, Mobil 🍴 Jimmy John's 🍴 Arby's, Dos Reales Mexican, Dunkin Donuts, LJ Silver 🛏 Days Inn, EconoLodge 🄾 $General, CarX, Home Depot, NAPA, Tire Barn, Walgreens
179b a	I-57, N to Chicago, S to Memphis
174	Lake of the Woods Rd, Prairieview Rd, **N** 🅖 BP, Casey's, Mobil/dsl 🄾 auto repair, Lake of the Woods SP, Tin Cup RV Park, **S** 🅖 Marathon/Subway/dsl 🍴 McDonald's
172	IL 47, Mahomet, **N** 🄾 R&S RV Sales, **S** 🅖 BP/dsl, Mobil/dsl, Shell/Domino's/dsl 🍴 Arby's, Azteca, DQ, HenHouse Rest., Jr's Burgers&Custard, Los Zarapes, Monical's Pizza, Peking House, Subway, The Wok 🛏 Heritage Inn 🄾 Ace Hardware, CVS Drug, IGA Foods, NAPA, vet, Walgreens

D A N V I L L E (vertical, left margin)

C H A M P A I G N (vertical, center margin)

IL (right margin tab)

INTERSTATE 74 Cont'd

Exit #	Services
166	Mansfield, S 🅿 BP/dsl 🅾 Mansfield Gen. Store/Rest.
159	IL 54, Farmer City, S 🅿 Casey's, Huck's/Quiznos/dsl 🍴 Family Rest. 🏠 Budget Motel, Days Inn 🅾 NAPA, to Clinton Lake RA, USPO
156mm	🆁🆂 both lanes, full ♿ facilities, litter larrels, petwalk, 📞, 🖼 playground, vending
152	US 136, to Heyworth
149	Le Roy, N 🅿 BP, Freedom/dsl, Loves/Arby's/dsl/scales/24hr 🍴 Jack's Cafe, McDonald's, Roma Ralph's Pizza, Subway 🏠 Holiday Inn Express 🅾 $General, Doc's Drug, IGA Foods, NAPA, to Moraine View SP, TrueValue, S 🅿 Shell/Woody's Rest./dsl/scales/24hr 🏠 Red Roof Inn 🅾 camping, Clinton Lake
142	Downs, N 🅿 BP/Pizza/Subs/dsl/24hr 🅾 USPO
135	US 51, Bloomington, N 🅿 BP/Circle K/dsl, Huck's/dsl, Mobil/dsl 🍴 McDonald's 🅾 $General, S 🅿 FastStop/dsl
134b[157]	N 🅾 H, to 🛬, Bloomington, Veterans Pkwy
134a	I-55, N to Chicago, S to St Louis, I-74 E
I-74 and I-55 run together 6 mi. See I-55, exits 157b-160b a	
127[163]	I-55, N to Chicago, S to St Louis, I-74 W to Peoria
125	US 150, to Bloomington, Mitsubishi Motorway
123mm	weigh sta wb
122mm	weigh sta eb
120	Carlock, N 🅿 BP/dsl/repair 🍴 Carlock Rest., S 🅾 Kamp Komfort Camping (Apr-Oct)
114.5mm	🆁🆂 both lanes, full ♿ facilities, litter barrels, petwalk, 📞, 🖼 vending
113.5mm	Mackinaw River
112	IL 117, Goodfield, N 🅿 Shell/Subway/dsl 🍴 Busy Corner Rest. 🅾 Eureka Coll, Jellystone Camping (1mi), Reagan Home, to Timberline RA, USPO
102b a	Morton, N 🅿 BP/rest./dsl, Mobil/Arby's/dsl/scales/24hr 🍴 Burger King, Cracker Barrel, Culver's, Hardee's, Ruby Tuesday, Steak'n Shake, Taco Bell 🏠 Baymont Inn, Best Value Inn, Best Western, Holiday Inn Express, Quality Inn, Travelodge 🅾 Chrysler/Dodge/Jeep, Farm&Fleet, Freightliner, Walmart/Subway S 🅿 BP/Circle K, Marathon/Circle K, Shell/Subway/dsl/24hr 🍴 China Dragon, Domino's, Great Harvest Bread, Jimmy John's, KFC, La Fiesta, Lin's Buffet, McDonald's, Monical's Pizza, Pizza Hut, Pizza Ranch 🅾 $Tree, Buick/GMC, CVS Drug, Ford, K-Mart, Kroger/dsl, O'Reilly Parts, Verizon
101	I-155 S, to Lincoln
99	I-474 W, 🅾 🛬
98	Pinecrest Dr
96	95c (from eb), US 150, IL 8, E Washington St, E Peoria, N 🅿 Fast Stop/dsl 🍴 Subway, Super Gyros 🏠 Super 8 🅾 O'Reilly Parts
95b	(from eb) IL 116, to Metamora, N 🅿 Shell/dsl 🍴 Burger King 🏠 Hampton Inn, Paradise Hotel 🅾 casino
95a	N Main St, Peoria, S 🅿 BP/Circle k 🍴 A&W/LJ Silver, Bob Evans, Chipotle Mexican, Firehouse Pizza/subs, Grand Village Buffet, Hardee's, IHOP, Jersey Mikes, Jimmy John's, Johnny's Italian Steaks, McDonald's, Noodles&Co, Panda Express, Papa Murphy's, Pizza Hut, Popeyes, Potbelly, Red Robin, Subway, Taco Bell, Tequilas Grill 🏠 Best Western, Fairfield Inn, Holiday Inn, Motel 6 🅾 $Tree, Advance Parts, Aldi Foods, AT&T, Costco/gas, CVS Drug, GNC, Goodyear/auto, Gordman's, Kohl's, Kroger, Ross, Target, Verizon, Walgreens

Exit #	Services
94	IL 40, RiverFront Dr, S 🅿 Hucks/Godfather's/dsl 🍴 Applebee's, Arby's, Buffalo Wild Wings, Chili's, Culver's, Granite City Grill, Logan's Roadhouse, Lorena's Mexican, Ming's Rest., Panera Bread, Papa John's, Qdoba Mexican, Steak'n Shake, TX Roadhouse, Uncle Buck's Grill 🏠 Embassy Suites 🅾 Bass Pro Sop, Lowe's, PetsMart, Radio Shack, Verizon, Walmart/Subway
93.5mm	Illinois River
93b	US 24, IL 29, Peoria, N 🅿 BP, S 🏠 Mark Twain Hotel 🅾 civic ctr
93a	Jefferson St, Peoria, N 🅿 BP, S 🍴 Two 25 Grill 🏠 Mark Twain Hotel, Marriott, Sheraton 🅾 to civic ctr
92b	Glendale Ave, Peoria, S 🅾 H, downtown
92a	IL 40 N, Knoxville Ave, Peoria, S 🏠 Sheraton 🅾 H,
91	University St, Peoria
90	Gale Ave, Peoria, S 🅿 Marathon 🅾 to Bradley U
89	US 150, War Memorial Dr, Peoria, N on War Memorial 🅿 BP/Circle K, Marathon/dsl, Shell 🍴 Arby's, Avanti's Rest., Baskin-Robbins/Dunkin Donuts, Biaggi's Ristorante, Bob Evans, Burger King, Chick-fil-A, Chipotle Mexican, ChuckeCheese, Dunkin Donuts, Five Guys, Golden Corral, Hokkaido Hibachi, Hometown Buffet, IHOP, Mango Grill, McDonald's, Panda Express, Panera Bread, Papa Murphy's, Perkins, Red Lobster, Sonic, Steak'n Shake, Subway, Wendy's, Wild Berries Rest. 🏠 Baymont Inn, Comfort Suites, Courtyard, EconoLodge, Extended Stay America, Grand Hotel, Quality Inn, Red Roof Inn, Residence Inn, SpringHill Suites, Super 8 🅾 $Tree, Aldi Foods, AT&T, AutoZone, Barnes&Noble, Best Buy, Chevrolet/Cadillac, Hobby Lobby, JC Penney, Lowe's, Macy's, mall, Midas, NAPA, PetsMart, Ross, Sears/auto, Shop'n Save Foods, Target, The Fresh Mkt, Tires+, U-Haul, Verizon, vet, Walgreens, Walmart/Subway
88	to US 150, War Memorial Dr, same as 89
87b a	I-474 E, IL 6, N to Chillicothe, S 🅾 🛬
82	Edwards Rd, Kickapoo, N 🅿 Mobil/dsl/service, Shell/Subway/dsl 🍴 Jubilee Café 🅾 to Jubilee Coll SP, S 🅾 USPO, Wildlife Prairie SP
75	Brimfield, Oak Hill, N 🅿 Casey's/dsl
71	to IL 78, to Canton, Elmwood
62mm	🆁🆂 both lanes, full ♿ facilities, litter barrels, petwalk, 📞, 🖼 vending
61.5mm	Spoon River
54	US 150, IL 97, Lewistown, N 🅾 TravL Park Camping (1mi), S 🅿 Mobil/dsl (2mi) 🍴 Alfano's Pizza (2mi)
51	Knoxville, S 🅿 BP/dsl, Phillips 66/Charley's Subs/dsl/scales 🍴 Hardee's, McDonald's 🏠 Super 8
48b a	E Galesburg, Galesburg, N 🏠 Best Western 🅾 Harley-Davidson, S 🅿 BP/Circle K/dsl, HyVee/dsl, Phillps 66/Beck's/dsl 🍴 DQ, Hardee's, Jalisco Mexican, KFC, Marco's Pizza, McDonald's, Pizza Hut, Subway, Taco Bell 🏠 Holiday Inn Express 🅾 Family$, Firestone, HyVee Foods, Lincoln-Douglas Debates, Sav-A-Lot Foods, to Sandburg Birthplace, Walgreens
46b a	US 34, to Monmouth, W 1 mi 🅾 Aldi Foods, N 🅾 Nichol's dsl Service, S 1 mi 🍴 Buffalo Wild Wings, Crazy Buffet 🅾 H, Menards, Radio Shack, Toyota/Scion, Verizon, vet, Walmart/Subway
32	IL 17, Woodhull, N 🅿 BP/dsl 🍴 Subway, S 🅿 ▢▢/dsl/scales/24hr 🅾 Shady Lakes Camping (8mi)
30mm	🆁🆂 wb, full ♿ facilities, litter barrels, petwalk, phones, 🖼 playground, RV dump, vending
28mm	🆁🆂 eb, full ♿ facilities, litter barrels, petwalk, phones, 🖼 playground, RV dump, vending

IL

BLOOMINGTON

PEORIA

GALESBURG

INTERSTATE 74 Cont'd

Exit #	Services
24	IL 81, Andover, N🍽 camping, Casey's (2mi)
14mm	I-80, E to Chicago, I-80/I-280 W to Des Moines
8mm	weigh sta wb
6mm	weigh sta eb
5b	US 6, Moline, S🅶 Shell/dsl 🍽 Bare Bones BBQ, McDonald's, MT Jack's 🛏 Best Inn, Country Inn&Suites, Hampton Inn, Holiday Inn Express, La Quinta, Motel 6, Quality Inn 🅾 🖨
5a	I-280 W, US 6 W, to Des Moines
4b a	IL 5, John Deere Rd, Moline, N🅶 BP/7-11, Phillips 66, Shell/dsl 🍽 Applebee's, Burger King, Chipotle Mexican, Culver's, Hungy Hobo, Osaka Buffet, Panera Bread, Ryan's, Starbucks, Steak'n Shake, Subway, Wendy's 🛏 Residence Inn 🅾 $Tree, Cadillac, Farm&Fleet, Honda, Hyundai, Lowe's, Menard's, Radio Shack, Sam's Club/dsl, Staples, Subaru, Tires+, Toyota/Scion, Volvo, Walmart/Subway S🅶 BP/7-11 🍽 A&W/LJ Silver, Arby's, Buffalo Wild Wings, China Cafe, Denny's, KFC, Los Agaves, McDonald's, New Mandarin Chinese, Qdoba Mexican, Taco Bell 🛏 Best Western, Comfort Inn, Fairfield Inn, Motel 6 🅾 $General, Best Buy, Buick/GMC, Chevrolet, Chrysler/Dodge/Jeep, Dillards, Firestone/auto, Ford/Lincoln, Goodyear/auto, Gordman's, Hancock Fabrics, JC Penney, mall, Mazda, Nissan, PetCo, Von Maur, Walgreens, Younkers
3	23rd Ave, Moline, N🛏 Economy Inn
2	7th Ave, Moline, S🅶 QuikStop 🍽 La Casa Mexican 🅾 riverfront, to civic ctr, USPO
1	3rd Ave (from eb), Moline, S🅶 QuickStop 🛏 Stoney Creek Inn
0mm	Illinois/Iowa state line, Mississippi River. **Exits 4-1 are in Iowa.**
4	US 67, Grant St, State St, Bettendorf, N🍽 Hardee's, McDonald's, Ross' Rest./24hr, Subway 🛏 Twin Bridges Motel, Waterfront Conv Ctr 🅾 CarQuest, S🍽 Village Inn Rest. 🛏 City Ctr Motel 🅾 $General
3	Middle Rd, Locust St, Bettendorf, S🅶 BP/dsl 🍽 China Taste, Grinders Rest., McDonald's, Pizza Ranch, Red Ginger Asian, Starbucks, Subway 🛏 Hilton Garden 🅾 🅷, AT&T, Burlington Coats, Hobby Lobby, Home Depot, Marshall's, Schuck's Foods, Verizon, Walgreens
2	US 6 W, Spruce Hills Dr, Bettendorf, N🅶 BP/dsl, Phillips 66 🍽 Domino's, Old Chicago Pizza 🛏 Courtyard, EconoLodge, Ramada Inn, Super 8, The Lodge Hotel/rest. 🅾 U-Haul, S🅶 Hyvee Gas 🍽 Applebee's, KFC, Panera Bread, Red Lobster 🛏 Days Inn, Fairfield Inn, Holiday Inn, La Quinta 🅾 Buick/GMC, Gander Mtn, Gordman's, Kohl's, Lowe's, PetCo, Sam's Club/gas, st patrol
1	53rd St, Hamilton, N🅶 BP 🍽 Bad Boyz Pizza, Biaggi's Italian, Buffalo Wild Wings, Chili's, Coldstone, Granite City Rest., Los Agaves, Maggie Moo's, Osaka Steaks, Panchero's Mexican, Red Lantern Chinese, Red Robin, TX Roadhouse 🛏 Hampton Inn, Staybridge Suites 🅾 🅷, Harley-Davidson, Hy-Vee Foods, Michael's, Old Navy, TJ Maxx, Walgreens, S🅶 Murphy USA/dsl, Shell/dsl 🍽 Arby's, Azteca Mexican, Burger King, Chick-fil-A, China Cafe, Chipotle Mexican, DQ, Dynasty Buffet, Golden Corral, HuHot, Hungry Hobo, IHOP, La Rancherita, Noodles&Co., PepperJax Grill, Quiznos, Sonic, Starbucks, Steak'n Shake, Subway, Taco Bell, Village Inn Rest., Wendy's 🛏 Sleep Inn 🅾 $Tree, Aldi Foods, AT&T, Best Buy, Dick's, Discount Tire, Meineke, PetsMart, Staples, Target, Verizon, Walmart
0mm	**I-74 begins/ends on I-80, exit 298. Exits 1-4 are in Iowa.**

INTERSTATE 80

Exit #	Services
163mm	Illinois/Indiana state line
161	US 6, IL 83, Torrence Ave, N🅶 BP 🍽 Burger King, Chili's, Culver's, Dixie Kitchen, Hooters, IHOP, Kenny's Ribs, Liang's Garden, New China Buffet, Oberweiss, Olive Garden, Shark's, Taco-Burrito's, Wendy's 🛏 Comfort Suites, Days Inn, Extended Stay America, Holiday Inn Express, Howard Johnson Express, Red Roof Inn, Sleep Inn, Super 8 🅾 $General, $Tree, Aldi Foods, AT&T, Best Buy, CarEx, Chrysler/Jeep, Curves, Dunkin Donuts, Fannie May Candies, Firestone/auto, Home Depot, Honda, JustTires, K-Mart, PepBoys, Radio Shack, Ultra Foods, Walmart S🅶 Citgo, Marathon, Mobil 🍽 Burger King, China Chef, DQ, Dunkin Donuts, Jonny's K's Cafe, McDonald's/playplace, Mr Gyros, Popolono's Italian, Subway 🛏 Pioneer Motel 🅾 Chevrolet, Petsmart, SunRise Foods, Tuesday Morning, vet, Walgreens
160b	I-94 W, to Chicago, **tollway begins wb/ends eb,**
160a	IL 394 S, to Danville
159mm	Oasis, 🍽 Mobil/dsl 🍽 McDonald's, Panda Express, Starbucks, Subway
157	IL 1, Halsted St, N🅶 Citgo/dsl, Marathon/dsl 🍽 Burger King 🛏 Chicago Southland Hotel, Clarion, Comfort Inn, Comfort Suites, EconoLodge, Regency Inn, S🅶 Citgo, Delta Sonic, Shell, Speedway 🍽 Applebee's, Arby's, Athens Gyros, Boston Mkt, Burger King, Chili's, Dunkin Donuts, Fannie May Candies, KFC, McDonald's, Panda Express, Pizza Hut, Popeye's, Starbucks, Subway, Taco Bell, Washington Square Rest., Wendy's, White Castle 🛏 Homewood Hotel, Super 8 🅾 $Tree, Aldi Foods, AT&T, Best Buy, Chevrolet, Discount Tire, Fanny May Candies, Firestone/auto, Goodyear/auto, Home Depot, Jewel-Osco, Jo-Ann Fabrics, K-Mart, Kohl's, Menards, PepBoys, PetCo, Radio Shack, Target, TJ Maxx, Walgreens
156	Dixie Hwy (from eb, no return), S🅶 Mobil 🍽 Leona's Rest. 🅾 golf
155	I-294 N, **Tri-State Tollway, toll plaza**
154	Kedzie Ave (from eb, no return), N🅶 Speedway, S🅾🅷,
151b a	I-57 (exits left from both directions), N to Chicago, S to Memphis
148b a	IL 43, Harlem Ave, N🅶 Speedway/dsl 🍽 Al's Beef, Buffalo Wild Wings, Burger King, Cracker Barrel, Culver's, Dunkin Donuts, Eggi Grill, Hamada of Japan, Pop's Italian Beef, Quizno's, Taco Fresco, Tin Fish Grill, Wendy's 🛏 Comfort Suites, Fairfield Inn, Hampton Inn, Holiday Inn, La Quinta, Sleep Inn, Wingate Inn, S🍽 Arby's, Boston's Grill, Subway, Taco Bell, TGIFriday's 🅾 ampitheater, Best Buy, Carmax, Kohl's, Michael's, PetsMart, SuperTarget

MOLINE

BETTENDORF

CHICAGO AREA

IL

🖲 = gas   🍴 = food   🏠 = lodging   ⊡ = other   🅟ₛ = rest stop   Copyright 2015 - the Next EXIT ®

INTERSTATE 80 Cont'd

Exit #	Services
147.5mm	weigh sta wb
145b a	US 45, 96th Ave, **N** 🍴 4K Asian, Arby's, Arrenello's Pizza, Baskin-Robbins/Dunkin Donuts, Quizno's, Tokyo Steaks, TX Roadhouse 🏠 Country Inn&Suites, Hilton Garden ⊡ Harley-Davidson, **S** **0-2 mi** 🖲 BP, Clark, Gas City, Shell/Circle K/dsl/24hr 🍴 A&W, Applebee's, Beggar's Pizza, Denny's, DQ, KFC, Mindy's Ribs, Nick's Rest., Rising Sun Chinese, Stoney Pt Grill, Subway, Wendy's, White Castle 🏠 Super 8 ⊡ Brookhaven Foods, CVS Drug, repair, Tuesday Morning
143mm	weigh sta eb
140	SW Hwy, **I-355 N Tollway**, US 6 S
137	US 30, New Lenox, **N** 🍴 Williamson's Rest. ⊡ K-Mart, **S** 🖲 Speedway/dsl 🍴 Beggar's Pizza, Burger King, KFC, LJ Silver/Papa Joe's, McDonald's/playplace, Paisono's Pizza, Pizza Hut, Subway, Taco Bell ⊡ Ace Hardware, city park, Goodyear/auto, Jewel-Osco/dsl, vet, Walgreens
134	Briggs St, **N** 🖲 Citgo, Speedway ⊡ 🅗, **S** 🖲 Shell/dsl, Valero/dsl ⊡ EZ Lube, Martin Camping, US RV Ctr
133	Richards St
132b a	US 52, IL 53, Chicago St
131.5mm	Des Plaines River
131	US 6, Meadow Ave, **N** ⊡ to Riverboat Casino
130b a	IL 7, Larkin Ave, **N** 🖲 Clark, Delta Sonic/dsl, Marathon/24hr, Mobil, Shell/24hr, Speedway 🍴 A&W/KFC, Baskin-Robbins/Dunkin Donuts, Bellagio Pizzaria, Bob Evans, Boston Mkt, Burger King, DQ, JJ Fish&Chicken, McDonald's, Quizno's, Steak'n Shake, Subway, Taco Bell, Wendy's, White Castle 🏠 Budget Inn, Comfort Inn, Holiday Inn, Motel 6, Red Roof Inn, Super 8 ⊡ 🅗, 7-11, Aldi Foods, Cadillac/Chevrolet, Discount Tire, Ford, Goodyear/auto, K-Mart, Pepboys, Radio Shack, Sam's Club/gas, to Coll of St Francis, vet, **S** 🖲 Citgo ⊡ auto repair
127	Houbolt Rd, to Joliet, **N** 🖲 7-11, BP/deli 🍴 Arby's, Burger King, China Kitchen, Cracker Barrel, Dunkin Donuts, Heros Sports Grill, Jimmy John's, McDonald's, Papa&Nana's Pizza 🏠 Fairfield Inn, Hampton Inn, Ramada Inn ⊡ Riverboat Casino
126b a	I-55, N to Chicago, S to St Louis
125.5mm	Du Page River
122	Minooka, **N** 🖲 Citgo/dsl, **S** 🖲 BP, 🍴 Arby's/scales/dsl/24hr 🍴 2-Fers Pizza, Baskin-Robbins/Dunkin Donuts, KFC, McDonald's/playplace, Rosati's Pizza, Subway, Taco Bell, Wendy's ⊡ $General, 7-11
119mm	🅟ₛ wb, full ♿ facilities, litter barrels, petwalk, phones, 🖾 playground, vending
117mm	🅟ₛ eb, full ♿ facilities, litter barrels, petwalk, 🖾 playground, vending
116	Brisbin Rd
112	IL 47, Morris, **N** 🖲 Marathon/dsl, 🍴 Subway/dsl/scales/24hr, TA/BP/Quiznos/scales/dsl/24hr/@ 🍴 Bellacino's, Chili's, IHOP 🏠 Comfort Inn, Days Inn, Holiday Inn Express, Quality Inn ⊡ $General, Menards, URGENT CARE, **S** 🖲 BP/dsl, Mobil/dsl, Shell, Spirit 🍴 Burger King, Culver's, DQ, Dunkin Donuts, Hong Kong Chinese, KFC/LJ Silver, Little Caesar's, Maria's Ristorante, McDonald's, Morris Diner, Pizza Hut, Rosati's Pizza, Subway, Taco Bell, Wendy's 🏠 Park Motel, Sherwood Oaks Motel, Super 8 ⊡ 🅗, $Tree, Aldi Foods, AT&T, AutoZone, Big R Store, Buick/Cadillac/Chevrolet, Chrysler/Dodge/Jeep, Fisher Parts, Ford, GMC, GNC, Jewel-Osco, Radio Shack, to Stratton SP, transmissions/repair, Verizon, Walgreens, Walmart/Subway

105	to Seneca
97	to Marseilles, **S** 🖲 Shell/dsl ⊡ Four Star Camping (5mi), Glenwood Camping (4mi), to Illini SP
93	IL 71, Ottawa, **N** 🍴 Road Ranger/Subway/dsl/scales/24hr, Shell/rest./dsl **S** 🍴 Hank's Farm Rest., New Chiam ⊡ 🅗,
92.5mm	Fox River
90	IL 23, Ottawa, **N** 🖲 BP/Subway 🍴 Arby's, Cracker Barrel, Taco Bell 🏠 Hampton Inn, Holiday Inn Express ⊡ AT&T, F&F, Honda, Toyota/Scion, Walmart/McDonald's **S** 🖲 BP/dsl/LP, Thornton's/dsl 🍴 Culver's, Dunkin Donuts, Hardee's, KFC/LJ Silver, Papa Murphy's, Sunfield Rest. 🏠 EconoLodge, Fairfield Inn, Super 8, Surrey Motel ⊡ 🅗, $Tree, Aldi Foods, Ford/Lincoln/Kia, Harley-Davidson, Kroger, O'Reilly Parts, Radio Shack, USPO
81	IL 178, Utica, **N** 🖲 Loves/McDonald's/Subway/dsl/scales/24hr ⊡ Hickory Hollow Camping, KOA (2mi), **S** 🖲 Shell/Jimmy Johns/dsl 🏠 Starved Rock Inn ⊡ repair, to Starved Rock SP, visitor info
79b a	I-39, US 51, N to Rockford, S to Bloomington
77.5mm	Little Vermilion River
77	IL 351, La Salle, **S** 🖲 FLYING J/Denny's/dsl/scales/24hr 🍴 UpTown Grill (3mi) 🏠 Daniels Motel (1mi) ⊡ st police
75	IL 251, Peru, **N** 🖲 BP, Shell/rest./dsl/24hr 🍴 4Star Rest., Arby's, McDonald's, Olive Garden, Starbucks, Taco Bell 🏠 Holiday Inn Express, Quality Inn, Super 8 ⊡ Kohl's, Petsmart, Walmart/Dunkin Donuts/Subway **S** 🖲 BP, Shell 🍴 Applebee's, Buffalo Wild Wings, Burger King, Culver's, DQ, IHOP, Jalepeno's Mexican, Jimmy John's, Master Buffet, McDonald's, Mi Margarita, Papa John's, Pizza Hut, Red Lobster, Steak'n Shake, Subway, Wendy's 🏠 Fairfield Inn, Hampton Inn, La Quinta ⊡ 🅗, $Tree, Advance Parts, Aldi Foods, AT&T, AutoZone, BigLots, Buick/GMC, Chevrolet/Mercedes, Chrysler/Dodge/Jeep, CVS Drug, Ford/Hyundai/Lincoln, Goodyear/auto, Hobby Lobby, Home Depot, HyVee Food/dsl, JC Penney, Jo-Ann Fabrics, Marshall's, Menards, Mercedes, Midas, NAPA, Nissan, O'Reilly Parts, Sears/auto, Staples, Target, Verizon, Walgreens
73	Plank Rd, **N** 🖲 Sapp Bros/Burger King/dsl/scales/@ 🍴 Big Apple Rest. ⊡ Barney's Lake Camping, Kenworth/Volvo
70	IL 89, to Ladd, **N** 🖲 Casey's, **S** 🖲 BP (3mi), Shell (3mi) 🏠 Spring Valley Motel ⊡ 🅗, golf
61	I-180, to Hennepin
56	IL 26, Princeton, **N** 🖲 Road Ranger/🍴/scales/dsl/@ 🏠 Super 8, **S** 🖲 BP/Beck's/dsl, Shell/dsl 🍴 Big Apple Rest., Burger King, Coffee Cup Rest., Culver's, KFC, McDonald's, Subway, Wendy's 🏠 AmericInn, Days Inn, EconoLodge ⊡ 🅗, $General, antiques, AutoZone, Buick/Cadillac/Chevrolet, O'Reilly Parts, Pennzoil, Sullivan's Food/gas/E-85, vet, Walmart
51mm	🅟ₛ both lanes, full ♿ facilities, litter barrels, petwalk, 🖾 playground, RV dump, vending
45	IL 40, **N** ⊡ antiques, to Ronald Reagan Birthplace (21mi), **S** ⊡ Hennepin Canal SP
44mm	Hennepin Canal
33	IL 78, to Kewanee, Annawan, **N** 🖲 Shabbona RV Ctr/Camp (3mi), **S** 🖲 Cenex/dsl, FS/dsl/E-85, Shell/Subway/dsl 🏠 Best Western ⊡ to Johnson-Sauk Tr SP
27	to US 6, Atkinson, **N** 🖲 Casey's (1mi)
19	IL 82, Geneseo, **N** 🖲 BP/dsl, Casey's/dsl 🍴 Culvers, DQ, Happy Joe's Pizza, Hardee's, McDonald's, New China, Pizza Hut, Subway, Sweet Pea's Grill 🏠 Best Western, Super 8 (2 mi) ⊡ 🅗, $General, Ford, SaveALot Foods, Verizon, Walgreens, Walmart **S** 🍴 Los Ranchitos Mexican
10	I-74, I-280, W to Moline, E to Peoria

IL

M O R R I S

P E R U

INTERSTATE 80 Cont'd

Exit #	Services
9	US 6, to Geneseo, **N** 🅕 Lavender Crest Winery/Cafe, **S** 🅞 Niabi Zoo
7	Colona, **N** 🅖 Shell/dsl 🅕 Country Fixins Rest.
5mm	Rock River
4b	I-88, IL 92, E to Rock Falls
4a	IL 5, IL 92, W to Silvis, **S** 🅞 Lundeen's Camping, st police
2mm	**weigh sta both lanes**
1.5mm	**Welcome Ctr eb, full 🅥 facilities, info, litter barrels, petwalk, 🅒, 🅙 scenic overlook**
1	IL 84, 20th St, Great River Rd, E Moline, **N** 🅖 BP/dsl 🅕 Bros Rest. 🅞 camping, The Great River Rd, **S 3 mi** 🅞 camping
0mm	Illinois/Iowa state line, Mississippi River

INTERSTATE 88

Exit #	Services
139.5mm	I-88 begins/ends on I-290.
139	I-294, S to Indiana, N to Milwaukee
138mm	**toll plaza**
137	IL 83 N, Cermak Rd, **N** 🅕 Clubhouse rest., Ditkas Rest., McDonald's 🅛 Marriott, Renaissance Inn 🅞 Barnes&Noble, Lord&Taylor, Macy's, Nieman-Marcus
136	IL 83 S, Midwest Rd (from eb), **N** 🅖 Shell/Circle K 🅕 All-Stars Rest., Burger King, Capri Ristorante, Chipotle Mexican, Denny's, Dunkin Donuts, Eggstacy, Giordano's Rest., Jamba Juice, McDonalds, Noodles&Co, Quizno's, Redstones, Starbucks, Subway, Subway 🅛 Holiday Inn, La Quinta 🅞 AT&T, Costco/gas, Home Depot, Nordstrom's, Old Navy, TJ Maxx, Walgreens, World Mkt
134	Highland Ave (no EZ wb return), **N** 🅕 Baker's Square, Bouna Beef, Brio Grille, Buca Italian, Burger King, Capital Grille, Champps Grill, Cheeseburger Paradise, Cici's, Claimjumper Rest., Fuddruckers, Harry Caray's, Hooters, Joe's Crabshack, Kona Grill, Kyoto, McCormick & Schmick's, Miller's Steakhouse, Olive Garden, Panera Bread, PF Chang's, Portilo's Hotdogs, Potbelly's, Qdoba, Red Lobster, Rockbottom Brewery, Ruby Tuesday, Starbucks, Subway, Taylor Brewing Co, TGIFriday's, Uncle Milio's, Weber Grill 🅛 Comfort Inn, Embassy Suites, Holiday Inn Express, Homestead Studios, Hyatt Place, Marriott, Red Roof Inn, Westin Hotel 🅞 🅗, Best Buy, Firestone/auto, Home Depot, JC Penney, Kohl's, mall, Marshall's, PetsMart, Vonmaur, **S** 🅕 Parkers Ocean Grill
132	I-355 N (from wb)
131	I-355 S (from eb)
130	IL 53 (from wb), **N 1 mi** 🅖 BP, Mobil 🅕 McDonald's 🅞 Walmart
127	Naperville Rd, **N** 🅕 Mullen's Grill 🅛 Hilton, Wyndam, **S** 🅖 Mobil 🅕 Buona Beef, Froots, HoneyBaked Ham, Jason's Deli, Maggiano's, McDonald's, Morton's Steaks, Pizza Hut, Subway, Taco Fresco, TGIFriday's, Wendy's, White Chocolate Grill 🅛 Best Western, Courtyard, Days Inn, Fairfield Inn, Hampton Inn, Holiday Inn Select 🅞 Dodge, Ford, Kia, Office Depot, Radio Shack, Subaru
125	Winfield Rd, **N** 🅖 BP, Mobil 🅛 Hamton Inn 🅞 🅗, Walgreens, **S** 🅕 Arby's, Atlanta Bread, Buffalo Wild Wings, CA Pizza Kitchen, Chipotle Mexican, Corner Bakery Cafe, Go-Roma, Jamba Juice, Max&Erma's, McDonald's, Potbelly's, Red Robin, Rockbottom Brewery, Starbucks, StirCrazy Grill 🅛 Hilton Garden, Springhill Suites 🅞 SuperTarget

123	IL 59, **N** 🅖 Gas City/dsl 🅕 Omega Rest 🅞 Carmax, **S** 🅖 BP, Mobil/dsl, Speedway 🅕 Baskin Robbins/Dunkin Donuts, Caribou Coffee, Cracker Barrel, Danny's Grill, Jimmy John's, Lee's Garden, Oberweis, Spicy Pickle, Starbucks, Steak'n Shake, Subway, TX Roadhouse, Wendy's 🅛 Extended Stay America, Fairfield Inn, Red Roof Inn, Sleep Inn, SpringHill Suites, Towneplace Suites 🅞 7-11, CVS Drug, Walgreens
119	Farnsworth Ave, **N** 🅖 BP, Shell 🅕 McDonald's, Millet's Grill, Papa Bear Rest., Quizno's, Sonic, Starbucks 🅛 Fox Valley Inn, Motel 6 🅞 Firestone/auto, Premium Outlets/Famous Brands, Walmart **S** 🅖 Marathon, Phillips 66/dsl, Shell, Speedway 🅕 Baskin-Robbins/Dunkin Donuts, Drive-Thru, Little Caesars, McDonald's, Mike&Denise's Pizza, Subway, Taco Bell 🅞 7-11, AutoZone, Family$, Goodyear, Walgreens
118mm	**toll plaza**
117	IL 31, IL 56, to Aurora, Batavia, **N** 🅖 Citgo/dsl 🅕 A&W 🅞 7-11, **S** 🅖 Mobil, Thornton's 🅕 Arby's, Baskin-Robbins/Dunkin Donuts, Burger King, Culver's, Denny's, KFC, LJ Silver, McDonald's, Nikary's, Popeye's, Quizno's, Rest., Subway, Taco Bell, White Castle 🅛 Baymont Inn 🅞 🅗, $Store, Ace Hardware, AutoZone, Cermak Foods, Firestone, GNC, Jewel/Osco, Murray's Parts, Radio Shack, U-Haul, Walgreens
115	Orchard Rd, **N** 🅕 McDonald's, Subway 🅞 Best Buy, Chrysler/Dodge/Jeep, Ford/Lincoln, Hyundai, JC Penney, Michaels, Nissan, PetCo, Subaru, Target, Woodman's/dsl, **S 0-2 mi** 🅖 7-11 🅕 A&W/KFC, Arby's, Buffalo Wild Wings, Chili's, Cold Stone, IHOP, Jimmy John's, Panera Bread, Papa Saverio's, Pizza Hut, Quizno's, Starbucks, Wendy's 🅛 Candlewood Suites, Hampton Inn, Holiday Inn 🅞 AT&T, CVS Drug, Discount Tire, Home Depot, Lowe's Whse, Office Depot, T-Moble
114	IL 56W, to US 30 (from wb, no EZ return), to Sugar Grove
109	IL 47 (from eb), Elburn
94	Peace Rd, to IL 38, **N** 🅞 🅗,
93mm	**Dekalb Oasis/24hr both lanes**, 🅖 Mobil/dsl 🅕 McDonald's, Panda Express, Subway
92	IL 38, IL 23, Annie Glidden Rd, to DeKalb, **N 2-3 mi** 🅖 BP, Marathon, Road Ranger/dsl, Shell 🅕 Aldorado, Baskin-Robbins, Blackstone Rest., Burger King, Chipotle Mexican, El Burrito Loco, Gyro's, Happy Wok Chinese, Jct Rest., KFC, LJ Silver, Lukulo's Rest., McDonald's, Molly's Eatery, Pagliai's Pizza, Pancake Rest., Panda Express, Papa John's, Pizza Hut, Pizza Pros, Pizza Villa, Potbelly, Quizno's, Starbucks, Subway, Taco Bell, Tom&Jerry's, Topper's Pizza, Vinny's Pizza, Wendy's 🅛 Best Western, Magneson Inn, Super 8, Travelodge 🅞 $General, Ford, Illini Tire, Schnuck's Food/Drug, to N IL U, Walgreens
86mm	**toll plaza**
78	I-39, US 51, S to Bloomington, N to Rockford

INTERSTATE 88 Cont'd

DIXON

Exit #	Services
76	IL 251, Rochelle, N 🅿 BP, Casey's, Shell 🍴 Olive Branch Rest. 🅾 🏥, Ford, GMC, tires/repair
56mm	**toll plaza**
54	IL 26, Dixon, N 🅿 BP/Subway/scales/dsl, Murphy USA/dsl 🍴 Culver's, Hardee's, Panda Chinese, Pizza Hut 🏨 Comfort Inn, Quality Inn, Super 8 🅾 🏥, $Tree, to John Deere HS, to Ronald Reagan Birthplace, to St Parks, Verizon, Walmart
44	US 30 (last free exit eb), N 🅾 Leisure lake RV Ctr (2mi), food, gas, lodging
41	IL 40, to Sterling, Rock Falls, N **1-2 mi** 🅿 Marathon, Mobil/dsl, Shell 🍴 American Grill, Arby's, Arthur's Deli, Burger King, Candlelight Rest., Culver's, El Tapatio Mexican, First Wok Chinese, Gazi's Rest., Hardee's, KFC, McDonald's/playplace, Perna's Pizza, Pizza Hut, Red Apple Rest., Subway 🏨 All Seasons Motel, Candlelight Inn, Country Inn&Suites, Holiday Inn, Super 8 🅾 🏥, $General, AutoZone, Country Mkt Foods, Curves, Harley-Davidson, O'Reilly Parts, Sav-a-Lot, Walgreens, Walmart

E MOLINE

36	to US 30, Rock Falls, Sterling
26	IL 78, to Prophetstown, Morrison, N 🅾 to Morrison-Rockwood SP
18	to Albany, Erie
10	to Port Byron, Hillsdale, S 🅿 Phillips 66/dsl, Shell/Mama J's Rest./scales/dsl/24hr
6	IL 92 E, to Joslin, N 🍴 Jammerz Roadhouse (2mi), S 🅾 Sunset Lake Camping (1mi)
2	Former IL 2
1b a	I-80, W to Des Moines, E to Chicago
0mm	IL 5, IL 92, W to Silvis. Lundeen's Camping, to Quad City Downs. **I-88 begins/ends on I-80, exit 4b.**

INTERSTATE 90

CHICAGO AREA

Exit #	Services
0mm	Illinois/Indiana state line, **Chicago Skyway Toll Rd begins/ends**
1mm	US 12, US 20, 106th St, Indianapolis Blvd, N 🅿 Citgo, Mobil, Shell/dsl 🅾 casino, S 🍴 Burger King, KFC, McDonald's 🅾 Aldi Foods, auto repair, Jewel-Osco
1.5mm	**Welcome Ctr/🆁🆂 eb, full 🏨 facilities, info, litter barrels, petwalk, 🚻, 🏨 playground, RV dump**
2.5mm	🅿 Skyway Oasis 🍴 McDonald's 🅾 **toll plaza**
3mm	87th St (from wb)
3.5mm	**S Beloit Toll Plaza,** phone
4mm	79th St, services on 79th St and Stoney Island Ave
5.5mm	73rd St (from wb)
6mm	State St (from wb), S 🅿 Citgo
7mm	I-94 N (mile markers decrease to IN state line)
I-90 E and I-94 E run together. See I-94, exits 43b - 59a.	
84	I-94 W, Lawrence Ave, N 🅿 BP
83b a	Foster Ave (from wb), N 🅿 BP 🍴 Checker's, Dunkin Donuts 🅾 Firestone/auto, Goodyear/auto, Walgreen
82c	Austin Ave, to Foster Ave
82b	Byrn-Mawr (from wb)
82a	Nagle Ave
81b	Sayre Ave (from wb)
81a	IL 43, Harlem Ave, S 🅿 BP, Shell
80	Canfield Rd (from wb), N 🅾 Walgreen
79b a	IL 171 S, Cumberland Ave, N 🅿 7-11, Marathon 🍴 Hooters, McDonald's, Outback Steaks, Starbucks 🏨 Holiday Inn, Marriott, SpringHill Suites, Westin Hotel 🅾 Dominick's Foods,

79b a	Continued
	S 🏨 Ramada, Renaissance
78.5mm	River Road Plaza, N 🍴 McDonald's 🏨 Marriott, Westin Hotel, S 🏨 Hyatt
78mm	I-294, I-190 W, 🅾 to O'Hare ✈
76mm	IL 72, Lee St (from wb), N 🏨 Extended Stay America, Quality Inn, Wyndham, S 🍴 McDonald's 🏨 Best Western, Holiday Inn Express, Holiday Inn Select, Sheraton Gateway, Studio+
74.5mm	**Des Plaines Oasis both lanes,** 🅿 Mobil/dsl/24hr 🍴 McDonald's/24hr, Panda Express, Starbucks, Subway
73.5mm	Elmhurst Rd (from wb), S 🅿 Shell 🍴 McDonald's 🏨 Best Western, Comfort Inn, Days Inn, La Quinta, Microtel, Motel 6
70.5mm	Arlington Hts Rd, N on Algonquin 🅿 Shell 🍴 Arby's, Baja Fresh, Birch River Grill, Buona Beef, Caribou Coffee, Chicago Pizza, Chili's, Chipotle Mexican, Denny's, Honey Baked Ham, Jimmy Johns, Magnum Steaks, McDonald's, Old Country Buffet, Panda Express, Pappadeaux Rest., Potbelly's, Steak'n Shake, Subway, Yanni's Greek Rest. 🏨 Courtyard, Double-Tree, Hyatt, Jameson Suites, Motel 6, Radisson, Red Roof Inn 🅾 AT&T, GNC, Lowe's Whse, Meijer, NTB, Staples, vet, Walmart S 🅿 Mobil, Shell 🍴 Subway 🏨 Sheraton

SCHAUMBURG

68mm	I-290, IL 53, N on Algonquin 🍴 Moretti's Italian 🏨 Best Western, Embassy Suites, Holiday Inn, Holiday Inn Express, Renaissance Inn, 🅾 mall, S **1 mi Golf Rd** 🍴 CA Pizza Kitchen, Cheesecake Factory, Hooters, Joe's Crabshack, Olive Garden, Panera Bread, Red Robin, Ruby Tuesday, Starbucks, Subway, TGI Friday's, Uno 🏨 Extended Stay America, Hyatt, Residence Inn 🅾 AT&T, Firestone, JC Penney, Lord&Taylor, Macy's, Marshall's, Nordstrom, Sears/auto
65.5mm	Roselle Rd (from wb, no return), N 🅾 Medieval Times Funpark, S 🅿 Mobil 🍴 Boston Mkt, Caribou Coffee, Chipotle Mexican, Denny's, Fox&Hound, Jimmy John's, KFC, La Magdalena, Melting Pot, Outback Steaks, Panda Express, Subway, Wendy's 🏨 Country Inn&Suites, Extended Stay America, Holiday Inn Express, Homestead Suites 🅾 7-11, Advance Parts, Audi, AutoZone, Buick/GMC, Carmax, Chrysler/Dodge/Jeep, Firestone, Hancock Fabrics, Jewel-Osco, Lexus, Mazda, Office Depot, O'Reilly Parts, PetCo, TJ Maxx, Walgreens
62mm	Barrington Rd (from wb), N 🍴 Apple Villa Pancake House, Hunan Beijing, Jersey's Grill, Jimmy John's, Lucky Monk, Millrose Rest., Quiznos, Subway 🏨 Hilton Garden 🅾 vet, S 🅿 BP 🍴 Chili's, IHOP, Macaroni Grill, McDonald's, Starbucks, Steak'n Shake, TGIFriday's 🏨 Candlewood Suites, Comfort Inn, Hampton Inn, Hyatt Place, La Quinta, Red Roof Inn 🅾 U-Haul
59.5mm	IL 59, N 🍴 Buffalo Wild Wings, Caribou Coffee, Chipotle Mexican, Claim Jumper Rest., Cooper's Hawk Rest., Jimmy John's, Moe's SW Grill, Noodles&Co, Panda Express, Panera Bread, Potbelly's, Red Robin, Ruth's Chris Steaks, Subway, Which Wich 🏨 Marriott 🅾 AT&T, Cabela's, CVS Drug, GNC, Michael's, Petsmart, Ross, Target, TJ Maxx, to Poplar Creek Music Theatre, Verizon, World Mkt
58mm	Beverly Rd (from wb)
56mm	IL 25, N 🏨 Lexington Inn, S 🅿 BP/dsl, Citgo, Shell/dsl, Speedway/dsl 🍴 Arby's, Baker Hill Pancakes, Wendy's 🅾 🏥, Advance Parts, city park, NAPA AutoCare

ELGIN

54.5mm	IL 31 N, N 🅿 BP, Thornton's 🍴 Alexander's Rest., Baskin-Robbins/Dunkin Donuts 🏨 Courtyard, Hampton Inn, Holiday Inn, Quality Inn, Super 8, TownePlace Suites, S 🍴 One for the Road Hotdogs
54mm	**Elgin Toll Plaza,** phone

INTERSTATE 90 Cont'd

Exit #	Services
52mm	Randall Rd, **N** 🅖 Shell 🍴 Big Sammy's Hot Dogs, Burnt Toast, Cafe Roma, DQ, Jimmy John's, Jimmy's Charhouse, Mr Wok, Panera Bread, Rookies Grill, Starbucks, Tilted Kilt, Village Pizza 🏨 Comfort Suites, Country Inn&Suites 🄾 Honda, **S** 🅖 7-11 🏨 Candlewood Suites 🄾 🄷,
46.5mm	IL 47, to Woodstock, **N** 🄾 Ford, General RV Ctr, Huntley Outlets/famous brands
42.5mm	US 20, Marengo, **N** 🅖 Citgo/Arrowhead Rest/dsl/scales/24hr, [Pilot]/Road Ranger/Subway/dsl/scales/24hr, TA/BP/Burger King/Popeye's/dsl/scales/24hr/@ 🍴 McDonald's, Wendy's 🏨 Super 8 🄾 **access to services at exit 46 (6mi)**, Ford, Huntley Outlets, museums
38mm	**Marengo Toll Plaza (from eb)**
25mm	Genoa Rd, to Belvidere, **N** 🅖 Murphy USA/dsl 🍴 Applebee's, Rosati's Pizza, Starbucks, Subway 🄾 camping, Verizon, Walmart/Blimpie
24mm	**Belvidere Oasis both lanes**, 🅖 Mobil/7-11/dsl/24hr 🍴 Food Court, McDonald's, Panda Express, 🅒, Starbucks, Subway, Taco Bell
23.5mm	**Belvidere Toll Plaza**
18mm	Kishwaukee River
17.5mm	I-39 S, US 20, US 51, to Rockford, **S** funpark
15mm	US 20, State St, **N** 🅖 Mobil/dsl, Phillips 66/Subway/dsl 🍴 Cracker Barrel 🏨 Baymont Inn, Clocktower Resort, Days Inn, **S** 0-2 mi 🅖 Mobil/dsl, Road Ranger/dsl 🍴 5 Guys Burgers, Applebee's, Buffalo Wild Wings, Burger King, Chick-fil-A, Chili's, Chipotle Mexican, City Buffet, Coldstone, Culver's, Denny's, Dos Reales, Fiesta Cancun, Gerry's Pizza, Giovanni's Rest., Hoffman House Rest., Hooters, IHOP, Jason's Deli, JerseyMike's, Jimmy John's, KFC/LJ Silver, Lino's Italian, LoneStar Steaks, Longhorn Steaks, Machine Shed Rest., McDonald's, Noodles&Co, Old Chicago Grill, Olive Garden, Outback Steaks, Panda Express, Panera Bread, Panino's Drive-Thru, Perkins, Pizza Hut/Taco Bell, PotBelly, Red Lobster, Red Robin, Ruby Tuesday, Starbucks, Steak'n Shake, Stone Eagle Tavern, Subway, ThunderBay Grille, TX Roadhouse, Wendy's 🏨 Candlewood Suites, Comfort Inn, Courtyard, Extended Stay America, Fairfield Inn, Hampton Inn, Hilton Garden, Holiday Inn, Motel 6, Quality Suites, Radisson, Red Roof Inn, Residence Inn, Sleep Inn, Staybridge Suites, Super 8 🄾 🄷, $Tree, Advance Parts, Aldi Foods, AT&T, Best Buy, BigLots, Burlington Coats, Cadillac, Chrysler/Dodge/Jeep, Dick's, Discount Tire, GNC, Gordman's, Hancock Fabrics, Hobby Lobby, Home Depot, Hyundai, JoAnn Fabrics, K-Mart, Kohl's, Lowe's, Marshall's, Mazda, Michael's, Nissan, Old Navy, Old Time Pottery, PetCo, Petsmart, Radio Shack, Ross, Sam's Club/gas, Schnuck's Foods, Subaru, Target, Tuesday Morning, Valli Foods, Verizon, Walgreens, Walmart/McDonald's
12mm	E Riverside Blvd, Loves Park, **S** 0-2 mi 🅖 BP, Mobil/dsl, Phillips 66/dsl, Road Ranger/[Pilot]/Subway/dsl, Shell/dsl 🍴 2nd Cousin's Grill, Arby's, BeefARoo, Ciaobella, Culver's, DQ, Greenfire Rest., India House, Japanese Express, KFC, McDonald's, RBI Rest., Rosatti's Pizza, Sam's Ristorante, Singapore Grill, Subway, Taco Bell, Wendy's 🏨 Holiday Inn Express, Quality Inn 🄾 Audi/Honda/Mercedes, Autowerks, Farm&Fleet, funpark, Lexus, to Rock Cut SP, Toyota/Scion, Tuffy Auto, Walgreens
8mm	Il 173, **S** to Rock Cut SP
3	Rockton Rd, **S** 🅖 Loves/Hardee's/dsl/scales/24hr

Exit #	Services
1	US 51 N, IL 75 W, S Beloit, **N** 🅖 Road Ranger/McDonald's/dsl, **S** 🅖 ⟋FLYING J/Denny's/dsl/scales/24hr, Road Ranger/[Pilot]/Subway/dsl/E85/scales/24hr 🏨 Best Western, Tollway Inn 🄾 Finnegan's RV Ctr, Pearl Lake camping (2mi)
0mm	Illinois/Wisconsin state line

INTERSTATE 94

Exit #	Services
161	US 6, IL 83, Torrence Ave, **N** 🅖 BP 🍴 Arby's, Bob Evans, Chili's, Dixie Kitchen, Hooters, IHOP, Olive Garden, On-the-Border, Oriental Palace, Wendy's 🏨 Comfort Suites, Days Inn, Extended Stay America, Fairfield Inn, Red Roof Inn, Sleep Inn, Super 8 🄾 Best Buy, Chrysler/Jeep, Dominick's Foods, Firestone/auto, Home Depot, JustTires, K-Mart, PepBoys, Radio Shack, **S** 🅖 Gas City, Marathon, Mobil 🍴 Al's Diner, Brown's Chicken/pasta, Burger King, Dunkin Donuts, Golden Crown Rest., McDonald's, Pappy's Gyro's 🄾 Auto Clinic, Chevrolet, Sam's Club, SunRise Foods, Walgreen
	I-94 and I-80 run together 3 mi.
77mm	Illinois/Indiana state line
74a	IL 394 S, to Danville
74[160]b	I-80/I-294 W
73b a	US 6,159th St, **N** 🅖 Mobil 🍴 Applebee's, Buffalo Wild Wings, Fuddrucker's, Outback Steaks, Panda Express, Quiznos, Rib Ribs, Sonic, Starbucks, Taco Bell, White Castle 🄾 BigLots, Hyundai, JC Penney, Kia, Lincoln, Macy's, Marshall's, Michael's, Nissan, Office Depot, Old Navy, PetCo, Target, Toyota/Scion, USPO, vet, **S** 🅖 BP, Marathon 🍴 Harold's Chicken, McDonald's, Popeye's, Rally's, Shark's, Subway 🏨 Cherry Lane Motel 🄾 Aldi Foods, Jewel-Osco, Stanfa Tire/repair
71b a	Sibley Blvd, **N** 🅖 Citgo, Mobil/dsl, Valero/dsl 🍴 McDonald's, Nicky's Gyros, Popeye's, Quiznos, Shark's, Subway 🏨 Baymont Inn 🄾 Family$, Pete's Mkt, **S** 🅖 Clark, Marathon/dsl, Shell 🍴 Baskin-Robbins/Dunkin Donuts, Burger King, Family Wendy's, KFC, Snapper's Chicken, White Castle 🏨 Best Motel 🄾 $General, Advance Parts, AutoZone, Fairplay Foods, Food4Less/gas, Menards, Radio Shack, Walgreens
70b a	Dolton
69	Beaubien Woods (from eb), Beaubien Woods Forest Preserve
68b a	130th St
66b	115th St, **S** 🅖 McDonald's
66a	111th Ave, **S** 🅖 Citgo/dsl, Shell 🄾 🄷, Firestone/auto
65	103rd Ave, Stony Island Ave
63	I-57 S (exits left from wb)
62	Wentworth Ave (from eb), **N** 🅖 Citgo, Mobil 🍴 Subway
61b	87th St, **N** 🅖 BP, Shell 🍴 Burger King, McDonald's, **S** 🍴 Stabucks, Subway 🄾 $Tree, AutoZone, Best Buy, Burlington

R O C K F O R D

C H I C A G O   A R E A

IL

INTERSTATE 94 Cont'd

Exit #	Services
61b	Continued
	Coats, Food4Less, Home Depot, Jewel-Osco, Marshall's, O'Reilly Parts, Staples, Verizon
61a	83rd St (from eb), N 🅟 Shell 🍴 Subway 🅾 st police
60c	79th St, N 🅟 Mobil, Shell 🍴 Brown's Chicken 🅾 Walgreens, S 🅟 Citgo/dsl 🍴 Church's
60b	76th St, N 🅟 BP, Mobil, Shell 🅾 Walgreens, S 🍴 KFC/Pizza Hut, Popeye's
60a	75th St (from eb), N 🅟 BP, Mobil, Shell 🅾 Aldi Foods, S 🍴 KFC, Pizza Hut, Popeye's 🅾 Walgreens
59c	71st St, N 🅟 BP, S 🍴 McDonald's
59a	I-90 E, to **Indiana Toll Rd**
58b	63rd St (from eb), N 🅟 Citgo, S 🅟 Mobil
58a	I-94 divides into local and express, 59th St, S 🅟 BP
57b	Garfield Blvd, N 🍴 Al's Beef, Checker's, Grand Chinese Kitchen, Subway 🅾 Family$, Walgreens, S 🅟 Citgo, Mobil, Shell/24hr 🍴 Wendy's 🅾 🏠
57a	51st St
56b	47th St (from eb)
56a	43rd St, S 🅟 BP/Subway/dsl, Citgo/dsl
55b	Pershing Rd
55a	35th St, S 🅾 to New Comiskey Park
54	31st St
53c	I-55, Stevenson Pkwy, N to downtown, Lakeshore Dr
53b	I-55, Stevenson Pkwy, S to St Louis
52c	18th St (from eb), 🅾 Dominick's Foods
52b	Roosevelt Rd, Taylor St (from wb), N 🅟 Citgo 🅾 Best Buy, Home Depot, Walgreens, Whole Foods Mkt
52a	Taylor St, Roosevelt Rd (from eb), N 🅟 Citgo
51h-i	I-290 W, to W Suburbs
51g	E Jackson Blvd, downtown
51f	W Adams St, downtown
51e	Monroe St (from eb), downtown, S 🏠 Crowne Plaza 🅾 Dominick's Foods, Walgreens
51d	Madison St (from eb), S 🏠 Crowne Plaza 🅾 Dominick's Foods, Walgreens, downtown
51c	E Washington Blvd, downtown
51b	W Randolph St, downtown
51a	Lake St (from wb)
50b	E Ohio St, S 🅟 Marathon, downtown
50a	Ogden Ave
49b a	Augusta Blvd, Division St, N 🅾 Lexus, S 🅟 BP, Shell 🍴 Pizza Hut
48b	IL 64, North Ave, N 🅟 BP, S 🅟 Valero 🅾 Mercedes
48a	Armitage Ave, N 🅾 Best Buy, Kohl's, S 🅟 Shell 🅾 Jaguar, Land Rover, Volvo
47c b	Damen Ave, N 🅟 car/vanwash, Citgo
47a	Western Ave, Fullerton Ave, N 🅟 Citgo 🍴 Burger King, Dunkin Donuts, Popeye's, Starbucks, Subway 🅾 Costco/gas, Home Depot, Jo-Ann Fabrics, Pepboys, Petsmart, Staples, Target, S 🅟 Marathon
46b a	Diversey Ave, California Ave, N 🅟 Citgo, S 🍴 IHOP/24hr, Popeye's 🅾 Walgreens
45c	Belmont Ave, N 🍴 Wendy's
45b	Kimball Ave, N 🅟 Marathon/dsl, S 🅟 Valero 🍴 Dunkin Donuts, Pizza Hut, Subway 🅾 Aldi Foods, Best Buy, Radio Shack, Walgreens
45a	Addison St
44b	Pulaski Ave, Irving Park Rd, N 🅟 BP, Mobil

Exit #	Services
44a	IL 19, Keeler Ave, Irving Park Rd, N 🅟 BP, Shell/24hr 🅾 to Wrigley Field
43c	Montrose Ave
43b	I-90 W
43a	Wilson Ave
42	W Foster Ave (from wb), S 🅟 Citgo, Marathon
41mm	Chicago River, N Branch
41c	IL 50 S, to Cicero, to I-90 W
41b a	US 14, Peterson Ave, N 🅾 Whole Foods Mkt
39b a	Touhy Ave, N 🅟 BP/dsl, Shell/Circle K 🅾 Cassidy Tire, Toyota/Scion, S 🅟 BP, Citgo, Shell 🍴 Baja Fresh, Baskin-Robbins/Dunkin Donuts, Buffalo Wild Wings, Burger King, Chili's, Chipotle Mexican, ChuckeCheese, Jack's Rest./24hr, McDonald's, Noodles&Co, Outback Steaks, Quiznos, Red Robin, Sander's Rest., Starbucks, Subway 🏠 Holiday Inn 🅾 Barnes&Noble, Best Buy, Dick's, GNC, Jewel-Osco, Lee's Parts, Nissan, Office Depot, PepBoys, PetCo, Petsmart, Radio Shack, vet, Walgreens, Walmart
37b a	IL 58, Dempster St
35	Old Orchard Rd, N 🅟 BP, Shell 🍴 Bloomingdale's, CA Pizza Kitchen, CheeseCake Factory, McCormick&Schmick's Rest 🅾 🏠, mall, Nissan, S 🍴 Ruby Tuesday 🏠 Extended Stay America, Hampton Inn
34c b	E Lake Ave, N 🅟 BP 🍴 Omaha Steaks, Panda Express, Starbucks 🅾 Fresh Mkt Foods, GNC, S 🅟 BP, Shell 🍴 DQ
34a	US 41 S, Skokie Rd (from eb)
33b a	Willow Rd, S 🅟 BP, Shell 🍴 Starbucks 🅾 Dominick's Foods, Walgreens
31	E Tower Rd, S 🅾 BMW, Carmax, Chrysler/Dodge/Jeep, Infiniti, Mercedes, Toyota/Scion, vet
30b a	Dundee Rd (from wb, no EZ return), S 🅟 Citgo, Marathon 🍴 Barnaby's Rest., Morton's Steaks, Potbelly's, Ruth's Chris Steaks, Starbucks 🏠 Renaissance
29	US 41, to Waukegan, to Tri-state tollway
28mm	IL 43, Waukegan Rd, N 🅟 BP, Shell 🍴 Baja Fresh, Old Country Buffet 🏠 Embassy Suites, Red Roof Inn 🅾 Best Buy, Home Depot, Jewel-Osco, NTB, Steinmart, TJ Maxx
26mm	I-294 S, Lake-Cook Rd (from sb), E 🍴 J-Alexander's Rest 🏠 Hyatt
25mm	**Deerfield Rd toll plaza,** phones
24mm	Deerfield Rd (from nb), W 🅟 Mobil 🏠 Marriott Suites
22mm	IL 22, Half Day Rd, E 🏠 La Quinta, W 🏠 Homewood Suites
19mm	IL 60, Town Line Rd, E 🅾 🏠, W 🏠 Hilton Garden, Residence Inn 🅾 Costco/gas
18mm	**Lake Forest Oasis both lanes,** E 🅟 Mobil/7-11/dsl 🍴 KFC, McDonald's, Panda Express, Starbucks, Subway, Taco Bell 🅾 info
16mm	IL 176, Rockland Rd (no nb re-entry), E 🅾 Harley-Davidson, to Lamb's Farm
14mm	IL 137, Buckley Rd, E 🅾 Chicago Med School, to VA 🏠
11mm	IL 120 E, Belvidere Rd (no nb re-entry), E 🅾 🏠
10mm	IL 21, Milwaukee Ave (from eb, no eb re-entry), E 🍴 Papa John's 🅾 🏠, Six Flags
8mm	IL 132, Grand Ave, E 🅟 Speedway/dsl 🍴 Baskin-Robbins/Dunkin Donuts, Burger King, ChuckeCheese, Cracker Barrel, Culver's, Golden Corral, Ichibahn, IHOP, Jimmy John's, Joe's Crabshack, KFC/LJ Silver, McDonald's, Moe's SW Grill, Oberweiss, Old Chicago Red Hots, Olive Garden, Outback Steaks, Rosati's Pizza, Starbucks, Subway 🏠 Best Western, Country Inn&Suites, Extended Stay America, Grand Hotel, Hampton Inn, Key Lime Cove Resort, La Quinta 🅾 Six Flags Park, W 0-2 mi 🅟 Mobil, Shell/Circle K 🍴 Bakers Square,

CHICAGO AREA · *IL* · *CHICAGO AREA* · *GURNEE*

🔼E INTERSTATE 94 Cont'd	
Exit #	Services
8mm	Cont'd
	Boston Mkt, Chili's, Chipotle Mexican, Denny's, Giordano's Pizza, Jersey Mike's Subs, Jimano's Pizza, LoneStar Steaks, McDonald's, Noodles&Co, Panda Express, Panera Bread, Penn Sta Subs, Pizza Hut, Potbelly's, Red Lobster, Red Robin, Ruby Tuesday, Starbucks, Steak'n Shake, Taco Bell, TGIFriday's, Uno Grill, Wendy's, White Castle 🏨 Comfort Inn, Fairfield Inn, Holiday Inn 🅾 $Tree, AT&T, AutoZone, Bass Pro Shops, Best Buy, Buick/GMC, Chrysler/Dodge/Jeep, Dominick's Foods, Firestone/auto, Goodyear, Gurnee Mills Outlet Mall/famous brands, Home Depot, Honda, Hyundai, Jewel-Osco, Kohl's, Macy's, Menards, Michael's, Nissan, Old Navy, Petsmart, Radio Shack, Ross, Sam's Club, Sears Grand/auto, Target, TJ Maxx, Tuesday Morning, Verizon, VW, Walgreens, Walmart
5mm	**Waukegan toll plaza**, phones
2mm	IL 173 (from nb, no return), Rosecrans Ave, E 🅾 to IL Beach SP
1b	US 41 S, to Waukegan (from sb), E 🅾 I-94 RV Ctr
1a	Russell Rd, W 🅿 Citgo/dsl/scales, TA/Country Pride/dsl/scales/24hr/@ 🅾 Peterbilt
0mm	Illinois/Wisconsin state line

🔼N INTERSTATE 255 (St Louis)	
Exit #	Services
I-255 begins/ends on I-270, exit 7.	
30	I-270, W to Kansas City, E to Indianapolis
29	IL 162, to Glen Carbon, to Pontoon Beach, Granite City
26	Horseshoe Lake Rd, E st police
25b a	I-55/I-70, W to St Louis, E to Chicago, Indianapolis
24	Collinsville Rd, E 🅿 BP/24hr 🍽 Jack-in-the-Box 🅾 Shop'n Save, W 🅾 Fairmount Racetrack
20	I-64, US 50, W to St Louis, E to Louisville, **services 1 mi E off I-64, exit 9.**
19	State St, E St Louis, E 🏨 Western Inn 🅾 Holten SP
17b a	IL 15, E St Louis, to Belleville, Centreville, E 🅿 ⊘FLYING J/Denny's/dsl/scales/24hr W 🅿 Phillips 66
15	Mousette Lane, E 🅾 🅷, W 🅾 Peterbilt
13	IL 157, to Cahokia, E 🅿 Phillips 66, W 🅿 BP/24hr, QT 🍽 Capt D's, China Express, Classic K Burgers, Domino's, DQ, Hardee's, Jade Garden, KFC, McDonald's, Pizza Hut, Popeye's, Rally's, Subway 🏨 Holiday Inn Express 🅾 $General, Advance Parts, Aldi Foods, AutoZone, Buick/GMC, Cahokia RV Park, Cahokia RV Parque (2mi), CarQuest, Curves, Dobb's Tires, Family$, Schnuck's, Shop'n Save Foods, Walgreens, Walmart/drugs
10	IL 3 N, to Cahokia, E St Louis, W 🅿 ZX/Subway/dsl
9	to Dupo, W 🅿 BP
6	IL 3 S, to Columbia (exits left from sb), E 🅿 Phillips 66, Shell/dsl/24hr 🏨 Hampton Inn (2mi) 🅾 Chevrolet
4mm	Missouri/Illinois state line, Mississippi River
3	Koch Rd
2	MO 231, Telegraph Rd, N 🅿 Conoco, Shell/Circle K 🍽 McDonald's, Pizza Hut/Taco Bell, Steak'n Shake, Waffle House 🅾 $Tree, Advance Parts, Jefferson Barracks Nat Cem, Radio Shack, Walmart S 🅿 CFM/dsl, Mobil, QT, Shell 🍽 China Wok, DQ, Imo's Pizza
1d c	US 50, US 61, US 67, Lindbergh Blvd, Lemay Ferry Rd, accesses same as I-55 exit 197 E, N 🅿 Phillips 66 🍽 Arby's, Buffalo Wild Wings, ChuckeCheese, CiCi's Pizza, Dillard's,

1d c	Continued
	Hometown Buffet, HoneyBaked Ham, Hooters, KFC, Krispy Kreme, Macaroni Grill, Noodles&Co, Qdoba Mexican, Quizno's, St Louis Bread Co, Station Subs, Steak'n Shake, Subway, Tucker's Place 🅾 Advance Parts, Best Buy, Costco/gas, Dillard's, Discount Tire, Dodge, Ford, Home Depot, JC Penney, Kia, K-Mart, Macy's, mall, Marshall's, NTB, Sears/auto, Tuesday Morning, S 🅿 Phillips 66 🍽 Jack-in-the-Box, McDonald's, Rich & Charlie's Italian, White Castle 🅾 $General, BigLots, Firestone, Old Navy, Petsmart, Sam's Club/gas, Walgreens
1b a	I-55 S to Memphis, N to St Louis. **I-255 begins/ends on I-55, exit 196.**

INTERSTATE 270 (St Louis)	
See Missouri Interstate 270 (St Louis)	

🔼E INTERSTATE 294 (Chicago)	
Exit #	Services
I-294 begins/ends on I-94. exit 71. Numbering descends from west to east.	
I-294 & I-80 run together 5 mi. See I-80, exits 155-160.	
5mm	I-80 W, access to I-57
5.5mm	167th St, **toll booth**, phones
6mm	US 6, 159th St, E 🅿 Citgo, Clark, Marathon, Mobil/dsl, Shell/dsl 🅾 Aldi Foods, AutoZone, Walgreen, W 🅿 BP 🍽 Baskin-Robbins/Dunkin Donuts, Burger King, McDonald's, Popeye's, Subway, Taco Bell, White Castle 🏨 Chicago Inn&Suites 🅾 $Tree, AutoZone, Family$, U-Haul, Walgreens
11mm	Cal Sag Channel
12mm	IL 50, Cicero Ave, E 🅿 7-11, BP, Shell/dsl 🍽 Dunkin Donuts, Subway, White Castle 🅾 Home Depot, W 🅿 Shell/dsl 🍽 Boston Mkt, IHOP, Panda Express, Pizza Hut, Popeye's, Portillo's Dogs, Potbelly, Subway 🏨 Baymont Inn, Hampton Inn, Holiday Inn Express 🅾 Best Buy, NTB, PepBoys
18mm	US 12/20, 95th St, E 🅿 Citgo, Marathon 🍽 Chick-fil-A, TX Corral 🅾 🅷, CarMax, Discount Tire, mall, Mazda, Sears/auto, W 🅿 7-11, BP, Shell, Speedway/dsl 🍽 Arby's, Baskin-Robbins, Burger King, Denny's, Dunkin Donuts, Jimmy John's, Les Bros Rest., McDonald's, Prime Time Rest., The Pit Ribhouse, Wendy's 🏨 Exel Inn 🅾 🅷, $Tree, Jewel-Osco, Walgreen
20mm	**toll booth**, phones
22mm	75th St, Willow Springs Rd
23mm	I-55, Wolf Rd, to Hawthorne Park
25mm	**Hinsdale Oasis both lanes**, 🅿 Mobil/7-11/dsl 🍽 KFC/Taco Bell, McDonald's, McDonald's, Panda Express, Sbarro, Subway

G U R N E E

C H I C A G O   A R E A

IL

IL

CHICAGO AREA
IL IN

⬆E INTERSTATE 294 (Chicago) Cont'd

Exit #	Services
28mm	US 34, Ogden Ave, **E** Ⓞ zoo, **W** ⓐ BP, Shell/deli ⑪ Dunkin Donuts, McDonald's, Starbucks Ⓞ Ⓗ, Ferrari/Maserati, Firestone/auto, LandRover, Whole Foods Mkt
28.5mm	Cermak Rd (from sb, no return)
29mm	**I-88 tollway**
30mm	**toll booth**, phones
31mm	IL 38, Roosevelt Rd (no EZ nb return), **E** ⓐ Citgo/dsl ⌂ Hillside Manor Motel
32mm	I-290 W, to Rockford (from nb)
34mm	I-290 (from sb), to Rockford
38mm	**O'Hare Oasis both lanes,** ⓐ Mobil/7-11/dsl ⑪ KFC, McDonald's, Panda Express, Sbarro, Starbucks, Subway, Taco Bell, TCBY
39mm	IL 19 W (from sb), Irving Park Rd, ⓐ BP/repair, Clark, Clark, Marathon/dsl ⑪ DQ, Dunkin Donuts, McDonald's, Subway, Wendy's ⌂ Comfort Suites Ⓞ 7-11, Aldi Foods, Walgreen, **W** ⌂ Candlewood Suites, Day's Inn, Hampton Inn, Howard Johnson, Sheraton
40mm	I-190 W, **E Services from I-90, exit 79** ⓐ Mobil ⑪ McDonald's ⌂ Courtyard, Doubletree, Embassy Suites, Holiday Inn, Hotel Softel, Hyatt, Marriott, Radisson, Rosemont Suites, Westin
41mm	**toll booth,** phones
42mm	Touhy Ave, **W** ⓐ Mobil/service ⑪ Tiffany's Rest. ⌂ Comfort Inn
43mm	Des Plaines River
44mm	Dempster St (from nb, no return), **E** Ⓞ Ⓗ, **W** ⑪ Dunkin Donuts, Subway
46mm	IL 58, Golf Rd, **E** ⓐ Citgo/dsl, Shell ⑪ Omega Rest., Senoya Oriental ⌂ Wyndham Ⓞ Ⓗ, auto repair, Best Buy, CVS Drug, Golf Mill Mall, Target
49mm	Willow Rd, **W 1 mi on Milwaukee** ⓐ BP ⑪ Burger King, Denny's, McDonald's, TGIFriday's ⌂ Courtyard, Doubletree Suites, Fairfield Inn, Motel 6, Wingate Inn
53mm	Lake Cook Rd (no nb re-entry), **E** ⌂ Embassy Suites, Hyatt
	I-294 begins/ends on I-94.

⬆N INTERSTATE 355

Exit #	Services
30mm	**I-355 begins/ends on I-290**
29	US 20 W Lakes St, **E** ⓐ Citgo/dsl, Marathon, Shell, ⑪ Applebee's, Baskin-Robbins/Dunkin Donuts, Culver's, Famous Dave's BBQ, Home Run Rest, IHOP, Jimmy John's, La Hacienda Mexican, Nana Hotdogs, Panera Bread, Ristorante de Marco's, Starbucks, Wok'n Fire, Zaza's Steaks, ⌂ Hampton Inn, Ⓞ Midas, Verizon, Walmart, **W** ⓐ Shell, ⑪ Venuti's Rest
28	IL 64, E North Ave, **E** ⓐ BP/Subway/dsl, Shell/Circle K, Burger King, McDonald's, Comfort Suites, Fairfield Inn, **W** ⓐ Phillips 66, Speedway/dsl, ⌂ Hilton Garden, Ramada, Ⓞ Art's RV Ctr, Goodyear
25	Roosevelt, **E** ⓐ Mobil, ⑪ Boston Mkt, Buffalo Wild Wings, Odyssey Greek, Pizza Hut, Roundhead Pizza, Starbucks, White Castle, Wolfy's Dogs, ⌂ Crowne Plaza, Ⓞ AutoZone, Cadillac, $General, Jewel-Osco, K-Mart, Toyota/Scion, **W** ⑪ Jimmy John's, Ⓞ Dominick's Foods, NAPA
22	IL 56, Butterfield Rd, **E** ⑪ Brick House Rest, Buona Beef, Burger King, Cheese Burger Paradise, Chipotle Mexican, CiCi's Pizza, Fuddrucker's, Hooters, Melting Pot, Olive Garden, Panera Bread, Portillo, Qdoba, Red Lobster, Rita's Mexican, Ruby Tuesday, Subway, ⌂ Comfort Inn, Holiday Inn Express, Marriott, Red Roof Inn, Ⓞ Best Buy, $Tree, Kohl's, Petsmart,

PEORIA

22	Continued
	Verizon, **W** ⑪ Carlucci Italian, ⌂ DoubleTree Suites, Ⓞ Home Depot, 7-11
20mm	**I-88 E/I-355 run together**
19	US 34, Ogden Ave, **E** ⓐ Shell, ⑪ Culver's, Jimmy John's, ⌂ InTown Suites, Ⓞ AT&T, Buick/GMC, Chrysler/Dodge/Jeep, **W** Speedway/dsl, ⑪ Baskin-Robbins/Dunkin Donuts, ⌂ Extended Stay America, Ⓞ Chevrolet
18	Maple Ave, **E 1 mi** ⓐ BP, ⑪ KFC/Taco Bell, McDonald's, Ⓞ Walgreens
16	63rd St, Hobson Rd, **E** ⓐ Mobil, Thornton's/McDonald's, ⑪ Steven's Rest, Subway, Ⓞ AutoZone, Dominick's Foods, GNC, Target, Walgreen's
15	W 75th St, **E** ⓐ Mobil, ⑪ Arby's, Bakers Square Rest, Ⓞ Home Depot, JC Penney Sam's Club/gas, **W** ⓐ Marathon, Phillips 66, ⑪ Dunkin-Donuts, El Burro Loco, McDonald's, Pizza Italiano, Sandpiper Rest, Ⓞ Jewel-Osco
14	87th St, Baughton Rd, **E** ⓐ BP, Shell, ⑪ Al's Pizza, Dunkin-Donuts, McDonald's, Subway, Wendy's, Ⓞ CVS Drug, Costco/gas, Staples, **W** ⓐ Mobil, ⑪ Buffalo Wild Wings, Famous Dave's BBQ, 5 Guys Burgers, Johnny Rockets, Longhorn Steaks, Panda Express, Potbelly, Starbucks, Ⓞ Barnes&Noble, Bass Pro Shops, Macy's, Meijer/gas, Verizon, Walgreens
12	I-55
8	127th St, **E** ⓐ Phillips 66/dsl, ⑪ Burger King, KFC, McDonald's, Starbucks, Subway, Taco Bell, Ⓞ Aldi Foods, Firestone/auto, Jewel-Osco, Jiffy Lube, Walgreens, USPO
6	IL 171, Archer Ave, 143rd St, **E** Ⓞ Kohl's, Target, vet
5	159th Ave, IL 7, Orland Park, Homer Glen, **E** ⓐ Speedway/dsl, **W** URGENT CARE
3mm	**toll booth,** both directions
1	US 6, **W** Ⓗ
0mm	I-80 E, W. **I-355 begins/ends on I-80 exit 140**

⬆E INTERSTATE 474 (Peoria)

Exit #	Services
15	I-74, E to Bloomington, W to Peoria
9	IL 29, E Peoria, to Pekin, **N** ⓐ Shell/Arby's/dsl, Thornton's ⑪ DQ, Driftwood Pizza, Taco John's ⌂ Ragon Motel Ⓞ $General, Riverboat Casino (6mi), **S** ⓐ Casey's, Shell/Subway/dsl ⑪ Denny's, KFC, Lian Wang, McDonald's, Mickie's Pizza Ⓞ Chrysler/Dodge/Jeep, Toyota/Scion
8mm	Illinois River
6b a	US 24, Adams St, Bartonville, **S** ⓐ BP/dsl, Shell/dsl ⑪ Hardee's, KFC, McDonald's, Tyroni's Café
5	Airport Rd, **S** ⓐ Phillips 66/e-85/dsl Ⓞ ☞
3a	to IL 116, Farmington, **S** Ⓞ Wildlife Prairie Park
0b a	I-74, W to Moline, E to Peoria. **I-474 begins/ends on I-74, exit 87.**

INDIANA

⬆E INTERSTATE 64

Exit #	Services
124mm	Indiana/Kentucky state line, Ohio River
123	IN 62 E, New Albany, **N** ⓐ Marathon/dsl, Shell/Circle K ⑪ DQ Ⓞ Ⓗ, Family$, Firestone/auto, Save-A-Lot, **S** ⓐ Shell/Circle K, Valero ⑪ Daisy's Cafeteria, Subway, Waffle House ⌂ Best Western, Hampton Inn
121	I-265 E, to I-65 (exits left from eb), **N** access to Ⓗ,
119	US 150 W, to Greenville, **N** ⓐ Marathon ⑪ Bean St Cafe, Bearno's Buffet, Beef O'Brady's, China Cafe, Domino's, DQ, El Nopal, McDonald's, Papa John's, Sam's Family Rest.,

↑E INTERSTATE 64 Cont'd

Exit #	Services
119	Continued Subway, Taco Bell, Tumbleweed SW Grill 🅾 AutoZone, JayC Foods, Rite Aid, URGENT CARE, Walgreens
118	IN 62, IN 64W, to Georgetown, **N** 🛢 Marathon/dsl/24hr, Shell/Circle K 🍴 Korner Kitchen, McDonald's 🏠 Motel 6 🅾 CashSaver Foods, Mr. Hardware, **S** 🛢 Marathon/dsl
115mm	**Welcome Ctr wb, full ♿ facilities, litter barrels, 🚮, 🧃 vending**
113	to Lanesville
105	IN 135, to Corydon, **N** 🛢 Marathon/dsl, Shell 🍴 Big Boy 🏠 Comfort Inn, **S** 🛢 5 Star, BP/dsl 🍴 Alberto's Italian, Arby's, Beef O'Brady's, Burger King, Cracker Barrel, Culver's, Domino's, DQ, El Nopal Mexican, Hong Kong Buffet, KFC, Lee's Chicken, LJ Silver, McDonald's, O'Charley's, Papa John's, Papa Murphy's, Pizza Hut, Ryan's, Subway, Taco Bell, Waffle House, Wendy's, White Castle 🏠 Baymont Inn, Hampton Inn, Holiday Inn Express, Super 8 🅾 🏥 $Tree, Advance Parts, AT&T, AutoZone, Big O Tire, Buick/Chevrolet, Chrysler/Dodge/Jeep, CVS Drug, Family$, Ford, Radio Shack, RV camping, Verizon, Walgreens, Walmart/Subway
100mm	Blue River
97mm	**parking area both lanes**
92	IN 66, Carefree, **N** 🅾 Marengo Caves, **S** 🛢 Marathon/dsl/rest./24hr, 🍴 Subway/dsl/scales/24hr 🍴 Big Dadd's Rest., Country Style Rest. 🏠 Old Stone Lodge/Grill 🅾 Carefree Truckwash, Harrison Crawford SF, repair, to Wyandotte Caves
88mm	Hoosier Nat Forest eastern boundary
86	IN 37, to Sulphur, **N** to Patoka Lake, **S** food, gas, 🚮, scenic route
79	IN 37, to Tell City, St Croix, **S** 🛢 Marathon/Subshop/pizza/dsl 🅾 🚮, Rec. Facilities, to Hoosier NF, to OH River Br
76mm	Anderson River
72	IN 145, to Birdseye, **N** 🅾 to Patoka Lake, **S** 🅾 St Meinrad Coll, winery (2mi), gas
63	IN 162, to Ferdinand, **N** 🛢 Sunoco/dsl 🍴 China Garden, McDonald's, Subway, Wendy's 🏠 Comfort Inn, Super 8 🅾 CVS Drug, Ferdinand SF, **S** 🅾 Lake Rudolph RV Camping (8mi)
58mm	🆁🆂 both lanes, full ♿ facilities, info, litter barrels, 🚮, 🧃 vending
57	US 231, to Dale, Huntingburg, **N** 🅾 🏥, **S** 🛢 Chuckles/dsl 🍴 Denny's, Wendy's 🏠 Baymont Inn, Motel 6 🅾 Lincoln Boyhood Home, Lincoln SP
54	IN 161, to Holland, Tennyson
39	IN 61, Lynnville, **N** 🛢 Marathon 🍴 Monterrey Mexican 🅾 USPO
32mm	**N** 🅾 Wabash & Erie Canal
29b a	I-69 N, IN 57 N&S, to Evansville
25b a	US 41, to Evansville, **N** 🛢 FLYING J/Denny's/dsl/scales/24hr, Loves/Wendy's/dsl/24hr, 🍴 Subway/Taco Bell/dsl/24hr 🏠 Baymont Inn 🅾 Blue Beacon, truck repair/lube, **S** 🛢 Marathon/dsl 🍴 Arby's, Denny's, McDonald's, Stoll's Amish Rest. 🏠 Apar Inn, Comfort Inn, Gateway Inn, Super 8 🅾 st police, to U S IN
18	IN 65, to Cynthiana, **S** 🛢 Motomart/dsl/24hr
12	IN 165, Poseyville, **S** 🛢 CountryMark/Subway/DSL 🍴 Red Wagon Rest 🅾 NAPA, New Harmonie Hist Area/SP
7mm	**Black River Welcome Ctr eb, full ♿ facilities, litter barrels, petwalk, 🚮, picnic tables**
5mm	Black River
4	IN 69 S, New Harmony, Griffin, **N** 1 mi USPO **S** Harmony St Park
2mm	Big Bayou River
0mm	Indiana/Illinois state line, Wabash River

↑N INTERSTATE 65

Exit #	Services
262	I-90, W to Chicago, E to Ohio, **I-65 begins/ends on US 12, US 20.**
261	15th Ave, to Gary, **E** 🅾 Mack/Volvo Trucks, **W** 🛢 Clark
259b a	I-94/80, US 6W
258	US 6, Ridge Rd, **E** 🛢 Marathon/dsl, Speedway/dsl 🍴 Country Lounge Diner, Diner's Choice Rest., **W** 🛢 Clark, Save Gas

CORYDON

IN

M E R R I L L V I L L E

🧭 Ⓝ	INTERSTATE 65 Cont'd
Exit #	Services
255	61st Ave, Merrillville, E 🅖 Speedway/dsl, Thornton's 🅕 Arby's, Cracker Barrel, McDonald's, Pizza Hut/Taco Bell, Wendy's 🅛 $Inn, Comfort Inn, EconoLodge 🅞 🅗, Chevrolet, I-65 Repair, Menards, Mr Tire, W 1 mi 🅖 Shell 🅕 Burger King, Subway
253b	US 30 W, Merrillville, W 🅖 Mobil/dsl, Shell, Speedway/dsl 🅕 Abuelo's Mexican, Applebee's, Barnelli's Rest., Baskin-Robbins/Dunkin Donuts, Denny's, DQ, Gino's Rest., Golden Corral, Hooters, House of Kobe, Ichiban Steaks, Johnnie's Rest., KFC, La Carreta's, Maloney's Grill, McDonald's, Old Chicago Pizza, Oriental Buffet, Outback Steaks, Panda Express, Panera Bread, Pepe's Mexican, Pizza Hut, Portillo's Hot Dogs, Starbucks, Steak'n Shake, Subway, TX Corral Steaks, Wendy's, White Castle 🅛 Courtyard, Deluxe Inn, Fairfield Inn, Hampton Inn, Holiday Inn Express, Radisson, Red Roof Inn, Residence Inn 🅞 🅗, $Tree, Aldi Foods, Buick/GMC, Cadillac, CarQuest, CarX, Chrysler/Dodge/Jeep, Discount Tire, Fanny May Candies, Ford, Goodyear/auto, Hyundai, Jo-Ann Fabrics, K-Mart, Lincoln, Mazda, Meijer/dsl, Midas, Mr Tire, NTB, Old Time Pottery, Staples, Subaru, U-Haul, Verizon, Walgreens
253a	US 30 E, E 🅖 BP/Noble Romans, Speedway/dsl 🅕 Arby's, Bakers Square, Bob Evans, Buffalo Wild Wings, Chick-fil-A, Chili's, Chipotle Mexican, ChuckeCheese, Culver's, Don Pablo, IHOP, Jamba Juice, Jimmy John's, Joe's Crabshack, KFC/LJ Silver, Longhorn Steaks, McDonald's, Olive Garden, Peking Buffet, Popeye's, Potbelly, Red Lobster, Red Robin, Ruby Tuesday, Sheffield's Rest., Starbucks, Taco Bell, Taco Depot, TGIFriday's, Wendy's 🅛 Best Value Inn, Best Western, Candlewood Suites, Comfort Suites, Country Inn&Suites, Economy Inn, Extended Stay America, Hilton Garden, La Quinta, Motel 6, Quality Inn, Super 8 🅞 AT&T, Audi/VW, AutoZone, Best Buy, BigLots, Carmax, Costco/gas, Dick's, Firestone/auto, Gander Mtn, Hobby Lobby, Home Depot, Honda, JC Penney, Kia, Kohl's, Lowe's, Macy's, mall, Michael's, Nissan, Office Depot, Old Navy, PetCo, Petsmart, Sam's Club/gas, Sears/auto, Target, Tire Barn, TJ Maxx, Toyota/Scion, Tuesday Morning, vet, Walmart/McDonald's
249	109th Ave, W 🅕 Beggars Pizza, China Garden, Golden Apple Rest., Jimmy John's, Oberweis Icecream 🅞 GNC, Verizon, Walgreens
247	US 231, Crown Point, W 🅖 Mobil/dsl 🅞 🅗, Vietnam Vet Mem
241mm	weigh sta sb
240	IN 2, Lowell, E 🅖 🅯FLYING J/Denny's/dsl/24hr/@, Mobil/Burger King, 🅛oves/McDonalds/dsl/scales/24hr 🅕 Arby's, Subway 🅛 Comfort Inn, Super 8 🅞 truck wash, W 🅞 st police
234mm	Kankakee River
231mm	🆁🆂 both lanes, full ♿ facilities, info, litter barrels, petwalk, phones, 🆅 vending
230	IN 10, Roselawn, E 🅖 Gas City/Kozy Kitchen/dsl/scales/24hr, 🅛oves/Arby's/dsl/scales/24hr W 🅖 Family Express/e85, Marathon/Subway 🅕 China Wok, J&J Pizza, Sycamore Drive-In 🅞 $General, CarQuest, CVS Drug, Fagen Drug, IGA Foods, Lake Holiday Camping, Oak Lake Camping, TrueValue
220	IN 14, Winamac, W 🅖 BP/Subway/dsl 🅞 Fair Oaks Farms Store
215	IN 114, Rensselaer, E 🅖 Family Express/dsl/e85/24hr 🅕 Arby's, DQ, KFC, McDonald's, Rensselaer Rest. 🅛 Holiday Inn Express, Knights Inn 🅞 🅗, W 🅖 Marathon/Trail Tree

L A F A Y E T T E

L E B A N O N

215	Continued Rest./dsl/24hr 🅕 Burger King 🅛 Economy Inn 🅞 fireworks, tires/repair/towing/24hr
212mm	Iroquois River
205	US 231, Remington, E 🅖 BP/dsl, Crazy D/dsl 🅞 🅗, to St Joseph's Coll
201	US 24/231, Remington, E 🅞 Caboose Lake RV Camping, W 🅖 Petro/Shell/Iron Skillet/dsl/scales/24hr/@, 🅛oves/Subway/dsl/scales/24hr 🅕 KFC, McDonald's 🅛 Sunset Inn, Super 8
196mm	🆁🆂 both lanes, full ♿ facilities, info, litter barrels, petwalk, 🅒, 🆅 vending
193	US 231, to Chalmers, E 🅖 BP/DQ/Stuckey's
188	IN 18, to Brookston, Fowler, many windmills
178	IN 43, W Lafayette, E 🅖 GA/Taco Bell, Phillips 66/Subway/dsl 🅕 McDonald's, Wendy's 🅛 EconoLodge 🅞 museum, st police, to Tippecanoe Bfd, W 🅞 to Purdue U
176mm	Wabash River
175	IN 25, Lafayette, E 🅖 BP/dsl, Family Express/dsl/e85, W 🅞 🅗,
172	IN 26, Lafayette, E 🅕 Cracker Barrel, DQ, El Rodeo, Starbucks, Steak'n Shake, Subway, Taj Mahal, White Castle 🅛 Baymont Inn, Candlewood Suites, Comfort Inn, Comfort Suites, Days Inn, La Quinta, Motel 6, TownePlace Suites 🅞 Meijer/dsl/e85, visitor's ctr, W 🅖 BP/Circle K/dsl/24hr, Citgo, Speedway/dsl 🅕 Arby's, Bob Evans, Burger King, Camille's Cafe, Chick-fil-A, Chili's, ChuckeCheese, Country Cafe, Culvers, Denny's, Don Pablo, Fazoli's, Golden Corral, Grindstone Charlie's, Hour Time Rest., IHOP, Jimmy John's, KFC, Logan's Roadhouse, McAlister's Deli, McDonald's, Moe's SW Grill, Mt Jack's, Olive Garden, Outback Steaks, Pizza Hut, Sonic, Spageddie's, Starbucks, Steak'n Shake, Subway, Taco Bell, TGIFriday's 🅛 Best Western, Clarion, Courtyard, Fairfield Inn, Hampton Inn, Homewood Suites, Knights Inn, Quality Inn, Red Roof Inn, Super 8 🅞 🅗, $General, $Tree, Aamco, Chevrolet, CVS Drug, Discount Tire, Gordman's, Hobby Lobby, Home Depot, Hyundai, Lowe's, Marsh Foods, Nissan, Office Depot, Sam's Club/gas, Target, TJ Maxx, to Purdue U, Toyota, USPO, Verizon, vet, Walgreens, Walmart/Subway
168	IN 38, IN 25 S, Dayton, E 🅖 BP/Subway, Pantry/dsl
158	IN 28, to Frankfort, E 🅖 BP/Subway/dsl 🅞 Harley-Davidson, Peterbilt, repair, W 2 mi 🅛 Lincoln Lodge Motel 🅞 🅗, camping
150mm	🆁🆂 sb, full ♿ facilities, info, litter barrels, petwalk, 🅒, 🆅 vending
148mm	🆁🆂 nb, full ♿ facilities, info, litter barrels, petwalk, 🅒, 🆅 vending
146	IN 47, Thorntown, W 🅞 🅗, camping
141	US 52 W (exits left from sb), Lafayette Ave, E 🅞 🅗,
140	IN 32, Lebanon, E 🅖 BP/repair, Marathon/dsl 🅕 Denny's, Depot Rest., McDonald's, White Castle 🅛 Comfort Inn 🅞 🅗, AutoZone, Goodyear/auto, Menards, O'Reilly Parts, Pomp's Tires, W 🅖 McClure/dsl/e85, Shell 🅕 Arby's, Flapjacks Pancakes, KFC, Steak'n Shake, Subway, Taco Bell 🅛 EconoLodge, Holiday Inn Express, Motel 6, Super 8 🅞 truckwash
139	IN 39, Lebanon, E 🅖 GA/dsl 🅕 Penn Sta Subs, Starbucks, Wendy's, W 🅖 🅯FLYING J/IHOP/dsl/LP/scales/24hr 🅞 Donaldson's Chocolates
138	to US 52, Lebanon, E 🅖 BP/dsl
133	IN 267, Whitestown, W 🅖 🅛oves/McDonald's/Subway/dsl/scales/24hr

⬆ INTERSTATE 65 Cont'd

Exit #	Services
130	IN 334, Zionsville, **E** 🅖 Marathon/Noble Roman's/Starbucks/Stuckey's/dsl/24hr, Shell/Circle K/Subway/dsl 🅕 Burger King, El Rodeo Mexican, Fox's Pizza, Hong Kong House, McDonald's, Taco Bell 🅞 🅗, CVS Drug, Lowe's, **W** 🅖 TA/BP/Popeye's/dsl/scales/24hr/@
129	I-865 E, to I-465 E, US 52 E (from sb)
126mm	Fishback Creek
124	71st St, **E** 1 mi 🅖 BP 🅕 Bob Evans, Starbucks, Steak'n Shake 🅛 Candlewood Suites, Courtyard, Hampton Inn, Hilton Garden, Residence Inn, Wingate Inn, **W** 🅞 Eagle Creek Park
123	I-465 S, **S** 🅞 to ✈
121	Lafayette Rd, **E** 🅖 GA, Speedway/dsl 🅛 Quality Inn, **W** 🅖 Shell/Circle K 🅕 Applebee's, Arby's, Church's, Fazoli's, La Bamba Burritos, Wendy's 🅛 Best Value Inn 🅞 🅗, $Tree, Batteries+, Discount Tire, Family$, Kia, Mazda, NAPA, Nissan, PepBoys, same as 119, Tire Barn, Toyota/Scion, Verizon, Walmart/Subway
119	38th St (no nb return), Dodge, **W** 🅖 Speedway/dsl 🅕 ChuckeCheese, Fiesta Mexican, Hooters, KFC, McDonald's, O'Charley's, Papa John's, Penn Sta Subs, Pizza Hut, Popeye's, Red Lobster, Taco Bell, WTT Buffet 🅞 Aldi Foods, Best Buy, Chevrolet, CVS Drug, Honda, Hyundai, Meijer/dsl, Radio Shack, same as 121, Staples, Tires+
117.5mm	White River
117	MLK St (from sb), **W** 🅖 Marathon/dsl
116	29th St, 30th St (from nb), **W** 🅞 Marian Coll
115	21st St, **E** 🅖 Shell/Circle K 🅞 🅗, **W** 🅞 museums, zoo
114	MLK St, West St, downtown
113	US 31, IN 37, Meridian St, to downtown, **E** 🅞 🅗,
112a	I-70 E, to Columbus
111	Market St, Michigan St, Ohio St, **E** 🅕 Hardee's, **W** 🅞 City Market, museum
110b	I-70 W, to St Louis
110a	Prospect St, Morris St, East St
109	Raymond St, **E** 🅞 🅗, **W** 🅖 BP, Speedway/dsl 🅕 Little Caesars, White Castle 🅞 CVS Drug, Family$, Safeway
107	Keystone Ave, **E** 🅖 Mystik 🅛 Best Value Inn 🅞 🅗, **W** 🅖 Phillips 66/dsl, Speedway/dsl, Valero 🅕 Big Kahuna Pizza, Burger King, Denny's, McDonald's, Subway, Wendy's 🅛 Comfort Inn 🅞 $General, U of Indianapolis, Walmart Mkt
106	I-465 and I-74
103	Southport Rd, **E** 🅖 BP/McDonald's, Shell/Circle K 🅕 Arby's, Chicago Grill, Chick-fil-A, El Puerto, Hardee's, Hong Kong, Jimmy John's, Longhorn Steaks, Noble Roman's, O'Charley's, Panda Express, Panera Bread, Penn Sta Subs, Qdoba, Quiznos, Rally's, Starbucks, Taco Bell 🅞 Aldi Foods, AT&T, Firestone/auto, Harley-Davidson, Home Depot, Kohl's, Meijer/dsl/e85, Menards, Radio Shack, Staples, Target, Verizon, **W** 🅖 Marathon/Circle K, Phillips 66, Speedway/dsl 🅕 Bob Evans, Burger King, Carrabba's, Cheeseburger Paradise, Cracker Barrel, JT Johnson's Grill, KFC, McDonald's, Starbucks, Steak'n Shake, Subway, TX Roadhouse, Waffle House, Wendy's 🅛 Best Western, Comfort Suites, Country Inn&Suites, Courtyard, Fairfield Inn, Hampton Inn, Jameson Inn, Quality Inn, Super 8 🅞 🅗, 7-11
101	CountyLine Rd, **E** 🅕 Candlewood Suites, **W** 🅖 Murphy USA/dsl 🅕 Buffalo Wild Wings, El Mason Mexican, Fireside Rest., Little Mexico, Pasquale's Pizza, Tokyo Buffet 🅛 Hilton Garden, Holiday Inn Express, Value Place Hotel 🅞 🅗, Gander Mtn, Kroger, Verizon, Walmart/Subway
99	Greenwood, **E** 🅖 Road Ranger/▥▥▥/Subway/dsl/scales/24hr **W** 🅖 Marathon, Shell/Circle K, Sunoco 🅕 Arby's, Bob Evans, Byrd's Cafeteria, China Wok, Denny's, McDonald's, Oaken Barrel Rest., Puerto Vallarta, Starbucks, Subway, Taco Bell, Waffle House, White Castle 🅛 Baymont Inn, In-Town Suites, Red Carpet Inn, Red Roof Inn 🅞 🅗, Camping World RV Ctr, Sam's Club, vet
95	Whiteland, **E** 🅖 ⬥FLYING J/Denny's/scales/dsl/LP/RV dump/24hr 🅞 Blue Beacon, SpeedCo, tires, **W** 🅖 ◆Loves /Arby's/dsl/scales/24hr, ▥▥▥/McDonald's/dsl/scales/24hr/@ 🅞 Family RV Ctr
90	IN 44, Franklin, **W** 🅖 Marathon/Chester's/Subway/dsl, Shell/Circle K 🅕 Burger King, El Torito, McDonald's/RV Parking, Waffle House 🅛 Comfort Inn, Howard Johnson, Quality Inn, Red Carpet Inn, Super 8 🅞 🅗, golf
85mm	Sugar Creek
82mm	Big Blue River
80	IN 252, to Flat Rock, Edinburgh, **W** 🅖 Shell/dsl, Sunoco/dsl
76b a	US 31, Taylorsville, **E** 🅖 Shell/Circle K/dsl, Speedway/dsl 🅕 A&W/KFC, Burger King, El Toreo Mexican, Waffle House 🅛 Red Roof Inn 🅞 🅗, $ General, Buick/Cadillac/Chevrolet/GMC, Toyota, **W** 🅖 Marathon, Thornton's/café/dsl 🅕 Arby's, Cracker Barrel, Hardee's, Max&Erma's, McDonald's, MT Mikes, Ruby Tuesday, Snappy Tomato Pizza, Subway, Taco Bell 🅛 Best Western, Comfort Inn, Hampton Inn, Hilton Garden, Holiday Inn Express 🅞 antiques, Driftwood RV Camp, Goodyear, Harley-Davidson, Premium Outlets/famous brands, repair
73mm	🆁🆂 both lanes, full ♿ facilities, info, litter barrels, petwalk, 🅲, 🖼 vending
68mm	Driftwood River
68	IN 46, Columbus, **E** 🅖 Shell/Circle K, Speedway/dsl 🅕 Buffalo Wild Wings, Burger King, Coldstone, Culver's, Dimitri's Rest., IHOP, Jimmy John's, McDonald's, RuYi Asian, Snappy Tomato Pizza, Starbucks, Subway, Wendy's 🅛 Comfort Inn&Suites, Holiday Inn/rest., Sleep Inn, Super 8 🅞 🅗, AT&T, Menards, Sam's Club/gas, Verizon, Walgreens, Walmart/Subway **W** 🅖 BP, Swifty 🅕 Arby's, Bob Evans, Casa del Sol, Denny's, El Nopal Mexican, KFC, Noble Roman's, Papa's Grill, Taco Bell 🅛 Courtyard, Days Inn, La Quinta, Motel 6, Residence Inn 🅞 $General, CVS Drug, Jay-C Foods, to Brown Co SP
64	IN 58, Walesboro, **W** 🅖 Marathon/dsl 🅞 to RV camping
55	IN 11, to Jonesville, Seymour
54mm	White River
51mm	weigh sta both lanes
50b a	US 50, Seymour, **E** 🅖 Marathon/Circle K/dsl, Swifty, TA/BP/Country Pride/dsl/24hr/@ 🅕 McDonald's, Waffle House 🅛 Allstate Inn, Days Inn, EconoLodge, Motel 6, Super 8,

Map labels: 74, Lebanon, 465, 70, Indianapolis, Greenwood, 70, 74, 65, Columbus, Seymour, Scottsburg, 64

IN

Side labels: INDIANAPOLIS AREA, GREENWOOD, COLUMBUS

⬆N INTERSTATE 65 Cont'd

Exit #	Services
50b a	Continued
	W 🅖 Citgo/dsl, Shell/Circle K/dsl, Speedway/dsl, Sunoco/dsl 🍴 Applebee's, Arby's, Buffalo Wild Wings, Buffet China, Burger King, Capt D's, Chili's, Cracker Barrel, Domino's, DQ, El Nopal Mexican, Hardee's, KFC, Little Caesars, LJ Silver, McDonalds, Papa John's, Pizza Hut, Rally's, Ryan's, Steak'n Shake, Subway, Taco Bell, Tumbleweed Grill, Wendy's, White Castle 🏨 Fairfield Inn, Hampton Inn, Holiday Inn Express, Knights Inn, Quality Inn 🅞 🏥 $General, $Tree, Advance Parts, Aldi Foods, AT&T, AutoZone, BigLots, Buick/Cadillac/Chevrolet/GMC, Chrysler/Dodge/Jeep, CVS Drug, Ford, GNC, Home Depot, Jay-C Foods, JC Penney, O'Reilly Parts, Radio Shack, Russell Stover Candies, st police, Staples, Walgreens, Walmart/Subway
41	IN 250, Uniontown, **E** 🅞 tires, **W** 🅖 UnionTown/rest./dsl 🅞 auto/truck repair
36	US 31, Crothersville, **E** 🅖 Shell, **W** 🅖 Marathon/dsl
34a b	IN 256, Austin, **E** 🅖 Shell/Circle K 🅞 Clifty Falls SP, to Hardy Lake, **W** 🅖 Fuelmart/dsl/scales, Sunoco/Huddle House/dsl
29b a	IN 56, to Salem, Scottsburg, **E** 🅖 MotoMart, Speedway/dsl 🍴 Burger King, Cracker Barrel, KFC, Mariann Rest., Papa John's, Ponderosa, Sonic, Subway, Taco Bell 🏨 Best Value Inn, Holiday Inn Express 🅞 🏥 Ace Hardware, Advance Parts, AutoZone, CVS Drug, O'Reilly Parts, **W** 🅖 Marathon, Murphy USA, Shell/Circle K 🍴 Arby's, LJ Silver, McDonald's, Pizza Hut, Roadhouse USA, Waffle House, Wendy's 🏨 Hampton Inn, Quality Inn, Super 8 🅞 Big O Tire, Jellystone Camping (4mi), Radio Shack, Verizon, Walmart/Subway
22mm	🆁🆂 both lanes, full 🚻 facilities, info, litter barrels, petwalk, 🅒, 🚰 vending
19	IN 160, Henryville, **E** 🅖 Marathon/Subway/dsl, Shell/Circle K 🍴 Schuler's Rest. 🅞 Family$
16	Memphis Rd, Memphis, **E** 🅖 Loves/McDonald's/Subway/dsl/scales/24hr 🍴 Fill'n Station Cafe, **W** 🅖 🏕/Arby's/dsl/scales/24hr/@ 🅞 Customers 1st RV Ctr
9	IN 311, to New Albany, Sellersburg, **E** 🅖 5 Star Gas, BP, Shell/Circle K, Swifty 🍴 Arby's, Cracker Barrel, DQ, Quiznos, Waffle House 🏨 Ramada Inn 🅞 Carmerica/repair, Ford, O'Reilly Parts, st police, **W** 🅖 Marathon/Circle K 🍴 Burger King, El Nopal Mexican, McDonald's, Taco Bell 🏨 Comfort Inn 🅞 city park
7	IN 60, Hamburg, **E** 🅖 Clark/dsl, **W** 🍴 Cricket's Cafe, KFC/Pizza Hut 🏨 Days Inn
6b a	I-265 W, to I-64 W, IN 265 E, New Albany
5	Veterans Parkway, **E** 🅖 Shell/Circle K 🍴 Beef'O Brady's 🅞 🏥 Tire Discounters, **W** 🍴 Buffalo Wild Wings, Cheddars, Chick-fil-A, Chuy's Mexican, DQ, Famous Dave's, IHOP, Krispy Kreme, Longhorn Steaks, McAlister's Deli, Moe's SW Grill, Olive Garden, Panera Bread, Papa Murphy's, Pizza Hut, Ruby Tuesday, Stevie B's Burgers, Studio Pizza, Subway, Taco Bell 🅞 AT&T, Bass Pro Shops, Best Buy, Chevrolet, Lowe's, Michael's, Old Navy, Old Time Pottery, Petsmart, Rite Aid, Sam's Club/gas, Staples, Target, Verizon, Walmart/Subway
4	US 31 N, IN 131 S,, Clarksville, New Albany, **E** 🅖 Thorntons/Dunkin Donuts/dsl 🍴 White Castle 🏨 Value Place Inn 🅞 Raben Tire, **W** 🅖 Speedway/dsl 🍴 Applebee's, Arby's, Bob Evans, Burger King, Capt D's, ChuckeCheese, Denny's, Don Pablo, El Caporal, Fazoli's, Frisch's, Golden Corral, Hooters, Iguana Rest., LJ Silver, Logan's Roadhouse, McDonald's,

CLARKSVILLE

4	Continued
	O'Charley's, Outback Steaks, Papa John's, Rally's, Red Lobster, Steak'n Shake, Wendy's 🏨 Best Western, Candlewood Suites, Hampton Inn, Suburban Lodge 🅞 $Tree, AT&T, AutoZone, BigLots, Books-A-Million, Buick/GMC, Dick's, Dillard's, Firestone/auto, Ford, Hobby Lobby, Home Depot, Honda, JC Penney, Jo-Ann Fabrics, Kia, Kroger/gas, Office Depot, O'Reilly Parts, PepBoys, Sears/auto, Toyota/Scion, Tuesday Morning, USPO, VW, Walgreens
2	Eastern Blvd, Clarksville, **E** 🍴 Comfort Suites, Days Inn, Motel 6, Super 8 🅞 🏥, U-Haul, **W** 🅖 Shell/Circle K 🏨 Best Inn
1	US 31 S, IN 62, Stansifer Ave, **E** 🅖 Thorntons 🍴 DQ 🅞 🏥 Advance Parts, info ctr, Walgreens, **W** 🏨 Holiday Inn 🅞 Stinnett RV Ctr
0	Jeffersonville, **E** 🅖 Thornton/Dunkin Donuts 🍴 Hardee's, McDonald's, Waffle House 🅞 🏥, Chrysler/Jeep, Hyundai, Nissan, to Falls of OH SP, Walgreens, **W** 🍴 Subway 🏨 Fairfield Inn, Sheraton, TownePlace Suites
0mm	Indiana/Kentucky state line, Ohio River

⬆N INTERSTATE 69

Exit #	Services
358mm	Indiana/Michigan state line
357	Lake George Rd, to IN 120, Fremont, Lake James, **E** 🅖 Petro/Iron Skillet/dsl/LP/scales/24hr/@ 🅞 Freightliner/Western Star Truck Repair, golf/rest, Kenworth, **W** 🅖 Marathon/dsl, 🏕/Wendy's/dsl/scales/24hr, Shell/Subway/dsl 🍴 McDonald's, Red Arrow Rest. 🏨 Holiday Inn Express, Redwood Inn 🅞 Freemont Outlets/Famous Brands, GNC, **E Services on IN 120** 🏨 Comfort Inn, Hampton Inn, Travelers Inn 🅞 golf/rest, **W** to Pokagon SP, Jellystone Camping (5mi)
356	I-80/90 Toll Rd, E to Toledo, W to Chicago
354	IN 127, to IN 120, IN 727, Fremont, Orland, **E** 🏨 Budgeteer Motel, Comfort Inn, Hampton Inn, Ramada, Travelers Inn 🅞 golf, Oak Hill RV camp, **W** 🅖 Marathon/dsl 🏨 Holiday Inn Express 🅞 Freemont Outlets/Famous Brands, Jellystone Camping (4mi), to Pokagon SP
350	rd 200 W, to Lake James, Crooked Lake, **E** 🅖 Sunoco/Subway/dsl 🅞 fireworks, **W** 🅖 Marathon, Shell 🍴 Caruso's Rest., Tasty Pizza 🅞 Marine Ctr
348	US 20, to Angola, Lagrange, **E** 🅖 Marathon/Subway/dsl, Speedway/Taco Bell/dsl 🍴 McDonald's 🏨 Happy Acres Camping (1mi), University Inn (2mi) 🅞 🏥, **W** 🅞 Circle B RV Prk (2mi)
345mm	Pigeon Creek
344mm	🆁🆂 sb, full 🚻 facilities, info, litter barrels, petwalk, 🅒, 🚰 vending
340	IN 4, to Hamilton, Ashley, Hudson, **W 1 mi** 🅖 Marathon/Ashley Deli/dsl
334	US 6, to Waterloo, Kendallville, **E** 🍴 Subway (1mi), **W** 🅖 BP/dsl, Marathon/dsl/24hr 🍴 Maria's Pancakes
329	IN 8, to Garrett, Auburn, **E** 🅖 BP, GA, Lassus, Speedway/dsl 🍴 Applebee's, Arby's, Bob Evans, Burger King, China Buffet, DQ, KFC, Little Caesars, McDonald's, Papa John's, Peking Buffet, Penguin Point Rest., Pizza Hut, Ponderosa, Richard's Rest., Starbucks, Steak'n Shake, Subway, Taco Bell, Wendy's 🏨 Comfort Suites, Days Inn, Holiday Inn Express, La Quinta, Quality Inn, Super 8 🅞 🏥, $General, $Tree, Ace Hardware, Advance Parts, AT&T, AutoZone, Buick/Chevrolet/RV Ctr, Chrysler/Dodge/Jeep, CVS Drug, Ford, GNC, Kroger/dsl, museum, Radio Shack, Staples, Walmart/Subway, **W** 🅖 Marathon/dsl 🍴 Buffalo Wild Wings, Cracker Barrel, Paradise Buffet 🏨 Hampton Inn 🅞 Home Depot, Verizon

Side labels: **SEYMOUR**, **SCOTTSBURG** (I-65 column); **CLARKSVILLE**, **AUBURN** (I-69 column); **IN**

INTERSTATE 69 Cont'd

Exit #	Services
326	rd 11A, to Garrett, Auburn, **E** 🅞 Kruse Auction Park, **W** 🅞 camping
321	🆁🆂 nb, full ♿ facilities, info, litter barrels, vending
317	Union Chapel Rd, 🅞 🅷
316	IN 1 N, Dupont Rd, **E** 🅖 Lassus/Elmo's/dsl, Phillips 66/Burger King 🅕 Arby's, Culver's 🅛 Comfort Suites, Hampton Inn 🅞 🅷, **W** 🅖 Speedway/dsl 🅕 Bandito's Mexican, Bob Evans, Cozy Nook Cafe, Jimmy John's, Mancino's Grinders, McDonald's, Pine Valley Grill, Starbucks, Trolley Grill 🅛 Baymont Inn, La Quinta
315	I-469, US 30 E, **W** 🅛 Value Place Hotel
312b a	Coldwater Rd, **E** 🅖 BP/dsl, Marathon, Sunoco 🅕 Arby's, Chappell's, Chili's, Cork'N Cleaver, Hall's Factory Rest., Hunan Chinese, IHOP, Jimmy John's, Koto Japanese, Papa John's, Quiznos, Rally's, Red Lobster, Red River Steaks, Steak'n Shake, Taco Bell, Wendy's 🅛 Hotel Ft Wayne, Hyatt Place 🅞 $Tree, Hobby Lobby, Hyundai, JoAnn Fabrics, NAPA, O'Reilly Parts, PetCo, Tuesday Morning, Tuffy Auto, U-Haul, Walmart/Subway **W** 🅕 Dunkin Donuts
311b a	US 27 S, IN 3 N, **E** 🅖 Shell/dsl, Sunoco/dsl 🅕 Arby's, Cheddar's, ChuckECheese's, DQ, Fazoli's, Golden Corral, Hall's Rest., McDonald's, Olive Garden, Quaker Steak&Lube, TGIFriday's 🅛 Candlewood Suites, Stay Inn, TownePlace Suites 🅞 Aldi Foods, Barnes&Noble, Chevrolet, Chrysler/Dodge/Jeep, Costco/gas, Discount Tire, Fiat, Ford/Lincoln, Hancock Fabrics, Honda, Infiniti, JC Penney, Macy's, Nissan, Sears, Toyota/Scion, Verizon, **W** 🅕 Lassus/Elmo's Pizza/dsl, Marathon 🅕 Applebee's, Burger King, Cracker Barrel, Culver's, Golden China, IHOP, Logan's Roadhouse, McDonald's, Panda Express, Starbucks, Subway, Taco Bell, TX Roadhouse 🅛 Best Value Inn, County Inn&Suites, Courtyard, Days Inn, EconoLodge, Extended Stay America, Fairfield Inn, Guesthouse Motel, Hampton Inn, Quality Inn, Super 8 🅞 CVS Drug, Gander Mtn, Home Depot, Lowe's, Meijer/dsl/E85, Sam's Club/gas, URGENT CARE, VW, Walgreens
309b a	US 33, Goshen Rd, Ft Wayne, **E** 🅖 ▭/dsl/scales/24hr, Sunoco/dsl 🅕 Liberty Diner, McDonald's, Pace Rest. 🅛 Clarion, Country Hearth Inn, Guest House Inn, Knights Inn, Motel 6, Red Roof Inn, Travel Inn 🅞 🅷, auto/dsl repair, Blue Beacon, NAPA
305b a	IN 14 W, Ft Wayne, **E** 🅖 Lassus, Murphy USA, Shell/Subway/dsl, Speedway/dsl/LP 🅕 Arby's, Biaggi's, Bob Evans, Burger King, Chick-fil-A, Chipotle Mexican, Coldstone, Eddy Merlot Rest., Firehouse Subs, Flat Top Grill, Great Wall Buffet, Logan's Roadhouse, McAlister's Deli, Noodles&Co., O'Charley's, Panda Express, Panera Bread, Papa Murphy's, Penn Sta Subs, Qdoba, Smokey Bones BBQ, Starbucks, Steak'n Shake, Subway, Tilted Kilt Eatery, Wendy's 🅛 Klopfenstein Suites 🅞 🅷, $Tree, Acura, Advance Parts, AT&T, Audi/Porsche, Barnes&Noble, Best Buy, BigLots, BMW, Buick/GMC, Cadillac, Chevrolet, Chrysler/Dodge/Jeep, Dick's, Ford/Lincoln, Hancock Fabrics, Harley-Davidson, Kia, Kohl's, Lexus, Lowe's, mall, Marshalls, Mazda, Meijer/dsl, Menards, Michael's, NAPA, Old Navy, Petsmart, Radio Shack, Staples, Subaru, Target, to St Francis U, Toyota/Scion, Tuesday Morning, Verizon, vet, Volvo, Walmart
302	US 24, to Jefferson Blvd, Ft Wayne, **E** 🅕 Subway (1mi), Taco Bell (1mi) 🅛 Extended Stay America, Hampton Inn, Residence Inn 🅞 🅷, to IN Wesleyan U, **W** 🅕 Lassus, Marathon/dsl 🅕 Applebee's, Arby's, Bob Evans, Buffalo Wild Wings,

FT WAYNE

302	Continued — Carlos O'Kelly's, Coventry Tavern Rest., McDonald's, Naked Chopstix, Outback Steaks, Pizza Hut, Sara's Rest., Starbucks, Wendy's, Zesto Drive-In 🅛 Best Western Luxury, Comfort Suites, Hilton Garden, Holiday Inn Express, Homewood Suites, Staybridge Suites 🅞 Kroger, Meineke, st police, Walgreens
299	Lower Huntington Rd, **E** 🅞 to
296b a	I-469, US 24 E, US 33 S, **E** to
286	US 224, to Huntington, Markle, **E** 🅖 Marathon (1mi), Phillips 66/Subway/dsl 🅕 Daily Diner, DQ, Vinatelli's 🅛 Guesthouse Inn, Super 8 🅷, repair/tires, **W** 🅞 Roush Lake, to Huntington Reservoir
280mm	weigh sta sb/parking area nb
278	IN 5, to Warren, Huntington, **E** 🅕 Phillips 66/dsl 🅛 Huggy Bear Motel, **W** 🅕 Marathon/Subway/dsl, Sunoco/HomeTown Diner/dsl/scales/24hr 🅕 McDonald's, Ugalde's Rest. 🅛 Best Value Inn, Comfort Inn 🅞 🅷, fireworks, RV Camping, to Salamonie Reservoir
276mm	Salamonie River
273	IN 218, to Warren
264	IN 18, to Marion, Montpelier, **E** 🅕 Loves/McDonalds/dsl/scales/24hr **W** 🅖 BP/Subway/dsl 🅕 Arby's 🅛 Best Value Inn 🅞 🅷, Chrysler/Jeep, Harley-Davidson
260mm	Walnut Creek
259	US 35 N, IN 22, to Upland, **E** 🅖 Valero/Subway 🅕 Burger King, Casa Grande Mexican, China 1, Cracker Barrel 🅛 Best Western, Super 8 🅞 Mar-Brook Camping, Taylor U, **W** 🅖 Marathon/dsl, McClure Trkstp/dsl/24hr, Phillips 66/dsl 🅕 Hardee's, KFC/Taco Bell, Starbucks 🅛 Holiday Inn Express 🅞 to IN Wesleyan
255	IN 26, to Fairmount
250mm	🆁🆂 both lanes, full ♿ facilities, info, litter barrels, pet walk, 🖐, vending
245	US 35 S, IN 28, to Alexandria, Albany, **E** 🅕 Petro/Shell/Iron Skillet/Subway/dsl/scales/24hr/@ 🅞 RV Camping
241	IN 332, to Muncie, Frankton, **E** 🅖 BP/dsl 🅞 🅷, to Ball St U
234	IN 67, to IN 32, Chesterfield, Daleville, **E** 🅖 ▭/Subway/dsl/scales/24hr, Shell 🅕 Arby's, Pizza Hut, Smokehouse BBQ, Taco Bell, Waffle House, White Castle 🅛 Budget Inn 🅞 🅷, **W** 🅖 McClure/dsl/E85, ▭/Denny's/dsl/scales/24hr, Speedway/dsl 🅕 3rd Generation Pizza, McDonald's, Subway, Wendy's 🅛 Travel Inn 🅞 flea mkt, Timberline Valley Camping (3mi)
226	IN 9, IN 109, to Anderson, **E** 🅕 A&W/KFC, Culver's, Golden Corral, MT Mike's 🅛 Deluxe Inn, Hampton Inn, Holiday Inn Express, Quality Inn 🅞 Meijer/dsl, Menards, visitors ctr, **W** 🅖 BP, Marathon/dsl, PayLess/dsl, Speedway/dsl 🅕 Applebee's,

🅖 = gas   🅗 = food   🅛 = lodging   🅞 = other   🆁🆂 = rest stop   Copyright 2015 - the Next EXIT ®

⬆N INTERSTATE 69 Cont'd

Exit #	Services
226	Continued
	Arby's, Bob Evans, Buffalo Wild Wings, Burger King, Cracker Barrel, Fazoli's, IHOP, Jimmy John's, LoneStar Steaks, Mayo Mexican, McDonald's, Olive Garden, Panda Express, Panera Bread, Papa Murphy's, Penn Sta Subs, Perkins, Pizza Hut, Poblanos Mexican, Qdoba, Quiznos, Red Lobster, Ruby Tuesday, Starbucks, Steak'n Shake, Subway, Taco Bell, Waffle House, Wendy's, White Castle 🅛 Best Western, Comfort Inn, Days Inn, Fairfield Inn, Motel 6, Super 8 🅞 🅗, $General, $Tree, Aldi Foods, AT&T, Cadillac/Chevrolet, Chrysler/Dodge/Jeep, Freightliner, GNC, Hobby Lobby, Kohl's, Lowe's, Marshalls, Office Depot, Old Navy, O'Reilly Parts, Petsmart, Radio Shack, Target, Tire Barn, to Anderson U, to Mounds SP, Toyota/Scion, Verizon, Walgreens, Walmart/Subway
222	IN 9, IN 67, to Anderson, W 🅖 Speedway/dsl 🅗 Skyline Chili 🅞 🅗, st police
219	IN 38, Pendleton, E 🅖 Marathon 🅗 Burger King, McDonald's, Subway, W 🅞 Pine Lakes Camping
214	IN 13, to Lapel, E 🅖 BP 🅗 Waffle House, W 🅖 🍔/Subway/dsl/scales/24hr 🅞 camping
210	IN 238, to Noblesville, Fortville, E 🅖 BP 🅗 DQ, Starbucks, Taco Bell, Wendy's 🅞 🅗, W 🅗 5 Guys Burgers, BBQ, Bella Pizzeria, Coldstone, Famous Dave's, Houlihan's, McAlister's Deli, McDonald's, Mo's Cafe, Olive Garden, Panda Express, Paradise Cafe, Qdoba, Red Robin, Stone Creek Rest. 🅛 Cambria Suites 🅞 $Tree, AT&T, CVS Drug, Dick's, Earth Fare Foods, Firestone/auto, GNC, JC Penney, Old Navy, Radio Shack, Sleepy Bear Camping, Steinmart, Verizon
205	IN 37 N, 116th St, to Noblesville, Fishers, E 🅖 BP 🅗 La Fuente Mexican, Penn Sta Subs, Sunrise Cafe 🅞 Fresh Mkt, Kroger, URGENT CARE, W 🅖 Shell/Circle K, Speedway 🅗 5 Guys Burgers, Coldstone, Friaco's Mexican Grill, Greek Pizzaria, Handel's Ice Cream, Happy Dragon, Jet's Pizza, Marco's Pizza, Maya Mexican, McAlister's Deli, McDonald's, Moe's SW Grill, O'Charley's, Qdoba, Starbucks, Steak'n Shake, Subway, Wendy's, Wild Ginger Asian 🅛 Hampton Inn 🅞 AT&T, CVS Drug, Firestone/auto, Target
203	96th St, E 🅖 Marathon/dsl, Murphy USA/dsl, Shell/Circle K 🅗 Applebee's, Blimpie, Cracker Barrel, Donato's Pizza, Dunkin Donuts, Extreme Pizza, IHOP, Jimmy John's, McDonald's, Noodles&Co., Panda Express, Panera Bread, Qdoba, Ruby Tuesday, Sahm's Grill, Starbucks, Steak'n Shake, Subway, Tiawana Flats, Wendy's 🅛 AmericInn, Baymont Inn, Hilton Garden, Holiday Inn, Studio 6 🅞 AT&T, Fry's, GNC, Kohl's, Marsh Food, Meijer/dsl, PepBoys, PetCo, Radio Shack, Staples, Tuesday Morning, Verizon, Walmart W 🅖 Marathon/dsl 🅗 Arby's, Bob Evans, Burger King, Cheeseburger Paradise, Culver's, DJ's Hotdogs, Izakya Japanese, La Cabana, Panda Express, Peterson's Steaks/seafood, Quiznos, Starbucks, Taco Bell, Wolfie's Grill 🅛 Comfort Suites, Residence Inn, SpringHill Suites, Staybridge Suites 🅞 $Tree, Aldi Foods, Home Depot, Menards, NAPA, Sam's Club/gas
201	82nd St, Castleton, E 🅖 Shell 🅗 Boston Mkt, Burger King, Golden Corral, Jet's Pizza, O'Charley's 🅛 $Inn, Drury Inn, Extended Stay, Hilton, Super 8 🅞 🅗, CVS Drug, Lowe's, Walgreens, W 🅖 Speedway/dsl 🅗 Applebee's, Arby's, Burger King, Castleton Grill, Charleston's Rest., Denny's, Domino's, Fazoli's, Formosa Buffet, Hooters, Houlihan's, Jimmy John's, Joe's Grille, KFC, LJ Silver, Longhorn Steaks, Los Cabos Mexican, McDonald's, Olive Garden, Penn Sta Subs,

Exit #	Services
201	Continued
	Pizza Hut, Rally's, Red Lobster, Skyline Chili, Starbucks, Stir Crazy, Subway, Taco Bell, Wendy's 🅛 Candlewood Suites, Days Inn, Hampton Inn, Magnuson Hotel, Motel 6 🅞 $Tree, Aamco, Advance Parts, AutoZone, Best Buy, CarX, Dick's, Discount Tire, Firestone/auto, fireworks, Goodyear/auto, JC Penney, Macy's, mall, Midas, O'Reilly Parts, Sears/auto, Tire Barn, Verizon
200mm	I-465 around Indianapolis. **I-69 begins/ends on I-465, exit 37, at Indianapolis.**

⬆E INTERSTATE 70

Exit #	Services
156.5mm	Indiana/Ohio state line, **weigh sta**
156b a	US 40 E, Richmond, N 🅖 Petro/BP/Iron Skillet/dsl/24hr/@ 🅛 Fairfield Inn 🅞 Blue Beacon, S 🅖 BP/White Castle, Murphy USA/dsl, Shell, Speedway/dsl 🅗 A&W/LJ Silver, Applebee's, Arby's, Big Boy, Bob Evans, Buffalo Wild Wings, Burger King, Chili's, Chipotle Mexican, Cracker Barrel, Fazoli's, Golden Corral, Hacienda Mexican, IHOP, Jade House Chinese, KFC, McDonald's, MCL Cafeteria, O'Charley's, Pizza Hut, Rally's, Red Lobster, Starbucks, Steak'n Shake, Subway, Super China, Taco Bell, TX Roadhouse 🅛 Best Western, Days Inn, Hampton Inn, Lee's Inn, Motel 6, Quality Inn 🅞 $General, $Tree, Advance Parts, Aldi Foods, AT&T, Best Buy, BigLots, Buick/GMC, CarQuest, Chevrolet, Chrysler/Jeep, Dillard's, Expert Tire, Family$, Ford, Hastings Books, Hobby Lobby, Hyundai, JC Penney, Jo-Ann Fabrics, Kohl's, Kroger, Lowe's, Menards, Save-A-Lot Foods, Sears/auto, Tires+, Toyota/Scion, Tuffy, U-Haul, Verizon, Walgreens, Walmart
153	IN 227, to Whitewater, Richmond, N 2 mi Grandpa's Farm RV Park (seasonal)
151b a	US 27, to Chester, Richmond, N 🅗 Fricker's Rest. 🅞 Honda, KOA, S 🅖 Shell 🅗 Bob Evans, Burger King, Carver's Rest., China Buffet, McDonald's, Rally's, Subway, Taco Bell, Wendy's 🅛 Comfort Inn, Super 8 🅞 🅗, CVS Drug, Harley-Davidson, Meijer/dsl/E85
149b a	US 35, IN 38, to Muncie, N 🅖 Loves/Hardee's/dsl/scales/24hr S 🅖 Shell/Quiznos/dsl 🅞 Raper RV Ctr
148mm	**weigh sta wb**
145mm	🅞 Nolands Fork Creek
145	Centerville, N 🅖 BP/DQ/Stuckey's 🅛 Super 8 🅞 Goodyear/truck repair, S 🅞 Warm Glow Candles
144mm	🆁🆂 wb, full 🅰 facilities, info, litter barrels, petwalk, 🕻, 🖷 vending
141mm	Greens Fork River
137	IN 1, to Hagerstown, Connersville, N 🅞 Amish Cheese, S 🅖 GA, Gas City/rest./dsl/24hr, Shell 🅗 Burger King, McDonald's
131	Wilbur Wright Rd, New Lisbon, S 🅖 Shell/KFC/Taco Bell/dsl/scales/24hr/@ 🅞 New Lisbon RV park
126mm	Flatrock River
123	IN 3, to New Castle, Spiceland, N 🅛 All American Inn (3mi), Holiday Inn Express (3mi) 🅞 🅗, S 🅖 FLYING J/Denny's/Subway/dsl/LP/scales/24hr 🅞 tires/repair
117mm	Big Blue River
115	IN 109, to Knightstown, Wilkinson, N 🅖 GA/rest/dsl/scales/24hr 🅗 Burger King 🅞 Jellystone Camping
107mm	🆁🆂 both lanes, full 🅰 facilities, litter barrels, petwalk, 🕻, 🖷 vending
104	IN 9, Greenfield, Maxwell, N 🅖 GA/Miami Grill/dsl, S 🅖 GA, Murphy USA/dsl, Shell/Circle K, Sunoco/dsl, Swifty 🅗 Applebee's, Arby's, Bamboo Garden, Bob Evans, Burger King,

A N D E R S O N

I N D I A N A P O L I S   A R E A

IN

R I C H M O N D

INTERSTATE 70 Cont'd

GREENFIELD

Exit #	Services
104	Continued China Inn, Cracker Barrel, Culver's, El Rodeo Mexican, Hardee's, KFC, Little Caesars, McDonald's, Mi Casa Mexican, Mozzi's Pizza, MT Mike's Steaks, O'Charley's, Papa John's, Papa Murphy's, Penn Sta Subs, Pizza Hut, Ponderosa, Qdoba, Quiznos, Starbucks, Steak'n Shake, Subway, Taco Bell, Wendy's, White Castle 🛏 $Inn, Comfort Inn, Country Inn&Suites, Hampton Inn, Holiday Inn Express, Quality Inn, Super 8 🅾 🄷, $General, $Tree, Advance Parts, Aldi Foods, Big O Tire, BigLots, CVS Drug, GNC, Home Depot, Kroger/dsl, Marsh Foods, Radio Shack, Walgreens, Walmart
96	Mt Comfort Rd, N 🅿 GA/Subway/dsl, 🏪/Pizza Hut/dsl/scales/24hr 🍴 Burger King, El Nopal, Wendy's, S 🅿 Shell/Circle K 🍴 McDonald's 🅾 KOA (seasonal), Mt Comfort RV Ctr

INDIANAPOLIS AREA

Exit #	Services
91	Post Rd, to Ft Harrison, N 🅿 7-11, Citgo 🍴 Cracker Barrel, Denny's, Joe's Crabshack, McDonald's, Outback Steaks, Steak'n Shake, Wendy's 🛏 InTown Suites, La Quinta 🅾 Lowe's, st police, S 🅿 Admiral, BP/dsl, Shell/dsl, Speedway 🍴 Hardee's, KFC/Taco Bell, Waffle House 🛏 Country Hearth Inn, Days Inn 🅾 CVS Drug, Family$, Home Depot, Marsh Foods
90	I-465 (from wb)
89	Shadeland Ave, I-465 (from eb), N 🅿 Marathon/dsl 🍴 Bob Evans 🛏 Comfort Inn, Hampton Inn, Holiday Inn Express, Motel 6 🅾 Toyota/Scion, U-Haul, S 🅿 Admiral/dsl, Circle K, Marathon, Shell, Speedway/dsl 🍴 4Seasons Diner, Arby's, Burger King, Damon's, Lincoln's Rest., McDonald's, Noble Roman's, Papa John's, Penn Sta Subs, Rally's, Red Lobster, Ryan's, Starbucks, Subway, Taco Bell, TX Roadhouse, Wendy's, White Castle, Zelma's Rest. 🛏 Best Value Inn, Candlewood Suites, Fairfield Inn, Knights Inn, La Quinta, Marriott, Quality Inn, Ramada Inn 🅾 Aamco, CarX, Chevrolet, Chrysler/Dodge/Jeep, CVS Drug, Honda, Kia, Kroger/gas, Mazda, Nissan
87	Emerson Ave, N 🅿 BP/McDonald's, Speedway/dsl, S 🅿 Shell 🅾 🄷
85b a	Rural St, Keystone Ave, N 🅾 fairgrounds
83b (112)	I-65 N, to Chicago
83a (111)	Michigan St, Market St, S 🍴 Hardee's, downtown
80 (110a)	I-65 S, to Louisville
79b	Illinois St, McCarty St, downtown
79a	West St, N 🅿 Speedway/dsl 🛏 Comfort Inn, Holiday Inn Express, Hyatt, Staybridge Suites 🅾 🄷, Govt Ctr, Lucas Oil Stadium, to Union Sta, zoo
78	Harding St, to downtown, S 🅿 Marathon 🍴 Wendy's
77	Holt Rd, N 🍴 Steak'n Shake, S 🅿 Shell 🍴 McDonald's 🅾 Ford Trucks
75	Airport Expswy, to Raymond St (no EZ wb return), N 🅿 Marathon, Speedway/dsl 🍴 Denny's, Indy's Rest., Library Rest., Waffle House 🛏 Adam's Mark, Candlewood Suites, Courtyard, EconoLodge, Extended Stay Deluxe, Fairfield Inn, Hyatt Place, La Quinta, Quality Inn, Ramada, Residence Inn 🅾 NAPA, to ✈
73b a	I-465 N/S, I-74 E/W
69	(only from eb) to I-74 E, to I-465 S
68	Six Points Rd, N 🍴 Subway 🛏 Hampton Inn, Hilton Garden 🅾 ✈
66	IN 267, to Plainfield, Mooresville, N 🅿 BP, Shell/Circle K, Speedway/dsl, Thornton's/dsl 🍴 Arby's, Bob Evans,

Exit #	Services
66	Continued Burger King, Coachman Rest., Cracker Barrel, Denny's, Golden Corral, Hog Heaven BBQ, McDonald's, Quiznos, Steak'n Shake, Subway, White Castle, Wood Fire Grill 🛏 Baymont Inn, Best Western, Budget Inn, Cambria Suites, Comfort Inn, Days Inn, Hampton Inn, Holiday Inn Express, Homewood Suites, Motel 6, Staybridge Suites, Super 8, ValuePlace Inn, Wingate Inn 🅾 Buick/GMC, Chateau Thomas Winery, Harley-Davidson
65mm	Rs both lanes, full 🛗 facilities, info, litter barrels, petwalk, 🄲, ⛽ vending
59	IN 39, to Belleville, N 🅿 ❤Love's/McDonald's/Subway/dsl/scales/24hr 🅾 🄷, S 🅿 TA/Country Pride/dsl/scales/24hr/@, truckwash
51	rd 1100W, S 🅿 Koger's/Sunoco/dsl/rest/24hr 🅾 repair/towing/24hr
41	US 231, to Greencastle, Cloverdale, S 🅿 BP/dsl, Casey's (2mi), Marathon/dsl/scales/24hr 🍴 Arby's, Chicago's Pizza, El Cantarito, Icebox Rest., KFC, McDonald's, Subway, Taco Bell, Wendy's 🛏 Days Inn, EconoLodge, Holiday Inn Express, Motel 6, Super 8 🅾 🄷, $General, Bill's Hardware, Discount Tire, NAPA, to Lieber SRA, Value Mkt Foods
37	IN 243, to Putnamville, S 🅿 Marathon/dsl 🍴 A-Frame Cafe 🅾 Misty Morning Campground (4mi), to Lieber SRA
23	IN 59, to Brazil, N 🅿 🏪/McDonald's/Subway/dsl/scales/24hr 🅾 🄷, S 🅿 AM Best/Brazil Grill/dsl/scales/24hr/@, BP/Rally's/dsl, Road Ranger/🏪/Subway/dsl/scales 🍴 Burger King, Family Table Rest 🛏 Knights Inn
15mm	Honey Creek
11	IN 46, Terre Haute, N 🅿 🏪/Subway/dsl/scales/24hr, Thornton/dsl 🍴 Burger King, Holiday Inn Express, 🛏, McDonald's 🅾 ✈, S 🅾 KOA

TERRE HAUTE

Exit #	Services
7	US 41, US 150, Terre Haute, N 🅿 Marathon/dsl, Thornton's/dsl 🍴 Applebee's, Beef o'Brady's, Bob Evans, China Buffet 8, Cracker Barrel, Fazoli's, IHOP, LoneStar Steaks, Pasta House, Pizza Hut, Real Hacienda Mexican, Starbucks, Steak'n Shake, Sunrise Rest., Tumbleweed SW Grill, TX Roadhouse 🛏 Best Value Inn, Comfort Suites, Days Inn, Drury Inn, EconoLodge, Fairfield Inn, PearTree Inn, Super 8 🅾 AutoZone, Chrysler/Jeep, Kia, Mike's Mkt, O'Reilly Parts, S 🅿 Speedway/dsl, Thornton's/mart 🍴 Arby's, Baskin-Robbins, Buffalo Wild Wings, Burger King, Cheeseburger Paradise, Crazy Buffet, Denny's, DQ, Garfield's Rest., Golden Corral, Hardee's, Ichiban Japanese, Jimmy John's, KFC, Little Caesar's, LJ Silver, Los Tres Caminos, McDonald's, Monical's Pizza, Olive Garden, Outback Steaks, Panda Garden, Panera Bread, Papa John's, Penn Sta. Subs, Rally's, Red Lobster, Ruby Tuesday, Ryan's, Starbucks, Subway, Taco Bell, TGIFriday's, Wendy's,

🅶 = gas 🍴 = food 🛏 = lodging Ⓞ = other 🆁🆂 = rest stop Copyright 2015 - the Next EXIT ®

INTERSTATE 70 Cont'd

TERRE HAUTE

Exit #	Services
7	Continued
	White Castle 🛏 Hampton Inn, Holiday Inn, Motel 6, SpringHill Suites Ⓞ 🛏, $Tree, Aldi Foods, AT&T, Best Buy, BigLots, BooksAMillion, Buick/Cadillac/GMC, Burlington Coats, Chevrolet, Dodge, Ford, Gander Mtn., Goodyear/auto, Harley-Davidson, Hobby Lobby, Hyundai/Nissan, Jo-Ann Fabrics, K-Mart/gas, Kohl's, Kroger/gas, Lowe's, Macy's, NAPA, Old Navy, Petsmart, Sam's Club/gas, Sears/auto, Staples, Tire Barn, TJ Maxx, Verizon, Walgreens, Walmart
5.5mm	Wabash River
3	Darwin Rd, W Terre Haute, N Ⓞ to St Mary of-the-Woods Coll
1.5mm	**Welcome Ctr eb, full 🅼 facilities, info, litter barrels, petwalk, 🅲, 🆁🆂 vending**
1	US 40 E (from eb, exits left), to Terre Haute, W Terre Haute
.5mm	**eb only, weigh sta**
0mm	Indiana/Illinois state line

INTERSTATE 74

Exit #	Services
171.5mm	Indiana/Ohio state line
171mm	**weigh sta wb**
169	US 52 W, to Brookville
168.5mm	Whitewater River
164	IN 1, St Leon, N 🅶 Exxon/Noble Romans, Shell/dsl, S 🅶 BP/Blimpie/dsl
156	IN 101, to Sunman, Milan, S 🅶 Exxon/dsl
152mm	**🆁🆂 both lanes, full 🅼 facilities, litter barrels, petwalk, 🅲, 🆁🆂 vending**
149	IN 229, to Oldenburg, Batesville, N 🅶 Marathon, Shell/dsl 🍴 China Wok, McDonald's, Pizza King, Subway, Toros Mexican, Wendy's 🛏 Hampton Inn Ⓞ $General, Advance Parts, Kroger/dsl, ShopKo, URGENT CARE, Verizon, S 🅶 BP 🍴 Arby's, DQ, KFC/Taco Bell, La Rosa's Pizza, Skyline Chili, Steak'n Shake 🛏 Comfort Inn Ⓞ 🛏, CVS Drug, O'Reilly Parts
143	to IN 46, New Point, N 🅶 Petro/Iron Skillet/Subway/dsl/scales/24hr/@ S 🅶 BP 🛏 Hwy 46 Inn

GREENSBURG

134b a	IN 3, to Rushville, Greensburg, S 🅶 BP/dsl, Marathon/DQ/Subway, Speedway/dsl, Swifty 🍴 A&W, Arby's, Big Boy, Buffalo Wings, Burger King, Chili's, El Reparo Mexican, Great Wall Buffet, Jimmy John's, KFC/LJ Silver, Little Caesars, McDonald's, Papa John's, Taco Bell, Waffle House, Wendy's 🛏 Baymont Inn, Holiday Inn Express, Quality Inn Ⓞ $General, $Tree, Aldi Foods, AutoZone, Buick/Chevrolet, Chrysler/Dodge/Jeep, CVS Drug, Ford, GNC, NTB, O'Reilly Parts, Radio Shack, repair, Staples, TrueValue, Verizon, vet, Walgreens, Walmart/Subway
132	US 421, to Greensburg, S 🅶 BP 🛏 Hampton Inn, Holiday Inn Express (2mi)
130mm	Clifty Creek
123	Saint Paul, S 🅶 ♥Loves/McDonald's/Subway/dsl/scales/24hr Ⓞ camping, repair
119	IN 244 E, to Milroy
116	IN 44, to Shelbyville, Rushville, N 🅶 Marathon/Circle K/dsl S 🅶 BP, Marathon, Murphy USA/dsl, Sunoco/dsl, Swifty 🍴 Applebee's, Arby's, Bellacino's, Bob Evans, Buffalo Wild Wings, Burger King, China Buffet, China Inn, Denny's, Domino's, DQ, Dunkin Donuts, Fazoli's, Golden Corral, KFC, King Buffet, LJ Silver, McDonald's, Papa John's, Penn Sta Subs, Pizza Hut, Rally's, Starbucks, Subway, Taco Bell, Wendy's, White Castle

SHELBYVILLE

116	Continued
	🛏 Quality Inn Ⓞ 🛏, $General, $Tree, Ace Hardware, Advance Parts, Aldi Foods, AT&T, AutoZone, BigLots, Chevrolet, Ford, GNC, Kroger/dsl, O'Reilly Parts, Radio Shack, Verizon, Walgreens, Walmart/McDonald's
115mm	Little Blue River
113mm	Big Blue River
113	IN 9, to Shelbyville, N 🅶 Speedway 🍴 Cracker Barrel, Wendy's, S 🅶 (1mi), Shell, Shell/Circle K/Subway/dsl 🍴 McDonald's, Waffle House 🛏 Comfort Inn, EconoLodge, Hampton Inn, Holiday Inn Express, Super 8 Ⓞ 🛏
109	Fairland Rd, N 🅶 ⟨Little⟩/McDonald's/dsl/scales/24hr Ⓞ Indiana Downs/casino, S Ⓞ Brownie's Marine
103	London Rd, to Boggstown
102mm	Big Sugar Creek
101	Pleasant View Rd, N 🅶 Country Mark/dsl/repair
99	Acton Rd
96	Post Rd, N 🅶 Marathon/Subway/dsl/24hr 🍴 McDonald's, S 🅶 Shell/Circle K/dsl 🍴 Wendy's Ⓞ Chevrolet
94b a	I-465/I-74 W, I-465 N, US 421 N
	I-74 and I-465 run together 21 miles. See I-465 exits 2-16, and 52-53.
73b	I-465 N, access to same services as 16a on I-465
73a	I-465 S, I-74 E
71mm	Eagle Creek
68	Ronald Reagan Pkwy

BROWNSBURG

66	IN 267, Brownsburg, N 🅶 Citgo/dsl, Shell/Circle K 🍴 Applebee's, Asia Wok, Buffalo Wild Wings, Dunkin Donuts, Hardee's, Steak'n Shake, Subway, Tequila Mexican 🛏 Hampton Inn, Holiday Inn Express Ⓞ Big O Tire, S 🅶 BP/dsl, Speedway/dsl 🍴 Arby's, Asian Fusion, Bob Evans, Burger King, China's Best, HoWah, Hurricane Grill, Jimmy John's, KFC, Little Caesars, Los Toros Mexican, McDonald's, Papa Murphy's, Penn Sta Subs, Starbucks, Taco Bell, Wendy's, White Castle 🛏 Comfort Suites, Super 8 Ⓞ $Tree, AT&T, Firestone/auto, Ford, K-Mart, Kohl's, Kroger/gas, Lowe's, Radio Shack, USPO, Walmart/Subway
61	to Pittsboro, S 🅶 ♥Loves/Godfather's/Subway/dsl/scales/24hr
58	IN 39, to Lebanon, Lizton, S Ⓞ 🛏
57mm	**🆁🆂 both lanes, full 🅼 facilities, litter barrels, petwalk, 🅲, 🆁🆂 vending**
52	IN 75, to Advance, Jamestown, S **2 mi** camping, food, gas
39	IN 32, to Crawfordsville, S 🅶 ⟨Little⟩/Subway/dsl/scales/24hr
34	US 231, to Linden, S 🅶 BP/Circle K, GA, Marathon/dsl 🍴 Burger King, McDonald's, Subway 🛏 Candlewood Suites, Comfort Inn, Hampton Inn, Holiday Inn Express, Motel 6, Quality Inn, Ramada Ltd., Super 8 Ⓞ 🛏, Buick/GMC, KOA (1mi), Sugar Creek Campground (4mi)
25	IN 25, to Wingate, Waynetown
19mm	**weigh sta eb/parking area wb**
15	US 41, to Attica, Veedersburg, S **1 mi** 🅶 Marathon/dsl 🍴 Apple Tree Diner Ⓞ camping, to Turkey Run SP
8	Covington, N 🅶 Marathon, Valero/dsl 🍴 Benjamin's, Overpass Pizza Ⓞ fireworks, Ford
7mm	Wabash River
4	IN 63, to Newport, N 🅶 ⟨Little⟩/Arby's/dsl/scales/24hr 🍴 Beefhouse Rest., Wendy's
1mm	**Welcome Ctr eb, full 🅼 facilities, info, litter barrels, petwalk, 🅲, 🆁🆂 vending**
0mm	Indiana/Illinois state line, Eastern/Central Time Zone

IN

INTERSTATE 80/90

Exit #	Services
157mm	Indiana/Ohio state line
153mm	**toll plaza**, litter barrels
146mm	**TP both lanes** 🅖 Mobil/dsl, 🍴 McDonald's
144	I-69, US 27, Angola, Ft Wayne, **N** 🅖 Petro/BP/dsl/scales/@, 🚚/Wendy's/dsl/scales, Shell/Subway/dsl 🍴 Clay's Family Rest., Lake George Rest., McDonald's, Red Arrow Rest. 🛏 Redwood Inn 🄾 Freightliner/Western Star/truck repair **S** 🅖 Marathon/dsl 🛏 Holiday Inn Express 🄾 Freemont Outlet Shops/famous brands, GNC, **Services on IN 120 E** 🛏 Comfort Inn, Hampton Inn, Travelers Inn 🄾 golf/rest, **W** to Pokagon SPJellystone Camping (5mi)
131.5mm	Fawn River
126mm	**Ernie Pyle TP both lanes**, 🍴 Hardee's 🅖 Mobil/dsl, 🍴 Red Burrito, 🄾 gifts, RV dump
121	IN 9, to Lagrange, Howe, **N 2 mi** 🅖 Golden Buddha, Marathon, Murphy USA/dsl, Speedway/dsl 🍴 Applebee's, Burger King, Fiesta Mexican, Hot'n Now, KFC, King Dragon, Little Caesar's, McDonald's, Pizza Hut, Subway, Taco Bell, Wendy's 🛏 American Inn, Best Western, Country Hearth Inn, Hampton Inn, Regency Inn, Sturgess Inn, Travel Inn 🄾 $Tree, AT&T, Cadillac/Chevrolet, CarQuest, Family$, Ford, GNC, Ⓗ, (4mi), K-Mart, Kroger, Radio Shack, Rite Aid, Walgreens, Walmart/Subway **S** 🅖 Valero/dsl 🛏 Holiday Inn Express, Super 8 🄾 Ⓗ, (8mi)
120mm	Fawn River
108mm	🆁🆂 both lanes, trucks only
107	US 131, IN 13, to Middlebury, Constantine, **N 0-3 mi** 🅖 Marathon/dsl, Speedway 🍴 Country Table Rest., McDonald's 🛏 Patchwork Quilt Inn, Plaza Motel, Tower Motel 🄾 $General, Family$, **S 1 mi** 🅖 BP/Blimpie/dsl 🍴 Yup's DairyLand 🛏 McKenzie House B&B 🄾 Eby's Pines RV Park, KOA (apr-nov)
101	IN 15, to Goshen, Bristol, **S 0-2 mi** 🅖 7-11, Speedway/dsl 🍴 River Inn Rest., Subway 🄾 Eby's Pines Camping (3mi), USPO
96	Rd 1, E Elkhart, **S 2 mi** 🅖 7-11, BP/dsl, Marathon 🍴 Arby's, China Star, DQ, McDonald's, Subway, Taco Bell 🄾 Ace Hardware, RV/MH Hall of Fame
92	IN 19, to Elkhart, **N** 🅖 7-11, Marathon, Phillips 66/Subway/dsl 🍴 Applebee's, Cracker Barrel, Golden Egg Pancakes, Perkins, Steak'n Shake 🛏 Best Western, Candlewood Suites, Comfort Suites, Country Inn&Suites, Diplomat Motel, EconoLodge, Fairway Inn, Hampton Inn, Hilton Garden, Holiday Inn Express, Microtel, Quality Inn, Sleep Inn, Staybridge Suites, Turnpike Motel 🄾 $General, Aldi Foods, CVS Drug, Elkhart Campground (1mi), GNC, K-Mart, Martin's Foods, tires, transmissions, Walgreens, **S 0-2 mi** 🅖 Marathon/dsl, Shell, Speedway 🍴 Arby's, Bob Evans, Burger King, Callahan's, Chicago Grill, Chubby Trout, Culver's, Da Vinci's Pizza, DQ, El Camino Royal, Jimmy John's, KFC, King Wha Chinese, LJ Silver, Marco's Pizza, Matterhorn Rest., McDonald's, North Garden Buffet, Olive Garden, Papa John's, Pizza Hut, Red Lobster, Ryan's, Subway, Taco Bell, TX Roadhouse, Wendy's, Wings Etc. 🛏 Budget Inn, Days Inn, Jameson Inn, Red Roof Inn, Super 8 🄾 Ⓗ, $Tree, Ace Hardware, Advance Parts, AT&T, AutoZone, CarQuest, Family$, Lowe's, Menards, O'Reilly Parts, Radio Shack, Verizon, vet, Walmart
91mm	Christiana Creek
90mm	**Schricker TP both directions** 🅖 BP/dsl, 🍴 Burger King, Pizza Hut, Starbucks, 🄾 RV Dump, USPO, Z Mkt

ELKHART

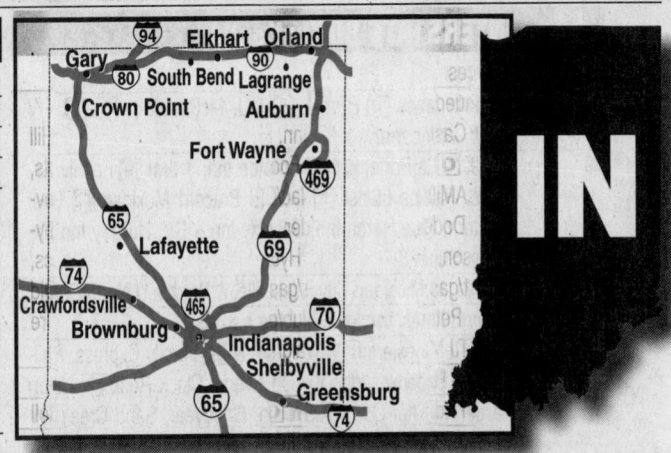

MISHAWAKA

83	to Mishawaka, **N** 🅖 BP/dsl, Phillips 66/Subway/dsl 🍴 Applebee's, Moe's SW Grill 🛏 Country Inn&Suites, Hampton Inn, Red Roof Inn 🄾 $Tree, CVS Drug, Marshall's, Martin's Foods/gas, Menards, PetCo, Target, vet, Walgreens, **N 1-2 mi on IN 23 W** 🍴 5 Guys Burgers, Barlouie, Famous Dave's BBQ, Granite City Grill, King's Buffet, Olive Garden, Papa Murphy's, Pizza Hut, Subway, Wendy's, Wings Etc 🛏 Fairfield Inn, Holiday Inn Express, Super 8 🄾 Best Buy, JC Penney, KOA (mar-nov), Macy's, mall, Michael's, Sears/auto, **S 2 mi on Grape Rd & Main St (off IN 23W)** 🍴 Arby's, Bob Evans, Buffalo Wild Wings, Burger King, Carraba's, Chick-fil-A, Chili's, Chipotle Mexican, CiCi's Pizza, Culver's, Del Taco, Hacienta Mexican, Hooters, Houlihan's, IHOP, Jimmy John's, Krispy Kreme, Logan's Roadhouse, Mancino's Pizza, Max&Erma's, McDonald's, Old Country Buffet, Outback Steaks, Panera Bread, Papa Vino's Italian, Quiznos, Red Lobster, Red Robin, Sonic, Starbucks, Steak'n Shake, Subway, Taste of Asia, TGIFriday's 🛏 Comfort Inn, Courtyard, Extended Stay America, Hyatt Place Hotel, Residence Inn, SpringHill Suites, Studio+ 🄾 Ⓗ Aldi Foods, Barnes&Noble, Buick/GMC/Hyundai, Christmas Tree Shop, Discount Tire, Hobby Lobby, Home Depot, Honda, Jo-Ann Fabrics, Kohl's, Lexus, Lowe's, Meijer/dsl, Meijer/gas, Mercedes, Nissan, Office Depot, Old Navy, Petsmart, Sam's Club, TJ Maxx, VW, Walmart

SOUTH BEND

77	US 33, US 31B, IN 933, South Bend, **N** 🅖 Admiral, Mobil/dsl 🍴 Arby's, DQ, Eleni's Rest., Fazoli's, Marco's Pizza, McDonald's, Papa John's, Ponderosa, Starbucks, Steak'nShake, Subway 🛏 Comfort Suites, Hampton Inn, Motel 6, Suburban Lodge, Waterford Lodge 🄾 AutoZone, BMW, Mazda, NAPA, O'Reilly Parts, TrueValue, Walgreens **N 2 mi on frtge rd** 🍴 Applebee's, Burger King, Hacienda Mexican, Jimmy John's, KFC, McDonald's, Quiznos, Sonic 🄾 $Tree, Aldi Foods, Meijer, Meijer/dsl/24hr, Murphy USA, Phillips 66/Subway/dsl, Walmart **S** 🅖 Marathon, Phillips 66/Subway/dsl 🍴 American Pancake House, Bob Evans, HoPing House, Mikados Japanese, Perkins, Taco Bell, Wendy's 🛏 Best Value Inn, Hilton Garden, Holiday Inn Express, Howard Johnson, Jameson Inn, Knights Inn, Microtel, Quality Inn, St Marys Inn 🄾 Ⓗ, to Notre Dame, vet,
76mm	St Joseph River
72	US 31, to Niles, South Bend, **N** 🅖 🚚/Subway/dsl/scales/24hr, Speedway/Subway/dsl 🛏 **S 2 mi on US 20** 🍴 4 Seasons Rest., Days Inn, McDonald's, Ponderosa, Quality Inn, Super 8, Taco Bell, Wendy's 🄾 ♿, RV Ctr, st police, to Potato Creek SP (20mi)
62mm	Eastern Time Zone/Central Time Zone

INTERSTATE 80/90 Cont'd

Exit #	Services
56mm	TP both lanes 🅖 BP/dsl, 🍴 DQ, McDonald's, 🅞 🅒, RV dump, litter barrel
49	IN 39, to La Porte, **N** 🛏 Hampton Inn, **S 3mi** 🅖 Family Express, Phillips 66/dsl 🍴 DQ, El Bracero Mexican 🛏 Best Western, Blue Heron Inn, Cassidy Inn & RV, Holiday Inn Express, Super 8
39	US 421, to Michigan City, Westville, **S** Purdue U North Cent
38mm	🆁🆂 both lanes, trucks only, litter barrels
31	IN 49, to Chesterton, Valparaiso, **N** 🅖 Family Express, Phillips 66, Speedway/dsl 🍴 Bob Evans, Clock Rest. 🛏 Hilton Garden 🅞 Apr-Oct), CVS Drug, Goodyear, Sand Creek RV Park (3mi, to IN Dunes Nat Lakeshore, WiseWay Foods, **S** 🛏 Hampton Inn (8mi), Super 8 (8mi)
24mm	toll plaza
23	Portage, Port of Indiana, **N 0-2 mi** 🅖 Marathon, Shell 🍴 Denny's, Mark's Grill 🛏 $Inn, Best Western, Comfort Inn, Country Inn&Suites, Days Inn, Holiday Inn Express, Ramada Inn, Super 8, **S** 🅖 BP, Marathon, Speedway 🍴 Burger King, CiCi's Pizza, DQ, Dunkin Donuts, El Contarito Mexican, First Wok Chinese, J&J's Pizza, Jimmy John's, KFC, Little Caesar's, McDonald's, Rosewood Rest., Starbucks, Subway, Wendy's 🅞 Ace Hardware, Advance Parts, AutoZone, Family$, GNC, Town&Country Mkt, USPO, Walgreens
22mm	TP both lanes, 🅖 BP/dsl, 🍴 Hardee's, Red Burrito, 🅞 info, scales
21mm	**I-90 and I-80 run together eb, separate wb. I-80 runs with I-94 wb. For I-80 exits 1 through 15, see Indiana Interstate 94.**
21	I-94 E to Detroit, I-80/94 W; US 6, IN 51, Lake Station, **N** 🅖 FLYING J/Denny's/dsl/scales/24hr/@, Blue Ox/Subway/dsl/scales/24hr, TA/BP/Popeye's/dsl/scales/24hr/@ 🅞 Blue Beacon, **S** 🅖 🏨 Road Ranger/Subway/dsl/scales 🍴 McDonald's
17	I-65 S, US 12, US 20, Dunes Hwy, to Indianapolis
14b	IN 53, to Gary, Broadway, **S** 🅖 Citgo
14a	Grant St, to Gary, **S** 🅞 🅷,
10	IN 912, Cline Ave, to Gary, **N** 🅞 🛏, casino
5	US 41, Calumet Ave, to Hammond, **S** 🅖 Nice'n Easy, Race-Co, Speedway/dsl 🍴 Arby's, Aurelio's Pizza, Dunkin Donuts, Johnel's Rest., KFC, McDonald's, Subway, Taco Bell, White Castle 🛏 Quality Inn, Ramada Inn, Super 8 🅞 Aldi Foods, AutoZone, Murray's Parts, Walgreens
3	IN 912, Cline Ave, to Hammond, **S** 🅖 BP, 🅞 to Gary Reg 🛩
1.5mm	toll plaza
1mm	US 12, US 20, 106th St, Indianapolis Blvd, **N** 🅖 Citgo, Mobil, Shell/dsl 🅞 casino, **S** 🅖 🍴 Burger King, KFC, McDonald's 🅞 Aldi Foods, auto repair, Jewel-Osco
0mm	Indiana/Illinois state line

INTERSTATE 94

Exit #	Services
46mm	Indiana/Michigan state line
43mm	**Welcome Ctr wb, full 🛏 facilities, info, litter barrels, petwalk, 🅒, 🛏 vending**
40b a	US 20, US 35, to Michigan City, **N** 🍴 McDonald's (3mi) 🅞 🅷 **S** 🅖 Speedway/dsl
34b a	US 421, to Michigan City, **N** 🅖 BP/dsl, Citgo/dsl, Family Express/e-85, Speedway/White Castle/dsl 🍴 Applebee's, Arby's, Asian Buffet, Baskin-Robbins/Dunkin Donuts, Bob Evans, Buffalo Wild Wings, Burger King, Chili's, Culver's,

34b a	Continued
	Damon's, Denny's, Dynasty Buffet, El Bracero Mexican, IHOP, KFC, LJ Silver, McDonald's, Olive Garden, Papa John's, Pizza Hut/Taco Bell, Quizno's, Red Lobster, Ryan's, Schoop's Rest., Sophia's Pancakes, Starbucks, Steak'n Shake, Subway, TX Corral, Wendy's 🛏 ABC Motel, Clarion, Comfort Inn, Country Inn&Suites, Knights Inn, Microtel, Milan Inn, Quality Inn, Red Roof Inn, Super 8, Travel Inn 🅞 🅷, $General, $Tree, Advance Parts, Aldi Foods, AutoZone, Big R, BigLots, CVS Drug, Fannie May Candies, Ford/Lincoln, Hobby Lobby, JC Penney, Jewel-Osco Drug/gas, JoAnn Fabrics, Lowe's, Meijer/dsl, Menards, NAPA, Office Depot, Radio Shack, Save-a-Lot, Sears/auto, Verizon, Walgreens, Walmart/Subway **S** 🅖 Gas City/Subway/dsl/scales/e-85 🅞 Buick/Chevrolet/GMC, Harley-Davidson
29mm	**weigh sta both lanes**
26b a	IN 49, Chesterton, **N** 🅞 to IN Dunes SP, **S** 🅖 BP/White Castle, Speedway/dsl 🍴 A&W/KFC, Applebee's, Arby's, Burger King, DQ, Dunkin Donuts, El Salto Mexican, Jimmy John's, Little Caesar's, LJ Silver, McDonald's, Pizza Hut, Quizno's, Subway, Sunrise Rest., Taco Bell, Tao Chins, Third Coast Cafe, Wendy's 🛏 Best Western, EconoLodge, Hilton Garden (3mi), Super 8 🅞 Advance Parts, AutoZone, Jewel-Osco, K-Mart, Sand Cr Camping (5mi), to Valparaiso, Walgreens
22b a	US 20, Burns Harbor, **N** 🅖 Steel City Express/dsl/e-85/scales/LP, TA/BP/Buckhorn Rest/Pizza Hut/Popeye's/Subway/Taco Bell/dsl/scales/24hr/@ 🛏 Comfort Inn 🅞 Blue Beacon, fireworks, **S** 🅖 Luke/dsl, 🏨/McDonald's/Subway/dsl/scales/24hr 🅞 Camp-Land RV Ctr, Chevrolet, fireworks, Ford, Nissan, repair, Toyota/Scion
19	IN 249, to Port of IN, Portage, **N** 🅖 Family Express/dsl/e-85 🍴 Deli Belly, Egg Face Grill, Longhorn Steaks, Quaker Steak&Lube, Starbucks 🛏 Country Inn&Suites 🅞 Bass Pro Shops, **S** 🅖 Marathon/dsl, Shell/Luke 🍴 Denny's, Lure Burgers, Shenanigans Grill 🛏 Best Western, Days Inn, Dollar Inn, Hampton Inn, Super 8, Travel Inn
16	access to **I-80/90 toll road E, I-90 toll road W**, IN 51N, Ripley St, same as 15b&a
I-94/I-80 run together wb	
15b	US 6W, IN 51, **N** 🅖 FLYING J/Denny's/dsl/scales/24hr/@, Blue Ox/Subway/dsl/scales/24hr, BP, TA/BP/Popeye's/Subway/dsl/scales/@ 🍴 McDonald's, 🅞 Blue Beacon, **N on US 20** 🅖 Dunes/Steel City/dsl/scales/dsl repair 🍴 Paradise Rest., Ponderosa, Wing Wah
15a	US 6E, IN 51S, to US 20, **S** 🅖 GoLo, Road Ranger/🏨/Subway/dsl/scales/24hr, Shell/Luke 🍴 Burger King, DQ, LJ Silver, Papa John's, Ruben's Café, Wendy's 🅞 Ace Hardware, Walgreens
13	Central Ave (from eb)
12b	I-65 N, to Gary and **toll road**
12a	I-65 S (from wb), to Indianapolis
11	I-65 S (from eb)
10b a	IN 53, Broadway, **N** 🅖 Citgo, Gas for Less 🍴 JJ Fish, **S** 🅖 Mobil 🍴 DQ, Rally's
9	Grant St, **N** 🅖 Clark 🍴 Chicago Hotdogs 🅞 County Mkt Foods, Sav-a-Lot Foods, Walgreens, **S** 🅖 Citgo, ♥Loves/Denny's/dsl/scales/LP/24hr/@, Steel City/dsl/scales/rest./24hr 🍴 A&W/KFC, Burger King, Church's, Dunkin Donuts, J&J Fish, McDonald's, Subway 🅞 $Tree, Aldi Foods, AutoZone, CarX, Fagen Drug, Firestone/auto, Midas
6	Burr St, **N** 🅖 🏨/Subway/dsl/scales/24hr/@, TA/Chester's/Pizza Hut/Taco Bell/dsl/scales/24hr/@ 🍴 J&J Fish

P O R T A G E — **IN**

G A R Y   A R E A

INTERSTATE 94 Cont'd

Exit #	Services
6	Continued
	& Chicken, Philly Steaks, Rico's Pizza 🅾 SpeedCo, S 🅶 Citgo/dsl/24hr
5	IN 912, Cline Ave, S 🅶 BP, Clark, Marathon, Speedway 🍴 Arby's, DQ, Jedi's Garden Rest., KFC, McDonald's, Pizza Hut, Popeye's, Taco Bell, Wendy's, White Castle 🛏 Best Western, Hometowne Lodge, Motel 6, Super 8 🅾 $Tree, Fannie May Candies, K-Mart, Radio Shack
3	Kennedy Ave, N 🅶 Clark, Mobil/dsl, Speedway 🍴 Burger King, Domino's, McDonald's 🅾 repair, Walgreens, S 🅶 Citgo 🍴 Cholie's Pizza, Cracker Barrel, Squigi's Pizza, Subway, Wendy's 🛏 Courtyard, Fairfield Inn, Residence Inn 🅾 IN Welcome Ctr, USPO
2	US 41S, IN 152N, Indianapolis Blvd, N 🅶 GoLo, Luke, SavA-Stop 🍴 Arby's, Dunkin Donuts, House Of Pizza, La Rosa, Papa John's, Pizza Hut, Popeye's, Rally's, Schoop's Burgers, Taco Bell, Wheel Rest., Woodmar Rest. 🅾 CarEx, Goodyear, Midas, vet, S 🅶 ⛽/scales/dsl/24hr 🍴 White Castle 🛏 Hammond Inn 🅾 Aldi Foods, Cabela's
1	US 41N, Calumet Ave, N 🅶 BP/dsl, Gas City 🍴 Barton's Pizza, Baskin-Robbins/Dunkin Donuts, Subway 🅾 Walgreens, S 🅶 BP, Marathon, Mobil/dsl, Shell 🍴 Arby's, Baskin-Robbins/Dunkin Donuts, Boston Mkt, Burger King, Canton House Chinese, Edwardo's Pizza, Fortune House, Munster Gyros, Subway, Taco Bell, Wendy's 🅾 $Jct, Jewel-Osco, Radio Shack, Staples, Target, vet
0mm	Indiana/Illinois state line

INTERSTATE 465 (Indianapolis)

Exit #	Services
	I-465 loops around Indianapolis. Exit numbers begin/end on I-65, exit 108.
53b a	I-65 N to Indianapolis, S to Louisville
52	Emerson Ave, N 🅶 Marathon, Shell/Circle K, Speedway 🍴 Asian Spice, Burger King, Denny's, Domino's, KFC, LJ Silver, Subway, Taco Bell, Wendy's 🛏 Motel 6 🅾 🄷, $General, Family$, S 🅶 Circle K, Shell/Circle K, Speedway/dsl 🍴 Applebee's, Arby's, Bamboo House, Buffalo Wild Wings, China Buffet, Donato's Pizza, DQ, El Puerto Mexican, Fazoli's, Fujiyama, Hardee's, Hunan House, McDonald's, Papa John's, Pizza Hut, Ponderosa, Rally's, Starbucks, Steak'n Shake, Subway, Waffle House, Wendy's, White Castle/24hr 🛏 Budget Inn, Holiday Inn, InnAmerica, La Quinta, Red Roof Inn 🅾 $Tree, Advance Parts, AutoZone, GNC, Goodyear/auto, K-Mart, Kroger, Lowe's Whse, Marsh Foods, NAPA, Radio Shack, vet, Walgreens
	I-74 W and I-465 S run together around S Indianapolis 21 miles
49	I-74 E, US 421 S
48	Shadeland Ave (from nb)
47	US 52 E, Brookville Rd, E 🅶 Marathon/Burger King, Speedway/dsl 🍴 Bugsy's Grill, McDonald's, Subway 🛏 Baymont Inn 🅾 CVS Drug, vet
46	US 40, Washington St, E 🅶 Marathon, Phillips 66, Shell/dsl, Speedway 🍴 Arby's, Blueberry Hill Pancakes, China Buffet, Church's, LJ Silver, Olive Garden, Skyline Chili, Steak'n Shake, Yen Ching Chinese 🅾 $General, Advance Parts, AutoZone, Ford, Meineke, O'Reilly Parts, Radio Shack, Target,

Exit #	Services
46	Continued
	W 🍴 Thornton's 🍴 Applebee's, Bob Evans, Fazoli's, McDonald's, Subway 🛏 Best Western 🅾 Buick/GMC, Hyundai, K-Mart, PepBoys
44b	I-70 E, to Columbus
44a	I-70 W, to Indianapolis
42	US 36, IN 67 N, Pendleton Pike, E 🍴 Chile Verde, Hardee's, Papa's Rest., Popeye's, Wendy's 🅾 $General, Family$, Meineke, Save-A-Lot Foods, U-Haul, W 🅶 Speedway/dsl, Thornton's 🍴 Arby's, Café Heidelberg, Domino's, Dunkin Donuts, KFC, LJ Silver, Los Rancheros, McDonald's, Pizza Hut/Taco Bell, Rally's, Subway, Waffle House, White Castle 🅾 🄷Advance Parts, Aldi Foods, CVS Drug, Family$, Menards, O'Reilly Parts
40	56th St, Shadeland Ave, E 🅶 Marathon, to Ft Harrison SP
37b a	I-69, N to Ft Wayne, IN 37, W 🅾 🄷, services on frontage rds
35	Allisonville Rd, N 🍴 Bravo Italian, Buca Italian, Buffalo Wild Wings, Dave&Buster's, Hardee's, Max&Erma's, MCL Cafeteria, Melting Pot, On-the-Border, Outback Steaks 🛏 Courtyard 🅾 Costco/gas, Firestone/auto, Gander Mtn, JC Penney, Jo-Ann Fabrics, Macy's, mall, Sear/auto, Target, Tires+, Van Maur, S 🅶 Shell, Speedway/dsl 🍴 5 Guys Burgers, China Buffet, ChuckeCheese, Panera Bread, Papa John's, Perkins/24hr, Qdoba, White Castle 🛏 Jameson Inn 🅾 Marsh Foods, Michael's, Petsmart, Radio Shack, TJ Maxx, Trader Joe's
33	IN 431, Keystone Ave, N 🅶 BP/McDonald's, Marathon/dsl 🍴 Arby's, Bob Evans, Burger King, Penn Sta Subs, Ruth Chris Steaks, Subway 🅾 Acura, Audi, BMW/Mini, Chevrolet, Ford, Harley-Davidson, Honda, Hyundai, Infiniti, Nissan, Porsche, Scion/Toyota, Subaru, S 🍴 Blimpie, Champ's, Cheesecake Factory, El Torito Grill, Fleming's Steaks, LePeep's Rest, Lulu's Rest, Maggiano's, Maggie Moo's Icecream, McAlister's Deli, PF Changs, Pizza Hut, Shanghai Lil, Starbucks, Sullivan's Steaks, TGIFriday's 🛏 Hyatt Place, Marriott, Sheraton 🅾 Kohl's, mall, Nordstrom's
31	US 31, Meridian St, N 🛏 Courtyard, Jameson Inn, Radisson 🅾 🄷, Cadillac, S 🅶 Shell/Circle K/dsl 🍴 Arby's, Granite City Rest, La Margarita, McAlister's Deli, McDonald's, Paradise Bakery/Cafe, Starbucks
27	US 421 N, Michigan Rd, N 🅶 Marathon, Phillips 66/dsl, Speedway/dsl 🍴 Applebee's, Bajio Mexican, Burger King, HoneyBaked Ham, Jimmy John's, Maggie Moo's Icecream, McDonald's, Noble Roman's, Red Robin, Subway, Wendy's, Wings Etc 🛏 Country Inn&Suites, Red Roof Inn 🅾 AT&T, Best Buy, Buick/GMC, Chevrolet, Chrysler/Dodge/Jeep, Ford, Home Depot, Kohl's, Marshall's, PetCo, Target, Walgreens, S 🅶 Citgo/dsl, Shell/Circle K 🍴 Arby's, Burger King, Chic-

INDIANAPOLIS AREA

INTERSTATE 465 (Indianapolis) Cont'd

Exit #	Services
27	Continued
	fil-A, China Buffet, Chipotle Mexican, Cici's, Cracker Barrel, Denny's, El Meson Mexican, Famous Dave's, Hardee's, McAlister's Deli, McDonald's, Noodles&Co, O'Charley's, Outback Steaks, Panda Express, Papa Murphy's, Pizza Hut, Qdoba, Rally's, Ruby Tuesday, Steak'n Shake, Subway, Taco Bell, TX Roadhouse, Wendy's, White Castle, Yen Ching Chinese 🛏 Best Western, Comfort Inn, Days Inn, Drury Inn, Embassy Suites, Extended Stay America, Extended Stay Deluxe, Holiday Inn, Homewood Suites, InTown Suites, La Quinta, Microtel, Residence Inn, Super 8 🅞 $General, $Tree, Aamco, Aldi Foods, BigLots, Costco/gas, Discount Tire, Firestone, GNC, JC Penney, Lowe's Whse, Office Depot, Radio Shack, Sam's Club/gas, Staples, Walgreens, Walmart
25	I-865 W, I-465 N to Chicago
23	86th St, E 🅖 BP, Speedway/dsl 🍴 Abuelo's, Applebee's, Arby's, Chili's, Coldstone Creamery, Jimmy John's, Longhorn Steaks, Macaroni Grill, Monical's Pizza, Noodles&Co, Panera Bread, Quizno's, Starbucks, Steak'n Shake, Subway, Taco Bell, Ted's MT Grill, Traders Mill Grill, Wendy's 🛏 Fairfield Inn, Homestead Suites, InTown Suites 🅞 🍴, AT&T, Big-O Tires, BookAMillion, Marsh Foods, Michael's, Old Navy, Petsmart
21	71st St, E 🅖 BP 🍴 Bella Chino's Italian, Hardee's, McDonald's, Steak'n Shake, Subway 🛏 Candlewood Suites, Clarion Inn, Courtyard, Hampton Inn, Holiday Inn Express, TownePlace Suites 🅞 Curves, W 🍴 Bob Evans, LePeep's Rest, Los Agave's Mexican, Max&Erma's, Quizno's, Starbucks 🛏 Hilton Garden, Residence Inn, Wingate Inn
20	I-65, N to Chicago, S to Indianapolis
19	56th St (from nb), E 🅖 Marathon, Speedway/dsl
17	38th St, E 🅖 BP, Marathon/dsl, Shell/Circle K/24hr, Speedway 🍴 ChuckECheese, Domino's, DQ, El Maguey Mexican, Ginzo Japanese, Golden Corral, Hooters, Little Caesar's, LJ Silver, LoneStar Steaks, Machu Pichu Peruvian, O'Charley's, Penn Sta Subs, Popeye's, Red Lobster, Starbucks, Steak'n Shake, Subway, White Castle, World Buffet 🛏 Best Value Inn 🅞 $Tree, AutoZone, Best Buy, Chevrolet, CVS Drug, Family$, Ford, Home Depot, Kroger/gas, Meijer, O'Reilly Parts, Radio Shack, Staples, Walgreens, W 🍴 Arby's, Burger King, Chili's, Cracker Barrel, McDonald's, Mike's Subs, Pizza Hut/Taco Bell, Ruby Tuesday, TGIFriday's 🛏 Jameson Inn, Ramada Ltd 🅞 Marsh Foods, Target

I-74 W and I-465 S run together around S Indianapolis 21 miles

Exit #	Services
16b	I-74 W, to Peoria
16a	US 136, to Speedway, E 🅖 Circle K, Shell/Circle K, Thornton's/dsl 🍴 Applebee's, Arby's, Buffalo Wild Wings, Denny's, Hardee's, KFC, LJ Silver, McDonald's, Papa Murphy's, Pizza Hut, Quizno's, Subway, Taco Bell, Wendy's 🛏 $Inn, Budget Inn, Motel 6, Red Roof Inn 🅞 $General, $Tree, CVS Drug, Firestone/auto, Goodyear/auto, Kroger, Marsh Foods, PetCo, Radio Shack, W 🛏 Clarion
14b a	10th St, E 🍴 Peking Chinese, Penn Sta, Pizza Hut, Wendy's 🅞 🍴, Lowe's Whse, W 🅖 GA/Subway, Shell/Circle K, Speedway/24hr 🍴 Arby's, Fazoli's, Hardee's, McDonald's, Rally's, Starbucks, Taco Bell 🅞 CVS Drug
13b a	US 36, Rockville Rd, E 🅖 Marathon 🛏 Comfort Inn, Microtel, Sleep Inn, Wingate Inn 🅞 Sam's Club, W 🅖 Speedway/dsl/24hr 🍴 Bob Evans 🛏 Best Western
12b a	US 40 E, Washington St, E 🍴 Burger King, China Buffet, Church's, Fazoli's, McDonald's, Papa John's, Pizza Hut, Taco Bell, Wendy's, White Castle 🅞 $Tree, Ace Hardware,

Exit #	Services
12b a	Continued
	Advance Parts, AutoZone, CVS Drug, Family$, Kroger/gas, repair, Speedway Parts, U-Haul, Walgreens, W 🍴 Marathon/Circle K, Phillips 66/Noble Roman's/dsl, Thornton's/24hr 🍴 Arby's, Hardee's, KFC, LJ Silver, McDonald's, Pizza Hut, Steak'n Shake, Subway 🛏 $Inn 🅞 Aamco, Goodyear, K-Mart, TireBarn
11b a	Sam Jones Expwy, E 🅖 Marathon 🍴 Denny's, Indy's Rest., Schlotzky's, Waffle House 🛏 Adam's Mark Hotel, Candlewood Suites, Courtyard, Day's Hotel, Econolodge, Extended Stay America, Extended Stay Deluxe, Fairfield Inn, Hyatt Place, La Quinta, Quality Inn, Ramada Inn, Residence Inn, W 🛏 Crowne Plaza, Radisson
9b a	I-70, E to Indianapolis, W to Terre Haute
8	IN 67 S, Kentucky Ave, E 🅞 🍴, W 🅖 BP/McDonald's/dsl, Shell, Speedway/dsl, Subway, Swifty 🍴 Burger King, Culver's, Damon's, Denny's, KFC 🛏 Country Inn&Suites
7	Mann Rd (from wb), E 🅞 🍴,
4	IN 37 S, Harding St, N 🅖 Mr Fuel/dsl/scales, 🚚🛏/Subway/dsl/scales/24hr 🍴 Omelette Shoppe 🛏 Best Inn, Quality Inn 🅞 🍴, Blue Beacon, S 🅖 ✈FLYING J/Denny's/dsl/LP/scales/24hr/@, Marathon 🍴 Hardee's, McDonald's, Taco Bell, White Castle 🛏 Knight's Inn 🅞 Freightliner, SpeedCo, TruckoMat/scales
2b a	US 31, IN 37, E 🅖 BP/24hr 🍴 Arby's, China Garden, CiCi's, Domino's, DQ, El Azabache, KFC, King Gyros, LJ Silver, MCL Cafeteria, Old Country Buffet, Penn Sta, Pizza Hut, Steak'n Shake, White Castle 🅞 $General, $Tree, Advance Parts, Aldi Foods, AutoZone, Chrysler/Jeep, Family$, Firestone, GNC, Goodyear, Jiffy Lube, Kroger/gas, Lincoln, Office Depot, Radio Shack, Save-A-Lot, U-Haul, W 🍴 Speedway 🍴 8Lucky Buffet, Bob Evans, Denny's, McDonald's, Red Lobster, Subway, Taco Bell, Wendy's 🛏 Best Value Inn, Comfort Inn, Holiday Inn Express, Ramada, Super 8, Travelers Inn, Travelodge 🅞 CVS Drug, Walgreens

I-465 loops around Indianapolis. Exit numbers begin/end on I-65 exit 108

🔼Ⓝ INTERSTATE 469 (Ft Wayne)

FT WAYNE

Exit #	Services
31c b a	I-69, US 27 S, Auburn Road. **I-469 begins/ends.**
29.5mm	St Joseph River
29b a	Maplecrest Rd, W 🅖 Lassus/DQ/Subway/dsl, Marathon/dsl
25	IN 37, to Ft Wayne, W 🅖 Murphy USA/dsl 🍴 Antonio's Pizza, Applebee's, Bob Evans, Buffalo Wild Wings, Cracker Barrel, DQ, Golden Corral, Steak'n Shake, Subway, Vince's Rest., Wendy's, Wings Etc, Zianos Italian 🅞 AT&T, Discount Tire, Kohl's, Marshall's, Meijer/dsl, Menards, Michael's, Office Depot, Petsmart, Walgreens, Walmart/McDonald's
21	US 24 E
19b a	US 30 E, to Ft Wayne, E 🅖 ✈FLYING J/Huddle House/Subway/dsl/LP/scales/24hr, Sunoco/Taco Bell/dsl 🅞 Freightliner, Mack, Peterbilt, truck/tire repair, W 🅖 Marathon 🍴 Garno's Italian, Golden Gate Chinese, Mancino's Grinders, Richard's Rest., Salvatori's Mexican, Zesto Drive-In 🛏 Holiday Inn Express
17	Minnich Rd
15	Tillman Rd
13	Marion Center Rd
11	US 27, US 33 S, to Decatur, Ft Wayne, E 🅖 BP/Subway/dsl
10.5mm	St Marys River
9	Winchester Rd
6	IN 1, to Bluffton, Ft Wayne, E 🅞 KOA, W 🅞 to 🍴
2	Indianapolis Rd, W 🅞 to 🍴
1	Lafayette Ctr Rd

	INTERSTATE 29
Exit #	**Services**
152mm	Iowa/South Dakota state line, Big Sioux River
151	IA 12 N, Riverside Blvd, E ⓖ Casey's 🄾 $General, Fareway Foods, Pecaut Nature Ctr, Riverside Park, to Stone SP
149	Hamilton Blvd, E ⓖ Conoco 🍴 Horizon Rest 🏠 Rodeway Inn 🄾 JiffyLube, to Briar Cliff Coll W **Iowa Welcome Ctr sb, full facilities** 🍴 Bev's on the River Rest. 🏠 Hilton Garden 🄾 Riverboat Museum,
148	US 77 S, to S Sioux City, Nebraska, W ⓖ Casey's, Conoco/dsl, Sam's 🍴 DQ, McDonald's, MiFamilia, Pizza Hut, Taco Bell 🏠 Marina Inn, Regency Inn 🄾 Advance Parts, camping/picnic area, Family $, O'Reilly Parts
147b	US 20 bus, Sioux City, E ⓖ Sam's 🍴 Arby's, Burger King, Chili's, Famous Dave's BBQ, Hardee's, IHOP, Perkins 🏠 Holiday Inn, Ramada, Stoney Creek Inn 🄾 🏥, Chevrolet, USPO, Walgreens
147a	Floyd Blvd, E ⓖ Valero 🄾 Home Depot, W 🄾 to Riverboat Casino
146.5mm	Floyd River
144b	I-129 W, US 20 W, US 75 S
144a	US 20 E, US 75 N, to Ft Dodge, E **1 mi on Lakeport Rd** ⓖ Casey's, Shell 🍴 5 Guys Burgers, A&W/LJ Silver, Applebee's, Black Bear Diner, Buffalo Wild Wings, Burger King, Carlos'o Kelly's, ChuckeCheese, Golden Corral, Hardee's, HuHot Chinese, Iron Hill Grill, Jimmy John's, McDonald's, Olive Garden, Outback Steaks, Red Lobster, Red Robin, Starbucks, Taco Del Mar, Tokyo Japanese, TX Roadhouse 🏠 Comfort Inn, Fairfield Inn, Holiday Inn Express, Quality Inn 🄾 Barnes&Noble, Best Buy, Buick/Honda, Gordman's, Hobby Lobby, Hy-Vee Foods/gas, JC Penney, Jiffy Lube, Kohls, Lowe's, Michael's, Old Navy, Petsmart, Scheel's, Sears/auto, Staples, Target, URGENT CARE, Verizon, Younkers
143	US 75 N, Singing Hills Blvd, E ⓖ Cenex/dsl, Murphy USA/dsl, 🍴 Moe's SW Grill/Subway/dsl/scales/24hr 🍴 China Buffet, Culver's, Eldon's Rest., KFC, McDonald's, Pizza Hut, Quiznos, Taco John's 🏠 AmericInn, Days Inn, Victorian Inn

143	Continued
	🄾 $Tree, AT&T, Cadillac/GMC, Ford/Kia, Mazda, Nissan, Sam's Club/gas, Sgt Floyd Mon, Subaru, Suzuki, Toyota/Scion, URGENT CARE, Verizon, vet, Walmart/Subway W ⓖ Loves/Subway/dsl/scales/24hr/@ 🍴 Wendy's 🏠 Super 8 🄾 Peterbilt, truckwash/repair
141	D38, Sioux Gateway 🛬, E ⓖ Cenex, Phillips 66/dsl, Shell/dsl 🍴 Aggies Rest., Pizza Ranch, Puerto Vallarta Mexican, Subway 🏠 EconoLodge 🄾 $General, W 🏠 Motel 6 🄾 🛬, museum
139mm	ⓇⓈ both lanes, full ♿ facilities, info, litter barrels, 🅟, 🚐 RV dump, wireless internet
135	Port Neal Landing
134	Salix, W 🄾 camping
132mm	ⓇⓈ parking only nb, weigh sta sb, litter barrels, 🅟
127	IA 141, Sloan, E ⓖ Casey's, Kum&Go/Subway/dsl 🏠 Homestead Inn, WinnaVegas Inn 🄾 RV Park, W 3 mi ⓖ Heritage Express 🄾 to Winnebago Indian Res/casino
120	to Whiting, W 🄾 camping
112	IA 175, Onawa, E ⓖ Conoco/Subway/dsl, Phillips 66/dsl 🍴 DQ, McDonald's, Michael's Rest. 🏠 Super 8 🄾 🏥, NAPA, On-Ur-Wa RV Park, Pamida, repair, W 2 mi 🄾 Keel Boat Exhibit, KOA, Lewis&Clark SP
110mm	ⓇⓈ both lanes, full ♿ facilities, info, litter barrels, petwalk, 🅟, 🚐 RV dump, wireless internet
105	E60, Blencoe
96mm	Little Sioux River
95	F 20, Little Sioux, E 🄾 Loess Hills SF (9mi), gas, W 🄾 Woodland RV Park
92mm	Soldier River
91.5mm	ⓇⓈ both lanes, litter barrels, parking only
89	IA 127, Mondamin, E 1 mi ⓖ Jiffy Mart/dsl 🍴 K Crossing Cafe
82	F50, Modale, W 1 mi ⓖ Cenex/dsl
79mm	ⓇⓈ both lanes, full ♿ facilities, info, litter barrels, 🅟, 🚐 RV dump, wireless internet

S I O U X   C I T Y

IA

⬆N   INTERSTATE 29 Cont'd

Exit #	Services
75	US 30, Missouri Valley, **E** Iowa Welcome Ctr (5mi), 🅿 Shell/dsl/24hr 🍴 Arby's, McDonald's, Penny's Diner, Subway 🏠 Oaktree Inn 🅾 �H, (2mi), to Steamboat Exhibit, **W** 🅿 BP/dsl, Phillips 66/Jctn Cafe/dsl 🍴 Burger King, Taco John's 🏠 Days Inn, Rath Inn, Super 8 🅾 Buick/Chevrolet
72.5mm	Boyer River
72	IA 362, Loveland, **E** 🅿 Phillips 66/dsl, **W** 🅾 to Wilson Island SP (6mi)
71	I-680 E, to Des Moines
I-29 S & I-680 W run together 10 mi.
66	**W** 🅾 RV Camping, Honey Creek
61b	I-680 W, to N Omaha, **W** Mormon Trail Ctr, **I-29 N & I-680 E run together 10 mi**
61a	IA 988, to Crescent, **E** to ski area
56	IA 192 S (sb only, exits left), Council Bluffs, **E** 🅾 �H,
55	N 25th, Council Bluffs, **E** 🅿 Cenex/dsl, Sinclair
54b	N 35th St (from nb), Council Bluffs
54a	G Ave (from sb), Council Bluffs
53b	I-480 W, US 6, to Omaha (exits left from nb)
53a	9th Ave, S 37th Ave, Council Bluffs, **E** 🅿 Phillips 66, Shell 🍴 Hog Stop BBQ 🏠 Days Inn, **W** 🅾 camping, Harrah's Hotel/Casino, RiverBoat Casino
52	Nebraska Ave, **E** 🅿 Phillips 66/dsl 🍴 Quaker Steak, Ruby Tuesday 🏠 Comfort Suites, Holiday Inn Express, Microtel, SpringHill Suites, ValuePlace Inn 🅾 Bass Pro Shops, **W**... 🏠 AmeriStar Hotel/casino, Hampton Inn, Holiday Inn
51	I-80 W, to Omaha
I-29 and I-80 run together 3 miles. See Iowa I-80, exits 1b-3.
48	I-80 E (from nb), to Des Moines, **E** 🅾 �H,
47	US 275, IA 92, Lake Manawa, **E** 🅾 Iowa School for the Deaf, **W** 🍴 Buffalo Wild Wings, Firehouse Subs, Freddy's, Longhorn Steaks, Olive Garden, Panda Express, Panera Bread, Pizza Ranch 🅾 $Tree, Hobby Lobby, Kohl's, Petsmart, Radio Shack, Target, TJ Maxx, Verizon
42	IA 370, to Bellevue, **W** 🅾 K&B Saddlery, to Offutt AFB, truck parts
38mm	Ⓡ🅂 both lanes, full ♿ facilities, info, litter barrels, petwalk, 🐾, 🚐 RV dump, wireless internet
35	US 34 E, to Glenwood, **E** 🍴 McDonalds (4mi) 🏠 Western Inn (4mi) 🅾 RV Park, **W** 🅿 BP/rest/dsl 🏠 Bluff View Motel 🅾 Harley-Davidson
32	US 34 W, Pacific Jct, to Plattsmouth
24	L31, to Tabor, Bartlett
20	IA 145, Thurman
15	J26, Percival, **E** 1-2 mi gas/dsl
11.5mm	**weigh sta nb**
10	IA 2, to Nebraska City, Sidney, **E** 🅾 to Waubonsie SP (5mi), **W** 🅿 Cenex/Godfathers/dsl/E85, 🛢/Subway/dsl/scales/24hr, Sapp Bros/Apple Barrel Rest/dsl/scales/24hr 🍴 Wendy's 🏠 Best Value Inn, Super 8 🅾 antiques, dsl/tire repair, IA Info, Lewis&Clark Ctr (3mi), to Arbor Lodge SP, Victorian Acres RV Park (3mi)
1	IA 333, Hamburg, **E** 1 mi 🅿 Casey's/dsl 🍴 Blue Moon Grill 🏠 Hamburg Motel 🅾 �H, NAPA, Soda Fountain
0mm	Iowa/Missouri state line

⬆N   INTERSTATE 35

Exit #	Services
219mm	Iowa/Minnesota state line
214	rd 105, to Northwood, Lake Mills, **E** 🏠 Royal Motel (7mi), **W** Welcome Ctr both lanes, full ♿ facilities, litter barrels, petwalk, 🚐 RV dump, vending, wireless internet 🅿 BP/Burger King/dsl 🏠 Country Inn&Suites, Holiday Inn Express 🅾 casino
212mm	Ⓡ🅂 nb, litter barrels, 🚐 weigh sta sb
208	rd A38, to Joice, Kensett, windmills
203	IA 9, to Manly, Forest City, to Pilot Knob SP
202mm	Winnebago River
197	rd B20, **E** 8 mi Lime Creek Nature Ctr
196mm	Ⓡ🅂 both lanes, litter barrels, parking only
194	US 18, to Mason City, Clear Lake, **E** 🅾 Chevrolet, Freightliner, �H, (8mi), truck repair, **W** 🅿 Casey's/dsl, Kum&Go/dsl, 🛢/Denny's/Subway/dsl/scales, Shell/Wendy's/dsl 🍴 Arby's, Cancun Mexican, Culver's, DQ, KFC/Taco Bell, McDonald's, Perkins, Pizza Hut, Rice House Chinese, Subway 🏠 AmericInn, Best Western/rest., Budget Inn, Microtel
193	rd B35, to Mason City, Emery, **E** 🅿 Kum&Go/Taco John's/dsl/E-85 🏠 Super 8 🅾 truckwash, **W** 🅾 Ford, to Clear Lake SP
190	US 18, rd 27 E, to Mason City
188	rd B43, to Burchinal
182	rd B60, to Rockwell, Swaledale
180	rd B65, to Thornton, **W** 🅿 Cenex (2mi) 🅾 camping
176	rd C13, to Sheffield, Belmond
170	rd C25, to Alexander
165	IA 3, **E** 🅿 Shell/dsl/rest. 🏠 AmericInn (9mi), Hampton Motel (9mi) 🅾 �H, (7mi)
159	rd C47, Dows, **W** Ⓡ🅂 both lanes, full ♿ facilities info, litter barrels, petwalk, 🐾, 🚐 RV dump, vending, wireless internet Shell/Arby's/Godfather's/dsl/24hr
155mm	Iowa River
151	rd R75, to Woolstock
147	rd D20, to US 20 E
144	rd D25, Williams, **E** 🅿 Boondocks Trkstp/cafe/dsl 🏠 Best Western, Boondocks Motel 🅾 RV camping, **W** 🅿 ⊕FLYING J/Trump's Rest/dsl/scales/24hr
142b a	US 20, to Webster City, Ft Dodge
139	rd D41, to Kamrar
133	IA 175, to Jewell, Ellsworth, **W** 🅿 Kum&Go/Subway/dsl
128	rd D65, to Stanhope, Randall, **W** 5 mi Little Wall Lake Pk
124	rd 115, Story City, **W** 🅿 Casey's, Kum&Go/dsl 🍴 DQ, Happy Chef/24hr, McDonald's, Pizza Ranch, Royal Cafe, Subway 🏠 Comfort Inn, Super 8, Viking Motel/rest 🅾 antiques, Ford, Story City RV Ctr, VF Factory Stores/famous brands, Whispering Oaks Camping
123	rd E18, to Roland, McCallsburg
120mm	Ⓡ🅂 nb, full ♿ facilities, info, litter barrels, 🐾, 🚐 RV dump/scenic prairie area sb, vending, wireless internet
119mm	Ⓡ🅂 sb, full ♿ facilities, litter barrels, 🐾, 🚐 RV dump, vending, wireless internet
116	rd E29, to Story, **W** 2 mi Story Co Conservation Ctr

COUNCIL BLUFFS

CLEAR LAKE

IA

▲N	INTERSTATE 35 Cont'd
Exit #	Services

113 — 13th St, Ames, W 🅖 Kum&Go/Burger King/dsl/E-85, Phillips 66/Arby's 🅕 Pizza Ranch 🅛 Holiday Inn Express, Quality Inn 🅞 H, Harley-Davidson, ISU, to USDA Vet Labs

111b a — US 30, to Nevada, Ames, E 🅛 Twin Acres Campground (11mi), W 🅖 Kum&Go/DQ/Subway/dsl 🅕 El Azteca Mexican 🅛 AmericInn, Comfort Inn, Country Inn&Suites, EconoLodge, Fairfield Inn, Hampton Inn, Microtel, Super 8, TownePlace Suites 🅞 to IA St U

109mm — S Skunk River

106mm — weigh sta both lanes

102 — IA 210, to Slater, W 3 mi 🅕 Subway

96 — to Elkhart, W Saylorville Lake, to Big Creek SP (11mi)

92 — 1st St, Ankeny, W 🅖 Kum&Go, QT 🅕 Ankeny Diner, Applebee's, Arby's, Burger King, Cazador Mexican, Fazoli's, Guadalajara Mexican, KFC, Quiznos, Tokyo Steaks, Village Inn 🅛 Best Western/rest., Days Inn, Fairfield Inn, Quality Inn, Super 8 🅞 H, auto repair, Goodyear/auto, O'Reilly Parts, Staples, Tires+

90 — IA 160, Ankeny, E 🅖 Casey's 🅕 Chip's Diner, Outback Steaks 🅛 AmericInn, Comfort Inn, Country Inn&Suites, Courtyard, Holiday Inn Express 🅞 Buick/GMC, W 🅖 Casey's/dsl 🅕 B-bops Rest., Buffalo Wild Wings, Burger King, Chili's, China Buffet, Culver's, El Charro, HuHot Chinese, IHOP, Jimmy John's, Marble Slab, McDonald's, Old Chicago, Panchero's Mexican, Panera Bread, SmashBurger, Starbucks, Subway, Tasty Tacos, Wendy's 🅞 AT&T, Best Buy, Big O Tires, Chevrolet, Chrysler/Dodge/Jeep, Ford, GNC, Home Depot, Jo-Ann Fabrics, Kohl's, Menards, Michael's, Petsmart, Radio Shack, Staples, Target, TJ Maxx, to Saylorville Lake (5mi), Tuesday Morning, Tuffy Auto, Verizon, vet, Walgreens, Walmart/Subway

89 — Corporate Woods Dr, E 🅛 Hampton Inn, W 🅛 ValuePlace

87b a — I-235, I-35 and I-80

72c — (124 from I-80) University Ave, See I-80, exit 124. E 🅖 BP/MaidRite, 🅕 Applebees, Bakers Square, Chili's, Huhot Mongolian, Jason's Deli, KFC, Little Caesars, Macaroni Grill, McDonald's, Mi Mexico, Outback Steaks, Qdoba Mexican, RockBottom Rest/Brewery, TCBY, 🅛 Chase Suites, Courtyard, Days Inn, Sheraton, Super 8, Wildwood Lodge, 🅞 AT&T, Barnes&Noble, Best Buy, Home Depot, Kmart, Kohl's, Lowes, Marshall's, Office Depot, Petsmart, Target, Horizon, Whole Foods Mkt, World Mkt, W 🅖 Kum&Go/Burger King, QT, 🅕 Biaggi's Rest, Boston's Caribou Coffee, Cracker Barrel, El Rodeo Mexican, Panera Bread, Red Rossa Pizza, Wendy's, Z'Marik's Cafe, 🅛 Best Western, Country Inn & Suites, La Quinta, 🅞 H Granite CityFood, Walgreen's

86 — Exits 124-136.

I-35 and I-80 run together 14 mi around NW Des Moines. See Iowa I-80, exits 124-138

72b — I-80 W

72a — I-235 E, to Des Moines

70 — Civic Pkwy, Mills E 🅖 Kum&Go/McDonald's 🅕 Fire Creek Grill, Legend's Grill 🅞 Hy-Vee Foods/gas, Verizon, Walgreens, W 🅖 Casey's/MaidRite/dsl 🅕 Applebee's, Bang-Bang Mongolian, BoneFish Grill, Buffalo Wild Wings, Caribou Coffee, Champp's Grill, Cheesecake Factory, Chick-fil-A, Cusina Italiana, Fleming's Rest., Fuddruckers, Iron Wok, Joe's Crabshack, Johnny's Italian Steaks, Joseph's Steaks, Mimi's Cafe, Monterrey Mexican, O'Charly's, On-the-Border,

70 Continued — Panda Express, Panera Bread, PF Chang's, Quiznos, Red Robin, Starbucks, Sticks Rest. 🅛 Courtyard, Drury Inn, Hilton Garden, Holiday Inn, Residence Inn 🅞 H, Barnes&Noble, Best Buy, Costco/gas, Dillards, Kohl's, Lowe's, Old Navy, PetCo, Scheel's Sports, Target, TJ Maxx, Trader Joe's, Walmart

69b a — Grand Ave, W Des Moines

68.5mm — Racoon River

68 — IA 5, E 7 mi to 🛩, to Walnut Woods SP

65 — G14, to Norwalk, Cumming, W 14 mi John Wayne Birthplace, Madison Co Museum

61mm — North River

56mm — Middle River

56 — IA 92, to Indianola, Winterset, W 🅖 Kum&Go/dsl 🅕 Hitchin Post Grill 🅞 Diamond Trail RV Ctr

53mm — 🆁🆂 nb, litter barrels

52 — G50, St Charles, St Marys, W 🅖 14 mi, Casey's/dsl, John Wayne Birthplace, Kum&Go, museum

51mm — 🆁🆂 sb, litter barrels, parking only

47 — rd G64, to Truro, W 🅖 Kum&Go (1mi)

45.5mm — South River

43 — rd 207, New Virginia, E 🅖 Kum&Go/Subway/dsl

36 — rd 152, to US 69, E 3 mi 🅛 Blue Haven Motel, Evergreen Inn, W st patrol

34 — Clay St, Osceola, W 🅖 ▥/Subway/dsl/scales/24hr 🅞 Lakeside Casino Resort/camping

33 — US 34, Osceola, E 🅖 Casey's/dsl/scales 🅕 McDonald's, Pizza Hut, Subway 🅛 Best Value Inn, Days Inn, Super 8 🅞 H, Ford, Goodyear, Hy-Vee Foods, O'Reilly Parts, st patrol, tires, W 🅖 BP/Arby's/dsl 🅕 KFC/Taco Bell 🅛 AmericInn 🅞 Harley-Davidson, Walmart

32mm — 🆁🆂 both lanes, full 🚿 facilities, litter barrels, petwalk, 📞, ♿ RV dump, vending, wireless internet

31mm — parking area sb, weigh sta nb

29 — rd H45

22 — rd J14, Van Wert

18 — rd J20, to Grand River

12 — rd 2, Decatur City, Leon, E 5 mi 🅖 Shell/dsl 🅛 Little River Motel 🅞 H,

7.5mm — Grand River

7mm — 🆁🆂 both lanes, full 🚿 facilities, info, litter barrels, petwalk, 📞, ♿ RV dump, vending, wireless internet

4 — US 69, to Davis City, Lamoni, E to 9 Eagles SP (10mi), W 🅖 Casey's (2mi), Kum&Go/dsl/E-85 🅕 Maid-Rite Cafe, Pizza Hut (2mi), QC Rest, Subway (2mi) 🅛 Best Value Inn, Chief Lamoni Motel 🅞 auto/truck repair, CarQuest, IA Welcome Ctr

0mm — Iowa/Missouri state line

↑E   INTERSTATE 80

Exit #	Services
307mm	Iowa/Illinois state line, Mississippi River
306	US 67, to Le Claire, **N** 🅟 BP/A&W (2mi), Shell/dsl 🍴 Bierstube Grill, Hungry Hobo, McDonald's, Pizza Hut, Steventon's Rest., Subway 🛏 Comfort Inn, Holiday Inn Express, Super 8 🅞 Buffalo Bill Museum, Slagles Foods, **S** 🅟 BP (2mi)
301	Middle Rd, to Bettendorf
300mm	🆁 both lanes, full 🚻 facilities, litter barrels, petwalk, 🅒, 🏕 RV dump, vending, WiFi
298	I-74 E, to Peoria, **S** 🅞 st patrol, to 🏥,
295b a	US 61, Brady St, to Davenport, **N** 🅟 BP/dsl 🅞 Fiat, Sears Auto Ctr, to Scott CP, **S** 0-2 mi 🅟 BP, KwikStar/dsl, Shell 🍴 Burger King, Cracker Barrel, Happy Joe's Pizza, Hardee's, Hooters, Los Agaves Mexican, McDonald's, Mo Brady's Steaks, Olive Garden, Papa John's, ThunderBay Grille, Village Inn Rest. 🛏 Baymont Inn, Best Western, Casa Loma Suites, Clarion, Country Inn&Suites, Motel 6, Quad City Inn, Quality Inn, Residence Inn, Super 8, Travelodge, Wickliffe Inn 🅞 $General, AutoZone, CarQuest, Firestone/auto, Hancock Fabrics, Honda, Hyundai, JC Penney, K-Mart, Lexus, mall, Menards, Nissan, Sears/auto, Tires+, Toyota, US Adventures RV Ctr, vet, Von Maur, VW
292	IA 130 W, Northwest Blvd, **N** 🅟 ⊕FLYING J/Denny's/dsl/LP/scales/24hr, ⬥Loves/Arby's/dsl/scales/24hr 🛏 Comfort Inn 🅞 Farm&Fleet, Interstate RV Park (1mi), Peterbilt, truckwash, **S** 🅟 BP/McDonald's/dsl, Sinclair 🍴 Machine Shed Rest. 🛏 Days Inn 🅞 Freightliner
290	I-280 E, to Rock Island
284	Y40, to Walcott, **N** 🅟 ▭▭▭/Arby's/dsl/24hr/scales, TA/IA 80/BP/DQ/Pizza Hut/Taco Bell/Wendy's/dsl/scales/24hr/@ 🍴 Gramma's Rest. 🛏 Comfort Inn, EconoLodge 🅞 Blue Beacon, IA 80 Trucking Museum, IA 80 Truck-o-Mat, SpeedCo Lube, tires, **S** 🅟 ▭▭▭/Subway/dsl/24hr 🍴 McDonald's 🛏 Days Inn 🅞 Cheyenne Camping Ctr, Walcott CB
280	Y30, to Stockton, New Liberty
277	Durant, **S** 2 mi 🅟 Sinclair/dsl/E-85
271	US 6 W, IA 38 S, to Wilton
270mm	🆁 both lanes, full 🚻 facilities, info, litter barrels, petwalk, 🅒, 🏕 RV dump, vending, WiFi
268mm	parking areas
267	IA 38 N, to Tipton, **N** 🅟 Kum&Go/Subway/dsl/E-85 🅞 Cedar River Camping
266mm	Cedar River
265	to Atalissa, **S** 🅟 ▭▭▭/Chester's/dsl only/scales/24hr
259	to West Liberty, Springdale, **S** 🅟 BP/dsl/24hr 🛏 EconoLodge 🅞 West Liberty Camping
254	X30, West Branch, **N** 🅟 BP/Quiznos/dsl, Casey's 🅞 Hoover NHS, Jack&Jill Foods, USPO, **S** 🅟 Kum&Go 🍴 McDonald's 🛏 Presidential Inn 🅞 Chrysler/Dodge/Jeep
249	Herbert Hoover Hwy, **N** 🅞 winery (2mi), **S** 🍴 Wildwood Smokehouse 🅞 golf
246	IA 1, Dodge St, **N** 🅟 BP/A&W/Subway/dsl 🛏 Clarion, **S** 🅟 Sinclair 🍴 Bob's Pizza 🛏 Travelodge
244	Dubuque St, Iowa City, **N** 🅟 Coralville Lake, **S** 🅞 🏥, museum, to Old Capitol
242	to Coralville, **N** 🍴 River City Grille 🛏 Hampton Inn, Holiday Inn, **S** 🅟 BP, Kum&Go/dsl 🍴 Applebee's, Arby's, Bandana's BBQ, Burger King, Delago Mexican Cafe, DQ, Edge Water Grill, Hardee's, IA Riverpower Rest., Jade Sisters Rest., McDonald's, Milio's Sandwiches, Mondo's Cafe, Old Chicago Grill, Papa John's, Peking Buffet, Perkins, Sonic,

I O W A   C I T Y

242	**Continued** Sparti's Gyros, Subway, Taco John's 🛏 Best Western, Big Ten Inn, Comfort Inn, Days Inn, Fairfield Inn, Heartland Inn, IA Lodge, Marriott, Motel 6, Super 8 🅞 🏥, Aamco, vet, Walgreens
240	IA 965, to US 6, Coralville, N Liberty, **N** 🅟 BP, Casey's/dsl 🍴 Buffalo Wild Wings, Culver's, Jimmy John's, McDonald's, Steak'n Shake, TX Roadhouse, Village Inn, Wendy's 🛏 AmericInn, Country Inn&Suites, Suburban Lodge 🅞 Colony Country Camping (3mi), Costco, Gordmans, Harley-Davidson, Kohl's, Michael's, PetCo, TJ Maxx, Walgreens, Walmart/Subway **S** 🅟 Casey's 🍴 Caribou Coffee, Chili's, Coldstone, Food Court, Huhot Mongolian, IHOP, Jimmy John's, Noodles&Co, Old Country Buffet, Olive Garden, Outback Steaks, Panchero's Mexican, Papa Murphy's, Pizza Hut, Red Lobster, Starbucks, Taste of China, Which Which 🛏 Comfort Suites, Holiday Inn Express, Residence Inn 🅞 Ace Hardware, Barnes&Noble, Best Buy, Dillard's, Hobby Lobby, HyVee Foods/dsl, JC Penney, Lowe's, mall, Radio Shack, Scheel's Sports, Sears/auto, Target, Tires+, U-Haul, Verizon, Younkers
239b	I-380 N, US 218 N, to Cedar Rapids
239a	US 218 S
237	Tiffin, **N** 🅟 Kum&Go/Subway/dsl 🍴 Jon's Rest (1mi) (seasonal)
236mm	🆁 full 🚻 facilities, litter barrels, petwalk, 🅒, 🏕, RV dump, vending, wireless internet
230	W38, to Oxford, **N** 🅞 Kalona Museum, Sleepy Hollow Camping
225	US 151 N, W21 S, **N** 🛏 Heritage Inn, to Amana Colonies, **S** **Welcome Ctr** 🅟 BP, Casey's 🍴 7 Villages Rest., Colony Village Rest., Little Amana Rest./Winery, MaidRite Cafe, Ox Yoke Rest. 🛏 Clarion, Motel 6
220	IA 149 S, V77 N, to Williamsburg, **N** 🅟 BP, Casey's/rest/dsl 🍴 Arby's, McDonald's, Subway 🛏 Best Western, Crest Motel, Super 8 🅞 factory outlets/famous brands, GNC, Old Navy, **S** 🛏 Days Inn
216	to Marengo, **N** 🅟 Kum&Go/Subway/dsl 🛏 Sudbury Court Motel (7mi) 🅞 🏥, (8mi)
211	to Ladora, Millersburg, **S** 🅞 Lake IA Park (5mi)
208mm	🆁 both lanes, full 🚻 facilities, litter barrels, petwalk, 🅒, 🏕 RV dump, vending, wireless internet
205	to Victor
201	IA 21, to Deep River, **N** 🅟 ▭▭▭/Subway/dsl/scales/24hr 🛏 Baymont Inn, **S** 🅟 KwikStar/Pinecone Rest./dsl/scales/24hr/@, truck repair
197	to Brooklyn, **N** RV camping
191	US 63, to Montezuma, **S** 🅞 to Diamond Lake SP (9mi)
182	IA 146, to Grinnell, **N** 0-2 mi 🅟 Casey's, Kum&Go/Subway/dsl/24hr 🍴 Casa Margaritas, DQ, Grinnell Steakhouse, KFC, McDonald's, Pizza Ranch, Taco John's 🛏 Best Western, Comfort Inn, Country Inn, Days Inn, Super 8 🅞 $General, Ace Hardware, Buick/Chevrolet/GMC, 🏥, (4mi), HyVee Foods, O'Reilly Parts, Verizon, vet, Walmart
180mm	🆁 both lanes, full 🚻 facilities, litter barrels, petwalk, 🅒 🏕 playground, RV dump (eb) wireless internet, vending, weather info
179	IA 124, to Oakland Acres, Lynnville
175mm	N Skunk River
173	IA 224, Kellogg, **N** 🅟 Phillips 66/Best Burger/dsl/24hr 🅞 Kellogg RV Park, Rock Creek SP (9mi), **S** 🅞 Pella Museum
168	SE Beltline Dr, to Newton, **N** 1 mi 🅟 Casey's/dsl, Murphy USA/dsl 🍴 Arby's 🛏 Mid-Iowa Motel 🅞 $Tree,

INTERSTATE 80 Cont'd

NEWTON

Exit #	Services
168	Continued KOA (seasonal), Radio Shack, Walmart S 🅿 ♥Loves /Chester's/McDonald's/dsl/scales 🏨 AmericInn ⊙ Iowa Speedway
164	US 6, IA 14, Newton, N 🅿 Casey's, Phillips 66/Subway/dsl 🍴 Country Kitchen, Culver's, KFC/Taco Bell, MT Mikes, Okoboji Grill, Perkins, Pizza Ranch, Senor Tequila Mexican 🏨 Days Inn, EconoLodge, Quality Inn, Super 8 ⊙ H, museum, S 🏨 Best Value Inn ⊙ Cadillac/Chevrolet, to Lake Red Rock
159	F48, to Jasper, Baxter
155	IA 117, Colfax, N 🅿 BP/McDonald's 🏨 Colfax Inn, Microtel ⊙ Pitstop RV Camping, truck repair, S 🅿 Casey's, Kum&Go/Subway/dsl/24hr
153mm	S Skunk River
151	weigh sta wb
149	Mitchellville
148mm	🆁🆂 both lanes, full ♿ facilities, litter barrels, petwalk, 🅒, 🚮 RV dump, vending, wireless internet
143	Altoona, Bondurant, S 0-2 mi 🅿 Casey's, Kum&Go 🍴 Pizza Ranch 🏨 Holiday Inn Express ⊙ HyVee Foods
142b a	US 65, Hubble Ave, Des Moines, S 🅿 ⊕FLYING J/Max's Diner/dsl/scales/24hr/@, Git'n Go 🍴 Big Steer Rest., Burger King, Culver's, Jethro's BBQ, KFC/Taco Bell, McDonald's/playplace, Pizza Hut, Subway, Taco John's 🏨 Adventureland Inn, Best Western, Motel 6, Regency Inn, Settle Inn ⊙ Adventureland Funpark, Blue Beacon, camping, casino, Freightliner, Peterbilt
141	US 6 W, US 65 S, Pleasant Hill, Des Moines, 🍴 Uncle Buck's Grill ⊙ Bass Pro Shops
137b a	I-35 N, I-235 S, to Des Moines

I-80 W and I-35 S run together 14 mi.

DES MOINES

Exit #	Services
136	US 69, E 14th St, Camp Sunnyside, N 🅿 BP/dsl, Casey's 🍴 Bonanza Steaks, MT Mikes 🏨 Budget Inn, Comfort Inn, Motel 6, Rodeway Inn ⊙ Allied Tire, antiques, Shoppers, Volvo, S 0-1 mi 🅿 Casey's/dsl, QT/Burger King/dsl/scales/24hr, Star Gas 🍴 Arby's, Fazoli's, Hardee's, KFC, McDonald's, Papa Murphy's, Pueblo Viejo Mexican, Subway, Taco Bell, Taco John's, Village Inn, Wendy's 🏨 Baymont Inn, Travelodge ⊙ $General, Advance Parts, Aldi Foods, AutoZone, CarX, Family$, O'Reilly Parts, Tires+, TruckLube, USPO
135	IA 415, 2nd Ave, Polk City, N 🍴 Smokey D's BBQ ⊙ antiques, Harley-Davidson, Rider Trucks, S 🅿 Git'n Go, QT, Shell ⊙ H, Earl's Tire, NAPA, st patrol
133mm	Des Moines River
131	IA 28 S, NW 58th St, N 🅿 Casey's, QT 🍴 Bandit Burrito, Chopsticks, DQ, El Mariachi Mexican, Greenbriar Rest., Jimmy John's, Pagliai's Pizza, Panera Bread, Sonic, Subway, VanDee's Icecream/Sandwiches 🏨 AmericInn ⊙ Ace Hardware, Acura, Audi/VW, Goodyear/auto, Hy-Vee Food, USPO, Verizon, vet, S 🅿 BP/dsl/LP/24hr, Casey's, QT 🍴 Applebee's, Arby's, Bamboo Buffet, Bennigan's, Buffalo Wild Wings, Burger King, Carlos O'Kelly's, Chipotle Mexican, Cici's Pizza, Daytona's Grill, Famous Dave's BBQ, Fazoli's, IHOP, Jimmy John's, KFC, McDonald's, Old Chicago, Panda Express, Perkins, Popeye's, Quiznos, Starbucks, Subway, Wendy's 🏨 Days Inn, EconoLodge, Holiday Inn, Quality Inn, Ramada/Rest., Super 8 ⊙ H, $General, $Tree, Advance Parts, AT&T, BigLots, CarQuest, CarX, Chevrolet, Dahl's Food/Fuel, Firestone/auto, Ford, Goodyear/auto, Hobby Lobby, Kohl's, mall, NAPA, Nissan, Office Depot, Sears/auto, Staples, Target, Tires+, Toyota/Scion, URGENT CARE, Verizon, vet, Younkers

DES MOINES

Exit #	Services
129	NW 86th St, Camp Dodge, N 🅿 Kum&Go 🍴 Burger King, Coldstone, Garden Grill, Legends Grill, Maid-Rite Cafe, McDonald's, Okoboji Grill, Panchero's Mexican, Planet Sub, Quiznos, Starbucks, TX Roadhouse, Village Inn 🏨 Hilton Garden, Stoney Creek Inn, TownePlace Suites ⊙ Dahl's Foods, Verizon, S 🅿 Casey's, Kum&Go/dsl 🍴 Arby's, B-Bops Burgers, Culver's, Friedrich's Coffee, Overtime Grill, Ruby Tuesday 🏨 Holiday Inn Express, Microtel ⊙ Walgreens
127	IA 141 W, Grimes, N 🅿 BP/dsl, QT/dsl 🍴 MaidRite Cafe, McCoy's Grill, Subway 🏨 AmericInn (3mi) ⊙ Kia/Suzuki, to Saylorville Lake, S 🅿 Kum&Go/E-85 🍴 McDonald's, Quiznos ⊙ Home Depot, Target
126	Douglas Ave, Urbandale, N 🅿 Kum&Go/dsl, ▦▦▦/Grandma Max's/Subway/dsl/scales/24hr/@ S 🅿 Dragon House 🏨 EconoLodge, Extended Stay America, Villa Lodge ⊙ Chevrolet
125	US 6, Hickman Rd, N 🅿 ♥Loves/Denny's/dsl/scales/LP/24hr ⊙ Chrysler/Dodge/Jeep, Menards, S 🍴 IA Machine Shed Rest., Starbucks 🏨 Clive Hotel, Comfort Suites, Sleep Inn ⊙ AAA, Honda, Hyundai, to Living History Farms
124	(72c from I-35 nb), University Ave, N 🅿 Kum&Go/Burger King, QT 🍴 Biaggi's Rest., Boston's, Caribou Coffee, Cracker Barrel, El Rodeo Mexican, Panera Bread, Red Rossa Pizza, Wendy's, Z'Marik's Cafe 🏨 Best Western, Country Inn&Suites, La Quinta ⊙ H, Granite City Food, Walgreens, S 🅿 BP/MaidRite 🍴 Applebee's, Bakers Square, Chili's, Huhot Mongolian, Jason's Deli, KFC, Little Caesars, Macaroni Grill, McDonald's, Mi Mexico, Outback Steaks, Qdoba Mexican, RockBottom Rest./brewery, TCBY 🏨 Chase Suites, Courtyard, Days Inn, Sheraton, Super 8, Wildwood Lodge ⊙ AT&T, Barnes&Noble, Best Buy, Home Depot, I-80 E and I-35 N run together 14 mi, K-Mart, Kohl's, Lowe's, Marshall's, Office Depot, Petsmart, Target, Verizon, Whole Foods Mkt, World Mkt

I-80 E and I-35 N run together 14 mi.

Exit #	Services
123b a	I-80/I-35 N, I-35 S to Kansas City, I-235 to Des Moines
122	(from eb)60th St, W Des Moines
121	74th St, W Des Moines, N 🍴 Biaggi's Rest., Panera Bread, Red Rossa Pizza 🏨 Hampton Inn, Staybridge Suites ⊙ H, Granite City Foods, HyVee Food/gas, Walgreens, S 🅿 Kum&Go/Subway 🍴 Arby's, Burger King, CK's, Culver's, McDonald's, Perkins, Quiznos, Taco John's 🏨 Candlewood Suites, Fairfield Inn, Marriott, Motel 6, SpringHill Suites, vet
119mm	🆁🆂 both lanes, full ♿ facilities, info, petwalk, 🅒, 🚮 RV dump, vending, Wireless Internet
117	R22, Booneville, Waukee, N 🍴 Organic Farm Rest. ⊙ Timberline Camping (2mi), S 🅿 Kum&Go/24hr 🍴 Rube's Steaks, Waveland Rest. (2mi)
115mm	weigh sta eb

(Map of central Iowa showing I-35, I-80, I-235, US 35 highways with locations: Camp Dodge, Grimes, Johnston, Urbandale, Crestwood, Des Moines, West Des Moines, Fort Des Moines, Carbondale, Hastie, Levey, Avon, Adelphi, Lakewood, Carlisle, Cumming, Scotch Ridge)

IA

⬆E INTERSTATE 80 Cont'd

Exit #	Services
113	R16, Van Meter, **S 1 mi** 🅖 Casey's 🅞 Feller Museum, Veteran's Cemetery
112mm	N Racoon River
111mm	Middle Racoon River
110	US 169, to Adel, DeSoto, **N** 🅞 camping (6mi), **S** 🅖 Casey's, Kum&Go/dsl/E-85 🛏 Countryside Inn, Edgetowner Motel 🅞 John Wayne Birthplace (14mi)
106	F90, P58, 🅞 KOA (apr-oct)
104	P57, Earlham, **S** 🅖 Casey's (2mi) 🍴 Master Griller (2mi)
100	US 6, to Redfield, Dexter, 🅖 Casey's (2mi) 🍴 Drew's Chocolate (2mi)
97	P48, to Dexter, **N** 🅖 camping, Casey's (2mi)
93	P28, Stuart, **N** 🅖 Casey's/dsl/scales, Kum&Go/dsl 🍴 Burger King, McDonald's/playplace, Subway 🛏 AmericInn, Super 8 🅞 $General, camping (7mi), Chevrolet, city park, Hometown Foods, **S** 🅖 Phillips 66/dsl 🍴 Country Kitchen 🛏 Economy Inn, Edgetowner Motel 🅞 NAPA
88	P20, Menlo
86	IA 25, to Greenfield, Guthrie Ctr, **S** 🅞 🅗, (13mi), to Spring Brook SP
85mm	Middle River
83	N77, Casey, **N 1 mi** 🅖 Kum&Go 🅞 camping
80.5mm	🆁🆂 both lanes, full 🅰 facilities, litter barrels, petwalk, 🅒, 🅐 RV dump, vending, wireless internet
76	IA 925, N54, Adair, **N** 🅖 Casey's/dsl, Kum&Go/Subway/dsl 🍴 Happy Chef 🛏 Adair Budget Inn, Super 8 🅞 camping, city park
75	G30, to Adair
70	IA 148 S, Anita, **S** to Lake Anita SP (6mi)
64	N28, to Wiota
61mm	E Nishnabotna River
60	US 6, US 71, to Atlantic, Lorah, **S** 🅖 Phillips 66/dsl/24hr 🛏 Best Value Inn
57	N16, to Atlantic, **S** 🅞 🅗, (7mi), Nelsen RV Ctr
54	IA 173, to Elk Horn, **N 6 mi Welcome Ctr/Wireless Internet,** 🛏 AmericInn, Windmill Museum
51	M56, to Marne
46	M47, Walnut, **N** 🅖 BP/McDonald's/dsl 🍴 Emma Jean's Rest. 🛏 Super 8, to Prairie Rose SP (8mi), **S** 🅖 Kum&Go/pizza/dsl 🛏 EconoLodge/RV Park, tires/repair
44mm	weigh sta wb/parking area eb
40	US 59, to Harlan, Avoca, **N** 🅖 🚛/Phillips 66/Taco John's/MaidRite Cafe/dsl/24hr/scales 🍴 CJ's Grill, Subway 🛏 Motel 6 🅞 🅗, (12mi), truckwash, **S** 🅖 Casey's/dsl, Shell/dsl 🍴 Embers Rest. 🛏 Acova Motel, Capri Motel 🅞 Avoca Foods, Farmall-Land Museum (seasonal), Nishna Museum
39.5mm	W Nishnabotna River
34	M16, Shelby, **N** 🅖 BP/rest/dsl/E-85, Shell/Cornstalk Cafe/dsl 🍴 DQ, Godfather's 🛏 Shelby Country Inn/RV Park
32mm	🆁🆂 both lanes, parking only
29	L66, to Minden, **S** 🅖 Phillips 66/A&W/dsl 🛏 Mid-Town Motel (2mi) 🅞 winery (4mi)
27	I-680 W, to N Omaha
23	IA 244, L55, Neola, **S** 🅖 Kum&Go/dsl 🅞 camping, to Arrowhead Park
20mm	Welcome Ctr eb/🆁🆂 wb, full 🅰 facilities, litter barrels, petwalk, 🅒, 🅐 RV dump, vending, Wireless Internet
17	G30, Underwood, **N** 🅖 Phillips 66/Subway/dsl/24hr 🛏 Underwood Motel 🅞 truck/tire repair
8	US 6, Council Bluffs, **N** 🅖 Phillips 66/dsl (1mi) 🅞 $General, 🅗 (3mi), K-Mart, **S** 🅞 st patrol

COUNCIL BLUFFS

5	Madison Ave, Council Bluffs, **N** 🅖 BP/dsl 🍴 Burger King, FoodCourt, Great Wall Chinese, KFC, McDonald's, Papa Murphy's, Pizza Hut, Starbucks, Subway 🛏 AmericInn 🅞 HyVee Foods/drug, Sears/auto, Verizon, Walgreens, **S** 🅖 Cenex/DQ/dsl, Phillips 66 🍴 Johnny's Cantina, Puerto Vallarta, Sam&Louie's Pizza, Village Inn Rest. 🛏 Western Inn 🅞 No Frills Mkt, TrueValue
4	I-29 S, to Kansas City
3	IA 192 N, Council Bluffs, **N** 🅞 to Hist Dodge House, **S** 🅖 Phillips 66/dsl, Shell/dsl, TA/dsl/scales/24hr@ 🍴 Applebee's, Beijing Rest., Burger King, Cracker Barrel, DQ, Fazoli's, Golden Corral, Hardee's, Huhot Mongolian, La Mesa Mexican, LJ Silver, McDonald's, Old River Pizza, Perkins, Red Lobster, Subway, Taco Bell 🛏 Days Inn, Fairfield Inn, Motel 6, Settle Inn 🅞 Advance Parts, Aldi Foods, Best Buy, Buick/GMC, Cadillac/Chevrolet, Chrysler/Jeep/Suzuki, Ford, Freightliner, Gordman's, Home Depot, Hyundai/Subaru, Kia, Menards, Nissan, Outdoor Recreation RV, Sam's Club/gas, truck/dsl repair, U-Haul, Verizon, Walmart/Subway
1b	S 24th St, Council Bluffs, **N** 🅖 BP, Casey's, 🚛/Arby's/scales/dsl/24hr, Sapp Bros/Shell/Burger King/dsl 🍴 Famous Dave's BBQ, Hooters, Quaker Steak&Lube, Ruby Tuesday, Uncle Buck's 🛏 American Inn, Best Western, Country Inn&Suites, Hilton Garden, Holiday Inn Express, Microtel, SpringHill Suites, Super 8 🅞 Bass Pro Shop, Blue Beacon, Camping World RV Ctr, casino, Horseshoe RV Park, Peterbilt, SpeedCo, **S Welcome Ctr, full facilities** 🍴 Culver's, TX Roadhouse 🅞 JC Penney, PetCo, ShopKO, Verizon
1a	I-29 N, to Sioux City
0mm	Iowa/Nebraska state line, Missouri River

⬆N INTERSTATE 235 (Des Moines)

Exit #	Services
15	I-80, E to Davenport
12	US 6, E Euclid Ave, **E** 🅖 Casey's 🍴 Burger King, Dragon House Chinese, Papa John's, Perkins, Tasty Tacos 🅞 $Tree, HyVee Foods/drug, Radio Shack, Walgreens, **W** 🅖 QT 🅞 NAPA
11	Guthrie Ave, **W** 🅖 Kum&Go/dsl 🅞 CarQuest
10a b	IA 163 W, E University Ave, Easton Dr
9	US 65/69, E 14th, E 15th, **N** 🅞 Walgreens, **S** 🅖 QT 🍴 McDonald's, Quiznos 🅞 🅗, st capitol, URGENT CARE, zoo
8a	3rd St, 5th Ave, **N** 🛏 Holiday Inn 🅞 🅗, **S** 🛏 Embassy Suites, Marriott, Quality Inn 🅞 Conv Ctr
7	Keo Way
6	MLK Blvd/31st St, **S** 🅞 🛏, 🅞 Drake U, Governor's Mansion
5b	42nd St, Science & Art Ctr, **N** 🅖 Git'n Go 🍴 Papa John's 🅞 Curves
5a	56th St (from wb), **N** 🅞 golf
4	IA 28, 63rd St, to Windsor Heights, **S** 🅞 Historic Valley Jct, zoo
3	8th St, W Des Moines, **N** 🅖 Kum&Go 🍴 B-Bop's Café, Burger King, Papa Murphy's, Starbucks 🅞 HyVee Foods, PetCo, Sam's Club/gas, Walmart/Subway **S** 🅖 BP, Kum&Go/dsl/E-85 🍴 Jimmy John's, Lemongrass Thai, Raul's Mexican, Taste of Oriental 🛏 Days Inn
2	22nd St, 24th St, W Des Moines, **N** 🅖 BP, Casey's, QT/dsl 🍴 Arby's, Culver's, Famous Dave's BBQ, Hardee's,

IA

INTERSTATE 235 (Des Moines) Cont'd

Exit #	Services
2	Continued
	Hooters, LoneStar Steaks, SmashBurger, Taco Bell, Village Inn 🏠 Studio+ 🅞 $Tree, Firestone/auto, Gordman's, Meineke, Michael's, Walgreens
1b	Valley West Dr W Des Moines, **N** 🅖 BP/dsl 🍴 Carlos O'Kelly's, Chipotle Mexican, Eastern Buffet, Hamilton's Rest., Jimmy John's, Noodles&Co, Olive Garden, Panera Bread, Red Lobster, Subway 🏠 Valley West Inn 🅞 AT&T, Best Buy, Home Depot, HyVee Foods, JC Penney, mall, Marshall's, Target, Von Maur, Whole Foods Mkt, Younker's
0mm	I-235 begins/ends on I-80, exit 123.

INTERSTATE 280 (Davenport)

Exit #	Services
18b a	I-74, US 6, Moline, **S** 🅖 Shell/dsl 🍴 Bare Bones BBQ, McDonald's, MT Jack's 🏠 Best Inn, Country Inn&Suites, Hampton Inn, Holiday Inn Express, La Quinta, Motel 6, Quality Inn 🅞🆁🆂
15	Airport Rd, Milan, **N 1 mi** 🍴 MaidRite Café, Hardee's, McDonald's, Subway 🅞 auto repair, Buick/Chevrolet, Firestone
11b a	IL 92, to Andalusia, Rock Island, **S** 🏠 Jumer's Hotel/casino/rest. 🅞 KOA Camping
9.5mm	Iowa/Illinois state line, Mississippi River
8	rd 22, Rockingham Rd, to Buffalo
6	US 61, W River Dr, to Muscatine, **W** 🅞 camping, 🅖
4	Locust St, rd F65, 160th St, **E** 🅞 🄷, St Ambrose U, to Palmer Coll, **W** 🅖 Shell/Subway/dsl
1	US 6 E, IA 927, Kimberly Rd, to Walcott, **E 3 mi** 🅖 Murphy USA/dsl 🍴 Applebee's, Culver's, Harlan's Rest., Steak'n Shake, Subway, Wendy's 🅞 Discount Tire, GNC, Walmart
0mm	I-280 begins/ends on I-80, exit 290.

INTERSTATE 380

W A T E R L O O

Exit #	Services
73mm	**I-380 begins/ends on US 218, 73mm in Waterloo, E** 🅖 BP/dsl, **W** 🅖 Clark 🍴 Pizza Hut
72	San Marnan Dr, **W** 🍴 A&W/LJ Silver, Applebee's, Bonanza, Burger King, Carlos O'Kelly's, Coldstone, Godfather's, Golden China, Hardee's, IHOP, Jimmy John's, Olive Garden, Panera Bread, Pizza Hut, Red Lobster, Starbucks, Subway, Taco John's 🏠 Baymont Inn, Candlewoods Suites, Comfort Inn, Country Inn&Suites, Days Inn, Fairfield Inn, Hampton Inn, Holiday Inn Express, Super 8 🅞 $General, Advance Parts, Aldi Foods, Barnes&Noble, Best Buy, Chevrolet, Chrysler/Dodge/Jeep, CVS Drug, Dillards, Ford, Gordman's, Hobby Lobby, HyVee Foods, JC Penney, Jo-Ann Fabrics, KIA, Menards, Old Navy, PetCo, PetsMart, Radio Shack, Sears/auto, Staples, Target, Tires+, TJ Maxx, Walmart
71	I-380, US 20, IA 27, Cedar Rapids, Cedar Falls, Dubuque, **S US 18** 🍴 Isle Hotel/Casino
70	River Forest Rd
68	Elk Run Heights, Evansdale Dr, **E** 🅖 ⊘FLYING J/Denny's/dsl/scales/24hr, 🚛/RR/Junie's/Subway/dsl/scales/24hr/@ 🍴 Arby's, McDonald's 🏠 Days Inn 🅞 Freightliner, Paine's RV Ctr, truckwash/repair
66	Gilbertville, Raymond
65	US 20 E, Dubuque
62	rd d-38, Gilbertville
55	rd v-65, Jesup, La Port, **W** 🅞 Hickory Hills Park, McFarlane Park
54mm	weigh sta sb
51mm	weigh sta nb
49	rd d-48, Brandon, **W 1 mi** food, gas
43	IA 150, Independence, Vinton, **E** 🅖 Phillips 66/dsl/24hr 🏠 Inn Suites 🅞 truckwash
41	Urbana, **E** 🅞 Lazy Acres RV Park, **W** 🅖 Casey's/dsl
35	rd w-36, Center Point, **E** 🅖 BP, Casey's, Sinclair/McDonald's/Subway/dsl/scales/24hr **W** 🅞 Pleasant Creek SRA (5mi)
28	rd e-34, Robins, Toddville, **W** 🅞 Wickiup Outdoor Learning Ctr (5mi)
25	Boyson Rd, Hiawatha, **E** 🅞 Ketelsen RV Ctr, **W** 🅖 BP, Casey's/Blimpie/Pizza 🍴 Culver's, Pizza Wagon 🅞 Toyota/Scion/VW
24	IA 100, Blairs Ferry Rd, **E** 🅖 KwikShop/dsl 🍴 Happy Chef, Hardee's, KFC, La Glorias Mexican, McDonald's 🏠 Days Inn, Hawthorn Suites 🅞 CVS Drug, HyVee Foods, **W** 🅖 Road Ranger 🍴 Arby's, Burger King, Metro Buffet, Pizza Hut, Subway, Taco Bell 🅞 Aldi Foods, AutoZone, GNC, Lowe's, Sam's Club/gas, Walmart
22	Glass Rd, 32nd st, **E** 🅖 KwikShop/dsl 🍴 Papa Johns
21	H St, Cedar Rapids, downtown
20b	7th St E, Cedar Rapids, **E** 🅞 🄷, downtown
20a	US 151 Bus., **E** 🅖 Crowne Plaza
19b	1st Ave W, **W** 🅖 Best Western 🅞 NAPA
18	Wilson Ave, 🅞 museums
17	33rd ave SW, Hawkeye Downs, **W** 🅖 Casey's 🍴 Burger King, McDonald's, Sonic, Taco Bell, Wendy's 🏠 Clarion, Comfort Inn, Economy Inn, Hampton Inn, Heartland Inn, Holiday Inn Express, Motel 6, Red Roof Inn, Super 8
16	US 30 W, US 151 S, US 218 N, Tama
13	Ely, **W** 🅖 Casey's/A&W/dsl, Casey's/dsl/scales 🍴 McDonald's 🏠 AmericInn, Country Inn&Suites 🅞🆁🆂
12mm	🆁🆂 both lanes, litter barrels, petwalk, 🄲, 🖐, RV Dump, vending, wireless internet
10	rd f-12, Shueyville, Swisher, **E** 🅖 BP/dsl 🅞 Lake Mcbride SP, **W** 🅖 Amana Colonies
8mm	Iowa River
4	rd f-28, North Liberty, **E** 🅖 BP/dsl, Casey's/Blimpie, Kum&Go/dsl (2mi) 🏠 Sleep Inn 🅞 Colony Country RV Park (5mi)
0b a	I-80 E to Iowa City, W to Des Moines, **I-380 begins/ends on I-80**

C E D A R R A P I D S

IA

⬆N INTERSTATE 35	
Exit #	**Services**
235mm	Kansas/Missouri state line
235	Cambridge Circle
234b a	US 169, Rainbow Blvd, E 🚰 Phillips 66, QT 🍴 Applebee's, Arby's, Burger King, McDonald's, Rosedale BBQ, Sonic, Wendy's 🛏 Best Western, Sun Inn ⬛ KU MED CTR, W 🍴 KFC, LJ Silver, Taco Bell
233b	37th Ave (from sb)
233a	SW Blvd, Mission Rd
232b	US 69 N, E 🚰 QT 🍴 Cici's, McDonald's, Taco Bell
232a	Lamar Ave, E 🚰 QT 🛏 ValuePlace Inn
231b a	I-635 (exits left from sb)
230	Antioch Rd (from sb), E 🚰 QT
229	Johnson Dr, E 🚰 Phillips 66 🍴 Arby's, Bob Evans, Chili's, Chipotle Mexican, McDonald's, Papa John's, Starbucks ⬛ GNC, Hen House Mkt, Home Depot, Marshall's, Old Navy, Petsmart, Walgreens, W 🚰 Cenex/dsl
228b	US 56 E, US 69, Shawnee Mission Pkwy, E 🚰 Shell 🍴 Caribou Coffee, Denny's, IHOP, Krispy Kreme, Pizza Hut, Taco Bell 🛏 Drury Inn, Homestead Suites, Winsteads Suites ⬛ BMW/Mini, Sears Grand, W 🚰 Valero 🍴 A&W, LJ Silver, Panera Bread, Pizza Hut, Subway, Wendy's ⬛ Cotman's Transmissions, Firestone, Ford, Goodyear/auto, Jo-Ann Fabrics, Office Depot, O'Reilly Parts, Russell Stover, Walgreens
228a	67th St, E 🛏 Quality Inn ⬛ CarMax, W 🚰 Phillips 66/Circle K/dsl 🍴 Hyundai, Jaguar, Land Rover, Maserati, Mercedes, Porsche Smart, Toyota/Scion
227	75th St, E 🍴 McDonald's 🛏 Extended Stay America ⬛ 🅷 Acura, vet, Walmart W 🚰 QT/dsl 🍴 2 Amigos Mexican, Domino's, Sonic, Subway, Taco Bell, Wendy's 🛏 Hampton Inn ⬛ Hyundai
225b	US 69 S (from sb), Overland Pkwy
225a	87th St, E 🚰 Phillips 66 🍴 Green Mill Rest 🛏 Holiday Inn, W 🚰 Phillips 66/Circle K/dsl 🍴 Taco Bell, Zarda BBQ ⬛ auto repair
224	95th St, E 🚰 Phillips 66/Circle K, Shell 🍴 Applebee's, BD Mongolian BBQ, Burger King, Chick-fil-A, Chipotle Mexican, Denny's, Houlihan's, KFC, McDonald's, Mimi's Café, On-the-Border, Outback Steaks, Panda Express, Subway, Taco Bell, TGIFriday's, Winstead's Cafe 🛏 Comfort Inn, Crowne Plaza, Days Inn, Extended Stay America, Knight's Inn, La Quinta, Motel 6, Super 8 ⬛ 🅷, Advance Parts, Barnes&Noble, Best Buy, Dillard's, Firestone/auto, Hy-Vee Foods, JC Penney, Kohl's, Macy's, mall, Nordstrom, Office Depot, PetCo, Sam's Club/gas, Target, W 🚰 Phillips 66 🍴 Costco/gas, Mi Ranchito, O'Reilly Parts, other:, U-Haul
222b a	I-435 W & E
220	119th St, E 🚰 Conoco/7-11, Phillips 66/Circle K, Shell 🍴 5 Guys Burgers, A&W, Buffalo Wild Wings, Burger King, Chick-fil-A, Chipotle Mexican, Coldstone, Cracker Barrel, Dodge City Steaks, Firehouse Subs, Granite City Cafe, Greek Rest., Haru's Steak, IHOP, Jersey Mike's, Jimmy John's, Joe's Crab-shack, La Parrilla, LJ Silver, Longhorn Steaks, McDonald's, Noodles&Co, OK Joe's BBQ, Old Chicago, Olive Garden, Panda Express, Panera Bread, Papa Murphy's, Pei Wei, Planet Sub, Popeye's, Red Lobster, Ruby Tuesday, Schlotzsky's, Starbucks, Steak'n Shake, Subway, Taco Bell, TX Roadhouse, Wei's Buffet, Zio's Italian 🛏 Comfort Suites, Fairfield Inn, Hampton Inn, Hilton Garden, Residence Inn, SpringHill Suites, ValuePlace Inn ⬛ AT&T, Best Buy, Chrysler/Dodge/Jeep, Dick's, Fiat, GNC, Goodyear/auto, Home Depot, Honda,

220	Continued
	Marshall's, Mazda, Michael's, NTB, Old Navy, Petsmart, Radio Shack, Target, U-Haul, Verizon, W 🍴 Houlihan's, Jason's Deli, Longhorn Steaks, Starbucks ⬛ Bass Pro Shops
218	135th, Santa Fe St, Olathe, E 🚰 Phillips 66/dsl, QT 🍴 Applebee's, Burger King, Chapala Mexican, China Buffet, Chucke-Cheese, Church's, Garozzo's Italian, McDonald's, Other Place Grill, Papa John's, Perkins, Pizza St, Quiznos, Sheridan's Custard, Subway, Taco Bell ⬛ $General, $Tree, Ace Hardware, Aldi Foods, AutoZone, BigLots, CVS Drug, Ford/Lincoln, GNC, Goodyear, Hobby Lobby, Hy-Vee Foods, K-Mart, Kohl's, Lowe's, Office Depot, PriceChopper Foods, Tuesday Morning, vet, W 🚰 QT 🍴 El Camino Real, Taco Bell, Waffle House, Wendy's 🛏 Rodeway Inn ⬛ Aamco, Advance Parts, Buick/GMC, Chevrolet, Harley-Davidson, Hyundai, Kia, Meineke, O'Reilly Parts, Radio Shack, Subaru, Toyota/Scion, VW
217	Old Hwy 56 (from sb), same as 215
215	US 169 S, KS 7, Olathe, E 🚰 Phillips 66/dsl, QT/dsl 🍴 China Inn, Chipotle Mexican, Cilantro Mexican, IHOP, Jimmy John's, Outback Steaks, Panera Bread, Red Robin, Ryan's 🛏 Candlewood Suites, Comfort Inn ⬛ Aldi Foods, AT&T, Home Depot, Jiffy Lube, NTB, Target, W 🚰 Shell/dsl/scales/24hr 🍴 54th St Grill, Applebee's, Burger King, Chili's, FoodCourt, McDonald's, Red Lobster, Taco Bell, Waffle House, Wendy's 🛏 Best Western, Days Inn, Holiday Inn, La Quinta ⬛ 🅷, mall, Mazda
214	Lone Elm Rd, 159th St
213mm	**weigh sta both lanes**
210	US 56 W, Gardner, W 🚰 Phillips 66/Circle K/dsl 🍴 Arby's, Burger King, KFC, McDonald's, Mr Goodcents Subs, Pizza Hut, Subway, Taco Bell, Waffle House 🛏 Super 8 ⬛ NAPA, Verizon, Walmart/Subway
207	US 56 E, Gardner Rd, E ⬛ Olathe RV Ctr, W 🚰 Phillips 66/dsl, Shell/dsl
202	Edgerton
198	KS 33, to Wellsville, W food, gas
193	Tennessee Rd, Baldwin
188	US 59 N, to Lawrence
187	KS 68, Ottawa, W 🚰 Zarco/Phillips 66/dsl/E-85 ⬛ Central RV Ctr, vet
185	15th St, Ottawa
183	US 59, Ottawa, E 🚰 Loves/Hardee's/dsl/scales/24hr W 🚰 BP, Conoco/dsl, Ottawa/dsl 🍴 Applebee's, Burger King, KFC, McDonald's, Old 56 Rest, Pizza Hut, Sirloin Stockade, Taco Bell, Wendy's 🛏 Best Western, Comfort Inn, Days Inn, EconoLodge, Super 8 ⬛ 🅷, $General, $Tree, Advance Parts, CountryMart Foods, Walmart
182b a	US 50, Eisenhower Rd, Ottawa
176	Homewood, W ⬛ RV camping
175mm	**🅿 both lanes, full 🛏 facilities, litter barrels, petwalk, 🍴, 🅿 RV dump, vending, wireless internet**
170	KS 273, Williamsburg, W food, gas
162	KS 31 S, Waverly
160	KS 31 N, Melvern
155	US 75, Burlington, Melvern Lake, E 🚰 BP/Subway/dsl, TA/Shell/Wendy's/dsl/scales/24hr/@ 🍴 Beto Jct Rest. 🛏 Wyatt Earp Inn ⬛ dsl repair
148	KS 131, Lebo, E 🚰 Casey's, Cenex/dsl 🍴 Lebo Diner 🛏 Universal Inn, W ⬛ to Melvern Lake
141	KS 130, Neosho Rapids, E ⬛ NWR (8mi)
138	County Rd U
135	County Rd R1, W ⬛ RV camping/phone

🧭**N**	**INTERSTATE 35 Cont'd**	

Exit #	Services
133	US 50 W, 6th Ave, Emporia, **E** 🅶 1-3 mi 🍴 Casey's 🍴 McDonald's, Pizza Hut 🏨 Budget Host
131	KS 57, KS 99, Burlingame Rd, **E** 🅶 Conoco/dsl 🍴 Hardee's, Mr Goodcents Subs 🅾 Dillon's Food, repair, tires
130	KS 99, Merchant St, **E** 🅶 Phillips 66/dsl 🍴 Subway 🅾 Emporia SU, Lyon Co Museum
128	Industrial Rd, **E** 🅶 FL 🍴 Arby's, Bruff's Steaks, Burger King, China Buffet, Gambino's Pizza, House of Ma, Spangles, Subway 🏨 EconoLodge, GuestHouse Inn, Motel 6 🅾 🅷 $General, Aldi Foods, AT&T, CarQuest, Family$, JC Penney, Walgreens, **W** 🅶 Phillips 66/Wendy's/dsl/LP 🍴 Applebee's, Braum's, Golden Corral, KFC, McDonald's, MT Mike's Steaks, Pizza Hut, Pizza Ranch, Planet Sub, Starbucks, Taco Bell, Village Inn 🏨 Candlewood Suites, Comfort Inn, Fairfield Inn, Holiday Inn Express 🅾 Medicine Shoppe, Radio Shack, Staples, Verizon, Walmart/Subway
127c	KS Tpk, I-335 N, to Topeka
127b a	US 50, KS 57, Newton, **E** 🅶 ⓕ FLYING J/Huddle House/dsl/LP/scales/24hr, Shell 🍴 Arby's, China Buffet, Papa John's 🏨 Best Inn, Best Western/rest., Days Inn, Knights Inn, Super 8 🅾 Buick/Chevrolet, Chrysler/Dodge/Jeep, dsl repair, Ford/Lincoln, Kenworth, NAPA, Nissan, PriceChopper Foods, Tires4Less, Toyota, **W** 🅾 Emporia RV Park
127mm	I-35 and I-335 KS Tpk
I-35 S and KS tpk S run together, toll plaza	
125	Cottonwood River
111	Cattle Pens
97.5mm	Matfield Green Service Area (both lanes exit left), 🅶 Phillips 66/dsl, 🍴 McDonald's
92	KS 177, Cassoday, **E** 🅶 Fuel'n Service, phone
76	US 77, El Dorado N, **E** 🅶 3 mi 🅶 Casey's 🍴 Pizza Hut, Taco Bell 🏨 Stardust Motel 🅾 $General, Ace Hardware, city park, Dillon's Foods/gas, El Dorado SP, Walgreens
71	KS 254, KS 196, El Dorado, **E** 🅶 Conoco/dsl, Phillips 66/dsl, QT 🍴 Arbys, Braum's, Burger King, China Star Buffet, DD Family Rest, Freddy's Frozen Custard, Gambino's Pizza,

71	Continued KFC, Kountry Kettle, LJ Silver, McDonald's, Papa Murphy's, Pizza Hut, Playa Azul Mexican, Sonic, Spangles, Subway, Taco Tico 🏨 Best Western, Heritage Inn, Holiday Inn Express, Sunset Inn, Super 8 🅾 🅷, $General, Buick/Cadillac, Bumper Parts, Deer Grove RV Park, KS Oil Museum, O'Reilly Parts, Radio Shack, Walmart
65mm	Towanda Service Area (both lanes exit left) 🅶 Phillips 66/dsl, 🍴 McDonald's
62mm	Whitewater River
57	21st St, Andover, **W** golf, phone
53	KS 96, Wichita, **W** 1 mi on Kellogg 🅶 Phillips 66
50	US 54, Kellogg Ave, **E** McConnell AFB, **W** on Kellogg Ave **East** 🅶 Conoco/Wendy's/dsl 🍴 Beijing Bistro, Burger King, Golden Corral, IHOP, McDonald's, Panda Express, Pizza Hut, Sonic, Subway, Taco Bell 🅾 Acura, AT&T, CarMax, Infiniti, Jaguar/Porsche, Lexus, Lowe's, Mazda, Michael's, Nissan, Suzuki, Verizon, VW, Walmart/Subway, **W** on Kellogg Ave **West** 🍴 BJ's Rest, Carlos Kelly's, Chipotle Mexican, Denny's, Green Mill Rest., LJ Silver, Logan's Roadhouse, Old Chicago Pizza, Red Lobster, Scotch&Sirloin Steaks, Super Buffet 🏨 Best Western, Comfort Inn, Days Inn, EconoLodge, Fairfield Inn, GuestHouse Inn, Hampton Inn, Hawthorn Suites, Holiday Inn, La Quinta, Marriott, Motel 6, Studio+, Super 8, Wichita Inn, Wichita Suites 🅾 BMW, Bosley Tires, Buick/GMC, Cadillac/Chevrolet, CarQuest, Chrysler/Dodge/Jeep, Dillard's, Fiat, Firestone/auto, Ford, Hancock Fabrics, Honda, JC Penney, Kia, Lincoln, Radio Shack, Ross, Sears/auto, Target, TJ Maxx, Toyota/Scion, VA 🅷, Von Maur
45	KS 15, Wichita, **E** 🅾 Spirit Aero Systems
44.5mm	Arkansas River
42	47th St, I-135, to I-235, Wichita, **W** 🅶 Phillips 66, QT 🍴 Applebee's, Braum's, Burger King, Carlos O'Kelly's, Godfather's, Heritage Rest, KFC, LJ Silver, McDonald's, Mr Goodcents, New China, Papa John's, Pizza Hut, Spangles Rest., Subway, Taco Bell, Wild Hog BBQ 🏨 AmericInn, Best Western, Days Inn, Quality Inn, Springfield Inn, ValuePlace 🅾 $General, $Tree, AutoZone, Dillon's Foods/dsl, K-Mart, O'Reilly Parts, Radio Shack

E M P O R I A   **W I C H I T A**

KS

⬆N   INTERSTATE 35 Cont'd

Exit #	Services
39	US 81, Haysville, **W** 🛏 Haysville Inn
33	KS 53, Mulvane, **E** 🅞 Mulvane Hist Museum, **W** 🍴 Kansas Star Casino/Hotel 🅞 Wyldewood Winery
26mm	**Belle Plaine Service Area (both lanes exit left),** 🍴 McDonald's, 🅖 Phillips 66/dsl
19	US 160, Wellington, **W 3 mi** 🍴 KFC, McDonald's, Penny's Diner 🛏 OakTree Inn, Sunshine Inn 🅞 KOA
17mm	**I-35N and KS TPK N run together, toll plaza**
4	US 166, to US 81, South Haven, **E** 🛏 Motel 6 🅞 repair/tires, **W** 🅞 Oasis RV Park
1.5mm	**weigh sta nb**
0mm	**Kansas/Oklahoma state line**

⬆E   INTERSTATE 70

Exit #	Services
423b	3rd St, James St
423a	5th St
422d c	Central Ave, service rd
422b a	US 69 N, US 169 S
421b	I-670
421a	**S** 🅞 railroad yard
420b a	US 69 S, 18th St Expswy, **N** 🅖 Cenex 🍴 China Town, Jack-in-the-Box, Tapatio Mexican 🅞 SunFresh Foods
419	38th St, Park Dr, access to 10 motels
418b	I-635 N (eb only)
418a	I-635 S
417	57th St
415b	to US 24 W, State Ave, Kansas City, **N on US 24** 🅖 Conoco Phillips 66/dsl 🍴 Papa John's, Perkins, Taco Bell 🛏 Gables Motel 🅞 Chrysler/Jeep, Ford, Lowe's, Toyota/Scion
415a	KS 32 E (from eb)
414mm	**parking area both lanes,** 🅒 **vehicle insp sta wb**
414	78th St, **N** 🅖 QT/dsl, 🍴 Wendy's, 🛏 Days Inn **N on US 40** 🅖 Phillips 66, 🍴 Arby's, Burger King, Capt D's, DQ, Hardee's, Lucky Chinese, McDonald's, Sonic, Subway, 🅞 🄷, $Tree, Advance Parts, BigLots, Buick/GMC, Firestone, Goodyear/auto, K-Mart, O'Reilly Parts, PriceChopper Foods, Tires+, Walgreens, **S** 🅖 BP 🛏 American Motel, Comfort Inn
411b	I-435 N, 🅞 to KCI ✈, access to Woodlands Racetrack
411a	I-435 S
410	110th St, **N** 🛏 Great Wolf Lodge 🅞 Cabela's, KS Speedway
225mm	**I-70 W and KS TPK W run together**
224	KS 7, to US 73, Bonner Springs, Leavenworth, **(last free exit wb before KS TPK)** **N** 🅖 Phillips 66/dsl, QT 🍴 KFC/Taco Bell, Mazzio's, Subway, Waffle House 🛏 Holiday Inn Express, Super 8 🅞 museum, **S** 🅖 BP 🍴 Arby's, Burger King, Evergreen Chinese, Goodcents Subs, McDonald's, Papa Murphy's, Pizza Hut, Subway, Taco John's 🅞 $Tree, AutoZone, Cottonwood RV Camp, Ford, PriceChopper Foods, Radio Shack, TrueValue, Walgreens, Walmart/Subway
217mm	**toll booth**
212	Eudora, Tonganoxie
209mm	**Lawrence Service Area (both lanes exit left), full facilities,** 🅖 Phillips 66/dsl, 🍴 McDonald's
204	US 24, US 59, to E Lawrence, **S** 🅖 Phillips 66/dsl, 🍴 Burger King, Sonic, 🛏 Motel 6, SpringHill Suites (1mi), 🅞 Harley-Davidson, Jellystone Camping, O'Reilly Parts

203mm	Kansas River
202	US 59 S, to W Lawrence, **S on US 40** 🅖 BP, Conoco/dsl, Phillips 66/dsl 🍴 Burger King, Domino's, McDonald's, Panda Garden, Sonic, Spangles, Subway, Taco Bell, Taco John's, Wendy's 🛏 Baymont Inn, Best Western, Days Inn, EconoLodge, Hampton Inn, Holiday Inn, Quality Inn, Rodeway Inn, Super 8 🅞 🄷, $General, Advance Parts, CarQuest, Dillon's Foods/gas, to Clinton Lake SP, to U of KS
197	KS 10, Lecompton, Lawrence, **N** 🅞 Perry Lake SP, **S** 🅞 Clinton Lake SP
188mm	**Topeka Service Area, full** 🅒 **facilities,** 🅖 Conoco/dsl 🍴 Dunkin Donuts Hardee's, Pizza Hut, Taco Bell
183	I-70 W (from wb), to Denver
367mm	**toll plaza**
366	I-470 W, to Wichita
I-70 E and KS TPK E run together	
365	21st St, Rice Rd, access to Shawnee Lake RA
364b	US 40 E, Carnahan Ave, to Lake Shawnee
364a	California Ave, **S 0-1 mi** 🅖 BP/dsl, Phillips 66/dsl 🍴 Arby's, Baskin-Robbins, Burger King, Domino's, DQ, McDonald's, Pizza Hut, Subway, Tacos Mexicano 🅞 $General, Ace Hardware, Advance Parts, AutoZone, Dillon's Food/gas, Family$, O'Reilly Parts, repair, TrueValue, vet, Walgreens
363	Adams St, downtown
362c	10th Ave (from wb), **N** 🛏 Ramada Inn, **S** 🅞 st capitol
362b a	to 8th Ave, **N** 🛏 Ramada, **S** 🅞 to St Capitol, downtown
361b	3rd St, Monroe St
361a	1st Ave, **S** Ryder
359	MacVicar Ave
358b a	Gage Blvd
357b a	Fairlawn Rd, 6th Ave, **S** 🅖 Conoco/dsl, Phillips 66 🛏 Best Western, Holiday Inn/rest., Motel 6 🅞 $General, NAPACare, vet, zoo-rain forest
356b a	Wanamaker Rd, **N** 🍴 Carino's, Red Robin 🛏 Hyatt Place 🅞 KS Museum of History, **S** 🅖 BP, Murphy Express/dsl, Phillips 66/dsl 🍴 Applebee's, Arby's, Boston Mkt, Buffalo Wild Wings, Chili's, Chipotle Mexican, ChuckECheese, CiCi's Pizza, Coldstone, Coyote Canyon Café, Cracker Barrel, Denny's, Famous Dave's BBQ, Freddy's Steakburgers, Golden Corral, Hooters, Huhot Chinese, IHOP, Jason's Deli, Jersey Mike's Subs, Jimmy John's, Jose Pepper's, Longhorn Steaks, McDonald's, Mr Goodcents, Mr Stirfry, Old Chicago, Olive Garden, On-the-Border, Panera Bread, Papa John's, Perkins, Pizza Hut, Qdoba, Red Lobster, Sonic, Spangles, Starbucks, Steak'n Shake, Taco Bell, Taco John's, TX Roadhouse, Wendy's 🛏 AmericInn, Baymont Inn, Candlewood Suites, Clubhouse Inn, Comfort Suites, Country Inn&Suites, Courtyard, Days Inn, Fairfield Inn, Hampton Inn, Holiday Inn Express, Homewood Suites, Motel 6, Quality Inn, Residence Inn, Sleep Inn, Super 8, ValuePlace 🅞 $Tree, AAA, Aldi Foods, AT&T, Barnes&Noble, Best Buy, Dick's, Dillard's, Ford/Lincoln, Goodyear/auto, Hobby Lobby, Home Depot, JC Penney, K-Mart, Kohl's, Lowe's, Macy's, mall, Menards, Michael's, Office Depot, Old Navy, PetCo, Radio Shack, Sam's Club/gas, Sears/auto, Suzuki, Target, Tuesday Morning, Verizon, Walmart/Subway
355	I-470 E, US 75 S, to VA MED CTR, Topeka, **S 1 mi** same as 356, air museum
353	KS 4 W, to Auburn Rd
351	frontage rd (from eb), Mission Creek
350	Valencia Rd
347	West Union Rd

INTERSTATE 70 Cont'd

Exit #	Services
346	Carlson Rd, to Rossville, Willard
343	Ranch Rd
342	Keene-Eskridge Rd, access to Lake Wabaunsee
341	KS 30, Maple Hill, S 🅿 24-7/Subway/café/dsl/RV dump
338	Vera Rd, 🅿 Valero/Baskin-Robbins/dsl
336mm	℞ₛ (exits left from both lanes), full ♿ facilities, litter barrels, petwalk, 🚻, 🚐 RV parking, wireless internet
335	Snokomo Rd, Paxico, Skyline Mill Creek Scenic Drive
333	KS 138, Paxico, N Ⓞ Mill Creek RV Park, winery
332	Spring Creek Rd
330	KS 185, to McFarland
329mm	weigh sta both lanes
328	KS 99, to Alma, S Wabaunsee Co Museum
324	Wabaunsee Rd, N Ⓞ Grandma Horners Store&Factory
322	Tallgrass Rd
318	frontage rd
316	Deep Creek Rd
313	KS 177, to Manhattan, N 8 mi 🅿 Phillips 66 🍴 Chili's, IHOP, Longhorn Steaks, McAlister's Deli, McDonald's, Olive Garden, Sonic, Taco Bell, TX Roadhouse, Wendy's 🛏 Best Western, Candlewood Suites, Comfort Inn, Fairfield Inn, Hampton Inn, Hilton Garden, Motel 6, Quality Inn, Super 8 Ⓞ Aldi Foods, JC Penney, Sears/auto, to KSU, Walmart/Subway
311	Moritz Rd
310mm	℞ₛ both lanes, full ♿ facilities, litter barrels, petwalk, 🚻, 🚐 RV dump
307	McDowell Creek Rd, scenic river rd to Manhattan
304	Humboldt Creek Rd
303	KS 18 E, to Ogden, Manhattan, N Ⓞ to KSU
301	Marshall Field, N Ⓞ Cavalry Museum, Custer's House, KS Terr Capitol, to Ft Riley
300	US 40, KS 57, Council Grove, S hist church
299	Flinthills Blvd, to Jct City, Ft Riley, N 🅿 Phillips 66/dsl 🍴 Stacy's Rest 🛏 EconoLodge, Great Western Inn, Red Carpet Inn, Super 8
298	Chestnut St, to Jct City, Ft Riley, N 🅿 Shell/dsl/24hr 🍴 Arby's, Cox Bros BBQ, Cracker Barrel, Family Buffet, Freddy's Steakburgers, La Fiesta, Mr Goodcents Subs, Pizza Hut, Taco Bell 🛏 Best Western, Candlewood Suites, Courtyard, Holiday Inn Express, Quality Inn Ⓞ $General, $Tree, Verizon, Walmart/Subway
296	US 40, Washington St, Junction City, N 🅿 Casey's, Cenex/dsl, Phillips 66, Shell/dsl 🍴 McDonald's, Peking Chinese, Senor Tequila Mexican, Sonic, Subway 🛏 Budget Host/RV park, Comfort Inn, Hampton Inn, Howard Johnson, Knights Inn, Ramada Ltd, ValuePlace Ⓞ Cadillac/Chevrolet, city park, Haas Tire, Harley-Davidson, vet
295	US 77, KS 18 W, Marysville, to Milford Lake, N 🅿 Phillips 66/Sapp Bro's/A&W/dsl/24hr 🛏 Motel 6 Ⓞ 🅷, Ford/Kia/Chrysler/Dodge/Jeep, RV Ctr, truckwash, S Ⓞ truckwash
294mm	℞ₛ both lanes, full ♿ facilities, litter barrels, petwalk, 🚻, 🚐 RV dump
290	Milford Lake Rd
286	KS 206, Chapman, S 1 mi 🅿 Casey's, Cenex/dsl Ⓞ KS Auto Racing Museum
281	KS 43, to Enterprise, N 🅿 Shell/dsl Ⓞ 4 Seasons RV Ctr/Park
277	Jeep Rd
275	KS 15, to Clay Ctr, Abilene, N 🍴 DQ 🛏 Brookville Hotel/rest., Holiday Inn Express, S 🅿 24-7/dsl, KwikShop

275	Continued
	🍴 Burger King, Green Acres Grill, M&R Grill, McDonald's, Pizza Hut, Sonic, Subway 🛏 Best Value Inn, Budget Inn, Super 8 Ⓞ 🅷, $General, Alco/gas, AutoZone, Buick/Cadillac/Chevrolet, CountryMart Foods, O'Reilly Parts, Ricco Drug, to Eisenhower Museum
272	Fair Rd, to Talmage, S Ⓞ Russell Stover Candies
266	KS 221, Solomon
265mm	℞ₛ both lanes, full ♿ facilities, litter barrels, petwalk, 🚻, 🚐 RV dump, vending
264mm	Solomon River
260	Niles Rd, New Cambria
253mm	Saline River
253	Ohio St, N Ⓞ RV park, S 🅿 ⚡FLYING J/Huddle House/dsl/LP/scales/24hr Ⓞ 🅷, Harley-Davidson, Kenworth
252	KS 143, 9th St, Salina, N 🅿 24-7/Subway/dsl/24hr, Petro/Shell/Starbucks/Wendy's/dsl/24hr/@ 🍴 IHOP, Iron Skillet, McDonald's 🛏 Best Inn, Days Inn, Holiday Inn Express, Howard Johnson, La Quinta, Motel 6, Super 8 Ⓞ Blue Beacon, dsl repair, Freightliner, KOA, S 🅿 ▭/Grandma Max/dsl/scales/24hr/@ 🛏 EconoLodge, Rodeway Inn
250b a	I-135, US 81, N to Concordia, S to Wichita
249	Halstead Rd, to Trenton
244	Hedville, N Ⓞ Sundowner West RV Park (seasonal), S Ⓞ Rolling Hills Park
238	to Brookville, Glendale, Tescott
233	290th Rd, Juniata
225	KS 156, to Ellsworth, S 🅿 D&S/pizza/dsl Ⓞ Ft Harker Museum, Ft Larned HS
224mm	℞ₛ both lanes, full ♿ facilities, litter barrels, petwalk, 🚻, 🚐 RV dump
221	KS 14 N, to Lincoln
219	KS 14 S, to Ellsworth, S 🅿 Conoco/dsl
216	to Vesper
209	to Sylvan Grove
206	KS 232, Wilson, N 🅿 Travel Shoppe/rest. Ⓞ RV Park, Wilson Lake (6mi), winery
199	Dorrance, N Ⓞ to Wilson Lake, S 🅿 Agco/dsl/food
197	KS 10, Lecompton, Lawrence, N Ⓞ Perry Lake SP, S Ⓞ Clinton Lake SP
193	Bunker Hill Rd, N 🅿 Conoco/Quiznos/dsl/24hr, to Wilson Lake WA
189	US 40 bus, Pioneer Rd, Russell
187mm	℞ₛ both lanes, litter barrels, petwalk, 🚐 RV dump
184	US 281, Russell, N 🅿 24-7/dsl, Phillips 66/Fossil Sta./dsl 🍴 A&W, McDonald's, Meridy's Rest., Pizza Hut, Sonic, Subway

⬆🅴 INTERSTATE 70 Cont'd

Exit #	Services
184	Continued
	🛏 Days Inn, Fossil Creek Hotel, Russell's Inn, Super 8 🅾 H $General, Alco, CarQuest, Fossil Creek RV Park, JJJ RV Park, st patrol
180	Balta Rd, to Russell
175	Gorham, N 1 mi 🅶 Co-Op/dsl
172	Walker Ave
168	KS 255, to Victoria, S 🅶 255 Diner/dsl, to Cathedral of the Plains
163	Toulon Ave
161	Commerce Parkway
159	US 183, Hays, N 🅶 Qwest/dsl 🍴 Applebee's, Carlos O'Kelly's, Golden Corral, IHOP, Subway, Wendy's 🛏 Best Western, Comfort Inn, Fairfield Inn, Hampton Inn, Holiday Inn Express, Sleep Inn 🅾 AT&T, Chrysler/Dodge/Jeep, Ford/Lincoln, Harley-Davidson, Home Depot, Radio Shack, Toyota, Walmart/Subway S 🅶 24-7/dsl, Conoco/dsl/24hr, ♥Loves Phillips 66/dsl, Shamrock 🍴 Arby's, Burger King, China Garden, Emperial Garden, Freddy's Steakburgers, Jimmy John's, KFC, K's Diner, LJ Silver, Lucky Buffet, McDonald's, MT Mike's Steaks, Pheasant Run Pancakes, Pizza Hut, Smoothie King, Sonic, Subway, Taco Bell, Taco Grande, Vagabond Rest., Wendy's, Whiskey Creek Grill 🛏 Baymont Inn, Best Value Inn, Days Inn, EconoLodge, Motel 6, Quality Inn, Ramada, Super 8 🅾 H $General, Ace Hardware, Advance Parts, Chevrolet, Dillon's Foods/gas, Firestone/auto, Hastings Books, JC Penney, O'Reilly Parts, st patrol, Tires 4 Less, Verizon, Walgreens
157	US 183 S byp, to Hays, S 🅾 museum, to Ft Hays St U, tourist info
153	Yocemento Ave
145	KS 247 S, Ellis, S 🅶 Casey's, ♥Loves/DQ/Subway/dsl/scales/24hr 🛏 Days Inn 🅾 Railroad Museum, RV camping, to Chrysler Museum, USPO
140	Riga Rd
135	KS 147, Ogallah, N 🅶 Frontier Selfserve/dsl, S 🅾 to Cedar Bluff SP (13mi)
132mm	🆁🆂 both lanes, full 🅰 facilities, litter barrels, petwalk, 🚐 RV dump
128	US 283 N, WaKeeney, N 🛏 Super 8
127	US 283 S, WaKeeney, N 🍴 El Dos De Oros, Jade Garden Rest., McDonald's, Pizza Hut 🛏 Best Western, KS Kountry Inn 🅾 $General, city park, S 🅶 24-7/Real Country Cafe/dsl/24hr, Conoco/Subway/dsl 🛏 EconoLodge 🅾 antiques, auto repair, KOA
120	Voda Rd
115	KS 198 N, Banner Rd, Collyer
107	KS 212, Castle Rock Rd, Quinter, N 🅶 Sinclair/dsl 🛏 Budget Host 🅾 H, repair, S 🅶 Conoco/dsl/24hr 🍴 DQ
99	KS 211, Park, N 1 mi 🅶 Sinclair/dsl
97mm	🆁🆂 both lanes, full 🅰 facilities, litter barrels, petwalk, 🚐 RV dump, vending
95	KS 23 N, to Hoxie
93	KS 23, Grainfield, N 🅶 Sinclair/dsl
85	KS 216, Grinnell
79	Campus Rd
76	US 40, to Oakley, S 🅶 TA/Shell/Buckhorn Rest./Subway/

76	Continued
	dsl/e-85/scales/24hr/@ 🛏 EconoLodge (2mi), Relax Inn, Sleep Inn 🅾 H, Blue Beacon, Fick Museum
70	US 83, to Oakley, N 🛏 Free Breakfast Inn, S 🅶 Phillips 66/dsl 🍴 Colonial Steaks 🅾 H, antiques, Fick Museum, High-Plains RV Park, Prairie Dog Town
62	rd K, Mingo, S 🅶 gas/dsl/phone
54	Country Club Dr, Colby, N 🅶 🚛/Subway/dsl/scales/24hr 🛏 Hampton Inn 🅾 H, truck/dsl repair
53	KS 25, Colby, N 🅶 24-7/Subway/dsl, Conoco 🍴 Arby's, Burger King, China Buffet, McDonald's, MT Mike's Steaks, Pizza Hut, Sonic, Subway, Taco John's 🛏 Days Inn, Holiday Inn Express, Motel 6, Quality Inn, Sleep Inn, Super 8 🅾 H $General, Dillon's Foods/dsl, dsl repair, Ford/Lincoln, Haas Tire, Prairie Museum, Quilt Cabin, Radio Shack, RV park/antiques, trucklube/wash, visitors ctr, Walmart S 🅶 Petro/Phillips 66/scales/dsl/@ 🍴 Baskin-Robbins, City Limits Grill, Quiznos, Starbucks, Village Inn 🛏 Comfort Inn, Knights Inn 🅾 Chrysler/Dodge/Jeep, truck repair/wash
48.5mm	🆁🆂 both lanes, full 🅰 facilities, litter barrels, petwalk, 🚻, 🚐 RV park/dump, vending
45	US 24 E, Levant
36	KS 184, Brewster, N 🅶 Fuel Depot/dsl
35.5mm	Mountain/Central time zone
27	KS 253, Edson
19	US 24, Goodland, N 🍴 Pizza Hut 🛏 Motel 7 🅾 $General, High Plains Museum, KOA
17	US 24, KS 27, Goodland, N 🅶 Cenex/dsl, Conoco, Phillips 66/dsl 🍴 DQ, McDonald's, Mexico #3, Reynaldo's Mexican, Subway, Taco John's, Wonderful House Chinese 🛏 Best Value Inn, Comfort Inn, Days Inn, Motel 6, Super 8 🅾 H, CarQuest/Firestone, Chevrolet, GMC, Walmart S 🅶 24-7/dsl/scales 🛏 Holiday Inn Express 🅾 Mid-America Camping
12	rd 14, Caruso
9	rd 11, Ruleton
7.5mm	Welcome Ctr eb/🆁🆂 wb, full 🅰 facilities, info, litter barrels, petwalk, 🚻, 🚐 RV dump, vending, wireless internet
1	KS 267, Kanorado, N food, gas
0.5mm	weigh sta eb
0mm	Kansas/Colorado State Line

⬆N INTERSTATE 135

Exit #	Services
95b a	I-135 begins/ends on I-70, exit 250. US 81 continues nb, I-70, E to KS City, W to Denver.
93	KS 140, State St, Salina, 🅾 art ctr, museum
92	Crawford St, E 🅶 24-7/dsl, Gas4Less/dsl, KwikShop, Shell, Sinclair 🍴 Arby's, Braum's, Cotijas Mexican, Daimaru Steaks, Great Wall Chinese, Gutierrez Mexican, Hickory Hut BBQ, Jim's Chicken, KFC, McDonald's, Russell's Rest., Spangles, Subway, Taco Bell, Western Sizzlin 🛏 AmericInn, Days Inn, Fairfield Inn, Knights Inn, Ramada Inn, Value Inn&Suites 🅾 $General, Advance Parts, Dillon's Foods, K-Mart, Midwest Tires, NAPA, O'Reilly Parts, Radio Shack, Walgreens, W 🅶 Phillips 66/dsl 🛏 Quality Inn
90	Magnolia Rd, E 🅶 Casey's, Phillips 66/dsl 🍴 AppleTree Rest., Burger King, Carlos O'Kelly's, Chili's, Coyote Canyon Café, Domino's, Freddy's Burgers, Hog Wild BBQ, Hong Kong Buffet, IHOP, Jalisco Mexican, Longhorn Steaks, McDonald's, Mr Goodcents Subs, Papa Murphy's,

Side tabs: HAYS, ELLIS, WAKEENEY, KS, COLBY, GOODLAND

INTERSTATE 135 Cont'd

Exit #	Services

SALINA

90 Continued
Poncho's Mexican, Schlotzsky's, Sonic, Spangles, Starbucks, Subway 🛏 Best Value Inn, Candlewood Suites 🔘 $General, $Tree, Aldi Foods, AutoZone, BigLots, Cadillac/Chevrolet, Dick's, Dillard's, Dillon's Foods/dsl, Hobby Lobby, Honda, JC Penney, Jo-Ann Fabrics, Kohl's, Menard's, Old Navy, O'Reilly Parts, PetCo, Sears/auto, Subaru, Toyota, Tuesday Morning, Verizon, vet, **W** 🔲 Cenex/dsl

89 Schilling Rd, **E** 🔲 KwikShop/dsl 🍴 Applebee's, Daimaru Steaks, Logan's Roadhouse, Olive Garden, Pizza Hut, Pop-eye's, Red Lobster, Tucson's Steaks, Wendy's 🛏 Country Inn&Suites, Courtyard, Hampton Inn 🔘 Lowe's, Sam's Club/gas, Target, Walmart/Subway **W** 🔲 Casey's 🛏 Best Western, Comfort Suites, Super 8

88 Water Well Rd, **E** 🛏 Sleep Inn 🔘 Ford, Nissan

86 KS 104, Mentor, Smolan

82 KS 4, Falun Rd, Assaria, **E** 🔘 RV Camping

78 KS 4 W, Lindsborg, **E** 🔘 to Sandz Gallery/Museum

72 Lindsborg, **E** **4 mi** 🔘 Maxwell WR, McPherson St Fishing Lake, **W** 🔘 🏥, camping, food, gas, lodging, museum

68mm 🆁🆂 (both lanes exit left), full ♿ facilities, litter barrels pet-walk, 📞, 🔘 RV dump

65 Pawnee Rd

MC PHERSON

60 US 56, McPherson, Marion, **W** 🔲 Midway Gas/dsl, Phillips 66/dsl 🍴 Applebee's, Arby's, Braum's, Freddy's Burgers, Golden Dragon Chinese, Hunan Chinese, KFC/LJ Silver, La Fiesta Mexican, McDonald's, MT Mike's, Perkins, Pizza Hut, Subway, Taco Bell, Taco John's, Woodie's BBQ 🛏 Best Value Inn, Best Western, Days Inn, EconoLodge, Holiday Inn Express 🔘 🏥, AutoZone, Buick/Cadillac/GMC, Chrysler/Dodge/Jeep, Ford, Walgreens, Walmart

58 US 81, KS 61, to Hutchinson, McPherson

54 Elyria

48 KS 260 E, Moundridge, **W 2 mi** 🍴 Block 2 Eatery, gas

46 KS 260 W, Moundridge, **W 2 mi** 🔘 truck repair, food, gas

40 Lincoln Blvd, Hesston, **E** 🍴 Panda Kitchen 🛏 AmericInn 🔘 Cottonwood Grove RV Camping, **W** 🔲 Casey's/dsl/24hr 🍴 El Cerrito Grill, Lincoln Perk Coffee, Pizza Hut, Sonic, Subway 🛏 Best Value Inn 🔘 city park

NEWTON

34 KS 15, N Newton, to Abilene, KS 15, **E** 🔘 RV camping, **W** 🍴 Subway (1mi), Taco Bell (1mi) 🔘 Kauffman Museum

33 US 50 E, to Peabody (from nb)

31 1st St, Broadway St, **E** 🔲 Conoco/dsl, Newell TC/dsl/@ 🍴 Applebee's, CJ's Rest., Huddle House, KFC 🛏 1st Inn, Days Inn, EconoLodge, Holiday Inn Express 🔘 Cadillac/Chevrolet, Chrysler/Dodge/Jeep, Ford/Lincoln, **W** 🔲 Braum's, MT Mike's 🛏 Best Western/rest., Comfort Inn

30 US 50 W, KS 15 (exits left from nb), to Hutchinson, Newton, **W** 🔲 KwikShop/dsl 🍴 Arby's, Papa Murphy's, Pizza Hut, Sonic, Subway 🔘 🏥, $Tree, AutoZone, Buick/GMC, Dillon's Foods, R Tires, Radio Shack, Verizon, Walmart

28 SE 36th St, **W** 🔲 Phillips 66/dsl 🍴 Burger King 🔘 Chisholm Trail Outlets/famous brands

25 KS 196, to Whitewater, El Dorado

23mm 🆁🆂s both lanes, full ♿ facilities, litter barrels, petwalk, 📞, 🔘 RV dump, vending

22 125th St

19 101st St, **W** 🔘 RV camping

17 85th St, **E** 🔘 KS Coliseum, Valley Ctr

16 77th St, **E** 🛏 Sleep Inn 🔘 Wichita Greyhound Park

14 61st St, **E** 🔲 QT/dsl 🍴 Applebee's, Chopstix, Cracker Barrel, Pizza Hut, Spangles Rest., Subway, Taco Bell, Wendy's 🛏 Comfort Inn 🔘 Chevrolet, TrueValue, vet, **W** 🔲 Phillips 66/dsl 🍴 KFC, McDonald's 🛏 Quality Inn, Super 8 🔘 Goodyear/auto

13 53rd St, **E** 🔘 Freightliner, Harley-Davidson, Mack Trucks, **W** 🔲 Phillips 66/dsl 🍴 Country Kitchen 🛏 Best Western, Days Inn

11b I-235 W, KS 96, to Hutchinson

11a KS 254, to El Dorado

10b 29th St, Hydraulic Ave

10a KS 96 E

9 21st St, **E** 🍴 Sonic 🔘 $General, Wichita St U

8 13th St, 🍴 Dad's BBQ, Mel's Carryout, Pig In Pig Out BBQ

7b 8th St, 9th St, Central Ave., **E** 🔘 School of Medicine

7a downtown

6b 1st St, 2nd St, downtown

5b US 54, US 400, Kellogg Ave, **E** 🔲 QT/dsl 🍴 Burger King, Chipotle Mexican, Jimmy John's, Subway, Taco Bueno 🛏 Wichata Suites

5a Lincoln St, **E** 🔲 DQ, **W** 🔲 QT

WICHITA

4 Harry St, **E 1 mi** 🔲 QT 🍴 Arby's, Bionic Burger, Burger King, Church's, Denny's, Jimmie's Diner, Jimmy's Egg, Little Caesars, LJ Silver, McDonald's, NuWay Drive-Thru, Poblano Mexican, Shanghai Chinese, Spangles Rest., Subway, Taco Bell, Wendy's 🔘 🏥, BigLots, CVS Drug, Firestone/auto, Goodyear/auto, **W** 🔲 BD-C/dsl

3 Pawnee Ave, **E** 🔲 QT 🔘 Family$, O'Reilly Parts, **W** 🔲 Jumpstart/dsl 🍴 Burger King, Pizza Hut, Spangles 🛏 Pawnee Inn (1mi) 🔘 $General, AutoZone

2mm Arkansas River

2 Hydraulic Ave, **E** 🔲 QT, **W** 🍴 McDonald's, Subway

1c I-235 N, **W 2 mi** 🛏 Hilton

1b a US 81 S, 47th St, **E** 🔲 QT 🛏 Days Inn, Quality Inn, Super 8, **W** 🔲 Phillips 66 🍴 Applebee's, Braum's, Burger King, Carlos O'Kelly's, Godfather's, Goodcents Subs, Heritage Rest, Hog Wild BBQ, KFC, LJ Silver, McDonald's, New China, Papa John's, Pizza Hut, Spangles Rest., Subway, Taco Bell 🛏 Best Western, Springfield Inn, ValuePlace 🔘 $Tree, Air Capital RV Park, AutoZone, Dillon's Foods/dsl, K-Mart, O'Reilly Parts, Radio Shack

0mm I-135 begins/ends on I-35, exit 42.

INTERSTATE 24

Exit #	Services
93.5mm	Kentucky/Tennessee state line
93mm	**Welcome Ctr wb, full ⓫ facilities, litter barrels, petwalk, phones, 🆚 vending**
91.5mm	Big West Fork Red River
89	KY 115, to Oak Grove, **N**🅞 to Jeff Davis Mon St HS, **S**🅟 ⛽/McDonald's/dsl/scales/24hr, Shell/dsl 🅞 truck repair
86	US 41A, to Ft Campbell, Pennyrile Pkwy, Hopkinsville, **N** 🅟 Marathon/Chester's/dsl/scales/24hr **S** 🅟 *FLYING J*/Denny's/dsl/LP/scales/24hr, BP/dsl/24hr, ⛽/Subway/Wendy's/dsl/scales/24hr 🅝 McDonald's, Waffle House 🛏 Comfort Suites, Days Inn, Holiday Inn Express, Quality Inn, Sleep Inn 🅞 🅷, truck wash
81	Pennyrile Pky N, to Hopkinsville
79mm	Little River
73	KY 117, to Gracey, Newstead
65	US 68, KY 80, to Cadiz, **S** 🅟 BP/dsl, Marathon/dsl, Shell/dsl/24hr 🅝 Cracker Barrel, KFC, McDonald's, Subway, Taco Bell, Wendy's 🛏 Broadbent Inn, Knights Inn, Super 7 Inn, Super 8 🅞 🅷, Chevrolet, golf, to NRA
56	KY 139, to Cadiz, Princeton, **S**🅟 Marathon/dsl 🅞 KOA (9mi), NRA
47mm	Lake Barkley
45	KY 293, to Princeton, Saratoga, **S**🅟 Marathon/dsl 🅞 Mineral Mound SP, RV Camping, to KY St Penitentiary
42	I-69, to W KY Pkwy, Elizabethtown
40	US 62, US 641, Kuttawa, Eddyville, **N** 🛏 Regency Inn, Relax Inn 🅞 camping, Mineral Mound SP, **S** 🅟 BP/Wendy's/dsl/24hr, Marathon, ⛽/Huck's/Quiznos/dsl/scales/24hr 🅝 Huddle House, SW Grill 🛏 Days Inn, Hampton Inn 🅞 camping, KY Lake Rec Areas, to Lake Barkley
36mm	**weigh sta both lanes, phones**
34mm	Cumberland River
31	KY 453, to Grand Rivers, Smithland, **N** 🅟 BP/dsl 🛏 Patti's Inn, **S** 🅟 Exxon/dsl 🅝 Miss Scarlett's 🛏 Best Value Inn, Grand Rivers Resort (3mi), Lighthouse Landing Resort 🅞 Exit 31 RV Park, NRA
29mm	Tennessee River
27	US 62, to KY Dam, Calvert City, **N** 🅟 BP/dsl 🅝 Cracker Barrel, DQ, KFC, Mama D's Italian, McDonald's, Waffle House, Willow Pond Rest. 🛏 Days Inn, KY Dam Motel, Super 8 🅞 Cypress Lakes Camp, Freightliner, KOA, vet, **S**🅟❤️*Love's*/Arby's/dsl/scales/24hr 🅝 Subway 🅞 truck repair
25b a	to Calvert City, Carroll/Purchase Pkwy, **S** KY Lake RA
16	US 68, to Paducah, **S** 🅟 BP/Southern Pride/Subway/dsl/scales/24hr 🅞 antiques, flea mkt
11	rd 1954, Husband Rd, to Paducah, **N**🅟 Parkway/dsl 🛏 Best Western 🅞 Duck Creek RV Park, **S** 🅞 Harley-Davidson
7	US 45, US 62, to Paducah, **N** 🅟 BP/dsl 🅝 Burger King, Taco Bell 🅞 🅷, **S Welcome Ctr both lanes, full ⓫ facilities, gas:, litter barrels, petwalk, phones, 🆚 vending** 🅟 BP, Marathon/dsl 🅝 Arby's, Backyard Burger, Chong's Chinese, Hardee's, KFC, Los Amigo's Mexican, McDonald's, Parker's Drive-In, Pizza Hut, Popeye's, Quiznos, Sonic, Waffle House 🛏 Denton Motel 🅞 K-Mart, O'Reilly Parts, Plaza Tires, SuperValu Foods/gas, Verizon,
4	US 60, to Paducah, **N** 🅟 BP 🅝 Applebee's, Bob Evans, Burger King, McDonald's, O'Charley's, Outback Steaks, Rafferty's 🛏 Candlewood Suites, Courtyard, Days Inn, Drury Inn, Fairfield Inn, Hampton Inn, Holiday Inn Express, Residence Inn, Westowne Inn 🅞 Hancock Fabrics, Toyota/Scion, **S** 🅟 BP, Murphy USA/dsl, Superway 🅝 Arby's, Backwoods BBQ,

4	**Continued** Backyard Burger, Buffalo Wild Wings, Capt D's, Chick-fil-A, Chong's Chinese, ChuckeCheese, Cracker Barrel, Domino's, El Chico's, Fazoli's, Hardee's, IHOP, Logan's Roadhouse, Los Amigos, McAlister's Deli, Olive Garden, Panera Bread, Pasta House, Penn Sta. Subs, Pizza Hut, Red Lobster, Ryan's, Sonic, Steak'n Shake, Taco Bell, TGIFriday's, Tokyo Hibachi, TX Roadhouse, Wendy's 🛏 Comfort Suites, Country Inn&Suites, Drury Suites, Motel 6, Paducah Inn, PearTree Inn, Thrifty Inn 🅞 AAA, Advance Parts, Aldi Foods, AT&T, Best Buy, Books-A-Million, Dick's, Dillard's, Gander Mtn, Goodyear, Hobby Lobby, Home Depot, JC Penney, Kohl's, Lowe's, mall, Michael's, Office Depot, Old Navy, Petsmart, Sam's Club/gas, Sears/auto, TJ Maxx, Tuesday Morning, Verizon, Walmart
3	KY 305, to Paducah, **N**🅟 Shell/dsl 🛏 Best Value Inn, Comfort Inn/rest., EconoLodge, **S**🅟 Cheers/Huddle House/pizza/subs/dsl/e85, ⛽/Subway/dsl/scales/24hr 🅝 Waffle Hut, Yu's Kitchen 🛏 Baymont Inn 🅞 Fern Lake Camping
0mm	Kentucky/Illinois state line, Ohio River

INTERSTATE 64

Exit #	Services
192mm	Kentucky/West Virginia state line, Big Sandy River
191	US 23, to Ashland, **N 1-2 mi**🅟 Exxon, Marathon/Subway/dsl, Speedway/dsl 🅝 Arby's, Little Caesars, McDonald's, Waffle House, Wendy's 🛏 Ramada Ltd 🅞 🅷, IGA Foods, Rite Aid, USPO
185	KY 180, Cannonsburg, **N 0-3 mi**🅟 Exxon/dsl, Marathon/dsl, Shell/McDonald's/USPO, Superquik 🅝 Arby's, Bob Evans, Burger King, DQ, Gatti's Pizza, Hermanos Nunez Mexican, KFC, Subway, Taco Bell, Waffle House, Wendy's 🛏 Days Inn, Fairfield Inn, Hampton Inn, Holiday Inn Express 🅞 $Tree, st police, Walmart/Subway, **S**🅟 *FLYING J*/Denny's/dsl/LP/scales/24hr 🅞 Hidden Valley Camping
181	181 US 60, to Princess, **N**🅟 BP/dsl, **S**🅟 Marathon/dsl
179	rd 67, industrial parkway, **N**🅞 KOA@
174mm	🆁🆂 eb, full ⓫ facilities, litter barrels, petwalk, 🅒, 🆚, vending
173mm	🆁🆂 wb, full ⓫ facilities, litter barrels, petwalk, 🅒, 🆚, vending
172	rd 1, rd 7, Grayson, **N**🅟 Marathon/dsl, Superquik/dsl/24hr🅝 A&W/LJ Silver, Huddle House, KFC, Pizza Hut, Subway 🛏 Days Inn, Guesthouse Inn, Quality Inn 🅞 $General, $Tree, Chrysler/Dodge/Jeep, Ford, K-Mart, Save-A-Lot Foods, URGENT CARE, **S** 🅟 BP, Exxon, Exxon/Hardees, ❤️*Love's*/Wendy's/scales/dsl/24hr, Marathon, Shell/dsl, Speedway/dsl 🅝 Arby's, Biscuit World, China House, DQ, Little Caesar's, McDonald's, Papa John's, Taco Bell, Toro Loco 🛏 Super 8 🅞 $General, Advance Parts, AT&T, AutoZone, Family$, Food Fair, Rite Aid, Verizon
161	US 60, to Olive Hill, **N** 🅟 BP 🛏 Spanish Manor Motel 🅞 camping, to Carter Caves SP
156	rd 2, to KY 59, to Olive Hill, **S**🅟 BP
148mm	weigh sta wb
141mm	🆁🆂 both lanes, full ⓫ facilities, litter barrels, petwalk, 🅒, 🆚 vending
137	KY 32, to Morehead, **N** 🅟 BP/dsl, Speedway/dsl 🅝 CiCi's Pizza, DQ, Huddle House, Reno's Roadhouse 🅞 AT&T, Big Lots, Kroger/dsl, Lowe's, Walmart/Subway, **S** 🅟 BP/McDonald's/dsl/24hr, Marathon/dsl 🅝 China Star, Cracker Barrel, Domino's, Don Señor, Hardee's, Lee's Chicken, Ponderosa 🛏 Days Inn, Hampton Inn, Holiday Inn Express, Red Roof Inn, Super 8 🅞 🅷, $General, Ace Hardware, auto repair, AutoZone, Radio Shack, st police

P A D U C A H (vertical, left margin)

G R A Y S O N (vertical, center margin)

◻ = gas ◻ = food ◻ = lodging ◻ = other ◻ = rest stop

⬆️E INTERSTATE 64 Cont'd

Exit #	Services
137	KY 32, to Morehead, **N** ⬜ BP/dsl, Speedway/dsl ⬜ CiCi's Pizza, DQ, Huddle House, Reno's Roadhouse ⬜ AT&T, Big Lots, Kroger/dsl, Lowe's, Walmart/Subway, **S** ⬜ BP/McDonald's/dsl/24hr, Marathon/dsl ⬜ China Star, Cracker Barrel, Domino's, Don Señor, Hardee's, Lee's Chicken, Ponderosa ⬜ Days Inn, Hampton Inn, Holiday Inn Express, Red Roof Inn, Super 8 ⬜ H, $General, Ace Hardware, auto repair, AutoZone, Radio Shack, st police
133	rd 801, to Sharkey, Farmers, **N** ⬜ Shell/dsl, **S** ⬜ BP/Subway/dsl ⬜ Comfort Inn ⬜ Outpost RV Park (4mi)
123	US 60, to Salt Lick, Owingsville
121	KY 36, to Owingsville, **N** ⬜ BP/dsl, Exxon/dsl, Valero/dsl ⬜ DQ, McDonald's, Subway ⬜ $General, Family$, **S** ⬜ Save-a-Lot Foods
113	US 60, to Mt Sterling, **N** ⬜ Shell/dsl, **S** ⬜ ⬜ 🏨/McDonald's/Subway/dsl/scales/24hr
110	US 460, KY 11, Mt Sterling, **N** ⬜ Shell/Krystal/Subway/dsl, Valero/dsl ⬜ Cattleman's Roadhouse, Cracker Barrel ⬜ Fairfield Inn, Ramada Ltd, **S** ⬜ Marathon/dsl, Speedway/dsl ⬜ Applebee's, Arby's, Asian Buffet, Burger King, El Camino Real, Jerry's Rest., KFC, Lee's Chicken, LJ Silver, McDonald's, Waffle House, Wendy's ⬜ Budget Inn, Days Inn ⬜ H AutoZone, Family$, O'Reilly Parts, Verizon, **S on KY 686** ⬜ Marathon, Murphy Express/dsl ⬜ Don Señor, Hardee's, Little Caesar's, Los Rodeos, Pizza Hut, Subway, Taco Bell ⬜ $Tree, Advance Parts, AT&T, Chevrolet, Chrysler/Dodge/Jeep, CVS Drug, Ford, JC Penney, Kroger, Lowe's, Walmart/Subway
101	US 60
98.5mm	⬜ eb, full ♿ facilities, litter barrels, petwalk, 🅒, 🚮, vending
98	KY 402 (from eb), **S** Natural Bridge Resort SP
96b a	KY 627, to Winchester, Paris, **N** ⬜ BP/dsl, Marathon/96 Truck Plaza/dsl/rest./scales, **S** ⬜ Hampton Inn, Quality Inn, Red Roof Inn ⬜ Buick/Chevrolet/GMC
94	KY 1958, Van Meter Rd, Winchester, **N** ⬜ Road Ranger/dsl/24hr, Shell/scales/dsl ⬜ Holiday Inn Express, Value Stay Inn, **S** ⬜ BP/dsl, Marathon/dsl, Murphy Express/dsl, She'll/dsl, Speedway/dsl ⬜ Applebee's, Arby's, Big Boy, Burger King, Capt D's, Domino's, Don Senor, DQ, El Camino Real, Fazoli's, Golden Corral, Great Wall Chinese, Hardee's, Jade Garden Chinese, KFC, Little Caesar's, McDonald's, Papa John's, Pizza Hut, Puerta Grande, Rally's, Sakura Express, Sir Pizza, Sonic, Starbucks, Subway, Taco Bell,

94	Continued Taste Of China, Waffle House, Wendy's ⬜ H, $Tree, Advance Parts, AT&T, auto repair, AutoZone, Chrysler/Dodge/Jeep, Kroger/dsl, Lowe's, Office Depot, O'Reilly Parts, Radio Shack, Rite Aid, Tire Discounters, to Ft Boonesborough Camping, Verizon, Walgreens, Walmart/Subway
87	KY 859, Blue Grass Sta
81	I-75 S, to Knoxville
	I-64 and I-75 run together 7 mi. See KY I-75, exits 113-115.
75	I-75 N, to Cincinnati, access to KY Horse Park
69	US 62 E, to Georgetown, **N** ⬜ antiques (6mi), to Georgetown Coll., **S** ⬜ Equus Run Vineyards (2mi)
65	US 421, Midway, **S** ⬜ Shell/dsl ⬜ McDonald's
60mm	⬜ both lanes, full ♿ facilities, litter barrels, petwalk, vending
58	US 60, Frankfort, **N** ⬜ BP/dsl, Shell/dsl, Speedway/dsl ⬜ Arby's, Buffalo Wild Wings, Capt. D's, Cattleman's Roadhouse, DQ, KFC, McDonald's, Miguel's Mexican, Starbucks, Subway, Taco Bell, Waffle House, Wendy's, White Castle, Zaxby's ⬜ Best Western, Bluegrass Inn, Fairfield Inn ⬜ $General, $Tree, Buick/Chevrolet/GMC, Chrysler/Dodge/Jeep, Dick's, ElkHorn Camping (5mi), Ford/Lincoln, GNC, Honda, Kohl's, Kroger/gas, KYSU, Michael's, Nissan, TireDiscounters, TJMaxx, to KY St Capitol, to Viet Vets Mem, Toyota/Scion, Walgreens, **S** ⬜ Cracker Barrel, Logan's Roadhouse
55mm	Kentucky River
53b a	US 127, Frankfort, **N** ⬜ Marathon, Speedway/dsl, Speedway/dsl ⬜ Applebee's, Arby's, Baskin-Robbins, Beef O'Brady's, Big Boy, Burger King, Capt D's, Carino's Italian, Chili's, China Buffet, CookOut, DQ, Fazoli's, Ginza Japanese, Hardee's, KFC, Longhorn Steaks, McDonald's, My Guadalajara, O'Charley's, Panera Bread, Penn Sta Subs, Qdoba Mexican, Sonic, Starbucks, Staxx BBQ, Steak'n Shake, Subway, Taco Bell, Tacos n More, Wendy's ⬜ Best Value Inn, Days Inn, Hampton Inn, Holiday Inn Express ⬜ H, $General, Advance Parts, Ancient Age Tour, AT&T, AutoZone, BigLots, Big-O Tire, Family$, GNC, Goodyear/auto, JC Penney, K-Mart, Kroger/gas, Lowe's, Midas, Office Depot, Petco, Radio Shack, Rite Aid, st police, Staples, to KY St Capitol, URGENT CARE, USPO, Verizon, Walgreens, Walmart/Subway, **S** ⬜ BP/dsl
48	KY 151, to US 127 S, **S** ⬜ BP/dsl, Valero/dsl
43	KY 395, Waddy, **N** ⬜ FLYING J/Denny's/dsl/LP/scales/24hr, **S** ⬜ Loves/McDonald's/Subway/dsl/scales/24hr
38.5mm	**weigh sta eb**

MT STERLING WINCHESTER

FRANKFORT

KY

⛽ = gas 🍴 = food 🏠 = lodging 🅾 = other ℞ = rest stop   Copyright 2015 - the Next EXIT ®

⬆E INTERSTATE 64 Cont'd

Exit #	Services
35	KY 53, Shelbyville, N ⛽ Marathon/dsl, Shell/Circle K/dsl, Speedway/dsl 🍴 Cracker Barrel, KFC, Little Caesar's, McDonald's (1mi), Subway, Taco Bell, Waffle House 🅾 $General, Advance Parts, Family$, Ford, Kroger/deli/dsl, Lake Shelby Camping (3mi), vet, S ⛽ Huck's/White Castle/dsl, Valero/Subway/dsl 🏠 Holiday Inn Express 🅾 golf
32b a	KY 55, Shelbyville, N 1-2 mi ⛽ Murphy USA/dsl, Valero/dsl 🍴 Arby's, Asian Buffet, Firefresh BBQ, Hardee's, McDonald's, Pizza Hut, Salgado's FreshMex, Subway, Waffle House, Wendy's, Zaxby's 🏠 Best Western, Country Hearth Inn, Red Roof Inn 🅾 H, $Tree, AutoZone, Big O Tire, Buick/Chevrolet/GMC, Chrysler/Dodge/Jeep, CVS Drug, Lowe's, Rolling Hills Camping (16mi), Verizon, Walgreens, Walmart, S 🍴 Cattleman's Roadhouse 🏠 Ramada 🅾 Taylorsville Lake SP
28mm	℞ eb, full 🏠 facilities, info, litter barrels, petwalk, 🚻, 🅿, vending
28	KY 1848, Veechdale Rd, Simpsonville, N ⛽ 🅿/Wendy's/dsl/scales/24hr 🍴 DQ, Subway 🅾 golf, S 🍴 Bob Evans, Culver's 🅾 Blue Grass Outlets/famous brands
19b a	I-265, Gene Snyder Fwy, N to Tom Sawyer SP
17	S Blankenbaker, N ⛽ Shell/Circle K/dsl 🍴 Mellow Mushroom Pizza, Zaxby's 🏠 Staybridge Suites 🅾 Harley-Davidson, S ⛽ Marathon, Speedway/Subway/dsl, Thornton's/dsl 🍴 Arby's, BackYard Burger, Burger King, Cracker Barrel, El Caporal Mexican, HomeTown Buffet, KFC, Kingfish Rest., LJ Silver/Taco Bell, Logan's Roadhouse, McDonald's, Penn Sta Subs, Qdoba, Ruby Tuesday, Starbucks, Waffle House, Wendy's 🏠 Comfort Suites, Country Inn&Suites, Extended Stay America, Fairfield Inn, Hampton Inn, Hawthorn Suites, Hilton Garden, Holiday Inn Express, La Quinta, Microtel, Quality Inn, Sleep Inn, ValuePlace, Wingate Inn 🅾 Lexus, Sam's Club/gas
15	Hurstbourne Pkwy, Louisville, N 0-2 mi ⛽ Shell/Circle K/dsl, Speedway, Thorton's/dsl 🍴 Arby's, Bob Evans, Bonefish Grill, Carrabba's, Chili's, Fazoli's, Firehouse Subs, IHOP, Jimmy John's, Macaroni Grill, McDonald's, Mimi's Cafe, Momma's BBQ, Noodles&Co, Olive Garden, Panda Express, Panera Bread, Papa John's, PF Changs, Pita Pit, Qdoba, Sichuan Garden, Skyline Chili, Smashburger, Starbucks, Subway, Waffle House 🏠 Baymont Inn, Courtyard, Days Inn, Drury Inn, Holiday Inn, Hyatt Place, Red Roof Inn, Residence Inn 🅾 Barnes&Noble, Kroger/gas, Lowe's, Towery's Auto, Tuesday Morning, Walgreens, S 🍴 Applebee's, BoomBozz Pizza, Buca Italian, Buffalo Wild Wing, Burger King, Cattleman's Roadhouse, Chick-fil-A, ChuckeCheese, Coldstone, DQ, El Marlin Seafood, El Torazo Mexican, Famous Daves, Happy China, Home Run Burgers, J Gumbo's Cajun, Jason's Deli, Jumbo Buffet, Kansai Japanese, Longhorn Steaks, McAlister's Deli, McDonald's, Melting Pot, Moe's SW Grill, O'Charley's, Old Chicago, Panera Bread, Penn Sta. Subs, Pizza Hut, Qdoba, Shogun Japanese, Smokey Bones BBQ, Starbucks, Steak'n Shake, Taco Bell, Tumbleweed SW Grill, Wendy's, White Castle, Yen Ching 🏠 Best Western, Extended Stay America, Marriott, Ramada, Red Carpet Inn 🅾 $Tree, Autozone, BMW, Buick/GMC, Cadillac, Carmax, Chevrolet, Discount Tire, GNC, Hancock Fabrics, Home Depot, Honda, Infiniti, Kroger/gas, Michael's, Office Depot, Radio Shack, Staples, Subaru, Target, Verizon, Volvo, VW, Walgreens, Walmart
12b	I-264 E, Watterson Expsway, N 1 exit on US 60 ⛽ Thornton's/dsl 🍴 Arby's, Big Boy, Bravo Cucina Italin, Buffalo Wild Wings, CA Pizza, Cheesecake Factory, Chick-Fil-A,

12b	Continued
	Chuy's Mexican, Jason's Deli, Logan's Roadhouse, McDonald's, Outback Steaks, Panera Bread, Red Robin, Speedway/dsl, Taco Bell, Wendy's 🅾 Acura, Best Buy, Dick's, Dillard's, Ford/Lincoln, Goodyear/auto, Hyundai, JC Penney, Jo-Ann, Kia, Kohl's, Macy's, mall, Old Navy, Sears/auto, Staples, SteinMart, Toyota/Scion, Von Maur, Whole Foods Mkt
12a	I-264 W, access to H
10	Cannons Lane
8	Grinstead Dr, Louisville, S 🍴 ⛽, Jim Porter's Rest., KT Cafe
7	US 42, US 62, Mellwood Ave, Story Ave
6	I-71 N (from eb), to Cincinnati
5b	3rd St, Louisville, N 🍴 Joe's CrabShack, S 🏠 Galt House Hotel, Marriott 🅾 H
5a	I-65, S to Nashville, N to Indianapolis
4	9th St, Roy Wilkins Ave, S 🅾 KY Art Ctr, science museum, downtown
3	US 150 E, to 22nd St, S ⛽ Marathon/dsl, Shell/Circle K 🍴 DQ, McDonald's 🅾 Family$
1	I-264 E, to Shively, S 🅾 🅿, zoo
0mm	Kentucky/Indiana state line, Ohio River

⬆N INTERSTATE 65

Exit #	Services
138mm	Kentucky/Indiana state line, Ohio River
137	I-64 W, I-71 N, I-64 E, W 🅾 to Galt House, downtown
136c	Jefferson St, Louisville, E 🅾 H, Walgreens, W ⛽ Shell 🍴 McDonald's, Papa John's, Subway, White Castle 🏠 Courtyard, EconoLodge, Fairfield Inn, Hampton Inn, Hyatt, Marriott, SpringHill Suites 🅾 Tires+
136b	Broadway St, Chestnut St (from nb), E 🅾 H, NAPA, Walgreens, W ⛽ Shell, Thornton's 🍴 McDonald's, Rally's, Subway, White Castle 🏠 Courtyard, Fairfield Inn, Hampton Inn, Hyatt, Marriott, Springhill Suites 🅾 same as 136c, Tires+
135	W St Catherine, E ⛽ Shell
134b a	KY 61, Jackson St, Woodbine St, W ⛽ Shell/Circle K 🏠 Days Inn, Quality Inn 🅾 Harley-Davidson
133b	US 60A, Eastern Pkwy, Taylor Blvd, E 🍴 Denny's, Pizza Mia, Snappy Tomato Pizza, Subway, W ⛽ Marathon 🍴 Cracker Barrel, McDonald's, Papa John's 🏠 Country Hearth Inn 🅾 Churchill Downs, museum, U of Louisville
133b	Crittenden Dr (132from sb), E 🍴 Denny's, same as 133, W ⛽ BP 🍴 Arby's, Burger King, Cracker Barrel, Hall of Fame Cafe 🏠 Country Inn&Suites, Hilton Garden, Holiday Inn, Ramada Inn, Super 8
131b a	I-264, Watterson Expsway, W 🅾 🅿, Cardinal Stadium, Expo Center
130	KY 61, Preston Hwy, E on Ky 61 ⛽ Shell/Circle K, Speedway/dsl, Thornton's 🍴 Bob Evans, Burger King, Domino's, Fazoli's, KFC, Little Caesars, McDonald's, Papa John's, Popeyes, Rally's, Royal Garden Buffet, Subway, Taco Bell, Waffle House, Wendy's 🏠 EconoLodge, Red Roof Inn, Super 8 🅾 $General, Aamco, AutoZone, Big O Tire, BigLots, Chevrolet/Kia, Dodge, Ford, O'Reilly Parts, PepBoys, Radio Shack, Sav-A-Lot Foods, Staples, Tires+, U-Haul
128	KY 1631, Fern Valley Rd, E ⛽ BP, Marathon/Circle K, Thornton's/dsl 🍴 Arby's, Big Boy, El Nopal Mexican, Hardee's, Indi's Rest., McDonald's, Outback Steaks, Shoney's, Subway, Taco Bell, Waffle House, Wendy's, White Castle 🏠 Comfort Suites, Days Inn, Fern Valley Hotel, Holiday Inn, InTown Suites, Jameson Inn 🅾 Sam's Club/gas, Walgreens, W 🅾 UPS Depot

⬆N INTERSTATE 65 Cont'd

Exit #	Services
127	KY 1065, outer loop, E 🍽 TX Roadhouse, W Ⓞ McDonald's/RV Parking, to Motor Speedway
125 b a	I-265 E, KY 841, Gene Snyder Fwy
121	KY 1526, Brooks Rd, E 🅟 BP, Marathon 🍽 Arby's, Burger King, Cracker Barrel, McDonald's, Tumbleweed Grill 🛏 Comfort Inn, Fairfield Inn, Holiday Inn Express Ⓞ 🅷 Tinker's RV Ctr, W 🅟 BP/dsl, ▱/Subway/Taco Bell/dsl/scales/24hr 🍽 Waffle House 🛏 Baymont Inn, EconoLodge, Hampton Inn, Quality Inn
117	KY 44, Shepherdsville, E 🅟 Gulf 🍽 Bearno's Pizza, Denny's 🛏 Best Western/rest., Days Inn Ⓞ KOA (2mi), W 🅟 Marathon, Speedway/dsl 🍽 Arby's, Big Boy, Cattlelands Roadhouse, China Buffet, DQ, El Nopal, Fazoli's, KFC, Little Caesars, LJ Silver, McDonald's/playplace, Mr Gatti's, Quiznos, Sonic, Subway, Taco Bell, Triple Crown Steaks, Waffle House, Wendy's, White Castle 🛏 Country Inn&Suites, Motel 6, Sleep Inn, Super 8 Ⓞ $General, Advance Parts, auto repair, AutoZone, BigLots, Family$, Kroger/gas, Lowe's, Radio Shack, Rite Aid, Sav-a-Lot, Walgreens
116.5mm	Salt River
116	KY 480, to KY 61, E 🅟 ❤Loves/Chester's/Subway/dsl/scales/24hr, Shell/dsl Ⓞ House of Quilts, W 🅟 Marathon/dsl Ⓞ Grandma's RV Park/flea mkt
114mm	🆁🆂 sb, full 🅰 facilities, litter barrels, petwalk, 🅲, 🔶 vending
112	KY 245, Clermont, E 🅟 Shell/dsl Ⓞ Bernheim Forest, Jim Beam Outpost, to My Old Kentucky Home SP
105	KY 61, Lebanon Jct, W 🅟 105 QuikStop/dsl, ▱/McDonald's/Subway/dsl/scales/24hr/@ 🍽 Vegas Lou's BBQ
102	KY 313, to KY 434, Radcliff, W to Patton Museum
94	US 62, Elizabethtown, E 🅟 BP/dsl, Marathon/dsl 🍽 Denny's, Waffle House, White Castle 🛏 Comfort Inn, Days Inn, Super 8, W 🅟 BP/dsl, Speedway/dsl 🍽 Arby's, Burger King, Chalupa's Mexican, Cracker Barrel, Gatti's Pizza, HoneyBaked Ham, KFC/Taco Bell, McDonald's, Papa John's, Ruby Tuesday, Ryan's, Shoney's, Snappy Tomato Pizza, Stone Hearth, Subway, TX Outlaw Steaks, TX Roadhouse, Wendy's 🛏 Baymont Inn, Best Western, Comfort Suites, Fairfield Inn, Hampton Inn, Holiday Inn Express, Howard Johnson, La Quinta, Motel 6, Ramada Inn Ⓞ 🅷, $General, $Tree, Advance Parts, AutoZone, Crossroads Camping, Kroger/gas, Skagg's RV Ctr, st police, USPO, visitors ctr, Walgreens
93	to Bardstown, to BG Pkwy, E Ⓞ Maker's Mark Distillery, to My Old KY Home SP
91	US 31 W, KY 61, WK Pkwy, Elizabethtown, E 🅟 Marathon/dsl 🍽 LJ Silver, Subway 🛏 Bluegrass Inn, Budget Motel, Commonwealth Lodge Ⓞ $General, to Lincoln B'Place, W 🅟 Doug's/dsl, Marathon 🍽 Jerry's Rest. 🛏 KY Cardinal Inn, Roadside Inn Ⓞ 🅷,
90mm	weigh sta sb only
86	KY 222, Glendale, E 🅟 ▱/McDonalds/dsl/scales/24hr Ⓞ Glendale Camping, trk repair, W 🅟 Petro/Dunkin Donuts/dsl/scales/24hr/@ 🛏 Glendale Economy Inn Ⓞ Blue Beacon
83mm	Nolin River
81	KY 84, Sonora, E 🅟 Marathon/dsl, ▱/Subway/scales/24hr Ⓞ Blue Beacon, to Lincoln B'Place, W 🅟 BP/dsl
76	KY 224, Upton, E 🅟 Marathon/dsl, W Ⓞ to Nolin Lake

(left margin vertical text:) **ELIZABETHTOWN**

Exit #	Services
75mm	eastern/central time zone
71	KY 728, Bonnieville
65	US 31 W, Munfordville, E 🅟 BP/Subway/dsl, FiveStar/dsl 🍽 DQ, El Mazatlan, King Buffet, McDonald's, Pizza Hut, Sonic 🛏 Super 11 Ⓞ $General, Advance Parts, Family$, Fred's Store, IGA Foods, Pamida, Save-A-Lot, W 🅟 Marathon/dsl, Shell 🍽 Country Kitchen, to Nolin Lake
61mm	🆁🆂 both lanes, full 🅰 facilities, Green River, info, litter barrels, petwalk, 🅲, 🔶 vending
58	KY 218, Horse Cave, E 🅟 ❤Loves/McDonald's/dsl/scales/24hr/@ Ⓞ 🅷, W 🅟 Gulf/dsl, Marathon/dsl/repair 🛏 Country Hearth Inn, Hampton Inn Ⓞ KOA, to Mammoth Cave NP
53	KY 70, KY 90, Cave City, E 🅟 BP/dsl, Gulf/dsl/repair, JR's, Marathon/dsl, Shell 🍽 A&W/LJ Silver, Cracker Barrel, El Mazatlan, El Patron, KFC, McDonald's, Pizza Hut, Subway, Wendy's 🛏 Best Value Inn, Best Western, Comfort Inn, Days Inn/rest., EconoLodge, Sleep Inn, Super 8 Ⓞ 🅷, $General, Barren River Lake SP (24mi), W 🍽 Watermill Rest. Ⓞ Jellystone Camping, Mammoth Cave NP, Onyx Cave
48	KY 255, Park City, E 🅟 Shell/dsl Ⓞ $General, Park Mammoth Resort, W Ⓞ Diamond Caverns Resort, to Mammoth Cave NP
43	Nun/Cumberland Pkwy, to Barren River Lake SP
38	KY 101, Smiths Grove, W 🅟 Exxon/dsl/scales, Marathon/Subway/dsl, Shell 🍽 Bestway Pizza, McDonald's, Wendy's 🛏 Bryce Motel Ⓞ $General, auto repair, city park, IGA Foods, Larry's Parts
36	US 68, KY 80, Oakland, (no nb return)
28	rd 446, to US 31 W, Bowling Green, W 🅟 Shell/dsl 🍽 Hardee's, Jerry's Rest., Wendy's 🛏 Continental Inn, Country Hearth Inn, Super 8, Value Lodge Ⓞ 🅷, Corvette Museum/cafe, to WKYU
26	KY 234, Bowling Green, W 🅟 Shell/dsl 🍽 Subway Ⓞ 🅷, IGA Foods
22	US 231, Bowling Green, E 🅟 Exxon/dsl Keystop Gas, Shell 🍽 Catfish House, Cracker Barrel, Culver's, Denny's, Domino's, Godfather's, Hardee's, Mancino's Pizza, Motor City Grill, Ryan's, Sonic, Waffle House, Zaxby's 🛏 Best Value Inn, Best Western, Comfort Inn, Days Inn, EconoLodge, Fairfield Inn, HomeTowne Suites, La Quinta, Microtel, Quality Inn, Ramada Inn, Sleep Inn Ⓞ $General, Camping World/Gander Mtn, Harley-Davidson, URGENT CARE, USPO, W 🅟 Gulf/dsl, RaceWay, Shell/dsl, Speedway/dsl 🍽 Applebee's, Arby's, Beijing Chinese, Bob Evans, Bruster's, Buffalo Wild Wings, Burger King, Capt D's, Chick-fil-A, China Buffet, ChuckeCheese, Double-Dog's Chowhouse, Fazoli's, Great Harvest Bread, Guadalajara Grill, KFC, Krystal,

(right margin vertical text:) **BOWLING GREEN**

⬆N INTERSTATE 65 Cont'd

Exit #	Services
22	Continued
	Kyoto Steaks, Linzie's Sandwiches, Logan's Roadhouse, Longhorn Steaks, McDonald's, Moe's SW Grill, MT Grille, O'Charley's, Olive Garden, Outback Steaks, Panera Bread, Pizza Hut, Rafferty's, Red Lobster, Ruby Tuesday, Shogun Japanese, Smokey Bones BBQ, Sonic, Starbucks, Steak'n Shake, Subway, Taco Bell, TGIFriday's, Toots Rest., Waffle House, Wendy's, White Castle, Zaxby's ⌂ Baymont Inn, Candlewood Suites, Country Inn&Suites, Courtyard, Drury Inn, Hampton Inn, Hilton Garden, Holiday Inn, Motel 6, News Inn, Red Roof Inn ⊙ Ⓗ, $General, Advance Parts, AT&T, Barnes&Noble, Best Buy, BMW/Mercedes, Buick/GMC, Chevrolet, Chrysler/Jeep, Curves, CVS Drug, Dillard's, Fisher Parts, Ford/Lincoln, Goodyear/auto, Hancock Fabrics, Hobby Lobby, Home Depot, Honda, JC Penney, Kia, K-Mart, KOA, Kohl's, Kroger/gas, Lowe's, mall, Nissan, Office Depot, Old Navy, PetCo, Sam's Club/gas, Sears, Staples, Target, TJ Maxx, Toyota, U-Haul, URGENT CARE, Walgreens, Walmart/McDonald's
20	**WH Natcher Toll Rd**, to Bowling Green, access to W KY U, ⊙ st police
6	KY 100, Franklin, E ⓖ BP/dsl, Shell/dsl/24hr ⊙ truckwash, W ⓖ 🚚/Subway/dsl/scales/24hr, 🚚/Wendy's/dsl/scales/24hr ⌂ Comfort Inn, Days Inn, Knights Inn ⊙ Ⓗ, Bluegrass RV Park, Petrolube, SpeedCo, truck&tires/repair, truckwash
4mm	weigh sta nb
2	US 31 W, to Franklin, E ⓖ ⊕FLYING J/Denny's/dsl/LP/scales/24hr, Keystop/Marathon/Burger King/dsl/24hr W ⓖ BP/dsl ⑪ Cracker Barrel, McDonald's, Oasis SW Grill, Waffle House ⌂ Best Western, EconoLodge, Hampton Inn, Holiday Inn Express, Quality Inn, Super 8 ⊙ Ⓗ, antiques
1mm	**Welcome Ctr nb, full ♿ facilities, litter barrels, petwalk, 🅲, vending**
0mm	Kentucky/Tennessee state line

⬆N INTERSTATE 71

Exit #	Services
100	Kentucky/Ohio state line, Ohio River
	I-71 and I-75 run together 19 miles. See I-75 exits 175-192.
77 [173]	I-75 S, to Lexington
75mm	weigh sta sb
72	KY 14, to Verona, E ⓖ BP/dsl, Marathon/dsl ⊙ Oak Creek Camping (5mi)
62	US 127, to Glencoe, E ⓖ 62 TrkPlaza/rest./dsl, W ⓖ Valero/dsl/rest. ⌂ 127 Motel
57	KY 35, to Sparta, E ⓖ Marathon/dsl ⊙ Eagle Valley Camping (10mi), Sparta RV Park (3mi), W ⓖ BP/dsl ⌂ Ramada ⊙ KY Speedway
55	KY 1039, W ⓖ ♥Loves/McDonald's/Subway/dsl/scales/24hr ⊙ casino, KY Speedway
44	KY 227, to Indian Hills, W ⓖ Marathon/dsl, Murphy USA/dsl, Valero/dsl ⑪ Arby's, Burger King, El Nopal, Hometown Pizza, KFC, McDonald's, Mi Viejo Mexican, New China, Sonic, Subway, Taco Bell, Waffle House ⌂ Best Western, Hampton Inn, Holiday Inn Express, Quality Inn, Super 8 ⊙ HOSPITAL, $General, $Tree, AutoZone, Chevrolet, Ford, Gen. Butler SP, Kroger/dsl, Save-a-Lot Foods, URGENT CARE, Verizon, Walmart

43.5mm	Kentucky River
43	KY 389, to KY 55, English
34	US 421, New Castle, Campbellsburg, W ⓖ Marathon/dsl, Valero/Subway/dsl ⊙ st police
28	KY 153, KY 146, to US 42, Pendleton, E ⓖ 🚚/Subway/dsl/scales/24hr/@, Valero/dsl, W ⓖ 🚚/McDonald's/scales/dsl/24hr ⊙ truck repair
22	KY 53, La Grange, E ⓖ Speedway/Rally's/dsl, Valero/dsl ⑪ Applebee's, Beef O'Brady's, Burger King, Jumbo Buffet, Papa John's, Papa Murphy's, Ponderosa, Subway, Waffle House, Wendy's ⌂ Best Western-Ashbury, Comfort Inn ⊙ Ⓗ, $General, AT&T, Big-O Tire, GNC, Kroger/gas, Radio Shack, Towery's Tire/auto, Verizon, Walgreens, Walmart/Subway, W ⓖMarathon/dsl ⑪ Arby's, Cracker Barrel, Domino's, DQ, El Nopal, Hometown Pizza, KFC, LJ Silver, McDonald's, Taco Bell ⌂ Comfort Suites, Super 8 ⊙ Advance Parts, Buick/Chevrolet/GMC, Lee Tires, NAPA, Rite Aid, USPO, vet, N ⊙ $Tree
18	KY 393, Buckner, W ⓖ Marathon/dsl ⑪ Subway ⊙ Ford
17	KY 146, Buckner, W ⓖ Thornton's/dsl/24hr ⊙ st police, USPO
14	KY 329, Crestwood, Pewee Valley, Brownsboro, E ⓖ BP/dsl ⑪ DQ, Hometown Pizza, McDonald's, Sonic, Starbucks, Subway
13mm	⅌ both lanes, full ♿ facilities, litter barrels, petwalk, 🅲, vending
9 b a	I-265, KY 841, Gene Snyder Fwy, E ⌂ Hilton Garden ⊙ Cabela's, Costco/gas, Ⓗ, to Sawyer SP
5	I-264, Watterson Expswy (exits left from sb), E ⊙ to Sawyer SP
2	Zorn Ave, E ⊙ VA Ⓗ, W ⓖShell/dsl, Valero ⑪ El Nopal Mexican, KingFish Rest. ⌂ Ramada Inn ⊙ WaterTower Art Museum
1b	I-65, S to Nashville, N to Indianapolis

⬆N INTERSTATE 75

Exit #	Services
193mm	Kentucky/Ohio state line, Ohio River
192	5th St (from nb), Covington, E ⓖ BP/dsl, Shell/Circle K, Speedway/dsl ⑪ Big Boy, Burger King, GoldStar Chili, McDonald's, Popeyes, Riverfront Pizza, Skyline Chili, Subway, Taco Bell, Waffle House, White Castle ⌂ Courtyard, Extended Stay America, Holiday Inn, Radisson ⊙ Lexus, Riverboat Casino, W ⌂ Hampton Inn
191	12th St, Covington, E ⊙ Ⓗ, museum, same as 192
189	KY 1072, Kyles Lane, W ⓖBP/dsl, Shell/dsl ⑪ Big Boy, Skyline Chili, Substation II Subs ⌂ Rodeway Inn ⊙ same as 188, Walgreens
188	US 25, US 42, Dixe Hwy, E ⓖ Marathon ⑪ Starbucks, Subway ⊙ GNC, Kroger/dsl, Tuesday Morning, W ⌂ Rodeway Inn ⊙ Mercedes, same as 189
186	KY 371, Buttermilk Pike, Covington, E ⓖ BP/dsl, Marathon/DQ/dsl ⑪ Graeter's Ice Cream, Oriental Wok, Papa John's ⌂ Montgomery Inn, Super 8, W ⓖ BP, Speedway/dsl, Sunoco/dsl ⑪ Arby's, Baskin-Robbins/Dunkin Donuts, Bonefish Grill, Burger King, Cancun Mexican, Chipotle Mexican, Domino's, Empire Buffet, Firehouse Subs, GoldStar Chili, Jimmy John's, La Rosa's Pizza, Marco's Pizza, McDonald's, Miyako Steaks, Outback Steaks, Skyline Chili, Subway, Sweet Basil Thai ⊙ $Tree, Field & Stream, Home Depot, Petco, Remke Foods, Staples, Verizon, Walgreens
185	I-275 E and W, W to 🍴

🧭N INTERSTATE 75 Cont'd

Exit #	Services
184	KY 236, Donaldson Rd, to Erlanger, **E** 🅖 BP, Erlanger/Dunkin Donuts 🍴 Double Dragon Oriental, **W** 🅖 Racers/Subway/dsl, Speedway/dsl 🍴 Peecox Grill, Waffle House 🛏 Country Hearth Inn, EconoLodge, Red Roof Inn, Wingate Inn 🅞 Goodyear/auto
182	KY 1017, Turfway Rd, **E** 🅖 BP/dsl, Shell/dsl 🍴 Bamboo Garden, Big Boy, China City, Lee's Chicken, McDonald's, Papa John's, Subway, Taco Bell 🛏 Baymont Inn, Courtyard, Days Inn, ValuePlace 🅞 BigLots, CVS Drug, Family$, Office Depot, Remke Foods, USPO, **W** 🍴 Applebee's, Chick-fil-A, Chili's, CiCi's Pizza, Cracker Barrel, Famous Dave's BBQ, Firebowl Grill, Longhorn Steaks, Noodles&Co., O'Charley's, Potbelly, Rafferty's, Skyline Chili, Steak'n Shake, Subway, Wendy's 🛏 Comfort Inn, Extended Stay America, Hampton Inn, Hilton, Hyatt Place, La Quinta, SpringHill Suites 🅞 🏨, Best Buy, Dick's, Home Depot, Jo-Ann, Kohl's, Lowe's, Meijer, Michael's, Petsmart, Radio Shack, Sam's Club, Target, Turfway Park Racing
181	KY 18, Florence, **E** 🅖 Speedway/dsl, TA/Valero/Pizza Hut/Popeye's/Subway/dsl/24hr/@ 🍴 Kiwha Korean, Waffle House 🛏 Best Value Inn, Best Western, Heritage Inn 🅞 Chevrolet, **W** 🅖 BP/dsl, Marathon/dsl, Speedway/dsl 🍴 Buffalo Wild Wings, Cheddar's, Chipotle Mexican, Chuy's Mexican, City BBQ, Currito Burrito, El Rio Grande, Fazoli's, Firehouse Subs, Fuji Steaks, Hooters, IHOP, Jersey Mike's, La Rosa's, Laughing Noodle, Logan's Roadhouse, Miyoshi Japanese, Panda Express, Panera Bread, Red Robin 🛏 Homewood Suites, Stay Lodge 🅞 AT&T, Buick/GMC, Chrysler/Jeep/Dodge, Ford, Honda, Hyundai, Mazda, Nissan, Tire Discounters, Toyota/Scion, URGENT CARE, Verizon, VW, Walmart/Subway
180a	Mall Rd (from sb), **W** 🍴 Asian Buffet, BJ's Rest., Buca Italian, ChuckeCheese, GoldStar Chili, HoneyBaked Ham, Jimmy John's, Olive Garden, Pizza Hut, Qdoba, Quaker Steak, Skyline Chili, Smokey Bones BBQ, Starbucks, Subway, Taco Bell, Which Wich? 🅞 $General, $Tree, AT&T, Barnes&Noble, Harley Davidson, Hobby Lobby, JC Penney, Kroger/dsl, Macy's, mall, Old Navy, same as 180, Sears/auto, Staples, TJ Maxx, Tuesday Morning
180	US 42, US 127, Florence, Union, **E** 🅖 BP/dsl, Speedway/dsl 🍴 Big Boy, Bob Evans, Capt D's, Chipotle Mexican, El Nopal Mexican, Mai Thai, McDonald's, Penn Sta Subs, Rally's, Red Lobster, Subway, Wendy's 🛏 Holiday Inn, Howard Johnson, Knights Inn, Motel 6, Quality Inn, Super 8 🅞 Cadillac, funpark, Subaru, **W** 🅖 Marathon/dsl, Murphy USA/dsl, Speedway/dsl 🍴 Arby's, KFC, Little Caesars, LJ Silver, Ponderosa, Waffle House, White Castle 🛏 Magnuson Hotel, Travelodge 🅞 CarX, Midas, O'Reilly Parts, PepBoys, Tire Discounters, Tires+, Walgreens
178	KY 536, Mt Zion Rd, **E** 🅖 Marathon/Rally's/dsl, Speedway/dsl, Sunoco/Subway/dsl 🍴 Buffalo Bob's, Chopsticks, GoldStar Chili, Hot Head Burritos, Jersey Mike's Subs, La Fuentes Mexican, La Rosa's Pizza, Mad Mike's Burgers, Sonic, Steak'n Shake, Taco Bell 🅞 AutoZone, Goodyear/auto, Kroger
177mm	**Welcome Ctr sb/🆁🆂 nb, full 🚻 facilities, litter barrels, ⊕, 🌳 RV dump, vending**
175	KY 338, Richwood, **E** 🅖 🚚/Subway/dsl/24hr, TA/BP/Country Pride/Taco Bell/dsl/24hr/@ 🍴 Arby's, Burger King, White Castle 🛏 Richwood Inn 🅞 RV Park, **W** 🅖 BP/dsl, 🚚/Subway/dsl/scales/24hr, Shell/dsl 🍴 GoldStar Chili, Gourmet Cafe, Hong Kong Cafe, McDonald's,

175	Continued
	Papa Dino's Pizza, Penn Sta Subs, Skyline Chili, Snappy Tomato Pizza, Waffle House, Wendy's 🛏 EconoLodge, Holiday Inn Express 🅞 to Big Bone Lick SP
173	I-71 S, to Louisville
171	KY 14, KY 16, to Verona, Walton, **E** 🅖 BP/dsl, Marathon/DQ/dsl 🍴 China Moon, El Toro Mexican, McDonald's, Pizza Hut, Starbucks, Subway, Waffle House 🅞 AT&T, AutoZone, Kohl's, Kroger/dsl, Tire Discounters, URGENT CARE, Walton Drug, **W** 🅖 FLYING J/Denny's/dsl/scales/24hr 🅞 Blue Beacon, Delightful Days RV Ctr, Oak Creek Camping (1mi), to Big Bone Lick SP, vet
168mm	**weigh sta/rest haven sb**
166	KY 491, Crittenden, **E** 🅖 BP/dsl, Marathon/dsl 🍴 McDonald's 🅞 Chrysler/Dodge/Jeep, Cincinnati S Camping (2mi), **W** 🅖 Marathon/dsl, Shell/Gold Star Chili 🍴 China Castle, Subway, Wendy's 🅞 $General, Grant Co Drugs
159	KY 22, to Owenton, Dry Ridge, **E** 🅖 BP, Shell/dsl, Speedway/dsl 🍴 Arby's, Burger King, Happy Dragon Chinese, KFC/Taco Bell, La Rosa's, LJ Silver, McDonald's, Pizza Hut, Skyline Chili, Subway, Waffle House, Wendy's 🛏 Microtel, Value Stay 🅞 🏨, $General, Buick/Chevrolet, O'Reilly Parts, Radio Shack, Verizon, Walmart **W** 🅖 Road Ranger/dsl, Speedway/dsl 🍴 Country Grill, Cracker Barrel, El Rio Grande Mexican 🛏 Comfort Inn, Hampton Inn 🅞 Camper Village, Dry Ridge TowneCtr, Sav-A-Lot, Tire Discounters, Toyota/Scion
156	Barnes Rd, **E** 🅞 🏨,
154	KY 36, Williamstown, **E** 🅖 Marathon/dsl, Shell/dsl 🅞 🏨, to Kincaid Lake SP, **W** 🅖 Marathon/dsl 🍴 El Jalisco Mexican 🛏 Best Value Inn, Sunrise Inn
144	KY 330, to Owenton, Corinth, **E** 🅖 Marathon/dsl, Noble's Trk Plaza/rest./dsl 🅞 camping, **W** 🅖 BP 🍴 Gary's Grill Inn 🛏 3 Springs Motel
136	KY 32, to Sadieville
130.5mm	**weigh sta nb**
129	rd 620, Cherry Blossom Wy, **E** 🅖 🚚/Wendy's/dsl/scales/24hr/@ 🍴 Waffle House 🛏 Days Inn, Motel 6, **W** 🅖 🚚/McDonald's/dsl/scales/24hr, Shell 🅞 Whispering Hills RV Park (3mi)
127mm	🆁🆂 both lanes, full 🚻 facilities, litter barrels, petwalk, ⊕, 🌳 vending
126	US 62, to US 460, Georgetown, **E** 🅖 Marathon/dsl, Murphy USA/dsl 🍴 Applebee's, Asian Royal Buffet, Big Boy, Buffalo Wild Wings, Gold Star Chili, Golden Corral, Jimmy John's, McDonald's, O'Charley's, Papa John's, Penn Sta Subs, Pepe's Mexican, Qdoba, Starbucks, Steak'n Shake, Subway 🛏 Holiday Inn Express 🅞 AT&T, Kohl's, Lowe's, Tire Discounters, URGENT CARE, Verizon, Walmart/Subway **W** 🅖 Marathon,

*(side tab: **KY**)*

🅿 = gas   🍴 = food   🛏 = lodging   🅾 = other   Ⓡ🅂 = rest stop

Copyright 2015 - the Next EXIT ®

INTERSTATE 75 Cont'd

Exit #	Services
126	**Continued** Shell/Subway, Speedway/dsl 🍴 Chick-fil-A, Cracker Barrel, Fazoli's, KFC, Ruby Tuesday, Waffle House 🛏 Baymont Inn, Best Western, Comfort Suites, Country Inn&Suites, Fairfield Inn, Hampton Inn, Hilton Garden, Microtel, Super 8 🅾 🏥, Buick/Chevrolet, Chrysler/Dodge/Jeep, same as 125, to Georgetown Coll
125	US 460 (from nb), Georgetown, E 🅿 Gulf, Shell 🍴 FatKats Pizza 🛏 Knights Inn, W 🅿 Swifty/dsl, Valero/dsl 🍴 Arby's, DQ, Little Caesars, LJ Silver, Taco Bell, Wendy's 🛏 Winner's Circle Motel 🅾 $Tree, Advance Parts, BigLots, K-Mart, Midas, Outlets/Famous Brands, Radio Shack, same as 126
120	rd 1973, to Ironworks Pike, KY Horse Park, E 🅾 KY Horse Park Camping, W 🅿 Shell/dsl 🅾 🏥,
118	I-64 W, to Frankfort, Louisville
115	rd 922, Lexington, E 🅿 Shell/Subway/dsl 🍴 Cracker Barrel, McDonald's, Waffle House 🛏 Fairfield Inn, Knights Inn, La Quinta, Sheraton 🅾 SaddleHorse Museum (4mi), W 🅿 Marathon/dsl 🍴 Cortland's Kitchen, Denny's, Happy Dragon Chinese 🛏 Clarion, Embassy Suites, Marriott/rest. 🅾 museum
113	US 27, US 68, to Paris, Lexington, E 🅿 BP/dsl, Speedway/dsl 🍴 Waffle House 🛏 Ramada Inn, W 🅿 Marathon/dsl, Shell, Shell/dsl 🍴 Arby's, Burger King, Capt D's, Donato's Pizza, DQ, Fazoli's, Golden Corral, Hardee's, Horseshoes Grill, Little Caesars, McDonald's, Penn Sta Subs, Rally's, Subway, Taco Bell, Wendy's, Zaxby's 🛏 Catalina Motel, Days Inn, Red Roof Inn 🅾 Advance Parts, AutoZone, Bluegrass RV Ctr, Chevrolet, CVS Drug, Northside RV Ctr, O'Reilly Parts, Rupp Arena, to UK, Walmart
111	I-64 E, to Huntington, WV
110	US 60, Lexington, W 🅿 Murphy USA/dsl, Shell/dsl, Speedway/dsl, Thorntons/dsl 🍴 A&W Cafe, Arby's, Bob Evans, Calistoga Cafe, Cane's Chicken, Cracker Barrel, FirstWatch Cafe, McDonald's, Smashing Tomato, Starbucks, Tom+Chee Rest., Waffle House, Wendy's 🛏 Baymont Inn, Comfort Inn, Country Inn&Suites, Guesthouse Inn, Hampton Inn, Holiday Inn Express, Howard Johnson, Microtel, Motel 6, Quality Inn, Super 8 🅾 🏥, Hobby Lobby, Lowe's, Rite Aid, Walmart/Subway
108	Man O War Blvd, E 🅿 Shell 🅾 Costco/gas, Rite Aid, W 🅿 Marathon/dsl, Meijer/dsl, Shell/KFC/Pizza Hut/Wendy's/dsl 🍴 Applebee's, Arby's, Asuka Grill, Backyard Burger, BD Mongolian Grill, Big Boy, BoneFish Grill, Carino's, Carrabba's, Cheddar's, Chick-fil-A, Chipotle Mexican, Coldstone, Culver's, Fazoli's, GoldStar Chili, IChing Asian, Logan's Roadhouse, Malone's, McDonald's, Old Chicago, Outback Steaks, Qdoba, Quiznos, Rafferty's, Red Lobster, Saul Good Rest., Starbucks, Steak'n Shake, Subway, Taco Bell, Ted's MT Grill, TGIFriday's, Waffle House 🛏 Courtyard, Hilton Garden, Homewood Suites, Hyatt Place, Residence Inn, Sleep Inn, TownePlace Suites 🅾 🏥, AT&T, Audi, Barnes&Noble, Best Buy, BigLots, Dick's, GNC, Gordmans, Harley-Davidson, Kohl's, Marshall's, Michael's, Old Navy, Petsmart, Radio Shack, Ross, Staples, Target, Tire Discounters, Verizon, Walgreens
104	KY 418, Lexington, E 🅿 BP/Arby's/dsl, Shell/McDonald's 🍴 Waffle House 🛏 Best Western, Comfort Inn, Days Inn, EconoLodge, La Quinta, W 🅿 Marathon/dsl, Speedway/dsl 🍴 Wendy's 🅾 🏥,

Exit #	Services
99	US 25 N, US 421 N, Clays Ferry
98mm	Kentucky River
97	US 25 S, US 421 S, Clay's Ferry
95	rd 627, to Boonesborough, Winchester, E 🅿 BP/dsl, Loves/Arby's/dsl/scales/24hr 🅾 camping, Ft Boonesborough SP, W 🅿 Shell/Subway/dsl
90	US 25, US 421, Richmond, E 🅿 Shell 🍴 Cracker Barrel 🛏 La Quinta, Red Roof Inn, Relax Inn, Super 7, W 🅿 BP, Exxon/Arby's/dsl, Marathon, Shell 🍴 Big Boy, DQ, Hanger's Rest., Hardee's, McDonald's, Pizza Hut, Subway, Waffle House, Wendy's 🛏 Days Inn, Super 8 🅾 $General, vet
87	rd 876, Richmond, E 🅿 BP/dsl, Marathon/dsl, Shell/dsl, Speedway/dsl 🍴 A&W/LJ Silver, Arby's, Casa Fiesta Mexican, CookOut, Domino's, Fazoli's, Fong's Chinese, Hardee's, Hooters, King Buffet, Lee's Chicken, Little Caesars, McAlister's Deli, McDonald's, Papa John's, Qdoba, Rally's, Subway, Taco Bell, Waffle House, Wendy's 🛏 Best Western, Country Hearth Inn, Quality Quarters Inn 🅾 🏥, $General, Aamco, Ace Hardware, AT&T, BigLots, Goodyear/auto, Rite Aid, to EKU, vet, W 🅿 Marathon/Circle K, Shell/dsl 🍴 Bob Evans, Buffalo Wild Wings, Burger King, Cane's, Chick-fil-A, Culver's, Firehouse Subs, IHOP, Koto Japanese, Logan's Roadhouse, Olive Garden, Panera Bread, Ryan's, Starbucks, Steak'n Shake, Subway 🛏 Comfort Suites, Hampton Inn, Holiday Inn Express, Quality Inn 🅾 Belk, Dick's, GNC, Hastings Books, JC Penney, Meijer/dsl, Michaels, Petsmart, Radio Shack, Tire Discounters, TJ Maxx, Verizon
83	to US 25, rd 2872, Duncannon Ln, Richmond, E 🅾 Bluegrass Army Depot
77	rd 595, Berea, E 🅾 🏥, KY Artisan Ctr/Cafe/Travelers Ctr, to Berea Coll, W 🅿 Shell/dsl, Valero/Subway/dsl 🍴 Back Porch BBQ, Dino's Italian, Smokehouse Grill 🛏 Motel 6, Red Roof Inn
76	KY 21, Berea, E 🅿 BP, Marathon/Circle K, Shell/Burger King, Speedway/dsl 🍴 A&W/LJ Silver, Cracker Barrel, Dinner Bell Rest., Gondolier Italian, Hong Kong Buffet, KFC, Mario's Pizza, McDonald's, Old Town Amish Rest., Papa John's, Pizza Hut, Subway, Taco Bell, WanPen Chinese/Thai, Wendy's 🛏 Best Value Inn, Holiday Motel, Knights Inn 🅾 🏥 $General, $Tree, Radio Shack, URGENT CARE, Walmart W 🅿 76 Fuel/dsl, BP/dsl, Marathon/dsl 🍴 Lee's Chicken 🛏 Comfort Inn, EconoLodge, Fairfield Inn 🅾 Oh! Kentucky Camping, tires, Walnut Meadow RV Park
62	US 25, to KY 461, Renfro Valley, E 🅿 Derby City/rest./dsl, Shell 🍴 Hardee's, Little Caesar's 🛏 Heritage Inn 🅾 KOA (2mi), Renfro Valley RV Park/rest, W 🅿 BP, Marathon/dsl, Marathon/Wendy's/dsl, Shell 🍴 Arby's, Denny's, Godfather's/Subway, KFC, Limestone Grill, McDonald's, Taco Bell 🛏 Days Inn, EconoLodge 🅾 🏥, Lake Cumberland, Rite Aid, to Big South Fork NRA
59	US 25, to Livingston, Mt Vernon, E 🅿 Shell, TravelCtr/dsl 🍴 El Cazador Mexican, Pizza Hut 🛏 Kastle Inn, W 🅿 BP 🛏 Mtn View Inn
51mm	Rockcastle River
49	KY 909, to US 25, Livingston, E 🅾 Camp Wildcat Bfd, W 🅿 49er/dsl/24hr 🅾 RV Park, truck/tire repair
41	rd 80, to Somerset, London, E 🅿 Speedway/dsl 🍴 Arby's, Azteca Mexican, Burger King, Gondolier Italian, KFC, McDonald's, Subway, White Castle 🛏 Days Inn, EconoLodge, Quality Inn, Red Roof Inn, Super 8 🅾 🏥, $General, Advance Parts, AutoZone, CVS Drug, Kroger/deli, Parsley's Tire/repair, st police, W 🅿 BP/Home Cooker/dsl/24hr,

Left margin vertical labels: GEORGETOWN · LEXINGTON · RICHMOND · BEREA · LONDON

⬆N INTERSTATE 75 Cont'd

Exit #	Services
41	Continued Marathon/McDonald's, Shell/pizza, Sunoco/dsl, Valero/dsl 🍴 Cheddar's, Cracker Barrel, LJ Silver, Old Town Grill, Shiloh Roadhouse, Subway, Taco Bell, Waffle House, Wendy's 🛏 Budget Host, Hampton Inn 🅾 Dog Patch Ctr, Westgate RV Camping
38	rd 192, to Rogers Pkwy, London, E 🅶 BP/dsl, Marathon, Shell/Mama's Subs/dsl, Speedway/dsl 🍴 Big Boy, Burger King, Capt D's, Dino's Italian, Domino's, DQ, El Dorado Mexican, Fazoli's, Golden Corral, Great Wall Chinese, Hardee's, Huddle House, Krystal, McDonald's, Penn Sta Subs, Pizza Hut, Ruby Tuesday, Starbucks, Steak'n Shake, Subway, Sun Buffet, Taco Bell 🛏 Baymont Inn, Comfort Suites, Country Inn&Suites, Holiday Inn Express, Microtel 🅾 $Tree, Advance Parts, 🛒, camping, E Kentucky RV Ctr, K-Mart, Kroger/dsl, Lowe's, NAPA, Nissan, Office Depot, Peterbilt, Radio Shack, Rogers Pkwy to Manchester/Hazard, to Levi Jackson SP, USPO, Verizon, Walgreens, Walmart/Subway W 🅾 🅷, to Laurel River Lake RA
34mm	truck haven, weigh sta both lanes
30.5mm	Laurel River
29	US 25, US 25E, Corbin, E 🅶 Marathon, Murphy USA, Pilot/McDonald's/Subway/dsl/scales/24hr, Spur Oil 🍴 David's Steaks, DQ, Huddle House, Mi Jalisco Mexican, Taco Bell 🛏 Super 8 🅾 Aldi Foods, AutoZone, Blue Beacon, Lowe's, to Cumberland Gap NP, Walmart/Subway W 🅶 BP/Krystal/dsl, Loves/Hardee's/dsl/scales/24hr/@, Marathon, Shell/dsl 🍴 Cracker Barrel, Sonny's BBQ 🛏 Baymont Inn, Comfort Suites, Fairfield Inn, Hampton Inn, Knights Inn 🅾 KOA, tires/repair, to Laurel River Lake RA
25	US 25W, Corbin, E 🅶 Speedway/dsl 🍴 Applebee's, Burger King, Cayenne SW Grill, CB's Grill, Dino's Italian, McDonald's, Wendy's 🛏 Country Inn&Suites, EconoLodge, Holiday Inn Express, Landmark Inn 🅾 🅷, auto repair/tires, W 🅶 Shell 🍴 Arby's, El Dorado Mexican, Subway, Waffle House 🛏 Best Western 🅾 to Cumberland Falls SP
15	US 25W, to Williamsburg, Goldbug, W 🅶 Xpress/dsl 🅾 Cumberland Falls SP
14.5mm	Cumberland River
11	KY 92, Williamsburg, E 🅶 BP/dsl, Shell 🍴 Arby's, El Dorado Mexican, Hardee's, KFC, Little Caesars, McDonald's, Pizza Hut, Subway, Taco Bell 🛏 Cumberland Inn, Scottish Inn, Super 8 🅾 $General, Advance Parts, AutoZone, Family$, museum, Sav-A-Lot, Windham Drug, W 🅶 Pilot/Wendy's/dsl/scales/24hr, Shell 🍴 Burger King, DQ, Huddle House, Krystal, LJ Silver 🛏 Hampton Inn 🅾 $Tree, Radio Shack, to Big South Fork NRA, Walmart
1.5mm	Welcome Ctr nb, full ♿ facilities, litter barrels, petwalk, 🄲, 🛒 vending
0mm	Kentucky/Tennessee state line

⬆N INTERSTATE 275 (Cincinnati)

Exit #	Services
84	I-71, I-75, Louisville, N to Cincinnati, S to Lexington
83	US 25, US 42, US 127, S 🅶 Shell/dsl, Speedway, Thorntons 🍴 5 Guys Burgers, Abuelo's Mexican, Burger King, Carrabba's, Coldstone, Donato's Pizza, John Phillip's Rest., KFC, Max&Erma's, McAlister's Deli, McDonald's, Moe's SW Grill, Panera Bread, Pizza Hut, Starbucks, Subway, Taco Bell, Wendy's 🅾 $Tree, Dillard's, GNC, K-Mart, Walgreens
82	rd 1303, Turkeyfoot Rd, S 🅾 🅷
80	KY 17, Independence, N 🅶 Speedway/dsl, Thorntons/dsl, United/dsl 🍴 Arby's, Big Boy, Bob Evans, Buffalo Wild Wings, Burger King, Golden Corral, Hot Wok, McDonald's, Penn Sta Subs, Snappy Tomato Pizza, Subway, TX Roadhouse, Wendy's 🅾 Chevrolet, TireDiscounters, Walmart
79	KY 16, Taylor Mill Rd, N 🅶 BP, Marathon, Speedway 🍴 Goldstar Chili, LJ Silver, McDonald's, Wendy's 🅾 $Tree, Big-Lots, CVS Drug, Kroger/gas, Radio Shack, Walgreens, S 🅶 BP/dsl 🍴 KFC/Taco Bell, McDonald's, Oriental Wok, Skyline Chili, Subway 🅾 Remke's Foods
77	KY 9, Maysville, Wilder, N 🛏 Hampton Inn, S 🅶 Mobil/dsl, Thorntons/dsl 🍴 DQ, Goldstar Chili, McDonald's, Waffle House
74b	I-471 N, Newport, Cincinnati, N 🅾 🅷
74a	Alexandria, (exits left from sb), to US 27
73mm	OH River, OH/KY state line
72	US 52 W, Kellogg Ave, S 🅶 🛒, Marathon
71	US 52 E, New Richmond
69	5 Mile Rd, W 🅶 BP/dsl 🍴 Big Boy, IHOP, La Rosa's Mexican, McDonald's, TGIFriday's, Wendy's 🅾 🅷 Kroger/gas
65	OH 125, Beechmont Ave, Amelia, E 🅶 Mobil/dsl, Shell, Speedway 🍴 Hibachi Grill, Hooters, Red Lobster, Wendy's 🛏 Motel 6 🅾 CarX, Ford, Lowe's, Tires+, Walgreens, W 🅶 BP, Marathon, Speedway/dsl 🍴 Big Boy, Bob Evans, Burger King, Butterbee's Grille, Chick-fil-A, Chipotle Mexican, Dos Amigo's Mexican, McDonald's, Olive Garden, Smokey Bones BBQ, Starbucks, White Castle 🛏 Best Western, Days Inn, Red Roof Inn 🅾 $Tree, Aldi Foods, AT&T, BigLots, Goodyear/auto, Hancock Fabrics, Home Depot, Honda, Kroger, Staples, Sumerel Tire/repair, Target, TireDiscounters, TJ Maxx, Toyota/Scion, Verizon
63b a	OH 32, Batavia, Newtown, E 🅶 Marathon, Mobil, Thornton's 🍴 Applebee's, Bob Evans, Burger King, Cheeseburger Paradise, Chick-fil-A, CiCi's Pizza, City BBQ, Fuji Steaks, Golden Corral, KFC, LJ Silver, Longhorn Steaks, Max&Erma's, McDonalds, Panera Bread, Penn Sta Subs, Perkins, Pizza Hut, Popeye's, Skyline Chili, Taco Bell, White Castle 🛏 Comfort Inn, Fairfield Inn, Hampton Inn, Holiday Inn 🅾 $Tree, Best Buy, Bigg's Foods, Dillard's, Hobby Lobby, Jo-Ann Fabrics, Kohl's, Kroger, Meijer/dsl, Michael's, PepBoys, Petsmart, Sam's Club/gas, Sears/auto, Walmart, W 🅶 Exxon, Marathon, Speedway/dsl, Sunoco 🍴 La Rosa's Mexican, Roy Rogers 🅾 Kroger
59	OH 452, US 50, Milford Pkwy, Hillsboro, S 🅶 Mobil 🍴 Buffalo Wild Wings, Cracker Barrel, Goldstar Chili, Mio's Pizza, Quaker Steak&Lube, Red Robin, Ruby Tuesday, Subway, TX Roadhouse, Wendy's 🛏 Homewood Suites 🅾 Office Depot, Petsmart, Target, Walmart

⬆N INTERSTATE 275 (Cincinnati)

Exit #	Services
57	OH 28, Blanchester, Milford, N 0-1 mi 🍴 Applebee's, Arby's, Burger King, Chipotle Mexican, DQ, Dunkin Donuts, Goldstar Chili, IHOP, Panera Bread, Skyline Chili, Sonic, Steak'n Shake, Subway, Taco Bell, Wendy's, White Castle 🅾 Home Depot, K-Mart, Kroger/gas, Lowe's, Meijer/dsl S 🅿 Exxon, Shell, Speedway, Thorntons/dsl 🍴 Big Boy, Bob Evans, Cazadore's Mexican, Hong Kong Wok, Little Caesar's, McDonald's, Putter's Grill, Quiznos, Roosters Grill 🛏 Holiday Inn Express 🅾 🏥, $Tree, BigLots, CVS Drug, Goodyear/auto, Kroger/gas, Tires+, USPO, vet
54	Wards Corner Rd, N 🅿 BP, S 🅿 Mobil/dsl 🍴 Big Boy, Dominos, Goldstar Chili, Subway 🛏 Hilton Garden
53mm	Little Miami River
52	Loveland, Indian Hill, N 🅿 Circle K/dsl, Marathon, Shell, Speedway/dsl 🍴 Arby's, Burger King, Dragon Wok, Penn Sta Subs, Pizza Hut, Starbucks, Subway, Taco Bell, Wendy's 🅾 CVS Drug, Verizon, VW, Walgreens
50	US 22, OH 3, Montgomery, N 🅿 Shell 🍴 Buffalo Wild Wings, Chili's, Donato's Pizza, DQ, Melting Pot, Panera Bread, Starbucks, Subway, Taco Casa 🅾 Acura, GNC, Hyundai, Kroger, S 🅿 BP/dsl, Shell 🍴 Goldstar Chili, La Rosa's, McDonald's, Merlot's Rest., Quiznos, Skyline Chili, Wendy's 🅾 🏥
49	I-71 N to Columbus, S to Cincinnati
47	Reed Hartman Hwy, Blue Ash, S 🍴 Chipotle, Jersey Mike's, Jimmy John's, Kanpai Japanese, Ruby Tuesday 🛏 DoubleTree, Hyatt Place, Residence Inn
46	US 42, Mason, N 🅿 BP 🍴 Chipotle, KFC, McDonald's, Skyline Chili, Taco Bell, Wendy's, White Castle 🛏 Holiday Inn, Motel 6, ValuePlace 🅾 Advance Parts, CVS Drug, Kroger, S 🅿 Marathon/dsl, Shell, Speedway/dsl, UDF/dsl 🍴 Arby's, Schezwan House, Waffle House 🛏 Days Inn 🅾 Midas, Mr Transmission, Tire Discounters
44	Mosteller Rd, N 🍴 Subway, S 🛏 Homewood Suites
43b a	I-75, N to Dayton, S to Cincinnati
42	OH 747, Springdale, Glendale, N 🅿 Sunoco, Thorntons 🅾 Staples, S 🅿 Shell 🍴 BJ's Brewhouse, Chipotle, Firehouse Subs, Jimmy John's, KFC, La Rositas, McDonald's, Skyline Chili, Steak'n Shake, TGIFriday's 🅾 BigLots, Chevrolet, Chrysler/Dodge/Jeep, Dillard's, Hobby Lobby, Macy's, Petsmart, Sears, Tires+
41	OH 4, Springdale Pkwy, N 🅿 Mobil, Shell, Speedway/dsl 🍴 Burger King, Hooters, Olive Garden, Pappadeaux, Roosters Rest., Skyline Chili, Wendy's 🛏 La Quinta 🅾 Tire Discounters, S 🅿 BP, UDF/dsl 🍴 Beef'O'Brady's, DQ, Goldstar Chili, Outback Steaks, Subway, White Castle 🛏 Extended Stay America, Howard Johnson, Super 8 🅾 CVS Drug, Family$,
41	Continued O'Reilly Parts, URGENT CARE
39	Winton Rd, Winton Woods, N 🅿 BP 🍴 Bob Evans, Chipotle, Golden Corral, IHOP, McDonald's, Old Spaghetti Factory, Panera Bread, Red Lobster, Steak'n Shake 🛏 Comfort Suites, Hampton Inn 🅾 Bass Pro Shops, CarMax, Home Depot, Kohl's, Meijer/dsl, PetCo, Tire Discounters, S 🅿 Marathon/dsl, Shell/dsl, UDF/dsl 🍴 Big Boy, Buffalo Wild Wings, Cancun Mexican, Cracker Barrel, Popeye's, Skyline Chili, Starbucks, Subway, Wendy's 🛏 Quality Inn, SpringHill Suites 🅾 $Tree, AAA, Aldi Foods, Kroger/gas, Tires+, Walgreens, Walmart
36	US 127, Hamilton, Mt Healthy, N 🅿 BP/Circle K, Speedway 🍴 Skyline Chili, Wendy's, S 🅿 Shell/dsl, Sunoco 🍴 Arby's, Big Boy, La Rosa's Pizza, Little Caesars, McDonald's, Rally's, Subway, Taco Bell 🅾 Advance Parts, Family$, O'Reilly Parts
33	US 27, US 126, Colerain Ave, N 🅿 Speedway 🍴 Burger King, Skyline Chili, Steak'n Shake, Wendy's 🅾 Colerain RV Ctr, Dick's, Hobby Lobby, Lowe's, Walmart/Subway, S 🅿 Shell 🍴 5 Guys Burgers, Arby's, Big Boy, Bob Evans, Burger King, Cheddar's, Chipotle, Firehouse Subs, IHOP, KFC, LJ Silver, Longhorn Steaks, McDonald's, Olive Garden, Outback Steaks, Panera Bread, Pizza Hut, Qdoba, Red Lobster, Starbucks, Taco Bell, TGIFriday's, White Castle 🅾 AT&T, Best Buy, JC Penney, Kia, Macy's, Marshalls, Meijer/dsl, Michael's, Old Navy, Tires+, URGENT CARE, Walgreens
31	Ronald Reagan Hwy, Blue Rock Rd
28	E to Cincinnati, I-74, US 52, W to Indianapolis
24	E to Cincinnati, I-74, W to Indianapolis
21	Kilby Rd, 🅾 Indian Springs Camping (3mi)
18mm	Ohio/Indiana State Line
16	US 50, Greendale, Lawrenceburg, W 🅿 Ameristop/dsl, Marathon/dsl, Shell/Circle K/Subway 🍴 Buffalo's Cafe, Burger King, KFC, McDonald's 🛏 Comfort Inn, Holiday Inn Express, Quality Inn, Riverside Inn 🅾 Buick/Chevrolet/GMC, casino, Chrysler/Dodge/Jeep, Ford, TireDiscounters, Walgreens
14mm	Kentucky/Indiana state line, Ohio River
11	Petersburg
8b a	KY 237, Hebron, N 🅿 BP/DQ/dsl, Mobil/dsl 🍴 Arby's, Beef'O'Brady's, China Wok, Edwardo's Pizza/Subs, El Mariachi, Jimmy John's, Penn Sta Subs, Vintage Deli, Wendy's 🅾 Remke's Foods, S 🅿 Shell/Subway/dsl 🍴 Bruster's, Burger King, Goldstar Chili, Waffle House
4a b	KY 212, KY 20, N 🅿 ValAir Gas 🛏 Comfort Suites, Country Inn&Suites, Hampton Inn, Marriott, S 🛏 DoubleTree 🅾 🏥, 🛩
2	Mineola Pike, N 🅿 Mobil/Rally's/Subway/dsl 🛏 Holiday Inn, Quality Inn, S 🛏 Courtyard Inn, Residence Inn

LOUISIANA

⬆E INTERSTATE 10

Exit #	Services
274mm	Louisiana/Mississippi state line, Pearl River
272mm	West Pearl River
270mm	**Welcome Ctr wb, full 🛏 facilities, info, litter barrels, pet-walk, 🔧, 🚻 RV dump**
267b	I-12 W, to Baton Rouge
267a	I-59 N, to Meridian
266	US 190, Slidell, N 🅿 RaceTrac/dsl, Shell/dsl, TA/Country Pride/dsl/scales/24hr/@, Valero/dsl 🍴 Arby's, Baskin-Robbins, Cane's Rest., Carreta's Mexican, Chesterfield Grill, Chick-fil-A, Copeland's Rest., Golden Dragon Chinese, KFC, Los Tres Amigos, McDonald's, NOLA Southern Grill, Panda Express, Retro Grill, Rotolo's Pizza, Shoney's, Sonic, Subway, Taco Bell, Wendy's, Zydecos Rest. 🛏 Best Value Inn, Best Western, Deluxe Motel, Motel 6 🅾 🏥, CVS Drug, Firestone/auto, Freightliner, GNC, Harley-Davidson, Hobby Lobby,

KY LA

Exit #	Services
251	Bayou Sauvage NWR, S ⊙ swamp tours
248	Michoud Blvd
246b a	I-510 S, LA 47 N, S to Chalmette, N to Little Woods
245	Bullard Ave, N ⛽ Chevron/dsl, Shell/dsl 🍴 Southern Smoque Diner, Waffle House 🛏 Comfort Suites, Holiday Inn Express ⊙ Family$, Honda, S ⛽ Chevron/dsl, Shell 🍴 Burger King, IHOP, KFC/Taco Bell, McDonald's, Papa John's, Super Cajun Seafood 🛏 Baymont Inn, Motel 6 ⊙ Chrysler/Dodge/Jeep, Home Depot, Nissan, PepBoys, Rite Aid, Tire Kingdom, Toyota/Scion, Walgreens, Walmart
244	Read Blvd, N ⛽ Shell/dsl 🍴 McDonald's ⊙ Walgreens, S ⛽ EZ Stop/dsl 🍴 Popeye's, Subway, Waffle House, Wendy's 🛏 Clarion, Days Inn, Knights Inn ⊙ 🏥, CVS, Lowe's, SaveALot Foods
242	Crowder Blvd, N ⛽ Chevron, S ⛽ Crowder Ctr, Exxon/dsl 🍴 Subway 🛏 Quality Inn ⊙ Walgreens
241	Morrison Rd, N ⛽ Big E-Z/dsl, FuelXpress/dsl
240b a	US 90 E, Chef Hwy, Downman Rd, N ⛽ Shell/dsl 🛏 Super 8 ⊙ Chevrolet, U-Haul, USPO, S ⛽ Chevron/dsl, DZ/dsl ⊙ Delta Tires
239b a	Louisa St, Almonaster Blvd, N ⛽ Big Easy TP/rest./dsl, Chevron/dsl, Exxon/dsl, FuelZone/dsl 🍴 Burger King, Church's, McDonald's, Min Moon Chinese, Popeyes, Rally's, Subway, Taco Bell, Waffle House, Wendy's 🛏 EconoLodge, Motel 6 ⊙ $General, Family$, Goodyear/auto, Walgreens, Walmart, Winn-Dixie, S ⛽ Day&Night/dsl
238b	I-610 W (from wb)
237	Elysian Fields Ave, N 🍴 Mardi Gras Trkstp/Subway/dsl ⊙ Lowe's
236c	St. Bernard Ave
236b	LA 39, N Claiborne Ave
236a	Esplanade Ave, downtown
235b	Poydras St, N ⊙ 🏥, S ⊙ to Superdome, downtown
235a	Orleans Ave, to Vieux Carre, French Qtr, S ⛽ Chevron/dsl 🛏 Clarion, Marriott, Sheraton
234a	US 90A, Claiborne Ave, to Westbank, S ⊙ Superdome
232	US 61, Airline Hwy, Tulane Ave, N 🍴 Burger King, S ⛽ Exxon, Shell 🍴 McDonald's, Popeye's, Rallys, Subway, Wendy's ⊙ Costco/gas, CVS, Family$, Firestone/auto, Pepboys, to Xavier U, USPO, vet
231b	Florida Blvd, WestEnd
231a	Metairie Rd
230	I-610 E (from eb), to Slidell

S L I D E L L

⛑E	**INTERSTATE 10 Cont'd**
Exit #	Services
266	Continued Office Depot, O'Reilly Parts, PepBoys, Petco, Radio Shack, Rouse's Mkt, U-Haul, Walgreens, S ⛽ Chevron/Subway/dsl, Murphy USA/dsl, RaceTrac/dsl 🍴 Applebee's, Big Easy Diner, Cracker Barrel, Fuji Yama Hibachi, Hooters, McAlister's Deli, Outback Steaks, Ruby Tuesday, Sonic, Starbucks, TX Roadhouse, Waffle House 🛏 Days Inn, La Quinta, Value Inn, Wingate Inn ⊙ 🏥, $General, $Tree, AT&T, CVS, Home Depot, Lowe's, repair/transmissions, Rite Aid, vet, Walmart/Subway
265	US 190, Fremaux Ave, N ⛽ Shell/Purple Cow/dsl 🍴 Cheddar's, Felipe's Mexican, Longhorn Steaks, Panera Bread, Starbucks ⊙ Best Buy, Dick's, Kohl's, Michaels, Petsmart, TJ Maxx, Verizon
263	LA 433, Slidell, N ⛽ Exxon/Circle K/dsl, Shell/dsl, Valero 🍴 Oishii Buffet, Waffle House 🛏 Hampton Inn, Super 8 ⊙ repair, S ⛽ Kangaroo/Subway/scales/dsl, Valero/dsl 🍴 McDonald's, Taco Bell, Wendy's 🛏 Holiday Inn ⊙ Buick/GMC, Chevrolet/Cadillac, Chrysler/Dodge/Jeep, Ford, Honda, Hyundai, Kia, Mazda, Nissan, NO East RV Park (1mi), Pinecrest RV Park, Toyota/Scion
261	Oak Harbor Blvd, Eden Isles, N ⛽ Exxon/Circle K/dsl 🍴 Waffle House 🛏 Sleep Inn, S ⛽ Shell/Subway/dsl ⊙ Bayou Country Store
255mm	Lake Pontchartrain
254	US 11, to Northshore, Irish Bayou, S ⛽ Texaco/dsl

LA

NEW ORLEANS AREA

INTERSTATE 10 Cont'd

Exit #	Services
229	Bonnabel Blvd
228	Causeway Blvd, N ⛽ Exxon/dsl, Shell/dsl 🍴 Buffalo Wild Wings, Cheesecake Factory, Cucina Italiana, Outback Steaks, PF Chang's, Red Lobster, Ruth's Chris Steaks, TGIFriday's 🛏 Best Western, Hampton Inn, Ramada ⊙ Dick's, Dillard's, JC Penney, Macy's, Whole Foods Mkt, S ⛽ DZ, Exxon/Circle K 🍴 IHOP, Little Tokyo 🛏 Courtyard, Days Inn, Extended Stay America, Holiday Inn, La Quinta, Residence Inn, Sheraton
226	Clearview Pkwy, Huey Long Br, N ⛽ Chevron/dsl, Exxon/Circle K/dsl 🍴 Cafe Dumonde, Cane's, Chili's, Copeland's Cheesecake Bistro, Corky's BBQ, Don's Seafood Hut, Hooters, Houston's Rest., Izzo's Burrito, Jimmy John's, Popeye's, Romano Italian, Starbucks, Taco Bell, Taco Tico, Zea Rotisserie 🛏 Sleep Inn ⊙ Hancock Fabrics, Sears/auto, Target, Tire Kingdom, Walgreens, S ⛽ Chevron, Danny&Clyde 🍴 Beijing Chinese, Burger King, Piccadilly, Smoothie King, Subway 🛏 Sun Suites, Super 8 ⊙ AT&T, Buick/GMC, Firestone/auto
225	Veterans Blvd, N ⛽ Chevron, DZ/dsl, Shell 🍴 Bonefish, Burger King, Coyote Blues, Denny's, Hooters, McDonald's, Panera Bread, Pei Wei 🛏 La Quinta ⊙ CVS Drug, Honda, Hyundai, Radio Shack, Rite Aid, Rouses Mkt, URGENT CARE, S ⛽ Shell/dsl 🍴 Burger King, Casa Garcia, Chuck-eCheese, Little Caesars, Louisiana Purchase Kitchen, New Orleans Burgers, O'Henry's, Popeye's, Starbucks, Subway, Tiffin Pancakes, Wendy's 🛏 Evergreen Inn, Sheraton ⊙ $General, Acura, Best Buy, BigLots, BMW, Chevrolet, GNC, Home Depot, Jo-Ann Fabrics, Kia, K-Mart, Lexus, Michaels, Nissan, Office Depot, PepBoys, Petsmart, TJ Maxx, Verizon, vet, VW, Walgreens, Walmart
224	Power Blvd (from wb)
223b a	LA 49, Williams Blvd, N ⛽ DZ/dsl, Exxon/dsl, Shell/dsl 🍴 Cafe Dumonde, Cane's Chicken, Casa Tequila, Fisherman's Cove, IHOP, Papa's Pizza, Popeye's, Rally's, Subway, Taco Bell, Wendy's 🛏 Fairfield Inn ⊙ $Tree, AutoZone, Dillards, Family$, Ford, Macy's, Office Depot, PetCo, Save-a-Lot Foods, Target, TrueValue, Walmart Mkt S ⛽ Exxon/Circle K/dsl, Shell 🍴 American Pie Diner, Brick Oven, Don Jose's Grill, Dot's Diner, KFC/LJ Silver, McDonald's, Pollo Campero, Prime Time Steaks/Seafood, Quiznos, Sonic, Subway, Taco Tico 🛏 Inn, Comfort Suites, Contempra Inn, Country Inn&Suites, Crowne Plaza, DoubleTree, EconoLodge, Extended Stay America, La Quinta ⊙ $General, CVS Drug, Family$, Firestone/auto, Goodyear/auto, NAPA, Tire Kingdom, Toyota/Scion, U-Haul, USPO, Winn-Dixie
221	Loyola Dr, N ⛽ Chevron, Circle K, Exxon/Circle K/dsl, Shell/dsl 🍴 Church's, Little Caesar's, McDonald's, Popeye's, Rally's, Subway, Taco Bell, VooDoo BBQ ⊙ Advance Parts, Sam's Club/gas, S ⛽ Citgo/dsl, DZ 🍴 Michelle's Rest., Wendy's 🛏 Sleep Inn ⊙ $General, Family$, info
220	I-310 S, to Houma
214mm	Lake Pontchartrain
210	I-55N (from wb)
209	I-55 N, US 51, to Jackson, LaPlace, Hammond, N ⛽ Shell/Huddle House/casino/dsl 🛏 Suburban Lodge, S ⛽ Chevron/dsl, Circle K/dsl, Pilot/Subway/dsl/24hr/scales 🍴 Burger King, McDonald's, Waffle House, Wendy's 🛏 Best Western, Days Inn, Hampton Inn, Holiday Inn Express, Quality Inn
207mm	weigh sta both lanes
206	LA 3188 S, La Place, S ⛽ Citgo/dsl, Shell/dsl ⊙ H, Chrysler/Dodge/Jeep, Ford, Goodyear/auto
194	LA 641 S, to Gramercy, S 4-6 mi ⛽ Chevron, Shell, Taylors/dsl 🍴 Golden Grove Rest, McDonald's, Popeye's ⊙ H, plantations
187	US 61, N to Sorrento, S to Gramercy
182	LA 22, Sorrento, N ⛽ Shell/Popeye's/dsl, Texaco/dsl, S ⛽ Chevron/Subway/dsl/scales/24hr, SJ/dsl 🍴 McDonald's, Waffle House ⊙ tourist info
179	LA 44, Gonzales, N 1 mi ⛽ Exxon/Popingo's Cafe/dsl, Murphy USA/dsl 🍴 Alabasha Cafe, Subway ⊙ $General, Buick/GMC, Fred's Store, Walgreens
177	LA 30, Gonzales, N ⛽ Cracker Barrel/dsl, Shell/dsl 🍴 Burger King, El Paso Mexican, Jack-in-the-Box, McDonald's, Outback Steaks, Taco Bell, Taco Bell, Waffle House 🛏 Best Inn, Best Western, Budget Inn, Clarion, Highland Inn, Western Inn ⊙ H, Home Depot, S ⛽ Chevron/dsl, RaceTrac/dsl, Shell/dsl 🍴 Chili's, Cracker Barrel, Don's Seafood Hut, KFC, Logan's Roadhouse, Popeye's, Sonic, Starbucks, Subway, Tang Buffet, Wendy's 🛏 Comfort Suites, Hampton Inn, Holiday Inn Express, La Quinta, SpringHill Suites, Supreme Inn, TownePlace Suites ⊙ Cabela's, Tanger/famous brands, Vesta RV Park
173	LA 73, to Geismar, Prairieville, N ⛽ Shell/dsl ⊙ vet, S ⛽ Chevron/dsl, Exxon/dsl, Mobil/McDonald's/dsl, RaveTrac/dsl, Sunoco/dsl 🍴 Athenos Cafe, Burger King, DeAngelo's Pizza, Griffin Grill, Hot Wok, Las Palmas Mexican, Papa Murphy's, Pizza Hut, Popeye's, Smoothie King, Sonic, Subway ⊙ Family$, Harvest Foods, repair, Twin Lakes RV Park (1mi), Walgreens
166	LA 42, LA 427, Highland Rd, Perkins Rd, N ⛽ Chevron/Church's/dsl, Exxon/Circle K/dsl 🍴 Las Palmas Mexican, Popeye's, Ruffino's Italian, Sonic, Starbucks, Waffle House ⊙ Alexander's Mkt, funpark, Goodyear/auto, Home Depot, Tire Pros, S ⛽ Shell/BBQ/dsl, Texaco/dsl 🍴 Subway
163	Siegen Lane, N ⛽ Chevron, RaceTrac/dsl, Shell/Circle K/dsl 🍴 Arby's, Burger King, Cane's, CC's Coffee, Chee Burger, Chick-fil-A, China 1, CiCi's Pizza, Hooters, IHOP, Jason's Deli, McAlister's, McDonald's, Olive Garden, PoBoy Express, Ribs Chophouse, Smoothie King, Subway, Taco Bell, Twin Peaks Rest., Waffle House, Whataburger, Which Witch? 🛏 Best Western, Days Inn, Hampton Inn, Holiday Inn Express, La Quinta, Microtel, Motel 6, Super 8 ⊙ $Tree, Advance Parts, AT&T, BigLots, Cadillac, CarMax, Firestone/auto, Harley-Davidson, Honda, Kia, Office Depot, PetCo, Radio Shack, Ross, Target, Verizon, S 🍴 Backyard Burger, Chili's, Chuck-eCheese, Honeybaked Ham, Joe's Crabshack, Teppanyaki, TX Roadhouse, Zapata's Mexican 🛏 Courtyard, Residence Inn ⊙ Jo-Ann, Kohl's, Lowe's/Subway, Old Navy, Petsmart, Sam's Club/gas, TJ Maxx, Walmart/Subway, World Mkt
162	Bluebonnet Rd, N ⛽ Chevron/dsl 🍴 Albasha Rest., Cadillac Cafe, Kabuki Japanese 🛏 Wyndham Garden ⊙ vet, S ⛽ Raceway 🍴 Bar Louie, BJ's Brewhouse, Copeland's Cheesecake Bistro, J Alexander's, King Buffet, Logan's Roadhouse, Pluckers Wing Bar, Ralph&Kacoo's, Red Lobster 🛏 Hyatt Place, Renaissance ⊙ H, Best Buy, Dick's, Dillard's, JC Penney, Macy's, Mall of LA, Sears/auto
160	LA 3064, Essen Lane, S ⛽ Exxon/Circle K/dsl, RaceTrac/dsl, Valero 🍴 Burger King, Copeland's Bistro, Domino's, Gatti's Pizza, Ichiban Japanese, India's Rest., McDonald's, Omi Japanese, Piccadilly, Popeye's, Quiznos, Smoothie King, Subway, Taco Bell, Times Grill, Wendy's 🛏 Drury Inn,

INTERSTATE 10 Cont'd

Exit #	Services
160	**Continued**
	Fairfield Inn, Springhill Suites 🅞 🅗, $General, Albertson's, O'Reilly Parts, Rite Aid, Tire Kingdom, URGENT CARE, Walgreens
159	I-12 E, to Hammond
158	College Dr, Baton Rouge, N 🅕 Valero 🅕 Broken Egg Cafe, Cane's, Firehouse Subs, Hooters, Izzo's Grill, Jason's Deli, Koto Rest., Mansurs Rest., Marble Slab Creamery, Melting Pot, On-the-Border, Pelican House Rest., Subway, Sullivan's Rest., Waffle House, Wendy's 🅛 Best Western, Chase Suites, Extended Stay America, Homewood Suites, Marriott 🅞 🅗, Barnes&Noble, Meineke, Midas, S 🅕 Chevron, Exxon/dsl, Shell/Circle K 🅕 Casa Maria Mexican, Chick-fil-A, Chili's, Gino's Rest., IHOP, Jingdu Japanese, Marina's Mexican, McDonald's, Ninfa's Mexican, Panda Express, Ruth's Chris Steaks, Sporting News Grill, Starbucks, Station Grill, Subway, Taco Bell 🅛 Aspen Suites, Comfort Inn, Comfort Suites, Crowne Plaza, DoubleTree, Embassy Suites, Hampton Inn, Holiday Inn, Holiday Inn Express 🅞 $Tree, Albertson's/Sav-On, AutoZone, Hobby Lobby, Office Depot, Radio Shack, USPO, Verizon, Walgreens, Walmart/Subway
157b	Acadian Thwy, N 🅕 Chevron/dsl, Shell/Circle K 🅕 Mestizo Grill, Rib's Rest. 🅛 La Quinta, Radisson 🅞 🅗, S 🅕 Shell/Circle K/dsl 🅕 Acme Oyster House, Coyote Blues Mexican, Galatoire's Bistro, Juban's Rest., Outback Steaks, Pei Wei 🅛 Courtyard 🅞 AT&T, PetCo, Trader Joe's, Tuesday Morning
157a	Perkins Rd (from eb), same as 157b
156b	Dalrymple Dr, S 🅞 to LSU
156a	Washington St
155c	Louise St (from wb)
155b	I-110 N, to Baton Rouge bus dist, 🅞 🖻
155a	LA 30, Nicholson Dr, Baton Rouge, N 🅛 Belle Hotel, S 🅕 Snell/Circle K/dsl 🅞 to LSU
154mm	Mississippi River
153	LA 1, Port Allen, N 🅕 Chevron, Shell/Circle K/dsl 🅕 Church's, Pizza Hut 🅞 AutoZone, Family$, Kenworth, NAPA, O'Reilly Parts, repair, Walgreens, S 🅕 Chevron, LA 1S TP/Exxon/Casino/dsl/scales/24hr, RaceTrac/dsl 🅕 Burger King, Domino's, Hardee's, Smoothie King, Waffle House 🅛 Magnuson Hotel 🅞 $General, $Tree, AT&T, Verizon, Walmart/Subway
151	LA 415, to US 190, N 🅕 Cash's Trk Plaza/dsl/scales/casino, Chevron/dsl, Emerald Plaza Trkstp/Champs Chicken/dsl, Exxon/dsl, Nino's/dsl/casino, Shell/Blimpie/dsl 🅕 Bergeron's Cajun, Burger King, KFC/Taco Bell, McDonald's, Popeye's, Subway, Waffle House 🅛 Best Western, Comfort Suites, Hampton Inn, Holiday Inn Express, Quality Inn, West Inn 🅞 $General, S 🅕 Valero/dsl/24hr, Loves/Arby's/dsl/scales/24hr 🅛 Audubon Inn, Motel 6, Super 8 🅞 truck repair
139	LA 77, Grosse Tete, N 🅕 Shell/Subway/dsl 🅕 Big Heads BBQ 🅞 Chevrolet, S 🅕 Tiger/Country Store/dsl/rest./@
135	LA 3000, to Ramah
127	LA 975, to Whiskey Bay
126.5mm	Pilot Channel of Whiskey Bay
122mm	Atchafalaya River
121	Butte La Rose, **visitors ctr/🆁🆂, both lanes, full facilities, litter barrels, petwalk, 🖻 tourist info, vending** S 🅕 Lazy Cajun Grill (2mi) 🅞 Frenchman's Wilderness Camground (.5mi)
115	LA 347, to Cecilia, Henderson, N 🅕 Shamrock/dsl, Texaco/dsl 🅕 Chicken on the Bayou, Landry's Seafood 🅛 Holiday Inn Express 🅞 casinos, S 🅕 Chevron/dsl,

115	**Continued**
	Exxon/Subway/dsl, Shell/McDonald's/dsl, Texaco/dsl, Valero/dsl 🅕 Popeye's, Waffle House, 🅞 Exxon/dsl/24hr
109	LA 328, to Breaux Bridge, N 🅕 Shell/dsl, Texaco/Quiznos/dsl/casino 🅛 Microtel, S 🅕 Conoco/dsl, Exxon/Domino's/dsl, Murphy USA/dsl, 🅞 Arby's/dsl/scales/24hr, Valero/Popeye's/dsl 🅕 Burger King, City Buffet, Crazy Bout Cajun, Hacienda Real, McDonald's, Pizza Hut, Sonic, Taco Bell, Waffle House, Wendy's, Zapote Mexican, Zeus 🅛 Sona Inn, Super 8 🅞 $General, $Tree, AT&T, AutoZone, Chevrolet, Chrysler/Dodge/Jeep, city park, Family$, Ford/Lincoln, O'Reilly Parts, Pioneer RV Park, USPO, Verizon, Walgreens, Walmart/Subway, Winn-Dixie
108mm	**weigh sta both lanes**
104	Louisiana Ave, S 🅕 Chick-fil-A, McDonald's, Subway, Taco Bell 🅞 AT&T, GNC, JC Penney, Office Depot, PetCo, Ross, Target, Verizon
103b	I-49 N, to Opelousas
103a	US 167 S, to Lafayette, S 🅕 Chevron/dsl, Murphy USA/dsl, RaceTrac/dsl, Shell/dsl, Valero 🅕 Checkers, KFC, McDonald's, Pizza Hut, Popeye's, Shoney's, Subway, Taco Bell, Waffle House, Wendy's 🅛 Baymont Inn, Best Western, Comfort Inn, EconoLodge, Fairfield Inn, Howard Johnson, La Quinta, Quality Inn, Ramada, Super 8, TravelHost Inn 🅞 🅗, $Tree, CVS Drug, Home Depot, Radio Shack, repair, Super 1 Foods/gas, transmissions, Walmart/Subway
101	LA 182, to Lafayette, N 🅕 Chevron/McDonald's, Shell/dsl, TA/Country Pride/dsl/scales/24hr/@, Valero/Subway/dsl 🅕 Burger King, Waffle House, Whataburger 🅛 Red Roof Inn, S 🅕 Exxon, RaceTrac/dsl, Shell/dsl, Shell/dsl, Texaco 🅕 Cracker Barrel, Popeyes 🅛 Days Inn, Drury Inn, Hilton Garden (2mi), Motel 6, Peartree Inn 🅞 🅗, $General, Advance Parts, Family$, Kia, O'Reilly Parts
100	Ambassador Caffery Pkwy, N 🅕 Exxon/Subway/dsl 🅞 Gauthier's RV Ctr, Peterbilt, Ryder Trucks, S 🅕 Chevron/dsl, RaceTrac/dsl, Shell/dsl 🅕 Burger King, McDonald's, Pizza Hut/Taco Bell, Sonic, Waffle House, Wendy's 🅛 Ambassador Inn, Hampton Inn, Microtel, Sleep Inn 🅞 🅗, Southern Tire Mart
97	LA 93, to Scott, S 🅕 Chevron/McDonald's, Shell/Church's/dsl 🅕 Billy's Cracklings, Fezzo's Seafood, Huddle House, Popeyes, Rochetto's Pizza 🅛 Comfort Inn, Holiday Inn Express, Howard Johnson 🅞 Harley-Davidson, KOA
92	LA 95, to Duson, N 🅕 Exxon/dsl/casino/RV dump/scales/24hr, Loves/Chester's/Wendy's/dsl/scales/24hr S 🅕 Chevron/dsl, Roadies/cafe/dsl/casino, Shell/Subway/dsl/casino 🅛 Super 8 🅞 Frog City RV Park

Side labels: **BATON ROUGE** (left), **LAFAYETTE** (right), **LA** (bottom right)

⬆️E   INTERSTATE 10 Cont'd

Exit #	Services
87	LA 35, to Rayne, **N** 🅰 Chevron/dsl, Shell/Subway/casino/dsl 🍴 Burger King, Chef Roy's Rest., McDonald's 🏠 Days Inn 🄾 $General, RV camping, **S** 🅰 Frog City/Exxon/Cajun Rest./dsl, Mobil/dsl, Shop Rite, Valero/dsl 🍴 Candyland Ice Cream, DQ, Gabe's Café, Great Wall Chinese, Pizza Hut, Popeye's, Sonic 🏠 Best Western 🄾 H, Advance Parts, Family$, O'Reilly Parts, Walgreens, Winn-Dixie
82	LA 1111, to E Crowley, **S** 🅰 Chevron/dsl, Murphy USA 🍴 Chili's, Wendy's 🄾 H, $Tree, AT&T, GNC, Lowe's, Radio Shack, Walgreens, Walmart/Subway
80	LA 13, to Crowley, **N** 🅰 Conoco/Exit 80/dsl/rest./24hr 🍴 Fezzo's Seafood/steaks, Waffle House 🏠 Crowley Inn, Days Inn, La Quinta 🄾 Buick/Chevrolet, vet, **S** 🅰 Chevron/dsl, Exxon, Raceway/dsl, Tobacco+/gas, Valero/dsl 🍴 Asian Buffet, Burger King, Cajun Way, China Dragon, El Dorado Mexican, Gatti's Pizza, Golden Seafood, McDonald's, Pizza Hut, PJ's Grill, Popeye's, Sonic, Subway, Taco Bell 🄾 $General, $General, AutoZone, Family$, Ford, O'Reilly Parts, Verizon, Winn-Dixie
76	LA 91, to Iota, **S** 🅰 Petro/Shell/Subway/dsl/scales/24hr
72	Egan, **N** 🄾 Cajun Haven RV Park
65	LA 97, to Jennings, **S** 🅰 Shell/dsl/casino 🏠 Howard Johnson
64	LA 26, to Jennings, **N** 🍴 Los Tres Potrillos 🄾 LA Oil & Gas Park, RV Park, **S** 🅰 Exxon/dsl, EZ Mart, Jennings Trvl Ctr/dsl/casino, Murphy USA/dsl, Valero/dsl 🍴 Burger King, Gatti's Pizza, General Wok Chinese, La Rumba Mexican, McDonald's, Pizza Hut, Popeye's, Shoney's, Sonic, Subway, Taco Bell, Waffle House, Wendy's 🏠 Days Inn, Hampton Inn, Red Carpet Inn 🄾 H, $General, $Tree, AT&T, AutoZone, Buick/GMC, Chrysler/Dodge/Jeep, Fred's Store, O'Reilly Parts, Radio Shack, Verizon, Walgreens, Walmart/Subway
59	LA 395, to Roanoke, **N** 🅰 Petos TrvlCtr/Chevron/dsl/scales/24hr
54	LA 99, Welsh, **S** 🅰 Cajun Lunch/dsl, Citgo/Perky's Pizza, Exxon/dsl/24hr 🍴 Cajun Tales Seafood, DQ
48	LA 101, Lacassine, **S** 🅰 Exxon
44	US 165, to Alexandria, **N** 🄾 Quiet Oaks RV Park (10mi), **S** 🍴 Rabideaux's Cajun 🄾 RV Park
43	LA 383, to Iowa, **N** 🅰 Exxon/Pit Grill/Quiznos/dsl/24hr, 🅛🅞🅥🅔🅢/Hardee's/dsl/scales/24hr 🍴 Burger King 🏠 Howard Johnson Express, La Quinta 🄾 United RV Ctr, **S** 🅰 Citgo/dsl, Shell/McDonald's/dsl, Valero 🍴 Boudreaux's Cajun, Sonic, Subway 🄾 $General, I-10 Outlet/famous brands, RV park
36	LA 397, to Creole, Cameron, **N** 🄾 I-10 RV Camping, Jean Lafitte RV Park (2mi), Jellystone Camping, **S** 🅰 Cash Magic/grill/dsl/RV Dump, Chevron/dsl 🏠 Red Roof Inn 🄾 casino, RV Camping
34	I-210 W, to Lake Charles
33	US 171 N, **N** 🅰 Chevron/dsl, Conoco/dsl, Exxon/dsl, Race-Way/dsl/E85, Shell/ dsl 🍴 Burger King, Church's, Subway, Taco Bell 🏠 Best Value, Best Western, Comfort Suites, Lake Charles Inn, Richmond Suites 🄾 $General, AutoZone, Family$, O'Reilly Parts, to Sam Houston Jones SP, **S** 🏠 EconoLodge, Holiday Inn Express, Motel 6
32	Opelousas St, **N** 🅰 Exxon, **S** 🏠 EconoLodge, Holiday Inn Express, Motel 6
31b	US 90 E, Shattuck St, to LA 14, **N** 🅰 Shell/Subway/dsl/casino, **S** 🅰 Valero/dsl
31a	US 90 bus, Enterprise Blvd, **S** 🍴 Popeye's

30b	downtown
30a	LA 385, N Lakeshore Dr, Ryan St, **N** 🅰 Exxon 🍴 Steamboat Bill's Rest., Waffle House 🏠 Days Inn, Oasis Inn, **S** 🍴 Wendy's 🏠 Best Suites
29	LA 385 (from eb), same as 30a
28mm	Calcasieu Bayou, Lake Charles
27	LA 378, to Westlake, **N** 🅰 Chevron/dsl, Conoco/dsl, Shell/dsl, Valero 🍴 Burger King, El Tapatia Mexican, McDonald's, Popeye's, RoundTop Burger, Sonic, Subway 🄾 $General, Bumper Parts, Family$, Fred's, MarketBasket, O'Reilly Parts, to Sam Houston Jones SP (6mi), **S** 🏠 Inn at the Isle 🄾 Riverboat Casinos
26	US 90 W, Southern Rd, Columbia, **N** 🅰 Exxon/dsl
25	I-210 E, to Lake Charles
23	LA 108, to Sulphur, **N** 🅰 Chevron, Circle K, Exxon/dsl, Murphy USA, Shell 🍴 Burger King, Cane's, Chili's, China Wok, Hollier's Cajun Diner, Japanese Steaks, McDonald's, Popeye's, Subway, Taco Bell, Wendy's 🏠 Quality Inn 🄾 $General, $Tree, AT&T, Bumper Parts, Lowe's, Radio Shack, Verizon, Walgreens, Walmart/Subway **S** 🅰 Chevron/Jack-in-the-Box/dsl, Citgo/Cash Magic/dsl, Sulphur Trkstp/Shell/Subway/dsl/casino 🍴 Cracker Barrel, Waffle House 🏠 Best Western, Comfort Suites, Crossland Suites, Days Inn, Holiday Inn Express, Studio 6, Super 8 🄾 Southern Tire Mart
21	LA 3077, Arizona St, **N** 🅰 Conoco/dsl, Shell 🍴 Boiling Point Cajun, China Taste, Papa John's, Starbucks 🄾 $General, AT&T, Chevrolet, CVS Drug, Ford, GNC, Kroger/gas, NAPA, Walgreens, **S** 🅰 Chevron/dsl, Valero/dsl/casino 🄾 H, Hidden Ponds RV Park
20	LA 27, to Sulphur, **N** 🅰 Chevron/dsl, Circle K, Conoco/dsl, Gulf, Valero/dsl 🍴 Burger King, Casa Ole Mexican, Checkers, Gatti's Pizza, Hollier's Cajun, Hong Kong Chinese, Joe's Pizza/pasta, Johnny T's Grill, La Rumba Mexican, LeBleu's Landing Cajun, Little Caesar's, McDonald's, Pitt Grill Cajun, Popeye's, Subway, Taco Bell, Wendy's 🏠 Best Value, Hampton Inn, Motel 6 🄾 Brookshire Bros/gas, Family$, Firestone/auto, Goodyear/auto, Jiffy Lube, **S** 🅰 Conoco/dsl, Shell/dsl 🍴 Navroskey's Burgers, Pizza Hut, Sonic, Waffle House 🏠 Baymont Inn, Candlewood Suites, Fairfield Inn, Holiday Inn, La Quinta, Super Inn, Wingate Inn 🄾 H, casino, Stine, to Creole Nature Trail
8	LA 108, Vinton, **N** 🅰 Chevron/dsl, Exxon/dsl 🍴 Cajun Cowboy's Rest. 🄾 V RV Park
7	LA 3063, Vinton, **N** 🅰 Exxon/dsl 🍴 Burger King, Sonic, Subway 🄾 $General, casino, **S** 🅰 🅛🅞🅥🅔🅢/Arby's/dsl/scales/24hr
4	US 90, LA 109, Toomey, **N** 🅰 Cash Magic/dsl/grill/casino, Chevron/dsl/casino 🄾 truck repair, **S** 🅰 Exxon/dsl, Shell/dsl/rest 🍴 Subway 🄾 casinos, RV Park
2.5mm	weigh sta wb lanes
1.5mm	Welcome Ctr eb, full ♿ facilities, litter barrels, petwalk, 🄲, picnic tables
1	(from wb), Sabine River Turnaround
0mm	Louisiana/Texas state line, Sabine River

⬆️E   INTERSTATE 12

Exit #	Services
85c	I-10 E, to Biloxi. **I-12 begins/ends on I-10, exit 267.**
85b	I-59 N, to Hattiesburg
85a	I-10 W, to New Orleans
83	US 11, to Slidell, **N** 🅰 Chevron/dsl, Exxon/dsl, Valero/dsl 🍴 Burger King, McDonald's, Sonic, Waffle House 🄾 $General, **S** 🅰 Shell/dsl 🄾 H,

Side markers (left): **CROWLEY · JENNINGS · LAKE CHARLES**

Side markers (right): **SULPHUR**

LA

➤E INTERSTATE 12 Cont'd

Exit #	Services

C O V I N G T O N (vertical label, left margin)

80 — Airport Dr, North Shore Blvd, N ⛽ Kangaroo/Krystal/dsl 🍴 IHOP, PJ's Coffee, Quiznos, Smoothie King, Sonic 🛏 Comfort Inn ⊙ AT&T, Petsmart, Ross, Target, S ⛽ Chevron, Shell/dsl 🍴 Burger King, Chili's, ChuckECheese's, McDonald's, Olive Garden, Pizza Hut/Taco Bell, Starbucks, Subway, Vera's Seafood, Wendy's, Zea Grill 🛏 Candlewood Suites, Homewood Suites, La Quinta ⊙ $Tree, Best Buy, Dillard's, Goodyear/auto, Home Depot, JC Penney, mall, Marshalls, Office Depot, Sam's Club/gas, Sears/auto, Walgreens, Walmart

74 — LA 434, to Lacombe, N ⛽ Chevron/Subway/dsl ⊙ 🏥, Steve's RV Ctr, S ⊙ Big Branch Marsh NWR

68 — LA 1088 to Mandeville

65 — LA 59, to Mandeville, N ⛽ Chevron/dsl, Danny&Clyde's/cafe, Shell 🍴 Popeye's, Sonic, Subway, Waffle House 🛏 Comfort Suites ⊙ tourist info, S ⛽ Kangaroo/Arby's/dsl, Texaco/Domino's/dsl 🍴 Liu's Wok, McDonald's, PJ's Coffee, Quiznos, Wow Cafe ⊙ camping, to Fontainebleau SP, vet, Winn-Dixie

63b a — US 190, Covington, Mandeville, N ⛽ Chevron, Exxon, RaceTrac, Shell/Circle K 🍴 4 Seasons Chinese, Acme Oyster House, Albasha Greek, Applebee's, Baskin-Robbins, Burger King, Cane's, Chick-fil-A, CiCi's Pizza, Copeland's Grill, Don's Seafood, Garcias Mexican, HoneyBaked Ham, IHOP, Isabella's Pizza, Lee's Hamburgers, Mellow Mushroom Cafe, Mi Casa Mexican, Osaka Japanese, Outback Steaks, Picadilly, Rolly Polly Sandwiches, Sonic, Subway, Thai Chili, Waffle House, Wendy's 🛏 Best Western, Clarion, Comfort Inn, Country Inn&Suites, Courtyard, Hampton Inn, Hilton Garden, Homewood Suites, Residence Inn, Staybridge Suites, Super 8 ⊙ Ace Hardware, AT&T, AutoZone, Books-A-Million, Chevrolet, Chrysler/Dodge/Jeep, CVS Drug, Firestone/auto, GNC, Home Depot, Honda, Hyundai, Lincoln, Lowe's, Nissan, Office Depot, Petsmart, Rouses Mkt, Subaru, Toyota, Verizon, Walmart S ⊙ 🏥, st police, **to New Orleans via toll causeway**

60 — Pinnacle Pkwy, to Covington, same as 59

59 — LA 21, to Covington, Madisonville, N ⛽ Chevron/dsl, Kangaroo, Shell 🍴 5 Guys Burgers, Buffalo Wild Wings, Cafe Du Monde, Carreta's Grill, Coldstone, Cracker Barrel, Firehouse Subs, Golden Wok, Isabella's Pizza, Italian Pie, Izzo's Burrito, Jerk's Island Grill, Lee's Hamburgers, McDonald's, Olive Garden, Panda Buffet, Panera Bread, Pek's Seafood Grill, PJ's Coffee, Sake Steaks, Smoothie King, Steak'n Shake, Subway, TX Roadhouse, Wow Cafe 🛏 La Quinta ⊙ 🏥, $Tree, AT&T, CVS Drug, Hobby Lobby, Kohl's, URGENT CARE, Walgreens, Winn-Dixie, S ⛽ Texaco/Domino's 🍴 Chick-fil-A, ChuckECheese's, Longhorn Steaks, Quiznos, Taco Bell, Wendy's 🛏 Hampton Inn, Holiday Inn Express ⊙ AT&T, Belk, Best Buy, Fairview Riverside SP, GNC, JC Penney, Marshall's, Michael's, Ross, Sam's Club/gas, Target, World Mkt

57 — LA 1077, to Goodbee, Madisonville, S ⛽ QuickWay/PoBoys/dsl 🍴 Best Wok, Pizza Hut, PJ's Coffee, Subway ⊙ Family RV Park, to Fairview Riverside SP

47 — LA 445, to Robert, N **1-3 mi** ⊙ Jellystone Camping, to Global Wildlife Ctr

42 — LA 3158, to 🔆, N ⛽ Chevron/Quiznos/dsl/24hr, Texaco/dsl 🍴 McDonald's 🛏 Friendly Inn, S ⛽ Shell/Chester's/dsl ⊙ 🏥, Berryland RV Ctr

40 — US 51, to Hammond, N ⛽ RaceTrac/dsl, Shell/Circle K 🍴 Burger King, Cane's, China Garden, Church's, Coldstone, Don's Seafood, IHOP, Jimmy John's, McDonald's,

---

H A M M O N D (vertical label)

40 — Continued
Nagoya Rest, Olive Garden, Pizza Hut, Quiznos, Ryan's, Santa Fe Steaks, Smoothie King, Sonic, Subway, Taco Bell, Wendy's 🛏 Best Western, Holiday Inn, Motel 6, Quality Inn, Supreme Inn ⊙ AT&T, Best Buy, Books-A-Million, Dillard's, Harley-Davidson, JC Penney, mall, Rite Aid, Sears/auto, Target, TJ Maxx, U-Haul, Verizon, Walgreens, S ⛽ Petro/Mobil/Subway/dsl/scales/24hr/@, 🍴Arby's/dsl/scales/24hr, Shell/dsl 🍴 Waffle House 🛏 Colonial Inn, Days Inn, La Quinta ⊙ 🏥, $General, Blue Beacon, SpeedCo

38b a — I-55, N to Jackson, S to New Orleans

37mm — weigh sta both lanes

35 — Pumpkin Ctr, Baptist, N ⛽ Exxon/dsl, Texaco ⊙ $General, Dixie Camping World RV Service/Supplies, Punkin RV Park (2mi), S ⛽ Chevron/Bayou Boyz/dsl

32 — LA 43, to Albany, N ⛽ Big River/dsl, Chevron/Subway/dsl, Exxon/dsl, S ⛽ Potluck/dsl ⊙ to Tickfaw SP (11mi), tourist info

29 — LA 441, to Holden, N ⛽ 1Stop/dsl ⊙ Berryland Campers

22 — LA 63, to Frost, Livingston, N ⛽ Chevron/dsl 🍴 Hi-Ho BBQ, Subway, Wayne's BBQ ⊙ Carters Foods, Family$, Thrift Town Drug, S ⊙ Lakeside RV Park (1mi)

19 — to Satsuma, Colyell, N ⛽ Exxon/dsl

15 — LA 447, to Walker, N ⛽ Murphy Express/dsl, Shell/Subway/dsl, Texaco/dsl 🍴 Burger King, Domino's, Jack-in-the-Box, McDonald's, Papa John's, Papa Murphy's, Pizza Hut, Popeye's, Quiznos, Sherwood PoBoy's, Sonic, Taco Bell, Waffle House, Wendy's 🛏 La Quinta ⊙ $General, $Tree, AutoZone, NAPA, O'Reilly Parts, Verizon, vet, Walgreens, Walmart/Subway, Winn-Dixie, S ⛽ Chevron/dsl

12 — LA 1036, Juban Rd, N **2 mi** ⛽ Valero/dsl

10 — LA 3002, to Denham Springs, N ⛽ Chevron, Circle K, RaceTrac/dsl, Shell/Circle K/dsl 🍴 Arby's, Baskin-Robbins, Burger King, Cactus Café, Cane's, Chili's, Domino's, Don's Seafood, Gatti's Pizza, IHOP, McDonald's, Papa John's, Papi's Fajita, Pizza Hut, Popeye's, Ron's Seafood, Ryan's, Sonic, Starbucks, Subway, Taco Bell, Waffle House, Wendy's 🛏 Best Western, Hampton Inn, Quality Inn, Western Inn ⊙ $General, $Tree, Advance Parts, Albertsons, AT&T, AutoZone, CVS Drug, Home Depot, Meineke, Office Depot, O'Reilly Parts, PetCo, Radio Shack, Rite Aid, Tire Kingdom, URGENT CARE, Verizon, Walgreens, Walmart S ⛽ 🍴/Subway/dsl/scales/24hr, Shell 🍴 Backyard Burger, Hooters, Islamorada Fish Co, Longhorn Steaks, Piccadilly, VooDoo BBQ 🛏 Days Inn, Highland Inn ⊙ Bass Pro Shops, Chrysler/Dodge/Jeep, Ford, KOA, Sam's Club/gas, Walgreens

8.5mm — Amite River

Map

Louisiana state map showing route highlights. Cities labeled: Minden, Monroe, Shreveport, Bawcomville, Stonewall, Mansfield, Coushatta, Pleasant Hill, Natchitoches, Provencal, Coifax, Flatwoods, Alexandria, Woodworth, Lecompte, Pine Prairie, Opelousas, Baton Rouge, Lake Charles, Lafayette. Highway markers: 20, 220, 49, 12, 10. Labels "LA" and state outline shown.

INTERSTATE 12 Cont'd

BATON ROUGE

Exit #	Services
7	O'Neal Lane, N 🅰 Mobil 🅻 La Quinta, Quality Inn 🅾 Hobby Lobby, Toyota/Scion, S 🅰 RaceTrac/dsl, Shell, Texaco/Subway/dsl 🅸 Backyard Burger, China King, Las Palmas Mexican, Little Caesars, LoneStar Steaks, McDonald's, Pizza Hut/Taco Bell, Popeye's, Sonic, Waffle House, Wendy's 🅾 🅷 $Tree, AutoZone, O'Reilly Parts, Radio Shack, Walgreens, Walmart/Subway
6	Millerville Rd, N 🅰 Chevron/dsl 🅸 Chick-fil-A, Chili's 🅾 Best Buy, Lowe's, Office Depot, Petsmart, Super Target, S 🅰 Texaco/dsl 🅸 Subway, Tiger Bait Grill 🅾 Ace Hardware
4	Sherwood Forest Blvd, N 🅰 Exxon, Shell/Circle K/dsl 🅸 Burger King, ChuckECheese, Egg Roll King, Jack-in-the-Box, Kung Fu Buffet, McDonald's, Popeye's, Sonic, Subway, Taco Bell, Waffle House 🅻 Crossland Suites, Red Roof Inn, Super 8, Value Place 🅾 Fred's, Goodyear/auto, Rite Aid, S 🅰 RaceTrac/dsl, Shell 🅸 Baskin-Robbins, Cane's, Dunkin Donuts, Nagoya, Picadilly, Podnuh's BBQ, Sherwood PoBoys 🅻 Calloway Inn 🅾 AT&T, auto care
2b	US 61 N, N 🅰 B-Quik/dsl, Chevron/dsl, Rende's/dsl 🅸 Applebee's, Chinese Inn, Cracker Barrel, Little Caesars, McDonald's, Panda Buffet, Pizza Hut/Taco Bell, Subway 🅻 Holiday Inn, Knights Inn, Magnuson Hotel, Microtel, Motel 6, Ramada Inn, Sleep Inn 🅾 $Tree, Albertsons/gas, Dodge, Marshall's, Michael's, Nissan, PepBoys, repair/transmissions, SteinMart, Toyota/Scion, Walgreens, Walmart Mkt
2a	US 61 S, S 🅰 Chevron, Circle K, Exxon/Circle K/dsl, Ride USA 🅸 Burger King, China 1, Isabella's Pizza, McDonald's, Subway, Waffle House 🅻 Deluxe Inn 🅾 Costco/gas, Home Depot, Hyundai, Volvo
1b	LA 1068, to LA 73, Essen Lane, N 🅰 Shell/Circle K/dsl 🅸 Cane's, McDonald's, VooDoo BBQ 🅾 🅷 Family$, Hancock Fabrics, Hi-Nabor Foods, Radio Shack, vet
1a	I-10 (from wb). **I-12 begins/ends on I-10, exit 159 in Baton Rouge**

INTERSTATE 20

Exit #	Services
189mm	Louisiana/Mississippi state line, Mississippi River
187mm	weigh sta both lanes
186	US 80, Delta, S 🅰 Chevron/Subway/dsl/24hr
184mm	🆁🆂 wb, full 🅳 facilities, litter barrels, petwalk, 🅲, 🅱 RV dump
182	LA 602, Mound
173	LA 602, Richmond
171	US 65, Tallulah, N 🅰 Chevron/Subway/dsl, Kangaroo/dsl 🅸 Chopsticks Buffet, McDonald's, Wendy's 🅻 Days Inn, Super 8 🅾 🅷, S 🅰 Exxon/dsl/scales, Loves/Arby's/dsl/scales/24hr, TA/Country Pride/dsl/scales/24hr/@, Texaco 🅸 Red Top Grill
164mm	Tensas River
157	LA 577, Waverly, N 🅰 Tiger Trkstp/rest./dsl/24hr 🅾 to Tensas River NWR, S 🅰 Chevron/Hunt Bros Pizza/dsl/24hr, Shell/rest./dsl/24hr 🅾 Casino
155mm	Bayou Macon
153	LA 17, Delhi, N 🅰 Chevron/Subway, Texaco/dsl 🅸 Boomers, Burger King, Pizza Hut, Sonic 🅾 🅷, $General, AT&T, Brookshire's Foods, Family$, Fred's, USPO, S 🅰 Valero/dsl 🅻 Best Western, Executive Inn
148	LA 609, Dunn

RAYVILLE

145	LA 183, rd 202, Holly Ridge
141	LA 583, Bee Bayou Rd
138	US 425, Rayville, N 🅰 Bud's, 🅸/Wendy's/dsl/scales/24hr 🅸 Fox's Pizza, McDonald's, Sonic 🅻 Days Inn 🅾 🅷, $General, $Tree, AutoZone, Brookshire's Foods, Buick/Chevrolet, Family$, repair, Verizon, Walmart S 🅰 Chevron/Subway/dsl/24hr, Exxon/Circle K/Quiznos/dsl, RaceWay/dsl 🅸 Big John's Rest., Popeye's, Waffle House 🅻 Super 8
135mm	Boeuf River
132	LA 133, Start, N 🅰 Exxon/dsl
128mm	Lafourche Bayou
124	LA 594, Millhaven, N 🅰 EZ Mart/dsl 🅾 st police, to Sage Wildlife Area
120	Garrett Rd, Pecanland Mall Dr, N 🅰 Chevron/dsl 🅸 Applebee's, ChuckECheese, Copeland's Rest., Eastern Empire Buffet, IHOP, Longhorn Steaks, McAlister's, O'Charleys, Olive Garden, Red Lobster, Ronin Habachi, Sonic 🅻 Courtyard, Residence Inn, TownePlace Suites 🅾 $Tree, AT&T, Belk, Best Buy, Dick's, Dillard's, Firestone/auto, Home Depot, JC Penney, Kohl's, mall, Michael's, Old Navy, PetCo, Petsmart, Ross, Sears/auto, Stein Mart, Target, TJ Maxx, S 🅰 Kangaroo/dsl 🅻 Best Western, Days Inn 🅾 Harley-Davidson, Hope's Campers, Lowe's, Ouachita RV Park, Pecanland RV Park, Sam's Club/gas
118b a	US 165, N 🅰 Valero/dsl 🅻 Clarion, Motel 6, Stratford House Inn 🅾 Hyundai, Kia, Nissan, to NE LA U, S 🅰 Chevron, Conoco/dsl, Exxon, Now Save/dsl, Shell/Circle K 🅸 Burger King, Capt D's, Church's, KFC, McDonald's, Popeye's, Sonic, Subway, Taco Bell, Wendy's 🅻 Comfort Suites, Hampton Inn, Motel 6, Super 8
117b	LA 594, Texas Ave, N 🅰 Now Save/deli/dsl
117a	Hall St, Monroe, N 🅾 🅷, Civic Ctr
116b	US 165 bus, LA 15, Jackson St, N 🅾 🅷,
116a	5th St, Monroe
115	LA 34, Mill St, N 🅰 Chevron

MONROE

114	LA 617, Thomas Rd, N 🅰 Murphy USA, RaceWay/dsl 🅸 5 Guys Burgers, Burger King, Cane's, Capt D's, Cheddar's, Chick-fil-A, El Chico, El Chile Verde, Grandy's, Hibachi Grill, IHOP, KFC, McAlister's Deli, McDonald's, Podnuh's BBQ, Popeye's, Subway, Taco Bell, Waffle House, Wendy's 🅻 Best Value Inn, Super 8, Wingate Inn 🅾 🅷 AT&T, BigLots, Hobby Lobby, Office Depot, Rite Aid, Walgreens, Walmart/McDonald's S 🅰 Chevron, Exxon/Circle K/Subway/dsl 🅸 Buffalo Wild Wings, Chili's, Cracker Barrel, El Sombrero, Four Bros Rest., Genghis Grill, Hooters, Logan's Roadhouse, Outback Steaks, Peking Chinese, Pizza Hut, Ronin Hibachi, Sonic, Waffle House 🅻 Best Western, Comfort Inn, Motel 6, Quality Inn, Red Roof Inn 🅾 Radio Shack
113	Downing Pines Rd, S 🅻 Hampton Inn, Hilton Garden, Holiday Inn Express 🅾 Chrysler/Dodge/Jeep
112	Well Rd, N 🅰 Conoco, Shell/Circle K/dsl, Texaco/dsl 🅸 Burger King, McDonald's, Sam's Eatery, San Francisco TexMex, Sonic, Subway, Taco Bell, Waffle House, Zaxby's 🅾 Advance Parts, CVS Drug, Mac's Fresh Mkt, vet, Walgreens, S 🅰 🅸/Subway/Wendy's/dsl/scales/24hr 🅾 Pavilion RV Park
108	LA 546, to US 80, Cheniere, N 🅰 Shell/dsl, Smart/dsl
107	Camp Rd, rd 25, Cheniere
103	US 80, Calhoun, N 🅰 Chevron, Shell/rest/dsl/24hr 🅸 Johnny's Pizza (1mi) 🅻 Avant Motel
101	LA 151, to Calhoun, S 🅰 Chevron/Huddle House/Subway/dsl, Exxon 🅸 Sonic
97mm	🆁🆂 wb, full 🅳 facilities, litter barrels, petwalk, 🅲, 🅱 RV dump

LA

INTERSTATE 20 Cont'd

Exit #	Services
95mm	🆁🆂 eb, full ♿ facilities, litter barrels, petwalk, 🚮, 🚐 RV dump
93	LA 145, Choudrant, S 🍴 American 🅾 camping, Jimmy Davis SP
86	LA 33, Ruston, N 🅿 Murphy USA, RaceWay/dsl, Shell/Circle K/Quiznos/dsl, Texaco/dsl 🍴 Arby's, Cane's Chicken, Cheeburger Cheeburger, Chili's, El Jarrito Mexican, Hot Rod BBQ, Huddle House, Log Cabin Grill, Logan's Roadhouse, Portico Grill, Ronin Hibachi, Ryan's, Sonic, Taco Bell, Whataburger, Z Buffet 🛌 Comfort Inn, Days Inn 🅾 $Tree, AT&T, Buick/GMC, Cadillac/Chevrolet, Chrysler/Dodge/Jeep, Ford/Lincoln, Fred's, GNC, Lowe's, Toyota, vet, Walmart/Subway S 🅿 Spirit/dsl 🛌 Fairfield Inn, Holiday Inn Express
85	US 167, Ruston, N 🅿 Chevron/Subway, Exxon, Shell/Circle K 🍴 Applebee's, Burger King, Capt D's, Little Caesars, McDonald's, Peking Chinese, Wendy's 🛌 Hampton Inn, Relax Inn 🅾 $General, Office Depot, Radio Shack, Super 1 Foods, TrueValue, Walgreens, S 🅿 Texaco, Valero/dsl 🍴 Pizza Hut 🛌 Best Value Inn, Sleep Inn 🅾 🏥 Advance Parts, Verizon
84	LA 544, Ruston, S 🅿 Chevron/dsl, Exxon 🍴 Domino's, Johny's Pizza, Pizza Inn, Smoothie King, Starbucks, Subway, Waffle House 🛌 Super 8
81	LA 149, Grambling, S 🅿 Chevron/Church's/dsl, Exxon 🅾 to Grambling St U
78	LA 563, Industry, S 🅿 Texaco/dsl
77	LA 507, Simsboro
69	LA 151, Arcadia, N 🅿 Mobil/Burger King/dsl 🍴 La Fogata Mexican, S 🅿 Exxon/dsl, Gulf/dsl, Shell/Church's/dsl 🍴 El Jarrito Mexican, McDonald's, Sonic, Subway 🛌 Days Inn 🅾 🏥, $General, Brookshire Foods, Bumper Parts, Factory Stores/famous brands, Fred's, tires/repair
67	LA 9, Arcadia, N 🅾 to Lake Claiborne SP, S 🅿 Shell/dsl/repair
61	LA 154, Gibsland, N 🅾 to Lake Claibourne SP
55	US 80, Ada, Taylor
52	LA 532, to US 80, Dubberly, N 🅿 Exxon/dsl, Texaco/CJ's Diner/dsl
49	LA 531, Minden, N 🅿 Loves/Arby's/dsl/scales/24hr, Minden TrkStp/Shell/dsl/rest./24hr, Murphy USA, QuickDraw/Subway/dsl 🍴 KFC (3mi), Pizza Hut (3mi), Taco Bell (3mi) 🅾 Walmart (3mi) S 🍴 truck/tire repair
47	US 371 S, LA 159 N, Minden, N 🅿 Chevron/dsl, Exxon/dsl, Valero/dsl 🍴 Beanie&Bubba's Grill 🛌 Best Western, Exacta Inn/rest., Holiday Inn Express, Southern Inn 🅾 🏥, Ford, S 🅾 camping, to Lake Bistineau SP
44	US 371 N, Cotton Valley, N 🅿 Exxon/Huddle House/dsl 🍴 Crawfish Hole #2, Nicky's Cantina, Sonic 🛌 Minden Motel (2mi) 🅾 Cinnamon Creek RV/camping, Family$, Lakeside RV Camping
38	Goodwill Rd, S 🅿 Gulf/Rainbow Diner/dsl/24hr 🅾 Ammo Plant, truck/trailer repair
33	LA 157, Fillmore, N 🅿 Texaco, S 🅿 Exxon, Loves/Arby's/dsl/scales/24hr 🍴 Pizza Hut, Waffle House 🅾 $General, Family$, Fred's, Lake Bistineau SP, USPO
26	I-220, Shreveport, N 1 mi 🅿 RaceWay/dsl 🛌 Comfort Suites, Holiday Inn, Springhill Suites 🅾 Casino
23	Industrial Dr, N 🅿 Exxon/dsl, Shell/Circle K, Valero/dsl 🍴 McDonald's, Popeye's, Sue's Country Kitchen, Taco Bell, Wendy's 🛌 Ramada Inn 🅾 O'Reilly Parts, RV Repair, st police, S 🅿 Mobil/dsl 🛌 EconoLodge 🅾 Peterbilt, Southern RV Ctr

22	Airline Dr, N 🅿 Citgo/dsl, Mobil/McDonald's/dsl, Shell/Circle K, Valero/dsl 🍴 5 Guys Burgers, Applebee's, Arby's, Burger King, Chili's, China Flag, DQ, Gatti's Pizza, IHOP, Johnny's Pizza, Logan's Roadhouse, Notini's Italian, Popeye's, Red Lobster, Shogun Steaks, Sonic, Starbucks, Subway, Taco Bell, TX Street Steaks, Waffle House 🛌 Country Hearth Inn, Crossland Suites, Rodeway Inn, Super 8 🅾 Albertsons, BigLots, Books-A-Million, CVS Drug, Dillard's, Firestone/auto, JC Penney, K-Mart, mall, Meineke, Michael's, Office Depot, PepBoys, Sears/auto, Tuesday Morning, Verizon, Walgreens, S 🅿 Exxon/dsl 🍴 Beard's Catfish/seafood, Capt John's, Church's, Griff's Burgers, Outback Steaks, Quizno's 🛌 Microtel, Quality Inn, Red Carpet Inn 🅾 🏥, AutoZone, Fred's, Super1 Foods, to Barksdale AFB
21	LA 72, to US 71 S, Old Minden Rd, N 🅿 Shell/Circle K/dsl, Valero 🍴 DAQ's Grill, Denny's, Johnny's Pizza, McDonald's, Pancho's Mexican, Podnah's BBQ, Posado's Mexican, Ralph&Kacoo's, Subway, TX Roadhouse, Whataburger 🛌 Best Value Inn, Hampton Inn, Hilton Garden, Homewood Suites, La Quinta, MainStay Suites, TownePlace Suites 🅾 $General, Bayou RV Ctr, O'Reilly Parts, USPO, VW, S 🅿 RaceWay 🍴 Waffle House, Wendy's 🛌 Days Inn, Motel 6, ValuePlace Inn 🅾 visitor info
20c	to US 71 S, to Barksdale Blvd
20b	LA 3, Benton Rd, same as 21
20a	Hamilton Rd, Isle of Capri Blvd, N 🅿 Circle K 🛌 Comfort Inn, Wingate Inn, S 🅿 Exxon 🛌 Bossier Inn, Travelodge 🅾 casino
19b	Traffic St, Shreveport, N 🛌 Courtyard 🅾 Bass Pro Shop, casino, Chevrolet, S 🅾 casino, downtown
19a	US 71 N, LA 1 N, Spring St, Shreveport, N 🛌 Best Western, Hilton, Shreveport Hotel
18b-d	Fairfield Ave (from wb), S 🅾 🏥, downtown Shreveport
18a	Line Ave, Common St (from eb), S 🅿 1st Stop 🅾 🏥, downtown
17b	I-49 S, to Alexandria
17a	Lakeshore Dr, Linwood Ave
16b	US 79/80, Greenwood Rd, N 🅾 🏥, S 🅿 Citgo/dsl 🍴 El Chico 🛌 Travelodge
16a	US 171, Hearne Ave, N 🅿 Shell/dsl 🍴 Subway 🅾 🏥, vet, S 🅿 Raceway/dsl 🍴 KFC, Wendy's 🛌 Cajun Inn
14	Jewella Ave, Shreveport, N 🅿 Clark/dsl, Phillips 66/dsl, Valero 🍴 Burger King, Church's, McDonald's, Popeye's, Sonic, Subway, Whataburger 🅾 AutoZone, County Mkt Foods, Family$, O'Reilly Parts, Rite Aid, Super 1 Foods, Walgreens
13	Monkhouse Dr, Shreveport, N 🅿 Bro's Cafe 🛌 Days Inn, Ramada, Residence Inn, Super 8, Value Inn, S 🅿 Citgo/dsl, Exxon/Subway/dsl, Valero/dsl 🍴 Waffle House

RUSTON

MINDEN

SHREVEPORT

LA

INTERSTATE 20 Cont'd

Exit #	Services
13	Continued
	🛏 Baymont Inn, Hampton Inn, Holiday Inn Express, Merryton Inn, Moonrider Inn, Motel 6, Quality Inn, Regency Inn Ⓞ to ✈
11	I-220 E, LA 3132 E, to I-49 S
10	Pines Rd, **N** ⛽ Chevron/dsl 🍴 DQ, Johnny's Pizza, Pizza Hut, Popeye's, Sam's Eatery, Subway Ⓞ Meineke, **S** ⛽ Circle K, Exxon/dsl, Murphy USA/dsl, Shell/Circle K/Quiznos/dsl 🍴 Burger King, CiCi's Pizza, Cracker Barrel, Domino's, Dragon Chinese, Great Wall Chinese, IHOP, KFC, McDonald's, Nicky's Mexican, Papa John's, Sonic, Taco Bell, Waffle House, Wendy's, Whataburger 🛏 Comfort Suites, Courtyard, Fairfield Inn, Hilton Garden, Holiday Inn, Homewood Suites, Howard Johnson, La Quinta, Sleep Inn, ValuePlace Inn Ⓞ $Tree, CVS Drug, Family$, GNC, Home Depot, O'Reilly Parts, Radio Shack, Rite Aid, USPO, Verizon, Walgreens, Walmart/Subway
8	US 80, LA 526 E, **N** 🛏 Motel 6 Ⓞ Freightliner, repair, tires, **S** ⛽ Chevron/dsl, Citgo/dsl, Petro/Shell/Iron Skillet/dsl/scales/@ 🍴 Wendy's Ⓞ Blue Beacon, Camper's RV Ctr/park, Tall Pines RV Park (1mi)
5	US 79 N, US 80, to Greenwood, **N** ⛽ Outpost Travel Ctr/dsl, TA/Valero/Country Pride/Subway/dsl/scales/24hr/@ 🛏 Country Inn, Mid Continent Motel Ⓞ RV park, **S** 🍴 Pizza Hut Ⓞ $General, Southern Living RV Park
3	US 79 S, LA 169, Mooringsport, **S** ⛽ ⭗ FLYING J/Denny's/dsl/LP/scales/24hr, ❤Loves/Arby's/dsl/scales/24hr 🍴 Sonic Ⓞ Alligator RV Park (4mi), SpeedCo
2mm	**Welcome Ctr eb, full** 🛏 **facilities, litter barrels, petwalk,** ⟨C⟩, 🚮 **RV dump**
1mm	**weigh sta both lanes**
0mm	Louisiana/Texas state line

INTERSTATE 49

Exit #	Services
	I-49 begins/ends in Shreveport on I-20, exit 17.
206	I-20, E to Monroe, W to Dallas
205	King's Hwy, **E** 🍴 Cane's, McDonald's, Piccadilly's, Taco Bell Ⓞ Dillard's, mall, Sears/auto, **W** ⛽ Valero/dsl 🍴 Burger King, LJ Silver, Subway 🛏 Sleep Inn Ⓞ Ⓗ,
203	Hollywood Ave, Pierremont Rd, **W** ⛽ Chevron/dsl
202	LA 511, E 70th St, **E** ⛽ RaceWay/dsl, **W** ⛽ Circle K 🍴 SC Chicken Ⓞ $General, Family$
201	LA 3132, to Dallas, Texarkana
199	LA 526, Bert Kouns Loop, **E** ⛽ Chevron/Arby's/dsl/24hr, Exxon/Circle K 🍴 Burger King, KFC, Taco Bell, Wendy's 🛏 Comfort Inn Ⓞ Home Depot, **W** ⛽ RaceWay/dsl, Shell/dsl 🍴 McDonald's, Sonic, Starbucks, Waffle House Ⓞ Brookshire Foods
196mm	Bayou Pierre
196	Southern Loop
191	LA 16, LA 3276, to Stonewall
186	LA 175, to Frierson, Kingston, **E** Ⓞ Trailerhood RV Park (3mi), **W** ⛽ Relay Sta./rest./casino/dsl/scales Ⓞ Heart of Haynesville RV Park (7mi)
177	LA 509, to Carmel, **E** ⛽ Texaco/Eagles Trkstp/casino/dsl/rest. **W** Ⓞ Hwy 509 RV Park (4mi)
172	US 84, to Grand Bayou, Mansfield, **W** Ⓞ Civil War Site, New Rockdale RV Park (4mi)
169	Asseff Rd
162	US 371, LA 177, to Evelyn, Pleasant Hill

Exit #	Services
155	LA 174, to Ajax, Lake End, **W** Ⓞ Country Livin' RV Pk, gas/dsl
148	LA 485, Powhatan, Allen
142	LA 547, Posey Rd
138	LA 6, to Natchitoches, **E** ⛽ French Mkt/cafe/dsl, RaceWay/dsl 🍴 Popeye's, Wendy's 🛏 Best Western, Comfort Suites, Days Inn, Holiday Inn Express Ⓞ Ⓗ, (5mi), Walmart **W** ⛽ Chevron/dsl, Exxon, Texaco/dsl 🍴 Burger King, Huddle House, McDonald's 🛏 EconoLodge, Hampton Inn, Quality Inn Ⓞ Nakatosh RV Park, to Kisatchie NF
132	LA 478, rd 620
127	LA 120, to Cypress, Flora, **E** ⛽ Exxon/dsl Ⓞ to Cane River Plantations
119	LA 119, to Derry, Cloutierville, **E** to Cane River Plantations
113	LA 490, to Chopin, **E** ⛽ Express Mart TrkStp/dsl
107	to Lena, **E** Ⓞ USPO
103	LA 8 W, to Flatwoods, **E** ⛽ Shell/dsl, **W** Ⓞ RV camping, to Cotile Lake
99	LA 8, LA 1200, to Boyce, Colfax, **W 6 mi** Ⓞ Cotile Lake RV Camping
98	LA 1 (from nb), to Boyce
94	rd 23, to Rapides Sta Rd, **E** ⛽ Rapides/dsl **W LA Welcome Ctr, full** 🛏 **facilities, litter barrels, petwalk,** 🚮 **vending** Ⓞ I-49 RV Ctr
90	LA 498, Air Base Rd, **W** ⛽ Chevron/dsl/CNG/24hr, Exxon/Subway/dsl, Shell/dsl, Texaco/Eddie's BBQ/dsl 🍴 Burger King, Cracker Barrel, McDonald's 🛏 Comfort Suites, Hampton Inn, La Quinta, Super 8, Travel Express Inn Ⓞ Cabana RV Park
86	US 71, US 165, MacArthur Dr, **W 0-2 mi** ⛽ Chevron, Conoco/dsl, Exxon/dsl, Mobil/dsl, Shell/Circle K/dsl, Texaco/dsl 🍴 Anchor's Seafood Rest, Applebee's, Arby's, Burger King, Cajun Landing Rest., Cane's, Chick-fil-A, Church's, CiCi's Pizza, Dominos, DQ, Eddie's BBQ, El Reparo Mexican, Little Caesars, McDonald's, Outlaw's BBQ, Picadilly, Popeye's, Ryan's, Schlotzsky's, Sonic, Subway, Taco Bell, Taco Bueno, TX Roadhouse 🛏 Alexandria Inn, Baymont Inn, Best Value Inn, Best Western, Candlewood Suites, Comfort Inn, EconoLodge, Guesthouse Inn, Holiday Inn Express, Motel 6, Quality Inn, Ramada Ltd, Super 8, Value Place Inn Ⓞ $General, Advance Parts, AutoZone, BigLots, Buick/GMC, Family$, Hastings Books, Kia, Kroger, NAPA, O'Reilly Parts, Rite Aid, Staples, Super 1 Foods
85b	Monroe St, Medical Ctr Dr (from nb), **E** Ⓞ Ⓗ,
85a	LA 1, 10th St, MLK Dr, downtown
84	US 167 N, LA 28, LA 1, Pineville Expswy, no ez return nb
83	Broadway Ave, **E** ⛽ gas, **W 1 mi** 🍴 Checker's, Sonic, Wendy's Ⓞ $Tree, AutoZone, Harley-Davidson, Radio Shack, Walmart
81	US 71 N, LA 3250, Sugarhouse Rd, MacArthur Dr (from sb), **W** same as 80 and 83
80	US 71 S, US 167, MacArthur Dr, Alexandria, **W 0-3 mi** ⛽ Chevron/dsl, Exxon/dsl, Shell 🍴 Buffalo Wild Wings, Burger King, Capt D's, Carino's Italian, Chili's, Copeland's Rest, IHOP, KFC, Logan's Roadhouse, McDonald's, Outback Steaks, Pizza Hut, Popeye's, Sonic, Subway, Taco Bell 🛏 Courtyard Ⓞ $General, Albertsons, Best Buy, Dillard's, Family$, Ford/Lincoln, Hyundai, JC Penney, mall, Marshall's, Mazda, Michael's, Old Navy, Petsmart, Sam's Club/gas, U-Haul
73	LA 3265, rd 22, to Woodworth, **E** Ⓞ dsl repair, **W** ⛽ Exxon/Coops/dsl Ⓞ LA Conf Ctr, RV camping, to Indian Creek RA
66	LA 112, to Lecompte, **E** ⛽ Chevron/dsl 🍴 Burger King, **W** ⛽ Exxon/dsl Ⓞ museum

Vertical side labels: **GREENWOOD**, **SHREVEPORT** (left); **NATCHITOCHES**, **ALEXANDRIA** (right); **LA**

🔼N INTERSTATE 49 Cont'd

Exit #	Services
61	US 167, to Meeker, E🅞 to Loyd Hall Plantation (3mi), Turkey Creek
56	LA 181, Cheneyville
53	LA 115, to Bunkie, E🅖 Sammy's/Chevron/dsl/casino/24hr 🛏 Howard Johnson
46	LA 106, to St Landry, W🅞 to Chicot SP
40	LA 29, to Ville Platte, E🅖 Exxon/Cafe Mangeur/casino/dsl
35mm	🆁🆂/rec area both lanes, full 🅰 facilities, litter barrels, pet-walk, 🚻 RV dump, vending
27	LA 10, to Lebeau
25	LA 103, to Washington, Port Barre, W🅖 Citgo, Mobil 🅞 Family$
23	US 167 N, LA 744, to Ville Platte, E🅖 Chevron/Subway/Stuckey's/dsl/scales/casino, Texaco/dsl/casino W🅖 Exxon/dsl/casino 🅞 visitors ctr
19b a	US 190, to Opelousas, E🅞 Evangeline Downs Racetrack, W🅖 Exxon/dsl, Mobil/dsl, RaceTrac/dsl 🅞 🍴, CVS Drug, Lowe's, tourist info, USPO
18	LA 31, to Cresswell Lane, E🅖 Murphy USA/dsl 🍴 Casa Ole's, Little Caesars 🛏 Comfort Inn, Holiday Inn 🅞 $Tree, Chrysler/Dodge/Jeep, Radio Shack, URGENT CARE, Verizon, Walmart/Subway W🅖 Chevron/dsl, Shell, Valero/dsl 🍴 Burger King, Cane's, Cresswell Lane, Domino's, Gatti's Pizza, Hacienda Mexican, McDonald's, Peking Buffet, Pizza Hut, Subway, Taco Bell, Wendy's 🛏 Days Inn, Super 8 🅞 AT&T, Buick/GMC, Family$, Nissan, Piggly Wiggly, repair, Save-A-Lot, Walgreens
17	Judson Walsh Dr, E🅖 Texaco/dsl
15	LA 3233, Harry Guilbeau Rd, E🅞 RV Brokers, W🛏 Best Value Inn 🅞 🍴, RV Ctr, Toyota/Scion
11	LA 93, to Grand Coteau, Sunset, E🅖 Chevron, Citgo/rest./dsl/24hr, Exxon/Popeye's/dsl 🍴 Beau Chere Rest., McDonald's, W🍴 Subway 🅞 $General, Family$, Janise's Foods
7	LA 182, W🅞 Primeaux RV Ctr
4	LA 726, Carencro, E🅞 Super 1 Foods/gas, URGENT CARE, W🅖 Chevron/Popeye's/dsl, Texaco/dsl 🍴 Burger King, King Wok, McDonald's 🛏 Economy Inn 🅞 $General, Don's Country Mart, Family$, Kenworth, Mack, USPO
2	LA 98, Gloria Switch Rd, E🅖 Chevron/deli/dsl 🍴 Chili's, IHOP, Prejean's Rest., Wendy's 🅞 Lowe's, W🅖 Shell, Church's/dsl 🍴 Domino's, Great Wall Buffet, Picante Mexican, Subway
1c	Pont Des Mouton Rd, E🅖 Exxon/dsl/LP, Texaco/dsl 🍴 Burger King 🛏 Motel 6, Plantation Inn 🅞 st police, Walgreens, W 🅞 Ford
1b a	I-10, W to Lake Charles, E to Baton Rouge, S US 167 🅖 Chevron/dsl, Murphy USA/dsl, RaceTrac/dsl, Shell/dsl, Valero 🍴 Checker's, KFC, McDonald's, Popeye's, Shoney's, Subway, Taco Bell, Waffle House, Wendy's 🛏 Best Western, Comfort Inn, EconoLodge, Fairfield Inn, Holiday Inn, Howard Johnson, Jameson Inn, La Quinta, Quality Inn, Super 8 🅞 🍴 CVS Drug, Home Depot, Radio Shack, Super 1 Foods/gas, transmissions, Walmart/Subway

I-49 begins/ends on I-10, exit 103.

🔼N INTERSTATE 55

Exit #	Services
66mm	Louisiana/Mississippi state line
65mm	Welcome Ctr sb, full 🅰 facilities, litter barrels, petwalk, 🍴, 🚻 tourist info
64mm	weigh sta nb

Exit #	Services
61	LA 38, Kentwood, E🅖 Chevron/dsl, Texaco 🍴 Jam Chicken, Popeye's, Sonic 🅞 🍴, $General, AutoZone, Family$, Fred's, IGA Foods, Super$, W🅖 Kangaroo/dsl, Kangaroo/Subway/dsl
58.5mm	weigh sta sb
57	LA 440, Tangipahoa, E🅞 to Camp Moore Confederate Site
53	LA 10, to Greensburg, Fluker, W🅞🍴,
50	LA 1048, Roseland, E🅖 Chevron/dsl 🍴 Subway (1mi)
46	LA 16, Amite, E🅖 Exxon/dsl, Murphy USA/dsl, RaceTrac/dsl 🍴 Burger King, Master Chef, McDonald's, Mike's Catfish, Panda Garden, Popeye's, Sonic, Subway, Waffle House, Wendy's 🛏 Comfort Inn 🅞 🍴, $Tree, AutoZone, Fred's, O'Reilly Parts, to Bogue Chitto SP, Walgreens, Walmart/Subway, Winn-Dixie, W🅖 Amite Trkstp/grill/dsl (2mi) 🍴 Ardillo's 🛏 Colonial Inn, Holiday Inn Express 🅞 Buick/Chevrolet/GMC
40	LA 40, Independence, E🅖 Best Stop 🅞 🍴, W🅞 Indian Cr Camping (2mi)
36	LA 442, Tickfaw, E🅖 Chevron/dsl 🅞 camping, to Global Wildlife Ctr (15mi), W🅖 Exxon/dsl
32	LA 3234, Wardline Rd, E🅖 Chevron, Kangaroo/dsl, Texaco 🍴 Burger King, McDonald's, Popeye's, Sarita Grill, Sonic, Subway, Taco Bell, Wendy's 🛏 Lexington Inn 🅞 Tony's Tire
31	US 190, Hammond, E🅖 Exxon/Subway/dsl, Murphy USA/dsl, RaceTrac/dsl, Shell/dsl/scales/24hr 🍴 Applebee's, Baskin-Robbins, Buffalo Wild Wings, Burger King, Cane's, Chili's, CiCi's Pizza, Cracker Barrel, Firehouse Subs, Hi-Ho 1 BBQ, Lee's Burgers, McDonald's, Pizza Hut, Sonic, Starbucks, Taco Bell, Voodoo BBQ, Waffle House, Wendy's 🛏 Comfort Inn, Hampton Inn, Super 8, ValuePlace, Western Inn 🅞 🍴, $General, $Tree, Aamco, Advance Parts, AT&T, AutoZone, Chrysler/Dodge/Jeep, CVS Drug, Family$, Hobby Lobby, LeBlanc's Foods Lowe's, Office Depot, Radio Shack, Ross, Sav-A-Lot Foods, Tuesday Morning, Walgreens, Walmart/Subway, Winn-Dixie
29b a	I-12, W to Baton Rouge, E to Slidell
28	US 51 N, Hammond, E🅖 Exxon, RaceTrac/dsl 🍴 Don's Seafood/Steaks, Great Wall Chinese 🛏 Magnuson Hotel, Motel 6 🅞 🍴, Buick/GMC, dsl repair, Mitchell RV Ctr, Toyota/Scion
26	LA 22, to Springfield, Ponchatoula, E🅖 Chevron/dsl, Exxon/dsl, Shell/dsl 🍴 Burger King, China King, Hi-Ho BBQ, McDonald's/playplace, Papa John's, Pizza Hut, Popeye's, Smoothie King, Sonic, Subway, Waffle House, Wendy's 🛏 Microtel 🅞 AutoZone, Bohning's Foods, CVS Drug, Family$, Ford, O'Reilly Parts, Walgreens, Winn-Dixie, W🅖 Kangaroo/Domino's/dsl 🅞 Tickfaw SP (13mi)
23	US 51, Ponchatoula

⬆N INTERSTATE 55 Cont'd

Exit #	Services
22	frontage rd (from sb)
15	Manchac, E 🍴 Middendorf Café 🅾 🚗, swamp tours
7	Ruddock
1	US 51, to I-10, Baton Rouge, La Place, S 🚗 Circle K/dsl 🍴/Subway/dsl/24hr/scales, Shell/Huddle House/casino/dsl 🍴 Bully's Seafood, Burger King, McDonald's, Shoney's, Waffle House, Wendy's 🏠 Best Western, Days Inn, Hampton Inn, Holiday Inn Express, Quality Inn, Suburban Lodge

I-55 begins/ends on I-10, exit 209

⬆N INTERSTATE 59

Exit #	Services
11	W to Bogue Chitto NWR, Pearl River Turnaround
5b	Honey Island Swamp
5a	LA 3081, Pearl River, E 🚗 Riverside TrvlCtr/dsl
3	US 11 S, LA 1090, Pearl River, W 0-1 mi 🚗 Chevron/dsl, Interstate Fuels/dsl, Shell/Subway/dsl, Texaco, 🍴 McDonald's, Sonic, Waffle House, 🏠 Microtel, 🅾 AutoZone, Family$, Jubilee Foods/drug, NAPA
1.5mm	Welcome Ctr sb, full ♿ facilities, info, 🚗, 🅂ᔆ, litter barrels, petwalk, RV dump
1c b	I-10, E to Bay St Louis, W to New Orleans
1a	I-12 W, to Hammond. **I-59 begins/ends on I-10/I-12.**

⬆E INTERSTATE 220 (Shreveport)

Exit #	Services
I-220 begins/ends on I-20, exit 26.	
17b	I-20, W to Shreveport, E to Monroe
17a	US 79, US 80, N 🚗 RaceWay/dsl, Shell/Circle K 🍴 Taco Bell, Waffle House 🏠 Comfort Suites, Holiday Inn, SpringHill Suites 🅾 Racetrack/casino, S 🚗 Chevron/Huddle House/dsl 🍴 Silver Star Smokehouse
15	Shed Rd
13	Swan Lake Rd
12	LA 3105, Airline Dr, N 🍴 Baskin-Robbins, Chick-fil-A, Dickey's BBQ, Firehouse Subs, Izzo's Burrito, McAlister's Deli, Newk's Eatery, Olive Garden, Papa Murphy's, Santa Fe Steaks, Starbucks, Subway, TaMolly's 🅾 🏥, AT&T, Belk, Best Buy, GNC,

ᔆ H R E V E P O R T

Exit #	Services
12	Continued
	Old Navy, Petsmart, Ross, Sam's Club/gas, Target, Verizon, Walgreens, S 🚗 Clark/Subway/dsl, Murphy USA/dsl, Valero/dsl 🍴 Applebee's, Burger King, Cane's, Capt D's, China Flag, McDonald's, Nicky's Rest., Ruby Tuesday, Ryan's, Smashburger, Sonic, Taco Bell, Trejo's Mexican, Wendy's 🏠 Hampton Inn 🅾 $Tree, Gateway Tire, Home Depot, Lowe's, Radio Shack, USPO, vet, Walmart
11	LA 3, Bossier City, N 🚗 RaceWay/dsl 🅾 🏥, Buick/GMC, Ford, Harley-Davidson, Lexus, RV Park, Subaru, Suzuki, Toyota/Scion, S 🚗 Valero/dsl 🅾 Chrysler/Dodge/Jeep, Nissan
7b a	US 71, LA 1, Shreveport, N 🚗 Exxon/dsl, Shell/dsl 🍴 Checkers, Domino's, Johnny's Pizza, Papa John's, Pizza Hut, Sonic, Subway, Waffle House, Whataburger/24hr 🅾 Brookshire Foods/gas, Family$, Walgreens, S 🚗 RaceWay/dsl, Shell, Valero/dsl 🍴 Burger King, Carl's Jr, Church's, KFC, McDonald's, Podnah's BBQ, Popeye's, Taco Bell, Wendy's 🏠 Royal Inn 🅾 Advance Parts, AutoZone, County Mkt Foods, CVS Drug, Family$, O'Reilly Parts, Radio Shack, repair/transmissions, Rite Aid, U-Haul
5	LA 173, Blanchard Rd, N 🚗 Citgo/dsl
2	Lakeshore Dr
1a	Jefferson Paige Rd, S 🏠 Days Inn, Hampton Inn, Merryton Inn, Ramada Inn, Residence Inn, Super 8, Value Inn
1b c	I-20, E to Shreveport, W to Dallas. **I-220 begins/ends on I-20, exit 11.**

⬆E INTERSTATE 610 (New Orleans)

Exit #	Services
I-610 begins/ends on I-10	
4	Franklin Ave (from eb)
3	Elysian fields, S 🚗 B Express, Shell 🍴 Burger King, McDonald's, Waffle House 🅾 🏥, Lowe's
2c	Paris Ave (from wb, no return), S 🚗 Jimmy's, Shell/24hr 🍴 Popeye's
2b	US 90, N Broad St, New Orleans St (from wb)
2a	St Bernard Ave (from eb), to LSU School of Dentistry, auto racetrack
1b	I-10, to New Orleans
1a	Canal Blvd
I-610 begins/ends on I-10	

MAINE

⬆N INTERSTATE 95

Exit #	Services
305mm	US/Canada border, Maine state line, US Customs. **I-95 begins/ends.**
305	US 2, to Houlton, E 🅾 DFA Duty Free Shop, Houlton 🗺
303mm	Meduxnekeag River
302	US 1, Houlton, E 🚗 Irving/Circle K/dsl/24hr 🍴 Amato's, Burger King, McDonald's, Pizza Hut, Tang's Chinese 🅾 🏥 IGA Foods, Mardens, O'Reilly Parts/VIP Service, Rite Aid, W 🅂ᔆ both lanes, full ♿ facilities, litter barrels, petwalk, 🚗, picnic tables 🚗 Citgo/Subway/dsl, Irving/Circle K/dsl/scales/@, Shell/Dunkin Donuts/dsl 🍴 Tim Hortons/Coldstone 🏠 Ivey's Motel, Shiretown Motel 🅾 Arrowstook SP, Family$, Ford, Shop'n Save, Toyota, Walmart
301mm	B Stream
291	US 2, to Smyrna, E 🏠 Brookside Motel/rest.

Exit #	Services
286	Oakfield Rd, to ME 11, Eagle Lake, Ashland, W 🚗 Irving/Circle K/dsl, Valero/dsl 🍴 A Place To Eat 🅾 USPO
277mm	Mattawamkeag River, W Branch
276	ME 159, Island Falls, E 🚗 Dysarts Fuel, Porter's/rest. 🅾 Bishop's Mkt, USPO, W 🅾 RV camping, to Baxter SP (N entrance)
264	to ME 11, Sherman, E 🚗 Shell/dsl/LP/rest., W 🚗 Irving/Circle K/dsl 🏠 Katahdin Valley Motel 🅾 to Baxter SP (N entrance)
259	Benedicta (from nb, no re-entry)
252mm	scenic view Mt Katahdin, nb
247mm	Salmon Stream
244mm	Penobscot River
244	ME 157, to Medway, E Millinocket, W 🚗 Irving/Circle K/dsl 🍴 The Bridge Rest. 🏠 Gateway Inn 🅾 🏥, city park, Pine Grove Camping (4mi), to Baxter SP (S entrance), USPO, vet
243mm	🅂ᔆ both lanes, full ♿ facilities, litter barrels, petwalk, 🚗, picnic tables

INTERSTATE 95 Cont'd

Exit #	Services
227	to US 2, ME 6, Lincoln, **E** 4 mi 🅞 🅗, RV camping, food, gas, lodging
219mm	Piscataquis River
217	ME 6, Howland, **E** 🅖 Irving/95 Diner/dsl 🅞 95er Towing/repair, camping, LP
201mm	Birch Stream
199	ME 16 (no nb re-entry), to LaGrange
197	ME 43, to Old Town, **E** gas/dsl
196mm	Pushaw Stream
193	Stillwater Ave, to Old Town, **E** 🅖 Citgo/dsl, Gulf/Subway/dsl, Irving/Circle K/dsl 🍴 Burger King, China Garden, Dunkin Donuts, Governor's Rest., McDonald's, Tim Horton, Wendy's 🛏 Black Bear Inn 🅞 $Tree, IGA Foods, O'Reilly Parts/VIP Service
191	Kelly Rd, to Orono, **E** 2-3 mi camping, food, gas, lodging
187	Hogan Rd, Bangor Mall Blvd, to Bangor, **E** 🅖 Citgo 🍴 Denny's 🛏 Courtyard, Hampton Inn, Hilton Garden, TownePlace Suites 🅞 🅗, Audi/VW, Buick/GMC, Cadillac/Chevrolet, Chrysler/Dodge/Jeep, Firestone/auto, Ford, Honda, Hyundai, Mazda, Mercedes, Nissan, Sam's Club/gas, Subaru, Volvo, **W** 🅖 Citgo/dsl, Irving/Circle K/dsl 🍴 Applebee's, Arby's, Buffalo Wild Wings, Bugaboo Creek Café, Burger King, Chicago Grill, Chili's, Dunkin Donuts, Five Guys, Green Tea Japanese, Happy China, KFC, Kobe Japanese, Las Palapas, Longhorn Steaks, McDonald's, Miguel's Mexican, Olive Garden, Papa Johns, Pizza Hut, Quiznos, Ruby Tuesday, Starbucks, Subway, TX Roadhouse, Wendy's 🛏 Bangor Motel, Comfort Inn, Country Inn, Quality Inn 🅞 $Tree, Advance Parts, AT&T, Best Buy, BigLots, BooksAMillion, Dick's, Goodyear/auto, Hannaford Foods, Harley-Davidson, Hobby Lobby, Home Depot, JC Penney, Jo-Ann Fabrics, Kia, K-Mart/Little Caesars, Kohl's, LL Bean, Lowe's, Macy's, mall, Old Navy, O'Reilly Parts/VIP Service, PetCo, Petsmart, Sears/auto, Staples, Target, Town Fair Tire, URGENT CARE, Verizon, Walmart
186	Stillwater Ave, same as 187
185	ME 15, to Broadway, Bangor, **E** 🅖 Irving/Circle K/dsl 🍴 Tri-City Pizza 🅞 🅗, **W** 🅖 Citgo 🍴 Amato's, BoBo Chinese, China Light, Coldstone/Tim Hortons, Governor's Rest., KFC, McDonald's, Moe's BBQ, Pizza Hut, Subway, Taco Bell 🅞 CarQuest, Family$, Hannaford Foods, Rite Aid, TJ Maxx, Walgreens
184	ME 222, Union St, to Ohio St, Bangor, **E** 🅖 Citgo, Irving 🅞 Rite Aid, **W** 🅖 Citgo, Gulf, Shell/dsl 🍴 Burger King, Capt Nick's Rest., Dunkin Donuts, McDonald's, Nicky's Rest., Wendy's 🛏 Sheraton 🅞 $Tree, Hannaford Foods, Marshall's, Midas, RV Camping, to ✈
183	US 2, ME 2, Hammond St, Bangor, **E** 🅖 Citgo, Shell 🍴 Angelo's Pizza, Papa Gambino's Pizza, Whoopie Pie Cafe 🅞 Corner Store, Fairmont Mkt, NAPA, TrueValue, **W** 🅞 ✈
182b	US 2, ME 100 W, **W** 🅖 Irving/Subway/dsl, Shell/dsl 🍴 Dunkin Donuts, Ground Round, Tim Hortons 🛏 Days Inn, EconoLodge, Fairfield Inn, Holiday Inn, Howard Johnson, Motel 6, Ramada Inn, Super 8, Travelodge 🅞 O'Reilly Parts/VIP Service, RV camping, Tire Whse
182a	I-395, to US 2, US 1A, Bangor, downtown
180	Cold Brook Rd, to Hampden, **E** 🅖 Citgo 🍴 Angler's Rest. (1mi), **W** 🅖 Citgo/dsl/24hr/@, Dysarts Fleet Fuel/dsl 🛏 Best Western 🅞 dsl repair, Mack, Volvo
178mm	🆁🆂 sb, full ♿ facilities, info, litter barrels, petwalk, ⓒ, 🚮 vending, wireless internet
177mm	Soudabscook Stream
176mm	🆁🆂 nb, full ♿ facilities, info, litter barrels, petwalk, ⓒ, 🚮 vending, wireless internet
174	ME 69, to Carmel, **E** 🅖 Citgo/dsl, **W** 🅞 RV camping
167	ME 69, ME 143, to Etna
161	ME 7, to E Newport, Plymouth, **W** 🅞 LP, RV camping
159	Ridge Rd (from sb), to Plymouth, Newport
157	to US 2, ME 7, ME 11, Newport, **W** 🅖 Irving/Circle K/dsl/24hr, Shell/dsl 🍴 Burger King, China Way, Dunkin Donuts, McDonald's, Pando Italian American, Pizza Hut, Sawyers Dairy Bar, Subway, Tim Hortons 🛏 Lovley's Motel 🅞 Aubuchon Hardware, Auto Value Parts, AutoZone, CarQuest, Chrysler/Dodge/Jeep, Rite Aid, Shop'n Save, Verizon, Walmart/Dunkin Donuts

BANGOR

NEWPORT

ME

INTERSTATE 95 Cont'd

Exit #	Services
151mm	Sebasticook River
150	Somerset Ave, Pittsfield, E 🅐 Irving/dsl 🍴 Subway 🛏 Pittsfield Motel 🅞 🅗, CarQuest, Chevrolet, Family$, Rite Aid, Shop'n Save Foods
138	Hinckley Rd, Clinton, W 🅐 95 One-Stop/dsl
134mm	Kennebec River
133	US 201, Fairfield, E 🍴 Purple Cow Pancakes
132	ME 139, Fairfield, W 🅐 Irving/Circle K/Subway/dsl/scales/24hr
130	ME 104, Main St, Waterville, E 🅐 Citgo 🍴 Cappza's Pizza, Coldstone, Dunkin Donuts, Friendly's, Governor's Rest., Little Caesar's, McDonald's, Ruby Tuesday, Starbucks, Subway, Tim Horton, Wendy's 🛏 Best Western, Comfort Inn, Fireside Inn 🅞 🅗, Advance Parts, Audi/Mazda/VW, GNC, Hannaford Foods, Home Depot, JC Penney, K-Mart, O'Reilly Parts/VIP Service, Radio Shack, Staples, Verizon, Walmart
129mm	Messalonskee Stream
127	ME 11, ME 137, Waterville, Oakland, E 🅐 Irving/dsl/24hr, Xpress/dsl 🍴 Applebee's, Burger King, DQ, Dunkin Donuts, KFC/Taco Bell, McDonald's, Pad Thai, Papa John's, Pizza Hut, Sam's Italian, Subway, Super Buffet, Weathervane Seafood 🛏 Budget Host, EconoLodge, Hampton Inn 🅞 🅗, AutoZone, Buick/Chevrolet, Chrysler/Dodge/Jeep, CVS Drug, Hannaford Foods, Jo-Ann Fabrics, Marden's, Shaw's Foods/Osco Drug, Tire Whse, TJ Maxx, Toyota/Scion, Verizon, W 🅐 Shell/dsl 🅞 Aubuchon Hardware, CarQuest, Ford/Lincoln
120	Lyons Rd, Sidney
117mm	weigh sta both lanes
113	ME 3, Augusta, Belfast
112	ME 27, ME 8, ME 11, Augusta, E 🅐 Citgo 🍴 Denny's, DQ, Dunkin Donuts, Longhorn Steaks, Olive Garden, Panera Bread, Red Robin, Rooster's, Ruby Tuesday, Sam's Italian, Subway 🛏 Best Western 🅞 Barnes&Noble, Dick's, GNC, Home Depot, Kohl's, Michaels, Old Navy, Radio Shack, Sam's Club, TownFair Tire, Verizon, Walmart W 🅐 Irving/Circle K/dsl/24hr 🍴 99 Rest., Great Wall Chinese, KFC/Taco Bell, Wendy's 🛏 Comfort Inn, Fairfield Inn 🅞 Advance Parts
109	US 202, ME 11, ME 17, ME 100, Augusta, E 🅐 Citgo/Dunkin Donuts/dsl, Irving/Circle K/dsl 🍴 Amato's Rest., Applebee's, Arby's, Burger King, China King, Damon's Italian, Domino's, DQ, Friendly's, KFC, Little Caesars, McDonald's, Pizza Hut, Subway, Tim Horton, Wendy's 🛏 Senator Inn 🅞 $Tree, Best Buy, BigLots, Family$, K-Mart, Lowe's, O'Reilly Parts/VIP Service, Petsmart, Radio Shack, Shaw's Foods/Osco Drug, Staples, Target, U-Haul, USPO, vet, Walgreens, W 🅐 Valero 🍴 Margarita's Mexican, TX Roadhouse 🛏 Hampton Inn, Motel 6, Quality Inn, Super 8 🅞 CarQuest, Chrysler/Dodge, Hannaford Foods, Honda, Hyundai, Jeep, Kia, Nissan, PetCo, Sears/auto, Subaru, TJ Maxx, Toyota/Scion
103	to I-295 S (from sb), ME 9, ME 126, to Gardiner, **Service plaza** 🅐 Citgo 🍴 Burger King, Hersheys, Quiznos, Starbucks 🅞 ZMkt
102	to I-295 S (from nb), rd 9, rd 106, **Service plaza** 🅐 Citgo 🍴 Burger King, Hersheys, Quiznos, Starbucks 🅞 ZMkt
100mm	toll plaza
86	to ME 9, Sabattus
84mm	Sabattus Creek
80	ME 196, Lewiston, W on ME 196 🅐 Coast Fuels, Gendron's/dsl, Mobil, Shell/dsl, Sunoco, XPress/dsl 🍴 Burger King, Cathay Hut Chinese, D'Angelo, Dunkin Donuts, Governor'sRest.,

80	Continued KFC/Taco Bell, McDonald's, Papa John's, Pepper&Spice Thai, Sam's Italian, Subway 🅞 Advance Parts, Motel 6, Ramada Inn, Super 8 🅞 🅗, $Tree, Family$, NAPA, Rite Aid, Staples, USPO
78mm	Androscoggin River
75	US 202, rd 4, rd 100, to Auburn, E 🅐 Irving/Circle K/dsl, Mobil/Subway/dsl 🍴 Danny Boy's Rest., Dunkin Donuts, Peking Chinese 🛏 Fireside Inn 🅞 RV Camping, W 🅞 🅗,
71mm	Royal River
66mm	toll plaza
63	US 202, rd 115, rd 4, to ME 26, Gray, E 🅐 Citgo, Gulf, Mobil, Sunoco 🍴 China Gray, Dunkin Donuts, Goody's Pizza, McDonald's, Subway 🅞 $Tree, Ace Hardware, Family$, NAPA, Shop'n Save Mkt
59mm	Service plaza both lanes 🅐 Citgo/dsl 🍴 Chicago Pizza, Starbucks 🅞 atm
55mm	Piscataqua River
53	to ME 26, ME100 W, N Portland, E 🅐 Irving/Circle K/Subway/dsl 🍴 Dunkin Donuts, Maddens Grill 🅞 🅗, Hannaford Foods
52	to I-295, US 1, Freeport
48	ME 25, to Portland, E 🅐 Citgo 🍴 Applebee's, Asian Bistro, Full Belly Deli, Little Caesar's, Subway 🛏 Portland Inn 🅞 $Tree, BigLots, BJ's Whse/gas, Chevrolet, CVS Drug, Fiat, Jo-Ann Fabrics, Lowe's, Radio Shack, Sullivan Tire, vet, W 🅐 Gulf, Irving/Circle K/dsl 🍴 Amato's Rest., Burger King, Chipotle, Denny's, Dunkin Donuts, Egg&I Cafe, KFC/Taco Bell, McDonald's, Panera Bread, Pizza Hut, Ruby Tuesday, Seasons Grille, Wendy's 🛏 Fireside Inn, Howard Johnson, Motel 6, Super 8, Travelodge 🅞 Advance Parts, AT&T, CarQuest, Chrysler/Dodge/Jeep, Ford, GNC, Harley-Davidson, Home Depot, Hyundai, Kohl's, Lexus/Toyota/Scion, Lincoln, Midas, NAPA, O'Reilly Parts/VIP Service, Shaw's Foods/Osco Drug, Sullivan Tire, Tire Whse, vet
47mm	Stroudwater River
47	to ME 25, Rand Rd
46	to ME 22, Congress St, same as 45
45	to US 1, Maine Mall Rd, S Portland, E 🅐 Citgo/dsl, Sunoco/dsl 🍴 Bugaboo Creek Steaks, Burger King, Chili's, Chipotle Mexican, Cracker Barrel, Dunkin Donuts, Five Guys, Food Court, Friendly's, Great Wall Chinese, Hokkaido Japanese, HomeTown Buffet, IHOP, Imperial China, Jimmy the Greek Rest., Longhorn Steaks, Macaroni Grill, McDonald's, Newick's Lobster House, Olive Garden, On the Border, Panera Bread, Pizza Hut, Qdoba, Ruby Tuesday, Sebago Brewing Rest., Starbucks, Tim Horton/Coldstone, UNO Pizzaria, Weathervane Seafood, Wendy's 🛏 Comfort Inn, Courtyard, Days Inn, DoubleTree, EconoLodge, Fairfield Inn, Hampton Inn, Homewood Suites 🅞 $Tree, Best Buy, BonTon, BooksAMillion, Dick's, Hannaford Foods, Honda, JC Penney, Macy's, mall, Michael's, Nissan, Old Navy, PetCo, Sears/auto, Staples, TJ Maxx, TownFair Tire, Verizon, W 🍴 Applebee's, Starbucks 🛏 Holiday Inn Express, Marriott 🅞 Target
44	I-295 N (from nb), to S Portland, Scarborough, E 1 mi on ME 114 🅐 Cumberland 🍴 Chia Sen Chinese, KFC/Taco Bell, Little Caesars, Red Robin, Shogun Japanese, Subway, TX Roadhouse 🛏 Homewood Suites, Residence Inn, TownePlace Suites 🅞 🅗, AT&T, Lowe's, NAPA, O'Reilly/VIP Parts/service, Sam's Club/gas, Shaw's Foods/Osco Drug, Walmart/Dunkin Donuts
42mm	Nonesuch River

INTERSTATE 95 Cont'd

Exit #	Services
42	to US 1, E🍴 Famous Dave's, Portland Pie 🅾 Cabela's, Scarborough Downs Racetrack (seasonal)
36	I-195 E, to Saco, Old Orchard Beach, E🛏 Hampton Inn 🅾 KOA, Paradise Park Resort RV
35mm	E🛏 Ramada Inn/Saco Hotel Conference Ctr
33mm	Saco River
32	ME 111, to Biddeford, E🅰 Irving/Circle K/Subway/dsl 🍴 Amato's Sandwiches, Dunkin Donuts, Ruby Tuesday, Wendy's 🛏 Best Value Inn, Holiday Inn Express 🅾 🏥, AAA, AutoZone, O'Reilly/VIP Parts/Service, Osco Drug, Shaw's Foods, Walmart W🅰 Cumberland/dsl 🍴 Applebees, Casa Fiesta Mexican, Kobe Japanese, Longhorn Steaks, Olive Garden, Panera Bread 🅾 GNC, Home Depot, Kohl's, Market-Basket Foods, Michaels, Petsmart, Staples, Target, TJ Maxx, TownFair Tire, Verizon
25mm	Kennebunk River
25	ME 35, Kennebunk Beach, E🛏 Turnpike Motel
24mm	**Service plaza both lanes** 🅰 Citgo/dsl, 🍴 Burger King, Hershey's, Popeye's, Starbucks, 🅾 atm, Z Mkt
19.5mm	Merriland River
19	ME 9, ME 109, to Wells, Sanford, W🅾 to Sanford RA
7mm	**Maine Tpk begins/ends, toll booth**
7	ME 91, to US 1, The Yorks, **(last exit before toll rd nb)** E🅰 Gulf, Irving/Circle K/dsl, Mobil/dsl, Shell 🍴 China Bistro, Norma's Rest., Ruby's Grill, Wild Willy's Burgers, York 54 Cafe 🛏 Best Western, Microtel, York Corner Inn 🅾🏥, Ford, Hannaford Foods, NAPA, Rite Aid, TrueValue, vet
5.5mm	**weigh sta nb**
5mm	York River
4mm	**weigh sta sb**
3mm	**Welcome Ctr nb, full** ♿ **facilities, info, litter barrels, petwalk,** 🚻, 🛏 **vending** 🅾 **wireless,**
2	(2 & 3 from nb), US 1, to Kittery, E on US 1 🅰 7-11/dsl, Irving/Circle K/dsl/scales 🍴 Burger King, DQ, McDonald's, Robert's Maine Grill, Starbucks, Subway, Sunrise Grill, Tasty Thai, Weathervane Seafood Rest. 🛏 Blue Roof Motel, Days Inn, Northeaster Hotel, Ramada Inn 🅾 Outlets/Famous Brands, vet
1	ME 103 (from nb, no re-entry), to Kittery
0mm	Maine/New Hampshire state line, Piscataqua River

INTERSTATE 295

Exit #	Services
52mm	**I-295 begins/ends on I-95, exit 103**
51	ME 9, ME 126, to Gardiner, Litchfield, **toll plaza W Service plaza** 🅰 Citgo 🍴 Burger King, Hersheys, Quiznos, Starbucks 🅾 ZMkt
49	US 201, to Gardiner
43	ME 197, to Richmond, E 🅰 Irving/Quincey's Deli/dsl 🍴 Dunkin Donuts, Subway, W🅾 KOA (5mi)
37	ME 125, Bowdoinham
31b a	ME 196, to Lisbon, Topsham, E🅰 Gibbs/dsl, Irving/Circle K/ Dunkin Donuts/Subway 🍴 99 Rest., Arby's, Fairground Cafe, Firehouse Subs, Little Caesars, McDonald's, Panera Bread, Romeo's Pizza, Ruby Tuesday, Starbucks, Tim Horton's, Wendy's 🅾 $Tree, AT&T, Best Buy, Dick's, Hannaford Foods, Home Depot, Jo-Ann Fabrics, Meineke, Nissan, O'Reilly Parts/

31b a	Continued VIP Service, PetCo, Radio Shack, Rite Aid, Target, Tire Whse, Town Fair Tire, Toyota/Scion, Verizon, W🅰 Xpress Stop/dsl
30mm	Androscoggin River
28	US 1, Bath, E 1 mi on US 1 🅰 Cumberland/dsl, Irving/dsl, Mobil/dsl, Shell 🍴 Amato's, Dunkin Donuts, McDonald's, Subway 🛏 Best Value Inn, Comfort Inn, Fairfield Inn, Knights Inn, Travelers Inn 🅾🏥, Chevrolet/Mazda, Chrysler/Dodge/Jeep, Ford
24	to Freeport (from nb), **services** E 1 mi on US 1
22	ME 125, to Pownal, E on US 1 🅰 Irving/Circle K 🍴 Azure Cafe, Corsican Rest., Jameson Rest., Linda Bean's ME Kitchen, McDonald's, Sam's Italian, Starbucks, Subway, Tuscan Bistro 🛏 Harraseeket Inn, Hilton Garden 🅾 CVS Drug, LL Bean, outlets/famous brands, USPO, W to Bradbury Mtn SP
20	Desert Rd, Freeport, E🅰 Irving/Circle K 🍴 Antonia's Pizza, Buck's BBQ, Dunkin Donuts, Thai Garden Rest. 🛏 Comfort Suites, Econolodge, Hampton Inn, Holiday Inn Express, Super 8 🅾 RV camping, Shaw's Foods
17	US 1, Yarmouth, E🆁🆂 both lanes, full ♿ facilities, info, 🍴 Day's Takeout, Muddy Rudder Rest. 🛏 Best Western 🅾 Delorme Mapping, Ford, W🅰 Citgo/dsl, Cumberland/dsl 🍴 McDonald's, Pat's Pizza 🅾 Ace Hardware, Hannaford Foods, O'Reilly Parts/VIP Service, Tire Whse
15	US 1, to Cumberland, Yarmouth, W🅰 Irving/dsl, Mobil 🍴 233 Grill, Chopstick Asian, Romeo's Pizza, Subway 🅾 AT&T, Rite Aid
11	to I-95, ME Tpk (from sb)
10	US 1, to Falmouth, E🅰 Citgo/dsl, Irving/dsl 🍴 Dunkin Donuts, Foreside Rest., House of Pizza, Leavitt & Sons Deli, McDonald's, Orchid Thai, Ricetta's Pizza, Starbucks, Subway, Wendy's 🛏 Falmouth Inn 🅾 Ace Hardware, Audi/VW, Goodyear/auto, Mazda, Radio Shack, Rite Aid, Shaw's Foods, Staples, vet, Walmart
9mm	Presumpscot River
9	US 1 S, ME 26, to Baxter Blvd
8	ME 26 S, Washington Ave, E🅾 U-Haul
7	US 1A, Franklin St, E🍴 Miss Portland Diner 🅾 AAA Car Care, AT&T, CarQuest, NAPA, Trader Joe's, Verizon, Walgreens, Whole Foods Mkt
6b a	US 1, Forest Ave, E🅰 Citgo 🅾🏥, Firestone/auto, USPO, W🅰 Mobil/dsl 🍴 Burger King, Leonardo's Pizza, Pizza Hut, Stavro's Pizza, Subway 🅾 CVS Drug, Hannaford Foods, U of SME, Walgreens
5b a	ME 22, Congress St, E🍴 Amato's Rest., D'Angelos, Denny's, Dunkin Donuts, Lang's Chinese, McDonald's, Subway 🛏 La

BIDDEFORD

KITTERY

FREEPORT

ME

INTERSTATE 295 Cont'd

Exit #	Services
5b a	Continued Quinta 🅾 �H, Sullivan Tire, **W** 🅖 Gulf/Dunkin Donuts, Mobil/dsl 🍴 Anania's Italian 🛏 Clarion
4	US 1 S, to Main St, to S Portland, US 1 S, **E services on US 1**
3mm	Fore River
3	ME 9, to Westbrook St, no sb return, **W** 🅖 Citgo/dsl, Irving/Circle K/dsl 🍴 Buffalo Wild Wings, El Rodeo Mexican, Olive

3	Continued Garden, Seadog Brew Co., Subway, Wild Willy's Burger 🅾 Chevrolet, Home Depot, Marshalls
2	to US 1 S, S Portland, **Services E on US 1** 🅖 7-11, Irving/Circle K/dsl, Mobil 🍴 Dunkin Donuts 🛏 Howard Johnson, Super 8, 🛏 Best Western, Knights Inn
1	to I-95, to US 1, **multiple services E on US 1**, same as 2

I-295 begins/ends on I-95, exit 44.

MARYLAND

INTERSTATE 68

Exit #	Services
82c	I-70 W, to Breezewood. **I-68 begins/ends on I-70, exit 1.**
82b	I-70 E, US 40 E, to Hagerstown
82a	US 522, Hancock, **N** 🅾 Chevrolet, Chrysler/Dodge/Jeep, **S** 🅖 Mobil/dsl, Sheetz 🍴 Hardee's, Park'n Dine, Pizza Hut, Subway, Weaver's Rest. 🛏 Best Value Inn, Super 8 🅾 $General, Happy Hills Camping, Save-A-Lot Foods
77	US 40, MD 144, Woodmont Rd, **S** 🅾 RV camping
75mm	**runaway truck ramp eb**
74mm	**Sideling Hill 🆁🆂/exhibit both lanes, full 🚻 facilities, vending, 1269 ft (seasonal)**
74	US 40, Mountain Rd (no return from eb)
73mm	Sideling Hill Creek
72mm	**truck ramp wb**
72	US 40, High Germany Rd, Swain Rd, **S** 🅖 Citgo/dsl
68	Orleans Rd, **N** 🅖 Exxon/dsl
67mm	Town Hill, elevation 940 ft
64	MV Smith Rd, **S** 🅖, scenic overlook 1040 ft, to Green Ridge SF HQ
62	US 40, 15 Mile Creek Rd, **N** 🅾 Billmeyer Wildlife Mgt Area
58.7mm	Polish Mtn, elevation 1246 ft
57mm	Town Creek
56mm	Flintstone Creek
56	MD 144, National Pike, Flintstone, **S** 🅖 Billi's Gas&Grub
52	MD 144, Pleasant Valley Rd (from eb), National Pike
50	Pleasant Valley Rd, **N** 🍴 Lakeside Grill, Signature's Grill 🛏 Rocky Gap Lodge/golf/rest. 🅾 to Rocky Gap SP
47	US 220 N, MD 144, Dehaven Rd (from wb), Old National Pike, Bedford, same as 46
46	US 220 N, Dehaven Rd, Baltimore Pike, Naves Crossroads, **N** 🛏 Cumberland Motel 🅾 Advance Parts, Shop'n Save, vet, **S** 🅖 Sheetz/dsl 🍴 Puccini's Rest.
45	Hillcrest Dr, **S** 🅖 Sunoco/dsl
44	US 40A, Baltimore Ave, Willow Brook Rd, to Allegany Comm Coll, 🅾 �H
43mm	Youghiogheny River
43d	Maryland Ave, **N** 🛏 Holiday Inn 🅾 �H, USPO, **S** 🅖 Gulf/7-11 🍴 Chick-fil-A, Papa John's, Quiznos 🅾 AT&T, AutoZone, Martin's Foods/gas
43c	downtown, same as 43b
43b	MD 51, Industrial Blvd, **N** 🍴 McDonald's 🛏 Holiday Inn 🅾 Family$, **S** 🅖 Gulf/dsl 🍴 Papa John's, Pizza Hut/Taco Bell, Roy Rogers, Wendy's 🛏 Fairfield Inn
43a	to WV 28A, Beall St, Industrial Blvd, to Cumberland, Johnson St, **N** 🅖 Sheetz
42	US 220 S, Greene St, Ridgedale
41mm	Haystack Mtn, elev 1240 ft

41	Seton Dr (from wb, no directory turn)
40	US 220 S, to US 40A, Vocke Rd, La Vale, **N** 🅖 BP/dsl, Sunoco 🍴 Arby's, Asian Garden, Bob Evans, Burger King, D'Atri Rest., Denny's, DQ, Gehauf Rest., Grand China, Henny's Grill, KFC, LJ Silver, McDonald's, Pizza Hut, Rio Grande Mexican, Rita's Custard, Ruby Tuesday, Subway, TX Grill, Wendy's 🛏 Best Western/rest, Comfort Inn, Slumberland Motel, Super 8 🅾 �H, $General, Advance Parts, CVS Drug, Harley-Davidson, Jo-Ann Fabrics, Lowe's, Mr Tire, st police, Staples, **S** 🍴 Applebee's, CiCi's Pizza, Dragon China Buffet, Ponderosa, Wasabi Japanese 🛏 EconoLodge 🅾 $Tree, BonTon, JC Penney, Kohl's, mall, Martin's Foods/gas, Sears/auto, Walmart/McDonald's
39	US 40A (from wb), same as 40
34	MD 36, to Westernport, Frostburg, **N** 🅖 Sheetz, Valero 🍴 Burger King, Fox's Pizza, McDonald's, Peking House, Pizza Hut, Subway 🛏 Days Inn, Hampton Inn 🅾 �H, $General, CarQuest, Food Lion, Rite Aid, Save-A-Lot, USPO, **S** 🅾 to Dans Mtn SP
33	Midlothian Rd, to Frostburg, **N** 🅾 �H, **S** 🅾 to Dans Mt SP
31mm	**weigh sta eb**
30mm	Big Savage Mtn, elevation 2800 ft
29	MD 546, Finzel, **N** 🍴 Hen House Rest. 🅾 Mason-Dixon Camping (4mi/seasonal), **S** 🍴 Savage River Lodge Rest.
25.8mm	eastern continental divide, elevation 2610 ft
24	Lower New Germany Rd, to US 40A, **S** 🅾 to New Germany SP, to Savage River SF
23mm	Meadow Mtn, elevation 2780 ft
22	US 219 N, to Meyersdale, **N** 🅖 🅿️/Arby's/dsl/scales/24hr, Sunoco/dsl 🍴 Burger King, Hilltop Rest., Penn Alps Rest., Subway 🅾 $Discount, $General, Ford, Hilltop Fruit Mkt, NAPA, Rite Aid, Shop'n Save, TrueValue, **S** 🅖 Valero/dsl 🛏 Comfort Inn 🅾 New Germany SP, Savage River SF
20mm	Casselman River
19	MD 495, to US 40A, Grantsville, **N** 🅖 Exxon/Subway/dsl, Sunoco/dsl 🛏 Casselman Motel/rest. 🅾 CarQuest, Medicine Shoppe, USPO
15mm	Mt Negro, elevation 2740 ft
14mm	Keyser's Ridge, elevation 2880 ft
14b a	US 219, US 40 W, Oakland, **N** 🅖 Liberty/Ridge/rest./dsl, Sunoco/7-11/dsl 🍴 McDonald's, repair
6mm	**Welcome Ctr eb, full 🚻 facilities, info, litter barrels, petwalk, 🅖, 🛏, vending**
4.5mm	Bear Creek
4	MD 42, Friendsville, **N** 🅖 Liberty/dsl, Marathon/dsl 🍴 Old Mill Rest. 🛏 Yough Valley Motel 🅾 S&S Mkt, USPO, **S** 🍴 Sunset Inn 🅾 camping, to Deep Creek Lake SP
0mm	Maryland/West Virginia state line

HANCOCK (vertical label)
FROSTBURG (vertical label)

ME
MD

⬆E INTERSTATE 70

Exit #	Services
I-70 begins/ends in Baltimore at Cooks Lane.	
94	Security Blvd N, **S** ⛽ Shell
91b a	I-695, **N** off exit 17 ⛽ Exxon, Sunoco 🍴 5 Guys Burgers, Burger King, McDonald's, Panera Bread, Popeye's, Quiznos 🛏 Best Western ⊙ Best Buy, Ford, Macy's, mall, Old Navy, Sears/auto, Weis Foods **S** ⛽ BP/repair, Shell 🍴 Dunkin Donuts, Subway, Wendy's 🛏 Days Inn, Leisure Inn, Motel 6 ⊙ Chevrolet, Nissan,
87b a	US 29 (exits left from wb)to MD 99, Columbia, **S 2 mi on US 40** ⛽ BP/dsl, Citgo/Subway, Exxon/dsl, Gulf, Shell, Sunoco 🍴 Arby's, Baskin-Robbins/Dunkin Donuts, Boston Mkt, Burger King, Checkers, Domino's, Dunkin Donuts, Jerry's Subs, Jimmy John's, McDonald's, Papa John's, Pizza Hut, Qdoba ⊙ 7-11, Acura/Infiniti, Advance Parts, Cadillac/Chevrolet, Carmax, CVS Drug, Giant Foods, Goodyear/auto, Home Depot, Honda, Mars Foods, Midas, Mr Tire, NAPA, Nissan, Rite Aid, Safeway Foods, Shoppers Foods, Verizon, Walmart
83	US 40, Marriottsville (no EZ wb return), **S 2 mi** 🛏 Turf Valley Hotel/Country Club/rest.
82	US 40 E (from eb), same as 83
80	MD 32, Sykesville, **N** ⊙ golf, **S** ⛽ Shell 🍴 Subway, Tony's Pizzeria
79mm	weigh/insp sta wb, ⊙
76	MD 97, Olney, **S** ⛽ High's/dsl 🍴 Subway
73	MD 94, Woodbine, **N** ⛽ Shell 🍴 Baskin Robbins, China Yee, Dunkin Donuts, Harvest Chicken, McDonald's, Pizza Hut, Subway ⊙ $Tree, Food Lion, Ramblin Pines RV Park (6mi), **S** ⛽ BP/dsl, Citgo 🍴 Town Grill
68	MD 27, Mt Airy, **N** ⛽ 7-11, Liberty/Blimpie/dsl, Shell 🍴 5 Guys Burgers, Arby's, Baskin-Robbns/Dunkin Donuts, Burger King, China Taste, Chipotle, Domino's, J&P Pizza, Jersey Mike' Subs, KFC/Taco Bell, Ledo's Pizza, McDonald's, Papa John's, Pizza Hut, Quick Fire Japanese, Starbucks, Subway, TCBY ⊙ Ace Hardware, Advance Parts, AT&T, Food Lion, GNC, Goodyear, Mr Tire, Radio Shack, Rite Aid, Safeway, vet, Walmart, **S** ⛽ Exxon/dsl, Shell 🛏 Budget Inn
66mm	truckers parking area eb
64mm	weigh/insp sta eb
62	MD 75, Libertytown, **N** ⛽ Classic Fuels, Shell 🍴 Asian Bistro, Baskin Robbins, Domino's, Dunkin Donuts, McDonald's, Morgan's Grill ⊙ CVS Drug, Food Lion, New Market Hist Dist, vet
59	MD 144
57mm	Monocacy River
56	MD 144, **N** ⛽ BP, Sheetz 🍴 Beijing, Burger King, JR's Pizza, McDonald's, Roy Rogers, Taco Bell, Waffle House, Wendy's ⊙ $General, to Hist Dist, **S** ⊙ Triangle RV Ctr
55	South St, **N 1 mi** ⛽ BP, Sheetz/dsl
54	Market St, to I-270, **N** ⛽ Costco/gas 🛏 Travelodge, **S** ⛽ 7-11, Sheetz, Shell, SouStates/dsl, Valero 🍴 Arby's,

54	Continued Bob Evans, Burger King, Checker's, Cracker Barrel, Jerry's Rest., KFC/Taco Bell, Longhorn Steaks, McDonald's, Papa John's, Popeye's, Red Robin, Roy Rogers, Ruby Tuesday, Subway, Waffle House, Wendy's 🛏 Courtyard, Days Inn, EconoLodge, Fairfield Inn, Hampton Inn, Holiday Inn, Holiday Inn Express, Sleep Inn ⊙ Aamco, Audi, Best Buy, Buick, Chrysler/Dodge/Jeep, Ford/Lincoln, Home Depot, Honda, Hyundai, JC Penney, Kia, Kohl's, Lowe's, mall, Michael's, Mr Tire, Nissan, Ross, Sam's Club/gas, Sears/auto, Staples, Tires+, TJMaxx, Toyota, Volvo, Walmart
53b a	I-270 S, US 15 N, US 40 W, to Frederick
52b a	US 15 S, US 340 W, Leesburg
49	US 40A, Braddock Heights, **N on US 40** ⛽ Citgo/dsl, Exxon/dsl, Freestate/dsl, GetGo, Shell, Sunoco 🍴 Arby's, Bob Evans, Boscov's, Boston Mkt, Burger King, Carrabba's, Casa Rico Mexican, City Buffet, Denny's, Dunkin Donuts, Famous Dave's BBQ, Flaming Grill, Fritchie's Rest., Ground Round, HoneyBaked Ham, Hunter's Rest., KFC, Los Trios, McDonald's, Mtn View Diner, Outback Steaks, Pizza Hut, Popeye's, Red Lobster, Roy Rogers, Ruby Tuesday, Starbucks, Subway, Taco Bell, Wendy's 🛏 Comfort Inn, Motel 6 ⊙ H, $General, 7-11, Advance Parts, Aldi Foods, AT&T, CVS Drug, Ford/Subaru, Giant Eagle Foods, Goodyear/auto, Home Depot, K-Mart, Merchant Tire, Mr Tire, PepBoys, PetCo, st police, Tire Pros, Toyota, Verizon, Weis Foods **S** ⊙ camping, to Washington Mon SP,
48	US 40 E, US 340 (from eb, no return), **N 1 mi** same as 49
42	MD 17, Myersville, **N** ⛽ Exxon, Sunoco/dsl 🍴 Burger King, McDonald's, Old Town Diner ⊙ Greenbrier SP (4mi), to Gambrill SP (6mi), **S** ⛽ Crown/dsl 🍴 Subway
39mm	🅿ₛ both lanes, full ♿ facilities, litter barrels, petwalk, ⊙, 🛏 vending
35	MD 66, to Boonsboro, **S** ⛽ Sheetz/dsl (1mi) ⊙ camping, to Greenbrier SP
32b a	US 40, Hagerstown, **N 0-3 mi** ⛽ 7-11, BP, Exxon/dsl, Sheetz/dsl, Sunoco 🍴 5 Guys Burgers, Baskin-Robbins/Dunkin Donuts, Bob Evans, Burger King, Checkers, Denny's, DQ, El Ranchero Mexican, Hall of Fame Rest., Hong Kong Chinese, Jimmy John's, KFC, Ledo's Pizza, Little Caesars, McDonald's, Papa John's, Papa Murphy's, Pizza Hut, Popeye's, Quiznos, Sonic, Subway, Super Buffet, Taco Bell, TX Roadhouse

MD

(Vertical label left margin: BALTIMORE)

(Vertical label right margin: FREDERICK)

🅿 = gas 🍴 = food 🛏 = lodging 🅾 = other 🆁🆂 = rest stop   Copyright 2015 - the Next EXIT ®

MD

HAGERSTOWN

INTERSTATE 70 Cont'd

Exit #	Services
32b a	Continued
	🛏 Best Western, Clarion, Comfort Suites, Days Inn, Hampton Inn, Super 8 🅾 🅷, $Tree, Advance Parts, Aldi Foods, AT&T, AutoZone, Cadillac/Chevrolet, Chrysler/Dodge/Jeep, CVS Drug, Family$, Firestone/auto, Martin's Foods, Mercedes, Midas, Mr Tire, Nissan, Tires+, Toyota/Scion, Walgreens, Weis Foods, S 🅾 Buick/GMC, Honda, Kia, Subaru, VW
29b a	MD 65, to Sharpsburg, N 🅿 Exxon/Subway/dsl, Sheetz 🍴 FoodCourt, Longhorn Steaks, Starbucks 🅾 🅷, Prime Outlets/famous brands, st police, S 🅿 Liberty/7-11/dsl 🍴 Burger King, Cracker Barrel, McDonald's, Waffle House, Wendy's 🛏 Sleep Inn 🅾 Safari Camping, to Antietam Bfd
28	MD 632, Hagerstown
26	I-81, N to Harrisburg, S to Martinsburg
24	MD 63, Huyett, N 🅿 ⬜⬜⬜/Subway/dsl/24hr, Sheetz/dsl (2mi), S 🛏 Red Roof Inn 🅾 C&O Canal, KOA (2mi)
18	MD 68 E, Clear Spring, N 🅿 BP, Liberty 🍴 McDonald's 🛏 Sleep Inn, S 🅿 Exxon/dsl 🍴 Wendy Hill Café
12	MD 56, Indian Springs, S 🅿 Exxon/dsl 🅾 Ft Frederick SP
9	US 40 E (from eb, exits left), Indian Springs
5	MD 615 (no immediate wb return), N 🅾 Log Cabin Rest. (2mi)
3	MD 144, Hancock (exits left from wb), S 🅿 ACT/Exxon/dsl, Liberty/rest./dsl/24hr 🍴 Hardee's, Park'n Dine 🛏 Hilltop Inn 🅾 Blue Goose Mkt
1b	US 522 (exits left from both lanes), Hancock, N 🅿 Mobil/dsl Sheetz/dsl, S 🅿 PitStop 🍴 Pizza Hut, Subway, Weaver's Rest. 🛏 Best Value Inn, Super 8 🅾 $General, Chevrolet, Chrysler/Dodge/Jeep, Happy Hills Camp, NAPA, Save-A-Lot Foods
1a	I-68 W, US 40, W to Cumberland
0mm	Maryland/Pennsylvania state line, Mason-Dixon Line

INTERSTATE 81

Exit #	Services
12mm	Maryland/Pennsylvania state line
10b a	Showalter Rd, E 🅾 ⟲
9	Maugans Ave, E 🅿 BP, Sheetz, Shell/Domino's/dsl 🍴 McDonald's, Papa Murphy's, Pizza Hut, Quiznos, Taco Bell, Waffle House 🛏 Hampton Inn 🅾 $General, AutoZone, CVS Drug, Food Lion, Martin's Foods/gas, vet, W 🍴 Burger King 🛏 Microtel 🅾 Kenworth, Volvo
7b a	MD 58, Hagerstown, same as 6
6b a	US 40, Hagerstown, E 🅿 Shell 🛏 Comfort Inn, Days Inn, Super 8 🅾 🅷, W 🍴 5 Guys Burgers, Arby's, Chipotle Mexican, IHOP, Jersey Mike's Subs, KFC, McDonald's, Panera Bread, Ryan's, Starbucks, Subway, TGIFriday's, Uno Pizza, Wendy's 🅾 $Tree, AT&T, Best Buy, Dick's, Home Depot, Marshall's, Petsmart, Walmart
5b a	Halfway Blvd, E 🅿 AC&T/dsl 🍴 Bob Evans, Boston Mkt, Buffalo Wild Wings, Burger King, Café Rio, Chick-fil-A, Chuck-ECheese's, CiCi's Pizza, Cinco de Mayo, Coldstone, Crazy Horse Steaks, El Ranchero Mexican, Garfield's Rest., Golden Corral, McDonald's, Olive Garden, Orchid Garden, Outback Steaks, Papa John's, Pizza Hut, Popeye's, Quizno's, Red Lobster, Roy Rogers, Ruby Tuesday, Sakura Steaks, Shoney's, Taco Bell, Tilted Kilt, Wendy's 🛏 Country Inn&Suites, Courtyard, Holiday Inn Express, Homewood Suites, Motel 6,

5b a	Continued
	Ramada, SpringHill Suites 🅾 $Tree, AT&T, BigLots, BonTon, CVS Drug, Firestone/auto, Ford, Hobby Lobby, Hyundai, JC Penney, K-Mart, Lowe's, Macy's, mall, Martin's Foods/gas, Michael's, PetCo, Ross, Sam's Club/gas, Sears/auto, Staples, Target, W 🅿 Exxon/dsl/scales/24hr, ⬜⬜⬜/McDonald's/Subway/dsl/scales/24hr 🛏 Super 8 🅾 Freightliner
4	I-70, E to Frederick, W to Hancock, to I-68
2	US 11, Williamsport, E 🅿 AC&T/dsl, W 🅿 Exxon/dsl, Sunoco/dsl 🍴 China 88, McDonald's, Subway, Waffle House 🛏 Red Roof Inn 🅾 auto repair, KOA (4mi)
1	MD 63, MD 68, Williamsport, E 🅿 Bowman/dsl 🅾 Jellystone, KOA, to Antietam Bfd, W 🅿 Citgo 🅾 $General, NAPA
0mm	Maryland/West Virginia state line, Potomac River

INTERSTATE 83

Exit #	Services
38mm	Maryland/Pennsylvania state line, Mason-Dixon Line
37	to Freeland (from sb)
36	MD 439, Bel Air, W 🅿 Filler-Up 🍴 Maryland Line Inn Grill 🅾 Holiday Travel Park (5mi), Morris Meadows Camping (5mi)
35mm	weigh/insp sta sb
33	MD 45, Parkton, E 🅾 USPO
31	Middletown Rd, to Parkton, E 🅾 golf
27	MD 137, Mt Carmel, Hereford, E 🅿 Exxon/dsl 🍴 Michael's Pizza, Monkton Grill, Subway 🅾 7-11, Graul's Foods, Hereford Drug, Mt Carmel Drug, USPO, vet
24	Belfast Rd, to Butler, Sparks
20	Shawan Rd, Hunt Valley, E 🅿 Exxon/dsl, Mobil 🍴 Burger King, CA Pizza, Carrabba's, Chick-fil-A, Chipotle Mexican, Coal Fire Cafe, Joe's Crabshack, McDonald's, Noodles&Co, Outback Steaks, Panera Bread, Pei Wei, Sakura Hibachi, Subway 🛏 Courtyard, Embassy Suites, Holiday Inn Express, Hunt Valley Inn, Residence Inn 🅾 Burlington Coats, Dick's, Giant Foods, Goodyear/auto, Marshall's, Sears/auto, Verizon, vet, Wegman's Foods
18	Warren Rd (from nb, no return), Cockeysville, E **services on York Rd** 🛏
17	Padonia Rd, Deereco Rd, E 🅿 7-11, BP/dsl, Gulf/dsl, Hess/dsl 🍴 Applebee's, Bob Evans, Chili's, Macaroni Grill, Wendy's 🛏 Extended Stay America, Hampton Inn, Holiday Inn 🅾 Audi/VW, Chevrolet, Goodyear/auto, Lowe's Whse, Mars Mkt, Mr Tire, Porsche, Rite Aid, Sam's Club, services E on York Rd, Subaru, Target, USPO
16b a	Timonium Rd, E **on York Rd** 🅿 Sunoco/dsl 🍴 Baja Fresh, Firehouse Subs, Little Caesar's, McDonald's 🛏 N Baltimore Plaza Hotel, Red Roof Inn 🅾 Infiniti/Nissan, Petsmart, REI, Rite Aid, ShopRite Foods
14	I-695 N
13	I-695 S, Falls Rd, 🅾 🅷, st police
12	Ruxton Rd (from nb, no return)
10b a	Northern Parkway, E 🅿 Exxon, Shell, W 🅾 🅷
9b a	Cold Spring Lane
8	MD 25 N (from nb), Falls Rd
7b a	28th St, E 🅾 🅷, W 🅾 Baltimore Zoo
6	US 1, US 40T, North Ave, downtown
5	MD Ave (from sb), downtown
3	Chase St, Gilford St, downtown
2	Pleasant St (from sb), downtown
1	Fayette St, **I-83 begins/ends, downtown Baltimore**

BALTIMORE

INTERSTATE 95

Exit #	Services
110mm	Maryland/Delaware state line
109b a	MD 279, to Elkton, Newark, **E** 🅖 ⊕*FLYING J*/Patriot Farms/dsl/scales/24hr/@, Shell/dsl 🍴 Cracker Barrel, KFC/Taco Bell, McDonald's, Waffle House 🛏 Days Inn, Elkton Lodge, Hampton Inn, Knights Inn, La Quinta, Motel 6 🅞 🅷, Blue Beacon, **W** 🅖 7-11, TA/Subway/dsl/24hr/@, WaWa 🛏 Comfort Suites 🅞 to U of DE
100	MD 272, to North East, Rising Sun, **E** 🅖 ⊕*FLYING J*/Denny's/dsl/LP/24hr, Sunoco/dsl 🍴 Burger King, Dunkin Donuts, Empire Rest., Frank's Pizza, McDonald's, Waffle House, Wendy's 🛏 Comfort Inn, Holiday Inn Express 🅞 $General, $Tree, Advance Parts, AT&T, auto repair, Food Lion, PetCo, Rite Aid, st police, to Elk Neck SP, Verizon, Walgreens, Walmart/Subway, **W** 🅖 Citgo 🛏 Best Western 🅞 zoo
96mm	**Chesapeake House service area** (exits left from both lanes) Exxon/dsl, Sunoco/dsl 🍴 Burger King, Popeye's, Quiznos, Starbucks 🅞 gifts
93	MD 275, to Rising Sun, US 222, to Perryville, **E** 🅖 Exxon/dsl, 🚛/Subway/dsl/scales/24hr 🍴 Denny's, KFC/Taco Bell 🛏 Ramada Inn 🅞 🅷, Perryville Outlets/famous brands, Riverview Camping
92mm	weigh sta/toll booth
91.5mm	Susquehanna River
89	MD 155, to Havre de Grace **(last nb exit before toll)**, **E** 1-3 mi 🍴 Burger King, Chesapeake Grill, Dunkin Donuts, MacGregor's Rest., McDonald's, Waffle House 🛏 Best Budget Inn, Super 8, Van Divers B&B 🅞 🅷, **W** 🅞 to Susquehanna SP
85	MD 22, to Aberdeen, **E** 🅖 7-11, BP/dsl, Royal Farms/dsl, Shell/dsl 🍴 Applebee's, Arby's, Baskin-Robbins/Dunkin Donuts, Bob Evans, Burger King, Durango's, Family Buffet, KFC, Korea House, Little Caesars, Mamie's Cafe, McDonald's, Olive Tree Italian, Panera Bread, Papa John's, Pizza Hut, Rita's Custard, Subway, Taco Bell, Wendy's 🛏 Clarion, Courtyard, Days Inn, Hilton Garden, Holiday Inn, La Quinta, Red Roof Inn, Residence Inn, Super 8, Travelodge 🅞 $General, $Tree, auto repair, Home Depot, Mars Foods, museum, Radio Shack, Rite Aid, ShopRite Foods, Target, Verizon, Walgreens
81mm	**MD House service area** (exits left from both lanes) 🅖 Exxon/dsl, Sunoco/dsl 🍴 Phillips Seafood, Roy Rogers, Sbarro's, Starbucks, TCBY 🅞 gifts
80	MD 543, to Riverside, Churchville, **E** 🅖 7-11, BP/Burger King, Shell/Quiznos/dsl, Sunoco 🍴 Arby's, China Moon, Cracker Barrel, McDonald's, Pizza Hut, Riverside Crabs, Riverside Grille, Riverside Pizzeria, Ruby Tuesday, Subway, Waffle House 🛏 Candlewood Suites, Country Inn&Suites, Extended Stay America, Homewood Suites, SpringHill Suites, Wingate Inn 🅞 Bar Harbor RV Park (4mi), Rite Aid, ShopRite Foods, Verizon
77b a	MD 24, to Edgewood, Bel Air, **E** 🅖 BP/dsl, Citgo/dsl, Exxon/dsl, Royal Farms/dsl 🍴 Denny's, Dimitri's Pizza, El Rodeo, My 3 Sons Rest., Waffle House 🛏 Best Western, Days Inn, Hampton Inn, Holiday Inn Express, Ramada Inn, Sleep Inn 🅞 URGENT CARE, **W** 🅖 Exxon/dsl, WaWa/dsl 🍴 Chick-fil-A, KFC/Taco Bell, McDonald's, Starbucks 🅞 🅷, $Tree, BJ's Whse, Lowe's, Target, Walmart/Subway, Wegman's Foods
74	MD 152, Fallston, Joppatowne, **E** 🅖 BP/dsl, Citgo/dsl, Exxon/dsl, Sheetz, Shell/dsl, WaWa/dsl 🍴 Dunkin Donuts, Friendly's, KFC, Subway, Venitian Palace, Wendy's 🛏 Edgewood Motel, Super 8 🅞 🅷, Toyota (1mi), **W** 🅖 Royal Farms/dsl

70mm	Big Gunpowder Falls
67b a	MD 43, to White Marsh Blvd, US 1, US 40, **E on MD 7** 🅖 BP/dsl 🍴 5 Guys Burgers, Chick-fil-A, McDonald's, Noodles&Co, Panera Bread, Qdoba Mexian, Starbucks, Subway 🅞 Best Buy, Carmax, Chevrolet, Dick's, Lowe's, Michael's, Nissan, Target, Tire Discounters **W on White Marsh Blvd**, 🅖 7-11, Exxon/dsl 🍴 Bertucci's, Buffalo Wild Wings, Burger King, Chili's, China Wok, Coldstone, Don Pablo, Lin's Chinese, McDonald's, Olive Garden, PF Chang's, Red Brick Sta., Red Lobster, Red Robin, Ruby Tuesday, Starbucks, Taco Bell, TGIFriday's, Wendy's, Zack's Hotdogs, Z-Burger 🛏 Fairfield Inn, Hampton Inn, Hilton Garden, Residence Inn 🅞 AT&T, Barnes&Noble, Giant Foods, JC Penney, Macy's, mall, Old Navy, Sears/auto, Staples, to Gunpowder SP, USPO, Verizon
64b a	I-695 (exits left), **E** to Essex, **W** to Towson
62	to I-895 (from sb)
61	US 40, Pulaski Hwy, **E** 🅖 BP, Shell/dsl 🍴 McDonald's
60	Moravia Rd
59	Eastern Ave, **W** 🅖 BP/dsl, Exxon, Royal Farms/dsl, WaWa 🍴 Broadway Diner, McDonald's, Subway, Wendy's 🅞 🅷, AT&T, Shoppers Foods
58	Dundalk Ave, (from nb), **E** 🅖 Citgo, Sunoco
57	O'Donnell St, Boston St, **E** 🅖 TA/Buckhorn/Subway/dsl/scales/motel/@ 🍴 McDonald's 🛏 Best Western
56mm	McHenry Tunnel, toll plaza (north side of tunnel)
56	Keith Ave
55	Key Hwy, to Ft McHenry NM, **last nb exit before toll**
54	MD 2 S, to Hanover St, **W** 🅞 🅷, Harris Teeter, downtown
53	I-395 N, to MLK, **W** 🅞 Oriole Park, downtown
52	Russell St N, **W** 🅞 🅷
51	Washington Blvd
50.5mm	inspection sta nb
50	Caton Ave, **E** 🅖 Hess/dsl, Shell/dsl, US/dsl 🍴 Caton House, Loafers Grill, McDonald's 🛏 Motel 6 🅞 7-11, Aldi Foods, auto repair, Midas, Toyota/Scion, **W** 🅞 🅷
49b a	I-695, **E** to Key Bridge, Glen Burnie, **W** to Towson, to I-70, to I-83
47b a	I-195, to MD 166, to BWI 🛫, to Baltimore
46	I-895, to Harbor Tunnel Thruway
43b a	MD 100, to Glen Burnie, **E** 1 mi on US 1 🅖 Exxon/Wendy's/dsl, Xtra 🛏 Best Western
41b a	MD 175, to Columbia, **E** 🅖 BP/dsl, Exxon/dsl, Shell/dsl, TA/Country Pride/Subway/dsl/scales/24hr/@ 🍴 Arby's, Burger King, Frank's Diner, IHOP, McDonald's, Panda Express, Starbucks 🛏 Comfort Suites, Holiday Inn, La Quinta, Red Roof Inn, Sleep Inn, Super 8 🅞 $Tree, Advance Parts, Mom's Organic Mkt, **W** 🅖 Exxon 🍴 Bob Evans, Fat Burger, Houlihan's, Jersey Mike's, McDonald's, Mimi's Cafe, Olive Garden,

A B E R D E E N (vertical, left margin)

B A L T I M O R E (vertical, middle margin)

MD (tab, right margin)

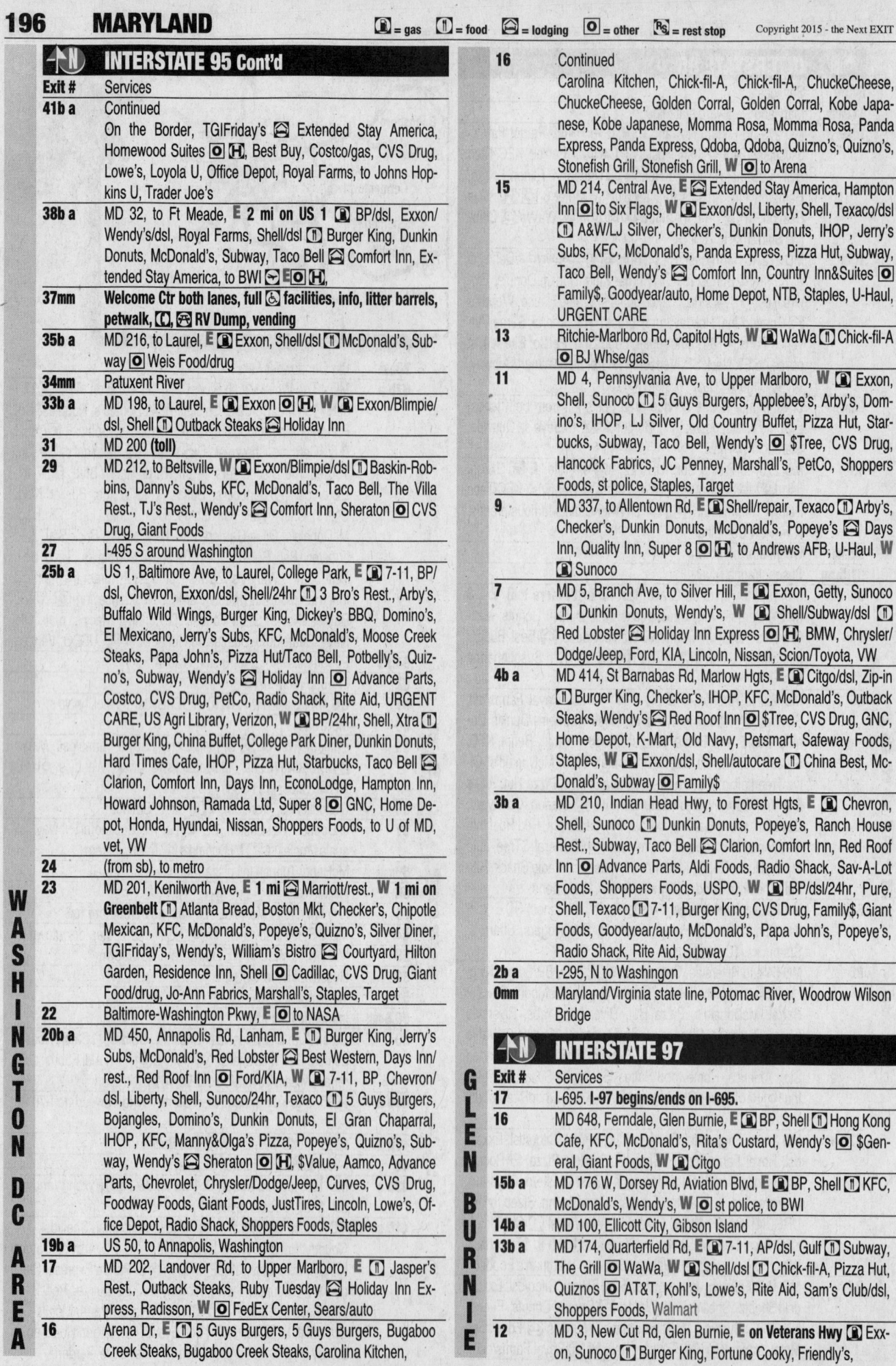

⬆N INTERSTATE 95 Cont'd

Exit #	Services
41b a	Continued On the Border, TGIFriday's 🏠 Extended Stay America, Homewood Suites 🅞 🏠, Best Buy, Costco/gas, CVS Drug, Lowe's, Loyola U, Office Depot, Royal Farms, to Johns Hopkins U, Trader Joe's
38b a	MD 32, to Ft Meade, **E 2 mi on US 1** 🅟 BP/dsl, Exxon/Wendy's/dsl, Royal Farms, Shell/dsl 🍴 Burger King, Dunkin Donuts, McDonald's, Subway, Taco Bell 🏠 Comfort Inn, Extended Stay America, to BWI 🖂🅞🏠,
37mm	**Welcome Ctr both lanes, full 🛇 facilities, info, litter barrels, petwalk, 🛈, 🚐 RV Dump, vending**
35b a	MD 216, to Laurel, **E** 🅟 Exxon, Shell/dsl 🍴 McDonald's, Subway 🅞 Weis Food/drug
34mm	Patuxent River
33b a	MD 198, to Laurel, **E** 🅟 Exxon 🅞 🏠, **W** 🅟 Exxon/Blimpie/dsl, Shell 🍴 Outback Steaks 🏠 Holiday Inn
31	MD 200 **(toll)**
29	MD 212, to Beltsville, **W** 🅟 Exxon/Blimpie/dsl 🍴 Baskin-Robbins, Danny's Subs, KFC, McDonald's, Taco Bell, The Villa Rest., TJ's Rest., Wendy's 🏠 Comfort Inn, Sheraton 🅞 CVS Drug, Giant Foods
27	I-495 S around Washington
25b a	US 1, Baltimore Ave, to Laurel, College Park, **E** 🅟 7-11, BP/dsl, Chevron, Exxon/dsl, Shell/24hr 🍴 3 Bro's Rest., Arby's, Buffalo Wild Wings, Burger King, Dickey's BBQ, Domino's, El Mexicano, Jerry's Subs, KFC, McDonald's, Moose Creek Steaks, Papa John's, Pizza Hut/Taco Bell, Potbelly's, Quizno's, Subway, Wendy's 🏠 Holiday Inn 🅞 Advance Parts, Costco, CVS Drug, PetCo, Radio Shack, Rite Aid, URGENT CARE, US Agri Library, Verizon, **W** 🅟 BP/24hr, Shell, Xtra 🍴 Burger King, China Buffet, College Park Diner, Dunkin Donuts, Hard Times Cafe, IHOP, Pizza Hut, Starbucks, Taco Bell 🏠 Clarion, Comfort Inn, Days Inn, EconoLodge, Hampton Inn, Howard Johnson, Ramada Ltd, Super 8 🅞 GNC, Home Depot, Honda, Hyundai, Nissan, Shoppers Foods, to U of MD, vet, VW
24	(from sb), to metro
23	MD 201, Kenilworth Ave, **E 1 mi** 🍴 Marriott/rest., **W 1 mi on Greenbelt** 🍴 Atlanta Bread, Boston Mkt, Checker's, Chipotle Mexican, KFC, McDonald's, Popeye's, Quizno's, Silver Diner, TGIFriday's, Wendy's, William's Bistro 🏠 Courtyard, Hilton Garden, Residence Inn, Shell 🅞 Cadillac, CVS Drug, Giant Food/drug, Jo-Ann Fabrics, Marshall's, Staples, Target
22	Baltimore-Washington Pkwy, **E** 🅞 to NASA
20b a	MD 450, Annapolis Rd, Lanham, **E** 🍴 Burger King, Jerry's Subs, McDonald's, Red Lobster 🏠 Best Western, Days Inn/rest., Red Roof Inn 🅞 Ford/KIA, **W** 🅟 7-11, BP, Chevron/dsl, Liberty, Shell, Sunoco/24hr, Texaco 🍴 5 Guys Burgers, Bojangles, Domino's, Dunkin Donuts, El Gran Chaparral, IHOP, KFC, Manny&Olga's Pizza, Popeye's, Quizno's, Subway, Wendy's 🏠 Sheraton 🅞 🏠, $Value, Aamco, Advance Parts, Chevrolet, Chrysler/Dodge/Jeep, Curves, CVS Drug, Foodway Foods, Giant Foods, JustTires, Lincoln, Lowe's, Office Depot, Radio Shack, Shoppers Foods, Staples
19b a	US 50, to Annapolis, Washington
17	MD 202, Landover Rd, to Upper Marlboro, **E** 🍴 Jasper's Rest., Outback Steaks, Ruby Tuesday 🏠 Holiday Inn Express, Radisson, **W** 🅞 FedEx Center, Sears/auto
16	Arena Dr, **E** 🍴 5 Guys Burgers, 5 Guys Burgers, Bugaboo Creek Steaks, Bugaboo Creek Steaks, Carolina Kitchen,

16	Continued Carolina Kitchen, Chick-fil-A, Chick-fil-A, ChuckeCheese, ChuckeCheese, Golden Corral, Golden Corral, Kobe Japanese, Kobe Japanese, Momma Rosa, Momma Rosa, Panda Express, Panda Express, Qdoba, Qdoba, Quizno's, Quizno's, Stonefish Grill, Stonefish Grill, **W** 🅞 to Arena
15	MD 214, Central Ave, **E** 🏠 Extended Stay America, Hampton Inn 🅞 to Six Flags, **W** 🅟 Exxon/dsl, Liberty, Shell, Texaco/dsl 🍴 A&W/LJ Silver, Checker's, Dunkin Donuts, IHOP, Jerry's Subs, KFC, McDonald's, Panda Express, Pizza Hut, Subway, Taco Bell, Wendy's 🏠 Comfort Inn, Country Inn&Suites 🅞 Family$, Goodyear/auto, Home Depot, NTB, Staples, U-Haul, URGENT CARE
13	Ritchie-Marlboro Rd, Capitol Hgts, **W** 🅟 WaWa 🍴 Chick-fil-A 🅞 BJ Whse/gas
11	MD 4, Pennsylvania Ave, to Upper Marlboro, **W** 🅟 Exxon, Shell, Sunoco 🍴 5 Guys Burgers, Applebee's, Arby's, Domino's, IHOP, LJ Silver, Old Country Buffet, Pizza Hut, Starbucks, Subway, Taco Bell, Wendy's 🅞 $Tree, CVS Drug, Hancock Fabrics, JC Penney, Marshall's, PetCo, Shoppers Foods, st police, Staples, Target
9	MD 337, to Allentown Rd, **E** 🅟 Shell/repair, Texaco 🍴 Arby's, Checker's, Dunkin Donuts, McDonald's, Popeye's 🏠 Days Inn, Quality Inn, Super 8 🅞 🏠, to Andrews AFB, U-Haul, **W** 🅟 Sunoco
7	MD 5, Branch Ave, to Silver Hill, **E** 🅟 Exxon, Getty, Sunoco 🍴 Dunkin Donuts, Wendy's, **W** 🅟 Shell/Subway/dsl 🍴 Red Lobster 🏠 Holiday Inn Express 🅞 🏠, BMW, Chrysler/Dodge/Jeep, Ford, KIA, Lincoln, Nissan, Scion/Toyota, VW
4b a	MD 414, St Barnabas Rd, Marlow Hgts, **E** 🅟 Citgo/dsl, Zip-in 🍴 Burger King, Checker's, IHOP, KFC, McDonald's, Outback Steaks, Wendy's 🏠 Red Roof Inn 🅞 $Tree, CVS Drug, GNC, Home Depot, K-Mart, Old Navy, Petsmart, Safeway Foods, Staples, **W** 🅟 Exxon/dsl, Shell/autocare 🍴 China Best, McDonald's, Subway 🅞 Family$
3b a	MD 210, Indian Head Hwy, to Forest Hgts, **E** 🅟 Chevron, Shell, Sunoco 🍴 Dunkin Donuts, Popeye's, Ranch House Rest., Subway, Taco Bell 🏠 Clarion, Comfort Inn, Red Roof Inn 🅞 Advance Parts, Aldi Foods, Radio Shack, Sav-A-Lot Foods, Shoppers Foods, USPO, **W** 🅟 BP/dsl/24hr, Pure, Shell, Texaco 🍴 7-11, Burger King, CVS Drug, Family$, Giant Foods, Goodyear/auto, McDonald's, Papa John's, Popeye's, Radio Shack, Rite Aid, Subway
2b a	I-295, N to Washingon
0mm	Maryland/Virginia state line, Potomac River, Woodrow Wilson Bridge

⬆N INTERSTATE 97

Exit #	Services
17	I-695. **I-97 begins/ends on I-695.**
16	MD 648, Ferndale, Glen Burnie, **E** 🅟 BP, Shell 🍴 Hong Kong Cafe, KFC, McDonald's, Rita's Custard, Wendy's 🅞 $General, Giant Foods, **W** 🅟 Citgo
15b a	MD 176 W, Dorsey Rd, Aviation Blvd, **E** 🅟 BP, Shell 🍴 KFC, McDonald's, Wendy's, **W** 🅞 st police, to BWI
14b a	MD 100, Ellicott City, Gibson Island
13b a	MD 174, Quarterfield Rd, **E** 🅟 7-11, AP/dsl, Gulf 🍴 Subway, The Grill 🅞 WaWa, **W** 🅟 Shell/dsl 🍴 Chick-fil-A, Pizza Hut, Quiznos 🅞 AT&T, Kohl's, Lowe's, Rite Aid, Sam's Club/dsl, Shoppers Foods, Walmart
12	MD 3, New Cut Rd, Glen Burnie, **E on Veterans Hwy** 🅟 Exxon, Sunoco 🍴 Burger King, Fortune Cooky, Friendly's,

⬆N INTERSTATE 97 Cont'd

Exit #	Services
12	Continued Hardee's, Squisto NY Pizza, Subway, Wendy's 🅾 🍴, Ace Hardware, Giant Foods, Goodyear/auto, Target, Walgreens, 🚗 BP, Gulf, Royal Farms, WaWa 🍴 Domino's, KFC, McDonald's, Taco Bell 🅾 CVS Drug, vet
10b a	Benfield Blvd, Severna Park, **E** 🚗 BP/dsl, Exxon/Quiznos/dsl, Transit/dsl/scales 🍴 Baskin-Robbins/Dunkin Donuts, Hella's Rest., Ledo's Pizza 🅾 7-11, access to same as 12, KOA
7	MD 3, MD 32, Bowie, Odenton, **E** 🛏
5	MD 178 (from sb, no EZ return), Crownsville
0mm	**I-97 begins/ends on US 50/301.**

⬆N INTERSTATE 270

Exit #	Services
32	**I-270 begins/ends on I-70, exit 53.**
31b a	MD 85, **N** 🚗 7-11, Lowest Price/dsl, Sheetz/24hr, Shell/24hr, SouStates/dsl 🍴 Applebee's, Arby's, Bob Evans, Burger King, Checker's, Chick-fil-A, El Ranchero Mexican, Golden Corral, Houlihan's, Jerry's Pizza, KFC, Longhorn Steaks, McDonald's, Olive Garden, Panera Bread, Papa John's, Peking Gourmet, Perkin's, Pizza Hut, Popeye's, Roy Rogers, Ruby Tuesday, Silver Diner, Subway, Taco Bell, UNO Grill, Waffle House, Wendy's 🛏 Days Inn, EconoLodge, Holiday Inn Express, Sleep Inn, Travelodge 🅾 Aamco, Audi, Barnes&Noble, Best Buy, Buick/GMC, Chrysler/Dodge/Jeep, Costco/gas, Harley-Davidson, Home Depot, Hyundai, JC Penney, Kohl's, Lincoln, Lowe's, Macy's, mall, Michael's, Mr Tire, Nissan, Office Depot, Ross, Sam's Club, Sears/auto, Staples, Tires+, vet, Volvo, Walmart, **S** 🚗 BP 🍴 Chipotle Mexican, Cracker Barrel, Firehouse Subs, IHOP, Macaroni Grill, Maggie Moo's, McDonald's, Mediterranean Grill, Mimi's Cafe, Panda Express, Quizno's, Starbucks, TGIFriday's 🛏 Comfort Inn, Courtyard, Extended Stay America, Fairfield Inn, Hampton Inn, Hilton Garden, MainStay Suites, Residence Inn 🅾 Honda, Toyota
30mm	Monocacy River
28mm	scenic view (wb only), no restrooms
26	MD 80, Urbana, **N** 🚗 7-11, Exxon 🍴 Buffalo Wild Wings, China Taste, Dunkin Donuts, Foster's Grill, Ledo's Pizza, McDonald's, Waffle House
22	MD 109, to Barnesville, Hyattstown, **N** 🚗 BP/dsl 🍴 Hyattstown Deli 🅾 Food+
21mm	weigh/insp sta both lanes
18	MD 121, to Clarksburg, Boyds, **N** camping, gas, Little Bennett Pk, **S** Blackhill Pk
16	MD 27, Father Hurley Blvd, to Damascus, **N** 🚗 Chevron, Exxon, Free State/dsl, Sunoco 🍴 Applebee's, Bob Evans, Burger King, Jersey Mike's Subs, McDonald's, Starbucks, Subway 🛏 Extended Stay America, Hampton Inn 🅾 AT&T, Best Buy, Giant Foods, GNC, Home Depot, Kohl's, Michael's, PepBoys, Petsmart, Target, TJ Maxx, Verizon, Walmart, **S** 🚗 7-11, BP, Exxon, Shell, Sunoco 🍴 5 Guys Burgers, Bailey's Grill, Baja Fresh, Burger King, Carrabba's, Chick-fil-A, Domino's, Dunkin Donuts, Hardtimes Cafe, IHOP, Jerry's Subs, Longhorn Steaks, McDonald's, Mi Rancho, Panera Bread, Pizza Hut, Quizno's, Red Robin, Ruby Tuesday, Starbucks, Subway, Taco Bell, Wendy's 🛏 Fairfield Inn, Homestead Suites 🅾 Giant Foods, Mercedes, NAPA, NTB, Office Depot, PetCo, Rite Aid, Safeway Foods, same as 15, SmartCar, USPO
15b a	MD 118, to MD 355, **S** 🅾 Honda, Nissan, same as 16
13b a	Middlebrook Rd (from wb)

GAITHERSBURG ROCKVILLE (vertical text)

11	MD 124, Quince Orchard Rd, **N** 🚗 Exxon, Shell 🍴 Boston Mkt, ChuckeCheese, Honeybaked Ham, Ichiban Rest., KFC, McDonald's, Panera Bread, Popeye's, Subway 🛏 Hilton, Holiday Inn, TownePlace Suites, Wyndham Garden 🅾 Aamco, Acura, AT&T, Costco, CVS Drugs, Ford, Hyundai, JC Penney, JustTires, Lincoln, Lord&Taylor, Macy's, mall, Mazda, NAPA, Nissan, Ross, Sam's Club, Sears/auto, Toyota, VW, **S** 🚗 Shell/dsl 🍴 Chevy's Mexican, CiCi's Pizza, Jerry's Subs, Rita's Ice Cream, Starbucks 🛏 Motel 6 🅾 Advance Parts, Chevrolet, Chrysler/Dodge/Jeep, Giant Foods, JoAnn Fabrics, McGruder's Foods, Rite Aid, Seneca Creek SP, Staples
10	MD 117, Clopper Rd (from wb), same as 11
9b a	I-370, to Gaithersburg, Sam Eig Hwy, **S on Washington Blvd** 🚗 Chevron 🍴 Joe's Crabshack, Macaroni Grill, Pizza Hut, Red Rock Grill, Subway, Uncle Julio's 🛏 Courtyard 🅾 Barnes&Noble, Kohl's, Target, Weis Mkt
8	Shady Grove Rd, **N** 🚗 Chevron, Shell/dsl 🍴 Bugaboo Creek Steaks, Burger King, Red Lobster 🛏 Sheraton 🅾 7-11, AT&T, Best Buy, Home Depot, Office Depot, vet, **S** 🍴 Thatsamore 🛏 Courtyard, Crowne Plaza, Marriott, Residence Inn, Sleep Inn, SpringHill Suites 🅾 🍴
6b a	MD 28, W Montgomery Ave, **N** 🅾 🍴, **S** 🚗 Shell 🛏 Best Western
5b a	MD 189, Falls Rd
4b a	Montrose Rd, **N** 🚗, **S** 🍴 Starbucks 🅾 Harris Teeter, Walgreens st police
2	I-270/I-270 spur diverges eb, converges wb
1b a	(I-270 spur)Democracy Blvd, **E** 🛏 Marriott, **W** 🚗 Exxon/dsl, Shell/dsl 🍴 Macy's, mall, Nordstrom's, Sears
1	MD 187, Old Georgetown Rd, **S** 🚗 Exxon 🍴 Hamburger Hamlet 🅾 🍴, Balducci's Foods, Giant Foods, GNC
0mm	**I-270 begins/ends on I-495, exit 35.**

INTERSTATE 495 (DC)

See Virginia Interstate 495 (DC)

⬆N INTERSTATE 695 (Baltimore)

Exit #	Services
48mm	Francis Scott Key Br, Patapsco River
44	MD 695 (from nb)
43mm	**toll plaza**
42	MD 151 S, Sparrows Point (last exit before toll sb), **E** 🚗 Citgo/dsl 🅾 North Point SP
41	MD 20, Cove Rd, **W** 🚗 Royal Farms, WaWa 🍴 Burger King, McDonald's, Subway
40	MD 150, MD 151, North Point Blvd, (nb only)
39	Merritt Blvd, **W** 🚗 BP 🍴 Burger King, McDonald's 🛏 $Tree, Aldi Foods, Ford, Giant Foods, Honda, Hyundai, JC Penney, Mazda, Mr Tire, Walmart

MD

⬆N INTERSTATE 695 (Baltimore) Cont'd

Exit #	Services
38b a	MD 150, Eastern Blvd, to Baltimore, **E** 🛢 Royal Farms, **W** ⏺ Applebee's, Arby's, Burger King, Cactus Willy's Steaks, Checker's, Chick-fil-A, Dunkin Donuts ⊙ AT&T, Kia/Nissan, mall, Sears/auto, Staples, Walgreens
36	MD 702 S (exits left from sb), Essex
35	US 40, **N** 🛢 Sunoco, WaWa/gas ⏺ Arby's, Bateman's Bistro, Chipotle Mexican, DQ, Dunkin Donuts, Grand Buffet, Longhorn Steaks, Panda Express, Panera Bread ⊙ Aldi Foods, Best Buy, Harley-Davidson, Home Depot, NTB, Office Depot, PetCo, same as 34, Sam's Club/gas, U-Haul, Walmart
34	MD 7, Philadelphia Rd, **N** ⏺ McDonald's, Wendy's 🏠 La Quinta ⊙ Ⓗ, $General, $Tree, Giant Foods, Goodyear/auto, Marshall's, **S** 🛢 Exxon ⊙ same as 35, Walgreens
33b a	I-95, N to Philadelphia, S to Baltimore
32b a	US 1, Bel Air, **N** 🛢 Exxon ⏺ Arby's, Bob Evans, Burger King, Denny's, Dunkin Donuts, Golden Corral, IHOP, McDonald's, Taco Bell ⊙ $Tree, 7-11, BJ's Whse, Giant Foods, K-Mart, Merchants Tire/auto, Mr Tire/auto, Toyota/Scion, Verizon, vet, **S** 🛢 Shell ⏺ Baskin-Robbins/Dunkin Donuts, Carrabba's, McDonald's, Rita's Custard, Subway, Szechuan Taste ⊙ 7-11, Goodyear/auto
31c	MD 43 E (from eb, exits left)
31b a	MD 147, Harford Rd, **N** 🛢 7-11, BP, CF/dsl, Shell/dsl ⏺ Dunkin Donuts, Wendy's ⊙ Chrysler/Jeep, CVS Drug, Goodyear/auto, Honda, Mars Foods, VW, Walgreens
30b a	MD 41, Perring Pkwy, **N** 🛢 Shell ⏺ 5 Guys Burgers, Burger King, Checker's, Chick-fil-A, Denny's, Dunkin Donuts, KFC, McDonald's, Popeye's, Rita's Custard, Subway, Taco Bell ⊙ Advance Parts, Chevrolet, Ford, Home Depot, Jo-Ann Fabrics, K-Mart, NTB, Office Depot, Ross, Safeway Foods, Shoppers Foods, Tuesday Morning, Verizon
29b	MD 542, Loch Raven Blvd, **S** 🛢 BP, Gulf, Hess ⏺ Bel-Loch Diner, Hooters, McDonald's, Pizza Hut, Subway 🏠 Comfort Inn, Ramada Inn ⊙ Mr Tire, PepBoys
29a	Cromwell Bridge Rd, **S** 🏠 Best Western
28	Providence Rd, **S** 🛢 Citgo ⊙ Royal Farms
27b a	MD 146, Dulaney Valley Rd, **N** ⊙ Hampton NHS, **S** 🛢 Exxon ⏺ Bahama Breeze, Cheesecake Factory, PF Chang's, Starbucks, Stoney River Steaks 🏠 Sheraton ⊙ Barnes&Noble, Fresh Mkt, Macy's, mall
26b a	MD 45, York Rd, Towson, **N** 🛢 BP, Exxon/dsl, Oceanic, Sunoco/dsl ⏺ Dunkin Donuts, Friendly's, Ocean Pride Rest., Pizza Hut, Subway ⊙ Best Buy, Kia, Mr Tire, NTB, Rite Aid, **S** 🛢 Exxon, Shell ⏺ 5 Guys Burgers, Burger King, McDonald's ⊙ CVS Drug, Goodyear/auto, Honda, Hyundai, Lexus, Safeway Foods, vet, Walgreens
25	MD 139, Charles St, **S** ⊙ Ⓗ
24	I-83 N, to York
23b	MD 25, Falls Rd, Baltimore, **N** 🛢 Exxon/dsl
23a	I-83 S, MD 25 N, Baltimore
22	Greenspring Ave
21	MD 129, to Stevenson Rd, Park Hghts Rd
20	MD 140, Reisterstown Rd, Pikesville, **N** 🛢 Exxon/7-11/dsl ⏺ Chipotle Mexican ⊙ AT&T, Barnes&Noble, Trader Joe's, **S** 🛢 BP/dsl, Shell/dsl, Sunoco/Subway ⏺ McDonald's, Olive Branch Italian 🏠 Hilton, Ramada Inn ⊙ Target, vet
19	I-795, NW Expswy
18b a	MD 26, Randallstown, Lochearn, **E** 🛢 Shell/dsl, Sunoco/dsl ⏺ Baskin-Robbins/Dunkin Donuts, KFC, Subway

Exit #	Services
18b a	Continued ⊙ $General, Family$, **W** 🛢 BP, Exxon/dsl Shell ⏺ Burger King, Dunkin Donuts, McDonald's, Sonic, Subway, Taco Bell ⊙ Ⓗ, 7-11, auto repair, Firestone/auto, Giant Foods, Shoppers Foods, Walgreens
17	MD 122, Security Blvd, **E** 🛢 BP/repair, Shell ⏺ City View Grill, Dunkin Donuts, McDonald's, Subway, Wendy's 🏠 Days Inn, Motel 6, Quality Inn ⊙ Chevrolet, Family$, Nissan, PriceRite Foods, Rite Aid, **W** 🛢 Exxon/dsl, Sunoco ⏺ 5 Guys Burgers, Burger King, McDonald's, Panera Bread, Popeye's, Quiznos, Rita's Custard 🏠 Best Western ⊙ Best Buy, Ford, Macy's, mall, Old Navy, Rite Aid, Sears/auto
16b a	I-70, E to Baltimore, W to Frederick
15b a	US 40, Ellicott City, Baltimore, **E** 🛢 BP ⏺ Burger King, Checker's, Chick-fil-A, ChuckECheese's, KFC, McDonald's, Panda Express, Quiznos, Shirley's Diner, Subway 🏠 Comfort Inn ⊙ $Tree, BigLots, CVS Drug, Dodge, Firestone/auto, Lowe's, Marshall's, Rite Aid, Ross, Safeway Foods/gas, Sam's Club/gas, Shoppers Foods, U-Haul, Walgreens, **W** 🛢 BP/dsl, Exxon, Gulf, Shell ⏺ Applebee's, Bob Evans, CiCi's Pizza, McDonald's, Old Country Buffet, Popeye's, Starbucks, Subway, Taco Bell, TT Diner 🏠 Ramada Ltd ⊙ $Tree, Aamco, Chrysler/Jeep, Firestone/auto, Giant Foods, Goodyear/auto, Home Depot, Hyundai, Mr Tire, NTB, Office Depot, PepBoys, Petsmart, Staples, Toyota/Scion, Verizon, Walgreens, Walmart/McDonald's
14	Edmondson Ave, **E** 🛢 Sunoco ⏺ Grilled Cheese&Co ⊙ Royal Farms, **W** 🛢 CF ⏺ Papa John's
13	MD 144, Frederick Rd, Catonsville, **W** 🛢 BP, CF, Gulf ⏺ Baskin-Robbins/Dunkin Donuts, McDonald's, Subway ⊙ 7-11
12c b	MD 372 E, Wilkens, **E** ⊙ Ⓗ
11b a	I-95, N to Baltimore, S to Washington
10	US 1, Washington Blvd (from wb only), **E** 🛢 Royal Farms/dsl ⏺ 3 Bros Pizza, Chick-fil-A, Dunkin Donuts, Quiznos, Wendy's 🏠 Beltway Motel/rest. ⊙ Goodyear/auto, Home Depot, Office Depot, PetCo, Radio Shack, Walmart, **W** ⏺ Burger King
9	Hollins Ferry Rd, Lansdowne, **E** 🛢 BP, Sunoco/7-11/dsl ⏺ Victor's Deli ⊙ Royal Farms
8	MD 168, Nursery Rd, **N** 🛢 Exxon, Shell ⏺ Hardee's, KFC, McDonald's, Taco Bell, Wendy's 🏠 Motel 6, **S** 🛢 BP, Citgo/dsl ⏺ G&M Rest., Happy Garden Chinese, Rita's Custard, Seasons Pizza
7b a	MD 295, **N** to Baltimore, **S** ⊙ BWI 🛫
6b a	Camp Mead Rd (from eb)
5	MD 648, Ferndale, 🛢 Shell, Xtra/7-11/dsl ⏺ Checker's, Dunkin Donuts, Hot Wok 🏠 Comfort Inn ⊙ NAPA, police
4b a	I-97 S, to Annapolis
3b a	MD 2, Brooklyn Park, **S** 🛢 Exxon, Hess, Royal Farms/dsl, Shell, Sunoco ⏺ 5 Guys Burgers, Best Buffet, Bob Evans, BoneFish Grill, Checker's, Chick-fil-A, ChuckECheese's, Coldstone, Denny's, Golden Corral, HipHop Fish&Chicken, KFC, McDonald's, Panera Bread, Pappas Rest., Pizza Hut, Qdoba, Quiznos, Starbucks, Subway, Taco Bell 🏠 Days Inn, Extended Stay America, Hampton Inn, La Quinta ⊙ $Tree, Aamco, Advance Parts, Aldi Foods, Best Buy, BigLots, Buick/GMC, Dick's, Giant Foods, Hyundai, Just Tires, Lowe's, Office Depot, PetCo, Radio Shack, Salvo Parts, ShopRite Foods, Subaru, Target, Tuesday Morning, Verizon, Walgreens, Walmart
2	MD 10, Glen Burnie
1	MD 174, Hawkins Point Rd, **S** 🛢 Citgo/deli/dsl

MD

INTERSTATE 84

Exit #	Services
4 (11)	**I-84 begins/ends on I-90, Exit 9.**
3b a (9)	US 20, Sturbridge, **N 0-2 mi** 📶 Citgo, Cumberland Farms 🍴 Admiral O'Brien's, Burger King, Dunkin Donuts, Empire Village, Friendly's, McDonald's, Rovezzi's Ristorante, Smokehouse BBQ, Thai Place, Village Pizza 🛏 EconoLodge, Hampton Inn, Quality Inn, Sturbridge Country Inn, Super 8 ⊙ 🄷 USPO, vet, **S 0-2 mi** 📶 NE TrkStp/dsl, S&S, Shell/Dunkin Donuts/Subway 🍴 Applebee's, Cracker Barrel, Uno Pizzaria, Wendy's 🛏 Comfort Inn ⊙ Marshall's, Michael's, Staples, Stop&Shop, Verizon, vet, Walmart
2 (5)	MA 131, to Old Sturbridge Village, Sturbridge, **S 2 mi** 🛏 Publick House, RV camping
4mm	🅡ₛ wb, litter barrels
1 (3)	Mashapaug Rd, to Southbridge, **S** 📶 Mobil/dsl, 🚛/deli/dsl/scales/24hr/@ 🍴 Roy Rogers, Sbarro's 🛏 Days Inn ⊙ 🄷
2mm	weigh sta both lanes
.5mm	🅡ₛ eb
0mm	Massachusetts/Connecticut state line

INTERSTATE 90

Exit #	Services
140mm	**I-90 begins/ends near Logan Airport.**
25	to I-93, to downtown Boston
24	to I-93, to downtown Boston
22 (134)	Presidential Ctr, downtown
20 (132)	MA 28, Alston, Brighton, Cambridge, **N** 🛏 Courtyard, Doubletree Inn ⊙ 🄷, **S** 📶 Sunoco
131mm	toll plaza
19 (130)	MA Ave (from eb), **N** 🍴 IHOP, McDonald's 🛏 Day's Inn
17 (128)	Centre St, Newton, **N** 🛏 Sheraton ⊙ Cadillac, Chevrolet, Honda, Nissan
16 (125)	MA 16, W Newton, **S** 📶 Mobil/repair
15 (124)	I-95, **N** 🛏 Marriott
123mm	toll plaza
14.5mm	Appalachian Trail
14 (122)	MA 30, Weston
117mm	**Natick Travel Plaza eb,** 📶 Gulf/dsl 🍴 Dunkin Donuts, McDonald's ⊙ info
13 (116)	MA 30, Natick, **S** 📶 Getty, Gulf, Shell 🍴 Bickford's, Boston Mkt, Bugaboo Creek Steaks, Burger King, Harvard's Steaks, Lotus Flower Chinese, McDonald's, Panera Bread, Papagino's, Quizno's 🛏 Best Western, Red Roof Inn ⊙ 🄷, BJ's Whse, Home Depot, Isuzu, Kohl's, Lowe's, Macy's, mall, Marshalls, Target, USPO, Walmart

BOSTON AREA

114mm	**Framingham Travel Plaza wb,** 📶 Gulf/dsl 🍴 Boston Mkt, McDonald's ⊙ info
12 (111)	MA 9, Framington, **N** 📶 Getty, Hess 🍴 Acapulco Mexican, Dunkin Donuts, Molly Malone's Grill, Tin Alley Grill 🛏 Motel 6, Sheraton ⊙ 🄷, **S** 🍴 Chef Orient ⊙ Chrysler/Isuzu/Jeep, mall, Target, Toyota/Scion
11a (106)	I-495, N to NH, S to Cape Cod
105mm	**Westborough Travel Plaza wb,** 📶 Gulf/dsl 🍴 Boston Mkt, D'angelo, Dunkin Donuts, Papagino's ⊙ gifts
11 (96)	MA 122, to Millbury, **N** ⊙ UMA Med Ctr
10a (95)	MA 146
94mm	Blackstone River
10 (90)	I-395 S, to Auburn, I-290 N, Worcester, **N** 📶 Shell 🍴 Piccadilly's 🛏 Comfort Inn, Holiday Inn Express, **S** 📶 Shell/repair/24hr 🍴 Applebee's, D'angelo's, Dunkin Donuts, Friendly's, Wendy's 🛏 Fairfield Inn ⊙ 🄷, CVS Drug, Hyundai, Park'n Shop, TJ Maxx
84mm	**Charlton Travel Plaza wb,** 📶 Gulf/dsl 🍴 McDonald's ⊙ info
80mm	**Charlton Travel Plaza eb,** 📶 Exxon/dsl 🍴 McDonald's ⊙ st police, info
79mm	toll plaza
9 (78)	I-84, to Hartford, NYC, Sturbridge, access to 🄷
67mm	Quaboag River
8 (62)	MA 32, to US 20, Palmer, **S on MA 32** 📶 Hess/Godfather's, Pride, Shell/dsl 🍴 Jenny Chan's Chinese, McDonald's, Subway, Wendy's ⊙ 🄷, Big Y Foods, Chevrolet, CVS Drug, repair/transmissions, Rite Aid
58mm	Chicopee River
56mm	**Ludlow Travel Plaza wb,** 📶 Gulf/dsl 🍴 Boston Mkt, D'angelo
55mm	**Ludlow Travel Plaza eb,** 📶 Gulf/dsl 🍴 McDonald's
7 (54)	MA 21, to Ludlow, **N** 📶 Gulf, Pride/dsl, Sunoco, Verizon 🍴 Burger King, Dunkin Donuts, Friendly's, McDonald's, Subway ⊙ 🄷, Ace Hardware, Big Y Foods, CVS Drug, Jo-Ann Fabrics, NAPA, repair, **S** 📶 Shell/dsl 🍴 Dominos, Taco Bell 🛏 Holiday Inn Express
6 (51)	I-291, to Springfield, Hartford CT, **N** 📶 Pride/50's Diner/Subway/dsl 🍴 Dr Deegan's Steaks, Dunkin Donuts, McDonald's,

MA

🔼🅴 INTERSTATE 90 Cont'd

Exit #	Services
6 (51)	Continued
	Po's Chinese 🏠 Econolodge, Motel 6 🅞 🏥, Basketball Hall of Fame, to Bradley Int 🆂
5 (49)	MA 33, to Chicopee, Westover AFB, **N** 🍴 99 Rest., Applebee's, Arby's, Chipotle Mexican, Denny's, Dunkin Donuts, Friendly's, Panera Bread, Popeye's, Royal Buffet, Starbucks, Subway, Wendy's 🏠 Days Inn, Hampton Inn, Quality Inn, Residence Inn 🅞 $Tree, Aldi Foods, Big Y Foods, BJ's Whse/gas, Chrysler/Dodge/Jeep, Home Depot, Honda, Marshall's, Monroe, Nissan, Staples, Stop&Shop/gas, TownFair Tire, U-Haul, Walmart, **S** 🅖 Pride/Dunkin Donuts/Subway/dsl 🅞 Buick/GMC
46mm	Connecticut River
4 (46)	I-91, US 5, to Holyoke, W Springfield, **N on US 5** 🅖 Shell 🍴 Dunkin Donuts 🏠 Welcome Inn, **S on US 5** 🅖 Pride/dsl 🍴 5 Guys, Donut Dip, Hooters, On the Border, Outback Steaks, Piccadilly's, Subway 🏠 Knights Inn, Red Roof Inn, Springfield Inn, Super 8 🅞 AAA, BMW, Honda/Lexus/Toyota/Scion, repair
41mm	st police wb
3 (40)	US 202, to Westfield, **N** 🅖 Mobil 🍴 Amalfi Pizza, Dunkin Donuts, **S** 🅖 Citgo/Subway/dsl 🍴 Friendly's, Wendy's 🏠 EconoLodge, Holiday Inn Express 🅞 🏥, repair
36mm	Westfield River
35.5mm	**runaway truck ramp eb**
29mm	**Blandford Travel Plaza wb**, Gulf/dsl, McDonalds, gifts, info
20mm	1724 ft, highest point on MA Tpk
14.5mm	Appalachian Trail
2 (11)	US 20, to Lee, Pittsfield, **N** 🅖 Citgo, Shell/dsl, Sunoco 🍴 Arizona Pizza, Athena's Rest., Dunkin Donuts, Friendly's, McDonald's, Red Apple Chinese, Subway 🏠 Morgan House/rest., Pilgrim Inn, Sunset Motel, Super 8 🅞 PriceChopper Foods, Rite Aid, True Value, **S** 🍴 Orient Taste, Simply Grillicious, Subway, Villa Pizza 🅞 Big Y Foods, Lee Outlets/famous brands
10.5mm	Hoosatonic River
8mm	**Lee Travel Plaza both lanes, vending, info** 🅖 Gulf/dsl 🍴 McDonald's 🅞 atm
4mm	**toll booth,** 🅒
1 (2)	MA 41 (from wb, no return), to MA 102, W Stockbridge, the Berkshires, **N** 🏠 Pleasant Valley Motel 🅞 to Bousquet Ski Area
0mm	Massachusetts/New York state line

🔼🅽 INTERSTATE 91

Exit #	Services
55mm	Massachusetts/Vermont state line, call boxes
54mm	**parking area both lanes,** 🆁🆂
28 (51)	US 5, MA 10, Bernardston, **E** 🏠 Fox Inn, **W** 🅖 Sunoco 🍴 Antonio's Il Ristorante, Four-leaf Clover Rest., Hillside Organic Pizza 🅞 Country Corner Store, RV camping, USPO
27 (45)	MA 2 E (exits left from sb), Greenfield, **E US 5** 🅖 Gulf, Hess/Dunkin Donuts, Stop&Shop, Sunoco/dsl 🍴 Burger King, Denny's Pantry, Domino's, Dunkin Donuts, Goodies Rest., McDonald's, Subway 🅞 🏥, $General, Aubuchon Hardware, AutoZone, Bond Parts, Chrysler/Dodge/Jeep, Honda, Walgreens
26 (43)	MA 2 W, MA 2A E, Greenfield, **E** 🅖 Planet/dsl, Shell/dsl 🍴 Applebee's, Athens Pizza, China Gourmet, D'Angelo, Dunkin Donuts 🏠 Quality Inn 🅞 🏥, Chevrolet, Ford/Lincoln, Toyota,

Exit #	Services
26 (43)	Continued
	W 🅖 Irving/Circle K, Valero 🍴 99 Rest., Asian Buffet, Friendly's, KFC/Pizza Hut/Taco Bell, McDonald's, Subway 🏠 Days Inn, Hampton Inn 🅞 $Tree, Big Y Foods, BJ's Whse, Family$, Home Depot, Radio Shack, Staples, to Mohawk Tr, Verizon
39mm	Deerfield River
37mm	**weigh sta both lanes**
25 (36)	MA 116 (from sb), S Deerfield, camping, hist dist, same as 24
24 (35)	US 5, MA 10, MA 116, Deerfield (no EZ return), **E** 🅖 Irving/Circle K/Dunkin Donuts/Subway/dsl 🏠 Red Roof Inn 🅞 Final Markdown, vet, Yankee Candle Co, **W** 🅖 Roady's Trkstp/diner/dsl/24hr 🍴 24hr Diner
34.5mm	**parking area both lanes**
23 (34)	US 5 (from sb), **E** 🍴 Tom's Hot Dog 🅞 Orchard Trailers, Rainbow Motel/camping
22 (30)	US 5, MA 10 (from nb), **N** Hatfield, **W** Diamond RV Ctr
21 (28)	US 5, MA 10, Hatfield, **W** 🅖 Sunoco/dsl 🍴 Subway 🏠 Scottish Inn 🅞 st police
20 (26)	US 5, MA 9, MA 10 (from sb), Northampton, **W** 🅖 Hess/dsl, Pride/Dunkin Donuts/dsl 🍴 Burger King, D'angelo's, KFC, McDonald's, PapaGino's Italian, Taco Bell 🅞 🏥, AutoZone, Big Y Food/Drug, BigLots, Chevrolet, CVS Drug, Firestone/auto, Ford, Goodyear/auto, Honda, Hyundai, Kia, NAPA, Radio Shack, Staples, Stop&Shop/gas, TownFair Tire, Toyota/Scion, U-Haul, Verizon, VW, Walgreens, Walmart/Subway
19 (25)	MA 9, to Amherst, Northampton, **E 0-2 mi** 🅖 Gulf, Phillips 66/Dunkin Donuts, Shell/dsl 🍴 Primo Pizza 🏠 Hampton Inn 🅞 🏥, Nissan, to Elwell SP, vet
18mm	scenic area both lanes
18 (22)	US 5, Northampton, **E** 🍴 Page's Loft Rest. 🏠 Clarion, Country Inn&Suites (5mi), **W** 🅖 Shell/Dunkin Donuts 🏠 Fairfield Inn, Quality Inn 🅞 to Smith Coll
17b a (16)	MA 141, S Hadley, **E** 🅖 Mobil/dsl, Shell/dsl 🍴 Dunkin Donuts, Real China, Subway 🏠 Days Inn 🅞 Meineke, Rite Aid, Walgreens, **W** 🅞 to Mt Tom Ski Area
16 (14)	US 202, Holyoke, **W** Soldier's Home
15 (12)	to US 5, Ingleside, **E** 🅖 Shell/Dunkin Donuts 🍴 Chicago Grill, Cracker Barrel, JP's Rest., Red Robin 🏠 Howard Johnson 🅞 🏥, Barnes&Noble, Best Buy, CVS Drug, Hobby Lobby, JC Penney, Macy's, mall, Old Navy, PetCo, Sears/auto, Target, TJ Maxx
14 (11)	to US 5, to I-90 (Mass Tpk), **E** to Boston, **W** to Albany, **E** 🅞 🏥
13b a (9)	US 5 N, W Springfield, **E** 🅖 Pride/dsl 🍴 Backyard Grill, Donut Dip, Five Guys, Hooters, On-the-Border, Outback Steaks, Shallot Thai, Subway 🏠 Knights Inn, Red Roof Inn, Residence Inn, Springfield Inn, Super 8 🅞 BMW, Lexus/Toyota/Scion, **W** 🅖 Mobil/dsl, Pride/dsl 🍴 99 Rest., Arby's, Bertucci's, Burger King, Cal's Grill, Carrabba's, Chili's, D'angelo's, Friendly's, IHOP, KFC, Longhorn Steaks, McDonald's, Nippon Grill, Olive Garden, Panera Bread, Pizza Hut, Tokyo Cuisine 🏠 Bel Air Inn, Candlewood Suites, Clarion, Days Inn, EconoLodge, Hampton Inn, Quality Inn, Red Carpet Inn, Travelodge 🅞 $Tree, Aldi Foods, AT&T, Chrysler/Dodge/Jeep, Costco, CVS Drug, Dick's, Fiat, GNC, Home Depot, Honda, Kohl's, Mazda, Michael's, Nissan, Staples, Stop&Shop, Subaru, TownFair Tire, Verizon
12 (8.5)	I-391 N, to Chicopee
11 (8)	Birnie Ave (from sb), **E** 🅖 Mobil 🅞 🏥
10 (7.5)	Main St (from nb), Springfield, **E** 🅖 Mobil
9 (7)	US 20 W, MA 20A E (from nb), **E** 🍴 McDonald's, **W** 🅖 Pride/Subway/dsl
8 (6.5)	I-291, US 20 E, to I-90, **E** downtown

P I T T S F I E L D

G R E E N F I E L D

N O R T H A M P T O N

S P R I N G F I E L D

MA

⬆N INTERSTATE 91 Cont'd

Exit #	Services
7 (6)	Columbus Ave (from sb), **E** 🄶 Pride/Subway/dsl 🄴 Marriott, Sheraton, **W** 🄾 to Basketball Hall of Fame
6 (5.5)	Springfield Ctr, **E** 🄶 Pride/Dunkin Donuts/Subway/dsl 🄵 Starbucks, **W** 🄵 Coldstone, Plan B Burger 🄾 Basketball Hall of Fame
5 (5)	Broad St, **E** 🄶 Mobil/dsl 🄴 Hampton Inn 🄾 Hyundai, **W** 🄶 Sunoco/dsl 🄵 Chicago Grill, Subway 🄴 Hilton Garden 🄾 Buick/GMC, same as 4
4 (4.5)	MA 83, Broad St, Main St, **E** 🄶 Mobil/dsl 🄵 Antonio's Grinders 🄾 Hyundai, **W** 🄶 Sunoco/dsl 🄵 Chicago Grill, Subway 🄴 Buick/GMC, Chevrolet, Hilton Garden, same as 5
3 (4)	US 5 N, to MA 57, Columbus Ave, W Springfield, **E** 🄶 Sunoco 🄵 Antonio's Pizza, **W** 🄾 Chevrolet
2 (3.5)	MA 83 S (from nb), to E Longmeadow, **E** 🄵 Friendly's
1 (3)	US 5 S (from sb)
0mm	Massachusetts/Connecticut state line, callboxes begin/end

⬆N INTERSTATE 93

Exit #	Services
47mm	Massachusetts/New Hampshire state line, callboxes begin/end
48 (46)	MA 213 E, to Methuen, **E** 🄾 🄷
47 (45)	Pelham St, Methuen, **E** 🄶 Sunoco 🄵 Dunkin Donuts, Heavenly Donuts, McDonald's, Outback Steaks, **W** 🄵 BP, Irving/Circle K/Subway/dsl 🄵 Fireside Rest., NE Seafood 🄴 Day's Hotel/rest. 🄾 Chrysler/Dodge/Jeep
46 (44)	MA 110, MA 113, to Lawrence, **E** 🄶 BP/repair, Mobil, Shell 🄵 Burger King, Dunkin Donuts, KFC/Taco Bell, McDonald's, PapaGino's, Pizza Hut 🄾 🄷, $Tree, MktBasket Foods, Rite Aid, **W** 🄶 Citgo, Super 🄵 Dunkin Donuts, Irish Cottage Rest., Jules Rest., Riverside Pizza, Royal Roast Beef 🄴 Passport Inn
45 (43)	Andover St, River Rd, to Lawrence, **E** 🄴 Courtyard, Homewood Suites, Wyndham, **W** 🄶 Mobil/Dunkin Donuts 🄵 Chateu Italian, Chili's 🄴 La Quinta, Residence Inn, SpringHill Suites 🄾 vet
44b a (40)	I-495, to Lowell, Lawrence, **E** 🄾 🄷
43 (39)	MA 133, N Tewksbury, **E** 🄶 Mobil/Dunkin Donuts, **W** 🄵 99 Rest.
42 (38)	Dascomb Rd, East St, Tewksbury, **W** 🄶 Citgo/dsl 🄵 Dunkin Donuts, Luna Rossa Italian, Subway 🄾 7-11
41 (35)	MA 125, Andover, 🄾 st police
40 (34)	MA 62, Wilmington
39 (33)	Concord St, **E** 🄵 Dunkin Donuts, Subway 🄾 Shriners Auditorium, URGENT CARE
38 (31)	MA 129, Reading, **W** 🄶 Mobil/Dunkin Donuts/Subway/dsl 🄵 Burger King, Pacific Grove Chinese, Red Heat Tavern
37c (30)	Commerce Way, Atlantic Ave, **W** 🄵 Chipotle Mexican, Firehouse Subs, Starbucks 🄴 Red Roof Inn, Residence Inn 🄾 PetCo, Petsmart, Target, Verizon
37b a (29)	I-95, S to Waltham, N to Peabody
36 (28)	Montvale Ave, **E** 🄶 Mobil 🄵 Deli Works, Dunkin Donuts, Kiotoya Japanese 🄴 Courtyard, **W** 🄶 BP, Gulf 🄵 Bickford's Grille, Dunkin Donuts, McDonald's, Polcari's Italian, Wendy's 🄴 Best Western, Comfort Inn 🄾 🄷
35 (27)	Winchester Highlands, Melrose, **E** 🄾 🄷 (no EZ return to sb)
34 (26)	MA 28 N (from nb, no EZ return), Stoneham, **E** 🄶 Mobil 🄵 Friendly's 🄾 🄷
33 (25)	MA 28, Fellsway West, Winchester, **E** 🄾 🄷

Exit #	Services
32 (23)	MA 60, Salem Ave, Medford Square, **W** 🄴 Hyatt Place 🄾 🄷 to Tufts U
31 (22)	MA 16 E, to Revere (no EZ return sb), **W** 🄶 Fred's Gas, Mr. C's/dsl 🄵 Avellino's Italian, Burger King, Dunkin Donuts, Pizza Hut 🄾 AutoZone, Chrysler/Dodge/Jeep, Kia, Nissan, Staples
30 (21)	MA 28, MA 38, Mystic Ave, Somerville, **W** 🄶 Mr. C's/dsl 🄵 Burger King 🄾 AutoZone, Lincoln
29 (20)	MA 28 (from nb), Somerville, **E** 🄵 99 Rest., Dunkin Donuts 🄴 La Quinta 🄾 Home Depot, K-Mart, mall, Staples, TJ Maxx, **W** 🄶 Gulf, Hess 🄾 Radio Shack, same as 30, Stop&Shop
28 (19)	Sullivans Square, Charles Town, downtown
27	US 1 N (from nb)
26 (18.5)	MA 28 N, Storrow Dr, North Sta, downtown
25	Haymarket Sq, 🄾 Gov't Center
24 (18)	Callahan Tunnel, **E** 🄾 ➡
23 (17.5)	High St, Congress St, **W** 🄴 Marriott
22 (17)	Atlantic Ave, Northern Ave, South Sta, 🄾 Boston World Trade Ctr
21 (16.5)	Kneeland St, ChinaTown
20 (16)	I-90 W, to Mass Tpk
19 (15.5)	Albany St (from sb), **W** 🄶 Mobil/dsl 🄾 🄷
18 (15)	Mass Ave, to Roxbury, **W** 🄾 🄷
17 (14.5)	E Berkeley (from nb), **E** 🄾 New Boston Food Mkt
16 (14)	S Hampton St, Andrew Square, **W** 🄵 Applebee's, Olive Garden 🄴 Holiday Inn Express 🄾 Best Buy, Home Depot, Marshall's, Old Navy, Stop&Shop/gas, Target, TJ Maxx
15 (13)	Columbia Rd, Everett Square, **E** 🄴 DoubleTree 🄾 JFK Library, to UMA, **W** 🄶 Shell
14 (12.5)	Morissey Blvd (from nb no return), **E** 🄾 JFK Library, **W** 🄶 Shell
13 (12)	Freeport St, to Dorchester, (from nb), **W** 🄶 7-11, BP 🄵 Boston Mkt, D'Angelo's, Deadwood Cafe, Freeport Tavern 🄴 Comfort Inn, Ramada 🄾 CVS Drug, Lambert's Mkt, NAPACare, Stop&Shop, Toyota/Scion
12 (11.5)	MA 3A S (from sb, no EZ return), Quincy, **E** 🄶 repair, Shell, **W** 🄶 Gulf/Dunkin Donuts, Hess 🄵 PapaGino's 🄾 AutoZone, CVS Drug, Lincoln, Staples, Verizon, Walgreens
11b a (11)	to MA 203, Granite Ave, Ashmont
10 (10)	Squantum Ave (from sb), Milton, **W** 🄾 🄷
9 (9)	Adams St, Bryant Ave, to N Quincy, **E** 🄶 Milton Fuel 🄵 Dunkin Donuts, **W** 🄶 Shell/repair
8 (8)	Brook Pkwy, to Quincy, Furnace, **E** 🄶 Gulf/dsl, Mobil/dsl
7 (7)	MA 3 S, to Cape Cod (exits left from sb), Braintree, **E** 🄴 Marriott
6 (6)	MA 37, to Holbrook, Braintree, **E** 🄶 Mobil/24hr 🄵 99 Rest., Boardwalk Café, CA Pizza Kitchen, Cheesecake Factory, Chicago Grill, D'angelo's, Legal Seafood, TGIFriday's,

MA

BOSTON AREA / AMESBURY / PEABODY

⬆N INTERSTATE 93 Cont'd

Exit #	Services
6 (6)	Continued
	Tokyo Japanese 🅞 Lord&Taylor, Macy's, mall, Nordstrom's, Sears/auto, Target, **W** 🅝 Citgo 🍴 Ascari Café, Wood Road Deli 🛏 Candlewood Suites, Extended Stay America, Hampton Inn, Holiday Inn Express 🅞 Ford, VW
5b a (4)	MA 28 S, to Randolph, Milton, **E** 🅝 Citgo, Mobil/dsl, Mutual, Shell/dsl/24hr 🍴 Domino's, Dunkin Donuts, La Scala, Lombardo's, Picadilly's Pub, Randolph Cafe, Sal's Calzone Rest., Stash's Pizza, Wong's Chinese 🛏 Comfort Inn 🅞 AT&T
4 (3)	MA 24 S (exits left from sb), to Brockton
3 (2)	MA 138 N, to Ponkapoag Trail, Houghtons Pond
2b a (1)	MA 138 S, to Stoughton, Milton, **E** 🅞 golf, **W** 🅝 BlueHill/dsl, Mobil, Shell/dsl 🍴 Dunkin Donuts 🛏 Homewood Suites
1 (0)	**I-95 N, S to Providence. I-93 begins/ends on I-95, exit 12.**

⬆N INTERSTATE 95

Exit #	Services
89.5mm	Massachusetts/New Hampshire state line, **Welcome Ctr/🅡ₛ sb, full ♿ facilities, litter barrels, 🚮**
60 (89)	MA 286, to Salisbury, beaches, **E** 🅝 Mobil/dsl 🍴 Cosmos Rest., Dunkin Donuts, Lena's Seafood Rest. 🅞 Black Bear Camping (seasonal)
59 (88)	I-495 S (from sb)
58b a (87)	rd 110, to I-495 S, to Amesbury, Salisbury, **E** 🅝 Sunoco/Dunkin Donuts/Subway/dsl 🍴 China Buffet, Niko's Place, Sylvan St Grille, Winner's Circle Rest. 🅞 Ford, U-Haul, vet, **W** 🅝 Irving Gas/Circle K, Mobil, Sunoco/dsl 🍴 Acapulco's Mexican, Burger King, Dunkin Donuts, Friendly's, McDonald's, PapaGino's 🛏 Fairfield Inn 🅞 AT&T, Chevrolet, Stop&Shop, Verizon
57 (85)	MA 113, to W Newbury, **E** 🅝 Mobil/dsl, Shell/dsl/repair, Sunoco 🍴 China One, D'angelo, Dunkin Donuts, Dunkin Donuts, Giuseppe's Italian, Hana Japan, McDonald's, Panera Bread, PapaGino's, Sal's Pizza, Wendy's 🅞 H, 7-11, GNC, K-Mart, Marshall's, Midas, MktBasket Foods, Radio Shack, Rite Aid, Shaw's Foods, Verizon, Walgreens
56 (83)	Scotland Rd, to Newbury, **E** 🅞 st police
55 (82)	Central St, to Byfield, **E** 🍴 Gen Store Eatery, Parker River Grille, **W** 🅝 Prime/dsl/repair
54b a (78)	MA 133, E to Rowley, W to Groveland, **E** 🅞 vet
77mm	**weigh sta both lanes**
53b a (76)	MA 97, S to Topsfield, N to Georgetown
52 (74)	Topsfield Rd, to Topsfield, Boxford
51 (72)	Endicott Rd, to Topsfield, Middleton
50 (71)	US 1, to MA 62, Topsfield, **E** 🅝 Gulf/dsl, Mobil/dsl 🅞 Honda, **W** 🅝 S&S 🍴 Supino's Rest., Timothy's Rest., TX Roadhouse 🛏 DoubleTree, Knights Inn 🅞 CVS Drug, st police, Staples, Stop&Shop
49 (70)	MA 62 (from nb), Danvers, Middleton, **W** same as 50
48 (69)	Hobart St (from sb), **W** 🍴 Calitri's Italian 🛏 Comfort Inn, Extended Stay America, Motel 6 🅞 Home Depot
47b a (68)	MA 114, to Middleton, Peabody, **E** 🅝 Gulf/Dunkin Donuts, Sunoco 🍴 Dunkin Donuts, Honey Dew Donuts, McDonald's, Olive Garden, Outback Steaks, PapaGino's, Pizza Hut, Subway 🅞 Audi, Chevrolet, Chrysler/Dodge/Jeep, Infiniti, Lexus, Lowe's, NTB, Petsmart, Porsche, Subaru, TJ Maxx, Toyota/Scion, Trader Joe's, Verizon, vet, VW, Walmart, **W on US 1** 🍴 Chili's, Hardcover Rest., TGIFriday's 🛏 Motel 6, Residence Inn, TownePlace Suites 🅞 Costco/gas, Hess/dsl, Home Depot, LandRover, Meineke, NAPA

READING / LEXINGTON

Exit #	Services
46 (67)	to US 1, **W** 🅝 Best, Global, Gulf/dsl, Sunoco/dsl 🍴 Dunkin Donuts, Honey Dew Donuts 🅞 auto repair
45 (66)	MA 128 N, to Peabody
44b a (65)	US 1 N, MA 129, **W** 🅝 7-11, Shell, Sunoco 🍴 Bertucci's, Bros Kouzina Rest., Carrabba's, Dunkin Donuts, Marco's Italian, Santarpio's Pizza, Sonic, Wendy's 🛏 Hampton Inn, Holiday Inn, Homewood Suites, Plaza Motel, SpringHill Suites 🅞 H
43 (61)	Walnut St, Lynnfield, **E** 🅞 to Saugus Iron Works NHS (3mi), **W** 🛏 Sheraton 🅞 golf
42 (62)	Salem St, Montrose, **E** 🍴 Irving/Circle K/Subway, Sunoco 🍴 Dunkin Donuts, **W** 🛏 Sheraton
41 (60)	Main St, Lynnfield Ctr, **E** 🅝 Shell
40 (59)	MA 129, Wakefield Ctr, N Reading, **E** 🍴 Bellino's Italian, Honey Dew Donuts 🅞 city park, vet, **W** 🅝 Gulf 🍴 Dunkin Donuts, Mandarin Chinese 🅞 Chevrolet, Mazda, REI
39 (58)	North Ave, Reading, **E** 🛏 Clarion 🅞 city park, Subaru, Volvo, **W** 🅝 Shell/dsl 🍴 Bertucci's, Chili's, Fuddrucker's, Longhorn Steaks, Macaroni Grill, Oye's Rest., Starbucks 🅞 H, Home Depot, Honda, Mkt Basket Foods, Staples, Stop&Shop Foods, URGENT CARE, Verizon
38b a (57)	MA 28, to Reading, **E** 🅝 Gulf/repair, Hess/dsl, Mobil 🍴 5 Guys Burgers, 99 Rest., Burger King, Burger King, D'Angelo's/PapaGino's, Dunkin Donuts, Dunkin Donuts, Subway, Uno Fresco Cafe 🅞 Advance Parts, AutoZone, CVS Drug, Ford, GNC, Marshall's, Michaels, Radio Shack, Stop&Shop/gas, Walgreens, **W** 🅝 Eleven Variety, Mobil/dsl, Shell, Sunoco 🍴 Anthony's Roastbeef, Burger King, Calariso's Farm Stand, Domino's, Dunkin Donuts, Harrow's Chicken Pies, McDonald's, Sam's Bistro, Starbucks 🅞 Meineke
37b a (56)	I-93, N to Manchester, S to Boston
36 (55)	Washington St, to Winchester, **E** 🅝 BP 🍴 Dunkin Donuts, Fresh City, Sal's Pizza, Starbucks, Subway 🛏 Hilton 🅞 Hogan's Tires, Jaguar, Nissan, Staples, Toyota, **W** 🅝 Sunoco 🍴 99 Rest., Bertucci's, Chicago Grill, China Pearl, d'Angelo's, Dunkin Donuts, Joe's Grill, On the Border, Panera Bread, Papa Gino's, Qdoba, Sarku Japan 🛏 Courtyard, Fairfield Inn, Hampton Inn, Red Roof Inn 🅞 $Tree, AT&T, CVS Drug, Kohl's, Lowe's, Mkt Basket Foods, NTB, Radio Shack, TJ Maxx, Town Fair Tire, USPO
35 (54)	MA 38, to Woburn, **E** 🍴 Scoreboard Grill 🛏 Crowned Plaza 🅞 H, **W** 🅝 Mobil/dsl 🍴 Applebee's, Dunkin Donuts, Sichuan Garden 🛏 Extended Stay America 🅞 city park, CVS Drug, Stop&Shop Foods
34 (53)	Winn St, Woburn
33b a (52)	US 3 S, MA 3A N, to Winchester, **E** 🍴 Bickford's Grille, Café Escadrille, Capital Grille, ChuckeCheese, Dunkin Donuts, Outback Steaks, Panera Bread, Paparazzi's, Subway 🅞 H AAA, CVS Drug, Honda, Marshall's, Michael's, Roche Bro's Foods, **W** 🅝 Hess, Prime 🛏 Marriott 🅞 H, Audi/Porsche, Kia, repair
32b a (51)	US 3 N, MA 2A S, to Lowell, **E** 🅝 Mobil, Shell 🍴 Burger King, d'Angelo's, Dunkin Donuts, McDonald's, Subway 🛏 Hilton Garden 🅞 Best Buy, Mkt Basket Foods, Old Navy, PetCo, Trader Joe's, Verizon, **W** 🍴 Border Cafe, Cheesecake Factory, Chicago Grill, Chili's, Legal Seafoods, Macaroni Grill, Pizzaria Regina 🛏 Candlewood Suites, Homestead Suites 🅞 Barnes&Noble, Macy's, mall, Nordstrom, Sears/auto, Staples
31b a (48)	MA 4, MA 225, Lexington, **E** 🅝 Gulf, Mobil/dsl/repair 🍴 Alexander's Pizza, Starbucks 🅞 Curves, Stop&Shop, Walgreens, **W** 🅝 Gulf, Shell 🍴 d'Angelo's, Dunkin Donuts, Firebox BBQ, Friendly's, Margarita's, McDonald's, Papa Gino's 🛏 Bedford Plaza Hotel, Quality Inn, Travelodge 🅞 Staples, TJ Maxx, vet

⬆🅽 INTERSTATE 95 Cont'd

Exit #	Services
30b a (47)	MA 2A, Lexington, **E** 🅖 Sunoco/Dunkin Donuts/dsl 🅞 🄷, **W** 🛏 ALoft, Element Hotel 🅞 Hanscom AFB, to MinuteMan NP
46.5mm	**travel plaza nb**, 🅖 Gulf/dsl 🍴 Honey Dew Donuts, McDonald's 🅞 gifts
29b a (46)	MA 2 W, Cambridge
28b a (45)	Trapelo Rd, Belmont, **E** 🅖 Gulf/dsl, Mobil/dsl 🍴 Boston Mkt, Burger King, Dunkin Donuts, Friendly's, McDonald's, Panera Bread, Papa Gino's 🅞 AT&T, city park, Radio Shack, Shaw's Foods/Osco Drugs
27b a (44)	Totten Pond Rd, Waltham, **E** 🅖 Shell 🍴 Naked Fish Rest. 🛏 Best Western, Courtyard, Hilton Garden, Holiday Inn Express, Home Suites, Westin Hotel, **W** 🍴 Bertucci's Rest., Green Papaya Thai 🛏 Embassy Suites/The Grill 🅞 AT&T, Costco, Home Depot
26 (43)	US 20, to MA 117, to Waltham, **E** 🅖 Sunoco/dsl, **W** 🅖 Mobil/dsl 🍴 Chicago Grill 🅞 NTB, vet
25 (42)	I-90, MA Tpk
24 (41)	MA 30, Newton, Wayland, **E** 🅖 Hess 🛏 Marriott/rest.
23 (40)	Recreation Rd (from nb), to MA Tpk
22b a (39)	Grove St, **E** 🛏 Holiday Inn Express 🅞 golf
38.5mm	**travel plaza sb**, 🅖 Gulf/dsl 🍴 HoneyDew Donuts, McDonald's 🅞 gifts
21b a (38)	MA 16, Newton, Wellesley, **E** 🅞 🄷, **W** 🅖 Sunoco 🍴 Dunkin Donuts, House of Pizza, Paparazzi, Starbucks
20b a (36)	MA 9, Brookline, Framingham
19 (35)	Highland Ave, Newton, Needham, **E** 🅖 Hess 🍴 Acupulcos, Chipotle Mexican, D'Angelo's, Mandarin Cuisine, Mighty Subs, Panera Bread, Pronto Bistro, Starbucks 🛏 Sheraton/rest. 🅞 AAA, CVS Drug, Marshall's, PetCo, Radio Shack, Staples, TJ Maxx, **W** 🍴 Bickford's 🅞 Chevrolet, Ford
18 (34)	Great Plain Ave, W Roxbury
33.5mm	**parking area sb, litter barrels,** 🚻
17 (33)	MA 135, Needham, Wellesley
32mm	**truck turnout sb**
16b a (31)	MA 109, High St, Dedham, **W** 🅖 Mobil/dsl
15b a (29)	US 1, MA 128, **E 0-2 mi** 🅖 Gulf, Monro/service 🍴 Bugaboo Creek Steaks, Chili's, Domino's, Joe's Grill, Panera Bread, PapaGino's, PF Chang's, TGIFriday's 🛏 Fairfield Inn, Holiday Inn, Residence Inn 🅞 AT&T, Best Buy, BJ's Whse, Costco, CVS Drug, Lincoln, LL Bean, NTB, PepBoys, PetCo, Staples, Star Foods, Tuesday Morning, Verizon, vet, Volvo, Walgreens, Whole Foods Mkt, **W 0-2 mi** 🅖 Irving/dsl, Shell/dsl/24hr 🍴 Burger King, Dunkin Donuts, Jade Chinese, McDonald's 🛏 Budget Inn 🅞 AAA, AT&T, Audi/Porsche, Buick/GMC, Chevrolet, Chrysler/Dodge/Jeep, Fiat, Honda, Kia, Mercedes, Toyota/Scion
14 (28)	East St, Canton St, **E** 🛏 Hilton
27mm	🆁🆂 **sb, full** 🚻 **facilities, litter barrels,** 🚰, 🐾
13 (26.5)	University Ave
12 (26)	I-93 N, to Braintree, Boston, motorist callboxes end nb
11b a (23)	Neponset St, to Canton, **E** 🅖 Citgo/repair, Sunoco 🍴 Dunkin Donuts, Rosario's Grill, **W 2 mi on US 1** 🅖 Gulf, Sunoco 🍴 Jake&Joe's 🛏 Hampton Inn, The Chateau 🅞 🄷, Chevrolet, Ferrari, Hyundai, Maserati, Nissan
22.5mm	Neponset River
10 (20)	Coney St (from sb, no EZ return), to US 1, Sharon, Walpole, **W 1 mi on US 1** 🅖 Mobil 🍴 5 Guys Burgers, 99 Rest., Bertucci's, Chili's, Chipotle Mexican, Dunkin Donuts, Friendly's, HoneyDew Donuts, IHOP, McDonald's, Old Country Buffet, Outback Steaks, Panda Express, Panera Bread, PapaGino's,

10 (20)	**Continued** Pizza Hut, Starbucks, Subway, Taco Bell, TGIFriday's, TX Roadhouse 🛏 Courtyard, Residence Inn, Sheraton 🅞 Acura, Advance Parts, Barnes&Noble, CVS Drug, Home Depot, Kohl's, Lexus, mall, Old Navy, PetCo, Radio Shack, Staples, Stop&Shop, TownFair Tire, VW, Walgreens
9 (19)	US 1, to MA 27, Walpole, **W** 🅖 Gulf, Mobil/dsl 🍴 Applebee's, Asia Treasures, Dunkin Donuts, Starbucks 🛏 Boston View, EconoLodge, Holiday Inn Express 🅞 BigY Foods/drug, same as 10, Stop&Shop, Walmart
8 (16)	S Main St, Sharon, **E** 🍴 Dunkin Donuts 🅞 Rite Aid, Shaw's Foods, whaling museum
7b a (13)	MA 140, to Mansfield, **E** 🍴 99 Rest., Domino's, Piccadilly's 🛏 Comfort Inn, Courtyard, Holiday Inn, Red Roof Inn, Residence Inn., **W** 🅖 Shell/HoneyDew Donuts/dsl 🍴 Dunkin Donuts, PapaGino's 🅞 AT&T
6b a (12)	I-495, S to Cape Cod, N to NH
10mm	**Welcome Ctr/🆁🆂 nb, full** 🚻 **facilities, info, litter barrels, petwalk,** 🚰, 🐾
9mm	**truck parking area sb**
5 (7)	MA 152, Attleboro, **E** 🅞 🄷, **W** 🅖 Gulf/dsl 🍴 Bill's Pizza, Piccadilly Rest., Wendy's 🅞 Shaw's Foods/Osco Drug
4 (6)	I-295 S, to Woonsocket
3 (4)	MA 123, to Attleboro, **E** 🅖 Shell/dsl 🍴 Dunkin Donuts 🅞 🄷 zoo
2.5mm	**parking area/weigh sta both lanes, litter barrels, no restrooms**
2b a (1)	US 1A, Newport Ave, Attleboro, **E** 🅖 Mobil/dsl, Shell 🍴 Archie's Pizza, HoneyDew Donuts, McDonald's, Olive Garden, Spumoni's Italian 🅞 Home Depot, K-Mart, Monroe's Service, **W** 🅖 BP
1 (.5)	US 1 (from sb), **E** 🛏 Days Inn 🅞 Kia, Rite Aid, Volvo, **W** 🅖 Hess
0mm	Massachusetts/Rhode Island state line

⬆🅽 INTERSTATE 195

Exit #	Services
22 (41)	I-495 N, MA 25 S, to Cape Cod. **I-195 begins/ends on I-495, exit 1.**
21 (39)	MA 28, to Wareham, **N** 🅖 Maxi/dsl/24hr 🍴 Longhorn Steaks, Pomodore's Italian, Qdoba Mexican, Red Robin 🅞 Best Buy, JC Penney, LL Bean, Lowe's, Michaels, Old Navy, PetCo, Staples, Target, TJ Maxx, **S** 🅖 Irving/dsl, Mobil/Dunkin Donuts/dsl 🅞 🄷, repair
37mm	**parking area eb, boatramp, info**
36mm	Sippican River
20 (35)	MA 105, to Marion, **S** 🅞 RV camping (seasonal)

[gas] = gas   [food] = food   [lodging] = lodging   [other] = other   [Rs] = rest stop   Copyright 2015 - the Next EXIT ®

↑N INTERSTATE 195 Cont'd

Exit #	Services
19b a (31)	to Mattapoisett, S [gas] Mobil [food] Nick's Pizza, Panino's Rest., Ying Dynasty [other] USPO
18 (26)	MA 240 S, to Fairhaven, S 1 mi [gas] 7-11, Valero/dsl [food] 99 Rest., Burger King, Dunkin Donuts, Jake's Diner, McDonald's, PapaGino's, Pasta House, Pizza Hut, Subway, Sweet Ginger Asian, Taco Bell, Wendy's [lodging] Hampton Inn [other] $Tree, AutoZone, Brahman Handbags, Buick/GMC, GNC, K-Mart, Marshalls, Mazda, Radio Shack, Shaw's Foods, Staples, Stop&Shop/gas, Sullivan Tire, TownFair Tire, Verizon, Walgreens, Walmart
25.5mm	Acushnet River
17 (24)	Coggeshall St, (from wb only), New Bedford, N [gas] 7-11/gas, Petro, Sunoco [food] Dunkin Donuts, HoneyDew Donuts, McDonald's, Papa Johns, Subway [other] Market Basket Foods, same as 16
16 (23)	Washburn St (from eb), N [gas] Sunoco [food] McDonald's, Papa John's
15 (22)	MA 18 S, New Bedford, S [gas] Lukoil [lodging] Fairfield Inn [other] hist dist, to downtown, Whaling Museum
14 (21)	Penniman St (from eb), New Bedford, downtown
13b a (20)	MA 140, N [other][food], S [gas] 1 Stop, Sunoco [food] Dunkin Donuts [other] [H], Buttonwood Park/zoo, CVS Drug, Honda, Shaw's Foods, Walgreens
12b a (19)	N Dartmouth, S [gas] Hess, Mobil/dsl [food] 5 Guys Burgers, 99 Rest., Applebee's, Azuma Asian, Burger King, Chucke-Cheese, Coldstone, Dunkin Donuts, Friendly's, IHOP, Jimmy's Pizza, McDonald's, Old Country Buffet, Olive Garden, Panera Bread, PapaGino's, Peking Garden, Quiznos, Rose&Vicki's Bistro, Ruby Tuesday, Subway, Taco Bell, TGIFriday's, Tropical Smoothie, TX Roadhouse, Wendy's [lodging] Residence Inn [other] $Tree, AT&T, Barnes&Noble, Best Buy, BJ's Whse/gas, Chevrolet, Curves, Dick's, Firestone/auto, JC Penney, Kohl's, Lowe's, Macy's, mall, Michael's, Nissan, Old Navy, PetCo, Sears/auto, st police, Stop&Shop/gas, Target, TJ Maxx, TownFair Tire, Toyota/Scion, USPO, Verizon, Walgreens, Walmart
11b a (17)	Reed Rd, to Dartmouth, S 2 mi [gas] Shell
10 (16)	MA 88 S, to US 6, Westport, S [gas] Gulf [other] CVS Drug, same as 9
9 (15.5)	MA 24 N (from nb), Stanford Rd, Westport, S [gas] Rte 6 Gas, Supreme, Valero [food] Dunkin Donuts, Galley Grill [lodging] Hampton Inn [other] White' Hospitality
8b	MA 24 N, (exits left from eb)
8a (15)	MA 24 S, Fall River, Westport
7 (14)	MA 81 S, Plymouth Ave, Fall River, N [gas] BP, Hess [food] 99 Rest., Boston Mkt, Burger King, D'angelo's Rest., Dunkin Donuts, HoneyDew Donuts, KFC, Subway, Wendy's [other] [H], CVS Drug, S [gas] Gulf, Shell [food] Applebee's, McDonald's [other] Stop&Shop, Sullivan Tire, Walgreens
6 (13.5)	Pleasant St, Fall River, downtown
5 (13)	MA 79, MA 138, to Taunton, S [gas] 7-11, Hess [food] Dunkin Donuts
12mm	Assonet Bay
4b a (10)	MA 103, to Swansea, Somerset, N [gas] BP [food] Rogers Rest. [other] repair, vet, S [gas] Shell/24hr [food] Jillian's Grill [lodging] Quality Inn, Super 8
3 (8)	US 6, to MA 118, Swansea, Rehoboth, N [gas] Citgo/dsl, Hess, Mobil/Dunkin Donuts [food] Friendly's, McDonald's, Subway, Thai Taste, Wendy's [other] $Tree, BigLots, CarQuest, Firestone/auto, Jo-Ann Fabrics, Macy's, mall, Marshall's, Old Navy, Price Rite Foods, Radio Shack, Sears/auto, Target, S [gas] Gulf [food] Anthony's Seafood [lodging] Swansea Motel [other] Kia, NAPA

(left margin: **FALL RIVER**)

(right margin: **SEEKONK / PROVIDENCE**)

Exit #	Services
6mm	[Rs] eb, full [handicap] facilities, litter barrels, petwalk, [other], [other]
5.5mm	parking area wb
2 (5)	MA 136, to Newport, S [gas] Mobil/24hr, Shell/24hr [food] Cathay Pearl Chinese, Dunkin Donuts, McDonald's, Michael's Rest., Subway [other] CVS Drug
3mm	weigh sta both lanes
1 (1)	MA 114A, to Seekonk, N [gas] Citgo, Gulf, Shell/24hr [food] 99 Rest., Dunkin Donuts, HoneyDew Donuts, Lums Sandwiches, Newport Creamery [lodging] Motel 6 [other] vet, S [gas] Hess/dsl, Mobil/24hr, Stop&Shop Gas/repair [food] 1149 E Rest., 5 Guys Burgers, Applebee's, BigLots, Buca Italian, Burger King, Chili's, D'Angelo's, Dicky's BBQ, Diparma Italian, Dunkin Donuts, Friendly's, McDonald's, Old Country Buffet, Outback Steaks, Panera Bread, PapaGino's, Starbucks, Subway, Taco Bell, TGIFriday's, Wendy's [lodging] Best Western, Comfort Inn, Extended Stay America, Hampton Inn, Knights Inn, Mary's Motel, Ramada Inn, Town&Country Motel [other] $Tree, Acura, Advance Parts, AT&T, Best Buy, BigLots, Bob's Stores, Dick's, Firestone/auto, Home Depot, Kohl's, Lowe's, Michael's, PepBoys, PetCo, Sam's Club, Staples, Stop&Shop Foods, Target, TJMaxx, TownFair Tire, Tuesday Morning, Verizon, Walmart
0mm	**Massachusetts/Rhode Island state line, Exits 8-1 are in RI.**
8 (5)	US 1A N, Pawtucket, S [gas] Mobil/dsl [food] Subway [other] CVS Drug
7 (4)	US 6 E, CT 114 S, to Barrington, Seekonk
6 (3)	Broadway Ave, N [gas] Speedy AutoService, S [gas] Shell, Sunoco/dsl
5 (2.5)	RI 103 E, Warren Ave
4 (2)	US 44 E, RI 103 E, Taunton Ave, Warren Ave, N [gas] Sunoco
3 (1.5)	Gano St, N [other] Wyndham Garden
2 (1)	US 44 W, Wickenden St, India Pt, N [gas] Shell/dsl [other] Wyndham Garden, downtown
1 (.5)	Providence, downtown
0mm	**I-195 begins/ends on I-95, exit 20 in Providence, RI, Exits 1-8 are in RI.**

↑E INTERSTATE 290

(right margin: **WORCHESTER**)

Exit #	Services
26b a (20)	I-495. I-290 begins/ends on I-495, exit 25.
25b a (17)	Solomon Pond Mall Rd, to Berlin, N [food] Bertucci's, Olive Garden, TGIFriday's [lodging] Comfort Inn, Residence Inn [other] Best Buy, JC Penney, Macy's, mall/foodcourt, Old Navy, Sears/auto, Target, S [food] Guiseppe's Grill
24 (15)	Church St, Northborough
23b a (13)	MA 140, Boylston, N [gas] Citgo/Dunkin Donuts/dsl
22 (11)	Main St, Worcester, N [food] Dunkin Donuts
21 (10)	Plantation St (from eb), N [food] Dunkin Donuts, same as 20
20 (8)	MA 70, Lincoln St, Burncoat St, N [gas] Gulf/Subway [food] 5 Guys Burgers, 5&Diner, Crown Chicken, Denny's, Dunkin Donuts, KFC, McDonald's, PapaGino's, Plaza Azteca, Ruby Tuesday, Taco Bell, TX Roadhouse, Wendy's [lodging] Quality Inn [other] $Tree, Aldi Foods, AutoZone, Barnes&Noble, CVS Drug, Dick's, Lowe's, Radio Shack, Staples, Stop&Shop, Target, USPO, Walgreens
19 (7)	I-190 N, MA 12
18	MA 9, Framingham, Ware, N [other], [H], [other] Worcester [other]
16	Central St, Worcester, N [food] 99 Rest., Starbucks [lodging] Crowne Plaza, Hilton Garden, mall
14	MA 122, Barre, Worcester, downtown
13	MA 122A, Vernon St, Worcester, downtown
12	MA 146 S, to Millbury
11	Southbridge St, College Square, N [gas] Shell/dsl [food] Golden House Chinese, Wendy's [other] Family$

INTERSTATE 290 Cont'd

Exit #	Services
10	MA 12 N (from wb), Hope Ave
9	Auburn St, to Auburn, E 🔲 BP, Shell 🔲 Arby's, Auburn Town Pizza, Dunkin Donuts, McDonald's, PapaGino's, Starbucks, Yong Shing 🔲 Comfort Inn, Holiday Inn Express (1mi), La Quinta 🔲 Acura, Macy's, mall, Sears/auto, Shaw's Foods, TownFair Tire
8	MA 12 S (from sb), Webster, W 🔲 Shell 🔲 Holiday Inn Express
7	I-90, E to Boston, W to Springfield. **I-290 begins/ends on I-90.**

INTERSTATE 395

Exit #	Services
	I-395 begins/ends on I-90, exit 10.
7 (12)	to I-90 (MA Tpk), MA 12, E 🔲 Shell 🔲 Piccadilly's 🔲 Holiday Inn Express
6b a (11)	US 20, E 🔲 BP, Gulf 🔲 Frank&Nancy's Cafe 🔲 Honda/VW, NAPA, truck tires/repair, W 🔲 Shell 🔲 Chuck's Steakhouse, Dunkin Donuts, Friendly's 🔲 Fairfield Inn, Hampton Inn 🔲 BJ's Whse, Buick/Cadillac/GMC, Chevrolet, Ford, Home Depot, Nissan, TJ Maxx, transmissions
5 (8)	Depot Rd, N Oxford
4b a (6)	Sutton Ave, to Oxford, E 🔲 MktBasket Foods, W 🔲 Cumberland Farms, Mobil/24hr 🔲 Dunkin Donuts, McDonald's, NE Pizza, Subway, Veranda Cafe 🔲 Cahill's Tire/repair, CVS Drug, Home Depot, MktBasket Foods, Verizon
3 (4)	Cudworth Rd, to N Webster, S Oxford
2 (3)	MA 16, to Webster, E 🔲 RV Camping, Subaru, W 🔲 BP/repair, Gulf, Hi-Lo Gas, Sunoco 🔲 Burger King, D'angelo's, Dunkin Donuts, Empire Wok, Friendly's, HoneyDew Donuts, KFC/Taco Bell, McDonald's, PapaGino's 🔲 🔲, Advance Parts, AT&T, Consumer Parts, CVS Drug, Ford, PriceChopper Foods, Rite Aid, Verizon, vet, Walgreens
1 (1)	MA 193, to Webster, E 🔲 🔲, W 🔲 Citgo/dsl 🔲 Golden Greek Rest., Wind Tiki Chinese 🔲 Goodyear/auto
0mm	Massachusetts/Connecticut state line

INTERSTATE 495

Exit #	Services
	I-495 begins/ends on I-95, exit 59
55 (119)	MA 110 (from nb, no return), to I-95 S, E 🔲 Irving/Circle K, Mobil, Sunoco/dsl 🔲 Acupulco Mexican, Burger King, Dunkin Donuts, Friendly's, McDonald's, PapaGino's 🔲 Fairfield Inn 🔲 AT&T, Chevrolet, Stop&Shop, Verizon, W 🔲 Gulf 🔲 CVS, NAPA
54 (118)	MA 150, to Amesbury, W 🔲 RV camping
53 (115)	Broad St, Merrimac, W 🔲 Citgo/repair 🔲 Dunkin Donuts
114mm	**parking area sb, (6am-8pm), litter barrels, 🔲, restrooms**
52 (111)	MA 110, to Haverhill, E 🔲 Seafood Etc 🔲 🔲, W 🔲 Racing Mart 🔲 Biggart Ice Cream, Dunkin Donuts
110mm	**parking area nb, litter barrels, 🔲**
51 (109)	MA 125, to Haverhill, E 🔲 Gulf 🔲 Bros Pizza, China King, Dunkin Donuts 🔲 🔲, Family$, W 🔲 Mobil/dsl 🔲 Applebee's, Burger King, Dunkin Donuts, Friendly's, Li's Asian, Longhorn Steaks, Lucky Corner Chinese, McDonald's, Mr Mikes Grill, Starbucks, Taco Bell, Tuscan House Pizza, Wendy's 🔲 Monro Service
50 (107)	MA 97, to Haverhill, W 🔲 Ford, Target
49 (106)	MA 110, to Haverhill, E 🔲 Gulf, Sunoco 🔲 99 Rest., Athens Pizza, Dunkin Donuts, McDonald's, Oriental Garden, PapaGino's 🔲 Best Western, Hampton Inn 🔲 Buick/Chevrolet/GMC,

49 (106)	Continued Chrysler/Dodge/Jeep, CVS Drug, Marshall's, MktBasket Foods, Walgreens
105.8mm	Merrimac River
48 (105.5)	MA 125, to Bradford, E 🔲 BJ's Whse/gas
47 (105)	MA 213, to Methuen, W **1-2 mi** 🔲 Burger King, ChuckeCheese, Friendly's, Joe's Crabshack, McDonald's, New Tokyo, Olive Garden, OrangeLeaf, Santana Rae's Mexican, Starbucks, TGIFriday's, Wendy's 🔲 🔲, Home Depot, Marshalls, MktBasket Foods, Old Navy, Radio Shack, Stop&Shop, Target, The Mann Orchards/Bakery, Walmart/Subway
46 (104)	MA 110, E 🔲 Giovanni's Deli, Pleasant Valley Gas, Sunoco, W 🔲 🔲
45 (103)	Marston St, to Lawrence, W 🔲 Chevrolet, Honda, Kia, Nissan, VW
44 (102)	Merrimac St, to Lawrence
43 (101)	Mass Ave
42 (100)	MA 114, E 🔲 Gulf, Mobil, Wave 🔲 Bertucci's, Boll Wood Grill, Boston Mkt, Burger King, Burtons Grill, Chipotle Mexican, Dunkin Donuts, Friendly's, Lee Chin Chinese, Panera Bread 🔲 Holiday Inn Express 🔲 Ace Hardware, CVS Drug, Kohl's, MktBasket Foods, PetCo, Staples, TJ Maxx, Walgreens, W 🔲 Denny's, Dunkin Donuts, KFC, Little Caesar's, Pizza Hut/Taco Bell, Subway, Wendy's 🔲 🔲, Advance Parts, Family$, Marshall's, Monroe Service, O'Reilly Parts/VIP Service, vet
41 (99)	MA 28, to Andover, E 🔲 Dunkin Donuts 🔲 Cadillac/Chevrolet
40b a (98)	I-93, N to Methuen, S to Boston
39 (94)	MA 133, to Dracut, E 🔲 Hess 🔲 Longhorn Steaks, McDonald's 🔲 Extended Stay America, W 🔲 Mobil/dsl 🔲 Cracker Barrel, Wendy's 🔲 Fairfield Inn, Holiday Inn/rest., Residence Inn
38 (93)	MA 38, to Lowell, E 🔲 Petroil/dsl, Shell/dsl 🔲 99 Rest., Applebee's, Burger King, Dunkin Donuts, IHOP, Jade East, Waffle House 🔲 Motel 6, Motel Caswell 🔲 Home Depot, Honda/VW, TownFair Tire, Walmart, W 🔲 Citgo, Mobil, Sunoco, USA/dsl 🔲 Dunkin Donuts, Jillie's Rest., McDonald's, Milan Pizza, Wendy's 🔲 Buick/GMC, Chevrolet, Chrysler/Dodge/Jeep, CVS Drug, Hannaford Foods, Marshalls, Mazda, MktBasket Foods, Sears Essentials, Staples
37 (91)	Woburn St, to S Lowell, W 🔲 Gulf/Dunkin Donuts/Subway
35c (90)	to Lowell SP, Lowell ConX, W **0-2 mi on US 3** 🔲 Burger King, Chili's, McDonald's, Outback Steaks, Wendy's 🔲 Courtyard 🔲 Kia, Lowe's, Shop&Save, Walgreens
35b a (89)	US 3, S to Burlington, N to Nashua, NH
34 (88)	MA 4, Chelmsford, E 🔲 Ampet, Mobil, Sunoco 🔲 Cafe Madrid, Domino's, Dunkin Donuts, Jimmy's Pizza, PapaGino's 🔲 Radisson 🔲 CVS Drug, Walgreens, W 🔲 Shell 🔲 Moonstone's Rest. 🔲 Best Western

OXFORD

HAVERHILL

LOWELL

MA

INTERSTATE 495 Cont'd

Exit #	Services
33	MA 4, N Chelmsford (from nb)
87mm	🆁🆂 both lanes, (8am-8pm), full 🅰 facilities, litter barrels, 🅒🅒 🔌, vending
32 (83)	Boston Rd, to MA 225, **E** 🅖 Cumberland Farms, Gulf, Mobil 🅕 Applebee's, British Beer Co Rest., Burger King, Chili's, D'angelo's, Dunkin Donuts, McDonald's, PapaGino's, Starbucks, Subway, Westford Grill 🅛 Hampton Inn, Residence Inn 🅞 🅷, CVS Drug, Jo-Ann Fabrics, MktBasket Foods, Radio Shack, Rite Aid, to Nashoba Valley Ski Area, Walgreens
31 (80)	MA 119, to Groton, **E** 🅖 Gulf, Mobil/dsl/24hr, Shell 🅕 Dunkin Donuts, Littleton's Subs, Subway, Tre Amici Ristorante 🅞 Aubuchon Hardware, CVS Drug, Donelan's Foods, Toyota/Scion, Verizon, vet
30 (78)	MA 110, to Littleton, **E 1 mi** 🅖 Shell/Dunkin Donuts 🅕 CVS Drug, RV Camping, USPO, vet, **W** 🅖 Shell/Dunkin Donuts 🅞 🅷, vet
29b a (77)	MA 2, to Leominster, **E** 🅞 to Walden Pond St Reserve
28 (75)	MA 111, to Boxborough, Harvard, **E** 🅖 Gulf/Dunkin Donuts 🅛 Holiday Inn
27 (70)	MA 117, to Bolton, **E** 🅖 Mobil/dsl 🅕 Subway, **W** 🅕 Bolton Pizza 🅞 vet
26 (68)	MA 62, to Berlin, **E** 🅖 Gulf/Dunkin Donuts 🅛 Holiday Inn Express 🅞 🅷, BJ's Whse/gas, Lowe's, **W** 🅖 Shell/dsl 🅕 Berlin Farms Cafe
66mm	Assabet River
25b (64)	I-290, to Worcester
25a	to MA 85, Marlborough, **E 1 mi** 🅖 Gulf, Mobil/dsl 🅕 99 Rest., Applebee's, Burger King, Checkerboards Rest., Domino's, HoneyDew Donuts, KFC/Taco Bell, PapaGino's 🅞 $Tree, AutoZone, Chevrolet, CVS Drug, Family$, Hannaford Foods, PetCo, Stop&Shop/gas, TJ Maxx, Verizon, Walgreens
24b a (63)	US 20, to Northboro, Marlborough, **E** 🅖 Mobil 🅕 Allora Rest., D'angelo's, Dunkin Donuts, Lake Williams Pizza 🅛 Holiday Inn, **W** 🅖 Gulf, Shell 🅕 5 Guys Burgers, 99 Rest., Boston Mkt, China Taste, Chipotle Mexican, Japan 1, Longhorn Steaks, McDonald's/playplace, Panera Bread, PapaGino's, Quiznos, Starbucks, Tandoori Grill, Wendy's 🅛 Best Western, Courtyard, Embassy Suites, Hampton Inn, Homestead Suites 🅞 $Tree, GNC, Hannaford Foods
23c (60)	Simrano Dr, Marlborough
23b a (59)	MA 9, to Shrewsbury, Framingham, **E** 🅖 Cumberland/Dunkin Donuts, Gulf 🅕 Wendy's 🅛 Red Roof Inn, **W 0-2 mi** 🅖 Mobil/dsl/24hr, Shell 🅕 Bertucci's, Burger King, Chateau Rest., Chengdu, Chipotle Mexican, D'angelo's, Dunkin Donuts, Friendly's, Harry's Rest., McDonald's, Piccadilly Cafe, Ruby Tuesday, Starbucks 🅛 Doubletree Inn, Extended Stay America, Extended Stay Deluxe, Residence Inn 🅞 🅷, Buick/GMC, Chrysler/Dodge/Jeep, Marshall's, Staples, Stop&Shop, VW
22 (58)	I-90, MA TPK, E to Boston, W to Albany
21b a (54)	MA 135, to Hopkinton, Upton, **E** 🅖 Cumberland, Mobil 🅕 Dino's Pizza, Dynasty Chinese, Golden Spoon Rest.
20 (50)	MA 85, to Milford, **W** 🅖 Gulf/dsl/LP, Mobil/dsl 🅕 99 Rest., Pizza 85/deli, TGIFriday's, Wendy's 🅛 Comfort Inn, Courtyard, Fairfield Inn, Holiday Inn Express 🅞 🅷, Best Buy, Lowe's, PetCo, Staples, Stop&Shop, Target, TJ Maxx, Toyota/Scion

19 (48)	MA 109, to Milford, **W** 🅖 Mobil/Dunkin Donuts/dsl, Shell 🅕 5 Guys Burgers, Alamo Mexican, Applebee's, Bugaboo Cr Steaks, Burger King, D'angelo's, Friendly's, KFC/Pizza Hut, Maria's Italian, McDonald's/playplace, Panera Bread, PapaGino's, Subway 🅛 Doubletree, La Quinta 🅞 $Tree, AutoZone, CVS Drug, Hannaford Foods, Jo-Ann Fabrics, K-Mart, Kohl's, Radio Shack, Rite Aid, TownFair Tire
18 (46)	MA 126, to Bellingham, **E** 🅕 Chili's, Coldstone, McDonald's 🅞 Barnes&Noble, Michael's, MktBasket Foods, Old Navy, Staples, Verizon, Walmart/Subway, Whole Foods Mkt, **W** 🅖 Hess/dsl, Mobil/24hr, Sunoco/dsl 🅕 Chicago Grill, DQ, Dunkin Donuts, Outback Steaks 🅞 Home Depot, Petsmart
17 (44)	MA 140, to Franklin, Bellingham, **E** 🅖 Mobil/dsl, Shell, Sunoco 🅕 Burger King, D'angelo's, Dunkin Donuts, Franklin Cafe, HoneyDew Donuts, Longhorn Steaks, Panera Bread, PapaGino's, Pepper Terrace Thai, Subway, Taco Bell, Tepanyaki Asian 🅞 AT&T, AutoZone, Buick/GMC, CVS Drug, GNC, Marshalls, Radio Shack, Stop&Shop, **W** 🅕 99 Rest., Encontro Rest. 🅛 Residence Inn 🅞 🅷, BJ's Whse/Subway/gas
16 (42)	King St, to Franklin, **E** 🅖 Sunoco 🅕 Dunkin Donuts, Joe's Grill, King St Cafe, Spruce Pond Creamery 🅛 Hampton Inn, **W** 🅛 Hawthorn Inn
15 (39)	MA 1A, to Plainville, Wrentham, **E** 🅖 Shell 🅕 Assisi Pizza 🅞 🅷, **W** 🅖 Mobil/dsl 🅕 Chicago Grill, Cracker Barrel, Dunkin Donuts, Friendly's, Ruby Tuesday 🅞 Premium Outlets/famous brands
14b a (37)	US 1, to N Attleboro, **E** 🅖 Interstate/D'angelo's/PapaGino's/dsl 🅕 Luciano's Rest. 🅛 Arbor Motel 🅞 Bass Pro Shops (4mi), **W** 🅖 Citgo/dsl, Mobil 🅕 Chili's, Dunkin Donuts, Panera Bread, The Tavern 🅛 Holiday Inn Express 🅞 Lowe's, Macdonald's RV Ctr, NTB, Stop&Shop, Stop&Shop, Target, TJ Maxx, vet
13 (32)	I-95, N to Boston, S to Providence, access to 🅷
12 (30)	MA 140, to Mansfield, **E** 🅕 Asian Grill, Bertucci's Italian, Chipotle Mexican, Friendly's Express, Longhorn Steaks, Qdoba Mexican, Sake Japanese, TGIFriday's, Wendy's 🅞 AT&T, Best Buy, Home Depot, Kohl's, LL Bean, Michael's, PetCo, Radio Shack, Shaw's Foods, Staples, Verizon
11 (29)	MA 140 S (from sb), **W 1 mi** 🅖 Gulf 🅕 Dunkin Donuts, Mandarin Chinese, McDonald's, Subway 🅞 $Tree
10 (26)	MA 123, to Norton, **E** 🅕 Dunkin Donuts 🅞 QuickStop, **W** 🅞 🅷
9 (24)	Bay St, to Taunton, **E** 🅕 Chateau Rest., **W** 🅕 Dunkin Donuts, Jaybo Cafe, NE Hotdog, Ruby Tuesday, Subway, Wendy's 🅛 Extended Stay America 🅞 $Tree, BJ's Whse, Tadeschi Foods, Watson Pond SP
8 (22)	MA 138, to Raynham, **E** 🅖 Hess/dsl, Mobil/dsl 🅕 Christopher's Pizza, HoneyDew Donuts, Yummyhouse Rest., **W** 🅖 Gulf/dsl, Shell/dsl/repair, Stop'n Go/dsl 🅕 Brothers Pizza, Cape Cod Cafe, China Garden, D'angelos, Dunkin Donuts, HoneyDew Donuts, Lucky Corner Chinese, McDonald's, Subway 🅞 🅷, Ace Hardware, CVS Drug, Mkt Basket Foods, USPO, vet
7b a (19)	MA 24, to Fall River, Boston, **E 1/2 mi** 🅖 Mobil/dsl 🅕 Burger King
18mm	weigh sta both lanes
17mm	Taunton River
6 (15)	US 44, to Middleboro, **E** 🅖 Super/dsl 🅕 Burger King, Dunkin Donuts, Fireside Grille, Friendly's, Hong Kong Taste, PapaGino's, Subway, **W** 🅖 Mobil/Dunkin Donuts/dsl 🅛 Fairfield Inn, Holiday Inn Express

(margin left, top to bottom) **MARLBORO**

(margin right, top to bottom) **MILFORD**

↑N	**INTERSTATE 495 Cont'd**
Exit #	Services
5 (14)	MA 18, to Lakeville, **E** 🅶 Shell, Super/dsl 🍽 D'Angelo's, Dave's Diner, Fireside Grille, Harry's Grille, Lorenzo's Rest, PapaGino's, Persy's Place Cafe 🅾 CVS Drug, Kelly's Tire, Stop&Shop, **W** 🅾 Massasoit SP, RV camping (seasonal)
4 (12)	MA 105, to Middleboro, **E** 🅶 Gulf/dsl, Shell/24hr, Sunoco/24hr 🍽 China Sails, DQ, Dunkin Donuts, McDonald's, Tuttabella Pizza 🏠 Days Inn 🅾 AutoZone, Rite Aid

11mm	parking area eb
10mm	parking area both lanes
3 (8)	MA 28, to Rock Village, S Middleboro, **E** 🅶 Irving/dsl 🅾 Fred's Repair, **W** 🅶 Mobil/Dunkin Donuts/Subway/dsl
2mm	Weweantic River
2 (3)	MA 58, W Wareham, **E** 🅾 RV camping, to Myles Standish SF, **W** 🅶 7-11
1 (0)	I-495 begins/ends on I-195, MA 25 S.

MICHIGAN

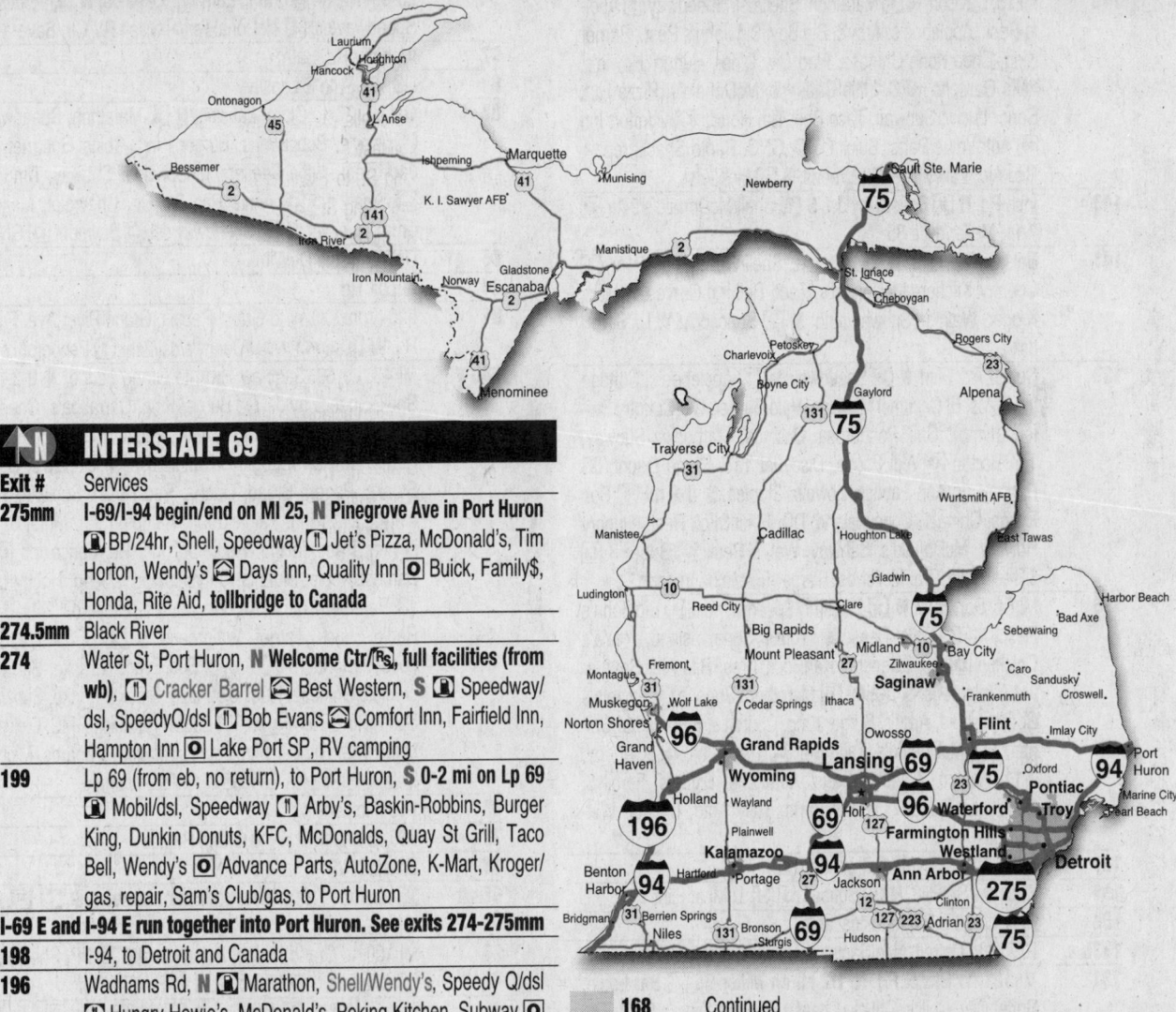

↑N	**INTERSTATE 69**
Exit #	Services
275mm	**I-69/I-94 begin/end on MI 25, N Pinegrove Ave in Port Huron** 🅶 BP/24hr, Shell, Speedway 🍽 Jet's Pizza, McDonald's, Tim Horton, Wendy's 🏠 Days Inn, Quality Inn 🅾 Buick, Family$, Honda, Rite Aid, **tollbridge to Canada**
274.5mm	Black River
274	Water St, Port Huron, **N** Welcome Ctr/🆁🆂, full facilities (from wb), 🍽 Cracker Barrel 🏠 Best Western, **S** 🅶 Speedway/dsl, SpeedyQ/dsl 🍽 Bob Evans 🏠 Comfort Inn, Fairfield Inn, Hampton Inn 🅾 Lake Port SP, RV camping
199	Lp 69 (from eb, no return), to Port Huron, **S** 0-2 mi on Lp 69 🅶 Mobil/dsl, Speedway 🍽 Arby's, Baskin-Robbins, Burger King, Dunkin Donuts, KFC, McDonalds, Quay St Grill, Taco Bell, Wendy's 🅾 Advance Parts, AutoZone, K-Mart, Kroger/gas, repair, Sam's Club/gas, to Port Huron
	I-69 E and I-94 E run together into Port Huron. See exits 274-275mm
198	I-94, to Detroit and Canada
196	Wadhams Rd, **N** 🅶 Marathon, Shell/Wendy's, Speedy Q/dsl 🍽 Hungry Howie's, McDonald's, Peking Kitchen, Subway 🅾 KOA (1mi), Vinckier Foods, Wadham's Drugs, **S** 🅾 golf
194	Taylor Rd, **N** 🅾 Goodells CP, RV camping
189	Wales Center Rd, to Goodells, **S** 🅾 golf
184	MI 19, to Emmett, **N** 🅶 Citgo/Steverino's/dsl/scales/24hr 🅾 repair, **S** 🅶 Marathon/dsl/24hr
180	Riley Center Rd, **N** 🅾 KOA
176	Capac Rd, **N** 🅶 BP/McDonald's/dsl/scales 🍽 Subway (2mi)
174mm	🆁🆂 wb, full ♿ facilities, litter barrels, petwalk, 🅲, 🏕, vending
168	MI 53, Imlay City, **N** 🅶 BP/dsl/24hr, Speedway/dsl 🍽 Big Boy, Big Joe's Pizza, Burger King, DQ, Hungry Howie's, John's Country Kitchen, Little Caesar's, Lucky's Steaks, McDonald's, New China, Taco Bell, Wah Wong Chinese,

168	Continued
	Wendy's/Tim Horton 🏠 Days Inn, M53 Motel, Super 8 🅾 $Discount, AutoZone, Chevrolet, Chrysler/Dodge/Jeep, Ford, GNC, Grocery Outlet, Kroger/gas, NAPA, Radio Shack, Sav-On Drug, ShopKO **S** 🅾 camping
163	Lake Pleasant Rd, to Attica
160mm	🆁🆂 eb, full ♿ facilities, litter barrels, petwalk, 🅲, 🏕, vending
159	Wilder Rd
158mm	Flint River
155	MI 24, Lapeer, **N** 1 mi 🅶 BP, Clark/dsl, FS, Speedy Q 🍽 Apple Tree Rest., Applebee's, Arby's, Blind Fish Rest., Brian's Rest., Burger King, Checker's, DQ, Farmhouse Rest., Jet's Pizza, Jimmy John's, KFC, Little Caesar's, Mancino's,

MI

LAPEER

INTERSTATE 69 Cont'd

Exit #	Services
155	Continued
	McDonald's, Mr Pita, Nick's Rest., Sonic, Starbucks, Subway, Taco Bell, Tim Horton, Wah Wong Chinese, Wendy's 🛏 Best Western, Lapeer Hotel ⊙ 🄷 $Tree, AutoZone, Home Depot, K-Mart, Kohl's, Kroger, Meijer/dsl, Office Depot, O'Reilly Parts, Radio Shack, Save-a-Lot, st police, vet, Walgreens, **S** 🅖 Mobil/dsl ⊙ Chrysler/Dodge/Jeep
153	Lake Nepessing Rd, **S** ⊙ camping, golf, to Thumb Correctional
149	Elba Rd, **N** ⊙ Torzwski CP, **S** ⊙ Country Mkt, RV/truck repair
145	MI 15, Davison, **N** 🅖 Marathon, Shell/dsl, Speedway 🍴 Apollo Rest., Applebee's, Arby's, Big Boy, Big John's Rest., Burger King, Chee Kong Chinese, Flag City Diner, Hungry Howie's, Italia Gardens, KFC, Little Caesar's, McDonald's, Pizza Hut, Senor Lucky, Subway, Taco Bell, Tim Horton 🛏 Comfort Inn ⊙ AutoValue Parts, Buick/GMC, GNC, Radio Shack, repair, Rite Aid, Valley Tire, Walgreens, **S** 🅖 Mobil/dsl
143	Irish Rd, **N** 🅖 Speedway/dsl, **S** 🅖 Shell/McDonald's/24hr ⊙ 7-11, Meijer/dsl/e-85
141	Belsay Rd, Flint, **N** 🅖 1 stop, Shell/Wendy's/dsl/24hr 🍴 Country Kitchen, McDonald's, Taco Bell ⊙ Curves, K-Mart, Kroger, Walmart/Subway/auto, **S** 🅖 Sunoco/A&W/LJ Silver/dsl

FLINT

139	Center Rd, Flint, **N** 🅖 Speedway/dsl 🍴 Applebee's, Cottage Inn Pizza, El Cazumel Mexican, Halo Burger, Old Country Buffet, Olympic Grill, Ponderosa, Quiznos, Starbucks, Subway, Tim Horton ⊙ Aldi Foods, Discount Tire, Home Depot, JC Penney, Jo-Ann Fabrics, Lowe's, Staples, **S** 0-2 mi 🍴 Bob Evans, China 1, Coney Island, DQ, Firkin&Fox Rest., Hungry Howie's, McDonald's, Subway, Walli's Rest. 🛏 Super 8 ⊙ $Tree, Belle Tire, Meijer/dsl, Target, TJ Maxx, Verizon
138	MI 54, Dort Hwy, **N** 🅖 BP/24hr, Speedway/dsl 🍴 Big John's Rest., KFC, Little Caesar's, Tom's Coney Island, YaYa's Chicken ⊙ 🄷 $General, KanRock Tires, Rite Aid, Save-a-Lot, Walgreens, **S** 0-2 mi 🅖 Marathon, Sunoco 🍴 Angelo's Coney Island, Arby's, Burger King, Church's, Empress of China, KFC, McDonald's, Taco Bell 🛏 Travel Inn ⊙ $General, 7-11, Aamco, Advance Parts, AutoZone, BigLots, Family$, Goodyear, K-Mart, O'Reilly Parts, Tuffy Auto, U-Haul, Walgreens
137	I-475, UAW Fwy, to Detroit, Saginaw
136	Saginaw St, Flint, **N** 🅖 Sunoco ⊙ 🄷, U MI at Flint
135	Hammerberg Rd, industrial area
133 b a	I-75, S to Detroit, N to Saginaw, US 23 S to Ann Arbor
131	MI 121, to Bristol Rd, **N** 1/2 mi on Miller Rd 🍴 Bar Louie, Buffet City, Chili's, ChuckeCheese, Famous Dave's BBQ, Fire Mtn, Golden Moon Chinese, Halo Burger, Leo's Coney Island, LJ Silver, Logan's Roadhouse, Mongolian BBQ, Old Country Buffet, Olive Garden, Outback Steaks, Red Robin, Ruby Tuesday, Subway, Taco Bell, Valley Diner ⊙ Barnes&Noble, Best Buy, BigLots, Discount Tire, Firestone/auto, Gander Mtn, Goodyear/auto, Hobby Lobby, JC Penney, Jo-Ann Fabrics, Macy's, mall, Michael's, Old Navy, PetCo, PetsMart, Sears/auto, Target, TJ Maxx
129	Miller Rd, **S** 🍴 Arby's, Burger King, McDonald's, Subway, Wendy's ⊙ Kroger/gas
128	Morrish Rd, **S** 🅖 Admiral/24hr, BP/dsl/24hr ⊙ Sports Creek Horse Racing
126mm	🆁🆂 **eb, full** ♿ **facilities, info, litter barrels, petwalk,** ⬜, ⛟

LANSING

123	MI 13, to Saginaw, Lennon, **N** 🅖 Speedway/dsl
118	MI 71, to Corunna, Durand, **N** ⊙ st police, **S** 🅖 QuikStop, Shell/dsl 🍴 McDonald's, Subway, Wendy's 🛏 Quality Inn ⊙ Ace Hardware, Chevrolet, Family$, golf, Rite Aid
115mm	Shiawassee River
113	Bancroft, **S** 🅖 BP/dsl ⊙ RV camping
105	MI 52, to Owosso, Perry, **S** 🅖 7-11, Mobil, PS/Subway/dsl, Sunoco/dsl/scales 🍴 Burger King, Café Sports, McDonald's, Taco Bell 🛏 Heb's Inn ⊙ Family$, Ford, IGA Foods, Rite Aid, RV camping, truck repair (1mi)
101mm	🆁🆂 **wb, full** ♿ **facilities, litter barrels, petwalk,** ⬜, ⛟
98.5mm	Looking Glass River
98	Woodbury Rd, to Laingsburg, Shaftsburg, **S** ⊙ RV camping
94	Lp 69, Marsh Rd, to E Lansing, Okemos, **S** 🅖 Admiral/dsl, Speedway/dsl 🍴 McDonald's ⊙ Gillett RV Ctr, Save-a-Lot
92	Webster Rd, Bath
89	US 127 S, to E Lansing
87	Old US 27, to Clare, Lansing, **N** 🅖 Marathon, Speedway/dsl 🍴 Arby's, Bob Evans, Burger King, China Gourmet, FlapJack Rest., Little Ceasars, McDonald's, Subway, Tim Horton 🛏 Sleep Inn ⊙ Annie Rae RV Ctr, Chevrolet, Meijer/dsl, TrueValue, vet, **S** 🅖 Speedway/dsl 🛏 Baymont ⊙ GNC
85	DeWitt Rd, to DeWitt
84	Airport Rd
91	I-96 (from sb), W to Grand Rapids, Grand River Ave, Frances Rd, **W** 🅖 ⛽FLYING J/Denny's/dsl/24hr 🍴 Pepperoni's Rest.
93b a	MI 43, Lp 69, Saginaw Hwy, to Grand Ledge, **N** 0-2 mi 🅖 Shell, Speedway/dsl 🍴 Burger King, Carrabba's, Cheddar's, Denny's, Fazoli's, Frank's Grill, Hibachi Grill, Honeybaked Ham, Houlihan's, Logan's Roadhouse, McDonald's, Outback Steaks, Panera Bread, Qdoba, Red Robin, Subway, Younkers 🛏 Days Inn, Fairfield Inn, Hampton Inn, Motel 6, Quality Inn, Ramada Inn, Red Roof Inn, Residence Inn ⊙ 🄷, Barnes&Noble, BigLots, Chrysler/Dodge/Jeep, Hobby Lobby, JC Penney, Kohl's, Kroger, Macy's, Meijer/dsl/24hr, NAPA, Radio Shack, Target, Walgreens, **S** 🅖 BP/24hr, QD, Sunoco/McDonald's 🍴 Arby's, Bob Evans, Cracker Barrel, Ingcredible Chinese, Rudino's Pizza, Steak'n Shake, Subway 🛏 SpringHill Suites ⊙ AT&T, Belle Tire, Buick/GMC, Dick's, Discount Tire, Gander Mtn, Lowe's, Mazda, Menards, Michael's, PetsMart, Staples, URGENT CARE, Walmart
95	I-496, to Lansing
72	I-96, E to Detroit, W to Grand Rapids
70	Lansing Rd
68mm	🆁🆂 **nb, full** ♿ **facilities, litter barrels, petwalk,** ⬜, ⛟, **vending**
66	MI 100, to Grand Ledge, Potterville, **W** 🅖 BP, Shell/Subway 🍴 Charlie's Grill, McDonald's, to Fox Co Park
61	Lansing Rd, **E** 🍴 Applebee's 🛏 Comfort Inn ⊙ $Tree, AutoZone, Buick/Chevrolet/GMC, Walmart/Subway, **W** 🅖 QD, Speedway/dsl 🍴 Arby's, Big Boy, Biggby Coffee, Burger King, Jersey Subs, Jet's Pizza, KFC, Little Caesars, McDonald's, Pizza Hut, Rally's, Taco Bell, Tasty Twist, Top Chinese, Wendy's ⊙ 🄷, Advance Parts, CarQuest, Charlotte Tires, Family$, Ford, TrueValue, vet
60	MI 50, Charlotte, **E** 🛏 Holiday Inn Express ⊙ Meijer/dsl, **W** 🅖 Admiral 🛏 Best Value Inn ⊙ 🄷, RV camping
57	Lp 69, Cochran Rd, to Charlotte, **E** ⊙ RV camping
51	Ainger Rd, **E** 1 mi 🅖, 🍴, ⊙ RV camping
48	MI 78, to Bellevue, Olivet, **E** 1 mi 🅖 BP/Subway/dsl ⊙ to Olivet Coll
42	N Drive N, Turkeyville Rd, **W** 🍴 Cornwell's Rest. (1mi)

MARSHALL / COLDWATER

INTERSTATE 69 Cont'd	
Exit #	**Services**
41mm	sb, full facilities, litter barrels, petwalk, ,
38	I-94, E to Detroit, W to Chicago
36	Michigan Ave, to Marshall, **E** Admiral, Citgo/dsl/E85, Shell/Subway Applebee's, Arby's, Biggby Coffee, Burger King, Little Caesars, McDonald's, Pizza Hut, Speedy Chick, Taco Bell, Wendy's, Yin Hai Chinese Comfort Inn , H, $General, $Tree, Ace Hardware, AutoZone, Chevrolet, Family Fare Foods, K-Mart, NAPA, Radio Shack, Rite Aid, Save-A-Lot, Tuffy Auto, **W** Arbor Inn Chrysler/Dodge/Jeep
32	F Drive S, **E** Shell (3/4 mi) Moonraker Rest. (3mi) **W** RV Camping
25	MI 60, to Three Rivers, Jackson, **E** BP/dsl, Sunoco/dsl, TA/Shell/Country Pride/dsl/scales/24hr/@ McDonald's, Subway $General, Auto Value Parts, auto/truck repair, RV camping
23	Tekonsha, **W** access to RV camping
16	Jonesville Rd, **W** Waffle Farm Camping (2mi)
13	US 12, to Quincy, Coldwater, **E** Speedway/dsl Applebee's, Biggby Coffee, Bob Evans, Buffalo Wild Wings, Grand Buffet, Papa Murphy's Hampton Inn, Red Roof Inn $Tree, Aldi Foods, AT&T, AutoZone, BigLots, Buick/Chevrolet/GMC, Gander Mtn., GNC, Haylett RV Ctr, Home Depot, Meijer/dsl, Radio Shack, Verizon, Walmart/Subway, Younkers, **W** Citgo, Speedway/dsl Arby's, Benedict's Steaks, Big Boy, Burger King, Coldwater Garden Rest., Cottage Inn Pizza, Culver's, Jimmy John's, KFC, Little Caesars, McDonald's, Pizza Hut, Ponderosa, Subway, Taco Bell, Wendy's Best Western, Comfort Inn , H, Advance Parts, auto repair, Ford/Lincoln, Rite Aid, st police, Walgreens
10	Lp 69, Fenn Rd, to Coldwater
8mm	weigh sta nb
6mm	**Welcome Ctr nb, full facilities, litter barrels, petwalk, , , vending**
3	Copeland Rd, Kinderhook, **W** BP/dsl camping
0mm	Michigan/Indiana state line

SAULT STE MARIE

INTERSTATE 75	
Exit #	**Services**
395mm	**US/Canada Border Michigan state line, I-75 begins/ends at toll bridge to Canada**
394	Easterday Ave, **E** Citgo/dsl McDonald's Holiday Inn Express , H, to Lake Superior St U, **W** Welcome Ctr/, info Admiral/dsl, Holiday/dsl/currency exchange Freighter's Rest (2mi) Ramada Inn (2mi)
392	3 Mile Rd, Sault Ste Marie, **E** Admiral/dsl, BP/dsl, Holiday/dsl, Marathon/dsl, Shell/dsl Ang-gio's Italian, Applebee's, Arby's, Buffalo Wild Wings, Burger King, Country Kitchen, Domino's, DQ, Great Wall Chinese, Indo China Garden, Little Caesars, McDonald's, Pizza Hut, Studebaker's Rest., Subway, Taco Bell, Wendy's Best Value Inn, Best Western, Comfort Inn, Days Inn, Park Inn, Plaza Motel, Skyline Motel, Soo Locks Lodge, Super 8, Superior Place Motel , H, $Tree, Advance Parts, AT&T, BigLots, Buick/Chevrolet/GMC, Family$, Glen's Mkt, Goodyear/auto, JC Penney, Jo-Ann Fabrics, K-Mart, NAPA, Radio Shack, Save-a-Lot, Soo Locks Boat Tours, st police, TJ Maxx, Verizon, Walgreens, Walmart/Subway
389mm	nb, full facilities, info, litter barrels, petwalk, ,
386	MI 28, **W** Clear Lake Camping (5mi), to Brimley SP
379	Gaines Hwy, **E** Clear Lake Camping, to Barbeau Area

MACKINAW CITY

378	MI 80, Kinross, **E** BP/dsl Frank&Jim's Diner , , golf, RV Camping, to Kinross Correctional
373	MI 48, Rudyard, **W 2 mi** gas/dsl ,
359	MI 134, to Drummond Island, **W** National Forest Camping
352	MI 123, to Moran, Newberry
348	H63, to Sault Reservation, St Ignace, **E 0-2 mi** Jose's Cantina Bavarian Haus, Bayview Motel, Bear Cove Inn, Best Value Inn, Birchwood Motel, Cedars Motel, Comfort Inn, Evergreen Motel, Great Lakes Motel, Holiday Inn Express, Kewadin Inn, NorthernAire Motel, Pines Motel, Quality Inn, Tradewinds Motel , H, , casino, Castle Rock Camping, st police, to Mackinac Trail, **W** Castle Rock Gifts
346mm	/scenic turnout sb, full facilities, litter barrels, petwalk,
345	Portage St (from sb), St Ignace
344b	US 2 W, **W** BP/dsl, Holiday/dsl, Shell/dsl Big Boy, Burger King, Clyde's Drive-In, McDonald's, Subway, Suzy's Pasties 4 Star Motel, Quality Inn, Sunset Motel, Super 8 Ford, golf, Lakeshore RV Park
344a	Lp 75, St Ignace, **E 0-2 mi** Shell BC Pizza, Bentley's Cafe, Galley Rest., Mackinac Grille, Marina Rest., Northern Lights Rest., Subway Aurora Borealis Motel, Boardwalk Inn, Colonial House, Moran Bay Motel, Normandy Motel, Thunderbird Motel, Village Inn/rest., Vitek's Motel, Voyager Motel , H, Ace Hardware, Bay Drug, Doud's Mkt, Family$, Glen's Mkt, NAPA, public marina, Radio Shack, st police, Straits SP, to Island Ferrys, TrueValue, USPO
343mm	**Welcome Ctr nb, full facilities, litter barrels, , , W museum, toll booth to toll bridge**
341mm	Lake Huron, Lake Michigan, toll bridge
339	US 23, Jamet St, **E** Audie's Rest. Days Inn, EconoLodge, LightHouse View Motel, Parkside Motel, Riviera Motel, Super 8, **W** Shell Darrow's Rest., Mackinaw Cookie Co Holiday Inn Express, Vindel Motel Wilderness SP
338	US 23 (from sb), **E** Marathon/dsl BC Pizza, Burger King, Cunningham's Rest., DQ, KFC, Mama Mia's Pizza, Pancake Chef, Subway Baymont Inn, Court Plaza Hotel IGA Foods/supplies, Mackinaw Outfitters, same as 337, USPO, **W** Ft Mackinaw Motel, Holiday Inn Express
337	MI 108 (from nb, no EZ return), Nicolet St, Mackinaw City, **E** **Welcome Ctr/**, Citgo/dsl/LP Admiral's Table Rest., Anna's Country Buffet, Bell's Melody Motel, Blue Water Grill, Embers Rest., Lakeside Grill, Lighthouse Rest., Mackinaw Pastie&Cookie Co, Mancino's Pizza Anchor Inn, Bayside Inn, Beach House Cottages, BeachComber Motel, Best Inn, Best Value Inn, Best Western, Bridge Vista Beach Motel, Bridgeview Motel, Budget Inn, Capri Motel, Clarion,

🅿 = gas 🍴 = food 🛏 = lodging 🅾 = other 🆁🆂 = rest stop   Copyright 2015 - the Next EXIT ®

MI

⬆N INTERSTATE 75 Cont'd

Exit #	Services
337	Continued
	Clearwater Lakeshore Motel, Comfort Inn, Comfort Suites, Days Inn, EconoLodge, Fairview Inn, Grand Mackinaw Resort, Great Lakes Inn, Hamilton Inn, Hampton Inn, Mackinaw Inn, North Winds Motel, Quality Inn, Rainbow Motel, Ramada Ltd, Sundown Motel, Sunrise Beach Motel, Super 8, Thunderbird Inn, Waterfront Inn 🅾 Harley-Davidson, Mackinaw Camping (2mi), Old Mill Creek SP, to Island Ferrys, **W** 🅾 KOA, Wilderness SP
336	US 31 S (from sb), to Petoskey
328mm	🆁🆂 sb, full ♿ facilities, info, litter barrels, petwalk, 📶, 🅿
326	C66, to Cheboygan, **E** 🅿 gas/dsl 🅾 🏥, Sea Shell City/gifts, st police
322	C64, to Cheboygan, **E** 🅾 🏥, 🚐, LP, st police
317mm	🆁🆂/scenic turnout nb, full ♿ facilities, info, litter barrels, petwalk, 📶, 🅿
313	MI 27 N, Topinabee, **E** 🏕 Indian River RV Resort/Camping, Johnson Motel
311mm	Indian River
310	MI 33, MI 68, **E** 🛏 Hometown Inn 🅾 Jellystone Park (3mi), **W** 🅿 Marathon, Shell/McDonald's 🍴 Burger King, DQ, Paula's Cafe, Subway, Wilson's Rest 🛏 Coach House Motel, Indian River Motel 🅾 auto repair, Family$, Ken's Mkt/gas, to Burt Lake SP, to Indian River Trading Post/RV Resort
301	C58, Wolverine, **E** 🅿 Marathon/dsl 🍴 Whistle Stop Rest. 🅾 Elkwood Campground (5mi), **W** 🅾 Sturgin Valley Campground (3mi)
297mm	Sturgeon River
290	Vanderbilt, **E** 🅿 BP/dsl/LP/RV dump, Spirit/dsl 🍴 Elk Horn Grill 🅾 USPO, Village Mkt Foods, **W** 🅿 Mobil/dsl 🅾 Black Bear Golf Resort (2mi)
287mm	🆁🆂 sb, full ♿ facilities, info, litter barrels, 📶, 🅿
282	MI 32, Gaylord, **E** 🅿 Holiday, Speedway/dsl 🍴 Arby's, Big Buck Steaks, Burger King, DQ, Gino's Italian, Jet's Pizza, KFC, La Senorita Mexican, McDonald's, Qdoba Mexican, Subway, Wendy's 🛏 Alpine Lodge, Baymont Inn, Quality Inn 🅾 🏥, Advance Parts, Ben Franklin, Family$, Glen's Mkt/gas, Harley-Davidson, Rite Aid, st police, **W** 🅿 BP/dsl, Marathon/dsl, Mobil/dsl, Shell/dsl 🍴 Applebee's, BC Pizza, Big Boy, Bob Evans, China 1, Coldstone/Tim Horton, Culver's, El Rancho Mexican, Little Caesars, Mancino's Pizza, Ponderosa, Ruby Tuesday, Taco Bell 🛏 Hampton Inn, Holiday Inn Express 🅾 $Tree, AT&T, BigLots, Chrysler/Dodge/Jeep, Hobby Lobby, Home Depot, International RV Ctr, Kenworth, Lowe's, Radio Shack, RV camping, Save-A-Lot Foods, tires, Verizon, Walgreens, Walmart/Subway
279mm	45th Parallel, halfway between the equator and north pole
279	Old US 27, Gaylord, **E** 🅿 Marathon/Subway/dsl, Mobil/dsl, Shell 🍴 Burger King, Mama Leone's 🛏 Best Value Inn 🅾 Ace Hardware, Buick/GMC, Chevrolet, Ford, st police, transmissions, **W** 🍴 Bennethums Rest, Stampede Saloon 🛏 KOA (3mi), Marsh Ridge Motel (2mi)
277mm	🆁🆂 nb, full ♿ facilities, info, litter barrels, petwalk, 📶, 🅿
270	Waters, **E** 🅿 BP/dsl 🍴 Hilltop Rest., **W** 🅿 Citgo/dsl 🛏, Waters Inn 🅾 to Otsego Lake SP, USPO, Waters RV Ctr
264	Lewiston, Frederic, **W** 🍴 access to food 🅾 camping
262mm	🆁🆂 sb, full ♿ facilities, litter barrels, petwalk, 📶, 🅿
259	MI 93, **E** 🅾 Hartwick Pines SP
256	(from sb), to MI 72, Grayling, access to same as 254

Exit #	Services
254	MI 72 (exits left from nb, no return), Grayling, **W 1 mi** 🅿 Admiral/dsl, Clark, Shell, Speedway, Valero 🍴 Big Boy, Burger King, DQ, Keg'O'Nails, McDonald's, Pizza Hut, Subway, Taco Bell, Wendy's 🛏 Days Inn, Ramada 🅾 🏥, $General, 7-11, Ace Hardware, Auto Value Parts, Family$, Ford, Glen's Mkt, K-Mart, NAPA, Rite Aid, Save-A-Lot Foods, Walgreens
251mm	🆁🆂 nb, full ♿ facilities, info, litter barrels, petwalk, 📶, 🅿, vending
251	4 Mile Rd, **E** 🅾 Jellystone RV Park (5mi), skiing, **W** 🅿 Marathon/Arby's/dsl/scales/RV Dump/24hr 🛏 Super 8
249	US 127 S (from sb), to Clare
244	MI 18, Roscommon, **E 3 mi** 🅿 Mobil/dsl, Shell/dsl 🍴 McDonald's, **W** 🅿 Valero/dsl 🅾 Higgins Lake SP, KOA (1mi), museum
239	MI 18, Roscommon, S Higgins Lake SP, **E 3 mi** 🅿 Marathon/McDonald's/dsl 🅾 camping, **W** 🅾 camping, Higgins Lake SP
235mm	🆁🆂 sb, full ♿ facilities, info, litter barrels, petwalk, 📶, 🅿, vending
227	MI 55 W, rd F97, to Houghton Lake, **W 5 mi** 🍴
222	Old 76, to St Helen, **E 2-4 mi** 🍴, 🛏, 🅾 camping
215	MI 55 E, West Branch, **E** 🅿 Shell/dsl 🍴 Wagon Wheel Rest. (6mi) 🅾 🏥
212	MI 55, West Branch, **E** 🅿 Citgo/7-11, Murphy USA/dsl, Shell/Subway/dsl 🍴 Applebee's, Arby's, Big Boy, Burger King, KFC, Lumberjack Rest., McDonald's, Ponderosa, Taco Bell, Tim Horton, Wendy's 🛏 Quality Inn, Super 8 🅾 🏥, Home Depot, st police, Tanger Outlet/famous brands, Walmart/Subway, **W** 🅿 Jaxx Snaxx/dsl
210mm	🆁🆂 nb, full ♿ facilities, info, litter barrels, petwalk, 📶, 🅿, vending
202	MI 33, to Rose City, Alger, **E** 🅿 Mobil/jerky outlet/dsl, Narski's Mkt/gas (1/2mi), Shell/Subway/dsl 🅾 camping
201mm	🆁🆂 sb, full ♿ facilities, litter barrels, petwalk, 📶, 🅿, vending
195	Sterling Rd, to Sterling, **E 6 mi** 🅿, 🅾 Riverview Camping (seasonal)
190	MI 61, to Standish, **E** 🅾 🏥, Standish Correctional, **W** 🅿 Marathon, Mobil/jerky
188	US 23, to Standish, **E 2-3 mi** 🅿, 🍴, 🅾 camping
181	Pinconning Rd, **E** 🅿 Shell/McDonald's/dsl, XWay 🍴 Cheesehouse Diner 🛏 Pinconning Inn (2mi) 🅾 Pinconning Camping, **W** 🅿 Sunoco/pizza/dsl/24hr
175mm	🆁🆂 nb, full ♿ facilities, litter barrels, petwalk, 📶, 🅿, vending
173	Linwood Rd, to Linwood, **E** 🅿 Mobil/dsl/jerky 🍴 Arby's (2mi)
171mm	Kawkawlin River
168	Beaver Rd, to Willard, **E** 🅾 to Bay City SRA, **W** 🅿 Mobil/jerky
166mm	Kawkawlin River
164	to MI 13, Wilder Rd, to Kawkawlin, **E** 🍴 Cracker Barrel, Lucky Steaks, Ponderosa, Uno 🛏 AmericInn, Holiday Inn Express 🅾 KanRock Tire, Meijer/dsl, Menards
162b a	US 10, MI 25, to Midland
160	MI 84, Delta, **E** 🅿 Mobil/Subway, **W** 🅿 Citgo/7-11, Speedway 🍴 Berger's Rest., Burger King, KFC/Taco Bell, McDonald's 🅾 RV World Super Ctr, to Saginaw Valley Coll
158mm	🆁🆂 sb, full ♿ facilities, litter barrels, petwalk, 📶, 🅿, vending
155	I-675 S, to downtown Saginaw, **W 4 mi** 🍴 Outback Steaks 🛏 Hampton Inn
154	to Zilwaukee
153mm	Saginaw River
153	MI 13 E Bay City Rd, Saginaw, **W 2-3 mi** 🅿, 🛏

GRAYLING (vertical, right column top)

SAGINAW (vertical, right column)

GAYLORD (vertical, left column)

INTERSTATE 75 Cont'd

Exit #	Services
151	MI 81, to Reese, Caro, **E** ⓖ Sunoco/McDonald's/dsl ⊙ Volvo Trucks, **W** ⓖ *FLYING J*/Wendy's/dsl/LP/24hr
150	I-675 N, to downtown Saginaw, **W 6 mi** 🍴 Outback Steaks 🛏 Hampton Inn
149b a	MI 46, Holland Ave, to Saginaw, **W** ⓖ Speedway/dsl, Sunoco 🍴 Arby's, Big John's Steaks, Burger King, McDonald's, Subway, Taco Bell, Texan Rest 🛏 Best Value Inn, Motel 6, Super 7 Inn ⊙ Ⓗ, Advance Parts, Save-A-Lot Foods, USPO
144b a	Bridgeport, **E** ⓖ Speedway/dsl ⊙ Jellystone Camping (9mi), **W** ⓖ Mobil/dsl/e-85, TA/Country Pride/dsl/scales/24hr/@ 🍴 Arby's, Big Boy, Cracker Barrel, Hungry Howie's, McDonald's, Subway, Taco Bell, Wendy's 🛏 Baymont Inn, Knights Inn ⊙ Family$, Kroger/gas, Rite Aid, st police, USPO
143mm	Cass River
138mm	**pull off both lanes**
136	MI 54, MI 83, Birch Run, **E** ⓖ Mobil/dsl/24hr 🍴 Exit Rest., Halo Burger, KFC, Subway 🛏 Best Value Inn, Best Western, Comfort Inn, Hampton Inn, Holiday Inn Express ⊙ Car-Quest, General RV Ctr, Mejier/dsl/E-85, Totten Tires, **W** ⓖ 7-11, Marathon, Sunoco/dsl 🍴 A&W, Applebee's, Arby's, Big Boy, Bob Evans, Culver's, DQ, Little Caesars, McDonald's, Quiznos, Sonic, Starbucks, Taco Bell, Tony's Rest., Uno, Victor&Merek's Pizza, Wendy's 🛏 Country Inn&Suites ⊙ Birch Run Drug, Birch Run Outlet/famous brands, Buick/Chevrolet, GNC, Harley-Davidson, Old Navy, USPO
131	MI 57, to Montrose, **E** ⓖ Citgo, Shell 🍴 Arby's, Big John's Steaks, Burger King, DQ, KFC, McDonald's, Oriental Express, Subway, Taco Bell, Tim Horton, Twins Pizza, Wendy's ⊙ AutoZone, Chevrolet, Chrysler/Dodge/Jeep, KanRock Tire, K-Mart, Tradewinds RV Ctr, vet, **W** ⓖ BP, Mobil/Rally's/dsl, Murphy USA/dsl 🍴 Big Boy, Lucky Steaks ⊙ $Tree, Menards, Walmart/Subway
129mm	Ⓡ **both lanes, full** ♿ **facilities, litter barrels, petwalk,** 🅲, 🚶 **vending**
126	to Mt Morris, **E** ⓖ B&B/Halo Burger/dsl/scales/24hr, **W** ⓖ BP/dsl
125	I-475 S, UAW Fwy, to Flint
122	Pierson Rd, to Flint, **E** ⓖ BP, Marathon/dsl 🍴 McDonald's, Papa's Coney's, Subway 🛏 EconoLodge ⊙ Kroger/gas, Murray's Parts, NW Tire, Tuffy Auto, **W** ⓖ Citgo, Shell/dsl 🍴 A&W/KFC, Applebee's, Arby's, Big John's Steaks, Bob Evans, Burger King, Cottage Inn Pizza, Cracker Barrel, Denny's, Halo Burger, LJ Silver, Red Lobster, Taco Bell, Tim Horton, Wendy's, YaYa Chicken 🛏 Baymont Inn, Great Western Inn ⊙ $Tree, Aldi Foods, AT&T, Discount Tire, Home Depot, Meijer/dsl
118	MI 21, Corunna Rd, **E** ⓖ Sunoco 🍴 Atlas Coney Island, Badawest Lebanese, Big John's Steaks, Burger King, Halo Burger, Hollywood Diner, Hungry Howie's, Little Caesar's, Taco Bell, Wing Fong Chinese, YaYa Chicken ⊙ Ⓗ, $Zone, CarQuest, Family$, Kroger/gas, Rite Aid, **W** ⓖ BP/dsl, Mobil, Shell/Wendy's, Speedway, Valero 🍴 A&W/KFC, Blue Collar Grill, Burger King, Fazoli's, Happy Valley Rest., McDonald's, Mega Diner, Tim Horton, White Castle 🛏 Economy Motel ⊙ $General, Aldi Foods, AutoZone, Buick, Chevrolet, GMC, Home Depot, KanRock Tire, Kroger/gas, Lowe's Whse, Rite Aid, Sam's Club/gas, st police, VG's Foods, Walgreens, Walmart/auto
117b	Miller Rd, to Flint, **E** ⓖ Speedway/dsl, Sunoco/dsl 🍴 Applebee's, Arby's, Cottage Inn, Don Pablo, Fuddrucker's, KFC,

117b	Continued LoneStar Steaks, McDonald's, Pizza, Qdoba, Sonic, Subway, West Side Diner 🛏 Comfort Inn, Motel 6, Sleep Inn ⊙ Belle Tire, K-Mart, Tuffy Auto, URGENT CARE, **W** ⓖ BP, Marathon 🍴 BD's BBQ, Big Boy, Bob Evans, Chili's, ChuckeCheese, Famous Dave's BBQ, Fire Mtn Grill, Happy's Pizza, Honey-Baked Ham, Hooters, Italia Garden, Logan's Roadhouse, Old Country Buffet, Olive Garden, Outback Steaks, Pizza Hut, Quizno's, Red Robin, Rib City, Salvatori's Ristorante, Starbucks, Subway, Taco Bell, Telly's Coney Island, Valley Rest. 🛏 Hometown Inn, Red Roof Inn, Super 8 ⊙ AT&T, Barnes&Noble, Best Buy, Dale's Foods, Discount Tire, Dodge, Gander Mtn, Goodyear, Hobby Lobby, JC Penney, Jo-Ann Fabrics, Macy's, mall, Michael's, Office Depot, Old Navy, PetCo, Radio Shack, Sears/auto, Target, U-Haul, Valley Tire, vet
117a	I-69, E to Lansing, W to Port Huron
116	MI 121, Bristol Rd, **E** ⓖ Citgo, Speedway/dsl 🍴 Capitol Coney Island, KFC, McDonald's 🛏 Days Inn, Rodeway Inn ⊙ AutoZone, **W** ⓖ Mobil/dsl ⊙ ☕
115	US 23 (from sb), **W on Hill Rd** ⓖ Citgo, Mobil 🍴 Arby's, McDonald's, Redwood Steaks, Subway, Taco Bell, Turkey Farm Deli 🛏 AmericInn, Best Value Inn, Courtyard, Hampton Inn, Holiday Inn, Residence Inn ⊙ $Tree, Meijer/dsl
111	I-475 N (from nb), UAW Fwy, to Flint
109	MI 54, Dort Hwy (no EZ return to sb)
108	Holly Rd, to Grand Blanc, **E** ⓖ Sunoco/dsl 🍴 Big Apple Bagels, Buffalo Wild Wings, Da Edoardo Ristorante, Quiznos, Taco Bell 🛏 Comfort Inn, Holiday Inn Express ⊙ BMW/Mercedes/Toyota, URGENT CARE, **W** ⓖ BP/McDonald's/dsl 🍴 Arby's ⊙ Ⓗ
106	Dixie Hwy (exits left from sb, no nb return), Saginaw Rd, to Grand Blanc
101	Grange Hall Rd, Ortonville, **E** ⊙ Holly RA, KOA, st police, **W** ⓖ Mobil/dsl ⊙ RV camping, to Seven Lakes/Groveland Oaks SP
98	E Holly Rd, **E** ⓖ Mobil/Subway/dsl/24hr ⊙ Ford, golf
96mm	Ⓡ **nb, full** ♿ **facilities, info, litter barrels, petwalk,** 🅲, 🚶 **vending**
95mm	Ⓡ **sb, full** ♿ **facilities, info, litter barrels, petwalk,** 🅲, 🚶 **vending**
93	US 24, Dixie Hwy, Waterford, **E** ⓖ BP/dsl ⊙ Chrysler/Dodge/Jeep, Kroger/gas (2mi), Nissan, **W 1-3 mi** ⓖ Speedway 🍴 Big Boy, McDonald's, Subway, Taco Bell, Wendy's ⊙ to Pontiac Lake RA, Walgreens
91	MI 15, Davison, Clarkston, **E** ⓖ Sunoco/dsl 🍴 Bullfrog's (5mi), Subway (5mi) ⊙ camping, **W** ⓖ BP 🍴 Mesquite Creek Café ⊙ Ⓗ, URGENT CARE

MI

Exit #	Services
89	Sashabaw Rd, **E** 🄟 Shell/dsl 🍴 Culvers, Ruby Tuesday, Tropical Smoothie Cafe 🄾 county park, **W** 🄟 BP, Citgo 🍴 Caribou Coffee, Chicken Shack, Dunkin Donuts, E Ocean Chinese, Guido's Pizza, Hong Kong Chinese, Hungry Howie's, Jimmy John's, Leo's Coney Island, Little Caesars, McDonald's, Quiznos, Rio Wraps, Subway, Tim Horton, Wendy's 🄾 $Tree, CVS Drug, Kroger, vet
86mm	weigh sta sb
84b a	Baldwin Ave, **E** 🄟 Shell 🍴 Arby's, Big Boy, Joe's Crabshack, Longhorn Steaks, Panera Bread, Taco Bell, Wendy's 🄾 $Tree, Best Buy, Costco/gas, Discount Tire, Kohl's, Michael's, Old Navy, PetCo, Staples, **W** 🄟 Mobil 🍴 5 Guys Burgers, Chili's, Jimmy John's, Kerry's Coney Island, Max&Erma's, McDonald's, On-the-Border, Oriental Forest Buffet, Qdoba Mexican, Quiznos, Rainforest Cafe, Starbucks, Steak'n Shake, Subway 🄾 AT&T, Bass Pro Shops, Batteries+, Great Lakes Crossing Outlet/famous brands, Hampton Inn, Holiday Inn Express, Marshall's, TJ Maxx, USPO, Vitamin Shoppe
83b a	Joslyn Rd, **E** 🍴 Applebee's, Logan's Roadhouse, Olive Garden 🄾 Belle Tire, Home Depot, Jo-Ann Fabrics, Meijer/dsl, Sam's Club/gas, Target, **W** 🄟 BP
81	MI 24, Pontiac (no EZ return), **E** 🄾 The Palace Arena, to Bald Mtn RA
79	University Dr, **E** 🄟 BP 🍴 BD Mongolian, Jimmy John's, Rio Wraps, Spargo Coney Island, Subway, Taste of Thailand 🛏 Homestead Suites, **W** 🄟 Mobil, Speedway/dsl 🍴 A&W/KFC, Burger King, Lelli's Steaks, McDonald's, Taco Bell, Wendy's/Tim Horton 🛏 Candlewood Suites, Comfort Suites, Courtyard, Crowne Plaza, Extended Stay America, Extended Stay Deluxe, Fairfield Inn, Hampton Inn, Hilton, Hyatt Place, Rodeway Inn, Staybridge Suites, Wingate Inn 🄾 🄷
78	Chrysler Dr, **E** 🄾 Chrysler, Chrysler Museum, Oakland Tech Ctr
77b a	MI 59, to Pontiac, **E 2 mi on Adams** 🍴 112 Pizza, 5 Guys Burgers, Kerry's Cone Island, McDonald's, Panera Bread 🄾 GNC, Meijer/dsl, Petsmart, Radio Shack, Walmart
75	Square Lake Rd (exits left from nb), to Pontiac, **W** 🄾 🄷, St Mary's Coll
74	Adams Rd
72	Crooks Rd, to Troy, **W** 🍴 Cedar Grill, Jimmy John's, Kerby's Coney Island, Loccino Italian, Papa Romano's Pizza, Red Robin, Starbucks 🛏 Embassy Suites
69	Big Beaver Rd, **E** 🍴 Champp's Grill, Kona Grill, Shula's Steaks, TGIFriday's 🛏 Drury Inn, Marriott, **W** 🄟 BP 🍴 Benihana, Caribou Coffee, Chipotle Mexican, Granite City Rest, Maggiano's Italian, Melting Pot Rest., Morton's Steaks, Noodles&Co, Papa Romano's Pizza, PF Chang's, Potbelly's, Ruth's Chris Steaks, Starbucks 🛏 Somerset Inn 🄾 Macy's, mall, Neiman Marcus, Nordstrom
67	Rochester Rd, to Stevenson Hwy, **E** 🄟 BP, Shell/dsl, Sunoco 🍴 Bahama Breeze, Burger King, Caribou Coffee, Dickey's BBQ, Domino's, El Charro, Hills Grille, Hooters, Hungry Howies, Jimmy John's, McDonald's, Mr Pita, Ntl Coney Island, Orchid Cafe, Panera Bread, Papa John's, PeiWei, Picano's Italian, Pizza Hut/Taco Bell, Qdoba, Subway, Tim Hortons, Troy Deli, Wendy's 🄾 Discount Tire, Nordstrom Rack, Office Depot, Petsmart, Radio Shack, transmissions, vet, **W** 🄟 BP 🛏 Courtyard, Quality Inn, Red Roof Inn 🄾 tires/repair
65b a	14 Mile Rd, Madison Heights, **E** 🄟 Mobil, Shell 🍴 Azteca Mexican, Bob Evans, Burger King, Chili's, ChuckeCheese,

65b a	Continued
	CiCi's Pizza, Coldstone, Krispy Kreme, Logan's Roadhouse, McDonald's, Panera Bread, Pizza Papalis, Red Robin, Rio Wraps, Sonic, Steak'n Shake, Taco Bell, Wendy's 🛏 Motel 6, Red Roof Inn 🄾 AT&T, auto repair, Barnes&Noble, Belle Tire, Best Buy, BigLots, CVS Drug, Dick's, Firestone/auto, Ford, JC Penney, Jo-Ann Fabrics, Kohl's, Macy's, Sears/auto, Target, TJ Maxx, Verizon, **W** 🄟 Mobil 🍴 Applebee's, Caribou Coffee, Dolly's Pizza, McDonald's, NY Coney Island, Outback Steaks 🛏 Courtyard, Days Inn, EconoLodge, Extended Stay America, Fairfield Inn, Hampton Inn, Residence Inn 🄾 Costco/gas, Value Ctr Foods
63	12 Mile Rd, **E** 🄟 Marathon/dsl 🍴 Culver's, Green Lantern Rest., Marinelli's Pizza, McDonald's, Red Lobster, Sero's Rest., Starbucks, Tim Hortons, TX Roadhouse 🄾 Home Depot, K-Mart/foods, Lowe's, Midas, Radio Shack, Sam's Club/gas, Uncle Ed's Oil, USPO, **W** 🄟 Marathon/Dunkin Donuts, Speedway 🍴 Col's Rest. 🄾 Chevrolet, Costco/gas
62	11 Mile Rd, **E** 🄟 Mobil 🍴 Albert's Coney Island, Boodles Rest., Happy's Pizza, Jets Pizza, Telway Burgers 🄾 7-11, Advance Parts, CVS Drug, repair/tires, Save-a-Lot, Tuffy Auto, vet, Walgreens, **W** 🄟 BP, Marathon/dsl, Mobil 🍴 KFC, Taco Bell, Tim Hortons, Tubby's Subs 🄾 Belle Tire
61	I-696 E, to Port Huron, W to Lansing, to Hazel Park Raceway
60	9 Mile Rd, John R St, **E** 🍴 Checkers, China 1 Buffet, Coney Craver's Diner, DQ, Hardee's, McDonald's, Subway, Tim Hortons 🄾 CVS Drug, Kroger/gas, USPO, **W** 🄟 Exxon, Marathon, Mobil 🍴 Tubby's Subs, Wendy's 🄾 Hasting's Parts, repair
59	MI 102, 8 Mile Rd, **W 3 mi** 🄾 st fairgrounds
58	7 Mile Rd, **W** 🄟 BP/dsl
57	McNichols Rd, **E** 🄟 Citgo/dsl, Shell/dsl 🍴 LA Coney Island 🄾 Auto Parts/Repair
56b a	Davison Fwy
55	Holbrook Ave, Caniff St, **E** 🄟 Mobil/dsl 🍴 Grandy's Coney Island
54	E Grand Blvd, Clay Ave, **W** 🄟 BP/dsl
53b	I-94, Ford Fwy, to Port Huron, Chicago
53a	Warren Ave, **E** 🄟 Mobil, Shell, **W** 🄟 BP
52	Mack Ave, **E** 🄟 Shell 🍴 McDonald's
51c	I-375 to civic center, tunnel to Canada, downtown
51b	MI 3 (exits left from nb), Gratiot Ave, downtown
50	Grand River Ave, downtown
49b	MI 10, Lodge Fwy, downtown
49a	Rosa Parks Blvd, **E** 🄾 Tiger Stadium, **W** 🄟 Mobil/dsl 🄾 Firestone
48	I-96 begins/ends
47b	Porter St, **E** bridge to Canada, **MI Welcome Ctr**, DutyFree/24hr
47a	MI 3, Clark Ave, **E** 🄟 Citgo, **W** 🄟 Marathon
46	Livernois Ave, to Hist Ft Wayne, **E** 🄟 Marathon 🍴 KFC/Taco Bell, Livernois Coney Island
45	Fort St, Springwells Ave, **E** 🄟 BP/dsl, Pure Petro/dsl, **W** 🄟 Mobil 🍴 McDonald's
44	Deerborn St (from nb)
43b a	MI 85, Fort St, to Schaefer Hwy, **E** 🄟 BP, **W** 🄟 Marathon Refinery 🄾 to River Rouge Ford Plant
42	Outer Dr, **E** 🄟 Marathon 🍴 Happy's Pizza 🄾 URGENT CARE, **W** 🄟 BP/Subway/dsl 🄾 Family$, truck tires
41	MI 39, Southfield Rd, to Lincoln Park, **E** 🄟 A&W, Tim Hortons, White Castle 🄾 Aldi Foods, O'Reilly Parts, Walgreens, **W** 🄟 Citgo/Tim Hortons, Mobil 🍴 Burger King, Checker's, Hungry Howie, LJ Silver, McDonald's, Pizza Hut, Starbucks,

MI

⬆🅝 INTERSTATE 75 Cont'd

Exit #	Services
41	Continiued
	Taco Bell, Wendy's 🅛 Sleep Inn 🄾 AT&T, Belle Tire, Kroger/gas, Radio Shack, Rite Aid, Walgreens
40	Dix Hwy, **E** 🅖 Citgo, Future/A&W/dsl, Marathon/A&W/dsl, Sunoco, Welcome 🅕 Baskin-Robbins/Dunkin Donuts, Toma's Coney Island 🄾 7-11, CVS Drug, Meijer, repair, URGENT CARE, **W** 🅖 Future, Marathon 🅕 Big Boy, Burger King, Checker's, DQ, LJ Silver, McDonald's, Pizza Hut, Starbucks, Taco Bell, Wendy's 🄾 AT&T, auto repair, Belle Tire, Family$, Kroger/gas, Rite Aid, Sears/auto, Walgreens
37	Allen Rd, North Line Rd, to Wyandotte, **E** 🅖 BP, Shell/Tim Hortons 🅛 Holiday Inn 🄾 🄷, Sam's Club/gas, **W** 🅖 Mobil, Sunoco 🅕 Arby's, Burger King, Mallie's Grill, McDonald's, Wendy's 🅛 Comfort Suites, La Quinta, Motel 6
36	Eureka Rd, **E** 🅖 BP 🅕 Bob Evans, Denny's, Fire Mtn Grill, Orleans Steaks 🅛 Ramada Inn, Super 8 🄾 vet, **W** 🅕 American Thai Grill, Big Boy, Coldstone, Culver's, HoneyBaked Ham, Hooters, Jimmy John's, Little Daddy's Rest., McDonald's, Ruby Tuesday, Starbucks, Subway, TX Roadhouse, Wendy's 🅛 Red Roof Inn 🄾 AT&T, Belle Tire, Best Buy, Discount Tire, Home Depot, JC Penney, Kohl's, Macy's, mall, Meijer/dsl, Petsmart
35	US 24, Telegraph Rd, (from nb, exits left)
34b	Sibley Rd, Riverview, **W** 🅖 Sunoco/Baskin-Robbins/Dunkin Donuts/Subway 🄾 General RV Ctr
34a	to US 24 (from sb), Telegraph Rd
32	West Rd, to Trenton, Woodhaven, **E** 🅖 ✈FLYING J/Detroiter/IHOP/dsl/LP/scales/24hr/@, Speedway/dsl 🅕 5 Guys Burgers, Applebee's, Baskin-Robbins/Dunkin Donuts, Blue Margarita Mexican, Bob Evans, Christoff's Rest., Coldstone, IHOP, Jersey Subs, Panera Bread, Pizza Hut, Steak'n Shake, Subway, Taco Bell, Tim Hortons, Wendy's, White Castle 🄾 Aldi Foods, Belle Tire, Chevrolet, Chrysler/Dodge/Jeep, Discount Tire, Firestone/auto, Ford, Home Depot, K-Mart, Kohl's, Kroger, Lowe's, Meijer/dsl, Michael's, Office Depot, O'Reilly Parts, Petsmart, Radio Shack, Target, transmissions, URGENT CARE, Verizon, Walmart, **W** 🅖 BP/Tim Hortons, Citgo, Shell 🅕 Andy's Pizza, Jimmy John's, Little Caesars, McDonald's, Milli's Rest, Subway 🅛 Best Western/rest., Holiday Inn Express, Westwood Inn 🄾 🄷, $Tree, CVS Drug, Kroger, SavOn Drug, Walgreens
29	Gilbralter Rd, to Flat Rock, Lake Erie Metropark, **E** 🅖 Citgo/dsl 🅕 Cottage Inn Pizza, McDonald's, Peking Chinese, Subway, Wendy's 🄾 🄷, Curves, GNC, Kroger, **W** 🅖 Marathon/dsl 🅛 Sleep Inn 🄾 Ford, st police
28	rd 85 (from nb), Fort St, **E** 🄾 🄷
27	N Huron River Dr, to Rockwood, **E** 🅖 Marathon/7-11/dsl 🅕 Benito's Pizza, Huron River Rest., Marco's Pizza 🄾 FoodTown Foods, Rite Aid, USPO, **W** 🅖 Speedway/dsl 🅕 Riverfront Rest.
26	S Huron River Dr, to S Rockwood, **E** 🅖 Sunoco/dsl 🅕 Dixie Cafe, Drift Inn 🄾 USPO
21	Newport Rd, to Newport, **E** 🅖 BP/Subway/dsl 🄾 repair, **W** 🅖 Marathon/Burger King/dsl/24hr
20	I-275 N, to Flint
18	Nadeau Rd, **W** 🅖 🛢/Taco Bell/dsl/scales/24hr 🄾 🄷, RV camping
15	MI 50, Dixie Hwy, to Monroe, **E** 🅖 Shell 🅕 Burger King, Red Lobster 🅛 Best Value Inn, Hampton Inn, Motel 6,

15	Continued
	Red Roof Inn 🄾 to Sterling SP, **W** 🅖 🛢/Subway/dsl/scales/24hr, TA/BP/Country Pride/Pizza Hut/Popeye's/Tim Hortons/dsl/scales/24hr/@ 🅕 Big Boy, Cracker Barrel, Denny's, El Maguey, McDonald's, Wendy's 🅛 Knights Inn, Quality Inn 🄾 🄷, to Viet Vet Mem
14	Elm Ave, to Monroe
13	Front St, Monroe
11	La Plaisance Rd, to Bolles Harbor, **W** 🅖 Marathon/Taco Bell/dsl, Speedway 🅕 McDonald's, Wendy's 🅛 Baymont Inn, Comfort Inn, Harbor Town RV Resort 🄾 Kroger/gas (2mi), st police
10mm	**Welcome Ctr nb, full 🅰 services, info, litter barrels, petwalk, 🄲, 🄴, vending**
9	S Otter Creek Rd, to La Salle, **W** 🄾 antiques
7mm	**weigh sta both lanes**
6	Luna Pier, **E** 🅖 Sunoco/dsl/scales 🅕 Beef Jerky UnLtd., Ganders Rest., Roma's Pizza 🅛 Super 8, **W** 🄾 KOA, st police
5	to Erie, Temperance
2	Summit St
0mm	Michigan/Ohio state line

➡🅔 INTERSTATE 94

Exit #	Services
275mm	I-69/I-94 begin/end on MI 25, **N Pinegrove Ave in Port Huron** 🅖 BP/24hr, Shell, Speedway 🅕 Jet's Pizza, McDonald's, Tim Horton, Wendy's 🅛 Days Inn, Quality Inn 🄾 Buick, Family$, Honda, Rite Aid, **tollbridge to Canada**
274.5mm	Black River
274	Water St, Port Huron, **N Welcome Ctr/🆁🆂, full facilities, (from wb only)**, 🅕 Cracker Barrel 🅛 Best Western, **S** 🅖 Speedway/dsl, SpeedyQ/dsl 🅕 Bob Evans 🅛 Comfort Inn, Fairfield Inn, Hampton Inn 🄾 Lake Port SP, RV camping
271	**I-69 E and I-94 E run together eb, Lp I-69, S 0-2 mi on Lp 69 S** 🅖 Mobil/dsl, Speedway 🅕 Arby's, Baskin-Robbins, Burger King, Dunkin Donuts, KFC, McDonalds, Quay St Grill, Taco Bell, Wendy's 🄾 Advance Parts, AutoZone, K-Mart, Kroger/gas, repair, Sam's Club/gas, to Port Huron
269	Dove St, Range Rd, **N** 🅖 Speedway/dsl/24hr 🅕 Billy Boy's Diner 🅛 Baymont Inn
266	Gratiot Rd, Marysville, **S 0-2 mi** 🅖 Admiral, BP/dsl/scales/24hr, Marathon/scales/dsl, Speedway 🅕 4 Star Rest., Arby's, Big Boy, Burger King, Dairy Boy, Daliono's, Hungry Howie's, Jimmy John's, KFC, Little Caesars, McDonald's, Mr Pita, Pelican Café, Pizza Hut, Seros, Subway, Taco Bell, Tim Horton 🅛 Super 8 🄾 🄷, $General, $Plus, AutoZone, CarQuest, CVS Drug, Meijer/dsl, Rite Aid, vet, Wally's Foods

M O N R O E (vertical, left margin)

P O R T H U R O N (vertical, center margin)

MI

⬆E INTERSTATE 94 Cont'd

Exit #	Services
262	Wadhams Rd, N 🅾 camping, S 🅶 Mobil/dsl
257	St Clair, Richmond, S 🅶 BP/dsl 🅾 st police
255mm	🆁🆂 eb, full 🚻 facilities, info, litter barrels, petwalk, 🅲, 🎮
251mm	🆁🆂 wb, full 🚻 facilities, info, litter barrels, petwalk, 🅲, 🎮
248	26 Mile Rd, to Marine City, N 🍽 McDonald's (2mi), S 🅶 7-11/gas, Speedy Q (1mi) 🍽 Asian Garden, My Place Cafe, Tim Horton 🅾 Mejier/dsl
247mm	Salt River
247	MI 19 (no eb return), New Haven
243	MI 29, MI 3, Utica, New Baltimore, N 🅶 BP, Marathon/dsl, Sunoco/dsl 🍽 Applebee's, Arby's, Buffalo Wings, Burger King, Chophouse, Coney Island, Dimitri's Rest., Empire Buffet, Little Caesars, McDonald's, Outback Steaks, Panera Bread, Ruby Tuesday, Starbucks, Stevie B's Pizza, Subway, Tim Horton, Waffle House, Wendy's, White Castle 🛏 Chesterfield Motel 🅾 $Tree, AutoZone, Best Buy, Dick's, Discount Tire, GNC, Home Depot, JC Penney, Jo-Ann Fabrics, K-Mart, Kohl's, Lowe's, Meijer/dsl/24hr, Michael's, NAPA, O'Reilly Parts, PetCo, PetsMart, Radio Shack, Rite Aid, Staples, Target, TJ Maxx, Walgreens, S 🅶 7-11/gas, Marathon/dsl/24hr, Speedway/dsl/24hr 🍽 Big Boy, Buscemi's Pizza, Hot'n Now Burgers, Taco Bell 🛏 LodgeKeeper
241	21 Mile Rd, Selfridge, N 🅶 Exxon/dsl, Speedway 🍽 China King, Hungry Howie's 🅾 Advance Parts, AT&T, CVS Drug, same as 240, Verizon, vet
240	to MI 59, N 🅶 7-11/gas, Marathon, Mobil 🍽 Arby's, Bob Evans, Burger King, Coney Island, KFC, McDonald's, O'Charley's, Taco Bell, Tim Horton 🛏 Hampton Inn, Holiday Inn Express 🅾 Ford, Harley-Davidson, Tuffy Auto, Walmart
237	N River Rd, Mt Clemens, N 🅶 BP/dsl, Mobil/Subway/dsl 🍽 McDonald's 🛏 Victory Inn 🅾 🏥, General RV Ctr, Gibraltar Trade Ctr
236.5mm	Clinton River
236	Metro Parkway, S 🍽 Big Apple Bagels, Empire Chinese, Little Caesars, McDonald's, Subway 🅾 🏥, Curves, CVS Drug, GNC, Kroger
235	Shook Rd (from wb)
234b a	Harper Rd, 15 Mile Rd, N 🅶 BP/McDonald's, Marathon/dsl, SpeedyQ, Sunoco/dsl/24hr 🍽 Dan Good Pizza, Gina's Cafe 🅾 vet, S 🅶 FL Gas 🍽 China Moon, Subway, Travis Rest., Winners Grill 🅾 URGENT CARE
232	Little Mack Ave (from wb only), N 🅶 7-11, Marathon, Shell, Speedway, Sunoco 🍽 Coldstone, Denny's, Hooters, Longhorn Steaks, McDonald's, Pizza Hut, Red Robin, Sea Breeze Diner, Woody's Grill 🛏 Holiday Inn Express, Red Roof Inn, Relax Inn, Super 8, Victory Inn 🅾 Advance Parts, Aldi Foods, Belle Tire, Discount Tire, Firestone, JC Penney, O'Reilly Parts, Sam's Club, Sears/Auto, Staples, Target, S 🅶 Marathon, Speedway/dsl 🍽 Cracker Barrel, Culvers, IHOP, Izzy's Cafe 🛏 Baymont Inn 🅾 Family$, Home Depot, Jo-Ann Fabrics, Meijer/dsl/24hr, PetsMart, same as 231
231	(from eb), MI 3, Gratiot Ave, N 🅶 Marathon, Sunoco 🍽 Applebee's, Arby's, Big Boy, Bob Evans, Burger King, Chili's, ChuckeCheese, Cici's, Del Taco, Denny's, Famous Dave's BBQ, Logan's Roadhouse, Longhorn Steaks, Marco's Italian, McDonald's, Panera Bread, PetCo, Pizza Hut, Ruby Tuesday, Sajo's Rest., Starbucks, Subway, Tim Horton, TX Roadhouse 🛏 Best Western, Days Inn, EconoLodge, Extended Stay America, Microtel 🅾 Best Buy, Discount Tire, Firestone/auto, Honda/Acura, Kia, Kohl's, Kroger, mall, Michael's, Nissan, Radio Shack, Sam's Club/gas, Staples, Toyota, U-Haul
230	12 Mile Rd, N 🅶 Mobil/dsl, Sunoco/dsl 🍽 BD's Mongolian, Jimmy John's, Noni's Grill, Outback Steaks, Starbucks, Taco Bell 🅾 $Tree, AT&T, CVS Drug, Marshall's, NAPA, Walmart/Subway
229	I-696 W, Reuther Fwy, to 11 Mile Rd, S 🅶 BP/dsl, Speedway 🅾 7-11
228	10 Mile Rd, N 🅶 BP/24hr, Mobil, Shell 🍽 Baskin-Robbins, Coney Island, Eastwind Chinese, Friendly Rest, Jet's Pizza 🅾 CVS Drug, Save More Drugs
227	9 Mile Rd, N 🅶 Mobil/dsl, Speedway/dsl, Sunoco 🍽 McDonald's, Papa John's, Pizza Hut/Taco Bell, Subway, Wendy's 🅾 $Tree, Aldi Foods, CVS Drug, Family$, Fresh Choice Foods, Office Depot, TrueValue, vet, S 🅶 Mobil/dsl 🛏 Shore Pointe Motel 🅾 Cadillac, Mercedes
225	MI 102, Vernier Rd, 8 Mile Rd, S 🅶 BP/Subway, Mobil, Sunoco/dsl 🍽 Coney Island, KFC, Taco Bell, Wendy's 🅾 Kroger, Walgreens
224b	Allard Ave, Eastwood Ave
224a	Moross Rd, S 🅶 Shell 🅾 🏥, Family Foods
223	Cadieux Rd, S 🅶 BP/Subway, Mobil, Shell, Sunoco 🍽 McDonald's, Papa's Pizza, Popeye's, Taco Bell, Tubby's Subs, Wendy's, White Castle 🅾 Rite Aid
222b	Harper Ave (from eb), S 🅾 Hastings Auto
222a	Chalmers Ave, Outer Dr, N 🅶 BP/Subway/dsl, Zoom 🍽 Coney Island, KFC, Little Caesars, White Castle 🅾 Family$
220b	Conner Ave, N 🅶 BP, Zoom
220a	French Rd, S 🅶 Marathon
219	MI 3, Gratiot Ave, N 🅶 Marathon/Subway, Speedy 🍽 Coney Island, KFC, McDonald's 🅾 Family$, Farmer John's Foods, S 🅶 GasMart 🍽 Burger King
218	MI 53, Van Dyke Ave, N 🅶 BP, Mobil/dsl
217b	Mt Elliott Ave, S 🅶 Marathon, Sunoco/dsl 🍽 Royal BBQ
217a	E Grand Blvd, Chene St, S 🅶 Marathon
216b	Russell St (from eb), to downtown
216a	I-75, Chrysler Fwy, to tunnel to Canada
215c	MI 1, Woodward Ave, John R St
215b	MI 10 N, Lodge Fwy
215a	MI 10 S, tunnel to Canada, downtown
214b	Trumbull Ave, 🅾 to Ford 🏥
214a	(from wb)Grand River Ave
213b	I-96 W to Lansing, E to Canada, bridge to Canada, to Tiger Stadium
213a	W Grand (exits left from eb)
212b	Warren Ave (from eb)
212a	Livernois Ave, S 🅶 Marathon/Subway/dsl, Sunoco
211b	Cecil Ave (from wb), Central Ave
211a	Lonyo Rd
210	US 12, Michigan Ave, Wyoming Ave, N 🅶 Mobil/dsl, S 🅶 BP/dsl, Sunoco/dsl, Valero
209	Rotunda Dr (from wb)
208	Greenfield Rd, Schaefer Rd, N 🅶 Mobil/dsl 🅾 7-11, S 🅾 River Rouge Ford Plant
207mm	Rouge River
206	Oakwood Blvd, Melvindale, N 🅶 Marathon, Shell 🍽 Applebee's, Carino's, Chili's, Coldstone, Coney Island, Famous Hamburger, Little Caesar's, Longhorn Steaks, Moe's SW Grill, On-the-Border, Panera Bread, Pottbelly, Quizno's, Starbucks, Taco Bell 🅾 AAA, Barnes&Noble, Best Buy, GNC, Greenfield Village Museum, Home Depot, Jo-Ann Fabrics, Lowe's, Meijer, Michael's, Old Navy, PetCo, Staples, Target, TJ Maxx, Verizon, S 🅶 BP/dsl 🍽 Burger King, McDonald's, Melvindale Coney Island, O'Henry's, Sabina's, Subway 🛏 Best Western,

*(vertical text in left margin)* DETROIT AREA

(vertical text in right margin) DETROIT AREA

MI

INTERSTATE 94 Cont'd

D E T R O I T   A R E A

Exit #	Services
206	Continued
	Holiday Inn Express 🅞 $General, 7-11, Curves, CVS Drug, Rite Aid
205mm	🅞 Largest Uniroyal Tire in the World
204b a	MI 39, Southfield Fwy, Pelham Rd, **N** 🅖 Marathon/dsl, Mobil, Valero/dsl 🅞 7-11, to Greenfield Village, **S** 🅖 Marathon/dsl 🅕 Papa's Pizza 🅞 Walgreens
202b a	US 24, Telegraph Rd, **N** 🅖 Citgo, Shell, Sunoco 🅕 Burger King, Checkers, Dunkin Donuts, KFC, McDonald's, Pizza Hut, Ram's Horn Rest., Subway, Taco Bell, Wendy's 🅞 Advance Parts, Aldi Foods, Rite Aid, True Value, Walgreen, **S 0-2 mi** 🅖 BP, Marathon/dsl, Valero/dsl 🅕 Arby's, Big Boy, Burger King, Hungry Howie's, KFC, Leon's, Leo's Coney Island, Little Caesar's, LJ Silver, Marina's Pizza, McDonald's, New Hong Kong, Old Country Buffet, Pizza Hut, Popeye's, Rest., Subway, Super China, Taco Bell, Wendy's, Yum Yum Donuts 🅛 Comfort Inn 🅞 $Tree, AT&T, AutoZone, Curves, Family$, Firestone/auto, Radio Shack, Rite Aid, st police, U-Haul, USPO, Walgreens, Walmart
200	Ecorse Rd, (no ez eb return), to Taylor, **N** 🅖 Marathon/Subway/dsl/scales, **S** 🅖 Rich, Speedy/dsl 🅕 Danny's Pizza, Norm's Subs, Webster's BBQ 🅞 USPO
199	Middle Belt Rd, **S** 🅖 BP/dsl/24hr 🅕 Checkers, McDonald's, Wendy's 🅛 Days Inn, Quality Inn, Super 8
198	Merriman Rd, **N** 🅖 Marathon, Speedway 🅕 Big Boy, Bob Evans, Leonardo's Italian, McDonald's, Merriman St Grill, Subway, Toramino's Pizza 🅛 Baymont Inn, Best Western, Clarion, Comfort Inn, Courtyard, Crowne Plaza Hotel, Embassy Suites, Extended Stay America, Fairfield Inn, Hampton Inn, Holiday Inn, Howard Johnson, La Quinta, Lee's Inn, Lexington Motel, Marriott, Metro Inn, Metropolitan Hotel, Ramada Inn, Red Roof Inn, Rodeway Inn, Sheraton, SpringHill Suites 🅞 USPO, **S** 🅞 Wayne Co 🚉
197	Vining Rd
196	Wayne Rd, Romulus, **N** 🅖 Shell/dsl 🅕 McDonald's, **S** 🅖 Mobil/dsl 🅕 Burger King, Subway
194b a	I-275, N to Flint, S to Toledo
192	Haggerty Rd, **N** 🅖 BP/Tubby's/dsl, Mobil/dsl, **S** 🅞 Lower Huron Metro Park
190	Belleville Rd, to Belleville, **N** 🅖 BP/dsl 🅕 Applebee's, Arby's, Big Boy, Coney Island, Cracker Barrel, Culver's, Happy's Pizza, McDonald's, Quiznos, Taco Bell, Tim Horton, Twisted Rooster, Wendy's 🅛 Holiday Inn Express, Red Roof Inn 🅞 $Tree, AT&T, Belle Tire, Camping World RV Ctr, CVS Drug, Firestone/auto, Ford, Meijer/dsl, National RV Ctr, O'Reilly Parts, Verizon, vet, Walgreens, Walmart, **S** 🅖 Shell 🅕 Burger King, China City, Dos Pesos Mexican, Mike's Kitchen, Subway 🅛 Comfort Inn, Super 8 🅞 URGENT CARE, USPO
189mm	🆁🆂 wb, full 🅰 facilities, info, litter barrels, petwalk, 🅲, 🅰, vending
187	Rawsonville Rd, **N** 🅞 Freightliner, **S** 🅖 Mobil/dsl, Speedway/dsl 🅕 Denny's, KFC, Little Caesars, McDonald's, Pizza Hut, Taco Bell, Tim Horton, Wendy's 🅞 $General, $Tree, Detroit Greenfield RV Park, GNC, K-Mart
185	US 12, Michigan Ave (from eb, exits left, no return), to frontage rds, 🅞 🚉
184mm	🅞 Ford Lake
183	US 12, Huron St, Ypsilanti, **N** 🅖 Marathon/pizza/dsl 🅞 to E MI U, **S** 🅕 Buffalo Wild Wings, Coney Island, Jet's Pizza, McDonald's 🅛 Marriott 🅞 🅷, Kroger/dsl, st police

A N N   A R B O R

Exit #	Services
181b a	US 12 W, Michigan Ave, Ypsilanti, **N** 🅖 Meijer/dsl, Speedway/dsl 🅕 Coney Island, Dunkin Donuts, Hong Kong Chinese, Roundtree Grill, Taco Bell, Tim Horton/Wendy's 🅞 🅷 $Tree, Aamco, BigLots, Firestone/auto, GNC, Meijer/dsl, Radio Shack, Rose Mkt, Walmart, **S 0-2 mi** 🅖 BP/Circle K, Citgo/Subway/dsl, Sunoco/dsl 🅕 Harvest Moon Cafe, McDonald's 🅞 Sam's Club/gas
180b a	US 23, to Toledo, Flint
177	State St, **N** 🅖 BP, Mobil, Shell 🅕 Burger King, Graham's Steaks, Los Amigos, Macaroni Grill, Max&Erma's, Mediterrano Rest., Olive Garden, Panda Express, Red Robin, Wendy's 🅛 Comfort Inn, Courtyard, Extended Stay America, Fairfield Inn, Hampton Inn, Hilton Garden, Holiday Inn, Holiday Inn Express, Kensington Court Inn, Red Roof Inn, Sheraton, TownePlace Suites 🅞 Firestone/auto, Honda, JC Penney, Macy's, mall, Porsche, Sears/auto, to UMI, Vaun Mar, VW, World Mkt, **S** 🅖 Citgo/Subway, Speedway/dsl 🅕 Coney Island, McDonald's, Taco Bell 🅛 Motel 6 🅞 Costco/gas, U-Haul
175	Ann Arbor-Saline Rd, **N** 🅖 Shell 🅕 Applebee's, Bella Italia, Dibella Subs, Moe's SW Grill, Panera Bread, Subway 🅛 Candlewood Suites 🅞 Office Depot, to UMI Stadium, vet, Whole Foods Mkt, **S** 🅕 ChuckECheese's, Godaik Japanese, Jet's Pizza, Joe's Crabshack, McDonald's, Nick's Pancakes, Outback Steaks, TGIFriday's 🅞 Best Buy, BigLots, Dick's, JoAnn Fabrics, Kohl's, Meijer/dsl/e-85, Petsmart, Target
172	Jackson Ave, to Ann Arbor, **N on Stadium Ave** 🅖 BP, Marathon, Shell, Sunoco/dsl 🅕 Burger King, McDonald's, Noodles&Co, Quarter Rest., Subway, Taco Bell, Zingerman's Roadhouse 🅞 🅷, $Tree, Discount Tire, Goodyear/auto, K-Mart, Rite Aid, Staples, Verizon, vet, Walgreens, **S** 🅖 Marathon 🅕 Weber's Rest. 🅛 Clarion 🅞 Chevrolet/Cadillac, Ford, Great Lakes Chocolate, Mini
171	MI 14 (from eb, exits left), to Ann Arbor, to Flint by US 23
169	Zeeb Rd, **N** 🅖 BP/dsl 🅕 Big Boy, Grand Pies Co, McDonald's, Metzger's Rest., **S** 🅖 Citgo/dsl 🅕 Arby's, Burger King, Creekside Grill, Culver's, Domino's, Panera Bread, Pizza Hut, Subway, Taco Bell, Wendy's, Westside Grill 🅞 CVS Drug, Discount Tire, Lowe's, Meijer/dsl, vet
167	Baker Rd, Dexter, **N** 🅖 [PILOT]/Subway/scales/dsl/24hr, **S** 🅖 [PILOT]/Arby's/dsl/scales/24hr, TA/BP/Popeye's/dsl/scales/24hr/@ 🅕 McDonald's 🅞 Blue Beacon
162	Jackson Rd, Fletcher Rd, **S** 🅖 BP/Subway/dsl/24hr 🅕 Stiver's Rest.
161mm	🆁🆂 eb, full 🅰 facilities, litter barrels, petwalk, 🅲, 🅰, vending
159	MI 52, Chelsea, **N** 🅖 Mobil/dsl, Rich Gas/dsl, Sunoco/dsl 🅕 Big Boy, Chelsea Grill, China Garden, Chinese Tonite, Jimmy John's, KFC/Taco Bell, McDonald's, Subway,

INTERSTATE 94 Cont'd

Exit #	Services
159	Continued
	Uptown Coney Island, Wendy's 🛏 Comfort Inn, Holiday Inn Express 🅞 🅗 AutoZone, Chrysler/Dodge/Jeep, Country Mkt Foods/drug, CVS Drug, Travel Land RV Ctr, USPO, Verizon, vet, S 🅞 Buick/Chevrolet
157	Jackson Rd, Pierce Rd, N 🅞 Gerald Eddy Geology Ctr
156	Kalmbach Rd, N 🅞 to Waterloo RA
153	Clear Lake Rd, N 🅖 Marathon/dsl
151.5mm	weigh sta both lanes
150mm	🆁🆂 wb, full ♿ facilities, litter barrels, petwalk, 🅒, 🏞, vending
150	to Grass Lake, S 🅖 Mobil/Subway
147	Race Rd, N 🅞 camping, Holiday RV Camp, to Waterloo RA, S 🛏 lodging
145	Sargent Rd, S 🅖 BP/dsl, Mobil/145 Rest/dsl/scales/rest./24hr 🅗 McDonald's, Wendy's 🛏 Colonial Inn
144	Lp 94 (from wb), to Jackson
142	US 127 S, to Hudson, S 3 mi 🅖 Meijer/dsl, Speedway 🅗 Domino's, McDonald's, Wendy's 🅞 Advance Parts, Kroger, Parts+, Rite Aid, to MI Speedway
141	Elm Rd, N 🛏 Travelodge 🅞 Chevrolet, Chrysler/Dodge/Jeep, Ford/Lincoln, Honda, Nissan, S 🅞 🅗
139	MI 106, Cooper St, to Jackson, N 🅞 st police/prison, S 🅖 Citgo/Subway 🅞 🅗
138	US 127 N, MI 50, to Lansing, Jackson, N 🅗 Red Lobster 🛏 Baymont Inn, Best Value Inn, Comfort Inn, Country Inn&Suites, Fairfield Inn, Hampton Inn, Super 8 🅞 vet, S 🅖 Admiral, BP, Shell/dsl 🅗 Arby's, Big Boy, Bob Evans, Burger King, Dunkin Donuts, Fazoli's, Ground Round, Jumbo Buffet, KFC, LJ Silver, Los Tres Amigos, McDonald's, Old Country Buffet, Outback Steaks, Panera Bread, Papa John's, Pizza Hut, Qdoba, Starbucks, Subway, Tim Horton, Wendy's 🛏 Best Value Inn 🅞 $Tree, Advance Parts, Aldi Foods, AT&T, AutoZone, Belle Tire, Best Buy, BigLots, Discount Tire, Family$, Home Depot, JoAnn Fabrics, Kohl's, Kroger/gas, Lowe's, Michael's, Midas, Office Depot, O'Reilly Parts, Petsmart, Sears/auto, Target, TJ Maxx, Verizon, Walgreens
137	Airport Rd, N 🅖 Marathon, Shell/Taco Bell 🅗 Burger King, Denny's, McDonald's, Steak'n Shake, Subway, Wendy's 🛏 Holiday Inn 🅞 7-11, Meijer/dsl, S 🅖 BP 🅗 Cracker Barrel, Culvers, LoneStar Steaks, Olive Garden 🛏 Country Inn&Suites 🅞 K-Mart, Sam's Club/gas, Save-A-Lot Foods
136	Lp 94, MI 60, to Jackson
135mm	🆁🆂 eb, full ♿ facilities, litter barrels, petwalk, 🅒, 🏞, vending
133	Dearing Rd, Spring Arbor, S 🅞 to Spring Arbor U
130	Parma
128	Michigan Ave, N 🅖 BP/Burger King/scales/dsl/24hr, Marathon/dsl/24hr 🅞 RV camping
127	Concord Rd, N 🅞 wineries
124	MI 99, to Eaton Rapids
121	28 Mile Rd, to Albion, N 🅖 Mobil/Subway/dsl 🅗 Arby's 🛏 Days Inn, S 🅖 BP, Clark/dsl, Speedway/dsl 🅗 Frosty Dan's, KFC, La Casa Mexican, Maria's Garden Rest., McDonald's, Pizza Hut 🛏 Super 9 🅞 🅗, $General, AutoZone, Buick/Chevrolet, Family Fare Foods, Family$, Ford, Radio Shack, RV camping, Tire City
119	MI 199, 26 Mile Rd
115	22.5 Mile Rd, N 🅖 Citgo/115 Rest./dsl/24hr
113mm	🆁🆂 wb, full ♿ facilities, litter barrels, petwalk, 🅒, 🏞, vending

Exit #	Services
112	Partello Rd, S 🅖 Loves/Hardee's/scales/dsl/24hr 🅗 Schuler's Rest.
110	Old US 27, Marshall, N 🅖 Shell/Country Kitchen/Subway/dsl/24hr, S 🅖 Citgo/dsl 🅗 Denny's, Pizza Hut (2mi), Schuler's Rest. (2mi) 🛏 Hampton Inn, Holiday Inn Express 🅞 🅗, sheriff
108	I-69, US 27, N to Lansing, S to Ft Wayne
104	11 Mile Rd, Michigan Ave, N 🅖 Pilot/McDonald's/dsl/scales/24hr, TA/Country Pride/dsl/scales/24hr/@, S 🅖 Citgo/Subway/dsl/e-85 🛏 Quality Inn/rest. 🅞 casino
103	Lp 94 (from wb, no return), to Battle Creek, N 🅞 🅗
102mm	Kalamazoo River
100	rd 294, Beadle Lake Rd, N 🅗 Moonraker Rest., S 🅖 Citgo/dsl/repair 🅞 Binder Park Zoo
98b	I-194 N, to Battle Creek
98a	MI 66, to Sturgis, S 🅖 Citgo/dsl 🅗 Chili's, Los Aztecas, McDonald's, Ruby Tuesday, Schlotzsky's, Starbucks, Steak'n Shake 🛏 Holiday Inn 🅞 AT&T, Best Buy, Discount Tire, Kohl's, Lowe's, Meijer/dsl, Menards, Michael's, PetCo, same as 97, Sam's Club/gas, Staples, TJ Maxx, Verizon, Walgreens, Walmart/Subway
97	Capital Ave, to Battle Creek, N 🅖 BP, Marathon 🅗 Arby's, LoneStar Steaks, Lux Cafe, McDonald's, Old China, Red Lobster 🛏 Comfort Inn, Knights Inn, S 🅖 Citgo/Subway, Shell 🅗 Applebee's, Bob Evans, Buffalo Wild Wings, Burger King, Canton Buffet, Coney Island, Cracker Barrel, Culver's, Denny's, Don Pablo, Fazoli's, Jimmy John's, La Cocina, Old Country Buffet, Panera Bread, Pizza Hut, Taco Bell, Wendy's 🛏 Baymont Inn, Best Value Inn, Best Western, Fairfield Inn, Hampton Inn, Howard Johnson, Travelers Inn, Travelodge 🅞 $Tree, AAA, Barnes&Noble, Belle Tire, BigLots, Firestone/auto, Goodyear/auto, Hobby Lobby, JC Penney, JoAnn Fabrics, Macy's, mall, Sears/auto, Target, vet
96mm	🆁🆂 eb, full ♿ facilities, litter barrels, petwalk, 🅒, 🏞, vending
95	Helmer Rd, N 2 mi 🅖 Citgo/dsl 🅗 Arby's, Big Boy 🅞 Meijer/dsl/e-85, st police
92	Lp 94, rd 37, to Battle Creek, Springfield, N 🅖 Citgo/Arlene's Trkstp/dsl/rest./24hr, Shell 🅞 RV camping, to Ft Custer RA
88	Climax, N 🅞 Galesburg Speedway
85	35th St, Galesburg, N 🅖 Shell/dsl 🅗 McDonald's, Subway 🅞 Galesburg Speedway, River Oaks CP, to Ft Custer RA, S 🅞 Colebrook CP, RV camping, Scottsville CP, Winery Tours
85mm	🆁🆂 wb, full ♿ facilities, litter barrels, petwalk, 🅒, 🏞, vending
81	Lp 94 (from wb), to Kalamazoo
80	Cork St, Sprinkle Rd, to Kalamazoo, N 🅖 Marathon/dsl, Speedway/dsl 🅗 Arby's, Burger King, Chicken Coop, Crew Rest., Denny's, Godfather's, Taco Bell 🛏 Best Western, Fairfield Inn, Holiday Inn Express, Red Roof Inn 🅞 vet, S 🅖 BP/dsl, Speedway/dsl 🅗 Derk's Rest., McDonald's, Nob Hill Grill, Subway, Wendy's 🛏 Candlewood Suites, EconoLodge, Motel 6, Quality Inn
78	Portage Rd, Kilgore Rd, N 🅖 BP/Circle K 🅗 China Hut, Summer Thyme Cafe, Uncle Ernie's Pancakes 🛏 AmericInn 🅞 🅗, repair, S 🅖 Marathon/dsl, Shell, Speedway 🅗 Angelo's Italian, Bravo Rest., Brewster's, Café Meli, McDonald's, Pizza King, Quiznos, Subway, Taco Bell, Theo&Stacy's Rest. 🛏 Best Value Inn, Country Inn&Suites, Days Inn 🅞 AutoValue Parts, Fields Fabrics, museum
76	Westnedge Ave, N 🅖 Admiral, Meijer/dsl, Speedway/dsl 🅗 Arby's, BD BBQ, Burger King, Hibachi Buffet, Hooters,

INTERSTATE 94 Cont'd

Exit #	Services
76	Continued
	IHOP, Lee's Chicken, McDonald's, Old Chicago Grill, Outback Steaks, Papa John's, Papa Murphy's, Pizza Hut, Root Beer Stand, Steak'n Shake, Stirmax Asian, Subway, Taco Bell, Theo&Stacy's Rest. 🔲 Courtyard 🔲 Advance Parts, BigLots, Discount Tire, Family$, Firestone/auto, Gander Mtn, Goodyear/auto, Lowe's, Meijer, Midas, Office Depot, **S** 🔲 Shell 🔲 5 Guys Burgers, Applebee's, Bilbo's Pizza, Bob Evans, Burger King, Carrabba's, Chili's, ChuckECheese's, Coldstone, Colonial Kitchen, Culver's, HoneyBaked Ham, Jimmy Johns, KFC, Krispy Kreme, Little Caesars, LJ Silver, Logan's Roadhouse, Los Amigos Mexican, MacKenzie's Bakery, McDonald's, Noodles&Co, Old Country Buffet, Olive Garden, Panchero's Mexican, Panera Bread, Penn Sta Subs, Pizza Hut, Qdoba Mexican, Red Lobster, Red Robin, Schlotzsky's, Subway, Taco Bell, Tim Horton, TX Roadhouse, Wendy's 🔲 Holiday Motel 🔲 $Tree, AT&T, AutoZone, Barnes&Noble, Belle Tire, Best Buy, Buick/Cadillac/GMC, Dick's, Fannie May Candies, Firestone/auto, Harding's Foods, Hobby Lobby, Home Depot, JoAnn Fabrics, K-Mart, Kohl's, Macy's, mall, Michael's, Old Navy, O'Reilly Parts, PepBoys, Sam's Club, Sears/auto, Target, TJMaxx, Tuesday Morning, Tuffy Auto, Uncle Ed's Oil Shoppe, Verizon, Walgreens, WorldMkt
75	Oakland Dr
74b a	US 131, to Kalamazoo, **N** 🔲 Kalamazoo Coll, to W MI U
72	9th St, Oshtemo, **N** 🔲 BP, Speedway/dsl 🔲 Arby's, Culver's, McDonald's, Taco Bell, Wendy's 🔲 Hampton Inn, **S** 🔲 Cracker Barrel 🔲 Fairfield Inn, Microtel, Towne Place Suites
66	Mattawan, **N** 🔲 Speedway/Subway/dsl/scales/24hr 🔲 Main St Grill, Mancino's Italian 🔲 Family$, Freightliner, R&S RV Service, Rossman Auto/repair, **S** 🔲 Shell/dsl 🔲 Pizza Hut
60	MI 40, Paw Paw, **N** 🔲 BP, Speedway/dsl 🔲 Arby's, Burger King, Chicken Coop, Copper Grille, Gallagher's Eatery, McDonald's, Pizza Hut, Root Beer Stand, Subway, Taco Bell, Wendy's 🔲 Comfort Inn, EconoLodge, StaAt 🔲 🔲, Advance Parts, AT&T, Buick/Chevrolet/GMC, Chrysler/Dodge/Jeep, Curves, Family Fare Foods, St Julian Winery, Walgreens
56	MI 51, to Decatur, **N** 🔲 st police, **S** 🔲 Citgo/dsl, Marathon/dsl/24hr
52	Lawrence, **N** 🔲 Waffle House of America
46	Hartford, **N** 🔲 Shell/dsl 🔲 McDonald's, Panel Room Rest., Subway, **S** 🔲 fruit stand
42mm	🔲 wb, full 🔲 facilities, litter barrels, petwalk, 🔲, 🔲, vending
41	MI 140, to Niles, Watervliet, **N** 🔲 Citgo, Marathon/dsl, Shell/dsl 🔲 Burger King, Chicken Coop, Millcreek Charlie's Rest., Subway, Taco Bell 🔲 Fairfield Inn 🔲 🔲, KOA (Apr-Oct)
39	Millburg, Coloma, Deer Forest, **N 0-1 mi** 🔲 BP/dsl, Marathon, Speedway/dsl, Wesco/dsl 🔲 Diggins Rest., DQ, Friendly Grill, J&P Cafe, McDonald's, Subway 🔲 Family$, Krenek RV Ctr, **S** 🔲 Jollay Mkt, wine tasting
34	I-196 N, US 31 N, to Holland, Grand Rapids
33	Lp I-94, to Benton Harbor, **N 2-4 mi** 🔲 🔲, sheriff's dept
30	Napier Ave, Benton Harbor, **N** 🔲 🔲/Wendy's/dsl/LP/24hr/@, Shell/dsl 🔲 Knights Inn 🔲 🔲, Blue Beacon
29	Pipestone Rd, Benton Harbor, **N** 🔲 Applebee's, Asian Grill, Burger King, IHOP, Isabella's Rest., Mancino's Pizza, McDonald's, Pizza Hut, Sophia's Pancake House, Steak'n Shake, Super Buffet, TX Corral 🔲 Courtyard, Motel 6, Red Roof Inn,

BENTON HARBOR

Exit #	Services
29	Continued
	Twin City Inn 🔲 Aldi Foods, Best Buy, Home Depot, JC Penney, JoAnn Fabrics, Lowe's, Meijer/dsl, Radio Shack, Staples, Walmart/Subway, **S** 🔲 Mobil/dsl/24hr 🔲 Bob Evans 🔲 Comfort Suites, Holiday Inn Express
28	US 31 S, MI 139 N, Scottsdale Rd, to Niles, **N** 🔲 Citgo/dsl, Marathon/dsl 🔲 Bejing House, Burger King, Chicken Coop, Country Kitchen, DQ, Henry's Burgers, KFC, Little Caesars, Pizza Hut, Taco Bell, Wendy's 🔲 Best Value Inn, Rodeway Inn 🔲 🔲, $Tree, AutoZone, BigLots, Chevrolet, Family$, Kohl's, M&W Tire, Michael's, Midas, NAPA, Office Depot, Old Navy, Petsmart, radiators/repair/transmissions, Rite Aid, Save-A-Lot, st police, Target, TJ Maxx, U-Haul, Walgreens
27mm	St Joseph River
27	MI 63, Niles Ave, to St Joseph, **N** 🔲 BP 🔲 Nye's Apple Barn, **S** 🔲 Moe's SW Grill, Panera Bread 🔲 Goodyear
23	Red Arrow Hwy, Stevensville, **N** 🔲 Admiral, BP, Marathon/dsl, Mobil, Shell/dsl 🔲 Big Boy, Burger King, Cracker Barrel, Culver's, DQ, HoneyBaked Ham, LJ Silver, McDonald's, Papa John's, Popeye's, Quizno's, Subway 🔲 Baymont Inn, Candlewood Suites, Comfort Suites 🔲 Honda, Walgreens, **S** 🔲 Five O'Clock Grill 🔲 Hampton Inn 🔲 Meijer/dsl
22	John Beers Rd, Stevensville, **N** 🔲 Chalet on the Lake 🔲 to Grand Mere SP, **S** 🔲 Marathon/dsl 🔲 Pizza Hut
16	Bridgman, **N** 🔲 BP/Quiznos/dsl 🔲 camping, to Warren Dunes SP, **S** 🔲 McDonald's, Olympus Rest., Pizza Hut, Roma Pizza, Sammies Rest., Subway 🔲 Bridgman Inn 🔲 auto repair, Chevrolet, st police, vet
12	Sawyer, **N** 🔲 Marathon/deli/dsl/scales/24hr 🔲 truck wash, **S** 🔲 TA/Burger King/Popeye's/Taco Bell/scales/dsl/24hr/@ 🔲 Super 8 🔲 Schlipp's Drug, USPO
6	Lakeside, Union Pier, **N** 🔲 antiques, St Julian's Winery, **S** 🔲 RV camping
4b a	US 12, to Three Oaks, New Buffalo, **N** 🔲 Pizza Hut, Roma Pizza 🔲 st police
2.5mm	weigh sta both lanes
1	MI 239, to Grand Beach, New Buffalo, **N 0-2 mi** 🔲 Shell/Quiznos 🔲 Bruster's Italian, Casey's Grille, Hannah's Rest., Jimmy's Grill, McDonald's, Nancy's, Rosie's Rest., Stray Dog Grill, Subway, Wheel Inn Rest. 🔲 Best Western, Comfort Inn, Fairfield Inn, Holiday Inn Express, Super Inn 🔲 $General, **S** 🔲 Plaza1/rest/dsl/scales/24hr 🔲 Harbor Country Kitchen, Wendy's 🔲 Obrien's Inn 🔲 casino
0.5mm	Welcome Ctr eb, full 🔲 facilities, info, litter barrels, petwalk, 🔲, 🔲, vending
0mm	Michigan/Indiana state line

MI

DETROIT AREA

⬆E INTERSTATE 96

Exit #	Services
	I-96 begins/ends on I-75, exit 48 in Detroit.
191	I-75, N to Flint, S to Toledo, US 12, to MLK Blvd, to Michigan Ave
190b	Warren Ave, N ⓡ BP/dsl, S ⓡ Marathon
190a	I-94 E to Port Huron
189	W Grand Blvd, Tireman Rd, N ⓡ BP/Subway, Mobil
188b	Joy Rd, N ⓕ Church's
188a	Livernois, N ⓡ Mobil, Shell/Subway ⓕ Burger King, KFC, McDonald's, Wendy's
187	Grand River Ave (from eb)
186b	Davison Ave, I-96 local and I-96 express divide, no exits from express
186a	Wyoming Ave
185	Schaefer Hwy, to Grand River Ave, N ⓡ BP/24hr, Mobil ⓕ Coney Island, McDonald's ⓞ CVS Drug, S ⓡ Sunoco
184	Greenfield Rd
183	MI 39, Southfield Fwy, exit from expswy and local
182	Evergreen Rd
180	Outer Dr, N ⓡ BP/dsl/lube
180mm	I-96 local/express unite/divide
179	US 24, Telegraph Rd, N ⓡ BP, Marathon/dsl ⓕ Arby's, Baskin-Robbins/Dunkin Donuts, China King, McDonald's, Wendy's, White Castle ⓞ Chevrolet, Family$, NAPA, S ⓡ BP, Marathon/dsl
178	Beech Daly Rd, N ⓡ gas
177	Inkster Rd, N ⓡ BP/Tim Horton ⓕ Subway ⌂ Best Value Inn ⓞ $General, 7-11, URGENT CARE
176	Middlebelt Rd, N ⓕ Bob Evans, IHOP, Olive Garden ⌂ Comfort Inn, S 0-1 mi ⓕ Biggby Coffee, Chili's, Logan's Roadhouse, Noodles&Co, Pottbelly, Qdoba, Red Lobster ⌂ Crossland Suites ⓞ $Tree, auto repair/transmissions, Big-Lots, Costco/gas, Firestone/auto, Home Depot, Marshall's, Meijer, Michael's, Office Depot, Petsmart, Target, Verizon, Walgreens, Walmart
175	Merriman Rd, N ⓡ Mobil/dsl, Speedway/dsl, S ⓡ Exxon/dsl ⓕ Blimpie, Royal Coney Island
174	Farmington Rd, N ⓡ Mobil/dsl, Sunoco ⓕ Looney Baker, S ⓡ BP ⓕ KFC
173b	Levan Rd, N ⓞ Ⓗ, to Madonna U
173a	Newburgh Rd
171mm	I-275 and I-96 run together 9 miles
170	6 Mile Rd, N ⓕ Big Boy, Buffalo Wild Wings, Jimmy John's, Red Robin, Taco Del Mar ⌂ Best Western, Courtyard, Holiday Inn, Marriott ⓞ Ⓗ, ACO Hardware, AT&T, Busch's Foods, GNC, mall, O'Reilly Parts, Rite Aid, Verizon, Walgreens, S ⓡ Marathon, Mobil ⓕ Applebee's, Baja Fresh, Brann's Steaks, Bravo Italian, Buca Italian, Charlie's Grill, Claddagh Rest., Flemings, McDonald's, Mitchell's Fishmarket, Panchero's, PF Chang, Potbelly, Subway, Tim Horton, Wendy's ⌂ Fairfield Inn, Residence Inn, TownePlace Suites ⓞ Barnes&Noble, Kroger, Office Depot, Petsmart
169b a	7 Mile Rd, N ⓕ Big Daddy's, Doc's Grill ⌂ Embassy Suites, S ⓕ Alexander's Rest., Andiamo's Cafe, Bahama Breeze Rest., Champp's Rest., Macaroni Grill ⌂ Hyatt Place ⓞ Home Depot
167	8 Mile Rd, to Northville, S ⓡ BP, Speedway/dsl ⓕ 5 Guys Burgers, Aubree's Pizza, Benihana, Big Boy, Chili's, Kerry's Koney Island, McDonald's, On-the-Border, Panera Bread, Qdoba, Starbucks, Taco Bell, TGIFriday's ⌂ Extended Stay America, Hampton Inn, Holiday Inn Express, Quality Inn,

Exit #	Services
167	Continued
	Sheraton ⓞ Best Buy, Costco/gas, Dick's, Firestone/auto, Kohl's, Meijer/dsl, Target, to Maybury SP, Trader Joe's, Verizon
165	I-696, I-275, MI 5, Grand River Ave.
	I-275 and I-96 run together 9 miles
163	I-696 (from eb)
162	Novi Rd, to Walled Lake, Novi, N ⓡ BP ⓕ Bar Louie, Black Rock Rest., Buffalo Wild Wings, Carrabba's, Cheesecake Factory, ChuckECheese's, Denny's, Hooters, McDonald's, Novi Chophouse, Red Lobster, Rojo Mexican, Subway, Tilted Kilt Eatery ⌂ Crowne Plaza, Hilton Garden, Renaissance, Residence Inn ⓞ Ⓗ, Best Buy, BigLots, Dick's, Gander Mtn, JC Penney, JoAnn Fabrics, Lord&Taylor, Macy's, mall, Marshalls, Michael's, Midas, Nordstrom, Old Navy, Radio Shack, Sears/auto, S ⓡ Mobil/dsl, Sunoco/dsl ⓕ Athenian Coney Island, Bagger Dave's Burgers, BD Mongolian BBQ, Big Boy, Biggby Coffee, Blue Fin Rest., Bonefish Grill, Boston Mkt, Famous Dave's, Kim's Chinese, Melting Pot, Olive Garden, Panera Bread, Pei Wei, Potbelly, Qdoba, Red Robin, Steve&Rocky's, TGIFriday's, Tony Sacco Pizza, Wendy's ⌂ Courtyard, DoubleTree, Towne Place Suites ⓞ Advance Parts, AT&T, Belle Tire, Better Health Foods, Chevrolet, Discount Tire, Firestone/auto, Kia, NAPA, TJ Maxx, URGENT CARE, vet, Walmart
160	Beck Rd, 12 Mile Rd, S ⓡ Shell/Tim Horton ⓕ Applebee's, Caribou Coffee, Guido's Pizza, La Herraduro Mexican, Olga's Kitchen, Outback Steaks, Subway, Zoup! ⌂ Hyatt Place, Staybridge Suites ⓞ Ⓗ, Home Depot, Kroger, Staples, to Maybury SP
159	Wixom Rd, Walled Lake, N ⓡ Marathon/dsl, Sunoco/dsl ⓕ Leon's Rest., Papa Romano's Pizza, Quiznos, Wendy's ⌂ Holiday Inn Express ⓞ to Proud Lake RA, S ⓡ Mobil/dsl, Shell, Valero/dsl ⓕ A&W/KFC, Arby's, Baskin-Robbins/Dunkin Donuts, Burger King, Don's Diner, Jimmy John's, McDonald's, Stinger's Grill, Taco Bell ⌂ Comfort Suites ⓞ Lincoln, Meijer/dsl, Sam's Club/gas, Target
155b a	to Milford, New Hudson, N ⓞ Camp Deerborn (5mi), Ford, to Lyon Oaks CP, S ⓡ Sunoco ⓕ Applebee's, Arby's, Jet's Pizza, KG Grill, Leo's Coney Island, McDonald's, Starbucks, Subway ⓞ AT&T, Belle Tire, Chevrolet, Discount Tire, Haws Lake RV Camping (Apr-Oct), Hyundai, Lowe's, URGENT CARE, Verizon, Walmart
153	Kent Lake Rd, N ⓞ Kensington Metropark, S ⓡ Mobil/dsl ⌂ Country Meadows Inn (3mi)
151	Kensington Rd, N ⓞ Kensington Metropark, S ⓕ food ⌂ lodging ⓞ Island Lake RA
150	Pleasant Valley Rd (no return wb)
148b a	US 23, N to Flint, S to Ann Arbor
147	Spencer Rd, N ⓡ Mobil/dsl ⓞ st police, S ⓕ Bagger Dave's Burgers (2mi) ⓞ to Brighton St RA
145	Grand River Ave, to Brighton, N ⓡ BP, Shell/dsl ⓕ Arby's, Baskin-Robbins/Dunkin Donuts, Cracker Barrel, Outback Steaks, Pizza Hut ⌂ Courtyard ⓞ Ⓗ, $General, Buick/GMC, camping, Ford, Honda, Mazda, URGENT CARE, S ⓡ Marathon/Subway ⓕ Big Boy, Border Cantina, Burger King, Chili's, Firehouse Subs, IHOP, Jimmy John's, Leo's Coney Island, Lil Chef, McDonald's, Olga's Kitchen, Panera Bread, Pi's Asian, Red Robin, Starbucks, Taco Bell, Tim Horton, Wendy's ⌂ Holiday Inn Express, Homewood Suites ⓞ $Tree, AAA, Aldi Foods, Belle Tire, Best Buy, Bob's Tire, CVS Drug, Home Depot, JoAnn Fabrics, Marshalls, Meijer/dsl/E85, Michael's, O'Reilly Parts, Petsmart, Radio Shack, Staples, Target, to Brighton Ski Area, USPO, Verizon, Walgreens

INTERSTATE 96 Cont'd

Exit #	Services
141	Lp 96 (from wb, return at 140), to Howell, **N 0-2 mi** 🅟 Shell, Speedway, Sunoco/dsl 🍴 Applebee's, Arby's, Biggby Coffee, Bluefin Steaks, Bob Evans, Buffalo Wild Wings, KFC, Little Caesars, McDonald's, New Century Buffet, Subway, Taco Bell, Wendy's, White Castle 🛏 Grandview Inn 🅞 $Tree, AT&T, Chevrolet, Discount Tire, Home Depot, Kohl's, Lowe's, Meijer, O'Reilly Parts, Staples, TJ Maxx, Walmart
140	S Latson Rd, same as 141
137	D19, to Pinckney, Howell, **N** 🅟 Mobil, Shell/dsl, Speedway/dsl, Sunoco/Baskin-Robbins/Dunkin Donuts/dsl 🍴 Jonna's ToGo, Mario Bros Pizza, Wendy's 🛏 Kensington Inn 🅞 🄷 Parts+, Spartan Tire, True Value, USPO, vet, **S** 🍴 Country Kitchen 🛏 Best Western
135mm	🅡ₛ eb, full ♿ facilities, litter barrels, petwalk, 🚽, 🛢, vending
133	MI 59, Highland Rd, **N** 🅟 Marathon/McDonald's/dsl 🍴 Arby's, Leo's Coney Island 🛏 Baymont, Holiday Inn Express 🅞 Tanger Outlets/famous brands
129	Fowlerville Rd, Fowlerville, **N** 🅟 BP, Shell/dsl, Sunoco/dsl 🍴 A&W/KFC, Great Lakes Rest., McDonald's, Pizza Hut/Taco Bell, Wendy's 🛏 Magnuson Hotel 🅞 Chevrolet, Walmart, **S** 🅟 Mobil/dsl 🍴 Subway 🅞 Chysler/Dodge/Jeep, Ford
126mm	weigh sta both lanes
122	MI 43, MI 52, Webberville, **N** 🅟 Mobil/dsl/24hr 🍴 McDonald's 🅞 MI Brewing Co
117	to Dansville, Williamston, **N** 🅟 Marathon/Jersey's Giant Subs/dsl 🍴 Spag's Grill (3mi), **S** 🅟 Sunoco/dsl
111mm	🅡ₛ wb, full ♿ facilities, litter barrels, petwalk, 🚽, 🛢, vending
110	Okemos, Mason, **N** 🅟 Marathon/dsl, Sunoco/Dunkin Donuts 🍴 Applebee's, Arby's, Backyard BBQ, Big John's Steaks, Biggby Coffee, Coldstone/Tim Horton, Cracker Barrel, Gilbert&Blake's, Grand Traverse Pie Co., Little Caesars, McDonald's, Ozzy Mediterranean, Panchero's Mexican, Starbucks, Stillwater Grill, Subway, Taco Bell 🛏 Comfort Inn, Fairfield Inn, Hampton Inn, Holiday Inn Express, Staybridge Suites 🅞 7-11, BMW/Porsche, Mercedes, to stadium
106b a	I-496, US 127, to Jackson, Lansing, **N** 🅞 St Police
104	Lp 96, Cedar St, to Holt, Lansing, **N** 🅟 Admiral, Speedway/dsl 🍴 Applebee's, Arby's, Asia's Finest, Big John's, Biggby Coffee, Blimpie, Bob Evans, Boston Mkt, Burger King, China King, Cici's, Fazoli's, Finley's Rest., Happy's Pizza, Hooters, Jersey Giant Subs, Jet's Pizza, KFC, Los Tres Amigos, Panda Gourmet, Pizza Hut, Steak'n Shake, Tim Horton, TX Roadhouse, Wendy's, Zeus Coney Island 🛏 Best Value Inn, Best Western, Magnuson Hotel, Super 8 🅞 🄷, $Tree, Aldi Foods, auto repair, Belle Tire, Cadillac, Chevrolet, Discount Tire, Dodge, Family$, Kia, Lexus, Meijer/dsl, Menards, Sam's Club/gas, Target, Toyota/Scion, Tuffy Auto, Verizon, vet, **S** 🅟 Marathon, Speedway/dsl 🍴 Aldaco's Taco Bar, Burger King, Champion's Grill, China East Buffet, Dairy Dan, Famous Dave's BBQ, Flapjack Rest., McDonald's, Ponderosa, Subway 🛏 Best Western 🅞 AutoZone, Budget Tire, CarQuest, CVS Drug, Family$, Kroger/gas, L&L Foods, Lowe's, Rite Aid
101	MI 99, MLK Blvd, to Eaton Rapids, **N 0-3 mi** 🅟 QD 🍴 Arby's, Tim Horton 🅞 Kroger/gas, Meijer/dsl, **S** 🍴 Speedway/Subway/dsl, Sunoco/dsl 🍴 Coach's Grill, McDonald's, Wendy's
98b a	Lansing Rd, to Lansing, **N** 🍴 Wendy's 🛏 Comfort Inn, Holiday Inn Express 🅞 Harley-Davidson, **S** 🅞 st police
97	I-69, US 27 S, S to Ft Wayne, N to Lansing

95	I-496, to Lansing
93b a	MI 43, Lp 69, Saginaw Hwy, to Grand Ledge, **N 0-2 mi** 🅟 Shell, Speedway/dsl 🍴 Burger King, Carrabba's, Cheddar's, Denny's, Fazoli's, Frank's Grill, Hibachi Grill, Honeybaked Ham, Houlihan's, Logan's Roadhouse, McDonald's, Outback Steaks, Panera Bread, Qdoba, Red Robin, Subway, Younkers 🛏 Days Inn, Fairfield Inn, Hampton Inn, Motel 6, Quality Inn, Ramada Inn, Red Roof Inn, Residence Inn 🅞 🄷, Barnes&Noble, BigLots, Chrysler/Dodge/Jeep, Hobby Lobby, JC Penney, Kohl's, Kroger, Macy's, Meijer/dsl/24hr, NAPA, Radio Shack, Target, Walgreens, **S** 🅟 BP/24hr, QD, Sunoco/McDonald's 🍴 Arby's, Bob Evans, Cracker Barrel, Incredible Chinese, Rudino's Pizza, Steak'n Shake, Subway 🛏 SpringHill Suites 🅞 AT&T, Belle Tire, Buick/GMC, Dick's, Discount Tire, Gander Mtn, Lowe's, Mazda, Menards, Michael's, Petsmart, Staples, URGENT CARE, Walmart
92mm	Grand River
91	I-69 N (from wb), US 27 N, to Flint, **S** 🅟 🚛FLYING J/Denny's/dsl/24hr 🍴 Pepperoni's Rest.
90	Grand River Ave, to 🚲 (from wb)
89	I-69 N, US 27 N (from eb), to Flint
87mm	🅡ₛ eb, full ♿ facilities, litter barrels, petwalk, 🚽, 🛢, vending
86	MI 100, Wright Rd, to Grand Ledge, **S** 🅟 Mobil/McDonald's/dsl, Speedway/Subway/24hr
84	to Eagle, Westphalia
79mm	🅡ₛ wb, full ♿ facilities, info, litter barrels, petwalk, 🚽, 🛢, vending
77	Lp 96, Grand River Ave, Portland, **N** 🅟 BP/24hr, Shell/Burger King, Speedway/dsl 🍴 Arby's, Biggby Coffee, Hungry Howie's, KFC/Taco Bell, Little Caesar's, McDonald's 🛏 Best Western 🅞 Curves, Family$, Rite Aid, Tom's Foods, **S** 🍴 Wendy's 🅞 Ford
76	Kent St, Portland
76mm	Grand River
73	to Lyons-Muir, Grand River Ave
69mm	weigh sta both lanes
67	MI 66, to Ionia, Battle Creek, **N** 🅟 🚛/Subway/dsl/scales/24hr 🍴 Corner Landing Grill 🛏 Midway Motel, Super 8 🅞 🄷, (4mi), Meijer/dsl (4mi), RV camping, st police, truck wash, Walmart
64	to Lake Odessa, Saranac, **N** 🅞 Ionia St RA, **S** 🅞 I-96 Speedway
63mm	🅡ₛ eb, full ♿ facilities, litter barrels, petwalk, 🚽, 🛢, vending
59	Clarksville
52	MI 50, to Lowell, **N** 🅟 Mobil/Subway/dsl 🅞 fairgrounds, **S** 🅟 Marathon/Noble Roman's/dsl (2mi) 🅞 RV camping

🅿 = gas 🍴 = food 🛏 = lodging 🅾 = other Ⓡˢ = rest stop   Copyright 2015 - the Next EXIT ®

MI

INTERSTATE 96 Cont'd

Exit #	Services
46	rd 6, to rd 37
46mm	Thornapple River
44	36 St, S 🅾 🛏 🍴
43b a	MI 11, 28th St, Cascade, N 🅿 Marathon/dsl 🍴 Biggby Coffee, Brann's Steaks, Burger King, Culver's, Jet's Pizza, Jimmy John's, Macaroni Grill, Panera Bread, Papa John's, Pizza Hut, Quizno's, Stabucks, Subway, Sundance Grill, Taco Boy, Wendy's 🛏 Baymont Inn, Best Western, Country Inn&Suites, Crowne Plaza, EconoLodge, Holiday Inn Express 🅾 Audi/Porsche/Subaru, Fresh Mkt, GNC, Meijer/dsl, Mercedes/Volvo/VW, True Value, Walmart, S 0-3 mi 🅿 BP, Citgo, Shell, Speedway/dsl 🍴 Applebee's, Arby's, Arnie's Rest., Baskin-Robbins/Dunkin Donuts, Burger King, Cantina Mexican, Carabba's, Carlos O'Kelley's, Chili's, Chipotle Mexican, ChuckeCheese, Coldstone, Denny's, Don Julio's, Grand Rapids Brewery, Honey Baked Ham, Hooters, Jimmy John's, Krispy Kreme, Longhorn Steaks, McDonald's, Moe's SW Grill, Noodles&Co, Old Chicago, Olive Garden, Outback Steaks, Panera Bread, Papa Vino's, Perkins, Pizza Hut, Quaker Steak&Lube, Red Lobster, Red Robin, Red Sun Buffet, Ruby Tuesday, Smokey Bones, Starbucks, Steak'n Shake, Subway, Taco Bell, TX Roadhouse, Wendy's, Yin Ching Chinese 🛏 Clarion, Comfort Inn, Courtyard, Hampton Inn, Hilton, Motel 6, Quality Inn, Ramada, Red Roof Inn, SpringHill Suites, Super 8 🅾 $Tree, Belle Tire, Best Buy, CarQuest, Costco/gas, Dick's, Ford, Gander Mtn, Hobby Lobby, Home Depot, Honda, Hyundai/KIA, Jo-Ann Fabrics, Lentz Automotive, Lowe's, Michael's, Nissan, Office Depot, Old Navy, Petsmart, Radio Shack, Sam's Club/gas, Sears/auto, Staples, Target, TJ Maxx, U-Haul
40b a	Cascade Rd, N 🅿 Forrest Hills Fuel, Marathon/dsl 🍴 Biggby Coffee, China Garden, Forrest Hills Rest, Great Harvest, Little Bangkok, Little Caesar's, Subway 🅾 7-11, vet, S 🅿 Shell/Quizno's/dsl, Speedway/dsl 🍴 Bonefish Grill, Jimmy John's, Zoup 🅾 🅷, Keystone Drug
39	MI 21 (from eb), to Flint
38	E Beltline Ave, to MI 21, MI 37, MI 44, N 🅿 BP 🍴 O'Charley's 🅾 Meijer/dsl, RV camping, S 🍴 Uno Pizzaria 🛏 Country Inn&Suites 🅾 🅷
37	I-196 (from wb, exits left), Gerald Ford Fwy, to Grand Rapids
36	Leonard St, S 2 mi 🍴 Arby's, Jimmy John's, McDonald's 🅾 sheriff's dept
33	Plainfield Ave, MI 44 Connector, N 🅿 BP, Speedway/dsl 🍴 Arby's, Baskin-Robbins, Blimpie, Charley's Grille, Cheers Grill, Fred's Italian, Golden Dragon, KFC, Little Caesar's, LJ Silver, McDonald's, Pizza Hut, Russ' Rest., Subway, Taco Bell, Tokyo Roadhouse, Wendy's 🛏 Grand Inn, Lazy T Motel 🅾 $Tree, AutoZone, Belle Tire, BigLots, Chevrolet, Chrysler/Jeep, Curves, Discount Tire, Dodge, Firestone/auto, Ford, Goodyear/auto, K-Mart, Lowe's, Meijer/dsl, NAPA, Nissan/VW, Radio Shack, Save-A-Lot Foods, Toyota, U-Haul, Walgreens, S 🅿 BP 🍴 Denny's
31mm	Grand River
31b a	US 131, N to Cadillac, S to Kalamazoo, N 1 mi 🅿 BP 🍴 McDonald's
30b a	Alpine Ave, Grand Rapids, N 🅿 7-11, BP, Marathon/dsl 🍴 Applebee's, Buffalo Wild Wings, Checkers, ChuckeCheese, Coldstone, Culvers, El Burrito Mexican, Empire Buffet,

GRAND RAPIDS

30b a	Continued Fire Mtn Grill, First Wok, Golden Corral, Hibachi Grill, IHOP, Jimmy John's, Little Caesar's, Logan's Roadhouse, Mafia Mike's Pizza, McDonald's, Olive Garden, Outback Steaks, Panera Bread, Perkins, Qdoba, Quizno's, Russ' Rest., Sonic, Starbucks, Steak'n Shake, Subway, Taco Bell, TGIFriday's, Thai Basil 🛏 Hampton Inn, Holiday Inn Express, SpringHill Suites 🅾 $Tree, Aldi Foods, AT&T, AutoZone, Belle Tire, Best Buy, CarQuest, Discount Tire, Ford/KIA, GNC, Hobby Lobby, Kohl's, Marshall's, Menards, Michael's, NAPA, Office Depot, PepBoys, PetCo, Radio Shack, Sam's Club/gas, Save-a-Lot Foods, Schuler Books, Target, TJ Maxx, Verizon, Walgreens, Walmart/auto, S 🅿 Admiral/dsl, Speedway/dsl 🍴 Arby's, Burger King, Fazoli's, First 1 Chinese, KFC, LJ Silver, McDonald's, Papa John's, Pizza Hut, Wendy's 🛏 Motel 6 🅾 auto repair, Goodyear/auto, Home Depot, Jo-Ann Fabrics, Meijer/dsl, Midas, Tuffy Auto, U-Haul
28	Walker Ave, S 🅿 Meijer/dsl/24hr 🍴 Bob Evans, McDonald's 🛏 Baymont Inn, Quality Inn
26	Fruit Ridge Ave, N 🅿 Citgo/dsl, S 🅿 Citgo/deli/dsl
25mm	Ⓡˢ eb, full ♿ facilities, litter barrels, petwalk, 🕭, 🐕
25	8th Ave, 4Mile Rd (from wb), S 🅿 Marathon/dsl 🛏 Wayside Motel
24	8th Ave, 4Mile Rd (from eb), S 🅿 Marathon/dsl 🛏 Wayside Motel
23	Marne, N 🅾 tires, S 🍴 Depot Café, Rinaldi's Café 🅾 Ernie's Mkt, fairgrounds/raceway, USPO
19	Lamont, Coopersville, N 🍴 food, S 🍴 Sam's Joint Rest. 🅾 LP
16	B-35, Eastmanville, N 🅿 BP/Subway/dsl, Shell/Burger King/dsl, Speedway/dsl/24hr 🍴 #1 Chinese, Arby's, Hungry Howie's, Little Caesar's, McDonald's, Taco Bell 🛏 Rodeway Inn 🅾 Buick/Chevrolet/Poniac, Curves, Family Fare Foods, Family$, Fun 'N Sun RV Ctr, Rite Aid, vet, S 🅿 Pacific Pride/dsl 🅾 RV camping
10	B-31 (exits left from eb), Nunica, N 🍴 Turk's Rest., S 🅾 Conestoga RV camping, golf course/rest.
9	MI 104 (from wb, exits left), to Grand Haven, Spring Lake, S 🅿 Marathon 🅾 to Grand Haven SP
8mm	Ⓡˢ wb, full ♿ facilities, litter barrels, petwalk, 🕭, 🐕, vending
5	Fruitport (from wb, no return)
4	Airline Rd, N 🅾 NAPA, S 🅿 Speedway/dsl, Wesco/dsl 🍴 Burger Crest Diner, Dairy Bar, McDonald's, Subway, Village Inn 🅾 auto/tire repair, Grover Drug, Orchard Mkt Foods, to PJ Hoffmaster SP, USPO, Water Park (5mi)
1c	Hile Rd (from eb), S 🍴 Arby's, Brann's Grille, Buffalo Wild Wings, ChuckeCheese, Dynasty Buffet, Golden Corral, KFC, Logan's Roadhouse, Perkins, Quizno's, Red Robin, TX Roadhouse 🛏 Baymont Inn, Fairfield Inn, Hampton Inn 🅾 AT&T, Barnes&Noble, Best Buy, Hobby Lobby, JC Penney, Jo-Ann Fabrics, Kohl's, mall, Meijer/dsl, Menards, Old Navy, PetCo, Target, TJ Maxx, VW, Younkers
1b a	US 31, to Ludington, Grand Haven, N 2 mi on Sherman Blvd 🍴 Applebee's, Arby's, Fazoli's, McDonald's, Pizza Ranch, Red Wok, Subway, Wendy's 🛏 Airline Motel, Alpine Motel, Bel-aire Motel, Comfort Inn/rest. 🅾 🅷, $Tree, All Seasons RV Ctr, Citgo/dsl, GNC, Lowe's, Petsmart, Radio Shack, Sam's Club/gas, Staples, Walmart/24hr, S same as 1c

I-96 begins/ends on US 31 at Muskegon.

INTERSTATE 196 (Grand Rapids)

Exit #	Services
81mm	I-196 begins/ends on I-96, 37mm in E Grand Rapids.
79	Fuller Ave, N ⊙ sheriff, S 📇 Shell/dsl, Speedway/dsl 🍴 Biggby Coffee, Bill's Rest., Checkers, Elbow Room, KFC, Subway, Taco Bell, Wendy's ⊙ H, Ace Hardware, Walgreens
78	College Ave, S 📇 Marathon/Circle K 🍴 McDonald's, Omelette Shop ⊙ H, Ford Museum
77c	Ottawa Ave, S ⊙ Gerald R Ford Museum, downtown
77b a	US 131, S to Kalamazoo, N to Cadillac
76	MI 45 E, Lane Ave, S 🍴 El Granjero Mexican ⊙ auto repair, Gerald R Ford Museum, John Ball Park&Zoo
75	MI 45 W, Lake Michigan Dr, N ⊙ to Grand Valley St U
74mm	Grand River
73	Market Ave, N ⊙ to Vanandel Arena
72	Lp 196, Chicago Dr E (from eb)
70	MI 11 (exits left from wb), Grandville, Walker, S 📇 BP/dsl, Shell 🛏 Days Inn ⊙ Auto Value Parts, USPO
69c	Baldwin St (from wb)
69b a	Chicago Dr, N 📇 Speedway 🍴 Culver's, Hungry Howie's, KFC, McDonald's, Papa John's, Peppino's Pizza, Perkins, Subway, Taco Bell, Youming Chinese ⊙ $Tree, Aldi Foods, AutoZone, Curves, Meijer/dsl, Radio Shack, Target, USPO, Walgreens, S 📇 Admiral, Speedway/dsl 🍴 Adobe Mexican, Arby's, Baskin-Robbins/Dunkin Donuts, Biggby Coffee, Burger King, Little Caesar's, Pizza Hut, Rainbow Grill, Russ' Rest., Subway, Wendy's 🛏 Best Western, Holiday Inn Express ⊙ USPO
67	44th St, N 📇 Mobil/dsl 🍴 Burger King, Cracker Barrel, Panera Bread, Steak'n Shake 🛏 Comfort Suites ⊙ Honda, Walmart/auto, S 0-2 mi 🍴 Famous Dave's, IHOP, Jimmy John's, Logan's Roadhouse, Max&Erma's, Qdoba, Quizno's, Starbucks, Subway, TX Roadhouse, Wendy's 🛏 Residence Inn ⊙ $Tree, Best Buy, Chrysler/Dodge/Jeep, Costco/gas, Dick's, Discount Tire, Fresh Mkt Foods, Gander Mtn., Hobby Lobby, Home Depot, JC Penney, Kohl's, Lowe's, Macy's, Marshall's, Michael's, Old Navy, Petsmart, Sear/auto, World Mkt
64	MI 6 E, to Lansing (exits left from wb)
62	32nd Ave, to Hudsonville, N 📇 BP/dsl/24hr, Citgo/dsl 🍴 Arby's, Burger King, Hudsonville Grill, Little Caesar's, McDonald's 🛏 Quality Inn ⊙ camping, Chevrolet, S 📇 Mobil/Subway/dsl/24hr 🍴 Rainbow Grill 🛏 Super 8 ⊙ Harley-Davidson, Harvest Foods
58mm	📇 eb, full 🚻 facilities, litter barrels, petwalk, 🔌, 🐾, vending
55	Byron Rd, Zeeland, N 📇 7-11 🍴 Blimpie, McDonald's ⊙ H to Holland SP
52	16th St, Adams St, N 2 mi 🍴 Wendy's 🛏 EconoLodge ⊙ H Meijer/dsl/e-85, S 📇 Mobil/Subway/dsl 🍴 Burger King
49	MI 40, to Allegan, N 📇 BP/McDonald's/dsl 🛏 Residence Inn, S 📇 Tulip City/Marathon/Subway/dsl/scales/24hr 🍴 Rock Island Rest. ⊙ truck repair, truck wash
44	US 31 N (from eb), to Holland, N 3-5 mi 🛏 Country Inn ⊙ H food, gas
43mm	📇 wb, full 🚻 facilities, info, litter barrels, petwalk, 🔌, 🐾, vending
41	rd A-2, Douglas, Saugatuck, N 📇 Marathon/dsl, Shell/Subway/dsl 🍴 Burger King, Spectators Grill 🛏 Best Western (1mi), Timberline Motel (3mi) ⊙ $General, NAPA, to Saugatuck SP, S 🍴 Belvedere Inn ⊙ Red Barn Gifts
38mm	Kalamazoo River
36	rd A-2, Ganges, N 📇 Shell 🍴 Christo's Rest., Kalico Kitchen 🛏 AmericInn

34	MI 89, to Fennville, N ⊙ to West Side CP, S 📇 Shell/24hr ⊙ Cranes Pie Pantry (4mi, Lyons Fruits, seasonal), Winery Tours
30	rd A-2, Glenn, Ganges, N ⊙ to Westside CP (4mi)
28mm	📇 eb, full 🚻 facilities, litter barrels, petwalk, 🔌, 🐾, vending
26	109th Ave, to Pullman, ⊙ Dutch Farm Mkt
22	N Shore Dr, N ⊙ Cousin's RV Camping/rest., to Kal Haven Trail SP
20	rd A-2, Phoenix Rd, N 📇 BP/dsl, Marathon/dsl 🍴 Arby's, China Buffet, Taco Bell ⊙ H, $Tree, AutoZone, st police, Walgreens, S 📇 Murphy USA/dsl, Shell/dsl 🍴 Big Boy, McDonald's, Sherman's Dairybar, Wendy's 🛏 Comfort Suites, Hampton Inn, Holiday Inn Express, Ramada ⊙ $General, Menards, Walmart
18	MI 140, MI 43, to Watervliet, N 0-2 mi 📇 BP/dsl, Shell/dsl/24hr, Xpress/dsl 🍴 50's Drive Inn, Burger King, Hungry Howie's, Little Caesar's, McDonald's, Pizza Hut, Willy O's Pizza 🛏 Great Lakes Inn, LakeBluff Motel ⊙ auto repair, AutoValue Parts, Buick/Cadillac/GMC, Chevrolet, Chrysler/Dodge/Jeep, Ford/Lincoln, st police, Village Mkt Foods, S 7 mi ⊙ KOA (Apr-Oct)
13	to Covert, N ⊙ RV camping, to Van Buren SP
7	MI 63, to Benton Harbor, N 🍴 DiMaggio's Pizza, Vitale's Mkt/subs ⊙ RV camping
4	to Coloma, Riverside, S 📇 Marathon/dsl ⊙ KOA (Apr-Oct)
2mm	Paw Paw River
1	Red Arrow Hwy, N ⊙ SW Michigan ⊙
0mm	I-94, E to Detroit, W to Chicago

I-196 begins/ends on I-94, exit 34 at Benton Harbor.

INTERSTATE 275 (Livonia)

Exit #	Services
	I-275 and I-96 run together 9 miles. See Michigan I-96, exits 165-170
29	I-96 E, to Detroit, MI 14 W, to Ann Arbor
28	Ann Arbor Rd, Plymouth, E 📇 BP/Dunkin Donuts, Mobil, Shell 🍴 Denny's, Little Caesars, McDonald's 🛏 Red Roof Inn ⊙ $Tree, Verizon, W 🍴 Burger King, Firehouse Subs, Grand Traverse Pie Co., McDonald's 🛏 Comfort Inn ⊙ Cadillac, CVS Drug, K-Mart, Lincoln, vet
25	MI 153, Ford Rd, Garden City, W 📇 BP, Shell, Speedway, Valero 🍴 5 Guys Burgers, Applebee's, Arby's, BD Mongolian BBQ, Bob Evans, Boston Mkt., Buffalo Wild Wings, Carrabba's, Chili's, ChuckeCheese, Coney Island, Dunkin Donuts/Baskin-Robbins, KFC, Olga's Kitchen, Outback Steaks, Panera Bread, Potbelly, Quiznos, Roman Forum Rest., Subway, TGIFriday's, Tim Horton, Wendy's, White Castle/Church's

🔳 = gas   🍴 = food   🏠 = lodging   🔲 = other   ℞ = rest stop   Copyright 2015 - the Next EXIT ®

MI

L I V O N I A

⬆N INTERSTATE 275 (Livonia) Cont'd

Exit #	Services
25	Continued
	🏠 Best Value Inn, Comfort Suites, Extended Stay America, Fairfield Inn, Hampton Inn, La Quinta 🔲 Advance Parts, Aldi Foods, AT&T, Discount Tire, Firestone/auto, Hobby Lobby, JC Penney, Kohl's, Lowe's, Midas, PetCo, Richardson Drug, Target, URGENT CARE, Verizon, vet, Walgreens
23	℞ nb, full 🚻 facilities, info, litter barrels, 🛢, 🎣
22	US 12, Michigan Ave, to Wayne, E 🔳 BP/dsl, Shell, Valero/dsl 🍴 Arby's, Jonathan's Rest., McDonald's, Quiznos, Subway, Wendy's 🏠 Days Inn, Fellows Cr Motel, Holiday Inn Express, Super 8, Willo Acres Motel, W 🔳 Marathon/dsl 🍴 Jimmy John's 🔲 Kia, Nissan, URGENT CARE
20	Ecorse Rd, to Romulus, E 🔳 7-11, W 🔳 Mobil/Burger King/scales/dsl/24hr
17	I-94 E to Detroit, W to Ann Arbor, E 🔲 🎣
15	Eureka Rd, E 🔳 🎣, Shell
13	Sibley Rd, New Boston, W 🔳 Fusion/Subway/dsl 🍴 LC's Chicken 🔲 to Lower Huron Metro Park
11	S Huron Rd, W 1 mi 🔳 Sunoco/Burger King/dsl 🍴 Jacob's Rest 🔲 RV LP (1mi)
8	Will Carleton Rd, to Flat Rock
5	Carleton, South Rockwood, W 🍴 food
4mm	℞ sb, full 🚻 facilities, litter barrels, 🛢, 🎣
2	US 24, to Telegraph Rd, W 🏠 lodging, Marathon/dsl
0mm	I-275 begins/ends on I-75, exit 20.

⬆N INTERSTATE 475 (Flint)

F L I N T

Exit #	Services
17mm	I-475 begins/ends on I-75, exit 125.
15	Clio Rd, W 🔳 BP 🔲 Chevrolet
13	Saginaw St, E 🔳 BP 🍴 McDonald's, Taco Bell 🔲 Advanced Parts, Family$, Kroger/gas, W 🔳 Marathon 🍴 Burger King, KFC, Little Caesars
11	Carpenter Rd
10	Pierson Rd
9	rd 54, Dort Hwy, Stewart Ave, E 🔳 Citgo 🔲 McDonald's
8mm	Flint River
8b	Davison Rd, Hamilton Ave
8a	Longway Blvd, W 🏠 Holiday Inn Express 🔲 🅗, farmers mkt, USPO
7	rd 21, Court St, downtown Flint
6	I-69, W to Lansing, E to Port Huron
5	Atherton Rd (from sb), E 🔳 Marathon/dsl
4	Hemphill Rd, Bristol Rd, E 🔳 Speedway/dsl 🍴 Rally's, Subway 🔲 Rite Aid, W 🔳 Speedway/dsl 🍴 Little Caesars, Tim Horton/Wendy's 🔲 Family$, Kroger/dsl, vet
2	Hill Rd, E 🔳 Speedway 🍴 Applebee's, Bob Evans 🏠 Wingate Inn 🔲 vet, W 🔳 Mobil/Tim Horton, Speedway/dsl 🍴 Arby's, Bangkok Peppers, Blimpie, Burger King, Burger St Grill, Little Caesars, McDonald's, Wendy's 🔲 Rite Aid
0mm	I-475 begins/ends on I-75, exit 111.

⬆E INTERSTATE 696 (Detroit)

Exit #	Services
	I-696 begins/ends on I-94.
28	I-94 E to Port Huron, W to Detroit, 11 Mile Rd, E 🔳 7-11, BP/dsl, Speedway

D E T R O I T

27	MI 3, Gratiot Ave, N 🔳 BP, Valero 🍴 Checkers, McDonald's, National Coney Island, Tubby's Subs 🔲 7-11, Costco/gas, S 🔳 Marathon, Mobil/McDonald's, Shell 🍴 8 China Buffet, Bigby Coffee, DQ, Subway, White Castle 🔲 GNC, Goodyear/auto, K-Mart, Kroger/gas, Radio Shack, Rite Aid, Sav-A-Lot Foods
26	MI 97, Groesbeck Ave, Roseville, N 🔳 Shell/dsl S 🍴 Omega Grill
24	Hoover Rd, Schoenherr Rd, N 🔳 BP 🍴 Burger King, KFC, S 🔳 BP, Mobil 🍴 Boston Mkt, Carlito's Pizza, Del Taco, Doc's Rest., Pizza Hut, Quizno's, Red Lobster, Subway, Taco Bell, Tim Horton 🏠 Holiday Inn Express 🔲 $Tree, Curves, CVS Drug, GNC, Home Depot, Kroger, Marshall's
23	MI 53, Van Dyke Ave, N 🔳 BP, Mobil/dsl 🍴 Angelo's Rest., Arby's, Baskin-Robbins/Dunkin Donuts, Juliano's Rest., McDonald's 🔲 $General, Cadillac, Dodge, Scion/Toyota, S 🔳 Citgo 🍴 Luca's Coney Island 🔲 Chevrolet, Discount Tire, Ford, Rite Aid, USPO, vet
22	Mound Rd, N 🔳 BP/Burger King
20	Ryan Rd, Dequindre Rd, N 🔳 7-11, BP, Citgo, Marathon, Shell 🍴 Azteca Mexican, Ponderosa 🏠 Knights Inn, Red Roof Inn 🔲 BigLots, vet, S 🍴 Bob Evans, Chicken Shack, Church's, LA Coney Island, McDonald's 🏠 Best Value Inn, Comfort Suites 🔲 Rite Aid, Sears, transmissions
19	Couzens St, 10 Mile Rd, S 🔲 Hazel Park Racetrack
18	I-75 N to Flint, S to Detroit
17	Campbell Ave, Hilton Ave, Bermuda, Mohawk, S 🔳 Marathon/dsl
16	MI 1, Woodward Ave, Main St, N 🔲 zoo, S 🔳 Sunoco
14	Coolidge Rd, 10 Mile Rd, S 🔳 Speedway 🍴 Hungry Howie's, Jade Palace Chinese, Little Caesar's, Subway 🔲 CVS Drug, Farm Fresh Foods
13	Greenfield Rd, N 🔳 Marathon, Mobil 🍴 Church's, L George Coney Island, McDonald's, Ponderosa, Popeye's, White Castle 🔲 Aldi Foods, Family$, K-Mart, Sav-A-Lot Foods, S 🔳 Mobil, Sunoco 🍴 Baskin-Robbins/Dunkin Donuts, Front Page Deli, Pita Cafe, Starbucks 🔲 Rite Aid
12	MI 39, Southfield Rd, 11 Mile Rd, N 🔲 Discount Tire, S 🔳 Shell 🍴 Happy's Pizza 🔲 AT&T
11	Evergreen Rd, S 🏠 Hawthorn Suites
10	US 24, Telegraph Rd, N 🔳 Marathon, Mobil, Sunoco 🍴 5 Guys Burgers, Baja Fresh, Copper Canyon Rest., Denny's, Fat Burger, Pottbelly, Quizno's, Starbucks, Wendy's 🏠 Embassy Suites, Hampton Inn, Red Roof Inn 🔲 AT&T, Belle Tire, Best Buy, Buick/GMC, Chrysler/Dodge/Jeep, Ford, Honda, Hyundai, Lexus, Lincoln, Lowe's, mall, Meijer/dsl, Michael's, Nissan, Office Depot, Petsmart, Subaru, Verizon, S 🔳 Mobil, Sunoco 🍴 Big Boy, Kerry's Koney Island 🏠 Best Western, Candlewood Suites, Courtyard, Holiday Resort Hotel, Marriott
8	MI 10, Lodge Fwy
7	American Dr (from eb), S 🏠 Extended Stay America, Hilton Garden
5	Orchard Lake Rd, Farmington Hills, N 🔳 Marathon, Mobil/dsl, Shell 🍴 Arby's, Camelia's Mexican, Coney Island, Hong Hua Chinese, Jet's Pizza, Jimmy John's, Roberto's Rest., Ruby Tuesday, Starbucks, Steak&Tavern, Subway, Wendy's 🏠 Comfort Inn, Courtyard, Extended Stay America, Fairfield Inn 🔲 Discount Tire, to St Mary's Coll
1	(from wb), I-96 W, I-275 S, to MI 5, Grand River Ave

INTERSTATE 35

Exit #	Services

I-35 begins/ends on MN 61 in Duluth.

259 MN 61, London Rd, to Two Harbors, North Shore, **W** 🅖 BP, Holiday/dsl, ICO/dsl 🍴 Blackwoods Grill, Burger King, Dunn Bros Coffee, KFC, McDonald's, Perkins, Pizza Hut, Subway, Taco John's, Wendy's 🛏 Edgewater Inn 🅞 vet

258 21st Ave E (from nb), to U of MN at Duluth, same as 259

256b Mesaba Ave, Superior St, **E** 🅖 ICO/DQ 🍴 Bellicio's, Caribou Coffee, Famous Dave's BBQ, Grandma's Grill, Greenmill Rest., Grizzly's, Little Angie's Cantina, Old Chicago, Red Lobster, Smokehouse Rest., Subway, Timberlodge Steaks 🛏 Canal Park Lodge, Comfort Suites, Hampton Inn, Hawthorn Suites, Inn at Lake Superior, Suites Motel, The Inn, **W** 🛏 Holiday Inn, Radisson, Sheraton

256a Michigan St, **E** 🅞 waterfront, **W** 🅞 🅷, downtown

255a US 53 N (exits left from nb), **W** 🅞 Auto Value Parts, Kia, 🅞 mall, downtown

255b I-535 spur, to Wisconsin

254 27th Ave W, **W** 🅖 Holiday/Burger King/dsl, Spur/dsl 🍴 Duluth Grill, Little Caesars, Quiznos, Subway 🛏 Motel 6 🅞 USPO

253b 40th Ave W, **W** 🅖 BP/dsl/24hr 🍴 Perkins 🛏 Comfort Inn, Super 8

253a US 2 E, US 53, to Wisconsin

252 Central Ave, W Duluth, **W** 🅖 Holiday/dsl, Little Store/dsl 🍴 China King Buffet, Domino's, Jade Fountain Rest., KFC, McDonald's, Mr D's Grill, Pizza Hut, Sammy's Café, Subway, Taco John's 🅞 $Tree, Advance Parts, K-Mart, Menards, O'Reilly Parts, Save-a-Lot Foods, Super 1 Foods, vet, Walgreens

251b MN 23 S, Grand Ave

251a Cody St, **E** 🛏 Allyndale Motel 🅞 zoo

250 US 2 W (from sb), to Grand Rapids, **W** 1/2 mi 🅖 Holiday/dsl, Mobil/dsl/LP 🍴 Blackwoods Grill 🛏 AmericInn

249 Boundary Ave, Skyline Pkwy, **E** 🅖 Holiday/McDonald's/dsl 🛏 Country Inn&Suites 🅞 to ski area, to Spirit Mtn RA, **W** 🆁🆂 both lanes, full 🅑 facilities, info, litter barrels, 🅒, 🅐, vending 🅖 Little Store/dsl/E-85/24hr 🍴 Blackwoods Grill 🛏 AmericInn, Best Value Inn

246 rd 13, Midway Rd, Nopeming, **W** 🅖 Armor/dsl 🍴 Dry Dock Rest.

245 rd 61, **E** 🍴 Buffalo House Rest./camping

242 rd 1, Esko, Thomson, **E** 🅖 BP/dsl

239.5mm St Louis River

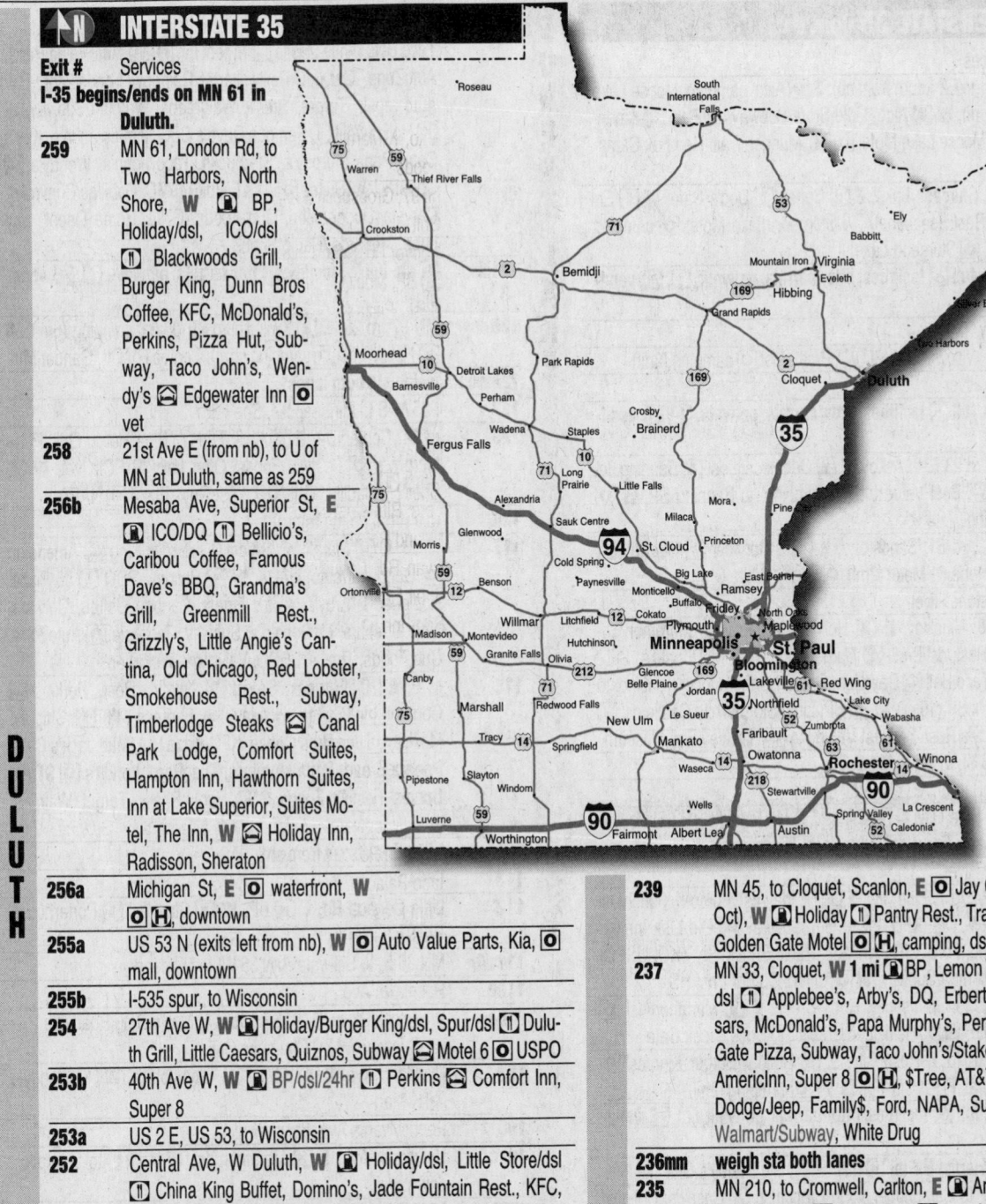

239 MN 45, to Cloquet, Scanlon, **E** 🅞 Jay Cooke SP, KOA (May-Oct), **W** 🅖 Holiday 🍴 Pantry Rest., Trapper Pete's Steaks 🛏 Golden Gate Motel 🅞 🅷, camping, dsl repair

237 MN 33, Cloquet, **W** 1 mi 🅖 BP, Lemon Tree/dsl, Murphy USA/dsl 🍴 Applebee's, Arby's, DQ, Erbert&Gerberts, Little Caesars, McDonald's, Papa Murphy's, Perkins, Pizza Hut, South Gate Pizza, Subway, Taco John's/Stake Escape, Wendy's 🛏 AmericInn, Super 8 🅞 🅷, $Tree, AT&T, AutoZone, Chrysler/Dodge/Jeep, Family$, Ford, NAPA, Super 1 Foods, Verizon, Walmart/Subway, White Drug

236mm weigh sta both lanes

235 MN 210, to Cromwell, Carlton, **E** 🅖 Armor Fuel, BP/rest./dsl, Spur/dsl/24hr 🍴 Spirits Rest 🛏 AmericInn, Royal Pines Motel 🅞 to Jay Cooke SP, **W** 🅞 Black Bear Casino/Hotel/rest.

235mm Big Otter Creek

233mm Little Otter Creek

227 rd 4, Mahtowa, **E** 🅞 camping, **W** 🅞 TJ's Country Store/gas (2 mi)

226mm 🆁🆂 nb, full 🅑 facilities, litter barrels, petwalk, 🅒, 🅐, vending

220 rd 6, Barnum, **E** 🅞 camping, **W** 🅖 BP/café/dsl/24hr 🍴 Lazy Bear Rest. 🛏 Northwoods Motel 🅞 Munger Tr

219mm Moose Horn River

218mm Moose Horn River

216 MN 27 (from sb, no EZ return), Moose Lake, **W** 1-2 mi 🅖 BP, Cenex/dsl, Holiday/dsl, Little Store (4mi), Rebel 🍴 Art's Café, DQ, Lazy Moose Grille, Poor Gary's Pizza 🛏 AmericInn (4mi), Moose Lake Motel 🅞 🅷, 1918 Museum, Ace Hardware, AutoValue Parts, Ford, Mkt Place Foods, O'Reilly Parts, repair, to Munger Trail, vet

MN

⬆N INTERSTATE 35 Cont'd

Exit #	Services
214	rd 73 (no EZ return from nb), **E** ⊙ Alco, camping, Moose Lake SP (2mi), **W** ⛽ Alco, Little Store/Subway/dsl/E-85 🏠 AmericInn, Moose Lake Motel ⊙ 🅷, Munger Trail, Red Fox Camping
209	rd 46, Sturgeon Lake, **E** ⛽ Cenex 🍴 Doc's Cafe, **W** 🍴 Ernie's Rest. (seasonal) 🏠 Sturgeon Lake Motel ⊙ camping (3mi), ⊙ Sturgeon Lake
209mm	🅁🅂 **sb, full** ♿ **facilities, litter barrels, petwalk,** 🚽, 🛈, **vending**
206.5mm	Willow River
205	rd 43, Willow River, **W** ⛽ BP/cafe/dsl ⊙ camping (2mi)
198.5mm	Kettle River
198mm	🅁🅂 **nb, full** ♿ **facilities, litter barrels, petwalk,** 🚽, 🛈, **vending**
195	rd 18, rd 23 E, to Askov, **E** ⛽ Cenex/cafe/dsl 🍴 Banning Jct Cafe 🏠 Best Value Inn ⊙ camping, to Banning SP, **W** ⊙ camping
191	MN 23, rd 61, Sandstone, **E** ⛽ Victory/dsl 🍴 Subway 🏠 Sandstone 61 Motel (2mi) ⊙ Thrifty White Drug
184mm	Grindstone River
183	MN 48, Hinckley, **E** ⛽ Holiday/Hardee's/dsl, Marathon/Tobie's Rest./dsl/E-85 🍴 Burger King, DQ, McDonald's, Subway, Taco Bell 🏠 Days Inn, Grand Northern Inn ⊙ casino, to St Croix SP (15mi), **W** ⛽ BP, Little Store/White Castle/dsl 🍴 Cassidy's Rest. 🏠 Best Value Inn ⊙ Hinckley Fire Museum
180	MN 23 W, rd 61, to Mora
175	rd 14, Beroun, **E** ⛽ Marathon/dsl
171	rd 11, Pine City, **E** ⛽ SA/dsl 🍴 McDonald's ⊙ $Stuff, Ace Hardware, Chrysler/Dodge/Jeep, **W** ⊙ camping
170mm	Snake River
169	MN 324, rd 7, Pine City, **E** ⛽ Holiday/dsl, Pump-n-Munch/dsl 🍴 A&W, DQ, KFC, Pizza Hut, Subway 🏠 Old Oak Inn ⊙ camping, Ford, O'Reilly Parts, Radio Shack, ShopKO, USPO, vet, Walmart/Subway, **W** ⊙ to NW Co Fur Post HS
165	MN 70, to Grantsburg, Rock Creek, **E** ⛽ Marathon/dsl ⊙ camping, **W** ⛽ Heidelbergers/dsl 🍴 Rock Creek Cafe
159	MN 361, rd 1, Rush City, **E** ⛽ Holiday/Burger King/dsl ⊙ $General, Rush City Foods, **W** ⊙ camping (2mi)
154mm	🅁🅂 **nb, full** ♿ **facilities, litter barrels, petwalk,** 🚽, 🛈, **vending**
152	rd 10, Harris, **E 1 mi** ⛽ gas/dsl 🍴 Big Daddy's Grill
147	MN 95, to Cambridge, North Branch, **E** ⛽ Casey's, Holiday/dsl, Marathon/dsl 🍴 China Taste, Domino's, DQ, KFC/Taco Bell, McDonald's, Oak Inn Rest, Perkins, Pizza Hut, Subway 🏠 AmericInn, Budget Host ⊙ Fisk Tire, NAPA, O'Reilly Parts, to Wild River SP (14mi), vet, **W** ⛽ Holiday/dsl/E-85 🍴 Burger King, Denny's, Papa Murphy's ⊙ County Mkt Foods, Ford, North Branch Outlets/famous brands, ShopKO, USPO, Verizon
143	rd 17, **E** ⛽ Tesoro/dsl
139	rd 19, Stacy, **E** ⛽ Gas+ 🍴 Rustic Inn Rest., Stacy Grill, Subway ⊙ city park, **W** ⛽ Shell ⊙ A-1 Tires
135	US 61 S, rd 22, Wyoming, **E** ⛽ BP/dsl, Casey's 🍴 DQ, Linwood Pizza, Subway, Tasty Asia ⊙ 🅷, Ace Hardware, CarQuest, WY Drug, **W** ⛽ Shell/dsl 🍴 McDonald's, Village Inn Rest. ⊙ camping (10mi), golf, vet
132	US 8 (from nb), to Taylors Falls
131	rd 2, Forest Lake, **E** ⛽ BP, Holiday/dsl, SA/dsl 🍴 Applebee's, Arby's, Burger King, Chueng Sing Chinese, Culvers, KFC, McDonald's, Papa John's, Perkins, Quack's Cafe, Subway,

F O R E S T   L A K E

131	Continued Taco Bell, White Castle 🏠 AmericInn ⊙ 🅷, AutoValue Parts, AutoZone, CarX, O'Reilly Parts, Rainbow Foods/24hr, RV/Auto repair, Target, Tires+, Walgreens, Walmart/Subway, **W** ⛽ Holiday/dsl 🍴 Famous Dave's BBQ, Jimmy John's, Key's Cafe, Papa Murphy's, Starbucks, Taco John's, Wendy's 🏠 Country Inn&Suites ⊙ AT&T, Buick/GMC, Cadillac/Chevrolet, Chrysler/Dodge/Jeep, Cub Foods, GNC, Home Depot, Jiffy Lube, Menards, Radio Shack
131mm	🅁🅂 **sb, full** ♿ **facilities, litter barrels, petwalk,** 🚽, 🛈, **vending**
129	MN 97, rd 23, **E** ⛽ Kwik Trip/dsl/E-85 ⊙ camping (6mi), **W** ⛽ Holiday/dsl ⊙ camping (1mi), Coates RV Ctr, Gander Mtn.
128mm	**weigh sta both lanes**
127	I-35W, S to Minneapolis. See I-35W.
123	rd 14, Centerville, **E** ⛽ Kwik Trip 🍴 Blue Heron Grill, Papa Murphy's ⊙ Festival Foods, Otter Lake RV Ctr, vet, **W** ⛽ Shell 🍴 Cadillac Grill, DQ, WiseGuys Pizza ⊙ NAPA
120	rd J (from nb, no return)
117	rd 96, **E** ⛽ Marathon, SA/dsl 🍴 Burger King 🏠 AmericInn ⊙ Goodyear/auto, NAPA, **W** ⛽ Holiday, PDQ 🍴 $5 Pizza, Applebee's, Arby's, Asia's Finest, Caribou Coffee, Culver's, Little Caesars, McDonald's, Subway, Zen Asia ⊙ AutoZone, Cub Foods, Tires+, USPO, Valvoline, Walgreens
115	rd E, **E** ⛽ BP/repair, SA/dsl 🍴 Jimmy's Rest., Perkins 🏠 Country Inn&Suites, Holiday Inn Express, **W** 🍴 Chipotle Mexican, Dunn Bros Coffee, KFC/Pizza Hut, Mad Jack's Cafe, Panera Bread, Papa Murphy's, Thai Pan, Wendy's ⊙ $Tree, Curves, Festival Foods, GNC, Radio Shack, Target, Walmart/auto
114	I-694 E (exits left from sb)
113	I-694 W
112	Little Canada Rd, **E** ⛽ BP, **W** ⛽ Clark/dsl 🍴 Porterhouse Rest
111a/b	MN 36 E, to Stillwater/MN 36 W, to Minneapolis
110b	Roselawn Ave
110a	Wheelock Pkwy, **E** ⛽ BP, Gulf 🍴 May's Deli, Roadside Pizza, Subway, **W** 🍴 Champps Grill
109	Maryland Ave, **E** ⛽ SA/dsl 🍴 Taco John's, **W** 🍴 Wendy's ⊙ K-Mart
108	Pennsylvania Ave, downtown
107c	University Ave, **E** ⛽ Marathon/dsl, **W** ⊙ 🅷, to st capitol, downtown
107b a	I-94, W to Minneapolis, E to St Paul.
	I-35 and I-94 run together.
106c	11th St (from nb), Marion St, downtown
106b	Kellogg Blvd (from nb), **E** 🍴 Eagle St. Grill, Subway 🏠 Holiday Inn ⊙ 🅷, downtown
106a	Grand Ave, **E** ⊙ 🅷
105	St Clair Ave
104c	Victoria St, Jefferson Ave
104b	Ayd Mill Rd (from nb)
104a	Randolph Ave
103b	MN 5, W 7th St, **E** 🍴 Burger King, **W** ⛽ SA/dsl ⊙ Midas, USPO
103a	Shepard Rd (from nb)
102mm	Mississippi River
102	MN 13, Sibley Hwy, **W** ⛽ BP, Holiday/Subway
101b a	MN 110 W, **E** ⛽ BP 🍴 Caribou Coffee, McDonald's, Subway, Teresa's Mexican ⊙ Tuesday Morning, **W** ⛽ SA
99b a	I-494 W/I-494 E

S T   P A U L

H I N C K L E Y

INTERSTATE 35 Cont'd

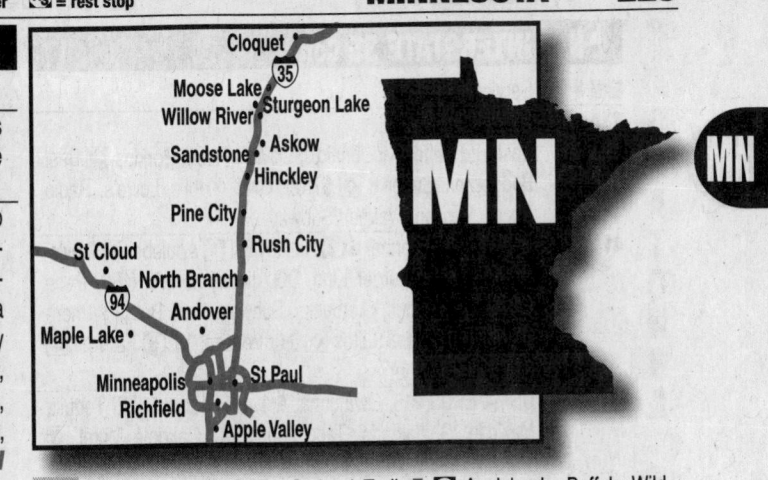

Exit #	Services
98	Lone Oak Rd, E 🅖 Homestead Suites, Microtel 🅞 Sam's Club/gas, USPO, W 🍴 Joe Senser's Grill, Magic Thai Café 🏠 Hampton Inn, Residence Inn 🅞 Lone Oak Mkt/gas
97b	Yankee Doodle Rd, E 🍴 Applebee's, Arby's, Buffalo Wild Wings, Burger King, Coldstone, Culver's, DQ, Houlihan's, Jake's Grill, Jimmy John's, KFC, New China Buffet, Noodles&Co, Old Chicago Pizza, Panera Bread, Papa Murphy's, Perkins, Pizza Hut, Pizza Man, Pot Bellys, Savoy Pizza, Taco Bell 🅞 AT&T, Barnes&Noble, Best Buy, BigLots, Byerly's Foods, Firestone, Goodyear, Home Depot, Kohl's, Michael's, Office Depot, Old Navy, Petsmart, Radio Shack, Rainbow Foods, TJ Maxx, Walgreens, Walmart/Subway, W 🅖 BP/dsl, SA/dsl 🍴 Al Baker's Rest., Dragon Palace Chinese, El Loro Mexican, Starbucks 🏠 Best Western, Extended Stay America 🅞 NAPA, Superior Auto
97a	Pilot Knob Rd, E 🅖 Holiday, SA 🍴 Chili's, McDonald's, Wendy's 🏠 SpringHill Suites, TownePlace Suites 🅞 Excel Repair, Kohl's, Tires+, W 🅖 BP, SA/dsl 🏠 Best Western, same as 97b
94	rd 30, Diffley Rd, to Eagan, E 🅖 Holiday/dsl 🅞 CVS Drug, Kowalski's Mkt/Starbucks, W 🅖 Sinclair/Goodyear
93	rd 32, Cliff Rd, E 🅖 Holiday 🍴 Bonfire Grill, Subway 🅞 Ace Hardware, W 🅖 Holiday/dsl 🍴 Burger King, Caribou Coffee, Caspers's Rest., Chipotle Mexican, Dolittle's Grill, DQ, Hong Wong Chinese, KFC, Leeann Chin's, McDonald's, Pizza Hut, Quiznos, Starbucks, Taco Bell, Wendy's 🏠 Hilton Garden, Holiday Inn Express, Staybridge Suites 🅞 Cub Foods, O'Reilly Parts, Target, USPO, Walgreens
92	MN 77, Cedar Ave, E 🅞 Zoo, W 1 mi access to Cliff Rd services
90	rd 11, E 🅖 KwikTrip 🍴 Subway 🅞 Valley Natural Foods, W 🅖 SA/dsl
88b	rd 42, Crystal Lake Rd, E 🅖 SA/dsl 🍴 Caribou Coffee, Chianti Grill 🅞 Byerly's Foods, Petsmart, Tuesday Morning, W 🅖 BP, Holiday/dsl, PDQ, SA/dsl 🍴 Applebee's, Arby's, Buca Italian, Burger Jones, Burger King, Cam Ranh Bay, Champp's Grill, Chipotle Mexican, Ernie's Grill, HoneyBaked Ham, IHOP, Jimmy John's, KFC, Kings Buffet, Little Caesars, Macaroni Grill, McDonald's, Noodles&Co, Old Country Buffet, Olive Garden, Outback Steaks, Panera Bread, Papa John's, Papa Murphy's, Porter Creek Grill, Red Lobster, Roasted Pear, Taco Bell, TGIFriday's, Wendy's 🏠 Best Western, Days Inn, Fairfield Inn, Hampton Inn, InTown Suites 🅞 🄷 Ace Hardware, AT&T, Barnes&Noble, Cadillac, Chevrolet, Cotco/gas, Cub Foods, Dick's, Discount Tire, Gordman's, Home Depot, JC Penney, K-Mart, Kohl's, Macy's, mall, Michael's, Office Depot, Old Navy, PetCo, Rainbow Foods, Sears/auto, Target, Tires+, TJ Maxx, USPO, Verizon, VW, Walgreens
88a	I-35W (from nb), N to Minneapolis. See I-35W.
87	Crystal Lake Rd (from nb), W 🅞 Honda/Nissan, Mazda, to Beaver Mtn ski area, Toyota/Scion
86	rd 46, E 🅖 KwikTrip, SA/dsl 🍴 KFC, Starbucks 🅞 Harley-Davidson, W 🅞 auto repair, O'Reilly Parts
85	MN 50, E 🅖 F&F/dsl, SA/dsl 🍴 Burger King, Caribou Coffee, Culver's, DQ, Greenmill Rest., Jimmy John's, Lakeville Chinese, Pizza Hut, Starbucks, Subway, Taco Bell, Wendy's 🏠 Comfort Inn 🅞 $Tree, CVS Drug, Goodyear/auto, NTB, O'Reilly Parts, Rainbow Foods, Verizon, Walgreens, W 🅖 Holiday/dsl 🍴 Cracker Barrel, Perkins, Pizza Ranch 🏠 AmericInn 🅞 Gander Mtn.
84	185th St W, Orchard Trail, E 🍴 Applebee's, Buffalo Wild Wings, Caribou Coffee, Quiznos, SawaJapan 🅞 Best Buy, Marshall's, Target
81	rd 70, Lakeville, E 🅖 Holiday/dsl 🍴 Baldy's BBQ, McDonald's, Subway, Tacoville 🏠 Holiday Inn/rest, Motel 6, W 🍴 Harry's Cafe 🅞 Walmart/Subway
76	rd 2, Elko, E 🅖 gas/dsl, W 🍴 Endzone Grill 🅞 Elko Speedway
76mm	🆁🆂 sb, full 🚻 facilities, litter barrels, petwalk, 🅒, 🎁, vending
69	MN 19, to Northfield, New Prague, E 7 mi 🅖 KwikTrip 🍴 Applebee's, Big Steer Rest., Caribou Coffee, McDonald's, Quarterback Rest., Subway, Taco Bell 🏠 AmericInn, College City Motel, Country Inn&Suites, Super 8 🅞 🄷 Carleton Coll, St Olaf Coll, W 🅖 🄵 FLYING J/Subway/dsl/scales/24hr
68mm	🆁🆂 nb, full 🚻 facilities, litter barrels, petwalk, 🅒, 🎁, vending
66	rd 1, to Dundas, W 1 mi 🍴 Boonie's Grill
59	MN 21, Faribault, E 0-2 mi 🅖 BP/rest./dsl/scales/24hr, KwikTrip 🍴 A&W, Arby's, Burger King, DQ, Hardee's, Joe's Cafe, KFC, Pizza Hut, Taco Bell, Taco John's 🏠 AmericInn, Best Value Inn, Days Inn, Grandstay 🅞 Aldi Foods, AT&T, Buick/Chevrolet/GMC, Chrysler/Dodge/Jeep, O'Reilly Parts, repair, Satakah St Trail, vet, W 🅞 camping, Harley-Davidson
56	MN 60, Faribault, E 🅖 KwikTrip 🍴 A&W, Arby's, Burger King, Great China Buffet, Hardee's, Jimmy John's, KFC, Little Caesars, McDonald's, Perkins, Pizza Hut, Subway, Taco John's 🅞 🄷, $Tree, Aldi Foods, AutoValue Parts, Buick/Chevrolet/GMC, Chrysler/Dodge/Jeep, Curves, Dodge, Family$, Goodyear/auto, Hy-Vee Foods/gas, JC Penney, mall, O'Reilly Parts, Radio Shack, Tires+, TrueValue, Verizon, Walmart, W 🅖 Petro/dsl 🍴 Country Kitchen, DQ 🏠 Regency Inn 🅞 camping, Sakatah Lake SP, same as 59
55	rd 48, (from nb, no return), E 1 mi 🅖 KwikTrip, Mobil/dsl, SA/dsl 🍴 A&W, Arby's, Broaster Rest., Burger King, DQ, KFC, Pizza Hut, Southern China Cafe, Subway, Taco John's 🏠 AmericInn
48	rd 12, rd 23, Medford, W 🍴 McDonald's 🅞 Outlet Mall/famous brands
45	rd 9, Clinton Falls, W 🅖 KwikTrip/dsl 🍴 Caribou Coffee, Famous Dave's BBQ, Sportsman's Grille, Subway, TimberLodge Steaks, Wendy's 🏠 Comfort Inn, Holiday Inn 🅞 Cabela's Sporting Goods, museum, Russell-Stover Candies
43	rd 34, 26th St, Owatonna, E 🅞 Noble RV Ctr, W 🅞 🄷
42b a	US 14 W, rd 45, to Waseca, Owatonna, E 🍴 Kernel Rest. 🏠 Budget Host 🅞 AutoZone, CashWise Foods, Chrysler/Dodge/Jeep, Ford/Lincoln, O'Reilly Parts, repair, vet, W 🅖 KwikTrip/dsl 🍴 Big 10 Rest., Buffalo Wild Wings, Culver's,

*(vertical label at left of second column:)* FARIBAULT

MN

O W A T O N N A

A L B E R T   L E A

⬆N INTERSTATE 35 Cont'd

Exit #	Services
42b a	Continued Eastwind Buffet, McDonald's, Olivia's Rest., Perkins ⊞ Best Budget Inn, Super 8 ⊡ $Tree, GNC, Kohl's, Lowe's, Radio Shack, Verizon, Walmart/Subway
41	Bridge St, Owatonna, E ⊞ Holiday/dsl ⊞ Applebee's, Arby's, Asian Kitchen, Burger King, DQ, Jimmy John's, KFC, Papa Murphy's, Quiznos, Starbucks, Subway, Taco Bell ⊞ AmericInn, Country Inn&Suites ⊡ H, Verizon, W ⊞ F&F/dsl ⊞ Microtel ⊡ Target
40	US 14 E, US 218, Owatonna, E 1 mi on rd 6 ⊞ El Tequila Mexican, Godfather's, Taco John's ⊞ Oakdale Motel ⊡ H Buick/Chevrolet, Curves, Hy-Vee Foods/dsl, Walgreens, WholesaleTire
38mm	Turtle Creek
35mm	⊞ both lanes, full ⊞ facilities, litter barrels, petwalk, ⊞, ⊞ vending
34.5mm	Straight River
32	rd 4, Hope, E 1/2 mi ⊡ camping, W 1 mi ⊞, ⊞
26	MN 30, to Blooming Prairie, Ellendale, E ⊞ Cenex/pizza/dsl
22	rd 35, to Hartland, Geneva, E 1 mi ⊞, ⊞
18	MN 251, to Hollandale, Clarks Grove, W ⊞ BP/dsl/LP ⊡ camping
17mm	weigh sta both lanes
13b a	I-90, W to Sioux Falls, E to Austin, W ⊡ H
12	US 65 S (from sb), Lp 35, Albert Lea, same as 11
11	rd 46, Albert Lea, E ⊞ ♥Loves/Wendy's/dsl/scales/24hr, TA/Coldstone/Pizza Hut/dsl/scales/24hr/@ ⊞ McDonald's ⊞ Comfort Inn, Holiday Inn Express ⊡ dsl repair, KOA (may-oct/6mi), W ⊞ KwikTrip, Shell/dsl ⊞ Big John's, Burger King, Casa Zamora Mexican, GreenMill Rest, KFC, Perkins, Pizza Hut, Subway, Taco John's, Trumble's Rest. ⊞ Best Value Inn, Country Inn&Suites, Countryside Inn, Knights Inn, Super 8 ⊡ H, $Tree, Advance Parts, AutoValue Parts, AutoZone, Buick/GMC, CarQuest, Chrysler/Dodge/Jeep, Ford, Home Depot, Honda, NAPA, Nissan/VW, O'Reilly Parts, Radio Shack, to Myre-Big Island SP, Volvo, Walmart/Subway
9mm	Albert Lea Lake
8	US 65, Lp 35US 65, Lp 35, Albert Lea, W 2 mi ⊞ Freeborn City Co-op/dsl ⊞ DQ, Hardee's
5	rd 13, to Glenville, Twin Lakes, W 3 mi ⊡ camping
2	rd 5
1mm	Welcome Ctr nb, full ⊞ facilities, litter barrels, petwalk, ⊞, ⊞, vending
0mm	Minnesota/Iowa state line

⬆N INTERSTATE 35 West

Exit #	Services
41mm	I-35W begins/ends on I-35, exit 127.
36	rd 23, E ⊞ Holiday/dsl ⊞ Country Inn&Suites, W ⊞ US/dsl ⊞ Caribou Coffee, DQ, McDonald's, Subway ⊞ Hampton Inn ⊡ Discount Tire, Kohl's, Super Target
33	rd 17, Lexington Ave, E 1 mi ⊞ F&F/dsl, Holiday ⊞ Burger King, McDonald's, W ⊞ Applebee's, Arby's, Bonfire Rest., Caribou Coffee, Green Mill Rest., Quizno's, Taco Bell/LJ Silver, Wendy's, Zantigo's Mexican ⊡ Cub Foods, GNC, Home Depot, Michael's, Radio Shack, Walgreens, Walmart
32	95th Ave NE, to Lexington, Circle Pines, W ⊡ Nat Sports Ctr
31b a	Lake Dr, E ⊞ Shell/dsl ⊞ Quizno's, Red Ginger Asian, Steamin Bean Coffee ⊞ Country Inn&Suites

M I N N E A P O L I S

30	US 10 W, MN 118, to MN 65
29	rd I
28c b	rd 10, rd H, W ⊞ BP ⊞ KFC, LJ Silver/Taco Bell, McDonald's, Mermaid Café, RJ Riches Rest. ⊞ AmericInn, Days Inn ⊡ carwash, NAPA
28a	MN 96
27b a	I-694 E and W
26	rd E2, W ⊞ Exxon/dsl ⊞ Jimmy John's, Limu Coffee
25b	MN 88, to Roseville (no EZ return to sb), same as 25a
25a	rd D (from nb), E ⊞ BP/dsl ⊞ Blimpie ⊞ Courtyard, Fairfield Inn, Residence Inn, W ⊞ PDQ, SA ⊞ Barley John's, Caribou Coffee, Jake's Café, McDonald's, New Hong Kong, Perkins/24hr, Sarpino's Italian, Subway
24	rd C, E ⊞ Burger King, India Palace Rest., Joe Senser's Rest. ⊞ Days Inn, Motel 6, Radisson ⊡ USPO, W ⊞ Holiday Inn Express ⊡ Chevrolet/GMC, Chrysler/Dodge/Jeep, Volvo
23b	Cleveland Ave, MN 36
23a	MN 280, Industrial Blvd (from sb)
22	MN 280, Industrial Blvd (from nb), E ⊞ Ramada Plaza
21b a	Broadway St, Stinson Blvd, E ⊡ Ford/Isuzu Trucks, W ⊞ Baja Sol, Burger King, Caribou Coffee, Cousins Subs, Leeann Chin, McDonald's, Pizza Hut/Taco Bell ⊡ GNC, Home Depot, Old Navy, Rainbow Foods/24hr, Target
19	E Hennepin (from nb)
18	US 52, 4th St SE, University Ave, to U of MN, E ⊞ BP/repair
17c	11th St, Washington Ave, E ⊞ Holiday Inn, W ⊞ Mobil ⊡ H , Goodyear, to Metrodome
17b	I-94 W (from sb)
17a	MN 55, Hiawatha
16b a	I-94 (from nb), E to St Paul, W to St Cloud, to MN 65
15	31st St (from nb), Lake St, E ⊞ McDonald's, Taco Bell ⊡ Auto Zone, W ⊡ H
14	35th St, 36th St
13	46th St
13mm	Minnehaha Creek
12b	Diamond Lake Rd
12a	60th St (from sb), W ⊞ Mobil ⊡ Cub Foods
11b	MN 62 E, to ⊞, ⊡ to ⊞
11a	Lyndale Ave (from sb)
10b	MN 62 W, 58th St
10a	rd 53, 66th St, E ⊞ SA
9c	76th St (from sb)
9b a	I-494, MN 5, to ⊞, ⊡ to ⊞
8	82nd St, E ⊡ BMW, W ⊞ Caribou Coffee, Jimmy Johns, Red Lobster, Sonic, Timberlodge Steaks, Wendy's ⊞ Embassy Suites ⊡ Chevrolet, Chrysler/Dodge/Jeep, Hyundai, Infiniti, Kia, Kohl's, TJ Maxx, Walgreens
7b	90th St
7a	94th St, E ⊡ Goodyear/auto, W ⊞ Holiday Inn
6	rd 1, 98th St, E ⊞ Holiday ⊞ Applebee's, Bakers Square, Burger King, Coldstone, Domino's, Golden Wok, Jimmy John's, Leeann Chen, McDonald's, Starbucks, Wendy's, White Castle ⊡ Bloomington Drug, Festival Foods, Ford, Radio Shack, URGENT CARE, Walgreens, W ⊞ SA/dsl ⊞ Denny's
5	106th St
5mm	Minnesota River
4b	113th St, Black Dog Rd
4a	Cliff Rd, E ⊡ Dodge, Subaru, W ⊡ VW
3b a	MN 13, Shakopee, Canterbury Downs, E ⊞ Select Inn
2	Burnsville Pkwy, E ⊞ BP, Marathon ⊞ Bumpers Grill, W ⊞ Holiday ⊞ Gourmet Chinese, Hooters, Perkins,

INTERSTATE 35 West Cont'd

Exit #	Services
2	Continued
	TimberLodge Steaks 🛏 Best Value Inn, LivInn, Prime Rate Motel, Travelodge Ⓞ Best Buy, Goodyear/auto, vet
1	rd 42, Crystal Lake Rd, **E** 🍴 Chianti Grill Ⓞ Byerly's Foods, PetsMart, Tuesday Morning, **W** Ⓞ Holiday/dsl, SA 🍴 Applebee's, Arby's/Sbarro's, Azteca Mexican, Buca Italian, Burger King, Cam Aranh Bay, Champp's Grill, Chili's, Dakota County Grill, HoneyBaked Ham, IHOP, Jimmy John's, KFC, Kings Buffet, Macaroni Grill, McDonald's, Old Country Buffet, Olive Garden, Outback Steaks, Panera Bread, Papa John's, Papa Murphy's, Qdoba Mexican, Red Lobster, Roasted Pear, Starbucks, Taco Bell/Pizza Hut, TGIFriday's, Wendy's 🛏 Days Inn, Fairfield Inn, Hampton Inn, Holiday Inn, InTown Suites Ⓞ Ⓗ, AT&T, Barnes&Noble, Best Buy, Cadillac, Chevrolet, Cub Foods, Discount Tire, Goodyear/auto, Home Depot, JC Penney, K-Mart, Kohl's, Macy's, mall, Michael's, PetCo, Rainbow Foods, Sears/auto, Target, Tires+, USPO, Walgreens
0mm	I-35W begins/ends on I-35, exit 88a.

INTERSTATE 90

Exit #	Services
278mm	Minnesota/Wisconsin state line, Mississippi River
276	US 14, US 61, to MN 16, La Crescent, **N** Welcome Ctr wb, full ♿ facilities, info, litter barrels, petwalk, 🚻, vending, **S** 🅿 Kwik Trip (1mi)
273b a	Dresbach
271	Dakota
270	US 14, US 61, to Winona (from wb), **N** to OL Kipp SP/camping
267	rd 12, Nodine, **N** Ⓞ camping, Great River Bluffs SP, **S** 🅿 Kwik Trip/Hearty Platter Rest./dsl/e-85/scales/24hr/@
261mm	weigh sta both lanes
258	MN 76, to Houston, Ridgeway, Witoka, **N** 🅿 gas, **S** Ⓞ camping
252	MN 43 N, to Winona, **N** 7 mi 🍴 Taco Bell 🛏 Express Inn, Holiday Inn Express, Plaza Hotel, Quality Inn Ⓞ Ⓗ, **S** Ⓞ get
249	MN 43 S, to Rushford, **N** Ⓞ Peterbilt Trucks/repair
244mm	℞ eb, full ♿ facilities, litter barrels, petwalk, 🚻, vending
242	rd 29, Lewiston
233	MN 74, to Chatfield, St Charles, **N** 🅿 Kwik Trip/LP/24hr (2mi) 🍴 A&W (2mi), Subway (2mi) Ⓞ Whitewater SP, **S** 🅿 BP/Amish Ovens Rest./dsl/RV dump/LP
229	rd 10, Dover
224	MN 42, rd 7, Eyota, **N** 🅿 KwikTrip/dsl/E-85 (3mi) 🍴 Country Cafe (3mi)
222mm	℞ wb, full ♿ facilities, litter barrels, petwalk, 🚻, vending
218	US 52, to Rochester, **S** 🅿 BP/dsl Ⓞ KOA (Mar-Oct) (1mi)
209b a	US 63, MN 30, to Rochester, Stewartville, **N** 8-10 mi 🛏 Clarion, Comfort Inn, EconoLodge, Hampton Inn, Holiday Inn, **S** 1 mi 🅿 KwikTrip/dsl 🍴 DQ, Pizza Ranch, Subway 🛏 Best Inn Ⓞ Family$, Verizon
205	rd 6
202mm	℞ eb, full ♿ facilities, litter barrels, petwalk, 🚻, vending
193	MN 16, Dexter, **N** 🅿 BP/Oasis Rest./dsl **S** 🛏 Windmill Motel
189	rd 13, to Elkton
187	rd 20, **S** 🛏 Jelly Stone Camping
183	MN 56, to Rose Creek, Brownsdale, **S** 🅿 Freeborn County Co-op/dsl/LP

AUSTIN

181	28th St NE
180b a	US 218, 21st St NE, to Austin, Oakland Place, **S** 🅿 Shell 🛏 Rodeway Inn
179	11th Dr NE, to Austin, **N** 🅿 KwikTrip/dsl/24hr
178b	6th St NE, to Austin, **S** Ⓞ Spam Museum
178a	4th St NW, **N** 🍴 Culver's, Jimmy John's, Perkins, Torge's Grille 🛏 AmericInn, Days Inn, Holiday Inn Ⓞ AutoValue Parts, Buick/Chevrolet/GMC, **S** 🅿 KwikTrip/dsl 🍴 Burger King, Subway Ⓞ Ⓗ
177	US 218 N, to Owatonna, Austin, Mapleview, **N** 🍴 Applebee's, Arby's, China Star, El Patron Mexican, KFC, King Buffet, Pizza Ranch, Quiznos, Wendy's Ⓞ $Tree, Aldi Foods, AT&T, AutoZone, Hy-Vee Foods/gas, JoAnn Fabrics, mall, O'Reilly Parts, Radio Shack, ShopKO, Target, Verizon, Walmart/Subway, Younkers, **S** 🅿 Sinclair/McDonald's/dsl 🛏 Super 8
175	MN 105, rd 46, to Oakland Rd, **N** 🛏 Econolodge, **S** 🅿 BP/dsl, Shell/dsl Ⓞ Chrysler/Dodge/Jeep, Ford/Lincoln, vet
171mm	℞ wb, full ♿ facilities, litter barrels, petwalk, 🚻, 🚻
166	rd 46, Oakland Rd, **N** Ⓞ golf (par3), KOA/LP
163	rd 26, Hayward, **S** 🅿 Freeborn County Co-op/dsl 🍴 Pizza Hut (4mi), Trails Rest. (4mi) Ⓞ camping, Myre-Big Island SP
161.5mm	℞ eb, full ♿ facilities, petwalk, 🚻, 🚻, litter barrels
159b a	I-35, N to Twin Cities, S to Des Moines
157	rd 22, Albert Lea, **N** Ⓞ Kenworth, **S** 🅿 HyVee/dsl 🍴 Applebee's, Arby's, Caribou Coffee, DQ, KwikTrip/dsl, McDonald's, Pizza Ranch, Plaza Morina Mexican 🛏 AmericInn, Best Western Ⓞ Ⓗ, Ace Hardware, Chevrolet, Harley-Davidson, Herberger's, Hy-Vee Foods, mall, ShopKO, Verizon
154	MN 13, to US 69, to Manchester, Albert Lea, **N** 🅿 SA/dsl, **S** 3 mi 🛏 BelAire Motel
146	MN 109, to Wells, Alden, **S** 🅿 BP/dsl/rest., Freeborn Co-Op Gas/dsl/E-85 Ⓞ truck/dsl repair
138	MN 22, to Wells, Keister, **N** 🅿 Casey's (6mi) **S** Ⓞ camping
134	MN 253, rd 21, to Bricelyn, MN Lake, **N** Ⓞ camping
128	MN 254, rd 17, Frost, Easton
119	US 169, to Winnebago, Blue Earth, **S** 🅿 Shell/dsl, Sinclair/dsl 🍴 Country Kitchen, DQ, McDonald's, Pizza Hut, Subway 🛏 AmericInn, Super 8 Ⓞ Ⓗ, $General, camping, Jolly Green Giant, Walmart
119mm	℞ both lanes, full ♿ facilities, litter barrels, petwalk, 🚻, 🚻 playground
113	rd 1, Guckeen
107	MN 262, rd 53, to East Chain, Granada, **S** Ⓞ camping (May-Oct) (1mi), gas/dsl
102	MN 15, to Madelia, Fairmont, **N** 🅿 Verizon, Walmart/Subway, **S** 0-2 mi 🅿 BP, Cenex/dsl, SA/dsl/24hr 🍴 Arby's, Bean Town a Grill, Burger King, China Buffet, DQ, Green Mill Rest., McDonald's, Perkins, Pizza Ranch, Ranch Family Rest.,

ALBERT LEA

MN

FAIRMONT

🔼E INTERSTATE 90 Cont'd

Exit #	Services
102	Continued
	Subway 🏨 Budget Inn, Comfort Inn, Hampton Inn, Holiday Inn, Super 8 🅾 🅷, $Tree, Ace Hardware, auto repair, camping, CarQuest, Chevrolet, Chrysler/Dodge/Jeep, Fareway Foods, Ford, Freightliner, Goodyear/auto, Hy-Vee Foods, JC Penney, NAPA, O'Reilly Parts, ShopKO, USPO, Walgreens
99	rd 39, Fairmont
93	MN 263, rd 27, Welcome, S 1/2 mi camping, Casey's/dsl
87	MN 4, Sherburn, N 🅾 Everett Park Camping (5mi) S 🅿 Casey's/dsl 🅿 Kum&Go/Subway/dsl/E-85
80	rd 29, Alpha
73	US 71, Jackson, N 🅿 SA/dsl 🍴 Burger King 🏨 EconoLodge, Super 8 🅾 KOA, to Kilen Woods SP, S 🅿 BP/DQ, Casey's/dsl 🍴 Embers Rest., Pizza Ranch, Subway 🏨 AmericInn, Earth Inn, Prairie Winds Motel 🅾 🅷, Ace Hardware, Buick/Chevrolet, Chrysler/Dodge/Jeep, city park, Family$, Sunshine Foods, to Spirit Lake
72.5mm	W Fork Des Moines River
72mm	🆁🆂 wb, full 🚻 facilities, litter barrels, petwalk, 🎁, 🅿, vending
69mm	🆁🆂 eb, full 🚻 facilities, litter barrels, petwalk, 🎁, 🅿, vending
64	MN 86, Lakefield, N 🅿 gas/dsl 🍴 food 🅾 🅷, camping, to Kilen SP (12mi)
57	rd 9, to Heron Lake, Spafford
50	MN 264, rd 1, to Brewster, Round Lake, S 🅾 camping
47	rd 3 (from eb), no return
46mm	weigh sta eb

WORTHINGTON

45	MN 60, Worthington, N 🅿 BP/Blueline Cafe/dsl/scales, S 🅿 Holiday/dsl/scales/24hr 🅾 camping, truckwash
43	US 59, Worthington, N 🅿 Casey's/dsl 🏨 Comfort Suites, Travelodge, S 🅿 Casey's, Cenex/dsl, Shell 🍴 Arby's, Burger King, DQ, Ground Round, Hardee's, KFC, McDonald's, Perkins, Pizza Hut, Pizza Ranch, Subway, Taco John's 🏨 AmericInn, Holiday Inn Express 🅾 🅷, $General, $Tree, Ace Hardware, CarQuest, Chevrolet, Fareway Foods, Ford, Hy-Vee Foods/dsl, NAPA, O'Reilly Parts, Radio Shack, ShopKO, Verizon, Walgreens, Walmart/Subway
42	MN 266, rd 25, to Reading, S 🏨 Days Inn, Super 8
33	rd 13, to Wilmont, Rushmore
26	MN 91, Adrian, S 🅿 Cenex/dsl, Kum&Go/Subway/dsl/E-85/24hr 🍴 Countryside Steaks 🅾 Adrian Camping, city park
25mm	🆁🆂 wb, full 🚻 facilities, litter barrels, petwalk, 🎁, 🅿
24mm	🆁🆂 eb, full 🚻 facilities, litter barrels, petwalk, 🎁, 🅿
18	rd 3, Kanaranzi, Magnolia, N 🅾 camping
12	US 75, Luverne, N 🅿 BP/dsl/E-85, Casey's/dsl, Holiday/Subway/dsl 🍴 China Inn, McDonald's, Papa's Place Rest., Taco John's, Tasty Drive-In 🏨 Cozy Rest Motel (1mi), GrandStay Hotel, Quality Inn 🅾 🅷, $General, Buick/Cadillac/Chevrolet/GMC, Chrysler/Dodge/Jeep, Ford, Lewis Drugs, Pipestone NM, Sturdevant's Parts, to Blue Mounds SP, S 🍴 Blue Stem Rest. 🏨 Super 8 🅾 ShopKO
5	rd 6, Beaver Creek, N 🅿 Local/dsl
3	rd 4 (from eb), Beaver Creek
1	MN 23, rd 17, to Jasper, N 🅾 access to gas/dsl, to Pipestone NM
0mm	**Welcome Ctr eb, full 🚻 facilities, info, litter barrels, 🎁, 🅿**
	Minnesota/South Dakota state line

🔼E INTERSTATE 94

Exit #	Services
259mm	Minnesota/Wisconsin state line, St Croix River
258	MN 95 N, to Stillwater, Hastings, Lakeland, N 🍴 Bungalow Rest.
257mm	**Welcome Ctr wb, full 🚻 facilities, litter barrels, petwalk, 🎁, 🅿, vending, weigh sta wb**
253	MN 95 S, rd 15, Manning Ave, N 🅾 StoneRidge Golf, S 🅾 ski area, to Afton Alps SP
251	rd 19, Keats Ave, Woodbury Dr, S 🅿 KwikTrip, SA/dsl 🍴 Applebee's, Arby's, Asia Bistro, Burger King, Caribou Coffee, Chili's, Chipotle Mexican, Dino's Rest, Dunn Bros Coffee, Lakes Grill, Las Margaritas, LeeAnn Chin, McDonald's, Outback Steaks, Quiznos, Ray J's Grill, SmashBurger, Subway 🏨 Extended Stay America, Holiday Inn Express 🅾 $Tree, AT&T, Gander Mtn, Hancock Fabrics, Michael's, Sam's Club/gas, Staples, Target, Trader Joe's, Tuesday Morning, Walmart/Subway, Woodbury Lakes Outlets/famous brands
250	rd 13, Radio Dr, Inwood Ave, N 🍴 5 Guys Burgers, Baja Sol, Buffalo Wild Wings, Caribou Coffee, Machine Shed Rest., Milio's Rest., Olive Garden, Red Lobster 🏨 Hilton Garden, Wild Wood Lodge 🅾 Best Buy, S 🅿 Holiday 🍴 Champp's, Domino's, DUK Vietnamese, Jamba Juice, Little Caesars, Pei Wei, Starbucks, Taco Bell, Wendy's, Wild Bill's Grill 🅾 Aldi Foods, BigLots, Cub Foods, CVS Drug, Dick's, Fannie May, GNC, Gordmans, Hepner's Auto Ctr, Home Depot, JC Penney, Jo-Ann, LandsEnd Inlet, Old Navy, Petsmart, Tires+, Verizon, vet
249	I-694 N & I-494 S

ST PAUL

247	MN 120, Century Ave, N 🍴 Denny's 🏨 AmericInn, LivInn 🅾 Harley-Davidson, S 🅿 SA 🍴 GreenMill Rest. 🏨 Country Inn/rest. 🅾 CarQuest, Chevrolet
246c b	McKnight Ave, N 🅾 3M, S 🏨 Holiday Inn
246a	Ruth St (from eb, no return), N 🅿 BP 🍴 Culver's, Domino's, Hoho Chinese, Jimmy John's 🅾 $Tree, Cub Foods, Firestone/auto, GNC, Radio Shack, TJ Maxx
245	White Bear Ave, N 🅿 BP, SA/dsl 🍴 Subway 🏨 Super 8 🅾 Walgreens, S 🅿 BP 🍴 Arby's, Davanni's Pizza/subs, Los Ocampo, McDonald's, Papa John's, Popeye's, Sonic, Taco Bell, Wendy's 🅾 Aldi Foods, Byerly's Foods, Family$, NAPA, O'Reilly Parts, Target
244	US 10 E, US 61 S, 🅾 Mounds/Kellogg
243	US 61, Mounds Blvd, S River Centre
242d	US 52 S, MN 3, 6th St, (exits left from wb), N 🅿 Holiday 🍴 Subway
242c	7th St, S 🅿 SA
242b a	I-35E N, US 10 W, I-35E S (from eb)
241c	I-35E S (from wb)
241b	10th St, 5th St, to downtown
241a	12th St, Marion St, Kellogg Blvd, N 🏨 Best Western Kelly Inn, S 🅾 St Paul's Cathedral
240	Dale Ave
239b a	Lexington Pkwy, Hamline Ave, N 🅿 BP, SA 🍴 Hardee's, Leeann Chin, Popeye's, White Castle 🅾 🅷, AutoZone, Cub Foods, Discount Tire, Herberger's, O'Reilly Parts, Target
238	MN 51, Snelling Ave, N 🍴 Applebee's, Culver's, Jimmy John's, Little Caesars, McDonald's, Perkins 🅾 CVS Drug, Family$, Radio Shack, Rainbow Foods, same as 239, Tires+, Walgreens, Walmart
237	Cretin Ave, Vandalia Ave, to downtown
236	MN 280, University Ave, to downtown

INTERSTATE 94 Cont'd

Exit #	Services
235b	Huron Blvd
235mm	Mississippi River
235a	Riverside Ave, 25th Ave, N 🅶 Tesoro 🍴 Starbucks, S 🍴 Perkins, Taco Bell
234c	Cedar Ave, downtown
234b a	MN 55, Hiawatha Ave, 5th St, N 🛏 Courtyard 🅾 to downtown
233b	I-35W N, I-35W S (exits left from wb)
233a	11th St (from wb), N downtown
231b	Hennepin Ave, Lyndale Ave, to downtown
231a	I-394, US 12 W, to downtown
230	US 52, MN 55, 4th St, 7th St, Olson Hwy, N 🅾 Metrodome, S 🅾 🏥, Int Mkt Square
229	W Broadway, Washington Ave, N 🅶 Holiday/dsl, Old Colony/dsl, S 🅶 Winner 🍴 Broadway Pizza, Burger King, KFC, Little Caesars, McDonald's, Subway, Taco Bell, Wendy's 🅾 $Tree, AutoZone, Cub Foods, Family$, Walgreens
228	Dowling Ave N
226	53rd Ave N, 49th Ave N
225	I-694 E, MN 252 N, to Minneapolis
	I-94 & I-494 run together. See I-494/694, exits 28-34.
216	I-94 W and I-494
215	rd 109, Weaver Lake Rd, N 🅶 SA/dsl, Shell 🍴 Anginos, Broadway Pizza, Burger King, Caribou Coffee, Champps, ChuckECheese's, Domino's, Don Pablo, DQ, El Rodeo Mexican, Famous Dave's BBQ, Frankie's Pizza, Great Harvest Bread Co., Jimmy John's, McDonald's, Old Country Buffet, Papa John's, Papa Murphy's, Starbucks, Subway, Taco Bell, Wendy's 🅾 AT&T, Barnes&Noble, Byerly's Foods, Cub Foods, Gander Mtn, GNC, Goodyear/auto, JC Penney, K-Mart, Kohl's, mall, Michael's, Midas, Old Navy, PetCo, Radio Shack, same as 28, Tires+, USPO, Verizon, Walgreens, S 🍴 Applebee's, IHOP
214mm	🆁🆂 eb, full ♿ facilities, litter barrels, 🅲, 🅿
213	rd 30, 95th Ave N, Maple Grove, N 🅶 SA/dsl 🍴 Chipotle Mexican, Subway 🛏 Cambria Suites 🅾 🏥, Aldi Foods, GNC, Home Depot, Target, S 🅶 Holiday/dsl 🍴 Culver's, Leeann Chin, Little Caesars, McDonald's, Starbucks, Which Wich, White Castle 🅾 Apr-Oct), BigLots, Discount Tire, Firestone, Goodyear/auto, KOA (2mi), Menards, Rainbow Foods, Sam's Club/gas, Verizon, Walgreens, Walmart/Subway
207	MN 101, to Elk River, Rogers, N 🅶 Holiday, SA/dsl, TA/Country Pride/dsl/scales/24hr/@ 🍴 Applebee's, Arby's, Burger King, China Kitchen, Culver's, Davanni's Pizza, Denny's, Dickey's BBQ, Domino's, DQ, Hardee's, Jimmy John's, Maynard's, McDonald's, Noodles&Co, Starbucks, Subway, Taco Bell, Wendy's 🛏 Hampton Inn, Holiday Inn Express, Super 8 🅾 $Tree, AT&T, Cabela's, Camping World, Cub Foods, Discount Tire, Gander Mtn, GNC, Kohl's, Lowe's, NAPA, NTB, O'Reilly Parts, Target, Tires+, Verizon, vet, Walgreens, S 🅶 BP/Circle K/dsl, Holiday 🍴 BoBo Asian, Guadalajara Mexican, Harvest Grill, Minne's Diner 🛏 AmericInn 🅾 Chevrolet, CVS Drug, TrueValue, URGENT CARE
205.5mm	Crow River
205	MN 241, rd 36, St Michael, S 🅶 QwikTrip/dsl, SA/dsl
202	rd 37, Albertville, N 🅶 Shell/dsl 🍴 Emma Krumbee's Rest., S 🅶 BP/dsl, same as 201, Sunoco/dsl
201	rd 19 (from eb), Albertville, St Michael, N 🅶 Shell/dsl 🍴 Andy's Pizza, Burger King, Michael B's Grill, Perkins, Subway 🛏 Country Inn&Suites 🅾 Albertville Outlets/famous brands, Old Navy, S 🅶 BP/dsl, Casey's, Mobil/Subway, Sunoco/dsl

Exit #	Services
201	Continued 🍴 Caribou Coffee, China Dragon, Culver's, Little Caesars, Papa Murphy's, Space Aliens Grill 🅾 Ace Hardware, auto repair, Coburn's/gas, Goodyear/auto, Verizon
194	rd 18, rd 39, Monticello, N 🅶 Cruiser's/dsl, Marathon/dsl/E85 🍴 Caribou Coffee, Little Caesars, McDonald's 🅾 🏥, GNC, Home Depot, Petsmart, Target, Verizon
193	MN 25, to Buffalo, Monticello, Big Lake, N 🅶 Holiday/dsl 🍴 5 Buck Pizza, Burger King, Caribou Coffee, KFC, Papa Murphy's, Perkins, Poncho Villa Mexican, Quiznos, Rancho Grande Mexican, Taco Bell 🛏 AmericInn 🅾 AutoValue Parts, Cub Foods, Radio Shack, USPO, Walgreens, S 🅶 Holiday/dsl, KwikTrip/dsl, SA/dsl 🍴 Applebee's, Arby's, Blue Stone Grill, Buffalo Wild Wings, Chatter's Grill, China Buffet, Culver's, DQ, Jimmy John's, McDonald's, Pizza Ranch, Subway, Taco John's 🛏 Best Western, Days Inn, Super 8 🅾 $Tree, Buick/GMC, Chevrolet, Goodyear/auto, Lake Maria SP, NAPA, O'Reilly Parts, Verizon, vet, Walmart/Subway
187mm	🆁🆂 eb, full ♿ facilities, litter barrels, petwalk, 🅲, 🅿, vending
183	rd 8, to Silver Creek, Hasty, Maple Lake, S 🅶 BP/rest./dsl/scales/24hr/@ 🅾 camping, to Lake Maria SP
178	MN 24, to Annandale, Clearwater, N 🅶 Holiday/Petro/dsl/scales/24hr/@ 🍴 Burger King, DQ, Keith's Kettle, Subway, Taco Gringo 🛏 Best Value Inn 🅾 Clearwater Hardware, Coburn's Foods/gas, GS Camping (1mi), Parts City, repair, USPO, vet, S 🅾 A-J Acres RV Camping (Apr-Oct)Recreation Outdoor RV Ctr
178mm	🆁🆂 wb, full ♿ facilities, litter barrels, petwalk, 🅲, 🅿, vending
173	Opportunity Dr
171	rd 7, rd 75, St Augusta, N 🅶 🈂/McDonald's/dsl/scales/24hr, Shell 🍴 Burger King, MadeRite Grill, RJ's Grill, Subway 🛏 AmericInn, Holiday Inn Express, Travelodge 🅾 🏥, Goodyear/auto, S 🅾 Freightliner, Pleasureland RV Ctr
167b a	MN 15, to St Cloud, Kimball, N 4 mi 🅶 Holiday, SA/dsl 🍴 5 Guys Burgers, Applebee's, Arby's, Bonanza, Boulder Taphouse, Buffalo Wild Wings, Burger King, Caribou Coffee, Chipotle, ChuckECheese's, Domino's, Famous Dave's BBQ, Granite City Grill, Grizzly's Grill, IHOP, La Casita Mexican, McDonald's, Noodles&Co, Old Chicago Pizza, Old Country Buffet, Olive Garden, Panda Express, Perkins, Pizza Hut, Pizza Ranch, Qdoba, Red Lobster, Sammy's Pizza, Starbucks, Subway, Taco Bell, Taco John's, TGIFriday's, Wendy's, White Castle 🛏 Country Inn&Suites, Days Inn, Fairfield Inn, Hampton Inn, Holiday Inn, Homewood Suites, Quality Inn, Super 8 🅾 🏥, AT&T, Barnes&Noble, Best Buy, BigLots, CashWise Foods, Gander Mtn, Home Depot, JC Penney,

MINNEAPOLIS

MONTICELLO

ST CLOUD

⬆E INTERSTATE 94 Cont'd

Exit #	Services
167b a	Continued Jo-Ann Fabrics, K-Mart, Kohl's, Macy's, Michael's, Office Depot, Old Navy, Petsmart, Sam's Club, Save-A-Lot, Scheel's Sports, Sears/auto, ShopKo, Subaru, Target, USPO, Walgreens, Walmart, S ⛽ Shell/dsl (2mi)
164	MN 23, to St Cloud, Rockville, N 4-6 mi ⛽ Holiday 🍴 Culver's, IHOP, KFC, Subway, Taco Bell, Wendy's 🛏 Motel 6 ⊙ Discount Tire, Gander Mtn, Grande Depot Gourmet Foods, Hyundai, Kia, Menards, Petsmart, same as 167, Toyota/Scion
162.5mm	Sauk River
160	rd 2, to Cold Spring, St Joseph, N ⛽ BP 🛏 Super 8 (3mi) ⊙ Coll of St Benedict
158	rd 75 (from eb exits left), to St Cloud, N 3 mi same as 160
156	rd 159, St Joseph, N ⊙ St Johns U
153	rd 9, Avon, N ⛽ Shell/dsl, Tesoro/McDonald's/dsl 🍴 Joseph's Rest., Subway 🛏 Budget Host ⊙ city park, picnic area, USPO, S ⊙ El Rancho Manana Camping (10mi)
152mm	℞ both lanes, full ♿ facilities, litter barrels, petwalk, 📞, 🐾 vending
147	MN 238, rd 10, Albany, N ⛽ Holiday/dsl, Shell/A&W/Subway/dsl 🍴 Chesters, DQ, Hillcrest Rest. 🛏 Norwood Inn&Suites ⊙ H, golf, S ⊙ Chrysler/Dodge/Jeep, NAPA, vet
140	rd 11, Freeport, N ⛽ Cenex/dsl, Clark/dsl 🍴 Ackie's Pioneer Rest., Charlie's Café ⊙ auto repair, USPO, vet
137	MN 237, rd 65, New Munich
137mm	Sauk River
135	rd 13, Melrose, N ⛽ Clark/dsl/repair, Tesoro/Subway/dsl 🍴 Burger King, Cornerstone Buffet ⊙ H, $General, S ⛽ Casey's/dsl 🍴 DQ, El Portal Mexican 🛏 Super 8 ⊙ Save Foods, vet
132.5mm	Sauk River
131	MN 4, to Paynesville, Meire Grove
128mm	Sauk River
127	US 71, MN 28, Sauk Centre, N ⛽ Casey's, Holiday/dsl 🍴 4 Seas Buffet, DQ, Hardee's, McDonald's, Pizza Hut, Subway 🛏 AmericInn, Best Value Inn, Guesthouse Inn ⊙ H Ace Hardware, Coborn's Foods, Ford, Lewis Ctr/℞, NAPA, O'Reilly Parts, Walmart/Subway, S ⛽ Shell/café/dsl/scales/24hr/@ ⊙ Buick/Chevrolet/Chrysler/Dodge/Jeep
124	Sinclair Lewis Ave (from eb), Sauk Centre
119	rd 46, West Union
114	MN 27, rd 3, to Westport, Osakis, N 3 mi 🍴 A&W, gas, lodging, Subway
105mm	℞ wb, full ♿ facilities, litter barrels, petwalk, 📞, 🐾 vending
103	MN 29, to Glenwood, Alexandria, N ⛽ F&F/dsl, Holiday, Tesoro 🍴 Arby's, Burger King, Caribou Coffee, China Buffet, Culver's, Dolittle's Grill, Dunn Bros Coffee, Godfather's Pizza, Great Hunan, Hardee's, Jimmy John's, KFC, McDonald's, Perkins, Subway, Taco Bell, TN Roadhouse, Wendy's 🛏 AmericInn, Best Western, Days Inn, Hampton Inn, Super 8 ⊙ H AT&T, Cadillac/Chevrolet/Mazda, County Mkt Foods, Goodyear/auto, Harley-Davidson, Jeep, Jo-Ann Fabrics, K-Mart, Menards, Radio Shack, Target, Tires+, Verizon, Walmart/Subway, S ⛽ Holiday/dsl 🛏 Country Inn&Suites, Holiday Inn ⊙ Alexandria RV Ctr
100mm	Lake Latoka
100	MN 27, N ⛽ 🍴/Subway/dsl/scales/24hr/@ 🛏 Best Inn/Alexandria RV Park ⊙ H, S ⊙ camping

FERGUS FALLS / **MOORHEAD** / **ALEXANDRIA** (side tabs)

Exit #	Services
99mm	℞ eb, full ♿ facilities, litter barrels, petwalk, 📞, 🐾, vending
97	MN 114, rd 40, to Lowry, Garfield
90	rd 7, Brandon, S camping, ski area
82	MN 79, rd 41, to Erdahl, Evansville, N 2 mi ⛽ BP/dsl, S ⊙ H camping
77	MN 78, rd 10, to Barrett, Ashby, N ⛽ gas/dsl ⊙ Prairie Cove Camping (May-Sept), S ⊙ camping
69mm	℞ wb, full ♿ facilities, litter barrels, petwalk, 📞, 🐾, vending
67	rd 35, Dalton, N ⊙ camping, S ⊙ camping
61	US 59 S, rd 82, to Elbow Lake, N ⛽ Tesoro/café/dsl/LP/24hr ⊙ H, camping (4mi), Pine Plaza RV Ctr, S ⊙ camping
57	MN 210 E, rd 25, Fergus Falls, N ⊙ H
55	rd 1, to Wendell, Fergus Falls, N ⊙ antiques
54	MN 210 W, Lincoln Ave, Fergus Falls, N ⛽ Cenex/dsl, F&F/dsl, Tesoro/dsl 🍴 Applebee's, Arby's, Burger King, Debbie's Kitchen, Family Diner, Hunan Spring Buffet, KFC, McDonald's, Papa Murphy's, Perkins, Pizza Hut, Pizza Ranch, Subway 🛏 AmericInn, Best Value Inn, Best Western, Comfort Inn, Motel 7, Super 8 ⊙ H, $Tree, AT&T, Chrysler/Dodge/Jeep, Ford/Lincoln, GMC, Herbergers, Home Depot, K-Mart, museum, NAPA, O'Reilly Parts, SunMart Foods, Target, Tires+, Toyota, S 🍴 Mabel Murphy's Rest. ⊙ Walmart
50	rd 88, rd 52, to US 59, to Fergus Falls, Elizabeth, ⊙ camping
38	rd 88, Rothsay, S ⛽ Tesoro/cafe/dsl/24hr 🍴 Ole&Lena's Pizza 🛏 Comfort Zone Inn ⊙ tires
32	MN 108, rd 30, to Pelican Rapids, Lawndale, N 19 mi Maplewood SP
24	MN 34, Barnesville, N 🍴 Renee's Drive-in, S 1 mi ⛽ Cenex/dsl, Tesoro/dsl 🍴 DQ, Subway 🛏 motel ⊙ city park, Wagner Park Camping (May-Oct)
22	MN 9, Barnesville, N 1 mi ⛽ Cenex/dsl, Tesoro/dsl 🍴 DQ, Subway 🛏 motel
15	rd 10, Downer
8mm	Buffalo River
6	MN 336, rd 11, to US 10, Dilworth, N ⊙ to Buffalo River SP
5mm	Red River weigh sta eb
2mm	Welcome Ctr eb, full ♿ facilities, info, litter barrels, 📞, 🐾, vending
2b a	rd 52, Moorhead, N 2 mi ⛽ Holiday/dsl/e-85, Tesoro 🍴 Arby's, McDonald's, Perkins, Pizza Ranch, Subway, Taco Bell 🛏 Travelodge ⊙ H, antiques, CVS Drug, K-Mart, KOA, Menards, Radio Shack, Target, Walmart
1b	20th St, Moorhead (from eb, no return)
1a	US 75, Moorhead, N ⛽ Clark/dsl 🍴 Burger King, Crave Burger Co., Little Caesars, Papa Murphy's, Qdoba, Sarpinos Pizza, Starbucks, Village Inn 🛏 Courtyard ⊙ Curves, SunMart Foods, Verizon, S ⛽ Casey's, Orton's Gas 🍴 DQ, Panchero's Mexican, Snapdragon Asian, Speak Easy Rest., Subway 🛏 Days Inn, Grand Inn, Super 8 ⊙ CVS Drug, vet, Walgreens
0mm	Minnesota/North Dakota state line, Red River

⬆E INTERSTATE 494/694

Exit #	Services
	I-494/I-694 loops around Minneapolis/St Paul.
71	rd 31, Pilot Knob Rd, N 🛏 Courtyard, Fairfield Inn, S 🍴 LoneOak Café 🛏 Best Western, Crowne Plaza
70	I-35E, N to St Paul, S to Albert Lea
69	MN 149, MN 55, Dodd Rd, N 🍴 Ziggy's Deli, S 🍴 Caribou Coffee, McDonald's, Subway 🛏 Budget Host, Country Inn&Suites

ST PAUL

INTERSTATE 494/694 Cont'd

Exit #	Services
67	MN 3, Roberts St, **N 1 mi** 🅿 BP, Holiday, Mobil 🍴 Acre's Rest., Arby's/Sbarro's, Baker's Square, Buffalo Wings, Burger King, Chipotle Mexican, ChuckeCheese, Culver's, Grand Buffet, KFC, Old Country Buffet, Pizza Hut, Taco Bell, Timber Lodge Steaks, White Castle 🅾 Aamco, Best Buy, Buick, Checker Parts, Chevrolet, Cub Foods, Dodge, Ford, Jo-Ann Fabrics, Kia, K-Mart, Lincoln, Mazda, NAPA, Nissan, Rainbow Foods/24hr, Target, Tires+, Toyota, VW, Walmart, **S** 🍴 PDQ
66	US 52, **S** 🅿 SA 🍴 Old World Pizza, Outback Steaks 🏠 Country Inn&Suites, Microtel
65	7th Ave, 5th Ave
64b a	MN 56, Concord St, **N** 🅿 Conoco/dsl 🅾 Best Western Drovers 🅾 Ford Trucks, Goodyear, Peterbilt, **S** 🍴 EZ Stop 🅾 Chrysler/Jeep/Dodge, Parts+
63mm	Mississippi River
63c	Maxwell Ave
63b a	US 10, US 61, to St Paul, Hastings, **S** 🅿 BP, SA 🍴 Burger King, Subway 🏠 Boyd's Motel 🅾 NAPA
60	Lake Rd, **E** 🅿 SA/dsl, **W** 🏠 Country Inn&Suites
59	Valley Creek Rd, **E** 🅿 BP/repair, SA/dsl/LP 🍴 America's Burger, Applebees, Broadway Pizza, Chipotle Mexican, DQ, Old Country Buffet, Papa Murphy's, Perkins, Potbelly's Rest., Yang's Chinese 🏠 Red Roof Inn 🅾 Barnes&Noble, Kohl's, Marshall's, Office Depot, PetCo, Rainbow Foods, Target, USPO, Walgreens, **W** 🅿 PBQ 🍴 Bonfire Rest., Burger King, McDonald's, Pizza Hut, Subway 🏠 Hampton Inn 🅾 🇭, Ace Hardware, Goodyear
58c	Tamarack Rd, **E** 🍴 Paisano's Cafe, Woodbury's Cafe 🏠 Sheraton
58b a	I-94, E to Madison, W to St Paul. **I-494 S begins/ends, I-694 N begins/ends**
57	rd 10, 10th St N, **E** 🅿 SA 🍴 IHOP, Quizno's 🏠 Wingate Inn, **W** 🅿 Holiday 🍴 Burger King, Hunan Buffet, KFC 🅾 $Tree, K-Mart, mall, Rainbow Foods/24hr, vet
55	MN 5, **E** 🅾 Target, **W** 🅿 Holiday/dsl 🍴 Subway 🅾 Menards, st patrol
52b a	MN 36, N St Paul, to Stillwater, **W** 🅿 F&F/dsl
51	MN 120, **E** 🅿 BP, SA/dsl 🍴 Jethro's, Starbucks, **W** 🅿 Kellie's Corner/gas
50	White Bear Ave, **E** 🅿 SA 🅾 K-Mart, Sam's Club/gas, **W** 🅿 BP, Shell 🍴 Acupulco Chicken, Arby's, Bakers Square, Buffalo Wild Wings, Caribou Coffee, Chili's, Denny's, Great Moon Buffet, IHOP, Jake's Grill, Jimmy John's, KFC, McDonald's, Noodles&Co, North China, Old Country Buffet, Outback Steaks, Peiwei Asian, Perkins/24hr, Red Lobster, Taco Bell, TGI Friday, Wendy's 🏠 Emerald Inn 🅾 Aamco, Best Buy, Goodyear/auto, JC Penney, Jo-Ann Fabrics, Kohl's, Macy's, mall, Marshall's, Michael's, PetCo, Sears/auto, Tires+, Tuesday Morning, Walgreens
48	US 61 (from wb), **E** 🅾 Acura, Chrysler/Dodge/Jeep, Ford, Honda, Hyundai, Isuzu/Subaru, Lincoln, **W** 🍴 Chili's, Gulden's Rest., McDonald's, Olive Garden 🏠 Best Western 🅾 🇭, Audi/Porsche, Lexus, Mercedes, Toyota, Venburg Tire, Volvo
47	I-35E, N to Duluth
46	I-35E, US 10, S to St Paul
45	rd 49, Rice St, **N** 🅿 Gas+, Marathon/dsl 🍴 Papa John's, Subway, Taco Bell 🅾 Checker Parts, **S** 🅿 Marathon/dsl 🍴 A&W, Burger King, Caribou Coffee, Taco John's 🅾 Kath Parts

MINNEAPOLIS

Exit #	Services
43b	Victoria St, **S** 🅾 Bill's Foods
43a	Lexington Ave, **N** 🍴 Greenmill Rest., Red Robin 🏠 Hampton Inn, Hilton Garden, **S** 🅿 Exxon, Sinclair 🍴 Blue Fox Grill, Burger King, Davanni's Pizza, Papa Murphy's, Perkins, Subway, Wendy's 🏠 Holiday Inn, Super 8 🅾 Cub Foods, Goodyear/auto, Target, transmissions
42b	US 10 W (from wb), to Anoka
42a	MN 51, Snelling Ave, **N 1 mi** 🅿 Shell 🍴 Flaherty's Grill, Lindey's Steaks, McDonald's 🏠 Country Inn&Suites, Holiday Inn
41b a	I-35W, S to Minneapolis, N to Duluth
40	Long Lake Rd, 10th St NW
39	Silver Lake Rd, **N** 🅿 BP 🍴 Acupulco Mexican, Champps, McDonald's, Subway 🅾 Fairview Drug, Ford, U-Haul
38b a	MN 65, Central Ave, **N** 🅿 Holiday/dsl 🍴 Subway, **S** 🅿 SA, SuperStop 🍴 A&W/KFC, Applebee's, Asia Rest., Big Marina Deli, Buffalo Wild Wings, Flameburger Rest., La Casita Mexican, McDonald's, Mr BBQ, Papa John's, Ricky's, Sonic, Subway, Taco Bell, Wendy's, White Castle 🏠 LivInn Hotel 🅾 $General, Advance Parts, AutoZone, Discount Tire, Menards, O'Reilly Parts, PetCo, Rainbow Foods, Target, Tires+, vet, Walgreens
37	rd 47, University Ave, **N** 🅿 Holiday, SA/dsl 🍴 Burger King, McDonald's, Papa Murphy's Pizza, Zantigo's Rest. 🅾 Cub Foods, CVS Drug, Goodyear, Home Depot, **S** 🅿 Bona Bros/repair, Shell
36	E River Rd
35mm	**I-494 W begins/ends, I-694 E begins/ends**
35c	MN 252, **N** 🅿 Holiday, SA
35b a	I-94 E to Minneapolis
34	to MN 100, Shingle Creek Pkwy, **N** 🍴 Denny's, Mr BBQ, Oak City Rest. 🏠 AmericInn, Comfort Inn, Country Inn&Suites, Crowne Plaza, Days Inn, Extended Stay America, Motel 6, Super 8, **S** 🍴 C1 Buffet, Global Kitchen, Ocean Buffet, Panera Bread 🏠 Embassy Suites 🅾 🇭, AT&T, Curves, Kohl's, PepBoys, Target, Tires+, Walmart
33	rd 152, Brooklyn Blvd, **N** 🅿 SA/dsl, Shell 🍴 Culver's, Slim's Café, Subway 🅾 Buick/GMC, Chevrolet, Honda, Toyota/Scion, USPO, **S** 🅿 BP 🍴 Applebee's, Arby's, IHOP, McDonald's, Popeye's, Starbucks, Subway, Taco Bell, Wendy's 🅾 AutoZone, Cub Foods, CVS Drug, Family$, NTB, Sun Foods, Walgreens
31	rd 81, Lakeland Ave, **N** 🅿 SA/dsl 🍴 Chipotle Mexican, Wagner's Drive-In, Wendy's 🅾 Target, U-Haul, **S** 🏠 Northstar Inn
30	Boone Ave, **N** 🏠 La Quinta, Marriott, **S** 🅾 Discount Tire, Home Depot
29b a	US 169, to Hopkins, Osseo

MN
MS

INTERSTATE 494/694 Cont'd

Exit #	Services
28	rd 61, Hemlock Lane, **N on Elm Creek** 5 Guys Burgers, Arby's, Benihana, Biaggi's Italian, Boston's Grill, Buca Italian, CA Pizza Kitchen, Chick-fil-A, Chipotle Mexican, Coldstone, Dave&Buster's, Dickey's BBQ, Granite City Rest., Houlihan's, Leeann Chin, Malone's Grill, Mongo's Grill, Noodles&Co, Olive Garden, Panera Bread, PF Chang's, Pittsburgh Blue, Potbelly's, Red Lobster, Redstone Grill, Starbucks, Subway, TGIFriday's, Wild Bill's Café Courtyard, Hampton Inn, Holiday Inn, Staybridge Suites $Tree, Best Buy, Costco/gas, Dick's, Jo-Ann Fabrics, Lowe's, Marshalls, Office Depot, Old Navy, URGENT CARE, Whole Foods Mkt, **S** BP Perkins Asteria Suites
27	I-94 W to St Cloud, I-94/694 E to Minneapolis
26	rd 10, Bass Lake Rd, **E** Freedom Caribou Coffee, Culver's, McDonald's, Subway Extended Stay America mall, vet, **W** BP, Marathon/dsl Dunn Bro's Cofee, Milio's Sandwiches, Pancake House, Pizza Hut Hilton Garden CVS Drug
23	rd 9, Rockford Rd, **E** Holiday Chili's, Peony's Chinese GNC, O'Reilly Parts, PetsMart, Rainbow Foods, Target, TJ Maxx, vet, Walgreens, **W** PDQ Cousins Subs, DQ, LeAnn Chin, Panchero's, Subway
22	MN 55, **E** Holiday/dsl Broadway Pizza, Caribou Coffee, Green Mill Rest., Jimmy John's, McDonald's, Red Robin, Solos Pizza, Starbucks Best Western Kelly, Radisson, Red Roof Inn, Residence Inn, **W** Holiday/dsl Arby's, Burger King, Davanni's Rest., Jake's Rest., Perkins, Wendy's Comfort Inn, Days Inn Goodyear/auto, Tires+
21	rd 6, **E** KwikTrip Discount Tire, Home Depot
20	Carlson Pkwy, **E** Holiday/dsl Pizza Hut, Subway, **W** Woody's Grill Country Inn&Suites
19b a	I-394 E, US 12 W, to Minneapolis, **E 1 mi off of I-394** Applebee's, Wendy's Barnes&Noble, Best Buy, Byerly's Foods, Ford, JC Penney, Jo-Ann Fabrics, Mazda, Mazerati, Mercedes, Sears/auto, Subaru, Target, Tires+ **W 1/2 mi** BP, Holiday KFC, McDonald's BMW, Chevrolet, Lexus, Mitsubishi, Nissan
17b a	Minnetonka Blvd, **W** US Gas Cousin's Subs, Dunn Bros Coffee
16b a	MN 7, **W 1 mi** Marathon Christo's Rest., Davanni's Rest., Famous Dave's BBQ, Taco Bell Goodyear
13	MN 62, rd 62
12	Valleyview Rd, rd 39 (from sb)
11c	MN 5 W, same as 11 a b
11b a	US 169 S, US 212 W, **N** Don Pablo, Subway Courtyard, Fairfield Inn, Hampton Inn, Hyatt Place, Residence Inn, **S** BP, Holiday, Marathon Caribou Coffee, Davanni's Rest.,Fuddruckers, Jake's Grill, Jason's Deli, KFC, Leeann Chin, Old Chicago, Panera Bread, Papa John's, Qdoba, Starbucks Best Western, Discount Tire, Homestead Suites, JC Penney, Office Depot, Sears/auto, SpringHill Suites, Target, Walgreens, Walmart
10	US 169 N, to rd 18
8	rd 28 (from wb, no return), E Bush Lake Rd, same as 7 a b
7b a	MN 100, rd 34, Normandale Blvd, **N** Shell/dsl Burger King, Caribou Coffee, Chili's, DQ, Subway, TGIFriday Days Inn, Sheraton, Sofatel, **S** Oak City Rest. Country Inn&Suites, Crowne Plaza, Hilton Garden, La Quinta, Staybridge Inn

Exit #	Services
6b	rd 17, France Ave, **N** Mobil Cattle Co Rest., ChuckeCheese, Fuddracker's, Hot Wok, Macaroni Grill, McDonald's, Perkins, Quizno's Best Western, Le Bourget, Park Plaza Hotel Michael's, Office Depot, **S** Denny's, Joe Senser's Grill, Olive Garden Hampton Inn, Hilton Buick/GMC, Ford, Mercedes, Nissan, Toyota/Scion
6a	Penn Ave (no EZ eb return), **N** Residence Inn Best Buy, Buick, Hyundai, Isuzu, **S** Applebee's, Atlantic Buffet, McDonald's, Starbucks, Steak&Ale, Subway Embassy Suites Chevrolet, Chrysler/Jeep/Plymouth, Dodge, Hancock Fabrics, Herberger's, Kohl's, Rainbow Foods, Target, TJ Maxx
5b a	I-35W, S to Albert Lea, N to Minneapolis
4b	Lyndale Ave, **N** Boston Mkt, Chipotle Mexican, Don Pablo's, DQ, Eddie Cheng's, Papa John's, Subway Candlewood Suites, Hampton Inn, Ramada Inn Best Buy, Honda, Lands End, PetsMart, Tires+, **S** Extended Stay America Lincoln, Mazda, Subaru
4a	MN 52, Nicollet Ave, **N** SA/dsl Burger King, Ember's, Jumbo Chinese, Rest Candlewood Suites Honda, Menards, **S** Mobil, Shell Big Boy, Culver's, Kwik Mart, McDonald's La Quinta, Super 8 Home Depot, Sam's Club
3	Portland Ave, 12th Ave, **N** PDQ Mart, Phillips 66, Sinclair Arby's AmericInn, **S** BP Denny's, Outback Steaks, Subway Comfort Inn/rest., Holiday Inn Express, Microtel, Quality Inn, Residence Inn, Travelodge Walgreens, Walmart
2c b	MN 77, **N** Motel 6, **S** BP, SA AmeriSuites, Best Western, Courtyard, Embassy Suites, Exel Inn, Fairfield Inn, Grand Motel, Marriott, Sheraton Mall of America, Nordstrom's, Sears
2a	24th Ave, same as 2c b
1b	34th Ave, Nat Cemetary, **S** Embassy Suites, Hilton, Holiday Inn
1a	MN 5 E, **N**
0mm	Minnesota River. **I-494/I-694 loops around Minneapolis/St Paul.**

MISSISSIPPI

INTERSTATE 10

Exit #	Services
77mm	Mississippi/Alabama state line, **weigh sta wb**
75	Franklin Creek Rd
75mm	**Welcome Ctr wb, full facilities, litter barrels, petwalk, , , RV dump, S weigh sta eb**
74mm	Escatawpa River
69	MS 63, to E Moss Point, **N** Raceway/dsl, Valero/Domino's/dsl/24hr Waffle House Best Value, Deluxe Inn, La Quinta, **S** Chevron/dsl, Exxon/Subway/dsl, /Moe's SW/dsl/scales/24hr, Shell Burger King, Cracker Barrel, Hardee's, KFC, McDonald's, Pizza Hut, Ruby Tuesday, San Miguel Mexican, Waffle House, Wendy's Best Western, Comfort Inn, Days Inn, Hampton Inn, Holiday Inn Express, Quality Inn, Shular Inn , Toyota
68	MS 613, to Moss Point, Pascagoula, **N** BP/Chester's, Chevron/dsl Coco Loco Mexican, Tugus' Rest. Super 8, **S** Marathon/dsl , Pelican Landing Conf Ctr
64mm	Pascagoula River
63.5mm	**both lanes, 24hr security, full facilities, litter barrels, petwalk, , , RV dump**

MOSS POINT

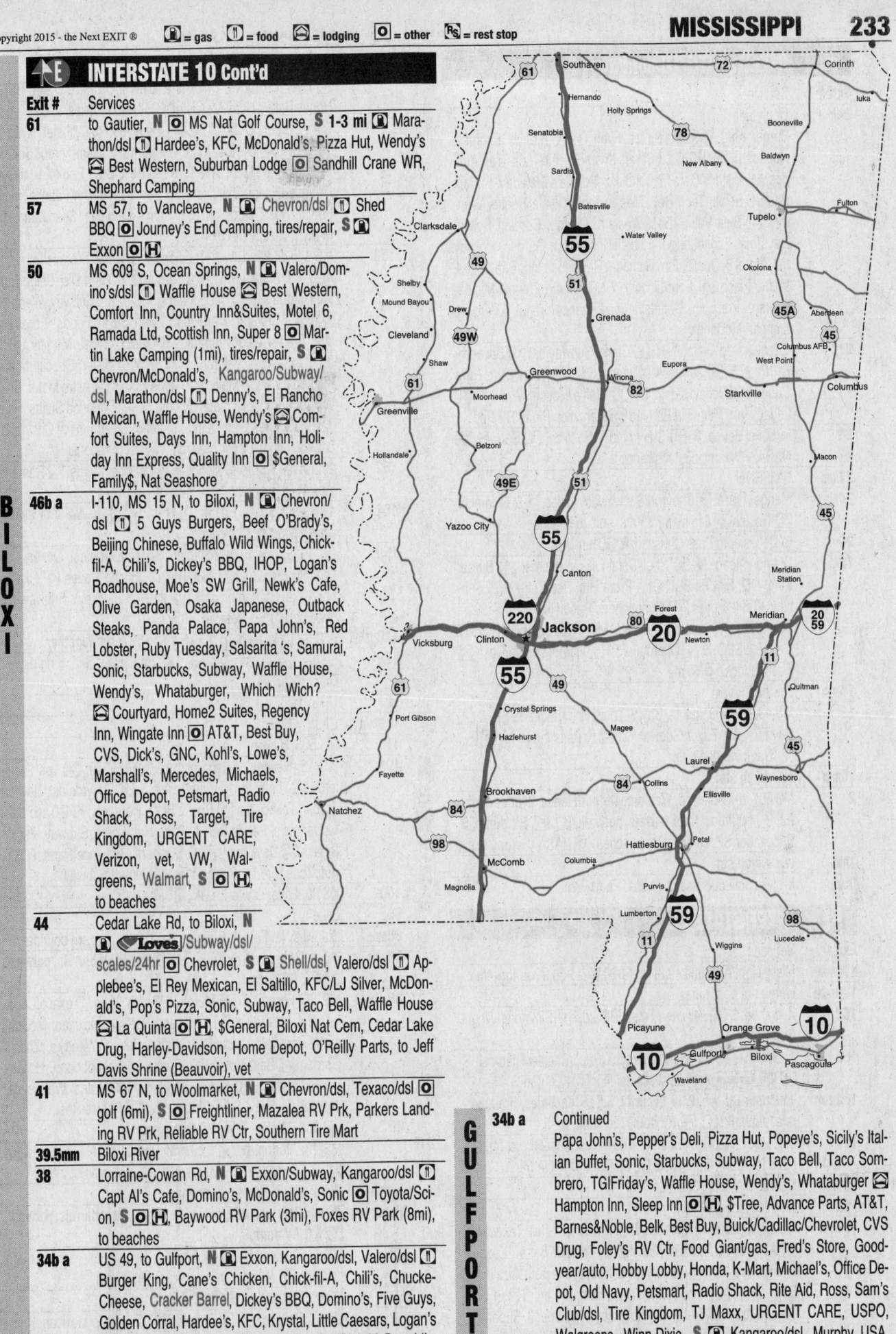

↑E INTERSTATE 10 Cont'd

Exit #	Services
61	to Gautier, **N** 🅞 MS Nat Golf Course, **S** **1-3 mi** 🅖 Marathon/dsl 🍴 Hardee's, KFC, McDonald's, Pizza Hut, Wendy's 🛏 Best Western, Suburban Lodge 🅞 Sandhill Crane WR, Shephard Camping
57	MS 57, to Vancleave, **N** 🅖 Chevron/dsl 🍴 Shed BBQ 🅞 Journey's End Camping, tires/repair, **S** 🅖 Exxon 🅞 🄷
50	MS 609 S, Ocean Springs, **N** 🅖 Valero/Domino's/dsl 🍴 Waffle House 🛏 Best Western, Comfort Inn, Country Inn&Suites, Motel 6, Ramada Ltd, Scottish Inn, Super 8 🅞 Martin Lake Camping (1mi), tires/repair, **S** 🅖 Chevron/McDonald's, Kangaroo/Subway/dsl, Marathon/dsl 🍴 Denny's, El Rancho Mexican, Waffle House, Wendy's 🛏 Comfort Suites, Days Inn, Hampton Inn, Holiday Inn Express, Quality Inn 🅞 $General, Family$, Nat Seashore
46b a	I-110, MS 15 N, to Biloxi, **N** 🅖 Chevron/dsl 🍴 5 Guys Burgers, Beef O'Brady's, Beijing Chinese, Buffalo Wild Wings, Chick-fil-A, Chili's, Dickey's BBQ, IHOP, Logan's Roadhouse, Moe's SW Grill, Newk's Cafe, Olive Garden, Osaka Japanese, Outback Steaks, Panda Palace, Papa John's, Red Lobster, Ruby Tuesday, Salsarita 's, Samurai, Sonic, Starbucks, Subway, Waffle House, Wendy's, Whataburger, Which Wich? 🛏 Courtyard, Home2 Suites, Regency Inn, Wingate Inn 🅞 AT&T, Best Buy, CVS, Dick's, GNC, Kohl's, Lowe's, Marshall's, Mercedes, Michaels, Office Depot, Petsmart, Radio Shack, Ross, Target, Tire Kingdom, URGENT CARE, Verizon, vet, VW, Walgreens, Walmart, **S** 🅞 🄷, to beaches
44	Cedar Lake Rd, to Biloxi, **N** 🅖 Loves/Subway/dsl/scales/24hr 🅞 Chevrolet, **S** 🅖 Shell/dsl, Valero/dsl 🍴 Applebee's, El Rey Mexican, El Saltillo, KFC/LJ Silver, McDonald's, Pop's Pizza, Sonic, Subway, Taco Bell, Waffle House 🛏 La Quinta 🅞 🄷, $General, Biloxi Nat Cem, Cedar Lake Drug, Harley-Davidson, Home Depot, O'Reilly Parts, to Jeff Davis Shrine (Beauvoir), vet
41	MS 67 N, to Woolmarket, **N** 🅖 Chevron/dsl, Texaco/dsl 🅞 golf (6mi), **S** 🅞 Freightliner, Mazalea RV Prk, Parkers Landing RV Prk, Reliable RV Ctr, Southern Tire Mart
39.5mm	Biloxi River
38	Lorraine-Cowan Rd, **N** 🅖 Exxon/Subway, Kangaroo/dsl 🍴 Capt Al's Cafe, Domino's, McDonald's, Sonic 🅞 Toyota/Scion, **S** 🅞 🄷, Baywood RV Park (3mi), Foxes RV Park (8mi), to beaches
34b a	US 49, to Gulfport, **N** 🅖 Exxon, Kangaroo/dsl, Valero/dsl 🍴 Burger King, Cane's Chicken, Chick-fil-A, Chili's, Chucke-Cheese, Cracker Barrel, Dickey's BBQ, Domino's, Five Guys, Golden Corral, Hardee's, KFC, Krystal, Little Caesars, Logan's Roadhouse, Longhorn Steaks, Marble Slab, McDonald's, Newk's Cafe, O'Charley's, O'Neal's PoBoy, Panda Palace,

G U L F P O R T

34b a Continued
Papa John's, Pepper's Deli, Pizza Hut, Popeye's, Sicily's Italian Buffet, Sonic, Starbucks, Subway, Taco Bell, Taco Sombrero, TGIFriday's, Waffle House, Wendy's, Whataburger 🛏 Hampton Inn, Sleep Inn 🅞 🄷, $Tree, Advance Parts, AT&T, Barnes&Noble, Belk, Best Buy, Buick/Cadillac/Chevrolet, CVS Drug, Foley's RV Ctr, Food Giant/gas, Fred's Store, Goodyear/auto, Hobby Lobby, Honda, K-Mart, Michael's, Office Depot, Old Navy, Petsmart, Radio Shack, Rite Aid, Ross, Sam's Club/dsl, Tire Kingdom, TJ Maxx, URGENT CARE, USPO, Walgreens, Winn-Dixie, **S** 🅖 Kangaroo/dsl, Murphy USA, RaceWay/dsl, Shell/dsl 🍴 Applebee's, Arby's,

B I L O X I

⬆E INTERSTATE 10 Cont'd

Exit #	Services
34b a	Continued
	Burger King, Dynasty Buffet, Food Court, Hibachi Express, Hooters, IHOP, KFC/LJ Silver, Krispy Kreme, Los Tres Amigos, McAlister's Deli, McDonald's, Morelia's Mexican, Shrimp Basket, Sonic, Taco Bell, Tres Amigos, Waffle House, Wendy's 🏨 Best Value, Best Western, Clarion, Comfort Suites, Days Inn, EconoLodge, Fairfield Inn, Hilton Garden, Holiday Inn, Motel 6, Quality Inn, Ramada, Residence Inn, Sun Suites, Value Place 🅾 Ford/Lincoln, GNC, Home Depot, Mazda, Nissan, Premium Outlets/famous brands, repair, Verizon, Walmart/McDonald's
31	Canal Rd, to Gulfport, N 🅶 Clarks/Subway/dsl 🅾 Bayberry RV Park, S 🅶 FLYING J/Denny's/dsl/LP/scales/24hr, Pure Country/McDonald's/dsl/24hr 🍴 Waffle House, Wendy's 🏨 Legacy Inn, Magnolia Bay Inn 🅾 Plantation Pines RV Prk
28	to Long Beach, S 🅶 Chevron/dsl, Shell/dsl 🍴 Subway 🅾 NAPA, RV camping, tires/repair
27mm	Wolf River
24	Menge Ave, N 🅶 Chevron/Subway/dsl/scales 🅾 $General, S 🅶 Texaco 🅾 flea mkt/RV Park, golf, to beaches
20	to De Lisle, to Pass Christian, N 🅶 Kin-Mart
16	Diamondhead, N 🅶 Shell/Domino's, Valero/dsl 🍴 Burger King, DQ, Fire Pit BBQ Grill, Pizza Hut, Red Zone Grill, Subway, Waffle House 🏨 Diamondhead Resort 🅾 Diamondhead Drug, Family$, repair, Rouse's Mkt, TrueValue, URGENT CARE, USPO, S 🅶 Giterdone/dsl 🍴 Harbor House Rest. 🏨 EconoLodge, 🅾 $Tree
15mm	Jourdan River
13	MS 43, MS 603, to Kiln, Bay St Louis, N 🅾 McLeod SP, S 🅶 Bay Fuel/dsl, Exxon/Subway/dsl 🏨 Knights Inn (6mi) 🅾 🅷, RV Camping (8-13mi)
10mm	eb, weigh sta
2	MS 607, to Waveland, **Welcome Ctr both lanes, 24hr security, full ♿ facilities, litter barrels, petwalk, 🚻, 🎁, RV dump, S** Buccaneer SP, camping, to beaches, 🅾 NASA Visitor Ctr
1mm	wb, weigh sta
0mm	Mississippi/Louisiana state line, Pearl River

⬆E INTERSTATE 20

Exit #	Services
172mm	Mississippi/Alabama state line. **I-20 W & I-59 S run together.**
170mm	weigh sta both lanes
169	Kewanee, S 🅶 Kewanee Trkstp/BBQ/dsl 🅾 Simmons-Wright Gen Store
165	Toomsuba, N 🅶 Shell/Subway, Texaco/ChesterFried/dsl, S 🅶 ❤Loves/Arby's/dsl/scales/24hr 🅾 KOA(2mi)
164mm	**Welcome Ctr wb, 24hr security, full ♿ facilities, litter barrels, petwalk, 🚻, 🎁, RV dump, vending, wi-fi**
160	to Russell, N 🅶 TA/Country Pride/dsl/scales/24hr/@ 🅾 Nanabe RV Camping(1mi), S 🅶 Shell/dsl 🅾 KOA (4mi)
157b a	US 45, to Macon, Quitman
156	Jimmie Rodgers Pkwy
154b a	MS 19 S, MS 39 N, Meridian, N 🅶 Pure/dsl, Shell, Texaco/dsl 🍴 Applebee's, Buffalo Wild Wings, Cracker Barrel, Logan's Roadhouse, Penn's Rest, Waffle House, Western Sizzlin 🏨 Days Inn, Drury Inn, Fairfield Inn, Hampton Inn, Hilton Garden, Holiday Inn, Relax Inn, Rodeway Inn, Super 8, Super Inn, Western Motel 🅾 auto repair, Back Country RV Ctr, Chrysler/Dodge/Jeep/Kia, U-Haul, S 🅶 Chevron/dsl, Texaco/dsl

NEWTON (vertical text in center margin)

Exit #	Services
154b a	Continued
	🍴 Beef 'O'Bradys, Chick-fil-A, Chili's, CiCi's, Dickey's BBQ, Honey Baked Ham, McAlister's Deli, McDonald's, O'Charley's, Olive Garden, Outback Steaks, Popeyes, Red Lobster, Ryan's, Taco Bell 🏨 Baymont Inn, Comfort Inn, Country Inn&Suites, Microtel 🅾 $Tree, AT&T, Belk, Best Buy, Books-A-Million, Dillard's, Harley-Davidson, JC Penney, Jo-Ann Fabrics, mall, PetCo, Ross, same as 153, Sam's Club/gas, Sears/auto, TJ Maxx, Tuesday Morning
153	MS 145 S, 22nd Ave, Meridian, N 🅶 Shell, Xpress Lane 🍴 Arby's, Bumper's Drive-In, Burger King, Capt D's, China Buffet, Hardee's, KFC, McDonald's, Pizza Hut, Subway, Wendy's 🅾 🅷, $General, CarQuest, Cash Saver Foods, Ford/Nissan, Fred's, Goodyear/auto, S 🅶 Exxon/dsl, Murphy USA/dsl, Texaco/dsl, Valero/dsl 🍴 A&W/LJ Silver, Checkerboard Kitchen, El Norte Mexican, Waffle House 🏨 Astro Motel, Best Western, Budget 8 Motel, EconoLodge, Extended Suites, Holiday Inn Express, La Quinta, Motel 6, Sleep Inn 🅾 Chevrolet, Lowe's, Office Depot, Verizon, Walmart/McDonald's
152	29th Ave, 31st Ave, Meridian, N 🅶 Chevron/dsl 🏨 Ramada Ltd, S 🏨 Royal Inn
151	49th Ave, Valley Rd, N 🅾 tires, S 🅶 🌀/Subway/dsl/scales/24hr 🅾 stockyards
150	US 11 S, MS 19 N, Meridian, N 🅶 Exxon/dsl, Queen City Trkstp/dsl/rest./@ 🍴 McDonald's, Waffle House 🅾 Okatibbee Lake, RV camping, S 🅶 Chevron/Stuckey's/Subway/dsl, Shell/dsl 🅾 🍴, Peterbilt
130 [149]	I-59 S, to Hattiesburg. **I-20 E and I-59 N run together.**
129	US 80 W, Lost Gap, S 🅶 Spaceway/Grill King/dsl/RV Dump/24hr
121	Chunky
119mm	Chunky River
115	MS 503, Hickory
109	MS 15, Newton, N 🅶 Shell/Jct Deli/dsl/24hr 🍴 Los Parrilleros 🏨 Thrifty Inn 🅾 lube/repair, S 🅶 Chevron/dsl, Newton Jct/dsl, Texaco/dsl 🍴 Cooks BBQ, Hardee's, KFC/Taco Bell, McDonald's, Panda Buffet, Pizza Hut, Sonic, Subway, Zack's Steaks 🏨 Days Inn 🅾 🅷, $General, Advance Parts, AT&T, AutoZone, Fred's, Piggly Wiggly, Walmart/Subway
100	US 80, Lake, Lawrence, N 🅶 BP/rest/dsl
96	Lake
95mm	Bienville Nat Forest, Bienville Nat Forest, eastern boundary
90mm	🆁🆂 eb, 24hr security, full ♿ facilities, litter barrels, petwalk, 🚻, 🎁, RV dump
88	MS 35, Forest, N 🅶 Murphy USA/dsl, Shell, Texaco/Chester's/dsl, Valero/dsl 🍴 KFC, Las Parrillas Mexican, McDonald's, Popeye's, Taco Bell, Waffle House, Wendy's, Zhen's Garden 🏨 Best Value Inn, Days Inn, EconoLodge, Holiday Inn Express 🅾 🅷, $Tree, AT&T, O'Reilly Parts, Walgreens, Walmart/Subway, S 🅶 Chevron/dsl 🍴 Penn's Rest.
80	MS 481, Morton, S 🅾 RV Camping
77	MS 13, Morton, N 🅶 Exxon/McDonald's/dsl, Texaco/dsl 🅾 🅷, RV camping, to Roosevelt SP, S 🅶 Shell/Subway/dsl
76mm	Bienville NF, western boundary
75mm	🆁🆂 wb, 24hr security, full ♿ facilities, litter barrels, petwalk, 🚻, 🎁, RV dump
68	MS 43, Pelahatchie, N 🅶 Chevron/Subway/dsl, Texaco/rest./dsl/24hr 🅾 Jellystone Camping, S 🅶 BP/dsl
59	US 80, E Brandon, **S 2 mi** 🅶 Shell/dsl
56	US 80, Brandon, N 🅶 Shell/dsl 🍴 El Potrillo Mexican, Krystal, Sonny's BBQ, Taco Bell 🏨 Microtel 🅾 AT&T, AutoZone, O'Reilly Parts, USPO, Verizon, S 🅶 BP, Chevron, Exxon,

INTERSTATE 20 Cont'd

BRANDON

Exit #	Services
56	Continued
	Mac's Gas, Texaco/dsl 🍴 DQ, Penn's Rest., Sonic, Waffle House, Wendy's 🛏 Best Value Inn, Red Roof Inn Ⓞ Auto+, to Ross Barnett Reservoir, vet
54	Crossgates Blvd, W Brandon, N Ⓡ Exxon, Kangaroo, Murphy USA 🍴 Abner's Chicken, Applebee's, Burger King, Chick-fil-A, China Buffet, Fernando's Fajita Factory, KFC, Little Caesars, Mazzio's, McAlister's Deli, McDonald's, Newk's Rest., Papa John's, Pizza Hut, Popeye's, Subway, Waffle House Ⓞ Ⓗ, $Tree, BigLots, Buick/GMC, Chevrolet, CVS Drug, Ford/Lincoln, Fred's, GNC, Hancock Fabrics, Kroger/dsl, Nissan, Office Depot, Piggly Wiggly, Radio Shack, Scotty's Tire/repair, Toyota/Scion, Tuesday Morning, Walgreens, Walmart/Subway, S Ⓡ Exxon/dsl, Kangaroo/dsl, Valero/Domino's/dsl 🍴 Steak Escape, Wendy's 🛏 La Quinta Ⓞ Home Depot, Honda, Tire Pros
52	MS 475, N Ⓡ RaceWay/dsl, Texaco/dsl, Valero/Subway/dsl 🍴 Waffle House 🛏 Quality Inn, Ramada, Sleep Inn, Super 8 Ⓞ Peterbilt, to Jackson ✈

PEARL

48	MS 468, Pearl, N Ⓡ Exxon/dsl, Snell/dsl, Texaco 🍴 Arby's, Baskin Robbins, Bumpers Drive-In, Cracker Barrel, Domino's, Dunkin Donuts, Jose's Rest., KFC, Kobe Japanese, Logan's Roadhouse, LoneStar Steaks, Los Parrilleros, McAlister's Deli, McDonald's, Mikado, Mikado Japanese, Moss Creek Fishouse, O'Charley's, Popeye's, Ruby Tuesday, Ryan's, Ryan's, Sonic, Subway, Waffle House, Wendy's 🛏 Baymont Inn, Best Western, Comfort Inn, Courtyard, Days Inn, Fairfield Inn, Hampton Inn, Hilton Garden, Holiday Inn Express, Motel 6 Ⓞ AT&T, CarCare, S Ⓡ Exxon/dsl, Valero/dsl 🛏 Candlewood Suites, Country Inn&Suites, La Quinta Ⓞ $General, Family$
47b a	US 49 S, Flowood, N Ⓡ 🚛FLYING J/Denny's/dsl/LP/RV dump/24hr, ♥Loves/Subway/dsl/scales/24hr 🍴 Western Sizzlin 🛏 Airport Inn, Holiday Inn Ⓞ Bass Pro Shop, MS Outlets/famous brands, Sam's Club/dsl, SpeedCo, S 2-3 mi Ⓡ RaceWay/dsl 🍴 Waffle House Ⓞ Freightliner, Kenworth, tires
46	I-55 N, to Memphis
45b	US 51, State St, to downtown

JACKSON

45a	Gallatin St, to downtown, N Ⓡ BP/dsl, Petro/Iron Skillet/dsl/scales/24hr/@, Shell Ⓞ Blue Beacon, tires/truck repair, vet, S Ⓡ 🚛/McDonald's/dsl/scales/24hr 🛏 Hilltop Inn Ⓞ Nissan
44	I-55 S (exits left from wb), to New Orleans
43b a	Terry Rd, N Ⓡ Exxon/dsl, Jasco Ⓞ Apache RV Ctr
42b a	Ellis Ave, Belvidere, N Ⓡ BP, Citgo/dsl, Shell 🍴 Capt D's, Church's, McDonald's, Pizza Hut, Popeye's, Sonny's BBQ, Wendy's 🛏 Best Inn, Metro Inn, Scottish Inn, Super 8 Ⓞ $Tree, Advance Parts, AutoZone, CarQuest, Family$, Firestone/auto, O'Reilly Parts, Sav-a-Lot Foods, transmissions, U-Haul, zoo, S Ⓡ Citgo/dsl, Exxon/dsl 🍴 DQ
41	I-220 N, US 49 N, to Jackson
40b a	MS 18 W, Robinson Rd, N Ⓡ Exxon/dsl, Jasco/dsl, Shell/dsl 🍴 Arby's, Krystal, Mazzio's, Piccadilly, Popeye's Ⓞ $General, AT&T, Office Depot, USPO, S Ⓡ Chevron, Citgo/dsl, Murphy USA, RaceWay/dsl, Shell/Church's/dsl 🍴 Chan's Garden, IHOP, McDonald's, Subway, Waffle House, Wendy's 🛏 Quality Inn Ⓞ Ⓗ, $Tree, GNC, Lowe's, Radio Shack, Walmart/Subway
36	Springridge Rd, Clinton, N Ⓡ Chevron/Burger King, Citgo/dsl, Murphy USA/dsl, Shell 🍴 Capt D's, Chick-fil-A,

CLINTON

36	Continued
	China Buffet, Chopstick Buffet, DQ, El Sombrero, Hungry Howie's, KFC, Kroger/dsl, Little Ceasars, Mazzio's, McAlister's, McDonald's, Newk's Cafe, Smoothie King, Sonic, Starbucks, Subway, Taco Bell, Waffle House, Wendy's, Zaxby's 🛏 Comfort Inn, Days Inn Ⓞ $Tree, Advance Parts, AT&T, BigLots, CVS Drug, Family$, Fred's, Home Depot, Kroger/gas, O'Reilly Parts, Radio Shack, Verizon, Walgreens, Walmart (2mi), S Ⓡ Exxon/Baskin-Robbins/Quiznos/dsl, Valero/dsl 🍴 Applebee's, Bonsai, Froghead Grill, Pizza Hut, Popeye's, Salsa's Mexican, Shoney's 🛏 Best Western, Econolodge, Hampton Inn, Holiday Inn Express, Quality Inn, Super 8 Ⓞ $General, Davis Tire, Springridge RV Park, vet
35	US 80 E, Clinton, N Ⓡ Chevron, Shell/dsl, Valero/dsl Ⓞ vet
34	Natchez Trace Pkwy
31	Norrell Rd
27	Bolton, S Ⓡ Chevron/dsl
19	MS 22, Edwards, Flora, N Ⓞ Askew's Landing Camping (2mi), S Ⓡ Exxon/dsl, Shell/dsl 🛏 Relax Inn
17mm	Big Black River
15	Flowers
11	Bovina, N Ⓡ Texaco/Subway/dsl/24hr Ⓞ RV camping
10mm	**weigh sta wb**
8mm	**weigh sta eb**
6.5mm	**parking area eb**
5b a	US 61, MS 27 S, N Ⓡ Exxon/dsl, Kangaroo/dsl 🍴 Sonic, S same as 4a
4b a	Clay St, N Ⓡ Valero/Kangaroo 🛏 Battlefield Inn, Hampton Inn, Motel 6, Quality Inn Ⓞ Ⓗ, RV Park, to Vicksburg NP, S Ⓡ Texaco, Valero/dsl 🍴 Bumper's Drive-In, China Buffet, Cracker Barrel, Little Caesars, McAlister's deli, Pizza Inn, Rowdy's Rest., Subway, Waffle House, Wendy's 🛏 Baymont Inn, Beechwood Inn/rest., Comfort Suites, Courtyard, Econolodge, Holiday Inn Express, La Quinta, Scottish Inn Ⓞ $General, Outlet Mall/famous brands/deli, same as 5, Toyota

VICKSBURG

3	Indiana Ave, N Ⓡ Valero/Subway/dsl 🍴 China King, McDonald's, Papa John's, Waffle House 🛏 Best Western, Deluxe Inn Ⓞ Chevrolet, Chrysler/Dodge/Jeep, Corner Mkt Foods, Ford/Lincoln, Honda, Mazda, Nissan, Rite Aid, S Ⓡ Kangaroo/dsl 🍴 Goldie's BBQ, Heavenly Ham, KFC 🛏 Best Inn Ⓞ Buick/Cadillac/GMC, Family$
1c	Halls Ferry Rd, N Ⓡ Exxon/dsl 🍴 Burger King, Sonic 🛏 Travel Inn Ⓞ Ⓗ, CVS Drug, Durst Drugs, S Ⓡ Kangaroo/dsl 🍴 Asian Kitchen, Capt D's, Chick-fil-A, El Sombrero Mexican, Garfield's Rest., Goldie's Express, Little Caesars, Newk's Eatery, Pizza Hut, Popeye's, Shoney's, Subway, Taco Bell, Taco Casa, Wendy's, Whataburger 🛏 Candlewood Suites, Fairfield Inn, Holiday Inn, Rodeway Inn, Super 8 Ⓞ $General,

| | = gas | = food | = lodging | = other | = rest stop   Copyright 2015 - the Next EXIT ® |

INTERSTATE 20 Cont'd

Exit #	Services
1c	Continued
	Advance Parts, AT&T, Belk, BigLots, Dillard's, Fred's, Hobby Lobby, Home Depot, JC Penney, Kroger/dsl, TJ Maxx, USPO, Walgreens
1b	US 61 S, S Kangaroo/Domino's/dsl, Murphy Express/dsl McDonald's, Panda Buffet, Waffle House $Tree, Radio Shack, same as 1c, Verizon, Walmart/Subway
1a	Washington St, Vicksburg, N Welcome Ctr both lanes, full facilities, Kangaroo/dsl, Shell/Subway/dsl AmeriStar Hotel/Casino/RV Park, S Waffle House Best Value Inn, Days Inn
0mm	Mississippi/Louisiana state line, Mississippi River

INTERSTATE 22 (Future)

Exit #	Services
118mm	Alabama/Mississippi State Line
115mm	Welcome Ctr/ wb, litter barrels, petwalk, , RV dump, vending
113	rd 23, Tremont, Smithville
108	rd 25 N, Belmont, Iuka
106mm	both lanes, weigh sta
104	rd 25 S, Fulton, Amory, N Shell/cafe/dsl/scales, Texaco/dsl Burger King, Hardee's, Homer's BBQ, Huddle House, McDonald's, Mi Toro Mexican, Sonic, Subway Days Inn, Holiday Inn Express $General, AutoZone, Food Giant/dsl, Fred's, O'Reilly Parts, RV camping, Whitten HS, Brown's Auto Repair, S Murphy USA/dsl Peking Palace AT&T, KFC, Los Compadres Mexican, Pizza Hut, URGENT CARE, Walmart, Wendy's
104mm	Tombigbee River/Tenn-Tom Waterway
101	rd 178, rd 363, Peppertown, Mantachie, N Exxon, S Dorsey Fuel/dsl (2mi)
97	Fawn Grove Rd
94	rd371, Mantachie, Mooreville, N Woco/Pizza Inn/dsl
90	Auburn Rd, N Dee's Oil/dsl
87	Veterans Blvd, N Shell/Chix Rest/dsl Huddle House Wingate Inn E. Presley Campground/Park, S Tombigbee SP
86	US 45 N, Tupelo, to Corinth, N 1 exit BP, Shell, Texaco Abner's Rest., Applebee's, Burger King, Capt D's, Chick-fil-A, Chili's, ChuckeCheese, Cici's Pizza, Cracker Barrel, IHOP, Kyoto Japanese, Lenny's Subs, Logan's Roadhouse, McDonald's, New China, O'Charley's, Olive Garden, Pizza Hut, Red Lobster, Ryan's, Sonic, Subway, Taco Bell, Wendy's Baymont Inn, Best Inn, Comfort Inn, Days Inn, Fairfield Inn, Hampton Inn, Jameson Inn, La Quinta $General, AutoZone, Barnes&Noble, Belk, Best Buy, Books-A-Million, Dick's, Ford/Lincoln, Hobby Lobby, Home Depot, Hyundai, JC Penney, Kohl's, Kroger/gas, Lowe's, Mazda, NAPA, Old Navy, Petsmart, Ross, Sam's Club/gas, Sears, Staples, Toyota, Tuesday Morning, Walgreens, Walmart
85	Natchez Trace Pkwy
81	rd 178, McCullough Blvd, N Loves/McDonald's/dsl/scales/24hr, S Exxon/dsl, Shell/dsl, Texaco/dsl Old Venice Pizza, Sonic Super 8 $General, USPO
76	rd 9 S, Sherman, Pontotoc, N Wild Bill's/dsl Sherman RV Ctr
73	rd 9 N, Blue Springs
64	rd 15, rd 30 E, Pontotoc, Ripley, N Eagle/dsl, S /Arby's/scales/dsl/24hr, Shell/dsl

63	New Albany, N Dee's Oil/dsl Buick/Chevrolet/GMC, Ford
62mm	Tallahatchie River
61	rd 30 W, W New Albany, N Express China Buffet, McAlister's Deli, McDonald's, Pizza Hut, Subway, Wendy's Hampton Inn , Rite Aid, Walgreens, S Exxon, Murphy USA/dsl, Shell Burger King, Capt D's, Huddle House, KFC, Mi Pueblo Mexican, Taco Bell, Wendy's, Western Sizzlin Comfort Inn, Economy Inn, Hallmarc Inn, Holiday Inn Express , $Tree, Lowe's, Radio Shack, to U of MS, Walmart
60	Glenfield, to Oxford, N Budget Inn, S to U of MS
55	Myrtle
48	rd 178, Hickory Flat, S Trkstp/rest/dsl/24hr
41	rd 346, Potts Camp, S Flicks/dsl $General, CarQuest
41mm	Tippah River
37	Lake Center, N Chewalla Lake/RV camping
30	rd 7, rd 4, Holly Springs, Oxford, N Exxon, Shell/Chester's/BBQ Capt D's, El Nopalito, Huddle House, KFC, McDonalds, Panda Buffet, Pizza Hut, Popeye's, Sonic, Subway, Taco Bell, Wendy's Magnolia Inn , $General, AutoZone, Libby's Drug, Save-a-Lot, Wall Doxey SP/RV camping, S Exxon Days Inn, Le Brooks Inn Walmart
26	W Holly Springs
21	Red Banks, N Dee's Oil/dsl, Texaco/dsl
18	Victoria, E Byhalia, N BP
14	rd 309, Byhalia, N Exxon, Shell/Chester's/dsl Best Value Inn
10	W Byhalia
6	Bethel Rd, Hacks Crossroad, N FLYING J/Denny's/dsl/scales/LP/RV dump/24hr, BP, Shell/Chesters/dsl JR's Grill, Tops BBQ Best Western, Super 8 truck repair
6mm	parking area both lanes
4	rd 305, Olive Branch, Independence, N BP/dsl, Mobil/Huddle House, Shell/Circle K Old Style BBQ, Pizza Hut Holiday Inn Express, S BP/Quiznos CVS Drug
3.5mm	both lanes, weigh sta
2	rd 302, Olive Branch, N Abbay's Rest., Baskin-Robbins, Buffalo Wild Wings, Chick-fil-A, Chili's, Colton's Steaks, IHOP, Krystal, Lenny's Subs, McAlisters Deli, O'Charley's, Starbucks, Subway, Wendy's Candlewood Suites, Comfort Suites $Tree, Ford, Home Depot, Lowe's, Radio Shack, Walmart, S Chevron/dsl, Shell/Circle K Applebees, Backyard Burger, Burger King, Casa Mexicana, Honeybaked Ham, Hunan Chinese, McDonald's, Panera Bread, Papa John's, Steak Escape, Subway, Taco Bell, Waffle House, Zaxby's Comfort Inn, Hampton Inn AutoZone, CVS Drug, GNC, Goodyear/auto, Kroger/dsl, Petco
1	Craft Rd, N American RV Ctr, Chevrolet, Hyundai, Suzuki
0mm	Mississippi/Tennessee state line, I-22 (future) begins/ends. US 78 continues wb.

INTERSTATE 55

Exit #	Services
291.5mm	Mississippi/Tennessee state line
291	State Line Rd, Southaven, E Exxon, RaceWay/dsl, Shell/dsl Interstate BBQ, Little Caesars, Subway, Tops BBQ Waffle House Days Inn, Holiday Inn Express, Quality Inn, Southern Inn, Super 8 Family$, Firestone/auto, Goodyear/auto, Kroger/dsl, Southaven RV Park, Walgreens, W Exxon Capt D's, Checker's, China Wok, Dales Rest, El Patron Mexican, Lucky China, Mainstreet Pizza, Sonic, Taco Bell, Wendy's BigLots, Fred's, Mainstreet Automotive, Rite Aid, tires, USPO

Side markers: OLIVE BRANCH, CORINTH, SOUTHAVEN

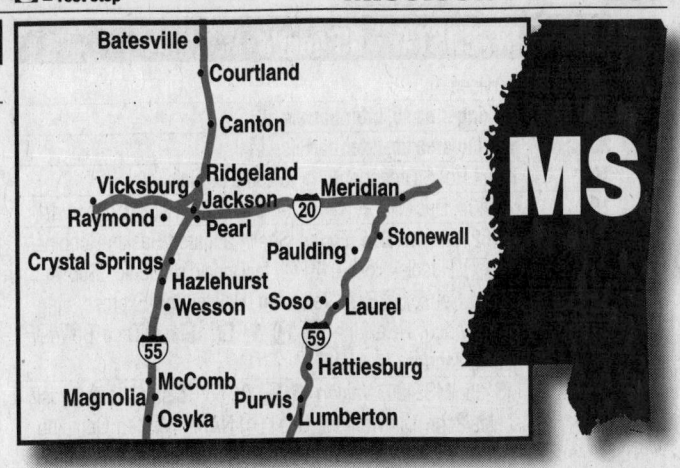

INTERSTATE 55 Cont'd

Exit #	Services
289	MS 302, to US 51, Horn Lake, **E** 🅟 BP/Circle K, Shell 🍴 Abbays Rest., Backyard Burger, Baskin-Robbins, Brusters, Buffalo Wild Wings, Burger King, Chick-fil-A, Chili's, Dunkin Donuts, Fazoli's, Firehouse Subs, Fox&Hound, Haru Japanese, Huey's Rest., Hunan Buffet, IHOP, Krystal, Kublai Khan, La Hacienda, Lenny's Subs, Logan's Roadhouse, Longhorn Steaks, Maria's Cantina, McDonald's, Mi Pueblo, Nagoya Japanese, O'Charley's, Olive Garden, On-the-Border, Outback Steaks, Red Lobster, Sonic, Starbucks, Steak'n Shake, Subway, TGIFriday's, Wendy's 🛏 Comfort Suites, Courtyard, Fairfield Inn, Hampton Inn, Hilton Garden, Holiday Inn, Home-2Suites, Residence Inn 🅾 🅗 $Tree, Aldi Foods, AT&T, Best Buy, Books-A-Million, Buick/GMC, Chevrolet, Chrysler/Dodge/Jeep, CVS Drug, Dillards, Ford, GNC, Gordman's, Hancock Fabrics, JC Penney, Jo-Ann Fabrics, Kroger/dsl, Lowe's, Marshall's, Nissan, Office Depot, Old Navy, PetCo, Radio Shack, Sam's Club/gas, Tuesday Morning, URGENT CARE, Verizon, Walmart/Subway, **W** 🅟 BP/Circle K, Phillips 66/dsl, Shell/Circle K/dsl 🍴 Applebee's, Arby's, ChuckECheese's, Country Home Buffet, Cracker Barrel, Grand Buffet, Holiday Deli, Hooters, KFC, McDonald's, Memphis BBQ, Mrs Winner's, Papa John's, Pizza Hut, Popeye's, Ryan's, Sekisui Japan, Taco Bell, TX Roadhouse, Waffle House, Wendy's, Zaxby's 🛏 Best Western, Comfort Inn, Drury Inn, EconoLodge, La Quinta, Motel 6, Ramada Ltd, Sleep Inn 🅾 CVS Drug, Family$, Gateway Tires/repair, Home Depot, Kroger, Meineke, Save-a-Lot Foods, Target, Verizon, Walgreens
287	Church Rd, **E** 🅟 Citgo/dsl 🍴 Domino's, Wadford's Grill 🅾 AutoZone, **W** 🅟 Citgo/dsl, Shell/Circle K/dsl 🍴 3 Guys Pizza, Boiling Point Seafood, Casa Mexicana, McDonald's, Sonic, Subway, Taco Bell, Waffle House 🛏 Keywest Inn, Magnolia Inn 🅾 El Daze RV Camping (1mi), Family$, Fred's, Harley-Davidson, Jellystone Camping, Southaven RV Ctr, Walgreens
285mm	**weigh sta both lanes**
284	to US 51, Nesbit Rd, **W** 🅟 Shell 🍴 Happy Daze Dairybar 🅾 USPO
283	I-69, MS 304, Tunica
280	MS 304, US 51, Hernando, **E** 🅟 Exxon, Murphy USA/dsl 🍴 Arby's, Asian Buffet, Capt D's, Dominos, Fins Grill, Guadalajara Mexican, KFC, Sonic, Steak Escape, Taco Bell, Zaxby's 🛏 Days Inn, Hampton Inn 🅾 $Tree, AT&T, Ultimate Tires/repair, URGENT CARE, Walgreens, Walmart, **W** 🅟 Mobil, Shell/Circle K/dsl 🍴 Brick Oven Rest., Coleman's BBQ, Lenny's Subs, Little Caesars, McDonald's, Mi Pueblo, Mr Chen's, Papa John's, Pizza Hut, Subway, Taco Felix, Waffle House, Wendy's 🛏 Super 8 🅾 AutoZone, Bryant Repair, Desoto Museum, Family$, Fred's, Kroger/gas, Memphis S Camping (2mi), NAPA, to Arkabutla Lake, USPO
279mm	**Welcome Ctr sb, 24hr security, full ♿ facilities, litter barrels, petwalk, 🚻, 🍽, RV dump**
276mm	**🆁🆂 nb, 24hr security, full ♿ facilities, litter barrels, petwalk, 🚻, 🍽, RV dump**
273mm	Coldwater River
271	MS 306, Coldwater, **W** 🅟 Shell/dsl 🍴 Subway 🅾 Lake Arkabutla, Memphis S RV Park
265	MS 4, Senatobia, **W** 🅟 BP/dsl, Exxon, ▦▦▦/Huddle House/dsl/scales/24hr, Shell/dsl 🍴 Backyard Burger, Coleman's BBQ, Domino's, KFC, McDonald's/playplace, New China Buffet, Pizza Hut, Popeye's, Rio Lindo Mexican, Sonic, Subway, Taco Bell, Waffle House, Wendy's 🛏 Best Value Inn,

Exit #	Services
265	Continued
	Days Inn 🅾 🅗, AT&T, CarQuest, City Drug, Curves, Fred's, Kaye Mkt, transmissions, truck repair, USPO
263	rd 740, S Senatobia
257	MS 310, Como, **E** 🅟 Dee's Oil 🅾 N Sardis Lake, **W** 🅟 Citgo/dsl 🍴 Windy City Grille (1mi)
252	MS 315, Sardis, **E** 🅟 Chevron/dsl, Local/dsl 🍴 McDonald's 🛏 Lake Inn, Super 8 🅾 NAPA, repair, RV camping, Sardis Dam, to Kyle SP, **W** 🅟 BP/Chester's/dsl, Shell/dsl 🍴 Sonic 🅾 🅗, $General, Family$, Fred's
246	MS 35, N Batesville, **E** 🅾 to Sardis Lake, **W** 🅟 ♥Loves/McDonald's/Subway/dsl/scales/24hr, Shell/dsl
243b a	MS 6, to Batesville, **E** 🅟 BP/dsl, Murphy USA/dsl, Shell/dsl 🍴 Backyard Burger, Chili's, Mi Pueblo Mexican, Zaxby's 🛏 Comfort Suites 🅾 🅗, $Tree, Lowe's, to Sardis Lake, U of MS, Walmart/Subway, **W** 🅟 BP, Exxon/dsl, Phillips 66/dsl, Shell/dsl, Valero/Kangaroo/dsl 🍴 Burger King, Burn's BBQ, Cafe Ole, Capt D's, Cracker Barrel, Domino's, Hardee's, Huddle House, KFC, McDonald's, New China, Pizza Hut, Popeye's, Sonic, Subway, Taco Bell, Waffle House, Wendy's, Western Sizzlin 🛏 Days Inn, EconoLodge, Hampton Inn, Holiday Inn, Quality Inn, Ramada Ltd 🅾 🅗, $General, AT&T, AutoZone, Curves, Factory Stores/famous brands, Family$, Fred's, Kroger, O'Reilly Parts, Piggly Wiggly, Save-a-Lot, URGENT CARE, USPO, Walgreens
240mm	🆁🆂 **both lanes, 24hr security, full ♿ facilities, litter barrels, petwalk, 🚻, 🍽, RV dump**
237	to US 51, Courtland, **E** 🅟 Pure/dsl, **W** 🅾 $General
233	to Enid Dam, **E** 🅾 RV camping, to Enid Lake
227	MS 32, Oakland, **E** 🅾 Sunrise RV Park, to Cossar SP, **W** 🅟 Exxon/Chester's/dsl, Shell/dsl 🅾 $General, antiques
220	MS 330, Tillatoba, **E** 🅟 Conoco/rest./dsl/@
211	MS 7 N, to Coffeeville, **E** 🅾 Frog Hollow RV Park, **W** 🅟 Shell/Chester's/dsl
208	Papermill Rd, **E** 🅾 Grenada 🛏
206	MS 8, MS 7 S, to Grenada, **E** 🅟 Exxon/dsl, Shell/dsl 🍴 Burger King, China Buffet, Church's, Clubhouse Rest., Domino's, Great Wall Chinese, Jake&Rip's Café, La Cabana Mexican, Lost Pizza Co., McAlister's Deli, McDonald's, Pizza Hut, Pizza Inn, Shoney's, Subway, Taco Bell, Wendy's, Western Sizzlin 🛏 Baymont Inn, Best Value Inn, Days Inn, EconoLodge, Hampton Inn, Holiday Inn Express, Quality Inn, Relax Inn, Super 8 🅾 🅗, $General, $Tree, Advance Parts, AT&T, AutoZone, Chrysler/Dodge/Jeep, Curves, CVS Drug, GNC, O'Reilly Parts, Radio Shack, to Grenada Lake/RV camping, USPO, Walmart/McDonald's, **W** 🅟 Exxon/Huddle House 🍴 Waffle House 🛏 Comfort Inn, Motel 6 🅾 Ford/Lincoln, Nissan, repair, Toyota

BATESVILLE

GRENADA

MS

⬆N INTERSTATE 55 Cont'd

Exit #	Services
204mm	parking area sb, litter barrels, ⌨
202mm	parking area nb, litter barrels, ⌨
199	Troutt Rd, S Grenada, E ⭕ to camp McCain
195	MS 404, Duck Hill, E ⭕ to Camp McCain, W 🗝 Conoco/dsl
185	US 82, Winona, E 🗝 Exxon, Shell/Kangaroo/Baskin-Robbins/dsl 🍴 Huddle House, KFC, McDonald's, Sonic, Subway, Waffle House 🛏 Best Value Inn, Holiday Inn Express, Magnolia Lodge, Relax Inn ⭕ 🛏, W 🗝 💼/Taco Bell/dsl/scales/24hr/@
174	MS 35, MS 430, Vaiden, E 🗝 35-55 Trkstp/Chester's/dsl/scales/24hr, Chevron/dsl, Shell ⭕ NAPA, Vaiden Camping, W 🗝 Exxon/dsl
173mm	℞ sb, 24hr security, full ♿ facilities, litter barrels, petwalk, ⌨, 🐾, RV dump
164	to West, W 🗝 West Trkstp/dsl
163mm	℞ nb, 24hr security, full ♿ facilities, litter barrels, petwalk, ⌨, 🐾, RV dump
156	MS 12, Durant, E 🗝 Shell/Chester's/dsl 🍴 Subway 🛏 Durant Motel/rest. (3mi), Super 8, W ⭕ 🛏 (7mi)
150	E ⭕ Holmes Co SP, RV camping
146	MS 14, Goodman, W ⭕ to Little Red Schoolhouse
144	MS 17, to Pickens, W 🗝 BP/Baskin-Robbins/dsl/24hr ⭕ to Little Red Schoolhouse
139	MS 432, to Pickens
133	Vaughan, E ⭕ to Casey Jones Museum
128mm	Big Black River
124	MS 16, to N Canton
119	MS 22, to MS 16 E, Canton, E 🗝 Canton Jct/dsl, Exxon, Kangaroo/Subway/dsl, Shell/Domino's, Valero/dsl 🍴 El Sombrero Mexican, McDonald's, Pizza Hut, Popeye's, Sonic, Waffle House, Wendy's, Western Sizzlin 🛏 Best Value Inn, Best Western, Brentwood Inn, Hampton Inn, Holiday Inn Express, La Quinta, Relax Inn, Studio 9 ⭕ 🛏, $General Mkt, Family$, O'Reilly Parts, to Ross Barnett Reservoir, W 🗝 Chevron/KFC/dsl, Citgo, 💙Loves/Arby's/dsl/scales/24hr/@, Texaco/Penn's/dsl 🍴 2 Rivers Steaks, Bumpers Drive-In
118a b	Nissan Parkway, E ⭕ to Nissan
114a b	Sowell Rd
112	US 51, Gluckstadt, E 🗝 Exxon/Krystal/dsl 🍴 Sonic 🛏 Super 8 ⭕ Goodyear/auto, W ⭕ Camper Corral RV Ctr
108	MS 463, Madison, E 🗝 Shell/dsl, Valero/dsl 🍴 Applebee's, Backyard Burger, Burger King, Chick-Fil-A, Chili's, Coldstone, Corner Bakery Café, Dickey's BBQ, El Potrillo, Haute Pig Café, Little Caesars ⭕ $Tree, AT&T, Best Buy, Dick's, GNC, Lowe's, Michael's, Office Depot, PetCo, SteinMart, Walmart, W 🗝 Exxon/KFC/dsl 🍴 BoneFish Grill, Nagoya Japanese, Papito's Grill, PieWorks, Pizza Inn, Subway, Tay's BBQ, Wendy's 🛏 Hilton Garden ⭕ 🛏, CVS Drug, Home Depot, Kroger
105c b	Old Agency Rd, E 🗝 Chevron/dsl 🛏 Home2Suites ⭕ Honda, Hyundai, W 🍴 5 Guys Burgers, Biaggi's Ristorante, Maggie Moo's, PF Changs, Ruth's Chris Steaks, Smoothie King, Sweet Peppers Cafe 🛏 Hyatt Place ⭕ Barnes&Noble, Fresh Mkt Foods
105a	Natchez Trace Pkwy
104	I-220, to W Jackson
103	County Line Rd, E 🗝 Chevron, Exxon/dsl, Murphy Express/dsl 🍴 Applebee's, Bop's Custard, Bulldog Grill, Burgers&Blues Cafe, Cane's, Chick-fil-A, ChuckECheese's, Cozumel Mexican, Grand China, HoneyBaked Ham, Huntington's Grille, Jason's Deli, KFC, King Buffet, Krispy Kreme, Mazzio's,

C A N T O N

M A D I S O N

103	Continued
	Papito's Grill, Peachtree Cafe, Pizza Hut, Popeye's, Shoney's, Taco Bell, Wendy's, Whataburger, Zaxby's 🛏 Cabot Lodge, Courtyard, Days Inn, EconoLodge, Hilton, Quality Inn, Red Roof Inn ⭕ $Tree, Acura, Belk, Best Buy, BigLots, Cadillac, Dillard's, JC Penney, Lowe's, Marshall's, Office Depot, Old Navy, Radio Shack, Sam's Club/gas, TJ Maxx, to Barnett Reservoir, Tuesday Morning, Verizon, Walgreens, Walmart, W 🍴 Logan's Roadhouse, Nagoya Japanese, Olive Garden, Red Lobster, Subway 🛏 Drury Inn, Holiday Inn Express, Motel 6, Studio 7 ⭕ Fred's, Home Depot, Jo-Ann Fabrics, Office Depot, Petsmart, Target, Upton Tire
102b	Beasley Rd, Adkins Blvd, E 🍴 Cracker Barrel, Outback Steaks, Twin Peaks Rest. 🛏 Super 8 ⭕ Chevrolet, Ford, Nissan, Toyota/Scion, W 🗝 Exxon/dsl, Shell/dsl 🍴 Baskin-Robbins, Burger King, Chili's, IHOP, McDonald's 🛏 Baymont Inn, Best Western, Fairfield Inn, Hampton Inn, Harmony Court, Howard Johnson, InTown Suites ⭕ CarMax, frontage rds access 102a, Mercedes, Save-A-Lot Foods
102a	Briarwood, E 🛏 La Quinta ⭕ Buick/GMC, W 🍴 Capt D's, Popeye's 🛏 Clarion, Hampton Inn ⭕ Chrysler/Dodge/Jeep, Porsche/Smart
100	North Side Dr W, E 🗝 BP/dsl, Chevron, Sprint 🍴 Burger King, Char Rest., Charokee Drive-In, McAlister's Deli, Papa John's, Piccadilly's, Pizza Hut, Starbucks, Subway, Wendy's 🛏 Extended Stay America ⭕ $Tree, AT&T, Audi, Books-A-Million, CVS Drug, Firestone/auto, Goodyear/auto, Jaguar/LandRover, Kroger/gas, Office Depot, SteinMart, vet, VW, Walgreens, W 🗝 Exxon/dsl FastLane, Shell 🍴 Domino's, Hooters, Waffle House 🛏 Select Motel, USA Inn
99	Meadowbrook Rd, Northside Dr E (from nb), E 🍴 Newk's Eatery
98c b	MS 25 N, Lakeland Dr, E 🗝 Shell/dsl 🛏 Parkside Inn ⭕ LaFleur's Bluff SP, museum, W ⭕ 🛏, ⛽
98a	Woodrow Wilson Dr (exits left from nb), downtown
96c	Fortification St, E 🛏 Studio 6 Suites, W ⭕ 🛏, Bellhaven College
96b	High St, Jackson, E ⭕ BMW, Chevrolet, Infiniti, Lexus, W 🗝 Shell/Subway/dsl, Valero/Kangaroo/dsl 🍴 Arby's, Chimneyville Cafe, Domino's, Popeye's, Shoney's, Taco Bell, Waffle House, Wendy's, Whataburger 🛏 Best Western, Comfort Inn, Days Inn, Hampton Inn, Jackson Hotel, Red Roof Inn, Regency Hotel, Travelodge ⭕ 🛏, fairgrounds, Honda, museum, st capitol, Subaru/Volvo
96a	Pearl St (from nb), Jackson, W access to same as 96b, downtown
94	(46 from nb), I-20 E, to Meridian, US 49 S
45b [I-20]	US 51, State St, N 🗝 BP, Petro, Shell, S 🗝 💼, to downtown
45a	Gallatin St (from sb), N 🗝 BP, Petro/dsl, Shell, S 🗝 💼/McDonald's/dsl ⭕ Nissan
92c	(44 from sb), I-20 W, to Vicksburg, US 49 N
92b	US 51 N, State St, Gallatin St
92a	McDowell Rd, E 🗝 Petro/dsl, 💼/McDonald's/dsl, W 🗝 BJ's/dsl, BP/dsl, Citgo/dsl, Exxon, Shell 🍴 McDonald's, Subway, Waffle House ⭕ Food Depot, Fred's, Rite Aid, Roses
90b	Daniel Lake Blvd (from sb), W 🗝 Shell ⭕ Harley-Davidson
90a	Savanna St, E ⭕ transmissions, W 🗝 BP ⭕ Caney Creek RV Ctr
88	Elton Rd, W 🗝 Exxon/dsl, Shell/Subway/dsl
85	Byram, E 🗝 Blue Sky/dsl, BP/Burns Grill/dsl 🍴 Krystal, Mexican Grill, Tin Shed BBQ 🛏 Comfort Inn, ValuePlace

J A C K S O N

⬆N INTERSTATE 55 Cont'd

Exit #	Services
85	Continued
	🅾 Swinging Bridge RV Park, **W** 🅿 Byram/dsl, Chevron, Exxon/dsl, Valero/Kangaroo/dsl 🍴 Backyard Burger, Burger King, Capt D's, Domino's, KFC, Mazzio's, McAlister's Deli, McDonald's, New China, Newk's Eatery, Papa John's, Pizza Hut, Popeye's, Sonic, Subway, Taco Bell, Waffle House, Wendy's 🏠 Days Inn, Holiday Inn Express 🅾 $General, AutoZone, Family$, Mkt Place Foods, NAPA, O'Reilly Parts, Tire Depot, Walgreens
81	Wynndale Rd, **E** 🅾 repair, **W** 🅿 Chevron/dsl
78	Terry, **E** 🅿 Citgo/dsl, Texaco/Subway/dsl 🅾 Buick/Chevrolet/GMC (1mi), Fred's, USPO, **W** 🅿 Mac's 🅾 $General
72	MS 27, Crystal Springs, **E** 🅿 Exxon/Subway/dsl, Phillips 66/dsl 🍴 Louise's Pit BBQ, McDonald's, Popeye's 🅾 Ford, vet
68	to US 51, S Crystal Springs, **E** 🅿 gas/dsl 🅾 Red Barn Produce, vet
65	to US 51, Gallman, **E** 🅿 Stuckey's/dsl
61	MS 28, Hazlehurst, **E** 🅿 BP, Exxon/Circle K/Subway/dsl, Murphy Express/dsl, Phillips 66/dsl, Pump&Save 🍴 Bumpers Drive Inn, Burger King, China Buffet, KFC/Taco Bell, McDonald's, Pizza Hut, Sonic, Waffle House, Wendy's 🏠 Best Value Inn, Claridge Inn, Western Inn 🅾 🏠, $General, $Tree, Advance Parts, Family$, Fred's, Walgreens, Walmart
59	to S Hazlehurst
56	to Martinsville
54mm	Ⓡ both lanes, 24hr security, full ♿ facilities, litter barrels, petwalk, 🐾, 🛢, RV dump, vending
51	to Wesson, **E** 🅾 Lake Lincoln SP, **W** 🅿 Country Jct Trkstp/rest/dsl
48	Mt Zion Rd, to Wesson
42	to US 51, N Brookhaven, **E** 🅿 Exxon/Subway, Shell/Gridiron Grill/dsl/scales/24hr 🅾 🏠, **W** 🏠 Super 8
40	to MS 550, Brookhaven, **E** 🅿 Blue Sky, BP/Domino's/dsl, Exxon/Subway, Murphy USA/dsl, Shell/dsl 🍴 Bowie BBQ, Burger King, China Buffet, Cracker Barrel, DQ, El Sombrero Little Caesars, Hudgey's Rest., KFC, Krystal, McDonald's, Mitchell's Steaks, Pizza Hut, Popeye's, Sonic, Taco Bell, Waffle House, Wards Burgers, Wendy's, Western Sizzlin 🏠 Best Inn, Best Value Inn, Comfort Inn, Hampton Inn, Holiday Inn Express, Lincoln Inn, Spanish Inn 🅾 🏠, $General, $Tree, AT&T, AutoZone, Buick/Cadillac/Chevrolet/GMC, CarQuest, Family$, Ford/Lincoln, Fred's, Gene's Tires, Honda, Nissan, O'Reilly Parts, Rite Aid, Save-A-Lot Foods, Toyota, Walgreens, Walmart, **W** 🅾 Home Depot
38	US 84, S Brookhaven, **W** 🅿 Chevron/dsl
30	Bogue Chitto, Norfield, **E** 🅿 Shell/BogueChitto/dsl, **W** 🅾 Bogue Chitto RV Park
24	Johnston Station, **E** 🅾 to Lake Dixie Springs
20b a	US 98 W, to Natchez, Summit, **E** 🅿 BP/dsl, Shell/dsl, Stop'n Shop/dsl, **W** 🅿 Exxon/Subway/dsl, ShawnMart/dsl
18	MS 570, Smithdale Rd, N McComb, **E** 🅿 BP 🍴 Burger King, McDonald's, Piccadilly's, Ruby Tuesday 🏠 Holiday Inn Express 🅾 🏠, AT&T, Belk, JC Penney, Kia, Lowe's, mall, Radio Shack, Walgreens, Walmart/Subway, **W** 🅿 Chevron/Mr Whiskers/dsl 🍴 Applebee's, Arby's, El Dorado Mexican, Santa Fe Steaks 🏠 Deerfield Inn, Hampton Inn, Ramada 🅾 Ford/Lincoln
17	Delaware Ave, McComb, **E** 🅿 Blue Sky, BP/Subway, Chevron/dsl, Exxon/Penn's Rest., Pump&Savor, RaceWay/dsl 🍴 Backyard BBQ, Burger King, Domino's, Golden Corral,

Exit #	Services
17	Continued
	Kyoto Steaks, Papa's Pizza, Popeye's, Smoothie King, Sonic, Taco Bell, Waffle House, Wendy's 🏠 Best Western, Comfort Inn, Executive Inn 🅾 🏠, $General, AutoZone, CVS Drug, Family$, Fred's, Kroger, Office Depot, O'Reilly Parts, Rite Aid, Verizon, **W** 🏠 Days Inn 🅾 Chrysler/Dodge/Jeep
15b a	US 98 E, MS 48 W, McComb, **E 1 mi** 🅿 BP, Citgo, Exxon/Subway, Presley QuikStop/dsl, Shell 🍴 Church's, KFC 🏠 Camellian Motel 🅾 $General, Advance Parts, Family$, tires, vet, **W** 🅿 BP/dsl
13	Fernwood Rd, **E** 🅾 truck repair, **W** 🅿 ♥Love's/Chester's/McDonald's/dsl/scales/24hr/@ 🅾 golf, to Percy Quin SP
10	MS 48, Magnolia, **E 1 mi** 🅿 Exxon, Shell/dsl 🍴 Subway 🅾 RV camping
8	MS 568, Magnolia
4	Chatawa
3mm	Welcome Center, nb, 24hr security, full ♿ facilities, litter barrels, petwalk, 🐾, 🛢, RV dump
2mm	weigh sta nb
1	MS 584, Osyka, Gillsburg
0mm	Mississippi/Louisiana state line

⬆N INTERSTATE 59

Exit #	Services
172mm	Mississippi/Alabama state line
149mm	I-59 N and I-20 E run together to AL state line. See I-20, exits 170mm-150
142	to US 11, Savoy, **W** to Dunns Falls
137	to N Enterprise, to Stonewall
134	MS 513, S Enterprise
126	MS 18, to Rose Hill, Pachuta, **E** 🅿 BB/dsl, Pachuta TP/dsl
118	to Vossburg, Paulding
113	MS 528, to Heidelberg, **E** 🅿 Chevron/dsl, Exxon/Subway/dsl, Shell 🍴 Ward's Burgers
109mm	parking area sb, litter barrels, no restrooms
106mm	parking area nb, litter barrels, no restrooms
104	Sandersville, **E** 🍴 Lucky's Rest. (4mi)
99	US 11, **E** 🅾 Sleepy Hollow RV Park (1mi)
97	US 84 E, **E** 🅿 Exxon/Huddle House/dsl/scales, Kangaroo/Subway/dsl 🍴 Hardee's, Ward's Burgers, **W** 🅿 Shell 🍴 KFC, Vic's Rest.
96b	MS 15 S, Cook Ave
96a	Masonite Rd, 4th Ave
95d	(from nb)
95c	Beacon St, Laurel, **W** 🍴 Burger King, Cane's, Church's, DQ, Little Caesars, McDonald's, Popeye's, Tokyo Grill 🏠 Town-House Motel 🅾 AT&T, Expert Tire, Family$, Grocery Depot,

MS

⬆N	**INTERSTATE 59 Cont'd**
Exit #	Services

LAUREL

Exit #	Services
95c	Continued JC Penney, museum of art, NAPA, Winn-Dixie
95b a	US 84 W, MS 15 N, 16th Ave, Laurel, **W 0-2 mi** 🅶 Alliance/dsl, Chevron, Exxon/dsl, Murphy Express/dsl, Pure, Shell 🍴 Applebee's, Arby's, Buffalo Wild Wings, Buffet City, Burger King, Capt D's, Checkers, China Town, China Wok, Dickey's BBQ, Domino's, Eatza Pizza, Hardee's, KFC, Laredo Grill, McDonald's, Mi Casita, Papa John's, Pizza Hut, Popeye's, Shipley's Donuts, Shoney's, Sonic, Subway, Sweet Peppers Deli, Taco Bell, Waffle House, Ward's Burgers, Wendy's, Western Sizzlin 🏠 Best Western, Comfort Suites, EconoLodge, Hampton Inn, Holiday Inn Express, Rodeway Inn, Super 8 🅾 🅷, $General, $Tree, Advance Parts, AutoZone, BigLots, Buick/GMC, Chevrolet, Chrysler/Dodge/Jeep, CVS Drug, Ford/Lincoln, Grocery Depot, Kia, Kroger/dsl, Lowe's, New South Tires, Nissan, Office Depot, O'Reilly Parts, Piggly Wiggly, Roses, Toyota, Tuesday Morning, Verizon, Walgreens, Walmart/Subway
93	US 11, S Laurel, **W** 🅶 Exxon/Subway/dsl, Shell/dsl 🍴 Hardee's 🅾 Southern Tires
90	US 11, Ellisville Blvd, **E** 🅶 Texaco/dsl 🍴 Huddle House, **W** 🅶 Dixie/dsl
88	MS 588, MS 29, Ellisville, **E** 🅶 Chevron/dsl, Fast Mkt/dsl, Shell 🍴 Domino's, KFC, McDonald's, Pizza Hut, Sonic, Subway, Ward's Burgers 🅾 $General, AutoZone, Ellisville Drug, Family$, Food Tiger, NAPA, O'Reilly Parts, URGENT CARE, **W** 🅶 Exxon/dsl 🏠 Best Western
85	MS 590, to Ellisville, **W** 🅾 auto repair
80	to US 11, Moselle, **E** 🅶 Chevron/dsl
78	Sanford Rd
76	**W** to Hattiesburg-Laurel Reg ✈
73	Monroe Rd, to Monroe
69	MS 42 E, Gandy Pkwy, to Petal, Eatonville

HATTIESBURG

Exit #	Services
67b a	US 49, Hattiesburg, **E** 🅶 Exxon, Shell, Texaco, Valero/Kangaroo/dsl/scales 🍴 Arby's, Burger King, Cracker Barrel, DQ, Krystal, McDonald's, Pizza Hut, Waffle House 🏠 Budget Inn, Comfort Inn, EconoLodge, Executive Inn, Howard Johnson, La Quinta, Motel 6, Quality Inn, Red Carpet Inn, Regency Inn, Sleep Inn, Sunset Inn, Super 8 🅾 $General, Hattiesburg Cycles, **W** 🅶 Chevron, MapleLeaf/dsl, Pure/dsl, Shell/Subway, Stuckey's Express/dsl, Texaco 🍴 Sonic, Waffle House, Ward's Burgers, Wendy's 🏠 Candlewood Suites, Holiday Inn, Northgate Inn
65b a	US 98 W, Hardy St, Hattiesburg, **E** 🅶 Shell/dsl 🍴 Applebee's, Bop's Custard, Buffalo Wild Wings, Caliente Grille, Cane's, Checkers, CiCi's Pizza, Domino's, IHOP, Izzo's Pizza, Jimmy John's, KFC, Kobe Japanese, Lenny's Subs, Little Caesars, Little Tokyo, McDonald's, Pizza Hut, Purple Parrot Cafe, Qdoba, Starbucks, Taco Bell, Ward's Burgers 🏠 Days Inn, Fairfield Inn, Residence Inn, Super 8, Western Motel 🅾 Corner Mkt Foods, CVS Drug, Goodyear/auto, Home Depot, to USM, Verizon, Walgreens, **W** 🅶 Exxon/Domino's, Kangaroo, Shell, Texaco 🍴 5 Guys Burgers, Arby's, Burger King, Cheddars, Chesterfield's Rest., Chick-fil-A, Chili's, China Buffet, ChuckECheese's, Coldstone, FireHouse Subs, Gatti Town Pizza, Grand China, Hardee's, HoneyBaked Ham, Hooters, Krispy Kreme, Logan's Roadhouse, Longhorn Steaks, McDonald's, Mellow Mushroom, Newk's Eatery, O'Charley's, Olive Garden, Outback Steaks, Papa Murphy's, Peking Garden, Pepper's Deli, Pizza Inn, Popeye's, Red Lobster, Subway, Super King Asian, Taco Bell, TGIFriday's, Waffle House, Ward's Burgers, Wendy's, Yamato Japan, Zaxby's 🏠 Baymont Inn, Comfort Suites, Hampton Inn, Hilton Garden, Microtel, Sun Suites

Exit #	Services
65b a	Continued 🅾 🅷, Aamco, Advance Parts, AT&T, AutoZone, Belk, Best Buy, BigLots, Books-A-Million, Dick's, Dillard's, Firestone/auto, Gander Mtn, Goodyear/auto, Hobby Lobby, JC Penney, Kohl's, Lowe's, mall, Michael's, Midas, Nissan, Office Depot, Old Navy, PetCo, Petsmart, Radio Shack, Ross, Sam's Club/gas, Sears/auto, SteinMart, Target, TJ Maxx, Tuesday Morning, Verizon, Walgreens, Walmart, Winn-Dixie
60	US 11, S Hattiesburg, **E** 🅶 Shell/dsl, **W** 🅶 Kangaroo/Subway/dsl/24hr, Texaco 🍴 Huddle House 🅾 Freightliner, Peterbilt
59	US 98 E, to US 49, Lucedale, MS Gulf Coast
56mm	**parking area both lanes, litter barrels, no restrooms**
51	rd 589, to Purvis, **W** 🅶 Chevron/dsl, Pinebelt Oil/dsl, Shell/dsl (2mi) 🍴 McDonald's (2mi), Pizza Hut (2mi), to Little Black Cr Water Park
48mm	Little Black Creek
41	MS 13, to Lumberton, **W** 🅾 $General, to Little Black Cr Water Park
35	Hillsdale Rd, **E** 🅶 Pitstop/dsl 🏠 to Kings Arrow Ranch, to Lake Hillside Resort
32mm	Wolf River
29	rd 26, to Poplarville, **W** 🅶 Pure/dsl 🍴 Burger King (2mi)
27	MS 53, to Poplarville, Necaise, **W** 🅶 Shell/dsl 🍴 McDonald's 🅾 RV Camping (2mi)
19	to US 11, Millard
15	to McNeill, **W** 🅶 McNeill Trkstop/rest./dsl
10	to US 11, Carriere, **E** 🅶 Texaco/Huddle House/dsl 🅾 Clearwater RV Camp (5mi), repair/tires
6	MS 43 N, N Picayune, **E** 🍴 Marble Slab, Paul's Pastries, **W** 🅶 Chevron/dsl 🍴 Dockside Rest. (1mi), McDonald's, Sonic, Subway 🏠 Picayune Motel (1mi) 🅾 🅷, CVS Drug, Family$, vet, Walgreens, Winn-Dixie
4	MS 43 S, to Picayune, **E** 🅶 Murphy USA/dsl, RaceTrac/dsl 🍴 McDonald's, Ryan's, Subway, Wow Wingery 🅾 $Tree, AT&T, Buick/Cadillac/Chevrolet/GMC, GNC, Home Depot, Nissan, Sun Roamers RV Park (1mi), Verizon, Walgreens, Walmart, **W** 🅶 Chevron/dsl, Exxon/dsl, Shell/dsl 🍴 Applebee's, Burger King, Domino's, Golden Dragon Buffet, Hardee's, IHOP, KFC, New Buffet City, Pizza Hut, Popeye's, Subway, Taco Bell, Waffle House, Wendy's 🏠 Days Inn, Heritage Inn, Holiday Inn Express 🅾 🅷, $General, Advance Parts, AutoZone, Family$, Firestone, Ford/Lincoln, Fred's, Midas, O'Reilly Parts, Paw Paw's RV Ctr, Radio Shack, Rite Aid, URGENT CARE, Winn-Dixie
3mm	**Welcome Ctr nb, full ♿ facilities, litter barrels, petwalk, 🅲, 🆁🆂, RV dump, vending**
1.5mm	**weigh sta both lanes**
1	US 11, MS 607, **E** 🅾 NASA, **W** 🅶 Chevron/dsl, Shell/Subway/dsl
0mm	**Mississippi/Louisiana state line, Pearl River. Exits 11-1 are in Louisiana**
11	Pearl River Turnaround. Callboxes begin sb.
5b	Honey Island Swamp
5a	LA 41, Pearl River, **E** 🅶 Riverside TrvlCtr/dsl
3	US 11 S, LA 1090, Pearl River, **W 0-1 mi** 🅶 Chevron/dsl, Shell/Subway/dsl, Texaco 🍴 McDonald's, Sonic, Waffle House 🏠 Microtel 🅾 AutoZone, Family$, Jubilee Foods/drug, NAPA
1.5mm	**Welcome Ctr sb, full ♿ facilities, info, litter barrels, petwalk, 🅲, 🆁🆂, RV dump**
1c b	I-10, E to Bay St Louis, W to New Orleans
1a	I-12 W, to Hammond. **I-59 begins/ends on I-10/I-12. Exits 1-11 are in Louisiana.**

PICAYUNE

⬆N INTERSTATE 220 (Jackson)

Exit #	Services
11mm	I-220 begins/ends on I-55, exit 104.
9	Hanging Moss Rd, County Line Rd, **E** 🅿 BP
8	Watkins Dr, **E** 🅿 Exxon/Subway, Shell/Chester's/dsl
5b a	US 49 N, Evers Blvd, to Yazoo City, **E** 🅿 BP 🍽 KFC, Sonic 🛏 Star Motel 🅾 Family$, Food Depot/gas, **W** 🍽 BP, Exxon/Burger King, Gas+, Shell/Subway/dsl

3	Industrial Dr
2b a	Clinton Blvd, Capitol St, **E** 🅾 to Jackson Zoo, **W** 🅿 Race-Way, Shell 🍽 McDonald's, Popeye's, Sonic 🅾 Family$
1b a	US 80, **E** 🅿 BP, Citgo/dsl, Shell 🍽 Capt D's, Hunan Garden, KFC, McDonald's, Pizza Hut, Popeye's, Sonny's BBQ, Taco Bell, Wendy's 🛏 Best Inn, Scottish Inn, Super 8 🅾 Mr Transmission, **W** 🅿 Exxon/dsl 🍽 Arby's, Krystal 🅾 $General
0mm	I-220 begins/ends on I-20, exit 41.

MISSOURI

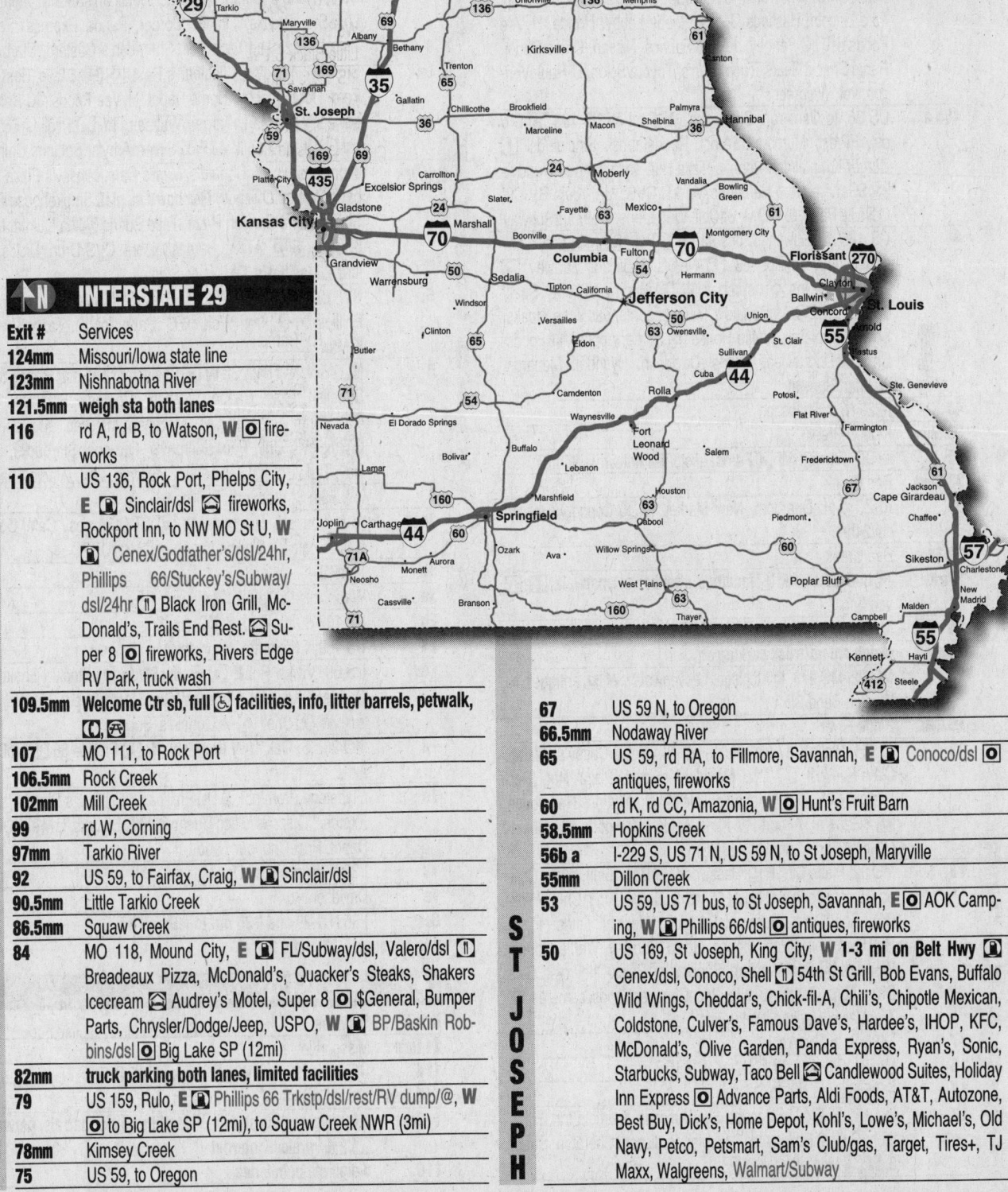

⬆N INTERSTATE 29

Exit #	Services
124mm	Missouri/Iowa state line
123mm	Nishnabotna River
121.5mm	weigh sta both lanes
116	rd A, rd B, to Watson, **W** 🅾 fireworks
110	US 136, Rock Port, Phelps City, **E** 🅿 Sinclair/dsl 🛏 fireworks, Rockport Inn, to NW MO St U, **W** 🅿 Cenex/Godfather's/dsl/24hr, Phillips 66/Stuckey's/Subway/dsl/24hr 🍽 Black Iron Grill, McDonald's, Trails End Rest. 🛏 Super 8 🅾 fireworks, Rivers Edge RV Park, truck wash
109.5mm	Welcome Ctr sb, full ♿ facilities, info, litter barrels, petwalk, 🅒, 🅿
107	MO 111, to Rock Port
106.5mm	Rock Creek
102mm	Mill Creek
99	rd W, Corning
97mm	Tarkio River
92	US 59, to Fairfax, Craig, **W** 🅿 Sinclair/dsl
90.5mm	Little Tarkio Creek
86.5mm	Squaw Creek
84	MO 118, Mound City, **E** 🅿 FL/Subway/dsl, Valero/dsl 🍽 Breadeaux Pizza, McDonald's, Quacker's Steaks, Shakers Icecream 🛏 Audrey's Motel, Super 8 🅾 $General, Bumper Parts, Chrysler/Dodge/Jeep, USPO, **W** 🅿 BP/Baskin Robbins/dsl 🅾 Big Lake SP (12mi)
82mm	truck parking both lanes, limited facilities
79	US 159, Rulo, **E** 🅿 Phillips 66 Trkstp/dsl/rest/RV dump/@, **W** 🅾 to Big Lake SP (12mi), to Squaw Creek NWR (3mi)
78mm	Kimsey Creek
75	US 59, to Oregon

67	US 59 N, to Oregon
66.5mm	Nodaway River
65	US 59, rd RA, to Fillmore, Savannah, **E** 🅿 Conoco/dsl 🅾 antiques, fireworks
60	rd K, rd CC, Amazonia, **W** 🅾 Hunt's Fruit Barn
58.5mm	Hopkins Creek
56b a	I-229 S, US 71 N, US 59 N, to St Joseph, Maryville
55mm	Dillon Creek
53	US 59, US 71 bus, to St Joseph, Savannah, **E** 🅾 AOK Camping, **W** 🅿 Phillips 66/dsl 🅾 antiques, fireworks
50	US 169, St Joseph, King City, **W** 1-3 mi on Belt Hwy 🅿 Cenex/dsl, Conoco, Shell 🍽 54th St Grill, Bob Evans, Buffalo Wild Wings, Cheddar's, Chick-fil-A, Chili's, Chipotle Mexican, Coldstone, Culver's, Famous Dave's, Hardee's, IHOP, KFC, McDonald's, Olive Garden, Panda Express, Ryan's, Sonic, Starbucks, Subway, Taco Bell 🛏 Candlewood Suites, Holiday Inn Express 🅾 Advance Parts, Aldi Foods, AT&T, Autozone, Best Buy, Dick's, Home Depot, Kohl's, Lowe's, Michael's, Old Navy, Petco, Petsmart, Sam's Club/gas, Target, Tires+, TJ Maxx, Walgreens, Walmart/Subway

🅖 = gas 🍴 = food 🏠 = lodging 🅞 = other 🆁🆂 = rest stop   Copyright 2015 - the Next EXIT ®

MO

⬆N INTERSTATE 29 Cont'd

Exit #	Services
47	MO 6, Frederick Blvd, to Clarksdale, St Joseph, **E** 🅖 Conoco 🍴 Bandanas BBQ 🏠 Days Inn, Drury Inn 🅞 🅗, **W** 🅖 Phillips 66/dsl, Sinclair/dsl 🍴 Applebee's, Arby's, Burger King, Cracker Barrel, Denny's, Dunkin Donuts, El Maguey Mexican, Fazoli's, Five Guys, Golden Corral, LJ Silver, McAlister's Deli, McDonald's, New China Super Buffet, Pancheros, Panera Bread, Papa John's, Papa Murphy's, Perkins, Pizza Hut, Red Lobster, Rib Crib BBQ, Sonic, Starbucks, Subway, Taco Bell, TX Roadhouse, Wendy's, Whiskey Creek Steaks 🏠 Best Value Inn, Comfort Suites, Hampton Inn, Motel 6, Ramada, Stoney Creek Inn 🅞 $General, Apple Mkt Foods, BigLots, Buick/GMC, Chevrolet, CVS Drug, Dillard's, Firestone/auto, Ford/Lincoln, Hastings Books, Hobby Lobby, Honda, HyVee Foods/dsl, JC Penney, Jo-Ann Fabrics, Nissan, Office Depot, Radio Shack, Sears, Taco John's, Toyota/Scion, U-Haul, Verizon, vet, Walgreens
46b a	US 36, to Cameron, St Joseph, **W 1 mi on US 169** 🅖 BP/dsl, FP/dsl, Murphy USA/dsl, Roadstar/dsl, Sinclair/dsl 🍴 Burger King, Jimmy John's, Pizza Hut, Taco John's, Wendy's 🅞 $General, Ace Hardware, AT&T, CVS, KIA, Klein RV Ctr, O'Reilly Parts, to MO W St Coll, Walgreens, Walmart/Subway
44	US 169, to Gower, St Joseph, **E** 🅖 ♥Loves/Arby's/dsl/scales/24hr, Phillips 66 🍴 Nelly's Mexican, Subway 🏠 Guesthouse Inn 🅞 dsl repair, **W** 🅖 Murphy USA/dsl, Shell/dsl/24hr 🍴 DQ, McDonald's, Mr Goodcents, San Jose Steaks, Sonic, Taco Bell, Waffle House 🅞 $Tree, Apple Mkt Foods, Chrysler/Dodge/Jeep, Harley-Davidson, Hyundai, Menards, Walmart/Subway
43	I-229 N, to St Joseph
39.5mm	Pigeon Creek
35	rd DD, Faucett, **W** 🅖 Farris Trkstp/dsl/motel/rest/24hr/@
33.5mm	Bee Creek
30	rd Z, rd H, Dearborn, New Market, **E** 🅖 Conoco/Subway/dsl/24hr
29.5mm	Bee Creek
27mm	🆁🆂 **both lanes, full** 🚻 **facilities, litter barrels, petwalk,** 📞, 🅿 **vending**
25	rd E, rd U, to Camden Point, **E** 🅖 Phillips 66/dsl
24mm	**weigh sta nb/truck parking sb**
20	MO 92, MO 273, to Atchison, Leavenworth, **W** 🅞 antiques, to Weston Bend SP
19.5mm	Platte River
19	rd HH, Platte City (sb returns at 18), **W** 🅖 Casey's, Platte-Clay Fuel/dsl 🍴 DQ, Maria's Mexican, Pizza Hut, Red Dragon Chinese, Roxanne's Cafe 🏠 Quality Inn, Travelodge 🅞 $General, Airport RV Park, Apple Mkt Foods, CarQuest, O'Reilly Parts, same as 18, USPO
18	MO 92, Platte City, **E** 🅞 Basswood RV Park (5mi), **W** 🅖 Conoco/Jimmy John's, QT/dsl 🍴 Arby's, Burger King, China Wok, DQ, GoodCents Subs, McDonald's, Mexicali Lindo, Pizza Hut/Taco Bell, Pizza Shoppe, Sonic, Subway, Waffle House, Wendy's 🏠 Best Western, Super 8 🅞 Buick/Chevrolet, CVS Drug, Ford, Goodyear/auto, PriceChopper Foods, same as 19, TrueValue, Verizon, Walgreens
17	I-435 S, to Topeka
15	Mexico City Ave, **W** 🏠 Marriott 🅞 🖨
14	I-435 E (from sb), to St Louis
13	to I-435 E, **E** 🏠 Extended Stay America, Fairfield Inn, Hawthorn Suites, Holiday Inn, Microtel, Radisson, Sheraton, Super 8, **W** 🏠 Marriott 🅞 KCI

P L A T T E   C I T Y

K A N S A S   C I T Y

Exit #	Services
12	NW 112th St, **E** 🅖 BP, Conoco/dsl 🏠 Candlewood Suites, Comfort Inn, Days Inn, Extended Stay America, Hampton Inn, Hilton, Holiday Inn Express, **W** 🏠 EconoLodge
10	Tiffany Springs Pkwy, **E** 🅖 Phillips 66 🍴 Cirque d'Alex, SmokeBox BBQ 🏠 Embassy Suites, Holiday Inn Express, Homewood Suites, Residence Inn, **W** 🍴 Cracker Barrel, Marco's Pizza, Ruby Tuesday, Waffle House, Wendy's 🏠 Chase Suites, Courtyard, Drury Inn, Homestead Suites, Hyatt Place, Sleep Inn 🅞 Buick/GMC, Harley-Davidson, Honda, Lexus, Nissan, Toyota
9b a	MO 152, to Liberty, Topeka
8	MO 9, rd T, NW Barry Rd, **E** 🅖 Valero/dsl 🍴 Applebee's, Boston Mkt, Chili's, China Wok, Chipotle Mexican, Honeybaked Cafe, Hong's Buffet, Hooters, Houlihan's, Kato Japanese, LoneStar Steaks, On the Border, Panda Express, Panera Bread, Pizza Hut/Taco Bell, Sheradon's Custard, Starbucks, Subway, Wendy's, Winstead's Rest. 🅞 🅗, $Tree, Best Buy, Ford, Hobby Lobby, Home Depot, HyVee Foods, JC Penney, Lowe's, SteinMart, Target, Walmart, **W** 🅖 Phillips 66, QT/dsl 🍴 54th St Grill, A&W/LJSilver, Arby's, BoLings Chinese, Jimmy John's, McDonald's, Mimi's Cafe, Minsky's Pizza, Outback Steaks, Quiznos, Rainbow Oriental, Smokehouse BBQ, Sonic, Stone Canyon Pizza, Taco Bueno 🏠 La Quinta, Motel 6, Super 8 🅞 AT&T, Barnes&Noble, CVS Drug, Dick's, Dillard's, Marshall's, Old Navy, Staples
6	NW 72nd St, Platte Woods, **E** 🅖 Sinclair/dsl 🅞 vet, **W** 🅖 Phillips 66 🍴 Iron Wok, KFC, Papa John's, Tasty Thai 🅞 K-Mart
5	MO 45 N, NW 64th St, **W** 🅖 Shell/dsl 🍴 All-star Pizza&Subs, Bonefish Grill, Caribou Coffee, Chamas Brazilian Grill, Goodcents Subs, IHOP, Mazatlan Mexican, McDonald's, O'Quigley's Grill, Papa Murphy's, Quiznos, Starbucks, Subway, Taco Bell 🅞 $General, CVS Drug, GNC, Radio Shack
4	NW 56th St (from nb), Phillips 66
3c	rd A (from sb), Riverside, **W** 🅖 QT 🍴 Argosy Café, Corner Café, Sonic 🏠 Skyline Inn, Super 8 🅞 USPO
3b	I-635 S
3a	Waukomis Dr, rd AA (from nb)
2b	US 169 S (from sb), to KC
2a	US 169 N (from nb), to Smithville
1e	US 69, Vivion Rd, **E** 🅖 Phillips66/dsl 🍴 Steak'n Shake 🅞 Cadillac/Chevrolet, Chrysler/Jeep, Home Depot, Lincoln, Suzuki, **W** 🅖 Shell 🍴 McDonald's, Subway
1d	MO 283 S, Oak Tfwy (from sb), **W** 🅖 Phillips 66 🍴 McDonald's
1c	Gladstone (from nb), **E** 🅖 Phillips 66 🍴 CiCi's Pizza, Panda Express, Quiznos, Taco Bueno 🅞 🅗, BigLots, Lowe's, Office Depot, PriceChopper Foods
1b	I-35 N (from sb), to Des Moines
1a	Davidson Rd
8mm	I-35 N. I-29 and I-35 run together 6 mi.

See Missouri I-35, exits 2-8a.

⬆N INTERSTATE 35

Exit #	Services
114mm	Missouri/Iowa state line
114	US 69, to Lamoni, **W** 🅖 Conoco/dsl/24hr
113.5mm	Zadie Creek
112mm	**MO Welcome Ctr sb, full** 🚻 **facilities, litter barrels, petwalk,** 📞, 🅿, **wireless internet**
110	**weigh sta both lanes**

INTERSTATE 35 Cont'd

Exit #	Services
106	rd N, Blythedale, E 🅖 Conoco/fireworks, Phillips 66/Dinner Bell Cafe/motel/dsl/24hr/@ 🅾 camping, dsl repair, W 🅖 Phillips 66/dsl/24hr 🛏 Eagle Ridge RV Park (2mi), fireworks
99	rd A, to Ridgeway, W 5 mi 🅾 camping
94mm	E Fork Big Creek
93	US 69, Bethany, W 🅾 RV dump
92	US 136, Bethany, E 🅖 FL/dsl 🅕 KFC/Taco Bell, McDonald's 🛏 Budget Inn, W 🅖 BP/dsl, Casey's, Kum&Go/Wendy's/dsl, MFA 🅕 Country Kitchen, DQ, Nopal Mexican, Sonic, Subway, TootToot Rest. 🛏 Comfort Inn, Super 8 🅾 🅗, Russell Stover, Walmart
90mm	Pole Cat Creek
88	MO 13, to Bethany, Gallatin
84	rds AA, H, to Gilman City, E 🅾 Crowder SP (24mi)
81mm	**truck parking, limited facilities**
80	rds B, N, to Coffey
78	rd C, Pattonsburg, W 🅖 Phillips 66/dsl
74.5mm	Grand River
72	rd DD
68	US 69, to Pattonsburg
64	MO 6, to Maysville, Gallatin
61	US 69, Winston, Gallatin, E 🅖 Shell/rest/dsl/24hr
54	US 36, Cameron, E 🅖 Shell/Baskin-Robbins/Wendy's/dsl/24hr, Sinclair/dsl/scales/24hr 🅕 McDonald's, Subway 🛏 Best Western, Budget Inn, Comfort Inn 🅾 Crossroads RV Park, W 🅖 Valero/dsl 🅕 Burger King, Chinese Chef, Domino's, DQ, El Maguey Mexican, KFC/Taco Bell, Ma&Pa's Kettle Rest, Pizza Hut, Sonic 🛏 Best Value Inn, Comfort Inn, Days Inn, EconoLodge, Super 8 🅾 🅗, Advance Parts, antiques, Buick/Chevrolet/GMC, CountryMart Foods, O'Reilly Parts, Radio Shack, tires, Twin Creeks Tire, USPO, Verizon, Walmart
52	rd BB, Lp 35, to Cameron, E 🅾 🅗, W 🅖 Casey's, same as 54
49mm	Brushy Creek
48.5mm	Shoal Creek
48	US 69, Cameron, E 🅾 to Wallace SP (2mi), W 🅖 Shamrock 🅾 fireworks
40	MO 116, Lathrop, E 🅾 antiques
34.5mm	🆁ₛ both lanes, full ♿ facilities, litter barrels, petwalk, 🚻, 🖼 vending
33	rd PP, Holt, E 🅕 Hilltop Grill, W 🅖 BP, Conoco/dsl 🛏 American Eagle Inn
30mm	Holt Creek
26	MO 92, Kearney, E 🅖 Casey's, Phillips 66/dsl, Shell/dsl 🅕 China Wok, McDonald's, Pizza Hut, Sonic 🛏 Comfort Inn, Super 8 🅾 CountryMart Foods, CVS Drug, Kramer Hardware, Red Cross Drug, to Watkins Mill SP, W 🅖 ▥▥/Taco Bell/dsl/scales/24hr 🅕 Arby's, Burger King, Hunan Garden Chinese, Pizza Shoppe, Stables Grill, Subway 🛏 EconoLodge, Quality Inn 🅾 Curves, Goodyear/auto, John's Foods, O'Reilly Parts, to Smithville Lake
22mm	**parking area sb, weigh sta nb**
20	US 69, MO 33, to Excelsior Springs, E 🅾 🅗
17	MO 291, rd A, E 1 mi 🅖 BP, QT 🅕 A&W, Arby's, CiCi's, LJ Silver, McDonald's, Minsky's Pizza, Papa John's, Papa Murphy's, Perkins, Sonic, Subway, Taco Bell 🅾 $General, Chevrolet, Days Inn, Firestone, Lifestyle RV Ctr, O'Reilly Parts, same as 16, Walgreens, W 🅖 Phillips 66/dsl, QT 🅕 McDonald's, Nicky's Pizza, Sonic, Subway, Wasabi Japanese

Exit #	Services
17	Continued 🛏 Sleep Inn, ValuePlace Inn 🅾 Price Chopper Foods, to KCI ➕, URGENT CARE, Walgreens
16	MO 152, Liberty, E 🅖 Phillips 66 🅕 5 Guys Burgers, Baskin-Robbins, Chick-fil-A, CiCi's Pizza, Culver's, IHOP, Jimmy John's, Margarita's, Olive Garden, Perkins, Pizza Hut, Planet Sub, Red Robin, Starbucks, TX Roadhouse, Wendy's 🛏 Days Inn, Super 8 🅾 🅗, Advance Parts, AutoZone, Chevrolet, CVS Drug, Dick's, Firestone/auto, Ford, Hy-Vee Foods, K-Mart, Lowe's, URGENT CARE, Walgreens, W 🅖 Phillips 66/Circle K/dsl 🅕 54th St Grill, Applebee's, Arby's, Bob Evans, Buffalo Wild Wings, Burger King, Chili's, Chipotle Mexican, Corner Cafe, Cracker Barrel, Freddy's Burgers, Golden Corral, Jose Peppers, KFC, LongHorn Steaks, McDonald's, Panda Express, Panera Bread, Schlotzsky's, SmokeBox BBQ, Steak'n Shake, Subway, Taco Bell, Waffle House 🛏 Comfort Suites, Fairfield Inn, Hampton Inn, Holiday Inn Express 🅾 Aldi Foods, AT&T, Best Buy, Christian Bros Auto, Ford, Home Depot, JC Penney, Jiffy Lube, Kohl's, Michael's, NAPA, NTB, Office Depot, Petsmart, Radio Shack, Target, TJ Maxx, Verizon, Walmart/Subway
14	US 69 (exits left from sb), Liberty Dr, to Glenaire, Pleasant Valley, E 🅖 Phillips 66, Shell, Sinclair 🅾 I-35 RV Ctr, W 🅖 QT/dsl
13	US 69 (from nb), to Pleasant Valley, E 🅖 Phillips 66/dsl, Shell, Sinclair/24hr 🅕 KFC, McDonald's 🅾 auto repair, W 🅖 QT/dsl
12b a	I-435, to St Louis
11	US 69 N, Vivion Rd, E 🅖 BP/dsl, Shell/dsl 🅕 Church's, McDonald's, W 🅖 QT 🅕 Sonic, Stroud's Rest.
10	N Brighton Ave (from nb), E 🅕 Church's, McDonald's
9	MO 269 S, Chouteau Trfwy, E 🅖 Phillips 66 🅕 IHOP, McDonald's, Ming Garden, Outback Steaks, Papa Murphy's, Popeye's, Subway, Wing Stop 🅾 AT&T, Food Festival, GNC, Harrah's Casino/rest., Radio Shack, Target, W 🅕 Wendy's (1mi)
8c	MO 1, Antioch Rd, E 🅖 7-11 🅕 Domino's 🛏 Best Western 🅾 auto repair, W 🅖 Phillips 66 🅕 Catfish Rest., Waffle House 🅾 Walgreens
8b	I-29 N, US 71 N, KCI ➕
	I-35 S and I-29 S run together 6 mi.
8a	Parvin Rd, E 🅖 BP, Shell 🅾 O'Reilly Parts, W 🛏 Super Inn
6b a	Armour Rd, E 🅖 Phillips 66/dsl 🅕 Arby's, Burger King, Denny's, McDonald's, Quiznos 🛏 EconoLodge, La Quinta 🅾 🅗, repair, to Riverboat Casino, W 🅖 Conoco/dsl, Phillips 66, QT 🅕 DQ, Lucky Dragon Chinese, Pizza Hut, Subway, Taco Bell, Wendy's 🛏 American Inn, Holiday Inn Express 🅾 USPO

⬆N INTERSTATE 35 Cont'd

Exit #	Services
5b	16th Ave, industrial district
5a	Levee Rd, Bedford St, industrial district
4.5mm	Missouri River
4b	Front St, E 🅞 Isle of Capri Riverboat Casino/rest.
4a	US 24 E, Independence Ave
3	I-70 E, US 71 S, to St Louis
2g	**I-35 N and I-29 N run together 6 mi**
2e	Oak St, Grand-Walnut St, E 🅖 Phillips 66 🛏 Marriott
2d	Main-Delaware, Wyandotte St, downtown
2a	I-70 W, to Topeka
2y	US 169, Broadway, to downtown
2w	12th St, Kemper Arena, to downtown
2v	14th St, to downtown
2u	I-70 E, to Broadway, E 🍴 Denny's
1e	US 69, Vivion Rd, E 🅖 Phillips66/dsl 🍴 Steak'n Shake 🅞 Cadillac/Chevrolet, Chrysler/Jeep, Home Depot, Lincoln, Suzuki, W 🅖 Shell 🍴 McDonald's, Subway
1d	20th St (from sb), W 🅖 Phillips 66 🍴 McDonald's
1c	27th St, SW Blvd, W Pennway (from nb), E 🅖 Phillips 66 🍴 CiCi's Pizza, Panda Express, Quiznos, Taco Bueno 🅞 🇭, BigLots, Lowe's, Office Depot, PriceChopper Foods
1b	I-29 (from nb), to Des Moines
1a	SW Trafficway (from sb)
0mm	Missouri/Kansas state line

⬆E INTERSTATE 44

Exit #	Services
293mm	**I-44 begins/ends on I-70, exit 249 in St Louis.**
290a	I-55 S, to Memphis
290c	Gravois Ave (from wb), 12th St, S 🍴 McDonald's
290b	18th St (from eb), downtown
289	Jefferson Ave, St Louis, N 🅖 Phillips 66 🛏 Holiday Inn Express, Residence Inn, S 🅖 Conoco 🍴 Lee's Chicken, McDonald's
288	Grand Blvd, St Louis, N 🅖 BP 🛏 Water Tower Inn 🅞 🇭, S 🍴 Jack-in-the-Box, Qdoba, St Louis Bread
287b a	Kingshighway, Vandeventer Ave, St Louis, N 🅖 BP 🅞 🇭 Jiffy Lube, U-Haul, S 🅖 BP 🅞 Chevrolet, to MO Botanical Garden, Walgreens
286	Hampton Ave, St Louis, N 🅖 BP, Mobil, Phillips 66, Shell/Circle K 🍴 Denny's, Jack-in-the-Box, McDonald's, Steak'n Shake, Subway, Taco Bell, S 🅖 Shell/Circle K 🍴 Hardee's 🛏 Drury Inn, Holiday Inn, Red Roof Inn 🅞 museums, zoo
285	SW Ave (from wb, no EZ return)
284b a	Arsenal St, Jamieson St
283	Shrewsbury (from wb), some services same as 282
282	Laclede Sta Rd, Murdock Ave (from eb), St Louis, N 🅖 Phillips 66 🍴 DQ, Front Row Grill, Imo's Pizza, McDonald's, Racanelli's Pizza, Starbucks, Subway, Webster Wok Chinese 🅞 Ben Franklin Crafts, Subaru, vet
280	Elm Ave, St Louis, N 🅖 BP/repair 🍴 Lenny's Subs 🅞 Schnuck's Food/24hr, S 🅖 BP (1mi), Circle K 🅞 Walgreens
279	(from wb), Berry Rd
278	Big Bend Rd, St Louis, N 🍴 Hardee's, Sonic 🅞 🇭, Sam's Club/gas, S 🅖 Mobil/dsl, QT
277b	US 67, US 61, US 50, Lindbergh Blvd, N 🅖 Shell 🍴 Arby's, Chili's, Chipotle Mexican, O'Charley's, Steak&Rice Chinese, TX Roadhouse, Uno, White Castle 🛏 Best Western 🅞 🇭 $Tree, AT&T, Hancock Fabrics, Harley-Davidson, Hobby Lobby, Lowe's Whse, Office Depot, PetCo, Target, TJ Maxx,

Exit #	Services
277b	Continued Verizon, Walmart, S 🅖 Phillips 66, Shell/Circle K 🍴 Burger King, Denny's, Fuddrucker's, Helen Fitzgerald's Grill, IHOP, Lion's Choice, Longhorn Steaks, Ruby Tuesday, St Louis Bread, Steak'n Shake, Viking Rest 🛏 Days Inn/rest., Hampton Inn, Holiday Inn, Quality Inn 🅞 Dobb's Auto/Tire, Home Depot, Marshall's, Old Navy, Petsmart, WorldMkt
277a	MO 366 E, Watson Rd, access to same as 277b S
276b a	I-270, N to Chicago, S Memphis
275	N Highway Dr (from wb), Soccer Pk Rd, N 🅖 ⛟/Road Ranger/rest/dsl
274a b	Bowles Ave, N 🅖 Road Ranger/⛟/Subway/dsl, S 🅖 Phillips 66/dsl, QT/dsl, ZX/dsl 🍴 Bandana's BBQ, Cracker Barrel, Denny's, Jack-in-the-Box, Krispy Kreme, Mandarin Cuisine, McDonald's, Quiznos, Sonic, White Castle 🛏 Drury Inn, Fairfield Inn, Holiday Inn Express, Motel 6, PearTree Inn, Rodeway Inn, Stratford Inn, Super 8, TownePlace Inn 🅞 Goodyear
272	MO 141, Fenton, Valley Park, N 🅖 Motomart, S 🅖 Phillips 66/dsl 🍴 Bob Evans, Burger King, Dickey's BBQ, Hardee's, Jimmy John's, McDonald's, Ruby Tuesday, Starbucks, Steak'n Shake, Subway, Taco Bell 🛏 Drury Inn, Hampton Inn 🅞 AT&T, Curves, Save-A-Lot Foods
269	Antire Rd, Beaumont
266	Lewis Rd, N 🅞 golf, Rte 66 SP
266mm	Meramec River
265	Williams Rd (from eb)
264	MO 109, rd W, Eureka, N 🅖 Phillips 66/dsl 🍴 Arby's, Burger King, Culver's, Domino's, El Nopal Mexican, McDonald's, Pizza Hut, Ponderosa, Smokers BBQ, St Louis Bread, Subway, Taco Bell, White Castle 🛏 Best Value Inn 🅞 AT&T, Byerly RV Ctr, O'Reilly Parts, Schnuck's Foods, to Babler SP, Valvoline, S 🅖 QT 🅞 Walgreens
261	Lp 44, to Allenton, N 🅖 Motomart/McDonald's/dsl 🍴 Applebee's, China King, Denny's, Imo's Pizza, Lion's Choice, Steak'n Shake, White Castle 🛏 Best Inn, Holiday Inn, Super 8 🅞 $Tree, AutoZone, GNC, Jellystone RV Camping, Radio Shack, same as 264, to Six Flags, Verizon, Walmart, S 🅖 Shell/Circle K/dsl 🅞 KOA, Long's RV Ctr
257	Lp 44, Pacific, N 🅖 Phillips 66, ⛟/Subway/dsl/scales/24hr 🍴 Huddle House 🛏 Comfort Inn 🅞 fireworks, S 🅖 BP/dsl, Mobil/dsl, Motomart 🍴 Hardee's, KFC, McDonald's, New China, Pizza Hut, Taco Bell 🛏 Quality Inn 🅞 $General, Chrysler/Dodge/Jeep, O'Reilly Parts, Queen's Foods, vet
253	MO 100 E, to Gray Summit, S 🅖 Phillips 66/dsl 🛏 Gardenway Motel, Travelodge 🅞 CarQuest, fireworks
251	MO 100 W, to Washington, N 🅖 BP/dsl, Mr Fuel/dsl/scales, Phillips 66/Burger King/dsl 🍴 Domino's 🅞 🇭, $General, antiques
247	US 50 W, rd AT, rd O, to Union, N 🅞 Harley-Davidson, S 🅞 to Robertsville SP
247mm	Bourbeuse River
242	rd AH, to Hist Rte 66
240	MO 47, St Clair, N 🅖 Phillips 66/Taco Bell/dsl 🍴 Burger King, Los Cabos 🅞 NAPA, Reed RV Ctr, S 🅖 Mobil/dsl 🍴 McDonald's, Subway 🛏 Budget Lodge, Super 8 🅞 $General, Save-A-Lot Foods, USPO
239	MO 30, rds AB, WW, St Clair, N 🅞 repair
238mm	**weigh sta both lanes**
235mm	**🆁🆂 both lanes (both lanes exit left), full 🛏 facilities, litter barrels, petwalk, 🍴, ♿, vending**
230	rds W, Stanton, S 🅖 Shell/fireworks 🅞 KOA, Meramec Caverns Camping (3mi)

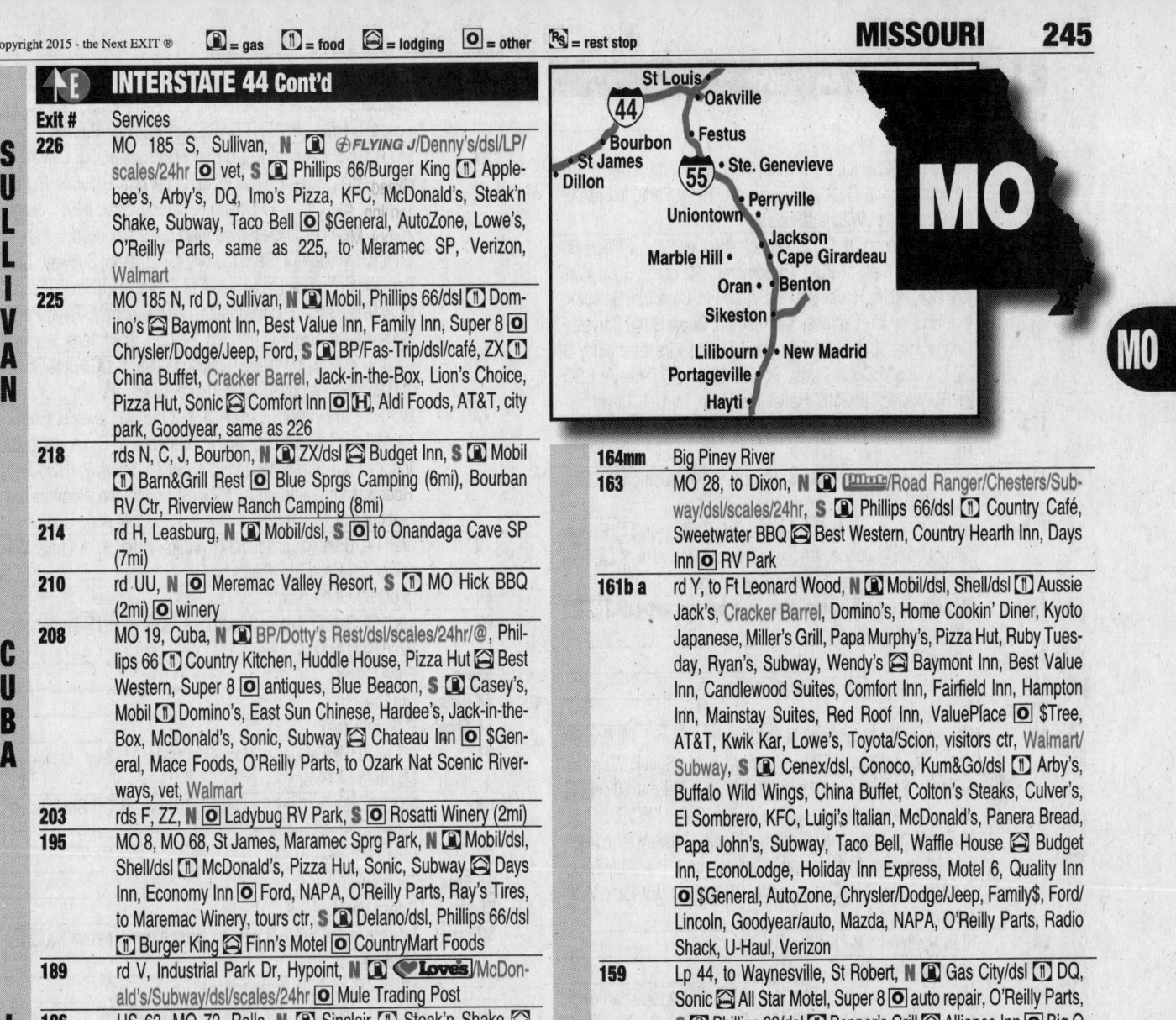

INTERSTATE 44 Cont'd

Exit #	Services
226	MO 185 S, Sullivan, **N** 🅖 *FLYING J*/Denny's/dsl/LP/scales/24hr 🅞 vet, **S** 🅖 Phillips 66/Burger King 🍴 Applebee's, Arby's, DQ, Imo's Pizza, KFC, McDonald's, Steak'n Shake, Subway, Taco Bell 🅞 $General, AutoZone, Lowe's, O'Reilly Parts, same as 225, to Meramec SP, Verizon, Walmart
225	MO 185 N, rd D, Sullivan, **N** 🅖 Mobil, Phillips 66/dsl 🍴 Domino's 🛏 Baymont Inn, Best Value Inn, Family Inn, Super 8 🅞 Chrysler/Dodge/Jeep, Ford, **S** 🅖 BP/Fas-Trip/dsl/café, ZX 🍴 China Buffet, Cracker Barrel, Jack-in-the-Box, Lion's Choice, Pizza Hut, Sonic 🛏 Comfort Inn 🅞 🏥, Aldi Foods, AT&T, city park, Goodyear, same as 226
218	rds N, C, J, Bourbon, **N** 🅖 ZX/dsl 🛏 Budget Inn, **S** 🅖 Mobil 🍴 Barn&Grill Rest 🅞 Blue Sprgs Camping (6mi), Bourban RV Ctr, Riverview Ranch Camping (8mi)
214	rd H, Leasburg, **N** 🅖 Mobil/dsl, **S** 🅞 to Onandaga Cave SP (7mi)
210	rd UU, **N** 🅞 Meremac Valley Resort, **S** 🍴 MO Hick BBQ (2mi) 🅞 winery
208	MO 19, Cuba, **N** 🅖 BP/Dotty's Rest/dsl/scales/24hr/@, Phillips 66 🍴 Country Kitchen, Huddle House, Pizza Hut 🛏 Best Western, Super 8 🅞 antiques, Blue Beacon, **S** 🅖 Casey's, Mobil 🍴 Domino's, East Sun Chinese, Hardee's, Jack-in-the-Box, McDonald's, Sonic, Subway 🛏 Chateau Inn 🅞 $General, Mace Foods, O'Reilly Parts, to Ozark Nat Scenic Riverways, vet, Walmart
203	rds F, ZZ, **N** 🅞 Ladybug RV Park, **S** 🅞 Rosatti Winery (2mi)
195	MO 8, MO 68, St James, Maramec Sprg Park, **N** 🅖 Mobil/dsl, Shell/dsl 🍴 McDonald's, Pizza Hut, Sonic, Subway 🛏 Days Inn, Economy Inn 🅞 Ford, NAPA, O'Reilly Parts, Ray's Tires, to Maremac Winery, tours ctr, **S** 🅖 Delano/dsl, Phillips 66/dsl 🍴 Burger King 🛏 Finn's Motel 🅞 CountryMart Foods
189	rd V, Industrial Park Dr, Hypoint, **N** 🅖 *Love's*/McDonald's/Subway/dsl/scales/24hr 🅞 Mule Trading Post
186	US 63, MO 72, Rolla, **N** 🅖 Sinclair 🍴 Steak'n Shake 🛏 Drury Inn, Hampton Inn, Sooter Inn 🅞 Big O Tire, Kia, Kohl's, Lowe's, Nissan, Plaza Tire, **S** 🅖 BP, Mobil/dsl, Phillips 66 🍴 Colton's Steaks, Domino's, Donut King, Koi Chinese, Lee's Chicken, Panera Bread 🛏 Budget Motel 🅞 🏥
185	rd E, to Rolla, **N** 🅞 hwy patrol, **S** 🅖 Delano, Phillips 66 🍴 Arby's, DQ, Gordoz Steaks, Hardee's, Huddle House, Jimmy John's, Kyoto Japanese, LJ Silver, Papa John's, Subway, Taco Bell, Wendy's 🅞 🏥, Ford/Lincoln, Kroger, UMO at Rolla, Walgreens
184	US 63 S, to Rolla, **N** 🛏 Comfort Suites, Holiday Inn Express, **S** 🅖 Delano, MotoMart, Route 66 🍴 Arby's, Burger King, Little Caesars, LJ Silver, Lucky House Chinese, Maid-Rite, McDonald's, Pizza Hut, Pizza Inn, Shoney's, Sirloin Stockade, Waffle House, Wendy's 🛏 Baymont Inn, Best Value Inn, Best Way Inn, Best Western, Days Inn, EconoLodge, Quality Inn, Sunset Inn, Super 8 🅞 🏥, Buick/Cadillac/GMC, Chevrolet, city park, Goodyear/auto, Kroger
179	rds T, C, to Doolittle, Newburg, **S** 🅖 Phillips 66 🍴 Cookin' From Scratch Rest.
178mm	**truck parking both lanes, restrooms**
176	Sugar Tree Rd, **N** 🛏 Vernelle's Motel, **S** 🅞 Arlington River Resort Camping (2mi)
172	rd D, Jerome, **N** 🅞 camping
169	rd J
166	to Big Piney

Exit #	Services
164mm	Big Piney River
163	MO 28, to Dixon, **N** 🅖 🚂/Road Ranger/Chesters/Subway/dsl/scales/24hr, **S** 🅖 Phillips 66/dsl 🍴 Country Café, Sweetwater BBQ 🛏 Best Western, Country Hearth Inn, Days Inn 🅞 RV Park
161b a	rd Y, to Ft Leonard Wood, **N** 🅖 Mobil/dsl, Shell/dsl 🍴 Aussie Jack's, Cracker Barrel, Domino's, Home Cookin' Diner, Kyoto Japanese, Miller's Grill, Papa Murphy's, Pizza Hut, Ruby Tuesday, Ryan's, Subway, Wendy's 🛏 Baymont Inn, Best Value Inn, Candlewood Suites, Comfort Inn, Fairfield Inn, Hampton Inn, Mainstay Suites, Red Roof Inn, ValuePlace 🅞 $Tree, AT&T, Kwik Kar, Lowe's, Toyota/Scion, visitors ctr, Walmart/Subway, **S** 🅖 Cenex/dsl, Conoco, Kum&Go/dsl 🍴 Arby's, Buffalo Wild Wings, China Buffet, Colton's Steaks, Culver's, El Sombrero, KFC, Luigi's Italian, McDonald's, Panera Bread, Papa John's, Subway, Taco Bell, Waffle House 🛏 Budget Inn, EconoLodge, Holiday Inn Express, Motel 6, Quality Inn 🅞 $General, AutoZone, Chrysler/Dodge/Jeep, Family$, Ford/Lincoln, Goodyear/auto, Mazda, NAPA, O'Reilly Parts, Radio Shack, U-Haul, Verizon
159	Lp 44, to Waynesville, St Robert, **N** 🅖 Gas City/dsl 🍴 DQ, Sonic 🛏 All Star Motel, Super 8 🅞 auto repair, O'Reilly Parts, **S** 🅖 Phillips 66/dsl 🍴 Pepper's Grill 🛏 Alliance Inn 🅞 Big O Tire, Cadillac/GMC, TrueValue
158mm	Roubidoux Creek
156	rd H, Waynesville, **N** 🅖 BP, Casey's, Conoco/dsl/E-85, Kum&Go/dsl 🍴 McDonald's, Starbucks, Subway 🅞 $General, Chevrolet, Price Cutter+, vet
153	MO 17, to Buckhorn, **N** 🅖 Whitmor Farms/dsl 🛏 Ft Wood Inn, **S** 🅖 Shell/dsl 🅞 Glen Oaks RV Park
150	MO 7, rd P to Richland, **S** 🍴 Roadhouse Steaks
145	MO 133, rd AB, to Richland, **N** 🅖 Sinclair/Oasis/cafe/dsl/24hr, **S** 🅞 camping
143mm	Gasconade River
140	rd N, to Stoutland, **S** 🅖 Phillips 66/pizza/dsl
139mm	Bear Creek
135	rd F, Sleeper
130	rd MM, **N** 🅖 Conoco/dsl, Phillips 66 🍴 Napoli's Italian 🛏 Best Western, Budget Inn, Munger Moss Inn, **S** 🅖 Kum&Go 🅞 🏥
129	MO 5, MO 32, MO 64, to Hartville, Lebanon, **N** 🍴 Applebee's, Arby's, Bamboo Garden, Burger King, DQ, Elm St Eatery, KFC, Little Caesars, LJ Silver, McDonald's, Papa John's, Shoney's, Sonic, Steak'n Shake, Subway, Taco Bell, Wendy's, Western Sizzlin 🅞 Aldi Foods, AT&T, AutoZone, Chevrolet, Ford, O'Reilly Parts, repair, Rte 66 Museum, Smitty's Foods, to Bennett Sprgs SP, Verizon, Walgreens, Walnut Bowl Factory, **S** 🅖 Conoco/dsl, Phillips 66/dsl 🍴 Capt D's, Domino's,

➤E INTERSTATE 44 Cont'd

Exit #	Services
129	Continued
	Hardee's, Pizza Hut, T's Steaks 🅞 🍴, $General, $Tree, FSA/Famous Brands, Goodyear, Lowe's, O'Reilly Parts, to Lake of the Ozarks, vet, Walmart/Subway
127	Lp 44, Lebanon, **N** 🅖 B&D/rest/dsl/scales/24hr, Phillips 66 🍴 Dowd's Catfish&BBQ, El Sombrero Mexican, Great Wall Chinese, Waffle House 🛏 Best Value Inn, Days Inn, Hampton Inn, Holiday Inn Express, Midwest Inn, Super 8 🅞 Chrysler/Dodge/Jeep, Cutlery/Walnut Bowl Outlet, Firestone/auto, **S** 🅖 Conoco/McDonald's/dsl, Phillips 66/dsl 🍴 Dickey's BBQ 🅞 Buick/Cadillac/GMC, Harley-Davidson, Russell Stover
123	County Rd, **S** 🅞 antiques, Happy Trails RV Ctr, Happy Trails RV Park
118	rds C, A, Phillipsburg, **S** 🅖 Phillips 66 🅞 Redmond's Gifts, tourist info
113	rds J, Y, Conway, **N** 🅖 Conoco/dsl, Phillips 66 🍴 Rockin Chair Café 🛏 Budget Inn 🅞 to Den of Metal Arts, **S** 🅖 Sinclair/dsl 🅞 $General, SummerFresh Foods, USPO
111mm	🆁🆂 both lanes, full 🚻 facilities, litter barrels, petwalk, 🅲, 🛢 playground, vending
108mm	Bowen Creek
107	Sparkle Brooke Rd, Sampson Rd
106mm	Niangua River
100	MO 38, rd W, Marshfield, **N** 🅖 Murphy USA/dsl, Phillips 66 🅞 AT&T, auto repair, Chevrolet, Ford, Radio Shack, Walmart/Subway, **S** 🅖 Conoco/dsl, Kum&Go/dsl, Phillips 66/dsl 🍴 DQ, El Charro, Golden China, Grillos Cafe, KFC/Rib Crib, McDonald's, Pizza Hut, Pizza Inn, Sonic, Subway, Taco Bell 🛏 Holiday Inn Express 🅞 $General, antiques, AutoZone, O'Reilly Parts, PriceCutter Foods, RV Express RV Park, Walgreens
96	rd B, Northview, **N** Paradise RV Park (2mi)
89mm	**weigh sta both lanes**
88	MO 125, to Fair Grove, Strafford, **N** 🅖 ♥Love's/Hardee's/dsl/scales/rv dump/24hr, Shell/scales TA/Country Pride/Subway/Taco Bell/dsl/scales/24hr/@ 🍴 McDonald's 🅞 Camping World RV Ctr, truckwash, vet, **S** 🅖 Conoco/dsl, Kum&Go 🍴 Fox's Pizza, Pizza Hut 🛏 Motel 8 🅞 $Station, Strafford RV Park
84	MO 744, **S** 🅞 Peterbilt
82b a	US 65, to Branson, Fedalia, **S** 🅖 Kum&Go, Phillips 66/dsl 🍴 Waffle House 🅞 Bass Pro Shops, Bull Shoals Lake, Kenworth, st patrol, to Table Rock Lake
80b a	rd H to Pleasant Hope, Springfield, **N** 🅖 Conoco/rest/dsl/24hr 🍴 Waffle House 🛏 Budget Lodge, Days Inn, Microtel, Super 8 🅞 to SWSU, **S** 🅖 Casey's, Kum&Go/dsl, Phillips 66/dsl, Shell 🍴 Andy's Custard, Applebee's, Backyard Burger, Bob Evans, Braum's, Buckingham BBQ, Burger King, Chicago Gyros, China Garden, Cracker Barrel, Culver's, El Maguey Mexican, Fazoli's, Hardee's, Hong Kong Garden, Houlihan's, Jade East Chinese, Krispy Kreme, Kyoto Japanese, La Mision Mexican, Little Tokyo, LJ Silver, McDonald's, Pizza Hut, Rib Crib, Ruby Tuesday, Schlotzsky's, Shanghai Chicken, Shoney's, Sonic, Steak'n Shake, Subway, Taco Bell, Ziggies Cafe 🛏 Best Value Inn, Best Western, Budget Inn, Candlewood Suites, Comfort Inn, Dogwood Park Inn, Doubletree Hotel, Drury Inn, EconoLodge, Economy Inn, Flagship Motel, Hampton Inn, Holiday Inn, Homestay Inn, La Quinta, Lamplighter Hotel, Motel 6, Ozark Inn, Plaza Inn, Quality Inn, Ramada, Rancho Motel 🅞 🍴, $General, Aamco, Aldi Foods, antiques,

80b a	Continued
	AutoZone, Goodyear/auto, K-Mart, O'Reilly Parts, PriceCutter Foods, U-Haul, URGENT CARE, vet, Walmart/Subway
77	MO 13, KS Expsy, **N** 🅖 Kum&Go/dsl/e-85 🅞 Lowe's, **S** 🅖 Casey's, Gas+, Phillips 66/dsl 🍴 Arby's, Braum's, Buffalo Wild Wings, CiCi's, El Charro, Golden Corral, IHOP, Jimmy John's, McAlister's Deli, McDonald's, Mr Goodcents, Panera Bread, Papa John's, Papa Murphy's, Pizza Inn, Subway, Taco Bell, Waffle House 🅞 $Tree, AT&T, BigLots, Dillon's Foods, Drug Mart, GNC, Goodyear/auto, Hobby Lobby, O'Reilly Parts, Radio Shack, ShopKO, Staples, Verizon, Walgreens, Walmart
75	US 160 W byp, to Willard, Stockton Lake, **S** 🅖 Kum&Go/dsl 🍴 Quiznos, Wendy's 🛏 Courtyard, La Quinta
72	MO 266, to Chesnut Expwy, **S 1-2 mi** 🅖 Casey's, Cenex, Kum&Go 🍴 Alli's Rest, Arby's, Hardee's, KFC, La Hacienda Mexican, LJ Silver, McDonald's, Sonic, Subway, Taco Bell, Taco Bueno, Waffle House 🛏 Best Budget Inn, Ramada Ltd, Redwood Motel 🅞 $General, AutoZone, city park, Curves
70	rds MM, B, **N** 🅞 antiques, fireworks, **S** 🅞 KOA (1mi), Wilson's Creek Nat Bfd (5mi)
69	to US 60, Springfield
67	rds N, T, Bois D' Arc, to Republic, **S** 🅖 Shell/dsl 🛏 AmericInn (5mi) 🅞 art glass
66mm	Pond Creek
64.6mm	Dry Branch
64.5mm	Pickerel Creek
61	rds K, PP, **N** 🅖 Cenex/Hoods/dsl/scales/LP/24hr, Phillips 66 🛏 Hood I-44 Motel
58	MO 96, rds O, Z, to Carthage, Halltown, **S** 🅖 Shell/dsl 🅞 antiques, truck/auto parts
57	to rd PP (from wb)
56.5mm	Turnback Creek
56mm	Goose Creek
52.5mm	🆁🆂 both lanes, full 🚻 facilities, litter barrels, petwalk, 🅲, 🛢 vending
49	MO 174E, rd CCW, Chesapeake
46	MO 39, MO 265, Mt Vernon, Aurora, **N** 🅖 Casey's/dsl, Kum&Go/dsl, Phillips 66/dsl, TA/Conoco/Country Pride/dsl/scales/24hr/@ 🍴 Bamboo Garden Chinese, KFC/LJ Silver, Mazzio's, McDonald's, Red Barn Cafe, Sonic, Subway, Taco Bell, TJ's BBQ 🛏 Super 8, USA Inn 🅞 $General, Family$, Hometown Drug, O'Reilly Parts, Summer Fresh Foods, True Value, **S** 🅖 Conoco/dsl 🛏 Relax Inn 🅞 antiques, Stockton Lake, to Table Rock Lake
44	rd H, to Monett, Mt Vernon, **N** 🍴 Subway (1mi) 🅞 Mid-America Dental/Hearing, RV Camping
43.5mm	Spring River
38	MO 97, to Stotts City, Pierce City, **N** 🅖 gas/dsl/repair/tires, **S** 🅞 U of MO SW Ctr
33	MO 97 S, to Pierce City, **S** 🍴 Hungry House Cafe
29	rd U, to La Russell, Sarcoxie, **N** 🅞 antiques, Beagle Bay RV Camping, Ozark Village Gifts, **S** 🅖 Casey's (1mi), Kum&Go/Subway/dsl
29mm	Center Creek
26	MO 37, to Reeds, Sarcoxie, **N** 🅞 Bill's Truck/trailer repair
22	rd 100 N, **N** 🅞 Colaw RV Ctr, **S** 🅞 Consignment RV Sales
21mm	Jones Creek
18b a	US 71 N, MO 59 S, to Carthage, Neosho, **N** 🅞 Big Barn Camping, Coachlight RV Ctr/Camping
15	MO 66 W, Lp 44 (from wb), Joplin, **N** 🛏 Tara Motel
15mm	Grove Creek
14mm	Turkey Creek

MO

MARSHFIELD

SPRINGFIELD

JOPLIN

INTERSTATE 44 Cont'd

Exit #	Services
11b a	US 71 S, MO 249 N, to Neosho, Ft Smith, S 🔲 ⊕FLYING J /Denny's/dsl/LP/scales/24hr/@, Phillips 66, Speedco 🔲 Blue Beacon, Kenworth
8b a	US 71, to Neosho, Joplin, N 🔲 Conoco/dsl, Kum&Go/dsl, Phillips 66/dsl 🔲 Applebee's, Backyard Burger, Bob Evans, Braum's, Cabo del Sol, Carino's Italian, Casa Montez Mexican, Cheddar's, Chick-fil-A, ChuckeCheese, Denny's, Domino's, Garfield's, Golden Corral, Golden Dragon, Hardee's, IHOP, Jimmy John's, KFC, King Palace, Logan's Roadhouse, Mazzio's, McAlister's, McDonald's, Noodle&Grill, Ocean Rest, Olive Garden, Outback Steaks, Pitcher's Grill, Pizza Hut, Quiznos, Red Hot&Blue Grill, Red Lobster, Rib Crib, Ruby Tuesday, Ryan's, Schlotzsky's, Sonic, Starbucks, Steak'n Shake, Subway, Taco Bell, Waffle House, Wendy's 🔲 Baymont Inn, Best Western, Candlewood Suites, Comfort Inn, Days Inn, Drury Inn, Fairfield Inn, Hallmark Inn, Hampton Inn, Hilton Garden, Holiday Inn, Homewood Suites, La Quinta, Motel 6, Quality Inn, Residence Inn, Sunrise Inn 🔲 $Tree, Aldi Foods, AT&T, AutoZone, Best Buy, Books-A-Million, Cadillac/Chevrolet, Dillon's Foods, Firestone/auto, Food4Less, Ford, Freightliner, Goodyear/auto, Hasting's, Hobby Lobby, Home Depot, Honda, Hyundai, JC Penney, Jo-Ann Fabrics, Kohl's, Lowe's, Macy's, Mercedes, Michael's, Nissan, Office Depot, O'Reilly Parts, Petsmart, Ross, Sam's Club/gas, Sears, Target, TJ Maxx, Toyota/Scion, Verizon, Walgreens, Walmart/Subway, S 🔲 Casey's 🔲 Cracker Barrel, Fazoli's 🔲 Microtel, TownePlace Suites 🔲 Wheelen RV Ctr
6	MO 86, MO 43 N, to Racine, Joplin, N 🔲 Phillips 66 🔲 KFC (1mi), Schlotzsky's (1mi) 🔲 Walgreens (2mi), S 🔲 🔲, Harley-Davidson
5.5mm	Shoal Creek
4	MO 43 to Seneca, N 🔲 ♥Loves▪/Hardee's/dsl/scales/24hr 🔲 antiques, Peterbilt, S 🔲 Conoco/Subway/dsl, Petro/Iron Skillet/dsl/scales/24hr/@, 🔲/Wendy's/dsl/scales/24hr 🔲 McDonald's 🔲 Sleep Inn 🔲 $General, fireworks, IA 80 Truckomat, KOA
3mm	weigh sta both lanes
2mm	🔲 Welcome Ctr eb, truck parking wb, litter barrels, 🔲, 🔲, full 🔲 facilities, restrooms, vending
1	US 400, US 166W, to Baxter Springs, KS, N 🔲 Downstream/dsl 🔲 Red Oak Steaks 🔲 Downstream Casino/RV Park, S 🔲 Sandstone Gardens
0mm	Missouri/Oklahoma state line

INTERSTATE 55

ST LOUIS

Exit #	Services
209mm	Missouri/Illinois state line at St. Louis, Mississippi River
209b	to I-70 W, to Kansas City
209a	to Arch, Busch Stadium
208	Park Ave, 7th St, W 🔲 BP 🔲 Rally's, Taco Bell, White Castle 🔲 Hilton
207c b	I-44W, Truman Pkwy, to Tulsa
207a	Gravois St (from nb), E 🔲 Midwest Petroleum, W 🔲 A-1 Chinese Wok, Jack-in-the-Box
206c	Arsenal St, E 🔲 Anheuser-Busch Tour Ctr, W 🔲 Shell
206b	Broadway (from nb), Broadway (from nb)
206a	Potomac St (from nb)
205	Gasconade, W 🔲🔲
204	Broadway, E 🔲 Phillips 66/repair, W 🔲 Sinclair/dsl 🔲 Hardee's, McDonald's, Subway 🔲 Radio Shack, Walgreen/24hr

203	Bates St, Virginia Ave, W 🔲 7-11, BP
202c	Loughborough Ave, W 🔲 St Louis Bread Co, Starbucks 🔲 Lowe's Whse, Schnuck's Foods
202b	Germania (from sb)
202a	Carondelet (from nb), Carondelet (from nb)
201b	Weber Rd
201a	Bayless Ave, E 🔲 BP 🔲 McDonald's, W 🔲 7-11/gas, Mobil 🔲 China Wok, DQ, Jack-in-the-Box, Pizza Hut/Taco Bell, Subway, Taco Bell 🔲 auto repair, Walgreens
200	Union Rd (from sb)
199	Reavis Barracks Rd, E 🔲 Shell 🔲 Pennie's BBQ 🔲 Hancock Fabrics
197	US 50, US 61, US 67, Lindbergh Blvd, E 🔲 Phillips 66 🔲 Arby's, Buffalo Wild Wings, ChuckeCheese, Dillard's, HoneyBaked Ham, Hooters, KFC, Krispy Kreme, Macaroni Grill, Noodles&Co, Qdoba, Quiznos, St Louis Bread Co, Station Subs, Steak'n Shake, Subway, Tucker's Place 🔲 Holiday Inn 🔲 Advance Parts, Best Buy, Dillard's, Discount Tire, Dodge, Ford, Home Depot, JC Penney, Jo-Ann Fabrics, Kia, K-Mart, Macy's, mall, Marshall's, NTB, Sears/auto, Tuesday Morning, W 🔲 QT 🔲 Bob Evans, Casa Gallardo, Culvers, Denny's, Lenny's Subs, O'Charley's, Ponderosa 🔲 Best Value Inn, Motel 6 🔲 Aldi Foods, AT&T, Costco/gas, Ford/Lincoln, Honda, Hyundai, Mazda, Office Depot, Target
196b	I-270 W, to Kansas City
196a	I-255 E, to Chicago
195	Butler Hill Rd, E 🔲 Phillips 66 🔲 Hampton Inn, Holiday Inn/rest. 🔲 Advance Parts, Walgreens, W 🔲 Phillips 66 🔲 Burger King, Hardee's, Pizza Hut/Taco Bell, Subway, Waffle House 🔲 Schnuck's Foods, tires/repair
193	Meramec Bottom Rd, E 🔲 Mobil/dsl, QT 🔲 Cracker Barrel 🔲 Best Western 🔲 Midwest RV Ctr
191	MO 141, Arnold, E 🔲 QT 🔲 5 Guys Burgers, 54th St Grill, Applebee's, Arby's, Bandana's BBQ, Capt D's, Casa Mexicana, Chick-fil-A, China King, CiCi's Pizza, Denny's, Fazoli's, Jack-in-the-Box, Lee's Chicken, Lion's Choice, LJ Silver, McDonald's, Pizza Hut, Rally's, Steak'n Shake, Super China Buffet, Taco Bell, Terrazza Grill 🔲 Drury Inn, Pear Tree Inn 🔲 Aldi Foods, AT&T, Dobbs Tire, Hobby Lobby, Kohl's, NAPA, O'Reilly Parts, PetCo, Shop'n Save Foods, vet, Walgreens, Walmart, W 🔲 Phillips 66/dsl 🔲 Chili's, Pasta House, Qdoba, St Louis Bread, TX Roadhouse 🔲 ValuePlace Hotel 🔲 $Tree, Dierberg's Foods, GNC, Lowe's, Office Depot, Petsmart, Verizon
190	Richardson Rd, E 🔲 Phillips 66/dsl, QT, Shell/Circle K/dsl 🔲 Culver's, Domino's, DQ, Pizza Hut, Ponderosa, Quiznos, Roly-Poly Sandwiches, Sonic, Taco Bell, White Castle 🔲 $Tree,

⬆N INTERSTATE 55 Cont'd

Exit #	Services
190	Continued Advance Parts, Auto Tire, Firestone, Ford, Save-A-Lot Foods, URGENT CARE, **W** 🅿 7-11, Phillips 66/dsl, Shell/Circle K/dsl 🍴 Burger King, Happy Wok, Imo's Pizza, McDonald's/playplace, Mr. Goodcents Subs, Pizza Den, Ruby Tuesday, Waffle House 🛏 Comfort Inn 🅾 Aamco, AutoZone, GNC, Home Depot, Plaza Tire, Radio Shack, Schnuck's Foods, Target, Walgreens
186	Imperial, Kimmswick, **E** 🅿 Mobil, Shell/Circle K 🍴 Blue Owl (1mi), Main St BBQ 🅾 auto repair, **W** 🅿 Phillips 66/Jack-in-the-Box/dsl 🍴 China Wok, Domino's, Gianno's Grill, O'aces Grill, Papa John's, Subway 🅾 to Mastodon SP, USPO
185	rd M, Barnhart, Antonia, **E** 🅿 BP/dsl 🍴 Ginny's Kitchen, **W** 🅿 7-11, BP, Phillips 66/dsl 🅾 Walgreens
184.5mm	**weigh sta both lanes**
180	rd Z, to Hillsboro, Pevely, **E** 🅿 Mobil/dsl 🍴 Burger King, China House, Domino's, Main St BBQ, Subway, Taco Bell, The Kitchen 🅾 $General, Queens Foods, **W** 🅿 Mr Fuel, Phillips 66/McDonald's/dsl/scales 🛏 Super 8 🅾 auto repair, rv camping
178	Herculaneum, **E** 🅿 QT/Wendy's/dsl/scales, Shell/Circle K 🍴 Cracker Barrel, Dog House Diner, DQ, Jack-in-the-Box, La Pachanga Mexican 🅾 Toyota/Scion, **W** 🅾 Buick/GMC, Cadillac/Chevrolet, Ford, vet
175	rd A, Festus, **E** 🅿 Mobil, Murphy USA/dsl, Phillips 66/dsl 🍴 Arby's, Bob Evans, Burger King, Capt D's, China 1, Fazoli's, Imo's Pizza, Jack-in-the-Box, McDonald's/playplace, Papa John's, Ryan's, Sonic, St. Louis Bread Co, Steak'n Shake, Subway, Taco Bell, Tanglefoot Steaks, White Castle 🛏 Best Western, Drury Inn 🅾 $Tree, Advance Parts, Aldi Foods/dsl, AutoZone, GNC, Home Depot, K-Mart, Plaza Tire, Radio Shack, Schnuck's Foods, URGENT CARE, Verizon, Walgreens, Walmart, **W** 🅿 7-11/dsl, Phillips 66/Domino's/dsl 🍴 Hardee's, Jimmy John's, Ruby Tuesday, Waffle House, Whittaker's Pizza 🛏 Comfort Inn, Holiday Inn Express 🅾 Chrysler/Dodge/Jeep, Lowe's
174b a	US 67, Lp 55, Festus, Crystal City, **E** 🅿 Phillips 66/dsl
170	US 61, **W** 🅿 BP/dsl/LP 🍴 Laddie Boy Rest
165	rd TT (from sb)
162	rds DD, OO
160mm	℞s **both lanes, full ♿ facilities, litter barrels, petwalk, phones, 🚮, vending**
157	rd Y, Bloomsdale, **E** 🅿 Phillips 66, **W** 🅿 ❤Loves/Chester's/McDonald's/dsl/scales/24hr
154	rd O, to St Genevieve
150	MO 32, rds B, A, to St Genevieve, **E** 🅿 BP 🍴 DQ 🅾 Ⓗ, Hist Site (6mi), **W** 🅿 Phillips 66/dsl 🍴 Hawn SP (11mi)
143	rds J, M, N, Ozora, **W** 🅿 Shell/dsl 🍴 Zone Grill 🛏 Regency Inn 🅾 truckwash
141	rd Z, St Mary
135	rd M, Brewer, **E** 🅾 propane depot
129	MO 51, to Perryville, **E** 🅿 MotoMart/McDonald's/dsl, Phillips 66/dsl 🍴 Burger King, KFC, Ponderosa, Taco Bell 🅾 Ⓗ, Ford, **W** 🅿 Rhodes/dsl 🍴 5 Star Chinese, China Buffet 🛏 Comfort Inn, Days Inn, Super 8 🅾 AT&T, Buick/Chevrolet, Chrysler/Dodge/Jeep, Walmart
123	rd B, Biehle, **W** 🅿 Rhodes/dsl 🍴 Missy's Country Kettle
119mm	Apple Creek
117	rd KK, to Appleton, **E** 🍴 Terri's Cafe 🅾 Ron's Grocery
111	rd E, Oak Ridge

110mm	℞s **both lanes, full ♿ facilities, litter barrels, petwalk, phones, 🚮, vending**
105	US 61, Fruitland, **E** 🍴 Casey's, Phillips 66/dsl, Rhodes/dsl 🅾 $General, Percull Tires/repair, Trail of Tears SP (11mi), **W** 🅿 D-Mart/dsl 🍴 Bavarian Halle, DQ, Pizza Inn 🛏 Drury Inn
102	LaSalle Ave, E Main St, no facilities
99	US 61, MO 34, to Jackson, **E** 🅾 RV camping, **W** 🛏 Comfort Suites 🅾 McDowell South RV Ctr
96	rd K, to Cape Girardeau, **E** 🅿 Phillips 66 🍴 Applebee's, Blimpie, Bob Evans, Buffalo Wild Wings, Burger King, Chick-fil-A, CiCi's Pizza, Cracker Barrel, Denny's, Dexter BBQ, DQ, El Acapulco, Great Wall Chinese, Honey Baked Ham, Logan's Roadhouse, O'Charley's, Olive Garden, Panera Bread, Papa Murphy's, Pizza Hut, Pizza Inn, Popeye's, Qdoba, Red Lobster, Ruby Tuesday, Ryan's, Schnucks, Starbucks, Steak'n Shake, Subway, Taco Bell, TX Roadhouse, Wendy's 🛏 Auburn Place, Drury Lodge/rest., Holiday Inn Express, PearTree Inn 🅾 Ⓗ, AT&T, Barnes&Noble, Best Buy, BigLots, Hancock Fabrics, Hobby Lobby, JC Penney, Macy's, Old Navy, Schnuck's Foods, to SEMSU, Verizon, **W** 🅿 Shell 🍴 McDonald's/playplace, Outback Steaks, Penn Sta Subs, Sonic, Subway, White Castle 🛏 Drury Suites, Hampton Inn 🅾 $Tree, Honda, Hyundai, Kohl's, Lowe's, Mazda, Nissan, PetCo, Plaza Tire, Sam's Club, Sears Grand, Staples, Target, TJ Maxx, Toyota, USPO, Walmart/Subway
95	MO 74 E, **E** 🛏 Candlewood Suites, **W** 🅾 Menards
93a b	MO 74 W, Cape Girardeau, **E** 🛏 Townhouse inn 🅾 diesel repair
91	rd AB, to Cape Girardeau, **E** 🅿 Rhodes/dsl 🍴 Huddle House 🅾 Harley-Davidson, tire repair, vet, **W** 🅾 🚂, Capetown RV Ctr, Youngbloods RV Ctr
89	US 61, rds K, M, Scott City, **E** 🅿 Rhodes, Store 24 🍴 Burger King, Ice Cream Corner, Las Brisas Mexican, Pizza Pro 🅾 $General, Bob's Foods, Medicap Drug, NAPA, Plaza Tires, repair
80	MO 77, Benton, **E** 🅿 Express/dsl, **W** 🅿 Phillips 66/McDonald's/dsl/fireworks 🅾 antiques, winery (8mi)
69	rd HH, to Sikeston, Miner, **E** 🅾 Peterbilt, **W** 🅿 Sinclair/dsl (1mi) 🅾 Ⓗ, golf
67	US 60, US 62, Miner, **E** 🅿 Breaktime/dsl 🛏 Best Value Inn, Holiday Inn Express, Motel 6 🅾 Hinton RV Park, **W 0-2 mi** 🅿 Cenex, Hucks, Jasper's Gas, QuickCheck 🍴 Bo's BBQ, Buffalo Wild Wings, Burger King, Dexter BBQ, El Tapatio Mexican, Lambert's Rest., Little Caesars, McDonald's, Pizza Hut, Pizza Inn, Ruby Tuesday, Sonic, Subway, Taco John's, Wendy's 🛏 Comfort Inn, Country Hearth Inn, Drury Inn, PearTree Inn, Super 8, Thrifty Inn 🅾 Ⓗ, $General, AutoZone, Buick/Chevrolet, Cadillac/GMC, Family$, Food Giant, Raben Tires, Sikeston Outlets/famous brands, Verizon, vet, Walgreens
66b	US 60 W, to Poplar Bluff, **W 3 mi on US 61/62** 🅿 Breaktime/E-85, Sinclair 🍴 A&W/LJ Silver, Applebee's, Arby's, China Buffet, DQ, El Bracero Mexican, Hardee's, KFC, McDonald's, Sonic, Subway, Taco Bell 🛏 Days Inn 🅾 $Tree, Aldi Foods, AT&T, Chrysler/Dodge/Jeep, Ford/Lincoln, GNC, JC Penney, Lowe's, O'Reilly Parts, Radio Shack, Walmart
66a	I-57 E, to Chicago, US 60 W
59mm	St Johns Bayou
58	MO 80, Matthews, **E** 🅿 TA/Taco Bell/dsl/scales/24hr/@ 🅾 to Big Oak Tree SP (24mi), truck repair, **W** 🅿 ✈FLYING J/Denny's/dsl/LP/RV dump/scales/24hr, ❤Loves/Chester's/Subway/dsl/scales/24hr 🅾 truckwash/repair
52	rd P, Kewanee, **E** 🅿 BJ Trvl Ctr/BBQ/dsl

*(side marginal labels: MO; CAPE GIRARDEAU; MINER; PERRYVILLE)*

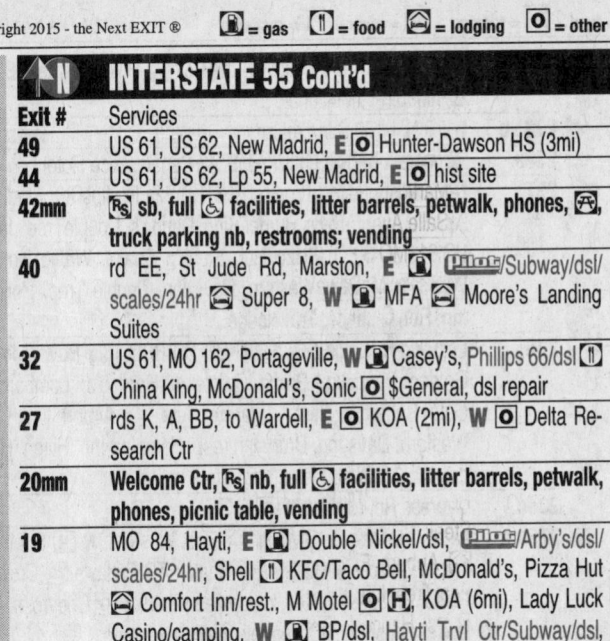

	⬆N	**INTERSTATE 55 Cont'd**
Exit #		Services
49		US 61, US 62, New Madrid, **E** 🅞 Hunter-Dawson HS (3mi)
44		US 61, US 62, Lp 55, New Madrid, **E** 🅞 hist site
42mm		🆁🆂 sb, full ♿ facilities, litter barrels, petwalk, phones, 🅿, truck parking nb, restrooms; vending
40		rd EE, St Jude Rd, Marston, **E** 🍴 ▥/Subway/dsl/scales/24hr 🛏 Super 8, **W** 🅖 MFA 🛏 Moore's Landing Suites
32		US 61, MO 162, Portageville, **W** 🅖 Casey's, Phillips 66/dsl 🍴 China King, McDonald's, Sonic 🅞 $General, dsl repair
27		rds K, A, BB, to Wardell, **E** 🅞 KOA (2mi), **W** 🅞 Delta Research Ctr
20mm		Welcome Ctr, 🆁🆂 nb, full ♿ facilities, litter barrels, petwalk, phones, picnic table, vending
19		MO 84, Hayti, **E** 🅖 Double Nickel/dsl, ▥/Arby's/dsl/scales/24hr, Shell 🍴 KFC/Taco Bell, McDonald's, Pizza Hut 🛏 Comfort Inn/rest., M Motel 🅞 🏨, KOA (6mi), Lady Luck Casino/camping, **W** 🅖 BP/dsl, Hayti Trvl Ctr/Subway/dsl, R&P/dsl 🍴 Apple Barrel, Chubby's BBQ, Los Portales, Patty Ann's BBQ 🛏 Drury Inn 🅞 🏨, $General, CarQuest, Fred's Store, Goodyear/auto, Hay's Foods, repair, USPO
17b a		I-155 E, US 412, to TN
14		rds J, H, U, to Caruthersville, Braggadocio
10mm		weigh sta nb
8		US 61, MO 164, Steele, **W** 🅖 BP/Chester's/Subway/dsl/scales 🛏 Deerfield Inn 🅞 truck repair
4		rd E, to Holland, Cooter
3mm		truck parking, restrooms
1		US 61, rd O, Holland, **W** 🅖 Shell/dsl/24hr
0mm		Missouri/Arkansas state line

	⬆N	**INTERSTATE 57**
Exit #		Services
22mm		Missouri/Illinois state line, Mississippi River
18.5mm		weigh sta both lanes
12		US 62, MO 77, Charleston, **E** 🅖 Exxon/Cheers/Quiznos/dsl/scales/24hr 🛏 Eagle Inn, **W** 🅖 ⒿFLYING J/Huddle House/dsl/scales/24hr 🍴 Las Brisas Mexican 🛏 EconoLodge
10		MO 105, Charleston, **E** 🅖 Conoco/Boomland/dsl, ▥/Subway/dsl/scales/24hr 🍴 Wally's Eatery 🅞 Boomland RV Park, **W** 🅖 Casey's 🍴 China Buffet, McDonald's, Pizza Hut 🛏 Quality Inn 🅞 Alco, city park, CountryMart Foods, Plaza Tire, Verizon
4		rd B, Bertrand
1b a		I-55, N to St Louis, S to Memphis. **I-57 begins/ends on I-55**

	⬆E	**INTERSTATE 64**
Exit #		Services
41mm		Missouri/Illinois state line, Mississippi River
40b a		Broadway St, to Stadium, to the Arch, **N** 🛏 Hilton, Sheraton, stadium, **S** 🅞 Dobb's Tire
40c		(from wb), I-44 W, I-55 S
39c		11th St (exits left), downtown
39b		14th St, **N** 🛏 Sheraton, **S** 🅖 BP, downtown
39a		21st St, Market St (from wb), **N** 🛏 Drury Inn, Hampton Inn
38d		Chestnut at 20th St, **N** 🛏 Drury Inn, Hampton Inn
38c		Jefferson Ave, St Louis Union Sta, **N** 🅞 Joplin House, **S** 🛏 Residence Inn
38a		Forest Park Blvd (from wb), **N** 🅖 Shell
37b a		Market St, Bernard St, Grand Blvd, **N** 🅖 Shell 🍴 Del Taco 🛏 Adam's Mark Hotel, Courtyard, Drury Inn, Hampton Inn, Hyatt, Marriott

Exit #		Services
36d		Vandeventer Ave, Chouteau Ave
36b a		Kingshighway, **N** 🅞 🏨, **S** 🅖 BP
34d c		Hampton Ave, Forest Park, **N** 🅞 museums, zoo, **S** 🅖 BP, Mobil, Phillips 66 🍴 Courtesy Diner, Hardee's, Imo's Pizza, Jack-in-the-Box, Smokin' Al's BBQ, Steak'n Shake, Subway, Taco Bell 🛏 Hampton Inn
34a		Oakland Ave, **N** 🅖 BP 🍴 Del Taco, Subway 🅞 🏨
33d		McCausland Ave, **N** 🅖 BP 🍴 Del Taco
33c		Bellevue Ave, **N** 🅞 🏨
33b		Big Bend Blvd
32b a		Eager Rd, Hanley Rd, **S** 🅖 Shell 🍴 Lion's Choice, Macaroni Grill, McDonald's, St Louis Bread Co, Subway 🅞 Best Buy, Dierberg's Foods, Home Depot, Target, Whole Foods Mkt
31b a		I-170 N, **N** 🅖 Shell 🍴 Burger King, Dillard's, DQ, IHOP, KFC, Steak'n Shake, TGIFriday 🅞 mall, **S** 🅖 BP 🍴 Macaroni Grill, Subway 🅞 Dierberg's Foods, Goodyear, Target
30		McKnight Rd
28c		Clayton Rd (from wb)
28b a		US 67, US 61, Lindbergh Blvd, **S** 🅖 BP 🍴 Brio Grill, Fleming's Rest., Schneithouse Rest., Starbucks 🛏 Hilton 🅞 Honda, mall, Shnuck's Foods
27		Spoede Rd
26		rd JJ, Ballas Rd, **N** 🅞 🏨, **S** 🅞 🏨
25		I-270, N to Chicago, S to Memphis
24		Mason Rd, **N** 🛏 Courtyard, Marriott 🅞 hwy patrol, LDS Temple
23		Maryville Centre Dr (from wb), **N** 🛏 Courtyard, Marriott
22		MO 141, **N** 🍴 Regatta Grille 🅞 🏨, **S** 🍴 5 Guys Burgers, Pizza Hut
21		Timberlake Manor Pkwy
20		Chesterfield Pkwy (from wb), same as 19b a
19b a		MO 340, Chesterfield Pkwy, Olive Blvd, **N** 🅖 BP, Shell 🍴 Applebee's, Pizzaria Uno, Sheridan's Custard, Taco Bell, Yaya's Cafe 🛏 DoubleTree Hotel, Hampton Inn, Homewood Suites, Residence Inn 🅞 Dobb's Tire, Schnucks Foods, USPO, Walgreens, **S** 🅖 Mobil 🍴 Bacana Cafe, Bahama Breeze Rest., California Pizza Kitchen, Casa Gallardo's, Chili's, Houlihans, Macaroni Grill, PF Chang's 🛏 Drury Plaza Hotel 🅞 Dillard's, mall
17		Boones Crossing, Long Rd, Chesterfield Airport Rd, **S** 1 mi 🅖 Mobil 🍴 Bob Evans, Chick-fil-A, Coldstone, Cousins Subs, Culver's, East Coast Pizza, Emperor's Buffet, Fox&Hound, Golden China, Hardee's, Hometown Buffet, IHOP, IMO's Pizza, Joe's Crabshack, Kaldi's Coffee, Lion's Choice, Longhorn Steaks, Matador Cafe., McDonald's, Mimi's Cafe, O'Charley's, Old Country Buffet, Old Spaghetti Factory, Olive Garden, Original Pancakes, Qdoba Mexican, Quiznos, Red Lobster, Red Robin, SmokeHouse Rest., Sonic, Starbucks, Steak'n Shake,

HAYTI

CHARLESTON

ST LOUIS

🅖 = gas   🍴 = food   🏨 = lodging   🅞 = other   🆁🆂 = rest stop   Copyright 2015 - the Next EXIT ®

INTERSTATE 64 Cont'd

Exit #	Services
17	Continued
	Subway, Taco Bell 🏨 Hampton Inn, Hilton Garden 🅞 $Tree, Best Buy, Dick's, Dobb's Tire, Firestone, Ford, Home Depot, KIA, Lowe's, Michael's, Petsmart, Radio Shack, Sam's Club, Target, vet, Walmart, WorldMkt
14	Chesterfield Airport Rd (from eb), S 🅖 Phillips 66 🏨 Comfort Inn
13mm	Missouri River
11	Research Park Ctr Dr
10	MO 94, St. Charles, N 🅖 Mobil, QT, Shell 🍴 Jack-in-the-Box, McDonald's 🅞 Busch Wildlife Area, Mercedes
9	rd k, O'Fallon, N 🅖 Mobil, QT 🍴 Cracker Barrel, Ruby Tuesday, Starbucks 🏨 Holiday Inn Express, Residence Inn, Staybridge Suites 🅞 Chevrolet, Honda, Volvo
6	rd DD, Wing Haven Blvd, N 🅖 Phillips 66 🍴 Bristol Seafood, Hunan King, Massa's Italian, Outback Steaks, Subway, VA BBQ 🏨 Hilton Garden
4	rd N, N 🅖 PetroMart, Phillips 66 🍴 McDonald's, Qdoba Mexican, Red Robin, St. Louis Bread Co., Steak'n Shake 🅞 JC Penney, Shop'n Save, Target, S 🅖 Murphy USA/dsl, Phillips 66 🍴 Dragon Buffet, El Maguay, Jack-in-the-Box, McDonald's, Sonic, Starbucks, Subway, Taco Bell, Wendy's, White Castle 🅞 $Tree, Aldi Foods, AutoZone, Dobb's Tire, Firestone, GNC, Lowe's, Radio Shack, Walmart
2	Lake St. Louis Blvd, N 🍴 BC's Rest., Max&Erma's 🅞 Old Navy, Schnuck's Foods, Von Maur, Walgreens
1	Prospect Rd, N 🅖 Shell
0mm	I-70 E to St Louis, W to Kansas City

INTERSTATE 70

Exit #	Services
252mm	Missouri/Illinois state line, Mississippi River
251a	I-55 S, to Memphis, to I-44, to downtown/no return
250b	Memorial Dr, downtown, Stadium S 🅖 Shell 🍴 McDonald's 🏨 Days Inn
250a	Arch, Riverfront, N 🅞 The Arch, S 🏨 Drury Inn, Hampton Inn, Hilton, Hyatt, Millineal Hotel, Renaissance 🅞 Edward Jones Dome
249b	Tucker Blvd, downtown St Louis, S 🅖 Mobil/dsl
249a	I-70 E, to I-64 E, I-55 E
248b	St Louis Ave, Branch St
248a	Salisbury St, McKinley Br, N 🅞 truck repair/24hr, S 🅖 BP, Phillips 66
247	Grand Ave, N 🅖 BP, Phillips 66/Subway/dsl 🏨 Western Inn
246b	Adelaide Ave
246a	N Broadway, O'Fallon Park, N 🅖 ♥Loves/McDonald's/ Subway/dsl/scales/24hr, Mobil/dsl 🅞 Freightliner
245b	W Florissant
245a	Shreve Ave, S 🅖 BP
244b	Kingshighway, S 3/4 mi 🍴 Burger King, McDonald's, Subway
244a	Bircher Blvd, Union Blvd
243b	(243c from eb)Bircher Blvd
243a	Riverview Blvd
243	Goodfellow Blvd, N 🅖 Shell
242b a	Jennings Sta Rd, S 🏨 Western Inn
241b	Lucas-Hunt Rd, N 🅖 Shell/Circle K, S 3/4 mi 🍴 Lee's Chicken, McDonald's
241a	Bermuda Rd, S 🅞 🅷
240b a	Florissant Rd, N 🅖 BP/McDonald's 🍴 DQ, Sonic, Taco Bell 🅞 Schnuck's Foods, Walgreens

---

ST LOUIS

Exit #	Services
239	N Hanley Rd, N 🍴 Jack-in-the-Box 🏨 Hilton Garden, S 🅖 BP, Mobil 🍴 McDonald's
238c b	I-170 N, I-170 S, no return
238a	N 🅞 Lambert-St Louis ✈, S 🏨 Renaissance Hotel
237	Natural Bridge Rd (from eb), S 🅖 BP, Phillips 66, Shell 🍴 Airport Diner, Arby's, Burger King, Denny's, DoubleTree, Jack-in-the-Box, KFC, Pizza Hut, Steak'n Shake, Waffle House, Wendy's 🏨 Best Western, Days Inn, Double Tree, Holiday Inn, Renaissance, Travelodge
236	Lambert-St Louis ✈, S 🅖 BP 🍴 BBQ, Big Boy, Coco's, Golden Pancake, Grone Cafeteria, Hardee's, Lombardo's Café Rafferty's Rest., Tiffany's Rest. 🏨 Airport Inn, Best Western, Days Inn, Drury Inn/rest., Hampton Inn, Hilton, Holiday Inn, Marriott, Motel 6, Peartree Inn
235c	Cypress Rd, rd B W, N 🅞 to ✈
235b a	US 67, Lindbergh Blvd, N 🏨 Best Western, S 🅖 Shell 🍴 Lion's Choice Rest., Steak'n Shake, TGIFriday's 🏨 Crowne Plaza, Embassy Suites, Homestead Studios 🅞 Chevrolet, Dillard's, Firestone, JC Penney, mall, Sears/auto
234	MO 180, St Charles Rock Rd, N 🅖 Phillips 66/dsl 🍴 Applebee's, Arby's, Fazoli's, HomeTown Buffet, Imo's Pizza, Jack-in-the-Box, LoneStar Steaks, McDonald's, New China Buffet, Ponderosa, Red Lobster, St Louis Bread, Subway, Wendy's, White Castle 🅞 🅷, $Tree, Aldi Foods, AutoZone, Best Buy, Kohl's, Lowe's, Meineke, NTB, Office Depot, Petsmart, Save-A-Lot Foods, Target, Tuesday Morning, Verizon, Walgreens, Walmart, S 🅖 QT 🍴 IHOP 🅞 Chrysler/Dodge/Jeep, Home Depot, Schucks, tires/repair, Walgreens
232	I-270, N to Chicago, S to Memphis
231b a	Earth City Expwy, N 🅖 Motomart, Phillips 66/Jack-in-the-Box/ dsl 🍴 McDonald's, Quiznos 🏨 Candlewood Suites, Courtyard, Holiday Inn, Residence Inn, SpringHill Suites, Studio+, S 🅖 Mobil 🍴 Burger King, Dave&Buster's 🏨 Holiday Inn Express, Homewood Suites, Wingate Inn 🅞 Harrah's Casino/ Hotel, Riverport Ampitheatre
230mm	Missouri River
229b a	5th St, St Charles, N 🅖 BP, Mobil/dsl 🍴 Bellacino's Italian, Buffalo Wild Wings, Denny's, El Tio Pepe, Jack-in-the-Box, KFC, Lee's Chicken, McDonald's, Waffle House 🏨 Best Value Inn, Best Western, Comfort Suites, Quality Inn 🅞 Aldi Foods, Ameristar Casino, Bass Pro Shops, Gordman's, Walgreens, S 🅖 QT/dsl 🍴 Cracker Barrel🏨 Embassy Suites, Fairfield Inn 🅞 malls
228	MO 94, to Weldon Springs, St Charles, N 🅖 Phillips 66, ZX/ dsl 🍴 Arby's, Chinatown Express, DQ, Imo's Pizza, Papa John's, Steak'n Shake 🅞 Advance Parts, Chevrolet, NAPA, Valvoline, Walgreen, S 🅖 QT 🍴 Chinese Express, Chuck-ECheese, Fazoli's, Gingham's Rest., Grappa Grill, McAlister's Deli, Outback Steaks, Pizza Hut 🏨 Days Inn, Intown Suites 🅞 access to 227, Dobb's Tire, vet
227	Zumbehl Rd, N 🅖 Phillips 66/dsl, ZX 🍴 Culpepper's Grill 🏨 Super 8 🅞 Lowe's, Sav-A-Lot Foods, S 🅖 BP, Hucks/dsl 🍴 Applebee's, Bob Evans, Boston Mkt, Capt D's, Chevy's Mexican, Chirco's Grill, CiCi's Pizza, El Mariachi Mexican, Fazoli's, Gingham's Rest., Golden Corral, Great Wall Chinese, Hardee's, Hoho Chinese, Jack-in-the-Box, McCalister's, McDonald's, Quiznos, Subway, Taco Bell/Pizza Hut, Wiliker's Cafe 🏨 Days Inn, Red Roof Inn, TownePlace Suites, Travelodge 🅞 $Tree, access to 228, BigLots, Dierberg's Foods, GNC, Jiffy Lube, Michael's, NTB, Petsmart, Radio Shack, Sam's Club/gas, Schnuck's Foods, vet, Walgreens, Walmart/Blimpie

ST CHARLES

MO

INTERSTATE 70 Cont'd

Exit #	Services

225 Truman Rd, to Cave Springs, N ⛽ BP, Casey's, Shell, ZX Gas 🛏 Hampton Inn, Motel 6 ⊙ Buick/GMC, Cadillac, Kenworth, Mazda, Subaru, U-Haul, VW, S ⛽ Conoco, Mobil, QT 🍴 Bandanas BBQ, Big Boy, Burger King, China Wok, Culver's, Denny's, DQ, El Tio Pepe, Hooters, IHOP, Jack-in-the-Box, Lion's Choice Rest., LJ Silver, Longhorn Steaks, McDonald's, O'Charley's, Pasta House, Pizza Hut, Pizza St, Red Lobster, Steak'n Shake, Subway, Taco Bell, Thai Kitchen, White Castle 🛏 Country Inn&Suites ⊙ 🅷, Batteries+, Chrysler/Dodge/ Jeep, Firestone, Home Depot, Kia, Office Depot, Shop'n Save, Target, TJ Maxx

224 MO 370 E

S T   P E T E R S

222 Mid-Rivers Mall Dr, rd C, St Peters, N ⛽ QT/dsl/24hr 🍴 Burger King ⊙ Chevrolet, Honda, Lincoln, Toyota/Scion, S ⛽ Mobil, ZX Gas/dsl 🍴 Arby's, Bob Evans, Buffalo Wild Wings, Chili's, China Wok, Domino's, HoneyBaked Ham, Jack-in-the-Box, Joe's Crabshack, Macaroni Grill, Max & Erma's, McDonald's/playplace, Olive Garden, Pizza Hut/Taco Bell, Qdoba, Red Robin, Ruby Tuesday, Steak'n Shake, Subway, Wendy's 🛏 Drury Inn, Extended Stay America ⊙ Aldi Foods, AutoZone, Barnes&Noble, Best Buy, BigLots, Costco/ gas, Dick's, Dillard's, Discount Tire, Hancock Fabrics, Hyundai/Nissan/VW, JC Penney, Jo-Ann Fabrics, Marshall's, NTB, Sears/auto, Tuesday Morning, Walgreens

220 MO 79, to Elsberry, N ⊙ Cherokee Lakes Camping (7mi), S ⛽ 7-11/gas, BP, Phillips 66/dsl 🍴 Caleco's Rest., El Mezon, Jack-in-the-Box, McDonald's/playplace, Pirrone's Pizzaria, Quiznos, Roly Poly Sandwiches, Sonic, Subway 🛏 Days Inn ⊙ Curves, Dierberg's Foods, O'Reilly Parts, Walgreens

219 T R Hughes Blvd, S ⛽ QT 🍴 Ethyl's Smokehouse 🛏 Comfort Inn

O' F A L L O N

217 rds K, M, O'Fallon, N ⛽ Hucks/dsl 🍴 Baskin-Robbins, Burger King, Jack-in-the-Box, Piggy's BBQ, Pizza Hut/Taco Bell, Rally's, Sonic, Waffle House ⊙ Firestone, Jiffy Lube, O'Reilly Parts, Radio Shack, S ⛽ Phillips 66/dsl, QT, ZX 🍴 Applebee's, Arby's, Bob Evans, Chick-fil-A, Domino's, Fazoli's, IHOP, KFC, Krieger's Grill, Lion's Choice Rest., McDonald's/playplace, Pantera's Pizza, Papa John's, Pizza Hut, Red Robin, Stefanina's Pizza, Subway ⊙ Advance Parts, Aldi Foods, Auto Tire, AutoZone, camping, GNC, Home Depot, K-Mart/drugs, Lowe's, Schnuck's Foods, Shop'n Save Foods, TrueValue, Walgreens, Walmart

216 Bryan Rd, N 🛏 Super 8 ⊙ CarQuest, Ford, Peterbilt, S ⛽ Conoco, Phillips 66/Jack-in-the-Box/dsl, QT 🍴 Cappuccino's, DQ, Mr. Goodcents, Wendy's

214 Lake St Louis, N ⛽ Phillips 66/McDonald's/dsl, Q-Stop 🍴 McDonald's, S ⛽ Phillips 66/dsl, Shell/Circle K 🍴 Denny's, El Maguey Mexican, Hardee's, Subway 🛏 Days Inn ⊙ 🅷, Wharf Drug

212 rd A, N 🛏 Economy Inn, S ⛽ Mobil 🍴 Imo's Pizza 🛏 Motel 6 ⊙ Chrysler/Dodge/Jeep

210b a to I-64, US 40 E, US 61 S, S ⊙ 🅷

209 rd Z, Church St, New Melle, N 🍴 DQ, S ⛽ Phillips 66/dsl

208 Pearce Blvd, Wentzville Pkwy, Wentzville, N ⛽ Mobil/dsl, QT/ dsl 🍴 54th St Grill, 88 China, Applebee's, Arby's, Bob Evans, Buffalo Wild Wings, Chick-fil-A, China Buffet, Culver's, Domino's, El Maguey, Fritz's Custard, Hardee's, Jack-in-the-Box, Jimmy John's, KFC, Lion's Choice, Little Caesar's, McDonald's, Olive Garden, Panda Express, Papa John's, Penn Sta., Pizza Hut, Pizza Pro, Ruby Tuesday, St Louis Bread,

208 Continued
Starbucks, Steak'n Shake, Subway, Sunny St Cafe, Taco Bell, Waffle House, Wendy's, White Castle 🛏 Fairfield Inn ⊙ 🅷, $General, AT&T, AutoZone, Best Buy, Chevrolet, Dick's, Dierberg's Foods, Dobb's Tire, GNC, Home Depot, Kohl's, Lowe's, Michael's, NAPA, O'Reilly Parts, Petsmart, Ross, Sam's Club/ dsl, Save-A-Lot, Schnuck's Food, Target, URGENT CARE, Verizon, Walgreens, Walmart, S ⛽ BP/dsl 🍴 Bandana's BBQ, Chimi's FreshMex, IHOP 🛏 Super 8 ⊙ Hyundai, Thomas RV Ctr

204mm weigh sta both lanes

W E N T Z V I L L E

203 rds W, T, Foristell, N ⛽ Mr Fuel/dsl/scales, TA/BP/Pizza Hut/ Popeye's/Taco Bell/dsl/scales/24hr/@ 🛏 Quality Inn, S ⛽ Phillips 66/McDonald's/dsl ⊙ dsl repair

200 rds J, H, F (from wb), Wright City, N ⛽ Phillips 66/dsl 🍴 Ruiz Castillo's Mexican (1mi), S 🍴 Subway 🛏 Super 7 Inn

199 rd J, H, F, Wright City, N ⛽ Shell/McDonald's/dsl ⊙ $General, S 🛏 Super 7 Inn ⊙ Volvo Trucks

198mm 🆁🆂 both lanes, full 🚻 facilities, litter barrels, petwalk, 🄲, 🅿

W A R R E N T O N

193 MO 47, Warrenton, N ⛽ Mobil/dsl, Phillips 66/Chester's/dsl 🍴 1st Wok, Applebee's, Burger King, China House, Dominos, DQ, El Jimador Mexican, Jack-in-the-Box, Little Caesar's, McDonald's, Pizza Hut, Subway, Waffle House, Wendy's 🛏 Best Value Inn, Holiday Inn Express, Super 8 ⊙ Aldi Foods, AT&T, Mosers Foods, Walmart, S ⛽ BP/dsl, Conoco/dsl, Phillips 66/ dsl 🍴 Denny's, Imo's Pizza, Papa John's, Taco Bell 🛏 Baymont Inn ⊙ AutoZone, CarQuest, Chevrolet, NAPA, O'Reilly Parts, Walgreens

188 rds A, B, to Truxton, S ⛽ ⛟FLYING J/Denny's/dsl/LP/RV Dump/scales/24hr 🛏 Budget Inn

183 rds E, NN, Y, Jonesburg, N 1 mi ⊙ Jonesburg Gardens Camping, S ⛽ Phillips 66/Chester's/dsl ⊙ USPO

179 rd F, High Hill, S 🛏 Budget Motel, Colonial Inn

175 MO 19, New Florence, N ⛽ BP/dsl, Shell/dsl/24hr 🍴 Dad's Jct Cafe, McDonald's 🛏 Best Inn, Best Value Inn, Days Inn ⊙ auto repair, Stone Hill Winery/gifts (15mi)

170 MO 161, rd J, Danville, N ⛽ Sinclair/dsl ⊙ Kan-Do RV Park, to Graham Cave SP, S ⊙ Lazy Day RV Park

169.5mm truck parking

168mm Loutre River

167mm truck parking eb

161 rds D, YY, Williamsburg, N ⛽ Cranes/mkt 🍴 Marlene's Rest. ⊙ USPO

155 rds A, Z, to Calwood, N ⊙ antiques

148 US 54, Kingdom City, N ⛽ BP/dsl, Phillips 66/Burger King/dsl 🍴 Taco Bell ⊙ MO Tourism Ctr, to Mark Twain Lake,

INTERSTATE 70 Cont'd

Exit #	Services
148	Continued
	S 〔gas〕 Conoco/Subway/dsl/scales/24hr, Petro/Mobil/Iron Skillet/dsl/scales/24hr/@, Phillips 66/dsl, Shell/Gasper's/Arby's/dsl/scales/@ 〔food〕 Denny's, McDonald's 〔lodging〕 Best Value Inn, Comfort Inn, Days Inn, Super 8 〔other〕 Ozarkland Gifts, Wheeler's Truckwash
144	rds M, HH, to Hatton, S 〔other〕 fireworks
137	rds DD, J, to Millersburg, Stephens, S 〔food〕 Ranch House BBQ 〔other〕 antiques, Freightliner, to Little Dixie WA (4mi)
133	rd Z, to Centralia, N 〔other〕 Camping World RV Ctr
131	Lake of the Woods Rd, N 〔gas〕 BP, Phillips 66/Subway/dsl 〔food〕 Buckingham BBQ, George's Rest, Sonic 〔lodging〕 Super 8 〔other〕 Harley-Davidson, S 〔gas〕 Conoco/dsl 〔food〕 Jimmy John's 〔lodging〕 Holiday Inn
128a	US 63, to Jefferson City, Columbia, N 〔gas〕 CNG, Mobil/dsl, QT 〔food〕 Bandanas BBQ, Bob Evans, Burger King, China Garden, Cracker Barrel, Golden Corral, Hooters, KFC, Lonestar Steaks, McDonald's, Pizza Hut, Ruby Tuesday, Steak'n Shake, Taco Bell, Wendy's, White Castle 〔lodging〕 Fairfield Inn, Hampton Inn, Hilton Garden, Red Roof Inn, Residence Inn, Super 8 〔other〕 Bass Pro Shop, Home Depot, Menard's, Pine Grove RV Park, S 〔gas〕 BreakTime/dsl 〔food〕 5 Guys Burgers, Applebee's, Baskin-Robbins, Chili's, Chipotle Mexican, CiCi's, Culver's, El Maguey, Firehouse Subs, Freddy's, Good Cents Subs, Houlihan's, IHOP, Kobe Japanese, Little Caesar's, Longhorn Steaks, Panda Express, Panera Bread, Sonic, Starbucks, Subway, TGIFriday's 〔lodging〕 Baymont Inn, Country Inn&Suites, Howard Johnson, Motel 6, Ramada, Staybridge Suites, Suburban Inn, Wingate Inn 〔other〕 H, $Tree, HyVee Foods, Lowe's/Subway, Patricia's Foods, Sam's Club, Staples, Verizon, Walmart/McDonald's
128	Lp 70 (from wb), Columbia, N 〔food〕 Hardee's, S 〔food〕 Capt D's 〔lodging〕 Eastwood Motel 〔other〕 H, Big O Tire, same as 128a
127	MO 763, to Moberly, Columbia, N 〔gas〕 BreakTime/dsl 〔food〕 Waffle House 〔lodging〕 Budget Host 〔other〕 $General, Chrysler/Dodge/Jeep, Fiat, Hyundai, Mazda, Mercedes, Toyota/Scion, transmissions, S 〔gas〕 Phillips 66/dsl 〔lodging〕 Super 7 Motel
126	MO 163, Providence Rd, Columbia, N 〔gas〕 Phillips 66/dsl 〔food〕 Chop Sticks, Country Kitchen 〔lodging〕 Best Value Inn, Quality Inn, Red Roof Inn 〔other〕 CarQuest, Honda, McKnight Tire, same as 127, S 〔gas〕 BreakTime/dsl 〔food〕 Burger King, Carlito's Mexican, Church's, DQ, LJ Silver, McDonald's, Pizza Hut, Sonic, Subway, Taco Bell 〔other〕 H, AutoZone, Buick/Cadillac/Chevrolet/GMC, Nissan, O'Reilly Parts, Transmissions+
125	Lp 70, West Blvd, Columbia, N 〔lodging〕 Comfort Suites, S 〔gas〕 Phillips 66/dsl, Shell/dsl 〔food〕 Cheddar's, Domino's, Fazoli's, JJ's Cafe, Olive Garden, Outback Steaks, Teppanyaki Grill 〔lodging〕 EconoLodge 〔other〕 Aldi Foods, BMW, Firestone/auto, Kia, Mosers Foods, same as 124, Subaru, U-Haul
124	MO 740, rd E, Stadium Blvd, Columbia, N 〔lodging〕 Extended Stay America, S 〔gas〕 BreakTime, Phillips 66/dsl 〔food〕 5 Guys Burgers, Applebee's, ChuckECheese, Denny's, Hardee's, Jazz Kitchen, KFC, Lee's Chicken, Macaroni Grill, McDonald's, Panera Bread, Pizza Hut, Quiznos, Red Lobster, Ruby Tuesday, Steak'n Shake, Subway, Taco Bell, TX Roadhouse, Wendy's 〔lodging〕 Days Inn, Drury Inn, Holiday Inn, La Quinta, Motel 6 〔other〕 $Tree, Barnes&Noble, Best Buy, Dick's, Dillard's, Ford, Hobby Lobby, Macy's, mall, Marshalls, Michael's, Natural Grocers, Old Navy, PetCo, Petsmart, Radio Shack, same as 125, Sears/auto, Target, to U of MO, Verizon
122mm	Perche Creek

Exit #	Services
121	US 40, rd UU, Midway, N 〔gas〕 Conoco/dsl/rest.; Phillips 66 〔lodging〕 Budget Inn 〔food〕 tires/repair, S 〔other〕 golf
117	rds J, O, to Huntsdale, Harrisburg
115	rd BB N, Rocheport, N 〔other〕 to Katy Tr SP, winery
114.5mm	Missouri River
111	MO 98, MO 179, to Wooldridge, Overton, S 〔gas〕 Phillips 66/dsl/repair 〔other〕 RV Park
106	MO 87, Bingham Rd, to Boonville, S 〔gas〕 Phillips 66/dsl
104mm	〔rest stop〕 both lanes, full 〔lodging〕 facilities, litter barrels, petwalk, 〔C〕, 〔vending〕 vending
103	rd B, Main St, Boonville, N 〔gas〕 Breaktime, Murphy USA/dsl, Phillips 66/dsl 〔food〕 Happy China, KFC/LJ Silver, La Hacienda Mexican, McDonald's, Pizza Hut, Sonic, Subway, Taco Bell 〔lodging〕 Days Inn, Super 8 〔other〕 H, Dave's Mkt, Radio Shack, RV Express Camping, to Katy Tr SP, Walmart/Subway, S 〔gas〕 Cenex/dsl 〔lodging〕 QT Inn
101	US 40, MO 5, to Boonville, N 〔food〕 〔gas〕/Wendy's/dsl/24hr 〔food〕 Arby's 〔lodging〕 Comfort Inn, Holiday Inn Express, Isle of Capri Hotel (3mi) 〔other〕 Buick/Cadillac/Chevrolet/GMC, Ford, Russell Stover Candies, S 〔gas〕 Love's/Hardee's/scales/dsl/24hr, to Lake of the Ozarks
98	MO 41, MO 135, Lamine, N 〔other〕 tires, to Arrow Rock HS (13mi), S 〔gas〕 Conoco/Dogwood Rest./dsl, Phillips 66/dsl 〔other〕 repair
93mm	Lamine River
89	rd K, to Arrow Rock, N 〔other〕 to Arrow Rock HS
84	rd J, N 〔food〕 truck repair, Valero/DQ/Stuckey's
78b a	US 65, to Marshall, N 〔gas〕 Conoco/dsl 〔other〕 fireworks, RV Park
77mm	Blackwater River
74	rd YY, N 〔gas〕 Shell/Betty's/cafe/dsl/repair/24hr 〔lodging〕 Welcome Motel
71	rds EE, K, to Houstonia
66	MO 127, Sweet Springs, N 〔other〕 H, S 〔gas〕 BreakTime/dsl, Casey's/dsl 〔food〕 Mi Pueblo 〔lodging〕 Rodeway Inn 〔other〕 $General, NAPA
65.5mm	Davis Creek
62	rds VV, Y, Emma
58	MO 23, Concordia, N 〔gas〕 TA/Country Pride/Subway/dsl/scales/24hr/@ 〔food〕 KFC/Taco Bell, McDonald's 〔other〕 $General, Patricia's Foods, truck/RV wash, S 〔gas〕 Breaktime/dsl, Casey's, Conoco/dsl, Phillips 66 〔food〕 Biffle's BBQ, Hardee's, Pizza Hut 〔lodging〕 Budget Inn, Days Inn, Travelodge 〔other〕 NAPA
57.5mm	〔rest stop〕 both lanes, full 〔lodging〕 facilities, litter barrels, petwalk, 〔C〕, 〔vending〕 vending
52	rd T, Aullville
49	MO 13, to Higginsville, N 〔gas〕 Casey's, 〔gas〕/McDonald's/Subway/dsl/scales/24hr 〔lodging〕 Camelot Inn/rest 〔other〕 to Confederate Mem, S 〔lodging〕 Super 8 〔other〕 Great Escape RV Park, Interstate RV Park
45	rd H, to Mayview
43mm	weigh sta both lanes
41	rds O, M, to Lexington, Mayview
38	MO 131 (from wb), Odessa, S 〔gas〕 BP/dsl, Phillips 66/dsl, Shell, Sinclair 〔food〕 McDonald's, Morgan's Rest., Pizza Hut, Sonic, Subway, Taco John's 〔other〕 $General, camping, O'Reilly Parts, same as 37
37	MO 131, Odessa, N 〔other〕 Country Gardens RV Park/dump, S 〔gas〕 BP/dsl, Shell, Sinclair 〔food〕 El Camino Real, McDonald's, Pizza Hut, Sonic, Subway, Taco John's 〔lodging〕 Parkside Inn 〔other〕 $General, fireworks, O'Reilly Parts, Patricia's Foods, same as 38
35mm	truck parking both lanes
31	rds D, Z, to Bates City, Napoleon, N 〔other〕 Bates City RV Camping, S 〔gas〕 Valero/dsl 〔food〕 Bates City BBQ 〔other〕 fireworks

MO (side tab)

COLUMBIA (side tab)

BOONVILLE (side tab)

CONCORDIA (side tab)

INTERSTATE 70 Cont'd

Exit #	Services
29.5mm	Horse Shoe Creek
28	rd H, rd F, Oak Grove, **N** 🅐 TA/Country Pride/Popeye's/dsl/scales/24hr/@ 🏠 Days Inn 🅞 Blue Beacon, KOA, **S** 🅐 Casey's, Petro/BP/DQ/Wendy's/scales/dsl/@, QT/dsl 🍴 China Buffet, Hardee's, KFC/Taco Bell, McDonald's, Pizza Hut, PJ's Rest., Subway, Waffle House 🏠 EconoLodge 🅞 Cash Saver Foods, Lake Paradise RV/Camping (9mi), O'Reilly Parts, SpeedCo Lube, Verizon, Walgreens, Walmart
24	US 40, rds AA, BB, to Buckner, **N** 🅐 McShop/dsl 🏠 Best Value Inn, Comfort Inn 🅞 auto/dsl repair, LifeStyle RV Ctr, **S** 🅐 Conoco/Subway/dsl/scales/24hr 🍴 Sonic 🅞 Trailside RV Park/Ctr
21	Adams Dairy Pkwy, **N** 🏠 Days Inn 🅞 Nationwide RV Ctr (1mi), **S** 🅐 Murphy USA/dsl, Phillips 66/Burger King/dsl 🍴 Arby's, Buffalo Wild Wings, Chick-fil-A, Chipotle Mexican, Olive Garden, Panda Express, Panera Bread, Planet Sub, Sonic, Taco Bell, TX Roadhouse 🏠 Courtyard 🅞 AT&T, GNC, Gordman's, Home Depot, Kohl's, Michael's, NTB, PetCo, Ross, Staples, Target, TJ Maxx, Verizon, Walmart
20	MO 7, Blue Springs, **N** 🅐 Phillips 66/dsl, QT/dsl 🍴 Backyard Burger, Bob Evans, China 1, Minsky's Pizza, Papa Murphy's, Pizza Shoppe, Pizza St, Rancho Grande, Sonic, Subway 🏠 Best Value Inn, Days Inn, Motel 6 🅞 $General, Ace Hardware, CVS Drug, O'Reilly Parts, PriceChopper Foods, Walgreens, **S** 🅐 BP/dsl, QT/dsl, Shell, Valero 🍴 Applebee's, Arby's, Cinco de Mayo, Denny's, Godfather's, Jack-in-the-Box, Jimmy John's, KFC, LJ Silver, McDonald's, Original Pizza, Sheridan's Custard, Starbucks, Subway, Taco Bueno, Wendy's, Winsteads Cafe, Zarda's BBQ 🏠 Hampton Inn, Quality Inn 🅞 H, Advance Parts, Aldi Foods, AutoZone, BigLots, Chevrolet, Firestone/auto, Goodyear/auto, Hobby Lobby, Hy-Vee Foods/gas, NAPA, Office Depot, Russell Stover, URGENT CARE
18	Woods Chapel Rd, **N** 🅐 BP 🏠 American Inn, La Quinta, Night's Inn, Super 8 🅞 Harley-Davidson, **S** 🅐 Conoco/dsl, Phillips 66/dsl, QT 🍴 China Kitchen, KFC/Taco Bell, Las Playas Mexican, McDonald's, Pizza Hut, Sonic, Subway, Taco John's, Waffle House 🅞 Ford/Lincoln, Hyundai, Nissan, same as 20
17	Little Blue Pkwy, 39th St, **N** 🍴 Buffalo Wild Wings, Coldstone, Hereford House, Jimmy John's, Joe's Crabshack, On the Border, Sonic 🏠 Hilton Garden 🅞 H, mall entrance, World Mkt, **S** 🅐 QT 🍴 Arby's, BD Mongolian, Carrabba's, Chipotle Mexican, Corner Cafe, Culver's, El Maguey Mexican, Golden Corral, Hooters, IHOP, Kobe Steaks, Outback Steaks, Red Robin, Rib Crib, Subway, Wendy's 🏠 Comfort Suites, Drury Inn, Holiday Inn Express 🅞 Carmax, Costco/gas, Lowe's
16mm	Little Blue River
15b	MO 291 N, Independence, **N** 1 exit on 39th St 🅐 Phillips 66, QT 🍴 54th St Grill, Applebee's, Bob Evans, Burger King, Chick-fil-A, Chili's, ChuckECheese, Fazoli's, Logan's Roadhouse, Longhorn Steaks, McDonald's, Noodles&Co, Perkins, Smokehouse BBQ, Taco Bell, Zio's Italian 🏠 Fairfield Inn, Staybridge Suites 🅞 H, AT&T, Barnes&Noble, Best Buy, Dick's, Dillard's, JC Penney, Kohl's, Macy's, mall, Marshalls, NTB, Petsmart, Ross, Sam's Club/gas, Sears/auto, Target, Verizon, Walmart
15a	I-470 S, MO 291 S, to Lee's Summit
14	Lee's Summit Rd, **N** 1 mi 🍴 Bob Evans, Longhorn Steaks, **S** 🍴 Cheddar's, Cracker Barrel 🅞 Bass Pro Shops, Hobby Lobby, Home Depot

12	Noland Rd, Independence, **N** 🅐 Conoco/dsl, QT, Shell 🍴 China Town, Denny's, Domino's, Hardee's, Mr Goodcents, Pizza St, Sheridan's Custard, Sonic 🏠 Best Western, Super 8 🅞 $General, Advance Parts, Buick/Chevrolet, Chrysler/Jeep, CVS Drug, Firestone/auto, Hancock Fabrics, Honda, K-Mart, Office Depot, to Truman Library, TrueValue, Walgreens, **S** 🅐 Phillips 66/Circle K 🍴 Arby's, Bandana's BBQ, Burger King, HoneyBaked Ham, KFC/Taco Bell, Krispy Kreme, McDonald's, Olive Garden, Pizza Hut, Quiznos, Red Lobster, Ruby Tuesday, Steak'n Shake, Wendy's 🏠 American Inn, Best Value Inn, EconoLodge, Quality Inn, Super 6 Motel 🅞 $Tree, BigLots, Gordman's, HyVee Foods/gas, Meineke, Savers, Tires+, U-Haul
11	US 40, Blue Ridge Blvd, Independence, **N** 🅐 QT 🍴 A&W/LJ Silver, Benny's BBQ, Sonic, Subway, V's Italian, **S** 🅐 7-11, Sinclair 🍴 Applebee's, Big Boy, Chipotle Mexican, Church's, East Buffet, Firehouse Subs, IHOP, McDonald's, Papa John's, Samurai Chef, Starbucks, Subway, Taco Bell 🅞 Cadillac, Family$, GNC, Lowe's, O'Reilly Parts, Radio Shack, Verizon, vet, Walmart/Subway
10	Sterling Ave (from eb), same as 11
9	Blue Ridge Cutoff, **N** 🍴 Denny's 🏠 Drury Inn, Holiday Inn 🅞 H, **S** 🅐 BP, Conoco/Subway 🍴 Taco Bell 🏠 Clarion 🅞 Sports Complex
8b a	I-435, N to Des Moines, S to Wichita
7mm	Blue River
7b	Manchester Trafficway
7a	US 40 E, 31st St
6	Van Brunt Blvd, **N** 🅐 Phillips 66/dsl, **S** 🅐 BP 🍴 McDonald's, Pizza Hut 🅞 NAPA, VA H
5c	Jackson Ave (from wb)
5b	31st St (from eb)
5a	27th St (from eb)
4c	23rd Ave
4b	18th St
4a	Benton Blvd (from eb), Truman Rd, **N** 🅐 Super Stop/Wendy's/dsl 🍴 Subway 🅞 Advance Parts, Save-A-Lot Foods
3c	Prospect Ave, **N** 🅐 BP 🍴 Bryant's BBQ, Church's, **S** 🍴 McDonald's
3b	Brooklyn Ave (from eb), **N** 🍴 Gates BBQ, **S** 🍴 Bryant's, Church's, McDonald's
3a	Paseo St, **S** 🅐 BP/dsl 🅞 tires
2m	US 71 S, downtown
2l	I-670, to I-35 S
2j	11th St, downtown
2h	US 24 E, downtown
2g	I-29/35 N, US 71 N, to Des Moines

*(Vertical margin labels, left column: BLUE SPGS, INDEPENDENCE; right column: KANSAS CITY)*

[gas] = gas [food] = food [lodging] = lodging [other] = other [rest stop] = rest stop Copyright 2015 - the Next EXIT ®

⬆E INTERSTATE 70 Cont'd

Exit #	Services
2e	MO 9 N, Oak St, **S** [gas] Phillips 66, Valero [lodging] Marriott
2d	Main St, downtown
2c	US 169 N, Broadway, **S** [gas] Phillips 66 [lodging] Marriott
2b	Beardsley Rd
2a	I-35 S, to Wichita
0mm	Missouri/Kansas state line, Kansas River

⬆N INTERSTATE 270 (St Louis)

Exit #	Services
15b a	I-55 N to Chicago, S to St Louis. **I-270 begins/ends in Illinois on I-55/I-70, exit 20.**
12	IL 159, to Collinsville, **N 1 mi** [gas] Conoco, Phillips 66 [food] Applebee's, China Rest., Denny's, DQ, Hardee's, Jack-in-the-Box, KFC, Papa John's, Ponderosa, Quizno's [other] Aldi Foods, Buick/GMC, Chrysler/Dodge/Jeep, Home Depot, Lowes Whse, PetsMart, Radio Shack, Walgreens, Walmart, **S** [other] [H]
9	IL 157, to Collinsville, **N** [food] Comfort Inn, **S** [gas] Phillips 66/24hr [lodging] Hampton Inn
7	I-255, to I-55 S to Memphis
6b a	IL 111, **N** [gas] ⟨FLYING J⟩/Denny's/dsl/scales/24hr, BP [food] Hen House Rest. [lodging] Magnuson Hotel [other] Blue Beacon/scales, Speedco, truck/trailer repair, **S** [gas] Mobil/dsl [food] Denny's, La Mexicana Rest., McDonald's/playplace, Taco Bell [lodging] Days Inn, Holiday Inn Express, Sleep Inn, Super 8 [other] [H], to Pontoon Beach
4	IL 203, Old Alton Rd, to Granite City
3b a	IL 3, **N** [other] Riverboat Casino, **S** [gas] Phillips 66 [food] Hardee's, Waffle House [lodging] Budget Motel, EconoLodge, Sun Motel [other] KOA, MGM Camping
2mm	Chain of Rocks Canal
0mm	Illinois/Missouri state line, Mississippi River, motorist callboxes begin eb
34	Riverview Dr, to St Louis, **N Welcome Ctr/[rest stop] both lanes, full [lodging] facilities, info, litter barrels**, [other], [rest stop], [gas] Moto Mart/Subway
33	Lilac Ave, **N** [other] USPO, **S** [gas] Phillips 66/Jack-in-the-Box/dsl, QT/dsl/scales/24hr [food] Hardee's
32	Bellefontaine Rd, **N** [gas] Mobil, QT, Shell [food] China King, KFC, McDonald's, Pizza Hut, Steak'n Shake [lodging] Economy Inn, Motel 6 [other] Advance Parts, Firestone, Schnuck's Foods, **S** [gas] BP [food] White Castle [other] Aldi Foods
31b a	MO 367, **N** [gas] BP, QT/dsl [food] Jack-in-the-Box, McDonalds, Subway [other] [H], $General, Chevrolet, Shop'n Save Foods, U-Haul, Walgreens
30b a	Hall's Ferry Rd, rd AC, **N** [gas] Mobil/dsl, Phillips 66/dsl, QT, ZX [food] Applebee's, Capt. D's, Popeye's, Waffle House, White Castle [lodging] Knights Inn [other] Ford/Lincoln, **S** [gas] BP/dsl, Conoco, Phillips 66 [food] China Wok, Church's, CiCi's Pizza, Cracker Barrel, IHOP, Steak'n Shake, Subway [other] $Buster, AutoZone, Family$, Home Depot, JoAnn Fabrics, O'Reilly Parts, Shop'n Save Foods
29	W Florissant Rd, **N** [food] Jack-in-the-Box, Lion's Choice, Pasta House [other] $General, Dobb's Tire/auto, Firestone, K-Mart, Office Depot, **S** [gas] Phillips 66 [food] Arby's, Burger King, Krispy Kreme, Malone's Grill, McDonald's, Pantera's Pizza, Sonic [other] $Tree, BigLots, Mazda, NTB, Radio Shack, Sam's Club/gas, Walgreens, Walmart
28	Elizabeth Ave, Washington St, **N** [gas] Phillips 66/dsl [food] Jack-in-the-Box, Jerome's Pizza, Pizza Hut/Taco Bell, Subway [other] Chevrolet, Schnuck's Foods, Walgreens, **S** [gas] BP

Exit #	Services
27	New Florissant Rd, rd N, **N** [gas] BP, Shell/Circle K
26b	Graham Rd, N Hanley, **N** [gas] 7-11/dsl [food] Arby's, LJ Silver, Starbucks [lodging] Hampton Inn, Motel 6 [other] [H], **S** [gas] QT [food] McDonald's [lodging] Days Inn [other] $General, Hancock Fabrics
26a	I-170 S
25b a	US 67, Lindbergh Blvd, **N** [gas] BP, Phillips 66, QT [food] Bandana's BBQ, Burger King, China Wok, Church's, Del Taco, IHOP, Imo's Pizza, Jack-in-the-Box, McDonald's, Outback Steaks, Papa John's, Pizza Hut/Taco Bell, Pueblo Nuevo Mexican, Quiznos, Rally's, Sonic, Starbucks, Waffle House, Wendy's [lodging] Comfort Inn, InTown Suites, La Quinta, Ramada Inn [other] AutoZone, Cadillac, Dierberg's Deli, Family$, Firestone/auto, Ford, GNC, Goodyear, NAPA, Nissan, Radio Shack, Sav-a-Lot Foods, Schnuck's Foods, Toyota/Scion, Walgreens, **S** [gas] 7-11 [food] Subway [lodging] Budget Inn, EconoLodge, Extended Stay America, Studio+ [other] Honda, transmissions, USPO, VW
23	McDonnell Blvd, **E** [food] Denny's, Quiznos [lodging] La Quinta, **W** [gas] BP, QT, ZX [food] Arby's, Jack-in-the-Box, Lion's Choice, McDonald's, Starbucks, Steak'n Shake [other] Buick/GMC
22b a	MO 370 W, to MO Bottom Rd
20c	MO 180, St Charles Rock Rd, **E** [gas] Phillips 66/dsl [food] A&W/LJ Silver, Arby's, Casa Gallardo's, Fazoli's, Hometown Buffet, Jack-in-the-Box, Lonestar Steaks, McDonald's, Ponderosa, Red Lobster, St. Louis Bread, Subway, Taco Bell, Wendy's, White Castle [lodging] Economy Inn [other] [H], $Tree, Aldi Foods, AutoZone, Best Buy, K-Mart, Kohl's, Lowe's, NTB, Office Depot, Petsmart, Target, Tuesday Morning, Verizon, vet, Walgreens, **W** [gas] QT, ZX [food] Bob Evans, Olive Garden, Waffle House [lodging] Best Value Inn, Motel 6, Super 8
20b a	I-70, E to St Louis, W to Kansas City
17	Dorsett Rd, **E** [gas] BP, QT [food] BBQ, Syberg's Grill [lodging] Best Western, Drury Inn, Hampton Inn, **W** [gas] Mobil, Phillips 66, Shell [food] Arby's, Denny's, Fuddrucker's, McDonald's, Steak'n Shake, Subway [lodging] Baymont Inn
16b a	Page Ave, rd D, MO 364 W, **E** [gas] BP, CFM, Citgo/7-11, QT, Sinclair [food] Blimpie, Copperfield's Rest., Hardee's, Hooters, Malone's Grill, McDonald's, Stazio's Café [lodging] Comfort Inn, Courtyard, DoubleTree, Holiday Inn, Homestead Suites, Red Roof Inn, Residence Inn, Sheraton
14	MO 340, Olive Blvd, **E** [gas] BP, Mobil [food] Applebee's, Bristol Cafe, Denny's, Domino's, KFC, Lion's Choice Rest., McDonald's, Pasta House, Steakout [lodging] Courtyard, Drury Inn [other] [H], BMW/Land Rover/Cadillac, Chevrolet, Crysler/Jeep, Lexus, **W** [gas] Schnucks [food] Coldstone Creamery, Culpepper's Café, House of Wong, Subway, TGIFriday [other] Dierberg's Foods, Kohl's, Walgreens
13	rd AB, Ladue Rd
12b a	I-64, US 40, US 61, E to St Louis, W to Wentzville, **E** [other] [H]
9	MO 100, Manchester Rd, **E** [gas] BP [food] Café America, Houlihan's Rest, IHOP, Lion's Choice Rest., McDonald's [other] Famous Barr, Galyan's, Lord&Taylor, mall, Nordstrom's, **W** [gas] Phillips 66, Shell [food] Applebee's, Casa Gallardo's Mexican, Olive Garden, Red Robin
8	Dougherty Ferry Rd, **S** [gas] Citgo/7-11, Mobil [food] McDonald's [other] [H]
7	Big Ben Rd, **N** [other] [H]
5b a	I-44, US 50, MO 366, E to St Louis, W to Tulsa
3	MO 30, Gravois Rd, **N** [gas] BP, Phillips 66 [food] Bandana BBQ, Olive Garden, Outback Steaks [lodging] Days Inn, Quality Inn [other] Ford

ST LOUIS

▲N | INTERSTATE 270 (St Louis) Cont'd

Exit #	Services
2	MO 21, Tesson Ferry Rd, N 🅿 BP 🍴 El Muguey Mexican, Jimmy John's, Panda Chinese, Pizza Hut ⊙ Acura, AutoZone, Buick, Dobb's Auto, O'Reilly Parts, Scion/Toyota, vet, S 🅿 Shell/Circle K/dsl 🍴 Little Caesar's, ⊙ Dierberg's Foods, N on Lindbergh 🍴 54th St Grill, Burger King, Church's, Jack-in-the-Box, Olive Garden, Outback Steaks, Quizno's, Red Lobster, Subway, Taco Bell, TGIFriday's, Waffle House, White Castle ⊙ Buick/GMC, Honda, Mobil, Schnuck's Foods, Shop'n Save, Walgreens
1b a	I-55 N to St Louis, S to Memphis

▲N | INTERSTATE 435 (Kansas City)

Exit #	Services
83	I-35, N to KS City, S to Wichita
82	Quivira Rd, Overland Park, N 🍴 Burger King, Old Chicago Pizza, Pizza Hut, Ponderosa, Taco Bell ⊙ Ⓗ, CVS Drug, S 🍴 McDonald's, Subway, Wendy's 🛏 Extended Stay America
81	US 69 S, to Ft Scott
80	Antioch Rd
79	Metcalf Ave, N 🅿 Conoco/7-11 🍴 Carrabba's, D'Bronx Pizza, Denny's, Hardee's, Hooters, Jack-in-the-Box, Jose Peppers, Krispy Kreme, Winstead's 🛏 Clarion, Comfort Inn, Days Inn, Embassy Suites, Hampton Inn, Super 8 ⊙ Ⓗ, AAA, Office Depot, Walmart Mkt, S 🍴 Applebee's, McDonald's, Panera Bread 🛏 Drury Inn, Marriott, PearTree Inn
77b a	Nall Ave, Roe Ave, N 🅿 BP, QT 🍴 DQ, Mr Goodcents, Sonic, Winstead's Grill 🛏 Best Value Inn, S 🍴 McDonald's, Wendy's 🛏 Courtyard, Hilton Garden, Holiday Inn, Homestead Suites, Hyatt Place, Sheraton
75b	State Line Rd, N 🅿 Phillips 66 🍴 Applebee's, Gate's BBQ, McDonald's, Taco Bell, Waid's Rest., Wendy's ⊙ Goodyear/auto, Lexus, Midas, O'Reilly Parts, PriceChopper Foods, Volvo, S 🅿 BP ⊙ Ⓗ, city park
75a	Wornall Rd, N 🅿 QT 🍴 Applebee's, China King, Coach's Grill, Dunkin Donuts, Fuzzy's Taco Shop, McDonald's, Pizza Hut, Subway ⊙ Acura, Audi, Chevrolet, Honda, Infiniti, Nissan, Toyota/Scion, URGENT CARE, Volvo, VW
74	Holmes Rd, N 🅿 Phillips 66/dsl 🍴 Subway, Thai House, S 🛏 Courtyard, Extended Stay America
73	103rd St (from sb)
71b a	I-470, US 71 S, US 50 E
70	Bannister Rd, E 🅿 Phillips 66 🍴 McDonalds, Wendy's ⊙ K-Mart, W 🍴 A&W/LJ Silver, Taco Bell ⊙ Firestone/auto, Home Depot
69	87th St., E 🅿 Conoco/dsl, QT 🛏 A-1 Motel, Capital Inn ⊙ Meineke, Suzuki, W 🛏 Baymont Inn
67	Gregory Blvd (same as 66a b), E 🅿 Shell 🍴 Applebee's, Niece's Rest., Wendy's ⊙ $General, BigLots, PriceChopper Foods, W ⊙ Nature Ctr, zoo
66	MO 350 E, 63rd st
65	Eastwood Tfwy, W 🅿 Conoco 🍴 Church's, McDonald's, Peachtree Rest., Pizza Hut
63c	Raytown Rd, Stadium Dr (nb only), E ⊙ to Sports Complex
63b a	I-70, W to KC, E to St Louis
61	MO 78, E 1 mi 🍴 Church's Chicken
60	MO 12 E, Truman Rd, 12th St, E 🅿 BP/dsl, Shamrock, W 🅿 QT
59	US 24, Independence Ave, E 🅿 QT 🍴 Hardee's ⊙ to Truman Library, W ⊙ CarQuest, Waffle House

Exit #	Services
57	Front St, E 🅿 ⊛FLYING J/Conoco/rest/dsl/scales/24hr ⊙ Blue Beacon, Freightliner, Kenworth, W 🅿 Phillips 66/dsl, QT 🍴 Denny's, McDonald's, Smugglers Rest, Subway, Taco Bell, Waffle House, Wendy's 🛏 Ramada ⊙ URGENT CARE, Walgreens
56mm	Missouri River
55b a	MO 210, E 🛏 Ameristar Hotel/Casino, Red Roof Inn ⊙ Ford/Volvo/GMC/Mercedes Trucks, Riverboat Casino, W 🍴 Arby's, Burger King, Denny's 🛏 La Quinta
54	48th St, Parvin Rd, E 🅿 Phillips 66 ⊙ RV Park, W 🅿 QT 🍴 Subway, Waffle House, Wendy's 🛏 Candlewood Suites, Crossland Suites, Days Inn, Fairfield Inn, Funpark Inn, Hampton Inn, Holiday Inn, Super 8
52b	I-35, S to KC
52a	US 69, E 🅿 Phillips 66, Shell, Sinclair, W 🅿 Fuel Outlet 🍴 McDonald's, Pizza Hut, Subway, Taco Bell ⊙ $General, CVS Drug, Save-A-Lot Foods
51	Shoal Creek Dr
49b a	MO 152 E, to I-35 N, Liberty, E 🍴 54th St Grill, Applebee's, Bob Evans, Buffalo Wild Wings, Cracker Barrel, Longhorn Steaks, Steak'n Shake 🛏 Best Western, Comfort Inn, Fairfield Inn, Hampton Inn, Holiday Inn Express, Super 8
47	NE 96th St
46	NE 108th St
45	MO 291, NE Cookingham Ave, E to I-35 N
42	N Woodland Ave
41b a	US 169, Smithville, N 🅿 Kum&Go 🍴 Burger King, McDonald's, Sonic 🛏 Super 8
40	NW Cookingham
37	NW Skyview Ave, rd C, N 🅿 Shamrock (1mi), S ⊙ golf (3mi)
36	to I-29 S, to KCI ✈, N 🅿 Shamrock, S 🅿 BP 🛏 Best Western, Clarion, Comfort Suites, Fairfield Inn, Hampton Inn, Hilton, Holiday Inn Express, Microtel, Radisson, Wyndham Garden
31mm	Prairie Creek
29	rd D, NW 120th St
24	MO 152, rd N, NW Berry Rd
22	MO 45, Weston, Parkville
20mm	Missouri River, Missouri/Kansas state line
18	KS 5 N, Wolcott Dr, E ⊙ to Wyandotte Co Lake Park
16	Donohoo Rd
15b a	Leavenworth Rd, E 🅿 Conoco/Subway/dsl 🛏 Comfort Suites, Woodlands Racetrack
14b a	Parallel Pkwy, E ⊙ Honda, Toyota/Scion, W 🅿 Phillips 66/Subway/dsl 🍴 Applebee's, Arby's, Bob Evans, Bryant's BBQ, Carino's Italian, Cheeseburger Paradise, Chili's, Chipotle Mexican, Culver's, Dave&Buster's, Granite City Rest, Hooters, IHOP, Jack-in-the-Box, Logan's Roadhouse, McDonald's, Olive Garden, Panda Express, Red Lobster,

INTERSTATE 435 (Kansas City) Cont'd

Exit #	Services
14b a	Continued
	Sheridan's Custard, Sonic, Taco Bell, Taco Bueno, Wendy's 🛏 Candlewood Suites, Country Inn&Suites, Holiday Inn Express 🅞 AT&T, Kohl's, NTB, Old Navy, Sam's Club/dsl, Target, TJ Maxx, Walmart
13b a	US 24, US 40, State Ave, E 🍴 Frontier Steaks, W 🍴 Famous Dave's BBQ, Lonestar Steaks 🛏 Best Western, Great Wolf Lodge, Hampton Inn 🅞 Cabela's, KS Race Track, Russell Stovers
12b a	I-70, KS Tpk, to Topeka, St Louis
11	Kansas Ave
9	KS 32, KS City, Bonner Springs, W 🍴 Phillips 66/dsl
8.8mm	Kansas River
8b	Woodend Rd, E 🅞 Peterbilt, W 🍴 Shell/food court/dsl/scales
8a	Holliday Dr, to Lake Quivira

6c	Johnson Dr
6b a	Shawnee Mission Pkwy, E 🍴 McDonald's, Subway 🅞 Home Depot, Kohl's, Lowe's, Michael's, museum, Old Navy, Petsmart, Radio Shack, Target, Walmart/Subway
5	Midland Dr, Shawnee Mission Park, E 🍴 Conoco, Phillips 66/Subway/dsl 🍴 Barley's Brewhaus, Chen's Kitchen, Eggct, Jose Pepper's Grill, Minsky's Pizza, Paula&Bill's Ristorante, Wendy's 🛏 Hampton Inn 🅞 vet, W 🍴 Hereford House 🛏 Courtyard
3	87th Ave, E 🍴 BP, Phillips 66/dsl 🍴 McDonald's, Panera Bread, Panzon's Rest, Papa John's, Papa Murphy's, Sonic, Taco Bell 🅞 Ace Hardware, Aldi Foods, Tuesday Morning, Walgreens
2	95th St
1b	KS 10, to Lawrence
1a	Lackman Rd, N 🍴 Phillips 66 🛏 Suburban Lodge
0mm	I-435 begins/ends on I-35.

MONTANA

INTERSTATE 15

SHELBY

Exit #	Services
398mm	Montana/US/Canada Border
397	Sweetgrass, W ℞ both lanes, full 🦽 facilities, litter barrels, petwalk, 🚻, 🏞 🍴 Gastrak 🛏 Glocca Morra Motel/cafe 🅞 Duty Free
394	ranch access
389	MT 552, Sunburst, W 🍴 CFN/dsl 🅞 Prairie Mkt/Chester Fried, Sunburst RV Park, USPO
385	Swayze Rd
379	MT 215, MT 343, to Kevin, Oilmont, W 🍴 Four Corners Café
373	Potter Rd
369	Bronken Rd
366.5mm	weigh sta sb
364	Shelby, E 🅞 Lewis&Clark RV Park, W 🅞 ✈
363	US 2, Shelby, to Cut Bank, Shelby, E 0-1 mi 🍴 Cenex, 🚚/Exxon/Country Skillet/dsl/scales/24hr, Sinclair/dsl 🍴 Cowloon Chinese, Dash Drive-In, Dixie Inn Steaks, Pizza Hut, Subway, The Griddle 🛏 Comfort Inn, Crossroads Inn, Glacier Motel/RV Park, O'Haire Motel 🅞 Ⓗ, Albertsons, CarQuest, city park, Mark's Tire, Parts+, TrueValue, USPO, visitor info, W 🛏 Best Western 🅞 ShopKo, to Glacier NP
361mm	parking area nb
358	Marias Valley Rd, to Golf Course Rd, E 🅞 camping
357mm	Marias River
352	Bullhead Rd
348	rd 44, to Valier, W 🅞 Lake Frances RA (15mi)
345	MT 366, Ledger Rd, E 🅞 to Tiber Dam (42mi)
339	Conrad, E ℞/weigh sta, both lanes, full 🦽 facilities, litter barrels, 🚻, 🏞 W 🍴 Calumet/dsl, Cenex/dsl, Exxon/Subway/dsl 🍴 A&W/Chester's, Home Cafe, Main Drive-In, Pizza House 🛏 Northgate Motel, Super 8 🅞 Ⓗ, Buick/Chevrolet/GMC, Conrad Tire/repair, Ford, IGA Foods, museum, Olson's Drug, Pondera RV Park, Radio Shack, TrueValue, USPO, vet, Westco RV Ctr,
335	Midway Rd, Conrad, W 4 mi 🍴, 🍴, 🛏, 🅞 Ⓗ, RV camping, 🚻
328	MT 365, Brady, W 🍴 Mtn View Co-op/dsl 🅞 city park, USPO
321	Collins Rd
319mm	℞ both lanes, full 🦽 facilities, litter barrels, petwalk, 🚻, 🏞 Teton River

GREAT FALLS

313	MT 221, MT 379, Dutton, W 🍴 Cenex/dsl 🍴 Café Dutton 🅞 city park, USPO
302	MT 431, Power
297	Gordon
290	US 89 N, rd 200 W, to Choteau, W 🍴 Conoco/dsl, Sinclair/dsl/LP/RV dump 🅞 USPO
288mm	parking area both lanes
286	Manchester, W 🅞 livestock auction, same as 290 (2mi)
282	US 87 N (from sb), NW bypass, E 2-3 mi 🍴 Conoco/dsl, Holiday/dsl 🍴 Arby's, Burger King, Little Caesars, McDonald's, New Peking, Pizza Hut, Subway, Taco Bell, Taco John's 🛏 Days Inn 🅞 $Tree, Albertsons/Osco, K-Mart, O'Reilly Parts, Sam's Club/gas, ShopKo, Staples, Tire-Rama, Walgreens, Walmart
280mm	Sun River
280	US 87 N, Central Ave W, Great Falls, E 🍴 Loaf 'N Jug 🍴 A&W/KFC, Ford's Drive-In, Lippi's Kitchen, Papa John's 🛏 Alberta Inn, Central Motel, Days Inn (3mi), Staybridge Suites 🅞 city park, to Giant Sprgs SP, U-Haul/LP, vet, Whalen Tire
278	US 89 S, rd 200 E, 10th Ave, Great Falls, E 1-3 mi 🍴 Calumet/dsl, Cenex/dsl, Conoco, Exxon/dsl, Holiday/Subway/dsl, Sinclair/dsl 🍴 4B's Rest., Applebee's, Arby's, Baskin-Robbins, Beef'O'Brady's, Best Wok, Boston's Pizza, Burger King, Café Rio, Chili's, China Buffet, Classic 50s Diner/casino, Coldstone, DQ, Fiesta Jalisco, Fuddrucker's, Golden Corral, Hardee's, Jaker's Rest., JB's Rest., Jimmy John's, KFC, Little Caesars, MacKenzie River Pizza, McDonald's, Ming's Chinese, Moonshine Grill, Noodle Express, On-the-Border Mexican, Papa John's, Papa Murphy's, Pita Pit, Pizza Hut, PrimeCut Rest., Quiznos, Sonic, Starbucks, Subway, Taco Bell, Taco John's, Taco Treat, Wendy's, Wheat MT 🛏 Best Western, Comfort Inn, Extended Stay America, Fairfield Inn, Hampton Inn, Hilton Garden, Holiday Inn, Holiday Inn Express, La Quinta, Motel 6, Plaza Inn, Super 8, Townhouse Inn, Western Motel 🅞 Ⓗ, $Tree, Ace Hardware, Albertsons/Osco, AT&T, AT&T, AutoZone, Barnes&Noble, BigLots, Cadillac/Chevrolet/Toyota, CarQuest, Chrysler/Dodge/Jeep, CVS Drug, Dick's RV Park, Discount Drug, Firestone/auto, Ford, Harley-Davidson, Hastings Books, Herberger's, Home Depot, Honda, Hyundai, JC Penney, Jo-Ann Fabrics, KOA, Michael's,

MT

INTERSTATE 15 Cont'd

Exit #	Services
278	Continued
	Midas, NAPA, Nissan, Old Navy, O'Reilly Parts, PetCo, Pierce RV Ctr, Ross, Scheels Sports, Sears/auto, Smith's/dsl, Target, Tire-Rama, to Malmstrom AFB, transmissions, Travel Time RV Ctr, USPO, Van's/IGA, Verizon, vet, VW, Walgreens
277	Airport Rd, E 🅖 ⓕFLYING J/Denny's/dsl/scales/24hr, 🍴🅖/Conoco/Subway/casino/dsl/scales/24hr 🛏 Crystal Inn, W 🅾 🔄
275mm	weigh sta nb
270	MT 330, Ulm, E 🅖 Conoco/dsl/LP 🅾 USPO, W 🍴 Beef'n Bone Steaks 🅾 to Ulm SP
256	rd 68, Cascade, E 1/2 mi 🅖 Sinclair 🍴 Badger Cafe 🅾 Tom's Foods, USPO
254	rd 68, Cascade, E 1/2 mi same as 256
250	local access
247	Hardy Creek, W 🅾 RV camping, to Tower Rock SP, food, phone
246.5mm	Missouri River
245mm	scenic overlook sb
244	Canyon Access, W 2 mi 🍴 MO Inn Rest. 🅾 Prewett Creek Camping, rec area, RV camping
240	Dearborn, E 🅾 RV park
239mm	℞ both lanes, full ♿ facilities, litter barrels, petwalk, 🚻, 🐾
238mm	Stickney Creek
236mm	Missouri River
234	Craig, E 🍴 Izaak's Cafe, Trout Shop Café/lodge 🅾 boating, camping, rec area
228	US 287 N, to Augusta, Choteau
226	MT 434, Wolf Creek, E 🅖 Exxon/dsl 🍴 Oasis Café 🅾 camping, MT River Outfitters/lodge/flyshop, to Holter Lake, W 🍴 Frenchman&Me Café 🅾 USPO
222mm	parking area both lanes
219	Spring Creek, Recreation Rd (from nb), Spring Creek, 🅾 boating, camping
218mm	Little Prickly Pear Creek
216	Sieben
209	E to Gates of the Mtns RA
205mm	turnout both directions
202mm	weigh sta sb

200	MT 279, MT 453, Lincoln Rd, W 🅖 Sinclair/Bob's Mkt/dsl 🍴 GrubStake Rest. 🅾 Lincoln Rd RV Park, to ski area
194	Custer Ave, E 🅖 Cenex, Conoco/dsl, Conoco/dsl, Exxon/dsl 🍴 Applebee's, Arby's, Buffalo Wild Wings, Burger King, Chili's, DQ, Hardee's, IHOP, Jade Garden, Macaroni Grill, McDonald's, Moonshine Grill, Panda Express, Pizza Hut, Quiznos, Taco Bell, Taco Del Mar 🛏 Comfort Suites, Holiday Inn Express, Residence Inn 🅾 $Tree, Albertson's, AT&T, AutoZone, Costco/gas, CVS Drug, Hastings Books, Helena RV Park (5mi), Home Depot, Lowe's, Macy's, Murdoch's, Natural Grocers, Office Depot, PetCo, Ross, ShopKo, Staples, Target, TJMaxx, Verizon, Whalen Tire
193	Cedar St, Helena, E 🚂, W 🅖 Cenex, Conoco/dsl, Exxon/dsl 🍴 Godfather's, Little Caesars, Perkins, Steffano's Pizza, Subway, Taco John's 🛏 Quality Inn, Wingate Inn 🅾 Ace Hardware, Chevrolet, K-Mart, O'Reilly Parts, Tire Rama, USPO, vet
192b a	US 12, US 287, Helena, Townsend, E 🅖 Cenex, Conoco/dsl 🍴 Burger King, Pizza Hut, Subway 🛏 Hampton Inn 🅾 Buick/GMC, Chrysler/Dodge/Jeep, D&D RV Ctr, Ford/Lincoln, Honda, Nissan, Schwab Tire, st patrol, Toyota, Walmart/Subway, W 🅖 Exxon/dsl, Holiday, Sinclair/dsl 🍴 A&W/KFC, DQ, Hunan Chinese, Jimmy John's, L&D Chinese, McDonald's, Overland Express Rest., Papa John's, Papa Murphy's, Quiznos, Starbucks, Steve's Cafe, Taco John's, Taco Treat, Village Inn Pizza, Wendy's 🛏 Comfort Inn, Days Inn, Fairfield Inn, Howard Johnson, Jorgenson's Inn, La Quinta, Motel 6, Red Lion Inn, Shilo Inn, Super 8 🅾 ♿, AAA, Albertsons, CVS Drug, GNC, JC Penney, Safeway/dsl, Tire Factory, Verizon, Walgreens
190	S Helena, W 🅾 ♿
187	MT 518, Montana City, Clancy, E 🍴 Hugo's Pizza/casino, W 🅖 Cenex/dsl 🍴 Jackson Creek Cafe, MT City Grill 🛏 Elkhorn Inn
182	Clancy, E 🅾 RV camping, W 🍴 Chubby's Grill 🅾 to NF, USPO
178mm	℞ both lanes, full ♿ facilities, litter barrels, petwalk, 🚻, 🐾
176	Jefferson City, NF access
174.5mm	chain up area both lanes
168mm	chainup area both lanes
164	rd 69, Boulder, E 🅖 Exxon/dsl/casino 🍴 Elkhorn Cafe, Gator's Pizza Parlour, Mtn Good Rest., The River Café 🅾 auto repair, L&P Foods, Parts+, RC RV camping, USPO

HELENA (vertical)

MT

⬆N   INTERSTATE 15 Cont'd

Exit #	Services
161mm	**parking area nb**
160	High Ore Rd
156	Basin, **E** 🅞 Merry Widow Health Mine/RV camping, **W** 🅞 Basin Cr Pottery, camping, USPO
154mm	Boulder River
151	to Boulder River Rd, Bernice, **W** 🅞 camping, 🏕
148mm	**chainup area both lanes**
143.5mm	**chainup area both lanes**
138	Elk Park, **W** 🅞 Sheepshead 🏕 Area, wildlife viewing
134	Woodville
133mm	Continental Divide, elev 6368
130.5mm	scenic overlook sb
129	I-90 E, to Billings

I-15 S and I-90 W run together 8 mi

127	Harrison Ave, Butte, **E** 🅖 Cenex/dsl, Conoco/dsl, Exxon/dsl 🍴 4B's Rest., A&W/KFC, Arby's, Burger King, MacKenzie River Pizza, McDonald's, MT Club Rest., Perkins, Pizza Hut, Silver Bow Pizza, Starbucks, Subway, Taco Bell, Wendy's 🏠 Best Western, Comfort Inn, Copper King Hotel, Hampton Inn, Super 8 🅞 $Tree, American Car Care, Buick/Chevrolet/GMC, CarQuest, casinos, Chrysler/Dodge/Jeep, Ford, Hart's RV Ctr, Herberger's, Honda, JC Penney, Jo-Ann Fabrics, Kia, K-Mart, Murdoch's, NAPA, Rocky Mtn RV Ctr, Staples, Subaru, Toyota/Scion, Verizon, Walmart/Subway, **W** 🅖 Cenex/dsl, Conoco/dsl 🍴 Derby Steaks, Domino's, DQ, El Taco Mexican, Hanging 5 Rest., John's Rest., L&D Chinese, Papa John's, Papa Murphy's, Quiznos, Royse's Burgers, Taco John's 🏠 Days Inn, Holiday Inn Express, La Quinta, Quality Inn, War Bonnet Inn 🅞 Ace Hardware, AutoZone, Hastings Books, Lisac's Tires, O'Reilly Parts, Safeway, Walgreens
126	Montana St, Butte, **E** 🅖 Conoco/dsl, Exxon/dsl, **W** 🍴 Chef's Garden Italian 🏠 Eddy's Motel 🅞 H, repair, Safeway, Schwab Tire
124	I-115 (from eb), to Butte City Ctr
123	**weigh sta sb**
122	Rocker, **E** 🅖 🅖Conoco/Arby's/McDonald's/Subway/dsl/scales/24hr 🏠 Motel 6 🅞 repair, **weight sta nb**, **W** 🅖 ✈FLYING J/Exxon/rest./dsl/LP/24hr 🏠 Best Value Inn 🅞 RV camping

I-15 N and I-90 E run together 8 mi

121	I-90 W, to Missoula, **W** 🅞 2 Bar Lazy-H RV Camping
119	Silver Bow, **W** 🅞 Port of MT Transportation Hub
116	Buxton
112mm	Continental Divide, elevation 5879
111	Feely
109mm	🅡ˢ both lanes, full 🚻 facilities, litter barrels, petwalk, ⛽, 🏕
102	rd 43, to Wisdom, Divide, **W** 🅞 rv camping (2mi), to Big Hole Nat Bfd (62mi)
99	Moose Creek Rd
93	Melrose, **W** 🍴 Hitchin Post Rest., Melrose Café/grill/dsl 🏠 Great Waters Inn (5mi), Pioneer Mtn Cabins 🅞 Sportsman Motel/RV Park, Sunrise Flyshop, USPO
85.5mm	Big Hole River
85	Glen, **E** 🅞 Willis Sta RV camping (3mi)
74	Apex, Birch Creek
64mm	Beaverhead River
63	Lp 15, rd 41, Dillon, Twin Bridges, **E** 🅖 Cenex/dsl/LP/RV Dump, Exxon/dsl, Phillips 66/dsl 🍴 Lions Den, McDonald's, Pizza Hut, Subway, Whistlestop Diner 🏠 Best Value Inn, Best Western/rest., Comfort Inn, GuestHouse Inn, Motel 6,

D I L L O N

63	Continued Sundowner Motel 🅞 H, auto repair/tires, Buick/Chevrolet, CarQuest, city park, Family$, KOA, Les Schwab Tire, Murdoch's, museum, NAPA, O'Reilly Parts, Safeway/dsl, W MT U
62	Lp 15, Dillon, **E** 🍴 DQ, El Toro Mexican, Sparky's Rest., Taco John's 🏠 Flyshop Inn 🅞 H, KOA, Southside RV Park, to W MT U, Van's/IGA Foods
60mm	Beaverhead River
59	MT 278, to Jackson, **W** 🅞 Bannack SP, Countryside RV Park/LP
56	Barretts, **E** 🅞 RV camping
55mm	**parking area sb, litter barrels**
52	Grasshopper Creek
51	Dalys (from sb, no return)
50mm	Beaverhead River
46mm	Beaverhead River
45mm	Beaverhead River
44	MT 324, **E** 🍴 Buffalo Lodge 🅞 Armstead RV Park, **W** 🅞 Clark Cyn Reservoir/RA, RV camping
38.5mm	Red Rock River
37	Red Rock
34mm	**parking area both lanes, litter barrels, restrooms**
29	Kidd
23	Dell, **E** 🅖 Cenex/dsl 🍴 Yesterdays Calf-a 🅞 USPO
16.5mm	**weigh sta both lanes**
15	Lima, **E** 🅡ˢ both lanes, 🚻 facilities, litter barrels, petwalk, 🅖 Exxon/dsl 🍴 Jan's Café 🏠 Mtn View Motel/RV Park 🅞 ambulance, Big Sky Tire/auto, Ralph's Tire, USPO
9	Snowline
0	Monida, **E** 🅞 ⛽, to Red Rock Lakes
0mm	Montana/Idaho state line, Monida Pass, elevation 6870

⬆E   INTERSTATE 90

Exit #	Services
559.5mm	**weigh sta both lanes**
554.5mm	Montana/Wyoming state line
549	Aberdeen
544	Wyola
530	MT 463, Lodge Grass, **S** 1 mi dsl, food, gas, lodging
517.5mm	Little Bighorn River
514	Garryowen, **N** 🅖 Conoco/Subway 🅞 Custer Bfd Museum, **S** 🅞 7th Ranch RV camp
511.5mm	Little Bighorn River
510	US 212 E, **N** 🅖 Exxon/café/dsl/gifts 🍴 Crows Nest Café 🅞 H, casino, to Little Bighorn Bfd, **S** 🅞 Little Bighorn RV Camp/dump
509.5mm	**weigh sta, both lanes exit left**
509.3mm	Little Bighorn River
509	Crow Agency, **N** 🅖 Conoco, **S** 🅞 to Bighorn Canyon NRA
503	Dunmore
498mm	Bighorn River
497	MT 384, 3rd St, Hardin, **S** 🏠 Western Motel 🅞 H, Bighorn Cty Museum, Casino Rest./lounge
495	MT 47, City Ctr, Hardin, **N** 🅖 Cenex/dsl 🍴 Purple Cow Rest. 🅞 KOA, **S** 🅖 Cenex/dsl, Exxon/dsl, ✈FLYING J/Conoco/Subway/dsl/LP/24hr, Soco/dsl 🍴 DQ, Farwest Rest., McDonald's, Pizza Hut, Taco John's 🏠 Rodeway Inn, Super 8, Western Motel 🅞 H, casinos, Chevrolet, Grand View Camping/RV Park, Sunset Village RV Park
484	Toluca
478	Fly Creek Rd
477mm	🅡ˢ both lanes, full 🚻 facilities, litter barrels, petwalk, ⛽, 🏕

H A R D I N

INTERSTATE 90 Cont'd

Exit #	Services
469	Arrow Creek Rd
462	Pryor Creek Rd
456	I-94 E, to Bismarck, ND
455	Johnson Lane, **N** 🅖 ▥▥▥/Conoco/McDonald's/dsl/scales/24hr, **S** 🅖 ⊕FLYING J/dsl/LP/scales/24hr, Exxon/A&W/dsl 🅕 Burger King, Domino's, DQ, Jin's Chinese, Subway 🛏 Holiday Inn Express 🅾 Bretz RV Ctr (1mi), Verizon, Whalen Tire
452	US 87 N, City Ctr, Billings, **N 2-4 mi on US 87** 🅖 Conoco/Arby's/dsl/LP, Exxon 🅕 Applebee's, Arby's, Bugz Rest./casino, Burger King, Domino's, DQ, Fuddrucker's, Golden Phoenix, Jimmy John's, KFC, Little Caesars, McDonald's, MT Jack's, Panda Express, Papa John's, Papa Murphy's, Pizza Hut, Shanghai Buffet, Sonic, Subway, Taco Bell, Taco John's, Wendy's 🛏 Best Western, Country Inn&Suites, Foothills Inn, Heights Motel 🅾 $Tree, Ace Hardware, Albertsons/Osco, American Spirit RV Ctr, AT&T, AutoZone, BigLots, CarQuest, Cenex/dsl, Conoco/dsl, CVS Drug, GNC, Holiday/dsl, Metra Rv Ctr, Office Depot, O'Reilly Parts, Radio Shack, Target, Tire Rama, transmissions, U-Haul, Verizon, vet, Walgreens, Walmart, **S** 🅖 Cenex/dsl 🅾 RV Camping
451.5mm	Yellowstone River
450	MT 3, 27th St, Billings, **N** 🅖 Conoco/dsl, Sinclair 🅕 Blondy's Cafe, Pizza Hut 🛏 Crowne Plaza, Vegas Motel 🅾 🅗, CarQuest, city park, USPO, visitor ctr, **S** 🅾 KOA, Yellowstone River Camping
447	S Billings Blvd, **N** 🅖 Conoco/Subway/dsl, Holiday/dsl 🅕 Burger King, DQ, El Corral Mexican, McDonald's 🛏 Best Western/Kelly, Days Inn, Extended Stay America, Hampton Inn, Sleep Inn, Super 8 🅾 Cabela's Sporting Goods, NAPA, Sam's Club/gas, **S** 🅾 Billings RV Park (2mi), Freightliner, Kenworth, KOA (2mi), Yellowstone River Campground
446	King Ave, Billings, **N on 24th** 🅖 Conoco/dsl, Conoco/dsl, Exxon, Exxon/Subway, Holiday/dsl/LP/RV dump 🅕 Applebee's, Arbys, Bruno's Italian, Buffalo Wild Wings, Burger King, Cactus Creek Steaks, Café Rio, Carino's Italian, Chuck-ECheese's, City Brew Coffee, Coldstone, Del Taco, Denny's, Dos Machos, DQ, Emporium Rest., Famous Dave's, Fuddrucker's, Golden Corral, Gusicks Rest., Hardee's, HuHot Mongolian, IHOP, Jade Palace, Jake's Grill, Japanese Steaks, KFC, Lemongrass Thai, Little Caesars, McDonald's, MooYah Burgers, Old Chicago, Olive Garden, Outback Steaks, Papa John's, Perkins, Pizza Hut, Pizza Ranch, Qdoba, Red Lobster, Rendezvous Grill, Starbucks, Subway, Taco Bell, Taco John's, TX Roadhouse, Wendy's 🛏 C'Mon Inn, Comfort Inn, Fairfield Inn, Hilton Garden, Lexington Inn, Quality Inn, Residence Inn, SpringHill Suites, Western Executive Inn 🅾 Albertsons/Osco, AutoZone, Barnes&Noble, Best Buy, Cadillac/GMC, Chevrolet, Chrysler/Dodge/Jeep, Costco/gas, Dillards, Ford, Hancock Fabrics, Hobby Lobby, Home Depot, JC Penney, JoAnn Fabrics, Kia, K-Mart, Lisac's Tire, Lowe's, mall, Mercedes, Michael's, Natural Grocers, Nissan, Office Depot, Old Navy, O'Reilly Parts, Petsmart, Ross, ShopKo, Subaru, Suzuki, Toyota, USPO, Verizon, Walmart/Subway, World Mkt, **S** 🅖 Conoco/dsl 🅕 Cracker Barrel, Emporium Rest. 🛏 Billings Hotel, EconoLodge, Holiday Inn, Howard Johnson, Kelly Inn, Motel 6 🅾 Volvo/Mack Trucks, water funpark
443	Zoo Dr, to Shiloh Rd, **N** 🅖 Holiday/dsl 🅕 MT Rib/Chophouse 🛏 Bighorn Resort/waterpark, Hampton Inn, Holiday Inn Express, Homewood Suites 🅾 Honda, Pierce RV Ctr, zoo, **S** 🅾 Harley-Davidson, vet
439mm	weigh sta both lanes
437	E Laurel, **S** 🅖 Sinclair/rest./dsl/scales/casino/motel/RV Park/24hr
434	US 212, US 310, to Red Lodge, Laurel, **N** 🅖 Cenex/dsl, Conoco/dsl, Exxon/dsl 🅕 City Brew Coffee, Hardee's, McDonald's, Pitts Pizza, Pizza Hut, Subway, Taco John's 🛏 Best Western, Locomotive Inn 🅾 Ace Hardware, AutoZone, Chevrolet, CVS Drug, Ford, IGA Foods, O'Reilly Parts, Rapid Tire, Verizon, Walmart/Subway, **S** 🅾 Riverside Park/RV Camping, to Yellowstone NP, vet
433	Lp 90 (from eb), same as 434
426	Park City, **S** 🅖 Cenex/café/dsl/24hr, KwikStop 🅕 The Other Cafe 🛏 CJ's Motel 🅾 auto/tire repair, USPO
419mm	🆁🆂 both lanes, full ♿ facilities, litter barrels, petwalk, 🎑, 🖼
408	rd 78, Columbus, **N** 🅾 Mtn Range RV Park, **S** 🅖 Conoco, ▥▥▥/Exxon/dsl/24hr 🅕 Apple Village Café/gifts, McDonald's, Subway 🛏 Big Sky Motel, Super 8 🅾 🅗, casino, city park, IGA Foods, museum, tires/repair, to Yellowstone
400	Springtime Rd
398mm	Yellowstone River
396	ranch access
392	Reed Point, **N** 🅾 Old West RV Park, USPO
384	Bridger Creek Rd
381mm	🆁🆂 both lanes, full ♿ facilities, litter barrels, petwalk, 🎑, 🖼
377	Greycliff, **S** 🅾 KOA, Prairie Dog Town SP
370	US 191, Big Timber, **N 1 mi** 🅖 Cenex/dsl, Sinclair/dsl 🛏 Grand Hotel, Lazy J Motel 🅾 🅗, Spring Creek RV Ranch (4mi), USPO, vet
369mm	Boulder River
367	US 191 N, Big Timber, **N** 🅖 Conoco/dsl, Exxon/dsl 🅕 Country Skillet 🛏 River Valley Inn, Super 8 🅾 CarQuest, historic site/visitor info, Spring Creek Camping (3mi)
362	De Hart
354	MT 563, Springdale
352	ranch access
350	East End access
343	Mission Creek Rd, **N** 🅾 Ft Parker HS
340	US 89 N, to White Sulphur Sprgs, **S** 🅾 ⊙
337	Lp 90, to Livingston, **N 2 mi** services
333mm	Yellowstone River
333	US 89 S, Livingston, **N** 🅕 Clark's Rest., DQ, Mark's In&Out, Pizza Hut, Taco John's 🛏 Best Western, Budget Host, Livingston Inn, Quality Inn, Rodeway Inn 🅾 🅗, Chrysler/Dodge/Jeep, Radio Shack, RV Park, ShopKo, Town&Country Foods, Verizon, Western Drug, **S** 🅖 Cenex/dsl, Conoco/dsl, Exxon/dsl 🅕 Arby's, McDonald's, Rosa's Pizza, Subway 🛏 Comfort Inn, Super 8 🅾 Albertsons/Osco, KOA (10mi), LP, Osen's RV Park, to Yellowstone, vet

BILLINGS

BILLINGS

LIVINGSTON

MT

🔼E	**INTERSTATE 90 Cont'd**
Exit #	Services
330	Lp 90, Livingston, **N 1 mi** 🅰 Cenex/Yellowstone Trkstp/dsl/rest./24hr
326.5mm	**chainup/chain removal area both lanes**
324	ranch access
323mm	**chainup/chain removal area wb**
322mm	Bridger Mountain Range
321mm	turnouts/hist marker both lanes
319mm	**chainup area both lanes**
319	Jackson Creek Rd
316	Trail Creek Rd
313	Bear Canyon Rd, **S** 🅾 Bear Canyon Camping
309	US 191 S, Main St, Bozeman, **N** 🅾 Subaru, Sunrise RV Park, VW, **S** 🅰 Cenex/dsl, Exxon/dsl 🍴 MT AleWorks 🛏 Continental Motel, Ranch House Motel, Western Heritage Inn 🅾 Ⓗ, Heeb's Foods, repair, Tire Rama, to Yellowstone, vet
306	MT 205, N 7th, to US 191, Bozeman, **N** 🅰 Cenex 🍴 McDonald's, Panda Buffet 🛏 Fairfield Inn, La Quinta, Microtel, Motel 6, Ramada Ltd, Super 8, TLC Inn 🅾 Merdoch's, ski area, Whalen Tire, **S** 🅰 Conoco/Arby's/dsl, Exxon 🍴 Applebee's, Bar-3 BBQ, Dominos, DQ, Famous Dave's BBQ, Papa John's, Santa Fe Red's Cafe, Taco John's, Tarintino's Pizza, The Wok Chinese 🛏 Best Western, Bozeman Inn, Comfort Inn, Days Inn, Hampton Inn, Holiday Inn, Homewood Suites, Royal 7 Inn 🅾 Big O Tire, Firestone/auto, K-Mart, Museum of the Rockies, U-Haul, Walmart/McDonald's
305	MT412, N 19th Ave, **N** 🅰 Exxon 🛏 Mountainview Inn, **S 0-2 mi** 🆁🆂 full ♿ facilities, petwalk, 🐾 litter barrels, 🅰 Conoco/dsl 🍴 A&W/KFC, Baja Fresh, Buffalo Wild Wings, Canyons Grill, Carino's Italian, City Brew Coffee, Clarks Fork Rest., IHOP, Jimmy John's, Mongolian BBQ, Old Chicago Pizza, Olive Garden, Outback Steaks, Papa Murphy's, Starbucks, Subway, Wasabi Grill, Wendy's 🛏 C'mon Inn, Comfort Suites, Hilton Garden, Holiday Inn Express, My Place Extended Stay, Residence Inn 🅾 AT&T, Costco/gas, Ford/Lincoln/RV Ctr, Home Depot, Lowe's, Michaels, Office Depot, Petsmart, Radio Shack, REI, Ross, Smith's Foods, Staples, Target, TJMaxx, UPS, USPO, Verizon, vet, World MKT
298	MT 291, rd 85, Belgrade, **N** 🅰 Cenex/dsl, Exxon/Subway/dsl 🍴 Burger King, DQ, McDonald's, Papa Murphy's, Pizza Hut, Rosa's Pizza, Starbucks, Taco Time 🛏 Holiday Inn Express 🅾 Albertson's/Osco, Lee&Dad's Foods, NAPA, Verizon, Whalen Tire, **S** 🅰 ⊕FLYING J/Conoco/dsl/scales/LP 🛏 La Quinta, Quality Inn, Super 8 🅾 Freightliner, Harley-Davidson, KOA (9mi), repair, Tire Factory, to Yellowstone NP, truckwash, TrueValue
292.5mm	Gallatin River
288	MT 288, MT 346, Manhattan, **N** 🅰 Conoco/Subway/dsl 🅾 RV camping
283	Logan, **S** 🅾 Madison Buffalo Jump SP (7mi)
279mm	Madison River
278	MT 205, rd 2, Three Forks, Trident, **N** 🅾 Missouri Headwaters SP, **S 1 mi** 🅰 Conoco/dsl 🛏 Broken Spur Motel, Lewis&Clark Motel, Sacajawea Hotel 🅾 camping, CarQuest, phone
277.5mm	Jefferson River
274	US 287, to Helena, Ennis, **N** 🅰 Conoco/dsl 🍴 Wheat MT Bakery/deli 🛏 Ft 3 Forks Motel 🅾 dsl repair, KOA (2mi), to Canyon Ferry SP, **S** 🅰🍴🛢/Exxon/Subway/dsl/scales/24hr 🅾 Camp 3 Forks, Lewis&Clark Caverns SP, to Yellowstone NP

267	Milligan Canyon Rd
261.5mm	chain-up area
257mm	Boulder River
256	MT 359, Cardwell, **S** 🅰 Cenex/dsl/RV Park 🅾 Lewis&Clark Caverns SP, RV camping, to Yellowstone NP
249	rd 55, to rd 69, Whitehall, **S** 🅰 Exxon/dsl 🍴 A&W/KFC, Subway 🛏 Rodeway Inn 🅾 camping, casino, Virginia City NHS
241	Pipestone
240.5mm	**chainup/chain removal area both lanes**
238.5mm	**runaway ramp eb**
237.5mm	pulloff eb
235mm	**truck parking both lanes, litter barrels, rest rooms**
233	Homestake, Continental Divide, elev 6393
230mm	**chain-up area both lanes**
228	MT 375, Continental Dr, **S** 🅰 Conoco/dsl 🅾 3 Bears Foods, Harley-Davidson
227	I-15 N, to Helena, Great Falls
I-90 and I-15 run together 8 mi. See Montana I-15, exits 122-127	
219	I-15 S, to Dillon, Idaho Falls
216	Ramsay
211	MT 441, Gregson, **S 3-5 mi** Fairmont RV Park (Apr-Oct), food, lodging
210.5mm	**Pintlar Scenic route info, parking area wb**
208	rd 1, Pintler Scenic Loop, Georgetown Lake RA, Opportunity, Anaconda, **S** 🆁🆂 both lanes, full ♿ facilities, 🐾 litter barrels, petwalk 🅾 Ⓗ, gas, food, lodging, RV camp/dump, ski area
201	Warm Springs, **S** 🅾 MT ST Ⓗ
197	MT 273, Galen, **S** 🅾 to MT ST Ⓗ
195	Racetrack
187	Lp 90, Deer Lodge (no wb return), **S 2 mi** 🅰 Calumet/dsl 🛏 Budget Inn 🅾 Ⓗ, KOA (seasonal), Old MT Prison/auto museum, same as 184, Valley Foods
184	Deer Lodge, **S 2 mi** 🅰 Conoco/dsl/casino, Exxon/dsl/casino 🍴 4B's Rest., A&W, McDonald's, Pizza Hut, Yak Yak Cafe 🛏 Travelodge, Western Big Sky Inn 🅾 Ⓗ, city park, Grant-Kohrs Ranch NHS, Indian Creek Camping, KOA, Safeway/deli, Schwab Tire, USPO
179	Beck Hill Rd
175mm	Little Blackfoot River
175	US 12 E, Garrison, **N** 🅾 hist site, Ⓒ, RiverFront RV Park
174	US 12 E (from eb), **S** 🍴 Ranch House Cafe/RV Park, same as 175
170	Phosphate
168mm	🆁🆂 both lanes, full ♿ facilities, hist site, litter barrels, petwalk, Ⓒ, 🐾
166	Gold Creek, **S** 🅾 Camp Mak-A-Dream, USPO
162	Jens
154	to MT 1 (from wb), Drummond, **S** 🅰 Cenex/dsl, Conoco/dsl 🍴 Parker's Rest., Wagon Wheel Café 🛏 Drummond Motel, Sky Motel, Wagon Wheel Motel 🅾 city park, Front St Mkt, Georgetown Lake RA, Goodtime RV Park (3mi), Pintler Scenic Lp
153	MT 1 (from eb), **N** 🅾 Garnet GhostTown, Goodtime RV Park (3mi), **S** same as 154
150.5mm	**weigh sta both lanes**
143mm	🆁🆂 both lanes, full ♿ facilities, litter barrels, petwalk, Ⓒ, 🐾
138	Bearmouth Area, **N** 🅾 Chalet Bearmouth Camp/rest., food, lodging, to gas
130	Beavertail Rd, **S** 🅾 camping (seasonal), rec area, to Beavertail Hill SP
128mm	**parking area both lanes, litter barrels/restrooms**

Exit #	Services
INTERSTATE 90 Cont'd	
126	Rock Creek Rd, **S** 🅶 Rock Creek Lodge/gas/casino 🅾 rec area
123mm	**weight sta wb**
120	Clinton, **N** 🅶 Conoco/dsl 🍴 Poor Henry's Café (1mi W on frtg rd) 🅾 Clinton Market, **S** 🅾 USPO
113	Turah, **S** Turah RV Park/gas
109.5mm	Clark Fork
109mm	Blackfoot River
109	MT 200 E, Bonner, **N** 🅶 ⛽Exxon/Arby's/Subway/dsl/scales/casino/LP/24hr 🍴 River City Grill 🅾 hist site, USPO
108.5mm	Clark Fork
107	E Missoula, **N** 🅶 Ole's Mkt/Conoco/diner/dsl, Sinclair 🍴 Reno Cafe 🛏 Aspen Motel 🅾 dsl repair
105	US 12 W, Missoula, **S** 🅶 Cenex/dsl, Conoco/dsl, Sinclair/dsl 🍴 5 Guys Burgers, Burger King, Finn &Porter Rest., McDonald's, Pizza Hut, Qdoba, Subway, Taco Bell 🛏 Budget Inn, Campus Inn, Comfort Inn, DoubleTree, Motel 6, Thunderbird Motel 🅾 Ace Hardware, Albertson's, Kingfisher Flyshop, O'Reilly Parts, U of MT, Verizon, Vietnam Vet's Mem
104	Orange St, Missoula, **S** 🅶 Conoco/dsl 🍴 Pagoda Chinese, Subway, Taco John's 🛏 Best Value Inn, Red Lion Inn 🅾 Ⓗ, TireRama, to City Ctr
101	US 93 S, Reserve St, **N** 🅶 Conoco/dsl 🍴 Cracker Barrel, MacKenzie River Pizza, Starbucks 🛏 Best Western, C'Mon Inn, Motel 6 🅾 ski area, **S** 0-2 mi 🅶 Cenex/dsl/LP, Conoco/dsl, Exxon/Subway/dsl, Sinclair/dsl 🍴 Arby's, Buffalo Wild Wings, Burger King, Cafe Rio, Carino's, China Bowl, Coldstone, DQ, Famous Dave's BBQ, Fuddrucker's, HoagiVille, Hooters, IHOP, Jimmy John's, Little Caesars, McDonald's, MT Club Rest./casino, Outback Steaks, Perkins, Pizza Hut, Quiznos, Rowdy's Cabin Rest., Stone Of Accord, Taco Bell, Taco Time/TCBY, Wendy's 🛏 Courtyard, EconoLodge, Hampton Inn, Hilton Garden, Holiday Inn Express, La Quinta, Quality Inn, Ruby's Inn/rest., Staybridge Suites, Super 8, TownePlace Suites, Travelers Inn 🅾 Albertson's, Barnes&Noble, Best Buy, Bretz RV/Marine, casinos, Chevrolet/Cadillac, Costco/gas, dsl repair, Firestone/auto, GNC, Home Depot, Lowe's, Michael's, Old Navy, Petsmart, Radio Shack, Ross, Staples, Target, TJ Maxx, Verizon, VW, Walgreens, Walmart/Subway
99	Airway Blvd, **S** 🅶 Mobil/dsl/24hr, Sinclair/dsl 🛏 Stone Creek Lodge, Wingate Inn 🅾 🖨, Chrysler/Dodge/Jeep, Harley-Davidson, Kia
96	US 93 N, MT 200W, Kalispell, **N** 🅶 Conoco/rest./dsl/scales/24hr/@, ⛽FLYING J/Exxon/McDonald's/dsl/scales/24hr 🍴 WheatMT/deli 🛏 Days Inn/rest. 🅾 Jellystone RV Park (1mi), Jim&Mary's RV Park (1mi), Peterbilt, to Flathead Lake&Glacier NP, **S** 🅶 Sinclair/dsl, TA/Sinclair/Country Pride/dsl/scales/24hr 🛏 Redwood Lodge 🅾 Kenworth
92.5mm	**inspection sta both lanes**
89	Frenchtown, **N** 🅾 to Frenchtown Pond SP, **S** 🅶 Conoco/dsl/café 🍴 Alcan Grill, Eugene's Cafe, Quiznos 🅾 Broncs Grocery/gas, USPO
85	Huson, **S** 🅶 🍴 cafe 🅾 phone
82	Nine Mile Rd, **N** 🍴 Mile House Rest. 🅾 food, Hist Ranger Sta/info, phone
81.5mm	Clark Fork
80mm	Clark Fork
77	MT 507, Petty Creek Rd, Alberton, **S** 🅶 access to gas, food, lodging 🅾 phone
75	Alberton, **N** 🅶 Cenex/dsl 🅾 USPO, **S** 🛏 River Edge Rest 🅾 casino, motel, RV camp
73mm	**parking area wb, litter barrels**
72mm	**parking area eb, litter barrels**
70mm	Clark Fork
70	Cyr
66mm	Clark Fork
66	Fish Creek Rd
61	Tarkio
59mm	Clark Fork
58mm	Ⓡⓢ **both lanes, full ♿ facilities, litter barrels, NF camping (seasonal), petwalk, 🐕, 🚮**
55	Lozeau, Quartz
53.5mm	Clark Fork
49mm	Clark Fork
47	MT 257, Superior, **N** 🅶 Conoco/dsl, Mtn West/LP 🍴 Durango's Rest./gas 🛏 Big Sky Motel, Hilltop Motel 🅾 Ⓗ, Family Foods, Mineral Drug, NAPA, USPO, **S** 🅶 ⛽Exxon/dsl/casino/24hr
45mm	Clark Fork
43	Dry Creek Rd, **N** 🅾 NP camping (seasonal)
37	Sloway Area
34mm	Clark Fork, Clark Fork
33	MT 135, St Regis, **N** 🅶 Conoco/rest/dsl/gifts, Exxon, Sinclair 🍴 Frosty Drive-In, Huck's Grill, Jasper's Rest., OK Café/casino, Subway (seasonal) 🛏 Little River Motel, St Regis Motel, Super 8 🅾 antiques, city park, Nugget Camground, St Regis Campground (seasonal), to Glacier NP, USPO
30	Two Mile Rd, **S** 🅾 fishing access
29mm	fishing access, wb
26	Ward Creek Rd (from eb)
25	Drexel
22	Camels Hump Rd, Henderson, **N** 🅾 antiques (1mi), camping (seasonal)
18	DeBorgia, **N** 🍴 O'aces Rest. 🅾 Black Diamond Guest Ranch, USPO
16	Haugan, **N** 🅶 Exxon/dsl/24hr 🛏 50000 Silver $/motel/rest./casino/RV park
15mm	**weigh sta both lanes, exits left from both lanes**
10mm	St Regis River
10	Saltese, **N** 🛏 Mangold's Motel
5	Taft Area, access to Hiawatha Trail
4.5mm	Ⓡⓢ **both lanes, chainup/removal, full ♿ facilities, 🚮, litter barrels, petwalk**
0	Lookout Pass, 🅾 access to Lookout Pass ski area/lodge, info
0mm	Montana/Idaho state line, Lookout Pass elev 4680, Central/Pacific time zone

MT

GLENDIVE

⬆E INTERSTATE 94

Exit #	Services
250mm	Montana/North Dakota state line
248	Carlyle Rd
242	MT 7 (from wb), Wibaux, S 📱 both lanes, full ♿ facilities, litter barrels, ⬛, 🚻, 🅿 Amsler's/dsl, Cenex/dsl/service 🍴 Tastee Hut 🏠 Beaver Creek Inn 🅾 RV camping,
241	MT 261 (from eb), to MT 7, Wibaux, S same as 242
240mm	weigh sta both lanes
236	ranch access
231	Hodges Rd
224	Griffith Creek, frontage road
222.5mm	Griffith Creek
215mm	Yellowstone River
215	MT 335, Glendive, City Ctr, N 🅿 Cenex 🍴 C's Family Café 🏠 Astoria Suites, Comfort Inn, Days Inn, Holiday Inn Express, Super 8, Yellowstone River Inn 🅾 Glendive Camping (apr-oct), museum, Running's Hardware, S 🅿 Exxon/dsl, Holiday/dsl 🍴 Mexico Lindo, Subway, Taco John's 🏠 El Centro Motel, Glendive Inn, Guesthouse Inn 🅾 Ⓗ, Radio Shack, to Makoshika SP
213	MT 16, to Sidney, Glendive, N 🅾 Green Valley Camping, st patrol, S 🅿 Cenex/dsl, Conoco/dsl, Sinclair/dsl 🍴 Dickey's BBQ, Pizza Hut 🏠 Riverside Inn 🅾 Albertson's/Osco, Ford, K-Mart, NAPA, Reynolds Mkt
211	MT 200S (from wb, no EZ return), to Circle
210	Lp 94, to rd 200 S, W Glendive, S 🅿 Cenex/dsl 🅾 Buick/Chevrolet, I-94 RV Park, Makoshika SP, Tire Rama
206	Pleasant View Rd
204	Whoopup Creek Rd
198	Cracker Box Rd
192	Bad Route Rd, S 📱/weigh sta both lanes, camping, full ♿ facilities, litter barrels, petwalk, ⬛, 🚻, weather info
187mm	Yellowstone River
185	MT 340, Fallon, S 🍴 café 🅾 phone
184mm	O'Fallon Creek
176	MT 253, Terry, N 🅿 4Corners/dsl, Conoco/dsl 🍴 Dizzy Diner 🏠 Kempton Hotel 🅾 Ⓗ, museum, Terry RV Oasis
170mm	Powder River
169	Powder River Rd
159	Diamond Ring
148	Valley Access
141	US 12 E, Miles City, N 🅾 RV Camping
138	rd 59, Miles City, N 🅿 Cenex/dsl, Conoco/dsl, ⬛/Exxon/dsl/24hr 🍴 4B's Rest., Arby's, Boardwalk Rest., DQ,

MILES CITY

FORSYTH

138	Continued
	Gallagher's Rest., Little Caesars, McDonald's, Mexico Lindo, Pizza Hut, R&B Chophouse, Subway, Taco John's, Wendy's 🏠 Best Western, EconoLodge, Motel 6, Sleep Inn 🅾 Ⓗ, Ace Hardware, Albertsons/Osco, casinos, Meadows RV Park, Murdoch's, O'Reilly Parts, Verizon, Walmart, S 🍴 New Hunan Chinese 🏠 Comfort Inn, Guesthouse Inn, Holiday Inn Express, Super 8
137mm	Tongue River
135	Lp 94, Miles City, N 🅾 KOA (Apr-Oct)
128	local access
126	Moon Creek Rd
117	Hathaway
114mm	📱 eb, full ♿ facilities, litter barrels, petwalk, ⬛, 🚻
113mm	📱 wb, full ♿ facilities, litter barrels, overlook, petwalk, ⬛, 🚻
106	Butte Creek Rd, to Rosebud, N 🍴 food 🅾 phone
103	MT 446, MT 447, Rosebud Creek Rd, N 🍴 food 🅾 phone
98.5mm	weigh sta both lanes
95	Forsyth, N 🅿 Exxon/dsl, Kum&Go 🍴 DQ, M&M Café 🏠 Magnuson Hotel 🅾 Ⓗ, Ford, museum, NAPA, to Rosebud RA, Van's/IGA, Yellowstone Drug, S 🅾 Wagon Wheel Camping
93	US 12 W, Forsyth, N 🅿 Exxon/dsl, Kum&Go 🍴 Fitzgerald's Rest., Top That Eatery 🏠 Rails Inn, Restwel Inn, WestWind Motel 🅾 Ⓗ, museum, RV camping, Tire Factory/repair
87	rd 39, to Colstrip
82	Reservation Creek Rd
72	MT 384, Sarpy Creek Rd
67	Hysham, N 1-2 mi gas 🍴 food 🅾 phone
65mm	📱 both lanes, full ♿ facilities, litter barrels, petwalk, ⬛, 🚻
63	ranch access
53	Bighorn, access to phone
52mm	Bighorn River
49	MT 47, to Hardin, Custer, S 🍴 Ft Custer Café 🅾 camping, to Little Bighorn Bfd
47	Custer, S 🅿 Custer Sta/dsl 🍴 Jct City Saloon/café 🅾 USPO
41.5mm	📱 wb, full ♿ facilities, litter barrels, petwalk, ⬛, 🚻
38mm	📱 eb, full ♿ facilities, litter barrels, petwalk, ⬛, 🚻
36	frontage rd, Waco
23	Pompeys Pillar, N 🅾 Pompeys Pillar Nat Landmark
14	Ballentine, Worden, S 🍴 Long Branch Café/casino
6	MT 522, Huntley, N 🅿 gas/phone 🍴 golf, Pryor Creek Café/casino
0mm	I-90, E to Sheridan, W to Billings, **I-94 begins/ends on I-90, exit 456.**

NEBRASKA

⬆E INTERSTATE 80

Exit #	Services
455mm	Nebraska/Iowa state line, Missouri River
454	13th St, N 🅿 BP/dsl, Midtown, Valero 🍴 Big Horn BBQ, Burger King, McDonald's/playplace 🏠 Comfort Inn 🅾 Family$, tires/repair, S 🍴 King Kong Burgers 🅾 Doorly Zoo, Imax, stadium
453	24th St (from eb)
452b	I-480 N, US 75 N, 🅾 Eppley Airfield, to Henry Ford's Birthplace
452a	US 75 S

451	42nd St, N 🅿 BP/dsl, S 🅿 Phillips 66 🍴 Burger King, McDonald's, Taco Bell 🅾 Ⓗ, Pitstop Lube
450	60th St, N 🅿 Phillips 66 🅾 NAPA, to U of NE Omaha, S 🅿 Omaha 66/dsl 🅾 transmissions
449	72nd St, to Ralston, N 🅿 BP, QT 🍴 Arby's, Burger King, Margarita's Mexican, Perkins, Spezia Italian 🏠 Comfort Inn, DoubleTree, Holiday Inn/rest., Omaha Executive Inn, Quality Inn, Super 8, Travelodge 🅾 Ⓗ, S 🅿 Cenex/dsl 🍴 Anthony's Steaks
448	84th St, N 🍴 Arby's, Denny's, Farmhouse Café, Husker Hounds, McDonald's, Subway, Taco Bell, Top of the World 🏠 Motel 6 🅾 Ace Hardware, Advance Parts, Curves,

🔼Ⓔ INTERSTATE 80 Cont'd

Exit #	Services
448	**Continued**
	Hancock Fabrics, Jensen's Tire/auto, Jo-Ann Fabrics, Mangelson's Crafts, ShopKO, USPO, **S** 🚗 QT, Shell/dsl 🍴 Wendy's Ⓞ Chevrolet, Kia
446	I-680 N, to Boystown
445	US 275, NE 92, I thru L St, **N** 🚗 Cenex 🍴 Famous Dave's BBQ, Hardee's, Jason's Deli, Smash Burger, Wendy's 🛏 Carol Hotel Ⓞ Best Buy, Book-A-Million, Buick/GMC, Home Depot, Michael's, Nelsen's RV Ctr, PetCo, Sam's Club/gas, Super Target, Verizon, Walmart/24hr, **S** 🍴 Brew Burgers, Perkins, Village Inn 🛏 Baymont Inn, Best Western, Carlisle Hotel, Comfort Inn, Days Inn, EconoLodge, Hawthorn Suites, Holiday Inn Express, Howard Johnson, La Quinta, Motel 6, Super 8 Ⓞ Goodyear, NE Beef Co, S on 108th 🍴 Arby's, Burger King, Godfather's Pizza, Hong Kong Café, Jimmy John's, LJ Silver, McDonald's, Pizza Hut/Taco Bell, Quizno's, Runza, Sonic, Subway, Valentino's, Wongs Hunan Garden Ⓞ Bag'n Save Foods, BP, O'Reilly Parts, QT/dsl
444	Q St, **N** 🚗 Cenex/dsl
442	126th St, Harrison St, **N** Ⓞ Chrysler/Dodge/Jeep, Toyota, VW, **S** 🚗 Phillips 66 🍴 Burger King, Jimmy John's, Pizza Gourmet, Runza 🛏 Courtyard, Embassy Suites, Hampton Inn, ValuePlace Hotel Ⓞ Cabela's
440	NE 50, to Springfield, **N** 🚗 Phillips 66, Shell/Sapp Bros/Subway/dsl/24hr/@ 🍴 Azteca Mexican, Cracker Barrel, Hardee's, McDonald's 🛏 Comfort Inn, Countryside Suites, Hometowne Lodge, Motel 6, Quality Inn, Red Carpet Inn Ⓞ Ⓗ, Ford, truckwash, **S** 🚗 BP/dsl, to Platte River SP
439	439 NE 370, to Gretna, **N** 🚗 Kum&Go/Quiznos/dsl, Phillips 66/dsl 🛏 Holiday Inn Express Ⓞ Walmart/Subway, **S** Ⓞ Ⓗ, museum, Volvo Trucks
432	US 6, NE 31, to Gretna, **N** 🚗 Sinclair/rest/dsl/24hr 🍴 McDonald's 🛏 Super 8 Ⓞ Curves, Nebraska X-ing/famous brands, **S** 🚗 ⓕFLYING J/Denny's/dsl/LP/24hr Ⓞ KOA, to Schramm SP
431mm	Ⓡ🇸 wb, full 🛏 facilities, info, litter barrels, petwalk, 🅲, 🅰
427mm	Platte River
426	NE 66, to Southbend, **N** Ⓞ museum, rv camping, to Mahoney SP
425.5	Ⓡ🇸 eb, full 🛏 facilities, litter barrels, petwalk, 🅲, 🅰, vending

Exit #	Services
420	NE 63, Greenwood, **N** 🚗 Cenex/cafe/dsl/scales/24hr Ⓞ Pine Grove RV Park, **S** 🚗 Shell/dsl 🛏 Big Inn Ⓞ antiques, to Platte River SP, WWII Museum
416mm	weigh sta both lanes
409	US 6, to E Lincoln, Waverly, **N** 🍴 McDonald's, **S** Ⓞ Ⓗ
405	US 77 N, 56th St, Lincoln, **S** 🚗 Phillips 66 🍴 Misty's Rest. 🛏 GuestHouse Inn, Star City Inn Ⓞ antiques, Freightliner, **truck parking**
403	27th St, Lincoln, **S** 0-3 mi 🚗 Conoco/Wendy's/dsl, Mobil, Phillips 66/Subway/dsl, Shell 🍴 Applebee's, Arby's, Beacon Hills Rest., Burger King, Carlos O'Kelly's, China Inn, CiCi's Pizza, Cracker Barrel, Culver's, daVinci's Italian, DQ, Godfather's Pizza, Golden Corral, IHOP, Jimmy John's, King Kong Burger, Mazatlan Mexican, McDonald's, Mr Goodcents, Papa John's, Popeye's/Taco Inn, Quizno's, Ruby Tuesday, Runza, Schlotzsky's, Sonic, Taco Bell, Taco John's, Village Inn 🛏 AmericInn, Best Western, Comfort Suites, Country Inn&Suites, Countryside Suites, Fairfield Inn, Hampton Inn, Holiday Inn Express, La Quinta, Microtel, Settle Inn, Staybridge Suites, Super 8, ValuePlace Inn Ⓞ $Tree, AutoZone, BMW, Cadillac/Chevrolet/GMC, Chrysler, Curves, Dodge/Jeep, Ford/Lincoln, GNC, Haas Tire, Home Depot, HyVee Foods, Lexus, Mazda, Menards, Mercedes, Petsmart, Sam's Club/gas, ShopKO, st fairpark, Super Saver Foods, to U NE, Toyota, URGENT CARE, Verizon, Walmart
401b	US 34 W, **S** Ⓞ RV camping
401a	I-180, US 34 E, to 9th St, Lincoln
399	Lincoln, **N** 🚗 BP/dsl, Phillips 66 🍴 Baskin-Robbins, McDonald's, Perkins, Quiznos 🛏 Comfort Inn, Days Inn, Hampton Inn, Holiday Inn Express, Horizon Inn, Luxury Inn, Motel 6, Quality Inn, Ramada Inn, Sleep Inn Ⓞ to ✈, **S** 🚗 Casey's 🍴 Subway 🛏 EconoLodge, Economy Lodge
397	US 77 S, to Beatrice
396	US 6, West O St (from eb), **S** 🚗 Sinclair/dsl 🛏 Rodeway Inn, Super 8
395	US 6, NW 48th St, **S** 🚗 Phillips 66/dsl, Shoemaker's/Shell/dsl/scales/@ 🛏 Cobbler Inn Ⓞ Harley-Davidson, truck repair
388	NE 103, to Crete, Pleasant Dale
382	US 6, Milford, **S** 🚗 Phillips 66/dsl
381mm	Ⓡ🇸 eb, full 🛏 facilities, litter barrels, petwalk, 🅲, 🅰, vending
379	NE 15, to Seward, **N** 2-3 mi 🍴 McDonald's 🛏 Super 8 Ⓞ Ⓗ antiques, Buick/Chevrolet/GMC, Ford, **S** 🚗 Shell/dsl
375mm	truck parking (wb)

Exit #	Services

🅝🅔 INTERSTATE 80 Cont'd

YORK / AURORA / KEARNEY

Exit #	Services
373	80G, Goehner, **N** 🅿 gas
369	80E, Beaver Crossing, **S 3 mi** 🅾 🇭, food, RV camping
366	80F, to Utica
360	93B, to Waco, **N** 🅿 Phillips 66/Waco Rest/dsl/24hr, **S** 🏨 Double Nickel Camping
355mm	🆁🆂 wb, full 🦽 facilities, info, litter barrels, petwalk, 🚰, 🌳, vending
353	US 81, to York, **N** 🅿 Conoco/dsl, Pump-N-Pantry/e85, SappBros/Sinclair/Subway/scales/dsl, Shell/dsl 🍴 Arby's, Burger King, China Buffet, Dickey's BBQ, Golden Gate Chinese, KFC/Taco Bell, McDonald's, Runza, Salsa's Mexican, Starbucks, Taco John's, The Kitchen, Wendy's 🏨 Best Value Inn, Comfort Inn, Days Inn, Hampton Inn, Holiday Inn Express, New Victorian Inn, Super 8, Yorkshire Motel 🅾 🇭, Buick/GMC, Chevrolet, Elms RV Park, Ford, Walmart/Subway, **S** 🅿 Petro/Phillips 66/Iron Skillet/Pizza Hut/dsl/24hr/@ 🍴 Applebee's 🏨 Best Western, Motel 6 🅾 Blue Beacon, Freightliner, tires/wash/lube
351mm	🆁🆂 eb, full 🦽 facilities, info, litter barrels, petwalk, 🚰, 🌳, vending
348	93E, to Bradshaw
342	93A, Henderson, **N** 🅾 Prairie Oasis Camping, **S** 🅿 Henderson Trkstp/dsl 🍴 Subway 🏨 Sun Motel 🅾 🇭
338	41D, to Hampton
332	NE 14, Aurora, **N 2-3 mi** 🅿 Casey's 🍴 McDonald's, Pizza Hut, Subway 🏨 Budget Host 🅾 🇭, to Plainsman Museum, **S** 🅿 ❤️Loves/Arby's/dsl/scales/24hr
324	41B, to Giltner
318	NE 2, to Grand Island, **S** 🅾 KOA (seasonal)
317mm	🆁🆂 wb, full 🦽 facilities, info, litter barrels, petwalk, 🚰, 🌳, vending
315mm	🆁🆂 eb, full 🦽 facilities, info, litter barrels, petwalk, 🚰, 🌳, vending
314mm	Platte River
314	Locust Street, to Grand Island, **N 4-6 mi** 🅾 food, gas, lodging
312	US 34/281, to Grand Island, **N** 🅿 Bosselman/Sinclair/Little Caesar's/Max's/Subway/scales/dsl/24hr, Fat Dogs 🍴 Quaker Steak 🏨 Motel 6, USA Inn 🅾 🇭, Mormon Island RA, to Stuhr Pioneer Museum, **S** 🅿 Phillips 66/Arby's/dsl 🏨 Days Inn, Quality Inn/Riverfront Grille 🅾 Hastings Museum (15mi), Peterbilt
305	40C, to Alda, **N** 🅿 Sinclair/dsl, TA/Country Pride/dsl/scales/24hr/@, **S** 🅾 Crane Meadows Nature Ctr/🆁🆂
300	NE 11, Wood River, **N** 🅾 to Cheyenne SRA, **S** 🅿 ❤️Loves/Subway/dsl/scales/24hr 🏨 motel/RV park
291	10D, Shelton, **N** 🅾 War Axe SRA
285	10C, Gibbon, **N** 🅿 Petro Oasis/dsl 🅾 RV camping, Windmill SP, **S** 🏨 Country Inn
279	NE 10, to Minden, **N** 🅿 Shell/dsl, **S** 🅾 Pioneer Village Camping (13mi)
275mm	The Great Platte River Road Archway Monument
275	Kearney, E Entrance, **N** 🅾 Great River Rd Mon
272	NE 44, Kearney, **N** 🅿 Casey's, Casey's/dsl, Cenex/Subway/dsl, Pump&Pantry/dsl, Shell/dsl 🍴 Amigo's, Arby's, Burger King, Carlos O'Kelly's, DQ, Egg&I, El Maguey, Gourmet House Japanese, Hunan's Rest., King's Buffet, LJ Silver, McDonald's, Old Chicago Rest, Perkins, Pizza Hut, Red Lobster, Ruby Tuesday, Runza, Taco Bell, Taco John's, USA Steaks, Wendy's, Whiskey Creek 🏨 AmericInn, Boarders Inn, Comfort Inn, Country Inn&Suites, EconoLodge, Fairfield Inn,

LEXINGTON / N PLATTE

Exit #	Services
272	Continued Hampton Inn, Holiday Inn, Howard Johnson, Microtel, Midtown Western Inn, Motel 6, New Victorian Inn, Quality Inn, Ramada Inn, Rodeway Inn, Super 8, Western Inn South, Wingate Inn 🅾 🇭, $General, Apache Camper Ctr, Boogaart's Foods, Buick/Cadillac, Chevrolet, Chrysler/Dodge/Jeep, Kearney RV Park/camping, Museum of NE Art, to Archway Mon, U NE Kearney, Verizon, Walmart (3mi), **S** 🅿 Qwest/dsl 🍴 Skeeter's BBQ 🏨 Best Western, Holiday Inn Express
271mm	🆁🆂 wb, full 🦽 facilities, info, litter barrels, petwalk, 🚰, 🌳
269mm	🆁🆂 eb, full 🦽 facilities, info, litter barrels, petwalk, 🚰, 🌳
263	Rd 10 b, Odessa, **N** 🅿 Sapp Bros./Apple Barrel Rest./dsl 🅾 UP Wayside
257	US 183, Elm Creek, **N** 🅿 ❤️Loves/Subway/dsl/scales/24hr 🏨 Royal Inn 🅾 Antique Car Museum, Sunny Meadows Camping, **S** 🅾 Nebraska Prarie Museum (9mi)
248	Overton, **N** 🅿 Jay Bros/dsl
237	US 283, Lexington, **N** 🅿 Casey's, Cenex/dsl, Conoco/dsl, Phillips 66/dsl 🍴 Arby's, Baskin-Robbins, Burger King, Delight Donuts, DQ, Hong Kong Buffet, Little Caesar's, McDonald's, Pizza Hut, San Pedro Mexican, Sonic, Wendy's 🏨 Comfort Inn, Days Inn, Econolodge, Holiday Inn Express, Minute Man Motel 🅾 🇭, $General, $Tree, Advance Parts, Buick/Chevrolet, Military Vehicle Museum, O'Reilly Parts, Plum Creek Foods, Verizon, Walmart/Subway, **S** 🅿 Sinclair/dsl/@ 🍴 Kirk's Café 🏨 Super 8 🅾 to Johnson Lake RA (6mi)
231	Darr Rd
227mm	🆁🆂 both lanes, full 🦽 facilities, info, litter barrels, petwalk, 🚰, 🌳, vending
222	NE 21, Cozad, **N** 🅿 Casey's/dsl, Cenex/dsl 🍴 Burger King, DQ, El Paraiso Mexican, Panda Buffet, Pizza Hut, Runza, Subway 🏨 Circle S Motel, Rodeway Inn 🅾 🇭, $General, Alco, Firestone/auto, museum
211	NE 47, Gothenburg, **N** 🅿 Cenex/dsl, Cenex/dsl/24hr 🍴 China Cafe, Lasso Espresso, McDonald's, Mi Ranchito Mexican, NE Grill, Pizza Hut, Runza 🏨 Comfort Suites, Howard Johnson, Travel Inn 🅾 🇭, Buick/Chevrolet, Carquest, Pony Express Sta Museum (1mi), ShopKO, **S** 🅾 KOA/Sinclair
199	Brady, **N** 🅿 Brady 1 Stop/DQ/dsl
194mm	🆁🆂 both lanes, full 🦽 facilities, litter barrels, petwalk, 🚰, 🌳, vending
190	Maxwell, **N** 🅿 Sinclair/dsl, **S** 🅾 RV camping, to Ft McPherson Nat Cemetary (2mi)
181mm	weigh sta both lanes 🚰
179	to US 30, N Platte, **N** 🅿 Pump&Pantry/dsl 🏨 La Quinta 🅾 RV camping, **S** 🅿 ⚡FLYING J/Denny's/dsl/scales/LP/RV dump/24hr, ❤️Loves/McDonald's/Subway/dsl/scales/24hr 🅾 tire/lube/repair, truckwash
177	US 83, N Platte, **N** 🅿 Cenex/dsl, Shell/dsl, Sinclair/dsl, U-Fillem 🍴 Amigo's Rest., Applebee's, Arby's, Burger King, Coldstone, DQ, Dunkin Donuts, Hunan Moon, Jimmy John's, KFC, King Buffet, Little Caesar's, LJ Silver/Taco Bell, McDonald's, Penny's Diner, Perkins, Pizza Hut, Quiznos, Ruby Tuesday, Runza, San Pedro Mexican, Sonic, Starbucks, Subway, Wendy's, Whiskey Creek Steaks 🏨 Blue Spruce Motel, Fairfield Inn, Hampton Inn, Howard Johnson, Knights Inn, Motel 6, Oak Tree Inn, Quality Inn 🅾 🇭, $General, $Tree, Advance Parts, Goodyear/auto, Harley-Davidson, Herberger's, Holiday RV Park, JC Penney, mall, museum, Staples, SunMart Foods, Tire Pros, to Buffalo Bill's Ranch, Verizon, Walgreens, Walmart/Subway, **S** 🅿 Cenex, Conoco/Taco Bell/dsl/24hr, U-Fillem/dsl/RV dump 🍴 Hunan Chinese, Taco John's

⬆E   INTERSTATE 80 Cont'd

Exit #	Services
177	Continued
	🏨 Comfort Inn, Days Inn, Holiday Inn Express, Ramada Ltd, Super 8 ⊙ Chevrolet/Cadillac, Chrysler/Dodge/Jeep, dsl repair, Ford/Lincoln, Honda, Menards, Nissan, to Lake Maloney RA, Toyota, vet, veterans memorial/info
164	56C, Hershey, N 🛢 Western/Western Cafe/dsl/24hr/@ ⊙ KJ's Ranch Store
160mm	🅟 both lanes, full 🅰 facilities, info, litter barrels, petwalk, 🚻, 🚮
158	NE 25, Sutherland, N 🏨 Park Motel (1mi) ⊙ RV camping, S 🛢 Sinclair/Godfather's Pizza/dsl ⊙ RV camping
149mm	Central/Mountain time zone
145	51C, Paxton, N 🛢 Shell/dsl/24hr 🏨 Days Inn ⊙ RV camping
133	51B, Roscoe
132mm	🅟 wb, full 🅰 facilities, info, litter barrels, petwalk, 🚻, 🚮
126	US 26, NE 61, Ogallala, N 🛢 Cenex/dsl, Kwik Stop, PetroMart/dsl, Sapp Bros/Shell/dsl/24hr, Watering Hole/dsl, Western/dsl 🍴 Arby's, Denny's, Front Street Cafe, Golden Village Chinese, Margarita's, McDonald's, Peking Chinese, Pizza Hut, Runza, Spur Steaks, Valentino's 🏨 Days Inn, Holiday Inn Express, Quality Inn, Stagecoach Inn ⊙ 🅷, $General, Alco, Buick/Chevrolet/GMC, Chrysler/Dodge/Jeep, Firestone/auto, Ford/Lincoln, NAPA, SunMart Foods, to Lake McConaughy, TrueValue, U-Save Drug, Verizon, S 🛢 Conoco/Subway/dsl, TA/Country Pride/dsl/scales/24hr/@ 🍴 DQ, KFC/Taco Bell, Mi Ranchito Mexican, Wendy's 🏨 Comfort Inn, Rodeway Inn, Super 8 ⊙ Ace Hardware, Countryview Camping, ShopKO, Sleepy Sunflower RV Park, truck repair, Walmart/dsl
124mm	🅟 eb, full 🅰 facilities, info, litter barrels, petwalk, 🚻, 🚮
117	51A, Brule, N 🛢 Happy Jack's/dsl ⊙ Riverside RV camping
107	25B, Big Springs, N 🛢 Big Springs/dsl, 🔶FLYING J/Grandma Max's/Subway/dsl/scales/24hr/@ 🍴 Sam Bass' Steaks 🏨 Motel 6 ⊙ truckwash, S ⊙ McGreer's Camping
102mm	S Platte River
102	I-76 S, to Denver
101	US 138, to Julesburg, S truck parking
99mm	scenic turnout eb
95	NE 27, to Julesburg
85	25A, Chappell, N 🛢 Cenex/dsl/repair, Pump&Pantrydsl, Shell/dsl ⊙ Creekside RV Park/Camping, Super Foods, USPO, wayside park
76	17F, Lodgepole, N 1 mi ⊙ gas/dsl, lodging
69	17E, to Sunol
61mm	🅟 wb, full 🅰 facilities, litter barrels, petwalk, 🚻, 🚮, vending
59	US 385, 17J, Sidney, N 🛢 Conoco/dsl, Sapp Bros/Shell/dsl/24hr 🍴 Arby's, Buffalo Point Rest., China 1 Buffet, DQ, McDonald's, Mi Ranchito Mexican, Perkins, Pizza Hut, Runza, Sonic, Subway 🏨 Best Western, Comfort Inn, Days Inn, Hampton Inn, Motel 6 ⊙ auto/dsl repair, Cabela's Outfitters/RV Park, Chrysler/Dodge/Jeep, Ford, Radio Shack, RV camping (2mi), visitor ctr, Walmart, S 🛢 Shamrock/dsl 🏨 Country Inn Suites ⊙ auto tire/truck repair, truckwash
55	NE 19, to Sterling, Sidney
51.5mm	🅟 hist marker eb, full 🅰 facilities, litter barrels, petwalk, 🚻, 🚮, vending
48	to Brownson
38	rd 17 b, Potter, N 🛢 Cenex/dsl/LP ⊙ repair
29	53A, Dix, N 1/2 mi ⊙ food, gas
22	53E, Kimball, N 1/2 mi 🛢 Kwik Stop, Vince's/dsl 🍴 Pizza Hut, Subway 🏨 Days Inn, Motel Kimball, Sleep4Less Motel ⊙ city park, Kimball RV Park (seasonal), Main St Mkt, NAPA
20	NE 71, Kimball, N 0-2 mi 🛢 Cenex/dsl, Kwk Stop, Vince's/dsl 🍴 O'Henry's Diner, Pizza Hut, Subway 🏨 1st Interstate Inn, Days Inn, Motel Kimball, Sleep4Less Motel, Super 8 ⊙ city park, Kimball RV Park (seasonal), Main St Mkt, NAPA, ShopKO
8	53C, to Bushnell
1	53B, Pine Bluffs, N 1 mi ⊙ RV camping
0mm	Nebraska/Wyoming state line

⬆E   INTERSTATE 680 (Omaha)

Exit #	Services
I-680 begins/ends on I-80, exit 27.	
29b a	I-80, W to Omaha, E to Des Moines.
28	IA 191, to Neola, Persia
21	L34, Beebeetown
19mm	🅟 wb, full 🅰 facilities, info, litter barrels, petwalk, 🚻, 🚮
16mm	🅟 eb, full 🅰 facilities, info, litter barrels, petwalk, 🚻, 🚮
15mm	scenic overlook
71	I-29 N, to Sioux City
66	W 🛢 Sinclair/dsl/rest. 🍴 Iowa Feed&Grain Co Rest., ⊙ Honey Creek
3b a	(61 b a from wb) I-29, S to Council Bluffs, IA 988, to Crescent, E 🛢 Phillips 66 ⊙ to ski area
1	County Rd
14mm	Missouri River, Mormon Bridge, Nebraska/Iowa state line
13	US 75 S, 30th St, Florence, E 🛢 Shell/dsl 🍴 Jimmy C's Cafe, Zesto Diner 🏨 Mormon Trail Motel ⊙ HyVee Drug, LDS Temple, Mormon Trail Ctr, vet, W 🛢 Florence
12	US 75 N, 48th St, E 🛢 Cenex/dsl 🍴 Burger King (2mi), Taco Bell (2mi)
9	72nd St, E 1-2 mi 🛢 QuikShop 🍴 Applebee's, Burger King, Famous Dave's BBQ, IHOP, Jimmy John's, Sonic, Taco Bueno, Village Inn ⊙ 🅷, W ⊙ Cunningham Lake RA
6	NE 133, Irvington, E 🛢 Phillips 66 🍴 Burger King, Jimmy John's, Wings'n Things ⊙ Walmart/Subway/drugs/24hr, W 🍴 Legend's Grill, Zesto Cafe 🏨 Holiday Inn Express
5	Fort St, W 🛢 KwikShop ⊙ CVS Drug, Goodyear/auto, HyVee Foods, URGENT CARE, USPO, Walgreens
4	NE 64, Maple St, E 🛢 BP, W 🛢 Kum&Go/dsl, Shell 🍴 Burger King, China 1, Godfather's Pizza, Jimmy John's, KFC, La Mesa Mexican, McDonald's, Pizza Hut, Runza, Subway, Taco Bell, Taco John's 🏨 Comfort Suites, La Quinta ⊙ $General, Bag'n Save, O'Reilly Parts, vet

O G A L L A L A

S I D N E Y

O M A H A

↑E INTERSTATE 680 (Omaha)

Exit #	Services
3	US 6, Dodge St, **E** ⓕ Cheesecake Factory, Granite City Rest., JC Manderin Chinese, Panera Bread, PF Chang's, TGI-Friday's 🛏 Hampton Inn, Marriott ⓞ AAA, Audi/VW, BMW, Hynundai, Jaguar/Land Rover, JC Penney, mall, Mazda, Mini, Subaru, Von Maur, Whole Foods Mkt, Younkers, **W** 🅿 BP, Phillips 66 ⓕ Boston Mkt, Burger King, DQ, Grand China Buffet. Grisanti's. McDonald's. Starbucks 🛏 Best Western.

3	Continued
	Crowne Plaza Motel, Holiday Inn, Super 8, TownPlace Suites ⓞ Bag'n Save Foods, Cadillac, Chevrolet, Costco/gas, Ford, Hummer, Menards, Nissan, Toyota
2	Pacific St, **E** 🅿 BP 🛏 Regency Lodge
1	NE 38, W Center Rd, **E** 🅿 Cenex/dsl ⓕ Don Carmelo's, Don&Millie's Rest., **W** 🅿 Phillips 66 ⓕ Arby's, Burger King, Godfather's Pizza, Krispy Kreme, Ozark BBQ, Táco Bell, Wendy's ⓞ $Tree, Baker's Foods, Haas Tire, TJ Maxx
0mm	I-680 begins/ends on I-80, exit 446

NEVADA

↑N INTERSTATE 15

Exit #	Services
123mm	Nevada/Arizona state line, Pacific/Mountain time zone
122	Lp 15, Mesquite, **E** NV Welcome Ctr both lanes, full ♿ facilities, petwalk, 🅿 Arco, Maverik/dsl, Shell/DQ/dsl ⓕ Alberto's Mexican, Canton Chinese, Cucina Italiano, Dominos, Golden West Rest./casino, Jack-in-the-Box, KFC, Los Lupes, Panda Garden, Taco Bell 🛏 Best Western ⓞ $General, Ace Hardware, AutoZone, Big O Tire, CarQuest, city park, Radio Shack, Smith's/Subway/dsl, Sun Resort RV Park, USPO, Walgreens **W** 🅿 Rebel/dsl/LP/RV park ⓕ McDonald's, Starbucks 🛏 Eureka Motel/casino, Virgin River Hotel/casino
120	Lp 15, Mesquite, Bunkerville, **E** 🅿 Shell/dsl, Terrible's ⓕ McDonald's 🛏 Casablanca Resort/casino/RV Park, Oasis Resort RV Park ⓞ USPO, **W** 🅿 Chevron/dsl ⓕ Del Taco, Popeye's, Roberto's Tacos 🛏 Holiday Inn Express ⓞ 🅷, $Tree, Beall's, Ford/RV Ctr, Verizon, Walmart/Subway
112	NV 170, Riverside, Bunkerville
110mm	litter barrels, truck parking both lanes
100	to Carp, Elgin
96mm	truck parking both lanes, litter barrels
93	NV 169, to Logandale, Overton, **E** 🅿 Chevron (3mi) ⓞ Lake Mead NRA, Lost City Museum
91	NV 168, Glendale, **W** 🅿 Arco/dsl ⓕ Muddy River Rest. ⓞ USPO
90.5mm	Muddy River
90	NV 168 (from nb), Glendale, Moapa, **W** 🅿 gas ⓞ Moapa Indian Reservation, USPO
88mm	parking area both lanes, litter barrels
88	Hidden Valley
84	Byron
80	Ute
75	Valley of Fire SP, Lake Mead NRA, **E** 🅿 Chevron/dsl ⓞ casino, fireworks
64	US 93 N, Great Basin Hwy, to Ely, Great Basin NP, **W** 🅿 Loves/Subway/Godfather's/dsl/scales/24hr
60mm	livestock check sta sb
58	NV 604, Las Vegas Blvd, to Apex, Nellis AFB
54	Speedway Blvd, Hollywood Blvd, **E** 🅿 Petro/Valero/dsl/scales/24hr/@ ⓕ Race Day Cafe ⓞ Las Vegas Speedway
52	rd 215 W
50	Lamb Ave, **E** 1-2 mi 🅿 Shell/dsl 🛏 Comfort Inn ⓞ Hitchin Post RV Park
48	Craig Rd, **E** 🅿 7-11, Arco, ███/KFC/Pizza Hut/dsl/scales/24hr, Shell, Sinclair/Subway/dsl ⓕ Burger King, Jack-in-the-Box, Zapata's Cantina ⓞ Firestone, to Nellis AFB, **W** 🅿 7-11 ⓕ Cannery Grill, Carl's Jr, Chipotle Mexican,

48	Continued
	Del Taco, Famous Dave's BBQ, In-N-Out, Jamba Juice, Marble Slab, Mulligan's, Panda Express, Poppa's Grill, Quiznos, Sonic, Starbucks, Subway 🛏 Best Western, Hampton Inn ⓞ dsl repair, Freightliner, Just Brakes, Lowe's, Sam's Club/gas
46	Cheyenne Ave, **E** 🅿 Arco/24hr ⓕ CiCi's Pizza, Lucy's Grill, Marianna's Mkt, Panda Express, Starbucks, Subway ⓞ $Tree, 7-11, NAPA, vet, **W** 🅿 /Mortons/dsl/LP/rest./24hr, 7-11, Sinclair/Jack-in-the-Box ⓕ Denny's, McDonald's 🛏 Comfort Inn ⓞ Blue Beacon, dsl repair, Kenworth, Mack, SpeedCo, tires, Volvo
45	Lake Mead Blvd, **E** 🅿 Chevron, Rebel/dsl ⓕ Burger King, Carl's Jr., Jack-in-the-Box, McDonald's ⓞ 7-11, PepBoys, **W** 🅿 Arco/dsl ⓕ Jack-in-the-Box, McDonald's ⓞ CVS Drug
44	Washington Ave (from sb), **E** ⓞ casinos
43	D St (from nb), same as 44
42b a	I-515 to LV, US 95 N to Reno, US 93 S to Phoenix
41b a	NV 159, Charleston Blvd, **E** 🅿 7-11, Arco/dsl ⓞ antiques, Walgreens, **W** 🅿 Rebel, Terrible's/E-85/dsl/casino ⓕ Bentley's Coffee, Carl's Jr, Del Taco, McDonald's, Wendy's ⓞ 🅷 CVS Drug, Smith's Foods
40	Sahara Ave, **E** 🛏 Artisan Hotel, Vagabond Inn ⓞ KOA, multiple casinos/hotels, NV Tire/Repair, The Strip, **W** 🅿 7-11, Chevron, Rebel/dsl, Shell ⓕ Carl's Jr, Chipotle Mexican, El Pollo Loco, In-N-Out, Jack-in-the-Box, Jimmy Johns, KFC, Landry's Seafood, Los Tacos, Macaroni Grill, McDonald's, Panda Express, Pizza Hut, Shilla BBQ, Starbucks, TGIFriday's, Wendy's 🛏 Palace Sta. Hotel/Casino ⓞ casinos, CVS Drug, Food4Less, Office Depot, Ross, TJ Maxx, Von's Foods, Walgreens
39	Spring Mtn Rd (from sb), **E** ⓞ multiple hotels/casinos, **W** ⓕ Multiple Asian Cuisine, Quiznos, Starbucks ⓞ Firestone/auto
38b a	Flamingo Rd, **E** ⓞ multiple casinos/hotels, The Strip, to UNLV, **W** 🅿 Chevron ⓕ Burger King, McDonald's, Sonic, Starbucks, Subway, Taco Bell, TGIFriday's, Wendy's 🛏 Gold Coast Hotel, Palms Hotel, Rio Hotel ⓞ Discount Tire
37	Tropicana Ave, **E** 🅿 Rebel ⓕ Coco's Rest., McDonald's 🛏 Bellagio, Excaliber Hotel, Hooters Hotel/casino, Mandalay Bay, MGM Grand, Monte Carlo, Motel 6, Tropicana Hotel ⓞ 🅷, multiple hotels/casinos, **W** 🅿 Rebel/dsl, Shell/Subway, Standard, Texaco ⓕ Burger King, Dennys, In-N-Out, Jack-in-the-Box, McDonald's, Taco's Mexico, Wendy's 🛏 Budget Suites, Days Inn, Hampton Inn, La Quinta, Motel 6, Orleans Hotel, Siegel Suites
36	Russell Rd, **E** ⓞ multiple hotels/casinos, to 🛩, **W** 🅿 Chevron/Herbst/dsl 🛏 Courtyard, Fairfield Inn, Holiday Inn Express, Residence Inn, Staybridge Suites
34	to I-215 E, Las Vegas Blvd, to The Strip, **E** ⓞ McCarran 🛩

(left margin vertical text: NE NV · MESQUITE · LAS VEGAS)

⬆N INTERSTATE 15 Cont'd

Exit #	Services
33	NV 160, to Blue Diamond, Death Valley, **E** 🅖 7-11/dsl, Chevron, Rebel/dsl 🍴 Bootlegger Bistro, Buffalo Wild Wings, Burger King, Cane's Rest, Chili's, Chipotle Mexican, Dickey's BBQ, Dunkin Donuts, IHOP, McDonald's, Outback Steaks, Panda Express, Popeyes, Quizno's, Starbucks, Subway, Wienerschnitzel 🛏 Budget Suites, Carib Resort, Crestwood Suites, Hilton Garden, Microtel Ⓞ CVS Drug, factory outlet/famous brands, Food4Less, Oasis RV Resort, Verizon, **W** 🅖 Chevron/dsl, Fills/dsl, Shell, TA/Burger King/Subway/TacoTime/dsl/LP/scales/24hr/@ 🍴 Bilbo's Grill, Cafe Rio, Carl's Jr, Del Taco, Famous Dave's BBQ, In-N-Out, Jack-in-the-Box, Panda Express, Quiznos, Taco Bell 🛏 Silverton Lodge/Casino Ⓞ $Tree, Albertson's, Bass ProShops, BigLots, Discount Tire, GNC, Kohl's, Office Depot, PetCo, Radio Shack, Ross, Target, Verizon, Walgreens, WorldMkt
31	Silverado Ranch Blvd, **E** 🍴 Steak'n Shake 🛏 South Point Hotel/Casino
27	NV 146, to Henderson, Lake Mead, Hoover Dam, **E 0-2 mi** 🅖 Arco, Chevron, Shell 🍴 Jack-in-the-Box, Starbucks, Subway 🛏 Hampton Inn, Wingate Inn Ⓞ Camping World, casino, USPO, **W** Ⓞ vet
25	NV 161, Sloan, **E 1 mi** Ⓞ Camping World
24mm	**bus/truck check sta nb**
12	NV 161, to Goodsprings, Jean, **E** 🅖 Shell/dsl Ⓞ Gold Strike Casino/hotel, NV Correctional, NV HP, skydiving, USPO, **W** 🅖 Shell
1	Primm, **E** 🅖 Chevron/dsl, Texaco/dsl 🍴 Carl's Jr, Dennys, KFC, Mad Greek Cafe, McDonald's, Panda Express, Starbucks, Taco Bell, Tony Roma Ⓞ Buffalo Bill's Resort/casino, factory outlets, Primm Valley Resort/casino, **W** 🅖 Chevron/dsl/scales 🛏 Whiskey Pete's Hotel/casino
0mm	Nevada/California state line

⬆E INTERSTATE 80

Exit #	Services
411mm	Nevada/Utah state line
410	US 93A, to Ely, W Wendover, **S NV Welcome Ctr/info, full** 🛏 **facilities,** 🆁🆂, 🅖 Chevron/dsl, Arby's/dsl/scales/24hr, Shell/Taco Time/dsl 🍴 Burger King, McDonald's, Pizza Hut, Subway 🛏 Knights Inn, Motel 6, Nugget Hotel/casino, Peppermill Hotel/casino/RV parking, Rainbow Hotel/casino, Red Garter Hotel/casino Ⓞ Best Hardware, city park, KOA, Smith's Foods/dsl, 407 Ola, W Wendover
405mm	Pacific/Mountain time zone
398	to Pilot Peak
390mm	Silverzone Pass, elev 5940
387	to Shafter
378	NV 233, to Montello, Oasis
376	to Pequop

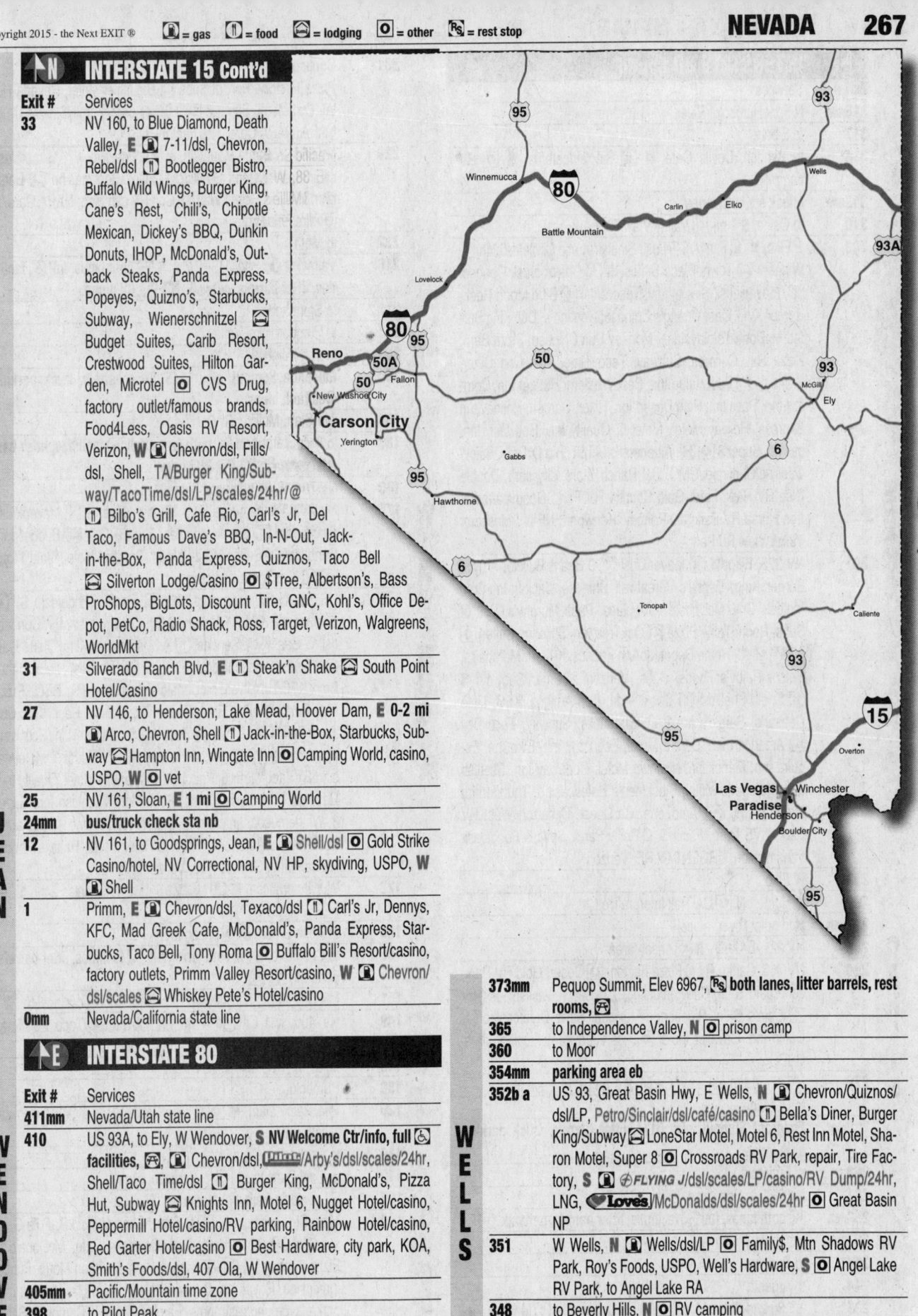

Exit #	Services
373mm	Pequop Summit, Elev 6967, 🆁🆂 **both lanes, litter barrels, rest rooms,** 🆁🆂
365	to Independence Valley, **N** Ⓞ prison camp
360	to Moor
354mm	**parking area eb**
352b a	US 93, Great Basin Hwy, E Wells, **N** 🅖 Chevron/Quiznos/dsl/LP, Petro/Sinclair/dsl/café/casino 🍴 Bella's Diner, Burger King/Subway 🛏 LoneStar Motel, Motel 6, Rest Inn Motel, Sharon Motel, Super 8 Ⓞ Crossroads RV Park, repair, Tire Factory, **S** 🅖 FLYING J/dsl/scales/LP/casino/RV Dump/24hr, LNG, Loves/McDonalds/dsl/scales/24hr Ⓞ Great Basin NP
351	W Wells, **N** 🅖 Wells/dsl/LP Ⓞ Family$, Mtn Shadows RV Park, Roy's Foods, USPO, Well's Hardware, **S** Ⓞ Angel Lake RV Park, to Angel Lake RA
348	to Beverly Hills, **N** Ⓞ RV camping
343	to Welcome, Starr Valley, **N** 🅖, Ⓞ 🍴, Welcome RV Park
333	Deeth, Starr Valley
328	to River Ranch
321	NV 229, Halleck, Ruby Valley

JEAN

WENDOVER

WELLS

NV

INTERSTATE 80 Cont'd

Exit #	Services
318mm	N Fork Humboldt River
317	to Elburz
314	to Ryndon, Devils Gate, N 🅿 Sinclair/cafe/dsl, S 🅾 RV camping
312mm	**check sta both lanes**
310	to Osino, S 4 mi 🅾 Valley View RV Park
303	E Elko, N 🅿 Flyers/CFN/dsl, Sinclair/Arctic Circle/dsl/24hr 🍴 Wingers 🛏 TownePlace Suites, S 🅿 Chevron/dsl, Conoco/dsl, Maverik/dsl, Sinclair/dsl, Tesoro/dsl 🍴 Blue Moon Rest., Burger King, Chef Cheng's Chinese, Domino's, DQ, King Buffet, McDonald's/playplace, Monkey Sun Chinese, Pizza Barn, Pizza Hut, Quiznos, Subway, Taco Time, Toki Ona Diner, Wendy's 🛏 Best Value Inn, Best Western, Budget Inn, Comfort Inn, Days Inn, High Desert Inn, Hilton Garden, Holiday Inn Express, Holiday Motel, Motel 6, Quality Inn, Red Lion Inn/casino, Super 8 🅾 🛏, Albertson's, AT&T, Big O Tires, Buick/Cadillac/Chevrolet/GMC, Cal Ranch Store, city park, Double Dice RV Park, Ford, Gold Country RV Park, Goodyear/auto, Iron Horse RV Park, JC Penney, Kenworth, NE NV Museum, Valley View RV Park
301	NV 225, Elko, N 🅿 Maverik/dsl 🍴 9 Beans/Burrito, Arby's, Burger King, Denny's, Greatwall Chinese, Jack-in-the-Box, Mattie's Grill, McDonald's/playplace, Papa Murphy's, Port of Subs, RoundTable Pizza 🛏 OakTree Inn, Shilo Inn Suites 🅾 AT&T, GNC, Home Depot, JoAnn Fabrics, K-Mart, Marshall's, Petco, Raley's Foods, Ross, Verizon, Walmart/Subway, S 🅿 Shell, Shell/dsl 🍴 Costa Vida, Dos Amigos, KFC, Little Caesar's, Sergio's Mexican, Starbucks, Subway, Taco Bell 🛏 American Inn, Centre Motel, Economy Inn, Elko Inn, Esquire Inn, Manor Inn, Midtown Motel, Rodeway Inn, Scottish Inn, Stampede Motel, Stockmen's Hotel/casino, Thunderbird Motel 🅾 🛏, 🔧, AutoZone, CarQuest, Cimarron West RV Park, CVS Drug, Family$, O'Reilly Parts, Smith's Foods/dsl, transmission, URGENT CARE, Verizon
298	W Elko
292	to Hunter, N 🅾 CA Trail Interpretive Ctr
285mm	Humboldt River, tunnel
282	NV 221, E Carlin, N 🅾 prison area
280	NV 766, Carlin, N 🍴 Pizza Factory 🅾 Desert Gold RV Park, dsl repair, S 🅿 Chevron/dsl, ▭▭▭/Subway/dsl/scales/24hr 🍴 Chin's Cafe, Rigobertos Mexican, State Café/casino 🛏 Carlin Inn, Cavalier Motel 🅾 Ace Hardware, Family$, tires, USPO
279	NV 278 (from eb), to W Carlin, S 1 mi 🅿 Flyers/dsl
271	to Palisade
270mm	**Emigrant Summit, elev 6114, litter barrels, truck parking both lanes**
268	to Emigrant
261	NV 306, to Beowawe, Crescent Valley
258mm	🆁🆂 **both lanes, full 🦽 facilities, litter barrels, petwalk, 🞉**
257mm	Humboldt River
254	to Dunphy
244	to Argenta
233	NV 304, to Battle Mountain, N 🅿 Conoco/dsl 🍴 Mama's Pizza/deli 🛏 Best Value Inn 🅾 🛏, FoodTown, Royal Hardware
231	NV 305, Battle Mountain, N 1 mi 🅿 ⚡FLYING J/76/Blimpie/dsl/casino/24hr, Chevron/dsl, Maverik/dsl 🍴 El Aguila Real, Hide-a-way Steaks, McDonald's, Ming Dynasty, Owl Rest.,

231	Continued
	Pizza Factory, Port of Subs 🛏 Big Chief Motel, Nevada Hotel, Owl Motel, Super 8 🅾 🛏, city park, Family$, Mills Drug, NAPA, NAPA Care, Tire Factory, USPO
229	NV 304, W Battle Mountain, N 🅿 ⚡FLYING J/76/Blimpie/dsl/casino/scales/24hr, Shell/dsl 🍴 Colt Rest./casino 🛏 Battle Mtn. Inn, Big Chief Motel 🅾 Colt RV camping, NAPA Care, S 🅾 Tire Factory
222	to Mote
216	Valmy, N 🅿 Shell/USPO/dsl, S 🆁🆂 both lanes, full 🦽 facilities, litter barrels, petwalk, 🞉, 🞉, RV dump
212	to Stonehouse
205	to Pumpernickel Valley
203	to Iron Point
200	**Golconda Summit, elev 5145, litter barrels, truck parking area both lanes**
194	Golconda, N 🅾 USPO
187	to Button Point, N 🆁🆂 both lanes, full 🦽 facilities, litter barrels, petwalk, 🞉, 🞉, RV dump
180	NV 794, E Winnemucca Blvd
178	NV 289, Winnemucca Blvd, Winnemucca, S 🅿 Maverik/dsl, Sinclair/dsl 🍴 Las Margaritas, Rte 66 Grill 🛏 Budget Inn, Candlewood Suites, Cozy Motel, Frontier Motel, Valu Motel 🅾 🛏, CarQuest, carwash
176	US 95 N, Winnemucca, N 🅿 Pacific Pride/dsl, S 🅿 ⚡FLYING J/dsl/LP/RV dump/24hr, Chevron/dsl/24hr, Conoco/dsl, G Gas, Kwik Serv/dsl 🍴 Arby's, Burger King, China Garden, Dos Amigos Mexican, Dotty's, Griddle Rest., Jack-in-the-Box, KFC/LJ Silver, McDonald's/playplace, Pig BBQ, Pizza Hut, Port of Subs, RoundTable Pizza, Sid's Rest., Subway, Taco Bell, Taco Time 🛏 Best Western, Days Inn, Economy Inn, Holiday Inn Express, Holiday Motel, Model T Motel/casino/RVPark, Motel 6, Park Hotel, Pyrenees Motel, Quality Inn, Regency Inn, Santa Fe Inn, Scott Motel, Scottish Inn, Super 8, Winnemucca Inn/casino, Winner Hotel/casino 🅾 🛏, auto/truck repair, AutoZone, Ford, O'Reilly Parts, Raley's Foods, RV camping, Schwab Tire, Verizon, Walmart/Subway
173	W Winnemucca, N 🅿 ▭▭▭/Subway/dsl/scales/24hr, S 🅾 ✈
168	to Rose Creek, S 🅾 prison area
158	to Cosgrave, S 🆁🆂 both lanes, full 🦽 facilities, litter barrels, petwalk, 🞉, 🞉
151	Mill City, N 🅿 TA/Subway/Taco Bell/Fork/dsl/casino/24hr/@
149	NV 400, Mill City, N 1 mi 🅿 TA/Subway/Taco Bell/Fork/dsl/24hr/@, S 🅾 Star Point Gen. Store/RV camping
145	Imlay, S 🅾 Star Peak RV Park
138	Humboldt
129	Rye Patch Dam, N 🅾 to Rye Patch SRA, S 🅿 Rye Patch Trkstp/dsl
119	to Rochester, Oreana
112	to Coal Canyon, S 🅾 to correctional ctr
107	E Lovelock (from wb), same as 106
106	Main St, Lovelock, N 🅿 2 Stiffs, Chevron/dsl/LP, PJ's Gas/subs/dsl 🍴 Black Rock Grill, Cowpoke Cafe, McDonald's, Pizza Factory 🛏 Cadillac Inn, Covered Wagon Motel, Punch Inn/casino, Royal Inn, Super 10 Motel 🅾 🛏, auto care, city park/playground/restrooms, Family$, Lazy K Camping, Safeway Foods, USPO, S 🅿 Conoco/Port of Subs/dsl24hr
105	W Lovelock (from eb), N 🅿 Shell/dsl, Shop'n Go/dsl 🍴 La Casita Mexican 🛏 Lovelock Inn 🅾 🛏, Brookwood RV Park, museum, NAPA, same as 106

Exit #	Services

🔼🄴 INTERSTATE 80 Cont'd

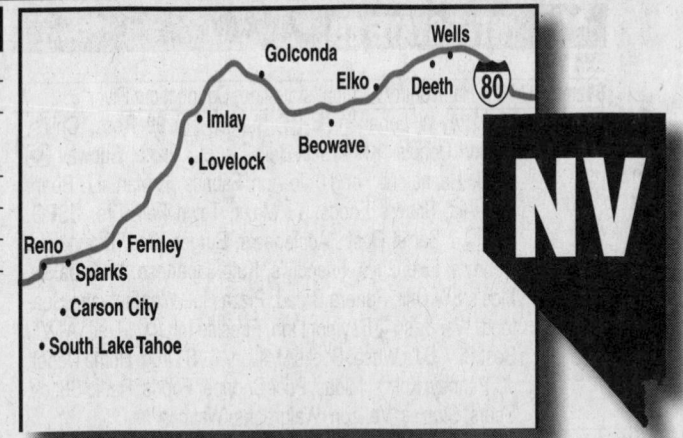

Exit #	Services
93	to Toulon, S 🅞 ⊟
83	US 95 S, to Fallon, S 🆁🆂 both lanes, full ♿ facilities, litter barrels, 🅲, ⊞
78	to Jessup
65	to Hot Springs, Nightingale
50	NV Pacific Pkwy, Fernley
48	US 50A, US 95A, to Fallon, E Fernley, N 🅖 ⊕FLYING J/ Denny's/dsl/scales/Lp/24hr, S 🅖 Shell/dsl, Silverado/dsl 🍴 Bully's Rest., Burger King, Dotty's Grill, Jack-in-the-Box, KFC, Louie's China, McDonald's, Moto Japanese, Papa Murphy's, Pizza Hut, Silverado Rest./casino, Starbucks, Taco Bell 🏠 Best Western, Super 8 🅞 $Tree, AutoZone, Lowe's, O'Reilly Parts, Scolari's Foods, tires, to Great Basin NP, URGENT CARE, USPO, Verizon, Walgreens, Walmart/Subway
46	US 95A, W Fernley, N 🅖 ⬤Loves/Arby's/dsl/scales/24hr, S 🅖 ⬛⬛⬛/DQ/Wendy's/dsl/scales/24hr 🍴 Chukars Grill/ Casino 🏠 Comfort Suties 🅞 Blue Beacon, SpeedCo
45mm	Truckee River
43	to Pyramid Lake, Wadsworth, N 🅖 Pyramid Lake gas/dsl/RV camping
42mm	🆁🆂 wb, check sta eb, full ♿ facilities, litter barrels, petwalk, 🅲, ⊞, wireless internet
40	Painted Rock
38	Orchard
36	Derby Dam
32	USA Pkwy, Tracy, Clark Station, S 🅖 Golden Gate/Port of Subs/dsl/scales 🍴 Phillys, Subway
28	NV 655, Waltham Way, Patrick
27mm	eb, scenic view
25mm	**check sta wb**
23	Mustang, S 🅖 truck repair
22	Lockwood
21	Vista Blvd, Greg St, Sparks, N 🅖 Chevron/McDonald's, Qwik-Stop 🍴 Del Taco 🏠 Fairfield Inn 🅞 🅷, S 🅖 Petro/Iron Skillet/dsl/24hr/@ 🏠 Super 8 🅞 Peterbilt, truckwash
20	Sparks Blvd, Sparks, N 🅖 7-11, Shell/dsl 🍴 BJ's Rest., Buffalo Wild Wings, Carl's Jr, Chipotle, Fuddruckers, Olive Garden, Outback Steaks, Panda Express, Popeye's, Starbucks, Subway, Taco Bell, Taco del Mar 🅞 AT&T, Best Buy, Discount Tire, GNC, Lowe's, Old Navy, Scheel's Sports, Schwab Tire, Target, Tires+, TJ Maxx, water funpark, S 🅖 Petro/Iron Skillet/dsl/scales/24hr/@ 🏠 Super 8 🅞 Freightliner
19	E McCarran Blvd, Sparks, N 🅖 Arco, Chevron/dsl, Sinclair/dsl, TA/Valero/Country Pride/dsl/scales/@ 🍴 Applebee's, Baskin-Robbins, BJ's BBQ, Black Bear Diner, Burger King, China King, Domino's, El Pollo Loco, Jack-in-the-Box, KFC, Little Caesar's, McDonald's, Pizza Hut, Pizza+, Port Of Subs, Sizzler, Taco Bell, Wendy's, Wienerschnitzel 🏠 Aloha Inn, Sunrise Motel, Windsor Inn 🅞 $Tree, 99¢ Store, AutoZone, BigLots, CVS Drug, Family$, O'Reilly Parts, Radio Shack, Ross, Savemart Foods, Victorian RV Park, S 🍴 Denny's, Super Burrito 🏠 Holiday Inn 🅞 NAPA
18	NV 445, Pyramid Way, Sparks, N 🅖 7-11 🍴 In-N-Out 🏠 Bourbon Square Casino, Nugget Courtyard, S 🏠 Nugget Hotel/casino
17	Rock Blvd, Nugget Ave, Sparks, N 🅖 Arco, Chevron, V/dsl 🏠 Safari Motel, Victorian Inn, Wagon Train Motel 🅞 casinos, O'Reilly Parts, S 🏠 Nugget Hotel/casino

SPARKS (vertical label)

RENO (vertical label)

Exit #	Services
16	B St, E 4th St, Victorian Ave, N 🅖 Arco 🍴 Jack's Cafe 🏠 Motel 6 🅞 Rail City Casino, S 🅖 Chevron/repair
15	US 395, to Carson City, Susanville, S 0-1 mi 🏠 Best Western, Holiday Inn Express, Hyatt Place, La Quinta 🅞 ⊟, Costco/ gas, Grand Sierra Resort, USPO, Walmart/McDonald's
14	Wells Ave, Reno, N 🏠 Motel 6, S 🅖 Chevron/dsl 🍴 Carrow's Rest., Denny's 🏠 America's Best Inn, Days Inn, Ramada Inn 🅞 auto repair, Big O Tire, Goodyear
13	US 395, Virginia St, Reno, N 🅖 Shell/dsl 🍴 Giant Burger, S 🅞 🅷, Circus Circus, to downtown hotels/casinos, to UNVReno, Walgreens
12	Keystone Ave, Reno, N 🅖 Arco 🍴 Pizza Hut, Starbucks 🏠 Gateway Inn, Motel 6 🅞 7-11, CVS Drug, Raley's Foods, S 🅖 Chevron/dsl 🍴 Burger King, Jack-in-the-Box, KFC, Little Caesar's, McDonald's, Port of Subs, Round Table Pizza, Taco Bell, Wendy's 🅞 casinos, Keystone RV Park, Meineke, NAPA, O'Reilly Parts, Radio Shack, SaveMart/drug
10	McCarran Blvd, Reno, N 🅖 7-11/dsl, Arco 🍴 Applebee's, Asian Wok, Baskin-Robbins, Bully's Grill, Burger King, Carl's Jr, Chili's, Del Taco, DQ, El Pollo Loco, Hacienda Mexican, Hawaiian BBQ, IHOP, Jack-in-the-Box, KFC, Little Caesar's, McDonald's, Papa Murphy's, Pizza+, Popeyes, Qdoba Mexican, RoundTable Pizza, Silver Chop Chinese, Starbucks, Subway, Taco Bell, Tacos el Rey 🅞 $Tree, AT&T, AutoZone, Big O Tire, Discount Tire, Kohl's, O'Reilly Parts, Petsmart, Radio Shack, Ross, Safeway/dsl, SaveMart Foods, Staples, Tires+, Walgreens, Walmart/McDonald's, S 🅖 7-11 🅞 Home Depot, URGENT CARE, vet
9	Robb Dr, N 🅖 Chevron/dsl, Maverik/dsl 🍴 Bully's Grill, Burger Me, Casa Grande, China Kitchen, Dickey's BBQ, Domino's, Jimmy John's, Moxie's Cafe, Port Of Subs, Starbucks, Subway 🏠 Hampton Inn 🅞 CVS Drug, Raley's Foods/dsl, Scolari's Foods
8	W 4th St (from eb), Robb Dr, Reno, S 🅞 RV camping
7	Mogul
6.5mm	**truck parking/hist marker/scenic view both lanes**
5	to E Verdi (from wb no return), N 🍴 Backstop Grill
4.5mm	scenic view eb
4	Garson Rd, Boomtown, N 🅖 Chevron/Boomtown Hotel/dsl/ casino 🍴 Peet's Rest. 🅞 Cabela's, KOA/RV dump
3.5mm	**check sta eb**
3	Verdi (from wb)
2.5mm	Truckee River
2	Lp 80, to Verdi, N 🅖 Sinclair/dsl/24hr 🍴 Jack-in-the-Box 🏠 Gold Ranch RV Resort/casino
0mm	Nevada/California state line

⬆N INTERSTATE 89

L E B A N O N

Exit #	Services
61mm	New Hampshire/Vermont state line, Connecticut River
20 (60)	NH 12A, W Lebanon, **E** 🅟 Sunoco 🍴 99 Rest., Chili's, Dunkin Donuts, KFC/Taco Bell, Lui Lui Pizza, Subway 🅞 GNC, Hannaford Foods, Jo-Ann Fabrics, K-Mart, LL Bean, Rite Aid, Shaw's Foods, TJ Maxx, Town Fair Tire, USPO, **W** 🍴 7 Barrel Rest., Applebee's, Burger King, D'angelo's, Denny's, Five Guys, Friendly's, Koto Japanese, McDonald's, Moe's SW Grill, Panera Bread, Pizza Hut, Weathervane Seafood, Wendy's 🏠 Baymont Inn, Fireside Inn 🅞 $Tree, AT&T, Best Buy, BJ's Whse, BooksAMillion, CVS Drug, Home Depot, JC Penney, Kohl's, Midas, PriceChopper Foods, Radio Shack, Sears, Staples, Verizon, Walgreens, Walmart
19 (58)	US 4, NH 10, W Lebanon, **E** 🅟 Gulf/dsl, Shell 🍴 China Station 🅞 AutoZone, Family$, Ford, Harley-Davidson, Honda, Pricechopper Foods, **W** 🅟 Maplewoods/dsl, Sunoco/repair 🅞 Bond Parts
57mm	Welcome Ctr/🆁🆂/weigh sta sb, weigh sta nb, full 🅑 facilities, litter barrels, petwalk, 🅒, 🅟🅰, vending
18 (56)	NH 120, Lebanon, **E** 🅟 Citgo/dsl/scales 🏠 Courtyard (3mi), Days Inn, Residence Inn (2mi) 🅞 🅷 Cadillac/Chevrolet, Chrysler/Dodge/Jeep, Freightliner, Nissan, to Dartmouth Coll, Volvo/VW, Wilson Tire/repair, **W** 🅟 Mobil/Subway/dsl, Shell 🅞 U-Haul
17 (54)	US 4, to NH 4A, Enfield, **E** 🅞 RV Camping, vet
16 (52)	Eastman Hill Rd, **E** 🅟 Gulf/Subway/dsl, **W** 🅟 Mobil/Dunkin Donuts/dsl 🅞 Whaleback Ski Area
15 (50)	Montcalm
14 (47)	NH 10 (from sb), N Grantham
13 (43)	NH 10, Grantham, **E** 🅟 Irving/Gen Store/dsl, **W** 🅟 Irving/Circle K 🍴 Dunkin Donuts, Pizza Chef 🅞 repair, vet
40mm	🆁🆂 nb, full 🅑 facilities, info, litter barrels, petwalk, 🅒, 🅟🅰, vending
12a (37)	Georges Mills, **W** 🅞 food, lodging, 🅒, RV camping, to Sunapee SP
12 (34)	NH 11 W, New London, **E 2 mi** 🅟 Irving/dsl 🍴 McKenna Rest. 🏠 Maple Hill Country Inn, New London Inn 🅞 🅷
11 (31)	NH 11 E, King Hill Rd, New London, **E 2-3 mi** 🍴 Hole in the Fence Cafe 🏠 Fairway Motel, New London Inn, ski area
10 (27)	to NH 114, Sutton, **E** 🅞 to Winslow SP, **W 1 mi** 🏠 lodging 🅞 to Wadleigh SB

W A R N E R

Exit #	Services
26mm	🆁🆂 sb, full 🅑 facilities, info, litter barrels, petwalk, 🅒, 🅟🅰, vending
9 (19)	NH 103, Warner, **E** 🅟 Irving/Circle K/Dunkin Donuts/dsl, Shell/Subway/pizza 🍴 McDonald's 🅞 Aubuchon Hardware, MktBasket Foods, Rollins SP, **W** 🅞 ski area, to Sunapee SP
8 (17)	NH 103 (from nb, no EZ return), Warner, **W 1 mi** 🅟 🍴 food 🅞 museum, to Rollins SP
15mm	Warner River
7 (14)	NH 103, Davisville, **E** 🅞 camping, **W** 🅞 Pleasant Lake Camping
12mm	Contoocook River
6 (10)	NH 127, Contoocook, **E** 🅟 Sunoco 🍴 Country Fair Cafe 🅞 vet, **W** 🅞 Elm Brook Park, Sandy Beach Camping (3mi)
5 (8)	US 202 W, NH 9 (exits left from nb), Hopkinton, **W** 🅞 food, RV camping (seasonal)
4 (7)	NH 103, Hopkinton (from nb, no EZ return), **E** 🅟, 🅞 Horse-Shoe Tavern
3 (4)	Stickney Hill Rd (from nb)
2 (2)	NH 13, Clinton St, Concord, **E** 🅞 🅷, **W** 🅞 NH Audubon Ctr
1 (1)	Logging Hill Rd, Bow, **E** 🅟 Mobil 🍴 Chen Yang Li Chinese 🏠 Hampton Inn
0mm	I-93 N to Concord, S to Manchester, **I-89 begins/ends on I-93, 36mm.**

⬆N INTERSTATE 93

L I T T L E T O N

Exit #	Services
2 (11)	I-91, N to St Johnsbury, S to White River Jct. **I-93 begins/ends on I-91, exit 19.**
1 (8)	VT 18, to US 2, to St Johnsbury, **E 2 mi** 🅟 🍴 food 🏠 camping, lodging
1mm	Welcome Ctr nb, full 🅑 facilities, info, litter barrels, petwalk, 🅒, 🅟🅰, vending
131mm	Vermont/New Hampshire state line, Connecticut River., exits 1-2 are in VT.
44 (130)	NH 18, NH 135, **W** Welcome Ctr (8am-8pm) /scenic vista both lanes, full 🅑 facilities, info, litter barrels, petwalk, 🅒, 🅟🅰
43 (125)	NH 135 (from sb), to NH 18, Littleton, **W 1-2 mi** 🅞 🅷, same as 42
42 (124)	US 302 E, NH 10 N, Littleton, **E** 🅟 Citgo/Quiznos, Gulf, Irving, Sunoco 🍴 Burger King, Deluxe Pizza, Dunkin Donuts, Littleton Diner, Pizza Hut, Subway 🏠 Beal House, Littleton Motel 🅞 Bond Parts, Family$, Rite Aid, USPO, Walgreens, **W** 🅟 Mobil 🍴 99 Rest., Applebee's, Asian Garden, McDonald's 🏠 Hampton Inn 🅞 $Tree, Aubuchan Hardware, Buick/Chevrolet, Chrysler/Dodge/Jeep, Home Depot, KOA (5mi), Lowe's, O'Reilly Parts/VIP Service, Shaw's Foods/Osco Drug, Staples, Tire Whse, TJ Maxx, Verizon, Walmart/Dunkin Donuts
41 (122)	US 302, NH 18, NH 116, Littleton, **E** 🅟 Irving/Circle K/dsl 🏠 Eastgate Motel/rest., Travel Inn 🅞 Littleton Food Co-op, **W** 🅞 NE Tire
40 (121)	US 302, NH 10 E, Bethlehem, **E** 🏠 Adair Country Inn/Rest. 🅞 to Mt Washington
39 (119)	NH 116, NH 18 (from sb), N Franconia, Sugar Hill, **W** 🏠 lodging
38 (117)	NH 116, NH 117, NH 142, NH 18, Sugar Hill, **E** 🏠 Best Western, **W** 🍴 DutchTreat Rest., Wendle's Deli 🅞 camping, Franconia Hardware, Franconia Village Store, Frost Museum, gifts, info, Mac's Mkt, USPO
37 (115)	NH 142, NH 18 (from nb), Franconia, Bethlehem, **W** 🏠 Cannon Mtn View Motel, Hillwinds Lodge 🅞 Franstead Camping
36 (114)	NH 141, to US 3, S Franconia, **W** 🅟 🏠 🅞 golf
35 (113)	US 3 N (from nb), to Twin Mtn Lake
112mm	S Franconia, Franconia Notch SP begins sb
34c	NH 18, S Franconia, Echo Beach Ski Area, info, view area
34b	Cannon Mtn Tramway, **W** 🅞 Boise Rock, Lafayette Place Camping, Old Man Viewing
109mm	trailhead parking
108mm	Lafayette Place Camping, trailhead parking
107mm	The Basin, The Basin
34a	US 3, The Flume Gorge, camping (seasonal), info, The Flume Gorge
104mm	Franconia Notch SP begins nb

W O O D S T O C K

Exit #	Services
33 (103)	US 3, N Woodstock, **E** 🅟 Irving/dsl 🍴 Dad's Rest., Fresolones Pizza, Longhorn Palace Rest., Notchview Country Kitchen 🏠 Beacon Lodge, EconoLodge, Franconia Notch Motel, Green Village Cottages, Indian Head Resort, Mt Coolidge Motel, Pemi Motel, Profile Motel, Rodeway Inn, Woodward's Resort/Rest. 🅞 Indian Head viewing, to Franconia Notch SP, waterpark, **W** 🍴 Sunny Day Diner 🏠 Country Bumpkin Cottages/Camping, Cozy Cabins, Mt Liberty Cabins, White Mtn Motel/Cottages 🅞 Arnold's NAPACare, Clark's Trading Post, Cold Springs Camping, Tim's Repair, vet
32 (101)	NH 112, Loon Mtn Rd, N Woodstock, **E** 🅟 Irving, Mobil, Tedeschi/dsl 🍴 3 Cultures Deli, Black Mtn Burger, Cafe Nacho's, Cheng Garden Chinese, Common Man Rest.,

NH

INTERSTATE 93 Cont'd

Exit #	Services
32 (101)	Continued Dunkin Donuts, Elvio's Pizza, Flapjack's Pancakes, GH Pizza, Gordi's Fish&Steaks, Gypsy Cafe, McDonald's, Subway, White Mtn Bagel Deli 🛏 Comfort Inn, Kancamagu's Lodge, Lincoln Sta. Lodge, Nordic Inn, South Mtn Resort Ⓞ Auburn Hardware, Family$, NAPA, PriceChopper Foods, Rite Aid, USPO, W ⛽ Citgo 🍴 Lafayette Dinner Train, Landmark II Rest., Peg's Café, Truant's Rest., Woodstock Inn Rest. 🛏 Alpine Lodge, Autumn Breeze Motel, Carriage Motel, Cascade Lodge Ⓞ candy/fudge/gifts, USPO
31 (97)	to NH 175, Tripoli Rd, E Ⓞ RV camping (seasonal), W Ⓞ KOA (2mi)
30 (95)	US 3, Woodstock, E 🍴 Lanterns End Grill, Tony's Rest. 🛏 Jack-O-Lantern Inn/rest. Ⓞ golf, W Ⓞ camping (seasonal)
29 (89)	US 3, Thornton, E Ⓞ Pemi River RV Park/LP, W 🛏 Gilcrest Motel
28 (87)	NH 49, Campton, E ⛽ Gulf, Mobil 🍴 Dunkin Donuts, Exit 28 Pizza Ⓞ Handy Man Hardware, RV camping, to ski area, USPO, W ⛽ Irving/dsl 🍴 Sunset Grill Ⓞ Branch Brook Camping, Chesley's Glory Sta., Mtn Vista RV Park, repair
27 (84)	Blair Rd, Beebe River, E 🍴 Country Cow Rest. 🛏 Days Inn, Red Sleigh Condos
26 (83)	US 3, NH 25, NH 3A, Tenney Mtn Hwy, W 🛏 Common Man Inn, EconoLodge, Pilgrim Inn Ⓞ Ⓗ
25 (81)	NH 175 (from nb), Plymouth, W ⛽ Citgo/dsl, Irving/Circle K/dsl 🍴 Downtown Pizza, Fracher's Diner, HongKong Garden, House of Pizza, Lucky Dog Grill, Subway, Thai Smile Ⓞ Ⓗ, Chase St Mkt, Plymouth State U, USPO
24 (76)	US 3, NH 25, Ashland, E ⛽ Gulf, Irving/Circle K/dsl, Mobil 🍴 Ashland Pizza, Burger King, Common Man Diner, Dot's Bistro, Dunkin Dounts, Lucky Dragon Chinese, Village Grill 🛏 Comfort Inn Ⓞ Bob's Mkt, Jellystone RV Camp (4mi), repair, USPO
23 (71)	NH 104, NH 132, to Mt Washington Valley, New Hampton, E ⛽ Irving/Circle K/dsl, Mobil/dsl 🍴 Dunkin Donuts, Rossi Italian, Subway Ⓞ Clearwater Campground, info, Jellystone, USPO, W 🍴 Homestead Rest. (2mi) Ⓞ RV Park (2mi), ski area
22 (62)	NH 127, Sanbornton, W 1-5 mi Ⓞ Ⓗ, food, gas/dsl, Ⓒ
61mm	Ⓡs sb, full ♿ facilities, info, litter barrels, petwalk, Ⓒ, 🏤, vending
20 (57)	US 3, NH 11, NH 132, NH 140, Tilton, E ⛽ Irving/Circle K/dsl/24hr, Shell/Subway/dsl 🍴 99 Rest., Applebees, Burger King, Dunkin Donuts, Green Ginger Chinese, KFC, McDonald's, Starbucks, Thai Cuisine, Tilt'n Diner, UNO, UpperCrust Pizza, Wendy's 🛏 Hampton Inn, Holiday Inn Express, Super 8 Ⓞ BJ's Whse/gas, Home Depot, Old Navy, O'Reilly Parts/VIP Service, Staples, Subaru, Tanger Outlet/famous brands, Walgreens, W 🍴 Chili's, Pizza Hut Ⓞ Chrysler/Dodge/Jeep, Ford, Kohl's, Lowe's, MktBasket Foods, Nissan, USPO, VW, Walmart/Subway
56mm	Winnipesaukee River
19 (55)	NH 132 (from nb no ez return), Franklin, W ⛽ Gulf 🍴 Ciao Italian Ⓞ Ⓗ, antiques, NH Vet Home
51mm	Ⓡs nb, full ♿ facilities, info, litter barrels, petwalk, Ⓒ, 🏤, vending
18 (49)	to NH 132, Canterbury, E ⛽ Gulf Ⓞ to Shaker Village HS
17 (46)	US 4 W, to US 3, NH 132, Boscawen, W 4 mi Ⓒ
16 (41)	NH 132, E Concord, E ⛽ Mobil/dsl Ⓞ Quality Cash Mkt

15W (40)	US 202 W, to US 3, N Main St, Concord, W ⛽ Citgo, Cumberland/Dunkin Donuts, Hess 🍴 Domino's, Friendly's 🛏 Courtyard/café
15E	I-393 E, US 4 E, to Portsmouth
14 (39)	NH 9, Loudon Rd, Concord, E ⛽ Shell/dsl 🍴 Boloco Burritos, Buffalo Wild Wings, Chicago Grill, El Rodeo Mexican, Five Guys, Moritomo Japanese, Panera Brea, Wok Inn Ⓞ $Tree, AAA, Ace Hardware, AutoZone, BooksAMillion, CVS, GNC, Hannaford Foods, LLBean, Lowe's, Meineke, Midas, Mkt Basket Foods, PetCo, Radio Shack, Rite Aid, Shaws Foods/24hr, Staples, TJ Maxx, URGENT CARE, USPO, E 1-2 mi on Loudon Rd ⛽ Irving/Circle K/Subway/ dsl, Mobil, 7-11, Shell/dsl, Sunoco/dsl 🍴 Applebee's, Arnie's Place, Burger King, D'angelo's, Dunkin Donuts, Friendly's, KFC, LJ Silver/Taco Bell, Longhorn Steaks, McDonald's, Newick's Lobster House, 99 Rest., Olive Garden, PapaGino's, Pizza Hut, Red Apple Buffet, Ruby Tuesday, Starbucks, Sunshine Oriental, TGIFriday's, Wendy's, Windmill Rest., Ⓞ Advance Parts, Best Buy, BonTon, Dick's, Home Depot, JC Penney Michael's, Petsmart, Sam's Club/gas, Sears/auto, Shaw's Foods/Osco Drug, Target, Town Fair Tire, Verizon, Walgreens, Walmart, city park, W ⛽ Citgo, Cumberland, Hess 🍴 Domino's, Gas Lighter Rest., Nonni's Rest., Siam Orchid, Tea Garden Rest. 🛏 Holiday Inn Ⓞ hist sites, Jo-Ann, Marshall's, MktBasket, museum, to state offices, vet

C O N C O R D

CONCORD

<table>
<tr><td colspan="2">⬆N **INTERSTATE 93 Cont'd**</td></tr>
<tr><td>Exit #</td><td>Services</td></tr>
<tr><td>13 (38)</td><td>to US 3, Manchester St, Concord, E 🅖 Cumberland, Sunoco/dsl/deli 🍽 Beefside Rest., Brookside Pizza, Cityside Grille, Dunkin Donuts, Ichiban Japanese, Kaylen's Pizza, Red Blazer Rest., Veano's Italian 🄾 Buick/GMC, Cadillac/Chevrolet, Chrysler/Dodge/Jeep, Harley-Davidson, Kia, Nissan, O'Reilly Parts/VIP Service, Outdoor RV Ctr Subaru, Subaru, Tire Whse, Volvo, W 🅖 Hess/dsl, Mobil/dsl 🍽 Burger King, Common Man Diner, D'angelo's, Dunkin Donuts, KFC, McDonald's 🛏 Best Western, Comfort Inn, Fairfield Inn, Residence Inn 🄾 🏥, Aubuchon Hardware, CVS Drug, Firestone, Goodyear/auto</td></tr>
<tr><td>12N (37)</td><td>NH 3A N, S Main, E 🅖 Gulf, Irving/Subway/dsl/24hr 🍽 Dunkin Donuts 🛏 Days Inn 🄾 Ford, Honda, Hyundai, Mazda, Toyota/Scion, W 🄾 🏥</td></tr>
<tr><td>12S</td><td>NH 3A S, Bow Junction</td></tr>
<tr><td>36mm</td><td>I-89 N to Lebanon, **toll road begins/ends**</td></tr>
<tr><td>31mm</td><td>🆁🆂 both lanes, full 🚻 facilities, info, 🄲, vending</td></tr>
<tr><td>11 (28)</td><td>NH 3A, to Hooksett, E 4 mi 🅖 ▨▨▨/dsl/rest., 🄲, **toll plaza**</td></tr>
<tr><td>28mm</td><td>I-293, Everett Tpk</td></tr>
</table>

MANCHESTER

<table>
<tr><td>10 (27)</td><td>NH 3A, Hooksett, E 🅖 Irving/Circle K/dsl 🍽 Dunkin Donuts, Subway, Wendy's 🄾 BJ's Whse, Home Depot, Kohl's, Petco, Target, W 🅖 Irving/Circle K/Dunkin Donuts/dsl, Mr Gas 🄾 Bass Pro Shop, MktBasket Foods, Walmart/Subway</td></tr>
<tr><td>26mm</td><td>Merrimac River</td></tr>
<tr><td>9N S (24)</td><td>US 3, NH 28, Manchester, E 🅖 Irving/Dunkin Donuts/Circle K/dsl 🛏 Fairfield Inn, W 🅖 Manchester/dsl, Sunoco/dsl 🍽 Burger King, Cheng Du Chinese, D'Angelo's, Happy Garden Chinese, La Carreta Mexican, Lusia's Italian, Mr Mac's Cafe, PapaGino's, Puritan Rest., Shorty's Mexican, Subway, Villaggio Ristorante 🄾 🏥, Chrysler/Dodge/Jeep, city park, Hannaford Foods, Kia, Lincoln, O'Reilly Parts/VIP Service, U-Haul</td></tr>
<tr><td>8 (23)</td><td>to NH 28a, Wellington Rd, W 🄾 Currier Gallery, VA 🏥</td></tr>
<tr><td>7 (22)</td><td>NH 101 E, to Portsmouth, Seacoast</td></tr>
<tr><td>6 (21)</td><td>Hanover St, Candia Rd, Manchester, E 🍽 Dunkin Donuts, Wendy's 🄾 vet, W 🅖 Mobil/dsl, Shell 🍽 Dunkin Donuts, McDonald's, Subway 🄾 🏥, GNC, Goodyear/auto, Hannaford Foods</td></tr>
<tr><td>19mm</td><td>I-293 W, to Manchester (from nb), 🄾 to ✈</td></tr>
<tr><td>5 (15)</td><td>NH 28, to N Londonderry, E 🅖 Irving/Dunkin Donuts/dsl, Sunoco/dsl 🍽 Poor Boy's Diner, W 🅖 Shell/dsl 🍽 Subway 🛏 Sleep Inn</td></tr>
</table>

DERRY

<table>
<tr><td>4 (12)</td><td>NH 102, Derry, E 🅖 Mobil/dsl, Mutual, Shell/dsl, Sunoco/dsl, Super 🍽 Burger King, Cracker Barrel, Derry Rest., Juliano's Pizza, Poorboys Drive-In, Subway 🄾 🏥, Advance Parts, R. Frost Farm, W 🅖 7-11, Global, Gulf/dsl/repair, Hess 🍽 99 Rest., Dunkin Donuts, Ginger Garden, KFC/Taco Bell, McDonald's, PapaGino's, Wendy's, Whippersnappers Rest. 🄾 AT&T, Ford, GNC, Hannaford Foods, Home Depot, Mkt Basket Foods, O'Reilly Parts/VIP Service, Shaw's Foods, Staples, TJ Maxx, USPO, Verizon</td></tr>
<tr><td>7mm</td><td>**weigh sta both lanes**</td></tr>
<tr><td>3 (6)</td><td>NH 111, Windham, E 🅖 Mobil/McDonald's 🍽 House of Pizza, Windham Rest. 🄾 URGENT CARE, vet, W 🅖 B&H 🍽 Capri Pizza, Dunkin Donuts, Klemm's Bakery, TJ's Roast Beef, Windham Deli 🄾 Castleton Conference Ctr, CVS Drug, Osco Drug, Shaw's Foods, USPO</td></tr>
<tr><td>2 (3)</td><td>to NH 38, NH 97, Salem, E 🍽 Tuscan Kitchen 🛏 Red Roof Inn, W 🍽 A&A Rest., Blackwater Grill, Dunkin Donuts, Margarita's Cafe 🛏 Holiday Inn, La Quinta 🄾 URGENT CARE</td></tr>
</table>

SALEM

<table>
<tr><td>1 (2)</td><td>NH 28, Salem, E 🅖 BP/dsl, Citgo/dsl, Gulf 🍽 99 Rest., Bickfords, Burger King, Chili's, Denny's, Grand China, LJ Silver, McDonald's, PapaGino's, Taco Bell, T-Bones 🛏 Park View Inn 🄾 AT&T, Barnes&Noble, Best Buy, Home Depot, JC Penney, K-Mart, Kohl's, Lord&Taylor, Macy's, mall, Marshall's, Meineke, Michael's, MktBasket Foods, NTB, PetCo, Petsmart, racetrack, Radio Shack, Sears/auto, Shaw's Foods, Staples, Target, TJ Maxx, TownFair Tire, vet, Walgreens</td></tr>
<tr><td>1mm</td><td>**Welcome Ctr nb, full** 🚻 **facilities, info, litter barrels, petwalk,** 🄲, 🅿, **vending, WiFi**</td></tr>
<tr><td>0mm</td><td>New Hampshire/Massachusetts state line</td></tr>
</table>

<table>
<tr><td colspan="2">⬆N **INTERSTATE 95**</td></tr>
<tr><td>Exit #</td><td>Services</td></tr>
<tr><td>17mm</td><td>New Hampshire/Maine state line, Piscataqua River</td></tr>
<tr><td>7 (16)</td><td>Market St, Portsmouth, Port Authority, E 🛏 Residence Inn, W 0-2 mi 🅖 BP, Mobil 🍽 Applebee's, D'Angelo, Dunkin Donuts, Panera Bread, Qdoba, Ruby Tuesday, Starbucks, Wendy's 🛏 Courtyard, Hampton Inn, Homewood Suites 🄾 $Tree, BJ's Whse/gas, Marshall's, MktBasket Foods, PepBoys, PetCo, Rite Aid, Shaw's Foods, TJ Maxx, Verizon, vet, 🄾 waterfront hist sites</td></tr>
<tr><td>6 (15)</td><td>Woodbury Ave (from nb), Portsmouth, E 🛏 Best Inn, W same as 7</td></tr>
<tr><td>5 (14)</td><td>US 1, US 4, NH 16, The Circle, Portsmouth, E 🅖 Gulf, Shell/dsl 🍽 Roudabout Diner 🛏 Anchorage Inn, Best Inn, Best Western, Fairfield Inn, Holiday Inn, Port Inn 🄾 🏥, Buick/Cadillac/GMC, Chevrolet, U-Haul, W 🍽 Chipotle, Longhorn Steaks, McDonald's 🛏 Hampton Inn, Motel 6, Residence Inn 🄾 Barnes&Noble, Best Buy, Dick's, Ford/Lincoln, Home Depot, Kohl's, Mazda, Michael's, Nissan, Old Navy, Staples, Sullivan Tire, Trader Joe's</td></tr>
<tr><td>4 (13.5)</td><td>US 4 (exits left from nb), to White Mtns, Spaulding TPK, E 🄾 🏥, W 🄾 to Pease Int Trade Port</td></tr>
<tr><td>3a (13)</td><td>NH 33, Greenland</td></tr>
<tr><td>3b (12)</td><td>NH 33, to Portsmouth, E 🄾 🏥, W 0-2 mi 🅖 Sunoco/dsl, TA/Country Pride/dsl/scales/24hr/@ 🍽 Dunkin Donuts, McDonald's 🄾 Lowe's, Mercedes, Target, VW</td></tr>
<tr><td>6.5mm</td><td>**toll plaza**</td></tr>
<tr><td>2 (6)</td><td>NH 101, to Hampton, E 🄾 🏥</td></tr>
<tr><td>4mm</td><td>Taylor River</td></tr>
</table>

SEABROOK

<table>
<tr><td>1 (1)</td><td>NH 107, to Seabrook, **toll rd begins/ends**, E 🅖 BP, Irving/Circle K/dsl, Monster Energy, Prime, Richdale, Sunoco/Subway/dsl, Xtra 🍽 99 Rest., Applebees, Chili's, Dunkin Donuts, Five Guys, HoneyDew Donuts, KFC/Taco Bell, McDonald's, PapaGino's, Pizza Hut, Sal's Pizza, Starbucks, Wendy's 🛏 Hampshire Inn, Holiday Inn Express 🄾 $Tree, Advance Parts, AutoZone, CVS Drug, Dick's, GNC, Home Depot, Jo-Ann Fabrics, Kohl's, Lowe's, Meineke, MktBasket Foods, NTB, Petsmart, Radio Shack, Staples, Sullivan Tire, TJ Maxx, to Seacoast RA, TownFair Tire, Verizon, Walmart, W 🅖 Citgo 🍽 McGrath's Dining 🛏 Seabrook Inn 🄾 NAPA, Sam's Club</td></tr>
<tr><td>.5mm</td><td>**Welcome Ctr nb, full** 🚻 **facilities, litter barrels, petwalk,** 🄲, 🅿, **vending**</td></tr>
<tr><td>0mm</td><td>New Hampshire/Massachusetts state line</td></tr>
</table>

<table>
<tr><td colspan="2">⬆N **INTERSTATE 293**</td></tr>
<tr><td>Exit #</td><td>Services</td></tr>
<tr><td>8 (9)</td><td>I-93, N to Concord, S to Derry. **I-293 begins/ends on I-93, 28mm.**</td></tr>
<tr><td>7 (6.5)</td><td>NH 3A N, Dunbarton Rd (from nb)</td></tr>
<tr><td>6 (6)</td><td>Amoskeag Rd, Singer Park, Manchester, E 🅖 Sunoco/dsl 🛏 La Quinta, W 🅖 Mobil, Shell/dsl 🍽 Dunkin Donuts, Hot Stone Pizza 🄾 🏥</td></tr>
</table>

🅽🅷 NH

INTERSTATE 293 Cont'd

MANCHESTER

Exit #	Services
5 (5)	Granite St, Manchester (from nb, no EZ return), **E** 🍴 World Sports Grill 🏨 Radisson, **W** 🅖 7-11, Gulf 🍴 Dunkin Donuts, Subway Ⓞ Ⓗ, tires, Walgreens
4 (4)	US 3, NH 3A, NH 114A, Queen City Br, **E** 🅖 7-11 Ⓞ Elliott Ⓗ **W on US 3** 🅖 Hess/dsl, Mobil/dsl, Z1 Gas/dsl 🍴 Applebee's, Burger King, Chen's Garden, D'angelo's, DQ, Dunkin Donuts, Ipswich Clambake, KC's Rib Shack, KFC, Little Caesars, McDonald's, Panera Bread, Subway, Taco Bell, T-Bones, Wendy's 🏨 Comfort Inn, EconoLodge Ⓞ Family$, Hannaford Foods, Subaru
3 (3)	NH 101, **W 0-2 mi on US 3** 🍴 Carrabba's, Chipotle, Dunkin Donuts, Fresh Mkt, IHOP, Outback Steaks, Panera Bread, Starbucks 🏨 Country Inn & Suites, Hampton Inn Ⓞ CVS Drug, Kohl's, Lexus, Lowe's, Macy's, Marshalls, Mini, O'Reilly Parts/VIP Service, Radio Shack, Rite Aid, Staples, Target, URGENT CARE, vet
2.5mm	Merrimac River
2 (2)	NH 3A, Brown Ave, **S** 🅖 Mobil/dsl, Shell/Subway/dsl 🍴 Airport Diner, Dunkin Donuts, McDonald's 🏨 Holiday Inn, Super 8 Ⓞ Manchester 🛫

NEW JERSEY

INTERSTATE 78

NEWARK

Exit #	Services
58b a	US 1N, US 9N, NJ Tpk
57	US 1S, US 9S, **N** 🏨 Doubletree, Ramada Inn, **S** 🏨 Courtyard, Fairfield Inn, SpringHill Suites Ⓞ to Newark 🛫
56	Clinton Ave (exits left from eb)
55	Irvington (from wb), **N** 🅖 Hess/dsl 🍴 Burger King, Wendy's, White Castle Ⓞ Ⓗ, AutoZone
54	Hillside, Irvington (from eb), **N** 🅖 Hess/dsl 🍴 Burger King, Wendy's, White Castle Ⓞ Ⓗ, AutoZone
52	Garden State Pkwy
50b a	Millburn (from wb), **N** 🅖 BP, Exxon, Lukoil 🍴 Manny's Wieners Ⓞ Best Buy, Firestone/auto, Ford/Lincoln, Home Depot Superstore, Target, USPO, Whole Foods Mkt
49b a	NJ 124 (from eb), to Maplewood, same as 50b a
48mm	I-78 eb divides into express & local
48	to NJ 24, to I-287 N, (exits left from eb), Springfield
45	NJ 527 (from eb), Glenside Ave, Summit
44	(from eb), to Berkeley Heights, New Providence
43	to New Providence, Berkeley Heights
41	to Berkeley Heights, Scotch Plains
40	NJ 531, The Plainfields, **S** 🅖 Valero Ⓞ Ⓗ
36	NJ 651, to Warrenville, Basking Ridge, **N** 🅖 Exxon 🍴 Dunkin Donuts Ⓞ A&P, **S** 🅖 Exxon
33	NJ 525, to Martinsville, Bernardsville, **N** 🍴 3West Rest., LingLing Chinese, Starbucks 🏨 Courtyard, Hotel Indigo, Somerset Hills Inn Ⓞ USGA Golf Museum, **S** 🅖 Exxon/7-11 🍴 Panera Bread Ⓞ Goodyear/auto, Verizon
32mm	scenic overlook wb
29	I-287, to US 202, US 206, I-80, to Morristown, Somerville, **S** Ⓞ Ⓗ
26	NJ 523 spur, to North Branch, Lamington
24	NJ 523, to NJ 517, to Oldwick, Whitehouse, **S 2-3 mi** 🅖 Exxon/dsl, Gulf/dsl 🍴 Readington Diner, Starbucks, Subway Ⓞ Kings Mkt, Rite Aid

CLINTON

1 (1)	NH 28, S Willow Rd, **N** 🅖 Mobil/dsl, Sunoco/dsl 🍴 5 Guys Burgers, Boston Mkt, Burger King, Cactus Jack's, Chipotle Mexican, Coldstone, D'angelo's, Dunkin Donuts, Friendly's, McDonald's, Panera Bread, Papa John's, PapaGino's, Pizza Hut, Sal's Pizza, Starbucks, Subway, Taco Bell, Wendy's, Yee Dynasty Chinese 🏨 Fairfield Inn, Holiday Inn Express, Sheraton Ⓞ Ⓗ, $Tree, AT&T, AutoZone, Batteries+Bulbs, Buick/GMC, Chevrolet, CVS Drug, Hannaford Foods, Harley-Davidson, Home Depot, Mazda, Mercedes, Michael's, Pep-Boys, PetCo, Petsmart, Radio Shack, Sam's Club, Sullivan Tire/repair, TJ Maxx, TownFair Tire, U-Haul, URGENT CARE, Verizon, vet, VW, **S** 🅖 Shell 🍴 99 Rest., Bertucci's, Chuck-eCheese, D'angelo's, FoodCourt, Great Buffet, La Carreta, Longhorn Steaks, Masa Japanese Steaks, Olive Garden, Red Robin, TGIFriday's, TX Roadhouse 🏨 Courtyard, TownePlace Suites Ⓞ Barnes&Noble, Best Buy, BMW, Ford, Hobby Lobby, Honda, Hyundai, JC Penney, LL Bean, Macy's, mall, Nissan, NTB, Old Navy, Sears/auto, Staples, Toyota/Scion, Walmart/Subway
0mm	I-93, N to Concord, S to Derry. **I-293 begins/ends on I-93.**
20b a	NJ 639 (from wb), to Cokesbury, Lebanon, **S** 🅖 Exxon, Shell/dsl, Sunoco 🍴 Cutting Board Deli, Dunkin Donuts, Janina Bistro, Kirsten's Italian 🏨 Courtyard Ⓞ to Round Valley RA, vet
18	US 22 E, Annandale, Lebanon, **N** same as 17, **S** Ⓞ Ⓗ, Honda
17	NJ 31 S, Clinton, **N** 🅖 Exxon, Hess, Valero/dsl 🍴 Baskin-Robbins/Dunkin Donuts, Blimpie, Country Griddle, Finnigal's, McDonald's Ⓞ STS Tire/auto, to Voorhees SP
16	NJ 31 N (from eb), Clinton, **N** same as 17
15	NJ 173 E, to Pittstown, Clinton, **N** 🅖 Express/repair, Shell/dsl 🍴 Subway 🏨 Holiday Inn Ⓞ museum, **S** 🍴 Cracker Barrel, Frank's Italian, Hunan Wok, Quiznos 🏨 Hampton Inn Ⓞ Ⓗ GNC, ShopRite Foods, TJMaxx, Verizon, Walmart/Dunkin Donuts
13	NJ 173 W (from wb), **N** 🍴 Clinton Sta Diner, same as 12
12	NJ 173, to Jutland, Norton, **N** 🅖 Clinton/dsl, Exxon/Dunkin Donuts/dsl, 🛢/Subway/dsl/scales/24hr 🍴 Grand Colonial Rest. Ⓞ to Spruce Run RA, vet, **S** 🅖 Shell 🍴 Bagelsmith Deli
11	NJ 173, West Portal, Pattenburg, **N** 🅖 Mobil, Shell/pizza/dsl 🍴 Chalet Rest., Landslide Rest. Ⓞ Jugtown Camping, st police
8mm	🅡ˢ **both lanes, litter barrels, no restrooms,** 🛳
7	NJ 173, to Bloomsbury, West Portal, **N** Ⓞ RV camping, **S** 🅖 Citgo/deli, 🛢/Subway/dsl/scales/24hr, TA/Burger King/Country Pride/dsl/scales/24hr/@
6mm	**weigh sta both lanes**
6	Warren Glen, Asbury (from eb)
4	Warren Glen, Stewartsville (from wb)
3	US 22, NJ 173, to Phillipsburg, **N 0-2 mi** 🅖 BP/dsl, Hess/dsl, Mobil/Subway/dsl, Penn Jersey Trkstp/dsl/scales/24hr, US/dsl, Wawa 🍴 Applebee's, Burger King, Chick-fil-A, Dunkin Donuts, Frank's Trattoria, Friendly's, Key City Diner, McDonald's, Panera Bread, Perkins, Pizza Hut, Quaker Steak, Ruby Tuesday, Taco Bell, Teppanyaki, White Castle 🏨 Best Value Ⓞ Ⓗ, $Tree, Advance Parts, AutoZone, Best Buy,

INTERSTATE 78 Cont'd

Exit #	Services
3	Continued
	BonTon, Hobby Lobby, Home Depot, Honda, Kohl's, Lowe's, Marshall's, Meineke, Michael's, PetCo, Sears/auto, ShopRite Foods, Staples, Stop&Shop, Target, Walmart/Subway, **S** 🔣 Hyundai
0mm	New Jersey/Pennsylvania state line, Delaware River

INTERSTATE 80

Exit #	Services
I-80 begins/ends on I-95, exit 69.	
68b a	I-95, N to New York, S to Philadelphia, to US 46
68	Leonia, Teaneck, **N** 🔣 Marriott 🔣 🔣
67	to Bogota (from eb)
66	Hudson St, to Hackensack
65	Green St, S Hackensack
64b a	NJ 17 S, to US 46 E, Newark, Paramus, **S** 🔣 BP/dsl 🔣 Crow's Nest Rest. 🔣 Hilton 🔣 PathMark Foods, Stop&Shop
63	NJ 17 N, **N** 🔣 BP, Exxon/dsl, Hess/dsl, Mobil/dsl, Sunoco, Wawa/dsl 🔣 Burger King, Five Guys, Longhorn Steaks, Outback Steaks 🔣 🔣, Acura, BMW, Harley-Davidson, Home Depot
62b a	GS Pkwy, to Saddle Brook, **N** 🔣 Dunkin Donuts 🔣 Holiday Inn, Marriott, **S** 🔣 Crowne Plaza
61	NJ 507, to Garfield, Elmwood Park, **N** Marcal Paper Co
60	NJ 20, N to Hawthorne, **N** 🔣 🔣, Lowe's, Michelin/Cooper Tires, Pepboys
59	Market St (from wb), to Paterson
58b a	Madison Ave, to Paterson, Clifton, **S** 🔣 🔣
57c	Main St (from wb), to Paterson
57b a	NJ 19 S, to Clifton, downtown Paterson
56b a	Squirrelwood Rd, to Paterson, **S** 🔣 Lukoil/Dunkin Donuts
55b a	Union Blvd (from wb, no EZ return), Totowa, **N** 🔣 Shell/dsl, **S** 🔣 Holiday Inn 🔣 Cadillac
54	Minnisink Rd, to Paterson, **S** 🔣 Dunkin Donuts 🔣 Home Depot, mall
53	US 46 E, to NJ 3 (no eb return), to Wayne, Cliffton, **S** 0-2 mi 🔣 Exxon 🔣 Applebee's, Bahama Breeze, Brio Tuscan Grill, CA Pizza, Chipotle, IHOP, Olive Garden, Ruby Tuesday, Sonic, TGIFriday's 🔣 Bloomingdale's, Costco/gas, Hobby Lobby, JC Penney, Lord&Taylor, Macy's, Nissan, Office Depot, Old Navy, Sears/auto
52	US 46, the Caldwells
48	to Montville (from wb), Pine Brook
47b	US 46 W, to Montclair, **N** 🔣 Sunoco 🔣 Five Guys, Longhorn Steaks, Wendy's 🔣 Holiday Inn 🔣 ShopRite Foods
47a	I-280 E, to The Oranges, Newark
45	to US 46, Lake Hiawatha, Whippany, **N** 0-2 mi on US 46 🔣 BP/dsl, Gulf/dsl, Sunoco/dsl 🔣 5 Guys Burgers, Applebee's, Buffalo Wild Wings, Burger King, Eccola Rest., Empire Diner, Franco's Pizza, IHOP, Jasper Chinese, KFC, Longhorn Steaks, McDonald's, Moe's SW Grill, Outback Steaks, Pure Rest., Quin Dynasty, Sakura Japanese, Smashburger, Subway, Taco Bell, Wendy's 🔣 Budget Inn, Holiday Inn/rest., Howard Johnson, Ramada Ltd, Red Roof Inn 🔣 $Tree, Firestone, Home Depot, K-Mart, Michael's, PathMark Foods, PepBoys, PetCo, Radio Shack, ShopRite Foods, Staples, Verizon, Walgreens

Exit #	Services
43b a	I-287, to US 46, Boonton, Morristown
42b a	US 202, US 46, to Morris Plains, Parsippany, **N** 0-1 mi on US 46 🔣 76/Dunkin Donuts/dsl, Exxon 🔣 Fuddrucker's, McDonald's, TGIFriday's, Wendy's 🔣 Courtyard, Days Inn, Fairfield Inn, Hampton Inn 🔣 Marshall's, same as 39, Subaru
39	(38 from eb), US 46 E, to NJ 53, Denville, **N** 0-2 mi on US 46 🔣 Citgo/dsl, Enrite Gas, Exxon, Hess/Dunkin Donuts, Sunoco 🔣 Burger King, Casa Bella Italian, Charlie Brown's Steaks, Dunkin Donuts, Moe's SW Grill, Paul's Diner, Wendy's 🔣 🔣 Chevrolet, Verizon, Walgreens, **S** 🔣 Delta
37	NJ 513, to Hibernia, Rockaway, **N** 🔣 Exxon/dsl, Shell 🔣 Barn Rest., Dunkin Donuts, Hibernia Diner 🔣 Hampton Inn, Rockaway Hotel, **S** 🔣 BP 🔣 🔣
35b a	to Dover, Mount Hope, **S** 🔣 Exxon 🔣 Buffalo Wild Wings, Chipotle, Coldstone, Dunkin Donuts, La Salsa Mexican, Olive Garden, Quiznos, Red Robin, Tiff's Burger 🔣 Hilton Garden, Homewood Suites 🔣 🔣, Best Buy, JC Penney, Lord&Taylor, Macy's, mall, Michael's, Sears/auto, Verizon
34b a	NJ 15, to Sparta, Wharton, **N** 🔣 Exxon/dsl 🔣 Fortune Buffet 🔣 Rite Aid, **S** 🔣 Dunkin Donuts, Good 5 Chinese, Panera Bread, Qdoba, Starbucks, Townsquare Diner 🔣 🔣, $Tree, Big Lots, Costco/gas, Dick's, Home Depot, Petsmart, ShopRite Foods, Target, Walmart
32mm	truck 🔣 wb
30	Howard Blvd, to Mt Arlington, **N** 🔣 Exxon/dsl 🔣 Blossom Asian, Cracker Barrel, Davy's Hotdogs, Dunkin Donuts, Frank's Pizza, Wingman 🔣 Courtyard, Holiday Inn Express 🔣 QuickChek Foods
28	US 46, to NJ 10, to Ledgewood, Lake Hopatcong, **S** 1-2 mi on US 46, NJ 10 🔣 Delta Gas, Hess/dsl, Sunoco/dsl 🔣 Boston Mkt, Domino's, Dunkin Donuts, Fuddruckers, KFC/LJ Silver, McDonald's, Muldoons Diner, Outback Steaks, Panera Bread, Pizza Hut, Red Lobster, Ruby Tuesday, Taco Bell, TGIFriday's, Wendy's, White Castle 🔣 AutoZone, Barnes&Noble, BJ's Whse, CVS Drug, Home Depot, Jo-Ann, Kohl's, Petco, ShopRite Foods, Walgreens, Walmart
27	US 206 S, NJ 182, to Netcong, Somerville, **N** 🔣 Valero/dsl 🔣 Dunkin Donuts 🔣 Ford, **S** 🔣 Shell/dsl 🔣 Applebee's, Chili's, Longhorn Steaks, Macaroni Grill, McDonald's, Panera Bread, Subway, Wendy's 🔣 Extended Stay America 🔣 $Tree, Lowe's, Michael's, Old Navy, Petsmart, Sam's Club, TJMaxx, Walmart
26	US 46 W (from wb, no EZ return), to Budd Lake, **S** 🔣 same as 27, Shell/dsl
25	US 206 N, to Newton, Stanhope, **N** 1-2 mi on US 206 🔣 Exxon/dsl, Shell/dsl 🔣 Blackforest Rest., Byram Diner, Byram Pizza, Dunkin Donuts, Empire Buffet, Frank's Pizza, McDonald's, Subway 🔣 Holiday Inn, Residence Inn 🔣 CVS Drug, GNC, Int Trade Ctr, Nissan, ShopRite Foods, STS tires/repair, to Waterloo Village, vet
23.5mm	Musconetcong River
21mm	scenic overlook (eb), 🔣 area both lanes, litter barrels, no facilities, petwalk, 🔣
19	NJ 517, to Hackettstown, Andover, **N** 🔣 Shell/dsl 🔣 RV camping, **S** 1-2 mi 🔣 Shell/dsl/repair 🔣 Terranova Pizza 🔣 Panther Valley Inn/rest. 🔣 🔣, 7-11, Stephen's SP, USPO
12	NJ 521, to Blairstown, Hope, **N** 🔣 Mediterranean Diner 🔣 Harley-Davidson, st police, **S** 🔣 US Gas 🔣 Hope Mkt Deli 🔣 Jenny Jump SF, Land of Make Believe, RV camping (5mi), USPO
7mm	🔣 eb, full 🔣 facilities, info, litter barrels, petwalk, 🔣, 🔣, vending

PATERSON (vertical side label left margin)
STANHOPE (vertical side label right margin)
NJ (tab marker left margin)

INTERSTATE 80 Cont'd

Exit #	Services
6mm	scenic overlook wb, no trailers
4c	to NJ 94 N (from eb), to Blairstown
4b	to US 46 E, to Buttzville
4a	NJ 94, to US 46 E, to Portland, Columbia, N 🅖 TA/Pizza Hut/Taco Bell/dsl/scales/24hr/@ 🍴 McDonald's 🅾 RV camping, S 🅾 USPO
3.5mm	Hainesburg Rd (from wb), accesses services at 4
2	weigh sta eb
1mm	Worthington SF
1	to Millbrook (from wb), N 🅾 Worthington SF
0mm	New Jersey/Pennsylvania state line, Delaware River

INTERSTATE 95

Exit #	Services
124mm	New Jersey/New York state line, Hudson River, Geo Washington Br.
123mm	Palisades Pkwy (from sb)
73	NJ 67, Lemoine Ave, W 🅖 Sunoco 🍴 Five Guys, McDonald's 🅾 A&P Mkt, GNC, Verizon, Walgreens
72 (122)	US 1, US 9, US 46, Ft Lee, E 🛏 Doubletree, W 🅖 Sunoco 🍴 McDonald's
71 (121)	Broad Ave, Leonia, Englewood, E 🅖 Lukoil, W 🛏 Holiday Inn
70 (120)	to NJ 93,, Leonia, Teaneck, W 🛏 Marriott
69 (119)	I-80 W (from sb), to Paterson
68 (118)	US 46, Challenger Blvd, Ridgefield Park, E 🅖 Exxon 🍴 Lan Garden Chinese 🛏 Day's Inn, Hampton Inn, Hilton Garden

I-95 and NJ Turnpike run together sb. See NJ TPK, exits 7a-18

I-95 nb becomes I-295 sb at US 1.

67b a	US 1, to Trenton, New Brunswick, E 🅖 Shell 🍴 Michael's Diner 🛏 Howard Johnson, Sleepy Hollow Motel 🅾 Acura, W 0-3 mi 🅖 Gulf, LukOil/dsl 🍴 Applebee's, Big Fish Bistro, Cheeburger Cheeburger, Chevy's Mexican, Chili's, ChuckE-Cheese's, Dunkin Donuts, Hooters, Houlihan's, Joe's Crabshack, Macaroni Grill, NY Deli, Olive Garden, On-the-Border, Panera Bread, PF Chang's, Princetonian Diner, Pure Rest., Red Lobster, Rita's Custard, Starbucks, Subway, TGIFriday's, Wendy's 🛏 Clarion, Comfort Inn, Extended Stay America, Hyatt Place, Hyatt Regency, Red Roof Inn, Residence Inn 🅾 AT&T, Barnes&Noble, Best Buy, Buick/Cadillac, Chevrolet, Dick's, Firestone/auto, Home Depot, JC Penney, Jo-Ann Fabrics, Kohl's, Lord&Taylor, Lowe's, Macy's, malls, Marshall's, Michael's, Mini, NTB, Office Depot, Old Navy, PepBoys, PetCo, Petsmart, Ross, Sam's Club, Sears/auto, ShopRite Foods, Staples, Target, TJ Maxx, Trader Joe's, Verizon, Walmart, Wegman's Foods, Whole Foods Mkt
8b a	NJ 583, NJ 546, to Princeton Pike
7b a	US 206, W 🅖 LukOil/dsl 🍴 Fox's Pizza, Tastee Subs
5b a	Federal City Rd (sb only)
4b a	NJ 31, to Ewing, Pennington, E 🅖 Citgo/repair, Exxon/repair, LukOil/Dunkin Donuts/dsl 🛏 SpringHill Suites 🅾 7-11, Robbins Drug, USPO, W 🅖 Exxon, LukOil/Blimpie/dsl 🍴 Mizuki Asian, Starbucks 🅾 AT&T, ShopRite Foods, Stop&Shop Foods
3b a	Scotch Rd, E 🛏 Courtyard, W 🅾 🅗

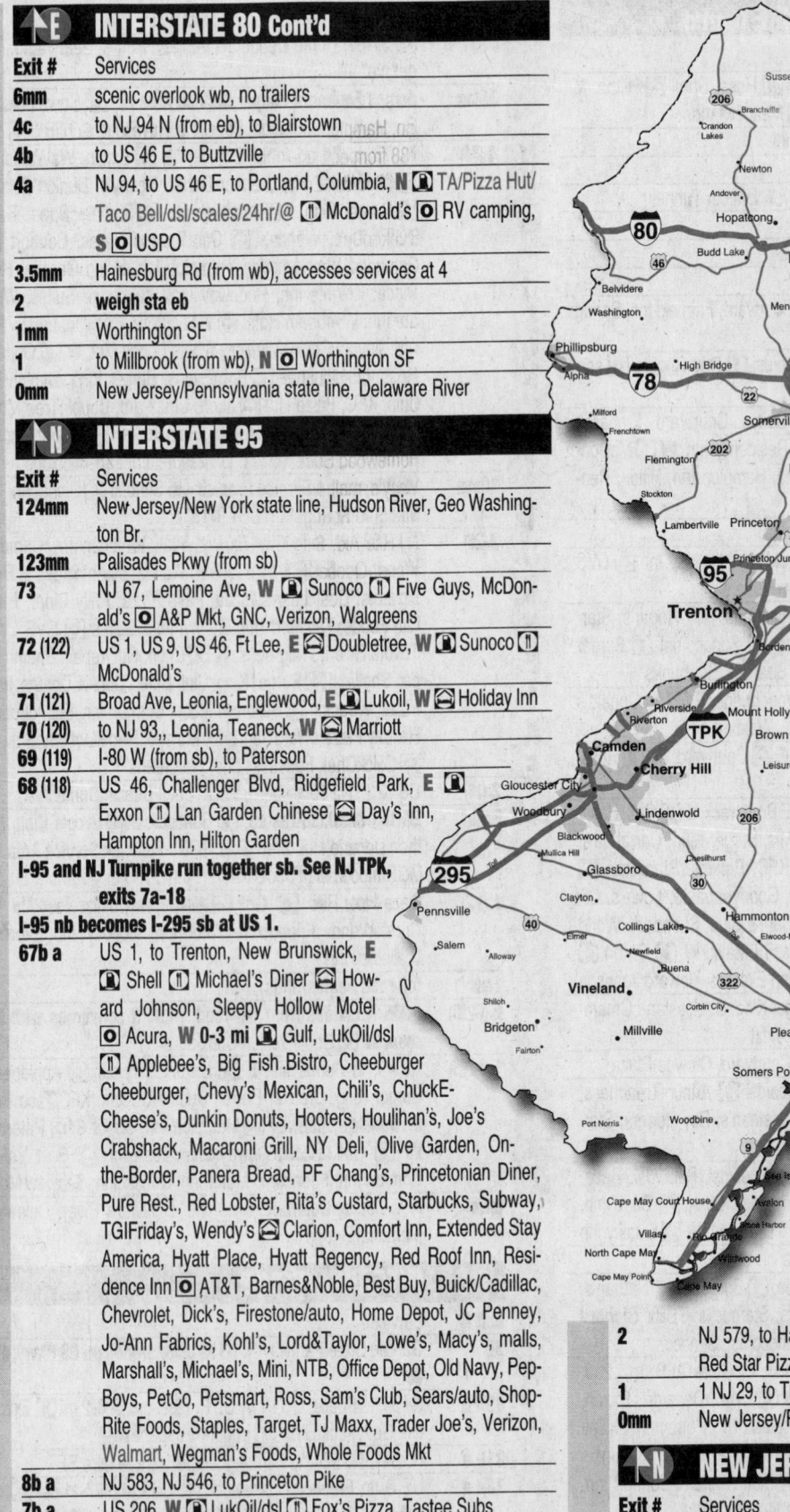

2	NJ 579, to Harbourton, E 🅖 LukOil (1mi) 🍴 Dunkin Donuts, Red Star Pizza 🅾 7-11, W 🅖 BP
1	1 NJ 29, to Trenton, W 2 mi 🅖 🅾 museum, st police
0mm	New Jersey/Pennsylvania state line, Delaware River

NEW JERSEY TURNPIKE

Exit #	Services
18 (117)	US 46 E, Ft Lee, Hackensack, last exit before toll sb
17 (116)	Lincoln Tunnel
115mm	**Vince Lombardi Service Plaza nb**, W 🅖 Sunoco/dsl, 🍴 Burger King, Nathan's, Popeye's
114mm	toll plaza, 🅒
112mm	**Alexander Hamilton Service Area sb**, 🅖 Sunoco/dsl 🍴 Roy Rogers 🅾 gifts

T R E N T O N

NJ

N | **NEW JERSEY TURNPIKE Cont'd**

NEW JERSEY TURNPIKE

Exit #	Services
16W (113)	NJ 3, Secaucus, Rutherford, **E** 🅕 Hess, Shell 🅛 Hilton, M Plaza Hotel, **W** 🅛 Sheraton 🅞 Meadowlands
16E (112)	NJ 3, Secaucus, **E** Lincoln Tunnel
15W (109)	I-280, Newark, The Oranges
15E (107)	US 1, US 9, Newark, Jersey City, **E** Lincoln Tunnel
14c	Holland Tunnel
14b	Jersey City
14a	Bayonne
14 (105)	I-78 W, US 1, US 9, **W 2 mi** 🅛 Courtyard, Fairfield Inn, Spring Hill Suites 🅞 🅓
102mm	**Halsey Service Area**, 🅖 Sunoco/dsl 🅕 Roy Rogers 🅞 services in Elizabeth
13a (102)	Elizabeth, **E** 🅛 Country Inn Suites, Courtyard, Embassy Suites, Extended Stay America, Residence Inn, **W** 🅕 McDonald's 🅛 Crowne Plaza, Days Inn, Hampton Inn, Hilton, Renaisance, services on US1/US9
13 (100)	I-278, to Verrazano Narrows Bridge
12 (96)	Carteret, Rahway, **E** 🅕 McDonald's 🅛 Holiday Inn 🅞 CVS Drug, Walgreens, **W** 🅛 Executive Suites
93mm	**Cleveland Service Area nb** 🅕 Nathans, Roy Roger's, Starbucks **T Edison Service Area sb** 🅖 Sunoco/dsl 🅕 Burger King, Dunkin Donuts, Popeye's, Sbarro's, Starbucks
11 (91)	US 9, Garden State Pkwy, to Woodbridge, **E** 🅕 McDonald's 🅛 Hampton Inn 🅞 Home Depot, Walmart
10 (88)	I-287, NJ 514, to Perth Amboy, **E** 🅛 Courtyard, **W** 🅖 Hess/dsl 🅛 Holiday Inn
9 (83)	US 1, NJ 18, to New Brunswick, E Brunswick, **E** 🅖 Gulf, Hess/dsl 🅕 Bone Fish Grill, Boston Mkt, Burger King, Carrabba's, Dunkin Donuts, Grand Buffet, KFC, Perkins, Starbucks 🅛 Days Inn, Motel 6 🅞 Best Buy, Goodyear/auto, Lowe's, Office Depot, Petsmart, Rite Aid, Sam's Club, Shopper's World Foods, ShopRite Foods, Staples, TJ Maxx, **W** 🅖 Exxon 🅕 Fuddruckers 🅛 Hilton, Holiday Inn Express, Howard Johnson
79mm	**Kilmer Service Area nb** 🅕 Burger King, Cookies and Creamery, Sbarro, Starbucks 🅞 Sunoco/dsl
8a (74)	to Jamesburg, Cranbury, **W** 🅛 Courtyard, Crowne Plaza
72mm	**Pitcher Service Area**, 🅖 Sunoco/dsl 🅕 Arthur Treacher's, Cinnabon, Dick Clark's AB Grill, Nathan's, Roy Rogers, Starbucks
8 (67)	NJ 33, NJ 571, Highstown, **E** 🅖 Hess/dsl, Petro/dsl, RaceWay, Shell/Dunkin Donuts 🅕 Prestige Diner 🅛 Days Inn, Hampton Inn, Holiday Inn 🅞 CVS Drug, vet, **W** 🅛 Quality Inn
7a (60)	I-195 W to Trenton, E to Neptune
59mm	**Woodrow Wilson Service Area nb** 🅕 Burger King, Nathan's, Pizza Hut, Quiznos, Roy Rogers, Starbucks, TCBY **Richard Stockton Service Area sb** 🅛 Sunoco/dsl, Sunoco
7 (54)	US 206, to Bordentown, to Ft Dix, McGuire AFB, to I-295, Trenton **W Services on US 206** 🅖 Citgo, Delta/dsl, Exxon, Gulf, 🅛Loves/Wendy's/dsl/scales/24hr, Petro/Iron Skillet/dsl/scales/24hr/@, Sunoco, Valero/dsl 🅕 Denny's, Dunkin Donuts, McDonald's, Wendy's 🅛 Best Western, Comfort Inn, Days Inn, Hampton Inn, Ramada Inn 🅞 WaWa
6 (51)	I-276, to PA Tpk
5 (44)	to Mount Holly, Willingboro, **E** 🅖 US Gas/dsl 🅕 Applebee's, Charlie Brown's Steaks, Cracker Barrel, McDonald's, Recovery Grill 🅛 Best Western, Hampton Inn, Hilton Garden, Quality Inn, **W** 🅖 BP, Exxon/dsl, Valero/dsl 🅕 Burger King, China House, ChuckECheese's, Dunkin Donuts, IHOP, Quiznos, Subway, TGIFriday's 🅛 Courtyard, Holiday Inn Express

Exit #	Services
5 (44)	Continued 🅞 $Tree, Home Depot, JC Penney, Kohl's, Sears/auto, Target, vet
39mm	**James Fenimore Cooper Service Area nb**, 🅖 Sunoco/dsl 🅕 Burger King, Cinnabon, Popeye's, Roy Rogers, TCBY 🅞 gifts
4 (34)	NJ 73, to Philadelphia, Camden, **E** 🅖 Exxon, WaWa/dsl 🅕 Chick-fil-A, Chili's, Cracker Barrel, Denny's, Dunkin Donuts, Macaroni Grill, McDonald's, On-the-Border, Sage Rest., TGIFriday's, Wendy's 🅛 Candlewood Suites, Comfort Inn, Extended Stay America, Hampton Inn, Hilton Garden, Hyatt Place, Knights Inn, Rodeway Inn, Staybridge Suites, Wingate Inn, Wyndham Hotel 🅞 7-11, BMW, Cadillac, Lexus, Rite Aid, Toyota/Scion, Verizon, Whole Foods Mkt, **W** 🅖 Gulf/dsl, Hess, Lukoil, Shell 🅕 Bob Evans, Burger King, Dunkin Donuts, KFC, Pizza Hut 🅛 aLoft, Courtyard, DoubleTree Motel, Fairfield Inn, Marriott, Motel 6, Ramada Inn, Red Roof Inn, Super 8 🅞 Lincoln, Mazda, to st aquarium, transmissions
30mm	**Walt Whitman Service Area sb**, 🅖 Sunoco 🅕 Cinnabon, Nathan's, Roy Rogers, TCBY 🅞 gifts
3 (26)	NJ 168, Atlantic City Expwy, Walt Whitman Br, Camden, Woodbury, **E** 🅖 7-11, Pioneer, WaWa 🅕 Antonietta's, Bella Rizzo's Pizza, Luigi's Pizza, Pat's Pizza, Phily Diner, Rita's Custard 🅛 Comfort Inn, Runnymead Suites 🅞 CVS Drug, Toyota/Scion, Walgreens, **W** 🅖 Citgo, Gulf/repair, Shamrock/dsl, Shell/dsl 🅕 Burger King, Club Diner, Dunkin Donuts, Italia Pizza, Wendy's 🅛 Bellmawr Motel, Comfort Inn, EconoLodge, Holiday Inn, Howard Johnson, Motel 6, Red Roof Inn, Super 8 🅞 CVS Drug, transmissions, Walgreens
2 (13)	US 322, to Swedesboro, **W** 🅖 Shell/Dunkin Donuts/dsl
5mm	**Barton Service Area sb**, 🅖 Sunoco/dsl 🅕 Burger King, Nathan's, Pizza Hut, Starbucks, TCBY **Fenwick Service Area nb**, 🅖 Sunoco/dsl 🅕 TCBY
1 (1.2)	Deepwater, **W** 🅖 Gulf,🚚/Subway/dsl/scales/24hr 🅛 Comfort Inn, Friendship Motor Inn, Holiday Inn Express, Wellesley Inn
1mm	**toll road begins/ends**
2 (I-295)	**I-295 N divides from toll road, I-295 S converges with toll road**, **W** 🅖 Shell/Dunkin Donuts/dsl
1 (I-295)	NJ 49, to Pennsville, **E** 🅖 Exxon/dsl/repair 🅕 Applebees, Burger King, Cracker Barrel, Dunkin Donuts, KFC/Taco Bell, McDonald's, Subway 🅛 Hampton Inn, Super 8 🅞 Peterbilt, **W** 🅖 Gulf,🚚/Subway/dsl/scales/24hr 🅛 Best Value, Comfort Inn, Friendship Motor Inn, Quality Inn, Seaview Motel
0mm	New Jersey/Delaware state line, Delaware River, Delaware Memorial Bridge

E | **INTERSTATE 195**

Exit #	Services
36	Garden State Parkway N. **I-195 begins/ends on GS Pkwy, exit 98.**
35b a	NJ 34, to Brielle, GS Pkwy S., Pt Pleasant, **S 0-2 mi** 🅖 Exxon/dsl, Getty, Lukoil/dsl 🅕 Legends Japanese
31b a	NJ 547, NJ 524, to Farmingdale, **N** 🅞 to Allaire SP
28b a	US 9, to Freehold, Lakewood, **N** 🅖 LukOil/7-11/dsl 🅕 Ivy League Grill, Stewart's Drive-In 🅛 At 9 Motel, **S** 🅖 Exxon, Getty, Gulf, LukOil, WaWa 🅕 5 Guys Burgers, Applebee's, Arby's, Baskin-Robbins/Dunkin Donuts, Boston Mkt, Burger King, Carino's, Chick-fil-A, China Moon, Coldstone, Domino's, Jersey Mike's Subs, Longhorn Steaks, Luigi's Pizza, McDonald's, Panera Bread, Pizza Hut, Rojo Loco, Ruby Tuesday, Sonic, Starbucks, Taco Bell 🅛 Capri Inn 🅞 Barnes&Noble, Best Buy, GNC, K-Mart, Kohl's, Lowe's, Michael's,

⬆️E INTERSTATE 195 Cont'd

Exit #	Services
28b a	Continued PathMark Foods, PepCo, PetCo, Petsmart, Radio Shack, repair, Staples, Stop&Shop, Target, TJ Maxx, USPO, Verizon, Walgreens, Walmart/McDonald's
22	to Jackson Mills, Georgia, **N** 🅞 to Turkey Swamp Park, **S 2 mi** 🍴 McDonald's 🅞 ShopRite Foods
21	NJ 526, NJ 527, to Jackson, Siloam
16	NJ 537, to Freehold, **N** ⛽ Remington/dsl/LP, Sunoco 🍴 DQ, FoodCourt, GianMarco's Pizza, Java Moon Café 🅞 🏠, Jackson Outlets/famous brands, **S** ⛽ WaWa/dsl 🍴 BellaV Pizzaria, Burger King, Chicken Holiday, Dunkin Donuts, KFC/LJ Silver, McDonald's, McGinns Pizzaria, Rio Grande Mexican, Tommy's Rest. 🅞 6Flags Themepark
11	NJ 524, Imlaystown, **S** 🅞 to Horse Park of NJ
8	NJ 539, Hightstown, Allentown, **S** ⛽ Shell (1mi), Valero/repair 🍴 American Hero Deli 🅞 Crosswicks HP, vet
7	NJ 526 (no eb return), Robbinsville, Allentown, **S 1 mi** 🍴 La Piazza Ristorante
6	NJ Tpk, N to NY, S to DE Memorial Br
5b a	US 130, **N** ⛽ Delta/dsl/repair, Valero/dsl 🍴 Domino's, Dunkin Donuts, Rusert's Deli, ShrimpKing Rest. 🅞 AAA, Harley-Davidson, vet, **S** ⛽ GS Fuel/dsl 🍴 Chick-fil-A, Chili's, China Grill, Cracker Barrel, DQ, Jersey Mike's Subs, Longhorn Steaks, McDonald's, Outback Steaks, Panera Bread, Red Robin, Ruby Tuesday, Subway, TGIFriday's, Wendy's 🏠 Hilton Garden 🅞 $Tree, AT&T, Barnes&Noble, BJ's Whse, GNC, Hamilton Shops/famous brands, Harry's Army Navy, Home Depot, Kohl's, Lowe's, mall, Michael's, Old Navy, Petsmart, Ross, ShopRite Foods, Staples, to state aquarium, USPO, Verizon, Walmart
3b a	Hamilton Square, Yardville, **N** 🅞 🏠
2	US 206 S, S Broad St, Yardville, **N** 🍴 Rosa's Ristorante, **S** ⛽ Shell, Valero 🍴 Subway 🅞 7-11, CVS Drug, Rite Aid
1b a	US 206 (eb only), **N** 🍴 Circle Deli, Taco Bell 🅞 Advance Parts, **S** 🍴 Papa John's 🅞 ShopRite Foods
0mm	**I-295, I-195 begins/ends.**

⬆️N INTERSTATE 287

Exit #	Services
68mm	New Jersey/New York state line
66	NJ 17 S, Mahwah, **E 1-3 mi** ⛽ Gulf, Liberty/dsl, Mobil/dsl, [illegible]/dsl, Sunoco/dsl, Valero/Subway/dsl 🍴 Boston Mkt, Burger King, Dunkin Donuts, McDonald's 🏠 Comfort Suites, Courtyard, Doubletree, Hampton Inn, Homewood Suites, Sheraton, Super 8 🅞 Buick/GMC, Cadillac, Chrysler/Dodge/Jeep, Home Depot, Honda, Hyundai
59	NJ 208 S, Franklin Lakes
58	US 202, Oakland, **E** ⛽ Lukoil/dsl 🍴 Jr's Pizza, Mike's Doghouse, Starbucks, Subway 🅞 $Tree, Staples, USPO, Walgreens, **W** ⛽ Exxon
57	Skyline Dr, Ringwood
55	NJ 511, Pompton Lakes, **E** 🍴 Frank's Pizza, Quizno's, Starbucks, Subway, Thatcher McGhee Eatery, Wendy's 🅞 A&P, **W** ⛽ Gulf/dsl 🍴 Baskin-Robbins, Burger King, Dunkin Donuts 🏠 Holiday Inn Express 🅞 CVS Drug, Stop'n Shop
53	NJ 511A, rd 694, Bloomingdale, Pompton Lakes, **E** ⛽ Sunoco, Valero 🍴 Blimpie 🅞 USPO
52b a	NJ 23, Riverdale, Wayne, Butler, **E 0-3 mi** ⛽ Delta, Gulf, Hess/dsl, Lukoil, Valero/dsl 🍴 23 Buffet, Moe's SW Grill,

Exit #	Services
52b a	Continued Pompton Queen Diner, Stefano's Pizza 🅞 🏠, GNC, Honda, Pepboys, Radio Shack, Stop&Shop, TJ Maxx, Toyota/Scion, VW, **W** ⛽ Lukoil, Lukoil 🍴 Applebees, Chili's, Dunkin Donuts, Mangia Pizza, NJ Buffet, Subway, Wendy's 🅞 Best Buy, BJ's Whse, Harley-Davidson, Home Depot, Jo-Ann, Lowes Whse, Staples, Target, Walmart
47	US 202, Montville, Lincoln Park, **E** ⛽ Exxon 🍴 Harrigan's Rest., Montville Inn Rest.
45	Myrtle Ave, Boonton, **W** ⛽ Hess, Shell/dsl 🍴 Dunkin Donuts, McDonald's, Subway 🅞 A&P Mkt, Buick/Chevrolet, Walgreens
43	Intervale Rd, to Mountain Lakes, **E** ⛽ Valero/dsl, **W** 🅞 Dodge
42	US 46, US 202 (from sb only), **W** ⛽ 76/Dunkin Donuts/dsl, Exxon 🍴 Fuddrucker's, McDonald's, TGIFriday's, Wendy's 🏠 Courtyard, Day's Inn, Embassy Suites, Fairfield Inn, Hampton Inn 🅞 Marshall's, Subaru, USPO
41b a	I-80, E to New York, W to Delaware Water Gap
40	NJ 511, Parsippany Rd, to Whippany, **W** ⛽ BP, Shell/dsl, Woroco Gas 🍴 Frank&Son Pizza, Subway, Wok's Chinese 🏠 Embassy Suites (1mi) 🅞 vet
39b a	NJ 10, Dover, Whippany, **E** ⛽ Exxon, Shell 🍴 Brookside Diner, Dunkin Donuts, Jersey Mike's, Melting Pot, Pancake House, Scallopini Rest., Whippany Diner 🅞 CVS Drug, Farmtastic Mkt, Tuesday Morning, **W** ⛽ Liberty/dsl, Lukoil, Raceway 🍴 Atlanta Bread, Dunkin Donuts, Panchero's Mexican, Smashburger, Subway, Wendy's 🏠 EconoLodge, Hilton, Hyatt House, Marriott 🅞 Barnes&Noble, Buick/GMC, GNC, Harley Davidson, Kohl's, Stop'n Shop, Verizon
37	NJ 24 E, Springfield
36b a	rd 510, Morris Ave, Lafayette
35	NJ 124, South St, Madison Ave, Morristown, **E** 🍴 Friendly's 🅞 Richie's Country Store, vet, **W** 🏠 Best Western 🅞 🏠, Rite Aid, Walgreens
33mm	truck Rs nb, full ♿ facilities, litter barrels, petwalk, 🅞, 🚻, vending
33	Harter Rd
30b a	to US 202, N Maple Ave, Basking Ridge, **E** 🏠 Dolce Resort, **W** ⛽ Gulf, Lukoil 🍴 GrainHouse Rest., Vine Rest. 🏠 Olde Mill Inn/rest.
26b a	rd 525 S, Mt Airy Rd, Liberty Corner, **E 3 mi** ⛽ Exxon 🏠 Courtyard, Somerset Hotel
22b a	US 202, US 206, Pluckemin, Bedminster, **E** ⛽ Exxon, Exxon/dsl 🍴 Burger King, Coldstone, Dunkin Donuts, Golden Palace, Panchero's, Rocco's Pizza, Starbucks, Subway 🅞 CVS Drug, Fresh Mkt, King's Foods, URGENT CARE, Verizon

NJ

NJ

⬆N INTERSTATE 287 Cont'd

Exit #	Services
21b a	I-78, E to NY, W to PA
17	US 206 (from sb), Bridgewater, **W** 🅖 Exxon, Hess 🍽 Buffalo Wild Wings, CA Pizza, Cheescake Factory, Chipotle Mexican, Dunkin Donuts, KFC, La Catena Ristorante, Maggiano's Italian, McCormick&Schmick's, McDonald's, TGIFriday, Wendy's 🏠 Marriott 🄾 Best Buy, Bloomingdale's, Lord&Taylor, Macy's, mall
14b a	US 22, to US 202/206, **E** 🅖 Hess/dsl 🄾 Chevrolet/Lexus, **W** 🅖 Sunoco/dsl, Valero/dsl 🍽 Houlihan's, Red Lobster 🏠 Day's Inn 🄾 Acura, Chrysler/Dodge/Jeep, Fiat, Ford, Infiniti, Kia, Mercedes, Nissan, Volvo
13b a	NJ 28, Bound Brook, **E** 🅖 76/dsl, BP/dsl 🍽 25 Burgers, Burger King, Dunkin Donuts, Frank's Pizza, Girasole Rest., Little Caesar's 🄾 7-11, AT&T, AutoZone, QuickChek Mkt, Radio Shack, ShopRite Foods, Walgreens, **W** 🍽 Applebees, ChuckeCheese, McDonald's, Panchero's 🏠 Hilton Garden 🄾 🄷, 7-11, Costco, Home Depot, Marshall's, Michael's, Old Navy, PepBoys, PetsMart, Target
12	Weston Canal Rd, Manville, **E** 🄾 ShopRite (3mi), USPO, **W** 🍽 Soho Grill 🏠 La Quinta
10	NJ 527, Easton Ave, New Brunswick, **E** 🏠 Hotel Somerset, **W** 🅖 Exxon 🍽 Dunkin Donuts, Lo Duca Pizza, Ruby Tuesday, Subway 🏠 Candlewood Suites, Comfort Inn, Courtyard, Doubletree, EconoLodge, Extended Stay America, Fairfield Inn, Holiday Inn, Homewood Suites, Madison Suites, Residence Inn, Sonesta Suites 🄾 🄷, Garden State Exhibit Ctr
9	NJ 514, River Rd, **W** 🅖 Gulf 🏠 Embassy Suites, Radisson
8.5mm	weigh sta nb
8	Possumtown Rd, Highland Park
7	S Randolphville Rd, Piscataway, **E** 🅖 Lukoil/dsl
6	Washington Ave, Piscataway, **E** 🅖 Shell/7-11/dsl 🍽 Popeye's, **W** 🍽 Applebees, Chand Palace, Gourmet Oizza, Healthy Garden, Longhorn Steaks, Olive Garden, Panera Bread, Piscataway Pizza, Starbucks, Subway, TGIFriday's, Thai Basil 🄾 99¢ Depot, Aldi Foods, GNC, Lowes Whse, PetCo, same as 5, ShopRite Foods, Walmart/McDonald's
5	NJ 529, Stelton Rd, Dunellen, **E** 🅖 BP/dsl, Gulf/dsl, Lukoil/dsl 🍽 Enzo's Pizza, KFC 🏠 Ramada Ltd. 🄾 Advance Parts, Goodyear/auto, Home Depot, Meineke, Stop'n Shop, STS Tire/auto, **W** 🅖 Exxon, Gulf 🍽 365 Bistro, Brickhouse Rest., Burger King, Chipotle, Corner Cafe, Dunkin Donuts, Five Guys, Fontainbleu Diner, Friendly's, Gabrieles Grill, Gianni Pizza, IHOP, Joe's Crabshack, Panda Express, Pizza Hut, Red Lobster, Red Robin, Ruby Tuesday, Taco Bell, Villa Pizza, Wendy's, White Castle 🏠 Best Western, Hampton Inn, Holiday Inn, Motel 6 🄾 $Tree, Burlington Coats, Dick's, Hobby Lobby, Kohl's, Macy's, Marshall's, NAPA, Pep Boys, Radio Shack, Staples, Target, Verizon, Walgreens
4	Durham Ave (from nb, no EZ return), S Plainfield, **E** 🅖 Full One/dsl 🍽 Subway 🄾 🄷, Firestone/auto
3	New Durham Rd (from sb), **E** 🅖 Shell, **W** 🍽 Dunkin Donuts, Red Onion Chinese 🏠 Fairfield Inn, Red Roof Inn 🄾 Walgreens
2b a	NJ 27, Metuchen, New Brunswick, **E** 🍽 Brownstone Grill, **W** 🅖 BP, Lukoil 🍽 Dunkin Donuts, Little Caesar's 🄾 Costco/gas, Petsmart, USPO, Walmart/Subway
1b a	US 1, **N** 🅖 Exxon/dsl, Raceway/dsl, Shell 🍽 Benihana, Champp's, Cheesecake Factory, Dunkin Donuts, Famous Dave's BBQ, Houlihan's, IHOP, Macaroni Grill, McDonald's, Menlo Park Diner, Panera Bread, Seasons Grill, Sonic, Uno,

Exit #	Services
1b a	Continued White Castle 🄾 Barnes&Noble, Firestone/auto, Goodyear/auto, Macy's, Midas, Nordstrom's, Target, **S** 🅖 Shell/7-11/dsl 🍽 Applebees, Boston Mkt, ChuckeCheese, McDonald's 🏠 Comfort Inn, Quality Inn 🄾 $Tree, BJ's Whse, Home Depot, Infiniti, Land Rover/Jaguar/Porche, Mercedes, Office Depot, PepBoys, PetCo, Sam's Club/gas, Staples, Stop&Shop Foods, Volvo
0mm	I-287 begins/ends on NJ 440, I-95, NJ Tpk.

⬆N INTERSTATE 295

Exit #	Services
67b a	US 1. I-295 nb becomes I-95 sb at US 1. See NJ I-95, exit 67b a
65b a	Sloan Ave, **E** 🅖 Exxon 🍽 Burger King, Dunkin Donuts, New China Buffet, Subway, Taco Bell, Uno Grill 🄾 Goodyear/auto, Rizoldi's Mkt
64	NJ 535 N (from sb), to NJ 33 E, same as 63
63b a	NJ 33 W, rd 535, Mercerville, Trenton, **E on rd 33** 🅖 Hess/dsl, Lukoil, Valero 🍽 Applebee's, Asia Buffet, McDonald's, Pizza Hut, Popeye's, Stewart's Rootbeer, Subway, Vincent's Pizza 🄾 Ace Hardware, auto repair, CVS Drug, Ford/Subaru, Rite Aid, Staples, USPO, **W** 🅖 Exxon 🍽 Dunkin Donuts, Hamilton Diner, Szechuan House 🄾 Advance Parts, Family$, transmissions, Walgreens, WaWa
62	Olden Ave N (from sb, no return), **W** 🅖 Delta
61b a	Arena Dr, White Horse Ave, **W** 🄾 7-11
60b a	I-195, to I-95, W to Trenton, E to Neptune
58mm	scenic overlook both lanes
57b a	US 130, to US 206, **E** 🅖 Shell, Valero 🍽 Denny's, McDonald's 🏠 Best Western, Comfort Inn, Days Inn, EconoLodge, Hampton Inn 🄾 Blue Beacon, **W** 🏠 Candlewood Suites 🄾 st police
56	to US 206 S (from nb, no return), to NJ Tpk, Ft Dix, McGuire AFB, **E** 🅖 ❤Love's/Wendy's/dsl/scales/24hr, Petro/Iron Skillet/dsl/scales/24hr/@ 🏠 Days Inn, Hampton Inn, same as 57, **W** 🏠 Candlewood Suites 🄾 st police
52b a	rd 656, to Columbus, Florence, **E 3 mi** 🅖 ❤Love's/Wendy's/dsl/scales/24hr, Petro/Iron Skillet/dsl/scales/24hr/@
47b a	NJ 541, to Mount Holly, NJ Tpk, Burlington, **E** 🅖 BP, Exxon/dsl, Valero/dsl 🍽 Applebee's, Burger King, China House, ChuckECheese's, Coldstone, Cracker Barrel, Dunkin Donuts, IHOP, Quiznos, Recovery Grill, TGIFriday's 🏠 Best Western, Budget Inn, Courtyard, Hampton Inn, Hilton Garden, Holiday Inn Express, Quality Inn 🄾 $Tree, AT&T, Dick's, Home Depot, JC Penney, Kohl's, mall, Sears/auto, Target, vet, **W** 🅖 Citgo/dsl, US Gas, WaWa/dsl 🍽 Checker's, Friendly's, Subway, Villa Pizza, Wedgewood Farms Rest., Wendy's 🄾 🄷, Acme Foods, AutoZone, Marshall's, Walmart
45b a	to Mt Holly, Willingboro, **W** 🅖 LukOil 🄾 🄷, auto repair
43b a	rd 636, to Rancocas Woods, Delran, **W** 🅖 Exxon 🍽 Carlucci's Rest.
40b a	NJ 38, to Mount Holly, Moorestown, **W** 🅖 Shell/dsl 🍽 Arby's, Baja Fresh, Chick-fil-A, Dunkin Donuts, Panera Bread, Ruby Tuesday, Starbucks, Subway, TGIFriday's 🏠 Residence Inn (4mi) 🄾 🄷, Costco, GNC, Jo-Ann Fabrics, Petsmart, Radio Shack, Target, TJ Maxx, U-Haul, Wegman's Foods
36b a	NJ 73, to NJ Tpk, Tacony Br, Berlin, **E** 🅖 Exxon, LukOil/dsl 🍽 Bob Evans 🏠 aLoft, Courtyard, EconoLodge, Fairfield Inn, Red Roof Inn, Super 8, **W** 🅖 Citgo, Shell 🍽 5 Guys Burgers, Bertucci's, Boscov's, Boston Mkt, Chick-fil-A, Chipotle Mexican, Don Pablo, Dunkin Donuts, Friendly's, Mikado Japanese, Old Town Buffet, Panera Bread, PeiWei, Perkins,

TRENTON

INTERSTATE 295 Cont'd

C H E R R Y   H I L L

Exit #	Services
36b a	Continued
	PJ Whelahin's, Popeye's, Uno Grill, Wendy's 🏠 Bel-Air Motel, Crossland Suites, Homewood Suites, Motel 6, Quality Inn 🅞 $Tree, Acura, AT&T, AutoZone, Barnes&Noble, Best Buy, Chevrolet, Dick's, Fiat, Firestone/auto, Ford/Lincoln, Home Depot, Infiniti, K-Mart, Lord&Taylor, Lowe's, Macy's, mall, Marshall's, Michael's, Old Navy, PepBoys, Petsmart, Ross, Sears/auto, ShopRite Foods, Staples
34b a	NJ 70, to Camden, Cherry Hill, **E** 🅖 BP, Exxon, WaWa 🍴 Big John's Steaks, Burger King, Dunkin Donuts, PJ Whelihans 🏠 Extended Stay America 🅞 Curves, Tires+, **W** 🅖 Exxon, Gulf/dsl, LukOil, US Gas 🍴 Dunkin Donuts, Famous Dave's BBQ, McDonald's, Mirabella Cafe, Norma's Cafe, Ponzio's Rest, Qdoba, Salad Works, Seasons Pizza, Starbucks, Steak&Ale, Subway 🏠 Crowne Plaza (3mi) 🅞 🅷, $Tree, AT&T, CVS Drug, Goodyear/auto, Rite Aid, vet, WaWa
32	NJ 561, to Haddonfield, Voorhees, **E 3 mi** 🅖 LukOil/dsl 🍴 5 Guys Burgers, Applebee's, Olive Garden, Panera Bread, Vito's Pizza 🏠 Hampton Inn, Wingate Inn 🅞 🅷, USPO, **W** 🅖 Pioneer/dsl, Sunoco 🍴 Burger King, Dunkin Donuts, Subway 🅞 7-11, Ford, vet
31	Woodcrest Station
30	Warwick Rd (from sb)
29b a	US 30, to Berlin, Collingswood, **E** 🅖 Astro/dsl, Citgo/dsl, Exxon, LukOil/dsl 🍴 Arby's, Church's, Dunkin Donuts, McDonald's, Popeye's, Subway, Wendy's 🅞 AutoZone, Home Depot, Lowe's, PathMark Foods, Petsmart, Sears Essentials
28	NJ 168, to NJ Tpk, Belmawr, Mt Ephraim, **E** 🅖 Citgo, Gulf/repair, Shamrock/dsl, Shell/dsl 🍴 Burger King, Club Diner, Dunkin Donuts, Italia Pizza, Wendy's 🏠 Bellmawr Motel, Comfort Inn, EconoLodge, Holiday Inn, Howard Johnson, Motel 6, Red Roof Inn, Super 8 🅞 CVS Drug, transmissions, Walgreens, **W** 🅖 BP, Exxon/LP, Hess/dsl, WaWa 🍴 5 Guys Burgers, Applebee's, Arby's, Black Horse Diner, Chick-fil-A, Domino's, Dunkin Donuts, Golden Corral, McDonald's, Sonic, Subway 🅞 Acme Foods, AutoZone, Chrysler/Dodge, CVS Drug, Firestone, Harley-Davidson, PepBoys, Staples, USPO, Walgreens, Walmart
26	I-76, NJ 42, to I-676 (exits left from sb), Walt Whitman Bridge, Walt Whitman Bridge
25b a	NJ 47, to Westville, Deptford
24b a	NJ 45, NJ 551 (no EZ sb return), to Westville, **E** 🅞 🅷, AutoZone, **W** 🅖 WaWa 🅞 Chevrolet, Family$

23	US 130 N, to National Park
22	NJ 644, to Red Bank, Woodbury, **E** 🅖 LukOil, **W 1 mi** 🅖 Crown Point Trkstp/dsl/@, WaWa 🍴 Wendy's
21	NJ 44 S, Paulsboro, Woodbury, **W** 🅖 WaWa, Wendy's 🏠 Westwood Motor Lodge
20	NJ 44, rd 643, to National Park, Thorofare, **E** 🏠 Best Western, **W** 🏠 Red Bank Inn
19	to NJ 44, rd 656, Mantua
18b a	rd 667, to rd 678, Clarksboro, Mt Royal, **E** 🅖 BP/dsl, TA/Exxon/Buckhorn Rest./dsl/scales/@ 🍴 Dunkin Donuts, KFC/Taco Bell, McDonald's, Wendy's 🅞 RV camping, **W** 🅖 Valero, WaWa/dsl
17	rd 680, to Mickleton, Gibbstown, **W** 🍴 Burger King, Domino's 🏠 Motel 6 🅞 Advance Parts, Family$, GNC, Rite Aid, ShopRite Foods, WaWa
16b	rd 551, to Gibbstown, Mickleton
16a	rd 653, to Paulsboro, Swedesboro
15	rd 607, to Gibbstown
14	rd 684, to Repaupo
13	US 130 S, US 322 W, to Bridgeport (from sb, no return)
11	US 322 E, to Mullica Hill
10	Ctr Square Rd, to Swedesboro, **E** 🅖 BP/dsl, WaWa/dsl 🍴 Applebee's, Dunkin Donuts, McDonald's, Subway, Wendy's 🏠 Hampton Inn, Holiday Inn 🅞 Acme Foods/Sav-On, Firestone/auto, Rite Aid, **W** 🅞 Camping World RV Supplies/service
7	to Auburn, Pedricktown
4	NJ 48, Woodstown, Penns Grove
3mm	**weigh sta nb**
2mm	**🆁🆂 nb, full ♿ facilities, info, litter barrels, 🅲, picnic table, RV dump, vending**
2c	to US 130 (from sb), Deepwater, **E** same as 2b, **W** 🅖 ⊘FLYING J/Denny's/dsl/scales/LP/24hr, Sunoco/Dunkin Donuts/dsl/scales/24hr 🅞 🅷
2b	US 40 E, to NJ Tpk, **E** 🅖 Gulf, 🚚/Subway/dsl/scales/24hr 🏠 Best Value, Comfort Inn, Friendship Motor Inn, Knights Inn, Quality Inn, **W** same as 2c
2a	to Delaware Bridge, US 40 W (from nb)
1c	NJ 551 S, Hook Rd, to Salem, **E** 🏠 White Oaks Motel, **W** 🅞 🅷
1b	US 130 N (from nb), Penns Grove
1a	NJ 49 E, to Pennsville, Salem, **E** 🅖 Exxon/dsl/repair 🍴 Applebees, Burger King, Cracker Barrel, Dunkin Donuts, KFC/Taco Bell, McDonald's, Subway 🏠 Hampton Inn, Super 8 🅞 Peterbilt, **W** 🅖 Coastal/dsl 🏠 Seaview Motel
0mm	New Jersey/Delaware state line, Delaware River, Delaware Memorial Bridge

NJ

NM

NEW MEXICO

INTERSTATE 10

Exit #	Services
164.5mm	New Mexico/Texas state line
164mm	**Welcome Ctr wb, full ♿ facilities, litter barrels, petwalk, 🅲, 🏕**
162	NM 404, Anthony, **S** 🅖 Alon/dsl 🅞 Family$, RV camping
160mm	**weigh sta wb**
155	NM 227 W, to Vado, **N** 🅞 Western Sky's RV Park, **S** 🅖 NTS/dsl/scales/24hr/@, Texaco/El Viajero/dsl/scales/24hr 🅞 $General, El Camino Real HS
151	Mesquite

L A S   C R U C E S

144	I-25 N, to Las Cruces
142	Rd 188, Rd 101, Valley Dr, Las Cruces, **N** 🅖 Chevron/dsl 🍴 Chilito's Mexican, Dick's Cafe, Whataburger 🏠 Best Western, EconoLodge, Holiday Inn Express, Motel 6, Quality Inn, Ramada Inn, Super 8, Teakwood Inn 🅞 🅷, auto/RV repair/tires, Cadillac/Chevrolet, Dalmont's RV Camping, Ford/Lincoln, Honda, Hyundai, Mazda, Nissan, NMSU, vet, **S** 🅖 Alon/dsl 🅞 USPO
140	NM 28, to Mesilla, Las Cruces, **N** 🅖 Alon/dsl 🍴 Applebee's, Blake's Lotaburger, BurgerTime, Cracker Barrel, Domino's, McDonald's, Murry Express, Starbucks, Subway 🏠 Best Value Inn, Days Inn, Drury Inn, La Quinta, SpringHill Suites

NM

◀▶ E	INTERSTATE 10 Cont'd
Exit #	Services
140	Continued
	⊙ Buick/GMC, Kia, Radio Shack, Toyota/Scion, VW, Walmart/McDonald's, S 🍴 LunaRossa Pizza 🛏 Comfort Inn ⊙ Harley-Davidson, Holiday World RV Ctr, Siesta RV Park, United RV Ctr
139	NM 292, Amador Ave, Motel Blvd, Las Cruces, N 📮 🍴 Subway/dsl/scales/24hr, TA/Burger King/Pizza Hut/Taco Bell/dsl/24hr/scales/@, S 🍴 PitStop Café 🛏 Coachlight Inn/RV Park ⊙ NAPACare
138mm	Rio Grande River
135.5mm	℞ˢ eb, full 🦽 facilities, litter barrels, petwalk, 🌲, RV dump, scenic view
135	US 70 E, to W Las Cruces, Alamogordo, N 1 mi ⊙ KOA
132	N ⊙ fairgrounds, to 🛫, S 📮 Loves/Subway/dsl/scales/24hr
127	Corralitos Rd, N 📮 Exxon ⊙ Bowlin's Trading Post, to fairgrounds
120.5mm	insp sta wb
116	NM 549
111mm	parking area wb, litter barrels
102	Akela, N 📮 Exxon/dsl/gifts
85	East Motel Dr, Deming, S 📮 Chevron/dsl, Save Gas/dsl 🛏 Hampton Inn, Holiday Inn Express, La Quinta, Motel 6, Quality Inn ⊙ Buick/Cadillac/Chevrolet/GMC, Chrysler/Dodge/Jeep, Dreamcatcher RV Park
82b	Railroad Blvd, Deming, N 📮 Chevron/dsl, S 📮 Fina/dsl 🍴 DQ, Golden Star Chinese, IHOP, KFC, Little Caesars, Ranchers Grill, Wendy's 🛏 Days Inn, Grand Motel ⊙ $General, $Tree, AutoZone, Big O Tire, Deming Visitors Ctr, Ford/Lincoln, K-Mart, Little Vinyard RV Park, NAPA, O'Reilly Parts, Roadrunner RV Park, st police, Sunrise RV Park, to Rock Hound SP, Verizon, Wagon Wheel RV Park, Walmart/Subway
82a	US 180, NM 26, NM 11, Deming, N 📮 Chevron/dsl 🍴 Blake's Lotaburger, S 📮 Exxon, Phillips 66 🍴 Burger King, China Rest., Denny's, Domino's, KFC, Palma's Italian, Pizza Hut, Rancher's Grill, Si Senor 🛏 Butterfield Stage Motel ⊙ Budget Tire, CarQuest, museum, Radio Shack, Rockhound SP, to Pancho Villa SP, Walgreens
81	NM 11, W Motel Dr, Deming, S 📮 Deming Truck Terminal/cafe/dsl/scales/24hr/@, Shamrock/dsl 🍴 Benji's Rest, Burger Time, El Camino Real, McDonald's, Sonic, Subway, Taco Bell 🛏 Best Western, Comfort Inn, Deming Motel, Executive Motel, Super 8, Western Motel ⊙ 81 Palms RV Park, city park, Hitchin Post RV Park, Rock Hound SP, to Pancho Villa SP
68	NM 418, S 📮 Petro/Iron Skillet/Starbucks/dsl/scales/24hr, tires/repair
62	Gage, S 📮 Butterfield Station/Exxon/DQ/dsl
61mm	℞ˢ wb, full 🦽 facilities, litter barrels, petwalk, 🌲, vending
55	Quincy
53mm	℞ˢ eb, full 🦽 facilities, litter barrels, petwalk, 🌲, vending
51.5mm	Continental Divide, elev 4585
49	NM 146 S, to Hachita, Antelope Wells
42	Separ, S ⊙ Bowlin's Continental Divide Trading Post/Gifts
34	NM 113 S, Muir, Playas
29	no services
24	US 70, E Motel Dr, Lordsburg, N 📮 FLYING J/Denny's/dsl/LP/scales/RV Dump/24hr, 📮 Arby's/dsl/scales/24hr 🛏 American Motel ⊙ Horseman RV Park
23.5mm	weigh sta both lanes

22	NM 494, Main St, Lordsburg, N 🍴 McDonald's 🛏 Comfort Inn, Hampton Inn ⊙ $General, Family$, NAPA, Saucedo's Foods, USPO, S 📮 Valero/dsl 🍴 Kranberry's Rest. 🛏 Best Western, EconoLodge, Motel 10, Plaza Inn ⊙ KOA
20b a	W Motel Dr, Lordsburg, N 📮 Loves/Godfather's Pizza/Subway/scales/dsl 🛏 Days Inn, S 📮 Chevron/dsl, Visitors Ctr/full 🦽 facilities, info
15	to Gary
11	NM 338 S, to Animas
5	NM 80 S, to Road Forks, S 🛏 Desert West Motel/rest. ⊙ dsl/tire repair, fireworks
3	Steins
0mm	New Mexico/Arizona state line

◀▶ N	INTERSTATE 25
Exit #	Services
460.5mm	New Mexico/Colorado state line
460	E ⊙ Cedar Rail Campground, Raton Pass Summit, elev 7834 weigh sta sb
454	2nd St, Lp 25, Raton, W 2 mi 📮 Crossroads 🛏 Budget Host ⊙ 🄷 CarQuest, Ford
452	NM 72 E, Raton, E ⊙ to Sugarite Canyon SP, W 📮 Conoco
451	US 64 E, US 87 E, Raton, E 📮 87 Express/dsl, Chevron/dsl, CR/dsl/24hr 🍴 Subway ⊙ Summerlan RV Park, to Capulin Volcano NM, W 📮 Conoco/dsl, CR/dsl, Loaf'n Jug/dsl, Phillips 66, Shell/dsl 🍴 All Seasons Rest., Arby's, Denny's, DQ, K-Bob's, McDonald's, Pizza Hut, Sand's Rest., Sonic 🛏 Best Value Inn, Best Western, Microtel, Motel 6, Oasis Motel/rest, Quality Inn, Robin Hood Motel, Super 8, Texan Motel, Travel Motel, Village Inn Motel ⊙ 🄷, $General, Ace Hardware, AutoZone, Family$, K-Mart, KOA, Super Save Foods, Visitor's Ctr/info
450	Lp 25, Raton, W 🛏 Holiday Inn Express, Oasis Motel/rest. ⊙ 🄷, AutoZone, KOA, vet
446	US 64 W, to Cimarron, Taos, W 4 mi ⊙ camping, NRA Whittington Ctr
440mm	Canadian River
435	Tinaja
434.5mm	℞ˢ both lanes, full 🦽 facilities, litter barrels, petwalk, 🌲, weather info
426	NM 505, Maxwell, W 📮 Maxwell Station/dsl ⊙ to Maxwell Lakes, USPO
419	NM 58, to Cimarron, E 📮 Chevron/Russell's/Subway/dsl/scales/24hr/@
414	US 56, Springer, E 1 mi 📮 Conoco/dsl, Crossroads/dsl 🍴 Minnie's Dairy Delite 🛏 Oasis Motel ⊙ Old Santa Fe Trail RV Park
412	US 56 E, US 412 E, NM 21, NM 468, Springer, E 1 mi 📮 Alon 🛏 Brown Hotel/cafe ⊙ CarQuest, Springer Foods, USPO
404	NM 569, Colmor, Charette Lakes
393	Levy
387	NM 120, to Roy, Wagon Mound, E 📮 Conoco/dsl, Phillips 66/dsl
376mm	℞ˢ sb, full 🦽 facilities, litter barrels, petwalk, 🅲, 🌲, RV camp
374mm	℞ˢ nb, full 🦽 facilities, litter barrels, petwalk, 🅲, 🌲, RV camp
366	NM 97, NM 161, Watrous, Valmora, W ⊙ Ft Union NM, Santa Fe Trail
364	NM 97, NM 161, Watrous, Valmora
361	no services
360mm	parking area both lanes, litter barrels

RATON

DEMING

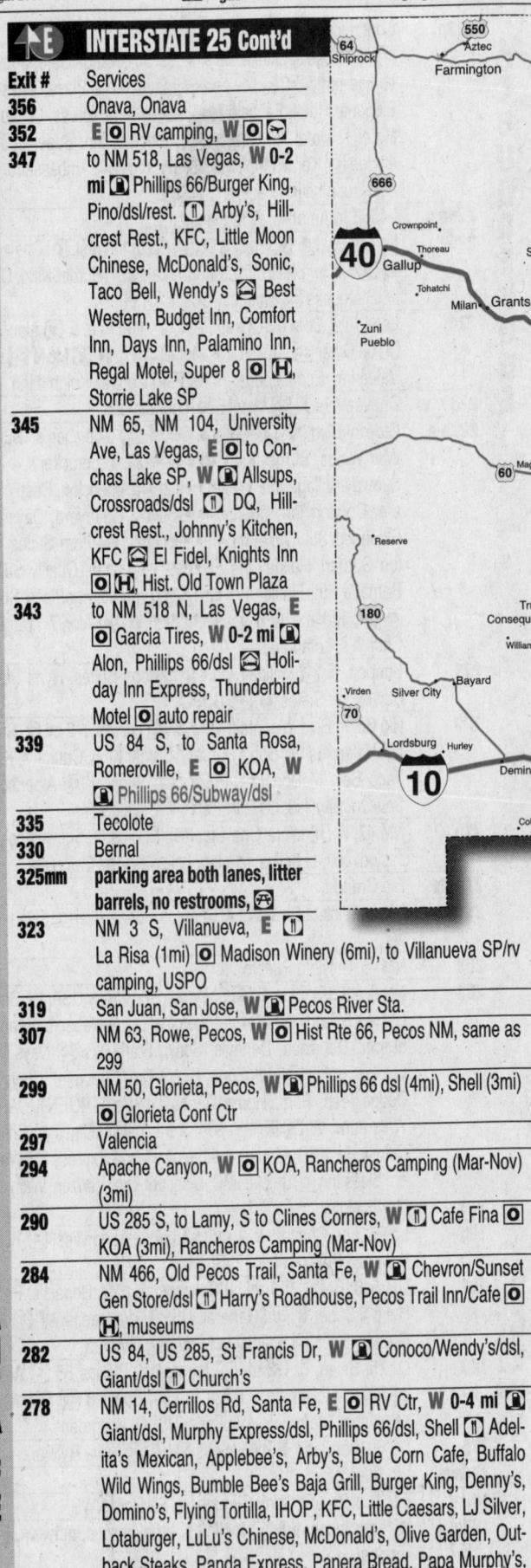

INTERSTATE 25 Cont'd

Exit #	Services
356	Onava, Onava
352	**E** 🅾 RV camping, **W** 🅾 ✈
347	to NM 518, Las Vegas, **W 0-2 mi** 🅶 Phillips 66/Burger King, Pino/dsl/rest. 🍴 Arby's, Hillcrest Rest., KFC, Little Moon Chinese, McDonald's, Sonic, Taco Bell, Wendy's 🛏 Best Western, Budget Inn, Comfort Inn, Days Inn, Palamino Inn, Regal Motel, Super 8 🅾 🅷, Storrie Lake SP
345	NM 65, NM 104, University Ave, Las Vegas, **E** 🅾 to Conchas Lake SP, **W** 🅶 Allsups, Crossroads/dsl 🍴 DQ, Hillcrest Rest., Johnny's Kitchen, KFC 🛏 El Fidel, Knights Inn 🅾 🅷, Hist. Old Town Plaza
343	to NM 518 N, Las Vegas, **E** 🅾 Garcia Tires, **W 0-2 mi** 🅶 Alon, Phillips 66/dsl 🛏 Holiday Inn Express, Thunderbird Motel 🅾 auto repair
339	US 84 S, to Santa Rosa, Romeroville, **E** 🅾 KOA, **W** 🅶 Phillips 66/Subway/dsl
335	Tecolote
330	Bernal
325mm	**parking area both lanes, litter barrels, no restrooms,** 🛆
323	NM 3 S, Villanueva, **E** 🍴 La Risa (1mi) 🅾 Madison Winery (6mi), to Villanueva SP/rv camping, USPO
319	San Juan, San Jose, **W** 🅶 Pecos River Sta.
307	NM 63, Rowe, Pecos, **W** 🅾 Hist Rte 66, Pecos NM, same as 299
299	NM 50, Glorieta, Pecos, **W** 🅶 Phillips 66 dsl (4mi), Shell (3mi) 🅾 Glorieta Conf Ctr
297	Valencia
294	Apache Canyon, **W** 🅾 KOA, Rancheros Camping (Mar-Nov) (3mi)
290	US 285 S, to Lamy, S to Clines Corners, **W** 🍴 Cafe Fina 🅾 KOA (3mi), Rancheros Camping (Mar-Nov)
284	NM 466, Old Pecos Trail, Santa Fe, **W** 🅶 Chevron/Sunset Gen Store/dsl 🍴 Harry's Roadhouse, Pecos Trail Inn/Cafe 🅾 🅷, museums
282	US 84, US 285, St Francis Dr, **W** 🅶 Conoco/Wendy's/dsl, Giant/dsl 🍴 Church's
278	NM 14, Cerrillos Rd, Santa Fe, **E** 🅾 RV Ctr, **W 0-4 mi** 🅶 Giant/dsl, Murphy Express/dsl, Phillips 66/dsl, Shell 🍴 Adelita's Mexican, Applebee's, Arby's, Blue Corn Cafe, Buffalo Wild Wings, Bumble Bee's Baja Grill, Burger King, Denny's, Domino's, Flying Tortilla, IHOP, KFC, Little Caesars, LJ Silver, Lotaburger, LuLu's Chinese, McDonald's, Olive Garden, Outback Steaks, Panda Express, Panera Bread, Papa Murphy's, Pizza Hut, Ranch House Steaks, Red Lobster, Schlotzsky's, Sonic, Starbucks, Taco Bell, Tortilla Flats 🛏 Best Western, Comfort Inn, Comfort Suites, Courtyard, Days Inn, Doubletree, EconoLodge, Fairfield Inn, Hampton Inn, Holiday Inn Express,

Exit #	Services
278	Continued Hyatt Place, La Quinta, Motel 6, Quality Inn, Santa Fe Inn, Super 8, Tranquilla Inn 🅾 AAA, Albertson's, AT&T, Best Buy, BigLots, BMW, Buick/GMC, Cadillac/Chevrolet, Chrysler/Dodge/Jeep, CVS Drug, Dillard's, Discount Tire, Firestone/auto, Ford/Lincoln, Harley-Davidson, Home Depot, Honda, JC Penney, Jo-Ann Fabrics, Kohl's, Land Rover, Lexus, Los Campos RV Park, Lowe's, Mazda, Mecedes/Smart, Meineke, Michaels, Natural Grocers, Peerless Tire, Penske, PepBoys, Petsmart, Ross, Sam's Club/gas, Santa Fe Outlets/famous brands, Sears/auto, Sprouts Mkt, Staples, Subaru/VW, Target, TJ Maxx, Tuesday Morning, Verizon, Volvo, Walgreens, Walmart
276b a	NM 599, to NM 14, to Madrid, **E** 🅶 Phillips 66/Allsup's 🅾 Santa Fe Skies RV Park, **W 4 mi** 🍴 Shell 🅾 Sunrise Springs
271	CR 50F, La Cienega
269mm	🆁 nb, full 🚻 facilities, litter barrels, petwalk, 🍴, 🛆
267	Waldo Canyon Rd, 🅾 insp sta., access to nb 🆁
264	NM 16, Pueblo, **W** 🅾 to Cochiti Lake RA
263mm	Galisteo River
259	NM 22, to Santo Domingo Pueblo, **W** 🅶 Phillips 66/cafe/dsl 🅾 to Cochiti Lake RA (11mi)
257	Budaghers, **W** 🅾 Mormon Battalion Mon
252	San Felipe Pueblo, **E** 🅶 Phillips 66/dsl 🍴 San Felipe Casino/rest.
248	Rte 66, Algodones
242	US 550, NM 44 W, NM 165 E, to Farmington, Aztec, **W 0-2 mi** 🅶 Chevron/dsl, Conoco/dsl, M&M/Burger King/dsl, Phillips

LAS VEGAS

SANTA FE

NM

⬆N INTERSTATE 25 Cont'd

Exit #	Services
242	Continued
	66/dsl, Valero/dsl 🍴 Denny's, Guang Dong Chinese, IHOP, KFC, Lotaburger, McDonald's, Pizza Hut, Sonic, Starbucks, Subway, Taco Bell, Twisters, Wendy's 🛏 Days Inn, Holiday Inn Express, Motel 6, Super 8 ⊙ $General, AutoZone, Casino, Home Depot, KOA, O'Reilly Parts, to Coronado SP, Walgreens, Walmart
240	NM 473, to Bernalillo, W 🚩 Conoco/dsl 🍴 Abuelita's Mexican, Range Café ⊙ KOA, to Coronado SP, USPO, vet
234	NM 556, Tramway Rd, E 🚩 Valero/Subway/dsl ⊙ casino, W 🚩 Phillips 66/dsl
233	Alameda Blvd, E 🚩 Chevron 🍴 Burger King 🛏 Comfort Suites, Motel 6, Staybridge Suites ⊙ Audi/Porsche, Lincoln, Meineke, Mercedes, Toyota/Scion, Volvo, W 🚩 Phillips 66/Circle K/dsl 🍴 Carl's Jr 🛏 Best Value, Holiday Inn Express ⊙ Balloon Fiesta Park, CarMax
232	Paseo del Norte, Paseo del Norte, E 🍴 Chick-fil-A, China Luck, Chipotle Mexican, Five Guys, Freddy's Steakburgers, Jason's Deli, Jimmy John's, McDonald's, Panda Express, Panera Bread, Starbucks, Subway, Tomato Cafe, Wendy's 🛏 Howard Johnson ⊙ Aloha RV Ctr, AutoZone, Discount Tire, Kohl's, Lowe's, Office Depot, Target, Verizon, Walgreens, W 🚩 Shell/Circle K 🍴 Arby's 🛏 Courtyard, Marriott
231	San Antonio Ave, E 🚩 Alon/7-11 🍴 Cracker Barrel, Denny's, Lotaburger 🛏 Comfort Suites, Hilton Garden, Homewood Suites, La Quinta, Quality Inn ⊙ H, USPO, W 🛏 Baymont Inn, Crossland Suites, LaQuinta ⊙ Mazda, VW
230	San Mateo Blvd, Osuna Rd, Albuquerque, E 🚩 Chevron, Circle K, Giant/dsl, Phillips 66/Circle K, Shell 🍴 Applebee's, Arby's, Azuma Grill, Bob's Burgers, Burger King, Chick-fil-A, Chili's, Cici's Pizza, Firehouse Subs, Furrs Buffet, Golden Corral, Hayashi, Hooters, Jack-in-the-Box, KFC, LJ Silver, McDonald's, Olive Garden, Papa John's, Pizza Hut/Taco Bell, Popeyes, Schlotzsky's, Sonic, Souper Salad, Starbucks, Subway, SweetTomatoes, Taco Bueno, Taco Cabana, Teriyaki Chicken, TX Roadhouse, Village Inn, Wendy's, Wienerschnitzel 🛏 Nativo Lodge ⊙ H, $Tree, Albertson's, AT&T, AutoZone, Brake Masters, Cadillac, CVS Drug, Fiat, Firestone, Firestone/auto, GNC, Just Brakes, Midas, NAPA, O'Reilly Parts, Peerless Tire, PepBoys, PetCo, Ross, Sprouts Mkt, Subaru, Tuesday Morning, U-Haul, Walgreens, W 🚩 Circle K/dsl, Valero/dsl 🍴 McDonald's, Quiznos, Weck's Breakfast/lunch, Whataburger 🛏 Studio 6 ⊙ BMW/Mini
229	Jefferson St, E 🍴 Carrabba's, ClaimJumper, Landry's Seafood, Outback Steaks 🛏 Holiday Inn ⊙ H, same as 230, W 🍴 Boston's Pizza, Chama River Rest., Cheddar's, Chile Rio, Coldstone, Fox&Hound, Fuddrucker's, Genghis Grill, Mimi's Café, Nick&Jimmy's Grill, Pappadeaux, Pars Cuisine, PF Chang's, Plum Cafe Asian, Red Robin, Subway, Twin Peaks Rest., TX Land&Cattle Steaks 🛏 Drury Inn, Hampton Inn, Residence Inn, TownePlace Suites ⊙ Lexus
228	Montgomery Blvd, E 🚩 Alon/7-11/dsl, Chevron/dsl, Conoco/dsl 🍴 Fiestas Cantina, Lotaburger 🛏 Best Western ⊙ H, Discount Tire, W 🚩 Shell/Circle K 🍴 Arby's, Carl's Jr, IHOP, McDonald's, Panda Express, Starbucks, Wendy's 🛏 InTowne Suite ⊙ Acura, Costco/gas, Ford, Home Depot, Infiniti, Office Depot, Petsmart, REI, Sam's Club/gas, Sportsman's Whse
227b	Comanche Rd, Griegos Rd, E ⊙ UPS Depot
227a	Candelaria Rd, Albuquerque, E 🚩 Circle K/dsl, Pump'n'Save/dsl, Shell, TA/Valero/Country Pride/dsl/scales/24hr/@

227a	Continued
	🍴 Applebee's, Little Anita's, Mesa Grill, Range Cafe, Subway, Village Inn 🛏 Candlewood Suites, Crowne Plaza, Days Inn, Elegante Hotel, Fairfield Inn, Holiday Inn Express, La Quinta, Motel 1, Motel 76, Quality Inn, Rodeway Inn, Super 8, Travelodge ⊙ Kenworth, W 🚩 Chevron/dsl 🛏 Ambassador Inn, Red Roof Inn ⊙ Penske
226b a	I-40, E to Amarillo, W to Flagstaff
225	Lomas Blvd, E 🚩 Phillips 66 🍴 Plaza Inn/rest. ⊙ Chevrolet, W 🚩 FillUp, Shell/Circle K/McDonald's 🍴 Burger King, Carl's Jr, Starbucks 🛏 Embassy Suites ⊙ H
224	Lead Ave, Coal Ave, Grand Ave, Central Ave, E 🚩 Alon/7-11 🍴 66 Diner 🛏 Crossroads Motel ⊙ H, W 🚩 M&M 🛏 Best Value Inn, EconoLodge, Hotwl Parq Central, Knights Inn
223	Chavez Ave, E 🛏 Motel 6 ⊙ sports arena
222b a	Gibson Blvd, E 🚩 Phillips 66/dsl 🍴 Applebee's, Buffalo Wild Wings, Burger King, Dion's Pizza, Fuddrucker's, IHOP, Subway, Village Inn, Waffle House 🛏 AmericInn, Best Western, Comfort Inn, Country Inn&Suites, Courtyard, Days Inn, Extended Stay America, Fairfield Inn, Hawthorn Suites, Hilton Garden, Holiday Inn Express, La Quinta, Quality Suites, Ramada Inn, Residence Inn, Sleep Inn, TownePlace Suites ⊙ H, Kirtland AFB, museum, vet, W 🚩 Alon/7-11/dsl 🍴 Church's, Lotaburger
221	Sunport, E 🛏 Holiday Inn, Homewood Suites, Hyatt Place, Staybridge Suites ⊙ ✈, USPO
220	Rio Bravo Blvd, Mountain View, E ⊙ golf, W 1-2 mi 🚩 Shell/dsl, Valero/dsl 🍴 Bob's Burgers, Burger King, Church's, KFC/Taco Bell, McDonald's, Pizza Hut, Subway ⊙ Albertsons/Sav-On, Family$, O'Reilly Parts, vet, Walgreens
215	NM 47, E 🚩 Isleta One Stop/dsl, Phillips 66/Subway/dsl ⊙ casino, golf, st police, to Isleta Lakes RA/RV Camping
214mm	Rio Grande
213	NM 314, Isleta Blvd, W 🚩 Chevron/Subway/dsl ⊙ $General, vet
209	NM 45, to Isleta Pueblo
203	NM 6, to Los Lunas, E 🚩 Chevron/dsl, Murphy USA/dsl, Shell/Circle K/Wendy's/dsl/24hr, Valero/dsl 🍴 Applebee's, Benny's Burger, Del Taco, Denny's, Sonic, Starbucks 🛏 Days Inn, Los Lunas Inn ⊙ AutoZone, Big O Tire, Chevrolet, Chrysler/Dodge/Jeep, Ford, Home Depot, Lowe's, URGENT CARE, Walgreens, W 🚩 Phillips 66/Subway/dsl 🍴 Carl's Jr, Chili's, Coldstone, KFC, Mariscos Altamar, Panda Express 🛏 Western Skies Inn ⊙ Buick/GMC, Discount Tire, Verizon, Walmart/McDonald's
195	Lp 25, Los Chavez, E 1 mi 🚩 Roadrunner/grill/dsl 🍴 Pizza Hut/Taco Bell ⊙ Walmart/Subway
191	NM 548, Belen, E 1 mi 🚩 Conoco/dsl 🍴 McDonald's, Pizza Hut 🛏 Super 8 ⊙ $General, USPO, Walgreens, W 🍴 Rio Grande Diner 🛏 Holiday Inn Express, RV park
190	Lp 25, Belen, E 1-2 mi 🚩 Conoco/dsl, Phillips 66 🍴 A&W/LJ Silver, McDonald's, Pizza Hut 🛏 Super 8 ⊙ $General, Affordable Tire/repair, AutoZone, USPO, Walgreens
175	US 60, Bernardo, E ⊙ Salinas NM, W ⊙ Kiva RV Park
174mm	Rio Puerco
169	E 🍴 La Joya St Game Refuge ⊙ Sevilleta NWR
167mm	Ⓡ both lanes, full 🛏 facilities, litter barrels, petwalk, ☕, vending
166mm	Rio Salado
165mm	weigh sta/parking area both lanes
163	San Acacia
156	Lemitar, W 🚩 Phillis 66/dsl/24hr

⬆N INTERSTATE 25 Cont'd

Exit #	Services
152	Escondida, W 🅞 to st police
150	US 60 W, Socorro, W 🅖 Chevron/dsl, Exxon/dsl, Phillips 66/dsl, Valero/dsl 🍴 Bodega Burger Co, Burger King, China Best, Denny's, Domino's, K-Bob's, Little Caesar's, Lotaburger, McDonald's, Pizza Hut, Socorro Springs Rest., Sofia's Kitchen, Sonic, Subway 🛏 Best Value, Best Western, Comfort Inn, Days Inn, EconoLodge, Economy Inn, Holiday Inn Express, Sands Motel, Super 8 🅞 $General, Ace Hardware, AutoZone, Brooks Foods, CarQuest, Family$, Ford, NAPA, Radio Shack, Smith's Foods, to NM Tech, Verizon, vet, Walmart
147	US 60 W, Socorro, W 🅖 Chevron/dsl, Conoco/dsl/LP, Pump-N-Save/dsl, Shell/Circle K/dsl 🍴 Arby's 🛏 Rodeway Inn 🅞 🅷, repair/transmissions, Socorro RV Park, to 🍴
139	US 380 E, to San Antonio, E 🅖, 🍴, 🅞 to Bosque Del Apache NWR
124	to San Marcial, E 🅞 Ft Craig, to Bosque del Apache NWR
115	NM 107, E 🅖 Truck Plaza/dsl/rest./24hr 🅞 to Camino Real Heritage Ctr
114mm	🆁🆂 both lanes, full ♿ facilities, litter barrels, petwalk, 🏞, RV parking, vending
107mm	🅞 Nogal Canyon
100	Red Rock
92	Mitchell Point
90mm	La Canada Alamosa
89	NM 181, to Cuchillo, to Monticello, 🅞 RV Park (4mi)
83	NM 52, NM 181, to Cuchillo, E 3 mi 🍴 Ivory Tusk Inn& Tavern 🛏 Elephant Butte Inn/rest. 🅞 Elephant Lake Butte SP, RV Park
82mm	insp sta nb
79	Lp 25, to Truth or Consequences, E 🅖 Chevron/dsl, Circle K, Shell/dsl 🍴 Blakes's Lotaburger, Denny's, K-Bob's, La Cocina Mexican, Los Arcos Steaks, McDonald's, Pizza Hut, Sonic, Subway 🛏 Ace Lodge, Comfort Inn, Desert View Motel, Holiday Inn Express, Hot Springs Inn, Motel 6, Oasis Motel 🅞 🅷, $General, AutoZone, O'Reilly Parts, to Elephant Butte SP, USPO, Verizon, Walmart
76	(75 from nb)Lp 25, to Williamsburg, E 🅖 Conoco/dsl, Fil-JUp/dsl, Phillips 66/dsl, Shell/dsl 🍴 Maria's Mexican 🛏 Rio Grande Motel 🅞 Alco, auto/tire repair, Buick/Chevrolet/GMC, Cielo Vista RV Park, city park, Rio Grande RV Park, RJ RV Park, Shady Corner RV Park
71	Las Palomas
63	NM 152, to Hillsboro, Caballo, E 🅞 Lakeview RV Park/dsl/LP
59	rd 187, Arrey, Derry, E 🅞 to Caballo-Percha SPs
58mm	Rio Grande
51	rd 546, to Arrey, Garfield, Derry
41	NM 26 W, Hatch, W 1 mi 🅖 Alon/Subway/dsl 🍴 Burgers&More, Sparky's Cafe 🛏 Kings Pillow Inn 🅞 Chile Pepper Outlets, Franciscan RV Ctr, USPO
35	NM 140 W, Rincon
32	Upham
27mm	scenic view nb, litter barrels, 🏞
26mm	insp sta nb
23mm	🆁🆂 both lanes, full ♿ facilities, litter barrels, petwalk, 🏞, vending
19	Radium Springs, W 🅞 Family$, Fort Selden St Mon, Leasburg SP, RV camping, USPO
9	Dona Ana, W 🅖 Chucky's/dsl, Circle K/dsl 🍴 Chachi's Mexican, Jake's Cafe 🅞 $General, Family$, RV camping, USPO

Exit #	Services
6	US 70, to Alamogordo, Las Cruces, E 🅖 Alon/dsl, Shell 🍴 Domino's, IHOP, Outback Steaks, Papa Johns, Peter Piper Pizza, Pizzaria Uno, Red Brick Pizza, Ruby Tuesday, Starbucks, Subway 🛏 Fairfield Inn, Holiday Inn Express, Motel 6, Staybridge Suites, Towneplace Suites 🅞 🅷, AT&T, K-Mart, Sam's Club/gas, USPO, vet, W 🅖 Alon/dsl, Chevron, Shell/dsl, Valero/dsl 🍴 Burger King, BurgerTime, China Express, Domino's, DQ, Dunkin Donuts, KFC, Little Caesar's, Lotaburger, McDonald's, Sonic, Spanish Kitchen, Subway, Taco Bell, Whataburger/24hr, Wienerschnitzel 🅞 $General, $Tree, Albertson's, AutoZone, CVS Drug, Family$, Kohl's, Lowe's, O'Reilly Parts, Radio Shack, Verizon, vet, Walgreens
3	Lohman Ave, Las Cruces, E 🅖 Alon/dsl, Shell 🍴 Applebee's, Buffalo Wild Wings, Burger King, Cattle Baron Steaks, Chili's, ChuckeCheese, Dumkin Donuts, Empire Buffet, Farley's Grill, Fidencio's Mexican, Five Guys, Genghis Grill, Golden Corral, Hooters, Jack-in-the-Box, Jason's Deli, KFC, McAlister's Deli, Olive Garden, Pecan Grill, Red Lobster, Sonic, Starbucks, Village Inn, Whataburger 🛏 Hotel Encanto 🅞 Albertsons, AutoZone, Barnes&Noble, Dick's, Dillard's, Discount Tire, Home Depot, JC Penney, mall, Marshalls, PetCo, Ross, Sears/auto, Target, W 🅖 Giant/dsl, Valero/dsl 🍴 Arby's, Carl's Jr, Corner Bakery Cafe, McDonald's, Papa Murphy's, Quiznos, Subway, Taco Bell, TX Roadhouse, Wendy's 🛏 Hampton Inn 🅞 AT&T, Best Buy, Big Lots, Brake Masters, Hastings Books, Hobby Lobby, NAPA, Old Navy, PepBoys, Petsmart, Staples, URGENT CARE, Verizon, vet, Walgreens, Walmart
1	University Ave, Las Cruces, E 🅖 AlonSubway/dsl 🛏 Hilton Garden 🅞 🅷, golf, museum, st police, W 🅖 Giant/dsl 🍴 Dublin's Cafe, Lorenzo's Italian, McDonald's, Schlotsky's 🛏 Comfort Suites, Sleep Inn, ValuePlace 🅞 $Tree, Jo-Ann Fabrics, NMSU, Tuesday Morning
0mm	I-25 begins/ends on I-10, exit 144 at Las Cruces.

⬆E INTERSTATE 40

Exit #	Services
373.5mm	New Mexico/Texas state line, Mountain/Central time zone
373mm	Welcome Ctr wb, full ♿ facilities, litter barrels, petwalk, 🅞 🏞
369	NM 93 S, NM 392 N, Endee, N 🅖 Chevron/Russell's Truck&Travel/Subway/dsl/scales/24hr
361	Bard
358mm	weigh sta both lanes
356	NM 469, San Jon, N 🅖 Dhillon/cafe/dsl 🅞 repair, to Ute Lake SP, S 🅖 Valero/dsl 🛏 San Jon Motel 🅞 city park, USPO
343	no services
339	NM 278, N 🅞 🍴

Exit #	Services

TUCUMCARI

INTERSTATE 40 Cont'd

335 Lp 40, E Tucumcari Blvd, Tucumcari, N 🔧 Conoco/dsl, Phillips 66 🏠 EconoLodge, Gateway Inn, Hampton Inn, Motel 6, Quality Inn, Rodeway Inn, Super 8 Ⓞ Empty Saddle RV Park, to Conchas Lake SP, S 🔧 KOA

333 US 54 E, Tucumcari, N 0-1 mi 🔧 ♥Loves/Arbys/Chester's/Godfather's/dsl/scales 🍴 Rockin Y's Roadhouse 🏠 Tucumcari Inn Ⓞ city park, K-Mart, Mtn Rd RV Park, truck repair, truckwash

332 NM 209, NM 104, 1st St, Tucumcari, N 0-2 mi 🔧 Phillips 66/Allsups, Shell/Circle K/Subway/dsl 🍴 Blake's Lotaburger, K-Bob's, McDonald's, Pizza Hut, Sonic 🏠 Best Western, Days Inn, Desert Inn, Holiday Inn Express, La Quinta Ⓞ H, $General, Ace Hardware, Dinosaur Museum, Family$, Lowe's Foods, st police, to Conchas Lake SP

331 Camino del Coronado, Tucumcari

329 US 54, US 66 E, W Tucumcari Ave

321 Palomas, S 🔧 Shell/DQ/Stuckey's/dsl

311 Montoya

302mm Ⓡˢ both lanes, full ♿ facilities, litter barrels, petwalk, Ⓒ, 🏠 RV dump

300 NM 129, Newkirk, N 🔧 Rte 66/dsl Ⓞ to Conchas Lake SP, USPO

291 to Rte 66, Cuervo, N 🔧 Cuervo Gas/repair

284 no services

SANTA ROSA

NM

277 US 84 S, to Ft Sumner, N 🔧 Phillips 66/dsl 🍴 Denny's, DQ, Silver Moon Café 🏠 Best Western, Budget Inn, Comfort Inn, Hampton Inn, Holiday Inn Express, Motel 6, Quality Inn Ⓞ NAPACare, Rte 66 Car Museum, RV/auto repair, S 🔧 ♥Loves/Carl's Jr/dsl/24hr, TA/Shell/Subway/dsl/24hr/@ Ⓞ truck/tire repair

275 US 54 W, Santa Rosa, N 🔧 Phillips 66 🍴 KFC/LJ Silver, McDonald's, Rte 66 Rest., Santa Fe Grill 🏠 Best Western, Days Inn, La Quinta, Travelodge Ⓞ Santa Rosa Camping, st police, S 🔧 Shell/Circle K/dsl 🍴 Joseph's Grill, Papo's Pizza 🏠 American Inn, Laloma Motel/RV Park, Sun'n Sand Motel/rest., Super 8, Tower Motel Ⓞ H, $General, CarQuest, city park, Family$, NAPA, USPO

273.5mm Pecos River

273 US 54 S, Santa Rosa, N Ⓞ Santa Rosa Lake SP, S 🔧 Phillips 66 🏠 Best Value Inn Ⓞ NAPACare, to Carlsbad Caverns NP

267 Colonias, N 🔧 Shell/Stuckey's/dsl/rest.

263 San Ignacio

256 US 84 N, NM 219, to Las Vegas

252 no services

251.5mm Ⓡˢ both lanes, full ♿ facilities, litter barrels, petwalk, Ⓒ, 🏠 RV dump

243 Milagro, N 🔧 Phillips 66/dsl

239 no services

234 N 🔧 Exxon/Flying C/DQ/dsl/gifts

230 NM 3, to Encino, N Ⓞ to Villanueva SP

226 no services

220mm parking area both lanes, litter barrels

218b a US 285, Clines Corners, N 🔧 Conoco/dsl/24hr, Phillips 66/dsl 🍴 Clines Corners Rest., Subway, S Ⓞ to Carlsbad Caverns NP

208 Wagon Wheel

207mm Ⓡˢ both lanes, full ♿ facilities, litter barrels, petwalk, 🏠

203 N Ⓞ RV Park

MORIARTY

197 to Rte 66, Moriarty, S 🔧 Lisa's TC/dsl/rest./@ Ⓞ auto/RV repair, Glider Museum, same as 194

196 NM 41, Howard Cavasos Blvd, S 🔧 Phillips 66/Circle K/dsl 🍴 Blakes Lotaburger, SuperChina Buffet 🏠 Comfort Inn, Sunset Motel Ⓞ auto repair, city park, Family$, NAPA, to Salinas NM (35mi), USPO

194 NM 41, Moriarty, S 🔧 Conoco, Pump'n Save, TA/Shell/Burger King/Country Pride/Pizza Hut/dsl/24hr/scales/@ 🍴 Arby's, El Comedor, KFC/Taco Bell, McDonald's, Subway 🏠 Best Value Inn, Best Western, Motel 6, Ponderosa Motel, Super 8 Ⓞ $General, Alco, Chevrolet/GMC, Moriarty Foods, RV Ctr, URGENT CARE

187 NM 344, Edgewood, N 🔧 Conoco/DQ/dsl Ⓞ Walmart/McDonald's, S 🔧 Phillips 66/dsl 🍴 Chili Hills Mexican, China Chef, Domino's, McDonald's, Pizza Barn, Sonic, Subway Ⓞ auto/rv repair, AutoZone, Family$, Ford, RV Camping, Smith's Foods/dsl, USPO, vet, Walgreens

181 NM 217, Sedillo, S 🔧 Route 66/dsl

178 Zuzax, S 🔧 Shelby's/dsl Ⓞ Hidden Valley RV Park, Leisure Mtn RV Park

175 NM 337, NM 14, Tijeras, N Ⓞ to Cibola NF, Turquoise Trail RV Park, S 🍴 Subway

170 Carnuel

ALBUQUERQUE

167 Central Ave, to Tramway Blvd, S 🔧 Alon/7-11, Phillips 66, Valvoline 🍴 Blakes Lotaburger, Carl's Jr, KFC, McDonald's, Pizza Hut/Taco Bell, Starbucks, Subway, Waffle House 🏠 Best Value, Budget Host, Comfort Inn, Deluxe Inn, EconoLodge, Edgwood Studios, Travelodge, Value Place Ⓞ $Tree, Albertsons, Rocky Mtn RV/marine, Smith's/gas, to Kirtland AFB

166 Juan Tabo Blvd, N 🔧 Phillips 66/Circle K, Texaco 🍴 AA Buffet, China King, Dominos, Fedrico's Mexican, Lin's Chinese, McDonald's, Olive Garden, Paul's Rest., Pizza Hut/Taco Bell, Twisters Diner, Village Inn Rest., Wendy's 🏠 Best Value, Super 8 Ⓞ $General, Albertson's, Big O Tire, Discount Tire, Family$, Hastings Books, Hobby Lobby, Sav-On Drug, transmissions, Tuesday Morning, vet, S 🍴 Little Caesars, Sonic, Wienerschnitzel Ⓞ $General, Holiday RV Ctr, KOA/LP, Meyer's RV Ctr, repair

165 Eubank Blvd, N 🔧 Chevron, Phillips 66/Circle K 🍴 Applebee's, Owl Cafe, Panda Express, Sadie's Rest., Sonic 🏠 Days Inn, EconoLodge, Guesthouse Inn, Holiday Inn Express, Quality Inn, Rodeway Inn Ⓞ Best Buy, CarQuest, PetCo, Radio Shack, Target, S 🔧 Conoco/dsl, Valero 🍴 Bob's Burgers, Boston Mkt, Chili's, Church's, Del Taco, Golden Corral, IHOP, Jack-in-the-Box, Pizza Hut, Starbucks, Subway, Taco Bell, Taco Cabana, Twister's Burritos, Wendy's Ⓞ AutoZone, Costco/gas, Home Depot, Office Depot, O'Reilly Parts, Peerless Tires, Petsmart, repair, Sam's Club/gas, Toyota, Walgreens, Walmart

164 Lomas Blvd, Wyoming Blvd, N 🔧 Circle K/dsl, Phillips 66/dsl 🍴 Dominos, Eloy's Mexican, South China, Wandy's Ⓞ H, NAPA, vet, Walgreens, S Ⓞ Dodge, Ford, Honda, Hyundai, Kia, Kirtland AFB, transmissions

162b a Louisiana Blvd, N 🍴 Bravo Italian, Buca Italian, CA Pizza Kitchen, Chili's, Elephant Bar Rest., Fuddrucker's, Garduno's, Jasons Deli, LePeep, Macaroni Grill, Marcello's, McAlister's Diner, Peiwei Asian, Shoney's, Starbucks 🏠 Hilton Garden, Homewood Suites, Hyatt Place, Marriott, Sheraton Ⓞ Barnes&Noble, Big O Tire, Dillard's, Firestone, JC Penney, Kohl's, Macy's, Sears/auto, Trader Joe's, Verizon, S 🔧 Shell 🍴 Burger King Ⓞ atomic museum

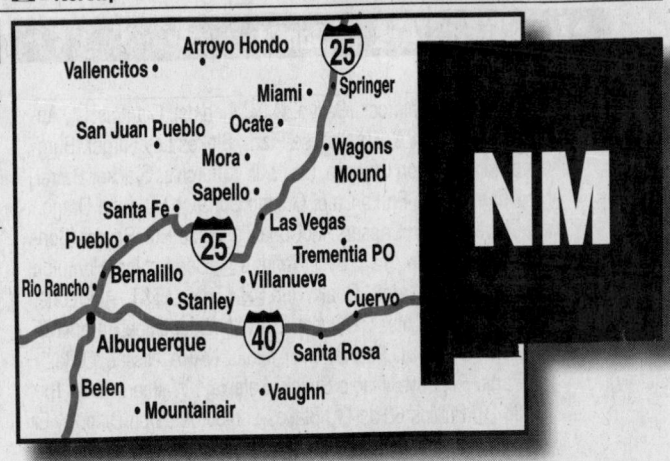
INTERSTATE 40 Cont'd

Exit #	Services
161b a	San Mateo Blvd, Albuquerque, **N** Giant/dsl, Shell Bob's Burgers, Boston Mkt, Carl's Jr., Denny's, KFC, Pizza Hut, Starbucks, Subway, Taco Bell, Wendy's La Quinta $Tree, Office Depot, Old Navy, **S** Chevron/dsl
160	Carlisle Blvd, Albuquerque, **N** Circle K/gas, Premier, Pump'n Save, Shell Applebee's, Blakes Lotaburger, Cheesecake Factory, China Wok, Little Anita's, McDonald's, Pizza Hut, Range Cafe, Rudy's BBQ, Sonic, Subway, Twisters Grill, Village Inn Rest., Whataburger Candlewood Suites, Days Inn, EconoLodge, Elegante Hotel, Hampton Inn, Hilton, Holiday Inn Express, La Quinta, Motel 6, Radisson, Residence Inn, Rodeway Inn, Suburban Motel, Super 8 Firestone/auto, JC Penney, Smith's Foods, Walgreens, **S** Chevron/Subway/dsl Burger King H, K-Mart, Whole Foods Mkt
159b c	I-25, S to Las Cruces, N to Santa Fe
158	6th St, 8th St, 12th St, Albuquerque, **N** Loves/Subway/dsl U-Haul, **S** Chevron Quality Inn
157b	12th St (from eb), **N** Alon/Arby's/dsl Holiday Inn Express Lowe's, Walgreens
157a	Rio Grande Blvd, Albuquerque, **N** Chevron, **S** Shell Ben Michaels, Blakes Lotaburger, Little Anita's, Starbucks Best Western/grill, Hotel Albuquerque repair
156mm	Rio Grande River
155	Coors Rd, Albuquerque, **N** Chevron, Circle K, Duke City/dsl, Giant Gas/dsl Applebee's, Arby's, Baskin-Robbins, Burger King, Chili's, Cracker Barrel, Golden Corral, IHOP, Krispy Kreme, McDonald's, Mimmo's Pizza, Panda Express, Papa Murphy's, Quiznos, Red Brick Pizza, Sonic, Subway, Taco Cabana, Twisters Burritos, Wendy's, Wing Stop $Tree, AutoZone, Brake Masters, Brook's Foods, Family$, Firestone, GNC, Home Depot, Jiffy Lube, Midas, Radio Shack, Staples, Verizon, vet, Walgreens, Walmart, **S** Phillips 66, Shell, Valero Altimar's Mexican, Blakes Lotaburger, Del Taco, Denny's, Federico's Mexican, McDonald's, New China, Papa John's, Pizza Hut/Taco Bell, Subway, Twisters Burritos, Village Inn Rest. Days Inn, EconoLodge, Hampton Inn, La Quinta, Motel 6, Motel 76, Quality Inn, Rodeway Inn, Super 8 BigLots, Discount Tire, dsl repair, O'Reilly Parts
154	Unser Blvd, **N** Valero to Petroglyph NM
153	98th St, **S** FLYING J/Denny's/dsl/LP/24hr, Valero Burger King, Little Caesars, McDonald's, Subway Microtel $Tree, AutoZone, truckwash/tire/lube
149	Central Ave, Paseo del Volcan, **N** Camping World, Enchanted Trails RV Camping, Freightliner, LaMesa RV Ctr, to Shooting Range SP, **S** American RV Park, High Desert RV Park
140.5mm	Rio Puerco River, **N** 66 Pit Stop
140	Rio Puerco, **N** 66 Pit Stop/dsl, **S** Rte 66 TC/DQ/Road Runner Cafe/hotel/casino/dsl/@
131	Canoncito
126	NM 6, to Los Lunas
120mm	Rio San Jose
117	Mesita
114	NM 124, Laguna, **N** 1/2 mi 66 Pit Stop/dsl
113.5mm	scenic view both lanes, litter barrels
108	Casa Blanca, Paraje, **S** Dancing Eagle TC/DQ/dsl/24hr Ace Hardware, casino, RV park
104	Cubero, Budville

Exit #	Services
102	Sky City Rd, Acomita, **N** Sky City/McDonald's/hotel/casino/dsl Huwak'a Rest. casino, RV Park/laundry, **S** H, both lanes, full facilities, litter barrels, petwalk,
100	San Fidel
96	McCartys
89	NM 117, to Quemado, **N** Skyway/Shell/Subway/dsl/gifts, **S** El Malpais NM
85	NM 122, NM 547, Grants, **N** Alon/dsl, Phillips 66/dsl, Shell/dsl Asian Buffet, Blakes Lotaburger, Canton Cafe, Denny's, Pizza Hut, Subway, Taco Bell Comfort Inn, Days Inn, Holiday Inn Express, Motel 6, Quality Inn, Red Lion Motel, Sands Motel, Super 8, Travelodge H, $Tree, AutoZone, Delta Tire, O'Reilly Parts, repair/transmissions/towing, Walmart, **S** Lavaland RV Park
81b a	NM 53 S, Grants, **N** Phillips 66 Domino's, KFC, McDonald's H, Ford, NAPA, USPO, **S** Blue Spruce RV Park, El Malpais NM, KOA/Cibola Sands RV Park
79	NM 122, NM 605, Milan, **N** Chevron/dsl, Loves/Chester's/Subway/dsl/scales/24hr DQ Crossroads Motel Bar-S RV Park, **S** Petro/Iron Skillet/dsl/scales/24hr/@ Speedco Lube, st police
72	Bluewater Village, **N** Exxon/DQ/dsl
63	NM 412, Prewitt, **S** to Bluewater Lake SP (7mi)
53	NM 371, NM 612, Thoreau; **N** Giant/Blimpie/dsl Family$, NAPA, USPO
47	Continental Divide, 7275 ft, **N** Phillips 66 Continental Divide Trdg Post, towing/repair, **S** USPO
44	Coolidge
39	Refinery, **N** /Subway/Dennys/dsl/scales/24hr/@
36	Iyanbito
33	NM 400, McGaffey, Ft Wingate, **N** museum, RV camping, to Red Rock SP
26	E 66th Ave, E Gallup, **N** Shell/Subway/dsl Denny's Comfort Suites, Holiday Inn Express, La Quinta, Sleep Inn museum, Red Rock Camping, st police, to Red Rock SP, **S** on Rte 66 Alon/dsl, Conoco/dsl, Giant, Shell/Ortega Gifts Aurelie's Diner, Blakes Lotaburger, Burger King, KFC, McDonald's, Sonic, Wendy's Days Inn, Hacienda Motel, Roadrunner Motel H, $General
22	Montoya Blvd, Gallup, **N** both lanes, full facilities, info **S** on Rte 66 Duke City, Gas Up, Phillips 66 Big Cheese Pizza, Church's, Domino's, DQ, Earl's Rest., Hong Kong Buffet, LJ Silver, Panz Alegra, Papa John's, Pizza Hut, Subway, Taco Bell Blue Spruce Motel, El Capitan Motel, El Rancho Motel/rest. Albertson's, Giant/dsl, O'Reilly Parts, Radio Shack, Walgreens

GRANTS

GALLUP

NM

Map locations: Arroyo Hondo, Vallencitos, Miami, Springer, San Juan Pueblo, Ocate, Wagons Mound, Mora, Sapello, Santa Fe, Las Vegas, Pueblo, Tremendia PO, Rio Rancho, Bernalillo, Villanueva, Cuervo, Stanley, Albuquerque, Santa Rosa, Belen, Vaughn, Mountainair

⬆E INTERSTATE 40 Cont'd

Exit #	Services
20	US 491, to Shiprock, Gallup, **N** 🅖 Alon/dsl, Giant/dsl 🍴 Applebee's, Arby's, Big Cheese Pizza, Blakes Lotaburger, Burger King, Canton Chinese, Carl's Jr., Church's, Cracker Barrel, Denny's, DQ, Furr's Café, Golden Corral, KFC, King Dragon Chinese, Little Caesars, McDonald's, Pizza Hut, Sizzler, Sonic, Super Buffet, Taco Bell, Wendy's 🏠 Comfort Inn, Hampton Inn, Hilton Garden, Quality Inn 🅞 $Tree, AT&T, AutoZone, Beall's, Big Lots, CarQuest, Chrysler/Dodge/Jeep, Family$, Home Depot, JC Penney, mall, Midas, NAPA, Nissan, O'Reilly Parts, PepBoys, Radio Shack, Safeway, Walmart, **S on Rte 66** 🅖 Phillips 66/dsl 🍴 Blakes Lotaburger, Don Diego's, El Dorado Rest., El Sombrero Mexican, Garcia's Rest., McDonald's, Rte 66 Diner, Sonic 🏠 Ambassador Motel, Best Value Inn, Days Inn, Desert Skies, Golden Desert Motel,

20	Continued Rodeway Inn, Royal Holiday Motel, Super 8 🅞 H, Ford/Lincoln, RV camping, Tire Factory
16	NM 118, W Gallup, Mentmore, **N** 🅖 ♥Love's/Chester's/Subway/dsl/24hr, Navajo/dsl/24hr, TA/Country Pride/dsl/scales/24hr/@, USave Trkstp/dsl 🅞 Blue Beacon, dsl repair, **S** 🅖 Alon, Conoco, Phillips 66/Allsup's, Thrift Way 🍴 Ranch Kitchen, Taco Bell 🏠 Baymont, Budget Inn, EconoLodge, Gallup Inn, Hampton Inn, Microtel, Motel 6, Red Lion, Red Roof Inn, Travelodge 🅞 USA RV Park
12mm	inspection/weigh sta eb
8	to Manuelito
3mm	**Welcome Ctr eb, full ♿ facilities, litter barrels, petwalk, ⟦C⟧, 🚮**
0mm	New Mexico/Arizona state line

NEW YORK

⬆N INTERSTATE 81

Exit #	Services
184mm	US/Canada border, New York state line. **I-81 begins/ends.**
183.5mm	US Customs (sb)
52 (183)	Island Rd, to De Wolf Point, **E** 🍴, last US exit nb
51 (180)	Island Rd, to Fineview, Islands Parks, **E 2-3 mi** 🏠 Seaway Island Resort, Thousand Islands Club/rest 🅞 camping, golf, Nature Ctr, USPO, **W** 🅖 Sunoco/dsl
179mm	St Lawrence River
178.5mm	**NY Welcome Ctr/🆁🆂 sb, full ♿ facilities, litter barrels, petwalk, ⟦C⟧, 🚮, Thousand Islands Toll Bridge Booth**
50NS (178)	NY 12, E to Alexandria Bay, W to Clayton, **E** 🅖 Mobil/dsl 🍴 Kountry Kottage Rest., Subway 🏠 Bonnie Castle Resort, Otter Creek Inn, PineHurst Motel, River Edge Inn 🅞 H, funpark (seasonal), st police, to Thousand Island Region, **W** 🅖 Mobil 🏠 Bridgeview Motel, PJ's Motel 🅞 **NY Welcome Ctr/🆁🆂** to RV camping
174mm	🆁🆂 nb, full ♿ facilities, litter barrels, petwalk, ⟦C⟧, 🚮, st police, vending
49 (171)	NY 411, to Theresa, Indian River Lake, **E** 🅖 Mobil/dsl (4mi), Sunoco/dsl, **W** 🍴 Trickey's Diner
168mm	parking area sb, picnic table
161mm	parking area nb
48a (159)	CR 16
48 (158)	US 11, NY 37, **E 1/4 mi** 🅖 Mobil/dsl, Nice'n Easy/dsl, Sunoco/dsl 🍴 Arby's, Longway's Diner, McDonald's, Papa John's, Subway 🏠 Allen's Budget Motel, Candlewood Suites, Fort Drum Studio-Tels, Microtel, Royal Inn 🅞 st police, Sugar Creek Stores
156.5mm	parking area both lanes
47 (155)	NY 12, Bradley St, Watertown, **E** 🅖 Nice'n Easy/Subway/dsl, Valero 🍴 Frosty Dairy Bar 🅞 H, **W** 🏠 Rainbow Motel
154.5mm	Black River
46 (154)	NY 12F, Coffeen St, Watertown, **E** 🅖 Mobil 🍴 Cracker Barrel, Shorty's Diner 🅞 Home Depot, URGENT CARE
45 (152)	NY 3, to Arsenal St, Watertown, **E** 🅖 Mobil, Sunoco 🍴 5 Guys Burgers, American Grill, Applebee's, Arby's, Buffalo Wild Wings, Burger King, Chipotle Mexican, CiCi's Pizza, Coldstone, Denny's, Dunkin Donuts, Friendly's, Jreck Subs, KFC, McDonald's, Panda Buffet, Ponderosa, Ruby Tuesday, Starbucks, Taco Bell, Tilted Kilt 🏠 Best Value Inn,

45 (152)	Continued Comfort Inn, EconoLodge, Fairfield Inn, Hampton Inn, Hilton Garden, Holiday Inn Express, Rodeway Inn 🅞 $General, $Tree, Advance Parts, Aldi Foods, AT&T, AutoZone, BigLots, Jo-Ann Fabrics, Kost Tire, Mavis Discount Tire, Michael's, Monro, PriceChopper Foods/24hr, Radio Shack, Staples, TJ Maxx, USPO, Walgreens, **W** 🅖 Fastrac 🍴 Bob Evans, Olive Garden, Panera Bread, Pizza Hut, Red Lobster, Subway, Teriyaki Experience, TGIFriday's, TX Roadhouse 🏠 Ramada Inn 🅞 Best Buy, BonTon, Dick's, Gander Mtn, Hannaford Foods, JC Penney, K-Mart, Kohl's, Lowe's, mall, Michael's, Old Navy, PetCo, Sam's Club, Sears/auto, Target, to Sackets Harbor, Verizon, Walmart
149mm	parking area nb, ⟦C⟧
44 (148)	NY 232, to Watertown Ctr, **E 3 mi** 🅖 Mobil 🍴 Subway 🏠 Best Western 🅞 H
147mm	🆁🆂 sb, full ♿ facilities, litter barrels, petwalk, ⟦C⟧, 🚮, vending
43 (146)	US 11, to Kellogg Hill
42 (144)	NY 177, Adams Center, **E** 🅖 Nice'n Easy/Mama Mia's Pizza/dsl, Sunoco/dsl 🍴 Depot Cafe 🅞 Harley-Davidson, Tugger's Camping (12mi)
41 (140)	NY 178, Adams, **E** 🅖 Sunoco/dsl 🍴 Dunkin Donuts, McDonald's, Subway 🅞 KOA, st police, Willows on the Lake RV Park
138mm	South Sandy Creek
40 (135)	NY 193, to Ellisburg, Pierrepont Manor
134mm	both lanes, parking area/picnic tables
39 (133)	Mannsville
38 (131)	US 11
37 (128)	Lacona, Sandy Creek, **E** 🍴 J&R Diner 🏠 Harris Lodge, **W** 🅖 Mobil, Valero 🍴 Sandy Creek Diner 🏠 Anglers Roost B&B 🅞 CarQuest, Colonial Court Camping, Sandy Island Beach SP, USPO
36 (121)	NY 13, Pulaski, **E** 🅖 Byrne Dairy/dsl, Valero 🍴 Ponderosa 🏠 Travelodge, **W** 🅖 KwikFill/dsl, Mobil/dsl, Nice'n Easy/Subway/dsl, Valero 🍴 Arby's, Burger King, Dunkin Donuts, Eddy's Place, Jreck Subs, McDonald's, Paulanjo's Pizza, River House Rest., Stefano's Rest. 🏠 1880 House B&B, Super 8 🅞 Aldi Foods, Buick/Chevrolet, camping, Family$, fish hatchery, Kinney Drug, NAPA, Rite Aid, to Selkirk Shores SP, Top's Foods, Verizon

NM
NY

WATERTOWN

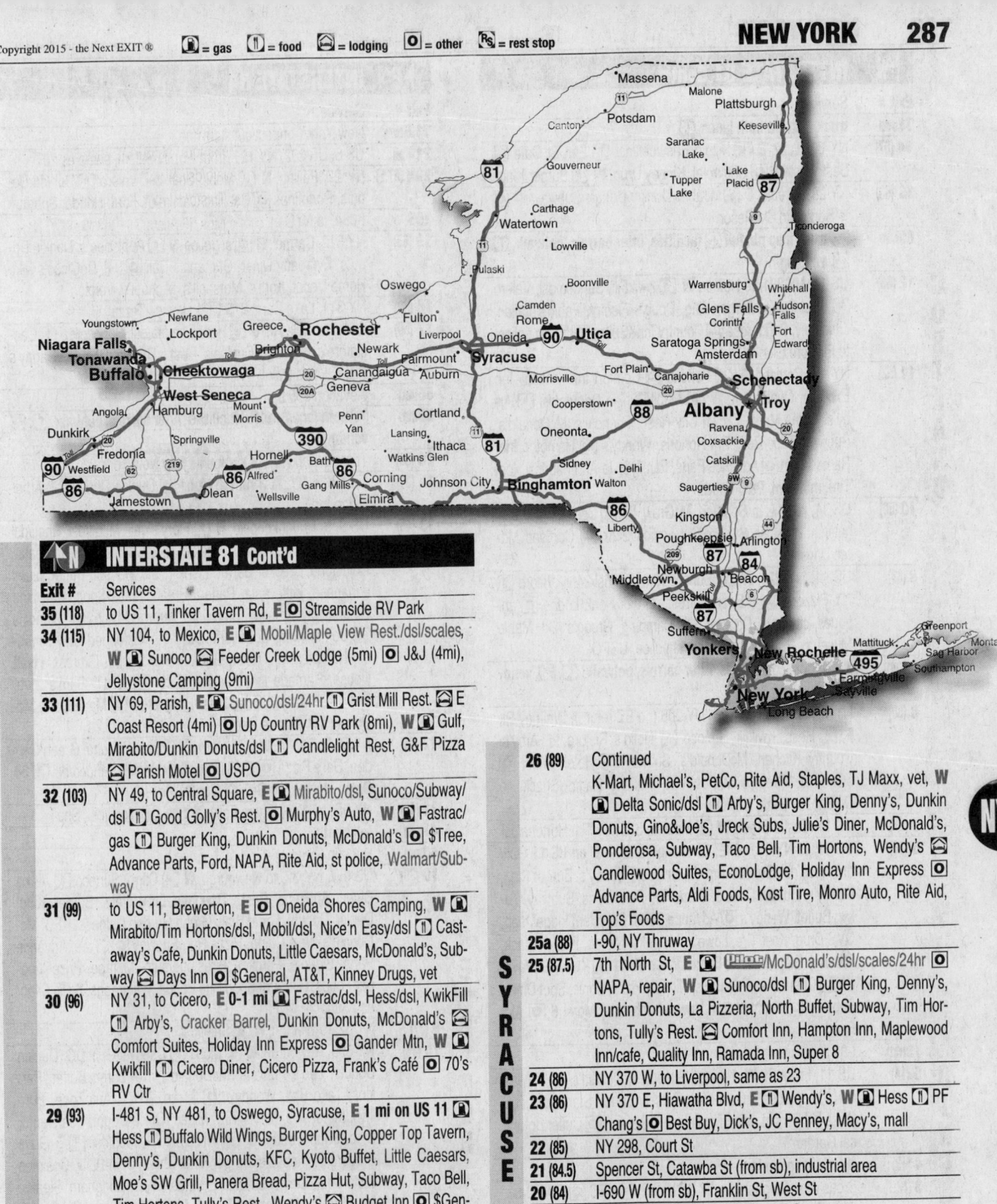

↖N INTERSTATE 81 Cont'd

Exit #	Services
35 (118)	to US 11, Tinker Tavern Rd, E Ⓞ Streamside RV Park
34 (115)	NY 104, to Mexico, E 🚗 Mobil/Maple View Rest./dsl/scales, W 🚗 Sunoco 🏨 Feeder Creek Lodge (5mi) Ⓞ J&J (4mi), Jellystone Camping (9mi)
33 (111)	NY 69, Parish, E 🚗 Sunoco/dsl/24hr 🍴 Grist Mill Rest. 🏨 E Coast Resort (4mi) Ⓞ Up Country RV Park (8mi), W 🚗 Gulf, Mirabito/Dunkin Donuts/dsl 🍴 Candlelight Rest, G&F Pizza 🏨 Parish Motel Ⓞ USPO
32 (103)	NY 49, to Central Square, E 🚗 Mirabito/dsl, Sunoco/Subway/dsl 🍴 Good Golly's Rest. Ⓞ Murphy's Auto, W 🚗 Fastrac/gas 🍴 Burger King, Dunkin Donuts, McDonald's Ⓞ $Tree, Advance Parts, Ford, NAPA, Rite Aid, st police, Walmart/Subway
31 (99)	to US 11, Brewerton, E Ⓞ Oneida Shores Camping, W 🚗 Mirabito/Tim Hortons/dsl, Mobil/dsl, Nice'n Easy/dsl 🍴 Castaway's Cafe, Dunkin Donuts, Little Caesars, McDonald's, Subway 🏨 Days Inn Ⓞ $General, AT&T, Kinney Drugs, vet
30 (96)	NY 31, to Cicero, E 0-1 mi 🚗 Fastrac/dsl, Hess/dsl, KwikFill 🍴 Arby's, Cracker Barrel, Dunkin Donuts, McDonald's 🏨 Comfort Suites, Holiday Inn Express Ⓞ Gander Mtn, W 🚗 Kwikfill 🍴 Cicero Diner, Cicero Pizza, Frank's Café Ⓞ 70's RV Ctr
29 (93)	I-481 S, NY 481, to Oswego, Syracuse, E 1 mi on US 11 🚗 Hess 🍴 Buffalo Wild Wings, Burger King, Copper Top Tavern, Denny's, Dunkin Donuts, KFC, Kyoto Buffet, Little Caesars, Moe's SW Grill, Panera Bread, Pizza Hut, Subway, Taco Bell, Tim Hortons, Tully's Rest., Wendy's 🏨 Budget Inn Ⓞ $General, $Tree, Advance Parts, AT&T, Audi/Porsche/VW, Chrysler/Dodge/Jeep, Dunn Tire, Firestone/auto, GNC, Home Depot, Hyundai, Kia, Lexus, Lincoln, Lowe's, Marshall's, NAPA, Nissan, PepBoys, PriceChopper Foods, Radio Shack, Rite Aid, Suzuki, Target, Toyota/Scion, Verizon, Walmart, Wegman's Foods
28 (91)	N Syracuse, Taft Rd, E 🚗 KwikFill, Sunoco/dsl Ⓞ U-Haul, W 🚗 Sunoco Ⓞ Auto Value Parts, USPO
27 (90)	N Syracuse, E Ⓞ 🚗
26 (89)	US 11, Mattydale, E 🚗 Mobil 🍴 Hofmann Rest., Pizza Hut 🏨 Red Carpet Inn Ⓞ $Tree, BigLots, GNC, Goodyear/auto,

26 (89)	**Continued** K-Mart, Michael's, PetCo, Rite Aid, Staples, TJ Maxx, vet, W 🚗 Delta Sonic/dsl 🍴 Arby's, Burger King, Denny's, Dunkin Donuts, Gino&Joe's, Jreck Subs, Julie's Diner, McDonald's, Ponderosa, Subway, Taco Bell, Tim Hortons, Wendy's 🏨 Candlewood Suites, EconoLodge, Holiday Inn Express Ⓞ Advance Parts, Aldi Foods, Kost Tire, Monro Auto, Rite Aid, Top's Foods
25a (88)	I-90, NY Thruway
25 (87.5)	7th North St, E 🚗 🍴/McDonald's/dsl/scales/24hr Ⓞ NAPA, repair, W 🚗 Sunoco/dsl 🍴 Burger King, Denny's, Dunkin Donuts, La Pizzeria, North Buffet, Subway, Tim Hortons, Tully's Rest. 🏨 Comfort Inn, Hampton Inn, Maplewood Inn/cafe, Quality Inn, Ramada Inn, Super 8
24 (86)	NY 370 W, to Liverpool, same as 23
23 (86)	NY 370 E, Hiawatha Blvd, E 🍴 Wendy's, W 🚗 Hess 🍴 PF Chang's Ⓞ Best Buy, Dick's, JC Penney, Macy's, mall
22 (85)	NY 298, Court St
21 (84.5)	Spencer St, Catawba St (from sb), industrial area
20 (84)	I-690 W (from sb), Franklin St, West St
19 (84)	I-690 E, Clinton St, Salina St, to E Syracuse
18 (84)	Harrison St, Adams St, E 🏨 Crowne Plaza Ⓞ Ⓗ, Civic Ctr, to Syracuse U
17 (82)	Brighton Ave, S Salina St, W 🚗 KwikFill, Valero/Chicken Basket
16a (81)	I-481 N, to DeWitt
16 (78)	US 11, to Nedrow, Onondaga Nation, W 1-2 mi 🍴 Fire Keepers Diner, McDonald's, Pizza Hut
15 (73)	US 20, La Fayette, E 🚗 Sunoco/dsl 🍴 La Fayette Inn, Old Tymes Rest. Ⓞ $General, NAPA, st police, USPO, vet, W 🍴 McDonald's

S Y R A C U S E

🅿 = gas 🍴 = food 🏨 = lodging 🅾 = other 🆁🆂 = rest stop   Copyright 2015 - the Next EXIT ®

⬆N	INTERSTATE 81 Cont'd
Exit #	**Services**
71mm	**truck insp sta both lanes, (🄲**
14 (67)	NY 80, Tully, **E** 🅿 Nice'n Easy/deli/dsl 🍴 Elm St Cafe 🏨 Best Western 🅾 Chevrolet, Kinney Drug, **W** 🍴 Burger King
13 (63)	NY 281, Preble, **E** 🅿 Mirabito/Dunkin Donuts/Subway/dsl 🅾 to Song Mtn Ski Resort
60mm	🆁🆂/truck insp nb, full 🚻 facilities, litter barrels, petwalk, (🄲 🖼, vending
12 (53)	US 11, NY 281, to Homer, **W** 🅿 KwikFill, Sunoco/dsl, Valero 🍴 Applebee's, Burger King, Doug's Fishfry, Fabio's Italian, Little Italy, Ponderosa 🏨 Country Inn&Suites 🅾 🄷, st police, to Fillmore Glen SP
11 (52)	NY 13, Cortland, **E** 🍴 Perkins 🏨 Comfort Inn, Holiday Inn Express, Quality Inn, **W** 🅿 Mobil/Dunkin Donuts/dsl 🍴 Arby's, China Moon, Crown City Rest., Friendly's, McDonald's, Subway, Taco Bell, Tim Hortons, Wendy's 🏨 Hampton Inn, Ramada Inn 🅾 Advance Parts, Family$, Jo-Ann Fabrics, Kost Tire, museum, P&C Foods
10 (50)	US 11, NY 41, to Cortland, McGraw, **W** 🅿 Citgo/Dunkin Donuts/Quiznos/dsl, Sunoco/Subway/dsl/24hr 🏨 Cortland Motel, Days Inn
9 (38)	US 11, NY 221, **W** 🅿 Sunoco/XtraMart/dsl/24hr, Valero 🍴 NY Pizzaria 🏨 3 Bear Inn/rest., Greek Peak Lodge 🅾 antiques, city park, Country Hills Camping, Gregg's Mkt, Maple Museum, Robinson's Repair, st police, USPO
33mm	🆁🆂 sb, full 🚻 facilities, litter barrels, petwalk, (🄲, 🖼, vending
8 (30)	NY 79, to US 11, NY 26, NY 206 (no EZ return), Whitney Pt, **E** 🅿 Hess, Kwikfill, Sunoco 🍴 Aiello's Ristorante, Arby's, Country Kitchen, McDonald's, Subway 🏨 Hotel Griffin 🅾 $General, Gregg's Mkt, NAPA, Parts+, Radio Shack, to Dorchester Park, USPO
7 (21)	US 11, Castle Creek, **W** 🅿 Mirabito/Subway/Tim Hortons/dsl
6 (16)	US 11, to NY 12, I-88E, Chenango Bridge, **E on US 11** Gulf/dsl, Hess/dsl, Sunoco/Tim Hortons/dsl 🍴 Arby's, Burger King, Denny's, Dunkin Donuts, Pizza Hut, Ponderosa, Subway, Tokyo Buffet, Wendy's 🅾 Advance Parts, Chrysler/Dodge/Jeep, CVS Drug, Kost Tire, Lowe's, Meineke, Monro, Radio Shack, Rite Aid, Staples, Weis Foods, **W on US 11** 🅿 KwikFill, Wave/dsl 🍴 China Star, Friendly's, Nirchi's Pizza, Sonic, Spot Diner, Subway 🏨 Comfort Inn, Howard Johnson, Motel 6 🅾 Aldi Foods
15mm	I-88 begins eb
5 (14)	US 11, Front St, **W 1 mi** 🅿 Sunoco/McDonald's/dsl, Valero/dsl 🍴 Applebee's, Coldstone, Cracker Barrel, Starbucks, TLC Pizza 🏨 EconoLodge, Fairfield Inn, Super 8 🅾 Cutler Botanical Garden
4 (13)	NY 17, Binghamton
3 (12)	Broad Ave, Binghamton, **W** 🅿 Valero 🍴 KFC 🅾 CVS Drug, Giant Foods
3 (10)	Industrial Park, same as 2
2 (8)	US 11, NY 17, **W 1-2 mi** 🅿 Gulf/dsl, Loves/Wendy's/dsl/scales/24hr, TA/dsl/rest./24hr/@ 🍴 Arby's, Burger King, McDonald's, Subway 🏨 Del Motel, Wright Motel
1 (4)	US 11, NY 7, Kirkwood, **W 1-2 mi** 🅿 Mirabito/dsl, Xtra 🍴 Hallo Berlin Rest 🏨 Kirkwood Motel
2mm	**Welcome ctr nb, full 🚻 facilities, litter barrels, petwalk, (🄲, 🖼, vending**
1mm	**truck insp sta nb**
0mm	New York/Pennsylvania state line

Left side vertical label: C O R T L A N D ... B I N G H A M T O N

NY

⬆E	INTERSTATE 84
Exit #	**Services**
71.5mm	New York/Connecticut state line
21 (69)	US 6; US 202, NY 121 (from wb), N Salem, same as 20
20N (67.5)	NY 22, Palling, **N** 🅿 Mobil, Shell/dsl, Valero 🍴 Dunkin Donuts, Portofinos 🅾 Cadillac/Chevrolet, Ford, Honda, Subaru
20S	I-684, to NYC
19 (65)	NY 312, Carmel, **N** 🅾 st police, **S** 🍴 Applebee's, Dunkin Donuts, Eveready Diner, Gaetano's Deli 🅾 🄷, DeCicco's Mkt, Home Depot, Kohl's, Marshall's, Michael's, Verizon
18 (62)	NY 311, Lake Carmel, **S** 🍴 Lakeview Pizza
17 (59)	Ludingtonville Rd, **S** 🅿 Hess/Blimpie/dsl, Sunoco/dsl 🍴 Cacciatore's Pizzaria, Cutiloo's Rest., Dunkin Donuts, Gappy's Pizza, Lou's Deli
56mm	elevation 965 ft
55mm	🆁🆂 both lanes, full 🚻 facilities, litter barrels, petwalk, (🄲, 🖼 vending
16 (53)	Taconic Parkway, N to Albany, S to New York
15 (51)	Lime Kiln NY, **N 3 mi** 🅿 Mobil 🍴 Dunkin Donuts 🏨 Arbor Ridge Inn
13 (46)	US 9, to Poughkeepsie, **N** 🅿 Flory's/deli, Mobil/dsl, Shell/dsl 🍴 5 Guys, A&W/KFC, Boston Mkt, Charlie Brown Steaks, Coldstone, Cracker Barrel, Fishkill Grill, Hudson Buffet, Izumi Japanese, Little Asia, Panera Bread, Pizza Shop, Red Line Diner, Ruby Tuesday, Starbucks, Subway, Taco Bell, Wendy's 🏨 Comfort Inn, Courtyard, Days Inn, Extended Stay America, Hampton Inn, Hilton Garden, Holiday Inn Express, Hyatt House, Ramada Inn, Residence Inn 🅾 AT&T, Sam's Club, Verizon, Walmart, **S** 🅿 Hess/Blimpie/dsl 🍴 Maya Cafe, McDonald's 🅾 Home Depot
12 (45)	NY 52 E, Fishkill, **N** 🅿 Valero 🍴 Golden Buddha, Green Garden, Sal's Pizza 🅾 CVS Drug, **S** 🅿 Mobil, Sunoco/dsl 🍴 84 Diner, Hometown Deli 🏨 Quality Inn
11 (42)	NY 9D, to Wappingers Falls, **N 1 mi** 🅿 Mobil/dsl, Shell
41mm	toll booth
40mm	Hudson River
10 (39)	US 9W, NY 32, to Newburgh, **N** 🅿 Citgo, Sunoco 🍴 Alexis Diner, Andiamo Rest., Bonura's Little Italy, Burger King, Dunkin Donuts, Great Wall, Green Garden Chinese, KFC, McDonald's, New China, Pizza Hut, Subway 🅾 $Tree, Advance Parts, BigLots, Family$, Firestone/auto, Monroe, PriceChopper Foods, Rite Aid, Shop Rite Foods, Walgreens, **S** 🅿 Citgo/dsl, Sunoco 🅾 🄷
8 (37)	NY 52, to Walden, **N** 🅿 Shell/dsl
7b (36)	NY 300, Newburgh, **N** 🅿 Mobil 🍴 Daddy's Grill, DQ, Dunkin Donuts, Leo's Pizzaria, McDonald's, Newburgh Buffet, Perkins, Taco Bell, Wendy's 🅾 $Tree, AT&T, AutoZone, Bon-Ton, Marshall's, Mavis Tire, Midas, Office Depot, Sears/auto, Stop&Shop Foods, **S** 🅿 Hess/dsl, Sunoco/dsl 🍴 5 Guys Burgers, Applebee's, Burger King, Chili's, China City, Cosimos Ristorante, Denny's, IHOP, Ikaros Diner, Longhorn Steaks, Neptune Diner, Panera Bread, Pizza Mia, Sonic, Starbucks, Steak'n Stein, Subway, TGIFriday's, Union Sq Rest., Yobo Asian 🏨 Days Inn, Hilton Garden, Howard Johnson, Ramada Inn, Super 8 🅾 $General, Adam's Farm Mkt, Aldi Foods, Barnes&Noble, Buick/GMC, Cadillac/Chevrolet, Chrysler/Dodge/Jeep, Ford/Lincoln, Home Depot, Honda, Kohl's, Lowe's, Meineke, Michael's, Nissan, Orange County Choppers/cafe, PetsMart, Radio Shack, Target, Verizon, Walmart
7a (35)	I-87, NY Thruway, Albany, to NYC
6 (34)	NY 17K, to Newburgh, **N** 🅿 Mobil, 🅿/Arby's/dsl/scales/24hr 🍴 Airport Diner 🏨 Comfort Inn, **S** 🅿 Shell/dsl 🏨 Courtyard, Days Inn, Hilton Garden, Howard Johnson

Right side vertical label: N E W B U R G H

INTERSTATE 84 Cont'd

Exit #	Services
5a (33)	NY 747, International Blvd, **S** 🏠 Homewood Suites 🅞 to Stewart ✈
5 (29)	NY 208, Maybrook, **N** 🅖 Mobil/dsl, Sunoco/dsl 🍴 Burger King, Dunkin Donuts, McDonald's 🅞 NAPA, Rite Aid, Shop-Rite Foods, Walgreens, Winding Hills Camping, **S** 🅖 Hess/dsl, TA/Valero/Country Pride/Pizza Hut/dsl/scales/24hr/@ 🍴 Prima's Deli, Renee's Deli, Subway 🏠 Super 8 🅞 Advance Parts, auto/truck repair, Blue Beacon, st police
24mm	🆁🆂 wb, full 🅰 facilities, litter barrels, petwalk, 🎁, 🍴, vending
4 (19)	NY 17, Middletown, **N** 🅖 Mobil/24hr 🍴 Americana Diner, Applebee's, Arby's, Baskin-Robbins/Dunkin Donuts, Boston Mkt, Burger King, Cheeseburger Paradise, ChuckeCheese, Denny's, Friendly's, KFC, McDonald's, Olive Garden, Panera Bread, Papa John's, Perkins, Pizza Hut, Red Lobster, Ruby Tuesday, Starbucks, Subway, Taco Bell, Wendy's, Youyou Japanese 🏠 Howard Johnson, Middletown Motel, Super 8 🅞 🏥, $Tree, Aldi Foods, AutoZone, Best Buy, Big Lots, Firestone/auto, Gander Mtn, Hannaford Foods, Home Depot, Honda, JC Penney, Jo-Ann Fabrics, Kohl's, Lowe's, mall, Marshall's, Michael's, Old Navy, PetCo, PetsMart, PriceChopper Foods, Rite Aid, Sam's Club/gas, Sears/auto, ShopRite Foods, Staples, Tire Discount, TJ Maxx, U-Haul, URGENT CARE, Verizon, vet, Walmart/24hr, **S** 🅖 Citgo/dsl 🍴 Chili's, El Bandido Mexican, Outback Steaks, TGIFriday 🏠 Courtyard, Hampton Inn, Holiday Inn, Microtel 🅞 st police
17mm	🆁🆂 eb, full 🅰 facilities, litter barrels, petwalk, 🎁, 🍴, vending
3 (15)	US 6, to Middletown, **N** 🅖 Citgo/dsl, Mobil, QuickChek/dsl, Shell, Valero 🍴 Bro Bruno's Pizza, Dunkin Donuts, IHOP, McDonald's, NY Buffet, Peking Chinese, Rita's Custard, Subway, Taco Bell, Wendy's 🅞 🏥, Acura, AutoZone, Buick/Chevrolet, CarQuest, Family$, Goodyear, Mavis Discount Tire, Mazda, Meineke, Radio Shack, Rite Aid, ShopRite Foods, Subaru, Verizon, VW, **S** 🅖 Citgo/dsl, Geo/Dunkin Donuts/dsl 🏠 Days Inn, Global Budget Inn 🅞 Kia, Nissan, Toyota/Scion
2 (5)	Mountain Rd, **S** 🍴 Greenville's Deli
4mm	1272 ft eb, elevation 1254 ft wb
3mm	**parking area both lanes**
1 (1)	US 6, NY 23, Port Jervis, **N** 🍴 Arlene'n Tom's Diner, Baskin-Robbins/Dunkin Donuts 🏠 Brookside Cottages 🅞 🏥, Ford, **S** 🅖 BP/dsl/LP, Citgo/dsl, Gulf/dsl, ⬜/Subway/dsl, Valero/dsl 🍴 DQ, McDonald's 🏠 Days Inn 🅞 🏥, $Tree, GNC, ShopRite Foods, TJ Maxx
0mm	New York/Pennsylvania state line, Delaware River

INTERSTATE 86

Exit #	Services
	I-86 begins/ends on I-87, exit 16, toll booth
131 (379)	NY 17, **N** 🍴 Applebee's 🅞 Outlets/famous brands, **S** 🅖 Gulf/dsl 🍴 Chili's, Dunkin Donuts, KFC, Outback Steaks, Panera Bread, TGIFriday's, Uno Grill, Wendy's 🏠 Days Inn, Hampton Inn 🅞 $Tree, Best Buy, BJ's Whse, BMW, GNC, Home Depot, Kohl's, Michael's, Old Navy, Petsmart, Radio Shack, Staples, Target, TJMaxx, Verizon, Walmart/Subway
130a (378)	US 6, Bear Mtn, to West Point (from eb, no return)
130 (377)	NY 208, Monroe, Washingtonville, **N** 🍴 Rambler's Rest, **S** 🅖 Mobil/dsl, Sunoco/dsl, Valero 🍴 Burger King, Dunkin Donuts, Monroe Diner 🅞 $Tree, ShopRite Foods, st police

Exit #	Services
129 (375)	Museum Village Rd
128 (374)	rd 51 (only from wb), Oxford Depot
127 (373)	Greycourt Rd (from wb only), Sugar Loaf, Warwick
126 (372)	NY 94 (no EZ wb return), Chester, Florida, **N** 🅖 Mobil, Shell, Sunoco/dsl 🍴 Bro Bruno Pizza, Chester Diner, Lobster Pier Rest, McDonald's, Wendy's 🏠 Holiday Inn Express 🅞 CVS Drug, GNC, Radio Shack, ShopRite Foods, USPO, **S** 🅞 Black Bear Camping, Lowe's
125 (369)	NY 17M E, South St, **N** 🍴 Hacienda Mexican
124 (368)	NY 17A, NY 207, **N** 🅖 Gulf/Subway/dsl, Mobil/dsl 🍴 Burger King, Dunkin Donuts, Friendly's, Goshen Diner, Pizza Hut 🅞 🏥, CVS Drug, Verizon, **S** 🏠 Comfort Inn 🅞 Chrysler/Dodge/Jeep, Hyundai, URGENT CARE
123	US 6, NY 17M (wb only), Port Jervis
122a (367)	Fletcher St, Goshen
122 (364)	rd 67, E Main St, Crystal Run Rd, **N** 🍴 Chili's, Outback Steaks, TGIFriday's 🏠 Courtyard, Hampton Inn, Holiday Inn, Microtel 🅞 URGENT CARE, **S** 🍴 El Bandido Rest.
121 (363)	I-84, E to Newburgh, W to Port Jervis
120 (363)	NY 211, **N** 🅖 Lukoil, Mobil, Sunoco 🍴 Buffalo Wild Wings, Cosimo's Ristorante, Olive Garden, Perkins 🏠 Howard Johnson, Middletown Motel, Super 8 🅞 Best Buy, Dick's, Gander Mtn, Hannaford's Foods, Honda, JC Penney, Lowe's, Macy's, Mavis Discount Tire, Old Navy, PetCo, Sam's Club/gas, Sears, Target, vet, **S** 🅖 Mobil 🍴 5 Guys Burgers, Americana Diner, Applebee's, Arby's, Boston Mkt, Burger King, Cheeseburger Paradise, Denny's, Dunkin Donuts, Franko Di Roma Italian, Friendly's, KFC, McDonald's, Panera Bread, Papa John's, Pizza Hut, Red Lobster, Ruby Tuesday, Starbucks, Subway, Taco Bell, TX Roadhouse, Wendy's, YouYou Chinese 🅞 $General, $Tree, Aldi Foods, AT&T, AutoZone, BigLots, Firestone/auto, Hobby Lobby, Home Depot, Kohl's, Marshall's, Michael's, Midas, Petsmart, PriceChopper, Rite Aid, ShopRite Foods, Staples, Tire Discount Ctr, TJMaxx, U-Haul, Verizon, Walmart/Subway
119 (360)	NY 309, Pine Bush, **S** 🅖 Citgo/dsl, Valero/Dunkin Donuts/dsl 🍴 Subway
118a (358)	NY 17M, Fair Oaks
118 (358)	Circleville, **N** 🏠 Economy Inn, **S** 🅖 Citgo/dsl, Mobil/dsl
116 (355)	NY 17K, Bloomingburg, **N** 🍴 Mtn View Rest, **S** 🅖 Citgo/dsl 🍴 Quickway Diner
115	Burlingame Rd
114	Wurtsboro, Highview (from wb)
113 (350)	US 209, Wurtsboro, Ellenville, **N** 🅖 Mobil/dsl, Stewarts/gas 🍴 Custar's Last Stand, Danny's Steaks 🏠 Days Inn, Gold Mtn Chalet, Honors Haven Resort, Valley Brook Motel 🅞 G-Mart Foods, Spring Glen Camping, **S** 🍴 Giovanni's Café (2mi)

↑E INTERSTATE 86 Cont'd

Exit #	Services
112 (347)	Masten Lake, Yankee Lake, N 🛏 Days Inn, ValleyBrook Motel 🅞 Catskill Mtn Ranch Camping, Yankee Lake
111 (344)	(eb only), Wolf Lake, S 🅟 Citgo/dsl
110 (343)	Lake Louise Marie
109 (342)	Rock Hill, Woodridge, N 🅟 Citgo/dsl 🍴 Angelo's Kitchen, Dutch's Cafe, Krust Italian, Pizza Rock, RockHill Diner 🛏 Sullivan Hotel 🅞 Ace Hardware, auto repair, Hilltop Farms Camping, Super Mkt Trading Post, USPO, S 🅟 Mobil/dsl 🍴 Dragon Garden Chinese
108 (341)	Bridgeville, same as 109
107 (340)	Thompsonville, S 🍴 Old Homestead Diner 🅞 Chevrolet, Chrysler/Dodge/Jeep, Toyota
106 (339)	(wb only), E. Broadway, N 🅞 Ford/Lincoln, S 🅟 Mobil/dsl 🛏 Super 8 (2 mi) 🅞 GMC Trucks, Hyundai
105 (337)	NY 42, Monticello, N 🅟 Mobil, Valero 🍴 Blue Horizon Diner, Bro Bruno's Pizza, Burger King, China 1, Dunkin Donuts, Giovanni's Rest, KFC, McDonald's, Subway 🅞 AutoZone, Home Depot, museum, Radio Shack, ShopRite Foods, Staples, Walmart/McDonald's, S 🅟 Citgo/dsl, Sunoco/dsl 🍴 Miss Monticello Diner, Nugget Rest, Pizza Hut, Pizza Hut, Stewart's, Wendy's 🛏 EconoLodge, Heritage Inn, Super 8 🅞 Advance Parts, Family$, NAPA, Rite Aid
104 (336)	NY 17B, Raceway, Monticello, S 🅟 Citgo/dsl, Mobil/dsl 🍴 Albella Rest, Bean Bag Cafe, Colosseo Rest. 🛏 Best Western, Raceway Motel, Travel Inn 🅞 AT&T, Swinging Bridge Camp, Woodstock Camping
103	Rapp Rd (wb only)
102 (332)	Harris, N 🅞 Ⓗ
101mm	🅡 eb, full 🅖 facilities, litter barrels, petwalk, 🅒, 🅐, vending
101 (327)	Ferndale, Swan Lake, S 🅟 Mobil/dsl 🅞 Swan Lake Camping (5mi)
100a	NY 52 W (no wb return), Liberty, S 🍴 McCabe's Rest 🅞 K&K Drug, st police
100 (327)	NY 52 E, Liberty, N 🅟 Citgo, Sam's, Sunoco 🍴 Albert's Diner, Burger King, Dunkin Donuts, Last Licks Cafe, Liberty Diner, McDonald's, Piccolo Italian, Pizza Hut, Subway, Taco Bell, Wendy's 🛏 Days Inn, Howard Johnson 🅞 $Tree, Ace Hardware, Advance Parts, Rite Aid, ShopRite Foods, USPO, S 🅟 XtraMart 🛏 Lincoln Motel 🅞 Buick/Cadillac, Chrysler/Dodge/Jeep, Ford/Lincoln, Southend Parts, Swan Lake Camping (5mi)
99 (325)	NY 52 W, to NY 55, Liberty, S 🅟 Sunoco 🛏 Catskill Motel
98 (321)	Cooley, Parksville, N 🅟 Mobil/dsl 🍴 Dari-King
97 (319)	Morsston
96 (316)	Livingston Manor, N 🅞 Covered Bridge Camping, S 🅟 Citgo, Sunoco 🍴 Lazy Beagle Grill, Robinhood Diner 🛏 Lanza's Country Inn 🅞 Covered Bridge Camping, Mongaup Pond Camping, Peck's Mkt, to Covered Bridge, USPO
313mm	🅡 eb, truck insp. sta (eb), full 🅖 facilities, litter barrels, petwalk, 🅒, 🅐, vending
94 (311)	NY 206, Roscoe, Lew Beach, N 🅟 Mobil/dsl, Sunoco/dsl 🍴 La Voglia, NYC Gyros, Raimondo's Diner, Roscoe Diner 🛏 Reynolds House Motel, Rockland House Motel, Roscoe Motel, Tennanah Lake Motel 🅞 Catskill Grocers, st police, S 🅟 Mobil/dsl 🅞 Beaverkill St Camping (8mi)
93 (305)	to Cooks Falls (from wb)
92 (303)	Horton, Cooks Falls, Colchester, S 🅟 Sunoco/dsl 🍴 Riverside Café/lodge 🅞 Russell Brook Camping

Exit #	Services
90 (297)	NY 30, East Branch, Downsville, N 🅟 Sunoco 🅞 Beaver-Del Camping, Oxbow Camping, Peaceful Valley Camping, S 🛏 E Branch Motel
295mm	🅡 wb, full 🅖 facilities, litter barrels, petwalk, 🅒, 🅐, vending
89 (293)	Fishs Eddy
87a (288)	NY 268 (from wb, no ez-return), same as 87
87 (284)	NY 97, to NY 268, to NY 191, Hancock, Cadosia, S 🅟 Getty, Mirabito/Subway/dsl, Valero 🍴 Bluestone Grill, Little Italy Pizza, McDonald's, McTigues Rest, New China 🛏 Capra Inn, Colonial Motel, Starlight Lake Inn 🅞 Family$, Grand Union Foods, NAPA, Rite Aid
276mm	parking area wb
84 (274)	Deposit, N 🅟 Citgo/dsl 🍴 BC Pizza, Grand Stand Rest., Pines Rest., Wendy's 🛏 Deposit Motel, Laurel Bank Motel 🅞 Family$, st police
83 (272)	Deposit, Oquaga Lake
82 (270)	NY 41, McClure, Sanford, N 🍴 Cornerstone Cafe 🅞 Kellystone Park, S 🅟 Sun/dsl 🛏 Scott's Family Resort 🅞 Guestward Camping (3mi), Oquaga Creek SP
265mm	parking area eb, litter barrels, 🅐
81 (263)	E Bosket Rd
80 (261)	Damascus, N 🅟 Gulf/Manley's/dsl 🅞 auto repair, Forest Hill Lake Park Camping
79 (259)	NY 79, Windsor, N 🅟 Extra, Sunoco/dsl 🍴 McBride's Rest, Subway, S 🍴 Marian's Pizza/Subs 🅞 Lakeside Camping (8mi)
78 (256)	Dunbar Rd, Occanum
77 (254)	W Windsor, N 🅟 Sunoco/dsl 🍴 McDonald's
76 (251)	Haskins Rd, to Foley Rd
75 (250)	I-81 S, to PA (exits left from wb)
I-86/I-81 run together 4 miles	
3	Colesville Rd (from eb), S 🅟 Loves/Wendy's, TA/dsl/scales /24hr
I-86/I-81 run together 4 miles	
3	Broad Ave (from wb, no return)
4NS	NY 7, **I-86/I-81 run together 4 miles**
72 (244)	I-81 N, US 11, Front St, Clinton St, (no wb re-entry), S 🅞 Aamco
71 (242)	Airport Rd, Johnson City, S 🅟 Valero 🅞 Walmart
70 (241)	NY 201, Johnson City, N 🅟 Hess/Blimpie/dsl, Valero 🍴 Arby's, Christy's Grill, Dunkin Donuts, Friendly's, Great China, Ground Round, Grub House Cafe, McDonald's, Papa John's, Pizza Hut, Ruby Tuesday, Taco Bell 🛏 Best Western, Hampton Inn, La Quinta, Red Roof Inn 🅞 Bon-Ton, JC Penney, Kost Tire, Macy's, mall, PetCo, Sears/auto, vet, Wegman's Foods, Wies Foods, S 🅞 Home Depot
69 (239)	NY 17C
238mm	Susquehanna River
68 (237)	NY 17C, Old Vestal Rd, (from eb, no re-entry)
67 (236)	NY 26, NY 434, Vestal, Endicott, S on NY 434 🅟 Hess, Stop'N Gas, Valero/dsl 🍴 A&W/LJ Silver, Arby's, Burger King, CA Grill, ChuckECheese, Dunkin Donuts, Friendly's, Grand Buffet, KFC, La Vita Bella, McDonald's, Moe's SW Grill, Old Country Buffet, Olive Garden, Outback Steaks, Panera Bread, Plaza Diner, Red Lobster, Starbucks, Subway, Taco Bell, TGIFriday's, Uno Grill, Wendy's 🛏 Comfort Suites, Courtyard, Hampton Inn, Holiday Inn Express, Homewood Suites, Parkway Motel, Vestal Motel 🅞 $General, $Tree, Advance Parts, Aldi Foods, AT&T, Barnes&Noble, Best Buy, BigLots, CarQuest, CVS Drug, Dick's, Firestone/auto, Ford/Lincoln, JoAnn Fabrics, Kohl's, Kost Tire, Lowe's, Meineke, Michael's,

WINDSOR

VESTAL

NY

INTERSTATE 86 Cont'd

Exit #	Services

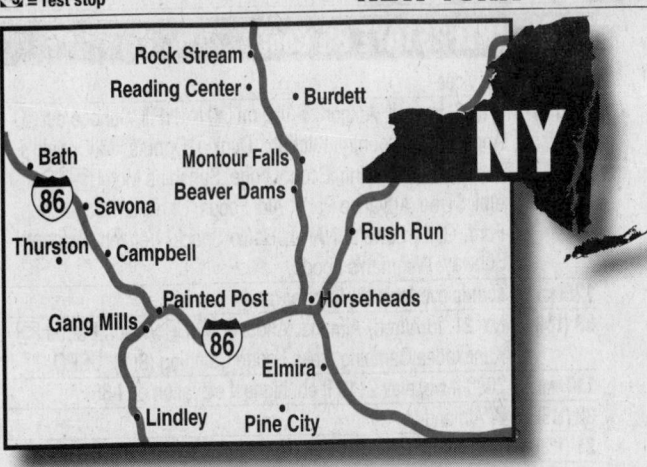

67 (236) Continued
Nissan, Old Navy, Petsmart, Price Rite Foods, Radio Shack, Rite Aid, Sam's Club, Staples, Suzuki, Target, TJ Maxx, U-Haul, Verizon, vet, Volvo, Walmart/Blimpie, Wies Foods

66 (231) NY 434, Apalachin, S 🅖 KwikFill, Mobil/dsl, Sunoco 🅕 Big Dipper Drive-In, Blue Dolphin Diner, Dunkin Donuts, McDonald's, Subway 🅛 Quality Inn

65 (225) NY 17C, NY 434, Owego, N 🅖 Sunoco 🅕 A&W/KFC, Arby's, Panda Wok, Pizza Hut, Subway, Wendy's 🅛 Hampton Inn, Holiday Inn Express, Treadway Inn/rest. 🅞 $General, Buick/GMC, Hickories Park Camping, Kost Tire, Top's Foods, Verizon, S 🅞 st police

64 (223) NY 96, Owego, N 🅕 Dunkin Donuts 🅞 AutoZone, CVS Drug, USPO, S 🅖 Valero

222mm 🆁🆂 wb, full 🅗 facilities, litter barrels, petwalk, 🅒, 🏕, vending

63 (218) Lounsberry, S 🅖 Valero/rest./dsl/24hr

62 (214) NY 282, Nichols, S 🅖 Citgo/pizza/dsl 🅞 Jim's RV Ctr, Tioga Downs Race Track (2mi)

212mm 🆁🆂 eb, full 🅗 facilities, litter barrels, petwalk, 🅒, 🏕, vending

208mm Susquehanna River

61 (206) NY 34, PA 199, Waverly, Sayre, N 🅞 $General, Goodyear/gas, S 🅖 Gulf, Sunoco/dsl 🅛 Best Western/rest. 🅞 Chrysler/Dodge/Jeep, Joe's RV Ctr, Kia, Nissan

60 (204) US 220, to Sayre, Waverly, N 🅛 O'brien's Inn 🅞 Clark's Foods, S 🅖 Citgo/dsl, Xtra/dsl 🅕 Wendy's (3mi) 🅛 Hampton Inn 🅞 Advance Parts, Aldi Foods, K-Mart, Rite Aid, Top's Foods

59a (202) Wilawana, S 🅖 Sunoco/Subway/dsl

59 (200) NY 427, Chemung, N 🅖 Dandy/dsl

58a (197) to CR 60

57 (195) rd 2, Lowman, Wellsburg, N 🅞 USPO, S 🅞 Gardiner Hill Campsites (4mi), st police

56 (190) Jerusalem Hill, S 🅖 Citgo/dsl, KwikFill, Sunoco/Pizza Hut/Subway/dsl 🅕 Hilltop Rest., McDonalds 🅛 Coachman Motel, Holiday Inn, Mark Twain Motel

54 (186) NY 13, to Ithaca

53 (185) Horseheads, S 🅖 Mobil, Sunoco 🅕 Burger King, Dunkin Donuts, Guiseppe's Pizza, Lin Buffet, McDonald's, Subway, Wendy's 🅛 Motel 6, Red Carpet Inn 🅞 Advance Parts, Family$, K-Mart, Radio Shack, Rite Aid, Save-A-Lot Foods

52b (184) NY 14, to Watkins Glen, N 🅕 Friendly's 🅛 Holiday Inn Express, Knights Inn, Landmark Inn, S 🅕 Denny's

52a (183) Commerce Ctr, S 🅕 Buffalo Wild Wings, CiCi's Pizza, Cracker Barrel, Empire Buffet, TX Roadhouse 🅞 Aldi Foods, AT&T, Dick's, Jo-Ann Fabrics, Kohl's, Mavis Discount Tire, Petsmart, Walmart/McDonald's

51a (182) Chambers Rd, N 🅖 Sunoco/Subway/dsl 🅕 Bon Ton, Chili's, Dunkin Donuts, McDonald's, Olive Garden, Outback Steaks, Red Lobster, Ruby Tuesday 🅛 Candlewood Suites, Country Inn&Suites, Hampton Inn, Hilton Garden 🅞 Firestone/auto, JC Penney, Macy's, mall, Nissan, Sears/auto, S 🅕 5 Guys Burgers, Applebee's, Charley's Subs, Mt Fuji Japanese, Old Country Buffet, Panera Bread, Taco Bell, TGIFriday's, Wendy's 🅛 EconoLodge 🅞 $Tree, Barnes&Noble, Best Buy, Buick/GMC, Hobby Lobby, Hyundai, Kost Tire, Lowe's, Michael's, museum, Old Navy, PetCo, Sam's Club, Staples, Subaru/Suzuki, Target, TJ Maxx, Top's Foods, Toyota/Scion, URGENT CARE, Verizon

50 (180) Kahler Rd, N 🅞 to ☎

49 (178) Olcott Rd, Canal St, Big Flats, N 🅞 ✈, antiques, S 🅖 Sunoco 🅕 Picnic Pizza 🅞 USPO

48 (171) NY 352, E Corning, N 🅖 Citgo 🅛 Budget Inn, Gate House Motel

47 (174) NY 352, Gibson, E Corning, N 🅛 Budget Inn, Gate House Motel

46 (171) NY 414, to Watkins Glen, Corning, N 🅞 Ferenbaugh Camping (5mi), KOA (14mi), Watkins Glen Camping, S 🅖 Sunoco 🅛 Comfort Inn, Days Inn, Radisson, Staybridge Suites 🅞 🅗 Corning Glass Museum

45 (170) NY 352, Corning, S 🅖 Fastrac 🅕 Bob Evans, EnEn Chinese, Friendly's, Subway, Wendy's 🅛 Fairfield Inn 🅞 AT&T, AutoZone, CarQuest, Rite Aid

44b a US 15 S, NY 417 W, Gang Mills, N 🅖 Sunoco 🅕 McDonald's, S 🅖 Citgo, Sunoco 🅕 Applebee's, Arby's 🅛 Best Value Inn, Corning Inn, Ramada Inn 🅞 Aldi Foods, Buick/GMC, Chevrolet, Harley-Davidson, Home Depot, Walmart

43 (167) NY 415, Painted Post, N 🅖 Citgo 🅕 Burger King 🅞 $General, AutoValue Parts, Firestone/auto, Verizon, S 🅖 Sunoco 🅕 Denny's 🅛 Hampton Inn

167mm parking area wb, litter barrels

42 (165) Coopers Plains, N 🅞 st police

41 (161) rd 333, Campbell, N 🅞 Camp Bell Camping (1mi), S 🅖 Sunoco 🅞 antiques, Cardinal Campsites (6mi)

160mm 🆁🆂 eb, full 🅗 facilities, litter barrels, petwalk, 🅒, 🏕, vending

40 (156) NY 226, Savona, N 🅖 Mobil/dsl 🅕 Savona Diner, Subway

39 (153) NY 415, Bath, N 🅕 Chat-a-Whyle Rest. (3mi) 🅛 Holland American Country Inn, National Hotel, S 🅞 Babcock Hollow Camping (2mi)

38 (150) NY 54, to Hammondsport, Bath, N 🅖 Citgo, KwikFill, Mobil, Sunoco/dsl 🅕 Arby's, Burger King, Dunkin Donuts, Ling Ling Chinese, McDonald's/playplace, Pizza Hut, Ponderosa, Rico's Pizza, Subway 🅛 Budget Inn, Days Inn, Microtel, Super 8 🅞 🅗, $General, Advance Parts, AT&T, Campers Haven Camping, Camping World RV Ctr, Family$, Hickory Hill Camping (3mi), K-Mart, museum, Rite Aid, st police, to Keuka Lake, Top's Foods/gas, Walgreens, winery

147mm 🆁🆂 wb, full 🅗 facilities, litter barrels, petwalk, 🅒, 🏕, vending

37 (146) NY 53, to Prattsburg, Kanona, S 🅖 🚚/Subway/dsl/scales/24hr/@, Sunoco/Smokey's/dsl/scales 🅞 st police, USPO, Wilkin's RV Ctr (1mi)

36 (145) I-390 N, NY 15, to Rochester

35 (138) Howard, S 🅞 🅒, to Lake Demmon RA

= gas   = food   = lodging   = other   = rest stop   Copyright 2015 - the Next EXIT ®

INTERSTATE 86 Cont'd

Exit #	Services
34 (130)	NY 36, Hornell, Arkport, **S 0-2 mi** KwikFill, Sunoco/dsl Applebee's, Country Kitchen, Dunkin Donuts, McDonald's, Subway Days Inn, EconoLodge, Sunshine Motel $General, $Tree, Advance Parts, Aldi Foods, Chrysler/Dodge/Jeep, Ford, GNC, Lowe's, NAPA, Radio Shack, Verizon, Walmart/Subway, Wegman's Foods
125mm	**scenic overlook eb, litter barrels**
33 (124)	NY 21, to Alfred, Almond, Andover, **S** Wilson Farms Kanakadea Camping, Lake Lodge Camping (8mi), USPO
117mm	2080 ft wb, elev 2110 ft eb, highest elevation on I-86.
32 (116)	W Almond
31 (108)	Angelica, **N** Valero/dsl Angelica Inn B&B
30 (104)	NY 19, Belmont, Wellsville, **N** 6-S Camping (3mi), Letchworth SP (27mi), **S** Iron Kettle Rest. H, st police
29 (99)	NY 275, to Bolivar, Friendship, **S** Miller&Brandes Gas, Mobil/Subway/dsl
28 (92)	NY 305, Cuba, **N** Moonwink's Rest. EconoLodge $General, Maple Lane RV Park, **S** Sunoco/dsl, Valero/dsl Charlie's Chicken Pizza, McDonald's, Subway H Cuba Cheese Shop, Cuba Drug, Family$, Giant Foods
27 (84)	NY 16, NY 446, Hinsdale, **N** **S** ,
26 (79)	NY 16, Olean, **S** Sunoco Burger King, Wendy's H
25 (77)	Buffalo St, Olean, **S** Citgo/dsl Country Fare H, **S 2 mi on NY 417** KwikFill, Applebee's, Burger King, Coldstone/Tim Hortons, Domino's, Dunkin Donuts, Friendly's, Little Caesars, McDonald's, Perkins, Ponderosa, Subway Best Western, Country Inn&Suites, Microtel H, $Tree, Advance Parts, Aldi Foods, AT&T, BJ's Whse/gas, GNC, Home Depot, Jo-Ann Fabrics, K-Mart, NAPA, Old Navy, Radio Shack, St Bonaventure U, Staples, Tops Foods/gas, Verizon, Walmart/Subway
24 (74)	NY 417, Allegany, **S 1 mi** Mobil/7-11/dsl to St Bonaventure U
73mm	**wb, full facilities, litter barrels, petwalk,**
23 (68)	US 219 S, **N** Allegany Jct./Subway/dsl
66mm	Allegheny River
21 (61)	US 219 N, Salamanca, **S** Red Garter Rest
20 (58)	NY 417, NY 353, Salamanca, **N** Antone's Gas, Nafco Quickstop/Burger King/24hr, Seneca OneStop/dsl/24hr, VIP Gas McDonald's Holiday Inn Express, Hotel Westgate AutoZone, Rail Museum, Seneca-Iroquis Museum, **S** casino
19 (54)	**S** Allegany SP, Red House Area
18 (51)	NY 280, **S** Allegany SP, Quaker Run Area
17 (48)	NY 394, Steamburg, **N** RV camping, **S** Seneca, WW/dsl RV camping
16 (41)	W Main St, Randolph, **N** Mobil/dsl R&M Rest. RV camping
40mm	**parking area,**
15 (39)	School House Rd
39mm	**parking area,**
14 (36)	US 62, Kennedy, **N 1 mi** Keystone Gas Office Pizza/Subs, **S** RV camping
32mm	Cassadaga Creek
13 (31)	NY 394, Falconer, **S** Mobil/dsl, Sunoco Burger King, McDonald's, Tim Hortons, Wendy's Budget Inn, Red Roof Inn CVS Drug, Harley-Davidson, Sugar Creek Stores
12 (28)	NY 60, Jamestown, **N** KwikFill/Dunkin Donuts/dsl, **S** Mobil/McDonald's/dsl Bob Evans Comfort Inn, Hampton Inn H, st police

11 (25)	to NY 430, Jamestown, **S** gas/dsl ,
22mm	**Welcome ctr/ eb, full facilities, litter barrels, petwalk, , vending**
10 (21)	NY 430 W, Bemus Point
9 (20)	NY 430 E (no EZ eb return), **N** Mobil, **S** ,
19mm	Chautauqua Lake
8 (18)	NY 394, Mayville, **N** lodging, Mobil/dsl RV camping, USPO
7 (15)	Panama
6 (9)	NY 76, Sherman, **N** Keystone Gas Main Street Diner, Murdock's Rest Morse Hotel, Plum B&B city park, NAPA, Sherman Drug, USPO
4 (1)	NY 430, Findley Lake, **N** Holiday Inn Express, **S** gas food Peek'n Peak Conference Ctr RV camping, to Peek'n Peak Ski Area
0mm	New York/Pennsylvania state line. **Exits 3-1 are in PA.**
3	PA 89, North East, Wattsburg, **N** ,
1 b a	I-90, W to Erie, E to Buffalo.
I-86 begins/ends on I-90, exit 37.	

INTERSTATE 87

Exit #	Services
176mm	US/Canada Border, NY state line, **I-87 begins/ends.**
43 (175)	US 9, Champlain, **E** Duty Free America, **W** Peterbilt Trkstp/deli/dsl/scales/24hr/@ repair
42 (174)	US 11 S, to Rouse's Point, Champlain, **E** Irving/dsl, Sunoco/Subway China Buffet, J-reck Subs, Pizza+ Ace Hardware, Chevrolet (3mi), Kinney Drug, PriceChopper, Rite Aid, USPO, **W** Mobil/dsl, Valero/dsl Dunkin Donuts, McDonald's, Papa John's
41 (167)	NY 191, Chazy, **E** st police, **W** Miner Museum
162mm	**both lanes, full facilities, info, litter barrels, petwalk, ,**
40 (160)	NY 456, Beekmantown, **E** Mobil/dsl Conroy's Organics Pt Auroche Lodge, Stonehelm Motel/café, **W** Twin Ells Camping
39 (158)	NY 314, Moffitt Rd, Plattsburgh Bay, **E** Mobil/dsl, Stewarts A&W, Dunkin Donuts, Gino's Pizza, Gus' Rest Rip van Winkle Motel, Super 8 Plattsburgh RV Park, to VT Ferry, **W** Shady Oaks Camping, to Adirondacks
38 (154)	NY 22, NY 374, to Plattsburgh, **E** Mobil/dsl Subway Kinney Drug
37 (153)	NY 3, Plattsburgh, **E** Stewarts, Sunoco #1 Chinese, Buffalo Wild Wings, Burger King, China Buffet, Chipotle, Domino's, Dunkin Donuts, Five Guys, Guiseppe's Pizza, Jade Buffet, KFC, Koto Japanese, McDonald's, Michigans+ Rest., Panera Bread, Perkins, Pizza Hut, Starbucks, Subway, Taco Bell, TX Roadhouse, Wendy's Comfort Inn, Holiday Inn H, Aldi Foods, BigLots, Buick/GMC, Family$, Ford, GNC, Kinney Drug, Michael's, Petsmart, Radio Shack, Rite Aid, Sam's Club, Staples, TJ Maxx, TrueValue, Verizon, vet, Walgreens, Walmart, **W** Mobil, Shell, Sunoco/Jreck Subs 99 Rest., Anthony's Rest., Applebee's, Butcher Block Rest., Dickey's BBQ, Dunkin Donuts, Friendly's, Ground Round, PriceChopper, Subway, Uno Best Value Inn, Best Western, Days Inn, EconoLodge, Hampton Inn, La Quinta, Microtel $Tree, Advance Parts, AT&T, AutoZone, Best Buy, Dick's, Gander Mtn, Harley-Davidson, Honda, JC Penney, Kinney Drug, K-Mart, Lowe's, Midas, Prays Mkt, Sears/auto, Target, vet
151mm	Saranac River
36 (150)	NY 22, Plattsburgh AFB, **E** Mobil/dsl st police, U-Haul, **W** Shell/Dunkin Donuts/dsl

Side labels: OLEAN, NY, JAMESTOWN, PLATTSBURGH

⬆N INTERSTATE 87 Cont'd

Exit #	Services
146mm	Ⓡ nb, full ♿ facilities, litter barrels, ©, petwalk, ⛫, truck insp sta both lanes
35 (144)	NY 442, to Port Kent, Peru, **E 2-8 mi** ⭕ Iroquois/Ausable Pines Camping, to VT Ferry, **W** 📷 Mobil/Dunkin Donuts/Subway/dsl, Mobil/repair 🍴 Livingood's Rest., McDonald's, Pasquale's Rest. ⭕ Auchuban Hardware, Tops Foods, USPO, vet
143mm	emergency phones at 2 mi intervals begin sb/end nb
34 (137)	NY 9 N, Ausable Forks, **E** 📷 Sunoco/dsl 🍴 Mac's Drive-in, Pleasant Corner Rest. ⭕ vet, **W** ⭕ Ausable River RV Camping, auto repair, Prays Mkt
136mm	Ausable River
33 (135)	US 9, NY 22, to Willsboro, **E** 📷 gas/dsl 🍴 food 🛏 lodging ⭕ RV camping, to Essex Ferry
125mm	N Boquet River
32 (124)	Lewis, **E** ⭕ RV Camping, **W** 📷 Lukoil/dsl, Pierce's/dsl 🍴 Trkstp Diner ⭕ RV Camping, st police
123mm	Ⓡ both ways, full ♿ facilities, info, no restrooms, petwalk, ©, ⛫
120mm	Boquet River
31 (117)	NY 9 N, to Elizabethtown, Westport, **E** 📷 Mobil 🛏 HillTop Motel ⭕ RV camp/dump, **W** ⭕ 🏥, st police, vet
111mm	Ⓡ nb, full ♿ facilities, litter barrels, petwalk, ©, ⛫, vending
30 (104)	US 9, NY 73, Keene Valley
99mm	parking area nb, litter barrels, ©, ⛫
29 (94)	N Hudson, **E** ⭕ Jellystone Camping, USPO, **W** ⭕ Blue Ridge Falls Camping
28 (88)	NY 74 E, to Ticonderoga, Schroon Lake, **E** 📷 Mt Severance Country Store, Sunoco/dsl 🛏 Maple Leaf Motel, Schroon Lake B&B ⭕ RV camp/dump, services on US 9, st police
27 (81)	US 9 (from nb, no EZ return), Schroon Lake, **E** 📷 to gas/dsl 🍴 food 🛏 lodging
26 (78)	US 9 (from sb, no EZ return), Pottersville, Schroon Lake, **E** 🍴 Cafe Adirondack, Family Deli 🛏 Lee's Corner Motel ⭕ RV Camping, **W** 📷 Valero/dsl 🍴 Black Bear Diner ⭕ USPO
25 (73)	NY 8, Chestertown, **E** 📷 Crossroads Country Store 🍴 Suzie Q's Rest. ⭕ Country Haven Camping, **W** 📷 Mobil/dsl
24 (67)	Bolton Landing, **E** ⭕ RV camping
67mm	Schroon River
66mm	parking area sb, ⛫
64mm	parking area nb, ⛫
23 (58)	to US 9, Diamond Point, Warrensburg, **W** 📷 Citgo/dsl, Cumberland, Mobil/Dunkin Donuts/e85, Stewarts 🍴 Dragon Lee Chinese, Geroge Henry's Rest., McDonald's, Subway 🛏 Super 8 ⭕ Central Adirondack Tr, Family$, Ford, PriceChopper Foods, Riverview Camping, Schroon River Camping (3mi), ski area, Tops Foods
22 (54)	US 9, NY 9 N, to Diamond Pt, Lake George, **E on US 9** 🍴 Big Smoke BBQ, Gino&Tony's, Guiseppe's Pizza, Mario's Italian, Monte Cristo's, Moose Tooth Grill 🛏 7 Dwarfs Motel, Admiral Motel, Balsam Motel, Barberry Ct, Best Value Inn, Blue Moon Motel, Brookside Motel, EconoLodge, Georgian Lakeside Resort, Georgian Motel, Heritage Motel, Lake Crest Inn, Lake George Inn, Lake Haven Motel, Lake Motel, Marine Village Resort, Motel Montreal, Nordick's Motel, Oasis Motel, O'Sullivan's Motel, Park Lane Motel, Sundowner Motel, Surfside Motel ⭕ multiple services, PriceChopper Foods, same as 21, **W parking area both lanes**

21 (53)	NY 9 N, Lake Geo, Ft Wm Henry, **E on US 9** 📷 Stewarts, Sunoco/dsl, Valero 🍴 A&W, Adirondack Brewery, Barnsider BBQ, Blacksmith Rest., Dining Room, DJ's Cafe, Gaslight Grill, Jasper's Steaks, Lobster Pot, Mama Riso's Italian, McDonald's, Mezzaluna's, Pizza Hut 🛏 Best Western, Ft William Henry Inn, Hampton Inn, Holiday Inn Resort, Lake View Inn, Lincoln Log Motel, Motel 6, Quality Inn, Rodeway Inn, Super 8, Tiki Hotel, Travelodge, Villager Motel, Windsor Hotel, Wingate Inn ⭕ city park, Harley-Davidson, King Phillip Camping, Lake George Camping, multiple services, Rite Aid, same as 22, USPO, waterpark, **W** 📷 Mobil/dsl/LP 🛏 Kathy's Cottages
20 (49)	NY 149, to Ft Ann, **E N on US 9** 📷 Mobil/Dunkin Donuts/dsl, Sunoco/dsl 🍴 Blue Moose Rest., Frank's Pizza, Johnny Rocket's, Logjam Rest., Olde Post Grille, Subway 🛏 Clarion, Comfort Suites, French Mtn Inn, Great Escape Lodge, Mohican Motel ⭕ 6 Flags Funpark, Factory Outlets/famous brands, Ledgeview RV Park (3mi), st police, **S on US 9** waterpark
51mm	**W** ⭕ Adirondack Park
19 (47)	NY 254, Glens Falls, **E** 📷 Hess, Mobil/dsl, Sunoco 🍴 5 Guys Burgers, 99 Rest., Ambrosia Diner, Burger King, Chicago Grill, Dickey's BBQ, Dunkin Donuts, Friendly's, Giavano's Pizza, Golden Corral, KFC, Liberty Pizza, McDonald's, Moe's SW Grill, Mr B's Rest., Old China Buffet, Olive Garden, Outback Steaks, Panera Bread, Papa John's, Pizza Hut, Red Lobster, Silo Rest., Starbucks, Subway, Taco Bell/LJ Silver, Wendy's 🛏 Alpen Haus Motel, Budget Inn, EconoLodge, Quality Inn, Red Roof Inn, Sleep Inn ⭕ $Tree, Ace Hardware, Advance Parts, AT&T, AutoZone, Bon Ton, Dick's, Goodyear, Hobby Lobby, Home Depot, JC Penney, Jo-Ann Fabrics, mall, Meineke, Petco, Price Rite Foods, PriceChopper Foods, Radio Shack, Rite Aid, Sears/auto, Staples, Target, TJ Maxx, Tuesday Morning, USPO, Verizon, Walmart, **W** 📷 Mobil/Dunkin Donuts/Subway/dsl 🛏 Ramada/rest. ⭕ st police
18 (45)	Glens Falls, **E** 📷 Gulf/Subway/e-85/dsl, Hess/dsl, Sunoco/dsl 🍴 Carl R's Café, Dunkin Donuts, Pizza Hut, Steve's Place Rest. 🛏 Days Inn ⭕ 🏥, CVS Drug, Hannaford Foods, Toyota/Scion, U-Haul, Walgreens, **W** 📷 Stewarts 🍴 McDonald's, Taco Bell ⭕ Super 8
43mm	Ⓡ both lanes, full ♿ facilities, litter barrels, petwalk, ©, ⛫ vending
42mm	Hudson River
17 (40)	US 9, S Glen Falls, **E** 📷 Citgo/dsl, Gulf, Hess/Blimpie/Dunkin Donuts, Sunoco/dsl, Valero/Subway/dsl 🍴 Dunkin Donuts, Fitzgerald's Steaks 🛏 Budget Inn, Landmark Motel (1mi) ⭕ Adirondack RV Camp, auto/truck repair/transmissions, Suzuki, vet, **W** ⭕ Moreau Lake SP

LAKE GEORGE

GLENS FALLS

= gas   = food   = lodging   = other   RS = rest stop   Copyright 2015 - the Next EXIT ®

↑N INTERSTATE 87 Cont'd

Exit #	Services
16 (36)	Ballard Rd, Wilton, **E** ◯ Coldbrook Campsites, golf, **W** Mobil, Stewart's, Sunoco/Scotty's Rest./dsl/scales/24hr 🛏 Mt View Acres Motel ◯ Alpin Haus RV Ctr
15 (30)	NY 50, NY 29, Saratoga Springs, **E** Hess/dsl, Sunoco 🍴 5 Guys Burgers, 99 Rest., Applebee's, Burger King, Chicago Grill, Chipotle Mexican, Denny's, Dunkin Donuts, Friendly's, Golden Corral, KFC/Taco Bell, McDonald's, Moe's SW Grill, Osaka, Panera Bread, Subway, Sunny Wok, TGIFriday's 🛏 Comfort Inn ◯ AT&T, Barnes&Noble, Best Buy, BJ's Whse, BonTon, Dick's, Ford, GNC, Hannaford Foods, Healthy Living Mkt, Home Depot, JC Penney, Kohl's, Lowe's, Mazda, Old Navy, Petsmart, PriceChopper Foods, Rite Aid, Sears/auto, Staples, Subaru, Target, TJ Maxx, Toyota/Scion, Walgreens, Walmart, **W** 🛏 Residence Inn ◯ H
14 (28)	NY 9P, Schuylerville, **W 2 mi** 🛏 Hampton Inn, Holiday Inn ◯ H, museum, racetrack
13 (25)	US 9, Saratoga Springs, **E** 🍴 Bentley's Rest., DeLucia's Deli, Saratoga Pizza Place 🛏 Budget Inn, Locust Grove Motel ◯ Ballston Spa SP, Nissan, **W** Mobil/Dunkin Donuts/dsl, Stewarts 🍴 Finish Line Rest., Hibachi Grill, Jack Dillon's Rest., PJ's BBQ 🛏 Best Western, Hilton Garden (4mi), Roosevelt Inn/rest., Top Hill Hotel ◯ Saratoga SP, vet
12 (21)	NY 67, Malta, **E** Getty/dsl, Sunoco/dsl 🍴 Bentley's Rest., Dunkin Donuts, KFC/Taco Bell, Malta Diner, McDonald's, Starbucks, Subway 🛏 Fairfield Inn ◯ AT&T, CVS Drug, GNC, PriceChopper Foods, Saratoga NHP, st police, Stewart's, Verizon, **W** 🛏 Hyatt Place ◯ URGENT CARE
11 (18)	Round Lake Rd, Round Lake, **W** Gulf/dsl, Sunoco/dsl 🍴 Mulligan's Rest. ◯ Hannaford Foods, Rite Aid, Stewarts
10 (16)	Ushers Rd, **E** Hess/Dunkin Donuts/dsl, Xtra/dsl 🍴 Ferretti's Rest. ◯ auto repair, **W** ◯ Stewarts
14mm	RS nb, full ♿ facilities, info, litter barrels, petwalk, 🅲, 🅰, vending
8 (10)	Crescent, Vischer Ferry, **E** Hess/Blimpie/Godfather's/dsl 🍴 McDonald's ◯ USPO, **W** Gulf/NY Pizza/dsl, Sunoco 🍴 Dunkin Donuts, Pancho's Mexican, Tufanos Pizza ◯ Ace Hardware, CVS Drug, Stewarts
9 (13)	NY 146, Clifton Park, **E** Hess/Dunkin Donuts/dsl, USA 🍴 Burger King, Caputo's Pizza, Chili's, Cracker Barrel, Delmonico's Steaks, Giffy's BBQ, Harborhouse Fish Fry, Mr Subb, Peddler's Grill, Pizza Hut, Red Robin, Snyder's Rest., Subway, Wheatfields Bistro 🛏 Comfort Suites, Holiday Inn Express, Residence Inn ◯ Advance Parts, Aldi Foods, Big-Lots, Goodyear/auto, Home Depot, Kohl's, Lowe's, Michael's, Midas, Petco, Rite Aid, Target, vet, **W** Mobil, Sunoco/dsl 🍴 5 Guys Burgers, 99 Rest., Bellini's Italian, Brick House Pizza, Buffalo Wild Wings, Chipotle Mexican, Dickey's BBQ, Dunkin Donuts, East Palace, East Wok, Friendly's, IHOP, La Fiesta, McDonald's, Moe's SW Grill, Olive Garden, Outback Steaks, Panera Bread, Pasta Pane, Ruby Tuesday, Salad Creations, Shane's Rib Shack, Starbucks, Subway, Taco Bell, TGIFriday's, Wendy's 🛏 Best Western, Hampton Inn, Hilton Garden ◯ $Tree, AT&T, Chevrolet, CVS Drug, Firestone/auto, GNC, Hannaford Foods, JC Penney, Jo-Ann Fabrics, Marshall's, Petsmart, PriceChopper Foods, st police, Staples, Verizon, Walgreens
8a (12)	Grooms Rd, to Waterford
8mm	Mohawk River

7 (7)	NY 7, Troy, **E** on US 9 N Hess/dsl 🍴 Century House, Mr Subb 🛏 Clarion, Comfort Inn, Days Inn, Holiday Inn Express, Sycamore Motel ◯ $General, Acura, Ford, Infiniti, Lexus, Nissan, Rite Aid, Volvo, **E** on US 9 S Sunoco 🍴 Dunkin Donuts, McDonald's, Red Robin, Subway ◯ Hobby Lobby, Marshall's
6 (6)	NY 2, to US 9, Schenectady, **E** Hess, Mobil 🍴 Applebee's, Boston Mkt, Chicago Grill, ChuckeCheese, Circle Diner, Firehouse Subs, Joe's Crabshack, Mr Subb, Panera Bread, Rafferty's, Red Robin, Sake Japanese, Starbucks, Wendy's 🛏 Cocca's Inn, La Quinta, Travelodge ◯ $Tree, CVS Drug, GNC, Hannaford Foods, Home Depot, Lowe's, Mavis Discount Tire, Michael's, Mkt Bistro, Petsmart, same as 7, Sam's Club, Staples, Toyota/Scion, VW, Walmart, **W** Mobil/dsl, Stewart's 🍴 Carrabba's, Chipotle Mexican, Denny's, DiBella's Subs, Dunkin Donuts, Kings Buffet, Ruby Tuesday, Subway 🛏 Microtel, Quality Inn, Super 8 ◯ Goodyear/auto, Target, TJ Maxx, Verizon
5 (5)	NY 155 E, Latham, **E** 🍴 DeeDee's Rest., Philly's Grill ◯ USPO
4 (4)	NY 155 W, Wolf Rd, **E** on Wolf Rd Hess/dsl, Mobil/Subway, Sunoco 🍴 99 Rest., Arby's, Buffalo Wagon, Burger King, Capital Buffet, Chipotle Mexican, CiCi's Pizza, Denny's, Dunkin Donuts, Macaroni Grill, Maxie's Grill, McDonald's, Moe's SW Grill, Olive Garden, Outback Steaks, Pizza Hut, Red Lobster, Reel Seafood Co, Samurai, Starbucks, Subway, Ted's Fishfry, TX Roadhouse, Wolf Rd Diner, Wolf Rd Diner, Wolfs 1-11 🛏 Best Western, Courtyard, Hampton Inn, Holiday Inn, Homewood Suites, Marriott, Red Roof Inn, Staybridge Suites ◯ Chevrolet, CVS Drug, Firestone/auto, Hannfords Foods, Trader Joe's, **W** 🍴 Bluestone Bistro, Koto Japanese 🛏 Desmond Hotel, Hotel Indigo ◯ to Heritage Park
2 (2)	NY 5, Central Ave, **E** on Wolf Rd Mobil/dsl, Sunoco 🍴 Bonefish Grill, Bucca Italian, Cheesecake Factory, Chili's, Delma's Diner, Five Guys, Honeybaked Ham, Hooters, IHOP, Panera Bread, PF Chang's, Starbucks, Taco Bell, Wendy's 🛏 Cocca's Inn, Comfort Inn, Scottish Inn, SpringHill Suites, Travelodge ◯ Barnes&Noble, BJ's Whse/gas, Goodyear/auto, Jo-Ann Fabrics, Kost Tire, LL Bean, Lowe's, Macy's, mall, Marshall's, PetCo, Sears/auto, Staples, Target, Whole Foods Mkt, **W** Gulf/dsl, Mobil, USA/dsl 🍴 Delmonico's Steaks, Domino's, Dunkin Donuts, La Fiesta Mexican, McDonald's, Moe's SW Grill, Smokey Bones BBQ, Subway, Truman's Grill, Wendy's 🛏 Days Inn, EconoLodge, Howard Johnson, Motel 6, Quality Inn, Super 8 ◯ Advance Parts, AT&T, Buick/GMC, Cadillac, Krause's Candy, Midas, PepBoys, ShopRite/gas, Subaru, Verizon, Walgreens
1W (1)	NY State Thruway (from sb), I-87 S to NYC, I-90 W to Buffalo
1E (1)	I-90 E (from sb), to Albany, Boston
1S (1)	to US 20, Western Ave, **E** on US 20 Getty 🍴 5 Guys Burgers, 99 Rest., Burger King, Chipotle Mexican, Coldstone, Creo, Dunkin Donuts, Starbucks, TGIFriday's 🛏 Best Western, CVS Drug, Days Inn, Holiday Inn Express ◯ AT&T, USPO, Verizon, vet **W** on US 20 Mobil, USA 🍴 Capital City Diner, Dunkin Donuts, Hana Grill, Ichiban Japanese, McDonald's ◯ Adirondack Tires, PriceChopper Foods
1N (1)	I-87 N (from nb), to Plattsburgh
24 (148)	I-90 and I-87 N
23 (142)	I-787, to Albany, US 9 W, **E** on US 9 W Cumberland Farms/Dunkin Donuts/dsl, Sunoco/dsl 🛏 Comfort Inn ◯ to Knickerbocker Arena, transmissions, **W** Stewarts 🛏 Days Inn
139mm	parking area sb, litter barrel, 🅲, 🅰

(vertical left margin) **SARATOGA SPGS**   NY

(vertical right margin) **ALBANY**

⬆N INTERSTATE 87 Cont'd

Exit #	Services
22 (135)	NY 396, to Selkirk
21a (134)	I-90 E, to MA Tpk, Boston
127mm	**New Baltimore Travel Plaza both lanes** 🅖 Mobil/dsl 🍴 Famous Famiglia, Quiznos, Roy Rogers, Starbucks, TCBY 🄾 atm, info, wi-fi
21b (124)	US 9 W, NY 81, to Coxsackie, **W** 🅖 Sunoco/dsl, Trvl Plaza/Citgo/rest./dsl/scales/24hr 🍴 McDonald's 🛏 Best Western, Budget Inn, Holiday Inn Express, Red Carpet Inn 🄾 $Tree, Boat'n RV Whse, repair, vet
21 (114)	NY 23, Catskill, **E** 🅖 Mobil, Sunoco/dsl 🛏 Catskill Motel/rest. (2mi), Pelokes Motel (2mi) 🄾 Home Depot, to Rip van Winkle Br, transmissions, visitors ctr, **W** 🍴 Anthony's Banquet Hall 🛏 Astoria Motel, Rip Van Winkle Motel 🄾 to Hunter Mtn/Windham Ski Areas
103mm	**Malden Service Area nb,** 🅖 Mobil/dsl 🍴 Carvel Ice Cream, Hotdogs, McDonald's 🄾 atm, parking area sb
20 (102)	NY 32, to Saugerties, **E** 🅖 Mobil/dsl, Stewarts, Sunoco 🍴 Dunkin Donuts, Giordano's Pizza, McDonald's, Pizza Star, Starway Café, Subway 🄾 Advance Parts, Big Lots, Chrysler/Dodge/Jeep, CVS Drug, Family$, PriceChopper Foods, Verizon, **W** 🅖 Hess/Blimpie/Dunkin Donuts/dsl, Sunoco/dsl 🍴 Land&Sea Grill, Saugerties Diner 🛏 Comfort Inn, Howard Johnson/rest. 🄾 Blue Mtn Campground (5mi), Brookside Campground (10mi), KOA (2mi), Rip Van Winkle Campground (3mi), to Catskills
99mm	🆁🆂 both lanes, full 🛏 facilities, litter barrels, petwalk, 🅲, 🄿🅰 trk insp sta
96mm	**Ulster Travel Plaza sb,** 🅖 Sunoco/dsl 🍴 Nathan's, Pizza Hut, Roy Rogers, Starbucks, TCBY 🄾 atm, 🅲, wi-fi
19 (91)	NY 28, Rhinecliff Br, Kingston, **E** 🅖 QuickChek/dsl 🍴 Blimpie, Olympic Diner, Picnic Pizza, Stadium Diner 🛏 Garden Plaza Hotel, Super 8 🄾 access to I-587 E, Advance Parts, CVS Drug, Hannaford Foods, Kia, Radio Shack, Walgreens, **W** 🍴 NY Pizza, Roudigan's Steaks 🛏 Motel 19, Quality Inn, Rodeway Inn, SuperLodge 🄾 access to US 209, Camping World RV Ctr, Ford, Nissan
18 (76)	NY 299, to Poughkeepsie, New Paltz, **E** 🅖 Mobil, Shell/dsl 🍴 College Diner 🛏 87 Motel, EconoLodge, Rodeway Inn 🄾 Lowe's, to Mid-Hudson Br, **W** 🅖 Sunoco 🍴 Burger King, Dunkin Donuts, Gabaletos Seafood, McDonald's, Pasquale's Pizza, Plaza Diner, Rino's Pizza, Rococo's Pizza, Subway 🛏 Best Value Inn 🄾 Advance Parts, AT&T, KOA (10mi), Midas, Radio Shack, Rite Aid, ShopRite Foods, Stop'n Shop, Verizon, vet
66mm	**Modena service area sb,** 🅖 Sunoco/dsl 🍴 Carvel's Ice Cream, Chicago Grill, McDonald's, Moe's SW Grill 🄾 atm, UPS, wi-fi
65mm	**Plattekill Travel Plaza nb** 🅖 Sunoco/dsl 🍴 Nathans, Roy Rogers, Starbucks 🄾 atm, UPS, wi-fi
17 (60)	I-84, NY 17K, to Newburgh, **E on NY 300 N** 🅖 Mobil 🍴 Daddy's Grill, DQ, Dunkin Donuts, Joe's Deli, McDonald's, Newburgh Buffet, Perkins, Taco Bell, Wendy's 🄾 $Tree, AT&T, AutoZone, BonTon, Marshall's, Mavis Tire, Midas, Office Depot, Sears/auto, Stop&Shop, **E on NY 300 S** 🅖 Hess/dsl, Sunoco/dsl 🍴 Applebee's, Burger King, Chili's, China City, Cosimos Ristorante, Denny's, Five Guys, IHOP, Ikaros Diner, Longhorn Steaks, Neptune Diner, Panera Bread, Pizza Mia, Sonic, Starbucks, Steak&Stein, Subway, TGIFriday's, Union Sq Rest., Yobo Asian 🛏 Days Inn, Howard Johnson, Ramada Inn, Super 8 🄾 $General, Adam's Food Mkt, Aldi Foods,

NEWBURGH

Map

Lewis •
🛡87 Olmstedville •
• Chestertown
• Glens Falls
Edinburg •
🛡90
• Saratoga Springs
Schenectady •
• Troy
Delmar • • Albany
• Davenport
• Pittsfield

NY

17 (60)	Continued Barnes&Noble, Buick/GMC, Cadillac/Chevrolet, Chrysler/Dodge/Jeep, Ford/Lincoln, Home Depot, Honda, Kohl's, Lowe's, Meineke, Michael's, Nissan, Petsmart, Radio Shack, Target, Verizon, Walmart/McDonald's **W on NY 17K** 🛏 Hilton Garden
16 (45)	US 6, NY 17, to West Point, Harriman, **W** 🅖 Gulf/dsl 🍴 Applebee's, Chicago Grill, Chili's, Dunkin Donuts, KFC, Outback Steaks, Panera Bread, TGIFriday's, Wendy's 🛏 Days Inn, Hampton Inn 🄾 $Tree, Best Buy, BJ's Whse, BMW, GNC, Home Depot, Kohl's, Michaels, Old Navy, Petsmart, Radio Shack, st police, Staples, Target, TJ Maxx, Verizon, Walmart/Subway, Woodbury Outlet/famous brands
34mm	**Ramapo Service Area sb,** 🅖 Sunoco/dsl 🍴 Carvel, McDonald's, Uno Pizza 🄾 atm, wi-fi
33mm	**Sloatsburg Travel Plaza nb,** 🅖 Sunoco/dsl 🍴 Burger King, Dunkin Donuts, Quiznos, Sbarro's 🄾 atm, gifts, info
15a (31)	NY 17 N, NY 59, Sloatsburg
15 (30)	I-287 S, NY 17 S, to NJ. **I-87 S & I-287 E run together.**
14b (27)	Airmont Rd, Montebello, **E** 🛏 Crowne Plaza, **W on NY9** 🅖 Gulf/Dunkin Donuts/dsl 🍴 Airmont Diner, Applebee's, Bagel Boys Cafe, Bella Vita Pizza, Friendly's, Pasta Cucina, Starbucks, Sutter's Mill Rest. 🛏 Howard Johnson 🄾 🄷, ShopRite Foods, Tall Man Tires, Walgreens, Walmart
14a (23)	Garden State Pkwy, to NJ, Chestnut Ridge
14 (22)	NY 59, Spring Valley, Nanuet, **E** 🅖 Citgo/dsl, Shell/dsl, Valero/dsl 🍴 Burger King, Deliziosa Pizza, Domino's, IHOP, McDonald's, Planet Wings, Subway 🛏 Fairfield Inn 🄾 BMW, CarQuest, GNC, Maserati/Ferrari, Michael's, Target, TJ Maxx, Verizon, **W** 🅖 Citgo, Gulf 🍴 Baskin-Robbins/Dunkin Donuts, Bonefish, ChuckeCheese, Corner Bakery Cafe, Dunkin Donuts, Franko's Pizza, KFC/Taco Bell, Nanuet Diner, Panera Bread, Red Lobster, Smashburger, Starbucks, White Castle 🛏 Days Inn, Hampton Inn, Hilton Garden 🄾 $Tree, AT&T, Barnes&Noble, Fairway Mkt, Home Depot, Hyundai, Macy's, Marshall's, Midas, PetCo, Sears/auto, Staples, Stop&Shop Foods, STS Tires, transmissions, Verizon
13 (20)	Palisades Pkwy, N to Bear Mtn, S to NJ
12 (19)	NY 303, Palisades Ctr Dr, W Nyack, **W** 🅖 Mobil 🍴 Cheesecake Factory, Outback Steaks, Panera Bread, Tony Roma's 🛏 Nyack Motel 🄾 Barnes&Noble, Best Buy, BJ's Whse, Dave&Buster's, Dick's, Home Depot, JC Penney, Lord&Taylor, Macy's, mall, Old Navy, Staples, STS Tire/repair, Target, Verizon
11 (18)	US 9W, to Nyack, **E** 🅖 Mobil, Shell/dsl 🛏 Best Western 🄾 Walgreens, **W** 🅖 Shell/dsl 🍴 Dunkin Donuts, McDonald's 🛏 Super 8 🄾 🄷, J&L Repair/tire, Midas, Old World Food Mkt, VW

NYACK

NY

🏪 = gas   🍴 = food   🛏 = lodging   ⭕ = other   🆁🆂 = rest stop   Copyright 2015 - the Next EXIT ®

⬆N INTERSTATE 87 Cont'd

Exit #	Services
10 (17)	Nyack (from nb), same as 11
14mm	Tappan Zee Br, Hudson River
13mm	**toll plaza**
9 (12)	to US 9, to Tarrytown, **E** 🏪 Hess/dsl, Shell ⭕ CVS Drug, **W** 🏪 Mobil 🍴 El Dorado West Diner 🛏 DoubleTree Hotel ⭕ Honda, Mavis Tire
8 (11)	I-287 E, to Saw Mill Pkwy, White Plains, **E** 🛏 Hampton Inn, Marriott
7a (10)	Saw Mill River Pkwy S, to Saw Mill River SP, ⭕ Taconic SP
7 (8)	NY 9A (from nb), Ardsley, **W** 🛏 Ardsley Acres Motel ⭕ H
6mm	**Ardsley Travel Plaza nb** 🏪 Sunoco/dsl 🍴 Burger King, Popeye's ⭕ vending
5.5mm	**toll plaza, phone**
6ba (5)	Stew Leonard Dr, to Ridge Hill, **W** ⭕ Costco, Home Depot, Stew Leonard's Farmfresh Foods
6 (4.5)	Tuckahoe Dr, Yonkers, **E** 🏪 Getty/repair 🍴 Marcellino's Pizza, McDonald's, Subway 🛏 Tuckahoe Motel ⭕ ShopRite Foods/drug, **W** 🏪 Gulf, Mobil/dsl 🍴 Domino's, Dunkin Donuts, Kim Wei Chinese 🛏 Ramada Inn, Royal Regency Hotel
5 (4.3)	NY 100 N (from nb), Central Park Ave, White Plains
4 (4)	Cross Country Pkwy, Mile Sq Rd, **E** ⭕ Ford/Lincoln/Subaru, Macy's, Marshall's, Sears/auto, TJ Maxx, **W** 🏪 BP, Shell/dsl, Shell/Dunkin Donuts/dsl 🍴 Burger King ⭕ Chevrolet, Mavis Tire
3 (3)	Mile Square Rd, **E** ⭕ GNC, mall, Stop&Shop, Thriftway Drug, **W** 🏪 BP, Citgo
2 (2)	Yonkers Ave (from nb), Westchester Fair, **E** 🏪 Mobil ⭕ Yonkers Speedway
1 (1)	Hall Place, McLean Ave, **E** 🍴 Dunkin Donuts ⭕ A&P Foods/Subway
0mm	**New York St Thruway and I-87 N run together to Albany**
14 (11)	McLean Ave, **E** 🏪 A&P/dsl 🍴 Dunkin Donuts, Subway
13 (10)	E 233rd, NE Tollway, **service plaza both lanes,** Gulf/Dunkin Donuts
12 (9.5)	Hudson Pkwy (from nb), Sawmill Pkwy
11 (9)	Van Cortlandt Pk S
10 (8.5)	W 230th St (from sb), W 240th (from nb), **W** 🏪 Getty 🍴 Dunkin Donuts ⭕ H, Marshall's, Target
9 (8)	W Fordham Rd, **E** 🏪 BP/dsl 🍴 Dallas BBQ ⭕ H
8 (7)	W 179th (from nb), **W** ⭕ Roberto Clemente SP
7 (6)	I-95, US 1, S to Trenton, NJ, N to New Haven, CT
6 (5)	E 153rd st, River Ave, Stadium Rd, **E** ⭕ Yankee Stadium
5 (5)	E 161st, Macombs Dam Br, (exit 4 from nb), **E** ⭕ AT&T, Best Buy, Michael's, Target, Yankee Stadium
3 (3)	E 138th St, Madison Ave Br, **E** 🏪 BP/dsl
2 (2)	Willis Ave, 3rd Ave Br, **E** 🏪 Mobil/dsl, **W** 🍴 McDonald's
1 (1)	Brook Ave, Hunts Point, **E** 🏪 BP, Hess
0mm	**I-87 begins/ends on I-278.**

⬆E INTERSTATE 88

Exit #	Services
25a	I-90/NY Thruway. **I-88 begins/ends on I-90, exit 25a.**
117mm	**toll booth** (to enter or exit NY Thruway)
25 (116)	NY 7, to Rotterdam, Schenectady, **S 3 mi** 🏪 Gulf, ⛟/Dunkin Donuts/Subway/dsl/scales/24hr 🍴 Burger King, McDonald's, Peppino's Pizza, Top's Diner, Wagon Train BBQ 🛏 L&M Motel, Quality Inn ⭕ Frosty Acres Camping
24 (112)	US 20, NY 7, to Duanesburg, **N** ⭕ Mobil, Stewarts 🍴 Dunkin Donuts ⭕ st police, **S** 🍴 Duanesburg Diner ⭕ USPO

Exit #	Services
23 (101)	NY 30, to Schoharie, Central Bridge, **N** ⭕ Apple Food/dsl 🛏 Holiday Motel ⭕ Hideaway Camping, Locust Park Camping, **S** 🏪 Mobil/Subway/dsl 🍴 Dunkin Donuts 🛏 Days Inn, Hyland House B&B (2mi), Wedgewood B&B (2mi)
22 (95)	NY 7, NY 145, to Cobleskill, Middleburgh, **N 2-5 mi** 🏪 Hess/dsl, Mobil, Sunoco 🍴 Dunkin Donuts, Pizza Hut, Subway 🛏 Colonial CT Motel, Holiday Motel, Super 8 ⭕ H, $General, Advance Parts, Buick/Chevrolet/GMC, Chrysler/Dodge/Jeep, Howe Caverns Camping, PriceChopper Foods, to Howe Caverns, Walmart/McDonald's, **S** ⭕ st police, Twin Oaks Camping (5mi)
21 (90)	NY 7, NY 10, to Cobleskill, Warnerville, **N 2-3 mi** 🏪 Hess/dsl, Mobil/dsl, Stewart's/dsl 🍴 Arby's, Burger King, Dairy Deli, Delaney's Rest., KFC/Taco Bell, McDonald's, Pizza Hut, Red Apple Rest., Sub Express 🛏 Best Western, Gables B&B ⭕ H, $General, Ace Hardware, CarQuest, CVS Drug, NAPA, PriceChopper Foods, TrueValue, Walmart/McDonald's
20 (87)	NY 7, NY 10, to Richmondville, **S** 🏪 Mobil/dsl, Sunoco/dsl 🍴 Reinhardt's Deli, Sub Express 🛏 Red Carpet Inn ⭕ USPO
79mm	🆁🆂 wb, full 🦽 **facilities, litter barrels, petwalk,** 🚻, 🚮, **vending**
19 (76)	to NY 7, Worcester, **N** 🏪 Stewarts, Sunoco/dsl
18 (71)	to Schenevus, **N** 🏪 Citgo 🍴 Schenevus Rest.
17 (61)	NY 7, to NY 28 N, Colliersville, Cooperstown, **N 2 mi** 🏪 Sunoco 🛏 Best Western (14mi), Red Carpet Inn ⭕ to Baseball Hall of Fame
16 (59)	NY 7, to Emmons, **N** 🍴 Arby's, Brooks BBQ, Farmhouse Rest., Morey's Rest., Pizza Hut, Sonny's Pizza 🛏 Amber Life Motel, Rainbow Inn ⭕ PriceChopper Foods, Rite Aid
15	NY 28, NY 23, Oneonta, **N** 🏪 Citgo, Hess, KwikFill 🍴 Dunkin Donuts, Friendly's, KFC 🛏 Clarion, Townhouse Inn ⭕ H, Advance Parts, to Soccer Hall of Fame, **S** 🏪 Hess/Dunkin Donuts, Mirabito/dsl 🍴 Applebee's, Burger King, Denny's, McDonald's, Neptune Diner/24hr, Quiznos, Sabatini's Italian, Subway, Taco Bell, Wendy's 🛏 Budget Inn, Christopher's Lodge/rest., Holiday Inn, Sun Lodge, Super 8 ⭕ $Tree, Aldi Foods, BJ's Whse/gas, Dick's, Ford, Hannaford Foods, Home Depot, JC Penney, Kost Tire, TJ Maxx, Verizon, Walmart
14 (55)	Main St (from eb), Oneonta, **N** 🏪 Citgo, Stewarts, Sunoco 🍴 Alfresco's Italian ⭕ CarQuest
13 (53)	NY 205, **N 1/2 mi** 🏪 Citgo, Hess, Valero/dsl 🍴 DQ, Dunkin Donuts, McDonald's 🛏 Celtic Motel, Hampton Inn, Motel 88 ⭕ Buick/Cadillac/Chevrolet/GMC, camping, Family$, Gilbert Lake SP (11mi), Honda, Jellystone Park Camping, Kia, NAPA, Nissan, Rite Aid, st police, Subaru, to Susquehanna Tr
12 (47)	NY 7, to Otego, **S** 🏪 Mirabito/Subway/Tim Hortons/dsl/24hr
11 (40)	NY 357, to Unadilla, Delhi, **N** ⭕ KOA
39mm	🆁🆂 eb, full 🦽 **facilities, litter barrels, petwalk,** 🚻, 🚮, **vending**
10 (38)	NY 7, to Unadilla, **N 2 mi** 🏪 KwikFill, Mirabito 🛏 Country Motel (4mi) ⭕ Great American Foods, st police, USPO
9 (33)	NY 8, to Sidney, **N** 🏪 Hess/dsl, Mobil/dsl, Sunoco 🍴 China Buffet, Little Caesars, McDonald's, Pizza Hut, Subway 🛏 Algonkin Motel, Country Motel, Super 8 ⭕ H, $General, Advance Parts, K-Mart, PriceChopper Foods, Tall Pines Camping, USPO
8 (29)	NY 206, to Bainbridge, **N** 🏪 Sunoco 🍴 Bob's Family Diner, Deli Joe's, Dunkin Donuts 🛏 Algonkin Motel, Susquehanna Motel ⭕ Chevrolet/GMC, Parts+, Riverside RV Park, to Oquage Creek Park, USPO
7 (22)	NY 41, to Afton, **N 1-5 mi** 🏪 Mobil, Sunoco/dsl 🍴 RiverClub Rest., Vincent's Rest. ⭕ Afton Golf/rest., Kellystone Park, Smith-Hale HS

NY (side tab)

N Y C A R E A (side label)

C O B L E S K I L L (side label)

O N E O N T A (side label)

⬆E INTERSTATE 88 Cont'd

Exit #	Services
6 (16)	NY 79, to NY 7, Harpursville, Ninevah, **S** 🅶 Mirabito/dsl 🍴 Gramma's Country Cafe, Tim Hortons 🅾 to Nathanial Cole Park, USPO
5 (12)	Martin Hill Rd, to Belden, **N** 🅶 Manley's Trstp/dsl 🅾 Belden Manor Camping
4 (8)	NY 7, to Sanitaria Springs, **S** 🅶 Hess/dsl
3 (4)	NY 369, Port Crane, **N** 🅾 to Chenango Valley SP, **S** 🅶 Fastrac/dsl, KwikFill
2 (2)	NY 12a W, to Chenango Bridge, **N** 🅶 Mirabito 🅾 USPO
1 (1)	NY 7 W (no wb return), to Binghamton
0mm	I-81, N to Syracuse, S to Binghamton.

I-88 begins/ends on I-81.

⬆E INTERSTATE 90

Exit #	Services
B24.5mm	New York/Massachusetts state line
B3 (B23)	NY 22, to Austerlitz, New Lebanon, W Stockbridge, **N** 🅶 Citgo/dsl/scales/24hr, **S** 🅶 Sunoco/dsl 🏠 Berkshire Travel Lodge 🅾 Woodland Hills Camp
B18mm	**toll plaza,** 🅲
B2 (B15)	NY 295, Taconic Pkwy, **S** 1/2 mi 🅶 gas
B1 (B7)	US 9, NY Thruway W, to I-87, 🅲, **toll booth**
12 (20)	US 9, to Hudson, **N** 🅶 🅿🅸🅻🅾🆃/McDonald's/Subway/dsl/scales/24hr, **S** 0-3 mi 🅾 to Van Buren NHS
18.5mm	🆁🆂/weigh sta wb,full 🚻 **facilities, litter barrels, petwalk,** 🅲, 🆀, **vending**
11 (15)	US 9, US 20, E Greenbush, Nassau, **N** 🅶 Hess/dsl, Sunoco/dsl 🍴 Dunkin Donuts 🅾 st police, **S** 🅶 Mobil (2mi), Stewarts 🍴 Lighthouse Rest. 🏠 Host Field Inn, Knights Inn 🅾 repair, Rite Aid, vet
10 (10)	Miller Rd, to E Greenbush, **S** 🅶 Mobil/dsl, Stewarts 🍴 Dunkin Donuts 🏠 Comfort Inn
9 (9)	US 4, to Rensselaer, Troy, **N** 🅶 Mobil 🍴 5 Guys Burgers, Applebee's, Domino's, Dunkin Donuts, McDonald's, OffShore Pier Rest., Panera Bread, Starbucks, Subway, The Sports Grill 🏠 Holiday Inn Express, Residence Inn 🅾 $Tree, Home Depot, PetsMart, Radio Shack, Staples, Target, Walmart, **S** 🅶 Mobil/dsl, Stewart's 🍴 Cracker Barrel, Denny's, Dunkin Donuts 🅾 Fairfield Inn
8 (8)	NY 43, Defreestville
7 (7)	Washington Ave (from eb), Rensselaer
6.5mm	Hudson River
6a	I-787, to Albany
6 (4.5)	US 9, Northern Blvd, to Loudonville, **N** 🅶 Stewarts 🍴 Forbidden City, Mr Subb, NY Pizza 🏠 Red Carpet Inn 🅾 🅷
5a (4)	Corporate Woods Blvd
5 (3.5)	Everett Rd, to NY 5, **S on NY 5, Central Ave** 🅶 Hess/dsl, ShopRite 🍴 Bob&Ron's Fishfry, Dunkin Donuts, Gateway Diner, Little Caesars, Mama Buffet, McDonald's, Popeye's, Subway, Taco Bell 🅾 🅷, $Tree, Aamco, Advance Parts, Chevrolet, Chrysler/Dodge/Jeep, CVS Drug, Fiat, Ford, Hannaford's Foods, Home Depot, Honda, Hyundai, Kia, Mavis Tire, Mazda, Monroe, Nissan, PepBoys, PriceChopper Foods, Radio Shack, Rite Aid, ShopRite Foods
4 (3)	NY 85 S, to Slingerlands
3 (2.5)	**N** 🅾 State Offices
2 (2)	Fuller Rd, Washington Ave, **S on Washington** 🅶 Sunoco/Subway 🍴 Dunkin Donuts 🏠 Courtyard, CrestHill Suites, Extended Stay America, Fairfield Inn, Hilton Garden, Red Carpet Inn, TownePlace Suites 🅾 same as 1S

1N (1)	I-87 N, to Montreal, to Albany 🆂
1S (1)	US 20, Western Ave, **S** 🅶 Mobil 🍴 5 Guys Burgers, 99 Rest., Burger King, Capital City Diner, Chipotle Mexican, Dunkin Donuts, Hana Grill, Ichiban Japanese, McDonald's, Moe's SW Grill, Panera Bread, Peaches Cafe, Starbucks, TGIFriday's, Uno Grill, Wendy's 🏠 Holiday Inn Express, Residence Inn 🅾 AT&T, Best Buy, CVS Drug, Dick's, Home Depot, JC Penney, Macy's, mall, Michael's, Old Navy, PetsMart, PriceChopper Foods, USPO, Verizon, vet, Walmart
24 (149)	I-87 N to Albany, Montreal, S to NYC
153mm	**Guilderland Service Area eb,** 🅶 Mobil/dsl 🍴 McDonald's
25 (154)	I-890, NY 7, NY 146, to Schenectady
25a (159)	I-88 S, NY 7, to Binghamton, 🅶 🅿🅸🅻🅾🆃/Dunkin Donuts/Subway/dsl/scales/24hr
26 (162)	I-890, NY 5 S, Schenectady
168mm	**Pattersonville Service Area wb,** 🅶 Mobil/dsl 🍴 Hershey's, Quiznos, Roy Rogers, Starbucks 🅾 atm, wi-fi
172mm	**Mohawk Service Area eb,** 🅶 Mobil/dsl 🍴 McDonald's
27 (174)	NY 30, Amsterdam, **N** 1 mi 🅶 Mobil/dsl, Valero 🏠 Best Value Inn, Super 8, Valleyview Motel 🅾 Alpin Haus RV Ctr (3mi)
28 (182)	NY 30A, Fonda, **N** 🅶 Citgo/rest/dsl/motel/24hr, Mobil (1mi), Sunoco/dsl, TA/Buck Hill Rest/dsl/motel/scales/24hr/@ 🍴 Dunkin Donuts, McDonald's 🏠 Holiday Inn (7mi), Microtel, Riverside Motel, Super 8 (8mi) 🅾 🅷, st police, truck repair
184mm	**parking area/truck insp area both lanes, litter barrels,** 🅲
29 (194)	NY 10, Canajoharie, **N** 🅶 Gulf, Stewarts 🍴 McDonald's, Subway 🅾 $General, Ace Hardware, BigLots, NAPA, Rite Aid, Riverfront Park, USPO, **S** 🅶 Citgo/dsl, Lukoil/dsl, Sunoco 🍴 Mercato Pizza, Village Rest. 🏠 Rodeway Inn 🅾 NAPACare, USPO
210mm	**Indian Castle Service area eb,** 🍴 Hershey's Ice Cream, Roy Rogers, Starbucks 🅾 atm, gifts, wi-fi **Iroquois Service Area wb,** 🍴 Burger King, Dunkin Donuts, wi-fi
29a (211)	NY 169, to Little Falls, **N** 🏠 Knights Inn (3mi) 🅾 🅷, to Herkimer Home
30 (220)	NY 28, to Mohawk, Herkimer, **N** 🅶 FasTrac/dsl, Mobil/Subway/dsl, Stewarts 🍴 Applebee's, Burger King, Denny's, Dunkin Donuts, KFC/Taco Bell, McDonald's, Pizza Hut, Tony's Pizzaria, Vinny's Pizza 🏠 Best Inn, Budget Motel, Herkimer Motel, Inn Towne Motel 🅾 $General, $Tree, Advance Parts, Aubuchon Hardware, AutoZone, Goodyear, Rite Aid, Verizon, Walmart, **S** 🅶 FasTrac 🍴 Little Caesars, Red Apple Chinese 🏠 Red Carpet Inn (2mi) 🅾 Factory Depot, Family$, to Cooperstown (Baseball Hall of Fame)
227mm	**Schuyler Service Area wb,** 🅶 Mobil/dsl 🍴 Breyer's, Fresh Fudge, McDonald's 🅾 atm, st police

A L B A N Y

N Y

▲E	**INTERSTATE 90 Cont'd**

U T I C A

Exit #	Services
31 (233)	I-790, NY 8, NY 12, to Utica, **N** ⛽ Citgo/dsl, Fastrac, Sunoco ⑪ Applebees, Burger King, Franco's Pizza, Good Friend Chinese ◙ $Tree, BigLots, BJ's Whse/gas, Curves, Lowe's, PriceChopper Foods, Rite Aid, Walmart/McDonald's, **S** ⛽ Hess/dsl ⑪ Babe's Grill, Delmonico's Steaks, Denny's, Dunkin Donuts, Friendly's, Knock-Out Pizza, McDonald's, Pizza Hut, Romeo's Italian, Subway, Taco Bell, Wendy's 🛏 Best Western, Days Inn, Hampton Inn, Happy Journey Motel, Red Roof Inn, Scottish Inn, Super 8 ◙ AT&T
236mm	I-790 (from eb), to Utica
237.5mm	Erie Canal
238mm	Mohawk River
32 (243)	NY 232, Westmoreland, **N 4-8 mi** 🛏 EconoLodge, Quality Inn, Red Carpet Inn, Scottish Inn, **S 5 mi** 🛏 Hampton Inn
244mm	**Oneida Service Area eb**, ⛽ Sunoco/dsl ⑪ Burger King, Sbarro's, Starbucks ◙ atm, gifts÷
250mm	parking area eb, litter barrel, ◙, ⛾, 🍽
33 (253)	NY 365, to Vernon Downs, Verona, **N** ⛽ SavOn Gas/dsl ⑪ Joel's Frontyard Steaks 🛏 Inn at Turning Stone, **S** ⛽ SavOn Gas/LP/repair ⑪ Dunkin Donuts, Recovery Grill 🛏 Fairfield Inn, La Quinta ◙ 🅷, Turning Stone Casino
256mm	parking area wb, litter barrel, ◙, 🍽
34 (262)	NY 13, to Canastota, **S** ⛽ KwikFill, SavOn/dsl, Sunoco ⑪ Dunkin Donuts, McDonald's 🛏 Days Inn, Graziano Motel/rest., Super 8 ◙ Boxing Hall of Fame, Verona Beach SP Camping
266mm	**Chittenango Service Area wb**, ⛽ Sunoco/dsl ⑪ Sbarro's, Starbucks ◙ arm, Wi-fi
34a (277)	I-481, to Syracuse, Chittenango

S Y R A C U S E

35 (279)	NY 298, The Circle, Syracuse, **S** ⛽ Mobil, Valero/dsl ⑪ Burger King, Denny's, Dunkin Donuts, East Wok, Green Onion Rest., Grimaldi's, Joey's Italian, Jreck Subs, Justin's Grill, McDonald's, Ruby Tuesday, Weigh Lock Cafe 🛏 Candlewood Suites, Comfort Inn, Courtyard, Cresthill Suites, Days Inn, Doubletree Inn, Embassy Suites, Extended Stay America, Hampton Inn, Hilton Garden, Holiday Inn, John Milton Inn, Microtel, Motel 6, Quality Inn, Ramada Ltd, Red Roof Inn, Residence Inn, Super 8 ◙ Goodyear/auto
280mm	**Dewitt Service Area eb**, ⛽ Sunoco/ds ⑪ Edy's Ice Cream, McDonald's
36 (283)	I-81, N to Watertown, S to Binghamton
37 (284)	7th St, Electronics Pkwy, to Liverpool, **N** 🛏 Best Western, **S** ⛽ Hess/Blimpie/Dunkin Donuts/Godfather's ⑪ KFC/Taco Bell 🛏 Holiday Inn, Homewood Suites, Knights Inn, Staybridge Suites ◙ Kinny Drug
38 (286)	NY 57, to Liverpool, Syracuse, **N** ⛽ Fastrac/dsl, Hess, KwikFill ⑪ Bangkok Thai, Hooligan's, Kirby's Rest., Pier 57 Diner, Pizza Hut, Quiznos, Salsarita's Grill 🛏 Hampton Inn (7mi), Super 8 ◙ $Tree, Aldi Foods, NAPA, Rite Aid
39 (290)	I-690, NY 690, Syracuse, **N** 🛏 Comfort Inn/rest. ◙ Camping World RV Ctr, **S** ⑪ Quaker Steak&Lube 🛏 Holiday Inn Express
292mm	**Warners Service Area wb**, ⛽ Mobil/dsl ⑪ Boston Pizza, Edy's Ice Cream, McDonald's
40 (304)	NY 34, to Owasco Lake, Weedsport, **N** ◙ Riverforest RV Park, **S** ⛽ Fastrac, KwikFill, Sunoco/dsl ⑪ Arby's, Arnold's Rest., Cj's Rest., DB's Drive-In, Jreck Subs, Lin Bo Chinese, Old Erie Diner 🛏 Best Western, Days Inn, Finger Lakes Inn, Holiday Inn (12mi) ◙ $General, Ace Hardware, Bass Pro Shops (12mi), Big M Foods, Kinney Drug, NAPA

310mm	**Port Byron Service Area eb**, ⛽ Mobil/dsl ⑪ Boston Pizza, Edy's Ice Cream, McDonald's
318mm	parking area wb, litter barrels, ◙
41 (320)	NY 414, to Cayuga Lake, Waterloo, **S** ⛽ Nice'n Easy/dsl, Petro/Iron Skillet/dsl/scales/24hr/@ ⑪ MaGee Country Diner 🛏 Hampton Inn (4mi), Holiday Inn (4mi), Microtel (4mi) ◙ Cayuga Lake SP/camping, Waterloo Outlets/famous brands (3mi)
324mm	**Junius Ponds Service Area wb**, ⛽ Sunoco/dsl ⑪ Dunkin Donuts, Roy Rogers ◙ atm, wi-fi
42 (327)	NY 14, to Geneva, Lyons, **N** ◙ RV camping, **S 6 mi** ⛽ Mobil/dsl/scales 🛏 Belherst, Best Value Inn, Days Inn, Hampton Inn, Ramada Inn, Red Carpet Inn ◙ Junius Ponds RV Camping, Waterloo Outlets/famous brands (3mi)
337mm	**Clifton Springs Service Area eb**, ⛽ Sunoco/dsl ⑪ Roy Rogers, Sbarro's, Starbucks ◙ atm, gifts÷
43 (340)	NY 21, to Palmyra, Manchester, **N** ◙ Hill Cumorah LDS HS (6mi), **S** ⛽ Sunoco/dsl ⑪ Lehigh Valley Rest., McDonald's 🛏 Scottish Inn ◙ KOA
44 (347)	NY 332, Victor, **S** ⛽ Getty/Subway/dsl, Sunoco/dsl ⑪ Dairy-Ann, Dunkin Donuts, KFC, King's Wok, McDonald's, NY Pizza 🛏 Best Value Inn, Budget Inn, Comfort Inn, Travelodge ◙ Aldi Foods, casino, CVS Drug, KOA (4mi), st police, Wade's Foods
350mm	**Seneca Service Area wb**, ⛽ Mobil/dsl ⑪ Checker's, Tim Hortons, Villa Pizza ◙ atm, wi-fi
45 (351)	I-490, NY 96, to Rochester, **N** ⛽ Mobil/dsl ⑪ Biaggi's Rest., BoneFish Grill, Champp's Grill, Distillery Rest., Longhorn Steaks, Moe's SW Grill, Olive Garden, PF Chang's, Starbucks, Subway, TGIFriday's, Uno Grill 🛏 Hampton Inn, Springdale Farm B&B ◙ $Tree, Best Buy, BJ's Whse/gas, Bonton, Dick's, Home Depot, JC Penney, K-Mart, Kohl's, Lord&Taylor, Macy's, Michael's, Old Navy, Petsmart, Rite Aid, Sears/auto, Staples, Target, Verizon, Walmart, **S** ⛽ KwikFill ⑪ Burger King, Chili's, Denny's, Wendy's 🛏 Best Western, Holiday Inn Express, Homewood Suites, Microtel, Royal Inn ◙ Ballantyne RV Ctr
353mm	parking area eb, litter barrels, ◙
46 (362)	I-390, to Rochester, **W on NY 253** ⛽ Gulf/dsl, Hess, Sunoco/dsl ⑪ Lehigh Rest., McDonald's, Peppermint's Rest., Tim Hortons, Wendy's 🛏 Country Inn&Suites, Days Inn, Fairfield Inn, Microtel, Red Carpet Inn, Red Roof Inn, Super 8 ◙ Buick/GMC
366mm	**Scottsville Service Area eb**, ⛽ Mobil/dsl ⑪ Arby's, Tim Horton ◙ atm, info, wi-fi
376mm	**Ontario Service Area wb**, ⛽ Sunoco/dsl ⑪ Boston Pizza, Edy's Ice Cream, McDonald's ◙ atm, wi-fi
47 (379)	I-490, NY 19, to Rochester, **N** ◙ Timberline Camping
48 (390)	NY 98, to Batavia, **N** 🛏 Comfort Inn, Hampton Inn, Holiday Inn Express, **S** ⛽ Citgo ⑪ Applebee's, Bob Evans, Peking Buffet 🛏 Best Western, Budget Inn, Clarion, Days Inn, Quality Inn, Red Roof Inn, Super 8 ◙ AT&T, AutoZone, BJ's Whse, Home Depot, K-Mart, Michael's, PetCo, Radio Shack, Target, Walmart
397mm	**Pembroke Service Area eb**, ⛽ Sunoco/dsl ⑪ Checker's, Tim Hortons ◙ atm, gifts, ◙, wi-fi÷
48a (402)	NY 77, Pembroke, **S** ⛽ ✈FLYING J/Denny's/Subway/dsl/LP/scales/24hr, TA/Valero/dsl/scales/24hr/@ ⑪ Subway 🛏 Darien Lake Lodge/camping, EconoLodge ◙ Sleepy Hollow Camping (8mi)
412mm	**Clarence Service Area wb**, full 🛏 facilities, info, wi-fi, ⛽ Sunoco/dsl ⑪ Arby's, Tim Hortons ◙ atm

R O C H E S T E R

NY

E **INTERSTATE 90 Cont'd**

Exit #	Services

DEPEW

49 (417) NY 78, Depew, **N** 0-3 mi 🅖 Delta Sonic, Mobil/dsl, Sunoco 🍴 Applebee's, Arby's, Burger King, Carmen's Rest., Chili's, Coldstone, Cracker Barrel, Denny's, Dibella's Subs, DQ, Dunkin Donuts, Friendly's, Frog Hair Grille, Just Pizza, KFC, La Tolteca, McDonald's, Mighty Taco, Moe's SW Grill, Mr Pita, Old Country Buffet, Panera Bread, Perkins, Picasso's Pizza, Pizza Hut, Pizza Plant, Pomegranate, Protocol Rest., Quaker Steak&Lube, Quiznos, Red Lobster, Russel's Steaks, Salsarita's, Spilio's Rest., Starbucks, Subway, Taco Bell, Ted's HotDogs, TGIFriday's, Tim Horton, Tully's Rest., Wendy's 🛏 Clarion, Microtel, Motel 6, Rodeway Inn, Salvatore's Hotel, Staybridge Suites, Super 8 🅾 $Tree, Acura, Aldi Foods, AT&T, Barnes&Noble, Best Buy, BigLots, BJ's Whse/gas, BonTon, Buick/GMC, Chrysler/Dodge/Jeep, Dick's, Dunn Tire, Firestone/auto, Ford, Goodyear, Home Depot, Honda, JC Penney, Jo-Ann Fabrics, Kohl's, Lowe's, mall, Michael's, PetCo, PetsMart, Rite Aid, Sears/auto, SteinMart, Suzuki, Target, TJ Maxx, Top's Food/deli, Tuesday Morning, vet, Walgreens, Walmart, Wegman's Foods, **S** 🅖 Kwikfill, Mobil 🍴 Bob Evans, China 1, Dunkin Donuts, John&Mary's Cafe, McDonald's, Salvatore's Italian, Subway, Tim Horton 🛏 Garden Place Hotel, Hospitality Inn, La Quinta, Red Roof Inn 🅾 $Tree, Aamco, CarQuest, Top's Foods

419mm toll booth
50 (420) I-290 to Niagara Falls
50a (421) Cleveland Dr (from eb)
51 (422) NY 33 E, Buffalo, **S** 🅾 🆁🆂, st police
52 (423) Walden Ave, to Buffalo, **N** 🍴 Applebees, Burger King, Famous Dave's BBQ, IHOP, McDonald's, Ruby Tuesday, Starbucks, Subway, TGIFriday's, Tim Horton 🛏 Hampton Inn, Residence Inn 🅾 $Tree, Aldi Foods, AT&T, Firestone, Ford, Goodyear/auto, Home Depot, Michael's, Office Depot, PetsMart, PriceRight, Target, Top's Foods, Walmart, **S** 🅖 Delta Sonic, Jim's Trk Plaza/Sunoco/dsl/rest./scales/24hr, KwikFill 🍴 Alton's Rest., Bar Louie's, Bravo Italiano, Cheesecake Factory, Dunkin Donuts, Fuddrucker's, Hyde Park Steaks, Jack Astor's Grill, McDonald's, Melting Pot, Mighty Taco, Milton's Rest., Olive Garden, PF Chang's, Pizza Hut, Smokey Bones BBQ, Zahng's Buffet 🛏 Millenium Hotel, Oak Tree Inn 🅾 Best Buy, Burlington Coats, Dick's, Dunn Tire, JC Penney, K-Mart, Lord&Taylor, Macy's, mall, NAPA, Niagara Hobby, Old Navy, Sears

52a (424) William St
53 (425) I-190, to Buffalo, Niagara Falls, **N** 🛏 Best Western
54 (428) NY 400, NY 16, to W Seneca, E Aurora
55 (430) US 219, Ridge Rd, Orchard Park, **S** 🅖 Delta Sonic, Valero 🍴 Denny's, Mighty Taco, Subway, Tim Horton, Wendy's 🛏 Country Inn&Suites, Hampton Inn, Staybridge Suites 🅾 $General, Aldi Foods, BigLots, Goodyear/auto, Home Depot, K-Mart, Mr Tire, Pepboys, to Wilson Stadium, Tops Foods, Wegman's Foods

431mm toll booth
56 (432) NY 179, Mile Strip Rd, **N** 🅖 Sunoco, Valero 🍴 Blasdale Pizza, China King, DiPallo's Rest., Odyssey Rest., Whse Rest. 🛏 EconoLodge 🅾 $General, CarQuest, CVS Drug, Family$, Jubilee Foods, repair, Rite Aid, USPO, **S** 🍴 Applebee's, Boston Mkt, Buffalo Wild Wings, ChuckeCheese, Friendly's, McDonald's, Mongolian Buffet, Olive Garden, Outback Steaks, Panera Bread, Pizza Hut, Red Lobster, Ruby Tuesday, Starbucks, Subway, TGIFriday's, Wasabi Japanese, Wendy's

BUFFALO

56 (432) Continued 🛏 Best Western, McKinley's Hotel, Red Carpet Inn (2mi) 🅾 $Tree, Aldi Foods, Barnes&Noble, Best Buy, BJ's Whse, BonTon, Dick's, Firestone/auto, Home Depot, JC Penney, Jo-Ann Etc, Macy's, mall, Old Navy, PepBoys, Sears, TJ Maxx, Wegman's Foods

57 (436) NY 75, to Hamburg, **N** 🅖 Mobil/Dunkin Donuts/dsl 🍴 Anthony's Diner, Bozanna's Pizza, Denny's, McDonald's, Tim Horton, Uncle Joe's Diner, Wendy's 🛏 Comfort Inn, Holiday Inn Express, Motel 6, Red Roof Inn 🅾 (3mi) Chevrolet, Chrysler/Dodge/Jeep, Ford, Lowe's, repair, transmissions, Wal-Mar, **S** 🅖 Go Gas, Kwikfill/dsl, Stop&Gas 🍴 Arby's, Burger King, Hideaways Rest., Pizza Hut, Subway, Tim Horton 🛏 Quality Inn, Super 8 🅾 $General, AutoZone, Goodyear/auto, USPO, vet

442mm parking area both lanes, litter barrels, 🆁🆂
57a (445) to Eden, Angola, **N** 2 mi 🅖 Sunoco/dsl
447mm Angola Service Area both lanes, 🅖 Sunoco/dsl 🍴 McDonald's, Moe's SW Grill, Subway 🅾 atm, gifts, wi-fi
58 (456) US 20, NY 5, to Silver Creek, Irving, **N** 🅖 Citgo, Kwikfill 🍴 Burger King, Colony Rest., Millie's Rest., Primo's Rest., Subway, Sunset Bay, Tim Hortons, Tom's Rest. 🛏 Lighthouse Inn 🅾 🏥, to Evangola SP
59 (468) NY 60, Fredonia, Dunkirk, **N** 🛏 Clarion (2mi), Dunkirk Motel (4mi) 🅾 Lake Erie SP/camping (7mi), **S** 🅖 Country Fair, Fuel Ctr/dsl, Kwikfill/dsl, Mobil/dsl 🍴 Applebee's, Arby's, Azteca Mexican, Best Buffet, Bob Evans, Burger King, Denny's, Dunkin Donuts, KFC/Taco Bell, McDonald's, Pizza Hut, Subway, Tim Hortons, Wendy's, Wing City Grille 🛏 Best Western, Comfort Inn, Days Inn 🅾 $General, $Tree, Advance Parts, Aldi Foods, AutoZone, BigLots, Ford/Lincoln, GMC, GNC, Home Depot, Radio Shack, Rite Aid, TJ Maxx, Tops Foods/gas, Walmart
60 (485) NY 394, Westfield, **N** 🛏 Webb's Motel 🅾 Brookside Beach Camping, KOA, to Lake Erie SP/camping, **S** 🛏 Holiday Motel 🅾 🏥
494mm toll booth
61 (495) Shortman Rd, to Ripley, **N** 🅾 Lakeshore RV Park
496mm New York/Pennsylvania state line

HAMBURG

N **INTERSTATE 95**

Exit #	Services
32mm	New York/Connecticut state line
22 (30)	Midland Ave (from nb), Port Chester, Rye, **W** 🍴 Subway 🅾 🏥, Home Depot, Staples
21 (29)	I-287 W, US 1 N, to White Plains, Port Chester, Tappan Zee
20 (28)	US 1 S (from nb), Port Chester, **E** 🅖 Shell 🅾 CVS Drug, Ford, Subaru, USPO

⬆N INTERSTATE 95 Cont'd

Exit #	Services
19.5mm	**toll plaza**
19 (27)	Playland Pkwy, Rye, Harrison
18b (25)	Mamaroneck Ave, to White Plains, **E** 🅖 Hess, Shell 🍴 Domino's 🅞 A&P Foods, Mavis Tire
18a (24)	Fenimore Rd (from nb), Mamaroneck, **E** 🅖 Citgo, Gulf
17 (20)	Chatsworth Ave (from nb, no return), Larchmont
16 (19)	North Ave, Cedar St, New Rochelle, **E** 🍴 Applebee's, Buffalo Wild Wings, TX Roadhouse 🏠 Radisson, Residence Inn 🅞 ShopRite, Toyota, USPO, **W** 🅞 🄷
15 (16)	US 1, New Rochelle, The Pelhams, **E** 🅖 GasTrack/dsl, SuperGas 🅞 AutoZone, Costco/gas, CVS Drug, Harley-Davidson, Home Depot, Walgreens, **W** 🅞 repair
14 (15)	Hutchinson Pkwy (from sb), to Whitestone Br
13 (16)	Conner St, to Mt Vernon, **E** 🅖 Gulf/dsl 🏠 Ramada Inn, **W** 🅖 BP 🍴 McDonald's 🏠 Holiday Motel 🅞 🄷, Goodyear/auto, Pepboys
12 (15.5)	Baychester Ave (exits left from nb)
11 (15)	Bartow Ave, Co-op City Blvd, **E** 🍴 Applebee's, Bartow Pizza, Burger King, Checker's, Dallas BBQ, Genarro's Pizza, McDonald's, Panera Bread, Popeye's, Red Lobster, Zinhi Chinese 🅞 $Tree, AT&T, Barnes&Noble, JC Penney, K-Mart, Marshall's, Old Navy, PathMark Foods, Staples, Verizon, **W** 🅖 BP/Dunkin Donuts, Sunoco/dsl, Wave/dsl 🍴 ChuckeCheese, Dunkin Donuts, Pizza Hut, TGIFriday's 🅞 Aldi Foods, Home Depot
10 (14.5)	Gun Hill Rd (exits left from nb), **W** 🏠 Pelham Bay Hotel/diner
9 (14)	Hutchinson Pkwy
8c (13.5)	Pelham Pkwy W
8b (13)	Orchard Beach, City Island
8a (12.5)	Westchester Ave (from sb)
7c (12)	Pelham Bay Park (from nb), Country Club Rd
7b (11.5)	E Tremont (from sb), **W** 🅞 Super FoodTown
7a (11)	I-695 (from sb), to I-295 S, Throgs Neck Br
6b (10.5)	I-278 W (from sb), I-295 S (from nb)
6a (10)	I-678 S, Whitestone Bridge
5b (9)	Castle Hill Ave, **W** 🅖 Sunoco 🍴 McDonald's
5a (8.5)	Westchester Ave, White Plains Rd
4b (8)	Bronx River Pkwy, Rosedale Ave, **E** 🅖 BP
4a (7)	I-895 S, Sheridan Expsy
3 (6)	3rd Ave, **W** 🅞 🄷
2b (5)	Webster Ave, **W** 🅞 🄷
2a (4)	Jerome Ave, to I-87
1c (3)	I-87, Deegan Expsy, to Upstate
1b (2)	Harlem River Dr
1a (1)	US 9, NY 9A, H Hudson Pkwy, 178th St, downtown
0mm	New York/New Jersey state line, Hudson River, Geo Washington Br

⬆E INTERSTATE 190 (Buffalo)

Exit #	Services
25.5mm	US/Canada Border, US Customs
25b a	R Moses Pkwy, NY 104, NY 265, Lewiston, **E** 🅞 🄷
24	NY 31, Witmer Rd, **E** 🅞 🄷, st police
23	NY 182, Porter Rd, Packard Rd, **E** 🅖 Sunoco 🍴 Applebees, Burger King, DQ, Mighty Taco, Perkins, Subway, Tim Horton 🅞 Big Lots, CarQuest, Chrysler/Jeep, Firestone/auto, Jo-Ann Fabrics, K-Mart, NAPA, Prime Outlets/famous brands, U-Haul, **W** 🍴 Wendy's 🅞 Aldi Foods, Sam's Club, Walmart/Subway

Exit #	Services
22	US 62, Niagara Falls Blvd, **E** 🅖 Sunoco 🍴 Bob Evans, Burger King, Denny's, Dunkin Donuts, KFC, McDonald's, Pizza Hut, Taco Bell, Wendy's 🏠 Budget Host, Caravan Motel, Holiday Motel, Howard Johnson, Knight's Inn, Pelican Motel, Quality Inn, Red Carpet Inn, Super 8, Swiss Cottage Inn 🅞 Advance Parts, Ford, Radio Shack, Rite Aid, Target, Top's Foods/gas, Toyota, **W** 🏠 Econolodge, Sunrise Inn 🅞 Home Depot
21a	NY 384, Buffalo Ave, R Moses Pkwy, **W** 🅖 Getty 🅞 American Falls, casino, to NY SP
21	La Salle Expswy
20.5mm	**toll booth sb**, Niagara River East
20b a	Long Rd, **E** 🏠 Budget Motel
19	Whitehaven Rd, **E** 🅖 Getty, Noco Gas 🍴 McDonald's, Subway 🏠 Chateu Motel (2mi), Holiday Inn (4mi) 🅞 $Tree, funpark, KOA (1mi), Top's Foods/gas, **W** 🅞 Chevrolet, Toyota/Scion, vet
18b a	NY 324 W, Grand Island Blvd, **E** 🍴 Asian Buffet, Burger King, Tim Horton, Wendy's 🏠 Chateu Motel, Grand Suites 🅞 NAPA, **W** 🅞 Beaver Island SP
17.5mm	Niagara River East, **toll booth**
17	NY 266, last free exit nb
16	I-290 E, to I-90, Albany
15	NY 324, Kenmore Ave, **E** 🅖 7-11, **W** 🅞 U-Haul
14	Ontario St, **E** 🅖 KwikFill 🍴 McDonald's, Tim Horton 🅞 Advance Parts, Family$, **W** 🍴 Harry's Grille
13	(from nb), same as 14
12	Amherst St, (from nb), downtown
11	NY 198, Buffalo, **E** 🅖 Sunoco
9	Porter Ave, to Peace Bridge, Ft Erie
8	NY 266, Niagara St, **E** 🏠 Adam's Mark Hotel, downtown
7	NY 5 W, Church St, Buffalo, downtown
6	Elm St, **E** 🅞 🄷, downtown, **W** 🅞 Arena
5	Louisiana St, Buffalo, downtown
4	Smith St, Fillmore Ave, Buffalo, downtown
3	NY 16, Seneca St, from sb, **W** 🅞 CarQuest
2	US 62, NY 354, Bailey Ave, Clinton St
1	Ogden St, **E** 🅖 Sunoco 🍴 Wendy's 🏠 Comfort Inn, Holiday Inn Express 🅞 CVS Drug, Tops Foods, Volvo/GMC Trucks
.5mm	**toll plaza nb**
0mm	I-90. I-190 begins/ends on I-90, exit 53.

⬆E INTERSTATE 287 (New York City)

Exit #	Services
	I-287 begins/ends on I-95, exit 21.
12	I-95, N to New Haven, S to NYC.
11	US 1, Port Chester, Rye, **N** 🅖 BP, Mobil, Sunoco 🍴 Burger King, Domino's, Dunkin Donuts, KFC, McDonald's, Port Chester Diner, Subway, Wendy's 🅞 🄷, Goodyear/auto, Kohl's, Mavis Discount Tire, Nissan, Petsmart, Staples, Verizon
10	Bowman Ave, Webb Ave
9N S	Hutchinson Pkwy, Merritt Pkwy, to Whitestone Br
9a	I-684, Brewster
8	Westchester Ave, to White Plains, **S** 🅖 BP, Cheesecake Factory, Mobil, Morton's Steaks, PF Chang's, Westchester Burger Co, White Plains Diner 🅞 Chrysler/Dodge/Jeep, Hyundai, Neiman Marcus, Nordstrom, Stop&Shop Foods, Westchester Mall Place, Whole Foods Mkt
7	Taconic Pkwy (from wb), to N White Plains
6	NY 22, White Plains
5	NY 100, Hillside Ave, **S** 🅖 Citgo, Gulf, Lukoil 🍴 Applebee's, Dunkin Donuts, Papa John's, Planet Pizza, Subway 🅞 Aamco, AutoZone, Barnes&Noble, GNC, K-Mart, Lexus, Mazda, Radio Shack, vet

NY (side tab — NYC AREA)

NIAGARA FALLS / BUFFALO / NYC AREA (side tabs)

⬆E INTERSTATE 287 (New York City) Cont'd

Exit #	Services
4	NY 100A, Hartsdale, **N** 🅖 Shell 🅞 🏥, **S** 🍴 Bamboo Garden Chinese, Burger King 🅞 BMW/Mini, Jaguar, Staples, Volvo
3	Sprain Pkwy, to Taconic Pkwy, NYC
2	NY 9A, Elmsford, **N** 🅖 BP, Citgo, Mobil, Sunoco 🍴 Dunkin Donuts, KFC/Taco Bell, Subway 🅞 Mavis Discount Tire, NAPA, Sam's Club, **S** 🅖 Shell 🍴 Wendy's
1	NY 119, Tarrytown, **N** 🅖 Gulf/dsl 🍴 Ruth's Chris Steaks 🏠 Marriott, Sheraton, **S** 🅖 Gulf/dsl 🍴 El Dorado Diner 🏠 Extended Stay America, Hampton Inn

I-287 runs with I-87 N.

⬆N INTERSTATE 290 (Buffalo)

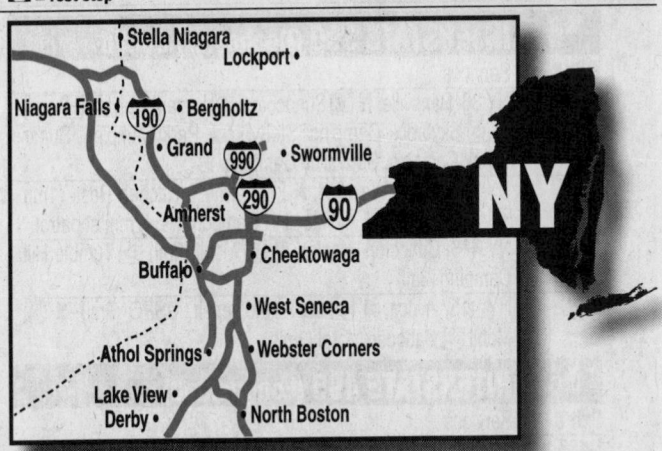

Exit #	Services
8	I-90, NY Thruway, **I-290 begins/ends on I-90, exit 50.**
7b a	NY 5, Main St, **N** 🅖 Mobil, Sunoco 🍴 La Nova Pizza/Wings, McDonald's, Pizza Plant, Subway, Tim Horton, Wendy's 🅞 Quality Mkt Foods, Walgreens, **S** 🅖 Valero 🍴 Sonoma Grille 🏠 Amherst Motel 🅞 vet
6	NY 324, NY 240, **N** 🅖 Getty 🏠 Courtyard, **S** 🅖 Valero 🍴 China Star, ChuckeCheese, Subway 🅞 Chrysler/Jeep, CVS Drug, Hyundai/Subaru, KIA/Mazda, Lexus, Nissan
5b a	NY 263, to Millersport, **N** 🍴 Houlihan's 🏠 Comfort Inn, Marriott, Red Roof Inn, **S** 🅖 Mobil 🏠 Homewood Suites 🅞 Scion/Toyota, VW, Walgreens
4	I-990, to St U
3b a	US 62, to Niagara Falls Blvd, **N** 🅖 Citgo, Valero 🍴 Bob Evans, Dunkin Donuts, Just Pizza, Max's Grill, Pancake House, Ted's Hot Dogs 🏠 Blvd Inn, Econolodge, Extended Stay America, Holiday Inn, Knight's Inn, Red Carpet Inn, Sleep Inn 🅞 Buick/GMC, CarQuest, Dodge, Home Depot, Honda, vet, Walmart/auto, **S** 🅖 Delta Sonic, Mobil 🍴 Applebee's, Arby's, BoneFish Grill, Burger King, Carrabba's, Chili's, Denny's, Dibella's Subs, John's Pizza, McDonald's, Moe's SW Grill, Montana's Grill, Outback Steaks, Panera Bread, Pizza Hut, Starbucks, Subway, Swiss Chalet Grill, TGIFriday, Tim Horton, Tulley's 🏠 Days Inn, Royal Inn 🅞 $Tree, Barnes&Noble, Best Buy, Firestone, Goodyear/auto, JC Penney, Jo-Ann Fabrics, Lowes Whse, Macy's, mall, Michael's, PetCo, PetsMart, Sears/auto, Target
2	NY 425, Colvin Blvd, **N** 🍴 Athena's Rest., KFC, McDonald's, Subway, Texas Roadhouse, Tim Horton, Wendy's 🅞 🏥, Big Lots, BJ's Whse/gas, Family$, Gander Mtn, Goodyear/auto, Top's Foods/gas, **S** 🅖 KwikFill
1b a	Elmwood Ave, NY 384, NY 265, **N** 🅖 KwikFill 🍴 John's Pizza/Subs, Sam's Cafe 🏠 Microtel 🅞 🏥, $Tree, NAPA, Rite Aid, **S** 🅖 Mobil/dsl 🍴 Arby's
0mm	I-190. **I-290 begins/ends on I-190 in Buffalo.**

⬆E INTERSTATE 390 (Rochester)

Exit #	Services
20b a	I-490. **I-390 begins/ends on I-490 in Rochester**
19 (75)	NY 33a, Chili Ave, **N** 🍴 Wishing Well Rest., **S** 🅖 Sunoco 🍴 Burger King, Pizza Hut, Subway 🏠 Motel 6, Quality Inn 🅞 $General
18b a	NY 204, Brooks Ave, **N** 🏠 Holiday Inn, **S** 🏠 Fairfield Inn 🅞 ✈
17 (73)	NY 383, Scottsville Rd, **W** 🅖 Sunoco/Subway/dsl
16 (71)	NY 15a, to E Henryetta, **S** 🍴 Basil's Rest 🏠 Courtyard, Hampton Inn 🅞 🏥
15 (70)	I-590, Rochester
14 (68)	NY 15a, NY 252, **E** 🍴 Domino's, Gray's Cafe, McDonald's, Outback Steaks, Papa John's, Perkins, Tully's Rest. 🏠 Extended Stay America 🅞 Staples, **W** 🅖 Mobil/dsl 🍴 Boston Mkt, Dunkin Donuts, Starbucks, Subway, Taco Bell 🏠 Best Western, DoubleTree Inn 🅞 Big Lots, Office Depot, Radio Shack, Top's Foods
13 (67)	Hylan Dr, **E** 🍴 Cracker Barrel 🏠 Comfort Suites, Homewood Suites, **W** 🅖 Mobil/dsl 🍴 Bonton, ChuckECheese, IHOP, McDonald's, Olive Garden, Panera Bread, Tim Hortons, Uno Grill, Wendy's 🅞 Aldi Foods, Best Buy, BJ's Whse, Gander Mtn, Goodyear/auto, JC Penney, Lowe's, Macy's, Michael's, Old Navy, PepBoys, PetCo, Sam's Club/gas, Sears, Target, Walmart, Wegman's Foods
12 (66)	I-90. NY Thruway, NY 253, **W** 🅖 Gulf/dsl/scales, Hess, Sunoco/dsl 🍴 Lehigh Rest, McDonald's, Peppermint's Rest., Tim Hortons, Wendy's 🏠 Country Inn&Suites, Days Inn, Fairfield Inn, Microtel, Red Carpet Inn, Red Roof Inn, Super 8 🅞 Buick/GMC
11 (62)	NY 15, NY 251, Rush, Scottsville, **N 2 mi** 🍴 McDonald's, Tim Hortons, Wendy's 🏠 Days Inn, Fairfield Inn, Red Roof Inn, RIT Inn
10 (55)	US 20, NY 5, Avon, Lima, **N** 🅖 Exxon 🍴 Countryside Diner 🏠 CrestHill Inn, Stratford Inn, **S 3 mi** 🅖 Sugar Creek/dsl 🍴 Avon Cafe, Dutch Hollow Cafe, McDonald's, Subway, Tom Wahls Cafe 🏠 Avon Cedar Lodge 🅞 Chrysler/Dodge/Jeep, Ford, Sugar Creek Camping
9mm	scenic area wb
9 (52)	NY 15, **N** 🅖 Mobil/Dunkin Donuts/dsl 🍴 Fratelli's Rest., Lakeville Rest., McDonald's, Tee&Gee Cafe 🏠 Conesus Motel 🅞 Chevrolet
8 (48)	US 20a, Geneseo, **N** 🏠 Oak Valley Inn 🅞 Conesus Lake Camping, **S** 🍴 Denny's, Dunkin Donuts, KFC/Taco Bell, McDonald's, Wendy's 🏠 Quality Inn
7 (39)	NY 63, NY 408, Geneseo, **S** 🅖 KwikFill, Mobil, Sunoco/dsl 🍴 Brian's Diner, McDonald's 🏠 Alligence B&B, Country Inn&Suites, Geneseo River Hotel/Rest., Greenway Motel 🅞 Bonadonna Auto, Family$, Letchworth SP, NAPA, Ridge Camping, Rite Aid, Save-A-Lot Foods, st police
38mm	🆁🆂 both lanes, full 🏠 facilities, litter barrels, petwalk, ✈, vending
6 (33)	NY 36, Mt Morris, Sonyea
5 (26)	NY 36, Dansville, **N** 🅖 KwikFill, Mobil/Subway 🍴 Arby's, Burger King, Dunkin Donuts, McDonald's, Pizza Hut, Subway 🅞 $Tree, Advance Parts, BigLots, Chevrolet, Chrysler/Dodge/Jeep, CVS Drug, Radio Shack, Rite Aid, Save-A-Lot Foods, Top's Foods/gas, Verizon, **S** 🅖 TA/Valero/Country Pride/dsl/scales/24hr/@ 🏠 TA Motel

⬆N INTERSTATE 390 (Rochester) Cont'd

Exit #	Services
4 (23)	NY 36, Dansville, N 🅖 Sunoco/dsl 🏠 Logan's Inn 🅞 H, vet, S 🅞 Skybrook Camping, Stonybrook Park Camping, Sugar Creek Camping, Sunvalley Camping
3 (17)	NY 15, NY 21, Wayland, N 🍴 Farmer's Kitchen Rest. (1mi) 🅞 CarQuest (1mi), Holiday Hill Campground (7mi), st patrol
2 (11)	NY 415, Cohocton, Naples, N 🅖 Mobil (2mi) 🅞 Tumble Hill Camping (3mi)
1 (2)	NY 415, Avoca, N 🅞 truck/auto repair, USPO (2mi), S 🅖 Mobil 🏠 Caboose Motel (3mi)

⬆E INTERSTATE 495 (Long Island)

Exit #	Services
	I-495 begins/ends on NY 25.
73	rd 58, Old Country Road, to Greenport, Orient, S 0-2 mi 🅖 Gulf, Hess/dsl, Lukoil/7-11, Mobil/dsl 🍴 Applebees, Boulder Creek Steaks, Panera Bread, Taco Bell, TGIFridays, Wendy's 🏠 Hilton Garden, Holiday Inn Express 🅞 AutoZone, Best Buy, Buick/GMC, Chevrolet, Chrysler/Jeep, Costco/gas, CVS Drug, Ford/Lincoln, Harley-Davidson, Home Depot, Honda, Kia/Mazda, Lowe's, Michael's, Nissan/Hyundai, PetCo, Stop&Shop, Subaru/VW, Tanger/famous brands, Target, Toyota/Scion, Volvo, Waldbaum's, Walgreens
72	NY 25, (no ez eb return), Riverhead, Calverton (no EZ eb return), N 🅞 funpark, S 🅖 Hess 🏠 Hotel Indigo 🅞 Tanger/famous brands/foodcourt
71	NY 24, to Hampton Bays (no ez eb return), Calverton, N 🅖 Hess/Subway/dsl
70	NY 111, to Eastport, Manorville, S 🅖 7-11, Mobil/dsl 🍴 McDonald's, Michelangelo's Rest., Starbucks 🅞 King Kullen Food/drug, Verizon
69	Wading River Rd, Center Moriches, to Wading River
68	NY 46, to Shirley, Wading River, S 🅞 7-11, golf
67	Yaphank Ave
66	NY 101, Sills Rd, Yaphank, N 🅖 Shell/24hr
65.5mm	**parking area**
65	Horse Block Rd, N 🍴 Baskin-Robbins/Dunkin Donuts, Kings Buffet 🅞 Ford/Kenworth/Mack, LI RV Ctr, S 🅞 funpark
64	NY 112, to Coram, Medford, N 🅖 Citgo/dsl, Hess 🍴 Subway 🅞 7-11, Lowe's, Michael's, Radio Shack, Sam's Club, Staples, Target, Walgreens, S 🅖 BP, Gulf, USA/dsl 🍴 J&R Steaks, Quiznos, Rita's Custard, Starbucks 🏠 Comfort Inn, Fairfield Inn 🅞 7-11, Aid Parts
63	NY 83, N Ocean Ave, N 🅖 Hess/dsl 🍴 Applebee's, Burger King, McDonald's, Taco Bell, TGIFriday's 🅞 7-11, CVS Drug, Hampton Inn, K-Mart, Stop'n Shop, S 🅖 Gulf/dsl, Lukoil/dsl 🍴 Yogi's Grill 🏠 Crowne Plaza
62	Nicolls Rd, rd 97, to Blue Point, Stony Brook, N 🅖 Gulf, S 🍴 Charlie Brown's Steaks, Chili's, La Capannina Italian, Wendy's 🏠 Residence Inn
61	rd 19, to Patchogue, Holbrook, N 🅖 Mobil, S 🅖 Gulf/dsl, Hess/dsl 🍴 China 4, Greek Islands Rest, Joe's Pizza/Pasta, Outback Steaks, Subway 🅞 7-11, CVS Drug, Waldbaums Foods
60	Ronkonkoma Ave, N 🅖 Gulf, S 🍴 Red Lobster, Smokey Bones BBQ 🏠 Courtyard
59	Ocean Ave, to Oakdale, Ronkonkoma, S 🅖 Gulf, Sunoco 🏠 Hilton Garden (2mi) 🅞 7-11
58	Old Nichols Rd, Nesconset, N 🅖 Gulf 🍴 Hooters 🏠 Marriott 🅞 BJ's Whse, S 🅖 BP
57	NY 454, Vets Hwy, to Hauppauge, N 🅖 Exxon/dsl 🍴 TGIFriday's, S 🅖 Getty's, Gulf/dsl, Shell, Sunoco 🍴 Dave&Buster's, Subway 🏠 Hampton Inn 🅞 7-11, Radio Shack, Rite Aid, Stop&Shop Foods, TJ Maxx, Walmart

Exit #	Services
56	NY 111, Smithtown, Islip, N 🅖 Gulf/Subway/Domino's/dsl, Mobil, S 🅖 Mobil 🍴 Café La Strada 🏠 Holiday Inn Express
55	Central Islip, N 🅖 Mobil, S 🅖 Exxon/dsl
54	Wicks Rd, N 🅖 BP 🏠 Sheraton, S 🅖 Mobil
53	Sunken Meadow Pkwy, to ocean beaches, Bayshore
52	rd 4, Commack, N 🅖 Mobil/dsl, Shell/repair 🍴 Conca d'Oro Pizza, Ground Round 🏠 Hampton Inn 🅞 Costco
51.5mm	**parking area both lanes, litter barrels,** Rs
51	NY 231, to Northport, Babylon
50	Bagatelle Rd, to Wyandanch
49S	NY 110 S, to Amityville
49N	NY 110 N, to Huntington, N 🏠 Marriott
48	Round Swamp Rd, Old Bethpage, S 🅖 Mobil/dsl 🍴 Old Country Pizza/deli 🏠 Homewood Suites, Palace Hotel, Sheraton 🅞 USPO
46	Sunnyside Blvd, Plainview, N 🏠 Holiday Inn
45	Manetto Hill Rd, Plainview, Woodbury
44	NY 135, to Seaford, Syosset
43	S Oyster Bay Rd, to Syosset, Bethpage, N 🅖 Mobil
42	Northern Pkwy, rd N, Hauppauge
41	NY 106, NY 107, Hicksville, Oyster Bay, S 🅖 BP, Mobil, Sunoco 🍴 Boston Mkt, Boulder Creek Steaks, Broadway Diner, Burger King, Dunkin Donuts, McDonald's, On the Border 🅞 Goodyear/auto, Sears/auto
40	NY 25, Mineola, Syosset, S 🅖 BP, Exxon, Hess/dsl, Shell 🍴 A&W, Burger King, Friendly's, IHOP, McDonald's, Wendy's 🏠 Howard Johnson 🅞 7-11, Home Depot, Kohl's, Staples
39	Glen Cove Rd, N 🅖 Mobil
38	Northern Pkwy E, Meadowbrook Pkwy, to Jones Beach
37	Willis Ave, to Roslyn, Mineola, N 🅖 Gulf, Shell 🍴 Dunkin Donuts, Skinny Pizza, S 🅖 Mobil/dsl 🍴 Tofu Chinese
36	Searingtown Rd, to Port Washington, S 🅞 H
35	Shelter Rock Rd, Manhasset, S 🅞 H
34	New Hyde Park Rd
33	Lakeville Rd, to Great Neck, N 🅞 H
32	Little Neck Pkwy, N 🅖 Gulf 🍴 Centre Pizza, Jain Rest., KFC/Taco Bell, Panera Bread, Starbucks
31	Douglaston Pkwy, S 🅖 BP/service 🍴 Burger King, Grimaldi's Pizza, Pinecourt Chinese, Subway 🅞 DR Drug, Macy's, USPO, Verizon, Waldbaum's Foods
30	E Hampton Blvd, Cross Island Pkwy
29	Springfield Blvd, S 🅖 Citgo, Gulf/Dunkin Donuts 🍴 McDonald's
27	I-295, Clearview Expswy, Throgs Neck, N 🅖 7-11, Gulf 🍴 Blue Bay Diner 🅞 drugstore
26	Francis Lewis Blvd
25	Utopia Pkwy, 188th St, N 🅖 Citgo, Gulf, S 🅖 Mobil, Quality/dsl, Savvy, Shell 🍴 5 Guys Burgers, Arby's, Baskin-Robbins, Dunkin Donuts, Subway 🅞 Radio Shack, USPO
24	Kissena Blvd, N 🅖 Gulf/dsl 🍴 Baskin-Robbins, Dunkin Donuts, S 🅖 Mobil
23	Main St, N 🍴 Palace Diner
22	Grand Central Pkwy, to I-678, College Pt Blvd, N 🏠 Holiday Inn Express
21	108th St, N 🅖 BP/7-11, Mobil
19	NY 25, Queens Blvd, Woodhaven Blvd, to Rockaways, N 🍴 McDonald's 🅞 JC Penney, Macy's, mall, S 🅖 BP 🍴 5 Guys Burgers, Applebees, Burger King, Dallas BBQ, Moe's SW Grill, Subway 🅞 Aldi Foods, Costco, Kohl's, Marshall's, Old Navy, Rite Aid, Sears, TJ Maxx
18.5	69th Ave, Grand Ave (from wb)
18	Maurice St, N 🅖 Exxon, S 🅖 BP 🍴 McDonald's 🏠 Holiday Inn Express 🅞 dsl repair
17	48th St, to I-278, N 🏠 Queensboro Hotel 🅞 Rs
16	**I-495 begins/ends in NYC.**

NC

INTERSTATE 26

Exit #	Services
71mm	North Carolina/South Carolina state line
69mm	N Pacolet River
67.5mm	**Welcome Ctr wb, full 🚻 facilities, litter barrels, Ⓒ, 🛒**
67	US 74 E, to NC 108, Columbus, Tryon, **N** 🅖 Shell/dsl, Vgo/dsl 🍴 Cocula Mexican, Joy Wok, Larkin's Carolina Grill, McDonald's, Subway, Waffle House, Wendy's Ⓞ Advance Parts, CVS Drug, Family$, Food Lion, **S** 🅖 Exxon/dsl 🍴 KFC/Taco Bell, Mtn View Deli 🛏 Days Inn Ⓞ Ⓗ, $General, Bi-Lo
59	Saluda, **N** 🛏 Saluda Mtn Lodge, **S** 🅖 BP/dsl, Marathon/Subway/dsl 🍴 Crust&Kettle Cafe, Saluda Rest. 🛏 Orchard Inn B&B (2mi) Ⓞ $General, AppleMill Outlet, Atkins Fruit, camping, repair, vet
56mm	Ⓞ Green River
54	US 25 (from eb), to Greenville, E Flat Rock, to Carl Sandburg Home
53.5mm	2130 ft, Eastern Continental Divide
53	Upward Rd, Hendersonville, **N** 🅖 Marathon/Dunkin Donuts/dsl 🍴 Waffle House, Zaxby's 🛏 Mtn Inn&Suites Ⓞ Bloomfields Giftshop, Lakewood RV Park, Wildflower RV Park, **S** 🅖 Exxon/McDonald's, Shell/pizza 🍴 Cracker Barrel, Poplar Leaf Cafe, Subway 🛏 Holiday Inn Express Ⓞ repair, to Carl Sandburg Home
49b a	US 64, Hendersonville, **N** 🅖 Marathon/dsl, Shell/dsl, Sunoco/dsl 🍴 Chick-fil-A, Golden Corral, Jack-in-the-Box, Moose Cafe, O'Charley's, Sonic, Starbucks, Waffle House, Zaxby's 🛏 Best Western, Hampton Inn, Quality Inn, Ramada Inn Ⓞ $Tree, Advance Parts, Ingles/gas, PetCo, Radio Shack, Sam's Club/gas, Staples, Walmart, World of Clothing, **S** 🅖 Exxon/dsl/LP, Shell/dsl 🍴 Applebee's, Arby's, Binion's Roadhouse, Bojangles, Burger King, China Buffet, Denny's, Fatz Café, Hardee's, Harry's Rest., HoneyBaked Ham, KFC, Krispy Kreme, LJ Silver, Lon Sen Chinese, McDonald's, Outback Steaks, Pizza Hut, Subway, Taco Bell, Tequila's Grill, Wendy's 🛏 Days Inn, EconoLodge, Red Roof Inn Ⓞ Ⓗ, Aldi Foods, Belk, BigLots, Bi-Lo Foods, Chrysler/Dodge/Jeep, Clark Tire/auto, CVS Drug, Family$, Home Depot, JC Penney, Jo-Ann, Lowe's, NAPA, TJ Maxx, Tuesday Morning, Verizon
46mm	**weigh sta both lanes, Ⓒ**
44	US 25, Fletcher, **N** 🅖 Exxon/dsl 🍴 Hardee's, Subway Ⓞ flea mkt/campground, vet, **S** 🅖 Citgo/dsl, Shell/DQ/dsl/scales/24hr, Sonny's/dsl 🍴 Bojangles, Burger King, McDonald's, Valentina's Mexican 🛏 Mountain Inn&Suites Ⓞ Ⓗ, Camping World RV Ctr, USPO
41mm	**℞ˢ both lanes, full 🚻 facilities, litter barrels, Ⓒ, 🛒, vending**
40	NC 280, Arden, **N** 🅖 Fastop/dsl, Shell/Arby's 🍴 Bojangles, Carrabba's, Casa Torres, Chili's, Cracker Barrel, Firehouse Subs, IHOP, Jersey Mike's, Little Caesar's, Lonestar Steaks,

ARDEN

40	**Continued** McDonald's, Moe's SW Grill, Olive Garden, Ruby Tuesday, Sonic, Tamarind Thai, Tokyo Express 🛏 Budget Motel, Clarion, Comfort Inn, Courtyard, EconoLodge, Hampton Inn, Knight's Inn Ⓞ Acura/Honda, Aldi Foods, Best Buy, BigLots, Dick's, Lowe's, Marshalls, Michael's, Old Navy, Petsmart, Ross, Rutledge Lake RV Park, Target, World Mkt, **S** 🅖 Citgo/dsl 🍴 Circle B Ranch BBQ, J&S Cafeteria 🛏 Fairfield Inn Ⓞ Asheville 🛒, BMW
37	NC 146, Skyland, **N** 🅖 BP 🍴 Arby's, Brixx Pizza, Broken Egg Cafe, Coldstone, Hickory Tavern, McDonald's, Neo Burrito, PF Changs, Starbucks, Waffle House, Which Wich 🛏 Hilton, Quality Inn Ⓞ Barnes&Noble, CVS Drug, Ingles/gas, REI, **S** Ⓞ Chevrolet
34mm	French Broad River
33	NC 191, Brevard Rd, **N** 2 mi Ⓞ Asheville Farmers Mkt, Bear Creek RV Camp, Toyota/Scion, **S** 🅖 Citgo, HotSpot/dsl 🍴 Apollo Flame, Harbor Inn Seafood, LJ Silver, McDonald's, Papa's Mexican, Ryan's, Shogun Buffet, Stoneridge Grill, Subway, Taco Bell, Waffle House 🛏 Comfort Suites, Country Inn&Suites, Fairfield Inn, Hampton Inn, Holiday Inn Express, Rodeway Inn Ⓞ $Tree, Asheville Outlets, Belk, Dillards, Ingles Foods, Kia, K-Mart/Little Caesar's, PetCo, to Blue Ridge Pkwy
31b a	I-40, E to Statesville, W to Knoxville
27mm	I-240 E, Patton Ave
I-26 and I-240 run together 3 mi. See NC I-240 exits 1-4	
25	rd 251, **N** Ⓞ to UNCA
24	Elk Mtn Rd, Woodfin
23	Merrimon Ave, N Asheville, **N** 🅖 BP/dsl, HotSpot 🍴 Bellagio Bistro, Frank's Pizza, Magnolia Ray Rest. 🛏 Days Inn Ⓞ camping, vet
21	New Stock Rd, **N** 🅖 Citgo/dsl, Shell 🍴 Granny's Kitchen, Pizza Hut Ⓞ $General, Campfire Lodge RV Park, CVS, Ingles/gas
19a b	N US 25, W US 70, Marshall, **N** 🅖 Shell/dsl 🍴 Arby's, Bojangles, Burger King, Chapala Mexican, KFC, La Carreta Mexican, Little Caesars, McDonald's, Subway, TCBY, Waffle House, Zaxby's Ⓞ Ace Hardware, Advance Parts, AutoZone, BigLots, Ingles/dsl, Kerr Drug, Roses, URGENT CARE, **S** 🅖 Shell/DQ/dsl 🍴 Steak'n Shake Ⓞ $Tree, CVS, Lowe's, Walmart/Subway
18	Weaverville (no EZ return from eb)
17	to Flat Creek

ASHEVILLE

⬆E INTERSTATE 26 Cont'd

Exit #	Services
15	rd 197, to Jupiter, Barnardsville
13	Forks of Ivy, N 🅖 Mkt Ctr/dsl, S 🅖 Shell/dsl
11	rd 213, to Mars Hill, Marshall, N 🅞 tires, S 🅖 Exxon//Hardee's/dsl, Shell/dsl, TriCo 🅕 Osaka Japanese, Subway, Waffle House, Wagon Wheel Rest. 🅛 Comfort Inn 🅞 $General, CVS, Ingles/dsl, NAPA, Radio Shack
9	Burnsville, Spruce Pine, N 🅞 to Mt Mitchell SP
7mm	**runaway truck ramp eb**, scenic overlook wb
6mm	**Welcome Ctr/🆁🆂 eb, full 🅛 facilities**
5.5mm	**runaway truck ramp eb**
5mm	Buckner Gap, elev. 3370
3	to US 23 A, Wolf Laurel, N 🅖 Exxon/dsl 🅕 Little Creek Cafe 🅞 to ski areas
2.5mm	**eb runaway truck ramp**
0.5mm	**eb brake insp sta**
0mm	North Carolina/Tennessee state line

⬆E INTERSTATE 40

Exit #	Services
420mm	I-40 begins/ends at Wilmington N Services on US 17 🅕 Buffalo Wild Wings 🅛 Hampton Inn 🅞 CarQuest, Home Depot, Hyundai, Kia, Kohl's, Land Rover, Mazda, Nissan, Subaru, Toyota/Scion, Volvo, S Services on US 17 🅖 BP, Exxon/dsl, Hugo's, Murphy USA/dsl 🅕 Arby's, Bojangles, Bonefish Grill, Carrabba's, Chick-fil-A, ChopStix, Church's, Cracker Barrel, Dunkin Donuts, Elizabeth's Pizza, Hardee's, Hooters, IHOP, Jason's Deli, McDonald's, Olive Garden, Sonic, Subway, Waffle House 🅛 Best Western, Budgetel, Comfort Suites, Days Inn, EconoLodge, Extended Stay America, Holiday Inn, MainStay Suites, Quality Inn, Ramada Inn, Red Roof Inn, Sleep Inn, Travel Inn, Wingate Inn 🅞 Advance Parts, AutoZone, Batteries+, Black's Tires/auto, Cadillac, Costco/gas, Marshall's, Petsmart, Radio Shack, Rite Aid, Target, Walgreens, Walmart, S Services 2-4 mi on US 117/NC 132 🅖 BP/dsl, Exxon/dsl 🅕 Applebee's, Bojangles, Burger King, Carolina Ale House, Chili's, CiCi's Pizza, College Diner, Cookout, Golden Corral, Hardee's, Hieronymus Seafood, HoneyBaked Ham, Jersey Mike's, Jimmy John's, Kickback Jack's, Little Caesars, McAlister's Deli, McDonald's, Mission BBQ, Okami Japanese, Outback Steaks, Starbucks, Taco Bell, Wendy's 🅛 Baymont Inn, Comfort Inn, Country Inn Suites, Courtyard, Holiday Inn Express, Jameson Inn, Staybridge Suites 🅞 $Tree, Acura/Honda, AT&T, Best Buy, Buick/GMC, Chevrolet, Chrysler/Dodge/Jeep, Dick's, Fiat, Harris-Teeter, Jo-Ann, K-Mart, Lowe's Foods, Lowe's Whse, Mercedes, Old Navy, PetCo, Ross, Sam's Club/gas, Staples, TJ Maxx, to UNCW, URGENT CARE, Verizon, VW
420b a	Gordon Rd, NC 132 N, N 2 mi 🅖 Hess/dsl, Kangaroo/dsl 🅕 Andy's, Domino's, Hardee's, KFC, McDonald's, Waffle House, Zaxby's 🅞 CVS Drug, KOA (4mi), Rite Aid, vet, Walgreens, S 🅖 BP/dsl, Go Gas/dsl, Kangaroo/dsl 🅕 Carolina BBQ, China Wok, McDonald's, Subway 🅞 $General, Family$, Lowe's Foods, Rite Aid
416b a	I-140, US 17, to Topsail Island, New Bern, Myrtle Beach
414	Holly Shelter Rd, to Brunswick Co beaches, Castle Hayne, S 🅖 BP, GoGas/dsl, Kangaroo/dsl 🅕 Carolina Cafe, Domino's, Hardee's, Subway 🅞 $General, Bo's Foods, CVS Drug, USPO
413mm	NE Cape Fear River

Exit #	Services
408	NC 210, N 🅞 Mack/Volvo/Isuzu, S 🅖 Hess/Wendy's/dsl/cafe/scales/24hr, Phoenix TC/Exxon/Subway/dsl/scales, Shell/Noble Roman's/dsl 🅕 Hardee's, McDonald's 🅞 Advance Parts, Family$, Food Lion, to Moore's Creek Nat Bfd/camping, USPO
398	NC 53, Burgaw, S 2 mi 🅖 Carolina Petro 🅕 Hardee's, KFC, McDonald's, Subway 🅛 Burgaw Motel 🅞🅗, Advance Parts, camping, Family$, Food Lion
390	to US 117, Wallace
385	NC 41, Wallace, N 🅖 Exxon/Village Subs 🅕 Bojangles, Mad Boar Rest. 🅛 Holiday Inn Express 🅞 Lake Leamon Camping, S 1.5 mi 🅖 Hess/dsl, Murphy USA/dsl 🅕 Burger King, Domino's, McDonald's, Subway, Taco Bell, Zaxby's 🅞 $General, $Tree, Food Lion, O'Reilly Parts, Verizon, Walgreens, Walmart/Subway
384	NC 11, Wallace
380	Rose Hill, S 🅖 BP/Subway/dsl (1mi), Marathon (1mi), Pure 🅞 Duplin Winery
373	NC 24 E, NC 903, Magnolia, N 🅖 BP/dsl, Exxon/dsl/e-85 🅞 🅗, Cowan Museum
369	US 117, Warsaw
364	NC 24, to NC 50, Clinton, 🆁🆂 **both lanes, full 🅛 facilities, litter barrels, petwalk, [C], [vending], N** 🅖 Wilco/Hess/Arby's/Dunkin Donuts/Stuckey's/dsl/24hr, S 🅖 BP/dsl, Kangaroo/dsl, Marathon, Sunoco/Bojangles 🅕 KFC, McDonald's, Smithfield's BBQ, Subway, Waffle House, Wendy's 🅛 Days Inn, Quality Inn
355	NC 403, to US 117, Goldsboro, Faison, N 3 mi 🅖 Exxon
348	Suttontown Rd
343	US 701, Newton Grove, N 1 mi 🅖 Exxon/dsl, to Bentonville Bfd
341	NC 50, NC 55, to US 13, Newton Grove, N 1.5 mi 🅖 Exxon/dsl 🅕 Hardee's 🅞 Food Lion, S 🅖 BP/McDonald's, Shell/Subway/dsl 🅕 Smithfield BBQ 🅞 Family Auto/tire
334	NC 96, Meadow, S 🅖 Short Stop/dsl
328b a	I-95, N to Smithfield, S to Benson
325	NC 242, to US 301, to Benson, S 🅖 Marathon/dsl
324mm	🆁🆂 **both lanes, full 🅛 facilities, litter barrels, no overnight parking, petwalk, [C], [vending]**
319	NC 210, McGee's Crossroads, N 🅖 BP/Papa's Subs&Pizza/dsl, Shell/BBQ/dsl/24hr 🅕 McDonald's 🅞🅗, vet, S 🅖 Mobil/CW's Cafe 🅕 Bojangles, China Star, Italian Pizza/Pasta, KFC/Taco Bell, Subway, Wendy's 🅞 $General, AutoZone, Food Lion, USPO
312	NC 42, to Clayton, Fuquay-Varina, N 🅖 Murphy Express/dsl, Wilco/Hess/Dunkin Donuts/Wendy's/dsl/24hr 🅕 Andy's, Applebee's, China King, Cookout, Cracker Barrel, Fiesta Mexicana, Golden Corral, Jersey Mike's Subs, King Chinese, Marco's Pizza, Papa Subs/Pizza, Pizza Inn, Ruby Tuesday, Smithfield BBQ 🅛 Comfort Inn, Holiday Inn Express, Super 8, ValuePlace Hotel 🅞 $Tree, JustTires, Lowe's, URGENT CARE, USPO, Verizon, Walmart/McDonald's, S 🅖 BP/Subway/dsl, Exxon/Burger King, Marathon/dsl, Shell/dsl 🅕 American Hero Rest, Bojangles, Domino's, DQ, Jumbo China, KFC/Taco Bell, McDonald's, Snoopy's Hotdogs, Waffle House 🅛 Hampton Inn, Sleep Inn 🅞 CVS Drug, Food Lion, vet, Walgreens
309	US 70 E, Goldsboro, Smithfield
306b a	US 70 E bus, to Smithfield, Garner, Goldsboro, N 1 mi 🅖 Kangaroo/Subway/dsl, Shell/dsl 🅞 Chrysler/Dodge/Jeep, S 🅕 Buffalo Wild Wings, Chick-fil-A, Chili's, Coldstone, Kaze Japanese, La Cocina Mexican, Logan's Roadhouse,

⬆E INTERSTATE 40 Cont'd

Exit #	Services
306b a	Continued
	McDonald's, Moe's SW Grill, New Japan Express, Prima Vera Pizza, Subway, TGIFriday's, Wendy's 🅞 AT&T, Best Buy, BJ's Whse/gas, Dick's, GNC, Kohl's, Michael's, Petsmart, Ross, Staples, Target, TJ Maxx
303	Jones Sausage Rd, **N** 🅟 Hess/Dunkin Donuts/dsl 🍴 Bojangles, Burger King, Smithfield BBQ, **S** 🅟 Hess/Dunkin Donuts/dsl
301	I-440 E, US 64/70 E, to Wilson
300b a	Rock Quarry Rd, **N** 🅞 Kroger/gas, **S** 🅟 Exxon, Valero 🍴 Burger King, Little Caesars, Subway 🅞 Food Lion, Rite Aid
299	Person St, Hammond Rd, Raleigh (no EZ return eb), **N 1 mi** 🅟 Exxon/dsl 🅞 to Shaw U
298b a	US 401 S, US 70 E, NC 50, **N** 🅟 Shell/dsl 🏠 Red Roof Inn, **S** 🅟 BP, Exxon/dsl, Hess/dsl, Hugo's, Raceway 🍴 Baskin-Robbins/Dunkin Donuts, Bojangles, Cinco de Mayo Mexican, Cook-Out, Domino's, Golden Seafood&Chicken, Taco Bell, Wendy's 🏠 Claremont Inn, Super 8 🅞 AutoZone, CarQuest, Family$, Meineke, Sam's Club/gas
297	Lake Wheeler Rd, **N** 🅟 Exxon 🍴 Subway 🅞 Ⓗ, Farmer's Mkt, **S** 🅟 Marathon
295	Gorman St, **N 1 mi** 🅟 Exxon/dsl 🍴 Hardee's, McDonald's, Subway 🏠 Holiday Inn Express 🅞 to NCSU, **S** 🅟 Kangaroo
293	to I-440, US 1, US 64 W, Raleigh, **S** 🅟 Exxon, Shell 🍴 Astor's Grill, Bob Evans, Chick-fil-A, China King, Coldstone, Cook-Out, Dickey's BBQ, Golden Corral, HoneyBaked Ham, Jason's Deli, Jersey Mike's Subs, McDonald's, Moe's SW Grill, Noodles&Co, Olive Garden, Panera Bread, Qdoba, Red Lobster, Red Robin, Remington Grill, Ruby Tuesday, Starbucks, Subway, Taco Bell, Waffle House, Wild Wing Cafe 🏠 Best Western, DoubleTree, Hilton Garden, Holiday Inn, Red Roof Inn 🅞 Best Buy, BJ's Whse, Dick's, Ford, GNC, Home Depot, Jo-Ann Fabrics, Kohl's, Lincoln, Lowe's, Marshalls, Mazda, Michael's, NTB, Office Depot, Old Navy, PetCo, Petsmart, SteinMart, Target
291	Cary Towne Blvd, Cary, **S 1 mi** 🅟 Circle K 🍴 5 Guys Burgers, Burger King, China 1, DQ, Jersey Mike's, Macaroni Grill, McDonald's, Mimi's Cafe, On-the-Border, Pei Wei, Ragazzi's, S Asian, Starbucks, Tomyum Thai 🅞 AT&T, Barnes&Noble, Belk, Dillard's, Firestone, Harris Teeter, JC Penney, Macy's, Sears, TJ Maxx
290	NC 54, Cary, **N** 🅟 Sheetz/dsl 🍴 McDonald's 🅞 Hyatt Place, Wingate Inn, **S** 🅟 Exxon (1mi) 🏠 Hampton Inn
289	to I-440, Wade Ave, to Raleigh, **N** 🅞 Ⓗ, Carter-Finley Stadium, museum, **S** 🅞 to fairgrounds
287	Harrison Ave, Cary, **N** 🅞 to Wm B Umstead SP, **S** 🅟 BP/dsl 🍴 An Cuisine, Bonefish Grill, Burger King, BurgerFi, Carolina Cafe, Chick-fil-A, Maggie Moo's, McDonald's, Moe's SW Grill, NY Pizza, Ruth's Chris Steaks, Starbucks, Subway, Thai Cuisine, Wendy's 🏠 Embassy Suites, Studio+, TownePlace Suites, Umstead Hotel 🅞 Colony Tire
285	Aviation Pkwy, to Morrisville, **N** 🅟 Sheetz/dsl 🏠 Hilton Garden 🅞 Raleigh/Durham ✈
284	Airport Blvd, **N** 🍴 Capital City Chophouse 🏠 Cambria Suites, Country Inn&Suites, Hyatt Place 🅞 to RDU ✈, **S** 🅟 BP/dsl, Mobil 🍴 Bojangles, Cracker Barrel, Hooters, KFC/Taco Bell, TX Steaks, Waffle House, Wendy's 🏠 Courtyard, Days Inn, Extended Stay America, Fairfield Inn, Hampton Inn, Holiday Inn, Holiday Inn Express, La Quinta, Microtel, Residence Inn, Sheraton, Staybridge Suites 🅞 Morrisville Outlets/famous brands/food court

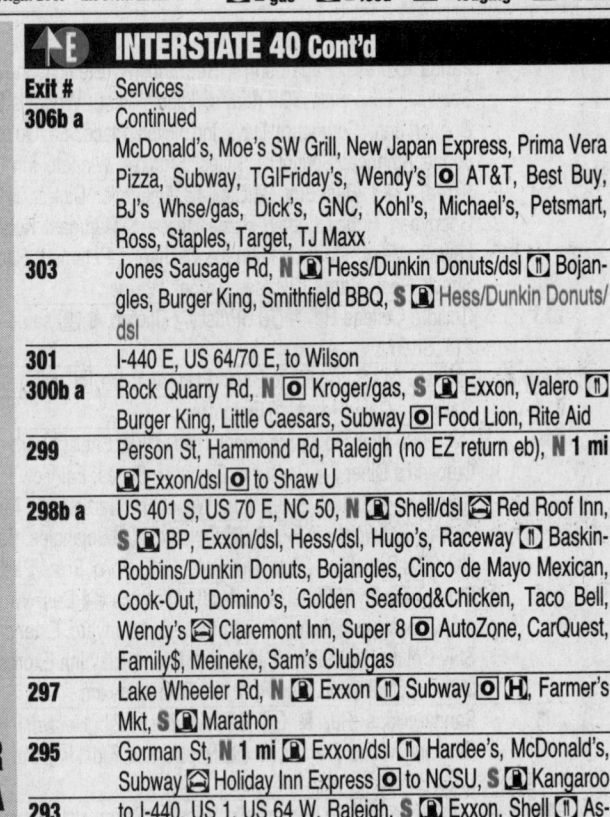

283	I-540 E, toll I-540 W, to US 70, Aviation Pkwy
282	Page Rd, **S** 🍴 Arby's, Bojangles, Jimmy John's, McDonald's, Mez Cafe, Starbucks 🏠 Comfort Suites, Hilton, Sheraton, Sleep Inn, Wingate Inn
281	Miami Blvd, **N** 🏠 Extended Stay Deluxe, Hilton Garden, Marriott, **S** 🅟 BP, Shell 🍴 Arby's, Bojangles, Burger King, McDonald's, Quiznos, Randy's Pizza, Rudino's Grill, Subway, Tropical Smoothie, Wendy's, Wok'n Grill 🏠 Extended Stay Deluxe, Holiday Inn Express, Homewood Suites, Hotel Indigo 🅞 Office Depot
280	Davis Dr, **N** 🅞 to Research Triangle, **S** 🏠 Radisson
279b a	NC 147 N, Triangle Expwy, to Durham, **N** 🅞 Ⓗ
278	NC 55, to NC 54, Apex, Foreign Trade Zone 93, **N** 🅟 Marathon 🍴 Sansui Grill, Waffle House 🏠 Comfort Inn, DoubleTree, EconoLodge, La Quinta, Red Roof Inn, **S** 🅟 BP, Exxon/dsl, Mobil/dsl 🍴 Arby's, Backyard BBQ, Bojangles, Capt D's, Chick-fil-A, El Agave Mexican, El Dorado Mexican, Golden Corral, Hardee's, Little Caesars, Papa John's, Pizza Hut, Quiznos, Sal's Italian, Starbucks, Subway, Taco Bell, Thai China, Wendy's, William's Kitchen 🏠 Candlewood Suites, Courtyard, Crossland Suites, Homestead Suites, Residence Inn 🅞 $Tree, AAA, Aamco, Advance Parts, AutoZone, BigLots, Colonial Tire, CVS Drug, Firestone, Food Lion, Jiffy Lube, Just Tires, Lube N'Tune, Meineke, O'Reilly Parts, Walgreens
276	Fayetteville Rd, **N** 🅟 Circle K/dsl, Exxon/dsl, Shell/Circle K 🍴 China Cafe, McDonald's, Orient Garden, Quiznos, Ruby Tuesday, Rudino's Pizza, Souper Salad, Waffle House, Wendy's, Wing Stop 🅞 GNC, Harris-Teeter, Kroger/dsl, to NC Central U, Walgreens, **S** 🍴 Bufflo Wild Wings, CA Pizza Kitchen, Champp's Rest, Cheesecake Factory, Chili's, Firebird's, Fork-in-the-Road Cafe, Los Portales Mexican, Maggiano's, McAlister's Deli, Melting Pot, Moe's SW Grill, PF Chang's, Rockfish Rest, Ruth's Chris Steaks, Starbucks, Ted's MT Grill 🏠 Hilton Garden 🅞 AT&T, Belk, Best Buy, JC Penney, Macy's, mall, Nordstrom, Old Navy, Sears/auto, World Mkt
274	NC 751, to Jordan Lake, **N** 🅟 BP, Marathon 🍴 Burger King, Char Grill, Dunkin Donuts, Jimmy John's, KFC, McDonald's, Taco Bell, Waffle House, Wendy's 🅞 Advance Parts, CVS Drug, Harris Teeter, Honda, Lexus, Rite Aid, URGENT CARE, Walgreens, **S** 🅟 BP 🍴 Bonefish Grill, Chick-fil-A, Subway 🏠 Sheraton 🅞 Aldi Foods, Michael's, PetCo, Target
273	NC 54, to Durham, UNC-Chapel Hill, **N** 🅟 BP/dsl, **S** 🅟 BP, Shell/dsl 🍴 Hardee's, Nantucket Grill 🏠 Courtyard (2mi), Hampton Inn, Holiday Inn Express 🅞 URGENT CARE, vet
270	US 15, US 501, Chapel Hill, Durham, **N** 🍴 Applebee's, Bob Evans, Carrabba's, Dickey's BBQ, Firehouse Subs, Jason's Deli, Lonestar Steaks, Longhorn Steaks, McAlister's, Moe's SW Grill, NY Pizza, Outback Steaks, Panera Bread,

Vertical left margin labels: **RALEIGH**, **CARY**

Vertical right margin labels: **CHAPEL HILL**, **NC**

INTERSTATE 40 Cont'd

Exit #	Services
270	Continued
	Philly Steaks, Red Robin, Starbucks, Xank's Japanese 🛏 Comfort Inn, Homewood Suites, SpringHill Suites, Staybridge Suites 🅾 $Tree, AT&T, Barnes&Noble, Best Buy, Dick's, Home Depot, 🆁🆂, Kohl's, Kroger, Marshalls, Michael's, Old Navy, Petsmart, to Duke U, Verizon, Walmart/Subway, S 🚗 BP, Exxon 🍴 Boston Mkt, Chick-fil-A, Hardee's, K&W Cafeteria, La Hacienda Mexican, McDonald's, Subway, Wendy's 🛏 Days Inn, Quality Inn, Red Roof Inn, Sheraton 🅾 Acura, Advance Parts, BMW, Chevrolet, Dillard's, Food Lion, Harris Teeter, Kia, Lowe's, Subaru, Trader Joe's
266	NC 86, to Chapel Hill, S 2 mi 🚗 BP, Exxon, Hess/dsl 🍴 Pop's Pizza, Subway
263	New Hope Church Rd
261	Hillsborough, N 1.5 mi 🚗 BP, Citgo/dsl, Shell 🍴 Hardee's, KFC/Taco Bell, McDonald's, Subway, Waffle House, Wendy's 🛏 Holiday Inn Express, Microtel
259	I-85 N, to Durham
I-40 and I-85 run together 30 mi. See I-85, exits 131-161.	
227	to I-85 S, to I-73 N, to US 421, Highpoint, Charlotte
226	McConnell Rd, S 🚗 Exxon
224	E Lee St, to US 29 N, to US 220 N, N 🚗 BP/dsl, Shell/dsl 🛏 Holiday Inn Express, Quality Inn
223	to N US 29, E US 70, N US 20, Reidsville
222	MLK Jr (from eb), Sanford, S 🚗 Arby's, Biscuitville, Burger King, McDonald's, Subway, Taco Bell 🅾 Advance Parts, CVS Drug, Food Lion, Hall Tire Co, Tom's Tire/auto
221	S Elm-Eugene St, N 🚗 Citgo/dsl, Crown/dsl, Shell 🛏 Homestead Lodge 🅾 AutoZone, CarQuest, Family$, Food Lion, O'Reilly Parts, S 🚗 BP, Shell/dsl 🛏 EconoLodge, Super 8 🅾 Home Depot
220	Randleman Rd, US 220 S, to Greensboro, Ashboro, N 🚗 BP, Solo 🍴 Biscuitville, Church's, KFC, McDonald's, Pizza Hut, Sub Sta 2 🛏 Budget Inn 🅾 Harley-Davidson, Rite Aid, Save-A-Lot, S 🚗 BP, Kangaroo 🍴 Cook-Out, Mayflower Seafood, Waffle House, Wendy's
219	US 29 S, W US 70, Highpoint (exits left from wb), Charlotte
218	US 220, Freeman Mill Rd, Ashboro
217	Highpoint Rd, Koury Blvd (from wb), N 🚗 Exxon, Shell/dsl 🍴 Biscuitville, Burger King, Chili's, China King, Fatz Cafe, Ham's Rest, Hooters, Little Caesars, Lonestar Steaks, Olive Garden, Sakura Japanese, Subway, Taco Bell 🛏 DoubleTree Hotel, Hampton Inn, Park Lane Hotel, Quality Inn, Red Roof Inn, Super 8 🅾 $General, Office Depot, S 🚗 Shell 🍴 Bonefish Grill, Carrabba's, Jimmy John's, Krispy Kreme, McDonald's, Smokey Bones BBQ, Waffle House, Wendy's 🛏 Baymont Inn, Comfort Suites, Drury Inn, Ramada Inn, Sheraton, Studio 6 🅾 Dillard's, Discount Tire, Gander Mtn, JC Penney, O'Reilly Parts
216	(from eb), Greensboro, 🅾 coliseum
214	Wendover Ave, N 🚗 Sheetz 🍴 Burger King, China Buffet, Coldstone, Mario's Pizza, Moe's SW Grill, Panera Bread, Penn Sta Subs, Waffle House 🛏 Extended Stay, Fairfield Inn, Hilton Garden, Holiday Inn Express, Microtel 🅾 Audi, Costco/gas, CVS Drug, Fiat, Ford, Nissan, PetCo, Staples, Verizon, VW, S 🍴 Applebee's, Arby's, Biscuitville, Bojangles, Chick-fil-A, Chipotle Mexican, Cracker Barrel, Elizabeth's Pizza, Fuddrucker's, Golden Corral, Golden Wok, IHOP, Jimmy John's, Kabuto Japanese, La Hacienda Mexican, Logan's Roadhouse, Longhorn Steaks, McDonald's, O'Charley's,

Exit #	Services
214	Continued
	Panda Express, Papa John's, Red Lobster, Steak'n Shake, Subway, Taco Bell, TGIFriday's, Tripp's Rest., Wendy's 🛏 Comfort Inn, Courtyard, Days Inn, Hyatt Place, La Quinta, Lodge America, SpringHill Suites, Studio+, Wingate Inn 🅾 $Tree, AT&T, Best Buy, Buick/GMC, Chevrolet, Dick's, GNC, Goodyear, Hobby Lobby, Home Depot, K-Mart/gas, Kohl's, Lowe's, Macy's, Mazda, Meineke, Michael's, Petsmart, Radio Shack, Ross, Sam's Club/gas, Target, Walmart
213	Guilford College Rd, N 🚗 BP/dsl 🛏 Clarion, S 🚗 same as 214, Sheetz
212b a	I-73, US 241 S, to I-85, to Bryan Blvd, Ashboro, 🅾 to ✈
211	Gallimore Dairy Rd, N 🅾 Freightliner
210	NC 68, to High Point, Piedmont Triad, N 🚗 Shell 🍴 Arby's, Carolina's Diner 🛏 Days Inn, Embassy Suites, Fairview Inn, Homewood Suites, Sleep Inn, Wyndham Garden 🅾 Ford Trucks, Kenworth, to ✈, S 🚗 Exxon/dsl 🍴 Bojangles, Fatz Cafe, McDonald's, Pizza Hut/Taco Bell, Pollo Pizza/Pasta, Ruby Tuesday, Shoney's, Subway, Wendy's 🛏 Best Western, Candlewood Suites, Comfort Suites, Courtyard, Extended Stay Deluxe, Fairfield Inn, Hampton Inn, Holiday Inn Express, Motel 6, Quality Inn, Red Roof Inn, Residence Inn
208	Sandy Ridge Rd, N 🚗 Exxon/Subway/dsl, Hess/dsl 🅾 Camping World RV Ctr, S 🚗 Shell/Circle K/dsl 🅾 Out Of Doors Mart
206	Lp 40 (from wb), to Kernersville, Winston-Salem, downtown
203	NC 66, to Kernersville, N 🚗 Citgo/McDonald's/dsl, Hess/dsl, QM/Subway/dsl 🍴 Capt Tom's Seafood, Clark's BBQ, Wendy's 🛏 Sleep Inn 🅾 🆁🆂, Curves, Ford, Merchant Tire/repair, S 🚗 Shell/dsl 🛏 Holiday Inn Express
201	Union Cross Rd, N 🚗 Citgo/dsl, QM/dsl 🍴 Blue Naples Pizza, Burger King, China Café, Subway 🅾 $Mart, CVS Drug, Food Lion
196	US 311 S, to High Point
195	US 311 N, NC 109, to Thomasville, S 🚗 Citgo, Hess/dsl 🅾 Family$
193c	Silas Creek Pkwy (from eb), same as 192
193b a	US 52, NC 8, to Lexington, S 🚗 Hess/dsl, Shell 🍴 Hardee's
192	NC 150, to Peters Creek Pkwy, N 🚗 Giant, Hess, Shell 🍴 Bojangles, Burger King, China Wok, Hero House Rest, Hong Kong Buffet, IHOP, KFC, Little Caesars, Monterrey Mexican, Mr BBQ, Sonic, Subway, Taco Bell, Tokyo Japanese, Tomo'E Steaks 🛏 Innkeeper 🅾 $General, $Tree, Acura/Subaru, Audi, AutoZone, BigLots, Ford, Hamrick's, Hyundai, Infiniti, Mazda, Office Depot, Radio Shack, Rite Aid, VW, S 🚗 BP, QM 🍴 Arby's, Baskin-Robbins/Dunkin Donuts, Cook-Out, K&W Cafeteria, McDonald's, Papa John's, Pizza Hut, Waffle House, Wendy's 🛏 Holiday Inn Express 🅾 Advance Parts, Aldi Foods, BMW/Mini, CVS Drug, Family$, Food Lion, Hancock Fabrics, Honda, K-Mart, Mock Tire, Toyota/Scion
190	Hanes Mall Blvd (from wb, no re-entry), N 🍴 Chipotle Mexican, Coldstone, Elizabeth's Pizza, Jimmy John's, McDonald's, Ruby Tuesday, TGIFriday's, Tripp's Rest. 🛏 Quality Inn 🅾 🆁🆂, Belk, Dick's, Dillard's, Firestone/auto, JC Penney, Macy's, mall, Marshalls, same as 189, Sears/auto, S 🍴 Burger King, ChuckECheese, Outback Steaks, Starbucks, Subway 🛏 Comfort Suites, Microtel 🅾 Office Depot
189	US 158, Stratford Rd, Hanes Mall Blvd, N 🍴 Bojangles, Chili's, Golden Corral, Olive Garden, Red Lobster, Taco Bell, TX Roadhouse 🛏 Courtyard, Fairfield Inn 🅾 🆁🆂, Belk, Buick/GMC, Cadillac, Chevrolet, Dillard's, JC Penney, Jo-Ann Fabrics, Macy's, mall, Sears/auto, Walgreens, S 🚗 BP, Shell

GREENSBORO

WINSTON•SALEM

NC

➤E INTERSTATE 40 Cont'd

Exit #	Services
189	Continued
	🍴 5 Guys Burgers, Applebee's, Bleu Rest., Brixx Pizza, Buffalo Wild Wings, Chick-fil-A, Firebirds Grill, Fuddruckers, Hooters, Jason's Deli, KFC/LJ Silver, Lonestar Steaks, Longhorn Steaks, Macaroni Grill, Moe's SW Grill, Nuke's Cafe, Panera Bread, Qdoba, Subway, Village Tavern, Which Wich 🏠 Extended Stay America, Hampton Inn, Hilton Garden, La Quinta, Sleep Inn, SpringHill Suites ⊡ $Tree, AT&T, Barnes&Noble, Best Buy, Costco/gas, CVS Drug, Discount Tire, Food Lion, Home Depot, Kohl's, Lowe's, Michael's, Petsmart, Ross, Sam's Club/gas, Target, Verizon
188	US 421, to Yadkinville, to WFU (no EZ wb return), Winston-Salem, N 1/2 mi off US 421 📱 BP, Exxon, Kangaroo, Shell 🍴 Arby's, Burger King, Cook-Out, Dickey's BBQ, McDonald's, Starbucks, Subway, Waffle House, Wendy's ⊡ CarMax, Mercedes, vet, Walmart
184	to US 421, Clemmons, N 📱 Mobil, Shell 🍴 Applebee's, Dunkin Donuts, IHOP, K&W Cafe, KFC, Panera Bread, Steak Escape 🏠 Holiday Inn Express, S 📱 BP/dsl, Hess, Kangaroo 🍴 Arby's, Biscuitville, Brick Oven Pizza, Burger King, Cozumel Mexican, Cracker Barrel, Domino's, Kimono Japanese, Little Richard's BBQ, McDonald's, Mi Pueblo Mexican, Mtn Fried Chicken, Pizza Hut, Sonic, Starbucks, Subway, Taco Bell, Time to Eat Cafe, Waffle House, Wendy's 🏠 Super 8 ⊡ $Tree, Advance Parts, BigLots, CVS Drug, GNC, K-Mart, Lowe's Foods, Meineke, Merchant Tire, O'Reilly Parts, Staples, USPO, Verizon, vet, Walgreens
182mm	Yadkin River
182	Bermuda Run, Tanglewood, S 🍴 Chang Thai, Lee's Chinese, Monte De Rey Mexican, Papa John's, Subway ⊡ Harris-Teeter, Tanglewood Camping
180	NC 801, Tanglewood, N 🍴 Capt's Galley Seafood, Chilo's Mexican, Domino's, Subway 🏠 Hampton Inn ⊡ Lowe's Foods/dsl, Rite Aid, S 📱 BP/McDonald's/dsl, Hess/dsl 🍴 Bojangles, Jimmy's Greek, Miyabi Japanese, Venezia Italian, Wendy's ⊡ $General, Ace Hardware, CVS Drug, Food Lion, Radio Shack, Walgreens
177mm	🅡 both lanes, full 🚻 facilities, litter barrels, petwalk, 🅲, 🖨 vending
174	Farmington Rd, N 📱 Shell/dsl ⊡ antiques, S ⊡ vineyards
170	US 601, Mocksville, N 📱 Citgo/dsl, Horn's TC/Marathon/DQ/Jersey Mike's/dsl/scales/24hr, Murphy USA/dsl 🍴 JinJin Chinese, La Carreta Mexican, Moe's Cafe, Subway ⊡ $Tree, Campers Inn RV Ctr, Verizon, Walmart, S 📱 Exxon, Hess, Taco Bell, Sheetz/dsl 🍴 Arby's, Blackbeard's Seafood Shack, Bojangles, Burger King, China Grill, Dunkin Donuts, Dynasty Chinese, KFC, Marco's Pizza, McDonald's, Papa John's, Pier 601, Pizza Hut, Sagebrush Steaks, Shiki Japanese, Wendy's 🏠 Days Inn, HighWay Inn, Quality Inn, Scottish Inn ⊡ 🏥 $General, Advance Parts, Lowe's, Mocksville Tire/auto, USPO, vet, Walgreens
168	US 64, to Mocksville, N 📱 Exxon/dsl ⊡ Lake Myers RV Resort (3mi), S 📱 BP/dsl ⊡ 🏥
162	US 64, Cool Springs, N ⊡ Lake Myers RV Resort (5mi), S 📱 Shell/dsl ⊡ KOA
161mm	S Yadkin River
154	to US 64, Old Mocksville Rd, N ⊡ 🏥, S 📱 Citgo/dsl 🍴 Jaybee's Hotdogs ⊡ repair/tires

153	US 64 (from eb), S 1/2 mi 📱 Citgo/dsl 🍴 Jaybee's Hotdogs ⊡ repair/tires
152b a	I-77, S to Charlotte, N to Elkin
151	US 21, E Statesville, N 📱 Hess/dsl, Marathon/DQ/dsl 🍴 Applebee's, Baskin-Robbins/Dunkin Donuts, Bojangles, Chick-fil-A, Chili's, Cook-Out, Cracker Barrel, Golden Corral, K&W Cafeteria, KFC, Logan's Roadhouse, McDonald's, Mi Pueblo Café, Pizza Hut/Taco Bell, Red Lobster, Ruby Tuesday, Shiki Japanese, Wendy's, Zaxby's 🏠 Days Inn, Sleep Inn ⊡ $Tree, Advance Parts, Aldi Foods, AutoZone, BigLots, Chevrolet, CVS Drug, GNC, Home Depot, Lowe's, Meineke, Michael's, Petsmart, Radio Shack, Staples, Tire Kingdom, TJ Maxx, URGENT CARE, Verizon, Walmart, S 📱 Exxon 🍴 Greg's BBQ, Lonestar Steaks, Sonic, Waffle House 🏠 Holiday Inn Express, Masters Inn, Quality Inn ⊡ 🏥 $General, URGENT CARE
150	NC 115, Statesville, N 📱 BP/dsl, Citgo, Sheetz/dsl, Shell/Subway 🍴 Amalfi's Italian, Little Caesars, Ol'Bob's BBQ, Waffle Shop ⊡ $General, CVS Drug, Food Lion, Fred's, museum
148	US 64, NC 90, W Statesville, N 📱 Citgo/dsl, Shell 🍴 Arby's, BoxCar Grille, Burger King, McDonald's, Shiki Japanese, Subway, Village Inn Pizza 🏠 Economy Inn ⊡ $General, CVS Drug, Ingles Foods
146	Stamey Farm Rd, N ⊡ truck repair
144	Old Mountain Rd, N 📱 BP/dsl/repair 🍴 Troy's Rest., S 📱 BP/dsl, Shell/dsl
143mm	weigh sta both lanes
141	Sharon School Rd, N 📱 Citgo/dsl
140mm	Catawba River
138	NC 10 W, Oxford School Rd, to Catawba, N 📱 Exxon/dsl
136mm	🅡 both lanes, full 🚻 facilities, litter barrels, petwalk, 🅲, 🖨 vending
135	Claremont, S 📱 Shell 🍴 BoxCar Grille, Burger King, Hannah's BBQ, Hardee's, New Panda, Subway 🏠 Super 8 ⊡ $General, Carolina Coach RV Ctr, Lowe's Foods
133	Rock Barn Rd, N 📱 Shell/dsl, S 📱 Wilco/Hess/Godfather's/Stuckey's/Subway/dsl/scales/24hr
132	to NC 16, Taylorsville, N 📱 BP, Shell/dsl 🍴 Burger King, JinJin's Buffet, Subway, Zaxby's 🏠 Holiday Inn Express ⊡ $Tree, Verizon, Walmart
130	Old US 70, N 🍴 Jack-in-the-Box, Subway ⊡ $General, K-Mart, repair, Verizon, vet, S 📱 Citgo, Pure ⊡ USPO
128	US 321, Fairgrove Church Rd, Hickory, N 📱 BP, Marathon/dsl, Shell 🍴 McDonald's, Waffle House ⊡ 🏥, to Catawba Valley Coll, S 📱 Citgo/dsl 🍴 Wendy's, Yukio Japanese 🏠 Days Inn, La Quinta ⊡ Chrysler/Dodge/Jeep, GMC/Volvo Trucks

Map sidebar: **74**, Pilot Mountain, Elkin, Winston-Salem, Durham, **40**, Greensboro, Hickory, Lexington, Raleigh, Statesville, **85**, **40**, Huntersville, Concord, Gastonia, Charlotte, Monroe, **77**, **NC**

(side markers) STATESVILLE, MOCKSVILLE, NC

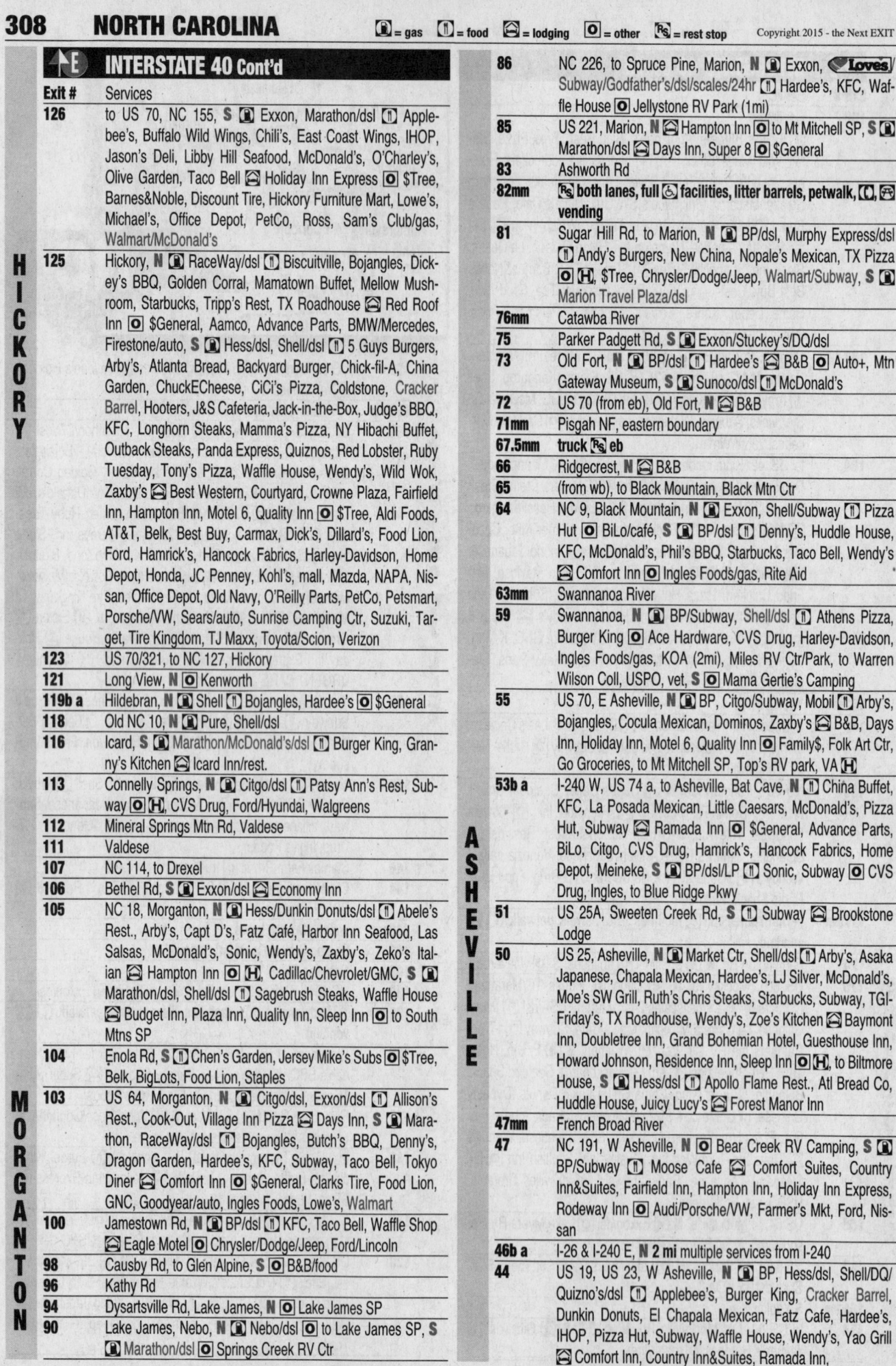

◀Ⓔ	**INTERSTATE 40 Cont'd**

HICKORY

Exit #	Services
126	to US 70, NC 155, S 🅖 Exxon, Marathon/dsl 🍴 Applebee's, Buffalo Wild Wings, Chili's, East Coast Wings, IHOP, Jason's Deli, Libby Hill Seafood, McDonald's, O'Charley's, Olive Garden, Taco Bell 🛏 Holiday Inn Express 🅾 $Tree, Barnes&Noble, Discount Tire, Hickory Furniture Mart, Lowe's, Michael's, Office Depot, PetCo, Ross, Sam's Club/gas, Walmart/McDonald's
125	Hickory, N 🅖 RaceWay/dsl 🍴 Biscuitville, Bojangles, Dickey's BBQ, Golden Corral, Mamatown Buffet, Mellow Mushroom, Starbucks, Tripp's Rest, TX Roadhouse 🛏 Red Roof Inn 🅾 $General, Aamco, Advance Parts, BMW/Mercedes, Firestone/auto, S 🅖 Hess/dsl, Shell/dsl 🍴 5 Guys Burgers, Arby's, Atlanta Bread, Backyard Burger, Chick-fil-A, China Garden, ChuckECheese, CiCi's Pizza, Coldstone, Cracker Barrel, Hooters, J&S Cafeteria, Jack-in-the-Box, Judge's BBQ, KFC, Longhorn Steaks, Mamma's Pizza, NY Hibachi Buffet, Outback Steaks, Panda Express, Quiznos, Red Lobster, Ruby Tuesday, Tony's Pizza, Waffle House, Wendy's, Wild Wok, Zaxby's 🛏 Best Western, Courtyard, Crowne Plaza, Fairfield Inn, Hampton Inn, Motel 6, Quality Inn 🅾 $Tree, Aldi Foods, AT&T, Belk, Best Buy, Carmax, Dick's, Dillard's, Food Lion, Ford, Hamrick's, Hancock Fabrics, Harley-Davidson, Home Depot, Honda, JC Penney, Kohl's, mall, Mazda, NAPA, Nissan, Office Depot, Old Navy, O'Reilly Parts, PetCo, Petsmart, Porsche/VW, Sears/auto, Sunrise Camping Ctr, Suzuki, Target, Tire Kingdom, TJ Maxx, Toyota/Scion, Verizon
123	US 70/321, to NC 127, Hickory
121	Long View, N 🅾 Kenworth
119b a	Hildebran, N 🅖 Shell 🍴 Bojangles, Hardee's 🅾 $General
118	Old NC 10, N 🅖 Pure, Shell/dsl
116	Icard, S 🅖 Marathon/McDonald's/dsl 🍴 Burger King, Granny's Kitchen 🛏 Icard Inn/rest.
113	Connelly Springs, N 🅖 Citgo/dsl 🍴 Patsy Ann's Rest., Subway 🅾 Ⓗ, CVS Drug, Ford/Hyundai, Walgreens
112	Mineral Springs Mtn Rd, Valdese
111	Valdese
107	NC 114, to Drexel
106	Bethel Rd, S 🅖 Exxon/dsl 🛏 Economy Inn
105	NC 18, Morganton, N 🅖 Hess/Dunkin Donuts/dsl 🍴 Abele's Rest., Arby's, Capt D's, Fatz Café, Harbor Inn Seafood, Las Salsas, McDonald's, Sonic, Wendy's, Zaxby's, Zeko's Italian 🛏 Hampton Inn 🅾 Ⓗ, Cadillac/Chevrolet/GMC, S 🅖 Marathon/dsl, Shell/dsl 🍴 Sagebrush Steaks, Waffle House 🛏 Budget Inn, Plaza Inn, Quality Inn, Sleep Inn 🅾 to South Mtns SP
104	Enola Rd, S 🍴 Chen's Garden, Jersey Mike's Subs 🅾 $Tree, Belk, BigLots, Food Lion, Staples

MORGANTON

103	US 64, Morganton, N 🅖 Citgo/dsl, Exxon/dsl 🍴 Allison's Rest., Cook-Out, Village Inn Pizza 🛏 Days Inn, S 🅖 Marathon, RaceWay/dsl 🍴 Bojangles, Butch's BBQ, Denny's, Dragon Garden, Hardee's, KFC, Subway, Taco Bell, Tokyo Diner 🛏 Comfort Inn 🅾 $General, Clarks Tire, Food Lion, GNC, Goodyear/auto, Ingles Foods, Lowe's, Walmart
100	Jamestown Rd, N 🅖 BP/dsl 🍴 KFC, Taco Bell, Waffle Shop 🛏 Eagle Motel 🅾 Chrysler/Dodge/Jeep, Ford/Lincoln
98	Causby Rd, to Glen Alpine, S 🅾 B&B/food
96	Kathy Rd
94	Dysartsville Rd, Lake James, N 🅾 Lake James SP
90	Lake James, Nebo, N 🅖 Nebo/dsl 🅾 to Lake James SP, S 🅖 Marathon/dsl 🅾 Springs Creek RV Ctr

86	NC 226, to Spruce Pine, Marion, N 🅖 Exxon, 🔵Loves/Subway/Godfather's/dsl/scales/24hr 🍴 Hardee's, KFC, Waffle House 🅾 Jellystone RV Park (1mi)
85	US 221, Marion, N 🛏 Hampton Inn 🅾 to Mt Mitchell SP, S 🅖 Marathon/dsl 🛏 Days Inn, Super 8 🅾 $General
83	Ashworth Rd
82mm	🆁🆂 both lanes, full 🚻 facilities, litter barrels, petwalk, Ⓒ, 🅿 vending
81	Sugar Hill Rd, to Marion, N 🅖 BP/dsl, Murphy Express/dsl 🍴 Andy's Burgers, New China, Nopale's Mexican, TX Pizza 🅾 Ⓗ, $Tree, Chrysler/Dodge/Jeep, Walmart/Subway, S 🅖 Marion Travel Plaza/dsl
76mm	Catawba River
75	Parker Padgett Rd, S 🅖 Exxon/Stuckey's/DQ/dsl
73	Old Fort, N 🅖 BP/dsl 🍴 Hardee's 🛏 B&B 🅾 Auto+, Mtn Gateway Museum, S 🅖 Sunoco/dsl 🍴 McDonald's
72	US 70 (from eb), Old Fort, N 🛏 B&B
71mm	Pisgah NF, eastern boundary
67.5mm	truck 🆁🆂 eb
66	Ridgecrest, N 🛏 B&B
65	(from wb), to Black Mountain, Black Mtn Ctr
64	NC 9, Black Mountain, N 🅖 Exxon, Shell/Subway 🍴 Pizza Hut 🅾 BiLo/café, S 🅖 BP/dsl 🍴 Denny's, Huddle House, KFC, McDonald's, Phil's BBQ, Starbucks, Taco Bell, Wendy's 🛏 Comfort Inn 🅾 Ingles Foods/gas, Rite Aid
63mm	Swannanoa River
59	Swannanoa, N 🅖 BP/Subway, Shell/dsl 🍴 Athens Pizza, Burger King 🅾 Ace Hardware, CVS Drug, Harley-Davidson, Ingles Foods/gas, KOA (2mi), Miles RV Ctr/Park, to Warren Wilson Coll, USPO, vet, S 🅾 Mama Gertie's Camping
55	US 70, E Asheville, N 🅖 BP, Citgo/Subway, Mobil 🍴 Arby's, Bojangles, Cocula Mexican, Dominos, Zaxby's 🛏 B&B, Days Inn, Holiday Inn, Motel 6, Quality Inn 🅾 Family$, Folk Art Ctr, Go Groceries, to Mt Mitchell SP, Top's RV park, VA Ⓗ
53b a	I-240 W, US 74 a, to Asheville, Bat Cave, N 🍴 China Buffet, KFC, La Posada Mexican, Little Caesars, McDonald's, Pizza Hut, Subway 🛏 Ramada Inn 🅾 $General, Advance Parts, BiLo, Citgo, CVS Drug, Hamrick's, Hancock Fabrics, Home Depot, Meineke, S 🅖 BP/dsl/LP 🍴 Sonic, Subway 🅾 CVS Drug, Ingles, to Blue Ridge Pkwy
51	US 25A, Sweeten Creek Rd, S 🍴 Subway 🛏 Brookstone Lodge
50	US 25, Asheville, N 🅖 Market Ctr, Shell/dsl 🍴 Arby's, Asaka Japanese, Chapala Mexican, Hardee's, LJ Silver, McDonald's, Moe's SW Grill, Ruth's Chris Steaks, Starbucks, Subway, TGI-Friday's, TX Roadhouse, Wendy's, Zoe's Kitchen 🛏 Baymont Inn, Doubletree Inn, Grand Bohemian Hotel, Guesthouse Inn, Howard Johnson, Residence Inn, Sleep Inn 🅾 Ⓗ, to Biltmore House, S 🅖 Hess/dsl 🍴 Apollo Flame Rest., Atl Bread Co, Huddle House, Juicy Lucy's 🛏 Forest Manor Inn
47mm	French Broad River
47	NC 191, W Asheville, N 🅾 Bear Creek RV Camping, S 🅖 BP/Subway 🍴 Moose Cafe 🛏 Comfort Suites, Country Inn&Suites, Fairfield Inn, Hampton Inn, Holiday Inn Express, Rodeway Inn 🅾 Audi/Porsche/VW, Farmer's Mkt, Ford, Nissan
46b a	I-26 & I-240 E, N 2 mi multiple services from I-240
44	US 19, US 23, W Asheville, N 🅖 BP, Hess/dsl, Shell/DQ/Quizno's/dsl 🍴 Applebee's, Burger King, Cracker Barrel, Dunkin Donuts, El Chapala Mexican, Fatz Cafe, Hardee's, IHOP, Pizza Hut, Subway, Waffle House, Wendy's, Yao Grill 🛏 Comfort Inn, Country Inn&Suites, Ramada Inn,

ASHEVILLE

NC

INTERSTATE 40 Cont'd

Exit #	Services
44	Continued
	Red Roof Inn, Rodeway Inn, Sleep Inn, Whispering Pines Motel 🅞 Chevrolet, Chrysler/Dodge/Jeep, Family$, Ingles Foods, Lowe's, Mazda/Mercedes, **S** 🍴 McDonald's, Zaxby's 🏨 Budget Motel, Holiday Inn, ValuePlace Inn 🅞 Bi-Lo Foods, CVS Drug, Home Depot
41mm	weigh sta both lanes
37	Candler, **N** 🅖 BP, TA/Buckhorn Rest./dsl/scales/24hr/@ 🅞 Goodyear/truck tires, **S** 🅖 Exxon/dsl 🏨 Days Inn, Plantation Motel 🅞 $General, KOA
33	Newfound Rd, to US 74, **S** 🅖 Exxon
31	Rd 215, Canton, **N** 🍴 Sagebrush Steaks 🏨 Best Value Inn 🅞 URGENT CARE, **S** 🅖 BP/dsl, Marathon/DQ, Shell/dsl 🍴 Arby's, Bojangles, Burger King, McDonald's, Starbucks, Subway, Taco Bell, Waffle House 🏨 Comfort Inn 🅞 Ford, Ingles Foods/dsl, RV/truck repair
27	US 19/23, to Waynesville, Great Smokey Mtn Expswy, **S 3 mi** 🍴 Burger King, Coffee Cup Cafe, Subway 🏨 Super 8 🅞 🅷 $Tree, Food Lion, GNC, Lowe's, to WCU (25mi)
24	NC 209, to Lake Junaluska, **N** 🚛/Subway/dsl/scales/24hr/@ 🏨 Midway Motel, **S** 🅖 Shell/cafe/dsl/24hr 🅞 🅷
20	US 276, to Maggie Valley, Lake Junaluska, **S** 🅖 BP/dsl, Exxon/dsl, Marathon (2mi) 🅞 Creekwood RV Park, Pride RV Resort, Winngray RV Park
16mm	Pigeon River
15	Fines Creek
13mm	Pisgah NF eastern boundary
10mm	🆁🆂 both lanes, full ♿ facilities, litter barrels, petwalk, 🅲, 🖼 vending
7	Harmon Den
4mm	tunnel both lanes
0mm	North Carolina/Tennessee state line

INTERSTATE 77

Exit #	Services
105mm	North Carolina/Virginia state line
105mm	**Welcome Ctr sb, full** ♿ facilities, info, litter barrels, petwalk, 🅲, 🖼, vending
103mm	weigh sta both lanes
101	I-74 E, to Mt Airy, Winston-Salem, Greensboro, **E** 🏨 Hampton Inn 🅞 🅷 (12mi)
100	NC 89, to Mt Airy, **E** 🅖 *FLYING J*/Brintle's Rest./dsl/scales/24hr/@, Marathon/Subway/dsl, Shell/Circle K/dsl 🍴 Copper Pot Rest. 🏨 Best Western 🅞 dsl repair, 🅷 (12mi)
93	to Dobson, Surry, **E** 🅖 BP/DQ/dsl, Marathon/dsl 🍴 BelloVino Italian 🏨 Hampton Inn, Surry Inn 🅞 camping
85	NC 118, CC Camp Rd, to Elkin, **W 1-3 mi** 🅖 Murphy Express/dsl, Neighbor's, Shell/Blimpie/Stuckey's/dsl, Wilco/Hess/dsl 🍴 Burger King, KFC, Mazzini's Italian, McDonald's, Sonic 🏨 Elk Inn, Fairfield Inn 🅞 $Tree, AT&T, BigLots, Food Lion, Lowe's, Rite Aid, Walmart/Subway
83	US 21 byp, to Sparta (from nb)
82.5mm	Yadkin River
82	NC 67, Elkin, **E** 🅖 BP/Subway/dsl, Citgo/Case Outlet/dsl, Exxon/dsl 🍴 Arby's, Cracker Barrel, Pop-Pops Grill 🏨 Best Western 🅞 Holly Ridge Camping (8mi), **W** 🅖 Wilco/Hess/Dunkin Donuts/dsl 🍴 Bojangles, Capt Galley, McDonald's, Valentino's Pizza, Waffle House, Wendy's 🏨 Comfort Inn, Days Inn, Hampton Inn, Rose's Motel 🅞 D-Rex Drug, Food Lion, vet

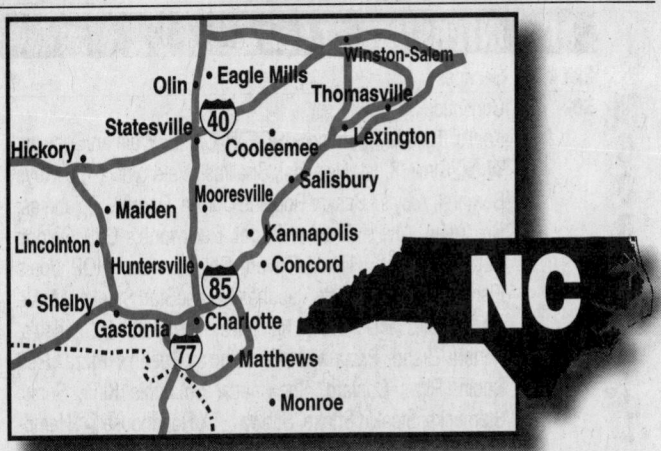

79	US 21 S, to Arlington, **E** 🅖 Citgo/Subway/dsl 🏨 Super 8, **W** 🅖 BP/dsl 🍴 Glenn's BBQ 🏨 Best Value Inn
73b a	US 421, to Winston-Salem (20mi), **E** 🅖 (1mi), Shell/Subway/dsl, USPO
72mm	🆁🆂 nb, full ♿ facilities, litter barrels, petwalk, 🅲, 🖼, vending
65	NC 901, to Union Grove, Harmony, **E** 🅞 Van Hoy Farms Camping, **W** 🅖 BP/dsl, Shell/Subway/dsl/24hr 🍴 Burger Barn 🏨 B&B 🅞 Ace Hardware, auto/tire repair, Fiddler's Grove Camping (2mi)
63mm	🆁🆂 sb, full ♿ facilities, litter barrels, petwalk, 🅲, 🖼, vending
59	Tomlin Mill Rd, **W** 🅖 Valero/dsl
56.5mm	S Yadkin River
54	US 21, to Turnersburg, **E** 🅖 Citgo, **W** 🅖 Shell/dsl 🍴 Arby's, Baskin-Robbins/Dunkin Donuts, Chick-fil-A, CookOut, Golden Corral, Zaxby's
51b a	I-40, E to Winston-Salem, W to Hickory
50	E Broad St, Statesville, **E** 🅖 Citgo, Kangaroo/dsl, Shell 🍴 Arby's, Bojangles, Burger King, Charanda Mexican, Domino's, Golden Dragon, IHOP, Jack-in-the-Box, Little Caesar's, McDonald's, Papa John's, Pizza Hut, Shanghai Buffet, Shoney's, Starbucks, Subway, Taco Bell, Wendy's 🏨 Brookwood Inn, Red Roof Inn 🅞 $General, $Tree, Ace Hardware, AT&T, Belk, Bi-Lo, Food Lion, JC Penney, JR Outlet, K-Mart, Rite Aid, URGENT CARE, USPO
49b a	US 70, G Bagnal Blvd, to Statesville, **E** 🅖 BP, Citgo/dsl, Kangaroo, Shell, Solo 🍴 KFC, Outback Steaks, Rice Fun Chinese, Subway, Waffle House 🏨 Best Value Inn, Best Western, Comfort Inn, Courtyard, Hampton Inn, Motel 6, Ramada Inn 🅞 auto repair, Camping World RV Ctr, Ford/Lincoln, Harley-Davidson, Honda, Nissan, Toyota/Scion, **W** 🅖 Citgo/dsl, Exxon/dsl 🏨 Microtel 🅞 Buick/GMC, Chrysler/Dodge/Jeep
45	to Troutman, Barium Springs, **E** 🅞 KOA, RV Repair, **W** 🅖 4 Bros (3mi)
42	US 21, NC 115, to Troutman, Oswalt, **E** 🅖 Hess/Wilco/Subway/dsl/scales/24hr 🍴 McDonald's, Wendy's 🅞 AutoZone, Lowe's, **W** 🅖 Citgo/dsl 🍴 Arby's 🅞 camping, to Lake Norman SP
39mm	🆁🆂 both lanes, full ♿ facilities, litter barrels, petwalk, 🅲, 🖼 vending
36	NC 150, Mooresville, **E** 🅖 Circle K/dsl, Exxon, Shell/dsl 🍴 Applebee's, China Buffet, CiCi's Pizza, CookOut, Denny's, FatBoy's Cafe, Italian, Pizza Hut, Pomodoro's, Sonny's BBQ, Taco Bell, Waffle House, Wendy's 🏨 Days Inn, Fairfield Inn, Holiday Inn Express, Quality Inn, Ramada Ltd 🅞 $Tree, Belk, Cadillac/Chevrolet, Gander Mtn, GNC, Jo-Ann Fabrics, Kia,

(vertical margin text) **STATESVILLE** · **ELKIN** · **NC**

⬆N	**INTERSTATE 77 Cont'd**
Exit #	Services

MOORESVILLE

36	Continued
	Kohl's, Tuesday Morning, URGENT CARE, Walmart/Subway, **W** 🅿 Circle K/dsl, Hess/dsl, Shell/dsl, Valero/dsl 🍴 5 Guys Burgers, Arby's, Baskin-Robbins/Dunkin Donuts, Bojangles, Chick-fil-A, Chili's, Cracker Barrel, Duckworth's Grill, Golden Corral, Hardee's, Hickory Tavern Grill, Hooters, IHOP, Joe's Fish Rest., KFC, Kyoto Japanese, LoneStar Steaks, McAlister's Deli, McDonald's, Monterrey Mexican, O'Charley's, Panera Bread, Pizza Vito, Portofino's, Queen's Pizza, Red Robin, Rita's Custard, Showmar's, Smoothie King, Sonic, Starbucks, Steak'n Shake, Subway, TX Roadhouse 🛏 Hampton Inn, Sleep Inn, Super 8, Wingate Inn 🅾 Advance Parts, AT&T, AutoZone, Best Buy, BJ's Whse/gas, CVS Drug, Dick's, Discount Tire, Food Lion, Lowe's, Michael's, Old Navy, PetCo, Petsmart, Ross, Staples, Target, Tire Kingdom, TJ Maxx, Verizon, Walgreens
35	Brawley School Rd.
33	US 21 N, **E** 🅿 Shell 🍴 Big League Hotdogs, China Express, DQ, Jeffrey's Rest., McDonald's, Quiznos, Starbucks, Subway 🛏 Candlewood Suites, Hilton Garden, SpringHill Suites, TownePlace Suites 🅾 Ⓗ, AT&T, **W** 🅿 BP, Citgo/dsl 🍴 Arby's, Baskin-Robbins/Dunkin Donuts, Sauza's Mexican 🅾 Food Lion, Lake Norman RV Resort (13mi), vet
31	Langtree Rd, **W** 🅿 Shell/dsl
30	Davidson, **E** 🅿 Exxon/dsl, Liberty 🍴 Char-Grill, Subway 🛏 Homewood Suites 🅾 Harris-Teeter, to Davidson College, **W** 🍴 North Harbor Rest
28	US 21 S, NC 73, Cornelius, Lake Norman, **E** 🅿 Cashion/dsl, Citgo 🍴 Acropolis Cafe 🛏 Days Inn, Hampton Inn 🅾 NAPA, **W** 🅿 Kangaroo 🍴 Asiana, Bojangles, Chicago Dog, Drifter's Grill, KFC, Kobe Japanese, Mac's BBQ, McAlister's Deli, McDonald's, Pizza Hut, Starbucks, Subway, Taco Bell, Waffle House, Wendy's 🛏 Clarion, Comfort Inn, EconoLodge, Microtel 🅾 $Tree, Chrysler/Dodge/Jeep, CVS Drug, Fresh Mkt, Hyundai, Rite Aid, SteinMart, USPO, Walgreens

CONCORD

25	NC 73, Concord, Lake Norman, **E** 🅿 Shell/dsl 🍴 Burger King, Chick-fil-A, Chili's, Donato's Pizza, IHOP, Longhorn Steaks, McDonald's, Melting Pot, Moe's SW Grill, O'Charley's, Panda Express, Papa John's, Starbucks 🛏 Country Inn&Suites, Holiday Inn Express, Quality Inn 🅾 AAA, Advance Parts, AT&T, GNC, Harris-Teeter, Home Depot, Kohl's, Lowe's, Marshall's, PetCo, Radio Shack, Staples, Target, Tuffy Auto, Verizon, vet, **W** 🅿 Shell/Circle K/dsl 🍴 Arby's, Bob Evans, Bojangles, Carrabba's, ColdStone, DQ, Fox&Hound, Hickory Tavern Grill, House of Tei Pei, Jason's Deli, Kabuto Japanese, Outback Steaks, Qdoba, Red Rock's Cafe, Starbucks, Subway, Taco Mac 🛏 Candlewood Suites, Courtyard, Residence Inn, Sleep Inn 🅾 Barnes&Noble, Dick's, Food Lion/deli, Office Depot, to Energy Explorium, Walgreens
23	Gilead Rd, to US 21, Huntersville, **E** 🅿 BP, Citgo/dsl, Shell/24hr 🍴 Baskin-Robbins/Dunkin Dounuts, Capt's Galley, Chico's Mexican, CookOut, Hardee's, Little Caesar's, Subway, Taco Bell, Waffle House, Wendy's 🛏 Best Western, Comfort Suites, Hampton Inn, Ramada Inn 🅾 AutoZone, Buick/GMC, Food Lion, Ford, Goodyear/auto, Hancock Fabrics, O'Reilly Parts, Rite Aid, Toyota, Tuesday Morning, USPO, vet, VW, **W** 🅿 Shell 🍴 5 Guys Burgers, Domino's, Firehouse Subs, McDonald's, Salsarita's, Starbucks 🅾 Ⓗ, Batteries+, Bi-Lo, CVS Drug, Earth Fare, Harris-Teeter, URGENT CARE, Walgreens

CHARLOTTE

19b a	S I-485 Outer, Rd 115, to Spartanburg
18	Harris Blvd, Reames Rd, **E** 🅿 BP/Arby's, Shell/7-11/dsl 🍴 Azteca Mexican, Bob Evans, Hickory Tavern, Jack-in-the-Box, Jimmy John's, Subway, Waffle House 🛏 Comfort Suites, Courtyard, Fairfield Inn, Hilton Garden, Holiday Inn Express, Suburban Lodge 🅾 Ⓗ, Advance Parts, Staples, to UNCC, Univ Research Park, URGENT CARE, **W** 🍴 5 Guys Burgers, Bravo Italian, Buffalo Wild Wings, Chick-fil-A, Chili's, East Coast Grill, Edomae Grill, Firebirds Grill, Firehouse Subs, Fox&Hound, Fox&Hound, Jersey Mike's, Mimi's Cafe, Moe's SW Grill, Olive Garden, Olive Garden, On-the-Border, Panera bread, PF Chang's, Red Robin, Shane's Rib Shack, TGI Friday's, Wendy's 🛏 Drury Inn 🅾 $Tree, AT&T, Belk, Best Buy, Dick's, Dillard's, Discount Tire, Lowe's, Macy's, mall, Old Navy, Petsmart, REI, Target, Verizon
16b a	US 21, Sunset Rd, **E** 🅿 Circle K, QT/dsl, Shell/7-11/dsl 🍴 Capt D's, Hardee's, KFC, McDonald's, Papa John's, Subway, Taco Bell, Wendy's 🛏 Days Inn, Super 8 🅾 $General, AutoZone, Just$ave Foods, NAPA, O'Reilly Parts, **W** 🅿 Circle K/dsl, Citgo/dsl, Shell/dsl/scales/24hr 🍴 Baskin-Robbins/Dunkin Donuts, Bojangles, Bubba's BBQ, CookOut, Denny's, Domino's, Jack-in-the-Box, Little Caesar's, Subway, Waffle House 🛏 Microtel, Sleep Inn 🅾 Advance Parts, Aldi Foods, CVS Drug, Family$, Food Lion, Meineke, Walgreens
13b a	I-85, S to Spartanburg, N to Greensboro
12	La Salle St, **W** 🅿 Marathon/dsl, Shell/dsl
11b a	I-277, Brookshire Fwy, NC 16
10b	Trade St, 5th St, **E** 🅾 to Discovery Place, **W** 🅿 Marathon 🍴 Bojangles, Church's 🅾 Family$
10a	US 21 (from sb), Moorhead St, downtown
9	I-277, US 74, to US 29, John Belk Fwy, downtown, **E** 🅾 Ⓗ, stadium
8	Remount Rd (from nb, no re-entry)
7	Clanton Rd, **E** 🅿 Marathon/dsl 🛏 EconoLodge, Super 8 🅾 Family$, **W** 🅿 BP, Shell/7-11/dsl
6b a	US 521, Billy Graham Pkwy, **E** 🅿 Citgo, QT/dsl, Shell/dsl 🍴 Arby's, Azteca Mexican, Bojangles, Capt D's, Carolina Prime Steaks, Domino's, Dragon House, Firehouse Subs, HoneyBaked Ham, IHOP, KFC, Papa John's, Tres Pesos Grill, Waffle House 🛏 Best Western, Days Inn, Ramada Ltd, Sheraton 🅾 CVS Drug, Family$, Home Depot, TJ Maxx, to Queens Coll, Walgreens, **W** 🅿 Kangaroo 🍴 Omaha Steaks 🛏 Courtyard, Embassy Suites, Extended Stay America, Hyatt House, InTowne Suites, La Quinta, Sleep Inn 🅾 ⛺
5	Tyvola Rd, **E** 🅿 Kangaroo, Shell 🍴 Chili's, China King, Denny's, McDonald's, Sonny's BBQ, Subway 🛏 Comfort Inn, Crowne Plaza, Extended Stay America, Hawthorn Suites, Hilton, Quality Inn, Residence Inn 🅾 Costco/gas, Family$, Jaguar, Maserati, Meineke, **E services 1 mi** Verizon, **W** 🛏 Extended Stay America, Home2 Suites, Wingate Inn
4	Nations Ford Rd, **E** 🅿 Citgo, Shell/Circle K 🍴 Floyd's Rest. 🛏 Knights Inn, La Casa Inn, **W** 🅿 Shell/Burger King
3	Arrowood Rd, **E** 🍴 Cafe South, Jack-in-the-Box, Sonic, Starbucks, Wendy's 🛏 Courtyard, Fairfield Inn, Holiday Inn Express, Hyatt Place, Mainstay Suites, Sonesta Suites, TownePlace Suites, **W** 🍴 Ruby Tuesday 🛏 Hampton Inn
2	I-485
1.5mm	**Welcome Ctr nb, full ♿ facilities, info, litter barrels, petwalk, 🍴, ⛺, vending**
1	Westinghouse Blvd, to I-485 (from nb), **E** 🅿 BP/dsl 🍴 Jack-in-the-Box, Subway, Waffle House 🛏 Super 8, **W** 🅿 Shell/7-11/dsl 🍴 Burger King
0mm	North Carolina/South Carolina state line

NC

↑N	**INTERSTATE 85**

Exit #	Services
234mm	North Carolina/Virginia state line
233	US 1, to Wise, **E** 🅖🍴 Budget Inn
231mm	**Welcome Ctr sb, full** 🚹 **facilities, litter barrels, petwalk,** 🅒, 🔄
229	Oine Rd, to Norlina, **E** 🅖 BP, **W** 🅞 SRA
226	Ridgeway Rd, **W** to Kerr Lake, to SRA
223	Manson Rd, **E** 🅖 BP/dsl 🅞 camping, **W** 🅞 to Kerr Dam
220	US 1, US 158, Flemingtown Rd, to Middleburg, **E** 🅖 Mobil/dsl, **W** 🅖 Exxon/dsl/scales/truck wash 🏠 Chex Motel/rest.
218	US 1 S (from sb exits left), to Raleigh
217	Nutbush Bridge, **E** 🅞 auto repair, **W** 🅖 Exxon/dsl 🅞 Kerr Lake RA

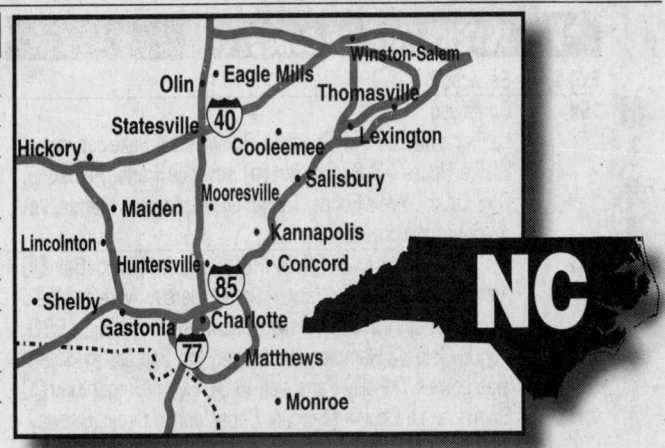

H E N D E R S O N	
215	US 158 BYP E, Henderson (no EZ return from nb), **E** 🅖 Hess/dsl, Shell, Sunoco 🍴 Burger King, Forsyth's BBQ, Nunnery-Freeman BBQ, Subway 🏠 Budget Host, EconoLodge, Scottish Inn 🅞 $General, Food Lion, repair/tires, Roses, services on US 158
214	NC 39, Henderson, **E** 🅖 BP 🍴 Waffle House 🅞 Verizon, **W** 🅖 Mobil/dsl, Shell 🅞 to Kerr Lake RA
213	US 158, Dabney Dr, to Henderson, **E** 🅖 Marathon, Valero 🍴 Bamboo Garden, Big Cheese Pizza, Bojangles, Denny's, Ichibar Chinese, KFC, McDonald's, Papa John's, Pino's Italian, Subway, Wendy's 🅞 Family$, Food Lion, Radio Shack, Roses, Save-a-Lot Foods, **W** 🅖 Shell 🍴 Chick-fil-A, Golden Corral, Mayflower Seafood, Pizza Hut, Ruby Tuesday, Smithfields BBQ, Taco Bell 🏠 Holiday Inn Express 🅞 Advance Parts, BigLots, Buick/Chevrolet/GMC, Chrysler/Dodge/Jeep, Ford/Lincoln, Lowe's, Rite Aid, Staples, Verizon
212	Ruin Creek Rd, **E** 🅖 Shell/dsl 🍴 Cracker Barrel, Mazatlan Mexican, Ribeye's, Waffle House 🏠 Knight's Inn 🅞 Toyota/Scion, **W** 🅖 Exxon/Burger King, Sheetz/dsl 🏠 Baymont Inn, Hampton Inn, Sleep Inn 🅞 🅗, $Tree, Belk, JC Penney, Walmart

O X F O R D	
209	Poplar Creek Rd, **W** 🅞 Vance-Granville Comm Coll
206	US 158, Oxford, **W** 🅖 BP/dsl 🅞 🔄
204	NC 96, Oxford, **E** 🅖 BP/dsl 🏠 Comfort Inn, King's Inn 🅞 Buick/Chevrolet/GMC, Ford, Honda, **W** 🅖 Hess, Shell, Valero 🍴 Burger King, China Wok, Cookout, Domino's, KFC/Taco Bell, McDonald's, Pizza Hut, Subway, Wendy's 🅞 🅗, GNC, Just Save
202	US 15, Oxford, **W** 🅖 Murphy Express/dsl 🍴 Bojangles, Hibachi, HWY 55 🏠 Crown Motel (2mi) 🅞 $Tree, Verizon, Walmart
199mm	🆁🆂 **both lanes, full** 🚹 **facilities, litter barrels, petwalk,** 🅒, 🔄
198mm	Tar River

B U T N E R	
191	NC 56, Butner, **E** 🅖 BP/dsl, Hess/dsl 🍴 Betty Lue's Rest., Bob's BBQ, Bojangles, Domino's, El Rio Mexican, KFC/Taco Bell, McDonald's, Pizza Hut, Pizza Mia, Sonic, Subway, Taste of China, Wendy's 🏠 Creedmor Inn 🅞 $General, $Tree, Advance Parts, AutoZone, Food Lion, M&H Tires, Rite Aid, to Falls Lake RA, vet, **W** 🅖 Exxon, Shell/dsl 🍴 Hardee's, Ribeye's 🏠 Best Western, EconoLodge, Ramada Ltd 🅞 auto repair
189	Butner, **W** 1 mi 🅖 BP/dsl, Citgo, Valero 🍴 Subway 🅞 repair
186b a	US 15, to Creedmoor, **E** 🅖 Variety Mart/dsl
185mm	Falls Lake
183	Redwood Rd
182	Red Mill Rd, **E** 🅖 Exxon/dsl 🅞 Kenworth/Isuzu Trucks
180	Glenn School Rd
179	E Club Blvd, **E** 🅖 Exxon

D U R H A M	
178	US 70 E, to Raleigh, Falls Lake RA, Research Triangle, **E** 🅞 RDU ✈
177	Avondale Dr, NC 55, **W** 🅖 BP, Shell 🍴 American Hero, Arby's, Hong Kong Buffet, Los Comales, McDonalds, Subway 🅞 Advance Parts, Family$
176b a	Gregson St, US 501 N, **E** 🅖 Biscuitville, Burger King, Hugo's, PanPan Diner, Randy's Pizza, Ruby Tuesday, Tripp's Diner 🏠 Hampton Inn 🅞 Macy's, mall, Museum of Life&Science, Sears/auto, **W** 🅞 🅗, museum
175	Guess Rd, **E** 🅖 Citgo 🅞 Doghouse Café, Hog Heaven BBQ 🏠 Holiday Inn Express, Super 8 🅞 Rite Aid, **W** 🅖 BP/dsl, Pure/dsl 🍴 Bojangles, Honey's Diner, IHOP, TX Roadhouse 🏠 Red Roof Inn 🅞 Family Dollar, GNC, Home Depot, Kroger, PetsMart, Ross, Verizon, vet
174b	US 15 S, US 501 S
174a	Hillandale Rd, **W** 🅖 BP 🍴 Blue Olive, China King, El Corral, Pomodoro Italian 🏠 Comfort Inn, Courtyard 🅞 Kerr Drug, URGENT CARE
173	US 15, US 501, US 70, Colemill Rd, W Durham, **E** 🅖 BP, Exxon/dsl, Mobil, Shell 🍴 Arby's, Biscuitville, Bojangles, Chick-fil-A, Cookout, Cracker Barrel, DogHouse Rest., Domino's, Japan Express, KFC/Taco Bell, McDonald's, Shanghai Chinese, Subway, Waffle House, Wendy's 🏠 Days Inn, Hilton, Motel 6, Quality Inn 🅞 🅗, $General, Advance Parts, Autozone, CVS Drug, Hancock Fabrics, Kroger, O'Reilly Parts, Rite Aid
172	NC 147 S, to US 15 S, US 501 S (from nb), Durham
170	to NC 751, to Duke U (no EZ return from nb), **E** 🏠 Durham Skyland Inn, Scottish Inn, **W** 🅞 to Eno River SP
165	NC 86, to Chapel Hill, **E** 🅖 Eagles/Burger King/dsl 🍴 China Fuji, Hwy 55, Papa John's, Subway 🅞 Home Depot, Walmart, **W** 🅖 BP/dsl 🅞 auto repair
164	Hillsborough, **E** 🅖 BP, Citgo/dsl 🍴 McDonald's 🏠 Holiday Inn Express, **W** 🅖 Shell 🍴 Bojangles, Domino's, Hardee's, KFC/Taco Bell, Pizza Hut, Pueblo Viejo Mexican, Russell's Steaks, Subway, Waffle House, Wendy's 🏠 Microtel 🅞 $General, $Tree, AutoZone, CarQuest, Food Lion, Ford, Goodyear/auto
163	I-40 E, to Raleigh.

I-85 S and I-40 W run together 38 mi.

161	to US 70 E, NC 86 N
160	to NC 86 N, Efland, **W** 🅖 Exxon/dsl 🅞 Andrew's Repair
158mm	**weigh sta both lanes**
157	Buckhorn Rd, **E** 🅖 BP/dsl, Petro/Valero/Dunkin Donuts/Iron Skillet/dsl/scales/24hr/@, **W** 🅖 Citgo
154	Mebane-Oaks Rd, **E** 🅖 Murphy USA/dsl, Sheetz/dsl 🍴 China Garden, Ciao Pizza, Subway, Wendy's, Zaxby's 🅞 $Tree, GNC, Radio Shack, Walmart/Subway, **W** 🅖 BP, Hess/dsl, Shell/dsl 🍴 Biscuitville, Blue Ribbon Diner, Bojangles,

🅖 = gas 🍴 = food 🛏 = lodging ◉ = other 🅡ˢ = rest stop   Copyright 2015 - the Next EXIT ®

⬆N	INTERSTATE 85 Cont'd
Exit #	Services

M E B A N E

154 Continued
La Fiesta Mexican, McDonald's, Roma Pizza, Sake Japanese, Waffle House 🛏 Budget Inn ◉ Advance Parts, AutoZone, CVS Drug, Lowe's Foods, Tanger Outlets/famous brands, Verizon, vet, Walgreens

153 NC 119, Mebane, **E** 🅖 BP/KFC/Pizza Hut/Taco Bell 🍴 Anna Maria's Pizza, Cracker Barrel, Jersey Mike's, Moe's SW Grill, Ruby Tuesday, Sakura Japanese, Smithfield's BBQ, Yogurt Café 🛏 Hampton Inn, Holiday Inn Express ◉ $General, Lowe's, O'Reilly Parts, vet, **W** 🅖 Exxon/Burger King 🍴 Domino's, La Cocina Mexican, Papa John's, Sonic, Subway, YumYum Chinese ◉ Curves, Food Lion

152 Trollingwood Rd, **E** 🅖🍴/McDonald's/dsl/scales/24hr

150 to Roxboro, Haw River, **W** 🅖 ✈FLYING J/Denny's/dsl/LP/scales/24hr, Hess/Wilco/DQ/Wendy's/dsl/scales/24hr, SpeedCo 🛏 Days Inn ◉ Blue Beacon

148 NC 54, Graham, **E** 🅖 BP/dsl, Marathon/dsl, Shell/dsl 🍴 Waffle House 🛏 Homestay Suites, **W** 🍴 AmMex 2 Cafe

147 NC 87, to Pittsboro, Graham, **E** 🅖 BP, Sheetz/dsl 🍴 Anna-Maria's Pizzeria, Arby's, Bojangles, Burger King, Domino's, Great Wall Chinese, Guerrero Mexican, Lucky Bamboo, Pizza Hut, Subway, Wendy's ◉ Advance Parts, AutoZone, Champion Tire/Repair, Curves, Family$, Food Lion, Ford, Just Save, O'Reilly Parts, Rite Aid, vet, **W** 🅖 Citgo/dsl, Exxon/dsl, Shell/dsl 🍴 Biscuitville, Cook-Out, Golden China, McDonald's, Taco Bell, Zaxby's ◉🅷, $General, CVS Drug, Verizon, Walgreens

B U R L I N G T O N

145 NC 49, Burlington, **E** 🅖 Marathon/dsl, Shell/dsl 🍴 Capt D's 🛏 EconoLodge, Microtel, Motel 6 ◉ Harley-Davidson, **W** 🅖 BP/dsl 🍴 Biscuitville, Bojangles, Burger King, China Inn, Hardee's, KFC, Subway 🛏 Quality Inn, Red Carpet Inn, Royal Inn ◉ $General, Chrysler/Dodge/Jeep, Family$, Food Lion, Radio Shack, Rite Aid

143 NC 62, Burlington, **E** 🅖 Sav-Way 🍴 Hardee's, Waffle House, Wendy's ◉ JR Outlet, to Alamance Bfd, **W** 🅖 Marathon, Sheetz/dsl 🍴 Biscuitville, Cutting Board Rest, K&W Cafeteria 🛏 Ramada Inn ◉ $General, auto repair, Cadillac, Chevrolet, Food Lion, Ford, Home Depot, Mazda, vet

141 Huffman Mill Rd, Burlington, **E** 🅖 BP, Marathon/Kangaroo 🍴 IHOP, Mayflower Seafood, Outback Steaks 🛏 Hampton Inn, Holiday Inn Express ◉🅷, Nissan, **W** 🅖 Raygo 🍴 5 Guys Burgers, Andy's, Applebee's, Arby's, Biscuitville, Bojangles, Cancun Mexican, Chick-fil-A, China Gate, Cook-Out, Cracker Barrel, Golden Corral, Good Times Cafe, Grill 584, Hibachi Buffet, HoneyBaked Ham, Hooters, KFC, La Cocina Mexican, Longhorn Steaks, Mellow Mushroom, O'Charley's, Panera Bread, Ruby Tuesday, Sal's Italian, Starbucks, Steak'n Shake, Subway, Taco Bell, Village Grill, Wholly Guacamole 🛏 Best Western, Country Inn&Suites, Courtyard, Super 8 ◉ $Tree, Hamrick's, Harris Teeter, Hyundai, K-Mart/gas, Lowe's, mall, Radio Shack, Sears/auto, TJ Maxx, to Elon Coll, Verizon, Walgreens, Walmart/McDonald's

140 University Ave, **E** ◉🅷, Toyota/Scion, **W** 🍴 Brixx Pizza, Buffalo Wing Wings, Burger King, Chick-fil-A, Chili's, Coldstone, Jimmy John's, Little Italy, McDonald's, Mimi's Cafe, Moe's SW Grill, Olive Garden, Peking House, Qdoba, Red Bowl Asian, Red Lobster, Red Robin, Starbucks, TX Roadhouse ◉ AT&T, Barnes&Noble, Belk, Best Buy, BJ's Whse/gas, Dick's, Dillard's, Discount Tire, GNC, Hobby Lobby, JC Penney, Kohl's, Michael's, Old Navy, Petsmart, Ross, Target, Verizon

G R E E N S B O R O

139mm 🅡ˢ both lanes, full 🚻 facilities, litter barrels, 🅒, 🐾, vending

138 NC 61, Gibsonville, **W** 🅖 TA/BP/Burger King/Popeye's/dsl/scales/24hr/@ ◉ truckwash

135 Rock Creek Dairy Rd, **W** 🅖 Citgo, Marathon/Kangaroo 🍴 Bojangles, China 1, Ciao Italian, Domino's, Guacamole Mexican, Jersey Mike's Subs, McDonald's, Pizza Hut/Taco Bell, Subway 🛏 Comfort Suites ◉ $General, Curves, CVS Drug, Food Lion, Midtown Drug, Verizon

132 Mt Hope Church Rd, **E** 🅖 Citgo/Subway/dsl 🍴 McDonald's, Pascali's Pizza, **W** 🅖 Exxon/dsl, Hess/Wendy's/dsl/24hr 🛏 Hampton Inn

131 to I-85 S, to I-73 N, to US 421, Highpoint, Charlotte

129 Youngsmill Rd, **W** ◉ Greensboro Camping (4mi)

128 Alamance Church Rd, **E** 🅖 Citgo/Subway/dsl

126b a US 421, to Sanford, **E** 🅖 Exxon/dsl, Hagan Stone Park Camping, Kangaroo/dsl

124 S Elm, Eugene St, **W** 🅖 Murphy Express/dsl 🍴 Andy's, Bamboo Grill, Bojangles, Cracker Barrel, McDonald's, Mi Casa, Smithfield's BBQ, Starbucks, Subway, Waffle House, Wendy's ◉ AT&T, Lowe's, Verizon, Walmart/McDonald's

122c b a US 220, to Greensboro, Asheboro (from sb)

121 I-40 W, I-73 N, to Winston-Salem

120 N US 29, E US 70, to I-40 W

119 Groometown Rd, from nb, **W** 🅖 Citgo/dsl

118 US 29 S, US 70 W, to High Point, Jamestown, **W** 🛏 Grandover Resort ◉🅷

115mm Deep River

113c I-74, US 311, Ashboro, to Winston-Salem

113a NC 62, Archdale, **E** 🅖 Citgo/dsl, **W** 🅖 BP/dsl 🛏 Quality Inn

111 US 311, to High Point, Archdale, **E** 🅖 Sheetz/dsl 🍴 Bamboo Garden, Bojangles, Hardee's, Pizza Hut, Subway, Wendy's 🛏 Days Inn ◉ $General, CVS Drug, Food Lion, Lowe's Foods/24hr, **W** 🅖 Citgo, Exxon/McDonald's, Marathon/dsl, Shell/Circle K/dsl 🍴 Biscuitville, J&S Cafe, Rancho Rest, Waffle House 🛏 Comfort Inn, Country Inn&Suites, Fairfield Inn, Hampton Inn, Holiday Inn Express ◉🅷, O'Reilly Parts, tires, USPO, vet

108 Hopewell Church Rd, Trinity

106 Finch Farm Rd, **E** 🅖 BP/dsl, **W** 🅖 Sheetz/dsl 🍴 Smokey T's BBQ, Subway (1mi)

T H O M A S V I L L E

103 NC 109, to Thomasville, **E** 🅖 Marathon/dsl, Murphy USA/dsl, Shell 🍴 Arby's, Chen's Kitchen, Cookout Burgers, Elizabeth's Pizza, Taco Bell 🛏 Hospitality Suites ◉ $Tree, CVS Drug, Ingles Foods, K-Mart, Radio Shack, Walmart/McDonald's, **W** 🅖 Exxon/Subway/dsl, Hess/Wilco/dsl, RaceWay, Shell 🍴 BBQ Shack, Biscuitville, Bojangles, Burger King, Captain Tom's, China Garden, Denny's, E Coast Grill, Hardee's, Hunan Chinese, KFC, La Carreta Mexican, Little Caesars, Mandarin Express, Mazatlan Mexican, McDonald's, Mr Gatti's, Papa John's, Pizza Hut, Ruby Tuesday, Sonic, Sunrise Diner, Waffle House, Wendy's 🛏 Davidson Lodge, Quality Inn ◉ $General, Advance Parts, Aldi Foods, AutoZone, Family$, Food Lion, Merchant's Tire, Mighty$, NAPA, O'Reilly Parts, Peebles, Rite Aid, Verizon, Walgreens

102 Lake Rd, **W** 🅖 Marathon/dsl, Sunoco/dsl 🛏 Comfort Inn, Microtel ◉🅷

100mm 🅡ˢ both lanes, full 🚻 facilities, litter barrels, petwalk, 🅒, 🐾, vending

96 US 64, to Asheboro, Lexington, **E** 🅖 Exxon/dsl ◉ Modern Tire, NC Zoo, **W** 🅖 Citgo/dsl, Gulf/dsl 🍴 Randy's Rest. ◉ to Davidson Co Coll

94 Old US 64, **E** 🅖 Shell, **W** ◉ Timberlake Gallery

INTERSTATE 85 Cont'd

Exit #	Services
91	NC 8, to Southmont, **E** 🅖 BP/dsl, Mobil/7-11, Shell/dsl 🍴 Biscuit King, Chrissy's Doghouse, Christo Rest., Hunan Express, Jimmy's BBQ, Kabuki, KFC, McDonald's, Ocean View Seafood, Subway, Wendy's 🏠 Days Inn, Hwy 8 Motel 🅞 Food Lion, High Rock Lake Camping (7mi), Kerr Drug, Mock Tire, **W** 🅖 Exxon/dsl, QM/dsl 🍴 Applebee's, Arby's, Burger King, Cagmey's Kitchen, Cracker Barrel, Golden Corral, La Carreta Mexican, Little Ceasars, Mi Pueblo, Pizza Hut (1mi), Subway, Taco Bell, Zaxby's 🏠 Country Hearth Inn, Quality Inn 🅞 H, $Tree, Belk, GNC, Lowe's (1mi), Radio Shack, Walmart
88	Linwood, **W** 🅖 Gulf/dsl 🅞 H
87	US 29, US 70, US 52 (from nb), High Point, **W** 🅞 H, ✈
86	Belmont Rd, **W** 🅖 Bill's Trkstp/dsl/scales/24hr/@
84	US 29 S, US 70 W, NC 150 (from nb), to Spencer
82	US 29, US 70 (from sb), to Spencer
81.5mm	Yadkin River
81	Long Ferry Rd, Spencer, **E** 🅖 Liberty/dsl
79	Spencer Shops SHS, Spencer, E Spencer, **W** 1 mi 🅖 Citgo 🍴 Bojangles, Subway 🅞 $General, Food Lion, Kerr Drug
76b a	US 52, to Albemarle, Salisbury, **E** 🅖 BP, Citgo, Pop Shoppe 🍴 Applebee's, Capriano's, ColdStone, E Coast Grill, Grand Asian, IHOP, Mr Gatti's Pizza, Pancho Villa Mexican, Top China, Zaxby's 🏠 Days Inn, Economy Inn, Happy Traveler Inn 🅞 $Tree, Aldi Foods, AT&T, CVS Drug, Food Lion, GNC, Harley-Davidson, Lowe's, Marshall's, Old Navy, Petsmart, Radio Shack, Rite Aid, Staples, Tire Kingdom, Verizon, vet, Walgreens, **W** 🅖 Murphy Express/dsl, Shell/Circle K/dsl, Wilco/Hess/dsl 🍴 Blue Bay Seafood, Bojangles, Burger King, Capt D's, Chick-fil-A, China Buffet, Christo's Rest., Cookout, Cracker Barrel, Hardee's, HoneyBaked Ham, KFC, McDonald's, O'Charley's, Outback Steaks, Papa John's, Pizza Hut, Starbucks, Subway, Taco Bell, Tokyo Express, Wendy's 🏠 Comfort Suites, Courtyard 🅞 H, Advance Parts, AutoZone, BigLots, Family$, Firestone/auto, Goodyear/auto, K-Mart, Office Depot, USPO, Walmart/Subway
75	US 601, Jake Alexander Blvd, **E** 🅖 Sheetz/dsl 🍴 Arby's, Farmhouse Rest. 🏠 EconoLodge 🅞 NAPA, to Dan Nicholas Park, **W** 🅖 BP, Citgo, Shell/dsl 🍴 Casa Grande Mexian, CiCi's Pizza, Ichiban Japanese, Nyoshi Japanese, Ryan's, Waffle House, Wendy's 🏠 Hampton Inn, Holiday Inn, Quality Inn 🅞 Buick, Cadillac/Chevrolet, Chrysler/Dodge/Jeep, Ford, GMC, Honda, Kia, Magic Mart, Nissan, Toyota/Scion
74	Julian Rd, **W** 🍴 Longhorn Steaks, Los Arcos, Olive Garden, Subway 🅞 $Tree, Belk, Kohl's, Michael's
72	Peach Orchard Rd
71	Peeler Rd, **E** 🅖 Loves/Chester's/McDonald's/dsl/scales/24hr, **W** 🅖 Hess/Wilco/Bojangles/Subway/dsl/scales/24hr 🅞 dsl repair
70	Webb Rd, **E** 🅞 flea mkt, **W** 🅖 Shell/dsl 🍴 Bebops BBQ 🅞 st patrol
68	US 29, US 601, to Rockwell, China Grove, **W** 🅖 BP 🍴 Domino's, Gary's BBQ, Hardee's, Jimmie's Rest., Pizza Hut, Subway 🅞 $General, AutoZone, Family$, Food Lion, Rite Aid
63	Kannapolis, **E** 🅖 [Liberty]/Subway/dsl/scales 🍴 Waffle House 🏠 Motel 6
60	Earnhardt Rd, Copperfield Blvd, **E** 🅖 Exxon/dsl, Marathon 🍴 Bojangles, Cracker Barrel, Waffle House 🏠 Country Inn&Suites, Hampton Inn, Sleep Inn 🅞 H, Discount Tire, **W** 🅖 Marathon/Kangaroo/dsl 🍴 Carino's Italian, Casa Grande Mexican, Dragon Wok, Firehouse Subs, Logan's Roadhouse,

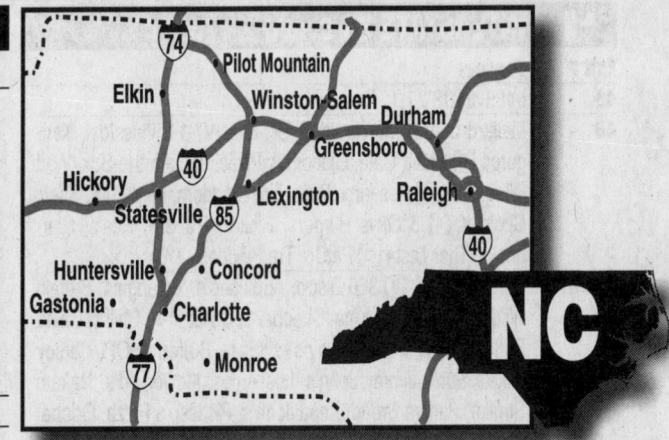

Exit #	Services
60	Continued McDonald's, Ruby Tuesday, Steak'n Shake, Subway, Taco Bell, Wendy's 🏠 Holiday Inn Express 🅞 Hobby Lobby, Kohl's, Lowe's, Sam's Club/gas, URGENT CARE, Walmart
59mm	🆁🆂 both lanes, full ♿ facilities, litter barrels, petwalk, 🄲, 🚻 vending
58	US 29, US 601, Concord, **E** 🅖 BP, Marathon/dsl, Shell/dsl 🍴 Applebee's, Capt D's, Chick-fil-A, Chili's, El Vallarta Mexican, Golden Corral, Jimmy John's, Mayflower Seafood, McDonald's, Moe's SW Grill, Mr C's Rest., O'Charley's, Popeye's, Starbucks, Subway, Wendy's 🏠 Best Value Inn, Howard Johnson, Rodeway Inn 🅞 H, Belk, Harris Teeter, JC Penney, mall, Sears/auto, st patrol, Staples, Verizon, Walgreens, **W** 🅖 BP, Hess 🍴 CiCi's, IHOP 🏠 Econolodge, Fairfield Inn, Microtel 🅞 $General, Ford, Hancock Fabrics, Home Depot, vet
55	NC 73, to Davidson, Concord, **E** 🅖 Shell 🍴 McDonald's, **W** 🅖 Shell/Circle K/dsl 🏠 Days Inn
54	Kannapolis Pkwy, George W Lyles Pkwy, **E** 🅖 Citgo 🍴 Bojangles, China Garden, Noodles&Co, Off-the-Grill 🅞 Advance Parts, AutoZone, CVS Drug, Firestone, Food Lion, Harris Teeter, URGENT CARE, vet, Walgreens, **W** 🅖 Marathon/Kangaroo 🍴 Arby's, Asian Cafe, Buffalo Wild Wings, Chick-fil-A, Fatz Cafe, Jersey Mike's, McDonald's, Mi Pueblo, Starbucks 🅞 $Tree, Best Buy, Dick's, Goodyear/auto, Marshall's, Steinmart, Super Target
52	Poplar Tent Rd, **E** 🅖 Shell/7-11/dsl 🍴 R&R BBQ 🅞 museum, to Lowe's Speedway, **W** 🅖 Exxon/7-11/dsl
49	Bruton Smith Blvd, Concord Mills Blvd, **E** 🅖 BP/McDonalds, Shell/7-11/dsl 🍴 5 Guys Burgers, Bojangles, Camila's Mexican, Carrabbas, ChuckECheese, Cinco de Mayo Mexican, Cookout, Cracker Barrel, Firehouse Subs, Hooters, Jack-in-the-Box, KFC/Taco Bell, Quaker Steak, Ruby Tuesday, Sonic, Sonny's BBQ, Starbucks, Subway, Taco Bell, TX Land&Cattle Steaks, TX Roadhouse, Waffle House, Wendy's, Zaxby's 🏠 Comfort Suites, Courtyard, Embassy Suites, Great Wolf Lodge, Hampton Inn, Hilton Garden, Holiday Inn Express, Residence Inn, Sleep Inn, SpringHill Suites, Suburban Lodge, Wingate Inn 🅞 BJ's Whse/gas, Fleetwood RV camping (1.5mi), Harley-Davidson, Honda, to Lowe's Motor Speedway, Tom Johnson RV Ctr (1.5mi), Toyota/Scion, **W** 🅖 Marathon/dsl, Texaco 🍴 Applebee's, Burger King, Charanda Mexican, Chick-fil-A, Foster's Grille, Jimmy John's, Mayflower Seafood, McAlisters Deli, Olive Garden, On-the-Border, Panera Bread, Razzoo's Cafe, Red Lobster, Steak'n Shake, Sticky Fingers, TGI Friday's 🅞 $Tree, AT&T, BassPro Shops, Best Buy, BooksAMillion, Concord Mills Mall, Discount Tire, Goodyear/auto, Lowe's, PetCo, Radio Shack, Ross, TJ Maxx, URGENT CARE, Verizon, Walmart/Subway

(Left margin: **SALISBURY** *)*
(Right margin: **CONCORD** *)*
(Right edge tab: **NC** *)*

⬆N INTERSTATE 85 Cont'd

Exit #	Services
48	I-485, to US 29, to Rock Hill
46	Mallard Creek Church Rd, E 📱 Exxon/7-11, Hess/dsl, Kangaroo 🍴 China Cafe, Giacomos Pizza, Jack-in-the-Box, Wild Wing Cafe ⦿ Research Park, Tire Kingdom, vet, W 📱 Shell/Circle K 🍴 5 Guys Burgers, Hickory Tavern, Rita's, Starbucks, Thai Taste ⦿ PetCo, Trader Joes
45b a	Harris Blvd, E 🍴 360 Bistro, Applebee's, Bojangles, Buffalo Wild Wings, Burger King, Cheddar's, Chick-fil-A, Chili's, China Buffet, China Palace, Chipotle, Fuse Buffet, IHOP, Jersey Mike's Subs, Jimmy John's, Los Arcos, McDonald's, Nakato Steaks, Panera Bread, Papa John's, Picasso's Pizza, Qdoba, Shane's Rib Shack, Shoney's, Showmar's Rest, Smokey Bones, Starbucks, T. Mac Grill, Taco Bell, TGIFriday's 🏠 Country Inn&Suites, Courtyard, Drury Inn, Extended Stay America, Hampton Inn, Hilton, Holiday Inn, Homewood Suites, Microtel, Residence Inn, Sleep Inn ⦿ 🏥 Dick's, Food Lion, Kohl's, Michael's, Office Depot, Ross, Sam's Club, TJ Maxx, to Miz Scarlett's, to UNCC, U Research Park, Verizon, Walgreens, Walmart/McDonald's, W 0-2 mi 🍴 Longhorn Steaks, Macaroni Grill, Red Robin, Tony's Pizza 🏠 SpringHill Suites, TownePlace Suites ⦿ Harris Teeter, Rite Aid
43	University City Blvd, E 📱 Marathon/Subway/dsl 🍴 Honeybaked Ham, Taco Bell, Zaxby's 🏠 Extended Stay America, InTowne Suites ⦿ Discount Tire, Firestone/auto, GNC, Hobby Lobby, IKEA, Marshall's, Old Navy, Petsmart, Walmart, World Mkt
42	US 29 (nb only)
41	Sugar Creek Rd, E 📱 RaceWay 🍴 Bojangles, McDonald's, Taco Bell, Wendy's 🏠 Brookwood Inn, Continental Inn, Motel 6, Travel Inn, W 📱 Shell/Circle K 🍴 Chicken Box Rest, Cookout, TX Ranch Steaks 🏠 Days Inn, Red Roof Inn, Rodeway Inn, Sunset Inn, Super 8, S 📱 7-11/gas
40	Graham St, E 📱 Exxon/7-11/dsl 🏠 Budget Inn ⦿ UPS, Volvo, Western Star, W 📱 Marathon/dsl ⦿ Freightliner, S ⦿ NAPA Autocare
39	Statesville Ave, E 📱 🚛/Subway/dsl/scales/24hr ⦿ CarQuest, repair, W 📱 Citgo/dsl, Shell/dsl 🍴 Bojangles ⦿ Family$
38	I-77, US 21, N to Statesville, S to Columbia
37	Beatties Ford Rd, E 📱 Marathon, Shell/7-11/dsl 🍴 Burger King, McDonald's, Subway ⦿ CVS Drug, Family$, Food Lion, USPO, W 📱 Citgo
36	NC 16, Brookshire Blvd, E 🏠 Rodeway Inn ⦿ 🏥, repair, W 📱 Hari/dsl, RaceWay/dsl, Shell/7-11/dsl, Sunoco/dsl 🍴 Burger King, Jack-in-the-Box, Mr C's Rest., Subway ⦿ Family$, Griffin Tire
35	Glenwood Dr, E 🏠 Knights Inn, W 📱 Shell/dsl
34	NC 27, Freedom Dr, E 📱 Citgo/dsl, Shell/Circle K 🍴 Beauregard's Rest, Bojangles, Capt D's, Cookout, McDonald's, Pizza Hut, Showmar's, Subway, Taco Bell, Wendy's ⦿ $Tree, Advance Parts, Aldi Foods, AutoZone, Family$, Goodyear, Rite Aid, Save-A-Lot Foods, URGENT CARE, vet, Walgreens, W 🏠 Charlotte Express ⦿ JiffyLube
33	US 521, Billy Graham Pkwy, E 📱 Shell/dsl 🍴 Bojangles, KFC/Taco Bell, McDonald's, Wendy's 🏠 Baymont Inn, Comfort Suites, Royal Inn, Sheraton, SpringHill Suites ⦿ 🚉, W 📱 Exxon/dsl 🍴 Cracker Barrel, Ichiban, Waffle House 🏠 EconoLodge, La Quinta, Microtel, Motel 6, Quality Inn, Red Roof Inn, Super 8

Exit #	Services
32	Little Rock Rd, E 📱 Shell/7-11/dsl 🏠 Airport Inn, Courtyard, Hampton Inn, Holiday Inn, W 📱 Citgo/dsl, Shell/7-11 🍴 Arby's, Bud's Chicken, Hardee's, Showmar's Rest., Subway 🏠 Country Inn&Suites, Day's Inn, Wingate Inn ⦿ Family$, Food Lion, Griffin Tire, Rite Aid
30b a	I-485, to I-77, Pineville
29	Sam Wilson Rd, E 📱 BP (1mi) ⦿ camping, W 📱 Shell/dsl
28mm	weigh sta both lanes
27.5mm	Catawba River
27	NC 273, Mt Holly, E 📱 BP/Dunkin Donuts/dsl, Murphy USA/dsl 🍴 Arby's, Captain's Cap Seafood, Chick-fil-A, KFC, Pizza Hut, Sake Japanese, Subway, Taco Bell, Waffle House, Wendy's ⦿ Big Lots, CVS Drug, Family$, Firestone/auto, Lowe's, NAPA, Walgreens, Walmart/Subway, W 📱 Citgo/dsl 🏠 Holiday Inn Express
26	NC 7, E 📱 BP/dsl, Marathon/dsl 🍴 Bojangles, Hardee's, King Buffet, McDonald's, New China, Papa John's 🏠 Hampton Inn ⦿ $Tree, Advance Parts, Aldi Foods, AT&T, AutoZone, BiLo, Ford, Verizon, W ⦿ Belmont Abbey Coll
24mm	South Fork River
23	NC 7, McAdenville, W 📱 Exxon/dsl, Shell/Subway/dsl 🍴 Hardee's, Hillbilly's BBQ/Steaks
22	Cramerton, Lowell, E 📱 Hess/dsl, Marathon 🍴 Applebee's, Chick-fil-A, CiCi's, Jack-in-the-Box, Jersey Mike's Subs, Popeyes, Portofino's, Sakura Japanese, Schlotzsky's, Zaxby's ⦿ Books-A-Million, Buick/Cadillac/Chevrolet/GMC, Gander Mtn, Honda, Kia, K-Mart, Kohl's, Lowe's, Old Navy, Petsmart, Sam's Club/gas, U-Haul
21	Cox Rd, E 📱 Marathon 🍴 Akropolis Cafe, Buffalo Wild Wings, Cheddar's, Chili's, Chipotle, ChuckeCheese, Cookout, Dynasty Buffet, Firehouse Subs, Five Guys, Golden Corral, Hibachi Buffet, Krispy Kreme, La Fuente, Logan's Roadhouse, Longhorn Steaks, McAlister's Deli, McDonald's, Olive Garden, On the Border, Panera Bread, Peking Garden, Qdoba, Ruby Tuesday, Starbucks, Steak'n Shake, Subway, Tijuana Flats ⦿ $Tree, AT&T, Best Buy, Chrysler/Dodge/Jeep, Dick's, Discount Tire, Ford/Subaru, GNC, Hobby Lobby, Home Depot, Lowes Foods, Mary Jo's Cloth, Michael's, Nissan, Office Depot, O'Reilly Parts, PepBoys, Petco, Ross, Target, Tire Kingdom, TJ Maxx, Verizon, vet, Walgreens, Walmart/Subway, W 📱 Marathon 🍴 Arby's, Brixx Pizza, IHOP 🏠 Super 8 ⦿ 🏥, $General, Medical Ctr Drug
20	NC 279, New Hope Rd, E 📱 United, World 🍴 Capt D's, Jackson's Cafeteria, Los Arcos Mexican, McDonald's, O'Charley's, Pizza Hut, Red Lobster, Sake Japanese, Showmar's Rest, Taco Bell, Wendy's ⦿ Advance Parts, AutoZone, Belk, Dillard's, Family$, Firestone/auto, JC Penney, Sears/auto, Tuesday Morning, W 🍴 Bojangles, Cracker Barrel, Honeybaked Ham, KFC, Outback Steaks, TX Roadhouse, Waffle House 🏠 Best Western, Comfort Suites, Courtyard, Fairfield Inn, Hampton Inn ⦿ 🏥, CarMax
19	NC 7, E Gastonia, E 📱 Shell
17	US 321, Gastonia, E 📱 Citgo/dsl/LP 🍴 Los Arcos Mexican 🏠 Days Inn, ValuePlace ⦿ Family$, W 📱 Marathon/dsl, QT/dsl 🍴 Dunkin Donuts, Hardee's, Papa John's 🏠 Holiday Inn Express, Motel 6, Red Carpet Inn
14	NC 274, E Bessemer, E 📱 Citgo/dsl, Murphy USA/dsl ⦿ Walmart, W 📱 BP/Subway, Citgo/dsl 🍴 Bojangles, Waffle House 🏠 Express Inn
13	Edgewood Rd, Bessemer City, E ⦿ to Crowders Mtn SP, W 📱 Exxon
10b a	US 74 W, US 29, Kings Mtn

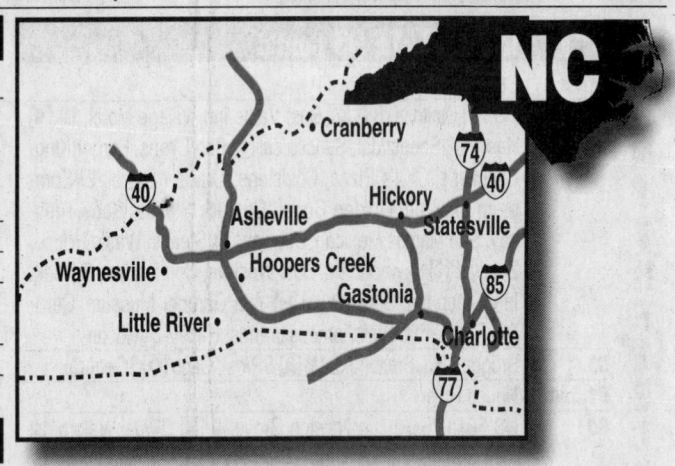

🅽 INTERSTATE 85 Cont'd

Exit #	Services
8	NC 161, to Kings Mtn, **E** 🍴 Holiday Inn Express 🅾 camping, **W** 🅶 BP/dsl 🍴 McDonald's, Mi Pueblito Mexican, Subway, Taco Bell, Waffle House, Wendy's 🛏 Quality Inn, Super 8 🅾 🅷, $General, Campers Inn RV Ctr
5	Dixon School Rd, **E** 🅶 Citgo/dsl/24hr 🅾 truck/tire repair
4	US 29 S (from sb)
2.5mm	Welcome Ctr nb, full 🅿 facilities, info, litter barrels, petwalk, 🅲, 🛐, vending
2	NC 216, Kings Mtn, **E** 🅾 to Kings Mtn Nat Military Park
0mm	North Carolina/South Carolina state line

🅽 INTERSTATE 95

Exit #	Services
181mm	Welcome Ctr sb, full 🅿 facilities, litter barrels, petwalk, 🅲, 🛐, vending, North Carolina/Virginia state line
180	NC 48, to Gaston, to Lake Gaston, Pleasant Hill, **W** 🅶 /Subway/dsl/scales/24hr
176	NC 46, to Garysburg, **W** 🅶 Shell/dsl 🍴 Burger King 🛏 Super 8
174mm	Roanoke River
173	US 158, Roanoke Rapids, Weldon, **E** 🅶 BP/dsl, Shell/dsl 🍴 Frazier's Rest., Ralph's BBQ, Waffle House 🛏 Days Inn, Orchard Inn, **W** 🅶 BP/dsl, Exxon/DQ/Stuckey's, Murphy USA/dsl, Shell/dsl 🍴 Applebee's, Arby's, Bojangles, Burger King, Carolina BBQ, Chick-fil-A, China Lin, Cookout, Cracker Barrel, Hardee's, Ichiban, KFC, Little Caesar's, Logan's Roadhouse, Mayflower Seafood, McDonald's, New China, Papa John's, Pizza Hut, Popeyes, Ruby Tuesday, San Jose Mexican, Starbucks, Subway, Subway, Taco Bell, TX Steaks, Waffle House, Wendy's 🛏 Hampton Inn, Holiday Inn Express, Motel 6, Quality Inn, Sleep Inn 🅾 🅷, $General, $Tree, Advance Parts, AutoZone, Belk, BigLots, Firestone/auto, Food Lion, GNC, Harley-Davidson, Honda, Lowe's, O'Reilly Parts, Radio Shack, Rite Aid, Save a Lot Foods, Staples, Toyota, URGENT CARE, Verizon, Walgreens, Walmart
171	NC 125, Roanoke Rapids, **E** 🛏 Hilton Garden 🅾 Carolina Crossroads RV Resort, Roanoke Rapids Theater, **W** 🅶 Shell/dsl 🛏 Best Western 🅾 st patrol
168	NC 903, to Halifax, **E** 🅶 Exxon/Subway/dsl, Shell/Burger King/dsl, **W** 🅶 Oasis/Dunkin Donuts/LP/dsl
160	NC 561, to Brinkleyville, **E** 🅶 Exxon, **W** 🅶 Shell/dsl
154	NC 481, to Enfield, **W** 1 mi 🅾 KOA
151mm	weigh sta both lanes
150	NC 33, to Whitakers, **E** 🅾 golf, **W** 🅶 BP/Subway/DQ/Stuckey's/dsl
145	NC 4, to US 301, Battleboro, **E** 🅶 BP/dsl, Exxon/dsl, Marathon/dsl, Shell 🍴 Carolina BBQ, Denny's, Hardee's, Waffle House 🛏 Ashburn Inn, Best Western, Deluxe Inn, EconoLodge, Economy Inn, Quality Inn, Red Carpet Inn, Travelers Inn
142mm	🆁🆂 both lanes, full 🅿 facilities, litter barrels, petwalk, 🅲, 🛐 vending
141	NC 43, Red Oak, **E** 🅶 BP/dsl, Exxon/dsl/LP 🅾 $General, Smith's Foods
138	US 64, **E** 1 mi on Winstead 🅶 BP/dsl, Hess/dsl 🍴 Bojangles, Cracker Barrel, Gardner's BBQ, Hardee's, Highway Diner, Outback Steaks, TX Steaks, Waffle House 🛏 Candlewood Suites, Comfort Inn, Country Inn&Suites, Courtyard, Doubletree, Hampton Inn, Holiday Inn, Residence Inn 🅾 🅷, Buick/GMC, Harley-Davidson, Honda, Rite Aid, to Cape Hatteras Nat Seashore, URGENT CARE

Exit #	Services
132	to NC 58, **E** 🅶 Pitstop/dsl, **W** 1 mi 🅶 BP/dsl
128mm	Tar River
127	NC 97, to Stanhope, **E** 🅾 🛐
121	US 264a, Wilson, **E** 0-4 mi 🅶 BP, Hess/dsl, Kangaroo/dsl/LP, Marathon, Murphy USA/dsl, Shell 🍴 Applebee's, Arby's, Buffalo Wild Wings, Burger King, Chick-fil-A, Chili's, Chopstix, Cookout, Denny's, El Tapatio, Golden Corral, Hardee's, Hibachi Buffet, Jersey Mike's, KFC/LJ Silver, Kobe Express, Mama Mia's Pizzaria, McDonald's, Moe's SW Grill, Olive Garden, Quizno's, Red Chileez Grill, Ruby Tuesday, San Jose Mexican, Sonic, Starbucks, Subway, Teppanyaki, TX Steaks, Waffle House, Wendy's, Zaxby's 🛏 Candlewood Suites, Hampton Inn, Quality Inn 🅾 🅷, $General, $Tree, Aldi Foods, AT&T, AutoZone, Belk, Best Buy, Big Lots, Chevrolet, Chrysler/Dodge/Jeep, Ford/Lincoln, GNC, Harris-Teeter, Hobby Lobby, Honda, Lowe's, Marshall's, Mr Tire, Nissan, O'Reilly Parts, Petsmart, Radio Shack, Ross, Staples, Target, Toyota/Scion, URGENT CARE, Verizon, vet, Walmart, White's Tires, **W** 🅶 BP 🍴 Best-N-Burgers, Bojangles, Burger King, Cracker Barrel, McDonald's, Pino's Pizza 🛏 Comfort Suites, Country Inn&Suites, Fairfield Inn, Hampton Inn, Holiday Inn Express, Jameson Inn, Microtel, Sleep Inn 🅾 to Country Dr Museum
119b a	I-795 S, US 264, US 117
116	NC 42, to Clayton, Wilson, **E** 🅶 Shell/dsl 🅾 🅷, **W** 🅶 BP/dsl 🅾 Rock Ridge Camping (2mi)
107	US 301, Kenly, **E** 🅶 BP/dsl, Citgo, Exxon/McDonald's/dsl, Fuel Doc, PitStop 🍴 Andy's Cafe, Golden China, Nik's Pizza, Norman's BBQ, Subway 🛏 Budget Inn, Deluxe Inn, Quality Inn 🅾 $General, CarQuest, Family$, Food Lion, Ford, O'Reilly Parts, Piggly Wiggly, Tobacco Museum
106	Truck Stop Rd, Kenly, **E** 🅶 ⓕFLYING J/Denny's/dsl/LP/scales/24hr, **W** 🅶 Kenly 95/Petro/DQ/Subway/Wendy's/dsl/scales/24hr/@, Wilco/Hess/Arby's/dsl/scales/24hr 🍴 Waffle House 🛏 Days Inn, Motel 6 🅾 Blue Beacon, Speedco Lube, Truck-o-Mat
105.5mm	Little River
105	Bagley Rd, Kenly, **E** 🅶 Big Boys/Shell/105 Pizza/dsl/scales/24hr 🍴 Lowell Mill Rest.
102	Micro, **W** 🅶 Shop'N-Go 🍴 Backdoor Cafe 🅾 $General, city park, USPO
101	Pittman Rd
99mm	🆁🆂 both lanes, full 🅿 facilities, hist marker, litter barrels, petwalk, 🅲, 🛐, vending
98	to Selma, **E** 🅾 RVacation
97	US 70 A, to Pine Level, Selma, **E** 🅶 Mobil/dsl 🍴 Denny's, Robbins Nest Rest. 🛏 Days Inn 🅾 J&R Outlet, **W** 🅶 BP/dsl, Exxon/dsl, Shell/dsl 🍴 Bojangles, Cookout, Don Beto's Tacos, KFC, McDonald's, Shoney's, Waffle House, Wendy's 🛏 EconoLodge, Hampton Inn, Masters Inn, Quality Inn 🅾 🅷

ROANOKE RAPIDS

WILSON

KENLY

NC

NC

⬆N INTERSTATE 95 Cont'd

Exit #	Services
95	US 70, Smithfield, **E** 🛏 Best Value Inn, Village Motel, **W** 🅟 Hess/dsl, Sheetz/dsl, Sunoco/dsl 🍽 Bob Evans, Burger King, Checker's, CiCi's Pizza, Coldstone, Cracker Barrel, El Sombrero Mexican, Golden Corral, Outback Steaks, Ruby Tuesday, San Marcos Mexican, Subway, TX Steaks, Waffle House, Zaxby's 🛏 Baymont Inn, Best Western, Comfort Inn, Fairfield Inn, Sleep Inn, Super 8 🅞 🏥 Ava Gardner Museum, Carolina Premium Outlets/famous brands, Harley-Davidson
93	Brogden Rd, Smithfield, **W** 🅟 BP/dsl, Citgo 🅞 $General
91.5mm	Neuse River
90	US 301, US 701, to Newton Grove, **E** 🅟 BP/dsl, Valero/dsl 🛏 Travelers Inn 🅞 Happy Trails RV Park, Raleigh Oaks RV Resort, Ronnie's Tires, to Bentonville Bfd (14mi), **W** 🅟 Exxon/dsl 🍽 Holt Lake BBQ 🛏 Four Oaks Motel/RV Park
87	NC 96, Four Oaks, **W** 🅟 BP/dsl, Hess/dsl, Walmart Express/dsl 🍽 McDonald's, Subway 🅞 $General
81b a	I-40, E to Wilmington, W to Raleigh
79	NC 50, to NC 27, to NC 242, Benson, Newton Grove, **E** 🅟 Short Stop/dsl 🍽 Char-Grill, Waffle House 🅞 auto repair, **W** 🅟 Exxon/Burger King/dsl, Mule City/dsl 🍽 China 8, Domino's, McDonald's, Pizza Hut, Subway, Taco Bell, White Swan BBQ 🛏 Days Inn 🅞 Advance Parts, auto repair, Family$, Food Lion, Walgreens
78mm	Neuse River, Neuse River
77	Hodges Chapel Rd, **E** 🅟 🛢Loves/Subway/dsl/scales/RV dump/24hr
75	Jonesboro Rd, **W** 🅟 Exxon/Milestone Diner, 🛢/Shell/DQ/Quiznos/dsl/scales/24hr/@
73	US 421, NC 55, to Dunn, Clinton, **E** 🍽 Cracker Barrel, McDonald's, Mi Casita Mexican, Panda House Chinese, Steak Escape 🅞 Chevrolet, Chrysler/Dodge/Jeep, Family$, Food Lion, **W** 🅟 Exxon/dsl, Hess/dsl, Shell 🍽 Bojangles, Burger King, Dairy Freeze, El Charro Mexican, Hot Dog&Hamburger Heavan, Sagebrush Steaks, Subway, Taco Bell, Triangle Waffle 🛏 Baymont Inn, Hampton Inn, Holiday Inn Express, Quality Inn, Super 8 🅞 Charlie C's IGA, museum, to Campbell U.
72	Pope Rd, **E** 🛏 Comfort Inn, Royal Inn, **W** 🅟 BP, Pure/dsl 🍽 Brass Lantern Steaks 🛏 Valley Motor Inn 🅞 Cadillac/GMC
71	Longbranch Rd, **E** 🅟 🛢/Kangaroo/Hardee's/dsl/scales/24hr, **W** 🅞 to Averasboro Bfd
70	SR 1811, **E** 🛏 Relax inn
65	NC 82, Godwin, **E** 🅞 Falcon Children's Home, **W** 🅟 Epco/dsl
61	to Wade, **E** 🅟 61 Trkstp/dsl 🅞 Fayetteville RV Resort Cottages, **W** 🅟 Exxon/dsl
58	US 13, to Newton Grove, I-295 to Fayetteville, **E** 🅟 Shell/dsl/scales 🍽 Quiznos, Waffle House 🛏 Days Inn
56	Lp 95, to US 301 (from sb), Fayetteville, **W** 🅟 Epco/dsl, Kangaroo/dsl 🅞 🏥 Pope AFB, to Ft Bragg
55	NC 1832, Murphy Rd, **W** 🅟 Epco/dsl, Kangaroo/dsl
52	NC 24, Fayetteville, **W** 🅞 botanical gardens, museum, Pope AFB, to Ft Bragg
49	NC 53, NC 210, Fayetteville, **E** 🅟 BP/dsl, Exxon/dsl, Kangaroo/dsl, Marathon 🍽 Burger King, McDonald's, Pizza Hut, Taco Bell, Waffle House 🛏 Days Inn, Deluxe Inn, Motel 6, **W** 🅟 BP/Subway/dsl, Exxon/dsl, Sunoco/dsl 🍽 Cracker Barrel, Ruby Tuesday, Shoney's 🛏 Comfort Inn, Country Hearth Inn, Doubletree, EconoLodge, Fairfield Inn, Hampton Inn, Holiday Inn, Quality Inn, Rodeway Inn, Sleep Inn, Super 8

Exit #	Services
48mm	🆁🆂 both lanes, full ♿ facilities, litter barrels, petwalk, 🕭, 🎰 vending
47mm	🅞 Cape Fear River
46b a	NC 87, to Fayetteville, Elizabethtown, **W** 🅞 🏥, Civic Ctr, museum, to Agr Expo Ctr
44	Claude Lee Rd, **W** 🅞 Lazy Acres Camping, to ⛲
41	NC 59, to Hope Mills, Parkton, **E** 🅟 Kangaroo/Subway/dsl 🍽 Bojangles, **W** 🅟 BP/dsl 🍽 Grandsons Buffet 🅞 Lake Waldo's Camping, Spring Valley RV Park
40	Lp 95, to US 301 (from nb), to Fayetteville, services on US 301 (5-7mi)
33	US 301, St Pauls, **E** 🅟 BP/dsl
31	NC 20, to St Pauls, Raeford, **E** 🅟 BP, Marathon/Huddle House/dsl, Mobil/McDonald's, Valero 🍽 Burger King, Hardee's 🛏 Days Inn 🅞 Volvo Trucks, Walgreens, Walmart Mkt, **W** 🅟 Exxon/dsl, Sunoco 🍽 Taco Bell 🅞 Food Lion
25	US 301, **E** 🅟 Sun-Do/dsl
24mm	weigh sta both lanes
22	US 301, **E** 🅟 Exxon, Marathon, Shell/DQ 🍽 Burger King, Chick-fil-A, China Wok, Denny's, Firehouse Subs, Golden Corral, Hardee's, IHOP, Outback Steaks, Papa John's, Pizza Hut, Ruby Tuesday, San Jose Mexican, Shogun, Smithfield BBQ, Starbucks, TX Steaks, Waffle House, Wendy's, Zaxby's 🛏 Best Western, Comfort Suites, Hampton Inn, Holiday Inn, Super 8 🅞 $Tree, AT&T, Chrysler/Dodge/Jeep, Goodyear/auto, Honda, Lowe's, Lowe's Foods, Office Depot, Radio Shack, SaveALot Foods, st patrol, Toyota/Scion, URGENT CARE, Verizon, Walmart/Subway, **W** 🅟 Gulf, Sun-Do/dsl, Sunoco/dsl 🍽 Bojangles, Uncle George's Rest. 🛏 Springhill Suites 🅞 Ford/Lincoln, Sam's Club/gas
20	NC 211, to NC 41, Lumberton, **E** 🅟 Exxon/dsl, Liberty/dsl 🍽 Arby's, Arnold's Rest., Bojangles, Burger King, Cape Fear BBQ, Capt D's, CiCi's Pizza, Cook Out, Hardee's, Hong Kong Chinese, Kami Japanese, KFC, Little Caesar's, McDonald's, Shoney's, Sonic, Subway, Taco Bell, Tokyo Japanese, Tuscan Garden Italian, Village Sta. Rest., Waffle House 🛏 Deluxe Inn, EconoLodge, Howard Johnson 🅞 🏥, Advance Parts, AutoZone, Belk, city park, CVS Drug, Food Lion/deli, JC Penney, K-Mart, Nissan, O'Reilly Parts, Verizon, Walgreens, **W** 🅟 Marathon/dsl, Sun-do/dsl 🍽 Cracker Barrel, Fuller's BBQ Buffet, San Jose Mexican 🛏 Best Value Inn, Comfort Inn, Country Inn&Suites, Days Inn/rest., Fairfield Inn, Quality Inn
19	Carthage Rd, Lumberton, **E** 🅟 BP 🛏 Rodeway Inn, **W** 🅟 Valero/dsl 🛏 Motel 6, Royal Inn
18mm	Lumber River
17	NC 72, Lumberton, Pembroke, **E** 🅟 Atkinson's/dsl, BP/dsl, Dobbs, Dobb's/dsl, Go-Gas/dsl 🍽 Burger King, Hardee's, Huddle House, Little China, McDonald's, Papa Bill's BBQ, Pizza Hut, Ruby Tuesday, Subway, Waffle House 🛏 Atkinson Inn, Budget Inn, Southern Inn, Southern Inn 🅞 $General, Advance Parts, AutoZone, CVS Drug, Family$, Food Lion, Walmart Mkt/dsl, **W** 🅞 Sleepy Bear's RV Park (3mi)
13	I-74, US 74, Rockingham, Wilmington, **E** 🅞 SE NC Beaches, U.S.S Wilmington
10	US 301, to Fairmont
7	to McDonald, Raynham
5mm	Welcome Ctr nb, full ♿ facilities, litter barrels, petwalk, 🕭, 🎰, vending
2	NC 130, to NC 904, Rowland
1b a	US 301, US 501, Dillon, **E** 🅟 Exxon, Mobil 🍽 Hot Tamale Rest., Peddler Steaks, Porky's Truckstp, Sombrero Rest.

(Left margin vertical labels: SMITHFIELD, DUNN; Right margin: LUMBERTON)

⬆🅽 INTERSTATE 95 Cont'd

Exit #	Services
1b a	Continued 🏨 Budget Motel, South of the Border Motel, South-of-the-Border Motel 🅾 Pedro's Campground, W 🅰 Shell/dsl 🍴 Waffle House 🏨 Night Inn, Super 8
0mm	North Carolina/South Carolina state line

⬆🅴 INTERSTATE 240 (Asheville)

Exit #	Services
9mm	I-240 begins/ends on I-40, exit 53b a.
8	Fairview Rd, N 🅰 Shell/dsl 🍴 Ay Carumba, Cheddar's, China Buffet, Coldstone, J&S Cafeteria, KFC, Little Caesar's, McDonald's, Papa John's, Subway 🏨 Ramada Inn 🅾 $General, Advance Parts, Aldi Foods, Bi-Lo Foods, CVS Drug, Discount Tire, Hamrick's, Hancock Fabrics, Kohl's, Petsmart, U-Haul, Walmart/McDonald's, S 🅰 Citgo 🍴 Pizza Hut 🅾 Home Depot
7.5mm	Swannanoa River
7	US 70, N 🅰 Enmark 🏨 Best Western 🅾 Hyundai, KIA, Subaru, S 🅰 Shell/dsl 🍴 Applebee's, Bonefish Grill, Buffalo Wild Wings, Burger King, Carrabba's, Chick-fil-A, Chili's, ChuckeCheese, Cici's Pizza, Cook Out, Cornerstone Rest., Cracker Barrel, DQ, Firehouse Subs, IHOP, Jersey Mike's Subs, Longhorn Steaks, McAlister's Deli, McDonald's, McDonald's, Mikado Japanese, O'Charley's, Olive Garden, Outback Steaks, Papa's Mexican, Red Lobster, Starbucks, Subway, Taco Bell, Waffle House, Wild Wok 🏨 Country Inn&Suites, Courtyard, Days Inn, EconoLodge, Extended Stay America, Hampton Inn, Holiday Inn, Homewood Suites, InTown Motor Inn, Mountaineer Inn, SpringHill Suites, Super 8 🅾 $Tree, AT&T, Barnes&Noble, Belk, Best Buy, BigLots, Clark Tire/auto, Dick's, Dillards, Firestone/auto, Ingles Foods/gas, JC Penney, Jo-Ann, Lowe's, Michael's, Midas, Office Depot, Old Navy, Ross, Sears/auto, Target, TJ Maxx, Walgreens, Whole Foods Mkt
6	Tunnel Rd (from eb), same as 7
5b	US 70 E, US 74A, Charlotte St, N 🅰 Exxon, Shell 🍴 Charlotte St. Grill, Fuddruckers, Starbucks, Two Guys Hogi 🏨 B&B 🅾 vet, S 🍴 Chop House Rest. 🏨 Renaissance Hotel, Sheraton 🅾 Civic Ctr
5a	US 25, Merrimon Ave, N 🅰 Enmark, Exxon/dsl, Shell/dsl 🍴 Bojangles, Chick-fil-A 🅾 Green Life Foods, Harris Teeter, Staples, Trader Joe's
4c	Haywood St (no EZ return to eb), Montford, S 🍴 Carmel's Rest., Isa's Bistro, Roman's Deli 🏨 B&B, Hotel Indigo 🅾 downtown
4b	Patton Ave (from eb), downtown
4a	US 19 N, US 23 N, US 70 W, to Weaverville
3b	Westgate, N 🍴 Green Sage Cafe, Jason's Deli, Oriental Pavillion 🏨 Crowne Plaza 🅾 CVS Drug, EarthFare Foods, Mr Transmission, Sam's Club/gas, Tuesday Morning
3a	US 19 S, US 23 S, W Asheville, N 🅰 Shell/dsl 🍴 A&W/LJ Silver, Bojangles, Burger King, CookOut, Denny's, Dragon China, El Que Pasa Mexican, Firehouse Subs, Green Tea Japanese, Jersey Mike's, KFC, Krispy Kreme, Little Caesar's, McDonald's, Neo Burrito, New 1 China, Papa John's, Pizza Hut, Sonic, Subway, Taco Bell, Wendy's, Yoshida Japanese, Zingers Cafe 🅾 $General, Advance Parts, Aldi Foods, AT&T, AutoZone, Clark Tire/auto, Ingles Foods, K-Mart, Radio Shack, Sav-Mor Foods, URGENT CARE, vet, Walgreens

2	US 19, US 23, W Asheville, N 🅰 Haywood Quickstop/dsl 🍴 Zia Mexican, S 🅾 B&B Drug
1c	Amboy Rd (from eb)
1b	NC 191, to I-40 E, Brevard Rd, S 🅾 camping, farmers mkt
1a	I-40 W, to Knoxville
0mm	I-240 begins/ends on I-40, exit 46b a.

⬆🅴 INTERSTATE 440 (Raleigh)

Exit #	Services
16	I-40
15	Poole Rd, E 🅰 Exxon 🍴 Quiznos, W 🅰 BP/dsl, Citgo/dsl 🍴 Burger King, Family$, Food Lion, KFC/Taco Bell, McDonald's, Subway
14	US 64, to Rocky Mount, limited access hwy
13b a	US 64, US 264 E, New Bern Ave, to Wilson, E 0-2 mi 🅰 76/Circle K, BP, Caroco/dsl, Exxon, Micro Mart, Murphy USA/dsl, Shell/dsl 🍴 Bojangles, Burger King, Golden Corral, Jumbo China, McDonald's, Papa John's, Quiznos, Roh Buffet, Ruby Tuesday, Starbucks, Subway, Waffle House, Wendy's 🏨 Best Western, Comfort Suites, Holiday Inn Express, Microtel, Super 8 🅾 Advance Parts, AutoZone, CVS Drug, Firestone/auto, Food Lion, Kroger, Office Depot, O'Reilly Parts, RV Ctr, U-Haul, Walgreens, Walmart, W 🅾 🅷
12	Yonkers Rd, Brentwood Rd
11b a	US 1, US 401, Capital Blvd N, N 🅰 BP, Citgo, Exxon, Kangaroo/dsl, Mobil, Shell 🍴 Baskin-Robbins/Dunkin Donuts, Buffalo Bro's, Burger King, ChuckeCheese, Cici's, Cookout, IHOP, Mayflower Seafood, McDonald's, Outback Steaks, Perkins, Taco Bell, Vallerta Mexican, Waffle House 🏨 Best Western, Days Inn, EconoLodge, Holiday Inn, Lodge America, Quality Inn, Sleep Inn, Super 8, Wingate Inn 🅾 Aamco, AutoZone, Food Lion, Pepboys, Rite Aid, U-Haul, Walgreens
10	Wake Forest Rd, N 🍴 Bahama Breeze, Denny's 🏨 Days Inn, Hilton, Homestead Suites, Hyatt Place 🅾 🅷, CVS Drug, S 🅰 BP 🍴 Applebee's, Arby's, Biscuitville, Burger King, Courtney's Cafe, Jersey Mike's, Jimmy John's, Jumbo China, KFC/Taco Bell, McDonald's, Melting Pot Rest., Papa John's, Pizza Hut, Qdoba, Quiznos, Subway 🏨 Courtyard, Extended Stay America, Hampton Inn, Studio+ 🅾 Advance Parts, AutoZone, Buick/GMC, Costco/gas, Curves, Discount Tire, Hancock Fabrics, Hyundai, Mazda, Nissan, Staples, Subaru, Trader Joe's, VW
8b a	6 Forks Rd, North Hills, N 🅰 Exxon/repair 🍴 5 Guys Burgers, Bonefish Grill, Chick-fil-A, Firebirds Grill, Fox&Hound Grille, Moe's SW Grill, Panera Bread, Pig Shack, Ruths Chris Steaks, Starbucks, Tiola Pizza, Zoe's Kitchen 🏨 Renaissance 🅾 AT&T, GNC, Harris Teeter, JC Penney, Kerr Drug, Target

⬆️Ⓔ INTERSTATE 440 (Raleigh) Cont'd

Exit #	Services
7b a	US 70, NC 50, Glenwood Ave, Crabtree Valley, N 🅖 BP, Shell 🍴 Brio Grill, Cheesecake Factory, Fleming's, McDonald's, PF Chang's 🏨 Crabtree Inn, Embassy Suites, Holiday Inn, Marriott, Residence Inn, Windsor Inn 🅞 Barnes&Noble, Belk, Best Buy, Just Tires, Macy's, mall, McCormick&Shmicks, Old Navy, Sears/auto
6	Ridge Rd (from nb), same as 7
5	Lake Boone Tr, W 🅖 Circle K 🍴 McDonald's, Starbucks, Subway, Wendy's 🅞 🏥 Food Lion, Tuesday Morning
4b a	to I-40 W, Wade Ave, to RDU
3	NC 54, Hillsboro St, E 🅖 BP, Exxon, Hugo's, Pure 🍴 Applebee's, Arby's, Bean Sprout Chinese, Burger King, Marco's Pizza, Quiznos, Snoopy's Hotdogs, Subway, Waffle House, Zaxby's 🅞 to Meredith Coll, to St Mary's, USPO
2b a	Western Blvd, E 🅖 76/Circle K, Hess, Hugo's 🍴 Bojangles, Cookout, Dunkin Donuts, Greek Fiesta, McDonalds, Pizza Hut, Subway, Taco Bell, Ten Ten Chinese, Wendy's 🅞 Advance Parts, BigLots, Food Lion, Shaw U, to NCSU, W 🅞 K-Mart
1d	Melbourne Rd (from sb)
1c	Jones-Franklin Rd
1b a	I-40. I-440 begins on I-40., W 1-2 mi on Walnut St 🅖 Exxon, Shell 🍴 Astor's Grill, Bob Evans, Chick-fil-A, China King, Coldstone, Cookout, Dickey's BBQ, Golden Corral, Honey-Baked Ham, Jasmin Bistro, McDonald's, Moe's SW Grill, Noodles&Co, Olive Garden, Panera Bread, Qdoba, Red Lobster, Red Robin, Remington Grill, Ruby Tuesday, Starbucks, Subway, Taco Bell, Waffle House 🏨 Best Western, Red Roof Inn 🅞 BJ's Whse, Ford, GNC, Home Depot, Jo-Ann Fabrics, Kohl's, Lowe's, mall, Marshall's, Michael's, NTB, Office Depot, Old Navy, PetsMart, Steinmart

⬆️N INTERSTATE 485 (Charlotte)

Exit #	Services
I-485 begins/ends	
67	I-77, US 21, to Charlotte, Columbia
65	South Blvd, N 🅖 Kangaroo 🍴 Chick-fil-A, Golden Corral, Hooters, McDonald's, Popeyes, Steak'n Shake, Wendy's 🅞 $Tree, Advance Parts, Big Lots, Chevrolet, Discount Tire, Honda, Jo-Ann, Kohl's, Nissan, Old Navy, Petsmart, Ross, Subaru, Target, Toyota/Scion, Verizon, VW, World Mkt, S 🍴 Arby's 🅞 Cadillac, CarMax, Mercedes, NAPA, TreadQtrs Auto/tire, vet
64b a	rd 51, N 🅖 Exxon/dsl, Shell/Circle K/dsl 🍴 Bojangles, Chili's, CiCi's, CookOut, Firehouse Subs, Jimmy John's, K&W Cafeteria, KFC, McDonald's, Outback Steaks, Pizza Hut, Starbucks, Wendy's 🏨 Extended Stay America 🅞 🏥 Aldi Foods, AutoZone, Bi-Lo, Family$, Firestone/auto, S 🅖 Kangaroo, Shell/7-11 🍴 Applebee's, Buca Italian, Burger King, Capt D's, China Buffet, Harper's Rest., IHOP, Jason's Deli, Longhorn Steaks, McAlister's Deli, Olive Garden, Red Lobster, Sky Asian, Subway, Taco Bell 🏨 Comfort Suites, Hampton Inn, Hilton Garden, Holiday Inn Express, Quality Inn 🅞 $General, Barnes&Noble, Belk, Best Buy, Dick's, Dillard's, Food Lion, Home Depot, JC Penney, K-Mart, Macy's, Meineke, Midas, Office Depot, REI, Rite Aid, Sam's Club/gas, Sears/auto, SteinMart, Tire Kingdom, TJ Maxx
61b a	US 521 S, Johnston Rd, N 🍴 Global Rest., Hickory Tavern, Red Robin, Ruby Tuesday, Sticky Fingers, Viva Chicken 🏨 Homewood Suites, SpringHill Suites 🅞 Earth Fare Foods,

Exit #	Services
61b a	Continued S 🅖 Kangaroo/dsl 🍴 5 Guys Burgers, Duckworth's Grill, Mellow Mushroom Rest., Pei Wei, Starbucks, Stone Mtn Grill, Subway, Tony's Pizza, Vine American Kitchen 🏨 Ballantyne Hotel, Courtyard, Staybridge Suites 🅞 CVS Drug
59	Rea Rd, E 🅖 Exxon/7-11 🍴 1511 Cantina, Applebee's, Boneheads Grill, Chick-fil-A, City Tavern, Firebirds Grill, Marble Slab, Noodles Rest., Qdoba, Smashburger, Starbucks, True Pizza, Wendy's 🏨 Residence Inn 🅞 GNC, Goodyear/auto, Harris-Teeter, Michaels, Radio Shack, Target, vet
57	Providence Rd, rd 16, E 🅖 Kangaroo/Wendy's 🍴 Hickory Tavern, Ilios Noche, Papa John's, Penn Sta, The Wok 🅞 Harris-Teeter, USPO, W 🅖 Exxon/7-11, Shell 🍴 BBQ Shack, BT Burgers, Macaroni Grill, On the Border, Red Bowl Rest., Showmars Rest., Starbucks, Subway, Wolfman Pizza 🅞 CVS Drug, Harris-Teeter, Home Depot, Lowes Whse, Rite Aid, Staples, SteinMart, vet
52	E John St, to Matthews
51b a	US 74, to Charlotte, Monroe, E 🅖 Circle K/dsl, Shell/dsl 🏨 Country Inn&Suites, InTown Suites, Quality Inn 🅞 Country Camping RV Ctr, Toyota/Scion, W 🅖 Citgo/dsl, Exxon/7-11, Shell 🍴 Bojangles, Pizza Hut, TX Roadhouse, Wendy's 🏨 Courtyard, EconoLodge, Microtel 🅞 🏥 Aamco, AutoZone, Best Buy, Costco/gas, Firestone/auto, Goodyear/auto, Goodyear/auto, Lowe's Whse, Radio Shack, Sam's Club/gas, Target, Tuesday Morning
49	Idlewild Rd, E 🅖 Exxon/7-11/dsl 🍴 Cactus Rose Mexican, China Cafe, Mama's Pizza 🅞 $Tree, GNC, Harris-Teeter, Meineke, Rite Aid
47	Lawyers Rd, E 🅖 Gate/dsl 🍴 Bellacino's Pizza, Best China, Carnita's Mexican, Domino's, McDonald's, Subway 🅞 CVS Drug, Firestone/auto, Harris-Teeter, vet
44	rd 218, to Mint Hill, W 🅖 BP/dsl, Shell/7-11 🅞 $General, city park, CVS
43	rd 51, to Mint Hill
41	rd 24, rd 27, to Albemarle, E 🅖 Hess/dsl 🍴 Bojangles
39	Harrisburg Rd, W 🅖 BP 🍴 China Garden, Papa John's, Wendy's 🅞 Food Lion
36	Rocky River Rd, N 🅖 Citgo/dsl, Gate/dsl 🍴 Best China, Bojangles, Capriccio Pizza, Subway 🅞 CVS Drug, Discount Tire, GNC, Harris-Teeter, Tuffy Auto
33	rd 49, to Harrisburg, E 🅞 USPO, W 🍴 Arby's, Chopsticks, Domino's, N 🅖 Hess/dsl 🍴 Cici's Pizza 🅞 Food Lion, S 🅖 BP, Circle K/dsl, Exxon/7-11, Shell/7-11/dsl 🍴 Little Caesar's, Wendy's 🅞 Family$
32	US 29, N 🅞 CVS Drug, S 🅖 Exxon/7-11/dsl, Hess/dsl, Kangaroo 🍴 Jack-in-the-Box 🅞 🏥 Tire Kingdom
30b a	I-85, N to High Point, S to Charlotte
23c	rd 115, to Huntersville, N 🅖 Shell/7-11/dsl 🅞 Audi, BMW, Lexus, Mercedes, Walmart
23b a	I-77, to Charlotte, Statesville
21	rd 24, Harris Blvd, S 🍴 5 Guys Burgers, Bravo Italian, Buffalo Wild Wings, Chick-fil-A, Chili's, East Coast Grill, Edomae Grill, Firebirds Grill, Firehouse Subs, Fox&Hound, Jersey Mike's, McDonald's, Mimi's Cafe, Moe's SW Grill, Olive Garden, On-the-Border, Panera bread, PF Chang's, Red Robin, Shane's Rib Shack, TGI Friday's, Wendy's 🏨 Drury Inn 🅞 $Tree, AT&T, Belk, Best Buy, Dick's, Dillard's, Discount Tire, Lowe's Whse, Macy's, mall, Old Navy, Petsmart, REI, Target, Verizon
16	rd 16, to Newton, Brookshire Blvd, E 🅞 city park, W 🍴 Bojangles, Bull&Barrister Grille, Chick-fil-A, Domino's, Los Arcos, McDonald's, Papa John's, Pizza Hut, Red Bowl Asian, Subway, Wendy's 🅞 AT&T, AutoZone, Harris-Teeter, Rite Aid, URGENT CARE, vet, Walmart/Subway

⬆️N   INTERSTATE 485 (Charlotte)

Exit #	Services
14	rd 27, to Mt Holly Rd, **W** 🅖 BP (2mi) 🍴 Sonic (2mi) 🅞 Food Lion (2mi), Meineke (2mi)
12	Moores Chapel Rd, **E** 🍴 Jin Jin Chinese, Subway 🅞 Advance Parts, CVS Drug, Family$, Food Lion
10b a	I-85, to Spartanburg, Greensboro
9	US 29, US 74, Wilkinson Blvd, **S** 🅖 BP 🅞 camping
6	West Blvd
4	rd 160, to Fort Mill, **N** 🅖 Exxon/7-11/dsl 🅞 CVS Drug, **S** 🅖 BP/dsl 🍴 Bojangles 🅞 Charlotte Premium Outlets/famous brands
3	Arrowood Rd, **S** 🍴 Quizno's, Siam Garden

1 — S Tryon St, NC 49, **N** 🅖 Citgo, Exxon/7-11 🍴 Arby's, Bojangles, Chick-fil-A, Chili's, Dragon Buffet, IHOP, Lenny's Subs, Luigi's Pizza, McDonald's, O'Charley's, Panera Bread, Qdoba, Showmars Rest., Waffle House, Zaxby's 🅞 Family$, GNC, Lowe's Whse, Radio Shack, Rite Aid, Walmart, **S** 🅖 Kangaroo/dsl, QT/dsl 🍴 Mac's BBQ, Applebee's, Baskin-Robbins/Dunkin Donuts, Burger King, Domino's, Don Pedro Mexican, Firehouse Subs, Fortune Cookie, Hungry Howie's, Joe Momma's Pizza, KFC, McAlister's Deli, Pan China, Portofino's, Starbucks, Subway, Taco Bell, Wild Wing Cafe 🏠 Hilton Garden, Homewood Suites 🅞 $Tree, AT&T, AutoZone, Discount Tire, Food Lion, NAPA, Office Depot, Tire Kingdom, Tuffy Auto, URGENT CARE

NORTH DAKOTA

⬆️N   INTERSTATE 29

Exit #	Services
218mm	North Dakota state line, US/Canada border
217mm	US Customs sb
216mm	historical site nb, tourist info sb
215	ND 59, rd 55, Pembina, **E** 🅖 Gastrak/DutyFree Store/dsl, Gastrak/pizza/dsl/scales/24hr 🅞 Pembina State Museum/info
212	no services
208	rd 1, to Bathgate
203	US 81, ND 5, to Hamilton, Cavalier, 🅞 to Icelandic SP (25 mi), **weigh sta both lanes**
200	no services
196	rd 3, Bowesmont
193	no services
191	rd 11, to St Thomas
187	ND 66, to Drayton, **E** 🅖 Cenex/pizza/dsl/E-85, Tesoro/dsl 🏠 Motel 66 🅞 city park, Drayton Drug, USPO
184	to Drayton, **E 2 mi** 🅖 gas/dsl 🅞 USPO
180	rd 9
179mm	🆁🆂 both lanes (both lanes exit left), full ♿ facilities, litter barrels, petwalk, 🚰, 🐾, vending
176	ND 17, to Grafton, **W 10 mi** 🅖 🍴 food 🏠 AmericInn 🅞 Ⓗ
172	no services
168	rd 15, to Minto, Warsaw

164	no services
161	ND 54, rd 19, to Ardoch, Oslo
157	no services
152	US 81, to Gilby, Manvel, **W** 🅖 Manvel/dsl/food
145	US 81 bus, N Washington St, to Grand Forks

G R A N D   F O R K S

141	US 2, Gateway Dr, Grand Forks, **E** 🅖 Cenex, Loaf'N Jug/dsl, Univ. Sta/dsl 🍴 Al's Grill, Burger King, DQ, Greatwall Buffet, Little Caesars, McDonald's, Northside Cafe, Papa Murphy's, Subway, Taco John's 🏠 Best Value Inn, Budget Inn, Clarion, EconoLodge, Howard Johnson, Ramada Inn, Select Inn, Super 8 🅞 Ⓗ, AT&T, auto repair, Ford/Lincoln, Freightliner, Hugo's Foods, Kia, O'Reilly Parts, Subaru, to U of ND, transmissions, U-Haul, **W** 🅖 Simonson/café/dsl/24hr, StaMart/Tesoro/dsl/RV dump/scales/24hr/@ 🍴 Perkins 🏠 Settle Inn 🅞 ♿, Budget RV Ctr, dsl repair, Mack/Volvo, NW Tire, to AFB
140	DeMers Ave, **E** 🅖 Cenex, Loaf'N Jug, Valley Dairy 🍴 Red Pepper Cafe 🏠 Canada Inn, Hilton Garden, Sleep Inn, Staybridge Suites 🅞 Ⓗ, Alerus Ctr, to U of ND
138	US 81, 32nd Ave S, **E** 🅖 Cenex, Holiday/dsl 🍴 5 Guys Burgers, Arby's, Buffalo Wild Wings, Burger King, Cherry Berry Yogurt, China Garden, Coldstone, Culver's, Golden Corral, Ground Round, IHOP, Jimmy John's, McDonald's, Noodles&Co, Olive Garden, Papa Murphy's, Pizza Hut, Pizza Ranch, Qdoba Mexican, Quiznos, Red Lobster,

🅝🅒 NC

⬆N INTERSTATE 29 Cont'd

Exit #	Services
138	Continued
	Ruby Tuesday, Space Alien's Rest, Starbucks, Subway, TX Roadhouse, Village Inn, Wendy's 🛏 C'mon Inn, Country Inn&Suites, Days Inn, Fairfield Inn, Holiday Inn Express, Lakeview Inn, Quality Inn, Roadking Inn, SpringHill Suites 🅞 $Tree, AT&T, Best Buy, Chrysler/Dodge/Jeep, CVS Drug, Ford/Lincoln, Gordman's, Hugo's Foods, JC Penney, Jo-Ann Fabrics, Kohl's, Lowe's, Macy's, Menards, Michael's, Old Navy, PetCo, Sam's Club/gas, Super 1 Foods, Target, Tire 1, Tires+, TJ Maxx, Toyota/Scion, Verizon, vet, Walmart/Subway, White Drug, **W** 🍴 ⊕FLYING J/Subway/dsl/LP/scales/RV dump/24hr 🅞 Grand Forks Camping
130	ND 15, rd 81, Thompson, **W 1 mi** 🅖🍴 food
123	to Reynolds, **E** 🅞 to Central Valley School
118	to Buxton
111	ND 200 W, to Cummings, Mayville, **W** 🅞 Big Top Fireworks, to Mayville St U
104	Hillsboro, **E** 🅖 Cenex/Burger King/dsl/LP/24hr, Tesoro/Stop-n-Go/dsl/24hr 🍴 Country Hearth Rest., Pizza Ranch, Subway 🛏 Hillsboro Inn 🅞 🏥, RV park, USPO
100	ND 200 E, ND 200A, to Blanchard, Halstad
99mm	🆁🆂 both lanes, full ♿ facilities, litter barrels, petwalk, 🅒, 🖼 vending
92	rd 11, Grandin, **W** 🅖 Stop&Shop/dsl
86	Gardner
78	Argusville
74.5mm	Sheyenne River
72	rd 17, rd 22, Harwood, **E** 🅖 Cenex/pizza/dsl/LP/café/24hr
69	rd 20
67	US 81 bus, 19th Ave N, **E 1 mi** 🍴 Applebee's, Buffalo Wild Wings, Burger King, McDonald's, Subway, Taco Bell 🛏 Candlewood Suites, Days Inn, Homewood Suites 🅞 CVS Drug, Hector Int ✈, VA 🏥
66	12th Ave N, **E** 🅖 StaMart/Tesoro/dsl/24hr/scales, Stop'n Go 🅞 🏥, to ND St U, truck wash, **W** 🅖 Cenex/dsl 🍴 Arby's 🛏 Super 8
65	US 10, Main Ave, W Fargo, **E** 🅖 Tesoro/dsl 🅞 NAPA, OK Tire, True Value, vet, **W** 🅖 Cenex/Subway/dsl, Simonson's/dsl 🍴 Hardee's, O'Kelly's Rest, Season Buffet Chinese 🛏 Kelly Inn 🅞 CarQuest, Honda, Lincoln, Mac's Hardware, Mazda, O'Reilly Parts, Recreation RV Ctr, Subaru, Toyota/Scion
64	13th Ave, Fargo, **E** 🅖 All-Stop, Don's, Kum&Go/dsl, PetroServe/dsl 🍴 Acapulco Mexican, Applebee's, Arby's, Buck's Rest, Burger King, ChuckeCheese, Dickey's BBQ, DQ, Erbert&Gerbert's Subs, Giant Panda Chinese, Green-Mill Rest., Ground Round, Hooters, Little Caesars, Perkins, Quiznos, Subway, Taco John's, Wendy's 🛏 AmericInn, Best Western, Comfort Inn, Comfort Suites, Country Inn&Suites, Days Inn, EconoLodge, Grand Inn, Motel 6, Super 8 🅞 AT&T, auto repair, CashWise Foods/drug/gas, CVS Drug, Family$, Goodyear/auto, O'Reilly Parts, Tires+/transmissions, Tuesday Morning, White Drug, **W** 🍴 All-Stop/dsl, Cenex, Tesoro 🍴 Applebee's, Arby's, Buffalo Wild Wings, Chili's, Culver's, Denny's, Domino's, DQ, Happy Joe's Pizza, KFC, Kobe Japanese, Kroll's Diner, LoneStar Steaks, Longhorn Steaks, McDonald's, Olive Garden, Osaka Japanese, Panchero's Mexican, Paradiso Mexican, Pizza Hut, Red Lobster, Ruby Tuesday, Santa Lucia Cafe, Schlotzsky's, Spitfire Grill, Subway, Taco Bell, Taco John's, TGIFriday's, TX Roadhouse 🛏 Days Inn, EconoLodge, Fairfield Inn, Fargo Inn, Holiday Inn,

Exit #	Services
64	Continued
	Holiday Inn Express, Kelly Inn, Ramada Inn, Red River Lodge 🅞 $Tree, Audi/VW, Barnes&Noble, Best Buy, BigLots, Cadillac/Chevrolet, Chrysler/Dodge/Jeep, GNC, Gordman's, Herberger's, Hobby Lobby, Hornbacher's Foods, Hyundai, JC Penney, Jo-Ann Fabrics, Kohl's, Lowe's, Macy's, Menards, Michael's, Nissan, Office Depot, Old Navy, PetCo, Petsmart, Sam's Club/gas, Sears/auto, SunMart Foods, Target, TJ Maxx, USPO, Walgreens, Walmart/Subway.
63b a	I-94, W to Bismarck, E to Minneapolis
62	32nd Ave S, Fargo, **E** 🅖 F&F/dsl, Holiday, Tesoro 🍴 Arby's, Country Kitchen, Culver's, Jimmy John's, KFC, Little Caesars, Moe's SW Grill, Papa John's, Quiznos, Starbucks, Subway, Taco John's, Village Inn 🅞 🏥, Buick/GMC, Ford, Freightliner, JiffyLube, SunMart Foods, Verizon, **W** 🅖 ⊕FLYING J /dsl/LP/scales/24hr/@, 🅻🅾🆅🅴🆂 /McDonald's/Subway/dsl/scales/24hr 🛏 Motel 6 🅞 Fargo Tire/repair, Peterbilt, Volvo
60	52nd Ave S, to Fargo, **W** 🅞 Walmart/Subway
56	to Wild Rice, Horace
54	rd 16, to Oxbow, Davenport
50	rd 18, Hickson
48	ND 46, to Kindred
44	to Christine, **E 1 mi** 🅖
42	rd 2, to Walcott
37	rd 4, to Abercrombie, Colfax, **E** 🅞 to Ft Abercrombie HS, **W 1 mi** 🅖
31	rd 8, Galchutt
26	to Dwight
24mm	weigh sta both lanes exit left
23b a	ND 13, to Wahpeton, Mooreton, **E 10 mi** 🅞 🏥, ND St Coll of Science
15	rd 16, to Mantador, Great Bend
8	ND 11, to Hankinson, Fairmount, **E** 🅖 Tesoro/dsl, **W 3 mi** 🅞 camping
3mm	Welcome Ctr nb, full ♿ facilities, litter barrels, petwalk, 🅒, 🖼
2	rd 22
1	rd 1E, **E** 🅞 Dakota Magic Casino/Hotel/rest./gas/dsl
0mm	North Dakota/South Dakota state line

⬆E INTERSTATE 94

Exit #	Services
352mm	North Dakota/Minnesota state line, Red River
351	US 81, Fargo, **N** 🅖 Loaf'n Jug, Stop'n Go 🍴 Duane's Pizza, Great Harvest Breads, Great Wall Chinese, Taco Shop 🅞 🏥 Hornbacher's Foods, Medicine Shoppe, Verizon, vet, **S** 🅖 Stop'n Go, Tesoro/dsl 🍴 A&W/LJ Silver, Burger King, Happy Joe's Pizza, McDonald's, Pepper's Café, Randy's Diner, Subway, Taco Bell 🛏 Rodeway Inn, Vista Inn 🅞 Hornbacher's/gas, K-Mart, O'Reilly Parts, USPO
350	25th St, Fargo, **N** 🅖 Stop'n Go, **S** 🅖 Cenex/dsl, Loaf'n Jug/dsl 🍴 Dolittle's Grill, Ruby Tuesday
349b a	I-29, N to Grand Forks, S to Sioux Falls, exit 64, **services 1 mi N**
348	45th St, **N 0-2 mi** Visitor Ctr/full facilities, litter barrels, 🖼 🅖 Holiday/dsl, Petro/dsl/Lp/24hrs/@ 🍴 Carino's, Coldstone, Culver's, Denny's, Dunn Bros Coffee, HuHot Mongolian, IHOP, Kroll's Diner, Little Caesar's, Longhorn Steaks, McDonald's, Noodles&Co, Papa Murphy's, Pizza Hut, Qdoba, Quaker Steak, Quiznos, Smashburger, Space Aliens Grill, Subway, Wendy's 🛏 Best Western, C'Mon Inn, Expressway Suites, Hilton Garden, MainStay Suites, Ramada Inn,

ND

FARGO (I-29 column, vertical)

FARGO (I-94 column, vertical)

INTERSTATE 94 Cont'd

Exit #	Services
348	Continued
	Red Roof Inn, Staybridge Suites, Wingate Inn ⊙ Blue Beacon, Hobby Lobby, Home Depot, Kohl's, NAPA, Office Depot, Old Navy, Sam's Club, Scheel's Sports, Target, Tuffy Auto, Verizon, Walmart, **S** ⛽ Holiday, Stop'n Go, Tesoro/DQ/dsl 🍽 5 Guys Burgers, Applebee's, Famous Dave's BBQ, Golden Corral, Hardee's, Korean BBQ, Mexican Village, Old Chicago Pizza, Pizza Ranch, Taco John's, Taco Shop 🛏 Arbuckle Lodge, Comfort Suites, Hampton Inn, La Quinta, Residence Inn, Sleep Inn ⊙ AT&T, Gander Mtn, Red River Zoo
347	9th St E, Veterans Blvd, **S** ⛽ Stop-N-Go/dsl 🍽 Taco Bell ⊙ Costco/gas
346b a	to Horace, W Fargo, **S** ⛽ repair, Tesoro/dsl
343	US 10, Lp 94, W Fargo, **N** ⛽ Cenex/dsl 🛏 Sunset Motel ⊙ Adventure RV Ctr, Harley-Davidson, Pioneer Village
342mm	**weigh sta wb**
342	no services
340	to Kindred
338	Mapleton, **N** ⛽ Tesoro/dsl
337mm	**truck parking wb, litter barrels**
331	ND 18, to Leonard, Casselton, **N** ⛽ Tesoro/Subway/dsl 🍽 Country Kitchen 🛏 Days Inn/RV park ⊙ NAPA, repair
328	to Lynchburg
327mm	**truck parking eb, litter barrels**
324	Wheatland, to Chaffee
322	Absaraka
320	to Embden
317	to Ayr
314	ND 38 N, to Alice, Buffalo, **N 3 mi** ⛽ 🍽
310	no services
307	to Tower City, **N** ⛽ Cenex/café/dsl/RV Park/24hr, motel
304mm	🅟🅢 **both lanes (both lanes exit left), full** ♿ **facilities, info, litter barrels, petwalk, ⊙, 🔧, vending**
302	ND 32, to Fingal, Oriska, **N 1 mi** ⊙ city park
298	no services
296	no services
294	Lp 94, to Kathryn, Valley City, **N** ⊙ 🄷, camping
292	Valley City, **N** ⛽ Tesoro/café/dsl 🍽 Sabir's Rest. 🛏 AmericInn, Super 8, Wagon Wheel Inn/rest. ⊙ 🄷, camping, to Bald Hill Dam, **S** ⊙ Ft Ransom SP (35mi)
291	Sheyenne River
290	Lp 94, Valley City, **N** ⛽ Tesoro/dsl 🍽 Burger King, Kenny's Rest., Roby's Rest., Subway ⊙ 🄷, Chrysler/Dodge/Jeep, Family$, Firestone/auto, Ford, NAPA, Radio Shack, ShopKo
288	ND 1 S, to Oakes, **S** ⊙ Fort Ransom SP (36 mi)
283	ND 1 N, to Rogers
281	to Litchville, Sanborn, **N 1-2 mi** ⛽ 🍽 🛏
276	Eckelson, **S** ⊙ Prairie Haven Camping/gas/dsl
275mm	continental divide, elev 1490
272	to Urbana
269	Spiritwood
262	Bloom, **N** ⊙ ⊙
260	Jamestown, **N** ⛽ Stop'n Go, Tesoro/café/dsl/@ 🛏 Starlite Motel ⊙ camping, to St 🄷
259mm	James River
258	US 52 W, US 281, Jamestown, **N** ⛽ Clark/TCBY/dsl, Tesoro/dsl 🍽 Arby's, DQ, Hardee's, McDonald's, Pizza Ranch, Subway, Taco Bell 🛏 Comfort Inn, Days Inn, Holiday Inn Express, Jamestown Motel ⊙ 🄷, Buffalo Herd/museum, Buick/Chevrolet/GMC, Firestone/auto, NW Tire, O'Reilly Parts, Toyota,

Exit #	Services
258	Continued
	vet, **S** ⛽ Shell/dsl 🍽 Applebee's, Burger King, Grizzly's Rest., Hong Kong Buffet, La Carreta Mexican, Paradiso Mexican, Perkins 🛏 EconoLodge, Hampton Inn, Quality Inn, Super 8 ⊙ $Tree, AT&T, Chrysler/Dodge/Jeep, Ford/Lincoln, GNC, Harley-Davidson, JC Penney, Mac's Hardware, mall, Radio Shack, Sears, USPO, vet, Walmart
257	Lp 94 (from eb, exits left), to Jamestown, **N** ⊙ dsl repair
256	US 52 W, US 281 N, **S 1 mi** ⊙ Jamestown Campground/RV dump, Wiest truck/trailer repair
254mm	🅟🅢 **both lanes, full** ♿ **facilities, litter barrels, petwalk, ⊙, 🔧, vending**
251	Eldridge
248	no services
245	no services
242	Windsor
238	to Gackle, Cleveland
233	no services
230	Medina, **N 1 mi** ⛽ Famer's Union/dsl/LP 🍽 DairyTreat ⊙ city park, Medina RV Park, USPO
228	ND 30 S, to Streeter
224mm	🅟🅢 **wb, full** ♿ **facilities, litter barrels, petwalk, ⊙, 🔧, vending**
221mm	🅟🅢 **eb, full** ♿ **facilities, litter barrels, petwalk, ⊙, 🔧, vending**
221	Crystal Springs
217	Pettibone
214	Tappen, **S** ⛽ gas/dsl/food
208	ND 3 S, Dawson, **N** ⊙ RV camping, **S 1/2 mi** ⛽ 🍽, ⊙ RV camping, to Camp Grassick
205	Robinson
200	ND 3 N, to Tuttle, Steele, **S** ⛽ Cenex/dsl 🍽 Beary Tweet&Tasty 🛏 OK Motel ⊙ truckwash
195	no services
190	Driscoll, **S** 🍽 food
182	US 83 S, ND 14, to Wing, Sterling, **S** ⛽ Cenex/dsl 🛏 Top's Motel (1mi)
176	McKenzie
170	Menoken, **S** ⊙ RV Park, to McDowell Dam
168mm	🅟🅢 **both lanes, full** ♿ **facilities, litter barrels, petwalk, ⊙, 🔧, vending, wifi**
161	Lp 94, Bismarck Expswy, Bismarck, **N** ⛽ Cenex/dsl/LP/24hr, Clark/dsl 🛏 My Place ⊙ Peterbilt, Toyota/Scion, **S** ⛽ Tesoro/Marlin's Rest./dsl/scales/24hr 🍽 McDonald's 🛏 Ramada Ltd ⊙ Capital RV Ctr, Dakota Zoo, dsl repair, Freightliner, Kenworth, OK Tires, truckwash, Volvo

B I S M A R C K

▲E INTERSTATE 94 Cont'd

Exit #	Services
159	US 83, Bismarck, N 🅿 Holiday/dsl, Simonson/dsl 🍴 Applebee's, Arby's, China Star, China Town, Golden Corral, Hooters, KFC, Kroll's Diner, Little Caesars, MacKenzie River Pizza, McDonald's, Olive Garden, Paradiso Mexican, Perkins, Pita Pit, Red Lobster, Ruby Tuesday, Space Alien Grill, Subway, Taco Bell, TCBY, Wendy's 🏠 AmericInn, Candlewood Suites, Comfort Inn, Comfort Suites, Country Suites, Fairfield Inn, Hampton Inn, Holiday Inn Express, Mainstay Suites, Motel 6, Residence Inn, Sleep Inn, Staybridge Suites, Wingate Inn Ⓞ AT&T, Chevrolet, CVS Drug, Dan's Foods, Hancock Fabrics, Hobby Lobby, Jo-Ann Fabrics, K-Mart, mall, Menards, NW Tire, Sears/auto, UHaul, USPO, Verizon, Walmart/Subway, S 🅿 PetroServe/dsl, Shell/dsl, Tesoro 🍴 Caspars Rest., DQ, Hardee's, Minerva's Rest., Pizza Hut, Schlotzsky's, Starbucks, Subway, Taco John's, Woodhouse Rest. 🏠 Best Value Inn, Days Inn, Kelly Inn, La Quinta, Ramada Inn, Super 8 Ⓞ 🅷, O'Reilly Parts
157	Divide Ave, Bismarck, N 🅿 Shell/dsl 🍴 5 Guys Burgers, Carino's, Coldstone, Cracker Barrel, Goodtimes Grill/Taco John's, Jimmy John's, McDonald's, Pancheros Mexican, Starbucks, Subway, TX Roadhouse, Wendy's Ⓞ $Tree, AT&T, Best Buy, GNC, Kohls, Lowe's, Old Navy, Petsmart, TJ Maxx, Verizon, visitor ctr, S 🅿 Cenex/dsl/E85/LP/RV Dump 🍴 Stadium Café 🏠 Hampton Inn Ⓞ Central Mkt Foods
156mm	Missouri River
156	I-194, Bismarck Expswy, Bismarck City Ctr, S 1/2 mi Ⓞ Dakota Zoo
155	to Lp 94 (exits left from wb), Mandan, City Ctr, same as 153
153	ND 1806, Mandan Dr, Mandan, S 1/2 mi 🅿 Cenex/dsl, PetroServe/dsl, Tesoro 🍴 Bonanza, Burger King, Dakota Farms Rest., Domino's, DQ, Hardee's, Papa Murphy's, Pizza Hut, Pizza Ranch, Subway, Taco John's 🏠 North Country Inn Ⓞ Central Mkt Foods, Chevrolet, Dacotah Centennial Park, Family$, Ft Lincoln SP (5mi), Goodyear/auto, NAPA, NW Tire, O'Reilly Parts, Subaru, Verizon
152mm	scenic view eb
152	Sunset Dr, Mandan, N 🅿 Tesoro 🍴 MT Mike's Steaks 🏠 Best Western, Walmart, S 🅿 Tesoro/RV dump 🍴 Fried's Rest. Ⓞ 🅷
147	ND 25, to ND 6, Mandan, S 🅿 Tesoro/Subway/cafe/dsl/scales/24hr
140	to Crown Butte
135mm	**scenic view wb, litter barrel**
134	to Judson, Sweet Briar Lake
127	ND 31 N, to New Salem, N Ⓞ Knife River Indian Village (35mi), S 🅿 Cenex/dsl, Tesoro/dsl 🍴 Sunset Cafe 🏠 Arrowhead Inn/café Ⓞ DFC/dsl, Food Pride, Gaebe Drug, vet, World's Largest Cow
123	to Almont
120	no services
119mm	🅿ˢ **both lanes, full ♿ facilities, litter barrels, petwalk, Ⓞ, 🏠**
117	no services
113	no services
110	ND 49, to Glen Ullin
108	to Glen Ullin, Lake Tschida, S 3 mi 🅿, 🍴, 🏠, Ⓞ camping
102	Hebron, to Glen Ullin, to Lake Tschida, S 3 mi 🅿, 🍴, 🏠, Ⓞ camping
97	Hebron, N 2 mi 🅿, 🍴, 🏠
96.5mm	central/mountain time zone

D I C K I N S O N

90	no services
84	ND 8, Richardton, N 🅿 Cenex/dsl Ⓞ 🅷, Schnell RA, to Assumption Abbey
78	to Taylor
72	to Enchanted Hwy, Gladstone
64	Dickinson, S 🅿 Cenex/Tiger Truckstop/rest./dsl/24hr, Dakota Diner, 🍴, Ⓞ dsl repair, Ford/Lincoln, Honda, NW Tire, Toyota/Scion
61	ND 22, Dickinson, N 🅿 Cenex/dsl/LP, Simonson/dsl 🍴 Applebee's, Arby's, Bonanza, Burger King, DQ, El Sombrero Mexican, Papa Murphy's, Pizza Ranch, Sakura Japanese, Sanford's Rest., Taco Bell, Taco John's, Wendy's 🏠 AmericInn, Astoria Suites, Best Western, Comfort Inn, Hampton Inn, Holiday Inn Express, Microtel, My Place, Ramada, Savannah Suites Ⓞ AT&T, Chevrolet, Dan's Foods, Goodyear/auto, Herberger's, JC Penney, K-Mart, Midas, O'Reilly Parts, Runnings Hardware, USPO, Verizon, Walmart/Subway, White Drug, S 🅿 Cenex/dsl, Conoco/repair, Holiday/dsl, Tesoro/dsl 🍴 A&W/KFC, Country Kitchen, Domino's, Don Pedro's Mexican, King Buffet, McDonald's, Perkins, Subway 🏠 La Quinta, Quality Inn, Relax Inn, Select Inn, Super 8 Ⓞ 🅷, Mac's Hardware, museum, visitor info
59	Lp 94, to Dickinson, N 🏠 Extended Stay, ValuePlace, S Ⓞ camping, to Patterson Lake RA, services in Dickinson
51	South Heart
42	US 85, to Grassy Butte, Belfield,Williston, N 🅿 MVP/dsl Ⓞ T Roosevelt NP (52mi), S 🅿 Cenex/dsl/24hr, Conoco/dsl 🍴 DQ, Trapper's Kettle Rest. 🏠 Trapper's Inn Ⓞ info, NAPA
36	Fryburg
32	T Roosevelt NP
27	Lp 94, Ⓞ Historic Medora (from wb), T Roosevelt NP
24.5mm	Little Missouri Scenic River
24	Medora, Historic Medora, S Ⓞ visitors ctr, Chateau de Mores HS, T Roosevelt NP
23	West River Rd (from wb)
22mm	scenic view eb
18	Buffalo Gap, N 🍴, 🏠, Ⓞ Buffalo Gap Camping (seasonal)
10	Sentinel Butte, Camel Hump Lake, S 🅿 gas
7	Home on the Range
1mm	**weigh sta eb, litter barrel**
1	ND 16, S 🅿 ⓕFLYING J/Subway/dsl/scales/LP/24hr, Cenex/dsl/LP/24hr 🏠 Buckboard Inn Ⓞ 🅷, Beach RV Park **Welcome/Visitor Ctr, full ♿ facilities, litter barrels, petwalk,** 🏠
0mm	North Dakota/Montana state line

OHIO

▲E INTERSTATE 70

Exit #	Services
225.5mm	Ohio/West Virginia state line, Ohio River
225	US 250 W, OH 7, Bridgeport, N 🅿 Marathon, StarFire, Sunoco/dsl 🍴 DQ, Papa John's, Pizza Hut, Wendy's (1mi) Ⓞ Advance Parts, AutoZone, Family$, Meineke, NAPA, S 🅿 Clark, Exxon, Gulf 🍴 Domino's
220	US 40, rd 214, N 🅿 Marathon, Sunoco/dsl 🍴 Mehlman Cafe 🏠 Comfort Inn, S 🏠 Days Inn Ⓞ vet
219	I-470 E, to Bel-Aire, Washington PA, (from eb)
218	Mall Rd, to US 40, to Blaine, N 🅿 BP, Exxon/dsl 🍴 Applebee's, Arby's, Buffalo Wild Wings, Burger King, DeFelice Pizza, Denny's, Eat'n Park, HoneyBaked Ham, King Buffet, Little Caesars, Outback Steaks, Pizza Hut, Red Lobster, Starbucks,

🅖 = gas 🍴 = food 🛏 = lodging Ⓞ = other 🆁🆂 = rest stop

BLAINE

◆E INTERSTATE 70 Cont'd

Exit #	Services
218	Continued Steak'n Shake, Taco Bell, Tlaque-paque Mexican, W Texas Steaks, Wendy's 🛏 Best Value Inn, EconoLodge, Hampton Inn, Holiday Inn Express, Microtel, Red Roof Inn, Super 8 Ⓞ $General, $Tree, AAA, Aldi Foods, AT&T, AutoZone, Buick/Cadillac/Chevrolet, Kroger, Lowe's, Sam's Club, Staples, Stewarts RV Ctr, URGENT CARE, Verizon, Walmart/McDonald's, S 🍴 Bob Evans, Bonanza, Cracker Barrel, Garfield's Rest., KFC/LJ Silver, Longhorn Steaks, McDonald's, Osaka Steaks, Panera Bread, Starbucks 🛏 Fairfield Inn Ⓞ Chrysler/Dodge/Jeep, Elder-Beerman, JC Penney, JoAnn Fabrics, K-Mart, Macy's, mall, NTB, Sears/auto

216	OH 9, St Clairsville, N 🅖 BP
215	National Rd, N 🍴 Burger King, Domino's, WenWu Chinese Ⓞ NAPA, Riesbeck's Foods, USPO
213	OH 331, Flushing, S 🅖 BP, Marathon/Subway/dsl, Sunoco/dsl
211mm	🆁🆂 both lanes, full 🛏 facilities, litter barrels, petwalk, 🚻, 🍴 vending
208	OH 149, Morristown, N 🅖 Exxon/McDonald's/dsl 🍴 Schlepp's Rest. 🛏 Arrowhead Motel (1mi), Holiday Inn Express Ⓞ $General, Cannonball Speedway, Ford/Lincoln, S 🅖 Marathon/Quiznos/dsl Ⓞ Barkcamp SP, Harley-Davidson
204	US 40 E (from eb, no return), National Rd
202	OH 800, to Barnesville, S 🅖 202 Gas/dsl Ⓞ Ⓗ
198	rd 114, Fairview
193	OH 513, Middlebourne, N 🅖 BP, FuelMart/dsl Ⓞ fireworks
189mm	🆁🆂 eb, full 🛏 facilities, litter barrels, petwalk, 🚻, 🍴 vending
186	US 40, OH 285, to Old Washington, N 🅖 BP, S 🅖 GoMart/dsl, Speedway/dsl/scales/24hr
180b a	I-77 N, to Cleveland, to Salt Fork SP, I-77 S, to Charleston
178	OH 209, Cambridge, N 0-1 mi 🅖 Marathon/dsl, Sheetz/dsl, Starfire/dsl 🍴 Bob Evans, China Village, Coldstone/Tim Hortons, Cracker Barrel, Denny's, DQ, Forum Rest, KFC, McDonald's, Papa John's, Pizza Hut, Ruby Tuesday, Subway, Wendy's 🛏 Comfort Inn, Days Inn, EconoLodge, Hampton Inn, Holiday Inn Express, Microtel, Southgate Hotel Ⓞ Ⓗ $General, Advance Parts, AutoZone, BigLots, Buick/Cadillac/GMC, Family$, Riesbecks Foods, Verizon, S 🅖 Murphy USA/dsl, 🚚🚚🚚/Subway/dsl/scales/24hr 🍴 Arby's, Burger King,

CAMBRIDGE

ZANESVILLE

178	Continued Great Chinese, Little Caesars, Taco Bell, Tlaquepaque Mexican 🛏 Baymont Inn Ⓞ $Tree, $Zone, Aldi Foods, K-Mart/gas, Radio Shack, Spring Valley RV Park, Verizon, Walmart/Subway
176	US 22, US 40, to Cambridge, N 🅖 Sunoco/dsl 🛏 Budget Inn Ⓞ RV camping, st patrol, Western Shop
173mm	weigh sta both lanes
169	OH 83, to Cumberland, New Concord, N Ⓞ John&Annie Glen Historic Site, RV camping, to Muskingum Coll
164	US 22, US 40, Norwich, N 🅖 BP 🛏 Baker's Motel, Zane Gray Museum, S Ⓞ antiques, pottery
163mm	🆁🆂 wb, full 🛏 facilities, litter barrels, petwalk, 🚻, 🍴 vending
160	OH 797, 🛻 Rd, N 🅖 ♥Loves/Arby's/dsl/scales/24hr, S 🅖 BP, Exxon/Subway/dsl 🍴 Denny's, McDonald's, Wendy's 🛏 Best Value Inn, Best Western, Ramada Inn Ⓞ🛻, st patrol
157	OH 93, Zanesville, N 🅖 BP, S 🅖 Marathon, Shell/dsl, st patrol
155	OH 60, OH 146, Underwood St, Zanesville, N 🍴 Bob Evans, Olive Garden, Oriental Buffet, Red Lobster, Steak'n Shake, Tumbleweed Grill 🛏 Comfort Inn, Fairfield Inn, Hampton Inn, Holiday Inn Express Ⓞ Ⓗ Pick'n Save Foods, USPO, visitor info, S 🅖 Exxon/dsl 🍴 Adornetto Pizza, Cracker Barrel, Subway, Wendy's 🛏 Baymont Inn, EconoLodge, Travelodge Ⓞ Rite Aid
154	5th St (from eb)
153mm	Licking River

OH

Exit #	Services
INTERSTATE 70 Cont'd	
153b	Maple Ave (no EZ return from wb), N 🅖 BP 🍴 DQ, Italian Eatery, Papa John's, Tee Jaye's Rest 🅞 🏥 CVS Drug, Family$
153a	State St, N 🅖 Speedway/dsl 🅞 to Dillon SP (8mi), S 🅖 Marathon
152	US 40, National Rd, N 🅖 Exxon/A&W/Blimpie/dsl, Starfire/dsl 🍴 McDonald's 🏠 Super 8
142	US 40 (from wb, no EZ return), Gratiot, N 🅞 RV camping
141	OH 668, US 40 (from eb, no return), to Gratiot, same as 142
132	OH 13, to Thornville, Newark, N 🅞 Dawes Arboretum (3mi), S 🅖 BP, Shell 🍴 Subway (2mi) 🅞 RV camping
131mm	🆁🆂 both lanes, full ♿ facilities, litter barrels, petwalk, 🚻, 🆖 vending
129b a	OH 79, to Buckeye Lake, Hebron, N 🏠 Best Western, S 🅖 BP, Valero 🍴 Donato's Pizza, McDonald's, Pizza Hut/Taco Bell, Wendy's 🏠 Super 8 🅞 Blue Goose Marina (2mi), CarQuest, KOA (2mi)
126	OH 37, to Granville, Lancaster, N 🅖 Marathon/dsl, 🏪 Chester's/Subway/dsl/scales/24hr, Sunoco/dsl, S 🅖 TA/BP/Popeye's/Sbarro's/dsl/scales/24hr/@, Valero/dsl 🏠 Deluxe Inn, Red Roof Inn 🅞 IA 80 Truckomat/truckwash, KOA
122	OH 158, to Baltimore, Kirkersville, N 🏠 Regal Inn, S 🅖 FLYING J/Denny's/dsl/LP/scales/24hr 🅞 fireworks
118	OH 310, to Pataskala, N 🅖 BP/McDonald's, Shell/dsl, Speedway/dsl 🍴 DQ, S 🅖 BP/Duke's/Subway/dsl 🅞 RCD RV Ctr
112c	OH 204, to Blecklick Rd (from eb)
112	OH 256, to Pickerington, Reynoldsburg, N 🅖 BP, Shell/McDonald's 🍴 5 Guys Burgers, Chipotle Mexican, Culver's, IHOP, Logan's Roadhouse, Noodles&Co, O'Charley's, Olive Garden, Panera Bread, Penn Sta, Rotolo's Pizza, Smokey Bones BBQ, Subway, TGIFriday's, Tim Horton's 🏠 Fairfield Inn, Holiday Inn Express 🅞 AT&T, Best Buy, Gander Mtn, Jo-Ann Fabrics, Marshall's, NTB, Radio Shack, Sam's Club/gas, Staples, Target, Tire Discounters, Verizon, Walgreens, Walmart/Subway, S 🅖 Speedway/dsl 🍴 Arby's, Bob Evans, CiCi's Pizza, Classic's Diner, Cold Stone, Cracker Barrel, Dragon China, Feta Greek Cafe, Graffiti Burger, Iron Chef, KFC, La Fogata Mexican, LJ Silver, Longhorn Steaks, Skyline Chili, Steak'n Shake, Uno, Wendy's 🏠 Best Western, Comfort Inn, Hampton Inn 🅞 Barnes&Noble, Kohl's, Kroger/E85, Tuesday Morning, URGENT CARE
110	Brice Rd, to Reynoldsburg, N 🅖 Speedway, Sunoco 🍴 Burger King, Donato's, Genji Japanese, Golden China, Popeye's, Subway, TeeJaye's Rest., Tim Horton's, Waffle House 🏠 Days Inn, Extended Stay America, La Quinta, Red Roof Inn, Super 8 🅞 BigLots, Goodyear/auto, Home Depot, O'Reilly Parts, S 🅖 BP, Speedway/dsl 🍴 Applebee's, Arby's, Asian Star, Big Boy, Boston Mkt, Burger King, Chipotle Mexican, Ichiban Steaks, KFC, McDonald's, Ruby Tuesday, Starbucks, Taco Bell, Waffle House, White Castle 🏠 Best Value Inn, Comfort Suites, EconoLodge, Motel 6 🅞 Acura, Advance Parts, Aldi Foods, Discount Tire, Family$, Fiat, Firestone/auto, GNC, Hobby Lobby, Honda, Lowe's, Michael's, NTB, Old Navy, Toyota/Scion, Walgreens
108b a	I-270 N to Cleveland, access to 🏥 I-270 S to Cincinnati
107a	OH 317, Hamilton Rd, to Whitehall, S 🅖 Shell/dsl, Valero/dsl 🍴 Arby's, Burger King, Capt D's, ChuckeCheese, Eastland Buffet, Ichiban Japanese, McDonald's, Papa John's, Pizza Hut, Red Lobster, Steak'n Shake, Taco Bell 🏠 Fort Rapids Resort, Hampton Inn, Hawthorn Inn, InTown Suites,

Exit #	Services
107a	Continued
	Knights Inn 🅞 $General, AT&T, JC Penney, Kohl's, Macy's, PepBoys, Staples
105b	US 33, James Rd, Bexley, N 🍴 Tat Italian
105a	US 33, to Lancaster, N 2 mi 🍴 Tat Italian
103b a	Livingston Ave, to Capital University, N 🅖 Exxon, Speedway/dsl 🍴 Mr Hero Subs, Peking Dynasty, Popeye's, Subway, Taco Bell, Wendy's 🅞 auto repair, S 🅖 Marathon, Shell 🍴 McDonald's, Rally's, White Castle
102	Kelton Ave, Miller Ave
101a	I-71 N, to Cleveland
100b	US 23, to 4th St, downtown
99c	Rich St, Town St (exits left from eb), N 🅖 Sunoco 🅞 Ford
99b	OH 315 N, downtown
99a	I-71 S, to Cincinnati
98b	Mound St (from wb, no EZ return), S 🅖 Speedway 🍴 Little Caesars, McDonald's, Rally's 🅞 Aldi Foods
98a	US 62, OH 3, Central Ave, to Sullivant, same as 98b
97	US 40, W Broad St, N 🅖 Valero/dsl 🍴 Arby's, Burger King, KFC, McDonald's, Pizza Hut/Taco Bell, Subway, Tim Horton's, Wendy's, White Castle 🏠 Knights Inn 🅞 Aamco, CVS Drug, U-Haul, USPO
96	I-670 (exits left from eb), 🅞 to ✈
95	Hague Ave (from wb), S 🅖 Sunoco
94	Wilson Rd, N 🅖 Marathon/Circle K/Subway/dsl, Mobil, S 🅖 BP, 🏪 /Wendy's/dsl/scales/24hr, Shell/dsl, Speedway 🍴 McDonald's, Waffle House, White Castle 🏠 EconoLodge
93b a	I-270, N to Cleveland, S to Cincinnati
91b a	to Hilliard, New Rome, N 🅖 GetGo, Shell, Speedway/dsl 🍴 5 Guys Burgers, AA China, Applebee's, Arby's, Big Boy, Buffalo Wild Wings, Burger King, Chick-fil-A, Cold Stone/Tim Horton's, Cracker Barrel, Culver's, Donato's Pizza, El Vaquero Mexican, Fazoli's, Golden Chopsticks, Hooters, KFC, McDonald's, Outback Steaks, Panera Bread, Perkins, Pizza Hut/Taco Bell, Red Robin, Ruby Tuesday, Salvi's Bistro, Skyline Chili, Smoothie King, TX Roadhouse, Wendy's, White Castle 🏠 Best Value Inn, Comfort Suites, Fairfield Inn, Hampton Inn, Hawthorn Inn, Holiday Inn, La Quinta, Motel 6, Red Roof Inn 🅞 Advance Parts, AT&T, Dick's, Discount Tire, Firestone/auto, Ford, Gander Mtn, Giant Eagle Foods/gas, GNC, Kohl's, Marshall's, Meijer/dsl, Michael's, Midas, Old Navy, Petsmart, Radio Shack, Sam's Club/gas, Target, URGENT CARE, Verizon, Walmart/Subway, S 🅖 BP/dsl, Marathon/dsl 🍴 Bob Evans, Handel's Icecream, Steak'n Shake 🏠 Best Western, Country Inn&Suites, Super 8
85	OH 142, to Plain City, W Jefferson, N 🅞 Prairie Oaks SP, S 🅞 Battelle Darby SP
80	OH 29, to Mechanicsburg, S 🅞 hwy patrol
79	US 42, to London, Plain City, N 🅖 🏪 /Arby's/dsl/scales/24hr 🍴 Waffle House 🅞 Raber's RV Ctr, truck/auto repair, S 🅖 Speedway/Subway/dsl, TA/BP/Pizza Hut/Popeye's/dsl/scales/24hr/@ 🍴 McDonald's, Taco Bell, Wendy's 🏠 Holiday Inn Express, Motel 6 🅞 🏥 truckwash
72	OH 56, to London, Summerford, N 🅖 Marathon, S 4 mi 🏠 🅞 🏥
71mm	🆁🆂 both lanes, full ♿ facilities, litter barrels, petwalk, 🚻, 🆖 vending
66	OH 54, to Catawba, South Vienna, N 🅖 Fuelmart/dsl/scales, S 🅖 Speedway/dsl
62	US 40, Springfield, N 🏠 Harmony Motel 🅞 antiques, auto repair, Harmony Farm Mkt, to Buck Creek SP, S 🅞 Beaver Valley Camping

COLUMBUS AREA

OH

COLUMBUS AREA

INTERSTATE 70 Cont'd

SPRINGFIELD

Exit #	Services
59	OH 41, to S Charleston, **N** Ⓞ H Harley-Davidson, st patrol, **S** Ⓖ antiques, BP, Clark/dsl
54	OH 72, to Cedarville, Springfield, **N** Ⓖ BP/dsl, Shell, Speedway/dsl, Sunoco/dsl 🍴 A&W/LJ Silver, Arby's, Bob Evans, Cassano's Pizza/subs, Cracker Barrel, Domino's, El Toro Mexican, Hardee's, Lee's Chicken, Little Caesars, McDonald's, Panda Chinese, Rally's, Rudy's Smokehouse, Subway, Taco Bell, Wendy's 🛏 Comfort Suites, Days Inn, Hampton Inn, Quality Inn, Ramada Ltd, Red Roof Inn, Super 8 Ⓞ H Advance Parts, BigLots, Family$, Kroger/deli, Rite Aid, Walgreens, **S** Ⓖ Marathon/dsl, Swifty
52b a	US 68, to Urbana, Xenia, **S** Ⓞ to John Bryan SP
48	OH 4 (from wb), to Enon, Donnelsville, **N** Ⓖ Speedway Ⓞ camping
47	OH 4 (from eb), to Springfield, **N** Ⓖ Speedway Ⓞ RV Camping
44	I-675 S, Spangler Rd, to Cincinnati
43mm	Mad River
41b a	OH 4, OH 235, to Dayton, New Carlisle, **N 1 mi** Ⓖ BP/dsl 🍴 KFC/LJ Silver, McDonald's, Wendy's Ⓞ Freightliner, Kenworth
38	OH 201, Brandt Pike, **N** Ⓖ Marathon/dsl Ⓞ Meijer/dsl/E85, **S** Ⓖ Shell, UDF/dsl 🍴 Bob Evans, Sonic, Tim Horton's, Waffle House, Wendy's 🛏 Best Value Inn, Comfort Inn Ⓞ vet, Walmart/McDonald's
36	OH 202, Huber Heights, **N** Ⓖ Speedway/dsl 🍴 Applebee's, Big Boy, Dragon City, El Toro Grill, Fazoli's, Steak'n Shake, Taco Bell, Waffle House 🛏 Baymont Inn Ⓞ $Tree, AT&T, Dick's, Elder Beerman, Gander Mtn., GNC, Hobby Lobby, Kia, Kohl's, Lowe's, Marshall's, Petsmart, Target, URGENT CARE, Verizon, vet, **S** Ⓖ BP/dsl, Marathon/dsl 🍴 Arby's, Buffalo Wild Wings, Burger King, Cadillac Jack's, Chipotle Mexican, CiCi's Pizza, El Dorado Mexican, La Rosa's Pizza, McDonald's, Skyline Chili, Subway, TGIFriday's, TX Roadhouse, White Castle 🛏 Days Inn, Hampton Inn, Holiday Inn Express Ⓞ Kroger/gas
33b a	I-75, N to Toledo, S to Dayton
32	to US 40, Vandalia, **N** to Dayton Intn'l ✈
29	OH 48, to Dayton, Englewood, **N** Ⓖ BP, Speedway/dsl, Sunoco/dsl, Valero 🍴 Arby's, Big Boy, Bob Evans, Company BBQ, Hot Head Burrito, KFC, Lee's Chicken, Perkins, Ponderosa, Skyline Chili, Taco Bell, Tim Horton's, Tony's Italian, Wendy's, Yen Ching Chinese 🛏 Best Value Inn, Best Western, Hampton Inn, Holiday Inn, Super 8 Ⓞ Advance Parts, Aldi Foods, BigLots, Family$, O'Reilly Parts, vet, **S** 🍴 McDonald's, Steak'n Shake, Tumbleweed SW Grill, Waffle House 🛏 Comfort Inn, Motel 6 Ⓞ H Meijer/dsl/E85
26	OH 49 S, **N** Ⓖ Murphy USA/dsl 🍴 Bob Evans, La Rosa's Pizza, Sonic Ⓞ Radio Shack, URGENT CARE, Walmart/Subway, **S** 🍴 Wendy's
24	OH 49 N, to Greenville, Clayton, **N** Ⓖ Sunoco/dsl Ⓞ KOA (seasonal)
21	Arlington Rd, Brookville, **N** Ⓖ GA/Subway, **S** Ⓖ Speedway/dsl, Swifty 🍴 Arby's, Brookville Grill, DQ, Great Wall Chinese, KFC/Taco Bell, K's Rest., McDonald's, Pizza Hut, Rob's Rest., Subway, Waffle House, Wendy's 🛏 Best Value Inn, Holiday Inn Express Ⓞ $General, Brookville Parts, Chevrolet, Curves, Family$, IGA Foods, Rite Aid
14	OH 503, to West Alexandria, Lewisburg, **N** Ⓖ Marathon/Subway/dsl 🍴 Dari Twist 🛏 Super Inn Ⓞ IGA Foods, **S** Ⓖ Valero/dsl

DAYTON

10	US 127, to Eaton, Greenville, **N** Ⓖ st patrol, TA/BP/Burger King/Subway/dsl/scales/24hr/@, **S** Ⓖ Pilot/Subway/dsl/scales/24hr 🛏 Budget Inn
3mm	Welcome Center 🆁🆂 both lanes, full 🦽 facilities, info, litter barrels, petwalk, 🅲, 🚰 vending
1	US 35 E (from eb), to Eaton, New Hope
0mm	Ohio/Indiana state line, Welcome Arch, **weigh sta eb**

INTERSTATE 71

Exit #	Services
	I-71 begins/ends on I-90, exit 170 in Cleveland.
247b	I-90 W, I-490 E.
247a	W 14th, Clark Ave
246	Denison Ave, Jennings Rd (from sb)
245	US 42, Pearl Rd, **E** Ⓖ BP, Gas&Go Ⓞ H zoo
244	W 65th, Denison Ave (exits left from nb)
242b a	W 130th, to Bellaire Rd, **W** Ⓖ Sunoco
240	W 150th, **E** Ⓖ Marathon, Speedway/dsl, Sunoco 🍴 Burger King, Denny's 🛏 Marriott Ⓞ AutoZone, Goodyear/auto, Marc's Foods, **W** Ⓖ BP/Subway/dsl 🍴 Nana's Italian, Somers Rest. 🛏 Holiday Inn, La Quinta
239	OH 237 S (from sb), **W** to ✈
238	I-480, Toledo, Youngstown, **W** ✈
237	Snow Rd, Brook Park, **E** Ⓖ BP, Marathon/Circle K, Shell 🍴 Bob Evans, Burger King, Dunkin Donuts, Goody's Rest., KFC, McDonald's, Rally's, Reddi's Pizza, Subway, Taco Bell 🛏 Best Western, Holiday Inn Express, Howard Johnson Ⓞ $General, Advance Parts, AutoZone, Conrad Tire/repair, O'Reilly Parts, Rite Aid, **W** to ✈
235	Bagley Rd, **E** 🍴 Bob Evans Ⓞ Mr Tire, vet, **W** Ⓖ BP/dsl, Shell, Speedway/dsl 🍴 5 Guys Burgers, Baskin-Robbins/Dunkin Donuts, Burger King, Caribou Coffee, Chipotle, Denny's, Friendly's, Jimmy John's, Max&Erma's, McDonald's, Olive Garden, Panera Bread, Perkins, Pizza Hut, Roadhouse Grill, Taco Bell 🛏 Comfort Inn, Courtyard, Crowne Plaza, Days Inn, Motel 6, Red Roof Inn, Residence Inn, TownePlace Suites Ⓞ H Aldi Foods, K-Mart
234	US 42, Pearl Rd, **E** Ⓖ Shell/dsl, Sunoco/dsl 🍴 3 Bros Pizza, Katherine's Rest., Wendy's Ⓞ Audi/Porsche, Honda, **W** Ⓖ Gas&Food/dsl 🍴 Buffalo Wild Wings, Jennifer's Rest 🛏 Kings Inn, La Siesta Motel, Metrick's Motel Ⓞ Circle K, Home Depot, Lowe's, Walmart
233	I-80 and Ohio Tpk, to Toledo, Youngstown
231	OH 82, Strongsville, **E** Ⓖ Shell 🛏 Holiday Inn, Super 8 Ⓞ Chevrolet, **W** Ⓖ BP/7-11/dsl, Marathon/dsl 🍴 Applebee's, Buca Italian, Chick-fil-A, DiBella's Subs, Houlihan's, Longhorn Steaks, Macaroni Grill, Panera Bread, Red Lobster, Rock Me's Grill, Rosewood Grill, Starbucks Ⓞ Best Buy,

STRONGSVILLE

OH

⬆N INTERSTATE 71 Cont'd

Exit #	Services
231	Continued
	Costco/gas, Dick's, Dillard's, Giant Eagle Foods, JC Penney, Kohl's, Macy's, mall, Midas, NTB, PetCo, Sears/auto, Target, Verizon
226	OH 303, Brunswick, **E** 🚹 Shell/dsl 🍴 Pizza Hut 🅾 Chrysler/Dodge/Jeep, Hyundai, Subaru, Toyota/Scion, VW, **W** 🚹 BP, Speedway, Sunoco/dsl 🍴 Applebee's, Arby's, Bob Evans, Burger King, Chipotle, CiCi's Pizza, McDonald's, Panera Bread, Panini's Grill, Sonic, Starbucks, Steak'n Shake, Subway, Taco Bell, Wendy's 🏠 Quality Inn 🅾 $General, Buehler's Foods, Ford, Giant Eagle Food, Home Depot, K-Mart, Radio Shack, Verizon
225mm	℞ nb, full ♿ facilities, litter barrels, petwalk, 📞, 🚮
224mm	℞ sb, full ♿ facilities, litter barrels, petwalk, 📞, 🚮
222	OH 3, Medina, Hinckley, **W** 🅾 st patrol
220	I-271 N, (from nb) to Erie, Pa
218	OH 18, to Akron, Medina, **E** 🚹 BP/dsl, Marathon/dsl, Sunoco/dsl 🍴 Alexandri's Rest., Ay Carumba, Baskin-Robbins/Dunkin Donuts, Burger King, DQ 🏠 Quality Inn, Rodeway Inn, Super 8 🅾 Kia, Nissan, **W** 🚹 Speedway/dsl 🍴 Arby's, Bob Evans, Buffalo Wild Wings, Denny's, McDonald's, Pizza Hut, Rocknes Rest., Waffle House, Wendy's 🏠 Hampton Inn, Motel 6, Red Roof Inn 🅾 🏥 Aldi Foods, Buehler's Foods, Buick/Cadillac/GMC, Dodge, Harley-Davidson, Honda, NTB
209	I-76 E, to Akron, US 224, **W** 🚹 ▦/Subway/dsl/scales/24hr, TA/Country Pride/Burger King/Popeye's/dsl/scales/24hr/@ 🍴 Arby's, McDonald's, Starbucks 🏠 Super 8 🅾 Blue Beacon, Chippewa Valley Camping (1mi), SpeedCo
204	OH 83, Burbank, **E** 🚹 BP/dsl, Duke/dsl, 🛒Loves/Hardee's/dsl/scales/24hr 🏠 Plaza Motel, **W** 🚹 ▦/Wendy's/dsl/scales/24hr 🍴 Bob Evans, Burger King, KFC/Taco Bell, McDonald's 🅾 🏥 Lodi Outlets/famous brands
198	OH 539, W Salem
196mm	℞ both lanes, full ♿ facilities, litter barrels, petwalk, 📞, 🚮 vending
196	OH 301 (from nb, no re-entry), W Salem
186	US 250, Ashland, **E** 🚹 Marathon 🍴 Grandpa's Village/cheese/gifts, Perkins 🅾 Hickory Lakes Camping (7mi), **W** 🚹 Goasis/BP/Pizza Hut/Popeye's/Starbucks/Taco Bell/dsl/24hr, Marathon 🍴 Brian Buffet, Denny's, Donato's Pizza, Jake's Rest., McDonald's, Wendy's 🏠 Ashland Inn, Days Inn, Holiday Inn Express, Super 8 🅾 🏥 Aldi Foods, Buehler's Foods, GNC, Home Depot, st patrol, to Ashland U, Walmart
176	US 30, to Mansfield, **E** 🏠 Heritage Inn 🅾 fireworks
173	OH 39, to Mansfield
169	OH 13, Mansfield, **E** 🚹 Marathon/dsl, Murphy USA/dsl 🍴 Applebee's, Cracker Barrel, Steak'n Shake, Subway, Wendy's 🏠 Best Western, La Quinta 🅾 Mohican SP, Walmart/Subway, **W** 🚹 Marathon 🍴 Arby's, Bob Evans, Burger King, El Compasino Mexican, McDonald's, Taco Bell 🏠 Hampton Inn, Super 8, Travelodge 🅾 🏥 st patrol
165	OH 97, to Bellville, **E** 🚹 BP, Shell/dsl, Speedway/dsl 🍴 Burger King, Dutch Heritage Rest., KC's Rib House, McDonald's 🏠 Comfort Inn, Days Inn, Economy Inn, Quality Inn 🅾 to Mohican SP, **W** 🍴 Wendy's
151	OH 95, to Mt Gilead, **E** 🚹 Duke/BP/deli, Marathon 🍴 Gathering Place Rest., McDonald's, Wendy's 🏠 Best Western 🅾 st patrol, **W** 🚹 Shell/dsl, Sunoco/dsl/E85 🍴 Subway 🏠 Knights Inn 🅾 🏥 Mt Gilead SP (6mi)

149mm	truck parking both lanes
140	OH 61, Mt Gilead, **E** 🚹 ▦/Arby's/dsl/scales/24hr, **W** 🚹 BP/Taco Bell, Marathon/Subway 🍴 Farmstead Rest. 🅾 Cardinal Ctr Camping
131	US 36, OH 37, to Delaware, **E** 🚹 🔷FLYING J/Denny's/dsl/LP/scales/24hr/@, ▦/Subway/dsl/scales/24hr 🍴 Burger King 🅾 Harley-Davidson, **W** 🚹 BP/dsl, Shell/Tim Hortons 🍴 Arby's, Bob Evans, Cracker Barrel, KFC/LJ Silver, McDonald's, Starbucks, Taco Bell, Waffle House, Wendy's, White Castle 🏠 Best Value Inn, Hampton Inn, Holiday Inn Express 🅾 🏥 Alum Cr SP, Cross Creek Camping (6mi)
128mm	℞ both lanes, full ♿ facilities, litter barrels, petwalk, 📞, 🚮 vending
121	Polaris Pkwy, to Gemini Pl, **E** 🚹 BP, Mobil, Shell 🍴 5 Guys Burgers, Bonefish Grill, Buffalo Wild Wings, Canes, Carfagna's, McDonald's, Mellow Mushroom Pizza, Pei Wei, Polaris Grill, Skyline Chili, Starbucks, Steak'n Shake 🏠 Best Western, Fairfield Inn, Hampton Inn, Holiday Inn Express, Wingate Inn 🅾 Firestone/auto, Polaris Ampitheatre, **W** 🚹 BP, Marathon/Circle K, Shell/Tim Horton 🍴 Applebee's, Arby's, Benihana, BJ's Rest., Brio Grille, Caribou Coffee, Carrabba's, Charley Subs, CheeseCake Factory, Chick-fil-A, Chipotle Mexican, City BBQ, Claddagh Rest., Coldstone, Cosi Cafe, Dave&Buster's, Domino's, El Vaquero Mexican, Hoggy's Grill, Honey Baked Ham, Hooters, House of Japan, Jimmy John's, Krispy Kreme, Marcella's Italian, Max&Erma's, McDonald's, Merlot's Rest., MiMi's Cafe, Mitchell Steaks, Noodles&Co, O'Charley's, Olive Garden, Panera Bread, Papa John's, Penn Sta Subs, Pizza Hut/Taco Bell, Planet Smoothie, Potbelly, Qdoba, Quaker Steak, Red Lobster, Red Robin, Rudedog Grill, Smokey Bones BBQ, Sonic, Starbucks, Subway, Tequilas Mexican, TGIFriday's, TX Roadhouse, Waffle House, Wendy's 🏠 Cambria Suites, Candlewood Suites, Comfort Inn, Extended Stay Deluxe, Hilton, Hilton Garden, Residence Inn 🅾 AutoZone, Barnes&Noble, Best Buy, BigLots, Cabela's, Costco/gas, Dick's, Earth Fare, funpark, GNC, JC Penney, Jo-Ann Etc, Kroger/gas, Lowe's, Macy's, mall, NTB, Old Navy, Petsmart, Sears/auto, Target, TireDiscounters, TJ Maxx, URGENT CARE, Walgreens, Walmart (3mi), World Mkt
119b a	I-270, to Indianapolis, Wheeling
117	OH 161, to Worthington, **E** 🚹 BP/dsl, Shell, Speedway/dsl, Sunoco/dsl 🍴 Burger King, Carfagna's, China Dynasty, Chipotle, KFC, LJ Silver, Max&Erma's, McDonald's, Rally's, Red Lobster, Subway, Super Seafood Buffet, Wendy's, White Castle 🏠 Comfort Inn, Days Inn, Knights Inn, Motel 6, Red Roof Inn 🅾 auto repair, CVS Drug, Family$, Staples, TireDiscounters, URGENT CARE, vet, Walgreens, **W** 🚹 GetGo, Shell, Speedway/dsl 🍴 Bob Evans, China Jade, Domino's, McDonald's, Pizza Hut, Skyline Chili, Starbucks, Subway, Tim Hortons, Waffle House, Wendy's 🏠 Baymont Inn, Best Western, Clarion, Columbus Inn, Country Inn&Suites, Crowne Plaza, Extended Stay America, Hawthorn Suites, Rodeway Inn, Super 8, Travelodge, ValuePlace 🅾 Advance Parts, Chevrolet, Family$, Giant Eagle Foods, NTB, Walgreens
116	Morse Rd, Sinclair Rd, **E** 🚹 BP, Marathon/dsl, Shell, Speedway, Turkey Hill/dsl 🍴 Chipotle, Jimmy John's, Little Caesars, McDonald's, Papa John's, Subway, Taco Bell, Tim Horton 🏠 Extended Stay America 🅾 $General, AT&T, Buick/GMC, CVS Drug, Family$, Firestone/auto, Ford, Kroger, Mendards, Pep-Boys, Save-A-Lot Foods, **W** 🚹 Sunoco 🏠 Best Value Inn, Motel 6, Ramada 🅾 NTB
115	Cooke Rd

AKRON

MANSFIELD

OH

COLUMBUS AREA

🧭 N   INTERSTATE 71 Cont'd

Exit #	Services
114	N Broadway, W 🚗 Sunoco 🍴 Broadway Mkt Cafe, Subway
113	Weber Rd, W 🚗 Speedway/dsl Ⓞ CarQuest
112	Hudson St, E 🚗 Marathon, Shell/dsl 🍴 Wendy's 🛏 Holiday Inn Express, W 🍴 Big Boy Ⓞ Aldi Foods, Lowe's, NTB
111	17th Ave, W 🍴 McDonald's 🛏 Comfort Inn, Days Inn
110b	11th Ave
110a	5th Ave, E 🚗 Sunoco 🍴 Royal Fish&Chicken, White Castle, W 🚗 Valero 🍴 Church's, KFC, Popeye's, Rally's, Wendy's Ⓞ AutoZone
109c	Spring St (exits left from sb)
109b	OH 3, Cleveland Ave
109a	I-670
108b	US 40, Broad St, downtown
108a	Main St
106b	OH 315 N, Dublin St, Town St
106a	I-70 W, to Indianapolis
105	Greenlawn, E 🚗 BP 🍴 White Castle, W 🚗 Shamrock
104	OH 104, Frank Rd
101b a	I-270, Wheeling, Indianapolis
101a[70]	I-70 E, US 23 N, to Wheeling
100b a[70]	US 23 S, Front St, High St, downtown
100	Stringtown Rd, E 🚗 BP 🍴 5 Guys Burgers, Bob Evans, Charley's Grilled Subs, Chick-fil-A, Chipotle, CiCi's Pizza, Coldstone, DQ, Jalapeno's Mexican, Longhorn Steaks, O'Charley's, Olive Garden, Panda Express, Red Robin, Roosters Grill, Smokey Bones BBQ, Sonic, Starbucks, Steak'n Shake, White Castle 🛏 Best Western, Drury Inn, Hampton Inn, Hilton Garden, Holiday Inn Express, La Quinta, Microtel, Red Roof Inn Ⓞ Best Buy, Dick's, Firestone/auto, Home Depot, Michael's, Petsmart, Staples, Target, TJ Maxx, Walmart, W 🚗 GetGo, Speedway/dsl, Sunoco/dsl, Turkey Hill/dsl 🍴 Applebee's, Arby's, Burger King, Cane's Chicken Fingers, China Bell, Cracker Barrel, Donato's Pizza, El Mesquite Mexican, Fazoli's, Golden Corral, KFC, Mariachi Mexican, McDonald's, Papa John's, Rally's, Ruby Tuesday, Starbucks, Taco Bell, TeeJaye's Rest., Tim Horton, Waffle House, Wendy's 🛏 Comfort Inn, Days Inn, Motel 6, Travelodge Ⓞ Ace Hardware, Advance Parts, Aldi Foods, AutoZone, BigLots, CVS Drug, Giant Eagle Foods, Goodyear/auto, K-Mart, Kroger, PetCo, Radio Shack, Tuffy Auto, Walgreens
97	OH 665, London-Groveport Rd, E 🚗 Marathon/Circle K 🍴 Arby's, McDonald's, Peking House, Quiznos, Sunny St Cafe, Tim Horton/Wendy's Ⓞ Ⓗ CVS Drug, Kroger/gas/E85, Meijer/E85, TireDiscounters, to Scioto Downs, URGENT CARE, W Ⓞ Eddie's Repair
94	US 62, OH 3, Orient, 🚗 Sunoco/dsl
84	OH 56, Mt Sterling, E 🚗 BP/Subway 🛏 Royal Inn Ⓞ to Deer Creek SP (9mi)
75	OH 38, Bloomingburg, E Ⓞ fireworks, W 🚗 Sunoco/dsl
69	OH 41, OH 734, Jeffersonville, E 🚗 ✈FLYING J/Denny's/dsl/scales/LP/24hr Ⓞ Ⓗ Walnut Lake Camping, W 🚗 BP, Shell/Subway 🍴 Arby's, Wendy's 🛏 Quality Inn Ⓞ Family$
68mm	Ⓡ both lanes, full ♿ facilities, litter barrels, petwalk, 🚙, 🐕 vending
65	US 35, Washington CH, E 🚗 Shell, TA/BP/Pizza Hut/Popeye's/dsl/scales/24hr/@ 🍴 A&W/KFC, Bob Evans, Chipotle Mexican, LJ Silver/Taco Bell, McDonald's, Subway, Waffle House, Wendy's, Werner's BBQ 🛏 Baymont Inn, Fairfield Inn, Hampton Inn Ⓞ Ⓗ AT&T, Tanger Outlets/famous brands, W 🚗 Loves/Hardee's/dsl/scales/24hr 🛏 EconoLodge

58	OH 72, to Sabina
54mm	weigh sta sb
50	US 68, to Wilmington, E Ⓞ Ⓗ W 🚗 BP/dsl, 🚚/Subway/dsl/scales/24hr, Shell/dsl 🍴 Max&Erma's, McDonald's, Wendy's 🛏 Budget Inn, Holiday Inn, repair/tires, Robert's Center
49mm	weigh sta nb
45	OH 73, to Waynesville, E 🚗 BP, Shell/dsl 🍴 73 Grill Ⓞ Ⓗ camping (3mi), RV Park, W Ⓞ Caesar Creek SP (5mi), flea mkt
36	Wilmington Rd, E Ⓞ RV camping, to Ft Ancient St Mem
35mm	Little Miami River
34mm	Ⓡ both lanes, scenic view, full ♿ facilities, litter barrels, petwalk, 🚙, 🐕, vending
32	OH 123, to Lebanon, Morrow, E 🚗 BP, Valero 🍴 Country Kitchen Ⓞ Morgan's Riverside Camping, W 3 mi 🍴 Bob Evans, Skyline Chili
28	OH 48, S Lebanon, E 🚗 Marathon/dsl 🍴 White Castle 🛏 Countryside Inn Ⓞ Kohl's, Lowe's, Target, Verizon, W Ⓞ hwy patrol, Lebanon Raceway (6mi)
25	OH 741 N, Kings Mills Rd, E 🚗 Shell/Popeye's, Speedway/dsl 🍴 McDonald's, Outback Steaks, Ruby Tuesday, Taco Bell 🛏 Comfort Suites, Great Wolf Lodge, Kings Island Resort Ⓞ Harley-Davidson, W 🚗 BP, Exxon/Subway 🍴 Arby's, Big Boy, Bob Evans, Burger King, Chipotle, Perkins, Pizza Hut, Skyline Chili, Tabby's Grill, Waffle House, Wendy's 🛏 Baymont Inn, Hampton Inn, Microtel, Super 8 Ⓞ CarX, CVS Drug, GNC, Kroger
24	Western Row, King's Island Dr (from nb), E 🚗 Sunoco 🍴 Fantastic Wok, MVPizza 🛏 King's Island Resort Ⓞ funpark, Jellystone Camping
19	US 22, Mason-Montgomery Rd, E 🚗 Speedway/dsl 🍴 Arby's, Asian Fusion, Big Boy, Boston Mkt, Burger King, Cracker Barrel, Fiesta Brava, Firehouse Subs, Golden Corral, HoneyBaked Ham, Iron Chef Grill, KFC, McDonald's, Olive Garden, Quiznos, Taco Bell, Taz Mediterranean Grill, TGIFriday's, Wendy's, White Castle 🛏 Clarion, Comfort Inn, SpringHill Suites, TownePlace Suites Ⓞ Aldi Foods, AT&T, AutoZone, Barnes&Noble, Best Buy, BigLots, Buick/GMC, Chevrolet, Chrysler/Dodge/Jeep, Costco/gas, Firestone/auto, Ford, GNC, Goodyear/auto, Hobby Lobby, Honda, Infiniti, JC Penney, Kia, Kohl's, Kroger, Lexus, Lincoln, Mazda, Meijer/dsl, Michael's, Nissan, Old Navy, O'Reilly Parts, Porsche, Radio Shack, Sam's Club/gas, Target, TireDiscounters, Toyota/Scion, Tuffy Auto, USPO, Verizon, vet, Walgreens, W 🚗 BP/dsl, Marathon/dsl/24hr 🍴 5 Guys Burgers, Abuelo's Mexican, Applebee's, BD Mongolian Grill, Bravo Italian, Burger King, Carrabba's, China City, Chipotle Mexican, Claddagh Irish, Dao Asian, Fox&Hound Grill, Graeter's Cafe, IHOP, Jimmy John's,

OH

🔼N INTERSTATE 71 Cont'd

Exit #	Services
19	Continued
	LoneStar Steaks, McAlister's Deli, MiMi's Cafe, O'Charley's, Panera Bread, Polo Grill, Qdoba, Red Robin, River City Grill, Skyline Chili, Steak'n Shake, Subway, Waffle House, Wendy's 🛏 Best Western, Days Inn, Hilton Garden, Holiday Inn Express, Hyatt Place, La Quinta, Marriott, Motel 6, Red Roof Inn 🅾 Bigg's Foods, Dick's, Home Depot, Lowe's, NAPA, Staples, vet, Walmart, Whole Foods Mkt
17b a	I-275, to I-75, OH 32
15	Pfeiffer Rd, E 🅾 🅷 W 🅖 BP, Shell/dsl, Sunoco/dsl/24hr 🍴 Applebee's, Bob Evans, Buffalo Wild Wings, Subway, Watson Bro's Bistro 🛏 Courtyard, Crowne Plaza, Embassy Suites, Hampton Inn, Holiday Inn Express, Red Roof Inn 🅾 Office Depot
14	OH 126, Reagan Hwy, Blue Ash
12	US 22, OH 3, Montgomery Rd, E 🅖 BP/dsl, Shell/24hr 🍴 Arby's, Bob Evans, Chipotle Mexican, Ember's, Jalapeno Cafe, KFC, LJ Silver, Outback Steaks, Panera Bread, Red Lobster, Ruby Tuesday, Subway, Taco Bell, TGIFriday, Wendy's 🛏 Best Western 🅾 Dodge, Firestone, Goodyear, Hyundai, Pep-Boys, Staples, Tuesday Morning, W 🅖 Chevron 🍴 Cheesecake Factory, IHOP, Johnny Rocket's, KFC, Macaroni Grill, Max&Erma's, McDonald's, Potbelly's, Starbucks, Wendy's 🅾 🅷 Barnes&Noble, Dillard's, Firestone/auto, Fresh Mkt Foods, Macy's, mall, Old Navy, Staples
11	Kenwood Rd, (from nb), W 🅾 🅷 same as 12
10	Stewart Rd (from nb), to Silverton, W 🅖 Marathon/dsl
9	Redbank Rd, to Fairfax, (no ez sb return), E 🅖 Mobil, Speedway 🅾 BMW
8	Kennedy Ave, Ridge Ave W, E 🅖 Meijer/dsl 🍴 IHOP 🛏 Motel 6 🅾 Dodge, Sam's Club/gas, Target, W 🅖 Marathon/dsl, Shell/Subway, Speedway 🍴 Denny's, Gold Star Chili, Golden Corral, KFC, LJ Silver, McDonald's, Old Country Buffet, Pizza Hut, Rally's, Taco Bell, Wendy's, White Castle 🅾 Big Lots, Bigg's Foods, Ford, Goodyear, Home Depot, Lowes Whse, Office Depot, Tire Discounter, transmissions, Walmart
7b a	OH 562, Ridge Ave E, Norwood, E 🅖 BP 🍴 Ponderosa 🅾 AutoZone
6	Edwards Rd, E 🅖 BP, Shell, Speedway 🍴 Boston Mkt, Buca Italian, Don Pablo, Donato's, Fuddrucker's, GoldStar Chili, J Alexander's Rest., Longhorn Steaks, Max&Erma's, Noodles, PF Chang's, Starbucks 🅾 GNC, SteinMart, W 🅖 Shell
5	Dana Ave, Montgomery Rd, W 🅾 Xavier Univ, Zoo
3	Taft Rd (from sb), W 🅾 U of Cincinnati
2	US 42, Reading Rd, Gilbert ave (from sb), W 🅾 🅷 art Museum, ballpark stadium arena, downtown
1k j	I-471 S
1d	Main St, downtown
1c b	Pete Rose Way, Fine St, downtown, stadium
1a	I-75 N, US 50, to Dayton
I-71 S and I-75 S run together	
0mm	Ohio/Kentucky state line, Ohio River

🔼E INTERSTATE 74

Exit #	Services
20	I-75 (from eb), N to Dayton, S to Cincinnati, **I-74 begins/ends on I-75.**
19	Gilmore St, Spring Grove Ave
18	US 27 N, Colerain Ave
17	Montana Ave (from wb), N 🅖 Circle K

CINCINNATI AREA

OH

14	North Bend Rd, Cheviot, N 🅖 Shell, Speedway/dsl 🍴 DQ, Dunkin Donuts, McDonald's, Papa John's, Perkins, Skyline Chili, Subway, Wendy's, White Castle 🅾 Curves, Family$, Kroger, Sam's Club/gas, Tire Discounters, Walgreens, S 🅖 BP 🍴 Bob Evans 🅾 vet
11	Rybolt Rd, Harrison Pike, S 🅖 BP 🍴 Longhorn Steaks, Marco's Pizza, McDonald's, Sakura Steaks, Skyline Chili, Wendy's, White Castle 🛏 Holiday Inn Express 🅾 Kohl's, Meijer/gas
9	I-275 N, to I-75, N to Dayton, (exits left from eb)
8mm	Great Miami River
7	OH 128, to Hamilton, Cleves, N 🅖 BP/dsl, Marathon/dsl 🍴 Wendy's
5	I-275 S, to Kentucky
3	Dry Fork Rd, N 🅖 BP, S 🅖 Marathon/dsl, Shell/Dunkin Donuts/dsl
2mm	weigh sta wb
1	New Haven Rd, to Harrison, N 🅖 BP/dsl 🍴 Buffalo Wild Wings, China Garden, Chipotle Mexican, Cracker Barrel, GoldStar Chili, Little Caesars, O'Charley's, Subway 🅾 Biggs Foods, Ford, Home Depot, Kia, Staples, Tires+, Verizon, S 🅖 Shell/Circle K, Speedway/dsl, Sunoco/White Castle 🍴 A&W/KFC, Arby's, Burger King, Domino's, DQ, El Mariachi, Happy Garden, McDonald's, Penn Sta Subs, Pizza Hut, Skyline Chili, Taco Bell, Waffle House, Wendy's 🛏 Holiday Inn Express 🅾 $General, $Tree, Advance Parts, AT&T, AutoZone, BigLots, CVS Drug, Family$, Firestone/auto, GNC, K-Mart, Kroger/dsl, Meineke, NAPA, O'Reilly Parts, Radio Shack, Tire Discounters, Walgreens
0mm	Ohio/Indiana state line

🔼N INTERSTATE 75

Exit #	Services
211mm	Ohio/Michigan state line
210mm	Ottawa River
210	OH 184, Alexis Rd, to Raceway Park, W 🅖 BP/Circle K/dsl, 🛏/Subway/dsl/scales/24hr 🍴 Arby's, Bob Evans, Burger King, McDonald's, Taco Bell, Wendy's 🛏 Fairfield Inn, Hampton Inn, Holiday Inn Express 🅾 AutoZone, Meijer/dsl, Menards, URGENT CARE
209	Ottawa River Rd (from nb), E 🅖 BP, Sunoco 🍴 China King, Little Caesars, Marco's Pizza, River Diner 🅾 Family$, Kroger/E85, Rite Aid, vet
208	I-280 S, to I-80/90, to Cleveland
207	Stickney Ave, Lagrange St, E 🅖 BP 🍴 Arby's, McDonald's, Wendy's 🅾 Family$, K-Mart, Rite Aid, Save-A-Lot Foods, USPO
206	to US 24, Phillips Ave, W 🅾 transmissions
205b	Berdan Ave, E 🅾 🅷 W 🅖 Marathon/dsl 🍴 Burger King, Subway
205a	to Willys Pkwy, to Jeep Pkwy
204	I-475 W, to US 23 (exits left fom nb), to Maumee, Ann Arbor
203b	US 24, to Detroit Ave, W 🅖 AP/dsl, BP 🍴 KFC, McDonald's, Rally's, Wendy's 🅾 Rite Aid, Save-A-Lot Foods, U-Haul
203a	Bancroft St, downtown
202	Washington St, Collingwood Ave (from sb, no EZ return), E 🅖 BP 🅾 🅷 Art Museum, W 🍴 McDonald's
201b a	OH 25, Collingwood Ave, W 🅾 Toledo Zoo
200mm	Maumee River
200	South Ave, Kuhlman Dr
199	OH 65, Miami St, to Rossford, E 🛏 Days Inn
198	Wales Rd, Oregon Rd, to Northwood, E 🅖 Shell/Subway/dsl

TOLEDO

INTERSTATE 75 Cont'd

Exit #	Services
198	Continued Sunoco/dsl Ⓕ Arby's, China Wok, Coney Is. Ⓛ Baymont Inn, Comfort Inn
197	Buck Rd, to Rossford, **E** Ⓖ Shell/dsl Ⓕ Tim Horton's, Wendy's, **W** Ⓖ BP, Sunoco/dsl Ⓕ Denny's, McDonald's Ⓛ American Inn, Knights Inn
195	to I-80/90, OH 795, OH Tpk (toll), Perrysburg, **E** Ⓖ BP/Subway/dsl Ⓛ Country Inn&Suites, Courtyard, Hampton Inn Ⓞ Bass Pro Shops
193	US 20, US 23 S, Perrysburg, **E** Ⓖ BP/dsl, GetGo, Sunoco Ⓕ 1st Wok, 5 Guys Burgers, Arby's, Big Boy, Bob Evans, Burger King, Chili's, China City, Coldstone, Cracker Barrel, Dragon Chef, Fricker's, IHOP, Jimmy John's, KFC, Mancino's Pizza, Ok Patron, Panera Bread, Penn Sta Subs, Sonic, Subway, Taco Bell Ⓛ Candlewood Suites, Comfort Suites, EconoLodge, Holiday Inn, Holiday Inn Express, Quality Inn Ⓞ $Tree, Belle Tire, Best Buy, Discount Tire, Giant Eagle Foods, GNC, Hobby Lobby, Home Depot, KOA (7mi), Kohl's, Kroger/gas/E85, Lowe's, Meijer/dsl, Michael's, Petsmart, Radio Shack, Target, TJ Maxx, Tuffy, Walgreens, Walmart/Subway, **W** Ⓖ Speedway/dsl Ⓛ La Quinta Ⓞ AutoZone, Harley-Davidson
192	I-475, US 23 N (exits left from nb), to Maumee, Ann Arbor
187	OH 582, to Luckey, Haskins
181	OH 64, OH 105, to Pemberville, Bowling Green, **E** Ⓛ Holiday Inn Express Ⓞ Meijer/dsl/E85, **W** Ⓖ BP/Circle K/Subway/dsl, Speedway Ⓕ Big Boy, Bob Evans, Buffalo Wild Wings, Burger King, Chipotle Mexican, Cinco de Mayo, Coldstone/Tim Horton's, Domino's, El Zarape Mexican, Fricker's Rest., Hunan Buffet, Jimmy John's, McDonald's, Padrone's Pizza, Starbucks, Waffle House, Wendy's Ⓛ Best Western, Days Inn, Hampton Inn, Quality Inn, Victory Inn Ⓞ Ⓗ to Bowling Green State U, USPO, Verizon
179mm	Ⓡˢ both lanes, full Ⓗ facilities, litter barrels, petwalk, Ⓒ, Ⓢ vending
179	US 6, to Fremont, Napoleon, **W** Ⓞ museum
175mm	weigh sta nb
171	OH 25, Cygnet
168	Eagleville Rd, Quarry Rd, **E** Ⓖ FuelMart/dsl
167	OH 18, to Fostoria, North Baltimore, **E** Ⓖ Petro/BP/Iron Skillet/dsl/scales/24hr/@ Ⓕ McDonald's Ⓞ Blue Beacon, truck repair, **W** Ⓖ ♥Love's/Arby's/dsl/scales/24hr, Sunoco Crown Inn Ⓞ $General, Great Scot Mkt
165mm	Rocky Ford River
164	OH 613, to McComb, Fostoria, **E** Ⓞ KOA, Van Buren SP, **W** Ⓖ 🚂/Subway/Taco Bell/dsl/scales/24hr
162mm	weigh sta sb, Ⓒ
161	rd 99, **E** Ⓖ Shell/Subway, Speedway/dsl Ⓛ Comfort Suites Ⓞ Ford/Lincoln, hwy patrol, Kia, **W** Ⓞ antiques
159	US 224, OH 15, Findlay, **E** Ⓖ BP/dsl, Speedway/dsl, Swifty Ⓕ Archie's Ice Cream, Burger King, Culver's, Dakota Grill, Fin's Seafood Grill, Jimmy John's, KFC/LJ Silver, McDonald's, Ming's Great Wall, Pizza Hut, Ralphie's, Spaghetti Shop, Steak'n Shake, Subway, Taco Bell, Wendy's Ⓛ Drury Inn, Motel 6, Red Roof Inn, Rodeway Inn Ⓞ Ⓗ auto/truck repair, **W** Ⓖ Murphy USA/dsl, Shell/dsl Ⓕ Bob Evans, China Garden, Coldstone/Tim Horton's, Cracker Barrel, Denny's, Hokkaido Steaks, Jac&Do's Pizza, Landing Pad, Max&Erma's, Outback Steaks, Tony's Rest., TX Roadhouse, Waffle House Ⓛ Country Inn&Suites, Hampton Inn, Holiday Inn Express,

	Quality Inn Ⓞ Best 1 Tires/repair, Chrysler/Dodge/Jeep, Peterbilt, Verizon, Walmart/Subway
158mm	Blanchard River
157	OH 12, Findlay, **E** Ⓖ GA/dsl, Marathon/Blimpie/Noble Roman's/dsl Ⓞ Findlay Convention Ctr, **W** Ⓕ Fricker's Rest. Ⓛ EconoLodge Ⓞ vet
156	US 68, OH 15, to Carey, **E** Ⓞ Ⓗ
153mm	Ⓡˢ both lanes, full Ⓗ facilities, litter barrels, petwalk, Ⓒ, Ⓢ vending
145	OH 235, to Ada, Mount Cory, **E** Ⓞ TwinLakes Camping
142	OH 103, to Arlington, Bluffton, **E** Ⓛ Knights Inn, **W** Ⓖ BP/dsl, Marathon/Circle K/dsl Ⓕ Arby's, Burger King, KFC, McDonald's/rv parking, Subway, Taco Bell Ⓛ Comfort Inn Ⓞ $General, auto repair, to Bluffton Coll, vet
140	Bentley Rd, to Bluffton, **W** Ⓞ Ⓗ
135	OH 696, to US 30, to Delphos, Beaverdam, **E** Ⓖ Speedway/dsl/24hr, **W** Ⓖ ✈FLYING J/Denny's/dsl/scales/LP/24hr/@, 🚂/McDonald's/Subway/dsl/24hr/@ Ⓕ Waffle House Ⓞ Blue Beacon, SpeedCo, tires, truck repair
134	Napolean Rd (no nb re-entry), to Beaverdam
130	Bluelick Rd, **E** Ⓛ Best Value Inn
127b a	OH 81, to Ada, Lima, **W** Ⓖ BP/dsl, Marathon/Subway/dsl Ⓕ Waffle House Ⓛ Comfort Inn, Days Inn/rest. Ⓞ Best 1 Tires/repair
126mm	Ottawa River
125	OH 309, OH 117, Lima, **E** Ⓖ BP/dsl, Murphy USA/dsl, Speedway/dsl Ⓕ Applebee's, Arby's, Bob Evans, Burger King, Capt D's, China Buffet, Cracker Barrel, Hunan Garden, J's Grill, McDonald's, Olive Garden, Panera Bread, Pizza Hut, Ralphie's, Red Lobster, Skyline Chili, Subway, Taco Bell, TX Roadhouse, Wendy's Ⓛ Courtyard, Hampton Inn, Howard Johnson, Motel 6 Ⓞ BigLots, Ford, K-Mart, Radio Shack, Ray's Foods, Sam's Club/gas, Verizon, Walgreens, Walmart/McDonald's, **W** Ⓖ Shell Ⓕ Kewpee Hamburger's, Yamato Steaks Ⓛ Country Inn&Suites, Holiday Inn, Travelodge Ⓞ Ⓗ $General, Advance Parts, Best 1 Tires/repair, Curves, Rite Aid, Save-A-Lot Foods
124	4th St, **E** Ⓞ hwy patrol
122	OH 65, Lima, **E** Ⓖ Speedway/dsl, **W** Ⓖ Marathon/Subway/dsl Ⓞ Freightliner, GMC, Mack, truck repair, vet, Volvo
120	Breese Rd, Ft Shawnee, **W** Ⓖ AP Trkstp/dsl Ⓞ Harley-Davidson
118	to Cridersville, **W** Ⓖ Fuelmart/Subway/dsl, Speedway/dsl Ⓕ Dixie Ley Diner Ⓞ $General
114mm	Ⓡˢ both lanes, full Ⓗ facilities, litter barrels, petwalk, Ⓒ, Ⓢ vending
113	OH 67, to Uniopolis, Wapakeneta

⬆N	**INTERSTATE 75 Cont'd**
Exit #	**Services**
111	Bellefontaine St, Wahpakeneta, **E** ☐ TA/Marathon/rest./dsl/scales/@ ☐ Country Charm Rest. ☐ Knights Inn ☐ KOA, truck tires, **W** ☐ BP/dsl, Murphy USA/dsl, Shell ☐ Arby's, Bob Evans, Burger King, Capt D's, Comfort Zone, DQ, El Azteca, King Buffet, Lucky Steer Rest., McDonald's, Pizza Hut, Taco Bell, Waffle House, Wendy's ☐ Best Western, Comfort Inn, Super 8, Western Inn ☐ Advance Parts, Aldi Foods, CVS Drug, Lowe's, Neil Armstrong Museum, O'Reilly Parts, Radio Shack, st patrol, Verizon, Walmart
110	US 33, to St Marys, Bellefontaine, **E** ☐ hwy patrol, KOA
104	OH 219, v, **W** ☐ Marathon/dsl, Shell/Circle K/Subway/dsl ☐ Larry's Pizza ☐ Budget Host
102	OH 274, to Jackson Ctr, New Breman, **E** ☐ bicycle museum, **W** ☐ air stream tours
99	OH 119, to Minster, Anna, **E** ☐ 99/dsl, **W** ☐ GA/Taco Bell, Shell ☐ Subway, Wendy's ☐ lube/wash/repair
94	rd 25A, Sidney, **E** ☐ Marathon/deli
93	OH 29, to St Marys, Sidney, **W** ☐ Lake Loramie SP, RV camping
92	OH 47, to Versailles, Sidney, **E** ☐ Shell, Speedway/dsl ☐ Arby's, China Garden, Coldstone, Subway, Time Horton, Wendy's ☐ ☐ $General, AutoZone, CVS Drug, DM, NAPA, Save-A-Lot Foods, URGENT CARE, Walgreens, **W** ☐ Murphy USA/dsl, Sunoco/dsl, Valero ☐ A&W/LJ Silver, Applebee's, Bob Evans, Buffalo Wild Wings, Burger King, Cazadores Mexican, Culver's, Highmarks Rest., KFC, McDonald's, Perkins, Pizza Hut, Quiznos, Smokin Joe's BBQ, Sonic, Taco Bell, Waffle House ☐ Comfort Inn, Country Hearth Inn, Days Inn, Travel Inn ☐ $Tree, Aldi Foods, AT&T, Best 1 Tires/repair, Buick/Cadillac/Chevrolet/GMC, Chrysler/Dodge/Jeep, Ford/Lincoln, Kroger/dsl, Lowe's, Menards, Radio Shack, Staples, Walmart/McDonald's
90	Fair Rd, to Sidney, **E** ☐ Sunoco/dsl, **W** ☐ Marathon/DQ/dsl ☐ Hampton Inn
88mm	Great Miami River
83	rd 25A, Piqua, **W** ☐ Marathon/MaidRite Cafe/Noble Roman's/dsl ☐ Red Carpet Inn ☐ Chrysler/Dodge/Jeep, Sherry RV Ctr, to Piqua Hist Area
82	US 36, to Urbana, Piqua, **E** ☐ Murphy USA/dsl, Valero ☐ A&W/LJ Silver, Arby's, China East, China Garden, DQ, KFC, Pizza Hut/Taco Bell, Subway, Waffle House, Wendy's ☐ $Tree, Aldi Foods, BigLots, Harley-Davidson, Home Depot, JoAnn Fabrics, Radio Shack, st patrol, Verizon, vet, Walmart/Subway, **W** ☐ Speedway ☐ Bob Evans, Cracker Barrel, El Tapatio Mexican, McDonald's, Red Lobster ☐ Comfort Inn, Knights Inn, La Quinta ☐ JC Penney
81mm	℞ both lanes, full ☐ facilities, litter barrels, ☐, ☐, vending
78	rd 25A, **E** ☐ ☐
74	OH 41, to Covington, Troy, **E** ☐ BP/dsl ☐ Al's Pizza, China Garden, Donato's Pizza, Fox's Pizza, Little Caesars, McDonald's, Pizza Hut, Subway, Taco Bell ☐ ☐ Radio Shack, Super Petz, to Hobart Arena, **W** ☐ Shell, Speedway/dsl ☐ Applebee's, Big Boy, Bob Evans, Buffalo Wild Wings, Burger King, Chipotle Mexican, Culver's, Fazoli's, Friendly's, KFC, Logan's Roadhouse, Los Pitayos Mexican, Outback Steaks, Panera Bread, Penn Sta Subs, Ruby Tuesday, Sakai Japanese, Skyline Chili, Sonic, Steak'n Shake ☐ Best Inn, Comfort Suites, Fairfield Inn, Hampton Inn, Holiday Inn Express, Residence Inn ☐ $General, $Tree, AT&T, AutoZone, GNC, Goodyear, Kohl's, Lowe's, Meijer/dsl, Staples, Tire Discounters, Verizon, Walmart/Subway

73	OH 55, to Ludlow Falls, Troy, **E** ☐ BP, Shell ☐ Boston Stoker Coffee House, Hot Head Burrito, Lincoln Sq Rest., Papa John's, Subway, Waffle House, Wendy's ☐ Quality Inn, Royal Inn, Super 8 ☐ ☐ $General, Kroger/e85
69	rd 25A, **E** ☐ BP/Circle K/Subway/dsl, Starfire/dsl ☐ Arbogast RV Ctr, Buick/GMC, Chrysler/Dodge/Jeep, Ford
68	OH 571, to West Milton, Tipp City, **E** ☐ BP/dsl, Shell, Speedway/dsl ☐ Burger King, Cassano's Pizza, Hickory River BBQ, Hong Kong Kitchen, McDonald's, Subway, Taco Bell ☐ AutoValue Parts, CVS Drug, Family$, FoodTown, Goodyear, Honda, Verizon, **W** ☐ Speedway/dsl ☐ Arby's, Big Boy, Bob Evans, Tipp' O the Town Rest., Wendy's ☐ Holiday Inn Express, La Quinta ☐ Main St Parts, Menards, vet
64	Northwoods Blvd, **E** ☐ El Toro Mexican, Emperial Palace ☐ $Tree, Kroger/dsl, **W** ☐ ✈FLYING J/Subway/dsl/scales/RV dump/24hr
63	US 40, to Donnelsville, Vandalia, **E** ☐ Speedway/dsl ☐ Bunker's Grill, Dragon China, Fricker's ☐ repair, **W** ☐ BP/dsl, Shell, Speedway/dsl ☐ Arby's, Burger King, Domino's, Hot Head Burrito, KFC/LJ Silver, McDonald's, Pizza Hut, Rib House, Subway, Taco Bell, Waffle House, Wendy's ☐ Super 8 ☐ Goodyear/auto, Rexall Drug, Rite Aid
61b a	I-70, E to Columbus, W to Indianapolis, to Dayton Int ☐
59	Wyse Rd, Benchwood Rd, **E** ☐ El Rancho Grande, Little York Pizza, Mr Lee's ☐ Dayton Inn, Hawthorne Suites ☐ BMW/Volvo/VW, Discount Tire, **W** ☐ Speedway/dsl, Valero ☐ Arby's, Asian Buffet, Big Boy, Bob Evans, Cassano's Pizza, Chick-fil-A, Chipotle Mexican, Coldstone, Cracker Barrel, Fricker's, Golden Corral, Hooters, LoneStar Steaks, Max&Erma's, McDonald's, O'Charley's, Olive Garden, Outback Steaks, Panera Bread, Pop's Diner, Red Lobster, Ruby Tuesday, Sake Japanese, Skyline Chili, SmashBurger, SmokeyBones BBQ, Steak'n Shake, Subway, Tim Horton ☐ Best Value Inn, Comfort Inn, Country Inn&Suites, Courtyard, Days Inn, Drury Inn, Extended Stay America, Fairfield Inn, Hampton Inn, Knights Inn, Red Roof Inn, Residence Inn, Rodeway Inn, TownePlace Suites ☐ Batteries+, Office Depot, Radio Shack, Sam's Club/gas, Verizon, Walmart/Subway
58	Needmore Rd, to Dayton, **E** ☐ BP/dsl, Shell/McDonald's ☐ Hardee's ☐ Goodyear/auto, to AF Museum, **W** ☐ Marathon/dsl, Speedway/dsl, Sunoco/dsl, Swifty ☐ A&W/LJ Silver, Church's, Domino's, Subway, Tim Horton, Waffle House, Wendy's ☐ $Tree, Advance Parts, AutoZone, Kroger/gas, O'Reilly Parts, repair/transmissions, USPO, Walgreens
57b	Wagner Ford Rd, Siebenthaler Rd, Dayton, **E** ☐ Sunoco ☐ Ramada Inn
57a	Neva Rd
56	Stanley Ave, Dayton, **E** ☐ Shell, **W** ☐ Clark ☐ Dragon City Chinese, Gold Star Chili, McDonald's, Taco Bell ☐ Dayton Motel ☐ truck repair
55b a	Keowee St, Dayton, downtown
54mm	Great Miami River
54c	OH 4 N, Webster St, to Springfield, downtown
54b	OH 48, Main St, Dayton, **E** ☐ Cadillac, Chevrolet, Honda, **W** ☐ BP ☐ ☐
54a	Grand Ave, Dayton, downtown
53b	OH 49, 1st St, Salem Ave, Dayton, downtown
53a	OH 49, 3rd St, downtown
52b a	US 35, E to Dayton, W to Eaton
51	Edwin C Moses Blvd, Nicholas Rd, **E** ☐ ☐Loves/Hardee's/dsl/scales/24hr ☐ Courtyard ☐ ☐ to U of Dayton, **W** ☐ BP/dsl ☐ McDonald's, Wendy's ☐ EconoLodge ☐ SunWatch Indian Village

Vertical labels: SIDNEY, TROY, OH, DAYTON

⛽ = gas 🍴 = food 🛏 = lodging 🄾 = other Ⓡ🅂 = rest stop

INTERSTATE 75 Cont'd

Exit #	Services
50b a	OH 741, Kettering St, Dryden Rd, **E** 🄾 Ⓗ vet, **W** 🍴 Marathon/dsl 🛏 Days Inn, Super 8 🄾 U-Haul
47	Dixie Dr, W Carrollton, Moraine, **E** 🍴 Sunoco, Valero 🍴 Big Boy, Waffle House 🄾 auto repair, transmissions, **W** 🍴 Shell, Speedway/dsl 🍴 El Mason, Ele Cake Co., KFC, McDonald's, Pizza Hut, Sonic, Taco Bell, Wendy's 🄾 $General, USPO
44	OH 725, to Centerville, Miamisburg, **E** 🍴 BP/dsl, Shell, Speedway 🍴 Applebee's, Baskin-Robbins, Big Boy, Bonefish Grill, Bravo Italiana, Burger King, Dunkin Donuts, El Toro Mexican, Fazoli's, Friendly's, Golden Corral, Hardee's, Jimmy John's, KFC, Logan's Roadhouse, Lonestar Steaks, McDonald's, O'Charley's, Olive Garden, Panera Bread, PF Chang's, Red Lobster, Rooster's Grill, Rusty Bucket Grill, Sake Japanese, Skyline Chili, SmashBurger, Starbucks, Steak'n Shake, Subway, Taco Bell, TGIFriday's, Waffle House, Wendy's 🛏 Comfort Suites, Courtyard, DoubleTree Suites, Garden Inn, Homewood Suites, InTowne Suites, SpringHill Suites, Studio 6 🄾 Ⓗ $Tree, Advance Parts, Aldi Foods, AT&T, Barnes&Noble, Best Buy, Cub Foods, Dick's, Elder Beerman, Hobby Lobby, Home Depot, Honda/Nissan/Mazda, JC Penney, JoAnn Fabrics, Kia, Lowe's, Macy's, mall, Michael's, NTB, Office Depot, PepBoys, Petsmart, Sears/auto, Super Petz, Target, Tire Discounters, TJ Maxx, Toyota/Scion, URGENT CARE, Verizon, Walmart, **W** 🍴 BP, Marathon, Shell/dsl 🍴 Bob Evans, LJ Silver, Perkins, Tim Horton 🛏 Knights Inn, Quality Inn, Red Roof Inn, Super 8 🄾 Ⓗ $General, Aamco, CarMax, Chevrolet, Ford, NAPA
43	I-675 N, to Columbus
41	Austin Blvd, **E** 🄾 Kohl's
38	OH 73, Springboro, Franklin, **E** 🍴 Shell, Speedway 🍴 Applebee's, Arby's, Bob Evans, Burger King, China Garden, Chipotle Mexican, KFC, LJ Silver, McDonald's, Papa John's, Pizza Hut, Skyline Chili, Subway, Taco Bell, Tim Horton, Wendy's 🛏 Comfort Inn, Hampton Inn 🄾 K-Mart, Kroger, Radio Shack, Tire Discounters, vet, **W** 🍴 Murphy USA/dsl, Road Ranger, Shell, Swifty 🍴 A&G Pizza, Big Boy, Cazadore's Mexican, Domino's, GoldStar Chili, Lee's Chicken, McDonald's 🛏 EconoLodge, Holiday Inn Express, Knights Inn 🄾 $General, $Tree, Advance Parts, AutoZone, Clark's Drug, Kemper Auto, Main St Mkt, NAPA, USPO, Walgreens, Walmart
36	OH 123, to Lebanon, Franklin, **E** 🍴 BP, ⛽/Subway/Pizza Hut/dsl/scales/24hr/@, Shell 🍴 McDonald's, Waffle House 🛏 Quail Inn, **W** 🍴 Marathon/White Castle/dsl, Sunoco
32	OH 122, Middletown, **E** 🍴 McDonald's 🛏 Best Value Inn, Days Inn, Reyton Inn, Super 8 🄾 Ⓗ CVS Drug, **W** 🍴 Applebee's, Arby's, Big Boy, Bob Evans, Cracker Barrel, El Rancho Grande, Golden Corral, GoldStar Chili, Hot Head Burrito, KFC, La Rosa's Pizza, LoneStar Steaks, O'Charley's, Olive Garden, Schlotzsky's, Sonic, Steak'n Shake, Wendy's, White Castle 🛏 Country Hearth Inn, Drury Inn, Fairfield Inn, Holiday Inn Express 🄾 Aldi Foods, AT&T, AutoZone, BigLots, Elder Beerman, Kohl's, Kroger/dsl, Lowe's, Meijer/dsl, PetMart, Sears/auto, Staples, Target, Tire Discounters, URGENT CARE, Verizon, Walmart
29	OH 63, to Hamilton, Monroe, **E** 🍴 Shell/Popeye's/dsl, Stony Ridge/dsl 🍴 Burger King, GoldStar Chili, Tim Horton/Wendy's, Waffle House 🛏 Comfort Inn 🄾 Premium Outlets/Famous Brands, Tire Discounters, Trader's World, **W** 🍴 Speedway/dsl 🍴 Froggy Blue's, McDonald's, Richard's Pizza, Sara Jane's Rest., Subway 🛏 Hampton Inn, Howard Johnson 🄾 Honda

MIDDLETOWN (vertical label)

Map of Ohio showing: Wauseon, Toledo (280), Bowling Green (80), Ottawa, Findlay, Elida, Lima, Mansfield (71), Marion, Sidney, Delaware, Huber Heights, Troy, Dublin, Columbus, Westerville, Dayton, Fairborn, Lancaster, Centerville, Zanesville (77), (70), (75), OH

27.5mm	Ⓡ🅂 both lanes, info, full ♿ facilities, litter barrels, petwalk, 🄲, 🔧, vending
24	OH 129 W, to Hamilton, **W** 🄾 Cincinnati Gardens
22	Tylersville Rd, to Mason, Hamilton, **E** 🍴 Sunoco, Thornton's/dsl 🍴 5 Guys Burgers, Arby's, Bob Evans, BoneFish Grill, Burger King, Caribou Coffee, Chick-fil-A, Chopsticks, City BBQ, Firehouse Subs, Geisha, GoldStar Chili, IHOP, Jimmy John's, KFC, LJ Silver, Longhorn Steaks, McAlister's Deli, McDonald's, Noodles&Co, Panera Bread, Perkins, Pizza Hut, Qdoba, Ruby Tuesday, Skyline Chili, SmashBurger, Soho Japanese, Starbucks, Subway, Taco Bell, TGIFriday's, Twin Dragon, Wendy's 🛏 Economy Inn 🄾 Ⓗ AT&T, BigLots, Firestone, GNC, Goodyear/auto, Home Depot, Kohl's, Kroger, Michael's, Office Depot, Petsmart, Radio Shack, Target, Tires+, TJ Maxx, Verizon, Walgreens, **W** 🍴 Shell, Speedway/dsl 🍴 O'Charley's 🛏 Wingate Inn 🄾 Aldi Foods, CarX, Lowe's, Meijer/dsl, Tire Discounters
21	Cin-Day Rd, **E** 🍴 Big Boy 🛏 Holiday Inn Express, **W** 🍴 Marathon/dsl, Mobil/Subway/dsl, Speedway/dsl 🍴 Arby's, Domino's, Guenther's Steaks, La Rosa's Pizza, Las Copas Mexican, Papa John's, Sonic, Waffle House, Wendy's, White Castle 🄾 Ace Hardware, AutoZone, Curves, PetMart, Walgreens, Walmart/Subway
19	Union Centre Blvd, to Fairfield, **E** 🍴 Bravo Italiana, Champps Rest., Mitchell's Fish Mkt, Original Pancakes, Panera Bread, PF Chang's, Red Robin, Smokey Bones BBQ, Steak'n Shake 🄾 Barnes&Noble, Verizon, **W** 🍴 BP/Subway/dsl, Marathon/Circle K, Shell 🍴 Aladdin's Eatery, Applebee's, Bob Evans, Buffalo Wild Wings, Burger King, Chipotle Mexican, Jag's Steaks, Jimmy John's, McDonald's, Qdoba, Quiznos, Rafferty's, Skyline Chili, Starbucks, Tazza Mia, Uno, Wendy's 🛏 Comfort Inn, Courtyard, Hampton Inn, Marriott, Residence Inn, Staybridge Suites 🄾 Mercedes, Volvo
16	I-275 to I-71, to I-74
15	Sharon Rd, to Sharonville, Glendale, **E** 🍴 Sunoco, Sunoco, Thornton's/dsl 🍴 5 Guys Burgers, Big Boy, Bob Evans, Burger King, Chick-fil-A, Chili's, ChuckeCheese, Cracker Barrel, IHOP, Jim Dandy BBQ, LJ Silver, Macaroni Grill, McDonald's, Panera Bread, Pizza Hut, Ruby Tuesday, Skyline Chili, Subway, Subway, Taco Bell, Tokyo Japanese, Vincenzo's, Waffle House, Wendy's 🛏 Baymont Inn, Country Inn&Suites, Crowne Plaza, Drury Inn, EconoLodge, Extended Stay America, Extended Stay Deluxe, Fairfield Inn, Hawthorn Suites, Hilton Garden, Holiday Inn Express, La Quinta, LivInn Suites, Red Roof Inn, Residence Inn, Travel Inn, Travelodge, Wyndham 🄾 Best Buy, Costco/gas, Dick's, Lowe's, Nissan, Sam's Club, Sears, Target

Ⓖ = gas   Ⓕ = food   🏠 = lodging   Ⓞ = other   Ⓡˢ = rest stop   Copyright 2015 - the Next EXIT ®

⬆N INTERSTATE 75 Cont'd

Exit #	Services
14	OH 126, to Woodlawn, Evendale, **E** 🏠 Wingate Inn (3mi) Ⓞ GE Plant, **W** Ⓖ Swifty
13	Shepherd Lane, to Lincoln Heights, **E** Ⓞ GE Plant, **W** Ⓕ Taco Bell, Wendy's Ⓞ Advance Parts
12	Wyoming Ave, Cooper Ave, to Lockland, **W** Ⓖ Marathon Ⓕ DQ, Subway
10b	Galbraith Rd (exits left from nb), Arlington Heights
10a	OH 126, Ronald Reagan Hwy
9	OH 4, OH 561, Paddock Rd, Seymour Ave, **E** Ⓞ to Cincinnati Gardens, **W** Ⓞ fairgrounds
8	Towne St, Elmwood Pl (from nb)
7	OH 562, to I-71, Norwood, Cincinnati Gardens
6	Mitchell Ave, St Bernard, **E** Ⓖ Marathon, Shell, Sunoco Ⓕ White Castle 🏠 Holiday Inn Express Ⓞ to Cincinnati Zoo, to Xavier U, Walgreens, **W** Ⓖ BP/Subway/dsl Ⓕ McDonald's, Rally's Ⓞ Advance Parts, Family$, Ford, Honda, Hyundai, Kia, Kroger, Tires+
4	I-74 W, US 52, US 27 N, to Indianapolis
3	to US 27 S, US 127 S, Hopple St, **E** Ⓖ BP/Subway/dsl Ⓕ Camp Washington Chili, Isador Italian, White Castle Ⓞ Ⓗ Family$, U of Cincinnati, **W** Ⓖ Shell Ⓕ Wendy's
2b	Harrison Ave, **W** Ⓖ BP Ⓕ McDonald's, industrial district
2a	Western Ave, Liberty St (from sb)
1g	Ezzard Charles Dr, **W** 🏠 Ramada Inn
1f	US 50W, Freeman Ave, **W** Ⓖ Sunoco Ⓕ Big Boy, Pizza Hut/ Taco Bell, Wendy's, White Castle 🏠 Ramada Inn Ⓞ Ford, GMC, NAPA, USPO
1e	7th St (from sb), downtown
1c	5th St, **E** 🏠 Crowne Plaza, Hyatt, Millenial Hotel, Sheraton Ⓞ Macy's, to Duke Energy Center, downtown
1a	I-71 N, to Cincinnati, downtown, to stadium
0mm	Ohio/Kentucky state line, Ohio River

⬆E INTERSTATE 76

Exit #	Services
	Ohio/Pennsylvania state line, See OH TPK exits 232-234
60mm	I-76 eb joins Ohio TPK (toll)
57	to OH 45, Bailey Rd, to Warren
54	OH 534, to Newton Falls, Lake Milton, **N** Ⓞ RV camping, **S** Ⓖ Sunoco/dsl Ⓞ camping, to Berlin Lake
52mm	Lake Milton
48	OH 225, to Alliance, **N** Ⓞ camping, to W Branch SP, **S** Ⓞ to Berlin Lake, to Lake Milton SP
45mm	Ⓡˢ both lanes, full ♿ facilities, litter barrels, petwalk, 📞, 🦮
43	OH 14, to Alliance, Ravenna, **N** Ⓞ to W Branch SP, **S** Ⓖ Marathon/Subway/dsl Ⓞ fireworks
38b a	OH 5, OH 44, to Ravenna, **N** Ⓖ BP/dsl, Speedway/dsl Ⓕ Arby's, McDonald's/rv parking, Wendy's, **S** Ⓖ Marathon/Circle K/Subway Ⓕ Cracker Barrel Ⓞ Ⓗ $General, auto parts, Giant Eagle Foods, RV camping
33	OH 43, to Hartville, Kent, **N** Ⓖ BP/dsl, Marathon Ⓕ Salsita's Mexican 🏠 Comfort Inn, Days Inn, EconoLodge, Hampton Inn, Holiday Inn Express, Super 8 Ⓞ to Kent St U, **S** Ⓖ Circle K, Speedway/dsl Ⓕ Gionino's Pizza, McDonald's, Pizza Hut, Subway, Wendy's Ⓞ $General, Goodyear Tire/brakes, vet
31	rd 18, Tallmadge, **N** Ⓖ Murphy USA/dsl Ⓕ #1 Chinese, Applebee's, Beef'O'Brady's, DQ, La Terraza Mexican, Panera Bread Ⓞ $Tree, AT&T, GNC, Kohl's, Lowe's, Marshall's, Petco, Verizon, Walmart/Subway

Exit #	Services
29	OH 532, Tallmadge, Mogadore
27	OH 91, Canton Rd, Gilchrist Rd, **N** Ⓕ Bob Evans, **S** Ⓖ Marathon/Subway/dsl Ⓕ Hardee's 🏠 Quality Inn
26	OH 18, E Market St, Mogadore Rd, **N** Ⓖ Marathon/dsl Ⓞ Hamad Tire/repair, **S** Ⓕ Arby's, McDonald's, Subway, Wendy's Ⓞ $General
25b a	Martha Ave, General St, Brittain, **N** Ⓖ Circle K/dsl 🏠 Hilton Garden Ⓞ Mercedes, Toyota/Scion, **S** Ⓞ Goodyear HQ
24	Arlington St, Kelly Ave, **S** Ⓞ Goodyear HQ
23b	OH 8, Buchtell Ave, to Cuyahoga (exits left from eb), to U of Akron
23a	I-77 S, to Canton
22b	Grant St, Wolf Ledges, Akron, **N** Ⓞ USPO, **S** Ⓖ BP Ⓕ McDonald's Ⓞ Family$, downtown
22a	Main St, Broadway, downtown
21c	OH 59 E, Dart Ave, **N** Ⓞ Ⓗ
21b	Lakeshore St, Bowery St (from eb)
21a	East Ave (from wb)
20	I-77 N (from eb), to Cleveland
19	Battles Ave, Kenmore Blvd
18	I-277, US 224 E, to Canton, Barberton
17b	OH 619, Wooster Rd, **S** Ⓖ Sunoco/dsl Ⓞ Ⓗ tires/repair
17a	(from eb, no return) State St, to Barberton, **S** Ⓕ Papa John's, Papa Roni's Pizza Ⓞ Ⓗ Walgreens
16	Barber Rd, **S** Ⓖ Rocky's/dsl/E85 Ⓕ DQ, Tomaso's Italian Ⓞ Chrysler/Dodge/Jeep, Fiat
14	Cleve-Mass Rd, to Norton, **S** Ⓖ BP/Blimpie/dsl, Circle K/dsl Ⓕ Arby's, Casa Del Mar Mexican, McDonald's, Pizza Hut, Subway, Wendy's Ⓞ $General, Ace Hardware, Acme Fresh Mkt, Advance Parts, CVS Drug, Family$, Radio Shack, Ritzman Drug, USPO, Verizon
13b a	OH 21, N to Cleveland, S to Massillon
11	OH 261, Wadsworth, **N** Ⓖ Speedway/dsl, **S** Ⓖ GetGo/E85, Giant Eagle Ⓕ Arabica Cafe, Beef'O'Brady's, Wayback Burger Ⓞ AAA, GNC, Kohl's, Lowe's, MC Sports, PetCo, Target, Verizon
9	OH 94, to N Royalton, Wadsworth, **N** Ⓖ Marathon/Circle K Ⓕ Applebee's, Arby's, Bob Evans, Burger King, China Express, Chipotle Mexican, Galaxy Rest., Marie's Cafe, McDonald's, Panera Bread, Patron's Mexican, Pizza Hut, Romeo's Pizza, Starbucks, Subway, Taco Bell, Wendy's 🏠 Comfort Inn, Holiday Inn Express Ⓞ $General, $Tree, BigLots, Buehler's Foods, DrugMart, Goodyear/auto, Home Depot, NTB, Radio Shack, Verizon, Walmart/Subway, **S** Ⓖ Marathon/DQ/dsl, Sunoco Ⓕ Casa Del Rio, Dunkin Donuts, Papa John's 🏠 Legacy Inn Ⓞ Advance Parts, auto repair, AutoZone, CVS Drug, NAPA, Rite Aid, vet
7	OH 57, to Rittman, Medina, **N** Ⓖ Marathon/dsl, **S** Ⓞ Ⓗ 🍽
6mm	**weigh sta eb**
2	OH 3, to Medina, Seville, **N** Ⓖ Marathon/Circle K/dsl Ⓕ DQ, Hardee's, Huddle House, Pizzazo's, Subway 🏠 Comfort Inn, Hawthorn Suites Ⓞ Maple Lakes Camping (seasonal), **S** Ⓖ Clark, Shell/dsl Ⓕ #1 Chinese, E of Chicago Pizza, El Patron Mexican Ⓞ $General, Ritzman Drug, Verizon
1	I-76 E, to Akron, US 224, **W** on US 224 Ⓖ Ⓕ/Subway/dsl/scales/24hr, TA/BP/Burger King/Popeye's/dsl/scales/24hr/@ Ⓕ Arby's, McDonald's, Starbucks 🏠 Super 8 Ⓞ Blue Beacon, Chippewa Valley Camping (1mi), SpeedCo
0mm	**I-76 begins/ends on I-71, exit 209.**

Side labels: CINCINNATI AREA • AKRON

⬆N   INTERSTATE 77

Exit #	Services
I-77 begins/ends on I-90 exit 172, in Cleveland.	
163c	I-90, E to Erie, W to Toledo
163b	E 9th St, Tower City
162b	E 22nd St, E 14th St (from nb)
162a	E 30th St, Woodland Ave, Broadway St (from nb), **W** 🅞 USPO
161b	I-490 W, to I-71, E 55th, **E** 🅞 🅷
161a	OH 14 (from nb), Broadway St
160	Pershing Ave (from nb), **W** 🅞 🅷
159b	Fleet Ave, **E** 🅖 BP/Subway/dsl
159a	Harvard Ave, Newburgh Heights, **W** 🅖 BP/Subway/dsl
158	Grant Ave, Cuyahoga Heights
157	OH 21, OH 17 (from sb), Brecksville Rd
156	I-480, to Youngstown, Toledo
155	Rockside Rd, to Independence, **E** 🅖 Shell, Sunoco/dsl 🍴 Aladdin's, Bob Evans, Bonefish Grill, Del Monico's Steaks, Denny's, DiBella's Subs, Jimmy John's, McDonald's, Melt Grill, Outback Steaks, Panera Bread, Red Robin, Shula's Steaks, Starbucks, Wendy's, Zoup 🏨 Comfort Inn, Double-tree, Embassy Suites, Holiday Inn, La Quinta, Red Roof Inn 🅞 Drugmart, to Cuyahoga Valley NP, Verizon, Walgreens, **W** 🅖 BP/dsl 🍴 Applebee's, Longhorn Steaks 🏨 Courtyard, Crowne Plaza, Hampton Inn, Hyatt Place, Residence Inn
153	Pleasant Valley Rd, to Independence, 7 Hills
151	Wallings Rd
149	OH 82, to Broadview Heights, Brecksville, **E 1 mi** 🅖 BP, Shell 🍴 Austin's Grille, McDonald's, Panera Bread, Sakura Japanese, Starbucks, Subway 🅞 CVS Drug, vet, **W** 🅖 BP, GetGo 🅞 Giant Eagle Foods
147	to OH 21, Miller Rd (from sb)
146	I-80/Ohio Tpk, to Youngstown, Toledo
145	OH 21 (from nb), **E** 🅖 🚚/Wendy's/dsl/scales 🍴 DQ, Memories Rest., Richfield Rest., Subway 🏨 Days Inn, Hampton Inn, Holiday Inn Express, Motel 6, Super 8
144	I-271 N, to Erie
143	OH 176, to I-271 S, **W** 🅖 Sunoco 🍴 McDonald's, Panda Chinese, Richfield Cafe, Subway, Teresa's Pizza
141mm	🆁🆂 both lanes, full ♿ facilities, litter barrels, petwalk, 🄲, 🕿 vending
138	Ghent Rd, **W** 🅖 Circle K/dsl 🍴 Gasoline Alley, Lanning's Rest.
137b a	OH 18, to Fairlawn, Medina, **E** 🅖 BP, GetGo, Shell, Speedway 🍴 5 Guys Burgers, Applebee's, A-Wok, Bob Evans, Boston Mkt, Chick-fil-A, Chili's, Chipotle Mexican, Coldstone, Cracker Barrel, Cusina Italian, Donato's Pizza, Fleming's Steaks, Friendly's, Gionino's Pizza, HoneyBaked Ham, Hudson's Rest., Hyde Park Grille, Macaroni Grill, Max&Erma's, McDonald's, Menchie's, Olive Garden, Pad Thai, Penn Sta Subs, PF Chang's, Rail Burger Bar, Red Lobster, Robeck's FruitJuice, Starbucks, Steak'n Shake, Subway, Swenson's Drive-In, Taco Bell, Wendy's 🏨 Baymont Inn, Courtyard, DoubleTree, EconoLodge, Hampton Inn, Hilton, Holiday Inn, Motel 6 🅞 $Tree, Acme Foods, Aldi Foods, AT&T, Barnes&Noble, Best Buy, Dick's, Dillard's, Earth Fare Foods, Ford, Giant Eagle Foods, Goodyear/auto, Hobby Lobby, Home Depot, JC Penney, Jo-Ann Fabrics, Lowe's, Macy's, Michael's, NTB, Old Navy, Petsmart, Sam's Club, Staples, TJ Maxx, Verizon, Walmart, World Mkt, **W** 🍴 Burger King, Don Pablo, Longhorn Steaks, Nicolinni's, Outback Steaks, Steak on a Stone, TGIFriday's, Tres Patrilios, Wasabi Grill 🏨 Best Western, Comfort Inn, Radisson, StayPlace Suites, Studio+ 🅞 🅷

Exit #	Services
136	(exits left from nb), OH 21S, to Massillon
135	Cleveland-Massillon Rd (from nb, no return)
133	Ridgewood Rd, Miller Rd, **E** 🅖 Circle K/dsl, **W** 🍴 Old Carolina BBQ, Tiffany's Bakery
132	White Pond Dr, Mull Ave
131	OH 162, Copley Rd, **E** 🅖 Circle K 🍴 Church's 🅞 Save-A-Lot Foods, USPO, Walgreens, **W** 🅖 BP/dsl/24hr 🍴 McDonald's, Pizza Hut
130	OH 261, Wooster Ave, **E** 🅖 Circle K, Marathon/dsl, Valero 🍴 Ann's Place, Burger King, Church's, New Ming Chinese, Rally's, Subway 🅞 Acme Foods, Advance Parts, AutoZone, Family$, O'Reilly Parts, **W** 🅞 Chevrolet, Toyota/Scion, U-Haul
129	I-76 W, to I-277, to Kenmore Blvd, Barberton
I-77 and I-76 run together, See I-76 exits 21a-22b	
125b	I-76 E, to Youngstown, I-77 and I-76 run together
125a	OH 8 N, to Cuyahoga Falls, 🅞 U of Akron
124b	Lover's Lane, Cole Ave
124a	Archwood Ave, Firestone Blvd (from sb), **E** 🅖 BP
123b	OH 764, Wilbeth Rd, **E** 🍴 DQ 🅞 to 📶
123a	Waterloo Rd (from sb), **W** 🅖 GetGo, Marathon 🍴 Burger King, Hungry Howies, Papa John's, Rally's, Subway 🅞 $Tree, Giant Eagle Foods, Goodyear/auto, Rite Aid, Walgreens
122b a	I-277, US 224 E, to Barberton, Mogadore
120	Arlington Rd, to Green, **E** 🅖 Speedway/dsl 🍴 Applebee's, Church's/White Castle, Denny's, Friendly's, Golden Corral, IHOP, Starbucks, Waffle House 🏨 Comfort Inn, Quality Inn, Red Roof Inn 🅞 $General, AutoZone, Home Depot, Kohl's, Staples, Walmart, **W** 🅖 BP 🍴 Bob Evans, Burger King, Chipotle Mexican, CiCi's Pizza, Lion Garden, Mariachi Mexican, McDonald's, Panera Bread, Subway, Taco Bell, Wendy's 🏨 Fairfield Inn, Hampton Inn, Holiday Inn Express, ValuePlace Inn 🅞 Acura, Buick/GMC, Chevrolet, GNC, Goodyear/auto, Honda, Hyundai, Lexus, Lowe's, Mazda, Meineke, Nissan, Sirpilla RV Ctr/Camping World, Subaru, Target
118	OH 241, to OH 619, Massillon, **E** 🅖 Sheetz, Speedway/dsl 🍴 Gionino's Pizza, Handel's Icecream, Subway, **W** 🅖 BP/Circle K, GetGo 🍴 Arby's, DQ, Grille 39, Hungry Howie's, Lucky Star Chinese, McDonald's, Menche's Rest., Quiznos, Subway 🏨 Cambria Suites, Super 8 🅞 🅷 $General, Advance Parts, AT&T, Curves, Giant Eagle Foods, Verizon, vet
113	**W** 🏨 Hilton Garden 🅞 Akron-Canton 🛫, General RV Ctr (2mi)
112	Shuffel St
111	Portage St, N Canton, **E** 🅖 Circle K, Marathon, Sunoco/dsl, TA/Country Pride/dsl/scales/24hr/@ 🍴 Burger King, Geisen Haus, Jimmy's Rest., KFC, Palombo's Italian, Quaker Steak, Subway, Sylvester's Italian 🅞 TrueValue, **W** 🅖 BP/dsl,

C L E V E L A N D

F A I R L A W N

A K R O N

OH

INTERSTATE 77 Cont'd

Exit #	Services
111	Continued

Speedway/dsl 🍴 5 Guys Burgers, Baskin-Robbins/Dunkin Donuts, Bonefish Grill, Carrabba's, ChuckeCheese, Coldstone, Cracker Barrel, Don Pablo, Donato's Pizza, Dunkin Donuts/Baskin-Robbins, Heavenly Ham, Hungry Howie's, IHOP, Longhorn Steaks, Lucky Star Chinese, McDonald's, Panera Bread, Philly Connection, Pizza Hut, Red Robin, Rockne's Cafe, Samantha's Rest., Subway, Taco Bell, Wasabi Japanese, Wendy's 🏠 Best Western, Microtel, Motel 6 🅾 At&T, Best Buy, BJ's Whse, Chevrolet, DrugMart, Gander Mtn, Giant Eagle Foods, GNC, Goodyear/auto, Harley-Davidson, Home Depot, Lowe's, Marshall's, Old Navy, Sam's Club/gas, Walgreens, Walmart/Subway/auto

109 b a Everhard Rd, Whipple Ave, **E** 🚗 Marathon/Subway, Speedway/dsl 🍴 Denny's, Fazoli's, McDonald's, Taco Bell, Waffle House 🏠 Comfort Inn, Fairfield Inn, Hampton Inn, La Quinta, Residence Inn 🅾 Ford, **W** 🚗 Marathon 🍴 Applebee's, Arby's, Bob Evans, Bravo Italian, Buffalo Wild Wings, Buffet Dynasty, Cheeseburger Paradise, Chick-fil-A, Chili's, Chipotle Mexican, Chips&Salsa Mexican, CiCi's Pizza, Damon's, Fox&Hound Grill, Friendly's, Golden Corral, HomeTown Buffet, HoneyBaked Ham, Jimmy John's, KFC, LoneStar Steaks, Macaroni Grill, Manchu Cafe, Max&Erma's, Mulligan's, Olive Garden, Outback Steaks, Panera Bread, Panini's Grill, Papa Bear's, Papa Gyros, Penn Sta. Subs, Perkin's, Red Lobster, Rita's Custard, Roadhouse Cafe, Robek's Cafe, Ruby Tuesday, Sahara Grill, Starbucks, Steak'n Shake, TGIFriday's, Wendy's 🏠 Courtyard, Holiday Inn, Knights Inn, Magnuson Hotel, Red Roof Inn 🅾 $Tree, Aamco, Advance Parts, Aldi Foods, AT&T, Dick's, Dillard's, Firestone/auto, Goodyear/auto, Jo-Ann Fabrics, Kohl's, Macy's, mall, Marc's Foods, NTB, Petsmart, Radio Shack, Sears/auto, Target, TJ Maxx, Tuesday Morning, USPO, Verizon, World Mkt

107 b a US 62, OH 687, Fulton Rd, to Alliance, **E** 🚗 Marathon/Circle K/Subway 🅾 city park, **W** 🚗 Circle K 🅾 Pro Football Hall of Fame

106	13th St NW, **E** 🅾 🅷
105b	OH 172, Tuscarawas St, downtown
105a	6th St SW (no EZ return from sb), **E** 🚗 Sunoco 🍴 McDonald's, **W** 🍴 Subway 🅾 🅷 AutoZone
104 b a	US 30, US 62, to E Liverpool, Massillon

103 OH 800 S, **E** 🚗 Marathon/Subway/dsl, Speedway 🍴 Arby's, DQ, Italo's Pizza, McDonald's, Peking Chinese, Taco Bell, Waffle House 🅾 Advance Parts, auto repair, Family$, Goodyear/auto, Rite aid, Save-A-Lot Foods

101 OH 627, to Faircrest St, **E** 🚗 🛻/Subway/dsl/scales/24hr, Speedway/McDonald's 🍴 Wendy's

99	Fohl Rd, to Navarre, **W** 🚗 Sunoco 🅾 KOA (4mi)

93 OH 212, to Zoar, Bolivar, **E** 🚗 Speedway/Subway/dsl 🍴 McDonald's, Pizza Hut, Wendy's 🏠 Sleep Inn 🅾 $General, Giant Eagle Foods, NAPA, to Lake Atwood Region, vet, Zoar Tavern HS (3mi), **W** 🚗 Marathon/DQ 🅾 KOA

87 US 250W, to Strasburg, **W** 🚗 Marathon/dsl 🍴 Hardee's, Manor Rest., McDonald's, Subway 🏠 Ramada Ltd 🅾 Verizon

85 Schneiders Crossing Rd, to Dover, **E** 🚗 Marathon 🍴 Arby's, Subway

83 OH 39, OH 211, to Sugarcreek, Dover, **E** 🚗 BP, Speedway/Subway/dsl 🍴 Bob Evans, KFC, McDonald's, Shoney's, Wendy's 🏠 Best Value Inn 🅾 🅷 Chrysler/Dodge/Jeep,

83	Continued

Flynn's Tires, Ford, Honda, Lincoln, Nissan, **W** 🏠 Comfort Inn, Country Inn&Suites

81 US 250, to Uhrichsville, OH 39, New Philadelphia, **E** 🚗 KwikFill, Sheetz/dsl, Speedway 🍴 Burger King, Denny's, El San Jose Mexican, Hog Heaven BBQ, LJ Silver, McDonald's, Pizza Hut, Taco Bell, TX Roadhouse 🏠 Best Western, Hampton Inn, Holiday Inn Express, Knights Inn, Motel 6, Schoenbrunn Inn 🅾 $General, $Tree, Advance Parts, Aldi Foods, BigLots, Walmart/Subway, **W** 🚗 Auto TP/rest./dsl/scales/24hr 🅾 Harley-Davidson

73	OH 751, to rd 53, Stone Creek, **W** 🚗 Marathon/dsl

65 US 36, Port Washington, Newcomerstown, **W** 🚗 BP, Duke TP/rest./dsl, Speedway/Wendy's 🍴 McDonald's 🏠 Hampton Inn, Super 8

64mm	Tuscarawas River
54	OH 541, rd 831, to Plainfield, Kimbolton, **W** 🚗 BP 🍴 Jackie's Rest.

47 US 22, to Cadiz, Cambridge, **E** 🏠, 🅾 RV camping, to Salt Fork SP (6mi), **W** 🚗 BP/repair 🅾, 🅷 info, to Glass Museum

46 b a US 40, to Old Washington, Cambridge, **W** 🚗 Clark, Marathon/Wendy's/dsl, Speedway/dsl 🍴 Burger King, Hunan Chinese, Lee's Rest., LJ Silver, McDonald's 🅾 Family$, Riesbeck's Food

44 b a	I-70, E to Wheeling, W to Columbus

41 OH 209, OH 821, Byesville, **W** 🚗 Circle K, Starfire 🍴 McDonald's, Subway 🅾 $General, Byesville Drug, Family$, museum, to Glenn HS

39mm 🆁🆂 sb, full 🦽 facilities, litter barrels, petwalk, 🅲, 🖼 vending

37 OH 313, Buffalo, **E** 🚗 BP 🍴 Coutos Pizza, Subway 🅾 to Senecaville Lake, truck repair, UPSO

36mm 🆁🆂 sb, full 🦽 facilities, litter barrels, petwalk, 🅲, 🖼 vending

28 OH 821, Belle Valley, **E** 🚗 Sunoco/dsl 🅾 RV camping, to Wolf Run SP, USPO

25 OH 78, Caldwel, **E** 🚗 BP, 🛻/Arby's/dsl/scales/24hr, Sunoco/Subway/dsl 🍴 DQ, Lori's Rest., McDonald's 🏠 Best Western

16	OH 821, Macksburg, **E** 🍴, 🅾 antiques

6 OH 821, to Devola, **E** 🚗 Exxon/dsl, **W** 🚗 Marathon/dsl/LP 🅾 🅷 RV camping

3mm 🆁🆂 nb, full 🦽 facilities, info, litter barrels, petwalk, 🅲, 🖼 vending

1 OH 7, to OH 26, Marietta, **E** 🚗 GoMart/dsl/24hr 🍴 Black Smith Grill, China Wind, DQ, Subway 🏠 Comfort Inn, Fairfield Inn, Holiday Inn 🅾 $Tree, Aldi Foods, Buick/GMC, Cadillac/Chevrolet, Chrysler/Dodge/Jeep, Ford/Lincoln, Lowe's, Radio Shack, Toyota/Scion, Walmart/McDonald's, **W** 🚗 BP/dsl, Duke/dsl, GetGo/dsl, Marathon/dsl, Speedway/dsl 🍴 Applebee's, Arby's, Bar-B-Cutie, Bob Evans, Burger King, Capt D's, China Fun, E Chicago Pizza, Empire Buffet, KFC, Little Caesar's, LJ Silver, McDonald's, Napoli's Pizza, Papa John's, Pizza Hut, Shoney's, Subway, Taco Bell, Tim Horton, Wendy's 🏠 Hampton Inn, Microtel, Super 8 🅾 Advance Parts, AT&T, AutoZone, BigLots, Curves, CVS Drug, Family$, Food4Less, JoAnn Fabrics, K-Mart, Kroger, museum, Rite Aid, Save-A-Lot Foods, st patrol, TrueValue, Verizon, Walgreens

0mm	Ohio/West Virginia state line, Ohio River

CANTON

MARIETTA

OH

INTERSTATE 80

Exit #	Services
237mm	Ohio/Pennsylvania state line
237mm	**Welcome Center wb, full facilities, info, litter barrels, pet-walk, vending**
234b a	US 62, OH 7, Hubbard, to Sharon, PA, Hubbard, N *FLYING J*/Denny's/dsl/LP/scales/24hr, Shell/rest./dsl/scales/motel/24hr/@ Arby's, Burger King, Dunkin Donuts, McDonald's, Waffle House Best Western, Travelodge Blue Beacon, Homestead RV Ctr., tire/dsl repair, S BP/dsl, Love's /Chester's/Subway/dsl/scales/24hr Chevrolet
232mm	weigh sta wb
229	OH 193, Belmont Ave, to Youngstown, N GetGo, Speedway/dsl Chad Anthony's Italian, Fortune Garden, Handel's Ice Cream, Sta Square Italian, Subway Hampton Inn, Motel 6, Super 8 Giant Eagle Foods, S BP/dsl, Shell Arby's, Bob Evans, Charley's Subs, Denny's, Fiesta Tapatia, Golden Hunan Chinese, Happy Buffet, Ianazones Pizza, Jimmy's Italian, KFC, Little Caesars, LJ Silver, McDonald's, Monteen's Southern Cuisine, Pizza Hut, Señor Jalapeño Mexican, Subway, Taco Bell, Uptown Pizza, Wendy's, Westfork Steaks, Youngstown Crab Co Days Inn, Quality Inn $General, Advance Parts, Aldi Foods, AutoZone, Family$, Firestone/auto, Goodyear/auto, O'Reilly Parts, Radio Shack, Rite Aid, SaveALot Foods, vet, Walgreens, Walmart/Subway
228	OH 11, to Warren (exits left from eb), Ashtabula
227	US 422, Girard, Youngstown, N Shell/dsl Burger King, DQ, Firegrill BBQ, JibJab Hotdogs, Subway
226	Salt Springs Rd, to I-680 (from wb), N BP/Dunkin Donuts/dsl, Sheetz/dsl McDonald's, Waffle House vet, S Mr Fuel/Road Rocket Diner/dsl/24hr, Petro/Shell/Iron Skillet/dsl/scales/24hr/@, Subway/dsl/scales/24hr Blue Beacon, dsl repair, Frank's Truckwash, SpeedCo
224b	I-680 (from eb), to Youngstown
224a	OH 11 S, to Canfield
223	OH 46, to Niles, N Country Fair/dsl, McDonald's/dsl/scales/24hr Bob Evans, Dunkin Donuts, IceHouse Rest., Salsita's Mexican Candlewood Suites, Comfort Inn, Holiday Inn Express, Hotel California, S BP/dsl, FuelMart/dsl/scales, Sunoco/Subway, TA/Counry Pride/dsl/scales/24hr/@ Arby's, Cracker Barrel, LJ Silver/Taco Bell, Los Gallos Mexican, Perkins, Quaker Steak&Lube, Starbucks, Wendy's Best Western, Country Inn&Suites, EconoLodge, Fairfield Inn, Hampton Inn, Sleep Inn, Super 8 Freightliner/24hr, Harley-Davidson
221mm	Meander Reservoir
219mm	**I-80 wb joins Ohio Tpk (toll)**
	For I-80 exits 2-218, see Ohio Turnpike.

INTERSTATE 90

Exit #	Services
244mm	Ohio/Pennsylvania state line
242mm	**/weigh sta wb, full facilities, info, litter barrels, pet-walk, vending**
241	OH 7, to Andover, Conneaut, N Burger King, McDonald's (2mi) Days Inn AutoZone, Evergreen RV Park, K-Mart, S Love's/McDonald's/Subway/dsl/scales/24hr Beef&Beer Café
235	OH 84, OH 193, to Youngstown, N Kingsville, N Grab&Go/gas, Marathon/Circle K Dav-Ed Motel Village Green Camping (2mi), S Circle K/Subway/dsl, TA/BP/Burger King/dsl/scales/24hr/@ Kay's Place Diner Kingsville Motel tire repair

228	OH 11, to Ashtabula, Youngstown, N (4mi)
223	OH 45, to Ashtabula, N *FLYING J*/Denny's/Shell/dsl/LP/scales/24hr Mr C's Rest. Best Value Inn, Holiday Inn Express, Ramada, Sleep Inn Buccaneer Camping, S /Subway/dsl/scales/24hr, SpeedCo Burger King, McDonald's, Quinn's Grille, Waffle House Hampton Inn auto repair
218	OH 534, Geneva, N GetGo Best Friend's Grill, Chop's Grille, McDonald's, Pizza Hut, Wendy's Motel 6 Goodyear/repair, Indian Creek Camping (8mi), to Geneva SP, S KwikFill/Subway/dsl/scales/24hr Kenisse's Camping
212	OH 528, to Thompson, Madison, N Cornerstone Rest., McDonald's Mentor RV Ctr, S Marathon/dsl Heritage Hills Camping (4mi), radiator repair
205	Vrooman Rd, S 0-2 mi BP/dsl, Marathon/dsl Capps Eatery, Subway Indian Point Park, Masons Landing Park
200	OH 44, to Painesville, Chardon, S BP/Subway/dsl, Sunoco/dsl Bellacino's, CK Steakhouse, McDonald's, Palmer's Bistro, Paninis, Red Hawk Grille, Teresa's Pizzaria, Waffle House Baymont Inn, Quail Hollow Resort Curves, hwy patrol, Reider's Foods, URGENT CARE
198mm	**both lanes, full facilities, litter barrels, petwalk, vending**
195	OH 615, Center St, Kirtland Hills, Mentor, N 1-2 mi BP El Rodeo Mexican, Yours Truly Rest. Best Western
193	OH 306, to Mentor, Kirtland, N 0-2 mi BP/Subway, Shell, Speedway Chipotle Mexican, McDonald's Best Value Inn, Comfort Inn, Super 8, S Speedway/dsl Burger King Days Inn, Red Roof Inn Kirtland Temple LDS Historic Site
190	Express Lane to I-271 (from wb)
189	OH 91, to Willoughby, Willoughby Hills, N BP/dsl, Shell Arby's (1mi), Bob Evans, Café Europa, Cracker Barrel, Eat'n Park, Peking Chef, Subway, TX Roadhouse, Wendy's Courtyard, Motel 6, Radisson (2mi), Travelodge CVS Drug, Walgreens, S BMW/Mini, Lexus
188	I-271 S, to Akron
187	OH 84, Bishop Rd, to Wickliffe, Willoughby, S BP/dsl, Shell Baker's Square, Golden Mtn Chinese, McDonald's, Mr Hero, Subway, Tony's Pizza Ramada Inn AT&T, Chevrolet, Curves, CVS Drug, Giant Eagle Foods, Marc's Foods, Mazda/VW, NTB, Verizon
186	US 20, Euclid Ave, N Sunoco McDonald's Mosley Suites, Quality Inn Ford, radiators/transmissions, Subaru, Suzuki, S Shell Arby's, KFC, Popeye's, R-Ribs, Sidewalk Cafe, Taco Bell $General, Advance Parts, Family$, Firestone/auto, Save-a-Lot Foods

E U C L I D

OH

INTERSTATE 90 Cont'd

Exit #	Services
185	OH 2 E (exits left from eb), to Painesville
184b	OH 175, E 260th St, N 🅿 Shell 🅾 USPO, S 🅾 auto/tire repair, vet
184a	Babbitt Rd, N Buick/GMC
183	E 222nd St, N 🅿 Sunoco/dsl, tires, S 🅿 BP, Sunoco 🅾 vet
182b a	185 St, 200 St, N 🍴 Subway 🅾 Home Depot, Honda, Hyundai, S 🅾 Marathon/dsl, Shell/dsl, Speedway/dsl
181b a	E 156th St, S 🅿 BP
180b a	E 140th St, E 152nd St
179	OH 283 E, to Lake Shore Blvd
178	Eddy Rd, to Bratenahl
177	University Circle, MLK Dr, N 🅾 Cleveland Lake SP, S 🅾 🏨 Rockefeller Park
176	E 72nd St
175	E 55th St, Marginal Rds
174b	OH 2 W, to Lakewood, downtown, Browns Stadium, Rock&Roll Hall of Fame
174a	Lakeside Ave
173c	Superior Ave, St Clair Ave, N 🅿 BP, downtown
173b	Chester Ave, S 🅿 BP
173a	Prospect Ave (from wb), downtown
172d	Carnegie Ave, S 🍴 Burger King 🅾 Cadillac, downtown
172c b	E 9th St, S 🅾 🏨 to Cleveland St U
172a	I-77 S, to Akron
171b a	US 422, OH 14, Broadway St, Ontario St, N 🅿 BP 🏨 Hilton Garden 🅾 to Browns Stadium
171	Abbey Ave, downtown
170c b	I-71 S, to I-490
170a	US 42, W 25th St, S 🅿
169	W 44th St, W 41st St, N 🅾 🏨
167b a	OH 10, West Blvd, 98th St, to Lorain Ave, N 🅾 🏨 S 🅿 BP/dsl 🅾 CVS Drug
166	W 117th St, N 🅿 BP/dsl, Get Go, Shell 🍴 KFC 🅾 Advance Parts, Giant Eagle Foods, Home Depot, Staples, Target, S 🍴 Church's/White Castle
165	W 140th St, Bunts Rd, Warren Rd, N 🅿 Marathon 🅾 🏨
164	McKinley Ave, to Lakewood
162	Hilliard Blvd (from wb), to Westway Blvd, Rocky River, S 🅿 BP, Shell
161	OH 2, OH 254 (from eb, no EZ return), Detroit Rd, Rocky River
160	Clague Rd (from wb), S 🅾 🏨 same as 159
159	OH 252, Columbia Rd, N 🍴 Carrabba's, Clubhouse Grille, Dave&Busters, Manero's, Outback Steaks 🏨 Courtyard, Super 8, TownePlace Suites 🅾 🏨 S 🅿 BP 🍴 Houlihan's, KFC, McDonald's, Taco Bell 🅾 Chevrolet, NTB
156	Crocker Rd, Bassett Rd, Westlake, Bay Village, N 🅿 BP, Shell 🏨 Extended Stay Deluxe, Holiday Inn, Red Roof Inn, Residence Inn, S 🅿 BP, Speedway 🍴 5 Guys Burgers, Applebee's, Baskin-Robbins, Blake's Seafood, Bob Evans, Cabin Club Steaks, Caribou Coffee, Cheesecake Factory, Chicago Grill, Chipotle Mexican, El Rodeo Mexican, Max&Erma's, McDonald's, Starbucks, Subway, TGIFriday's, Vieng's Asian, Wendy's 🏨 Hampton Inn 🅾 🏨 Aldi Foods, CVS Drug, Giant Eagle, GNC, mall, Marc's Foods, Radio Shack, Sears Grand, Trader Joes
155	new exit
153	OH 83, Avon Lake, N 🅿 GetGo/dsl, Marathon/Dunkin Donuts/dsl 🍴 Arby's, Bubba's BBQ, Buffalo Wild Wings, Perkins 🅾 AutoZone, Best Buy, Firestone/auto, JC Penney, Lowe's, PetCo, Walmart/auto, S 🍴 5 Guys Burgers, Applebees,

AVON

153	**Continued** Bob Evans, Burger King, Caribou Coffee, CiCi's Pizza, Coldstone, Hot Dog Heaven, IHOP, Mandarin House, Moe's SW Grill, Panera Bread, Quiznos, Red Robin, Subway, Wendy's 🅾 AT&T, Costco/gas, Curves, CVS Drug, GNC, Home Depot, Kohl's, Marc's Foods, Marshall's, Michael's, Old Navy, Radio Shack, Target, World Mkt
151	OH 611, Avon, N 🅿 BP/dsl, ⛽/Subway/dsl/24hr 🍴 McDonald's 🏨 Fairfield Inn, Value Place Hotel 🅾 Chevrolet, Goodyear/repair, Harley-Davidson, S 🅿 BJ's Whse/gas 🍴 Mulligan's Grille
148	OH 254, Sheffield, Avon, N 🍴 Quaker Steak&Lube 🅾 Ford, GMC, KIA, Mazda, Mitsubishi, Nissan, S 🅿 BP, Get-Go, Sheetz, Speedway 🍴 Arby's, Burger King, China Star, Cracker Barrel, KFC, McDonald's, Pizza Hut, Ruby Tuesday, Steak'n Shake, Subway, Taco Bell, Wendy's 🅾 $General, $Tree, Aldi Foods, CVS Drug, Drug Mart, Gander Mtn, Giant Eagle, NTB, Sam's Club/gas
147mm	Black River
145	OH 57, to Lorain, I-80/Ohio Tpk E, Elyria, N 🅿 Speedway 🍴 George's Rest., Hunan King, Red Lobster, Wendy's 🏨 Country Inn&Suites 🅾 Chevrolet, Save-a-Lot, U-Haul, vet, S 🅿 Speedway 🍴 #1 Buffet, Applebee's, Arby's, Bob Evans, Buffalo Wild Wings, Burger King, Chipotle Mexican, Denny's, Eat'n Park, Golden Corral, Harry Buffalo, McDonald's, Old Century Buffet, Olive Garden, Red Lobster, Subway, Wasabi Grill, Wendy's 🏨 Best Western, Comfort Inn, Country Inn&Suites, EconoLodge, Red Carpet Inn, Red Roof Inn, Super 8 🅾 $General, AT&T, Best Buy, Curves, Dick's, Firestone/auto, Giant Eagle, Home Depot, Honda, Hyundai, JC Penney, Jo-Ann Fabrics, Lowe's, Macy's, Marc's Foods, NTB, Petsmart, Radio Shack, Sears, Staples, Target, Tuffy Repair, Verizon, Walmart/auto
144	OH 2 W (from wb, no return), to Sandusky, N **1 mi on Broadway Ave** E 🅿 Marathon, Shell/24hr 🍴 McDonald's 🅾 🏨
143	**I-90 wb joins Ohio Tpk. WB exits to Ohio/Indiana state line are on Ohio Turnpike, exits 142-0.**
142	I-90 (from eb, exits left), OH 2, to W Cleveland
140	OH 58, Amherst, N **0-2 mi** 🅿 BP, GetGo, Speedway, Sunoco/Subway/dsl 🍴 Blue Sky Rest., Bob Evans, Donato's Pizza, DQ, KFC, Marco's Pizza, McDonald's, Moosehead Grill, Mr Hero, Taco Bell, Wendy's 🏨 Days Inn, Motel 6 🅾 Advance Parts, Aldi Foods, Chevrolet, Chrysler/Dodge, Drug Mart, Giant Eagle Foods, K-Mart, repair, Rite Aid, USPO, VW, Walgreens, S 🅾 Ford
139mm	**Service Plaza both lanes,** 🅿 Sunoco/dsl/24hr 🍴 Burger King, Great Steak&Potato, Hershey's, Panera Bread, Popeye's, Starbucks 🅾 gifts, phone, RV parking
135	rd 51, Baumhart Rd, to Vermilion
132mm	Vermilion River
118	US 250, to Norwalk, Sandusky, N 🅿 BP/Circle K/Dunkin Donuts, Marathon/dsl 🍴 Italian Gardens, McDonald's, Subway 🏨 Days Inn, Hampton Inn, Motel 6, Quality Inn, Red Roof Inn, Super 8 🅾 Milan RV Park, to Edison's Birthplace, S 🏨 Colonial Inn
110	OH 4, to Bellevue
100mm	**Service Plaza both lanes,** 🅿 Sunoco/dsl/24hr 🍴 Burger King, Cinnabon, Einstein Bros Bagels, Sbarro's, Starbucks 🅾 🅲
93mm	Sandusky River
91	OH 53, to Fremont, Port Clinton, N 🏨 Days Inn, S **0-2 mi** 🅿 BP/Subway/dsl/24hr, Murphy USA/dsl 🍴 Applebee's, Bob Evans, Burger King, Fricker's, Hibachi Buffet, McDonald's,

CLEVELAND

OH

INTERSTATE 90 Cont'd

Exit #	Services
91	Continued
	Pizza Hut, Subway, Taco Bell 🏠 Clarion, Comfort Inn, De-lux Inn, Hampton Inn 🅾️ 🏥 $Tree, Aldi Foods, Ford/Lincoln, Lowe's, Rutherford B. Hayes Library, Staples, USPO, Verizon, vet, Walmart
81	OH 51, Elmore, Woodville, Gibsonburg
80.5mm	Portage River
77mm	**Service Plaza both lanes,** 🛢️ Sunoco/dsl/24hr 🍴 Hardee's, Mancino's, Red Burrito 🅾️
71	I-280, OH 420, to Stony Ridge, Toledo, N 🛢️ *FLYING J*/Denny's/dsl/scales/LP/24hr, *Loves*/Arby's/dsl/scales/24hr, Petro/BP/Iron Skillet/dsl/scales/24hr/@ 🏠 Budget Inn, Crown Inn, Super 8, Travel Inn 🅾️ Blue Beacon, KOA, SpeedCo, S 🛢️ FuelMart/Roadeez Rest./dsl/scales, McDonald's/dsl/scales/24hr, TA/BP/Burger King/Taco Bell/dsl/scales/24hr/@ 🍴 Sunrise Grill 🅾️ truckwash
64	I-75 N, to Toledo, Perrysburg, S 🏠 Country Inn&Suites, Courtyard, Hampton Inn 🅾️ Bass Pro Shops, BP/Subway/dsl
63mm	Maumee River
59	US 20, to I-475, Maumee, Toledo, N 🛢️ BP, Shell, Speedway/dsl 🍴 Bob Evans, Golden Lily, McDonald's, Olive Garden, Pizza Hut, Steak'n Shake, Subway, Waffle House 🏠 Clarion, Motel 6 🅾️ Family$, Goodyear/auto, Jo-Ann Fabrics, K-Mart, NAPA, O'Reilly Parts, Radio Shack, Rite Aid, Savers, to Toledo Stadium, Walgreens, S 🛢️ Speedway/dsl 🍴 Big Boy, Chipotle Mexican, Donato's Pizza, El Azteca, Fricker's, Friendly's, Jed's BBQ, La Fiesta Mexican, Red Lobster, Schlotzsky's, Taco Bell 🏠 Best Value Inn, Budget Inn, Comfort Inn, Hampton Inn, Holiday Inn, Red Roof Inn 🅾️ AT&T, Ford, Honda, Meijer/gas, Toyota/Scion
52	OH 2, to Toledo, N 🛢️ Shamrock/dsl 🍴 Loma Linda Mexican, S 🏠 Days Inn 🅾️, RV/truck repair
39	OH 109, S 🛢️ Country Corral/Valero/Winchesters Rest/dsl/scales/wi-fi/24hr
34	34 OH 108, to Wauseon, S 🛢️ Shell/Subway/dsl/24hr 🍴 Smith's Rest., 🏠 Wendy's Arrowhead Motel, Best Western, Holiday Inn Express, Super 8 🅾️ Toledo RV Ctr, Woods Trucking/repair (1mi), S **2 mi on US 20A** 🛢️ BP/Circle K, 🍴 A&W/KFC, Arby's, Burger King, DQ, Grasshopper Rest., Kamwa Chinese, McDonald's, Pizza Hut, Subway, Taco Bell 🅾️ $General, Ace Hardware, AutoZone, Circle K, Marathon, Murphy USA/dsl, O'Reilly Parts, Rite Aid, Valero, Walmart
25	OH 66, Burlington, N 🅾️ Harrison Lake SP, S **3 mi** 🅾️ Sauder Village Museum
24.5mm	Tiffen River
18	**Indian Meadow Service Plaza both lanes,** 🛢️ Sunoco/dsl 🍴 Burger King, Sbarro's, Starbucks
13	OH 15, to Bryan, Montpelier, S 🛢️ Marathon/dsl, Sunoco 🍴 4Seasons Rest. 🏠 EconoLodge, Holiday Inn Express, Rainbow Motel, Ramada Inn 🅾️ Hutch's dsl Repair
11.5mm	St Joseph River
3mm	toll plaza, 🅿️
2	OH 49, to US 20, N 🍴 Burger King, Subway 🅾️ info, truck tires
0mm	Ohio/Indiana state line

INTERSTATE 270 (Columbus)

Exit #	Services
55	I-71, to Columbus, Cincinnati

Exit #	Services
52b a	US 23, High St, Circleville, N 🛢️ Marathon/Circle K, Speedway/dsl 🍴 A&W/KFC, Arby's, Bob Evans, Burger King, China Town, LJ Silver, Los Campero's, McDonald's, Pizza Hut, Ponderosa, Roadhouse Grill, Skyline Chili, Subway, Taco Bell, Tim Horton, Waffle House, Wendy's, White Castle 🏠 Kozy Inn 🅾️ $General, AutoZone, Curves, Firestone, Kroger/gas, Lowe's, Walgreens, Walmart, S 🛢️ BP/dsl 🏠 Budget Inn 🅾️ Kioto Downs
49	Alum Creek Dr, N 🛢️ Duke/dsl, Sunoco/dsl 🍴 Donato's Pizza, KFC/LJ Silver, Subway, S 🛢️ BP/dsl 🍴 Arby's, McDonald's, Taco Bell, Wendy's 🏠 Comfort Inn, Sleep Inn
46b a	US 33, Bexley, Lancaster
43b a	I-70, E to Cambridge, W to Columbus
41b a	US 40, E 🛢️ BP, Shell 🍴 Bob Evans, Boston Mkt, Hooters, McDonald's, Outback Steaks, Rally's, Steak'n Shake, Texas Roadhouse 🅾️ Walgreens, W 🛢️ Mobil, Shell, Speedway 🍴 Fuddruckers, Golden Corral, Hunan Chinese, LoneStar Steaks
39	OH 16, Broad St, E 🛢️ Meijer/dsl, Speedway/dsl 🍴 Arby's, Chipotle Grill, Church's, Quizno's, Waffle House, White Castle 🏠 Country Inn&Suites 🅾️ 🏥 W 🛢️ Shell 🍴 Applebee's 🏠 Ramada Inn
37	OH 317, Hamilton Rd, E 🛢️ BP/dsl, Marathon, Speedway/dsl 🍴 Big Boy, Bob Evans, Burger King, Chinese Express, Damon's, Donato's Pizza, Hickory House, KFC, Pizza Hut/Taco Bell, Starbucks 🏠 Holiday Inn Express, SpringHill Suites 🅾️ Firestone, GNC, Kroger, W **2 mi** 🏠 Comfort Suites, Hampton Inn, Hilton Garden
35b a	I-670W, US 62, E 🛢️ Speedway/dsl 🍴 City BBQ, Donato's Pizza, McDonald's, Tim Horton 🅾️ CVS Drug, W I-670
33	no services
32	Morse Rd, E 🛢️ Marathon/DM, Speedway/dsl 🍴 Donato's Pizza 🅾️ Mazda, Toyota, W 🛢️ BP, Mobil/dsl, Shell/Subway 🍴 Applebee's, Champp's Grill, HomeTown Buffet, Kobe Japanese, Logan's Roadhouse, McDonald's, On-the-Border, Pizza Hut/Taco Bell, Steak'n Shake, Wendy's 🏠 Extended Stay America, Hampton Inn 🅾️ Best Buy, BMW, Cadillac, Carmax, Discount Tire, Jo-Ann Fabrics, Lexus, Lowe's Whse, Macy's, mall, Mercedes, Nordstrom's, NTB, Sam's Club, Target, Walmart/24hr
30	OH 161 E to New Albany, W to Worthington
29	OH 3, Westerville, N 🛢️ BP/dsl, Shell 🍴 Applebee's, Arby's, Chipotle Mexican, Fazoli's, McDonald's, Pizza Hut, Tim Horton 🏠 Baymont Inn, Knight's Inn 🅾️ CarQuest, Firestone/auto, Kroger, S 🛢️ Speedway/dsl, Sunoco/dsl 🍴 Carsoni's Italian, China House, Domino's, Subway 🅾️ Aldi Foods, Family$, Midas

TOLEDO *(vertical left margin)*

OH *(right margin tab)*

INTERSTATE 270 (Columbus) Cont'd

Exit #	Services
27	OH 710, Cleveland Ave, **N** 🅡 Speedway 🍴 Subway, Tim Horton, Wendy's 🏠 Quality Inn, Ramada Inn, Signature Inn Ⓞ CVS Drug, NAPA, Tuffy, **S** 🍴 Bob Evans, McDonald's, O'Charley's, Steak'n Shake 🏠 Embassy Suites Ⓞ Home Depot
26	I-71, S to Columbus, N to Cleveland
23	US 23, Worthington, **N** 🍴 Alexander's, Amazon Grill, Bob Evans, Bravo Italian, Buffalo Wild Wings, Champp's Grill, Chipotle Mexican, Columbus Fish Mkt, El Acapulco, Gilbert's Steaks, Lotus Grill, Mitchell's Steaks, Panera Bread, Quizno's, Ruth's Chris Steaks, Starbucks, Sushiko Japanese, Tutt's Italian 🏠 AmeriSuites, Courtyard, Days Inn, DoubleTree, Extended Stay America, Homewood Suites, Motel 6, Red Roof Inn, Residence Inn, Sheraton, **S** 🅡 BP 🍴 Buca Italian, Cosi Grill, Jimmy John's, McDonald's 🏠 Econolodge, Holiday Inn
22	OH 315, **N** 🅡 Marathon/dsl
20	Sawmill Rd, **N** 🅡 BP, Marathon/dsl 🍴 Burger King, McDonald's, Olive Garden, Subway, Taco Bell, Wendy's Ⓞ Buick/GMC, CVS Drug, Ford, Hyundai, Lincoln, Mazda, NTB, Subaru, Tire Kingdom, **S** 🅡 Meijer, Shell, Speedway 🍴 Applebee's, Arby's, Asian Star, BajaFresh, Bob Evans, Boston Mkt, Burger King, Charlie's Subs, Chili's, Chipotle Mexican, Cosi Grill, Don Pablo, Golden Corral, HoneyBaked Cafe, Joe's Crabshack, KFC, Krispy Kreme, McDonald's, Mongolian BBQ, Red Lobster, Ruby Tuesday, Steak'n Shake, Ted's MT Grill 🏠 Hampton Inn, Quality Inn, Woodfin Suites Ⓞ $Tree, Barnes&Noble, Big Lots, Cadillac/Honda, Discount Tire, Firestone, Jo-Ann Fabrics, Kohl's, Lowe's Whse, PetCo, Sam's Club, Staples, SteinMart, Target, Toyota/Scion, Trader Joe's
17b a	US 33, Dublin-Granville Rd, **E** 🅡 Marathon, Sunoco 🍴 Bob Evans, Donato's, Max&Erma's, McDonald's, Subway 🏠 Best Value Inn, Courtyard, Crowne Plaza, Embassy Suites, Hilton Garden, Red Roof Inn, Residence Inn Ⓞ BMW/Mini, CVS Drug, Kroger, Mitsubishi, Mr Tire, USPO
15	Tuttle Crossing Blvd, **E** 🅡 BP, Mobil 🍴 Bob Evans, Boston Mkt, Chipotle Mexican, Cozymel's, Longhorn Steaks, Macaroni Grill, McDonald's, PF Chang's, Pizza Hut/Taco Bell, River City Grill, TGIFriday, Wendy's 🏠 Drury Inn, Homewood Suites, Hyatt Place, La Quinta, Marriott Ⓞ JC Penney, Macy's, mall, Sears/auto, **W** 🅡 Exxon/Subway/dsl, Shell 🍴 Quizno's, Steak'n Shake, Uno Pizzaria 🏠 Staybridge Suites Ⓞ Best Buy, NTB, Walmart/auto, World Mkt
13	Cemetery Rd, Fishinger Rd, **E** 🅡 Shell/Subway, Speedway 🍴 Burger King, CheeseBurger Paradise, Chili's, Chiotle Mexican, Damon's, Dave&Buster's, Donato's Pizza, KFC, Panera Bread, Quizno's, Skyline Chili, Spaghetti's, TGIFriday, Tropical Bistro 🏠 Comfort Suites, Homewood Suites Ⓞ CVS Drug, Home Depot, Lowe's Whse, Radio Shack, Staples, Target, Tire Dicounters, **W** 🅡 BP, Mobil, Speedway, Sunoco 🍴 Bob Evans, Max&Erma's, McDonald's, Tim Horton, Wendy's 🏠 Hampton Inn, Motel 6 Ⓞ Nissan
10	Roberts Rd, **E** 🅡 Marathon, Thornton's/dsl 🍴 Subway, Tim Horton, Wendy's, **W** 🅡 Speedway 🍴 Waffle House 🏠 Courtyard, Quality Inn, Royal Inn Ⓞ Kroger/gas
8	I-70, E to Columbus, W to Indianapolis
7	US 40, Broad St, **E** 🅡 BP, Speedway 🍴 Bob Evans, Boston Mkt, Burger King, McDonald's, Popeye's, TeeJay's, Wendy's, White Castle Ⓞ Buick/GMC, Chevrolet, Chrysler/Jeep, Family$, Firestone/auto, Kohl's, NTB, Pepboys, Sears/auto, Staples, Suzuki, Target, Tuffy, **W** 🅡 GetGo, Speedway/dsl, Thornton's 🍴 A&W/LJ Silver, Arby's, Big Boy, KFC,

Exit #	Services
7	Continued Papa John's, Waffle House 🏠 Holiday Inn Express, Hometown Inn Ⓞ 🅗 CVS Drug, Giant Eagle Foods, Goodyear, Home Depot, Jo-Ann Fabrics
5	Georgesville, **E** 🅡 Marathon, Mobil, Sunoco/dsl Ⓞ Walmart, **W** 🍴 Applebee's, Arby's, Bob Evans, Buffalo Wild Wings, Chipotle Mexican, DQ, Fazoli's, Fiesta Mariachi, KFC/LJ Silver, LoneStar Steaks, McDonald's, O'Charley's, Red Lobster, Steak'n Shake, Subway, Wendy's, White Castle Ⓞ Advance Parts, GNC, Hyundai/Isuzu/Subaru, KIA, Kroger/gas, Lowe's Whse, NTB, Toyota/Scion, VW
2	US 62, OH 3, Grove City, **N** 🅡 BP, **S** 🅡 Shell, Speedway, Sunoco 🍴 Big Boy, Brewster's, Burger King, Domino's, Donato's Pizza, McDonald's, Quizno's, Subway, Tim Horton/Wendy's, Waffle House 🏠 Knight's Inn
0mm	I-71

⬆N INTERSTATE 271 (Cleveland)

Exit #	Services
39mm	I-271 begins/ends on I-90, exit 188
38mm	I-271/I-480, Express Lanes
36	Wilson Mills Rd, Highland Hts, Mayfield, **E** 🅡 Shell 🍴 Austin's Steaks 🏠 Hilton Garden, Holiday Inn Ⓞ CVS Drug, vet, **W** 🅡 BP, Marathon/dsl 🍴 Denny's, Hibachi Steaks, Panera Bread, Qdoba Ⓞ Dick's, DrugMart, Home Depot, Kohl's, Tuesday Morning, Verizon
34	US 322, Mayfield Rd, **E** 🅡 BP/7-11, Sunmart 🍴 5 Guys Burgers, DiBella's Subs, Fox&Hound Grille, HotHead Burritos, Jimmy John's, Potbelly, Starbucks, Subway, Wendy's Ⓞ 🅗 CVS Drug, Marc's Foods, Michael's, Mr Tire, Old Navy, Rite Aid, Target, Walgreens, Walmart, **W** 🅡 Marathon, Shell, Speedway 🍴 Arby's, Bob Evans, Burger King, El Rio Grande, McDonald's, Panera Bread, Panini's Grill, Penn Sta Subs, Sonic, Subway, TGI Friday's 🏠 Comfort Inn Ⓞ 🅗 Advance Parts, AT&T, Best Buy, Costco/gas, CVS Drug, Ford/Lincoln, Giant Eagle Foods, GNC, JoAnn Fabrics, Marshalls, Midas, Nissan, NTB, O'Reilly Parts, Petsmart, Radio Shack, Staples, Verizon, vet, World Mkt
32	Brainerd Rd, **E** 🍴 Champp's Rest., J Alexander's Ⓞ 🅗
29	US 422 W, OH 87, Chagrin Blvd, Harvard Rd, **E** 🅡 Shell, Speedway, Sunoco 🍴 Bahama Breeze, Bob Evans, Bravo Italian, Corky&Lenny's Rest., Firehouse Subs, Flemings, McDonald's, Mitchell's Fish Mkt, Paladar Latin Kitchen, Red Lobster, Starbucks, Stone Oven, Wasabi Japanese, Wendy's 🏠 Courtyard, Extended Stay America, Fairfield Inn, Hampton Inn, Homestead Suites, Super 8 Ⓞ 🅗 AT&T, Barnes&Noble, CVS Drug, Rite Aid, TJ Maxx, Trader Joe's, Verizon, Whole Foods Mkt, **W** 🅡 BP/Subway, Shell 🍴 Hyde Park Steaks, PF Chang's, The Pit Steaks, Yours Truly 🏠 Clarion, DoubleTree, Embassy Suites, Homewood Suites, Residence Inn Ⓞ Buick/GMC, Cadillac, NTB, Porsche
28b	Harvard Rd, **E** 🍴 Red Robin, **W** 🍴 5 Guys Burgers, Abuelo's, Buffalo Wilds Wings, Chick-fil-A, Chipotle, DiBella's Subs, Olive Garden, Panera Bread, River City Grille, Robeks Cafe, Zoup! 🏠 Aloft, Marriott Ⓞ 🅗
28a	OH 175, Richmond Rd, Emery Rd, **E** 🅡 BP, GetGo, Marathon/Circle K/Subway/dsl 🍴 Baskin-Robbins/Dunkin Donuts, Jimmy John's, Marianne's Bakery, McDonald's, Quiznos, **W** 🍴 BJ's Whse
27b	I-480 W
27a	US 422 E, **E** Ⓞ Lowe's
26	Rockside Rd, 🅡 Speedway/dsl, Sunoco 🍴 Burger King, Subway

🧭 INTERSTATE 271 (Cleveland) Cont'd

Exit #	Services
23	OH 14 W, Forbes Rd, Broadway Ave, **E** 🚗 Sunoco 🍴 Double Dragon Chinese, McDonald's, Subway, Wendy's 🛏 Holiday Inn Express ⊙ Sam's Club/gas, **W** 🚗 Marathon/Circle K/dsl ⊙ 🅗
21	I-480 E, OH 14 E (from sb), to Youngstown
19	OH 82, Macedonia, **E** 🚗 Speedway/dsl/E85 🍴 Papa John's, Penn Sta Subs, **W** 🚗 Sunoco 🍴 Applebee's, Arby's, Chick-fil-A, Chili's, Chipotle, Coldstone, Fuji Japanese, Golden Corral, KFC, McDonald's, Outback Steaks, Panera Bread, Pizza Hut, Popeye's, Steak'n Shake, Subway, Taco Bell, Wendy's ⊙ Best Buy, Chevrolet, Discount Tire, Giant Eagle Foods, GNC, Hobby Lobby, Home Depot, Kohl's, Lowe's, NTB, O'Reilly Parts, PetCo, Petsmart, Radio Shack, Target, Verizon, Walgreens, Walmart
18b a	OH 8, Boston Hts, to Akron, (exits left from sb), **E** 🚗 BP/dsl, GetGo, Speedway/dsl 🍴 Bob Evans, Dos Coronas Mexican, Pacific Chinese 🛏 Country Inn&Suites, Days Inn, Knights Inn, La Quinta, Motel 6, **W** same as 19
12	OH 303, Richfield, Peninsula
10	I-77, to I-80, OH Tpk (from nb), to Akron, Cleveland
9	I-77 S, OH 176 (from nb), to Richfield
8mm	🅿 both lanes, full 🛏 facilities, litter barrels, petwalk, (🚗, 🚮)
3	OH 94, to I-71 N, Wadsworth, N Royalton, **W** 🚗 Marathon/dsl
0mm	I-271 begins/ends on I-71, exit 220.

INTERSTATE 275 (Cincinnati)

See Kentucky Interstate 275

🧭 INTERSTATE 280 (Toledo)

Exit #	Services
13	I-280 begins/ends on I-75, exit 208
12	Manhattan Blvd, **E** 🚗 Sunoco 🛏 Classic Inn, **W** 🚗 Sunoco 🍴 Arby's, McDonald's
11	OH 25 S, Eerie St, **W** ⊙ Huntington Ctr
10mm	Maumee River
9	OH 65, Front St, **E** 🚗 Sunoco, **W** 🚗 Sunoco
8	Starr Ave, (from sb only)
7	OH 2, Oregon, **E** 🚗 Sunoco 🍴 Arby's, Burger King, Coldstone/Tim Horton's, Empire Chinese, McDonald's, Wendy's 🛏 Comfort Inn ⊙ 🅗 Ford, K-Mart, to Maumee Bay SP, Walgreens
6	OH 51, Woodville Rd, Curtice Rd, **E** 🚗 BP/dsl 🍴 Bob Evans, Burger King ⊙ Menards, **W** 🚗 Meijer/dsl, Speedway/dsl 🍴 Applebee's, Arby's, Big Boy, Gino's Pizza, KFC, LJ Silver, McDonald's, Pizza Hut, Subway, Taco Bell 🛏 Sleep Inn ⊙ 🅗 $General, $Tree, Advance Parts, Jo-Ann Fabrics, O'Reilly Parts, Rite Aid, Tires+
4	Walbridge
2	OH 795, Perrysburg, **W** 🚗 Sunoco/Subway/dsl
1b	Bahnsen Rd, **E** 🚗 🚩FLYING J/Denny's/dsl/LP/scales/24hr 🛏 Crown Inn, Executive Inn, Regency Inn, **W** 🚗 💙Loves/Arby's/dsl/scales/24hr, Petro/BP/Iron Skillet/dsl/scales/24hr/@ 🍴 McDonald's ⊙ Blue Beacon, SpeedCo, Super 8
1a	I-280 begins/ends on I 80/90, OH Tpk, exit 71 services, **S** 🚗 FuelMart/Subway/dsl/scales, 🚩McDonald's/dsl/scales/24hr, TA/BP/Burger King/Taco Bell/dsl/scales/24hr/@ 🍴 Sunrise Cafe

🧭 INTERSTATE 475 (Toledo)

Exit #	Services
20	I-75. I-475 begins/ends on I-75, exit 204.
19	Jackman Rd, Central Ave, **S** 🍴 Subway ⊙ 🅗
18b	Douglas Rd (from wb)
18a	OH 51 W, Monroe St
17	Secor Rd, **N** 🚗 Shell/dsl, Valero 🍴 Applebee's, Bob Evans, Boston Mkt, Burger King, China Crown, Famous Dave's BBQ, Hooters, Penn Sta. Subs, Red Robin, Rudy's Hot Dogs, Tim Horton ⊙ 🅗 AT&T, Best Buy, Kohl's, Kroger/dsl, O'Reilly Parts, Verizon, Walgreens, **S** 🚗 BP 🍴 5 Guys Burgers, Big Boy, Chipotle Mexican, Del Taco, El Nuevo Vallarta, El Vaquero, McDonald's, Original Pancakes, Pizza Hut, Popeye's, Ritter's Custard, Sonic, Starbucks, Subway, Taco Bell, Uncle John's Pancakes 🛏 Comfort Inn, Ramada Inn ⊙ Batteries+, Costco/gas, Fresh Mkt, Home Depot, Radio Shack, Rite Aid, Sears/auto, Steinmart, U of Toledo
16	Talmadge Rd (from wb, no return), **N** 🚗 BP/dsl, Speedway/dsl 🍴 Aladdin's Eatery, Bravo Italiana, Coldstone, J Alexander's Rest., Jimmy John's, Longhorn Steaks, Panera Bread, Potbelly ⊙ Dick's, JC Penney, Kohl's, Macy's, mall, Old Navy
15	Corey Rd (from eb, no return)
14	US 23 N, to Ann Arbor
13	US 20, OH 120, Central Ave, **E** 🚗 Speedway/dsl 🍴 Bob Evans, Magic Wok, McDonald's, Rally's, Subway ⊙ BMW, Cadillac, Chrysler/Dodge/Jeep, Fiat, Ford, Honda, Kia, Nissan, Radio Shack, Subaru, Toyota/Scion, Walmart, **W** 🚗 BP, Shell, Speedway ⊙ Lowe's
8b a	OH 2, **E** 🚗 BP/dsl 🍴 Don Pablo, TGIFriday's, TX Roadhouse 🛏 Extended Stay America, Hawthorn Suites, Knights Inn, Red Roof Inn ⊙ 🅗 Gander Mtn, Home Depot, Kohl's, Old Navy, PetCo, to OH Med Coll, **W** 🚗 BP, Speedway/dsl, Sunoco/dsl 🍴 Arby's, Bob Evans, Boston Mkt, Burger King, Chili's, Chipotle Mexican, DQ, IHOP, Little Caesar's, Mancino's Pizza, McDonald's, Subway, Wendy's 🛏 Courtyard, EconoLodge, Quality Inn ⊙ Best Buy, BigLots, Dick's, Firestone/auto, Kroger, Petsmart, Rite Aid, Sam's Club/gas, Target, TJ Maxx, Verizon, Walmart/Subway
6	Dussel Dr, Salisbury Rd, to I-80-90/tpk, **E** 🚗 BP, Speedway 🍴 Applebee's, Arby's, Bankok Kitchen, Bluewater Grill, Buffalo Wild Wings, Coldstone, Cracker Barrel, El Camino Royal, Gino's Pizza, Jimmy John's, Longhorn Steaks, Marie's Diner, Max&Erma's, McDonald's, Outback Steaks, Panera Bread, Salsarita's Cantina, Smokey Bones BBQ, Subway, Tim Horton, Yoko Japanese 🛏 Country Inn&Suites, Courtyard, Fairfield Inn, Homewood Suites, Residence Inn, Studio+, Super 8, **W** 🚗 BP 🍴 Abuelo's, Bob Evans, Briarfield Café, Carraba's 🛏 Baymont Inn ⊙ Churchill's Foods, vet

OH

MACEDONIA

TOLEDO

🅖 = gas 🍽 = food 🛏 = lodging 🅞 = other ℞ₛ = rest stop Copyright 2015 - the Next EXIT ®

↑N INTERSTATE 475 (Toledo) Cont'd

Exit #	Services
4	US 24, to Maumee, Napolean, N 🅞 🔰 Toledo Zoo
3mm	Maumee River
2	OH 25, to Bowling Green, Perrysburg, N 🍽 BP/dsl, Circle K/dsl, Shell 🍽 American Table Rest., Beaner's Coffee, Buffalo Wild Wings, Charlie's Rest., El Vaquero, Gino's Pizza, Lee Garden Chinese, Marco's Pizza, McDonald's, Subway, Wendy's 🅞 Auto Value, Churchill's Mkt, GMC, Goodyear/auto, Hyundai, Toms Tire/auto, Volvo, VW, S 🍽 Exxon, Speedway/dsl 🍽 Bar Louie's, Biaggi's, Blue Pacific Grill, Bob Evans, JB's Shoppe, Marie's Scrambler, Max&Erma's, Starbucks, Tea Tree Asian, Waffle House 🛏 Economy Inn, Hilton Garden 🅞 AT&T, Books-A-Million, GNC, Tireman, URGENT CARE, Verizon, vet
0mm	I-475 begins/ends on I-75, exit 192.

↑E INTERSTATE 480 (Cleveland)

Exit #	Services
42	I-80, PA Tpk, I-480 begins/ends, S 0-2 mi 🍽 BP, Marathon/Circle K, Sheetz/24hr, Shell, Speedway 🍽 Applebees, Arby's, Baskin Robbins/Dunkin Dounts, Big Boy, Bob Evans, Brown Derby Roadhouse, Buffalo Wild Wings, Burger King, CiCi's Pizza, Denny's, DQ, Eat'n Park, KFC, McDonald's, Mr Hero, New Peking Chinese, Pizza Hut, Quizno's, Rockney's Grill, Ruby Tuesday, Sonic, Steak'n Shake, Taco Bell, Wendy's, Zeppe's Pizza 🛏 Best Value Inn, Comfort Inn, Econolodge, Fairfield Inn, Hampton Inn, Holiday Inn Express, Microtel, TownePlace Suites, Wingate Inn 🅞 🔰 $General, Aldi Foods, AutoZone, Buick/GMC, Curves, Defer Tire, Giant Eagle, Home Depot, Honda, Hyundai, K-Mart, Lowes Whse, mall, Midas, NAPA, NTB, Save-a-Lot Foods, Staples, Target, to Kent St U, U-Haul, USPO, Van's Tires, vet, Walgreens, Walmart
41	Frost Rd, Hudson-Aurora
37	OH 91, Solon, Twinsburg, N 🍽 Arby's, Pizza Hut, Taco Bell 🅞 Comfort Suites, Giant Eagle, S 🍽 BP
36	OH 82, Aurora, Twinsburg, N 🍽 BP/dsl, Get'n Go 🍽 Burger King 🛏 Super 8, S 🍽 Bob Evans, Cracker Barrel, Damon's, Donato's Pizza, Marathon, McDonald's, Wendy's 🛏 Hilton Garden
26	I-271, to Erie, PA
25a b c	OH 8, OH 43, Northfield Rd, Bedford, N 🅞 Harley-Davidson, S 🍽 McDonald's, Rally's, White Castle
23	OH 14, Broadway Ave, N 🍽 Gulf/dsl 🍽 Burger King, KFC
22	OH 17, Garanger, Maple Hts, Garfield Hts
21	Transportation Blvd, to E 98th St, S 🅞 Giant Eagle Foods, JoAnn Fabrics, Walmart
20b a	I-77, Cleveland
17	OH 176, Cleveland
16	OH 94, to OH 176 S, State Rd, N 🅞 Convenient Mart, transmissions, S 🍽 BP, Sunoco/dsl 🅞 KIA
15	10 US 42, Ridge Rd, N 🍽 BP 🍽 Applebee's, Baskin-Robbins/Dunkin Donuts, Boston Mkt, CiCi's Pizza, Coldstone Creamery, Hong Kong Buffet, McDonald's, Quizno's, Rockney's Rest., Starbucks, TX Roadhouse 🅞 Chevrolet, GNC, Lowe's, Marc's Foods, Radio Shack, TJMaxx, S 🍽 Speedway 🍽 Arby's, Denny's, DQ, Wendy's 🅞 $Tree, Best Buy, Hyundai, K-Mart, Staples
13	Teideman Rd, Brooklyn, S 🍽 BP, Speedway 🍽 Burger King, Carrabba's, Chipotle Mexican, Cracker Barrel, Don Pablo's, IHOP, LJ Silver, Panera Bread, Perkin's, Pizza Hut, Steak 'n Shake, TGIFriday's, Wild Ginger China Bistro

Exit #	Services
13	Continued 🛏 Extended Stay America, Hampton Inn 🅞 Aldi Foods, Home Depot, Jaguar, LandRover, Mazda, Sam's Club/gas, Volvo, Walmart
12	W 150th, W130th, Brookpark, N 🍽 Subway, S 🍽 Marathon, Shell 🍽 Arby's, Big Boy, Bob Evans 🛏 Best Value Inn, Park Brook Inn 🅞 Acura, Infiniti, Lexus, Toyota, U-Haul
11	I-71, Cleveland, Columbus
10	S rd 237, Airport Blvd, (wb only)
9	OH 17, Brookpark Rd, N 🛏 Hilton Garden 🅞 🔰 S 🛏 🛏 Sheraton
7	(wb only) Clague Rd, to WestLake
6	OH 252, Great Northern Blvd, to N Olmsted, N 🍽 BP, Shell, Speedway 🍽 Applebee's, Arby's, Bamboo Garden, Boston Mkt, Brown Bag Burgers, Burger King, Chick-fil-A, Chili's, ChuckeCheese, Daishin Japanese, Famous Dave's, Fat Burger, Great Wall Buffet, Harry Buffalo, Jimmy John's, Lonestar Steaks, Macaroni Grill, Moe's SW Grill, Olive Garden, Panera Bread, Penn Sta Subs, Red Lobster, Red Robin, Ruby Tuesday, Smokey Bones BBQ, Wendy's 🛏 Candlewood Suites, Courtyard, Homestead Suites, La Quinta, Radisson, Studio+ 🅞 $Tree, Aldi Foods, AT&T, Best Buy, Chipotle Mexican, Dillard's, Firestone/auto, Home Depot, JC Penney, Jo-Ann Etc, Macy's, mall, Marc's Foods, Mr Tire, NTB, Petsmart, Radio Shack, Sears/auto, Target, TJ Maxx, Toyota, Walmart
3	Stearns Rd, N 🅞 🔰 S 2 mi 🍽 Razzle's Cafe
2	OH 10, Lorain Rd, to OH Tpk, S 🍽 BP, Sheetz/24hr, Speedway/dsl 🍽 Ace's Grille, Gourme Rest., McDonald's, Pizza Pan 🛏 Motel 6, Super 8
1	OH 10 W, to US 20 (from wb), Oberlin
0mm	OH 10, to Cleveland, I-480 begins/ends on exit 151, OH Tpk

↑E INTERSTATE 680 (Youngstown)

Exit #	Services
14	OH 164, to Western Reserve Rd, I-680 begins/ends on OH Tpk, exit 234, S 🍽 Shell/Subway/dsl 🍽 Cafe 422, Carmella's Cafe, Dunkin Donuts, McDonald's, Pizza Hut, Wendy's 🅞 🔰
11b a	US 224, S 🍽 BP, GetGo, Shell/dsl 🍽 Applebee's, Burger King, Carabba's, Chick-fil-A, Chipotle, Dunkin Donuts, Honeybaked Ham, IHOP, KFC, LJ Silver, Longhorn Steaks, McDonald's, Nicolinni's Italian, O'Charley's, Olive Garden, Outback Steaks, Papa John's, Perkins, Red Lobster, Smokey Bones, Springfield Grill, Starbucks, Subway, Taco Bell, TGIFriday's, TX Roadhouse 🛏 Best Western, Days Inn, Fairfield Inn, Hampton Inn, Holiday Inn, Red Roof Inn, Residence Inn 🅞 🔰 $Tree, Aldi Foods, AT&T, Best Buy, Big Lots, Giant Eagle, GNC, K-Mart, Lowe's, Marc's Foods, NTB, Petsmart, Radio Shack, Sam's Club/gas, Staples, URGENT CARE, Walmart/Subway
9b a	OH 170, Midlothian Blvd, Struthers, S 🍽 Shell/dsl, Speedway/dsl 🍽 McDonald's, Subway 🅞 $General, Rite Aid, Walgreens
8	Shirley Rd, downtown
7	US 62, OH 7, South Ave, downtown
6b a	US 62, OH 7, Mkt St, downtown
5	Glenwood Ave, Mahoning Ave, downtown
4b a	OH 193, to US 422, Salt Springs Rd, N 🅞 🔰 museum
3c b	Belle Vista Ave, Connecticut Ave
3a	OH 711 E, to I-80 E
2	Meridian Rd, S 🅞 Ford/Peterbilt Trucks
1	OH 11

OH

⬆️Ⓔ OHIO TURNPIKE

Exit #	Services
241mm	Ohio/Pennsylvania state line
239mm	**toll plaza,** Ⓒ
237mm	**Mahoning Valley Travel Plaza eb, Glacier Hills Travel Plaza wb,** ⊞ Sunoco/dsl/24hr 🍴 McDonald's ⊙ gifts, Ⓒ
234	I-680 (from wb), to Youngstown
232	OH 7, to Boardman, Youngstown, **N** ⊞ Sheetz, Valero/dsl 🍴 DQ, Los Gallos Mexican, Rita's Custard, Steamer's Stonewall Tavern 🛏 Best Value Inn, Budget Inn, Holiday Inn Express, Super 8 ⊙ $General, antiques, **S** ⊞ 📶/McDonald's/dsl/scales/24hr 🛏 Davis Motel, Liberty Inn
218	I-80 E, to Youngstown, Niles. **OH Tpk runs with I-76 eb, I-80 wb. Services S on Mahoning.**
216	Lordstown (from wb), **N** GM Plant
215	Lordstown (from eb), **N** GM Plant
210mm	Mahoning River
209	OH 5, to Warren, **N** 🛏 Rodeway Inn, **S** ⊞ Marathon/dsl 🛏 EconoLodge, Holiday Inn Express
197mm	**Portage Service Plaza wb, Bradys Leap Service Plaza eb,** ⊞ Sunoco/dsl/24hr 🍴 McDonald's, Sbarro's, Starbucks ⊙ gifts, Ⓒ
193	OH 44, to Ravenna
192mm	Cuyahoga River
187	OH 14 S, I-480, to Streetsboro, **S 0-2mi** ⊞ BP, Marathon/Circle K, Sheetz, Shell, Speedway 🍴 Applebee's, Arby's, Baskin Robbins/Dunkin Dounts, Big Boy, Bob Evans, Brown Derby Roadhouse, Buffalo Wild Wings, Burger King, CiCi's Pizza, Denny's, DQ, Eat'n Park, KFC, McDonald's, Mr Hero, New Peking Chinese, Pizza Hut, Quiznos, Rockney's Grill, Ruby Tuesday, Sonic, Steak'n Shake, Taco Bell, Wendy's, Zeppe's Pizza 🛏 Best Value Inn, Comfort Inn, EconoLodge, Fairfield Inn, Hampton Inn, Holiday Inn Express, Microtel, TownePlace Suites, Wingate Inn ⊙ Ⓗ $General, Aldi Foods, AutoZone, Buick/GMC, Curves, Defer Tire, Giant Eagle Foods, Home Depot, Honda, Hyundai, K-Mart, Lowe's, mall, Midas, NAPA, NTB, Save-a-Lot Foods, Staples, Target, to Kent St U, U-Haul, USPO, Van's Tires, vet, Walgreens, Walmart
180	OH 8, to I-90 E, **N** 🛏 Comfort Inn, Holiday Inn ⊙ Harley-Davidson, **S** ⊞ BP/dsl ⊙ to Cuyahoga Valley NRA
177mm	Cuyahoga River
173	OH 21, to I-77, **N** ⊞ 📶/Wendy's/dsl/scales 🛏 Holiday Inn Express, Motel 6, **S** 🍴 DQ, Memories Rest., Richfield Rest., Subway 🛏 Days Inn, Hampton Inn, Super 8
170mm	**Towpath Service Plaza eb, Great Lakes Service Plaza wb,** ⊞ Sunoco/dsl/24hr 🍴 Burger King, FoodCourt, Panera Bread, Pizza Hut, Starbucks ⊙ gifts, Ⓒ
161	US 42, to I-71, Strongsville, **N on US 42** ⊞ AP/dsl 🍴 Buffalo Wild Wings, Jennifer's Rest., Mad Cactus Mexican 🛏 Days Inn, Kings Inn, La Siesta Motel, Metrick's Motel, Village Motel ⊙ Circle K, Home Depot, Lowe's, vet, Walmart, **S on US 42** 🛏 Elmhaven Motel ⊙ Burger King, Dodge, DQ, J-Bella Rest., KFC, La Volte Grill, Marco's Pizza, NAPA, Olympia's Cafe, Staples
152	OH 10, to Oberlin, I-480, Cleveland, **N** ⊞ BP, Sheetz, Speedway/dsl 🍴 Ace's Grille, Gourme Rest., McDonald's, Pizza Pan 🛏 Motel 6, Super 8
151	I-480 E (from eb), to Cleveland, ⊙ ♿
146mm	Black River
145	OH 57, to Lorain, to I-90, Elyria, **N** ⊞ Speedway 🍴 Applebee's, Arby's, Bob Evans, Buffalo Wild Wings, Burger King, Chipotle Mexican, Denny's, Eat'n Park, Golden Corral,

L O R A I N

145	Continued Harry Buffalo, Hunan King, McDonald's, Old Century Buffet, Olive Garden, Qdoba Mexican, Red Lobster, Subway, Wasabi Grill, Wendy's 🛏 Best Western, Comfort Inn, Country Inn&Suites, EconoLodge, Holiday Inn, Red Carpet Inn, Red Roof Inn ⊙ $General, $Tree, AT&T, Best Buy, Curves, Firestone/auto, Home Depot, Honda, JC Penney, Jo-Ann Fabrics, Lowe's, Macy's, Marc's Foods, NTB, Petsmart, Radio Shack, Sears/auto, Staples, Target, Walmart/auto, **S** ⊞ Shell, Speedway 🛏 Howard Johnson
142	I-90 (from eb, exits left), OH 2, to W Cleveland
140	OH 58, Amherst, **N 0-2 mi** ⊞ BP, GetGo, Speedway, Sunoco/Subway/dsl 🍴 Blue Sky Rest., Bob Evans, Donato's Pizza, DQ, KFC, Marco's Pizza, McDonald's, Moosehead Grill, Mr Hero, Taco Bell, Wendy's 🛏 Days Inn, Motel 6 ⊙ Advance Parts, Aldi Foods, Chevrolet, Chrysler/Dodge, Drug Mart, Giant Eagle Foods, K-Mart, repair, Rite Aid, USPO, VW, Walgreens, **S** ⊙ Ford
139mm	**Service Plaza both lanes,** ⊞ Sunoco/dsl/24hr 🍴 Burger King, Great Steak&Potato, Hershey's, Panera Bread, Popeye's, Starbucks ⊙ gifts, phone, RV parking
135	rd 51, Baumhart Rd, to Vermilion
132mm	Vermilion River
118	US 250, to Norwalk, Sandusky, **N** ⊞ BP/Circle K/Dunkin Donuts, Marathon/dsl 🍴 Italian Gardens, McDonald's, Subway 🛏 Days Inn, Hampton Inn, Motel 6, Quality Inn, Red Roof Inn, Super 8 ⊙ Milan RV Park, to Edison's Birthplace, **S** 🛏 Colonial Inn
110	OH 4, to Bellevue
100mm	**Service Plaza both lanes,** ⊞ Sunoco/dsl/24hr 🍴 Burger King, Cinnabon, Einstein Bros Bagels, Sbarro's, Starbucks ⊙ Ⓒ
93mm	Sandusky River
91	OH 53, to Fremont, Port Clinton, **N** 🛏 Days Inn, **S 0-2 mi** ⊞ BP/Subway/dsl/24hr, Murphy USA/dsl 🍴 Applebee's, Bob Evans, Burger King, Fricker's, Hibachi Buffet, McDonald's, Pizza Hut, Subway, Taco Bell 🛏 Clarion, Comfort Inn, Delux Inn, Hampton Inn ⊙ Ⓗ $Tree, Aldi Foods, Ford/Lincoln, Lowe's, Rutherford B. Hayes Library, Staples, USPO, Verizon, vet, Walmart
81	OH 51, Elmore, Woodville, Gibsonburg
80.5mm	Portage River
77mm	**Service Plaza both lanes,** ⊞ Sunoco/dsl/24hr 🍴 Hardee's, Mancino's, Red Burrito ⊙ Ⓒ
71	I-280, OH 420, to Stony Ridge, Toledo, **N** ⊞ FLYING J/Denny's/dsl/scales/LP/24hr, Loves/Arby's/dsl/scales/24hr, Petro/BP/Iron Skillet/dsl/scales/24hr/@ 🛏 Budget Inn, Crown Inn, Super 8, Travel Inn ⊙ Blue Beacon, KOA, Speed-Co, **S** ⊞ FuelMart/Roadeez Rest./dsl/scales, 📶/

🔺E   OHIO TURNPIKE Cont'd

Exit #	Services
71	Continued
	McDonald's/dsl/scales/24hr, TA/BP/Burger King/Taco Bell/dsl/scales/24hr/@ 🍴 Sunrise Grill 🅞 truckwash
64	I-75 N, to Toledo, Perrysburg, S 🛏 Country Inn&Suites, Courtyard, Hampton Inn 🅞 Bass Pro Shops, BP/Subway/dsl
63mm	Maumee River
59	US 20, to I-475, Maumee, Toledo, N 🅖 BP, Shell, Speedway/dsl 🍴 Bob Evans, Golden-Lily, McDonald's, Olive Garden, Pizza Hut, Steak'n Shake, Subway, Waffle House 🛏 Clarion, Motel 6 🅞 Family$, Goodyear/auto, Jo-Ann Fabrics, K-Mart, NAPA, O'Reilly Parts, Radio Shack, Rite Aid, Savers, to Toledo Stadium, Walgreens, S 🅖 Speedway/dsl 🍴 Big Boy, Chipotle Mexican, Donato's Pizza, El Azteca, Fricker's, Friendly's, Jed's BBQ, La Fiesta Mexican, Red Lobster, Schlotzsky's, Taco Bell 🛏 Best Value Inn, Budget Inn, Comfort Inn, Hampton Inn, Holiday Inn, Red Roof Inn 🅞 AT&T, Ford, Honda, Meijer/gas, Toyota/Scion
52	OH 2, to Toledo, N 🅖 Shamrock/dsl 🍴 Loma Linda Mexican, S 🛏 Days Inn 🅞 🔧, RV/truck repair

39	OH 109, S 🅖 Country Corral/Valero/Winchesters Rest/dsl/scales/wi-fi/24hr
34	34 OH 108, to Wauseon, S 🅖 Shell/Subway/dsl/24hr 🍴 Smith's Rest., 🛏 Wendy's Arrowhead Motel, Best Western, Holiday Inn Express, Super 8 🅞 Toledo RV Ctr, Woods Trucking/repair (1mi), S 2 mi on US 20A 🅖 BP/Circle K, 🍴 A&W/KFC, Arby's, Burger King, DQ, Grasshopper Rest., Kamwa Chinese, McDonald's, Pizza Hut, Subway, Taco Bell 🅞 $General, Ace Hardware, AutoZone, Circle K, Marathon, Murphy USA/dsl, O'Reilly Parts, Rite Aid, Valero, Walmart
25	OH 66, Burlington, N 🅞 Harrison Lake SP, S 3 mi 🅞 Sauder Village Museum
24.5mm	Tiffen River
18	**Indian Meadow Service Plaza both lanes,** 🅖 Sunoco/dsl 🍴 Burger King, Sbarro's, Starbucks
13	OH 15, to Bryan, Montpelier, S 🅖 Marathon/dsl, Sunoco 🍴 4Seasons Rest. 🛏 EconoLodge, Holiday Inn Express, Rainbow Motel, Ramada Inn 🅞 Hutch's dsl Repair
11.5mm	St Joseph River
3mm	**toll plaza,** 🅒
2	OH 49, to US 20, N 🍴 Burger King, Subway 🅞 info, truck tires
0mm	Ohio/Indiana state line

OKLAHOMA

🔺N   INTERSTATE 35

Exit #	Services
236mm	Oklahoma/Kansas state line
232	weigh sta, sb only
231	US 177, Braman, E 🅖 Conoco/deli/dsl
230	Braman Rd
229mm	Chikaskia River
225mm	**Welcome Ctr sb, full** ♿ **facilities, litter barrels, petwalk,** 🅒, 🔁, vending
222	OK 11, to Blackwell, Medford, Alva, Newkirk, E 🅖 Conoco/dsl, Shell/dsl 🍴 Braum's, KFC/Taco Bell, Los Potros Mexican, McDonald's, Plains Man Rest., Subway 🛏 Best Way Inn, Best Western, Comfort Inn 🅞 🏥
218	Hubbard Rd
217mm	weigh sta both lanes
214	US 60, to Tonkawa, Lamont, Ponka City, N OK Coll, W 🅖 Casey's/dsl, Shell/dsl 🛏 New Western Inn 🅞 RV Park
213mm	Salt Fork of Arkansas River
211	Fountain Rd, E 🅖 💟Loves/Chester's/Subway/dsl/scales/24hr/RV Dump
209mm	parking area, litter barrels
203	OK 15, to Marland, Billings, E 🅖 Phillips 66/DQ/dsl/scales/24hr
199mm	Red Rock Creek
195mm	parking area both lanes, litter barrels
194b a	US 412, US 64 W, Cimarron Tpk, to Cimarron, Enid, W 🅞 Phillips U
193	Airport Rd (from nb, no return)
191mm	Black Bear Creek
186	US 64 E, to Fir St, Perry, E 🅖 Mobil/Subway/dsl 🍴 Braum's, McDonald's, Taco Mayo 🛏 Super 8 🅞 🏥 museum, W 🅖 Exxon/dsl 🛏 Comfort Suites, Holiday Inn Express, Regency Inn
185	US 77, to Covington, Perry, E 🛏 American Inn, W 🅖 Phillips 66/rest/motel/dsl/24hr 🅞 RV camping

180	Orlando Rd
174	OK 51, to Stillwater, Hennessee, E 🅖 Conoco/dsl 🍴 Smokey Pokey Cafe 🛏 Fairfield Inn (12mi), Hampton Inn (12mi), Motel 6 (12 mi) 🅞 Lake Carl Blackwell RV Park, to OSU
173mm	parking area sb, litter barrels
171mm	parking area nb, parking only, litter barrels
170	Mulhall Rd
166mm	Cimarron River
157	OK 33, to Cushing, Guthrie, W 🅖 K&L/dsl, Love's/Subway/dsl, Road Star, Shell/dsl, Valero 🍴 Arby's, Braum's, El Rodeo Mexican, KFC (2mi), LJ Silver, Mazzio's, McDonald's (3mi), Pizza Hut, Sonic, The Ribshack 🛏 Best Western, Holiday Inn Express, Interstate Motel, Sleep Inn 🅞 🏥 Langston U, OK Terr Museum, RV camping
153	US 77 N (exits left from nb), Guthrie, W 🍴 McDonald's (3mi), Taco Bell (3mi) 🅞 Buick/Cadillac/GMC, Chevrolet, Chrysler/Dodge/Jeep
151	Seward Rd, E 🅖 Shell/cafe/dsl 🅞 Lazy E Arena (4mi), Pioneer RV park
149mm	weigh sta both lanes
146	Waterloo Rd, E 🅖 Shell/Subway/dsl
143	Covell Rd
142	Danforth Rd (from nb)
141	US 77 S, OK 66E, to 2nd St, Edmond, Tulsa, W 🅖 Conoco/dsl, Phillips 66/dsl 🛏 Best Western, Comfort Suites, Fairfield Inn, Hampton Inn, Holiday Inn Express 🅞 🏥 vet
140	SE 15th St, Spring Creek, Arcadia Lake, Edmond Park, W 🅖 Phillips 66/Circle K/Subway 🍴 Braum's, McDonald's 🅞 Walmart/McDonald's
139	SE 33rd St
138d	Memorial Rd
138c	Sooner Rd (from sb)
138b	Kilpatrick Tpk
138a	I-44 Tpk E to Tulsa
I-35 S and I-44 W run together 8 mi.	
137	NE 122nd St, to OK City, E 🅖 Shamrock/dsl, Shell/dsl

🏪 = gas 🍴 = food 🛏 = lodging 🅾 = other Rs = rest stop

INTERSTATE 35 Cont'd

Exit #	Services
137	Continued
	🍴 Charly's Rest., IHOP 🛏 Knights Inn, Sleep Inn, W 🏪 / Huddle House/dsl/scales/LP/24hr, ♥Loves/Godfathers/Subway/ dsl/24hr, Phillips 66/dsl/scales 🍴 Cracker Barrel, McDonald's, Sonic, Waffle House 🛏 Comfort Inn, Days Inn, EconoLodge, Economy Inn, Holiday Inn Express, Motel 6, Red Carpet Inn, Super 8 🅾 Abe's RV Park, Frontier City Funpark, Oklahoma Visitors Ctr/info/ restrooms, truckwash
136	Hefner Rd, W 🅾 Conoco/dsl, same as 137
135	Britton Rd
134	Wilshire Blvd, W 🛏 Executive Inn 🅾 Blue Beacon
I-35 N and I-44 E run together 8 mi	
133	I-44 W, to Amarillo, W 🅾 Cowboy Hall of Fame, st capitol
132b	NE 63rd St (from nb), E 1/2 mi 🏪 Conoco/dsl 🍴 Braum's 🛏 Remington Inn
132a	NE 50th St, Remington Pk, W 🅾 funpark, info, museum, zoo
131	NE 36th St, W 🏪 Phillips 66/dsl/24hr 🅾 45th Inf Division Museum
130	US 62 E, NE 23rd St, E 🏪 Shell/dsl, W 🅾 to st capitol
129	NE 10th St, E 🏪 Conoco/McDonald's/dsl
128	I-40 E, to Ft Smith
127	Eastern Ave, OK City, W 🏪 JR's Trvl Ctr/Wendy's/dsl/ scales/24hr/@, Petro/rest/dsl/24hr/@ 🍴 Waffle House 🛏 Best Western, Brick-Town Hotel, Central Plaza Hotel, EconoLodge, Quality Inn 🅾 Blue Beacon, Lewis RV Ctr
126b	I-35 S to Dallas
126a	I-40, W to Amarillo, I-235 N, to st capitol
125d	SE 15th St, E 🏪 Conoco/dsl
125b	SE 22nd St (from nb)
125a	SE 25th, same as 124b
124b	SE 29th St, E 🍴 China Queen, Denny's, McDonald's, Sonic, Taco Bell 🛏 Best Value Inn, Days Inn, Plaza Inn, Royal Inn, W 🏪 Phillips 66/Circle K 🍴 Mama Lou's Rest. 🛏 Executive Inn, same as 125a
124a	Grand Blvd, E 🛏 Studio 6, Super 8, W 🛏 Drover's Inn
123b	SE 44th St, E 🏪 Shell 🍴 Domino's, Sonic 🛏 Best Value Inn, Courtesy Inn, Motel 6, W 🏪 Phillips 66 🍴 Subway, Taco Mayo 🅾 $General, Family$, USPO
123a	SE 51st St, E 🏪 Conoco/dsl 🛏 Best Value Inn
122b	SE 59th St, E 🏪 Phillips 66/dsl, W 🏪 Shell, Valero/dsl 🅾 U-Haul
122a	SE 66th St, E 🍴 Burger King, Luby's, McDonald's, Subway, TX Roadhouse, Zeke's Rest. 🛏 Fairfield Inn, Ramada Inn, Residence Inn 🅾 Tires+, W 🏪 7-11 🍴 Arby's
121b	US 62 W, I-240 E
121a	SE 82nd St, (from sb), W 🛏 Baymont Inn, Days Inn
120	SE 89th St, E 🏪 Valero/dsl/scales 🛏 Ford, W ♥Loves /Subway/dsl/24hr 🅾 Classic Parts
119b	N 27th St, E 🏪 Shell/Circle K/dsl, W 🍴 Pickles Rest.
119a	Shields Blvd (exits left from nb)

118	N 12th St, E 🍴 Mazzio's, Peking Buffet 🛏 Super 8, W 🏪 Shell 🍴 A&W/LJ Silver, Arby's, Braum's, Grandy's, KFC, La Fajitas, Mamma Lou's, McDonald's, Papa John's, Subway, Taco Bell, Wendy's, Western Sizzlin 🛏 Best Western, Candlewood Suites, Comfort Inn, SpringHill Suites 🅾 $General, 7-11, AutoZone, Family$, vet
117	OK 37, S 4th St, W 🏪 7-11 🍴 Van BBQ 🅾 USPO
116	S 19th St, E 🏪 Conoco, Shell 🍴 Braum's, Genghis Grill, McDonald's, Ricky's Cafe, Taco Bell, Waffle House, Whataburger 🅾 AT&T, Best Buy, Firestone/auto, GNC, Hobby Lobby, JC Penney, Office Depot, Petsmart, Ross, W 🏪 Murphy USA 🍴 5 Guys Burgers, Alfredo's Mexican, Applebee's, Arby's, Buffalo Wild Wings, Burger King, Cane's, Carl's Jr, Chicken Express, Chick-fil-A, Chili's, China House, Earl's Ribs, Freddy's Custard, Furr's Buffet, Harry Bears, Hollies Steaks, IHOP, Jack-in-the-Box, Jersey's Mike's Subs, Jimmy's Egg, Mazzio's, McAlister's Deli, Panda Express, Poblano Grill, Qdoba Mexican, Quiznos, Schlotzsky's, Sonic, Starbucks, Subway, Taco Mayo 🛏 La Quinta 🅾 $Tree, Aldi Foods, AT&T, Discount Tire, Gordman's, Harley-Davidson, Home Depot, Kohl's, Lowe's, Radio Shack, Target, Tires+, Walmart
114	Indian Hill Rd, E 🍴 Double Dave's Pizza 🛏 ValuePlace Hotel 🅾 Cadillac, funpark
113	US 77 S (from sb, exits left), Norman
112	Tecumseh Rd, E 🅾 Nissan, Toyota/Scion, W 🍴 McDonald's, Sonic 🅾 🅷 CVS Drug, URGENT CARE
110b a	Robinson St, E 🍴 5 Guys Burgers, Carl's Jr, Cheddar's, Logan's Roadhouse, Panda Express, Pei Wei, Qdoba Mexican, Taco Bell, Wing Stop, Zio's Italian 🛏 Embassy Suites, Motel 6 🅾 🅷 $Tree, AT&T, Buick/GMC, Discount Tire, Ford, GMC, Homeland Foods/gas, Honda, Hyundai, Kohl's, Lincoln, Mazda, Office Depot, PetCo, Target, Tires+, TJ Maxx, Verizon, VW, W 🏪 Conoco/Subway 🍴 Arby's, Braum's, Cafe Escondido, Chuy's Mexican, Cracker Barrel, Domino's, Jersey Mike's, Outback Steaks, Papa John's, Papa Murphy's, Pizza Hut, Rib Crib, Saltgrass Steaks, Waffle House, Yamato Steaks 🛏 Comfort Inn, Courtyard, Hilton Garden, Holiday Inn 🅾 7-11, Kia, Suzuki
109	Main St, E 🏪 Murphy USA, Phillips 66/dsl, Shell/Circle K, Sinclair 🍴 Chick-fil-A, Golden Corral, Panera Bread,

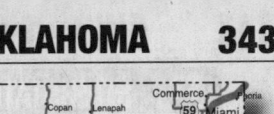

OK

NORMAN

⬆N INTERSTATE 35 Cont'd

Exit #	Services
109	Continued
	Prairie Kitchen, Taco Cabana, Waffle House, Wendy's, Whataburger 🛏 EconoLodge, Guest Inn, Motel 6, Super 8, Travelodge Ⓞ AT&T, AutoZone, Best Buy, BigLots, Cadillac, Chevrolet, Chrysler/Dodge/Jeep, Hastings Books, Hobby Lobby, Kwik Kar, Lowe's, Nissan, Tires+, Walmart/McDonald's, W 🅐 Conoco/Circle K/dsl 🍴 Applebee's, BJ's Brewhouse, Burger King, Charleston's Rest. Chili's, McDonald's, Olive Garden, On the Border, Red Lobster 🛏 Fairfield Inn, Hampton Inn, La Quinta Ⓞ Barnes&Noble, Dillard's, JC Penney, Michael's, Old Navy, Sam's Club, Sears/auto
108b a	OK 9 E, Norman, E 🅐 Conoco/Circle K 🍴 Arby's, Braum's, Del Rancho Steaks, Schlotzsky's, Taco Bell 🛏 Sooner Legends Inn/rest Ⓞ $General, NAPA, O'Reilly Parts, to U of OK, W 🍴 Cajun King Buffet, Carino's Italian, IHOP, Interurban Grill, Jasons Deli, Red Robin 🛏 Country Inn&Suites, La Quinta Ⓞ Chevrolet, Home Depot, Petsmart, Ross
107mm	Canadian River
106	OK 9 W, to Chickasha, E Ⓞ Casino, W 🅐 ❤Loves/Subway/dsl/24hr, Shell 🍴 McDonald's, Sonic 🛏 Sleep Inn Ⓞ casino, vet
104	OK 74 S, Goldsby, E Ⓞ Floyd's RV Ctr, W 🅐 Shamrock/dsl 🍴 Libby's Cafe
101	Ladd Rd
98	Johnson Rd, E 🅐 Shamrock/dsl Ⓞ Sooner RV Ctr
95	US 77 (exits left from sb), Purcell, E 1-3 mi 🅐 Shell 🍴 Braum's, KFC, Mazzio's, Pizza Hut, Subway Ⓞ 🏥 Ford
91	OK 74, to OK 39, Maysville, E 🅐 Conoco/dsl, Murphy USA/dsl, Phillips 66/dsl 🍴 Braum's, McDonald's, New China, Subway, Taco Mayo 🛏 EconoLodge, Executive Inn, Ruby's Inn/rest. Ⓞ AT&T, Walmart/Subway, W 🅐 Shell/dsl 🍴 A&W/LJ Silver, Taco Bell
86	OK 59, Wayne, Payne, E Ⓞ American RV Park
79	OK 145 E, Paoli, E 🅐 Phillips 66
76mm	Washita River
74	Kimberlin Rd, to OK 19
72	OK 19, Paul's Valley, E 🅐 Conoco/dsl, Murphy USA/dsl, Valero/dsl/rest/24hr 🍴 Arby's, Braum's, Chicken Express, Green Tea Chinese, Happy Days Diner, KFC/Taco Bell, McDonald's, Sonic, Stevenson BBQ, Subway, Taco Mayo, Tio's Mexican 🛏 American Inn, Best Value Inn, Comfort Inn, Days Inn, Holiday Inn Express, Relax Inn Ⓞ AT&T, Buick/Cadillac/GMC, Chrysler/Dodge/Jeep, Ford/Lincoln, Walmart, W 🅐 Phillips 66/dsl/24hr Ⓞ truckwash
70	Airport Rd, E 🅐 ❤Loves/Burger King/dsl/LP/scales/24hr/@ Ⓞ 🏥
66	OK 29, Wynnewood, E 🛏 Kent's Motel, W 🅐 Shell/dsl
64	OK 17A E, to Wynnewood, E Ⓞ GW Exotic Animal Park
60	Ruppe Rd
59mm	🆁🆂 both lanes, full ♿ facilities, litter barrels, petwalk, 🅲, 📶, RV dump
55	OK 7, Davis, E 🅐 Conoco, Phillips 66/A&W/dsl/24hr Ⓞ to Chickasaw NRA, Treasure Valley Casino/Inn, W Ⓞ **Chickasaw Nation Welcome Ctr**, to Arbuckle Ski Area
54.5mm	Honey Creek Pass
53mm	**weigh sta both lanes**
51	US 77, Turner Falls, E 🛏 Arbuckle Mtn Motel, Mtnview Inn (3mi) Ⓞ RV camping, to Arbuckle Wilderness, W 🅐 Sinclair/rv park 🍴 Cliff Steaks Ⓞ Botanic Gardens

ARDMORE

Exit #	Services
49mm	scenic turnout both lanes
47	US 77, Turner Falls Area
46mm	scenic turnout both lanes
42	OK 53 W, Springer, Comanche, W 🅐 Exxon/dsl
40	OK 53 E, Gene Autry, E 🅐 Shell/dsl/café/24hr 🍴 Broaster Rest Ⓞ Gene Autry Museum (8mi)
33	OK 142, Ardmore, E 🅐 Phillips 66/dsl 🍴 IHOP, Jimmy's Egg Cafe 🛏 Guest Inn, Holiday Inn, La Quinta, SpringHill Suites, Super 8 Ⓞ regional park, tires, W 🅐 ✈FLYING J/Huddle House/dsl/LP/scales/24hr
32	12th St, Ardmore, E 🅐 Conoco/dsl, Shell 🍴 Braum's, CiCi's Pizza, Cotton Patch Cafe, Quiznos, Santa Fe Steaks, Starbucks, Whataburger 🛏 Candlewood Suites, Holiday Inn, La Quinta Ⓞ $Tree, Hyundai, Lowe's, PetCo, Ross, Toyota, W 🅐 ❤Loves/Godfather's/Subway/dsl/24hr/@ 🍴 McDonald's 🛏 Microtel
31b a	US 70 W, OK 199 E, Ardmore, E 🅐 Shell/dsl, Valero/dsl 🍴 2Frogs Grill, Applebee's, Burger King, Cattle Rustlers, Denny's, El Chico, El Tapatio, Interurban Grill, Jack-in-the-Box, KFC, Mazzio's, McDonald's, Papa John's, Pizza Hut, Prairie Kitchen 🛏 Best Western, Comfort Inn, Days Inn, Motel 6, Quality Inn, Rodeway Inn Ⓞ AutoZone, Honda, O'Reilly Parts, W 🅐 Conoco/dsl Ⓞ Ardmore RV Park, Chrysler/Dodge/Jeep, Ford/Lincoln, Nissan, vet
29	US 70 E, Ardmore, E Ⓞ to Lake Murray SP/lodge (8mi), W Ⓞ Hidden Lake RV Park
24	OK 77 S, E Ⓞ Red River Livestock Mkt, to Lake Murray SP
22.5mm	Hickory Creek
21	Oswalt Rd, W 🅐 Valero/dsl Ⓞ Ardmore Marietta RV Park, Lazy Man's Corner RV Park
15	OK 32, Marietta, E 🅐 Valero/dsl/24hr 🍴 Carl's Jr, McDonald's, Pizza Hut, Robertson's Sandwiches, Sonic, Subway Ⓞ 🏥 $General, to Lake Texoma SP, W 🅐 Phillips 66 🍴 Hickory House BBQ
5	OK 153, Thackerville, W Ⓞ Red River Ranch RV Park, Shorty's Foods/gas
3.5mm	**Welcome Ctr nb, full ♿ facilities, litter barrels, petwalk, 🅲, 📶**
1	US 77 N, E 🅐 Phillips 66/dsl 🛏 Best Western, The Inn Ⓞ RV park, Winstar Casino, W Ⓞ Red River RV Resort (3mi)
0mm	Oklahoma/Texas state line, Red River

⬆E INTERSTATE 40

Exit #	Services
331mm	Oklahoma/Arkansas state line
330	OK 64D S (from eb), Ft Smith
325	US 64, Roland, Ft Smith, N 🅐 Cherokee Trkstp/Valero/Subway/dsl/scales/24hr 🍴 Four Star Diner 🛏 Cherokee Inn, Travelodge Ⓞ casino, S 🅐 ▮▮▮▮/Wendy's/dsl/scales/24hr, Shell/dsl/scales, Valero/dsl 🍴 Arby's, El Celaya Mexican, Mazzio's, McDonald's, Sonic, Subway, Taco Bell 🛏 Interstate Inn Ⓞ $General, Marvin's Foods
321	OK 64b N, Muldrow, N 🍴 Sonic (1mi), S 🅐 Shell/dsl 🛏 Best Value Inn Ⓞ auto/dsl repair
316mm	🆁🆂 eb, full ♿ facilities, info, litter barrels, petwalk, 🅲, 📶, vending
313mm	🆁🆂 wb, full ♿ facilities, info, litter barrels, petwalk, 🅲, 📶, RV dump, vending
311	US 64, Sallisaw, N 🅐 Cox's/dsl, Ed's Truckstop/Phillips 66/diner/dsl 🍴 Hardee's, KFC/Taco Bell, Pizza Hut, Taco Mayo 🛏 Motel 6, Sallisaw Inn Ⓞ 🏥 $General, AutoZone, Brushy Lake SP (10mi), city park, NAPA, Sequoya's Home (12mi), USPO

OK

⬆E INTERSTATE 40 Cont'd

Exit #	Services
308	US 59, Sallisaw, **N** 🅿 Murphy USA/dsl, Phillips 66/dsl 🍴 A&W/LJ Silver, Arby's, Braum's, China Panda, Gino's Pizza, Mazzio's, McDonald's, Roma's Italian, Sonic, Subway, Taco Pronto, Western Sizzlin 🏠 Best Value Inn, Blue Ribbon Inn, Days Inn, Golden Spur Motel, Super 8 🅾 🏥 $General, $Tree, antiques, AT&T, casino, Verizon, Walmart, **S** 🅿 Shell/dsl 🍴 Emma B's Diner 🅾 Buick/Chevrolet/GMC, Chrysler/Dodge/Jeep, Ford, KOA, to Kerr Lake, truck/tire repair
303	Dwight Mission Rd
297	OK 82 N, Vian, **N** 🅿 FL/dsl 🍴 Subway 🅾 Cherokee Landing SP (24 mi), IGA Foods, to Tenkiller Lake RA (12 mi), USPO, **S** 🅾 Sequoia NWR
291	OK 10 N, to Gore, **N** 🅾 Greenleaf SP (10mi), Tenkiller SP (21mi)
290mm	Arkansas River
287	OK 100 N, to Webbers Falls, **N** 🅿 ♥Love's/Burger King/Subway/dsl/24hr 🍴 Charlie's Chicken, Godfather's Pizza 🏠 Sleepy Traveler Motel 🅾 Greenleaf SP, parts/tires/repair, Tenkiller SP
286	Muskogee Tpk, to Muskogee
284	Ross Rd
283mm	**parking area both lanes, litter barrels**
278	US 266, OK 2, Warner, **N** 🅿 Conoco, Phillips 66/dsl, Sinclair/McDonald's/dsl 🍴 Duke's Diner, Simon's Pizza, Sonic, Subway 🏠 Sleepy Traveler Motel 🅾 $General, city park, Parts+
270	Texanna Rd, to Porum Landing, **S** 🅿 Sinclair
265	US 69 bus, Checotah, **N** 🅿 Quick'n Easy 🍴 Pizza Hut, Sonic, **S** 🅿 Shell/dsl 🏠 Budget Inn 🅾 Chevrolet/Chrysler/Dodge/Jeep
264b a	US 69, to Eufaula, **N 1 mi** 🅿 ⊘FLYING J/dsl/LP/scales/24hr, Phillips 66/dsl/24hr 🍴 Charlie's Chicken, El Jarocho Pizza, McDonald's, Simple Simon's Pizza, Subway 🏠 Best Value Inn 🅾 $General, Ace Hardware, O'Reilly Parts, repair, TrueValue, Walmart/Subway
262	to US 266, Lotawatah Rd, **N** 🅿 Sinclair
261mm	Lake Eufaula
259	OK 150, to Fountainhead Rd, **S** 🅿 Shell 🏠 Lake Eufaula Inn 🅾 to Lake Eufaula SP
255	Pierce Rd, **N** 🅾 KOA
251mm	🆁🆂 both lanes
247	Tiger Mtn Rd, **S** 🅾 Quilt Barn/antiques
240b a	US 62 E, US 75 N, Henryetta, **N** 🅿 Conoco/dsl, ♥Love's/dsl, Phillips 66, Shell, Sinclair 🍴 Arby's, Braum's, El Charro Mexican, KFC, Mazzio's, McDonald's, Sonic, Subway 🏠 Best Value Inn, Colonial Motel, Economy Inn, Henryetta Inn/rest., Relax Inn 🅾 Chevrolet, Chrysler/Dodge/Jeep, Ford, O'Reilly Parts, tires/repair, Walmart, **S** 🅾 Indian Nation Tpk
237	US 62, US 75, Henryetta, **N** 🅿 Shell/dsl/24hr 🍴 Char Crushers BBQ 🏠 Green Country Inn 🅾 🏥 Henryetta RV Park (2mi), **S** 🏠 Super 8
231	US 75 S, to Weleetka, **N** 🅿 Phillips 66/dsl 🍴 Cowpoke's Cafe
227	Clearview Rd, **S** 🅾 casino
221	US 62, OK 27, Okemah, **N** 🅿 Phillips 66/McDonald's, Valero/Subway/dsl/24hr 🍴 Mazzio's, Sonic 🏠 Days Inn 🅾 🏥 $General, Chevrolet, Homeland Foods, NAPA, TrueValue, **S** 🅿 ♥Love's/Chester Fried/dsl/24hr, Shell/dsl 🍴 Kellogg's Rest 🅾 casino, truck repair
217	OK 48, to Bristow, Bearden, **S** 🅿

216mm	N Canadian River
212	OK 56, to Cromwell, Wewoka, **N** 🅾 auto/tire repair, **S** 🅿 Shell/cafe/dsl, to Seminole Nation Museum
208mm	Gar Creek
202mm	Turkey Creek
200	US 377, OK 99, to Little, Prague, **N** 🅿 Bar H Bar TC/Shell/dsl/RV park, **S** 🅿 Conoco/dsl, ♥Love's/Subway/dsl/24hr, Sinclair/dsl 🍴 Robertson's Ham Sandwiches, Roundup Rest/RV Park 🅾 🏥
197mm	🆁🆂 both lanes, full ♿ facilities, litter barrels, petwalk, 🚙, 🚐
192	OK 9A, Earlsboro, **S** 🅿 Shell/dsl 🍴 Biscuit Hill
189mm	N Canadian River
186	OK 18, to Shawnee, **N** 🅿 Phillips 66, Sinclair 🍴 Denny's 🏠 American Inn, Best Value Inn, Comfort Inn, Days Inn, La Quinta, Motel 6, Super 8, **S** 🅿 Sonic, Van's BBQ 🅾 Cadillac/Chevrolet/GMC, Chrysler/Dodge/Jeep, Ford, Homeland Foods, vet
185	185 OK 3E, Shawnee Mall Dr, to Shawnee, **N** 🅿 Murphy USA/dsl 🍴 Buffalo Wild Wings, Chili's, KFC, Red Lobster, Santa Fe Steaks, Taco Bueno, Wendy's 🏠 Holiday Inn Express 🅾 $Tree, AT&T, Dillard's, JC Penney, Jo-Ann, Kohl's, mall, Radio Shack, Ross, Walgreens, Walmart/McDonald's, **S** 🅿 Phillips 66/Circle K/Quiznos/dsl 🍴 Braum's, Burger King, Cracker Barrel, Delta Cafe, IHOP, Mazzio's, McAlister's Deli, McDonald's, Popeye's, Rib Crib BBQ, Sonic, Starbucks, Subway, Taco Bell, Whataburger 🏠 Hampton Inn 🅾 CVS Drug, Kwik Kar, Lowe's, Staples, Verizon
181	US 177, US 270, to Tecumseh, **S** 🏠 Budget Inn
180mm	N Canadian River
178	OK 102 S, Dale, **N** 🅿 Firelake/dsl/casino
176	OK 102 N, McLoud Rd, **S** 🅿 ♥Love's/Subway/dsl/24hr, Sinclair/dsl 🍴 Curtis Watson Rest.
172	Newalla Rd, to Harrah
169	Peebly Rd
166	Choctaw Rd, to Woods, **N** 🅾 KOA, **S** 🅿 ♥Love's/McDonald's/Subway/dsl/scales/24hr, Ⓗⓘⓛⓣ/Wendy's/dsl/scales/24hr 🍴 Sonic 🅾 to Lake Thunderbird SP (11mi)
165	I-240 W (from wb), to Dallas
162	Anderson Rd, **N** 🅾 Leisure Time RV Ctr, LP
159b	Douglas Blvd, **N** 🅿 Conoco, Shell 🍴 Denny's, LJ Silver, McDonald's, Sonic, Subway, Taco Bell 🅾 Eastland Hills RV Park, **S** 🅾 🏥 Tinker AFB
159a	Hruskocy Gate, **N** 🅿 Shell 🍴 Cheddar's, Denny's, McDonald's, Taco Bell 🅾 Dodge, Family$, Nissan, same as 157, U-Haul, **S** 🅾 Tinker AFB, Gate 7
157c	Eaker Gate, 🅾 Tinker AFB, same as 159

SALLISAW (left margin, top)

HENRYETTA (left margin, bottom)

SHAWNEE (right column margin)

OK (right margin)

INTERSTATE 40 Cont'd

Exit #	Services
157b	Air Depot Blvd, **N** 🅿 Shell/Circle K 🍴 Chick-fil-A, Chili's, Jack-in-the-Box, Logans Roadhouse, Old Chicago Grill, Panda Express, Pizza Inn, Qdoba Grill, Santa Fe Steaks, Starbucks, Steak&Shake 🏨 Super 8 🅾 Best Buy, Dick's, Firestone, JC Penney, Kohl's, Lowe's, Marshall's, O'Reilly Parts, Petsmart, Target, **S** 🅾 Tinker AFB, Gate 1
157a	SE 29th St, Midwest City, **N** 🅿 Conoco/dsl, Shell 🏨 Best Western, Traveler's Inn 🅾 O'Reilly Parts, **S** 🅾 Ford, Sam's Club/gas
156b a	Sooner Rd, **N** 🅿 Conoco/Circle K 🍴 Primo's Rest., Waffle House 🏨 Comfort Inn, Hampton Inn, Hawthorn Suites, Holiday Inn Express, La Quinta, Sheraton, Studio 6 🅾 Home Depot, Nissan, Radio Shack, Walmart/Subway, **S** 🍴 Buffalo Wild Wings, Carl's Jr 🏨 Candlewood Suites, Motel 6 🅾 Chevrolet/GMC, Discount Tire, Tires+, Toyota/Scion
155b	SE 15th St, Del City, **N** 🅿 Shell 🅾 Family$, **S** 🍴 Madison's Kitchen
155a	Sunny Lane Rd, Del City, **N** 🅿 Conoco/dsl 🅾 Hyundai, U-Haul, **S** 🅿 Shamrock, Shell 🍴 Braum's, Dunkin Donuts, Sonic 🅾 $General, Ace Hardware
154	Reno Ave, Scott St, **N** 🅿 Sinclair 🏨 Value Place Motel, **S** 🅿 7-11
152	(153 from wb)I-35 N, to Wichita
151b c	I-35, S to Dallas, I-235 N, to downtown, 🅾 st capitol
151a	Lincoln Blvd, **N** 🅿 Conoco/Subway/Circle K/dsl 🍴 Earl's Rib Palace, Falcon's Pizza, IHOP, Sonic 🏨 Hampton Inn, Residence Inn 🅾 Bass Pro Shop, Bricktown Stadium
150c	Robinson Ave (from wb), OK City, **N** 🍴 Spaghetti Whse, Zio's Italian 🏨 Courtyard, Residence Inn, Westin Hotel 🅾 Ford Ctr, U-Haul
150b	Harvey Ave (from eb), **N** 🏨 Courtyard, Renaissance Hotel, Sheraton, Westin Hotel 🅾 Ford, downtown
150a	Walker Ave (from eb), **N** 🍴 La Luna Mexican 🅾 Ford/Lincoln, **S** 🅾 transmissions
149b	Classen Blvd (from wb), same as 149a, to downtown
149a	Western Ave, Reno Ave, **N** 🅿 Valero/Subway/dsl 🍴 China Queen, McDonald's, Sonic, Taco Bell, **S** 🅿 Conoco/dsl, Shell 🍴 Sweis Gyros
148c	Virginia Ave (from wb), to downtown
148b	Penn Ave (from eb), **N** 🅿 Shamrock, **S** 🅾 Isuzu Trucks
148a	Agnew Ave, Villa Ave, **N** 🅿 Phillips 66/dsl
147c	May Ave
147b a	I-44, E to Tulsa, W to Lawton
146	Portland Ave (from eb, no return), **N** 🅿 Conoco/Subway/dsl 🅾 water funpark
145	Meridian Ave, OK City, **N** 🅿 Conoco/Circle K/dsl, Shell/Circle K/dsl 🍴 Cimarron Steakhouse, Denny's, Jin Wei Aisan, Louie's Grill, Mango's, McDonald's, On the Border, Portofinos Italian, Shorty Small's Rest., Trapper's Rest. 🏨 Best Western, Biltmore Hotel, Days Inn, Extended Stay America, Howard Johnson, Red Roof Inn, Residence Inn, Super 8 🅾 USPO, **S** 🅿 Phillips 66/Circle K/dsl, Sinclair 🍴 Arby's, Burger King, Charleston Rest., Chili's, Cracker Barrel, El Sombrero, Golden Palace Chinese, IHOP, Kona Ranch Steaks, Mackie's Steaks, Panera Bread, Pearl's Fish House, Poblano's, Quiznos, Rib Crib, Riggin's Grill, Sonic, Subway, Taco Bell, Taco Bueno, Waffle House, Whataburger, Zapata's, Zio's Italian 🏨 Baymont Inn, Best Value Inn, Candlewood Suites, Caountry Inn&Suites, Clarion Hotel, Comfort Suites, Courtyard, Embassy Suites, Fairfield Inn, Governors Suites, Hampton Inn,

145	Continued Hilton Garden, Holiday Inn, Holiday Inn Express, Hyatt Place, La Quinta, Meridian Inn, Motel 6, Oak Tree Inn, Ramada Ltd, Regency Inn, Sleep Inn, Staybridge Suites, Wingate Inn, Wyndham Garden 🅾 Celebration Sta., Shepler's
144	MacArthur Blvd, **N** 🅿 Shell/Circle K/dsl 🍴 Applebee's, Coldstone, Golden Corral, Jack-in-the-Box, KFC, Lin's Buffet, McDonald's, Panda Express, Quiznos, Sonic, Starbucks, Steak'n'Shake, Taco Cabana, TX Roadhouse 🏨 SpringHill Suites 🅾 $Tree, AT&T, GNC, Hobby Lobby, Office Depot, Petsmart, Radio Shack, Ross, Walmart, **S** 🏨 Comfort Inn, Green Carpet Inn, Microtel, Super 10 Motel, Travelers Inn 🅾 dsl repair, Kenworth, Sam's Club/gas
143	Rockwell Ave, **N** 🅿 Shell/dsl 🍴 Buffalo Wild Wings, Mike's Subs, Taco Bell 🏨 Homewood Suites, Rodeway Inn 🅾 Best Buy, Dick's, Discount Tire, Harley Davidson, Home Depot, McClain's RV Ctr, Tires+, **S** 🏨 Sands Motel/RV Park/LP 🅾 A-OK RV Park, Rockwell RV Park
142	Council Rd, **N** 🅿 Shell, Sinclair 🍴 BJ's Rest., Braum's, McDonald's, Subway, Taco Bell 🏨 Super 40 Inn 🅾 Goodyear/auto, **S** 🅿 TA/Country Pride/dsl/scales/24hr/@ 🏨 EconoLodge 🅾 Council Rd RV Park, dsl repair, Ford/Peterbilt, truckwash
140	Morgan Rd, **N** 🅿 🚛/McDonald's/dsl/24hr/@, TA/Popeye's/dsl/24hr/@ 🅾 Blue Beacon, **S** 🅿 ⊘FLYING J/dsl/LP/scales/24hr, ❤Loves/Subway/dsl/scales/24hr 🍴 Ricky's Cafe, Sonic 🅾 Speedco
139	Kilpatrick Tpk
138	OK 4, to Yukon, Mustang, **N** 🅿 Best Value Inn, Comfort Suites 🅾 Chrysler/Dodge/Jeep, **S** 🅿 Conoco/Circle K/dsl 🍴 Braum's, Burger King, Hunan Express, IHOP, Interurban Grill, McDonald's, Sonic, Subway, Taco Bell 🏨 Best Western, La Quinta 🅾 Cottman Transmissions, CVS Drug, Homeland Food/drug, URGENT CARE
137	Cornwell Dr, Czech Hall Rd, **N** 🅾 Homeland Food/drug
136	OK 92, Garth Brooks Blvd, Yukon, **N** 🅿 Murphy USA/dsl, Shell/Circle K 🍴 A&W/LJ Silver, Braum's, CiCi's Pizza, Harry's Rest., KFC, McDonald's, Primo's Italian, Subway, Taco Mayo, Waffle House, Wendy's, Yukon Buffet 🏨 Hampton Inn 🅾 $Tree, AutoZone, Big Lots, Big O Tire, GNC, Hancock Fabrics, Hastings Books, Radio Shack, repair, Tuesday Morning, USPO, Verizon, Walgreens, Walmart, **S** 🍴 Alfredo's, Carino's Italian, Chick-fil-A, Chili's, Jimmy's Egg Café, Logan's Roadhouse, Louie's Grill, Mike's Subs, Pizza Hut, Quiznos, Rib Crib, Santa Fe Steaks, Starbucks, Taco Bueno 🏨 Holiday Inn Express 🅾 🄷 Discount Tire, Ford, Kohl's, Kwik Kar, Lowe's, PetsMart, Staples, Target, Tires+
132	Cimarron Rd, **S** 🅾 🖅
130	Banner Rd, **N** 🅿 Shell/dsl/rest.
129mm	weigh st both lanes
127	Eastern Ave (from eb), Okla City, **N** 🅿 JR's Trvl Crt/Corky's Grill/dsl/24hr, Petro/Mobil/dsl/scales/rest./@, Shamrock 🍴 Waffle House 🏨 Bricktown Hotel, Econolodge, Quality Inn 🅾 Blue Beacon, Lewis RV Ctr
125	US 81, to El Reno, **N** 🅿 Conoco/dsl, Love's/Subway/dsl 🍴 China King, Serapio's Mexican, Taco Mayo 🏨 Deluxe Inn, Economy Express, Super 8 🅾 $General, Buick/GMC, Chevrolet, Chrysler/Dodge/Jeep, Ford/Lincoln, **S** 🅾 truck repair
123	Country Club Rd, to El Reno, **N** 🅿 Murphy USA/dsl, Phillips 66, Shell, Valero 🍴 Arby's, Braum's, Burger King, Greatwall Chinese, KFC, Little Caesar's, Mazzio's, McDonald's, Pizza Hut, Subway, Taco Bell 🏨 Motel 6 🅾 🄷 AutoZone,

⬆🅴 INTERSTATE 40 Cont'd

Exit #	Services
123	Continued
	Radio Shack, Walgreens, Walmart, S 🍴 Denny's, MT Mikes Steaks 🛏 Baymont Inn, Best Western/RV Park, Days Inn, Regency Motel
119	Lp 40, to El Reno
115	US 270, to Calumet
111mm	🅿 eb, litter barrels
108	US 281, to Geary, N ⛽ Shell/Subway/dsl/24hr ⊡ KOA/Indian Trading Post, to Roman Nose SP, S ⛽ Phillips 66/dsl
105mm	S Canadian River
104	Methodist Rd
101	US 281, OK 8, Hinton, N ⊡ to Roman Nose SP, S ⛽ 💗Loves/Chester's/Godfather's/Sonic/dsl/scales 🍴 Subway 🛏 Hinton Travel Inn ⊡ casino, Chevrolet, 🅿, to Red Rock Canyon SP
95	Bethel Rd
94.5mm	🅿 wb, litter barrels
88	OK 58, to Hydro, Carnegie
84	Airport Rd, N ⛽ Phillips 66/dsl/scales/24hr 🍴 Lucille's Roadhouse 🛏 Holiday Inn Express, Travel Inn ⊡ 🏥 Buick/Cadillac/Chevrolet/GMC, Chrysler/Dodge/Jeep, S ⊡ Stafford Aerospace Museum
82	E Main St, Weatherford, N ⛽ Conoco/dsl, Phillips 66/dsl, Shell/dsl, Sinclair, Valero/dsl 🍴 Arby's, Braum's, Carl's Jr, Jerry's Rest., KFC/Taco Bell, Little Caesars, Mark Rest., Mazzio's, McDonald's, Pizza Hut, Quiznos, Sonic, Subway, Taco Mayo, T-Bone Steaks, Vinicio's Mexican 🛏 Best Western, Comfort Inn, Fairfield Inn, Scottish Inn ⊡ 🏥 $General, Ace Hardware, GNC, O'Reilly Parts, to SW OSU, Walgreens, S ⊡ Walmart
80a	(from eb), N ⛽ Conoco ⊡ Ford
80	W Main St, Mountainview, Thomas, N 🛏 Best Value Inn
71	Custer City Rd, N ⛽ 💗Loves/Subway/dsl/24hr ⊡ Cherokee Trading Post/rest.
69	Lp 40 (from wb), to Clinton, N 2 mi 🍴 DQ 🛏 Travel Inn
67.5mm	Washita River
66	US 183, Clinton, S ⛽ Shell/dsl ⊡ Buick/Chevrolet/GMC, Ford
65a	10th St, Neptune Dr, Clinton, N 🍴 Branding Iron Rest., China King, Oakwood Steaks, Picante Grille, Pizza Hut 🛏 Days Inn, Relax Inn, Super 8 ⊡ United Foods, S 🛏 EconoLodge ⊡ Hargus RV Park
65	Gary Blvd, Clinton, N ⛽ Conoco, Shell/dsl 🍴 Braum's, Del Rancho, KFC/Taco Bell, LJ Silver, Mazzio's, McDonald's, MT Mike's, Placio Mexican, Subway, Taco Mayo 🛏 Budget Inn, Hampton Inn, Ramada Inn, Tradewinds Inn ⊡ 🏥 $General, K-Mart, Rte 66 Museum, S 🛏 Holiday Inn Express
62	Parkersburg Rd, S ⊡ Hargus RV Ctr
61	Haggard Rd
57	Stafford Rd
53	OK 44, Foss, N ⊡ to Foss SP, S ⛽ gas/ds
50	Clinton Lake Rd, N ⊡ KOA/LP/dsl
47	Canute, S ⛽ Shell 🛏 Sunset Inn
41	OK 34 (exits left from eb), Elk City, N ⛽ 💗Loves/Subway/dsl, Shell 🍴 Home Cooking Rest. 🛏 Best Value Inn (3mi), Best Western (3mi), Economy Express, Elk City Motel, Home-Towne Inn, La Quinta, Motel 6, Sleep Inn, Super 8, Travel Inn ⊡ 🏥 Elk Run RV Park, Rte 66 Museum
40	E 7th St, Elk City, N 🍴 Portobello Grill 🛏 Holiday Inn Express, S ⛽ Hutch's/dsl/CNG 🍴 Huddle House 🛏 Hampton Inn ⊡ same as 41, Walmart

38	OK 6, Elk City, N ⛽ Conoco/dsl, Phillips 66/dsl 🍴 Arby's, China Super Buffet, Denny's, LJ Silver, McDonald's, Quizno's, Western Sizzlin 🛏 Bedford Inn, Days Inn ⊡ Ace Hardware, Elk Creek RV Park, tires, vet, S ⛽ Phillips 66/dsl 🛏 Clarion Inn, Comfort Inn, Ramada Inn, Rodeway Inn ⊡ to Quartz Mtn SP
34	Merritt Rd
32	OK 34 S (exits left from eb), Elk City
26	Cemetery Rd, N ⛽ Shell/dsl ⊡ dsl repair, S ⛽ TA/Taco Bell/Subway/dsl/scales/24hr/@
25	Lp 40, Sayre, N 1 mi ⛽ Shell/dsl 🛏 Western Motel ⊡ 🏥 $General, Chevrolet/GMC, Deep Creek RV Park, Ford
23	OK 152, Sayre, S ⛽ Shell/dsl
22.5mm	N Fork Red River
20	US 283, Sayre, N ⛽ ⊕FLYING J/Denny's/dsl/LP/RV dump/scales/24hr 🛏 AmericInn ⊡ to Washita Bfd Site (25mi), truckwash
14	Hext Rd
13.5mm	**check sta both lanes**
11	Lp 40, to Erick, Hext
10mm	**Welcome Ctr/rest area both lanes full ♿ facilities, litter barrels, petwalk, ⊙, RV dump**
7	OK 30, Erick, N 🛏 Premier Inn, S ⛽ 💗Loves/Subway/dsl/scales 🍴 Simple Simon's Pizza 🛏 Days Inn
5	Lp 40, Honeyfarm Rd
1	Texola, S ⛽ gas/dsl/rest. ⊡ RV camping
0mm	Oklahoma/Texas state line

⬆🅴 INTERSTATE 44

Exit #	Services
329mm	Oklahoma/Missouri state line
321mm	Spring River
314mm	**Oklahoma Welcome Center wb, full ♿ facilities, info, restrooms**
313	OK 10, Miami, N ⛽ Conoco, 💗Loves/dsl, Phillips 66 🍴 Donut Palace, Okie Burger 🛏 Best Value Inn, Deluxe Inn, EconoLodge, Hampton Inn, Holiday Inn Express, Legacy Inn, Microtel ⊡ 🏥 auto repair, Miami RV Park, to NE OK A&M Coll, S ⊡ casino, Chrysler/Dodge/Jeep
312mm	Neosho River
302	US 59, US 69, Afton, S ⛽ Buffalo Ranch/Subway/dsl 🛏 Rte 66 Motel (3mi)
289	US 60, Vinita, N ⛽ Murphy USA/dsl 🍴 Braum's, Clanton's Cafe, McDonald's, Pizza Hut, Sonic, Subway, Woodshed Deli 🛏 Holiday Inn Express, Vinita Inn ⊡ 🏥 $General, Ace Hardware, Chevrolet, O'Reilly Parts, Radio Shack, st patrol, USPO, Walmart

OK

Side tabs (left): W E A T H E R F O R D · C L I N T O N · E L K C I T Y

Side tabs (right): S A Y R E · V I N I T A

☐ = gas ☐ = food ☐ = lodging ☐ = other ☐ = rest stop Copyright 2015 - the Next EXIT ®

INTERSTATE 44 Cont'd

Exit #	Services
288mm	**Service Plaza both lanes**
286mm	**toll plaza**
283	US 69, Big Cabin, N ☐ Big Cabin/dsl/rest./scales/24hr/@ ☐ Super 8 ☐ Cabin RV Park, trk repair
269	OK 28 (from eb, no re-entry), to Adair, Chelsea, S ☐ Sinclair
255	OK 20, to Pryor, Claremore, N 0-2 mi ☐ Kum&Go/dsl/e-85, Murphy USA/dsl, QT/dsl ☐ Carl's Jr, Chili's, Red's Coney Island ☐ Clairmore Inn, Super 8, Travel Inn, Will Rogers Inn ☐ ☐ museum, to Rogers U, Walgreens, Walmart, Will Rogers Memorial
248	to OK 266, Port of Catoosa, N ☐ QT ☐ Comfort Inn, Will Rogers Inn ☐ Dave's RV Ctr
244mm	Kerr-McClellan Navigation System
241mm	**Will Rogers Tpk begins eb, ends wb, ☐**
241	OK 66 E, to Catoosa
240b	US 412 E, Choteau
240a	OK 167 N, 193rd E Ave, N ☐ IHOP, McDonald's, Taco Bueno, Waffle House, Wendy's ☐ Cherokee Inn/Casino, Hampton Inn, Hardrock Hotel/Casino, La Quinta ☐ KOA, Walgreens, S ☐ QT ☐ Mazzio's, PortCity Diner, Sonic, Subway ☐ Holiday Inn Express ☐ $General, O'Reilly Parts, tires/repair
238	161st E Ave, N ☐ Sinclair/rest/dsl/scales/24hr ☐ Goodyear Trk Tires, truckwash, S **OK Welcome Ctr**, ☐ QT/dsl/scales/24hr ☐ Arby's, Burger King ☐ Microtel ☐ truckwash
236b	I-244 W, to downtown Tulsa, ☐ ☐
236a	129th E Ave, N ☐ ☐ FLYING J/Denny's/dsl/LP/24hr, S ☐ McDonald's
235	E 11th St, Tulsa, N ☐ Big Daddy's BBQ, Mazzio's, Rioberto's Mexican, Sonic, Subway ☐ Economy Inn, Executive Inn, Knights Inn, Super 8 ☐ $General, Drug Whse, O'Reilly Parts, S ☐ QT ☐ Braum's, Taco Bueno ☐ EconoLodge ☐ Whse Mkt
234b a	US 169, N to Owasso, to ☐, S to Broken Arrow
233	E 21st St, S ☐ El Chico ☐ Comfort Suites ☐ Dean's RV Ctr, K-Mart, vet
231	US 64, OK 51, to Muskogee, E 31st St, Memorial Dr, N ☐ Speedy Gonzales Mexican, Whataburger ☐ Days Inn, Ramada Inn, Tulsa Inn, S ☐ Shell ☐ Cracker Barrel, IHOP, McDonald's, Pizza Hut, Ruby Tuesday, Village Inn ☐ Best Value Inn, Best Western, Comfort Suites, Courtyard, EconoLodge, Embassy Suites, Extended Stay America, Fairfield Inn, Hampton Inn, Holiday Inn Express, Quality Inn, Sleep Inn, Studio+, Super 8 ☐ Cavender's Boots, Chevrolet, Harley-Davidson, Nissan, URGENT CARE
230	E 41st St, Sheridan Rd, N ☐ Shell ☐ Carl's Jr, Desi Wok, On-the-Border, Panera Bread, Schlotzsky's, Subway, TGI-Friday's, Whataburger ☐ AT&T, Barnes&Noble, Curves, Dillard's, JC Penney, Jo-Ann Fabrics, Michael's, Old Navy, Petco, Petsmart, Reasor's Foods, Ross, Verizon, S ☐ Buffalo Wild Wings, Carino's Italian ☐ La Quinta ☐ Batteries+, Home Depot
229	Yale Ave, Tulsa, N ☐ Shell ☐ McDonald's, Subway ☐ Firestone, JC Penney, Macy's, mall, PetCo, S ☐ Phillips 66/dsl, QT ☐ Applebee's, Arby's, Braum's, Charlie Mitchell's Grill, Delta Cafe, Jack-in-the-Box, Outback Steaks, Qdoba, Red Lobster, Smoothie King, Sonic, Taco Bell, Village Inn ☐ Baymont Inn, Hilton Garden, Red Roof Inn, Tulsa Select Hotel ☐ ☐ Kia, vet
228	Harvard Ave, Tulsa, N ☐ El Tequila Mexican, NYC Pizza ☐ Tradewinds Motel, S ☐ Express ☐ A&W/LJ Silver, Chili's,
228	Continued Chimi's Mexican, Freckle's Frozen Custard, Jamil's Rest, Mario's Pizza, Osaka Steaks, Papa John's, Starbucks, Subway ☐ Stratford House Hotel, Wingate Inn ☐ $Tree, Food Pyramid, Hobby Lobby, K-Mart, SteinMart
227	Lewis Ave, Tulsa, S ☐ Goldie's Grill ☐ Walgreens
226b	Peoria Ave, Tulsa, N ☐ Kum&Go, QT/dsl ☐ Arby's, Burger St., CiCi's, Egg Roll Express, Jimmy's Egg, KFC, La Hacienda Mexican, Little Caesars, Mazzio's, Pizza Hut, Ron's Burgers/Chili, Sonic, Subway, Super Buffet, Taco Bell, Taco Bueno ☐ Peoria Inn ☐ Advance Parts, Food Pyramid, Harley-Davidson, O'Reilly Parts, Robertson Tire, Verizon, Walmart Mkt, Whole Foods Mkt, S ☐ Braum's, Corner Cafe, Golden Palace ☐ $General, AutoZone, Drug Whse, Family$
226a	Riverside Dr
225mm	Arkansas River
225	Elwood Ave, N ☐ Chevrolet, Ford, S ☐ Budget Inn
224b a	US 75, to Okmulgee, Bartlesville, N ☐ QT/dsl ☐ KFC, Mazzio's, Sonic, Subway ☐ $General, Whse Mkt, S ☐ Royal Inn ☐ RV park
223c	33rd W Ave, Tulsa, N ☐ Braum's, Domino's, S ☐ Conoco ☐ Rib Crib BBQ
223b	51st St (from wb)
223a	I-244 E, to Tulsa, downtown
222c	(from wb), S ☐ Value Inn
222b	55th Place, N ☐ Capri Motel, Crystal Motel, S ☐ Days Inn, Economy Inn
222a	49th W Ave, Tulsa, N ☐ Carl's Jr, Kelly's Country Cooking, Monterey Mexican, Subway ☐ Gateway Motel, Interstate Inn, Motel 6, Rest Inn ☐ $General, BigLots, Mack Trucks, S ☐ QT/Wendy's/dsl/scales/24hr ☐ Arby's, McDonald's, Taco Bueno, Village Inn, Waffle House ☐ Super 8 ☐ Buick/GMC, Freightliner, Kenworth, Peterbilt, Volvo Trucks
221mm	**Turner Tkp begins wb, ends eb**
221a	57th W Ave, (from wb), S ☐ Go West Rest ☐ Buick/GMC
218	Creek Tkp E (from eb)
215	OK 97, to Sand Sprgs, Sapulpa, S ☐ Kum&Go ☐ Arby's, Freddy's, Subway, Whataburger ☐ Super 8 ☐ ☐ Hunter RV Ctr, Route 66 RV Park
211	OK 33, to Kellyville, Drumright, S ☐ Shell/dsl ☐ Heyburn Lake SP
207mm	**service plaza wb**, ☐ Phillips 66/dsl
197mm	**service plaza eb**, ☐ McDonald's
196	OK 48, Bristow, S ☐ Conoco/dsl, Phillips 66 ☐ Mazzio's, McDonald's, Pizza Hut, Sonic, Steak'nEgg Rest, Taco Mayo ☐ Carolyn Inn ☐ ☐ Buick/Chevrolet, Ford, O'Reilly Parts, Walmart
182mm	**toll plaza**
179	OK 99, to Drumright, Stroud, N ☐ Best Western/rest, S ☐ Kids/dsl, Phillips 66/Subway/dsl ☐ 5Star BBQ, Mazzio's, McDonald's, Mi Casa Mexican, Sonic, Vallarta's Rest ☐ Skyliner Motel, Sooner Motel ☐ ☐ auto/tire repair, USPO
178mm	**Hoback Plaza both lanes (exits left)**, ☐ Phillips 66/dsl ☐ McDonald's
171mm	**picnic area eb, litter barrels**
167mm	**service plaza (from eb)**, S ☐ Phillips 66/dsl
166	OK 18, to Cushing, Chandler, N ☐ Chrysler/Dodge/Jeep, S ☐ Phillips 66/dsl ☐ B's Rest, Sonic ☐ EconoLodge, Lincoln Motel ☐ Chandler Tire, Ford
158	OK 66, to Wellston, N ☐ Kum&Go/Subway/dsl/24hr ☐ $General
146	Luther-Jones (from eb, no return)

TULSA

TULSA

OK

INTERSTATE 44 Cont'd

Exit #	Services
138d	to Memorial Rd, to Enterprise Square
138a	I-35, I-44 E to Tulsa, Turner Tpk
I-44 and I-35 run together 8 mi.	
137	NE 122nd St, to OK City, **E** 🅿 Shamrock/dsl, Shell/dsl 🍴 Charly's Rest., IHOP 🛏 Knights Inn, Sleep Inn, **W** 🅿 Huddle House/dsl/scales/LP/24hr, 🍴Loves/Godfathers/Subway/dsl/24hr, Phillips 66/dsl/scales 🍴 Cracker Barrel, McDonald's, Sonic, Waffle House 🛏 Comfort Inn, Days Inn, EconoLodge, Economy Inn, Holiday Inn Express, Motel 6, Red Carpet Inn, Super 8 ⊙ Abe's RV Park, Frontier City Funpark, Oklahoma Visitors Ctr/info/restrooms, truckwash
136	Hefner Rd, **W** 🅿 Conoco/dsl, same as 137
135	Britton Rd
135mm	**Turner Tpk begins eb, ends wb**
134	Wilshire Blvd, **E** 🅿 Drivers/dsl, 🍴 Braum's ⊙ Gordon Indland Marine, **W** 🛏 Executive Inn ⊙ Blue Beacon
I-44 and I-35 run together 8 mi.	
130	I-35 S, to Dallas, access to services on I-35 S
129	MLK Ave, Remington Park, **N** 🅿 Park Hill Inn ⊙ Cowboy Museum, **S** 🍴 McDonald's, Sonic ⊙ Family$
128b	Kelley Ave, OK City, **N** 🅿 Conoco, Valero/Subway/dsl 🍴 44 Diner
128a	Lincoln Blvd, **S** 🅿 Lincoln Mart/dsl 🛏 Lincoln Inn/Express, Oxford Inn ⊙ st capitol
127	I-235 S, US 77, City Ctr, Broadway St, **N on 63rd St** 🅿 Conoco/Circle K, Shell/Circle K 🛏 Best Western, Clarion
126	Western Ave, **N** 🍴 Camille's Cafe, Flip's Rest, Sonic, **S** 🛏 Sleep Inn
125c	NW Expressway (exits left from sb)
125a	OK 3A, Penn Ave, to NW Expswy, **N** 🅿 Express 🍴 Lion's Choice Rest, **S** 🅿 Shell/Circle K 🍴 Braum's, Coit's Cafe 🛏 Habana Inn ⊙ auto/tire repair, Family$, Super Save Foods
125	Classen Blvd, (exits left from wb), OK City, **N** 🍴 Cheesecake Factory, Chili's, Elephant Bar Rest., Jamba Juice, Milegro Mexican, Moe's SW Grill, Olive Garden, Pei Wei, Quiznos ⊙ AT&T, Dillard's, JC Penney, Macy's, Old Navy, Radio Shack, Ross, Verizon, Walmart/McDonald's, **S** 🍴 IHOP, McDonald's 🛏 Courtyard, Hawthorn Suites, Hyatt Place ⊙ auto repair
124	N May, **W** 🅿 Shell/Circle K/Subway 🍴 San Marco's Mexican 🛏 Days Inn, Motel 6, Super 8 ⊙ O'Reilly Parts, **S** 🅿 Shell 🍴 Jersey Mike's Subs, Starbucks, Wendy's ⊙ Aamco, Advance Parts, Ford, Lowe's
123b	OK 66 W, NW 39th, to Warr Acres, **N** 🅿 7-11, Shell, Valero, McDonald's/dsl 🍴 Braum's, Carl's Jr, Jimmy's Egg, Los Mariachi's, Sonic, Taco Bueno 🛏 Carlyle Motel, Hospitality Inn ⊙ $General, Advance Parts, U-Haul
123a	NW 36th St, **S** ⊙ Value Place Hotel
122	NW 23rd St, **N** 🅿 7-11 🍴 Church's, EggRoll King, Taco Mayo ⊙ Tires+, **S** 🅿 Conoco 🍴 Arby's, Sonic ⊙ Family$
121b a	NW 10th St, **N** 🅿 Shell, **S** 🅿 7-11, Sinclair ⊙ $General, antiques, fairgrounds, Family$, Whittaker's Foods
120b a	I-40, W to Amarillo, E to Ft Smith
119	SW 15th St
118	OK 152 W, SW 29th St, OK City, **E** 🅿 7-11 🍴 A&W/LJ Silver, Burger King, CiCi's Pizza, KFC/Taco Bell, McDonald's, Pizza Hut, Sonic, Subway, Taco Bueno ⊙ $General, $Tree, Advance Parts, AutoZone, Buy-4-Less Foods, city park, O'Reilly Parts, Walgreens, **W** 🅿 Shell ⊙ city park, transmissions, U-Haul/LP

117	SW 44th St, **W** ⊙ auto repair
116b	Airport Rd (exits left from nb), **W** ⊙ ✈
116a	SW 59th St, **E** 🅿 Conoco/Circle K 🍴 Pizza Inn, Taco Mayo ⊙ Family$, **W** ⊙ Will Rogers ✈
115	I-240 E, US 62 E, to Ft Smith
114	SW 74th St, OK City, **E** 🅿 Valero 🍴 Braum's, Burger King, Perry's Rest. 🛏 Cambridge Inn, Ramada Ltd ⊙ $General
113	SW 89th St, **E** 🅿 7-11, Loves/Subway/dsl, OG, Valero/dsl 🍴 Sonic ⊙ Ⓗ CVS Drug
112	SW 104th St, **E** 🅿 Valero
111	SW 119th St, **E** 🍴 Sonic ⊙ General Store RV Ctr
110	OK 37 E, to Moore, **E** ⊙ Ⓗ
109	SW 149th St, **E** 🍴 JR's Grill
108mm	S Canadian River
108	OK 37 W, to Tuttle, **W** 🅿 Conoco/dsl, Phillips 66 🍴 Arby's, Braum's, Carlito's Mexican, Jimmy's Egg, Little Caesars, Mazzio's, McDonald's, New China, Sonic, Taco Bell ⊙ $General, AT&T, O'Reilly Parts, URGENT CARE, Walgreens, Walmart/Subway
107	US 62 S (no wb return), to Newcastle, **E** 🛏 Newcastle Motel ⊙ casino/gas, Newcastle RV
99	H E Bailey Spur, rd 4, to Blanchard, Tuttle, Norman
97mm	**toll booth,** 🅿
96mm	🛏 wb, litter barrels
85.5mm	**Service Plaza, both lanes exit left,** 🅿 Phillips 66/dsl 🍴 McDonald's
83	US 62, Chickasha, **W** 🅿 Jay's/dsl, Valero/dsl ⊙ Indian Museum
80	US 81, Chickasha, **E** 🅿 Phillips 66/dsl, Shell/dsl 🍴 Eduardo's Mexican, La Fiesta Mexican, Western Sizzlin 🛏 Best Value Inn, Hampton Inn, Holiday Inn Express, Maverick Inn, Super 8 ⊙ Ⓗ $Tree, Buick/GMC, Cadillac/Chevrolet, Chrysler/Dodge/Jeep, vet, **W** 🅿 Griffith's, Love's/dsl, Murphy USA/dsl, Valero 🍴 Arby's, Braum's, Chicken Express, China Moon, Domino's, KFC, Little Caesars, LJ Silver, Mazzio's Pizza, McDonald's, Napoli's Rest., New China, Pizza Hut, Quiznos, Sonic, Taco Bell, Taco Mayo 🛏 Best Western, Budget Inn, Ranch House Motel ⊙ $General, Ace Hardware, AT&T, AutoZone, Chickasha RV Park, CVS Drug, Family$, Ford, O'Reilly Parts, Ralph&Son's Tires/repair, Save-A-Lot Foods, Staples, Verizon, Walgreens, Walmart/Subway
78mm	**toll plaza,** 🅿
63mm	🛏 wb, litter barrels
62	to Cyril (from wb)
60.5mm	🛏 eb, litter barrels
53	US 277, Elgin, Lake Ellsworth, **E** 🅿 Shamrock, Valero/McDonald's/dsl 🍴 Billy Sim's BBQ, China Garden, Sonic, Subway ⊙ Family$, tires, **W** 🅿 Fina/dsl

OKLAHOMA CITY (vertical, left margin)

CHICKASHA (vertical, center margin)

OK (right margin tab)

INTERSTATE 44 Cont'd

Exit #	Services
46	US 62 E, US 277, US 281, to Elgin, Apache, Comanche Tribe, last free exit eb
45	OK 49, to Medicine Park, W 🅟 Loves/Subway/dsl/24hr 🅕 Burger King, Sonic 🅞 Whichita NWR
41	to Ft Sill, Key Gate, W 🅞 Ft Sill Museum
40c	Gate 2, to Ft Sill
40a	to Cache
39b	US 281 (from sb), W 🅕 Pizza Hut 🅛 Super 9 Motel 🅞 transmissions, U-Haul
39a	US 281, Cache Rd (exits left from nb), Lawton, W 1-3 mi 🅟 Valero/dsl 🅕 Bianco's Italian, Pizza Hut 🅛 Best Value Inn, Super 9 Motel 🅞 Family$, Nissan, transmissions, U-Haul
39	US 62 W, to Cache, E 🅟 Alon/dsl, W 🅛 Super 8
38	Cache Rd (exits left from nb)
37	Gore Blvd, Lawton, E 🅕 Braum's, Los Tres Amigos, Papa John's, Sonic, Taco Mayo 🅛 Best Western 🅞 casino, Curves, USPO, W 🅕 Cracker Barrel, Mike's Grille 🅛 Fairfield Inn, Holiday Inn Express, Homewood Suites, Sleep Inn, SpringHill Suites 🅞 Harley-Davidson, Nissan
36a	OK 7, Lee Blvd, Lawton, E 🅟 Phillips 66, W 🅟 Alon/dsl/repair, Shamrock/dsl 🅕 Big Chef Rest., Braum's, Burger King, KFC/Taco Bell, Leo&Ken's Rest., McDonald's, Salas Mexican, Sonic 🅛 Motel 6 🅞 🅗 🖭, vet
33	US 281, 11th St, Lawton, W 🅞 🖭
30	OK 36 (last free exit sb), Geronimo
20.5mm	Elmer Graham Plaza (both lanes exit left), info 🅟 Phillips 66/dsl 🅕 McDonald's
20	OK 5, to Walters
19.5mm	toll plaza
5	US 277 N, US 281, Randlett, last free exit nb
1	OK 36, to Grandfield
0mm	Oklahoma/Texas state line, Red River

INTERSTATE 240 (Oklahoma City)

Exit #	Services
16mm	I-240 begins/ends on I-40.
14	Anderson Rd, S 🅟 Conoco
11b a	Douglas Blvd, N 🅞 Tinker AFB

9	Air Depot Blvd
8	OK 77, Sooner Rd, N 🅟 Shell/dsl 🅕 Sonic, S 🅟 Phillips 66/Popeye's/dsl, Valero/McDonald's/dsl 🅞 🅗
7	Sunnylane Ave, S 🅟 Valero/Subway/dsl 🅛 Value Place Motel
6	Bryant Ave
5	S Eastern Ave
4c	Pole Rd, N 🅕 Burger King, Subway, TX Roadhouse, Zeke's Grill 🅛 Fairfield Inn, Ramada Inn, Residence Inn 🅞 Best Buy, Tires+, URGENT CARE
4b a	I-35, N to OK City, S to Dallas, US 77 S, US 62/77 N
3b	S Shields, N 🅟 Valero/dsl 🅞 Dodge, Home Depot, S 🅞 Discount Tire, Nissan, Subaru
3a	S Santa Fe, S 🅟 Murphy USA/dsl, Shell 🅕 Chili's, IHOP, Mike's Subs 🅞 Buick, Lowe's, Staples, Walmart
2b	S Walker Ave, N 🅟 7-11, Shell/Circle K 🅕 Rib Crib, S 🅕 Carino's, ChuckeCheese, City Bites, Coach's Grill, Jimmy's Egg Grill, On-the-Border, Primo's Italian 🅞 PepBoys, URGENT CARE
2a	S Western Ave, N 🅟 7-11, Conoco 🅕 Burger King, CiCi's Pizza, House of Szechwan, Nino's Mexican, Taste of China 🅞 $General, Advance Parts, Hyundai, Tires+, vet, S 🅟 7-11, Valero/dsl 🅕 A&W/LJ Silver, Arby's, Grandy's, Hibachi Buffet, KFC, Krispy Kreme, McDonald's, Red Lobster 🅛 Best Western, Comfort Inn, Hampton Inn, Quality Inn 🅞 Big O Tire, Chevrolet, Home Depot, Honda, Office Depot, Tire Factory
1c	S Penn Ave, N 🅟 Conoco 🅕 Carl's Jr, Charleston's Rest., Denny's, Golden Corral, Harrigan's Rest., Hooters, Old Chicago Pizza, Olive Garden, Outback Steaks, Pioneer Pies, Salt-Grass Steaks, Santa Fe Grill, Schlotsky's 🅞 AT&T, BigLots, GNC, Hobby Lobby, Marshall's, Michaels, Old Navy, Radio Shack, Ross, Verizon, S 🅟 Shell/Circle K 🅕 August Moon, Hunan Buffet, Joe's Crabshack, Mazzio's, Pancho's Mexican, Papa John's, Starbucks, Subway, Taco Bueno, Wendy's, Western Sizzlin 🅞 $Tree, Hancock Fabrics
1b	S May Ave, N 🅟 7-11/gas 🅕 Abel's Mexican, Durango Mexican, Taco Bell, Waffle House 🅞 O'Reilly Parts, S 🅟 Valero 🅕 Burger King, Perry's Rest. 🅛 Cambridge Inn, Ramada Ltd 🅞 $General
1a	I-44, US 62, I-240 begins ends on I-44.

OREGON

INTERSTATE 5

Exit #	Services
308.5mm	Oregon/Washington state line, Columbia River
308	Jansen Beach Dr, E 🅟 Chevron/dsl 🅕 Burger King, Hooters, Starbucks, Taco Bell 🅛 Oxford Suites, Red Lion 🅞 Safeway, W 🅕 BJ's Rest., Bradley's Grill, CJ's Deli, Denny's, Jersey Mike's, Jimmy John's, McDonald's, Panera Bread, Stanford's Rest., Starbucks, Subway 🅞 Best Buy, Burlington Coats, GNC, Home Depot, Jansen Beach RV Park, Michael's, Michael's, Old Navy, PetCo, Ross, Staples, Target, TJ Maxx, Verizon
307	OR 99E S, MLK Blvd, Union Ave, Marine Dr (sb only), E 🅟 76/dsl, Jubitz Trvl Ctr/rest/dsl/@ 🅕 Pizza Mia, Portland Cascade Grill, Subway 🅛 Courtyard, Fairfield Inn, Portlander Inn, Residence Inn 🅞 Blue Beacon, truck repair, W 🅞 Expo Ctr
306b	Interstate Ave, Delta Park, E 🅟 Arco 🅕 Burger King, Burrito House, Elmer's, Mars Meadows Chinese, Shari's

306b	Continued 🅛 Best Western, Days Inn, Motel 6 🅞 $Tree, Baxter Parts, Dick's, Lowe's, Portland Meadows, vet, Walmart
306a	Columbia (from nb), same as 306b
305b a	US 30, Lombard St (from nb, no return), E 🅕 Little Caesar's 🅞 Knecht's Parts, W 🅟 Astro/dsl, Shell/dsl 🅕 Panda Express, Subway, Wendy's 🅞 Fred Meyer
304	Rosa Parks Way, W 🅟 76/dsl, Arco 🅕 Nite Hawk Cafe 🅛 Viking Motel 🅞 U of Portland
303	Alberta St, Swan Island, E 🅞 🅗 W 🅕 Subway, Taco Bell 🅛 Monticello Motel, Westerner Motel 🅞 CarQuest
302b	I-405, US 30 W, W to ocean beaches
302a	Rose Qtr, City Ctr, E 🅟 76/Circle K/dsl, Shell/dsl 🅕 Bellagio's Pizza, Burger King, Chipotle Mexican, Jersey Mike's, McDonald's, Muchas Gracias, Qdoba Mexican, Starbucks, Wendy's 🅛 Courtyard, Crowne Plaza, Shiloh Inn 🅞 🅗 7-11, Kia, Radio Shack, Schwab Tire, Toyota/Scion, Verizon, Walgreens, W 🅞 coliseum

↑N INTERSTATE 5 Cont'd	

Exit #	Services
301	I-84 E, US 30 E, **E** services off I-84 exits
300	US 26 E (from sb), Milwaukie Ave, **W** 🛏 Hilton, Marriott
299b	I-405, US 26 W, to city ctr
299a	US 26 E, OR 43 (from nb), City Ctr, to Lake Oswego
298	Corbett Ave
297	Terwilliger Blvd, **W** 🍴 Baja Fresh, KFC, La Costita, Starbucks 🅞 🄷 Fred Meyer, to Lewis and Clark Coll.
296b	Multnomah Blvd (from sb), **W** 🅞 Safeway, same as 296a
296a	(from sb), Barbur, **W** 🅖 76/dsl, Chevron/dsl 🍴 Bellagio's Pizza, Frack Burger, Subway 🛏 Aladdin Inn, Budget Lodge, Capitol Hill Motel 🅞 7-11, AT&T, Schwab Tire
295	Capitol Hwy (from sb), Taylors Ferry Rd (from nb), **E** 🅖 Shell/dsl 🍴 McDonald's, Sho Japanese, Starbucks, Thai Orchid 🛏 Hospitality Inn, **W** 🍴 Taco Time, Wendy's 🅞 Walgreens
294	Barbur Blvd, OR 99W, to Tigard, **E** 🛏 Comfort Suites, **W** 🅖 76, Chevron, Shell 🍴 Arby's, Baja Fresh, Banning's Rest., Baskin-Robbins, Burger King, Buster's BBQ, Carl's Jr, Chang's Mongolian Grill, Gators Eatery, Jimmy John's, Mazatlan Mexican, McDonald's, Starbucks, Subway, Taco Bell 🛏 Quality Inn, Regency Inn 🅞 $Tree, Americas Tire, auto repair, Baxter Parts, Costco, Fred Meyer, JoAnn Fabrics, NAPA, PetCo, Petsmart, Radio Shack, Schwab Tire, transmissions, U-Haul, vet, Walmart/Subway, Winco Foods
293	Haines St, **W** 🅞 Ford/Lincoln
292	OR 217, Kruse Way, Lake Oswego, **E** 🅖 Shell/dsl 🍴 Applebee's, Chevy's Mexican, Chipotle, Olive Garden, Oswego Grill, Potbelly, Stanford's Rest., Starbucks 🛏 Crowne Plaza, Fairfield Inn, Hilton Garden, Phoenix Inn, Residence Inn 🅞 LDS Temple, **W** 🛏 Extended Stay America 🅞 Lowe's
291	Carman Dr, Carman Dr, **W** 🅖 76/dsl, Chevron 🍴 Burgerville, Domino's, El Sol De Mexico, Starbucks, Subway, Sweet Tomatoes 🛏 Courtyard, Holiday Inn Express 🅞 Home Depot, Office Depot
290	Lower Boonsferry Rd, Lake Oswego, **E** 🅖 Chevron/dsl, Space Age/dsl/LP 🍴 Arby's, Baja Fresh, Baskin-Robbins, Burger King, Cafe Yumm, Carl's Jr., Fuddruckers, Miller's Rest., Nicoli's Grill, Panda Express, Starbucks, Subway, Taco Bell 🛏 Motel 6 🅞 Dick's, Safeway Foods, See's Kitchen, Walgreens, **W** 🍴 CA Pizza Kitchen, Claim Jumper, Jamba Juice, Jimmy John's, McCormick&Schmick's, Pastini Pastaria, PF Chang's, Qdoba Mexican, Royal Panda, Starbucks, Twigs Bistro, Village Inn 🛏 Grand Hotel 🅞 Barnes&Noble, Verizon, Whole Foods Mkt
289	Tualatin, **E** 🅖 76, Shell/dsl 🍴 Chipotle Mexican, Famous Dave's BBQ, Jamba Juice, McDonald's, Panera Bread, Starbucks, Subway 🅞 🄷 7-11, Best Buy, Old Navy, Petsmart, vet, **W** 🍴 Applebee's, Buffalo Wild Wings, Carl's Jr, Coldstone, Dickie Jo's Burgers, Hayden's Grill, Jack-in-the-Box, McDonald's, Outback Steaks, Pieology Pizzaria, Pizza Hut, Shari's, Starbucks, Subway, Taco Bell, Thai Rest., Wendy's 🛏 Century Hotel, Comfort Inn 🅞 Cabela's, Fred Meyer, Haggen's Foods, Michael's, New Seasons Mkt, O'Reilly Parts, PetCo, Radio Shack, Staples, TJ Maxx
288	I-205, to Oregon City
286	Elligsen Rd, Boonsferry Rd, Stafford, **E** 🅖 76/dsl 🍴 Burger King, Cafe Yumm!, Moe's SW Grill, Panda Express, Pizza Schmizza, Starbucks, Subway, Zoup! 🛏 La Quinta, Super 8 🅞 America's Tire, Chrysler/Dodge/Jeep, Costco/gas, Ferrari/Maserati, Mercedes, Office Depot, Petsmart, Pheasant Ridge RV Resort, Target, **W** 🅖 Chevron/dsl 🍴 Boone Town Bistro, Carl's Jr 🛏 Holiday Inn/rest. 🅞 Audi, Camping World RV Ctr, Chevrolet, Nissan, Toyota/Scion
283	Wilsonville, **E** 🅖 76 🍴 Abella Italian, Arby's, Bellagio's Pizza, Denny's, Jamba Juice, Jimmy John's, Juan Colorado, McDonald's, Papa Murphy's, Red Robin, Shari's, Starbucks, Subway, Taco Bell, Thai Rest., Wanker's Café, Wendy's, Wong's Chinese 🛏 GuestHouse Inn, Quality Inn, SnoozInn 🅞 $Tree, Ace Hardware, AT&T, Fry's Electronics, funpark,

WILSONVILLE (vertical text, center)

OR (tab, right margin)

⬆N INTERSTATE 5 Cont'd

Exit #	Services
283	Continued
	GNC, Honda, Lamb's Mkt., NAPA, Rite Aid, Schwab Tire, UR- GENT CARE, USPO, vet, **W** 🛢 Fred Meyer/dsl 🍴 Baskin- Robbins, Biscuits Cafe, Boone's Jct Pizza, Burger King, Dom- ino's, Hunan Kitchen, Little Caesar's, McMenamin's Rest., Oswego Grill, Perfect Pizza, Qdoba, RAM Rest., Sonic, Star- bucks, Subway, Wow Burger 🏠 Best Western Wilsonville 🅾 7-11, Albertson's, auto repair, Fred Meyer/dsl, O'Reilly Parts, Verizon, Walgreens
282.5mm	Willamette River
282	Charbonneau District, **E** 🍴 Langdon Farms Rest. 🅾 Lang- don Farms Golf
281.5mm	🅿️ both lanes, coffee, full ♿ facilities, info, litter barrels, petwalk, 🚬, 🐾, vending
278	Donald, **E** 🛢 76/dsl/LP 🍴 Aurora Acres RV Park, **W** 🛢 ✈FLYING J/Subway/dsl/scales/24hr, TA/Country Pride/Pop- eye's/dsl/scales/24hr/@ 🅾 NAPA Truck Parts, SpeedCo Lube, to Champoeg SP, truckwash
274mm	weigh sta both lanes
271	OR 214, Woodburn, **E** 🛢 Arco/dsl, Chevron 🍴 Burger King, Denny's, DQ, KFC, McDonald's/playplace, Subway, Taco Bell, Yun Wah Chinese 🏠 Best Western, Super 8 🅾 76/repair, vet, Walgreens, Walmart/McDonald's, Yun Wah Chinese, **W** 🛢 Shell/dsl 🍴 Arby's, Elmer's, Jack-in-the-Box, Jamba Juice, Starbucks 🏠 La Quinta 🅾 Ford, Woodburn Outlets/famous brands, Woodburn RV Park
263	Brooks, Gervais, **E** 🛢 Chevron/dsl 🅾 Brooks Mkt/deli, **W** 🛢 🚂/Subway/Taco Bell/dsl/LP/scales/24hr 🍴 Chalet Rest. 🅾 Antique Powerland Museum, Freightliner, Willamette Mis- sion SP (4mi)
260b a	OR 99E, Chemawa Rd, Keizer, **E 2 mi** 🅾 Silver Spur RV Park, **W** 🍴 Burger King, Jamba Juice, McDonald's, Outback Steaks, Panda Express, Panera Bread, RoundTable Pizza, Starbucks, Subway, Taco Bell, Taco del Mar 🅾 AT&T, GNC, Lowe's, Marshall's, Michael's, Old Navy, PetCo, REI, Ross, Staples, Target, Verizon, World Mkt
259mm	45th parallel, halfway between the equator and N Pole
258	N Salem, **E** 🛢 76 🍴 Figaro's Italian, Guesthouse Rest., Mc- Donald's, Original Pancake House, Subway 🏠 Best Western, Rodeway Inn 🅾 5 Star RV Park, Al's RV Ctr, Hwy RV Ctr, Roth's Foods, **W** 🛢 76, Arco, Pacific Pride/dsl, Shell/dsl 🍴 Don Pedro Mexican, Jack-in-the-Box, LumYuen Chinese 🏠 Budget Lodge, Travelers Inn 🅾 Stuart's Parts, to st capitol
256	to OR 213, Market St, Salem, **E** 🍴 5 Guys Burgers, Apple- bee's, Arby's, Baja Fresh, Blue Willow Rest., Burger King, Carl's Jr, China Buffet, Chipotle, Denny's, Elmer's, Izzy's Rest., Jack-in-the-Box, KFC, La Hacienda Mexican, McDon- ald's, Olive Garden, Sizzler, Skipper's, Starbucks, Subway, Taco Bell 🏠 Best Value Inn, Days Inn 🅾 Americas Tire, Big- Lots, Buick/GMC, Firestone/auto, Fred Meyer/dsl, Kia, Midas, Schwab Tires, Sears/auto, Verizon, Walgreens, **W** 🛢 Arco, Pacific Pride/dsl, Shell/dsl 🍴 Almost Home Rest., Baskin- Robbins, DQ, McDonald's, Newport Bay Seafood, Pietro's Pizza, Rockin-Rogers Diner, Subway 🏠 Comfort Inn, Double- Tree, Holiday Lodge, Motel 6, Red Lion Hotel, Shilo Inn, Super 8 🅾 Mazda, vet
253	OR 22, Salem, Stayton, **E** 🛢 Chevron, Shell/dsl, Space Age/ dsl 🍴 Burger King, Carls Jr, Las Polomas Mexican, McDon- alds/playplace, Shari's, Subway 🅾 $Tree, Home Depot, Sa- lem Camping/RV Park, ShopKO, to Detroit RA, WinCo Foods,

Exit #	Services
253	Continued
	W 🛢 Shell/dsl 🍴 Carl's Jr, Denny's, DQ, Jack-in-the-Box, Panda Express, Popeyes, Taco Del Mar 🏠 Best Western, Comfort Suites, Hampton Inn, La Quinta, Residence Inn 🅾 🚑 AAA, Chrysler/Jeep, Costco/gas, K-Mart, Lowe's, Nissan, Schwab Tire, st police, Walmart
252	Kuebler Blvd
249	to Salem, **W 2 mi** 🛢 76, Arco 🍴 Arby's, Burger King, Carl's Jr, Kwan's Cuisine 🏠 Phoenix Inn 🅾 Safeway
248	Sunnyside, **E** 🅾 Enchanted Forest Themepark, Willamette Valley Vineyards, **W** 🛢 Pacific Pride/dsl
244	to N Jefferson, **E** 🅾 Emerald Valley RV Park
243	Ankeny Hill
242	Talbot Rd
241mm	🅿️ both lanes, info, full ♿ facilities, info, litter barrels, pet- walk, 🚬, 🐾, vending
240.5mm	Santiam River
239	Dever-Conner, Dever-Conner
238	S Jefferson, Scio
237	Viewcrest (from sb)
235	Millersburg
234	OR 99E, Albany, **E** 🍴 Cascade Grill 🏠 Comfort Suites, Holi- day Inn Express 🅾 🚑, Knox Butte Camping/RV dump, **W** 🛢 Chevron 🍴 Burger King, Carl's Jr, DQ, Golden Town Buffet, McDonald's, Muchas Gracias, Subway, Taco Bell 🏠 Budget Inn, La Quinta, Motel 6, Super 8 🅾 🚑 Costco/gas, Kohl's, NAPA, to Albany Hist Dist
233	US 20, Albany, **E** 🛢 76/dsl, Chevron/dsl/LP 🍴 Denny's, Lu- mYuen Chinese 🏠 Best western, EconoLodge, Phoenix Inn 🅾 Blue Ox RV Park, Chevrolet, Home Depot, Honda, Lassen RV Ctr, st police, Toyota/Scion, Walmart, **W** 🛢 76/dsl, Shell/ dsl 🍴 Abby's Pizza, Arby's, Baskin-Robbins, Burgerville, Carl's Jr, Elmer's, Fox Den Pizza, Golden Wok, Jack-in-the- Box, Los Dos Amigos, Los Tequilos Mexican, Original Break- fast Cafe, Pizza Hut, Sizzler, Skipper's, Starbucks, Sweetwa- ters Rest., Taco Time, Wendy's 🏠 Valu Inn 🅾 🚑 $Tree, Bi-Mart, CarQuest, Chrysler/Dodge/Hyundai/Jeep/Subaru, Fred Meyer/dsl, Hyundai, JoAnn Fabrics, Knechts's Parts, Old Navy, O'Reilly Parts, Rite Aid, Ross, Schwab Tires, Staples, Target, Walgreens
228	OR 34, to Lebanon, Corvallis, **E** 🛢 76/dsl, Leather's/dsl 🍴 Pine Cone Cafe 🅾 Mallard Creek Golf/RV Resort, **W** 🛢 Arco/dsl, Chevron/CFN/A&W/dsl, Shell/dsl 🍴 Subway 🅾 KOA (5mi), to OSU
222mm	Butte Creek
216	OR 228, Halsey, Brownsville, **E** 🛢 76/Pioneer Villa TrkStp/ deli/dsl/24hr/@ 🏠 Travelodge, **W** 🛢 Shell/dsl 🅾 parts/re- pair/towing
209	to Jct City, Harrisburg, **W** 🅾 Diamond Hill RV Park
206mm	🅿️ both lanes, info, full ♿ facilities, info, litter barrels, pet- walk, 🚬, 🐾, vending
199	Coburg, **E** 🛢 Fuel'n Go/dsl 🅾 Premier RV Resort, **W** 🛢 Shell/McDonald's/dsl, TA/Country Pride/Truck'n'Travel Motel/ dsl/scales/24hr/@ 🍴 Coburg Crossing Cafe 🅾 Camping World, dsl repair, Eugene Kamping RV Park, Evert RV Ctr, Freightliner, hist dist, Volvo
197mm	McKenzie River
195b a	N Springfield, **E** 🛢 Arco, Chevron/dsl 🍴 5 Guys Burgers, Applebee's, Buffalo Wild Wings, Cafe Yummi, Carl's Jr, China Sun, Ciao Pizza, Denny's, Elmer's Rest., FarMan Chinese, Hacienda Amigo Mio, HomeTown Buffet, Hop Valley Rest., IHOP, Jack-in-the-Box, Jimmy John's, KFC, McDonald's,

ALBANY

SALEM

OR

SPRINGFIELD · EUGENE

🅽 INTERSTATE 5 Cont'd

Exit #	Services
195b a	Continued
	Outback Steaks, Panda Express, Quiznos, Roadhouse Grill, Shari's, Sizzler, Starbucks, Subway, Taco Bell, Taco Grande 🛏 Best Western, Comfort Suites, Courtyard, Hilton Garden, Holiday Inn, Holiday Inn Express, Motel 6, Quality Inn, Super 8 🅞 🅗 Best Buy, Cabela's, Kohl's, mall, Michael's, Ross, Sears/auto, st police, Staples, Target, USPO, Walmart Mkt, W 🅕 Taco Bell 🅞 Costco/gas, Office Depot, Petsmart, Shop-KO, to 🈁
194b a	OR 126 E, I-105 W, Springfield, Eugene, W 1 mi 🅖 76, Chevron, Mobil 🅕 Carl's Jr, PF Chang's, Starbucks 🛏 La Quinta, Residence Inn 🅞 Albertson's, Natural Grocers, Nissan, Old Navy, Subaru, U Of O
193mm	Willamette River
192	OR 99 (from nb), to Eugene, W 🅖 76 🅕 House Of Chen, Subway, Wendy's 🛏 Best Western, Days Inn, Holiday Inn Express, University Inn 🅞 Mkt Of Choice, to U of O
191	Glenwood, W 🅖 76/dsl, Shell/dsl/LP 🅕 Denny's 🛏 Comfort Suites, Motel 6
189	30th Ave S, Eugene, E 🅖 Shell/dsl/LP 🅞 Harley-Davidson, NW RV Supply, Shamrock RV Park, W 🅖 Chevron/dsl, Se-Quntial/dsl
188b	OR 99 S (nb only), Goshen
188a	OR 58, OR 99 S to Oakridge, E 🅞 Deerwood RV Park, W 🅖 Pacific Pride/dsl 🅞 tires
186	Dillard Rd, to Goshen (from nb)
182	Creswell, E 🅕 DQ, Subway 🛏 Comfort Inn 🅞 Bi-Mart, golf, OR RV Ctr, W 🅖 76/dsl, Arco/dsl 🅕 China Wok, Creswell Cafe, Joe's Diner, My Boys Pizza, TJ's Rest. 🛏 Super 8 🅞 Dari Mart, Knecht's Parts, NAPA, Sherwood Forest RV Park, Tire Factory
180mm	Coast Fork of Willamette River
178mm	🆁🆂 both lanes, coffee, full ♿ facilities, info, litter barrels, petwalk, 🐾, 🛻, vending
176	Saginaw
175mm	Row River
174	174 Cottage Grove, E 🅖 Chevron/dsl/repair, Pacific Pride/dsl 🅕 Chalerm Thai, Subway, Taco Bell 🛏 Village Resort/RV park 🅞 🅗 AutoZone, Chevrolet/GMC, Chrysler/Dodge/Jeep, Walmart, W 🅖 76/dsl, Chevron/dsl/LP, Shell/dsl 🅕 Burger King, Carl's Jr, Figaro's Pizza, Jack-in-the-Box, KFC, McDonald's/RV parking, Papa Murphy's, Pinocchio's Pizza, Torero's Mexican, Vintage Rest. 🛏 Best Western, Comfort Inn, Relax Inn 🅞 $Tree, Bi-Mart Foods, Grocery Outlet, Safeway/dsl, Walgreens
172	6th St (from sb), Cottage Grove Lake (from sb), W 2 mi 🅞 Cottage Grove RV Village
170	to OR 99, London Rd (nb only), Cottage Grove Lake, W 6 mi 🅞 Cottage Grove RV Village
163	Curtin, E 🛏 Stardust Motel 🅞 antiques, W 🅞 Pass Creek Park/camping
162	OR 38, OR 99, to Drain, Elkton
161	Anlauf (from nb)
160	Salt Springs Rd
159	Elk Creek, Cox Rd
154	Yoncalla, Elkhead
150	OR 99, to OR 38, Yoncalla, Red Hill, W 🅞 Trees of Oregon RV Park
148	Rice Hill, E 🅖 Arco/LP, Pacific Pride/dsl, ⛽Denny's/Subway/dsl/scales/24hr 🅕 Ranch Rest. 🛏 Motel 6,

SUTHERLIN · ROSEBURG

148	Continued
	Ranch Motel 🅞 Rice Hill RV Park, towing/dsl repair, W 🅕 K-R Drive-In
146	Rice Valley
144mm	🆁🆂 sb, full ♿ facilities, litter barrels, petwalk, 🐾, 🛻
143mm	🆁🆂 nb, full ♿ facilities, litter barrels, petwalk, 🐾, 🛻
142	Metz Hill
140	OR 99 (from sb), Oakland, E 🅕 Tolly's Rest. 🅞 Oakland Hist Dist
138	OR 99 (from nb), Oakland, E 🅕 Tolly's Rest. 🅞 Oakland Hist Dist
136	OR 138W, Sutherlin, E 🅖 76/dsl, Chevron/A&W/dsl 🅕 Abby's Pizza, Apple Peddler Rest., Burger King, Hong Kong Chinese, McDonald's, Papa Murphy's, Pedotti's Italian, Sol de Sutherlin 🛏 Best Western, Guesthouse Inn, Relax Inn 🅞 Autocare, I-5 RV Ctr, NAPA, W 🅖 Shell/dsl 🅕 Dakota St Pizza, DQ, Si Casa Flores, Subway, Taco Bell 🅞 Hi-Way Haven RV Camp, Umpqua RV Park
135	Wilbur, Sutherlin, E 🅖 CFN/dsl, Shell/dsl/LP 🅞 vet
129mm	N Umpqua River, N Umpqua River
129	OR 99, Winchester, E 🅕 Del Ray Cafe 🅞 Kamper Korner RV Ctr (1mi), Rivers Edge RV Park, st police
127	Stewart Pkwy, Edenbower Rd, N Roseburg, E 🅖 Shell/dsl 🅕 Shari's Rest., Subway 🛏 Motel 6, Super 8 🅞 Costco/gas, Home Depot, Lowe's, Mt Nebo RV Park, Verizon, W 🅖 Mobil, Valero/dsl 🅕 Applebee's, Del Taco, Jack-in-the-Box, McDonald's/playplace, Red Robin, Subway, Yummy Chinese 🛏 Sleep Inn 🅞 🅗 Albertson's, Big O Tire, K-Mart, Macy's, Sherm's Foods, vet, Walmart
125	Garden Valley Blvd, Roseburg, E 🅕 Abbey's Pizza, Brutke's Rest., Casey's Rest., China Buffet, Elmer's, Gilberto's Mexican, Jack-in-the-Box, KFC, Los Dos Amigo's Mexican, McDonald's, Smokin' Friday BBQ, Sonic, Subway, Taco Bell 🛏 Fairbridge Express Inn, Quality Inn, Windmill Inn/rest. 🅞 AT&T, AutoZone, BigLots, Buick/Chevrolet/GMC, Ford/Lincoln, NAPA, Safeway/dsl, Toyota, U-Haul, Verizon, vet, Walgreens, W 🅖 Shell/LP/repair 🅕 Burger King, Burrito Vaquero, Carl's Jr, Fox Den Pizza, Panda Express, Pita Pit, Rodeo Steaks, RoundTable Pizza, Si Casa Flores Mexican, Sizzler, Starbucks, TomTom Rest., Wendy's 🛏 Best Value Inn, Best Western 🅞 🅗 $Tree, Bi-Mart Foods, Fred Meyer/dsl, JC Penney, JoAnn Fabrics, mall, Marshall's, Michael's, O'Reilly Parts, PetCo, Rite Aid, Ross, Staples, Walgreens
124	OR 138, Roseburg, City Ctr, E 🅖 Chevron/dsl, Texaco/dsl 🅕 Chi's Chinese, Denny's 🛏 Dunes Motel, Holiday Inn Express, Rodeway Inn, Travelodge 🅞 Honda, Rite Aid, W 🅖 76/dsl, Shell/dsl 🅕 Charley's BBQ, Domino's, Gay 90's Deli, KFC/LJ Silver, Pete's Drive-In, Subway, Taco Time 🅞 Grocery Outlet, Harvard Ave Drug

Map: Eugene • Springfield, Cottage Grove, Yoncalla, Sutherlin • Oakland, Green • Roseburg, Myrtle Creek, Canyonville • Azalea, Wolf Creek, Grants Pass, Medford, Talent • Ashland — **OR**

↑N INTERSTATE 5 Cont'd

CANYONVILLE

Exit #	Services
123	Roseburg, E Ⓞ camping, museum, to Umpqua Park
121	McLain Ave
120.5mm	S Umpqua River
120	OR 99 N (no EZ nb return), Green District, Roseburg, E 🛏 Shady Oaks Motel, W Ⓞ auto repair
119	OR 99 S, OR 42 W, Winston, E Ⓞ Ingram Dist., W 🚗 Chevron/A&W/dsl, **Loves**/Arby's/dsl/scales/LP/24hr, Shell/dsl 🍴 McDonald's, Ocampos Mexican, Papa Murphy's, Subway Ⓞ Ray's Foods, Rising River RV Park, Western Star RV Park
113	Clarks Branch Rd, Round Prairie, W 🛏 Quikstop Motel Ⓞ On the River RV Park (2mi)
112.5mm	S Umpqua River
112	OR 99, OR 42, Dillard, E Ⓞ Rivers West RV Park
111mm	**weigh sta both directions**
110	Boomer Hill Rd
108	Myrtle Creek, E 🚗 Chevron 🍴 DQ, El Azteca, Golf Course Cafe, Subway Ⓞ city park, Myrtle Creek RV Park, Ray's Foods
106	Weaver Rd
103	Tri City, Myrtle Creek, E Ⓞ Tri-City RV Park, W 🚗 Chevron/A&W/dsl, Pacific Pride 🍴 McDonald's
102	Gazley Rd, E Ⓞ Surprise Valley RV Park (1mi)
101.5mm	S Umpqua River
101	Riddle, Stanton Park, W Ⓞ camping
99	Canyonville, E Ⓡs, 🚗 Penny Pincher 🍴 Burger King, El Paraiso 🛏 7 Feathers Hotel/casino, Riverside Motel Ⓞ Canyon Mkt, city park, W 🚗 7 Feathers Trkstp/café/dsl/scales/24hr/@ 🍴 Creekside Rest. 🛏 Holiday Inn Express Ⓞ 7 Feathers RV Resort
98	OR 99, Canyonville, Days Creek, E 🚗 Arco/dsl, Shell/dsl 🍴 Ken's Cafe, Marla Kay's Cafe, Serafino's Italian, Subway 🛏 Leisure Inn Ⓞ Ace Hardware, auto repair, NAPA, Ray's Foods, USPO, vet, W Ⓞ museum
95	Canyon Creek
90mm	Canyon Creek Pass, elev 2020
88	Azalea
86	Barton Rd, Quine's Creek, E Ⓞ Heaven on Earth Rest./rest., Meadow Wood RV Park (3mi)
83	Barton Rd (from nb), E Ⓞ Meadow Wood RV Park/camping
80	Glendale, W 🚗 Cow Creek/Lp/Rest.
79.5mm	Stage Road Pass, elev 1830
78	Speaker Rd (from sb)
76	Wolf Creek, W 🚗 76/deli/dsl, Pacific Pride/dsl, Shell/dsl 🍴 Wolf Creek Inn Rest. Ⓞ Creekside RV park, USPO
74mm	Smith Hill Summit, elev 1730
71	Sunny Valley, E Ⓞ Covered Bridge Store/gas, W Ⓞ Sunny Valley RV Park
69mm	elev 1960, Sexton Mtn Pass
66	Hugo, E Ⓞ Joe Creek Waterfalls RV Park, W Ⓞ Pottsville Museum (3mi)
63mm	Ⓡs both lanes, info, full ♿ facilities, info, litter barrels, petwalk, 🚻, 🐾, vending
61	Merlin, W 🚗 Shell/dsl Ⓞ Almeda RV Park, Beaver Creek RV Resort (2mi), OR RV Ctr, Ray's Foods, repair
58	OR 99, to US 199, Grants Pass, W 🚗 76/dsl/RV dump, CFN/dsl, Chevron, Fireball Gas, Shell/dsl/repair, Texaco/dsl, TownePump Gas 🍴 Angela's Mexican, Beacon Cafe, Black Bear Diner, Burger King, Carl's Jr, China Hut, Denny's, DQ, Jack-in-the-Box, McDonald's, Muchas Gracias Mexican,

GRANTS PASS

58	Continued
	Orchid Thai, Papa Murphy's, Sizzler, Subway, Taco Bell, Wendy's 🛏 Best Way Inn, Buona Sera Inn, Comfort Inn, Hawks Inn, La Quinta, Motel 6, Redwood Motel, Royal Vue Motel, Shilo Inn, Sunset Inn, Super 8, SweetBreeze Inn, Travelodge Ⓞ 🏥 $Tree, AutoZone, Chevrolet/Honda, Chrysler/Dodge/Jeep, Jack's RV Resort, Radio Shack, repair, Rouge Valley RV Park, Schwab Tire, st police, towing
55	US 199, Redwood Hwy, E Grants Pass, W 🚗 Arco/dsl, Mobil/dsl 🍴 Abby's Pizza, Applebee's, Arby's, Carl's Jr, Elmer's, KFC, Kobe Buffet, La Burrita, McDonald's, Pizza Hut, Shari's, Si Casa Flores Mexican, Subway, Taco Bell 🛏 Best Western, Holiday Inn Express Ⓞ 🏥 $Tree, Albertson's, AT&T, BigLots, Fred Meyer/dsl, Grocery Outlet, Home Depot, Jo-Ann, Moon Mtn RV Park (2mi), O'Reilly Parts, Petco, Rite Aid, RiverPark RV Park (4mi), Ross, Siskiyou RV Ctr, Staples, Verizon, Walmart
48	Rogue River, E 🚗 76/dsl, Chevron/Circle K/dsl 🍴 Abby's Pizza, Cottage Cafe, Homestead Rest. Ⓞ Ace Hardware, auto repair, Rogue River RA, vet, W 🍴 La Guayacama, Mkt Basket Deli 🛏 Bella Rosa Inn, Best Western Ⓞ Bridgeview RV Park, Chinook Winds RV Park, visitors ctr/info, Whispering Pines RV Park
45mm	Rogue River
45b	**Valley of the Rogue SP/Ⓡs both lanes, info, full ♿ facilities, info, litter barrels, petwalk, 🚻, 🐾**
45a	OR 99, Savage Rapids Dam, E Ⓞ Cypress Grove RV Park
43	OR 99, OR 234, to Crater Lake, Gold Hill, E 🛏 Lazy Acres Motel/RV Park, RoadRiver B&B
40	OR 99, OR 234, Gold Hill, E 🍴 Figaro's Pizza Ⓞ KOA, Lazy Acres Motel/RV Park, Running Salmon RV Park, W 🚗 Dardanelle's/gas Ⓞ Dardanelle's Trailer Park
35	OR 99, Blackwell Rd, Central Point, W 2-4 mi 🚗, 🍴, 🛏, Ⓞ Jacksonville Nat Hist Landmark, st police
33	Central Point, E 🚗 Chevron, LNG, 🚛/Subway/Taco Bell/dsl/scales/24hr 🍴 Burger King, KFC, Quiznos, Shari's Rest., Sonic 🛏 Candlewood Suites (2mi), Courtyard (2mi), Holiday Inn Express, Medford Inn, Super 8 Ⓞ funpark, W 🚗 76/Circle K/dsl, Shell/dsl 🍴 Abby's Pizza, Little Caesar's, Mazatlan Mexican, McDonald's Ⓞ Albertson's, AT&T, USPO
30	OR 62, to Crater Lake, Medford, E 🚗 Arco, Chevron/dsl, Witham Trkstp/rest./dsl/24hr/@ 🍴 Abby's Pizza, Applebee's, Asian Grill, Baskin Robbins, Buffalo Wild Wings, Burger King, Carl's Jr, Del Taco, Denny's, DQ, Elmer's, McDonald's, Olive Garden, Outback Steaks, Panda Express, Papa John's, Papa Murphy's, Pita Pit, Pizza Hut, Red Robin, RoundTable Pizza, Si Casa Flores Mexican, Sizzler, Sonic, Starbucks, Subway, Taco Bell, Taco Delite, Thai Bistro, TX Roadhouse, Wayback Burger, Wendy's 🛏 Comfort Inn, Hampton Inn, Motel 6, Quality Inn, Ramada, Rogue Regency Hotel, Shilo Inn Ⓞ 🏥 $Tree, AT&T, AutoZone, Barnes&Noble, Best Buy, BigLots, BiMart, Chevrolet/Buick/GMC, Costco/gas, Food4Less, Ford/Lincoln, Fred Meyer/dsl, JoAnn, Lowe's, Mazda, Mercedes, Michael's, NAPA, Office Depot, Old Navy, O'Reilly Parts, Petsmart, Radio Shack, Ross, Safeway, Schwab Tire, Sears/auto, st police, Subaru, TJ Maxx, Tuesday Morning, USPO, Verizon, vet, Walmart/Subway, W 🚗 76/dsl, Shell/dsl, Spirit/dsl 🍴 Chipotle, Jack-in-the-Box, Kaleidoscope Pizza, KFC, King Wah Chinese, Red Lobster, Wendy's Ⓞ CarQuest, JC Penney, Kohl's, Macy's, mall, Natural Grocers, Petco, REI, Target, Toyota/Scion, Trader Joe's, Verizon

MEDFORD

⬆N   INTERSTATE 5 Cont'd

Exit #	Services
27	Barnett Rd, Medford, **E** 🍽 Blackbear Diner, DQ 🛏 Best Western, Days Inn/rest., Homewood Suites, Motel 6, Travelodge 🅾 🅷 **W** 🅶 76/Circle K/dsl, Chevron/dsl, Texaco/dsl 🍽 Abby's Pizza, Arby's, Burger King, Carl's Jr, Domino's, El Arriero Mexican, HomeTown Buffet, Jack-in-the-Box, KFC, McDonald's, McGrath's FishHouse, Panda Express, Pizza Hut, Quiznos, Rooster's Rest., Shari's, Starbucks, Subway, Taco Bell, Wendy's 🛏 Comfort Inn, Holiday Inn Express, Medford Inn, Royal Crest Motel, Sovana Inn, SpringHill Suites, TownePlace Suites 🅾 $Tree, AT&T, Fred Meyer/dsl, GNC, Grocery Outlet, Harry&David's, O'Reilly Parts, Radio Shack, Staples, Verizon, Walgreens, Walmart/McDonald's, WinCo Foods
24	Phoenix, **E** 🅶 Petro/Iron Skillet/dsl/scales/RV dump/24hr/@, Shell/dsl 🛏 Best Inn/PearTree RV park 🅾 Home Depot, Peterbilt, **W** 🅶 Chevron/Circle K/dsl 🍽 Angelo's Pizza, Jack-in-the-Box, Joe's Rest., McDonald's, Si Casa Flores Mexican 🛏 Bavarian Inn 🅾 CarQuest, Harley Davidson, Holiday RV Park, Ray's Foods, Tire Pros
22mm	🆁🆂 **sb, full ♿ facilities, litter barrels, petwalk, 🚻, 🔌 vending**
21	Talent, **W** 🅶 Chevron/dsl, Circle K/dsl 🍽 Subway 🛏 GoodNight Inn 🅾 American RV Resort, vet
19	Valley View Rd, Ashland, **W** 🅶 76/dsl, Pacific Pride/dsl, Shell/dsl/LP 🍽 Burger King, El Tapatio Mexican 🛏 EconoLodge/RV Park, La Quinta 🅾 Acura, Chevrolet, Ford, Suzuki
18mm	**weigh sta both lanes**
14	OR 66, to Klamath Falls, Ashland, **E** 🅶 76/dsl/LP, Chevron/dsl, Valero/dsl 🍽 Caldera Rest., El Pariso Mexican, OakTree Rest. 🛏 Ashland Hills Inn & Suites, Best Western, Holiday Inn Express, Relax Inn 🅾 Emigrant Lake Camping (3mi), Glenyan RV Park (3mi), **W** 🅶 Arco, Texaco 🍽 Little Caesar's, Panda Garden Chinse, Señor Sam's Mexican, Subway, Taco Bell, Wendy's, Wild Goose Cafe 🛏 Rodeway Inn, Super 8 🅾 🅷 $Tree, Albertson's, AT&T, Bi-Mart, NAPA, Radio Shack, Rite Aid, Schwab Tire, Shop'n Kart, U-Haul, vet
11	OR 99, Siskiyou Blvd (nb only, no return)
6	to Mt Ashland, **E** 🍽 Callahan's Siskiyou Lodge/rest. 🅾 🚻, ski area
4mm	**Siskiyou Summit, elev 4310, brake check both lanes**
1	to Siskiyou Summit (from nb, no return)
0mm	Oregon/California state line

⬆E   INTERSTATE 84

Exit #	Services
378mm	Oregon/Idaho state line, Snake River
377.5mm	**Welcome Center wb, full ♿ facilities, info, litter barrels, petwalk, 🚻, 🔌 vending**
376b a	US 30, to US 20/26, Ontario, Payette, **N** 🅶 Chevron/dsl 🍽 A&W/KFC, Burger King, Carl's Jr, China Buffet, Country Kitchen, Denny's, Domino's, DQ, McDonald's, Quiznos, Taco Del Mar, Taco Time, Wingers 🛏 Best Value Inn, Best Western, Clarion, Colonial Inn, Motel 6, Sleep Inn, Super 8 🅾 $Tree, GNC, Home Depot, K-Mart, st police, Staples, Toyota/Scion, Verizon, Walgreens, Walmart/Subway, **S** 🅶 🚛/Arby's/dsl/scales/24hr, Shell/dsl 🍽 DJ's, East Side Cafe, Far East Chinese, Gandolfo's Deli, Ogawa's Japanese, Rusty's Steaks, Sizzler, Subway, Taco Bell 🛏 Economy Inn, Holiday Inn Express, OR Trail Motel, Rodeway Inn, Stockman's Motel 🅾 🅷 4 Wheeler Museum, Commercial Tire, Les Schwab Tire, NAPA, Radio Shack

Exit #	Services
374	US 30, OR 201, to Ontario, **N** 🅾 to Ontario SP, **S** 🅶 Loves/Chester's/Subway/dsl/scales/24hr/@, Pacific Pride 🛏 Budget Inn 🅾 🅷
373.5mm	Malheur River
371	Stanton Blvd, **S** 2 mi 🅾 to correctional institution
362	Moores Hollow Rd
356	OR 201, to Weiser, ID, **N** 3 mi 🅾 Catfish Junction RV Park, Oasis RV Park
354.5mm	weigh sta wb
353	US 30, to Huntington, **N** 🅾 info, RV camping, to Farewell Bend SP, **weigh sta wb**
351mm	Pacific/Mountain time zone
345	US 30, Lime, Huntington, **N** 1 mi 🅶, 🍽, 🛏, 🅾 to Snake River Area, Van Ornum BFD
342	Lime (from eb)
340	Rye Valley
338	Lookout Mountain
337mm	Burnt River
335	to Weatherby, **N** 🆁🆂 **both lanes, full ♿ facilities, litter barrels, Oregon Trail Info petwalk, 🚻, 🔌 vending**
330	Plano Rd, to Cement Plant Rd, **S** 🅾 cement plant
329mm	**pulloff eb**
327	Durkee, **N** 🅶 Co-op/dsl/LP/café
325mm	Pritchard Creek
321mm	Alder Creek
317	to Pleasant Valley (from wb)
315	to Pleasant Valley (from wb)
313	to Pleasant Valley (from eb)
306	US 30, Baker, **S** 2-3 mi 🅶 Chevron/dsl 🍽 DQ 🛏 Baker City Motel/RV Park, Bridge Street Hotel, OR Trail Motel/rest. 🅾 🅷 Les Schwab Tire, same as 304, to st police
304	OR 7, Baker, **N** 🅶 Chevron/dsl 🛏 Super 8, Welcome Inn, **S** 🅶 Maverik/dsl, Shell/dsl, Sinclair/rest./dsl/scales/24hr, USA/dsl 🍽 Arceo's Mexican, DQ, Golden Crown, McDonald's, Papa Murphy's, Pizza Hut, Raceo's Mexican, Rising Sun Chinese, Starbucks, Subway, Sumpter Jct Rest., Taco Time 🛏 Best Western, Budget Inn, Eldorado Inn, Geyser Grand Motel, Rodeway Inn, Western Motel 🅾 🅷 $Tree, Albertson's/gas, Bi-Mart, CarQuest, city park, Ford, Mtn View RV Park/LP (3mi), museum, Paul's Transmissions/repair, Rite Aid, Safeway Foods, to hist dist, Verizon
302	OR 86 E to Richland, **S** 🅾 🅷 OR Tr RV Park/LP, st police
298	OR 203, to Medical Springs
297mm	Baldock Slough
295mm	🆁🆂 **both lanes, full ♿ facilities, info, litter barrels, petwalk, 🚻, 🔌 vending**
289mm	Powder River

ASHLAND · **ONTARIO** (side tab, left margin)

BAKER (side tab, right margin)

OR (side tab, right margin)

INTERSTATE 84 Cont'd

Exit #	Services
287.5mm	45th parallel - halfway between the equator and north pole
286mm	N Powder River
285	US 30, OR 237, North Powder, N 🛏 North Powder Motel/cafe, S 🅞 ski area, to Anthony Lakes
284mm	Wolf Creek
283	Wolf Creek Lane
278	Clover Creek
273	Frontage Rd
270	Ladd Creek Rd (from eb, no return)
269mm	🆁🆂 both lanes, full 🚻 facilities, info, litter barrels, petwalk, 🅲, 🆅 vending
268	Foothill Rd
265	OR 203, LaGrande, N 🅞 🔧, Eagles Hot Lake RV Park, S 🅖 ✈FLYING J/Shell/res./dsl/scales/24hr 🍴 SmokeHouse Rest. (2mi) 🅞 Freightliner
261	OR 82, LaGrande, N 🅖 Chevron/dsl, Shell/dsl 🍴 Denny's, Pizza Hut, Primo's Pizza, Quiznos, Starbucks, Taco Bell 🛏 LaGrande Inn 🅞 Chrysler/Dodge/Jeep, Ford/Lincoln, Grocery Outlet, Les Schwab Tire, st police, Thunder RV Ctr, Verizon, vet, Walmart/Subway, S 🅖 76/Baskin-Robbins/Subway/dsl, Chevron, Texaco/dsl 🍴 Bear Mtn. Pizza, China Buffet, DQ, Dutch Bro's Coffee, KFC, La Fiesta Mexican, McDonald's, Moy's Dynasty, Nell's Steakburger, Papa Murphy's, Taco Time, Wendy's 🛏 Best Value Inn, Best Western, Royal Motel, Sandman Inn, Super 8 🅞 🅷 $General, $Tree, Ace Hardware, Albertson's, E OR U, Rite Aid, Safeway/gas, Schwab Tire, vet, Wallowa Lake
260mm	Grande Ronde River
259	US 30 E (from eb), to La Grande, S 1-2 mi 🅖 Chevron, Shell/dsl 🍴 Burger King, KFC 🛏 Greenwell Motel/rest., Rodeway Inn, Royal Motel, same as 261
257	Perry (from wb)
256.5mm	weigh sta wb
256	Perry (from eb)
255mm	Grande Ronde River
254mm	scenic wayside
252	OR 244, to Starkey, Lehman Springs, S 🅞 camping, chainup area, Hilgard SP
251mm	Wallowa-Whitman NF, eastern boundary
248	Spring Creek Rd, to Kamela, N 3 mi 🅞 Oregon Trail Visitors Park
246mm	Wallowa-Whitman NF, western boundary
243	Summit Rd, Mt Emily Rd, to Kamela, N 2 mi 🅞 Emily Summit SP, 🅞 Oregon Trail info
241mm	Summit of the Blue Mtns, elev 4193
238	Meacham
234	Meacham, S 🅞 Emigrant Sprs SP, RV camping
231.5mm	Umatilla Indian Reservation, eastern boundary
228mm	Deadman Pass, 🆁🆂 both lanes, full 🚻 facilities, litter barrels, **Oregon Trail info, petwalk, 🅲 wb, RV dump (wb)** 🆅 vending
227mm	**brake check area, weigh sta wb**
224	Poverty Flats Rd, Old Emigrant Hill Rd, to Emigrant Springs SP
223mm	wb viewpoint, no restrooms
221.5mm	eb viewpoint, no restrooms
220mm	wb runaway truck ramp
216	Mission, McKay Creek, N 🅖 Arrowhead Trkstp/Pacific Pride/McDonald's/dsl/24hr 🅞 Wildhorse Casino/RV Park
213	US 30 (from wb), Pendleton, N 3-5 mi 🅖 Chevron/dsl, Shell 🛏 Travelers Inn 🅞 🅷 Pendleton NHD

(side tab: LA GRANDE)

(side tab: OR)

212mm	Umatilla Indian Reservation western boundary
210	OR 11, Pendleton, N 🅞 🅷 museum, st police, S 🅖 Chevron/Circle K/dsl, Shell/dsl/LP 🍴 Shari's/24hr 🛏 Best Western, Hampton Inn, Holiday Inn Express, Motel 6, Red Lion Inn/rest., Super 8 🅞 KOA
209	US 395, Pendleton, N 🅖 Arco 🍴 Jack-in-the-Box, KFC, Little Caesars, Pizza Hut, Quiznos, Taco Bell 🛏 Oxford Suites, Travelodge 🅞 $Tree, Dean's Mkt, O'Reilly Parts, Radio Shack, Rite Aid, Safeway/dsl, Verizon, Walmart/Subway, S 🅖 76/dsl, Astro/dsl 🍴 Abby's Pizza, Burger King, Denny's, McDonald's, Rooster's Rest, Starbucks, Subway, Wendy's 🛏 EconoLodge 🅞 Les Schwab, Thompson RV Ctr
208mm	Umatilla River
207	US 30, W Pendleton, N 🅖 Shell/dsl/LP 🅞 Lookout RV Park, truck repair
202	Barnhart Rd, to Stage Gulch, N 🅞 Woodpecker Truck Repair, S 🛏 Rodeo City Inn 🅞 Oregon Trail info
199	Stage Coach Rd, Yoakum Rd
198	Lorenzen Rd, McClintock Rd, N 🅞 trailer/reefer repair
193	Echo Rd, to Echo, 🅞 Oregon Trail Site
188	US 395 N, Hermiston, N 5 mi 🅖 Chevron/dsl (1mi), 🚆/Subway/McDonald's/dsl/24hr/RV park 🍴 Denny's/24hr, Jack-in-the-Box, McDonald's, Shari's/24hr 🛏 Best Western, Economy Inn, Oak Tree Inn, Oxford Suites 🅞 🅷 S 🅞 Echo HS, Henrietta RV Park (1mi)
187mm	🆁🆂 both lanes, full 🚻 facilities, litter barrels, petwalk, 🅲, 🆅 vending
182	OR 207, to Hermiston, N 🅖 Space Age/A&W/dsl/LP/24hr 🛏 Comfort Inn
180	Westland Rd, to Hermiston, McNary Dam, N 🅞 Freightliner, trailer repair
179	I-82 W, to Umatilla, Kennewick, WA
177	Umatilla Army Depot
171	Paterson Ferry Rd, to Paterson
168	US 730, to Irrigon, N 8 mi 🅞 Green Acres RV Park, Oasis RV Park, Oregon Trail info
165	Port of Morrow, S 🅖 Pacific Pride/dsl
164	Boardman, N 🅖 Chevron/Circle K/dsl, Shell/dsl 🍴 C&D Drive-In, Lynard's Cafe, Sunrise Cafe 🛏 Fair Deal Inn, Riverview Motel 🅞 Boardman RV/Marina Park, city park, USPO, S 🅖 Shell/dsl 🛏 Michael's Repair, NAPA, Oregon Trail Library, Rodeway Inn, Select Mkt
161mm	🆁🆂 both lanes, full 🚻 facilities, litter barrels, petwalk, 🅲, 🆅 vending
159	Tower Rd
151	Threemile Canyon
147	OR 74, to Ione, Blue Mtn Scenic Byway, Heppner, 🅞 Oregon Trail Site
137	OR 19, Arlington, S 🅖 Shell/Circle K/dsl 🍴 Happy Canyon Cafe, Village Inn 🛏 Village Inn Motel 🅞 Ace Hardware, Arlington RV Park, city park, Thrifty Foods, USPO
136.5mm	view point wb, litter barrels, 🆅
131	Woelpern Rd (from eb, no return)
129	Blalock Canyon, 🅞 Lewis&Clark Trail
123	Philippi Canyon, 🅞 Lewis&Clark Trail
114.5mm	John Day River
114	S LePage Park
112	S **John Day Dam, both lanes, litter barrels, parking area**
109	Pendleton, N 🅞 John Day Visitor Ctr, S 🅖 Shell/dsl 🍴 Bob's T-Bone 🛏 Hillview Motel, Tyee Motel 🅞 Ed's RV Park, Rufus RV Park

(side tab: PENDLETON)

(side tab: BOARDMAN)

INTERSTATE 84 Cont'd

Exit #	Services
104	US 97, Biggs, **N** 🅞 Des Chutes Park Bridge, **S** 🅖 76/Circle K/Noble Roman's/dsl/24hr, 🅿/McDonald's/dsl/scales/24hr, Shell/Subway/dsl 🍴 Linda's Rest. 🏠 3 Rivers Inn, Biggs Motel/café, Dinty's Motel 🅞 Dinty's Mkt, dsl repair, Maryhill Museum
100mm	Columbia River Gorge Scenic Area, Deschutes River
97	OR 206, Celilo, **N** 🅞 Celilo SP, restrooms, **S** 🅞 Deschutes SP, Indian Village
92mm	**pullout eb**
88	**S** to The Dalles Dam
87	US 30, US 197, to Dufur, **N** 🅖 76/dsl/24hr, Chevron 🍴 McDonald's, Portage Grill 🏠 Comfort Inn, Shilo Inn/rest. 🅞 Columbia Hills RV Park, Lone Pine RV Park, st police, **S** 🍴 Big Jim's Drive-In 🏠 Celilo Inn
85	The Dalles, **N Riverfront Park, litter barrels, marina, 🍴🏠 playground, restrooms, S** 🅖 76/dsl, Chevron, Shell 🍴 Burgerville, Clock Tower Rest., Domino's, Taco Del Mar 🏠 Dalles Inn, Oregon Motel 🅞 🅷 AJ's Radiators, camping, Dalles Parts, NAPA, to Nat Hist Dist, TrueValue, USPO, Verizon, vet
83	(84 from wb)W The Dalles, **N** 🍴 Casa El Mirador 🅞 Tire Factory, **S** 🅖 Astro/dsl, Shell/dsl 🍴 Arby's, Burger King, Denny's, DQ, Dutch Bro's Coffee, Ixtapa Mexican, KFC, McDonald's, Papa Murphy's, Quiznos, Shari's Rest., Skipper's, Starbucks, Subway, Taco Bell, Taco Time, The BBQ, Wendy's 🏠 Cousin's Inn/rest., Motel 6, Super 8 🅞 🅷 $Tree, AT&T, Buick/Chevrolet/GMC, Chrysler/Dodge/Jeep, Ford, Fred Meyer/gas, Grocery Outlet, Honda, Jo-Ann Fabrics, K-Mart, Nissan, Oil Can Henry's, O'Reilly Parts, PetCo, Radio Shack, Rite Aid, Safeway/dsl, Save-a-Lot Foods, Staples, Subaru, Toyota/Scion, Walgreens
82	Chenowith Area, **S** 🅖 76/dsl 🍴 Spooky's Café 🅞 Bi-Mart Foods, Columbia Discovery Ctr, Home Depot, museum, same as 83
76	Rowena, **N** 🅞 Lewis & Clark info, Mayer SP, Memaloose SP, windsurfing
73mm	**Memaloose SP, 🆁🆂 both lanes, full ♿ facilities, litter barrels, petwalk, 🍴🏠 vending, RV dump** 🅞 camping
69	US 30, Mosier, **S** 🍴 10 Speed East Rest., Thirsty Woman 🅞 USPO
66mm	**Koberg Beach SP, N 🆁🆂 wb, full ♿ facilities, litter barrels, 🏠**
64	US 30, OR 35, to White Salmon, Hood River, **N** 🅖 Chevron, Shell/24hr 🍴 McDonald's, Riverside Grill, Starbucks 🏠 Best Western 🅞 marina, museum, st police, visitors info
63	Hood River, City Ctr, **N** 🅖 76/dsl, **S** 🅖 Astro 🍴 3 River's Grill, Andrew's Pizza, Big Horse Rest., Hood River Rest., Pietro's Pizza, Sage's Cafe, Taco Del Mar 🏠 Hood River Hotel, Oakstreet Hotel 🅞 🅷 same as 64, USPO
62	US 30, Westcliff Dr, W Hood River, **N** 🍴 Charburger, Cliff House Rest. 🏠 Columbia Gorge Hotel, Vagabond Lodge, **S** 🅖 76/dsl, Chevron/dsl/LP 🍴 Domino's, DQ, Egg River Cafe, HoHo Chinese, McDonald's, Pizzicato, Quiznos, Red Carpet Cafe, Starbucks, Subway, Taco Bell 🏠 Comfort Suites, Lone Pine Motel, Prater's Motel, Riverview Lodge, Sunset Motel 🅞 🅷 AT&T, Les Schwab, Oil Can Henry's, Rite Aid, Safeway, Walmart
61mm	pulloff wb
60	service rd wb (no return)

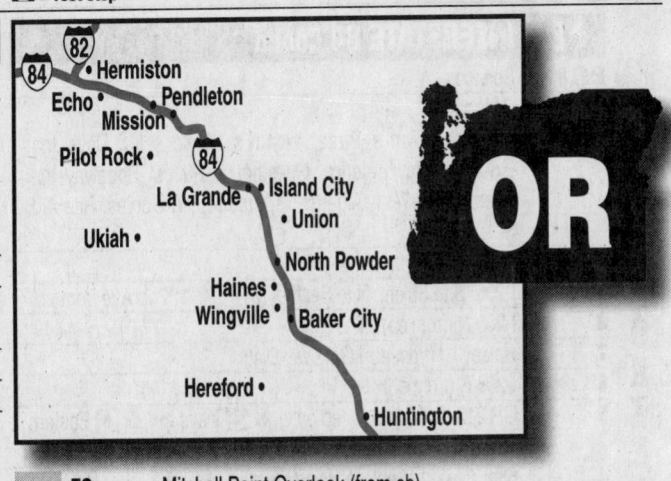

58	Mitchell Point Overlook (from eb)
56	Viento SP, 🅞 🍴, RV camping,
55	Starvation Peak Tr Head (from eb), restrooms
54mm	**weigh sta wb**
51	Wyeth, **S** camping
49mm	**pulloff eb**
47	Forest Lane, Hermon Creek (from wb), 🅞 camping
45mm	**weigh sta wb**
44	US 30, to Cascade Locks, **N** 🅞 CFN, Chevron/dsl, Shell/dsl 🍴 Cascade Inn Rest., Charburger, Pacific Crest Pub, Waterfront Cafe 🏠 Best Western, Bonneville Hot Spring Hotel, Bridge of the Gods Motel, Cascade Motel, Columbia Gorge Inn, Rodeway Inn, Skamania Springs Hotel 🅞 Columbia Mkt, KOA, Stern Wheeler RV Park, to Bridge of the Gods, USPO
41	Eagle Creek RA (from eb), to fish hatchery
40	**N** Bonneville Dam NHS, info, to fish hatchery
37	Warrendale (from wb)
35	Historic Hwy, 31 Multnomah Falls (exits left from both lanes), **S** 🅞 Ainsworth SP, Fishery RV Park, scenic loop highway, waterfall area
31	Multnomah Falls (exits left from both lanes), **S** 🍴 Multnomah Falls Lodge/Rest. (hist site) 🅞 camping
30	**S** Benson SRA (from eb)
29	Dalton Point (from wb)
28	to Bridal Veil (7 mi return from eb), **S** 🅞 USPO
25	**N** Rooster Rock SP
23mm	hist marker, viewpoint wb
22	Corbett, **S 2 mi** 🅖 Corbett Mkt 🍴 View Point Rest. 🅞 Crown Point RV Camping
19mm	Columbia River Gorge scenic area
18	Lewis&Clark SP, to Oxbow SP
17.5mm	Sandy River
17	Marine Dr, Troutdale, **N** 🏠 Holiday Inn Express, **S** 🅖 Chevron/24hr, 💙Loves/Chester's/dsl/LP/scales/24hr, TA/Shell/Buckhorn Rest./Popeye's/Subway/dsl/scales/24hr/@ 🍴 Arby's, McDonald's, Shari's/24hr, Subway, Taco Bell 🏠 Comfort Inn, Motel 6 🅞 Premium Outlets/famous brands, Sandy Riverfront RV Resort
16	238th Dr, Fairview, **N** 🅖 Arco/dsl/24hr 🍴 Bronx Eatery, Burger King, Jack-in-the-Box, Taco Del Mar 🏠 Travelodge 🅞 Camping World, Walmart/Subway, **S** 🅖 76 🏠 Best Western 🅞 🅷
14	207th Ave, Fairview, **N** 🅖 Shell/dsl 🍴 Europa Grill 🅞 American Dream RV Ctr, auto repair, NAPACare, Portland RV Park, Rolling Hills RV Park
13	181st Ave, Gresham, **N** 🅖 Chevron/dsl 🏠 Hampton Inn, **S** 🅖 Arco, Texaco 🍴 Burger King, Carl's Jr, Jung's Chinese, McDonald's, Quiznos, RoundTable Pizza, Shari's/24hr,

THE DALLES

HOOD RIVER

OR

Ⓖ = gas   Ⓕ = food   ⛺ = lodging   Ⓞ = other   Ⓡˢ = rest stop   Copyright 2015 - the Next EXIT ®

OR

INTERSTATE 84 Cont'd

Exit #	Services
13	Continued Starbucks, Tom's Pizza, Wendy's, Xavier's ⛺ Days Inn, Extended Stay America, Guesthouse Suites, Rodeway Inn, Sheraton Ⓞ 7-11, Albertson's, auto repair, Curves, Rite Aid, Safeway, vet
10	122nd Ave (from eb)
9	I-205, S to Salem, N to Seattle, to 🛫, (to 102nd Ave from eb)
8	I-205 N (from eb), N to 🛫
7	Halsey St (from eb), Gateway Dist
6	I-205 S (from eb)
5	OR 213, to 82nd Ave (eb only), N ⛺ Days Inn, S Ⓕ Eastern Cathay ⛺ Comfort Inn
4	68th Ave (from eb), to Halsey Ave
3	58th Ave (from eb), S Ⓖ Shell Ⓞ Ⓗ Fred Meyer
2	43rd Ave, 39th Ave, Halsey St, N Ⓖ 76, Chevron, Shell, Texaco Ⓕ Baja Fresh, Burger King, China Kitchen, McDonald's, Panera Bread, Poor Richard's Rest., Quizno's, Subway ⛺ Banfield Motel, Rodeway Inn Ⓞ Radio Shack, Rite Aid, Trader Joe's, S Ⓞ Ⓗ Buick/Jeep, same as 1
1	33rd Ave, Lloyd Blvd (eb only), downtown, N Ⓕ Applebee's ⛺ DoubleTree Inn, Residence Inn Ⓞ $Tree, JC Penney, Macy's, Marshall's, Sears, S Ⓕ Pizza Hut Ⓞ Cadillac, same as 2
1	to downtown (wb only)
0mm	**I-84 begins/ends on I-5, exit 301.**

INTERSTATE 205 (Portland)

Exit #	Services
37mm	**I-205 begins/ends on I-5. Exits 36-27 are in Washington.**
36	NE 134th St (from nb), E Ⓖ Chevron/dsl ⛺ Holiday Inn Express Ⓞ Ⓗ W Ⓖ 7-11, Arco, Mobil, Shell Ⓕ Applebee's, Baskin-Robbins, Billygan's Roadhouse, Burger King, Burgerville, El Tapatio, Jack-in-the-Box, McDonald's, Muchas Gracias, Panda Express, Papa Murphy's, PizzaSchmitzza, Round Table Pizza, Starbucks, Subway, Taco Bell ⛺ La Quinta, Shilo Inn, Vancouver Inn Ⓞ 99 RV Park, Albertson's, Fred Meyer, Safeway/dsl, Verizon, Walgreens
32	NE 83rd St, Andreson Rd, Battle Ground, W Ⓖ Shell/dsl/24hr Ⓕ Burger King, Emporor Chinese, Krispy Kreme, Panda Express, Starbucks, Subway, Taste of China, Weinerschnitzel, Wendy's Ⓞ Costco/gas, Home Depot, vet
30c b a	WA 500, Orchards, Vancouver, E Ⓖ 76, Shell, Shell, USA Ⓕ ABC Buffet, Applebee's, Burger King, Burgerville, DQ, Imperial Palace, KFC, McDonald's, Papa Murphy's, Subway, Wendy's Ⓞ 7-11, GNC, Jo-Ann Crafts, Midas, Office Depot, PetCo, repair, Sportsman's Whse, Toyota/Scion, Walgreens, W Ⓖ 7-11/dsl, Chevron/dsl, Shell/dsl Ⓕ Burgerville, ChuckeCheese, Golden Tent BBQ, Great Taste Chinese, Hometown Buffet, IHOP, Jack-in-the-Box, Jamba Juice, LaCosta Mexican, Muchas Gracias, Olive Garden, Outback Steaks, Popeyes, Red Lobster, Red Robin, RoundTable Pizza, Shari's, Starbucks, Subway, Taco Bell ⛺ Best Western, Comfort Suites, Day's Inn, Heathman Lodge, Holiday Inn Express, Howard Johnson's, Residence Inn, Staybridge Inn Ⓞ $Tree, Americas Tire, auto repair, Barnes&Noble, GNC, JC Penney, Macy's, mall, Old Navy, Petsmart, Ross, Sears/auto, Target, TJ Maxx, URGENT CARE, Verizon, Walmart Mkt
28	Mill Plain Rd, E Ⓖ 76/, Chevron Ⓕ Applebee's, Baskin-Robbins, Breakfast At Valerie's, Burger King, Burgerville, DQ, Elmer's Rest., Irishtown Grill, Jimmy John's, Kings Buffet,

---

28	Continued McDonald's, McGrath's Fish House, Muchas Gracias Mexican, Pizza Hut, Shari's, Starbucks, Starbucks, Sweet Tomatoes, Taco Bell, Yummy Mongolian ⛺ Best Western, DoubleTree Hotel, Extended Stay America, The Guesthouse Motel Ⓞ $Tree, 7-11, Fred Meyer/dsl, O'Reilly Parts, PetCo, Schwab Tire, Trader Joe's, W Ⓖ 7-11, 76 Ⓕ Arby's, Jack-in-the-Box, Little Caesar's, Subway Ⓞ Ⓗ auto/tire repair, Walgreens, Walmart/McDonald's
27	WA 14, Vancouver, Camas, Columbia River Gorge
25mm	Oregon/Washington state line, Columbia River, **exits 27-36 are in Washington.**
24	122nd Ave, 🛫 Way, E Ⓖ 7-11/dsl Ⓕ Burger King, China Wok, Dutch Bros Coffee, Jack-in-the-Box, McDonald's, Panera Bread, Shari's, Subway ⛺ Candlewood Suites, Clarion, Comfort Suites, Courtyard, Fairfield Inn, Hilton Garden, Holiday Inn Express, La Quinta, Shilo Inn/rest., SpringHill Suites, Staybridge Suites, Super 8 Ⓞ Home Depot, Michaels, W Ⓕ Buffalo Wild Wings, Famous Dave's, Red Robin ⛺ Embassy Suites, Hampton Inn, Hyatt Place, Loft Hotel, Red Lion Hotel, Residence Inn, Sheraton/rest. Ⓞ 🛫, Best Buy, Marshall's, PetsMart, Ross, Staples
23b a	US 30 byp, Columbia Blvd, E Ⓖ Leather's Fuel/dsl, Shell/dsl Ⓕ Bill's Steaks, Elmer's Rest. ⛺ Best Western, Comfort Inn, Econolodge, Quality Inn, Rodeway Inn, W ⛺ Best Value Inn, Holiday Inn, Radisson, Ramada Inn
22	I-84 E, US 30 E, to The Dalles
21b	I-84 W, US 30 W, to Portland
21a	Glisan St, E on NE 102nd St Ⓖ 76, Arco Ⓕ Applebee's, Carl's Jr, Izzy's Pizza, Jamba Juice, Starbucks, Subway Ⓞ Fred Meyer, Kohl's, Office Depot, Ross, WinCo Foods
20	Stark St, Washington St, E Ⓖ 76/7-11, Chevron/dsl Ⓕ Arby's, Baja Fresh, Burger King, Denny's, Elmer's Rest., Hometown Buffet, Jack-in-the-Box, McMenamin's Rest., Old Chicago Pizza, Olive Garden, Panda Express, Portland Seafood Co, Red Robin, Saylor's, Starbucks, Subway, Village Inn ⛺ Chestnut Tree Inn, Ramada Ⓞ $Tree, Big Lots, Home Depot, Target, Tuesday Morning, Verizon, W Ⓕ Stark St Pizza, Taco Bell ⛺ Motel 6 Ⓞ 7-11
19	US 26, Division St, E Ⓖ Space Age/dsl Ⓞ Ⓗ W Ⓖ Shell Ⓕ Burgerville, Campbell's BBQ, ChuckeCheese, McDonald's Ⓞ Jo-Ann Fabrics, Wal-Mart
17	Foster Rd, W 1 mi Ⓖ Chevron Ⓕ Copper Penney Grill
16	Johnson Creek Blvd, W Ⓖ 76, Arco Ⓕ Applebee's, Bajio, Burger King, Carl's Jr, Five Guys, Hog Wild BBQ, Jack-in-the-Box, Jimmy John's, Krispy Kreme, McDonald's, McDonald's, Outback Steaks, Panda Express, RoundTable Pizza, Starbucks, Taco Bell Ⓞ 7-11, Best Buy, Dick's, Firestone/auto, Fred Meyer/dsl, Home Depot, Knecht's Parts, O'Reilly Parts, PetsMart, Radio Shack, RV Ctrs, Trader Joe's, Walgreens, Walmart/Subway
14	Sunnyside Rd, E Ⓖ 76/dsl Ⓕ A&W/KFC, Baja Fresh, Domino's, Garlic Jim's Pizza, Gustav's Grill, McMenamin's, Starbucks, Subway, TCBY, Thai BBQ ⛺ Days Inn, Motel 6 Ⓞ Ⓗ Office Depot, W Ⓖ Chevron/dsl Ⓕ Burger King, CA Pizza Kitchen, Chipotle, Claim Jumper, Dave&Buster's, Denny's, DQ, Jimmy John's, McDonald's, Muchas Gracias, Noodles&Co, Old Spaghetti Factory, Olive Garden, Panera Bread, Pieology Pizzaria, Pizza Hut, RAM Rest., Red Robin, Stanford's Rest., Wendy's ⛺ Courtyard, Monarch Hotel/rest. Ⓞ America's Tire, Barnes&Noble, JC Penney, Kohl's, Macy's, mall, Nordstroms, Old Navy, PetCo, REI, Sears/auto, Target, U-Haul, Verizon, Walgreens, World Mkt

PORTLAND AREA

⬆N INTERSTATE 205 (Portland) Cont'd

Exit #	Services
13	OR 224, to Milwaukie, W 🅞 CarMax, Lowe's
12	OR 213, to Milwaukie, E 🅖 Chevron/dsl, Pacific Pride, Shell 🅕 Denny's, Elmer's, KFC, McDonald's, New Cathay Chinese, Pronto Pizza, Subway, Taco Bell, Wendy's 🅛 Clackamas Inn, Hampton Inn 🅞 $Tree, 7-11, Fred Meyer, USPO, W 🅛 Comfort Suites
11	82nd Dr, Gladstone, W 🅖 Arco, Chevron 🅕 High Rocks Rest., McDonald's, Starbucks, Subway 🅛 Holiday Inn Express 🅞 Harley-Davidson, Safeway
10	OR 213, Park Place, E 🅖 Chevron/dsl 🅞 🅷 Home Depot, to Oregon Trail Ctr
9	OR 99E, Oregon City, E 🅖 76, Chevron/dsl 🅕 KFC 🅞 🅷 repair, Subaru, W 🅕 La Hacienda Mexican, McDonald's, Shari's, Starbucks, Subway, Thai Rest. 🅛 Best Western/rest

Exit #	Services
9	Continued 🅞 $Tree, AT&T, Firestone/auto, Michael's, Rite Aid, Ross, URGENT CARE
8.5mm	Willamette River
8	OR 43, W Linn, Lake Oswego, E 🅖 76 🅞 museum, W 🅖 Chevron/dsl, Shell/dsl 🅕 BJ Willy's Pizza, Starbucks, Taco Del Mar, Thai Linn 🅞 Mkt of Choice, USPO, Verizon, vet
7mm	hist marker, viewpoint nb
6	10th St, W Linn St, E 🅖 Chevron/LP 🅕 5 Guys Burgers, Ixtapa Mexican, McDonald's, McMenamin's Rest., Papa Murphy's, Shari's/24hr, Wilamet Coffee House 🅞 Ace Hardware, Les Schwab, Oil Can Henry's, W 🅕 Biscuit's Cafe, Jack-in-the-Box, Starbucks, Subway 🅞 Albertsons/Sav-On
4mm	Tualatin River
3	Stafford Rd, Lake Oswego, W 🅕 Corner Saloon 🅞 🅷
0mm	**I-205 begins/ends on I-5, exit 288.**

PENNSYLVANIA

⬆E INTERSTATE 70

Exit #	Services
171mm	Pennsylvania/Maryland state line. **Welcome Center wb, full** 🅰 **facilities, info, litter barrels, petwalk,** 🅲, 🆅 **vending,**
168	US 522 N, Warfordsburg, N 🅖 Exxon/dsl, S 🅞 fireworks
163	PA 731 S, Amaranth
156	PA 643, Town Hill, N 🅛 Days Inn 🅞 NAPA
153mm	🆁🆂 eb, full 🅰 facilities, litter barrels, petwalk, 🅲, 🆅 vending
151	PA 915, Crystal Spring, N 🅞 auto repair, S 🅞 Country Store/ USPO
149	US 30 W, to Everett, S Breezewood (no immediate wb return), S 3 mi 🅕 McDonald's 🅛 Penn Aire Motel, Redwood Motel, Wildwood Motel
147	US 30, Breezewood, Services on US 30 🅖 Exxon/dsl, Ⓕ FLYING J/Perkins/dsl/scales/24hr, Sheetz/dsl, Shell/Dunkin Donuts/Subway/dsl, Sunoco/café/dsl, TA/Gateway Rest/dsl/ scales/24hr/@, Valero/dsl 🅕 Bob Evans, Denny's, DQ, Hardee's, McDonald's, Pizza Hut, Quiznos, Starbucks, Taco Bell, Wendy's 🅛 Best Western, EconoLodge, Holiday Inn Express,

B R E E Z E W O O D

Exit #	Services
147	Continued Howard Johnson, Penn Aire Motel, Quality Inn, Village Motel, Wiltshire Motel 🅞 Blue Beacon, camping, **I-70 W and I-76/PA Turnpike W run together**, museum, Radio Shack, truck/auto repair
	I-70 and I-76/PA Tpk run together 71 mi. For I-70 and I-76/PA Tpk 148mm-75, see Pennsylvania I-76 PA/Tpk.
57b a	I-70 W, US 119, PA 66 **(toll)**, New Stanton, N 🅖 Exxon, Sheetz 🅕 Bob Evans, Campy's Pizza, Eat'n Park, McDonald's, Pagano's Rest., Pizza Hut, Subway, Szechuan Wok, Wendy's 🅛 Budget Inn, Comfort Inn, Days Inn, EconoLodge, Express Inn, Fairfield Inn, Howard Johnson, Super 8, S 🅖 BP/dsl, Sunoco/dsl 🅕 Cracker Barrel, La Tavola Risorante, TJ's Rest. 🅞 USPO
54	Madison, N 🅞 KOA, S 🅞 truck repair
53	Yukon
51b a	PA 31, West Newton, S 🅞 Volvo/Mack
49	Smithton, N 🅖 Citgo/rest./dsl/scales/@, Ⓕ FLYING J/Denny's/dsl/LP/scales/24hr/@

OR PA

FAYETTE CITY

▲E INTERSTATE 70 Cont'd

Exit #	Services
46b a	PA 51, Pittsburgh, N 🗓 Sunoco/dsl 🍴 Burger King 🛏 Comfort Inn 🅾 Buick/Cadillac/Chevrolet, Ford/Kia, S 🗓 GetGo/dsl, PP/dsl 🍴 Clubhouse Grille 🛏 Belle Vernon Hotel, Budget Inn 🅾 golf
44	Arnold City
43b a	(43 from eb) PA 201, to PA 837, Fayette City, S 🗓 Exxon/dsl 🍴 A&W/LJ Silver, Burger King, Denny's, Eat'n Park, Hibachi Buffet, Hoss' Rest., Italian Village Pizza, KFC, Little Bamboo, McDonald's, Old Mexico, Pizza Hut, Rita's Custard, Starbucks, Subway, Taco Bell, Wendy's 🛏 Hampton Inn, Holiday Inn Express 🅾 $General, $Tree, Advance Parts, Aldi Foods, AT&T, BigLots, CVS Drug, Giant Eagle Foods, GNC, JoAnn Fabrics, K-Mart, Lowe's, Radio Shack, Rite Aid, Staples, Verizon, Walmart
42a	Monessen
42	N Belle Vernon, S 🗓 BP/McDonald's/7-11, Sunoco/dsl 🍴 DQ
41	PA 906, Belle Vernon
40mm	Monongahela River
40	PA 88, Charleroi, N 🗓 BP/dsl, Gulf, Sunoco 🍴 McDonald's, My Girl's Rest., Subway/TCBY 🅾 �H Rite Aid, Save-A-Lot Foods, Valley Tire
39	Speers, N 🍴 Lorraine's Rest., S 🗓 Exxon/dsl
37b a	PA 43 (toll), N to Pittsburgh, S to CA
36	Lover (from wb, no re-entry)
35	PA 481, Centerville
32b a	PA 917, Bentleyville, N 🍴 King of the Hill Steaks, S 🗓 BP/dsl, 🍴/DQ/Subway/dsl/scales/24hr 🍴 Burger King, King Rest., McDonald's, Pizza Hut 🛏 Best Western, Holiday Inn Express 🅾 $General, Advance Parts, Blue Beacon, Giant Eagle Foods, Rite Aid
31	to PA 136, Kammerer, N 🛏 Carlton Motel
27	Dunningsville, S 🛏 Avalon Motel
25	PA 519, to Eighty Four, S 🗓 BP/7-11 Diner/dsl/24hr, Sunoco/dsl
21	I-79 S, to Waynesburg.
I-70 W and I-79 N run together 3.5 mi.	
20	PA 136, Beau St, S 🅾 to Washington&Jefferson Coll

WASHINGTON

19b a	US 19, Murtland Ave, N 🗓 GetGo 🍴 Applebee's, Arby's, Bruster's, Cracker Barrel, Fusion Steaks, Jimmy John's, Krispy Kreme, Max&Erma's, McDonald's, Moe's SW Grill, Outback Steaks, Panera Bread, Ponderosa, Quiznos, Red Lobster, Red Robin, Rita's Custard, Starbucks, Subway, TGIFriday's, TX Roadhouse, Wong's Wok 🛏 SpringHill Suites 🅾 $Tree, Aldi Foods, AT&T, Dick's, Ford, Giant Eagle Foods, GNC, Honda, Hyundai, Kohl's, Lowe's, Mercedes, Michael's, Nissan, PetCo, Petsmart, Radio Shack, Sam's Club/gas, Save-A-Lot Foods, Target, Toyota/Scion, URGENT CARE, vet, Walmart/McDonald's, S 🗓 BP/dsl, Exxon/dsl, Sunoco, Valero 🍴 A&W/LJ Silver, Bob Evans, CiCi's Pizza, Donut Connection, Eat'n Park, Evergreen Chinese, Grand China, KFC, Old Mexico, Papa John's, Pizza Hut, Waffle House 🛏 Hampton Inn, Motel 6 🅾 �H BigLots, Buick/GMC, Chevrolet, Curves, Firestone/auto, Home Depot, JC Penney, Jo-Ann Fabrics, Mazda, Pepboys, Staples, Subaru
18	I-79 N, to Pittsburgh.
I-70 E and I-79 S run together 3.5 mi.	
17	PA 18, Jefferson Ave, Washington, N 🗓 GetGo/dsl 🍴 DQ, McDonald's 🅾 Family$, Rite Aid, S 🗓 Valero/dsl 🍴 4Star Pizza, Burger King, China Express, DeFelice Bros Pizza,

PHILADELPHIA

17	Continued
	Domino's, Little Caesars, Subway 🅾 $General, Advance Parts, AutoZone, CVS Drug, Shop'n Save Foods, USPO, Walgreens
16	Jessop Place, N 🗓 Citgo, S 🅾 auto/truck repair
15	US 40, Chesnut St, Washington, N 🍴 USA Steaks 🅾 Food Land, S 🗓 BP, Exxon, Sunoco/dsl, Valero 🍴 Bob Evans, Denny's, El Paso Mexican, Garfield's Rest., LJ Silver, McDonald's, Pizza Hut, Taco Bell, Wendy's 🛏 Best Value Inn, Comfort Suites, Days Inn, Ramada Inn, Red Roof Inn 🅾 BonTon, Gander Mtn, Macy's, mall, Marshalls, Rite Aid, Sears/auto
11	PA 221, Taylorstown, N 🗓 BP/dsl 🅾 truck repair
6	PA 231, to US 40, Claysville, N 🗓 Exxon, S 🗓 Petro/Sunoco/Huddle House/Subway/dsl/scales/24hr/@
5mm	Welcome Center/weigh sta eb, full ♿ facilities, info, litter barrels, petwalk, 🚮, 🖼 vending
1	W Alexander
0mm	Pennsylvania/West Virginia state line

▲E INTERSTATE 76

Exit #	Services
354mm	Pennsylvania/New Jersey state line, Delaware River, Walt Whitman Bridge
351	Front St, I-95 (from wb), N to Trenton, S to Chester
350	Packer Ave, 7th St, to I-95 (fromeb), S 🛏 Holiday Inn 🅾 to sports complex
349	to I-95, PA 611, Broad St, N 🗓 Citgo
348	PA 291, W to Chester (exits left from wb)
347b	Passyunk Ave, Oregon Ave, N 🍴 Burger King, McDonald's 🅾 BJ's Whse, Home Depot, Ross, ShopRite, S 🅾 sports complex
347a	to I-95 S (exits left from wb)
346c	28th St, Vare Ave, Mifflin St (from wb)
346b	Grays Ferry Ave, University Ave, N 🍴 Little Caesars, McDonald's 🅾 PathMark Foods, Radio Shack, USPO, S 🗓 Citgo, Hess/dsl 🅾 �H
346a	South St (exits left from wb)
345	30th St, Market St, downtown
344	I-676 E, US 30 E, to Philadelphia (no return from eb)
343	Spring Garden St, Haverford
342	US 13, US 30 W, Girard Ave, S 🅾 E Fairmount Park, Philadelphia Zoo
341	Montgomery Dr, W River Dr, W Fairmount Park, S 🅾 W Fairmount Park
340b	US 1 N, Roosevelt Blvd, to Philadelphia
340a	Lincoln Dr, Kelly Dr, to Germantown
339	US 1 S, S 🍴 CA Pizza Kitchen, Chipotle Mexican, Houlihans, PeiWei Asian, Potbelly's, Starbucks, TGIFriday's 🛏 Crowne Plaza 🅾 Target, Verizon
338	Belmont Ave, Green Lane, S 🗓 Sunoco 🅾 St Police, WaWa
337	Hollow Rd (from wb), Gladwyne
332	PA 23 (from wb), Conshohocken, N 🛏 Marriott
331b a	I-476, PA 28 (from eb), to Chester, Conshohocken
330	PA 320, Gulph Mills, S 🅾 to Villanova U
329	Weadley Rd (from wb), N 🗓 Exxon
328b a	US 202 N, to King of Prussia, N 🗓 Citgo, Exxon/dsl, Lukoil, Shell, Sunoco, WaWa 🍴 Bahama Breeze, Baja Fresh, Burger King, CA Pizza Kitchen, Capital Grille, Champp's, Cheesecake Factory, Chili's, Fox&Hound, Gino's, Joe's Crabshack, Lonestar Steaks, Maggiano's, Morton's Steaks, Panera Bread, Red Lobster, Ruby's Diner, Sullivan's Steaks, TGIFriday's, Uno Grill 🛏 Best Western, Clarion, Comfort Inn,

🔼🄴 INTERSTATE 76 Cont'd

Exit #	Services
328b a	Continued Crowne Plaza, Fairfield Inn, Hampton Inn, Holiday Inn, Hotel Sierra, Motel 6 🅞 Acme Foods, Best Buy, Bloomingdale's, Costco, Home Depot, JC Penney, Lord&Taylor, Macy's, mall, Neiman Marcus, Nordstrom, Old Navy, Sears/auto, vet
327	US 202 S, to US 420 W, Goddard Blvd, Valley Forge Park, 🅞 Valley Forge Park
326	I-76 wb becomes I-76/PA Tpk to Ohio

For I-76 westbound to Ohio, see I-76/PA Turnpike.

🔼🄴 INTERSTATE 76 (Turnpike)

Exit #	Services
PA Tpk runs wb as I-276.	
359	Pennsylvania/New Jersey state line, Delaware River Bridge I-276 continues to NJ, connecting with NJ TPK
358	US 13, Delaware Valley, **N** 🅖 BP, WaWa 🍴 Dallas Diner 🛏 Comfort Inn, Day's Inn, Ramada Inn 🅞 7-11, auto repair, U-Haul, vet, **S** 🅖 LukOil/dsl, Sunoco/dsl, Valero 🍴 Burger King, Gigi's Pizza, Golden Eagle Diner, Italian Family Pizza 🛏 Villager Lodge 🅞 $General, Buick, Mr. Transmission
352mm	**Neshaminy Service Plaza, Welcome Ctr wb** 🅖 Sunoco/dsl/24hr 🍴 Breyer's, Burger King, HotDog Co, McDonald's, Nathan's, Starbucks
351	US 1, to I-95, to Philadelphia, **N** 🍴 99, Bob Evans, Chick-fil-A, Cracker Barrel, Longhorn Steaks, On The Border, Red Robin, Ruby Tuesday, Starbucks, Wendy's 🛏 Courtyard, Hampton Inn, Holiday Inn Select 🅞 Buick/GMC, Home Depot, Lowes Whse, Macy's, mall, Sears/auto, Target, Walmart, **S** 🅖 Exxon/Subway, LukOil, Sunoco/dsl 🍴 Dunkin Donuts 🛏 Comfort Inn, Howard Johnson, Knight's Inn, Neshaminy Inn, Radisson, Red Roof Inn, Sunrise Inn 🅞 Toyota/Scion
343	PA 611, Willow Grove, **N** 🅖 Shell 🍴 Carrabba's 🛏 Candlewood Suites (5mi), Courtyard 🅞 🄷 **S** 🅖 Hess/dsl, Shell, Sunoco 🍴 Bonefish Grill, China Garden, Domino's, Dunkin Donuts, Friendly's, McDonald's, Nino's Pizza, Ooka Japanese, Starbucks, Williamson Rest. 🛏 Hampton Inn 🅞 7-11, Audi/Infiniti, Best Buy, PepBoys, repair, Staples, transmissions
340	to VA Dr, EZ tagholder only, no return eb, no trucks
339	PA 309, Ft Washington, **N** 🅖 Gulf, LukOil/dsl 🍴 Dunkin Donuts, Friendly's, Subway 🛏 Best Western, Hilton Garden, Holiday Inn 🅞 BMW, Mercedes, Volvo, WaWa
334	PA Tpk NE Extension, I-476, S to Philadelphia, N to Allentown
333	Germantown Pike, to Norristown, **N** 🅖 LukOil/dsl, Sunoco/Dunkin Donuts 🍴 California Pizza Kitchen, Houlihan's, PF Chang's, Red Stone Grill, Starbucks 🛏 Courtyard, Double-Tree, Extended Stay America, SpringHill Suites 🅞 🄷 Boscov's, Macy's, **S** 🅖 LukOil
328mm	**King of Prussia Service Plaza wb** 🅖 Sunoco/dsl/24hr 🍴 Breyer's, McDonald's
PA Tpk runs eb as I-276, wb as I-76.	
326	I-76 E, to US 202, I-476, Valley Forge, **N** 🅖 Shell 🍴 Burger King, Cracker Barrel, Hooters, Hoss' Rest. 🛏 MainStay Suites, Radisson, Sleep Inn, **S** 🅖 Exxon, LukOil, Shell, Sunoco, WaWa 🍴 CA Pizza Kitchen, Cheesecake Factory, Chili's, Denny's, Houlihan's, Lone Star Steaks, Maggiano's, McDonald's, Red Lobster, Ruth's Chris Steaks, Sullivan Steaks 🛏 Best Western, Clarion, Comfort Inn, Hampton Inn, Holiday Inn Express, Motel 6 🅞 Best Buy, Costco, Home Depot, JC Penney, Macy's, mall, Neiman Marcus, Nordstrom, Sears/auto, Walmart

325mm	**Valley Forge Service Plaza eb**, 🅖 Sunoco/dsl/24hr 🍴 Burger King, Starbucks
312	PA 100, to Downingtown, Pottstown, **N** 🅖 WaWa/dsl 🅞 CarSense, Harley-Davidson, **S** 🅖 Sunoco/dsl, WaWa 🍴 Applebee's, Chick-fil-A, Hoss's, Isaac's Deli, Red Robin, Starbucks, Uno Grill 🛏 Comfort Suites, Extended Stay America, Fairfield Inn, Hampton Inn, Residence Inn 🅞 🄷 Genuardi's Foods, Giant Foods, Walgreens
305mm	**Camiel Service Plaza wb**, 🅖 Sunoco/dsl/24hr 🍴 Roy Rogers, Sbarro's, Starbucks
298	I-176, PA 10, to Reading, Morgantown, **N** 🍴 Arby's, DQ, Dunkin Donuts, Sonic, Subway 🛏 Economy Lodge, Heritage Motel/rest. 🅞 🄷 $Tree, GNC, Lowe's, Verizon, Walmart, **S** 🅖 Exxon, Sheetz 🍴 Heritage Rest., McDonald's, Rita's Custard 🛏 Holiday Inn 🅞 Chevrolet, Rite Aid
290mm	**Bowmansville Service Plaza eb**, 🅖 Sunoco/dsl/24hr 🍴 Burger King, Hershey's, Starbucks
286	US 322, PA 272, to Reading, Ephrata, **N** 🅖 Citgo/dsl, Turkey Hill 🍴 Baskin-Robbins/Dunkin Donuts, Subway 🛏 Black Horse Inn/rest., Comfort Inn, Red Carpet Inn, Red Roof Inn, **S** 🛏 Hampton Inn (11mi)
266	PA 72, to Lebanon, Lancaster, **N** 🅖 Hess/Blimpie/dsl, Sunoco/Chester's 🍴 Farmer's Hope Inn Rest 🛏 Holiday Inn Express (17 mi), Penns Woods Inn, Red Carpet Inn 🅞 🄷 auto repair, Harley-Davidson, NAPA, **S** 🍴 Hitz Mkt/deli 🛏 Hampton Inn 🅞 Mt Hope Winery, Pinch Pond Camping
259mm	**Lawn Service Plaza wb**, 🅖 Sunoco/dsl/24hr 🍴 Burger King, Starbucks 🅞 RV dump
250mm	**Highspire Service Plaza eb**, 🅖 Sunoco/dsl/24hr 🍴 Hershey's Ice Cream, Sbarro's, Starbucks
247	I-283, PA 283, to Harrisburg, Harrisburg East, Hershey, **N** 🅖 Exxon/dsl, Sunoco 🍴 Bob Evans, Capitol Diner, Eat'n Park, McDonald's, Taco Bell, Wendy's 🛏 Best Western, Courtyard, Days Inn, EconoLodge, Holiday Inn Express, Howard Johnson, La Quinta, Red Roof Inn, Rodeway Inn, Sheraton, Super 8, Travelodge, Wingate Inn, Wyndham 🅞 Harrisburg East Camping, JC Penney, Kia, Target
246mm	Susquehannah River
242	I-83, Harrisburg West, **N** 🅖 Hess/Dunkin Donuts, Shell/dsl 🍴 Bob Evans, Doc Holliday's Rest, John's Diner, McDonald's, Pizza Hut 🛏 Best Western, Comfort Inn, Fairfield Inn, Holiday Inn, Motel 6, Quality Inn, Rodeway Inn, Travel Inn 🅞 vet, **S** 🛏 Days Inn, Keystone Inn
236	US 15, to Gettysburg, Gettysburg Pike, Harrisburg, **N** 🅖 Exxon, Gulf/dsl 🍴 Isaac's Rest, McDonald's, Papa John's, Peppermill Rest, Subway 🛏 Comfort Inn, Country Inn&Suites, Courtyard, EconoLodge, Hampton Inn/rest., Holiday Inn, Homewood Suites 🅞 🄷 U-Haul, vet, **S** 🅖 Sheetz 🍴 Arby's,

(sidebar, vertical text): HARRISBURG

🅰 = gas   🍴 = food   🏠 = lodging   🅾 = other   🆁🆂 = rest stop   Copyright 2015 - the Next EXIT ®

INTERSTATE 76 (Turnpike) Cont'd

Exit #	Services
236	Continued Burger King, Cracker Barrel, Quiznos, Wendy's 🏠 Best Western, Wingate Inn 🅾 Giant Food/gas, GNC, Rite Aid
226	US 11, to I-81, to Harrisburg, Carlisle, **N** 🅰 ✈FLYING J/Denny's/dsl/LP/scales/24hr/@, Gulf, ♥Loves/Wendy's/dsl/scales/24hr, Petro/Iron Skillet/dsl/scales/24hr/@, Pioneer/dsl, Shell/dsl/scales, Sunoco/Subway/dsl 🍴 Arby's, Bob Evans, Carelli's Subs, Country Club Diner, Dunkin Donuts, Embers Steaks, McDonald's, Middlesex Diner, Waffle House 🏠 Best Inn, Best Value Inn, EconoLodge, Hampton Inn, Hotel Carlisle, Howard Johnson, Motel 6, Quality Inn, Residence Inn, Rodeway Inn, Super 8, Travelodge 🅾 🏥 Blue Beacon, **S** 🅰 Rutter's/dsl, Sheetz/E85 🍴 Hoss' Rest. 🏠 Best Western, Motel 6 🅾 🏥 U-Haul, vet
219mm	**Plainfield Service Plaza eb**, 🅰 Sunoco/dsl/24hr 🍴 Hershey's Ice Cream, Roy Rogers 🅾 gifts
203mm	**Blue Mtn Service Plaza wb**, 🅰 Sunoco/dsl/24hr 🍴 Hershy's Ice Cream, Nathan's, Roy Rogers, Uno
201	PA 997, to Shippensburg, Blue Mountain, **S** 🏠 Johnnie's Motel/rest., Kenmar Motel
199mm	Blue Mountain Tunnel
197mm	Kittatinny Tunnel
189	PA 75, Willow Hill, **S** 🏠 Willow Hill Motel/rest.
187mm	Tuscarora Tunnel
180	US 522, Mt Union, Ft Littleton, **N** 🅰 Gulf/dsl, Noname/dsl 🍴 The Family Rest. 🏠 Downes Motel 🅾 🏥 st police
172mm	no services
161	US 30, Breezewood, **Services on US 30** 🅰 Exxon/dsl, ✈FLYING J/Perkins/dsl/scales/24h, Sheetz/dsl, Shell/Dunkin Donuts/Subway/dsl, Sunoco/café/dsl, TA/Gateway Rest/dsl/scales/24hr/@, Valero/dsl 🍴 Bob Evans, Denny's, DQ, Hardee's, McDonald's, Pizza Hut, Quiznos, Starbucks, Taco Bell, Wendy's 🏠 Best Western, EconoLodge, Holiday Inn Express, Howard Johnson, Penn Aire Motel, Quality Inn, Village Motel, Wiltshire Motel 🅾 Blue Beacon, camping, museum, Radio Shack, truck/auto repair
161mm	**I-70 W and I-76/PA Turnpike W run together**
148mm	**Midway Service Plaza both lanes**, 🅰 Sunoco/dsl/24hr 🍴 Hershey's Ice Cream, Quiznos, Sbarro's, Starbucks 🅾 gifts
146	I-99, US 220, Bedford, **N** 🅰 GetGo/McDonald's/dsl, PP/dsl, Sheetz/dsl/24hr, Shell/Subway/dsl 🍴 Bedford Diner, Clara's Place, Denny's, Ed's Steaks, Hoss' Rest., LJ Silver, Pizza Hut, Salsa's Mexican, Wendy's 🏠 Best Value Inn, Budget Host, Fairfield Inn, Quality Inn, Rodeway Inn, Travelodge 🅾 Blue Knob SP (15mi), to Shawnee SP (10mi), **S** 🏠 Hampton Inn
123mm	Allegheny Tunnel
112mm	**Somerset Service Plaza both lanes**, 🅰 Sunoco/dsl/24hr 🍴 Famiglia Pizza, Hershey's Ice Cream, Quiznos, Roy Rogers, Starbucks 🅾 gifts÷
110	PA 601, to US 219, Somerset, **N** 🅰 KwikFill/dsl, Sheetz 🍴 Hog Father's BBQ, Hoss' Rest., King's Rest., Pizza Hut 🏠 $Inn, Economy Inn 🅾 Advance Parts, Chrysler/Jeep, Ford, tires, **S** 🅰 Somerset TravelCtr/dsl/@, Turkey Hill 🍴 Arby's, Bruster's Ice Cream, Donut Connection, DQ, Eat'n Park, KFC, LJ Silver, Maggie Mae's Café, McDonald's, Pine Grill, Ruby Tuesday, Starbucks, Subway, Summit Diner, Wendy's 🏠 Best Value Inn, Best Western, Budget Host, Budget Inn, Comfort Inn, Days Inn, Hampton Inn, Holiday Inn, Quality Inn, Super 8 🅾 Dodge, Harley-Davidson, Volvo

91	PA 711, PA 31, to Ligonier, Donegal, **N** 🍴 Tall Cedars Rest., **S** 🅰 BP/McDonald's, Exxon/Subway/dsl, Sunoco/dsl 🍴 DQ 🏠 Days Inn 🅾 camping, golf
78mm	**New Stanton Service Plaza wb**, 🅰 Sunoco/dsl/24hr 🍴 Burger King, Hershey's Ice Cream, Quiznos, Starbucks

I-70 E runs with I-76/PA Turnpike eb.

75	I-70 W, US 119, PA 66 (toll), New Stanton, **S** 🅰 BP/7-11/dsl, Exxon, Sheetz, Sunoco 🍴 Bob Evans, Campy's Pizza, Cracker Barrel, Eat'n Park, La Tavola Risorante, McDonald's, Pagano's Rest., Pizza Hut, Subway, Szechuan Wok, TJ's Rest., Wendy's 🏠 Best Value Inn, Budget Inn, Comfort Inn, Days Inn, EconoLodge, Fairfield Inn, Howard Johnson, Super 8 🅾 USPO
74.6mm	**Hemphill Service Plaza eb**, 🅰 Sunoco/dsl/24hr 🍴 Breyer's, McDonald's 🅾 atm
67	US 30, to Greensburg, Irwin, **N** 🅰 BP/dsl, Sheetz/24hr 🅾 🏥 Ford, tires, vet, **S** 🅰 Marathon/7-11, Sunoco/24hr 🍴 Arby's, Bob Evans, Burger King, CiCi's Pizza, Denny's, DQ, Dunkin Donuts, Eat'n Park, KFC, LJ Silver, Los Campesinos Mexican, McDonald's, Panera Bread, Pizza Hut, Subway, Taco Bell, Teddy's Rest., Wendy's 🏠 Conley Inn, Holiday Inn Express 🅾 $Tree, Advance Parts, Aldi Foods, CarQuest, Giant Eagle Foods/24hr, GNC, Kohl's, Radio Shack, Rite Aid, Target
61mm	**parking area eb**
57	I-376, US 22, to Pittsburgh, Monroeville, **S** 🅰 Citgo/dsl, Exxon, Sheetz, Sunoco 🍴 A&W/LJ Silver, Arby's, Baskin-Robbins, Bob Evan's, Chick-fil-A, China Palace, ChuckeCheese, CiCi's Pizza, Damon's, Denny's, Golden Corral, Honeybaked Ham, Max&Erma's, McDonald's, Olive Garden, Outback Steaks, Panera Bread, Park Diner, Pizza Hut, Primanti Bro's, Quizno's, Red Lobster, Starbucks, Taco Bell, TGIFridays, Wendy's 🏠 Comfort Suites, Courtyard, Day's Inn, Extended Stay America, Hampton Inn, Holiday Inn, Radisson Inn, Red Roof Inn, Springhill Suites 🅾 🏥 Aamco, Big Lots, Firestone/auto, Honda, Jaguar/Land Rover, Jo-Ann Fabrics, Lowes Whse, Marshall's, Michael's, NTB, Office Depot, Old Navy, Pet Land, PetCo, Radio Shack, Rite Aid, to Three Rivers Stadium
49mm	**Oakmont Service Plaza eb**, 🅰 Sunoco/dsl/24hr 🍴 FoodCourt 🅾 litter barrels, 🍴, 🆁🆂
48.5mm	Allegheny River
48	PA 28, to Pittsburgh, Allegheny Valley, New Kensington, **N** 🅰 Shell/24hr, Sunoco 🍴 Pizza Hut, Subway 🅾 CarQuest, Rite Aid, **S** 🅰 Exxon/dsl, GetGo 🍴 Bob Evans, Bruster's, Denny's, Gino Bro's Pizza, KFC, King's Rest., McDonald's, Ponderosa, Primanti Bro's, Subway, Taco Bell, Wendy's 🏠 Comfort Inn, Day's Inn, Holiday Inn Express, Super 8, Valley Motel 🅾 Advance Parts, Ford, Target
41mm	**parking area/call box eb**
39	PA 8, to Pittsburgh, Butler Valley, **N** 0-1 mi 🅰 Exxon/7-11/dsl, GetGo, Sheetz/24hr, Sunoco 🍴 Applebees, Atria's Rest., Bruno's Pizza, Buffalo Wild Wings, Eat'n Park, King's Rest., Max&Erma's, McDonald's, Sonic, Starbucks, Taco Bell, Wendy's 🏠 Comfort Inn, Pittsburgh N Motel/rest 🅾 $Tree, Advance Parts, Curves, Dodge, Giant Eagle Foods, GNC, Kohl's, Lowes Whse, Rite Aid, Shop'n Save Foods, Target, TJ Maxx, Walmart/auto/drugs, **S** 🅰 BP, Sunoco/dsl 🍴 Arby's, Brusters, Burger King, China Bistro, KFC, McDonald's, Panera Bread, Pasquales Pizza, Pizza Hut, Subway, Vocelli Pizza, Wendy's 🅾 🏥 AutoZone, Firestone/auto, Goodyear/auto, Home Depot, Mr. Tire, Radio Shack, Rite Aid, USPO
31mm	**toll plaza wb**

BREEZEWOOD

PA

P I T T S B U R G

⬆E INTERSTATE 76 (Turnpike) Cont'd

Exit #	Services
28	to I-79, to Cranberry, Pittsburgh, **N** 🅖 BP/dsl, Exxon/dsl/24hr, GetGo, Sheetz/24hr, Sunoco/dsl 🍴 5 Guys Burgers, A&W/LJ Silver, Adrian's Pizza, Arby's, Bob Evans, Boston Mkt, Bravo Italian, Burger King, Chipotle Mexican, CiCi's Pizza, Denny's, Dominichi's Rest., DQ, Dunkin Donuts, Dynasty, Eat'n Park, Hartner's Rest., HotDog Shoppe, Houlihan's, Ichiban Steakhouse, King's Rest., Krispy Kreme, LoneStar Steaks, Mad Mex, Max&Erma's, McDonald's, Montecello's Grill, Panera Bread, Perkins, Pizza Hut, Pizza Roma, Primanti Bros, Quaker Steak, Saga Steaks, Subway, UNO, Vocelli Pizza, Wendy's 🛏 Comfort Inn, Fairfield Inn, Hampton Inn, Holiday Inn Express, Hyatt Place, Motel 6, Red Roof Inn, Residence Inn, Sheraton, Super 8 🅾 $Tree, Barnes&Noble, Best Buy, Costco/gas, Dick's, Giant Eagle Foods, GNC, Home Depot, Jo-Ann Fabrics, Kuhn's Foods, mall, Marshall's, Michael's, NAPA, Old Navy, PepBoys, PetCo, Radio Shack, Rite Aid, Toyota/Scion, transmissions, Tuesday Morning, USPO, vet, Walgreens, Walmart
23.5mm	pulloff eb
22mm	**Zelienople Service Plaza eb, Welcome Ctr,** 🅖 Sunoco/dsl/24hr 🍴 FoodCourt 🅾 crafts, gifts
17mm	**parking area eb**
13.4mm	**parking area eb**
13mm	Beaver River
13	PA 8, to Ellwood City, Beaver Valley, **N** 🅖 Al's Corner 🍴 Subway 🛏 Alpine Inn, Beaver Falls Motel, HillTop Motel, Holiday Inn, Lark Motel 🅾 🛏 🅖 Super 8
10	PA 60 **(toll)**, to New Castle, Pittsburgh, **S** 🅾 to ✈, services (6mi)
6mm	pulloff eb
2mm	pulloff eb
1mm	**toll plaza eb,** 🅾 🍴, call boxes located at 1 mi intervals,
0mm	Pennsylvania/Ohio state line

⬆E INTERSTATE 78

Exit #	Services
77mm	Pennsylvania/New Jersey state line, Delaware River
76mm	**Welcome Center wb, full** ♿ **facilities, litter barrels, petwalk,** 🍴, ✉ **vending, toll booth wb**
75	to PA 611, Easton, **N** 🅖 TurkeyHill/dsl 🍴 Dunkin Donuts, McDonald's (1mi), Subway 🛏 Quality Inn 🅾 Crayola Factory, CVS Drug, **S** 🅖 Exxon/dsl
71	PA 33, to Stroudsburg, **N 1 mi on Freemansburg Ave** 🍴 CJT Asian, Frank's Pizza, Panera Bread, Ruby Tuesday, TGIFriday's, TX Roadhouse, Wayback Burgers 🛏 Courtyard 🅾 Barnes&Noble, Best Buy, Dick's, 🏠 Lowe's, Michael's, Pet Supplies+, ShopRite Mkt, Staples
67	PA 412, Hellertown, **N** 🅖 TurkeyHill/gas 🍴 Wendy's 🛏 Comfort Suites (3mi) 🅾 🏠 Chevrolet, **S** 🅖 Citgo/dsl, Exxon/dsl, Sunoco 🍴 Bella's Ristorante, Dunkin Donuts, Papa John's, Rocco's Pizza, Roma Pizza, Vassi's Drive-In, Waffle House 🛏 Holiday Inn Express 🅾 7-11, CVS Drug, repair
60b a	PA 145 N, PA 309 S, South Fort St, Quakertown
59	to PA 145 (from eb), Summit Lawn
58	Emaus St (from wb), **S** 🅖 Gulf 🅾 $General
57	Lehigh St, **N** 🅖 Sunoco/dsl, WaWa/dsl 🍴 China House, IHOP, Palumbo Pizza, Queen City Diner, Subway, Willy Joe's Rest. 🛏 Best Value Inn 🅾 $Tree, AAA, BigLots, CVS Drug, Family$, Ford/Lincoln, Home Depot, Infiniti, Kia, Radio Shack, Redner's Whse, STS Tires/repair, Toyota/Scion, VW,

A L L E N T O W N

Exit #	Services
57	Continued **S** 🅖 Sunoco, TurkeyHill, Valero 🍴 A1 Japanese, Bangkok, Brass Rail Rest., Domino's, Dunkin Donuts, McDonald's, Papa John's, Perkins, Pizza Hut/Taco Bell, Rodizio Grill, Rossi's Pizza, Starbucks, Subway, Tilted Kilt Eatery, Wendy's 🅾 Acura, AT&T, Audi/Mercedes/Porsche, BonTon, Bottom$ Mkt, Buick/GMC, Cadillac/Chevrolet, Chrysler/Dodge/Jeep, Honda, Hyundai, Kost Tire, Mazda, Midas, Ross, Staples, SteinMart, Verizon, Volvo, Williams Tire/auto
55	PA 29, Cedar Crest Blvd, **N** 🅖 Shell, **S** 🅾 🏠
54b a	US 222, Hamilton Blvd, **N** 🅖 Hess 🍴 Bamboo Asian, Baskin-Robbins/Dunkin Donuts, Boston Mkt, Carrabba's, Friendly's, Gourmet Buffet, Ice Cream World, McDonald's, Menchie's, Perkins, Pistachio Cafe, Pizza Hut, Subway, Teppan Steaks, TGIFriday's, Wendy's 🛏 Comfort Suites/rest., Holiday Inn Express, Howard Johnson 🅾 Bottom$ Mkt, Dorney Funpark, Dorneyville Drug, Office Depot, Rite Aid, Weis Foods, **S** 🅖 WaWa 🍴 Dunkin Donuts, Hunan Springs 🛏 Wingate Inn 🅾 Queen City Tire, repair, Subaru
53	PA 309 (wb only)
51	to I-476, US 22 E, PA 33 N (eb only), Whitehall
49b a	PA 100, Fogelsville, **N** 🍴 Arby's, Cracker Barrel, Joe's Pizza, LJ Silver, Panda&Fish Chinese, Pizza Hut, Winger Deli 🛏 Comfort Inn, Hawthorn Inn 🅾 KOA (7mi), Rite Aid, STS Tire/repair, **S** 🅖 Shell/Dunkin Donuts, Sunoco, WaWa/dsl 🍴 Boston's Grill, Burger King, Florence Italian, Starlite Diner, Taco Bell, Yocco's Hotdogs 🛏 Hampton Inn, Hilton Garden, Holiday Inn, Sleep Inn, Staybridge Suites 🅾 Clover Hill Winery, st police, Toyota/Scion
45	PA 863, to Lynnport, **N** 🅖 Exxon/Subway/dsl, Sunoco/New Smithville Diner/dsl 🅾 truck service, **S** 🛏 Super 8
40	PA 737, Krumsville, **N** 🅾 Pine Hill Campground, Robin Hill RV Park (4mi)
35	PA 143, Lenhartsville, **S 3 mi** 🅾 Robin Hill Park
30	Hamburg, **S** 🍴 Hamburg Mkt
29b a	PA 61, to Reading, Pottsville, **N** 🅖 Shell//Subway/dsl, WaWa/dsl 🍴 Baskin-Robbins/Dunkin Donuts, Burger King, Cracker Barrel, Five Guys, JA Buffet, LJ Silver/Taco Bell, Logan's Roadhouse, McDonald's, Pappy T's, Pizza Hut, Red Robin, Wendy's 🛏 Microtel 🅾 $Tree, Advance Parts, AT&T, Boat'n RV Ctr RV, Cabela's Outdoor, GNC, Harley-Davidson (8mi), Hyundai, Lowe's, Pet Supplies+, Russell Stover, Toyota/Scion, Verizon, Walmart/Subway
23	Shartlesville, **N** 🅖 Chromeshop/dsl, Loves/McDonald's/Subway/dsl/scales/24hr 🍴 Dunkin Donuts 🛏 Dutch Motel 🅾 Appalachian Campsites, **S** 🍴 Blue Mtn Family Rest. 🛏 Scottish Inn 🅾 antiques, camping, Dutch Haus/gifts, USPO

PA

🅖 = gas   🍴 = food   🛏 = lodging   🄾 = other   🆁🆂 = rest stop   Copyright 2015 - the Next EXIT ®

INTERSTATE 78 Cont'd

Exit #	Services
19	PA 183, Straussown, N 🅖 Lukoil 🛏 Sheepskin Motel, S 🅖 Power/dsl
17	PA 419, Rehrersburg, N 🅖 Best 🄾 truck/tire repair
16	Midway, N 🅖 Exxon/dsl, Sunoco/dsl 🍴 J&S Pizza, Midway Diner 🛏 Comfort Inn, S 🄾 auto/truck repair
15	Grimes
13	PA 501, Bethel, N 🅖 Valero/dsl, S 🅖 Bethel/dsl 🄾 dsl repair
10	PA 645, Frystown, S 🅖 ⊘FLYING J/Huddle House/Subway/dsl/scales/24hr/@ 🛏 Travel Inn
6	(8 from wb, US 22) PA 343, Fredricksburg, S 1 mi 🅖 PP/dsl, Redner's Whse/mkt 🍴 Esther's Rest. 🄾 KOA (5mi)
1	I-81. **I-78 begins/ends on I-81, exit 89.**

INTERSTATE 79

Exit #	Services
183b a	PA 5, 12th St, Erie, E 🄾 🅗 Valley Tire, W 🅖 Country Fair/dsl, Sunoco/dsl 🍴 5 Guys, Applebee's, Bob Evans, Dominos, Eat'n Park, El Canelo Mexican, Hibachi Japanese, KFC, McDonald's, Panera Bread, Pizza Hut, Taco Bell, Taki Rest., Tim Hortons, Wendy's 🛏 Comfort Inn (2mi) 🄾 $General, $Tree, Aamco, Advance Parts, Aldi Foods, BigLots, CVS Drug, Dunn Tire, Family$, Giant Eagle Foods, GNC, Monro, NAPA, Rite Aid, Save-a-Lot Foods, Tires-4-Less, to Presque Isle SP, Tuesday Morning, U-Haul, vet
182	US 20, 26th St, E 🅖 Country Fair, KwikFill 🍴 Subway 🄾 🅗 CVS Drug, Family$, Tops Foods/gas/24hr, W 🅖 Country Fair, GetGo/dsl 🍴 Applebee's (2mi), Arby's, Burger King, DQ, Hong Kong Chinese, Hoss's Steaks, LJ Silver, McDonald's, Pizza Pete's, Subway, Tim Hortons 🛏 Glass House Inn 🄾 $General, AT&T, AutoZone, Family$, Ford, Giant Eagle Foods, K-Mart/Little Caesar's, Meineke, Shack, TrueValue, URGENT CARE, vet, Volvo
180	US 19, to Kearsarge, E 🍴 Aoyama Japanese, Arby's, Buffalo Wild Wings, Cheddars, Coldstone, Firebirds Grill, Fox&Hound, KFC, Max&Erma's, McDonald's, Moe's SW Grill, O'Charley's, Olive Garden, Outback Steaks, Red Lobster, Ruby Tuesday, Smokey Bones BBQ, Starbucks, Wendy's 🛏 Fairfield Inn, Homewood Suites, SpringHill Suites, TownePlace Suites 🄾 🅗 Audi/Cadillac, Barnes&Noble, Bon-Ton, Chrysler/Dodge/Jeep, Dick's, Firestone/auto, Gander Mtn, JC Penney, Macy's, mall, Michael's, Old Navy, PetCo, Ross, Sears/auto, TJ Maxx, Toyota/Scion, Verizon, W 🅖 Country Fair/dsl 🄾 camping
178b a	I-90, E to Buffalo, W to Cleveland
174	to McKean, E 🅖 access to gas/dsl, W 🄾 camping
166	US 6N, to Edinboro, E 🅖 Country Fair/dsl, Sheetz 🍴 McDonald's (3mi), Perkins (2mi), Subway, Wendy's 🛏 Comfort Suites 🄾 Advance Parts, Verizon, vet, Walmart
163mm	🆁🆂 both lanes, full ♿ facilities, litter barrels, petwalk, 🍴🚶, vending
154	PA 198, to Saegertown, Conneautville, 🄾 Erie NWR (17mi)
147b a	US 6, US 19, US 322, to Meadville, E 🅖 All American Gas/wash, Country Fair, GetGo, Sheetz/dsl 🍴 5 Guys Burgers, Applebee's, Arby's, Chovy's Italian, Cracker Barrel, DQ, Hoss's Rest., KFC, Perkins, Pizza Hut, Super Buffet, Taco Bell 🛏 Days Inn/rest., EconoLodge, Holiday Inn Express 🄾 🅗 Advance Parts, Eddie's Hotdogs, Family$, Giant Eagle Foods, Home Depot, Jo-Ann Fabrics, Radio Shack, Save-a-Lot Foods, W 🅖 Sheetz/dsl 🍴 Burger King, Compadres Mexican, King's Rest., McDonald's, Red Lobster, Subway, Tim Hortons, Yuen's Garden 🛏 Hampton Inn, Quality Inn

Exit #	Services
147b a	**Continued** 🄾 $Tree, Aldi Foods, AutoZone, Buick/Cadillac/GMC, Chevrolet, GNC, K-Mart, st police, Staples, to Pymatuning SP, Toyota/Scion, URGENT CARE, Verizon, visitor info, Walmart
141	PA 285, to Geneva, E 🄾 to Erie NWR (20mi), W 🅖 Aunt Bee's Rest./dsl, Citgo/dsl
135mm	🆁🆂/weigh both lanes, full ♿ facilities, litter barrels, petwalk, 🍴🚶, vending
130	PA 358, to Sandy Lake, W 🄾🅗 (13mi), to Goddard SP
121	US 62, to Mercer, E 🄾 Valley Tire, W 🅖 Sunoco/dsl 🄾 st police
116b a	I-80, E to Clarion, W to Sharon
113	PA 208, PA 258, to Grove City, E 🅖 BP, Country Fair/dsl 🍴 Compadres Mexican 🄾 🅗 W 🅖 KwikFill/Subway, Sheetz/dsl 🍴 Eat'n Park, Elephant&Castle Rest., Hoss' Rest., King's Rest., McDonald's, My Bro's Place, Primanti Bros; Taco Bell, Wendy's 🛏 Best Western, Comfort Inn, Hampton Inn, Holiday Inn Express, Microtel, Super 8 🄾 KOA (3mi), Premium Outlets/famous brands, tires
110mm	🆁🆂/weigh sta sb, full ♿ facilities, litter barrels, petwalk, 🍴🚶, vending
107mm	🆁🆂/weigh sta nb, full ♿ facilities, litter barrels, petwalk, 🍴🚶, vending
105	PA 108, to Slippery Rock, E 🍴 DQ 🛏 Evening Star Motel 🄾 Slippery Rock Camping, to Slippery Rock U
99	US 422, to New Castle, E 🄾 to Moraine SP, W 🅖 🚂 McDonald's/Subway/dsl/scales/24hr 🄾 Coopers Lake Camping, to Rose Point Camping
96	PA 488, Portersville, E 🄾 Bear Run Camping, Moraine SP, W 🍴 Brown's Country Kitchen, gas/dsl, McConnell's Mill SP (3mi)
88	(87 from nb) US 19, PA 68, Zelienople, E 🍴 Log Cabin Inn Rest., W 🅖 BiLo/dsl 🍴 Burger King, Pizza Hut
85	(83 from nb), PA 528 (no quick return), to Evans City, W 🄾 Buick
80mm	weigh sta both lanes
78	(76 from nb, exits left from nb), US 19, PA 228, to Mars, access to I-76, PA TPK, E 🅖 GetGo/dsl, Gulf/7-11/dsl 🍴 Applebee's, Chick-fil-A, Coldstone, DiBella's Subs, Echo Rest., Jimmy Wan's Chinese, Longhorn Steaks, McDonald's, Moe's SW Grill, Noodles&Co, Olive Garden, On-the-Border, Red Robin, Smokey Bones BBQ, Starbucks, Subway 🛏 Courtyard, Hilton Garden, Marriott 🄾 🅗 AT&T, Dick's, GNC, Kohl's, Lowe's, Petsmart, Staples, Target, TJ Maxx, W on US 19 🅖 BP/dsl, GetGo, Marathon/dsl, Sheetz, Sunoco/dsl 🍴 5 Guys Burgers, A&W/LJ Silver, Alladin's Eatery, Arby's, Bob Evans, Boston Mkt, Bravo Italian, Buffalo Wild Wings, Burger King, Chipotle Mexican, Denny's, DQ, Dunkin Donuts, Dynasty, Eat'n Park, Emiliano's Mexican, Firehouse Subs, HotDog Shoppe, Houlihan's, Ichiban Steakhouse, Jimmy John's, LoneStar Steaks, Mad Mex, Max&Erma's, McDonald's, Monte Cello's Grill, Panera Bread, Perkins, Pizza Roma, Primanti Bros, Quaker Steak, Saga Steaks, Sports Grille, Subway, Wendy's 🛏 Candlewood Suites, Comfort Inn, Fairfield Inn, Hampton Inn, Holiday Inn Express, Hyatt Place, Motel 6, Red Roof Inn, Residence Inn, Sheraton, Super 8 🄾 $Tree, AAA, AT&T, Autozone, Barnes&Noble, Best Buy, Costco/gas, Firestone/auto, Giant Eagle Foods, GNC, Home Depot, Jo-Ann Fabrics, Kuhn's Foods, mall, Marshall's, Michael's, NAPA, Old Navy, PepBoys, PetCo, Radio Shack, Rite Aid, Toyota/Scion, transmissions, Tuesday Morning, USPO, Verizon, vet, Walgreens, Walmart

ERIE

MEADVILLE

CRANBERRY

PA

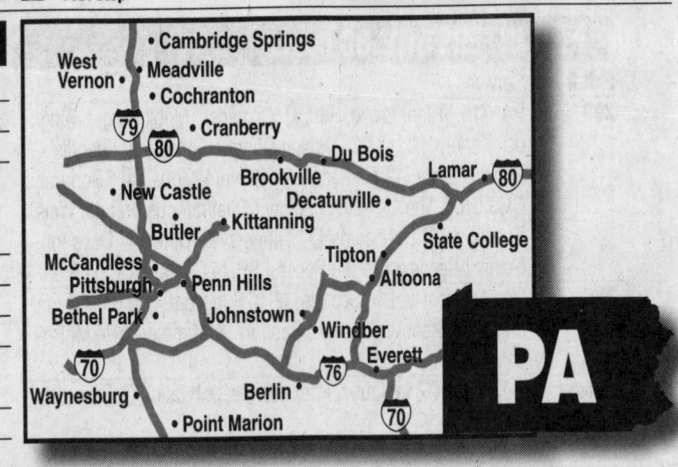

INTERSTATE 79 Cont'd

Exit #	Services
77	I-76/Tpk, to Youngstown
75	US 19 S (from nb), to Warrendale, services on US 19
73	PA 910, to Wexford, **E** 🅶 BP 🍴 Eat'n Park, King's Family Rest., Starbucks 🛏 EconoLodge, **W** 🅶 Exxon/Subway/dsl 🍴 Carmody's Rest.
72	I-279 S (from sb, exits left), to Pittsburgh
68	Mt Nebo Rd, **E** 🅶 Sheetz/dsl **W** 🅾 🅷
66	to PA 65, Emsworth
65	to PA 51, Coraopolis, Neville Island, **E** 🍴 Kings Grille 🛏 Fairfield Inn 🅾 Penske Trucks, **W** 🍴 Subway
64.5mm	Ohio River
64	PA 51 (from nb), to Coraopolis, McKees Rocks
60	PA 60, Crafton, **E** 🍴 King's Rest, Primanti Bros 🛏 Comfort Inn, EconoLodge, Motel 6, Travelodge 🅾 🅷 **W** 🍴 Juliano's Rest. 🅾 Meineke
59b	I-376 W, US 22 W, US 30 (from nb), **W** 🅾 🍽
59a	I-376 E, to Pittsburgh
57	to Carnegie
55	PA 50, to Heidelberg, **E on PA 50** 🅶 BP, Marathon, Sunoco 🍴 Arby's, Bob Evans, ChuckeCheese, Damon's, Eat'n Park, Firestone/auto, KFC, LJ Silver, McDonald's, Pizza Hut, Sonic, Starbucks, Taco Bell, TX Roadhouse, Wendy's 🅾 $Tree, BigLots, Ford, Giant Eagle Foods, GNC, Home Depot, Jo-Ann Fabrics, K-Mart/Little Caesar's, Lowe's, Mr Tire, Pepboys, Radio Shack, Rite Aid, TJ Maxx, Walgreens, Walmart
54	PA 50, to Bridgeville, **E** 🅶 BP/dsl, Fuel Stop/dsl, GetGo 🍴 King's Rest., McDonald's 🛏 Holiday Inn Express 🅾 🅷 Chevrolet, Midas, Monro, NAPA, Rite Aid, USPO, **W** 🅶 Sunoco/dsl 🛏 Hampton Inn, Knights Inn
50mm	🆁🆂/weigh sta both lanes, full ♿ facilities, litter barrels, petwalk, 🚻, 🐾, vending
48	South Pointe, **W** 🍴 Jackson's Rest. 🛏 Hilton Garden, Homewood Suites
45	to PA 980, Canonsburg, **E** 🅶 Sheetz, **W** 🅶 BP, Citgo 🍴 Hogfathers BBQ, KFC/Taco Bell, LJ Silver, McDonald's, Papa John's, Pizza Hut, Quiznos, Starbucks, Subway, WaiWai Grill, Wendy's 🛏 Super 8 🅾 $General, Advance Parts, auto/transmission repair, Verizon, Walgreens
43	PA 519, Houston, **E** 🅶 BP/dsl, **W** 🅶 Sunoco 🅾 Freightliner
41	Race Track Rd, **E** 🅶 Marathon/dsl 🍴 Buger King, McDonald's, Waffle House, Wendy's 🛏 Cambria Suites, Candlewood Suites, Comfort Inn, Country Inn&Suites, Courtyard, Doubletree, Hampton Inn, Holiday Inn 🅾 Audi, Old Navy, racetrack, Tanger Outlets/famous brands, **W** 🅶 BP/dsl 🛏 Microtel 🅾 Trolley Museum
40	Meadow Lands, **W** 🅾 golf, racetrack, Trolley Museum (3mi)
38	I-70 W, to Wheeling
I-79 and I-70 run together 3.5 mi. See I-70, exits 19b a - 20.	
34	I-70 E, to Greensburg
33	US 40, to Laboratory, **W** 🅾 KOA
31mm	weigh sta sb
30	US 19, to Amity, **W** 🅶 Exxon/Subway/dsl
23	to Marianna, Prosperity
20	(I-77) PA 136, to Beau St, **S** to Washington&Jefferson Coll
19	US 19, to PA 221, Ruff Creek, **W** 🅶 BP/dsl
14	PA 21, to Waynesburg, **E** 🅶 BP 🍴 Bob Evans 🛏 Comfort Inn, Microtel 🅾 Walmart/Subway, **W** 🅶 BP/7-11/dsl, Exxon/dsl, GetGo, Marathon, Sheetz, Sunoco 🍴 Burger King, DQ, Golden Wok, Hardee's, KFC, Little Caesars, McDonald's, Pizza Hut, Scotty's Pizza, Subway, Vocelli Pizza, Wendy's

WAYNESBURG

14	Continued
	🛏 EconoLodge, Hampton Inn, Super 8 🅾 🅷 $General, $Tree, Ace Hardware, Advance Parts, Aldi Foods, AT&T, AutoZone, BigLots, Cadillac/Chevrolet/Subaru, Chrysler/Dodge/Jeep, CVS Drug, Family$, Giant Eagle Foods, Radio Shack, Rite Aid, st police, Verizon, Walgreens
7	to Kirby
6mm	Welcome Center/weigh sta nb, full ♿ facilities, litter barrels, petwalk, 🚻, 🐾, vending
1	Mount Morris, **E** 🅶 Sunoco/Huddle House/dsl/scales/24hr 🅾 Honda/Mazda, **W** 🅶 BFS/dsl 🅾 Mt Morris Campground
0mm	Pennsylvania/West Virginia state line

INTERSTATE 80

Exit #	Services
311mm	Pennsylvania/New Jersey state line, Delaware River
310.5	toll booth wb, 🚻
310	PA 611, Delaware Water Gap, **S** 🅶 Fuel On, Gulf 🍴 Apple Pie Bakery, Doughboys Pizza, Water Gap Diner
309	US 209 N, PA 447, to Marshalls Creek, **N** 🅶 Gulf 🍴 Blue Tequila Mexican, DQ, Dunkin Donuts, Landmark Cafe, Wendy's (2mi) 🛏 Days Inn, Staybridge Suites 🅾 🅷
308	East Stroudsburg, **N** 🅶 Exxon/Subs Now 🅾 🅷 vet, WaWa, **S 1 mi** 🍴 Arby's, Burger King, CiCi's, Friendly's, Holy Guacamole, Ichiban Asian, KFC, McDonald's, Roasted Tomato Grill 🛏 Budget Motel, Super 8 🅾 K-Mart, Radio Shack, ShopRite Foods, Walmart/McDonald's
307	PA 191, Broad St, **N** 🛏 Hampton Inn 🅾 🅷 **S** 🅶 Sunoco 🍴 Compton's Rest. 🛏 EconoLodge
306	Dreher Ave (from wb, no EZ return), **N** 🅾 WaWa
305	US 209, Main St, **N** 🅶 Gulf/dsl, Shell 🍴 Perkins 🛏 Quality Inn, **S** 🅶 Exxon/dsl 🛏 Holiday Inn Express
304	US 209, to PA 33, 9th St (from wb)
303	9th St, (from eb), **N** 🍴 5 Guys Burgers, Burger King, Dunkin Donuts, Fume Asin, Garfield's Rest., McDonald's, Olive Garden, Panera Bread, Popeye's, Ruby Tuesday, TX Roadhouse, Wendy's 🅾 $Tree, Best Buy, BJ's/Subway/gas, Bon Ton, Buick/GMC, Chevrolet, CVS Drug, Home Depot, Hyundai, JC Penney, Kia, Michaels, Midas, Old Navy, Petsmart, Radio Shack, Staples, Target, Target, TJ Maxx, URGENT CARE, Walgreens, Weis Foods/gas
302	PA 611, to Bartonsville, **N** 🅶 Exxon/dsl 🍴 Big Daddy's BBQ, Chili's, Dickey's BBQ, Dunkin Donuts, East Gourmet Buffet, Frank's Pizza, Ichiban Steaks, Longhorn Steaks, Moe's SW Grill, Red Lobster, Red Robin, Sonic, Studebaker's, Subway 🛏 Comfort Inn, Hampton Inn, Howard Johnson 🅾 $Tree, Advance Parts, AT&T, Dick's, Giant Foods/gas, Kohl's, Lowe's, URGENT CARE, Verizon

STROUDSBURG

PA

INTERSTATE 80 Cont'd

Exit #	Services
299	PA 715, Tannersville, N 🅖 Citgo/dsl, Mobil/Burger King/dsl, Turkey Hill 🍴 DQ, Dunkin Donuts, FoodCout, Friendly's, Pocono Diner 🏠 Ramada Ltd, Scotrun Motel 🅾 $General, CVS Drug, The Crossing Factory Outlet/famous brands, Weis Foods, S 🅖 Sunoco/dsl 🍴 Tannersville Diner 🏠 Days Inn, Summit Resort 🅾 to Big Pocono SP, to Camelback Ski Area
298	PA 611 (from wb), to Scotrun, N 🅖 Sunoco/dsl 🍴 Brick Oven Pizza 🏠 Great Wolf Lodge, Scotrun Diner/motel 🅾 to Mt Pocono
295mm	🆁🆂 eb, full ♿ facilities, litter barrels, petwalk, 🚻🕭, 🖼 vending
293	I-380 N, to Scranton, (exits left from eb)
284	PA 115, to Wilkes-Barre, Blakeslee, N 🅖 WaWa/dsl 🏠 Best Western, Blakeslee Inn (2mi) 🅾 Fern Ridge Camping, st police, S 🅖 Exxon/dsl 🍴 Ray's Tuscan Villa 🅾 to Pocono Raceway
277	PA 940, to PA Tpk (I-476), to Pocono, Lake Harmony, Allentown, N 🅖 WaWa 🍴 A&W/LJ Silver, Arby's, McDonald's, Subway 🏠 Comfort Inn, EconoLodge, Holiday Inn Express, Mtn Laurel Resort, Pocono Inn/Resort, Quality Inn, Split Rock Resort
274	PA 534, N 🅖 Hickory Run/Valero/rest./dsl/scales/24hr, Sunoco/Subs Now/dsl/24hr 🅾 towing/repair, S 🅾 to Hickory Run SP (6mi)
273mm	Lehigh River
273	PA 940, PA 437, to Freeland, White Haven, N 🅖 Exxon, Fuel One, S 🍴 Forks Rest., Powerhouse Eatery
270mm	🆁🆂 eb, full ♿ facilities, litter barrels, petwalk, 🚻🕭, 🖼 vending
262	PA 309, to Hazleton, Mountain Top, N 🅖 Citgo 🍴 Mary's Rest., Wendy's 🏠 EconoLodge 🅾 auto/truck repair, S 🅖 Valero/dsl 🏠 Holiday Inn Express 🅾 Nescopeck SP (5mi)
260b a	I-81, N to Wilkes-Barre, S to Harrisburg
256	PA 93, to Nescopeck, Conyngham, N 🅖 🚂/Subway/dsl/scales/24hr, Sunoco/repair, S 🍴 Tom's Kitchen (2mi) 🏠 Best Value Inn, Hampton Inn (4mi) 🅾 🚑 towing/truck repair
251mm	Nescopeck River
246mm	🆁🆂/weigh sta both lanes, full ♿ facilities, litter barrels, petwalk, 🚻🕭, 🖼 vending, weather info
242	PA 339, to Mainville, Mifflinville, N 🅖 Loves/Arby's/dsl/scales/24hr, Sunoco/Subway/dsl 🍴 McDonald's 🏠 Super 8, S 🅖 Exxon/dsl 🏠 Comfort Inn
241mm	Susquehanna River
241b a	US 11, to Berwick, Lime Ridge, Bloomsburg, N 🏠 Red Maple Inn (2mi) 🅾 🚑 S 2-5 mi 🅖 Sheetz/dsl, SunocoSubs Now/dsl 🍴 Applebee's, Arby's, Burger King, Domino's, Dunkin Donuts, Kemlar's Rest., Marley's Grill, McDonald's, Morris Rest., Oliran Japanese, Pizza Hut, Rita's Custard, Subway, Taco Bell, Taste of Italy, Wendy's 🏠 Budget Host, Relax Inn 🅾 AAA, Ace Hardware, Advance Parts, BigLots, Buick/GMC, Cadillac/Chevrolet, CVS Drug, Ford/Honda, Giant Foods/gas, Kost Tire, Rite Aid, Staples, U-Haul, Weis Foods/gas
236	PA 487, to Bloomsburg, Lightstreet, S 🅖 Sunoco 🍴 Denny's 🏠 Hampton Inn, Relax Inn (2mi), Turkey Hill Inn 🅾 🚑 to Bloomsburg U
232	PA 42, Buckhorn, N 🅖 Exxon/Subs Now, TA/Country Pride/Subway/dsl/scales/24hr/@ 🍴 Burger King, Cracker Barrel, KFC, Perkins, Quaker Steak&Lube, Ruby Tuesday, Wendy's 🏠 EconoLodge, Holiday Inn Express 🅾 AT&T, BonTon, Home Depot, JC Penney, mall, Sears/auto, S 🍴 Carini's

232	Continued Italian, Gourmet Buffet, Olive Garden, Panera Bread 🏠 Comfort Suites 🅾 $Tree, Indian Head Camping (3mi), Lowe's, PetCo, Verizon, Walmart/McDonald's
224	PA 54, to Danville, N 🅖 Exxon/Subway/dsl 🏠 Quality Inn, S 🍴 Friendly's, McDonald's, Mom's Dutch Kitchen 🏠 Best Western, Hampton Inn, Red Roof Inn, Super 8 🅾🚑
219mm	🆁🆂 both lanes, full ♿ facilities, litter barrels, petwalk, 🚻🕭, 🖼 vending
215	PA 254, Limestonevill, N 🅖 Milton 32 Trkstp/rest./dsl/24hr, S 🅖 🟠FLYING J/Penn 80 Rest./Subway/dsl/scales/24hr/@ 🅾 Eagle Truckwash
212b a	I-180 W, PA 147 S, to Muncy, Williamsport, S 🅖 Sunoco (1mi)
210.5mm	Susquehanna River
210b a	US 15, to Williamsport, Lewisburg, S 🅖 Sunoco/dsl 🍴 Bonanza 🏠 Comfort Inn, Holiday Inn Express 🅾🚑 KOA (5mi)
199	Mile Run
194mm	🆁🆂/weigh sta both lanes, full ♿ facilities, litter barrels, petwalk, 🚻🕭, 🖼 vending
192	PA 880, to Jersey Shore, N 🅖 Sunoco/dsl 🅾🚑 S 🅖 Valero/dsl 🅾 towing/truck repair
185	PA 477, Loganton, N 🅖 Valero 🅾 camping, S 🍴 RB Winter SP (12mi), Twilight Diner
178	US 220, Lock Haven, N 5 mi 🅖 KwikFill/dsl, Sheetz/dsl 🍴 Little Caesar's, Pizza Hut, Ruby Tuesday 🅾🚑 $General, $Tree, Advance Parts, K-Mart, Lowe's, Walmart/Subway, Weis Foods
173	PA 64, Lamar, N 🅖 🚂/Subway/dsl/scales/24hr 🍴 Cottage Rest., McDonald's 🏠 Comfort Inn/rest., Hampton Inn 🅾 repair, S 🅖 🟠FLYING J/Denny's/dsl/LP/scales/24hr, TA/Country Pride/dsl/scales/24hr/@, Valero
161	I-99, US 220 S, PA 26, to Bellafonte, N 🅾 Bellefonte Camping, KOA (2mi), S 🅾 to PSU
158	US 220 S, PA 150, to Altoona, Milesburg, N 🅖 Bestway/rest./dsl/motel/24hr/@, Shell/Subway, TA/Country Pride/dsl/scales/24hr/@, Valero/dsl 🍴 McDonald's 🏠 Quality Inn, S st police
147	PA 144, to Snow Shoe, N 🅖 Exxon/dsl/repair/24hr, Sunoco/dsl/24hr 🍴 Snow Shoe Rest., Snow Shoe Sandwich Shop, Subway 🅾 Hall's Foods, USPO
146mm	🆁🆂 both lanes, full ♿ facilities, litter barrels, petwalk, 🚻🕭, 🖼 vending
138mm	Moshannon River
133	PA 53, to Philipsburg, Kylertown, N 🅖 KwikFill/motel/dsl/scales 🍴 Roadhouse Rest. 🅾 Black Moshannon SP (9mi), dsl repair, Mtn View Mkt, USPO, S 🅾🚑
123	PA 970, to Shawville, Woodland, N 🅾 Woodland Camping, S 🅖 Gio's BBQ/dsl (2mi), PP/dsl 🅾 st police, USPO
120mm	Susquehanna River, W Branch
120	PA 879, Shawville, Clearfield, N 🅖 Sapp Bros/rest./dsl/scales/24hr/@ 🏠 EconoLodge 🅾 Peterbilt, S 🅖 BP/dsl, Sheetz, Snappy's 🍴 Arby's, Burger King, Chinese buffet, Dunkin Donuts, Dutch Pantry, KFC/Taco Bell, McDonald's 🏠 Best Western, Comfort Inn, Hampton Inn, Holiday Inn Express, Super 8, Travelodge 🅾🚑 Lowe's, Walmart/Subway
111mm	2250 ft, highest point on I-80 east of Mississippi River
111	PA 153, to Penfield, N 🅾 to Parker Dam, to SB Elliot SP, S 🅾🚑
101	PA 255, Du Bois, N 🅖 Snappy's/Quiznos/dsl 🅾 camping, S 1-2 mi 🅖 Sheetz/dsl 🍴 A&W/LJ Silver, Arby's, Burger King, Dubois Buffet, Eat'n Park, Italian Oven, Japan One, McDonald's, Napoli Pizzeria, Perkins, Pizza Hut, Ponderosa,

Sidebar markers: HAZLETON, LAMAR, PA

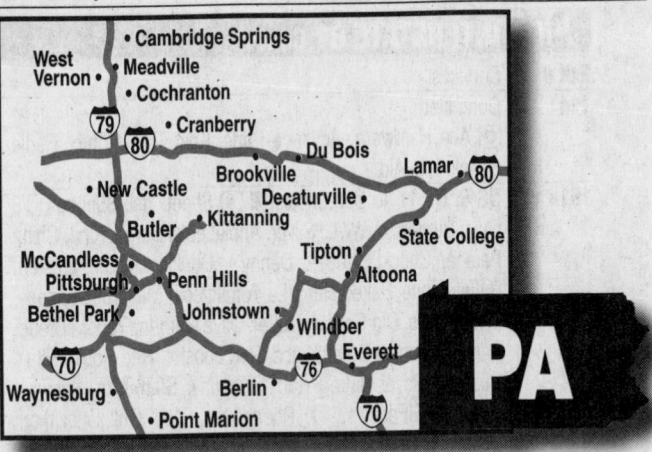

DU BOIS / BROOKVILLE

🔼E INTERSTATE 80 Cont'd

Exit #	Services
101	Continued
	Red Lobster, Ruby Tuesday, Station 101 Grill, Subway, Taco Bell, Valley Dairy Rest., Wendy's 🛏 Fairfield Inn, Hampton Inn, Homewood Suites 🄾 🄷 $General, $Tree, Aldi Foods, BigLots, BonTon, CVS Drug, JC Penney, Jo-Ann Fabrics, K-Mart, Lowe's, mall, Old Navy, PetCo, Radio Shack, Rite Aid, Ross, Sears/auto, Shop'n Save Foods, st police, Staples, TJ Maxx, URGENT CARE, Verizon, Walmart/Subway
97	US 219, to Brockway, Du Bois, S 2 mi 🍴/Arby's/dsl/scales/24hr, Sheetz/dsl/24hr 🍴 Dutch Pantry Rest., Hoss' Rest. 🛏 Best Western, Clarion, Holiday Inn Express 🄾 🄷 Advance Parts, Freightliner, st police
90	PA 830 E, N 🄾 Du Bois Regional ✈
87.5mm	🆁🆂 both lanes, full 🦽 facilities, litter barrels, petwalk, 🄲, 🖼 vending
86	PA 830, to Reynoldsville
81	PA 28, to Brookville, Hazen, S Brookville, hist dist (2mi)
78	PA 36, to Sigel, Brookville, N 🍴 ⊕FLYING J/Denny's/dsl/LP/scales/24hr, TA/BP/Taco Bell/dsl/scales/Howard Johnson/24hr/@ 🍴 DQ, McDonald's, Pizza Hut 🛏 Super 8 🄾 NAPA, to Cook Forest SP, S 🍴 GetGo/dsl, Oring CNG, Sheetz 🍴 Arby's, Burger King, China Wok, Plyler's Buffet, Subway 🛏 Gold Eagle Inn, Quality Inn 🄾 Chrysler/Dodge/Jeep, Family$, truckwash
73	PA 949, Corsica, N 🄾 to Clear Creek SP, S 🄾 USPO
70	US 322, to Strattanville
64	PA 66 S, to New Bethlehem, Clarion, N 🄾 to Clarion U
62	PA 68, to Clarion, N 🍴 BP, KwikFill/dsl 🍴 A&W/LJ Silver, Applebee's, Arby's, Eat'n Park, Hunan King, McDonald's, Perkins, Pizza Hut, RRR Roadhouse, Sakura Buffet, Subway, Taco Bell 🛏 Comfort Inn, Hampton Inn, Holiday Inn/rest., Microtel, Quality Inn, Super 8 🄾 🄷 $Tree, Advance Parts, Aldi Foods, AT&T, AutoZone, JC Penney, K-Mart, Verizon, Walmart/Subway
61mm	Clarion River
60	PA 66 N, to Shippenville, N 🍴 Jiffy/dsl 🄾 camping, to Cook Forest SP
56mm	weigh sta both lanes
53	to PA 338, to Knox, N 🍴 Satterlee Gas/dsl (cardlock) 🍴 BJ's Eatery 🄾 Countryside Crafts/Quilts, Wolf's Camping Resort, S 🄾 Good Tire Service
45	PA 478, to St Petersburg, Emlenton, S 4 mi 🄾 Golf Hall of Fame
44.5mm	Allegheny River
42	PA 38, to Emlenton, N 🍴 Exxon/Subway/dsl, Shell/Trkstp/rest./dsl/scales/24hr 🛏 Emlenton Motel 🄾 Gaslight RV Park, truck/RV repair
35	PA 308, to Clintonville
30.5mm	🆁🆂 both lanes, full 🦽 facilities, litter barrels, petwalk, 🄲, 🖼 vending
29	PA 8, to Franklin, Barkeyville, N 🍴 Arby's, Burger King, King's Rest. 🛏 Motel 6, Quality Inn 🄾 Freightliner, S 🍴 Heath/dsl, KwikFill/dsl/scales/motel/24hr, TA/BP/Subway/dsl/scales/24hr/@ 🄾 to Slippery Rock U, truckwash
24	PA 173, to Grove City, Sandy Lake, S 🄾 🄷 Grove City Coll, Wendell August Forge/gifts (3mi)
19b a	I-79, N to Erie, S to Pittsburgh
15	US 19, to Mercer, N 🍴 PP/dsl, Shell 🍴 Burger King, Margarita King Mexican, McDonald's/rv parking 🛏 Comfort Inn 🄾 st police, S 2 mi 🍴 Iron Bridge Rest., Springfield Grill 🄾 KOA (4mi)

Exit #	Services
4b a	I-376, PA 60, to PA 18, to Sharon-Hermitage, New Castle, N 🍴 Sheetz/dsl, Sunoco/Subway/dsl 🛏 EconoLodge, Hampton Inn, Holiday Inn Express, Park Inn, Quality Inn, Red Roof Inn, Super 8, S 🍴 DQ, MiddleSex Diner 🄾 $General
2.5mm	Shenango River
1mm	Welcome Center eb, full 🦽 facilities, litter barrels, petwalk, 🄲, 🖼 vending
0mm	Pennsylvania/Ohio state line

🔼N INTERSTATE 81

Exit #	Services
233mm	Pennsylvania/New York state line
232mm	Welcome Center/weigh sta sb, full 🦽 facilities, litter barrels, petwalk, 🄲, 🖼 vending
230	PA 171, Great Bend, E 🍴 Valero 🄾 Lakeside Camping (5mi), W 🍴 Exxon/Tim Hortons/dsl, Sunoco/dsl 🍴 Burger King, Dobb's Country Kitchen, Dunkin Donuts, Golden China, McDonald's, Subway 🛏 Colonial Brick Motel 🄾 Family$, Reddon's Drugs, Rob's Foods
223	PA 492, New Milford, E 🍴 🄾 East Lake Camping/RV Park (3mi), W 🍴 Gulf/dsl, Sunoco, Valero 🍴 Green Gables Rest. 🛏 Blue Ridge Motel, Lynn Lee B&B
219	PA 848, to Gibson, E 🍴 Sunoco/dsl, W 🍴 ⊕FLYING J/Denny's/dsl/scales/24hr, Exxon/McDonald's/dsl/24hr 🛏 Holiday Inn Express, st police
217	PA 547, Harford, E 🍴 Exxon/Subway/dsl/24hr, Mobil/dsl/24hr
211	PA 92, Lenox, E 🄾 Elk Mtn Ski Area, Shady Rest Camping (3mi), W 🍴 Pump-N-Pantry/dsl, Shell/dsl 🍴 Bingham's Rest. 🄾 Lenox Drug
209mm	🆁🆂 sb, full 🦽 facilities, litter barrels, petwalk, 🄲, 🖼 vending
206	PA 374, to Glenwood, Lenoxville, E 🍴 Sunoco/dsl 🄾 to Elk Mountain Ski Resort
203mm	🆁🆂 sb, full 🦽 facilities, litter barrels, petwalk, 🄲, 🖼 vending
202	PA 107, to Fleetville, Tompkinsville
201	PA 438, East Benton, W 🍴 Duchniks/dsl/repair 🍴 B&B Rest
199	PA 524, Scott, E 🍴 Delta/Eat'n Go Rest/dsl, Mobil/dsl, W 🍴 Exxon/Subway 🛏 Motel 81 🄾 to Lackawanna SP
197	PA 632, Waverly, E 🄾 Rite Aid, Weis Foods, W 🍴 Sunoco, Doc's Deli 🛏 Camelot Inn/rest
194	US 6, US 11, to I-476/PA Tpk, Clarks Summit, W 🍴 Exxon/dsl, Sheetz/dsl, Sunoco/dsl 🍴 Burger King, Damon's, Dino&Francesco's, Domino's, Dunkin Donuts, Gourmet Rest, Hibachi Steaks, Krispy Kreme, Kyoto, La Tonalteca, McDonald's, Moe's SW Grill, New Century Chinese, Pizza Hut, Starbucks, Taco Bell, Waffle House, Wendy's 🛏 Comfort Inn, EconoLodge, Hampton Inn, Nichols Village Inn, Ramada Inn,

▲N INTERSTATE 81 Cont'd

Exit #	Services
194	Continued
	◻ Ace Hardware, Advance Parts, Kost Tire, Monro, Radio Shack, Rite Aid
191b a	US 6, US 11, to Carbondale, E ◻ Sheetz/dsl, Sunoco ◻ 5 Guys Burgers, A&W/LJ Silver, Applebee's, Burger King, China Palace, ChuckECheese, Denny's, Dunkin Donuts, Eastern Buffet, HoneyBaked Ham, La Tonalateca, Masaru Japanese, McDonald's, Old Country Buffet, Olive Garden, Panera Bread, Perkins, Quaker Steak&Lube, Red Lobster, Red Robin, Rita's Custard, Royal Buffet, Ruby Tuesday, Starbucks, Subway, TCBY, TGIFriday's, TX Roadhouse, Uno Grill, Viewmont Diner ◻ Days Inn, Holiday Inn Express ◻ $Tree, Aldi Foods, AT&T, Books-A-Million, Dick's, Firestone/auto, Harley-Davidson, Hobby Lobby, Home Depot, Hyundai, JC Penney, Jo-Ann Crafts, K-Mart, Kohl's, Macy's, mall, Marshall's, Michael's, Old Navy, PepBoys, Petsmart, Rite Aid, Sears/auto, Target, TJ Maxx, Verizon, Walmart, William's Tires, W ◻ to Anthracite Museum
190	Main Ave, Dickson City, E ◻ Teppanyaki Buffet, Wendy's ◻ Fairfield Inn, Microtel, Residence Inn ◻ auto repair, Best Buy, Gander Mtn, Lowe's, Sam's Club/gas, Staples, vet, W ◻ Schiff's Foods, Toyota/Scion
188	PA 347, Throop, E ◻ Sheetz, Sunoco/dsl ◻ China Buffet, McDonald's, Wendy's ◻ Dunmore Inn, Quality Inn, Scottish Inn, Sleep Inn ◻ Advance Parts, BigLots, Kost Tire, Monro, PriceChopper Foods, st police, URGENT CARE, W ◻ Exxon/Subway/dsl ◻ Burger King, Dunkin Donuts, Friendly's
187	to I-84, I-380, US 6 (no return from nb)
186	PA 435, Drinker St (from nb), E ◻ Valero/dsl ◻ Best Western, W ◻ Exxon
185	Central Scranton Expwy (exits left from nb), W ◻ ◻
184	to PA 307, River St, W ◻ Exxon/Subway/dsl, Valero, Vamco ◻ Dunkin Donuts, House of China ◻ Clarion ◻ ◻ $Tree, CVS Drug, Gerrity Foods
182	Davis St, Montage Mtn Rd, E ◻ Exxon/Coldstone/Subway/dsl ◻ Doc's Oyster House, Johnny Rockets Cafe, Longhorn Steaks, Panchero's Mexican, Panera Bread, Quiznos, Ruby Tuesday, Starbucks ◻ Comfort Suites, Courtyard, Hampton Inn, Springhill Suites, TownePlace Suites ◻ AT&T, GNC, W ◻ Sunoco ◻ Dunkin Donuts, Waffle House, Wendy's ◻ EconoLodge ◻ CVS Drug, USPO
180	to US 11, PA 502, to Moosic, (exits left from nb), W on US 11 ◻ Exxon, Sunoco ◻ McDonalds, Subway ◻ Rodeway Inn
178b a	to US 11, Avoca, E ◻ Holiday Inn Express, W ◻ Petro/Valero/Iron Skillet/dsl/scales/24hr/@
175b a	PA 315 S, to I-476, Dupont, E ◻ Exxon/Subway/dsl, Sunoco ◻ Arby's, McDonald's, Perkins ◻ Knights Inn, Super 8 ◻ Volvo, W ◻ ◻/Wendy's/dsl/scales/24hr ◻ Burger King ◻ Best Value ◻ truck repair, Walmart/Subway
170b a	PA 115, PA 309, Wilkes-Barre, E ◻ Exxon/Subway/dsl, Sunoco/dsl ◻ Best Western ◻ to Pocono Downs, W ◻ Citgo, Sunoco/dsl ◻ Burger King, Denny's, Friendly's, LJ Silver, Lonestar Steaks, McDonald's, Pizza Hut, Red Lobster, Sonic, TGIFriday's, Wendy's ◻ Days Inn, Extended Stay America, Fairfield Inn, Holiday Inn Express, Quality Inn, Red Roof Inn ◻ ◻ $General, BonTon, Chevrolet, Goodyear, Harley-Davidson, JC Penney, Macy's, mall, Sears/auto
168	Highland Park Blvd, Wilkes-Barre, W ◻ Sheetz, Sunoco, TurkeyHill ◻ Applebee's, Arby's, Bob Evans, Chili's, ChuckeCheese, Cracker Barrel, King's Buffet, La Tolteca Mexican,

(side marker: SCRANTON)
(side marker: WILKES BARRE)
(side marker: PA)

168	Continued
	Logan's Roadhouse, Lucky's SportHouse, Olive Garden, Outback Steaks, Panera Bread, Red Robin, Smokey Bones BBQ, Starbucks, Subway, Wendy's ◻ Hampton Inn, Hilton Garden ◻ AT&T, Barnes&Noble, Best Buy, Dick's, Firestone/auto, Kohl's, Kost Tire, Lowe's, Marshall's, Michael's, Nissan, Old Navy, PepBoys, PetCo, Petsmart, PriceChopper, Radio Shack, Ross, Sam's Club/gas, Staples, Target, TJ Maxx, U-Haul, URGENT CARE, Verizon, Walgreens, Walmart, Wegman's Foods
165b a	PA 309 S, (exits left from nb), Wilkes-Barre, W ◻ Citgo/dsl, Gulf ◻ Dunkin Donuts, McDonald's, Perkins, Taco Bell ◻ Comfort Inn, EconoLodge ◻ $Tree, Advance Parts, K-Mart
164	PA 29, to Nanticoke, Ashley
159	Nuangola, W ◻ UniMart ◻ camping (10mi)
157mm	◻/weigh sta sb, full ◻ facilities, litter barrels, petwalk, ◻ ◻, vending
156mm	◻/weigh sta nb, full ◻ facilities, litter barrels, petwalk, ◻ ◻, vending
155	to Dorrance, E ◻ Sunoco/dsl ◻ EconoLodge (2mi), W ◻ Blue Ridge Plaza/dsl
151b a	I-80, E to Mountaintop, W to Bloomsburg
145	PA 93, W Hazleton, E ◻ Sunoco/dsl, TurkeyHill/dsl ◻ 5 Stars Chinese, Applebee's, Arby's, Bonanza, Damon's, Denny's, Friendly's, LJ Silver, McDonald's, Perkins, Pizza Hut, Taco Bell, Wendy's ◻ Best Western (2mi), Comfort Inn, Fairfield Inn, Forest Hill Inn, Ramada Inn (2mi) ◻ ◻ $Tree, Advance Parts, Aldi Foods, AT&T, Big Lots, Boscov's, Buick/Cadillac/GMC, Chrysler/Dodge/Jeep, JC Penney, K-Mart, Lowe's, Mazda, Michael's, Old Navy, Petsmart, Radio Shack, st police, Staples, Weis Foods, W ◻ Shell, Top of the 80's ◻ Candlewood Suites, Hampton Inn
143	PA 924, to Hazleton, W ◻ Fuelon/Subs Now/dsl, Shell/Subway, TurkeyHill/dsl ◻ Burger King, Sonic ◻ Residence Inn
141	PA 424, S Hazleton Beltway, ◻ Mt Laurel Motel
138	PA 309, to McAdoo, E 2 mi ◻ Pines Motel
134	to Delano
132mm	parking area/weigh sta both lanes
131b a	PA 54, Mahanoy City, E ◻ to Tuscarora/Locust Lake SP, W ◻ Shell/dsl, Sunoco/dsl
124b a	PA 61, to Frackville, E ◻ Cracker Barrel, McDonald's ◻ Holiday Inn Express ◻ BigLots, BonTon, K-Mart, mall, Sears/auto, W ◻ Exxon, Gulf, Hess ◻ Anthony's Pizza, Dutch Kitchen, Subway ◻ EconoLodge, Granny's Motel, Rodeway Inn ◻ ◻ Rite Aid, st police
119	High Ridge Park Rd, to Gordon, E ◻ Country Inn&Suites ◻ ◻
116	PA 901, to Minersville, E ◻ 901 Rest.
112	PA 25, to Hegins, W ◻ camping
107	US 209, to Tremont
104	PA 125, Ravine, E ◻ Exxon/Burger King/dsl/scales/24hr ◻ Echo Valley Campground
100	PA 443, to Pine Grove, E ◻ Exxon/dsl ◻ Arby's, McDonald's ◻ Comfort Inn, EconoLodge ◻ $General, W ◻ ◻/DQ/Subway/dsl/scales/24hr ◻ Gooseberry Farms Diner ◻ Hampton Inn ◻ KOA (5mi), truckwash
90	PA 72, to Lebanon, E ◻ Exxon/Subway, Hess/Blimpie ◻ Dunkin Donuts/dsl, ◻ Loves/McDonald's/dsl/scales/24hr ◻ DQ, Sbarro's, Wendy's ◻ Best Western, Days Inn ◻ KOA, repair, st police, W ◻ Quality Inn
89	I-78 E, to Allentown
85b a	PA 934, to Annville, W 2 mi ◻ Exxon/dsl ◻ Funck's Rest. ◻ to IndianTown Gap Nat Cem

(side marker: HAZLETON)
(side marker: LEBANON)

⬆N INTERSTATE 81 Cont'd

Exit #	Services
80	PA 743, Grantville, **E** 🖪 Shell/dsl 🛏 Days Inn, Hampton Inn, **W** 🖪 Exxon/dsl 🍴 Italian Delight 🛏 Comfort Suites, Holiday Inn 🄾 camping, racetrack
79mm	🅡🅢/weigh sta both lanes, full 🧑‍🦽 facilities, litter barrels, petwalk, 🚻, 🐾, vending
77	PA 39, to Hershey, **E** 🖪 Exxon/dsl 🄿🄸🄻🄾🅃/Pizza Hut/dsl/scales/24hr, Valero/dsl 🍴 Hershey Rd Rest. 🛏 Country Inn&Suites, EconoLodge, La Quinta, Motel 6, Scottish Inn 🄾 st police, to Hershey Attractions, **W** 🖪 Exit 77 TP/Subway/dsl, TA/Country Pride/dsl/scales/24hr/@, Wilco/Hess/Perkins/Stuckey's/dsl/24hr/@ 🍴 McDonald's 🛏 Holiday Inn Express 🄾 Goodyear, SpeedCo, truck repair
72	to US 22, Linglestown, **E** 🖪 Hess/dsl, Sheetz/dsl, Sunoco/dsl 🍴 5 Guys Burgers, Burger King, Chipotle Mexican, McDonald's, Red Robin, Starbucks, Subway, Tonino's Pizza 🛏 Comfort Inn, Quality Inn 🄾 Advance Parts, Chrysler/Dodge/Jeep, Costco/gas, CVS Drug, Giant Foods, Harley-Davidson, Karn's Foods, Target, Toyota/Scion, U-Haul, **W** 🍴 Turkey Hill 🍴 Mikado Japanese, Sindbaad Diner, Subway 🛏 Candlewood Suites, Ramada Inn 🄾 $General
70	I-83 S, to York, 🄾🐾
69	Progress Ave, **E** 🍴 Cracker Barrel, Fox&Hound, Macaroni Grill, Starbucks, Tonino's Grill 🛏 Hampton Inn 🄾 AT&T, CVS Drug, st police, Susquehanna Shoppes, **W** 🍴 Turkey Hill/dsl 🍴 Arby's, YP Rest. 🛏 EconoLodge, Red Roof Inn, SpringHill Suites
67b a	US 22, US 322 W, PA 230, Cameron St, to Lewistown
66	Front St, **E** 🄾🄷 **W** 🖪 Exxon, Sunoco 🍴 Bro's Pizza, Front St Diner, McDonald's, Pizza Hut, Taco Bell, Wendy's 🛏 Best Value, Days Inn
65	US 11/15, to Enola, **E 1 mi** 🖪 Sunoco/dsl, Tom's 🍴 Al's Pizza, China Taste, DQ, Dunkin Donuts, McDonald's, Subway, Summerdale Diner, Wendy's 🛏 Quality Inn 🄾 $Tree, Advance Parts, Fischer Parts, K-Mart, Radio Shack, Rite Aid, Sure Fine Foods
61	PA 944, to Wertzville, **E** 🛏 Holiday Inn Express 🄾🄷 Weiss Mkt, **W** 🍴 Turkey Hill/dsl 🛏 Microtel
59	PA 581, to US 11, to I-83, Harrisburg, **E 3 mi on Carlisle Pk E** 🖪 Sunoco 🍴 Bob Evans, Burger King, Carrabba's, Denny's, Dunkin Donuts, McDonald's, Outback Steaks, TGIFriday's 🛏 Comfort Inn, Park Inn 🄾 AutoZone, Buick/GMC, Dick's, GNC, Home Depot, Hyundai, K-Mart, Lowe's, Nissan, Pepboys, Petsmart, Radio Shack, Staples, TJ Maxx
57	PA 114, to Mechanicsburg, **E 2 mi** 🖪 Sheetz/dsl 🍴 Alfredo's Pizza, Arby's, Great Wall Chinese, Isaac's Rest., KFC/LJ Silver, McDonald's, Olive Garden, Pizza Hut, Red Robin, Silver Spring Diner, Subway, Taco Bell 🛏 Ramada Ltd 🄾 Giant Foods/gas, Marshall's, Verizon, Walmart
52b a	US 11, to I-76/PA Tpk, Middlesex, **E** 🖪 🄵🄻🅈🄸🄽🄶 J/Denny's/dsl/scales/24hr/@ 🍴 Bob Evans, Dunkin Donuts, Ember's Steaks, Middlesex Diner 🛏 Best Value Inn, Days Inn, Hotel Carlisle, Red Roof Inn, Super 8 🄾🄷 **W** 🖪 Gulf, 🄻🄾🅅🄴🅂 /Wendy's/dsl/24hr, Petro/dsl/24hr/@, Sunoco/Subway 🍴 Arby's, Carelli's Subs, McDonald's, Rte 11 Diner, Waffle House 🛏 Best Western, EconoLodge, Hampton Inn, Holiday Inn Express, Howard Johnson, Motel 6, Quality Inn, Residence Inn, Rodeway Inn, Travelodge 🄾🄷 Blue Beacon, truckwash
49	PA 74 (no EZ sb return), **E** 🛏 same as 48, Sheetz, **W** 🖪 Citgo 🍴 Trindle Grill 🄾 AAA
48	PA 74, York Rd (no EZ nb return), **E** 🖪 Gulf/dsl, Hess 🍴 Burger King, Little Caesars, Mama Sprigg's Rest., McDonald's, Pizza Hut, Red Robin, Starbucks, Subway, Taco Bell 🄾 $Tree, Aldi Foods, BonTon, CVS Drug, Dunkin Donuts, Ford, Kohl's, Lowe's, Michael's, Midas, Old Navy, Petsmart, Radio Shack, Rite Aid, Target, Verizon, Weis Foods
47	PA 34, Hanover St, **E** 🍴 Chili's, Cracker Barrel 🛏 Sleep Inn 🄾 Home Depot, **W** 🍴 Applebee's, Bruster's/Nathan's, DQ, Palace China, Panera Bread, Papa John's, Rita's Custard, Subway, Super Buffet, Vinny's Rest., Wendy's 🄾 AT&T, CVS Drug, Rite Aid, Ross, Staples, TJ Maxx, Walmart
45	College St, **E** 🖪 Gulf/dsl 🍴 Alfredo Pizza, Arby's, Bonanza, Great Wall Buffet, McDonald's, Subway 🛏 Days Inn, Super 8 🄾🄷 K-Mart, Nell's Foods, Tire Pros, Verizon
44	PA 465, Allen Rd, to Plainfield, **E** 🛏 Country Inn&Suites, Fairfield Inn 🄾 st police, **W** 🖪 Sheetz 🍴 Subway
38.5mm	🅡🅢 both lanes, full 🧑‍🦽 facilities, litter barrels, petwalk, 🚻, 🐾 vending
37	PA 233, to Newville, **E** 🄾 Pine Grove Furnace SP, **W** 🄾 Col Denning SP
29	PA 174, King St, **E** 🖪 Sunoco/dsl 🛏 Rodeway Inn, **W** 🖪 Gulf, Rutter's/dsl 🍴 Bro's Pizza, Burger King, China House, Domino's, KFC, Subway, Taco Bell, Wendy's 🛏 Best Western, Theo's Motel 🄾 $General, Advance Parts, Cadillac/Chevrolet, CVS Drug, Ford, Lowe's, Verizon, vet, Walmart
24	PA 696, Fayette St, **W** 🖪 Pacific Pride
20	PA 997, Scotland, **E** 🖪 Citgo/dsl 🍴 Bonanza, McDonald's 🛏 Comfort Inn, Super 8 🄾 BonTon, Gander Mtn, JC Penney, mall, Sears/auto, **W** 🖪 Sunoco 🛏 Sleep Inn
17	Walker Rd, **W** 🖪 Sheetz 🍴 Aki Steaks, Bruster's/Nathan's, Chipotle Mexican, Fuddrucker's, Longhorn Steaks, Moe's SW Grill, Olive Garden, Panera Bread, Pizza Boxx, Red Robin, Sonic, Subway, TGIFriday's, TX Roadhouse 🛏 Buick/Chevrolet/GMC, Candlewood Suites, Country Inn&Suites, Ford, Giant Foods/gas, Kohl's, Michael's, 🄾 AT&T, Petsmart, Staples, Target, Verizon
16	US 30, to Chambersburg, **E** 🖪 Fuel Ctr, Sheetz 🍴 Arby's, Benny's Italian, Broadway Deli, Bro's Pizza, Burger King, Chris' Country Kitchen, Hoss's Rest., KFC, Little Caesars, Meadow's Custard, Montezuma Mexican, Perkins, Popeye's, Rita's Custard, Ryan's, Supreme Buffet, Waffle House, Wendy's 🛏 Days Inn 🄾 $Tree, AAA, Aldi Foods, AT&T, Curves, Harley-Davidson, Hobby Lobby, Jo-Ann Fabrics, Lowe's, Midas, NAPA, Nissan/Toyota/Scion, st police, transmissions, U-Haul, Verizon, vet, Walmart/Subway, **W** 🖪 Hess/dsl 🍴 Big Oak Cafe, Burger King, Chambersburg Diner, Copper Kettle, Hardee's, LJ Silver, McDonald's, Pat&Carla Italian, Ruby Tuesday, Starbucks, Subway, Taco Bell 🛏 Best Western,

PA

Vertical side labels: HARRISBURG, CARLISLE, CHAMBERSBURG

◻ = gas ◻ = food ◻ = lodging ◻ = other ◻ = rest stop   Copyright 2015 - the Next EXIT ®

INTERSTATE 81 Cont'd

Exit #	Services
16	Continued
	La Quinta, Sheraton, Travelodge ◻ H Advance Parts, AutoZone, Lincoln, URGENT CARE, Walgreens
14	PA 316, Wayne Ave, E ◻ Sheetz/dsl ◻ Bob Evans, Cracker Barrel ◻ Fairfield Inn, Hampton Inn, Red Carpet Inn, W ◻ KwikFill, Sheetz, Shell ◻ Applebee's, Arby's, China Buffet, China Wok, Denny's, Mario's Italian, Montezuma Mexican, Papa John's, Red Lobster, SteviB's Pizza, Subway, Twin Dragon Chinese, Wendy's ◻ Best Value, Holiday Inn Express, Quality Inn ◻ $Tree, AT&T, CVS Drug, Giant Foods/gas, GNC, K-Mart, Mr Tire, Save-a-Lot Foods, Verizon, Weis Foods
12mm	**weigh sta sb**
10	PA 914, Marion
7mm	**weigh sta nb**
5	PA 16, Greencastle, E ◻ Shell/dsl, Sunoco/dsl, Sunoco/grill/dsl, TA/Country Pride/dsl/scales/24hr/@ ◻ Arby's, McDonald's, Subway ◻ Star Inn, TA Motel ◻ Whitetail Ski Resort, W ◻ Exxon/dsl, Sheetz/dsl ◻ Castle Green Motel/rest
3	US 11, E ◻ Sunoco/dsl ◻ Bro's Pizza ◻ Comfort Inn ◻ Goodyear/auto
2mm	**Welcome Center nb, full ◻ facilities, litter barrels, petwalk, ◻, ◻, vending**
1	PA 163, Mason-Dixon Rd, W ◻ Stateline Inn, Stateline Motel ◻ Keystone RV Ctr
0mm	Pennsylvania/Maryland state line, Mason-Dixon Line

INTERSTATE 83

Exit #	Services
51b a	**I-83 begins/ends on I-81, exit 70.**
50b a	US 22, Jonestown Rd, Harrisburg, E ◻ Hess/dsl, Sunoco/dsl, USA ◻ 5 Guys Burgers, Applebee's, Arby's, Buffalo Wild Wings, Chipotle Mexican, Cold Stone, Colonial Park Diner, Domino's, El Rodeo Mexican, Gilligan's Grill, Hibachi Grill, LJ Silver, Longhorn Steaks, McDonald's, Old Country Buffet, Olive Garden; Panera Bread, Pizza Hut, Red Lobster, Red Robin, Shogun Asian, Starbucks, Subway, Taco Bell, Tonino's Pizza, Wendy's ◻ Aamco, Advance Parts, AutoZone, Best Buy, BonTon, Boscov's, Coscto/gas, Dick's, Ford, Gander Mtn, Giant Foods, Goodyear/auto, Home Depot, Jo-Ann, K-Mart, Kohl's, mall, Marshall's, Meineke, Michael's, NTB, Old Navy, PepBoys, PetCo, Radio Shack, Ross, Sears/auto, Shannon Tire/auto, Target, Tires+, U-Haul, Verizon, vet, Weis Foods, William's Tires/repair, W ◻ Sunoco/dsl ◻ DQ, Dunkin Donuts, Friendly's, Gabriella's Italian, KFC, Roberto's Pizza ◻ Rite Aid
48	Union Deposit Rd, E ◻ Sunoco ◻ Arby's, Burger King, Infinito's Buffet, Panera Bread ◻ Best Western, Hampton Inn ◻ H $Tree, Giant Foods/gas, Rite Aid, Staples, URGENT CARE, W ◻ Gulf/dsl, Sheetz/dsl ◻ ChuckeCheese, Empire Asian Bistro, Great Wall Chinese, Jimmy John's, JoJo's Pizza, McDonald's, Naples Pizza, New China, Outback Steaks, Rita's Ice Cream, Starbucks, Subway, TGIFriday's, TX Roadhouse, Waffle House, Wendy's ◻ Country Inn&Suites, EconoLodge, Fairfield Inn, Holiday Inn Express ◻ $Tree, BigLots, Family$, Hancock Fabrics, Lowe's, PriceRite Foods, Tuesday Morning, Weis Foods
47	(46b from nb), US 322 E, to Hershey, Derry St, E ◻ Hess ◻ Papa John's, Pizza Hut ◻ Home Depot, Petsmart
46b a	I-283 S, to I-76/PA Tpk, E services off I-283 S ◻ Exxon/dsl, Sunoco/dsl ◻ Bob Evans, Capitol Diner, Chili's, Five Guys, Friendly's, Lancaster Brewing Rest., Leeds Rest., McDonald's, Moe's SW Grill, Subway ◻ Courtyard, EconoLodge, Holiday Inn, Howard Johnson, La Quinta, Red Roof Inn, Sheraton, Sleep Inn, Super 8, Wyndham Garden ◻ $General, GNC, JC Penney, Kia, Target, Verizon W ◻ Taco Bell, Wendy's ◻ Days Inn
45	Paxton St, E ◻ Sheetz/dsl ◻ Applebees, Burger King, Cafe Fresco, Fiesta Mexico, Hibachi Buffet, Isaac's Rest., McDonald's, Melting Pot, Papa Joe's Pizza, Pizza Hut, Qdoba, Ruby Tuesday, Starbucks, Tomato Pie Cafe ◻ Hilton Garden, Homewood Suites, Towneplace Suites ◻ Advance Parts, Bass Pro Shops, Macy's, mall, Mazda/Subaru, Meineke, Nissan, Toyota/Scion
44b	17th St, 19th St, E ◻ Sunoco, Turkey Hill ◻ Benihana Japanese, Dunkin Donuts, Hardee's ◻ Advance Parts, AutoZone, Buick/GMC, Firestone/auto, Honda, Hyundai, Midas
44a	PA 230, 13th St, Harrisburg, E ◻ Family$, W ◻ Chevrolet, VW, downtown
43	2nd St, Harrisburg, W ◻ Crowne Plaza, Hilton ◻ H st capitol, downtown
42.5mm	Susquehanna River
42	Lemoyne
41b	Highland Park, E ◻ Turkey Hill ◻ Burger King, KFC, W ◻ Sunoco ◻ Papa Joe's ◻ Ace Hardware, Weis Foods
41a	US 15, PA 581 W, to Gettysburg
40b	New Cumberland, W ◻ Gulf/dsl ◻ Cedar Cliff Pizza, McDonald's, New China, Subway ◻ $General, CVS Drug
40a	Limekiln Rd, to Lewisberry, E ◻ Shell/dsl, Sunoco ◻ Bob Evans, John's Diner, McDonald's, Pizza Hut ◻ Budget Inn, Clarion, Comfort Inn, Fairfield Inn, Quality Inn, W ◻ Hess ◻ Best Western, Motel 6, Scottish Inn ◻ vet
39b	I-76/PA Tpk
39a	PA 114, Lewisberry Rd, E ◻ Rutter's/dsl ◻ Days Inn, Highland Inn, Red Carpet Inn
38	Reesers Summit
36	PA 262, Fishing Creek, E ◻ Hess/Dunkin Donuts ◻ Bruster's, Mamma's Pizza ◻ CVS Drug
35	PA 177, Lewisberry, E ◻ 601 Pizzaria, W ◻ Exxon ◻ Francescos, Summit Rest. ◻ Alpine Inn
34mm	**parking area/weigh sta sb**
34	Valley Green (from nb), same as 33
33mm	**parking area/weigh sta nb**
33	PA 392, Yocumtown, E ◻ Hess/Dunkin Donuts/dsl, Rutter's ◻ Brothers Pizzaria, Burger King, Golden Plate Diner, Hong Kong Buffet, KFC/Taco Bell, Maple Donuts, McDonald's, New China Buffet, Subway ◻ Super 8 ◻ $Tree, Advance Parts, Darrenkamp's Mkt, GNC, Radio Shack, Rite Aid, Verizon, Walmart/Subway
32	PA 382, Newberrytown, E ◻ Rutter's/deli/dsl/24hr, Sunoco/dsl, W ◻ Exxon/dsl
28	PA 295, Strinestown, W ◻ Rutter's/24hr ◻ 83 Diner, Wendy's
24	PA 238, Emigsville, W ◻ Sunoco/dsl ◻ 4 Bros Rest.
22	PA 181, N George St, E ◻ Rutter's ◻ Comfort Inn, Homewood Suites, W same as 21b
21b a	US 30, Arsenal Rd, to York, E ◻ Sheetz/dsl ◻ Cheddar's, Clock Diner, Qdoba, San Carlo's Rest., Starbucks ◻ Days Inn, EconoLodge, Motel 6, Sheraton ◻ AT&T, Buick/GMC, W ◻ Royal Farms/dsl, Rutter's/dsl, Sheetz/dsl ◻ 5 Guys Burgers, Arby's, Bob Evans, Burger King, Chick-fil-A, Chili's,

(side margins: **HARRISBURG**, **LEWISBERRY**, **YORK**)

⬆N INTERSTATE 83 Cont'd

Exit #	Services
21b a	Continued
	China Buffet, CiCi's, Denny's, Domino's, DQ, Dunkin Donuts, El Rodeo Mexican, Friendly's, Great Wall, Hardee's, Hoss's, Jimmy John's, KFC, Little Caesars, LJ Silver, Logan's Roadhouse, Lyndon Diner, Maple Donuts, McDonald's, Mission BBQ, Old Country Buffet, Olive Garden, Panera Bread, Pizza Hut, Quaker Steak, Rita's Custard, Ruby Tuesday, Smokey Bones BBQ, Subway, Taco Bell, Wendy's 🏠 Best Western, Motel 6, Super 8, Wingate Inn 🅞 $General, $Tree, Acura, Advance Parts, Aldi Foods, AutoZone, BJ's Whse/gas, BMW, Cadillac/Chevrolet, Chrysler/Dodge/Jeep, CVS Drug, Dick's, Gander Mtn, Giant Foods/gas, Harley-Davidson, Honda, Kia, Kohl's, Lowe's, Macy's, NTB, Old Navy, PepBoys, PetCo, Petsmart, Radio Shack, Ross, Staples, Subaru, Target, TJ Maxx, URGENT CARE, Verizon, Walmart/McDonald's, Weis Foods/gas
19	PA 462, Market St, **E** 🅖 Rutter's/dsl 🍴 Applebee's, Arby's, Aroma Buffet, Buffalo Wild Wings, Chick-fil-A, Chuck-ECheese's, DQ, Fiesta Mexico, Fuddruckers, Jimmy John's, KFC, Outback Steaks, Panera Bread, Papa John's, Perkins, Red Lobster, Rita's Custard, Starbucks, Taco Bell, Tokyo Diner, Wendy's 🏠 Quality Inn 🅞 $General, $Tree, Aamco, Advance Parts, Aldi Foods, Burlington Coats, Firestone/auto, Giant Foods/gas, Goodyear/auto, Home Depot, Lowe's, Nissan, NTB, Petco, Sam's Club/gas, Volvo, Walgreens, Walmart, Weis Foods, **W** 🅞 🎗
18	PA 124, Mt Rose Ave, Prospect St, **E** 🅖 Pacific Pride/dsl, Rutters 🍴 5 Guys Burgers, Arooga's Grille, Burger King, Nino's Pizza, Parma Pizza Grill, Pizza Hut, Subway, Sweet House Chinese 🅞 Amelia's Groceries, K-Mart, Nello Tire
16b a	PA 74, Queen St, **E** 🅖 Sunoco 🍴 Baskin-Robbins/Dunkin Donuts, Cracker Barrel, Imperial Gourmet, Isaac's Rest., John's Pizza Shop, Maple Donuts, Ruby Tuesday, Starbucks, Stone Grill 🏠 Country Inn&Suites, Hampton Inn 🅞 Giant Foods/gas, **W** 🅖 Sheetz/dsl 🍴 Chipotle, Infinito's Pizza, Jimmy John's, Little Caesar's, McDonald's, Pizza Hut/Taco Bell, S Yorke Diner, Subway, Wendy's 🅞 $General, $Tree, AT&T, BonTon, CVS Drug, Jo-Ann Fabrics, Price Rite Foods, Tuesday Morning, vet, Walgreens, Weis Mkt
15	S George St, I-83 spur into York, **W** 🅞 🎗
14	PA 182, Leader Heights, **E** 🍴 Arby's, Domino's, First Wok, Subway 🅞 vet, **W** 🅖 Rutter's 🍴 McDonald's 🏠 Holiday Inn Express 🅞 Rite Aid
10	PA 214, Loganville, **W** 🅖 Rutter's/dsl 🍴 Mamma's Pizza 🏠 Midway Motel 🅞 st police, TrueValue
8	PA 216, Glen Rock, **W** 🅞 Shrewsbury Mkt (2mi)
4	PA 851, Shrewsbury, **E** 🅖 Tom's/dsl/24hr 🍴 Bill Bateman's Grill, Cracker Barrel, Papa John's, Ruby Tuesday 🏠 Hampton Inn 🅞 Home Depot, TrueValue, **W** 🅖 Exxon/dsl 🍴 Arby's, Chick-fil-A, Coachlight Rest., Emerald Garden Chinese, Ginza Japanese, KFC/Taco Bell, McDonald's, Rita's Custard, Sons of Italy Pizzaria, Starbucks, Subway, Wendy's 🅞 $Tree, AAA, Advance Parts, Giant Foods, GNC, Mr Tire, Radio Shack, Saubel's Foods, Verizon, Walmart
2mm	**Welcome Center nb, full** ♿ **facilities, litter barrels, petwalk,** 🎗, 🖼, **vending**
0mm	Pennsylvania/Maryland state line

⬆E INTERSTATE 84

Exit #	Services
54mm	Pennsylvania/New York state line, Delaware River
53	US 6, PA 209, Matamoras, **N Welcome Ctr both lanes, full** ♿ **facilities, litter barrels, petwalk,** 🎗, 🖼, **vending** 🅖 Go24, Shell, TurkeyHill/dsl 🍴 Polar Bear Rest, Stewart's Drive-Inn, The Grill 🏠 Appl Inn 🅞 auto repair, AutoZone, fireworks, PriceChopper, **S** 🅖 Sunoco/dsl 🍴 Dunkin Donuts, McDonald's, Perkins, Roma Pizza, Subway, Village Diner, Wendy's 🏠 Best Western, Hampton Inn, Scottish Inn 🅞 $Tree, Advance Parts, Home Depot, K-Mart, Lowe's, Staples, Tristate RV Park, Walmart/Subway
46	US 6, to Milford, **N** 🅖 Sunoco/dsl, **S** 0-2 mi 🅖 Exxon/dsl, Gulf, TurkeyHill, Xtra 🍴 Apple Valley Rest., Chang Mao Chinese, China Buffet 🏠 Black Walnut B&B, Red Carpet Inn 🅞 Grand Union Foods, NAPA, Rite Aid, USPO
34	PA 739, to Lords Valley, Dingmans Ferry, **S** 🅖 Sunoco/Dunkin Donuts/dsl, Xtra/dsl 🍴 Bruno's Pizza, McDonald's, Panda Chinese, Subway 🅞 Family$, Rite Aid, USPO, Weis Foods
30	PA 402, to Blooming Grove, **N** 🅞 st police, to Lake Wallenpaupack
26mm	🆁🆂/weigh sta both lanes, full ♿ facilities, litter barrels, petwalk, 🎗, 🖼, vending
26	PA 390, to Tafton, **N** 🅖 Exxon/dsl 🅞 Tanglewood Ski Area (4mi), to Lake Wallenpaupack, **S** 🅞 to Promised Land SP
20	PA 507, Greentown, **N** 🅖 Exxon/dsl, Shell/Subway 🍴 John's Italian 🅞 Animal Park (5mi)
17	PA 191, to Newfoundland, Hamlin, **N** 🅖 Howe's/Exxon/dsl/scales/24hr 🍴 Twin Rocks Diner 🏠 Comfort Inn 🅞 dsl repair
8	PA 247, PA 348, Mt Cobb, **N** 🅖 Gulf/dsl, Sunoco/Burger King/Tim Hortons/dsl, **S** 🅖 Exxon/Subway/dsl
4	I-380 S, to Mount Pocono
2	PA 435 S, to Elmhurst
1	Tigue St, **N** 🅖 Best Western, **S** 🅖 Valero/dsl
0mm	**I-84 begins/ends on I-81, exit 54.**

⬆E INTERSTATE 90

Exit #	Services
46mm	Pennsylvania/New York state line, **Welcome Ctr/weigh sta wb, full** ♿ **facilities, litter barrels, petwalk,** 🎗, 🖼, **vending**
45	US 20, to State Line, **N** 🅖 KwikFill/dsl/scales 🍴 McDonald's, **S** 🅖 BP/Subway/dsl 🏠 Red Carpet Inn 🅞 fireworks, Niagara Falls Info
41	PA 89, North East, **N** 🅖 Shell/repair 🍴 New Harvest Rest. 🏠 Holiday Inn Express, Super 8, Vineyard B&B, **S** 🅞 Family Affair Camping (4mi), winery

PA

🅖 = gas 🍽 = food 🛏 = lodging 🅞 = other Ⓡ🅢 = rest stop   Copyright 2015 - the Next EXIT ®

⬆E INTERSTATE 90 Cont'd

Exit #	Services
37	I-86 E, to Jamestown
35	PA 531, to Harborcreek, N 🅖 TA/Country Pride/Pizza Hut/Subway/dsl/scales/24hr/@ 🛏 Rodeway Inn 🅞 Blue Beacon, dsl repair
32	PA 430, PA 290, to Wesleyville, N 🅖 Country Fair, st police, S 🅞 camping
29	PA 8, to Hammett, N 🅖 Country Fair 🍽 Wendy's 🅞🅗 S 🛏 Best Value 🅞 dsl repair, Peterbilt
27	PA 97, State St, Waterford, N 🅖 Country Fair/dsl, Kwikfill 🍽 Arby's, Barbato's Italian, Doc Holiday's Grill, McDonald's 🛏 Days Inn, La Quinta, Red Roof Inn, Tallyho Inn 🅞🅗 S 🅖 ⛽/Subway/dsl/scales/24hr, Shell/Tim Hortons/dsl 🛏 Quality Inn, Super 8 🅞 casino
24	US 19, Peach St, to Waterford, N 🅖 Country Fair, KwikFill 🍽 5 Guys Burgers, Applebee's, Burger King, Chick-fil-A, Chipotle Mexican, ChuckeCheese, Cracker Barrel, Dunkin-Donuts, Eat'n Park, Famous Dave's BBQ, Golden Corral, KFC, Krispy Kreme, Longhorn Steaks, McDonald's, Old Country Buffet, Olive Garden, Panera Bread, Qdoba, Quaker Steak&Lube, Quiznos, S&S Buffet, Safari Grill, Steak'n Shake, Subway, Taco Bell, TGIFriday's, Tim Hortons, TX Roadhouse 🛏 Courtyard, Hilton Garden 🅞🅗 $Tree, Advance Parts, AT&T, Best Buy, Giant Eagle Foods, Hobby Lobby, Home Depot, Jo-Ann Fabrics, Kohl's, Lowe's, Marshall's, Petsmart, Sam's Club/gas, Staples, Target, URGENT CARE, Verizon, Walmart/Subway, Wegman's Foods, S 🅖 BP/dsl, Country Fair, Shell/dsl 🍽 Bob Evans, Boston's Rest. 🛏 Comfort Inn, Country Inn&Suites, EconoLodge, Hampton Inn, Holiday Inn Express, Microtel, Residence Inn, Wingate Inn 🅞 waterpark
22b a	I-79, N to Erie, S to Pittsburgh, N 3-5 mi services in Erie
18	PA 832, Sterrettania, N 🅖 Marathon/dsl 🍽 Burger King 🅞 Presque Passage RV Park, to Presque Isle SP, Waldameer Park (8mi), S 🍽 Beechwood Rest. 🛏 Quality Inn 🅞 golf, KOA
16	PA 98, to Franklin Center, Fairview, S 🅞 Follys Camping (2mi), Mar-Da-Jo-Dy Camping (5mi)
9	PA 18, to Girard, Platea, N 🅞 Fiesler's Service/repair/tires, st police, S 🛏 Green Roof Inn (2mi)
6	PA 215, to Albion, East Springfield, N 🛏 lodging
3	US 6N, to Cherry Hill, West Springfield, N 🛏 lodging on US 20, S 🅖 State Line/deli/dsl/scales/24hr
2.5mm	Ⓡ🅢/weigh sta eb, info, full ♿ facilities, litter barrels, petwalk, 🅒, 🚮, vending
0mm	Pennsylvania/Ohio state line

⬆N INTERSTATE 95

Exit #	Services
51mm	Pennsylvania/New Jersey state line, Delaware River
51	PA 32, to New Hope, W Washington Crossing Hist Park
50mm	Welcome Center sb, full ♿ facilities, litter barrels, petwalk, 🅒, 🚮, vending
49	PA 332, to Yardley, Newtown, W 🍽 Dunkin Donuts 🛏 Hampton Inn 🅞🅗 to Tyler SP
46b a	US 1 to I-276, PA TPK, Langhorne, Oxford Valley, E 🅞🅗
44	US 1, PA 413, to Penndel, Levittown, E 🅖 Shell/7-11/dsl 🍽 Arrano Hibachi Steaks, Blue Fountain Diner, Buffalo Wild Wing, ChuckECheese's, Dunkin Donuts, Friendly's, Great American Diner, Hong Kong Pearl, Langhorne Ale House, Ming's Asian, Olive Garden, Panera Bread, Red Lobster, Ruby Tuesday, Subway, Wendy's 🛏 Sheraton 🅞🅗 $Tree,

---

44	Continued Acura, Chrysler/Dodge/Jeep, Firestone/auto, Ford, Goodyear/auto, Harley-Davidson, Honda, Hyundai/Suzuki, Kia, K-Mart, Lincoln, Lowe's, Marshall's, Mazda, PepBoys, Redner's Whse Mkt, Sam's Club, Staples, Subaru, Target, TJ Maxx, VW/Volvo, W 🅖 LukOil/dsl 🍽 Denny's, McDonald's 🅞 Toyota/Scion, U-Haul
40	PA 413, I-276, to Bristol Bridge, Burlington, E 🅖 Hess/Dunkin Donuts/dsl, WaWa 🍽 Fish Factory Rest., Golden Eagle Diner, KFC, McDonald's 🅞🅗 Chevrolet
37	PA 132, to Street Rd, W 🅖 BP/dsl, Sunoco/dsl 🍽 Burger King, Chili's, China Sun Buffet, Dunkin Donuts, Gino's Burgers/Chicken, Golden Corral, IHOP, McDonald's, Old Country Buffet, Popeye's, Sonic, TX Roadhouse, Wendy's 🅞 $Tree, 7-11, Advance Parts, Aldi Foods, Giant Foods, GNC, Goodyear/auto, K-Mart, Kohl's, PepBoys, Radio Shack, Ross, Save-A-Lot, U-Haul, Walgreens, WaWa
35	PA 63, to US 13, Woodhaven Rd, Bristol Park, W 🅖 BP, Exxon, Liberty, LukOil, Sunoco/dsl 🍽 Arby's, Bob Evans, Boston Mkt, Burger King, Champs Pizza, Dave&Buster's, Dunkin Donuts, Dynasty Rest., Grand China Buffet, Hibachi Buffet, Joe Santucci's, KFC, McDonald's, McDonald's, Mr V's Steaks, Old Haven Pizza, Panda King, Pizza Hut, Rita's Custard, Ruby Tuesday, Supreme Buffet, Taco Bell, Uno, Wendy's 🛏 Hampton Inn 🅞🅗 $Tree, Acme Foods, BigLots, Burlington Coats, Dick's, Home Depot, Marshall's, NTB, Old Navy, Pathmark Foods, Rite Aid, Sam's Club, Tires+, Verizon, Walmart, WaWa
32	Academy Rd, W 🅞🅗 K-Mart
30	PA 73, Cottman Ave, W 🅖 Sunoco
27	Bridge St, W 🅖 7-11, BP, Exxon, LukOil 🍽 Dunkin Donuts 🅞🅗 Rite Aid
26	to NJ 90, Betsy Ross Brdg, W 🅖 BP, Hess, Sunoco/dsl 🍽 Applebee's, Burger King, KFC, McDonald's, Wendy's 🅞 Home Depot, Lowe's, ShopRite Foods, Target
25	Allegheny Ave, W 🅖 Sunoco 🅞🅗 WaWa
23	Lehigh Ave, Girard Ave, E casino, W 🅖 Exxon 🍽 Applebee's, Arby's, Coldstone, Dunkin Donuts, Pizza Hut, Rita's Custard 🅞🅗 AutoZone, CVS Drug, Family$, GNC, PepBoys, Radio Shack, Rite Aid, WaWa
22	I-676, US 30, to Central Philadelphia, Independence Hall
20	Columbus Blvd, Penns Landing, E 1-2 mi on Columbus 🅖 BP, Liberty/WaWa/dsl, LukOil/dsl 🍽 Burger King, Champp's Rest., ChartHouse Rest., Chick-fil-A, Dave&Buster's, Famous Dave's BBQ, IHOP, La Veranda Italian, Longhorn Steaks, McDonald's, Moshulu Rest., Ruby Buffet, Wendy's 🛏 Comfort Inn, Hyatt Hotel (1mi), Sheraton 🅞 $Tree, Best Buy, Home Depot, Lowe's, Marshall's, PepBoys, ShopRite Foods, Staples, Target, Verizon, Walmart
19	I-76 E, to Walt Whitman Bridge, E 🅖 BP, Exxon/dsl, Sunoco 🍽 Burger King, Dunkin Donuts, KFC, Little Caesars, McDonald's, Pizza Hut 🛏 Holiday Inn, to stadiums 🅞 Aldi Foods
17	PA 611, to Broad St, Pattison Ave, W 🅞🅗 to Naval Shipyard, to stadium
15mm	Schuylkill River
15	Enterprise Ave, Island Ave (from sb)
14	Bartram Ave, Essington Ave (from sb)
13	PA 291, to I-76 W (from nb), to Central Philadelphia, E 🅖 Exxon/dsl 🛏 Days Inn, Guest Quarters, Hilton, Marriott, Renaissance Inn, Residence Inn, Sheraton, Sheraton Suites, Westin Suites
12	E Philadelphia Intl 🛫, services same as 10

Side labels: LEVITTOWN · ERIE · PHILADELPHIA AREA

PA

INTERSTATE 95 Cont'd

Exit #	Services
10	PA 291, Bartrom Ave, (from nb), Cargo City, **E** 🛏 Marriott, Renaissance Hotel, **W** 🅖 WaWa/dsl 🍴 Ruby Tuesday 🛏 Courtyard, Embassy Suites, Extended Stay America, Extended Stay Deluxe, Fairfield Inn, Hampton Inn, Microtel, Studio+ 🅞 Heins NWR
9b a	PA 420, to Essington, Prospect Park, **E** 🅖 Sunoco/dsl, Valero/dsl 🍴 Denny's, Lehmans Rest., Mel's Diner, Philly Diner 🛏 Comfort Inn, Motel 6, Ramada Inn, Red Roof Inn, Residence Inn, SpringHill Suites, Wyndham Garden 🅞 USPO, WaWa
8	to Chester Waterfront, Ridley Park, **W** on US 13 🍴 Stargate Diner
7	I-476 N, to Plymouth, Meeting
6	PA 352, PA 320, to Edgmont Ave, **E** 1 mi on US 13 🍴 McDonald's, Popeye's 🅞 Radio Shack, Walmart/Subway **W** 🛏 Days Inn/Dawn's Diner
5	Kerlin St (from nb), **E** 🅖 Gulf
4	US 322 E, to NJ, to Barry Bridge, **W** 🛏 Highland Motel
3	(from nb, no EZ return)US 322 W, Highland Ave, **E** 🅖 Sunoco/dsl 🅞 Ford, Goodyear
2	PA 452, to US 322, Market St, 🅖 Exxon 🍴 McDonald's, Subway
1	Chichester Ave, **E** 🅖 Sunoco 🅞 fireworks, **W** 🅖 BP 🅞 transmissions, WaWa
0mm	Pennsylvania/Delaware state line, **Welcome Ctr/weigh sta nb, full 🅫 facilities, litter barrels, petwalk, 🅲, 🅟, vending**

INTERSTATE 99

Exit #	Services
I-99 begins/ends on I-80, exit 161	
83	PA 350, Bellefonte, Bellafonte, **E** 🅖 Weis Foods/gas, **W** 🅖 Lyken's Mkt 🍴 Bonfatto's Rest., Burger King, Pizza Hut 🅞 Rite Aid, TrueValue
81	PA 26 S, to PA 64, to Pleasant Gap
80	Harrison Rd (from nb, no re-entry)
78b a	PA 150, to Bellafonte, **W** 🅖 Sheetz/dsl 🍴 Bro's Pizza, Colts Rest. 🛏 EconoLodge 🅞 auto repair, Ford
76	Shiloh Rd, **E** 🅖 Sheetz/dsl 🍴 Garfields, McDonald's, Perkins, Quaker Steak, Rey Azteca 🛏 Best Western 🅞 $Tree, AAA, Advance Parts, Barnes&Noble, BigLots, BonTon, Chevrolet, JC Penney, Jo-Ann Fabrics, Macy's, Office Depot, Ross, Sam's Club, Sears, Subaru, Walmart/Subway
74	Innovation Park, Beaver Stadium, Penn State U
73	US 322 E, Lewiston, State College
71	Woodycrest, Tofftrees, **E** 🍴 Applebee's, Chick-fil-A, Cracker Barrel, Eat'n park, McDonald's, Olive Garden, Outback Steaks, Red Lobster, Starbucks, TX Roadhouse 🛏 Hampton Inn, Holiday Inn Express, SpringHill Suites 🅞 $Tree, Best Buy, Dick's, Kohl's, Michael's, PetCo, Radio Shack, Target, Verizon, Walmart, Wegman's Foods, **W** 🍴 Down Under Cafe 🛏 Marriott Golf Resort
69	US 322 E, Valley Vista Dr, **E** 🅖 Sheetz/dsl 🅞 Home Depot, Lowe's
68	Skytop Mtn Rd, Grays Woods, Waddle
62	US 322 W, to Phillipsburg (from sb)
61	to US 322 W, Port Matilda, **E** 🅖 Lykens Mkt/Sub Express/dsl 🍴 Brother's Pizza 🛏 Port Matilda Hotel 🅞 USPO
52	PA 350, **W** 🅖 Snappy's/Subway/dsl
48	PA 453, Tyrone, **W** 🅖 Sheetz/dsl 🍴 Burger King, Nino's Pizza, Subway 🅞 a USPO, Rite Aid

STATE COLLEGE (vertical label)

South Carolina state map showing Interstate routes including I-26, I-77, I-20, I-95 and cities: Monticello, Lugoff, Bishopville, Darlington, Florence, Columbia, Forest Acres, Rimbert, Ashwood, Sumter, Hopkins, Fort Motte, Sardinia, Alcolu, Manning, North, Summerton, Orangeburg, Santee, Barnwell, Bamberg, Holly Hill, St George, Harleyville. **SC**

Exit #	Services
45	Tipton, Grazierville, **W** 🅖 Rossi's 🍴 Aunt Nettie's Cafe 🅞 🅗 DelGrosso's Funpark, Ford
41	PA 865 N, Bellwood, **E** 🅞 Ft Roberdeau HS (6mi), **W** 🅖 Martin Gen Store/dsl, Sheetz/dsl 🅞 DelGrosso's Funpark (3 mi)
39	PA 764 S, Pinecroft, **W** 🍴 La Scalia Rest. 🛏 Comfort Inn, Days Inn 🅞 Martin's Foods, Oak Spring Winery
33	17th St, Altoona, **E** same as 32, **W** 🅖 Sheetz/dsl 🅞 Aldi Foods, Lowe's, Railroader Museum, U-Haul
32	PA 36, Frankstown Rd, Altoona, **E** 🅖 GetGo, Sheetz/dsl 🍴 Chili's, Chipotle, DQ, Millie's Pizza, Panera Bread, Subway, TX Roadhouse 🅞 Barnes&Noble, Best Buy, Boscov's, Canoe Cr SP, Dick's, Giant Eagle Foods, GNC, Home Depot, Kohl's, Michael's, PetCo, Ross, Staples, Verizon, **W** 🅖 Sheet/dsl 🍴 ChuckeCheese, Dunkin Donuts, El Campesino Mexican, Five Guys, Honeybaked Ham, HongKong Buffet, McDonald's, Olive Garden, Papa John's, Perkins, Pizza Hut, Red Lobster, Subway, Wendy's 🛏 EconoLodge, Holiday Inn Express, Super 8 🅞 🅗 $Tree, AT&T, AutoZone, Chrysler/Dodge/Jeep, CVS Drug, Jo-Ann Fabrics, Nissan, Rite Aid, Save-A-Lot, URGENT CARE, USPO, Walgreens
31	Plank Rd, Altoona, **E** 🍴 Friendly's, Jethro's Rest., King's Rest., Montezuma Mexican, Outback Steaks, TGIFriday's 🛏 Altoona Grand Hotel 🅞 Field&Stream, Firestone/auto, Radio Shack, Sam's Club/gas, st police, Target, TJ Maxx, Walmart/McDonald's, **W** 🅖 GetGo 🍴 Applebee's, Arby's, Bob Evans, Burger King, Casa Valadez, Champs Grill, Coldstone, Cracker Barrel, Denny's, Eat'n Park, Gourmet Buffet, KFC, Little Ceasars, LJ Silver, Longhorn Steaks, Taco Bell 🛏 Hampton Inn, Motel 6 🅞 Advance Parts, BigLots, Buick/GMC, Hobby Lobby, JC Penney, K-Mart, Macy's, Martin's/gas, Petco, Sears/auto, Verizon, Weis Foods
28	US 22, to Ebensburg, Holidaysburg
23	PA 36, PA 164, Roaring Spring, Portage, **E** 🅖 GetGo/dsl, Sheetz/24hr, Turkey Hill 🍴 Backyard Burger 🅞 🅗 truck repair, Walmart/Subway
15	Claysburg, King, Claysburg, King, **W** 🅖 Sheetz/dsl 🍴 Subway 🅞 $General
10	to Imler, **W** 🍴 Slick's Ivy Stone Rest. (2mi), Blue Knob SP (8mi)
7	PA 869, Osterburg, St Clairsville, **W** 🍴 Slick's Ivy Stone Rest. (2mi), Blue Knob SP
3	PA 56, Johnstown, Cessna, **E** 🅞 st police, truck parts
1	I-70/76, **E** 🅖 GetGo/McDonald's/dsl, Pacific Pride/dsl, Sheetz/dsl, Shell/Subway/dsl 🍴 Bedford Diner, Clara's Place, Denny's, Ed's Steaks, Hoss' Rest., LJ Silver, Pizza Hut, Salsa's Mexican, Wendy's 🛏 Best Value, Budget Host, Fairfield Inn, Hampton Inn, Quality Inn, Rodeway Inn, Travelodge
0	**I-99 begins/ends on US 220.**

ALTOONA (vertical label)

PA (tab marker)

🅟 = gas 🍽 = food 🛏 = lodging Ⓞ = other 🆁🆂 = rest stop   Copyright 2015 - the Next EXIT ®

INTERSTATE 476

Exit #	Services
131	US 11, US 6. **I-476 begins/ends on I-81**, services same as I-81, exit 194.
122	Keyser Ave, Old Forge, Taylor
121mm	toll plaza
115	I-81, PA 315, Wyoming Valley, Pittston, **W** 🅟 Mobil, (🅿🍽)/ Wendy's/dsl/scales/24hr, Sunoco 🍽 Arby's, McDonald's, Perkins 🛏 Knight's Inn, Ramada Inn Ⓞ Chevrolet
112mm	toll plaza
105	PA 115, Wilkes-Barre, Bear Creek, **E** 🅟 BP, Exxon, PSC
97mm	parking areas both lanes
95	I-80, PA 940, Pocono, Hazleton, **W** 🅟 WaWa 🍽 A&W/ LJ Silver, Arby's, McDonald's, Subway 🛏 Comfort Inn, EconoLodge, Holiday Inn Express, Mtn Laurel Resort, Pocono Inn/Resort, Quality Inn, Split Rock Resort
90mm	parking area sb
86mm	**Hickory Run Service Plaza both lanes**, 🅟 Sunoco/dsl 🍽 Breyer's, hot dogs, McDonald's
74	US 209, Mahoning Valley, Lehighton, Stroudsburg, **W** 🅟 Shell/Subway/dsl 🍽 Trainer's Inn Rest. 🛏 Country Inn&Suites, Hampton Inn
71mm	Lehigh Tunnel
56mm	**Allentown Service Plaza both lanes**, 🅟 Sunoco/dsl 🍽 Big Boy, Hershey's Ice Cream, Pizza Hut, Roy Rogers
56	I-78, US 22, PA 309, Lehigh Valley, **E** 🅟 Gulf 🍽 Dunkin Donuts, Quiznos, Red Robin, Trivet Diner, Wendy's 🛏 Comfort Inn, Days Inn, McIntosh Inn Ⓞ BMW, CVS Drug, Infiniti, Jaguar, K-Mart, Land Rover, Staples, **W on US 22** 🅟 Mobil, Sunoco 🍽 Chris Rest., Parma Pizza 🛏 Best Western Ⓞ CVS Drug

44	PA 663, Quakertown, Pottstown, **E** 🅟 BP, Mobil/dsl 🍽 Avanti Grill, Faraco's Pizza 🛏 Best Western (3mi), Comfort Suites, Hampton Inn, Holiday Inn Express, Rodeway Inn Ⓞ 🅷
37mm	parking area sb
31	PA 63, Lansdale, **E** 🅟 Exxon, Lukoil, WaWa 🍽 Bones Grill 🛏 Best Western, Courtyard, Lansdale Motel, Residence Inn Ⓞ 🅷
20	Germantown Pike W, to I-276 W, PA Tpk W
19	Germantown Pike E
18b a	(18 from sb), Conshoshocken, Norristown, **E** 🅟 Lukoil, Sunoco 🍽 Andy's Diner, Baja Fresh, Burger King, Domino's, Dunkin Donuts, Illiano's Pizza, McDonald's, Outback Steaks, Panera Bread, Rita's Ice Cream, Salad Works, Starbucks 🛏 Hampton Inn Ⓞ Barnes&Noble, Best Buy, Cracker Barrel, Dick's, Genuradi's Foods, Giant Foods, Giant Foods, Lowe's, Marshall's, Office Depot, Old Navy, Petsmart, Ross, Ruby Tuesday, Target, Toyota/Scion, **W** 🍽 Papa John's, Uno, Wendy's Ⓞ BJ's Whse, Ford, Home Depot, Honda, Hyundai, Kia, Mazda, Michael's, Nissan, Porsche
16b a	(16 from sb), I-76, PA 23, to Philadelpia, Valley Forge
13	US 30, **E** 🅟 Shell 🍽 Campus Pizza, Nova Grill, Winger's Ⓞ 🅷 Staples, to Villanova U, USPO
9	PA 3, Broomall, Upper Darby, **E** 🍽 Barnaby's Rest Ⓞ 🅷
5	US 1, Lima, Springfield, **E** 🍽 Dragon Garden, Mesa Mexican Ⓞ AT&T, Giant Foods, Jo-Ann Fabrics, Marshall's, Old Navy, Petsmart, Verizon, Walmart
3	Baltimore Pike, Media, Swarthmore, **E** 🅟 Lukoil 🍽 Ruby Tuesday Ⓞ 🅷 Macy's, Swarthmore Coll, Target
1	McDade Blvd, **E** 🅟 Exxon 🍽 Dunkin Donuts, KFC, McDonald's, Panda Chinese Ⓞ CVS Drug, Rite Aid
0mm	**I-476 begins/ends on I-95, exit 7.**

RHODE ISLAND

INTERSTATE 95

Exit #	Services
43mm	Rhode Island/Massachusetts state line
30 (42)	East St, to Central Falls, **E** 🍽 Dunkin Donuts, Subway
29 (41)	US 1, Cottage St, **W** 🍽 d'Angelo's
28 (40)	RI 114, School St, **E** 🅟 Sunoco Ⓞ 🅷 Car Pros, to hist dist, Yarn Outlet
27 (39)	US 1, RI 15, Pawtucket, **W** 🅟 Shell/repair, Sunoco/dsl/24hr 🍽 Burger King, Dunkin Donuts, Ground Round 🛏 Comfort Inn
26 (38)	RI 122, Lonsdale Ave (from nb), **E** Ⓞ U-Haul
25 (37)	US 1, RI 126, N Main St, Providence, **E** 🅟 Gulf, Hess, Shell 🍽 Chili's, Dunkin Donuts, Gregg's Rest., Subway Ⓞ 🅷 PepBoys, Rite Aid, URGENT CARE, Walgreens, **W** 🅟 Gulf/dsl, Hess 🍽 Burger King, Chelo's Rest. Ⓞ AAA, Aamco, Suzuki
24 (36.5)	Branch Ave, Providence, **W** 🅟 Mobil 🍽 Wendy's Ⓞ Stop&Shop, URGENT CARE, Walmart/Subway, downtown
23 (36)	RI 146, RI 7, Providence, **E** 🅟 Mobil/dsl 🛏 Marriott Ⓞ 🅷 **W** Ⓞ USPO
22 (35.5)	US 6, RI 10, Providence, **E** 🍽 Cheesecake Factory, Dave&Buster's Ⓞ CVS Drug, JC Penney, Macy's, mall, Nordstrom's
21 (35)	Broadway St, Providence, **E** 🛏 Hilton, Regency Plaza
20 (34.5)	I-195, to E Providence, Cape Cod
19 (34)	Eddy St, Allens Ave, to US 1, **W** 🍽 Dunkin Donuts, Wendy's Ⓞ 🅷

18 (33.5)	US 1A, Thurbers Ave, **W** 🅟 Shell/dsl 🍽 Burger King Ⓞ 🅷
17 (33)	US 1 (from sb), Elmwood Ave, **W** Ⓞ Cadillac, Tires Whse
16 (32.5)	RI 10, Cranston, **W** Ⓞ Williams Zoo/park
15 (32)	Jefferson Blvd, **E** 🅟 Mobil 🍽 Bugaboo Creek Steaks, Dunkin Donuts, Shogun Steaks 🛏 Courtyard, La Quinta, Motel 6, **W** Ⓞ Ryder Trucks
14 (31)	RI 37, Post Rd, to US 1, **W** 🅟 Shell, Sunoco 🍽 Burger King Ⓞ 🅷 CVS Drug, Ford/Lincoln, Mazda, Volvo
13 (30)	**E 1 mi** 🅟 Shell, Sunoco/Dunkin Donuts 🍽 Chelo's Grill, Legal Seafood, Wendy's 🛏 Best Western, Comfort Inn, Hampton Inn, Hilton Garden, Holiday Inn Express, Homestead Suites, Homewood Suites, Radisson, Residence Inn Ⓞ TF Green 🔁
12b (29)	RI 2, I-295 N (from sb)
12a	RI 113 E, to Warwick, **E** 🅟 Shell/Dunkin Donuts/dsl 🛏 Crowne Plaza Hotel Ⓞ Lowe's, Stop&Shop, **W** 🅟 Sunoco 🍽 ChuckeCheese, Wendy's Ⓞ Kohl's, mall, Sears/auto, Walmart/Subway
11 (29)	I-295 N (exits left from nb), to Woonsocket
10b a (28)	RI 117, to Warwick, **W** Ⓞ 🅷
9 (25)	RI 4 S, E Greenwich
8b a (24)	RI 2, E Greenwich, **E** 🅟 Shell/dsl 🍽 China Buffet, Coldstone, Dunkin Donuts, McDonald's, Outback Steaks, Panera Bread, Ruby Tuesday, TX Roadhouse 🛏 Extended Stay America Ⓞ AT&T, CVS Drug, Dave's Mkt, Walgreens, **W 0-2 mi** 🅟 Citgo, Sunoco/dsl 🍽 5 Guys Burgers, Agave's Mexican, Applebee's, Carrabba's, Chili's, Denny's, KFC, Olive Garden, PapaGino's Pizza, Smokey Bones BBQ, TGIFriday's, Wen

PROVIDENCE

E GREENWICH

PA

RI

🔼N INTERSTATE 95 Cont'd

Exit #	Services
8b a (24)	Continued
	dy's 🏠 SpringHill Suites 🅞 Acura, Aldi Foods, Arlington RV Ctr, Audi/Bentley/BMW/Inifinti/Lexus/Mini/Porsche/Smart, Barnes&Noble, Best Buy, Cadillac, Dick's, GNC, Goodyear/auto, Home Depot, Honda, Hyundai, Jaguar, Jo-Ann Fabrics, Land Rover, Lowe's, mall, Mercedes, Michael's, Nissan, Pep-Boys, Petco, Petsmart, Staples, Stop&Shop, Target, vet, VW
7 (21)	to Coventry, E 🅖 Mobil/dsl, W 🍴 Applebee's, Cilantro Mexican, Cracker Barrel, Denny's, Dunkin Donuts, Honeydew Donuts, Riccotti's Subs, Wendy's 🏠 Fairfield Inn, Hampton Inn, Residence Inn 🅞 BJ's Whse/gas, CVS Drug, GNC, Home Depot, Radio Shack, Walmart/Subway
6mm	Welcome Ctr/rest area nb, full ♿ facilities, litter barrels, pet-walk, 🅞, 🅞 vending
6a (20)	Hopkins Hill Rd, W 🍴 Dunkin Donuts 🅞 park&ride
6 (18)	RI 3, to Coventry, W 🅖 Lukoil, Shell/dsl/24hr, Sunoco/dsl 🍴 Dunkin Donuts, Europa Pizza, Gentleman Farmer Diner, Subway, Venus Pizza 🏠 Best Western, Super 8 🅞 TrueValue
5b a (15)	RI 102, W 🅖 R.I.'s Only Trkstp/dsl/scales/24hr 🍴 Dan's Rest. 🏠 Classic Motor Lodge
10mm	rest area/weigh sta both lanes
4 (9)	RI 3, to RI 165 (from nb), Arcadia, W 🅞 Arcadia SP, camping
3b a (7)	RI 138 E, to Kingston, Wyoming, E 🍴 Dunkin Donuts, Mc-Donald's, Wendy's 🅞 Rite Aid, Stop&Shop/gas, vet, W 🅖 Gulf, Hess, Mobil 🍴 Bali Village Chinese, Dragon Palace, Subway, Village Pizza, Wood River Inn Rest. 🏠 Stagecoach House B&B 🅞 CVS Drug, Family$, NAPA, USPO, Walgreens
2 (4)	Hope Valley
1 (1)	RI 3, to Hopkinton, Westerly, E 🅞 🏥 beaches, RV camping, to Misquamicut SP
0mm	Rhode Island/Connecticut state line

🔼N INTERSTATE (Providence)

Exit #	Services
2b a (4)	I-95, N to Boston, S to Providence. I-295 begins/ends on I-95, exit 4 in MA. Exits 2-1 are in MA.
1b a (2)	US 1, E 🅖 Mobil/Dunkin Donuts/dsl 🍴 99 Rest., Chicago Grill, ChuckeCheese, d'Angelo's, Friendly's, Hearth'n Kettle, Longhorn Steaks, Panera Bread, PapaGino's Italian, Ruby Tuesday, TGIFriday's 🅞 $Tree, Best Buy, BJ's Whse, Buick/Chevrolet/GMC, CVS Drug, Dick's, JC Penney, Jo-Anne Fabrics, Lowe's, Macy's, mall, Marshalls, Michael's, Office Depot, Old Navy, Petsmart, Sears/auto, Staples, Stop&Shop, Target, TJMaxx, Walmart, W 🅖 Emerald/dsl, Gulf, Shell/dsl 🍴 Applebee's, Dunkin Donuts 🏠 Holiday Inn Express, Pineapple Inn, Super 8 🅞 CVS Drug, Nissan, Toyota/Scion
0mm	Rhode Island/Massachusetts state line, Exits 1-2 are in MA
11 (24)	RI 114, to Cumberland, E 🅖 Shell/dsl, Sunoco 🍴 Dunkin Donuts, HoneyDew Donuts 🅞 CVS Drug, Dave's Foods, USPO, W 🍴 J's Deli, Pizza Pasta&More, Saki's Pizza/subs 🅞 Diamond Hill SP
10 (21)	RI 122, E 🅖 Gulf, Lukoil 🍴 Burger King, Dunkin Donuts, Forno Pizza, Jacky's Rest., McDonald's, Ronzio Pizza 🅞 Verizon, W 🍴 Forno Pizza, Fortune House Chinese, Pamfilios Deli, Subway 🅞 Ace Hardware, Curves, CVS Drug, Rite Aid, Seabra Foods, URGENT CARE
20mm	Blackstone River
19.5mm	weigh sta/🆁🆂 (full facilities) nb 🍴 Baskin-Robbins/Dunkin Donuts
9b a (19)	RI 146, Woonsocket, Lincoln, E 🏠 Courtyard
8b a (16)	RI 7, N Smithfield, E 🍴 European Cafe, W 🅖 7-11/dsl, Shell 🍴 Decarlo's Italian, Dunkin Donuts, House of Pizza, Parentes

PROVIDENCE

8b a (16)	Continued
	Rest. 🏠 Comfort Suites, Hampton Inn, Holiday Inn Express 🅞 Smith-Appleby House
7b a (13)	US 44, Centerdale, E 🅖 Hess, Valero 🍴 Ball's Grill, Cancun Mexican, La Cocina Italian 🅞 🏥 CarQuest, NAPA, repair, W 🅖 Gulf/dsl, Mobil, Shell 🍴 A&W, Applebee's, Burger King, Chelo's Grill, Chicago Grill, Chili's, D'angelo's, Dominos, Dunkin Donuts, KFC/Taco Bell, McDonald's, Panera Bread, PapaGino's, Subway, TinTsin Chinese, Wendy's, Yamato Steaks 🅞 $Tree, AAA, AT&T, Barnes&Noble, Curves, CVS Drug, Dave's Foods, Dick's, Home Depot, Kohl's, Michael's, Old Navy, Radio Shack, Rite Aid, Staples, Stop&Shop, Target, TJ Maxx, to Powder Mill Ledges WR, URGENT CARE, Verizon
6b c (10)	US 6, to Providence, E 🅖 7-11, Shell 🍴 Atwood Grill, Burger King, D'Angelo's, Dunkin Donuts, Jacky's Rest., KFC, Newport Creamery, Noble House Chinese, Ruby Tuesday, Subway, Wendy's 🅞 AT&T, BJ's Whse, Buick/Chevrolet/GMC, Chrysler/Dodge/Jeep, CVS Drug, Honda, Kia, Office Depot, PetsMart, Rite Aid Stop&Shop, USPO
6a (9)	US 6 E Expswy, E 1 mi 🍴 McDonald's, Ribs&Co, Ruby Tuesday, Taco Bell 🅞 BJ's Whse, Home Depot, Petsmart
5 (8)	🅞 RI Resource Recovery Industrial Park
4 (7)	RI 14, Plainfield Pk, E 🅖 Hess, W 🅖 Gulf, Mobil/dsl/24hr 🍴 Dunkin Donuts, Palmieri Pizza 🅞 CVS Drug, repair
3b a (4)	rd 37, Phenix Ave, E 🅞 TF Green ✈
2 (2)	RI 2 S, to Warwick, E 🍴 Chicago Grill, Longhorn Steaks, Red Robin 🅞 JC Penney, Macy's, mall, Marshalls, Old Navy, Verizon, Walgreens, W 🅖 Mobil, Sunoco 🍴 Burger King, Chili's, Chipotle Mexican, ChuckeCheese, Dunkin Donuts, Hometown Buffet, McDonald's/playplace, Olive Garden, On-the-Border, Panera Bread, Starbucks, Subway, Taco Bell, Wendy's 🅞 AT&T, Barnes&Noble, Best Buy, Chrysler/Dodge/Keep/Kia, Home Depot, Jaguar, Kohl's, mall, PetsMart, Price Rite Foods, Rite Aid, Sears/auto, Staples, Subaru, Target, TJMaxx, Town-Fair Tire, Trader Joe's, Verizon, Walmart/Subway
1 (1)	RI 113 W, to W Warwick, same as 2
0mm	I-295 begins/ends on I-95, exit 11.

RI

INTERSTATE 20

Exit #	Services
141b a	I-95, N to Fayetteville, S to Savannah. **I-20 begins/ends on I-95, exit 160. See I-95, exit 160a for services.**
137	SC 340, to Timmonsville, Darlington, N 🅖 BP/dsl (1mi) 🅾 $General, S 🅖 Marathon
131	US 401, SC 403, to Hartsville, Lamar, N 🅖 Exxon/dsl 🅾 to Darlington Int Raceway, S 🅖 Shell/Markette/dsl
129mm	parking area both lanes, commercial vehicles only
123	SC 22, N 🅾 camping, Lee SP
121mm	Lynches River
120	SC 341, Bishopville, Elliot, N 🅖 BP/dsl 🅾 to Cotton Museum, S 🅖 Exxon/dsl 🍴 Taste of Country Rest. 🛏 Best Value Inn
116	US 15, to Sumter, Bishopville, N 🅖 Shell/KFC/dsl/24hr 🍴 McDonald's, Pizza Hut, Subway (1mi), Waffle House, Zaxby's 🛏 EconoLodge 🅾 to Cotton Museum, S 🅖 Wilco/Hess/DQ/Wendy's/dsl/scales/24hr 🍴 Huddle House, 🅾 Shaw AFB
108	SC 34, to SC 31, Manville, N 🅖 BP/dsl, S 🅖 Exxon/dsl
101	rd 329
98	US 521, to Camden, N 🅖 BP/dsl, Exxon/McDonald's, Marathon, Shell/dsl 🍴 Fatz Cafe, Waffle House 🛏 Comfort Suites, Holiday Inn Express 🅾 🅷 to Revolutionary War Park
96mm	Wateree River
93mm	**rest area both lanes, full ♿ facilities, litter barrels, petwalk, 🅲, 🛏, vending**
92	US 601, to Lugoff, N 🅖 Marathon, 🚚/DQ/Subway/dsl/scales/24hr, Shell/Bojangles/dsl 🍴 Hardee's, Waffle House 🛏 EconoLodge, Ramada Ltd
87	SC 47, to Elgin, N 🅖 BP/dsl, Shell/dsl
82	SC 53, to Pontiac, N 🅖 Mobil, Shell 🍴 Blimpie, Burger King, Egg Roll Express, Quaker Steak & Lube 🛏 ValuePlace Inn 🅾 $General, Harley-Davidson, vet, S 🅖 BP/dsl 🅾 Clothing World Outlet
80	Clemson Rd, N 🅖 Circle K, Exxon/dsl, Shell/Bojangles/dsl 🍴 China Garden, D's, Dunkin Donuts, Groucho's Deli, Henry's, Krispy Kreme, Maurice's BBQ, McDonald's, San Jose Mexican, Subway, Sumo Japanese, Travinia Italian, Waffle House, Zaxby's 🛏 Hampton Inn, Holiday Inn Express 🅾 CVS Drug, Firestone/auto, S 🍴 Wendy's 🅾 Chevrolet, Ft Jackson Nat Cem, Hyundai
76b	Alpine Rd, to Ft Jackson, N Sesquicentennial SP
76a	(76 from eb), I-77, N to Charlotte, S to Charleston
74	US 1, Two Notch Rd, to Ft Jackson, N 🅖 Mobil/dsl 🍴 Chili's, Fazoli's, Hooters, IHOP, Lizard's Thicket, Outback Steaks, Waffle House 🛏 Best Western, Comfort Suites, EconoLodge, Fairfield Inn, Hampton Inn, La Quinta, Microtel, Motel 6, Red Roof Inn 🅾 Home Depot, to Sesquicentennial SP, USPO, S 🅖 BP, Exxon, Shell 🍴 Applebee's, Bojangles, Brickhouse, China Garden, Church's, Harbor Inn Seafood, Hardee's, Honeybaked Ham, Jasmine Buffet, Maurice's BBQ, McDonald's, Monterrey Mexican, Substaion II 🛏 Days Inn 🅾 Advance Parts, AT&T, AutoZone, Best Buy, Firestone/auto, K-Mart, Lowe's, mall, Marshalls, Sears/auto, Verizon
73b	SC 277 N, to I-77 N
73a	SC 277 S, to Columbia, S 🅾 🅷
72	SC 555, Farrow Rd
71	US 21, N Main, to Blythewood, Columbia, N 🅖 Citgo/dsl, Save-a-Ton/dsl, TravelPlaza/Subway/dsl/scales/24hr/@ 🍴 McDonald's 🛏 Days Inn 🅾 tires/repair, truckwash, S 🅖 Shell
70	US 321, Fairfield Rd, S 🅖 FLYING J/Denny's/dsl/LP/24hr, Exxon 🍴 Hardee's 🛏 Super 8 🅾 Blue Beacon, truck repair
68	SC 215, Monticello Rd, to Jenkinsville, N 🅖 Exxon/dsl, Shell/dsl, S 🅖 Shell/dsl
66mm	Broad River
65	US 176, Broad River Rd, to Columbia, N 🅖 BP, El Cheapo, Exxon, Shell/Circle K 🍴 Applebee's, Bojangles, Rush's BBQ, Sonic, Subway, Waffle House 🛏 Economy Inn 🅾 $Tree, Aamco, CVS Drug, U-Haul, Walgreens, S 🅖 Hess/Godfather's Pizza, RaceWay/dsl 🍴 Arby's, Atlantic Seafood, Baskin-Robbins/Dunkin Donuts, Chick-fil-A, Church's, KFC, Lizard's Thicket, McDonald's, Nick's, Ocean View Seafood, Ruby Tuesday, Sandy's HotDogs, Scholtzsky's, Taco Bell, Wendy's, Zaxby's 🛏 American Inn, InTown Suites, Quality Inn, Ramada Ltd, Royal Inn 🅾 $General, Advance Parts, Belk, Office Depot, PepBoys, Rite Aid
64b a	I-26, US 76, E to Columbia, W to Greenville, Spartanburg
63	Bush River Rd, N 🅖 Shell/Circle K 🍴 Burger King, Cracker Barrel, Real Mexican, Subway 🛏 Travelodge 🅾 CVS Drug, S 🅖 Marathon, Murphy USA/dsl, RaceWay, Sunoco/dsl 🍴 Fuddrucker's 🛏 Best Western, DoubleTree, Knights Inn, Sleep Inn 🅾 Hamrick's, Walmart
61	US 378, W Cola, N 🅖 Exxon/Hardee's 🍴 Chick-Fil-A, Chili's, McDonald's, Taco Bell 🛏 Wingate Inn 🅾 Honda, S 🅖 BP/dsl, Shell/Burger King/dsl 🍴 Waffle House
58	US 1, W Columbia, N 🅖 Exxon, Shell/Subway/dsl 🍴 Waffle House, S 🅖 Murphy Express/dsl 🍴 Bojangles, San Jose Mexican 🛏 ValuePlace Inn 🅾 auto repair, County Tire
55	SC 6, to Lexington, N 🅖 Shell/dsl 🍴 Chicken Shack 🛏 Hampton Inn (2mi) 🅾 CarQuest, John's RV Ctr, S 🅖 BP/dsl, Kangaroo/DQ/dsl, Pops 🍴 Bojangles, Dunkin Donuts, Great Wall Chinese, Maurice's BBQ, McDonald's, Waffle House, Wendy's 🛏 Ramada Ltd 🅾 $General, CVS Drug, Piggly Wiggly
52.5mm	weigh sta wb
51	SC 204, to Gilbert, N 🅖 Exxon/dsl, Shell/Subway/dsl/24hr 🍴 Burger King, S 🅖 Loves/Chester's/McDonald's/dsl/scales/24hr, Mobil/dsl 🅾 $General
44	SC 34, to Gilbert, N 🅖 44Trkstp/rest/dsl/24hr, BP/Blimpie/dsl
39	US 178, to Batesburg, N 🅖 Exxon/dsl, S 🅖 Marathon/dsl/scales 🍴 Hillview Rest.
35.5mm	weigh sta wb
33	SC 39, to Wagener, N 🅖 Cheapway/dsl, S 🅖 KK/Huddle House/dsl/scales
29	SC 49, Wire Rd
22	US 1, to Aiken, S 🅖 BP/dsl, RaceWay/dsl, Shell/Circle K/dsl 🍴 Baynham's, Hardee's, McDonald's, Waffle House 🛏 Days Inn, Quality Inn 🅾 $General, Palmetto Lake RV Camping, to USC Aiken
20mm	parking area both lanes (commercial vehicles only)
18	SC 19, to Aiken, S 🅖 Exxon/Subway/dsl, Shell 🍴 Waffle House 🛏 Deluxe Inn, Guesthouse Inn 🅾 🅷
11	Bettis Academy Rd, SC 144, Graniteville, N 🅖 BP/Huddle House/dsl/scales/24hr, S 🅖 Wilco/Hess/Dunkin Donuts/Subway/dsl/scales/24hr
6	I-520 to N Augusta
5	US 25, SC 121, N 🅖 BP/repair/dsl, Circle K/dsl, Shell/Circle K/dsl 🍴 Bojangles, Burger King, Checkers, Little Caesars, McDonald's, Sonic, Subway, Zaxby's 🅾 $General, Advance Parts, Food Lion, Walmart, S 🅖 Marathon 🍴 Waffle House 🛏 Sleep Inn
1	SC 230, Martintown Rd, N Augusta, N 🅖 Gas+/dsl, S 🅖 Shell/Circle K/Subway/dsl 🍴 Waffle House 🅾 to Garn's Place

COLUMBIA

[Map of South Carolina showing interstate highways I-85, I-26, I-385, I-77, I-20, I-95 and cities including Greenville, Spartanburg, Gaffney, Rock Hill, Columbia, Florence, Myrtle Beach, Charleston, Beaufort, Hilton Head Island]

⬆E INTERSTATE 20 Cont'd

Exit #	Services
0.5mm	Welcome Center eb, full ♿ facilities, litter barrels, petwalk, 🚰, 📷, vending
0mm	South Carolina/Georgia state line, Savannah River

⬆E INTERSTATE 26

Exit #	Services

I-26 begins/ends on US 17 in Charleston, SC.

221b	US 17 N, to Georgetown
221a	US 17 S, to Kings St, to Savannah, N ⊙ 🅗
221	Meeting St, Charleston, E 2 mi 🍴 Church's, KFC 🏨 Hampton Inn ⊙ Family$, Piggly Wiggly, Visitors Ctr
220	Romney St (from wb)
219b	Morrison Dr, East Bay St (from eb), N 🚗 Exxon
219a	Rutledge Ave (from eb, no EZ return), to The Citadel, ⊙ College of Charleston
218	Spruill Ave (from wb), N Charleston
217	N Meeting St (from eb)
216b a	SC 7, Cosgrove Ave, to US 17 S
215	SC 642, Dorchester Rd, N Charleston, N 🚗 El Cheapo/dsl 🏨 Clarion, S 🚗 BP/dsl 🍴 Alex's Rest ⊙ Rodeway Inn
213b a	Montague Ave, Mall Dr, N 🍴 Piccadilly's, Red Lobster 🏨 Courtyard, Sheraton, ValuePlace ⊙ Charles Towne Square, S 🚗 BP/dsl, Mobil, Spinx/dsl 🍴 5 Guys Burgers, Arby's, Big Billy's Burgers, Bufflo Wild Wings, Burger King, Chick-fil-A, Ci-Ci's Pizza, Fatz Cafe, Firehouse Subs, Golden Corral, Grand Buffet, Gringos, Hardee's, IHOP, Jimmy John's, Jim'N Nick's BBQ, Kamille's Cafe, La Hacienda, McAlister's Deli, McDonald's, Panda Express, Panera Bread, Qdoba, Rita's Custard, Sake Japanese, Starbucks, Steak'n Shake, Waffle House 🏨 ALoft, Crowne Plaza, Days Inn, EconoLodge, Embassy Suites, Extended Stay Deluxe, Fairfield Inn, Hampton Inn, Hilton Garden, Holiday Inn Express, HomePlace Suites, Homestead Suites, Homewood Suites, Hyatt Place, InTown Suites, N Charleston Inn, Residence Inn, Sleep Inn ⊙ $Tree, AT&T, Old Navy, Radio Shack, Sam's Club/gas, Staples, Tanger Outlet/Framous Brands, Verizon, vet, Walmart/Subway
212c b	I-526, E to Mt Pleasant, W to Savannah, ⊙ 📷
212a	Remount Rd, Hanahan, N on US 52/78 🍴 KFC, Taco Bell ⊙ Advance Parts, AutoZone, Ford, Suzuki
211b a	Aviation Pkwy, N on US 52/78 🚗 Citgo, Exxon 🍴 Arby's, Burger King, Capt D's, Church's, KFC, McDonald's, Papa John's, Popeye's, Sonic, Subway, Super Buffet, Taco Bell, Zaxby's 🏨 Masters Inn, Radisson ⊙ O'Reilly Parts, PepBoys, PetCo, U-Haul, USPO, S 🚗 Kangaroo/dsl 🍴 Waffle House 🏨 Budget Inn
209a	to US 52 (from wb), to Goose Creek, Moncks Corner
209	Ashley Phosphate Rd, to US 52, N 🚗 Exxon, Kangaroo 🍴 Applebee's, Cane's, Carrabba's, Chick-fil-A, China Buffet, Chipotle Mexican, ChuckECheese, Denny's, Hardee's, Hooters, Jason's Deli, Jersey Mike's Subs, Jimmy John's, King Street Grill, Longhorn Steaks, Los Reyes, Moe's SW Grill, O'Charley's, Olive Garden, Outback Steaks, Perkins, Smokey Bones BBQ, Starbucks, Taco Bell, Waffle House, Wendy's, Wild Wing Cafe 🏨 Candlewood Suites, Country Hearth Inn, Country Inn&Suites, Hawthorn Inn, Holiday Inn Express, InTown Suites, Red Roof Inn, Studio+ ⊙ 🅗 $General, $Tree, AT&T, Barnes&Noble, Belk, Best Buy, BigLots, Books-A-Million, Dillard's, Firestone/auto, GNC, Hancock Fabrics, Home Depot, JC Penney, Lowe's, Marshalls, Michael's, Nissan, Office Depot, Old Navy, Ross, Sears/auto, Target, Tire Kingdom, Toyota/Scion, Verizon, Walgreens, Walmart, S 🚗 BP, Hess/dsl, RaceWay/dsl 🍴 Bojangles, Cracker Barrel, IHOP, McDonald's, Osaka Asian, Ruby Tuesday, Waffle House 🏨 Best Western, Hampton Inn, Hyatt Place, InTown Suites, La Quinta, Motel 6, Quality Inn, Relax Inn, Residence Inn, Sleep Inn, Staybridge Suites, Value Place Inn
205b a	US 78, to Summerville, N 🚗 BP, Hess/dsl 🍴 Arby's, Atl Bread Co, Bruster's, Cook-Out, Dunkin Donuts, Fortune Garden, Sonic, Subway, Waffle House, Wendy's, Zaxby's 🏨 Fairfield Inn, Hampton Inn, Holiday Inn Express, Wingate Inn

[Vertical text left margin: CHARLESTON]

[Vertical text center margin: NORTH CHARLESTON]

SC

INTERSTATE 26 Cont'd

Exit #	Services
205b a	Continued
	Ⓞ Ⓗ Charleston Southern U, CVS Drug, S Ⓖ Hess/dsl, Sunoco/dsl Ⓕ Burger King, KFC Ⓞ Advance Parts, KOA, Piggly Wiggly
204mm	Ⓡⓢ eb, full ♿ facilities, litter barrels, petwalk, Ⓒ, Ⓐ vending
203	College Park Rd, Ladson, N Ⓖ BP, Sunoco/dsl Ⓕ McDonald's, Waffle House Ⓛ Best Western, Days Inn, S Ⓞ KOA (2mi)
202mm	Ⓡⓢ wb, full ♿ facilities, litter barrels, petwalk, Ⓒ, Ⓐ vending
199b a	US 17 A, to Moncks Corner, Summerville, N Ⓖ BP, Hess/Dunkin Donuts/Godfather's Pizza/dsl, Kangaroo/dsl, ⓛⓞⓥⓔⓢ/McDonald's/dsl/scales/24hr, Shell Ⓕ China Chef, China Wok, KFC, Subway Ⓞ $General, Advance Parts, AutoZone, BiLo, Buick/GMC, CVS Drug, Family$, O'Reilly Parts, vet, S Ⓖ Shell/Circle K Ⓕ 5 Guys Burgers, Applebee's, Arby's, Atlanta Bread, Bojangles, Burger King, Chick-fil-A, China Token, Cracker Barrel, Domino's, Firewater Grille, Hardee's, IHOP, Jersey Mike's Subs, La Hacienda, Logan's Roadhouse, Marble Slab, McAlisters Deli, McDonald's, Moe's SW Grill, O'Charleys, Panera Bread, Papa John's, Perkins, Ruby Tuesday, Ryan's, Santi's Taqueria, Shoney's, Starbucks, Sticky Fingers, Waffle House, Ye Ole Fashioned Cafe, Zaxby's Ⓛ Comfort Suites, Country Inn&Suites, EconoLodge, Economy Inn, Hampton Inn, Holiday Inn Express, Quality Inn, Sleep Inn Ⓞ AT&T, Belk, Best Buy, Chrysler/Jeep, Dick's, GNC, Home Depot, Kohl's, Lowe's, Petsmart, Radio Shack, Ross, Staples, Target, Tire Kingdom, TJ Maxx, Verizon, Walgreens, Walmart, World Mkt
194	SC 16, to Jedburg, access to Foreign Trade Zone 21
187	SC 27, to Ridgeville, St George, N Ⓖ Shell, S Ⓖ BP/dsl Ⓞ Francis Beidler Forest (10mi)
177	SC 453, to Holly Hill, Harleyville, S Ⓖ Shell/dsl Ⓛ Ashley Lodge
174mm	weigh sta both lanes
172b a	US 15, to Santee, St George, S Ⓖ Horizon/Domino's/Subway/dsl/e-85/scales/24hr
169b a	I-95, N to Florence, S to Savannah
165	SC 210, to Bowman, N Ⓖ Exxon/dsl, S Ⓖ BP/dsl
159	SC 36, to Bowman, N Ⓖ ⓛⓞⓥⓔⓢ/McDonald's/dsl/scales/24hr/@, S Ⓖ Exxon
154b a	US 301, to Santee, Orangeburg, N Ⓛ Days Inn, S Ⓖ Exxon, Loves/Chesters/Subway/dsl/scales/24hr, Shell/dsl Ⓕ Waffle House
152mm	Ⓡⓢ wb, full ♿ facilities, litter barrels, petwalk, Ⓒ, Ⓐ vending
150mm	Ⓡⓢ eb, full ♿ facilities, litter barrels, petwalk, Ⓒ, Ⓐ vending
149	SC 33, to Cameron, to SC State Coll, Orangeburg, Ⓞ Claflin Coll
145b a	US 601, to Orangeburg, St Matthews, S Ⓖ BP/dsl, Exxon, Shell, Sunoco/dsl, United/dsl Ⓕ Burger King, Chick-fil-A, Cracker Barrel, Fatz Café, Hardee's, McDonald's, Ruby Tuesday, Seafood Academy, Subway, Waffle House, Wendy's, Zaxby's Ⓛ Carolina Lodge, Comfort Inn, Country Inn&Suites, Days Inn, Fairfield Inn, Hampton Inn, Holiday Inn Express, Howard Johnson, Quality Inn, Sleep Inn, Southern Lodge Ⓞ Ⓗ $General, Cadillac/Chevrolet, Chrysler/Dodge/Jeep, Ford, Nissan, Toyota/Scion

139	SC 22, to St Matthews, S Ⓖ Horizon/e-85, Mobil, Wilco/Hess/Arby's/dsl/scales/24hr Ⓞ Sweetwater Lake Camping (2.5mi)
136	SC 6, to North, Swansea, N Ⓖ Exxon/dsl
129	US 21, N Ⓖ Shell/dsl
125	SC 31, to Gaston, N Ⓞ Wolfe's Truck/trailer repair
123mm	Ⓡⓢ both lanes, full ♿ facilities, litter barrels, petwalk, Ⓒ, Ⓐ vending
119	US 176, US 21, to Dixiana, S Ⓖ BP/Subway/dsl, Exxon/dsl
116	I-77 N, to Charlotte, US 76, US 378, to Ft Jackson
115	US 176, US 21, US 321, to Cayce, N Ⓖ BP, Gulf, RaceWay, Shell/dsl Ⓕ Pizza Hut, Waffle House Ⓞ $General, $Tree, Advance Parts, Bi-Lo, CVS Drug, Family$, Reid's Foods, S Ⓖ ⓛⓞⓥⓔⓢ/DQ/Wendy's/dsl/scales/24hr, Shell/dsl Ⓕ Bojangles, Carolina Wings, Great China, Hardee's, McDonald's, Sonic, Subway Ⓛ Country Hearth Inn Ⓞ Firestone, Piggly Wiggly
113	SC 302, Cayce, N Ⓖ A1, Mobil/Burger King, Sunoco/dsl Ⓕ Waffle House Ⓛ Ⓢ Inn, Knights Inn, Masters Inn Ⓞ $General, AutoZone, O'Reilly Parts, Rite Aid, Save-A-Lot, Toyota/Scion, Walgreens, S Ⓖ BP/dsl, RaceWay, Shell/Circle K Ⓕ Lizard's Thicket, Shoney's, Subway, Waffle House Ⓛ Carolina Lodge, Country Inn&Suites, Days Inn, Sleep Inn, Travelers Inn Ⓞ Ⓢ, NAPA
111b a	US 1, to W Columbia, N Ⓖ Murphy USA/dsl, RaceWay, Shell/Circle K/dsl Ⓕ Chick-fil-A, Domino's, Dragon City Chinese, Hardee's, Little Caesars, Maurice's BBQ, Moe's SW Grill, Ruby Tuesday, San Jose, Sonic, Subway, Tokyo Grill, Waffle House, Zaxby's Ⓛ Clarion, Delta Motel, Quality Inn Ⓞ $General, $Tree, AT&T, Bi-Lo, GNC, Hobby Lobby, Pet Supplies+, Radio Shack, to USC, Walgreens, Walmart, S Ⓖ Hess/Dunkin Donuts/dsl Ⓕ Applebee's, China Chef, Fat Boy Greek, Popeye's, Wendy's Ⓞ Aldi Foods, BigLots, Family$, Lowe's, U-Haul
110	US 378, to W Columbia, Lexington, N Ⓕ Grecian Gardens, Happy China, Lizard's Thicket, McDonald's, Rush's Rest., Subway, Waffle House Ⓛ America's Inn, Hampton Inn, Holiday Inn Ⓞ CVS Drug, Family$, Food Lion, Toyota, S Ⓖ Mobil/dsl, Shell/Circle K Ⓕ Atlanta Bread, Bojangles, China Dragon, Firehouse Subs, La Fogata, Pizza Hut Ⓛ Executive Inn Ⓞ Ⓗ URGENT CARE
108b a	I-126 to Columbia, Bush River Rd, N Ⓖ BP, Exxon/dsl, Shell/dsl Ⓕ Capt D's, Chick-fil-A, Hardee's, Ruby Tuesday, Schlotzsky's, Waffle House, Wendy's, Zaxby's Ⓛ Comfort Inn, Embassy Suites, Extended Stay America, Homewood Suites, Studio+, Western Inn Ⓞ $General, Advance Parts, Belk, Chrysler/Jeep/Dodge, Dodge/Ram, Firestone/auto, Ford/Lincoln, Hyundai, Kia, Mazda, Midas, Office Depot, Rite Aid, N services off I-126, (Greystone Blvd), Verizon, S Ⓖ City Gas, Murphy USA/dsl, RaceWay/dsl, Sunoco/dsl Ⓕ Bamboo House, Fuddrucker's, Pizza Hut, Tokyo Grill Ⓛ Baymont Inn, Best Western, DoubleTree, Knights Inn, Sleep Inn Ⓞ GNC, Hamrick's, Radio Shack, Riverbanks Zoo, Walmart
107b a	I-20, E to Florence, W to Augusta
106b a	St Andrews Rd, N Ⓖ Exxon/dsl Ⓕ ChuckECheese, IHOP, Papa John's, Sonic, Top China Buffet Ⓛ Motel 6 Ⓞ $Tree, Bi-Lo, Camping World RV Ctr, CVS Drug, Infiniti, Jaguar, Nissan, Walgreens, S Ⓖ BP/dsl, Hess/Dunkin Donuts/dsl, Shell Ⓕ Domino's, King Buffet, Maurice's BBQ, McDonald's, Nick's Grill, Pizza Hut, Sandy's Hot Dogs, Substation II, Waffle House, WG's Wings, Zaxby's Ⓛ EconoLodge, Red Roof Inn Ⓞ $General, KJ's IGA, Tire Kingdom, vet
104	Piney Grove Rd, N Ⓖ Sunoco/dsl Ⓕ Hardee's, San Jose Mexican, Waffle House Ⓛ Quality Inn Ⓞ Sportsmans Whse, vet, S Ⓖ Exxon, Shell/dsl Ⓛ Country Inn&Suites, Microtel Ⓞ Carmax, Land Rover

CAYCE

COLUMBIA

SC

🅔 INTERSTATE 26 Cont'd

Exit #	Services
103	Harbison Blvd, N 🅕 Applebee's, Hooters, Wendy's 🅛 Hampton Inn 🅞 Chevrolet, funpark, Home Depot, Lowe's, S 🅖 Hess/Dunkin Donuts/dsl, Shell/Circle K 🅕 5 Guys Burgers, Bojangles, BoneFish Grill, Buffalo Wild Wings, Carolina Alehouse, Carrabba's, Casa Linda, Chick-fil-A, Chili's, Chipotle Mexican, Coldstone, Copper River Grill, Denny's, Fazoli's, Firehouse Subs, Flaming Grill, Honey Baked Ham, Huhot Mongolian, Jimmy John's, Longhorn Steaks, Macaroni Grill, Marble Slab, McAlister's Deli, McDonald's, Miyabi Japanese, Miyo's, Olive Garden, Outback Steaks, Panera Bread, Rioz Brazilian, Rita's Custard, Ruby Tuesday, Rush's BBQ, Ryan's, Sonic, Starbucks, Subway, Tilted Kilt, Tokyo Grill, Tsunami Steaks, TX Roadhouse, Which Wich, Wild Wing Cafe, Yamato Japanese 🅛 Comfort Suites, Fairfield Inn, Hilton Garden, Holiday Inn Express, Home Towne Suites, InTown Suites, Wingate Inn 🅞 $Tree, AT&T, Belk, Best Buy, Buick/GMC, Dick's, Dillard's, Firestone/auto, Goodyear/auto, Hancock Fabrics, JC Penney, Kohl's, mall, Marshalls, Michael's, Midas, Old Navy, Petsmart, Publix, Ross, Sam's Club/dsl, Staples, SteinMart, Target, Tire Kingdom, TJ Maxx, Verizon, Walmart
102	SC 60, Ballentine, Irmo, N 🅕 Cracker Barrel 🅛 Extended Stay Deluxe, Hyatt Place 🅞 🅗 S 🅖 JP/dsl, Shell 🅕 Arby's, Bellacino's Pizza, Dunkin Donuts, Groucho's Deli, Marco's Pizza, Maurice's BBQ, Moe's SW Grill, Papa John's, Smashburger, Taco Bell, Zaxby's, Zoe's Kitchen 🅛 Residence Inn 🅞 AAA, CVS Drug, Jiffy Lube, same as 103
101b a	US 76, US 176, to N Columbia, N 1/2 mi 🅖 Exxon/Subway/dsl 🅕 Bojangles, China House, Fatz Café, Fuji Cafe, HotDog Heaven, Jersey Mike's Subs, Zorba's 🅞 $General, AutoZone, Food Lion, Harley-Davidson, Publix, Rite Aid, Walgreens, S 🅖 BP, Hickory Point/dsl, Mobil, Shell/dsl 🅕 Burger King, Lucky's BurgerShack, Waffle House 🅞 $General, Bi-Lo, Toyota/Scion
97	US 176, to Ballentine, Peak, N 🅕 China 1, Subway 🅞 Food Lion, S 🅖 Exxon/dsl
94mm	weigh sta wb
91	SC 48, to Chapin, S 🅖 BP/dsl, Exxon/Taco Bell/dsl, Shell/dsl 🅕 Bojangles, Farm Boys BBQ, McDonald's, Waffle House 🅞 to Dreher Island SP, URGENT CARE
85	SC 202, Little Mountain, Pomaria, S 🅞 to Dreher Island SP
82	SC 773, to Prosperity, Pomaria, N 🅖 Marathon/Kangaroo/Subway/dsl/24hr, Wilco/Hess/Wendy's/dsl/scales/24hr 🅕 Waffle House
81mm	weigh sta wb
76	SC 219, to Pomaria, Newberry, N 🅖 ♥Loves/McDonald's/Chester's/dsl/scales/24hr, S 0-2 mi 🅖 BP, Murphy USA 🅕 Burger King, Wendy's 🅛 Hampton Inn (4mi), Holiday Inn Express 🅞 to Newberry Opera House, Walmart
74	SC 34, to Newberry, N 🅖 BP/dsl, Shell/dsl 🅕 Bill&Fran's Café, S 2-4 mi 🅖 Citgo/dsl 🅕 Arby's, Capt D's, Hardee's, McDonald's, Waffle House 🅛 Days Inn, EconoLodge, Economy Inn 🅞 🅗 to NinetySix HS
72	SC 121, to Newberry, S 🅖 Citgo/dsl 🅞 🅗 to Newberry Coll
66	SC 32, to Jalapa
63.5mm	🆁🆂 both lanes, full 🅗 facilities, litter barrels, petwalk, 🅒, 🅐 vending
60	SC 66, to Joanna, S 🅖 BP/dsl 🅞 Magnolia RV Park
54	SC 72, to Clinton, N 🅖 BP/dsl, S 🅖 Citgo/dsl 🅕 Fatz Cafe 🅛 Hampton Inn 🅞 🅗 to Presbyterian Coll
52	SC 56, to Clinton, N 🅖 🍔/Subway/dsl/scales/24hr 🅕 Blue Ocean Rest., McDonald's 🅛 Comfort Suites, Quality Inn, S 🅖 Citgo/dsl 🅕 Hardee's, Waffle House, Wendy's 🅛 Days Inn 🅞 🅗
51	I-385, to Greenville (from wb)
45.5mm	Enoree River
44	SC 49, to Cross Anchor, Union
41	SC 92, to Enoree, N 🅖 Valero
38	SC 146, to Woodruff, N 🅖 HotSpot/Shell/Hardee's/Stuckey's/dsl/scales/24hr
35	SC 50, Walnut Grove Rd, to Woodruff, S 🅖 BP/dsl
33mm	S Tyger River
32mm	N Tyger River
28	US 221, to Spartanburg, N 🅖 Kangaroo/dsl/24hr, Shell/Subway/dsl 🅕 Bojangles, Burger King, Italian Pizza, Waffle House 🅞 🅗 Pine Ridge Camping (3mi), to Walnut Grove Plantation
22	SC 296, Reidville Rd, to Spartanburg, N 🅖 Exxon/dsl, Marathon/Kangaroo/dsl, Spinx/dsl 🅕 Arby's, Blue Bay Rest., Bruster's, Chief's Rest., Fatz Cafe, Fuddrucker's (1mi), Little Caesars, McDonald's, Outback Steaks, Substation II, Waffle House, Wasabi Japanese, Wayback Burger, Zaxby's 🅞 $General, Advance Parts, to Croft SP, USPO, vet, S 🅖 7-11/dsl, Sunoco/dsl 🅕 Clock Rest., Denny's, Domino's, Dunkin Donuts, El Limon Mexican, Hardee's, Hong Kong Express, Hunan K, Panda Garden, Papa John's, Subway 🅛 Sleep Inn, Southern Suites, Super 8 🅞 $General, Abbott Farms, Bi-Lo, CVS Drug, Hyundai, Midas, Rite Aid, Toyota/Scion, vet, VW, Walgreens
21b a	US 29, to Spartanburg, N 🅖 Marathon/Kangaroo, Spinx/dsl 🅕 A&W/LJ Silver, Bojangles, Brasilia Steaks, Buffalo Wild Wings, Burger King, Chick-fil-A, Chipotle Mexican, ChuckECheese, CiCi's, City Range Steaks, Corona Mexican, DQ, Firehouse Subs, FoodCourt, Golden Corral, Jack-in-the-Box, Jason's Deli, Jin Jin Buffet, Kanpai Tokyo, KFC, La Taverna Italian, Longhorn Steaks, McAlister's Deli, Moe's SW Grill, O'Charley's, Olive Garden, Panera Bread, Pizza Hut, Red Bowl Asian, Red Lobster, Ruby Tuesday, Ryan's, Starbucks, Subway, Wendy's 🅛 Comfort Suites, Hampton Inn, Holiday Inn Express 🅞 AT&T, Barnes&Noble, Belk, Best Buy, Costco/gas, Dick's, Dillard's, Discount Tire, Firestone/auto, Hamrick's, Home Depot, JC Penney, Jo-Ann Fabrics, Lowe's, mall, Meineke, Michael's, Office Depot, Old Navy, Petsmart, Rite Aid, Ross, Sears/auto, TJ Maxx, Tuesday Morning, USPO, Verizon, Walmart/McDonald's, S 🅖 Marathon/dsl, Shell/dsl 🅕 Apollo's Pizza, Applebee's, Compadre's TexMex, IHOP, McDonald's, Shogun Japanese, Starbucks, Taco Bell, Waffle House 🅞 $Tree, Advance Parts, CarQuest, Hobby Lobby, Ingles Foods/gas, Kohl's, Sam's Club/gas, Target, TrueValue

Map of South Carolina showing: Gramling, Greer, Greenville, Piedmont, Gray Court, Laurens, Joanna, Newberry, Prosperity, Saluda, Batesburg-Leesville, Gaffney, Saxon, Spartanburg, Roebuck, Buffalo, Enoree, Carlisle, Whitmire, Monticello, Irmo, Columbia, Rock Hill, Chester, Great Falls, Winnsboro, with I-85, I-26, I-385, US 77, I-20

SC

SPARTANBURG

INTERSTATE 26 Cont'd

Exit #	Services
19b a	Lp I-85, Spartanburg, **N** 🛢 BP/dsl, Valero 🍴 Cracker Barrel, Subway 🏠 Residence Inn **S** 🛢 Valero 🏠 Brookwood Inn
18b a	I-85, N to Charlotte, S to Greenville
17	New Cut Rd, **S** 🛢 BP/dsl, Virk/dsl 🍴 Burger King, Fatz Café, McDonald's, Waffle House 🏠 Days Inn, EconoLodge, Howard Johnson, Rodeway Inn
16	John Dodd Rd, to Wellford, **N** 🛢 Marathon/Kangaroo/Aunt M's/dsl Ⓞ Camping World RV Ctr
15	US 176, to Inman, **N** 🛢 Breakers, Shell/Circle K/dsl/scales 🍴 Waffle House Ⓞ Ⓗ **S** 🛢 Citgo/dsl
10	SC 292, to Inman, **N** 🛢 Shell/Hot Spot/Subway/dsl/scales/24hr
7.5mm	Lake William C. Bowman
5	SC 11, Foothills Scenic Dr, Chesnee, Campobello, **N** 🛢 Kangaroo/Pilot/Subway/dsl/scales/24hr, **S** 🛢 Marathon/Li'l Cricket/dsl
3mm	**Welcome Center eb, full** ♿ **facilities, litter barrels, petwalk,** Ⓒ, 🖥 **vending**
1	SC 14, to Landrum, **S** 🛢 Shell/Burger King/dsl 🍴 Bojangles, China Cafe, Papa John's, Pizza Hut (1mi), Starbucks, Subway Ⓞ $General, Bi-Lo Foods, Ingles/café/gas, Verizon, vet
0mm	South Carolina/North Carolina state line

INTERSTATE 77

Exit #	Services
91mm	South Carolina/North Carolina state line
90	US 21, Carowinds Blvd, **E** 🛢 Gulf/Quizno's/dsl, Kangaroo/dsl, QT/dsl 🍴 Bojangles, McDonald's Ⓞ Ⓗ Carowinds Camping (4mi), fireworks, **W** 🛢 Exxon/7-11, Kangaroo/Subway, Shell/Circle K/Wendy's/dsl 🍴 Cracker Barrel, Culver's, KFC, La Unica Mexican 🏠 Best Western, Clarion, Comfort Inn, EconoLodge, Motel 6, Quality Inn Ⓞ Carowinds Funpark
89.5mm	**Welcome Center sb, full** ♿ **facilities, litter barrels, petwalk,** Ⓒ, 🖥 **vending**
88	Gold Hill Rd, to Pineville, **E** Ⓞ URGENT CARE, **W** 🛢 QT/dsl, Shell/dsl, Valero/dsl 🍴 Hardee's 🏠 WingBonz Cantina Ⓞ Chrysler/Dodge/Jeep, Fiat, Ford, Hyundai, KOA, Publix
85	SC 160, Ft Mill, Tega Cay, **E** 🛢 Exxon 🍴 Subway Ⓞ Bi-Lo, Ft Mill Drug, The Drug Store, **W** 🛢 BP/dsl, QT/dsl, Shell/Circle K/dsl 🍴 Akahana Asian, Beef O'Brady's, Big Wok, Burger King, Charanda Mexican, Chick-fil-A, Empire Pizza, Fratelli's Italian, Jimmy John's, McAlister's Deli, Moe's SW Grill, Papa John's, Pizza Hut, Starbucks, Wendy's, Zaxby's Ⓞ CVS Drug, Firestone/auto, Goodyear/auto, Harris-Teeter, Lowe's, Meineke, vet, Walgreens
84.5mm	**weigh sta sb**
83	SC 49, Sutton Rd, **W** 🛢 Love's/Chester/Subway/dsl/scales/24hr
82.5mm	Catawba River
82c	US 21, SC 161, Rock Hill, Ft Mill, **E** 🛢 Exxon 🍴 IHOP, Sonny's BBQ, Steak'n Shake, Zaxby's Ⓞ Home Depot, Petsmart, **W** 🛢 Corner Stop, Kangaroo/dsl, QT/dsl, Shell/Circle K, Shell/dsl 🍴 Big Wok, Chinese Bistro Deli, Empire Grill, Hooters, Krispy Kreme, McDonald's, Outback Steaks, Sonic, Starbucks 🏠 Courtyard Ⓞ Ⓗ $General, Food Lion, TreadQtrs Auto, Walgreens
82b a	**E** 🛢 Exxon 🏠 Ramada Inn, **W** 🛢 Kangaroo, RaceWay 🍴 Arby's, Bojangles, Burger King, Chick-fil-A, China Kitchen, CiCi's Pizza, Cookout, Golden Corral, HoneyBaked Ham,

Exit #	Services
82b a	Continued HongKong Chinese, Italian Island Pizza, Jack-in-the-Box, Little Caesar's, Luigi& Sons Italian, Mario's Pizza, McDonald's, Penn Sta. Subs, Pizza Hut, Popeyes, Sake Express, Sakura Japanese, Señor Nachos Mexican, Subway, Taco Bell, Waffle House, Wendy's 🏠 Baymont Inn, Best Way, Country Inn&Suites, Days Inn, EconoLodge, Economy Express Inn, Howard Johnson, Microtel, Motel 6, Quality Inn, Regency Inn, Super 8 Ⓞ $General, Advance Parts, Aldi Foods, AutoZone, BigLots, Cadillac/Chevrolet, city park, Family$, Firestone/auto, Hancock Fabrics, K-Mart, Midas, NAPA, Office Depot, O'Reilly Parts, PepBoys, Publix, Verizon, York Co Museum
79	SC 122, Dave Lyle Blvd, to Rock Hill, **E** 🛢 BP/dsl, Murphy USA/dsl 🍴 Amber Buffet, Applebee's, Buffalo Wild Wings, Charanda Mexican, Chick-fil-A, Cracker Barrel, Five Guys, Hardee's, Jersey Mike's, Longhorn Steaks, Newk's Eatery, O'Charley's, Ruby Tuesday, TX Roadhouse 🏠 Comfort Suites, Hampton Inn, Holiday Inn, TownePlace Suites, Wingate Inn Ⓞ $Tree, Belk, Discount Tire, Food Lion, Hobby Lobby, Honda, JC Penney, Kohl's, Lowe's, mall, Meineke, Nissan, Sam's Club/dsl, Sears/auto, Staples, Tire Kingdom, Toyota/Scion, Verizon, Walmart, **W** 🛢 Kangaroo/dsl 🍴 Bob Evans, Chili's, DQ, Jack-in-the-Box, McAlister's Deli, McDonald's, Mellow Mushroom Pizza, Moe's SW Grill, Olive Garden, Panera Bread, Pizza Cafe, Quiznos, Subway, Taco Bell, Wendy's 🏠 Hilton Garden Ⓞ Best Buy, Books-A-Million, Dick's, Ford, Michael's, Ross, Target, TJ Maxx, URGENT CARE, visitor ctr
77	US 21, SC 5, to Rock Hill, **E** 🛢 BP/Subway/dsl, Wilco/Hess/dsl Ⓞ to Andrew Jackson SP (12mi), **W** 🛢 Exxon/dsl, Valero/dsl 🍴 Waffle House Ⓞ to Winthrop Coll
75	Porter Rd, **E** 🛢 Sunoco/dsl
73	SC 901, to Rock Hill, York, **E** 🛢 FLYING J/Denny's/dsl/scales/LP/24hr, Exxon/dsl, **W** Ⓞ Ⓗ
66mm	Ⓡˢ **both lanes, full** ♿ **facilities, litter barrels, petwalk,** Ⓒ, 🖥 **vending**
65	SC 9, to Chester, Lancaster, **E** 🛢 BP/dsl, Citgo/dsl, Liberty/Subway/dsl 🍴 Bojangles, China Wok, Waffle House 🏠 Days Inn, EconoLodge, Relax Inn Ⓞ $General, IGA Foods/gas, **W** 🛢 Exxon/dsl 🍴 Burger King, Country Omelette, Front Porch Cafe, KFC/Taco Bell, McDonald's, Zaxby's 🏠 Comfort Inn, Motel 6, Super 8 Ⓞ Ⓗ vet
62	SC 56, to Fort Lawn, Richburg
55	SC 97, to Chester, Great Falls, **E** 🛢 Exxon/dsl, **W** Ⓞ Ⓗ to Chester SP
48	SC 200, to Great Falls, **E** 🛢 Shell/Grand Central Rest./dsl/@, **W** 🛢 Wilco/Hess/DQ/Wendy's/dsl/scales/24hr/
46	SC 20, to White Oak
41	SC 41, to Winnsboro, **E** Ⓞ to Lake Wateree SP
34	SC 34, to Winnsboro, Ridgeway, **E** 🛢 Am Pm/dsl 🏠 Ridgeway Motel (1mi) Ⓞ Bryan's Auto/tire, Ridgeway Camping (1mi), **W** 🛢 Exxon/dsl 🍴 Waffle House 🏠 Ramada Ltd
32	Peach Rd, Ridgeway, Ⓞ Little Cedar Creek Camping (2mi)
27	Blythewood Rd, **E** 🛢 BP/Dunkin Donuts, Exxon/Bojangles/dsl/24hr 🍴 Carolina Wings, China King, Hardee's, KFC/Pizza Hut, McDonald's, San Jose Mexican, Subway, Valentina's Greek, Waffle House, Wendy's 🏠 Comfort Inn, Days Inn, Holiday Inn Express Ⓞ $General, IGA Foods, repair/tires, USPO, vet, **W** 🍴 Lizard's Thicket Ⓞ Food Lion, Groucho's Deli
24	US 21, to Wilson Blvd., **E** 🛢 BP/dsl, Shell/Subway/dsl Ⓞ auto repair, **W** 🛢 Exxon/dsl
22	Killian Rd, **E** 🛢 Mobil/Burger King/dsl, Murphy Express/

⬆N INTERSTATE 77 Cont'd

Exit #	Services
22	Continued
	dsl 🍴 Bojangles, Taco Bell, Zaxby's 🅾 Acura, Aldi Foods, AutoZone, CVS Drug, Discount Tire, Firestone, Honda, Kia, Lowe's, Mazda, Rite Aid, Toyota/Scion, VW, Walgreens, **W** 🍴 China Dragon, Monterrey's Mexican 🅾 AT&T, Lexus/Buick/GMC/Cadillac, Verizon, Walmart/McDonald's
19	SC 555, Farrow Rd, **E** 🆁 BP/dsl, Exxon, Shell/dsl 🍴 Bojangles, Cracker Barrel, Sonic, Wendy's 🛏 Courtyard, Hilton Garden, Residence Inn 🅾 🄷 Carquest, Longs Drug, **W** 🆁 Shell/dsl 🍴 Waffle House 🅾 SC Archives
18	to SC 277, to I-20 W (from sb), Columbia
17	US 1, Two Notch Rd, **E** 🆁 BP, Citgo, Kangaroo, Shell/Circle K 🍴 Arby's, Burger King, TX Roadhouse, Waffle House 🛏 Holiday Inn, InTown Suites, Quality Inn, Wingate Inn 🅾 Bi-Lo, Family$, Rite Aid, to Sesquicentennial SP, U-Haul, USPO, vet, Walgreens, **W** 🆁 Mobil 🍴 Chili's, Fazoli's, Hooters, IHOP, Lizard's Thicket, Outback Steaks, Waffle House 🛏 Best Western, Comfort Suites, EconoLodge, Fairfield Inn, Hampton Inn, La Quinta, Microtel, Red Roof Inn 🅾 Home Depot
16b a	I-20, W to Augusta, E to Florence, Alpine Rd
15b a	SC 12, to Percival Rd, **W** 🆁 Shell
13	Decker Blvd (from nb), **W** 🆁 El Cheapo, Spinx/dsl
12	Forest Blvd, Thurmond Blvd, **E** to Ft Jackson, **W** 🆁 BP/dsl, Shell/dsl/24hr 🍴 Chick-fil-A, Cookout, Domino's, Eastern Buffet, Fatz Café, Golden Corral, McDonald's, Pancho's, Sonic, Subway, Wendy's 🛏 Extended Stay America, Super 8 🅾 🄷 $Tree, AT&T, Hobby Lobby, museum, Radio Shack, Sam's Club/gas, T Heard Ins, Tuesday Morning, Verizon, vet, Walmart
10	SC 760, Jackson Blvd, **E** to Ft Jackson, **W 2 mi** 🆁 Shell 🍴 Applebee's, Bojangles, Buffalo Wild Wings, Maurices BBQ, Moe's SW, Ruby Tuesday, Smashburger, Subway 🛏 EconoLodge 🅾 Bilo, Staples, Walgreens, Whole Foods Mkt
9b a	US 76, US 378, to Sumter, Columbia, **E 0-2 mi** 🆁 BP, Citgo, Murphy USA/dsl, Shell, Shell/Burger King, Sunoco/dsl 🍴 Arby's, Bojangles, Capt D's, Chick-fil-A, Ichiban, KFC, McDonald's, Pizza Hut, Popeye's, Ruby Tuesday, Rush's Rest., Shoney's, Subway, Taco Bell, Waffle House, Waffle House, Wendy's, Zaxby's 🛏 Best Western, Candlewood Suites, Comfort Inn, Country Inn&Suites, Days Inn, Hampton Inn, Hampton Inn, Holiday Inn Express, La Quinta, Microtel, Quality Inn, Sleep Inn, TownePlace Suites 🅾 $Tree, Advance Parts, Aldi Foods, AutoZone, CVS Drug, Family$, Firestone/auto, Interstate Batteries, Lowe's, O'Reilly Parts, Tire Kingdom, Verizon, Walgreens, Walmart, **W** 🆁 Circle K, Shell 🍴 CiCi's Pizza, Eric's Mexican, Hardee's, Jimmy John's, Krispy Kreme, Panera Bread, Sonic, Starbucks, Sub Station, Wendy's 🛏 Best Value Inn 🅾 🄷 $General, BigLots, GNC, Goodyear/auto, Radio Shack, Rite Aid, Sav-A-Lot Foods, Target
6b a	Shop Rd, **W** 🅾 fairgrounds, to USC Coliseum
5	SC 48, Bluff Rd, **W** 🆁 Shell/Burger King/dsl 🍴 Bojangles (2mi) 🅾 $General
3mm	Congaree River
2	Saxe Gotha Rd
1	US 21, US 176, US 321 (from sb), Cayce, **W** accesses same as SC I-26, exit 115.
0mm	I-77 begins/ends on I-26, exit 116.

⬆N INTERSTATE 85

Exit #	Services
106.5mm	South Carolina/North Carolina state line
106	US 29, to Grover, **E** 🆁 BP/dsl, **W** 🆁 Exxon/dsl, Hickory Point/gas, Mobil/dsl/fireworks, Wilco/Hess/DQ/Wendy's/dsl/scales/24hr
104	SC 99, Tribal Rd, **E** 🆁 Loves/McDonald's/Subway/dsl/scales/24hr, **W** 🅾 fireworks
103mm	Welcome Center sb, full ♿ facilities, info, litter barrels, petwalk, 🚻, 🛒 vending
102	SC 198, to Earl, **E** 🆁 BP/dsl, Shell 🍴 Hardee's, **W** 🆁 FLYING J/Denny's/dsl/scales/LP/24hr, Citgo/dsl 🍴 McDonald's, Waffle House
100mm	Buffalo Creek
100	SC 5, to Blacksburg, Shelby, **W** 🆁 Citgo, Subway/dsl/scales/24hr
98	Frontage Rd (from nb)
97mm	Broad River
96	SC 18, **E** 🆁 Kangaroo/Krystal/dsl
95	SC 18, to Gaffney, **E** 🆁 Kangaroo/Aunt M's Rest/dsl, PetroMax/dsl 🍴 Italian Grill/Pizzaria, Mr Waffle 🛏 Gaffney Inn, Shamrock Inn 🅾 🄷 to Limestone Coll
92	SC 11, to Gaffney, **E** 🆁 Fast Point/dsl, Marathon/Subway/dsl, Murphy USA/dsl 🍴 Aegean Pizza, Applebee's, Bojangles, Burger King, Chick-fil-A, China Express, CookOut, Daddy Joe's BBQ, Domino's, Firehouse Subs, KFC, Little Caesars, McDonald's, Olive Garden, Papa John's, Pizza Hut, Sagebrush Steaks, Sonic, Taco Bell, Waffle House, Wendy's, Zaxby's 🛏 Baymont Inn, Super 8 🅾 $General, $Tree, Advance Parts, Aldi Foods, Belk, BigLots, BiLo, Ingles Foods, Lowe's, O'Reilly Parts, Radio Shack, Rite Aid, to Limestone Coll, USPO, Verizon, Walgreens, Walmart, **W** 🆁 BP 🍴 Fatz Cafe 🛏 Homestead Lodge, Quality Inn 🅾 Chevrolet, Foothills Scenic Hwy, to The Peach
90	SC 105, SC 42, to Gaffney, **E** 🆁 Marathon/Kangaroo/DQ/dsl, Hess/Arby's/dsl/scales/24hr, QT/dsl 🍴 Bojangles, Bronco Mexican, Clock Rest., Starbucks, Subway, Waffle House 🛏 Red Roof Inn, Sleep Inn, **W** 🆁 Citgo/dsl, Kangaroo/Burger King 🍴 Cracker Barrel, Cruisers, Food Court, Outback Steaks 🛏 Hampton Inn 🅾 fruit stand, Hamrick's, Prime Outlets/famous brands
87	SC 39, **E** 🅾 KOA
83	SC 110, **E** 🅾 fruit stand, **W** 🆁 Westar/dsl/scales/24hr@ 🅾 fruitstand, to Cowpens Bfd
82	Frontage Rd (from nb)
80.5mm	Pacolet River
80	SC 57, to Gossett, **E** 🆁 Hot Spot/Shell/dsl

(left margin, vertical) COLUMBIA

(right margin, vertical) GAFFNEY

INTERSTATE 85 Cont'd

Exit #	Services
78	US 221, Chesnee, **E** 🅖 Citgo/dsl 🍴 Hardee's 🛏 Motel 6, **W** 🅖 QT/dsl, RaceWay/dsl, Sunoco/Burger King/dsl 🍴 Arby's, Bojangles, McDonald's, Southern BBQ, Subway, Waffle House, Wendy's 🛏 Hampton Inn, Holiday Inn Express 🅞 $General, Advance Parts, Harley-Davidson, Ingles Foods/cafe/dsl
77	Lp 85, Spartanburg, services along Lp 85 exits E
75	SC 9, Spartanburg, **E** 🍴 Denny's 🛏 Best Value Inn, **W** 🅖 Marathon/Burger King/dsl, Pure, QT/dsl, RaceWay/dsl 🍴 Bruster's, Capri's Italian, CookOut, Copper River Grill, Fatz Café, Grapevine Rest, Jade House Asian, La Paz Mexican, McDonald's, Pizza Hut, Waffle House, Zaxby's 🛏 Comfort Inn, Days Inn 🅞 CVS Drug, Ingles/cafe/gas, Parr 3 Automotive, USPO
72	US 176, to I-585, **E** 🅞 to USCS, Wofford/Converse Coll, **W** 🅖 Kangaroo/dsl, RaceWay/dsl 🍴 China Fun, El Limon Mexican, Subway, Waffle House 🅞 $General, Ingles Foods/cafe/gas
70b a	I-26, E to Columbia, W to Asheville
69	Lp 85, SC 41 (from nb), to Fairforest
68	SC 129, to Greer
67mm	N Tyger River
66	US 29, to Lyman, Wellford, **E** 🅖 Exxon/Subway/dsl 🍴 Waffle House
63	SC 290, to Duncan, **E** 🅖 Circle K/dsl, Citgo/dsl, QT/dsl, Spinx/Dunkin Donuts/dsl 🍴 Chick-Fil-A, Clock Rest., Cracker Barrel, El Primo Mexican, Firehouse Subs, KFC, Paisanos Italian, Pizza Inn, Sake Japanese, Taco Bell, Thai Garden, Waffle House, Zaxby's 🛏 Baymont Inn, Hampton Inn, Microtel, **W** 🅖 BP, Marathon/dsl, 🚛Wendy's/dsl/scales/24hr, TA/BP/DQ/rest./dsl/scales/24hr/@ 🍴 Bojangles, Demetre's Grill, El Molcajete Mexican, Hardee's, McDonald's 🛏 Day's Inn, Holiday Inn Express, Quality Inn, ValuePlace Inn 🅞 Blue Beacon, Sonny's RV Ctr, Speedco
62.5mm	S Tyger River
60	SC 101, to Greer, **E** 🅖 Citgo/dsl, Marathon, Sunoco/dsl 🍴 Landmark Diner, Subway, Theo's Rest, **W** 🅖 Spinx/Burger King/dsl 🍴 Bojangles, Waffle House 🛏 Super 8 🅞 BMW Visitor Ctr
58	Brockman-McClimon Rd
57	**W** Greenville-Spartanburg ✈
56	SC 14, to Greer, **E** 🅖 Citgo/dsl 🅞 🅷 **W** 🅖 QT/dsl, Spinx/dsl 🅞 Goodyear Truck Tires, Ledford's Adventure RV Ctr
55mm	Enoree River
54	Pelham Rd, **E** 🅖 Marathon/Kangaroo, Stop-A-Minute/dsl 🍴 Burger King, Corona Mexican, Skin's Hotdogs, Waffle House 🛏 Best Western, **W** 🅖 BP/dsl 🍴 5 Guys Burgers, Acapulcos Mexican, Atlanta Bread Co, Bellacino's, Bertolos Pizza, Bojangles, California Dreaming Rest., Chick-fil-A, China Kitchen, Chophouse 47, Dunkin Donuts, Firehouse Subs, Frankie's Pizza, Hardee's, Joe's Crabshack, Joy of Tokyo, Logan's Roadhouse, Macaroni Grill, McDonald's, Moe's SW Grill, On the Border, Palmetto Alehouse, Papa Murphy's, PDQ Rest., Ruby Tuesday, Schlotzsky's, Starbucks, Subway 🛏 Courtyard, EconoLodge, Extended Stay America, Fairfield Inn, Hampton Inn, Holiday Inn Express, Home2 Suites, MainStay Suites, Marriott, Quality Inn, Residence Inn, Wingate Inn 🅞 Advance Parts, Bi-Lo, CVS Drug, EarthFare Foods, Goodyear/auto, Radio Shack, Verizon, Walgreens, Walmart
51	I-385, SC 146, Woodruff Rd, **E** 🍴 Brixx Pizza, Buffalo Wild Wings, Chipotle Mexican, Coldstone, Cracker Barrel, Fuddrucker's, IHOP, Lieu's Bistro, Longhorn Steaks, Monterrey Mexican, Oriental House, Panera Bread, PF Chang's, Red Robin, Sticky Fingers 🛏 Drury Inn, Hampton Inn, Hilton Garden, Homewood Suites, Staybridge Suites 🅞 Barnes&Noble, Best Buy, Dick's, Goodyear/auto, Hamrick's Outlet, Lowe's, Marshalls, PetCo, Petsmart, Ross, Verizon, vet, Whole Foods Mkt, **W** 🍴 Marathon/Kangaroo, QT/dsl, RaceWay/dsl 🍴 Bad Daddy's Burger, Carolina Alehouse, Carrabba's, Cheddars, Chuy's Mexican, Dave&Busters's, Firebirds, HuHot Mongolian, Krystal, Krystal, McDonald's, MidTown Deli, Ruby Tuesday, Ruth's Chris Steaks, Starbucks, Subway, TGIFriday's, Tucanos Brazilian Grill, Twin Peaks Rest, Waffle House, Yardhouse Rest., Zoe's Kitchen 🛏 Candlewood Suites, Comfort Inn, Crowne Plaza, Days Inn, Embassy Suites, Holiday Inn Express, La Quinta, Micotel 🅞 AT&T, Cabela's, Costco/gas, Firestone/auto, Home Depot, Old Navy, Target, Trader Joe's
48b a	US 276, Greenville, **E** 🅖 BP/dsl 🍴 Waffle House 🛏 Red Roof Inn 🅞 BMW/Mini, CarMax, to ICAR, **W** 🅖 Exxon/dsl 🍴 Arby's, Bojangles, Burger King, Happy China, Hooters, McDonald's, Olive Garden, Pizza Hut/Taco Bell, Ryan's, Subway 🛏 Comfort Inn, Embassy Suites 🅞 $Tree, Acura, Audi/Porsche/VW, Bi-Lo, Buick/GMC, Chevrolet/Cadillac, Chrysler/Dodge/Jeep, CVS Drug, Ford/Lincoln, GNC, Hancock Fabrics, Honda, Infiniti, Jaguar, Kia, Lexus, Mazda, Meineke, Mercedes, Michael's, Nissan, Office Depot, Old Time Pottery, PepBoys, Petsmart, SteinMart, Subaru, Toyota/Scion, Volvo
46c	rd 291, Pleasantburg Rd, Mauldin Rd, **W** 🅖 BP, Citgo/dsl 🍴 Jack-in-the-Box, Papa John's, Subway 🛏 InTown Suites, Quality Inn, Super Lodge, ValuePlace 🅞 Aamco, Advance Parts, Bi-Lo/gas, CVS Drug, Home Depot, same as 46ba, Tire Kingdom
46b a	US 25 bus, Augusta Rd, **E** 🅖 Mike&Jack/dsl, QT/dsl, Spinx/dsl, Sunoco, Vgo 🍴 Burger King, Waffle House 🛏 Camelot Inn, Country Hearth Inn, Holiday Inn, Southern Suites, **W** 🛏 Economy Inn, Traveler's Inn 🅞 Home Depot, same as 46c
44a	SC 20 (from sb), to Piedmont
44	US 25, White Horse Rd, **E** 🅖 Spinx/Subway/dsl, **W** 🅖 Citgo/McDonald's, RaceWay/dsl 🍴 Waffle House 🅞 🅷 Freightliner
42	I-185, to Greenville, I-185 S **(toll)**, Columbia, **W** 🅞🅷
40	SC 153, to Easley, **E** 🅖 BP/dsl 🍴 Waffle House, **W** 🅖 BP, Citgo/dsl, Hickory Point, RaceWay/dsl, Spinx/dsl 🍴 Arby's, Bojangles, Burger King, Cracker Barrel, El Sureno Mexican, Huddle House, KFC, Little Caesars, Los Amigos, McDonald's, Pizza House, Pizza Hut/Taco Bell, Sonny's BBQ, Subway, Zaxby's 🛏 Best Western, Executive Inn, Hampton Inn (4mi), Super 8 🅞 $General, Advance Parts, Bi-Lo, CVS Drug, GNC, Rite Aid, Verizon, Walgreens
39	SC 143, to Piedmont, **W** 🅖 Shell/dsl 🅞 antiques, 🅖 Vgo/dsl
35	SC 86, to Easley, Piedmont, **E** 🅖 🚛/McDonald's/dsl/scales/24hr 🍴 Hardee's (1.5mi), Mozzerelli's Pizza, Ole Carolina Smokehouse, Subway (1.5mi) 🅞 repair/tires, **W** 🅖 Spinx/Pete's Grill/dsl
34	US 29 (from sb), to Williamston
32	SC 8, to Pelzer, Easley, **E** 🅖 Hickory Point/dsl, Shell/dsl
27	SC 81, to Anderson, **E** 🅖 BP/dsl, Exxon, Zooms 🍴 Arby's, Charlie's Wings, KFC/Pizza Hut, McDonald's, Waffle House 🛏 Hampton Inn, Holiday Inn Express 🅞🅷
23mm	🆁🆂 sb, full 🛉 facilities, litter barrels, petwalk, 🅒, 🆅 vending

SPARTANBURG

GREENVILLE

SC

A N D E R S O N

🔼N INTERSTATE 85 Cont'd

Exit #	Services
21	US 178, to Anderson, **E 2 mi** 🅖 QT/dsl, Shell/dsl 🍴 Applebee's, Chick-fil-A, Chili's, Longhorn Steaks, O'Charley's, Waffle House 🛏 HomeTowne Suites, Quality Inn 🅾 Publix/deli
19b a	US 76, SC 28, to Anderson, **E 2 mi** 🅖 Exxon/dsl, QT/dsl, Shell 🍴 5 Guys Burgers, Applebee's, Chick-fil-A, Chili's, CookOut, Fuddruckers, Golden Corral, Grand China, Hardee's, Hardee's, Jack-in-the-Box, Logan's Roadhouse, Longhorn Steaks, O'Charley's, Olive Garden, Panera Bread, Red Lobster, Rita's Custard, Ryan's, Sonny BBQ, TX Roadhouse, Zaxby's 🛏 Best Value Inn, Days Inn, Hilton Garden, Holiday Inn, La Quinta, Royal American Motel, Super 8 🅾 $General, $Tree, Advance Parts, Aldi Foods, AT&T, Best Buy, Chrysler/Dodge/Jeep, Dick's, Ford/Mazda, Goodyear, Hancock Fabrics, Harley-Davidson, Hobby Lobby, Home Depot, Honda, K-Mart, Kohl's, Lowe's, Michael's, Nissan, Office Depot, Old Navy, O'Reilly Parts, Petsmart, Publix/deli, Ross, Russell Stover, Sam's Club/gas, Staples, Target, Toyota/Scion, Verizon, vet, Walmart, **W** 🅖 HotSpot/McDonald's, RaceWay/dsl 🍴 Arby's, Cracker Barrel, Fatz Cafe, Hooters, Outback Steaks, Subway, Waffle House, Wendy's, Wild Wing Cafe 🛏 Comfort Suites, Country Inn&Suites, Fairfield Inn, Hampton Inn, Holiday Inn Express, Jameson Inn, Microtel 🅾 to Clemson U
18mm	🆁🆂 **sb, full** ♿ **facilities, litter barrels, petwalk,** 🚮, 🅿 **vending**
15mm	Lake Hartwell
14	SC 187, to Clemson, Anderson, **E** 🅖 Marathon/dsl 🍴 Huddle House 🅾 camping (1mi), **W** 🅖 Hickory Point/dsl 🍴 Famous Pizza Grill 🛏 Budget Inn 🅾 to Clem Research Pk
12mm	Lake Hartwell, Seneca River
11	SC 24, SC 243, to Townville, **E** 🅖 Exxon/dsl, Sunoco/dsl/24hr 🍴 Subway 🅾 to Savannah River Scenic Hwy, **W** 🅖 Shell/dsl 🍴 Townville Cafe 🅾 RV camping
9mm	**weigh sta nb**
4	SC 243, to SC 24, Fair Play, **E** 🅖 **Loves**/Arby's/dsl/scales/24hr, Mobil/dsl/scales/LP/24hr
2	SC 59, to Fair Play, **W** 🅾 fireworks
1	SC 11, to Walhalla, **W** 🍴 Gazebo Rest. 🅾 fireworks, to Lake Hartwell SP
.5mm	**Welcome Center nb, full** ♿ **facilities, info, litter barrels, petwalk,** 🚮, 🅿 **vending**
0mm	South Carolina/Georgia state line, Tagaloo River, Lake Hartwell

🔼N INTERSTATE 95

Exit #	Services
198mm	South Carolina/North Carolina state line
196mm	**Welcome Center sb, full** ♿ **facilities, info, litter barrels, petwalk,** 🚮, 🅿 **vending**
195mm	Little Pee Dee River
193	SC 9, SC 57, to N Myrtle Beach, Dillon, **E** 🅖 Exxon/dsl, Mobil/dsl, Murphy Express/dsl, Sunoco/dsl 🍴 B&C Steak/BBQ, Burger King, Huddle House, Papa John's, Pizza Hut, Popeyes, Shoney's, Subway, Tokyo Cafe, Waffle House, Wendy's, Zaxby's 🛏 Best Value Inn, Days Inn, Quality Inn, Red Roof Inn, Royal Regency Inn 🅾 Ⓗ $General, $Tree, Advance Parts, CVS Drug, fireworks, Food Lion, O'Reilly Parts, SaveALot Foods, Walgreens, Walmart, **W** 🍴 Eastern Cafe Chines 🛏 EconoLodge, Super 8 🅾 Bass Lake RV Camp/LP
190	SC 34, to Dillon, **W** 🅖 **Loves**/Arby's/dsl/scales/24hr

D I L L O N

F L O R E N C E

181	SC 38, Oak Grove, **E** 🅖 🛢FLYING J/dsl/LP/scales/24hr, BP/Subway/dsl/24hr, Shell/McDonald's/dsl/24hr 🅾 fireworks, **W** 🅖 Wilco/Hess/DQ/Wendy's/dsl/scales/24hr 🛏 Best Western
175mm	Pee Dee River
170	SC 327, **E** 🅖 BP, 🛢/Wendy's/dsl/scales/24hr 🍴 McDonald's, Subway, Waffle House, Zaxby's 🛏 Holiday Inn Express 🅾 Missile Museum, to Myrtle Beach
169	TV Rd, to Florence, **E** 🅾 dsl repair, Florence RV Park, **W** 🅖 BP, Petro/Shell/Iron Skillet/dsl/scales/24hr/@ 🛏 Best Value Inn 🅾 Blue Beacon, dsl repair, Peterbilt
164	US 52, to Darlington, Florence, **E** 🅖 Exxon/dsl, RaceWay, Shell/Huddle House/dsl 🍴 Angelo's Seafood Rest., Cracker Barrel, Hardee's, McDonald's, Quincy's, Quiznos, Ruby Tuesday, Waffle House, Wendy's 🛏 Baymont Inn, Best Western, EconoLodge, Motel 6, Ramada Inn, Suburban Lodge, Super 8, Travel Inn 🅾 Ⓗ Chrysler/Dodge/Jeep, Hyundai, **W** 🅖 🛢/Subway/Taco Bell/dsl, TA/BP/Popeye's/dsl/scales/@ 🍴 Arby's, Calabria Mexican, Dickey's BBQ, Dunkin Donuts, Fatz Café, Krispy Kreme, Shoney's, Young's Pecans, Zaxby's 🛏 Comfort Suites, Country Inn&Suites, Days Inn, Hampton Inn, Howard Johnson, La Quinta, Microtel, Sleep Inn, Thunderbird Inn, Travel House Inn 🅾 to Darlington Raceway, transmissions
160b	I-20 W, to Columbia
160a	Lp 20, to Florence, **E** 🅖 Exxon/dsl 🍴 Arby's, Bruster's Ice Cream, Buffalo Wild Wings, Burger King, Chick-fil-A, Chili's, Chipotle, ChuckeCheese, Firehouse Subs, Golden Corral, Hibachi Grill, IHOP, La Bamba Mexican, Longhorn Steaks, Mellow Mushroom, Olive Garden, Outback Steaks, Percy & Willy, Red Bowl Asian, Red Lobster, Ruby Tuesday, San Jose's, Waffle House, Western Sizzlin 🛏 Courtyard, Fairfield Inn, Hampton Inn, Hilton Garden, Holiday Inn Express, Home2 Hilton, Quality Inn, Red Roof Inn, Residence Inn, SpringHill Suites 🅾 $Tree, AT&T, Barnes&Noble, Belk, Best Buy, Big Lots, Dick's, Hamricks, Hobby Lobby, Home Depot, JC Penney, Kohl's, Lowes Whse, mall, Petsmart, Sam's Club/gas, Sears/auto, Target, Walmart
157	US 76, Timmonsville, Florence, **E** 🅖 BP/dsl/repair, Citgo/dsl, Kangaroo/dsl, Shell/McDonald's 🍴 Peking Asian, Waffle House 🛏 Day's Inn, Florence Inn, Travelodge 🅾 Abbott Farms Peaches, **W** 🅖 Bull/dsl 🛏 Ramada/rest., Swamp Fox Camping (1mi), Tree Top Inn 🅾 auto repair
153	Honda Way, **W** 🅖 Palmetto Express/dsl 🅾 Honda Plant
150	SC 403, to Sardis, **E** 🅖 BP/dsl/scales 🍴 Hotplate Cafe 🛏 Budget Inn, **W** 🅖 Exxon/dsl
147mm	Lynches River
146	SC 341, to Lynchburg, Olanta, **E** 🛏 Relax Inn

🚗 = gas ⬜ = food 🛏 = lodging Ⓞ = other 🅿️ = rest stop Copyright 2015 - the Next EXIT ®

⬆N INTERSTATE 95 Cont'd

Exit #	Services
141	SC 53, SC 58, to Shiloh, **E** 🚗 Exxon Ⓞ DonMar RV Ctr, to Woods Bay SP, **W** 🚗 Shell
139mm	🅿️ **both lanes, full** ♿ **facilities, litter barrels, petwalk,** 📞, ☎ **vending**
135	US 378, to Sumter, Turbeville, **E** 🚗 Citgo/dsl/24hr ⬜ Compass Rest. 🛏 Day's Inn, **W** 🚗 Exxon/Subway/dsl
132	SC 527, to Sardinia, Kingstree
130mm	Black River
122	US 521, to Alcolu, Manning, **W** 🚗 Exxon/dsl ⬜ Paradise Cafe
119	SC 261, to Paxville, Manning, **E 0-1 mi** 🚗 Mobil, Murphy USA/dsl, Shell/dsl, TA/BP/Pizza Hut/Popeye's/dsl/scales/24hr/@ ⬜ Arby's, Bojangles, Golden Chick, Huddle House, Mariachi's Mexican, McDonald's, Shoney's, Sonic, Subway, Waffle House, Wendy's, Yucatan Mexican, Zaxby's 🛏 Baymont Inn, Days Inn, Hampton Inn, Quality Inn, Ramada Inn Ⓞ Ⓗ $General, AutoZone, Chrysler/Dodge/Jeep, CVS Drug, Ford, O'Reilly Parts, Radio Shack, truckwash, Verizon, Walmart, **W** 🚗 Horizon/dsl/e-85, Paxville 🛏 Super 8 Ⓞ auto repair
115	US 301, to Summerton, Manning, **W** 🚗 Shell/dsl ⬜ Georgio's Rest. 🛏 Knights Inn
108	rd 102, Summerton, **E** 🚗 BP/DQ, Travel Depot/dsl Ⓞ Taw-Caw Camping (6m), **W** 🛏 Days Inn, Deluxe Inn
102	US 15, US 301 N, to N Santee, **E** 🚗 StopSpot/dsl 🛏 Santee Resort/Motel Ⓞ Bigwater RV Camping, Santee Lakes Camping, **W** 🚗 Horizon/dsl/e-85 Ⓞ to Santee NWR
100mm	Lake Marion
99mm	🅿️ **both lanes, full** ♿ **facilities, litter barrels, petwalk,** 📞, ☎ **vending**
98	SC 6, to Eutawville, Santee, **E** 🚗 BP/Bojangles, Citgo, Exxon, Mobil ⬜ Coaster's Seafood, Huddle House, Pizza Hut, Shoney's, Subway 🛏 Best Value Inn, Best Western, Econolodge, Hampton Inn, Rodeway Inn, Super 8, Whitten Inn Ⓞ $General, IGA Foods, **W** 🚗 Hess/dsl; Horizon/dsl/e-85, Shell ⬜ Burger King, Cracker Barrel, Domino's, Maurice's BBQ, McDonald's, Waffle House, Wendy's 🛏 Clark Inn/rest., Comfort Inn, Holiday Inn, Howard Johnson, Lake Marion Inn, Quality Inn Ⓞ CarQuest, CVS Drug, Family$, Food Lion, Rivers Country Store, to Santee SP (3mi), USPO
97	US 301 S (from sb, no return), to Orangeburg
93	US 15, to Santee, Holly Hill
90	US 176, to Cameron, Holly Hill, **W** 🚗 Exxon/dsl
86b a	I-26, W to Columbia, E to Charleston
82	US 178, to Bowman, Harleyville, **E** 🚗 BP, Wilco/Hess/Stuckey's/Wendy's/DQ/dsl/scales/24hr 🛏 Peachtree Inn, **W** 🚗 Shell/dsl Ⓞ tires/truck repair
77	US 78, to Bamberg, St George, **E** 🚗 ⊘FLYING J/Denny's/dsl/scales/24hr, Horizon/Subway/dsl/e-85, Monoco, Sunoco ⬜ Georgio's Rest., Hardee's, KFC, McDonald's, Pizza Hut, Skynyrd's Grill, Waffle House 🛏 Best Value Inn, Comfort Inn/RV Park, EconoLodge, Quality Inn Ⓞ $General, Ace Hardware, CarQuest, Chevrolet/GMC, CVS Drug, Family$, Ford, Reid's Foods, St George RV Park, USPO, **W** 🚗 BP, Shell/Taco Bell/dsl 🛏 Country Hearth Inn, Days Inn, Southern Inn, Super 8
74mm	**weigh sta nb, parking area commercial vehicles only sb**
68	SC 61, Canadys, **E** 🚗 BP, Circle C/scales, Shell/Subway/dsl Ⓞ to Colleton SP (3mi), truck lube/repair

62	McLeod Rd
57	SC 64, Lodge, Walterboro, **E** 🚗 Horizon/e-85, Mobil/dsl, Shell/DQ, Sunoco/dsl ⬜ Arby's, Bojangles, Burger King, Capt D's, Dimitrio's Rest., Domino's, Hardee's, Huddle House, KFC, McDonald's, Olde House Café, Quiznos, Subway, Taco Bell, Waffle House, Wendy's 🛏 Carolina Lodge, Sleep Inn, Southern Inn Ⓞ Ⓗ $General, Ace Hardware, Advance Parts, AutoZone, Belk, Ford, GNC, O'Reilly Parts, Reid's Foods, Rite Aid, **W** 🚗 BP, Murphy USA/dsl ⬜ China Buffet, Zaxby's 🛏 Super 8 Ⓞ $Tree, PetCo, Radio Shack, Verizon, Walmart
53	SC 63, to Varnville, Walterboro, Hampton, **E** 🚗 BP/McDonald's, El Cheapo, Exxon, Petro Express/dsl, Shell/DQ ⬜ Glasshouse Rest., KFC, Ruby Tuesday, Shoney's, Waffle House 🛏 Best Western, Comfort Inn, EconoLodge, Motel 6, Palms Inn, Quality Inn, Ramada Inn, Rice Planter's Inn Ⓞ fireworks, **W** 🚗 Horizon/dsl ⬜ Cracker Barrel 🛏 Country Hearth Inn, Days Inn, Hampton Inn, Holiday Inn Express, Microtel Ⓞ Green Acres Camping
47mm	🅿️ **both lanes, full** ♿ **facilities, litter barrels, petwalk,** 📞, ☎ **vending**
42	US 21, to Yemassee, Beaufort
40mm	Combahee River
38	SC 68, to Hampton, Yemassee, **E** 🚗 Horizon/dsl/e-85 Ⓞ Family$, **W** 🚗 BP/Subway/TCBY, Exxon/dsl, Shell/dsl 🛏 Palmetto Lodge/rest., Super 8
33	US 17 N, to Beaufort, **E** 🚗 BP/dsl, Exxon/McDonald's, Marathon/Subway/TCBY, Shell ⬜ Denny's, Waffle House, Wendy's 🛏 Baymont Inn, Best Western, EconoLodge, Hampton Inn, Knights Inn Ⓞ Confederate Railroad Museum, Encore RV Camping, KOA
30.5mm	Tullifinny River
29mm	Coosawhatchie River
28	SC 462, to Coosawhatchie, Hilton Head, Bluffton, **W** 🚗 Citgo, El Cheapo, Exxon/Chester Fried/dsl
22	US 17, Ridgeland, **W** 🚗 Sunoco 🛏 Ridgeland Inn Ⓞ Ⓗ
21	SC 336, to Hilton Head, Ridgeland, **E** 🚗 Liberty/dsl ⬜ McDonald's, Wendy's Ⓞ Boat'n RV Whse, **W** 🚗 BP/DQ/dsl, Exxon, Gulf/dsl, Shell ⬜ BBQ Buffet, Bella Pizza, Burger King, Hong Kong Chinese, Huddle House, Jasper's Porch, KFC, Subway, Waffle House 🛏 Carolina Lodge, Comfort Inn/rest., Days Inn, Quality Inn Ⓞ Ⓗ $General, Harvey's Foods, Rite Aid
18	SC 13, to US 17, US 278, to Switzerland, Granville, Ridgeland
17mm	**parking area both lanes, commercial vehicles only**
8	US 278, to Bluffton, Hardeeville, **E** 🚗 BP/Huddle House/Wendy's/dsl/scales, Exxon, Kangaroo/McDonald's ⬜ Dunkin Donuts Ⓞ Ⓗ Hilton Head info, **W** 🚗 Horizon/Domino's/Krispy Kreme/Subway/dsl 🛏 Holiday Inn Express, Motel 6
5	US 17, US 321, to Savannah, Hardeeville, **E** 🚗 Citgo/dsl, Exxon/Blimpie, Gulf/dsl, Shell ⬜ Mi Tierrita Mexican, Waffle House 🛏 Days Inn, Economy Inn, Sleep Inn Ⓞ fireworks, to Savannah NWR, **W** 🚗 Butlers/dsl/repair, Marathon/dsl, Octane/dsl, Sunoco/dsl ⬜ Burger King, New China, Wendy's 🛏 Clean Stay USA, Country Hearth Inn, Deluxe Inn, Knights Inn, Magnolia Motel, Quality Suites, Red Roof Inn, Super 8, Travelodge Ⓞ $General, fireworks, NAPA
4.5mm	**Welcome Center nb, full** ♿ **facilities, litter barrels, petwalk,** 📞, ☎ **vending, wi-fi**
4mm	**weigh sta both lanes**
0mm	South Carolina/Georgia state line, Savannah River

MANNING

SANTEE

SC

WALTERBORO

HARDEEVILLE

INTERSTATE 385 (Greenville)

Exit #	Services
42	US 276, Stone Ave, to Travelers Rest, **E** 🅾 CarQuest, vet, **W 1-2 mi** 🅟 Spinx/dsl 🅾 multiple services on US 276, to Greenville Zoo, **I-385 begins/ends on US 276.**
40b a	SC 291, Pleasantburg Dr, **E** 🅟 Sunoco 🍴 Jack-in-the-Box, Little Caesar's, Olive Tree, S&S Cafeteria, Sonic, Starbucks, Subway, Taco Casa, Wendy's 🅾 $Tree, CVS Drug, Family$, Furman U, to BJU, Walgreens, **W** 🅟 Citgo/dsl, QT/dsl 🍴 Domino's, Krispy Kreme 🏠 Phoenix Inn/Rest., Sleep Inn 🅾 Cottman Transmissions, Midas
39	Haywood Rd, **E** 🅟 Spinx 🍴 Noodleville, Outback Steaks, Portofino's, Tony's Pizzeria 🏠 Clarion, Courtyard, Hawthorn Inn, Hilton, Hyatt Place, La Quinta 🅾 Firestone/auto, USPO, **W** 🅟 Spinx/dsl 🍴 Applebee's, Backyard Burger, Burger King, Chick-fil-A, Chili's, Chipotle, ChuckeCheese, CiCi's Pizza, CityRange Steaks, Clock Rest., Copper River Grill, Don Pablo, Firehouse Subs, Five Guys, Fried Green Tomatoes, Grille 33, Habiba Mediterranean, Halton Country Buffet, Harbor Inn Seafood, Jason's Deli, Jimmy John's, Kanpai Tokyo, McAlister's Deli, Miyabi Japanese, Moe's SW Grill, Monterrey Mexican, Panera Bread, Papa's&Beer, Rafferdi's, Saskatoon Rest,, Starbucks, Stax Grill, Steak'n Shake, Waffle House 🏠 Baymont Inn, Extended Stay America, Hampton Inn 🅾 AT&T, Barnes&Noble, Belk, Dillard's, Discount Tire, JC Penney, Jo-Ann, Macy's, mall, Sears/auto, TJ Maxx, Verizon, vet
37	Roper Mtn Rd, **W** 🅟 Marathon/Kangaroo/dsl, QT/dsl, RaceWay/dsl 🍴 Carrabba's, Cheddar's, Chuy's Mexican, Dave&Busters, HuHot Mongolian, Krystal, McDonald's, Mid-Town Deli, Ruby Tuesday, Ruths Chris Steaks, Starbucks, Strossner's Cafe, Subway, TGI Friday's, Tucnos Brazilian Grill, Twin Peaks Rest., Waffle House, Yardhouse Rest. 🏠 Candlewood Suites, Comfort Inn, Crowne Plaza, Days Inn, Embassy Suites, Holiday Inn Express, La Quinta, Microtel 🅾 AT&T, Cabela's, Costco/gas, Firestone/auto, Home Depot, Hyundai, Old Navy, Target, Trader Joe's
36b a	I-85, N to Charlotte, S to Atlanta
35	SC 146, Woodruff Rd, **E 0-2 mi** 🅟 Marathon, QT/dsl, Spinx 🍴 Applebee's, Bojangles, Bone Fish Grill, Boston Pizzeria, Bruster's, Chick-fil-A, Chili's, China Buffet, CookOut, Culver's, Dunkin Donuts, Epic Curean Rest., Firehouse Subs, Great Harvest Bread, Green Tomato Buffet, Hardee's, Hibachi Grill, Jersey Mike's, JP's 4 Corners SW Rest., KFC, Krispy Kreme, Little Caesar's, McAlister's Deli, McDonald's, Mimi's Japanese Steaks, Moe's SW Grill, Pizza Inn, Sonic, Starbucks, Stevi B's, Subway, Taco Bell, Topper's Rest., Travinia Italian, Waffle House, Wendy's, Your Pizza Pie, Zaxby's 🅾 $Tree, AAAAZ, Ace Hardware, Aldi Foods, BigLots, Bi-Lo Foods, Discount Tire, GNC, Hobby Lobby, Kohl's, O'Reilly Parts, Publix, Radio Shack, Rite Aid, Sam's Club/gas, Save-a-Lot Foods, Staples, Tire Kingdom, URGENT CARE, USPO, Walmart, **W** 🅟 Red Robin 🍴 Brixx Pizza, Buffalo Wild Wings, Chipotle Mexican, Coldstone, Cracker Barrel, Fuddrucker's, Genghis Grill, IHOP, La Parrilla Mexican, Lieu's Bistro, Longhorn Steaks, Monterrey Mexican, Oriental House, Panera Bread, PF Chang's, Red Robin, Salsarita's, Sticky Fingers, Which Wich? 🏠 Drury Inn, Hampton Inn, Hilton Garden, Homewood Suites, Staybridge Suites 🅾 Barnes&Noble, Best Buy, Dick's, Goodyear/auto, Hamrick's Outlet, Lowe's, Marshall's, Petco, Petsmart, REI,

35	Continued Ross, Verizon, vet, Whole Foods Mkt, World Mkt
34	Butler Rd, Mauldin, **E** 🅟 Spin/dsl 🍴 Arby's, **W** 🍴 Bojangles, Dino's Rest., Moretti's Pizzeria, Sub Sta. 2 🅾 $General
33	Bridges Rd, Mauldin
31	I-185 toll, SC 417, to Laurens Rd, **E** 🅟 Marathon, Shell/dsl 🍴 Hardee's, McDonald's, Subway 🅾 BiLo, SaveALot Foods, **W** 🅟 Spinx/dsl
30	I-185 toll, US 276, Standing Springs Rd
29	Georgia Rd, to Simpsonville, **W** 🏠 ValuePlace Inn
27	Fairview Rd, to Simpsonville, **E** 🅟 Shell 🍴 Carolina Rest., CoachHouse Rest., JB's BBQ, Little Caesar's, McDonald's, Milano Pizzeria, Subway 🏠 Palmetto Inn 🅾 🅗 $General, Advance Parts, AutoZone, Big Lots, CVS Drug, O'Reilly Parts, **W** 🅟 Exxon, Murphy USA, Spinx/dsl 🍴 5 Guys Burgers, Anthony's Pizza, Applebee's, Arby's, AZ Steaks, Baskin-Robbins, Bellacino's, Bruster's, Burger King, Chick-fil-A, Cracker Barrel, Epic Buffet, Firehouse Subs, Hibachi House, Hungry Howie's, IHOP, Jack-in-the-Box, Jersey Mike's, KFC, La Fogata Mexican, Mad Cuban, McDonald's, Mei Mei House, Moe's SW Grill, O'Charley's, Panera Bread, Pizza Hut, Ruby Tuesday, Sonic, Starbucks, Subway, Taco Bell, Tequila's Mexican, Waffle House, Wendy's, Zaxby's 🏠 Comfort Suites, Days Inn, Hampton Inn, Holiday Inn Express, Motel 6, Quality Inn 🅾 $Tree, AT&T, Belk, Bi-Lo, CVS Drug, GNC, Goodyear/auto, Home Depot, Howe Home, Ingles Foods, Kohl's, Lowe's, Publix, Radio Shack, Ross, Target, Tire Kingdom, TJ Maxx, URGENT CARE, USPO, Verizon, Walgreens, Walmart
26	Harrison Bridge Rd, **W** 🅟 7-11/dsl, same as 27
24	Fairview St, **E** 🅟 Marathon 🍴 Hardee's, Waffle House
23	SC 418, to Fountain Inn, Fork Shoals, **E** 🅟 Exxon/pizza/subs/dsl 🍴 Bojangles 🅾 $General, O'Reilly Parts, USPO, **W** 🅟 Sunoco/dsl
22	SC 14 W, Old Laurens Rd, to Fountain Inn
19	SC 14 E, to Gray Court, Owings
16	SC 101, to Woodruff, Gray Court
10	rd 23, Barksdale, Ora
9	US 221, to Laurens, Enoree, **E** 🅟 Citgo/Subs/dsl 🍴 Waffle House 🏠 Budget Inn, **W** 🅾 Walmart Dist Ctr
6mm	🆁🆂 both lanes (both lanes exit left), full ♿ facilities, litter barrels, petwalk, 🅲, 🛒 vending
5	SC 49, to Laurens, Union
2	SC 308, to Clinton, Ora, **W** 🅾 🅗 to Presbyterian Coll in Clinton
0mm	I-26 S to Columbia, I-385 begins/ends on I-26 at 52mm.

GREENVILLE

SIMPSONVILLE

SC

SD

↑E INTERSTATE 526 (Charleston)

Exit #	Services
33mm	I-526 begins/ends.
32	US 17, **N 0-1 mi** 🔲 Hess/dsl, Shell 🔲 Atl Bread, Bojangles, Burger King, Burton's Grill, Cane's, Five Guys, Grimaldi's Brick Oven, IHOP, PF Chang's, Qdoba, Sonic, Taco Bell, TGIFriday, Zoe's Kitchen 🔲 Courtyard, Hampton Inn 🔲 Advance Parts, AT&T, Barnes&Noble, Belk, BiLo, Chevrolet, CVS Drug, GNC, Lowes Whse, Midas, Old Navy, Rite Aid, Tire Kingdom, TrueValue, Verizon, Walgreens, **S 0-1 mi** 🔲 Shell/Circle K, Sunoco/dsl 🔲 Applebees, Arby's, Chick-fil-A, Cici's, Firehouse Subs, Hardee's, Huddle House, Jimmy John's, La Hacienda Mexicana, Liberty Rest., McDonald's, Melvin's Ribs& Cue, Moe's SW Grill, Momma Goldberg's Deli, Outback Steaks, Sticky Fingers, Subway, Wendy's, Zeus Grill 🔲 Best Western, Clarion, Day's Inn, Extended Stay America, Hampton Inn, Hilton Garden, Holiday Inn, Holiday Inn Express, Mainstay Suites, Quality Inn, Red Roof Inn, Sleep Inn 🔲 $Tree, Bi-Lo, CVS Drug, Firestone/auto, Harris Teeter, Jiffy Lube, Marshall's, Michaels, NAPA, Office Depot, O'Reilly Parts, Petco, Publix, Radio Shack, Staples, TJ Maxx, Trader Joe's, USPO, Verizon, vet, VW, Walmart, Whole Foods Mkt
28	Long Point Rd, **N** 🔲 BP, Exxon 🔲 Bamboo Garden, Beef'o Brady's, McAlister's, Moe's SW Grill, Sonic, Starbucks, Subway, Waffle House, Wendy's 🔲 Charles Pinckney NHS, CVS Drug, Food Lion, Harris Teeter Foods, PetsMart, Ross, Steinmart
26mm	Wando River
24	Daniel Island, **S** 🔲 Texaco 🔲 Dragon Palace, Lana's Mexican, Queen Anne's Steaks/seafood, Subway 🔲 Hampton Inn 🔲 Publix
23b a	Clements Ferry Rd
21mm	Cooper River
20	Virginia Ave (from eb), **S** 🔲 Hess Depot
19	N Rhett Ave, **N** 🔲 Hess, Kangaroo/Subway/dsl 🔲 Hardee's 🔲 Family$, Food Lion, Rite Aid, **S** 🔲 BP
18b a	US 52, US 78, Rivers Ave, **N** 🔲 BP/dsl, Hess, Kangaroo/dsl 🔲 KFC, Peking Gourmet, Pizza Hut/Taco Bell 🔲 auto repair,

18b a	Continued
	AutoZone, Dodge, Family$, Ford, H&L Foods, **S** 🔲 Exxon
17b a	I-26, E to Charleston, W to Columbia
16	Montague Ave, 🔲 Rd, **S** 🔲 Bonefish Grill, Chili's, Denny's, Jersey Mike's, La Hacienda, Panera Bread, Starbucks, Wendy's 🔲 Embassy Suites, Hilton Garden, Holiday Inn, Homewood Suites, Residence Inn 🔲 Sam's Club/gas, Staples, Tanger Outlet/famous brands, Walmart/Subway
15	SC 642, Dorchester Rd, Paramount Dr, **N** 🔲 Shell/Circle K 🔲 auto service, Family$, **S** 🔲 Citgo/dsl, Sunoco 🔲 Burger King, Checker's, Domino's, East Bay Deli, Huddle House, Little Caesars, Pizza Hut, Subway 🔲 🔲 Inn 🔲 Advance Parts, Bi-Lo Foods, CVS Drug, Family$, Food Lion, Harley-Davidson, U-Haul
14	Leeds Ave, **S** 🔲 Value Place Inn 🔲 boat marina
13mm	Ashley River
11b a	SC 61, Ashley River Rd , **N** 🔲 Baron's Pizza, Chick-fil-A, McDonald's, O'Charley's 🔲 🔲 Food Lion, Home Depot, Jo-Ann, Kohl's, Lowes Whse, Marshall's
10	US 17, SC 7, **E** services from US 17 🔲 BP 🔲 5 Guys Burgers, Bessinger's BBQ, Capt D's, Chick-fil-A, CookOut, Dunkin Donuts, Hopsing's Asian, IHOP, King St Grille, Krispy Kreme, La Fontana Italian, McDonald's, Panera Bread, Red Lobster, Ruby Tuesday, Taco Bell 🔲 Best Western, Evergreen Motel, Holiday Inn Express, Motel 6, Sleep Inn, Town & Country Suites 🔲 AutoZone, Belk, BiLo, BMW/Mini, Buick/GMC/Cadillac, Chevrolet, Chrysler/Dodge/Jeep, Dick's, Dillard's, Ford/Lincoln, Honda, Hyundai, Hyundai, Infiniti, Jaguar/Range Rover/Porsche, JC Penney, Maserati, Mercedes, Nissan, Pepboys, Petsmart, Ross, Sears/auto, Smart, Target, Tire Kingdom, vet, Volvo, **W** services from US 17 🔲 AMFlag, Hess/dsl, Shell/Circle K 🔲 China Fun, Hardees, Inyabi Japanese, Subway, Waffle House 🔲 Comfort Suites, Econolodge, Hampton Inn, Hawthorn Suites, InTown Suites 🔲 Acura, Advance Parts, Audi, Carmax, Costco/gas, CVS Drug, DriveTime, Family$, Food Lion, Kia, Lexus, Toyota

I-526 begins/ends on US 17.

SOUTH DAKOTA

↑N INTERSTATE 29

Exit #	Services
253mm	South Dakota/North Dakota state line
251mm	**Welcome Center sb, full 🔲 facilities, litter barrels, petwalk, 🔲, 🔲**
246	SD 127, to Rosholt, New Effington, **W 3 mi** 🔲, 🔲, 🔲 RV camping, Sica Hollow SP (24mi)
242	no services
235mm	weigh sta sb
232	SD 10, Sisseton, **E** 🔲 Dakota Connection/dsl/casino/24hr 🔲 Crossroads Cafe, **W 1-3 mi** 🔲 Amstar/dsl, FuelMax/dsl, Sinclair/dsl/E-85, Tesoro 🔲 Cottage Rest, DQ, Pizza Hut, Subway, Taco John's 🔲 Holiday Motel, I-29 Motel, Super 8 🔲 HOSPITAL, Alco, Buick, Camp Dakotah, Family$, Ft Sisseton SP(35mi), NAPA, ShopKO, SuperValu Foods/gas, Teals Mkt, to Roy Lake SP(25mi)
224	Peever, Sioux Tribal Hqtrs, **E** 🔲 I-29 Food'n Fill/dsl, **W** 🔲 Pickerel Lake(16mi)

213	SD 15, to Wilmot, **E** 🔲 **both lanes, full 🔲 facilities, litter barrels, petwalk, 🔲, 🔲, RV dump, vending 7 mi** 🔲, 🔲, 🔲 to Hartford Beach SP (17mi); st patrol
207	US 12, Summit, **E** 🔲 Sinclair/dsl/24hr 🔲 County Line Rest (1mi), **W** 🔲 Blue Dog Fish Hatchery (15mi), Waubay NWR (19mi)
201	to Twin Brooks
193	SD 20, to South Shore, Stockholm
185	to Waverly, **W 4 mi** 🔲 Dakota Sioux Casino/rest.
180	US 81 S, to Watertown, **W 5 mi** 🔲 Sinclair 🔲 🔲, Bramble Park Zoo
177	US 212, Watertown, **E** 🔲 Tesoro/Grainery Cafe/dsl/24hr 🔲 Holiday Inn Express 🔲 fireworks, truck repair, truck wash, WW Tires, **W 0-2 mi** 🔲 Cenex/Subway/dsl, Clark/dsl, Freedom/dsl, Sinclair/dsl, Tesoro/dsl 🔲 Applebee's, Arby's, Buffalo Wild Wings, Burger King, China Buffet, Culver's, Domino's, DQ, Godfather's, Guadalajara Mexican, Italian Garden, Jimmy John's, KFC, McDonald's, Papa Murphy's, Perkins, Pizza Hut, Quiznos, Senor Max's Mexican, Starbucks, Subway, Taco John's 🔲 Days Inn, Hampton Inn, Quality Inn,

SC

Charleston (vertical text, left side)

Watertown (vertical text, bottom right)

W A T E R T O W N B R O O K I N G S	⬆️N **INTERSTATE 29 Cont'd**			

INTERSTATE 29 Cont'd

Exit #   Services

Exit #	Services
177	Continued Rodeway Inn, Travelers Inn 🅞 $Tree, Advance Parts, AT&T, Chrysler/Dodge/Jeep, Ford/Lincoln, Goodyear/auto, Harley-Davidson, Herberger's, Hy-Vee Foods, JC Penney, Menards, NAPA, O'Reilly Parts, Radio Shack, ShopKO, Target, Tires+, to Sandy Shore RA(10mi), Verizon, Walgreens, Walmart/Subway
164	SD 22, to Castlewood, Clear Lake, E 9 mi 🅖 Cenex/dsl 🅞 🅷
161mm	🆁🆂 both lanes, full ♿ facilities, litter barrels, petwalk, 🚻, 🐾 vending
157	to Brandt, no services
150	SD 28, SD 15 N, to Toronto, W 7 mi 🅖, 🍴, 🏠, 🅞 Lake Poinsett RA, SD Amateur Baseball Hall of Fame
140	SD 30, to White, Bruce, W 🅞 Oakwood Lakes SP(12mi)
133	US 14 byp, Brookings, E 🅞 WW Tires, W 🅞 Laura Ingalls Wilder Home, museums, to SD St U
132	US 14, Lp 29, Brookings, E 🅖 Cenex/dsl 🍴 Applebee's 🏠 Fairfield Inn, Hampton Inn, Holiday Inn Express, Super 8, W 🅖 BP 🍴 Arby's, Buffalo Wild Wings, Burger King, Culver's, DQ, Ground Round, Guadalajara Mexican, Hardee's, Jimmy John's, KFC, King's Wok, McDonald's, Papa John's, Papa Murphy's, Perkins, Pizza Ranch, Qdoba Mexican, Subway 🏠 Comfort Inn, Days Inn, Staurolite Inn 🅞 🅷, Advance Parts, Buick/Chevrolet/GMC, CarQuest, city park, Lowe's, Radio Shack, Walmart/Subway
127	SD 324, to Elkton, Sinai
124mm	Big Sioux River
121	to Nunda, Ward, E 🆁🆂 both lanes, full ♿ facilities, litter barrels, petwalk, 🚻, 🐾, RV dump, vending st patrol W 🍴 RV camping
114	SD 32, to Flandreau, E 7 mi 🅖 Cenex 🍴 Subway 🏠 Sioux River Motel/RV park 🅞 Royal River Casino/hotel, Santee Tribal Hqtrs
109	SD 34, to Madison, Colman, W 🅖 BP/rest/dsl, Shell/rest/dsl 🅞 Dakota St U, museum, to Lake Herman SP
104	to Trent, Chester
103mm	parking area both lanes
98	SD 115 S, Dell Rapids, E 3 mi 🅖 Cenex, Shell 🍴 DQ, Pizza Ranch 🏠 Bilmar Inn 🅞 🅷, Chevrolet

S I O U X F A L L S	

Exit #	Services
94	SD 114, to Baltic, E 10 mi 🅞 to EROS Data Ctr, US Geological Survey
86	to Renner, Crooks
84b a	I-90, W to Rapid City, E to Albert Lea
83	SD 38 W, 60th St, E 🅖 ⬨FLYING J/Denny's/dsl/LP/scales/24hr/@ 🏠 Quality Suites 🅞 Freightliner, Harley-Davidson, Indian Motorcycles, Truckwash, W 🅞 fireworks, hwy patrol, Walmart/Subway
82	Benson Rd, E 🍴 BeefOBrady's 🏠 Fairfield Inn
81	SD 38 E, Russell St, Sioux Falls, E 🅖 BP, Food'n Fuel/Quiznos 🍴 Roll'n Pin Rest. 🏠 Arena Motel, Best Western/Ramkota, Dakotah Lodge, Guesthouse Inn, Motel 6, Ramada Inn, Sheraton, Sioux Falls Inn, Sleep Inn, Super 8 🅞 golf, Schaap's RV Ctr, W 🍴 Subway
80	Madison St, E 🅖 Sinclair/dsl 🅞 to fairgrounds
79	SD 42, 12th St, E 🅖 BP, Freedom 🍴 Burger King, Burger Time, Fry'n Pan, Golden Harvest Chinese, KFC, McDonald's, Pizza Hut, Sneaky's Chicken, Subway, Taco Bell, Taco John's, Tomacelli's Pizza, Wendy's 🏠 Ramada, ValuePlace Inn 🅞 🅷, $General, Ace Hardware, BMW/Cadillac/Mercedes, Chevrolet, city park, K-Mart, Lewis Drug, NAPA, Nissan, to Great Plains Zoo/museum, Toyota/Scion, USPO, Walgreens, W 🅖 BP/dsl, Cenex/Chester's/dsl, Food'n Fuel 🍴 Hardee's 🅞 Meineke, Tower RV Park
78	26th St, Empire St, E 🅖 BP/dsl/E85 🍴 Buffalo Wild Wings, Carino's Italian, Carnaval Brazillian Grill, Chevy's Mexican, ChuckeCheese, Coldstone, Cracker Barrel, Culver's, Domino's, Granite City Rest, Outback Steaks, Puerto Vallarta, Ruby Tuesday, Sonic 🏠 ClubHouse Suites, Hampton Inn, Holiday Inn Express, StayBridge Suites 🅞 BigLots, Home Depot, Michael's, Petsmart, Sam's Club/gas, USPO, World Mkt, W 🍴 DQ, Papa John's, Starbucks 🏠 TownePlace Suites 🅞 Hy-Vee Foods/gas, Lowe's, Tuffy Auto, Verizon
77	41st St, Sioux Falls, E 🅖 BP, SA/dsl, Shell, Sinclair/dsl 🍴 Applebee's, Arby's, Burger King, Chili's, Firehouse Subs, Fry'n Pan Rest., Fuddrucker's, HuHot Mongolian, KFC, Lonestar Steaks, McDonald's, Old Chicago Pizza, Olive Garden, Pancake House, Panda Express, Papa Murphy's, Perkins,

🚘 = gas 🍴 = food 🛏 = lodging ⊙ = other Ⓡ = rest stop Copyright 2015 - the Next EXIT ®

SD

🔼N INTERSTATE 29 Cont'd

Exit #	Services
77	Continued
	Pizza Hut, Pizza Ranch, Qdoba Mexican, Red Lobster, Starbucks, Subway, Szechwan Chinese, Taco Bell, Taco John's, TX Roadhouse, Valentino's, Wendy's 🛏 Best Western, Comfort Suites, Courtyard, Fairfield Inn, Microtel, MyPlace Hotel, Red Rock Inn, Residence Inn, SpringHill Suites, Super 8 ⊙ Advance Parts, Barnes&Noble, Best Buy, Dick's, Ford/Lincoln, Goodyear/auto, Gordman's, Hyundai, Hy-Vee Foods/dsl, JC Penney, Kohl's, Macy's, Mazda, Menards, Old Navy, PetCo, Radio Shack, Sears/auto, ShopKO, Target, Tires+, TJ Maxx, Verizon, Walgreens, Walmart/Subway, Younkers, W 🚘 Shell/dsl 🍴 Burger King, Godfather's, IHOP, Little Caesars, Perkins, Subway 🛏 AmericInn, Baymont Inn, Days Inn ⊙ Lewis Drug, USPO
75	I-229 E, to I-90 E
73	Tea, E 🚘 Sinclair/dsl 🍴 Marlin's Rest, W 1.5mi ⊙ Red Barn Camping
71	to Harrisburg, Lennox, E ⊙ repair, W ⊙ RV camping
68	to Lennox, Parker
64	SD 44, Worthing, W ⊙ Buick/Chevrolet, Great Plains RV Ctr
62	US 18 E, to Canton, E 🚘 Shell/pizza/dsl ⊙ Countryside RV park/motel
59	US 18 W, to Davis, Hurley
56	to Fairview, E ⊙ to Newton Hills SP(12mi)
53	to Viborg
50	to Centerville, Hudson
47	SD 46, to Irene, Beresford, E 🚘 BP/Burger King, Casey's/dsl, Sinclair/dsl 🍴 Emily's Café, Subway 🛏 Crossroads Motel, Super 8 ⊙ $General, Chevrolet, Fiesta Foods, Jet Auto Repair, W 🚘 Clark/Godfather's/dsl/scales/24hr
42	to Alcester, Wakonda
41mm	**truck check (from sb)**
38	to Volin, E ⊙ to Union Grove SP(3mi)
31	SD 48, to Akron, Spink
26	SD 50, to Vermillion, E **Welcome Center**/Ⓡ **both lanes, full** ♿ **facilities, info, litter barrels, petwalk,** 🚻, 🚮 W 🚘 BP/dsl 🍴 Burger King, Godfather's Pizza, Red Steakhouse, Subway, Taco John's 🛏 Comfort Inn, Holiday Inn Express, Prairie Inn, Super 8, Westside Inn ⊙ H, Hy-Vee Foods, to Lewis & Clark RA, to U of SD, Walmart/deli
18	Lp 29, to Burbank, Elk Point, E 🚘 A-1/dsl, Casey's 🛏 Home-Towne Inn
15	to Elk Point, E 🚘 Kum&Go/Subway/dsl, W ⊙ fireworks
13mm	**parking area sb, weigh sta nb**
9	SD 105, Jefferson, E 🚘 BP/Choice Cut Rest.
4	McCook, W 1 mi ⊙ Adams Homestead/nature preserve, KOA (seasonal)
2	N Sioux City, E 🚘 Goode/casino/dsl/E10/20/30 🍴 McDonald's, Subway, Taco John's ⊙ fireworks, USPO, W 🚘 Casey's, Clark 🛏 Days Inn, Hampton Inn, Red Carpet Inn, Super 8 ⊙ KOA, to Sodrac Dogtrack
1	E ⊙ Dakota Dunes Golf Resort, W 🚘 Dunes Gen. Store/dsl 🍴 Graham's Grill 🛏 Country Inn&Suites
0mm	South Dakota/Iowa state line, Big Sioux River

🔼E INTERSTATE 90

Exit #	Services
412.5mm	South Dakota/Minnesota state line
412mm	**Welcome Center wb**/Ⓡ **eb, full** ♿ **facilities, info, litter barrels, petwalk,** 🚻, 🚮 **RV dump (wb), weigh sta (wb)**

SIOUX FALLS

Exit #	Services
410	Valley Springs, N ⊙ Palisades SP (7mi), S 🚘, 🍴, ⊙ Beaver Creek Nature Area
406	SD 11, Brandon, Corson, N ⊙ Palisades SP(10mi), S 🚘 BP/dsl, Holiday/McDonald's/dsl, Local 🍴 Brandon Steaks, DQ, Great Wall, Pizza Hut, Pizza Ranch, Subway, Taco John's, Tailgater's Grill 🛏 Comfort Inn, Holiday Inn Express ⊙ Ace Hardware, Lewis Drug, Sturdevant's Parts, Sunshine Foods, to Big Sioux RA (4mi), Verizon
402	EROS Data Ctr, N ⊙ Jellystone RV Park, tires
400	I-229 S, no services
399	SD 115, Cliff Ave, Sioux Falls, N 🚘 TC's/BP/dsl ⊙ KOA, Spader RV Ctr, S 🚘 BP, Get'n Go/DSL, Holiday/dsl/e-85, Loves/GrandmaMax's/Subway/dsl/scales/24hr/@, Sinclair 🍴 Arby's, Burger King, McDonald's/truck parking, Perkins, Taco Bell, Taco John's 🛏 Cloud Nine Motel, Days Inn, EconoLodge, Super 8 ⊙ H Graham Tire, Kenworth, Peterbilt, Volvo
398mm	Big Sioux River
396b a	I-29, N to Brookings, S to Sioux City
395	Marion, S ⊙ Walmart/Subway
390	SD 38, Hartford, N 🍴 Pizza Ranch (3mi) ⊙ Camp Dakota RV Park, Goos RV Ctr, S 🍴 Cowboy Town/dsl
387	rd 17, Hartford, N 🚘 BP/dsl 🍴 Midway Grill, Pizza Ranch (1.6mi) 🛏 AmericInn
379	SD 19, Humboldt, N 🚘 Clark/dsl ⊙ USPO
375mm	E Vermillion River
374	to SD 38, Montrose, S 5 mi ⊙ Battle Creek Res., Lake Vermillion RA, RV camping
368	Canistota, S 4 mi 🛏 Best Western, Canistota Depot Inn, Ortman Hotel
364	US 81, to Yankton, Salem, S 1 mi 🚘 Cenex 🛏 Home Motel ⊙ Camp America
363.5mm	W Vermillion River
363mm	Ⓡ **both lanes, full** ♿ **facilities, litter barrels, petwalk,** 🚻, 🚮 **RV dump, vending,** st patrol
357	to Bridgewater, Canova
353	Spencer, Emery, S 🚘 FuelMart/Subway/dsl/casino/24hr
352mm	Wolf Creek
350	SD 25, Emery, Farmer, N ⊙ Home of Laura Ingalls Wilder, to DeSmet
344	SD 262, to Fulton, Alexandria, S 🚘 Shell/dsl
337mm	**parking area both lanes**
335	Riverside Rd, N ⊙ KOA(1mi)
334.5mm	James River
332	SD 37 S, to Parkston, Mitchell, N 🚘 Cenex/Chester's/dsl, Clark, I-90/Holiday/Marlin's Rest./Subway/dsl/scales/24hr, Mobil/Jimmy John's, Sinclair 🍴 Arby's, Cattleman's Club Steaks, Chef Louie Steaks, Corona Village Mexican, McDonald's, Perkins, Pizza Hut, Pizza Ranch, Twin Dragon Chinese 🛏 AmericInn, Best Value Inn, Days Inn, Quality Inn, Super 8/truck parking, Thunderbird Motel ⊙ H Advance Parts, AutoZone, Chrysler/Dodge/Jeep, K-Mart, Museum of Pioneer Life, O'Reilly Parts, Rondee's Campground, to Corn Palace, transmissions, URGENT CARE, Verizon, Walgreens, S 🚘 Shell/Godfather's/Taco Bell/dsl/24hr 🍴 Culver's, Hardee's, Quiznos, Ruby Tuesday, Whiskey Creek Grill 🛏 Comfort Inn, Hampton Inn, Holiday Inn Express, Kelly Inn ⊙ $Tree, AT&T, Cabela's, Menards, Verizon, Walmart/Subway
330	SD 37 N, Mitchell, N 🚘 Cenex/Chester's/dsl, Shell/dsl, Sinclair/dsl 🍴 DQ, Phoenix & Dragon Chinese 🛏 Budget Inn, EconoLodge, Motel 6, Ramada Inn, Siesta Motel ⊙ H County Fair Foods, Jack's Campers/RV Ctr, Lewis Drug, Mr. Tire, museum, to Corn Palace, **weigh sta,** S ⊙ Dakota RV Park

MITCHELL

SD

SD

INTERSTATE 90 Cont'd

Exit #	Services
325	Betts Rd, S 🅞 Famil-e-Fun Camping
319	Mt Vernon, N 1 mi 🅟 Sinclair/dsl, Westey's One Stop/dsl
310	US 281, to Stickney, S 🅟 Sinclair/Deli Depot/dsl/24hr 🅞 to Ft Randall Dam
308	Lp 90, to Plankinton, N 🅟 Sinclair/Al's Cafe/dsl 🛏 Cabin Fever Motel/RV Park, Smart Choice Inn 🅞 Gordy's Camping, Hills RV Park, repair, USPO
301.5mm	🆁🆂 both lanes, full ♿ facilities, info, litter barrels, 🄲, 🅰, RV dump
296	White Lake, N 1 mi 🅟 Hillman's/DSL 🛏 A-Z Motel 🅞 USPO, S 🅞 Siding 36 Motel/RV Park
294mm	Platte Creek
289	SD 45 S, to Platte, S 🅞 to Snake Cr/Platte Cr RA (25mi)
284	SD 45 N, Kimball, N 🅟 Clark, Conoco/Ditty's/Diner/dsl 🍴 Frosty King 🛏 Dakota Winds Motel, Regency Inn 🅞 Parkway Campground, repair/tires, S 🅞 tractor museum
272	SD 50, Pukwana, N 2 mi 🅟, 🍴, S 🅞 Snake/Platte Creek Rec Areas (25mi)
265	SD 50, Chamberlain,, N 🅟 Cenex/DQ/dsl 🛏 AmericInn 🅞 🅷 Alco, St Joseph Akta Lakota Museum(4mi), vet, S 🅟 SA/dsl 🅞 Happy Camper Campground
264mm	🆁🆂 both lanes, full ♿ facilities, info, litter barrels, 🄲, 🅰, scenic views
263	Chamberlain, N 🅟 Sinclair/dsl 🍴 McDonald's, Pizza Hut, Subway(1mi), Taco John's 🛏 Bel Aire Motel(1mi), Best Western(1mi), Riverview Inn, Super 8 🅞 Crow Creek Sioux Tribal Hqtrs, SD Hall of Fame
262mm	Missouri River
260	SD 50, Oacoma, N 🅟 Cenex/Arby's/dsl, Clark/dsl, Shell/dsl 🛏 Al's Oasis/Motel/Camping/cafe/mkt, Cedar Shore Motel/Camping (3mi), Days Inn, Howard Johnson, Quality Inn 🅞 antiques, Buick/Chevrolet, Dakota Camping, Oasis Camping, Old West Museum
251	SD 47, to Winner, Gregory
248	SD 47, Reliance, N 🅟 Cenex(1mi), Farmer's Union/dsl(1mi) 🅞 Sioux Tribal Hqtrs, to Big Bend RA
241	to Lyman
235	SD 273, Kennebec, N 🅟 Clark/dsl 🍴 Hot Rods Steaks 🛏 Budget Host, Kings Inn 🅞 auto repair, KOA, USPO
226	US 183 S, Presho, N 🅟 Cenex/dsl, Sinclair/dsl 🛏 Hutch's Motel/café 🅞 New Frontier RV Park, pioneer museum, repair, vet
225	lp 90, Presho, same as 226
221mm	🆁🆂 wb, full ♿ facilities, info, litter barrels, 🄲, 🅰, RV dump
220	no services
218mm	🆁🆂 eb, full ♿ facilities, info, litter barrels, 🄲, 🅰, RV dump
214	Vivian
212	US 83 N, SD 53, to Pierre, N 🅟 Sinclair/dsl 🅞 🅷 (34mi)
208	no services
201	Draper
194mm	parking area both lanes
192	US 83 S, Murdo, N 🅟 🚛/Subway/dsl/Lp/scales/24hr, Pioneer/dsl 🍴 Buffalo Rest., Murdo Drive-In, Prairie Pizza, Rusty Spur Steaks, Star Rest., The Diner 🛏 American Inn, Anchor Inn, Best Western, Iversen Inn, Range Country Lodge, Sioux Motel, Super 8 🅞 American RV Park/camping, auto museum, city park, Ford, Murdo Foods, USPO, N 🛏 Country Inn 🅞 to Rosebud
191	Murdo, N same as 192
188mm	parking area both lanes, litter barrels

Exit #	Services
183	Okaton, S 🅞 Ghost Town
177	no services
175mm	central/mountain timezone
172	to Cedar Butte
170	SD 63 N, to Midland, N 🅟 Shell/dsl 🅞 1880's Town, KOA
167mm	🆁🆂 wb, full ♿ facilities, litter barrels, pet walk, 🄲, 🅰, RV dump
165mm	🆁🆂 eb, full ♿ facilities, litter barrels, pet walk, 🄲, 🅰, RV dump
163	SD 63, Belvidere, S 🅟 Belvidere Store/dsl 🍴 JR's Grill
152	Lp 90, Kadoka, N 🅟 Conoco/rest./dsl/24hr, S 🅞 Badlands Petrified Gardens, camping
150	SD 73 S, Kadoka, N Dakota Inn/rest., S 🅟 Conoco/DSL, Sinclair/pizza/dsl 🍴 Subway, Sunset Grill 🛏 Best Value Inn, Budget Host, Ponderosa Motel/RV Park, Rodeway Inn, Wagon Wheel Motel 🅞 Kadoka Kampground, repair, to Buffalo Nat Grasslands
143	SD 73 N, to Philip, N 15 mi 🅞 🅷
138mm	scenic overlook wb
131	SD 240, N 🅞 Minuteman Missle NHS, S 🅟 Conoco 🛏 Badlands Inn(9mi), Cedar Pass Lodge/rest. (9mi) 🅞 Circle 10 Camping, KOA(11mi), Prairie Home NHS, to Badlands NP
129.5mm	scenic overlook eb
127	no services
121	Bigfoot Rd
116	239th St
112	US 14 E, to Philip
110	SD 240, Wall, N 🅟 Conoco/dsl, Exxon, Phillips 66/Subway 🍴 Cactus Cafe, DQ, Red Rock Rest., Roadtrip Cafe, Wall Drug Rest. 🛏 Ann's Motel, Best Value Inn, Best Western, Days Inn, EconoLodge, Fountain Hotel, Motel 6, Sunshine Inn, Super 8, The Wall Motel, Welsh Motel 🅞 Ace Hardware, Arrow Campground, Harley Davidson, National Grasslands Visitor Ctr, Pronto Parts, Sleepy Hollow RV Park/Camping, Wall Drug, Wall Foods, Wounded Knee Museum, N 🛏 Frontier Cabins Motel 🅞 RV camping, to Badlands NP
109	W 4th Ave, Wall, N 1-2 mi access to same as 110
107	Cedar Butte Rd
101	Jensen Rd, to Schell Ranch
100mm	🆁🆂 both lanes, full ♿ facilities, litter barrels, pet walk, 🄲, 🅰, RV dump, vending
99.5mm	Cheyenne River
98	Wasta, N 🅟 Mobil/dsl 🅞 24 Express RV Camping, USPO
90	173rd Ave, to Owanka
88	171st Ave (from eb, no re-entry)
84	167th Ave, N 🅞 Olde Glory Fireworks

🅶 = gas 🍴 = food 🛏 = lodging 🅾 = other 🆁🆂 = rest stop

SD

⬆E INTERSTATE 90 Cont'd

Exit #	Services
78	161st Ave, New Underwood, **S** 🅶 Sinclair/dsl, Steve's General Store/dsl/motel/rest. 🍴 Harry's Hideaway Rest, 🛏 BJ's Motel 🅾 Boondocks Camping
69mm	**parking area both lanes**
67	to Box Elder, **N** 🅶 ♥Love's/Subway/dsl/scales/24hr 🅾 Air&Space Museum, Ellsworth AFB
63	(eb only), 🅾 Ellsworth AFB, to Box Elder
61	Elk Vale Rd, **N** 🅶 ✈FLYING J/Conoco/CountryMkt/dsl/e-85/LP/RV dump/scales/24hr/@ 🍴 Quaker Steak 🛏 Cambrian Suites, MainStay Suites 🅾 Black Hills Visitor Ctr, Cabela's, Dakota RV Ctr, **S** 🅶 Conoco/dsl, Mobil/dsl/e-85 🍴 Arby's, Dakotah Steakhouse, Marco's Pizza, McDonalds 🛏 Baymont Inn, Comfort Suites, Fairfield Inn, La Quinta, Residence Inn, Sleep Inn 🅾 KOA (2mi seasonal)
60	Lp 90, to Mt Rushmore, Rapid City, **N** 🅾 Buick/GMC, Chevrolet, Ford, Great Western Tire, Kenworth/Volvo, Toyota, **S** 🍴 Blaze Pizza, Culver's, Famous Dave's, Five Guys, Fuji Japanese Steaks, HuHot Mongolian, Longhorn Steaks, On the Border, Pizza Ranch, Popeyes, Qdoba Mexican, Smiling Moose Deli, Starbucks 🅾 H, $Tree, Aamco, Gordman's, Menards, Michael's, Nat Coll of Mines/Geology, PetCo, Sam's Club/dsl, Scheel's Sports, Target, TJ Maxx, Verizon
59	La Crosse St,, Rapid City, **N** 🅶 Mobil/dsl, Phillips 66 🍴 Boston's Rest., Burger King, Denny's, Fuddrucker's, Minerva's Rest., Outback Steaks, Starbucks, TGIFriday's, TX Roadhouse 🛏 Best Western, Country Inn&Suites, EconoLodge, Hilton Garden, Holiday Inn Express, Super 8 🅾 Herberger's, Hobby Lobby, mall, Sears/auto, st patrol, **S** 🅶 Exxon/24hr, Sinclair 🍴 Arnold's Diner, China Wok, Golden Corral, Little Caesar's, MillStone Rest., Mongolian Grill, Pacific Rim Cafe, Perkins, Philly Ted's, Subway 🛏 AmericInn, Comfort Inn, Days Inn, Fair Value Inn, Foothills Inn, Grand Gateway Hotel, Hampton Inn, Microtel, Motel 6, Ramada, Travelodge 🅾 AT&T, URGENT CARE, Walgreens, Walmart/McDonald's
58	Haines Ave, Rapid City, **N** 🅶 Fresh Start/dsl 🍴 Applebee's, Chili's, Hardee's, IHOP, Olive Garden, Red Lobster 🛏 Best Value Inn, Grand Stay Motel 🅾 BAM!, Best Buy, Hancock Fabrics, Herbergers, JC Penney, Kohl's, Lowe's, Petsmart, Tires+, to Rushmore Mall, **S** 🅶 Loaf'n Jug 🍴 Dickey's BBQ, Jimmy John's, Papa John's, Taco John's, Wendy's 🅾 H, Family$, ShopKO, URGENT CARE
57	I-190, US 16, to Rapid City, Mt Rushmore, **S 1 mi on North St** 🅶 Exxon 🍴 Panchero's Mexican 🛏 Adoba Eco Hotel, Holiday Inn, Howard Johnson 🅾 Ace Hardware, Family Thrift Foods, Office Depot
55	Deadwood Ave, **N** 🅾 Dakota RV Ctr, Harley-Davidson/cafe, **S** 🅶 📠/Subway/dsl/scales/24hr/@ 🍴 Marlin's Rest. 🅾 Cadillac/Chevrolet, dsl repair
52	Peaceful Pines Rd, Black Hawk, **N** 🅾 Lazy JD RV Park(4mi), Three Flags Camping(1mi), **S** 🍴 BJ's/dsl, Godfather's Pizza, Longhorn Rest. 🅾 Family$, USPO
48	Stagebarn Canyon Rd, **N** 🅾 RV camping, **S** 🅶 Conoco/Haggar's Mkt/food, PitStop/dsl 🍴 Pizza Hut 🛏 Ramada 🅾 Mid-States RV Ctr
46	Piedmont Rd, Elk Creek Rd, **N** 🍴 Elk Creek Steakhouse 🅾 Elk Creek RV Park, to Petrified Forest, **S** 🅶 Mobil/Country Corner Cafe/Papa John's/dsl 🍴 Sacora Sta Rest. 🅾 Sacora Sta Camping
44	Bethlehem Rd, **S** 🅾 Jack's RV Ctr(2mi)

RAPID CITY

42mm	🆁🆂 both lanes, full ♿ facilities, info, litter barrels, pet walk, 📞, 🅾, RV dump, vending
40	Tilford, **S** 🅾 RV Park
39mm	**weigh sta eb**
37	Pleasant Valley Rd, **N** 🅾 Elkview Camp, **S** 🅾 Bulldog Camping, Rush-No-More Camping
34	**S** 🅾 Black Hills Nat Cemetary, No Name City RV Park
32	SD 79, Jct Ave, Sturgis, **N** 🅶 Conoco/dsl, Exxon/dsl 🍴 Caddy's Grill, Taco John's 🛏 Best Western, Knight's Inn 🅾 HOSPITAL, Ford, Grocery Mart, NAPA, to Bear Butte SP, vet
30	US 14A W, SD 34E, to Deadwood, Sturgis, **N** 🅶 Cenex/dsl, Fresh Start/dsl 🍴 McDonald's, Pizza Hut, Shanghai Chinese 🅾 CarQuest, Day's End Camping, Famliy$, Indian Motorcycles, Mr Tire, O'Reilly Parts, ShopKo, USPO, **S** 🅶 Conoco/dsl, RanchMart 🍴 Burger King, DQ, Kangeroo San Asian, Pizza Ranch, Subway 🛏 Days Inn, Holiday Inn Express, Super 8 🅾 BMW Motorcycles, Chevrolet, Verizon
23	SD 34 W, to Belle Fourche, Whitewood, **N** 🅾 Northern Hills RV Ctr, **S** 🅶 Howdy's/dsl, Sonset Sta/dsl 🍴 Hideaway Diner 🛏 Tony's Motel 🅾 USPO
17	US 85 S, to Deadwood, **S 9-17 mi in Deadwood** 🍴 Brown Rock, Deadwood Grill, Silverado Café 🛏 Deadwood Lodge, Elkhorn Ridge Motel, Holiday Inn Express, Mineral Palace Motel, SpringHill Suites, Super 8 🅾 Deadwood NLH, Elkhorn Ridge RV Resort, Whistler Gulch Camping
14	US 14A, Spearfish Canyon, **N** 🅶 FreshStart/dsl 🍴 Applebee's, Culver's, Subway 🛏 Fairfield Inn, Hampton Inn, Holiday Inn/rest., Quality Inn 🅾 AutoZone, Verizon, Walmart, **S** 🅶 Phillips 66/dsl 🍴 KFC/LJ Silver, Perkins, Pizza Ranch, Roma's Rest. 🛏 Howard Johnson, Rodeway Inn, Super 8 🅾 Ace Hardware, camping, Ford/Lincoln, K-Mart, transmissions
12	Jackson Blvd, Spearfish, **S** 🅶 Conoco/dsl, Exxon, Loaf'n Jug, Phillips 66/dsl 🍴 Arby's, Barbacoa's, Domino's, Jade Palace Chinese, McDonald's, Millstone Rest., Papa Murphy's, Pizza Hut, Taco John's 🛏 Best Western 🅾 H, Black Hills St U, CarQuest, Chrysler/Dodge/Jeep, historic fish hatchery, Radio Shack, same as 10
10	US 85 N, to Belle Fourche, **S** 🍴 Burger King, Cedar House Rest., Golden Dragon Chinese, Little Caesar's, McDonald's, Philly Ted's, Subway, Taco Bell 🛏 Days Inn 🅾 H, Buick/Chevrolet, Cadillac/GMC, KOA, Safeway/dsl, same as 12, USPO, Walgreens
8	McGuigan Rd, W Spearfish, **S** 🅾 KOA (1mi)
2	**N 1 mi** 🅾 McNenny St Fish Hatchery
1mm	**Welcome Center eb, full** ♿ **facilities, info, litter barrels, petwalk,** 📞, 🛏 **RV dump**
0mm	South Dakota/Wyoming state line

STURGIS **SPEARFISH** **SIOUX FALLS**

⬆N INTERSTATE 229 (Sioux Falls)

Exit #	Services
10b a	I-90 E and W. **I-229 begins/ends on I-90, exit 400.**
9	Benson Rd, **W** 🅶 Sinclair/pizza/dsl 🍴 DQ, Jimmy John's, Marlin's Rest. 🅾 Ford Trucks, Western Star
7.5mm	Big Sioux River
7	Rice St, **E** winter sports, **W** to stockyards
6	SD 38, 10th St, **E** 🅶 Sinclair 🍴 A&W, Applebee's, Arby's, Denny's, Domino's, DQ, Fryn' Pan Rest., Jimmy John's, KFC, Pizza Hut, Pizza Ranch, Taco Bell, Tokyo Hibachi, Tomacelli's Italian 🛏 Super 8 🅾 AT&T, AutoZone, Family$, Hy-Vee Foods, K-Mart, O'Reilly Parts, ShopKO, Sturdevant's Parts, USPO, Valvoline, vet, **W** 🅶 BP/dsl, Casey's/dsl, Shell 🍴 Burger King, BurgerTime, Hardee's, Little Caesar's,

S I O U X   F A L L S

⬆N   INTERSTATE 229 (Sioux Falls) Cont'd

Exit #	Services
6	Continued
	McDonald's, Pita Pit, Pizza Inn, Pizza Man, Puerto Vallarta, Qdoba Mexican, Subway, Taco John's 🔲 Rushmore Motel 🔲 Lewis Drug, vet
5.5mm	Big Sioux River
5	26th St, E 🔲 Holiday/dsl 🔲 Burger King, Cherry Creek Grill, Dario's Pizza, McDonald's, SaiGon Panda 🔲 city park, W 🔲 H
4	Cliff Ave, E 🔲 BP
3	SD 115, Lp 229, Minnesota Ave, E 🔲 city park, W 🔲 BP/dsl, Sinclair 🔲 Arby's, Burger King, Camilles Cafe, Culver's, DQ, Famous Dave's BBQ, Golden Bowl Chinese, Hardee's, Little Caesar's/TCBY, McDonald's, Subway 🔲 $Tree, Ace Hardware, Acura, Buick/GMC, Costco/gas, Hy-Vee Foods/dsl, Kia, Lewis Drug, Staples, tires, USPO, ver

2	Western Ave, E 🔲 Holiday/dsl 🔲 Bracco Cafe, DQ, Scooters Coffee, Siarbucks, W 🔲 Cenex/dsl, Holiday 🔲 Buck's Roadhouse, Burger King, China Buffet, Huhot Mongolian, Lone Star Steaks, Papa Murphy's, PepperJax Grill, Perkins, Qdoba Mexican, Redrossa Pizza, Scheell's, Valentino's 🔲 H Advance Parts, AutoZone, Best Buy, Goodyear/auto, Hancock Fabticks, Radio Shack, Tuesday Morning
1.5mm	Big Sioux River
1c	Louise Ave, E 🔲 Holiday/dsl 🔲 Comfort Suites, Holiday Inn Express, Homewood Suites 🔲 H Chrysler/Dodge/Jeep, Fiat, Lewis Drug, W 🔲 BP 🔲 Burger King, Jimmy John's, Marco's Pizza, McDonald's, Noodles&Co, Panera Bread, Qdoba Mexican, Royal Palace, Spezia's Rest, Taco John's, Wendy's 🔲 Hilton Garden Inn 🔲 Barnes&Noble, Dick's, Honda, Hy-Vee Foods/dsl, JC Penney, Jo-Ann Fabrics, Kohl's, mall, Target, Verizon, Walgreens
1b a	I-29 N and S. **I-229 begins/ends on I-29, exit 75.**

TENNESSEE

C H A T T A N O O G A

⬆E   INTERSTATE 24

Exit #	Services
185b a	I-75, N to Knoxville, S to Atlanta.
	I-24 begins/ends on I-75, exit 2 in Chattanooga.
184	Moore Rd, S 🔲 Chef Lin's Buffet, Provino's Italian 🔲 $Tree, Radio Shack
183	(183a from wb), Belvoir Ave, Germantown Rd
181a	US 41 S, to East Ridge (from eb), S 🔲 Sugar's Ribs 🔲 King's Lodge 🔲 Ford Trucks
181	Fourth Ave, to TN Temple U, Chattanooga, N 🔲 Citgo/dsl, Exxon/dsl, Hi-Tech Fuel, Stop'n Save 🔲 Bojangles, Burger King, Capt D's, Hardee's, Krystal, Subway, Waffle House 🔲 Chatt Inn 🔲 $General, BiLo, Mack/Volvo Trucks, O'Reilly Parts, repair, vet, S 🔲 Mystik
180b a	US 27 S, TN 8, Rossville Blvd, N 🔲 tires, to UT Chatt, U-Haul, S 🔲 Mapco/dsl, RaceWay/dsl 🔲 Hamilton Inn 🔲 auto repair, Family$, NTB, to Chickamauga Battlefield
178	US 27 N, Market St, to Lookout Mtn, Chattanooga, N 🔲 BP/dsl, Citgo 🔲 Country Hearth Inn, La Quinta, Marriott, Staybridge Suites 🔲 Chevrolet, Ford/Lincoln, Midas, Nissan, to aquarium, to Chattanooga ChooChoo, U-Haul, S 🔲 RaceWay/dsl 🔲 KFC 🔲 Comfort Suites, Motel 6
175	Browns Ferry Rd, to Lookout Mtn, N 🔲 BP, Exxon/dsl 🔲 China Gourmet 🔲 Best Value Inn 🔲 $General, CVS Drug, vet, S 🔲 Mapco/dsl 🔲 Hardee's, McDonald's 🔲 Comfort Inn, EconoLodge, Quality Inn
174	US 11, US 41, US 64, Lookout Valley, N 🔲 Waffle House 🔲 Days Inn 🔲 Racoon Mtn Camping (1mi), S 🔲 BP/dsl,

174	Continued
	Kangaroo 🔲 Cracker Barrel, Logan's Roadhouse, Los 3 Amigos, New China, Taco Bell, Waffle House, Wendy's 🔲 Baymont Inn, Best Western, Budget Motel, Country Inn&Suites, Fairfield Inn, Hampton Inn, Holiday Inn Express, Knights Inn, Ramada Ltd, Super 8 🔲 $Tree, Ace Hardware, AT&T, Lookout Valley Camping, st patrol, Verizon, Walmart/Subway
172mm	℞s eb, full ♿ facilities, litter barrels, petwalk, 🔲, 🔲 vending
171mm	Tennessee/Georgia state line
169	GA 299, to US 11, N 🔲 Mapco/dsl, S 🔲 BP/Krispy Chicken/dsl/24hr, 🔲/Subway/dsl/scales/24hr, RaceWay 🔲 Granny's Rest. 🔲 repair
167mm	Tennessee/Georgia state line, Central/Eastern time zone
167	I-59 S, to Birmingham
161	TN 156, to Haletown, New Hope, N 🔲 BP/dsl (1mi) 🔲 Hales Bar RV Park, S 🔲 Chevron/fireworks
160mm	Tennessee River/Nickajack Lake
159mm	**Welcome Center wb, ℞s eb, full ♿ facilities, litter barrels, petwalk, 🔲, 🔲 vending**
158	US 41, TN 27, Nickajack Dam, N 🔲 ❤Love's/McDonald's/Subway/dsl/scales/24hr, 🔲 BP/dsl/fireworks 🔲 Shellmound Camping (2.5mi)
155	TN 28, Jasper, N 🔲 BP/dsl (1mi), Hi-Tech 🔲 DQ (1mi) Hardee's, Western Sizzlin, S 🔲 BP/Quiznos/dsl 🔲 H
152	US 41, US 64, US 72, Kimball, S Pittsburg, N 🔲 BP/fireworks, RaceWay/dsl, Shell/dsl 🔲 A&W/LJ Silver, Arby's, China Buffet, Cracker Barrel, Domino's, El Toril, KFC, Krystal, Los Amigos, McDonald's, Pizza Hut, Shoney's, Subway,

🅟 = gas 🍴 = food 🛏 = lodging 🅞 = other 🆁 = rest stop   Copyright 2015 - the Next EXIT ®

TN

INTERSTATE 24 Cont'd

Exit #	Services
152	Continued
	Taco Bell, Waffle House, Wendy's 🛏 Best Value Inn, Comfort Inn, Hampton Inn, Holiday Inn Express, Super 8 🅞 🅷 $Tree, Buick/Chevrolet/GMC, GNC, Lowe's, Radio Shack, to Russell Cave NM, Walmart, **S 3 mi** 🅞 Lodge Cast Iron
143	Martin Springs Rd, **N** 🅟 Chevron/dsl/fireworks
135	US 41 N, Monteagle, **N** 🅟 BP/dsl, Wilco/Hess/Wendy's/dsl/scales/24hr 🍴 Shan Chinese, Smok'n B's BBQ 🅞 Family$, Laurel Trails Camping, USPO, **S** 🅟 Days Inn
134	US 64, US 41A, to Sewanee, Monteagle, **N** 🅟 Mapco/Mc-Donald's 🍴 Sonic 🛏 American Eagle Inn 🅞 CVS Drug, to S Cumberland SP, **S** 🅟 Marathon/Kangaroo, Shell/dsl 🍴 Hardee's, Monteagle Diner, Pizza Hut, Smokehouse BBQ, Subway, Waffle House 🛏 Best Western, Mtn Inn, Super 8 🅞 $General, Fred's, Monteagle Winery, Piggly Wiggly, to U of The South
133mm	🆁 both lanes, full 🅰 facilities, litter barrels, petwalk, 🅒, 🛏 vending
128mm	Elk River
127	US 64, TN 50, to Winchester, Pelham, **N** 🅟 BP, Phillips 66, **S** 🅟 Gulf/dsl 🅞 to Tims Ford SP/RV camping
119mm	trucks only parking area both lanes
117	to Tullahoma, 🅞 USAF Arnold Ctr, UT Space Institute
116mm	weigh sta both lanes
114	US 41, Manchester, **N** 🅟 BP/24 Truckers/scales/dsl, Marathon/dsl, Murphy USA/dsl, Shell/dsl 🍴 El Potrillo, Great Wall Chinese, Logan's Roadhouse, O'Charley's, Starbucks 🛏 Comfort Suites, Holiday Inn Express, Motel 6, Quality Inn, Scottish Inn, Sleep Inn, Truckers Inn 🅞 $Tree, Country Cabin Camping, Home Depot, KOA, Nissan, Toyota, Verizon, Walmart/Subway, **S** 🅟 Marathon, RaceWay/dsl 🍴 Arby's, Baskin-Robbins, Burger King, Capt D's, Hong Kong Buffet, KFC, Krystal, McDonald's/playplace, Pizza Hut, Shoney's, Subway, Taco Bell, Waffle House, Wendy's 🛏 Best Value Inn, Country Inn&Suites, Days Inn, Microtel, Royal Inn 🅞 Advance Parts, AutoZone, Family$, Ford/Lincoln, O'Reilly Parts, Russell Stover, USPO
111	TN 55, Manchester, **N** 🅟 BP/dsl, Co-op gas/dsl, Marathon/Kangaroo 🅞 to Rock Island SP, **S** 🅟 BP 🍴 Hardee's, J&G Pizza/Steaks, Sonic 🅞 🅷 Gateway Auto, Old Stone Fort, Rite Aid, to Jack Daniels Dist HS, vet, Walgreens
110mm	Duck River
110	TN 53, Manchester, **N** 🅟 BP, Marathon, Shell/dsl 🍴 Cracker Barrel, Emma's Rest., Oak Rest. 🛏 Ambassador Inn, Economy Inn, Super 8, **S** 🅟 Shell/dsl/24hr 🍴 Los 3 Amigos, Waffle House 🅞 🅷
105	US 41, **N** 🅟 BP/dsl, Shell/dsl, **S** 🅞 Dickle HS, tire/repair, to Normandy Dam, Whispering Oaks Camping
97	TN 64, to Shelbyville, Beechgrove, **S** 🅟 BP/dsl
89	Buchanan Rd, **N** 🅟 ♥Loves/McDonald's/dsl/scales/24hr, **S** 🅟 Shell/dsl 🍴 Fiesta Grill 🅞 $General
84	Joe B. Jackson Pkwy, **N** 🍴 Subway
81	US 231, Murfreesboro, **N** 🅟 BP/dsl, Exxon, Shell 🍴 Cathay Asian, Cracker Barrel, Krystal, Parthenon Grille, Sal's Pizza, Shoney's, Waffle House, Wendy's 🛏 Best Value Inn, Knights Inn, Quality Inn, Ramada Ltd, Regal Inn 🅞 🅷 antiques, Chrysler/Dodge/Jeep, Honda, **S** 🅟 Kangaroo, Mapco/dsl, Marathon, 🚚Arby's/scales/dsl/24hr 🍴 Bojangles, Burger King, Dick's Hamburgers, La Siesta Mexican, McDonald's/playplace, Pizza Hut/Taco Bell, Sonic, Starbucks, Subway,

Exit #	Services
81	Continued
	Waffle House, Zaxby's 🛏 Safari Inn, Select Inn, Vista Suites 🅞 Advance Parts, AutoZone, Discount Tire, Gateway Auto, Kroger/gas, Rite Aid, Toyota/Scion, U-Haul, vet
80	New Salem Hwy, rd 99, **S** 🅞 Domino's, Subway
78	TN 96, to Franklin, Murfreesboro, **N** 🅟 BP, Marathon, Murphy USA/dsl, Phillips 66/Church's/White Castle/dsl, Shell/Jack-in-the-Box 🍴 Arby's, Baskin-Robbins, Bonefish Grill, Buffalo Wild Wings, Carrabba's, Cheddar's, Chick-fil-A, ChuckECheese, Coconut Bay Cafe, Cracker Barrel, Fazoli's, IHOP, Jason's Deli, Jimmy John's, Jim'n Nick's BBQ, KFC, McDonald's, Mi Patria, Old Chicago, Olive Garden, Outback Steaks, Panda Express, Panera Bread, Red Lobster, Red Robin, Sam's Grill, Samurai's Cuisine, SmashBurger, Starbucks, Steak'n Shake, Subway, TGIFriday's, Waffle House, Wendy's, Zaxby's 🛏 Baymont Inn, Best Western, Candlewood Suites, Clarion, Comfort Suites, Country Inn&Suites, Days Inn, DoubleTree, EconoLodge, Fairfield Inn, Hampton Inn, Holiday Inn Express, Microtel, Motel 6, Red Roof Inn, Sleep Inn, Super 8 🅞 $Tree, Aldi Foods, AT&T, Books-A-Million, Dillard's, Discount Tire, Firestone, Hobby Lobby, Home Depot, JC Penney, Jo-Ann Fabrics, Lowe's, Marshalls, NTB, Petsmart, Ross, Sears/auto, Staples, Target, Thornton's/dsl, TJ Maxx, to Stones River Bfd, Verizon, vet, Walgreens, Walmart, **S** 🅟 Kangaroo, Mapco, Marathon/dsl, Shell 🍴 Capt D's, China Garden, Hardee's, Jersey Mike's Subs, Las Palmas, Little Caesars, McDonald's, O'Charley's, Papa Murphy's, Pizza Hut, Sonic, Subway, Taco Bell, Waffle House, Wasabi Japanese 🛏 ValuePlace Inn 🅞 $General, AutoZone, Kohl's, Kroger/dsl, Old Time Pottery, O'Reilly Parts, Rite Aid, Sam's Club/gas, Walgreens
76	Fortress Blvd, Manson Pike, Medical Center Pkwy, **N** 🍴 Bar Louie, Chili's, Culver's, Genghis Grill, Longhorn Steaks, Macaroni Grill, Mimi's Cafe, Subway, Which Wich 🛏 Embassy Suites 🅞 🅷 Barnes&Noble, Belk, Best Buy, Dick's, Michael's, Old Navy, Thornton's/dsl, to Stones River Nat. Bfd, World Mkt, **S** 🅟 Exxon/dsl
74b a	TN 840, to Lebanon, Franklin
70	TN 102, Lee Victory Pkwy, Almaville Rd, to Smyrna, **N** 🅟 Shell/dsl/scales, **S** 🅟 BP, Kangaroo/Quiznos/dsl, Mapco 🍴 Legends Steaks, McDonald's, Mi Camino Mexican, Sonic, Subway 🛏 Deerfield Inn 🅞 $General, Tennessee Expo
66	TN 266, Sam Ridley Pkwy, to Smyrna, **N** 🅟 Shell/dsl 🍴 5 Guys Burgers, A&W/LJ Silver, Arby's, Buffalo Wild Wings, Catfish House, Cheddar's, Chick-fil-A, Chili's, CiCi's Pizza, Famous Dave's BBQ, Golden China, Hickory Falls Cafe, IHOP, Jersey Mike's Subs, Jim'n Nick's BBQ, Krispy Kreme, La Fiesta, Logan's Roadhouse, Longhorn Steaks, Panda Express, Panera Bread, Papa John's, Razz Grill, Sonic, Starbucks, Subway, Tody's Grill, Uncle Bud's Catfish, Waffle House, Wendy's, Zaxby's 🅞 🅷 $Tree, AT&T, CVS Drug, Dicount Tire, GNC, Home Depot/gas, Kohl's, Kroger/dsl, Lowe's, Nashville I-24 Camping (3mi), Petsmart, Publix, Ross, Staples, Target, URGENT CARE, Verizon, Walgreens, **S** 🍴 Cracker Barrel, O'Charley's, Ruby Tuesday 🛏 Comfort Suites, Fairfield Inn, Hampton Inn, Hilton Garden, Holiday Inn Express, La Quinta, Sleep Inn
64	Waldron Rd, to La Vergne, **N** 🅟 Kangaroo, Kwik Sak, 🚚Subway/dsl/scales/24hr 🍴 Arby's, Hardee's, Krystal, McDonald's, Waffle House 🛏 Comfort Inn, Quality Inn, Ramada Inn 🅞 RV ctr, **S** 🅟 Mapco/dsl
62	TN 171, Old Hickory Blvd, **N** 🅟 Citgo/Subway/dsl, Shell/dsl, TA/BP/Burger King/Popeye's/dsl/scales/24hr@ 🍴 Acapulco Burrito 🛏 Best Western

Vertical labels: **MONTEAGLE**, **MANCHESTER** (left column); **MURFREESBORO**, **NASHVILLE** (right column)

INTERSTATE 24 Cont'd

Exit #	Services
60	Hickory Hollow Pkwy, **N** 🅡 BP, Exxon/dsl, Mapco 🍴 Applebee's, Burger King, ChuckECheese, El Patron, KFC/LJ Silver, Logan's Roadhouse, McDonald's/Playplace, O'Charley's, Red Lobster, Starbucks, Subway, Taco Bell, Wendy's, Zaxby's 🛏 Country Inn&Suites, Hampton Inn, Nashville Hotel 🅾 $Tree, Chevrolet, Chrysler/Dodge/Jeep, Family$, Firestone/auto, Kroger/gas, Mazda, NTB, Office Depot, TJ Maxx, **S** 🅡 BP/Quiznos/dsl, Shell/Dunkin Donuts 🍴 Camino Royale Mexican, Casa Fiesta Mexican, Evergreen Chinese, Fox's Pizza, IHOP, Olive Garden, Shoney's, Steak'n Shake 🛏 Knights Inn, Super 8 🅾 Home Depot, Kia, Target, vet
59	TN 254, Bell Rd, same as 60
57	Haywood Lane, **N** 🅡 Kwik Sak/dsl 🍴 Hardee's, Pizza Hut, Whitt's BBQ 🅾 $General, CarQuest, Walgreens, **S** 🅡 Kangaroo, Shell
56	TN 255, Harding Place, **N** 🅡 Exxon, Mapco, Shell/dsl 🍴 Applebee's, Bar-B-Cutie, Dunkin Donuts, Hardee's, KFC, McDonald's, Pizza Hut/Taco Bell, Subway, Waffle House, Wendy's 🛏 Executive Inn, Harding Inn, M Motel, Stay Lodge, Thrifty Inn 🅾 Sam's Club/gas, **S** 🅡 Mapco, Shell/dsl 🍴 Burger King, Hooters, Jack-in-the-Box, La Fiesta 🛏 Best Value Inn, Travelodge 🅾 Ⓗ
54b a	TN 155, Briley Pkwy, 🅾 to Opryland
53	I-440 W, to Memphis
52	US 41, Murfreesboro Rd, **N** 🅡 Mapco, Phillips 66/dsl, Shell 🍴 Picadilly's, Pizza Hut, Taco Bell, Waffle House 🛏 Days Inn, Executive Inn, Holiday Inn Express, Rodeway Inn, Super 8 🅾 AutoZone, Family$, Wagreens, **S** 🅾 NAPA
52b a	I-40, E to Knoxville, W to Memphis
I-24 and I-40 run together 2 mi. See I-40 exits 212-213	
50b	I-40 W
49	Shelby Ave, (from wb only), 🅾 to LP Field
48	James Robertson Pkwy, **N** 🅡 Citgo, **S** 🅡 Exxon, TA/Subway/dsl/24hr/@ 🍴 Shoney's 🛏 Ramada, Stadium Inn 🅾 LP Stadium, st capitol
47a	US 31E
47	N 1st St, Jefferson St, **N** 🅡 BP/Subway, Phillips 66 🅾 Family$, **S** 🅡 Mystic Gas 🛏 Days Inn, Knights Inn 🅾 U-Haul
I-24 and I-65 run together. See I-65 exit 87 b a.	
87b a	US 431, Trinity Lane, **E** 🅡 BP, ♥Loves/Subway/dsl/scales/24hr 🍴 Church's/White Castle, Krystal, Sonic 🛏 Cumberland Inn, Delux Inn 🅾 Piggly Wiggly, **W** 🅡 BCP/dsl, BP, Exxon, Mapco 🍴 Fat Mo's, Jack-in-the-Box, Jack's BBQ, McDonald's, Subway, Taco Bell, Waffle House 🛏 Best Value Inn, Comfort Inn, Days Inn, EconoLodge, Halmark Inn, Howard Johnson, King's Inn, Quality Inn, Ravin Hotel, Regency Inn, Rodeway Inn 🅾 $General, Family$
44b a	I-65, N to Louisville, S to Nashville
43	TN 155, Briley Pkwy, Brick Church Pike
40	TN 45, Old Hickory Blvd, **N** 🅡 BP/Subway/dsl, Phillips 66/dsl/24hr, Shell/dsl 🛏 Super 8
35	US 431, to Joelton, Springfield, **N** 🅾 Ⓗ **S** 🅡 Heritage TC/DQ/Subway/dsl, Shell 🍴 Family Rest., Mazatlan Mexican, McDonald's 🛏 Days Inn 🅾 auto repair, Curves, Family$, OK Camping
31	TN 249, New Hope Rd, **N** 🅡 Shell/Taco Tico/dsl, **S** 🅡 BP/dsl, Shell/dsl/24hr
24	TN 49, to Springfield, Ashland City, **N** 🅡 BP/dsl, Mapco/dsl/24hr, Phillips 66/dsl/24hr 🅾 Ⓗ repair, **S** 🅡 Shell/dsl, SS/Dunkin Donuts/Wendy's 🍴 Dragon Buffet, KFC/Taco Bell, Sonic, Subway 🅾 $General, city park, Hill Foods, USPO, vet

CLARKSVILLE

19	TN 256, Maxey Rd, to Adams, **N** 🅡 BP/dsl, **S** 🅡 Shell
11	TN 76, to Adams, Clarksville, **N** 🅡 Shell/dsl/24hr, **S** 🅡 BP/dsl/24hr 🍴 McDonald's, Subway, Waffle House 🛏 Days Inn, Holiday Inn Express, Quality Inn, Super 8 🅾 Ⓗ
9mm	Red River
8	TN 237, Rossview Rd, **S** 🅾 Dunbar Cave SP
4	US 79, to Clarksville, Ft Campbell, **N** 🅡 BP/dsl/24hr, Exxon/dsl 🍴 Cracker Barrel 🛏 Hilton Garden 🅾 Sam's Club/gas, Spring Creek Camping (2mi), **S** 🅡 BP/dsl/24hr, Murphy USA/dsl, Shell/dsl 🍴 Applebee's, Arby's, Baskin-Robbins, Buffalo Wild Wings, Burger King, Capt D's, Chili's, Chopsticks, ChuckeCheese, Church's/White Castle, DQ, Fazoli's, Golden Corral, Harbor Cafe, IHOP, KFC, Krystal, LJ Silver, Logan's Roadhouse, Longhorn Steaks, McDonald's, O'Charley's, Old Chicago Pizza, Olive Garden, Outback Steaks, Papa Murphy's, Quiznos, Rafferty's, Red Lobster, Ryan's, Shogun Japanese, Shoney's, Starbucks, Steak'n Shake, Subway, Taco Bell, Waffle House, Wendy's, Zaxby's 🛏 AT&T, Best Inn, Best Value Inn, Best Western, Candlewood Suites, Comfort Inn, Country Inn&Suites, Courtyard, Days Inn, EconoLodge, Fairfield Inn, Guesthouse Inn, Hampton Inn, Hawthorn Suites, Hometowne Suites, Mainstay Suites, Microtel, Quality Inn, Ramada Ltd, Red Roof Inn, Super 8, ValuePlace Hotel, Wingate Inn 🅾 Ⓗ $Tree, Advance Parts, Belk, Best Buy, Books-A-Million, Buick/GMC, Dick's, Dillard's, Firestone/auto, Goodyear/auto, Hancock Fabrics, Hobby Lobby, Home Depot, Hyundai, JC Penney, K-Mart, Kohl's, Kroger/dsl, Lowe's, mall, Mazda, Office Depot, Petsmart, Sears/auto, Subaru, Target, TJ Maxx, to Austin Peay St U, to Land Between the Lakes, U-Haul, Verizon, Walmart, winery
1	TN 48, to Clarksville, Trenton, **N** 🅡 Shell/dsl 🅾 Clarksville RV Camping, **S** 🅡 BP 🍴 Coldstone, El Tapatio Mexican, Gatti's Pizza, Sonic, Wendy's 🅾 $General, AutoZone, Walgreens
.5mm	**Welcome Center eb, full** 🅰 **facilities, litter barrels, petwalk,** 🅒, 🆃 **vending**
0mm	Tennessee/Kentucky state line

INTERSTATE 26

Exit #	Services
54.5mm	Tennessee/North Carolina state line
54mm	**runaway truck ramp wb**
52mm	**runaway truck ramp wb, scenic overlook eb (no trucks)**
50	Flag Pond Rd
47.5mm	scenic overlook wb (no trucks)
46mm	**Welcome Center/**🆁🆂 **both lanes, full** 🅰 **facilities, litter barrels, petwalk,** 🅒, 🆃 **vending**

INTERSTATE 26 Cont'd

Exit #	Services
44mm	Higgins Creek
43	US 19 W, rd 352, Temple Hill Rd
42mm	S Indian Creek
40	Jackson-Love Hwy, Erwin, Jonesborough, N 🅿 Valero/dsl 🏠 Mtn Inn 🅾 🏥 Nolichucky Gorge Camping (2mi)
37	TN 81, rd 107, Erwin, Jonesborough, N 🅿 Shell 🍴 Huddle House, McDonald's 🅾 🏥 USPO, Walgreens, S 🏠 Super 8 🅾 A. Johnson NHS, River Park Camping (5mi)
36	Main St, Erwin, N 🅿 BP/dsl, Exxon/dsl/e-85 🍴 Azteca Mexican, Hardee's, KFC, Little Caesars, Pizza Hut, Subway, Wendy's 🅾 $General, Advance Parts, AutoZone, Firestone, IGA Foods, Rite Aid
34	Tinker Rd, N 🅿 Murphy USA/dsl 🍴 Los Jalapenos, Primo's Pizza 🅾 Walmart
32	rd 173, Unicoi Rd, to Cherokee NF, N 🅿 Unicoi Mkt 🍴 Clarence's Drive-In, Maple Grove Café 🅾 Grandview Ranch Camping (7mi), S 🅾 Woodsmoke Camping
27	rd 359 N, Okolona Rd, N 🅿 BP 🍴 Kozy Kitchen 🏠 Budget Inn (3mi) 🅾 truck repair
24	US 321, TN 67, Elizabethton, N 🅿 Shell/dsl, S 🅿 BP/dsl 🍴 Arby's, Burger King, Fox's Pizza, Little Caesars, LJ Silver, Subway 🏠 Comfort Inn 🅾 🏥 Advance Parts, CVS, Food City/gas, Price Less Foods, Roan Mtn SP, to ETSU, Walgreens
23	rd 91, Market St, N 🍴 DQ, McDonald's, S 🅾 museum
22	rd 400, Unaka Ave, Watauga Ave
20b a	US 11 E, US 19 N, to Roan St, N 🅿 Shell/dsl, Sunoco 🍴 Arby's, Cootie Brown's Rest., El Rancon, Empire Buffet, Fred's, Harbor House Seafood, Hardee's, Hibachi Grill, Little Caesars, LJ Silver, Mellow Mushroom Pizza, Moto Japanese, Papa John's, Peerless Rest., Perkins, Popeye's, Rainbow Asian, Sonic 🏠 Best Western, Holiday Inn, Ramada Ltd, Super 8 🅾 Acura, Advance Parts, AT&T, AutoZone, BigLots, Ford, Honda, Hyundai, Mazda, O'Reilly Parts, Subaru, Tuesday Morning, VW, S 🍴 5 Guys Burgers, Applebees, Bailey's Grille, Bonefish Grill, Fazoli's, Hooters, Jack's City Grill, Jersey Mike's Subs, KFC, Longhorn Steaks, McAlister's Deli, McDonald's, O'Charley's, Olive Garden, Papa Murphy's, Red Lobster, Red Pig BBQ, Shoney's, Smokey Bones BBQ, Starbucks, Subway, Taco Bell, TX Roadhouse, Zaxby's 🏠 Motel 6, Red Roof Inn 🅾 $General, $Tree, Belk, Books-A-Million, CVS, Dick's, Hancock Fabrics, JC Penney, Kroger, Office Depot, Sears/auto, Target, TJ Maxx, Verizon, Walgreens
19	TN 381, to St of Franklin Rd, to Bristol, N 🅿 Murphy USA/dsl, Valero/McDonald's 🍴 Golden Corral, Honeybaked Ham, Logan's Roadhouse, Outback Steaks, Subway 🏠 Comfort Suites 🅾 Hyundai, Radio Shack, VW, Walmart, S 0-2 mi 🍴 Atlanta Bread, Barberito's Grille, Buffalo Wild Wings, Carrabba's, Cheddar's, Chick-fil-A, Chili's, ChuckECheese's, Cocula Mexi, Fuddruckers, IHOP, Marble Slab, Ming's Asian, Panera Bread, Rita's Custard, Wendy's, Which Wich 🏠 Courtyard, Hampton Inn, Sleep Inn 🅾 🏥 AT&T, Barnes&Noble, Best Buy, Home Depot, K-Mart, Kohl's, Lowe's, Michael's, Natural Foods Mkt, Old Navy, PetsMart, Ross, Sam's Club/gas, Steinmart, USPO, Verizon, vet
17	Boone St, N 🅿 BP 🍴 Beef'o Brady's, Bob Evans, Burger King, Giovanni's Italian, McDonald's, Pal's Drive-in, Pizza+ 🅾 Ingles Foods, S 🅿 Exxon/e-85, Shell/Subway 🍴 Cracker Barrel, Domino's, Poblano's Mexican, Waffle House, Wendy's 🏠 Holiday Inn Express, Quality Inn, Value Place

13	rd 75, Bobby Hicks Hwy, N 🅿 BP, Shell 🍴 Burger King, China Luck, DQ, Gino's Italian, La Carreta, McDonald's, Papa John's, Pizza Hut, Subway, Taco Bell, Yong Asian 🅾 $General, Advance Parts, Food City/gas, O'Reilly Parts, USPO, Walgreens, S 🅿 Exxon/dsl
10	Eastern Star Rd, N 🍴 Phil's Dream Pit
8b a	I-81, to Bristol, Knoxville
6	rd 347, Rock Springs Rd, S 🅿 Rite Quik
5	Pond Springs Rd.
4	TN 93, Wilcox Dr, N 🅿 BP/Subway, Shell/McDonald's/dsl 🍴 Burger King, Hardee's, La Carreta Mexican, Pizza Hut, Wendy's 🏠 Comfort Suites, Hampton Inn, Holiday Inn Express, Quality Inn 🅾 $General, Cave's Drug, Price Less Foods, S 🅿 BP, Zoomerz/Arby's/dsl/e-85 🍴 Pizza+
3	Meadowview Pkwy, N 🏠 Marriott
1	US 11 W, West Stone Dr, N 🅿 Shell 🍴 Little Caesars, Molcajete's Mexican 🏠 Super 8 🅾 🏥 Walgreens, S 🅿 Exxon, Murphy USA 🍴 Bojangles, China Star, Fatz Cafe, Sonic, Subway 🅾 $Tree, Lowe's, Walmart
0mm	I-26 begins/ends on US 23.

INTERSTATE 40

Exit #	Services
451mm	Tennessee/North Carolina state line
451	Waterville Rd
447	Hartford Rd, N 🅿 Citgo/dsl, S 🅿 BP/dsl 🍴 Bean Tree Cafe, Pigeon River Smokehouse 🅾 Foxfire Camping, Shauan's Riverside RV Park, USPO, whitewater rafting
446mm	Welcome Center wb, No Trucks, full ♿ facilities, litter barrels, petwalk, 🚰 vending
443mm	Pigeon River
443	Foothills Pkwy, to Gatlinburg, S 🅾 camping, 🅾 Great Smoky Mtns NP
440	US 321, to Wilton Spgs Rd, Gatlinburg, N 🅿 440 Trkstp/cafe/dsl, S 🅿 Marathon 🍴 Broasted Chicken 🅾 Arrow Creek Camping (14mi), CrazyHorse Camping (14mi), Jellystone Camping (12mi)
439mm	Pigeon River
435	US 321, to Gatlinburg, Newport, N 🅿 Exxon/Biodsl/e-85, Marathon, Mobil, Shell/dsl, Weigel/dsl 🍴 Arby's, Burger King, Hardee's, KFC, Lois' Country Kitchen, McDonald's, Pizza Hut, SageBrush Steaks, Subway, Taco Bell 🏠 Motel 6, Parkway Inn 🅾 🏥 CVS Drug, O'Reilly Parts, Town&Country Drug, USPO, Walgreens, S 🅿 Mobil/dsl, Murphy USA/dsl 🍴 Bojangles, Brooklyn Pizza, Cracker Barrel, Monterrey Mexican, New China, Papa John's, Ruby Tuesday, Waffle House, Wendy's 🏠 Best Western, Days Inn, Family Inn, Holiday Inn Express, Super 8 🅾 $General, $Tree, AT&T, Lowe's, Save-A-Lot Foods, Verizon, Walmart/Subway
432b a	US 70, US 411, US 25W, to Newport, N 🅿 Exxon/dsl, Marathon/dsl, TimeOut TC/BP/Huddle House/dsl/scales/ 🍴 Brandywine Creek Steaks 🏠 Comfort Inn, Relax Inn 🅾 Buick/Chevrolet, Chrysler/Dodge/Jeep, Ford, KOA (2mi), Tana-See RV Park, truck service, Westgate Tire, S 🅿 BP/pizza, Citgo/dsl, Marathon/dsl, Shell/dsl 🏠 Family Inn/rest. 🅾 $General
426mm	℞ wb, full ♿ facilities, litter barrels, petwalk, 🚰 vending
425mm	French Broad River
424	TN 113, Dandridge, N 🅿 Marathon/dsl
421	I-81 N, to Bristol
420mm	℞ eb, full ♿ facilities, litter barrels, petwalk, 🚰 vending

INTERSTATE 40 Cont'd

D A N D R I D G E

Exit #	Services
417	TN 92, Dandridge, N 🅖 Marathon/dsl, Pilot/Subway/dsl/scales/24hr/@ 🍴 Capt's Galley, Hardee's, McDonald's, Perkins, Ruby Tuesday, Taste of Dandridge 🏠 EconoLodge, S 🅖 Marathon/dsl, Shell/Wendy's/dsl, Weigel's/dsl 🍴 Arby's, Bojangles, LJ Silver/Taco Bell, Shoney's, Waffle House 🏠 Hampton Inn, Holiday Inn Express, Jefferson Inn, Quality Inn, Super 8 🅞 Advance Parts
415	US 25W, US 70, to Dandridge, S 🅖 Marathon/dsl 🍴 Sonic (3mi)
412	Deep Sprgs Rd, to Douglas Dam, N 🅖 Loves/Chester's/Subway/dsl/scales/24hr
407	TN 66, to Sevierville, Pigeon Forge, Gatlinburg, N 🅖 Shell/Subway/dsl 🍴 Chophouse, Cracker Barrel, McDonald's, Uncle Buck's Grill 🏠 Best Value Inn, Fairfield Inn, Hampton Inn, Holiday Inn Express 🅞 Bass Pro Shops, RV Camping, Smoky Mtn Visitor's Ctr, S 🅖 BP/Subway/dsl, Exxon/Subway/dsl, Mobil/Dunkin Donuts/dsl, Shell/Krystal/dsl 🍴 Burger King, FlapJack's, Wendy's 🏠 Comfort Suites, Days Inn, Motel 6, Quality Inn 🅞 Chrysler/Dodge/Jeep, flea mkt, Russell Stover, RV Camping, TN Tourist Info, USPO, multiple services/outlets
402	Midway Rd
398	Strawberry Plains Pk, Strawberry Plains Pk, N 🅖 BP/dsl, Citgo/dsl, Exxon/dsl, Shell/dsl 🍴 Aubrey's Rest., McDonald's, Outback Steaks, Waffle House, Wendy's 🏠 EconoLodge, Hampton Inn, Holiday Inn Express, Knight's Inn, Quality Inn, Red Roof Inn, Rodeway Inn, Super 8 🅞 TN RV Ctr, S 🅖 Pilot/Subway/dsl/scales/24hr, Weigel's 🍴 Arby's, Burger King, Cracker Barrel, Golden Wok Chinese, KFC, Krystal, Puleo's Grille, Taco Bell 🏠 Best Western, Comfort Suites, Fairfield Inn, La Quinta, Motel 6
395mm	🅞 Holston River
394	US 70, US 11E, US 25W, Asheville Hwy, N 🅖 Pilot/dsl, Shell/Quizno's/dsl 🍴 Papa John's, Subway, Wendy's 🏠 Gateway Inn 🅞 Advance Parts, AutoZone, city park, S 🅖 Exxon, Mapco/dsl 🍴 Habaneros Mexican, Pizza Hut, Scott's Place, Waffle House 🏠 Relax Inn 🅞 $General, CVS Drug, Family$, Kroger/gas, vet, Walgreens
393	I-640 W, to I-75 N
392	US 11W, Rutledge Pike, N 🅖 Citgo/dsl 🅞 $General, truck repair, U-Haul, S 🅖 Shell 🍴 Buddy's BBQ, Hardee's, Shoney's 🅞 NAPA, Sav-A-Lot Foods, to Knoxville Zoo, transmissions
390	Cherry St, Knoxville, N 🅖 Marathon/dsl, Top Fuel Mart, Weigel's/Subway 🍴 Happy Garden Chinese 🏠 Knoxville Inn 🅞 tires, S 🅖 Exxon 🍴 Arby's, Little Caesar's, LJ Silver, McDonald's 🏠 Regency Inn 🅞 Advance Parts, Family$, O'Reilly Parts, vet, Walgreens
389	US 441 N, Broadway, 5th Ave, N 🅖 Pilot/dsl, Shell/dsl, Star 🍴 Burger King, KFC, Krystal, McDonald's, Sonic, Subway, Taco Bell, Wendy's 🅞 $General, Ace Hardware, Belew Drug, CVS Drug, Family$, Firestone/auto, Kroger/dsl, Radio Shack, Save-A-Lot Foods, USPO, Walgreens/24hr
388	US 441 S (exits left from wb), S 🏠 Crowne Plaza, Hilton, Holiday Inn 🅞 downtown, to Smokey Mtns, to U of TN
387b	TN 62, 17th St, N 🅖 Gas'N Go, Pilot/dsl 🏠 Economy Inn, Royal Inn 🅞 $General, Food City/gas
387a	I-275 N, to Lexington
386b a	US 129, University Ave, to UT
385	I-75 N, I-640 E
	I-40 W and I-75 S run together 17 mi.

K N O X V I L L E

383	Papermill Rd, N 🏠 Red Roof Inn, S 🅖 BP, Citgo, Pilot/dsl, Spur Gas 🍴 5 Guys Burgers, Buddy's BBQ, Burger King, Krispy Kreme, Sonic, TGIFriday's, Waffle House 🏠 Super 8 🅞 Food City, same as 380, Walgreens
380	US 11, US 70, West Hills, S 🅖 Shell, Weigel's 🍴 Applebee's, Arby's, Brazeiro's Brazilian Steaks, Brixx Pizza, Chick-fil-A, Chili's, Dunkin Donuts, Firehouse Subs, Hardee's, Honeybaked Ham, Jet's Pizza, Macaroni Grill, McAlister's Deli, McDonald's, Mr Gatti's, O'Charley's, Olive Garden, Papa John's, Petro's Chili, PF Chang's, Pizza Hut, PlumTree Chinese, Puleo's Grille, Qdoba Mexican, Ray's Grille, Red Lobster, Salsarita's Cantina, Spice Rack Grill, Starbucks, Subway, Taco Bell, Tropical Smoothie Cafe, TX Roadhouse, Wishbone Wings 🏠 Extended Stay America, Magnuson Hotel, Ramada Inn 🅞 $Tree, AT&T, Barnes&Noble, Belk, Dillards, Food City, JC Penney, Kohl's, mall, NTB, Office Depot, Old Navy, O'Reilly Parts, Petsmart, Ross, Sears/auto, st patrol, Staples, Steinmart, Target, TJ Maxx, U-Haul, Walgreens
379	Bridgewater Rd, N 🅖 Exxon/Subway, Pilot/McDonald's, Shell 🍴 McDonald's, Taco Bell 🅞 Sam's Club/gas, Walmart, S 🅖 BP/dsl, Citgo/dsl, Conoco 🍴 Buddy's BBQ, Burger King, China Buffet, ChuckeCheese, CiCi's Pizza, Krystal, Makino's Japanese, Shoney's, Sonic, Wendy's 🏠 InTown Suites 🅞 Aamco, Advance Parts, AutoZone, Books-A-Million, Buick/GMC, Chrysler/Dodge/Jeep, Firestone/auto, Ford/Lincoln, Hyundai, Mazda, Nissan Subaru, Tire Barn, Transmission World
378	Cedar Bluff Rd, N 🅖 Pilot/Taco Bell, Shell, Weigel's 🍴 Arby's, Burger King, Cracker Barrel, Dunkin Donuts, KFC, Little Caesar's, McDonald's, Old Mill Bread Co., Papa John's, Quiznos, Starbucks, Subway, Waffle House, Wendy's 🏠 Country Inn&Suites, Days Inn, Hampton Inn, Holiday Inn, Ramada Inn, Sleep Inn 🅞 🏥 $General, S 🅖 Exxon, Phillips 66 🍴 Applebee's, Bob Evans, Carrabba's, Corky's Ribs/BBQ, Denny's, Famous Dave's BBQ, Fazoli's, Firehouse Subs, Friendly's, Fuddrucker's, Grady's Grill, IHOP, Krystal, Outback Steaks, Panera Bread, Parkside Grill, Peerless Grill, Penn Sta. Subs, Pizza Hut, Puleo's Grill, Rafferty's, Rubio's Grill, Sunny's BBQ 🏠 Best Western, Clubhouse Inn, Comfort Inn, Courtyard, Extended Stay America, Guesthouse Suites, Hilton Garden, Jameson Inn, La Quinta, Microtel, Red Roof Inn, Residence Inn, Signature Inn, Towne Place Suites 🅞 Best Buy, Cadillac, Celebration Sta, Chevrolet, Chrysler, CVS Drug, Dick's, Food City, Ford, Jo-Ann Fabrics, KIA, Lowe's, Michael's, Staples, Tuesday Morning, Walgreens
376	I-140 E, TN 162 N, to Maryville, N to Oak Ridge Museum

TN

⬆E INTERSTATE 40 Cont'd

Exit #	Services
374	TN 131, Lovell Rd, **N** 🚗 Shell/dsl, TA/Country Pride/dsl/scales/24hr/@ 🍴 Bojangles; McDonald's, Subway, Waffle House 🏨 Guesthouse Inn, Travelodge 🅾 Harley-Davidson, **S** 🚗 ⬛⬛⬛/Wendy's/dsl/24hr 🍴 Arby's, Baskin-Robbins, Bonefish Grill, Brixx Pizza, Buffalo Wild Wings, Calhoun's Rest., Chick-fil-A, Connor's Rest., Flemings, Genghis Grill, IHOP, Jimmy John's, Jim'N Nick's BBQ, Kabuki Japanese, Krystal, Mangia Pizza, Marble Slab, McAlister's Deli, McDonald's, Mike's Subs, Mimi's Cafe, Noodles&Co, O'Charley's, Olive Garden, Pei Wei, Pimento's Cafe, Red Robin, Salsarita's Cantina, Shoney's, Smokey Mtn Brewery, Sonic, Starbucks, Steak'n Shake, Subway, TX Roadhouse, Wasabai Japanese 🏨 Candlewood Suites, Homewood Suites, Motel 6, SpringHill Suites 🅾 $Tree, Advance Parts, Belk, Best Buy, BMW/Mini, CarMax, Costco/gas, EarthFare Foods, GNC, Hobby Lobby, Honda, Lexus, Marshall's, Mercedes, Old Navy, Petsmart, Radio Shack, Ross, Target, Toyota/Scion, Walgreens, Walmart
373	Campbell Sta Rd, **N** 🚗 Marathon/dsl, Shell/dsl 🏨 Comfort Suites, Country Inn&Suites, Holiday Inn Express, Super 8 🅾 Buddy Gregg RV Ctr, **S** 🚗 BP, Pilot, Weigel's 🍴 Border Tacos, Capt Ernie's Fishouse, Cracker Barrel, Dunkin Donuts, Gatti's Pizza, Hardee's, Kasumi Japanese, Mellow Mushroom, Newk's Grill, Vietnamese Bistro, Wild Wings Cafe 🏨 Baymont Inn, EconoLodge, Hampton Inn 🅾 AT&T, Gander Mtn, JC Penney, Verizon, Walgreens
372mm	weigh sta both lanes
369	Watt Rd, **N** 🚗 ⛛FLYING J/Denny's/dsl/LP/scales/RV dump/24hr, Speedco, **S** 🚗 Exxon/dsl, Petro/Iron Skillet/dsl/scales/24hr/@, TA/BP/Burger King/Pizza Hut/Popeye's/Subway/dsl/24hr/@ 🅾 Blue Beacon, Knoxville Coach/RV
I-40 E and I-75 N run together 17 mi.	
368	I-75 and I-40
364	US 321, TN 95, Lenoir City, Oak Ridge, **N** 🚗 Melton Hill Mkt/gas 🅾 Crosseyed Cricket Camping (2mi), **S 4-5 mi** 🚗 ❤Loves/McDonald's/Subway/dsl/24hr 🍴 KFC, Krystal, Ruby Tuesday 🏨 Comfort Inn, Days Inn, EconoLodge, Hampton Inn, Holiday Inn Express, Ramada Ltd
362	Industrial Park Rd
360	Buttermilk Rd, **N** Soaring Eagle RV Park
356	TN 58 N, Gallaher Rd, to Oak Ridge, **N** 🚗 BP/dsl, Weigels/dsl 🍴 Gallaher Grill 🏨 Budget Inn, Motel 6 🅾 4 Seasons Camping
355	Lawnville Rd, **N** 🚗 ⬛⬛⬛/Subway/dsl
352	TN 58 S, Kingston, **N** 🏨 Knights Inn, **S** 🚗 Exxon/dsl, RaceWay, Shell 🍴 Buddy's BBQ, Hardee's, McDonald's, Sonic, Subway, Taco Bell 🏨 Super 8 🅾 Family$, Marina RV Park, Piggly Wiggly, to Watts Bar Lake, USPO
351mm	Clinch River
350	US 70, Midtown, **N** 🅾 **H** **S** 🍴 Gondolier Italian 🅾 Caney Creek Camping (3mi), Kroger, Lowe's, Patterson RV Supplies, Walgreens
347	US 27, Harriman, **N** 🚗 Phillips 66/dsl 🍴 Hardee's, KFC, LJ Silver, Los Primos Mexican, McDonald's, Pizza Hut, Ruby Tuesday, Subway, Taco Bell, Wendy's 🏨 Days Inn 🅾 Big S Fork NRA, to Frozen Head SP, Verizon, **S 2-3 mi** 🚗 BP, Murphy USA/dsl, Shell/Krystal/dsl/24hr, Sunoco/dsl 🍴 Cancun Mexican, Capt D's, China King, Cracker Barrel, Domino's, Shoney's, Sonic 🏨 Comfort Inn, Holiday Inn Express, Quality Inn, Rodeway Inn 🅾 **H** Ace Hardware, BigLots, Radio Shack, vet, Walmart/Subway

340	TN 299 N, 🔄 Rd
339.5mm	eastern/central time zone line
338	TN 299 S, Westel Rd, **N** 🚗 BP/dsl, **S** 🚗 Shell/dsl 🅾 Boat-N-RV Ctr/Park
336mm	parking area/weigh sta eb, litter barrel
329	US 70, Crab Orchard, **N** 🚗 BP/dsl, Liberty/dsl 🅾 KOA (4mi), **S** 🅾 Cumberland Trails SP, Wilson SP
327mm	🅟ₛ wb, full 🚻 facilities, litter barrels, petwalk, 🅲, 🖻 vending
324mm	🅟ₛ eb, full 🚻 facilities, litter barrels, petwalk, 🅲, 🖻 vending
322	TN 101, Peavine Rd, Crossville, **N** 🚗 BP/Bean Pot Rest., Exxon/dsl, Volunteer/dsl 🍴 Hardee's, McDonald's, Quiznos, Subway 🏨 Holiday Inn Express 🅾 Deer Run RV Resort, KOA Camping, Roam-Roost RV Campground, to Fairfield Glade Resort, **S** 🚗 Phillips 66/dsl 🍴 Cancun Mexican, Taco Bell 🏨 Comfort Suites, Hampton Inn, Super 8 🅾 **H** Chestnut Hill Winery, Cumberland Mtn SP, RV Camping, Vallyhoo
320	TN 298, Crossville, **N** 🚗 ⬛⬛⬛/Wendy's/dsl/scales/24hr 🍴 Halcyon Days Rest. 🅾 antiques, golf, winery, **S** 🚗 BP/DQ/Pizza Hut/dsl, Shell/dsl 🅾 **H** antiques, auto repair/tires, Crossville Outlet/famous brands, Save-A-Lot Foods
318mm	Obed River
317	US 127, Crossville, **N** 🚗 Exxon/dsl/24hr, Shell/dsl 🍴 Shoney's, Subway 🏨 Best Western, La Quinta, Motel 6 🅾 repair, to Big South Fork RA, to York SP, **S 0-2 mi** 🚗 Citgo/dsl, Jiffy, Marathon, Murphy USA/dsl, Shell 🍴 Arby's, Burger King, Cancun Mexican, Cracker Barrel, La Costa Mexican, McDonalds, Papa John's, Peking Buffet, Ruby Tuesday, Ryan's, Sonic, Subway, Taco Bell, Vegas Steaks, Waffle House, Zaxby's 🏨 Best Value Inn, Days Inn, Economy Inn 🅾 **H** $General, $Tree, AT&T, Buick/Cadillac/Chevrolet/GMC, Chrysler/Dodge/Jeep, GNC, Lowe's, Rite Aid, Shadden Tires, Staples, to Cumberland Mtn SP, Verizon, vet, Walgreens, Walmart
311	Plateau Rd, **N** 🚗 Sunoco/Papa Lorenzo's Pizza/dsl, **S** 🚗 BP/dsl, Exxon/Hunt Bro's Pizza 🅾 rv service
307mm	parking area/weigh sta wb, litter barrels
301	US 70 N, TN 84, Monterey, **N** 🚗 Phillips 66, Shell 🍴 Burger King, DQ, Subway 🏨 Super 8
300	US 70, Monterey, **N** 🚗 Citgo/dsl 🍴 DQ, Hardee's
291mm	Falling Water River
290	US 70, Cookeville, **N** 🚗 BP (1mi), **S** 🚗 Citgo 🏨 Alpine Suites
288	TN 111, to Livingston, Cookeville, Sparta, **N** Hull SP, **S** 🚗 Sunoco/dsl, TN TravelCtr/dsl/24hr 🍴 Mona's Rest. 🏨 Knights Inn
287	TN 136, Cookeville, **N** 🚗 BP, Exxon, Murphy USA 🍴 Applebee's, Arby's, Baskin-Robbins, Bully's Rest., Burger King, Capt D's, Cheddars, Chick-fil-A, Chili's, Cracker Barrel, DQ, Fazoli's, Golden Corral, IHOP, King Buffet, Krystal, LJ Silver, Logan's Roadhouse, Longhorn Steaks, Mandarin Palace, McDonald's, Mike's Subs, Nick's Rest., O'Charley's, Olive Garden, Outback Steaks, Papa Murphy's, Pizza Hut, Puleo's Grill, Quiznos, Red Lobster, Ruby Tuesday, Shoney's, Sonic, Starbucks, Steak'n Shake, Subway, Taco Bell, Wendy's 🏨 Best Value Inn, Best Western, Clarion, Comfort Inn&Suites, Days Inn, Hampton Inn, Red Roof Inn, Super 8 🅾 Aldi Foods, BigLots, Firestone/auto, Harley-Davidson, JC Penney, K-Mart, Kroger/gas, Lowe's, Nissan, Radio Shack, st patrol, transmissions, Verizon, Walmart, **S** 🚗 Marathon/dsl, ⬛⬛⬛/dsl 🍴 Gondola, KFC, Waffle House 🏨 Baymont Inn, Country Hearth Inn, Country Inn&Suites, Fairfield Inn, Holiday Inn Express 🅾 Sam's Club/gas, URGENT CARE

(vertical margin labels: CROSSVILLE, COOKEVILLE, HARRIMAN)

↑E INTERSTATE 40 Cont'd

Exit #	Services
286	TN 135, Burgess Falls Rd, **N** 🅶 BP, Exxon, RaceWay/dsl, Shell/dsl 🍴 Arby's, Beef'O'Brady's, Christy's Cafe, Hardee's, Waffle House 🅾 🔧 Chrysler/Dodge/Jeep, Ford/Lincoln, Goodyear/auto, Hyundai, KIA, to TTU, Toyota/Scion, USPO, vet, **S** 🅶 Sunoco/dsl 🏠 Star Motor Inn 🅾 Burgess Falls SP (8mi)
280	TN 56 N, Baxter, **N** 🅶 🛑Loves/McDonalds/Subway/dsl/scales/24hr 🍴 Huddle House 🅾 Camp Discovery (2mi), Twin Lakes RV Park (2mi)
276	Old Baxter Rd
273	TN 56 S, to Smithville, **S** 🅶 BP/dsl, Phillips 66 🍴 Rose Garden Rest. 🅾 USPO
268	TN 96, Buffalo Valley Rd, **N** Grandville Marina Camping (11mi), **S** to Edgar Evins SP/RV camping
267mm	Caney Fork River
267mm	🆁🆂 both lanes, full ♿ facilities, litter barrels, petwalk, 🅲, 🚰 vending
266mm	Caney Fork River
263mm	Caney Fork River
258	TN 53, Gordonsville, **N** 🅶 Exxon/KFC/Taco Bell, Shell/dsl 🍴 McDonald's, Timberloft Café, Waffle House 🏠 Comfort Inn 🅾 to Cordell Hull Dam, **S** 🅶 Hess/Wendy's/dsl/scales/24hr, Mobil/dsl 🍴 Arby's, Cornerstone Cafe, El Corral Mexican 🅾 $General
254	TN 141, to Alexandria
252mm	parking area/truck sta both lanes, litter barrels, 🚰
245	Linwood Rd, **N** 🅶 BP/dsl
239	US 70, Lebanon, **N** 🅶 Citgo/dsl, Citgo/dsl, RaceWay, RaceWay, **S** 🅶 Phillips 66/Uncle Pete's/dsl/scales 🍴 Jalisco Mexican
238	US 231, Lebanon, **N** 🅶 Exxon, Mapco, Shell 🍴 Applebee's, Arby's, Cici's Pizza, Cracker Barrel, Demo's Steaks, El Molino Mexican, Gondola Rest., Hardee's, Jack-in-the-Box, KFC, King Buffet, McDonald's, Pizza Hut, Ponderosa, Ryan's, Shoney's, Subway, Sunset Rest., Taco Bell, Waffle House, Wendy's, White Castle, Whitt's BBQ, Zaxby's 🏠 Best Value Inn, EconoLodge, Executive Inn, Holiday Inn Express, Quality Inn, Ramada 🅾 🔧 $Tree, Aldi Foods, Discount Tire, Lowe's, to Bledsoe SP, Walgreens, Walmart, **S** 🅶 Citgo/Pizza Inn/Quiznos/dsl, 🛑/Chester's/Subway/dsl/scales/24hr, Shell/dsl 🍴 O'Charley's, Sonic 🏠 Comfort Suites, Country Inn&Suites, Days Inn, Knights Inn, Super 8 🅾 Family RV Ctr, Lebanon Outlets/famous brands, RV camping, Shady Acres Camping, Timberline Campground, to Cedars of Lebanon SP
236	S Hartmann Dr, **N** 🅶 Mapco, Shell/dsl 🍴 Chili's, Outback Steaks, Pizza Inn, Ruby Tuesday, Sonic, Subway 🅾 🔧 Hampton Inn, Home Depot, Rose Tire
235	TN 840 W, to Murfreesboro
232	TN 109, to Gallatin, **N** 🅶 Citgo, Mapco/Quiznos/dsl, Shell/McDonald's/dsl/24hr, Thornton's/dsl 🍴 Bellacino's Pizza, Coach's Grill, Sonic, Subway, Waffle House, Wendy's 🏠 Sleep Inn, ValuePlace Inn, **S 2 mi** 🅾 Countryside Resort Camping
229b a	Beckwith Rd
228mm	truck sta, wb only
226mm	truck sta
226	TN 171, Mt Juliet Rd, **N** 🅶 BP/McDonald's/dsl, Exxon/dsl, Shell/dsl/24hr 🍴 5 Guys Burgers, Arby's, Capt D's, Cheddars, Don Pancho Mexican, Far East Buffet, Subway 🏠 Comfort Suites 🅾 $Tree, Aldi Foods, Lowe's, NTB, Walmart,

226	Continued S 🅶 Mapco/Quiznos/dsl 🍴 Buffalo Wild Wings, Chick-fil-A, Cori's Dog House, Cracker Barrel, Fulin's Asian, Hacienda Del Sol, Logan's Roadhouse, NY Pizza, O'Charley's, Olive Garden, Panera Bread, Red Lobster, Red Robin, Ruby Tuesday, Salsarita's Cantina, Sonic, Steak'n Shake, Taco Bell, Waffle House, Wasabi Steaks, Wendy's, Zaxby's 🏠 Hampton Inn, Holiday Inn Express, Quality Inn 🅾 AT&T, Belk, Best Buy, Books-A-Million, Curves, Dick's, Discount Tire, Ford, GNC, JC Penney, JoAnn Fabrics, Kroger/dsl, Old Navy, Petsmart, Publix, Ross, Staples, Target, TJ Maxx, to Long Hunter SP, Verizon, Walgreens
221	TN 45 N, Old Hickory Blvd, to The Hermitage, **N 0-2 mi** 🅶 BP, Exxon, Mapco/dsl, RaceWay/dsl, Shell/24hr 🍴 Applebee's, Baskin-Robbins/Dunkin Donuts, Buffalo Wild Wings, Burger King, Chick-fil-A, Chili's, DQ, Famous Dave's, Fazoli's, Firehouse Subs, Golden Corral, Hardee's, IHOP, Jack-in-the-Box, Mike's Subs, O'Charley's, Outback Steaks, Panera Bread, Qdoba Mexican, Starbucks, Steak'n Shake, Subway, Waffle House 🏠 Best Value Inn, Suburban Lodge, Super 8, Vista Inn 🅾 🔧 Hobby Lobby, Home Depot, Kroger, Lowe's, PetCo, Staples, Walgreens, **S** 🅶 Phillips 66/White Castle, Qwiksak/dsl, Shell/McDonald's
219	Stewart's Ferry Pike, **N** 🅶 Mapco, **S** 🅶 Mapco/dsl, Shell/dsl, Thornton's/dsl 🍴 China King, Cracker Barrel, Epic Pizza, La Hacienda Mexican, Sal's Pizza, Subway, Waffle House 🏠 Best Western, Comfort Suites, Country Inn&Suites, Days Inn, EconoLodge, Family Inn, Sleep Inn 🅾 $General, Food Lion, Fred's, vet
216b a	(from eb), **S** Nashville Intn'l ✈
216	(216 c from eb)TN 255, Donaldson Pk, **N** 🅶 BP/dsl, Mapco, RaceWay/dsl, Shell/dsl/24hr 🍴 Arby's, Backyard Burger, Bar-B-Cutie, Darfon's, Domino's, Jalisco Mexican, KFC, McDonald's, New China, Pizza Hut/Taco Bell, Ruby Tuesday, Shoney's, Subway, Waffle House, Wendy's 🏠 Country Inn&Suites, Drury Inn, Fairfield Inn, Hampton Inn, Holiday Inn Express, Hyatt Place, La Quinta, Radisson, Red Roof Inn, SpringHill Suites, Super 8, Wingate Inn 🅾 Advance Parts, K-Mart, USPO, Walgreens, **S** ✈
215b a	TN 155, Briley Pkwy, to Opryland, **N on Elm Hill** 🅶 Citgo, Mapco 🍴 Casta Fiesta Mexican, Jack-in-the-Box, Waffle House 🏠 Alexis Inn, Baymont Inn, Comfort Suites, Courtyard, Embassy Suites, Extended Stay, Hilton Garden, Holiday Inn, Homestead Suites, Homewood Suites, La Quinta, Marriott, Ramada, Residence Inn, Sheraton, Studio+, **S** 🅶 Phillips 66/dsl 🍴 Dunkin Donuts, Mazatlan Mexican, Panda House, Subway 🏠 Hamilton Inn, Hotel Preston

TN

INTERSTATE 40 Cont'd

Exit #	Services
213b	I-24 W
213a	I-24 E/I-440, E to Chattanooga
213	US 41 (from wb no return), to Spence Lane, N Ⓞ Kenworth, S ⛽ Phillips 66/dsl, Shell 🍴 Waffle House 🛏 Days Inn, Holiday Inn Express, Rodeway Inn, same as 212, Super 8
212	Fessler's Lane (from eb, no return), N Ⓞ Freightliner, Harley-Davidson, S ⛽ Mapco/dsl, Shell/Dunkin Donuts 🍴 Burger King, McDonald's, Sonic, Wendy's 🛏 Scottish Inn Ⓞ Chevrolet, same as 213
211mm	Cumberland River
211b	I-24 W
211a	I-24E, I-40 W
210c	US 31 S, US 41A, 2nd Ave, 4th Ave, N 🛏 Hilton, Sheraton, Stouffer Hotel, S museum
210b a	I-65 S, to Birmingham
209b a	US 70 S, Charlotte Ave, Nashville, N ⛽ Exxon 🍴 McDonald's 🛏 Sheraton Ⓞ Conv Ctr, Country Music Hall of Fame, Firestone, transmissions, S ⛽ Exxon 🍴 Burger King, Krystal, Sonic, Subway, White Castle 🛏 Comfort Inn, Guesthouse Inn Ⓞ URGENT CARE, Walgreens
208b a	I-65, N to Louisville, S to Birmingham
207	28th Ave, Jefferson St, Nashville, N ⛽ BP, Citgo 🍴 Subway, Wendy's, Wing Zone Ⓞ 🅷 Family$, to TN St U
206	I-440 E, to Knoxville
205	46th Ave, W Nashville, N Ⓞ Harley-Davidson, S ⛽ Mapco, Shell 🍴 McDonald's, Mrs. Winners
204	TN 155, Briley Pkwy, S ⛽ BP/dsl, Citgo 🍴 Burger King, China Buffet, Church's/White Castle, Cinco De Mayo, Domino's, Jack-in-the-Box, KFC, Krystal, Las Palmas, Papa John's, Shoney's, Subway, Waffle House 🛏 Baymont Inn, Best Western, Comfort Inn, Days Inn Ⓞ CarQuest, CVS Drug, Firestone/auto, Kroger/gas, NTB, O'Reilly Parts, PepBoys, Sav-a-lot Foods, Walgreens
201b a	US 70, Charlotte Pike, N ⛽ Exxon, Shell/dsl/24hr 🍴 Bojangles, China Buffet, Cracker Barrel, Jim 'N Nick's BBQ, Krystal, Subway, Waffle House, Wendy's 🛏 Super 8 Ⓞ $Tree, GNC, Kwik Kar, Lowe's Whse, Radio Shack, Walmart, S ⛽ BP, Mapco, Shell 🍴 Arby's, McDonald's, Pizza Hut, Red Robin, Taco Bell Ⓞ Best Buy, Big Lots, BigLots, Books-A-Million, Costco/gas, Firestone/auto, Marshall's, Old Navy, PetsMart, Ross, Staples, Target, Uhaul, World Mkt
199	rd 251, Old Hickory Blvd, N ⛽ Shell, S ⛽ BP, Mapco 🍴 Sonic, Subway Ⓞ Sam's Club/gas
196	US 70, to Bellevue, Newsom Sta, N ⛽ Mapco/dsl 🍴 Shoney's, S ⛽ BP, Mapco/dsl, Shell/dsl/24hr 🍴 Arby's, Asihi Asian, O'Charley's, Pizza Hut, Sir Pizza, Sonic, Subway, Taco Bell, Waffle House, Wendy's 🛏 Hampton Inn, Microtel Ⓞ $Tree, Firestone/auto, Home Depot, Michael's, PetCo, Publix, Sears/auto, Staples, USPO, Walgreens
195mm	Harpeth River
192	McCrory Lane, to Pegram, N ⛽ Eddie's Mkt (1mi), S 4 mi 🍴 Loveless Cafe Ⓞ Natchez Trace Pkwy
190mm	Harpeth River
188mm	Harpeth River
188	rd 249, Kingston Springs, N ⛽ BP, Mapco/Quiznos/dsl, Shell/Arby's/dsl 🍴 El Jardin Mexican, McDonald's/playplace, Sonic, Subway 🛏 Best Western, Mid-Town Inn, Relax Inn Ⓞ CB Foods, USPO, S ⛽ Petro/BP/Quick Skillet/dsl/scales/showers/24hr/@ Ⓞ vet

D I C K S O N

182	TN 96, to Dickson, Fairview, N ⛽ BP/dsl 🛏 Fairview Inn Ⓞ M Bell SP (16mi), S ⛽ FLYING J/Denny's/dsl/LP/scales/24hr, Shell/Backyard Burger/Dunkin Donuts/dsl 🛏 Deerfield Inn
176	TN 840
172	TN 46, to Dickson, N ⛽ Citgo/Subway, Exxon, 🍴 Wendy's/dsl/scales/24hr, Shell 🍴 Arby's, Cracker Barrel, Farmer's Rest., Logan's Roadhouse, McDonald's, Ruby Tuesday, Waffle House/24hr, Wang's China 🛏 Best Western, Comfort Inn, EconoLodge, Hampton Inn, Motel 6, Quality Inn, South-Aire Inn, Super 8 Ⓞ 🅷 Chappell's Foods, Chevrolet, Dickson RV Park, Ford, Nissan, to M Bell SP, truck repair, S ⛽ BP, Shell/dsl 🍴 O'Charley's, Sonic 🛏 Days Inn, Dickson Inn, Holiday Inn Express
170	🅿️ both lanes, full 🛏 facilities, litter barrels, petwalk, 📞, 🖼 vending
166mm	Piney River
163	rd 48, to Dickson, N ⛽ Loves/McDonald's/Subway/dsl/scales/24hr, Phillips 66/dsl Ⓞ tire repair, S ⛽ Shell Ⓞ Pinewood Camping (7mi), Tanbark Camping
152	rd 230, Bucksnort, N ⛽ Citgo 🍴 Rudy's Rest. 🛏 Travel Inn
149mm	Duck River
148	rd 50, Barren Hollow Rd, to Turney Center
143	TN 13, to Linden, Waverly, N ⛽ BP, 🍴 Arby's/dsl/scales/24hr, Shell 🍴 Hot Spot BBQ, Log Cabin Rest., Loretta Lynn's Kitchen, McDonald's, Subway 🛏 Best Western, Days Inn, Holiday Inn Express, Knights Inn Ⓞ KOA/LP, tires, S ⛽ Fast Fuel/dsl 🛏 Scottish Inn
141mm	Buffalo River
137	Cuba Landing, N Ⓞ TN River RV Park, S 🍴 Cuba Landing Rest./gas
133mm	Tennessee River
133	rd 191, Birdsong Rd, N 9 mi ⛽ Birdsong RV Resort/marina, Good Sam RV Park
131mm	🅿️ both lanes, full 🛏 facilities, litter barrels, petwalk, 📞, 🖼 vending
126	US 641, TN 69, to Camden, N ⛽ Marathon/Subway/dsl, Phillips 66/North 40/dsl, Shell/dsl Ⓞ Paris Landing SP, tire/truck repair, to NB Forrest SP, S ⛽ BP/dsl, Shell/dsl 🛏 Days Inn Ⓞ 🅷 Mouse-tail Landing SP (24mi)
116	rd 114, S Ⓞ RV camping, to Natchez Trace SP
110mm	Big Sandy River
108	TN 22, to Lexington, Parkers Crossroads, N ⛽ BP/McDonald's/24hr/dsl, Citgo/dsl/24hr, Phillips 66/dsl 🍴 Bailey's Rest., DQ, Subway 🛏 Knights Inn Ⓞ city park, USPO, S ⛽ Exxon 🍴 Po' Boys Pizza 🛏 Best Value Inn Ⓞ 🅷 Parkers Crossroads Bfd Visitors Ctr, RV camping, to Shiloh NMP (51mi)
103mm	parking area/truck sta eb, litter barrels
102mm	parking area/truck sta wb, litter barrels
101	rd 104, N ⛽ 101 TP/rest/dsl/tires/24hr Ⓞ golf (3mi)
93	rd 152, Law Rd, N ⛽ Phillips 66/deli/dsl/24hr, S ⛽ BP/dsl, Super Way/dsl
87	US 70, US 412, Jackson, N ⛽ Coastal/dsl, S ⛽ BP/dsl, Loves/Hardee's/dsl/scales/24hr
85	Christmasville Rd, to Jackson, N ⛽ BP/dsl, Exxon/dsl/24hr, 🍴 Denny's/dsl/scales/24hr 🛏 Comfort Inn Ⓞ $General, S ⛽ Horizon/Baskin-Robbins/Pizza Pro 🍴 Jiang Jun Chinese, Lenny's Subs, Los Portales, McDonald's, Reggi's BBQ, Sonic, Sparky's, Taco Bell 🛏 Holiday Inn Express Ⓞ $Tree, Food Giant
83	Campbell st, N ⛽ Exxon/Old Madina Mkt/dsl 🛏 Residence Inn, S 🛏 Courtyard, Hampton Inn

INTERSTATE 40 Cont'd

Exit #	Services

JACKSON

82b a US 45, Jackson, **N** 🅖 BP 🍴 Cracker Barrel 🛏 Knights Inn, Microtel 🅞 Batteries+, Curves, Smallwoods RV Ctr (4mi), **S** 🅖 BP, Clark/dsl, Exxon 🍴 Baskin-Robbins, Burger King, Catfish Galley, ChuckeCheese, DQ, KFC, Krystal, Little Caesar's, LJ Silver, McDonald's/playplace, Niko's Creek, Pizza Hut, Popeye's, Sakura Japanese, Shoney's, Sonic, Subway, Taco Bell, Tulum Mexican, Waffle House, Wendy's 🛏 Executive Inn, La Quinta, Ramada Ltd, Super 8, Travellers Motel 🅞 $General, $Tree, Advance Parts, AT&T, AutoZone, BigLots, Firestone/auto, Fred's, Goodyear/auto, JC Penney, Kroger/24hr, Macy's, mall, Office Depot, Radio Shack, Sears/auto, TJ Maxx, vet

80b a US 45 Byp, Jackson, **N** 0-2 mi 🅖 BP, Exxon 🍴 Arby's, Asahi Japanese, Backyard Burger, Baskin-Robbins, Buffalo Wild Wings, Capt D's, Chick-fil-A, Chili's, El Comal Mexican, Fazoli's, Fujiyama Japanese, HoneyBaked Ham, IHOP, Jason's Deli, KFC, Lenny's Subs, Longhorn Steaks, Los Portales, Maggie Moo's, McAlisters Deli, Moe's SW Grill, Olive Garden, Outback Steaks, Panera Bread, Peking Chinese, Perkins, Popeye's, Quiznos, Red Robin, Ruby Tuesday, Sonic, Starbucks, Steak'n Shake, Subway, TGIFriday's, Wendy's, Zaxby's 🛏 Baymont Inn, Jameson Inn, SigNature Hotel 🅞 AT&T, Best Buy, Books-A-Million, Buick/Cadillac/Chevrolet/GMC, Dick's, Firestone/auto, Gateway Tires/repair, Hobby Lobby, Home Depot, JoAnn Fabrics, Kohl's, Lowe's, Marshall's, Mazda, Nissan, Old Navy, Petsmart, Ross, Sam's Club/gas, Steinmart, Target, Verizon, Walmart/gas, **S** 🅖 BP/Circle K, G/dsl, Phillips 66/dsl 🍴 Arby's, Asia Garden, Barnhill's Buffet, Burger King, Double D Ranch Rest., Heavenly Ham, Logan's Roadhouse, McDonald's, Mrs Winner's, O'Charley's, Old Hickory Steakhouse, Old Town Spaghetti, Red Bones Grill, Subway, Taco Bell, Waffle House 🛏 Best Western, Casey Jones Motel, Comfort Suites, Days Inn, DoubleTree, EconoLodge, Guesthouse Inn, Holiday Inn, Motel 6, Old Hickory Inn, Quality Inn 🅞 🏥 $General, Chickasaw SP, Chrysler/Dodge/Jeep, Ford/Lincoln, Harley-Davidson, Honda, Hyundai, K-Mart, to Pinson Mounds SP, Toyota/Scion, Tuesday Morning

79 US 412, Jackson, **N** 🅞 Gander Mtn., **S** 🅖 BP/dsl, Citgo/dsl, Exxon 🛏 Days Inn 🅞 Jackson RV Park

78mm Forked Deer River

76 rd 223, **S** 🍴 McKenzie BBQ 🅞 McKellar-Sites ✈, Whispering Pines RV Park

74 Lower Brownsville Rd

73mm 🆁🆂 both lanes, full ♿ facilities, info, litter barrels, petwalk, 🅲, 🅥 vending

68 rd 138, Providence Rd, **N** 🅖 BP/dsl 🛏 Ole South Inn, **S** 🅖 TA/Citgo/Subway/dsl/scales/24hr/@, Valero/dsl 🅞 Joy-O RV Park

66 US 70, to Brownsville, **N** 🅞 Ft Pillow SHP (51mi), **S** 🅖 Exxon/dsl 🛏 Motel 6

60 rd 19, Mercer Rd

56 TN 76, to Brownsville, **N** 🅖 BP, Shell/dsl/24hr 🍴 DQ, KFC, McDonald's/playplace, Pizza Hut/Taco Bell 🛏 Best Value Inn, Comfort Inn, Days Inn, Econolodge, **S** 🅖 Exxon/Huddle House/dsl/24hr

55mm Hatchie River

52 TN 76, rd 179, Koko Rd, to Whiteville, 🅖 Koko/dsl

50mm weigh sta both lanes, 🅲

47 TN 179, to Stanton, Dancyville, **S** 🅖 Exit 47 Trkstp/dsl

42 TN 222, to Stanton, **N** 🛏 Best Value Inn, **S** 🅖 Exxon/dsl, 🍴 Chester's/Subway/dsl/scales/24hr 🛏 Deerfield Inn

35 TN 59, to Somerville, **S** 🅖 BP/dsl/scales 🍴 Longtown Rest.

29.5mm Loosahatchie River

25 TN 205, Airline Rd, to Arlington, **N** 🅖 Shell/dsl, **S** 🅖 Exxon/Backyard Burger/dsl 🅞 vistor ctr

24 TN 385, rd 204, to Arlington, Millington, Collierville

20 Canada Rd, Lakeland, **N** 🅖 BP/McDonald's, Shell 🍴 Cracker Barrel, Waffle House 🛏 Motel 6, Relax Inn, Super 8, **S** 🅖 Exxon/Subway/dsl, 🍴 TCBY 🅞 Memphis East Camping

18 US 64, to Bartlett, **N** 🅖 Shell 🍴 Abuelo's, Bob Evans, Buffalo Wild Wings, El Porton Mexican, Firebird's Grill, Hooters, Longhorn Steaks, McAlister's Deli, O'Charley's, Olive Garden, Steak'n Shake, TGI Friday's, TX Roadhouse 🛏 Best Western, Fairfield Inn, Holiday Inn, La Quinta, SpringHill Suites 🅞 Buick/GMC, Firestone/auto, Goodyear/auto, Lowe's, same as 16, Sam's Club/gas, Walmart, **S** 🅖 BP/Circle K, Citgo/dsl 🍴 Backyard Burger, KFC, Lenny's Subs, Papa John's, Pizza Hut, Subway, Zaxby's 🅞 Kroger, Schnuck's Foods/gas, Walgreens, Zaxby's

16b a TN 177, to Germantown, **N** 🅖 BP/Circle K, Shell/Circle K 🍴 Abuelo's, Arby's, Bahama Breeze, Burger King, Casa Mexicana, Chick-fil-A, Chili's, Danver's, IHOP, J. Alexander's, Joe's Crabshack, Logan's Roadhouse, Macaroni Grill, McDonald's/playplace, On-the-Border, Red Lobster, Taco Bell, TCBY, Tellini's Italian, Waffle House, Wendy's 🛏 Extended Stay Deluxe, Hampton Inn, Hyatt Place 🅞 🏥 $Tree, Barnes&Noble, Best Buy, BigLots, Chevrolet, Chrysler/Dodge/Jeep, Dillard's, Ford, Hancock Fabrics, Hobby Lobby, Home Depot, Honda, JC Penney, Macy's, mall, Michael's, Nissan, Office Depot, Old Navy, Petsmart, Sears/auto, Target, TJ Maxx, Walgreens, **S** 0-2 mi 🅖 BP/Circle K, Shell/Circle K 🍴 Abbay's Rest., Arby's, Backyard Burger, Burger King, ChuckeCheese, Corky's BBQ, El Porton Mexican, Genghis Grill, Honeybake Ham, Howard's Doughnuts, Jason's Deli, Jimmy John's, Jim'n Nick's BBQ, Lenny's Subs, McDonald's, Newk's Cafe, Pei Wei Chinese, Qdoba Mexican, Shogun Japanese, Slim Skillets, Smoothie King, Waffle House, Wendy's 🛏 Comfort Suites, Microtel, Quality Inn, Quality Suites, Studio+, Wingate Inn 🅞 Aldi Foods, AT&T, AutoZone, Costco/gas, Dick's, GNC, Gordman's, Kohl's, Kroger/gas, Marshall's, Rite Aid, Ross, Steinmart, Toyota/Scion, Tuesday Morning, Verizon, vet

15b a Appling Rd, **N** 🅖 BP/Circle K/dsl, Shell/dsl 🅞 🏥

14 Whitten Rd, **N** 🅖 Citgo/dsl, Mapco, Shell/Burger King 🍴 McDonald's, Sidecar Café 🅞 Harley-Davidson, **S** 🅖 BP/Circle K, Shell/Backyard Burger/dsl 🍴 Dunkin Donuts, Subway, Supreme Hot Wings 🅞 Walgreens

TN

M E M P H I S

⬆E INTERSTATE 40 Cont'd

Exit #	Services
12c	(from eb) I-240 W, to Jackson, I-40 E to Nashville
12b	Sam Cooper Blvd (from eb)
12a	US 64/70/79, Summer Ave, N 🅖 Mapco/dsl, Shell 🍴 Asian Palace, Waffle House 🛏 Welcome Inn 🅞 U-Haul, S 🅖 Exxon 🍴 Arby's, McDonald's 🅞 $Tree, Firestone/auto, Fred's, Goodyear/auto, Sav-A-Lot Foods
12	Sycamore View Rd, N 🅖 Citgo/dsl, Texaco/dsl 🍴 Cajun Catfish Co., Capt D's, Church's, Cracker Barrel, IHOP, McDonald's, Mrs Winner's, Perkins, Ruby Tuesday, Shoney's, Sonic, Starbucks, Taco Bell, Waffle House 🛏 Baymont Inn, Best Value Inn, Clarion, Drury Inn, EconoLodge, Extended Stay America, Memphis Plaza, Red Roof Inn 🅞 $General, AutoZone, Family$, Fred's, Walgreens, S 🅖 BP/Circle K/dsl, Exxon, Mapco 🍴 Beijing Chinese, Burger King, Popeye's, Subway, Tops BBQ, Wendy's 🛏 Best Western, Budgetel, Comfort Inn, Days Inn, Fairfield Inn, La Quinta, Memphis Inn, Motel 6, Super 8 🅞 Bass Pro Shops, Parts+
10.5mm	Wolf River
10b a	(from wb) I-240 W around Memphis, I-40 E to Nashville
10	TN 204, Covington Pike, N 🅖 BP/Circle K 🍴 McDonald's, Wendy's 🅞 Audi/VW, Buick/GMC, Chevrolet, Chrysler/Dodge/Jeep, Honda, Hyundai, KIA, Mazda, Nissan, Sam's Club, Subaru, SuperLo Food/gas, Suzuki, Volvo
8b a	TN 14, Jackson Ave, N 🅖 Citgo/dsl, Shell 🛏 Motel 6, Sleep Inn 🅞 Raleigh Tire, vet, S 🅖 Citgo/dsl, Mapco 🅞 AutoZone, Family$, O'Reilly Parts, transmissions
6	Warford Rd
5	Hollywood St, N 🅖 BP, Q-Mart/dsl 🍴 Burger King, Mother's Rest., S 🅞 Memphis Zoo
3	Watkins St, N 🅖 BP, Chevron/dsl, Coastal/dsl, Oil City USA/dsl, Texaco/dsl 🅞 Family$, U-Haul
2a	rd 300, to US 51 N, Millington, N 🅞 Meeman-Shelby SP
2	Smith Ave, Chelsea Ave, N 🅖 Citgo, S 🅖 BP
1e	I-240 E
1d c b	US 51, Danny Thomas Blvd, N 🅖 Exxon 🍴 KFC; Wendy's 🅞 Ronald McDonald House, St Jude Research Ctr
1a	2nd St (from wb), downtown, S 🛏 Crowne Plaza, Holiday Inn, Marriott, Sheraton, Wyndham Garden 🅞 Conv Ctr
1	Riverside Dr, Front St (from eb), Memphis, S 🛏 Comfort Inn 🅞 Conv Ctr, Riverfront, **Welcome Ctr**
0mm	Tennessee/Arkansas state line, Mississippi River

⬆N INTERSTATE 55

Exit #	Services
13mm	Tennessee/Arkansas state line, Mississippi River
12c	Delaware St, Memphis
12b	Riverside Dr, E **TN Welcome Ctr**, downtown Memphis
12a	E Crump Blvd (from nb), E 🅖 Exxon 🍴 Capt D's, KFC, LJ Silver, Taco Bell, Wendy's 🅞 Family$, museum
11	McLemore Ave, Presidents Island, industrial area
10	S Parkway, E 1/2 mi 🅖 BP/dsl
9	Mallory Ave, industrial area
8	Horn Lake Rd (from sb)
7	US 61, 3rd St, E 🅖 BP, Exxon 🍴 Church's, Interstate BBQ 🅞 $Tree, AutoZone, Family$, Kroger, NAPA, Rose's, Save-A-Lot Foods, Walgreens, W 🅖 BP/dsl, MapCo 🍴 KFC, McDonald's, Subway 🛏 Rest Inn 🅞 Fuller SP, Indian Museum
6b a	I-240

M E M P H I S

5b	US 51 S, Elvis Presley Blvd, to Graceland, W **0-2 mi on US 51** 🅖 BP, Citgo/dsl, Dodge's/dsl, Exxon, Shell/dsl 🍴 Baskin-Robbins, BJ's Wings, Burger King, Checker's, Exline Pizza, KFC, Krispy Kreme, Little Caesars, McDonald's, Piccadilly's, Subway, Taco Bell 🛏 American Inn, Days Inn, EconoLodge, Heartbreak Hotel/RV Park, Value Place Inn 🅞 H $General, $Tree, Advance Parts, Aldi Foods, D&N RV Ctr, Family$, Memphis Visitors Ctr, Presley RV Park, Radio Shack, to Graceland, Walgreens
5a	Brooks Rd, E 🅖 BP, Exxon, Mapco/dsl 🍴 Blimpie, Burger King, Popeye's 🛏 Inn, Best Value Inn, Budget Lodge, Clarion, Motel 6 🅞 Freightliner, Peterbilt
2b a	TN 175, Shelby Dr, Whitehaven, E 🅖 BP/dsl, Citgo/Subway, Exxon, Shell/dsl, Texaco 🛏 Colonial Inn, W 🅖 BP, Exxon/dsl, Shell/dsl 🍴 Burger King, Dixie Queen Burgers, IHOP, McDonald's, Popeye's 🅞 $General, Family$, Goodyear/auto, Kroger/gas, Macy's, Save-a-Lot Foods, Sears/auto, Toyota/Scion, U-Haul, Walgreens
0mm	Tennessee/Mississippi state line

⬆N INTERSTATE 65

Exit #	Services
121.5mm	Tennessee/Kentucky state line
121mm	**Welcome Center sb, full ♿ facilities, litter barrels, petwalk, ⓒ, 🛏 vending**
119mm	**weigh/insp sta both lanes**
117	TN 52, Portland, E 🅖 BP/Godfather's/Quiznos/dsl, Shell/dsl, fireworks 🛏 Comfort Suites 🅞 H Bledsoe Cr SP, W 🅖 BP/dsl 🛏 Budget Host 🅞 fireworks
116mm	Red River
113mm	Red River
112	TN 25, Cross Plains, E 🅖 BP/dsl 🍴 Sad Sam's Deli 🅞 antiques, Bledsoe Cr SP, fireworks, W 🅖 Mapco/dsl, Shell/Godfather's/dsl 🍴 Sweet&Savory Diner
108	TN 76, White House, E 🅖 Nervous Charlie's/dsl, Shell 🍴 A&W/KFC, China Spring, Cracker Barrel, Hardee's, Little Caesars, Los Agave's, McDonald's, Mr Wok, Sonic, Subway, Taco Bell, Waffle House, Wendy's 🛏 Best Western, Comfort Inn, Holiday Inn Express, Quality Inn 🅞 $Tree, Ace Hardware, city park/playground, Kroger/gas, O'Reilly Parts, Rite Aid, USPO, Walgreens, Walmart/Subway, W 🅖 BP/dsl 🍴 Greek Gyro 🛏 Days Inn
104	rd 257, Bethel Rd, E 🅖 BP/rest./dsl, W 🅖 Shell/dsl 🅞 Owl's Roost Camping
98	US 31 W, Millersville, E 🅖 Citgo/dsl, RaceWay, Shell/dsl 🍴 Subway, Waffle House 🅞 $General, auto repair, Nashville Country RV Park, W 🅖 BP 🛏 Economy Inn 🅞 fireworks
97	rd 174, Long Hollow Pike, E 🅖 BP/dsl, Exxon, Mapco 🍴 Arby's, Capt D's, China Express, Cracker Barrel, Domino's, Kabuto Japanese, KFC, McDonald's, Papa Murphy's, Quiznos, Shoney's, Subway, Waffle House, Wendy's 🛏 Best Western, Courtyard, Days Inn, Executive Inn, Hampton Inn, Quality Inn, Red Roof Inn 🅞 K-Mart, Kroger, Walgreens, W 🅖 Shell/dsl 🍴 Buck's BBQ, DQ, Hardee's, Krystal, Poncho Villa Grill, Sonic 🛏 Holiday Inn Express, Motel 6 🅞 Rite Aid, vet, Walgreens
96	Rivergate Pky, E 🅖 Citgo/dsl, Shell/dsl 🍴 Bailey's Grill, Dougie Ray's Grill, El Chico, Fuji Steaks, HoneyBaked Ham, Hooters, Las Palmas Mexican, McDonald's, Pizza Hut, Subway, Waffle House, Wendy's 🛏 Baymont Inn, Best Value Inn, Comfort Suites, Rodeway Inn 🅞 H Best One Tires, Dillard's, JC Penney, Macy's, mall, Sears/auto, W 🅖 Marathon,

N A S H V I L L E

N

INTERSTATE 65 Cont'd

NASHVILLE

Exit #	Services
96	Continued
	Volunteer, **E** on Gallatin **N** 🍴 A&W/LJ Silver, Arby's, Bar-B-Cutie, Burger King, Calhoun's Cafe, Checker's, Chick-fil-A, Chili's, ChuckeCheese, Fazoli's, IHOP, Krispy Kreme, Las Fiestas, Logan's Roadhouse, Longhorn Steaks, Olive Garden, Outback Steaks, Panera Bread, Popeye's, Rafferty's, Ryan's, Sonic, Starbucks, Steak'n Shake, Taco Bell, TGI Friday's 🅾 $General, AAA, AT&T, Best Buy, Books-A-Million, CarMax, Chevrolet, Chrysler/Dodge/Jeep, CVS Drug, Dick's, Discount Tire, Firestone/auto, Goodyear/auto, Harley-Davidson, Hobby Lobby, Home Depot, Honda, Jo-Ann's Etc, Kia, Lexus, Lincoln, Lowe's, Mazda, Michael's, Nissan, Office Depot, Old Navy, PepBoys, Petsmart, Sam's Club/gas, Staples, Target, TJ Maxx, Toyota/Scion, URGENT CARE, Verizon, VW, Walgreens, Walmart
95	TN 386, Vietnam Veterans Blvd (from nb)
92	rd 45, Old Hickory Blvd, **E** 🅾 🇭 to Old Hickory Dam
90b	TN 155 E, Briley Pkwy, **E** 🅾 to Opreyland
90a	US 31W, US 41, Dickerson Pike, **E** 🅿 Citgo/dsl, Exxon/dsl, Mapco/dsl, Shell 🍴 Arby's, Capt D's, Chicago Gyros, China King, Church's, Domino's, Jay's Rest., KFC, McDonald's, Pizza Hut, Subway, Taco Bell, Waffle House, Wendy's 🏨 Days Inn, EconoLodge, Sleep Inn, Super 8 🅾 $General, Advance Parts, AutoZone, CVS Drug, Family$, Kroger, O'Reilly Parts, Walgreens, **W** 🅾 Lowe's, Walmart
88b a	I-24, W to Clarksville, E to Nashville
87b a	US 431, Trinity Lane, **E** 🅿 BP, ❤Loves/Subway/dsl/scales/24hr 🍴 Church's/White Castle, Krystal, Sonic 🏨 Cumberland Inn, Delux Inn 🅾 Piggly Wiggly, **W** 🅿 BCP/dsl, BP, Exxon, Mapco 🍴 Fat Mo's, Jack-in-the-Box, Jack's BBQ, McDonald's, Subway, Taco Bell, Waffle House 🏨 Best Value Inn, Comfort Inn, Days Inn, EconoLodge, Halmark Inn, Howard Johnson, King's Inn, Quality Inn, Ravin Hotel, Regency Inn, Rodeway Inn 🅾 $General, Family$
86mm	Cumberland River
86	I-24 E, to I-40 E, to Memphis
85	US 41A, 8th Ave, **E** 🅿 BP 🅾 O'Reilly Parts, tires, to st capitol, **W** 🅿 Exxon 🍴 Arby's, Jersey Mike's, McDonald's, Pizza Hut, Starbucks, Subway, Taco Bell, Wendy's, Wise Burger 🏨 Millennium Hotel, SpringHill Suites 🅾 Cadillac/Honda
84b a	I-40, E to Knoxville, W to Memphis
209 [I-40]	US 70, Charlotte Ave, Church St, **E** 🅿 Exxon 🍴 McDonald's 🅾 Firestone, **W** 🅿 Exxon, Shell 🍴 Burger King, Krystal, Sonic, Subway, White Castle 🏨 Comfort Inn 🅾 URGENT CARE, Walgreens
82b a	I-40, W to Memphis, E to Nashville
81	Wedgewood Ave, **W** 🅿 BP, Exxon, Shell 🍴 Burger King, Subway 🅾 $General, U-Haul
80	I-440, to Memphis, Knoxville
79	Armory Dr, **E** on Powell 🅿 Shell 🍴 Applebee's, Jersey Mike's, Logan's Roadhouse, Panda Express, Panera Bread, Rafferty's, Subway, Wendy's 🅾 BMW, CarMax, Home Depot, Michael's, Petsmart, Ross, Staples, TJ Maxx
78b a	rd 255, Harding Place, **E** 🅿 Mapco, Pure, Shell 🍴 Beijing Chinese, Cracker Barrel, Mama Mia's Italian, Sub House, Waffle House 🏨 La Quinta, Red Roof Inn, Traveler's Rest Hist Home 🅾 CVS Drug
74	TN 254, Old Hickory Blvd, to Brentwood, **E** 🍴 Capt D's, Coldstone, Longhorn Steaks, Panera Bread, Qdoba Mexican, Shoney's, Waffle House 🏨 Best Western,

BRENTWOOD

74	Continued
	Holiday Inn Express, Hyatt Place, Sheraton 🅾 GNC, Target, **W** 🅿 BP, Gulf, Shell/dsl 🍴 5 Guys Burgers, Backyard Burger, Chick-fil-A, Chili's, Chipotle Mexican, Church's, Corky's BBQ, Jimmy John's, Maggie Moo's, Mazatlan Mexican, McAlister's Deli, McDonald's, Moe's SW Grill, Mrs Winner's, O'Charley's, Papa John's, Pei Wei, Pizza Hut, Ruby Tuesday, Starbucks, Subway, Taco Bell, Wendy's 🏨 Courtyard, Extended Stay America, Hampton Inn, Hilton Suites, Homestead Suites, Studio+ 🅾 Cadillac, CVS Drug, Fresh Mkt Foods, Harris-Teeter, Land Rover, Office Depot, PetCo, Publix, Rite Aid, SteinMart, TJ Maxx, USPO, Walgreens
71	TN 253, Concord Rd, to Brentwood
69	rd 441, Moores Lane, Galleria Blvd, **E** 🅿 MapCo/dsl, Shell 🍴 Amerigo's Grill, Baskin-Robbins, Cozymel's, Dunkin Donuts, Fuji Japanese, Greek Cafe, Outback Steaks, Papa Murphy's, Shogun Japanese, Sonic, Starbucks 🏨 Hilton Garden, Hyatt Place, Red Roof Inn, Wingate Inn 🅾 Acura/Lexus, CVS Drug, Home Depot/gas, Michael's, Petsmart, Publix, Walgreens, **W** 🅿 BP, Shell/dsl 🍴 Backyard Burger, Buca Italian, Burger King, Capt D's, Chili's, Cracker Barrel, Famous Dave's, HoneyBaked Ham, J Alexander's Rest., Krispy Kreme, Logan's Roadhouse, Macaroni Grill, McDonald's, Peking Palace, Pizza Hut/Taco Bell, Red Lobster, Schlotzsky's, Stoney River Steaks 🏨 Sleep Inn 🅾 $Tree, Barnes&Noble, Belk, Best Buy, Costco/gas, Dillard's, Discount Tire, JC Penney, Macy's, mall, NTB, Old Navy, Ross, Sears/auto, Target
68b a	Cool Springs Blvd, **E** 🍴 Jersey Mike's 🏨 Courtyard, Embassy Suites, Marriott, Residence Inn, **W** 🅿 Exxon, Shell 🍴 5 Guys Burgers, BoneFish Grill, Bread&Co, Canton Buffet, Carrabba's, Chick-fil-A, ChuckeCheese, Chuy's Mexican, Genghis Grill, Golden Corral, Greek Cafe, J Christopher's, Jack-in-the-Box, Jason's Deli, Jersey Mike's, KFC, McAlister's Deli, McDonald's, Moe's SW Grill, Newk's Cafe, Omikoshi Japanese, Otter's Chicken Tenders, Panera Bread, PF Chang's, Pizza Hut, Quiznos, Royal Thai, Starbucks, Subway, TGIFriday's, Wendy's 🏨 ALoft, Country Inn&Suites, Hampton Inn 🅾 Acura, AT&T, Dick's, GNC, Harley-Davidson, Jo-Ann Fabrics, Kohl's, Kroger, Lowe's, Marshall's, Office Depot, Sam's Club/gas, Staples, TJ Maxx, to Galleria Mall, Verizon, Walgreens
67	McEwen Dr, 🍴 Blue Coast Burrito, Brick Top's, Little Caesars, Marco's Pizza, Sonic, Subway, Tazikis Mediterranean Cafe 🏨 Drury Inn 🅾 Toyota/Scion, Walmart/Blimpie, Whole Food Mkt
65	TN 96, to Murfreesboro, Franklin, **E** 🅿 Mapco, Shell/Krystal 🍴 Cracker Barrel, Sonic, Steak'n Shake 🏨 Best Value Inn, Comfort Inn, Days Inn, Holiday Inn Express, La Quinta, Ramada Inn 🅾 auto repair, Buick/GMC, Chevrolet, Honda,

🅖 = gas 🍴 = food 🏠 = lodging 🅞 = other 🆁🆂 = rest stop Copyright 2015 - the Next EXIT ®

TN

F R A N K L I N

⬆N	INTERSTATE 65 Cont'd
Exit #	Services
65	Continued
	Kia, Subaru, URGENT CARE, Volvo, Walgreens, W 🅖 BP/dsl, Shell, Shell/dsl 🍴 Arby's, Backyard Burger, Bar-B-Cutie, Bleachers Sports Grill, Franklin Chophouse, Hardee's, IHOP, KFC, La Terraza Mexican, McDonald's, Nashville Pizza, O'Charley's, Pancho's Mexican, Papa John's, Shoney's, Starbucks, Subway, Taco Bell, Waffle House, Wendy's, Whitts BBQ, Zaxby's 🏠 Best Western, Best Western, Quality Inn 🅞 $General, $Tree, Aldi Foods, BigLots, Chrysler/Dodge/Jeep, Discount Tire, Fiat, Ford/Lincoln, Hobby Lobby, Home Depot, K-Mart, Kroger/gas, Publix/gas, Radio Shack, Rite Aid, SteinMart, to Confederate Cem at Franklin, Tuesday Morning, Verizon, vet, Walgreens
64mm	Harpeth River
61	TN 248, Peytonsville Rd, to Spring Hill, E 🅖 TA/BP/Country Pride/dsl/scales/24hr/@, W 🅖 Mapco, Shell/dsl 🏠 Goose Creek Inn
59b a	TN 840, to Nashville
58mm	W Harpeth River
53	TN 396, Saturn Pkwy, Spring Hill, Columbia, W TN Scenic Pkwy
48mm	truck insp/weigh sta nb, litter barrels
46	US 412, TN 99, to Columbia, Chapel Hill, E 🅖 BP/dsl, ❤Loves/Arbys/dsl/scales/24hr 🅞 Harley-Davidson, Henry Horton SP, W 🅖 Citgo/dsl, Phillip 66/Subway/dsl, Shell, TJ's/Burger King 🍴 Cracker Barrel, McDonald's, Stan's Rest, Waffle House 🏠 Best Value Inn, Comfort Inn, Fairfield Inn, Hampton Inn, Holiday Inn Express, Relax Inn, Super 8 🅞 🏥
40.5mm	Duck River
37	TN 50, to Columbia, Lewisburg, E 🅞 🏥 TN Walking Horse HQ, W 🅖 Phillips 66dsl 🅞 to Polk Home
32	rd 373, to Lewisburg, Mooresville
27	rd 129, to Lynnville, Cornersville, E 🅞 Texas T Camping
25mm	W parking area sb, litter barrels
24mm	E parking area nb, litter barrels
22	US 31A, to Pulaski, E 🅖 Tennesseean Trkstp/Exxon/Pop's BBQ/dsl/scales/24hr/@ 🍴 McDonald's, Subway 🏠 EconoLodge, W 🅖 /dsl/scales/24hr, Shell/dsl
14	US 64, to Pulaski, E 🅖 BP/dsl, Shell/dsl 🍴 Sarge's Shack Rest. 🏠 Super 8 🅞 to Jack Daniels Distillery, W 🅞 🏥
6	rd 273, Bryson, E 🅖 Shell/rest./dsl/repair 🏠 Best Value Inn 🅞 dsl repair, W 🅖 Marathon/dsl (2mi)
5mm	E weigh sta nb
4mm	Elk River
3mm	Welcome Center nb, full ♿ facilities, info, litter barrels, petwalk, 📞, 🥤 vending
1	US 31, rd 7, Ardmore, Ardmore, E 1-2 mi 🅖 Chevron/dsl, Exxon/dsl, Shell 🍴 $General, El Olmeca Mexican, Hardee's, KFC/Taco Bell, McDonald's, Pizza Hut, Sonic, Subway, Whitts BBQ 🅞 $General Mkt, Ardmore Tire, O'Reilly Parts
0	Tennessee/Alabama state line

⬆E	INTERSTATE 75
Exit #	Services
161.5mm	Tennessee/Kentucky state line
161mm	Welcome Center sb, full ♿ facilities, litter barrels, petwalk, 📞, 🥤 vending
160	US 25W, Jellico, E 🅖 Exxon/dsl, Marathon/dsl, W 🅖 BP/Wendy's/dsl, Shell/Arby's/dsl 🍴 Hardee's, Heritage Pizza, McDonald's, Subway 🏠 Days Inn, Parkway Inn 🅞 🏥 camping, fireworks, to Indian Mtn SP

B E T H E L

156	Rarity Mtn Rd
144	Stinking Creek Rd, E 4 mi E 🅞 Ride Royal Blue Camping
141	TN 63, to Royal Blue, Huntsville, E 🅖 Shell/dsl 🍴 El Rey Azteca, W 🅖 /Subway/dsl/scales/24hr, Shell/dsl 🏠 Comfort Inn 🅞 fireworks, repair/truckwash, to Big South Fork NRA
134	US 25W, TN 63, Caryville, E 🅖 Shell 🍴 Takumi Japanese, Waffle House 🏠 Hampton Inn, Holiday Inn Express, Super 8, Travelodge 🅞 🏥 $General, Cumberland Gap NHP, to Cove Lake SP, W 🅖 BP/dsl 🍴 Scotty's Hamburgers, Shoney's 🏠 Budget Host 🅞 USPO
129	US 25W S, Lake City, W 🅖 Exxon/dsl, Marathon/Sonic/dsl, Pilot/dsl, Shell/dsl 🍴 Cracker Barrel, Domino's, Glen's Pizza, KFC/Taco Bell, La Fiesta Mexican, McDonald's, Subway 🏠 Blue Haven Motel, Days Inn, Lamb's Inn/rest., Scottish Inn 🅞 $General, Family$, fireworks, same as 128
128	US 441, to Lake City, E 🅖 Sunoco 🅞 Mtn Lake Marina Camping (4mi), W 🅖 Exxon/dsl, Marathon, Weigel's/dsl 🏠 Blue Haven Motel 🅞 $General, Advance Parts, antique cars, Family$, same as 129, to Norris Dam SP
126mm	Clinch River
122	TN 61, Bethel, Norris, E 🅖 Shell/dsl, Wiegel's/dsl 🍴 Shoney's 🅞 antiques, KOA, Museum of Appalachia, Toyota/Scion, W 🅖 BP/dsl, Exxon/Burger King/Subway/dsl, Git'n Go/dsl, Phillips 66/dsl, Shell/Baskin-Robbins 🍴 Arby's, Bojangles, Golden Girls Rest., Gondolier Italian, Hardee's, Harrison's Grill, Krystal, LJ Silver, McDonald's, Waffle House, Wendy's, Zaxby's 🏠 Comfort Inn, Country Inn&Suites, Hampton Inn, Holiday Inn Express, Red Roof Inn, Super 8 🅞 AT&T, Big Pine Ridge SP, Ford, Verizon, Walgreens, Walmart/McDonald's
117	rd 170, Racoon Valley Rd, E 🅖 /dsl/scales/24hr, W 🏠 Valley Inn 🅞 Racoon Valley RV Park, Volunteer RV Park
112	rd 131, Emory Rd, to Powell, E 🅖 Marathon/Buddy's BBQ/dsl, /DQ/Taco Bell/dsl 🍴 5 Guys Burgers, Arby's, Aubrey's Rest., Bruster's, Chick-fil-A, Firehouse Subs, Jets Pizza, Krystal, McDonald's/playplace, Petro's Cafe, Ruby Tuesday, Starbucks, Steak'n Shake, Subway, Wendy's, Zaxby's 🏠 Comfort Inn, Country Inn&Suites, Holiday Inn Express 🅞 🏥 CVS Drug, Ingles/gas, O'Reilly Parts, Rigg's Drug, Verizon, W 🅖 Exxon/dsl, Shell/dsl, Weigel's/dsl 🍴 Hardee's, Shoney's, Waffle House 🏠 Super 8
110	Callahan Dr, E 🅖 Weigel's/dsl 🍴 Archer's BBQ, Asian Cafe 🏠 Express Inn, Knights Inn 🅞 Honda, W 🏠 Scottish Inn 🅞 Kia, Mack/Volvo
108	Merchants Dr, E 🅖 Delta/dsl, Marathon/dsl, Mobil/dsl, Pilot/dsl 🍴 Applebee's, Cracker Barrel, El Chico, Hooters, Monterrey Mexican, O'Charley's, Pizza Hut, Puelo's Grill, Starbucks, Waffle House 🏠 Best Western, Comfort Suites, Days Inn, Hampton Inn, Mainstay Suites, Quality Inn, Relax Inn, Sleep Inn 🅞 Ingles, Valvoline, W 🅖 Exxon/dsl, Pilot/Domino's/dsl 🍴 Austin's Steaks, Burger King, Capt D's, IHOP, Mandarin House, McDonald's, Nixon's Deli, Outback Steaks, Red Lobster, Subway, Taco Bell 🏠 Best Value Inn, Clarion Inn, EconoLodge, Motel 6, Super 8 🅞 CVS Drug, Radio Shack, Walgreens
107	I-640 & I-75
3b [I-640]	US 25W, (from nb), W 🅞 Chevrolet, Ford, Nissan
1 [I-640]	rd 62, Western Ave, E 🍴 Hardee's, Krystal 🅞 Advance Parts, Family$, O'Reilly Parts, W 🅖 Exxon/dsl, Marathon/dsl, RaceWay/dsl 🍴 Central Park, Firehouse Subs, KFC, Little Caesars, LJ Silver, McDonald's, Panda Chinese, Shoney's, Subway, Taco Bell, Wendy's 🅞 CVS Drug, Kroger/dsl, Walgreens

I-75 and I-40 run together 17 mi. See I-40, exits 369-385.

Exit #	Services

INTERSTATE 75 Cont'd

84ba [368] I-40, W to Nashville, E to Knoxville

81 US 321, TN 95, to Lenoir City, **E** 🅿 BP/Buddy's BBQ/TCBY/ dsl, Exxon/Subway/dsl, Marathon/dsl, Mobil, Murphy USA/dsl, Shell/dsl 🍴 5 Guys Burgers, Angelo's Brick Oven, Bojangles, Burger King, Capt D's, Chili's, China Buffet, Cracker Barrel, Dunkin Donuts, Hardee's, KFC, McDonald's, Monterrey Mexican, Panda Buffet, Pizza Hut, Quiznos, Shoney's, Snappy Tomato Pizza, Taco Bell, Waffle House, Wendy's, Zaxby's 🏠 Days Inn, Hampton Inn, Holiday Inn Express, King's Inn/ rest. 🅾 $General Mkt, $Tree, Advance Parts, AT&T, AutoZone, CVS Drug, Food City/gas, Ford, Ft Loudon Dam, Great Smokies NP, Home Depot, Lazy Acres RV Park (7mi), O'Reilly Parts, Radio Shack, Verizon, Walmart/Subway, **W** 🅿 Citgo/dsl, Shell/dsl 🍴 Krystal, Ruby Tuesday 🏠 Comfort Inn, EconoLodge, Knights Inn 🅾 Crosseyed Cricket Camping (6mi), Matlock Tires/Repair

76 rd 324, Sugar Limb Rd, **W** 🅾 to TN Valley Winery

74mm Tennessee River

72 TN 72, to Loudon, **E** 🅿 BP/McDonald's, Shell/Wendy's 🍴 Cabin Rest., KFC, Taco Bell 🏠 Country Inn&Suites, Super 8 🅾 to Ft Loudon SP, Weigel's/dsl, **W** 🅿 Marathon 🏠 Best Value Inn 🅾 Express RV Park

68 rd 323, to Philadelphia, **E** 🅿 BP/dsl, Sunoco (2mi) 🍴 cheese factory/store (2mi)

62 RD 322, Oakland Rd, to Sweetwater, **E** 🍴 Dinner Bell Rest., **W** 🅾 KOA

60 TN 68, Sweetwater, **E 0-2 mi** 🅿 BP, RaceWay, Shell/dsl 🍴 A&W/LJ Silver, Bradley's BBQ, Burger King, Hardee's, KFC, McDonald's, Pizza Hut, Sonic, Subway, Taco Bell 🏠 Comfort Inn, Days Inn, EconoLodge, Economy Inn, Hilltop Motel 🅾 🅷 $General, $General, Ace Hardware, Advance Parts, Family$, Ford/Lincoln, K-Mart, O'Reilly Parts, to Lost Sea Underground Lake, Verizon, Walgreens, **W** 🅿 Kangaroo/dsl, Marathon 🏠 Magnuson Hotel, Quality Inn 🅾 flea mkt, tires/repair, to Watts Bar Dam, vet

56 rd 309, Niota, **E** 🅿 Wilco/Stuckey's/Wendy's/dsl/scales/24hr 🅾 TN Country Camping, **W** 🅾 tires

52 rd 305, Mt Verd Rd, to Athens, **E** 🅿 Marathon/dsl (2mi) 🍴 Subway (2mi) 🅾 Overniter RV Park, **W** 🅿 BP 🏠 Athens Lodge

49 TN 30, to Athens, **E** 🅿 BP, Kangaroo, Marathon, Murphy USA/dsl, RaceWay, Shell/dsl 🍴 Applebee's, Arby's, Buddy's BBQ, Burger King, Capt D's, China Wok, Firehouse Subs, Hardee's, KFC, Krystal, McDonald's, Monterrey Mexican, Papa John's, Pizza Hut, Ruby Tuesday, Shoney's, Sonic, Subway, Taco Bell, Waffle House, Wendy's, Western Sizzlin, Zaxby's 🏠 Days Inn, Hampton Inn, Holiday Inn Express, Homestead Inn, Motel 6, Scottish Inn, Super 8 🅾 🅷 $General, Advance Parts, Athens I-75 Camping, BigLots, Food Lion, K-Mart, Lowe's, Russell Stover, Staples, to TN Wesleyan Coll, Verizon, Walgreens, Walmart/Subway, **W** 🅿 Shell 🍴 Cracker Barrel 🏠 Best Value Inn, Comfort Inn

45mm ℞ₛ both lanes, full 🚻 facilities, info, litter barrels, petwalk, 🍴, 🚬 vending

42 rd 39, Riceville Rd, **E** 🅿 Citgo/dsl 🏠 Relax Inn, Rice Inn (2mi)

36 rd 163, to Calhoun, **E** 🍴 Hardee's (3mi) 🅾 Hiwassee/Ocoee River SP

35mm Hiwassee River

33 rd 308, to Charleston, **E** 🅿 Marathon/dsl, **W** 🅿 Loves/ McDonald's/Subway/dsl/scales/24hr, Shell/rest./dsl

27 Paul Huff Pkwy, **E 1 mi** 🅿 Murphy USA, Phillips 66 🍴 5 Guys Burgers, Applebee's, Capt D's, Chili's, CiCi's, DQ, Fazoli's, Firehouse Subs, Golden Corral, IHOP, McDonald's,

---

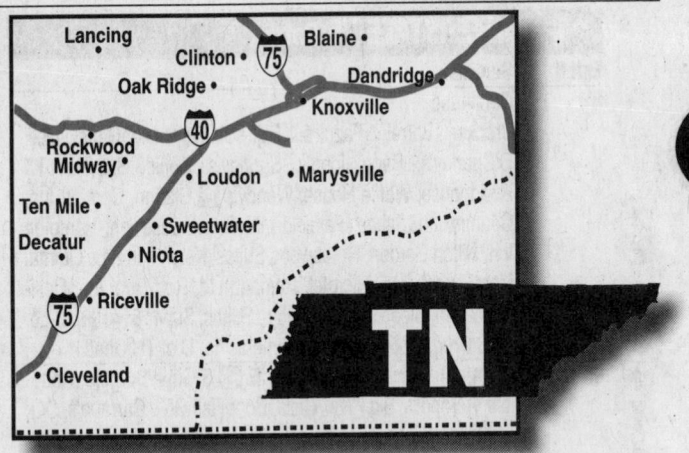

27 Continued
O'Charley's, Outback Steaks, Panera Bread, Pizza Hut, Ryan's, Sonic, Steak'n Shake, Taco Bell, Takoyaki 🏠 Jameson Inn 🅾 $Tree, Aldi Foods, auto repair/tires, AutoZone, Belk, Buick/Cadillac/GMC, CVS Drug, Food Lion, Hobby Lobby, Home Depot, JC Penney, K-Mart, Lowe's, mall, PetCo, Radio Shack, Rite Aid, Sears, Staples, TJ Maxx, Verizon, Walgreens, Walmart, **W** 🅿 BP/dsl, Exxon/dsl, Shell/Subway 🍴 Denny's, Fulin's Asian, Hardee's, Shane's Ribshack, Stevi B's Pizza, Waffle House, Wendy's 🏠 Classic Suites, Hampton Inn, Quality Inn, Ramada Ltd, Royal Inn, Super 8 🅾 AT&T, Books-A-Million, Kohl's, Michael's, Ross, Target

25 TN 60, Cleveland, **E** 🅿 Chevron/dsl, RaceWay/dsl, Shell/dsl 🍴 Bojangles, Burger King, Checker's, Cracker Barrel, Hardee's, McDonald's, Sonic, Waffle House, Wendy's, Zaxby's 🏠 Colonial Inn, Days Inn, Douglas Inn, EconoLodge, Economy Inn, Fairfield Inn, Howard Johnson, Knights Inn, Travel Inn 🅾 🅷 $General, Ace Hardware, BigLots, Cherokee Drug, to Lee Coll, Tuesday Morning, vet, **W** 🅿 Shell 🏠 Comfort Inn, Mtn View Inn, Wingate Inn

23mm truck/weigh sta nb

20 US 64 byp, to Cleveland, **E 1-4 mi** 🅿 FuelMart 🅾 Ford, Honda, **W** 🅿 BP/DQ/Pizza Hut/dsl, Exxon/dsl 🍴 McDonald's 🅾 fireworks, KOA (1mi), Toyota/Scion

16mm scenic view sb

13mm truck/weigh sta sb, litter barrels

11 US 11 N, US 64 E, Ooltewah, **E** 🅿 BP, Murphy USA/dsl, RaceWay/dsl, Shell 🍴 Arby's, Bojangles, Burger King, Capt D's, China Rose, Cracker Barrel, El Matador Mexican, Hardee's, Little Caesars, McDonald's, Sonic, Subway, Taco Bell, Wendy's, Zaxby's 🏠 Hampton Inn, Holiday Inn Express 🅾 Ace Hardware, Bi-Lo, GNC, O'Reilly Parts, Verizon, Walgreens, Walmart/Subway, **W** 🅿 BP/Quiznos/dsl 🍴 Krystal, Waffle House 🏠 Super 8 🅾 Publix, to Harrison Bay SP

9 Volkswagon Dr

7b a US 11, US 64, Lee Hwy, **E** 🅿 Exxon/dsl, **W** 🅿 Shell 🍴 City Cafe, Waffle House 🏠 Best Inn, Best Value Inn, Best Western, Comfort Inn, EconoLodge, Motel 6 🅾 Harley-Davidson, Jaguar/Land Rover/Porsche, repair

5 Shallowford Rd, **E** 🍴 Alexander's, Arby's, Capt. D's, Chili's, Chophouse Rest., CiCi's, Country Place Rest., DQ, Famous Dave's, J. Alexanders, Krystal, Logan's Roadhouse, Macaroni Grill, McAlister's Deli, McDonald's/playplace, Outback Steaks, Smokey Bones BBQ, Souper Salad, Starbucks, Steak'n Shake, Taco Bell, Zaxby's 🏠 Courtyard, Quality Inn, Wingate Inn 🅾 AAA, Barnes&Noble, Best Buy, Books-A-Million, Firestone/auto, Ford, FreshMkt Foods, Hobby Lobby, Home Depot, Lowe's, Office Depot, Old Navy, Petsmart, SteinMart, Target, Walgreens, Walmart/Subway, World Mkt, **W** 🅿 BP, Citgo/dsl, Exxon, Shell 🍴 Applebee's, Blimpie,

SWEETWATER
*(middle column vertical text: CLEVELAND)*

⬆N INTERSTATE 75 Cont'd

Exit #	Services
5	Continued
	Cracker Barrel, Fazoli's, Fuji Steaks, GlenGene Deli, O'Charley's, Papa John's, Shoney's, Sonic, Subway, TX Roadhouse, Waffle House, Wendy's 🏠 Clarion, Comfort Inn, Country Inn&Suites, Fairfield Inn, Guesthouse Inn, Hampton Inn, Hilton Garden, Homewood Suites, Knights Inn, La Quinta, MainStay Suites, Microtel, Ramada Ltd, Red Roof Inn, Residence Inn, Sleep Inn, Staybridge Suites, Super 8 🅞 🅗 Bi-Lo, CVS Drug, Goodyear/auto, same as 4a, U of TN/Chatt
4a	(from nb) Hamilton Place Blvd, E 🍴 5 Guys Burgers, Abuelo's, Acropolis, Big River Grille, BoneFish Grill, Carraba's, DQ, El Mason, Firehouse Subs, Fox&Hound Grill, Golden Corral, Jason's Deli, Kampai Of Tokyo, Moe's SW Grill, Olive Garden, Outback Steaks, Panera Bread, PF Chang's, Piccadilly's, Red Lobster, Ruby Tuesday, Salsarita's Mexican, Shogun Japanese, Starbucks, Sticky Fingers BBQ 🏠 InTown Suites 🅞 AAA, Belk, Dillard's, Firestone, JC Penney, Kohl's, mall, Marshall's, Michael's, Ross, same as 5, Sears/auto, Staples, Target, TJ Maxx
4	TN 153, Chickamauga Dam Rd, ✈
3b a	TN 320, Brainerd Rd, E 🅖 BP 🍴 Baskin-Robbins, Subway, W 🅞 BMW
2	I-24 W, to I-59, to Chattanooga, Lookout Mtn
1.5mm	**Welcome Center nb, full ♿ facilities, litter barrels, petwalk, 🚻, 🏧 vending**
1b a	US 41, Ringgold Rd, to Chattanooga, E 🅖 BP, Texaco/dsl 🍴 Wendy's 🏠 Best Value Inn, Best Western, Clarion, Knights Inn, Motel 6 🅞 Bi-Lo, Camping World RV Ctr/park, Family$, W 🅖 Conoco/dsl, Mapco/Quiznos/dsl 🍴 A&W/LJ Silver, Arby's, Baskin-Robbins, Burger King, Central Park Burger, Cracker Barrel, Hardee's, Krystal, McDonald's, PortoFino Italian, Subway, Taco Bell, Teriyaki House, Waffle House, Wally's Rest. 🏠 Days Inn, Fairfield Inn, Holiday Inn Express, Super 8, Superior Creek Lodge, Waverly Motel 🅞 O'Reilly Parts, U-Haul
0mm	Tennessee/Georgia state line

⬆N INTERSTATE 81

Exit #	Services
75mm	Tennessee/Virginia state line, **Welcome Center sb, full ♿ facilities, litter barrels, petwalk, 🚻, 🏧 vending**
74b a	US 11W, to Bristol, Kingsport, E 🏠 Hampton Inn 🅞 🅗 W 🅖 Valero 🏠 Super 8, Travelodge
69	TN 394, to Blountville, E 🅖 BP/Subway/dsl 🍴 Arby's, Domino's 🅞 Advance Parts, Bristol Int Speedway, Lakeview RV Park (8mi)
66	rd 126, to Kingsport, Blountville, W 🅖 Shell 🍴 McDonald's
63	rd 357, E 🅖 BP/Krystal/dsl, Shell/Subway/dsl 🍴 Cracker Barrel, Wendy's 🏠 La Quinta, Sleep Inn 🅞 Hamricks, W 🏠 Best Value Inn 🅞 dsl repair, KOA, Rocky Top Camping, 🅞 Tri-City ✈
60mm	Holston River
59	rd 36, to Johnson City, Kingsport, E 🅖 BP/dsl 🏠 Super 8, W 🅖 BP, Shell/dsl, Sunoco, Zoomerz 🍴 Arby's, Crazy Tomato, Domino's, Fisherman's Dock Rest., Hardee's, HotDog Hut, Jersey Mike's Subs, La Carreta Mexican, Little Caesars, McDonald's, Moto Japanese, Pal's Drive-Thru, Perkins, Pizza Hut, Raffaele's Pizza, Subway, The Shack BBQ 🏠 Colonial Inn, Comfort Inn 🅞 $General, $Tree, Advance Parts, Curves, CVS Drug, Firestone/auto, Ingles/deli, O'Reilly Parts, to Warrior's Path SP, URGENT CARE, USPO, Verizon, vet, Walgreens

Exit #	Services
57b a	I-26
56	Tri-Cities Crossing, E 🅞 regional shopping complex
50	TN 93, Fall Branch, W 🅞 auto auction, st patrol
44	Jearoldstown Rd, E 🅖 Marathon
41mm	🅡ₛ sb, full ♿ facilities, litter barrels, petwalk, 🚻, 🏧 vending
38mm	🅡ₛ sb, full ♿ facilities, litter barrels, petwalk, 🚻, 🏧 vending
36	rd 172, to Baileyton, E 🅖 ⛽/Subway/dsl/scales/24hr, W 🅖 BP/dsl, Shell/Subway/dsl/24hr, TA/Country Pride/dsl/scales/24hr/@ 🍴 Pizza+ 🏠 36 Motel 🅞 $General, Around Pond RV Park, Baileyton Camp (2mi), Family$
30	TN 70, to Greeneville, E 🅖 Exxon/DQ/Stuckey's/dsl
23	US 11E, to Greeneville, E 🅖 Marathon/Wendy's, Zoomerz/Subway 🅞 Crockett SP, to Andrew Johnson HS, Tri-Am RV Ctr, W 🅖 Exxon/DQ/dsl, Phillips 66/rest./scales 🍴 McDonald's, Pizza+, Taco Bell, Tony's BBQ 🏠 Best Western, Super 8
21mm	weigh sta sb
15	rd 340, Fish Hatchery Rd
12	TN 160, to Morristown, E 🅖 Phillips 66, W 🅖 Shell/dsl 🏠 Days Inn (6mi), Hampton Inn (12mi), Holiday Inn Express (5mi), Super 8 (5mi) 🅞 to Crockett Tavern HS
8	US 25E, to Morristown, E 🍴 Sonic (2mi), W 🍴 Cracker Barrel, Fastop/dsl, Hardee's 🏠 Best Western, Parkway Inn, Super 8 🅞 to Cumberland Gap NHP
4	rd 341, White Pine, E 🅖 ⛽/McDonald's/dsl/scales/24hr, W 🅖 Wilco/Hess/Wendy's/dsl/scales/24hr 🏠 Days Inn 🅞 to Panther Cr SP
2.5mm	🅡ₛ sb, full ♿ facilities, litter barrels, petwalk, 🚻, 🏧 vending
1b a	I-40, E to Asheville, W to Knoxville.
	I-81 begins/ends on I-40, exit 421.

⬆E INTERSTATE 640 (Knoxville)

Exit #	Services
9mm	**I-640 begins/ends on I-40, exit 393.**
8	Millertown Pike, Mall Rd N, N 🅖 Exxon/DQ, Shell 🍴 Applebee's, Burger King, China Wok, Don Pablos, Honeybaked Ham, KFC, Krystal, Mandarin Palace, McDonald's, Pizza Hut, Taco Bell, TX Roadhouse, Wendy's 🅞 $Tree, AT&T, Belk, Food City/dsl, JC Penney, Jo-Ann, Kohl's, mall, Marshall's, Old Navy, Ross, Sam's Club/dsl, Sears/auto, Target, Walmart, S 🅖 Shell/Quiznos/dsl 🍴 Cracker Barrel, Little Caesars, O'Charley's, Sonic 🅞 Home Depot, Lowe's Whse, PepBoys
6	US 441, to Broadway, N 🅖 Phillips 66, Pilot/dsl 🍴 Arby's, Cancun Mexican, Chick-fil-A, Chop House, CiCi's, Firehouse Subs, Hardee's, Krispy Kreme, Lenny's Subs, LJ Silver, McDonald's, Panera Bread, Papa John's, Papa Murphy's, Penn Sta Subs, Ruby Tuesday, Sonic, Subway, Taco Bell 🅞 $General, Advance Parts, AutoZone, BigLots, CVS Drug, Firestone, Food City/gas, Kroger, O'Reilly Parts, repair/tires, Verizon, Walgreens, S 🍴 Buddy's BBQ, Little Caesars, Shoney's 🅞 $General, $Tree, Food City, K-Mart, Office Depot
3b	US 25W, Clinton Hwy, N 🅞 Chevrolet, Ford, Nissan, services on frontage rds
3a	I-75 N to Lexington, I-275 S to Knoxville
1	TN 62, Western Ave, N 🅖 Exxon/dsl, Marathon/dsl, Raceway/dsl 🍴 Central Park, Firehouse Subs, KFC, Little Caesars, LJ Silver, McDonald's, Panda Chinese, Shoney's, Subway, Taco Bell, Wendy's 🅞 CVS Drug, Kroger/dsl, Walgreens, S 🍴 Hardee's, Krystal 🅞 Advance Parts, Family$, O'Reilly Parts
0mm	**I-640 begins/ends on I-40, exit 385.**

TX

↑E	**INTERSTATE 10**
Exit #	Services
880.5mm	Texas/Louisiana state line , Sabine River
880	Sabine River Turnaround, **N** 🅞 RV camping
879mm	**Welcome Center wb, full ♿ facilities, litter barrels, petwalk, 🗑, 🥤 vending**
878	US 90, Orange, **N** 🅖 Gulf/dsl 🅞 airboat rides, RV Park, **S** 🅞 Western Store
877	TX 87, 16th St, Orange, **N** 🅖 Exxon/dsl, Shamrock/dsl 🍴 Little Caesar's, Pizza Hut, Subway 🏠 Hampton Inn 🅞 Ace Hardware, Market Basket/deli, **S** 🅖 Get'n Go/dsl, Kwik Stop/dsl, Shell/dsl, Valero/dsl 🍴 2 Amigo's Mexican, Casa Ole, Church's, DQ, General Wok, Jack-in-the-Box, McDonald's, Popeye's, Sonic, Taco Bell 🅞 $General, CVS Drug, Family$, Goodyear/auto, HEB Foods, Kroger/dsl, Modica Tires, O'Reilly Parts, Verizon, Walgreens
876	Adams Bayou, frontage rd, Adams Bayou, **N** 🍴 Gary's Café, Señor Toro's Mexican, Taste of Orange Rest., Waffle House 🏠 Best Price Motel, Best Texan Inn, Days Inn, EconoLodge, Executive Inn, Knights Inn, Value Inn 🅞 Toyota, **S** 🅖 Chevron/dsl 🏠 Holiday Inn Express 🅞 same as 877
875	FM 3247, MLK Dr, **S** 🅞 🏥 Chrysler/Dodge/Jeep
874	US 90, Womack Rd, to Orange, **S** 🅞 🏥
873	TX 62, TX 73, to Bridge City, **N** 🅖 FLYING J/Denny's/dsl/LP/scales/24hr, Exxon/dsl/24hr 🏠 Studio 6 🅞 Oak Leaf RV Park, **S** 🅖 ⛽/Subway/Wendy's/dsl/scales/24hr, Shell/Church's/dsl, Valero/dsl 🍴 McDonald's, Sonic, Waffle House, Whataburger 🏠 Comfort Inn, La Quinta, Sleep Inn
872	N Mimosa Ln, Jackson Dr, from wb
870	FM 1136
869	FM 1442, to Bridge City, **S** 🅖 Chevron/dsl
867	frontage rd (from eb)
865	Doty Rd (from wb), frontage rd
864	FM 1132, FM 1135, **N** 🏠 Budget Inn 🅞 TX Star RV Park
862	Lakeside St, Timberlane Dr, **N** 🅖 Conoco
861	FM 105, Vidor, **N** 🅖 Citgo/dsl, Conoco/dsl, Shell/dsl, Valero/dsl 🍴 Casa Ole, Domino's, DQ, Jack-in-the-Box, Little Caesars, McDonald's/playplace, Ming's Buffet, Novrosky's Burgers, Popeye's, Waffle House 🅞 AutoZone, CVS, Mktbasket Foods, Modica Bros Tires, O'Reilly Parts, Radio Shack, Verizon, Walgreens, Walmart, **S** 🅖 Citgo/dsl, Exxon/dsl 🍴 Burger King, Pizza Hut, Sonic, Subway, Taco Bell, Whataburger 🏠 Best Western, Holiday Inn Express 🅞 auto repair, Family$
860	Dewitt Rd, frontage rd, W Vidor, **S** 🅖 Citgo, Exxon, Mobil/dsl 🍴 Burger King, Pizza Hut, Sonic, Subway, Taco Bell, Whataburger 🏠 Best Western, Holiday Inn Express 🅞 Family$, repair
859	Bonner Turnaround (from eb), Asher Turnaround (from wb), **N** 🅞 Boomtown RV Park, **S** 🅖 Chevron/Spindletop/dsl/24hr
858	Rose City
856	Old Hwy 90 (from eb), Rose City
855b	Magnolia St (from wb)

855a	US 90 bus, to downtown, Port of Beaumont
854	ML King Pkwy, Beaumont, **N** 🅖 Jack-in-the-Box, **S** 🅖 Exxon/dsl, Shamrock/dsl 🍴 McDonald's
853b	11th St, **N** 🅖 Valero/dsl 🍴 Cafe Del Rio, Red Lobster, Starving Marvin Grill, Waffle House 🏠 Beaumont Lodge, Days Inn, Red Carpet Inn, Sleep Inn, Studio 6, Travel Inn 🅞 MktBasket, **S** 🅖 Chevron/dsl, Shamrock 🍴 Checker's, Chula Vista Mexican, Dunkin Donuts, Jack-in-the-Box, Luby's 🏠 Oaks Lodge, Rodeway Inn 🅞 🏥
853a	US 69 N, to Lufkin
852	Harrison Ave, Calder Ave, Beaumont, **N** 🅖 Shell/dsl, Valero/dsl 🍴 Casa Ole Mexican, Casa Tapatia Mexican, Chili's, Frankie's Italian, Olive Garden, Saltgrass Steaks, Tony's BBQ, **S** 🍴 Church's, McDonald's 🏠 La Quinta, Scottish Inn 🅞 🏥
851	US 90, College St, **N** 🅖 Chevron/dsl, Exxon/dsl, Raceway/dsl 🍴 Carrabba's, Chicken Express, Floyd's Cajun Cafe, Golden Corral, Hooters, Lupe Tortilla, Outback Steaks, Sartin's Seafood, Tokyo Japanese, Waffle House 🏠 Quality Inn, Quality Inn, Ramada, Red Roof Inn 🅞 Advance Parts, AutoZone, Harley-Davidson, Indian Motorcycles, O'Reilly Parts, URGENT CARE, Verizon, Volvo Trucks, **S** 🅖 Exxon/dsl, Mobil, Shell/dsl 🍴 Catfish Seafood, China Hut, DQ, IHOP, Pizza Hut, Sonic, Taco Bell, Wendy's, Whataburger 🏠 Best Value, Courtyard, Elegante Motel, Fairfield Inn, Regency Inn, ValuePlace Hotel 🅞 🏥 $Tree, BMW, Chrysler/Dodge/Jeep, CVS Drug, Discount Tire, Firestone/auto, HEB Foods, Honda, Mercedes, Nissan, NTB, Office Depot, Radio Shack, Sam's Club/gas, U-Haul, VW, Walgreens
850	same as 851, wb only
849	US 69 S, Washington Blvd, to Port Arthur, 🅞 ✈

ORANGE

VIDOR

BEAUMONT

TX

WINNIE

BAYTOWN

INTERSTATE 10 Cont'd

Exit #	Services
848	Walden Rd, N 🅖 Shell/dsl 🍴 Pappadeaux Seafood, Sonic, Subway 🏠 Comfort Suites, Holiday Inn/rest., La Quinta 🅞 USPO, S 🅖 Chevron/dsl, Petro/Iron Skillet/dsl/scales/24hr/@, Shell/dsl 🍴 Carino's Italian, Cheddar's, Cracker Barrel, Jack-in-the-Box, Joe's Crabshack, Waffle House 🏠 Candlewood Suites, Hampton Inn, Hilton Garden, Homewood Suites, Knights Inn, Residence Inn, Super 8 🅞 Blue Beacon
847	Brooks Rd (from wb), (845 from eb), S 🅞 Gulf Coast RV Resort, Hidden Lake RV Park
843	Smith Rd
838	FM 365, Fannett, N 🍴 Alligator Park/Rest., Bar-H BBQ/gas 🅞 T&T RV Park
837.5mm	no services
833	Hamshire Rd, N 🅖 Chevron/dsl
829	FM 1663, Winnie, N 🅖 Exxon/dsl, Shell/dsl/24hr, Texaco/Burger King/dsl 🍴 McDonald's, Taco Bell, Whataburger/24hr 🏠 Days Inn 🅞 RV Park, S 🅖 Chevron/Chester's/dsl, Gulf/Subway/Pizza Hut/dsl/scales/24hr, Texaco/dsl 🍴 Al-T's Seafood, Denny's, Exxon/dsl, Hart's Chicken, Hunan Chinese, Jack-in-the-Box, Waffle House 🏠 Comfort Inn, EconoLodge, Hampton Inn, Holiday Inn, Home Suites, La Quinta, Winnie Inn/RV Park 🅞 🏥 Chrysler/Jeep/Dodge
828	TX 73, TX 124 (from eb), to Winnie, S 🅞 🏥 same as 829
827	FM 1406
822	FM 1410
821	insp sta wb
819	Jenkins Rd, S 🅖 Exxon/Stuckey's/Chester's/dsl
817	FM 1724
814	frontage rd, 🆁🆂 eb, full 🏠 facilities, litter barrels, petwalk, 🆊 🆋 vending
813	TX 61 (from wb), Hankamer, N 🅖 Shell/dsl 🏠 TX Country Inn, S 🅖 Exxon/DJ's Diner/dsl 🍴 McDonald's 🅞 same as 812
812	TX 61, Hankamer
811	Turtle Bayou Turnaround, S 🅖 Gator Jct/dsl 🅞 Turtle Bayou RV Park
810	FM 563, to Anahuac, Liberty, S 🅖 Chevron/Blimpie/dsl, Texaco/Jack-in-the-Box/dsl
807	to Wallisville, S 🅞 Heritage Park
805.5mm	Trinity River
804mm	Lost Rivers, Old
803	FM 565, Cove, Old River-Winfrey, N 🅞 Paradise Cove RV Park, S 🅖 Valero/dsl
800	FM 3180, N 🅖 Exxon/dsl
799	TX 99, Grand Pkwy
797	(798 from wb) TX 146, 99 toll, Baytown, N 🅖 Chevron/Subway/dsl/scale, Conoco/dsl/scales, Shell/dsl 🍴 DQ, El Hacendado, Iguana Joe's Mexican, McDonald's, Waffle House 🏠 Crystal Inn, Motel 6, Super 8 🅞 L&R RV Park, Value RV Park, S 🅖 Exxon, RaceWay/dsl, Stripes/Taco Co/dsl, Texaco/Popeye's/dsl 🍴 Baytown Seafood, Jack-in-the-Box, KFC/Taco Bell, Sonic 🏠 Magnuson Hotel 🅞 🏥 Houston East RV Park, vet, Walmart
796	frontage rd, N 🅖 Chevron/Phillips/Chemical Refinery
795	Sjolander Rd
793	N Main St, S 🅖 Valero/Hartz Chicken/dsl/24hr
792	Garth Rd, N 🅖 Chevron/dsl 🍴 Chicken Express, Cracker Barrel, Denny's, Jack-in-the-Box, Red Lobster, Richard's Cajun, Sonic, Starbucks, Subway, Tuscany Italian, Waffle House, Whataburger 🏠 Baymont Inn, Comfort Suites, Days Inn,

792	Continued EconoLodge, Hampton Inn, Holiday Inn, La Quinta, Motel 6, SpringHill Suites 🅞 Buick/GMC, Chrysler/Jeep/Dodge, Honda, Hyundai, Kia, Nissan, O'Reilly Parts, Toyota/Scion, Walgreens, S 🅖 RaceWay/dsl, Shell/dsl 🍴 Buffalo Wild Wings, Carino's Italian, Carl's Jr, Chili's, Firehouse Subs, Lee Palace, McDonald's, Olive Garden, Outback Steaks, Panera Bread, Pizza Hut/Taco Bell, Popeye's, Subway, Tortuga Mexican, TX Rodehouse, Wendy's 🏠 Palace Inn, Quality Inn, Scottish Inn 🅞 🏥 $General, AT&T, JC Penney, Kohl's, Macy's, Marshall's, Michael's, Sears/auto, Tuesday Morning, Verizon
791	John Martin Rd, S 🍴 Cheddars 🏠 ValuePlace 🅞 Cadillac/Chevrolet, Ford
790	Ellis School Rd, N 🏠 Super 8
788.5mm	🆁🆂 eb, full 🏠 facilities, litter barrels, petwalk, 🆊, 🆋 vending
788	sp 330 (from eb), to Baytown
787	sp 330, Crosby-Lynchburg Rd, to Highlands, N 🅖 Exxon/Domino's/dsl 🅞 RV Camping (1mi), S 🅖 Phillips 66/dsl 🍴 Four Corners BBQ 🅞 camping, to San Jacinto SP
786.5mm	San Jacinto River
786	Monmouth Dr
785	Magnolia Ave, to Channelview, N 🅖 Shell/dsl/scales, S 🅖 Exxon/dsl 🅞 truckwash
784	Cedar Lane, Bayou Dr, N 🅖 Valero/dsl 🏠 Budget Lodge, TX Inn
783	Sheldon Rd, N 🅖 Chevron/dsl, Shell/dsl, Valero/dsl 🍴 Burger King, Church's, Jack-in-the-Box, Pizza Hut, Pizza Inn, Popeye's, Subway, Taco Bell, Whataburger 🏠 Days Inn, Grand Inn, Holiday Inn, Leisure Inn, Palace Inn, Parkway Inn, Travelers Inn 🅞 AutoZone, Discount Tire, Family$, FoodFair, USPO, S 🅖 Chevron/dsl, Texaco/dsl 🍴 McDonald's, Wendy's 🏠 Deluxe Inn, Fairfield Inn, Scottish Inn 🅞 auto repair
782	Dell-Dale Ave, N 🅖 Exxon/dsl 🏠 Dell-Dale Motel, Luxury Inn 🅞 🏥 S 🅞 Channelview RV Ctr
781b	Market St, N 🏠 Clarion 🅞 🏥
781a	TX 8, Sam Houston Pkwy, S 🅖 Gulf/dsl
780	(779a from wb)Uvalde Rd, Freeport St, N 🅖 Chevron/dsl, Texaco/dsl 🍴 Capt Tom's Seafood, China Dragon, IHOP, Panda Express, Shipley Donuts, Sonic, Subway, Taco Cabana 🅞 🏥 $Tree, Aamco, Ace Hardware, Office Depot, S 🍴 Baytown Seafood, Golden Corral, Whataburger 🅞 Firestone/auto, Home Depot, Sam's Club/gas, U-Haul, Verizon, Walmart/McDonald's
779b	N 🅖 Gulf, Valero/dsl 🍴 China Dragon, IHOP, Panda Express, Shipley's Donuts, Sonic, Subway, Taco Cabana 🏠 Interstate Motel 🅞 $Tree, Aamco, Ace Hardware, Office Depot
778b	Normandy St, N 🅖 Shell/Jack-in-the-Box, Texaco/dsl 🏠 La Quinta, S 🅖 Citgo/dsl 🍴 Cafe Ko, Church's 🏠 Normandy Inn
778a	FM 526, Federal Rd, Pasadena, N 🍴 Burger King, Casa Ole Mexican, KFC/Taco Bell, Pizza Hut, Popeye's, Subway, S 🅖 Shell/dsl 🍴 James Coney Island, Pappadeaux Seafood Kitchen, Pappas BBQ, Pappa's Seafood, Peking Bo Chinese, Saltgrass Steaks, Sonic, Swamp Shack Rest. 🏠 Lamplight Inn, Super 8 🅞 AutoZone, Discount Tire, O'Reilly Parts, Scottish Inn
776b	John Ralston Rd, Holland Ave, N 🅖 Chevron/dsl, Exxon, Texaco 🍴 Chulas Mexican, Denny's, Fuddruckers, Luby's, Mambo Seafood, Pappasito's Cantina, Subway 🏠 Candlewood Suites, Comfort Inn, Day Inn, Palace Inn, Regency Inn 🅞 Family$, Fiesta Foods, NTB, URGENT CARE, S same as 778

INTERSTATE 10 Cont'd

Exit #	Services
776a	Mercury Dr, **N** 🅕 Aranda's Mexican, Burger King, McDonald's, Tepatillan Mexican, TX Grill 🅛 Best Western, Hampton Inn, Motel 6, Premier Inn, Quality Inn 🅞 Volvo Trucks, **S** 🅖 Shell/dsl, Valero/dsl 🅕 Chili's, Cici's Pizza, Murphy's Deli 🅛 Holiday Inn Express 🅞 CVS Drug, URGENT CARE
775b a	I-610
774	Gellhorn (from eb) Blvd, **S** 🅞 Anheuser-Busch Brewery
773b	McCarty St, **N** 🅖 Chevron/dsl, Shell
773a	US 90A, N Wayside Dr, **N** 🅖 Speedy/dsl 🅕 Jack-in-the-Box, Whataburger, **S** 🅖 Chevron/dsl, Shell/dsl, Valero 🅕 Church's, Subway
772	Kress St, Lathrop St, **N** 🅖 Conoco, Exxon 🅕 Popeye's, **S** 🅕 7 Mares Seafood, Burger King
771b	Lockwood Dr, **N** 🅖 Chevron/Subway/dsl 🅕 McDonald's 🅞 Family$, Walgreens, **S** 🅖 Shell/dsl 🅛 Palace Inn
771a	Waco St
770c	US 59 N
770b	Jenson St, Meadow St, Gregg St
770a	US 59 S, to Victoria
769c	McKee St, Hardy St, Nance St, downtown
769a	Smith St (from wb), to downtown
768b a	I-45, N to Dallas, S to Galveston
767b	Taylor St
767a	Studemont Dr, Yale St, Heights Blvd, **S** 🅖 Shell/dsl 🅕 Chick-fil-A, Chili's, Dickey's BBQ, KFC/Taco Bell, Panda Express, Subway 🅞 AT&T, Petsmart, Staples, Target
766	(from wb), Heights Blvd, Yale St
765b	N Durham Dr, N Shepherd Dr, **N** 🅖 Shell/dsl 🅕 Wendy's 🅛 Howard Johnson 🅞 vet, **S** 🅖 Valero/dsl 🅕 Saltgrass Steaks
765a	TC Jester Blvd, **S** 🅖 Exxon/dsl, Texaco/dsl 🅕 Golden Hunan, Starbucks 🅞 vet
764	Westcott St, Washington Ave, Katy Rd, **N** 🅕 Denny's 🅛 Hampton Inn, **S** 🅖 Chevron 🅕 IHOP, McDonald's 🅛 Scottish Inn
763	I-610
762	Silber Rd, Post Oak Rd, **N** 🅕 Chick-fil-A, Dave&Buster's, Jimmy John's, Panda Express, Red Robin, SteaKountry 🅞 Chrysler/Dodge/Jeep, Fiat, Firestone/auto, IKEA, Walmart, **S** 🅕 Jack-in-the-Box, Shipley Donuts 🅛 Crowne Plaza, Holiday Inn Express
761b	Antoine Rd, **S** 🅖 Exxon/dsl 🅞 CVS Drug
761a	Wirt Rd, Chimney Rock Rd, **S** 🅖 Exxon/dsl 🅞 CVS Drug
760	Bingle Rd, Voss Rd, **N** 🅕 Burger Shack, Hunan Chef, Pueblo Viejo, Starbucks, Subway 🅞 AT&T, Home Depot, **S** 🅖 Shell/dsl 🅕 Sweet Tomatoes
759	Campbell Rd (from wb), **N** 🅞 Ranch Mkt, same as 758b
758b	Blalock Rd, Campbell Rd, **N** 🅕 Sonic 🅞 🅷 Lowe's, **S** 🅖 Chevron/McDonald's/dsl 🅕 Baskin-Robbins, Goode Co TX BBQ, Pappy's Cafe, Saltgrass Steaks, Starbucks 🅞 cleaners, Kroger, Walgreens
758a	Bunker Hill Rd, **N** 🅕 Boudreaux's Cajun, Dennys, Egg&I, Five Guys, Freebirds Burritos, Genghis Grill, Jimmy John's, Marble Slab, Olive Garden, Panda Express, Which Wich? 🅞 Best Buy, Costco/gas, GNC, HEB Foods/dsl, Jo-Ann, Lowe's, Michael's, PepBoys, **S** 🅕 American Island Grill, Buffalo Wild Wings, Ciro's Italian, Corner Bakery Cafe, Denis Seafood, Firehouse Subs, Guadalajara Mexican, Kobe Japanese, Longhorn Steaks, Lupe Tortilla, Russo's NY Pizza, Subway 🅛 Memorial Inn 🅞 Marshall's, Ross, Verizon
757	Gessner Rd, **N** 🅕 Chili's, Chulas Grill, McDonald's, Murphy's Deli, Taco Bell, Wendy's, Whataburger 🅞 AT&T, CVS Drug, Hobby Lobby, Home Depot, Honda, Radio Shack, Sam's Club/gas, U-Haul, **S** 🅕 59 Diner, Cheesecake Factory, Fuddrucker's, Goode Co. Seafood, Jason's Deli, Pappadeaux Seafood, Pappasito's, Perry's Steaks 🅛 Westin Hotel 🅞 🅷 Firestone/auto, Ford, Macy's, mall, Office Depot, Target
756	**TX 8, Sam Houston Tollway**
755	Willcrest Rd, **N** 🅞 Discount Tire, Lincoln, Mazda, NTB, U-Haul, **S** 🅖 Citgo/dsl, Exxon/dsl 🅕 Brenner's Steaks, Denny's, IHOP, McDonald's, Subway, Taste of TX 🅛 Candlewood Suites, Extended Stay America, Hampton Inn, Sheraton
754	Kirkwood Rd, **N** 🅛 Embassy Suites 🅞 Audi/Porsche, Lincoln, Toyota/Scion, **S** 🅖 Shell/dsl 🅕 Carrabba's, Prince's Burgers, Shipley Do-Nuts, Spicy Pickle, Starbucks, Taco Cabana, Twin Peaks, Whataburger 🅞 Chevrolet
753b	Dairy-Ashford Rd, **N** 🅞 Infiniti, Lexus, Nissan, Volvo, **S** 🅖 Exxon/dsl 🅕 Chili's, Hibachi Grill, Subway, TX Cattle Steaks 🅛 Courtyard, Hilton Garden, Holiday Inn Express 🅞 Cadillac, URGENT CARE
753a	Eldridge Pkwy, **N** 🅖 Conoco/dsl 🅛 Omni Hotel, **S** 🅖 Valero/dsl 🅞 Kwik Kar
751	TX 6, to Addicks, **N** 🅖 Shell 🅕 Bros Pizza, Cattlegard Rest., Quiznos, Waffle House 🅛 Drury Inn, Homewood Suites, Studio 6, Wyndham, **S** 🅕 North China, Salata, Subway 🅛 Beat Value, Extended Stay America, Fairfield Inn, Hyatt House, La Quinta, Motel 6, TownePlace Suites 🅞 USPO
750	Park Ten Blvd, eb only, **N** 🅛 Red Roof Inn, **S** 🅛 Marriott 🅞 Acura, BMW, Buick/GMC, Hoover RV Ctr
748	Barker-Cypress Rd, **N** 🅖 Exxon/Subway 🅕 BurgerTex Grill, Coaches Grill, El Rancho Mexican, Firehouse Subs, Popeyes, Smoothie Factory, Tony's Mexican 🅛 Residence Inn 🅞 🅷 **S** 🅕 Cracker Barrel 🅞 Hyundai, Subaru, vet, VW
747b a	Fry Rd, **N** 🅖 Gulf/dsl, Shell/dsl 🅕 5 Guys Burgers, Applebee's, Arby's, Buffalo Wild Wings, Burger King, Chipotle, Denny's, DQ, Jimmy John's, McDonald's, Panda Express, Panera Bread, Pizza Hut, Smoothie King, Sonic, Souper Salad, Subway, Taco Bell, Waffle House, Whataburger 🅛 Candlewood Suites 🅞 AAA, Best Buy, HEB Food/gas, Hobby Lobby, Home Depot, Jo-Ann, Kohl's, Kroger/dsl, Ross, Sam's Club/gas, URGENT CARE, Verizon, vet, Walgreens, Walmart, **S** 🅖 Shell/dsl 🅕 Captain Tom's Seafood, Fazoli's, IHOP, McDonald's, Outback Steaks, Potbelly, Quiznos, Smashburger, Star Chinese, Starbucks, Starbucks, TX Mesquite Grill, Wendy's, Willie's 🅛 ValuePlace Hotel 🅞 🅷 A&T, Katy Drug, Lowe's, NTB, Office Depot, Petsmart, Radio Shack, Randall's Mkt, Target, TJ Maxx, U-Haul

🚩E INTERSTATE 10 Cont'd

Exit #	Services
746	W Green Blvd, N 🅖 RaceWay/dsl 🍴 BJ's Rest., Chang's Chinese, Cheddar's, Chuy's Mexican, Firehouse Subs, Kublai Khan Stirfry, Longhorn Steaks, Nagoya Japanese, Olive Garden, Orleans Seafood Kitchen, Springcreek BBQ, Stadia Grill, Steak'n Shake, TX Roadhouse, Wild Wings Cafe 🛏 Holiday Inn Express, Palace Inn, S 🍴 Carl's Jr, Jimmy Changas TexMex 🛏 Home2 🅞 Christian Bros Automotive, CVS Drug, Ford, Honda
745	Mason Rd, N 🅞 CarMax, S 🅖 Shell/dsl, Valero/dsl 🍴 Babin's Seafood, Blackeyed Pea, Burger King, Carino's Italian, Chick-fil-A, Chili's, CiCi's, Dickey's BBQ, DQ, El Patron Mexican, Freebirds Burrito, Hooters, Jack-in-the-Box, Jason's Deli, KFC, Landry's Seafood, Luby's, McDonald's, Panda Express, Papa John's, Pizza Hut, Popeye's, Rudy's BBQ/gas, SaltGrass Steaks, Schlotzsky's, Subway, Taco Bell, Taco Cabana, Whataburger, Which Wich? 🛏 Comfort Inn&Suites, Hampton Inn, La Quinta, Motel 6, Super 8 🅞 $Tree, 99c Store, AutoZone, Chevrolet, Chrysler/Dodge/Jeep, Discount Tire, Fiesta Foods, Firestone/auto, Goodyear/auto, Hancock Fabrics, HEB Food/gas, Kia, Toyota/Scion, transmissions, Walgreens
743	TX 99, Grand Pkwy, Peek Rd, N 🍴 La Madeleine, Red Robin 🅞 🅗 JC Penney, S 🍴 Freddy's Steakburgers, Subway 🅞 Costco/gas, URGENT CARE
741	(742 from wb) Katy-Fort Bend County Rd, Pin Oak Rd, S 🅖 Murphy USA/dsl, Shell/dsl, Texaco/dsl 🍴 Alegra Brazilian, Alicia's Mexican, Antonia's Rest, Chick-fil-A, ChuckECheese, CiCi's Pizza, Denny's, Fuddruckers, Jack-in-the-Box, Jimmy John's, JoJo's Mongolian Grill, KFC, LJ Silver/Taco Bell, Los Cucos, Pizza Hut, Popeyes, Rainforest Cafe, Red Lobster, Smashburger, Starbucks, Subway, Subway, TGIFriday's, Whataburger 🛏 Best Western, Comfort Suites, Coumtry Inn & Suites, Hilton Garden, Residence Inn, SpringHill Suites 🅞 🅗 $Tree, AT&T, BassPro Shops, BooksAMillion, Discount Tire, HEB/dsl, Katy Mills Outlet/famous brands, Marshall's, Nissan, Ross, URGENT CARE, Verizon, Walgreens, Walmart/McDonald's
740	FM 1463, N 🅖 Exxon/dsl, S 🅖 Shell/McDonald's/dsl
737	Pederson Rd, N 🅖 Loves/Arby's/dsl/scales/24hr, S 🅞 Camping World RV Super Ctr, Holiday World RV Ctr
735	Igloo Rd
732	FM 359, to Brookshire, N 🅖 FLYING J/Denny's/dsl/LP/scales/24hr/@, Exxon/Chester's/dsl, Shell 🍴 Church's, Orlando's Pizza, Subway 🛏 Executive Inn 🅞 RV camping, S 🅖 Chevron/dsl, Shell/McDonald's/dsl 🍴 Burger King, Jack-in-the-Box, Popeyes, Taco Bell 🛏 Super 8 🅞 truck lube, truckwash
731	FM 1489, to Koomey Rd, N 🅖 Exxon/dsl 🍴 Ernesto's Mexican 🛏 Brooke Hotel 🅞 RV Park, S 🛏 La Quinta
729	Peach Ridge Rd, Donigan Rd (730 from wb)
726	Chew Rd (from eb), S 🅞 golf
725	Mlcak Rd (from wb)
723	FM 1458, to San Felipe, N 🅖 Exxon/Subway/dsl/scales/24hr 🅞 Peterbilt, to Stephen F Austin SP (3mi), S 🅞 Riverside Tire
721	(from wb) US 90, N 🅖 Shell/Chester's/dsl 🅞 Ford
720a	Outlet Ctr Dr, N 🅖 Shell/Chester's/dsl
720	TX 36, to Sealy, N 🅖 Shell/dsl 🍴 China Buffet, DQ, Hartz Chicken, McDonald's, Sonic, Tony's Rest. 🅞 $General, Jones RV Ctr, O'Reilly Parts, Walgreens, S 🅖 Chevron/dsl,

720	Continued Murphy USA/dsl, Shell/dsl, Texaco/dsl 🍴 Cazadore's Mexican, Hinze's BBQ, Jack-in-the-Box, Jin's Asian, Maribelli Italian, Pizza Hut, Subway, Whataburger 🛏 Best Value Inn, Countryside Inn, Holiday Inn Express, Super 8 🅞 Verizon, Walmart/Subway
718	US 90 (from eb), to Sealy
716	Pyka Rd, N 🅖 Exxon/dsl/rest./showers/24hr/@
713	Beckendorff Rd
709	FM 2761, Bernardo Rd
704	FM 949, N 🅞 Happy Oaks RV Park (3mi)
699	FM 102, to Eagle Lake, N 🅞 Happy Oaks RV Park, S 🅞 Eagle Lake SP (14mi)
698	Alleyton Rd, N 🍴 Mikeska's BBQ 🛏 Lone Star Inn, S 🅖 Shell/Taco Bell/BBQ/dsl 🅞 Chrysler/Dodge/Jeep, Ford
697mm	Little Colorado River
696	TX 71, Columbus, N 🅖 Chevron/dsl, Shell/dsl 🍴 #1 Buffet, Cantus Rest., El Rey Mexican, Jack-in-the-Box, Pizza Hut, Schobel's Rest., Whataburger 🛏 Columbus Inn, Holiday Inn Express 🅞 🅗 AT&T, AutoZone, HEB Foods, Walmart, S 🅖 Conoco/Church's/Subway/dsl, Phillips 66/dsl, Valero/dsl 🍴 Los Cabos Mexican, McDonald's, Nancy's Steaks, Sonic 🛏 Best Value, Comfort Inn, LaQuinta 🅞 Columbus RV Park
695	TX 71 (from wb), to La Grange
693	FM 2434, to Glidden
692mm	🆁ⓢ both lanes, full 🚻 facilities, litter barrels, petwalk, 🕭, 🚐 RV dump, vending
689	US 90, to Hattermann Lane, N 🅞 Whispering Oaks RV Park
682	FM 155, to Wiemar, N 🅖 Shell/dsl, Valero/dsl 🍴 DQ, McDonald's, Subway/Texas Burger 🛏 Scottish Inn 🅞 🅗 $General, Lowe's Mkt, Tire Pros, S 🅖 Chevron/Church's/dsl/24hr, Loves/Chester's/Wendy's/dsl/scales/24hr 🅞 Buick/Chevrolet/GMC
678mm	E Navidad River
677	US 90
674	US 77, Schulenburg, N 🅖 Exxon/dsl, Stripes/Taco Co 🍴 McDonald's, Oak Ridge Smokehouse 🛏 Executive Inn, Oak Ridge Motel 🅞 Ford, Potter Country Store, S 🅖 Shell/dsl, Valero/Subway 🍴 Chez Grill, DQ, Frank's Rest., Guadalajara Mexican, Whataburger 🛏 Best Western, Holiday Inn Express 🅞 $General, Family$, Schulenberg RV Park
672mm	W Navidad River
668	FM 2238, to Engle
661	TX 95, FM 609, to Flatonia, N 🅖 Citgo/dsl 🍴 Joel's BBQ, Robert's Steaks, San Jose Mexican 🅞 Flatonia RV Ranch (1mi), S 🅖 Exxon/dsl, Shell/McDonald's/Grumpy's Rest./motel/dsl, Valero 🍴 DQ, Subway 🛏 Carefree Inn, Hampton Inn 🅞 $General, NAPA
658mm	🆁ⓢ both lanes, litter barrels
653	US 90, Waelder, N 🅖 Shell/dsl
649	TX 97, to Waelder
642	TX 304, to Gonzales
637	FM 794, to Harwood
632	US 90/183, to Gonzales, N 🅖 Loves/Subway/dsl/scales/24hr 🛏 Best Western, Coachway Inn (2mi), S 🅖 Bucee's/dsl 🅞 camping, to Palmetto SP (5mi)
630mm	San Marcos River
628	TX 80, to Luling, N 🅖 Citgo (2mi), Valero/pizza/dsl/24hr 🍴 DQ (2mi) 🅞 🅗 Riverbend RV Park
625	Darst Field Rd
624.5mm	Smith Creek
621mm	weigh sta both lanes

INTERSTATE 10 Cont'd

Exit #	Services
620	FM 1104
618mm	🆁🆂 both lanes, full ♿ facilities, litter barrels, petwalk, 🔄, 📷 vending
617	FM 2438, to Kingsbury
614	toll 130 N, to Austin, Waco
612	US 90
611mm	Geronimo Creek
610	TX 123, to San Marcos, **N** 🗋 Exxon/dsl, Shell/Subway/dsl 🍴 Bella Sera Italian, Chili's, IHOP, Los Cucos Mexican 🏠 Comfort Inn, Days Inn, Hampton Inn, Holiday Inn Express, TownePlace Suites 🅾 Carters Tires, **S** 🗋 Valero/dsl 🍴 Taco Cabana 🅾 🏥
609	TX 123, Austin St, **S** 🗋 Phillips 66/dsl 🅾 Chevrolet, Home Depot
607	TX 46, FM 78, to New Braunfels, **N** 🗋 Valero/Jack-in-the-Box/dsl 🏠 Motel 6 🅾 Ford, **S** 🗋 Chevron/dsl, Exxon/dsl 🍴 Bill Miller BBQ, Dixie Grille, McDonald's, Subway, Whataburger 🏠 La Quinta, Super 8 🅾 Chrysler/Dodge/Jeep
605mm	Guadalupe River
605	FM 464, **N** 🅾 Twin Palms RV Park
604	FM 725, to Lake McQueeney, **N** 🗋 ♥Love's/Arby's/dsl/scales/24hr 🅾 Explore USA RV Ctr, Twin Palms RV Park
603	US 90 E, US 90A, to Seguin, **N** 🅾 D&A RV Park, Seguin RV Ctr
601	FM 775, to New Berlin, **N** 🗋 Chevron/Subway/dsl/scales/24hr
600	Schwab Rd
599mm	Santa Clara Creek
599	FM 465, to Marion
597	Santa Clara Rd, **N** 🅾 auto racetrack
595	Zuehl Rd
594mm	Cibolo Creek
593mm	Woman Hollering Creek
593	FM 2538, Trainer Hale Rd, **N** 🗋 Texaco/dsl 🅾 tires, **S** 🗋 Exxon/Lucille's Rest./dsl/24hr
591	FM 1518, to Schertz, **N** 🗋 Alamo Trvl Ctr/Shell/dsl 🅾 repair
589mm	Salatrillo Creek
589	Pfeil Rd, Graytown Rd
587	LP 1604, Randolph AFB, to Universal City
585.5mm	Escondido Creek
585mm	Martinez Creek
585	FM 1516, to Converse, **N** 🗋 Shell/Church's/dsl/scales/24hr 🏠 Best Western, **S** 🅾 Kenworth, Peterbilt/GMC/Freightliner
583	Foster Rd, **N** 🗋 ⭐FLYING J/Denny's/dsl/LP/scales/24hr/@, Valero/Subway/dsl/24hr 🍴 Jack-in-the-Box 🏠 La Quinta 🅾 Blue Beacon, Speedco Lube, Tire Mart, **S** 🗋 TA/Chevron/Burger King/Pizza Hut/Popeye's/dsl/24hr/@
582.5mm	Rosillo Creek
582	Ackerman Rd, Kirby, **N** 🗋 PILOT/Subway/dsl/scales/24hr, **S** 🗋 Petro/Iron Skillet/dsl/scales/24hr/@ 🍴 El Rodeo Mexican 🏠 Knights Inn 🅾 Blue Beacon, Petrolube
581	I-410
580	LP 13, WW White Rd, **N** 🗋 Chevron/dsl 🍴 El Jacalito, La Playa Seafood, Wendy's 🏠 Motel 6, Red Roof Inn, Rodeway Inn 🅾 tires, **S** 🗋 Exxon/7-11 🍴 Bill Miller BBQ, El Rodeo Mexican, Lazaritas Mexican, McDonald's, Pizza Hut, Popeye's, Sonic, Subway 🏠 Best Value, EconoLodge, Super 8 🅾 $General, Ford/Volvo Trucks, tires/repair
579	Houston St, **N** 🗋 Valero/dsl 🏠 Travelodge 🅾 Penske, **S** 🗋 Chevron 🏠 Comfort Inn, Days Inn, Passport Inn

578	Pecan Valley Dr, ML King Dr, **S** 🗋 Shell/Subway/dsl
577	US 87 S, to Roland Ave, **S** 🍴 Whataburger 🏠 Super 8
576	New Braunfels Ave, Gevers St, **S** 🗋 Valero 🍴 McDonald's
575	Pine St, Hackberry St, **S** 🍴 Little Red Barn Steaks
574	I-37, US 281
573	Probandt St, **N** 🍴 Jack-in-the-Box, Miller's BBQ, **S** 🗋 Valero 🅾 tires/repair, to SA Missions HS

I-10 and I-35 run together 3 miles See I-35, exits 156-154a.

569c	Santa Rosa St, 🅾 to Our Lady of the Lake U, downtown
568	spur 421, Culebra Ave, Bandera Ave, **S** 🅾 to St Marys U
567	Lp 345, Fredericksburg Rd (from eb upper level accesses I-35 S, I-10 E, US 87 S, lower level accesses I-35 N)
566b	Fresno Dr, **S** 🗋 Exxon/dsl 🏠 Galaxy Inn
566a	West Ave, **N** 🗋 Exxon/7-11 🍴 DQ, Subway, Whataburger 🅾 CarCare
565c	(from wb), access to same as 565 a b, **S** 🗋 Shell 🍴 Jimador Mexican, Starbucks 🏠 La Quinta
565b	Vance Jackson Rd, **N** 🗋 Murphy USA/dsl 🍴 Bill Miller BBQ, IHOP 🏠 Comfort Inn, Days Inn, EconoLodge 🅾 Walmart, **S** 🗋 Shell/dsl 🏠 Holiday Inn Express
565a	Crossroads Blvd, Balcone's Heights, **N** 🗋 Shell/dsl 🏠 Howard Johnson 🅾 vet, **S** 🗋 Valero/dsl 🍴 Crossroads BBQ, Dave&Buster's, Denny's, El Pollo Loco, McDonald's, Whataburger 🏠 SpringHill Suites 🅾 Firestone/auto, Hobby Lobby, mall, Mazda, Office Depot, Target
564b a	I-410, services off of I-410 W, Fredericksburg Rd
563	Callaghan Rd, **N** 🗋 Valero 🍴 Las Palapas Mexican, Subway 🏠 Embassy Suites, Marriott 🅾 $General, Ford, Sprouts Mkt, Toyota/Scion, **S** 🗋 Exxon/7-11 🍴 Mamacita's Rest. 🅾 Lowe's
561	Wurzbach Rd, **N** 🗋 Texaco/dsl 🍴 Bolo's Grille, Broadway 5050 Grill, County Line BBQ, Egg&I, Firehouse Subs, Fuddrucker's, Honeybaked Ham, Jason's Deli, Pappasito's Cantina, Popeye's, Sea Island Shrimphouse, Taste Of China, TX Land&Cattle, Wasabi Grill 🏠 Extended Stay America, Homewood Suites, Hyatt Place, Motel 6, Staybridge Suites 🅾 AutoZone, BigLots, HEB Food/gas, Office Depot, Porsche, Tuesday Morning, **S** 🗋 Shell/dsl 🍴 210 Ceviche Seafood, Alamo Café, Arby's, Chester's Burgers, China Sea, Church's, Denny's, El Taco Tote, Jack-in-the-Box, Mamma Margie's Mexican, McDonald's, Pizza Hut, Ruby Tuesday, Sumo Japanese, Taco Bell, Wendy's 🏠 Baymont Inn, Best Western, Candlewood Suites, Drury Inn, Hawthorn Suites, La Quinta, Motel 6, Sleep Inn 🅾 🏥 CarMax
560b	frontage rd (from eb), same as 561
560a	Huebner Rd, **N** 🍴 CA Pizza Kitchen, Chipotle, Fare Wok, Genghis Grill, La Madeleine, Macaroni Grill, Panera Bread, Pericos Mexican, Salata, SaltGrass Steaks 🅾 Cadillac,

⊞ = gas ⊕ = food ⊟ = lodging ⊙ = other ℞ = rest stop   Copyright 2015 - the Next EXIT ®

▲E INTERSTATE 10 Cont'd

TX

Exit #	Services
560a	Continued
	Chrysler/Jeep/Dodge, Fiat, Nissan, Old Navy, Ross, **S** ⊞ Chevron, Exxon, Shell/Jack-in-the-Box/dsl ⊕ Cracker Barrel, Jim's Rest., Miller's BBQ ⊟ Days Inn, Quality Inn, TownePlace Suites
559	Lp 335, US 87, Fredericksburg Rd, **N** ⊕ Pearl Inn ⊟ Holiday Inn Express ⊙ Acura, **S** ⊕ Krispy Kreme, Shell/Jack-in-the-Box/dsl ⊟ Comfort Suites, Days Inn, HomeGate Studios, Rodeway Inn, SpringHill Suites ⊙ Infiniti
558	De Zavala Rd, **N** ⊞ Chevron, Shell/Subway ⊕ Bill Miller BBQ, Burger King, Carrabba's, Chick-fil-A, Chili's, Five Guys, Fox&Hound, Joe's Crabshack, KFC/Taco Bell, Logan's Roadhouse, McDonald's, Outback Steaks, Sonic, Starbucks, Taco Cabana, The Earl of Sandwich, Wendy's ⊙ HEB Foods, Home Depot, Marshall's, PetCo, Petsmart, Steinmart, Target, **S** ⊕ IHOP, Popeyes, Schlotzsky's ⊟ Days Inn, SpringHill Suites, Studio6 ⊙ Discount Tire, Sam's Club/gas, Verizon, Walmart
557	Spur 53, **N** ⊞ Exxon/dsl ⊕ Cheddar's, Chuy's Mexican ⊟ Best Western, EconoLodge, Howard Johnson, Super 8 ⊙ Audi, Chevrolet, Hyundai, Jaguar/Mazerati/Ferrari, **S** ⊞ Valero/Subway/dsl ⊕ A&W/LJ Silver, Cici's Pizza, Huhot Chinese, IHOP, Matamoro's Cantina, Quiznos, Twin Peaks, Whataburger, Zio's Italian ⊟ Holiday Inn ⊙ Costco/gas, Land Rover, Sams Club/gas, Univ of TX at San Antonio, Walmart
556b	frontage rd
556a	to Anderson Lp, **S** ⊙ to Seaworld, Six Flags
555	La Quintera Pkwy, **N** ⊕ 54th St Rest., BJ's Rest., Bob's Chophouse, Chick-fil-A, Coldstone, Freddy's Steakburger, Hofbrau at the Rim, Islamorada Rest., Maggiano's Little Italy, McDonald's/playplace, Mimi's Cafe, Popeyes, Red Robin, Starbucks, TGIFriday's, Tiago's, Whataburger ⊟ Courtyard, Hilton Garden, Residence Inn ⊙ $Tree, AT&T, Bass Pro Shops, Best Buy, Dick's, GNC, JC Penney, Lowe's, Michaels, Old Navy, Ross, Staples, Target, TJ Maxx, World Mkt, **S** ⊕ Applebee's, Longhorn Steaks, Olive Garden, Red Lobster ⊟ Drury Inn, La Quinta, Motel 6 ⊙ Honda, to La Cantera Pkwy
554	Camp Bullis Rd, **N** ⊞ Texaco/dsl ⊙ Russell CP, **S** ⊞ Shell/dsl ⊟ Rodeway Inn
551	Boerne Stage Rd (from wb), to Leon Springs, **N** ⊞ Shamrock/dsl ⊕ Rudy's BBQ, Sonic, **S** ⊕ Bourbon St Seafood, Las Palapas Mexican, Longhorns Rest., Papa Nacho's, Starbucks, Subway ⊙ CarX, GNC, HEB Foods/dsl
550	FM 3351, Ralph Fair Rd, **N** ⊞ Exxon/McDonald's/dsl, Valero/dsl ⊕ Willie's Cafe ⊟ La Quinta, **S** ⊞ Shell/Domino's/dsl ⊕ Schlotsky's, Taco Cabana ⊙ Walgreens
546	Fair Oaks Pkwy, Tarpon Dr, **N** ⊕ Papa John's ⊙ American Dream RV Ctr, Harley-Davidson, vet, **S** ⊞ Chevron/dsl/café, Exxon/dsl/café ⊙ Fair Oaks Automotive, Goodyear/auto, Hoover RV Ctr
543	Boerne Stage Rd, to Scenic LP Rd, **N** ⊞ Valero/Subway/dsl ⊟ Fairfield Inn ⊙ Ancira RV Ctr, Buick/GMC, Chevrolet, Chrysler/Dodge/Jeep, Ford, NAPA, tires/repair, to Cascade Caverns/camping (3mi), **S** ⊙ Explore USA RV Ctr, Mercedes, Nissan, Toyota/Scion
542	(from wb), **N** ⊞ Shamrock ⊕ Domino's, Pizza Hut, Subway, Wendy's ⊙ $Tree, Alamo Fiesta RV Park, same as 540, Verizon
540	TX 46, to New Braunfels, **N** ⊞ Exxon/Taco Bell/dsl, Murphy USA/dsl, Shell/dsl ⊕ Burger King, Centinela Mexican,

Exit #	Services
540	Continued
	Church's, Denny's, DQ, Guadalajara Mexican, Little Caesars, Papa Murphy's, Pizza Hut, Shanghai Chinese, Sonic, Subway, Taco Cabana, Wendy's ⊟ Best Value, Comfort Inn, Motel 6 ⊙ AutoZone, HEB Food/dsl, Radio Shack, Verizon, vet, Walgreens, Walmart, **S** ⊕ Chili's, Starbucks, Whataburger ⊟ Hampton Inn ⊙ Ⓗ Home Depot
539	Johns Rd, **N** ⊟ La Quinta, **S** ⊞ Valero/dsl/LP
538mm	Cibolo Creek
538	Ranger Creek Rd
537	US 87, to Boerne
533	FM 289, Welfare, **N** ⊕ PoPo Family Rest. ⊙ Top of the Hill RV Park (1mi)
532mm	Little Joshua Creek
531mm	℞ wb, litter barrels
530mm	Big Joshua Creek
529.5mm	℞ eb, litter barrels
527	FM 1621 (from wb), to Waring
526.5mm	Holiday Creek
524	TX 27, FM 1621, to Waring, **N** ⊙ vet, **S 1mi** ⊞ Chevron, Shell/dsl
523.5mm	Guadalupe River
523	US 87 N, to Comfort, **N** ⊞ Chevron/Chicken Express/dsl, ♥Loves/McDonald's/Subway/dsl/scales/24hr, **S** ⊞ Exxon/dsl ⊕ DQ ⊟ Executive Inn ⊙ $General, RV Park/LP
521.5mm	Comfort Creek
520	FM 1341, to Cypress Creek Rd
515mm	Cypress Creek
514mm	℞ both lanes, full ♿ facilities, litter barrels, petwalk, play area, ⊞, RV dump, vending, wireless internet
508	TX 16, Kerrville, **N** ⊞ Exxon/dsl ⊙ Buick/Cadillac/Chevrolet, **S 0-2 mi** ⊞ Exxon, Shell/McDonald's/dsl/24hr, Stripes/Taco Co, Valero/dsl/e-85 ⊕ Bamboo Asian, Bella Sera Italian, Chicken Express, Cracker Barrel, DQ, IHOP, Jack-in-the-Box, Little Caesars, McDonald's, Schlotzsky's, Sonic, Taco Bell, Taco Casa, Valentino's Italian ⊟ Best Value Inn, Best Western, Big Texas Inn, Days Inn, Hampton Inn, Holiday Inn Express, La Quinta, Motel 6, Quality Inn, Super 8, Yo Ranch Hotel ⊙ Ⓗ $Tree, Advance Parts, BigLots, Hastings Books, Home Depot, Kerrville RV Ctr, Lowe's, O'Reilly Parts, vet, Walgreens
505	FM 783, to Kerrville, **S** ⊞ Exxon/dsl, **S 3 mi on TX 27** ⊞ Exxon/dsl, Phillips 66/dsl, Stripes/Taco Co/dsl ⊕ Billy Gene's Rest., Chili's, CiCi's, Culver's, Del Norte Rest., Dickey's BBQ, DQ, Fuddruckers, Mamacita's, McDonald's, Pizza Hut, Popeyes, Sonic, Starbucks, Subway, Taco Casa, Wendy's, Whataburger ⊟ Inn of the Hills ⊙ $General, AT&T, AutoZone, Chrysler/Dodge/Jeep, CVS Drug, Discount Tire, HEB Foods/gas, Take It Easy RV Resort, Tuesday Morning, Walmart/McDonald's
503.5mm	scenic views both lanes, litter barrels
501	FM 1338, **N** ⊙ Buckhorn RV Resort, **S** ⊙ KOA (2mi)
497mm	℞ both lanes, litter barrels
492	FM 479
490	TX 41
488	TX 27, to Ingram, Mountain Home
484	Midway Rd
477	US 290, to Fredericksburg
476.5mm	service rd eb
472	Old Segovia Rd
465	FM 2169, to Segovia, **S** ⊞ Phillips 66/rest./dsl ⊟ EconoLodge/RV park

SAN ANTONIO

KERRVILLE

INTERSTATE 10 Cont'd

Exit #	Services
464.5mm	Johnson Fork Creek
462	US 83 S, to Uvalde
461mm	🏠 eb, litter barrels
460	(from wb), to Junction
459mm	🏠 wb, litter barrels
457	FM 2169, to Junction, N 🚗 Shell/dsl S 🏠 Days Inn ⊙ RV camping, S. Llano River SP
456.5mm	Llano River
456	US 83/377, Junction, N 🚗 Alon/dsl, Chevron/dsl, Valero/McDonald's/dsl/24hr 🍴 Cooper's BBQ, Tia Nina's Mexican 🏠 Motel 6, S 🚗 Big Star/dsl, Conoco/dsl, Exxon/Church's/dsl, Shell/Quizno's/dsl 🍴 DQ, Isaack Rest., La Familia Mexican, Lum's BBQ, Sonic 🏠 Best Western, Lazy T Motel, Legends Inn, Rodeway Inn, Sun Valley Motel, The Hills Motel ⊙ H $General, Best Hardware, CarQuest, Family$, Lowe's Mkt, Plumley's Store, Radio Shack, S Llano RV Park, to S Llano River SP
452.5mm	Bear Creek
451	RM 2291, to Cleo Rd
448mm	North Creek
445	RM 1674, S ⊙ camping
444.5mm	Stark Creek
442mm	Copperas Creek
442	RM 1674, to Ft McKavett, N ⊙ to Ft McKavett SHS
439mm	N Llano River
438	Lp 291 (from wb), to Roosevelt, same as 437
437	Lp 291 (from eb, no EZ return), to Roosevelt, N 1 mi 🚗 Simon Bros Mercantile/dsl ⊙ USPO
429	RM 3130, to Harrell
423mm	parking area both lanes, litter barrels
420	RM 3130, to Baker Rd
412	Allison Rd, RM 3130
404	RM 3130, RM 864, N ⊙ to Ft McKavett St HS, S 3 mi 🚗 Stripes/Taco Co 🏠 Holiday Host Motel ⊙ H
400	US 277, Sonora, N 🚗 Shell/dsl 🍴 Sutton Co Steaks 🏠 Days Inn, S 🚗 Alon/7-11/dsl, Chevron/dsl, Stripes/dsl 🍴 DQ, La Mexicana Rest., Pizza Hut, Sonic, Taco Grill 🏠 Best Western, Comfort Inn, Economy Inn ⊙ Alco, Family$, USPO
399	(from eb)LP 467, Sonora, N 🏠 Days Inn, S 🚗 Chevron/dsl, Stripes/Taco Co 🍴 DQ ⊙ H RV camping
394mm	℞ both lanes, full ♿ facilities, litter barrels, petwalk, 🚶, 🏠 vending
392	RM 1989, Caverns of Sonora Rd, S 8 mi ⊙ Caverns of Sonora Camping
388	RM 1312 (from wb)
381	RM 1312 (from eb)
372	Taylor Box Rd, N 🚗 Exxon/rest./dsl/scales/24hr 🏠 Super 8 ⊙ auto museum, Circle Bar RV Park
368	LP 466, N same as 365 & 363
365	TX 163, Ozona, N 🚗 Chevron/dsl, Stripes/Godfather's/Taco Co/dsl, Valero/dsl 🍴 Cafe Next Door, DQ, Sonic, Subway 🏠 Best Value Inn, Best Western, Economy Inn/RV Park, Hillcrest Inn, Holiday Inn Express ⊙ H $General, dsl/auto repair, NAPA, to David Crockett Mon, S 🚗 Chevron, 🚃/dsl 🍴 El Chato's ⊙ city park
363	Lp 466, to Ozona
361	RM 2083, Pandale Rd
357mm	Eureka Draw
351mm	Howard Draw
350	FM 2398, to Howard Draw
349mm	parking area wb, litter barrels
346mm	parking area eb, litter barrels
343	TX 290 W, S ⊙ Ft. Lancaster Historic Site
337	Live Oak Rd
336.5mm	Live Oak Creek
328	River Rd, Sheffield
327.5mm	Pecos River
325	TX 290, TX 349, to Iraan, Sheffield, N ⊙ H
320	frontage rd
314	frontage rd
309mm	℞ both lanes, full ♿ facilities, litter barrels, petwalk, 🚶, 🏠 vending
307	US 190, FM 305, to Iraan, N ⊙ H
298	RM 2886
294	FM 11, Bakersfield, N 🚗 Exxon, S 🚗 Chevron/café/dsl ⊙ phone
288	Ligon Rd, N many windmills
285	McKenzie Rd, S ⊙ Domaine Cordier Ste Genevieve Winery
279mm	🏠 eb, litter barrels
277	FM 2023
273	US 67/385, to McCamey, 🏠 wb, litter barrels
272	University Rd
264	Warnock Rd, N ⊙ Fort Stockton RV Park/Roadrunner Cafe
261	US 290 W, US 385 S, N 🚗 Exxon/dsl, S 🚗 ♥ Loves/ Carl's Jr/dsl/scales/24hr, Shell/dsl, Stripes/dsl 🍴 DQ, Pizza Hut, Sonic, Subway 🏠 All Inn, Budget Inn, Deluxe Inn, Executive Inn ⊙ H RV camping, to Big Bend NP
259b a	(259 from eb)TX 18, FM 1053, Ft Stockton, N 🚗 Alon/dsl, Apache Fuel Ctr/dsl, Shell/Burger King/dsl 🍴 John Chihuahua's Mexican ⊙ I-10 RV Park, tires, S 🚗 FLYING J/Subway/dsl/scales/24hr ⊙ H
257	US 285, to Pecos, Ft Stockton, N 🚗 Stripes/Exxon/Taco Co/dsl/scales24hr ⊙ Comanche Land RV Park, golf, S 🚗 Alon/dsl, Chevron/dsl, Exxon/dsl, Shell/dsl 🍴 DQ, KFC/Taco Bell, McDonald's, Pecos Roadhouse, Pizza Hut, Pizza Pro, Sonic, Steak House, Subway 🏠 Atrium Inn, Best Western, Candlewood Suites, Days Inn, Hampton Inn, La Quinta, Quality Inn, Texan Inn ⊙ $General, Ace Hardware, AutoZone, Buick/ Chevrolet, CarQuest, Family$, Firestone/auto, Lowe's Foods, McKissick Tires, O'Reilly Parts
256	to US 385 S, Ft Stockton, N ⊙ HillTop RV, S 1 mi 🚗 Shell/ dsl 🍴 Dragon Buffet, Howard's Drive-In, K-Bob's Steaks, Subway 🏠 Comfort Suites, Holiday Inn Express, Motel 6, Sleep Inn, Super 8 ⊙ auto/RV repair, Big Bend NP, Ford, to Ft Stockton Hist Dist, vet, Walmart
253	FM 2037, to Belding

(Left margin vertical labels: JUNCTION, SONORA, OZONA)
(Right margin vertical label: FT STOCKTON)

Map of West Texas showing cities: Lamesa, Big Spring, Stanton, Midland, Odessa (I-20), Monahans, Pyote, Thorntonville, Pecos, Barstow, Toyah, McCamey, Iraan, Ozona, Balmorhea, Fort Stockton, Sheffield, Fort Davis (I-10). TX

TX

▲E INTERSTATE 10 Cont'd

Exit #	Services
248	US 67, FM 1776, to Alpine, S 🅞 to Big Bend NP
246	Firestone
241	Kennedy Rd
235	Mendel Rd
233mm	🆁🆂 both lanes, full ♿ facilities, litter barrels, petwalk, 🄲, 🚰 vending
229	Hovey Rd
222	Hoefs Rd
214	(from wb), FM 2448
212	TX 17, FM 2448, to Pecos, N 🅞 litter barrels, 🚰, S 🅟 I-10 Fuel/café/dsl, Saddleback RV Camping
209	TX 17, S 🅞 Ft Davis NHS, to Balmorhea SP, to Davis Mtn SP
206	FM 2903, to Balmorhea, Toyah, S **2 mi** 🅟 GasCard 🍴 Uncles Rest. (2mi) 🅞 to Balmorhea SP
192	FM 3078, to Toyahvale, S 🅞 to Balmorhea SP
188	Giffin Rd
187	I-20, to Ft Worth, Dallas
186	I-10, E to San Antonio (from wb)
185mm	🚰 both lanes, litter barrels
184	Springhills
181	Cherry Creek Rd, S 🅟 Chevron/dsl
176	TX 118, FM 2424, to Kent, S 🅞 Davis Mtn SP, Ft Davis, to McDonald Observatory
173	Hurd's Draw Rd
166	Boracho Sta
159	Plateau, N 🅟 Exxon/rest./dsl/24hr
153	Michigan Flat
146mm	weigh sta wb
146	Wild Horse Rd
145mm	🆁🆂 both lanes, full ♿ facilities, litter barrels, petwalk, 🄲, 🚰 vending, wireless internet

VAN HORN

Exit #	Services
140b	Ross Dr, Van Horn, N 🅟 Chevron/dsl, Exxon/dsl, ♥Loves/Subway/dsl/scales/24hr 🛏 Days Inn, Desert Inn, Sands Motel/rest. 🅞 Desert Willow RV Park, repair, S 🅞 Mountain View RV Park/dump
140a	US 90, TX 54, Van Horn Dr, N 🛏 Hotel El Capitan 🅞 🅗 NAPA, S 🅟 ▬▬▬/Wendy's/dsl/scales/24hr, Valero/dsl 🍴 Papa's Pantry 🅞 dsl/tire repair, KOA, RV Dump
138	Lp 10, to Van Horn, N 🍴 Chuy's Rest. 🛏 Budget Inn, EconoLodge, King's Inn, Knights Inn, Motel 6, Plaza Inn, Value Inn, Whitten Inn 🅞 $General, auto/dsl repair, city park, Eagles Nest RV Park, Oasis RV Park, Pueblo Foods, UPSO, visitor info, S 🅟 Chevron/dsl/24hr 🍴 McDonald's 🛏 Hampton Inn, Quality Inn, Super 8 🅞 tires/repair
137mm	weigh sta wb
136mm	scenic overlook wb, litter barrels, 🚰
135mm	Mountain/Central time zone line
133	(from wb)frontage rd
129	to Hot Wells, Allamore
108	to Sierra Blanca (from wb), same as 107
107	FM 1111, Sierra Blanca Ave, N 🅟 Exxon/Subway/dsl/24hr 🅞 to Hueco Tanks SP, truck/tire repair, USPO, S 🅟 Chevron/dsl 🛏 Americana Inn 🅞 Stagecoach Trading Post
105	(106 from wb) Lp 10, Sierra Blanca, same as 107
102.5mm	insp sta eb
99	Lasca Rd, N 🅞 🚰 both lanes, litter barrels, no restrooms
98mm	🚰 eb, litter barrels, no restrooms
95	frontage rd (from eb)
87	FM 34

Exit #	Services
85	Esperanza Rd
81	FM 2217
78	TX 20 W, to McNary
77mm	truck parking area wb
72	spur 148, to Ft Hancock, S 🅟 Shell/dsl 🍴 Angie's Rest. 🛏 Ft Hancock Motel 🅞 USPO
68	Acala Rd
55	Tornillo
51mm	🆁🆂 both lanes, full ♿ facilities, litter barrels, petwalk, 🚰 vending
49	FM 793, Fabens, S 🅟 FastTrak/dsl 🍴 Church's, Little Caesars, McDonald's, Subway 🛏 Fabens Inn/Cafe 🅞 Family$, San Eli Foods
42	FM 1110, to Clint, S 🅟 Express/dsl 🍴 Cotton Eyed Joe's, Mamacita's Rest. 🛏 Adobe Inn, Cotton Valley Motel/RV Park/ rest./dump, Super 8
37	FM 1281, Horizon Blvd, N 🅟 ✈FLYING J/Denny's/dsl/ scales/24hr/@, ♥Loves/Chester's/Subway/dsl/scales/ 24hr/@ 🛏 Americana Inn 🅞 Freightliner, RV Camping, Speedco Lube, S 🅟 Petro/Valero/Iron Skillet/Subway/dsl/ scales/24hr/@ 🍴 McDonald's 🛏 Deluxe Inn 🅞 Blue Beacon
35	Eastlake Blvd.
34	TX 375, Americas Ave, N 🅟 Chevron/dsl, Valero/Subway/dsl 🛏 Microtel, ValuePlace 🅞 Mission RV Camping, Peterbilt, U-Haul, S 🅞 El Paso Museum of Hist

E L P A S O

Exit #	Services
32	FM 659, Zaragosa Rd, N 🅟 Alon/7-11 🍴 Applebee's, Barrigos Mexican, BJ's Rest., Cheddar's, Chico's Tacos, Chipotle Mexican, Corner Bakery Cafe, Famous Dave's, Five Guys, Furr's Buffet, Genghis Grill, Great American Steaks, IHOP, Jaci-in-the-Box, Jason's Deli, Krispy Kreme, La Malinche Mexican, Logan's Roadhouse, Macaroni Grill, Mama Fu's Asian, McDonald's, Outback Steaks, Pei Wei, Peter Piper Pizza, Potbelly, Sonic, Starbucks, Taco Bell, Village Inn, Whataburger 🛏 Courtyard, Hampton Inn, Holiday Inn Express 🅞 AT&T, Chevrolet, Discount Tire, GNC, Kohl's, Lowe's, Michaels, Nissan, Office Depot, Ross, Walgreens, Which Wich, World Mkt, S 🅟 Valero/dsl 🍴 Gallego's Mexican 🅞 city park, vet, Volvo/ Mack
30	Lee Trevino Dr, N 🅟 Exxon 🍴 Denny's, Los Canarios Mexican, Whataburger 🛏 La Quinta, Motel 6, Red Roof Inn, Studio 6 🅞 Discount Tire, Firestone/auto, Ford, Home Depot, Kenworth/Ford Trucks, Lexus, Mazda, Toyota/Scion, S 🅞 Chrysler/Dodge/Jeep
29	Lomaland Dr, S 🅟 Alon/7-11 🛏 Ramada 🅞 Harley-Davidson
28b	Yarbrough Dr, El Paso, N 🅟 Murphy USA, Shell/Coldstone/ dsl 🍴 Buffalo Wild Wings, Burger King, ChuckECheese, Corner Bakery, Dunkin Donuts, Grandy's, Hayashi Japanese, Hong Kong Buffet, LJ Silver, McDonald's, Peter Piper Pizza, Sonic, Subway, TX Roadhouse, Wendy's, Whataburger, Wienerschnitzel 🛏 Days Inn 🅞 🅗 AT&T, Big Lots, Office Depot, Radio Shack, Ranch Mkt, Ross, Walmart, S 🅟 Rudy's BBQ, Valero/dsl 🍴 Applebee's, Fuddrucker's, Julio's Cafe, La Malinche Mexican, Lin's Buffet, Pizza Hut, Rudy's BBQ/gas, Shangri-La, Villa Del Mar 🛏 Comfort Inn, InTown Suites, La Quinta 🅞 🅗 🅟 Texaco
28a	FM 2316, McRae Blvd, N 🅟 Texaco/dsl, Valero 🍴 Pizza Hut 🛏 La Quinta 🅞 🅗 Jo-Ann Fabrics, K-Mart, Murphy USA/dsl, S 🅟 Circle K/dsl 🍴 Fuddruckers, Gabriel's Mexican, Pizza Hut 🛏 La Quinta, Quality Inn 🅞 NAPA, vet
27	Hunter Dr, Viscount Blvd, N 🅟 Alon/7-11, Valero/dsl 🍴 Grand China Buffet, Taco Bell 🛏 La Quinta 🅞 $General,

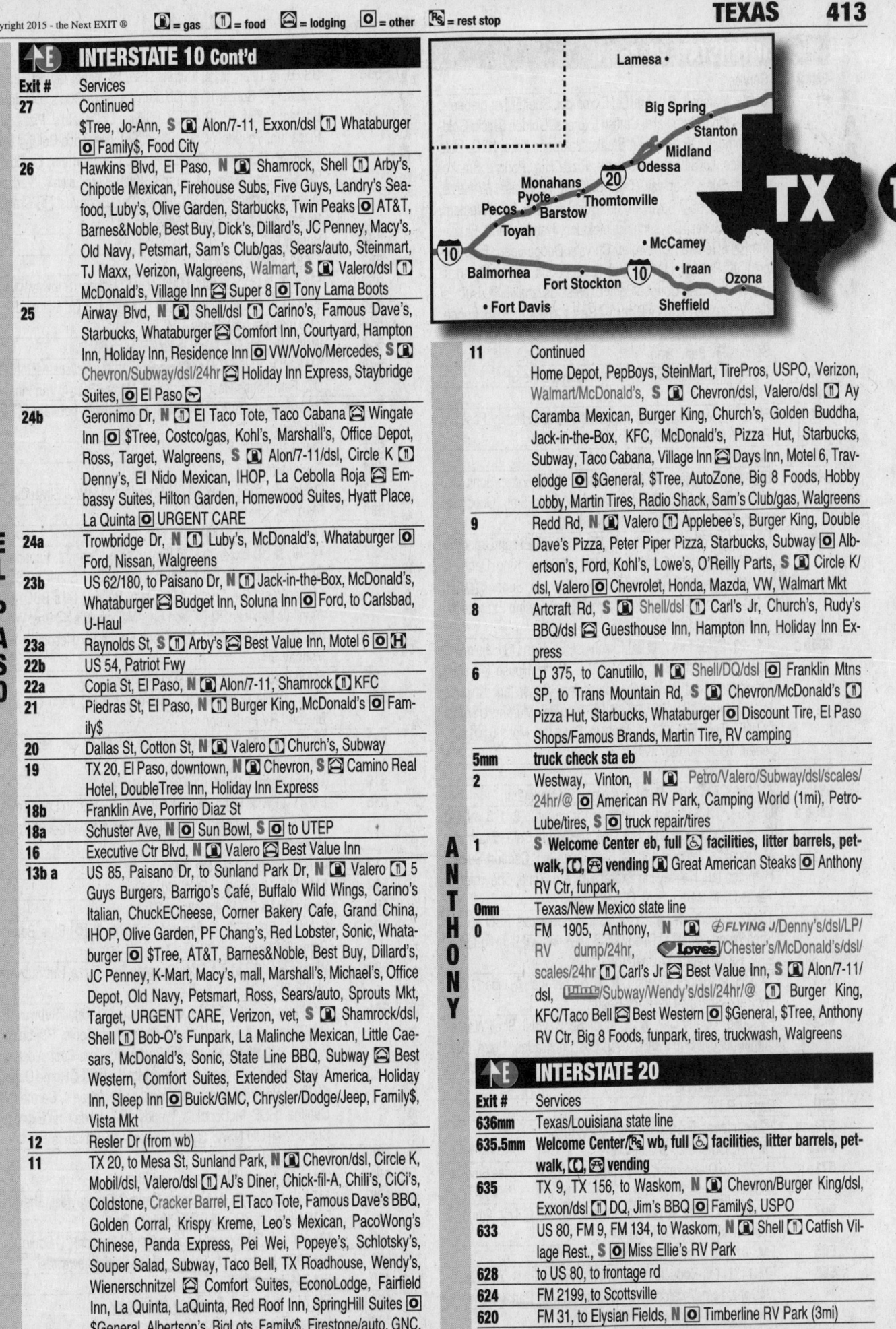

INTERSTATE 10 Cont'd

Exit #	Services
27	Continued $Tree, Jo-Ann, **S** 🅶 Alon/7-11, Exxon/dsl 🍴 Whataburger 🅾 Family$, Food City
26	Hawkins Blvd, El Paso, **N** 🅶 Shamrock, Shell 🍴 Arby's, Chipotle Mexican, Firehouse Subs, Five Guys, Landry's Seafood, Luby's, Olive Garden, Starbucks, Twin Peaks 🅾 AT&T, Barnes&Noble, Best Buy, Dick's, Dillard's, JC Penney, Macy's, Old Navy, Petsmart, Sam's Club/gas, Sears/auto, Steinmart, TJ Maxx, Verizon, Walgreens, Walmart, **S** 🅶 Valero/dsl 🍴 McDonald's, Village Inn 🏨 Super 8 🅾 Tony Lama Boots
25	Airway Blvd, **N** 🅶 Shell/dsl 🍴 Carino's, Famous Dave's, Starbucks, Whataburger 🏨 Comfort Inn, Courtyard, Hampton Inn, Holiday Inn, Residence Inn 🅾 VW/Volvo/Mercedes, **S** 🅶 Chevron/Subway/dsl/24hr 🏨 Holiday Inn Express, Staybridge Suites, 🅾 El Paso ✈
24b	Geronimo Dr, **N** 🍴 El Taco Tote, Taco Cabana 🏨 Wingate Inn 🅾 $Tree, Costco/gas, Kohl's, Marshall's, Office Depot, Ross, Target, Walgreens, **S** 🅶 Alon/7-11/dsl, Circle K 🍴 Denny's, El Nido Mexican, IHOP, La Cebolla Roja 🏨 Embassy Suites, Hilton Garden, Homewood Suites, Hyatt Place, La Quinta 🅾 URGENT CARE
24a	Trowbridge Dr, **N** 🍴 Luby's, McDonald's, Whataburger 🅾 Ford, Nissan, Walgreens
23b	US 62/180, to Paisano Dr, **N** 🍴 Jack-in-the-Box, McDonald's, Whataburger 🏨 Budget Inn, Soluna Inn 🅾 Ford, to Carlsbad, U-Haul
23a	Raynolds St, **S** 🍴 Arby's 🏨 Best Value Inn, Motel 6 🅾 🎗
22b	US 54, Patriot Fwy
22a	Copia St, El Paso, **N** 🅶 Alon/7-11, Shamrock 🍴 KFC
21	Piedras St, El Paso, **N** 🍴 Burger King, McDonald's 🅾 Family$
20	Dallas St, Cotton St, **N** 🅶 Valero 🍴 Church's, Subway
19	TX 20, El Paso, downtown, **N** 🅶 Chevron, **S** 🏨 Camino Real Hotel, DoubleTree Inn, Holiday Inn Express
18b	Franklin Ave, Porfirio Diaz St
18a	Schuster Ave, **N** 🅾 Sun Bowl, **S** 🅾 to UTEP
16	Executive Ctr Blvd, **N** 🅶 Valero 🏨 Best Value Inn
13b a	US 85, Paisano Dr, to Sunland Park Dr, **N** 🅶 Valero 🍴 5 Guys Burgers, Barrigo's Café, Buffalo Wild Wings, Carino's Italian, ChuckECheese, Corner Bakery Cafe, Grand China, IHOP, Olive Garden, PF Chang's, Red Lobster, Sonic, Whataburger 🅾 $Tree, AT&T, Barnes&Noble, Best Buy, Dillard's, JC Penney, K-Mart, Macy's, mall, Marshall's, Michael's, Office Depot, Old Navy, Petsmart, Ross, Sears/auto, Sprouts Mkt, Target, URGENT CARE, Verizon, vet, **S** 🅶 Shamrock/dsl, Shell 🍴 Bob-O's Funpark, La Malinche Mexican, Little Caesars, McDonald's, Sonic, State Line BBQ, Subway 🏨 Best Western, Comfort Suites, Extended Stay America, Holiday Inn, Sleep Inn 🅾 Buick/GMC, Chrysler/Dodge/Jeep, Family$, Vista Mkt
12	Resler Dr (from wb)
11	TX 20, to Mesa St, Sunland Park, **N** 🅶 Chevron/dsl, Circle K, Mobil/dsl, Valero/dsl 🍴 AJ's Diner, Chick-fil-A, Chili's, CiCi's, Coldstone, Cracker Barrel, El Taco Tote, Famous Dave's BBQ, Golden Corral, Krispy Kreme, Leo's Mexican, PacoWong's Chinese, Panda Express, Pei Wei, Popeye's, Schlotsky's, Souper Salad, Subway, Taco Bell, TX Roadhouse, Wendy's, Wienerschnitzel 🏨 Comfort Suites, EconoLodge, Fairfield Inn, La Quinta, LaQuinta, Red Roof Inn, SpringHill Suites 🅾 $General, Albertson's, BigLots, Family$, Firestone/auto, GNC,

Exit #	Services
11	Continued Home Depot, PepBoys, SteinMart, TirePros, USPO, Verizon, Walmart/McDonald's, **S** 🅶 Chevron/dsl, Valero/dsl 🍴 Ay Caramba Mexican, Burger King, Church's, Golden Buddha, Jack-in-the-Box, KFC, McDonald's, Pizza Hut, Starbucks, Subway, Taco Cabana, Village Inn 🏨 Days Inn, Motel 6, Travelodge 🅾 $General, $Tree, AutoZone, Big 8 Foods, Hobby Lobby, Martin Tires, Radio Shack, Sam's Club/gas, Walgreens
9	Redd Rd, **N** 🅶 Valero 🍴 Applebee's, Burger King, Double Dave's Pizza, Peter Piper Pizza, Starbucks, Subway 🅾 Albertson's, Ford, Kohl's, Lowe's, O'Reilly Parts, **S** 🅶 Circle K/dsl, Valero 🅾 Chevrolet, Honda, Mazda, VW, Walmart Mkt
8	Artcraft Rd, **S** 🅶 Shell/dsl 🍴 Carl's Jr, Church's, Rudy's BBQ/dsl 🏨 Guesthouse Inn, Hampton Inn, Holiday Inn Express
6	Lp 375, to Canutillo, **N** 🅶 Shell/DQ/dsl 🅾 Franklin Mtns SP, to Trans Mountain Rd, **S** 🅶 Chevron/McDonald's 🍴 Pizza Hut, Starbucks, Whataburger 🅾 Discount Tire, El Paso Shops/Famous Brands, Martin Tire, RV camping
5mm	**truck check sta eb**
2	Westway, Vinton, **N** 🅶 Petro/Valero/Subway/dsl/scales/24hr/@ 🅾 American RV Park, Camping World (1mi), Petro-Lube/tires, **S** 🅶 truck repair/tires
1	**S Welcome Center eb, full ♿ facilities, litter barrels, petwalk, 🚻, 🖨 vending** 🅶 Great American Steaks 🅾 Anthony RV Ctr, funpark,
0mm	Texas/New Mexico state line
0	FM 1905, Anthony, **N** 🅶 *FLYING J*/Denny's/dsl/LP/RV dump/24hr, *Loves*/Chester's/McDonald's/dsl/scales/24hr 🍴 Carl's Jr 🏨 Best Value Inn, **S** 🅶 Alon/7-11/dsl, *Circle K*/Subway/Wendy's/dsl/24hr/@ 🍴 Burger King, KFC/Taco Bell 🏨 Best Western 🅾 $General, $Tree, Anthony RV Ctr, Big 8 Foods, funpark, tires, truckwash, Walgreens

INTERSTATE 20

Exit #	Services
636mm	Texas/Louisiana state line
635.5mm	**Welcome Center/🆁🆂 wb, full ♿ facilities, litter barrels, petwalk, 🚻, 🖨 vending**
635	TX 9, TX 156, to Waskom, **N** 🅶 Chevron/Burger King/dsl, Exxon/dsl 🍴 DQ, Jim's BBQ 🅾 Family$, USPO
633	US 80, FM 9, FM 134, to Waskom, **N** 🅶 Shell 🍴 Catfish Village Rest., **S** 🅾 Miss Ellie's RV Park
628	to US 80, to frontage rd
624	FM 2199, to Scottsville
620	FM 31, to Elysian Fields, **N** 🅾 Timberline RV Park (3mi)

El Paso

Anthony

INTERSTATE 20 Cont'd

MARSHALL

Exit #	Services
617	US 59, Marshall, **N 0-2 mi** 🅟 Exxon/dsl, Shell 🍴 Applebee's, Burger King, Cafe Italia, Catfish Express, Golden Chick, Golden Corral, IHOP, In Japan Steaks, Jalapeño Tree, KFC, Little Caesars, LJ Silver, McDonald's, Pizza Hut, Porky's Smokehouse, Sonic, Subway, Taco Bell, Waffle House, Wendy's, Whataburger 🛏 Baymont Inn, Best Western, Best Western, Comfort Suites, Days Inn, Fairfield Inn, Hampton Inn, Quality Inn 🄾 $General, Chevrolet, Chrysler/Dodge/Jeep, Ford/Lincoln, JC Penney, NAPA, Save-A-Lot Foods, Toyota/Scion, **S** 🅟 Chevron/dsl, Conoco/Pony Express/dsl/scales/@, Rudy's/dsl, Valero/dsl 🍴 JW's Diner 🛏 Best Value Inn, EconoLodge, Holiday Inn Express, La Quinta, Motel 6, Super 8 🄾 Holiday Springs RV Park (2mi)
614	TX 43, to Marshall, **S** 🄾 to Martin Creek Lake SP
610	FM 3251
604	FM 450, Hallsville, **N** 🅟 Valero/dsl 🄾 450 Hitchin' Post RV Park, to Lake O' the Pines
600mm	Mason Creek
599	FM 968, Longview, **N** 🄾 Kenworth, **S** 🅟 Exxon/Sonic/dsl, Valero Travel Plaza@ 🄾 Cowboy RV Park (5mi), Goodyear Truck Tire, truck repair, truck/rv wash
596	US 259 N, TX 149, to Lake O' Pines, **N** 🅟 Exxon/Grandy's/dsl, Shell/Sonic/TX Smokehouse/dsl 🍴 Burger King, Denny's, Whataburger 🛏 Centerstone Suites, Microtel, Super 8 🄾 🅷 **S** 🅟 Valero/dsl 🍴 Cracker Barrel 🛏 Holiday Inn Express 🄾 to Martin Lake SP
595b a	TX 322, Estes Pkwy, **N** 🅟 Exxon/dsl, EZ Mart 🍴 Hajalmer's Rest., Jack-in-the-Box, McDonald's, Waffle House 🛏 Best Value Inn, Best Western, Express Inn, Guest Inn, Knight's Inn, La Quinta 🄾 Family$, **S** 🅟 Alon/dsl, Murphy USA/dsl 🍴 KFC/Taco Bell 🛏 Baymont Inn, Days Inn, Motel 6 🄾 auto repair, Walmart/Subway
593mm	Sabine River
591	FM 2087, FM 2011, **S** 🄾 Fernbrook RV Park (2mi)
589b a	US 259, TX 31, Kilgore (exits left from wb), **S 1-3 mi** 🅟 Chevron/dsl, Exxon/dsl 🍴 Chili's, Kilgore Café, Mazzio's, McDonald's, Taco Bueno 🛏 Best Value Inn, Comfort Suites, Hampton Inn, Holiday Inn Express 🄾 AutoZone, Chevrolet, E Texas Oil Museum, Ford, O'Reilly Parts
587	TX 42, Kilgore, **N** 🅟 Exxon/dsl 🍴 Bodacious BBQ, **S** 🅟 Shell/Wendy's/dsl 🍴 Denny's 🛏 Days Inn 🄾 Big Rig Lube, E TX Oil Museum, Walmart (3mi)
583	TX 135, to Kilgore, Overton, **N** 🅟 EZmart/dsl 🄾 Liberty City RV Park, Shallow Creek RV Resort
582	FM 3053, Liberty City, **N** 🅟 Mobil/Subway/dsl, Shell/Whataburger/dsl 🍴 Bob's BBQ, DQ, Los Enchiladas, Pizza Boy, Sonic
579	Joy-Wright Mtn Rd
575	Barber Rd
574mm	🛏 both lanes, ♿ accessible, litter barrels
571b	FM 757, Omen Rd, to Starrville
571a	US 271, to Gladewater, Tyler, **S** 🅟 Shell/Sonic/Texas Smokehouse/dsl/scales/24hr
567	TX 155, Winona, **N** 🅟 Valero/dsl/24hr, **S** 🍴 DQ (2mi) 🛏 Best Value Inn 🄾 🅷 Freightliner
565	FM 2015, to Driskill-Lake Rd
562	FM 14, **N** 🍴 Bodacious BBQ 🄾 to Tyler SP, **S** 🅟 McDonald's/dsl/scales/24hr 🄾 Northgate RV Park (4mi)
560	Lavender Rd, **S** 🄾 5 Star RV Park (2 mi)

TYLER / CANTON / TERRELL

Exit #	Services
557	Jim Hogg Rd, **N** 🅟 Shell/dsl 🄾 TX Rose RV Park
556	US 69, to Tyler, **N** 🅟 Murphy USA/dsl, RaceWay/dsl, Shamrock/dsl 🍴 Burger King, Chicken Express, Chili's, Domino's, Eastern Buffet, IHOP, KFC\LJ Silver, McDonald's, Pizza Hut, Pizza Inn, Posado's Cafe, Sonic, Subway, Taco Bell 🛏 Best Western, Comfort Suites, Days Inn, Hampton Inn, La Quinta 🄾 $General, Family$, Fred's, Kwik Kar, Lowe's, Verizon, Walmart/Subway, **S** 🅟 Chevron/DQ, Exxon/dsl 🍴 Cracker Barrel, Wendy's 🛏 Best Value Inn
554	Harvey Rd
553	TX 39 S (toll), CR 411
552	FM 849, **N** 🅟 Valero/dsl 🍴 Collin St Bakery, Subway 🄾 vet
548	TX 110, to Grand Saline, **N** 🅟 Exxon/dsl, **S** 🅟 Valero/dsl
546mm	cmv insp sta both lanes
544	Willow Branch Rd, **N** 🄾 Willow Branch RV Park
540	FM 314, to Van, **N** 🅟 Loves/Carl's Jr/dsl/scales/24hr 🍴 DQ, Farmhouse Rest, Sonic, Soul Mans BBQ 🛏 Van Inn
538mm	Ⓡ both lanes, full ♿ facilities, litter barrels, petwalk, 🕭, 🚰 vending
537	FM 773, FM 16
536	Tank Farm Rd
533	Oakland Rd, to Colfax, **N** 🅟 Shell/Pilot/A&W/LJ Silver/dsl
530	FM 1255, Canton
528	FM 17, to Grand Saline
527	TX 19, **N** 🅟 Exxon/dsl 🍴 Burger King, Denny's, Papadales Grill, Whataburger 🛏 Motel 6, Quality Inn, Super 8, **S** 🅟 Circle K/dsl/24hr, Shell/dsl 🍴 Dairy Palace, DJ's BBQ, DQ, Juanita's Mexican, KFC/Taco Bell, McDonald's 🛏 Best Western, Days Inn 🄾 Ford, Mill Creek Ranch RV Resort, to First Monday SP
526	FM 859, to Edgewood, **N** 🄾 water park
523	TX 64, Wills Point, **N** 🅟 Shell/dsl/24hr 🍴 Taco Casa 🄾 Bluebird RV Park, repair
521	Myrtle Springs Rd, **S** 🄾 Explore USA RV Ctr, repair, RV camp/dump
519	Turner-Hayden Rd, **S** 🄾 Canton RV Park
516	FM 47, to Wills Point, **N** 🍴 Fourwinds Steaks, to Lake Tawakoni, **S** 🅟 Texaco/dsl 🍴 Robertson's Café/gas 🛏 Interstate Motel
512mm	cmv inspection sta both lanes
512	FM 2965, Hiram-Wills Point Rd
509	Hiram Rd, **S** 🅟 Shell/dsl/cafe/24hr
506	FM 429, FM 2728, College Mound Rd, **N** 🄾 Blue Bonnet Ridge RV Park
503	Wilson Rd, **S** 🅟 TA/Shell/Country Fare/Pizza Hut/Subway/dsl/LP/24hr/@
501	TX 34, to Terrell, **N** 🅟 Exxon/dsl, QT/dsl, Shell/Subway/dsl 🍴 Church's, Italrican Cafe, Schlotzsky's, Sonic, Starbucks, Steak&Grill, Waffle House 🛏 Best Value Inn, Best Western, Comfort Inn, Days Inn, La Quinta, Motel 6 🄾 🅷 Home Depot, **S** 🅟 Circle K/dsl, Valero/dsl/24hr 🍴 Applebee's, Carmona's Cantina, IHOP, McDonald's, Wendy's 🛏 Holiday Inn Express, Super 8 🄾 Old Navy, Tanger Outlet/famous brands
499b	Rose Hill Rd, to Terrell
499a	to US 80, W to Dallas, same as 498
498	FM 148, to Terrell, **N** 🅟 Exxon/Denny's/Subway/dsl, Shell/dsl 🍴 Soulman's BBQ, **S** 🄾 Terrell RV Park
493	FM 1641, **S** 🅟 Exxon/Pizza Inn/Taco Mayo/dsl 🍴 Sonic
491	FM 2932, Helms Tr, to Forney, **N** 🅟 Shell/Subway/dsl
490	FM 741, to Forney
487	FM 740, to Forney, **S** 🄾 Forney RV park
483	Lawson Rd, Lasater Rd

INTERSTATE 20 Cont'd

D A L L A S

Exit #	Services
482	Belt Line Rd, to Lasater, **N** 🅖 Exxon/dsl 🍴 Smokehouse BBQ, Sonic, **S** 🅖 Shell/KFC/Pizza Hut/Subway 🅞 RV park
481	Seagoville Rd, **N** 🅖 Shell/Church's/Dickey's BBQ, Valero/dsl 🛏 La Quinta, **S** 🍴 Lindy's Rest.
480	I-635, N to Mesquite
479b a	US 175, **S** 🅖 Marlow/dsl
477	St Augustine Rd, **S** 🅖 Shell/dsl 🍴 Sonic
476	Dowdy Ferry Rd
474	TX 310 N, Central Expsy
473b a	JJ Lemmon Rd, I-45 N to Dallas, S to Houston
472	Bonnie View Rd, **N** 🅖 ⛽FLYING J/Denny's/dsl/LP/24hr, Shell 🍴 Jack-in-the-Box 🛏 Ramada Ltd 🅞 Blue Beacon, Kenworth, Speedco Lube, **S** 🅖 TA/Exxon/Burger King/Taco Bell/dsl/scales/24hr/@
470	TX 342, Lancaster Rd, **N** 🅖 Chevron/dsl, USA/Popeye's/Subway/dsl/scales/24hr 🍴 Soulman's BBQ, **S** 🅖 ⛽/Wendy's/dsl/scales/24hr, Shell 🍴 LJ Silver/Taco Bell, McDonald's, Sonic, Whataburger, William's Chicken 🛏 Days Inn
468	Houston School Rd, **S** 🅖 Exxon/dsl 🍴 Whataburger
467b a	I-35E, N to Dallas, S to Waco, **N** 1 mi off of I-35E 🅖 Chevron, Shell 🍴 McDonald's
466	S Polk St, **N** 🅖 Exxon/dsl, Texaco/dsl 🍴 DQ, Sonic, Subway 🅞 Family$, **S** 🅖 ⛽Loves/Carl's Jr/dsl/scales/24hr
465	Wheatland/S Hampton Rds, **N** 🅖 Shell/Subway 🍴 Chick-fil-A, Chili's, Furr's Cafeteria 🅞 $Tree, Aldi Foods, CVS Drug, GNC, Office Depot, Petsmart, Ross, Target, **S** 🅖 Chevron/McDonald's, Murphy USA/dsl, QT/dsl, RaceWay/dsl 🍴 Arby's, Burger King, Cheddar's, Jack-in-the-Box, Panda Express, Popeye's, Sonic, Spring Creek BBQ, Taco Bell, Wendy's 🛏 Super 8 🅞 Ⓗ Home Depot, Honda, Hyundai, Kia, Lowe's, Nissan, Sam's Club/gas, Toyota/Scion, Walmart
464b a	US 67, Love Fwy
463	Camp Wisdom Rd, **N** 🅖 Chevron/7-11, Exxon 🍴 Catfish King Rest., Denny's, Taco Bell/LJ Silver, Taco Cabana 🛏 Best Value Inn, Royal Inn, Super 7 🅞 $Tree, Chrysler/Dodge/Jeep, **S** 🅖 Shamrock 🍴 Burger King, Chubby's Rest., Dave's BBQ, Olive Garden, Red Lobster, Subway, Tortilla Factory
462b a	Duncanville Rd (no EZ wb return), **S** 🅖 QT, Shell/dsl 🍴 Church's, Jack-in-the-Box, Los Lupes Mexican, Popeye's, Whataburger 🛏 Hilton Garden, Motel 6 🅞 Firestone/auto, Kroger, Radio Shack
461	Cedar Ridge Rd, **S** 🅖 RaceWay/dsl
460	TX 408
458	Mt Creek Pkwy
457	FM 1382, to Grand Prairie, **N** 🅖 Shell/7-11/dsl, Valero/dsl 🍴 Waffle House, **S** 🅖 RaceTrac/dsl 🍴 Jack-in-the-Box 🅞 to Joe Pool Lake
456	Carrier Pkwy, to Corn Valley Rd, **N** 🅖 QT 🍴 Chick-fil-A, Dickey's BBQ, Domino's, Don Pablo, Popeyes, Sonic, Starbucks, Taco Cabana, Whataburger 🅞 AutoZone, Home Depot, Kohl's, Radio Shack, Target, **S** 🅖 Shell 🍴 Baskin-Robbins, Boston Mkt, Chapp's Cafe, Cheddar's, Chili's, Chipotle, Denny's, IHOP, Little Caesar's, McDonald's, Spring Creek BBQ, Subway 🛏 Holiday Inn Express 🅞 Albertsons/gas, CVS Drug, GNC, Tom Thumb Foods/gas, Verizon, vet, Walgreens
455	TX 151
454	Great Southwest Pkwy, **N** 🅖 Chevron/7-11/dsl, Exxon/dsl 🍴 Beto's, Carino's Italian, China Dragon, ChuckeCheese, DQ, Golden Corral, KFC, McDonald's, Pizza Hut/Taco Bell,

454	Continued Taco Bueno, TX Roadhouse, Waffle House, Wendy's, Wiener-schnitzel 🛏 Comfort Suites, Heritage Inn, Quality Inn 🅞 Ⓗ Firestone/auto, Harley-Davidson, U-Haul, **S** 🅖 7-11, Shell/Subway/dsl, Valero/dsl 🍴 Applebee's, Arby's, Buffalo Wild Wings, Burger King, Schlotzsky's, Sonic 🛏 La Quinta, Super 8 🅞 $Tree, AT&T, Discount Tire, Kroger, Office Depot, Petsmart, RaceTrac/dsl, Sam's Club, to Joe Pool Lake, Walgreens, Walmart/McDonald's
453b a	TX 360
452	Frontage Rd
451	Collins St, New York Ave, **N** 🅖 Exxon/dsl, RaceTrac/dsl, Rudy's Store/BBQ/dsl 🍴 Cotton Patch Cafe, Golden Corral, Jack-in-the-Box, Whataburger 🅞 Chrysler/Dodge/Jeep, Gander Mtn, Kia/Mazda/VW, URGENT CARE, **S** 🅖 QT, Shell, Valero/dsl 🍴 Chicken Express, KFC/Taco Bell, McDonald's, Sonic, Subway, Taco Bueno 🛏 Hampton Inn 🅞 Buick/GMC, Nissan
450	Matlock Rd, **N** 🍴 Abuelo's Mexican, Bar Louie, BJ's Rest., Black-eyed Pea, Bone Daddy's, Boomer Jack's Grill, Chuy's Mexican, Coldstone, Dave&Buster's, Genghis Grill, Houlihan's, India Grill, Jason's Deli, Kincaide's Burgers, McAlister's Deli, Melting Pot, Mercado Juarez, Mimi's Cafe, PF Changs, Pluckers's Wings, Potbelly, Red Robin, Starbucks, Sweet Tomatoes, The Keg Steaks, Wendy's, Which Wich 🛏 Courtyard, Quality Inn, Residence Inn 🅞 Ⓗ AT&T, Costco/gas, Jo-Ann Fabrics, Lowe's, Old Navy, Petsmart, Staples, World Mkt, **S** 🅖 7-11, RaceWay/dsl, Shell/7-11 🍴 Joe's Pizza, Pizza Patron, Starbucks 🅞 Fry's Electronics, O'Reilly Parts
449	FM 157, Cooper St, **N** 🅖 Shell/dsl 🍴 Cane's, Cheesecake Factory, Chili's, Corner Bakery, Grandy's, Honeybaked Ham, IHOP, In-N-Out, McDonald's, Nagoya Japanese, On-the-Border, Outback Steaks, Pei Wei, Razzoo's Cajun Café, Red Lobster, Rockfish Seafood, Salt Grass Steaks, Souper Salad, Spaghetti Whse, Spring Creek BBQ, Whataburger 🛏 Best Western, Days Inn, Holiday Inn Express, La Quinta, Studio 6, Super 8 🅞 Barnes&Noble, Best Buy, Dick's, Dillard's, Discount Tire, JC Penney, Macy's, mall, Michael's, Office Depot, Sears/auto, Target, TJ Maxx, Verizon, **S** 🅖 Shell 🍴 Applebee's, Arby's, Boston Mkt, Burger St, Carl's Jr, Chick-fil-A, Chipotle, Denny's, El Arroyo, El Fenix Mexican, Lin's Buffet, LJ Silver, Macaroni Grill, McDonald's, Olive Garden, Panda Express, Peter Piper Pizza, Schlotsky's, Starbucks, Subway, Taco Bueno, Taco Cabana, TGIFriday 🛏 InTown Suites, Microtel 🅞 $Tree, AAA, Acura, Chevrolet, Ford, Hobby Lobby, Home Depot, Honda, Hyundai, NTB, Ross, Suzuki, Toyota, Walmart/McDonald's

INTERSTATE 20 Cont'd

Exit #	Services
448	Bowen Rd, **N** 🅖 QT, RaceTrac/dsl 🍴 Cracker Barrel, Sonic, **S** 🅖 Shell
447	Kelly-Elliott Rd, Park Springs Blvd, **N** 🅖 7-11, Valero, **S** 🅖 Exxon/Subway 🅾 city park
445	Green Oaks Blvd, **N** 🅖 Conoco/dsl, Shell/7-11/dsl 🍴 Arby's, Boston Mkt, Braum's, Burger St, Cafe Acapulco, Chapp's Cafe, Chick-fil-A, Church's, CiCi's, Colter's BBQ, Fuzzy's Tacos, Hooters, Jack-in-the-Box, Jay Jay Rest., Joe's Pizza, Mijo's Cafe, Quizno's, Schlotzsky's, Starbucks, Taco Bell, Taco Cabana, Taco Casa, Tai-Pan, Wendy's, Whataburger 🅾 $Tree, Ace Hardware, Albertsons, AT&T, CVS Drug, Firestone, Kroger/dsl, Meineke, Office Depot, Radio Shack, Verizon, Walgreens, **S** 🅖 7-11, Murphy Express/dsl, QT/dsl, Valero/dsl 🍴 Cheddar's, Corky's Pizza, Golden Buffet, IHOP, McDonald's, Pancho's Mexican, Panda Express, Sonic, Subway, Taco Bueno, Waffle House 🅾 $General, AutoZone, BigLots, Discount Tire, O'Reilly Parts, Tuesday Morning, vet, Walmart/Subway
444	US 287 S, to Waxahatchie, from eb, same as 445
443	Bowman Springs Rd (from wb)
442b a	I-820 to Ft Worth, US 287 bus, **N** 🅖 Valero 🏠 Great Western Inn, Knights Inn, **S** 🅖 QT/dsl
441	Anglin Dr, Hartman Lane, **N** 🏠 ValuePlace Inn, **S** 🅖 Conoco/dsl
440b	Forest Hill Dr, **S** 🅖 Shell/7-11/dsl 🍴 Braum's, Capt D's, CiCi's Pizza, Jack-in-the-Box, Luby's, Sonic, Starbucks, Subway, Taco Bell 🏠 La Quinta 🅾 $General, $Tree, AutoZone, CVS Drug, Discount Tire, O'Reilly Parts, Super 1 Foods, Walgreens
440a	Wichita St, **N** 🅖 Chevron/dsl 🍴 #1 Chinese, Taco Casa, Wendy's, **S** 🅖 Texaco/dsl, Valero 🍴 Chicken Express, Denny's, Domino's, McDonald's, Pizza Hut, Schlotzsky's, Taco Bueno, Whataburger 🏠 Best Western, Comfort Inn, Hampton Inn
439	Campus Dr, **N** 🅾 Chrysler/Dodge/Jeep, Ford, **S** 🅾 Sam's Club/gas
438	Oak Grove Rd, **S** 🅖 Valero
437	I-35W, **N** to Ft Worth, **S** to Waco
436b	Hemphill St, **N** 🅖 Shell/dsl, **S** 🅾 Chevrolet
436a	FM 731 (from eb), to Crowley Ave, **N** 🅖 Conoco/dsl, Valero/dsl 🍴 China Express 🅾 $General, Sav-a-Lot Foods, **S** 🍴 BurgerBox, Pizza Hut/Taco Bell, Subway 🅾 transmissions
435	McCart St, **N** 🅖 Shamrock, Shell/dsl, **S** 🅖 Mobil/dsl
434b	Trail Lakes Dr, **S** 🅖 Shell 🍴 Sonic, Starbucks, Subway, Wendy's 🅾 CVS Drug, Family$
434a	Granbury Rd
433	Hulen St, **N** 🅖 Shell/dsl 🍴 Chef Chen, ChuckECheese, Honeybaked Ham, Hooters, Olive Garden, Papa Murphy's, Souper Salad, Subway, TX Roadhouse 🏠 TownePlace Suites 🅾 Albertsons, Home Depot, NTB, Petsmart, Sprouts Mkt, TJ Maxx, **S** 🍴 Abuelo's Mexican, BJ's Rest., Denny's, Five Guys, In-N-Out, Jack-in-the-Box, Kincaide's Burgers, McDonald's, Panera Bread, Pizza Inn, Potbelly, Red Lobster, Red Robin 🏠 Hampton Inn 🅾 Barnes&Noble, Dillard's, Hobby Lobby, Macy's, mall, Michael's, Office Depot, Old Navy, Ross, Sears/auto
431	(432 from wb), TX 183, Bryant-Irvin Rd, **N** 🅖 Chevron 🍴 Chipotle Mexican, Genghis Grill, Keg Steaks, Mimi's Café, On-the-Border, Taste of Asia 🅾 Best Buy, Cavender's Boots, Kohl's, Lowe's, Petsmart, Sam's Club/gas, **S** 🅖 Chevron,

431	Continued Shell/dsl 🍴 Blackeyed Pea, Chicken Express, Chick-fil-A, Cousin's BBQ, Fox & Hound, Fuddruckers, IHOP, Jimmy John's, Lonestar Oysters, Outback Steaks, Pei Wei, Pizza Hut, Razzoo's Cajun, Rio Mambo, SaltGrass Steaks, Schlotzsky's, Sonic, Starbucks, Subway, Szechuan 🏠 Courtyard, Extended Stay America, Holiday Inn Express, Homewood Suites, Hyatt Place, La Quinta 🅾 AT&T, Costco/gas, Firestone/auto, Ford, Goodyear/auto, Infiniti, Kwik Kar, Lexus, Mazda, PetCo, Staples, Target, Verizon, Walgreens
430mm	Clear Fork Trinity River
429b	Winscott Rd, **N** 🅖 Circle K/dsl 🍴 Cracker Barrel 🏠 Best Western, Comfort Suites
429a	US 377, to Granbury, **S** 🅖 QT/dsl, RaceTrac/dsl, Shell/dsl, Valero 🍴 7-11/dsl, Arby's, Braum's, Burger King, Chicken Express, Chick-fil-A, Domino's, Golden Chick, Jack-in-the-Box, KFC/Taco Bell, McDonald's, NY Pizza, Panda Express, Pizza Hut, Ricky's BBQ, Sonic, Starbucks, Subway, Taco Casa, Taco Villa, Waffle House, Waffle House, Whataburger 🏠 Motel 6 🅾 $General, Albertsons, AutoZone, CVS Drug, O'Reilly Parts, USPO, Walgreens, Walmart
428	I-820, **N** around Ft Worth
426	RM 2871, Chapin School Rd
425	Markum Ranch Rd
421	I-30 E (from eb), to Ft Worth
420	FM 1187, Aledo, Farmer, parking & ride
419mm	weigh sta wb
418	Ranch House Rd, Willow Park, Willow Park, **N** 🅖 Exxon/Taco Casa, Shell/dsl 🍴 Pizza Hut, Sonic, Subway, Whataburger, **S** 🅖 Shell/ChickenExpress/dsl 🍴 Domino's, McDonald's, Milano's Italian, Mr Jim's Pizza, Railhead BBQ 🏠 Knights Inn 🅾 $General, Ace RV Ctr., Brookshire Foods, Cowtown RV Park
417mm	no services
415	FM 5, Mikus Rd, Annetta, **S** 🅖 Chevron/dsl, Shell/dsl 🍴 Drivers Diner 🅾 415 RV Ctr
413	(414 from wb), US 180 W, Lake Shore Dr, **N** 🅖 Murphy USA/dsl, RaceTrac/dsl, Shell/dsl 🍴 DQ, Golden Chick, McDonald's, Sonic, Subway, Taco Bell, Waffle House 🅾 Buick/Cadillac/Chevrolet/GMC, Ford, Hyundai, Lincoln, Nissan, Suzuki, Toyota/Scion, Walgreens, Walmart/Subway, **S** 🅖 Valero/dsl
410	Bankhead Hwy, **S** 🅖 Loves/Subway/dsl/24hr
409	FM 2552 N, Clear Lake Rd, **N** 🅖 Petro/Valero/Iron Skillet/dsl/24hr/@ 🍴 Antonio's Mexican, Granny's Kitchen, Jack-in-the-Box, Little Panda Chinese, Popeyes 🏠 Heritage Inn, SleepGo Motel 🅾 Blue Beacon, **S** 🅖 Shell/dsl
408	TX 171, FM 1884, FM 51, Tin Top Rd, Weatherford, **N** 🅖 Exxon, Mobil, Murphy USA/dsl 🍴 Applebee's, Baker's Ribs, Braum's, Buffalo Wild Wings, Chicken Express, China Harbor, CiCi's Pizza, Cotton Patch Cafe, Denny's, IHOP, Kincade's Burgers, LJ Silver, Logan's Roadhouse, McAlister's Deli, McDonald's, MT Rest., Olive Garden, Rosa's Cafe, Schlotzsky's, Starbucks, Subway, Taco Bell, Taco Bueno, Taco Cabana, Whataburger, Wild Mushroom Steaks 🏠 La Quinta, Sleep Inn, Super 8 🅾 $Tree, AT&T, AutoZone, Belk, Christian Bros Auto, Discount Tire, Firestone/auto, JC Penney, Just Brakes, Michael's, Radio Shack, TJ Maxx, Verizon, Walgreens, Walmart/Subway, **S** 🅖 Exxon/Subway/dsl, Shell/Burger King/dsl 🍴 Chick-fil-A, Chili's, Cracker Barrel, Honey Bee Ham, On-the-Border, Tokyo Japanese Steaks, Waffle House, Whataburger 🏠 Best Western, Candlewood Suites, Comfort Suites, Fairfield Inn, Hampton Inn, Holiday Inn Express, Motel 6, Quality Inn, Super Value Inn 🅾 Best Buy, GNC, Kohl's, Lowe's, NTB, Petsmart, Ross, Target, URGENT CARE

(side tabs: TX / FT WORTH / WEATHERFORD)

INTERSTATE 20 Cont'd

Exit #	Services
407	Tin Top Rd (from eb), N ⊙ Home Depot, S ⊙ KOA, same as 408
406	Old Dennis Rd, N 🍴 Truck&Travel/dsl 🍴 Chuck Wagon Rest. 🛏 Quest Inn, S 🍴 [illeg]/Wendy's/dsl/scales/24hr 🛏 EconoLodge, Quality 1 Motel ⊙ Boss Shop Repair
404	Williams Memorial Dr
402	(403 from wb), TX 312, to Weatherford
397	FM 1189, to Brock, N 🍴 Valero/dsl ⊙ Oak Creek RV Park
394	FM 113, to Millsap
393mm	Brazos River
391	Gilbert Pit Rd
390mm	🅁🅂 both lanes, full ♿ facilities, litter barrels, petwalk, 🚻, 🏪 vending
386	US 281, to Mineral Wells, Stephenville, N 🍴 Shell/Subway/dsl ⊙ Gilbert Pecans, S 🍴 Chevron/Maverick TC/Taco Casa/dsl, Stripes/dsl/rest. 🍴 DQ
380	FM 4, Santo, S ⊙ RVPark
376	Blue Flat Rd, Panama Rd
373	TX 193, Gordon
370	TX 108 S, FM 919, Gordon, N 🍴 Texaco/Bar-B/dsl, S 🍴 Exxon/dsl ⊙ Cactus Rose RV Park, Longhorn Inn/Country Store
367	TX 108 N, Mingus, N 🍴 Smoke Stack Café ⊙ Thurber Sta, S 🍴 NY Hill Rest.
364mm	Palo Pinto Creek
363	Tudor Rd, litter barrels, 🏪
362mm	Bear Creek, litter barrels, 🏪
361	TX 16, to Strawn, N 🅁🅂 wb, full ♿ facilities, litter barrels, petwalk, 🏪 vending
358	(from wb), frontage rd
356mm	Russell Creek
354	Lp 254, Ranger
353	S 🅁🅂 wb, full ♿ facilities, litter barrels, petwalk, 🏪 vending
351	(352 from wb), College Blvd
349	FM 2461, Ranger, N 🍴 Love's/Godfather's/Subway/dsl/scales/24hr 🍴 DQ 🛏 Best Inn ⊙ RL RV Park, S 🍴 Shell/dsl ⊙ repair
347	FM 3363 (from wb), Olden, S ⊙ TX Steakhouse
345	FM 3363 (from eb), Olden, S 🍴 TX Steakhouse
343	TX 112, FM 570, Eastland, Lake Leon, N 🍴 Alon/7-11/Subway, Murphy USA/dsl, Shell/dsl 🍴 Chicken Express, DQ, Golden Chick, McDonald's, Pizza Heaven, Sonic, Taco Bell 🛏 Holiday Inn Express, La Quinta, Super 8/RV park ⊙ $General, AT&T, AutoZone, Buick/Cadillac/Chevrolet/GMC, Chrysler/Dodge/Jeep, Ford, O'Reilly Parts, TrueValue, Walmart, S 🍴 Exxon/dsl 🍴 Pulido's Mexican 🛏 Budget Host, Days Inn
340	TX 6, Eastland, N 🍴 Valero/dsl ⊙ 🏥 S 🍴 Shell/dsl
337	spur 490, N ⊙ The Wild Country RV Park
332	US 183, Cisco, N 🍴 Alon/Allsups/dsl, Cow Pokes/dsl 🍴 Chicken Express, DQ, Pizza Heaven, Sonic, Subway 🛏 Cisco Inn, Executive Inn/RV Park ⊙ $General, Family$, Hilton Mon (1mi), NAPA
330	TX 206, Cisco, N 🍴 Stripes/Tacos/dsl/scales/24hr 🛏 Best Value Inn ⊙ 🏥 S 🍴 Flying J/rest./dsl/scales/24hr (2015)
329mm	N 🅁🅂 wb, full ♿ facilities, litter barrels, 🏪
327mm	S 🅁🅂 wb, full ♿ facilities, litter barrels, 🏪
324	Scranton Rd
322	Cooper Creek Rd
320	FM 880 N, FM 2945 N, to Moran
319	FM 880 S, Putnam, N 🍴 Fillin Sta/café ⊙ USPO
316	Brushy Creek Rd
313	FM 2228
310	Finley Rd
308	Lp 20, Baird
307	US 283, Clyde, N 🍴 DQ 🛏 Baird Motel/RV park/dump, S 🍴 Alon/Allsups/7-11, Conoco/dsl 🍴 Robertson's Café
306	FM 2047, Baird, N ⊙ Chevrolet/GMC, Hanner RV Ctr
303	Union Hill Rd
301	FM 604, Cherry Lane, N 🍴 Exxon/Subway/dsl 🍴 McDonald's, Sonic, Whataburger, S 🍴 Alon/7-11/dsl, Shell/dsl 🍴 Chicken Express, Pizza House ⊙ Family$, Lawrence Bros Mkt
300	FM 604 N, Clyde, N ⊙ Chrysler/Dodge/Jeep, S 🍴 Conoco/dsl ⊙ White's RV Park/dump
299	FM 1707, Hays Rd
297	FM 603, Eula Rd
296.5mm	🅁🅂 both lanes, full ♿ facilities, litter barrels, petwalk, 🏪 vending, wireless internet
294	Buck Creek Rd, N ⊙ Big Country RV Ctr/park, Buck Creek RV Park/dump, S ⊙ Abilene RV Park
292b	Elmdale Rd
292a	Lp 20 (exits left from wb)
290	TX 36, Lp 322, S ⊙ 🏪, zoo
288	TX 351, N 🍴 Alon/7-11/dsl, Alon/7-11/dsl, Murphy USA/dsl 🍴 Chick-fil-A, Chili's, Cracker Barrel, DQ, Golden Chick, Jason's Deli, Oscar's Mexican, Panda Express, Subway, Taco Casa, Wendy's 🛏 Comfort Suites, Days Inn, Executive Inn, Holiday Inn Express, Quality Inn, Residence Inn, Whitten Inn ⊙ $Tree, AT&T, Lowe's, Radio Shack, Walmart/Subway, S 🛏 Super 8 ⊙ 🏥
286c	FM 600, Abilene, N 🍴 Alon/7-11/dsl, Alon/Allsups/dsl 🍴 Denny's 🛏 Best Western, Hampton Inn, La Quinta, S 🍴 Alon/7-11/dsl 🛏 Sleep Inn ⊙ Russell Stover Candies
286	US 83, Pine St, Abilene, S 🍴 Alon/Allsups 🛏 Frontier Inn ⊙ 🏥
285	Old Anson Rd, S 🍴 Alon/Allsups/dsl 🛏 Best Value Inn
283b	N US 277, U83, Anson
283a	US 277 S, US 83 (exits left from wb)
282	FM 3438, Shirley Rd, S 🛏 Motel 6 ⊙ KOA
281	Fulwiler Rd, to Dyess AFB, ⊙ to Dyess AFB
279	US 84 E, to Abilene, S 1-3 mi access to facilities
278	Lp 20, N 🍴 Conoco/dsl/24hr ⊙ dsl repair, S 🍴 Westgo TC/Conoco/rest/dsl/scales/24hr/@ ⊙ Mack Trucks/Volvo
277	FM 707, Tye, N 🍴 Flying J/Denny's/dsl/LP/24hr ⊙ Peterbilt, truck lube, Tye RV Park, S 🍴 Alon/7-11/dsl ⊙ USPO

Map labels: Greenville, Mount Vernon, Plano, Royse City, Garland, Dallas, Terrell, Mineola, Kaufman, Canton, Gladewater, Palmer, Ben Wheeler, Tyler, Ennis, Rice, Athens, Corsicana, TX

ABILENE

🅶 = gas   🍴 = food   🏠 = lodging   🅾 = other   🆁🆂 = rest stop   Copyright 2015 - the Next EXIT ®

INTERSTATE 20 Cont'd

Exit #	Services
274	Wells Lane
272	Wimberly Rd
270	FM 1235, Merkel, N 🅶 Conoco/dsl, Shell/dsl/24hr
269	FM 126, N 🍴 Sonic, Subway 🏠 Scottish Inn, S 🅶 Alon/7-11/dsl, Shell/dsl 🍴 DQ, Skeet's BBQ 🅾 CarQuest, Family$
267	Lp 20, Merkel, S 1 mi access to 🅶, 🍴, 🏠
266	Derstine Rd
264	Noodle Dome Rd
263	Lp 20, Trent, N 🅾 RV Park
262	FM 1085, S 🅶 Alon/7-11/dsl
261	Lp 20, Trent
259	Sylvester Rd
258	White Flat Rd, oil wells
257mm	🆁🆂 both lanes, full 🅱 facilities, litter barrels, petwalk, 🏕 vending
256	Stink Creek Rd
255	Adrian Rd
251	Eskota Rd
249	FM 1856, N 🅾 Lonestar RV Park
247	TX 70 N, Sweetwater
246	Alabama Ave, Sweetwater
245	Arizona Ave (from wb), same as 244
244	TX 70 S, Sweetwater, N 🅶 Alon/7-11/dsl/24hr, Chevron/Subway/dsl, Murphy USA/dsl 🍴 Domino's, DQ, Golden Chick, McDonald's, Subway, Wendy's 🏠 Best Western, Budget Inn, La Quinta, Motel 6 🅾 H AutoZone, Medicine Place Drug, Verizon, Walmart, S 🅶 Shell/dsl 🍴 Big Boy's BBQ, Buck's BBQ, Great Wall Buffet, Schlotzsky's, Skeet's Grill, Taco Bell 🏠 Country Hearth Inn, Hampton Inn, Holiday Inn Express, Ranch House Motel/rest., Stay Express Inn 🅾 Chaparral RV Park, Ford, K-Mart, Rainbolt RV Park
243	Hillsdale Rd, Robert Lee St, N 🅾 Family RV Ctr
242	Hopkins Rd, N 🅶 ♥Loves/Arby's/dsl/scales/24hr, S 🅶 TA/Pizza Hut/Popeye's/dsl/scales/24hr/@ 🅾 Rolling Plains RV Park, truck wash, truck/tire repair
241	Lp 20, Sweetwater, N 🅶, 🍴, 🏠 S 🅾 RV camping
240	Lp 170, N 🅾 🖴, camping
239	May Rd
238b a	US 84 W, Blackland Rd
237	Cemetery Rd
236	FM 608, Roscoe, N 🅶 Shell/dsl, Stripes/Taco Co/dsl 🅾 NAPA, S 🍴 Retta Mae's Rest
235	to US 84, Roscoe
230	FM 1230, many wind turbines
229mm	🆁🆂 wb, full 🅱 facilities, litter barrels, 🏕
228mm	🆁🆂 eb, full 🅱 facilities, litter barrels, 🏕
227	Narrell Rd
226b	Lp 20 (from wb), Loraine
226a	FM 644 N, Wimberly Rd
225	FM 644 S, S 1 mi 🅶 access to gas 🍴
224	Lp 20, to Loraine, S 1 mi 🅶 gas 🍴
223	Lucas Rd, S 🅾 223 RV Park
221	Lasky Rd
220	FM 1899
219	Lp 20, Country Club Rd, Colorado City
217	TX 208 S
216	TX 208 N, N 🅶 Chevron/Subway/dsl 🍴 DQ 🏠 Days Inn, S 🅶 Stripes/Taco Co/dsl 🍴 Golden Chick, Pizza Hut, Sonic 🏠 American Inn, Western Suites 🅾 H $General, Alco, City RV Park, Medicine Place Drug, Parts+

215	FM 3525, Rogers Rd, S 2 mi 🅶 access to gas 🍴 🅾 H
214.5mm	Colorado River
213	Lp 20, Enderly Rd, Colorado City
212	FM 1229
211mm	Morgan Creek, Morgan Creek
210	FM 2836, S 🅾 camping, 🏕 to Lake Colorado City SP
209	Dorn Rd
207	Lp 20, Westbrook
206	FM 670, to Westbrook
204mm	N 🆁🆂 wb, full 🅱 facilities, litter barrels, petwalk, 🛗 🏕
200	Conaway Rd
199	Iatan Rd
195	frontage rd (from eb)
194a	E Howard Field Rd
192	FM 821, many oil wells
191mm	🆁🆂 eb, full 🅱 facilities, litter barrels, petwalk, 🛗 🏕
190	Snyder Field Rd
189	McGregor Rd
188	FM 820, Coahoma, N 🅶 Stripes/Taco Co/dsl 🍴 DQ 🏠 Coahoma Inn 🅾 Coahoma RV Park, USPO
186	Salem Rd, Sand Springs
184	Moss Lake Rd, Sand Springs, N 🅶 Alon/dsl, S 🅾 RV camping
182	Midway Rd
181b	Refinery Rd, N 🅾 Alon Refinery
181a	FM 700, N 🖴, RV camping, S 2 mi H, N 🅾 🖴, RV camping, S 2 mi 🅾 H
179	US 80, Big Spring, S 🅶 Alon/7-11 🍴 Denny's 🏠 Camlot Inn, Quality Inn, Super 8 🅾 $General, Buick/Cadillac/Chevrolet
178	TX 350, Big Spring, N 🅶 Shell/dsl 🅾 tire/truck service, S 🅶 Pilot/McDonald's/dsl/scales/24hr
177	US 87, Big Spring, N 🅶 Exxon/dsl, TA/Subway/Popeye's/dsl/scales/24hr/@ 🍴 Texas Cajun Cafe 🏠 Advantage Inn, La Quinta, Motel 6, Plaza Inn, S 🅶 Alon/dsl, Stripes/dsl 🍴 Casa Blanca Mexican, DQ 🏠 Best Western, Hampton Inn, Holiday Inn Express
176	TX 176, Andrews
174	Lp 20 E, Big Springs, S 🅶 Shell/dsl 🅾 H 🖴, Big Spring SP
172	Cauble Rd
171	Moore Field Rd
169	FM 2599
168mm	🆁🆂 both lanes, litter barrels, 🏕
165	FM 818
158	Lp 20 W, to Stanton, N 🅾 RV camping
156	TX 137, Lamesa, S 🅶 Phillips 66/Stripes/Subway/dsl/24hr 🍴 Sonic 🏠 Cobblestone Inn, Comfort Inn
154	US 80, Stanton, S 2 mi access to 🅶, 🍴, 🏠
151	FM 829 (from wb)
144	Loop 250, N 2-3 mi facilities in Midland
143mm	frontage rd (from eb)
142mm	🆁🆂 both lanes, historic marker, litter barrels, 🏕
140	FM 307 (from eb)
138	TX 158, FM 715, Greenwood, N 🅶 Pilot/dsl, Shell/dsl 🍴 KD's BBQ, Whataburger, S 🅶 Stripes/Subway/dsl, Stripes/Taco Co/dsl
137	Old Lamesa Rd
136	TX 349, Midland, N 🅶 Murphy USA/dsl, Stripes/Taco Co/dsl 🍴 Cici's Pizza, Domino's, IHOP, Jack-in-the-Box, Little Caesars, McAlister's Deli, McDonald's, Sonic, Starbucks 🏠 Best Western, Candlewood Suites, Comfort Inn, Country Inn&Suites, Holiday Inn Express, Microtel, Quality Inn, West Texas Inn 🅾 $General, $Tree, Advance Parts, AutoZone,

TX

SWEETWATER

BIG SPRING

MIDLAND

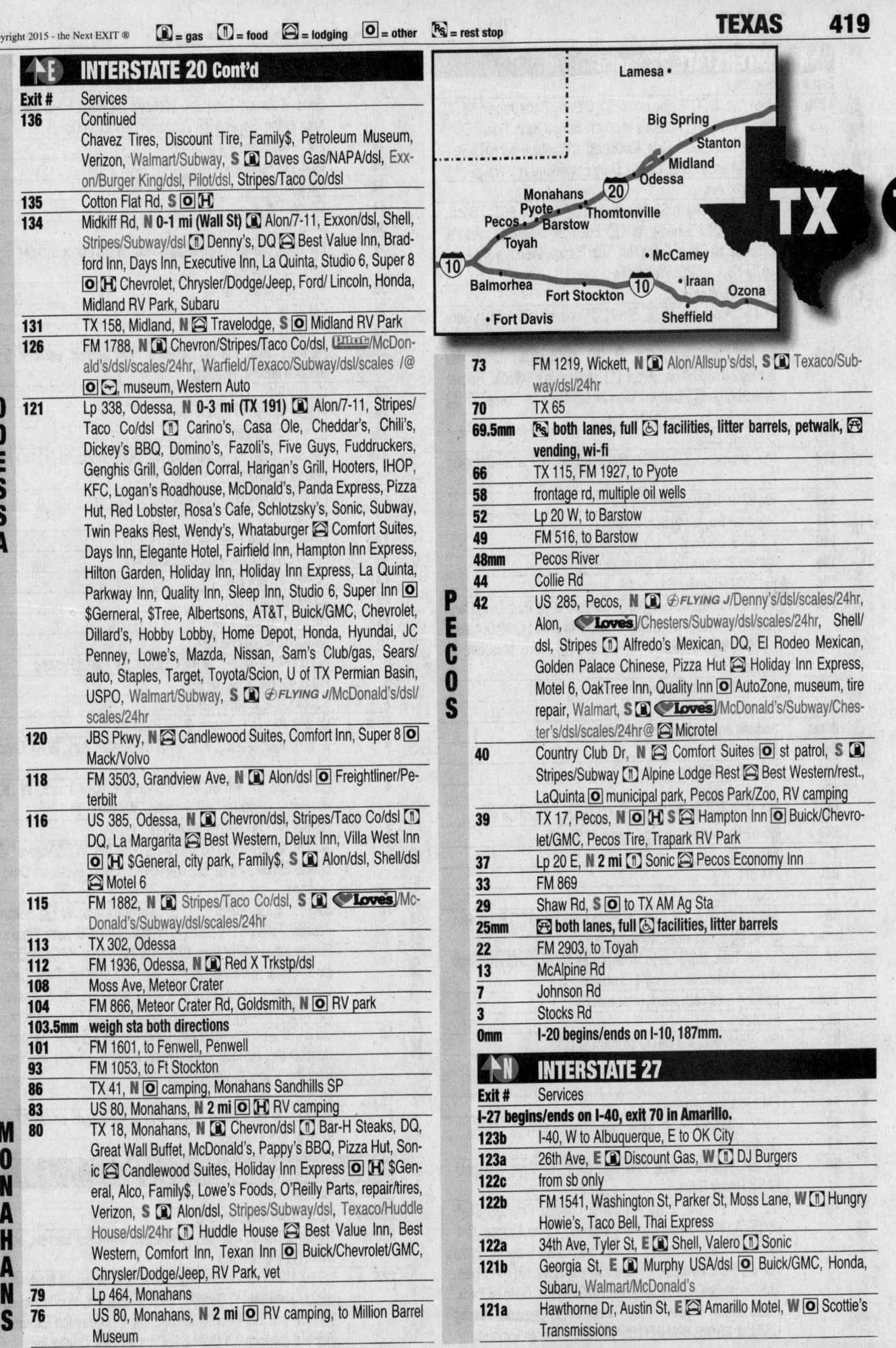

🄴 INTERSTATE 20 Cont'd

Exit #	Services
136	Continued
	Chavez Tires, Discount Tire, Family$, Petroleum Museum, Verizon, Walmart/Subway, **S** 🅿 Daves Gas/NAPA/dsl, Exxon/Burger King/dsl, Pilot/dsl, Stripes/Taco Co/dsl
135	Cotton Flat Rd, **S** 🅾 🄷
134	Midkiff Rd, **N** 0-1 mi (Wall St) 🅿 Alon/7-11, Exxon/dsl, Shell, Stripes/Subway/dsl 🍴 Denny's, DQ 🛏 Best Value Inn, Bradford Inn, Days Inn, Executive Inn, La Quinta, Studio 6, Super 8 🅾 🄷 Chevrolet, Chrysler/Dodge/Jeep, Ford/ Lincoln, Honda, Midland RV Park, Subaru
131	TX 158, Midland, **N** 🛏 Travelodge, **S** 🅾 Midland RV Park
126	FM 1788, **N** 🅿 Chevron/Stripes/Taco Co/dsl, ⛽McDonald's/dsl/scales/24hr, Warfield/Texaco/Subway/dsl/scales /@ 🅾 Ⓡ🆂, museum, Western Auto
121	Lp 338, Odessa, **N** 0-3 mi (TX 191) 🅿 Alon/7-11, Stripes/Taco Co/dsl 🍴 Carino's, Casa Ole, Cheddar's, Chili's, Dickey's BBQ, Domino's, Fazoli's, Five Guys, Fuddruckers, Genghis Grill, Golden Corral, Harigan's Grill, Hooters, IHOP, KFC, Logan's Roadhouse, McDonald's, Panda Express, Pizza Hut, Red Lobster, Rosa's Cafe, Schlotzsky's, Sonic, Subway, Twin Peaks Rest, Wendy's, Whataburger 🛏 Comfort Suites, Days Inn, Elegante Hotel, Fairfield Inn, Hampton Inn Express, Hilton Garden, Holiday Inn, Holiday Inn Express, La Quinta, Parkway Inn, Quality Inn, Sleep Inn, Studio 6, Super Inn 🅾 $Gerneral, $Tree, Albertsons, AT&T, Buick/GMC, Chevrolet, Dillard's, Hobby Lobby, Home Depot, Honda, Hyundai, JC Penney, Lowe's, Mazda, Nissan, Sam's Club/gas, Sears/auto, Staples, Target, Toyota/Scion, U of TX Permian Basin, USPO, Walmart/Subway, **S** 🅿 ⊕FLYING J/McDonald's/dsl/scales/24hr
120	JBS Pkwy, **N** 🛏 Candlewood Suites, Comfort Inn, Super 8 🅾 Mack/Volvo
118	FM 3503, Grandview Ave, **N** 🅿 Alon/dsl 🅾 Freightliner/Peterbilt
116	US 385, Odessa, **N** 🅿 Chevron/dsl, Stripes/Taco Co/dsl 🍴 DQ, La Margarita 🛏 Best Western, Delux Inn, Villa West Inn 🅾 🄷 $General, city park, Family$, **S** 🅿 Alon/dsl, Shell/dsl 🛏 Motel 6
115	FM 1882, **N** 🅿 Stripes/Taco Co/dsl, **S** 🅿 Loves/McDonald's/Subway/dsl/scales/24hr
113	TX 302, Odessa
112	FM 1936, Odessa, **N** 🅿 Red X Trkstp/dsl
108	Moss Ave, Meteor Crater
104	FM 866, Meteor Crater Rd, Goldsmith, **N** 🅾 RV park
103.5mm	weigh sta both directions
101	FM 1601, to Fenwell, Penwell
93	FM 1053, to Ft Stockton
86	TX 41, **N** 🅾 camping, Monahans Sandhills SP
83	US 80, Monahans, **N** 2 mi 🅾 🄷 RV camping
80	TX 18, Monahans, **N** 🅿 Chevron/dsl 🍴 Bar-H Steaks, DQ, Great Wall Buffet, McDonald's, Pappy's BBQ, Pizza Hut, Sonic 🛏 Candlewood Suites, Holiday Inn Express 🅾 🄷 $General, Alco, Family$, Lowe's Foods, O'Reilly Parts, repair/tires, Verizon, **S** 🅿 Alon/dsl, Stripes/Subway/dsl, Texaco/Huddle House/dsl/24hr 🍴 Huddle House 🛏 Best Value Inn, Best Western, Comfort Inn, Texan Inn 🅾 Buick/Chevrolet/GMC, Chrysler/Dodge/Jeep, RV Park, vet
79	Lp 464, Monahans
76	US 80, Monahans, **N** 2 mi 🅾 RV camping, to Million Barrel Museum

73	FM 1219, Wickett, **N** 🅿 Alon/Allsup's/dsl, **S** 🅿 Texaco/Subway/dsl/24hr
70	TX 65
69.5mm	Ⓡ🆂 both lanes, full ♿ facilities, litter barrels, petwalk, 🏧 vending, wi-fi
66	TX 115, FM 1927, to Pyote
58	frontage rd, multiple oil wells
52	Lp 20 W, to Barstow
49	FM 516, to Barstow
48mm	Pecos River
44	Collie Rd
42	US 285, Pecos, **N** 🅿 ⊕FLYING J/Denny's/dsl/scales/24hr, Alon, Loves/Chesters/Subway/dsl/scales/24hr, Shell/dsl, Stripes 🍴 Alfredo's Mexican, DQ, El Rodeo Mexican, Golden Palace Chinese, Pizza Hut 🛏 Holiday Inn Express, Motel 6, OakTree Inn, Quality Inn 🅾 AutoZone, museum, tire repair, Walmart, **S** 🅿 Loves/McDonald's/Subway/Chester's/dsl/scales/24hr@ 🛏 Microtel
40	Country Club Dr, **N** 🛏 Comfort Suites 🅾 st patrol, **S** 🅿 Stripes/Subway 🍴 Alpine Lodge Rest 🛏 Best Western/rest., LaQuinta 🅾 municipal park, Pecos Park/Zoo, RV camping
39	TX 17, Pecos, **N** 🅾 🄷 **S** 🛏 Hampton Inn 🅾 Buick/Chevrolet/GMC, Pecos Tire, Trapark RV Park
37	Lp 20 E, **N** 2 mi 🍴 Sonic 🛏 Pecos Economy Inn
33	FM 869
29	Shaw Rd, **S** 🅾 to TX AM Ag Sta
25mm	🏧 both lanes, full ♿ facilities, litter barrels
22	FM 2903, to Toyah
13	McAlpine Rd
7	Johnson Rd
3	Stocks Rd
0mm	I-20 begins/ends on I-10, 187mm.

🄽 INTERSTATE 27

Exit #	Services
	I-27 begins/ends on I-40, exit 70 in Amarillo.
123b	I-40, W to Albuquerque, E to OK City
123a	26th Ave, **E** 🅿 Discount Gas, **W** 🍴 DJ Burgers
122c	from sb only
122b	FM 1541, Washington St, Parker St, Moss Lane, **W** 🍴 Hungry Howie's, Taco Bell, Thai Express
122a	34th Ave, Tyler St, **E** 🅿 Shell, Valero 🍴 Sonic
121b	Georgia St, **E** 🅿 Murphy USA/dsl 🅾 Buick/GMC, Honda, Subaru, Walmart/McDonald's
121a	Hawthorne Dr, Austin St, **E** 🛏 Amarillo Motel, **W** 🅾 Scottie's Transmissions

⬆N INTERSTATE 27 Cont'd

AMARILLO

Exit #	Services
120b	45th Ave, **E** ⊞ Waffle House ⊡ O'Reilly Parts, repair, **W** ⊞ Shell, Valero ⊞ Abuelo's Mexican, Burger King, Donut Stop, Gatti's Pizza, GJ's Cafe, McDonald's, Whataburger ⊡ $General, Advance Parts, Dodge, Drug Emporium, vet, Walgreens
120a	Republic Ave
119b a	(from sb), Western St, 58th Ave, **E** ⊞ Phillips 66 ⊞ Sonic, Subway ⊡ $General, **W** ⊞ Shell/dsl, Valero ⊞ Arby's, Braum's, LJ Silver, Pizza Hut, Thai Palace, Wendy's ⊡ Aamco, U-Haul, USPO, Walgreens
119a	(from nb), W Hillside
117	Bell St, Arden Rd, **W** ⊞ Shell ⊞ Popeye's, Sonic ⊡ $General
116	Lp 335, Hollywood Rd, **E** ⊞ Loves/Subway/dsl/scales/24hr, Phillips 66/dsl ⊞ McDonald's, Waffle House, Whataburger ⊟ Canyon View Motel, Comfort Suites, **W** ⊟ Holiday Inn Express ⊡ Ⓗ (8mi)
115	Sundown Lane
113	McCormick Rd, **E** ⊡ $General, Ford, **W** ⊡ Family Camping Ctr
112	FM 2219, **E** ⊡ Stater's RV Ctr
111	Rockwell Rd, **W** ⊡ Buick/GMC
110	US 87 S, US 60 W, Canyon
109	Buffalo Stadium Rd, **W** ⊡ stadium
108	FM 3331, Hunsley Rd
106	TX 217, to Palo Duro Cyn SP, Canyon, **E** ⊡ Palo Duro Canyon SP (10 mi), Palo Duro RV Park, **W 3 mi** ⊞ McDonald's ⊟ Buffalo Inn, Holiday Inn Express ⊡ Plains Museum, to WTA&M
103	FM 1541 N, Cemetery Rd
99	Hungate Rd
98mm	**parking area both lanes, litter barrels**
96	Dowlen Rd
94	FM 285, to Wayside
92	Haley Rd
90	FM 1075, Happy, **W** ⊞ gas/dsl ⊞ Happy Place Cafe
88b a	US 87 N, FM 1881, Happy, same as 90
83	FM 2698
82	FM 214
77	US 87, Tulia
75	NW 6th St, Tulia, **E 1 mi** ⊞ Phillips 66, Shell ⊞ Pizza Hut, Sonic ⊟ Lasso Motel, **W** same as 74
74	TX 86, Tulia, **E** ⊟ Lasso Motel ⊡ Ⓗ **W** ⊞ Rip Griffin/Shell/Subway/dsl/scales/24hr ⊟ Executive Inn
70mm	**parking area both lanes, litter barrels**
68	FM 928
63	FM 145, Kress, **E 1 mi** ⊞ gas/dsl ⊞, Ⓒ

PLAINVIEW

61	US 87, County Rd
56	FM 788
54	FM 3183, to Plainview
53	Lp 27, Plainview, **E** ⊡ Ⓗ access to gas, camping, ⊞, ⊟
51	Quincy St
50	TX 194, Plainview, **E** ⊞ Phillips 66 ⊡ Ⓗ to Wayland Bapt U, **W** ⊟ Reddy Hotel
49	US 70, Plainview, **E** ⊞ Allstar/dsl, Conoco, Fina/dsl, Shell/dsl ⊞ A&W/LJ Silver, Carlito's Mexican, China Dragon, Cotton Patch Café, Domino's, Furr's Café, Leal's Mexican, Pizza Hut ⊟ Best Western, Comfort Suites, Days Inn ⊡ $Tree, AutoZone, Beall's, Ford/Lincoln, GNC, NAPA, O'Reilly Parts, Radio Shack, Toyota, United Foods, **W** ⊞ Chevron, Murphy USA/dsl, Phillips 66/dsl ⊞ Burger King, Chicken Express,

49	Continued
	Chili's, Empire Buffet, IHOP, McDonald's, Monterrey Mexican, Sonic, Subway, Taco Bell, Wendy's ⊟ Holiday Inn Express, Knights Inn, Super 8 ⊡ Verizon, Walmart/McDonald's
48	FM 3466, Plainview (from nb)
45	Lp 27, to Plainview
43	FM 2337
41	County Rd
38	Main St
37	FM 1914, Cleveland St, **E** ⊞ Co-op, **W** ⊞ Conoco ⊡ Ⓗ city park, Lowe's Foods
36	FM 1424 , Hale Center
32	FM 37 W
31	FM 37 E
29mm	ℝ𝕤 both lanes, full & facilities, litter barrels, petwalk, tornado shelter, vending
27	County Rd
24	FM 54, **W** ⊡ RV park/dump
22	Lp 369, Abernathy
21	FM 597, Main St, Abernathy, **W** ⊞ Conoco/dsl ⊞ DQ ⊡ $General, USPO
20	FM 597, Abernathy (from nb)
17	CR 53
15	Lp 461, to New Deal, same as 14
14	FM 1729, ⊞ Fina/rest/dsl/scales/24hr
13	Lp 461, to New Deal
12	access rd (from nb)
11	FM 1294, Shallowater
10	Keuka St, **E** ⊡ Fed Ex
9	Airport Rd, **E** ⊡ ⊟, **W** ⊡ Lubbock RV Park/LP/dump
8	FM 2641, Regis St, ⊡ ⊟
7	Yucca Lane, **E** ⊡ Pharr RV Ctr
6b a	Lp 289, Ave Q, Lubbock, **E** ⊡ Pharr RV
5	B. Holly Ave, Municipal Dr, **E** ⊡ Mackenzie Park, **W** ⊡ Civic Ctr
4	US 82, US 87, 4th St, to Crosbyton, **E** ⊡ funpark, **W** ⊞ ⊘FLYING J/Subway/dsl/LP/scales/24hr ⊡ to TTU
3	US 62, TX 114, 19th St, Floydada
2	34th St, **E** ⊞ Phillips 66 ⊞ Pete's Drive Inn, **W** ⊞ Valero ⊞ Simple Simon's Pizza, Subway ⊡ AutoZone, Raff&Hall Drug, U-Haul

LUBBOCK

1c	50th St, **E** ⊞ Buddy's ⊞ El Jalapeno Café, **W** ⊞ Bolton Fuel/dsl, Fina/7-11, Valero ⊞ A&W/LJ Silver, Bryan's Steaks, Burger King, China Star, Church's, Domino's, KFC, McDonald's, Pizza Hut/Taco Bell, Subway, Taco Villa, Tech Cafe, Whataburger, Wienerschnitzel ⊟ Travelodge ⊡ $General, Family$, O'Reilly Parts, United Food/gas, USPO, Walgreens
1b	US 84, **E** ⊟ Best Value Inn, Days Inn, **W** ⊟ Best Western, Comfort Inn, Holiday Inn Express, Motel 6, Quality Inn, Red Roof Inn, Super 8, Value Place
1a	Lp 289
1	82nd St, **W** ⊞ Phillips 66/dsl. **I-27 begins/ends on US 87 at 82nd St in S Lubbock.**

⬆E INTERSTATE 30

Exit #	Services
223mm	Texas/Arkansas state line
223mm	**Welcome Center wb, full & facilities, info, litter barrels, petwalk, Ⓒ, ⊟ vending**
223b a	US 59, US 71, State Line Ave, Texarkana, **N** ⊞ EZ Mart, Mobil/dsl, Shell/dsl ⊞ Denny's, IHOP, Pizza Inn, Waffle House ⊟ Baymont Inn, Best Western, Clarion, Holiday Inn Express, Howard Johnson, La Quinta, LaCrosse Hotel, Quality Inn,

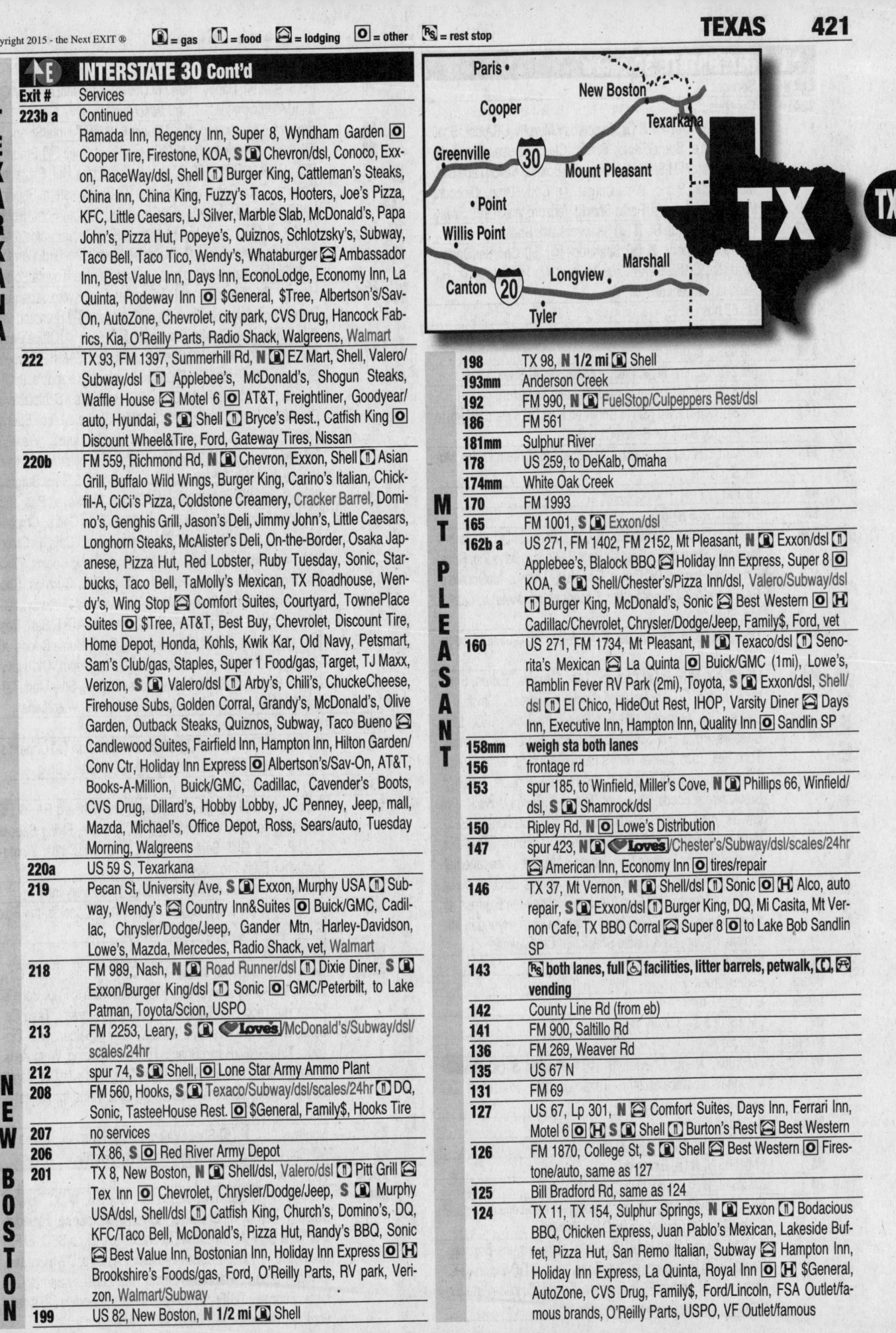

INTERSTATE 30 Cont'd

T E X A R K A N A

Exit #	Services
223b a	Continued
	Ramada Inn, Regency Inn, Super 8, Wyndham Garden 🄾 Cooper Tire, Firestone, KOA, **S** ⛽ Chevron/dsl, Conoco, Exxon, RaceWay/dsl, Shell 🍴 Burger King, Cattleman's Steaks, China Inn, China King, Fuzzy's Tacos, Hooters, Joe's Pizza, KFC, Little Caesars, LJ Silver, Marble Slab, McDonald's, Papa John's, Pizza Hut, Popeye's, Quiznos, Schlotzsky's, Subway, Taco Bell, Taco Tico, Wendy's, Whataburger 🛏 Ambassador Inn, Best Value Inn, Days Inn, EconoLodge, Economy Inn, La Quinta, Rodeway Inn 🄾 $General, $Tree, Albertson's/Sav-On, AutoZone, Chevrolet, city park, CVS Drug, Hancock Fabrics, Kia, O'Reilly Parts, Radio Shack, Walgreens, Walmart
222	TX 93, FM 1397, Summerhill Rd, **N** ⛽ EZ Mart, Shell, Valero/Subway/dsl 🍴 Applebee's, McDonald's, Shogun Steaks, Waffle House 🛏 Motel 6 🄾 AT&T, Freightliner, Goodyear/auto, Hyundai, **S** ⛽ Shell 🍴 Bryce's Rest., Catfish King 🄾 Discount Wheel&Tire, Ford, Gateway Tires, Nissan
220b	FM 559, Richmond Rd, **N** ⛽ Chevron, Exxon, Shell 🍴 Asian Grill, Buffalo Wild Wings, Burger King, Carino's Italian, Chick-fil-A, CiCi's Pizza, Coldstone Creamery, Cracker Barrel, Domino's, Genghis Grill, Jason's Deli, Jimmy John's, Little Caesars, Longhorn Steaks, McAlister's Deli, On-the-Border, Osaka Japanese, Pizza Hut, Red Lobster, Ruby Tuesday, Sonic, Starbucks, Taco Bell, TaMolly's Mexican, TX Roadhouse, Wendy's, Wing Stop 🛏 Comfort Suites, Courtyard, TownePlace Suites 🄾 $Tree, AT&T, Best Buy, Chevrolet, Discount Tire, Home Depot, Honda, Kohls, Kwik Kar, Old Navy, Petsmart, Sam's Club/gas, Staples, Super 1 Food/gas, Target, TJ Maxx, Verizon, **S** ⛽ Valero/dsl 🍴 Arby's, Chili's, ChuckeCheese, Firehouse Subs, Golden Corral, Grandy's, McDonald's, Olive Garden, Outback Steaks, Quiznos, Subway, Taco Bueno 🛏 Candlewood Suites, Fairfield Inn, Hampton Inn, Hilton Garden/Conv Ctr, Holiday Inn Express 🄾 Albertson's/Sav-On, AT&T, Books-A-Million, Buick/GMC, Cadillac, Cavender's Boots, CVS Drug, Dillard's, Hobby Lobby, JC Penney, Jeep, mall, Mazda, Michael's, Office Depot, Ross, Sears/auto, Tuesday Morning, Walgreens
220a	US 59 S, Texarkana
219	Pecan St, University Ave, **S** ⛽ Exxon, Murphy USA 🍴 Subway, Wendy's 🛏 Country Inn&Suites 🄾 Buick/GMC, Cadillac, Chrysler/Dodge/Jeep, Gander Mtn, Harley-Davidson, Lowe's, Mazda, Mercedes, Radio Shack, vet, Walmart
218	FM 989, Nash, **N** ⛽ Road Runner/dsl 🍴 Dixie Diner, **S** ⛽ Exxon/Burger King/dsl 🍴 Sonic 🄾 GMC/Peterbilt, to Lake Patman, Toyota/Scion, USPO
213	FM 2253, Leary, **S** ⛽ ♥Love's/McDonald's/Subway/dsl/scales/24hr
212	spur 74, **S** ⛽ Shell, 🄾 Lone Star Army Ammo Plant
208	FM 560, Hooks, **S** ⛽ Texaco/Subway/dsl/scales/24hr 🍴 DQ, Sonic, TasteeHouse Rest. 🄾 $General, Family$, Hooks Tire
207	no services
206	TX 86, **S** 🄾 Red River Army Depot
201	TX 8, New Boston, **N** ⛽ Shell/dsl, Valero/dsl 🍴 Pitt Grill 🛏 Tex Inn 🄾 Chevrolet, Chrysler/Dodge/Jeep, **S** ⛽ Murphy USA/dsl, Shell/dsl 🍴 Catfish King, Church's, Domino's, DQ, KFC/Taco Bell, McDonald's, Pizza Hut, Randy's BBQ, Sonic 🛏 Best Value Inn, Bostonian Inn, Holiday Inn Express 🄾 🄷 Brookshire's Foods/gas, Ford, O'Reilly Parts, RV park, Verizon, Walmart/Subway
199	US 82, New Boston, **N** 1/2 mi ⛽ Shell

N E W   B O S T O N

198	TX 98, **N** 1/2 mi ⛽ Shell
193mm	Anderson Creek
192	FM 990, **N** ⛽ FuelStop/Culpeppers Rest/dsl
186	FM 561
181mm	Sulphur River
178	US 259, to DeKalb, Omaha
174mm	White Oak Creek
170	FM 1993
165	FM 1001, **S** ⛽ Exxon/dsl
162b a	US 271, FM 1402, FM 2152, Mt Pleasant, **N** ⛽ Exxon/dsl 🍴 Applebee's, Blalock BBQ 🛏 Holiday Inn Express, Super 8 🄾 KOA, **S** ⛽ Shell/Chester's/Pizza Inn/dsl, Valero/Subway/dsl 🍴 Burger King, McDonald's, Sonic 🛏 Best Western 🄾 🄷 Cadillac/Chevrolet, Chrysler/Dodge/Jeep, Family$, Ford, vet
160	US 271, FM 1734, Mt Pleasant, **N** ⛽ Texaco/dsl 🍴 Senorita's Mexican 🛏 La Quinta 🄾 Buick/GMC (1mi), Lowe's, Ramblin Fever RV Park (2mi), Toyota, **S** ⛽ Exxon/dsl, Shell/dsl 🍴 El Chico, HideOut Rest, IHOP, Varsity Diner 🛏 Days Inn, Executive Inn, Hampton Inn, Quality Inn 🄾 Sandlin SP
158mm	weigh sta both lanes
156	frontage rd
153	spur 185, to Winfield, Miller's Cove, **N** ⛽ Phillips 66, Winfield/dsl, **S** ⛽ Shamrock/dsl
150	Ripley Rd, **N** 🄾 Lowe's Distribution
147	spur 423, **N** ⛽ ♥Love's/Chester's/Subway/dsl/scales/24hr 🛏 American Inn, Economy Inn 🄾 tires/repair
146	TX 37, Mt Vernon, **N** ⛽ Shell/dsl 🍴 Sonic 🄾 🄷 Alco, auto repair, **S** ⛽ Exxon/dsl 🍴 Burger King, DQ, Mi Casita, Mt Vernon Cafe, TX BBQ Corral 🛏 Super 8 🄾 to Lake Bob Sandlin SP
143	🆁🆂 both lanes, full ♿ facilities, litter barrels, petwalk, 🄲, 🖼 vending
142	County Line Rd (from eb)
141	FM 900, Saltillo Rd
136	FM 269, Weaver Rd
135	US 67 N
131	FM 69
127	US 67, Lp 301, **N** ⛽ Comfort Suites, Days Inn, Ferrari Inn, Motel 6 🄾 🄷 **S** ⛽ Shell 🍴 Burton's Rest 🛏 Best Western
126	FM 1870, College St, **S** ⛽ Shell 🛏 Best Western 🄾 Firestone/auto, same as 127
125	Bill Bradford Rd, same as 124
124	TX 11, TX 154, Sulphur Springs, **N** ⛽ Exxon 🍴 Bodacious BBQ, Chicken Express, Juan Pablo's Mexican, Lakeside Buffet, Pizza Hut, San Remo Italian, Subway 🛏 Hampton Inn, Holiday Inn Express, La Quinta, Royal Inn 🄾 🄷 $General, AutoZone, CVS Drug, Family$, Ford/Lincoln, FSA Outlet/famous brands, O'Reilly Parts, USPO, VF Outlet/famous

MT PLEASANT

TX

🔼E INTERSTATE 30 Cont'd

Exit #	Services
124	Continued
	brands, Walgreens, **S** 🅖 Exxon/dsl, Murphy USA/dsl, Shell 🍴 Braum's, Burger King, Chili's, China House, Domino's, Furr's Rest., H-H Steaks, Jack-in-the-Box, LJ Silver/Taco Bell, McDonald's, Sonic, Whataburger 🅞 Cody Drug, Discount Wheel&Tire, Lowe's, Radio Shack, Verizon, Walmart/Subway
123	FM 2297, League St, **N** 🅖 Shamrock/dsl, Shell
122	TX 19, to Emory, **N** 🅖 Shamrock 🅞 🏥 Chrysler/Dodge/Jeep, **S** 🅖 🆃🅰 /Arby's/dsl/scales/24hr 🅞 dsl repair, RV Park, to Cooper Lake SP, vet
120	US 67 bus
116	FM 2653, Brashear Rd
112	FM 499 (from wb)
110	FM 275, Cumby, **N** 🅖 Phillips 66/dsl, **S** 🅖 Shell
104	FM 513, FM 2649, Campbell, **S** to Lake Tawakoni
101	TX 24, TX 50, FM 1737, to Commerce, **N** 🅖 Valero/dsl 🅞 to E TX St U, **S** 🍴 TX Beach Club Grill
97	Lamar St, **N** 🅖 Exxon/dsl 🏠 Budget Inn, Dream Lodge Motel, **S** 🅞 vet
96	Lp 302
95	Division St, **S** 🅞 🏥
94b	US 69, US 380, Greenville, **N** 🅖 Valero/dsl 🍴 Senorita's Mexican, Shumardii's Rest 🏠 Best Value Inn, Days Inn, Royal Inn, Travelodge, **S** 🅖 Exxon, Fina/dsl 🍴 Arby's, McDonald's, Racho Viejo 🏠 EconoLodge, Economy Inn, Motel 6, Quality Inn, Super 8
94a	US 69, US 380 , Greenville, **S** 🅖 Valero 🅞 Chrysler/Dodge/Jeep
93b a	US 67, TX 34 N, **N** 🅖 Chevron/Taco Casa/dsl, Exxon, Shell/dsl, Texaco 🍴 Applebee's, Chicken Express, Chick-fil-A, CiCi's, DQ, Grandy's, IHOP, Jack-in-the-Box, KFC, Little Caesars, Pizza Hut, Schlotzsky's, Sonic, Starbucks, Subway, Taco Bell, Taco Bueno, Tony's Italian, Wendy's, Whataburger 🏠 Hampton Inn 🅞 🏥 AT&T, Beall's, Belk, BigLots, Braum's, Brookshire's Foods, Discount Tire, JC Penney, Kwik Kar, Lowe's, mall, O'Reilly Parts, Staples, transmissions, USPO, Verizon, Walgreens, **S** 🅖 Exxon/dsl, Valero/dsl 🍴 Chili's, Cracker Barrel, Jersey's Grill, Molino's Mexican, Paesano Italian, Papa Murphy's, Red Lobster, Soulman's BBQ, Subway, TaMolly's Mexican 🏠 Best Western, Holiday Inn Express 🅞 $Tree, Buick/GMC, Ford/Lincoln, Home Depot, Hyundai, Mitsubishi, Nissan, NTB, Radio Shack, RV Ctr, Walmart
92	Stratton Pkwy
90mm	Farber Creek
89mm	E Caddo Creek
89	FM 1570, **S** 🏠 Luxury Inn
87mm	Elm Creek
87	FM 1903, **N** 🅖 Chevron/dsl 🅞 fireworks, **S** 🅖 🆃🅰 /McDonald's/dsl/scales/24hr, Texaco/Huddle House/dsl 🍴 Baker's Ribs 🅞 tire repair
85mm	W Caddo Creek
85	FM 36, Caddo Mills, **N** 🅞 KOA
83	FM 1565 N, **N** 🅖 Exxon/dsl
79	FM 2642, **N** 🅞 Budget RV Ctr, **S** 🅞 vet
77b	FM 35, Royse City, **N** 🅖 Exxon/dsl, Texaco/Subway/dsl/scales/24hr 🍴 Soulman's BBQ 🅞 Family$
77a	TX 548, Royse City, **N** 🅖 Shell/dsl 🍴 Jack-in-the-Box, McDonald's 🏠 Royse Inn 🅞 AutoZone, tires, **S** 🅖 Exxon/KFC/Quiznos 🍴 Denny's, Rice Express, Sonic 🏠 Holiday Inn Express

GREENVILLE

73	FM 551, Fate
70	FM 549, **N** 🅞 Happy Trails RV Ctr, Hyundai, McLains RV Ctr, **S** 🅖 💚Love's/Carl's Jr./dsl/scales/24hr
69	(from wb), frontage rd, **N** 🅞 Super 8, **S** 🅞 Toyota/Scion
68	TX 205, to Rock Wall, **N** 🅖 RaceWay, Shell 🍴 Braum's, DQ, Jowilly's Grill, KFC, Luigi's Italian, Pizza Hut, Pizza Inn, Subway, Taco Casa, Whataburger 🏠 Best Western, Super 8, Value Place 🅞 Buick/GMC, Chevrolet, Dodge, Ford, Hobby Lobby, **S** 🅖 RaceTrac, TA/Burger King/Starbucks/dsl/24hr/scales/@, Valero/dsl 🍴 Firehouse Subs, Freebird Burritos, In-N-Out 🅞 Belk, Costco/gas, Jo-Ann Fabrics, Toyota/Scion
67a	Horizon Rd, Village Dr, **N** 🍴 Genghis Grill, Kyoto Japanese, Saltgrass Steaks, Snuffer's Rest, Starbucks 🏠 Hampton Inn, **S** 🍴 Culpepper Steaks, Oar House 🏠 Hilton 🅞 Office Depot
67	FM 740, Ridge Rd, **N** 🅖 Chevron, Murphy USA/dsl 🍴 Arby's, Burger King, Carabba's, Culver's, Domino's, Grandy's, IHOP, Logan's Roadhouse, McDonald's, Popeye's, Schlotzsky's, Smoothie King, Starbucks, Steak'n Shake, Taco Bueno, Taco Cabana, Trevino's Mexican, Waffle House, Wendy's 🏠 Hampton Inn 🅞 Firestone/auto, Goodyear/auto, Kwik Kar, Walmart, **S** 🅖 Exxon, Shell, Valero 🍴 5 Guys Burgers, Applebee's, Bahama Buck's Ice Cream, Blackeyed Pea, Buffalo Wild Wings, Carino's Italian, Chick-fil-A, Chili's, Chipotle Mexican, ChuckeCheese, CiCi's, Cotton Patch Cafe, El Chico, Jack-in-the-Box, La Madelein, McDonald's, Mi Cocina, Olive Garden, On-the-Border, Pizza Hut/Taco Bell, Quiznos, Shogun Steaks, Sonic, Soulman's BBQ, Starbucks, Subway, TGIFriday's 🏠 La Quinta 🅞 $Tree, Albertson's, AT&T, Belk, Best Buy, CVS Drug, Dick's, Discount Tire, GNC, Home Depot, JC Penney, Kohl's, Lowe's, Michael's, Office Depot, Old Navy, PetCo, Petsmart, Radio Shack, Ross, Staples, SteinMart, Target, TJ Maxx, to Lake Tawakoni, Verizon, vet, Walgreens
66mm	Ray Hubbard Reservoir
64	Dalrock Rd, Rowlett, **N** 🅖 Shell/dsl, Valero/dsl 🍴 Church's, Dickey's BBQ 🏠 Comfort Suites 🅞 🏥 Express Drug
63mm	Ray Hubbard Reservoir
62	Bass Pro Dr, **N** 🅖 Best Western 🅞 to Hubbard RA, **S** 🅖 Shell/dsl, Texaco, Valero/dsl 🍴 CiCi's Pizza, Flying Saucer Grill, Primo's Grill, Sonic, TexMex, TX Land&Cattle, Whataburger 🅞 Bass Pro Shops
61	Zion Rd (from wb), **N** 🅖 Exxon/dsl 🏠 Discovery Inn
60b	Bobtown Rd (eb only), **N** 🅖 Texaco/7-11 🍴 Jack-in-the-Box 🏠 La Quinta, **S** 🅖 Shell 🍴 Subway
60a	Rose Hill Dr
59	Beltline Rd, Garland, **N** 🅖 7-11, QT 🍴 Chili's, China City, Denny's, IHOP, India Garden, KFC, McDonald's, Papa John's, Pizza Hut/Taco Bell, Quiznos, Starbucks, Subway, Taco Cabana, Taco Casa, Wendy's, Whataburger 🅞 Albertson's, Discount Tire, GNC, Radio Shack, Tuesday Morning, Walgreens, Walmart, **S** 🍴 Baker's Ribs, Buffet King, Carl's Jr, DQ, Sonic, Waffle House, Williams Chicken 🏠 Best Value Inn, Motel 6, Super 8 🅞 Kroger
58	Northwest Dr, **N** 🅖 Shell, Valero/dsl 🅞 Hyundai, Nissan, **S** 🅖 Fina, Texaco 🍴 Jack-in-the-Box 🅞 Lowe's
56c b	I-635 S-N
56a	Galloway Ave, Gus Thomasson Dr (from eb), **N** 🅖 Texaco, Valero 🍴 KFC, McDonald's, Sonic 🅞 AutoZone, Hyundai, USPO, **S** 🅖 7-11, Chevron 🍴 Church's, Dickey's BBQ, El Fenix, Grandy's, Hooters, Jack-in-the-Box, Luby's, Olive Garden, Outback Steaks, Razzoo's Cajun, Red Lobster, Sports City Cafe, Subway, TGIFriday's, Tops Buffet, Wendy's 🏠 Courtyard, Crossland Suites, Delux Inn, Fairfield Inn

ROCKWALL

GARLAND

⬆E INTERSTATE 30 Cont'd

Exit #	Services

D A L L A S

56a Continued
🅞 🅗 Aldi Foods, BigLots, Celebration Sta Funpark, Firestone/auto, Kroger/dsl, Nichols RV Ctr, NTB

55 Motley Dr, **N** 🅖 Shell/dsl 🛏 Astro Inn, Executive Inn, **S** 🅖 Chevron 🛏 Microtel 🅞 🅗 to Eastfield Coll

54 Big Town Blvd, **N** 🍴 Valero/dsl 🛏 Mesquite Inn, **S** 🅞 dsl repair, Explore RV Ctr, Holiday World RV Ctr

53b US 80 E (from eb), to Terrell

53a Lp 12, Buckner, **N** 🅖 RaceTrac, Texaco 🍴 Burger King, Circle Grill 🛏 Holiday Inn Express, Luxury Inn, Super 8 🅞 Chevrolet, Toyota/Scion, **S** 🍴 Pizza Hut, Taco Cabana, Whataburger 🅞 $Tree, Radio Shack, Sam's Club/gas, Staples, Walmart

51 (52 a from wb), Highland Rd, Jim Miller Blvd, **N** 🍴 Exxon 🍴 Country China, Denny's, JP's Cafe, McDonald's 🛏 Holiday Inn Express, La Quinta, **S** 🅖 RaceWay/dsl, Shell/dsl 🍴 Burger King, Capt D's, CiCi's Pizza, Furr's Cafe, Grandy's, KFC, Subway, Taco Bell, Wendy's 🛏 Motel 6, Super 7 Inn 🅞 AutoZone, CVS Drug, O'Reilly Parts

50b a Longview, Ferguson Rd, **N** 🍴 Texaco, **S** 🅞 Brake-O, U-Haul

49b Dolphin Rd, Lawnview Ave, Samuell Ave, **N** 🅖 Shell 🛏 Best Value Inn

49a Winslow St, **N** 🍴 Circle K, Shell/dsl/repair 🍴 Jack-in-the-Box; McDonald's, **S** 🅖 Circle K, Shell 🅞 tires

48b TX 78, E Grand, **S** 🅞 arboretum, fairpark

48a Carroll Ave, Central Ave, Peak St, Haskell Ave, **N** 🍴 7-11, Shamrock, Valero 🅞 🅗 Hamm's Tires, **S** 🍴 Joe's Rest

47 2nd Ave, **S** 🅖 Shell 🍴 McDonald's 🅞 Cotton Bowl, fairpark

46b I-45, US 75, to Houston

46a Central Expswy, downtown

45 I-35E, N to Denton, to Commerce St, Lamar St, Griffin St, **S** 🍴 Gulf/dsl 🍴 McDonald's 🛏 Ambassador Inn

44b I-35E S, Industrial Blvd

44a I-35E N, Beckley Ave (from eb)

43b a Sylvan Ave (from wb), **N** 🍴 Valero/dsl 🅞 🅗 Family$, USPO

42 Hampton Rd

41 Westmoreland Ave

39 Cockrell Hill Rd, **N** 🅖 Shell/dsl 🍴 Grand China, IHOP, KFC/Taco Bell, Pollo Campero, Sonic, Wing Stop 🛏 Comfort Suites, Hampton Inn 🅞 Staples, **S** 🍴 Murphy USA 🍴 Chili's, Del Taco, Dickey's BBQ, Golden Corral, Lucky Rice, McDonald's, Panda Express, Starbucks, Subway, Taco Cabana, Wendy's, Whataburger 🛏 Holiday Inn Express 🅞 $Tree, Best Buy, Lowe's, Radio Shack, Ross, Walmart/McDonald's

38 Lp 12, **N 1 mi** 🍴 Exxon/7-11, Whip-In/dsl 🍴 Burger King, Popeye's

36 MacArthur Blvd, **S** 🅞 U-Haul

34 Belt Line Rd, **N** 🅖 Chevron, RaceTrac 🛏 Studio 6, Super 8 🅞 Ford, Ripley's Museum, **S** 🍴 RaceTrac/dsl, Shell/Subway, Valero 🍴 Burger King, Popeye's, Schlotzsky's, Starbucks 🅞 city park, vet

32b a George Bush Tpk, **toll**, **N** 🍴 Shamrock

30 TX 360, Six Flags Dr, Arlington Stadium, **N** 🍴 Mobil/dsl, Shell 🍴 Boston's, Cracker Barrel, Grand Buffet, Saltgrass Steaks, Steak'n Shake, TrailDust Steaks, Wendy's 🛏 Best Inn, Budget Suites, Candlewood Suites, Crowne Plaza, Extended Stay America, Fairfield Inn, Hawthorn Suites, Hilton, Hilton Garden, Residence Inn, Studio 6, Wingate Inn, **S** 🍴 Shell/7-11/dsl, Valero 🍴 Denny's, Jack-in-the-Box, Mariano's Mexican, McDonald's, Pancho's Mexican, Red Neck Heaven Rest, Subway

---

30 Continued
🛏 Baymont Inn, Holiday Inn Express, Homewood Suites, Hyatt Place, Knight's Inn, La Quinta, Ranger Inn, Sleep Inn 🅞 Ford/Lincoln, Six Flags Funpark

29 Ball Park Way, **N** 🍴 Chevron, QT, Valero 🍴 Dicky's BBQ, Sonic 🛏 Hampton Inn, Springhill Suites, Towneplace Suites 🅞 Toyota/Scion, USPO, **S** 🍴 On-the-Border 🛏 Howard Johnson, Sheraton 🅞 Six Flags Funpark

28b a FM 157, Collins St, **N** 🍴 Chevron/dsl 🍴 Arby's, Chipotle, IHOP, Waffle House 🛏 EconoLodge, Holiday Inn 🅞 BMW, Cadillac, Chrysler/Dodge/Jeep, Whole Foods Mkt, **S** 🍴 Asian Buffet, Blackeyed Pea, Chick-fil-A, Chili's, Colter's BBQ, El Fenix, Hooters, Jason's Deli, Joe's Crab Shack, Panera Bread, Pappasito's Cantina, Poppadeaux, Souper Salad, Taco Bueno, TGIFriday's, Wendy's 🛏 Comfort Suites, Courtyard 🅞 $Tree, Barnes&Noble, Best Buy, Home Depot, Michael's, PepBoys, Petsmart, Save-A-Lot Foods, SteinMart, TX Stadium

27 Lamar Blvd, Cooper St, **N** 🍴 Texaco 🍴 Jack-in-the-Box 🅞 BigLots, Family$, Kroger/dsl, vet, **S** 🍴 7-11, Shell 🍴 Burger King, Denny's, Tom's Burgers

26 Fielder Rd, **S** 🅞 to Six Flags (from eb)

25mm Village Creek

F T   W O R T H

24 Eastchase Pkwy, **N** 🍴 Jack-in-the-Box, Panda Express 🅞 CarMax, Lowe's, Sam's Club/gas, Verizon, Walmart/McDonald's, **S** 🍴 Chevron/dsl, RaceTrac, Shell/7-11/dsl 🍴 Burger King, Chicken Express, CiCi's Pizza, IHOP, McDonald's, No Frills Grill, Schlotzsky's, Subway, Taco Bell, Wendy's, Whataburger 🅞 AT&T, GNC, Office Depot, Radio Shack, Ross, Target

23 Cooks Lane, **S** 🍴 Shell

21c b I-820

21a Bridgewood Dr, **N** 🍴 Chevron 🍴 Braums, Church's, Jack-in-the-Box, KFC, Luby's, Subway, Wendy's 🅞 $General, Albertson's, Discount Tire, Firestone, Home Depot, U-Haul, **S** 🍴 Conoco, Phillips 66, QT 🍴 Domino's, Taco Bueno, Whataburger/24hr

19 Brentwood Stair Rd (from eb), **N** 🍴 Shell, **S** 🍴 Shamrock, Texaco 🅞 Family$

18 Oakland Blvd, **N** 🍴 Circle K, Shell/dsl 🍴 Taco Bell, Waffle House 🛏 Motel 6

16c Beach St, **S** 🍴 7-11 🛏 Ambassador Hotel, Inn Suites

16b a Riverside Dr (from wb), **S** 🛏 Great Western Inn

15b a I-35W N to Denton, S to Waco

14b Jones St, Commerce St, Ft Worth, downtown

14a TX 199, Henderson St, Ft Worth, downtown

13b TX 199, Henderson St, **N** 🛏 Omni, Sheraton

13a 8th Ave, **N** 🛏 Holiday Inn Express

▲E INTERSTATE 30 Cont'd

Exit #	Services
12b	Forest Park Blvd, N 🍴 Pappadeaux Café, Pappa's Burgers, Pappasito's, S 🅞 �H URGENT CARE
12a	University Dr, City Parks, S 🛏 SpringHill Suites
11	Montgomery St, S 🅖 Shell/7-11/dsl 🍴 Taco Bell, Whataburger 🅞 visitor info
10	Hulen St, Ft Worth, S 🍴 Chick-fil-A, McDonald's, Smoothie King, Starbucks 🅞 Central Mkt, WorldMkt
9b	US 377, Camp Bowie Blvd, Horne St, N 🍴 Uncle Julio's Mexican, S 🅖 7-11, Exxon, Texaco/dsl 🍴 Jack-in-the-Box, Jason's Deli, Mexican Inn Cafe, Qdoba, Schlotzsky's, Sonic, Subway, Taco Bueno, Wendy's 🅞 AT&T, Batteries+, Radio Shack, Verizon, Walgreens
9a	Bryant-Irvin Rd, S 🅖 same as 9b, Shell
8b	Ridgmar, Ridglea, N 🅖 Valero/dsl
8a	TX 183, Green Oaks Rd, N 🍴 Applebee's, Arby's, Chick-fil-A, Del Taco, Don Pablo, Grand Buffet, Jack-in-the-Box, McDonald's, Olive Garden, Panda Express, Sonic, Starbucks, Subway, Taco Bueno 🛏 Courtyard 🅞 $Tree, Albertson's, Aldi Foods, AT&T, Best Buy, BigLots, Dillard's, Firestone/auto, JC Penney, Jo-Ann Fabrics, Lowe's, Macy's, Neiman Marcus, NTB, Office Depot, Old Navy, PetCo, Petsmart, Radio Shack, Ross, Sam's Club/gas, Sears/auto, Target, U-Haul, Verizon, Walmart/Subway, S 🛏 Fairfield Inn, Hampton Inn
7b a	Cherry Lane, TX 183, spur 341, to Green Oaks Rd, N 🅖 Shell/7-11, Texaco/dsl, Valero/dsl 🍴 ChuckECheese, IHOP, Popeye's, Ryan's, Subway, Wendy's 🛏 La Quinta, Motel 6 🅞 O'Reilly Parts, same as 8a, U-Haul, S 🛏 Holiday Inn Express, Quality Inn, Super 8
6	Las Vegas Trail, N 🅖 Chevron/McDonald's/dsl, Conoco/dsl 🍴 Jack-in-the-Box, Waffle House 🛏 Days Inn 🅞 Hyundai, Suzuki, S 🅖 Alon, Shell/7-11/dsl, Valero/dsl 🛏 Best Value Inn, Knights Inn, Relax Inn 🅞 AutoZone, Kia
5b c	I-820 N and S
5a	Alemeda St (from eb, no EZ return)
3	RM 2871, Chapel Creek Blvd, S 🅖 Exxon/Church's/Subway 🍴 Sonic
2	spur 580 E
1b	Linkcrest Dr, S 🅖 Gulf/dsl
0mm	I-20 W. I-30 begins/ends on I-20, exit 421.

▲N INTERSTATE 35

Exit #	Services
504mm	Texas/Oklahoma state line, Red River
504	frontage rd, access to Texas Welcome Ctr
503mm	parking area both lanes
502mm	Welcome Center sb, full 🛏 facilities, litter barrels, 🅲, 🚗 TX Tourist Bureau/info, vending, wireless internet
501	FM 1202, Prime Outlets Blvd, E 🅞 Chrysler/Dodge/Jeep, Ford, W 🅖 Conoco/café/dsl 🍴 Applebee's, Cracker Barrel, Serna's Mexican 🛏 Hampton Inn, La Quinta 🅞 Prime Outlets/famous brands, RV camping, Western Outfitter
500	FM 372, Gainesville, W 🍴 Hitchin' Post/Shell/dsl
498b a	US 82, to Wichita Falls, Gainesville, Sherman, E 🅖 Chevron/dsl, Exxon, Shell/dsl, Valero/dsl 🍴 TX Border Rest, Waffle Inn 🛏 12 Oaks Inn, Bed&Bath Inn, Budget Host, Super 8 🅞 �H W 🅖 Exxon/dsl 🛏 Atria Inn, Comfort Suites, Days Inn
497	frontage rd, W 🅖 Valero/dsl
496mm	Elm Fork of the Trinity River
496b	TX 51, FM 51, California St, Gainesville, E 🍴 Arby's, Braum's,

496b	Continued
	Fera's Mexican, IHOP, McDonald's, Sonic, Starbucks, Starbucks, Taco Bell, Taco Casa, Wendy's 🛏 Holiday Inn Express, Quality Inn 🅞 Goodyear/auto, N Central TX Coll, W 🅖 Valero 🍴 Chili's
496a	to Weaver St
495	frontage rd
494	FM 1306
492mm	🚻 sb, litter barrels
491	Spring Creek Rd
490mm	🚻 nb, litter barrels
489	FM 1307, to Hockley Creek Rd
487	FM 922, Valley View, W 🅖 Valero/dsl/24hr 🍴 DQ 🅞 USPO
486	Fm 1307, W 🅖 Texaco/dsl 🛏 Motel 6 🅞 $General
485	frontage rd (from sb)
483	FM 3002, Lone Oak Rd, E 🅖 Shell/Church's/Subway/dsl 🅞 Roberts Lake SP
482	Chisam Rd
481	View Rd, W 🅞 McClain's RV Ctr
480	Lois Rd, E 🅞 Walmart Dist Ctr
479	Belz Rd, Sanger, same as 478
478	FM 455, to Pilot Pt, Bolivar, E 🅖 QuickTrack, Shell 🍴 DQ, Fuzzy's Tacos, Miguelitos, Sonic, Subway, Taco Bell 🛏 Sanger Inn 🅞 RV park, USPO, W 🅖 Chevron/dsl, Fuel 4 TX/Chicken Express/dsl 🍴 Jack-in-the-Box, McDonald's 🅞 Chevrolet, Family$, IGA Foods, Kwik Kar Lube, O'Reilly Parts, Ray Roberts Lake and SP, RV Park
477	Keaton Rd, E 🅖 Exxon 🅞 Curves
475b	Rector Rd
475a	FM 156, to Krum (from sb)
474	Cowling rd (from nb)
473	FM 3163, Milam Rd, E 🅖 Loves/Subway/dsl/scales/24hr
472	Ganzer Rd, W 🅞 Best Value RV Ctr, Crandell RV Ctr
471	US 77, FM 1173, Lp 282, to Denton, Krum, E 🅖 TA/Pizza Hut/Taco Bell/dsl/scales/24hr/@ 🅞 �H W 🅞 Foster's Western Shop, to Camping World RV Supply, truckwash
470	Lp 288, same services as 469 from sb
469	US 380, University Dr, to Decatur, McKinney, E 🅖 Chevron/Subway, RaceTrac/dsl 🍴 Braum's, Catfish King, Chick-fil-A, ChinaTown Café, Cowboy Chicken, Cracker Barrel, Freebird's Burrito, Luigi's Pizza, McDonald's, Panda Express, Taco Casa, Villa Grande, Whataburger, Which Wich, Wing Stop 🛏 Best Western, Fairfield Inn 🅞 Albertson's/Sav-On, AT&T, GNC, Jo-Ann Fabrics, Kohl's, Kwik Kar, PetCo, Ross, Sam's Club/gas, Walmart/McDonald's, W 🅖 QT/dsl, Shell/dsl 🍴 Denny's, DQ, Sonic, Waffle House 🛏 Comfort Inn, Days Inn, Holiday Inn Express, Howard Johnson, La Quinta, Motel 6, ValuePlace Inn 🅞 �H Camping World RV Supply, I-35 RV Ctr, to TX Woman's U
468	FM 1515, 🔄 Rd, W Oak St, E 🅞 �H
467	I-35W, S to Ft Worth
I-35 divides into E and W sb, converges into I-35 nb. See Texas I-35W.	
466b	Ave D, E 🅖 Exxon/dsl 🍴 IHOP, McDonald's, Pancho's Mexican, Taco Cabana 🛏 Comfort Suites 🅞 $General, Sack'n Save Foods, to NTSU
466a	McCormick St, E 🅖 EKon, Shell/7-11/dsl 🍴 Poncho's Mexican, Taco Cabana 🛏 Comfort Suites, Royal Inn 🅞 Sack&Save, W 🅖 Fina/dsl
465b	US 377, Ft Worth Dr, E 🅖 RaceTrac/dsl, Valero 🍴 Michael's Kitchen, Taco Bell, Taco Bueno, Whataburger 🛏 La Quinta, W 🅖 EKon, QuickTrack 🍴 Outback Steaks, Sonic 🛏 Knights Inn

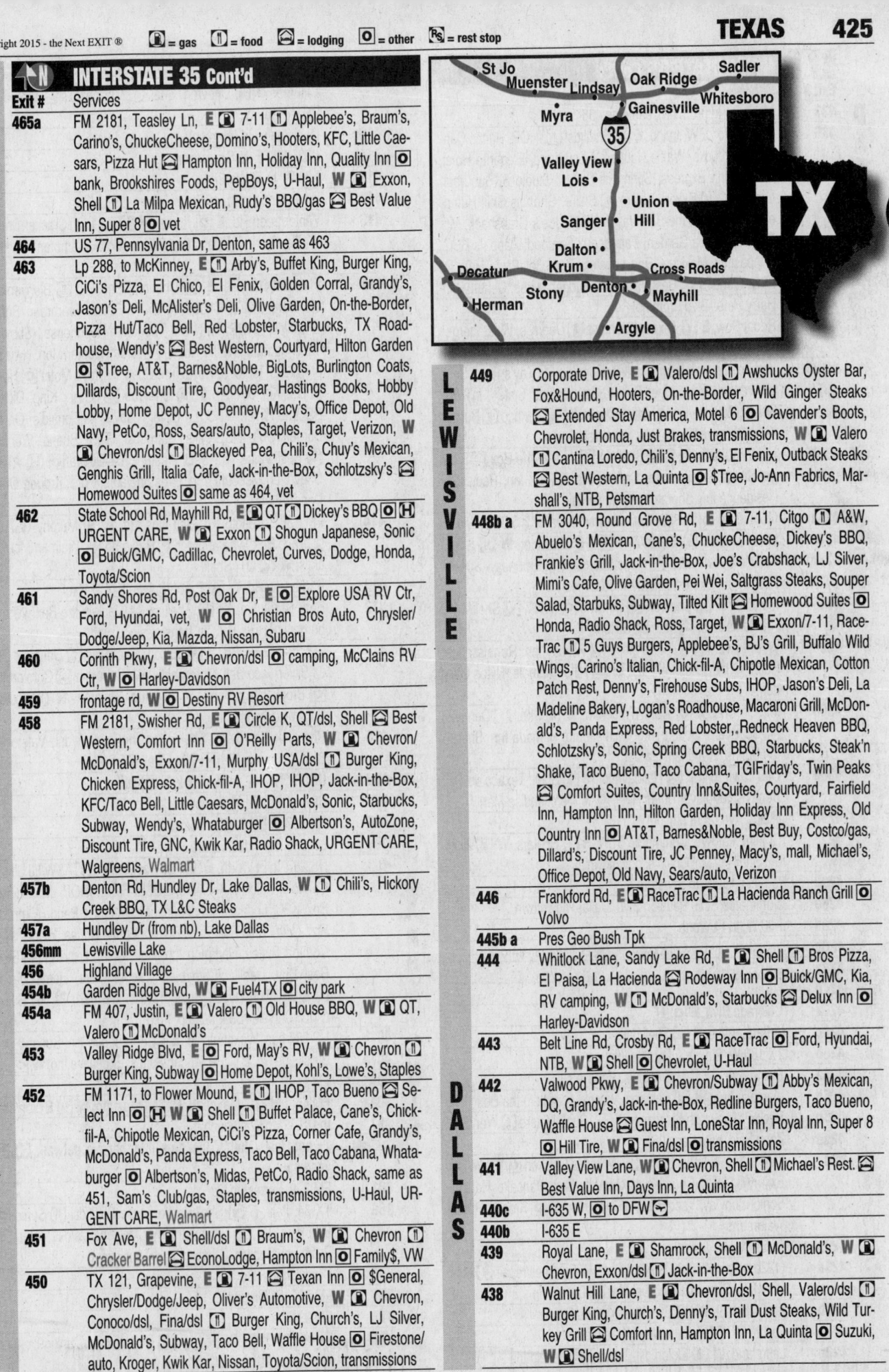

⬆N **INTERSTATE 35 Cont'd**

Exit #	Services
465a	FM 2181, Teasley Ln, **E** 🅿 7-11 🍴 Applebee's, Braum's, Carino's, ChuckeCheese, Domino's, Hooters, KFC, Little Caesars, Pizza Hut 🏠 Hampton Inn, Holiday Inn, Quality Inn 🄾 bank, Brookshires Foods, PepBoys, U-Haul, **W** 🅿 Exxon, Shell 🍴 La Milpa Mexican, Rudy's BBQ/gas 🏠 Best Value Inn, Super 8 🄾 vet
464	US 77, Pennsylvania Dr, Denton, same as 463
463	Lp 288, to McKinney, **E** 🍴 Arby's, Buffet King, Burger King, CiCi's Pizza, El Chico, El Fenix, Golden Corral, Grandy's, Jason's Deli, McAlister's Deli, Olive Garden, On-the-Border, Pizza Hut/Taco Bell, Red Lobster, Starbucks, TX Roadhouse, Wendy's 🏠 Best Western, Courtyard, Hilton Garden 🄾 $Tree, AT&T, Barnes&Noble, BigLots, Burlington Coats, Dillards, Discount Tire, Goodyear, Hastings Books, Hobby Lobby, Home Depot, JC Penney, Macy's, Office Depot, Old Navy, PetCo, Ross, Sears/auto, Staples, Target, Verizon, **W** 🅿 Chevron/dsl 🍴 Blackeyed Pea, Chili's, Chuy's Mexican, Genghis Grill, Italia Cafe, Jack-in-the-Box, Schlotzsky's 🏠 Homewood Suites 🄾 same as 464, vet
462	State School Rd, Mayhill Rd, **E** 🅿 QT 🍴 Dickey's BBQ 🄾 🄷 URGENT CARE, **W** 🅿 Exxon 🍴 Shogun Japanese, Sonic 🄾 Buick/GMC, Cadillac, Chevrolet, Curves, Dodge, Honda, Toyota/Scion
461	Sandy Shores Rd, Post Oak Dr, **E** 🄾 Explore USA RV Ctr, Ford, Hyundai, vet, **W** 🄾 Christian Bros Auto, Chrysler/Dodge/Jeep, Kia, Mazda, Nissan, Subaru
460	Corinth Pkwy, **E** 🅿 Chevron/dsl 🄾 camping, McClains RV Ctr, **W** 🄾 Harley-Davidson
459	frontage rd, **W** 🄾 Destiny RV Resort
458	FM 2181, Swisher Rd, **E** 🅿 Circle K, QT/dsl, Shell 🏠 Best Western, Comfort Inn 🄾 O'Reilly Parts, **W** 🅿 Chevron/McDonald's, Exxon/7-11, Murphy USA/dsl 🍴 Burger King, Chicken Express, Chick-fil-A, IHOP, IHOP, Jack-in-the-Box, KFC/Taco Bell, Little Caesars, McDonald's, Sonic, Starbucks, Subway, Wendy's, Whataburger 🄾 Albertson's, AutoZone, Discount Tire, GNC, Kwik Kar, Radio Shack, URGENT CARE, Walgreens, Walmart
457b	Denton Rd, Hundley Dr, Lake Dallas, **W** 🍴 Chili's, Hickory Creek BBQ, TX L&C Steaks
457a	Hundley Dr (from nb), Lake Dallas
456mm	Lewisville Lake
456	Highland Village
454b	Garden Ridge Blvd, **W** 🅿 Fuel4TX 🄾 city park
454a	FM 407, Justin, **E** 🅿 Valero 🍴 Old House BBQ, **W** 🅿 QT, Valero 🍴 McDonald's
453	Valley Ridge Blvd, **E** 🄾 Ford, May's RV, **W** 🅿 Chevron 🍴 Burger King, Subway 🄾 Home Depot, Kohl's, Lowe's, Staples
452	FM 1171, to Flower Mound, **E** 🍴 IHOP, Taco Bueno 🏠 Select Inn 🄾 🄷 **W** 🅿 Shell 🍴 Buffet Palace, Cane's, Chick-fil-A, Chipotle Mexican, CiCi's Pizza, Corner Cafe, Grandy's, McDonald's, Panda Express, Taco Bell, Taco Cabana, Whataburger 🄾 Albertson's, Midas, PetCo, Radio Shack, same as 451, Sam's Club/gas, Staples, transmissions, U-Haul, URGENT CARE, Walmart
451	Fox Ave, **E** 🅿 Shell/dsl 🍴 Braum's, **W** 🅿 Chevron 🍴 Cracker Barrel 🏠 EconoLodge, Hampton Inn 🄾 Family$, VW
450	TX 121, Grapevine, **E** 🅿 7-11 🍴 Texan Inn 🄾 $General, Chrysler/Dodge/Jeep, Oliver's Automotive, **W** 🅿 Chevron, Conoco/dsl, Fina/dsl 🍴 Burger King, Church's, LJ Silver, McDonald's, Subway, Taco Bell, Waffle House 🄾 Firestone/auto, Kroger, Kwik Kar, Nissan, Toyota/Scion, transmissions

Exit #	Services
449	Corporate Drive, **E** 🅿 Valero/dsl 🍴 Awshucks Oyster Bar, Fox&Hound, Hooters, On-the-Border, Wild Ginger Steaks 🏠 Extended Stay America, Motel 6 🄾 Cavender's Boots, Chevrolet, Honda, Just Brakes, transmissions, **W** 🅿 Valero 🍴 Cantina Loredo, Chili's, Denny's, El Fenix, Outback Steaks 🏠 Best Western, La Quinta 🄾 $Tree, Jo-Ann Fabrics, Marshall's, NTB, Petsmart
448b a	FM 3040, Round Grove Rd, **E** 🅿 7-11, Citgo 🍴 A&W, Abuelo's Mexican, Cane's, ChuckeCheese, Dickey's BBQ, Frankie's Grill, Jack-in-the-Box, Joe's Crabshack, LJ Silver, Mimi's Cafe, Olive Garden, Pei Wei, Saltgrass Steaks, Souper Salad, Starbucks, Subway, Tilted Kilt 🏠 Homewood Suites 🄾 Honda, Radio Shack, Ross, Target, **W** 🅿 Exxon/7-11, RaceTrac 🍴 5 Guys Burgers, Applebee's, BJ's Grill, Buffalo Wild Wings, Carino's Italian, Chick-fil-A, Chipotle Mexican, Cotton Patch Rest, Denny's, Firehouse Subs, IHOP, Jason's Deli, La Madeline Bakery, Logan's Roadhouse, Macaroni Grill, McDonald's, Panda Express, Red Lobster, Redneck Heaven BBQ, Schlotzsky's, Sonic, Spring Creek BBQ, Starbucks, Steak'n Shake, Taco Bueno, Taco Cabana, TGIFriday's, Twin Peaks 🏠 Comfort Suites, Country Inn&Suites, Courtyard, Fairfield Inn, Hampton Inn, Hilton Garden, Holiday Inn Express, Old Country Inn 🄾 AT&T, Barnes&Noble, Best Buy, Costco/gas, Dillard's, Discount Tire, JC Penney, Macy's, mall, Michael's, Office Depot, Old Navy, Sears/auto, Verizon
446	Frankford Rd, **E** 🅿 RaceTrac 🍴 La Hacienda Ranch Grill 🄾 Volvo
445b a	Pres Geo Bush Tpk
444	Whitlock Lane, Sandy Lake Rd, **E** 🅿 Shell 🍴 Bros Pizza, El Paisa, La Hacienda 🏠 Rodeway Inn 🄾 Buick/GMC, Kia, RV camping, **W** 🍴 McDonald's, Starbucks 🏠 Delux Inn 🄾 Harley-Davidson
443	Belt Line Rd, Crosby Rd, **E** 🅿 RaceTrac 🄾 Ford, Hyundai, NTB, **W** 🅿 Shell 🄾 Chevrolet, U-Haul
442	Valwood Pkwy, **E** 🅿 Chevron/Subway 🍴 Abby's Mexican, DQ, Grandy's, Jack-in-the-Box, Redline Burgers, Taco Bueno, Waffle House 🏠 Guest Inn, LoneStar Inn, Royal Inn, Super 8 🄾 Hill Tire, **W** 🅿 Fina/dsl 🍴 transmissions
441	Valley View Lane, **W** 🅿 Chevron, Shell 🍴 Michael's Rest. 🏠 Best Value Inn, Days Inn, La Quinta
440c	I-635 W, 🄾 to DFW ➡
440b	I-635 E
439	Royal Lane, **E** 🅿 Shamrock, Shell 🍴 McDonald's, **W** 🅿 Chevron, Exxon/dsl 🍴 Jack-in-the-Box
438	Walnut Hill Lane, **E** 🅿 Chevron/dsl, Shell, Valero/dsl 🍴 Burger King, Church's, Denny's, Trail Dust Steaks, Wild Turkey Grill 🏠 Comfort Inn, Hampton Inn, La Quinta 🄾 Suzuki, **W** 🅿 Shell/dsl

(vertical text, left margin) **LEWISVILLE**

DALLAS

DALLAS / **TX**

INTERSTATE 35 Cont'd

Exit #	Services
437	Manana Rd (from nb), same as 438
436	TX 348, to DFW, Irving, E ⛽ Shell/dsl 🍴 IHOP, Rucas Cantina, Starbucks, Waffle House 🛏 Courtyard, Elegante Hotel, Holiday Inn Express, SpringHill Suites, Studio 6, Suburban Lodge, W ⛽ Exxon, Valero 🍴 Chili's, Ghengis Grill, Humperdinks, Jack-in-the-Box, Jason's Deli, Joe's Crabshack, McDonald's, Olive Garden, Papadeaux Seafood, Pappa's BBQ, Pappasito's Mexican, Red Lobster, Taco Bell/Pizza Hut, TX L&C, Wendy's 🛏 Best Value Inn, Budget Suites, Century Inn
435	Harry Hines Blvd (from nb)
434b	Regal Row, E ⛽ Texaco/Grandy's 🍴 Denny's, Whataburger 🛏 Motel 6, W 🛏 Ramada Inn
434a	Empire, Central, E ⛽ Shell/McDonald's 🍴 Kay's Rest, Sonic, Wendy's 🛏 Budget Suites, Candlewood Suites, InTown Suites, Wingate Inn ⊙ Office Depot, W ⛽ Texaco 🍴 Burger King, Pizza Hut/Taco Bell, Schlotzsky's
433b	Mockingbird Lane, E ⛽ Shell/dsl 🍴 Jack-in-the-Box 🛏 Budget Suites, Comfort Inn, Crowne Plaza, Park Inn, Radisson, Residence Inn, Sheraton, ⊙ Love Field ✈
433a	(432b from sb)TX 356, Commonwealth Dr, W 🛏 Delux Inn
432a	Inwood Rd, E ⛽ Exxon/7-11 ⊙ 🄷 Chevrolet, W ⛽ Shell, Texaco/Subway/dsl 🍴 Whataburger 🛏 Embassy Suites, Holiday Inn Express, Homewood Suites
431	Motor St, E ⛽ Chevron 🍴 Denny's ⊙ 🄷 W ⛽ Shell/7-11 🍴 Alamo Rest 🛏 Marriott Suites
430c	Wycliff Ave, E 🍴 JoJo's Rest. 🛏 Holiday Inn, Renaissance Hotel ⊙ Intn'l Apparel Mart, W 🛏 Hilton Anatole, Hilton Garden
430b	Mkt Ctr Blvd, E ⊙ World Trade Ctr, W ⛽ Shell 🍴 Denny's 🛏 Courtyard, DoubleTree, Fairfield Inn, Ramada Inn, Sheraton Suites, Wyndham Garden
430a	Oak Lawn Ave, E 🛏 Holiday Inn, W ⛽ Shell, Texaco/dsl 🍴 Denny's, Medieval Times Rest. ⊙ to Merchandise Mart
429c	HiLine Ave (from nb)
429b	Continental Ave, Commerce St W, E 🍴 Hooters, W ⛽ Exxon, Shell 🍴 McDonald's, downtown
429a	to I-45, US 75, to Houston
428e	Commerce St E, Reunion Blvd, Dallas, downtown
428d	I-30 W, to Ft Worth
428b	Industrial Blvd, E ⛽ Exxon, W ⛽ Gulf/dsl, Shamrock
428a	I-30 E, to I-45 S
427b	I-30 E
427a	Colorado Blvd, E ⊙ 🄷
426c	Jefferson Ave, E ⛽ Shell/dsl
426b	TX 180 W, 8th St, E ⛽ Shell/dsl
426a	Ewing Ave, E 🍴 McDonald's, Popeye's
425c	Marsalis Ave, W ⛽ Chevron, Valero 🍴 Jack-in-the-Box
425b	Beckley Ave, 12th St, sb only, W ⛽ Shell, Valero 🍴 Wendy's
425a	Zang Blvd, same as 425b
424	Illinois Ave, E ⛽ Chevron 🍴 William's Chicken ⊙ 🄷 W ⛽ Exxon/7-11 🍴 Church's, Jack-in-the-Box, Pancake House, Sonic, Subway, Taco Bell 🛏 Oak Tree Inn ⊙ Kroger, Ross, Walgreens
423b	Saner Ave
423a	(422b from nb)US 67 S, Kiest Blvd, W ⛽ Shell/repair 🍴 McDonald's, Subway, Taco Del Mar 🛏 Dallas Inn
421b	Ann Arbor St, W ⛽ Exxon/dsl ⊙ L&L Repair
421a	Lp 12E W, E ⛽ RaceWay 🛏 Delux Inn
420	Laureland, W ⛽ Exxon/dsl, Texaco 🛏 Linfield Inn

WAXAHATCHIE

Exit #	Services
419	Camp Wisdom Rd, E ⛽ Exxon 🍴 Jack-in-the-Box 🛏 Oak Cliff Inn, W ⛽ Chevron, Shell 🍴 McDonald's 🛏 Grand Inn ⊙ U-Haul
418c	Danieldale Rd (from sb)
418b	I-635/I-20 E, to Shreveport
418a	I-20 W, to Ft Worth
417	Wheatland Rd (from nb)
416	Wintergreen Rd, E ⊙ repair, W ⛽ 7-11 🍴 Cracker Barrel, Waffle House 🛏 Days Inn, Grande Hotel, Hampton Inn, Holiday Inn Express
415	Pleasant Run Rd, E ⛽ Chevron, Shell/dsl 🍴 Bienvenidos Mexican, Chili's, Chubby's, CiCi's Pizza, Evergreen Buffet, Grandy's, IHOP, In-N-Out, Logan's Roadhouse, Subway, Taco Cabana, Waffle House 🛏 Great Western Inn, Hwy Express Inn, Motel 6, Royal Inn, Spanish Trails Motel ⊙ Home Depot, Kia, NAPA, W ⛽ Chevron 🍴 Burger King, Dicky's BBQ, El Chico, KFC, LJ Silver, Luby's, McDonald's, On the Border, Outback Steaks, Starbucks, Taco Bueno, Wendy's 🛏 Best Value Inn, Best Western, La Quinta ⊙ 🄷 AT&T, Chevrolet, Discount Tire, Firestone/auto, Ford, Kroger, Office Depot, Ross
414	FM 1382, Desoto Rd, Belt Line Rd, E ⛽ Murphy USA/dsl 🍴 Taco Bell, Whataburger ⊙ Radio Shack, Walmart/McDonald's, W ⛽ QT, Shell
413	Parkerville Rd, W ⛽ Exxon/Subway ⊙ U-Haul
412	Bear Creek Rd, W ⛽ Shell/dsl 🍴 Jack-in-the-Box, Whataburger ⊙ HiHo RV Ctr, transmissions, vet
411	FM 664, Ovilla Rd, E ⛽ Exxon, RaceTrac 🍴 Denny's, DQ, LJ Silver/Taco Bell, McDonald's, Whataburger 🛏 Comfort Inn ⊙ Brookshire's Foods, CVS Drug, Walmart, W ⛽ Exxon/Subway, Shamrock
410	Red Oak Rd, E ⛽ Shell/Pizza Inn/Subway/dsl, Valero 🛏 Best Value Inn, W ⊙ Hilltop Travel Trailers
408	US 77, TX 342, to Red Oak, E ⊙ golf
406	Sterrett Rd, E ⊙ fireworks
405	FM 387, E ⛽ Phillips 66/dsl
404	Lofland Rd, industrial area
403	US 287, to Ft Worth, E ⛽ RacTrac, Valero 🍴 A&W/LJ Silver, Carino's, Chick-fil-A, Chili's, DQ, El Fenix, IHOP, Jack-in-the-Box, KFC, Logan's Roadhouse, McDonald's, Panda Express, Pizza Hut, Taco Bell, Taco Bueno, Waffle House, Wendy's 🛏 Comfort Suites, Hampton Inn, Holiday Inn Express ⊙ Belk, Best Buy, Cadillac/Chevrolet, Discount Tire, Home Depot, Lowe's, Office Depot, Ross, Target, Walmart, W ⊙ Buick/GMC, Chrysler/Dodge/Jeep, Ford
401b	US 287 bus, Waxahatchie, E 🛏 Best Value Inn, Super 8
401a	Brookside Rd, E 🛏 American Suites, Executive Inn, W ⊙ vet
399b	FM 1446
399a	FM 66, FM 876, Maypearl, E 🛏 Texas Inn, W ⛽ Exxon/dsl
397	to US 77, to Waxahachie
393mm	℞ both lanes, full ♿ facilities, litter barrels, petwalk, 🛏, 🅿 vending
391	FM 329, Forreston Rd
386	TX 34, Italy, E ⛽ Shell/Smokehouse BBQ/dsl 🍴 Sonic ⊙ $General, W ⛽ Exxon/Grandy's/McDonald's/dsl/scales 🍴 Pizza Inn, Subway 🛏 Italy Inn ⊙ truckwash
384	Derrs Chapel Rd
381	FM 566, Milford Rd
377	FM 934
374	FM 2959, Carl's Corner, W ⛽ Petro/Exxon/Dunkin Donuts/Iron Skillet/dsl/scales/24hr

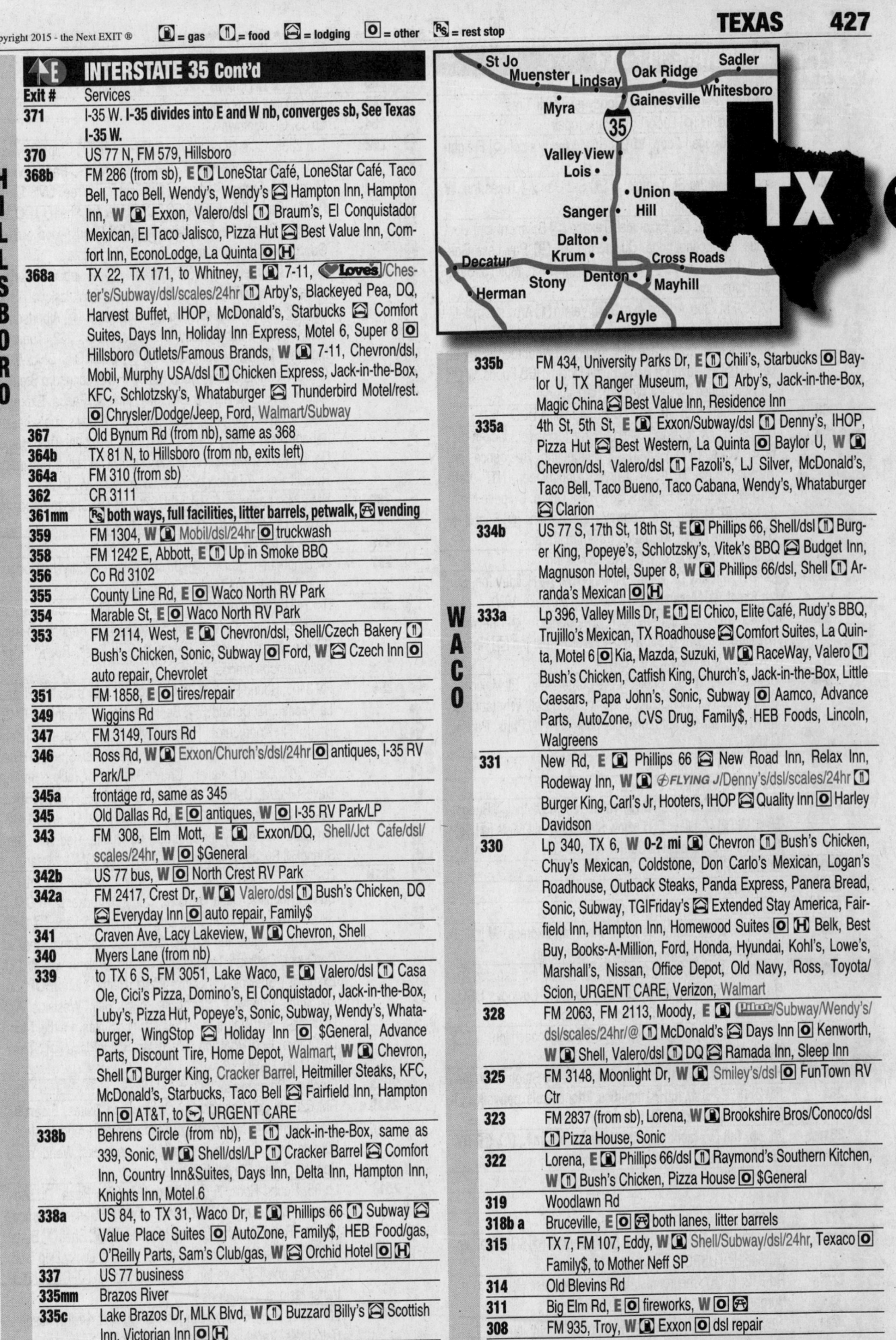

Exit #	Services
INTERSTATE 35 Cont'd	
371	I-35 W. **I-35 divides into E and W nb, converges sb, See Texas I-35 W.**
370	US 77 N, FM 579, Hillsboro
368b	FM 286 (from sb), E 🛢🍴 LoneStar Café, LoneStar Café, Taco Bell, Taco Bell, Wendy's, Wendy's 🏠 Hampton Inn, Hampton Inn, W 🛢 Exxon, Valero/dsl 🍴 Braum's, El Conquistador Mexican, El Taco Jalisco, Pizza Hut 🏠 Best Value Inn, Comfort Inn, EconoLodge, La Quinta ◎ H
368a	TX 22, TX 171, to Whitney, E 🛢 7-11, ♥Love's/Chester's/Subway/dsl/scales/24hr 🍴 Arby's, Blackeyed Pea, DQ, Harvest Buffet, IHOP, McDonald's, Starbucks 🏠 Comfort Suites, Days Inn, Holiday Inn Express, Motel 6, Super 8 ◎ Hillsboro Outlets/Famous Brands, W 🛢 7-11, Chevron/dsl, Mobil, Murphy USA/dsl 🍴 Chicken Express, Jack-in-the-Box, KFC, Schlotzsky's, Whataburger 🏠 Thunderbird Motel/rest. ◎ Chrysler/Dodge/Jeep, Ford, Walmart/Subway
367	Old Bynum Rd (from nb), same as 368
364b	TX 81 N, to Hillsboro (from nb, exits left)
364a	FM 310 (from sb)
362	CR 3111
361mm	🅿s both ways, full facilities, litter barrels, petwalk, 🍴 vending
359	FM 1304, W 🛢 Mobil/dsl/24hr ◎ truckwash
358	FM 1242 E, Abbott, E 🍴 Up in Smoke BBQ
356	Co Rd 3102
355	County Line Rd, E ◎ Waco North RV Park
354	Marable St, E ◎ Waco North RV Park
353	FM 2114, West, E 🛢 Chevron/dsl, Shell/Czech Bakery 🍴 Bush's Chicken, Sonic, Subway ◎ Ford, W 🏠 Czech Inn ◎ auto repair, Chevrolet
351	FM 1858, E ◎ tires/repair
349	Wiggins Rd
347	FM 3149, Tours Rd
346	Ross Rd, W 🛢 Exxon/Church's/dsl/24hr ◎ antiques, I-35 RV Park/LP
345a	frontage rd, same as 345
345	Old Dallas Rd, E ◎ antiques, W ◎ I-35 RV Park/LP
343	FM 308, Elm Mott, E 🛢 Exxon/DQ, Shell/Jct Cafe/dsl/scales/24hr, W ◎ $General
342b	US 77 bus, W ◎ North Crest RV Park
342a	FM 2417, Crest Dr, W 🛢 Valero/dsl 🍴 Bush's Chicken, DQ 🏠 Everyday Inn ◎ auto repair, Family$
341	Craven Ave, Lacy Lakeview, W 🛢 Chevron, Shell
340	Myers Lane (from nb)
339	to TX 6 S, FM 3051, Lake Waco, E 🛢 Valero/dsl 🍴 Casa Ole, Cici's Pizza, Domino's, El Conquistador, Jack-in-the-Box, Luby's, Pizza Hut, Popeye's, Sonic, Subway, Wendy's, Whataburger, WingStop 🏠 Holiday Inn ◎ $General, Advance Parts, Discount Tire, Home Depot, Walmart, W 🛢 Chevron, Shell 🍴 Burger King, Cracker Barrel, Heitmiller Steaks, KFC, McDonald's, Starbucks, Taco Bell 🏠 Fairfield Inn, Hampton Inn ◎ AT&T, to 🏠, URGENT CARE
338b	Behrens Circle (from nb), E 🍴 Jack-in-the-Box, same as 339, Sonic, W 🛢 Shell/dsl/LP 🍴 Cracker Barrel 🏠 Comfort Inn, Country Inn&Suites, Days Inn, Delta Inn, Hampton Inn, Knights Inn, Motel 6
338a	US 84, to TX 31, Waco Dr, E 🛢 Phillips 66 🍴 Subway 🏠 Value Place Suites ◎ AutoZone, Family$, HEB Food/gas, O'Reilly Parts, Sam's Club/gas, W 🏠 Orchid Hotel ◎ H
337	US 77 business
335mm	Brazos River
335c	Lake Brazos Dr, MLK Blvd, W 🍴 Buzzard Billy's 🏠 Scottish Inn, Victorian Inn ◎ H
335b	FM 434, University Parks Dr, E 🍴 Chili's, Starbucks ◎ Baylor U, TX Ranger Museum, W 🍴 Arby's, Jack-in-the-Box, Magic China 🏠 Best Value Inn, Residence Inn
335a	4th St, 5th St, E 🛢 Exxon/Subway/dsl 🍴 Denny's, IHOP, Pizza Hut 🏠 Best Western, La Quinta ◎ Baylor U, W 🛢 Chevron/dsl, Valero/dsl 🍴 Fazoli's, LJ Silver, McDonald's, Taco Bell, Taco Bueno, Taco Cabana, Wendy's, Whataburger 🏠 Clarion
334b	US 77 S, 17th St, 18th St, E 🛢 Phillips 66, Shell/dsl 🍴 Burger King, Popeye's, Schlotzsky's, Vitek's BBQ 🏠 Budget Inn, Magnuson Hotel, Super 8, W 🛢 Phillips 66/dsl, Shell 🍴 Arranda's Mexican ◎ H
333a	Lp 396, Valley Mills Dr, E 🍴 El Chico, Elite Café, Rudy's BBQ, Trujillo's Mexican, TX Roadhouse 🏠 Comfort Suites, La Quinta, Motel 6 ◎ Kia, Mazda, Suzuki, W 🛢 RaceWay, Valero 🍴 Bush's Chicken, Catfish King, Church's, Jack-in-the-Box, Little Caesars, Papa John's, Sonic, Subway ◎ Aamco, Advance Parts, AutoZone, CVS Drug, Family$, HEB Foods, Lincoln, Walgreens
331	New Rd, E 🛢 Phillips 66 🏠 New Road Inn, Relax Inn, Rodeway Inn, W 🛢 ⊕FLYING J/Denny's/dsl/scales/24hr 🍴 Burger King, Carl's Jr, Hooters, IHOP 🏠 Quality Inn ◎ Harley Davidson
330	Lp 340, TX 6, W 0-2 mi 🛢 Chevron 🍴 Bush's Chicken, Chuy's Mexican, Coldstone, Don Carlo's Mexican, Logan's Roadhouse, Outback Steaks, Panda Express, Panera Bread, Sonic, Subway, TGIFriday's 🏠 Extended Stay America, Fairfield Inn, Hampton Inn, Homewood Suites ◎ H Belk, Best Buy, Books-A-Million, Ford, Honda, Hyundai, Kohl's, Lowe's, Marshall's, Nissan, Office Depot, Old Navy, Ross, Toyota/Scion, URGENT CARE, Verizon, Walmart
328	FM 2063, FM 2113, Moody, E 🛢 ▦/Subway/Wendy's/dsl/scales/24hr/@ 🍴 McDonald's 🏠 Days Inn ◎ Kenworth, W 🛢 Shell, Valero/dsl 🍴 DQ 🏠 Ramada Inn, Sleep Inn
325	FM 3148, Moonlight Dr, W 🛢 Smiley's/dsl ◎ FunTown RV Ctr
323	FM 2837 (from sb), Lorena, W 🛢 Brookshire Bros/Conoco/dsl 🍴 Pizza House, Sonic
322	Lorena, E 🛢 Phillips 66/dsl 🍴 Raymond's Southern Kitchen, W 🍴 Bush's Chicken, Pizza House ◎ $General
319	Woodlawn Rd
318b a	Bruceville, E ◎ 🅿s both lanes, litter barrels
315	TX 7, FM 107, Eddy, W 🛢 Shell/Subway/dsl/24hr, Texaco ◎ Family$, to Mother Neff SP
314	Old Blevins Rd
311	Big Elm Rd, E ◎ fireworks, W ◎ 🅿s
308	FM 935, Troy, W 🛢 Exxon ◎ dsl repair

Map labels: St Jo, Muenster, Lindsay, Oak Ridge, Sadler, Myra, Gainesville, Whitesboro, Valley View, Lois, Sanger, Union Hill, Dalton, Krum, Cross Roads, Decatur, Stony, Denton, Mayhill, Herman, Argyle, TX, 35

INTERSTATE 35 Cont'd

Exit #	Services
306	FM 1237, Pendleton, W Ⓞ Goodyear Truck Tires
305	Berger Rd, W Ⓞ Lucky's RV Park, repair
304	Lp 363, Dodgen Loop, W 🅿 Shell/Wendy's/dsl Ⓞ Freightliner
303	spur 290, N 3rd St, Temple, E 🅿 S-2 Gas 🛏 Texas Inn, W 🛏 Continental Inn
302	Nugent Ave, E 🅿 Exxon/dsl, Texaco 🛏 Baymont Inn, Best Value Inn, EconoLodge, Quality Inn, W 🅿 Pay Less Gas, Shell/dsl 🍴 Denny's 🛏 Days Inn, Knights Inn, Motel 6, Stratford House Inn
301	TX 53, FM 2305, Adams Ave, E 🅿 Valero 🍴 Arby's, Chick-fil-A, KFC, LJ Silver, Mad Mongo's Grill, McDonald's, Pizza Hut, Starbucks, Subway, Taco Bell, Wendy's, Whataburger 🛏 La Quinta Ⓞ H Advance Parts, Ford/Lincoln, HEB Foods, W 🍴 TX Roadhouse 🛏 Best Western Ⓞ Hyundai
300	Ave H, 49th –57th Sts, E 🍴 Clem Mikeskas BBQ
299	US 190 E, TX 36, E 🅿 Shell 🍴 Cracker Barrel, Jack-in-the-Box, Luby's, Olive Garden 🛏 Budget Inn, Residence Inn, Travelodge Ⓞ H AT&T, Chrysler/Dodge/Jeep, NTP, Verizon, W 🍴 5 Guys Burgers, BJ's Rest, Chili's, Chipotle Mexican, IHOP, McDonald's, Subway, Taco Cabana Ⓞ Best Buy, GNC, Home Depot, Michael's, Petsmart, Target
298	nb only, to frontage rd, E 🛏 Residence Inn
297	FM 817, Midway Dr, E 🅿 Phillips 66/dsl 🛏 Holiday Inn, Super 8/rest. Ⓞ Nissan, W 🅿 Valero Ⓞ Meineke, VW
294b	FM 93, 6th Ave, E 🅿 Shell/dsl 🍴 McDonald's Ⓞ Chevrolet, Toyota/Scion, W 🍴 Subway 🛏 River Forest Inn Ⓞ Harley-Davidson, U of Mary Hardin Baylor
294a	Central Ave, W 🅿 Shell/dsl 🍴 Burger King, El Mexicano Grill, Pizza Hut, Schlotzsky's, Sonic, Taco Bell, Whataburger 🛏 Knights Inn Ⓞ AutoZone, city park, O'Reilly Parts, Parts+, USPO
293b	TX 317, FM 436, Main St
293a	US 190 W, to Killeen, Ft Hood
292	Lp 121 (same as 293a), E 🅿 Valero/rest./dsl/24hr 🛏 Budget Host, W 🅿 Mobil/dsl 🍴 Oxbow Steaks 🛏 La Quinta Ⓞ Belton RV Park, Sunbelt RV Ctr
290	Shanklin Rd
289	Tahuaya Rd
287	Amity Rd
286	FM 2484, E 🛏 Best Western, Holiday Inn Express, W Ⓞ to Stillhouse Hollow Lake, Tranquil RV Park (2mi)
285	FM 2268, Salado, E 🍴 Subway 🛏 Holiday Inn Express Ⓞ Brookshire Foods/gas, W 🅿 Pay Less 🍴 Cowboys BBQ, Robertson's Rest., Rush's Chicken, Sonic
284	Stagecoach Rd, E 🅿 Exxon/Arby's 🛏 Stagecoach Inn, W 🍴 DQ, Johnny's Steaks
283	FM 2268, FM 2843, to Holland, Salado, E 🛏 Stagecoach Inn
282	FM 2115, E 🆁🆂 sb, full ♿ facilities, litter barrels, petwalk, 🅲 🚗 RV dump, vending 🅿 Valero/dsl
281mm	🆁🆂 nb, full ♿ facilities, litter barrels, petwalk, 🅲, 🚗 RV dump, vending
280	Prairie Dell
279	Hill Rd
277	Rd 305
275	FM 487, to Florence, Jarrell, E 🅿 Exxon/dsl Ⓞ $General, W 🅿 Shell Ⓞ USPO
274	Rd 312, E 🅿 Chevron/dsl, Exxon/Subway/dsl, ⛽FLYING J/Burger King/Denny's/dsl/scales 🍴 McDonald's
271	Theon Rd, Rd 311, W 🅿 Shell/Subway/dsl/24hr
268	fm 972, Walburg, E Ⓞ Crestview RV Ctr
266	TX 195, E 🅿 Phillips 66/dsl, W 🅿 Shell/dsl
265	TX 130 Toll S, to Austin
264	Lp 35, Georgetown
262	RM 2338, Lake Georgetown, E 🅿 Valero 🍴 Chipotle Mexican, Duke's Smokehouse, KFC, McDonald's, Papa John's, Pizza Hut, Sonic, Starbucks, Subway Ⓞ $Tree, CVS Drug, Parts+, Radio Shack, URGENT CARE, W 🅿 Shell 🍴 DQ, La Tapatia, Placa Greek, Whataburger 🛏 Candlewood Suites, Georgetown Inn, Holiday Inn Express, La Quinta
261	TX 29, Georgetown, E 🅿 Shell/dsl 🍴 Applebee's, Burger King, Chili's, KFC, Luby's, McDonald's, Schlotzsky's, Taco Bell 🛏 Comfort Suites, Country Inn&Suites Ⓞ Albertson's, HEB Foods, Hobby Lobby, Midas, same as 262, Tuesday Morning, W 🅿 Murphy USA/dsl 🍴 Casa Ole, Chick-fil-A, CiCi's, Genghis Grill, Ichyban Buffet, IHOP, Longhorn Steaks, Mama Fu's, McAlister's Deli, MT Mike's, Panda Express, Souper Salad, Subway, Taco Cabana, Wendy's, Zio's Italian Ⓞ antiques, AT&T, Beall's, Best Buy, Discount Tire, Home Depot, Kohl's, Michael's, Office Depot, Old Navy, Petsmart, Ross, Target, TJ Maxx, Verizon, Walgreens, Walmart
260	RM 2243, Leander, E Ⓞ H USPO, W 🅿 Chevron, Exxon, Texaco 🍴 Jack-in-the-Box 🛏 Quality Inn
259	Lp 35, W Ⓞ RV Outlet Ctr, to Interspace Caverns
257	Westinghouse Rd, E Ⓞ Buick/Chevrolet, Chrysler/Dodge/Jeep, Ford/Lincoln, Mazda, Subaru/Volvo, VW
256	RM 1431, Chandler Rd, E 🍴 BJ Rest, Chili's, Jamba Juice, La Madeline, Mimi's Cafe, Panda Express Ⓞ JC Penney, Jo-Ann Fabrics, Mazda, Mazda, Petsmart, REI, Ross, Round Rock Outlet/famous brands, Volvo
254	FM 3406, Round Rock, E 🅿 Chevron 🍴 Arby's, Gatti's Pizza, La Tapatia, McDonald's 🛏 Best Western Ⓞ $General, CVS Drug, Firestone/auto, Harley-Davidson, Honda, Hyundai, Smart Car, Toyota/Scion, W 🅿 Phillips 66/dsl, Shell 🍴 Blue Oak Grill, Carino's Italian, Chuy's Mexican, Cracker Barrel, Dave's Pizza, Denny's, Mesa Rosa Mexican, Rudy's BBQ/gas, SaltGrass Steaks 🛏 Country Inn&Suites, Courtyard, Hilton Garden, Holiday Inn Express, La Quinta, Red Roof Inn, SpringHill Suites, ValuePlace Ⓞ CVS Drug, GMC, Nissan
253b	US 79, to Taylor, E 🅿 Chevron, Shell, Texaco 🍴 Arby's, Baskin-Robbins, Casa Garcia's, DQ, Fuddrucker's, KFC, LJ Silver, Pizza Hut, Short Stop Dogs, Sirloin Stockade 🛏 Best Western, Wingate Inn Ⓞ H $General, AutoZone, Beall's, CarQuest, Cottman Transmissions, Just Brakes, vet, W 🅿 Exxon/dsl, Shell/dsl 🍴 Gatti's Pizza, Hunan Lion, IHOP, La Margarita, Popeye's, Starbucks, Taco Bell, Westside Ale House 🛏 Best Value Inn, Country Inn&Suites, Fairfield Inn, La Quinta, Red Roof Inn, Sleep Inn, ValuePlace Ⓞ $Tree, CVS Drug, USPO
253a	Frontage Rd, same as 253 b
252b a	RM 620, E 🅿 Shell/dsl 🛏 Candlewood Suites, Extended Stay America Ⓞ NAPA, W 🅿 Texaco/dsl 🍴 Freddy's Steakburgers, Little Caesars, McDonald's, Starbucks, Wendy's 🛏 Comfort Suites, Staybridge Suites
251	Lp 35, Round Rock, E 🅿 Valero 🍴 CiCi's Pizza, Outback Steaks, Whataburger 🛏 Residence Inn Ⓞ $General, Aamco, BigLots, Brake Check, Tuesday Morning, W 🅿 Shell 🍴 Burger King, China Wall, Jack-in-the-Box, Luby's, Lucky Dog Grill, Taco Cabana 🛏 Days Inn, Mariott, Sleep Inn Ⓞ GNC, NTB, transmissions, Walgreens
250	FM 1325, E 🍴 5 Guys Burgers, Chick-fil-A, Chili's, Jason's Deli, Joe's Crabshack, Macaroni Grill, McDonald's,

TEMPLE

GEORGETOWN

ROUND ROCK

TX

N INTERSTATE 35 Cont'd

Exit #	Services
250	Continued

Panda Express, Subway, Twin Peaks Rest. 🛏 Hampton Inn, Homewood Suites, Residence Inn Ⓞ $Tree, AT&T, Best Buy, Discount Tire, Home Depot, Michael's, Petsmart, Radio Shack, Ross, Steinmart, Target, URGENT CARE, Walmart, **W** 🅖 Shell 🍴 Antonio's Cantina, ChuckeCheese, Fast Eddie's, Hooters, Jimmy John's, Mongolian Grill, Olive Garden, Schlotzsky's, Starbucks 🛏 Extended Stay America, La Quinta Ⓞ Barnes&Noble, Hobby Lobby, Kohl's, Lowe's, Marshall's, Old Navy, PetCo, Ross, Sam's Club, World Mkt

248 Grand Ave Pkwy, **E** 🅖 Citgo, Shell, Texaco/Subway/dsl 🍴 Chucho's Mexican, Posados Cafe, Thundercloud Subs, TX Roadhouse 🛏 Comfort Suites Ⓞ Firestone, URGENT CARE, **W** 🅖 Chevron/McDonald's

247 FM 1825, Pflugerville, **E** 🅖 Texaco 🍴 Cheddar's, Fish Daddy's Grill, Jack-in-the-Box, Sonic, Subway, Taco Cabana, Wendy's 🛏 Comfort Suites Ⓞ Firestone/auto, HEB Foods/gas, **W** 🅖 Exxon, Shell/Church's 🍴 KFC, Miller's BBQ, Sonic 🛏 Holiday Inn Express Ⓞ Goodyear, Tires4Less

246 Howard Lane, **E** 🅖 Citgo, Shell/dsl 🍴 Arby's, Baby Acapulco, McDonald's, Subway, Wings'n More Ⓞ Home Depot, Kohl's, NTB, **W** 🅖 Valero/dsl 🍴 IHOP, Whataburger 🛏 Sleep Inn

245 FM 734, Parmer Lane, to Yager Lane (244 from nb), **E** 🍴 Carino's, Chick-fil-A, Chili's, Golden Wok, Jimmy John's, Pei Wei, Schlotzsky's, Souper Salad, Subway, Zed's Rest 🛏 Courtyard Ⓞ $Tree, HEB Food/E-85, Hobby Lobby, JC Penney, Kohl's, Office Depot, PetCo, Petsmart, Ross, Sears Grand, Target, Verizon, **W** 🅖 Conoco/dsl, Exxon, Murphy USA/dsl 🍴 Buffalo Wild Wings, Golden Corral, Hoho Chinese, Red Robin, Starbucks 🛏 Courtyard, Fairfield Inn, Hilton Garden, Residence Inn, SpringHill Suites Ⓞ AT&T, CarMax, Discount Tire, Lowe's, Walmart

243 Braker Lane, **E** 🅖 Valero 🍴 Jack-in-the-Box, Whataburger Ⓞ U-Haul, **W** 🅖 Citgo, Shell/dsl 🛏 Austin Motel, ValuePlace Ⓞ $General

241 Rundberg Lane, **E** 🅖 Exxon 🍴 Grand China Buffet, Jack-in-the-Box, Mr Gatti's, Old San Francisco Steaks 🛏 Extended Stay Deluxe, Ramada Inn Ⓞ $General, Albertson's, Chevrolet, U-Haul, Walmart, **W** 🅖 Chevron, Conoco, Shell, Texaco 🛏 Austin Suites, Budget Inn, Budget Lodge, Economy Inn, Holiday Inn Express, Motel 6, Red Roof Inn, Super 8, Wingate Inn

240a US 183, Lockhart, **E** 🅖 Exxon 🍴 DQ, Jack-in-the-Box, Old San Francisco Steaks 🛏 Days Inn, Ramada Inn, **W** 🅖 Chevron/dsl, Texaco/dsl 🛏 Motel 6, Red Roof Inn, Super 8, Wingate Inn

239 St John's Ave, **E** 🅖 Shell 🍴 Burger King, Chili's, Japon Japanese, Pappadeaux, Pappasito's Mexican 🛏 Crowne Plaza, Days Inn, DoubleTree, Drury Inn, Hampton Inn, North Austin Plaza, Studio 6 Ⓞ USPO, **W** 🅖 Conoco/dsl, Exxon, Valero/dsl 🍴 Antonio's Texmex, Applebee's, Buffalo Wild Wings, Carrabba's, Denny's, IHOP, Panda Express, Quiznos, Verona Italian, Wendy's 🛏 Baymont Inn, Best Value Inn, Comfort Inn, Country Inn&Suites, Courtyard, Holiday Inn Express, Hyatt Place, La Quinta, Radisson, Ramada Inn, Sheraton, Sumner Suites Ⓞ Ford, Office Depot

238b US 290 E, RM 222, frontage rds connect several exits, same as 238a

238a 51st St, **E** 🅖 Chevron/dsl, Exxon, Shell 🍴 Buffet King, Burger King, Church's, McDonald's, TX Steaks

---

238a Continued

🛏 DoubleTree Hotel, Drury Inn, EconoLodge, Embassy Suites, North Austin Suites Ⓞ $Tree, Advance Parts, AutoZone, Best Buy, Firestone, FoodLand, Home Depot, Jo-Ann Crafts, Marshall's, Old Navy, Petsmart, Ross, Staples, Target, Walgreens, **W** 🍴 Baby Acapulco, Capt Benny's Seafood 🛏 Capital Inn, Courtyard, Fairfield Inn, Hilton, Motel 6, Super 8 Ⓞ Dillard's

237b 51st St, same as 238a

237a Airport Blvd, **E** 🍴 BBQ, **W** 🍴 Jack-in-the-Box, Quiznos, Wendy's Ⓞ GNC, Goodyear, HEB Foods, Old Navy, PetCo, Sears/auto

236.7 lower level accesses downtown, upper level is I-35 thru

236b 39th St, **E** 🅖 Chevron/dsl 🍴 Short Stop Burgers, Subway Ⓞ Fiesta Foods, O'Reilly Parts, U-Haul, **W** 🅖 Shell/dsl Ⓞ tires, to U of TX, Tune&Lube

236a 26th-32nd Sts, **E** 🍴 Los Altos Mexican, Subway 🛏 Days Inn, **W** 🛏 Rodeway Inn Ⓞ 🄷

235b Manor Rd, **E** 🍴 Denny's 🛏 DoubleTree, **W** 🛏 Rodeway Inn Ⓞ st capitol, U of TX, vet, same as 236a

235a MLK, 15th St, **W** Ⓞ 🄷

234.9 lower level accesses downtown, upper level is I-35 thru

234c 11th St, 12th St, **E** 🅖 Chevron/dsl, Shell/dsl 🍴 Denny's, Wendy's 🛏 DoubleTree Hotel, Super 8 Ⓞ CVS Drug, **W** 🅖 Chevron, Shell, Texaco 🍴 Wendy's 🛏 Crowne Plaza, Hilton Garden, La Quinta, Marriott, Omni Motel, Radisson, Sheraton Ⓞ 🄷 museum, st capitol, downtown

234b 8th-3rd St, **W** 🍴 IHOP

234a Cesar Chavez St, Holly St, downtown

233 Riverside Dr, Town Lake, **E** 🅖 Shell/dsl, **W** 🅖 Chevron/dsl 🛏 Holiday Inn

232mm Little Colorado River

232b Woodland Ave

232a Oltorf St, **E** 🅖 Gulf, Shell/dsl 🍴 Luby's, Sonic 🛏 Country Garden Inn, Garden West, Howard Johnson, La Quinta, Motel 6, Parkwest Inn, **W** 🅖 Conoco/dsl, Exxon 🍴 Denny's, Starbucks 🛏 Clarion

231 Woodward St, **E** 🅖 Shell/dsl 🛏 same as 232, Wyndham Garden, **W** Ⓞ Home Depot

230b a US 290 W, TX 71, Ben White Blvd, St Elmo Rd, **E** 🅖 Shell 🍴 Domino's, Jim's Rest., McDonald's, Sigon Kitchen, Subway, Western Choice Steaks 🛏 Baymont Inn, Best Western, Comfort Suites, Courtyard, Fairfield Inn, Hampton Inn, Marriott, Omni Hotel, Red Roof Inn, Residence Inn, SpringHill Suites Ⓞ Acura, **W** 🍴 Burger King, Furr's Cafeteria, IHOP, Pizza Hut 🛏 Candlewood Suites, Days Inn, La Quinta Ⓞ 🄷 Audi, CarMax, Chrysler/Dodge/Jeep, Ford, Hyundai, Kia, Mazda, Nissan, NTB, Suzuki, Toyota/Scion

(map labels, reading left to right top to bottom): Libery Hill, Weir, Georgetown, Leander, Taylor, 35, Hutto, Cedar Park, Round Rock, Jollyville, Pflugerville, Burbank Acres, River Hills, Abercrombie, Littig, Elgin, Butler, Bee Cave, McDade, Rollingwood, **Austin**, Del Valle, Pleasant Hill, Garfield, San Leanna, Wyldwood, Bastrop, Buda, Creedmoor

A U S T I N

⬆N INTERSTATE 35 Cont'd

Exit #	Services
229	Stassney Lane, **W** 🍴 Buffalo Wild Wings, Chili's, Krispy Kreme, Logan's Roadhouse, Macaroni Grill, Pizza Hut, Rockfish Grill, Twin Peaks Rest., TX Cattle Co Steaks 🅞 Albertson's/gas, Fiesta Foods/gas, Kia, Lowe's
228	Wm Cannon Drive, **E** 🅖 Exxon, Valero 🍴 Applebee's, McDonald's, Taco Bell 🅞 Brake Check, Chrysler, Discount Tire, HEB Foods, Mitsubishi, Nissan, Radio Shack, Target, **W** 🅖 Shell/dsl, Texaco 🍴 Arby's, Burger King, China Harbor, Gatti's Pizza, Jack-in-the-Box, KFC, LJ Silver, Peter Piper Pizza, Taco Cabana, Wendy's, Whataburger 🅞 $General, Advance Parts, BigLots, Chevrolet, CVS Drug, Firestone, Hyundai/Subaru
227	Slaughter Lane, Lp 275, S Congress, **E** 🅖 Shell/dsl 🍴 Don Dario's, IHOP 🅞 Home Depot, Lone Star RV Resort, U-Haul, **W** 🅖 Murphy USA/dsl, Texaco, Valero/dsl 🍴 Carino's, Chick-fil-A, Chili's, Chipotle Mexican, Gatti's, Jack-in-the-Box, Jason's Deli, Longhorn Steaks, Mama Fu's, Miller BBQ, Panda Express, Sonic, Starbucks, Steak'n Shake, Subway, Taco Bell, TGIFriday's, TX Roadhouse, Wendy's, Whataburger 🅞 Best Buy, Firestone/auto, GNC, Hobby Lobby, JC Penney, Marshall's, Petsmart, Ross, Sam's Club/gas, Target, Walgreens, Walmart
226	Slaughter Creek Overpass
225	FM 1626, Onion Creek Pkwy, **E** 🅖 Texaco, Valero 🍴 Subway 🅞 Harley-Davidson
224	frontage rd (from nb)
223	FM 1327, rd 45 toll
221	Lp 4, Buda, **E** 🅖 Chevron/McDonald's, Shell/dsl 🍴 Starbucks 🛏 Best Value Inn, Comfort Suites, Holiday Inn Express 🅞 Ford, Kenworth, **W** 🅖 Chevron, Murphy USA/dsl, Shell 🍴 Arby's, Chili's, Cracker Barrel, Dan's Burgers, Jack-in-the-Box, KFC/LJ Silver, Little Caesars, Logan's Roadhouse, Miller BBQ, Papa John's, Pizza Hut, Sonic, Subway, Taco Bell, Whataburger 🛏 Hampton Inn, Microtel 🅞 AT&T, Cabela's, HEB Food/dsl/E-85, O'Reilly Parts, Radio Shack, USPO, Walgreens, Walmart
220	FM 2001, Niederwald, **E** 🅖 Shell 🅞 Camper Clinic RV Ctr, Marshall's RV Park, **W** 🅞 Crestview RV Ctr/Park, Peterbilt
217	Lp 4, Buda, **E** 🅖 Conoco/dsl/24hr 🛏 La Quinta 🅞 Mack/Volvo, **W** 🅖 Valero/dsl 🍴 Burger King 🛏 Best Western 🅞 Christian Bros Auto, Home Depot
215	Bunton Overpass, **E** 🅖 Exxon/KFC/LJ Silver 🅞 🏥 AT&T, Discount Tire, Lowe's, Walgreens, **W** 🅖 Shell/dsl 🍴 Jack-in-the-Box, McDonald's, Papa Murphy's, Starbucks, Subway, Whataburger 🅞 $Tree, Explore USA RV Ctr, GNC, HEB Foods/dsl, Kohl's, PetCo, Target
213	FM 150, Kyle, **E** 🅖 Valero/dsl 🍴 DQ 🅞 AutoZone, Goodyear/auto, **W** 🅖 Conoco/dsl 🍴 Casa Maria Mexican 🅞 CVS Drug, repair
210	Yarrington Rd, **E** 🅞 Hyundai, **W** 🅞 Buick/Chevrolet/GMC, Plum Creek RV Park
209	weigh sta (sb only)
208mm	Blanco River
208	Frontage Rd, Blanco River Rd, **W** 🅞 Buick/Chevrolet/GMC
206	Lp 82, Aquarena Springs Rd, **E** 🅖 Conoco, Valero 🅞 San Marcos RV Park, **W** 🅖 Citgo/dsl, Exxon/dsl, Shell, Texaco 🍴 Pancake House, Popeye's, Sonic 🛏 Best Value Inn, Howard Johnson, La Quinta, Motel 6, Ramada Ltd, Rodeway Inn, Summit Inn, Super 8, Travelodge 🅞 to SW TX U

205	TX 80, TX 142, Bastrop, **E** 🅖 Exxon, Quix, RaceWay, Shell/dsl, Valero/dsl 🍴 Arby's, China Palace, DQ, Fazoli's, Jason's Deli, Subway, Wing Stop 🛏 Executive Inn 🅞 $General, AutoZone, CVS Drug, Hastings Books, Hobby Lobby, Kwik Kar, Verizon, vet, Walmart, **W** 🅖 Valero 🍴 A&W/LJ Silver, Burger King, Church's, KFC, Kobe Japanese, Logan's Roadhouse, McDonald's, Pizza Hut, Taco Cabana, Wendy's 🛏 Best Western, Budget Inn, Days Inn, Gateway Inn, Knights Inn, Red Roof Inn, Rodeway Inn 🅞 Brake Check, city park, GNC, HEB Foods, JC Penney, Office Depot, Radio Shack, Walgreens
204mm	San Marcos River
204b	CM Allen Pkwy, **W** 🅖 Shell/dsl, Spirit 🍴 DQ, Krispy Kreme, La Fonda Rest, Mazatlan Mexican, Plucker's Grill, Sonic 🛏 Best Western, EconoLodge 🅞 AutoZone, O'Reilly Parts, transmissions
204a	Lp 82, TX 123, to Seguin, **E** 🅖 Conoco, Exxon/dsl, Valero 🍴 Burger King, Carino's, Chicken Express, Chili's, Golden Corral, Luby's, McDonald's, Red Lobster, Whataburger 🛏 Comfort Suites, Hampton Inn, Holiday Inn Express 🅞 🏥 Aamco, Ford
202	FM 3407, Wonder World Dr, **E** 🅖 Exxon, Shell/Church's 🍴 Carl's Jr, Chick-fil-A, Fuschaks BBQ, Jack-in-the-Box, Taco Bueno, Taste of China, Wienerschnitzel 🅞 🏥 $Tree, Best Buy, Discount Tire, Lowe's, Marshall's, Petsmart, Ross, Sams Club/gas, **W** 🅖 Valero/dsl 🍴 TX Roadhouse 🛏 Candlewood Suites, Country Inn&Suites 🅞 repair
201	McCarty Lane, **E** 🛏 Embassy Suites, **W** 🍴 Panda Express, Sonic 🅞 AT&T, Beall's, Chrysler/Dodge/Jeep, Firestone/auto, JC Penney, Nissan, Target
200	Centerpoint Rd, **E** 🍴 Cracker Barrel, Food Court, Outback Steaks, River City Grill, Subway, Taco Bell, Wendy's 🅞 GNC, Old Navy, San Marcos Outlets/famous brands, Tanger Outlet/famous brands, VF Outlets/famous brands, **W** 🅖 Valero/dsl 🍴 McDonald's, Quiznos, Starbucks, Whataburger 🛏 Baymont Inn 🅞 Honda
199	Posey Rd, **E** 🅞 same as 200, Tanger Outlets/famous brands, Toyota/Scion
196	FM 1106, York Creek Rd, **W** 🅞 Canyon Trail RV Park
195	Watson Lane, Old Bastrop Rd
193	Conrads Rd, Kohlenberg Rd, **W** 🅖 TA/Country Fare Rest/Popeye's/Subway/dsl/scales/24hr/@ 🅞 Camping World RV Ctr
191	FM 306, FM 483, Canyon Lake, **E** 🅖 Buc-ee's 🍴 BJ's Rest, Longhorn Steaks, Subway, Whataburger 🅞 AT&T, Best Buy, Dick's, I-35 RV Camping, JC Penney, Petsmart, Ross, Target, URGENT CARE, Verizon, Walmart Dist Ctr, **W** 🅖 Chevron, Exxon/dsl 🍴 Burger King, Quiznos 🛏 Wingate Inn 🅞 transmissions
190c	Post Rd
190b	frontage rd, New Braunfels
190a	frontage rd, same as 189
189	TX 46, Seguin, **E** 🅖 Shell/dsl 🍴 Chili's, Denny's, Golden Corral, Logan's Roadhouse, Olive Garden, Peter Piper Pizza, Taco Bueno 🛏 Best Value Inn, EconoLodge, Hampton Inn, La Quinta, Super 8 🅞 Discount Tire, Home Depot, Kohl's, Office Depot, vet, **W** 🅖 Texaco, Valero 🍴 Applebee's, Chili's, Chipotle Mexican, El Tapatio, IHOP, Mama Fu's, McDonald's, MT Mike's, Pizza Hut, Subway, Taco Bell, Taco Cabana, TJ's Burgers, Wendy's 🛏 Baymont, Best Western, Comfort Suites, Days Inn, Edelweiss Inn, Fairfield Inn, Hilton Garden, Howard Johnson, Microtel, Motel 6, Quality Inn, Ramada Inn, Rodeway Inn, Sleep Inn 🅞 🏥 Walgreens

SAN MARCOS

NEW BRAUNFELS

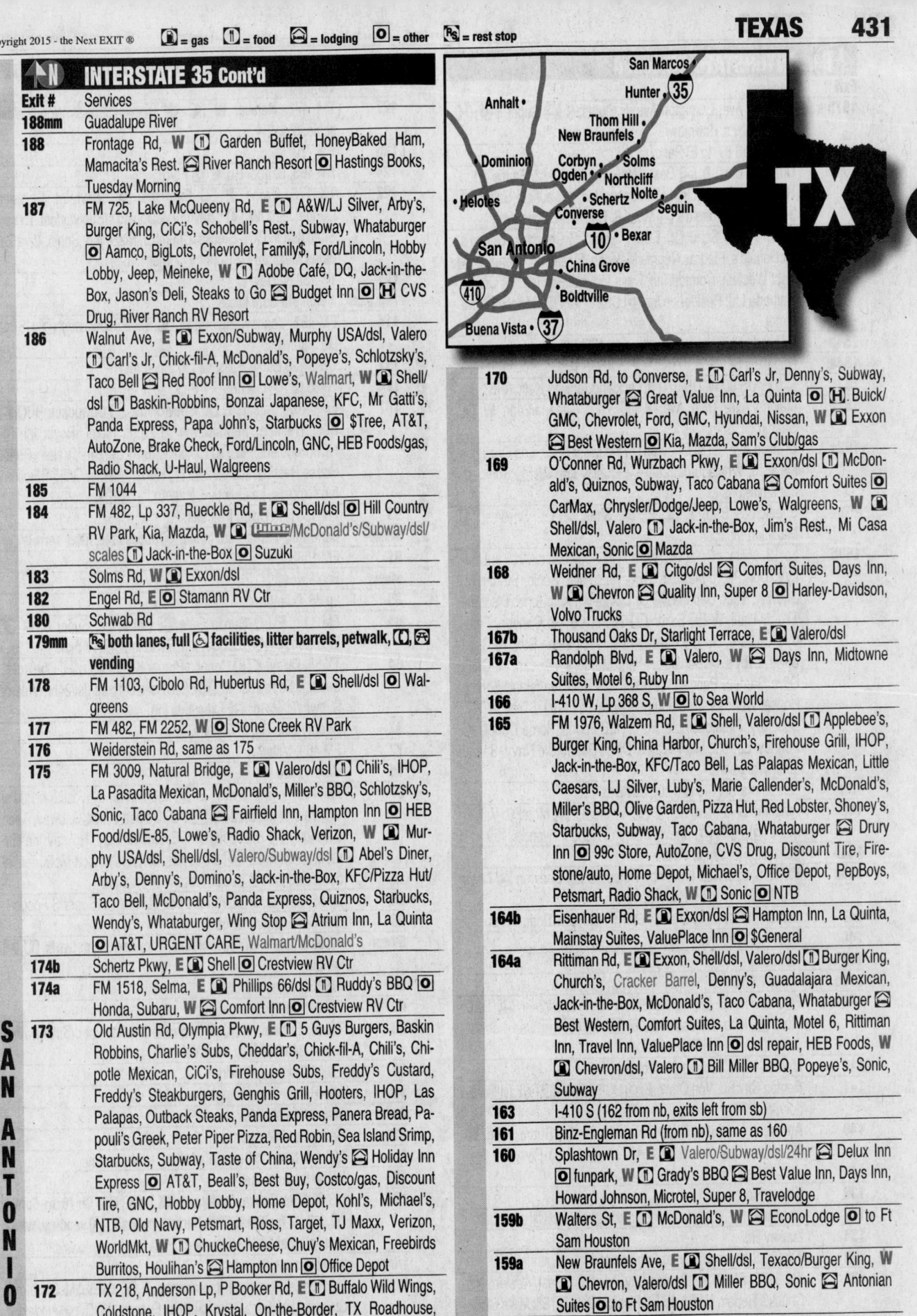

INTERSTATE 35 Cont'd

Exit #	Services
188mm	Guadalupe River
188	Frontage Rd, W 🅕 Garden Buffet, HoneyBaked Ham, Mamacita's Rest. 🅛 River Ranch Resort 🅞 Hastings Books, Tuesday Morning
187	FM 725, Lake McQueeny Rd, E 🅕 A&W/LJ Silver, Arby's, Burger King, CiCi's, Schobell's Rest., Subway, Whataburger 🅞 Aamco, BigLots, Chevrolet, Family$, Ford/Lincoln, Hobby Lobby, Jeep, Meineke, W 🅕 Adobe Café, DQ, Jack-in-the-Box, Jason's Deli, Steaks to Go 🅛 Budget Inn 🅞 🅷 CVS Drug, River Ranch RV Resort
186	Walnut Ave, E 🅖 Exxon/Subway, Murphy USA/dsl, Valero 🅕 Carl's Jr, Chick-fil-A, McDonald's, Popeye's, Schlotzsky's, Taco Bell 🅛 Red Roof Inn 🅞 Lowe's, Walmart, W 🅖 Shell/dsl 🅕 Baskin-Robbins, Bonzai Japanese, KFC, Mr Gatti's, Panda Express, Papa John's, Starbucks 🅞 $Tree, AT&T, AutoZone, Brake Check, Ford/Lincoln, GNC, HEB Foods/gas, Radio Shack, U-Haul, Walgreens
185	FM 1044
184	FM 482, Lp 337, Rueckle Rd, E 🅖 Shell/dsl 🅞 Hill Country RV Park, Kia, Mazda, W 🅖 [HESS]/McDonald's/Subway/dsl/scales 🅕 Jack-in-the-Box 🅞 Suzuki
183	Solms Rd, W 🅖 Exxon/dsl
182	Engel Rd, E 🅞 Stamann RV Ctr
180	Schwab Rd
179mm	🆁🆂 both lanes, full ♿ facilities, litter barrels, petwalk, ⧈, 🅛 vending
178	FM 1103, Cibolo Rd, Hubertus Rd, E 🅖 Shell/dsl 🅞 Walgreens
177	FM 482, FM 2252, W 🅞 Stone Creek RV Park
176	Weiderstein Rd, same as 175
175	FM 3009, Natural Bridge, E 🅖 Valero/dsl 🅕 Chili's, IHOP, La Pasadita Mexican, McDonald's, Miller's BBQ, Schlotzsky's, Sonic, Taco Cabana 🅛 Fairfield Inn, Hampton Inn 🅞 HEB Food/dsl/E-85, Lowe's, Radio Shack, Verizon, W 🅖 Murphy USA/dsl, Shell/dsl, Valero/Subway/dsl 🅕 Abel's Diner, Arby's, Denny's, Domino's, Jack-in-the-Box, KFC/Pizza Hut/Taco Bell, McDonald's, Panda Express, Quiznos, Starbucks, Wendy's, Whataburger, Wing Stop 🅛 Atrium Inn, La Quinta 🅞 AT&T, URGENT CARE, Walmart/McDonald's
174b	Schertz Pkwy, E 🅖 Shell 🅞 Crestview RV Ctr
174a	FM 1518, Selma, E 🅖 Phillips 66/dsl 🅕 Ruddy's BBQ 🅞 Honda, Subaru, W 🅛 Comfort Inn 🅞 Crestview RV Ctr
173	Old Austin Rd, Olympia Pkwy, E 🅕 5 Guys Burgers, Baskin Robbins, Charlie's Subs, Cheddar's, Chick-fil-A, Chili's, Chipotle Mexican, CiCi's, Firehouse Subs, Freddy's Custard, Freddy's Steakburgers, Genghis Grill, Hooters, IHOP, Las Palapas, Outback Steaks, Panda Express, Panera Bread, Papouli's Greek, Peter Piper Pizza, Red Robin, Sea Island Srimp, Starbucks, Subway, Taste of China, Wendy's 🅛 Holiday Inn Express 🅞 AT&T, Beall's, Best Buy, Costco/gas, Discount Tire, GNC, Hobby Lobby, Home Depot, Kohl's, Michael's, NTB, Old Navy, Petsmart, Ross, Target, TJ Maxx, Verizon, WorldMkt, W 🅕 ChuckeCheese, Chuy's Mexican, Freebirds Burritos, Houlihan's 🅛 Hampton Inn 🅞 Office Depot
172	TX 218, Anderson Lp, P Booker Rd, E 🅕 Buffalo Wild Wings, Coldstone, IHOP, Krystal, On-the-Border, TX Roadhouse, Zio's 🅛 Comfort Inn, ValuePlace 🅞 Nissan, to Randolph AFB, W to SeaWorld
171	Topperwein Rd, same as 170

170	Judson Rd, to Converse, E 🅕 Carl's Jr, Denny's, Subway, Whataburger 🅛 Great Value Inn, La Quinta 🅞 🅷 Buick/GMC, Chevrolet, Ford, GMC, Hyundai, Nissan, W 🅖 Exxon 🅛 Best Western 🅞 Kia, Mazda, Sam's Club/gas
169	O'Conner Rd, Wurzbach Pkwy, E 🅖 Exxon/dsl 🅕 McDonald's, Quiznos, Subway, Taco Cabana 🅛 Comfort Suites 🅞 CarMax, Chrysler/Dodge/Jeep, Lowe's, Walgreens, W 🅖 Shell/dsl, Valero 🅕 Jack-in-the-Box, Jim's Rest., Mi Casa Mexican, Sonic 🅞 Mazda
168	Weidner Rd, E 🅖 Citgo/dsl 🅛 Comfort Suites, Days Inn, W 🅖 Chevron 🅛 Quality Inn, Super 8 🅞 Harley-Davidson, Volvo Trucks
167b	Thousand Oaks Dr, Starlight Terrace, E 🅖 Valero/dsl
167a	Randolph Blvd, E 🅖 Valero, W 🅛 Days Inn, Midtowne Suites, Motel 6, Ruby Inn
166	I-410 W, Lp 368 S, W 🅞 to Sea World
165	FM 1976, Walzem Rd, E 🅖 Shell, Valero/dsl 🅕 Applebee's, Burger King, China Harbor, Church's, Firehouse Grill, IHOP, Jack-in-the-Box, KFC/Taco Bell, Las Palapas Mexican, Little Caesars, LJ Silver, Luby's, Marie Callender's, McDonald's, Miller's BBQ, Olive Garden, Pizza Hut, Red Lobster, Shoney's, Starbucks, Subway, Taco Cabana, Whataburger 🅛 Drury Inn 🅞 99c Store, AutoZone, CVS Drug, Discount Tire, Firestone/auto, Home Depot, Michael's, Office Depot, PepBoys, Petsmart, Radio Shack, W 🅕 Sonic 🅞 NTB
164b	Eisenhauer Rd, E 🅖 Exxon/dsl 🅛 Hampton Inn, La Quinta, Mainstay Suites, ValuePlace Inn 🅞 $General
164a	Rittiman Rd, E 🅖 Exxon, Shell/dsl, Valero/dsl 🅕 Burger King, Church's, Cracker Barrel, Denny's, Guadalajara Mexican, Jack-in-the-Box, McDonald's, Taco Cabana, Whataburger 🅛 Best Western, Comfort Suites, La Quinta, Motel 6, Rittiman Inn, Travel Inn, ValuePlace Inn 🅞 dsl repair, HEB Foods, W 🅖 Chevron/dsl, Valero 🅕 Bill Miller BBQ, Popeye's, Sonic, Subway
163	I-410 S (162 from nb, exits left from sb)
161	Binz-Engleman Rd (from nb), same as 160
160	Splashtown Dr, E 🅖 Valero/Subway/dsl/24hr 🅛 Delux Inn 🅞 funpark, W 🅕 Grady's BBQ 🅛 Best Value Inn, Days Inn, Howard Johnson, Microtel, Super 8, Travelodge
159b	Walters St, E 🅕 McDonald's, W 🅛 EconoLodge 🅞 to Ft Sam Houston
159a	New Braunfels Ave, E 🅖 Shell/dsl, Texaco/Burger King, W 🅖 Chevron, Valero/dsl 🅕 Miller BBQ, Sonic 🅛 Antonian Suites 🅞 to Ft Sam Houston
158c	N Alamo St, Broadway
158b	I-37 S, US 281 S, to Corpus Christi, to Alamo
158a	US 281 N (from sb), to Johnson City

SAN ANTONIO

🅖 = gas   🍴 = food   🏠 = lodging   🅞 = other   🆁🆂 = rest stop   Copyright 2015 - the Next EXIT ®

Exit #	Services
INTERSTATE 35 Cont'd	
157b a	Brooklyn Ave, Lexington Ave, N Flores, **E** 🏠 Super 8 🅞 🅷 **W** 🍴 Luby's, downtown
156	I-10 W, US 87, to El Paso
155b	Durango Blvd, **E** 🏠 Best Western, Courtyard, Fairfield Inn, Holiday Inn, La Quinta, Residence Inn, Woodfield Suites 🅞 🅷 **W** 🍴 McDonald's 🏠 Motel 6, Radisson, downtown
155a	South Alamo St, **E** 🅖 Exxon, Shell 🍴 Church's, Denny's, McDonald's, Piedras Negras Mexican, Pizza Hut, Wendy's 🏠 Best Western, Comfort Inn, Days Inn, Holiday Inn, La Quinta, Ramada Ltd, Residence Inn 🅞 USPO, **W** 🅖 Conoco 🏠 Microtel
154b	S Laredo St, Ceballos St, same as 155b
154a	Nogalitos St
153	I-10 E, US 90 W, US 87, 🅞 Lackland AFB, to Kelly AFB
152b	Malone Ave, Theo Ave, **E** 🍴 Taco Cabana/24hr, **W** 🅖 Shamrock, Shell
152a	Division Ave, **E** 🅖 Chevron 🍴 Bill Miller BBQ, Las Cazuelas Mexican, Whataburger/24hr 🏠 Quality Inn, **W** 🍴 Sonic 🅞 transmissions
151	Southcross Blvd, **E** 🅖 Exxon, Shell, **W** 🅖 Shell/dsl 🍴 Mazatlan Mexican
150b	Lp 13, Military Dr, **E** 🅖 Valero 🍴 Applebee's, Arby's, Denny's, Don Pedro Mexican, KFC, Pizza Hut, Sonic, Starbucks, Subway, Taco Cabana 🏠 La Quinta 🅞 AutoZone, Discount Tire, U-Haul, **W** 🅖 Exxon 🍴 Chili's, Coyote Canyon, Freddy's Custard, Hungry Farmer Rest, Jack-in-the-Box, KFC, LJ Silver, Luby's, McDonald's, Moma Margie's Mexican, Mr Gatti, Olive Garden, Panda Express, Pizza Hut, Sea Island Shrimp House, Wendy's, Whataburger 🏠 La Quinta 🅞 $Tree, AT&T, Best Buy, Firestone/auto, Ford, HEB Foods, Home Depot, JC Penney, Lowe's, Macy's, mall, Office Depot, Old Navy, Sears/auto, Walgreens
150a	Zarzamora St (149 fom sb), same as 150b
149	Hutchins Blvd (from sb), **E** 🅖 Valero/dsl 🏠 Motel 6, ValuePlace 🅞 🅷 **W** 🅞 Chevrolet, Ford, Honda, Hyundai, Kia
148b	Palo Alto Rd, **W** 🅖 Valero
148a	TX 16 S, spur 422 (from nb), Poteet, **E** 🅖 Chevron 🏠 Days Inn, **W** 🅖 Phillips 66 🅞 $General
147	Somerset Rd, **E** 🅖 Shell/dsl, **W** 🅞 Chrysler/Dodge/Jeep
146	Cassin Rd (from nb)
145b	Lp 353 N
145a	I-410, TX 16
144	Fischer Rd, **E** 🅖 Valero/Subway/dsl/scales/24hr 🏠 D&D Motel 🅞 lube, RV camping, **W** 🅖 **♥Loves**/Carl's Jr/dsl/scales/24hr/@ 🅞 Toyota/Scion
142	Medina River Turnaround (from nb)
141	Benton City Rd, Von Ormy, **E** 🅞 USPO, **W** 🅖 Shell/dsl/Parador Café
140	Anderson Lp, 1604, **E** 🅖 Exxon/dsl/24hr 🍴 Burger King, **W** 🅖 Valero/Church's/dsl/scales/24hr 🅞 Alamo River RV Resort, to Sea World
139	Kinney Rd
137	Shepherd Rd, **E** 🅞 truck repair, **W** 🅖 gas/dsl 🅞 dsl repair
135	Luckey Rd
133	TX 132 S (from sb), Lytle, same as 131
131	FM 3175, FM 2790, Benton City Rd, **E** 🏠 Best Western 🅞 Chuck's Repair, NAPA, **W** 🅖 Pico/dsl/24hr 🍴 Bill Miller BBQ, McDonald's, Sonic, Subway, Whataburger 🏠 Days Inn/cafe 🅞 $General, AutoZone, Crawford Drug, Family$, HEB Food/dsl, USPO

Exit #	Services
129mm	🆁🆂 both lanes, full 🚻 facilities, litter barrels, petwalk, 🄲, 🖼 vending
127	FM 471, Natalia, **W** 🅖 **♥Loves**/Subway/Wendy's/dsl/scales/24hr/@
125	FM 770
124	FM 463, Bigfoot Rd, **E** 🅞 Ford
122	TX 173, Divine, **E** 🅖 Exxon/dsl 🅞 Chevrolet, Chrysler/Dodge/Jeep, **W** 🅖 Chevron/McDonald's/Subway/dsl, Exxon, Shell/dsl 🍴 CCC Steaks, Church's, Pizza Inn, Sonic, Viva Zapatas Mexican 🏠 Country Corner Inn
121	TX 132 N, Devine
118.5mm	weigh sta both lanes
114	FM 462, Yancey, Bigfoot, **W** 🅖 Shell/Subway/dsl 🅞 USPO, 🅖 Lucky/dsl
111	US 57, to Eagle Pass, **W** 🅖 Valero/dsl
104	Lp 35, **E** 🅞 Gilendo RV Park
101	FM 140, Pearsall, **E** 🅖 Chevron/dsl 🍴 Cowpokes BBQ 🏠 Best Western, Pearsall Inn, Rio Frio Motel, Royal Inn 🅞 HEB Foods/dsl, **W** 🅖 Exxon/Subway/dsl/24hr, Valero/Porter House Rest/dsl/scales/24hr 🍴 Hungry Hunter Grill 🏠 Holiday Inn Express, La Quinta, Southern Inn 🅞 🅷
99	FM 1581, to Divot, Pearsall
93mm	parking/🆁🆂 area both lanes, 🚻 accessible, litter barrels
91	FM 1583, Derby
90mm	Frio River
86	Lp 35, Dilley
85	FM 117, **E** 🍴 Garcia Café 🏠 Relax Inn, Super 8, **W** 🅖 Exxon 🍴 DQ 🏠 Budget Inn, Sona Inn 🅞 RV park
84	TX 85, Dilley, **E** 🅖 Conoco/Burger King/dsl 🅞 🅷 Chevrolet, Super S Foods/dsl, **W** 🅖 Shell/Pollo Grande/dsl/24hr, Valero/Subway/dsl/24hr 🏠 Executive Inn
82	County Line Rd, to Dilley, Dilley
77	FM 469, Millett
74	Gardendale
67	FM 468, to Big Wells, **E** 🅖 Exxon/Wendy's/dsl/24hr, JJ's/dsl, Valero/deli/dsl/24hr 🍴 DQ, Golden Chick, Subway, Taco Palenque 🏠 Executive Inn, Extended Stay, Holiday Inn Express, Village Inn 🅞 tire repair, **W** 🅖 Chevron/McDonald's/dsl/scales/24hr 🏠 Best Western 🅞 rv park
65	Lp 35, Cotulla, **E** 🅖 Phillips 66 🅞 Family$, Super S Foods
63	Elm Creek Interchange
59mm	🆁🆂 both lanes, full 🚻 facilities, litter barrels, petwalk, 🄲, 🖼 vending
56	FM 133, Artesia Wells
48	Caiman Creek Interchange
39	TX 44, Encinal, **E** 🅖 **♥Loves**/Chester Fried/Subway/dsl/scales/24hr, **W** 🅖 Exxon/dsl
38	TX 44 (from nb), Encinal
32	San Roman Interchange
29mm	inspection sta nb
27	Callaghan Interchange
24	255 toll, **Camino Colombia toll rd**, to Monterrey
22	Webb Interchange
18	US 83 N, to Carrizo Springs, **E** 🅖 **TX Travel Info Ctr (8am-5pm)/** 🆁🆂, full 🚻 facilities, litter barrels, petwalk, 🖼 vending, wireless internet **W** RV Camping
14mm	parking area sb
12b	(13 from sb) Uniroyal Interchange, **E** 🅖 ▦/McDonald's/Subway/dsl/scales/24hr 🅞 Blue Beacon, **W** 🅖 ✈FLYING J/Denny's/dsl/scales/24hr, TA/Burger King/Subway/Taco Bell/dsl/scales/24hr/@
12a	Port Loredo

PEARSALL

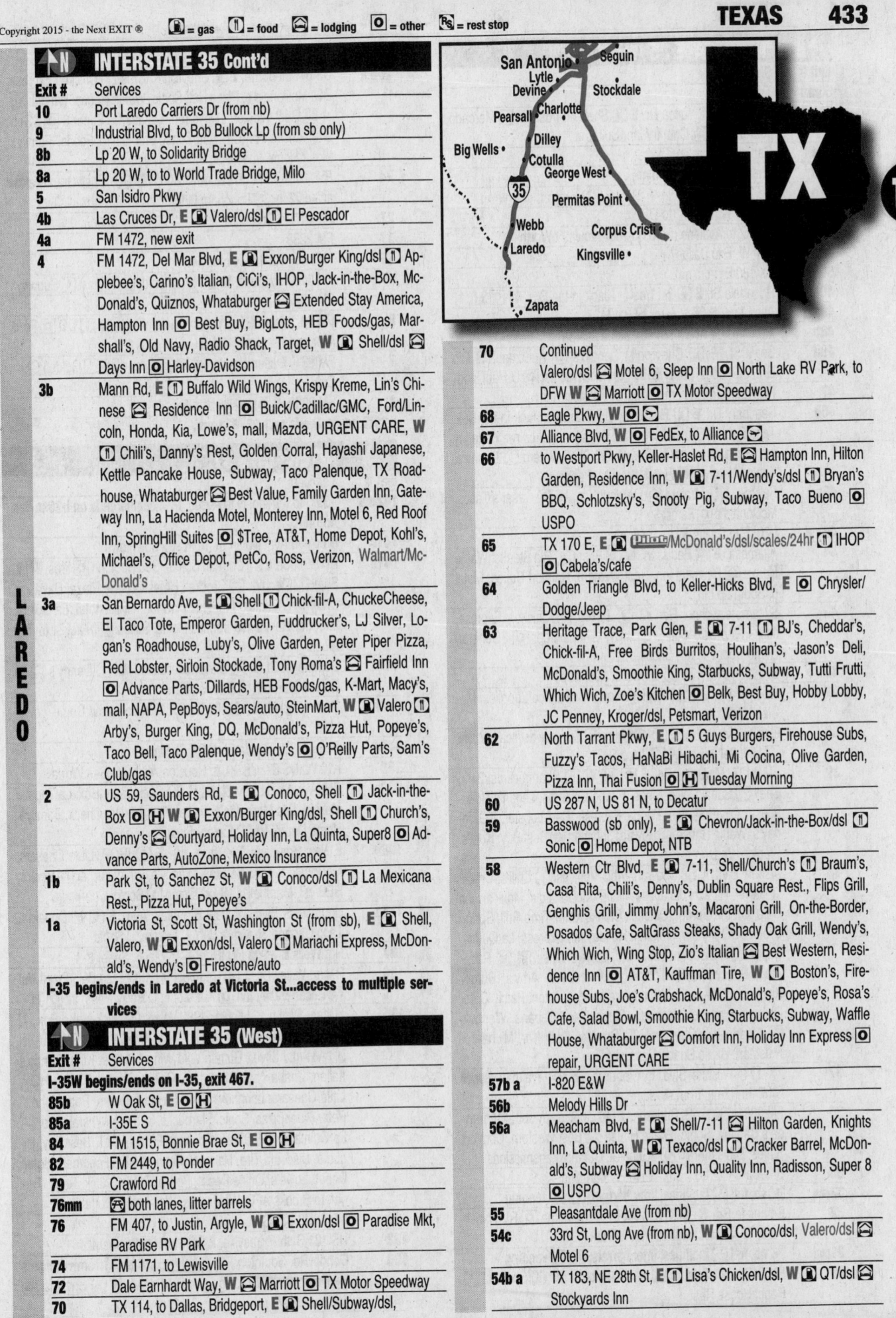

⬆N INTERSTATE 35 Cont'd

Exit #	Services
10	Port Laredo Carriers Dr (from nb)
9	Industrial Blvd, to Bob Bullock Lp (from sb only)
8b	Lp 20 W, to Solidarity Bridge
8a	Lp 20 W, to to World Trade Bridge, Milo
5	San Isidro Pkwy
4b	Las Cruces Dr, E 🅖 Valero/dsl 🍴 El Pescador
4a	FM 1472, new exit
4	FM 1472, Del Mar Blvd, E 🅖 Exxon/Burger King/dsl 🍴 Applebee's, Carino's Italian, CiCi's, IHOP, Jack-in-the-Box, McDonald's, Quiznos, Whataburger 🛏 Extended Stay America, Hampton Inn 🅞 Best Buy, BigLots, HEB Foods/gas, Marshall's, Old Navy, Radio Shack, Target, W 🅖 Shell/dsl 🛏 Days Inn 🅞 Harley-Davidson
3b	Mann Rd, E 🍴 Buffalo Wild Wings, Krispy Kreme, Lin's Chinese 🛏 Residence Inn 🅞 Buick/Cadillac/GMC, Ford/Lincoln, Honda, Kia, Lowe's, mall, Mazda, URGENT CARE, W 🍴 Chili's, Danny's Rest, Golden Corral, Hayashi Japanese, Kettle Pancake House, Subway, Taco Palenque, TX Roadhouse, Whataburger 🛏 Best Value, Family Garden Inn, Gateway Inn, La Hacienda Motel, Monterey Inn, Motel 6, Red Roof Inn, SpringHill Suites 🅞 $Tree, AT&T, Home Depot, Kohl's, Michael's, Office Depot, PetCo, Ross, Verizon, Walmart/McDonald's
3a	San Bernardo Ave, E 🅖 Shell 🍴 Chick-fil-A, ChuckeCheese, El Taco Tote, Emperor Garden, Fuddrucker's, LJ Silver, Logan's Roadhouse, Luby's, Olive Garden, Peter Piper Pizza, Red Lobster, Sirloin Stockade, Tony Roma's 🛏 Fairfield Inn 🅞 Advance Parts, Dillards, HEB Foods/gas, K-Mart, Macy's, mall, NAPA, PepBoys, Sears/auto, SteinMart, W 🅖 Valero 🍴 Arby's, Burger King, DQ, McDonald's, Pizza Hut, Popeye's, Taco Bell, Taco Palenque, Wendy's 🅞 O'Reilly Parts, Sam's Club/gas
2	US 59, Saunders Rd, E 🅖 Conoco, Shell 🍴 Jack-in-the-Box 🅞 🏥 W 🅖 Exxon/Burger King/dsl, Shell 🍴 Church's, Denny's 🛏 Courtyard, Holiday Inn, La Quinta, Super8 🅞 Advance Parts, AutoZone, Mexico Insurance
1b	Park St, to Sanchez St, W 🅖 Conoco/dsl 🍴 La Mexicana Rest., Pizza Hut, Popeye's
1a	Victoria St, Scott St, Washington St (from sb), E 🅖 Shell, Valero, W 🅖 Exxon/dsl, Valero 🍴 Mariachi Express, McDonald's, Wendy's 🅞 Firestone/auto

I-35 begins/ends in Laredo at Victoria St...access to multiple services

⬆N INTERSTATE 35 (West)

Exit #	Services
I-35W begins/ends on I-35, exit 467.	
85b	W Oak St, E 🅞 🏥
85a	I-35E S
84	FM 1515, Bonnie Brae St, E 🅞 🏥
82	FM 2449, to Ponder
79	Crawford Rd
76mm	🆁🆂 both lanes, litter barrels
76	FM 407, to Justin, Argyle, W 🅖 Exxon/dsl 🅞 Paradise Mkt, Paradise RV Park
74	FM 1171, to Lewisville
72	Dale Earnhardt Way, W 🛏 Marriott 🅞 TX Motor Speedway
70	TX 114, to Dallas, Bridgeport, E 🅖 Shell/Subway/dsl,

L
A
R
E
D
O

70	Continued Valero/dsl 🛏 Motel 6, Sleep Inn 🅞 North Lake RV Park, to DFW W 🛏 Marriott 🅞 TX Motor Speedway
68	Eagle Pkwy, W 🅞 🆁🆂
67	Alliance Blvd, W 🅞 FedEx, to Alliance 🆁🆂
66	to Westport Pkwy, Keller-Haslet Rd, E 🛏 Hampton Inn, Hilton Garden, Residence Inn, W 🅖 7-11/Wendy's/dsl 🍴 Bryan's BBQ, Schlotzsky's, Snooty Pig, Subway, Taco Bueno 🅞 USPO
65	TX 170 E, E 🅖 🚛 /McDonald's/dsl/scales/24hr 🍴 IHOP 🅞 Cabela's/cafe
64	Golden Triangle Blvd, to Keller-Hicks Blvd, E 🅞 Chrysler/Dodge/Jeep
63	Heritage Trace, Park Glen, E 🅖 7-11 🍴 BJ's, Cheddar's, Chick-fil-A, Free Birds Burritos, Houlihan's, Jason's Deli, McDonald's, Smoothie King, Starbucks, Subway, Tutti Frutti, Which Wich, Zoe's Kitchen 🅞 Belk, Best Buy, Hobby Lobby, JC Penney, Kroger/dsl, Petsmart, Verizon
62	North Tarrant Pkwy, E 🍴 5 Guys Burgers, Firehouse Subs, Fuzzy's Tacos, HaNaBi Hibachi, Mi Cocina, Olive Garden, Pizza Inn, Thai Fusion 🅞 🏥 Tuesday Morning
60	US 287 N, US 81 N, to Decatur
59	Basswood (sb only), E 🅖 Chevron/Jack-in-the-Box/dsl 🍴 Sonic 🅞 Home Depot, NTB
58	Western Ctr Blvd, E 🅖 7-11, Shell/Church's 🍴 Braum's, Casa Rita, Chili's, Denny's, Dublin Square Rest., Flips Grill, Genghis Grill, Jimmy John's, Macaroni Grill, On-the-Border, Posados Cafe, SaltGrass Steaks, Shady Oak Grill, Wendy's, Which Wich, Wing Stop, Zio's Italian 🛏 Best Western, Residence Inn 🅞 AT&T, Kauffman Tire, W 🍴 Boston's, Firehouse Subs, Joe's Crabshack, McDonald's, Popeye's, Rosa's Cafe, Salad Bowl, Smoothie King, Starbucks, Subway, Waffle House, Whataburger 🛏 Comfort Inn, Holiday Inn Express 🅞 repair, URGENT CARE
57b a	I-820 E&W
56b	Melody Hills Dr
56a	Meacham Blvd, E 🅖 Shell/7-11 🛏 Hilton Garden, Knights Inn, La Quinta, W 🅖 Texaco/dsl 🍴 Cracker Barrel, McDonald's, Subway 🛏 Holiday Inn, Quality Inn, Radisson, Super 8 🅞 USPO
55	Pleasantdale Ave (from nb)
54c	33rd St, Long Ave (from nb), W 🅖 Conoco/dsl, Valero/dsl 🛏 Motel 6
54b a	TX 183, NE 28th St, E 🍴 Lisa's Chicken/dsl, W 🅖 QT/dsl 🛏 Stockyards Inn

TX

🅿 = gas   🍴 = food   🏨 = lodging   🅾 = other   🆁🆂 = rest stop   Copyright 2015 - the Next EXIT ®

⬆N INTERSTATE 35 (West) Cont'd

Exit #	Services
53mm	Trinity River
53	North Side Dr, Yucca Dr, E 🅿 Shell/7-11/dsl, W 🍴 Mercado Juarez Café 🏨 Country Inn&Suites
52e	Carver St (from nb)
52d	Pharr St (exits left from nb)
52b	US 377N, Belknap
52a	US 377 N, TX 121, to DFW
51a	I-30 E, to Avalene (from nb), downtown Ft Worth
50c a	I-30 W, E to Dallas
50b	TX 180 E (from nb)
49b	Rosedale St, E 🅿 7-11/dsl 🍴 Jack-in-the-Box, W 🅾 H
49a	Allen Ave, E 🅿 Valero, W 🅾 H
48b	Morningside Ave (from sb), same as 48a
48a	Berry St, E 🅿 Chevron/McDonald's 🅾 Autozone, El Rio Grande Foods, Family$, W 🅿 RaceTrac/dsl 🅾 U-Haul, zoo
47	Ripy St, E 🅾 transmissions, W 🏨 Astro Inn
46b	Seminary Dr, E 🅿 RaceWay 🍴 Grandy's, Jack-in-the-Box, Taco Cabana, Whataburger 🏨 Days Inn, Delux Inn, Regency Inn, Super 7 Inn 🅾 NAPA, W 🅿 Shell, Valero 🍴 Denny's, Sonic, Wendy's 🅾 Firestone/auto, Pepboys
46a	Felix St, E 🅿 Valero 🏨 Dalworth Inn, W 🍴 Cesar's Tacos, McDonald's 🅾 Family$
45b a	I-20, E to Dallas, W to Abilene
44	Altamesa, E 🏨 Radisson, W 🅿 Prism 🍴 Rig Steaks, Waffle House 🏨 Baymont Inn, Best Western, Comfort Suites, Motel 6, South Lp Inn
43	Sycamore School Rd, W 🅿 Exxon 🍴 Chicken Express, Jack-in-the-Box, Sonic, Subway, Whataburger 🅾 $General, Home Depot, Radio Shack, repair
42	Everman Pkwy, W 🅿 QT/dsl/scales, Shell
41	Risinger Rd, W 🅾 Camping World RV Service/Supplies, McClain's RV Ctr
40	Garden Acres Dr, E 🅿 Loves/Subway/dsl/scales/24hr 🏨 Microtel 🅾 H W 🍴 Taco Bell
39	FM 1187, McAlister Rd, E 🅾 H W 🅿 Shamrock/dsl/24hr, Shell 🍴 Buffalo Wild Wings, Firehouse Subs, Logan's Roadhouse, Olive Garden, Panda Express, Red Lobster, TGIFriday's, Waffle House 🏨 Howard Johnson 🅾 Best Buy, Kohl's, Staples, Verizon
38	Alsbury Blvd, E 🅿 Chevron/24hr, Mobil/dsl 🍴 Chili's, Cracker Barrel, Hibachi Japanese, IHOP, McDonald's, Mexican Inn Cafe, On-the-Border, Outback Steaks, Over Time Grill, Spring Creek BBQ 🏨 Hampton Inn, Holiday Inn Express, La Quinta, Super 8 🅾 Discount Tire, Ford, Lowe's Whse, W 🅿 RaceTrac, Shamrock, Shell/24hr 🍴 Applebees, Arby's, Burger King, Chick-fil-A, Coldstone Creamery, Cotton Patch Cafe, Denny's, Pancho's Mexican, Sonic, Taco Cabana, Wendy's 🅾 Albertson's, Chevrolet, JC Penney, Kwik Kar, Michael's, PetsMart, Radio Shack, Ross, vet
37	TX 174, Wilshire Blvd, to Cleburne, W 🅾 Walmart Super Ctr/24hr, (2mi), from sb, same as 36
36	FM 3391, TX 174S, Burleson, E 🅿 Chevron, Mobil 🍴 Miranda's Cantina, Sonic, Waffle House 🏨 Best Western, Comfort Suites, Days Inn, W 🅾 $General, Curves, transmissions
35	Briaroaks Rd (from sb), W 🅾 RV camping
33mm	🆁🆂 sb, full 🚻 facilities, litter barrels, 🔧, 🆚 vending
32	Bethesda Rd, E 🅿 Valero 🏨 Best Value Inn 🅾 RV Ranch Park, W 🅾 Mockingbird Hill RV Park
31mm	🆁🆂 nb, full 🚻 facilities, litter barrels, 🔧, 🆚 vending
30	FM 917, Mansfield, E 🅿 Shell/Sonic/dsl, W 🅿 Shell/dsl 🍴 RanchHouse Rest.

27	Rd 604, Rd 707
26b a	US 67, Cleburne, E 🅿 Chevron/KFC/dsl 🍴 Chicken Express, DQ, McDonald's, Pizza Hut, Sonic, Waffle House, Whataburger 🏨 Best Western, Days Inn, La Quinta, Super 8 🅾 $General, Ancira RV Ctr, AutoZone, Brookshire Foods, Family$, Motor Home Specialist, Parts+, Walmart
24	FM 3136, FM 1706, Alvarado, E 🅿 Shell/Grandy's/dsl/scales/24hr 🍴 Longhorn Grill
21	Rd 107, to Greenfield
17	FM 2258
16	TX 81 S, Rd 201, Grandview
15	FM 916, Maypearl, W 🅿 Chevron/dsl, Mobil/dsl 🍴 Subway
12	FM 67
8	FM 66, Itasca, E 🅿 Valero/dsl/café/24hr, W 🍴 DQ 🅾 Ford, litter barrels, picnic tables
7	FM 934, E litter barrels, 🆁🆂 W 🅿 Exxon/dsl 🍴 Golden Chick Cafe
3	FM 2959, E 🅾 to Hillsboro 🔜

I-35W begins/ends on I-35, 371mm.

⬆N INTERSTATE 37

Exit #	Services
142b a	I-35 S to Laredo, N to Austin. **I-37 begins/ends on I-35 in San Antonio.**
141c	Brooklyn Ave, Nolan St (from sb), downtown
141b	Houston St, E 🏨 Comfort Suites, Red Roof Inn 🅾 tires, W 🅿 Shell 🍴 Denny's 🏨 Crockett Hotel, Crowne Plaza, Days Inn, Drury Inn, Fairfield Inn, Hampton Inn, Hyatt Hotel, La Quinta, Marriott, Residence Inn, SpringHill Suites 🅾 Macy's, to The Alamo
141a	Commerce St, E 🏨 Staybridge Suites, W 🍴 Denny's 🏨 La Quinta, Marriott 🅾 Macy's
140b	Durango Blvd, E 🍴 Bill Miller BBQ 🅾 to Alamo Dome, downtown
140a	Carolina St, Florida St, E 🅿 Shell/dsl
139	I-10 W, US 87, US 90, to Houston, W 🅾 to Sea World
138c	Fair Ave, Hackberry St, E 🍴 DQ, Jack-in-the-Box, La Tapatia Mexian, Las Margarita's, Popeye's 🅾 Brake Check, Family$, Home Depot, W 🅿 Exxon, Shell
138b	E New Braunfels Ave (from sb), E 🍴 IHOP, Little Caesars, McDonald's, Taco Cabana, Wendy's, Whataburger 🅾 Beall's, HEB/dsl, Marshall's, W 🅿 Exxon 🍴 Sonic
138a	Southcross Blvd, W New Braunfels Ave, E 🅿 McDonald's, Taco Cabana, Wendy's, W 🅿 Exxon 🍴 Sonic
137	Hot Wells Blvd, W 🍴 IHOP 🏨 Motel 6, Super 8
136	Pecan Valley Dr, E 🅿 Citgo/dsl 🍴 KFC/Taco Bell, Pizza Hut 🏨 Pecan Valley Inn 🅾 AutoZone, O'Reilly Parts, W 🅾 H
135	Military Dr, Lp 13, E 🅿 Shell, Valero 🍴 Jack-in-the-Box 🏨 Quality Inn 🅾 Mission Trail RV park, W 🅿 Valero/Subway/dsl 🍴 A&W/LJ Silver, Buffalo Wild Wings, Burger King, Carino's Italian, Chaba Thai, Chick-fil-A, Chili's, Cracker Barrel, IHOP, Little Caesars, Longhorn Cafe, Panda Express, Papa John's, Peter Piper Pizza, Sonic, Starbucks, Subway, Whataburger 🏨 La Quinta 🅾 H $Tree, Advance Parts, AT&T, Best Buy, BigLots, Discount Tire, Hancock Fabrics, HEB Food/gas, Home Depot, Lowe's, Office Depot, PetCo, Radio Shack, Ross, Target, to Brooks AFB, Walgreens, Walmart/McDonald's
133	I-410, US 281 S
132	US 181 S, to Floresville, E 🅿 Shell 🅾 $General
130	Donop Rd, Southton Rd, E 🅿 Valero/dsl 🍴 Tom's Burgers 🏨 Days Inn 🅾 Braunig Lake RV Resort, W 🅿 Shell/dsl 🅾 car/truckwash

SAN ANTONIO

INTERSTATE 37 Cont'd

Exit #	Services
127mm	San Antonio River
127	San Antonio River Turnaround (from nb), Braunig Lake
125	FM 1604, Anderson Lp, **E** 🅖 Conoco/dsl/24hr 🅕 Burger King 🅞 fireworks, **W** 🅖 Exxon/dsl, Shell/dsl 🅕 Miller's BBQ, Whataburger 🅞 fireworks, tires
122	Priest Rd, Mathis Rd, **E** 🅖 Valero
120	Hardy Rd
117	FM 536
113	FM 3006
112mm	🆁🆂 both lanes, litter barrels
109	TX 97, to Floresville, **E** 🅖 Chevron/dsl 🅕 Portrillo's Mexican 🅞 Chrysler/Dodge/Jeep
106	Coughran Rd
104	spur 199, Leal Rd, to Pleasanton (no immediate sb return), same as 103
103	US 281 N, Leal Rd, to Pleasanton, **E** 🅖 Valero/dsl 🅕 DQ, K&K Cafe 🅛 Kuntry Inn
98	TX 541, McCoy
92	US 281A, Campbellton
88	FM 1099, to FM 791, Campbellton
83	FM 99, Whitsett, Peggy, **E** 🅖 Shell/cafe/dsl, **W** 🅖 Chevron/dsl, Exxon/dsl 🅕 Choke Canyon BBQ
82mm	🆁🆂 sb, full 🅳 facilities, litter barrels, 🅲, 🆅 vending
78mm	🆁🆂 nb, full 🅳 facilities, litter barrels, 🅲, 🆅 vending
76	US 281A, FM 2049, Whitsett
75mm	truck weigh sta sb
74mm	truck weigh sta nb
72	US 281 S, Three Rivers, **W** 4 mi 🅖 Loves/McDonald's/Subway/dsl/scales/24hr/@, Valero 🅕 DQ, Staghorn Rest, Van's BBQ 🅛 Best Western, EconoLodge 🅞 to Rio Grande Valley
69	TX 72, Three Rivers, **W** 🅖 Valero/café/dsl/24hr 🅞 RV park, tires, to Choke Cyn SP
65	FM 1358, Oakville, **E** 🅕 Van's BBQ
59	FM 799
56	US 59, George West, **E** 🅖 Valero/dsl/24hr, **W** 🅖 Shell/Subway/dsl/24hr, Valero/Burger King/dsl/24hr
51	Hailey Ranch Rd
47	FM 3024, FM 534, Swinney Switch Rd, **W** 🅕 Swinney Switch Cafe 🅞 Mike's Mkt/gas (1mi), to KOA (4mi)
44mm	parking area sb
42mm	parking area nb
40	FM 888
36	TX 359, to Skidmore, Mathis, **W** 🅖 Citgo/Subway/dsl, Shell/McDonald's/dsl, Valero/dsl (1mi) 🅕 Pizza Hut 🅛 Mathis Inn 🅞 Lake Corpus Christi SRA
34	TX 359 W, **E** 🅞 Adventure TX RV Ctr/LP, **W** 🅖 Shell, Valero/dsl 🅛 DQ, Pizza Hut 🅞 $General, O'Reilly Parts, to Lake Corpus Christi SP
31	TX 188, to Sinton, Rockport
22	TX 234, FM 796, to Odem, Edroy
20b	Cooper Rd
19.5mm	🆁🆂 both lanes, 🅳 accessible, litter barrels
17	US 77 N, to Victoria
16	LaBonte Park, **W** info, litter barrels, 🆁🆂
15	Sharpsburg Rd (from sb), Redbird Ln
14	I-69, US 77 S, Redbird Ln, to Kingsville, Robstown, **W** 1 mi on FM 624 🅖 RaceWay/dsl, Shell/dsl, Valero/Burger King/dsl 🅕 Chili's, CiCi's, Denny's, Good'n Crisp Chicken, Miller's BBQ, Papa John's, Pizza Hut, Popeye's, Sonic, Subway,

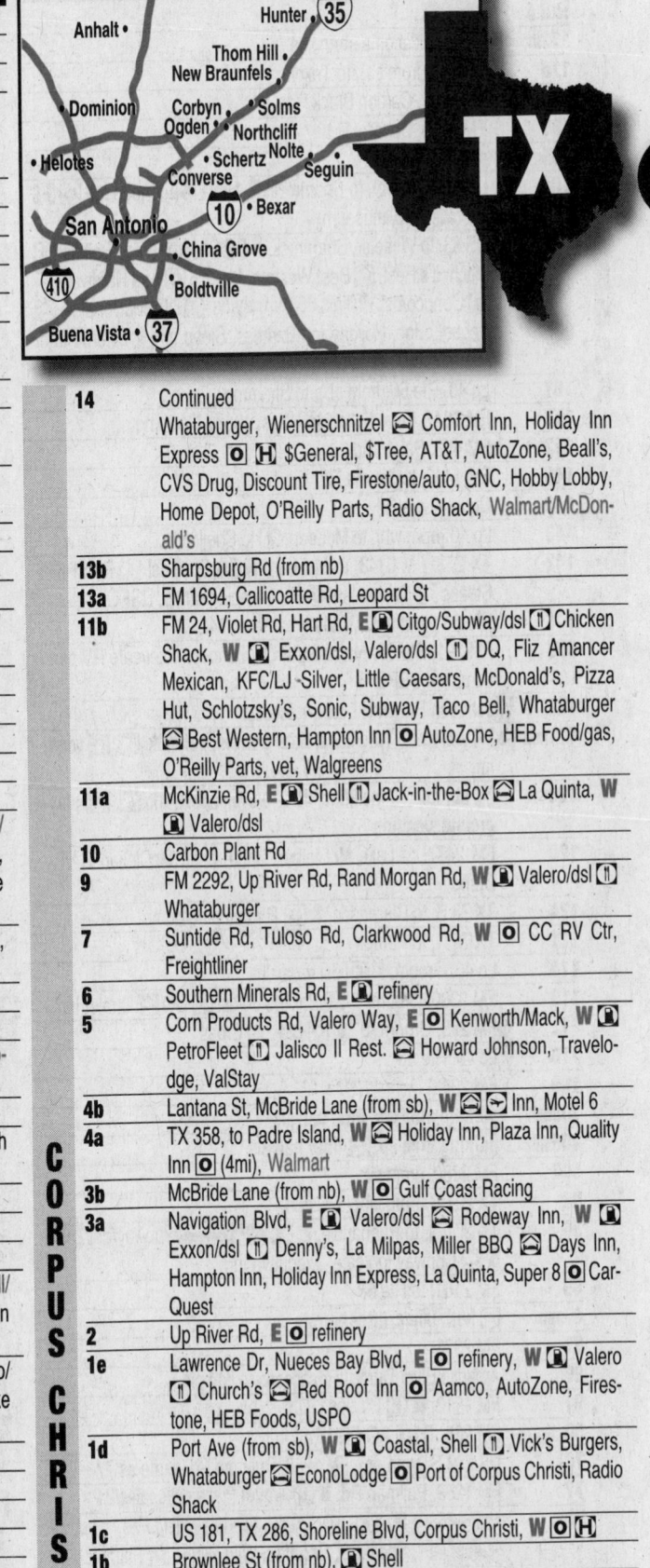

14	Continued Whataburger, Wienerschnitzel 🅛 Comfort Inn, Holiday Inn Express 🅞 🅷 $General, $Tree, AT&T, AutoZone, Beall's, CVS Drug, Discount Tire, Firestone/auto, GNC, Hobby Lobby, Home Depot, O'Reilly Parts, Radio Shack, Walmart/McDonald's
13b	Sharpsburg Rd (from nb)
13a	FM 1694, Callicoatte Rd, Leopard St
11b	FM 24, Violet Rd, Hart Rd, **E** 🅖 Citgo/Subway/dsl 🅕 Chicken Shack, **W** 🅖 Exxon/dsl, Valero/dsl 🅕 DQ, Fliz Amancer Mexican, KFC/LJ Silver, Little Caesars, McDonald's, Pizza Hut, Schlotzsky's, Sonic, Subway, Taco Bell, Whataburger 🅛 Best Western, Hampton Inn 🅞 AutoZone, HEB Food/gas, O'Reilly Parts, vet, Walgreens
11a	McKinzie Rd, **E** 🅖 Shell 🅕 Jack-in-the-Box 🅛 La Quinta, **W** 🅖 Valero/dsl
10	Carbon Plant Rd
9	FM 2292, Up River Rd, Rand Morgan Rd, **W** 🅖 Valero/dsl 🅕 Whataburger
7	Suntide Rd, Tuloso Rd, Clarkwood Rd, **W** 🅞 CC RV Ctr, Freightliner
6	Southern Minerals Rd, **E** 🅖 refinery
5	Corn Products Rd, Valero Way, **E** 🅞 Kenworth/Mack, **W** 🅖 PetroFleet 🅕 Jalisco II Rest. 🅛 Howard Johnson, Travelodge, ValStay
4b	Lantana St, McBride Lane (from sb), **W** 🅛 🔄 Inn, Motel 6
4a	TX 358, to Padre Island, **W** 🅛 Holiday Inn, Plaza Inn, Quality Inn 🅞 (4mi), Walmart
3b	McBride Lane (from nb), **W** 🅞 Gulf Coast Racing
3a	Navigation Blvd, **E** 🅖 Valero/dsl 🅛 Rodeway Inn, **W** 🅖 Exxon/dsl 🅕 Denny's, La Milpas, Miller BBQ 🅛 Days Inn, Hampton Inn, Holiday Inn Express, La Quinta, Super 8 🅞 CarQuest
2	Up River Rd, **E** 🅞 refinery
1e	Lawrence Dr, Nueces Bay Blvd, **E** 🅞 refinery, **W** 🅖 Valero 🅕 Church's 🅛 Red Roof Inn 🅞 Aamco, AutoZone, Firestone, HEB Foods, USPO
1d	Port Ave (from sb), **W** 🅖 Coastal, Shell 🅕 Vick's Burgers, Whataburger 🅛 EconoLodge 🅞 Port of Corpus Christi, Radio Shack
1c	US 181, TX 286, Shoreline Blvd, Corpus Christi, **W** 🅞 🅷
1b	Brownlee St (from nb), 🅖 Shell
1a	Buffalo St (from sb), **W** 0-1 mi on Shoreline 🅖 Valero/dsl 🅕 Burger King, Joe's Crabshack, Landry's Seafood, Subway, Waterstreet Seafood, Whataburger 🅛 Bayfront Inn, Best Western, Omni Hotel, Super 8 🅞 I-37 begins/ends on US 181 in Corpus Christi., U-Haul, USPO

I-37 begins/ends on US 181 in Corpus Christi.

(vertical text along center:) CORPUS CHRISTI

↑E   INTERSTATE 40

Exit #	Services
177mm	Texas/Oklahoma state line
176	spur 30 (from eb), to Texola
169	FM 1802, Carbon Black Rd
167	FM 2168, Daberry Rd
165mm	**check sta wb**
164	Lp 40 (from wb), to Shamrock, **S 1 mi** ⊙ EconoLodge ⊙ 🅗 check sta eb, museum
163	US 83, to Wheeler, Shamrock, **N** 📶 Chevron/Taco Bell/dsl 🍴 Mitchell's Rest. 🛏 Best Western, Motel 6 ⊙ Ace Hardware, **S** 📶 Conoco/dsl, Phillips 66/Subway/dsl 🍴 DQ, McDonald's 🛏 EconoLodge, Holiday Inn Express, Sleep Inn, Western Motel ⊙ Family$
161	Lp 40, Rte 66 (from eb), to Shamrock
157	FM 1547, Lela, **S 1 mi** ⊙ West 40 RV Camping
152	FM 453, Pakan Rd
148	FM 1443, Kellerville Rd
146	County Line Rd
143	Lp 40 (from wb), to McLean, 📶 to Shell/dsl
142	TX 273, FM 3143, to McLean, **N** 📶 Shell/dsl 🍴 Red River Steaks 🛏 Cactus Inn ⊙ RV Camping/dump, USPO
141	Rte 66 (from eb), McLean, same as 142
135	FM 291, Rte 66, Alanreed, **S** 📶 Conoco/motel/café/RV park/dump ⊙ USPO
132	Johnson Ranch Rd, ranch access
131mm	🅿️ wb, full 🚻 facilities, litter barrels, petwalk, 📞, 🚮 vending
129mm	🅿️ eb, full 🚻 facilities, litter barrels, petwalk, 📞, 🚮 playground, vending
128	FM 2477, to Lake McClellan, **N** ⊙ Lake McClellan RA/RV Dump
124	TX 70 S, to Clarendon, **S** ⊙ RV camping/dump
121	TX 70 N, to Pampa
114	Lp 40, Groom, **N** ⊙ dsl repair
113	FM 2300, Groom, **S** 📶 Phillips 66/dsl 🍴 DQ 🛏 Chalet Inn
112	FM 295, Groom, **S** 📶 ⊙ Biggest Cross
110	Lp 40, Rte 66
109	FM 294
108mm	**parking area wb, litter barrels**
106mm	**parking area eb, 🚮, litter barrels**
105	FM 2880, grain silo
98	TX 207 S (from wb), to Claude
96	TX 207 N, to Panhandle, **N** 📶 Loves/Subway/dsl/24hr, **S** 🛏 Conway Inn/cafe, Executive Inn
89	FM 2161, to Rte 66
87mm	🚮 both lanes, litter barrels
87	FM 2373
85	Amarillo Blvd, Durrett Rd, access to camping
81	FM 1912, **N** 📶 Phillips 66/dsl
80	FM 228, **N** ⊙ AOK RV Park
78	US 287 S (from eb), FM 1258, Pullman Rd, same as 77
77	FM 1258, Pullman Rd, **N** 📶 Travel Plaza/dsl/scales/24hr
76	spur 468, **N** 📶 FLYING J/Denny's/dsl/LP/RV dump/scales/24hr, Shell/dsl 🍴 Buffalo Wild Wings 🛏 Fairfield Inn, Holiday Inn Express ⊙ Mack/Volvo Trucks, tourist info, **S** 📶 Speedco ⊙ Custom RV Ctr, TX info
75	Lp 335, Lakeside Rd, **N** 📶 McDonald's/dsl/scales/24hr/@ 🍴 Waffle House 🛏 Plaza Hotel, Best Value Inn, Super 8 ⊙ KOA (2mi), Peterbilt Trucks, UPS, **S** 📶 Petro/dsl/rest./scales/@ ⊙ Blue Beacon

74	Whitaker Rd, **N** 🍴 Big Texan Inn ⊙ RV camping, **S** 📶 Loves/Subway/dsl/scales/@, TA/Exxon/FoodCourt/dsl/scales/24hr/@ 🛏 Budget Inn ⊙ Blue Beacon
73	Eastern St, Bolton Ave, Amarillo, **N** 📶 Shell/dsl 🛏 Dean Motel, Motel 6, Value Place, **S** 📶 Chevron/dsl 🛏 Best Western
72b	Grand St, Amarillo, **N** 📶 Shell 🍴 Henk's BBQ 🛏 Value Inn ⊙ Family$, O'Reilly Parts, **S** 📶 Murphy USA/dsl, Phillips 66, Valero 🍴 Braum's, Chicken Express, McDonald's, Pizza Hut, Sonic, Starbucks, Subway, Taco Villa, Whataburger 🛏 Motel 6 ⊙ $General, Advance Parts, Amigo's Foods, AutoZone, BigLots, same as 73, URGENT CARE, Walmart
72a	Nelson St, **N** 🍴 Cracker Barrel 🛏 La Kiva Hotel, Luxury Inn, Sleep Inn, Super 8, Travelodge ⊙ Qtrhorse Museum, **S** 📶 Shell/dsl 🛏 Camelot Suites ⊙ transmissions
71	Ross St, Osage St, Amarillo, **N** 📶 Shell/dsl, Valero 🍴 A&W/LJ Silver, Burger King, IHOP, KFC, McDonald's, Schlotsky's, Subway, Wienerschnitzel 🛏 Comfort Inn, Days Inn, Holiday Inn, Microtel, Quality Inn, **S** 🍴 Arby's, Denny's, Fiesta Grande Mexican, Sonic, Taco Bell, Wendy's 🛏 Hampton Inn, La Quinta, Magnuson Hotel ⊙ Chevrolet, Ford Trucks, Hyundai, Sam's Club/gas, USPO
70	I-27 S, US 60 W, US 87, US 287, to Canyon, Lubbock, to downtown Amarillo
69b	Washington St, Amarillo, **S** 🍴 DQ, Subway ⊙ CVS Drug
69a	Crockett St, access to same as 68b
68b	Georgia St, **N** 📶 Shell/Subway 🍴 Schlotzky's, TGIFriday 🛏 Ambassador Hotel, **S** 📶 Valero 🍴 Baker Bro's Deli, Burger King, Church's Chicken, Coldstone, Denny's, Furr's Café, LJ Silver, Pizza Hut, Red Lobster, Sonic, Starbucks, Taco Bueno, TX Roadhouse, Whataburger 🛏 Baymont Inn, Holiday Inn Express, Quality Inn, Travelodge ⊙ 🅗 Hastings Books, Home Depot, Office Depot, Radio Shack, Walgreens
68a	Julian Blvd, Paramount Blvd, **N** 📶 Shell 🍴 Arby's, Chili's, Nick's Rest., Pizza Hut, Schlotzsky's, TGIFriday's, Wendy's 🛏 Ambassador Inn, same as 67, **S** 📶 Valero 🍴 Baker Bro's Deli, Burger King, Furr's Buffet, Kushiyama, Red Lobster, Ruby Tequila's Mexican, TX Roadhouse 🛏 Best Value, Comfort Suites, Holiday Inn Express, Motel 6, Super 8, Travelodge ⊙ Home Depot, Office Depot
67	Western St, Amarillo, **N** 📶 Phillips 66, Shell 🍴 Braum's, Burger King, Cattle Call BBQ, Chili's, McDonald's, Rosa's Cafe, Sonic, Taco Bell, Wendy's, **S** 📶 Rudy's/BBQ/dsl, Valero 🍴 Blue Sky Rest., Cheddar's, IHOP, Olive Garden, Waffle House, Willy's Grill 🛏 Baymont Inn ⊙ Discount Tire, Firestone, Michael's, Petco, same 68
66	Bell St, Amarillo, **N** 📶 Shell/dsl, Valero/dsl 🛏 Fairfield Inn, Quality Inn, Relax Inn, Residence Inn ⊙ Harley-Davidson, **S** 🍴 Doughnut Stop, King & I Chinese, Taco Bueno ⊙ Albertson's/Sav-On
65	Coulter Dr, Amarillo, **N** 📶 Phillips 66/dsl 🍴 Arby's, Carino's Italian, Country Barn BBQ, Golden Corral, Kabuki Japanese, SaltGrass Steaks, Subway, Taco Bell, Waffle House 🛏 Courtyard, Days Inn, Executive Inn, La Quinta ⊙ 🅗 Cadillac/Chevrolet, Cavender's Boots, Discount Tire, Dodge, Firestone/auto, Nissan, **S** 📶 Chevron/Chicken Express/dsl, Shell 🍴 ChinaStar, CiCi's, Hoffbrau Steaks, Jason's Deli, McDonald's, Outback Steaks, Pizza Hut, Wendy's, Whataburger 🛏 5th Season Inn, Hampton Inn, Sleep Inn ⊙ AT&T, Goodyear/auto, Verizon
64	Soncy Rd, to Pal Duro Cyn, **N** 🍴 Famous Dave's BBQ, Furr's Buffet, Jimmy John's, Lin's Chinese, Logan's Roadhouse, Plaza Rest., Red Robin 🛏 Comfort Inn, Country Inn&Suites,

SHAMROCK (side tab, left)

AMARILLO (side tab, right)

AMARILLO (side tab, right lower)

TX (left margin tab)

⬆E INTERSTATE 40 Cont'd

Exit #	Services
64	Continued
	Drury Inn, Extended Stay America, Hilton Garden, Holiday Inn, Holiday Inn Express, Homewood Suites 🅞 USPO, **S** 🅖 Valero/dsl/24hr 🍴 Applebee's, Baker Bros Deli, Chuck-eCheese, DQ, Fazoli's, Hooters, Jake's Grill, Marble Slab Creamery, McAlisters Deli, McDonald's, On-the-Border, Pei Wei, Ruby Tequila's Mexican, Starbucks, Subway 🅞 $Tree, Barnes&Noble, Best Buy, Dillard's, Ford, Home Depot, JC Penney, Jo-Ann Fabrics, Kohl's, Lincoln, mall, Old Navy, PetsMart, Ross, Sears/auto, Target, World Mkt
62b	Lp 40, Amarillo Blvd, **N** 🅞 Gander Mtn, **S** 🅞 Sundown RV Resort
62a	Hope Rd, Helium Rd, **S** 🅞 antiques, RV camping
60	Arnot Rd, **S** 🅖 ♥Love's/Subway/dsl 🅞 Oasis RV Resort/dump
57	RM 2381, Bushland, **N** grain silos, **S** 🅖 Phillips 66/dsl 🍴 BBQ Barn 🅞 RV camping/dump (1mi), USPO
55mm	**parking area wb, litter barrels**
54	Adkisson Rd
53.5mm	**parking area eb, litter barrels**
49	FM 809, Wildorado, **S** 🅖 Crist Fuel/dsl/LP 🛏 Royal Inn
42	Everett Rd
37	Lp 40 W, to Vega, **N** 1 mi 🅖 Bonanza Motel 🅞 same as 36, Walnut RV Park
36	US 385, Vega, **N** 🅖 Alon/dsl, Conoco/dsl/24hr, Shamrock 🍴 Boothill Grill, DQ, Wooden Spoon Cafe 🛏 Days Inn 🅞 RV Park, **S** 🅖 Shell/cafe/dsl
35	to Rte 66, to Vega, **N** 🛏 Best Western, Bonanza Motel (1mi) 🅞 same as 36, Walnut RV Park (1mi)
32mm	🆁🆂 area both lanes, litter barrels
28	to Rte 66, Landergin
23	to Adrian, Vega, same as 22
22	TX 214, Adrian, **N** 🍴 Midpoint Cafe 🅞 auto repair, USPO, **S** 🅖 Phillips 66/dsl/Tommy's Café
18	FM 2858, Gruhlkey Rd, **S** 🅖 Shell/Stuckey's/cafe/dsl
15	Ivy Rd
13mm	🆁🆂 area both lanes, litter barrels
5.5mm	turnout
0	Lp 40, to Glenrio
0mm	Texas/New Mexico state line, Central/Mountain time zone

⬆E INTERSTATE 44

Exit #	Services
15mm	Red River, Texas/Oklahoma state line
14	Lp 267, E 3rd St, **W** 🅞 Burk RV Park, historical marker
13	Glendale St, **W** 🍴 Subway 🅞 Beall's
12	Burkburnett, **E** 🛏 Hampton Inn, **W** 🅖 Fina/7-11/dsl 🍴 Braum's, Chicken Express, Feedlot Rest., Lite Pan Asian, Mazzio's, McDonald's, Whataburger 🅞 CarQuest, Chevrolet, Ford
11	FM 3429, Daniels Rd
9mm	🆁🆂 area both lanes, litter barrels, petwalk
7	East Rd
6	Bacon Switch Rd
5a	FM 3492, Missile Rd, **E** 🍴 El Mejicano Rest., Hunan Chinese, Marco's Pizza 🅞 st patrol, **W** 🅖 Exxon/dsl
5	Access Rd
4	City Loop St
3c	FM 890, **W** 🅖 Murphy USA/dsl 🍴 Cracker Barrel, Jack-in-the-Box, KFC/Taco Bell, Papa Murphy's, Subway 🅞 vet, Walmart/Subway

Exit #	Services
3b	sp 325, Sheppard AFB
3a	US 287 N, to Amarillo, **W** 🅖 Shell 🍴 Carl's Jr 🛏 Ramada Ltd
2	Maurine St, **E** 🅖 Fina/7-11/dsl, Shell/dsl 🛏 Best Value Inn, Executive Inn, Quality Inn 🅞 Chevrolet, Mazda, **W** 🅖 Fina/7-11 🍴 China Star, Denny's, El Chico, LJ Silver, Whataburger 🛏 Candlewood Suites, Comfort Inn, La Quinta, Red Roof Inn, Super 8
1d	US 287 bus, Lp 370, **W** 🅖 FuelStop/dsl 🛏 Travelodge
1c	**Texas Travel Info Ctr**, **E** 🅖 $Saver, **W** 🛏 Holiday Inn
1b	Scotland Park (from nb)
1a	US 277 S, to Abilene, **E** 🛏 Howard Johnson, **W** 🍴 Arby's 🛏 EconoLodge
1	Holliday St, **W** 🅖 Valero/dsl 🍴 Arby's, Burger King, Carl's Jr, McDonald's, Subway 🛏 Holiday Inn, Motel 6 🅞 🏥 Walgreens
0mm	Witchita Falls, **I-44 begins/ends on US 287**

⬆N INTERSTATE 45

Exit #	Services
286	to I-35 E, to Denton. **I-45 begins/ends in Dallas.**
285	Bryan St E, US 75 N
284b a	I-30, W to Ft Worth, E to Texarkana, access to 🏥
283b	Pennsylvania Ave, to MLK Blvd, **E** 🅖 Shamrock
283a	Lamar St
281	Overton St (from sb), **W** 🅖 Chevron
280	Illinois Ave, Linfield St, **E** 🛏 Star Motel, **W** 🅖 Exxon, Shell/dsl
279b a	Lp 12
277	Simpson Stuart Rd, **W** 🅞 to Paul Quinn Coll
276b a	I-20, W to Ft Worth, E to Shreveport
275	TX 310 N (from nb, no re-entry)
274	Dowdy Ferry Rd, Hutchins, **E** 🅖 Exxon/Subway/dsl, Shell/McDonald's/dsl 🛏 Gold Inn, La Quinta, Motel 6 🅞 auto repair, **W** 🍴 DQ, Jack-in-the-Box, Whataburger
273	Wintergreen Rd, 🅖 QT/dsl/scales/24hr
272	Fulghum Rd, **E** 🅖 ♥Love's/Carl's Jr/dsl/scales/24hr, **W** weigh sta, both lanes
271	Pleasant Run Rd
270	Belt Line Rd, to Wilmer, **E** 🅖 Texaco/Pizza Inn/dsl, **W** 🅖 Exxon/Sonic/dsl, Shell/Church's/Subway/dsl 🅞 $General, Family$, USPO
269	Mars Rd
268	Malloy Bridge Rd
267	Frontage Rd
266	FM 660, **E** 🍴 Jack-in-the-Box, **W** 🅖 Shamrock/dsl 🍴 DQ, Pizza Hut
265	Lp 45, Ferris, nb only

VEGA (vertical left margin)

DALLAS (vertical left margin, I-45 section)

⬆N	**INTERSTATE 45 Cont'd**

ENNIS

Exit #	Services
263 a b	Lp 561
262	frontage rd
260	Lp 45, **E** 🍴 Trailor RV Park, **W** 🗜 Shell/Sonic/dsl
259	FM 813, FM 878, Jefferson St, **W** 🅾 Goodyear
258	Lp 45, Palmer, **E** 🗜 Chevron/Subway/dsl/scales/24hr 🅾 golf
255	FM 879, Garrett, **E** 🗜 Exxon/dsl, **W** 🗜 Chevron/dsl
253	Lp 45, **W** 🗜 Shell/Subway/dsl
251b	TX 34, Ennis, **E** 🗜 Fina/dsl, Shell/dsl, Valero/dsl 🍴 Bubba's BBQ, McDonald's 🛏 Baymont Inn, Comfort Suites, Days Inn, Holiday Inn Express 🅾 Ford, **W** 🗜 Chevron/dsl, Exxon/dsl/24hr, Murphy USA/dsl, Valero 🍴 Braum's, Burger King, Chili's, Denny's, Domino's, DQ, Golden Chick, Grand Buffet, Hilda's Kitchen, IHOP, Jack-in-the-Box, Jungle Jack's Pizza, KFC, Little Caesars, Sonic, Starbucks, Subway, Taco Bell, Taco Cabana, Waffle House, Wall Chinese, Wendy's, Whataburger 🛏 Ennis Inn, Quality Inn 🅾 Ⓗ $Tree, AutoZone, Beall's, Chevrolet, Chrysler/Dodge/Jeep, Radio Shack, RV camping, Walmart/McDonald's
251a	Creechville Rd, FM 1181, Ennis, **W** 🅾 Ⓗ
249	FM 85, Ennis, **E** 🗜 Budget Inn, **W** 🗜 Exxon/Subway 🅾 Blue Beacon, repair
247	US 287 N, to Waxahatchie
246	FM 1183, Alma, **W** 🗜 Chevron
244	FM 1182
243	Frontage Rd
242	Calhoun St, Rice, **W** 🗜 Shell/Sonic/dsl
239	FM 1126, **W** 🗜 45 Kwik Stop 🅾 Rendell RV Ctr
238	FM 1603, **E** 🗜 Exxon/rest/dsl/24hr 🅾 Casita RV Trailers
237	Frontage Rd
235b	Lp I-45 (from sb), to Corsicana
235a	Frontage Rd
232	Roane Rd, E 5th Ave

CORSICANA

231	TX 31, Corsicana, **E** 🗜 Phillips 66/dsl 🍴 Jack-in-the-Box 🛏 Best Western, Colonial Inn, La Quinta 🅾 Buick/Cadillac/Chevrolet/GMC, **W** 🗜 Exxon/Subway/dsl, Shell/Arby's 🍴 Bill's Fried Chicken, DQ, McDonald's 🛏 Comfort Inn 🅾 Ⓗ Chrysler/Dodge/Jeep, Ford/Lincoln, to Navarro Coll
229	US 287, Palestine, **E** 🗜 Exxon/Wendy's/dsl, Shell/dsl 🍴 Applebee's, Chili's, Collin St Bakery, Denny's, Sonic, Subway, Taco Bell 🛏 Hampton Inn, Holiday Inn Express 🅾 Corsicana Outlets, Gander Mtn, Home Depot, Office Depot, Russell Stover Candies, **W** 🍴 Waffle House 🛏 Corsicana Inn, EconoLodge, Motel 6, Traveler's Inn
228b	Lp 45 (exits left from nb), Corsicana, **W** 2 mi services in Corsicana
228a	15th St, Corsicana, 🅾 Scion/Toyota
225	FM 739, Angus, **E** 🗜 Conoco/dsl 🅾 RV park, to Chambers Reservoir
221	Frontage Rd
220	Frontage Rd
219b	Frontage Rd
219a	TX 14 (from sb), to Mexia, Richland, **W** 🗜 Shell
218	FM 1394 (from nb), Richland, **W** 🗜 Shell
217mm	🆁🆂 **both lanes, full** 🦽 **facilities, litter barrels, petwalk,** ⒸⒶ **vending**
213	TX 75 S, FM 246, to Wortham, **W** 🗜 Exxon/dsl
211	FM 80, to Streetman, Kirvin
206	FM 833, **3 mi**, I-45 RV Park
198	FM 27, to Wortham, **E** 🗜 Shell/Cole's BBQ 🍴 Gilberto's Mexican 🛏 La Quinta 🅾 Ⓗ **W** 🗜 Cooper Farms/dsl,

FAIRFIELD

198	Continued 🗜 Loves/Burger King/dsl/scales/24hr 🛏 Budget Inn 🅾 I-45 RV Park (4mi)
197	US 84, Fairfield, **E** 🗜 Chevron/dsl, Exxon/dsl, Shell/dsl 🍴 Bush's Chicken, DQ, Jack-in-the-Box, McDonald's, Sam's Rest., Something Different Rest, Sonic, Subway/TX Burger 🛏 Days Inn, Holiday Inn Express, Super 8 🅾 Brookshire Foods/gas, Chevrolet, Chrysler/Dodge/Jeep, Fred's Store, **W** 🗜 Exxon/dsl, Shell/dsl, Texaco/dsl 🍴 I-45 Rest., KFC/Taco Bell, Lonestar Grill, Pizza Hut, Ponte's Diner 🛏 Best Value Inn, Regency Inn 🅾 Ace Hardware, Ford
189	TX 179, to Teague, **E** 🗜 Citgo/Shirley's Cafe/dsl, Exxon/Dinner Bell Rest/dsl
180	TX 164, to Groesbeck
178	US 79, Buffalo, **E** 🗜 Chevron, Conoco/dsl, Shell/dsl 🍴 Pizza Hut, Subway/TX Burger 🅾 $General, Brookshire Foods/gas, Family$, **W** 🗜 Exxon/Church's/Subway/dsl/scales, Shamrock/dsl/24hr, Texaco/dsl 🍴 Dickey's BBQ, DQ, Mexican, Pitt Grill, Rancho Viejo, Sonic 🛏 Comfort Inn, Craig's Inn, Economy Inn, Hampton Inn
175mm	Bliss Creek
166mm	**weigh sta sb**
164	TX 7, Centerville, **E** 🗜 Chevron, Shell/Woody's BBQ/dsl 🍴 Country Cousins BBQ, Subway/TX Burger 🛏 Days Inn, **W** 🗜 Exxon/dsl, Shell/Woody's BBQ/dsl 🍴 DQ, Jack-in-the-Box, Roble's Mexican
160mm	🅿 **sb, litter barrels**
159mm	Boggy Creek
156	FM 977, to Leona, **W** 🗜 Exxon/dsl
155mm	🅿 **nb, litter barrels**
152	TX OSR, to Normangee, **W** 🗜 Chevron/dsl, Shell/Arby's/dsl
146	TX 75
142	US 190, TX 21, Madisonville, **E** 🗜 Exxon/BBQ/dsl, Shell/Buc-ees/dsl 🛏 Best Western, Carefree Inn, **W** 🗜 Chevron/Church's/dsl, Shell/Subway 🍴 Castanedas Mexican, Jack-in-the-Box, Lakeside Rest, McDonald's, Pizza Hut, Sonic, Taco Bell, TX Burger 🛏 Budget Motel, Western Lodge 🅾 Ⓗ Ford, Toyota
136	spur 67, **E** 🍴 Shrimpy's Seafood 🅾 Home on the Range RV camping/LP (3mi)
132	FM 2989
124mm	🆁🆂 **both lanes, full** 🦽 **facilities, litter barrels, petwalk,** Ⓒ🅿 **vending**
123	FM 1696

HUNTSVILLE

118	TX 75, **E** 🗜 Shell/Hitchin Post/dsl/24hr/@ 🅾 Texas Prison Museum, truckwash, **W** 🗜 Wendy's/dsl/scales/24hr, Shell/Dickey's BBQ/Subway/dsl 🍴 Chicken Express
116	US 190, TX 30, **E** 🗜 Conoco/dsl, Phillips 66/dsl, Valero/dsl 🍴 Arby's, Bandera Grill, Church's, El Chico, Golden Corral, Imperial Garden Chinese, Jct Steaks, McDonald's, Popeye's, Schlotzsky's, Sonic, Whataburger 🛏 Days Inn, EconoLodge, Holiday Inn Express, La Quinta, Motel 6 🅾 Ⓗ AutoZone, Brookshire Foods/gas, Buick/Cadillac/Chevrolet/GMC, Cavander's Boots, Chrysler/Dodge/Jeep, CVS Drug, Family$, Firestone/auto, Hastings Books, O'Reilly Parts, vet, Walgreens, **W** 🗜 Exxon/dsl, Murphy USA/dsl, Shell 🍴 5 Guys Burgers, Bob Luby's Seafood, Burger King, Chili's, Denny's, Grand Buffet, IHOP, Jack-in-the-Box, Little Caesars, Olive Garden, Pizza Hut, Starbucks, Subway, Taco Bell, Tinsley's Chicken, Wing Stop 🅾 $Tree, AT&T, Discount Tire, GNC, Home Depot, JC Penney, Kroger, Marshall's, Office Depot, Radio Shack, Target, USPO, Verizon, Walmart

↑N   INTERSTATE 45 Cont'd

Exit #	Services
114	FM 1374, **E** 🅖 Exxon/dsl, Shell 🍴 DQ, Margaritas Rest. 🛏 Gateway Inn, Super 8, **W** 🅖 Texaco/dsl, Valero/dsl 🍴 Country Inn Steaks 🛏 Best Value Inn, Comfort Suites 🅞 Ⓗ Ford, Hyundai
113	TX 19 (from nb), Huntsville
112	TX 75, **E** 🅖 Citgo 🛏 Baker Motel 🅞 Houston Statue, museum, to Sam Houston St U
109	Park 40, **W** 🅞 to Huntsville SP
103	FM 1374/1375 (from sb), to New Waverly, **W** 🅖 Chevron/Burger King/dsl
102	FM 1374/1375, TX 150 (from nb), to New Waverly, **E** 🅖 Valero/dsl (1mi), **W** 🅖 (1mi), Chevron/Burger King/dsl 🍴 Waverly Rest.
101mm	weigh sta nb
98	TX 75, Danville Rd, Shepard Hill Rd, **E** 🅞 Convenience RV Ctr/repair
97	Calvary Rd
95	Longstreet Rd, Calvary Rd, Willis, **W** 🅖 ♥Loves/Subway/Wendy's/dsl/scales/24hr
94	FM 1097, Longstreet Rd, to Willis, **E** 🅖 Kwik Stop/dsl 🍴 Jack-in-the-Box, Sonic, Taco Bell 🅞 $General, AutoZone, **W** 🅖 Chevron/Popeye's, Shell/dsl 🍴 Burger King, Chick-fil-A, Little Caesars, McDonald's, Pizza Hut, Rico's Grill, Scholtzsky's, Subway, Whataburger 🛏 Best Western 🅞 Kroger/dsl, vet, Walgreens
92	FM 830, Seven Coves Dr, **W** 🅞 Omega Farms RV Park, RV Park on the Lake (3mi), Thousand Trails Resort
91	League Line Rd, **E** 🅖 Chevron/McDonald's, Shell/dsl 🍴 Mamma Juanita's Mexican, Waffle House, Wendy's 🛏 Comfort Inn, Days Inn, La Quinta 🅞 Conroe Outlets/famous brands, **W** 🅖 Shell/Jack-in-the-Box 🍴 Cracker Barrel
90	FM 3083, Teas Nursery Rd, Montgomery Co Park, **E** 🅖 Exxon/dsl 🍴 Applebee's, Buffalo Wild Wings, Popeye's, Red Lobster, Smokey Mo's BBQ 🛏 Fairfield Inn 🅞 AT&T, convention center (4mi), Kohl's, Old Navy, Petsmart, Ross, TJ Maxx, **W** 🍴 Firehouse Subs, Olive Garden, Subway, Wings Wok 🛏 ValuePlace Inn 🅞 JC Penney, Verizon
88	Lp 336, to Cleveland, Navasota, **E** 🅖 Mobil/Chester's/dsl, Shell/dsl, Valero/dsl 🍴 A&W/LJ Silver, Arby's, Burger King, Chili's, China Delight, Denny's, Domino's, Los Cucos Mexican, Marble Slab Creamery, Margarita's Mexican, McDonald's, Papa John's, Pizza Hut, Quizno's, Sonic, TX Roadhouse, Whataburger, Wing Stop 🛏 Hampton Inn, Holiday Inn Express 🅞 $Tree, Advance Parts, Buick, CVS Drug, Discount Tire, GNC, HEB Foods/gas, Hobby Lobby, Just Brakes, Kroger/gas, Michael's, vet, Walgreens, **W** 🅖 Chevron/24hr 🍴 Blackeyed Pea, Casa Ole Mexican, Culver's, Dickie's BBQ, El Bosque Mexican, Jack-in-the-Box, KFC, Ryan's, Subway 🅞 99Cent Store, Hancock Fabrics, Lowe's, PetCo, Sam's Club/gas, Tuesday Morning, Walmart
87	TX 105, Conroe, **E** 🍴 Burger King, Jack-in-the-Box, Kettle, Luther's BBQ, McDonald's, Outback Steaks, Popeye's, Saltgrass Steaks, Sonic, Taco Bell, Tast of China 🛏 Super 8 🅞 Ⓗ $General, CVS Drug, Firestone/auto, Hyundai, Kia, NTB, **W** 🅖 Exxon 🍴 Chick-fil-A, Coney Island, Luby's, Panda Express, Panera Bread, Quizno's, Schlotzsky's, Shogun Japanese, Smoothie King, Starbucks, Subway, Taco Bell, Taco Bueno, Whataburger 🅞 Best Buy, Buick/GMC, Hastings Books, Home Depot, Office Depot, Radio Shack, Target, Tiremaxx

(left margin, vertical: CONROE)

85	FM 2854, Gladstell St, **E** 🅖 Citgo/dsl 🛏 Motel 6 🅞 Ⓗ Honda, Nissan, **W** 🅖 Shell/dsl, Valero 🍴 IHOP 🛏 Baymont Inn, Days Inn 🅞 Cadillac, Chrysler/Dodge/Jeep, Fun Country RV Ctr, Mazda, Scion/Toyota
84	TX 75 N, Frazier St, **E** 🅖 Chevron 🛏 Corporate Inn, Ramada Ltd 🅞 Ford, U-Haul, **W** 🅖 Shell 🍴 China Buffet, Incredible Pizza, Subway, Taco Cabana, Waffle House 🅞 Ⓗ Albertson's, Discount Tire, K-Mart, Kroger
83	Crighton Rd, Camp Strake Rd
82mm	San Jacinto River
82	River Plantation Dr
81	FM 1488, to Hempstead, Magnolia, **E** 🅖 Citgo, **W** 🅖 Valero/Subway 🅞 CamperLand RV Ctr
80	Needham Rd (from sb)
79	TX 242, Needham, **E** 🅖 Shell/McDonald's 🍴 Mama Juanita's Mexican, Quizno's 🛏 Best Western 🅞 Batteries+, **W** 🅖 Chevron, Murphy USA/dsl 🍴 Adobe Cafe, Arby's, Burger King, ChuckeCheese, Domino's, Outback Steaks, Popeye's, Sonic, Subway, Taco Cabana, Wendy's, Whataburger, Willie's Grill, Wings'N More 🛏 Country Suites, Fairfield Inn, TownPlace Suites 🅞 Ⓗ BMW/Mini, Firestone/auto, Kohl's, Lowe's Whse, Walgreens, Walmart
78	Needham Rd (from sb), Tamina Rd, access to same as 77
77	Woodlands Pkwy, Robinson, Chateau Woods, **E** 🅖 Chevron, Conoco/dsl 🍴 Babin's Seafood, Buca Italian, Buffalo Wild Wings, Church's, Chuy's, Hooters, Lupe Tortilla, Melting Pot, Pancho's Mexican, Pappadeaux, Pappa's BBQ, PeiWei, Pizza Hut, Red Robin, Saltgrass Steaks, Subway, Tom's Steaks 🛏 Best Value Inn, Budget Inn 🅞 Discount Tire, funpark, Home Depot, Jo-Ann Fabrics, Michael's, NTB, Office Depot, Old Navy, Petsmart, Sam's Club/gas, SteinMart, vet, Walgreens, **W** 🅖 Exxon, Shell, Texaco, Valero/dsl 🍴 A&W/KFC, Black-eyed Pea, Cane's, Chick-fil-A, Chili's, Chipotle Mexican, Culver's, Denny's, El Bosque Mexican, Guadalajara Mexican, Jack-in-the-Box, Jason's Deli, Jimmy John's, Kabab House, Kirby's Steakhouse, La Madeliene, Landry's Seafood, Luby's, Macaroni Grill, Olive Garden, Red Lobster, Sweet Tomatos, TGIFriday's 🛏 Comfort Suites, Days Inn, Drury Inn, Hampton Inn, Homewood Suites, La Quinta, Marriott, Shenandoa Inn 🅞 Ⓗ auto repair, Best Buy, Dillard's, HEB Foods, Macy's, mall, Marshall's, Ross, Sears, Target, World Mkt
76	Research Forest Dr, Tamina Rd, **E** 🅖 Chevron/dsl 🍴 LJ Silver, Pappa's BBQ 🅞 Firestone/auto, JustBrakes, Tiremaxx, URGENT CARE, vet, **W** 🅖 Shell 🍴 Carrabba's, Denny's, El Chico, IHOP, Jack-in-the-Box, Kyoto Japanese, Macaroni Grill, Olive Garden, TGIFriday's, Tortuga Mexican 🛏 Courtyard, Crossland Suites, Residence Inn 🅞 Goodyear/auto, JC Penney, Sears/auto, Woodlands Mall

(right margin, vertical: HOUSTON)

🅰 = gas   🍴 = food   🛏 = lodging   🅾 = other   🆁🆂 = rest stop   Copyright 2015 - the Next EXIT ®

⬆N   INTERSTATE 45 Cont'd

Exit #	Services
73	Rayford Rd, Sawdust Rd, **E** 🅰 Conoco, Shell, Valero 🍴 Hartz Chicken, Jack-in-the-box, McDonald's, Popeye's, Sonic, Taqueria Arandas, Thomas BBQ 🛏 Holiday Inn Express, La Quinta 🅾 Aamco, AutoZone, O'Reilly Parts, U-Haul, **W** 🅰 Mobil/dsl, Shell, Texaco 🍴 Carrabba's, Cici's Pizza, Grand Buffet, IHOP, Subway, Taipei Chinese, Tortuga 🛏 Extended Stay America, Red Roof Inn, Super 8 🅾 Brake Check, Discount Tire, GNC, Goodyear/auto, Harley-Davidson, HEB Foods, Kroger, Walgreens
72b	to Hardy Toll Rd from sb
72a	Spring Crossing Dr, **W** 🅰 Texaco/dsl
70b	Spring-Stuebner Rd, **E** 🅾 Vaughn RV Ctr
70a	FM 2920, to Tomball, **E** 🅰 Exxon, Murphy USA/dsl, Rudy's BBQ/dsl, Shell 🍴 Arby's, Chick-fil-A, El Palenque Mexican, Godfather's Pizza, Golden Jade Chinese, Hartz Chicken, McDonald's, Pizza Hut, Quizno's, Subway, Taco Cabana, Wendy's, Whataburger 🅾 $General, $Tree, BigLots, Kohl's, Kroger, Lincoln, Michael's, O'Reilly Parts, Radio Shack, Ross, Scion/Toyota, transmissions, Vaughn's RV Ctr, Walmart/24hr, **W** 🅰 Chevron, RaceTrac, Texaco 🍴 Burger King, Taco Bell, Tuscan Sun Coffee, Whataburger/24hr 🛏 Travelodge 🅾 Ford, U-Haul
68	Holzwarth Rd, Cypress Wood Dr, **E** 🅰 Texaco/dsl 🍴 Burger King, Pizza Hut/Taco Bell, Sonic, Starbucks, Wendy's 🅾 Albertson's, AT&T, Gander Mtn, GNC, Tiremaxx, **W** 🅰 Chevron/dsl 🍴 Cheddar's, Denny's, Jack-in-the-Box, Lenny's Subs, Pizza Hut, Popeye's, Starbucks 🛏 Motel 6, Spring Lodge 🅾 Advance Parts, Best Buy, Chrysler/Dodge/Jeep, Firestone/auto, Ford, Home Depot, Lowe's Whse, Office Depot, PetCo, Target, Walgreens
66	FM 1960, to Addicks, **E** 🅰 Chevron, RaceTrac, Shell 🍴 Hick's Rest., Jack-in-the-Box, Sonic, Subway, TX Roadhouse 🅾 Acura, AT&T, BMW, Chevrolet, Honda, Mercedes, Mistubishi, Petsmart, Radio Shack, Subaru, **W** 🅰 Exxon, Shell/dsl/24hr, Texaco/dsl, Valero 🍴 Cici's Pizza, Hooters, Jack-in-the-Box, James Coney Island, McDonald's, Outback Steaks, Panda Express, Red Lobster, Subway, Taco Bell, Taquiera Arendas 🛏 Baymont Inn, Comfort Suites, Fairfield Inn, Hampton Inn, Studio 6 🅾 🏥 Audi, Infiniti, Jaguar/LandRover, Lexus, mall, NTB, U-Haul
64	Richey Rd, **E** 🍴 Atchafalaya River Café 🛏 Best Value Inn, Holiday Inn, Lexington Suites, Rmada 🅾 CarMax, Discount Tire, Sam's Club/gas, **W** 🅰 ⚑FLYING J/Denny's/dsl/scales/24hr 🍴 Cracker Barrel, House of Creole, Jack-in-the-Box, Joe's Crabshack, Lupe Tortilla, Mamacita's Mexican, Michoacan Rest, SaltGrass Steaks, Tokyohana, Whataburger, Wings'n More, Zio's Italian 🅾 Jones RV Ctr
63	Airtex Dr, **E** 🅰 Texaco/Subway, Valero/Church's 🍴 China Bear, Pappasito's Cantina 🛏 ValuePlace Inn 🅾 Acura, Cadillac, LoneStar RV Ctr, Nissan, **W** 🍴 Cracker Barrel, Jack-in-the-Box, Whataburger 🛏 Best Western, Guesthouse Suites
62	Rankin Rd, Kuykendahl, **E** 🛏 Best Classic Inn, Scottish Inn, **W** 🅰 Chevron/McDonald's, RaceTrac, Shell 🍴 Luby's, Shiply Donuts 🛏 Palace Inn, Studio+, SunSuites 🅾 Buick/GMC, Demontrono RV Ctr, Hummer, Hyundai, Kia, Lamborghini, Mercedes, Volvo, VW
61	Greens Rd, **E** 🅰 Texaco 🍴 Brown Sugar's BBQ, IHOP, Imperial Dragon, Luna's 🛏 Knights Inn 🅾 Dillard's, JC Penney, Macy's, mall, Sears/auto, **W** 🍴 Burger King, Luby's, Subway 🛏 Baymont Inn, Comfort Inn 🅾 $General, Burlington Coat Factory, Kroger

Exit #	Services
60c	Beltway E
60	(b a from nb) TX 525, **W** 🍴 Pappas Seafood 🅾 U-Haul
59	FM 525, West Rd, **E** 🅰 Shell/dsl 🍴 A&W/LJ Silver, Burger King, China Border, Denny's, Domino's, Mambo Seafood, McDonald's, Michoacan Rest, Moon Palace Chinese, Pizza Hut, Taco Cabana 🅾 CarQuest, Chrysler/Dodge/Jeep, Firestone, Honda, Office Depot, **W** 🅰 Exxon, Shell 🍴 Chili's, Jalisco's Mexican, Panda Express, Papa John's Pizza, Quizno's, Starbucks, Subway, Taco Bell, Taco Cabana, Wendy's, Whataburger, Wing Stop 🛏 Best Value Inn, Best Western 🅾 $Tree, AT&T, Best Buy, Discount Tire, Fry's Electronics, Home Depot, NTB, Office Depot, PepBoys, Radio Shack, Ross, Verizon, Walmart/24hr
57	(b a from nb) TX 249, Gulf Bank Rd, Tomball, **E** 🅰 Chevron, Mobil/dsl, Texaco/Church's 🍴 Wings'n More, **W** 🅰 Shell 🍴 Sonic, Tombico Seafood 🛏 Greenchase Motel, La Quinta, Quality Inn 🅾 CVS Drug, Family$, Giant$, Mas Club/dsl
56	Canino Rd, **E** 🛏 Taj Inn Suites, **W** 🅰 Shell, Texaco 🍴 Capt D's, Denny's, Jack-in-the-Box, KFC, Luby's 🛏 Best Value Inn, EconoLodge, Gulfwind Motel, Passport Inn 🅾 Ford, Isuzu, USPO
55	(b a from nb) Little York Rd, Parker Rd, **E** 🅰 Chevron, Texaco 🍴 Burger King, China Panda, McDonald's, Whataburger 🅾 Advance Parts, Family$, FoodTown, **W** 🅰 Shell 🍴 Popeye's 🛏 Symphony Inn 🅾 🏥 Family$, Walgreens
54	Tidwell Rd, **E** 🅰 Exxon/dsl 🍴 Aunt Bea's Rest, Burger King, Chacho's Mexican, China Border, Frenchys, Pancho's Mexican, Subway, Thomas BBQ, Wings'N More 🅾 CVS Drug, Discount Tire, Radio Shack, transmissions, **W** 🅰 Chevron 🍴 McDonald's 🛏 Guest Motel, Scottish Inn, Southwind Motel, Town Inn 🅾 U-Haul
53	Airline Dr, **E** 🅰 Citgo 🍴 Popeye's 🅾 Fiesta Foods/drug, **W** 🅰 Citgo, Shell 🍴 Little Mexico, Wendy's 🛏 Luxury Inn, Palace Inn
52	(b a from nb) Crosstimbers Rd, **E** 🍴 Baskin-Robbins, Burger King, Chick-fil-A, China Star, ChuckeCheese, Cici's, IHOP, Jack-in-the-Box, James Coney Island, KFC, Pappas BBQ, Pizza Hut, Pollo Rico, Sonic, Subway, Taco Bell 🅾 $Tree, AT&T, CVS Drug, Discount Tire, Firestone, GNC, mall, Marshall's, Office Depot, Ross, Verizon, Walmart, **W** 🅰 Chevron/dsl 🍴 Whataburger/24hr 🛏 Texan Inn
51	I-610
50	(b a from nb) Patton St, Calvacade St, Link Rd, **E** 🅰 Citgo, Exxon, ❤Loves/Wendy's/dsl/scales/24hr, Shell 🛏 Best Value Inn, Luxury Inn, **W** 🛏 Astro Inn 🅾 NAPA
49b	N Main St, Houston Ave, **E** 🅰 Citgo 🍴 Casa Grande Mexican 🛏 Best Value Inn, Luxury Inn, **W** 🅰 Exxon/dsl 🍴 Domino's, McDonald's, Subway, Whataburger/24hr 🛏 Sleep Inn 🅾 O'Reilly Parts
48b a	I-10, E to Beaumont, W to San Antonio
47d	Dallas St, Pierce St (from sb), **E** 🅾 🏥
47c	McKinney St (from sb, exits left)
47b	Houston Ave, Memorial Dr, **W** 🛏 Double Tree Hotel, downtown
47a	Allen Pkwy (exits left from sb)
46b a	US 59, N to Cleveland, S to Victoria, **E** 🅰 Chevron, **W** 🅰 Texaco 🍴 McDonald's, Taco Bell 🅾 BMW
45b a	South St, Scott St, Houston, **E** 🅰 Shell/Blimpie, to TSU
44	Cullen Blvd, Houston, **E** 🅰 to U of Houston, Valero/dsl
43b	Telephone Rd, Houston
43a	Tellepsen St, **E** 🍴 Luby's, **W** 🅾 U of Houston

H O U S T O N

⬆N INTERSTATE 45 Cont'd

Exit #	Services
41b	US 90A, Broad St, S Wayside Dr, **E** 🅖 Phillips 66 🅕 Arranda's Mexican 🅛 Houston Inn, Red Carpet Inn, **W** 🅖 Chevron, Exxon, Mobil 🅕 Jack-in-the-Box, McDonald's, Monterrey Mexican, Subway, Taquiera Mexican, Wings and More 🅞 $Tree, K-Mart, Sellars Foods
41a	Woodridge Dr, **E** 🅖 Shell 🅕 Bonnie's Rest., China Star, Denny's, James Coney Island, McDonald's, Pappa's Seafood House, Schlotsky's 🅞 King$, **W** 🅖 Citgo 🅕 BoneBreak BBQ, IHOP, Pappas BBQ, Sonic, Subway, Wendy's, Whataburger 🅞 Chevrolet/Buick, Dillard's, HEB Food/gas, Home Depot, Lowe's, mall, Marshall's, Office Depot, Old Navy, Radio Shack, Ross
40c	I-610 W
40b	I-610 E, to Pasadena
40a	Frontage Rd (from nb)
39	Park Place Blvd, Broadway Blvd, **E** 🅖 Shell/dsl, **W** 🅖 Shell 🅕 Kelley's Rest., Papa John's, Red Panda, Subway 🅞 Chevrolet/Dodge/Jeep, Family$, transmissions
38b	Howard Dr, Bellfort Dr (from sb), **E** 🅖 Shell 🅕 Jack-in-the-Box, Wendy's, **W** 🅖 Citgo, Shell, Texaco 🅕 Chilo's Seafood 🅛 Camelot Inn, Moonlight Inn, Mustang Inn, Palace Inn 🅞 PepBoys
38	TX 3, Monroe Rd, **E** 🅖 Chevron/dsl, Shell/dsl, Valero 🅕 DQ, Jack-in-the-Box, Ninfa, Starbucks, Wendy's 🅞 Family$, Firestone, NTB, TX Campers, U-Haul, **W** 🅖 Chevron/dsl, Texaco/dsl 🅕 Manny's Seafood, Pappa's BBQ, Subway 🅛 Holiday Inn Express, Sheraton 🅞 Firestone, U-Haul
36	College Ave, 🔁 Blvd, **E** 🅖 Valero 🅕 Arranda's Bakery, Burger House, DQ, Jack-in-the-Box, Shipley Do-Nuts, Waffle House 🅛 Knights Inn, **W** 🅖 Shell/dsl, Valero/dsl 🅕 Denny's, Paco Joe's, Taco Cabana 🅛 Baymont Inn, Comfort Suites, Courtyard, Days Inn, Drury Inn, Hampton Inn, La Quinta, Marriott, Motel 6, SpringHill Suites, Super 8, Travel Inn 🅞 Discount Tire
35	Edgebrook Dr, **E** 🅖 Chevron, RaceWay 🅕 Arranda's Mexican, Burger King, Chilo's Rest., Jack-in-the-Box, KFC, Popeye's, Subway, Taco Bell 🅛🅛 Inn 🅕 Family$, Fiesta Foods, Firestone, Office Depot, vet, **W** 🅖 Mobil 🅕 James Coney Island, Mambo Seafood, McDonald's, Pizza Hut, Whataburger 🅞 Verizon
34	S Shaver Rd, **E** 🅖 Conoco 🅕 McDonald's 🅛 Island Suites 🅞 Ford, Kia, Nissan, Toyota/Scion, **W** 🅖 MurphyUSA/dsl 🅕 Arby's, China Star Buffet, Chopstix, KFC, Pancho's Mexican, Piccadilly's, Pizza Patron, Starbucks, Subway, Taco Bell, Wendy's 🅞 AT$T, Discount Tire, Firestone, GNC, Honda, Macy's, Marshall's, PetsMart, Ross, Staples, Walmart/McDonald's
33	Fuqua St, **E** 🅕 Chili's, Denny's, Fuddrucker's, Las Haciendas, Luby's, Olive Garden, Schlotzky's, TGIFriday's 🅛 Studio 6, Sun Suites 🅞 Hyundai, Lincoln, Volvo, **W** 🅕 Bayou City Wings, Blackeyed Pea, Boudreaux's, Casa Ole, Cici's Pizza, Fox&Hound, Golden Corral, Gringo's Mexican, IHOP, Joe's Crabshack, Kimhai Asian, McDonald's, Murphy's Deli, Outback Steaks, Subway, Taco Cabana, TX Land&Cattle Steaks, Whataburger, Wings&More 🅞 Buick/GMC, CarMax, Chevrolet, Home Depot, JC Penney, mall, Old Navy, Radio Shack, Sam's Club/gas, Subaru
32	**Sam Houston Tollway**
31	FM 2553, Scarsdale Blvd, **W** 🅞 Chevrolet

Exit #	Services
30	FM 1959, Dixie Farm Rd, Ellington Field, **E** 🅖 Shell/dsl 🅕 El Nopalito, Subway 🅛 Howard Johnson 🅞 🅷 Chrysler/Dodge/Jeep, Fiat, Infiniti, **W** 🅖 RaceWay, Shell/dsl 🅕 McDonald's, Popeye's 🅛 Palace Inn 🅞 Lonestar RV, VW
29	FM 2351, Clear Lake City Blvd, to Clear Lake RA, Friendswood, **W** 🅞 Hyundai
27	El Dorado Blvd, **E** 🅖 Exxon, Shell 🅕 Taco Bell 🅞 Home Depot, **W** 🅕 Sonic, TX Roadhouse, Whataburger 🅞 Cadillac, Kohl's, Lexus, Radio Shack, Sam's Club/gas, Walmart/McDonald's
26	Bay Area Blvd, **E** 🅖 Chevron 🅕 Chick-fil-A, Panera Bread, Peiwei, Potbelly's, Red Lobster, TGIFriday's, Zio's Kitchen 🅞 🅷 Barnes&Noble, Best Buy, Lowe's, Michael's, Staples, to Houston Space Ctr, World Mkt, **W** 🅕 5 Guys, Cafe Adobe, Chick-fil-A, ChuckeCheese, Denny's, McDonald's, Olive Garden, Panda Express 🅛 Holiday Inn Express 🅞 AT&T, Dillard's, JC Penney, Jo-Ann Fabrics, Macy's, mall, Marshall's, Office Depot, Old Navy, Sears/auto, Target, U of Houston, Verizon
25	FM 528, NASA rd 1, **E** 🅖 Chevron, Conoco 🅕 Big Ben Rest., Cheddar's, Chili's, Chuy's Mexican, Las Hacienda Mexican, Marble Slab, McAlister's Deli, Michiru Asian, Pappa's Seafood, Pappasito's Cantina, Rudy's BBQ/gas, Saltgrass Steaks, Steak'n Shake, Twin Peaks Rest., Vito's, Waffle House 🅛 Motel 6, Springhill Suites 🅞 🅷 BigLots, Fry's Electronics, Hobby Lobby, Home Depot, Honda, Mazda, Volvo, **W** 🅕 Cici's Pizza, Floyd's Cajun, Han's BBQ, Hooters, Hot Wok Chinese, James Coney Island, Pappa's Cafe, Subway 🅞 Tuesday Morning
23	FM 518, League City, **E** 🅖 RaceWay/dsl 🅕 Center Buffet, KFC, La Brisa, Subway, Sudie's Seafood 🅞 Just Brakes, Kroger, **W** 🅖 Chevron/dsl, Valero 🅕 Cracker Barrel, McDonald's, Taco Bell, Waffle House, Wendy's 🅛 Super 8 🅞 Discount Tire, Space Ctr RV Park, U-Haul
22	Calder Dr, Brittany Bay Blvd, **E** 🅕 Wings'n More 🅞 BMW/Mini, Mercedes, Nissan, Toyota/Scion, URGENT CARE, **W** 🅞 Acura, Holiday World RV Ctr
20	FM 646, Santa Fe, Bacliff, **E** 🅖 MurphyUSA/dsl 🅕 5 Guys, Chick-fil-A, Cici's Pizza, Denny's, Jack-in-the-Box, Logan's Roadhouse, Marble Slab, McDonald's, Panda Express, Schlotzky's, Spring Creek BBQ, Subway, Whataburger 🅛 Candlewood Suites, Hampton Inn 🅞 $Tree, Best Buy, Hobby Lobby, Home Depot, JC Penney, Lowe's, Michael's, NTB, PetsMart, Radio Shack, Ross, Staples, Target, TJ Maxx, Walmart/McDonald's, **W** 🅖 Chevron/dsl 🅕 Badabing, Chili's, Chinese Rest., Subway, Taco Cabana 🅞 HEB Foods/gas, Kohl's, PetCo, Verizon

(vertical text) LEAGUE CITY

INTERSTATE 45 Cont'd

Exit #	Services
19	FM 517, Dickinson Rd, Hughes Rd, **E** 🍴 Jack-in-the-Box, Monterey Mexico, Shipley Do-Nuts 🅞 Buick/GMC, CVS Drug, Due's RV Ctr, Family$, Kia, **W** 🅖 Conoco/dsl, Shell/dsl 🍴 Burger King, Dickenson's Seafood, KFC, McDonald's, Pizza Hut, Sonic, Subway, Taco Bell, Wendy's, Whataburger/24hr 🛏 Days Inn, Economy Inn 🅞 Chrysler/Dodge/Jeep, Curves, Ford, Kroger, Walgreens
17	Holland Rd, **W** 🅞 Tanger Outlets/Famous Brands, to Gulf Greyhound Park
16	FM 1764 E (from sb), Texas City, same as 15
15	FM 2004, FM 1764, Hitchcock, **E** 🅖 Shell 🍴 Gringo's Cafe, Jack-in-the-Box, Olive Garden, Popeye's, Ryan's, Uncle Chan's 🛏 Best Western, Fairfield Inn, Hampton Inn, Holiday Inn Express, Value Place Inn 🅞 🅷 Chevrolet/Toyota/RV Ctr, DeMontrond RV Ctr, Dillard's, JC Penney, Lowe's, Macy's, mall, Sam's Club/gas, Sears/auto, Toyota/Scion, **W** 🅖 Gulf/Subway, MurphyUSA/dsl, Shell 🍴 IHOP, Little Caesars, Pizza Hut, Sonic, Waffle House, Wendy's, Whataburger, WingStop 🅞 AT&T, Gulf Greyhound Park, Radio Shack, Verizon, Walmart/McDonald's
13	Century Blvd, Delany Rd, **W** 🍴 Barcema's Mexican 🛏 Best Value Inn, Super 8 🅞 Lazy Days RV Park, VF Factory Outlet/famous brands
12	FM 1765, La Marque, **E** 🅖 Chevron/24hr 🍴 Domino's, Jack-in-the-Box, Kelley's Rest., Sonic, **W** 🅖 Texaco 🅞 Little Thicket RV Park
11	Vauthier Rd
10	**E** 🅖 Exxon, Valero 🍴 KFC, McDonald's, PitStop BBQ, Subway, **W** 🅖 Shell/dsl 🅞 Hoover RV Ctr, Oasis RV Park
9	Frontage Rd (from sb, no return/turnaround)
8	Frontage Rd (from nb)
7c	Frontage Rd
7b	TX 146, TX 6 (exits left from nb), Texas City
7a	TX 146, TX 3
6	Frontage Rd (from sb)
5	Frontage Rd
4mm	West Galveston Bay
4	Frontage Rd, Village of Tiki Island, **W** 🅖 Valero 🅞 public boat ramp, Welcome Ctr
1c	TX 275, FM 188 (from nb), Port Ind Blvd, Teichman Rd, Port of Galveston, **E** 🅖 Citgo, Exxon, Valero 🛏 Motel 6 🅞 Buick/Chevrolet/GMC, Ford, Toyota/Scion
1b	71st St (from sb), **E** 🅖 EZ Mart/gas, same as 1c
1a	TX 342, 61st St, to W Beach, **E** 🍴 WingStop 🛏 Candlewood Suites 🅞 BigLots, Home Depot, NTB, PetsMart, Target, **W** 0-2 mi 🅖 Chevron, Citgo, Exxon, RaceWay, Valero 🍴 Cici's Pizza, Happy Buddah, Healthy Chinese, Hibachi Grill, Jack-in-the-Box, KFC, Little Caesars, Mario's, McDonald's, Pizza Hut, Popeye's, Quiznos, Sonic, Starbucks, Subway, Taco Bell, Taco Cabana, Wafflehouse, Whataburger, Yamato Japanese 🛏 Best Western, Comfort Inn, Days Inn, Quality Inn, Springhill Suites, Super 8 🅞 $Tree, AT&T, AutoZone, CVS Drug, Family$, Firestone, Kroger/dsl, KwikCar, Marshall's, Office Depot, O'Reilly Parts, Randall's Food/gas, Ross, Tuesday Morning, USPO, Verizon

I-45 begins/ends on TX 87 in Galveston.

INTERSTATE 410 (San Antonio)

Exit #	Services
53	I-35, S to Laredo, N to San Antonio
51	FM 2790, Somerset Rd
49	TX 16 S, spur 422, **N** 🅖 Chevron, Texaco/dsl 🍴 Church's, Domino's, Sonic, Subway, Whataburger 🛏 Days Inn 🅞 🅷 to Palo Alto Coll, **S** 🅖 Valero/dsl 🍴 Jack-in-the-Box 🛏 Best Western
48	Zarzamora St
47	Turnaround (from eb)
46	Moursund Blvd
44	US 281 S, spur 536, Roosevelt Ave, **N** 🅖 Shell/McDonald's/dsl, Valero/dsl, **S** 🛏 Holiday Inn Express
43	Espada Rd (from eb)
42	spur 122, S Presa Rd, **S** 🅖 Citgo/dsl, to San Antonio Missions Hist Park
41	I-37, US 281 N
39	spur 117, WW White Rd
37	Southcross Blvd, Sinclair Rd, Sulphur Sprs Rd, **N** 🅖 Valero 🍴 Capparelli's Pizza 🅞 🅷
35	US 87, Rigsby Ave, **E** 🅖 Exxon, Murphy USA/dsl, Valero/dsl 🍴 A&W, BorderTown Mexican, Cici's Pizza, Denny's, Jack-in-the-Box, LJ Silver, McDonald's, Subway, Taco Bell 🅞 $Tree, Radio Shack, Walmart/24hr, **W** 🅖 Chevron 🍴 Barnacle Bill's Seafood, Bill Miller BBQ, Domino's, El Tapito Mexican, Luby's, Sonic, Taco Cabana, Whataburger 🛏 Days Inn 🅞 $General, Aamco, Advance Parts, auto/dsl repair, O'Reilly Parts, U-Haul, vet, Walgreens
34	FM 1346, E Houston St, **W** 🅖 Valero/dsl
33	I-10 E, US 90 E, to Houston, I-10 W, US 90 W, to San Antonio
32	Dietrich Rd (from sb), FM 78 (from nb), to Kirby
31b	Lp 13, WW White Rd
31a	FM 78, Kirby, 🅖 Citgo, Valero/dsl 🅞 Family$
30	Binz-Engleman, Space Center Dr (from nb)
I-410 and I-35 run together 7 mi, See I-35 exits 161 thru 165	
27	I-35, N to Austin, S to San Antonio
26	Lp 368 S, Alamo Heights
25b	FM 2252, Perrin-Beitel Rd, **N** 🅖 Chevron/dsl, Valero 🍴 Carl's Jr, KFC/Taco Bell, Quizno's, Schlotsky's, Tastee-Freez/Wienerschnitzel, Wendy's 🛏 Best Value Inn 🅞 Brake Check, **S** 🍴 Jim's Rest.
25a	Starcrest Dr, **N** 🅖 Valero 🍴 Jack-in-the-Box, Los Patios Mexican 🅞 🅷 Toyota
24	Harry Wurzbach Hwy, **N** 🍴 Taco Cabana, **S** 🅖 Chevron 🍴 BBQ Sta. 🅞 VW
23	Nacogdoches Rd, **N** 🅖 Shell 🍴 Bill Miller BBQ, Church's, IHOP, Jack-in-the-Box, Luby's, Mamma's Cafe, Pizza Hut, Sonic, Wendy's 🛏 Crowne Plaza, **S** 🅖 Chevron
22	Broadway St, **N** 🅖 Shell/dsl 🍴 Chili's, Las Palapas, McDonald's 🛏 Cambria Suites, Courtyard 🅞 vet, **S** 🅖 Citgo, Valero 🍴 Chesters Hamburgers, Jim's Rest., Little Caesar's, Martha's Mexican, Quizno's, Taco Palenque, Whataburger 🛏 Residence Inn, TownHouse Motel
21	US 281 S, 🆁🆂 Rd, Jones Maltsberger Rd, **N** 🍴 Applebee's, Bubba's Rest 🛏 Best Western, Drury Suites, Hampton Inn, Holiday Inn, Holiday Inn Express, PearTree Inn, **S** 🅖 Murphy USA/dsl 🍴 Pappadeaux, Red Lobster, Texas Land&Cattle, Whataburger 🛏 Best Western, Courtyard, Days Inn, Fairfield Inn, La Quinta, Renaissance Hotel, Staybridge Suites, TownePlace Suites 🅞 Hyundai/Kia, Mitsubishi, Subaru, Target, TJ Maxx, Walmart/McDonald's/24hr

SAN ANTONIO

GALVESTON

TX

↑N INTERSTATE 410 (San Antonio) Cont'd

Exit #	Services
20	TX 537, **N** ⛽ Valero 🍴 Arby's, Chick-fil-A, Jack-in-the-Box, Jason's Deli, McDonald's, Subway, TGIFriday's 🏨 Double-Tree Hotel, Hilton 🅾 Barnes&Noble, Bealls, Best Buy, Brake Check, Cavender's Boots, Chevrolet, Honda, Jo-Ann Fabrics, Lexus, Lincoln, Marshall's, Mazda, Office Depot, PetCo, Ross, WorldMkt, **S** 🍴 Cheesecake Factory, El Pollo Loco, La Madeleine, Luby's, Taco Cabana 🅾 AT&T, CVS Drug, Dillard's, Dodge, JC Penney, Macy's, mall, Saks 5th, Sears/auto, Target, Verizon
19b	FM 1535, FM 2696, Military Hwy, **N** 🍴 Guajillos Mexican, Souper Salad, **S** 🍴 Denny's, Jim's Rest.
19a	Honeysuckle Lane, Castle Hills
17b	(18 from wb), **S** ⛽ Shell 🍴 Bill Miller BBQ, Subway 🅾 Firestone/auto, HEB Foods/gas
17	Vance Jackson Rd, **N** ⛽ Valero/dsl 🍴 Jack-in-the-Box, McDonald's, Sonic, Taco Cabana, Whataburger 🏨 Embassy Suites, Marriott 🅾 Aamco, Discount Tire, **S** ⛽ Citgo, Shell 🍴 Church's, Subway 🅾 U-Haul
16b a	I-10 E, US 87 S, to San Antonio, I-10 W, to El Paso, US 87 N
15	Lp 345, Fredericksburg Rd, **E** ⛽ Citgo 🍴 Church's, Dave&Buster's, Denny's, El Pollo Loco, Jack-in-the-Box, Jim's Rest., Luby's, McDonald's, Taco Cabana, Wendy's, Whataburger 🏨 Best Value Inn, SpringHill Suites 🅾 AT&T, Family$, Firestone/auto, Hobby Lobby, Jo-Ann Fabrics, SteinMart, Target, transmissions, **W** ⛽ Chevron/dsl 🅾 CVS Drug
14	(c b a from sb) Callaghan Rd, Babcock Ln, **E** ⛽ Chevron/dsl, Valero 🍴 Marie Callender's, Popeye's 🏨 Comfort Inn, Hampton Inn, Travelodge Suites 🅾 AT&T, GMC, Hyundai, **W** ⛽ Shell, Valero 🍴 Burger King, Chili's, ChopSticks Chinese, DingHow Chinese, Golden Corral, Henry's Tacos, IHOP, Jack-in-the-Box, Jim's Rest, Joe's Crabshack, Las Palapas Mexican, McDonald's, Quizno's, Red Lobster, Taco Cabana, Wendy's 🅾 Ⓗ Cavander's Boots, Chevrolet, Home Depot, NTB, Petsmart, Sam's Club/gas, vet,Walmart/Subway/24hr
13	(b a from sb) TX 16 N, Bandera Rd, Evers Rd, Leon Valley, **E** 🍴 Outback Steaks, Panda Express 🅾 Audi, HEB Foods/dsl, Office Depot, Old Navy, Toyota, U-Haul, **W** 🍴 Bill Miller BBQ, Henry's Tacos, Jim's Rest., Schlotzsky's, Sea Island Rest, Taco Cabana 🅾 BigLots, Chevrolet
12	(from sb) **W** 🍴 Fortune Cookie Chinese, Jason's Deli, Sea Island Shrimp House, Starbucks 🅾 $Tree, AT&T, Barnes&Noble, Best Buy, Marshall's, Michael's, Ross
11	Ingram Rd, **E** ⛽ Shell/dsl 🍴 KFC/Taco Bell, Krystal, Panda Buffet, TX Roadhouse 🏨 Comfort Suites, Courtyard, Days Inn, EconoLodge, Holiday Inn Express, Red Roof Inn, Residence Inn 🅾 Aamco, BrakeCheck, Chrysler/Dodge/Jeep, Mazda, **W** 🍴 Applebee's, Casa Real Mexican, Chick-fil-A, ChuckeCheese, Denny's, Fuddrucker's, Jack-in-the-Box, Whataburger 🏨 Best Western 🅾 Dillard's, Firestone/auto, JC Penney, Macy's, mall, Sears/auto
10	FM 3487, Culebra Rd, **E** 🍴 Bill Miller BBQ, Denny's, J Anthony's Seafood, McDonald's, Wendy's 🏨 La Quinta, Ramada Ltd 🅾 Harley-Davidson, to St Mary's U, **W** ⛽ Phillips 66 🅾 Ford, Mitsubishi
9	(b a from sb) TX 151, **W** ⛽ Murphy USA/dsl 🍴 Buffalo Wild Wings, Carino's Italian, Cheddar's, Chili's, Chipotle Mexican, Cracker Barrel, IHOP, McAlister's Deli, Panda Express, Starbucks, Taco Bueno, TGIFriday's 🏨 Alamo City Hotel, Quality Inn, Sleep Inn 🅾 Home Depot, Lowe's Whse, Office Depot, Petsmart, Ross, Target, to Sea World, Verizon, Walmart/24hr, ⛽

Exit #	Services
7	(8 from sb) Marbach Dr, **E** ⛽ Exxon 🍴 Church's, IHOP 🅾 PepBoys, **W** ⛽ Chevron/dsl, Shell 🍴 Acadiena Café, Asia Kitchen, Burger King, Coyote Canyon, Golden Wok, Jack-in-the-Box, Jim's Rest., KFC, LJ Silver, McDonald's, Mr Gatti's, Pancho's Mexican, Peter Piper Pizza, Pizza Hut, Red Lobster, Sonic, Subway, Taco Bell, Taco Cabana, Whataburger/24hr 🏨 Motel 6, Super 8 🅾 $General, $Tree, Advance Parts, Bealls, BigLots, BrakeCheck, Discount Tire, Firestone/auto, HEB Foods/gas
6	US 90, **E** 🏨 Country Inn Motel, **W** ⛽ Shell/dsl, Valero/dsl 🍴 Andrea's Mexican 🏨 Best Western 🅾 Explore USA RV Ctr, 🅾 to Lackland AFB
4	Valley Hi Dr, to Del Rio, San Antonio, **E** ⛽ Valero 🍴 Burger King, Church's, McDonald's, Pizza Hut, Sonic 🅾 AutoZone, HEB Food/gas, Radio Shack, **W** ⛽ Valero 🍴 Jack-in-the-Box 🅾 to Lackland AFB, Walgreens
3	(b a from sb) Ray Ellison Dr, Medina Base, **E** ⛽ Chevron/dsl, **W** ⛽ Valero/Subway/dsl
2	FM 2536, Old Pearsall Rd, **E** ⛽ Shell/dsl, Valero/dsl 🍴 Bill Miller BBQ, Church's, McDonald's, Mexico Taqueria, Sonic, Subway 🅾 O'Reilly Parts
1	Frontage Rd, 🅾 Scion/Toyota

↑N INTERSTATE 610 (Houston)

Exit #	Services
38c a	TX 288 N, access to zoo, downtown
37	Scott St, **N** ⛽ Citgo, Valero
36	FM 865, Cullen Blvd, **N** 🏨 Crystal Inn, **S** ⛽ Chevron/McDonald's, Mobil, Shell, Valero 🍴 Timmy Chan 🏨 Crown Inn, Cullen Inn
35	Calais Rd, Crestmont St, MLK Blvd, **N** ⛽ Exxon, Valero 🍴 Burger King
34	S Wayside Dr, Long Dr, **N** ⛽ Chevron, Phillips 66, Shell 🍴 Church's, Wendy's, **S** ⛽ Shell, Valero 🅾 NAPA
33	Woodridge Dr, Telephone Rd, **N** ⛽ Shell/dsl 🍴 ChuckeCheese, Cici's Pizza, IHOP, KFC/Taco Bell, McDonald's, Papa John's, Starbucks, Wendy's 🏨 South Lp Inn 🅾 Best Buy, Brake Check, HEB Foods, Lowe's, Marshall's, Old Navy, Ross, Staples, **S** ⛽ Texaco/dsl 🍴 Burger King, Gabby's BBQ, KFC, Piccadilly's Cafeteria, Spanky's Pizza, Whataburger 🅾 Dodge, Ford, mall
32b a	I-45, S to Galveston, N to Houston, 🅾 to 🆁🆂
31	Broadway Blvd, **S** ⛽ Texaco/dsl, Valero/dsl
30c b	TX 225, to Pasadena, San Jacinto Mon
29	Port of Houston Main Entrance
28	Clinton Dr, to Galina Park
27	Turning Basin Dr, industrial area

SAN ANTONIO

HOUSTON

TX

TX / UT

⬆N INTERSTATE 610 (Houston) Cont'd

Exit #	Services
26b	Market St
26a	I-10 E, to Beaumont, I-10 W, to downtown
24	(b a from sb) US 90 E, Wallisville Rd, E 🅖 Citgo/dsl, Loves/Arby's/dsl/scales/24hr, Pilot/McDonald's/dsl/scales, Texaco/dsl, Valero/Heart's Chicken/dsl/scales/24hr 🍴 Luby's, Wendy's 🄾 Blue Beacon, W 🅖 Citgo/dsl
23b	N Wayside, N 🅖 Valero
23a	Kirkpatrick Blvd
22	Homestead Rd, Kelley St, N 🅖 Shell/dsl 🍴 Whataburger 🏨 Super 8, S 🅖 Chevron/Subway/dsl/scales
21	Lockwood Dr, N 🅖 Chevron/McDonald's, Shell 🍴 Church's, Popeye's, Timmy Chan Chinese 🄾 🄷 Family$, Fiesta Foods
20a b	US 59, to downtown
19b	**Hardy Toll Rd**
19a	Hardy St, Jensen Dr (from eb)
18	Irvington Blvd, Fulton St, N 🅖 Chevron, S 🅖 Shell/dsl
17b c	I-45, N to Dallas, S to Houston
17a	(eb only) Airline Dr, S 🅖 Shell 🍴 Jack-in-the-Box 🏨 Western Inn
16	(b a from eb) Yale St, N Main St, Shamrock, N 🅖 Exxon 🄾 Harley-Davidson, S 🅖 Texaco 🍴 Burger King, Church's, KFC/Taco Bell, Starbucks
15	TX 261, N Shepherd Dr, N 🍴 Sonic, Taco Cabana, S 🅖 Chevron, Shell 🍴 Wendy's, Whataburger 🄾 Home Depot, PepBoys
14	Ella Blvd, N 🅖 Exxon, Texaco 🍴 A&W, KFC, McDonald's, Popeye's, Taco Bell, S 🅖 Shell 🍴 Thomas BBQ 🄾 🄷 BrakeCheck, Lowe's Whse, Office Depot
13c	TC Jester Blvd, N 🅖 Mobil, Shell 🍴 Denny's, Juanita's Mexican, Po' Boys Sandwiches 🏨 Courtyard, SpringHill Suites, S 🅖 Phillips 66/dsl
13b a	US 290 (exits left from nb)
12	W 18th St, E 🍴 Applebee's, Whataburger, W 🅖 Shell 🍴 Burger King 🏨 Sheraton
11	I-10, W to San Antonio, E to downtown Houston
10	Woodway Dr, Memorial Dr, W 🅖 Chevron/Pizza Inn/dsl, Shell/dsl 🄾 Goodyear

HOUSTON

9b	Post Oak Blvd, E 🏨 Drury Inn, Hampton Inn, La Quinta, W 🍴 Champp's Rest., McCormick&Schmick's Café
9a	San Felipe Rd, Westheimer Rd, FM 1093, E 🅖 Mobil, Shell 🍴 Omaha Steaks 🏨 Courtyard, Extended Stay America, Hampton Inn, La Quinta 🄾 CVS Drug, NTB, Target, W 🅖 Shell 🍴 Jamba Juice, Luke's Burgers 🏨 Crowne Plaza Hotel, HomeStead Suites, Marriott, Sheraton 🄾 Best Buy, Dillard's, Nieman-Marcus
8a	US 59, Richmond Ave, E 🏨 Extended Stay America, Holiday Inn 🄾 CVS Drug, W 🅖 Shell 🄾 Dillards
7	Bissonet St, West Park Dr, Fournace Place, E 🍴 Beudreax's Kitchen 🏨 Candlewood Suites 🄾 Home Depot, W 🅖 Shell/dsl/repair
6	Bellaire Blvd
5b	Evergreen St
5a	Beechnut St, E 🅖 Chevron 🍴 Boston Mkt, IHOP, Lowe's, McDonald's, Outback Steaks, W 🅖 Citgo, Shell 🍴 Escalante Mexican Grill, James Coney Island, Saltgrass Steaks, Smoothie King 🄾 GNC, mall, Marshall's, Ross
4a	S Post Oak Rd, Brasswood, E 🅖 Citgo 🍴 Outback Steaks 🏨 Days Inn, W 🄾 Target, Walmart .
3	Stella Link Rd, N 🅖 Chevron 🍴 Jack-in-the-Box 🄾 Discount Tire, Food City, Radio Shack, S 🅖 Exxon, Phillips 66/dsl, Shell, Valero 🄾 Brake Check
2	US 90A, N 🅖 Chevron, Conoco, Valero 🍴 Arby's, Burger King, Church's, Denny's/24hr, KFC, McDonald's, Shoney's, Taco Bell, Wendy's 🏨 Grand Plaza Hotel, Howard Johnson, Villa Motel 🄾 CVS Drug, Discount Tire, Ford, Honda, Walgreen, S 🅖 Chevron, Shell 🍴 Golden Corral, Pizza Hut/Taco Bell, Whataburger/24hr 🏨 Candlewood Suites, CareFree Inn, La Quinta, Motel 6, Speedway Inn, Super 8 🄾 Chevrolet, Firestone, Mazda, Nissan, to Buffalo Speedway, Toyota, U-Haul
1c	Kirby Dr (from eb), N 🍴 Burger King, Shell 🏨 Crowne Plaza, Holiday Inn, Radisson, S 🍴 Joe's Crabshack, Pappadeaux Seafood, Pappasito's Cantina 🄾 Cavender's Boots, Chevrolet, NTB, Toyota/Scion
1b a	FM 521, Almeda St, Fannin St, N 🅖 Chevron, Shell 🍴 Burger King 🏨 Scottish Inn 🄾 Astro Arena, S 🅖 Shell 🍴 McDonald's 🄾 Aamco, Chrysler/Dodge/Jeep, Sam's Club, to Six Flags

UTAH

⬆N INTERSTATE 15

Exit #	Services
400.5mm	Utah/Idaho state line
398	Portage
392	UT 13 S, Plymouth, E 🅖 United/A&W/dsl
385	UT 30 E, to Riverside, Fielding, E 1 mi 🅖 Sinclair/Riverside Grill/dsl
381	Tremonton, Garland, E 2 mi 🄾 🄷, 🍴, 🅖, 🏨
379	I-84 W, to Boise
376	UT 13, to Tremonton, E 2-3 mi 🅖 Texaco/Arby's/dsl/scales/24hr 🍴 Arctic Circle, JC'S Diner, Subway, Taco Time 🏨 Marble Motel, N 🏨 Sandman Motel (3mi)
372	UT 240, to UT 13, to rec area, Honeyville, E 🄾 Crystal Hot Springs Camping
370mm	🆁🅂 sb, full 🏨 facilities, info, litter barrels, petwalk, 🄲, 🄵, vending
365	UT 13, Brigham City, W 🄾 to Golden Spike NHS
363	Forest St, Brigham City, W 🄾 Bear River Bird Refuge

BRIGHAM CITY

362	US 91, to US 89, Brigham City, Logan, E 🅖 Chevron/dsl, Exxon, Phillips 66/dsl, USA 🍴 Arby's, Burger King, China Hua Guan, Domino's, Floriberto's Mexican, Hunan Chinese, J&D's Rest., KFC/Taco Bell, McDonald's, Old Grist Mill Bread, Pizza +, Pizza Hut, Sonic, Subway, Taco Time, Wendy's, Wingers 🏨 Crystal Inn, Howard Johnson Express 🄾 🄷 Verizon, $General, $Tree, 7-11, AT&T, AutoZone, Buick/Cadillac/Chevrolet, Family$, Golden Spike RV Park, KOA (4mi), O'Reilly Parts, Schwab Tires, ShopKO, to Yellowstone NP via US 89, Walmart/Subway, W 🅖 Pilot/DQ/dsl/scales/24hr 🏨 Days Inn
361mm	🆁🅂 sb, full 🏨 facilities, litter barrels, petwalk, 🄲, 🏨 vending
359	Port of Entry both lanes
357	UT 315, to Willard, Perry, E 🅖 FLYING J/Subway/dsl/LP/scales/24hr 🄾 KOA (2mi), Willard Peak Camping
351	UT 126, to US 89, to Utah's Fruit Way, Willard Bay, W 🄾 Smith & Edwards Hardware
349	UT 134, N Ogden, Farr West, E 🅖 7-11, Exxon/Wendy's/dsl,

INTERSTATE 15 Cont'd	
Exit #	**Services**

O G D E N

349   Continued
Maverik/dsl 🍴 Arby's, Bella's Mexican, Del Taco, Domino's, Jumbo Burger, McDonald's, Subway 🏠 Comfort Inn ⭕ Jiffylube, **W** 🅖 Chevron/dsl ⭕ Wasatch View RV park

346   to Harrisville, **W** 🅖 Chevron/Subway/dsl, dsl repair, Maverik/dsl 🍴 GriDeli's, Taco Time, Zhang's Chinese ⭕ Cal Store

344   UT 39, 12th St, Ogden, **E** 🅖 7-11/dsl, Chevron/dsl, Old Frontier 🏠 Best Western/rest. ⭕ to Ogden Canyon RA, **W** 🅖 🍴/Subway/Taco Bell/dsl/24hr 🍴 Uncle Lee's Cafe 🏠 Sleep Inn

343   UT 104, 21st St, Ogden, **E** 🅖 *FLYING J*/Denny's/dsl/LP/24hr, Phillips 66/dsl 🍴 Big Z Rest, Cactus Red's SW Grill, McDonalds 🏠 Comfort Suites, Holiday Inn Express, Motel 6, ValuePlace Inn ⭕ RV Repair, **W** 🅖 Texaco/Blimpie/dsl 🏠 Super 8 ⭕ Bideaux RV Ctr, Century RV Park

342   (from nb, no return) UT 53, 24th St, Ogden

341b a   UT 79 W, 31st St, Ogden, **E** 🍴 Longhorn Steaks ⭕ Ford, **E 1-2 mi on Wall St** ⭕ 🅷 Big O Tires, Chevrolet, Costco/gas, Dillard's, Firestone/auto, Hyundai, mall, to Weber St U **W** ⭕ 🍴

340   I-84 E (from sb), to Cheyenne, Wyo

339   UT 26 (from nb), to I-84 E, Riverdale Rd, **E** 🅖 Exxon/dsl, Sinclair/dsl 🍴 Applebee's, Arby's, Bajio Grill, Buffalo Wild Wings, Carl's Jr, Chili's, Honeybaked Ham, IHOP, Jamba Juice, Lucky Buffet, McDonald's, Starbucks, Subway, Wendy's 🏠 Motel 6 ⭕ $Tree, Best Buy, Buick/GMC, Cadillac, Chrysler/Dodge/Jeep, Good Earth Natural Foods, Gordman's, Harley-Davidson, Home Depot, Honda, Jo-Ann Fabrics, Kia, Mazda, Nissan, Petsmart, Sam's Club/gas, Schwab Tire, Target, Toyota/Scion, Verizon, Walmart

338   UT 97, Roy, Sunset, **E** ⭕ Air Force Museum, **W** 🅖 7-11, Exxon/dsl, Sinclair/dsl 🍴 A&W/KFC, Arby's, Beez Cafe, Blimpie, Chinese Gourmet, Five Star Chinese, Greek Island Broiler, Japanese Wasabi, La Frontera Mexican, McDonald's, Panda Express, Papa Murphy's, Rancherito's Mexican, Subway, Taco Bell, Village Inn Rest., Warren's Drive-In, Wendy's ⭕ AutoZone, Citte RV Ctr, CVS Drug, Discount Tire, Family$, Firestone/auto, Harmon's Mkt, Midas, O'Reilly Parts, RiteAid, Sacco's Fresh Mkt, Schwab Tires, Smith's/dsl, transmissions, vet, vet, Walgeens

335   UT 103, Clearfield, **E** ⭕ Hill AFB, **W** 🅖 Conoco, Phillips 66/dsl, Tesoro/dsl, Texaco/dsl 🍴 Carl's Jr, KFC, McDonald's, Subway, Taco Bell, Winger's 🏠 Days Inn, EconoLodge ⭕ C&M Tires, Sierra RV Ctr

334   UT 193, Clearfield, **E** 🅖 Chevron/dsl, Maverik ⭕ to Hill AFB, **W** 🅖 7-11, Maverik/dsl 🍴 Domino's ⭕ AutoZone

332   UT 108, Syracuse, **E** 🍴 Applebee's, Bandidos Border Grill, Boston's Rest., Brick Oven, Cafe Rio, Carl's Jr., Chick-fil-A, Chili's, Cracker Barrel, Famous Dave's, Five Guys, Golden

L A Y T O N

332   Continued
Corral, Jimmy John's, Koi Asian, MacCool's Grill, Marie Callender's, Mimi's Cafe, Noodles&Co, Outback Steaks, Panda Express, Papa Murphy's, Red Robin, Rumbi Island Grill, Sonic, Tepanyaki, Zupas Cafe 🏠 Courtyard, Fairfield Inn, Hampton Inn, Hilton Garden, Holiday Inn Express, Home2Home, La Quinta, TownePlace Suites ⭕ Barnes&Noble, Big O Tires, Lowe's Whse, Michaels, Office Depot, Petco, Ross, Target, URGENT CARE, Walgreens, **W** 🅖 Conoco/dsl 🍴 Arby's, Burger King, Crown Burger, McDonald's ⭕ 🅷 7-11, Ford, Kmart, to Antelope Island

331   UT 232, UT 126, Layton, **E** 🍴 Buffalo Wild Wings, Costa Vida, Denny's, Garcia's, McDonald's, Olive Garden, Red Lobster, Sizzler, Training Table Rest., TX Roadhouse, Wendy's 🏠 Best Western, Comfort Inn ⭕ $Tree, Dick's, JC Penney, Macy's, mall, to Hill AFB S Gate, Tuesday Morning, **W** 🅖 Exxon/dsl 🍴 Asian Buffet, Bajio Mexican, Burger King, Cantina SW Grill, ChuckeCheese, Coldstone, Del Taco, IHOP, KFC, Krispy Kreme, La Puente Mexican, Maid Rite Diner, Moon Dog Cafe, Pace's Rest., Rancheritos Mexican, Starbucks, Taco Bell, Taco Time ⭕ AT&T, Batteries+Bulbs, Big Lots, Buick/GMC, Chevrolet, Chrysler/Dodge/Jeep, Discount Tire, Hancock Fabrics, Hobby Lobby, Home Depot, Petsmart, Sam's Club/gas, ShopKO, Staples, Verizon, Walmart/McDonald's, 🍴 Iggy's Grill

330   Layton Pkwy, to UT 126, Layton, **E** 🍴 Little Orient Chinese ⭕ Tire Pros, **W** ⭕ Camping World RV Ctr

⬆N INTERSTATE 15 Cont'd

KAYSVILLE · N SALT LAKE

Exit #	Services
328	UT 273, Kaysville, **E** 🅖 7-11/dsl, Chevron/McDonald's 🍴 Arby's, Big Daddy's Pizza, Domino's, Dylan's Drive-In, Granny Annie's Rest., Pizza Hut, Subway, Taco Time, Wendy's, Winger's 🅞 AutoZone, Big O Tire, Fresh Mkt Foods, O'Reilly Parts, Schwab Tire, USPO, Walgreens, **W** 🅞 Camping World, Kia
325mm	**parking area both lanes**
325	UT 225, Lagoon Dr , Farmington, **E** 🍴 Subway 🅞 camping, funpark, **W** 🍴 Costa Vida, Dickey's BBQ, Habit Burger, Panda Express, Starbucks, Subway, Zupas 🅞 Gordmans, Harmon's Mkt, Marshalls, Old Navy, Petco, Ross
324	US 89 N, UT 225, Legacy Pkwy (from sb), **E 1 mi** 🅖 Maverik/dsl, Smith's Foods/dsl 🍴 Burger King, Chevron/dsl, Chopstix Chinese, Javier's Mexican, Papa John's, Subway 🏠 Hampton Inn 🅞 Aunt Pam's, Burt Bros/Goodyear/auto, RV Park, to I-84
322	UT 227 (from nb), Lagoon Dr, to Farmington, **E** 🍴 Subway 🅞 Lagoon Funpark/RV Park
319	UT 105, Parrish Lane, Centerville, **E** 🅖 7-11/dsl, Chevron/dsl, Phillips 66/dsl 🍴 Arby's, Carl's Jr, Chick-fil-A, Chili's, Costa Vida, DQ, Iggy's Grill, IHOP, In-N-Out, La Puente Mexican, Little Caesar's, McDonald's, Papa Murphy's, Ruby River Steaks, Starbucks, Subway, Taco Bell, TacoMaker, Wendy's 🅞 $Tree, Ace Hardware, Big O Tire, Dave's Auto Repair, Dick's Mkt, GNC, Home Depot, Jo-Ann, Kohl's, Land Rover, O'Reilly Parts, Petsmart, Schwab Tire, Target, Walmart
317	US 89 S (exits left from sb), UT 131, 500W, , S Bountiful, **E** 🅖 Chevron/dsl, Exxon/dsl, Sinclair/7-11/dsl 🍴 Starbucks 🏠 Country Inn Suites 🅞 Chrysler/Dodge/Jeep, Costco/gas, Office Depot, Parts+, PetCo
316	UT 68, 500 S, W Bountiful, Woods Cross, **E** 🅖 Texaco 🍴 Applebee's, Barbacoa Mexican, Cafe Rio, Carl's Jr, Chipotle, ChuckaRama, Coldstone, Del Taco, Five Guys, Jimmy John's, KFC, McDonald's, Mikado Japanese, Panda Express, Pei Wei, Pizza Factory, Pizza Hut, Sizzler, Starbucks, Subway, Taco Bell, TX Roadhouse, Wendy's 🅞 🅷 $Tree, AT&T, AutoZone, Barnes&Noble, Costco/gas, Firestone/auto, GNC, Lowe's, Michael's, Midas, Office Depot, O'Reilly Parts, Petco, Radio Shack, Ross, ShopKO, Tire Pros, TJ Maxx, Walgreens, **W** 🅖 Phillips 66/A&W/dsl 🏠 InTown Suites 🅞 vet
315	26th S, N Salt Lake, **E** 🅖 Chevron/dsl, Tesoro, Texaco 🍴 Arby's, Best Burger, Empire Chinese, Kneaders Bakery Cafe, McDonald's, Nielsen's Frozen Custard, Pappa's Steaks, Subway, Taco Time, Village Inn, Wendy's 🏠 Best Western, Comfort Inn 🅞 Buick/GMC, Burt Bros Tires, Chevrolet, Discount Tire, Ford/Lincoln, Honda, K-Mart, Mazda, Nissan, Schwab Tire, Smith's Foods, Southfork Hardware, Toyota/Scion, Tunex, U-Haul, Walgreens, **W** 🍴 Lorena's Mexican 🏠 Hampton Inn, Motel 6
314	Center St, Cudahy Lane (from sb), N Salt Lake, **E** 🅖 gas
313	I-215 W (from sb), 🅞 to 🆁🆂
312	US 89 S, to Beck St, N Salt Lake
311	2300 N
310	900 W (from sb), **W** 🏠 Salt City Motel
309	600 N, **E** 🅞 🅷 downtown, LDS Temple, to UT State FairPark
308	I-80 W, to Reno, 🅞 🆁🆂
307	400 S, downtown
306	600 S, SLC City Ctr, **E 1 mi** 🅖 Chevron, Phillips 66/dsl, Sinclair 🍴 Alberto's Mexican, Denny's, McDonald's, Starbucks, Subway, Wendy's 🏠 Crystal Inn, Comfort Inn, DoubleTree, Grand America, Hampton Inn, Hilton Garden, Little America, Motel 6, Red Lion Inn, Rodeway Inn, Sheraton,

SALT LAKE · SANDY · DRAPER

Exit #	Services
306	Continued SpringHill Suites 🅞 Hyundai, LDS Church Offices, to Temple Square, Toyota
305c-a	1300 S, 2100 S UT 201 W, SLC, downtown, **E** 🅖 Chevron/Subway/dsl, Shell 🍴 Carl's Jr, ChuckECheese, Dickey's BBQ, IHOP, Jimmy John's, McDonald's, Starbucks, Tepanyaki Japanese 🅞 $Tree, Best Buy, Costco/gas, Home Depot, Office Depot, PetsMart, Sams Club/dsl, U-Haul, Walmart, **W** 🅖 ⛽FLYING J/Denny's/dsl/LP/24hr 🍴 El Pasa Mexican 🅞 Blue Beacon, Kia
304	I-80 E, to Denver, Cheyenne
303	UT 171, 3300 S, S Salt Lake, **E** 🅖 7-11, Maverik/dsl, Sinclair/dsl 🍴 Apollo Burgers, Burger King, Crown Burger, Jimmy John's, McDonald's, Starbucks, Taco Bell 🏠 Day's Inn, InTowne Suites, **W** 🅖 Maverik 🅞 Buick/GMC
301	UT 266, 4500 S, Murray, Kearns, **E** 🍴 McDonald's, Subway, Super Grinders 🅞 Discount Tire, **W** 🅖 Chevron/Burger King/dsl, Conoco/dsl, Texaco/dsl 🍴 Denny's, Subway, Wendy's 🏠 Baymont Inn, Fairfield Inn, Hampton Inn 🅞 Lowe's Whse
300	UT 173, 5300 S, Murray, Kearns, **E** 🅞 🅷 **W** 🅖 Chevron/dsl, Conoco/dsl, Sinclair/dsl 🍴 Papa Murphy's, Subway, Taco Time 🏠 Pavilion Inn 🅞 Smith's Foods
298	I-215 E and W
297	UT 48, 7200 S, Midvale, **E** 🅖 Chevron, Phillips 66/dsl 🍴 Arctic Circle, Cafe Silvestre, Denny's, Hooters, McDonald's, Mezquite Mexican, Midvale Mining Cafe, Sweet Ginger Chinese, Taco Bell 🏠 Best Western, Day's Inn, Discovery Inn, InTowne Suites, La Quinta, Motel 6 🅞 Family$, Schwab Tire, Solitude Ski Areas, to Brighton, vet, Walgreens, **W** 🅖 Sinclair/dsl 🍴 Culver's, Dunkin Donuts, Jimmy John's, Subway, WinCo Foods 🏠 Staybridge Suites 🅞 GNC
295	UT 209, 9000 S, Sandy, **E** 🅖 Chevron/dsl, Sinclair/dsl 🍴 Arby's, Burger King, Ichiban Asian, Schlotzsky's, Sconecutter's Rest., Sizzler, Subway 🏠 Comfort Inn 🅞 Alta Ski Areas, Discount Tire, Firestone/auto, Ford/Lincoln, NAPA, Rio Rinto Stadium, to Snowbird, **W** 🅖 Maverik 🅞 🅷 Aamco, BMW Motorcycles, Harley-Davidson, URGENT CARE
293	106th S, Sandy, S Jordan, **E** 🅖 Conoco, Shell//dsl 🍴 A&W/KFC, Buffalo Wild Wings, Carl's Jr., Carver's Steak & Seafood, Chick-fil-A, Chili's, Chipotle Mexican, ChukECheese, Costa Vida, Firehouse Subs, Five Guys, Habit Burger, Iggy's Grill, IHOP, Jim's Rest., La Frontera, Los Cucos Mexican, McDonald's, McGrath's Fishhouse, Mimi's Cafe, Olive Garden, Pei Wei, Rumbi Island Grill, Sampan Chinese, Starbucks, Subway, Sweet Tomatoes, Taco Bell, TGIFriday, Training Table, TX Roadhouse, Village Inn, Wendy's 🏠 Best Western, Courtyard, Extended Stay America, Hampton Inn, Hilton Garden, Holiday Inn Express, Hyatt Summerfield, Marriott, Residence Inn, TownePlace Suites 🅞 Best Buy, Chevrolet, Chrysler/Dodge/Jeep, Costco/gas, Dillard's, Goodyear/auto, Home Depot, Honda, Hyundai, JC Penney, Macy's, mall, Petsmart, Scheels Sports, Staples, Subaru, Target, USPO, **W** 🍴 Denny's 🏠 Country Inn Suites, Sleep Inn, Super 8 🅞 Buick/GMC/Kia, CarMax, Nissan, Sam's Club/dsl, VW, Walmart,
291	UT 71, 12300 S, Draper, Riverton, **E** 🅖 Chevron, Common Cents/dsl 🍴 Arby's, Arctic Circle, Café Rio Mexican, Carl's Jr, Del Taco, Fazoli's, Guadalahonky's Mexican, In-N-Out, Jamba Juice, KFC, McDonald's, Panda Express, Pizza Hut, Quizno's, Ruby Tuesday, Sonic, Teriyaki Express, Wendy's, Wienerschnitzel, Wingers Diner 🏠 Comfort Inn, Fairfield Inn, Ramada Ltd 🅞 Brown RV, Camping World RV Supplies (1mi), Discount Tire, FSA Outlets/famous brands,

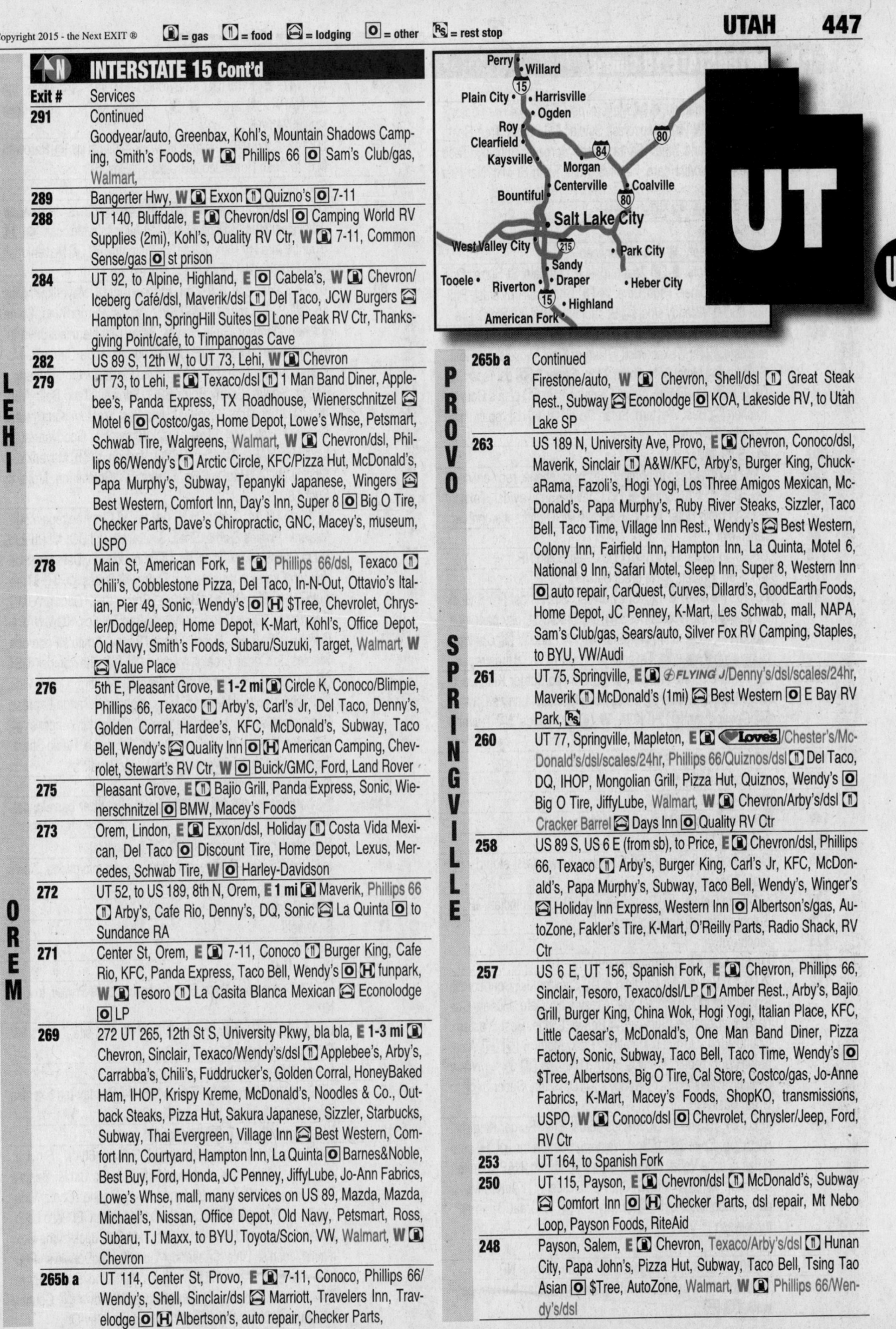

⬆N   INTERSTATE 15 Cont'd

Exit #	Services
291	Continued
	Goodyear/auto, Greenbax, Kohl's, Mountain Shadows Camping, Smith's Foods, W 🅶 Phillips 66 Ⓞ Sam's Club/gas, Walmart,
289	Bangerter Hwy, W 🅶 Exxon 🍴 Quizno's Ⓞ 7-11
288	UT 140, Bluffdale, E 🅶 Chevron/dsl Ⓞ Camping World RV Supplies (2mi), Kohl's, Quality RV Ctr, W 🅶 7-11, Common Sense/gas Ⓞ st prison
284	UT 92, to Alpine, Highland, E Ⓞ Cabela's, W 🅶 Chevron/ Iceberg Café/dsl, Maverik/dsl 🍴 Del Taco, JCW Burgers 🛏 Hampton Inn, SpringHill Suites Ⓞ Lone Peak RV Ctr, Thanks-giving Point/café, to Timpanogas Cave
282	US 89 S, 12th W, to UT 73, Lehi, W 🅶 Chevron
279	UT 73, to Lehi, E 🅶 Texaco/dsl 🍴 1 Man Band Diner, Apple-bee's, Panda Express, TX Roadhouse, Wienerschnitzel 🛏 Motel 6 Ⓞ Costco/gas, Home Depot, Lowe's Whse, Petsmart, Schwab Tire, Walgreens, Walmart, W 🅶 Chevron/dsl, Phillips 66/Wendy's 🍴 Arctic Circle, KFC/Pizza Hut, McDonald's, Papa Murphy's, Subway, Tepanyki Japanese, Wingers 🛏 Best Western, Comfort Inn, Day's Inn, Super 8 Ⓞ Big O Tire, Checker Parts, Dave's Chiropractic, GNC, Macey's, museum, USPO
278	Main St, American Fork, E 🅶 Phillips 66/dsl, Texaco 🍴 Chili's, Cobblestone Pizza, Del Taco, In-N-Out, Ottavio's Ital-ian, Pier 49, Sonic, Wendy's Ⓞ Ⓗ $Tree, Chevrolet, Chrys-ler/Dodge/Jeep, Home Depot, K-Mart, Kohl's, Office Depot, Old Navy, Smith's Foods, Subaru/Suzuki, Target, Walmart, W 🛏 Value Place
276	5th E, Pleasant Grove, E 1-2 mi 🅶 Circle K, Conoco/Blimpie, Phillips 66, Texaco 🍴 Arby's, Carl's Jr, Del Taco, Denny's, Golden Corral, Hardee's, KFC, McDonald's, Subway, Taco Bell, Wendy's 🛏 Quality Inn Ⓞ Ⓗ American Camping, Chev-rolet, Stewart's RV Ctr, W Ⓞ Buick/GMC, Ford, Land Rover
275	Pleasant Grove, E 🍴 Bajio Grill, Panda Express, Sonic, Wie-nerschnitzel Ⓞ BMW, Macey's Foods
273	Orem, Lindon, E 🅶 Exxon/dsl, Holiday 🍴 Costa Vida Mexi-can, Del Taco Ⓞ Discount Tire, Home Depot, Lexus, Mer-cedes, Schwab Tire, W Ⓞ Harley-Davidson
272	UT 52, to US 189, 8th N, Orem, E 1 mi 🅶 Maverik, Phillips 66 🍴 Arby's, Cafe Rio, Denny's, DQ, Sonic 🛏 La Quinta Ⓞ to Sundance RA
271	Center St, Orem, E 🅶 7-11, Conoco 🍴 Burger King, Cafe Rio, KFC, Panda Express, Taco Bell, Wendy's Ⓞ Ⓗ funpark, W 🅶 Tesoro 🍴 La Casita Blanca Mexican 🛏 Econolodge Ⓞ LP
269	272 UT 265, 12th St S, University Pkwy, bla bla, E 1-3 mi 🅶 Chevron, Sinclair, Texaco/Wendy's/dsl 🍴 Applebee's, Arby's, Carrabba's, Chili's, Fuddrucker's, Golden Corral, HoneyBaked Ham, IHOP, Krispy Kreme, McDonald's, Noodles & Co., Out-back Steaks, Pizza Hut, Sakura Japanese, Sizzler, Starbucks, Subway, Thai Evergreen, Village Inn 🛏 Best Western, Com-fort Inn, Courtyard, Hampton Inn, La Quinta Ⓞ Barnes&Noble, Best Buy, Ford, Honda, JC Penney, JiffyLube, Jo-Ann Fabrics, Lowe's Whse, mall, many services on US 89, Mazda, Mazda, Michael's, Nissan, Office Depot, Old Navy, Petsmart, Ross, Subaru, TJ Maxx, to BYU, Toyota/Scion, VW, Walmart, W 🅶 Chevron
265b a	UT 114, Center St, Provo, E 🅶 7-11, Conoco, Phillips 66/ Wendy's, Shell, Sinclair/dsl 🛏 Marriott, Travelers Inn, Trav-elodge Ⓞ Ⓗ Albertson's, auto repair, Checker Parts,

Exit #	Services
265b a	Continued
	Firestone/auto, W 🅶 Chevron, Shell/dsl 🍴 Great Steak Rest., Subway 🛏 Econolodge Ⓞ KOA, Lakeside RV, to Utah Lake SP
263	US 189 N, University Ave, Provo, E 🅶 Chevron, Conoco/dsl, Maverik, Sinclair 🍴 A&W/KFC, Arby's, Burger King, Chuck-aRama, Fazoli's, Hogi Yogi, Los Three Amigos Mexican, Mc-Donald's, Papa Murphy's, Ruby River Steaks, Sizzler, Taco Bell, Taco Time, Village Inn Rest., Wendy's 🛏 Best Western, Colony Inn, Fairfield Inn, Hampton Inn, La Quinta, Motel 6, National 9 Inn, Safari Motel, Sleep Inn, Super 8, Western Inn Ⓞ auto repair, CarQuest, Curves, Dillard's, GoodEarth Foods, Home Depot, JC Penney, K-Mart, Les Schwab, mall, NAPA, Sam's Club/gas, Sears/auto, Silver Fox RV Camping, Staples, to BYU, VW/Audi
261	UT 75, Springville, E 🅶 ⓕˡʸⁱⁿᵍ J/Denny's/dsl/scales/24hr, Maverik 🍴 McDonald's (1mi) 🛏 Best Western Ⓞ E Bay RV Park, Ⓡˢ
260	UT 77, Springville, Mapleton, E 🅶 ♥Loves/Chester's/Mc-Donald's/dsl/scales/24hr, Phillips 66/Quiznos/dsl 🍴 Del Taco, DQ, IHOP, Mongolian Grill, Pizza Hut, Quiznos, Wendy's Ⓞ Big O Tire, JiffyLube, Walmart, W 🅶 Chevron/Arby's/dsl 🍴 Cracker Barrel 🛏 Days Inn Ⓞ Quality RV Ctr
258	US 89 S, US 6 E (from sb), to Price, E 🅶 Chevron/dsl, Phillips 66, Texaco 🍴 Arby's, Burger King, Carl's Jr, KFC, McDon-ald's, Papa Murphy's, Subway, Taco Bell, Wendy's, Winger's 🛏 Holiday Inn Express, Western Inn Ⓞ Albertson's/gas, Au-toZone, Fakler's Tire, K-Mart, O'Reilly Parts, Radio Shack, RV Ctr
257	US 6 E, UT 156, Spanish Fork, E 🅶 Chevron, Phillips 66, Sinclair, Tesoro, Texaco/dsl/LP 🍴 Amber Rest., Arby's, Bajio Grill, Burger King, China Wok, Hogi Yogi, Italian Place, KFC, Little Caesar's, McDonald's, One Man Band Diner, Pizza Factory, Sonic, Subway, Taco Bell, Taco Time, Wendy's Ⓞ $Tree, Albertsons, Big O Tire, Cal Store, Costco/gas, Jo-Anne Fabrics, K-Mart, Macey's Foods, ShopKO, transmissions, USPO, W 🅶 Conoco/dsl Ⓞ Chevrolet, Chrysler/Jeep, Ford, RV Ctr
253	UT 164, to Spanish Fork
250	UT 115, Payson, E 🅶 Chevron/dsl 🍴 McDonald's, Subway 🛏 Comfort Inn Ⓞ Ⓗ Checker Parts, dsl repair, Mt Nebo Loop, Payson Foods, RiteAid
248	Payson, Salem, E 🅶 Chevron, Texaco/Arby's/dsl 🍴 Hunan City, Papa John's, Pizza Hut, Subway, Taco Bell, Tsing Tao Asian Ⓞ $Tree, AutoZone, Walmart, W 🅶 Phillips 66/Wen-dy's/dsl

Left margin vertical labels: LEHI, OREM (left column); PROVO, SPRINGVILLE (right column)

🔼 N INTERSTATE 15 Cont'd

Exit #	Services
244	US 6 W, Santaquin, **E** ⛽ Maverik/dsl 🍴 DQ Ⓞ Tire Factory, TrueValue, **W** ⛽ Conoco/dsl, Sinclair 🍴 Family Tree Rest., One Man Band Diner, Santa Queen Burgers, Subway, Taco Time Ⓞ auto/tire care, Family$, Ford, Main St Mkt, Nat Hist Area, USPO
242	to S Santaquin, **W** ⛽ Chevron/dsl
233	UT 54, Mona
228	UT 28, to Nephi, **W 2-4 mi** services
225	UT 132, Nephi, **E** ⛽ Tesoro/dsl/LP 🍴 Main St Pizza, One Man Band Diner, Taco Time, **W** ⛽ Chevron/Arby's/dsl, Phillips 66/7-11/Wendy's/dsl 🏨 Economy Inn Ⓞ 🏨 Big O Tire
222	UT 28, to I-70, Nephi, **E** ⛽ Chevron/dsl, Sinclair/Hogi Yogi/scales/dsl/24hr, Texaco/dsl 🍴 Burger King, Mickelson's Rest., Subway 🏨 Motel 6, National 9 Inn, Super 8 Ⓞ dsl repair, **W** ⛽ 🚛 FLYING J/Denny's/dsl/LP/scales/24hr 🍴 Lisa's Country Kitchen 🏨 Best Western, Safari Motel Ⓞ 🏨 dsl repair, High Country RV Park
207	to US 89, Mills
202	Yuba Lake, access to boating, camping, phone, rec services
188	US 50 E, to I-70, Scipio, **E** ⛽ Chevron/Subway/dsl, Texaco/dsl 🏨 Scipio Hotel, **W** ⛽ 🚛 FLYING J/DQ/dsl/rest stop/24hr
184	ranch exit
178	US 50, to Delta, **W** ⛽ Ⓞ 🆁🆂 to Great Basin NP
174	to US 50, Holden, Ⓞ to great Basin NP
167	Lp 15, Fillmore, **E** ⛽ Chevron/dsl, Sinclair/dsl 🍴 5 Buck Pizza 🏨 Best Western/rest. Ⓞ 🏨 CarQuest, city park, golf, Goodyear, KOA (3mi), WagonsWest RV Park, **W** ⛽ Chevron/Subway/rest stop/dsl, Texaco/dsl 🍴 Carl's Jr Ⓞ tires/repair
163	Lp 15, to UT 100, Fillmore, **E** ⛽ Conoco/Burger King/Costa Vida/dsl, Maverik/dsl 🍴 Hong Kong Chinese, Larry's Drive-In 🏨 Comfort Inn Ⓞ 🏨 KOA, **W** ⛽ Texaco/dsl 🏨 Travel & Rest Inn
158	UT 133, Meadow, **E** ⛽ Conoco/dsl, Shell/dsl
153mm	view area sb
151mm	view area nb
146	Kanosh, **E 2 mi** ⛽ Ⓞ chainup area
138	ranch exit
135	Cove Fort Hist Site, **E** ⛽ Chevron/Subway/rest stop/dsl Ⓞ repair/tires
132	I-70 E, to Denver, Ⓞ Capitol Reef NP, Fremont Indian SP
129	Sulphurdale, Ⓞ chainup area
125	ranch exit
120	Manderfield, Ⓞ chainup area nb
112	to UT 21, Beaver, Manderfield, **E** ⛽ Chevron/dsl, Conoco/dsl, Sinclair/dsl 🍴 Arshel's Café, Crazy Cow Cafe, Hunan Chinese, McDonald's, Subway 🏨 Beaver Lodge, Best Western, Country Inn, De Lano Motel/RV Park, Motel 6 Ⓞ 🏨 Alco, auto/RV/dsl repair, Family$, KOA (1mi), **W** ⛽ 🚛 FLYING J/cafe/dsl/scales/24hr 🍴 Wendy's 🏨 Days Inn, Super 8 Ⓞ to Great Basin NP
109	to UT 21, Beaver, **E** ⛽ Phillips 66/dsl, Shell/Burger King/dsl/RV dump, Spirit/dsl 🏨 Best Western, Comfort Inn Ⓞ 🏨 auto repair, Cache Valley Cheese, Mike's Foodtown, NAPA, United Camping, **W** ⛽ Blu LNG, Chevron/DQ/dsl 🍴 KanKun Mexican, Timberline Rest. 🏨 Quality Inn Ⓞ to Great Basin NP, truck wash
100	ranch exit
95	UT 20, to US 89, to Panguitch, Ⓞ Bryce Canyon NP
88mm	🆁🆂 both lanes, full ♿ facilities, hist site, litter barrels, petwalk, 🚻, 🎍

Exit #	Services
82	UT 271, Paragonah
78	UT 141, **E 1 mi** ⛽ Chevron/dsl, Maverik 🏨 Days Inn Ⓞ NAPA, ski areas, **W** ⛽ TA/Subway/Taco Bell/LP/dsl/scales/24hr/@
75	UT 143, **E 2 mi** ⛽ Chevron, Maverik 🏨 Days Inn Ⓞ Parowan Mkt, to Brian Head/Cedar Breaks Ski Resorts
71	Summit
62	UT 130, Cedar City, **E** ⛽ ❤Loves/Carl's Jr/Subway/dsl/scales/24hr, Phillips 66/dsl 🍴 Allberto's Mexican Ⓞ 🏨 Country Aire RV Park, KOA (2mi), st patrol, **W** ⛽ Maverik/dsl, Shell/dsl/24hr/dsl repair@ 🏨 Travelodge
59	UT 56, Cedar City, **E 0-2 mi** ⛽ Chevron/dsl, Maverik, Phillips 66/dsl/LP, Texaco 🍴 A&W/KFC, Arby's, Burger King, China Kitchen, Denny's, Great Harvest Bread Co., Hermie's Drive-In, Hong Kong Buffet, IHOP, Jimmy John's, Little Caesars, McDonald's/playplace, Papa Murphy's, Pizza Factory, Roberto's Tacos, Sizzler, Sonny Boy's BBQ, Subway, Taco Bell, Wendy's 🏨 Abbey Inn, Best Value Inn, Best Western, Quality Inn, Stratford Hotel Ⓞ $Tree, Buick/Chevrolet, Goodyear/auto, Lin's Mkt, NAPA, Tire Co., USPO, Verizon, **W** ⛽ Maverik/dsl, Sinclair/dsl 🍴 Bard's Cafe, Subway 🏨 Crystal Inn, Motel 6, Super 8
57	Lp 15, to UT 14, Cedar City **E 0-2 mi** ⛽ Chevron/repair/24hr, Maverik, Phillips 66/dsl, Shell, Sinclair/dsl 🍴 DQ, Mi Pueblo, Pizza Hut, Subway, Taco Time 🏨 Comfort Inn, Days Inn, Holiday Inn Express, Knights Inn, SpringHill Suites Ⓞ 🏨 $Tree, AutoZone, Big O Tire, BigLots, Bryce Cyn, Cadillac/GMC, CAL Ranch, Duck Crk, Family$, Jo-Ann Fabrics, KOA, NAPA-Care, Navajo Lake, O'Reilly Parts, Parts+, Smith's Food/gas, Staples, to Cedar Breaks, Verizon, **W** ⛽ Chevron/dsl, USA 🍴 5 Buck Pizza, Applebee's, Cafe Rio, Chili's, Costa Vida, Del Taco, Lupita's Mexican, Ninja Japanese, Panda Express, Papa John's, Quiznos, Starbucks, Subway, Winger's 🏨 Hampton Inn Ⓞ GNC, Home Depot, Jiffy Lube, Radio Shack, Tunex, Verizon, Walgreens, Walmart/McDonald's
51	Kanarraville, Hamilton Ft
44mm	🆁🆂 both lanes, full ♿ facilities, hist site, litter barrels, petwalk, 🚻, 🎍
42	New Harmony, Kanarraville, **W** ⛽ Texaco/dsl
40	to Kolob Canyon, **E** Ⓞ scenic drive, tourist info/phone, Zion's NP
36	Black Ridge
33	Snowfield
31	Pintura
30	Browse
27	UT 17, Toquerville, **E** Ⓞ Grand Canyon, Lake Powell, to Zion NP
23	Leeds, Silver Reef (from sb), **E 3 mi** Ⓞ hist site, Leed's RV Park/gas, museum
22	Leeds, Silver Reef (from nb), same as 23
16	UT 9, to Hurricane, **E** ⛽ Texaco/dsl 🏨 Holiday Inn Express Ⓞ Harley-Davidson, Walmart Dist Ctr
13	Washington Pkwy, **E** ⛽ Maverik/dsl
10	Middleton Dr, Washington, **E** ⛽ Phillips 66/dsl, Sinclair/dsl, USA 🍴 Alvero's Mexican, Arby's, Arctic Circle, Benja's Thai, Bishop's Cafe, Buca Italian, Burger King, Costa Vida, Del Taco, Dickey's BBQ, Don Pedro's Mexican, El Pollo Loco, Freddy's, Hungry Howie's, IHOP, In-N-Out, Jack-in-the-Box, Jimmy John's, Little Caesars, Mad Pita, McDonald's, Peppers Cantina, Pizza Factory, Pizza Hut, Red Robin, Royal Thai, Sonic, Subway, TX Roadhouse, Wendy's 🏨 Country Inn&Suites, Quality Inn Ⓞ AAA, Albertsons/Sav-On,

Vertical side labels: NEPHI, FILLMORE, BEAVER, CEDAR CITY

⬆N INTERSTATE 15 Cont'd

Exit #	Services
10	Continued

AutoZone, Barnes&Noble, Best Buy, Costco/gas, Dillard's, Discount Tire, Home Depot, JC Penney, Jo-Ann Fabrics, Kohl's, Natural Grocers, O'Reilly Parts, PetCo, Sears/auto, Tunex, Verizon, vet, Walmart/Subway, W 🅖 Chevron/dsl/LP, Texaco/dsl 🅞 auto repair, St George RV Park/camping

8   St George Blvd, St George, E 🅖 Chevron/Subway/dsl, Texaco/dsl 🍴 5 Guys Burgers, Apollo Burger, Applebee's, Brick Oven, Buffalo Wild Wings, Carl's Jr, Chick-fil-A, Chili's, Chuck-aRama, Coldstone, Firehouse Subs, Golden Corral, Habit Burger, Iggy's Grill, Jimmy John's, Mongolian BBQ, Olive Garden, Outback Steaks, Panda Express, Paradise Bakery & cafe, Red Lobster, Smashburger, Starbucks, Subway, Village Inn Rest., Winger's 🏠 Best Inn, Courtyard, Hampton Inn, Ramada Inn, TownePlace Suites 🅞 🏨 $Tree, AT&T, Dick's, Harmon's Foods, Lowe's, Old Navy, Petsmart, Ross, Staples, Sunrise Tire, Target, TJ Maxx, Tuesday Morning, Verizon, Zion Outlets/famous brands, W 🅖 Conoco/dsl, Maverik, Shell/dsl, Sinclair/dsl, Texaco/dsl 🍴 A&W/KFC, Burger King, Cafe Rio, Denny's, Iceberg Drive-Inn, Larsen's Drive-Inn, McDonald's, Ocean Buffet, Panda Garden, Papa John's, Port of Subs, Red Ginger Asian, Sakura Japanese, Taco Bell, Taco Time, Tropical Smoothie, Wendy's 🏠 Best Western, Chalet Motel, Coronada Inn, Days Inn, EconoLodge, Economy Inn, Knights Inn, Motel 6, Rodeway Inn, Sands Motel, SunTime Inn, Super 8 🅞 Auto Tech/tires, Big O Tire, Desert Coach RV Ctr, NAPA, O'Reilly Parts, Rite Aid, to LDS Temple, vet

6   UT 18, Bluff St, St George, E 🅖 Chevron/dsl, Sinclair/dsl, Texaco/dsl 🍴 Cracker Barrel, Culver's, Jack-in-the-Box, Player's Grill, Rib Chop House, Subway 🏠 Ambassador Inn, Comfort Inn, Fairfield Inn, Hilton Garden 🅞 Buick/GMC, Hyundai, Kia, museum, Subaru, VW, W 🅖 Shell, Texaco 🍴 Arby's, Beijing Buffet, Black Bear Diner, Burger King, Denny's, Domino's, DQ, Jimmy John's, McDonald's, Pizza Hut, Ricardo's Rest., SF Pizza 🏠 Best Value Inn, Best Western, Claridge Inn, Clarion Suites, Crystal Inn, Howard Johnson, Lexington Hotel, Quality Inn, St George Inn 🅞 🏨 auto/truck repair, AutoZone, Big O Tire, Cadillac/Chevrolet, Camping World RV Ctr, Chrysler/Dodge/Jeep, Ford/Lincoln, funpark, Goodyear/auto, Honda, K-Mart, Mazda, Nissan, Radio Shack, TempleView RV Park, Toyota, U-Haul

5   Dixie Dr

4   Brigham Rd, 4 Bloomington, E 🅖 ⛽/Burger King/dsl/scales/24hr 🏠 La Quinta, W 🅖 Chevron/Subway/Taco Time/dsl, USA/dsl 🍴 Dickey's BBQ, Hungry Howie's, Peppers Cantina, Wendy's 🏠 Wingate Inn 🅞 Walmart/Subway

2   UT 7 E, Southern Pkwy, E 🅞 📶

1   Port of Entry/**weigh sta both lanes**

0mm   Utah/Arizona state line

⬆E INTERSTATE 70

Exit #	Services
232mm	Utah/Colorado state line
228mm	view area wb, litter barrels
227	Westwater
221	ranch exit
214	to Cisco
204	UT 128, to Cisco
193	Yellowcat Ranch Exit

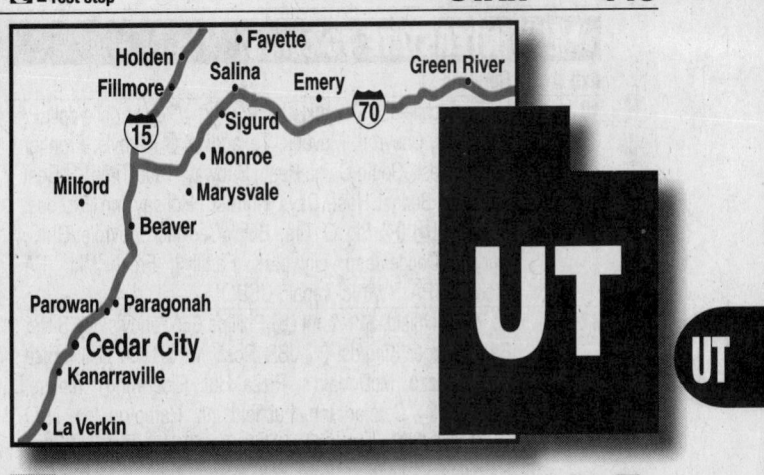

190mm	Welcome Center wb, full ♿ facilities, info, litter barrels, 🏕, vending
187	Thompson, N 🅖 Shell/dsl 🅞 café, camping, lodging
185mm	parking area eb
182	US 191 S, Crescent Jct, to Moab, N 🍴 Papa Joe's, S 🅞 to Arches/Canyonlands NP
181mm	🆁🆂 eb, full ♿ facilities, litter barrels, 🏕, 🏕, scenic view, vending
175	ranch exit
164	UT 19, Green River, N 1-3 mi 🅖 Phillips 66/Burger King/dsl, ⛽/Westwinds/rest/dsl/scales/24hr, Silver Eagle/Blimpie/dsl 🍴 Tamarisk Rest. 🏠 Bookcliff Motel/rest., Comfort Inn, Holiday Inn Express, Knights Inn, Motel 6, Ramada Ltd, River Terrace Inn, Super 8 🅞 KOA, Powell River Museum, same as 160, tires/repair
160	UT 19, Green River, N 0-2 mi 🅖 Chevron/Subway/dsl, Conoco/Arby's/dsl 🍴 Ben's Cafe, Chowhound, Ray's Rest. 🏠 Budget Inn, Green River Inn, Robbers Roost, Sleepy Hollow Motel 🅞 Ace Hardware, AG Mkt, city park, Green River SP, NAPA/repair, same as 164, Shady Acres RV Park, USPO
157	US 6 W, US 191 N, to Price, Salt Lake
149	UT 24 W, to Hanksville, to Capitol Reef, Lake Powell, 🅞 Goblin Valley SP
146	view area, restrooms wb
144mm	runaway truck ramp eb
143mm	view area both lanes, restrooms
142mm	runaway truck ramp eb
138mm	brake test area, restrooms eb
131	Temple Mt Rd
122mm	Ghost Rock View Area both lanes, restrooms
116	to Moore, N view area both lanes
115	N view area eb
108	ranch exit
105mm	Salt Wash View Area both lanes
99	ranch exit
91	UT 10 N, UT 72, to Emery, Price, N 12 mi 🅖 gas, S to Capitol Reef NP
86mm	S 🆁🆂 both lanes, full ♿ facilities, litter barrels, petwalk
73	ranch exit
63	Gooseberry Rd
56	US 89 N, to Salina, US 50 W, to Delta, N 0-1 mi 🅖 Conoco/dsl, Maverik, Phillips 66/dsl, Sinclair/Burger King/dsl 🍴 Denny's, El Mexicano Mexican, Losta Motsa Pizza, Mom's Cafe, Subway 🏠 EconoLodge, Rodeway Inn, Super 8 🅞 Barretts Foods, Butch Cassidy RV Camp, NAPA, NEXT SERVICES 109 MI EB, truck/RV/auto repair
48	UT 24, to US 50, Sigurd, Aurora, S 1-2 mi 🅖 🍴 🅞 Capitol Reef NP, to Fishlake NF

S T GEORGE   **GREEN RIVER**

🅟 = gas 🍴 = food 🛏 = lodging 🅞 = other 🆁🆂 = rest stop   Copyright 2015 - the Next EXIT ®

R I C H F I E L D

UT

🅔	INTERSTATE 70 Cont'd
Exit #	**Services**
40	Lp 70, Richfield, **S 0-2 mi** 🅟 ✈*FLYING J*/Pepperoni's/dsl/LP/rest./24hr, Chevron, Maverik, Texaco/dsl 🍴 Arby's, Frontier Village Rest., South China Rest., Subway, Taco Time 🛏 Best Western, Budget Host, Days Inn/rest., Holiday Inn Express, Super 8 🅞 🄷 Big O Tire, Buick/Cadillac/Chevrolet/GMC, Chrysler/Dodge/Jeep, city park, Family$, Fresh Mkt, IFA Store, NAPA, RV/truck repair, USPO
37	Lp 70, Richfield, **S 1-2 mi** 🅟 Phillips 66/Wendy's/dsl, Silver Eagle/Burger King/dsl 🍴 JB's Rest., KFC/Taco Bell, Lotsa Motsa Pizza, McDonald's, Pizza Hut, Rice King Chinese, Wingers 🛏 Comfort Inn, Fairfield Inn, Hampton Inn, New West Motel, Quality Inn, Royal Inn, Travelodge 🅞 $Tree, Ace Hardware, AutoZone, Ford, golf, Home Depot, K-Mart, KOA, O'Reilly Parts, Pearson Tire, st patrol, to Fish Lake/Capitol Reef Parks, Verizon, Walmart/Subway
31	Elsinore, Monroe, **S** 🅟 Silver Eagle/gas
25	UT 118, Joseph, Monroe, **S** 🅟 Diamond D Travel Plaza 🅞 Flying U Country Store/dsl/RV park
23	US 89 S, to Panguitch, Bryce Canyon
17	**N** 🅞 camping, **chain-up area (WB)**, Fremont Indian SP, info, museum, 🅲
13mm	**brake test area eb**
7	Ranch Exit
3mm	Western Boundary Fishlake NF
1	**N** 🅟 Chevron/Subway/rest stop (2mi) 🅞 Historic Cove Fort
0mm	I-15, N to SLC, S to St George.
I-70 begins/ends on I-15, exit 132.	

K I M B A L L   J C T

🅔	INTERSTATE 80
Exit #	**Services**
197mm	Utah/Wyoming state line
191	Wahsatch
187	ranch exit
185	Castle Rock
182mm	**Port of Entry/weigh sta wb**
178	Emery (from wb)
170	**Welcome Center wb/🆁🆂 eb, full 🅰 facilities, info, litter barrels, petwalk, 🅲, 🅰, RV dumping, vending**
169	Echo
168	I-84 W, to Ogden, I-80 E, to Cheyenne
166	view area both lanes, litter barrels
162	164 Coalville, **N** 🅟 Phillips 66/dsl/mart 🛏 Best Western 🅞 CamperWorld RV Park, Holiday Hills RV Camp/LP, **S** 🅟 Chevron/dsl, Sinclair/dsl 🍴 Polar King, Subway 🅞 Griffith's Foods, NAPA, to Echo Res RA, USPO
155	UT 32 S, Wanship, **S** 🅟 Sinclair/dsl 🅞 to Rockport SP
150	**toll gate promontory**
146b a	US 40 E, to Heber, Provo, **N** 🅟 Sinclair/Blimpie/Pizza Hut/dsl, **S** 🅟 Phillips 66/7-11/dsl 🅞 Burt Bros Tires, Home Depot
146	view area/chain up wb
145	UT 224, Kimball Jct, to Park City, **N** 🅞 Chevrolet, Ford, Park City RV Park, vet, **S** 🅟 Chevron/dsl 🍴 Arby's, Coldstone, Del Taco, Five Guys, Freebirds Burrito, Ghidottis Italian, Great Harvest Bread Co, Jimmy John's, Loco Lizard Cantina, McDonald's, Panda Express, Papa John's, Pizza Hut, Red Rock Cafe, Ruby Tuesday, Starbucks, Subway, Szechwan Chinese, Taco Bell, Wendy's, Whole Foods Mkt 🛏 Best Western, Hampton Inn, Holiday Inn Express 🅞 Best Buy, GNC, Michaels, Outlet Mall/famous brands, Petco, RV camping, Smith's Foods/dsl, Staples, TJ Maxx, to ski areas, USPO, visitors info, Walmart

S A L T   L A K E

144mm	view area eb
141	ranch exit, **N** 🅟 Phillips 66/Subway/dsl 🅞 Burt Bros Tires, to Jeremy Ranch, **S** 🍴 Billy Blanco Mexican 🅞 camping, Fresh Mkt, ski area
140	Parley's Summit, Parley's Summit, **S** 🅟 Sinclair/dsl 🍴 No Worries Café
137	Lamb's Canyon
134	UT 65, Emigration Canyon, East Canyon, 🅞 Mountaindale RA
133	utility exit (from eb)
132	ranch exit
131	(from eb) Quarry
130	I-215 S (from wb)
129	UT 186 W, Foothill Dr, Parley's Way, **N** 🅞 🄷
128	I-215 S (from eb)
127	UT 195, 23rd E St, to Holladay
126	UT 181, 13th E St, to Sugar House, **N** 🅟 Chevron 🍴 A&W/KFC, Cael's Jr, Chick-fil-A, Olive Garden, Red Lobster, Sizzler, Taco Bell, Training Table, Wendy's 🛏 Extended Stay America 🅞 ShopKO, Verizon
125	UT 71, 7th E St, **N** 🍴 Dee's Rest., Jimmy John's, Little Caesar's, Olympian Rest., Starbucks 🅞 AT&T, Firestone, Pepboys
124	US 89, S State St, **N** 🅟 7-11 🍴 Astro Burgers, Burger King, Starbucks, Subway, Taco Bell 🅞 Access RV Ctr, Chrysler/Dodge/Jeep, Discount Tire, vet, **S** 🍴 A&W/KFC 🛏 Ramada Inn
123mm	I-15, N to Ogden, S to Provo
I-80 and I-15 run together approx 4 mi. See I-15, exits 308-310.	
121	600 S, to City Ctr
120	I-15 N, to Ogden
118	UT 68, Redwood Rd, to N Temple, **N 0-1 mi on N Temple** 🅟 Chevron/Subway/dsl, 🔵*Love's*/Arby's/dsl/scales/24hr, Shell/dsl 🍴 A&W/KFC, Apollo Burger, Burger King, Carls Jr, Denny's, Taco Bell, Wendy's 🛏 🛏 Inn, Baymont Inn, Candlewood Suites, Comfort Suites, Holiday Inn Express, Motel 6, Radisson, Salt Lake Inn, **S** 🅟 Maverik/dsl 🅞 🄷
117	I-215, N to Ogden, S to Provo
115b a	Bangerter Hwy, **N** to Salt Lake 🅞
114	Wright Bros Dr (from wb), **N** same as 113
113	5600 W (from eb), **N** 🅟 Phillips 66/dsl 🍴 Perkins, Port of Subs, Subway 🛏 Comfort Inn, Courtyard, DoubleTree, Fairfield Inn, Hampton Inn, Hilton Garden, Holiday Inn, Hyatt Place, La Quinta, Microtel, Quality Inn, Ramada Inn, Residence Inn, SpringHill Suites, Super 8
111	7200 W
104	UT 202, Saltair Dr, to Magna, **N** 🅞 beaches, Great Salt Lake SP
102	UT 201 (from eb), to Magna
101mm	view area wb
99	UT 36, to Tooele, **S** 🅟 ✈*FLYING J*/Denny's/dsl/scales/LP/24hr, Chevron/Subway/dsl, TA/Burger King/Taco Bell/dsl/scales/24hr/@, Texaco/dsl 🍴 Del Taco, McDonald's 🛏 Comfort Inn/Suites, Oquirrh Motel/RV Park 🅞 🄷 Mamie's Place, SpeedCo
88	to Grantsville
84	UT 138, to Grantsville, Tooele
77	UT 196, to Rowley, Dugway
70	to Delle, **S** 🅟 Delle/Tesoro/café/dsl
62	to Lakeside, Eagle Range, 🅞 military area
56	to Aragonite
55mm	🆁🆂 both lanes, full 🅰 facilities, litter barrels, petwalk, 🅲, 🅰 vending

⬆E INTERSTATE 80 Cont'd

Exit #	Services
49	to Clive
41	Knolls
26mm	architectural point of interest
10mm	🆁🆂 both lanes, full ♿ facilities, litter barrels, observation area, petwalk, 🅲, 🗑 vending
4	Bonneville Speedway, N 🅿 Sinclair/dsl/café/24hr
3mm	Port of Entry, **weigh sta both lanes**
2	UT 58 (no EZ wb return), Wendover, S 🅿 Shell/Taco Time/dsl, Sinclair/dsl 🍴 Subway 🏠 Best Western, Bonneville Inn, Knights Inn, Motel 6, Nugget Hotel/casino, Quality Inn, Super 8, Western Ridge Motel Ⓞ auto repair, Carquest, Family$, KOA, Montego Bay Hotel/Casino, USPO
0mm	Utah/Nevada state line, Mountain/Pacific time zone

⬆E INTERSTATE 84

Exit #	Services
120	**I-84 begins/ends on I-80, exit 168 near Echo, Utah.**
115	Ut 65 S, to Henefer, Echo, to Henefer, Echo, S 1/2 mi Ⓞ Grump's Gen Store/gas, to E Canyon SP, USPO
112	UT 86 E, Henefer, S 🅿 🍴 🏠
111mm	Devil's Slide Scenic View
111	Croydon
108	Taggart
106	ranch exit
103	UT 66, Morgan, N Ⓞ Ford, S 🅿 Phillips 66/7-11/dsl, Texaco/dsl 🍴 J's Drive-in, Spring Chicken Café, Subway Ⓞ Ace Hardware, city park, E Canyon SP, Family$, Ridley's Mkt, URGENT CARE, USPO
96	Peterson, N 🅿 Sinclair/dsl (3mi) Ⓞ Nordic Valley Ski Areas, Powder Mtn, to Snow Basin, S 🅿 Phillips 66/dsl
94mm	N 🆁🆂 wb, full ♿ facilities, litter barrels, petwalk, 🗑
92	UT 167 (from eb), to Huntsville, N 🅿 Sinclair/dsl (2mi) Ⓞ city park (2mi), to ski areas
91mm	S 🆁🆂 eb, full ♿ facilities, litter barrels, petwalk, 🗑
87b a	US 89, to Ogden, Layton, Ogden, N 🍴 McDonald's (2mi), Wendy's (2mi) 🏠 Best Western Ⓞ Cheese Outlet, Goodyear/auto, S Ⓞ to Hill AFB
85	S Weber, Uintah
81	to I-15 S, UT 26, Riverdale Rd, N 🅿 Exxon/dsl, Sinclair/dsl 🍴 Applebee's, Arby's, Bajio Grill, Buffalo Wild Wings, Carl's Jr, Chili's, Honeybaked Ham, IHOP, Jamba Juice, Lucky Buffet, McDonald's, Starbucks, Subway, Wendy's Ⓞ $Tree, Best Buy, Buick/GMC, Cadillac, Good Earth Foods, Gordman's, Harley-Davidson, Home Depot, Honda, Jo-Ann, Kia, Lowe's Whse, Mazda, Nissan, PepBoys, Petsmart, Sam's Club/gas, Schwab Tire, Target, Toyota/Scion, Verizon, Walmart/McDonald's, S 🏠 Motel 6 Ⓞ Chrysler/Dodge/Jeep
	I-84 and I-15 run together. See I-15 exits 344 through 379.
41	I-15 N to Pocatello
40	UT 102, Tremonton, Bothwell, N 1 mi 🅿 Chevron/Poblano's/dsl/wash/24hr, Maverik/dsl, Sinclair/Burger King/dsl/scales/@ 🍴 Denny's, Grille Rest., McDonald's, Wendy's 🏠 Hampton Inn, Western Inn Ⓞ Alco, C&R Rv Ctr, Ⓗ (4mi), O'Reilly Parts, RV/truck/tire repair, S Ⓞ to Golden Spike NHS
39	to Garland, Bothwell, N Ⓞ Ⓗ
32	ranch exit
26	UT 83 S, to Howell, to Golden Spike NSH
24	to Valley
20	to Blue Creek
17	ranch exit
16	to Hansel Valley (from wb)
12	ranch exit
7	Snowville, N 🅿 ⓕFLYING J/Pepperoni's/dsl/LP/24hr 🍴 Mollie's Café, Ranch House Diner 🏠 Outsiders Inn Ⓞ city park, Lotti-Dell RV camping, USPO
5	UT 30, to Park Valley
0mm	Utah/Idaho state line

⬆N INTERSTATE 215 (Salt Lake)

Exit #	Services
29	**I-215 begins/ends on I-15.**
28	UT 68, Redwood Rd, E Ⓞ Pony Express RV Park, W 🅿 ⓕFLYING J/Pepperoni's/dsl/LP/24hr/@, Maverik/dsl 🍴 Lotus Chinese
26	Legacy Pkwy
25	22nd N
23	7th N, E 🅿 Exxon/dsl, ❤Loves/Arbys/dsl/scales/24hr (1.5 mi), Maverik 🍴 Denny's, KFC, McDonald's, Papa Murphy's, Subway, Taco Bell, Wendy's 🏠 Motel 6 Ⓞ $Tree, Family$, Super Saver Mkt, W 🏠 Inn, Baymont Inn, Candlewood Suites, Comfort Suites, Holiday Inn Express, Radisson
22 a	I-80, W to Wendover, E to Cheyenne
21	California Ave, E 🅿 Sapp Bros/Sinclair/Burger King/dsl/@, Tesoro/7-11/dsl Ⓞ RV/Truckwash, W 🅿 Chevron/dsl 🍴 Port of Subs
20b a	UT 201, W to Magna, 21st S, W 🅿 Maverik/dsl 🍴 Del Taco Ⓞ Goodyear, Kenworth
18	UT 171, 3500 S, W Valley, E 🅿 7-11 🍴 Applebee's, Chili's, Costa Vida Mexican, Cracker Barrel, Greek Souvlaki, IHOP, Kowloon Cafe 🏠 Baymont Inn, Country Inn Suites, Crystal Inn, Extended Stay America, Holiday Inn Express, La Quinta, Sleep Inn, Staybridge Suites Ⓞ Ⓗ PepBoys, W 🍴 Cafe Rio, In-N-Out, Jimmy John's, Olive Garden, Pizza Hut, Red Robin, Smashburger, TGIFriday's, Wendy's, Winger's, Zupas 🏠 Embassy Suites Ⓞ AT&T, Big O Tire, Costco/gas, CVS Drug, JC Penney, Macy's, Office Depot, Petco, Ross, Staples, Verizon
15	UT 266, 47th S, E 🅿 7-11, Conoco/dsl 🍴 Dee's Rest., KFC, Mad Greek, Pizza Hut, Taco Time, Village Inn, Wendy's Ⓞ Fresh Mkt, Goodyear/auto, Rite Aid, Walgreens, W 🅿 Chevron/dsl 🍴 Arby's, Arctic Circle, Tammie's Diner Ⓞ vet, 🅿 Sinclair/dsl
13	UT 68, Redwood Rd, E 🅿 Chevron, Shell/dsl 🍴 Apollo Burger, Applebee's, Arby's, Burger King, Carl's Jr, City Buffet, Dickey's BBQ, Domino's, Francesco's Rest., Freebirds Burrito, Honey Baked Ham, McDonald's/playplace, Panda Express, Starbucks, Subway, TX Roadhouse 🏠 Extended Stay America Ⓞ $Tree, AT&T, Harmon's Mkt, Jo-Ann Fabrics, PetsMart, Radio Shack, Ross, ShopKO, Verizon, Walmart/McDonald's

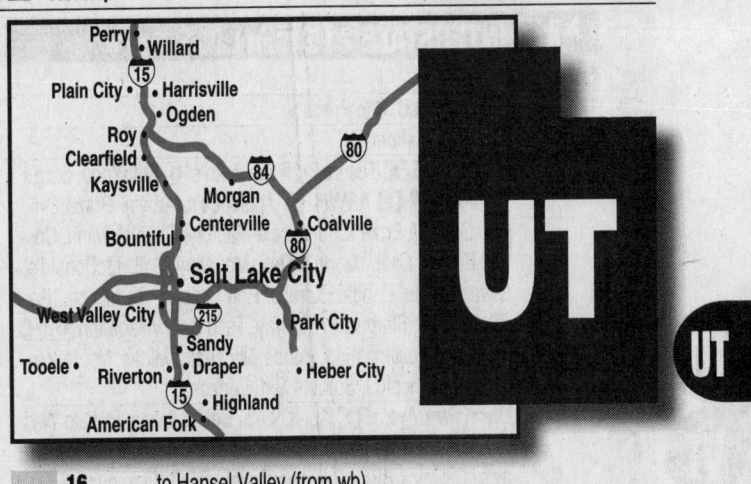

SALT LAKE CITY (vertical side text)

⬆N   INTERSTATE 215 (Salt Lake) Cont'd

Exit #	Services
12	I-15, N to SLC, S to Provo
11	same as 10 (from eb)
10	UT 280 E, **E** 🗛 Tesoro 🍴 Papa John's ⊙ AutoZone, Sam's Club/gas, **W** 🍴 A&W/KFC, Applebee's, Arby's, Braza Grill, Brio Grill, CA Pizza, Cheesecake Factory, ChuckARama, Corner Bakery Cafe, Jason's Deli, Macaroni Grill, McDonald's, Olive Garden, Panda Express, Red Lobster, Red Robin, RedRock Cafe, Starbucks, Subway, Taco Bell, Village Inn ⊙ 🄷 Dillard's, Firestone/auto, Honda, Marshalls, Midas, Nordstrom, Pepboys, ShopKO, Sprouts Mkt, Verizon
9	Union Park Ave, **E** 🍴 Applebee's, Bucca Italian, Buffalo Wild Wings, Cafe Rio, Carl's Jr, Chick-fil-A, Chili's, Chipotle, Denny's, Dickey's BBQ, Famous Dave's BBQ, Firehouse Subs, Five Guys, Longhorn Steaks, Noodles&Co, Panda Express, Pei Wei, Smashburger, Subway, Wendy's 🛏 Hawthorn Suites, Super 8 ⊙ $Tree, Barnes&Noble, Dick's, GNC, Gordman's, Home Depot, Michaels, Old Navy, Petco, Ross,

9	Continued Smith's Foods, Target, TJ Maxx, Verizon, Walmart/Subway, **W** 🗛 Shell 🛏 Crystal Inn, Motel 6 Extended ⊙ Firestone/auto, ⊙ Office Depot
8	UT 152, 2000 E, **E** 🗛 Chevron 🍴 KFC, McDonald's, Sonic, Taco Bell ⊙ Whole Foods Mkt, **W** 🗛 Phillips 66/dsl 🍴 Subway, Wendy's ⊙ Discount Tire
6	6200 S, **E** 🍴 Jimmy John's, Luna Blanca, Pie Five, Starbucks, Trio Cafe, Zupas 🛏 Hyatt Place, Residence Inn ⊙ Alta, Brighton, Snowbird, Solitude/ski areas
5	UT 266, 45th S (from sb), Holladay, **W** 🗛 Sinclair
4	39th S, **E** 🗛 Chevron/dsl, Sinclair/dsl 🍴 Barbacoa Grill, Rocky Mtn Pizza, Subway ⊙ Ace Hardware, Dan's Mkt, **W** ⊙ 🄷
3	33rd S, Wasatch, **W** 🗛 Smith's/dsl 🍴 Cafe Rio, Five Guys, KFC/Taco Bell, McDonald's, Shivers Burgers, Wendy's ⊙ Petsmart, REI, Smith's Mkt
2	I-80 W
0	**I-215 begins/ends on I-80, exit 130.**

VERMONT

⬆N   INTERSTATE 89

Exit #	Services
130mm	US/Canada Border, Vermont state line, **I-89 Begins/Ends.**
22 (129)	US 7 S, Highgate Springs, **E** 🗛 Irving/dsl ⊙ DutyFree
129mm	Latitude 45 N, midway between N Pole and Equator
128mm	Rock River
21 (123)	US 7, VT 78, Swanton, **E** 🗛 Shell/dsl, **W** 🗛 Mobil/Subway/dsl, Shell, Sunoco/dsl 🍴 Dunkin Donuts, McDonald's, Pam's Pizza, Shaggy's Snack Bar ⊙ Aubuchon Hardware, Hannaford Foods, NAPA
20 (118)	US 7, VT 207, St Albans, **E** ⊙ Chevrolet, Toyota, **W** 🗛 Mobil/Subway/dsl, Sunoco 🍴 Burger King, Dunkin Donuts, Hibachi Buffet, KFC/Taco Bell, McDonald's, Oriental Kitchen, Pizza Hut ⊙ 🄷 Advance Parts, AT&T, Aubuchon Hardware, Buick/GMC/Cadillac, Ford, Hannaford Foods, Jo-Ann Fabrics, Kinney Drug, PriceChopper Foods, Radio Shack, Staples, TJ Maxx, Verizon, Walmart/Subway
19 (114)	US 7, VT 36, VT 104, St Albans, **W** 🗛 Mobil/dsl, Shell/dsl 🍴 Dunkin Donuts, Subway 🛏 La Quinta ⊙ 🄷 st police, vet
111mm	🆁🆂 eb, full 🚻 facilities, info, litter barrels, petwalk, 🅲, 🖼, vending, Wi-Fi
18 (107)	US 7, VT 104A, Georgia Ctr, **E** 🗛 Mobil/dsl, Shell 🍴 GA Farmhouse Rest. ⊙ GA Auto Parts, Homestead RV Park, repair, USPO
17 (98)	US 2, US 7, **E** 🗛 Mobil, Shell/dsl ⊙ camping (4mi), **W** ⊙ camping (6mi), to NY Ferry, Lake Champlain Islands
96mm	**weigh sta both lanes**
16 (92)	US 7, US 2, Winooski, **E** 🗛 Mobil 🍴 Lighthouse Rest. 🛏 Hampton Inn ⊙ Costco, CVS Drug, Osco Drug, Shaw's Foods, **W** 🗛 Citgo, Irving, Shell/dsl 🍴 Athens Diner, Burger King, Jr's Italian, McDonald's, Subway 🛏 Motel 6, Quality Inn
15 (91)	VT 15 (from nb no return), Winooski, **E** 🛏 Days Inn, Handys Extended Stay Suites ⊙ to St Michael's Coll., **W** 🗛 Mobil/dsl, Shell ⊙ USPO
90mm	Winooski River
14mm	White River
14 (89)	US 2, Burlington, **E** 🗛 Gulf, Mobil, Shell/dsl, Sunoco, Valero 🍴 Al's Cafe, Applebee's, Chicken Charlie's, Dunkin Donuts, Hana Japanese, Leonardo's Pizza, McDonald's,

14 (89)	Continued Moe's SW Grill, Outback Steaks, Pulcinella's, Quiznos, Rotisserie, Starbucks, Subway, Trader Dukes, Wind Jammer Rest., Zachary's Pizza 🛏 Anchorage Inn, Best Western, Comfort Inn, DoubleTree Hotel, Holiday Inn, Homewood Suites, La Quinta ⊙ Aubuchon Hardware, Barnes&Noble, BonTon, Hannaford Foods, Healthy Living Mkt, JC Penney, Jo-Ann Fabrics, Kohl's, mall, Midas, PriceChopper, Rite Aid, Sears/auto, Trader Joe's, USPO, **W** 🗛 Mobil/dsl, Shell 🛏 Sheraton ⊙ 🄷 Advance Parts, Michael's, PetCo, Staples, to UVT, Verizon
13 (87)	I-189, to US 7, Burlington, **N** 🗛 Citgo/dsl, Sunoco/dsl 🍴 Buffalo Wild Wings, China Express, Five Guys, Starbucks, Subway ⊙ $Tree, GNC, Hyundai/Subaru, Kinney Drug, PriceChopper Foods, Radio Shack, Shaw's Foods, TJ Maxx, USPO, Walgreens, **W 2 mi on US 7 S** 🗛 Gulf, Irving, Mobil/dsl, Shell/dsl, Sunoco 🍴 Burger King, Chicago Grill, Denny's, Koto Japanese, Lakeview House Rest., McDonald's, Olive Garden, Panera Bread, Pauline's Cafe, Subway, Zen Garden 🛏 Comfort Suites, Ho-Hum Hotel, Holiday Inn Express, Maple Leaf Motel, North Star Motel, Travelodge ⊙ Acura/Audi/VW, Advance Parts, Buick/Cadillac/GMC, Chevrolet, Chrysler/Dodge, Ford, Hannaford Foods, Jeep, K-Mart, Lowe's, Nissan, Tire Whse, Toyota/Scion, URGENT CARE, Verizon, VW
12 (84)	VT 2A, to US 2, to Essex Jct, Williston, **E** 🗛 Mobil, Sunoco/Dunkin Donuts/dsl 🍴 99 Rest., Chili's, Friendly's, Longhorn Steaks, Moe's SW Grill, Panera Bread, Starbucks, TX Roadhouse, VT Taphouse 🛏 Fairfield, TownePlace Suites ⊙ Best Buy, CVS Drug, Dick's, Hannaford Foods, Home Depot, Marshall's, Natural Provisions Mkt, Old Navy, Petsmart, Shaws Foods/Osco, st police, Staples, Verizon, Walmart, **W** 🛏 Courtyard, Residence Inn
82mm	🆁🆂 **both lanes (7am-11pm), full** 🚻 **facilities, litter barrels, petwalk, 🅲, 🖼, vending, Wi-Fi**
11 (79)	US 2, to VT 117, Richmond, **W** 🗛 Mobil/dsl
67mm	parking area/weigh sta sb
66mm	weigh sta nb
10 (64)	VT 100, to US 2, Waterbury, **E** 🗛 Mobil/dsl, Shell/dsl 🍴 Pizza Shoppe 🛏 Best Western/rest ⊙ Shaws Foods/Osco Drug, TrueValue, **W** 🗛 Citgo/dsl 🍴 Maxi's Rest., Zachary's Pizza ⊙ USPO

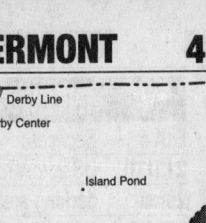

INTERSTATE 89 Cont'd

Exit #	Services
9 (59)	US 2, to VT 100B, Middlesex, **W** Red Hen Baking Co museum, st police
8 (53)	US 2, Montpelier, **E 1 mi** Citgo, Gulf/dsl, Mobil, Shell/dsl, Shell/dsl China Star, Dunkin Donuts, Julio's, Sarducci's Rest., Simply Subs, Village Pizza Capitol Plaza Hotel Aubuchon Hardware, Bond Parts, camping (6mi), Rite Aid, Shaw's Foods, Sunoco/repair, to VT Coll
7 (50)	VT 62, to US 302, Barre, **E** Irving/dsl Applebee's Comfort Suites, Hilltop Inn camping (7mi), Honda, JC Penney, Shaw's Foods, Subaru, Toyota/Scion, Walmart,
6 (47)	VT 63, to VT 14, S Barre, **E 4 mi** camping, info,
5 (43)	VT 64, to VT 12, VT 14, Williamstown, **E 6 mi** camping, food, gas/dsl, lodging, **W** to Norwich U
41mm	1752 ft, highest elevation on I-89
34.5mm	weigh sta both lanes
4 (31)	VT 66, Randolph, **E** RV camping (seasonal 1mi), **W** Mobil/dsl lodging (3mi), McDonald's RV camping (5mi)
30mm	parking area sb
3 (22)	VT 107, Bethel, **E** Mobil/dsl Eaton's Rest., Village Pizza to Jos Smith Mon (8mi), **W 1 mi** Irving/dsl/LP Rite Aid, st police, vet
14mm	White River
2 (13)	VT 14, VT 132, Sharon, **W** Gulf/dsl Jos Smith Mon (6mi), Sharon Country Store, USPO
9mm	(7am-11pm), weigh sta both lanes, full facilities, info, litter barrels, , vending, Wi-Fi
7mm	White River
1 (4)	US 4, to Woodstock, Quechee, **E 3 mi** Irving Hampton Inn, Holiday Inn Express, Super 8, **N 3 mi** Fairfield Inn
1mm	I-91, N to St Johnsbury, S to Brattleboro
0mm	Vermont/New Hampshire state line, Connecticut River

INTERSTATE 91

Exit #	Services
178mm	I-91 begins/ends., US Customs, US/Canada Border, Vermont state line
29 (177)	US 5, Derby Line, **E** Dutyfree, **W 1 mi** Irving/Circle K/dsl city park
176.5mm	Welcome Center sb, full facilities, info, litter barrels, petwalk, , , Midpoint between the Equator and N Pole
28 (172)	US 5, VT 105, Derby Ctr, **E** Gulf, Shell/dsl, Sunoco/repair Cow Palace Rest. auto/tire service, USPO, **W** Irving/Hoagie's Pizza, Mobil/dsl China Moon, McDonald's, Penn's Rest., Pizza Hut, Roasters Cafe, Village Pizza, VT Pie&Pasta 4 Seasons, Pepin's Motel $Tree, Advance Parts, Bond Parts, Chrysler/Dodge/Jeep, CVS Drug, Family$, Kinney Drug, Parts+, PriceChopper Foods, Rite Aid, RV camping, Shaw's Foods, st police, Verizon
27 (170)	VT 191, to US 5, VT 105, Newport, **W 3 mi** Border Patrol, camping, info
167mm	parking area/weigh sta both directions

Exit #	Services
26 (161)	US 5, VT 58, Orleans, **E** Irving, Sunoco Subway Austin's Drugs, Family$, Thibaults Mkt, TrueValue, USPO, **W** camping (5mi)
156.5mm	Barton River
25 (156)	VT 16, Barton, **E 1 mi** Gulf, Irving/Circle K/dsl Ming's Chinese, Parson's Corner Rest. C&C Foods, camping (2mi), Kinney Drug, USPO
154mm	parking area nb
150.5mm	1856 ft, highest elevation on I-91
143mm	scenic overlook nb
141mm	sb, full facilities, info, litter barrels,
24 (140)	VT 122, Wheelock, **E 2 mi**
23 (137)	US 5, to VT 114, Lyndonville, **E** Gulf/dsl, Mobil/Dunkin Donuts Hoagie's Pizza, Lyndon Buffet, McDonald's, Miss Lyndonville Diner, Pizza Man Colonnade Inn $General, CarQuest, Kinney Drug, Rite Aid, TrueValue, White Mkt Foods, **W** Lyndon Motel
22 (132)	to US 5, St Johnsbury, **E 1-2 mi** Sunoco/dsl KFC/Taco Bell, Kham's Cuisine, Pizza Hut Aubuchon Hardware, Bond Parts, Buick/GMC, Kinney Drug, NAPA, PriceChopper Foods, repair, Subaru

ST JOHNSBURY

VT VA

⬆N INTERSTATE 91 Cont'd

Exit #	Services
21 (131)	US 2, to VT 15, St Johnsbury, **E 1-2 mi** services
20mm	**parking area nb**
20 (129)	US 5, to US 2, St Johnsbury, **E** 🅖 Irving/dsl, Mobil, Shell/dsl 🍴 Anthony's Diner, Dunkin Donuts, East Garden Chinese, McDonald's, Subway, Winegate Rest. 🅞 Family$, Kevin's Repair, museum, Rite Aid, welcome ctr, **W** 🏠 Comfort Inn 🅞 st police
19 (128)	I-93 S to Littleton NH
122mm	scenic view nb
18 (121)	to US 5, Barnet, **E** 🅞 camping (5mi), **W** 🅞 camping (5mi)
115mm	**parking area sb**
113mm	**parking area nb**
17 (110)	US 302, to US 5, Wells River, NH, **W** 🅖 P&H Trkstp/rest./dsl/scales/24hr 🅞 camping (9mi), 🏠 (5mi)
100mm	🆁🆂 nb, parking area sb, full ♿ **facilities, info, litter barrels, petwalk,** 🚻, 🅰
16 (98)	VT 25, to US 5, Bradford, **E** 🅖 Mobil/dsl/LP/café 🍴 Hungry Bear Grill, Oasis Grill 🏠 Bradford Motel 🅞 Bond Parts, Family$, Hannafords Foods, Kinney Drug, NAPA, Pierson Farm Mkt, **W** st police
15 (92)	Fairlee, **E** 🅖 Gulf, Irving/dsl, Sunoco/dsl 🍴 Fairlee Diner, Subway 🅞 camping, USPO, Wings Mkt/deli, **W** 🅞 golf
14 (84)	VT 113, to US 5, Thetford, **E 1 mi** 🅞 camping, food, **W** 🅞 camping
13 (75)	US 5, VT 10a, Hanover, NH, **E** 🅞 🏠 to Dartmouth, **W** 🅖 Citgo 🍴 Norwich Inn Rest. 🅞 Subaru, USPO
12 (72)	US 5, White River Jct, Wilder, **E** 🅖 Gulf/dsl, Mobil
11 (71)	US 5, White River Jct, **E** 🅖 Mobil/dsl, Shell/Subway/dsl 🍴 China Moon, Crossroads Country Café, McDonald's 🏠 Comfort Inn 🅞 Ford/Lincoln, Hyundai, Toyota, USPO, **W** 🅖 Citgo, Irving/Dunkin Donuts, Sunoco/dsl 🏠 Fairfield Inn, Hampton Inn, Holiday Inn Express, Super 8, White River Inn 🅞 🏠
10N (70)	I-89 N, to Montpelier
10S	I-89 S, to NH, 🖼
68mm	**weigh sta both lanes**
9 (60)	US 5, VT 12, Hartland, **E** 🅞 🏠 **W** 🅖 Mobil (1mi) 🍴 Hartland Diner 🅞 info
8 (51)	US 5, VT 12, VT 131, Ascutney, **E** 🅖 Citgo/dsl, Gulf/dsl, Irving/Circle K, Sunoco/Dunkin Donuts/dsl 🍴 Ascutney House

BRATTLEBORO

8 (51)	Continued
	Rest., Mr G's Rest. 🏠 Yankee Village Motel 🅞 🏠 Getaway Camping (2mi), USPO, **W** 🅞 auto repair/tires
7 (42)	US 5, VT 106, VT 11, Springfield, **W** 🅖 Irving/Circle K/Subway/dsl/scales/24hr 🏠 Holiday Inn Express 🅞 camping, 🏠 (5mi)
39mm	**weigh sta sb**
6 (34)	US 5, VT 103, to Bellows Falls, Rockingham, **E** 🅖 Shell/dsl 🍴 Leslie's Rest. 🏠 Rodeway Inn, **W** 🅖 Sunoco/dsl 🅞 st police (6mi)
5 (29)	VT 121, to US 5, to Bellows Falls, Westminster, **E 3 mi** 🍴 🅖 🏠 🚻
24mm	**parking area both lanes**
22mm	**weigh sta sb**
20mm	**parking area nb**
4 (18)	US 5, Putney, **W** 🅖 Rod's/repair, Sunoco/dsl/LP/24hr 🍴 Katy's Cafe, Putney Diner, Putney Food Coop/deli, Putney Village Pizza 🅞 camping (3mi), Putney Gen Store/deli, USPO
3 (11)	US 5, VT 9 E, Brattleboro, **E** 🅖 Agway/dsl, Citgo/dsl, Mobil/dsl, Sunoco 🍴 99 Rest., China Buffet, Dunkin Donuts, Fast Eddy Cafe, House of Pizza, KFC, McDonald's, Panda North, Taco Bell, Thin Crust Pizzaria, Village Pizza, Wendy's 🏠 Best Inn, Colonial Motel, Hampton Inn, Holiday Inn Express, Motel 6, Quality Inn, Super 8 🅞 Advance Parts, Aldi Foods, AT&T, Bond Parts, Buick/Chevrolet/GMC, Chrysler/Dodge/Jeep, Family$, Ford, GNC, Hannaford Foods, Radio Shack, Rite Aid, Staples, Subaru, TrueValue, USPO, Verizon
2 (9)	VT 9 W, to rd 30, Brattleboro, **W** 🍴 VT Country Deli 🅞 st police, to Marlboro Coll
1 (7)	US 5, Brattleboro, **E** 🅖 Gulf/dsl, Irving/Circle K/dsl, Mobil/Dunkin Donuts, Shell/Subway/dsl 🍴 Burger King, FC Chinese, Georgio's Pizza, VT Inn Pizza 🏠 EconoLodge 🅞 🏠 PriceChopper Foods, Rite Aid, to Ft Dummer SP, vet, Walgreens
6mm	Welcome Center nb, full ♿ facilities, info, litter barrels, petwalk, 🚻, 🅰, playground, vending
0mm	Vermont/Massachusetts state line

⬆N INTERSTATE 93

See New Hampshire Interstate 93.

VIRGINIA

⬆E INTERSTATE 64

Exit #	Services
299b a	I-264 E, to Portsmouth. **I-64 begins/ends on I-264.**
297	US 13, US 460, Military Hwy, **N** 🅖 7-11, Exxon 🍴 McDonald's
296b a	US 17, to Portsmouth, **N** 🅖 7-11 🍴 Hardee's, McDonald's, Papa John's, Subway, Zino's Cafe 🏠 Comfort Inn 🅞 $General, Food Lion, USPO, vet
294mm	S Br Elizabeth River
292	VA 190, to VA 104 (from eb, no EZ return), Dominion Blvd, **S** 🅖 7-11 🍴 #1 China, Burger King, Royal China, Subway 🅞 Family$, Food Lion
291b a	I-464 N, VA 104 S, to Elizabeth City, Outer Banks, same services as 292
290b a	VA 168, Battlefield Blvd, to Nag's Head, Manteo, **N** 🍴 Burger King 🏠 ValuePlace 🅞 $General, BigLots, Hancock Fabrics, K-mart, Merchant's Auto Ctr, NAPA, **S** 🅖 7-11, BP/DQ, Shell

NORFOLK

290b a	Continued
	🍴 5 Guys Burgers, Applebee's, Baskin-Robbins, Burger King, Carrabba's, Chick-fil-A, ChuckECheese's, Denny', Dunkin Donuts, Firehouse Subs, Golden Corral, Grand China Buffet, Hardee's, Hunan Wok, Jade Garden, McDonald's, Salsarita's Cantina, Sonic, Starbucks, Taco Bell, TGIFriday's, Tropical Smoothie Café, TX Roadhouse, Waffle House, Wendy's, Wildwing Café, Woodchick's BBQ 🏠 Days Inn, Hampton Inn, Quality Inn, Savannah Suites 🅞 🏠 $Tree, Goodyear/auto, Home Depot, Kohl's, Lowe's, Nissan, Rite Aid, Sam's Club/gas, USPO, vet, Walgreens, Walmart,
289b a	Greenbrier Pkwy, **N** 🅖 7-11, Citgo, WaWa 🍴 Burger King, Cugini's Pizza, McDonald's, Subway, Taco Bell, Wendy's 🏠 Cedar Tree Inn, Extended Stay, Hampton Inn, Marriott, Red Roof Inn, Staybridge Suites, Wingate Inn 🅞 Acura, auto repair, Chevrolet, Chrysler/Jeep, Dodge, Ford, Hyundai, JoAnn Fabrics, Kia, Lincoln, Mazda, Scion/Toyota, U-Haul, vet,

VA

◆E   INTERSTATE 64 Cont'd

Exit #	Services
289b a	Continued
	S 🞖 7-11 🞖 Abuelo's Mexican, Baker's Crust, Boston Mkt, Buffalo Wild Wings, Chipotle, Coldstone, Cracker Barrel, Fazoli's, Firehouse Subs, Friendly's, Greenbrier Buffet, Hooters, Jason's Deli, Jersey Mike's Subs, Jimmy John's, Joe's Crabshack, Kyoto Japanese, LoneStar Steaks, McDonald's, Olive Garden, Panera Bread, Paradocks Grill, Pizza Hut, Pop's Diner, Qdoba, Red Robin, Ruby Tuesday, Smokey Bones BBQ, Starbucks, Subway, Zero's Subs, Zoot's Cafe 🞖 Aloft Hotel, Comfort Suites, Courtyard, Extended Stay America, Fairfield Inn, Hilton Garden, Homewood Suites, Residence Inn, SpringHill Suites, Sun Suites 🞖 AT&T, Barnes&Noble, Best Buy, Dillard's, Food Lion, Harris Teeter, Macy's, mall, Marshall's, Michael's, Office Depot, Old Navy, Petsmart, Ross, Sears/auto, Steinmart, Target, TJ Maxx, Verizon, Walgreens
286b a	Indian River Rd, N 🞖 BP/dsl, Gulf, Hess/dsl, SkyMart/dsl 🞖 Dunkin Donuts, Golden China, Hardee's 🞖 CVS, S 🞖 Sunoco/dsl 🞖 Capt D's, Oriental Cuisine, Shoney's, Top's China, Waffle House 🞖 7-11
285mm	E Branch Elizabeth River
284b	Newtown Rd
284a	I-264, to Norfolk, to VA Beach (exits left from eb)
282	US 13, Northampton Blvd, N 🞖 Quality Inn, Sleep Inn 🞖 to Chesapeake Bay Br Tunnel
281	VA 165, Military Hwy (no EZ eb return), N 🞖 Shell/dsl 🞖 EconoLodge 🞖 Aamco, Chysler/Dodge/Jeep, Fiat, S 🞖 7-11, Citgo 🞖 Burger King, Chick-fil-A, Cook-Out, Frank'n Bubba's BBQ, Hooters, IHOP, Jersey Mike's Subs, Jimmy John's, KFC, Logan's Roadhouse, Max&Erma's, Panera Bread, Qdoba, Sonic, Starbucks, Taco Bell, Wendy's 🞖 Candlewood Suites, Hampton Inn, Hilton, Holiday Inn, Holiday Inn Express, La Quinta, Ramada, Residence Inn, Savannah Suites 🞖 BJ's Whse, FarmFresh Foods, Firestone/auto, Food Lion, Home Depot, Lowe's, Nissan, Pep Boys, Petco, Petsmart, Target, TJ Maxx, Verizon, Walgreens, Walmart/Subway
279	Norview Ave, N 🞖 K Express, Shell/repair, WaWa 🞖 China House, Franco's Italian, Golden Corral, Pizza Hut, Wendy's 🞖 $General, $Tree, 7-11, Food Lion, K-Mart/gas, Tire City, to 🞖 & botanical garden
278	VA 194 S (no EZ return)

H A M P T O N

Exit #	Services
277b a	VA 168, to Tidewater Dr, N 🞖 7-11, Shell 🞖 Bojangles, Hardee's, Ruby Tuesday 🞖 Advance Parts, Food Lion, Radio Shack, Walmart/Subway, S 🞖 BP
276c	to US 460 W, VA 165, Little Creek Rd, (from wb only), N 🞖 Race Coast Gas, S 🞖 BP, Shell 🞖 KFC, McDonald's, Papa John's, Pizza Hut, Starbucks, Taco Bell, Wendy's 🞖 AutoZone, FarmFresh Foods, Kroger, Rite Aid, USPO, Walgreens
276b a	I-564 to Naval Base (exits left from wb)
274	Bay Ave (from wb), to Naval Air Sta
273	US 60, 4th View St, Oceanview, N 🞖 7-11 🞖 Economy Inn 🞖 Oceanview Pier, S 🞖 info, to Norfolk Visitors Ctr
272	W Ocean View Ave, N 🞖 Willoughby Seafood, S 🞖 Sunset Grill
270mm	Chesapeake Bay Tunnel
269mm	weigh sta wb
268	VA 169 E, to Buckroe Beach, Ft Monroe, N 🞖 Citgo 🞖 Hardee's, McDonald's 🞖 to VA Air&Space Ctr
267	US 60, to VA 143, Settlers Ldg Rd, S 🞖 Golden City Chinese, Subway, Tropical Smoothie 🞖 🞖 to Hampton U
265c	(from eb), N 🞖 Armistead Ave, to Langley AFB
265b a	VA 134, VA 167, to La Salle Ave, N 🞖 Citgo, RaceWay 🞖 Super 8 🞖 Home Depot, S 🞖 BP 🞖 KFC/Taco Bell, McDonald's 🞖 🞖 Advance Parts, Family$
264	I-664, to Newport News, Suffolk
263b a	US 258, VA 134, Mercury Blvd, to James River Br, N 🞖 7-11, BP, Exxon/dsl, Shell 🞖 5 Guys Burgers, Abuelo's Mexican, Applebee's, Bojangles, Boston Mkt, Burger King, Chick-fil-A, Chili's, China Wok, Chipotle Mexican, Denny's, Dog House, El Azteca, Firehouse Subs, Golden Corral, Hooters, IHOP, Jason's Deli, KFC, McDonald's, New Garden Buffet, Olive Garden, Outback Steaks, Panera Bread, Parklane Rest., Pizza Hut, Quizno's, Rally's, Red Lobster, Starbucks, Subway, Taco Bell, Tokyo Japanese, Waffle House, Wendy's 🞖 Comfort Inn, Courtyard, Days Inn, Embassy Suites, Holiday Inn Express, Quality Inn, Red Roof Inn, Rodeway Inn 🞖 $Tree, AT&T, Chevrolet/Mazda, FarmFresh Foods, Food Lion Ford, GNC, Goodyear/auto, JC Penney, Jo-Ann Fabrics, Macy's, Marshall's, Michael's, NAPA, Nissan, Office Depot, PetCo, Ross, Target, U-Haul, USPO, Verizon, Volvo, Walgreens, Walmart, S 🞖 Citgo/dsl, Miller's 🞖 Chick-fil-A, CiCi's Pizza, Coldstone, Cracker Barrel, Domino's, Joe's Crabshack, Lonestar Steaks, Longhorn Steaks, Pizza Hut, Rita's, Sonic,

INTERSTATE 64 Cont'd

Exit #	Services
263b a	Continued

Sports Grill, Waffle House, Zaxby's 🛏 Hampton Bay Suites, Hilton Garden, La Quinta, Relax Inn, Savannah Suites, SpringHill Suites 🅞 7-11, Aamco Advance Parts, BassPro Shop, BigLots, BJ's Whse/Subway/gas, CVS Drug, Firestone/auto, Hancock Fabrics, Lowe's, PepBoys, Radio Shack, Toyota/Scion

262 VA 134, Magruder Blvd (from wb, no EZ return), N 🅖 7-11, Exxon 🛏 Country Inn&Suites, Suburban Lodge 🅞 Hyundai, Mercedes

261b a Center Pkwy, to Hampton Roads, N 🛏 Hampton Inn (2mi), S 🅖 7-11, Shell 🍽 Anna's Italian, ChuckECheese's, Fortune Garden Chinese, McDonald's, Peking Chinese, Pizza Hut/Taco Bell, Plaza Azteca, Ruby Tuesday, Subway 🅞 $Tree, FarmFresh Foods, Food Lion, GNC, Rite Aid, TJMaxx

258b a US 17, J Clyde Morris Blvd, N 🅖 BP, Shell/dsl 🍽 Domino's, Fiorello Italian, New China, Waffle House 🛏 BudgetLodge, Country Inn&Suites, Holiday Inn, Host Inn, PointPlaza Hotel, Quality Inn 🅞 7-11, Advance Parts, Family$, Food Lion, S 🅖 BP, Kangaroo, WaWa 🍽 Angelo's Steaks, Burger King, DQ, KFC/Taco Bell, McDonald's, Papa John's, Starbucks, Subway, Vinny's Pizza, Wendy's 🛏 Motel 6 🅞 🄷 museum, Rite Aid, Subaru, VW

256b a Victory Blvd, Oyster Point Rd, N 🅖 BP, Citgo/dsl, Murphy USA/dsl 🍽 3 Amigos Mexican, Arby's, Burger King, Chick-fil-A, China Ocean, Hardee's, McDonald's, NY Pizza, Pizza Hut, Ruby Tuesday, Saisaki Asian, Sonic, Starbucks, Subway, TX Roadhouse, Uno Grill 🛏 CandleWood Suites, Courtyard, Hampton Inn, Hilton Garden, Staybridge Suites, TownePlace Suites 🅞 $Tree, FarmFresh Foods, GNC, Goodyear, K-Mart, Kroger, RadioShack, Walgreens, Walmart, S 🛏 Crestwood Suites, Jameson Inn

255b a VA 143, to Jefferson Ave, N 🅖 Shell/dsl 🍽 5 Guys Burgers, Chili's, Cookout, Donato's Pizza, Firehouse Subs, Golden Corral, HoneyBaked Ham, Hooters, Jason's Deli, Longhorn Steaks, McDonald's, Moe's SW Grill, Olive Garden, Panera Bread, Papa John's, Red City Buffet, Red Lobster, Smokey Bones BBQ, Starbucks 🛏 Comfort Suites 🅞 🄷 Acura, Buick/Cadillac/GMC, Chrysler/Dodge/Jeep, FarmFresh Foods/deli, Fiat, GNC, Home Depot, Kohl's, Lincoln, Lowe's, Michael's, PetCo, Ross, Sam's Club/gas, TJ Maxx, Trader Joe's, Tuesday Morning, Walmart, S 🅖 BP/dsl, Citgo/dsl, Exxon/dsl 🍽 Applebee's, Bailey's Grille, Buffalo Wild Wings, Carrabba's, Cheddar's, Cheeseburger Paradise, Chick-fil-A, Chipotle Mexican, Coldstone, Cracker Barrel, KFC, McDonald's, Outback Steaks, Red Robin, Starbucks, Subway, Taco Bell, TGIFriday's, Waffle House, Wendy's 🛏 Best Western, Comfort Inn, Courtyard, Extended Stay America, Hampton Inn, Microtel, Residence Inn 🅞 7-11, Barnes&Noble, Best Buy, Costco, Dick's, Dillard's, Fresh Mkt, JC Penney, Macy's, mall, Petsmart, Sears Auto Ctr, Target, Verizon, World Mkt

250b a to US Army Trans Museum, N 🅖 7-11/gas, Dodge's Store, Exxon/dsl, Sunoco 🍽 China Dragon, Hardee's, Little Italy, Subway 🅞 B&L Auto Repair, to Yorktown Victory Ctr, S 🛏 Ft Eustis Inn, Holiday Inn Express, Mulberry Inn 🅞 7-11, Newport News Campground/Park (1mi)

247 VA 143, to VA 238 (no EZ return wb), N 🅖 7-11/gas 🅞 to Yorktown, S 🅞 to Jamestown Settlement

243 VA 143, to Williamsburg, exits left from wb, S same as 242a

242b a VA 199, to US 60, to Williamsburg, N 🛏 Day's Hotel/rest. 🅞 Best Buy, Dick's, JC Penney, Kohl's, Target, to Yorktown NHS, water funpark, S 1 mi 🅖 7-11/gas, Shell, Sunoco 🍽 China's Cuisine, Doraldo's Italian, KFC, McDonald's, Sportsmans Grille, Starbucks, Subway, Taco Bell, Wendy's, Whaling Co Rest. 🛏 Country Inn&Suites, Courtyard, Marriott/rest., Quality Inn 🅞 Busch Gardens, camping, to Jamestown NHS, to William&Mary Coll

238 VA 143, to Colonial Williamsburg, Camp Peary, S 2-3 mi on US 60 🅖 7-11/gas, Shell, Sunoco 🍽 5 Guys Burgers, Aberdeen Barn Rest., Applebee's, Arby's, Chili's, Chipotle Mexican, Cracker Barrel, DQ, Firehouse Subs, Golden Corral, Hooters, IHOP, Jefferson Steaks, KFC, Kyoto, McDonald's, Pancake House, Pizza Hut, Plaza Azteca, Red Hot&Blue, Ruby Tuesday, Sal's Rest., Seafare Rest, Smokehouse Grill, Subway, Taco Bell, Uno Grille, Wendy's 🛏 1776 Hotel, America's Inn, Best Western, Comfort Inn, Comfort Suites, Country Inn&Suites, Days Inn, EconoLodge, Embassy Suites, Fairfield Inn, Hampton Inn, Hilton Garden, Holiday Inn Express, Holiday Inn/rest., Homewood Suites, La Quinta, Quality Inn, Sleep Inn, SpringHill Suites, Travelodge 🅞 🄷 Anvil Camping (4mi), CVS Drug, Goodyear, K-Mart

234 VA 646, to Lightfoot, N 1-2 mi 🅞 KOA, S 2-3 mi 🅖 BP/dsl, Exxon/dsl, Shell/dsl 🍽 Burger King, Chick-fil-A, China Wok, Hardee's, IHOP, McDonald's, Quiznos, Sonic, Starbucks, Subway 🛏 Greatwolf Lodge, Holiday Inn Express, Super 8 🅞 🄷 $Tree, Ford, Home Depot, Lowe's, PetCo, Pottery Camping (3mi), Ross, Toyota/Scion, USPO, Walmart,

231b a VA 607, to Norge, Croaker, N 🅖 7-11/gas 🅞 to York River SP, S 1-3 mi on US 60 🅖 Shell/dsl 🍽 Candle Light Kitchen, China Star, Daddy-O's Pizza, Jimmy's Grill, Pizza Hut 🛏 EconoLodge 🅞 American Heritage RV Park, CVS Drug, FarmFresh Deli/gas, Food Lion, Honda, Hyundai, USPO

227 VA 30, to US 60, to West Point, Toano, S 🅖 BP/dsl (2mi), Shell/dsl, Star/Subway/dsl 🍽 McDonald's

220 VA 33 E, to West Point, N 🅖 Exxon/dsl, Mobil/Circle K/dsl

214 VA 155, to New Kent, Providence Forge, S 🅖 Exxon/DQ/dsl 🍽 Antonio's Pizza, Tops China 🅞 camping (8mi), Colonial Downs Racetrack

213mm 🆁ⓢ both lanes, full ♿ facilities, litter barrels, petwalk, 🎔, 🅿 vending

211 VA 106, to Talleysville, to James River Plantations, S 🅖 ⛽/Subway/dsl/scales/24hr

205 VA 33, VA 249, to US 60, Bottoms Bridge, Quinton, N 🅖 Exxon/dsl, Star Express, Valero 🍽 Julio's Mexican, Maria's Italian, Panda Garden, Pizza Hut, Subway, Wendy's 🅞 Food Lion, S 🅖 FasMart, Shell/dsl 🍽 Bojangle's, McDonald's 🛏 Star Motel (3mi) 🅞 Food Lion, Rite Aid

204mm Chickahominy River

203mm weigh sta both lanes

200 I-295, N to Washington, S to Rocky Mount, to US 60

197b a VA 156, 🆕 Dr, to Highland Springs, N 🅖 Shell/dsl, Valero 🍽 Antonio's Pizza, Domino's, Hardee's, Subway, Tops China 🅞 7-11, Advance Parts, CVS Drug, Farmers Foods, S 🅖 7-11, BP, Chubby's/dsl, WaWa 🍽 Arby's, Aunt Sarah's Pancakes, Burger King, Mexico Rest., Pizza Hut, The Patron, Waffle House 🛏 Best Value Inn, Best Western, Comfort Inn, Courtyard, EconoLodge, Hampton Inn, Hilton Garden, Holiday Inn, Holiday Inn Express, Homewood Suites, Microtel, Motel 6, Quality Inn, Red Roof Inn, Super 8 🅞 $General, to 🆕

195 Laburnum Ave, N 🅖 Citgo 🅞 auto repair, S 🅖 7-11, BP, Exxon, WaWa 🍽 5 Guys Burgers, Applebee's, Capt D's,

WILLIAMSBURG

INTERSTATE 64 Cont'd

RICHMOND

Exit #	Services
195	Continued
	Chick-fil-A, China King, CiCi's Pizza, Cracker Barrel, Firehouse Subs, Hardee's, IHOP, KFC, Little Caesars, Longhorn Steaks, McDonald's, Olive Garden, Panera Bread, Papa John's, Qdoba Mexican, Red Lobster, Steak'n Shake, Subway, Taco Bell, Tepanyaki Grill, TGIFriday's, Wendy's 🛏 Hyatt Place, Sheraton, Wyndham Hotel 🅞 $General, $Tree, AT&T, CarQuest, CVS Drug, GNC, JC Penney, Kroger, Lowe's, Martin's Foods, Michael's, Petsmart, Radio Shack, Sam's Club/gas, Target, Walgreens
193b a	VA 33, Nine Mile Rd, **N** 🅖 Exxon/Subway/dsl, Sunoco/dsl 🅞 PepBoys, **S** 🅞 🅷
192	US 360, to Mechanicsville, **N** 🅖 Citgo/dsl, Shell 🍴 McDonald's 🅞 Tuffy Repair, **S** 🅖 Citgo, Shell 🍴 Church's
190	I-95 S, to Petersburg, 5th St, **N** 🅞 Richmond Nat Bfd Park, **S** 🛏 Hilton Garden, Marriott 🅞 coliseum., st capitol
	I-64 E and I-95 S run together. See I-95, exits 76-78.
187	I-95 N (exits left from eb), to Washington.
186	I-195, to Powhite Pkwy, from wb, Richmond
185b a	US 33, Staples Mill Rd, Dickens Rd
183c	from wb, US 250 W, Broad St, Glenside Dr N, same as exit 183
183b a	US 250, Broad St E, Glenside Dr S., **N** 🅖 Chevron, Sheetz 🍴 Bob Evans, Famous Dave's, McDonald's, Olive Garden, Pizza Hut, Taco Bell, TGIFriday's, Waffle House 🛏 Baymont Inn, Best Western, Embassy Suites, Hampton Inn, Super 8, ValuePlace 🅞 AutoZone, Honda, Hyundai, K-Mart, same as 181, vet, Volvo, **S** 🍴 Denny's, Plaza Azteca 🛏 Courtyard, Sheraton, Westin 🅞 🅷 Home Depot, Target, to U of Richmond
181b a	Parham Rd, **N** 2 mi on Broad 🅖 BP/dsl, Citgo, Exxon, Hess, Shell, Wawa 🍴 Arby's, Bailey's Grill, Buffalo Wild Wings, Burger King, Casa Grande Mexican, Chick-fil-A, Chucke-Cheese, CiCi's Pizza, Coldstone, Domino's, Friendly's, Gyros & Subs, Hooters, KFC, LoneStar Steaks, Ma Ma Wok, McDonald's, Nanking Rest., Outback Steaks, Penn Sta Subs, Piccadilly, Quaker Steak, Red Lobster, Shoney's, Starbucks, Superking Buffet, Valacino's, Wendy's, Zorba's Rest. 🛏 Country Inn&Suites, EconoLodge, Quality Inn, Rodeway Inn, Suburban Lodge 🅞 🅷 $General, $Tree, Aamco, Acura, Audi/VW, BigLots, BMW/Mini, Books-A-Million, Cadillac, Chrysler/Dodge/Jeep, CVS Drug, Food Lion, Hancock Fabrics, Infiniti, Jo-Ann Fabrics, KIA, Marshall's, Mercedes, Merchant's Tire, NAPA, PepBoys, Scion/Toyota, Steinmart, Subaru, TJ Maxx, Tuffy Repair, Verizon, Walgreens
180	Gaskins Rd, **N** 🅖 BP, Shell/dsl 🍴 Applebee's, Cracker Barrel, Golden Corral, IHOP, McDonald's, O'Charley's, Pizza Hut, Qdoba, Ruby Tuesday, Starbucks, Subway, Taco Bell, Tripp's Rest. 🛏 7-11, East Coast, Exxon, Fairfield Inn, Holiday Inn Express, SpringHill Suites 🅞 $Tree, Advance Parts, AutoZone, Costco/gas, Goodyear/auto, Kroger/gas, Lowe's, Martin's Foods, Mazda, Michael's, Sam's Club/gas
178b a	US 250, Broad St, Short Pump, **N** 🅖 7-11, Exxon, Wawa 🍴 5 Guys Burgers, BurgerWorks, Capital Alehouse, Chipotle Mexican, DQ, Firehouse Subs, Hondo's Rest., Joey's Hotdogs, Leonardo's Pizza, Moe's SW Grill, Panera Bread, Silver Diner, Starbucks 🛏 Comfort Suites, Courtyard, Extended Stay America, Hampton Inn, Hilton Garden, Homestead Suites, Hyatt Place, Marriott, Residence Inn 🅞 CarMax, CVS Drug, Firestone/auto, Ford, Kia, Marshall's, Ross, Verizon,

Exit #	Services
178b a	Continued
	S 🅖 7-11, Shell 🍴 Arby's, Bertucci's, Bonefish Grill, Buffalo Wild Wings, Burger King, Capt D's, Cheesecake Factory, Chick-fil-A, Chili's, Chipotle Mexican, Chuy's Mexican, Dave&Buster's, Domino's, Genghis Grill, HoneyBaked Ham, Jason's Deli, Jersey Mike's Subs, Jimmy John's, Kanpai, KFC, Kona Grill, LJSilver, Longhorn Steaks, Maggiano's Italian, McAlister's Deli, McDonald's, Mexico Rest., Mimi's Cafe, Olive Garden, Panera Bread, Plaza Azteca, Quiznos, Shula's Steaks, Sonic, Starbucks, Taco Bell, TGIFriday's, Wendy's 🛏 Candlewood Suites, Hilton, Wingate Inn 🅞 $Tree, AT&T, Barnes&Noble, Best Buy, Buick/Chevrolet/GMC, CarQuest, Crate&Barrel, Dick's, Dillard's, GNC, Hobby Lobby, Home Depot, Kohl's, Kroger, Lowe's, Macy's, Martin's Foods, Merchant's Tires, Nissan, Nordstrom, Petco, Petsmart, Radio Shack, Staples, Steinmart, Target, Tom Leonard's Mkt, Trader Joe's, Verizon, Walmart, Whole Foods Mkt, World Mkt
177	I-295, to I-95 N to Washington, to Norfolk, VA Beach, Williamsburg
175	VA 288, Chesterfield
173	VA 623, to Rockville, Manakin, **S** 0-2 mi 🅖 Exxon/dsl, Shell/dsl, Valero/Subway/dsl 🍴 BBQ, Sunset Grill 🅞 $General, Food Lion
169mm	🆁🆂 both lanes, full ♿ facilities, litter barrels, petwalk, 🆅, 🆂🅓 vending
167	VA 617, to Goochland, Oilville, **N** 🅖 Exxon/dsl, **S** 🅖 BP/Bullets/dsl
159	US 522, to Goochland, Gum Spring, **N** 🅖 Exxon/dsl, **S** 🅖 BP/DQ/dsl, Citgo
152	VA 629, Hadensville, **S** 1 mi 🅖 BP, Liberty 🅞 repair
148	VA 605, Shannon Hill
143	VA 208, to Louisa, Ferncliff, **N** 7 mi 🅞 Small Country Camping, **S** 🅖 Citgo/dsl, Exxon/dsl
136	US 15, to Gordonsville, Zion Crossroads, **N** 🅖 Sheetz/dsl 🍴 Arby's, IHOP, Subway 🛏 Best Western 🅞 Lowe's, Walmart, **S** 🅖 BP/McDonald's/dsl/24hr, Exxon/Burger King/dsl, Shell/Blimpie/dsl/scales 🍴 Crescent Rest.
129	VA 616, Keswick, Boyd Tavern
124	US 250, to Shadwell, **N** 2 mi 🅖 BP, Exxon, Hess, Shell 🍴 Applebee's, Burger King, Guadalajara Mexican, Hardee's, McDonald's, Quiznos, Starbucks, Taco Bell, TipTop Rest., Topeka's Steaks 🛏 Hilton Garden 🅞 🅷 Audi/VW, BMW, CarMax, Ford, Giant Foods, KIA, Mercedes, Porsche, Rite Aid, Toyota/Scion, **S** 🛏 Comfort Inn
123mm	Rivanna River
121	VA 20, to Charlottesville, Scottsville, **N** 🅖 BP/Blimpie, **S** 🅞 KOA (10mi), to Monticello

RICHMOND

CHARLOTTESVILLE

INTERSTATE 64 Cont'd

Exit #	Services
120	VA 631, 5th St, to Charlottesville, N Exxon/dsl Burger King, Domino's, Hardee's, Pizza Hut/Taco Bell, Waffle House 🛏 Holiday Inn, Sleep Inn Ⓞ CVS Drug, Food Lion, vet
118b a	US 29, to Lynchburg, Charlottesville, N 🅿 BP Ⓞ 🅷 services N on US 220, to UVA
114	VA 637, to Ivy
113mm	🆁ˢ wb, full 🔩 facilities, litter barrels, petwalk, ⓒ, 🖼 vending
111mm	Mechum River
108mm	Stockton Creek
107	US 250, Crozet, N 1 mi 🅿 Citgo, Shell/dsl S 1 mi Ⓞ Misty Mtn Camping
105mm	🆁ˢ eb, full 🔩 facilities, litter barrels, petwalk, ⓒ, 🖼 vending
104mm	scenic area eb, no truck or buses, litter barrels
100mm	scenic area eb, hist marker, litter barrels, no trucks or buses
99	US 250, to Waynesboro, Afton, N 🛏 Colony Motel Ⓞ ski area, Skyline Drive, to Blue Ridge Pkwy, to Shenandoah NP, S 🛏 Afton Inn
96	VA 622, to Lyndhurst, Waynesboro, N 3 mi 🅿 Hess, Shell ⓕ Tastee Freez 🛏 Quality Inn Ⓞ Waynesboro Camping
95mm	South River
94	US 340, to Stuarts Draft, Waynesboro, N 🅿 7-11/dsl, Exxon/dsl ⓕ Applebee's, Buffalo Wild Wings, Cracker Barrel, Giovanni's Pizza, Golden Corral, KFC, King Garden, Logan's Roadhouse, Outback Steaks, Panera Bread, Plaza Azteca, Ruby Tuesday, Shoney's, Sonic, Starbucks, Waffle House, Wendy's 🛏 Best Western, Comfort Inn, Days Inn, Holiday Inn Express, Residence Inn, Super 8 Ⓞ 🅷 Home Depot, Lowe's, Martin's Food/Drug, Radio Shack, vet, Walmart, Waynesboro N 340 Camping (9mi), S 🅿 Shell/dsl ⓕ Chick-fil-A, McAlister's Deli, McDonald's Ⓞ Books-A-Million, GNC, Kohl's, Michael's, museum, Petsmart, Ross, Target, Verizon
91	Va 608, to Stuarts Draft, Fishersville, N 🅿 Exxon/Subway (1mi), Shell/dsl 🛏 Hampton Inn Ⓞ 🅷 Eaver's Tires, S 🅿 Sheetz/dsl ⓕ McDonald's, Wendy's Ⓞ Shenadoah Acres Camping (8mi), Walnut Hills Camping (9mi)
89mm	Christians Creek
87	I-81, N to Harrisonburg, S to Roanoke
	I-64 and I-81 run together 20 miles. See I-81 exits 195-220
55	US 11, to VA 39, N 🅿 Exxon ⓕ Burger King, Crystal Chinese, Naples Pizza, Ruby Tuesday, Waffle House 🛏 Best Western, Sleep Inn, Super 8, Wingate Inn Ⓞ $Tree, Lowe's, Radio Shack, Stonewall Jackson Museum, Verizon, Walmart, S 🅿 BP/DQ, Marathon/7-11/Subway ⓕ Applebee's, Country Cookin, Redwood Rest. 🛏 Best Western, Comfort Inn, Country Inn&Suites, Holiday Inn Express, Motel 6 Ⓞ Cool Spring Mkt/cafe
50	US 60, rd 623, to Kerrs Creek, Lexington, S 5 mi 🛏 Days Inn
43	rd 780, to Goshen
35	VA 269, rd 850, Longdale Furnace
33mm	truck rest area eb
29	VA 269, VA 42 E, S 🅿 Sunoco/dsl
27	US 60 W, US 220 S, VA 629, Clifton Forge, N Ⓞ to Douthat SP, S 🅿 BP/dsl, Exxon ⓕ Bella Pizza, Pizza Hut (2mi) Ⓞ Alleghany Highlands Arts/crafts
24	US 60, US 220, Clifton Forge, S 1 mi 🅿 Shell/dsl ⓕ DQ, Hardee's, Vick's Cafe
21	to rd 696, Low Moor, S 🅿 Exxon ⓕ Penny's Diner, Quiznos 🛏 Oak Tree Inn Ⓞ 🅷

16	US 60 W, US 220 N, to Hot Springs, Covington, N 🅿 BP/Subway, Exxon/dsl, Shell ⓕ Burger King, Cucci's, Mtn View Rest., Western Sizzlin 🛏 Best Value Inn, Best Western, Holiday Inn Express, Pinehurst Hotel Ⓞ to ski area, S ⓕ McDonald's 🛏 Compare Inn Ⓞ K-Mart, Radio Shack
14	VA 154, to Hot Springs, Covington, N 🅿 Exxon/Arby's, Sunoco ⓕ Hong Kong Chinese, KFC, Little Caesars, LJ Silver, Subway, Wendy's Ⓞ $General, Advance Parts, AutoZone, CVS Drug, Family$, Food Lion, S ⓕ Applebee's, China House, Petron Mexican, Trani's Grille Ⓞ $Tree, Walmart,
10	US 60 E, VA 159 S, Callaghan, S 🅿 Marathon/dsl/LP
7	rd 661
2.5mm	Welcome Center eb, full 🔩 facilities, litter barrels, no trucks, petwalk, ⓒ, 🖼
1	Jerry's Run Trail, N to Allegheny Trail
0mm	Virginia/West Virginia state line

INTERSTATE 66

Exit #	Services
77mm	Constitution Ave, to Lincoln Mem. **I-66 begins/ends in Washington, DC.**
76mm	Potomac River, T Roosevelt Memorial Bridge
75	US 50 W (from eb), to Arlington Blvd, G Wash Pkwy, I-395, US 1, S Iwo Jima Mon
73	US 29, Lee Hwy, Key Bridge, to Rosslyn, N 🛏 Marriott, S 🛏 Holiday Inn
72	to US 29, Lee Hwy, Spout Run Pkwy (from eb, no EZ return), N 🅿 Shell 🛏 Virginia Inn, S ⓕ Starbucks, Tarbouch Grill Ⓞ CVS Drug, Giant Foods, Rite Aid, Starbucks, Walgreens
71	VA 120, Glebe Rd (no EZ return from wb), N Ⓞ 🅷 S 🅿 Sunoco ⓕ Booeymonger Grill, IHOP, Melting Pot, PF Chang's 🛏 Comfort Inn, Holiday Inn
69	US 29, Sycamore St, Falls Church, N 🅿 Exxon/7-11, S ⓕ Rock Cafe 🛏 EconoLodge
68	Westmoreland St (from eb), same as 69
67	to I-495 N (from wb), to Baltimore, Dulles 🛫
66b a	VA 7, Leesburg Pike, to Tysons Corner, Falls Church, N 🅿 Exxon, Sunoco ⓕ Jason's Deli, Ledo's Pizza, Olive Garden (2mi), Starbucks, Subway, Tara Thai Ⓞ 7-11, Trader Joe's, Whole Foods Mkt, S 🅿 Citgo ⓕ Baja Fresh, LJ Silver, McDonald's, Starbucks Ⓞ CVS Drug, Giant Foods, GNC, Kia, Staples, vet, Volvo
64b a	I-495 S, to Richmond
62	VA 243, Nutley St, to Vienna, S 🅿 Citgo ⓕ Chick-fil-A, Dunkin Donuts, IHOP, McDonald's, Starbucks Ⓞ S 1 mi on Lee Hwy 🅿 7-11, Advance Parts, Chrysler/Dodge/Jeep, Citgo, CVS Drug, Harley-Davidson, Home Depot, Jeep, Liberty, Michael's, Radio Shack, Safeway Foods/gas, Shell, Subaru, Sunoco/dsl, Walgreens
60	VA 123, to Fairfax, S 🅿 Exxon, Shell, Sunoco ⓕ 29 Diner, Denny's, Freddy's Steakburgers, Fuddruckers, Hooters, McDonald's, Outback Steaks, Panera Bread, Papa John's, Red Lobster, Smashburger, Subway 🛏 Best Western, Hampton Inn, Holiday Inn Express, Residence Inn Ⓞ Chevrolet, CVS Drug, Kia, Mazda, Rite Aid, Subaru, to George Mason U, Toyota/Scion
57b a	US 50, to Dulles 🛫, N ⓕ Cheesecake Factory 🛏 Extended Stay America, Marriott Ⓞ access to same as 55, JC Penney, Lord&Taylor, Macy's, mall, Sears/auto, S 🅿 BP, Shell/dsl ⓕ Ruby Tuesday, Wendy's 🛏 Comfort Inn/rest., Courtyard, SpringHill Suites Ⓞ Ford, Giant Foods, Honda, K-Mart, NRA Museum, Volvo, VW, Walmart,

WAYNESBORO · LEXINGTON

DC AREA

⬆️🄴	**INTERSTATE 66 Cont'd**

Exit # Services

55 Fairfax Co Pkwy, to US 29, **N** 🅖 Exxon, Sunoco 🍴 Applebees, Blue Iguana Café, Burger King, Cantina Italiana, Cooker Rest., Joe's Crabshack, Logan's Roadhouse, Malibu Grill, Olive Garden, Pizza Hut/Taco Bell, Red Robin, Sakura Japanese, Starbucks, Wendy's 🛏 Hyatt Hotel, Residence Inn 🅞 🄷 Best Buy, BJ's Whse, Bloom's Foods, GNC, Kohl's, Michael's, Petsmart, Radio Shack, Target, Walmart, Whole Foods Mkt, World Mkt, 4 Lakes Mall

53b a VA 28, to Centreville, **S** same as 52, Dulles ✈️, Manassas Museum

52 US 29, to Bull Run Park, Centreville, **N** 🅖 Sunoco/dsl 🅞 Bull Run Park/RV Dump, Goodyear/auto, **S** 🅖 Exxon, Sunoco/dsl 🍴 5 Guys Burgers, IHOP, Panda Express, Pizza Hut, Starbucks, Subway, Thai Rest., Tien Asia 🅞 $Tree, Advance Parts, AT&T, Giant Foods, Grand Mart, Radio Shack, SpringHill Suites, Trader Joe's, vet, Walgreens

49mm 🆁🆂 both lanes, full ♿ facilities, litter barrels, petwalk, 🄲, 🐾

47b a VA 234, to Manassas, **N** 🅖 Shell/dsl 🍴 5 Guys Burgers, Cracker Barrel, Golden Corral, Hershey's Ice Cream, Jerry's Subs, Uno, Wendy's 🛏 Courtyard, Fairfield Inn, Holiday Inn Express, Sheraton 🅞 Kohl's, Manassas Nat Bfd, Old Navy, **S** 🅖 7-11, BP, Exxon, RaceWay/dsl, Shell/repair, Sunoco 🍴 Arby's, Backyard Grill, Baja Fresh, Bob Evans, Burger King, CA Tortilla, Cafe Rio, Casa Chimayo, Checker's, Chick-fil-A, Chili's, China Jade, Chipotle Mexican, ChuckECheese's, City Grille, Coldstone, Denny's, Domino's, Don Pablo's, El Tolteca, Firehouse Subs, Great American Buffet, Hibachi Buffet, Hooters, KFC, Logan's Roadhouse, Marlin Ray's Grill, McDonald's, Olive Garden, Panda Express, Panera Bread, Papa John's, Pizza Hut, Pollo Campero, Popeye's, Potbelly's, Red Hot&Blue BBQ, Red Lobster, Starbucks, Subway, Taco Bell, TGIFriday's, Wendy's, Wok'n Roll 🛏 Best Western, Comfort Suites, Hampton Inn, Holiday Inn, Quality Inn, Red Roof Inn, Residence Inn, Super 8 🅞 $Tree, Advance Parts, Aldi Foods, AT&T, AutoZone, Barnes&Noble, Best Buy, Bottom$ Foods, Buick/GMC, Burlington Coats, Chevrolet, Costco/gas, CVS Drug, Dick's, Family$, Giant Foods, Home Depot, Honda, Jo-Ann Fabrics, K-Mart, Lowe's, Macy's, Marshall's, Merchant Auto Ctr, Michael's, NTB, Office Depot, PepBoys, PetCo, Petsmart, Radio Shack, Reines RV Ctr, Ross, Sears/auto, Shopper's Foods, Staples, Toyota, Tuesday Morning, Verizon, vet, Walgreens, Walmart,

44 VA 234 S, Manassas, **N** to Bristoe Sta Bfd SP

43b a US 29, to Warrenton, Gainesville, **N** 🅖 WaWa, **S** 🅖 7-11, Sunoco/dsl, WaWa 🍴 5 Guys Burgers, Burger King, Chick-fil-A, Chili's, Coldstone, Domino's, IHOP, Joe's Pizza/Subs, KFC/Pizza Hut/Taco Bell, McDonald's, Mimi's Cafe, MVP Grill, Papa John's, PeiWei, Potbelly, Qdoba, Subway, Wendy's 🛏 Hampton Inn, ValuePlace 🅞 Best Buy, CVS Drug, Giant Food/drug, GNC, Goodyear/auto, Lowe's, Petsmart, Target/food, Walgreens

40 US 15, Haymarket, **N** 🅞 Greenville Farms Camping, **S** 🅖 Sheetz/dsl 🍴 Foster's Grill, Giuseppe's Italian, McDonald's, Papa John's, Subway, Young Chow Cafe 🅞 Bloom Foods, CVS Drug

31 VA 245, to Old Tavern, **N** 1 mi 🅖 BP 🅞 USPO

28 US 17 S, Marshall, **N** 🅖 7-11, BP/McDonald's/dsl 🍴 Anthony's Pizza, Foster's Grille, Great Wall Chinese, Subway 🅞 🄷 Bloom Foods, Radio Shack, vet

27 VA 55 E, Rd 647, Marshall, **N** 1 mi 🅖 Citgo, Exxon/dsl/LP 🍴 Marshall Diner 🅞 IGA Foods

---

M A N A S S A S (left margin)

---

23 US 17 N, VA 55, Delaplane (no re-entry from eb)

20mm Goose Creek

18 VA 688, Markham

13 VA 79, to VA 55, Linden, Front Royal, **S** 🅖 Exxon/dsl, Shell/7-11 🍴 Applehouse Rest./BBQ/gifts 🅞 Skyline Drive, to Shenandoah NP

11mm Manassas Run

7mm Shenandoah River

6 US 340, US 522, to Winchester, Front Royal, **N** 🅖 7-11, Quarle's/Bullet's/dsl 🍴 Applebee's, Checkers, Cracker Barrel, Foster's Grille, Ledo's Pizza, Los Potrillo's, McAlister's Deli, Mikado, Panda Express, Quiznos, Starbucks, TGIFriday's, Vocelli Pizza 🅞 $Tree, Buick/GMC, Ford, GNC, Lowe's, PetCo, Staples, Target, Walmart, **S** 🅖 7-11, Exxon/Dunkin Donuts, Shell 🍴 McDonald's 🛏 Hampton Inn 🅞 Poe's Southfork Camping (2mi)

1b a I-81, N to Winchester, S to Roanoke

0mm I-66 begins/ends on I-81, exit 300.

⬆️🄽	**INTERSTATE 77**

Exit # Services

67mm Virginia/West Virginia state line, East River Mtn

66 VA 598, to East River Mtn

64 US 52, VA 61, to Rocky Gap

62mm **Welcome Center sb, full ♿ facilities, info, litter barrels, petwalk, 🄲, 🐾 vending**

62 VA 606, to South Gap

59mm 🆁🆂 sb, full ♿ facilities, litter barrels, petwalk, 🄲, 🐾 vending

58 US 52, to Bastian, **E** 🅖 BP/pizza/dsl, **W** 🅖 Citgo/dsl, Kangaroo

56mm runaway ramp nb

52 US 52, VA 42, Bland, **E** 🅖 Citgo 🍴 Subway 🅞 $General, IGA Foods, **W** 🅖 Kangaroo/DQ/dsl 🛏 Big Walker Motel

51.5mm weigh sta both lanes

48mm Big Walker Mtn

47 VA 717, **W** 6 mi 🅞 to Deer Trail Park/NF Camping

41 VA 610, Peppers Ferry, Wytheville, **E** 🍴 Sagebrush Steaks 🛏 Best Western, Sleep Inn, Super 8, **W** 🅖 Kangaroo/dsl/scales/24hr, TA/BP/Country Pride/Popeye's/Subway/Taco Bell/dsl/scales/24hr/@ 🍴 Southern Diner 🛏 Comfort Suites, Country Inn&Suites, Fairfield Inn, Hampton Inn, Ramada Inn

40 I-81 S, to Bristol, US 52 N

I-77 and I-81 run together 9 mi. See I-81, exits 73-80

32 I-81 N, to Roanoke

26mm New River

24 VA 69, to Poplar Camp, **E** 🅖 Pure 🅞 New River Trail Info Ctr, to Shot Tower HP, **W** 🅖 Marathon/Kangaroo/Subway/dsl

---

W Y T H E V I L L E (right column margin)

Manquin, Buckeye, Mechanicsville, Tuckahoe, 95, 64, Richmond, 295, Quinton, 64, Lee Park, Oakland, Brookbury, Glendale, Beulah, Fair Hill, Chester, Walthall, Hopewell, Colonial Heights, Petersburg, Prince George, Fort Davis, Burgess, **VA**

VA

🔼N	**INTERSTATE 77 Cont'd**
Exit #	Services
19	VA 620, 🆁🆂
14	US 58, US 221, to Hillsville, Galax, **E** 🅖 Citgo/Subway 🍴 Peking Palace 🏠 Red Carpet Inn 🅞 🅷 LakeRidge RV Resort (14mi) **W** 🅖 BP, Exxon/dsl, Gulf/dsl/24hr 🍴 Countryside Rest., McDonald's, Pizza Inn, Shoney's, TCBY, Wendy's 🏠 Best Western, Comfort Inn, Hampton Inn, Holiday Inn Express, Quality Inn, Super 8 🅞 Chevrolet
8	VA 148, VA 775, to Fancy Gap, **E** 🅖 Gulf, Marathon/dsl 🍴 Fancy Gap Cafe (2mi) 🏠 Lakeview Motel/rest. 🅞 $General, Chance's Creek RV Ctr, to Blue Ridge Pkwy, **W** 🅖 BP, Marathon/Kangaroo/dsl 🏠 Countryview Inn, Days Inn 🅞 KOA (2mi)
6.5mm	**runaway truck ramp sb**
4.5mm	**runaway truck ramp sb**
3mm	**runaway truck ramp sb**
1	VA 620, **E** 🅖 ♥Love's/McDonald's/Subway/dsl/scales/24hr
.5mm	**Welcome Center nb, full ♿ facilities, info, litter barrels, petwalk, 🅲, 🆂🆂**
0mm	Virginia/North Carolina state line

🔼N	**INTERSTATE 81**
Exit #	Services
324mm	Virginia/West Virginia state line
323	rd 669, to US 11, Whitehall, **E** 🅖 Exxon, **W** 🅖 ✈FLYING J/Denny's/Subway/dsl/LP/scales/24hr
321	rd 672, Clearbrook, **E** 🅖 Citgo/Old Stone Cafe/dsl 🅞 vet
320mm	**Welcome Center sb, full ♿ facilities, litter barrels, petwalk, 🅲, 🆂🆂, vending**
317	US 11, Stephenson, **E** 🍴 Chick-fil-A, Guan's Garden, Las Trancas, McDonald's, Subway, Tropical Smoothie Café, TX Roadhouse 🅞 AT&T, Lowe's, Target, Verizon, **W** 🅖 7-11/Burger King, Exxon/dsl, Sheetz, Sunoco/dsl 🍴 Denny's, Pizza Hut/Taco Bell 🏠 Comfort Inn, EconoLodge, Holiday Inn Express (3mi) 🅞 🅷 Candy Hill Camping
315	VA 7, Winchester, **E** 🅖 Exxon, Sheetz 🍴 Bamboo Garden, Ledo's Pizza, Little Caesars, Sansui Japanese, Sonic, Starbucks, Waffle House 🏠 TownePlace Suites 🅞 $Tree, Chrysler/Dodge/Jeep, Goodyear/auto, Martin's Foods/gas, PetCo, URGENT CARE, Walgreens, **W** 🅖 Exxon/Dunkin Donuts/Subway, Liberty/dsl, Shell/dsl 🍴 5 Guys Burgers, Arby's, Bros Pizza, Camino Real Mexican, KFC, McDonald's, Pizza Hut, Shoney's, Wendy's 🏠 Best Value Inn, Hampton Inn 🅞 CVS Drug, Family$, Food Lion, Food Maxx, TrueValue
314mm	Abrams Creek
313	US 17/50/522, Winchester, **E** 🅖 Exxon/Baskin-Robbins/Dunkin Donuts/Subway, Liberty/dsl, Shell/dsl 🍴 Asian Garden, Chinatown, Cracker Barrel, Golden Corral, Hibachi Grill, IHOP, Los Tolteco's Mexican, TX Steaks 🏠 Aloft Hotel, Candlewood Suites, Fairfield Inn, Holiday Inn, Red Roof Inn, Sleep Inn, Super 8, Travelodge 🅞 BigLots, Costco/gas, Food Lion, Jo-Ann Fabrics, Nissan, **W** 🅖 Sheetz 🍴 5 Guys Burgers, Bob Evans, Chick-fil-A, Chili's, China Jade, China Wok, Chipotle Mexican, ChuckECheese's, CiCi's Pizza, Glory Days Grill, Jimmy John's, KFC, Longhorn Steaks, McDonald's, Olive Garden, Panera Bread, Perkins, Pizza Hut/Taco Bell, Rancho Mexican, Red Lobster, Ruby Tuesday, TGIFriday's, Waffle House, Wendy's 🏠 Best Western, Hampton Inn, Hilton Garden, Wingate Inn 🅞 $Tree, Belk, Best Buy, Books-A-Million, Hobby Lobby, Home Depot, JC Penney, K-Mart, Kohl's,

Exit #	Services
313	Continued
	Lowe's, mall, Martin's Foods, Merchants Tire, Michael's, Old Navy, PepBoys, Petsmart, Radio Shack, Ross, Sears/auto, Staples, Target, TJ Maxx, to Shenandoah U, URGENT CARE, Verizon, Walgreens, Walmart,
310	VA 37, to US 50W, **W** 🅖 Citgo/dsl, Shell/7-11/dsl 🍴 Carrabba's, McDonald's, Outback Steaks, Subway 🏠 Best Value Inn, Budget Motel, Country Inn&Suites, Motel 6 🅞 🅷 Aldi Foods, Camping World, Candy Hill Camping (6mi), CarQuest, Gander Mtn, Honda, NAPA, Volvo, VW
307	VA 277, Stephens City, **E** 🅖 7-11, Gulf, Shell/Subway/dsl 🍴 Arby's, Burger King, Butcher Block Cafe, China House, Del Rio Mexicna, Domino's, Ginger Asian, KFC/Taco Bell, McDonald's, Pizza Hut, Roma Italian, Waffle House, Wendy's 🏠 Comfort Inn, Holiday Inn Express 🅞 Advance Parts, AutoZone, Curves, Food Lion, Martin's Foods/gas, Rite Aid, vet, **W** 🅖 Exxon/Dunkin Donuts, Sheetz
304mm	**weigh sta both lanes**
302	rd 627, Middletown, **E** 🅖 Exxon/dsl, **W** 🅖 7-11, Liberty/dsl 🅞 $General, to Wayside Theatre
300	I-66 E, to Washington, Shenandoah NP, Skyline Dr
298	US 11, Strausburg, **E** 🅖 Exxon/McDonald's/dsl/LP, Shell/7-11/dsl 🍴 Anthony's Pizza, Arby's, Burger King, Castiglia Italian, Ciro's Pizza, Denny's, Golden China, Great Wall Buffet 🏠 Fairfield Inn, Hotel Strasburg/rest., Ramada Inn 🅞 Family$, Food Lion, vet, **W** 🅞 Battle of Cedar Grove Camping, to Belle Grove Plantation
296	US 48, VA 55, Strausburg, **E** 🅞 museums
291	rd 651, Toms Brook, **E** 🏠 Budget Inn (3mi), **W** 🅖 ♥Love's/Arby's/dsl/scales/24hr, Wilco/Hess/DQ/Stuckey's/Subway/dsl/scales/24hr 🅞 truckwash/repair
283	VA 42, Woodstock, **E** 🅖 Liberty/7-11, Sheetz, Shell/Dunkin Donuts 🍴 Arby's, Burger King, China Wok, KFC, Las Trancas, McDonald's, Pizza Hut, Taco Bell, Wendy's 🏠 Comfort Inn, Hampton Inn, Holiday Inn Express 🅞 🅷 CVS Drug, Family$, Food Lion, Rite Aid, to Massanutten Military Academy, **W** 🅖 Exxon/dsl, Sunoco 🍴 China Wok, Cracker Barrel, Domino's, Subway 🅞 $Tree, Ford Lowe's, NAPA Care, Radio Shack, Walmart,
279	VA 185, rd 675, Edinburg, **E** 🅖 Exxon/dsl, Shell/dsl 🍴 Sal's Italian Bistro 🅞 auto repair, Creekside Camping (2mi), USPO
277	rd 614, Bowmans Crossing
273	VA 292, RD 703, Mt Jackson, **E** 🅖 7-11, Exxon/dsl, Liberty/dsl/scales/24hr, Sheetz/dsl/scales/24hr 🍴 Burger King, China King, Denny's, Subway 🏠 Super 8 🅞 $General, Food Lion, to Mt Jackson Hist Dist, USPO
269mm	N Fork Shenandoah River
269	rd 730, to US 11, Shenandoah Caverns, **E** 🅖 Shell/dsl
264	US 211, New Market, **E** 🅖 Exxon/Subway/dsl, Liberty/dsl, Mobil/dsl, Shell/dsl 🍴 Appleseed's Rest., Burger King, Italian Job, McDonald's, Publick House Rest. 🏠 Budget Inn, Quality Inn 🅞 Endless Caverns Camping, NAPA Care, Skyline Dr, to Shenandoah NP, USPO, **W** 🅖 7-11 🏠 Days Inn 🅞 to New Market Bfd SHP
262mm	**🆁🆂 both lanes, full ♿ facilities, litter barrels, petwalk, 🅲, 🆂🆂 vending**
257	US 11, VA 259, to Broadway, **E** 3-5 mi 🅖 Liberty/7-11/Burger King/dsl 🅞 Endless Caverns Camping, KOA
251	US 11, Harrisonburg, **W** 🅖 Exxon/dsl, ⬛⬛⬛/Subway/dsl/scales/24hr 🏠 Economy Inn
247b a	US 33, Harrisonburg, **E** 🅖 Citgo/dsl, Exxon/dsl, Royal/dsl, Sheetz/dsl, Shell/dsl, Walmart 🍴 5 Guys Burgers, Applebee's,

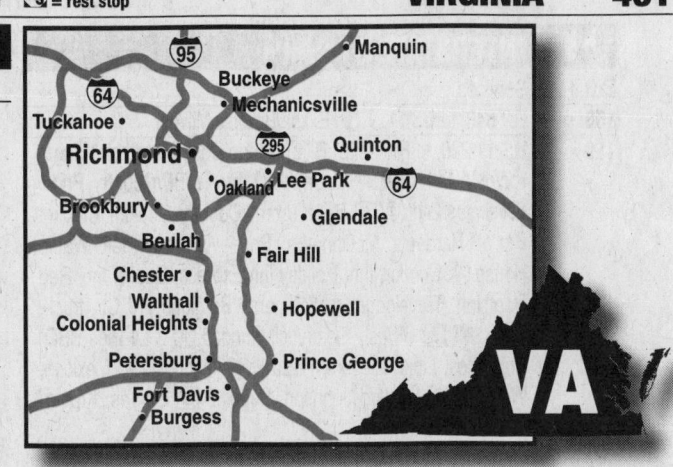

INTERSTATE 81 Cont'd

Exit #	Services

HARRISONBURG

247b a — Continued

Aroma Buffet, Bob Evans, Bruster's, Burger King, Chick-fil-A, Chili's, China Jade, Chipotle, CiCi's Pizza, Cook Out, Country Cookin, Domino's, El Charro Mexican, Firehouse Subs, Golden Corral, Great Wok, IHOP, Jess' Lunch, Jimmy John's, LJ Silver, McAlister's Deli, O'Charley's, Outback Steaks, Panera Bread, Qdoba, Quaker Steak&Lube, Red Lobster, Ruby Tuesday, Shoney's, Subway, Taco Bell, Tilted Kilt, TX Roadhouse, Waffle House, Wendy's, Wood Grill Buffet 🛏 Best Western, Candlewood Suites, Comfort Inn, Courtyard, EconoLodge, Fairfield Inn, Hampton Inn, Holiday Inn, Motel 6, Quality Inn, Residence Inn, Sleep Inn 🅞 $Tree, AT&T, Barnes&Noble, Belk, Best Buy, Books-A-Million, Cadillac/Chevrolet, Costco/gas, Dick's, Firestone/auto, Home Depot, JC Penney, K-Mart, Kohl's, Kroger, Lowe's, Martin's Foods/gas, Michael's, Nissan, Old Navy, PetCo, Petsmart, Ross, Skyline Dr, Staples, Target, TJ Maxx, to Shenandoah NP, Verizon, Walmart/McDonald's, **W** 🅖 Exxon/dsl, Liberty, Sheetz 🍴 Arby's, DQ, Dragon Palace, El Rancho Mexican, Golden China, Hardee's, KFC, Kyoto, Little Caesars, McDonald's, Sam's Hotdogs, Subway 🅞 🄷 Advance Parts, BigLots, CVS Drug, Food Lion

245 — VA 659, Port Republic Rd, **E** 🅖 Campus Corner, Exxon/dsl, Liberty/dsl, Royal/dsl 🍴 El Charro, Log Cabin BBQ, McDonald's, Subway 🛏 Days Inn 🅞 CVS Drug, Food Lion, **W** 🍴 Asian City, Jimmy John's, Starbucks 🅞 🄷 to James Madison U

243 — US 11, to Harrisonburg, **W 0-2 mi** 🅖 BP/dsl, Exxon/dsl, Harrisonburg Travel Ctr/diner/dsl/scales, Liberty, Sheetz/dsl, Shell/7-11/dsl 🍴 Burger King, Cracker Barrel, McDonald's, Pano's Rest., Pizza Hut, Subway, Taco Bell 🛏 Come On Inn, Hampton Inn, Holiday Inn Express, Microtel, Ramada Inn, Super 8 🅞 $General, Advance Parts, AutoZone, CarMax, Family$, Ford, Honda, Hyundai, Kia, Lincoln, Subaru, Toyota/Scion

240 — VA 257, rd 682, Mount Crawford, **E** 🅖 Shell/7-11/dsl 🍴 McDonald's, **W** 🅖 Exxon/Burger King/dsl (1mi)

235 — VA 256, Weyers Cave, **E** 🅖 Shell/dsl, **W** 🅖 BP/Subway/dsl, Exxon/dsl 🅞 antiques, Freightliner, to Grand Caverns

232mm — 🆁🆂 **both lanes, full** 🦽 **facilities, litter barrels, petwalk,** 🚻, 🏕 **vending**

227 — rd 612, Verona, **E** 🅖 BP/Subway/dsl 🍴 Waffle Inn, **W** 🅖 Citgo/Wendy's/dsl, Exxon/Dunkin Donuts, Shell/dsl 🍴 Burger King, China City, Ciro's Pizza, Hardee's, McDonald's 🛏 Knights Inn 🅞 $General, antiques, Food Lion, Good Sam RV Park (3mi), Rite Aid

225 — VA 262, Woodrow Wilson Pkwy, **E** 🛏 Motel 6, **W** 🛏 Days Inn, Holiday Inn/rest.

STAUNTON

222 — US 250, Staunton, **E** 🅖 BP, Royal/dsl 🍴 Cracker Barrel, Hometown Grill, McDonald's, Mrs Rowe's Rest., TX Steaks 🛏 Best Western, Red Roof Inn, Sleep Inn, **W** 🅖 Hess/dsl, Sheetz 🍴 5 Guys Burgers, Baskin-Robbins, Burger King, Chili's, Dunkin Donuts, Firehouse Subs, KFC, Massaki Japanese, Starbucks, Waffle House 🛏 Comfort Inn, EconoLodge, Microtel 🅞 American Frontier Culture Museum, AT&T, auto repair, AutoZone, Lowe's, Martin's Foods/gas, Toyota/Scion, URGENT CARE, Walmart/Subway

221 — I-64 E, to Charlottesville, Skyline Dr, Shenandoah NP

I-81 and I-64 run together 20 mi.

220 — VA 262, to US 11, Staunton, **W 1 mi** 🅖 Citgo, Exxon, Shell 🍴 88 Buffet, A&W/LJ Silver, Applebee's, Arby's, Burger King,

---

220 — Continued

CiCi's Pizza, El Puerto, Jimmy John's, Kathy's Rest., Kline's Dairy Bar, Maria's Italian, McDonald's, Papa John's, Red Lobster, Sam's HotDogs, Subway, Taco Bell, Wendy's 🛏 Budget Inn, Hampton Inn 🅞 $General, $Tree, Advance Parts, Belk, Buick/GMC, Cadillac/Chevrolet, Chrysler, CVS Drug, Dodge/Jeep, Food Lion, Ford, Harley-Davidson, Honda, Hyundai, JC Penney, Kia/Mazda, Kroger, Merchant's Tire/auto, Nissan, Obaugh RV Ctr, Petco, Staples, Subaru, TJ Maxx, Verizon, vet, VW

217 — Rd 654, to Mint Spring, Stuarts Draft, **E** 🅖 BP/Subway/dsl 🛏 Days Inn, **W** 🅖 Liberty/LP, Marathon/Kangaroo/dsl/24hr 🛏 Relax Inn 🅞 KOA

213b a — US 11, US 340, Greenville, **E** 🅖 BP/Subway, 🚚/Arby's/scales/dsl/24hr, Shell 🍴 Edelweiss Rest. 🛏 Hometown Inn 🅞 KOA

205 — Rd 606, Raphine, **E** 🅖 Fuel City/Smiley's BBQ/dsl/24hr, Petro/Exxon/Burger King/dsl/scales/24hr/@, Sunoco/dsl, **W** 🅖 Wilco/Hess/Wendy's/dsl/scales/24hr 🛏 Days Inn/rest. 🅞 Peterbilt

200 — RD 710, Fairfield, **E** 🅖 BP/McDonald's/dsl, Pure, **W** 🅖 Exxon/Subway/dsl, Shell/dsl

199mm — 🆁🆂 **sb, full** 🦽 **facilities, litter barrels, petwalk,** 🚻, 🏕 **vending**

195 — US 11, Lee Hwy, **E** 🛏 Maple Hall Country Inn, **W** 🅖 Exxon/dsl, TA/Shell/Berky's Rest./dsl/scales/24hr/@ 🛏 Days Inn, Howard Johnson, Quality Inn 🅞 Lee-Hi Camping, repair

191 — I-64 W (exits left from nb), US 60, to Charleston

I-81 and I-64 run together 20 mi.

LEXINGTON

188b a — US 60, to Lexington, Buena Vista **E 3-5 mi** 🅖 BP, Exxon 🍴 Burger King, Hardee's 🛏 Buena Vista Inn 🅞 🄷 $General, Family$, Food Lion, Marshall Museum, to Blue Ridge Pkwy, to Glen Maury Park, to Stonewall Jackson Home, **W** 🅖 Exxon/dsl 🅞 to Washington&Lee U, VMI

180 — US 11, Natural Bridge, **E** 🛏 Relax Inn 🅞 Cave Mtn NF, Jellystone Camping, **W** 🅖 Shell/dsl 🍴 Pink Cadillac Diner 🛏 Budget Inn 🅞 (180a exits left from sb), KOA

175 — US 11 N, to Glasgow, Natural Bridge, **E** 🅖 Exxon 🛏 Natural Bridge Hotel/rest. (2mi) 🅞 Jellystone Camping, to James River RA

168 — VA 614, US 11, Blue Ridge Pkwy, Arcadia, **E** 🅖 Shell 🍴 Mtn View Rest. 🛏 Wattstull Inn 🅞 Middle Creek Camping (6mi), **W 2 mi** 🅖 Exxon 🍴 Burger King, Rancho Veijo

167 — US 11 (from sb), Buchanan

162 — US 11, Buchanan, **E** 🅖 Exxon/dsl 🅞 to BR Pkwy, **W** 🅖 Citgo/Subway

158mm — 🆁🆂 **sb, full** 🦽 **facilities, litter barrels, petwalk,** 🚻, 🏕 **vending**

🧭N   INTERSTATE 81 Cont'd

Exit #	Services
156	RD 640, to US 11, **E** 🅖 Exxon/Brugh's Mill/dsl
150	US 11/220, to Fincastle, **E** 🅖 Dodge's/dsl, Marathon/Kangaroo/dsl/24hr, ⛽/Subway/dsl/24hr, TA/BP/Country Pride/dsl/scales/24hr/@ 🍴 Bella Pizza, Country Cookin', Cracker Barrel, Hardee's, McDonald's, Shoney's, Taco Bell, Waffle House 🛏 Comfort Inn, Holiday Inn Express, Quality Inn, Red Roof Inn, Travelodge 🅾 $General, Berglund RV Ctr, truckwash, **W** 🅖 BP/dsl, Exxon/dsl, Sunoco 🍴 3 Lil Pigs BBQ, Bojangles, Little Caesars, Pizza Hut, Rancho Viejo Mexican, Wendy's 🛏 Howard Johnson, Super 8 🅾 Curves, Kroger/gas, Verizon, vet
149mm	**weigh sta both lanes**
146	VA 115, Cloverdale, **E** 🅖 BP, Exxon, Shell/dsl 🍴 El Rodeo Mexican, Hardees, McDonald's, Subway 🛏 Country Inn&Suites, Days Inn/rest., Fairfield Inn, Hampton Inn 🅾 Camping World, CVS, Gander Mtn, to Hollins U
143	I-581, US 220, to Roanoke, Blue Ridge Pkwy (exits left from sb), **E 1 mi** 🅖 Kroger Gas/dsl 🍴 El Toreo, Subway, Waffle House 🛏 Howard Johnson, Quality Inn, Super 8 🅾 Honda, **E 2-3 mi on Hershberger** 🍴 Abuelo's Mexican, Applebee's, Buffalo Wild Wings, Carrabba's, Cheddar's, Chick-fil-A, Coldstone, Hardee's, IHOP, Logan's Roadhouse, Longhorn Steaks, O'Charley's, Olive Garden, Panera Bread, Penn Sta Subs, Red Palace Chinese, Red Robin, Ruby Tuesday, Shaker's, Smokey Bones BBQ, Starbucks, TGIFriday's, Zaxby's 🛏 Best Western, Comfort Inn, Courtyard, Extended Stay America, Hampton Inn, Holiday Inn, Hyatt Place, MainStay Suites, Residence Inn, Sheraton 🅾 $Tree, AT&T, Barnes&Noble, Belk, Best Buy, BigLots, Dick's, Exxon, Home Depot, JC Penney, Macy's, mall, Murphy USA/dsl, NTB, Old Navy, Petsmart, Sears/auto, Shell, Staples, Target, U-Haul, Verizon, Walmart
141	VA 419, Salem, **E** 🅖 BP, Liberty/7-11/dsl, Marathon/Burger King 🍴 Hardee's, IHOP, Starbucks, Subway 🛏 Days Inn, Holiday Inn Express, La Quinta, Quality Inn 🅾 🅷 Chevrolet, GNC, Kroger/gas, **W** 🅖 BP/Subway/dsl, Citgo
140	VA 311, Salem, **E 1 mi** 🍴 Mac&Bob's Cafe, **W 1 mi** 🍴 Hanging Rock Grill/golf
137	VA 112, VA 619, Salem, **E** 🅖 BP, Citgo/dsl, Exxon/dsl, Go-Mart, Marathon, Sheetz 🍴 Anthony's Cafe, Applebees, Arby's, Bojangles, Burger King, Chick-fil-A, Denny's, Dynasty Buffet, El Rodeo Mexican, Firehouse Subs, Hardee's, K&W Cafeteria, KFC, Mamma Maria Italian, McDonald's, Omelette Shoppe, Pizza Hut, Quiznos, Rancho Veijo, Shoney's, Starbucks, Subway, Taco Bell, Tokyo Express, Wendy's, Zaxby's 🛏 Comfort Suites, EconoLodge, Quality Inn, Super 8 🅾 $General, $Tree, Aamco, Advance Parts, AutoZone, BigLots, Food Lion, Goodyear, K-Mart, Kroger/gas, Lowe's, Merchant's Tire, O'Reilly Parts, Snyder's RV, Verizon, vet, Walgreens, Walmart/Subway, **W** 🛏 Holiday Inn, Howard Johnson
132	VA 647, to Dixie Caverns, **E** 🅖 Shell (2mi) 🛏 Blue Jay Hotel 🅾 Dixie Caverns Camping, st police
129mm	🆁🆂 sb, full ♿ facilities, litter barrels, petwalk, 🅲, 🚮 vending
128	US 11, VA 603, Ironto, **E** 🅖 Shell, **W** 🅖 Exxon/Dixie's/Subway/dsl/24hr
118c b a	US 11/460, Christiansburg, **E** 🅖 Shell/dsl 🍴 Cracker Barrel, Denny's 🛏 Days Inn, Fairfield Inn, Holiday Inn Express, Quality Inn, Super 8, **W** 🅖 Exxon/dsl, Liberty/7-11/dsl, Shell 🍴 Country Cookin', Hardee's, McDonald's, Pizza Hut, Ruby Tuesday, Waffle House, Wendy's 🛏 EconoLodge,
118c b a	Continued Rodeway Inn 🅾 🅷 $General, Advance Parts, Chevrolet, Chrysler/Dodge/Jeep, Food Lion, Ford, Honda, Hyundai, Kia, Subaru, to VA Tech, Toyota/Scion
114	VA 8, Christiansburg, **E** to Blue Ridge Pkwy, **W 0-1 mi** 🅖 Citgo/dsl 🍴 Burger King, Pizza Inn, Subway 🛏 Budget Inn 🅾 $General Mkt, Family$, tires, USPO
109	VA 177, VA 600, **E** 🅾 🅷 **W 0-2 mi** 🅖 Marathon, Sunoco/dsl 🛏 Best Western, Comfort Inn, La Quinta, Super 8 (2mi) 🅾 Buick/Cadillac/Chevrolet
107mm	🆁🆂 both lanes, full ♿ facilities, litter barrels, petwalk, 🅲, 🚮 vending
105	VA 232, RD 605, to Radford, **W 2-4 mi** 🅖 Citgo, Marathon/dsl 🍴 Sal's Italian 🛏 Executive Motel 🅾 museum
101	RD 660, to Claytor Lake SP, **E** 🛏 Claytor Lake Inn, Sleep Inn 🅾 repair, **W** 🅖 Marathon/DQ/dsl, Shell/Omelette Shoppe/Taco Bell/dsl/scales/@
98	VA 100 N, to Dublin, **E** 🅖 Exxon/Subway/dsl, Marathon 🍴 Bojangles, Shoney's 🛏 Comfort Inn, Hampton Inn, Holiday Inn Express, **W** 🅖 Liberty/Blimpie/dsl, Marathon/dsl 🍴 Arby's, Burger King, El Ranchero Mexican, Fatz Cafe, McDonald's, Subway, Waffle House, Wendy's 🛏 Super 8 🅾 🅷 $General, O'Reilly Parts, to Wilderness Rd Museum, vet, Walmart/Subway
94b a	VA 99 N, to Pulaski, **W 0-3 mi** 🅖 BP, Exxon/dsl, Hess 🍴 China Wall, Compadre's Mexican, Domino's, Hardee's, KFC, Kimono Japanese, Little Caesars, McDonald's, Pizza Hut, Sonic, Subway, Taco Bell, Wendy's 🅾 🅷 $General, Advance Parts, Curves, CVS, Family$, Food Lion, Goodyear/auto, O'Reilly Parts, Rite Aid
92	Rd 658, to Draper, **E** 🅖 BP 🅾 to New River Trail SP
89b a	US 11 N, VA 100, to Pulaski, **E** auto/truck repair
86	Rd 618, Service Rd, **W** 🅖 Sunoco/Appletree Rest./dsl 🅾 repair
84	Rd 619, to Grahams Forge, **W** 🅖 Kangaroo/DQ/dsl/24hr, ⛽Love's/Chester Fried/Subway/dsl/scales/24hr 🍴 Italian Garden 🛏 Fox Mtn Inn, Trail Motel
81	I-77 S, to Charlotte, to Blue Ridge Pkwy. Galax
	I-81 S and I-77 N run together 9 mi.
80	US 52 S, VA 121 N, to Ft Chiswell, **E** 🅖 ⛽FLYING J/Denny's/dsl/scales/24hr/@, BP/Burger King/dsl 🍴 Wendy's 🛏 Hampton Inn, Super 8 🅾 Blue Beacon, Ft Chiswell RV Park, NAPA, **W** 🅖 Kangaroo/dsl, Marathon/dsl, Valero 🍴 McDonald's 🛏 Comfort Inn 🅾 Speedco
77	Service Rd, **E** 🅖 ⛽FLYING J/Denny's/dsl/scales/LP/RV Dump/24hr, Kangaroo/Subway/dsl/24hr, Wilco/Hess/dsl/LP 🍴 Burger King 🅾 KOA, **W** 🅖 Exxon/dsl, Wilco/Hess/Arby's/DQ/dsl/scales/24hr 🅾 st police, Truck'o Mat
73	US 11 S, Wytheville, **E** 🅖 BP, Citgo/Quiznos/dsl, Go-Mart, Kangaroo/dsl 🍴 Applebee's, Bob Evans, Cracker Barrel, El Puerto Mexican, Hardee's, LJ Silver, Ocean Bay Rest., Papa John's, Peking Chinese, Pizza Hut, Shoney's, Smokey's BBQ, Sonic, Waffle House, Wendy's 🛏 Budget Host, Days Inn, EconoLodge, Knights Inn, La Quinta, Motel 6, Quality Inn, Red Roof Inn, Travelodge 🅾 🅷 $General, AutoZone, Buick/Chevrolet/GMC, CVS Drug, Food Lion, Ford, Goodyear/auto, Harley-Davidson, K-Mart, Nissan, Rite Aid, Subaru
	I-81 N and I-77 S run together 9 mi
72	I-77 N, to Bluefield, **1 mi N, I-77 exit 41 E** 🍴 Sagebrush Steaks 🛏 Best Western, Sleep Inn, Super 8, **1 mi N, I-77 exit 41 W** 🅖 Kangaroo/dsl/24hr, TA/Country Pride/Popeye's/Subway/Taco Bell/dsl/scales/24hr/@ 🍴 Southern Diner

(left margin, vertical) **VA**   **R O A N O K E**   **S A L E M**   **W Y T H E V I L L E**

⬆N INTERSTATE 81 Cont'd

Exit #	Services
72	Continued 🛏 Comfort Suites, Country Inn&Suites, Fairfield Inn, Hampton Inn, Ramada/rest.
70	US 21/52, Wytheville, E ⛽ BP/dsl, Sheetz/dsl 🍴 Bojangles, China Wok, El Patio Mexican, KFC/Taco Bell, Little Caesars, McDonald's, Ruby Tuesday, Starbucks, Subway, Tokyo Japanese, Wendy's Ⓞ 🍴 $Tree, AT&T, Food Lion, Lowe's, Pet-Co, Verizon, Walmart/Subway, W ⛽ Kangaroo 🛏 Comfort Inn
67	US 11 (from nb, no re-entry), to Wytheville
61mm	Ⓡˢ nb, full 🚻 facilities, litter barrels, No Trucks, petwalk, 🄲 🖵 vending
60	VA 90, Rural Retreat, E ⛽ Shell/dsl, Spirit/dsl 🍴 Dutch Pantry, El Ranchero, McDonald's Ⓞ $General, camping, to Rural Retreat Lake
54	rd 683, to Groseclose, E ⛽ Sunoco/dsl 🍴 The Barn Rest. 🛏 Relax Inn Ⓞ Settler's Museum
53.5mm	Ⓡˢ sb, full 🚻 facilities, litter barrels, petwalk, 🄲, 🖵 vending
50	US 11, Atkins, W ⛽ Exxon, Marathon/Subway/dsl/24hr 🛏 Comfort Inn Ⓞ NAPA Care
47	US 11, to Marion, W ⛽ Gas'N Go, Shell/dsl, Valero/Subway 🍴 Arby's, KFC/Taco Bell, Little Caesars, LJ Silver, McDonald's, Pizza Hut, Puerto Mexican, Sonic, Wendy's 🛏 Best Value Inn, EconoLodge, Travel Inn Ⓞ 🍴 $General, $Tree, Advance Parts, AutoZone, Buick/Chevrolet/GMC, CVS Drug, Family$, Food City, Food Lion, Ford, Ingles, Marion Drug, O'Reilly Parts, Rite Aid, to Hungry Mother SP (4mi), Walgreens, Walmart,
45	VA 16, Marion, E ⛽ Valero/dsl 🍴 AppleTree Rest. Ⓞ Mt Rogers NRA, to Grayson Highlands SP, W ⛽ Sunoco 🍴 Hardee's Ⓞ NAPA, USPO
44	US 11, Marion, W ⛽ Marathon/dsl
39	US 11, rd 645, Seven Mile Ford, E 🛏 Budget Inn, W Ⓞ Interstate Camping
35	VA 107, Chilhowie, E 🍴 Chilhowie Pizza, Hardees 🛏 Knights Inn, W ⛽ Exxon/dsl, Gas'N Go, Shell/dsl 🍴 McDonald's, Riverfront Rest., Subway 🛏 Budget Inn (1mi) Ⓞ $General, Curves, Food City, Greever's Drugs, USPO
32	US 11, to Chilhowie
29	VA 91, to Damascus, Glade Spring, E ⛽ Marathon/Subway/dsl, Petro/rest./dsl/24hr/@, Valero/Wendy's 🍴 Giardino's Italian, Pizza+ 🛏 EconoLodge, Super 8 Ⓞ $General, Peterbilt, W ⛽ Exxon, Shell/dsl, Spirit Ⓞ CarQuest, vet
26	rd 737, Emory, W 🍴 Mikado's (1mi) Ⓞ to Emory&Henry Coll
24	VA 80, Meadowview Rd, W auto repair
22	rd 704, Enterprise Rd, E ⛽ Brown's Pantry/dsl Ⓞ 🍴
19	US 11/58, to Abingdon, E ⛽ Shell/Subway/dsl 🍴 DQ, McDonald's, Pizza+ Ⓞ Lowe's, to Mt Rogers NRA, URGENT CARE, vet, W ⛽ BP/dsl, Citgo/Huddle House, Exxon/dsl 🍴 Bella's Pizza, Burger King, Cracker Barrel, DaVinci's Cafe, Harbor House Seafood, Wendy's 🛏 Alpine Motel, Best Value Inn, Holiday Inn Express, Quality Inn
17	US 58A, VA 75, Abingdon, E 🍴 Domino's, LJ Silver 🛏 Hampton Inn, W ⛽ Exxon, Gas'n Go 🍴 Arby's, Charley's Subs, China Wok, Hardee's, KFC, Los Arcos, McDonald's, Papa John's, Pizza Hut, Shoney's, Subway, Taco Bell, Wendy's 🛏 Super 8 Ⓞ 🍴 Advance Parts, Food City, GNC, K-Mart, Kroger, Radio Shack

Side tab: **MARION**

Side tab: **ABINGDON**

Exit #	Services
14	US 19, VA 140, Abingdon, W ⛽ BP/dsl, Exxon, Shell/dsl 🍴 McDonald's, Milano's Italian, Moon Dog Cafe, Subway 🛏 Comfort Inn, Comfort Suites Ⓞ Chevrolet, Ford/Lincoln, Riverside Camping (10mi)
13.5mm	Ⓡˢ nb Truckers Only, full 🚻 facilities, litter barrels, 🖵 vending
13	VA 611, to Lee Hwy, W ⛽ Shell/dsl Ⓞ Kenworth, Mack, Volvo
10	US 11/19, Lee Hwy, W ⛽ BP/dsl, Exxon, Shell/dsl 🛏 Deluxe Inn, Economy Inn, Evergreen Inn, Red Carpet Inn
7	Old 🛏 Rd, E ⛽ Shell/dsl 🍴 Bojangles, Cheddar's, Cracker Barrel, Sonic 🛏 La Quinta, W ⛽ Marathon, Sunoco/Wendy's, Valero/dsl 🍴 Bellecino's, Charley's Subs, Chick-fil-A, Chili's, Cook-Out, Domino's, DQ, El Patio Mexican, Golden Corral, IHOP, Jersey Mike's Subs, Kobe Japanese, Logan's Roadhouse, Los Arcos, Mellow Mushroom, O'Charley's, Olive Garden, Outback Steaks, Pal's Drive-In, Perkins, Pizza Hut, Red Lobster, Ruby Tuesday, Starbucks, Subway, Taco Bell 🛏 Courtyard, Holiday Inn, Microtel, Motel 6 Ⓞ $General, $Tree, Advance Parts, AutoZone, Best Buy, Books-A-Million, Food City, Home Depot, Lowe's, Office Depot, Old Navy, Petsmart, Ross, Sam's Club/gas, Sugar Hollow Camping, Target, TJ Maxx, Verizon, Walmart,
5	US 11/19, Lee Hwy, E ⛽ BP, Shell 🍴 Arby's, Burger King, Hardee's, KFC, LJ Silver, McDonald's, Shoney's 🛏 Budget Inn, Super 8 Ⓞ Family$, Harley-Davidson, USPO, W ⛽ Exxon/dsl 🛏 Comfort Inn Ⓞ Blevins Tire, Buick/GMC, Lee Hwy Camping
3	I-381 S, to Bristol, E 1 mi ⛽ Shell/dsl, Zoomers/dsl 🍴 Applebee's, Arby's, Krystal 🛏 EconoLodge
1b a	US 58/421, Bristol, E 1 mi ⛽ 5 Mart, Exxon, Shell, Zoomers 🍴 Burger King, Capt D's, Chick-fil-A, Chinese Family Buffet, KFC, McDonald's, Pizza Hut, Sonic, Subway, Taco Bell, Wendy's 🛏 Knights Inn Ⓞ 🍴 Belk, Chrysler/Dodge/Jeep, CVS Drug, Family$, JC Penney, K-Mart, Kroger/dsl, mall, Sears/auto, Toyota/Scion, URGENT CARE, Verizon, vet, Walgreens
0mm	Welcome Center nb, No Trucks, full 🚻 facilities, info, litter barrels, petwalk, 🄲, 🖵 vending, Virginia/Tennessee state line

⬆N INTERSTATE 85

Exit #	Services
69mm	I-85 begins/ends on I-95.
69	US 301, I-95 N, Wythe St, Washington St, Petersburg
68	I-95 S, US 460 E, to Norfolk, Crater Rd
65	Squirrel Level Rd, E Ⓞ to Richard Bland Coll, W ⛽ BP
63b a	US 1, to Petersburg, E ⛽ Chubby's/dsl, Exxon/KFC/dsl, Shell/Burger King/dsl 🍴 Hardee's, Waffle House 🛏 Holiday Inn Express, W ⛽ BP 🍴 McDonald's

Side tab: **VA**

⬆N INTERSTATE 85 Cont'd

Exit #	Services
61	US 460, to Blackstone, E 🅐 EastCoast/Subway/dsl/LP/e85 🍴 Huddle House, W 🍴 Giuseppe's Pizza 🅾 ♿, auto repair
55mm	🆁 both lanes, full ♿ facilities, litter barrels, petwalk, 📞, 🔧 vending
53	VA 703, Dinwiddie, W 🅐 Exxon/dsl 🍴 Fats BBQ 🅾 to 5 Forks Nat Bfd
52mm	Stony Creek
48	VA 650, DeWitt
42	VA 40, McKenney, W 🅐 Citgo, Exxon 🅾 auto repair
40mm	Nottoway River
39	VA 712, to Rawlings, W 🅐 Davis TC/Exxon/Dunkin Donuts/Subway/dsl/scales/24hr, Racine 🏠 Nottoway Motel/rest.
34	VA 630, Warfield, W 🅐 Exxon/dsl
32mm	🆁 both lanes, full ♿ facilities, litter barrels, petwalk, 📞, 🔧 vending
28	US 1, Alberta, W 🅐 Exxon 🅾 Family Dollar
27	VA 46, to Lawrenceville, E 🅾 to St Paul's Coll
24	VA 644, to Meredithville
22mm	weigh sta both lanes
20mm	Meherrin River
15	US 1, to South Hill, E 🅐 Citgo, W 🅐 Loves/Subway/McDonald's/dsl/scales/24hr, Valero/dsl 🍴 Kahill's Rest.
12	US 58, VA 47, to South Hill, E 🅐 BP/Quizno's/Stucky's/dsl, RaceWay, Shell/dsl 🍴 Applebee's, Arby's, Bojangles, Domino's, Glass House Grill, Sonic 🏠 Best Western, Comfort Inn, Fairfield Inn, Hampton Inn 🅾 $Tree, Verizon, Walmart/Subway, W 🅐 Exxon/dsl, Kangaroo/dsl 🍴 Brian's Steaks, Burger King, Cracker Barrel, Down Home Buffet, Hardee's, KFC/Taco Bell, McDonald's, New China, Pizza Hut, Subway, Wendy's 🏠 Quality Inn 🅾 🏥 $General, AutoZone, CVS Drug, Family$, Food Lion, Home Depot, Roses
4	VA 903, to Bracey, Lake Gaston, E 🅐 BP/Subway/dsl, Exxon/Simmon's/dsl/scales/24hr/@ 🍴 Huddle House, K St. Café 🅾 Americamps Camping (5mi), W 🅐 Shell/Pizza Hut/Quizno's 🏠 Lake Gaston Inn
3mm	Lake Gaston
1mm	Welcome Center nb, full ♿ facilities, litter barrels, petwalk, 📞, 🔧 vending
0mm	Virginia/North Carolina state line

⬆N INTERSTATE 95

Exit #	Services
178mm	Virginia/Maryland state line, Potomac River, Wilson Mem Br
177c b a	US 1, to Alexandria, Ft Belvoir, E 🍴 Great American Steaks 🏠 Budget Host, Hampton Inn, Red Roof Inn, Relax Inn 🅾 Chevrolet, Chrysler/Dodge/Jeep, W 🅐 Hess, Liberty/repair
176b a	VA 241, Telegraph Rd, E 🅐 Hess/dsl, W 🏠 Courtyard, Holiday Inn, Homestead Suites 🅾 Staples
174	Eisenhower Ave Connector, to Alexandria
173	rd 613, Van Dorn St, to Franconia, E 🏠 Comfort Inn, W 1 mi 🅐 Exxon, Shell 🍴 Dunkin Donuts, Jerry's Subs, McDonald's, Quizno's, Red Lobster 🅾 Aamco, Giant Foods, NTB
170b	I-395 N, to Washington
170a	I-495 N, I-495 & I-95 N run together to MD., to Rockville
169b a	rd 644, Springfield, Franconia, E 🍴 Bertucci's, Dunkin Donuts, Houlihan's, Silver Diner, Starbucks, Subway, TGIFriday's 🏠 Best Western, Comfort Inn, Courtyard, Extended Stay America, Hampton Inn, Hilton 🅾 🏥 AT&T, Barnes&Noble, Best Buy, Dick's, Firestone/auto, Ford, Home Depot, JC Penney, Macy's, mall, Michael's, Nissan, Old Navy, Petsmart,

169b a	Continued
	Staples, Subaru, Target, W 🅐 BP, Shell, Sunoco 🍴 5 Guys Burgers, Blue Pearl Buffet, Chick-fil-A, Chipotle Mexican, Deliah's Grill, Domino's, Dunkin Donuts, Hard Times Cafe, KFC, McDonald's, Noodles&Co, Outback Steaks, Panda Express, Popeye's, Starbucks, Subway 🏠 Holiday Inn Express, Homewood Suites, Motel 6, Residence Inn, TownePlace Suites 🅾 7-11, Advance Parts, CarQuest, Chrysler/Dodge/Jeep, CVS Drug, Giant Foods, GNC, Goodyear/auto, K-Mart, Mr Tire, Radio Shack, Toyota/Scion, Trader Joe's, USPO, Verizon, vet, VW
167	VA 617, Backlick Rd (from sb), W 🅐 InterFuel/dsl
166b a	VA 7100, Newington, to Ft Belvoir, E 🅐 Pkwy Express 🍴 Wendy's 🏠 Embassy Suites 🅾 NTB, Toyota/Scion, U-Haul, W 🅐 Exxon/7-11/dsl 🍴 McDonald's 🅾 Costco
163	VA 642, Lorton, E 🅐 Shell/repair, Sunoco/dsl 🅾 auto repair, W 🅐 Shell/dsl 🍴 Antoneli's Pizza, Burger King, Gunston Wok, Kabob Factory Rest. 🏠 Comfort Inn
161	US 1 S (exits left from sb, no reentry nb), to Ft Belvoir, Mt Vernon, Woodlawn Plantation, Gunston Hall
160.5mm	Occoquan River
160b a	VA 123 N, Woodbridge, Occoquan, E 🅐 Sunoco 🍴 Taco Bell 🏠 Hampton Inn, Quality Inn 🅾 Aldi Foods, Food Lion, Mr Transmissions, W 🅐 Exxon/repair/dsl, Fast Fuels, Shell/dsl 🍴 KFC, Madigan's Waterfront Rest., McDonald's, VA Grill, Wendy's 🅾 7-11, same as 161
158b a	VA 294, Prince William Pkwy, Woodbridge, W 🅐 7-11, Exxon, Shell, Sunoco/dsl 🍴 Bonefish Grill, Boston Mkt, Bungalow Alehouse, Chick-fil-A, Chipotle Mexican, ChuckeCheese, Coldstone, Famous Dave's BBQ, Firehouse Subs, Hooters, IHOP, Macaroni Grill, McDonald's, Noodles&Co, Old Country Buffet, On-the-Border, Panda Express, Panera Bread, Qdoba, Red Lobster, Red Robin, Smokey Bones BBQ, Starbucks, Taco Bell, TGIFriday's, Wendy's 🏠 Country Inn&Suites, Courtyard, Fairfield Inn, Holiday Inn Express, Residence Inn, SpringHill Suites 🅾 $Tree, Advance Parts, Best Buy, CarMax, Dick's, GNC, JC Penney, Lowe's, Michael's, Office Depot, Petsmart, Sam's Club/gas, Shopper's Foods, Target, Verizon, Walmart/Subway
156	VA 784, Potomac Mills, E 🍴 Brixx Woodfired Grill, Firebirds Grill, PF Chang's, Potbelly, Starbucks, Travinia Italian, Uncle Julio's Grill, Zoe's Kitchen 🏠 Hilton Garden, Homewood Suites 🅾 🏥 AT&T, Old Navy, REI, to Leesylvania SP, Wegman's Mkt, W 🅐 Mobil/dsl, Shell/dsl, Sunoco/dsl 🍴 Bahama Breeze, Bob Evans, Bobby's Burger, Buffalo Wild Wings, Burger King, Char Broil Grill, Cheesecake Factory, Chili's, China King Buffet, Denny's, Domino's, DQ, Guapo's, Hard Times Cafe, Los Amigos, McDonald's, Olive Garden, Outback Steaks, Paisano's, Popeye's, Sakura Japanese, Silver Diner, Subway, Wendy's 🏠 Best Western, Wytestone Suites 🅾 Costco/gas, Family$, Firestone/auto, IKEA, Jo-Ann Fabrics, K-Mart, Marshalls, Nordstrom Rack, NTB, Potomac Mills Outlets/Famous Brands, Staples, Tuesday Morning, U-Haul, vet
154mm	🆁/weigh sta both lanes
152	VA 234, Dumfries, to Manassas, E 🅐 BP/dsl, Express, Exxon/dsl, Shell/dsl, Valero/Subway 🍴 Applebee's, China One, KFC, McDonald's, Ruby Tuesday, Taco Bell 🏠 Sleep Inn, Super 8 🅾 7-11, Food Lion, Meineke, NAPA Autocare, Walmart, Weems-Botts Museum, W 🅐 7-11, Exxon 🍴 Asian Pan, Chick-fil-A, Cracker Barrel, Five Guys, IHOP, Jerry's Subs, MontClair Rest., Panera Bread, Starbucks, Subway, Tiziano Italian, Waffle House 🏠 Comfort Inn, Days Inn, EconoLodge,

(left margin, vertical) VA

(left margin, vertical) SOUTH HILL

(left margin, vertical) DC AREA

(right margin, vertical) DUMFRIES

	INTERSTATE 95 Cont'd
Exit #	**Services**
152	Continued
	Hampton Inn, Holiday Inn 🅞 AT&T, Prince William Camping, Rite Aid, Shoppers Foods, Target, URGENT CARE
150	VA 619, Quantico, to Triangle, **E** 🍴 Dunkin Donuts, McDonald's 🛏 Ramada Inn 🅞 7-11, to Marine Corps Base, **W** Prince William Forest Park
148	to Quantico (2mi) **E** 🅖 Gulf/dsl 🍴 Subway 🛏 Courtyard 🅞 to Marine Corps Base
143b a	to US 1, VA 610, Aquia, **E** 🅖 7-11, Exxon/Circle K/dsl, Valero 🍴 Carlos O'Kelly's, El Gran Charro, KFC, McDonald's, Mick's Rest., Papa John's, Pizza Hut, Ruby Tuesday, Subway 🛏 Best Western, Fairfield Inn, Hampton Inn, Staybridge Suites, Suburban Extended Stay, Towne Place Suites 🅞 Aquia Pines Camping, Nissan, Rite Aid, Tires+, **W** 🅖 7-11, Exxon/dsl, Kangaroo, WaWa 🍴 5 Guys Burgers, Applebee's, Baskin-Robbins/Dunkin Donuts, Bob Evans, Buffalo Wild Wings, Burger King, Chick-fil-A, Chili's, China Wok, CiCi's, Firehouse Subs, Hardee's, Hibachi Buffet, IHOP, Jersey Mike's, Jimmy the Greek, Kobe Japanese, Little Caesar's, McDonald's, Moe's SW Grill, Outback Steaks, Pancho Villa, Panera Bread, Popeye's, Starbucks, Taco Bell, Umi Japanese, Wendy's 🛏 Comfort Inn, Country Inn&Suites, Quality Inn, Super 8, Wingate Inn 🅞 $General, $Tree, Aldi Foods, AutoZone, Best Buy, CVS Drug, Giant Foods, GNC, Home Depot, Kohl's, Lowe's, Merchant's Tire, Michael's, PetCo, Petsmart, Ross, Shopper's Foods, Staples, Target, TJ Maxx, Toyota/Scion, URGENT CARE, Verizon, Walmart/McDonald's
140	VA 630, Stafford, **E** 🅖 7-11, Sunoco/dsl, Valero 🍴 McDonald's 🅞 🅗 **W** 🅖 Exxon/dsl, Shell/dsl
137mm	Potomac Creek
136	rd 8900, Centreport, **E 2 mi** 🅖 Valero/dsl, **W** 🆁🆂
133b a	US 17 N, to Warrenton, **E** 🅖 Exxon/dsl 🍴 Arby's 🛏 Knights Inn, Motel 6 🅞 7-11, auto/truck repair, CarQuest, **W** 🅖 EastCoast/Subway/dsl, Shell/dsl, WaWa/dsl 🍴 Aladin Grill, Burger King, Dunkin Donuts, Hardee's, McDonald's, Pancho Villa Mexican, Panera Bread, Perkins, Ponderosa, Popeye's, Sam's Pizza&Subs, Subway, Taco Bell, Waffle House, Wendy's 🛏 Best Value Inn, Clarion, Comfort Suites, Country Inn&Suites, Days Inn, Holiday Inn Express, Quality Inn, Sleep Inn, Super 8, Super Value Inn, Wingate Inn 🅞 Advance Parts, AutoZone, Blue Beacon, Food Lion, Honda, Petsmart, Target, Verizon
132.5mm	Rappahannock River
132mm	🆁🆂 sb, full 🚻 facilities, litter barrels, petwalk, 🅲, 🖼 vending
130b a	VA 3, to Fredericksburg, **E** 🅖 BP/dsl, Gulf/dsl, Shell/dsl, Wawa 🍴 Aladin Cafe, Arby's, Bob Evans, Dixie Bones BBQ, Dunkin Donuts, Friendly's, Honeybaked Ham, KFC, Lonestar Steaks, McDonald's, Pizza King, Popeye's, Shoney's, Starbucks, Subway, Teppanyaki Buffet, Wendy's 🛏 Best Western, Quality Inn 🅞 🅗 AutoZone, Batteries+Bulbs, BigLots, Home Depot, PepBoys, Staples, Tuesday Morning, U-Haul, Verizon, **W** 🅖 Exxon/dsl, Murphy USA, Sheetz/dsl, Valero, WaWa 🍴 5 Guys Burgers, A&W/LJ Silver, Applebee's, BoneFish Grill, Bravo!, Buffalo Wild Wings, Burger King, Cancun Mexican, Carrabba's, Checker's, Cheeburger Cheeburger, Chick-fil-A, Chili's, Chipotle Mexican, ChuckeCheese, CiCi's Pizza, Cracker Barrel, Dunkin Donuts, Firebirds Grill, Firehouse Subs, Hibachi Buffet, IHOP, Jimmy John's, Joe's Crabshack, Krispy Kreme, Logan's Roadhouse, McDonald's, Melting Pot, Noodles&Co, O'Charley's, Olive Garden,

130b a	Continued
	Outback Steaks, Pancho Villa, Panda Express, Panera Bread, Park Lane Grill, Peter Chang, Potbelly, Qdoba, Quaker Steak, Red Lobster, Ruby Tuesday, Ryan's, Sam's Pizza, Santa Fe Grill, Shane's Ribshack, Smokey Bones BBQ, Starbucks, Subway, Taco Bell, TGIFriday's, Tito's Diner, TX Roadhouse 🛏 Best Western, Hampton Inn, Hilton Garden, Homewood Suites, 🅗ity House, Residence Inn, Super 8, ValuePlace Inn 🅞 $General, $Tree, AAA, Aldi Foods, AT&T, AutoZone, Barnes&Noble, Belk, Best Buy, BJ's Whse, Books A Million, Costco/gas, CVS Drug, Dick's, Food Lion, Gander Mtn, GNC, Hancock Fabrics, Hobby Lobby, JC Penney, K-Mart, Kohl's, Lowe's, Macy's, mall, Meineke, Mercedes, Merchants Tire, Michael's, NTB, Office Depot, Old Navy, Petsmart, Radio Shack, Sears/auto, Target, Verizon, vet, Volvo, Walmart, Wegman's Foods, Yankee Candle
126	US 1, US 17 S, to Fredericksburg, **E** 🅖 7-11/dsl, BP/dsl, Exxon/Circle K, Gulf/dsl, Shell/dsl, Wawa 🍴 Arby's, Denny's, DQ, Friendly's, Golden Corral, Hardee's, Hooters, McDonald's, Pizza Hut, Poncho Villa Mexican, Ruby Tuesday, Subway, Taco Bell, Vita Felice Italian, Waffle House 🛏 Best Value Inn, Country Inn&Suites, Days Inn/rest., EconoLodge, Fairfield Inn, Hampton Inn, Howard Johnson, Knights Inn, Motel 6, Royal Inn, TownePlace Suites 🅞 🅗 $General, $Tree, Advance Parts, Aldi Foods, AutoZone, BMW Cycles, Buick/GMC, Chrysler/Dodge/Jeep, CVS Drug, Family$, Fiat, Food Lion, Hyundai, Kia, Little Tires, Mazda, Midas, Nissan, Rite Aid, Subaru, Tires+, VW, **W** 🅖 7-11, 95 Fuel Stop/dsl, Exxon/Circle K, WaWa/dsl 🍴 5 Guys Burgers, Applebee's, Arby's, Asian Diner, Bob Evans, Buffalo Wild Wings, Burger King, Chick-fil-A, Chili's, China King, Chipotle Mexican, Coldstone Creamery, Cracker Barrel, Dickey's BBQ, El Charro Mexican, Famous Dave's BBQ, Firehouse Subs, Golden China, KFC, Kobe Japanese, Legends Grill, Longhorn Steaks, Mad Crab Grill, McDonald's, Mexico Rest., Mimi's Cafe, Panera Bread, Papa John's, Red Robin, Salsarita's Cantina, Sonic, Starbucks, Steak'n Shake, Subway, Taco Bell, Wendy's 🛏 Candlewood Suites, Holiday Inn Express, Sleep Inn, WyteStone Suites 🅞 AT&T, Carmax, CVS Drug, Dick's, Firestone/auto, GNC, Jo-Ann Fabrics, Kohl's, Lowe's, Marshalls, Merchant Tire/auto, Petsmart, Radio Shack, Rite Aid, Ross, Staples, Target, URGENT CARE, USPO, Verizon, vet, Walmart/Subway, World Mkt
118	VA 606, to Thornburg, **E** 🅖 Shell/dsl 🅞 Safford RV Ctr, to Stonewall Jackson Shrine, **W** 🅖 7-11, Citgo/dsl, Exxon, Shell/DQ/dsl, Valero 🍴 Angela's Italian, Burger King, Domino's, McDonald's, Subway 🛏 Holiday Inn Express, Quality Inn 🅞 $General, Family$, Food Lion, KOA (7mi), to Lake Anna SP, USPO

🅐 = gas 🍴 = food 🅗 = lodging 🅞 = other 🆁🆂 = rest stop   Copyright 2015 - the Next EXIT ®

INTERSTATE 95 Cont'd

Exit #	Services
110	VA 639, to Ladysmith, **E** 🅐 Citgo, Shell/dsl, **W** 🅐 Citgo/dsl, Exxon/dsl 🍴 Domino's, Guiseppe's Rest., Lin's Gourmet, McDonald's, Subway, Timbers Rest. 🅞 $General, Family$, Food Lion, Lady Smith Drug, Lady Smith Tire/repair, Verizon
108mm	🆁🆂 both lanes, full 🅗 facilities, litter barrels, petwalk, 🅒, 🅐 vending
104	VA 207, to US 301, Bowling Green, **E** 🅐 Exxon/dsl, ✈FLYING J/Golden Corral/dsl/Lp/scales/24hr/@, Gulf/7-11/dsl, ❤Loves/DQ/Subway/dsl/scales/24hr, Mr Fuel/dsl, Valero/dsl 🍴 Arby's, McDonald's, Wendy's 🅗 Knights Inn, Super 8 🅞 Blue Beacon, SpeedCo, to Ft AP Hill, **W** 🅐 ✈FLYING J/Denny's/dsl/scales/RV dump/24hr, Exxon/dsl 🍴 Waffle House 🅗 City Studio, Comfort Inn, Days Inn/rest., EconoLodge 🅞 CarQuest, USPO
98	VA 30, Doswell, **E** 🅐 7-11, Doswell TP/motel/dsl/scales/24hr/@, Exxon 🍴 Burger King, Denny's 🅗 Best Western, Country Inn&Suites, Days Inn, La Quinta 🅞 Camp Wilderness, King's Dominion Camping, to King's Dominion Funpark, truckwash/service
92	VA 54, Ashland, **E** 🅐 Sunoco, **W** 🅐 7-11/dsl, EC/Krispy Kreme/dsl, Exxon/Subway, Kangeroo/dsl, Shell/dsl, Sunoco/Circle K/dsl, TA/Valero/Country Pride/dsl/scales/24hr/@ 🍴 Anthony's Pizza, Applebee's, Arby's, Brickoven Rest., Burger King, Capt D's, Chick-fil-A, China Wok, Cracker Barrel, DQ, El Azteca, GNC, Hardee's, Jersey Mike's Subs, KFC/LJ Silver, McDonald's, New China Buffet, Pizza Hut, Ponderosa, Ruby Tuesday, Starbucks, Taco Bell, Tops China, Waffle House, Wendy's 🅗 Apple Garden Inn, Ashland Inn, Days Inn, EconoLodge, Hampton Inn, Holiday Inn Express, Howard Johnson, Motel 6, Sleep Inn, Super 8 🅞 $General, $Tree, Ace Hardware, Advance Parts, AutoZone, Buick/GMC, CarQuest, CVS Drug, Family$, Food Lion, Martin's Foods/dsl, O'Reilly Parts, Radio Shack, Rite Aid, Tuesday Morning, Verizon, Walmart/Subway
89	VA 802, to Lewistown Rd, **E** 🅐 Shell, TA/Pizza Hut/Popeye's/dsl/scales/24hr/@ 🅞 Americamps RV Camp, **W** 🍴 Bojangles, Dunkin Donuts, Subway, Wendy's 🅗 Country Inn Suites 🅞 Bass Pro Shops, Harley Davidson, Kosmo Village Camping, McGeorge's RV Ctr
86b a	VA 656, Elmont, to Atlee, **E** 🅐 Sheetz/dsl, Valero/dsl 🍴 Burger King, Mario's Italian, McDonald's, Pizza Hut, Subway 🅞 CVS Drug, Food Lion, tire/auto repair, vet, **W** 🅐 Wawa/dsl 🍴 Applebee's, Arby's, BBQ, Buffalo Wild Wings, Chick-fil-A, Chili's, Chipotle Mexican, CiCi's Pizza, Coldstone Creamery, Famous Dave's BBQ, Firehouse Subs, Halligan BBQ, Jade Chinese, Jersey Mike's Subs, McDonald's, O'Charley's, O'Dragon Buffet, Panera Bread, Papa John's, Pizzaro, Plaza Azteca Mexican, Red Robin, Roda Japanese, Shoney's, Sonic, Starbucks, Subway, TX Roadhouse, Wendy's 🅗 Candlewood Suites, Comfort Suites, Courtyard, Hampton Inn, SpringHill Suites 🅞 $Tree, 7-11, AT&T, Barnes&Noble, Best Buy, Burlington, Dick's, Firestone/auto, GNC, Goodyear/auto, Home Depot, JC Penney, Macy's, mall, Martin's Foods, Merchant's Tire, Michael's, Petsmart, Ross, Sears/auto, Shell/dsl, Target, Tire America, Walgreens
84b a	I-295 W, to I-64, to Norfolk
83b a	VA 73, Parham Rd, **W** 🅐 7-11, Exxon/DQ, Shell/dsl, Wawa 🍴 Aunt Sarah's, Burger King, Firehouse Subs, Frida's Cafe, Hardee's, Hawks BBQ, KFC/Taco Bell, McDonald's, Popeyes, River City Diner, Starbucks, Subway, Waffle House, Wendy's

ELMONT

Exit #	Services
83b a	Continued 🅗 Best Value Inn, Best Western, Cavalier Motel, Days Inn, EconoLodge, Knights Inn, Quality Inn, Sleep Inn 🅞 $Tree, BigLots, Food Lion, Lowe's, Verizon, Walmart
82	US 301, Chamberlayne Ave, **E** 🅐 BP/dsl, Sunoco/dsl, Valero/dsl, Wawa 🍴 KFC, McDonald's, Pizza Hut/Taco Bell, Subway 🅗 Super 8 🅞 $Tree, Family$, Food Lion, USPO, 🅐 Exxon/Circle K
81	US 1, Chamberlayne Ave (from nb), same as 82
80	Hermitage Rd, Lakeside Ave (from nb, no return), **W** 🅐 Citgo/Subway 🅞 Ginter Botanical Gardens, Goodyear/auto
79	I-64 W, to Charlottesville, I-195 S, to U of Richmond
78	Boulevard (no EZ nb return), **E** 🅐 BP 🅗 Clarion, **W** 🅞 🅗 stadium, to VA HS
76	Chamberlayne Ave, Belvidere, **E** 🅞 🅗 VA Union U
75	I-64 E, VA Beach, to Norfolk, 🔜
74c	US 33, US 250 W, to Broad St, **W** 🅞 🅗 Museum of the Confederacy, st capitol
74b	Franklin St, **E** 🅞 Richmond Nat Bfd Park
74a	I-195 N, to Powhite Expsy, downtown
73.5mm	James River
73	Maury St, to US 60, US 360, industrial area
69	VA 161, Bells Rd, **E** Port of Richmond, **W** 🅐 Exxon/dsl, Shell/dsl 🍴 McDonald's, Subway 🅗 Candlewood Suites, Hampton Inn, Holiday Inn, Red Roof Inn
67b a	VA 895 (toll E), VA 150, to Chippenham Pkwy, Falling Creek, **W** 🅐 BP/dsl, RaceWay/dsl, Shell/dsl 🍴 Burger King, Hardee's 🅞 Food Lion, U-Haul
64	VA 613, to Willis Rd, **E** 🅐 BP, Exxon/Circle K/dsl 🍴 Waffle House 🅗 Best Value Inn, EconoLodge, **W** 🅐 7-11, Citgo/dsl, Shell/dsl, Sunoco 🍴 Burger King, Maury's BBQ, McDonald's, Subway 🅗 Country Inn&Suites, La Quinta, Sleep Inn, VIP Inn 🅞 Drewry's Bluff Bfd, flea mkt
62	VA 288 N, to Chesterfield, Powhite Pkwy, to 🔜
61b a	VA 10, Chester, **E** 🅐 RaceWay/dsl 🍴 Don Pepe Mexican, Hardee's 🅗 Comfort Inn, Courtyard, Hampton Inn, Holiday Inn Express, Homewood Suites, Quality Inn 🅞 🅗 City Point NHS, Petersburg NBF, to James River Plantations, **W** 🅐 Exxon/Circle K/dsl, Gulf/dsl, Mobil/Circle K/dsl, Shell/dsl, Sunoco/dsl 🍴 Applebee's, Bojangles, Brass Monkey Grill, Buffalo Wild Wings, Burger King, Capt D's, Chili's, Chipotle, CiCi's Pizza, Cracker Barrel, Denny's, Don Papa Mexican, Friendly's, Hardee's, Hooters, IHOP, KFC, Logan's Roadhouse, McDonald's, O'Charley's, Panera Bread, Peking Chinese, Pizza Hut, Shoney's, Sonic, Starbucks, Subway, Taco Bell, The Patron Cantina, Wendy's 🅗 Country Inn&Suites, Days Inn, Fairfield Inn, InTowne Suites, Suburban Lodge, Super 8 🅞 $General, $Tree, Aamco, AT&T, Big Lots, Chevrolet, CVS Drug, Food Lion, GNC, Home Depot, K-Mart, Kohl's, Kroger/gas, Lowe's, Martin's Foods, NAPA, PetCo, Radio Shack, Rite Aid, Target, to Pocahontas SP, Verizon
58	VA 746, to Ruffinmill Rd, **E** 🅐 🍴/Wendy's/dsl/scales/24hr 🅞 Honda, Hyundai, Kia, Nissan, Toyota/Scion, VW, **W** 🅐 7-11, Exxon/Subway/dsl, Wawa/dsl 🍴 McDonald's 🅗 Candlewood Suites, Days Inn, EconoLodge 🅞 Family$
54	VA 144, Temple Ave, Hopewell, to Ft Lee, **E** 🅐 Exxon/Subway, Sheetz/dsl, Shell/Burger King, Sunoco/Circle K/dsl, Wawa/dsl 🍴 5 Guys Burgers, Applebee's, Arby's, Buffalo Wild Wings, Chick-fil-A, China Buffet, Chipotle, CiCi's Pizza, Denny's, Firehouse Subs, Golden Corral, Great China, IHOP, Jimmy John's, LoneStar Steaks, McDonald's, Olive Garden, Outback Steaks, Panera Bread, Picadilly, Pizza Hut,

RICHMOND

CHESTER

🔼N   INTERSTATE 95 Cont'd

Exit #	Services
54	Continued
	Quiznos, Red Lobster, Ruby Tuesday, Sagebrush Steaks, Sonic, Starbucks, Subway, Taco Bell, TX Roadhouse, Wendy's 🛏 Comfort Suites, Hampton Inn, Hilton Garden, Holiday Inn, ValuePlace Inn ⭕ $Tree, AAA, AT&T, Best Buy, BooksAMillion, Dick's, Home Depot, JC Penney, Jo-Ann Fabrics, K-Mart, Macy's, mall, Marshall's, Merchant's Tire, Michael's, Old Navy, Petsmart, Radio Shack, Sam's Club/gas, Sears/auto, Staples, Target, Verizon, Walmart/Subway, **W** 📷 Kangaroo/dsl 🍴 DQ, Hardee's, Hardee's, Waffle House ⭕ to VSU, U-Haul
53	S Park Blvd, **E** same as 54
52.5mm	Appomattox River
52	Washington St, Wythe St, **E** 📷 Exxon/dsl, Valero/dsl 🍴 Jade Garden 🛏 Knights Inn, Royal Inn, Super 8 ⭕ Petersburg Nat Bfd, **W** 📷 Liberty 🍴 Neptune's Rest. ⭕🏥
51	I-85 S, to South Hill, US 460 W
50d	Wythe St, (from nb), same as 52
50b c	**E** 📷 7-11 🛏 Flagship Inn
50a	US 301, US 460 E, to Crater Rd, County Dr, **E** 📷 BP, Race-Way/dsl, Star Express 🍴 Hardee's 🛏 American Inn, Budget Inn, California Inn, EconoLodge ⭕🏥
48b a	Wagner Rd, **W on Crater Rd** 📷 Gulf/dsl, Wawa 🍴 Arby's, Bojangles, Burger King, Capt D's, KFC, King's BBQ, Little Caesar's, Pizza Hut, Plaza Mexico, Subway, Taco Bell, Taste of China 🛏 Country Inn&Suites, Super 8 ⭕ $General, $Tree, Advance Parts, Martin's Foods, O'Reilly Parts, PepBoys, Radio Shack, USPO, Verizon, Walgreens, Walmart
47	VA 629, to Rives Rd, **W** 📷 Citgo, Shell/dsl 🍴 Bojangles, KFC, Outlaw's Rest. 🛏 Heritage Motel ⭕ Ace Hardware, same as 48 on US 301, Softball Hall of Fame Museum, Walmart
46	I-295 N (exits left from sb), to Washington
45	US 301, **E** 📷 Shell/dsl, **W** 📷 Exxon/Circle K 🍴 Lighthouse Rest., Nanny's Rest., Steven Kent Rest. 🛏 Comfort Inn, Days Inn, Hampton Inn, Holiday Inn Express, Howard Johnson, Quality Inn
41	US 301, VA 35, VA 156, **E** 📷 Exxon/dsl/scales/24hr 🍴 Nino's N Italian Rest. 🛏 EconoLodge ⭕ South 40 camp resort, **W** 🛏 Travelers Inn
40mm	**weigh sta both lanes**
37	US 301, Carson, **W** 📷 BP/dsl, Shell/dsl
36mm	Ⓡˢ **nb, full ♿ facilities, litter barrels, petwalk, 📞, 🖼 vending**
33	VA 602, **W** 📷 Davis/Exxon/Subway/Starbucks/dsl/scales/24hr 🍴 Burger King, Denny's, Little Italy 🛏 Hampton Inn, Sleep Inn
31	VA 40, Stony Creek, to Waverly, **W** 📷 Shell/dsl, Sunoco/dsl 🍴 Tastee Hut ⭕ Family$
24	VA 645
20	VA 631, Jarratt, **W** 📷 Exxon/Blimpie/Pizza Hut/dsl/24hr, Race-in/dsl ⭕ $General, Ford
17	US 301, **E 1 mi** 🛏 Knights Inn, Reste Motel ⭕ Jellystone Park Camping
13	VA 614, to Emporia, **E** 📷 Exxon/Chester's/dsl, Shell/dsl
12	US 301 (from nb)
11b a	US 58, Emporia, to South Hill, **E** 📷 Citgo/Burger King, Exxon/Blimpie/LJ Silver, Shell/dsl 🍴 Applebee's, Arby's, Carolina BBQ, Cracker Barrel, Domino's, Hardee's, KFC, McDonald's, Pizza Hut, Taco Bell, Wendy's, Wong's Garden 🛏 Country Inn&Suites, Fairfield Inn, Rodeway Inn ⭕🏥 Advance Parts,

Exit #	Services
11b a	Continued
	Buick/Chevrolet/GMC, CVS Drug, Family$, Food Lion, NAPA, O'Reilly Parts, Rite Aid, Verizon, Walmart, **W** 📷 Exxon, 📷/Sadler/5 Guys Burgers/dsl/scales/24hr/@, Race-In/Quiznos/dsl 🍴 Bojangles, Pino's Pizza, Shoney's 🛏 Best Western, Days Inn, Hampton Inn, Holiday Inn Express, Quality Inn, Sleep Inn
8	US 301, **E** 📷 Citgo, Simmons/Exxon/Huddle House/dsl/scales/24hr 🛏 Motel 6, Red Carpet Inn ⭕ truck repair
4	VA 629, to Skippers, **E** 📷 ❤Loves/McDonald's/dsl/scales/24hr, Wilco/Hess/Dunkin Donuts/Subway/dsl/scales/24hr, **W** 📷 Foodmart/gas 🛏 AmericanInn ⭕ camping (3mi)
3.5mm	Fountain's Creek
0.5mm	**Welcome Center nb, full ♿ facilities, litter barrels, petwalk, 📞, 🖼 vending**
0mm	Virginia/North Carolina state line

🔼E   INTERSTATE 264 (Norfolk)

Exit #	Services
23mm	**I-264 begins/ends,** 📷 BP, Shell ⭕ convention ctr
22	Birdneck Rd, **I-264 begins/ends, S** 📷 Shell/dsl 🍴 LJ Silver, Max&Erma's, McDonald's/playplace, Subway 🛏 Double Tree ⭕ Family$, Food Lion, museum
21	VA Beach Blvd, First Colonial Rd, **N** 📷 BP, Shell 🍴 5 Guys Burgers, Applebee's, Arby's, Burger King, Burton's Grill, Chick-fil-A, China Wok, DQ, IHOP, KFC, McDonald's, Moe's SW Grill, Otani Japanese, Outback Steaks, Panera Bread, Pizza Hut, Plaza Azteca, Qdoba, Schlotzsky's, Shogun Japanese, Sonic, Starbucks, Subway, Taco Bell, Virginian Steaks, Wendy's ⭕ Advance Parts, CVS, GNC, Infiniti, JoAnn Fabrics, K-Mart, Kroger/dsl, Michael's, Office Depot, Petsmart, Radio Shack, Rite Aid, SteinMart, Target, Toyota/Scion, Trader Joe's, USPO, vet, Whole Foods Mkt, **S** 📷 Shell, Wawa/dsl ⭕ 7-11, CarQuest, NAPA
20	US 58 E, to VA Beach Blvd (eb only), **N** 📷 Citgo, Kangaroo, Wawa 🍴 Bojangle's, Capt. George's Seafood, China Moon, Hardee's, Ruby Tuesday, Subway ⭕ 7-11, Family$, Food Lion, KIA/Lincoln, Lowe's, PepBoys, TJ Maxx, Tuesday Morning, vet
19	Lynnhaven Pkwy, **N** 📷 7-11, Wawa 🍴 Ensenda Mexican, Iggle's, Lucky Express, Subway ⭕ Audi, Chevrolet, FarmFresh Foods, Ford, Hyundai, Jaguar, Porsche, Subaru, URGENT CARE, VW, **S** 🍴 McDonald's
18	Rosemont, **N** 📷 Exxon 🍴 Bonefish Grill, Burger King, Denny's, Hardee's, Jade Garden, KFC, LJ Silver, McDonald's, Mi Casita Mexican, Papa John's, Starbucks, Taco Bell, Wendy's, Zero's Subs 🛏 EconoLodge ⭕ $Tree, Acura, AutoZone, BJ's Whse/gas, CarMax, Chrysler/Dodge/Jeep, Food Lion,

↑E INTERSTATE 264 (Norfolk) Cont'd

Exit #	Services
18	Continued Harris Teeter, Home Depot, Honda, Kroger, Merchant's Tire/Auto, Nissan, Petsmart, Radio Shack, Rite Aid, Sam's Club/gas, Walgreens, **S** 🅿 Hess/dsl, Wawa 🍴 4 Seasons Chinese 🅾 $General, CVS
17.5mm	inspection sta, wb only
17a b	Independence Blvd, **N** 🅿 Exxon 🍴 Cheesecake Factory, Chipotle, IHOP, Jason's Deli, Macaroni Grill, Max&Erma's, McDonald's, Panera Bread, PF Chang's, Ruby Tuesday, Smokey Bones BBQ, Starbucks, Taco Bell, Tripps Rest., Village Inn, Wendy's 🏠 Candlewood Suites, Crowne Plaza, Days Inn, Extended Stay, Hilton Garden, Motel 6, Westin 🅾 Barnes&Noble, Best Buy, Dick's, K-Mart, Kohl's, Michael's, Old Navy, Sears/auto, Steinmart, Target, Walgreens, **S** 🅿 7-11, Exxon, Wawa 🍴 Arby's, Azteca Mexican, Domino's, Firehouse Subs, Golden Corral, Hardee's, KFC, Panda China, Quiznos, Starbucks, Subway, TX Roadhouse, Zero Subs 🏠 InTown Suites 🅾 $General, auto repair, Food Lion, Mazda, Rite Aid, vet
16	Witchduck Rd
15a b	Newtown Rd, **N** 🅿 BP, Citgo 🍴 McDonald's, Shoney's, Wendy's 🏠 Homewood Suites, TownePlace Suites 🅾 AutoZone, **S** 🅿 BP, Shell 🍴 Denny's, Ruby Tuesday 🏠 Courtyard, Hampton Inn, Holiday Inn, La Quinta, Red Roof Inn, SpringHill Suites 🅾 7-11, Rite Aid
14b a	I-64, US 13, to Military Hwy
13	US 13, Military Hwy, **N** 🅿 Shell 🍴 Arby's, Boston Mkt, Lonestar Steaks, Mongolian BBQ, Norfolk Garden Korean, Piccadilly, Schlotzsky's 🏠 Days Inn, EconoLodge, Motel 6, Ramada Ltd 🅾 CVS, Firestone/auto, JC Penney, Macy's, Ross
12	Ballentine Blvd, **N** 🅾 🎓 Norfolk SU
11b a	US 460, VA 166/168, Brambleton Ave, Campostello Rd, **N** 🅿 7-11, Shell
10	Tidewater Dr, City Hall Ave, exits left from eb, 🅿 7-11, Shell
9	St Paul's Blvd, Waterside Dr, to Harbor Park Stadium
8	I-464 S, to Chesapeake
7.5mm	tunnel
7b a	VA 141, Effingham St, Crawford St, **N** 🅿 Shell 🅾 Naval 🎓 **S** 🅾 Shipyard
6.5mm	weigh sta wb
6	Des Moines Ave (from eb)
5	US 17, Frederick Blvd, **N** 🅾 🎓 **S** 🅿 BP 🅾 Harley-Davidson, Midtown Tunnel
4	VA 337, Portsmouth Blvd
3	Victory Blvd, **N** 🅿 7-11, Exxon, Shell, WaWa 🍴 Bojangles, Capt D's, Domino's, DQ, Firehouse Subs, KFC, McDonald's, Pizza Hut, Ruby Tuesday, Taco Bell, Wendy's 🅾 $Tree, Advance Parts, AutoZone, BigLots, Lowe's, PepBoys, Radio Shack, Walgreens, **S** 🅿 Valero/dsl
2b a	Greenwood Dr
0mm	I-264 begins/ends on I-64, exit 299.

↑N INTERSTATE 295 (Richmond)

Exit #	Services
53b a	I-64, W to Charlottesville, E to Richmond, to US 250, **I-295 begins/ends.**
51b a	Nuckols Rd, **N 1 mi** 🅿 Miller's/dsl, Valero 🍴 Bruster's, Casa Grande, Cheeburger, Chen's Chinese, Home Team Grill, McDonald's, Nonna's Pizzaria, Rico's Mexican, Samurai Japanese, Starbucks, Subway, Tropical Smoothie Cafe

Exit #	Services
51b a	Continued 🅾 CVS Drug, Food Lion, vet, Walgreens, **S** 🅿 Exxon/Mkt Cafe 🅾 USPO
49b a	US 33, Richmond, **S 2 mi** 🍴 Carvel's Ice Cream, Little Szechuan, Quiznos 🅾 7-11, Martin's Foods
45b a	Woodman Rd, **S 1-2 mi** 🅿 7-11, Valero 🍴 Little Caesar's 🅾 $General, CVS Drug, Meadow Farm Museum
43	I-95, US 1, N to Washington, S to Richmond (exits left from nb), **N on US 1** 🅿 Shell/dsl 🍴 Applebee's, Arby's, BBQ, Buffalo Wild Wings, Chick-fil-A, Chili's, Chipotle Mexican, Coldstone, Famous Dave's BBQ, Firehouse Subs, McDonald's, O'Charley's, O'Dragon buffet, Panera Bread, Papa John's, Pizzaro, Plaza Azteca Mexican, Red Robin, Roda Japanese, Shoney's, Starbucks, Subway, TX Roadhouse, Wendy's 🏠 Candlewood Suites, Comfort Suites, Courtyard, Hampton Inn, SpringHill Suites 🅾 $Tree, AT&T, Barnes&Noble, Best Buy, Burlington, Dick's, Firestone/auto, GNC, Goodyear/auto, Home Depot, JC Penney, Macy's, mall, Martin's Foods, Merchant's Tire, Michael's, Petsmart, Ross, Sears/auto, Target, Tire America, Walgreens, **S 1-2 mi** 🅿 7-11, Shell, WaWa 🍴 Aunt Sarah's, Burger King, Frida's Mexican, Hardee's, KFC/Taco Bell, McDonald's, Ming's Dynasty, Starbucks, Subway, Waffle House, Wendy's 🏠 Best Value Inn, Cavalier Motel, Days Inn, EconoLodge, Knights Inn, Sleep Inn 🅾 $Tree, Food Lion, Lowe's, Walmart,
41b a	US 301, VA 2, **E** 🅿 BP/dsl, Valero/dsl, WaWa/dsl 🍴 Burger King, McDonald's, Popeye's, Tropical Smoothie Cafe, Zheng's Chinese 🅾 $General, Kroger/gas, Walgreens, **W 0-4 mi** 🅿 Exxon/dsl 🍴 Friendly's 🏠 Holiday Inn, Super 8, Travelodge
38b a	VA 627, Pole Green Rd, **E 0-1 mi** 🅿 7-11, BP/Miller's Mkt/dsl, Exxon 🍴 Antonio's Pizza, Bruster's, Chen's Rest., Coffee Lane, Mimmo's Rest., Plaza Tapatia, Subway 🅾 Curves, Food Lion, vet, **W** 🅿 7-11, Valero 🅾 Padon's Hams
37b a	US 360, **E 1 mi** 🅿 BP, Shell/dsl, Valero 🍴 Applebee's, Arby's, Buffalo Wild Wings, Burger King, Chick-fil-A, China Buffet, Cracker Barrel, DQ, Gus' Italian, IHOP, KFC, McDonald's, Mexico Rest., Moe's SW Grill, Noodles&Co, Outback Steaks, Panera Bread, Papa John's, Pizza Hut, Ruby Tuesday, Shoney's, Starbucks, Taco Bell, Waffle House, Wendy's 🏠 Hampton Inn, Holiday Inn Express 🅾 $Tree, AT&T, Best Buy, BJ's Whse/gas, GNC, Home Depot, Kohl's, Marshall's, Martin's Foods, Old Navy, Petsmart, Radio Shack, Target, Verizon, Walmart, **W** 🅿 7-11, Sunoco/dsl, Valero/dsl 🅾 $General, to Mechanicsville
34b a	VA 615, Creighton Rd, **E** 🅿 7-11, Valero
31b a	VA 156, **E** 🅿 Citgo/dsl 🅾 to Cold Harbor Bfd, **W 4 mi** 🅿 Shell, Valero 🍴 Hardee's 🏠 Courtyard, EconoLodge, Holiday Inn Express, Motel 6
28	I-64, to US 60, **W** 🅾 museum
25	Rd 895 W **(toll)**, to Richmond
22b a	VA 5, Charles City, **E** 🅿 Exxon/dsl 🍴 DQ 🅾 Shirley Plantation, **W** 🅿 Valero/dsl 🍴 China Taste, Portabella's Cafe 🅾 Food Lion, Richmond Nat Bfd, Rite Aid
18mm	James River
16	Rivers Bend Blvd
15b a	VA 10, Hopewell, **E** 🅿 BP/dsl 🅾 🎓 James River Plantations, **W** 🅿 EC/Subway/dsl, Exxon/McDonald's/dsl, Sheetz, WaWa 🍴 Cesare's Ristorante, Chen's Rest., Jalapeno's, Wendy's, Wing's Pizza 🏠 Hyatt Place, Residence Inn 🅾 7-11, Curves, CVS Drug, Food Lion
13mm	Appomattox River

Vertical side labels: **MECHANICSVILLE**, **HOPEWELL**

VA

INTERSTATE 295 (Richmond) Cont'd

Exit #	Services
9b a	VA 36, Hopewell, **E** 🅖 Gulf, Petrol, WaWa 🍴 A&W, Bojangles, El Nopal Mexican, Hardee's, Hong Kong's Rest., Huddle House, KFC, Little Caesar's, LJ Silver, McDonald's, Rosa's Italian 🛏 Best Western, EconoLodge, Fairfield Inn, StayOver Suites 🅞 Advance Parts, AutoZone, Family$, O'Reilly Parts, vet, Walgreens, **W** 🅖 BP/dsl/24hr, Shell, Valero/dsl 🍴 Burger King, Denny's, DQ, Dragon Express, Dunkin Donuts, Kanpai Japanese, McDonald's, Papa John's, Pizza Hut, Ruby Tuesday, Shoney's, Subway, Taco Bell, Top's China, Waffle House, Wendy's 🛏 Baymont Inn, Candlewood Suites, Hampton Inn, Quality Inn 🅞 $General, Chevrolet, Family$, Farmer's Foods, Food Lion, Rite Aid, to Petersburg Nat Bfd, U-Haul, US Army Museum
5.5mm	Blackwater Swamp
3b a	US 460, Petersburg, to Norfolk, **E** 🅖 EC/Subway/dsl, Wilco/Hess/Wendy's/dsl/scales/24hr 🍴 Prince George BBQ, **W 1-2 mi** 🅖 BP/dsl 🍴 McDonald's
1	I-95, N to Petersburg, S to Emporium, **I-295 begins/ends.**

INTERSTATE 495 (DC)

Exit #	Services
57	I-95 S, I-395 N, I-95 N. **I-495 & I-95 N run together. See MD I-95, exits 25b a-2b a.**
54b a	VA 620, Braddock Rd, **S** 🅖 Sunoco 🍴 Hong Kong Express 🅞 7-11, Ctr for the Arts, Geo Mason U, NTB, Rite Aid, Safeway Foods, USPO
52b a	VA 236, Little River Tpk, Fairfax, **E** 🅖 Liberty/dsl, Sunoco/repair 🍴 Chicken Loco, KFC/Taco Bell, Little Caesar's, McDonald's, Wendy's 🅞 $Tree, 7-11, Advance Parts, GNC, Petco, Safeway Foods
51	VA 657, Gallows Rd, **W** 🅖 Exxon 🅞 🅷 7-11
50b a	US 50, Arlington Blvd, Fairfax, Arlington, **E** 🛏 Marriott, **W** 🅖 Shell, Sunoco/dsl 🍴 5 Guys Burgers, Chevy's Mexican, Grevey's Rest, Jasmine Garden, McDonald's, Panda Express, Panera Bread, Papa John's, Starbucks, Sweetwater Tavern, UNO Grill, Wendy's 🛏 Residence Inn 🅞 🅷 CVS Drug, Midas, Staples, Target, URGENT CARE, vet
49c b a	I-66 (exits left from both lanes), to Manassas, Front Royal
47b a	VA 7, Leesburg Pike, Tysons Corner, Falls Church, **E** 🛏 Westin, **W** 🅖 BP/dsl, Exxon, Shell/dsl 🍴 BJ's Rest., Chili's, Jimmy John's, McDonald's, Olive Garden, On-the-Border, Panera Bread, Silver Diner, Starbucks, Subway, Wendy's 🛏 Embassy Suites, Hilton Garden 🅞 AT&T, Best Buy, Bloomingdale's, Buick/Chevrolet/GMC, Chrysler/Dodge/Jeep, CVS Drug, mall, Marshall's, Mr Tire, PetCo, Petsmart, Radio Shack, Staples, Subaru/VW, TJ Maxx
46b a	VA 123, Chain Bridge Rd, **W** 🅖 Gulf/dsl, Sunoco/dsl 🍴 Cheesecake Factory, Maggiano's, PF Chang's 🛏 Courtyard, Crowne Plaza 🅞 Macy's
45b a	VA 267 W (toll), to I-66 E, to Dulles 🅞
44	VA 193, Langley
43	G Washington Mem Pkwy, no trucks
42mm	Virginia/Maryland state line.Potomac River, **Exits 41-27 are in Maryland.**
41	Clara Barton Pkwy, Carderock, Great Falls, no trucks
40	Cabin John Pkwy, Glen Echo (from sb), no trucks
39	MD 190, River Rd, Washington, Potomac
38	I-270, to Frederick
36	MD 187, Old Georgetown Rd, **S** 🅞 🅷
35	I-270 (from wb)
34	MD 355, Wisconsin Ave, Bethesda
33	MD 185, Connecticut Ave, **N** 🅞 LDS Temple, **S** 🅖 Citgo/repair, Giant/dsl, Liberty 🍴 Chevy Chase Mkt, Starbucks
31b a	MD 97, Georgia Ave, Silver Springs, **N** 🅞 🅷 **S** 🅖 BP/dsl, Exxon/dsl, Shell, **W** Express/dsl 🍴 Armand's Pizza, Domino's, Mayflower Chinese 🅞 CVS Drug, Snider's Foods, Staples, vet
30b a	US 29, Colesville, **N** 🅖 BP/dsl, Citgo, Shell 🍴 Chipotle, McDonald's, Papa John's, Red Maple Asian, Starbucks, Subway 🅞 7-11/Jerry's Subs, CVS Drug, Safeway Foods
29b a	MD 193, University Blvd
28b a	MD 650, New Hampshire Ave, **N** 🅖 BP, Exxon/dsl, Shell/repair 🍴 Domino's, Quizno's, Starbucks, Urban BBQ 🅞 7-11, CVS Drug, Radio Shack, Safeway Foods
27	I-95, N to Baltimore, S to Richmond.
	I-495 & I-95 S run together. See Virginia, exits 173-177

INTERSTATE 664 (Norfolk)

Exit #	Services
15b a	I-64 to Chesapeake, I-264 E to Portsmouth & Norfolk. **I-664 begins/ends on I-64, exit 299.**
13b a	US 13, US 58, US 460, Military Hwy, **E** 🅖 Shell/dsl 🛏 Bowers Hill Inn
12	VA 663, Dock Landing Rd
11.5mm	insp sta nb
11b a	VA 337, Portsmouth Blvd, **E** 🅖 7-11, Citgo, Exxon/dsl, Hess, Shell/dsl 🍴 5 Guys Burgers, Applebee's, Arby's, Buffet City, Burger King, Chick-fil-A, ChuckECheese, Golden Corral, IHOP, Jalapeno's, McDonald's, Olive Garden, Outback Steaks, Piccadilly, Pizza Hut, Plaza Azteca, Red Lobster, Red Robin, Rita's Custard, Subway, Taco Bell, Wendy's 🛏 Extended Stay 4 Less, Hampton Inn, Holiday Inn Express 🅞 $Tree, $Tree Mkt, AutoZone, Best Buy, BJ's Whse/gas, Buick, Firestone Auto, Food Lion, Ford, Home Depot, JC Penney, K-Mart, Macy's, Merchant's Auto Ctr, Michael's, Old Navy, Petsmart, Ross, Sam's Club/gas, Sears/auto, Target, Tuesday Morning, Walmart, **W** 🅖 7-11 🍴 Burger King, Cracker Barrel, Subway, Waffle House 🛏 Baymont Inn, Candlewood Suites 🅞 Lowe's
10	VA 659, Pughsville Rd, **E** 🅖 7-11, Shell 🅞 Food Lion, Rite Aid
9mm	James River
8mm	tunnel
9b a	US 17, US 164, **E** 🅖 7-11, Hess, Wawa 🍴 Burger King, Capt D's, Domino's, DQ, Dunkin Donuts, Great Wall Chinese, KFC, McDonald's, Pizza Hut, Sonic, Taco Bell, Waffle House, Wendy's 🛏 Best Western, Budget Lodge, Extended Stay America,

WASHINGTON DC AREA

PORTSMOUTH

VA

INTERSTATE 664 (Norfolk) Cont'd

Exit #	Services
9b a	Continued Sleep Inn, Super 8 🅾 $Tree, Advance Parts, Chevrolet, Farm-Fresh Foods, Honda, Hyundai, NAPA, Nissan, O'Reilly Parts, tires, Toyota/Scion, **W** 🍴 Buffalo Wild Wings, Subway 🏠 Comfort Suites, Hilton Garden 🅾 🅷 Harris Teeter, museum, to James River Br
8b a	VA 135, College Dr, **E** 🅰 7-11, Exxon 🍴 Applebee's, Arby's, Chick-fil-A, Firehouse Subs, McDonald's, Panera Bread, Ruby Tuesday, Subway, Wendy's 🅾 Dick's, Food Lion, GNC, Kohl's, Petsmart, Radio Shack, TJ Maxx, Walmart,

8b a	Continued **W** 🍴 Riverstone Chophouse 🏠 Courtyard, TownePlace Suites
7	Terminal Ave
6	25th St, 26th St, **E** 🅰 7-11 🍴 McDonald's
5	US 60 W, 35th St, Jefferson Ave, **E** 🅰 Fast&Easy 🍴 #1 Chinese, Church's, King's Pizza 🅾 Hornsby Tire
4	Chesnut Ave, Roanoke Ave
3	Aberdeen Rd, **W** 🅰 7-11 🍴 Hardee's, McDonald's, Wendy's
2	Powhatan Pkwy, **E** 🅰 7-11, **W 1-2 mi** 🍴 Coldstone, Joe's Crabshack, Lonestar Steaks 🏠 Hilton Garden, SpringHill Suites 🅾 Bass Pro Shop, BJ's Whse/gas, Lowe's
1b a	I-64, W to Richmond, E to Norfolk. **I-664 begins/ends on I-64.**

WASHINGTON

VA / WA

BLAINE

INTERSTATE 5

Exit #	Services
277mm	USA/Canada Border, Washington state line, customs
276	WA 548 S, Blaine, **E** 🅰 Shell/dsl, Tank'n Tote/DSL, Texaco/dsl, USA/dsl 🍴 Big Al's Diner 🏠 Northwoods Motel 🅾 Duty Free, NAPA, to Peace Arch SP, **W** 🅰 Chevron/dsl/repair 🍴 Black Forest Steaks, Chada Thai, Little Red Caboose Cafe, Ocean Bay Chines, Pasa Del Norte, Pizza Factory, Seaside Bakery Cafe, Subway, Tony's Cafe 🏠 Anchor Inn, Bay Side Motel, Cottage by the Bay B&B, International Motel, Sunset Inn 🅾 Blaine Marine Park, USPO
275	WA 543 N (from nb, no return), **E** 🅰 Chevron/dsl, Mkt/dsl, Shell/dsl 🍴 Burger King, Little Caesars, Subway 🅾 $Tree, Ace Hardware, Border Tire, CostCutter Foods, Rite Aid, vet, truck customs
274	Peace Portal Drive (from nb, no return), Blaine, **W** 🅰 Shell/dsl 🅾 camping, Semi-ah-moo Resort
270	Birch Bay, Lynden, **W** 🅰 Shell/Domino's/Subway/dsl 🍴 Bob's Burgers, Jack-in-the-Box, Subway 🏠 Semi-ah-moo Resort 🅾 Birch Bay Mkt, Thousand Trails Camping, vet
269mm	**Welcome Center sb, full** ♿ **facilities, info, litter barrels, pet-walk,** 🚻, 🅿 **vending**
267mm	🆁🆂 **nb, full** ♿ **facilities, info, litter barrels, petwalk,** 🚻, 🅿 **vending**
266	WA 548 N, Grandview Rd, Custer, **W** 🅰 Arco 🅾 Birch Bay SP
263mm	Nooksack River
263	Portal Way, **E** 🅰 Pacific Pride/dsl, Shell/dsl 🍴 El Nopal Mexican 🅾 AA RV Park, Cedars RV Park
262	Main St, Ferndale, **E** 🅰 Chevron/dsl, 🅿🅿🅿/Subway/dsl/scales/24hr 🍴 Denny's, McDonald's 🏠 Super 8 🅾 RV Park, TDS Tires, vet, **W** 🅰 Gull/dsl, Shell/dsl 🍴 Bob's Burgers, Domino's, DQ, Jack-in-the-Box, Papa Murphy's, Quiznos, Sonic, Starbucks 🏠 Scottish Lodge 🅾 $Tree, Costcutter Foods, Haggen's Foods, NAPA, O'Reilly Parts, Schwab Tire, Verizon, vet, Walgreens
260	Slater Rd, Lummi Island, **E** 🅰 Arco/dsl 🅾 antiques, El Monte RV Ctr, **W 4 mi** 🏠 Silver Reef Hotel/Casino 🅾 Lummi Ind Res
258	Bakerview Rd, **E** 🍴 5 Guys Burgers, Asian Fusion, Baskin-Robbins, Jack-in-the-Box, Papa Murphy's, Starbucks, Subway 🏠 La Quinta 🅾 Fred Meyer/dsl, Verizon, **W** 🅰 76/7-11, Arco, Mkt/dsl 🍴 Mykono's Greek Rest. 🏠 Hampton Inn, Shamrock Motel 🅾 🖨, Bellingham RV Park, st patrol
257	Northwest Ave, **E** 🏠 Home 2 Hilton, SpringHill Suites, TownePlace Suites 🅾 Cadillac/Chevrolet

BELLINGHAM

256b	Bellis Fair Mall Pkwy, **E** 🅾 JC Penney, mall, Target
256a	WA 539 N, Meridian St, **E** 🅰 Shell/dsl, Super Gas/dsl 🍴 Arby's, Asian 1, Boston's Rest., Buffalo Wild Wings, Burger King, China Palace, Chipotle Mexican, Coldstone, Denny's, DQ, Lorenzo's Mexican, McDonald's, Mi Mexico, Old Country Buffet, Olive Garden, Quiznos, Red Robin, Shari's, Starbucks, Subway, Taco Bell, Taco Time, Thai House Rest., Wendy's, Wonderful Buffet 🏠 Baymont Inn, Best Western, Comfort Inn, Holiday Inn Express, Oxford Suites, Quality Inn 🅾 $Tree, AAA, AT&T, Barnes&Noble, Best Buy, Costco/gas, Home Depot, JC Penney, Kohl's, Macy's, mall, Marshall's, Michael's, Midas, Office Depot, O'Reilly Parts, PetCo, Petsmart, Rite Aid, Ross, Schwab Tire, st patrol, Target, TJ Maxx, to Nooksack Ind Res, U-Haul, vet, Walgreens, Walmart/McDonald's, WinCo Foods, **W** 🍴 Slo Pitch Grill 🏠 EconoLodge, Rodeway Inn, 🍴 Super Buffet
255	WA 542 E, Sunset Dr, Bellingham, **E** 🅰 76, Chevron/dsl, Shell/Subway/Domino's/dsl 🍴 A&W/KFC, Applebee's, El Gitano Mexican, Hawaii BBQ, Jack-in-the-Box, Panda Express, Panda Palace, Port of Subs, RoundTable Pizza, Starbucks, Taco Bell 🅾 Jo-Ann Fabrics, K-Mart, Lowe's, Rite Aid, Safeway, to Mt Baker, Tuesday Morning, USPO, Walgreens, **W** 🅾 🅷
254	Iowa St, State St, Bellingham, **E** 🅰 76, Valero 🅾 Audi/VW, Chrysler/Dodge/Jeep, Honda, Hyundai, Kia, Mercedes, Nissan, Subaru/Buick/GMC, Toyota/Scion, VacationLand RV Ctr, Volvo, **W** 🅰 Chevron/dsl, Shell 🍴 DQ, McDonald's, Subway 🅾 AutoZone, Ford/Lincoln, Midas, NAPA, O'Reilly Parts
253	Lakeway Dr, Bellingham, **E** 🍴 Little Caesars, Papa Murphy's, Port of Subs, Rhodes Cafe, Sol de Mexico, Subway 🏠 Best Western, Guesthouse Inn 🅾 7-11, Discount Tire, Fred Meyer/dsl, Radio Shack, **W** same as 252
252	Samish Way, Bellingham, **E** same as 253, **W** 🅰 76, Chevron, SuperGas/dsl 🍴 Boomers Drive-In, Busara Thai Cuisine, Diego's Mexican, Domino's, El Agave, El Albanil Mexican, Kyoto Steaks, McDonald's, Pizza Hut, Sehome Diner, Starbucks, Subway, Taco Time, Wendy's 🏠 Aloha Motel, Bay City Motel, Bellingham Lodge, Cascade Inn, Coachman Inn, Days Inn, Motel 6, Villa Inn 🅾 $Tree, 7-11, Ace Hardware, AT&T, Haggen Foods, REI, Rite Aid, vet
250	WA 11 S, Chuckanut Dr, Bellingham, Fairhaven Hist Dist, **W** 🅰 Arco, Shell/repair 🅾 to Alaska Ferry, to Larrabee SP, True Value
246	N Lake Samish, **E** 🅾 Lake Padden RA, **W** 🅰 Shell/dsl 🅾 RV camping
242	Nulle Rd, S Lake Samish

INTERSTATE 5 Cont'd

Exit #	Services

240 Alger, **E** 📱 Shell/dsl/LP/RV dump 🍴 Alger Grille 🏠 Whispering Firs Motel/RV Parking

238mm Ⓡ both lanes, full 🏠 facilities, litter barrels, petwalk, 📱, 📷 vending

236 Bow Hill Rd, **E** Ⓞ Skagit Hotel Casino/rest./dsl/LP

235mm weigh sta sb

234mm Samish River

232 Cook Rd, Sedro-Woolley, **E** 📱 76/dsl, Shell/dsl 🍴 Bob's Burgers, Jack-in-the-Box, Starbucks, Subway 🏠 Fairfield Inn Ⓞ Ⓗ KOA (3mi)

231 WA 11 N, Chuckanut Dr **E** Ⓞ Camping World RV Ctr, Dreamchasers RV Ctr, Kia, **W** Ⓞ st patrol, to Larrabee SP (14mi)

230 WA 20, Burlington, **E** 📱 Chevron, Shell/dsl 🍴 Applebee's, Carino's Italian, Jack-in-the-Box, Mi Mexico, Outback Steaks, Papa Murphy's, Pizza Factory, Pizza Hut/Taco Bell, Popeye's, Red Robin 🏠 Cocusa Motel, Sterling Motel Ⓞ Ⓗ $Tree, 7-11, AutoZone, Fred Meyer/dsl, Haggen Foods, JC Penney, Macy's, mall, Schwab Tire, Sears/auto, Skagit Transmissions, Target, to N Cascades NP, Verizon, Walgreens, **W** 📱 Pacific Pride/dsl 🍴 McDonald's 🏠 Holiday Inn Express Ⓞ Harley-Davidson, Hyundai, to San Juan Ferry

229 George Hopper Rd, **E** 📱 Arco, USA/dsl 🍴 Chipotle Mexican, Five Guys, Jamba Juice, McDonald's, Olive Garden, Panera Bread, Sakura Japanese, Shari's, Starbucks, Subway, Taco Del Mar, Wendy's 🏠 Candlewood Suites, Hampton Inn Ⓞ Best Buy, Costco/gas, Dick's, Discount Tire, Home Depot, K-Mart/Little Caesars, Kohl's, Michael's, Old Navy, Outlet Shops/famous brands, Petsmart, Ross, See's Candies, Verizon, vet, **W** Ⓞ Chrysler/Jeep/Dodge, Ford/Lincoln, Honda, Mazda, Nissan, Subaru, Suzuki, Toyota/Scion, VW

228mm Skagit River

227 WA 538 E, College Way, Mt Vernon, **E** 🍴 A&W, Big Scoop Rest., Cocina 18 Mexican, Denny's, Dragon Inn, El Gitano, Hong Kong Rest., Jack-in-the-Box, Jersey Mike's, KFC, Max

227 Continued
Dale's Steak Chops, Moreno's Mexican, Papa Murphy's, Pizza Hut/Taco Bell, Riverside Cafe, RoundTable Pizza, Sahara Pizza, Starbucks, Subway, Taco Time 🏠 Days Inn, West Winds Motel Ⓞ $Tree, Ace Hardware, AT&T, AutoZone, Goodyear/auto, Grocery Outlet, Hobby Lobby, Jo-Ann Fabrics, Midas, Office Depot, O'Reilly Parts, PetCo, Rite Aid, Safeway/dsl, Tire Factory, **W** 📱 APP/dsl, Shell/dsl 🍴 Arby's, Burger King, Cranberry Tree Rest., DQ, Fortune Chinese, IHOP, Los Compadres, Panda Express, Royal Star Buffet 🏠 Best Western, Quality Inn, Tulip Inn Ⓞ Blade RV Ctr, Chevrolet, Lowe's, Riverbend RV Park, URGENT CARE, Walmart/Subway

226 WA 536 W, Kincaid St, **E** Ⓞ Ⓗ RV camping, **W** 🍴 Old Towne Grainery Rest., Skagit River Brewing Co Ⓞ City Ctr, NAPA, Red Apple Mkt, visitor info

225 Anderson Rd, **E** 📱 76/dsl, Fuel Express/dsl Ⓞ CarQuest, Country Motorhomes, vet, **W** 📱 Chevron, Truck City Trkstp/dsl Ⓞ Evert's RV Ctr, Freightliner, Poulsbo RV Ctr, Poulsbo RV Ctr

224 WA 99 S (from nb, no return), S Mt Vernon, **E** food, gas/dsl

221 WA 534 E, Conway, Lake McMurray, **E** 📱 76/dsl 🍴 farmers mkt, **W** 📱 76/dsl, Chevron/dsl/LP 🍴 Conway Deli 🏠 Channel Lodge/Rest. (11mi) Ⓞ Blake's RV Park/marina (6mi), USPO

218 Starbird Rd

215 300th NW, **W** 📱 Interstate/dsl

214mm weigh sta nb

212 WA 532 W, Stanwood, Bryant, **W** 📱 76/dsl, Shell/Burger Stop/dsl Ⓞ Camano Island SP (19mi)

210 236th NE, **E** Ⓞ Angel Winds Casino, River Rock/dsl

209mm Stillaguamish River

208 WA 530, Silvana, Arlington, **E** 📱 76, A1/dsl, Arco/dsl, Tesoro/dsl 🍴 Denny's, Patty's Eggnest&Turkeyhouse, Subway 🏠 Arlington Motel Ⓞ to N Cascades Hwy, **W** 📱 76/dsl

207mm Ⓡ both lanes, coffee, full 🏠 facilities, litter barrels, petwalk, 📱, 📷 RV dump, vending

📬 = gas 🍴 = food 🛏 = lodging ⊙ = other 🅿 = rest stop   Copyright 2015 - the Next EXIT ®

	INTERSTATE 5 Cont'd
Exit #	**Services**
206	WA 531, Lakewood, **E** 📬 7-11, 76/dsl, 76/dsl, Arco, Shell 🍴 Alfy's Pizza, Buzz Inn Steaks, Domino's, Jack-in-the-Box, Jersey Mike's, Jersey Mike's, Jimmy John's, Jimmy John's, KFC, Little Caesar's, Little Caesar's, McDonald's, Moose Creek BBQ, Olympia Pizza, Olympia Pizza, Panda Express, Panda Express, Papa Murphy's, Papa Murphy's, Peking Palace, Peking Palace, Starbucks, Subway, Taco Del Mar, Taco Time, Wendy's 🛏 Best Western, Best Western, Medallion Hotel, Quality Inn, Quality Inn, Smokey Point Motel ⊙ $Tree, AT&T, Chrysler/Dodge/Jeep, Ford, Ford, Harley-Davidson, Honda, Honda, Jo-Ann Fabrics, Lowe's, O'Reilly Parts, Radio Shack, Radio Shack, Rite Aid, Safeway/dsl, Schwab Tire, Smokey Point RV Park, vet, Walmart/Subway, **W** 🍴 5 Guys Burgers, Boston's, Buffalo Wild Wings, Burger King, Coldstone, Hot Iron Mongolian, IHOP, Jamba Juice, Pizza Hut, Red Robin, Starbucks, Subway, Taco Bell, Teriyaki Wok, Wonderful Buffet ⊙ AT&T, Best Buy, Costco/gas, Discount Tire, Firestone/auto, Marshall's, Michael's, Office Depot, PetCo, Target, to Wenburg SP, Verizon
202	116th NE, **E** 📬 Shell/dsl 🍴 Blazing Onion Burger, Carl's Jr, Magic Dragon Chinese, Papa John's, Starbucks, Subway, Taco Bell, Tres Hermanos Mexican ⊙ Kohl's, Petsmart, Rite Aid, Ross, Verizon, WinCo Foods, **W** 📬 Chevron/dsl, Donna's Trkstp/Gull/dsl/scales/24hr/@ 🍴 McDonald's, Olive Garden, Ram Rest. ⊙ Seattle Outlets/famous brands, st patrol, Tulalip Resort/Casino
200	88th St NE, Quil Ceda Way, **E** 📬 7-11, Shell/dsl/LP 🍴 Applebee's, Mkt St Cafe, Starbucks 🛏 Holiday Inn Express ⊙ Haggen's Foods, **W** 📬 USA 🍴 Bob's Burgers, Port of Subs, Taco Del Mar ⊙ Cabela's, casino, Home Depot, Walmart/McDonald's
199	WA 528 E, Marysville, Tulalip, **E** 📬 76, Arco, Chevron/dsl, Shell/dsl 🍴 Burger King, Don's Rest./24hr, DQ, Jack-in-the-Box, Las Margaritas Mexican, Maxwell's Rest., Subway 🛏 Village Motel/Rest. ⊙ Albertson's, Big Lots, JC Penney, O'Reilly Parts, PepBoys, Petco, Rite Aid, Staples, Verizon, Walgreens, **W** 📬 76, Chevron/dsl 🍴 Arby's, McDonald's, Taco Time, Wendy's 🛏 Comfort Inn ⊙ casino, Chevrolet, Robinson RV Ctr, Subaru, to Tulalip Indian Res
198	Port of Everett (from sb), Steamboat Slough, st patrol
195mm	Snohomish River
195	Port of Everett (from nb), Marine View Dr
194	US 2 E, Everett Ave, **W** 📬 Shell/dsl ⊙ Schwab Tire, City Ctr
193	WA 529, Pacific Ave (from nb), **W** 📬 76 🍴 Denny's, Hunan Palace 🛏 Best Western, Holiday Inn, Travelodge ⊙ 🏥 Lowe's
192	Broadway, to 41st St, **W** 📬 76/dsl, Chevron, Shell 🍴 Buzz Inn Steaks, IHOP, Little Caesars, Quiznos, Starbucks, Subway 🛏 Travelodge ⊙ City Ctr
189	WA 526 W, WA 527, Everett Mall Way, Everett, **E** 📬 Arco, Chevron, Shell/dsl 🍴 Alfy's Pizza, Burger King, Buzz Inn Steaks, Subway, Wendy's 🛏 EconoLodge, Extended Stay America ⊙ Costco/gas, vet, WinCo Foods, **W** 📬 Shell/dsl 🍴 Bob's Burgers, Famous Dave's, Jack-in-the-Box, Jimmy John's, Olive Garden 🛏 Days Inn, Extended Stay America ⊙ Best Buy, Goodyear/auto, Macy's, mall, Michaels, Petsmart, Sears/auto, TJ Maxx, Verizon, Walmart,
188mm	🅿 weigh sta sb, coffee, full 🛏 facilities, info, litter barrels, ⊙, 🅿 RV dump

186	WA 96, 128th SW, **E** 📬 76/dsl, Shell/dsl, Texaco 🍴 O'Donnells Rest. 🛏 Quality Inn ⊙ Lakeside RV Park, **W** 📬 Arco, Chevron, Shell 🍴 A&W/KFC, Acropolis Pizza, Denny's, Dickey's BBQ, DQ, McDonald's, Ming Dynasty, Papa John's, Pizza Hut, Skipper's, Starbucks, Subway, Taco Bell, Taco Time 🛏 Holiday Inn Express, La Quinta, Motel 6 ⊙ $Tree, Albertson's/Sav-on, Goodyear/auto, Maple RV Park, vet
183	164th SW, **E** 📬 Arco, Shell/dsl 🍴 Jack-in-the-Box, Panda Express, Quiznos, Starbucks, Subway, Taco Del Mar, Taco Time ⊙ Walgreens, Walmart, **W** 📬 Chevron/dsl 🍴 5 Guys Burgers, MOD Pizza, Subway ⊙ Fred Meyer/dsl, vet
182	WA 525, Alderwood Mall Blvd, to Alderwood Mall, **E** I-405 S, to Bellevue, **W** 📬 Arco 🍴 Anthony's SeafoodGrill, Azteca Mexican, Buffalo Wild Wings, Cafe Rio, Claim Jumper, Fatburger, Jersey Mike's, Keg Steaks, Macaroni Grill, Panera Bread, PF Chang's, Qdoba Mexican, Red Robin, TCBY 🛏 Homewood Suites, Residence Inn ⊙ JC Penney, Kohl's, Macy's, Nordstrom, REI, Rite Aid, Ross, Sears/auto, See's Candies, Target, vet, World Mkt
181	44th Ave W, to WA 524, Lynnwood, **E** 📬 76/dsl, Arco, Shell 🍴 Jimmy John's, Little Caesar's, McDonald's/playplace, Old Spaghetti Factory, Starbucks 🛏 Embassy Suites, Extended Stay America, Hampton Inn, Holiday Inn Express ⊙ Albertson's, Barnes&Noble, Best Buy, Jaguar, Land Rover, Lowe's, Old Navy, O'Reilly Parts, PetCo, Staples, Verizon, vet, Whole Foods Mkt, **W** 📬 76/dsl, Arco, Chevron, Shell/repair 🍴 Applebee's, Arby's, Black Angus, Buca Italian, Chipotle Mexican, ChuckeCheese, Denny's, Ezell's Chicken, IHOP, Jack-in-the-Box, KFC, McDonald's, Old Country Buffet, Olive Garden, Panda Express, Red Lobster, Rock Woodfire Pizza, Starbucks, Subway, Taco Bell, Taco del Mar, Todo Mexico, Wendy's 🛏 Best Western, Courtyard, Days Inn, La Quinta ⊙ 7-11, Fred Meyer/dsl, Goodyear/auto, Radio Shack, Schwab Tire, Tuesday Morning, URGENT CARE, USPO, vet
179	220th SW, Mountlake Terrace, Mountlake Terrace, **W** 📬 Shell/dsl 🍴 Azteca Mexican, Port of Subs, Subway ⊙ 🏥 vet
178	236th St SW (from nb), Mountlake Terrace
177	WA 104, Edmonds, **E** 📬 Chevron/dsl, Shell/dsl 🍴 Gabriel's Fire BBQ, Mazatlan Mexican, McDonald's/playplace, Pagliacchi Pizza, Starbucks, Subway, Time Out Burger, Todo Mexico 🛏 Motel 6 ⊙ Office Depot, O'Reilly Parts, RiteAid, Thriftway Foods, URGENT CARE
176	NE 175th St, Aurora Ave N, to Shoreline
175	WA 523, NE 145th, 5th Ave NE
174	NE 130th, Roosevelt Way
173	1st Ave NE, Northgate Way, **E** 📬 76 🍴 5 Guys Burgers, Azteca Mexican, BlueFin Grill, CA Pizza Kitchen, Chipotle Mexican, Domino's, Jimmy John's, Macaroni Grill, Mama Sportini's, Marie Callender's, Panera Bread, Quiznos, Ram Rest., Red Robin, Stanford's Rest., Super Buffet ⊙ Barnes&Noble, Best Buy, Discount Tire, JC Penney, Macy's, mall, Nordstrom, Old Navy, Ross, Target, Verizon, **W** 📬 76, Chevron, Shell/dsl 🍴 Arby's, McDonald's, Saffron Grill, Starbucks 🛏 Hotel Nexus ⊙ 7-11
172	N 85th, Aurora Ave
171	WA 522, Lake City Way, Bothell
170	Ravenna Blvd, **E** 📬 Shell/dsl
169	NE 45th, NE 50th, **E** 📬 76, Shell 🍴 Subway ⊙ 🏥 PetCo, U of WA, vet, **W** ⊙ to Seattle Pacific U, zoo
168b	WA 520, to Bellevue
168a	Lakeview Blvd, downtown
167	Mercer St (exits left from nb), Fairview Ave, Seattle Ctr

SEATTLE

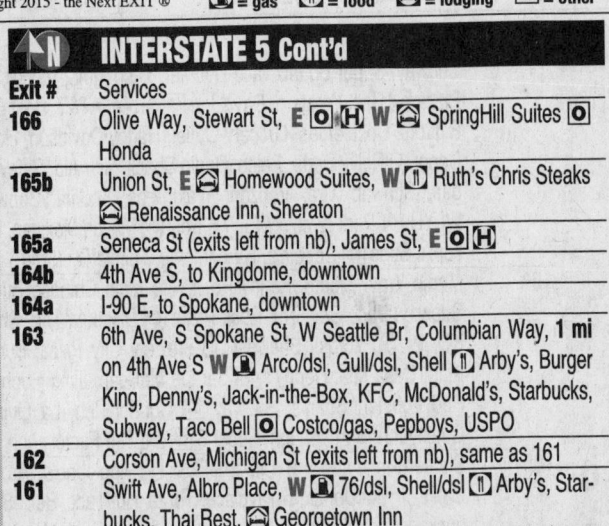

INTERSTATE 5 Cont'd	
Exit #	**Services**
166	Olive Way, Stewart St, **E** ⓞ 🛏️ **W** 🛏️ SpringHill Suites ⓞ Honda
165b	Union St, **E** 🛏️ Homewood Suites, **W** 🍽️ Ruth's Chris Steaks 🛏️ Renaissance Inn, Sheraton
165a	Seneca St (exits left from nb), James St, **E** ⓞ 🛏️
164b	4th Ave S, to Kingdome, downtown
164a	I-90 E, to Spokane, downtown
163	6th Ave, S Spokane St, W Seattle Br, Columbian Way, **1 mi** on 4th Ave S **W** 🛢️ Arco/dsl, Gull/dsl, Shell 🍽️ Arby's, Burger King, Denny's, Jack-in-the-Box, KFC, McDonald's, Starbucks, Subway, Taco Bell ⓞ Costco/gas, Pepboys, USPO
162	Corson Ave, Michigan St (exits left from nb), same as 161
161	Swift Ave, Albro Place, **W** 🛢️ 76/dsl, Shell/dsl 🍽️ Arby's, Starbucks, Thai Rest. 🛏️ Georgetown Inn
158	Pacific Hwy S, E Marginal Way, **W** 🛢️ Chevron/dsl ⓞ NAPA
157	ML King Way
156	WA 539 N, Interurban Ave (no EZ return to sb), Tukwila, **E** 🛢️ Pacific Pride/dsl 🍽️ Billy Baroos Rest., **W** 🛢️ 76/dsl, Shell/dsl 🍽️ Jack-in-the-Box, Quiznos, Starbucks, Sunny Teriyaki 🛏️ Days Inn
154b	WA 518, Burien, **W** 🛏️ Extended Stay America
154a	I-405, N to Bellevue
153	S Center Pkwy, (from nb), **E** 🛢️ Chevron/dsl 🍽️ Applebee's, Azteca Mexican, Bahama Breeze, BJ's Rest., Buffalo Wild Wings, Burger King, CA Pizza Kitchen, Cheesecake Factory, Chipotle Mexican, ClaimJumper, Coldstone, Duke's Chowder-House, Famous Dave's, Five Guys, Grazie Ristorante, IHOP, Jamba Juice, Mayflower of China, McDonald's, Mizuki Buffet, Mizuki Japanese Steaks, Mongolian Grill, Old Spaghetti Factory, Olive Garden, Outback Steaks, Panda Express, Panera Bread, Qdoba Mexican, Red Robin, Simply Thai, Sizzler, Stanford's Rest., Starbucks, Subway, Thai Cuisine, Zoopa 🛏️ DoubleTree Inn ⓞ $Tree, Acura, AT&T, Barnes&Noble, Best Buy, Big Lots, Firestone/auto, JC Penney, Jo-Ann Fabrics, Kohl's, Macy's, mall, Michael's, Nordstrom, Nordstrom Rack, Office Depot, Old Navy, PetCo, Petsmart, REI, Ross, Sears/auto, See's Candies, Target, Tuesday Morning, Verizon, World Mkt
152	S 188th, Orillia Rd, **W** 🛢️ 76/dsl 🍽️ Dave's Diner, Denny's, Jack-in-the-Box, Taco Bell 🛏️ DoubleTree Hotel, Hampton Inn, La Quinta, Motel 6 ⓞ city park, to 🛩️
151	S 200th, Military Rd, **E** 🛢️ 76/Subway/dsl 🛏️ Motel 6, **W** 🛢️ 7-11, 76, Chevron 🍽️ IHOP 🛏️ Best Value Inn, Best Western, Comfort Inn, Days Inn, Fairfield Inn, Hampton Inn, Holiday Inn Express, Sleep Inn, Super 8 ⓞ AutoZone, city park, NAPA, O'Reilly Parts, U-Haul
149	WA 516, to Kent, Des Moines, **E** 🛏️ Century Motel ⓞ Poulsbo RV Ctr, **W** 🛢️ Arco, Chevron/dsl, Shell/dsl 🍽️ Baskin Robbins, Burger King, Church's, Los Cabos Mexican, McDonald's, Starbucks, Subway 🛏️ Garden Suites, Kings Arms Motel ⓞ $Tree, Lowe's, Meineke, Radio Shack, to Saltwater SP, Walgreens
147	S 272nd, **E** 🛢️ 76/Circle K/dsl, **W on Pacific Hwy** 🛢️ Arco, Shell/dsl 🍽️ Jack-in-the-Box, Little Caesar's, McDonald's, Papa Murphy's, Quiznos, Starbucks, Subway, Taco Bell ⓞ Ace Hardware, AutoZone, Bartell Drug, Safeway
143	S 320th, Federal Way, **W** 🛢️ 76/dsl, Arco, Shell/dsl 🍽️ Applebee's, Azteca Mexican, Black Angus, Black Bear Diner, Buffalo Wild Wings, Chipotle Mexican, Church's, Coldstone, Costa Vida, Denny's, Domino's, Grand Buffet, Grand Peking,
143	Continued Ivar's Seafood, Jasmine Mongolian, Jimmy John's, McDonald's, McGrath's Fishouse, Mika Japanese Buffet, Old Country Buffet, Outback Steaks, Panda Express, Panera Bread, Papa Murphy's, Qdoba Mexican, Ram Rest., Red Lobster, Red Robin, Starbucks, Subway, Taco Time, Tokyo Japanese Steaks, Village Inn, Wendy's 🛏️ Best Western, Clarion, Comfort Inn, Courtyard, Extended Stay America, Hampton Inn ⓞ Albertson's, AT&T, Barnes&Noble, Best Buy, Dick's, Jo-Ann Fabrics, Kohl's, Macy's, mall, Marlene's Natural Mkt, Michael's, O'Reilly Parts, PetCo, Petsmart, Radio Shack, Rite Aid, Ross, Safeway/dsl, Sears/auto, See's Candies, Target, TJ Maxx, to Dash Point SP, Trader Joe's, Tuesday Morning, Verizon, Walmart/McDonald's
142b a	WA 18 E, S 348th, Enchanted Pkwy, **E** ⓞ funpark, **W** 🛢️ Chevron, Shell/dsl 🍽️ Arby's, Biscuits Cafe, Burger King, Del Taco, Denny's, Fatburger, Jack-in-the-Box, Jamba Juice, Jimmy Mac's Roadhouse, KFC, LJ Silver, McDonald's, Olive Garden, Panda Express, Popeye's, Puerta Vallarta, Quiznos, RoundTable Pizza, Shari's, Starbucks, Subway, Taco Bell, Taco Del Mar, Taco Time, Thai Bistro, The Rock Pizza, Time Out Grill 🛏️ Day's Inn, Quality Inn, Red Lion Inn ⓞ 🛏️ Chevrolet, Costco/gas, Discount Tire, Hobby Lobby, Home Depot, Lowe's, Office Depot, O'Reilly Parts, Pepboys, Schwab Tire, UHaul, Verizon, Walmart/Subway
140mm	🅿️ both lanes, coffee, full ♿ facilities, litter barrels, nb, pet-walk, 🚻, RV dump, weigh sta
137	WA 99, Fife, Milton, **E** 🛢️ Chevron/dsl, Shell, Tahoma Express/dsl 🍽️ DQ, Johnny's Rest., Warthog BBQ 🛏️ Motel 6 ⓞ Acura, Cadillac, Evert's RV Ctr, visitor info, **W** 🛢️ 76/dsl, Shell/dsl 🍽️ A&W/KFC, Arby's, Denny's, Fife Thai Rest., McDonald's, Mitzel's Kitchen, Pick Quick Burgers, Pizza Hut, Pizza Hut/Taco Bell, Poodle Dog, Quiznos, Sapporo Japanese, Starbucks, Subway, Taco Time, Wendy's 🛏️ Days Inn, EQC Motel/casino, Quality Inn ⓞ 7-11, Audi/Porsche, Infiniti, Mercedes, O'Reilly Parts, Schwab Tire, Sumner RV Ctr, Sunset RV Ctr, Tacoma RV Ctr, Verizon
136b a	Port of Tacoma, **E** 🛢️ CFN/dsl ⓞ Baydos RV Ctr, BMW, Costco, Honda, I-5 Motors, Mini, Peterbilt, Tacoma RV Ctr, **W** 🛢️ Chevron/dsl, Gull/dsl, Loves/Chester's/Subway/dsl/scales/LP/RV dump/24hr, Shell/dsl 🍽️ Jack-in-the-Box 🛏️ Best Night Inn, EconoLodge, Extended Stay America, Rodeway Inn, Sunshine Motel, Travelodge ⓞ Fife RV Ctr, Goodyear/biodsl, Harley-Davidson, Land Rover/Jaguar/Lexus, Meineke, NAPA, Nissan, Poulsbo RV Ctr, truck repair, Volvo
135	Bay St, Puyallup, **E** 🛢️ Shell/Tahoma Express ⓞ Majestic RV Park (4mi), **W** 🛢️ Chevron/dsl/scales 🍽️ Subway 🛏️ La Quinta ⓞ to Tacoma Dome

S E A T T L E

T A C O M A

INTERSTATE 5 Cont'd	
Exit #	**Services**
134	Portland Ave (from nb), same as 135
133	WA 7, I-705, **W** 🛏 Best Western, Courtyard, Holiday Inn Express 🅞 museum, Tacoma Dome, City Ctr
132	WA 16 W, S 38th, Gig Harbor, to Bremerton, **W** 🍴 Adriatic Grill, BJ's Rest., Buffalo Wild Wings, Chipotle, Five Guys, Jamba Juice, Jimmy John's, Krispy Kreme, Panera Bread, Red Robin, Wendy's 🅞 $Tree, Best Buy, Costco/gas, Firestone/auto, Ford/Toyota, Goodyear/auto, JC Penney, JoAnn Fabrics, Macy's, mall, Nordstrom, Old Navy, PetCo, REI, Sears/auto, to Pt Defiance Pk/Zoo, Verizon, World Mkt
130	S 56th, Tacoma Mall Blvd, **W** 🅖 Shell/dsl 🍴 Axteca Mexican, ChuckeCheese, Jack-in-the-Box, Subway, Wingers 🛏 Extended Stay America
129	S 72nd, S 84th, **E** 🅖 Chevron, Valero 🍴 Applebee's, Burger King, DQ, Elmer's, Famous Dave's, IHOP, Jack-in-the-Box, Mongolian Grill, Olive Garden, Popeyes, Red Lobster, RoundTable Pizza, Shari's, Starbucks, Subway 🛏 Motel 6, Shilo Inn 🅞 Bass Pro Shops, WinCo Foods, **W** 🍴 Hooters 🛏 Days Inn 🅞 Home Depot, to Steilacoom Lake
128	S 84th St (from nb)same as 129, **E** 🅖 76, Shell/dsl 🍴 Denny's, Ginger Palace, Greatwall Chinese, Subway 🛏 American Lodge, Comfort Inn, Crossland Suites, Econolodge, Hampton Inn, Holiday Inn Express, Howard Johnson, Red Lion Hotel, Rothem Inn, **W** 🅖 Shell/dsl 🅞 Discount Tire
127	WA 512, S Tacoma Way, Puyallup, Mt Ranier, **W** 🅖 7-11, 76/7-11, Arco/dsl, Eagle 🍴 AAA Buffet, DQ, Ivar's Seafood, Mazatlan Mexican, McDonald's, Sizzler, Starbucks, Subway, Taco Guaynas, Taco Time, Wendy's 🛏 Candlewood Suites, Western Inn 🅞 Grocery Outlet, O'Reilly Parts
125	to McChord AFB, Lakewood, **W** 🅖 76/Circle K/dsl, Chevron, Shell 🍴 A&W/KFC, Carr's Rest., Church's, Denny's, Greek Cafe, Pizza Hut, Subway, Wendy's 🛏 Holiday Inn Express, Home Motel 🅞 🅗 7-11, Aamco, Ford, NAPA, O'Reilly Parts, tires/repair, U-Haul
124	Gravelly Lake Dr, **W** 🅖 76/Circle K, Arco/repair 🍴 El Toro Mexican, Pizza Casa, Red Robin (2mi), same as 125
123	Thorne Lane, Tillicum Lane
122	Berkeley St, Camp Murray, **W** 🅖 Chevron/repair 🍴 Gertie's Grill, Jack-in-the-Box, KFC, McDonald's, Papa John's, Pizza Hut, Popeyes, Subway, Taco Bell, Teryaki House, Wok In Wok Out 🅞 7-11, AutoZone
120	Ft Lewis, **E** 🅞 Ft Lewis Military Museum
119	Du Pont Rd, Steilacoom, **E** to Ft Lewis, **W** 🅖 76 🍴 Happy Teriyaki, Starbucks, Subway 🛏 Hampton Inn
118	Center Dr, **W** 🅖 Chevron/dsl 🍴 Domino's, Farrelli's Pizza, Fortune Cookie Chinese, Jack-in-the-Box, Koko's Wok, McDonald's, McNamara's Eatery, Quiznos, Starbucks, Subway, Super Buffet, Viva Mexico 🛏 GuestHouse Inn, Liberty Inn
117mm	**weigh sta nb**
116	Mounts Rd, Old Nisqually, **E** golf, **W** 🍴 Caddy Shack Grill
115mm	**Nisqually River**
114	Nisqually, **E** 🅖 Arco/dsl, Chevron/repair/Lp 🍴 Nisqually Grill, Norma's Burgers 🅞 Nisqually Auto Repair, Nisqually RV Park, River Bend RV Park (3mi), WLYH RV Park (2mi)
111	WA 510 E, Marvin Rd, to Yelm, **E** 🅖 76/Circle K, Chevron/dsl, Shell/dsl 🍴 Burger King, Coldstone, Hawk's Prairie Rest./casino, Jack-in-the-Box, Jamba Juice, KFC/LJ Silver, Lemon Grass Rest., Little Caesar's, McDonald's, Panda Express, Panera Bread, Papa Murphy's, Popeyes, Puerto Vallarta, RAM Rest., Red Robin, RoundTable Pizza, Starbucks,

111	Continued
	Subway, Super Buffet, Taco Del Mar, Taco Time, Vinny's NY Pizza 🛏 Best Western, Day's Inn 🅞 $Tree, AT&T, Best Buy, BigLots, Costco/gas, Grocery Outlet, Harley Davidson, Home Depot, O'Reilly Parts, Petco, Radio Shack, Rite Aid, Safeway/gas, Schwab Tire, Verizon, Walgreens, Walmart/Subway, WLYH RV Park (2mi), **W** 🅖 7-11/dsl 🍴 Mayan Mexican, Meconi's Subs 🅞 Cabela's, RV camping, Tolmie SP (5mi)
109	Martin Way, Sleator-Kenny Rd, **E** 🍴 Main Chinese Buffet, Subway, Taco Bell, The Rock Pizza 🅞 Discount Tire, Shop-KO, **W** 🅖 76/dsl, Shell/dsl 🍴 Brewery City Pizza, Burger King, Casa Mia, Denny's, El Serape Mexican, Jimmy John's, Red Lobster, Shari's, Subway 🛏 Comfort Inn, La Quinta, Quality Inn, Ramada Inn, Super 8 🅞 🅗 Tire Factory
108	Sleater-Kinney Rd, **E** 🅖 Shell/dsl 🍴 Applebee's, Arby's, Carl's Jr, McDonald's/playplace, Pizza Hut/Taco Bell, Starbucks, Wendy's 🅞 $Tree, Firestone/auto, Fred Meyer/dsl, GNC, Kohl's, Marshall's, Michael's, Office Depot, Petsmart, Radio Shack, Rite Aid, Sears/auto, Target, Tuesday Morning, Verizon, **W** 🅖 Arco/dsl, Shell 🍴 Casa Mia, Dirty Dave's, El Sarape Mexican, Jack-in-the-Box, Panda Express, Starbucks, Subway 🛏 Ramada Inn 🅞 🅗 AT&T, Lowe's, Safeway/gas, same as 109, Tire Factory
107	Pacific Ave, **E** 🅖 Shell/dsl/E-85 🍴 DQ, Fajita a Grill, Izzy's Pizza, Jimmy's Thai/Chinese, Shari's, Subway, Taco Time 🅞 🅗 Albertson's, Home Depot, Ross, vet, **W** 🅞 Coumbs RV Ctr, Ford
105	St Capitol, **W** 🅖 76/Subway/dsl, Chevron/dsl 🛏 Quality Inn 🅞 to St Capitol
104	US 101 N, W Olympia, to Aberdeen, **W** 🅖 7-11, Chevron/dsl, Shell/Oly Burger/dsl 🍴 Jack-in-the-Box 🛏 Extended Stay America, Red Lion Hotel 🅞 Buick/GMC, Chevrolet/Cadillac, Ford, Honda, Hyundai, Kia, Lincoln/Mazda, Nissan, Subaru, to Capitol Mall, Toyota/Scion, VW
103	2nd Ave, Deschutes Ave, to hist dist
102	Trosper Rd, Black Lake, **E** 🅖 Shell 🍴 Brewery City Pizza, Burger King, DQ, El Sarape Mexican, Happy Teriyaki, Jack-in-the-Box, KFC, McDonald's, Plaza Jalisco Mexican, Starbucks, Subway, Taco Bell, Taco Time 🛏 Best Western, Tumwater Inn 🅞 Ace Hardware, Goodyear/auto, O'Reilly Parts, Schwab Tire, Verizon, **W** 🅖 Chevron, Mobil 🍴 Best Buffet, Nickelby's Rest., Panda Express, Papa Murphy's, Pizza Hut, Starbucks, Subway, Taco Del Mar, The Brick Rest. 🅞 Albertson's, Alderbrook RV Park, AutoZone, Costco/gas, Fred Meyer/dsl, GNC, Home Depot, Radio Shack, Tumwater Auto Repair, Walgreens, Walmart,
101	Tumwater Blvd, **E** 🅖 Chevron, Shell/dsl 🍴 DQ (1mi), Inferno's Pizza, Meconi's Pizza, Red Wagon Burgers 🛏 Comfort Inn, GuestHouse Inn, Olympia Camping 🅞 7-11, USPO
99	WA 121 S, 93rd Ave, Scott Lake, **E** 🍴 McDonald's/Subway/dsl/scales/24hr 🅞 Ace Hardware, American Heritage Camping, Olympia Camping
95	WA 121, Littlerock, **E 3 mi** 🅞 Millersylvania SP, RV camping, **W** 🅖 Chevron/dsl (3mi) 🍴 Farmboy Drive-In 🅞 Freightliner
93.5mm	🅁🅂 **sb, coffee, full 🛁 facilities, info, litter barrels, petwalk, 🆑, 🅿 vending**
91mm	🅁🅂 **nb, coffee, full 🛁 facilities, info, litter barrels, petwalk, 🆑, 🅿 vending**
88	US 12, Rochester, **E** 🅖 Blair's I-5 RV Ctr, I-5 Truckwash, **W** 🅖 Arco, CFN/dsl, Chevron/dsl, Shell 🍴 Burger Claim, DQ, Figaro's Pizza, Jack-in-the-Box, Mariachi Mexican, McDonald's, Quiznos, Starbucks 🛏 Great Wolf Lodge 🅞 auto repair, Outback RV Park (2mi)

WA

O L Y M P I A

Exit #	Services

⬆N INTERSTATE 5 Cont'd

82mm Skookumchuck River

82 Harrison Ave, Factory Outlet Way, Centralia, **E** 🅖 Arco 🍴 Burger King, Burgerville, Casa Ramos Mexican, Centralia Deli, DQ, Panda Chinese, Papa Pete's Pizza, Peking House Chinese, Pizza Hut, Quiznos, Thai Dish, Wendy's 🛏 Centralia Inn, King Oscar Motel, Quality Inn, Travelodge 🅞 AutoZone, VF/famous brands, **W** 🅖 Chevron/dsl, Shell/dsl, Texaco 🍴 Arby's, Bill&Bea's, Country Cousin Rest., Denny's, Domino's, Jack-in-the-Box, McDonald's, Papa Murphy's, Starbucks, Subway, Taco Bell 🛏 Motel 6 🅞 AT&T, Centralia Outlets/ famous brands, Midway RV Park, O'Reilly Parts, Rite Aid, Safeway/dsl, Schwab Tire, Verizon, 🅞 city park

81 WA 507, Mellen St, **E** 🅖 Chevron/dsl, Shell/dsl 🍴 Subway 🛏 Empress Inn, Lakeview Inn, Pepper Tree Motel/RV Park/ dump, **W** 🅞 🏥

79 Chamber Way, **E** 🅖 Shell/dsl 🍴 Jalisco Mexican 🅞 Good-year/auto, museum, vet, visitor info, **W** 🅖 Texaco/dsl/LP/e85 🍴 Applebee's, McDonald's, Starbucks, Subway, Taco Del Mar, Wendy's 🅞 $Tree, GNC, Grocery Outlet, Home Depot, K-Mart/Little Caesar's, Michael's, O'Reilly Parts, Radio Shack, st patrol, Toyota/Scion, Verizon, Walgreens, Walmart/McDonald's

77 WA 6 W, Chehalis, **E** 🅖 76/dsl, Cenex/dsl/LP 🍴 Dairy Bar, Jeremy's Cafe 🛏 Holiday Inn Express 🅞 NAPA, Schwab Tire, USPO, **W** 🅞 Rainbow Falls SP (16mi), truck parts, veterans museum

76 13th St, **E** 🅖 Arco, Chevron/dsl 🍴 Denny's, Jack-in-the-Box, Kit Carson Rest., South Pacific Bistro, Subway 🛏 Best Western, Econolodge, Relax Inn 🅞 Baydo's RV Ctr, Ford, Uhlmann's I-5 RV Ctr/RV dump, **W** 🅞 RV park/dump

74 Labree Rd, **W** 🅞 Emerald RV Ctr

72mm Newaukum River

72 Rush Rd, Napavine, **E** 🅖 Shell/dsl/scales 🍴 Burger King, Mc-Donald's, RibEye Rest., Subway 🅞 Country Canopy RV Ctr/ repair, RV park, **W** 🅖 Loves/Carl's Jr/dsl/scales/24hr, Shell/dsl 🍴 Starbucks

71 WA 508 E, Onalaska, Napavine, **E** 🅖 76/dsl 🅞 KC Truck Parts

68 US 12 E, Morton, **E** 🅖 Arco/dsl, Texaco/dsl 🍴 Spiffy's Rest. 🅞 Gateway RV Ctr, Mt Ranier NP, RV Park, to Lewis&Clark SP, **W** 🅖 76/rest./dsl

63 WA 505, Winlock, **W** 🅖 Shell/Chesters/dsl/LP

60 Toledo Vader Rd, Toledo

59mm Cowlitz River

59 WA 506 W, Vader, **E** 🅖 Shell/dsl 🍴 Beesley's Cafe 🅞 RV Park, **W** 🅖 Chevron/Subway/dsl 🍴 Country House Rest.

57 Jackson Hwy, Barnes Dr, **E** 🅞 R&R Tires, **W** 🅖 Texaco/ GeeCee's/café/dsl/scales/24hr/@ 🅞 repair, RV camping

55mm 🆁🆂 both lanes, full ♿ facilities, litter barrels, petwalk, 🐕, 🖼 vending

52 Barnes Dr, Toutle Park Rd, **E** 🅞 Paradise Cove RV Park/ general store, **W** 🅞 Toutle River RV Resort

50mm Toutle River

49 WA 504 E, Castle Rock, **E** 🅖 Chevron/dsl/LP, Shell/dsl 🍴 49er Diner, Burger King, C&L Burgers, El Compadre Mexican, Papa Pete's Pizza, Parker's Rest., Subway 🛏 7 West Motel, Mt St Helens Motel, Timberland Inn 🅞 Seaquest SP (5mi), **W** 🍴 McDonald's

48 Castle Rock, **E** 🅞 Cedars RV Park/dump, **W** 🅞 city park

46 Pleasant Hill Rd, Headquarters Rd, **E** 🅞 Cedars RV Park/ dump

44mm weigh sta sb, 🅞

42 Bridge Dr, Lexington, **W** 🅖 Chevron/dsl 🍴 Subway 🅞 auto repair

40 to WA 4, Kelso-Longview, **W** 🅖 Texaco 🛏 Econolodge

39 WA 4, Kelso, to Longview, **E** 🅖 Arco, Shell 🍴 Denny's, Jack-in-the-Box, McDonald's, Shari's, Starbucks, Subway, Taco Time 🛏 Motel 6, Red Lion Hotel, Super 8 🅞 Brook Hollow RV Park, city park, Rite Aid, Verizon, **W** 🍴 Burger King, DQ, Fiesta Bonita Mexican, Izzy's Pizza, Red Lobster, Taco Bell 🛏 Comfort Inn, GuestHouse Inn 🅞 JC Penney, Macys, mall, museum, Safeway/dsl, Target

36 WA 432 W, to WA 4, to US 30, Kelso, **E** 🅞 U-Neek RV Ctr, **W** 🅞 RV Camping, Toyota/Scion

32 Kalama River Rd, **E** 🍴 Fireside Café 🅞 Camp Kalama RV Park/camping/gifts

31mm Kalama River

30 Kalama, **E** 🅖 Chevron/dsl 🍴 Burger Bar, Columbia Rest., Lucky Dragon Chinese, Playa Azul Mexican, Poker Pete's Pizza, Subway 🛏 Kalama River Inn 🅞 antiques, Godfrey's Drug, USPO, **W** 🅖 Spirit/dsl 🅞 RV camping

27 Todd Rd, Port of Kalama, **E** 🅖 Rebel/Shell/café/dsl/24hr

22 Dike Access Rd, **W** 🅞 Columbia Riverfront RV Park, O'Reilly Parts, Schwab Tire, Walmart/Subway

21 WA 503 E, Woodland, **E** 🅖 Arco/dsl, Chevron, Pacific Pride/ dsl, Shell/LP/dsl 🍴 America's Diner, Burgerville, Casa Tapatia, DQ, Fat Moose Grill, Guilliano's Pizza, Mali Thai, OakTree Rest., Rosie's Rest. 🛏 Lewis River Inn, Motel 6, Quality Inn 🅞 Ace Hardware, Hi-School Drug, Woodland Shores RV Park, **W** 🅖 Astro, Shell/dsl 🍴 Antony's Pizzaria, Guadalajara Mexican, Los Pepes Mexican, McDonald's, Papa Murphy's, Starbucks, Subway 🛏 Hansen's Motel 🅞 $Tree, NAPA, Oil Can Henry's, repair/tires, Safeway/dsl, Verizon

20mm N Fork Lewis River

18mm E Fork Lewis River

16 NW La Center Rd, La Center, **E** 🅖 Shell/dsl 🍴 Twin Dragons Rest. (2mi) 🅞 Paradise Point SP, Tri-Mountain Golf/rest.

15mm weigh sta nb

14 WA 501 S, Pioneer St, Ridgefield, **E** 🅖 Arco 🍴 Country Café, Papa Pete's Pizza, Subway, Teriyaki Thai 🅞 Big Fir RV Park (4mi), Ridgefield WR, to Battleground Lake SP (14mi), Tri-Mountain RV Park, vet, **W** 🅖 Chevron/dsl

13mm 🆁🆂 sb, full ♿ facilities, info, litter barrels, petwalk, 🐕, 🖼, RV dump, vending

11 WA 502, Battleground, 🆁🆂 nb, full ♿ facilities, info, litter barrels, petwalk, 🐕, 🖼, RV dump, vending

9 NE 179th St, **E** 🍴 Jollie's Rest., **W** 🅖 Chevron/dsl 🅞 RV Park

🅖 = gas   🍴 = food   🏠 = lodging   🅞 = other   ♿ = rest stop   Copyright 2015 - the Next EXIT ®

⬆N   INTERSTATE 5 Cont'd

Exit #	Services
87	I-205 S (from sb), to I-84, WA 14, NE 134th St, **E** 🅖 7-11, Arco, Mobil 🍴 Applebee's, Billygan's Roadhouse, Burger King, Burgerville, Jack-in-the-Box, McDonald's, Muchas Gracias, Panda Express, Round Table Pizza, Starbucks, Subway, Taco Bell 🏠 Holiday Inn Express, Shilo Inn, Vancouver Inn 🅞 🏥 99 RV Park, Albertson's, Safeway/dsl, Verizon, Walgreens, **W** 🅖 Shell 🍴 Baskin-Robbins, Bruchi's, El Tapatio, Garlic Jim's Pizza, Papa Murphy's, PizzaSchmitzza, Planet Thai, Starbucks, Subway 🏠 La Quinta 🅞 AT&T, Fred Meyer, URGENT CARE
5	NE 99th St, **E** 🍴 Burgerville, Carl's Jr, Del Taco, Domino's, Fat Dave's Rest., Popeyes, Quiznos 🅞 7-11, AutoZone, Harley-Davidson, Walgreens, Walmart/Subway, Winco Foods/gas, **W** 🅖 Arco/dsl, Chevron/dsl 🍴 Applebee's, Bortolami's Pizza, McDonald's, Subway, Taco Del Mar 🅞 $Tree, Grocery Outlet, Kohl's, Office Depot, PetCo, Target, Verizon
4	NE 78th St, Hazel Dell, **E** 🅖 7-11, 76 🍴 Baja Fresh, Baskin Robbins, Burger King, Canton Chinese, Don Pedro Mexican, Dragon Buffet, Izzy's Grill, KFC, McDonald's, Muchas Gracias Mexican, PeachTree Rest., Pizza Hut, Skipper's, Starbucks, Subway, Taco Bell 🏠 Quality Inn 🅞 Aamco, AT&T, CarQuest, CostLess Parts, Firestone, Fred Meyer, Jo-Ann, O'Reilly Parts, Radio Shack, Tire Factory, U-Haul, **W** 🅖 Shell/dsl/LP 🍴 Buffalo Wild Wings, Chipotle Mexican, Five Guys, Jack-in-the-Box, Jazzy John's BBQ, Jimmy John's, Little Caesar's, Panda Express, Pita Pit, RoundTable Pizza, Starbucks, Wendy's 🅞 GNC, Hancock Fabrics, Natural Grocers, Petsmart, Ross, Safeway, Tuesday Morning
3	NE Hwy 99, Main St, Hazel Dell, **E** 🅖 7-11 🍴 Muchas Gracias Mexican, Pizza Hut, Skippers, **W** 🅖 Arco/dsl, Chevron/dsl 🍴 Papa Murphy's 🅞 Safeway, transmissions
2	WA 500 E, 39th St, to Orchards
1d	E 4th, Plain Blvd W, to WA 501, Port of Vancouver
1c	Mill Plain Blvd, City Ctr, **E** 🅞 Clark Coll, **W** 🅖 Chevron 🍴 Black Angus 🏠 Comfort Inn 🅞 st patrol
1b	6th St, **E** 🍴 Joe's Crabshack, Who Song & Larry's Mexican, **W** 🏠 EconoLodge, Hilton, Red Lion Hotel
1a	WA 14 E, to Camus, **E** 🅞 🏥 **W** 🏠 EconoLodge, Hilton
0mm	Washington/Oregon state line, Columbia River

⬆E   INTERSTATE 82

Exit #	Services
11mm	**I-82 Oregon begins/ends on I-84, exit 179.**
10	Westland Rd, **E** 🅞 to Umatilla Army Depot
5	Power Line Rd
1.5mm	Umatilla River
1	US 395/730, Umatilla, **E** 🍴 Jack-in-the-Box (5mi) 🏠 Best Western (8mi), Desert Inn/rest. (2mi), Motel 6 (8mi), Oxford Inn (5mi) 🅞 Hatrock Camping (8mi), to McNary Dam, **W** 🅖 Shell/Crossroads Trkstp/dsl/rest./24hr, Tesoro/Subway/dsl, Texaco/dsl 🏠 Tillicum Motel, Umatilla Inn 🅞 Harvest Foods, st police, Umatilla Marina/RV Park, USPO, weigh sta, Welcome Ctr
132mm	Washington/Oregon state line, Columbia River
131	WA 14 W, Plymouth, **N** 🅞 RV camping, to McNary Dam
130mm	**weigh sta wb**
122	Coffin Rd
114	Locust Grove Rd
113	US 395 N, to I-182, Kennewick, Pasco, st patrol, **N 2-4 mi** 🅖 Exxon/Circle K/dsl, Metro/dsl, USA/dsl 🍴 A&W/KFC, Azteca Mexican, Bob's Burgers, Burger King, Carl's Jr, Costa Vida,

113	Continued
	Denny's, Dickey's BBQ, DQ, Fujiyama Japanese, Jack-in-the-Box, Little Caesars, McDonald's, Osaka Asian, Panda Express, Starbucks, Subway, Taco Bell, Tesoro/dsl, The Rock Kitchen 🏠 Baymont Inn, Best Western, Comfort Suites, Days Inn, La Quinta 🅞 🏥 AT&T, Blue Dog RV Ctr, Fred Meyer/dsl, GNC, Harley-Davidson, Home Depot, PetCo, Radio Shack, Rite Aid, Safeway/dsl, st patrol, Traveland RV Ctr, Verizon, vet, Walgreens, Walmart/Subway
109	Badger Rd, W Kennewick, **N** 🅖 Exxon/Subway/dsl 🍴 Country Gentleman's Rest. 🏠 Guesthouse Suites, Quality Inn, Red Lion Hotel, Super 8, **S** 🅞 RV Park
104	Dallas Rd, **N 3 mi** 🅖 Conoco/dsl
102	I-182, US 12 E, to US 395, Spokane, 🅞 🏥 Pasco, services in Richland
96	WA 224 E, Benton City, **N** 🅖 Conoco/cafe/dsl 🅞 Beach RV Park
93	Yakitat Rd
88	Gibbon Rd
82mm	Yakima River
82	WA 22, WA 221, Mabton, **S** 🅖 Conoco/dsl 🅞 🏥 museum, to WAS U Research, to Wine Tasting
80	Gap Rd, **S** ♿ both lanes, full ♿ facilities, litter barrels, 🚐 RV dump 🅖 Chevron/dsl, Pacific Pride/dsl, Shell/dsl/scales 🍴 Barn Rest., Burger King, El Rancho Alegre, Garcia's Mexican, Golden Horse Chinese, KFC/Taco Bell, McDonald's, Starbucks, Subway 🏠 Best Western, Vintners Inn 🅞 🏥 Ford, Schwab Tire, Verizon, Wine Country RV Park
76mm	**weigh sta wb**
75	County Line Rd, Grandview, **S** 🅖 Cenex/dsl, Conoco/dsl (1mi) 🍴 Country Deli, Papa Murphy's 🅞 O'Reilly Parts, same as 73
73	Stover Rd, Wine Country Rd, Grandview, **S** 🅖 Chevron/Subway/dsl, Conoco/dsl 🍴 10-4 Café, DQ, Eli&Kathy's Rest., Garcia's Mexican, New Hong Kong 🏠 Apple Valley Motel, Grandview Motel 🅞 Chrysler/Dodge/Jeep, IGA Mercado, RV park/dump, Safeway/dsl, Schwab Tire
69	WA 241, to Sunnyside, **N** 🅖 Arco/dsl, Shell/dsl/scales/24hr, USA/dsl 🍴 A&W, Burger King, China Buffet, El Charrito Mexican, Green Olive Cafe, KFC, Little Caesars, McDonald's, Mongolian BBQ, Panda Garden, Papa Murphy's, Pizza Hut, Skipper's, Subway, Taco Bell 🏠 Best Western, Quality Inn 🅞 $Tree, AT&T, auto repair, AutoZone, Buick/Chevrolet, Fiesta Foods, GNC, JC Penney, Nissan, O'Reilly Parts, Radio Shack, Rite Aid, Walmart/Subway
67	Sunnyside, Port of Sunnyside, **N** 🅖 Chevron/CFN/dsl, Conoco/dsl/e85 🍴 Jack-in-the-Box 🅞 🏥 BiMart Foods, **S** 🅞 DariGold Cheese
63	Outlook, Sunnyside, **N 3 mi** 🍴 Snipe's Rest. 🏠 Country Inn&Suites, Travel Inn 🅞 Sunnyside RV Park
58	WA 223 S, to Granger, **S** 🅖 Arco/dsl/tacos, Conoco/dsl
54	Division Rd, Yakima Valley Hwy, to Zillah, **S** 🅞 Teapot Dome NHS
52	Zillah, Toppenish, **N** 🅖 76/dsl, Chevron/Circle K/dsl, Shell/Circle K/dsl 🍴 El Porton Mexican, McDonald's, Pizza Hut, Subway 🏠 Vintage Valley Inn
50	WA 22 E, to US 97 S, Toppenish, **S 3-4 mi** 🍴 Legends Buffet/casino, McDonald's 🏠 Days Inn, Quality Inn 🅞 🏥 Murals Museum, RV Park, to Yakima Nation Cultural Ctr
44	Wapato, **N** 🅖 Shell/dsl
40	Thorp Rd, Parker Rd, Yakima Valley Hwy, **N** 🅞 Sagelands Vineyard/Winery, **S** 🅞 Windy Point Vineyard

Side labels (vertical): **VANCOUVER**, **WA**, **KENNEWICK**, **SUNNYSIDE**

Y A K I M A

⬆N INTERSTATE 82 Cont'd

Exit #	Services
39mm	Yakima River
38	Union Gap (from wb), S 1 mi 🅾 🍴 🏠 museum
37	US 97 (from eb), S 🅖 Conoco/dsl, Shell
36	Valley Mall Blvd, Yakima, S 🅖 Arco/dsl, Cenex/dsl, Shell/Gearjammer/Subway/dsl/scales/24hr/@ 🍴 A&W/KFC, Applebee's, Burger King, Carl's Jr, Denny's, El Porton Mexican, Famous Dave's, Jack-in-the-Box, McDonald's, Miner's Drive-In, Old Country Buffet, Old Town Sta Rest., Outback Steaks, SeaGalley Rest., Shari's, Starbucks, Subway, Taco Bell 🏠 Best Western, Quality Inn, Super 8 🅾 AT&T, Best Buy, Cabela's, Canopy RV Ctr, Costco/gas, dsl/repair, Gap Autoparts, Hobby Lobby, Home Depot, JC Penney, Kohl's, Lowe's, Macy's, mall, Michaels, Office Depot, Old Navy, PetCo, Petsmart, Rite Aid, Ross, Sears/auto, ShopKO, st patrol, Tire Factory, TJ Maxx, Toyota/Scion, Verizon
34	WA 24 E, Nob Hill Blvd, Yakima, N 🅾 dsl/repair, K-Mart, Sportsman SP, S 🅖 7-11, 76/dsl, Arco/dsl, CFN/dsl, Time/dsl 🅾 🅷 19th Hole RV Park, Fiesta Foods, Freightliner, Kenworth, O'Reilly Parts, Peterbilt, Volvo
33	Yakima Ave, Yakima, N 🅖 Chevron/dsl, Shell/dsl 🍴 Burger King, El Mirador Mexican 🏠 Oxford Inn&Suites 🅾 Chevrolet, Honda, Mazda, Walmart/McDonald's, S 🅖 7-11, Arco 🍴 Bob's Burgers, Domino's, DQ, Pizza Hut, Taco Bell 🏠 Fairfield Inn, Guesthouse Suites, Hilton Garden, Holiday Inn, Holiday Inn Express, Howard Johnson, Ledgestone Hotel, Red Lion Hotel 🅾 $Tree, BigLots, Schwab Tire, Target
31b a	US 12 W, N 1st St, to Naches, S 🅖 Arco/dsl, Conoco/dsl, Shell 🍴 Black Angus Steaks, El Rinconsito, Golden Moon Chinese, Jack-in-the-Box, Mel's Diner, NY Teryaki, Peking Palace, Red Lobster, Subway, Tammy's Mexican, Waffle's Cafe, Yakima Rest. 🏠 Best Western, Budget Inn, Days Inn, Economy Inn, Holiday Lodge, Red Apple Motel, Sun Country Inn, Sunshine Motel, Yakima Inn, Yakima Valley Hotel 🅾 Harley-Davidson, Trailer Inns RV Park
30	WA 823 N, Rest Haven Rd, to Selah
29	E Selah Rd, N 🅾 fruits/antiques
26	WA 821 N, to WA 823, Canyon Rd, N 🅾 Chevrolet/Noble Romans/Subway/dsl
24mm	🆁🆂 eb, full ♿ facilities, litter barrels, 🚯, RV dump
23mm	Selah Creek
22mm	🆁🆂 wb, full ♿ facilities, litter barrels, 🚯, RV dump
21mm	2265 elev, S Umptanum Ridge
19mm	Burbank Creek
17mm	2315 elev, N Umptanum Ridge
15mm	Lmuma Creek
11	Military Area, Military Area
8mm	2672 elev, Manastash Ridge, view point both lanes
3	WA 821 S, Thrall Rd
0mm	I-90, E to Spokane, W to Seattle. **I-82 begins/ends on I-90, exit 110.**

⬆E INTERSTATE 90

Exit #	Services
300mm	Washington/Idaho state line, Spokane River
299	State Line, Port of Entry, N 🅾 Cabela's, Walmart/Subway
297	weigh sta wb
296	Otis Orchards, Liberty Lakes, N 🅖 Conoco/dsl 🍴 Legend's Grill 🏠 Best Western 🅾 Buick/GMC, Kia, Mercedes, Porsche, S 🅖 Cenex/dsl, Chevron/LP 🍴 Barlow's Rest., Carl's Jr, Ding How Asian, Domino's, Jimmy John's, McDonald's,

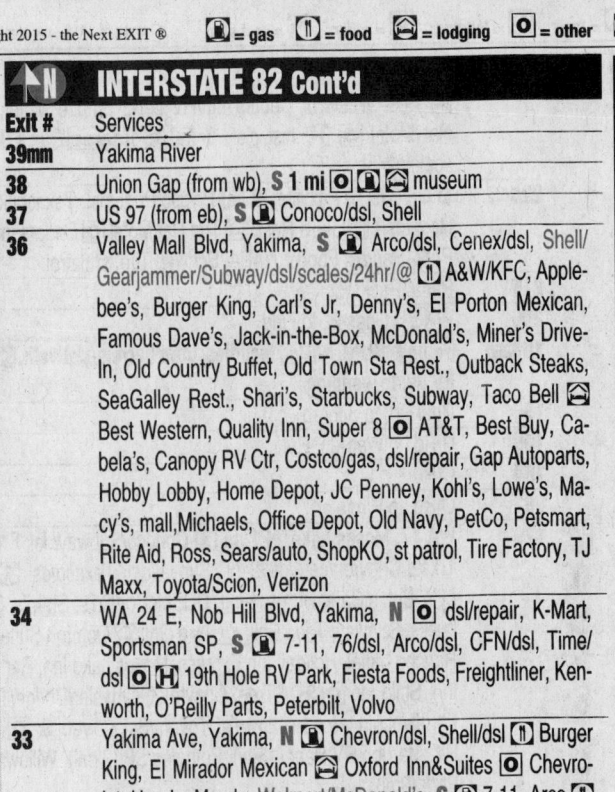

296	Continued Papa Murphy's, Pizza Hut, Quiznos, Starbucks, Subway, Taco Bell, Taco Time 🏠 Quality Inn 🅾 Albertson's/Sav-On, Home Depot, O'Reilly Parts, Peterbilt, RnR RV Ctr, Safeway, Tire-Rama, URGENT CARE, Verizon, vet, Walgreens
294	Country Vista Dr, Appleway Ave
293	Barker Rd, Greenacres, N 🅖 Chevron/Trkstp/dsl/scales, Conoco/dsl 🍴 Wendy's 🅾 Camping World RV Ctr, Freedom RV Ctr, Harley-Davidson, S 🅖 Exxon/Subway/dsl, Mobil/dsl 🅾 NW RV Ctr, repair, USPO

V E R A D A L E

291b	Sullivan Rd, Veradale, N 🍴 Arby's, Hong Kong Buffet, Krispy Kreme, Outback Steaks 🏠 Hampton Inn, My Place, Oxford Suites, Residence Inn 🅾 AT&T, Barnes&Noble, Best Buy, Jo-Ann Fabrics, mall, Verizon, S 🅖 Chevron/dsl, Conoco/dsl, Tesoro/dsl 🍴 5 Guys Burgers, DQ, Jack-in-the-Box, Jimmy John's, KFC, Little Caesars, Max' Rest., McDonald's, Mongolian BBQ, Noodle Express, Panda Express, Pizza Hut, Pizza Pipeline, RoundTable Pizza, Schlotzsky's, Shari's, Starbucks, Subway, Taco Bell, Wendy's, Zelia's Cafe 🏠 Mirabeau Park Hotel, Ramada Inn 🅾 $Tree, Ace Hardware, Fred Meyer/dsl, GNC, Hancock Fabrics, Hastings Books, Kohl's, Lowe's, Michael's, NAPA, PetCo, Petsmart, Ross, Schwab Tire, USPO, Walgreens, Walmart/McDonald's
291a	Evergreen Rd, N 🍴 Azteca Mexican, Black Angus, Boston's Rest, Buffalo Wild Wings, Cafe Rio, Honeybaked Ham, IHOP, Red Robin, Twigs Bistro 🅾 Dick's, Hobby Lobby, JC Penney, Macy's, mall, Old Navy, Sears/auto, Staples, TJ Maxx, S 🅖 Exxon/dsl, Maverik/dsl
289	WA 27 S, Pines Rd, Opportunity, N 🅖 Sam's/dsl 🍴 Black Pearl Rest., Subway 🅾 7-11, S 🅖 Cenex, Conoco/dsl, Holiday/dsl 🍴 Applebee's, DQ, Jack-in-the-Box, Qdoba Mexican, Quiznos 🏠 Comfort Inn 🅾 🅷 NW Auto, repair, Walgreens
287	Argonne Rd, Millwood, N 🅖 Holiday/dsl, Tesoro/dsl 🍴 Burger King, Caruso's Sandwiches, Denny's, Domino's, DQ, Jack-in-the-Box, Longhorn BBQ, McDonald's, Panda Express, Papa Murphy's, Pizza Hut, Starbucks, Subway, Taco Time, Timber Creek Grill, Wendy's 🏠 Motel 6, Super 8 🅾 $Tree, Albertson's, O'Reilly Parts, Savon, URGENT CARE, Verizon, vet, Walgreens, Yoke's Foods, S 🅖 Cenex/dsl, Conoco 🍴 Casa de Oro Mexican, Jimmy John's, Little Caesars, Starbucks 🏠 Holiday Inn Express, Quality Inn 🅾 Ace Hardware, Rite Aid, Safeway
286	Broadway Ave, N 🅖 ✈FLYING J/Conoco/rest./dsl/LP/scales/24hr/@, Chevron/dsl 🍴 Goodyear, Smacky's Cafe, Zip's Burgers 🏠 Rodeway Inn 🅾 International Trucks, Kenworth, Schwab Tire, S 🅾 7-11

Ⓖ = gas Ⓕ = food Ⓛ = lodging Ⓞ = other Ⓡ = rest stop   Copyright 2015 - the Next EXIT ®

WA

↑E INTERSTATE 90 Cont'd

S P O K A N E

Exit #	Services
285	Sprague Ave, N Ⓕ Dragon Garden Chinese, IHOP, Jack-in-the-Box, McDonald's, Panda Express, Starbucks, Subway, Wendy's Ⓛ ParkLane Motel/RV Park Ⓞ $Tree, AT&T, AutoZone, Costco/gas, Grocery Outlet, Home Depot, K-Mart/Little Caesars, Lowe's, O'Reilly Parts, Radio Shack, Verizon, Volvo Trucks, Walmart, S Ⓖ Conoco Ⓕ Bag of Burgers, Cottage Cafe, Puerta Vallarta Mexican, Starbucks, Taco Time Ⓞ Acura, CarMax, Chevrolet, Chrysler/Dodge, Ford, Honda, Hyundai, Mazda, Nissan, Toyota/Scion, transmissions, vet
284	Havana St (from eb, no EZ return), N Ⓖ Tesoro/dsl Ⓕ Wolf Lodge Steaks, S Ⓖ Conoco/dsl Ⓞ Fred Meyer/dsl
283b	Freya St, Thor St, N Ⓖ Chevron/dsl, Tesoro/dsl Ⓕ Wolf Lodge Steaks, S Ⓖ Conoco/dsl Ⓞ Fred Meyer/dsl
283a	Altamont St, S Ⓖ Cenex
282b	2nd Ave, N Ⓖ Conoco/dsl Ⓛ Comfort Inn Ⓞ Office Depot
282a	WA 290 E, Trent Ave, Hamilton St, N Ⓖ Conoco/dsl Ⓛ Comfort Inn Ⓞ Office Depot
281	US 2, US 395, to Colville, N Ⓖ 7-11, Conoco, Exxon, Tesoro/dsl Ⓕ Arby's, Dick's Hamburgers, Frankie Doodles Rest., Starbucks, Subway, Taco Time Ⓛ Days Inn, FairBridge Inn Ⓞ Firestone/auto, Schwab Tire, U-Haul, S Ⓛ Quality Inn Ⓞ Ⓗ URGENT CARE
280b	Lincoln St, N Ⓖ Chevron, Conoco/dsl Ⓕ Atilano's Mexican, Carl's Jr, Chapala Mexican, Domino's, Jack-in-the-Box, McDonald's, Molly's Rest., Taco Bell, Thai Cuisine, Zip's Burgers Ⓛ Tradewinds Motel Ⓞ Fiat, Honda, Lexus, Toyota/Scion, Troy's Tire, S Ⓞ Ⓗ
280a	Spokane, downtown, N Ⓖ Chevron/McDonald's/dsl, Conoco/dsl Ⓕ Frank's Diner, Pizza Hut, Subway Ⓞ AAA, Grocery Outlet
279	US 195 S, Pullman, to Colfax, no facilites
277b a	US 2 W (no ez wb return), to Grand Coulee Dam, N Ⓛ Blvd Motel, EconoLodge, Hampton Inn, Knight's Inn Ⓞ Fairchild AFB
276	Geiger Blvd, N Ⓖ ✈FLYING J/dsl/LP/24hr Ⓕ Denny's, Subway Ⓛ Airway Express Inn, Best Western Ⓞ st patrol, USPO, S Ⓖ Conoco/dsl
272	WA 902, Medical Lake, N Ⓖ Mobil/dsl Ⓞ Overland Sta/RV Park, S Ⓖ Exxon/Subway/dsl, Petro/Iron Skillet/dsl/scales/24hr/@ Ⓕ McDonald's Ⓛ Super 8 Ⓞ Freightliner, Ponderosa Falls RV Resort, truck repair

C H E N E Y

270	WA 904, Cheney, Four Lakes, S Ⓖ 76 Ⓛ Holiday Inn Express (4mi), Willow Springs Motel (6mi) Ⓞ E WA U, Peaceful Pines RV Park (7mi)
264	WA 902, Salnave Rd, to Cheney, Medical Lake, N 2 mi camping
257	WA 904, Tyler, to Cheney, S Ⓞ Peaceful Pines RV Park (10mi), to Columbia Plateau Trail SP, Tyler RV Park
254	Fishtrap, S Ⓞ Fishtrap RV camping/tents
245	WA 23, Sprague, S Ⓖ Chevron/dsl Ⓕ Viking Drive-In Ⓛ Sprague Motel/RV park Ⓞ 4 Seasons RV Park (6mi), Sprague Lake Resort/RV Park
242mm	Ⓡ both lanes, full ♿ facilities, litter barrels, petwalk, 📞, 🚮 RV dump eb, Tourist/weather info
231	Tokio, N Ⓞ weigh sta both lanes, S Ⓖ Templin's Café/CFN/dsl Ⓞ RV Park
226	Schoessler Rd
221	WA 261 S, Ritzville, City Ctr, N Ⓖ Chevron/McDonald's, Conoco/dsl, Exxon/Circle K/Subway/dsl Ⓕ Cow Creek Cafe/gifts, Ritz Roadhouse, Starbucks, Taco Del Mar, Zip's Rest.

M O S E S L A K E

221	Continued Ⓛ Best Western, Cedars Inn/RV park, Empire Motel, Top Hat Motel Ⓞ Ⓗ hist dist, S Ⓖ 💙Loves/Carl's Jr/dsl/scales/24hr
220	to US 395 S, Ritzville, N Ⓖ Pacific Pride/dsl, Texaco/Jake's Rest./dsl Ⓕ Jake's Rest. Ⓛ Top Hat Motel Ⓞ Cedars Inn RV Park, Harvest Foods, NAPA, Schwab Tire, st patrol
215	Paha, Packard
206	WA 21, Odessa, to Lind
199mm	Ⓡ both lanes, full ♿ facilities, litter barrels, petwalk, 📞, 🚮 RV dump, vending
196	Deal Rd, to Schrag
188	U Rd, to Warden, Ruff
184	Q Rd
182	O Rd, to Wheeler
179	WA 17, Moses Lake, N 1 mi Ⓖ Conoco/Subway/dsl, Ernie's Trkstp/Chevron/café/dsl/24hr, Sunval/dsl, Texaco/dsl Ⓕ Arby's, Bob's Cafe, Burger King, DQ, McDonald's, Shari's, Starbucks, Subway, Taco Bell, Y Guy's Grill Ⓛ Comfort Suites, El Rancho Motel, Holiday Inn Express, Moses Lake Inn, Ramada Inn, Shilo Inn Ⓞ Ⓗ $Tree, Chevrolet, Chrysler/Dodge/Jeep, Ford/Lincoln, Honda, Lowe's, Toyota/Scion, vet, S Ⓞ I-90 RV, Mardon RV Park (15mi), Potholes SP (22mi), Willows RV Park (2mi)
177mm	Moses Lake
176	WA 171, Moses Lake, N Ⓖ 76/dsl, Cenex/dsl, Chevron/dsl, Conoco, Exxon/dsl, Sunval/dsl Ⓕ El Rodeo Mexican, Michael's Rest., Subway, Taco Del Mar Ⓛ Best Western/rest., Interstate Inn, Motel 6, Oasis Motel, Super 8 Ⓞ Ⓗ AAA RV Park, Ace Hardware, auto repair, Harvest Foods, Lake Front RV Park, transmissions, vet, S Ⓛ Lakeshore Motel
175	Westshore Dr (from wb), to Mae Valley, N Ⓞ Moses Lake SP, S Ⓞ st patrol
174	Mae Valley, N Ⓞ Suncrest Resort/RV, S Ⓖ Conoco/dsl Ⓞ Pier 4 RV Park, st patrol
169	Hiawatha Rd
164	Dodson Rd, N Ⓞ Sunbasin RV park/camp (1mi)
162mm	Ⓡ wb, full ♿ facilities, litter barrels, petwalk, 📞, 🚮, RV dump
161mm	Ⓡ eb, full ♿ facilities, litter barrels, petwalk, 📞, 🚮, RV dump
154	Adams Rd
151	WA 281 N, to Quincy, N Ⓖ Shell/pizza/subs/dsl Ⓞ Ⓗ (12mi), Shady Grove RV park, to Grand Coulee Dam
149	WA 281 S, George, N Ⓞ Ⓗ (12mi), S Ⓖ BW&M/DSL, Shree's Trkstp/Subway/dsl/scales/24hr Ⓞ RV camp
143	Silica Rd, N Ⓞ to The Gorge Ampitheatre
139mm	N Wild Horses Mon, scenic view both lanes
137mm	Columbia River
137	WA 26 E, to WA 243, Othello, Richland
136	Huntzinger Rd, Vantage, N Ⓖ Spirit, Texaco/dsl Ⓕ Blustery's Burger Drive-in, Golden Harvest Rest. Ⓞ auto repair, Riverstone Vantage Resort/RV Park, to Ginkgo SP, Vantage Gen. Store, S Ⓞ to Wanapum SP (3mi)
126mm	Ryegrass, elev 2535 Ryegrass Ⓡ both lanes, full ♿ facilities, litter barrels, petwalk, 📞, 🚮
115	Kittitas, N Ⓖ Shell/dsl/LP Ⓕ Main Stop Rest. Ⓞ Olmstead Place SP, UHaul
110	I-82 E, US 97 S, to Yakima
109	Canyon Rd, Ellensburg, N Ⓖ 76, Astro/dsl, Chevron, Exxon/Circle K Ⓕ Arby's, Baskin Robbins, Burger King, Carl's Jr, Fiesta Mexican, KFC, Los Cabos Mexican, McDonald's,

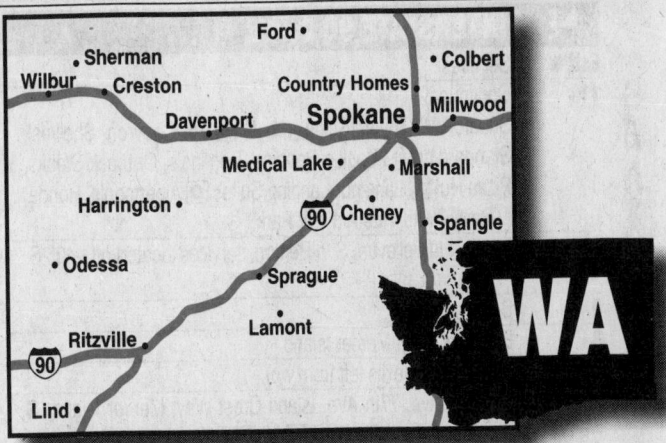

ELLENSBURG	**INTERSTATE 90 Cont'd**

Exit #	Services
109	Continued
	Oyama Japanese, Papa Murphy's, Quiznos, RanchHouse Rest., Roadhouse Grill, Rodeo City BBQ, Starbucks, Subway, Taco Del Mar, Teriyaki Wok, Wendy's 🏠 Best Western, Comfort Inn, Holiday Inn Express, Quality Inn, Super 8 🔲 H AutoZone, CarQuest, Chevrolet, NAPA, O'Reilly Parts, Rite Aid, Schwab Tire, Super 1 Foods, TrueValue, **S** 🚗 Conoco/ Ⓕ FLYING J/Sak's/dsl/scales/LP/24hr 🍴 Buzz Inn Steaks 🏠 Days Inn/RV park
106	US 97 N, to Wenatchie, **N** 🚗 76/dsl, Chevron/dsl, Conoco/ dsl, ➤Loves/Subway/dsl/scales/24hr 🍴 DQ, IHOP, Perkins 🏠 Cedars Inn, Hampton Inn 🔲 Buick/Cadillac/GMC, Canopy Country RV Ctr, Chrysler/Dodge/Jeep, Truck/RV Wash, **S** 🔲 KOA, st patrol
101	Thorp Hwy, **N** 🚗 Arco/dsl 🔲 antiques/fruits/vegetables
93	Elk Heights Rd, Taneum Creek
92.5mm	Elk Heights, elev 2359
89mm	Indian John Hill, elev 2141, Rs **both lanes, full** 🚻 **facilities, litter barrels, petwalk,** Ⓒ, 🔲, **RV dump, vending**

CLE ELUM	

Exit #	Services
85	WA 970, WA 903, to Wenatchie, **N** 🚗 76/dsl, Gas Save/dsl, Shell/dsl 🍴 Cottage Café, Giant Burger, Homestead BBQ 🏠 Aster Inn, Chalet Motel, Cle Elum Traveler's Inn, EconoLodge 🔲 vet
84	Cle Elum (from eb, return at 85), **N** 🚗 Chevron/dsl, Shell/Subway/dsl, Warrior's/dsl 🍴 Beau's Pizza, Burger King, Caboose Grill, DQ, El Caporal Mexican, Los Cabos Mexican, MaMa Vallones, McDonald's, New Cam Chinese, Sahara Pizza, Sunset Café, Taco Bell 🏠 Best Western Snowcap, Stewart Lodge, Timber Lodge Inn 🔲 Cle Elum Drug, Cle Elum Hardware, museum, Radio Shack, Safeway/dsl, Trailer Corral RV Park, URGENT CARE, USPO
81mm	Cle Elum River
80mm	**weigh sta both lanes**
80	Roslyn, Salmon la Sac, **N** 🏠 Suncadia Resort/rest. (4mi)
78	Golf Course Rd, **S** 🔲 Sun Country Golf/RV Park
74	W Nelson Siding Rd
71mm	Yakima River
71	Easton, **S** 🚗 Easton Store/dsl/LP 🏠 Easton Motel 🔲 Iron Horse SP, John Wayne Tr, USPO
70	Sparks Rd, Easton, Lake Easton SP, **N** 🚗 Shell/RV Town/dsl/ café 🍴 Backwoods Cafe, Mtn High Burger 🔲 repair, Silver Ridge Ranch RV Park, **S** 🔲 Lake Easton RV Camping, Lake Easton SP
63	Cabin Creek Rd
62	Stampede Pass, elev 3750, to Lake Kachess, **N** Lake Kachess Lodge
54	Hyak, Gold Creek, **S** Ski Area
53	Snoqualmie Pass, elev 3022, **S** 🚗 Chevron 🍴 Summit Pancake House 🏠 Summit Lodge 🔲 info, Lee's Summit Mkt, to rec areas
52	W Summit (from eb), same as 53
47	Tinkham Rd, Denny Creek, Asahel Curtis, **N** 🔲 chain area, **S** 🔲 RV camping/dump
45	USFS Rd 9030, **N** to Lookout Point Rd
42	Tinkham Rd
38	**N** fire training ctr
35mm	S Fork Snoqualmie River
34	468th Ave SE, Edgewick Rd, **N** 🚗 Gull/dsl/deli, Shell/dsl, TA/ Country Pride/Popeyes/dsl only/24hr/@ 🏠 Edgewick Inn 🔲 Norwest RV Park

Exit #	Services
32	436th Ave SE, **N 1 mi** 🔲 Snoqualmie Ranger Sta, 🚗🚻🏠 **S** 🍴 Riverbend Cafe, Iron Horse SP (3mi)
31	WA 202 W, North Bend, Snoqualmie, **N** 🚗 Chevron/dsl, Shell/dsl 🍴 Arby's, Blimpie, Burger King, Los Cabos, McDonald's, Mongolian Grill, Papa Murphy's, Starbucks, Subway, Taco Time 🏠 North Bend Motel, Sallish Lodge, Sunset Motel 🔲 H museum, NorthBend Outlets/famous brands, O'Reilly Parts, Safeway/dsl, st patrol
27	North Bend, Snoqualmie (from eb), **N** 🍴 Woodman's Steaks 🔲 H
25	WA 18 W, Snoqualmie Pkwy, Tacoma, to Auburn, **N** 🚗 Shell/ dsl/e85 (1.5mi) 🍴 Bayan Mongolian 🔲 **weigh sta**
22	Preston, **N** 🚗 Shell/dsl 🍴 Rhodes BBQ, Subway 🔲 LP, Snoqualmie River RV Park (4mi), USPO, **S** 🔲 Blue Sky RV Park
20	High Point Way
18	E Sunset Way, Issaquah, **S** 🚗 Shell (1mi) 🍴 Flying Pie Pizza, Jak's Grill, Mandarin Garden, Stan's BBQ, Sunset Alehouse 🔲 Front St Mkt
17	E Sammamish Rd, Front St, Issaquah, **N** 🚗 76 🍴 Coho Cafe, Coldstone, Fatburger, Jamba Juice, Krispy Kreme, McDonald's, Panda Express, Papa John's, Qdoba Mexican, Starbucks, Subway 🔲 AT&T, Bartell Drug, Best Buy, Fred Meyer, Home Depot, URGENT CARE, Walgreens, **S** 🚗 Arco/ dsl, Cenex/dsl, Chevron/dsl, Shell/dsl 🍴 Boehms Chocolates, Domino's, Shanghai Garden Rest., Stan's BBQ, Subway, XXX Rootbeer 🔲 Big O Tire, Staples, transmissions
15	WA 900, Issaquah, Renton, **N** 🚗 Arco/dsl, Chevron 🍴 Georgio's Subs, IHOP, O'Char Thai, Red Robin, Taco Time, Tully's Coffee 🏠 Holiday Inn, Motel 6 🔲 Barnes&Noble, Big Lots, Costco/gas, Lowe's, Michael's, Office Depot, PCC Natural Mkt, Petsmart, to Lk Sammamish SP, **S** 🚗 Shell/dsl 🍴 12th Ave Cafe, Baskin-Robbins, Burger King, Cascade Garden Chinese, Chipotle Mexican, Denny's, Five Guys, Franky's Pizza, Issaquah Cafe, Jack-in-the-Box, Jamba Juice, KFC/Taco Bell, La Venadita, McDonald's, Panera Bread, Papa Murphy's, Potbelly, RoundTable Pizza, Starbucks, Subway, Taco Time, The Egg&Us Rest., Tuttabella Pizza, WildFin Grill 🏠 Hilton Garden, Homewood Suites 🔲 Chevrolet, Firestone/auto, Ford, GNC, O'Reilly Parts, PetCo, QFC Foods, Radio Shack, REI, Rite Aid, Ross, Safeway, See's Candies, Target, Trader Joe's, USPO, Verizon
13	SE Newport Way, W Lake Sammamish, **S** 🚗 76/dsl 🍴 Starbucks, Subway 🔲 Matthew's Thriftway Mkt, vet
11	SE 150th, 156th, 161st, Bellevue, **N** 🚗 Shell 🍴 Dalian House Chinese, DQ, Jack-in-the-Box, Lil' Jon Rest., McDonald's, Starbucks, Subway, Tulley's Coffee 🏠 Days Inn, Embassy Suites, Hyatt House, Silver Cloud Inn 🔲 7-11, LDS Temple,

Side tabs: **ELLENSBURG**, **CLE ELUM**, **ISSAQUAH**, **SEATTLE**

WA (tab)

🅖 = gas 🍽 = food 🛏 = lodging 🅾 = other 🆁🆂 = rest stop   Copyright 2015 - the Next EXIT ®

SEATTLE

🚩E INTERSTATE 90 Cont'd

Exit #	Services
11	Continued
	Subaru/VW, Toyota/Scion, vet, **S** 🅖 76, Chevron, Shell/dsl, Standard/dsl 🍽 Baskin-Robbins, Domino's, Outback Steaks, Pizza Hut 🛏 Larkspur Landing Suites 🅾 Albertson's, Honda, O'Reilly Parts, Rite Aid, RV Park
10	I-405, N to Bellevue, S to Renton, services located off I-405 S, exit 10
9	Bellevue Way
8	E Mercer Way, Mercer Island
7c	80th Ave SE (exits left from wb)
7b a	SE 76th Ave, 77th Ave, Island Crest Way, Mercer Island, **S** 🅖 Chevron/dsl, Shell/dsl 🍽 McDonald's, Qdoba, Starbucks, Subway, Thai Rest., Tully's Coffee 🅾 Albertson's, TrueValue, Walgreens
6	W Mercer Way (from eb), same as 7
5mm	Lake Washington
3b a	Ranier Ave, Seattle, downtown, **N** 🅖 Shell/dsl 🅾 Vet
2c b	I-5, N to Vancouver, S to Tacoma
2a	4th Ave S, to King Dome
I-90 begins/ends on I-5 at exit 164.	

RICHLAND

🚩E INTERSTATE 182 (Richland)

Exit #	Services
14b a	US 395 N, WA 397 S, OR Ave, **N** 🅖 ⦿FLYING J/dsl/scales/24hr, King City/Shell/rest/dsl/@ 🍽 Burger King, Subway 🅾 Freightliner, Peterbilt, RV Park, **S** 🛏 Motel 6, **I-182 begins/ends on US 395 N**
13	N 4th Ave, Cty Ctr, **N** 🅖 CFN/dsl 🛏 🍽 Motel, Starlite Motel, **S** 🅖 76/dsl, Chevron/dsl 🅾 🏥 museum, RV park, Tire Pros, vet
12b	N 20th Ave, **N** 🛏 Best Western, Red Lion Hotel
12a	US 395 S, Court St, **S on Court St.** 🅖 Chevron, Conoco, Exxon/Jack-in-the-Box, Mobil/Circle K/dsl, Shell/dsl, Texaco, USA 🍽 A&W/KFC, Andy's Rest., Baskin-Robbins, Burger King, Domino's, El Mirador Mexican, Little Caesars, McDonald's, Oriental Express, Papa Murphy's, Pizza Hut, Quiznos, RoundTable Pizza, Subway, Taco Bell, Wendy's 🅾 $Tree, Albertson's, AutoZone, Cadillac/Chevrolet, Chief RV Ctr, Dean RV Ctr, Ford, Hyundai, Mazda, Nissan, Rite Aid, Subaru, U-Haul, USPO, Walgreens
9	rd 68, Trac, **N** 🅖 Exxon/Circle K/dsl, Maverik/dsl, Tesoro/dsl 🍽 Antonio's Pizza, Applebee's, Arby's, Bruchi's, Cousin's Rest., DQ, Fiesta Mexican, Figaro's Pizza, Hacienda del Sol, IHOP, Jack-in-the-Box, Little Caesar's, McDonald's, Panda Express, Pier 39 Seafood, Pita Pit, Pizza Hut, Shakey's Pizza, Sonic, Starbucks, Subway, Taco Bell, Teriyaki Grill 🛏 Holiday Inn Express, MyPlace 🅾 AT&T, Discount Tire, Firestone/auto, Franklin County RV Park, Lowe's, O'Reilly Parts, Schwab Tire, URGENT CARE, Verizon, Walgreens, Walmart/Subway, Yokes Foods, **S** 🅖 Maverik/dsl
7	Broadmoor Blvd, **N** 🛏 Sleep Inn 🅾 GNC, vet, **S** 🅖 Exxon/dsl 🅾 Broadmoor RV Ctr, KOA
6.5mm	Columbia River
5b a	WA 240 E, Geo Washington Way, to Kennewick, **N** 🅖 Conoco/dsl 🍽 Anthony's Rest., Applebee's, Jack-in-the-Box, Starbucks 🛏 Courtyard, Days Inn, Economy Inn, Hampton Inn, Red Lion Hotel, Shilo Inn, TownePlace Suites 🅾 $Tree, AT&T, Winco Foods
4	WA 240 W, **N** 🅖 Shell/dsl 🍽 El Porton Mexican, McDonald's, Starbucks 🅾 BMW, Fred Meyer/dsl, vet

3.5mm	Yakima River
3	Keene Rd, Queensgate, **N** 🅖 Exxon/Circle K, Maverik/dsl, USA/dsl 🍽 A&W/KFC, Bob's Burgers, Burger King, Costa Vida, El Rancho Alegre, Five Guys, Fujiyama Steaks, LJ Silver, McDonald's, Panda Express, Starbucks, Stick+Stone Pizza, Subway, Taco Bell 🅾 GNC, Home Depot, Marshall's, PetCo, Schwab Tire, Target, Tire Factory, Verizon, Walmart/Subway, **S** 🅖 Chevron/dsl 🅾 RV Park (3mi), tires/repair
0mm	I-182 begins/ends on I-82, exit 102.

🚩N INTERSTATE 405 (Seattle)

SEATTLE

Exit #	Services
30	I-5, N to Canada, S to Seattle, **I-405 begins/ends on I-5, exit 182.**
26	WA 527, Bothell, Mill Creek, **E** 🍽 Canyon's Rest., McDonald's 🛏 Extended Stay America 🅾 Lake Pleasant RV Park, **W** 🅖 Shell/dsl 🍽 Applebee's, Arby's, Bamboo House, Baskin-Robbins, Bonefish Grill, Crystal Creek Cafe, D.Thai, Denny's, Five Guys, Grazie Ristorante, Imperial Wok, Jack-in-the-Box, Jimmy John's, Little Caesar's, Mongolian Grill, Outback Steaks, Papa Murphy's, Qdoba Mexican, Quiznos, Starbucks, Subway, Taco Bell, Taco Time, Tully's Coffee, Wendy's, Zeek's Pizza 🛏 Comfort Inn, Extended Stay America, Hilton Garden, Holiday Inn Express 🅾 7-11, Bartell Drug, Goodyear/auto, QFC Foods, Radio Shack, Rite Aid, URGENT CARE, vet
24	NE 195th St, Beardslee Blvd, **E** 🅖 Shell/Quiznos/dsl 🍽 Subway, Teryaki Etc. 🛏 Country Inn&Suites, Residence Inn, SpringHill Suites 🅾 Exotic vet
23b	WA 522 W, Bothell
23a	WA 522 E, to WA 202, Woodinville, Monroe
22	NE 160th St, **E** 🅖 Chevron, Shell/dsl 🍽 Top Mkt/deli
20	NE 124th St, **E** 🅖 Arco, Chevron, Shell/dsl 🍽 Brown Bag Cafe, Cafe Veloce, Chan's Place, Denny's, Jack-in-the-Box, KFC, Pizza Hut, Santa Fe Mexican, Shari's, Subway, Taco Bell, Thai Kitchen 🛏 Baymont Inn, Comfort Inn, Motel 6 🅾 🏥 7-11, AutoZone, Big O Tire, Chrysler/Dodge/Jeep, Discount Tire, Fiat, Firestone/auto, Ford, Hyundai, Infiniti, NAPA, O'Reilly Parts, Radio Shack, Rite Aid, Ross, Schwab Tire, Toyota/Scion, Trader Joe's, Verizon, VW, **W** 🅖 76/dsl 🍽 Azteca Mexican, Burger King, Five Guys, Hunan Wok, Izumi Japanese, Jimmy John's, McDonald's, Mediterranean Kitchen, Olive Garden, Papa Murphy's, Picnics Hotdogs, Romio's Pizza, Starbucks, Subway, Taco Del Mar, Taco Time, Wendy's 🛏 Courtyard 🅾 AT&T, Buick/GMC, Fred Meyer/dsl, GNC, QFC Foods
18	WA 908, Kirkland, Redmond, **E** 🅖 76/Circle K/dsl, Chevron, Shell/dsl 🍽 Baskin-Robbins, Garlic Jim's, Little Caesar's, McDonald's, Outback Steaks, Pegasus Grill, Starbucks, Subway, Taco Time, Tres Hermanos, Valhalla Grill 🅾 Chevrolet, Costco, Goodyear/auto, Hancock Fabrics, Honda, Kia, Mazda, O'Reilly Parts, PetCo, Safeway, Tuesday Morning, U-Haul, URGENT CARE, vet, Walgreens, **W** 🅖 Shell/dsl 🍽 Acropolis Pizza, Original Pancakes, Papa John's, Starbucks, Subway, Wendy's 🅾 QFC Foods, Tire Factory
17	NE 70th Pl
14b a	WA 520, Seattle, Redmond
13b	NE 8th St, **E** 🅖 Arco, Chevron/dsl, Shell/dsl 🍽 Burger King, Taco del Mar 🛏 Coast Hotel 🅾 🏥 Bartell Drugs, Best Buy, Cadillac, Chevrolet, Ford, Home Depot, Mercedes, Nissan, Porsche, Volvo, Whole Foods Mkt, **W** 🍽 Starbucks, Subway 🛏 Courtyard, Hyatt

INTERSTATE 405 (Seattle) Cont'd

Exit #	Services
13a	NE 4th St, **E** 🛏 Extended Stay America, Hampton Inn 🅞 Chrysler/Dodge/Jeep, Lexus, **W** 🍴 Azteca Mexican, Subway 🛏 Hilton, Hotel Bellevue, Marriott, Red Lion/Bellevue Inn, Residence Inn, Sheraton
12	SE 8th St, **W** 🛏 Residence Inn
11	I-90, E to Spokane, W to Seattle
10	Cold Creek Pkwy, Factoria **E on Factoria Blvd** 🅖 76, Chevron 🍴 Applebee's, Burger King, Coldstone, El Tapatio Mexican, Goldberg's Rest., Great Harvest Bread, Jamba Juice, Jimmy John's, Keg Steaks, KFC, McDonald's, Novilhos Brazilian Steaks, Old Country Buffet, Panda Express, Panera Bread, Peking Wok, Ricardo's Mexican, Romio's Pizza, Shanghai Cafe, Starbucks, Subway, Taco Bell, Taco Time, Thai Ginger, Tokyo Japanese, Tony Maroni's Pizza 🅞 7-11, AT&T, Bartell Drug, Midas, Old Navy, O'Reilly Parts, PetCo, QFC Foods, Radio Shack, Rite Aid, Safeway, Target, TJ Maxx, Verizon, vet, Walmart,
9	112th Ave SE, Newcastle, phone
7	NE 44th St, **E** 🍴 Denny's, McDonald's, Starbucks, Subway, Teriyaki Wok 🛏 EconoLodge
6	NE 30th St, **E** 🅖 Arco, **W** 🅖 Chevron/dsl, Shell/dsl 🅞 7-11
5	WA 900 E, Park Ave N, Sunset Blvd NE, **W** 🍴 Jimmy John's, Panda Express, Panera Bread, Potbelly, Red Robin, Torero's Mexican 🅞 Dick's, Fry's Electronics, GNC, Lowe's,

5	Continued
	Marshall's, Petsmart, Ross, Staples, Target, Verizon, World Mkt
4	WA 169 S, Wa 900 W, Renton, **E** 🍴 Shari's 🛏 Quality Inn 🅞 Aqua Barn Ranch Camping, **W** 🍴 Burger King, Pizza Dudes, Stir Rest., Subway 🛏 Renton Inn 🅞 $Tree, 7-11
2	WA 167, Rainier Ave, to Auburn, **E** 🛏 Hilton Garden, Larkspur Landing, SpringHill Suites, TownePlace Suites 🅞 🏥 **W** 🅖 Arco/dsl, Chevron, Chevron, Mobil/dsl, Shell/dsl 🍴 A&W/KFC, Applebee's, Baskin-Robbins, IHOP, Jack-in-the-Box, Jimmy John's, Jimmy Mac's Roadhouse, King Buffet, Little Caesar's, Mazatlan Mexican, McDonald's, Papa Murphy's, Pizza Hut, Popeyes, Starbucks, Subway, Taco Bell, Taco Time, Wendy's, Yankee Grill 🛏 Red Lion Hotel 🅞 AutoZone, Buick/Cadillac/GMC, Chevrolet, Chrysler/Dodge/Jeep, Fiat, Firestone/auto, Ford, Fred Meyer/dsl, Honda, Hyundai, Kia, Mazda, Midas, O'Reilly Parts, Radio Shack, Safeway/gas, Sam's Club/gas, Schwab Tire, Subaru, Toyota/Scion, vet, Walgreens, Walmart,
1	WA 181 S, Tukwila, **E** 🅖 76/dsl 🍴 Jack-in-the-Box, Taco Bell, Teriyaki Wok 🛏 Courtyard, Embassy Suites, Extended Stay America, Hampton Inn, Ramada, Residence Inn 🅞 7-11, mall, **W** 🅖 76 🍴 Subway 🛏 Comfort Suites, Homewood Suites 🅞 fun center
0mm	I-5, N to Seattle, S to Tacoma, WA 518 W. **I-405 begins/ends on I-5, exit 154.**

SEATTLE

WA
WV

WEST VIRGINIA

INTERSTATE 64

Exit #	Services
184mm	West Virginia/Virginia state line
183	VA 311, (from eb, no reentry), Crows (from eb)
181	US 60, WV 92 (no ez wb return), White Sulphur Springs, **N** 0-2 mi 🅖 BP/Godfather's, Exxon/Quiznos, Shell 🍴 April's Pizzaria, Hardee's 🛏 Budget Inn, Greenbrier Resort, Old White Motel 🅞 Family$, Food Lion, Rite Aid, ski area, to Midland Trail, USPO, **S** 🛏 Black Bear Lodge 🅞 Twilight Camping
179mm	**Welcome Center wb, full ♿ facilities, info, litter barrels, pet-walk, 🅞**
175	US 60, WV 92, Caldwell, **N** 🅖 Exxon, Mountaineer Mart/dsl, Shell/Subway/dsl 🍴 Carlitos, McDonald's, Wendy's 🛏 Village Inn 🅞 $General, **S** 🅞 Greenbrier SF, Mountainaire Camping
173mm	Greenbrier River
169	US 219, Lewisburg, Hist Dist, **N** 🅖 Shell 🍴 Biscuit World 🅞 Federated Parts, **S** 🅖 Exxon/dsl, Gomart, Shell 🍴 Applebee's, Arby's, Bob Evans, China Palace, Hardee's, Papa John's, Ruby Tuesday, Shoney's, Subway, Taco Bell 🛏 Fairfield Inn, Hampton Inn, Holiday Inn Express, Quality Inn, Super 8 🅞 $Tree, AT&T, AutoZone, Buick/Chevrolet, Ford, Lowe's, URGENT CARE, Verizon, Walmart,
161	WV 12, Alta, **S** 🅖 Citgo/dsl 🍴 Alta Sta/cafe 🅞 Greenbrier River Camping (14mi)
156	US 60, Midland Trail, Sam Black Church, **N** 🅖 Citgo/dsl, Shell/dsl
150	rd 29, rd 4, Dawson, **S** 🅖 Exxon 🍴 Cheddar's Cafe 🛏 Dawson Inn 🅞 RV camping
147mm	**runaway truck ramp wb**
143	WV 20, Green Sulphur Springs, **N** 🅖 Liberty/dsl

LEWISBURG

139	WV 20, Sandstone, Hinton, **S** 🅖 Citgo/dsl 🅞 Blue Stone SP (16mi), Richmonds Store/USPO, to Pipestem Resort Park (25 mi)
138mm	New River
136mm	**eb runaway truck ramp**
133	WV 27, Pluto Rd, Bragg, **S** RV camping, mandatory truck stop eb, Sandstone Mtn (Elev. 2765)
129	WV 9, Shady Spring, **N** 🅞 to Grandview SP, **S** 🅖 Exxon/dsl, Shell/dsl 🍴 Subway 🅞 Little Beaver SP
125	WV 307, 📷 Rd, Beaver, **N** 🅖 Shell/dsl 🍴 Biscuit World 🛏 Sleep Inn, **S** 1 mi 🅖 BP/dsl, GoMart/gas, Sheetz/dsl 🍴 Bellacino's, DQ, El Mariachi, Hardee's, KFC, Little Caesars, LJ Silver, McDonald's, Pizza Hut, Subway, Wendy's 🅞 Advance Parts, Adventure RV Ctr, CVS Drug, Family$, Kroger, Radio Shack, USPO, Walgreens
124	US 19, Eisenhower Dr, E Beckley, **N** 1-2 mi 🅖 GoMart/gas 🍴 Capt D's, Huddle House 🛏 Green Bank Motel, Microtel 🅞 🏥 $General, last exit before toll rd wb
121	I-77 S, to Bluefield
	I-64 and I-77 run together 61 mi. See I-77, exits 42 - 100
59	I-77 N (from eb), to I-79
58c	US 60, Washington St, **N** 🅖 BP, Exxon, GoMart/dsl 🅞 Family$, **S** 🍴 5th Quarter Steaks, Capt D's, Panera Bread, Shoney's, Wendy's 🛏 Courtyard, Embassy Suites, Hampton Inn, Holiday Inn Express, Marriott 🅞 🏥 civic ctr, Goodyear/auto, Macy's, mall, Sears
58b	US 119 N (from eb), Charleston, downtown, same as 58c
58a	US 119 S, WV 61, MacCorkle Ave
56	Montrose Dr, **N** 🅖 Exxon/dsl, Marathon/dsl, Speedway/dsl 🍴 Hardee's, Los Agaves Mexican 🛏 Holiday Inn, Microtel, Wingate Inn 🅞 $General, Acura, Advance Parts, Chevrolet, Dodge, Hyundai, KIA, NAPA, Rite Aid, VW

CHARLESTON

🅿 = gas 🍴 = food 🏨 = lodging 🅾 = other 🆁🆂 = rest stop   Copyright 2015 - the Next EXIT ®

INTERSTATE 64

Exit #	Services
55	Kanawha Tpk (from wb)
54	US 60, MacCorkle Ave, N 🅿 🍴 Burger King, Casa Garcia, Graziano's Pizza, Krispy Kreme, Subway 🅾 $Tree, AT&T, Kroger/dsl, TJ Maxx, S 🍴 Bob Evans, Husson's Pizza, KFC, LJ Silver, McDonald's, Pizza Hut, Schlotzsky's, Taco Bell, Wendy's 🅾 H Aamco, Family$, Harley-Davidson, Honda, Mazda, URGENT CARE
53	Roxalana Rd, to Dunbar, S 🅿 GoMart/dsl 🍴 BiscuitWorld, Capt D's, Gino's Pizza, Graziano's Pizza, Los Agaves, McDonald's, Subway, Wendy's 🏨 Dunbar Plaza Motel, Super 8 🅾 $General, Advance Parts, Aldi Foods, CVS Drug, Family$, Jo-Ann Fabrics, Kroger/dsl, NTB, Rite Aid
50	VW 25, Institute, S 🅿 GoMart/dsl
47b a	WV 622, Goff Mtn Rd, N 🅿 Exxon/dsl, GoMart, Speedway/dsl 🍴 BiscuitWorld, Bob Evans, Capt D's, Domino's, Gino's Pizza, Little Caesar's, McDonald's, Papa John's, Pizza Hut, Subway, Taco Bell, Wendy's 🏨 Motel 6 🅾 Advance Parts, AT&T, Autozone, Family$, Kroger/gas, Rite Aid, Save-a-Lot, URGENT CARE, Walgreens, S 🍴 Arby's, Asian Buffet, Barnyard BBQ, Buffalo Wild Wings, Burger King, Cracker Barrel, Golden Corral, HoneyBaked Ham, La Roca Mexican, Sakura Japanese, TGIFriday's 🏨 Comfort Inn, Holiday Inn Express, Sleep Inn 🅾 $Tree, Lowe's, Radio Shack, Staples, Walmart
45	WV 25, Nitro, N 🅿 🍴/Arby's/dsl/scales/24hr 🅾 Chevrolet, S 🅿 Exxon/dsl, GoMart, Speedway/dsl 🍴 BiscuitWorld, Checker's, DQ, Gino's Pizza, McDonald's, Subway, Wendy's 🅾 $General
44.3mm	Kanawha River
44	US 35, St Albans, S 🅿 Shell/7-11/dsl
40	US 35 N, Winfield, Pt Pleasant, S 🅿 Sheetz/dsl, Speedway/dsl 🍴 DQ
39	WV 34, Winfield, N 🅿 BP/Arby's, GoMart/dsl 🍴 Applebee's, Bob Evans, Rio Grande Mexican, Taste of Asia 🏨 Holiday Inn Express, Red Roof Inn 🅾 $General, $Tree, Advance Parts, Aldi Foods, BigLots, Elder-Beerman, GNC, Home Depot, Radio Shack, USPO, S 🅿 GoMart, TA/Country Pride/dsl/scales/24hr/@ 🍴 Biscuit World, Burger King, Capt D's, China Chef, El Rancho Grande, Fat Patty's, Fireside Grille, Gino's Pizza, Graziano's Pizza, KFC, McDonald's, Penn Sta., Subway, Taco Bell, TCBY, Wendy's 🏨 Hampton Inn 🅾 AT&T, AutoZone, K-Mart, Kroger/dsl, Rite Aid, URGENT CARE, Verizon
38mm	weigh sta both lanes
35mm	🆁🆂 both lanes, full ♿ facilities, litter barrels, petwalk, 🅲, 🏕 vending
34	WV 19, Hurricane, N 🍴 Arby's, KFC, Taco Bell 🅾 $Tree, Chevrolet, Chrysler/Dodge/Jeep, Ford, Martin RV Ctr, Walmart/Subway, S 🅿 Exxon/Dunkin Donuts, Go-Mart, Sheetz/dsl 🍴 BiscuitWorld/Gino's Pizza, China Wok, Little Caesar's, McDonald's, Mi Pueblito, Pizza Hut, Subway 🏨 American Inn, Budget Inn 🅾 Rite Aid, USPO, vet, Walgreens
28	US 60, Milton, S 0-2 mi 🅿 Exxon, Go-Mart, Marathon/dsl, Sheetz/dsl 🍴 Biscuit World, McDonald's, Pizza Hut, Subway, Taco Bell, Wendy's 🅾 $General, Advance Parts, AutoZone, CVS Drug, Family$, Jim's Camping (2mi), KOA (3mi), NAPA, Piggly Wiggly, Rite Aid, Save-A-Lot foods, USPO
20	US 60, Mall Rd, Barboursville, N 🍴 Applebee's, Bob Evans, Buffalo Wild Wings, Burger King, Chick-fil-A, Chili's, Chipotle, IHOP, Logan's Roadhouse, McDonald's, Olive Garden, Panera Bread, Qdoba Mexican, Ruby Tuesday, Super China,

H U N T I N G T O N

20	Continued Wendy's 🏨 Comfort Inn 🅾 BAM!, Best Buy, Dick's, Drug Emporium, Elder-Beerman, Firestone/auto, Hobby Lobby, JC Penney, Jo-Ann Fabrics, Kohl's, Lowe's, Macy's, mall, Michael's, NTB, Old Navy, Sears/auto, Walmart/Subway, S 🅿 BP/dsl, Sheetz/dsl 🍴 Cracker Barrel, Fat Patty's, Outback Steaks, Shogun Japanese, Sonic, Steak&Shake, Subway, Taco Bell 🏨 Best Western, Hampton Inn, Holiday Inn 🅾 Toyota
18	US 60, to WV 2, Barboursville, N 🍴 Bellacino's, O'Charley's, Starbucks 🅾 $Tree, Home Depot, Marshall's, Office Depot, Petco, Target, S 🅿 Shell/7-11 🍴 Biscuit World, Gino's, Giovanni's Pizza, Hardee's, Papa John's 🅾 Food Fair, Kia, Kroger/gas, NAPA, Rite Aid, Walgreens
15	US 60, 29th St E, N 🅿 GoMart/dsl, Shell/dsl, Speedway/dsl 🍴 #1 Kitchen, Arby's, Biscuit World, Burger King, Honeybaked Ham, Ponderosa, Subway, Waffle House, Wendy's 🏨 Huntington Motel, Quality Inn 🅾 H $General, AT&T, Big-Lots, NAPA, Save-a-Lot Foods, st police, Verizon, Walmart/McDonald's, S 🅿 Exxon 🍴 Fazoli's, Golden Corral, KFC, Little Caesar's, Marco's Pizza, McDonald's, Penn Sta., Taco Bell 🏨 Days Inn, Red Roof Inn 🅾 Buick/Cadillac/GMC, CVS Drug, Honda, Nissan, Subaru, VW
11	WV 10, Hal Greer Blvd, N 0-2 mi 🅿 Marathon/Subway 🍴 Arby's, Baskin-Robbins, Biscuit World, Bob Evans, El Ranchito Mexican, Frostop Drive-In, McDonald's, Papa John's, Ritzy's Cafe, Wendy's 🏨 Hampton Inn, Ramada Ltd, Super 8, TownePlace Suites 🅾 H AutoZone, Chrysler/Dodge/Jeep, Rite Aid, S 🅾 Beech Fork SP (8mi)
10mm	Welcome Center eb, full ♿ facilities, litter barrels, petwalk, 🅲, 🏕, vending
8	WV 152 S, WV 527 N, N 🅾 URGENT CARE, vet, S 🅿 GoMart/dsl, Speedway/dsl
6	US 52 N, W Huntington, Chesapeake, N 🅿 Sheetz/dsl, Speedway/dsl 🍴 Pizza Hut, Shoney's, Wendys 🅾 H $General, AutoZone, BigLots, Family$, Save-A-Lot Foods
1	US 52 S, Kenova, N 0-1 mi 🅿 Exxon, Shell/dsl 🍴 Burger King, Evaroni's Pizza, Gino's Pizza, Hermanos Nunez Mexican, McDonald's, Stewart's Hotdogs, Taco Bell 🏨 Hollywood Motel 🅾 $General, Advance Parts, CVS Drug, NAPA, Save-A-Lot, USPO
0mm	West Virginia/Kentucky state line, Big Sandy River

INTERSTATE 68

Exit #	Services
32mm	West Virginia/Maryland state line
31mm	Welcome Center wb, full ♿ facilities, litter barrels, petwalk, 🅲, 🏕, vending
29	rd 5, Hazelton Rd, N 🅿 Sunoco/dsl 🏨 Microtel (1mi), S 🅾 Big Bear Camping (3mi), Pine Hill RV Camp (4mi)
23	WV 26, Bruceton Mills, N 🅿 BFS/Subway/dsl/24hr, Sunoco/Little Sandy's Rest./dsl/24hr 🍴 Mills Rest. 🏨 Maple Leaf Motel 🅾 antiques, Family$, Hostetler's Store, USPO
18mm	Laurel Run
17mm	runaway truck ramp eb
16mm	weigh sta wb
15	WV 73, WV 12, Coopers Rock, N 🅾 Chestnut Ridge SF, Sand Springs Camping (2mi)
12mm	runaway truck ramp wb
10	WV 43 N, to rd 857, Fairchance Rd, Cheat Lake, N 🅿 BFS/Charlie's/Little Ceasars/dsl, Exxon/dsl 🍴 Anthony's Pizza, China Kitchen, Subway 🏨 Lakeview Resort 🅾 USPO, vet, S 🍴 Burger King

M O R G A N T O W N

WV

⬆E INTERSTATE 68 Cont'd

Exit #	Services
9mm	Cheat Lake
7	rd 705, Pierpont Rd, N ⛽ BFS/Little Ceasars/Subway/ TCBY, Exxon/Taco Bell/dsl 🍴 Bob Evans, Fujiyama Steaks, Honeybaked Ham, IHOP, Outback Steaks, Ruby Tuesday, Wendy's 🛏 Euro Suites, Hilton Garden (3mi), Holiday Inn Express, Residence Inn, Super 8 ⊡ Ⓗ Books-A-Million, Family$, GNC, Harley-Davidson, Lowe's, Michael's, Shop'n Save Foods, to WVU Stadium, Verizon, S ⛽ Sunoco/dsl 🍴 Don Patron Mexican, Fox's Pizza Den, Rita's Custard ⊡ Chrysler/ Dodge, Fiat
4	rd 7, to Sabraton, N ⛽ BFS/Subway/dsl, Sheetz/dsl 🍴 Ar- by's, Burger King, Dunkin Donuts, Hardee's, KFC, LJ Silver, McDonald's, Wendy's 🛏 Spring-Hill Suites, Suburban Lodge ⊡ $General, Ad-vance Parts, AutoZone, CVS Drug, Ford/Lincoln, Kroger/dsl, NAPA, Save-A-Lot Foods, USPO, Walgreens, S ⛽ Marathon/Circle K, Su-noco/dsl 🍴 China City
3mm	Decker's Creek
1	US 119, Morgantown, N ⛽ Go-Mart/dsl 🛏 Comfort Inn, Ramada Inn/rest. ⊡ tires, S 🍴 Mariachi Loco, Subway ⊡ $Tree, to Tygart L SP, Walmart,
0mm	I-79, N to Pittsburgh, S to Clarksburg. **I-68 begins/ends on I-79, exit 148.**

⬆E INTERSTATE 70

Exit #	Services
14mm	West Virginia/Pennsylvania state line
13.5mm	**Welcome Center wb, full 🛏 facilities, litter barrels, petwalk, ⊡, 🚻, vending**
11	WV 41, Dallas Pike, N TA/Country Pride/dsl/scales/24hr/@ 🛏 Comfort Inn, S ⛽ Exxon, Marathon/DQ/dsl 🛏 EconoLodge ⊡ RV camping
10	rd 65, to Cabela Dr, N ⛽ Sheetz/dsl 🍴 Applebee's, Bob Evans, Cheddar's, Coldstone, Cracker Barrel, Eat'n Park, El Paso Mexican, Fusion Steaks, Logan's Roadhouse, McDon-ald's, Olive Garden, Panera Bread, Quaker Steak, Wendy's 🛏 Hampton Inn, Microtel ⊡ AT&T, Best Buy, Books-A-Million, Cabela's, JC Penney, Kohl's, Michael's, Old Navy, PetCo, Russell Stover Candies, Target, TJ Maxx, Verizon, Walmart/Subway, WV travel info, S 🛏 Holiday Inn Express, Suburban Lodge ⊡ Buick/GMC, Chevrolet, Ford, Honda, Hyundai, Nissan, Toyota/Scion
5a	I-470 W, to Columbus
5	US 40, WV 88 S, Tridelphia, N ⛽ Marathon/dsl 🍴 Pizza Hut, Subway, Wendy's 🛏 Super 8 ⊡ Chrysler/Dodge/Jeep, Fam-ily$, Riesbeck's Foods, Rite Aid, Subaru, URGENT CARE, vet, S ⛽ Drive/dsl, Marathon/dsl 🍴 Arby's, DQ, McDonald's, Undo's Rest. ⊡ Advance Parts, AT&T, museum, Rite Aid
4	WV 88 N (from eb), Elm Grove, same as 5

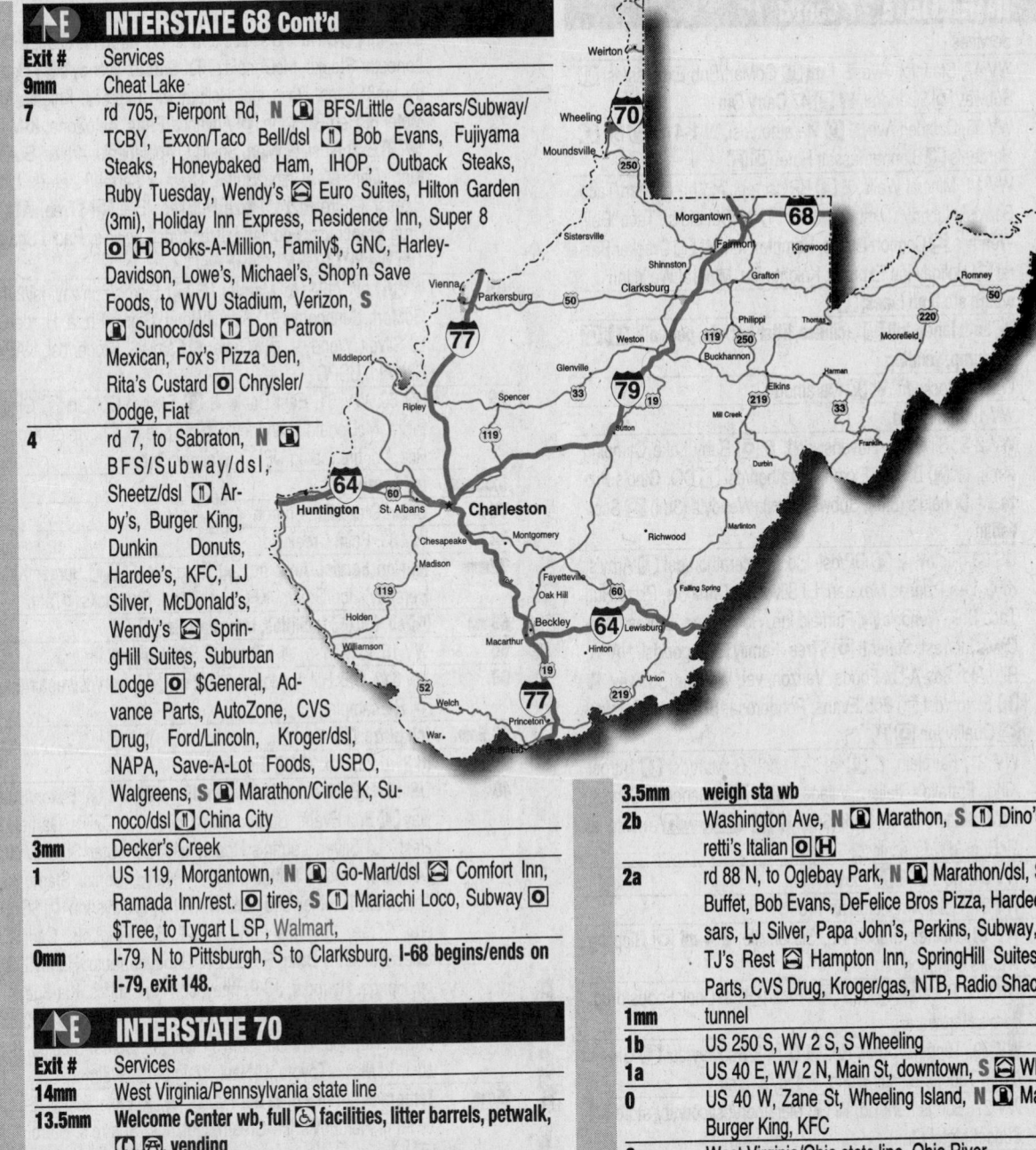

3.5mm	weigh sta wb
2b	Washington Ave, N ⛽ Marathon, S 🍴 Dino's Pizza, Figa-retti's Italian ⊡ Ⓗ
2a	rd 88 N, to Oglebay Park, N ⛽ Marathon/dsl, Sheetz 🍴 AC Buffet, Bob Evans, DeFelice Bros Pizza, Hardee's, Little Cae-sars, LJ Silver, Papa John's, Perkins, Subway, Tim Hortons, TJ's Rest 🛏 Hampton Inn, SpringHill Suites ⊡ Advance Parts, CVS Drug, Kroger/gas, NTB, Radio Shack, Verizon
1mm	tunnel
1b	US 250 S, WV 2 S, S Wheeling
1a	US 40 E, WV 2 N, Main St, downtown, S 🛏 Wheeling Inn
0	US 40 W, Zane St, Wheeling Island, N ⛽ Marathon/dsl 🍴 Burger King, KFC
0mm	West Virginia/Ohio state line, Ohio River

⬆N INTERSTATE 77

Exit #	Services
186mm	West Virginia/Ohio state line, Ohio River
185	WV 14, WV 31, Williamstown, W **WV Welcome Center**/Ⓡₛ, **full facilities, info, litter barrels,** 🚻 ⛽ GoMart/dsl, Shell 🍴 Dutch Pantry, Subway (1mi) 🛏 Magnuson Inn ⊡ Glass Fac-tory Tours
179	WV 2 N, WV 68 S, to Waverly, E ⛽ Exxon ⊡ 🚻, W ⛽ BP, OneStop 🍴 Burger King, Hardee's (3mi) 🛏 Red Carpet Inn ⊡ Ⓗ
176	US 50, 7th St, Parkersburg, E to North Bend SP, W ⛽ 7-11, BP, GoMart 🍴 Bob Evans, Burger King, Domino's, DQ, LJ Sil-ver, McDonald's, Mountaineer Rest./24hr, Omelette Shoppe, Wendy's 🛏 Economy Inn, Knights Inn, Red Roof Inn, Trav-elodge ⊡ Advance Parts, CVS Drug, Family$, Ford, Hyundai, Kroger/dsl, Lincoln, Mercedes, NAPA, Rite Aid, to Blennerhas-sett Hist Park, Toyota, vet
174mm	Little Kanawha River

W H E E L I N G
P A R K E R S B U R G
WV

⬆N INTERSTATE 77 Cont'd

Exit #	Services
174	WV 47, Staunton Ave, **E 1 mi** 🅖 GoMart/Sub Express/dsl 🍴 Subway Ⓞ $General, **W** 🅖 47 Carry Out
173	WV 95, Camden Ave, **E** 🅖 Marathon/dsl **W 1-4 mi** 🅖 BP 🍴 Hardee's 🛏 Blennerhassett Hotel Ⓞ ⊞
170	WV 14, Mineral Wells, **E** 🅖 BP/dsl/repair/24hr, GoMart/Taco Bell/dsl, Liberty Trkstp/dsl/24hr 🍴 McDonald's, Taco Bell, Wendy's 🛏 Comfort Suites, Hampton Inn, **W** 🍴 Cracker Barrel 🛏 Holiday Inn Express, Knights Inn, Mineral Wells Inn
169mm	**weigh sta both lanes,** Ⓒ
166mm	🅡ˢ **both lanes, full** ♿ **facilities, litter barrels, petwalk,** Ⓒ, 🚐 **RV dump, vending**
161	WV 21, Rockport, **W** 🅖 Marathon
154	WV 1, Medina Rd
146	WV 2 S, Silverton, Ravenswood, **E** Ⓞ Ruby Lake Camping (4mi), **W** 🅖 BP/dsl, Exxon, Marathon/dsl 🍴 DQ, Gino's Pizza, McDonald's (3mi), Subway (4mi), Wendy's (3mi) 🛏 Scottish Inn
138	US 33, Ripley, **E** 🅖 BP/dsl, Exxon, Marathon/dsl 🍴 Arby's, KFC, Las Trancas Mexican, LJ Silver, McDonald's, Pizza Hut, Taco Bell, Wendy's 🛏 Fairfield Inn, Holiday Inn Express, McCoy's Inn/rest, Super 8 Ⓞ $Tree, Family$, Kroger/dsl, NAPA, Rite Aid, Sav-A-Lot Foods, Verizon, vet, Walmart/Subway, **W** 🅖 Exxon/dsl 🍴 Bob Evans, Ponderosa, Shoney's, Subway 🛏 Quality Inn Ⓞ ⊞
132	WV 21, Fairplain, **E** 🅖 BP/7-11/dsl, GoMart/dsl 🍴 Burger King, Fratello's Italian, Village Pizza Ⓞ $General, Curves, Ford, Statts Mills RV Park (6mi), **W** 🅖 ♥Love's/Chester's/McDonald's/dsl/scales/24hr
124	WV 34, Kenna, **E** 🅖 Exxon
119	WV 21, Goldtown, same as 116
116	WV 21, Haines Branch Rd, Sissonville, **E 4 mi** Ⓞ Rippling Waters Camping
114	WV 622, Pocatalico Rd, **E** 🅖 BP/dsl Ⓞ FasChek Foods/drug, Tom's Hardware
111	WV 29, Tuppers Creek Rd, **W** 🅖 BP/Subway/dsl 🍴 Gino's (2mi), Tudor's Biscuit World, Wendy's (2mi)
106	WV 27, Edens Fork Rd, **W** 🅖 Marathon/dsl/country store 🛏 Sunset Motel (3mi)
104	I-79 N, to Clarksburg
102	US 119 N, Westmoreland Rd, **E** 🅖 BP/7-11, GoMart 🍴 Hardee's Ⓞ Foodland
101	I-64, E to Beckley, W to Huntington
100	Broad St, Capitol St, **W** 🛏 Best Western, Fairfield Inn, Marriott Ⓞ ⊞ Cadillac/GMC, CVS Drug, Family$, Firestone, Rite Aid
99	WV 114, Capitol St, **E** Ⓞ ⬚, **W** 🅖 BP/7-11, Exxon/Noble Roman's 🍴 Domino's, McDonald's, Wendy's Ⓞ st capitol, to museum
98	35th St Bridge (from sb), **W** 🍴 Husson's Pizza, McDonald's, Shoney's, Steak Escape, Subway, Taco Bell, Wendy's Ⓞ ⊞ Rite Aid, to U of Charleston
97	US 60 W (from nb), Kanawha Blvd
96mm	**W Va Turnpike begins/ends**
96	US 60 E, Midland Trail, Belle, **W** 🍴 Biscuit World, Gino's 🛏 Budget Host
95.5mm	Kanawha River
95	WV 61, to MacCorkle Ave, **E** 🅖 BP/Subway/dsl, GoMart/

95	Continued dsl/24hr 🍴 Bellacino's, Bob Evans, El Patron Mexican, IHOP, Lonestar Steaks, McDonald's, TX Steaks, Wendy's 🛏 Country Inn&Suites, Days Inn, Holiday Inn Express, Knights Inn, Motel 6, Red Roof Inn Ⓞ Advance Parts, AutoZone, K-Mart, **W** 🅖 Exxon/dsl, GoMart, Shell 🍴 Applebee's, Arby's, Burger King, Capt D's, China Buffet, Cracker Barrel, Hooters, Little Caesar's, Piro Pizza, Pizza Hut/Taco Bell Ⓞ $Tree, AT&T, Drug Emporium, Foodland, Kroger/dsl, Lowe's, Radio Shack, Tire World, URGENT CARE, vet
89	WV 61, WV 94, to Marmet, **E** 🅖 Exxon/Subway/dsl/24hr, GoMart, Sunoco/dsl 🍴 BiscuitWorld, Gino's Pizza, Hardee's, LJ Silver, Wendy's Ⓞ $General, Family$, Kroger/dsl, NAPA, Rite Aid, USPO
85	US 60, WV 61, East Bank, **E** 🅖 Exxon, GoMart 🍴 Gino's Pizza, McDonald's, Shoney's Ⓞ $General, Chevrolet, Kroger, Rite Aid, tire repair, USPO, Walmart/Subway
82.5mm	**toll booth**
79	Cabin Creek Rd, Sharon
74	WV 83, Paint Creek Rd
72mm	**Morton Service Area nb,** 🅖 Exxon/dsl 🍴 ⊞ Burger King, Hershey's Ice Cream, KFC, Pizza Hut, Starbucks Ⓞ atm
69mm	🅡ˢ **sb, full** ♿ **facilities, litter barrels,** Ⓒ, 🚐
66	WV 15, to Mahan, **W 1/2 mi** 🅖 Sunoco/dsl/24hr
60	WV 612, Oak Hill, to Mossy, **E 1/2 mi** 🅖 Exxon/dsl/repair/24hr Ⓞ RV camping
56.5mm	**toll plaza,** Ⓒ
54	rd 2, rd 23, Pax, **E** 🅖 Citgo/dsl
48	US 19, N Beckley, **E 1-4 mi on US 19/WV 16** 🅖 Exxon/Subway 🍴 Bob Evans, Burger King, Chick-fil-A, Chili's, Garfield's Rest., LJ Silver, Logan's Roadhouse, LoneStar Steaks, McDonald's, Peking Buffet, Rally's, Ryan's, Sonic, Starbucks, Taco Bell, Tumbleweed Grill, Wendy's 🛏 Days Inn Ⓞ $General, $Tree, Advance Parts, AT&T, Belk, BigLots, Cadillac/Chevrolet, CVS Drug, Food Lion, Goodyear/auto, Hobby Lobby, Honda, Hyundai, JC Penney, Jo-Ann Fabrics, Kia/Subaru, K-Mart, Kohl's, Kroger/gas, Lowe's, NAPA, Nissan, Radio Shack, Rite Aid, RV Ctr, Sam's Club/gas, Sears, Staples, Suzuki, TJ Maxx, Toyota, U-Haul, Walgreens, Walmart
45mm	**Tamarack Service Area both lanes, W** 🅖 Exxon/dsl 🍴 Burger King, Hershey's Ice Cream, Quiznos, Sbarro's. Starbucks Ⓞ gifts
44	WV 3, Beckley, **E** 🅖 Exxon, Marathon/dsl, Shell/Hardee's/24hr 🍴 Applebee's, Campestre Mexican, DQ, Hibachi Japanese, Hooters, IHOP, McDonald's, Omelette Shoppe, Outback Steaks, Pizza Hut 🛏 Best Value Inn, Courtyard, EconoLodge, Fairfield Inn, Howard Johnson, Quality Inn/rest, Super 8 Ⓞ ⊞ Advance Parts, CVS Drug, Kroger/gas, Rite Aid, Tires, URGENT CARE, **W** 🅖 BP/Subway/dsl, Go-Mart/dsl 🍴 Bob Evans, Cracker Barrel, Pasquale Mira Italian, Ruby Tuesday, Sam's Hotdogs, TX Steaks, Wendy's 🛏 Baymont Inn, Comfort Inn, Country Inn&Suites, Hampton Inn, Holiday Inn, Microtel
42	WV 16, WV 97, to Mabscott, **E 2 mi** 🍴 BiscuitWorld 🛏 Budget Inn Ⓞ ⊞ **W** 🅖 BP/dsl, Go-Mart 🍴 Godfather's Pizza, Subway Ⓞ AutoValue Repair, USPO, Walmart,
40	I-64 E, to Lewisburg
30mm	**toll booth,** Ⓒ
28	WV 48, to Ghent, **E** 🅖 Exxon/dsl, Marathon/dsl 🍴 Subway 🛏 Appalachian Resort Inn (12mi), Glade Springs Resort (1mi) Ⓞ to ski area, **W** 🛏 Knight's Inn

⬆N INTERSTATE 77 Cont'd

Exit #	Services
26.5mm	Flat Top Mtn, elevation 3252
20	US 19, to Camp Creek, E 🅿 Exxon/dsl, W 🅾 Camp Creek SP/RV camping
18.5mm	Bluestone River, **scenic overlook/parking area/weigh sta sb**
17mm	**Bluestone Service Area/weigh sta nb, atm/fax, full ♿ facilities, scenic view,** 🖼 🅿 Exxon/dsl 🍴 Blimpie, Hershey's Ice Cream, Starbucks, Uno Pizza
14	WV 20, Athens Rd, E 🅾 Pipestem Resort SP, to Concord U
9mm	**WV Turnpike begins/ends**
9	US 460, Princeton, E **Welcome Ctr/Rest Area, full ♿ facilities, litter barrels,** 🚻, 🖼, 🍴 Campestre Mexican, Kimono Japanese, Outback Steaks, Ryan's, Subway 🏠 $Tree, AT&T, Country Inn&Suites, 🅾 Radio Shack, URGENT CARE, Verizon, Walmart/Subway, W 🅿 BP/dsl, Exxon, Marathon, Sheetz/dsl, Shell/Subway 🍴 Applebee's, Arby's, Bob Evans, Capt D's, Chili's, Cracker Barrel, DQ, Hardee's, McDonald's, Omelette Spot, Shoney's, Starbucks, Taco Bell, TX Steaks, Wendy's 🏠 Budget Inn, Comfort Inn, Days Inn, Eden Rock Motel, Hampton Inn, Holiday Inn Express, Microtel, Sleep Inn, Turnpike Motel 🅾 🅗 Hyundai, Lowe's, Suzuki
7	WV 27, Twelve Mile Rd
5	WV 112 (from sb, no re-entry), to Ingleside
3mm	East River
1	US 52 N, to Bluefield, W 4 mi 🍴 KFC/LJ Silver, Wendy's 🏠 EconoLodge, Knights Inn, Quality Inn 🅾 🅗 to Bluefield St Coll
0mm	West Virginia/Virginia state line, East River Mtn

⬆N INTERSTATE 79

Exit #	Services
160mm	West Virginia/Pennsylvania state line
159	**Welcome Center sb, full ♿ facilities, info, litter barrels, petwalk,** 🚻, 🖼 vending
155	US 19, WV 7, E 0-3 mi 🅿 GetGo, Sheetz/dsl 🍴 Cheddars, Chili's, CiCi's Pizza, Cracker Barrel, Evergreen Buffet, Golden Corral, Longhorn Steaks, McDonald's, Olive Garden, Red Lobster, Shoney's, TX Roadhouse 🏠 Best Western, EconoLodge, Fairfield Inn, HM Hotel 🅾 🅗 $Tree, Barnes&Noble, Best Buy, Buick/Chevrolet/GMC, CVS Drug, Dick's, Giant Eagle Foods, Old Navy, PetCo, Sam's Club/gas, Target, TJ Maxx, to WVU, Walmart, W 🅾 Harley-Davidson
152	US 19, to Morgantown, E 🅿 BFS/dsl, Exxon, Getty 🍴 Arby's, China Wok, McDonald's, Pizza Hut, Subway, Taco Bell 🏠 EconoLodge 🅾 Advance Parts, BigLots, Monro, URGENT CARE, W 🍴 Bob Evans, Burger King, Garfield's Rest. 🏠 Microtel 🅾 Belk, Elder-Beerman, JC Penney, K-Mart, Lowe's, mall, Sears/auto
150mm	Monongahela River
148	I-68 E, to Cumberland, MD, E 1 mi 🅿 Go-Mart/dsl 🍴 Mariachi Loco, Subway 🏠 Comfort Inn, Morgantown Motel, Ramada Inn 🅾 $Tree, tires, to Tygart Lake SP, Walmart,
146	WV 77, to Goshen Rd, W 🅿 ⛟deli/dsl/scales/24hr
141mm	**weigh sta both lanes**
139	WV 33, E Fairmont, E 🅿 Sunoco, W 🅿 (1 mi), Exxon, K&T/BP/dsl/scales 🅾 repair, RV camping, to Prickett's Ft SP
137	WV 310, to Fairmont, E 🅿 Exxon/dsl, Sunoco 🏠 Clarion 🅾 to Valley Falls SP, vet, W 🅿 Shell/dsl 🍴 Domino's, KFC, McDonald's, Subway, Wendy's 🅾 🅗 $General, Advance Parts, Family$, Shop'n Save Foods

136	rd 273, Fairmont
135	WV 64, Pleasant Valley Rd
133	Kingmont Rd, E 🅿 Exxon/Fazoli's/dsl, Marathon/Subway/dsl 🍴 Cracker Barrel 🏠 Holiday Inn Express, Super 8, W 🅿 Shell/Quiznos/dsl 🍴 DJ's Diner 🏠 Comfort Inn
132	US 250, S Fairmont, E 🅿 BFS/DQ/dsl 🍴 Applebee's, Arby's, Bob Evans, Colasessano's Italian, Dutchman's Daughter, Firehouse Subs, Grand China Buffet, Hardee's, Little Caesars, McDonald's, Oldie's Diner, Subway, Taco Bell 🏠 Days Inn, Fairfield Inn, Red Roof Inn 🅾 $General, Ace Hardware, Advance Parts, Chrysler/Dodge/Jeep, GNC, mall, NAPA, Sav-A-Lot Foods, Shop'n Save, to Tygart Lake SP, Walmart, W 🅿 Exxon/dsl, GoMart/dsl, Sunoco/dsl 🍴 Steak Escape 🏠 Country Club Motel (4mi) 🅾 🅗 Buick/GMC, Ford/Lincoln, Toyota/Scion, Trailer City RV Ctr
125	WV 131, Saltwell Rd, to Shinnston, E 🍴 Oliverio's Rest. (4mi), W 🅿 Exxon/Circle K/Dunkin Donuts/Subway/dsl
124	rd 279, Jerry Dove Dr, E 🅿 BFS, Exxon/Dunkin Donuts/dsl 🍴 Buffalo Wild Wings, DQ, Little Caesars 🏠 Microtel, Wingate Inn, W 🅿 Sheetz/dsl 🍴 IHOP, Subway 🏠 Courtyard, Holiday Inn Express 🅾🅗
123mm	℞ **both lanes, full ♿ facilities, info, litter barrels, petwalk,** 🚻, 🖼, RV dump, vending
121	WV 24, Meadowbrook Rd, E 🅿 GoMart, Sheetz 🍴 Biscuit World, Bob Evans, Gino's Pizza 🏠 Hampton Inn 🅾 Hyundai/Subaru, URGENT CARE, W 🅿 Exxon/dsl 🍴 Burger King, Garfield's Rest., Outback Steaks 🏠 Super 8 🅾 Dick's, JC Penney, Jo-Ann Fabrics, mall, Marshall's, NTB, Old Navy, Sears/auto, Target
119	US 50, to Clarksburg, E 🍴 A&W/LJ Silver, Brickside Grille, Chick-fil-A, Coldstone, Denny's, Eat'n Park, Grand China, Hank's Deli, KFC, Las Trancas, Little Caesar's, Maxey's Rest., McDonald's, Panera Bread, Pizza Hut, Red Hot Buffet, Starbucks, Taco Bell, TX Roadhouse, Wendy's 🏠 Best Western, Days Inn, Sleep Inn, Sutton Inn, Townplace Suites, Travelodge 🅾 🅗 Advance Parts, Autozone, BigLots, Family$, GNC, Home Depot, K-Mart, Kohl's, Kroger/dsl, Lowe's, Monro, Radio Shack, Sam's Club/gas, USPO, Walgreens
117	WV 58, to Anmoore, E 🅿 BFS/dsl 🍴 Applebee's, Arby's, Burger King, Honeybaked Ham, Ruby Tuesday, Ryan's, Subway 🏠 Hilton Garden 🅾 Aldi Foods, AT&T, Kia, Staples, Walmart,
115	WV 20, Nutter Fort, to Stonewood, E 🅿 BP/7-11/dsl, Exxon/dsl 🅾 Stonewood Bulk Foods, W 🏠 Greenbrier Motel (5mi)
110	Lost Creek, E 🅿 BP/dsl
105	WV 7, to Jane Lew, E 🅿 Jane Lew Trkstp/dsl/rest, Valero/dsl/rest 🏠 Plantation Inn, W 🅿 GoMart, Shell 🅾 $General, glass factory tours, Kenworth/Mack/Volvo

INTERSTATE 79 Cont'd

Exit #	Services
99	US 33, US 119, to Weston, E 🅖 Marathon/DQ/Little Caesars/dsl, Sheetz/dsl 🍴 Burger King, Gino's Pizza, McDonald's, Patron Mexican, Peking Buffet, Steer Steakhouse, Subway 🛏 Comfort Inn/rest., Hampton Inn (9mi), Holiday Inn Express, Super 8 🅞 Advance Parts, Curves, Family$, GNC, Kroger/dsl, Radio Shack, Walmart, W 0-2 mi 🅖 Exxon, Go-Mart, Shell/7-11 🍴 Domino's, Giovanni's, Hardee's, KFC, LJ Silver, Pizza Hut, Subway, Wendy's 🅞 🏥 $General, Blackwater Falls, Chrysler/Dodge, CVS Drug, Ford, NAPA, NAPACare, Rite Aid, Save-a-Lot, to Canaan Valley Resort
96	WV 30, to S Weston, E 🅞 Broken Wheel Camping, to S Jackson Lake SP
91	US 19, to Roanoke, E 🅖 Marathon/dsl 🍴 Stillwaters Rest 🅞 camping, to S Jackson Lake SP
85mm	🆁🆂 both lanes, full ♿ facilities, info, litter barrels, petwalk, 🚻, 📞, RV dump, vending
79.5mm	Little Kanawha River
79	WV 5, Burnsville, E 🅖 Exxon 🛏 79er Motel/rest. 🅞 Burnville Dam RA, W 🅖 GoMart 🅞 Cedar Cr SP
76mm	Saltlick Creek
67	WV 4, to Flatwoods, E 🅖 BP/Arby's/dsl, Exxon, Go-Mart/dsl, Shell/dsl 🍴 Custard Stand, KFC/Taco Bell, McDonald's, Subway 🛏 Day's Hotel, Sutton Lake Motel 🅞 antiques, Buick/Chevrolet, camping, to Sutton Lake RA, W 🅖 🛢Moe's SW Grill/dsl/scales/24hr, Sunoco 🍴 China Buffet, Shoney's, Wendy's 🅞 Bulk Foods, farmer's mkt, Flatwood Factory Stores
62	WV 4, Gassaway, to Sutton, E 🛏 Elk Motel 🅞 Sutton Lake Camping, W 🅖 GoMart 🍴 LJ Silver, Pizza Hut 🛏 Microtel 🅞 🏥 Chrysler/Dodge/Jeep, CVS Drug, Ford, Kroger/deli
57	US 19 S, to Beckley
52mm	Elk River
51	WV 4, to Frametown, E antiques, food
49mm	🆁🆂 both lanes, full ♿ facilities, litter barrels, petwalk, 🚻, 📞 RV dump, vending
46	WV 11, Servia Rd
40	WV 16, to Big Otter, E 🅖 GoMart/dsl, W 🅖 Exxon/dsl
34	WV 36, to Wallback, E 10 mi 🍴 BiscuitWorld, Gino's Diner, Subway
25	WV 29, to Amma, E 🅖 Exxon/dsl
19	US 119, VW 53, to Clendenin, E 🅖 BP/dsl 🍴 BiscuitWorld, Gino's Diner 🅞 7-11, Shafer's Superstop
9	WV 43, to Elkview, E 🅖 GoMart/dsl 🍴 Burger King 🅞 AutoZone, W 🅖 Exxon/Arby's/dsl, Speedway/dsl 🍴 Bob Evans, La Carreta, McDonald's, Pizza Hut, Ponderosa, Subway 🛏 Inn&Suites 🅞 $Tree, Advance Parts, CVS Drug, K-Mart, Kroger/dsl, Radio Shack
5	WV 114, to Big Chimney, E 1 mi 🅖 Exxon 🍴 Hardee's 🅞 Rite Aid, Smith's Foods
1	US 119, Mink Shoals, E 🍴 Harding's Family Rest. 🛏 Sleep Inn
0	I-77, S to Charleston, N to Parkersburg.
	I-79 begins/ends on I-77, exit 104.

INTERSTATE 81

Exit #	Services
26mm	West Virginia/Maryland state line, Potomac River
25mm	**Welcome Center sb, full ♿ facilities, info, litter barrels, petwalk, 🚻, 📞**
23	US 11, Marlowe, Falling Waters, E 🅖 Exxon/AC&T/Subway/

Exit #	Services
23	Continued dsl 🍴 Kings Rest., Red Lantern Chinese 🅞 $General, Falling Waters Camping (1mi), Food Lion, W 🅖 BP/dsl 🅞 7-11, Outdoor Express RV Ctr
20	WV 901, Spring Mills Rd, E 🅖 Sheetz 🍴 Barney's Rest., China Spring, Cinco de Mayo, McDonald's, Pizza Montese, Tokyo Cafe 🛏 Motel 6 🅞 $Tree, Advance Parts, AT&T, Walmart/Subway, W 🅖 Shell/dsl 🍴 Burger King, Domino's 🛏 Holiday Inn Express
16	WV 9, N Queen St, Berkeley Springs, E 🅖 Crown/dsl, Exxon/Subway/dsl, Sheetz 🍴 American Icecream, Arby's, Casa Gonzales Mexican, China King, Domino's, DQ, Dunkin Donuts, East Moon Asian, Hibachi Grill, Hoss's, KFC, LJ Silver, McDonald's, Pizza Hut, Rita's Custard, Subway, Waffle House 🛏 Comfort Inn, Knights Inn, Rodeway Inn, Super 8 🅞 Advance Parts, Aldi Foods, AT&T, AutoZone, BigLots, CVS Drug, Family$, Food Lion, URGENT CARRE, USPO, Walgreens, W 🅖 Shell/Subway/dsl
14	rd 13, Dry Run Rd, E 🅞 🏥 W 🅞 Butler's Farm Mkt (1mi)
13	rd 15, Kings St, Martinsburg, E 🅖 BP/Subway/dsl, Sheetz/dsl 🍴 Applebee's, Buffalo Wild Wings, Burger King, Cracker Barrel, Daily Grind, Jerry's Subs, Kobe Japanese, Las Trancas, Outback Steaks, Pizza Hut, Wendy's 🛏 Days Inn, Holiday Inn/rest. 🅞 🏥 Chevrolet/Scion/Toyota, Walmart,
12	WV 45, Winchester Ave, E 🅖 Sheetz/dsl, Shell/dsl 🍴 Arby's, Asian Garden, Bob Evans, Chick-fil-A, China City Buffet, McDonald's, Olive Garden, Papa John's, Ruby Tuesday, Ryan's, Taco Bell, TX Steaks, Waffle House 🛏 Hampton Inn 🅞 Advance Parts, AutoZone, BonTon, Food Lion, JC Penney, K-mart/Little Caesars, Lowe's, Martin's Foods/gas, Nahkeeta Camping, W 🍴 Ledo's Pizza, Logan's Roadhouse, Subway 🅞 $Tree, AT&T, Best Buy, Books-A-Million, Dick's, GNC, Michael's, Petsmart, Staples, Target, TJ Maxx
8	rd 32, Tablers Sta Rd
5	WV 51, Inwood, to Charles Town, E 🅖 7-11, BP, Liberty, Sheetz/dsl, Shell/dsl 🍴 Burger King, Domino's, DQ, KFC, McDonald's, Pizza Hut, Pizza Oven, Subway, Waffle House 🛏 Hampton Inn 🅞 Advance Parts, CVS Drug, Family$, Food Lion, NAPA, Rite Aid, W 🅞 Lazy-A Camping (9mi)
2mm	**Welcome Center/weigh sta nb, full ♿ facilities, info, litter barrels, petwalk, 🚻, 📞, vending**
0mm	West Virginia/Virginia state line

WISCONSIN

INTERSTATE 39

Exit #	Services
211	US 51, rd K, Merrill, W 2 mi 🅖 Cenex 🍴 Chip's Burgers, Hardee's, Pizza Hut 🅞 💬
208	WI 64, WI 17, Merrill, E 🍴 KFC, Taco Bell, W 🅖 Cenex/dsl, KwikTrip/dsl, Mobil/dsl 🍴 3's Company Rest., Culver's, Los Mezcales, McDonald's, Pine Ridge Rest., Pizza Now, Subway 🛏 Americinn, Best Inn, EconoLodge 🅞 🏥 $Tree, Chrysler/Dodge/Jeep, O'Reilly Parts, Piggly Wiggly, to Council Grounds SP, Walmart,
206mm	Wisconsin River
205	US 51, rd Q, Merrill, E 🅖 BP/Hwy 51/rest./dsl/24hr 🅞 Buick/Cadillac/Chevrolet, fireworks
197	rd WW, to Brokaw
194	US 51, rd U, rd K, Wausau, E 🅖 F&F/dsl, KwikTrip/dsl 🍴 McDonald's, Taco Bell, W 🍴 BP/Arby's 🅞 Ford, Nissan,

Side tab: **M A R T I N S B U R G**

Side tab: **WV**

Side tab: **C H A R L E S T O N**

WV

🧭 N   INTERSTATE 39 Cont'd

Exit #	Services
194	Continued Subaru, Toyota/Scion
193	Bridge St, E 🅾 CVS Drug, W 🅾 H
192	WI 29 W, WI 52 E, Wausau, to Chippewa Falls, same as 191 b
191b	Sherman St, E 🚪 BP 🍴 Applebee's, Dickey's BBQ, Great Dane Rest., Hudson's Grill, Jimmy John's, King Buf- fet, Little Caesars, McDonald's, Noodles&Co, Panera Bread, Papa Murphy's, Qdoba, Star- bucks, Subway, Toppers Pizza 🏠 Courtyard, Days Inn, Hampton Inn, La Quinta, Plaza Hotel, Super 8 🅾 County Mkt Foods, ShopKo, Trig's Foods, Walgreens, W 🚪 KwikTrip/dsl 🍴 2510 Deli, Hardee's 🅾 H Cadillac, Home De- pot, Honda, Menards
191a	WI 29, Chippewa Falls
190mm	Rib River
190	rd NN, E 🚪 Mobil/Burger King 🍴 Bo-Jo's Grill, IHOP, Krum- bee's Bakery 🏠 Howard Johnson, W 🚪 The Store/Subway/ dsl 🏠 Best Western 🅾 Granite Mtn Ski Area, Rib Mtn Ski Area, st patrol
188	rd N, E 🚪 BP/dsl/scales/24hr, KwikTrip/dsl, Phillips 66/dsl 🍴 Burracho's Mexican, Fazoli's, Hibachi Buffet, McDon- ald's, Olive Garden, Rococo Pizza, Ropa Pizza, Starbucks, TX Roadhouse, Wendy's 🏠 Days Inn 🅾 $Tree, Aldi Foods, AT&T, Barnes&Noble, Best Buy, Chevrolet, GNC, Gordman's, Hobby Lobby, Hyundai, JoAnn Fabrics, King's RV Ctr, Kohl's, Michael's, Old Navy, PetCo, Petsmart, Radio Shack, Sam's Club/gas/dsl, Tires+, TJ Maxx, Tuesday Morning, Volvo, Walmart/Subway, W 🅾 Rib Mtn SP
187mm	**I-39 begins/ends. Freeway continues N as US 51.**
187	WI 29 E, to Green Bay
186mm	Wisconsin River
185	US 51, Rothschild, Kronenwetter, E 🚪 BP/dsl 🍴 Arby's, Cul- ver's, Denny's, Green Mill Rest., Master Buffet, Subway 🏠 Candlewood Suites, Cedar Creek Lodge, EconoLodge, Holi- day Inn, Motel 6, Stoney Creek Inn 🅾 Cedar Creek Factory Stores/famous brands, Gander Mtn, Harley-Davidson, mall, Pick'n Save Foods, visitor ctr
181	Maple Ridge Rd, Kronenwetter, Mosinee, E 🅾 Peterbilt, vet, Volvo, W Kenworth
179	WI 153, Mosinee, W 🚪 BP/Subway/dsl, KwikTrip, Shell/dsl 🍴 McDonald's, StageStop Rest. 🏠 Quality Inn
175	WI 34, Knowlton, to WI Rapids, W 1 mi 🅾 Mullins Cheese Factory
171	rd DB, Knowlton, E Rivers Edge Camping, W 🅾 camping, food, lodging, to gas
165	US 10 W, to Marshfield (no nb re-entry)
163	Casimir Rd
161	US 51, Stevens Point, W 🚪 BP, Quik Mart/dsl, Shell/dsl/E85, The Store 🍴 China Wok, Coldstone, Cousins Subs, Culver's, Dosirak Korean, Hardee's, Jimmy John's, KFC, McDonald's, Michele's Rest., Natalie's Rest., Noodles&Co, Perkins, Ro- coco's Pizza, Starbucks, Subway, Taco Bell, Tokyo Steaks, Topper's Pizza 🏠 Comfort Suites, Country Inn&Suites, Days Inn, Point Motel 🅾 $Tree, AT&T, K-Mart, Radio Shack, Trig's Foods, visitors ctr

Exit #	Services
159	WI 66, Stevens Point, W 🚪 KwikTrip/dsl 🅾 H Ford, Honda, Hyundai, Nissan, VW
158	US 10, Stevens Point, E 🚪 F&F/dsl, KwikFill/dsl, Mobil/ dsl, The Store/Subway/dsl 🍴 Amber Grille, Applebee's, Ar- by's, Buffalo Wild Wings, Culver's, DQ, El Mezcal Mexican, Fazoli's, Grazie's Italian, Hibachi Buffet, McDonald's, Taco Bell, Wendy's 🏠 Fairfield Inn, Holiday Inn Express 🅾 Aldi Foods, Copp's Foods, Frank's Hardware, Hancock Fabrics, Target, vet, W 🚪 BP/dsl 🍴 Hilltop Grill, Parkridge Rest. 🏠 EconoLodge, La Quinta
156	rd HH, Whiting, E 🚪 The Store/Subway/dsl 🍴 Charcoal Grill, Chili's, Denny's, Golden Corral, McDonald's, Starbucks 🅾 $Tree, Best Buy, GNC, JoAnn Fabrics, Kohl's, Lowe's, Mi- chael's, PetCo, Staples, TJ Maxx, Walmart/Subway
153	rd B, Plover, W 🚪 BP, Fueling Depot, Mobil/Dunkin Donuts/ dsl 🍴 Bamboo House, Burger King, Happy Wok, IHOP, KFC, McDonald's, Subway, Taco Bell, Tempura House Asian 🏠 AmericInn, Comfort Inn, Hampton Inn 🅾 city park, Copp's Foods, dsl repair, Menards, NAPA, ShopKo, Toyota/Scion, vet, Younkers
151	WI 54, to Waupaca, E 🚪 KwikTrip/rest./dsl/scales/24hr 🍴 4Star Family Rest., Shooter's Rest. 🏠 Best Western, Eliza- beth Inn/Conv Ctr 🅾 tires/repair
143	rd W, Bancroft, to WI Rapids, E 🚪 Citgo/dsl 🍴 Area 51 Rest.
139	rd D, Almond
136	WI 73, Plainfield, to WI Rapids, E 🚪 BP/dsl 🍴 Hooligan's Grill 🅾 NAPA Care, W 🚪 Citgo/dsl
131	rd V, Hancock, E 🚪 Citgo 🍴 Country Kettle
127mm	**weigh sta both lanes (exits left)**
124	WI 21, Coloma, E 🚪 Mobil/A&W/dsl 🍴 Subway 🏠 Mecan Inn 🅾 Buick/Chevrolet, Caloma Camping, W 🚪 BP/dsl
120mm	🆁🆂 sb, full 🏠 facilities, litter barrels, petwalk, 🚻, 🏠 vend- ing

(Wisconsin state map showing Interstate routes: I-94, I-90, I-39, I-43, US 41, with cities Superior, Eau Claire, Menomonie, La Crosse, Chippewa Falls, Wausau, Marshfield, Stevens Point, Green Bay, Appleton, De Pere, Kaukauna, Oshkosh, Fond Du Lac, Sheboygan, Beaver Dam, West Bend, Waukesha, Milwaukee, West Allis, Madison, Janesville, Beloit, Monroe, Racine, Kenosha, Menominee, Marinette, Two Rivers, Manitowoc)

WAUSAU

STEVENS PT

WI

PORTAGE

⬆N INTERSTATE 39 Cont'd

Exit #	Services
118mm	🆁🆂 nb, full ♿ facilities, litter barrels, petwalk, 🅒, 🅿 vending
113	rd E, rd J, Westfield, **W** 🅖 BP/Burger King, Marathon, Mobil/dsl 🅕 McDonald's, Subway 🛏 Pioneer Motel/rest. 🅞 city park, Curves, Family$
106	WI 82 W, WI 23 E, Oxford, **E** 🛏 Crossroads Motel, **W** 🅖 Citgo/dsl
104	(from nb, no EZ return) rd D, Packwaukee
100	WI 23 W, rd P, Endeavor, **E** 🅖 BP/dsl 🅕 KW's Grill
92	US 51 S, Portage, **E** 🅖 KwikTrip/dsl, Mobil 🅕 Chi-pan Asian, Culver's, Dino's Rest., Golden Cup 2 Cafe, Jimmy John's, KFC, La Tolteca Mexican, McDonald's, Papa Murphy's, Pizza Ranch, Subway, Suzy's Steaks, Taco Bell, World Buffet 🛏 Best Western, Ridge Motel, Sunset Motel, Super 8 🅞 $Tree, Ace Hardware, AutoZone, Chrysler/Dodge/Jeep, Curves, Ford/Lincoln, GNC, K-Mart, Pierce's Foods, Radio Shack, Staples, Verizon, Walgreens, Walmart,
89b a	WI 16, to WI 127, Portage, **E** 🅖 BP/dsl 🅕 Hitching Post Eatery, Murph's Chop Shop
88.5mm	Wisconsin River
87	WI 33, Portage, **W** ski area
86mm	Baraboo River
85	Cascade Mt Rd
84	I-39, **I-90 & I-94 run together sb/eb**

GREEN BAY

⬆N INTERSTATE 43

Exit #	Services
192mm	**I-43 begins/ends at Green Bay on US 41.**
192b	US 41 S, US 141 S, to Appleton, services on Velp Ave, **S 1 mi** 🅖 BP/A&W/dsl, Express/dsl, Mobil/Arby's, Shell/dsl 🅕 Burger King, Gilligan's Rest, Julie's Cafe, McDonald's, Riverstreet Rest, Subway, Taco Bell, Watering Hole Rest 🛏 AmericInn 🅞 Bay Parts, Bumper Parts, Family$, Good Wrench Auto, Harley-Davidson
192a	US 41 N, US 141 N
189	Atkinson Dr, to Velp Ave, Port of Green Bay
188mm	Fox River
187	East Shore Dr, Webster Ave, **W** 🅖 Shell/dsl/24hr 🅕 McDonald's, Mi Pueblo Mexican, Wendy's 🛏 Clarion, Hyatt 🅞 🅗
185	WI 54, WI 57, University Ave, to Algoma, **W** 🅖 Mobil, Shell/A&W 🅕 Green Bay Pizza, Subway, Taco Bell 🅞 Family$, U of WI GB, University Foods, Walgreens
183	Mason St, rd V, **E** 🅕 Culver's, Makinaw's Grill 🛏 Country Inn&Suites, Super 8 🅞 🅗 **W 1 mi** 🅖 BP, Mobil/dsl, Shell 🅕 Applebee's, Arby's, Burger King, China Buffet, Fazoli's, Grand Buffet, Great Lakes Sandwiches, KFC, Little Caesars, McDonald's, Papa John's, Papa Murphy's, Perkins, Pizza Hut, Pizza Ranch, Sonic, Starbucks, Taco Bell 🅞 $General, Advance Parts, Aldi Foods, AT&T, AutoZone, Batteries+, Copps Foods, Family$, Goodyear/auto, Hobby Lobby, Kohl's, Mazda, O'Reilly Parts, PetCo, ShopKO, Subaru, Tires+, Verizon, Walgreens, Walmart/Subway
181	Eaton Rd, rd JJ, **E** 🅖 BP/McDonald's/dsl 🅕 Hardee's, Jimmy John's, Luigi's, Taco John's 🅞 Ford/Kia, Harley-Davidson, Home Depot, **W** 🅖 Mobil/Subway/dsl, Shell 🅕 A&W, Ravine Grill 🛏 AmericInn 🅞 Farm&Fleet/gas, Festival Foods, Menards
180	WI 172 W, to US 41, **W 1 exit** 🅖 BP/Taco Bell/24hr, Citgo/Country Express/dsl/scales/24hr, KwikTrip, Shell/Subway 🅕 Burger King, McDonald's, Tuscon's Rest.

MANITOWAC

180	Continued 🛏 Holiday Inn Express 🅞 🅗 Copps Foods, Target, to stadium, Walgreens, multiple services
178	US 141, to WI 29, rd MM, Bellevue, **E** 🅖 Shell/Arby's/dsl, **W** repair
171	WI 96, rd KB, Denmark, **E** 🅖 BP/dsl 🅕 deGrande Rest, McDonald's, Smurava Cafe, Steve's Cheese, Subway 🅞 Shady Acres Camping
168mm	🆁🆂 both lanes, full ♿ facilities, litter barrels, petwalk, 🅒, 🅿 vending
166mm	Devils River
164	WI 147, rd Z, Maribel, **W** 🅖 BP/dsl 🅕 Ridge Rest
160	rd K, Kellnersville
157	rd V, Hillcrest Rd, Francis Creek, **E** 🅖 Citgo/Subway/dsl, Marathon/diner/dsl
154	US 10 W, WI 310, Two Rivers, to Appleton, **E** 🅖 Mobil 🅞 🅗 **W** 🅖 Cenex
153mm	Manitowoc River
152	US 10 E, WI 42 N, rd JJ, Manitowoc, **E** 🅕 TimeOut Grill 🅞 🅗 antiques, maritime museum
149	US 151, WI 42 S, Manitowoc, **E** 🅖 BP, Exxon, Grand Central Sta, KwikTrip/dsl, Mobil/dsl, Shell/dsl 🅕 4 Seasons Rest., A&W, Applebee's, Arby's, Burger King, Charcoal Grill, China Buffet, Culver's, DQ, Fork&Knife Rest, Frier Tuck's Sandwiches, Jimmy John's, Las Carretas Mexican, Little Caesars, McDonald's, Papa Murphy's, Perkins, Pizza Ranch, Starbucks, Taco Bell, Wendy's 🛏 Birch Creek Inn, Comfort Inn, Holiday Inn, Super 8 🅞 🅗 $Tree, Advance Parts, Aldi Foods, AutoZone, Buick/Cadillac/Chevrolet/GMC, Chrysler/Dodge/Jeep, Copps Foods, Family$, Festival Foods, GNC, Hobby Lobby, Kohl's, Lowe's, museum, O'Reilly Parts, PetCo, Radio Shack, ShopKO, Tires+, USPO, Verizon, vet, Walgreens, Walmart/Subway, **W** 🅖 Express/McDonald's 🅕 Subway 🛏 AmericInn 🅞 Harley-Davidson, Menards
144	rd C, Newton, **E** 🅖 Mobil/dsl 🅞 antiques
142mm	**weigh sta sb,** 🅒
137	rd XX, Cleveland, **E** 🅖 Citgo/Subway/dsl 🅕 Cleveland Family Rest. 🛏 Kessler's Old World Guesthouse 🅞 Wagner's RV Ctr
128	WI 42, Howards Grove, **E** 🅖 BP/dsl/24hr, KwikTrip 🅕 Culver's, Hardee's, Harry's Diner, Shuff's Rest, TX Roadhouse 🛏 Quality Inn 🅞 Gander Mtn, Pomp's Tire, **W** 🅖 Mobil/dsl 🅞 Menards, Walmart/Subway
126	WI 23, Sheboygan, **E** 🅖 BP, KwikTrip 🅕 Applebee's, Cousins Subs, Culver's, McDonald's, New China, Pizza Hut/Taco Bell, Pizza Ranch 🛏 La Quinta 🅞 🅗 Aldi Foods, Batteries+, BigLots, Festival Foods, Firestone/auto, Ford/Kia, Goodyear/auto, Hobby Lobby, Honda/Mazda, Kohl's, NAPA, Sears/auto, ShopKO, Subaru, Toyota/Scion
123	WI 28, rd A, Sheboygan, **E** 🅖 Citgo/dsl/24hr, Mobil/McDonald's/dsl 🅕 Coldstone, Jimmy John's, Perkins, Starbucks, Wendy's 🛏 AmericInn, Holiday Inn Express 🅞 Harley-Davidson/Cruisers Burgers, Walmart/Subway, **W** 🅕 Arby's, Century Buffet, Chili's 🅞 $Tree, AT&T, Best Buy, Boston's Store, GNC, Home Depot, Jo-Ann Fabrics, Petsmart, Radio Shack, Target, TJ Maxx
120	rds OK, V, Sheboygan, **E** 🅖 Citgo/dsl 🅕 Hwy Ridge Rest 🛏 Sleep Inn 🅞 camping, Nissan, to Kohler-Andrae SP, VW, **W 1 mi** 🅞 Horn's RV Ctr
116	rd AA, Foster Rd, Oostburg, **W 1 mi** 🅕 Judi's Place Rest, Pizza Ranch, Subway
113	WI 32 N, rd LL, Cedar Grove, **W** 🅖 Citgo/dsl/repair, Fueling Depot, Mobil 🅕 Country Grove Rest, Cousins Subs 🛏 Lakeview Motel

↑N INTERSTATE 43 Cont'd

Exit #	Services
107	rd D, Belgium, **E** 🏠 Lake Church Inn/grill 🅾 Harrington Beach SP, **W** 🅿 BP/McDonald's/dsl/24hr, How-Dea Trkstp/ Hobo's Korner Kitchen/dsl/scales, Mobil/dsl/24hr 🍴 Bic's Place, Say Cheese Outlet, Subway 🏠 Regency Inn 🅾 repair, USPO
100	WI 32 S, WI 84 W, Port Washington, **E** 🅿 Citgo/dsl, Mobil 🍴 Arby's, McDonald's, Pizza Hut, Subway 🏠 Country Inn&Suites, Holiday Inn 🅾 Allen-Edmonds Shoes, Goodyear/ auto, Sentry Foods, ShopKO Express, True Value, **W** 🏠 Nisleit's Country Rest.
97	Fredonia, WI 57, (from nb, exits left),
96	WI 33, to Saukville, **E** 🅿 Citgo 🍴 Culver's, KFC/LJ Silver 🅾 Best Hardware, Buick/Cadillac/Chevrolet, Chrysler/Dodge/ Jeep, Ford, Pick'n Save Foods, Piggly Wiggly, Walgreens, Walmart, **W** 🅿 Exxon/McDonald's 🍴 Domino's, DQ, La Chimenea, Lam's Chinese, Papa Murphy's, Subway, Taco Bell 🏠 Super 8 🅾 repair/tires
93	WI 32 N, WI 57 S, Grafton, **E 1-2 mi** 🅿 BP 🍴 George Webb Rest, Mamma Mia's Cafe, **W** 🍴 Flannery's Cafe
92	WI 60, rd Q, Grafton, **E** 🅿 BP 🍴 GhostTown Rest., Water St Rest 🏠 Hampton Inn, **W** 🅿 Citgo/DQ/dsl 🍴 Charcoal Grill, Noodles&Co, Qdoba, Quiznos, Starbucks, Subway 🏠 Baymont Inn 🅾 🏥 Aldi Foods, AT&T, Best Buy, Costco/gas, Dick's, Home Depot, Kohl's, Michael's, Petsmart, Target, Verizon, vet
89	rd C, Cedarburg, **W** 🅿 Mobil/dsl 🍴 Cedar Crk Settlement Café (6mi) 🏠 StageCoach Inn, Washington House Inn 🅾 🏥
85	WI 57 S, WI 167 W, Mequon Rd, **W** 🅿 BP, Citgo/dsl, Mobil, Shell 🍴 Caribou Coffee, Chancery Rest., Cousins Subs, Culver's, DQ, Hong Palace Chinese, Jimmy John's, Leonardo's Pizza, McDonald's, Panera Bread, Papa Murphy's, Pizza Hut, Starbucks, Subway 🏠 Best Western, Chalet Motel 🅾 🏥 Ace Harware, Kohl's, Office Depot, Sendik's Foods, Verizon, vet, Walgreens
83	rd W, Port Washington Rd (from nb only)
82b a	WI 32 S, WI 100, Brown Deer Rd, **E** 🅿 BP, Sendik's/dsl 🍴 Baskin-Robbins, Benji's Deli, Jimmy John's, La Paisa Mexican, Maxfield's Pancakes, McDonald's, Noodles&Co, Peking Chef, Qdoba, Starbucks, Subway, Toppers Pizza 🅾 Best Buy, CVS Drug, Fresh Mkt, GNC, Land's Inlet, Verizon, Walgreens
80	Good Hope Rd, **E** 🅿 BP 🍴 Jimmy John's, King's Wok, Nick-n-Willy's Pizza, Samurai Japanese 🏠 Radisson, Residence Inn 🅾 Pick'n Save Foods, to Cardinal Stritch U
78	Silver Spring Dr, **E** 🅿 BP, Citgo 🍴 5 Guys Burgers, Applebee's, Bar Louie, BD Mongolian, Boston Mkt, Bravo Italian, Buffalo Wild Wings, Burger King, CA Pizza Kitchen, Carabou Coffee, Cheesecake Factory, COA Mexican, Cousins Subs, Devon Steaks, Food Court, McDonald's, Panera Bread, Perkins, Pizza Hut, Qdoba, Taco Bell 🏠 Baymont Inn, La Quinta, Super 8 🅾 AT&T, Barnes&Noble, Batteries+, CarX, Goodyear/auto, Kohl's, mall, Nissan, Radio Shack, Sears/auto, Trader Joe's, USPO, Verizon, Walgreens, **W** 🅾 🏥
77b a	(from nb), **E** 🍴 Anchorage Rest., Solly's Grille 🏠 Hilton
76b a	WI 57, WI 190, Green Bay Ave, **E** 🅾 Home Depot, **W** 🅿 CTrip 🍴 Burger King 🅾 Volvo
75	Atkinson Ave, Keefe Ave, **E** 🅿 Mobil, **W** 🅿 BP
74	Locust St
73c	North Ave (rom sb), **E** 🍴 Wendy's, **W** 🍴 McDonald's
73b	North Ave (from nb), downtown
73a	WI 145 E, 4th St (exits left from sb), Broadway, downtown
72c	Wells St, **E** 🏠 Hilton 🅾 🏥 Civic Ctr, museum
72b	(from sb), I-94 W, to madison
72a	(310c from nb, exits left from sb), I-794 E, I-94 W to Madison, to Lakefront, downtown
311	WI 59, National Ave, 6th St, downtown
312a	Lapham Blvd, Mitchell St, **W** 🅿 BP, Citgo, Shell
312b	(from nb), Becher St, Lincoln Ave
314a	Holt Ave, **E** 🅿 Andy's/dsl 🍴 Applebee's, Arby's, China King, Jimmy John's, Little Caesars, Starbucks, Subway, Wendy's 🅾 $General, Home Depot, Pick'n Save Foods, Piggly Wiggly, Target, vet, **W** 🅾 🏥 to Alverno Coll
314b	Howard Ave
10b	(316 from sb), I-94 S to Chicago, 🖂
15	US 14, Darien, **E** 🅿 Mobil/dsl 🍴 West Wind Diner
9b a	WI 241, 27th St, **E** 🅿 BP/dsl, Clark, Happy Gas, Supreme/dsl 🍴 Arby's, Burger King, Chancery Rest., Famous Dave's, Pizza Hut, Sonic, Subway 🏠 Suburban Motel 🅾 AutoZone, Carquest, Curves, K-Mart, Subaru, Target, USPO, Walgreens, **W** 🍴 Boston Mkt, Buffalo Wild Wings, Chipotle Mexican, Denny's, Jimmy John's, Los Burritos Tapatios, McDonald's, New China, Omega Rest., Rich's Cakes, Taco Bell, Wong's Wok, Zebb's Rest 🏠 Quality Inn, Rodeway Inn 🅾 🏥 $Tree, AAA, Advance Parts, CarX, Chevrolet, CVS Drug, Firestone/auto, Ford, Goodyear/auto, Kohl's, Marshall's, Michael's, Pick'n Save Foods, Radio Shack, Save-A-Lot Foods, Walmart,
8a	WI 36, Loomis Rd, **E** 🅿 BP, Citgo 🍴 Los Mariachi's 🅾 Aldi Foods, Walgreens, **W** 🍴 Griddler's Cafe 🅾 to Alverno Coll
7	60th St, **E** 🅿 Speedway/dsl 🍴 Subway, Wendt's Grille 🅾 Harley-Davidson, **W** 🅿 Speedway
5b	76th St (from sb, no EZ return), **E** 🍴 Applebee's, Bakers Square, Breadsmith, Burger King, Carrabba's Italian, Cousins Subs, El Beso, Griddler's Cafe, Hooters, Kopp's Burgers, Kyoto Japanese, McDonald's, Noodles&Co, Old Country Buffet, Olive Garden, Outback Steaks, Panera Bread, Qdoba, Red Lobster, Red Robin, Ruby Tuesday, Starbucks, TGIFriday's, Topper's Pizza, Traditional Pancake House, Wendy's 🅾 $Tree, AT&T, Barnes&Noble, Best Buy, CarX, F&F Tire, Firestone/auto, Goodyear, Jo-Ann Fabrics, Office Depot, PetCo, Petsmart, Sears/auto, Sendik's Food, Tuesday Morning, Valvoline, Verizon, **W** 🍴 Arby's, Pizza Hut, Popeye's 🅾 Pick'n Save Foods, TJ Maxx, USPO, Walgreens
5a	WI 24 W, Forest Home Ave, **E** 🅿 Citgo 🅾 Boerner Botanical Gardens, Welk's Auto
61	(4 from sb), I-894/US 45 N, I-43/US 45 S
60	US 45 S, WI 100, 108th St (exits left from sb), **E** 🅿 BP, Citgo, Marathon, Mobil 🍴 A&W, Amore Italian, Chipotle Mexican, Confucius Chinese, Cousins Subs, Culver's, DQ,

MILWAUKEE

🅖 = gas 🍴 = food 🛏 = lodging 🅞 = other 🆁🆂 = rest stop   Copyright 2015 - the Next EXIT ®

⬆N INTERSTATE 43 Cont'd

Exit #	Services
60	Continued
	Fortune Chinese, George Webb Rest, McDonald's, McGuire's Grill, Noodles&Co, Open Flame Grill, Pizza Hut, Starbucks, Subway, Taco Bell 🅞 $Tree, AutoZone, Chevrolet, K-Mart, Midas, O'Reilly Parts, Pick'N Save, Radio Shack, URGENT CARE, USPO, vet, W 🅖 Andy's/dsl 🍴 Forum Rest., Goody's Rest, McDonald's, Organ Piper Pizza, Subway 🅞 Aldi Foods, Badger Transmissions, Goodyear, NAPA, Nissan, vet, Walgreens, Walmart,
59	WI 100, Layton Ave (from nb, exits left) , Hales Corner, W 🅖 BP, same as 60
57	Moorland Rd, E 🅖 KwikTrip/dsl 🍴 Applebee's, Stonefire Pizza Co, TX Roadhouse 🛏 La Quinta, W 🅖 Speedway/dsl 🍴 Buffalo Wild Wings, Cosina Real, Quaker Steak&Lube, Quiznos 🛏 Holiday Inn Express 🅞 Firestone/auto, GNC, Michael's, Target
54	rd Y, Racine Ave, E 1-2 mi 🅖 Citgo/dsl, KwikTrip 🅞 Cousins Subs, Culver's, McDonald's
50	WI 164, Big Bend, W 🅖 Mobil/dsl 🍴 McDonald's
44mm	Fox River
43	WI 83, Mukwonago, E 🅖 BP/dsl 🅞 Home Depot, Walmart, W 🅖 Citgo 🍴 Antigua Real Cafe, Chen's Kitchen, Domino's, DQ, Taco Bell 🛏 Rodeway Inn 🅞 Verizon
38	WI 20, East Troy, W 🅖 BP, ▭▭▭/Road Ranger/Subway/dsl/24hr, Shell/McDonald's 🍴 Burger King, Cousins Subs, Genoa Pizza, Golden Dragon, Roma Ristorante 🅞 $General, Carquest, Chrysler/Dodge/Jeep
36	WI 120, East Troy, E 🛏 Alpine Valley Resort, W 🛏 Country Inn&Suites
33	Bowers Rd, E to Alpine Valley Music Theatre
32mm	🆁🆂 both lanes, full ♿ facilities, litter barrels, petwalk, 🚱, 🖃 vending
29	WI 11, Elkhorn, fairgrounds
27b a	US 12, to Lake Geneva, E 🅞 🛏
25	WI 67, Elkhorn, E 🅖 BP/dsl 🛏 AmericInn 🅞 Buick/Chevrolet/GMC, Chrysler/Dodge/Jeep, vet, W 🅖 Speedway/dsl/24hr 🍴 Burger King, Subway 🛏 Hampton Inn (2mi) 🅞 Dehaan Auto/RV Ctr
21	WI 50, Delavan, E 🍴 Brodie's Beef, Chili's, China 1, Culvers, Domino's, Panera Bread, Papa Murphy's, Starbucks, Subway, Yoshi Japanese 🅞 Aldi Foods, AT&T, F&F Tires, golf, Kohl's, Lowe's, Petsmart, Radio Shack, Staples, Verizon, Walmart, W 🅖 Mobil, Speedway/dsl 🍴 KFC, McDonald's, Perkins, Pizza Hut, Taco Bell, Wendy's 🛏 Comfort Suites, Super 8 🅞 $Tree, Ace Hardware, AutoZone, Cadillac/Chevrolet, Ford/Lincoln, GNC, NAPA, Piggly Wiggly, ShopKO, Walgreens
17	rd X, Delavan, Darien, W 🅖 BP/dsl
6	WI 140, Clinton, E 🅖 Citgo/Subway/TCBY/dsl 🅞 Ford
2	rd X, Hart Rd, E 🍴 Butterfly Fine Dining
1b a	I-90, E to Chicago, W to Madison, S 🅖 BP, Mobil/McDonald's, ▭▭▭/Taco Bell/dsl/scales/24hr, Shell, Speedway/dsl 🍴 Applebee's, Arby's, Asia Buffet, Atlanta Bread, Burger King, Culver's, Jimmy John's, Little Caesars, Papa Murphy's, Road Dawg Rest, Starbucks, Subway, Wendy's 🛏 Comfort Inn, EconoLodge, Fairfield Inn, Hampton Inn, Holiday Inn Express, Rodeway Inn 🅞 $Tree, Aldi Foods, Buick/GMC, Cadillac/Chevrolet, GNC, Menards, NTB, O'Reilly Parts, Radio Shack, Staples, Walmart,
I-43 begins/ends on I-90, exit 185 in Beloit.	

(side tab) WI

(side tab) D E L A V A N

⬆E INTERSTATE 90

Exit #	Services
187mm	Wisconsin/Illinois state line, I-90 & I-39 run together nb.
187mm	**Welcome Center wb, full ♿ facilities, info, litter barrels, petwalk, 🚱, 🖃, vending**
185b	I-43 N, to Milwaukee
185a	WI 81, Beloit, S 🅖 Mobil/McDonald's/dsl, ▭▭▭/Taco Bell/dsl/scales/24hr, Shell, Speedway/dsl 🍴 Applebee's, Arby's, Asia Buffet, Burger King, Culver's, Jimmy John's, Little Caesars, Little Mexico, Papa Murphy's, Qdoba, Road Dawg Rest, Starbucks, Subway, Wendy's 🛏 Baymont Inn, Fairfield Inn, Hampton Inn, Holiday Inn Express, Quality Inn, Rodeway Inn 🅞 $Tree, Aldi Foods, AT&T, Buick/GMC, Cadillac/Chevrolet, GNC, Menards, NTB, O'Reilly Parts, Radio Shack, Staples, Walmart,
183	Shopiere Rd, rd S, to Shopiere, S 🅖 BP/Rollette/dsl/24hr 🅞 🛏 camping, repair
181mm	wb, weigh sta
177	WI 11 W, Janesville, S 2 mi 🅖 KwikTrip/dsl 🅞 S WI ☕, to Blackhawk Tec Coll
175b a	WI 11 E, Janesville, to Delavan, N 🅖 BP/Subway/dsl 🛏 Baymont Inn 🅞 🛏 bet, S 🛏 Lannon Stone Motel 🅞 city park
171c b	US 14, WI 26, Janesville, N 🅖 TA/Mobil/Wendy's/dsl/scales/24hr/@ 🍴 Coldstone, Cozumel Mexican, Fuddruckers, HomeTown Buffet, IHOP, Quaker Steak, Starbucks, Subway, TX Roadhouse 🛏 Holiday Inn Express, Microtel 🅞 Aldi Foods, Best Buy, Gander Mtn, GNC, Home Depot, Michael's, NTB, Old Navy, PetCo, Staples, TJ Maxx, S 🅖 Citgo, Exxon/dsl, Kwik Trip/dsl 🍴 Applebee's, Arby's, Buffalo Wild Wings, Burger King, ChuckeCheese, Culver's, Dunkin Donuts, Famous Dave's, Fazoli's, Fuji Steaks, Hacienda Real, Hardee's, Hooters, Jimmy John's, KFC, Mac's Pizza, McDonald's, Milio's Sandwiches, Milwaukee Grill, Noodles&Co, Olive Garden, Panda Express, Panera Bread, Papa Murphy's, Peking Chinese, Perkins, Pizza Hut, Prime Quarter Steaks, Qdoba Mexican, Red Robin, Road Dawg Eatery, Subway, Taco Bell, Taco John's, Toppers Pizza, World Buffet 🛏 EconoLodge, Super 8 🅞 🛏 $Tree, Aldi Foods, AT&T, AutoZone, Big Lots, CarQuest, CVS Drug, F&F, Ford/Lincoln, Harley-Davidson, Hobby Lobby, Hyundai, JC Penney, K-Mart/Little Caesar's, Kohl's, mall, Mazda, Menards, Nissan/Kia/Subaru, O'Reilly Parts, Sears/auto, ShopKO, Target, Toyota/Scion, USPO, Verizon, Walgreens
171a	WI 26, N 🅖 BP/dsl 🍴 Cracker Barrel 🛏 Hampton Inn, Motel 6, Ramada/rest. 🅞 Chrysler/Dodge/Jeep, Sam's Club, URGENT CARE, VW, Walgreens, Walmart, S same as 171c b
168mm	🆁🆂 eb, full ♿ facilities, litter barrels, petwalk, 🚱, 🖃 vending
163.5mm	Rock River
163	WI 59, Edgerton, to Milton, N 🅖 Mobil/Subway/dsl, Shell/Dunkin Donuts/Taco John's/dsl 🍴 Blue Gilly's Rest., Culver's, McDonald's, WI Cheese Store 🛏 Comfort Inn 🅞 marina
160	US 51S, WI 73, WI 106, Oaklawn Academy, to Deerfield, S 🅖 BP/dsl/scales/24hr/@ 🅞 🛏 Creek View Camping (2mi)
156	US 51N, to Stoughton, S 🛏 Coachman's Inn/rest. 🅞 🛏
147	rd N, Cottage Grove, to Stoughton, S 🅖 BP/Arby's/dsl, Road Ranger/Pilot/Subway/dsl/scales 🅞 Lake Kegonsa SP
146mm	weigh sta wb
142b a	(142a exits left from wb) US 12, US 18, Madison, to Cambridge, N 🅖 BP/dsl 🍴 Roadhouse Rest 🛏 Best Value Inn, Magnuson Grand Hotel 🅞 casino, Harley-Davidson, S 🅖 Citgo/dsl, Phillips 66/Arby's/dsl, Shell/dsl 🍴 Denny's 🛏 Days Inn, Sleep Inn 🅞 🛏 Menards, UWI
138b	WI 30, Madison, S ☕

(side tab) B E L O I T

(side tab) J A N E S V I L L E

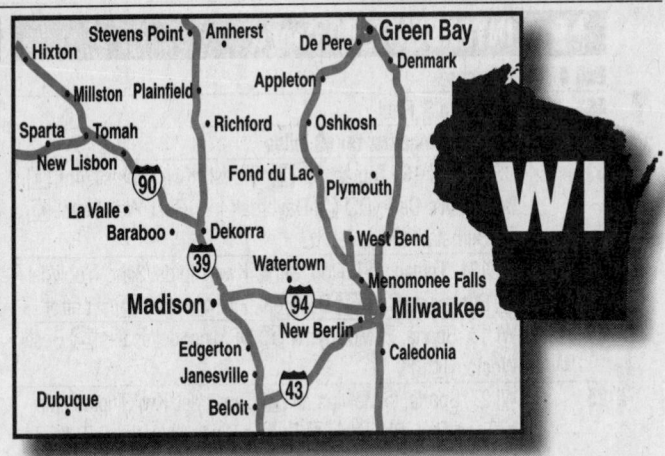

WI

MADISON

Exit #	Services
138a	I-94, E to Milwaukee, W to La Crosse, **I-90 W and I-94 W run together for 93 miles,** (exits left from eb)
135c b	US 151, Madison, N 🅖 BP/dsl 🍴 Erin's Cafe, Happy Wok, Milio's Sandwiches, Uno Grill 🏠 Cambria Suites, Courtyard, Fairfield Inn, GrandStay Suites, Holiday Inn, Staybridge Suites 🅞 Buick/GMC, Chrysler/Dodge/Jeep, Ford, Honda, Hyundai, Kia, Mazda, Nissan, Subaru, Toyota/Scion
135a	US 151, Madison, S 🅖 BP, Citgo, Mobil, Shell 🍴 Applebee's, Arby's, Buffalo Wild Wings, Chili's, Chipotle Mexican, Cracker Barrel, Culver's, Denny's, Dickey's BBQ, DoLittle's Woodfire Grill, Fazoli's, Hardee's, Hometown Buffet, Hooters, IHOP, Imperial Garden, Jimmy John's, KFC, McDonald's, Milio's, Noodles&Co, Olive Garden, Outback Steaks, Panera Bread, Perkins, Pizza Hut, Potbelly, Qdoba, Red Lobster, Red Robin, Rocky's Pizza, Starbucks, Taco Bell, Takumi Japanese, TGI-Friday's, Toppers's Pizza, TX Roadhouse, Wendy's 🏠 Best Western, Comfort Inn, Crowne Plaza Hotel/rest., EconoLodge, Hampton Inn, Howard Johnson, Microtel, Motel 6, Red Roof Inn, Residence Inn, Rodeway Inn, Super 8 🅞 $Tree, Aldi Foods, AT&T, Barnes&Noble, Best Buy, Burlington Coats, city park, Dick's, Firestone/auto, Goodyear/auto, Gordman's, Hobby Lobby, Home Depot, Hy-Vee Foods, JC Penney, JoAnn Fabrics, Kohl's, mall, Marshalls, Menards, Michaels, Office Depot, Old Navy, Petsmart, Savers, Sears/auto, ShopKO, st patrol, Target, Verizon
132	US 51, Madison, De Forest, N 🅖 Shell/Pinecone Rest/dsl/24hr 🅞 Camping World RV Ctr, Gander Mtn, S 🍴 TA/BP/Subway/Taco Bell/dsl/scales/24hr/@ 🅞 Freightliner/GMC/Volvo/White, Goodyear, Peterbilt, WI RV World
131	WI 19, Waunakee, N 🅖 Kwik Trip/dsl, Mobil/dsl, Speedway/dsl 🍴 A&W, McDonald's, Rodeside Grill 🏠 Days Inn, Super 8 🅞 fireworks, Kenworth, Mousehouse Cheesehaus, truckwash
126	rd V, De Forest, to Dane, N 🅖 BP/A&W/Rococo's/dsl, Phillips 66/Arby's/dsl 🍴 Burger King, Culver's, McDonald's, Subway, Taco Bell 🏠 Holiday Inn Express 🅞 Cheese Chalet, KOA, S 🅖 Exxon, Shell 🏠 Comfort Inn 🅞 dsl repair
119	WI 60, Arlington, to Lodi, S 🅖 Mobil/A&W/Cousins Subs/dsl 🍴 A&W, Rococo's Pizza 🏠 Quality Inn 🅞 dsl/tire repair
115	rd CS, Poynette, to Lake Wisconsin, N 🅖 BP/dsl 🍴 McDonald's, Subway 🅞 auto repair, dsl truck/trailer repair, Smokey Hollow Camping, trout fishing
113mm	🆁🆂 **both lanes, full** 🏠 **facilities, litter barrels, petwalk,** 🅞, 🔄 **vending**
111mm	Wisconsin River
108b a	I-39 N, WI 78, to US 51 N, Portage, N 🅞 🅷 to WI Dells, S 🅖 BP, Mobil, Petro/Iron Skillet/DQ/Subway/dsl/24hr/@ 🏠 Comfort Suites, Days Inn 🅞 Blue Beacon
106mm	Baraboo River
106	WI 33, Portage, N 🅞 🅷 S 🅖 BP 🅞 Circus World Museum, Devil's Lake SP, Kamp Dakota, SkyHigh Camping, to Cascade Mtn Ski Area, Wayside Park
92	US 12, to Baraboo, N 🅖 BP/dsl, Citgo/Subway/dsl, Exxon, Mobil/Dunkin Donuts/dsl/24hr 🍴 Buffalo Phil's Grille, Burger King, Cheese Factory Rest, Cracker Barrel, Culver's, Denny's, Domino's, Famous Dave's BBQ, Field's Steaks, Green Owl Pizza, Marley's Rest., McDonald's, Milio's, Monk's Grill, Noodles&Co, Pizza Ranch, Ponderosa, R Place Italian, Sarento's Italian, Starbucks, Taco Bell, Uno Grill, Wintergreen Grill 🏠 Alakai Hotel, Country Squire Motel, Dell Creek Motel, Glacier Canyon Lodge, Grand Marquis Inn, Great Wolf Lodge,

WISCONSIN DELLS

92	Continued Holiday Inn Express, Kalahari Resort, Ramada, Wilderness Hotel, Wintergreen Hotel 🅞 Mkt Square Cheese, museum, Tanger Outlets Famous Brands, URGENT CARE, Verizon, S 🏠 Motel 6 🅞 🅷 Jellystone Camping, Mirror Lake SP, Red Oak Camping, Scenic Traveler RV Ctr
89	WI 23, Lake Delton, N 🅖 Phillips 66, Shell/dsl 🍴 Brathouse Grill, Denny's Diner, Howie's Rest., KFC, Moosejaw Pizza 🏠 Hilton Garden, Kings Inn, Malibu Inn, Olympia Motel, Travelodge 🅞 Crystal Grand Music Theatre, Jellystone Camping, Springbrook Camping, USPO, S 🍴 McDonald's 🅞 $Tree, Country Roads RV Park, Home Depot, Jo-Ann, Kohl's, Walmart/Subway
87	WI 13, Wisconsin Dells, N 🅖 Citgo/dsl, Mobil/Arby's/dsl, Shell/Dunkin Donuts 🍴 Applebee's, Bunyan's Rest., Burger King, Coldstone, Culver's, Denny's, IHOP, Jimmy John's, McDonald's, Mexicali Rose Rest., Perkins, Starbucks, Taco Bell, Wei's Chinese 🏠 Ambers Resort, AmericInn, Baymont Inn, Best Western, Econolodge, Polynesian Hotel, Quality Inn, Super 8 🅞 golf, info, KOA, Sherwood Forest Camping, Walgreens, waterpark
85	US 12, WI 16, Wisconsin Dells, N 🏠 Fairway Motel 🅞 KOA, Sherwood Forest Camping, Standing Rock Camping, to Rocky Arbor SP, S 🅖 BP 🍴 Piccadilly's 🏠 Arrowhead Camping, Days End Motel, Edge-O-the-Dell RV Camping, Summer Breeze Resort
79	rd HH, Lyndon Sta, S 🅖 BP/Subway/dsl/24hr
76mm	🆁🆂 wb, full 🏠 facilities, litter barrels, petwalk, 🅞, 🔄 vending
74mm	🆁🆂 eb, full 🏠 facilities, litter barrels, petwalk, 🅞, 🔄 vending
69	WI 82, Mauston, N 🅖 Mauston TP/BP/Taco Bell/24hr, Pilot/Wendy's/dsl/scales/24hr, Shell/24hr 🍴 China Buffet, Family Rest. 🏠 Best Western Oasis, Quality Inn, Super 8 🅞 Carr Valley Cheese, to Buckhorn SP, S 🅖 KwikTrip/Hearty Platter Rest/dsl/scales/24hr, Mobil 🍴 Culver's, Log Cabin Deli, McDonald's, Pizza Hut, Roman Castle Rest., Subway 🏠 Alaskan Inn 🅞 🅷 $General, Buick/Chevrolet, Family$, Festival Foods, K-Mart, Verizon, vet, Walgreens
61	WI 80, New Lisbon, to Necedah, N 🅖 Mobil/A&W/Subway/dsl/scales/24hr 🏠 Edge O' the Woods Motel, Travelers Inn 🅞 Buckhorn SP, Chrysler/Dodge/Jeep, fireworks, Ford, S 🅖 KwikTrip/24hr 🅞 city park, Elroy-Sparta ST Tr, USPO
55	rd C, Camp Douglas, N 🅞 to Camp Williams, Volk Field, wayside, S 🅖 BP/dsl, Mobil/Home Front Cafe/dsl 🏠 K&K Motel 🅞 to Mill Bluff SP
48	rd PP, Oakdale, N 🅖 Road Ranger/Pilot/Subway/dsl/scales/24hr 🅞 antiques, Granger's Camping, KOA, truck/car wash, S 🅖 Loves/Hardee's/dsl/scales/24hr 🅞 Mill Bluff SP, repair

492 WISCONSIN   🅶 = gas 🍴 = food 🛏 = lodging 🅾 = other 🆁🆂 = rest stop   Copyright 2015 - the Next EXIT ®

INTERSTATE 90 Cont'd

Exit #	Services
45	I-94 W, to St Paul
	I-90 E and I-94 E run together for 93 miles
43	US 12, WI 16, Tomah, N 🅶 BP/dsl, KwikTrip/dsl/24hr 🍴 Burnstadt's Café, DQ 🛏 Daybreak Inn, Rest Well Motel 🅾 �H Burnstadt's Mkt, vet
41	WI 131, Tomah, to Wilton, N 🅶 KwikTrip/dsl/24hr, Mobil/dsl 🍴 Burnstadts Cafe 🛏 Daybreak Inn 🅾 vet, S 🅾 st patrol
28	WI 16, Sparta, Ft McCoy, N 🅶 BP/diner/dsl/scales 🛏 Best Western 🅾 �H
25	WI 27, Sparta, to Melvina, N 🅶 Cenex/dsl, KwikTrip/dsl, Mobil/Taco Bell, Shell/dsl 🍴 Burger King, Culver's, DQ, KFC, McDonald's, Pizza Hut, Sparta Rest., Subway 🛏 Country Inn, Super 8 🅾 �H $General, Buick/Chevrolet, Family$, Ford, Hansens IGA, O'Reilly Parts, Walgreens, Walmart/Subway, S 🅾 camping
22mm	🆁🆂 wb, full 🚻 facilities, litter barrels, petwalk, 🅲, 🖼 vending
20mm	🆁🆂 eb, full 🚻 facilities, litter barrels, petwalk, 🅲, 🖼 vending
15	WI 162, Bangor, to Coon Valley, N 🅶 S 🅾 Chevrolet
12	rd C, W Salem, N 🅶 Cenex/cafe/dsl/24hr 🅾 Coulee Region RV Ctr, NAPA, Neshonoc Camping, S 🅶 BP/Subway/dsl 🛏 AmericInn
10mm	weigh sta wb
5	WI 16, La Crosse, N 🍴 BA Burrito, Buffalo Wild Wings, Ciatti's Italian, Coldstone, Manny's Mexican, Outback Steaks 🛏 Baymont Inn, Hampton Inn, Microtel 🅾 $Tree, Aldi Foods, Freightliner, Home Depot, Walmart/Subway, Woodman's Foods/gas/lube, S 🅶 Kwik Trip/dsl/24hr 🍴 Bamboo House, Burracho's Mexican Grill, Carlos O'Kelly's, ChuckeCheese, Culver's, Fazoli's, Hong Kong Buffet, HuHot Grill, Jimmy John's, McDonald's, Old Country Buffet, Olive Garden, Perkins, Starbucks, TGIFriday's, TX Roadhouse 🛏 Holiday Inn Express 🅾 �H Barnes&Noble, Best Buy, Chevrolet, Dick's, F&F, Ford/Lincoln, Hobby Lobby, JC Penney, Kohl's, Macy's, mall, Michael's, Sears/auto, ShopKO, Target, Walgreens
4	US 53 N, WI 16, to WI 157, La Crosse, N 🅾 Harley-Davidson, S 🅶 Kwik Trip, TO 🍴 Applebee's, Burger King, Caribou Coffee, China Inn, Cousins Subs, Famous Dave's BBQ, Grizzly's Rest, Panera Bread, Papa Murphy's, Red Lobster, Rococo's Pizza, Shogun Hibachi, Subway, Taco Bell, Wendy's 🛏 Comfort Inn 🅾 �H Festival Food/24hr, Gander Mtn, GNC, Goodyear/auto, Hancock Fabrics, La Crosse River St Trail, Office Depot, Old Navy, PetCo, Petsmart, Sam's Club, Tires+, TJ Maxx, Verizon
3	US 53 S, WI 35, to La Crosse, S 🅶 Clark/dsl, Kwik Trip 🍴 Burger King, Coney Island, Edwardo's Pizza, Hardee's, KFC, La Crosse Rest., McDonald's, North Country Steaks, Perkins, Pizza Hut, Subway 🛏 Best Value Inn, Best Western, Motel 6, Quality Inn, Settle Inn, Super 8 🅾 ShopKO, to Great River St Trail, U-Haul, Viterbo Coll, Walgreens
2.5mm	Black River
2	rd B, French Island, N 🅾 🖼, S 🅶 BP/dsl 🛏 Days Inn/rest. 🅾 IGA Foods
1mm	**Welcome Center eb, full 🚻 facilities, info, litter barrels, petwalk, 🅲, 🖼 vending**
0mm	Wisconsin/Minnesota state line, Mississippi River

INTERSTATE 94

Exit #	Services
349mm	Wisconsin/Illinois state line, **weigh sta nb**
347	WI 165, rd Q, Lakeview Pkwy, **E Welcome Ctr, full facilities** 🅶 BP/dsl 🍴 Chancery Rest., Culver's, McDonald's 🛏 Radisson 🅾 Old Navy, Prime Outlets/famous brands
345mm	Des Plaines River
345	rd C, E 🛏 Holiday Inn Express (1mi)
344	WI 50, Lake Geneva, to Kenosha, **E 1 mi** 🍴 Buffalo Wild Wings, Cheddar's, Citgo/dsl, Cousins Subs, Dickey's BBQ, Famous Dave's, Nick-N-Willy's, Noodles&Co, Olive Garden, Panda Express, Perkins, Pizza Hut, Shell/dsl, Sparti's Gyros, Starbucks, Tuscany Bistro, TX Roadhouse, White Castle, Woodman's/gas 🛏 Candlewood Suites, Holiday Inn Express, La Quinta, Super 8 🅾 �H AT&T, Best Buy, Chevrolet, Dick's, Gander Mtn, GNC, JC Penney, Petsmart, Target, Verizon, Walgreens, W 🅶 BP, Speedway/dsl 🍴 Arby's, Birchwood Grill, Cracker Barrel, KFC, McDonald's, Pheonix Rest., Wendy's 🛏 Best Western, Country Inn&Suites, Quality Inn, Value Inn 🅾 BratStop Cheese Store, CarMax, Honda, Nissan, Toyota/Scion
342	WI 158, to Kenosha, E Harley-Davidson, W antiques
340	WI 142, rd S, to Kenosha, E 🅶 Kenosha TP/BP/Subway/dsl/E85/LP/scales/24hr 🅾 �H W 🍴 Mars Cheese Castle Rest. 🛏 Oasis Inn 🅾 Fun Time RV Ctr, to Bong RA
339	rd E
337	rd KR, to Mt Pleasant, W 🍴 Apple Holler Rest/orchard
335	WI 11, to Mt Pleasant, Burlington, to Racine
333	WI 20, Waterford, to Racine, E 🅶 KwikTrip/dsl/24hr, Shell/Cousins Subs/dsl 🍴 Burger King, McDonald's 🛏 Days Inn, Holiday Inn Express 🅾 �H W 🅶 Citgo/Wendy's/dsl/24hr, Petro/Mobil/Iron Skillet/dsl/scales/24hr/@ 🍴 Culver's, Route 20 Outhouse Grill, Subway 🛏 Travelodge 🅾 Burlington RV Ctr, visitor info
329	rd K, Thompsonville, to Racine, E 🅶 Loves/Arby's/Subway/dsl/scales/24hr, W 🍴 A&W 🅾 dsl repair
328mm	weigh sta wb
327	rd G, W fireworks
326	7 Mile Rd, E 🅶 BP, Mobil/dsl 🅾 Jellystone Park, W 🅾 antiques
325	WI 241 N (from wb), to 27th St
322	WI 100, to Ryan Rd, E 🅶 KwikTrip/dsl 🍴 McDonald's, Wendy's 🅾 dsl repair, W 🅶 Loves/Denny's/dsl/LP/scales/RV dump/24hr, Mobil, Loves/Subway/dsl/LP/scales/24hr, Shell/A&W/KFC/dsl 🍴 Arby's, Cousins Subs, Perkins, Yen Hwa Chinese 🛏 Staybridge Suites, Value Inn 🅾 AutoZone, Blue Beacon, Freightliner/repair, Pick'n Save, vet, Walgreens
321	Drexel Ave
320	rd BB, Rawson Ave, E 🅶 BP, Mobil 🍴 Applebee's, Burger King 🛏 La Quinta
319	rd ZZ, College Ave, E 🅶 Shell/Subway, Speedway/dsl 🍴 Branded Steer Rest., McDonald's 🛏 Candlewood Suites, Comfort Suites, Country Inn&Suites, Crowne Plaza, Days Inn, EconoLodge, Fairfield Inn, Hampton Inn, Holiday Inn Express, MainStay Suites, Ramada, Red Roof Inn, W 🅶 BP, FoodMart
318	WI 119, 🖼
317	I-43, I-894 (from wb)
316	I-43 S, I-894 W (I-94 exits left from eb), to Beloit
314b	Howard Ave, to Milwaukee, W to Alverno Coll
314a	Holt Ave, E 🅶 Andy's/dsl 🍴 Applebee's, Arby's, China King, Little Caesars, Quiznos, Starbucks, Subway, Wendy's 🅾 $General, Home Depot, Pick'n Save Foods, Sentry Foods,

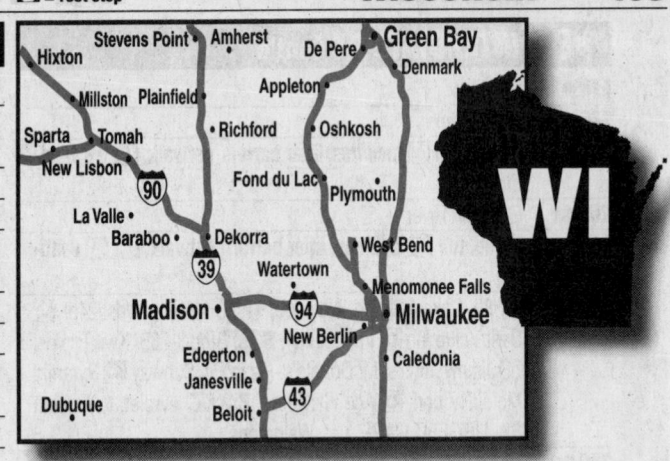

M I L W A U K E E

INTERSTATE 94 Cont'd

Exit #	Services
314a	Continued
	Target, vet, W 🅞 H to Alverno Coll
312b a	Becher St, Mitchell St, Lapham Blvd, W 🅖 BP, Citgo, Shell
311	WI 59, National Ave, 6th St, downtown
310c	I-794 E, E 🏠 Hilton, Holiday Inn 🅞 Lake Michigan Port of Entry, to downtown
310b	I-43 N, to Green Bay
310a	13th St (from eb), E 🅞 H
309b	26th St, 22nd St, Clybourn St, St Paul Ave, N 🅞 H to Marquette U
309a	35th St, N 🅖 BP, Speedway 🅞 URGENT CARE
308c b	US 41
308a	VA Ctr, N 🅞 Miller Brewing, S 🅞 Miller Park
307b	68th-70th St, Hawley Rd
307a	68th-70th St
306	WI 181, to 84th St, N 🅞 H S 🅞 Olympic Training Facility
305b	US 45 N, to Fond du Lac, N 🅞 H
305a	I-894 S, US 45 S, to Chicago, to ✈
304b a	WI 100, N 🅖 7-11, BP, Clark/dsl, Shell/dsl 🍴 Cousins Subs, Edwardo's Pizza, Ghengis Khan BBQ, Habanero's Mexican, HoneyBaked Cafe, Jimmy John's, Mo's Irish Grill, Peony Chinese, Qdoba, Rococo's, Starbucks, Subway, Taco Bell 🏠 Days Inn 🅞 H zoo, S 🍴 MiniMart 100, Mobil, Speedway/dsl 🍴 Culver's, DQ, Fazoli's, McDonald's, Pallas Rest., Starbucks, Wendy's 🏠 Days Inn 🅞 Midas, O'Reilly Parts, Sam's Club, U-Haul, Walgreens
301b a	Moorland Rd, N 🅖 Mobil 🍴 Bakers Square, Bravo Italiano, Buffalo Wild Wings, Caribou Coffee, Chili's, Claim Jumper, Cooper's Hawk, Culver's, Firehouse Subs, Fleming's Rest., Fuddrucker's, Hooters, McDonald's, Mitchell's Fish Mkt, Noodles&Co, Original Pancake House, Qdoba, Red Robin, Starbucks, Starbucks, Stir Crazy, TGIFriday's 🏠 Courtyard, Sheraton, TownePlace Suites 🅞 Barnes&Noble, CVS Drug, Fresh Mkt Foods, Goodyear/auto, JC Penney, Jo-Ann Fabrics, mall, Metro Mkt, Michael's, Office Depot, PetCo, Petsmart, Sears/auto, SteinMart, TJ Maxx, vet, Walgreens, S 🍴 Champp's Grill, Charcoal Grill, Maxwell's Rest., Outback Steaks, Panera Bread 🏠 Best Western Midway, Brookfield Suites, Country Inn&Suites, Residence Inn 🅞 golf, Pick'n Save Foods, Walgreens
297	WI 164 S, US 18, rd JJ, Blue Mound Rd, Barker Rd, N 0-2 mi 🅖 Clark 🍴 Applebee's, BoneFish Grill, Boston Mkt, Brookfield Rest., Bullwinkle's Rest., Carrabba's, ChuckECheese's, Cousins Subs, George Webb Rest., HoneyBaked Ham, Jose's Mexican, KFC, Kopp's Custard, Loredos Mexican, McDonald's, Melting Pot, Olive Garden, Perkins, Potbelly, Subway 🏠 DoubleTree, Extended Stay America, Hampton Inn, La Quinta, Motel 6, Quality Inn 🅞 $Tree, Acura, Advance Parts, Aldi Foods, Best Buy, GNC, K-Mart, Lexus/Mazda/VW, Meineke, Metro Mkt, S 🅖 Clark, F&F/dsl, PDQ 🍴 Arby's, Burger King, Cousin's Subs, Culver's, Famous Dave's BBQ, McDonald's, Milio's, New China, Oscar's Burgers, Papa Murphy's, Sonic, Starbucks, Taco Bell, Topper's Pizza, TX Roadhouse, Wendy's 🏠 Ramada Ltd, Super 8 🅞 AT&T, Buick/GMC, Cadillac, CarMax, CarX, Chevrolet, Firestone/auto, Ford, Gander Mtn, Home Depot, Honda, Hyundai, Infiniti/Maserati/Mercedes/Porsche, Jaguar/Land Rover/Volvo, Kia, Kohl's, Menards, Midas, Nissan, Pick'n Save Foods, Radio Shack, Sam's Club, st patrol, Target, Tires+, Volvo, Walgreens

W A U K E S H A

295	rd F, to WI 74, Waukesha, N 🅖 KwikTrip/dsl 🍴 Jimmy John's 🏠 Marriott, S 🅞 H to Carroll Coll
294	WI 164, rd J S, to Waukesha, N 🅖 Mobil/Subway/dsl 🍴 Machine Shed Rest., Thunder Bay Grille 🏠 Holiday Inn, Wildwood Lodge, S 🅞 Expo Ctr, Peterbilt
293c	WI 16 W, Pewaukee (from wb), N 🅞 GE Plant
293b a	rd T, Wausheka, Pewaukee, S 🅖 KwikTrip, Mobil 🍴 Arby's, Asian Fusion, Canyon City Wood Grill, Caribou Coffee, Cousins Subs, Culver's, Denny's, Dunkin Donuts, Feng's Kitchen, Jimmy John's, McDonald's, Mr. Wok, Papa Murphy's, Peking House, Primos Pizza, Qdoba, Rococo's Pizza, Rox Grill, Spring City Rest., Subway, Taco Amigo, Topper's Pizza, Weissgerber's Gasthaus Rest., Wendy's 🏠 Best Western 🅞 $Tree, AT&T, AutoZone, CVS Drug, Firestone/auto, GNC, Goodharvest Mkt, JoAnn Fabrics, Office Depot, Pick'n Save Foods, Radio Shack, Verizon, Walgreens
291	rd G, rd TT, N 🏠 Country Springs Inn
290	rd SS, Pewaukee
287	WI 83, Hartland, to Wales, N 🍴 5 Guys Burgers, Applebee's, Hardee's, McDonald's, Noodles&Co, Panera Bread, Perkins, Qdoba, Starbucks, Water St Brewery/rest. 🏠 Country Pride Inn, Holiday Inn Express 🅞 Albrecht's Mkt, Amish Barn Gifts, Best Buy, GNC, Kohl's, Marshalls, Radio Shack, Verizon, Walgreens, S 🅖 BP/dsl, PDQ/dsl/24hr 🍴 Burger King, Coldstone, DQ, Jimmy John's, Marty's Pizza, Pacific Asian Bistro, Pizza Hut, StoneCreek Coffee, Subway 🏠 La Quinta 🅞 $Tree, Ace Hardware, Home Depot, PetCo, Target, Tires+, vet, Walmart,
285	rd C, Delafield, N 🅖 BP/dsl, Mobil/deli 🏠 Delafield Hotel 🅞 to St John's Military Academy, S 🅞 to Kettle Moraine SF
283	rd P, to Sawyer Rd
282	WI 67, Dousman, to Oconomowoc, N 0-2 mi 🅖 KwikTrip/dsl, Mobil 🍴 Chili's, Cousins Subs, Culver's, Feng's Kitchen, Jimmy John's, Pizza Hut, Quiznos, Rococo's Pizza, Rosati's Pizza, Sammy's Taste Of Chicago, Schlotzsky's, Starbucks, Stone Creek Coffee, Subway 🏠 Hilton Garden, Olympia Resort 🅞 Ace Hardware, Aldi Foods, AT&T, Brennan's Mkt, Ford, GNC, K-Mart, Pick'n Save, Radio Shack, vet, Walgreens, S 🏠 Staybridge Suites 🅞 H Harley-Davidson, Old World WI HS (13mi), to Kettle Morraine SF (8mi)
277	Willow Glen Rd (from eb, no return)
275	rd F, Ixonia, to Sullivan, N 🅖 Mobil/dsl 🅞 Concord Gen Store, S 🅞 camping
267	WI 26, Johnson Creek, to Watertown, N 🅖 BP/McDonald's/dsl, Shell/dsl/rest./scales/24hr 🍴 Arby's, Hwy Harry's Cafe 🏠 Comfort Suites, Days Inn 🅞 Goodyear/auto, Johnson Creek Outlet Ctr/famous brands, Old Navy, S 🅖 KwikTrip/dsl 🍴 Culver's, Subway 🅞 H Kohl's, Menards, to Aztalan SP

WI

Exit #	Services

⬆E   INTERSTATE 94 Cont'd

Exit #	Services
266mm	Rock River
264mm	🆁🆂 wb, full 🚻 facilities, litter barrels, petwalk, 🕾, 🖼 vending
263mm	Crawfish River
261mm	🆁🆂 eb, full 🚻 facilities, litter barrels, petwalk, 🕾, 🖼 vending
259	WI 89, Lake Mills, to Waterloo, N 🅿 Mobil/rest/dsl/24hr 🛏 Best Value Inn 🅾 truck repair, S 🅿 BP/dsl/E85, KwikTrip/dsl 🍴 Jimmy John's, McDonald's, Pizza Pit, Subway 🛏 Pyramid Motel/RV park 🅾 Ace Hardware, Buick/Chevrolet, to Aztalan SP, URGENT CARE, vet, Walgreens
250	WI 73, Deerfield, to Marshall
244	rd n, Sun Prairie, Cottage Grove, N 🅿 BP, S 🅿 BP, KwikTrip 🍴 Arby's, Subway
240	I-90 E.

I-90 W and I-94 W run together for 93 miles. See I-90, exits 48-138.

Exit #	Services
138a	I-94, E to Milwaukee, W to La Crosse, (exits left from eb)
135c b	US 151, Madison, N 🅿 BP/dsl 🍴 Erin's Cafe, Happy Wok, Milio's Sandwiches, Uno Grill 🛏 Cambria Suites, Courtyard, Fairfield Inn, GrandStay Suites, Holiday Inn, Staybridge Suites 🅾 Buick/GMC, Chrysler/Dodge/Jeep, Ford, Honda, Hyundai, Kia, Mazda, Nissan, Subaru, Toyota/Scion
135a	US 151, Madison, S 🅿 BP, Citgo, Mobil, Shell 🍴 Applebee's, Arby's, Buffalo Wild Wings, Chili's, Chipotle Mexican, Cracker Barrel, Culver's, Denny's, Dickey's BBQ, DoLittle's Woodfire Grill, Fazoli's, Hardee's, Hometown Buffet, Hooters, IHOP, Imperial Garden, Jimmy John's, KFC, McDonald's, Milio's, Noodles&Co, Olive Garden, Outback Steaks, Panera Bread, Perkins, Pizza Hut, Potbelly, Qdoba, Red Lobster, Red Robin, Rocky's Pizza, Starbucks, Taco Bell, Takumi Japanese, TGI-Friday's, Toppers's Pizza, TX Roadhouse, Wendy's 🛏 Best Western, Comfort Inn, Crowne Plaza Hotel/rest., EconoLodge, Hampton Inn, Howard Johnson, Microtel, Motel 6, Red Roof Inn, Residence Inn, Rodeway Inn, Super 8 🅾 $Tree, Aldi Foods, AT&T, Barnes&Noble, Best Buy, Burlington Coats, city park, Dick's, Firestone/auto, Goodyear/auto, Gordman's, Hobby Lobby, Home Depot, Hy-Vee Foods, JC Penney, JoAnn Fabrics, Kohl's, mall, Marshalls, Menards, Michaels, Office Depot, Old Navy, Petsmart, Savers, Sears/auto, ShopKO, st patrol, Target, Verizon
132	US 51, Madison, De Forest, N 🅿 Shell/Pinecone Rest/dsl/24hr 🅾 Camping World RV Ctr, Gander Mtn, S 🅿 TA/BP/Subway/Taco Bell/dsl/scales/24hr/@ 🅾 Freightliner/GMC/Volvo/White, Goodyear, Peterbilt, WI RV World
131	WI 19, Waunakee, N 🅿 Kwik Trip/dsl, Mobil/dsl, Speedway/dsl 🍴 A&W, McDonald's, Rodeside Grill 🛏 Days Inn, Super 8 🅾 fireworks, Kenworth, Mousehouse Cheesehaus, truckwash
126	rd V, De Forest, to Dane, N 🅿 BP/A&W/Rococo's/dsl, Phillips 66/Arby's/dsl 🍴 Burger King, Culver's, McDonald's, Subway, Taco Bell 🛏 Holiday Inn Express 🅾 Cheese Chalet, KOA, S 🅿 Exxon, Shell 🛏 Comfort Inn 🅾 dsl repair
119	WI 60, Arlington, to Lodi, S 🅿 Mobil/A&W/Cousins Subs/dsl 🍴 A&W, Rococo's Pizza 🛏 Quality Inn 🅾 dsl/tire repair
115	rd CS, Poynette, to Lake Wisconsin, N 🅿 BP/dsl 🍴 McDonald's, Subway 🅾 auto repair, dsl truck/trailer repair, Smokey Hollow Camping, trout fishing
113mm	🆁🆂 both lanes, full 🚻 facilities, litter barrels, petwalk, 🕾, 🖼 vending
111mm	Wisconsin River
108b a	I-39 N, WI 78, to US 51 N, Portage, N 🅾 🛏 to WI Dells, S 🅿 BP, Mobil, Petro/Iron Skillet/DQ/Subway/dsl/24hr/@ 🛏 Comfort Suites, Days Inn 🅾 Blue Beacon
106mm	Baraboo River
106	WI 33, Portage, N 🅾 🛏 S 🅿 BP 🅾 Circus World Museum, Devil's Lake SP, Kamp Dakota, SkyHigh Camping, to Cascade Mtn Ski Area, Wayside Park
92	US 12, to Baraboo, N 🅿 BP/dsl, Citgo/Subway/dsl, Exxon, Mobil/Dunkin Donuts/dsl/24hr 🍴 Buffalo Phil's Grille, Burger King, Cheese Factory Rest, Cracker Barrel, Culver's, Denny's, Domino's, Famous Dave's BBQ, Field's Steaks, Green Owl Pizza, Marley's Rest., McDonald's, Milio's, Monk's Grill, Noodles&Co, Pizza Ranch, Ponderosa, R Place Italian, Sarento's Italian, Starbucks, Taco Bell, Uno Grill, Wintergreen Grill 🛏 Alakai Hotel, Country Squire Motel, Dell Creek Motel, Glacier Canyon Lodge, Grand Marquis Inn, Great Wolf Lodge, Holiday Inn Express, Kalahari Resort, Ramada, Wilderness Hotel, Wintergreen Hotel 🅾 Mkt Square Cheese, museum, Tanger Outlets Famous Brands, URGENT CARE, Verizon, S 🛏 Motel 6 🅾 🛏 Jellystone Camping, Mirror Lake SP, Red Oak Camping, Scenic Traveler RV Ctr
89	WI 23, Lake Delton, N 🅿 Phillips 66, Shell/dsl 🍴 Brathouse Grill, Denny's Diner, Howie's Rest., KFC, Moosejaw Pizza 🛏 Hilton Garden, Kings Inn, Malibu Inn, Olympia Motel, Travelodge 🅾 Crystal Grand Music Theatre, Jellystone Camping, Springbrook Camping, USPO, S 🍴 McDonald's 🅾 $Tree, Country Roads RV Park, Home Depot, Jo-Ann, Kohl's, Walmart/Subway
87	WI 13, Wisconsin Dells, N 🅿 Citgo/dsl, Mobil/Arby's/dsl, Shell/Dunkin Donuts 🍴 Applebee's, Bunyan's Rest., Burger King, Coldstone, Culver's, Denny's, IHOP, Jimmy John's, McDonald's, Mexicali Rose Rest., Perkins, Starbucks, Taco Bell, Wei's Chinese 🛏 Ambers Resort, AmericInn, Baymont Inn, Best Western, Econolodge, Polynesian Hotel, Quality Inn, Super 8 🅾 golf, info, KOA, Sherwood Forest Camping, Walgreens, waterpark
85	US 12, WI 16, Wisconsin Dells, N 🛏 Fairway Motel 🅾 KOA, Sherwood Forest Camping, Standing Rock Camping, to Rocky Arbor SP, S 🅿 BP 🍴 Piccadilly's 🛏 Arrowhead Camping, Days End Motel, Edge-O-the-Dell RV Camping, Summer Breeze Resort
79	rd HH, Lyndon Sta, S 🅿 BP/Subway/dsl/24hr
76mm	🆁🆂 wb, full 🚻 facilities, litter barrels, petwalk, 🕾, 🖼 vending
74mm	🆁🆂 eb, full 🚻 facilities, litter barrels, petwalk, 🕾, 🖼 vending
69	WI 82, Mauston, N 🅿 Mauston TP/BP/Taco Bell/24hr, 🅿/Wendy's/dsl/scales/24hr, Shell/24hr 🍴 China Buffet, Family Rest. 🛏 Best Western Oasis, Quality Inn, Super 8 🅾 Carr Valley Cheese, to Buckhorn SP, S 🅿 KwikTrip/Hearty Platter Rest/dsl/scales/24hr, Mobil 🍴 Culver's, Log Cabin Deli, McDonald's, Pizza Hut, Roman Castle Rest., Subway 🛏 Alaskan Inn 🅾 🛏 $General, Buick/Chevrolet, Family$, Festival Foods, K-Mart, Verizon, vet, Walgreens
61	WI 80, New Lisbon, to Necedah, N 🅿 Mobil/A&W/Subway/dsl/scales/24hr 🛏 Edge O' the Woods Motel, Travelers Inn 🅾 Buckhorn SP, Chrysler/Dodge/Jeep, fireworks, Ford, S 🅿 KwikTrip/24hr 🅾 city park, Elroy-Sparta ST Tr, USPO
55	rd C, Camp Douglas, N 🅾 to Camp Williams, Volk Field, wayside, S 🅿 BP/dsl, Mobil/Home Front Cafe/dsl 🛏 K&K Motel 🅾 to Mill Bluff SP
48	rd PP, Oakdale, N 🅿 Road Ranger/🅿/Subway/dsl/scales/24hr 🅾 antiques, Granger's Camping, KOA, truck/car wash, S 🅿 Loves/Hardee's/dsl/scales/24hr 🅾 Mill Bluff SP, repair

Left margin: **MADISON**   **EAU CLAIRE**   **WI**

INTERSTATE 94 Cont'd

Exit #	Services
147	I-90 W, to La Crosse
	I-94 and I-90 run together 93 miles.
143	US 12, WI 21, Tomah, N 📷 Mobil/dsl 🍴 A&W/LJ Silver, Perkins 🛏 AmericInn, Best Western, Microtel, Super 8 📷 Humbird Cheese/gifts, truckwash, S 📷 BP, KwikTrip/rest./dsl/scales/24hr 🍴 Arby's, China Buffet, Culver's, Ground Round, KFC, McDonald's, Pizza Hut, Subway, Taco Bell 🛏 Cranberry Lodge, EconoLodge, Hampton Inn, Quality Inn 📷 🅷 $Tree, Advance Parts, Aldi Foods, U-Haul, Verizon, Walmart/Subway, to Ft McCoy (9mi) **S on US 12** 🍴 Burger King 📷 Ace Hardware, Chrysler/Dodge/Jeep, Firestone/auto, Ford, GMC, NAPA, O'Reilly Parts
135	rd EW, Warrens, N 📷 Cenex/dsl 🛏 3 Bears Resort 📷 Jellystone Camping, S 🍴 Bog Rest.
128	rd O, Millston, N 📷 Black River SF, camping, S 📷 Cenex/dsl 📷 USPO
123mm	Rs/scenic view both lanes, full ♿ facilities, litter barrels, petwalk, 🚻, 🐾, vending
116	WI 54, N 📷 Cenex/Subway/Taco Johns/dsl/LP 🍴 Perkins 🛏 Best Western Arrowhead/rest., Comfort Inn, Super 8 📷 Black River RA, casino, Parkland Camp, S 📷 ⊕FLYING J/Denny's/dsl/24hr/@, KwikTrip/dsl 🍴 Burger King, Culver's, McDonald's, Oriental Kitchen, Pizza Hut 🛏 Days Inn 📷 $General, Buick/Chevrolet/GMC, Walmart/Subway
115mm	Black River
115	US 12, WI 27, Black River Falls, to Merrillan, S 📷 BP, Holiday/dsl 🍴 Hardee's, KFC, Subway, Sunrise Rest. 📷 🅷 Ace Hardware, Harley-Davidson, vet
105	to WI 95, Hixton, to Alma Center, N 🛏 Motel 95/camping 📷 KOA (3mi), S 📷 Cenex/dsl, Clark/dsl/24hr 🍴 Timber Valley Rest. 📷 city park
98	WI 121, Northfield, Pigeon Falls, to Alma Center, S 📷 Cenex/dsl 🍴 Crazy Jerry's Burgers
88	US 10, Osseo, to Fairchild, N 📷 BP/DQ, Exxon/Webb Rest./dsl/scales/24hr, Mobil/dsl 🍴 Hardee's, Moe's Diner 🛏 10-7 Inn, Super 8 📷 Chevrolet, Ford, Stoney Cr RV Park, S 📷 SA/dsl 🍴 McDonald's, Subway, Taco John's 🛏 Osseo Inn 📷 🅷 Family$
81	rd HH, rd KK, Foster, S 📷 BP/dsl/LP 🍴 Foster Cheesehaus
70	US 53, Eau Claire, N-off Golf Rd 📷 Mobil/dsl 🍴 Applebee's, Asia Palace, Buffalo Wild Wings, Burracho's Mexican, Caribou Coffee, Chipotle, Coldstone, Culver's, Fazoli's, Firehouse Subs, Fuji Steaks, Grizzly's Grill, HuHot Chinese, Jade Garden, Jimmy John's, Mancino's, Manny's Grill, McDonald's, Noodles&Co, Olive Garden, Panera Bread, TGIFriday's, TX Roadhouse 🛏 Baymont Inn, Country Inn&Suites, Grandstay, Holiday Inn 📷 $Tree, Aldi Foods, AT&T, Bam!, Best Buy, Hancock Fabrics, JC Penney, Jo-Ann Fabrics, Kohl's, Macy's, mall, Menards, Michael's, Office Depot, PetCo, Petsmart, Sam's Club, Scheel's Sports, Sears/auto, Target, TJ Maxx, Tuesday Morning, Verizon, Walmart/Subway, Younkers S 📷 Gander Mtn, st police
68	WI 93, to Eleva, N 📷 Holiday, KwikTrip/dsl 🍴 Burger King, Cousins Subs, DQ, Famous Dave's BBQ, Quiznos, Red Robin 🛏 EconoLodge 📷 BigLots, Chrysler/Dodge/Jeep, County Mkt Foods, Festival Foods, Firestone/auto, Goodyear/auto, Kia, NAPA, Nissan, Subaru, Suzuki, transmissions, vet, S 📷 Holiday/dsl 🛏 Metropolis Resort 📷 Audi/VW, Ford/Lincoln, Honda, Hyundai

Exit #	Services
65	WI 37, WI 85, Eau Claire, to Mondovi, N 📷 Exxon, Holiday/dsl, KwikTrip/dsl 🍴 Arby's, Godfather's Pizza, Green Mill Rest., Hardee's, Jimmy John's, Mancino's, McDonald's, Pizza Hut, Randy's Rest., Red Lobster, Starbucks, Subway, Taco Bell 🛏 Best Value Inn, Best Western, Clarion, Comfort Inn, Days Inn/rest., Hampton Inn, Highlander Inn, Plaza Hotel, Super 8 📷 🅷 County Mkt Foods, dsl repair, Radio Shack, ShopKo, Verizon, Walgreens
64mm	Chippewa River
59	to US 12, rd EE, to Eau Claire, N 📷 Holiday/Burger King/dsl/24hr, Holiday/Subway/dsl/24hr 🍴 Dana's Grill, El Mariachi, McDonald's 🛏 AmericInn, Days Inn, Knights Inn 📷 🅷 auto repair/towing, Freightliner, Mack/Volvo Trucks, Peterbilt, S 📷 dsl repair
52	US 12, WI 29, WI 40, Elk Mound, to Chippewa Falls, S 📷 U-Fuel/E85
49mm	weigh sta wb
45	rd B, Menomonie, N 📷 Cenex/Subway/dsl/scales/24hr, S 📷 KwikTrip/dsl/scales/24hr 🍴 Red Cedar Steaks 🛏 Quality Inn 📷 🅷 AOK RV Ctr, dsl repair, Kenworth, truckwash, Walmart Dist Ctr
44mm	Red Cedar River
43mm	Rs both lanes, full ♿ facilities, litter barrels, petwalk, 🚻, 🐾 vending, weather info
41	WI 25, Menomonie, N 📷 Cenex/E85 🍴 Applebee's, Caribou Coffee, China Buffet, Los Cabos Mexican, Pizza Hut, Subway 📷 🅷 $Tree, Aldi Foods, AT&T, Radio Shack, Twin Springs Camping, Walmart/Subway, S 📷 F&F/dsl, Holiday, SA/dsl 🍴 Arby's, Denny's, Dickey's BBQ, Jimmy John's, McDonald's, Perkins, Taco Bell, Taco John's, Wendy's 🛏 AmericInn, Country Inn&Suites, EconoLodge, Motel 6, Super 8 📷 Advance Parts, Buick/GMC, Chevrolet, Chrysler/Dodge/Jeep, K-Mart, Mkt Place Foods, O'Reilly Parts, to Red Cedar St Tr, Walgreens
32	rd Q, to Knapp
28	WI 128, Wilson, Elmwood, to Glenwood City, N 📷 KwikTrip/rest./dsl/24hr, S 📷 camping, dsl repair, Eau Galle RA
24	rd B, to Baldwin, N 📷 BP 🛏 Woodville Motel, S 📷 camping, Eau Galle RA
19	US 63, Baldwin, to Ellsworth, N 📷 Freedom/dsl, KwikTrip/Subway/dsl 🍴 A&W, DQ, Hardee's, McDonald's 🛏 AmericInn 📷 🅷 Mobil/rest./dsl 🛏 Super 8 📷 fireworks
16	rd T, Hammond
10	WI 65, Roberts, to New Richmond, 📷 BP/dsl (2mi), ⊕FLYING J /McDonald's/dsl/scales/24hr 🍴 Barnboard Rest. (2mi), Freightliner
8mm	weigh sta wb

M E N O M O N I E

⬆E INTERSTATE 94 Cont'd

Exit #	Services
4	US 12, rd U, Somerset, **N** 🅖 BP/dsl, TA/Country Pride/dsl/scales/24hr/@ 🛏 Regency Inn 🅞 to Willow River SP, vet
3	WI 35 S, to River Falls, U of WI River Falls
2	rd F, Carmichael Rd, Hudson, **N** 🅖 BP/repair, F&F/dsl, Freedom/dsl, Holiday, Holiday/dsl, KwikTrip/dsl, Shell 🍴 Applebee's, Arby's, Buffalo Wild Wings, Burger King, Caribou Coffee, Chipotle Mexican, Coldstone, Culver's, Denny's, Domino's, Fiesta Locà, Green Mill Rest., Jimmy John's, KFC, Kingdom Buffet, Little Caesars, McDonald's, Noodles&Co,

H U D S O N

2	Continued
	Papa Murphy's, Perkins, Pizza Hut, Starbucks, Subway, Taco Bell, Taco John's, Wendy's 🛏 Comfort Suites, Fairfield Inn, Holiday Inn Express, Hudson House Hotel, Royal Inn, Super 8 🅞 🎗 $Tree, Aldi Foods, Chevrolet/GMC, Chrysler/Dodge/Jeep, County Mkt Foods, Family Fresh Foods, Ford, GNC, Home Depot, Menards, NAPA, O'Reilly Parts, Radio Shack, repair, Target, TirePros, Tires+, to Kinnickinnic SP, USPO, Verizon, Verizon, Walgreens, Walmart
1	WI 35 N, Hudson, **N** 1 mi 🅖 Freedom/dsl, Holiday 🍴 Carbones Pizzeria, DQ
0mm	Wisconsin/Minnesota state line, St Croix River

WYOMING

⬆N INTERSTATE 25

Exit #	Services
300	I-90, E to Gillette, W to Billings. **I-25 begins/ends on I-90, exit 56.**
299	US 16, Buffalo, **E** 🅖 Cenex/dsl, Exxon/dsl, Maverik/dsl 🍴 Winchester Steaks 🛏 Buffalo Inn, Comfort Inn, Hampton Inn, Holiday Inn Express 🅞 Bighorn Tire, Deer Park Camping, KOA, vet, **W** 🅖 Cenex/dsl/24hr 🍴 Bozeman Tr Steaks, Dash Inn Rest., Hardee's, McDonald's, Pizza Hut, Sub Shop, Subway, Taco John's 🛏 Days Inn, Quality Inn, Rodeway WYO Motel, Super 8 🅞 🎗 Ace Hardware, Family$, Indian RV Camp, O'Reilly Parts, to Yellowstone, Verizon
298	US 87, Buffalo, **W** Nat Hist Dist Info
291	Trabing Rd
280	Middle Fork Rd
274mm	**parking area both lanes, litter barrels**
265	Reno Rd
254	Kaycee, **E** 🅖 Exxon/dsl 🍴 Country Inn Diner, Invasion Rest. 🛏 Cassidy Inn Motel, Siesta Motel 🅞 Kaycee Gen. Store, museum, NAPA Repair, Powder River RV Park, USPO, **W** 🆁🆂 **both lanes, full ♿ facilities, litter barrels, petwalk,** 🅞🎗 🅖 Sinclair/pizza/subs/dsl/LP/motel 🅞 KC RV Park,
249	TTT Rd
246	Powder River Rd
235	Tisdale Mtn Rd
227	WY 387 N, Midwest, Edgerton, Oil Field Museum
223	no services
219mm	**parking area both lanes, litter barrel**
216	Ranch Rd
210	Horse Ranch Creek Rd, Midwest, Edgerton
197	Ormsby Rd
191	Wardwell Rd, to Bar Nunn, **W** 🅖 Loaf'N Jug/dsl 🅞 KOA
189	US 20, US 26 W, to Shoshone, **W** 🅞 🚉, Port of Entry
188b	WY 220, Poplar St, **E** 🍴 McDonald's, The Fort Eatery 🛏 Best Western, Hampton Inn, Hilton Garden, La Quinta, Motel 6, Quality Inn, **W** 🅖 Exxon 🍴 Burger King, Casper's Rest., DQ 🅞 Harley-Davidson, to Ft Casper HS
188a	Center St, Casper, **E** 🅖 Conoco/dsl, Shell/dsl 🍴 Poor Boys Steaks, Taco John's 🛏 National 9 Inn, Ramada, Showboat Motel, **W** 🍴 La Cocina, Starbucks, Subway 🛏 Days Inn, Parkway Plaza Motel/cafe 🅞 USPO
187	McKinley St, Casper, **E** 🅖 Loaf'N Jug/dsl 🛏 Ranch House Motel

B U F F A L O

**WI
WY**

C A S P E R

186	US 20, US 26, US 87, Yellowstone St, **E** 🅞 city park, dsl repair, transmissions/repair, **W** 🅖 Exxon 🅞 🎗 auto repair, Chevrolet/Subaru, Kia, O'Reilly Parts
185	WY 258, Wyoming Blvd, E Casper, **E** 🅖 Kum&Go/dsl, Loaf'n Jug/dsl 🍴 Applebee's, Hacienda Mexican, IHOP, Outback Steaks, Southern BBQ HQ, TX Roadhouse 🛏 Baymont Inn, C'mon Inn, Comfort Inn, Hotel 🅞 bet, Murdoch's Ranch Store, RV camping, Smith RV Ctr, **W** 🅖 ✈FLYING J/Conoco/Subway/dsl/LP/scales/24hr, Exxon/dsl, Loaf'n Jug 🍴 Arby's, Buffalo Wild Wings, Burger King, Denny's, DQ, Five Guys, Golden Corral, Hamburger Stand, Hardee's, KFC/LJ Silver, McDonald's, Mongolian Grill, Old Chicago Grill, Olive Garden, On The Border, Perkins, Pizza Hut, Pizza Ranch, Qdoba, Red Lobster, Sanford's Cafe, Starbucks, Taco Bell, Taco John's, Village Inn, Wendy's 🛏 1st Interstate Motel, Candlewood Suites, Courtyard, Holiday Inn Express 🅞 AutoZone, Best Buy, Dick's, Home Depot, JC Penney, K-Mart, Macy's, mall, Natural Grocers, Nissan, PetCo, Plains Tire, Ross, Safeway Foods/dsl, Sam's Club/gas, Sears/auto, Staples, Target, to Oregon Tr, Verizon, Walgreens, Walmart,
182	WY 253, Brooks Rd, Hat Six Rd, **E** 🅖 Sinclair/Lou's Rest/dsl 🍴 Sonic 🛏 Sleep Inn 🅞 Rivers Edge Camping, to Wilkins SP, **W** 🍴 Famous Dave's BBQ, FireRock Rest., Keg&Cork Rest., Subway 🛏 Best Western, Holiday Inn, Mainstay Suites 🅞 🎗 Buick/Cadillac/GMC, Chrysler/Dodge/Jeep, Kohl's, Marshall's, Menards, Toyota, VW
171mm	**parking area both lanes, litter barrels**
165	Glenrock, **E** dinosaur museum, same as 160
160	US 87, US 20, US 26, E Glenrock, **E** 🍴 G-Rock's, Paisley Shawl 🛏 All American Inn, Hotel Higgins B&B 🅞 Deer Creek Village Camping, to Johnston Power Plant
156	Bixby Rd
154	Barber Rd
153mm	**parking area both lanes, litter barrels**
151	Natural Bridge
150	Inez Rd
146	La Prele Rd
140	WY 59, Douglas, **E** 🅖 Conoco/Subway/dsl, Maverik/dsl, Shell/dsl 🍴 Arby's, La Costa Mexican, McDonald's, Taco John's 🛏 Douglas Inn, Holiday Inn Express, La Quinta, Sleep Inn, Super 8 🅞 🎗 Chrysler/Dodge/Jeep, city park, Ford, KOA, Lone Tree Village RV Park, Pioneer Museum, vet, WY St Fair
135	US 20, US 26, US 87, Douglas, **E** 🅖 Loaf'n Jug/dsl, Sinclair/

D O U G L A S

WY

	🔼Ⓝ INTERSTATE 25 Cont'd
D O U G L A S	**Exit #** Services
	135 Continued
	dsl, Sinclair/rest./dsl/24hr 🍴 4 Seasons Chinese, Pizza Hut, Plains Trading Post Rest., Village Inn 🏠 1st Interstate Inn, 4 Winds Motel, Budget Inn Express, Plains Motel 🅞 🅷 auto repair, Douglas Hardware, Family$, O'Reilly Parts, Safeway Foods/dsl, Shopko, Verizon
	129mm **parking area both lanes**
	126 US 18, US 20 E, Orin, **E** Orin Jct 🆁🆂 both lanes, **both lanes, full 🚻 facilities, litter barrels, petwalk, 🛢, 🎣, RV dump** 🅖 Sinclair/Orin Jct Trkstp/dsl/café,
	125mm N Platte River
	111 Glendo, **E** 🅖 Sinclair/dsl 🍴 Glendo Marina Café 🅞 Glendo Lakeside RV camping, to Glendo SP, USPO
	104 to Middle Bear
	100 Cassa Rd
	94 El Rancho Rd
	92 US 26 E, Dwyer, **E** 🆁🆂 **both lanes, full 🚻 facilities, litter barrels, petwalk, 🎣, RV dump**, Ft Laramie NHS, to Guernsey SP
	87 Johnson Rd
	84mm Laramie River
	84 Laramie River Rd
	80 US 87, Laramie Power Sta, Wheatland, Laramie Power Sta, **E** 🅖 Sinclair/A&W/Chester's/dsl 🍴 Pizza Hut 🏠 Best Western, Super 8 🅞 Arrowhead RV Park, Buick/Cadillac/Chevrolet, CarQuest, Chrysler/Dodge/Jeep, Family$, Ford, museum, Safeway Foods, same as 78, ShopKo
	78 US 87, Wheatland, **E** 🅖 Cenex/dsl, Maverik/dsl, Shell/dsl 🍴 Arby's, Burger King, Subway, Taco John's,

78	Continued
	Western Sky's Diner 🏠 All American Motel, Motel 6, West Winds Motel, WY Motel 🅞 🅷 **visitors ctr**, Wheatland Country Store, **W** 🅖 Exxon/dsl, Pitstop/dsl 🅞 Mtn View RV Park
73	WY 34 W, to Laramie
70	Bordeaux Rd
68	Antelope Rd
66	Hunton Rd
65.5mm	**parking area both lanes, litter barrels**
65	Slater Rd
64mm	Richeau Creek
57	TY Basin Rd, Chugwater
54	Lp 25, Chugwater, **E** 🆁🆂 **both lanes, full 🚻 facilities, litter barrels, petwalk, 🛢, 🎣, RV dump** 🏠 Buffalo Lodge/Grill 🅞 RV camping
47	Bear Creek Rd
39	Little Bear Community
36mm	Little Bear Creek
34	Nimmo Rd
33mm	Horse Creek
29	Whitaker Rd
25	ranch exit
21	Ridley Rd
17	US 85 N, to Torrington, **W** 🍴 Little Bear Rest. (2mi)
16	WY 211, Horse Creek Rd
13	Vandehei Ave, **E** 🅖 Loaf'n Jug/Subway, Maverik/dsl 🍴 Mr Gem's Pizza, Silvermine Subs, **W** 🅖 Shamrock/dsl
12	Central Ave, Cheyenne, **E** 🅖 Exxon/dsl 🏠 Rodeway Inn 🅞 Frontier Days Park, museum, **E on Yellowstone Rd** 🅖 Loaf'n Jug, 🍴 Arby's, Godfather's, Great Harvest Bread, McDonald's, Pizza Hut, Starbucks, Subway, Taco John's 🅞

C H E Y E N N E

🢁N	INTERSTATE 25 Cont'd
Exit #	Services
12	Continued
	🚹 Albertsons, Big O Tire, Peerless Tire
11b	Warren AFB, Gate 1, Randall Ave, E 🅾 museum, to WY St Capitol
10b d	Warren AFB, Gate 2, Missile Dr, WY 210, HappyJack Rd, W 🅾 to Curt Gowdy SP
9	US 30, W Lincolnway, Cheyenne, E 🅖 Exxon/Downhome Diner/dsl 🍴 Outback Steaks, Village Inn 🛏 Best Value Inn, Candlewood Suites, Days Inn, Hampton Inn, Holiday Inn Express, La Quinta, Luxury Inn, Motel 6, My Place, Super 8, Towne Place Suites 🅾 Buick/Cadillac/GMC, Chevrolet, Ford/Lincoln, Home Depot, Honda, Hyundai, Mazda, Nissan, Subaru, Toyota, W 🅖 Little America/Sinclair/dsl/rest./motel/@
8d b	I-80, E to Omaha, W to Laramie
7	WY 212, College Dr, E 🅖 Loves/Wendy's/dsl/scales/24hr/@, Shamrock/Subway/dsl/24hr 🍴 Arby's 🅾 A-B RV Park (2mi), W 🅖 FLYING J/Denny's/dsl/LP/scales/24hr/@ 🍴 McDonald's 🛏 Quality Inn
6.5mm	nb, Port of Entry
4	High Plains Rd, WY Welcome/info Center both lanes, full ♿ facilities, litter barrels, petwalk, 🚻, 🛢
2	WY 223, Terry Ranch Rd, E 2 mi 🅾 Terry Bison Ranch RV camping
0mm	Wyoming/Colorado state line

🢁E	INTERSTATE 80
Exit #	Services
402mm	Wyoming/Nebraska State line
401	WY 215, Pine Bluffs, N 🅖 Exxon/Subway/dsl, Sinclair/A&W/dsl/24hr/@ 🍴 Cafe 307, Rock Ranch Grill 🛏 Gator's Motel 🅾 NAPA, Pine Bluff RV Park, USPO, S Welcome Center/🆁🆂 both lanes, full ♿ facilities, info, litter barrels, playground, nature trail, 🚻, 🛢
391	Egbert
386	WY 213, WY 214, Burns, N Antelope Trkstp/dsl/cafe
377	WY 217, Hillsdale, N 🅖 TA/Burger King/Taco Bell/dsl/scales/24hr/@ 🅾 Wyo RV Camping
372mm	Port of Entry wb, truck insp
370	US 30 W, Archer, N 🅖 Sapp Bros/Sinclair/T-Joe's Rest./dsl/scales/24hr/@ 🛏 Rodeway Inn 🅾 fireworks, repair, RV park
367	Campstool Rd, N 🅖 ⬛⬛/Subway/dsl/scales/24hr 🛏 Best Western 🅾 KOA (seasonal), Volvo Trucks, S 🅾 to Wyoming Hereford Ranch
364	WY 212, to E Lincolnway, Cheyenne, S 🅾 AB Camping (4mi), Peterbilt, N 1-2 mi on Lincoln way 🅖 Exxon/dsl, Kum&Go/dsl, Loaf'n Jug/Subway 🍴 Burger King, KFC, McDonald's, Shari's Rest., Subway, Taco Bell, Wendy's 🅾 🚹 $Tree, AutoZone, Big O Tire, BigLots, Family$, Harley-Davidson, Hobby Lobby, Murdoch's Ranch Store, O'Reilly Parts, Sierra Trading Post, Walgreens
362	US 85, I-180, to Central Ave, Cheyenne, Greeley, N 1 mi 🅖 Kum&Go/dsl, Sinclair 🍴 Arby's, Carls' Jr, Hacienda Mexican, Jimmy John's, Los Abuelo's Mexican, Papa John's, Quiznos, Village Inn 🅾 🚹 CarQuest, Family$, museum, st capitol, Verizon, S 🅖 Exxon/dsl, Loaf'n Jug/dsl, Shamrock/dsl 🍴 Burger King, Little Caesar's, Pizza Hut, Sonic, Subway,

362	Continued
	Taco John's 🛏 Comfort Inn, Holiday Inn, Roundup Motel, SpringHill Suites 🅾 Family$, Hideaway RV Village, Safeway Foods/gas, transmissions
359c a	I-25, US 87, N to Casper, S to Denver
358	US 30, W Lincolnway, Cheyenne, N 🅖 Exxon/dsl/24hr, Little America/Sinclair/dsl/motel/@ 🍴 Outback Steaks, Village Inn 🛏 Best Value Inn, Candlewood Suites, Days Inn, Hampton Inn, Holiday Inn Express, La Quinta, Luxury Inn, My Place Inn, Super 8, TownPlace Suites 🅾 🚹 Buick/GMC/Cadillac, Chevrolet, Ford/Lincoln, Home Depot, Honda, Hyundai, Mazda, Nissan, Subaru, Toyota
357	Wy 222, Roundtop Rd
348	Otto Rd
345	Warren Rd, N truck parking
342	Harriman Rd
339	Remount Rd
335	Buford, S 🅖 Phin Deli/dsl
333mm	parking area both lanes, point of interest
329	Vedeauwoo Rd, N camping, S Nat Forest RA, to Ames Monument
323	WY 210, Happy Jack Rd, N 🆁🆂 both lanes, full ♿ facilities, Lincoln Monument, litter barrels, petwalk, 🚻, 🛢, to Curt Gowdy SP
322mm	chain up area both lanes
316	US 30 W, Grand Ave, Laramie, N 0-2 mi 🅖 Exxon/dsl, Loaf'N Jug 🍴 Almanza's Mexican, Applebee's, Arby's, Burger King, Chili's, Hong Kong Buffet, Jimmy John's, Luciano's Italian, McAlister's Deli, McDonald's, Mr Jim's Pizza, Papa Murphy's, Perkins, Sonic, Starbucks, Subway, Taco Bell, Taco John's, Village Inn, Wendy's 🛏 AmericInn, Comfort Inn, Hampton Inn, Hilton Garden, Holiday Inn 🅾 🚹 $Tree, Albertsons/Osco/gas, AT&T, Buick/Chevrolet/GMC, Ford/Lincoln, GNC, Staples, to UW, Toyota, URGENT CARE, Verizon, Walgreens, Walmart/Subway
313	US 287, to 3rd St, Laramie, Port of Entry, N 🅖 Exxon, Gasa-Mat, Loaf'N Jug, Phillips 66/dsl, Shell/dsl 🍴 Chuck Wagon Rest., Corona Village Mexican 🛏 Laramie Valley Inn, Motel 8, Sunset Inn 🅾 🚹 Honda, Laramie Plains Museum, NAPA, Nissan, S 🛏 Motel 6, Ramada Inn 🅾 USPO
312mm	Laramie River
311	WY 130, WY 230, Snowy Range Rd, Laramie, N 🅾 WY Terr Park, S 🅖 Conoco/dsl, Phillips 66/dsl, Sinclair/dsl/LP 🍴 McDonald's, Subway 🛏 Best Value Inn 🅾 repair/tires, to Snowy Range Ski Area
310	Curtis St, Laramie, N 🅖 ⬛⬛/Wendy's/dsl/scales/24hr/@, Shamrock/café/dsl 🛏 Best Western, Days Inn, EconoLodge, Super 8 🅾 🚹 KOA, repair, S 🅖 Blue Beacon, Petro/Iron Skillet/dsl/scales/24hr/@ 🛏 Fairfield Inn, Quality Inn
307mm	parking area both lanes, litter barrels
297	WY 12, Herrick Lane
290	Quealy Dome Rd, S 🅖 A&C Truckstop/dsl
279	Cooper Cove Rd
272mm	Rock Creek
272	WY 13, to Arlington, N gas, RV camping
267	no services
262mm	parking area both lanes
260	CR 402
259mm	E Fork, Medicine Bow River

INTERSTATE 80 Cont'd

Exit #	Services
257mm	Medicine Bow River
255	WY 72, Elk Mtn, to Hanna, N Conoco/dsl, S Elk Mtn Hotel/rest
238	Peterson Rd
235	WY 130, S US 30/87, N Shell/dsl
229mm	N Platte River
228	no services
221	E Sinclair, N Sinclair/rest/dsl/24hr camping, to Seminoe SP
219	W Sinclair, N camping, to Seminoe SP
215	Cedar St, Rawlins, N Conoco/dsl, Shell/KFC/Taco Bell/dsl, Sinclair/dsl Burger King, China House, McDonald's, Penny's Diner, Pizza Hut, Subway, Taco John's 1st Choice Inn, Comfort Inn, Days Inn, Fairfield Inn, Hampton Inn, Holiday Inn Express, OakTree Inn, Rodeway Inn, The Key Motel $Tree, Alco, Buick/Chevrolet/GMC, CarQuest, Chrysler/Dodge/Jeep, City Mkt/dsl, Do-It Hardware, Frontier Prison NHS, museum, O'Reilly Parts, ShopKO, to Yellowstone/Teton NP, Walmart/dsl
214	Higley Blvd, Rawlins, N Pronghorn Suites KOA, S TA/Shell/Subway/dsl/scales/24hr/@ Best Value Inn
211	WY 789, to US 287 N, Spruce St, Rawlins, N Conoco/dsl, Exxon/dsl, Loaf'n Jug, Sinclair/dsl Cappy's Rest., Dragon Gate Chinese Best Western, EconoLodge, Express Inn, La Bella, Motel 7, Sunset Motel, Super 8, Travelodge Family$, Ford, RV World Camping, V1/LP, Verizon
209	Johnson Rd, N FLYING J/Denny's/dsl/LP/scales/24hr
206	Hadsell Rd (no return)
205.5mm	continental divide, elev 7000
204	Knobs Rd
201	Daley Rd
196	Riner Rd
190mm	parking area wb, litter barrels
189mm	parking area eb, litter barrels,
187	WY 789, Creston, Baggs Rd
184	Continental Divide Rd
173	Wamsutter, N Loves/Chester's/Subway/dsl/24hr/@; S Conoco/dsl/repair/café/24hr, Phillips 66/dsl Broadway Café, Southern Comfort Cafe Wamsutter Motel
165	Red Desert
158	Tipton Rd, continental divide, elev 6930
156	GL Rd
154	BLM Rd
152	Bar X Rd
150	Table Rock Rd
146	Patrick Draw Rd
144mm	both lanes, full facilities, litter barrels, petwalk, ,
143mm	parking area both lanes, litter barrels
142	Bitter Creek Rd
139	Red Hill Rd
136	Black Butte Rd
133mm	parking area both lanes
130	Point of Rocks, N Conoco/dsl RV Park
122	WY 371, to Superior
111	Airport Rd, Baxter Rd, S
107	Pilot Butte Ave, Rock Springs, S Kum&Go/dsl/e-85, Mobil/dsl Pizza Hut, Pizza Hut Sands Inn/cafe, Springs Motel

104	US 191 N, Elk St, Rock Springs, N FLYING J/Denny's/dsl/LP/24hr, Conoco/dsl, Exxon, Kum&Go/dsl/e-85, Phillips 66/dsl, Texaco/Burger King/dsl McDonald's, Renegade Rest., Santa Fe SW Grill, Subway, Taco Time Best Western, EconoLodge/rest. Buick/GMC, to Teton/Yellowstone Nat Parks via US 191, truck repair, S Exxon/dsl Days Inn
103	College Dr, Rock Springs, S Loaf'n Jug/dsl Domino's W WY Coll
102	WY 430, Dewar Dr, Rock Springs, N Exxon, Loaf'N Jug/dsl, Sinclair/dsl Applebee's, China King, KFC/LJ Silver, Taco Time Best Value Inn, Comfort Inn, LaQuinta, Motel 6 $Tree, Cadillac/Chevrolet, Chrysler/Dodge, Herberger's, Home Depot, JC Penney, Jo-Ann, K-Mart, Murdoch's, Smith's Foods, S Dickey's BBQ, Kum&Go/dsl, Loaf'N Jug/dsl, Mobil Arby's, Bonsai Chinese, Burger King, Cafe Rio, Chopstix Chinese, Golden Corral, IHOP, Jimmy John's, McDonald's, Papa Murphy's, Pizza Hut, Quizno's, Starbucks, Subway, Taco Bell, Village Inn, Wendy's, Winger's, Wonderful House Chinese Hampton Inn, Holiday Inn, Holiday Inn Express, Homewood Suites, Motel 8, Quality Inn, Super 8, Western Inn Albertsons/Sav-on, AutoZone, Big O Tire, Family$, Ford/Lincoln, Hastings Books, NAPA, Nissan, O'Reilly Parts, Radio Shack, Staples, Verizon, Walgreens, Walmart/Subway
99	US 191 S, E Flaming Gorge Rd, N KOA (1mi), S Sinclair/dsl/rest./24hr/@ Log Inn Rest., Ted's Rest. fireworks, truck repair
94mm	Kissing Rock
91	US 30, to WY 530, Green River, S 2 mi Loaf'N Jug/dsl, Maverik/dsl Arctic Circle, McDonald's, Pizza Hut, Subway, Taco Time Coachman Inn, Mustang Inn, Super 8 Expedition NHS, Family$, same as 89, to Flaming Gorge NRA
89	US 30, Green River, S Exxon/dsl, Sinclair/dsl Penny's Diner, Pizza Hut Hampton Inn, OakTree Inn, Super 8, Western Inn Adam's RV Service, The Travel Camp, to Flaming Gorge NRA
87.5mm	Green River
85	Covered Wagon Rd, S Adams RV parts/service, The Travel Camp
83	WY 372, La Barge Rd, N to Fontenelle Dam
78	(from wb)
77mm	Blacks Fork River
72	Westvaco Rd
71mm	parking area both lanes
68	Little America, N Sinclair/Little America Hotel/rest./dsl/24hr RV camping
66	US 30 W, to Teton, Yellowstone, Fossil Butte NM, Kemmerer

RAWLINS

ROCK SPGS

GREEN RIVER

🅿 = gas ⊓ = food 🏠 = lodging ⊡ = other 🆁🆂 = rest stop   Copyright 2015 - the Next EXIT ®

⬆️🅴 INTERSTATE 80 Cont'd

Exit #	Services
61	Cedar Mt Rd, to Granger
60mm	**parking area both lanes, litter barrels**
54mm	**parking area eb, litter barrels**
53	Church Butte Rd
49mm	**parking area wb, litter barrels**
48	Lp 80, Lyman, Ft Bridger, Hist Ft Bridger
45mm	Blacks Fork River
41	WY 413, Lyman, N 🆁🆂 **both lanes, full** ♿ **facilities, litter barrels, petwalk,** 🚰, 🅿️ **RV dump** 🅿 Gas'n Go/cafe/dsl, S ⊓ Taco Time ⊡ Gateway Inn (2mi), KOA (1mi)
39	WY 412, WY 414, to Carter, Mountain View
34	Lp 80, to Ft Bridger, S 🏠 Wagon Wheel Motel ⊡ Ft Bridger NHS, Ft Bridger RV Camp, to Flaming Gorge NRA
33.5mm	**parking area eb, litter barrels**
33	Union Rd
30	Bigelow Rd, N 🅿 TA/Tesoro/Burger King/Taco Bell/Fork In the Road/dsl/scales/24hr/@, S fireworks
28mm	French Rd, **parking area both lanes**
28	French Rd
24	Leroy Rd
23	Bar Hat Rd
21	Coal Rd
18	US 189 N, to Kemmerer, to Nat Parks, Fossil Butte NM
15	Guild Rd (from eb)
14mm	**parking area both lanes**
13	Divide Rd
10	Painter Rd, to Eagle Rock Ski Area
6	US 189, Bear River Dr, Evanston, N 🅿 🄻🄾🄾🄵/Subway/dsl/scales/24hr, Sinclair/dsl ⊓ Jody's Diner 🏠 Econolodge, Motel 6, Prairie Inn, Vagabond Motel ⊡ Phillips RV Park, repair/tires, truck wash, Wyo Downs Racetrack (10mi), S **Welcome Center both lanes, full** ♿ **facilities, litter barrels, petwalk,** 🚰 🅿️ **playground, RV dump seasonal**, Bear River SP
5	WY 89, Evanston, N 🅿 Chevron/Taco Time/dsl, Maverik/dsl ⊓ Arby's, DragonWall Chinese, McDonald's, Papa Murphy's, Subway, Wendy's 🏠 EconoLodge ⊡ 🄷 $Tree, AutoZone, Chevrolet, GNC, Jiffy Lube, Murdoch's, NAPA, O'Reilly Parts, Verizon, Walmart/Subway, S ⊡ WY St 🄷
3	US 189, Harrison Dr, Evanston, N 🅿 ⨁FLYING J/Subway/dsl/scales/24hr, Chevron/dsl, Shell, Sinclair ⊓ JB's, Lotty's Rest., TC's Rest., Wally's Burgers 🏠 Best Western/rest., Comfort Inn, Days Inn, Hampton Inn, HillCrest Motel, Holiday Inn Express, Howard Johnson, Quality Inn, Super 8 ⊡ Chrysler/Dodge/Jeep, USPO, S ⊓ KFC/Taco Bell ⊡ 🄷 fireworks
0.5mm	**Port of Entry eb, weigh sta wb**
0mm	Wyoming/Utah state line

⬆️🅴 INTERSTATE 90

Exit #	Services
207mm	Wyoming/South Dakota state line
205	Beulah, N 🅿 Sinclair/dsl/LP ⊓ Buffalo Jump Rest. ⊡ Sand Creek Trading Post/gas/cafe, USPO, S Ranch A NHP (5mi)
204.5mm	Sand Creek
199	WY 111, to Aladdin, ⊡ Red Water Creek RV Park, to Devil's Tower NM, to Vore Buffalo Jump NHP, **Welcome Center/**🆁🆂 **both lanes, full** ♿ **facilities, litter barrels, petwalk,** 🚰, 🅿️
191	Moskee Rd

189	US 14 W, Sundance, N 🅿 Conoco/dsl/24hr 🏠 Best Western ⊡ 🄷 Mt View Camping, museum, to Devil's Tower NM, S 🆁🆂 **both lanes, full** ♿ **facilities, info, litter barrels, petwalk,** 🚰, 🅿️, **playground, port of entry/weigh sta, RV dump**
187	WY 585, Sundance, N 🅿 Fresh Start/dsl, Sinclair/dsl ⊓ Aro Rest., Higbee's Cafe, Subway 🏠 Bear Lodge, Best Western, Budget Host Arrowhead, Rodeway Inn ⊡ 🄷 auto repair, Decker's Foods, museum, NAPA, to Devil's Tower
185	to WY 116, to Sundance, S **2 mi** 🅿 Conoco/dsl, same as 187
178	Coal Divide Rd
177mm	**parking area both lanes**
172	Inyan Kara Rd
171mm	**parking area both lanes, litter barrels**
165	Pine Ridge Rd, to Pine Haven, N Cedar Ridge RV Park (10mi), to Keyhole SP
163mm	**parking area both lanes**
160	Wind Creek Rd
154	US 14, US 16, S 🅿 Cenex/dsl ⊓ Donna's Diner, Subway 🏠 Cozy Motel, Moorcourt Motel, Rangerland Motel/RV Park, Wyo Motel ⊡ city park, Diehl's Foods/gas, museum, USPO
153	US 16 E, US 14, W Moorcroft, N 🆁🆂 **both lanes, full** ♿ **facilities, litter barrels, petwalk,** 🚰, 🅿️ S same as 154
152mm	Belle Fourche River
141	Rozet, S ⊡ All Seasons RV Park (3.5mi)
138mm	**parking area both lanes**
132	Wyodak Rd
129	Garner Lake Rd, S 🏠 Arbuckle Lodge ⊡ auto repair, Crazy Woman Camping (3mi), Harley-Davidson, High Plains Camping
128	US 14, US 16, Gillette, N 🅿 Conoco/Papa John's/dsl, Kum&Go, Maverik/dsl ⊓ Mona's American/Mexican, Taco John's, Village Inn 🏠 Howard Johnson, Mustang Motel, National 9 Inn ⊡ Crazy Woman Camping (2mi), East Side RV Ctr., Port of Entry, S 🏠 Arbuckle Lodge ⊡ High Plains Camping
126	WY 59, Gillette, N 🅿 Cenex/dsl, Conoco/Papa John's/dsl, Loaf'N Jug ⊓ China King Buffet, Hardee's, Little Caesar's, McDonald's, Pokey's BBQ, Prime Rib Rest., Starbucks, Subway 🏠 Best Value Inn ⊡ city park, Family$, Radio Shack, Smith's Foods, Tire Factory, Verizon, S 🅿 ⨁FLYING J/dsl/24hr, Exxon, Loaf'N Jug/dsl ⊓ A&W/LJ Silver, Adriano's Italian, Applebee's, Arby's, Buffalo Wild Wings, Burger King, DQ, Goodtimes Grill/Taco John's, Great Wall Chinese, Hibachi Buffet, Ice Cream Cafe, Jimmy John's, Jordan's Rest., KFC, Las Margarita's Mexican, Old Chicago Grill, Papa Murphy's, Perkins, Pizza Hut, Qdoba Mexican, Quiznos, Smiling Moose Deli, Subway, Taco Bell, Wendy's 🏠 Candlewood Suites, Clarion, Country Inn&Suites, Days Inn, Fairfield Inn, Holiday Inn Express, Wingate Inn ⊡ $Tree, Albertson's, AT&T, AutoZone, bet, Big O Tire, city park, GNC, Goodyear Truck Tire, Hastings Books, Home Depot, Jo-Ann, K-Mart, Midas, Office Depot, O'Reilly Parts, Osco Drug, Petco, Plains Tire, Tire-O-Rama, Verizon, Walgreens, Walmart/Subway
124	WY 50, Gillette, N 🅿 Conoco/Papa John's/dsl, Kum&Go/dsl, Shell/Burger King/dsl ⊓ Hong Kong Rest., Los Compadres Mexican, Pizza Hut, Rooster's Rest., Subway 🏠 Best Western/rest., Budget Inn, Comfort Inn, Hampton Inn, Motel 6, Super 8 ⊡ 🄷 Crazy Woman Camping, Don's Foods, Ford, S 🅿 Kum&Go/dsl ⊓ McDonald's ⊡ Bighorn Tire, Buick/Chevrolet/GMC, Chrysler/Dodge/Jeep

Sidebar markers (top to bottom): **SUNDANCE**, **EVANSTON**, **WY**, **GILLETTE**

INTERSTATE 90 Cont'd

Exit #	Services
116	Force Rd
113	Wild Horse Creek Rd
106	Kingsbury Rd
102	Barber Creek Rd
91	Dead Horse Creek Rd
89mm	Powder River
88	Powder River Rd, N Ⓡₛ both lanes, full ♿ facilities, litter barrels, petwalk, 🄲, 🄿, 🄾 RV Park
82	Indian Creek Rd
77	Schoonover Rd
73.5mm	Crazy Woman Creek
73	Crazy Woman Creek Rd
69	Dry Creek Rd
68.5mm	parking area wb, litter barrels (wb only)
65	Red Hills Rd, Tipperary Rd
60mm	parking area both lanes, litter barrels
58	US 16, to Ucross, Buffalo, S 0-3 mi 🅖 Cenex/dsl/24hr, Exxon/dsl, Maverik/dsl 🍴 Bozeman Tr Steaks, Dash Inn Rest., Hardee's, McDonald's, Pizza Hut, Sub Shop, Subway, Taco John's, Winchester Steaks 🛏 Buffalo Inn, Comfort Inn, Days Inn, Hampton Inn, Holiday Inn Express, Quality Inn, Rodeway WYO Motel, Super 8 🄾 🏥 Ace Hardware, Bighorn Tire, Deer Park Camping, Family$, Indian RV Camp, KOA, Nat Hist Dist, O'Reilly Parts, Verizon, vet
56b	I-25 S, US 87 S, to Buffalo
56a	25 Bus, 90 Bus, to Buffalo, services S 2 mi (from eb)
53	Rock Creek Rd
51	Lake DeSmet, N 1 mi Lake De Smet RV park, Lake Stop gas/motel/cafe
47	Shell Creek Rd
44	US 87 N, Piney Creek Rd, to Story, Banner, N 🄾 Ft Phil Kearney, museum, S 5 mi Wagon Box Cabins/Rest.
39mm	scenic turnout wb

37	Prairie Dog Creek Rd, to Story
33	Meade Creek Rd, to Big Horn
31mm	parking area eb
25	US 14 E, Sheridan, N 🛏 Quality Inn 🄾 Dalton's RV Ctr, S Exxon/dsl, Holiday/dsl, Loaf'n Jug/dsl, Maverik/dsl 🍴 Arby's, Burger King, Goodtimes/Taco John's, JB's, Jimmy John's, Los Agaves, McDonald's, Ole's Pizza, Papa John's, Papa Murphy's, Perkins, Qdoba, Starbucks, Subway, Taco Bell, Wendy's 🛏 Candlewood Suites, Days Inn, Holiday Inn, Holiday Lodge, Mill Inn 🄾 $Tree, Ace Hardware, ⊖, Albertson's/Osco Drug, Buick/GMC, Chrysler/Dodge/Jeep, Firestone/auto, Ford/Lincoln, Goodyear/auto, Home Depot, Jeep, Meineke, Midas, NAPA, O'Reilly Parts, Sheridan Coll, Tire-Rama, to Hist Dist, Toyota, vet, Walgreens, Walmart/Subway
23	WY 336, 5th St, Sheridan, N Ⓡₛ both lanes, full ♿ facilities, info, litter barrels, petwalk, 🄲, 🄿, RV dump 🅖 Rock Stop/Subway/dsl 🛏 Wingate Inn, S 1-2 mi 🅖 Cenex, Holiday/dsl 🍴 DQ, El Tapatio Dos, Olivia's Kitchen, Quiznos, WYO Rib&Chop House 🛏 Alamo Motel, Best Value Inn, Best Western, Hampton Inn, Motel 6, Sheridan Inn 🄾 🏥 Honda, park, Peter D's RV Park, radiators, Sheridan Cty Museum
20	Main St, Sheridan, S 🅖 Exxon/dsl/scales/24hr, Gasamat/dsl, Maverik 🍴 Country Kitchen, Domino's, Firewater Grill, Kim's Rest., Little Ceasars, McDonald's, Pizza Hut 🛏 Aspen Inn, Bramble Motel, Budget Host, Rodeway Inn, Stage Stop Motel, Super 8, Super Saver Motel, Trails End Motel/rest. 🄾 🏥 K-Mart, KOA, Peerless Tires
16	to Decker, Montana, port of entry
15mm	Tongue River
14	WY 345, Acme Rd
9	US 14 W, Ranchester, S 1 mi 🅖 Cenex/dsl 🄾 Conner Bfd NHS, Foothills Campground, Lazy R Campground, Ski Area, Teton NPs, to Yellowstone, Western Motel
1	Parkman
0mm	Wyoming/Montana state line

BUFFALO   **SHERIDAN**

WY

NOTES

NOTES

Assist A Fellow Traveler with...

Published annually,
the Next EXIT®
provides the best
USA Interstate Highway Information available.
Use this form to order another copy of the Next EXIT®
for yourself or someone special.

Please send _____ copies of the Next Exit® to the address below.
I've enclosed my check or money order for $23.95 US/$26.95 Canadian per copy.

Name:_____

Address:_____ Apt./Suite # _____

City: _____ State: _____ Zip:_____

THREE EASY ORDER OPTIONS:

1. *MAIL ORDER FORM TO:*
   the Next EXIT®, Inc.
   PO Box 888
   Garden City, Utah 84028

2. *ORDER ON THE WEB AT:*
   www.theNextExit.com

3. *Give Us A Call & Use Your Charge Card*
   1-800-NEX-EXIT or 1-800-639-3948

the Next EXIT® digital options are available at:
www.theNextExit.com